SECOND EDITION

BLOODSTAIN PATTERN ANALYSIS

LEVEL 1 LAB MANUAL

R. Craig Gravel

cognella | ACADEMIC PUBLISHING

Bassim Hamadeh, CEO and Publisher
Carrie Baarns, Senior Manager, Revisions and Author Care
Kaela Martin, Project Editor
Rachel Kahn, Production Editor
Jess Estrella, Senior Graphic Designer
Alexa Lucido, Licensing Manager
Natalie Piccotti, Director of Marketing
Kassie Graves, Senior Vice President, Editorial
Jamie Giganti, Director of Academic Publishing

cognella® | ACADEMIC PUBLISHING
3970 Sorrento Valley Blvd., Ste. 500, San Diego, CA 92121

CONTENTS

Introduction to Bloodstain Pattern Analysis

The focus of bloodstain pattern analysis (BPA) is to examine the **size**, **shape**, and **distribution** of bloodstains following a bloodshed event, to establish the types of activities and mechanisms that produced them.

- Bloodstain pattern analysis is the study of "static" bloodstains.
- These bloodstains are normally associated with the aftermath of a violent event and they provide information specific to the events that occurred.
- Bloodstain patterns are predictable and reproducible.
- You can determine the direction a bloodstain was moving by its appearance (shape).
    - A bloodstain will always point in the direction it is moving.
- The size of a projected bloodstain has a direct relationship with the speed at which it is traveling.
    - A small drop is moving much faster than a larger one.

The majority of forensic disciplines provide information regarding the "WHO" of the crime.

- Examples:
    - DNA
    - Fingerprints

Forensic pathology oftentimes answers the "WHAT" of the crime.

- Bloodstain pattern analysis also provides information regarding the "WHAT" of the crime.
    - Bloodstain pattern analysis brings to the investigation the ability to define those events that could or could not have occurred during bloodshed.

Blood as a fluid is four times thicker than water. This is due to the viscosity of the blood and the molecular bonding. In flight, blood occupies the smallest space possible, which is a sphere.

- Force applied to blood creates spatter. The greater the force, the smaller the spatter.
- Once a blood drop is in flight, it retains its volume until the blood drop impacts a surface. The only exception is when the blood drop ricochets off an object while still in flight.

- Due to the surface tension and viscosity, when a blood drop impacts a surface, the blood will attempt to hold together, unlike water.
- Bloodstain patterns are reproducible.
- These factors allow a Bloodstain Pattern Analyst to feel confident when examining a scene.

The primary functions of a BPA analyst are the following:

1. To define or categorize specific stains and patterns found.
2. To attempt to identify the nature of the event causing the pattern.

Using the information available through bloodstain pattern analysis, certain objectives can be met and conclusions made.

- This includes observing and identifying the following:
    - The direction a given blood drop was traveling
    - The angle of impact
    - The area above the target surface from which the droplet originated
    - The nature/type of the force
    - The direction from which the force was delivered
    - The nature of an object used in applying force
    - The minimum number of blows struck during the incident
    - The relative position of the suspect, victim, and related objects during the incident
    - The possible sequencing of multiple events associated with the incident

CHAPTER 1

Brief History

Bloodstain evidence is not new to the criminalist, as references exist as far back as 1894 in Germany. The 150-year written scientific history is longer than the history of fingerprint analysis. The importance of history is that it allows a person to understand the present, and to forecast the future because of events of the past. The discipline is constantly evolving and becoming better defined over time.

Historical Development

1856: J. B. Lassaigne

- Discussed fly spots.

1863: John and Theodric Beck

- Discussed specific patterns and correlation of patterns to wounds.

1880: Henry Faulds

- Discussed the use of bloody fingerprints.

1882: Charles Tidy

- "Few things hold so important a place as, or involve of greater nicety, than determining the precise nature of various [blood] spots or stains found on fabrics and instruments." In 1882, Professor Charles M. Tidy of London published "Legal Medicine" in which he made the above statement

1895: Eduard Piotrowski

- His work has been translated to English as *Concerning the Origin, Shape, Direction and Distribution of Bloodstains Following Head Wounds Caused by Blows.*
- Sought to understand spatter and expiratory blood.
- Discussed and defined directionality of droplets based on shapes and tails.
- Recognized and explained cast-off patterns.

1901: Albert Florence

- Created a complete system (taxonomy) for classifying bloodstains.

1904: Hans Gross

- Authored the *Handbook for Investigators.*
- Original version in German, and subsequent translation in English.
- Spent 30 pages describing the use of bloodstain patterns.

1914: Ernest Ziemke

- Authored the chapter "Bloodstain Patterns" in Theodor Lochte's *Techniques of Police Investigation.*
    - "Blood tracks are the most important tracks that stay behind after a crime is committed. Very often they alone have been of significant importance for the conviction of the suspect."
    - "Based on our experience and experiments we want to point out that it is necessary to be cautious and not draw conclusions from a single or very few blood tracks. This happens quite often. Only when a large number of bloodstains are examined and compared, is it possible to exclude errors."
- Discussed wave cast-off (satellite stains) and directionality of stains.
- Discussed cast-off patterns and pattern transfers, and described a case in which he compared a bloody shoe mark and found where the 14 shoe nails left the pattern.
- Discussed spatter and whether spatter would be found on a suspect in all cases.

1935: Svennson and Wendel

- Published Rikospaikka-Tutkimus "Criminal Investigation."
- Finnish criminal investigation reference.
- Called on the work of Hans Gross and spent significant number of pages explaining the use of bloodstain patterns.

1939: Victor Balthazard et al.

- Made a presentation to the Congress of Forensic Medicine.
- Described and explained spatter, the parabolic nature of blood flight paths.
- Introduced "stringing" concepts, although he did not use the word "stringing."

1941: John Gohringer

- Doctoral studies at the University of Heidelberg.
- Thesis "Is It Possible to Establish the Falling Height and Directionality of Dropped Down Blood from the Appearance of the Stain and Various Targets."
    - Gohringer's inspiration was Balthazard's effort and paper.
    - Gohringer was a U.S. citizen. Before completing his study, he spent seven months as an "internee" of the German government before being released.

1947: J. G. Wilhelm

- Study in the Practice of Criminalistics.
- Gave mention to bloodstain pattern, including the following:
    - Stain shape and impact angle
    - Pattern transfers

1953: Paul Kirk

- In 1953, he included a chapter entitled "Blood Physical Investigation" in his book *Criminal Investigation*.
- Worked on the Sam Sheppard case in Ohio in 1955.
- His affidavit in support of Sheppard is a very detailed description of some of his beliefs on bloodstain pattern analysis related to cast-off patterns, spatter patterns, and blood trails

1960: Jozef Radzicki

- Published *Bloodstain Prints in the Practice of Technology* in Warsaw, Poland.
    - Developed a more effective taxonomy based on the following:
        - Bloodstain from extravasations—drops, gushes, and pools
        - Bloodstains from application of instruments—spatter, cast-off, pattern transfers
        - Bloodstains from wiping or removal of blood
- Commented on the importance of target surface as it affects the resulting stain.

1970: MacDonell/Bialousz

- Authored *Flight Characteristics and Stain Patterns of Human Blood*.
- LEAA funded study (the Orange Book).

1983: International Association of Bloodstain Pattern Analysts (IABPA) was formed.

- Expressed need to enhance knowledge and education in the discipline.
- Provided yearly training conferences and committee effort to evaluate issues related to bloodstain pattern analysis.

1984: Laber and Epstein

- Authored *Experiments and Practical Exercises in Bloodstain Pattern Analysis*.
- Lab manual used in the Minnesota course

1989: Eckert and James

- Authored *Interpretation of Bloodstain Evidence at Crime Scenes*.
- Original publisher was Elsevier Press.
- CRC Press picked up the 2nd edition.
- 2nd edition was significantly expanded and enhanced.

1990: International Association for Identification (IAI)

- Removed bloodstain pattern analysis from the crime scene discipline and identified it as a separate discipline.
- IAI now offers Bloodstain Pattern Examiner certification.

1996: Stuart James (Editor)

- Authored *Scientific and Legal Applications of Bloodstain Pattern Interpretation.*

1997: Tom Bevel and Ross Gardner

- Authored *Bloodstain Pattern Analysis with an Introduction to Crime Scene Reconstruction.*
- Third edition published in 2007

2000: SWGSTAIN

- Originated as the FBI Scientific Working Group for Bloodstain Pattern Analysis (SWGSTAIN).
- Formed in March 2000, with express purpose of developing "best practices" for the discipline and create common ground (e.g., differences between IABPA, IAI).
- Now located at the Midwest Forensic Resource Center, Ames, Iowa.

2001: Anita Wonder

- Authored *Blood Dynamics.*
- Good document but interjected non-Newtonian fluids (manmade liquids, such as paint and other chemicals).

2015: National Institute of Standards and Technology

- A metrology laboratory and a non-regulatory agency of the United States Department of Commerce.
- The mission is to promote innovation and industrial competitiveness.
- NIST has subcommittees for a variety of forensic science disciplines, including bloodstain pattern analysis, known as The Organization of Scientific Area Committees for Forensic Science (OSAC).

Historical Development Timeline

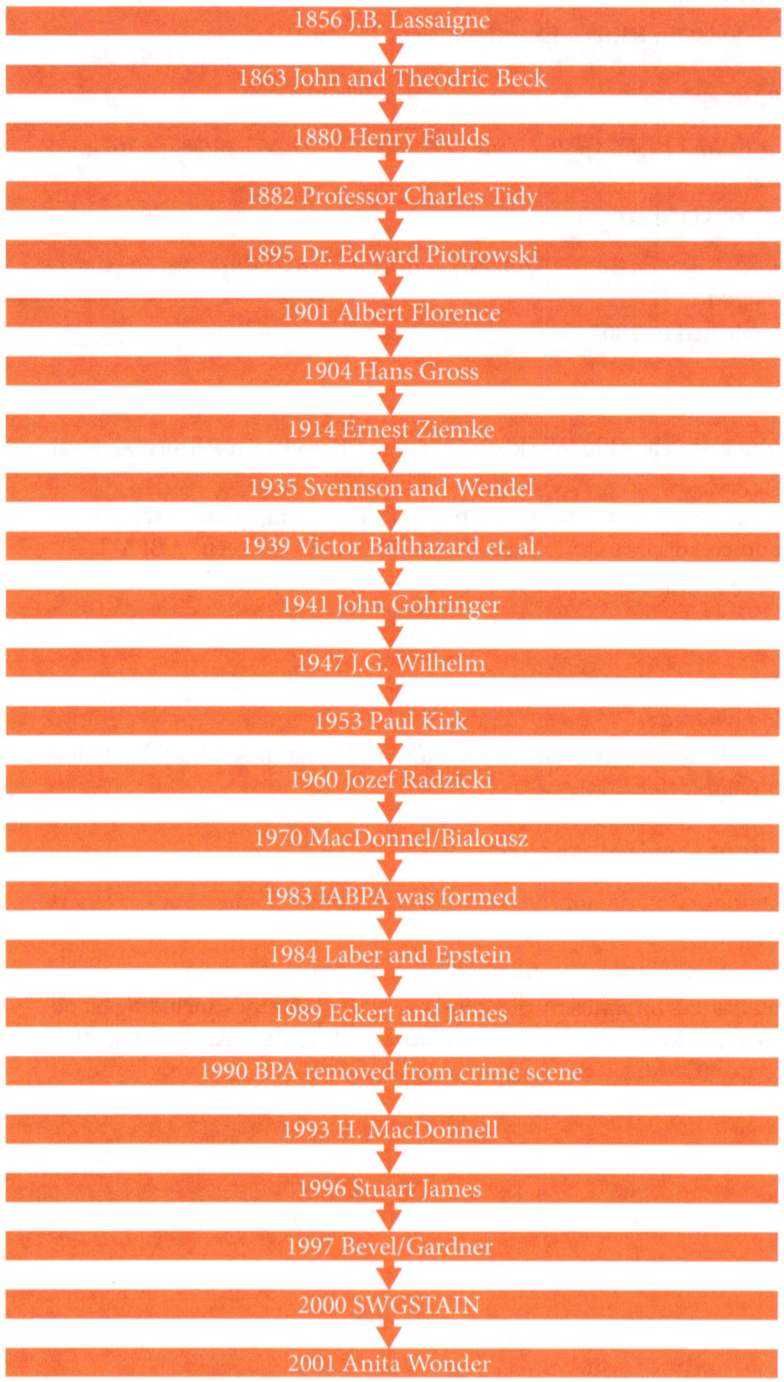

FIGURE 1.1 Historical Development Timeline

Figure Credit

Fig. 1.1: Tom Bevel and Ross M. Gardner, *Bloodstain Pattern Analysis with an Introduction to Crime Scene Reconstruction*. Copyright © 2001 by CRC Press.

CHAPTER 2

Bloodstain Pattern Classification

Classification Systems

- LVIS, MVIS, HVIS (MacDonell): Spatter size is the primary issue.
- Passive/dynamic (Bevel/Gardner): Focuses on the underlying nature of the event.
- Spatter/non-spatter (Wonder): Free flight stains versus all others (taxonomic in nature).
- Taxonomic: Physical characteristic-based, with established parent–child hierarchy.
- Low-energy impact spatter, medium-energy impact spatter, and high-energy impact spatter (Gravel/White): The preponderant stain size identifies the energy levels.
- Fine and coarse spatter used by Florida Department of Law: Size of spatter determines whether fine or coarse.

Each system has its own perspective and each system is valuable, as they primarily *each define the same reproducible pattern types.*

Tom Bevel and Ross M. Gardner introduced a taxonomic classification system in their third edition of *Bloodstain Pattern Analysis with an Introduction to Crime Scene Reconstruction.*

The taxonomy is a set of rules based on observable stain characteristics for classification. Their idea was derived from biology, where organisms are classified by shared characteristics. The taxonomy reduces subjectivity, as it provides recognizable decision points for the analyst.

In 2019, the taxonomic classification system was validated by a graduate student at the Forensic Science Institute at the University of Central Oklahoma. Fifty individuals in law enforcement, commissioned and non-commissioned, participated in a survey. They were provided 15 bloodstain photographs and asked to identify the various stains. One half of the participants was provided with a taxonomic classification decision map and the other group was not. The final results revealed that the participants with the decision map accurately identified 10 more bloodstains than those without the map. These two groups tied in identifying three identifications and the participants without the decision map identified two bloodstains that the other misidentified.

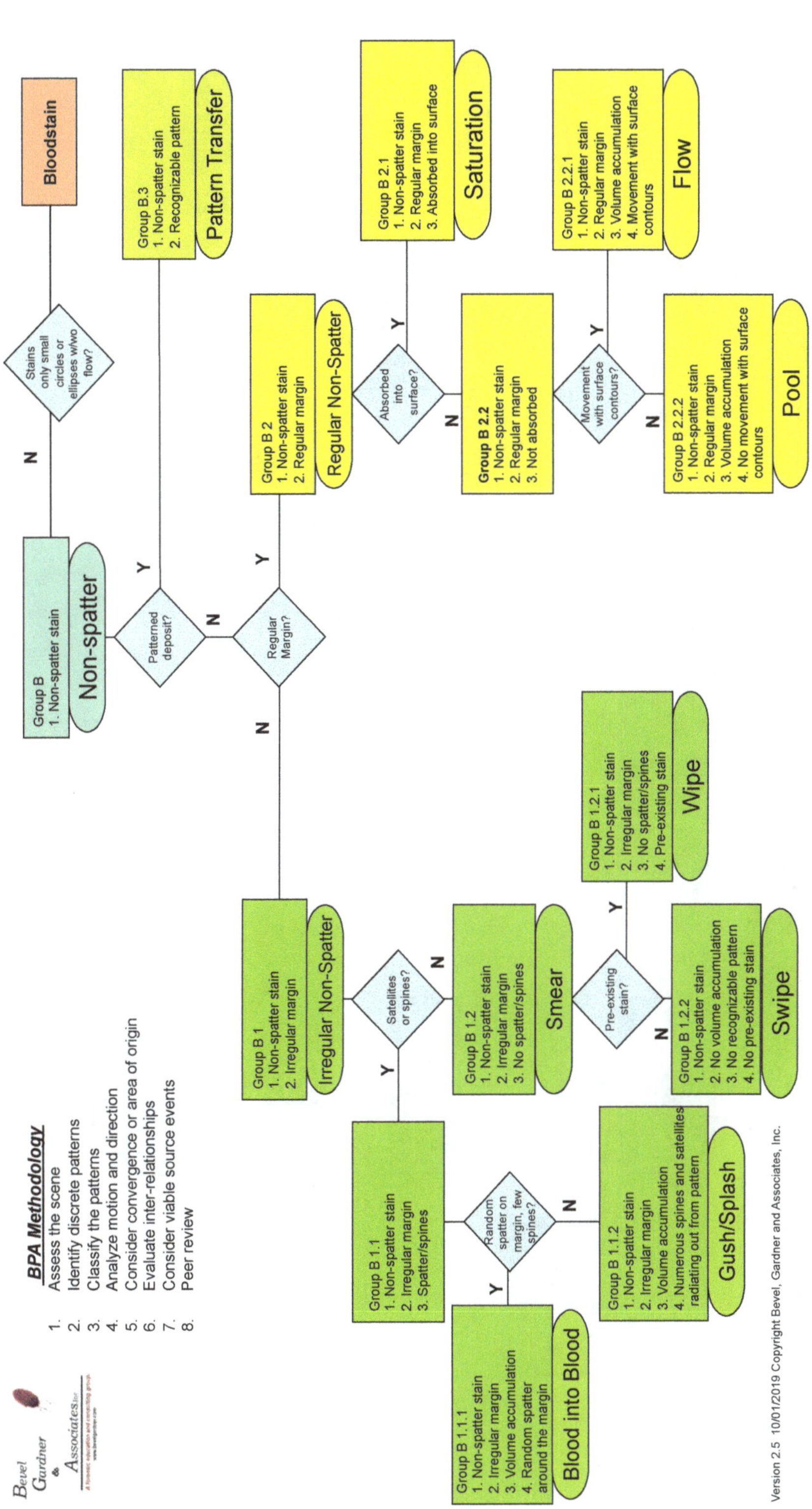

FIGURE 2.1 BPA Map

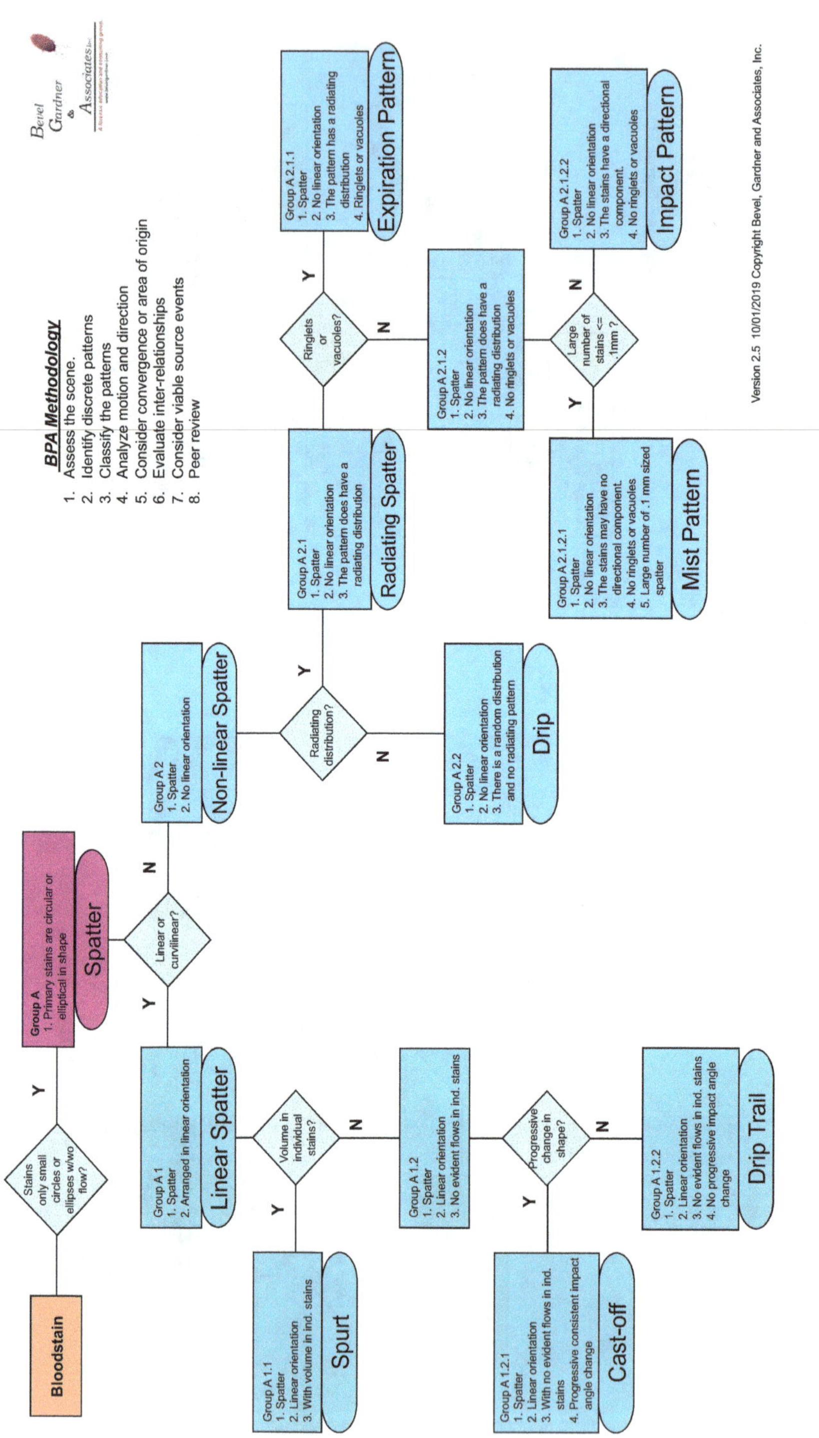

FIGURE 2.1 BPA Map *(continued)*

Reference

Bevel, T., & Gardner, R. M. (2008). *Bloodstain pattern analysis with an introduction to crime scene reconstruction* (3rd ed.). CRC Press.

CHAPTER 3

Categories of Bloodstain Patterns

Grouping Stains

All bloodstains generally fit into one of four categories. These groupings allow a basic categorization of a stain or pattern for the purpose of discussion early on in the investigation. (*Note:* Jozef Radziki was the first to suggest this grouping. Bevel and Gardner included the miscellaneous category.)

1. Passive stains
2. Transfer stains
3. Projected or impact stains
4. Miscellaneous

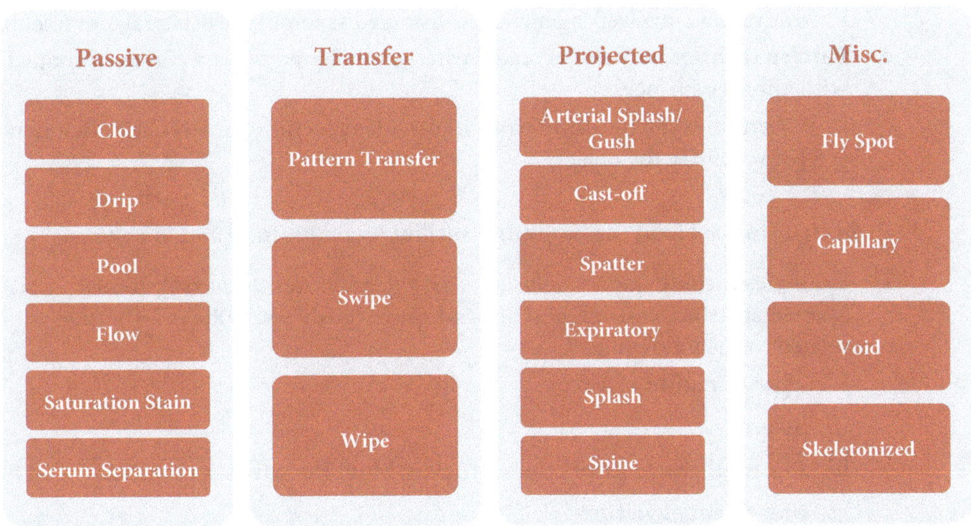

FIGURE 3.1 Categories of Bloodstain Patterns

1. **Passive stains**: result of **bleeding.**
   a. Examples include *clots, drops, flows,* and *pools.*
   b. Clots, drops, flows, and pools provide information related to the following:
      i. Time of bloodshed.
      ii. Disturbances after bloodshed.
   c. **Clots:** a gelatin mass.
      i. The mass will usually exhibit separation of the liquid and solid materials.
   d. **Drops:** referred to as passive bleeding and low-energy spatter.
      i. **Passive blood flows:** created by gravity alone with no circulatory action involved.

2. **Transfer stains:** result of a **bloody object coming in contact with a surface.**
   a. Examples include *wipes, swipes, pattern transfer,* and *other contact bloodstains.*
   b. Wipes, swipes, and pattern transfers provide information related to the following:
      i. Movement of victim and/or suspect.
      ii. Sequencing.
      iii. Identification of weapon.
   c. **Wipe:** a stain created when an object moves through a preexisting bloodstain.
      i. The motion is assumed to be a lateral movement.
   d. **Swipe:** the transfer of blood onto a surface by a moving object that is bloodstained.
      i. The motion involved is generally considered as some type of lateral movement.
   e. **Pattern transfer:** any stain created when a wet, bloody object comes in contact with another surface.
      i. Oftentimes the resulting pattern provides specific characteristics that may help identify the object.

3. **Projected stains:** blood that *impacts a surface under pressure and in volume.*
   a. Examples include *spatter, splashes, cast-off,* and *arterial spurts/gushes.*
   b. Spatter, splashes, cast-off, and arterial spurts/gushes provide information related to the following:
      i. Type or nature of force
      ii. Staging
      iii. Minimum number of blows struck in blunt force trauma injuries
      iv. Movement of victim
   c. **Spatter:** result of force being applied to blood.
      i. The greater the force, the smaller the individual blood drops will be.
      ii. The more elliptical (or longer) the individual blood drops are, the closer the blood source was to the target surface.

d. **Splash:** created when a volume of blood impacts a surface with minimal force.
e. **Cast-off:** stains created when blood is flung or projected from an object either in motion or when the motion suddenly stops.
f. **Arterial spurts/gushes:** the escape of blood under pressure from any breach in an artery or heart, showing pressure, pressure fluctuations, or both.

4. **Miscellaneous stains:** stains that don't fit neatly into any one group.
   a. Examples include *fly spots, capillary action, voids,* and *skeletonized stains.*
   b. Fly spots, capillary action, voids, and skeletonized stains provide information related to (1) movement, (2) time, and (3) sequencing.

Figure Credit

Fig. 3.1: Tom Bevel and Ross M. Gardner, *Bloodstain Pattern Analysis with an Introduction to Crime Scene Reconstruction*. Copyright © 2001 by CRC Press.

CHAPTER 4

Energy Pattern Groups

The method used by Gravel and White to categorize spatter is observing the *energy pattern*, which refers to the speed of the object creating the spatter/injury.

- Energy does not refer to the speed of the blood drops in flight.
    - The speed refers to the force or energy of the wounding agent.

General Sequence of Events

- The location of the greatest blood shed will most likely be the ending point of the event.
- The location with the least blood spatter will be at or near where the violence began.

When categorizing patterns, the analyst should look at the *preponderant stain size* in a pattern.

- The preponderant stain size represents the average size for the majority of spatter or stains present.
    - There are no perfect patterns.
- There is no specific separation between the three energy patterns.
    - Some overlap in stain size will be present.
    - No clear demarcation within the pattern.

As the energy increases on the blood source, there is a corresponding decrease in the size of the spatter.

- The dynamic nature of the impact, force, contact areas, angle of contact, and so on all affect the pattern.

The three energy patterns are **low-energy, medium-energy,** and **high-energy stains.**

Low-Energy Stains

- Considered to result from a normal gravitational pull up to 5 ft per second.
- Resulting stains are relatively large: **4 mm in diameter or larger.**
- Normally associated with **bleeding injury.**
- Assists in showing movement of person within a scene.

FIGURE 4.1 Low-Energy Stains

Medium-Energy Stains

- Considered to result from a force or energy of 5 ft to 25 ft per second.
- Resulting stains range in size from **1 mm to 4 mm.**
- Normally associated with **blunt force trauma** injuries.
    - *Exclusions to medium-energy stains:*
        - Blood dripping into blood (produces satellite spatter that looks similar to what would occur in a beating incident).

FIGURE 4.2 Medium-Energy Stains

High-Energy Stains

- Results from a force or energy in excess of 100 ft per second.
- Stains considered *mist-like*: **1 mm in diameter or smaller.**
- Normally associated with **gunshot wounds,** but are also found in explosions and high-speed machinery accidents.
    - *Exclusions to high-energy stains*:
        - Expiratory blood
            - Less vivid in color due to saliva
        - High-speed machinery
        - Explosions

FIGURE 4.3 High-Energy Stains

(*Note*: **Expiratory blood** is associated with injuries or bleeding that interferes with breathing. The spatter may be less vivid in color due to saliva.)

CHAPTER 5

Terminology

The terms listed in this chapter were adopted by the International Association of Bloodstain Pattern Analysts (IABPA).

Accompanying Drop: A small drop produced as a by-product of drop formation.

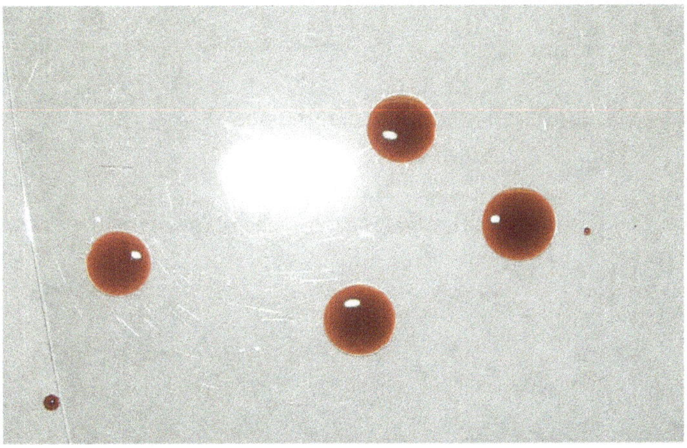

FIGURE 5.1 Accompanying Drop.

Altered Stain: A bloodstain with characteristics that indicate a physical change has occurred (i.e., *skeletonized stains, blood into blood, dried stains, wipes, swipes,* etc.).

FIGURE 5.2 Altered Stains Blood into Blood.

Angle of Impact: The acute angle (alpha), relative to the plane of a target, at which a blood drop strikes the target.

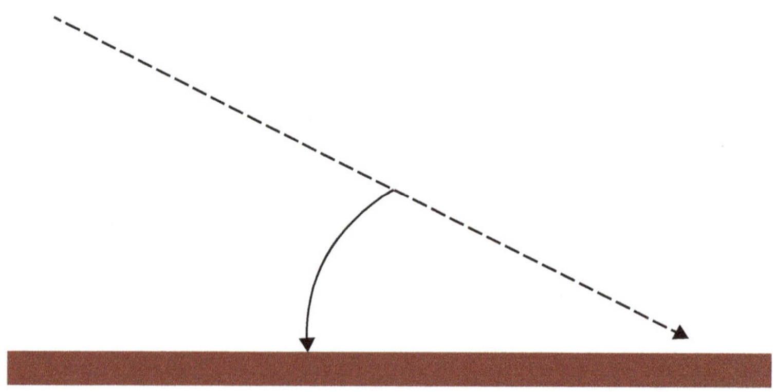

FIGURE 5.3 Angle of Impact.

Area of Convergence: The area containing the intersections generated by lines drawn through the long axes of individual stains that indicates in two dimensions the location of the blood source.

FIGURE 5.4 Area of Convergence, Also Known as Roadmapping.

Area of Origin: The three-dimensional (3D) location from which spatter originated.

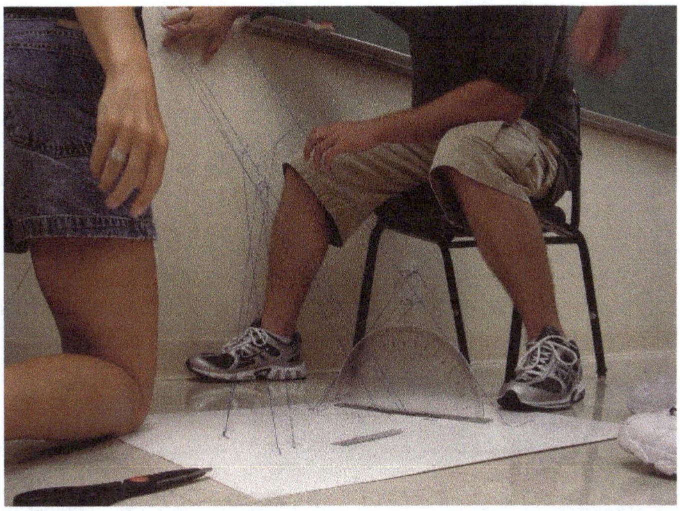

FIGURE 5.5 Area of Origin.

Backspatter Pattern: A bloodstain pattern resulting from blood drops that traveled in the opposite direction of the external force applied; associated with an entrance wound created by a projectile.

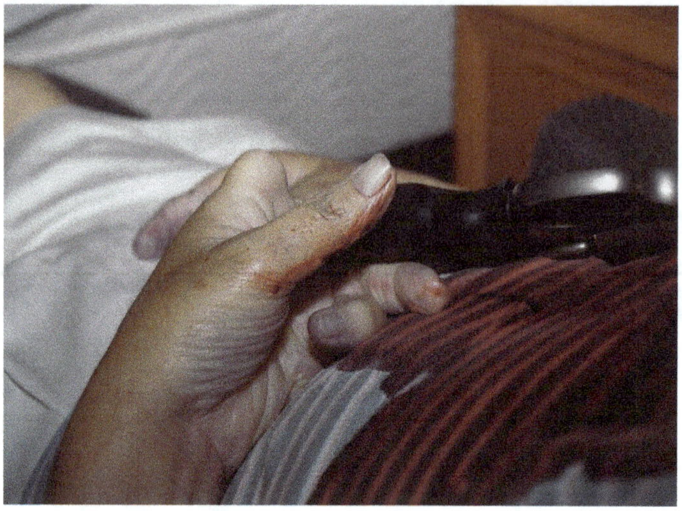

FIGURE 5.6 Backspatter Pattern

Blood Clot: A gelatinous mass formed by a complex mechanism involving red blood cells, fibrinogen, platelets, and other clotting factors.

FIGURE 5.7 Blood Clot.

Bloodstain: A deposit of blood on a surface.

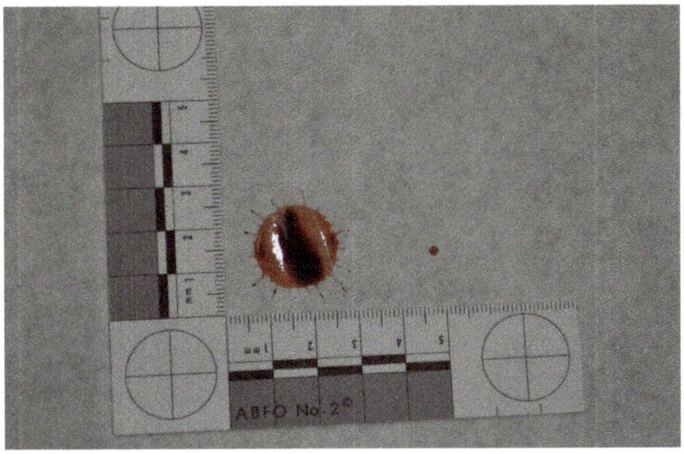

FIGURE 5.8 Bloodstain

Bloodstain Pattern: A grouping or distribution of bloodstains that indicates, through regular or repetitive form, the manner in which the pattern was deposited.

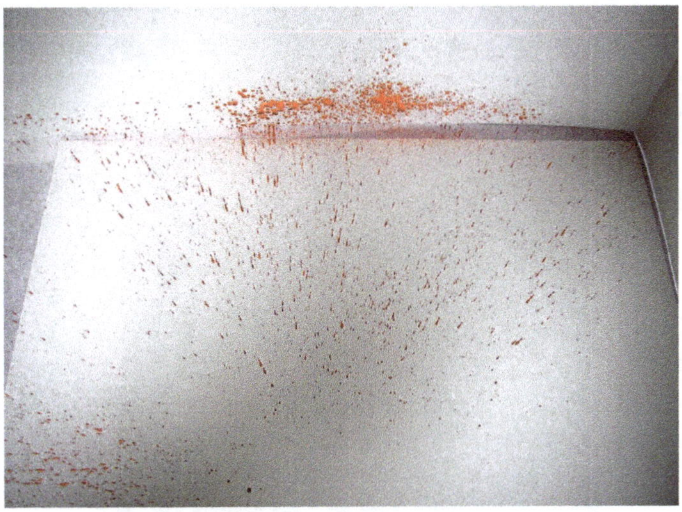

FIGURE 5.9 Bloodstain Pattern

Bubble Ring: An outline within a bloodstain resulting from air in the blood.

FIGURE 5.10 Bubble Ring

Cast-Off Pattern: A bloodstain pattern resulting from blood drops released from an object due to its motion.

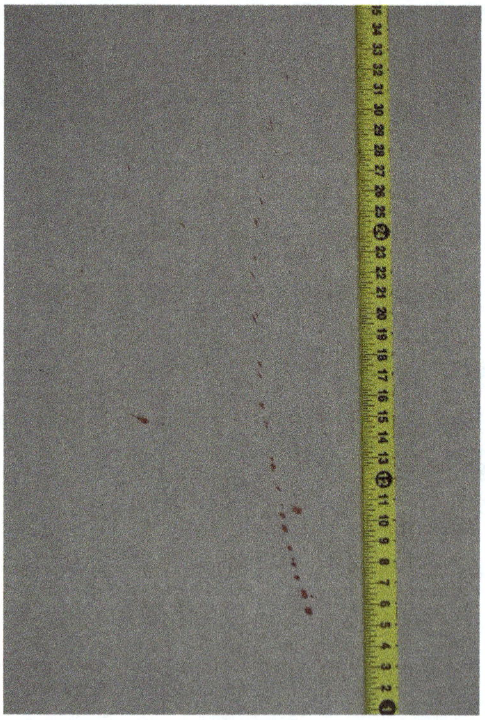

FIGURE 5.11 Cast-Off Pattern

Cessation Cast-Off Pattern: A bloodstain pattern resulting from blood drops released from an object due to its rapid deceleration.

FIGURE 5.12 Cessation Cast-Off Pattern.

Directionality: The characteristic of a bloodstain that indicates the direction blood was moving at the time of deposition.

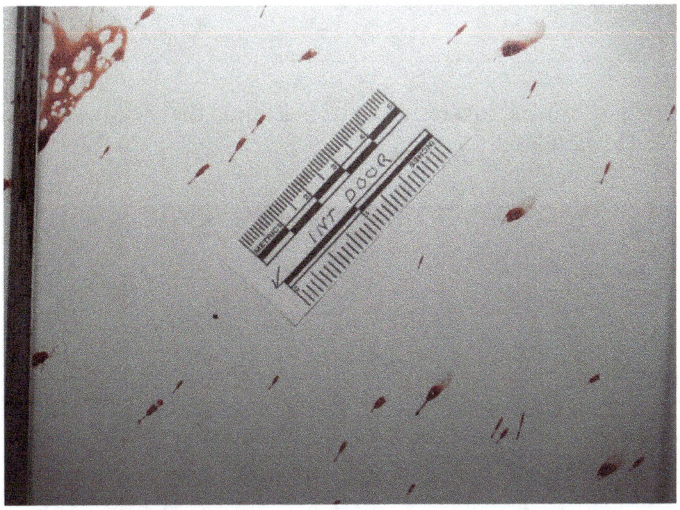

FIGURE 5.13 Directionality.

Directional Angle: The angle (gamma) between the long axis of a spatter stain target and a defined reference line on the target.

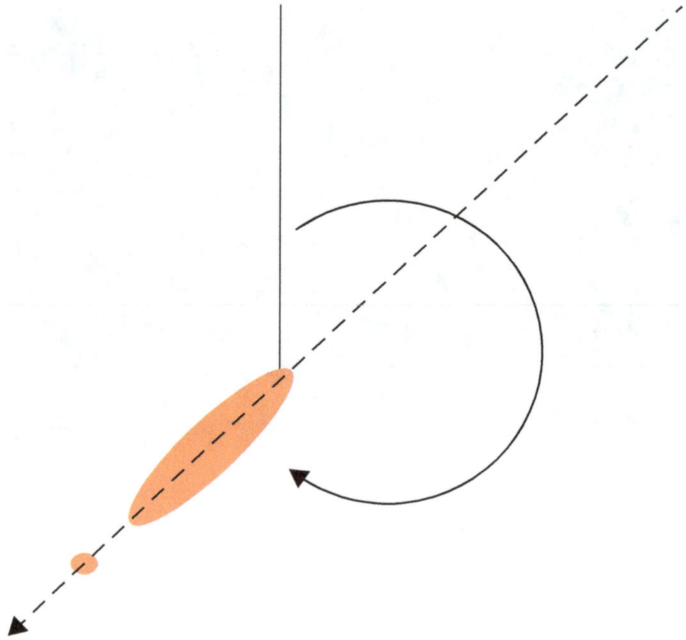

FIGURE 5.14 Directional Angle

Drip Pattern: A bloodstain pattern resulting from a liquid that dripped into another liquid, at least one of which was blood.

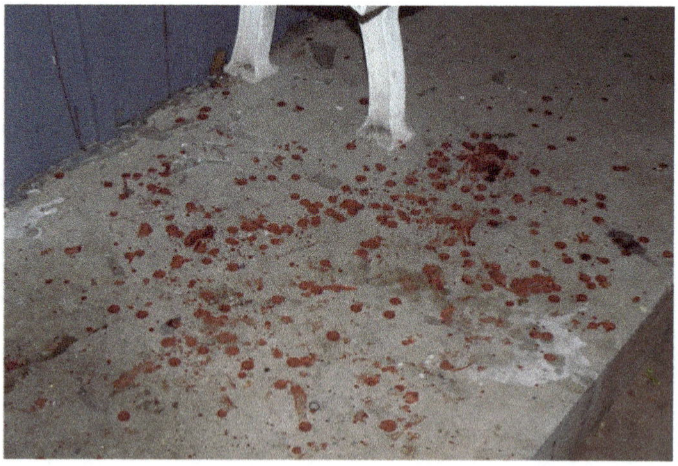

FIGURE 5.15 Drip Pattern

Drip Stain: A bloodstain resulting from a falling drop that formed due to gravity.

FIGURE 5.16 Drip Stain.

Drip Trail: A bloodstain pattern resulting from the movement of a source of drip stains between two points.

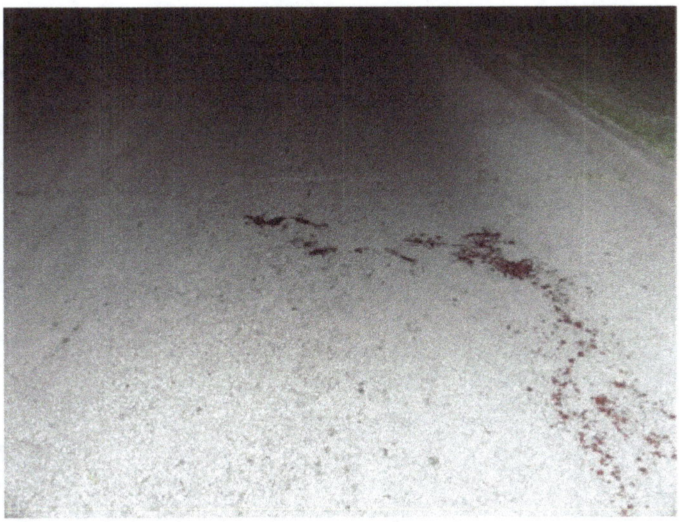

FIGURE 5.17 Drip Trail.

Edge Characteristics: A physical feature of the periphery of a bloodstain (i.e., *spines, smooth, scalloped*, etc.).

FIGURE 5.18 Edge Characteristics

Expiration Pattern: A bloodstain pattern resulting from blood forced by airflow out of the nose, mouth, or a wound.

FIGURE 5.19 Expiration Pattern

Flow: A bloodstain pattern resulting from the movement of a volume of blood on a surface due to gravity or movement of the target.

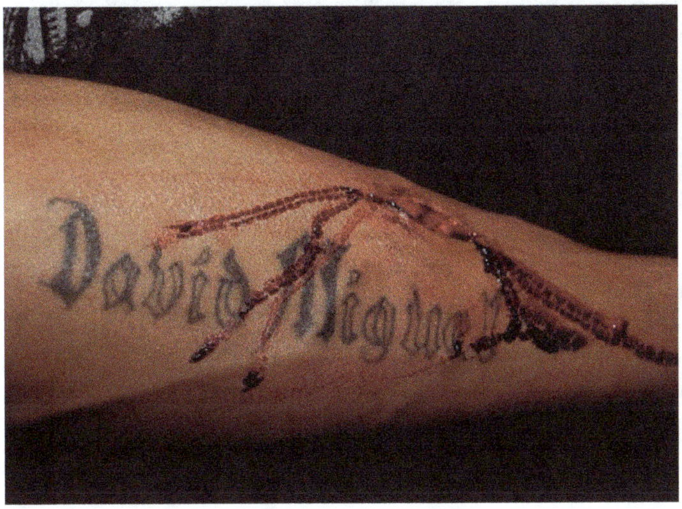

FIGURE 5.20 Flow.

Forward Spatter Pattern: A bloodstain pattern resulting from blood drops that traveled in the same direction as the impact force.

FIGURE 5.21 Forward Spatter Pattern.

Impact Pattern: A bloodstain pattern resulting from an object striking liquid blood.

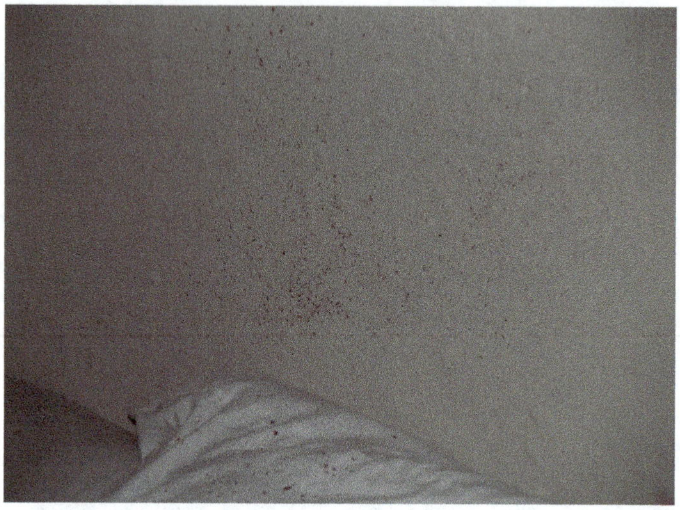

FIGURE 5.22 Impact Pattern.

Insect Stain: A bloodstain resulting from fly activity.

FIGURE 5.23 Insect Stain.

Parent Stain: A bloodstain from which a satellite stain originated.

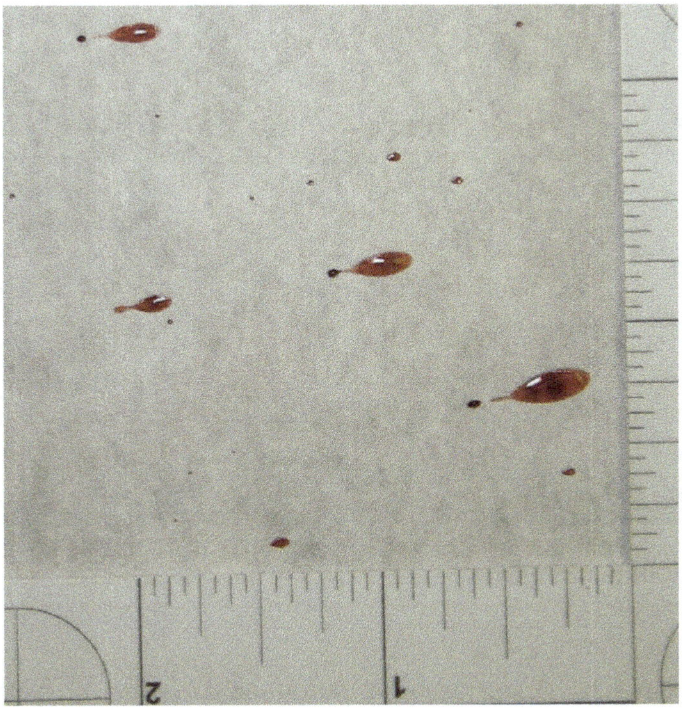

FIGURE 5.24 Parent Stain

Perimeter Stain: An altered stain that consists of the peripheral characteristics of the original stain (i.e., *skeletonized stains*).

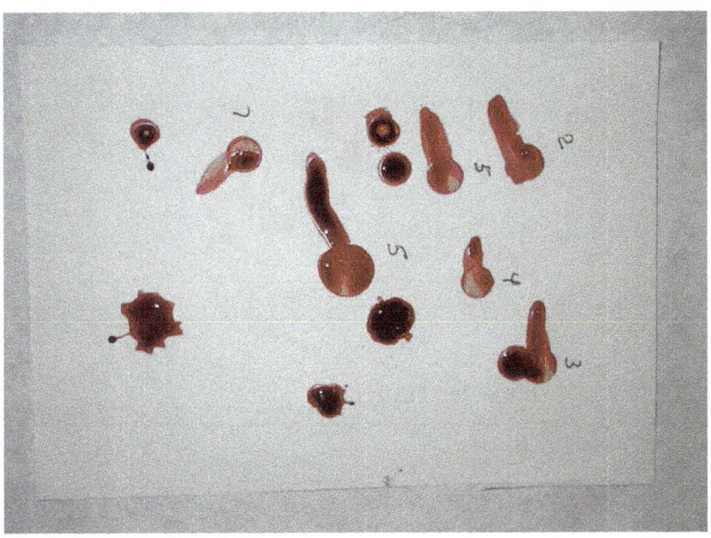

FIGURE 5.25 Perimeter Stain

Pool: A bloodstain resulting from an accumulation of liquid blood on a surface.

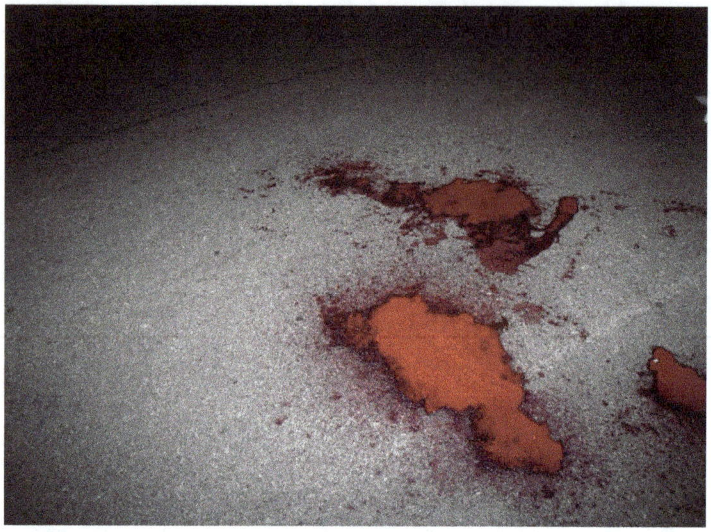

FIGURE 5.26 Pool

Projected Pattern: A bloodstain pattern resulting from the ejection of a volume of blood under pressure (i.e., *arterial gushing/spurts*).

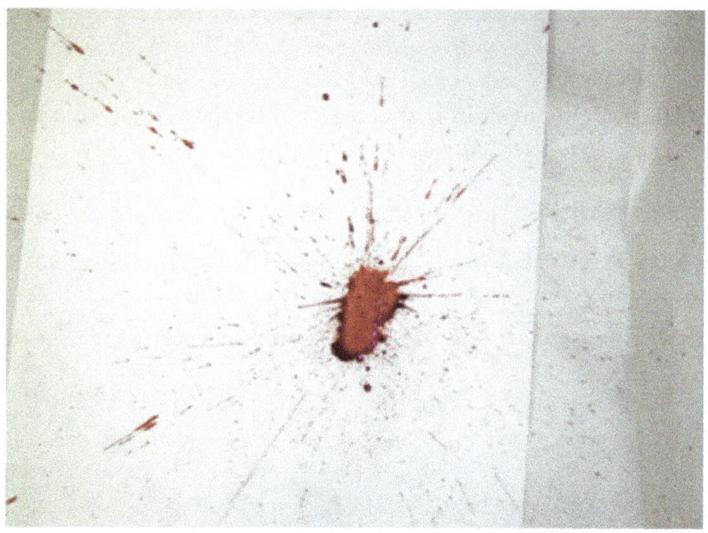

FIGURE 5.27A Projected Pattern

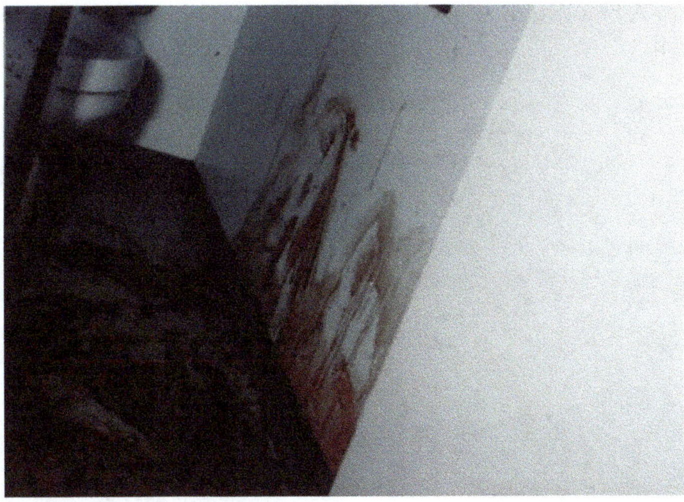

FIGURE 5.27B Projected Pattern.

Satellite Stain: A smaller bloodstain that originated during the formation of the parent stain as a result of blood impacting a surface.

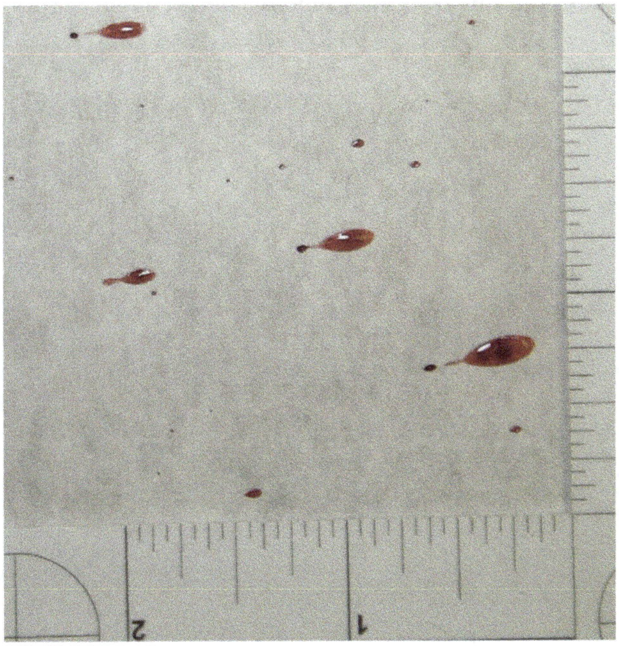

FIGURE 5.28 Satellite Stain

Saturation Stain: A bloodstain resulting from the accumulation of liquid blood in an absorbent material.

FIGURE 5.29 Saturation Stain

Serum Stain: The stain resulting from the liquid portion of blood (serum) that separates during coagulation.

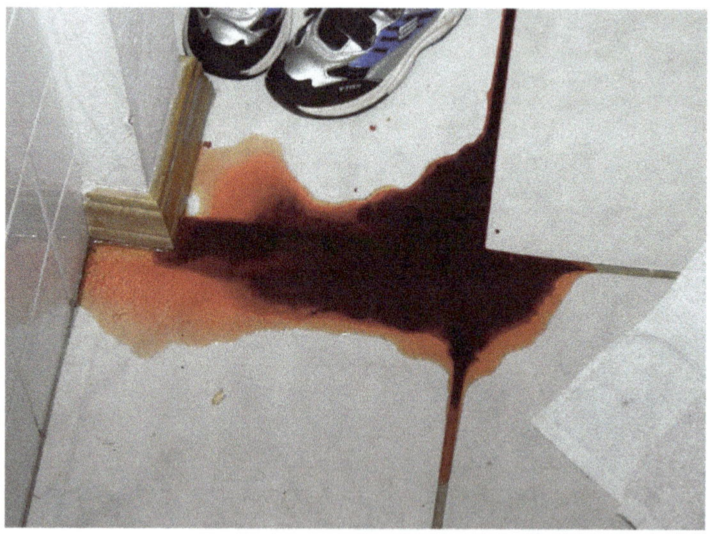

FIGURE 5.30 Serum Stain

Spatter Stain: A bloodstain resulting from a blood drop dispersed through the air due to an external force applied to a source of liquid blood.

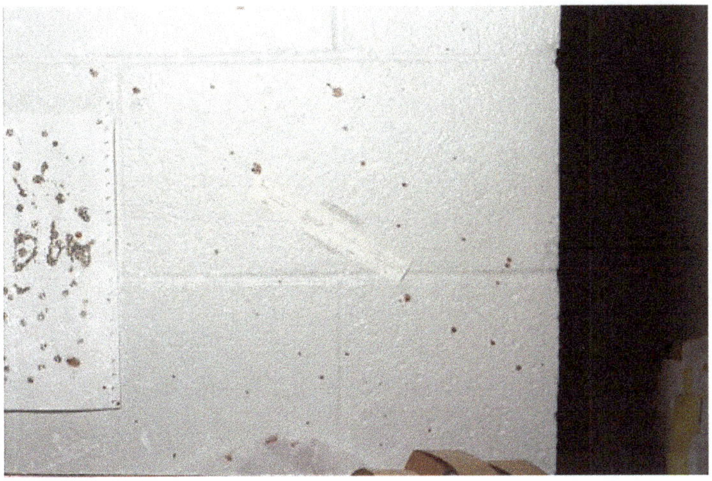

FIGURE 5.31 Spatter Stain

Splash Pattern: A bloodstain pattern resulting from a volume of liquid blood that falls or spills onto a surface.

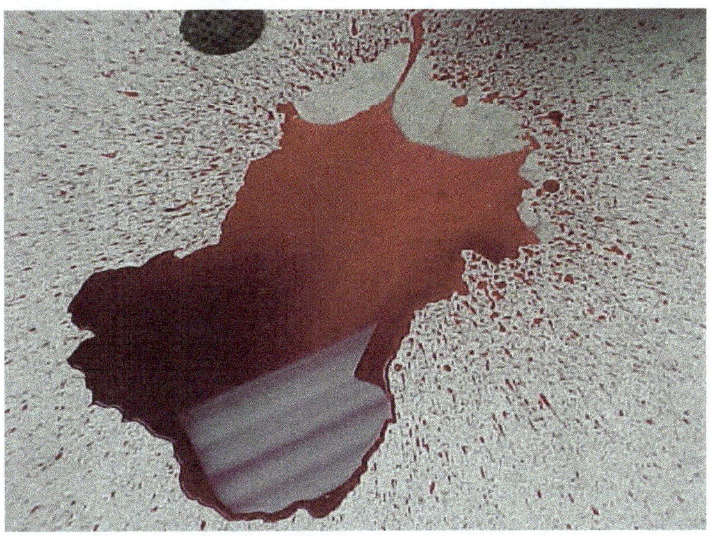

FIGURE 5.32 Splash Pattern

Swipe: A bloodstain pattern resulting from the transfer of blood from a blood-bearing surface onto another surface, with characteristics that indicate relative motion between the two surfaces.

FIGURE 5.33 Swipe

Target: A surface onto which blood has been deposited.

FIGURE 5.34 Target

Transfer Stain: A bloodstain resulting from contact between a blood-bearing surface and another surface.

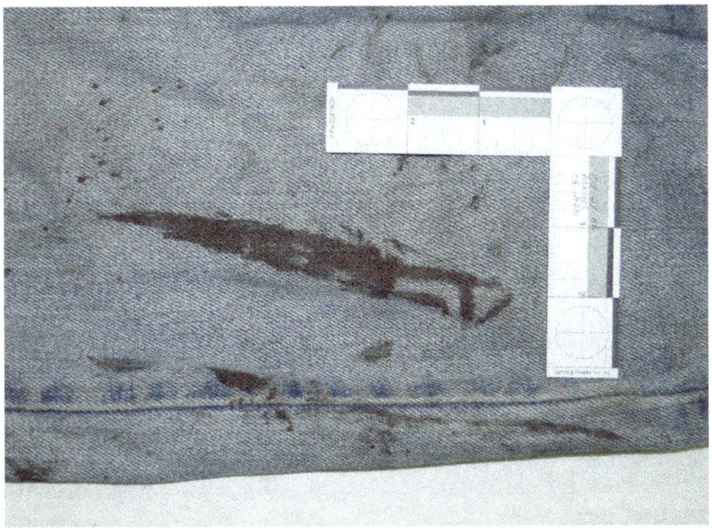

FIGURE 5.35 Transfer Stain.

Void: An absence of blood in an otherwise continuous bloodstain or bloodstain pattern.

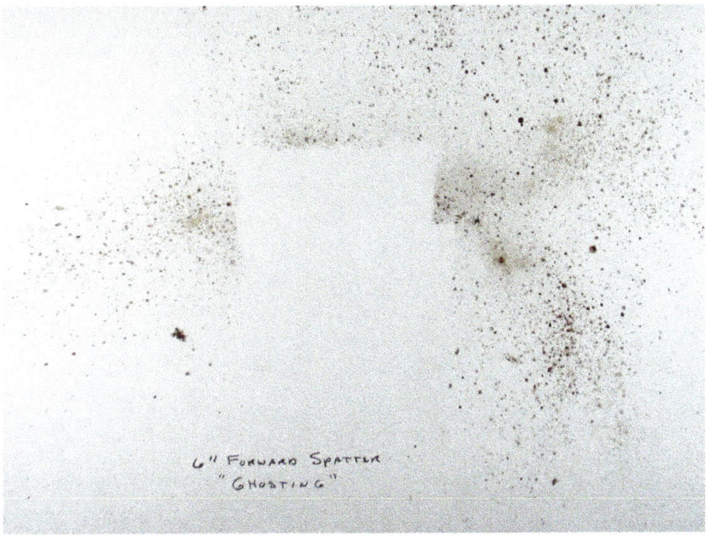

FIGURE 5.36 Void

Wipe: An altered bloodstain pattern resulting from an object moving through a preexisting wet bloodstain.

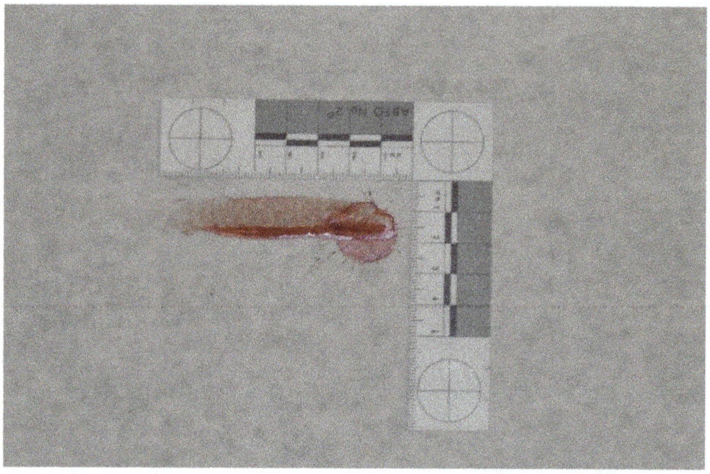

FIGURE 5.37 Wipe

Note: The Organization of Scientific Area Committees (OSAC) subcommittee for Bloodstain Pattern Analysis proposed the following changes to SWGSTAIN terminology: (1) elimination of the term "mist pattern," (2) changing "fly spot" to "insect activity," and (3) changing the term "flow pattern" to "flow."

CHAPTER 6

Factors Related to Bloodstain Evidence

Blood as a Fluid

- Blood as a fluid makes up 8 percent of the total body weight. Blood is more resistant to flow than water due to its viscosity; that is, blood is 4.4 parts to 1 part water (4.4:1), which is due to the proportion of cellular material to the fluid. Blood also has an adhesive quality. This stickiness results in pattern transfers in the crime scene.
- Fluids are generally incompressible, as they must displace in some fashion in response to force. This is the basis of hydraulics. The displacement of blood by force results in spatter.
- Twenty percent of the body's total volume of blood is in a passive flow.

Bloodstain Evidence Is a Reproducible Phenomenon

- The same physical laws apply to blood as to other fluids.
- Surface tension, viscosity, gravitational pull, and the laws of physics are applied equally.
- You don't have to understand the physical laws that are in effect to recognize the results.

Blood droplets retain spherical shape in flight due to the following:

- Surface tension
- Molecular bonding, which causes the liquid to occupy the smallest space possible (a sphere)
- Retention of shape until acted upon by other forces

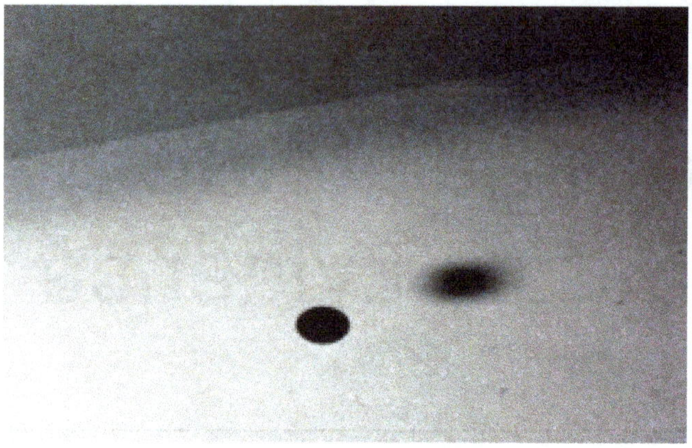

FIGURE 6.1 Example of blood droplets retaining spherical shape in flight.

Blood in Flight

- Viscosity or thickness of blood along with surface tension help control the oscillation.
    - Simply stated, viscosity is the *resistance to flow.*
- The damping, or the time it takes blood to stop oscillating, is immediate for small drops upon leaving the body. Larger drops, however, require more time for oscillation to stop.
- **Terminal velocity** occurs when gravity offsets air resistance.
    - Research has shown that dropping distance affects overall stain size.
        - Velocity increases as the droplet falls.
        - As distance increases, the speed also increases until the stain reaches terminal velocity.
            - The average-sized stain reaches (0.05 ml) terminal velocity at approximately 25 ft per second.

Impact angles are based on the belief that a blood droplet impacting a surface is in the shape of a sphere.

- Target surface is the most critical element.
    - The smoother the surface, the more probable that the stain will be usable.
    - A rougher surface will cause the stain to distort.
        - Distorted stains eliminate the ability to decipher anything of value.

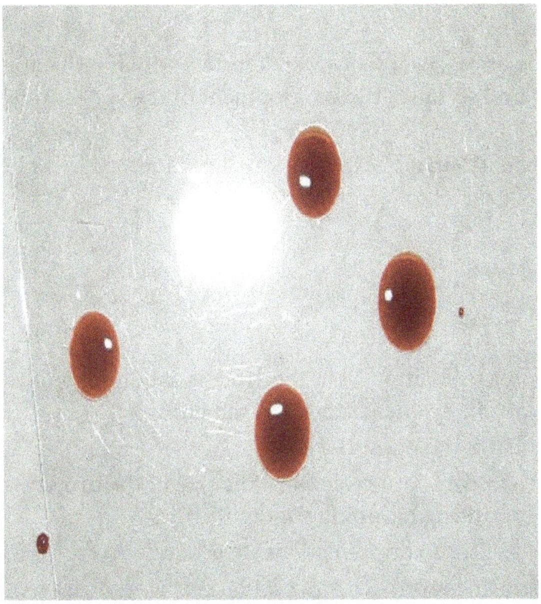

FIGURE 6.2 Smooth Target Surface

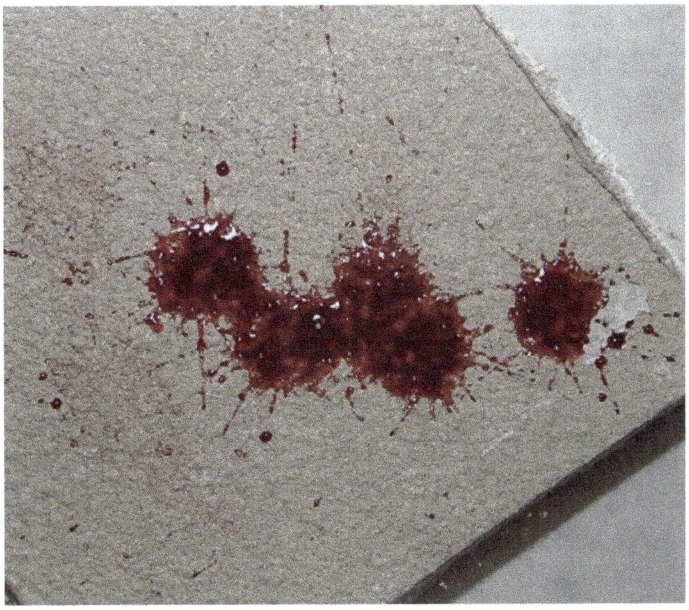

FIGURE 6.3 Rough Target Surface

- A 90° stain will have a rim that is equal on all sides.
- A 20° stain will be more elliptical, because the expanding boundary of the blood flow is primarily into the areas of the rim opposite the direction from which the droplet originated.
    - If sufficient force (inertia) is present, the droplet will break apart, causing satellite spatter.

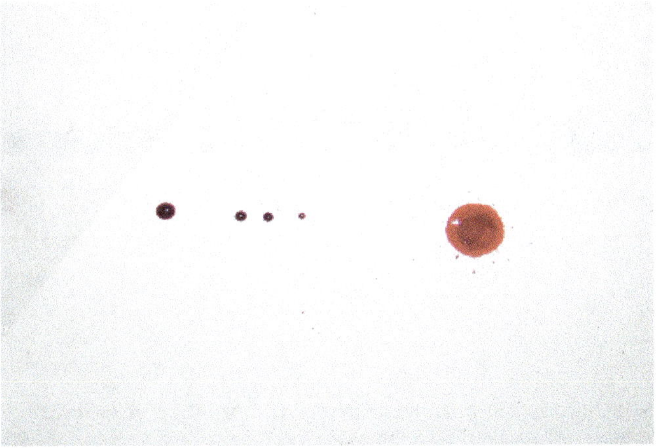

FIGURE 6.4 90° Stain

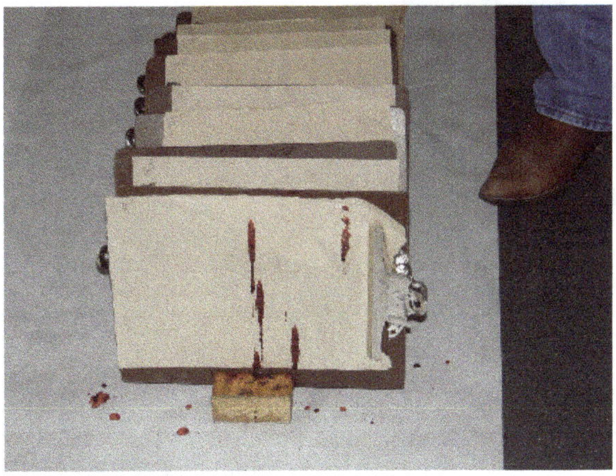

FIGURE 6.5 10° Stain

Oscillation

- When a fluid is disrupted by outside forces, oscillations are created, which influence the spherical nature of the droplet and initiates the development of the sphere into other forms (see Figures 6.6 and 6.7).
- Primary concerns related to the formation and perpetuation of oscillations include the following:
  - The means of disruption
  - The size of the droplet
  - The time in flight before impact
  - The viscosity of the fluid
- Surface tension plays a role in damping oscillations, but the process of damping time has demonstrated an inverse relationship to the viscosity of the fluid.
  - The greater the viscosity, the faster the damping time.
- Research on raindrops has suggested a correlation between the size of the droplets, the size of the oscillations, and the resulting damping time.
  - In droplets of 0.5 mm in diameter, little to no oscillations were found to be present.
  - In droplets of 5 mm in diameter, however, distinct oscillations were observed.
- Over time, oscillations will be damped.
  - The greater the time in flight, the longer the droplet has to return to its spherical shape.

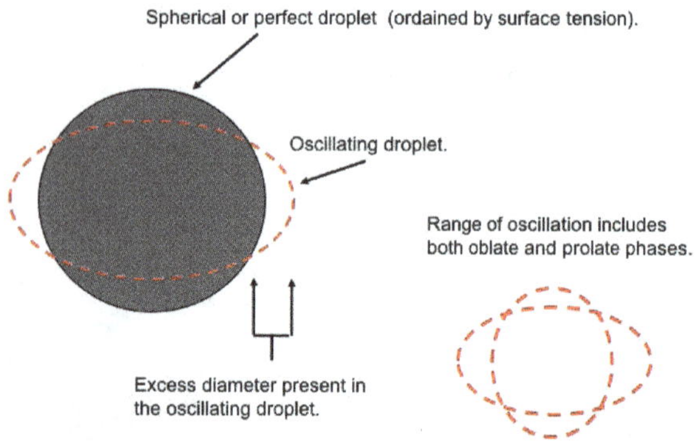

FIGURE 6.6 Oscillation Diagram

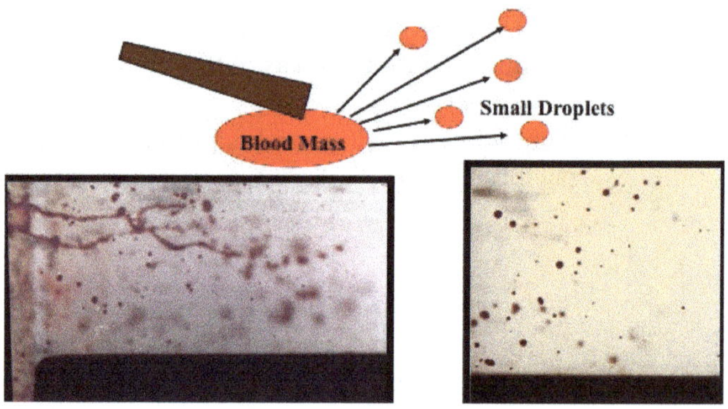

FIGURE 6.7 Oscillation Photo with Diagram.

References

Bevel, T., & Gardner, R. M. (1990). *Bloodstain pattern analysis and practice: A laboratory manual.* CRC Press.

Peterson, I. (n.d.). Raindrop oscillations: Raindrops do more than just fall; they also appear to oscillate during their downward plunge. *Science News, 127,* 136–137.

Figure Credits

Fig. 6.6: Tom Bevel and Ross M. Gardner, *Bloodstain Pattern Analysis with an Introduction to Crime Scene Reconstruction*. Copyright © 2008 by CRC Press.

Fig. 6.7: Tom Bevel and Ross M. Gardner, *Bloodstain Pattern Analysis with an Introduction to Crime Scene Reconstruction*. Copyright © 2008 by CRC Press.

CHAPTER 7

Uses of Bloodstain Evidence

Primary uses include the following:

- Directionality
- Impact angle
- Types of force
- Number of blows struck
- Positioning of the victim/assailant during the assault

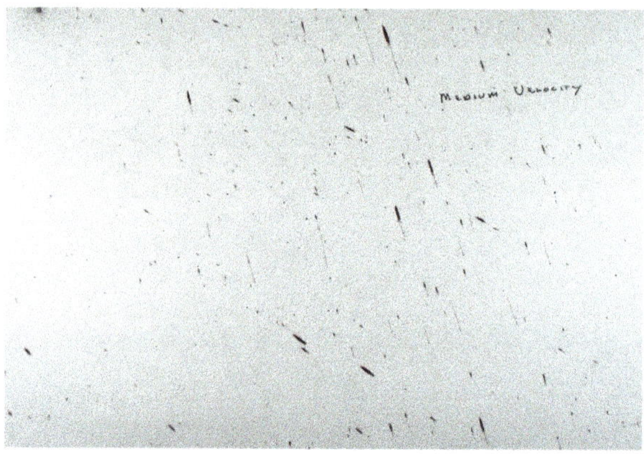

FIGURE 7.1 Directionality (Medium-Energy Spatter)

Example of medium-energy spatter—the stain will point in the direction of the force.

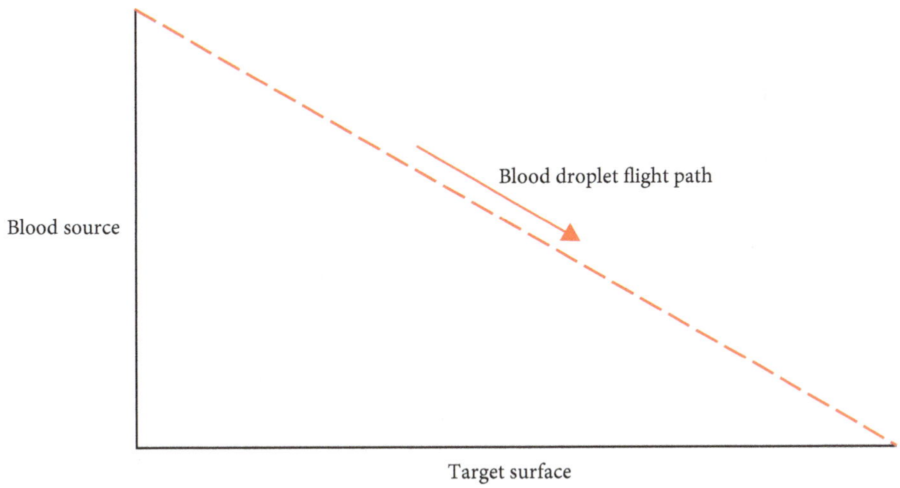

FIGURE 7.2 Directionality

Directionality

- Inertia caused by the motion of the droplet forces a wave of blood to form.
  - The wave wells up on the opposite point from where the stain struck.
  - The stain will point in the direction of the force.
    - If a wave breaks off from the parent stain, a satellite stain is formed.
    - The satellite stain will point back toward the parent stain.
- The pointed end of the resulting bloodstain will always *point in the direction of travel.*

Impact Angle

- When blood strikes a surface, a right triangle is created.
  - The triangle exists between the target surface and the line of travel.
  - Using mathematical principles, the impact angle can be determined by the following formula: width divided by length, then taking the second sine to determine the impact angle.

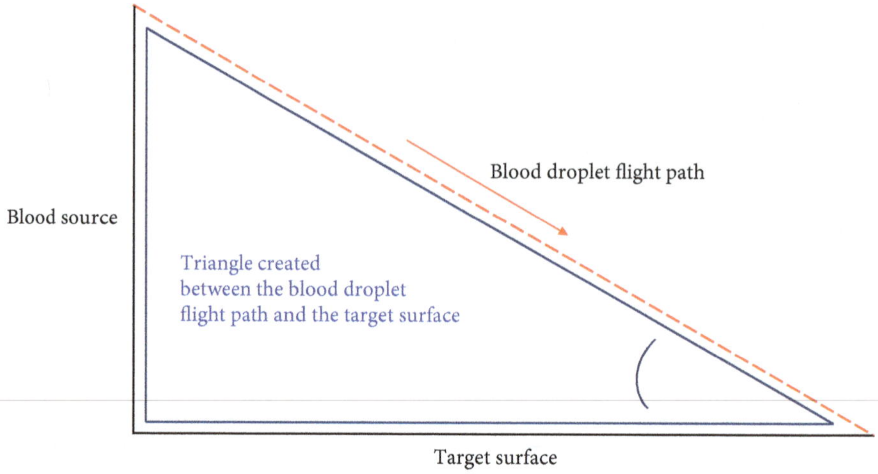

FIGURE 7.3 Impact Angle Diagram Example

Impact Droplet Size

- The volume of blood in a droplet determines its stain size.
- The force/energy transferred from impact to blood mass is what causes a droplet.
- Once in flight, a droplet maintains its volume.
- Smaller droplets attain and hold a true spherical shape quicker.
- A blood droplet of 2 mm in diameter will result in spatter 4 mm to 5 mm in size.

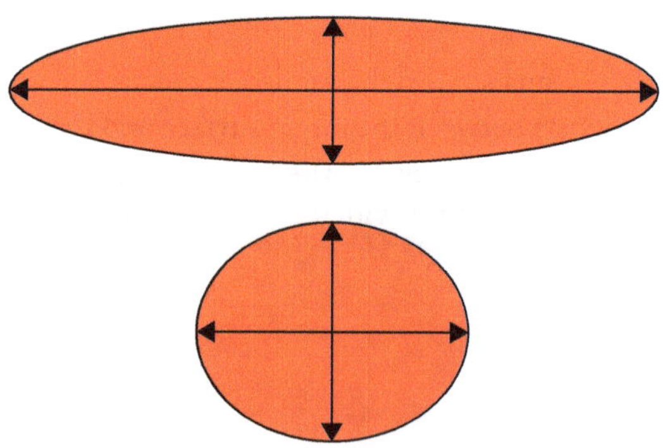

FIGURE 7.4 Well-Formed Stains Diagram

Well-Formed Stains

- A well-formed stain is one that, if divided along its axis, has opposite sides that are approximately equal.

Using a number of well-formed stains, you can establish parameters under which the stain was created.

- Minimum of four well-formed stains

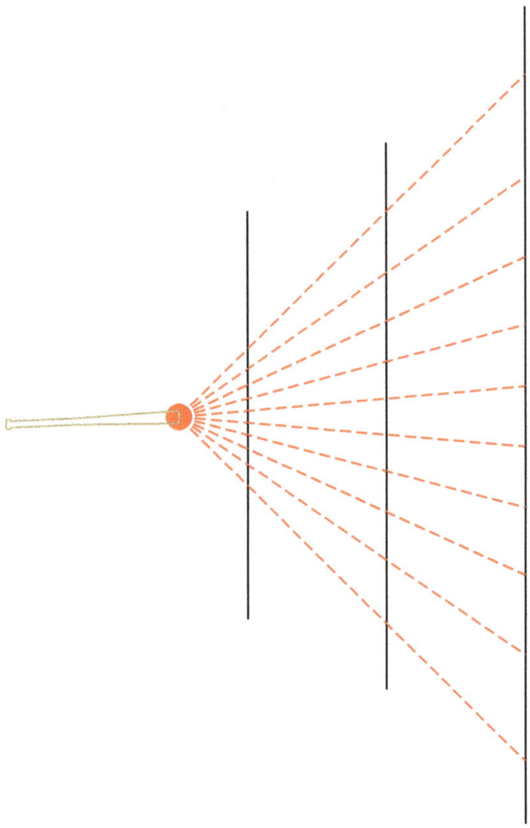

FIGURE 7.5 Impact Spatter Pattern Configuration Diagram

Impact Pattern Configuration

- Patterns disperse or radiate outward.
- The closer the impact site is to the target, the more stains you will find per square inch.
- The greater the distance, the fewer stains per square inch.
- Smaller droplets do not carry as far as large ones.
- The angle and surface of the weapon may cause significant variations in the resulting stains.

Blood does not travel in a straight line. Both gravity and air resistance affect the droplet, creating distinct arched parabolas.

- Analysts use straight-line geometry and basic trigonometry to determine the end and beginning of these parabolas. This strategy should not be viewed as inaccurate; instead, it is important to understand that it provides the investigator with a set of parameters.
    - Studies indicate this method is accurate to within +/- **5 degrees**.
- Computer software, such as BackTrack, takes this into consideration and modifies the parabolic arc when it's calculating the impact angle.

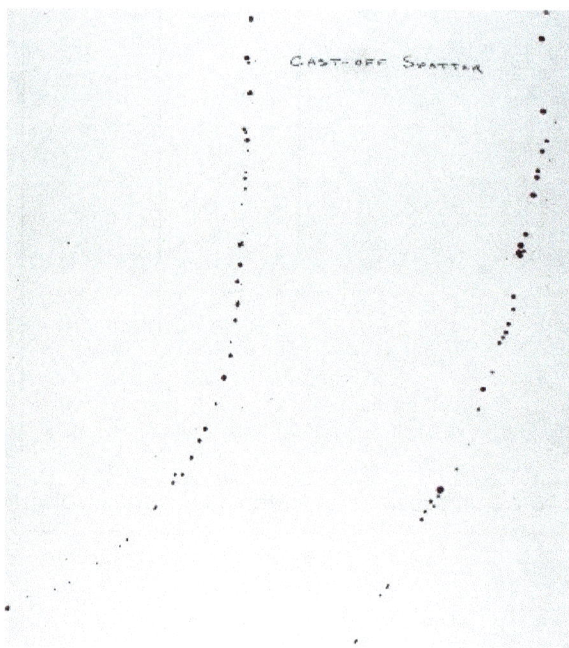

FIGURE 7.6 Cast-Off Stains

Cast-Off Stains

Cast-off stains occur from two actions:

1. Centrifugal force: as the bloody object is swung
2. Inertia: the cessations of the swing

Number of Blows Struck

- In blunt force trauma injuries, cast-off stains help determine the minimum number of blows.
- They are produced from blood coming off the swinging object.
- Cast-off stains occur as trails.
- Counting the cast-off trails and grouping them into forward and backward swings, the number of blows is apparent.
    - Add an additional blow to the number because the first blow is unlikely to have bloodied the object.
        - Using cast-off stains, it is possible to tell in which hand the assailant held the object.
- A 90° cast-off spatter gives an indication of the assailant's pivot point, which oftentimes can position the assailant at the time of the assault.

Gunshot Spatter

- Forward spatter occurs when the projectile exits.
- Back spatter is always possible.
- The closer the target surface is to the blood source, the more spatter per square inch.
- The stain from a close target will have a mist or spray-painted look.
    - There is a lack of agreement on what forces cause spatter during gunshot injuries:
        - The temporary stretching and then collapsing of the surrounding tissue back to the final defect is one consideration.
        - Two or more successive shots will result in the first blood-filled wound to squirt out its blood, resulting in heavier volume stains.
    - *Forward spatter* tends to be more symmetrical than back spatter due to the force projecting the spatter traveling in the same direction.
    - *Back spatter* is less defined. It travels up to 4 ft and quickly loses speed. It has been known to dry in the air before hitting the ground, leaving blood flakes. The flakes may float in the air and be found further than 4 ft away from where they originated. Suspects within 4 ft of victim can expect to find bloodstains on both the clothing and the gun.

Distinguishing spatter from contact stains on clothing.

- Incidental contact: the deeper weaves of material are normally left untouched in a lateral motion.
- Projected spatter: the deeper weaves are likely to have staining (back spatter).
    - *Always recover the clothing.*

FIGURE 7.7 Sequencing Using Multiple Events

Things to remember:

- Do not make an evaluation based on one stain.
- It is not always possible to obtain all the various types of information.
- Conclusion must be considered against the relationship of other evidence.

Sequencing of Events

- Transfer patterns and the drying times associated with them are good indicators of assessing the sequence of events at a crime scene.
    - Contact transfers offer information concerning objects that have been in contact with other items at a scene.
        - Examples include swipes and wipes
- Evaluating the drying time of droplets is a practical assessment tool in the sequencing of events, because a ring begins to form on the outer edge of a droplet within the first 50 s of its creation.
    - This process is called skeletonization.
- Additional considerations:
    - Generally, the location with the greatest bloodshed depicts the ending point of an event; whereas the location with the least blood spatter represents the point at or near where the violence began.

CHAPTER 8

Angle of Impact

Bloodstain mathematics is used to assist with the reconstruction of a crime scene.

- In most instances, this will be used with medium-energy spatter to determine the position of the victim and/or assailant during the assault.
- To determine the area of origin (a range), a trigonometric formula is used.

Angle of Impact Formula

- Before the area of origin is found, the angle of impact of several suitable stains must be found.
    - When blood strikes a surface, a right triangle is created.
    - The triangle exists between the target surface and the line of travel.
- Using mathematical principles, the impact angle can be determined.
    - Sine-1 W/L = angle of impact
        - Example:
            - Width = 5 mm
            - Length = 7 mm
            - Sin-1 5/7 = 45.58
            - Angle of Impact = 45–46°
    - L/W (number greater than 1), then use sine chart to find the angle of impact (see Appendix).

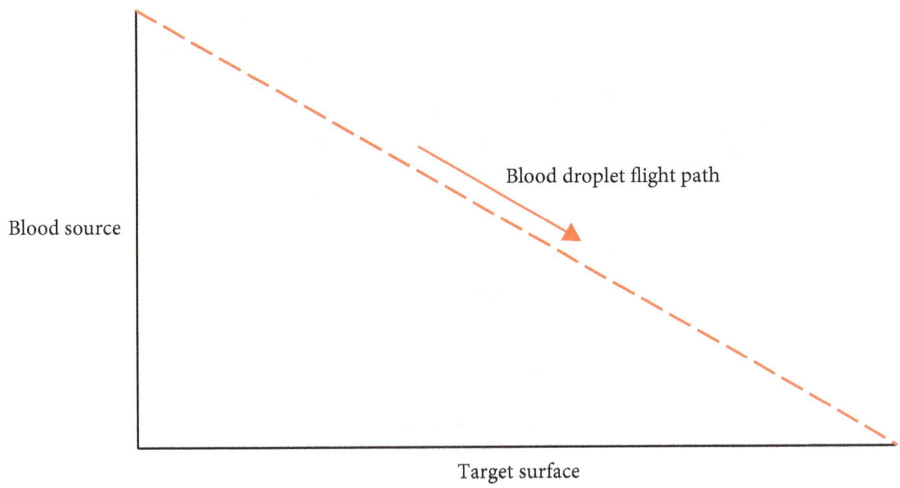

FIGURE 8.1 Impact Angle Diagram Example

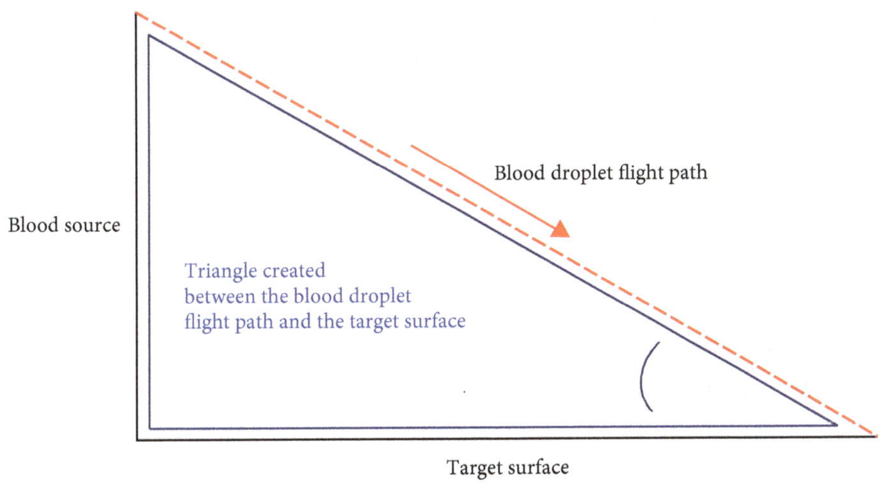

FIGURE 8.2 Impact Angle Diagram Example

(*Note*: Remember that blood falls in parabolic arcs that are affected by volume, gravity, and air resistance.)

- The area of origin is considered a range, but provides parameters to give insight into the position of the victim/assailant, and their relationship within the scene.

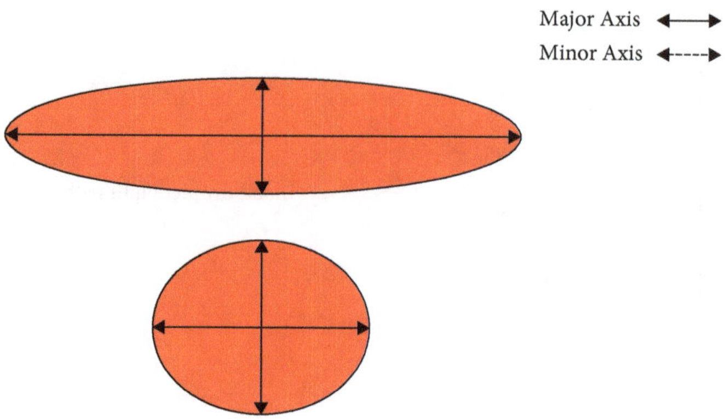

FIGURE 8.3 Well-Formed Stains Diagram

Well-Formed Stains

- A well-formed stain is one that, when divided along its axis, the opposite sides are approximately equal.
    - Not all bloodstains are truly elliptical in shape.
        - To measure a bloodstain correctly, one must find the true ellipse.

Tools Needed

- A drafting divider
- A ruler or micrometer
- A photographic loupe

First Step

- Measure the width of the bloodstain at its widest point.
    - Measure from side to side.

FIGURE 8.4 Measuring Bloodstains Diagram—"First Step"

Second Step

- Place a mark on each side of the bloodstain at the widest point.

FIGURE 8.5 Measuring Bloodstains Diagram—"Second Step"

Third Step

- Keep the divider tip that is in the center stationary.
- Rotate the divider tip from the top edge of the bloodstain to the bottom edge of the bloodstain.

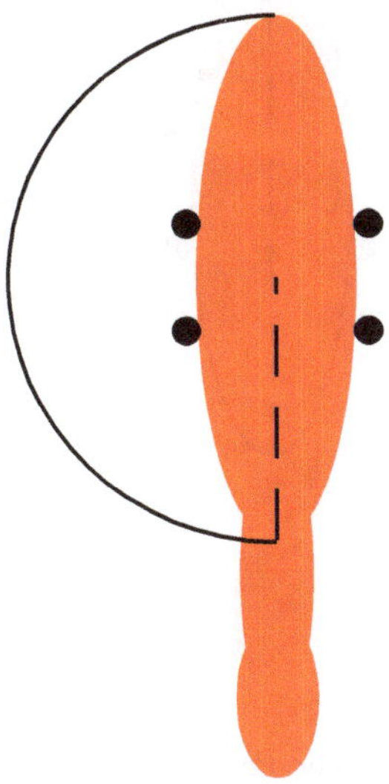

FIGURE 8.6 Measuring Bloodstains Diagram—"Third Step"

Fourth Step

- Extend the center divider tip to the top of the bloodstain.

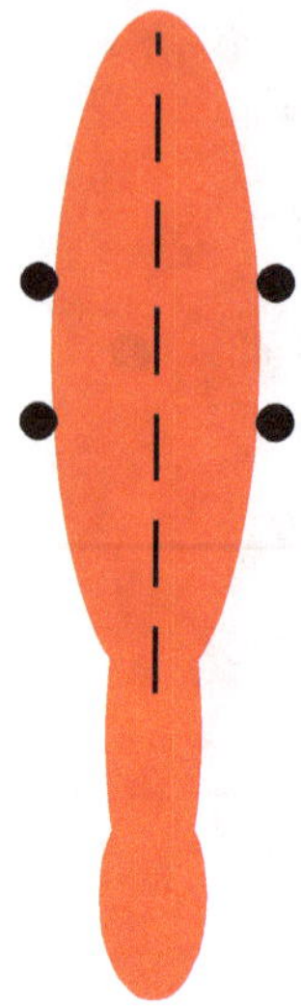

FIGURE 8.7 Measuring Bloodstains Diagram—"Fourth Step"

Fifth Step

- This closes the ellipse out and gives the analyst a length measurement.
    - For example, see the 9 mm in Figure 8.9.

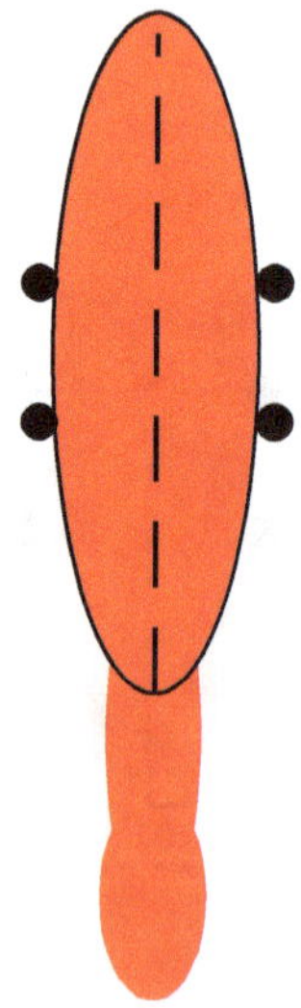

FIGURE 8.8 Measuring Bloodstains Diagram—"Fifth Step"

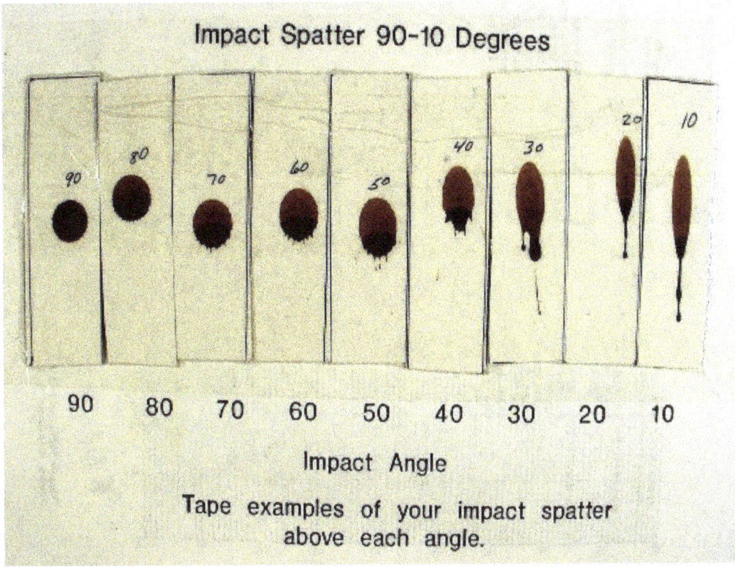

FIGURE 8.9 Impact Spatter Measured 90°-10°

Example:

- Bloodstain measures 3 mm wide and 9 mm long.
    - 3 mm divided by 9 mm = 0.33333
    - 0.33333 inverse or 2nd sin = 19.47°

Reference

Bevel, T., & Gardner, R. M. (1990). *Bloodstain pattern analysis and practice: A laboratory manual*. CRC Press.

CHAPTER 9

Blood-Borne Pathogens

Biological Hazards

- The BPA analyst must be aware of potential hazards associated with human biological evidence.
- They must follow precautionary measures to ensure their safety.
- Biological hazards are substances that pose a threat to human health, which can include:
    - Bacteria
    - Viruses
    - Fungi
    - Parasites
- Primary biohazards are the following:
    - Hepatitis (C in particular)
    - AIDS

Transmission Potential

- Direct contact with blood or a bodily fluid that may contain the pathogen.
- Airborne exposure through a mucous membrane.
    - Eyes
    - Mouth
    - Nose
- Contact through non-intact skin (e.g., prior open injuries).
    - Contact through injury with contaminated sharp instruments and needles. (*Note*: Direct and mucous membrane contact is low risk; injury site exposure is a greater risk.)

Universal Precautions

- Use proper personal protective equipment (PPE).
- Treat all blood and bodily fluids as if they were contaminated.
- Use proper cleanup and decontamination procedures.
- Dispose of all contaminated material in the proper manner.

Personal Protective Equipment (PPE)

- Anything that is used to protect a person from exposure.
- Tyvek, nitrile gloves, goggles, mouth barriers, aprons, and respirators.

PPE Rules to Remember

- Always check PPE for defects or tears before using.
- If PPE becomes torn or defective, remove and get a replacement.
- Remove PPE before leaving contaminated area.
- Do not reuse disposable equipment.

Decontamination

- When cleaning up surfaces, use prepared mixture (10% bleach or 1:10).
- Do an initial wipe up (small stains).
- Spray and allow it to stand for 10 min, then wipe up.
- Dispose of all wipes in biohazard containers.
- PPE should be removed and disposed of in biohazard containers.
- Call security for large stains.

Regulated Medical Waste

- Liquid or semi-liquid blood or other potentially infectious material (OPIM).
- Contaminated items that would release blood or OPIM when compressed.
- Contaminated sharps
  - Pathological and microbiological waste containing blood or OPIM

Reference

Bevel, T., & Gardner, R. M. (1990). *Bloodstain pattern analysis and practice: A laboratory manual*. CRC Press.

CHAPTER 10

The Scientific Method

The scientific method should be applied to any situation in which reconstruction is pursued. The implementation of the scientific method is used to maintain uniformity of standards in the field. Lucien Haag developed the most widely utilized technique, referred to as **PhD ic,** for the purpose of recall and application of the steps involved in the process. Ross Gardner and Tom Bevel (Gardner & Bevel, 2009) later expanded on the acronym, replacing the "ic" with "etc" to emphasize the testing of expectations and predictions before arriving at an ultimate conclusion.

PHD IC (Haag)

- Problem
- Hypothesis
- Data
- Interpretations
- Conclusions

PHD ETC (Gardner and Bevel)

- Problem
- Hypothesis
- Data
- Expectations/Predictions
- Testing
- Conclusions

PHD ETC

Problem

- The investigative questions being considered.

Hypothesis

- Identify all the viable ways an action could have been accomplished, based on the incident review and observations.

Data

- Collect all data that relates to the specific investigative question for potential resolution of the problem.

Expectations/Predictions (*Interpretations in Haag)*

- Identify predictions of what one would expect to find.
- Simple if "this" then "that" statements regarding the scene or the evidence.

Testing

- Test each hypothesis against all data developed from the investigation (scene context, lab analysis), seeking to falsify each hypothesis.

Conclusions

- State an opinion based on the results of this analysis.
- Repeat for each variable.

Reference

Gardner, R., & Bevel, T. (2009). *Practical crime scene reconstruction.* CRC Press.

CHAPTER 11

Laboratory Experiments

When close to a wall it creates a "V" pattern.

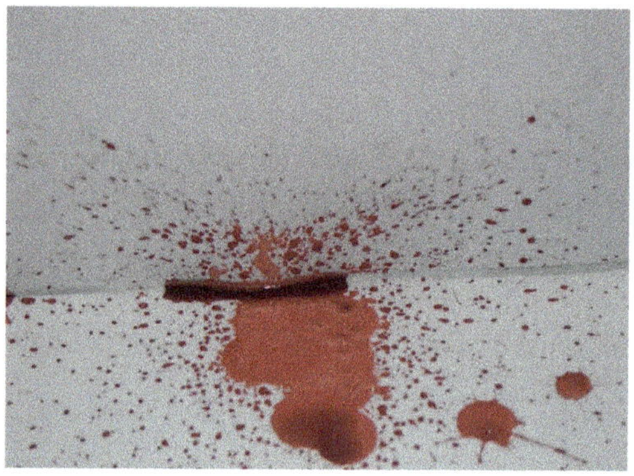

FIGURE 11.1 Blood Dripping into Blood.

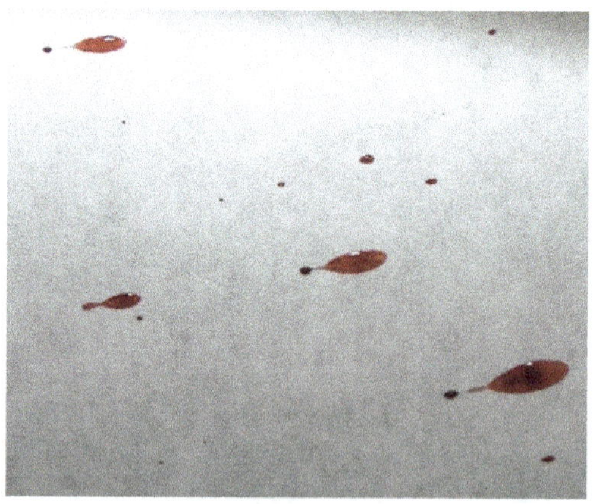

FIGURE 11.2 Medium-Energy Spatter Showing Directionality.

EXPERIMENT 1

Stain Shape Versus Angle of Impact

Objective: To produce stains in which the blood is dropped from a known distance onto target surfaces affixed at known angles between 10° and 90°. The resulting stains will be measured and the angles of impact calculated. The calculated angles will then be compared with the known angles.

Procedure

1. Place smooth-surface white targets into known angle slots from 10° to 90°.
2. Mark each target surface with its known angle and identity of examiner(s).
3. Fill a pipette with liquid blood.
4. Position the pipette 4 ft over the target surfaces.
5. Allow several drops to fall on each target, forming separate stains.
6. Allow each target to set for a minimum of 5 min after the last drop prior to target movement.
7. After the bloodstains have set, remove each target from its angled slot.
8. Measure the length and width of the stains, and record those measurements in the table provided. (*Note*: See instructor before measuring stains.)
9. Calculate the length/width ratio for stains at each known angle.
10. Plot those ratios on the graph paper provided.
11. Use a flexible guide to graph the ratio plots.
12. Repeat the above process with the rough-surface blotter targets. These targets can be measured prior to drying.
13. After the smooth-surface stains have dried completely, cut samples of stains from each angle. Tape the samples in order to the provided page.
14. When the instructor advises, calculate the angles of impact from the bloodstain measurements.

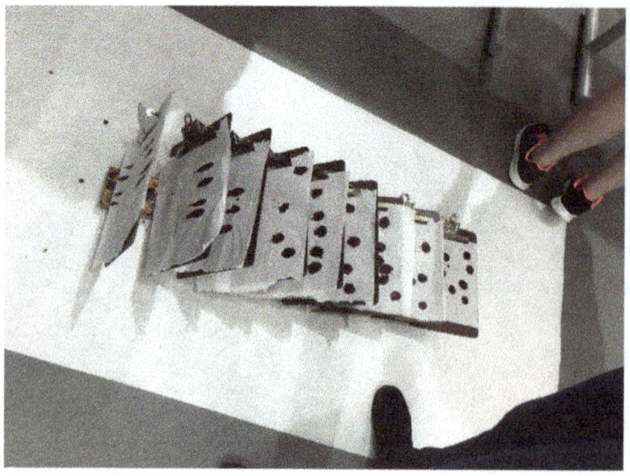

FIGURE 11.3 Experiment 1—Stain Shape Versus Angle of Impact.

FIGURE 11.4 Experiment 1—Stain Shape Versus Angle of Impact.

Equipment Needed

1. A sheet of 36″ × 48″ butcher paper
2. 2″ × 4″ board with known angles cut into it
3. Nine clipboards placed on top of the butcher paper
4. Poster board
5. Paper towel cut into 8″ × 11″ targets
6. Pipette
7. Container for blood

Data Paper Targets

Impact Angle	Width (mm)	Length (mm)	Calculated Angle (width/length)	Length/Width Ratio
90°				
80°				
70°				
60°				
50°				
40°				
30°				
20°				
10°				

Blotter Targets

Impact Angle	Width (mm)	Length (mm)	Calculated Angle (width/length)	Length/Width Ratio
90°				
80°				
70°				
60°				
50°				
40°				
30°				
20°				
10°				

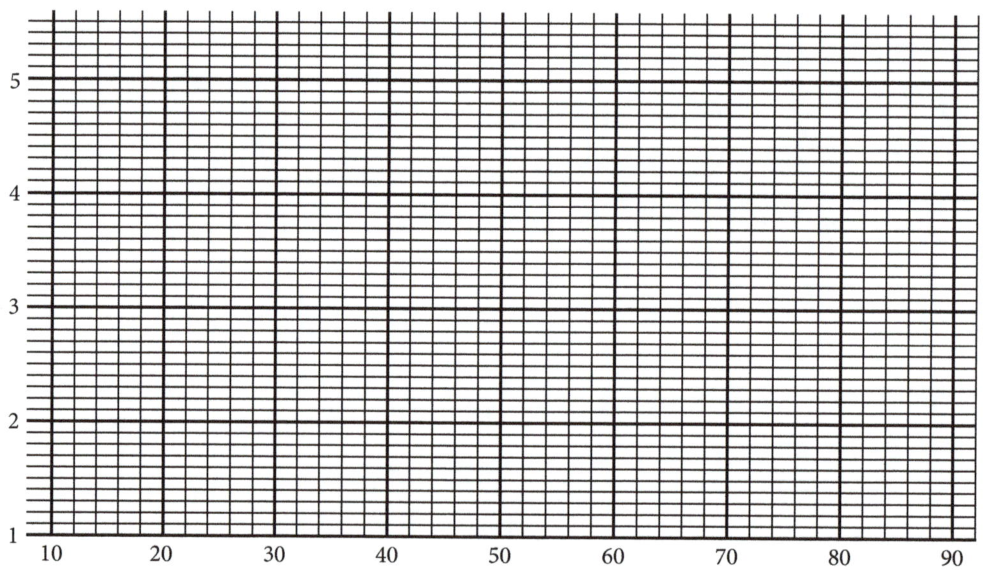

10°	20°	30°	40°	50°	60°	70°	80°	90°

Observations

Questions

1. Describe any observed correlation between the shapes of the stains at 10°, 30°, 60°, and 90°.

2. What is the shape of the graph produced by the length/width ratios?

3. How did the stain shapes on the smooth paper compare with the stain shapes on the blotter target?

4. Can you confidently calculate the angle of impact for stains on the blotter?

EXPERIMENT 2

Stain Diameter Versus Distance Fallen

Objective: To produce stains of a generally consistent volume from varying heights onto targets of glass or Plexiglas, paper, carpet and blotter paper.

Procedure

1. Affix a vertical strip of masking tape on a wall. Be sure the strip is of tape is straight.
2. Mark the tape at 3″, 12″, 36″, 72″, and 96″.
3. Place glass on the floor near the masking tape strip.
4. Fill the pipette with blood.
5. Hold the pipette steady and vertical, with the tip of the pipette 96″ above the floor.
    1. Allow a single blood drop to fall onto the glass.
6. Measure the diameter of the resulting bloodstain. Record that measurement on the provided table.
7. Clean the glass and repeat the procedure, holding the pipette at each of the marked measurements.
8. Repeat the procedure using the paper, blotter, and carpet, respectively.
9. Repeat the procedure by allowing blood to drop from two objects, one with a small surface area, such as an ice pick, and one with a large surface area, such as a hammer. Allow blood to fall from the objects at 3″, 12″, and 36″ above the floor. Measure the resulting stains and compare with stains produced by the pipette.

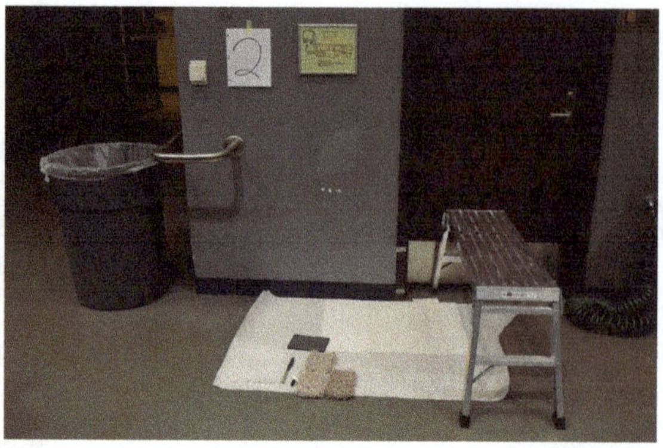

FIGURE 11.5 Experiment 2—Stain Diameter Versus Distance Fallen

FIGURE 11.6 Experiment 2—Stain Diameter Versus Distance Fallen

Equipment Needed

1. 36″ × 36″ piece of butcher paper
2. Masking tape
3. Tape measure
4. Marker
5. Wall or flat surface
6. Butcher paper to be placed on the floor below the tape
7. Targets can vary but need to include a smooth surface (glass, mirror, poster board, carpet) and rough surface (blotter paper, paper towel).
8. Pipette
9. Container for blood
10. Any object that blood can be transferred to and then dripped onto targets (i.e.: hammer, knife, screwdriver, etc.)

Stain Diameter

	Distance	Paper	Blotter	Glass	Carpet
Pipette	3 in.				
	12 in.				
	36 in.				
	72 in.				
	96 in.				
Object:	3 in.				
	12 in.				
	36 in.				
Object:	3 in.				
	12 in.				
	36 in.				

Observations

Questions

1. Describe any observed correlation between the distance fallen and the stain diameter.

2. Describe any observed correlation between distance fallen and the shape of the resulting stain.

3. Compare the stains formed on each of the different target surfaces.

4. What factors determine the size of the bloodstain?

5. What is *terminal velocity*?

Cast-Off Stains

Objective: To produce stains by the motion of bloodied objects.

Procedure

1. Hang lengths of paper to simulate two walls and a ceiling.
2. Place liquid blood on one end of an object.
3. Face one "wall," such that the second "wall" is behind you.
4. Swing the bloodstained object using forceful forward and backward motions.
5. The bloodstained object should not contact the "walls" or "ceiling."
6. Repeat three or four successive swings of the object. Replenish blood on the object between swings.
7. Note the size and distribution of bloodstains produced by the motion.
8. Mark the bloodstain patterns to indicate the type of object and whether it was made using the right hand or the left hand.
9. Repeat the procedure, using the same object and technique, while holding the object in the opposite hand.
10. Replace the target paper and repeat the procedure with an object with a different surface area.

FIGURE 11.7 Experiment 3—Cast-Off Stains

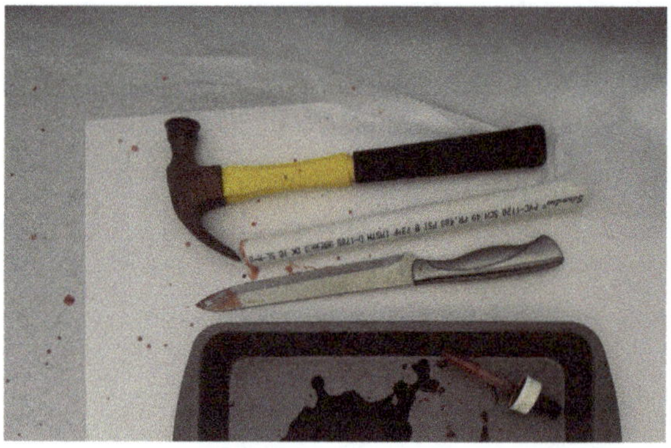

FIGURE 11.8 Experiment 3—Cast-Off Stains

FIGURE 11.9 Experiment 3—Cast-Off Stains

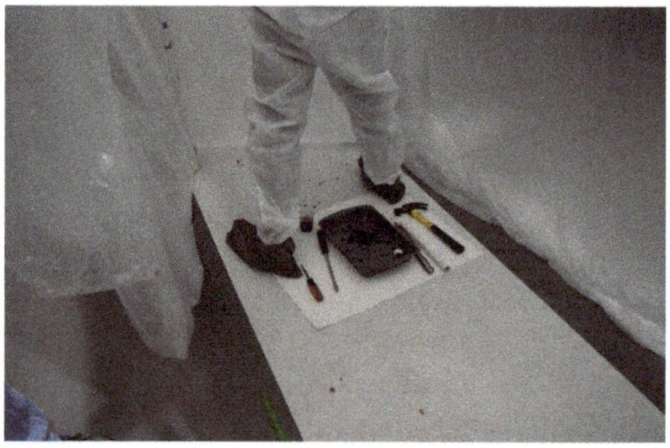

FIGURE 11.10 Experiment 3—Cast-Off Pattern

Equipment Needed

1. PVC pipe
   a. Build a cast-off frame with ¾″ PVC pipe that measures 7′ tall × 7′ long × 36″ wide.
2. Butcher paper
   a. Drape 36″ butcher paper over the frame, creating two walls and a ceiling. Place a clear plastic drop cloth on both sides of the frame, using clamps to contain the cast-off stains. Place 36″ × 7′ piece of butcher paper on the floor inside the cast-off frame. Place a baking pan in the center of the floor to catch the blood dripping off the objects used. Place several objects with various surface widths, along with a pipette and container of blood, next to the baking pan.

Setup for Alternate Cast-Off Frame

1. Two pieces of ¾″ PVC pipe cut at 36″ lengths.
2. Two pieces of small rope with "S" hooks on each end.
   a. The "S" hooks can be attached to the ceiling; the length of the rope will depend on the ceiling height to reach a 7′ ceiling height and 7′ length inside the cast-off frame.
3. Butcher paper will be draped over the frame to create two walls and a ceiling.

Cast-Off Data

Object	Right or Left Hand	Number of Forward Swing Trails	Approx. Stain Width	Locations of Stains

Observations

Questions

1. Explain the location and cause of any 90° stains in the patterns formed.

2. Can the directionality of the swing be determined from the stain pattern? Explain.

3. Was there a difference in stains produced by the forward swing and stains produced by the back swing? Explain the nature and cause of any differences noted.

4. What differences, if any, were produced by the right-hand swing versus the left-hand swing?

EXPERIMENT 4

Impact Spatter from Forceful Impacts

Objective: To produce spatter patterns by applying "medium-energy" force to blood.

Procedure

1. Tape together three pieces of poster board end-to-end and position the paper to form three sides of a box.
2. Place the mousetrap 12 in. from the center paper. Place a piece of poster board on the horizontal surface inside the vertical walls.
3. Fill the pipette with blood.
4. Deposit blood onto the open front edge of the mousetrap to produce a blood pool about 1 in. diameter.
5. Allow the top of the mousetrap to drop closed, impacting the blood pool.
6. Record observed bloodstains.
7. Turn the paper over to expose the unstained surfaces.
8. Wipe remaining blood from mousetrap and then prepare another blood pool as described above.
9. Slam the mousetrap closed.
10. Record observed bloodstains.
11. Repeat the observed procedure, placing the mousetrap 18 in. from the target surface.

FIGURE 11.11 Experiment 4—Impact Spatter from Forceful Impacts

Equipment Needed

1. Butcher paper to be placed under the mouse trap
2. Three poster boards taped together at the edges with masking tape to create three vertical walls
3. One poster board under the mouse trap to represent a floor
    a. The mousetrap can be constructed with two pieces of 2″ × 4″ board connected at one end with a door hinge.
4. Pipette
5. Container for blood
6. Paper towel for cleaning mouse trap between experiments
7. Tape measure
8. Marker

Setup

1. Measure a distance of 12″ and 18″ from the back wall and mark the distance on the floor of the experiment.
2. The poster board walls should be marked **12 D** on the bottom of the simulated wall and **12 S** on the top of the wall.
3. Repeat this on the opposite side of the poster board with **18 D** and **18 S.**
4. The 12″ drop is first and a bloodstain pattern will be created along the bottom of the wall.
5. Turn the wall over so the bottom of the wall is now the top of the wall.
6. Repeat the experiment with the 12″ slam.

7. Once this is completed, turn the poster board walls inside out and repeat the experiment at 18″.

Range of Spatter Diameter

Impact Distance	Largest Spatter Diameter	Smallest Spatter Diameter	Preponderant Diameter
12" Drop			
12" Slam			
18" Drop			
18" Slam			

Observations

____

____

____

____

____

____

Questions

1. Was there an observable difference in the range of stain sizes between the drop impact and the slam impact? If so, what caused the difference?

____

____

____

____

____

____

2. Was there an observable relationship between the shape of the overall stain pattern and the location of the mousetrap? Explain.

____

____

____

____

____

____

3. Describe the size, shape, and distribution of bloodstain patterns.

4. Define "medium-energy impact" as it relates to bloodstain patterns.

EXPERIMENT 5

Impact Spatter from Explosive Force

Objective: To produce spatter patterns by applying an explosive force to blood.

Procedure

1. Secure the revolver in the rack such that the revolver is aimed down range through the target.
2. Fill the pipette with blood. Place the blood on a sponge until the sponge is saturated.
3. Suspend the blood-soaked sponge from the center of the rack, such that the sponge is in the trajectory line of the revolver barrel.
4. Hang a paper target 6" behind and in front of the sponge.
5. Clear all participants from the area around and in front of the experiment area.
6. Load one .22 short cartridge in the cylinder of the revolver.
7. Fire one shot through the paper targets and sponge.
8. Remove the fired cartridge case from the revolver cylinder, leaving the cylinder in the open position.
9. Remove the targets and record observed bloodstains on each target.
10. Repeat the procedure with targets 12″ from the sponge.
11. Repeat the procedure with targets 18″ from the sponge.
12. Attach a denim swatch to the center of a paper target. Hang that target 6″ in front of the sponge and fire a .22 short cartridge into the sponge. There are two observations to be made:
    a. High-energy spatter into clothing versus a paper target.
    b. Removing the denim from the paper target to expose the void where the denim was.

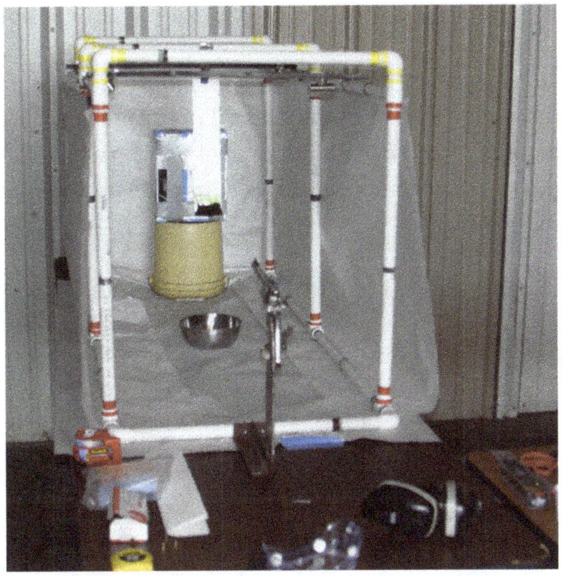

FIGURE 11.12 Experiment 5—Impact Spatter from Explosive Force

Alternative Procedure

1. A **pump pellet gun** can be used in place of the .22 caliber revolver. You can also saturate the **bristles of a toothbrush** with blood and point it toward a target.
2. Using your thumb drag it across the top of the toothbrush bristles and the resulting bloodstains will simulate a high-energy impact spatter. (*This method is used by the authors when teaching at the University of Central Oklahoma due to the banning of any firearms on campus.*)

Equipment

1. Pipette
2. Sponge
3. Revolver, toothbrush, or pellet gun
4. Poster board
5. Denim swatch
6. ¾″ PVC pipe
7. Paper clips
8. Commercial firearm trap, two large telephone books or two packets of plain paper

Setup for Using a Firearm

1. Use ¾″ PVC pipe to build a 72″ L × 28″ W × 24″ H frame. Along both sides of the width, the top of the frame should have grooves to support removable target holders.
2. The center of the frame should have a hanger for a blood-soaked sponge. The sponge is held in place by a larger paper clip.
3. Grooves on both sides of the sponge at 6″, 12″, and 18″.

4. The target holders should have two larger paper clips attached to hold the targets in place.
5. A gun support should be placed at one end of the frame to secure a firearm or pellet gun. Make sure the firearm is secured in the holder.
6. The firearm should be in alignment with a trap at the other end of the frame.
7. A commercial trap can be purchased, or two large telephone books or two packets of plain paper can be taped together. The .22 caliber short ammunition will not penetrate the paper traps.
8. Once the firearm and trap are in alignment, position the sponge between them. The sponge can be taped to poster board on one end. The other end of the poster board should be placed in the paper clip at the correct height.

Range of Spatter Diameter

Impact Distance	Largest Spatter Diameter	Smallest Spatter Diameter	Describe Pattern Dispersal
6" back spatter			
6" forward spatter			
12" back spatter			
12" forward spatter			
18" back spatter			
18" forward spatter			
6" denim back spatter			

Observations

Questions

1. Was a preponderant range of size produced by the high-energy experiment? If so, what was the range of diameters of those stains?

2. Was there an observable difference in distribution of stains in the patterns made at 6″, 12″, and 18″ impacts? If so, what caused the difference?

3. What differences exist between the forward spatter stain patterns and the back spatter stain patterns if a firearm was used?

4. How did the stain pattern on the denim compare with the pattern on the surrounding paper?

EXPERIMENT 6

Streaming Ejections/ Projected Blood

Objective: To produce stains created by a streaming ejection of blood volume.

Procedure

1. Draw 3 cc liquid blood into a syringe.
2. Hold the syringe level at a distance of 24″ from a vertical target.
3. Apply constant pressure to the syringe, forcing the blood out of the syringe.
4. Record observed blood motion and stains.
5. Repeat the procedure at a distance of 60″ from the vertical target.
6. Repeat the procedure with horizontal targets at 24″ and 60″ distances.
7. Record observed blood motion and stains.
8. Pour 3 cc liquid blood onto a horizontal target to form a blood pool.
9. Stomp on the blood pool, and then walk across the target away from the blood pool.
10. Record observed bloodstains.
11. Pour 3 cc liquid blood onto a gloved hand.
12. Slap the gloved hand onto a horizontal target.
13. Slap an unstained portion of the target with the bloodied gloved hand.
14. Record observed bloodstains.

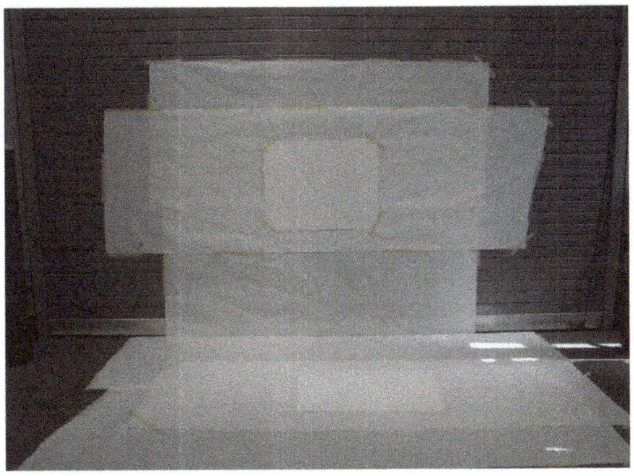

FIGURE 11.13 Experiment 6—Streaming Ejections/Projected Blood

FIGURE 11.14 Experiment 6—Streaming Ejections/Projected Blood

Equipment Needed

1. Poster board
2. Butcher paper
3. Masking or painter's tape
4. Tape measure
5. Marker
6. Syringe
7. Container to hold blood
8. Rubber gloves
9. Pair of old shoes

Setup

1. Take three 36″ × 96″ sheets of butcher paper and tape them on a wall horizontally, slightly overlapping each sheet.
   a. Repeat this process on the floor below the wall.
2. Place a second sheet of butcher paper over the middle sheet of butcher paper.
   a. This sheet will be changed out after each group has completed the experiment and new sheets of butcher paper will be put up for the next group.
3. Place a full sheet of poster board in the center of the second sheet of butcher paper on both the vertical and horizontal surfaces.
4. The poster board represent your targets.
5. Measure 24″ and 60″ using a tape measure and place a mark on one edge of the butcher paper on both the vertical and horizontal surfaces.

Observations

Pressure Source	Impact Distance	Description of Stains
Syringe	24"	
Syringe	60"	
Stomp	contact	
Walk	contact	
1st slap to target	contact	
2nd slap to target	contact	

Observations

____

____

____

____

____

____

Questions

1. Was a difference in patterns evident between the 24″ projection and the 60″ projection? If so, describe the difference.

   ____

   ____

   ____

   ____

   ____

   ____

2. Describe the appearance of the resulting satellite spatter.

   ____

   ____

   ____

   ____

   ____

   ____

3. Identify the source of any capillary action that affected stains produced by the stomp and slap.

   ____

   ____

   ____

   ____

   ____

   ____

4. Describe the size, shape, and distribution of the bloodstain patterns.

Stomp:

Slap:

EXPERIMENT 7

Low-Pressure Ejections/ Blood into Blood

Objective: To produce stains by allowing blood volumes to fall on target surfaces.

Procedure

1. Place 3 cc liquid blood into the beaker.
2. Hold the beaker 24″ above a horizontal paper target.
3. Turn the beaker over in a single motion, allowing the entire volume of blood in the beaker to fall to the target.
4. Record observed blood motion and stains.
5. Repeat the procedure at a distance of 60″ above a target.
6. Record observed blood motion and stains.
7. Hold the beaker 24″ from a vertical target.
8. Flip the wrist to allow the entire volume of blood in the beaker to splash onto the vertical target. (Do not throw the blood from the beaker.)
9. Record observed bloodstains.
10. Attach two targets to form a vertical and horizontal surface.
11. Fill the pipette with liquid blood.
12. Position the pipette 24″ above the horizontal target and about ½″ in front of the vertical target.
13. Allow blood to drip from the pipette onto the horizontal target, forming a blood pool on the horizontal target and a bloodstain pattern on the vertical target.
14. Record the observed bloodstains.

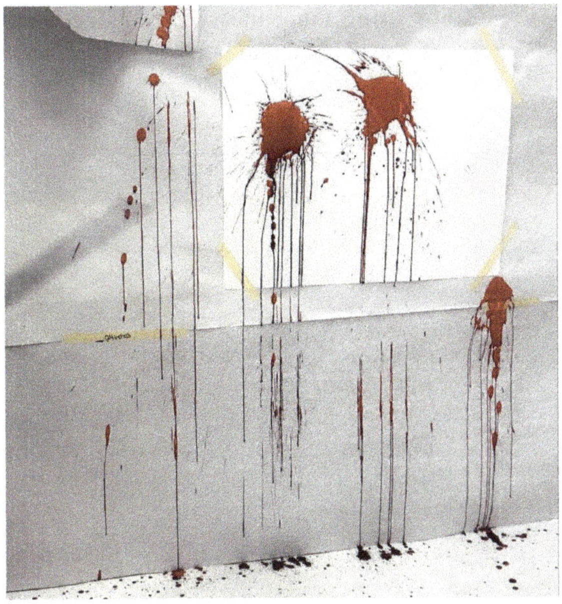

FIGURE 11.15 Experiment 7—Low Pressure Ejections/Blood into Blood

Equipment Needed

1. Poster board
2. Butcher paper
3. Masking or painter's tape
4. Tape measure
5. Marker
6. Syringe
7. Container to hold blood
8. Rubber gloves

The same equipment used in Experiment 6 will be used in this experiment. The only difference is that instead of using a syringe you will need a **small beaker.**

Setup

1. Take three 36″ × 96″ sheets of butcher paper and tape them on a wall horizontally, slightly overlapping each sheet.
   a. Repeat this process on the floor below the wall.
2. Place a second sheet of butcher paper over the middle sheet of butcher paper.
   a. This sheet will be changed out after each group has completed the experiment and new sheets of butcher paper will be put up for the next group.
3. Place a full sheet of poster board in the center of the second sheet of butcher paper, on both the vertical and horizontal surfaces. The poster board represents your targets.

4. Measure 24″ and 60″ using a tape measure and place a mark on one edge of the butcher paper on both the vertical and horizontal surfaces.

Observations

	Overall Dimensions of Pattern	Description of Stains
Pour 24"		
Pour 60"		
Splash		
Blood into Blood		

Observations

____

____

____

____

____

____

Questions

1. What scenarios could explain splashed blood in a crime scene?

2. Compare the splashed bloodstains with the projected bloodstains produced in Experiment 6. What are the differences, if any?

3. Compare the blood-into-blood pattern with blunt-impact spatter. What is the cause of any similarities in pattern? How can they be distinguished?

4. Describe the size, shape, and distribution of bloodstains in the following patterns.

Pour:

Splash:

Blood-into-blood:

Transfer Stains

Objective: To produce transfer stains by contact of bloodied surfaces with unstained surfaces.

Procedure

1. Place blood on the surface of an object.
2. Strike the object onto a paper target.
3. Replenish the blood on the object surface.
4. Press the object onto an unstained target surface.
5. Replenish the blood on the object surface.
6. Fold a cloth target around the bloodied object, as if preparing to wipe the object.
7. Replenish the blood on the object surface.
8. Wipe the object with an unstained cloth target.
9. Record observed bloodstains.
10. Repeat with other objects.

FIGURE 11.16 Experiment 8—Transfer Stains.

Equipment Needed

1. 6″ × 6″ pieces of clothing material.
   a. White cotton fabric is most commonly used.
   b. T-shirts can be purchased at Goodwill for $1.00 and then cut up into squares.
2. Butcher paper
3. One sheet of poster board
4. Telephone book
5. Various tools or kitchen utensils that blood can be placed on, then transferred to the clothing items
6. Eye dropper
7. Container to hold blood

Observations

Object	Mechanism	Description of Stains
	Paper strike	
	Paper contact	
	Cloth contact	
	Cloth wipe	
	Paper strike	
	Paper contact	
	Cloth contact	
	Cloth wipe	
	Paper strike	
	Paper contact	
	Cloth contact	
	Cloth wipe	
	Paper strike	
	Paper contact	
	Cloth contact	
	Cloth wipe	

	Paper strike	
	Paper contact	
	Cloth contact	
	Cloth wipe	
	Paper strike	
	Paper contact	
	Cloth contact	
	Cloth wipe	

Observations

____
____
____
____
____
____

Questions

1. What patterns were present that might help identify the bloodied item?

____

2. What information from the cloth wipe patterns could be used to identify the item?

____

3. Did every stain have sufficient recognizable characteristics for recognition of the object that produced the stain? Explain.

____

4. Do repetitive contacts with the same object produce identical stains? Why or why not?

Determining Directionality in Blood Trails

Objective: To produce blood trails similar to those created by bleeding wounds on mobile victims, and to determine directionality, if possible.

Procedure

1. Prepare a target area by rolling out a length of butcher paper.
2. Fill an eyedropper with blood. Produce a blood trail by dropping the blood from a point waist high, while walking along the target.
3. Repeat the experiment utilizing a faster horizontal motion (running or walking at a fast pace).
4. Repeat the experiment a third time, walking, but this time include a significant swinging motion (back and forth) of the arm holding the eyedropper.

FIGURE 11.17 Experiment 9—Determining Directionality in Blood Trails.

Equipment Needed

1. Butcher paper 36″ × 120″
2. Eye dropper
3. Container to hold blood
4. An area where a person can walk and run next to the butcher paper, *not* on the butcher paper

Observations

Questions

1. Can you define overall directionality in a blood trail based on the shape of the resulting stains?

2. Did all stains point in a single direction? If not, why not?

3. What differences are observed in the shape of the stains between the walking and running target? What other type of pattern was observed in the drip trail produced by "swinging"?

EXPERIMENT 10

Drying Time of Blood

Objective: To evaluate the period of time required for blood to begin to dry, and for skeletonization to occur.

Procedure

1. Using pre-marked poster board, deposit a single drop into the areas marked for 0, 15, 30, 45, 60, 75, and 90 s. Begin timing this series of droplets as they are created.
2. Once deposited, immediately disrupt the 0-second stain. Do this by drawing a gloved finger through the stain (you are not trying to wipe the entire stain away, you simply wish to disrupt the edges of the stain). Repeat the disruption process for stains timed at intervals of 15, 30, 45, 60, 75, and 90 s.
3. Once completed, repeat this process for stains timed at intervals of 5, 10, 20, 30, and 40 min. This can be done at the same time as you continue the remainder of the experiment.
4. Have part of your group repeat the entire experiment in an area dissimilar to the original location. Consider an area that has greater air circulation, more/less heat, or direct sunlight.
5. Once complete and the stain has dried, measure the width of the skeletonized ring that is present. (You are not measuring the diameter of the stain, but rather the width of the widest section of dried skeleton.)
6. Record your observations in the table provided.

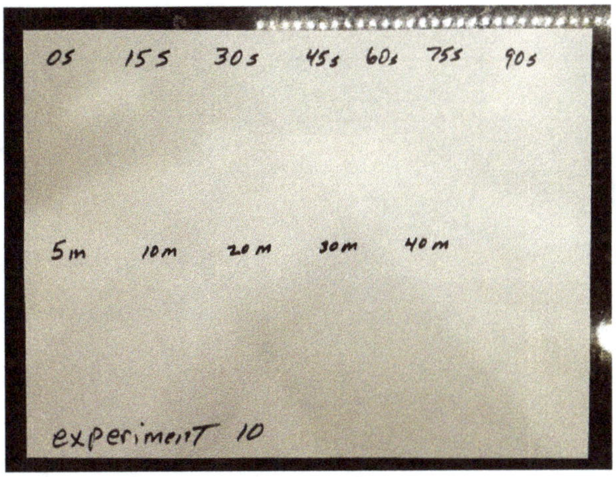

FIGURE 11.18 Experiment 10—Drying Time of Blood

Equipment Needed

1. Poster board
2. Timer
3. Eyedropper
4. Gloved finger to wipe through the stains

Drying Time/Stain Condition

Time	Paper Target	
	Ring Visible	Ring Width
0 s		
15 s		
30 s		
45 s		
60 s		
75 s		
90 s		
5 min		
10 min		
20 min		
30 min		
40 min		

Dissimilar Environment

Time	Paper Target	
	Ring Visible	Ring Width
0 s		
15 s		
30 s		
45 s		
60 s		
75 s		
90 s		
5 min		
10 min		
20 min		
30 min		
40 min		

Observations

____

____

____

____

____

____

Questions

1. Is there a point in time when the ring appears after blotting the droplets?

____

____

____

____

____

____

2. How long does the droplet take to dry completely? Is that consistent in dissimilar environments?

____

____

____

____

____

____

3. Could experimental effort provide a general time frame for drying time if environment and volume were known?

Reference

Bevel, T., & Gardner, R. M. (1990). *Bloodstain pattern analysis and practice: A laboratory manual.* CRC Press.

CHAPTER 12

Enhancement of Faint and Dilute Bloodstains with Chemical Reagents

Locating bloodstain evidence is not necessarily a simple process, as it's not always visible to the naked eye. This process can also be challenging when assessing whether the stains being examined are actually blood. Several chemical enhancement processes exist to assist the examiner in overcoming these hindrances and can be beneficial to the examination process in its entirety.

(*Note:* When using these chemical enhancements, always remember they are presumptive tests only. *They will not differentiate animal blood from human blood!*)

Enhancement reagents provide valuable assistance in crime scene processing and laboratory examinations. These enhancement reagents are designed for the following applications:

- Assists in the enhancement of pattern evidence found at a crime scene, on an item of evidence, clothing, or a body.
    - It assists in the recognition and identification of physical evidence.
- Assists in the interpretation and recognition of events, and identifies samples to be collected for further laboratory examination.
- Screens evidence and materials at a crime scene so valuable resources are not wasted on unwarranted laboratory analysis.
    - It provides the investigator with preliminary results in a timely manner, such as the fact that blood-like material was present.
- Provides a general indication of the existence of a chemical, physical, or biological substance and offers investigative leads.

Sources used to detect blood are the following:

- Alternate light source (ALS)
- Hemastix
- Luminol
- Fluorescein
- Blue Star
- Lueco Crystal Violet
- Fuchsin acid

Alternate Light Source (ALS)

- Blood will appear black on most surfaces under certain light ranges. An ALS should be employed before any chemicals are utilized and any indications should be photographed.
    - If the indication is of a fingerprint, shoe impression, or possible weapon, a scale should be used in the photograph.

Hemastix

- Simply rub the Hemastix across the sample in question and the response should be immediate. The Hemastix will turn a shade of green if hemoglobin is present, and this reaction should occur instantaneously. It is important to photograph any positive reaction.
    - The original purpose of Hemastix was to detect the presence of blood in urine.

Luminol

- Luminol is a presumptive test for blood. It reacts with the iron in the hemoglobin of blood and produces a blue glow when a reaction occurs. The location in which the process is conducted must be completely dark.
    - It can produce false positives.

Fluorescein

- The typical application of fluorescein is after a bloody crime scene has been cleaned up. Fluorescein produces a brighter and stronger image than Luminol, in addition to having a longer shelf life.
    - The solution is sprayed onto a target, allowed to dry briefly, and then sprayed with hydrogen peroxide solution.
        - The U.S. Food and Drug Administration (FDA) has accepted the use of Fluorescein for medical purposes on humans.

Blue Star

- The purpose of Blue Star is to reveal stains invisible to the naked eye.
    - The solution is sprayed onto a target, and a bluish color suggests a positive result.
        - The luminescence will fade quickly.
        - The technician must also perform this procedure on an unstained area to serve as a negative control.

Lueco Crystal Violet (LCV)

- LCV is a catalytic test specific to blood that produces a purple-colored stain when it reacts with blood. It should only be applied to dried blood impressions.

Fuchsin Acid

- Fuchsin acid is a water-soluble dye that reacts to the proteins found in blood. The purpose is to obtain a contrast with the background a technician may be presented with at a crime scene.

References

Bevel, T., & Gardner, R. M. (1990). *Bloodstain pattern analysis and practice: A laboratory manual.* CRC Press.

The Metropolitan Police Forensic Science Laboratory. (1980). *New presumptive test for blood.* Press FS 11.

CHAPTER 13

Bloodstain Documentation

Sufficient documentation of all evidence present in the crime scene is one of the most crucial aspects of processing a scene. It serves several functions, including the following:

- Verifying the scene's security.
- Providing a quality court presentation.
- Allowing outside analysis.
- Providing for independent defense evaluation.
- Recording relationships of evidence.

Several techniques, such as photographs, video photography, and sketches collected by the crime scene technician, assist in the subsequent evaluation process and courtroom presentation.

Outside Experts

- An outside expert is limited by the quality of the documentation that they are provided with.
- (Everyone else, you included, is also limited by the quality of your documentation.)

Defense Evaluations

- Police agencies are in constant pursuit of *the truth*! Objectivity is vital to the credibility of the BPA analyst.
- Proper documentation will provide less ammunition for the defense to question the evidence.

The following areas define proper documentation:

- Collection and detection of bloodstains and traces
- Photography of bloodstains, including videotape recordings
- Sketching techniques
- Written reports for bloodstain documentation

Collection

- The BPA analyst must recognize a pattern as defining some specific action.
- The bloodstains within the pattern must all be related to the action.
- This recognition must also consider collecting samples for DNA analysis.

Five issues in collecting stains for subsequent serology analysis are the following:

- Proper discrimination between stains
- Sufficient identification of samples to patterns
- Sufficient collection of samples
- Precluding cross-contamination of samples
- Sample collection prior to destructive testing

Proper Discrimination between Stains

- Failing to discriminate if a given stain belongs to a specific pattern will cause the serology information to be useless.
- The BPA analyst needs to be confident that the stains selected are representative of that pattern and only that pattern.
- Carefully documenting the location of each collected bloodstain insures that you will be able to relate it back to a specific pattern.
- Give each bloodstain collected an identifying number.
- Your narrative report might reflect the following:
    - Stain #1 from group A is approximately 2 × 2 mm. It is found on the west wall 2 ft up from the floor and 3 ft north of the south wall. This stain is scraped into a pharmacist's fold, sealed, and properly marked.
- Collection from each pattern group will give direction as to which bloodstains should be collected.
- Care must be given to insure there is no cross-contamination between stains that are collected.

Detection of Blood

- Never spray enhancement chemicals on any item of evidence until proper serology specimens are collected.
- Carry and use presumptive tests to assist you at the scene.

Documenting for What?

- If you are only documenting that there was blood loss, then a few photographs and a verbal description in your report is all that is needed.
- Even with minimal documentation, you should be able to estimate size.
    - Always put a scale of reference in your photos.
- If documentation that indicates the number of cast-off trails and spatter is warranted, then greater detail is required.

Minimum Photography Guidelines

- Document the entire scene.
- Take photos of evident pattern transfers, flows, and other fragile patterns early.
- Document all identified pattern groups or stains using evidence establishing shots.
- Take macro photos of all stains of interest; include a reference scale in each photo.
- In instances of spatter patterns, where point of origin determinations are made, document some of the individual spatter used in the determination.

Photographic Documentation

- First series has no identifiers.
- Second series has identifiers.
    - Overall
    - Mid-range (establishing shot)
    - Close-up (macro)

Overall (first series)

- The overall shot should be far enough back so that you are able to identify where in the room you are looking and should show the interrelationships between objects in the room.
- The first series will not have identifiers or scales of reference.

Mid-range (first series)

- The midrange picture should be an evidence establishing shot. It should be at a 90° angle.
- It should direct your attention to the area in question or of interest.
- It is still far enough back that you are able to tell where it is in relation to other objects.
- Again, the first series of photographs will not have any identifiers.

Place identifiers.

- Use place cards with either alpha or numeric identifiers.
- Mark each area associated with an occurrence with an identifier, such as "A," etc.
- So an "A", "B," and "C" would show three areas where a different blood-producing action occurred.

Select a minimum of four stains.

- Select a minimum of four well-formed bloodstains from each different occurrence.
- Select from a good range of coverage within each occurrence.
- Identify each selected bloodstain with group an individual identifier (A-1, etc.).

Overall (second series)

- The overall shot should be far enough back so that you are able to identify where in the room you are looking. Identifiers should be large enough to be readable in this shot.
  - It should show the relationships of objects in the room.
  - The overall should show the relationship of each occurrence group area to the others.

Mid-range (second series)

- The intermediate picture should be an establishing shot of each marked area.
  - It should be at a 90° angle.
  - It should direct your attention to the area in question or of interest.
  - This shot should show the relationship or location of each stain selected with this occurrence area.

Close-ups (second series)

- Within the pattern area, a minimum of four close-ups should be taken.
- These should be from throughout the pattern area and not all from the same area.
- The stains should be well formed.
- Each stain should have a stain of reference.
- Each stain should be identified (A-1).
- A-1 would indicate this stain is from group A and is number 1.
- Each stain should have information as to where it is (28″ up from the floor and 14″ E. of the W. wall).
- Each stain should show direction using a 360° protractor.

Run the three-dimensional (3D) strings.

- Following the determined impact angle for each stain selected, run a string from the leading edge of the stain to some object where the end of the string can be taped at the correct angle of flight path.

Documenting

- Each action that produced spatter was identified through using a different colored string.
  - In this case, one event is shown in blue, one in yellow, and one in red. The white strings on the yard stick show how far out from the wall the events occurred.
- Convergence: two dimensions on surface
- Origin: three dimensions out from surface

Roadmapping

- Roadmapping is a documentation strategy that is generally completed after the scene has been processed.
  - It was established by Toby Wolson in Dade County, Florida.

1. Label each pattern (i.e., Pattern A)

2. Add reference scales to outline the patterns.
3. Take overall photographs that demonstrate the relationships between the patterns.
4. Take overall photographs that demonstrate the overall pattern in question.
5. Take evidence-establishing shots (midrange) photographs to establish individual stains within the pattern.
   a. At least one label should be distinct in the photograph.
6. All close-up photographs should include a label.

Additional Methods

- Clothing items often require some means of pointing out the bloodstains.
  - Three ring reinforcements
    - Example: using circular ring reinforcements to illustrate the location of spatters on denim jean material.

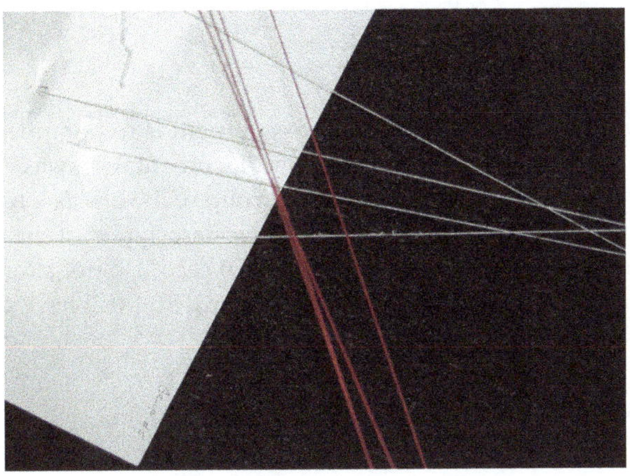

FIGURE 13.1 Roadmapping

Collecting Original Item of Evidence

- After properly documenting with photographs and measurements, representative samples of bloodstains from the same occurrence area should be collected for serological analysis.
  - Collect the clothing.
  - Swab the stains.

Forensic Software

- Point of origin information can also be analyzed using programs such as BackTrack and BackTrack/Strings. These programs were developed by Dr. Alfred Carter of Carleton University.
  - BackTrack utilizes point of origin determinations on vertical surfaces.
  - Whereas BackTrack utilizes a parabolic approach to determining flight paths, BackTrack/Strings relies on the stringing approach.

EXPERIMENT 11

Bloodstain Pattern Documentation Exercise

Objective: Use photography and a written narrative description to properly document the crime scene.

Procedure

A mock crime scene has been created. Your assignment is to document the scene using photography and narrative description, as if your documentation was going to be used by an outside analyst to do a reconstruction. Each group will work as a team to photograph the various bloodstain patterns and write a narrative description of the scene. When completed, turn in your narrative and secure digital (SD) card. Do not alter the scene or leave any materials behind that will distract the other groups. You will have 45 min to complete the exercise.

Equipment Needed

1. Camera
2. Scales
3. Evidence markers

CHAPTER 14

Cognitive Bias

Kelsey Backry

In bloodstain pattern analysis, the examiner may use the previously mentioned sources as a means to detect blood; however, once past the presumptive test, the examiner becomes the source of expert analysis. Psychology plays a role in this forensic discipline and it is crucial to use only facts when performing a reconstruction. Before discussing the possible cognitive biases which may arise, we must first understand the nature from which they develop. Cognitive psychology is the study of how individuals perceive, process, and store information (APA, 2014). Our brains operate in such ways that they create cognitive shortcuts for memory information, so it is easily accessible. Contingent upon one's previous encounters with a stimulus, one will most likely construct a predisposed emotion toward it. A cognitive bias may derive from environmental, situational, or emotional factors—all of which can affect the judgement of the expert. In this chapter we will discuss the different types of bias which may arise in a forensic investigation.

Types of Bias

Confirmation Bias

Confirmation bias is the tendency for an individual to look for or favor information which conforms to their preexisting beliefs (Kassin et al., 2013). As previously mentioned, biases are pervasive psychological phenomena which prevent an individual from interpreting information objectively (Noor, 2020). A confirmation bias serves somewhat as an efficient way for our brains to process and organize the information we are exposed to by constructing mental outlines called schemas. According to cognitive psychologist Jean Piaget's theory of cognitive development, a schema is a mental framework which helps us organize and interpret information. Prior encounters may influence the way in which information was encoded or how it is retrieved from memory. Schemas are acquired during cognitive development and continue to be modified throughout life (Huitt & Hummel, 2003). An example of such would be going to a new restaurant out of town. Though one has never been to this restaurant, they know what to expect while there because previous knowledge built their schema. As another example, when homicide detectives are called to crime scenes, they know generally what to assume. Though the environment may differ, the involvements are typically the same and they know what to expect.

Moving forward, in forensic science, keeping an unbiased opinion toward the matter at hand is extremely important. Bloodstain pattern analysis uses the scientific method as a guide for an examiner to keep their reconstruction unbiased; however, it is the expert's responsibility to not postulate when drawing a conclusion. For example, a bloodstain expert reconstructs a crime scene which is believed to be a suicide. Evidence was previously shared that the victim had particles of back spatter on his dominant hand and the firearm was found within close proximity to the body at the crime scene. After studying crime scene photos and reports, the examiner begins the reconstruction. Strung angles of impact confirm the blood spatter is consistent with a self-inflicted injury. All the blood spatter can be justified except a few passive blood drops. The expert's initial hypothesis of suicide was confirmed with the overwhelming majority of blood evidence, however challenged with the seemingly unexplainable drops. Research from Kassin et al. (2013) explains that, through forensic confirmation bias, weak evidence can be given more consideration, the direction of the investigation may become biased, and evidence to the contrary can be discounted or even ignored. In this example, if the expert were to discount the passive drops in favor of the suicide theory, the neglected information could be detrimental for the trajectory of the investigation. One can see using the scientific method to perform reconstructions is crucial in the way it makes one work in a deductive-type way; thus, there is less room for bias.

Contextual Bias

Contextual bias occurs when the circumstance, the context, of a scenario has an effect on the way in which it is interpreted. Research indicates contextual details can influence the expectations and cognitions of an analyst (Gardner et al., 2019). This was shown to be true in many disciplines, including bloodstain pattern analysis. Likewise, the National Commission on Forensic Science (NCFS) recommends task-relevant information be solely relied upon when performing forensic analyses (U.S. DOJ, n.d.). NCFS broadly defines such information to be anything *necessary* for drawing a conclusion. Task-irrelevant information believed to produce a contextual bias would include that of a suspect's criminal history, a prior confession, or other expert conclusions. Gardner et al. (2019) find that, because forensic science relies on human perception and judgement, experts are more vulnerable to bias.

As discussed in confirmation bias, it is vital to remember that developing a bias is normal, especially when one's schema has developed a blueprint of a similar scenario. This is important to keep in mind when you are part of the investigative team examining a crime, to ensure bias is not a driving force behind the decision drawn. As we learned in confirmation bias, one will look for supporting evidence for their initial inclinations, which can affect the way one interprets the context of the information being presented. Risinger et al. (2002) gives an example of an odontologist who investigates a bitemark on a deceased victim. He concludes the evidence is insufficient to identify the source of the bite. Later, the odontologist is informed the victim was assaulted and DNA evidence was recovered. He then concludes there is a high probability the source of the bitemark could be assigned to the defendant. In this instance, the odontologist was influenced by task-irrelevant information to his domain of the investigation, resulting in inductive reasoning. This person assaulted the victim, so they were the one who bit the victim.

Motivational Bias

The following two biases may be interpreted as sub-category biases, which coincide with contextual bias, though can also happen independently. As formerly mentioned, the context of a scenario can be very influencing, but the following will further illuminate the magnitude of subjectivity in contextual bias. Beginning with motivational bias, Ask and Granhag (2007) describe a few motivating derivatives which might encourage bias during a criminal investigation. **Motivational biases** include the context of the crime, time pressures, workload, and even personal desires (Siller et al., 2015). Ask and Granhag (2007) go on to say that in these types of situations, attention is focused on attributes deemed most important. In the aforementioned example of cognitive bias, the bloodstain expert was unable to explain the passive blood drops through the theory of self-inflicted injury. Adding a motivating factor to the equation, such as a time constraint, can enhance pressure on an investigation. As time becomes scarce, attention is given most to that which is perceived to be most important, whereas subjectively less pertinent information receives less consideration (Edland & Svenson, 1993). *The reconstruction needs to be completed before the investigation may move forward.* In their research, Ask and Granhag (2007) similarly state that investigators working under time pressure become more selective toward hypothesis-consistent evidence, becoming less likely to generate alternative explanations of criminal evidence, remaining persistent in their initial beliefs. *The passive blood was not deemed as pertinent to the crime as the vast amount of other blood evidence.* The expert could also have a motivating personal bias. They could want to keep their solved cases high, their caseload low, or simply be looking for gratification.

Expectation Bias

Expectation bias is most comparable to confirmation bias because what one looks for in a situation is what one expects to get out of the experience. Again, confirmation bias occurs when an individual looks for or favors information that conforms to preexisting beliefs (Kassin et al., 2013). Siller et al. (2015) discuss the study of Mossbridge et al. (2014), which describes anticipatory activity (AA). They explain how accounting for expectation effects is crucial in understanding reported outcomes. For instance, in the schema example from the discussion of cognitive bias, one visits a new restaurant they have never been to. They have a blueprint of what to expect, but at this point no other information to create an opinion. The individual revisits the restaurant another time because their experience was enjoyable. This time, there is a formed expectation for the experience at the restaurant. At this point, the individual expects to enjoy themselves as they did the first time. If the individual enjoys the visit a second time, the expectation becomes reinforced; however, if they are disappointed, they can experience cognitive dissonance. Cognitive dissonance is a term used to describe mental discomfort which occurs when one holds two conflicting thoughts, feelings, or beliefs, which then leads to an adjustment in one of the attitudes (McLeod, 2018).

Forensic examples of such would be a homicide detective who has a great record of solving cases. The detective is assigned a case and expects to solve it just as the other cases. The detective soon realizes there are no leads, evidence, or anything pointing to a suspect. The detective begins to feel cognitive dissonance because what they expect from prior experiences does not reflect the current situation.

It is important to remember that the above topics and chapters, and the ones to follow, are all based on scientific evidence. Though cognitive biases are inevitable, being aware of them can greatly minimize the unforeseen damage they may cause. This can be executed by following the scientific method, employing deductive-type thinking, and using facts to form opinions. When an examiner stays true to facts, no bias will misconstrue their findings. From a law enforcement perspective, these jobs will always be held to a higher standard of social and moral ethics. A forensic expert becomes such because they have proven themselves to be highly qualified and truly objective in their discipline, and that is where the standards should remain.

References

American Psychological Association (APA). (2014). *APA dictionary of psychology: Confirmation bias.* https://dictionary.apa.org/confirmation-bias

Ask, K., & Granhag, P. A. (2007). Motivational bias in criminal investigators' judgments of witness reliability. *Journal of Applied Social Psychology, 37*(3), 561–591.

Edland, A., & Svenson, O. (1993). Judgment and decision making under time pressure. In O. Svenson & J. Maule (Eds.), *Time pressure and stress in human judgment and decision making* (pp. 27–40). Plenum.

Gardner, B. O., Kelley, S., Murrie, D. C., & Dror, I. E. (2019), What do forensic analysts consider relevant to their decision making? *Science & Justice, 59*(5), 516–523.

Huitt, W., & Hummel, J. (2003). Piaget's theory of cognitive development. *Educational Psychology Interactive*, Valdosta State University. http://www.edpsycinteractive.org/topics/cognition/piaget.html

Kassin, S. M., Dror, I. E., & Kukucka, J. (2013). The forensic confirmation bias: Problems, perspectives and proposed solutions. *Journal of Applied Research in Memory and Cognition, 2*(1), 42–52.

McLeod, S. (2018, February 5). *Cognitive dissonance.* Simply Psychology. https://www.simplypsychology.org/cognitive-dissonance.html

Mossbridge, J. A., Tressoldi, P., Utts, J., Ives, J. A., Radin, D., and Jonas, W. B. (2014, March 25). Predicting the unpredictable: Critical analysis and practical implications of predictive anticipatory activity. *Frontiers in Human Neuroscience, 8*, Article 146.

Noor, I. (2020, June 10). *Confirmation bias.* Simply Psychology. https://www.simplypsychology.org/confirmation-bias.html

Risinger, D. M., Saks, M. J., Thompson, W. C., & Rosenthal, R. (2002, January). The Daubert/Kumho implications of observer effects in forensic science: Hidden problems of expectation and suggestion. *California Law Review, 90*(1), 1–56.

Siller, A., Ambach, W., Vaitl, D. (2015), Investigating expectation effects using multiple physiological measures. *Frontiers in Psychology, 6*, Article 1553.

U.S. Department of Justice (U.S. DOJ). (n.d.) *National Commission on Forensic Science.* U.S. Department of Justice Archives. https://www.justice.gov/archives/ncfs

CHAPTER 15

Written Reports

The bloodstain pattern analysis (BPA) written report is the foundation of the investigative documentation. The report has to be organized and understandable to other readers. When writing a BPA report, the author should have an eye on the courtroom. The information written in the report and those conclusions may be tested in court.

The American National Standards Institute (ANSI) and the American Academy of Forensic Science Academy Standards Board (ASB) list the following considerations when writing a BPA report:

- The report should be written clearly, without misleading language or jargon.
- The report format should be designed to minimize confusion.
- Reports authored by multiple parties shall be identified and define the role of each contributor.
- Headings should be standardized with the agency.
- ASB TR 033 shall be used for bloodstain pattern analysis terminology; all terminology references shall be defined and referenced. This may be accomplished by the use of footnotes, an appendix or glossary, or defined within the body of the report.
- When conclusions rely in part on the results of examinations reported by third parties (e.g., DNA, pathology, and fingerprint) a reference to these results shall be included in the BPA report. Quotations from associated documents (e.g., witness statements) shall be clearly defined and referenced.
- Case-related experimentation and findings shall be reported.
- The page number should appear on each page of the report and total numbers of pages should be defined.
- Abbreviations and acronyms not commonly recognized should be fully defined upon first use (e.g., bloodstain pattern analysis [BPA]).
- Any additions to the original report shall be issued as a supplemental report.
- Any corrections to the original report shall be identified and issued as an amended report.

When writing a report, include the following:

- date the report was written
- whom the report is to and the agency information
- reference information (e.g., case number or victim/defendant name)
- introductory statement
- disclaimer
- list of the information you were provided to conduct the analysis

Here is a disclaimer example.

- The analyst's opinion is based on all available evidence and relies on his education, experience, and training. Although all events, stains, and patterns may not be identified, those that are offer the best explanation for the variables considered in creating these stains. Should additional information become available, the analyst will consider its importance and *may* revise the analysis.

Here is an example of a list of information used in forming your opinions.

- 8″ × 10″ color photographs—109 pages
- Autopsy protocol—11 pages
- Police investigative reports—387 pages
- Diagrams of scene—7 pages
- DNA report—7 pages
- Firearms report—5 pages

The report should be complete, methodical, and as objective as possible. The true test of a good report is what it conveys to the reader. Does it leave them guessing what your opinions are, or what the foundation is based on?

- Is your report
    - reviewable?
    - testable?
    - repeatable?

Reviewable

- In reading your report, the reader should be able to understand what your opinions are and learn what the foundation in physical evidence or information is based on.

Testable

- By knowing your opinions and the basis for your opinion, the reader can test your opinions against the stain photographs, scene, lab reports, autopsy, and all other information to determine if they concur with or dissent from your opinions.

Repeatable

- If your opinions are tested, they should be repeatable.
    - In testing your opinions, the reader should be able to repeat your findings.
    - If they need to do experiments, they should be able to replicate your results.

Breakdown of a Scene

- A common practice is to break down the scene into areas that will be described.
    - Example: The Living Room
        - The west wall of the living room had multiple spatter patterns to the south of the entry door.
        - Stain group 1: Is a spatter pattern present on the west wall to the south side of the door. It contains approximately 100+ stains measuring from 0.5 mm to 3.8 mm in diameter. The center of the general pattern is 4′ 6″ up from the floor and 1′ 2″ left of the left edge of the door. The direction of travel is generally upward and to the north.
- This section of the report is just descriptive with **no opinions.**
    - This section is just to record each room and section of each room, to document and describe each pattern group and location.

Conclusion or Opinion Section

- Once the documentation section for each room and area is complete, you can begin describing your opinions of what the documentation means.
    - Example:
        - Pattern group 1 on the west wall of the living room is consistent with the type, size, and direction of travel as the spatter found on and around the victim's body. The range in size are also consistent with the type and number of wounds found on the victim and as documented in the autopsy report on page 4. These stains are consistent with blunt trauma to the victim while standing or bent over in front of this wall.
- All opinions you offer should also state the foundation they are based on.
    - Example:
        - *The above event is based on the following.*
        - *List the evidence that gives your foundation.*

Closing the Report

- If you have any questions on this report, please contact me at the above listed telephone numbers.

  Respectfully,

Bloodstain Pattern Analysis Report Format

Date

Normal Agency Information Header

Reference
Introductory statement
Disclaimer

List the items of information used to form the opinion of this report.

Examples:

Photographs:	The number of photos	Lab reports: Number of pages
Diagrams:	The number of diagrams	Autopsy reports: Number of pages
Police reports:	List number of pages	Videos: Length of time

General case information:

- Crime
- Date
- Location
- Victim information
- Defendant information

Brief synopsis of the case
Victim's injuries
Defendant's injuries
Statements
Evidence
Describe the scene room by room.

- Describe the blood within the scene.

Analysis

- Explain what events may or may not have occurred to create the bloodstains.

Conclusion
Signature

Reference

ANSI/ASB (2020). *Standard for report writing in bloodstain pattern analysis.* Standard 031, First Edition 2020.

CHAPTER 16

Courtroom Testimony

Bloodstain pattern analysts use applied sciences to determine the series of events based solely on blood evidence.

Qualifying for Court

- Expert testimony is admissible in court based on the following qualifications:
  - Training
  - Education
  - Experience
  - Objectivity

Admissibility Standards

The United States provides three court cases that address requirements for admissibility of expert testimony and evidence in court.

1. ***Frye v. United States* (1923)**
   a. Expert testimony must be "generally accepted" within the relevant scientific discipline.
   b. Frye-based admissibility hearings seek to accomplish the following:
      i. "Determine if the expert testimony will assist the jury in trying the case."
      ii. "Establish that the expert testimony is based on scientific principles that have been widely accepted in the field."
      iii. "Establish that the witness is qualified as an expert in the relevant field."
      iv. "Establish credibility of the witness."
2. **Federal Rule 702 (Federal Criminal Code and Rules, 1975, 2011)**
   a. Evaluates the admissibility of expert testimony.
      i. "Determine that the testimony is based upon sufficient facts or data."

ii. "Determine that the testimony is a product of reliable scientific principles and methods."

iii. "Determine that the witness has applied the scientific principles and methods reliably to the facts of the case."

3. ***Daubert v. Merrell Dow Pharmaceuticals* (1993)**

   a. The judge must determine the validity of expert testimony and an expert witness.

   b. Daubert-based admissibility hearings seek to accomplish the following:

      i. "Provide evidence that the methodology has been tested."

      ii. "Provide evidence that the methodology has been subjected to peer review and publication."

      iii. "Determine the known/potential error rate associated with the theory or technique when applied."

      iv. "Provide evidence that the standards controlling the technique are in place and maintained."

      v. "Provide evidence that the methodology has been generally accepted by the relevant scientific community."

Ethics in Testimony

- Experts should rely on comprehensive research *before* making a conclusion.
  - *Do not* form a firm conclusion in the beginning and work backward to find research that supports the conclusion.
- Expert witnesses should *not* play the advocate role.
  - *Your job is to be **objective** and speak **truth.***
    - i. Make a conscious effort to remain impartial.

Taking the Stand

- The first few moments on the witness stand cause the most distress.
  - It is during this time that the jury is forming their first impression, so as an expert you must remain comfortable and confident.
- Prepare for questions beforehand.
  - This preparation will allow you to relax before questioning begins.
  - Create your own qualifying questions to provide the attorneys.
  - No one knows your qualifications better than you. These questions should place you in a positive light but should not be embellished.

Qualifying questions should cover the following:

1. Training and years in the discipline
2. Position in and years with a given agency
3. Articles published or studies conducted
4. Schools taught on the subject
5. The number of times previously qualified as an expert witness
6. Memberships in professional organizations related to the field

Presenting in Court

- Your goal is to educate the jury.
- Testimony should be clear, logical, concise, and without inaccuracies, exaggerations, or unsupported theories.
- Speak to the jury in a language they can understand (explain jargon if necessary and use layman's terms).

References

Bevel, T., & Gardner, R. (1997). *Bloodstain pattern analysis: An introduction to crime scene reconstruction*. CRC Press.

Daubert v. Merrell Dow Pharmaceuticals, Inc., 509 U.S. 579 (1993).

Federal Criminal Code and Rules, Title 28, Section VII, 702 (1975).

Frye v. United States, 54 App. D.C. 46, 293 F. 1013, 1014 (1923).

Scientific Working Group on Bloodstain Pattern Analysis. (2014, December 16). *Admissibility resource kit on bloodstain pattern analysis*. http://www.swgstain.org/resources/ark

CHAPTER 17

Area of Convergence

The **area of convergence** is defined as the point at which the path of two bloodstains intersect, or *converge*. When determining area of convergence, it is important to identify where the majority of the stains appear to radiate within the impact pattern.

Determining Area of Convergence

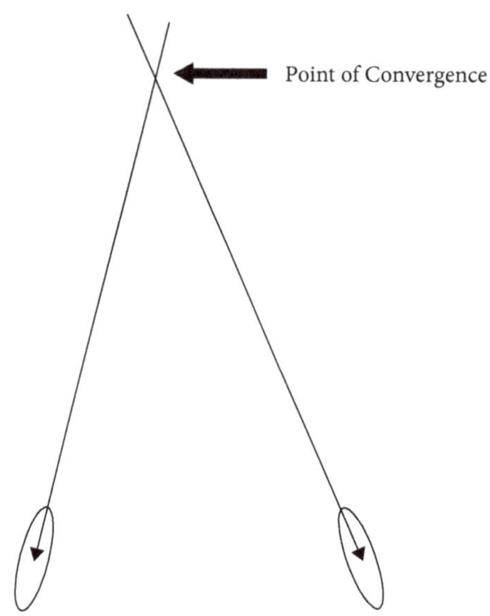

FIGURE 17.1 Point of Convergence Diagram Example

- There are several methods that can be used when determining area of convergence, including the use of string, a rubber band, a ruler, and so on. If the directionality of several well-formed bloodstains have been identified, draw a line back in the opposite direction and duplicate this process on a number of stains within the spatter pattern. When choosing bloodstains within the spatter pattern, choose bloodstains on each edge and in the center of the pattern. This results in a more accurate area of convergence.

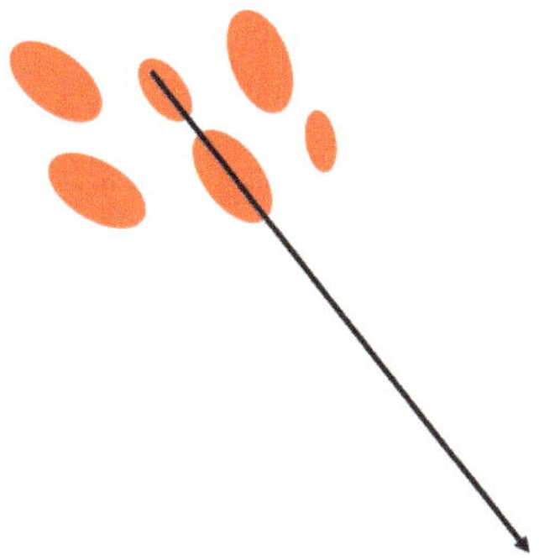

FIGURE 17.2 Area of Convergence Diagram Example

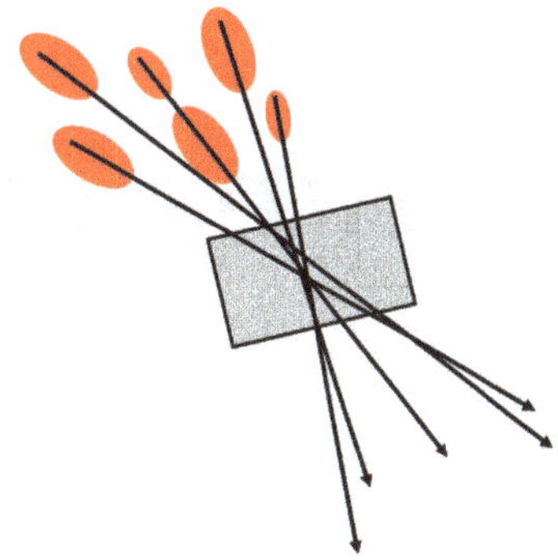

FIGURE 17.3 Area of Convergence Diagram Example

- When there are multiple spatter patterns in an area, use different colored lines or string to represent each occurrence in order to distinguish them.
- The only way to determine which occurrence happened first is to identify overlapping bloodstains. The one on the bottom occurred first.

Coincidental Convergence

- Coincidental convergence is the result of two different occurrences overlapping, giving the appearance that the convergence may have resulted from one spatter pattern.

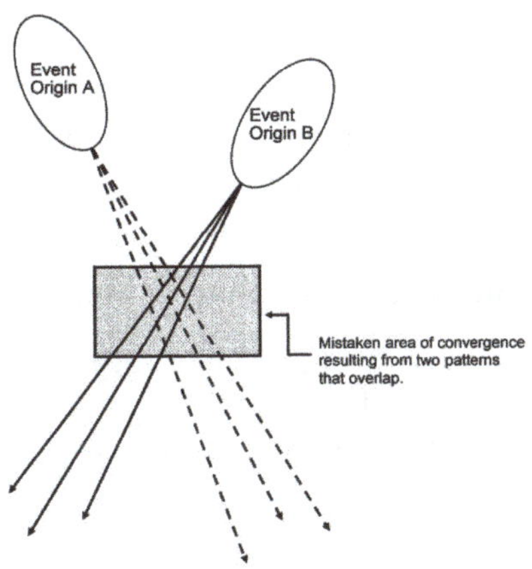

FIGURE 17.4 Coincidental Convergence Diagram Example

FIGURE 17.5 Coincidental Convergence Example

CHAPTER 18

Area of Origin

The **area of origin** is defined as the distance from the surface at which a blood source received impact. When determining area of origin, it is important to select stains from the spatter pattern that are well formed and oval in shape. It is recommended that no less than four stains are utilized. (*Note:* If no well-formed stains are present in the scene, the stains could still be utilized for DNA testing, so it is important to take a sample from the pattern that is being analyzed.)

Methods of Defining Area of Origin

- **Graphing** is a paper procedure. It requires impact angle and convergence point information.
- **Tangent** is a mathematical or paper procedure that requires impact angle and convergence point information.
- **Stringing** is a physical procedure that requires impact angle and directionality.
- **Backtrack win/Images** is a virtual procedure that requires photographs of the stains and their locations.

Determining Area of Origin with the Mathematical Model (Tangent Method)

- One method of determining area of origin is "stringing," but this method is time consuming and may not always be necessary. This process can be simplified by utilizing a mathematical approach (tangent method) to measure the distance from these stains to a common area of convergence.
  - Step 1: Choose your stains.
  - Step 2: Identify the impact angle for each stain.
  - Step 3: Identify the area of convergence and measure the distance to the area of convergence.
  - Step 4: Determine the tangent of the angle.
  - Step 5: Multiply the tangent by the distance.
  - Step 6: Repeat for a number of stains and define an average for the sum. The average is the height above the convergence (area of origin).

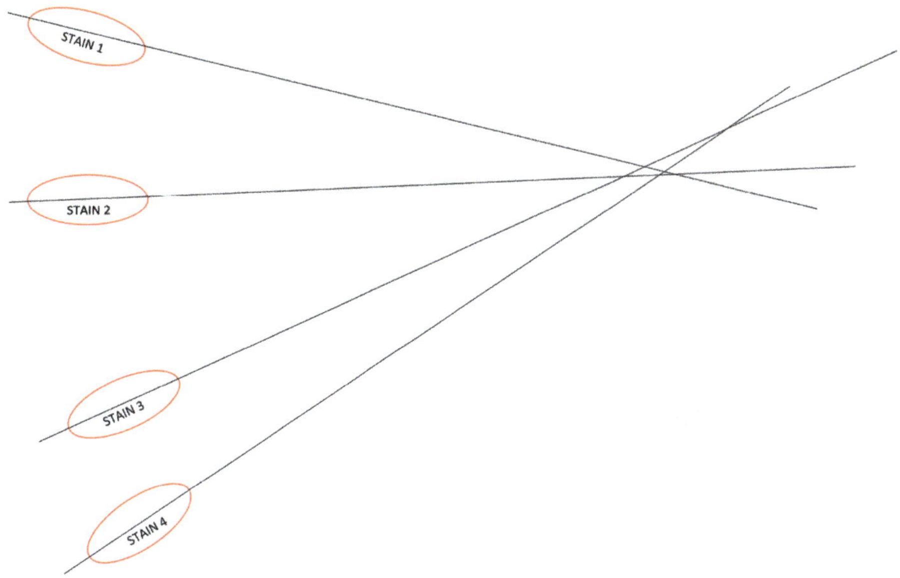

FIGURE 18.1 Determining Area of Origin Diagram

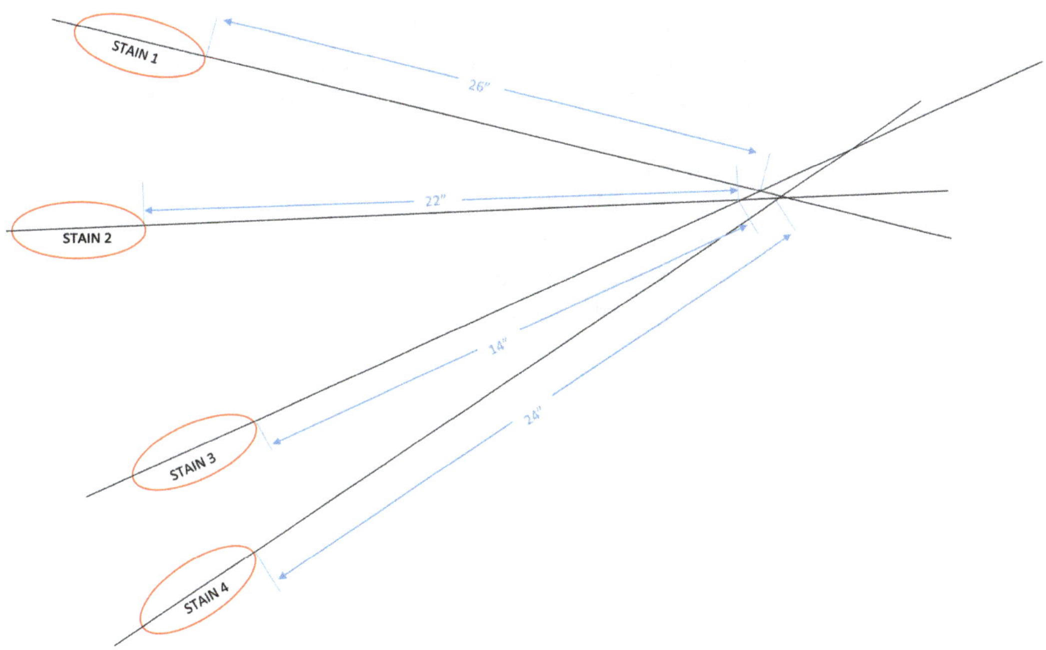

FIGURE 18.2 Determining Area of Origin Diagram

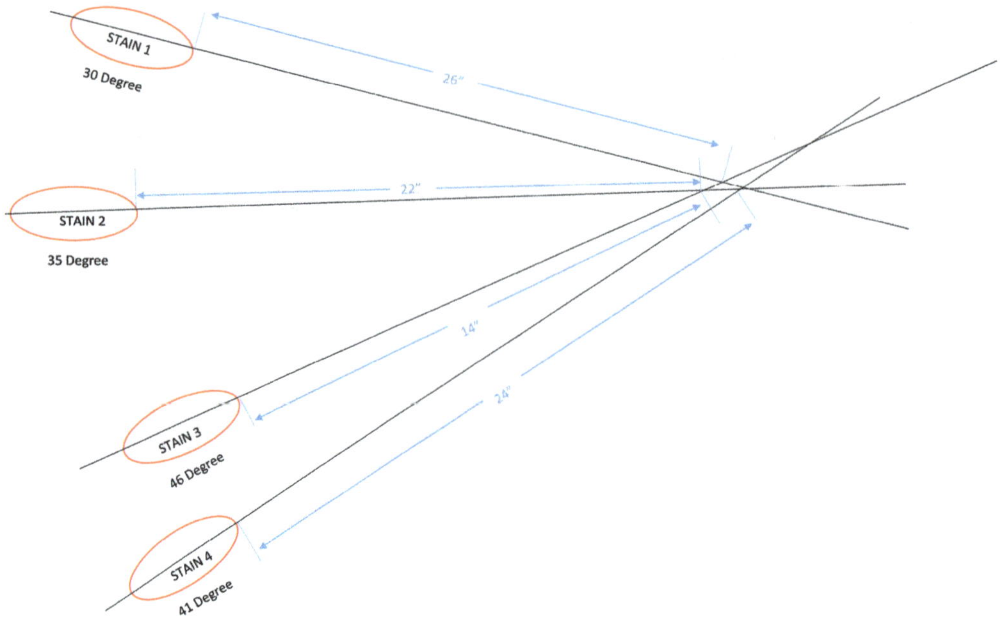

FIGURE 18.3 Determining Area of Origin Diagram

- Step 1: Measure from the base of the bloodstain to the first intersecting line.
- Step 2: Using a calculator, enter the degree, then the tangent.
- Step 3: Multiply the number by the length in inches, and that will equal the height above the target.
    - Example:
        - Stain 1 = 30° tan. × 26″ = 15″
        - Stain 2 = 35° tan. × 22″ = 15.4″
        - Stain 3 = 46° tan. × 14″ = 14.4″
        - Stain 4 = 41° tan. × 24″ = 3.8″

FIGURE 18.4 Stringing bloodstains showing direction using 360°

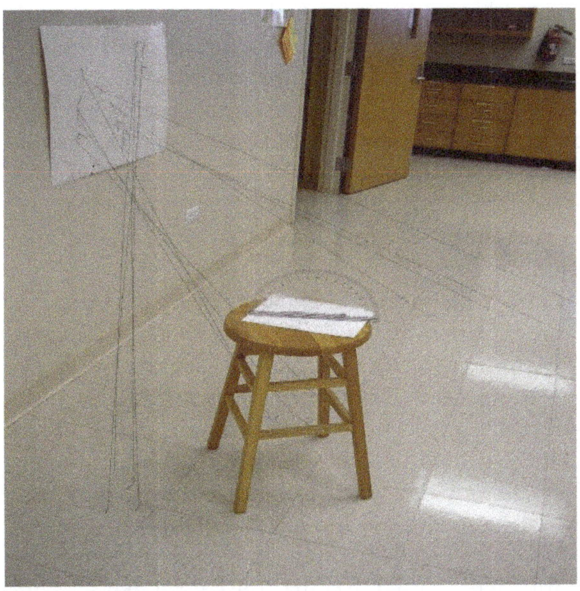

FIGURE 18.5 Stringing

CHAPTER 19

Conclusion

You have now completed the first-level bloodstain pattern analysis course. This International Association for Bloodstain Pattern Analysis (IABPA)–compliant course serves as an introduction to the discipline.

Students should now understand that bloodstain pattern analysis is the study of static bloodstains in a crime scene to determine what may or may not have occurred. BPA analysts study the size, shape, number, and distribution of the stains to form their opinion. The same law of physics applies to blood as it does to all fluids. An analyst does not have to be a physicist to be an expert in bloodstain pattern analysis, but only recognize that the law of physics exists. The history and terms in bloodstain pattern analysis were reviewed, as well as the categories of various bloodstains and patterns, and the uses of bloodstain pattern analysis. Students participated in a number of experiments that replicate the types of bloodstain patterns found in actual crime scenes.

The methods used to measure bloodstains to determine the angle of impact and the mathematical formula to obtain that angle were explained and demonstrated. Students displayed their understanding by working paper exercises as well as completing a stringing exercise.

Another critical area in bloodstain pattern analysis is knowing how to properly document blood in crime scenes with photography. The lecture, demonstration, and hands-on experiment were completed to demonstrate how important documentation is. To complement photographic documentation, an analyst will provide a written narrative report. The report will contain a written description of bloodstain patterns and will be used in conjunction with the photographs. The two forms of documentation complement each other but can stand alone. Oftentimes the documentation will be used in court. The court's expectations of a BPA expert were also discussed.

To tie all of this information together, students will process a mock crime scene to demonstrate their knowledge of the discipline and how to apply what has been learned.

The assignment is to enter the mock crime scene to form an opinion as to what may or may not have occurred based on the "static" bloodstains. Each group will have 45 min to observe the scene, write notes, and form an opinion. This exercise does not require you to photograph, measure stains, or create a sketch, due to time constraints.

When analyzing this crime scene, remember to be open minded and objective. When you first enter the crime scene as an analyst, it may be overwhelming. The analyst's responsibility is to look at the blood to determine what it tells you. The rule of thumb is, *"the area where there is the least amount of blood is likely near the location where the assault began and the area where there is the most amount of blood is near the end of where the assault occurred."*

Remember, you will not be able to explain how all the blood was created within the scene, so look for patterns that are familiar to you and then other patterns may become clearer. When observing the bloodstain patterns, remember your training. The experiments you conducted in this course are patterns typically observed in a crime scene.

Scenario

Patrol officers responded to a trouble unknown call at a service bay. The dispatcher informed you that a customer arrived at the shop this morning to have work performed on their vehicle. No one was in the office when the customer arrived. The customer waited for about 15 min and no one came into the office so the customer went out into the bay to look for the employees. Once in the bay he did not find anyone but he did see a lot of blood and an overturned chair. The customer exited the business and called 911.

When the officers arrived they were briefed by the customer. The officers went into the business and found no one was there and they saw the blood that the customer was talking about. The officer believed something bad must have happened in the bay but weren't sure what, since they had no training in bloodstain pattern analysis. The officers requested dispatch to contact you, because you are the department's BPA expert, to come to the scene to conduct an analysis.

Scene

FIGURE 19.1 (left) Overall Scene Photographs of the Bay

FIGURE 19.2 (right) Overall Scene Photographs of the Bay

FIGURE 19.3 (left) Overall Scene Photographs of the Bay

FIGURE 19.4 (right) Overall Scene Photographs of the Bay

In front of the overturned chair is a blood drop. Just feet away from the blood drop is medium-energy spatter, a transfer pattern, expectorant blood spatter and two lineal bloodstain patterns. Leading away from the chair toward the back door is a blood trail, and within this trail is a drip pattern.

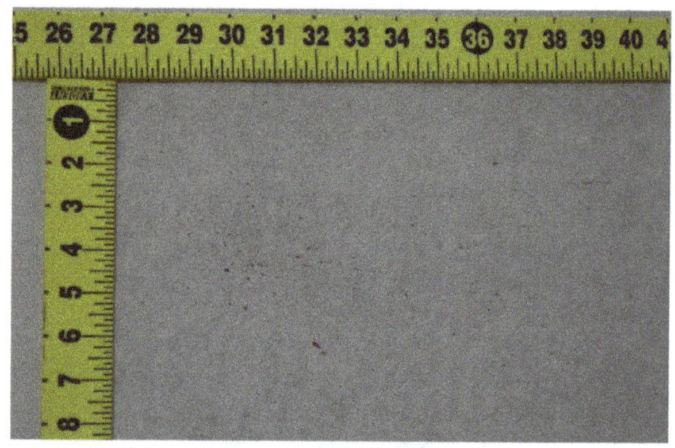

FIGURE 19.5 (left) Impact Pattern

FIGURE 19.6 (right) Expiration Pattern

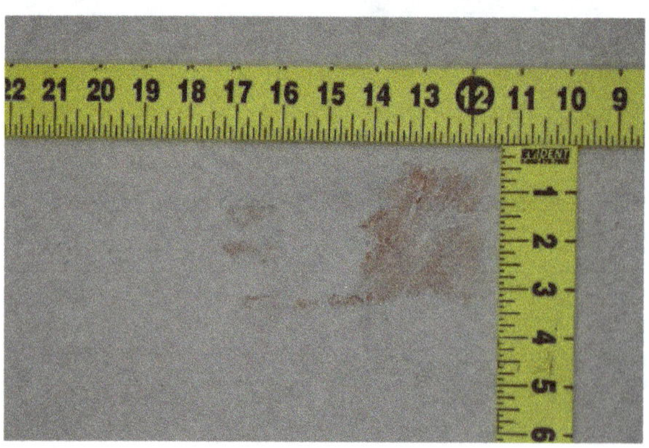

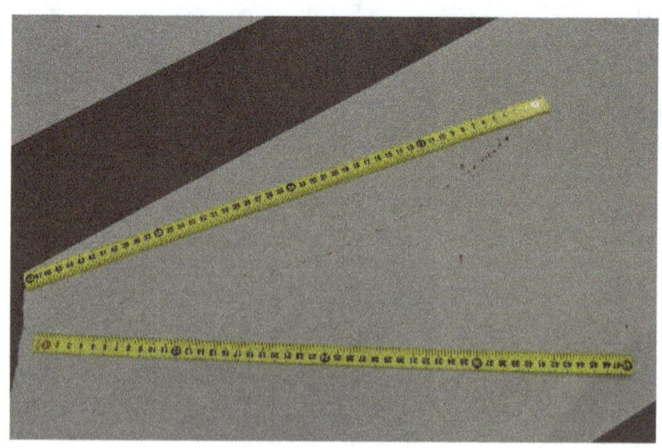

FIGURE 19.7 (left) Transfer Pattern

FIGURE 19.8 (right) Cast-Off Pattern

FIGURE 19.9 (left) Drip Trail

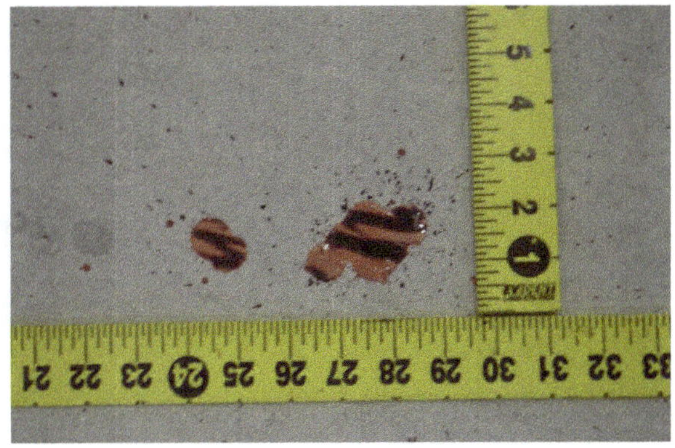

FIGURE 19.10 (right) Drip Pattern

The drip trail ends at the overhead garage door. At that location is another impact spatter, expectorant pattern, transfer stain, and two linear bloodstain patterns.

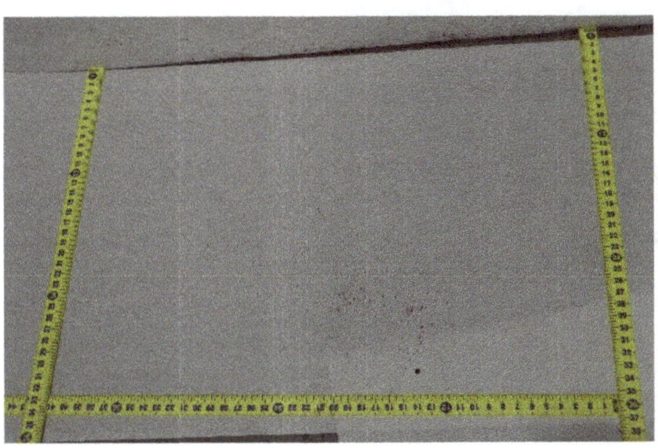

FIGURE 19.11 (left) Impact Pattern

FIGURE 19.12 (right) Expiration Pattern

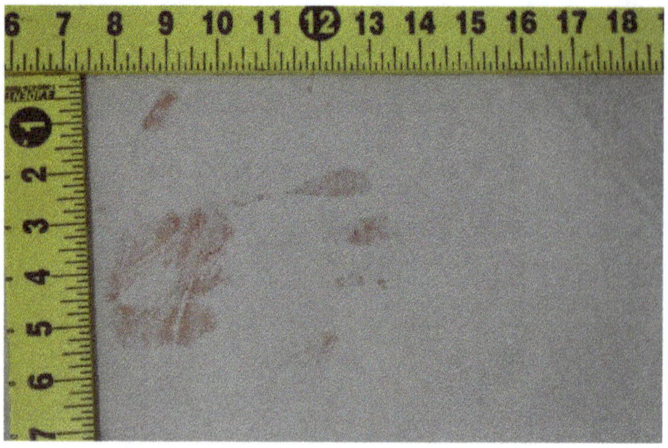

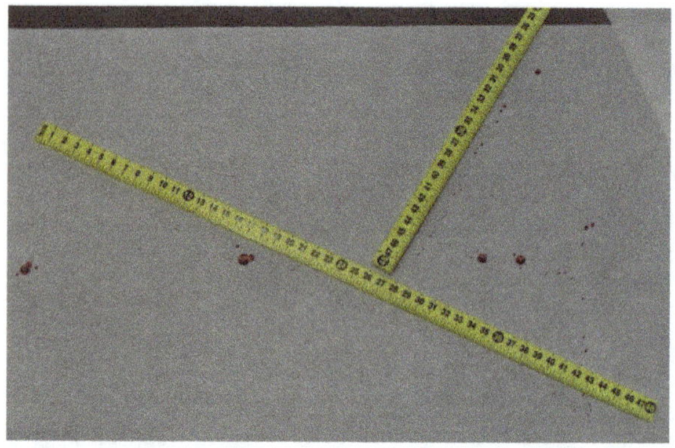

FIGURE 19.13 (left) Transfer Pattern

FIGURE 19.14 (right) Cast-Off Pattern

Between the overhead door and the back door is an altered blood pool, and two transfer stains, one on the floor and one on the door.

FIGURE 19.15 Altered Blood Pool

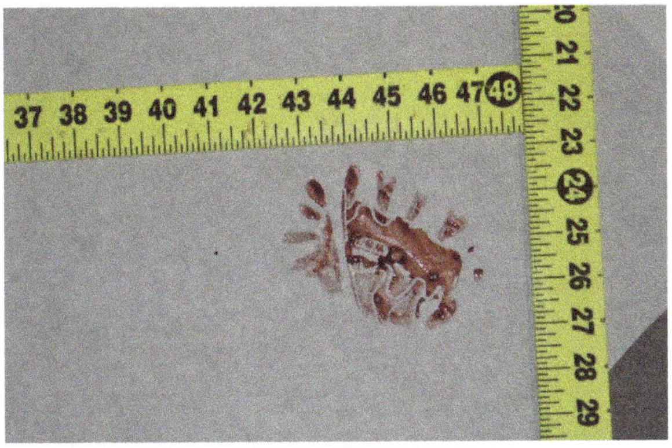

FIGURE 19.16 (left) Transfer Pattern

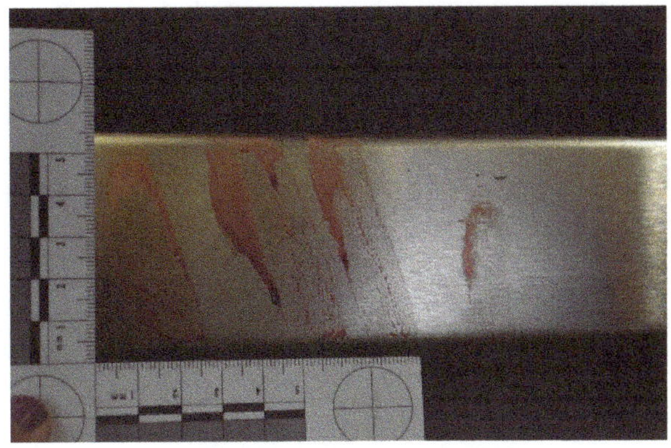

FIGURE 19.17 (right) Transfer Pattern

Glossary

Accompanying Drop: A small drop produced as a by-product of drop formation.

Altered Stain: A bloodstain with characteristics that indicate a physical change has occurred (i.e., skeletonized stains, blood into blood, dried stains, wipes, swipes, etc.).

Angle of Impact: The acute angle (alpha), relative to the plane of a target, at which a blood drop strikes the target.

Area of Convergence: The area containing the intersections generated by lines drawn through the long axes of individual stains that indicates in two dimensions the location of the blood source.

Area of Origin: The three-dimensional (3D) location from which spatter originated.

Back Spatter Pattern: A bloodstain pattern resulting from blood drops that traveled in the opposite direction of the external force applied; associated with an entrance wound created by a projectile.

Blood Clot: A gelatinous mass formed by a complex mechanism involving red blood cells, fibrinogen, platelets, and other clotting factors.

Bloodstain: A deposit of blood on a surface.

Bloodstain Pattern: A grouping or distribution of bloodstains that indicates through regular or repetitive form the manner in which the pattern was deposited.

Bubble Ring: An outline within a bloodstain resulting from air in the blood.

Cast-Off Pattern: A bloodstain pattern resulting from blood drops released from an object due to its motion.

Cessation Cast-Off Pattern: A bloodstain pattern resulting from blood drops released from an object due to its rapid deceleration.

Directional Angle: The angle (gamma) between the long axis of a spatter stain target and a defined reference line on the target.

Directionality: The characteristic of a bloodstain that indicates the direction blood was moving at the time of deposition.

Drip Pattern: A bloodstain pattern resulting from a liquid that dripped into another liquid, at least one of which was blood.

Drip Stain: A bloodstain resulting from a falling drop that formed due to gravity.

Drip Trail: A bloodstain pattern resulting from the movement of a source of drip stains between two points.

Edge Characteristics: A physical feature of the periphery of a bloodstain (i.e., spines, smooth, scalloped, etc.).

Expiration Pattern: A bloodstain pattern resulting from blood forced by airflow out of the nose, mouth, or a wound.

Flow Pattern: A bloodstain pattern resulting from the movement of a volume of blood on a surface due to gravity or movement of the target. (*Note:* The Organization of Scientific Area Committees [OSAC] subcommittee for Bloodstain Pattern Analysis proposed to change the verbiage from "flow pattern" to "flow.")

Fly Spot: A bloodstain resulting from fly activity. (*Note:* The Organization of Scientific Area Committees [OSAC] subcommittee for Bloodstain Pattern Analysis proposed to change the verbiage from "fly spot" to "insect activity.")

Forward Spatter Pattern: A bloodstain pattern resulting from blood drops that traveled in the same direction as the impact force.

Impact Pattern: A bloodstain pattern resulting from an object striking liquid blood.

Mist Pattern: A bloodstain pattern resulting from blood reduced to a spray of micro-drops as a result of the force applied. (*Note:* The Organization of Scientific Area Committees [OSAC] subcommittee for Bloodstain Pattern Analysis proposed to eliminate this term).

Parent Stain: A bloodstain from which a satellite stain originated.

Perimeter Stain: An altered stain that consists of the peripheral characteristics of the original stain (i.e., skeletonized stains).

Pool: A bloodstain resulting from an accumulation of liquid blood on a surface.

Projected Pattern: A bloodstain pattern resulting from the ejection of a volume of blood under pressure (i.e., arterial gushing/spurts).

Satellite Stain: A smaller bloodstain that originated during the formation of the parent stain as a result of blood impacting a surface.

Saturation Stain: A bloodstain resulting from the accumulation of liquid blood in an absorbent material.

Serum Stain: The stain resulting from the liquid portion of blood (serum) that separates during coagulation.

Spatter Stain: A bloodstain resulting from a blood drop dispersed through the air due to an external force applied to a source of liquid blood.

Splash Pattern: A bloodstain pattern resulting from a volume of liquid blood that falls or spills onto a surface.

Swipe Pattern: A bloodstain pattern resulting from the transfer of blood from a blood-bearing surface onto another surface, with characteristics that indicate relative motion between the two surfaces.

Target: A surface onto which blood has been deposited.

Transfer Stain: A bloodstain resulting from contact between a blood-bearing surface and another surface.

Void: An absence of blood in an otherwise continuous bloodstain or bloodstain pattern.

Wipe Pattern: An altered bloodstain pattern resulting from an object moving through a preexisting wet bloodstain.

www.ingramcontent.com/pod-product-compliance
Lightning Source LLC
LaVergne TN
LVHW080356011026
849161LV00009B/2323

Commentar

zur

Prozeßordnung

in

bürgerlichen Rechtsstreitigkeiten

für das

Königreich Bayern.

Von

J. Wernz,
Rath am kgl. Oberappellationsgerichte.

Erste Abtheilung,
enthaltend Buch I und II.

München 1871.
Rudolph Oldenbourg.

Inhaltsverzeichniß zur ersten Abtheilung.

Erstes Buch.

Allgemeine Bestimmungen.

V. Hauptstück.

Allgemeine Vorschriften über das Verfahren.

Zweites Buch.

Verfahren im ersten Rechtszuge.

Erster Abschnitt.

Ordentliches Verfahren vor den Bezirksgerichten.

VI. Hauptstück.

Verfahren im Allgemeinen.

VII. Hauptstück.

Urtheil.

VIII. Hauptstück.

Versäumungsurtheil.

IX. Hauptstück.

Beweis.

X. Hauptstück.

Urkunden.

XI. Hauptstück.

Augenschein.

XII. Hauptstück.

Zeugen.

XIII. Hauptstück.

Sachverständige.

XIV. Hauptstück.

Eid.

XV. Hauptstück.

Zwischenstreit und Betheiligung dritter Personen.

XVI. Hauptstück.

Unterbrechung und Aufhebung der Verhandlung.

XXIV. Hauptstück.

Vorsichtsverfügungen.

XXV. Hauptstück.

Verfahren bei gerichtlichen Entscheidungen auf einfache Vorstellungen.

XXVI. Hauptstück.

Verfahren bei den protestantischen Ehegerichten in den Landestheilen diesseits des Rheins.

Ende der ersten Abtheilung.

I. Buch.

Allgemeine Bestimmungen.

I. Hauptstück.

Zuständigkeit der Gerichte.

(Zuständigkeit der Gerichte überhaupt.)

Art. 1. — Die bürgerlichen Rechtsstreitigkeiten sind, soweit nicht gesetzlich anders bestimmt ist, vor den bürgerlichen Gerichten zu verhandeln und durch dieselben zu entscheiden.

Ges. Ausschr. der K. d. Abg. I S. 1—6, IV S. 4. — K. d. R. I S. 10 u. 11.

Das Gesetzbuch wird hier mit einem allgemeinen Satze eingeleitet, welcher besagt, daß im Civilprozesse die Civilgerichte zuständig seien; Aufschluß über die Frage zu geben, was zum Civilprozesse gehöre, ist nicht seine Absicht. — Da nun aber laut Einführungsgesetzes Art. 2 die neue Prozeßordnung nur bestimmt ist, das Verfahren in bürgerlichen Rechtsstreitigkeiten, d. h. den Civilprozeß, zu regeln, alle andern Rechtsgebiete aber unberührt bleiben sollen, so erscheint es sachgemäß, die bezüglichen Prinzipien hier in Kürze hervorzuheben. Dieselben ergeben sich aus der Natur der Sache und dem Gesammtinhalte des Gesetzbuches.

Im Allgemeinen läßt sich der Satz aufstellen, daß jedes Verfahren zum Civilprozesse gehöre, dessen Zweck direkt darauf gerichtet ist, ein Privatrecht, einem bestimmten Gegner gegenüber, zur Anerkennung oder zum Vollzuge zu bringen.

Obgleich daher die richterliche Thätigkeit nach dem neuen Verfahren erst beginnt mit Anmeldung des Prozesses zum Hauptverzeichnisse (Art. 235) und schon endigt mit Verkündigung und Eintrag des Urtheils, während das vorausgehende und das nachfolgende Verfahren, insbesondere auch der Urtheilsvollzug in den Händen der Gerichtsboten, Anwälte und Gerichtschreiber liegt, so erleidet es doch nicht den mindesten Zweifel, daß auch letzteres Verfahren in das Gebiet des Civilprozesses gehört.

Nach der geschichtlichen Entwicklung des französischen Prozesses, welcher unserer neuen Prozeßordnung als Muster gedient hat, sowie nach der inneren Natur der Funktionen, ist die Amtsthätigkeit der Anwälte, Gerichtsboten, Gerichtschreiber, ja der Notäre, nur als ein Theil der richterlichen Thätigkeit zu betrachten, welcher Theil Nebenbeamten, Gehülfen des Richters, zur selbständigen Verwaltung übertragen ist, während der Richter selbst, sich auf den Kern der richterlichen Thätigkeit, auf Finden und Sprechen des Rechts (die jurisdictio im engeren Sinne) beschränkt. — Was diese Nebenbeamten — die officiers ministeriels im Gegensatze zu den magistrats — auf dem Gebiete der streitigen und unstreitigen Rechtspflege thuen, geschieht im Grunde statt der Gerichte, zu deren Entlastung, d. h. in abgeleiteter richterlicher Thätigkeit.

Betrachtet man die Sache von diesem Standpunkte, so ist klar, daß unter dem neuen Prozesse, so gut wie unter dem alten, das ganze Vollstreckungsverfahren seiner Natur nach zum Civilprozesse gehört, mögen auch die Gerichte selbst den Vollzug nicht mehr anordnen und leiten. Es gilt dies nicht nur vom Vollstreckungsverfahren, welches auf Grund richterlichen Urtheils stattfindet, sondern auch von demjenigen, welches sich auf Notariatsurkunden gründet.

Ebenso gehören ins Gebiet des Civilprozesses auch Rechtshandlungen, welche dem Beginne eines Rechtsstreites, eines Vollstreckungsverfahrens vorausgehen, sich jedoch direkt darauf beziehen, wie z. B. Vergleichsversuche, Ermächtigung zur Ladung mit kurzer Frist, zur Beschlagnahme, Vorsichtsverfügungen 2c.

Alles, was der Zweck des Prozesses mit sich bringt, liegt im Zweifel in der Zuständigkeit der Gerichte, also namentlich auch Beurkundungen von Zugeständnissen, Verzichten, Vergleichen, sei es, daß sie in die Geschichtserzählung des Urtheils, sei es, daß sie in den Urtheilssatz selbst aufgenommen sind.

Fremd ist dem Civilprozesse, was nicht zur streitigen Rechtspflege gehört, d. h. das Gebiet der sog. freiwilligen Gerichtsbarkeit (jurisdictio voluntaria — juridiction volontaire ou gracieuse). Dieses Gebiet wird, soweit nicht ausdrücklich anders verfügt ist, von der neuen Prozeßordnung nicht berührt, vielmehr behaupten die betreffenden älteren Gesetze nach wie vor ihre Geltung.

Der Begriff der nichtstreitigen Rechtspflege ist nach französischem, gemein deutschem und bayrischem Rechte der nemliche.

Was den Ausdruck: »juridiction gracieuse« betrifft, welcher von der dem Richter selbst vorbehaltenen nichtstreitigen Rechtspflege gebraucht wird, so ist derselbe offenbar nicht sachentsprechend und sein Ursprung ein geschichtlicher. Carré, de l'organisation et de la compet. t. III p. 442, sagt:

»C'est pour cela, que nos anciens auteurs »ont appellé l'intervention légale du juge, dans »les affaires ou il n'existe point de litige, juri»diction gracieuse, parceque le législateur n'étant »rigoureusement obligé, à garantir aux citoyens »cette intervention, que dans les matières con»tentieuses, ne l'accorde en toutes autres, que »par faveur.«

Zimlich ebenso ungeeignet als der Ausdruck: »juridiction gracieuse« sind übrigens auch die Ausdrücke: »jurisdictio voluntaria« oder „freiwillige Gerichtsbarkeit", denn es ist von einem eigentlichen Rechtsprechen (jus dicere) nicht die Rede und hängt auch in der Regel nicht von der Willkür der Parteien ab, ob sie sich zu einem gewissen Zwecke einer Amtsthätigkeit bedienen wollen oder nicht. Sachentsprechend ist jedoch der Ausdruck: „nichtstreitige Rechtspflege".

Die nichtstreitige Rechtspflege wird geübt:

1) von den **Gerichten** und zwar vorzugsweise von den Landgerichten, insofern dieselben berufen sind, zum Schutze Rechtsunfähiger oder Abwesender thätig zu sein, zur Wahrung der Rechte Dritter Verlassenschafts-Verhandlungen zu leiten, Hypothekenbücher zu führen ꝛc. G. V. G. v. 10. Nov. 1861 Art. 18.

Hieraus folgt z. B., daß Entscheidungen in Verlassenschaftssachen ꝛc. nicht die Kraft von Urtheilen beanspruchen können. s. Seuff. Comm. zur G. O. Cap. XV § 5. Das Gleiche gilt in der Pfalz bei Homologationen von Familienraths-Beschlüssen, Theilungen, sofern sie letzteren Falls nur zur Ergänzung der Zustimmung Rechtsunfähiger stattfinden, bei Adoptionen ꝛc. s. Bioche v. adoption Nr. 31 u. v. cons. de famille Nr. 84.

Die nichtstreitige Rechtspflege wird ferner geübt:

2) von den **Notären**, insofern ihnen die Beurkundung aller auf Rechtsverhältnisse sich beziehenden Erklärungen übertragen ist. Ges. v. 10. Nov. 1861 Art. 11. — Ges. v. 25. Vent. XI Art. 1;

3) von den **Gerichtsboten**, insofern dieselben auch außer den Prozessen, Zustellungen von Aufforderungen, Erklärungen, Anerbieten vornehmen dürfen;

4) von den **Gerichtsschreibern**, insofern denselben in der Pfalz verschiedene Beurkundungen, z. B. von Erbverzichten, Erbannahmen, anvertraut sind und sie dort nebst den Gerichtsboten sogar Mobiliar-Versteigerungen abhalten dürfen;

5) von den **Hypotheken-Beamten** der Pfalz.

Ein weiteres Erforderniß für die Zuständigkeit der Civilgerichte ist, daß die Rechtsstreitigkeiten **bürgerliche** seien, d. h. daß sie Privatrechtsverhältnisse betreffen.

Ausgeschlossen sind daher weiter:

a) alle **Strafsachen**;

b) alle Streitsachen, welche auf dem **öffentlichen Rechte** beruhen.

Es tritt hier die Frage entgegen, was Verwaltungs-, was Justiz-Sache sei, eine Frage, welche zu den schwierigsten zählt, die im Rechtsgebiete vorkommen und welche namentlich in neuerer Zeit beim Streben, Justiz und Verwaltung sowohl ihren Gebieten als ihren Organen nach möglichst scharf zu trennen, von besonders großer Bedeutung ist. Im Hinblicke hierauf möchte es nicht ungeeignet sein, eine kurze Uebersicht der bezüglichen Prinzipien zu geben und zwar insbesondere mit Rücksicht auf die Rechtsprechung in Bayern und die Jurisprudenz des obersten Gerichtshofes für Competenzconflikte.

Ueber Ausscheidung von Justiz- und Verwaltungs-Sachen.

§ 1.

Richterliche Gewalt und Regierungsgewalt.

Rechte und Pflichten der Staatsbürger sind entweder durch Gesetze und Rechtsnormen im Voraus bestimmt und die Staatsgewalt ist nur berufen, sie in Fällen, wo Zweifel entsteht oder böser Wille herrscht, zur Anerkennung und zum Vollzuge zu bringen, oder aber es ist der Staatsgewalt die Macht verliehen, in einzelnen Fällen nach Rücksichten der Zweckmäßigkeit und des öffentlichen Wohls regelnd und bestimmend einzuschreiten.

Ersteres bildet das Wesen der richterlichen, Letzteres das Wesen der Regierungsgewalt.

Uebrigens genügt dieser Gesichtspunkt nicht, um die Grenzen der Zuständigkeit zwischen Gerichten und Verwaltungsbehörden zu finden, vielmehr ist noch ein fernerer sehr wichtiger Gesichtspunkt maßgebend, nemlich, daß die Wahrung der **Privatrechte** (Vermögen, persönliche Freiheit, Familienrechte) die besondere, den Gerichten zugewiesene Aufgabe ist. — Auf dem Gebiete der Privatinteressen sind die Gerichte daher auch dort zuständig, wo es sich bloß um Verwaltungsmaßregeln handelt, z. B. bei Bestellung und Ueberwachung von Pflegschaften, überhaupt bei der nicht streitigen Rechtspflege ihrem ganzen Umfange nach. Anderseits entscheiden in Fällen, wo das öffentliche Recht in Frage ist, die Verwaltungsbehörden in der Regel auch dann, wenn nach Maßgabe bestehender Gesetze, also richterlich zu entscheiden ist.

Der Gegensatz zwischen öffentlichen und Privatinteressen tritt, bei Entscheidung der Competenzfragen, so stark hervor, daß es den Anschein hat, als liege in ihm das einzig wesentliche Unterscheidungsmerkmal, dennoch aber macht sich der Grundcharakter der Funktionen immer sichtbar. Man verkennt nicht, daß die Verwaltung in vielen Beziehungen aus ihrer Sphäre heraustritt und richterliche Funktionen ausübt und spricht daher von „administrativer Justiz" (Ges. v. 17. Nov. 1837 Art. 1); man findet es ferner nöthig, derartige Funktionen theilweise besonderen Behörden zuzuweisen, welche mehr in der Weise und im Sinne von Richtern entscheiden. — In Frankreich z. B. wird die Administrativ-Justiz geübt vom Präfekturrath (conseil de prefecture) oder den Ministern in erster und vom Staatsrathe in höchster Instanz. — Auch in Bayern ist vielfach die höchste Entscheidung nicht den reinen Verwaltungsbehörden zugewiesen, sondern dem Staatsrathe. In andern Fällen sind besondere Organe geschaffen, wie die Ausschüsse zur Entscheidung über Kapital- und Einkommen-Steuer. — Aehnlichen Erwägungen liegt die Ueberzeugung von der Nothwendigkeit eines Verwaltungs-Gerichtshofes zu Grunde.

In gleicher Weise scheiden sich anderseits die den Gerichten obliegenden Verwaltungs-Funktionen von den rein richterlichen. — Man findet es z. B. unbedenklich, erstere Funktionen besonderen Beamten ohne richterliche Eigenschaft zu übertragen, wie dies bei uns in Bayern theilweise geschehen ist und in andern Ländern, z. B. in Frankreich, nahezu bezüglich der gesammten nicht streitigen Rechtspflege schon längst der Fall ist. — Allerdings sind auch diese besonderen Beamten Justizbeamte, allein es würde offenbar nicht so viel Ungehöriges darin liegen, das Vormundschaftswesen, Hypothekenwesen, die Civilstandsregister ꝛc. reinen Verwaltungsbeamten zu übertragen, als darin lag, daß früher die Polizeigerichtsbarkeit, die Entscheidungen von Miethstreitigkeiten ꝛc. zur Zuständigkeit der Verwaltung gehörten.

Das Verhältniß der richterlichen zur Regierungs-Gewalt ist je nach der Natur des Staates ein verschiedenes. — Im rein despotischen Staate ist die Justiz nur Dienerin der Verwaltung, eine Art der Ausübung der Verwaltung. Der Regent kann im Grunde nach Ermessen über alles verfügen und wenn er Richter aufstellt, welche nach gewissen Vorschriften urtheilen sollen, so sind dies eigentlich nur Verwaltungsbeamte und das, was man Gesetz nennt, sind Instruktionen, welche ihnen gegeben sind.

Umgekehrt ist es im vollkommenen Rechtsstaate. — Hier ist das Gesetz der oberste Herr, der Richter ist dessen Wächter und die Verwaltung bewegt sich nur innerhalb der Schranken, welche das Gesetz für die einzelnen Gebiete aufstellt. — Je schärfer und klarer die Gränzen der Verwaltung gezogen sind, desto ausgebildeter ist der Rechtsstaat. Es brauchen diese Gränzen nicht gerade allzu enge zu sein; im Gegentheile, je bestimmter sie sind und je besser gegen Ueberschreitungen gesorgt ist, um so freiere Bewegung kann der Verwaltung gegönnt werden.

Ein Mittelding bildet der Polizeistaat, d. h. derjenige Staat, in welchem die Regierungsgewalt übermächtig ist und ihre Zuständigkeit die Regel bildet.

In Bayern besteht der Rechtsstaat und hat daher als Grundsatz zu gelten, daß die Verwaltung nichts verfügen darf, was, sei es die Freiheit der Person, sei es die Vermögens- und Familienrechte von Personen beeinträchtigt, ohne vom Gesetze, sei es durch ausdrückliche Verfügung, sei es nach dem Geiste desselben, ermächtigt zu sein.

§ 2.

Competenz-Conflikte.

Innerhalb ihres Gebietes ist die Verwaltung selbständig und steht den Gerichten, der Regel nach, gleichberechtigt gegenüber. — Es ist nun natürlich, daß bei den vielfachen Berührungspunkten beider Gewalten häufig Streit über die Zuständigkeit entsteht und weil die Ansicht der einen für die andere nicht bindend ist, so wird ein besonderes Organ nöthig, um solche Conflikte zu entscheiden.

In vielen Ländern ist zur Entscheidung dieser Competenz-Conflikte eine Verwaltungsbehörde berufen (in Frankreich z. B. der Staatsrath), eine Einrichtung, welche mehr für den Polizeistaat, als für den Rechtsstaat sich eignet. — In Bayern ist durch das Gesetz vom 28. Mai 1850 ein besonderer Gerichtshof bestellt, von dessen Mitgliedern 4 der Justiz und 3 der Verwaltung angehören.

Dieses Gesetz gibt der Verwaltung das Recht, ihr Partei-Interesse, etwaigen Uebergriffen der Gerichte gegenüber, durch Erhebung eines bejahenden Competenz-Conflikts zu wahren. — Der richterlichen Gewalt ist ein solches Recht nicht eingeräumt; sie kann vielmehr, wie es ihre Natur mit sich bringt, nur thätig auftreten, wenn Betheiligte ihre Hülfe anrufen.

Es erklärt sich diese verschiedene Stellung beider Gewalten in Bezug auf Competenz-Conflikte aus der Thatsache, daß Verwaltungsbeschlüsse nicht in der Art, wie richterliche Erkenntnisse in Rechtskraft erwachsen. Ebenhieraus folgt aber nothwendig, daß die Gerichte, falls sie angerufen werden, an die Beschlüsse der Verwaltung nicht gebunden sind und ihnen frei steht, ganz ohne Rücksicht auf die Ansicht der Verwaltung auszusprechen, was Rechtens sei. In der Kritik von Verwaltungshandlungen allein kann eine Ueberschreitung der richterlichen Competenz nicht liegen, vielmehr ist nur dann eine solche gegeben, wenn die Gerichte mit Unrecht der Competenz der Verwaltung entgegentreten. Würde dies nicht zugegeben, so wäre die Priorität der administrativen Entscheidung immer hinreichend, die richterliche Competenz zu gefährden (Bl. f. R. Bd. XXII S. 390). — Deßhalb ist es denn auch für die richterliche Beurtheilung völlig gleichgültig, ob die Verwaltung in ihren Beschlüssen den Rechtsweg vorbehalten hat, oder nicht; dieser Vorbehalt ist selbstverständlich.

Der Competenz-Confliktshof war im Falle, in einer Reihe von Erkenntnissen diesen Grundsatz auszusprechen; s. Erk. v. 18 Jan. 1853 (Reg. Bl. S. 114), 26 Juni 1858 (S. 969), 10 Nov. 1862 (S. 2583), 20 März 1864 (S. 865) und 24 April 1865 (S. 483).

Insofern die Urtheile der Gerichte fähig sind, rechtskräftig zu werden, d. h. für den entschiedenen Fall das Gesetz zu bilden, überwiegt die richterliche Gewalt.

Auch noch in anderen Beziehungen kann dies gesagt werden. — So entscheidet in streitigen Fällen der Richter über die Thatfragen, von welchen die Zuständigkeit abhängt, allein und in einer der Verwaltung gegenüber bindenden Weise; er ist Herr des Faktums. — Falls daher nach dem Vortrage des Klägers, d. h. nach seiner Darstellung der Thatsachen, sein Anspruch sich zur Beurtheilung durch die Gerichte eignet, sind diese unbedingt zuständig und wenn später die Gerichte jene Thatsachen als erwiesen erklären, so ist es ohne Belang, wenn etwa die Verwaltung eine andere, ihre eigene Zuständigkeit begründende, Ansicht vom Sachverhalte hat, z. B. behauptet, es handele sich um Gemeinde-Eigenthum, an welchem dem Kläger bloß in seiner Eigenschaft als Gemeindeglied Nutzrechte zustünden.

Auch darin, daß die Gerichte berufen sind, den verletzten Rechtszustand wieder herzustellen, falls die Verwaltung in rechtswidriger Weise sich Eingriffe in Privatrechte erlaubt, sollte dies auch nur durch Zuspruch einer Entschädigung geschehen, liegt ein Uebergewicht der richterlichen Gewalt.

Eine bestreitbare Frage ist, ob die Gerichte ausschließlich befugt sind, den Rechtsbegriff eines Privatrechtes festzustellen, d. h. die Frage zu entscheiden, ob die behaupteten Thatsachen ein unter dem Schutze der Gerichte stehendes, klagbares Privatrecht begründen. Mit andern Worten: Gehört die Entscheidung, ob bei gegebenen Thatsachen ein Privatrechtsverhältniß vorliege, zur Competenz oder aber zum Grunde der Sache?

Vor Errichtung des Competenz-Conflikts-Hofes war man ziemlich einig darüber, daß diese Frage zur ausschließlichen Entscheidung der Gerichte gehöre. s. Bl. f. R., Bd. XI S. 329, Bd. XVIII Anhang S. 15, Bd. XX S. 303 und 327, Bd. XXII S. 150 und Seuff. Archiv Bd. IV Nr. 81 und VI Nr. 253. Die nemliche Ansicht wird in einer gegen die sich gestaltende abweichende Ansicht des C. C. Hofs gerichteten Abhandlung in den Bl. für R., Bd. XX S. 81, sehr energisch vertreten.

Der C. C. Hof hat, wie angedeutet, die entgegengesetzte Meinung angenommen und bis in die neueste Zeit festgehalten. s. Erkenntniß von 18. Jan. 1853 (S. 126 u. 155), 20. Juni 1854 (S. 504 u. 512), 3. Okt. 1854 (S. 950), 19. Juni 1855 (S. 823), 16. Jan., 14. März und 14. Okt. 1859 (S. 107, 291 und 989), 6. Mai 1861 (S. 467), 24. April und 18. Dez. 1865 (S. 483 u. 37) und 4. Februar 1867 (S. 171). Er hat sogar vielfach den Satz ausgesprochen, daß bei Bemessung der Competenz der Gerichtshof nicht gebunden sei, die thatsächlichen Behauptungen der Parteien nackt, wie sie gegeben werden, zu Grunde zu legen, daß es vielmehr statthaft sei, unter Zusammenhalt aller Umstände und Herbeiziehung der in den Akten liegenden notorischen Thatsachen, diesen Behauptungen ihren wahren Gehalt zu geben. — s. obige Erk. vom 14. Okt. 1859, 24. April 1865, 18. Dez. 1865 und 4. Februar 1867.

Offenbar ist diese Ansicht auch begründet und beruht auf einer richtigen Würdigung der dem Gerichtshofe für Competenz-Conflikte gewordenen Aufgabe.

Es ist erklärlich, wenn zur Zeit, als noch kein eigner, überwiegend aus richterlichen Elementen zusammengesetzter Gerichtshof für solche Conflikte bestand, das Streben der Jurisprudenz dahin gerichtet war, die Entscheidung der Frage, ob ein klagbares Privatrecht vorliege, unbedingt den Gerichten zu vindiziren, denn nur hiedurch erschien eine wirksame Garantie gegen Uebergriffe der Verwaltung gegeben und waren die dem Schutze der Gerichte anvertrauten Privatrechte den Verfügungen der Regierungsgewalt gegenüber genügend sichergestellt. Man stellte auf, daß die Gerichte in fraglicher Beziehung über ihre Competenz selbst zu entscheiden hätten.

Daß nemlich es sich vorliegenden Falles um eine wirkliche Competenzfrage handele, ist außer Zweifel. Ebensogut als es z. B. eine Competenzfrage für ein Handelsgericht bildet, ob ein gewisses Geschäft ein Handelsgeschäft sei, ob aus demselben eine Handelsklage entspringe, ebensogut ist es auch eine Competenzfrage für die Gerichte überhaupt, ob eine gewisse Thatsache einen privatrechtlichen Anspruch begründe. Man verrückt den wahren Standpunkt, wenn man einseitig hervorhebt, daß es sich darum handele, ob ein Privatrecht begründet sei, denn in dieser Art der Begründung liegt eben auch die Competenz. Besteht nemlich gesetzlich ein Privatrecht nicht, so liegt eben eine Streitsache vor, für welche nach dem Willen des Gesetzes eine gerichtliche Klage nicht gestattet ist, über welche vielmehr (falls überhaupt ein Anspruch erhoben werden kann) nur die Verwaltungsbehörden erkennen sollen. Es ist nun offenbar nach Zweck und Geist des Gesetzes vom 28. Mai 1850 die Aufgabe des Gerichtshofs für Competenz-Conflikte in solch' zweifelhaften Streitfällen zu entscheiden, welches der Wille des Gesetzes sei und jeder Gewalt dasjenige zuzutheilen, was ihr von Rechtswegen gehört.

Für die Richtigkeit dieser Anschauung zeugt, daß sie sogar in Staaten, wo nicht, wie bei uns, ein eigener C. C. Hof besteht, als maßgebend gilt. s. Seuff. Archiv Bd. XII Nr. 194, vgl. jedoch auch Bd. VI Nr. 253.

§ 3.
Allgemeine Merkmale zur Bestimmung der Competenz.

Erhebt sich die Frage, ob ein vor Gericht gebrachter Anspruch als Justizsache zu betrachten sei, so ist zweierlei ins Auge zu fassen, nemlich 1) das Begehren und 2) dessen Begründung.

I. Das Begehren muß der Natur der richterlichen Gewalt entsprechen, es dürfen also nur Aussprüche über Rechtsverhältnisse und Verfügungen zum Vollzuge solcher Aussprüche und dies zwar einem bestimmten Gegner gegenüber vom Richter verlangt werden und ferner muß es sich um Privatrechtsverhältnisse handeln, um Anerkennung von Familienrechten, dinglichen Rechten, um den Zuspruch von Forderungen.

Auch in Fällen, wo die richterliche Zuständigkeit an sich gegeben wäre, erleidet sie aus Rücksichten für die konkurrirende Zuständigkeit der Verwaltung manche Beschränkungen in der Art, daß Begehren nicht zulässig sind, über welche zu erkennen nach gewöhnlichen Prinzipien die Gerichte zuständig wären.

Aus der Gleichberechtigung der Gerichte und der Verwaltung ergibt sich nemlich, daß keine dieser beiden Gewalten befugt ist, direkt gegen die andere einzuschreiten und sie in Ausübung ihrer Amtsthätigkeit zu hemmen. — Jede Gewalt weiß in ihrer Sphäre die Sachlage am besten zu würdigen, die Gerichte die strengen Rechtsprinzipien, die Verwaltung die Gründe der Zweckmäßigkeit; das Wohl des Staates erheischt daher, daß eine jede auf ihrem Gebiete möglichst frei walte und keine sich die Oberherrschaft über die andere anmaße.

Wenn daher die Gerichte unbestritten die Befugniß haben, selbst der Regierungsgewalt gegenüber die Privatrechte zu schützen, so dürfen sie doch zu diesem Schutze nicht alle Mittel anwenden, welche ihnen Privaten gegenüber zu Gebote stehen würden; sie müssen auf jene Mittel verzichten, welche die Verwaltung in Abhängigkeit von der Justiz stellen, sie in die Stellung einer Untergebenen herabdrücken und hierdurch ihre Wirksamkeit wesentlich beeinträchtigen würde.

Eine Folgerung hieraus ist, daß den Amtshandlungen der Verwaltung die Rechtsvermuthung zur Seite steht, sich auf gesetzlichem Boden zu bewegen und daß die Einschreitung der Gerichte gegen Akte der Verwaltung, insofern sie überhaupt zulässig ist, jedenfalls nur stattfinden kann nach erschöpfender Prüfung des Rechtsverhältnisses. — Die Verwaltung ist befugt, überall provisorisch einzuschreiten, wo sie sich zuständig erachtet, vorbehaltlich der Verantwortlichkeit, welche sie den konstitutionellen Organen gegenüber vertreten muß und der Entschädigungspflicht, über welche der Richter erkennt.

Hieraus folgt, daß die sonst im Prozesse statthaften provisorischen Anordnungen, sofern sie die Hemmung der Verwaltung in einer Amtsthätigkeit bezwecken, nicht statthaft sind. — Aus gleichen Gründen ist auch die possessorische Klage, wenn sie sich nicht blos auf Feststellung der Thatsache des juristischen Besitzes beschränkt, sondern die Aenderung eines auf amtlicher Aenderung beruhenden Besitzstandes bezweckt, für unstatthaft zu erklären. Erk. des C. C. H. vom 26. Juli 1852 (S. 867), 12. Juli 1853 (S. 1075) und 31. Juli 1854 (S. 673), diese 3 Erk. pfälzisch, 30. März 1857 (S. 377), 12. März 1860 (S. 301), 15. Februar 1864 (S. 223), 10. April 1865 (S. 443), 24. April 1865 (S. 492), 18. Sept. und 13. Nov. 1865 (S. 1073 und 1379), 25. Juni 1866 (S. 973) und 18. Sept. 1866 (S. 1499). Seuff. Archiv Bd. VI Nr. 252, Bd. XIII Nr. 96. Pfeifer prakt. Erörterungen Bd. III Nr. X § 27 und § 8 (S. 313).

Allerdings ist richtig, daß nach diesen Prinzipien ein vollkommener Schutz der Privatrechte nicht gegeben ist, denn eine nachfolgende Geldentschädigung, ja selbst eine spätere Anerkennung des Rechtes selbst, enthält nicht immer die volle Wiederherstellung des gestörten Rechtszustandes; allein bei der selbständigen Stellung der Verwaltung den Gerichten gegenüber, wie sie im öffentlichen Interesse nöthig ist, lassen sich Prinzipien, welche die Gerichte ermächtigen würden, fortwährend kontrolirend einzugreifen, nicht aufrecht erhalten. Wo das öffentliche Wohl überwiegend betheiligt ist, muß eben das Privatinteresse sich Beschränkungen gefallen lassen. s. jedoch Erk. des C. C. H. vom 27. Juli 1863 (S. 1951).

Eine weitere Folgerung aus obigen Prinzipien ist, daß sich die Gerichte in der Regel auf Anerkennung und Zuspruch des Rechts beschränken und es ihnen nicht zusteht, ihre Urtheile der Verwaltung gegenüber zum Vollzuge zu bringen, d. h. durch ihre Organe Zwang gegen die Verwaltung üben zu lassen. — Den Verwaltungsbehörden allein steht es in der Regel zu, die gegen den Fiskus oder öffentliche Corporationen ergangenen Urtheile in Vollzug zu setzen; sie sind hiezu durch ihre Amtspflicht gezwungen und sind in der Lage, den Vollzug so zu bethätigen, daß das öffentliche Interesse dadurch nicht geschädigt wird. Dieser Punkt ist übrigens jetzt durch die Bestimmungen des Art. 882 geregelt.

Wo es sich daher um provisorische Einschreitung irgend einer Art gegen Regierungsmaßregeln oder um Vollzug eines Urtheils handelt, dürfen die Gerichte nicht befehlend, sondern nur im Wege des Ersuchens den Verwaltungsbehörden gegenüber auftreten, falls dieser Weg der Natur des bestehenden Gerichtsverfahrens entspricht, wie es nach dem seitherigen Prozesse der Fall war. s. Erk. d. C. C. H. vom 13. Nov. 1865 (S. 1379) und 25. Juni 1866 (S. 973). — Nach dem neuen Prozesse fällt dieses Auskunftsmittel weg, da die Gerichte nicht mehr berufen sind, in Vertretung der Parteiinteressen solche Schritte zu thun, vielmehr diese den

Parteien selbst überlassen bleiben und der Richter sich auf den Urtheilsspruch beschränkt.

Selbstverständlich erscheint, daß die Gerichte befugt sind, die weiteren Verpflichtungen festzustellen, welche sich im Falle des Nichtvollzuges rechtlich ergeben.

Eine weitere Frage ist, ob die Gerichte in Fällen, wo sie nach erschöpfender Verhandlung erkennen, daß durch eine Regierungshandlung ein Privatrecht verletzt sei, sich ausschließlich bloß auf Zuspruch einer Geldentschädigung zu beschränken haben, oder aber ob es ihnen zusteht, die Verpflichtung zur Wiederherstellung des Rechtszustandes auszusprechen, d. h. die Verwaltungshandlung unter Umständen rückgängig zu machen.

Nach den Prinzipien, wie sie der C. C. Hof in verschiedenen Erkenntnissen namentlich demjenigen vom 25. Juni 1866 ganz allgemein aufgestellt hat, so daß sie ebenso die petitorische als die possessorische Klage umfassen, wäre den Gerichten (mit Ausnahme der speziell im Gesetze vorgesehenen Fälle) unbedingt das Recht versagt, in die Amtshandlungen der Verwaltung einzugreifen, sei es indem sie den Vollzug von Verwaltungsmaßregeln hemmen, sei es indem sie Wiederherstellung des Rechtszustandes anordnen.

Man kann hierfür geltend machen, einerseits, daß die Verwaltung keine Privatpartei sei, sondern eine gleich berechtigte öffentliche Gewalt, welche ebensogut wie die Gerichte, die Amtspflicht habe, die Gesetze zu beobachten, anderseits, daß den Gerichten eine übermächtige, die Energie der Verwaltung lähmende Stellung eingeräumt würde, falls man sie befugt erachtete, Verwaltungsbeschlüsse für wirkungslos zu erklären. Es wird ferner darauf hingewiesen, daß deßhalb die Unterthanen nicht schutzlos seien, indem ihnen konstitutionelle Garantien, nemlich das Recht der Beschwerde bei den Kammern und beim Staatsrathe (Verordnung v. 18. Nov. 1825 § 7 Nr. 11) zur Seite stünden, sowie das Recht auf Schadenersatz bliebe.

Es enthalten diese Erwägungen ohne Zweifel viel Richtiges, allein sie wurzeln mehr in den Ideen des Polizeistaates als des Rechtsstaates.

Vor Allem ist darauf hinzuweisen, daß die Verwaltung, sofern sie innerhalb ihrer Amtssphäre handelt, kein Unrecht zufügen kann, mag sie immerhin Privatinteressen verletzen und den Unterthanen Schaden am Vermögen oder an der persönlichen Freiheit zufügen. Auch für sie gilt der Grundsatz: qui jure suo utitur, neminem laedit. — s. Erk. des C. C. H. vom 25. Juli 1854 (S. 649.)

Es kann sich in solchen Fällen nur noch darum handeln, ob im Sinne des Gesetzes ihre Amtsgewalt eine unbedingte war, oder ob ihr blos unter der Bedingung der Entschädigung der Eingriff in Privatrechte gestattet sein sollte.

Die Hauptschwierigkeit liegt in der Frage: „Wie weit gehen die Amtsbefugnisse der Verwaltung?" — Allerdings wäre es bedenklich, den Gerichten allein die Entscheidung über diese Frage einzuräumen, und sie zu ermächtigen, alle Verwaltungsmaßregeln, welche sie für ungesetzlich halten, sofern dieselben in Privatrechte eingreifen, außer Wirksamkeit zu setzen.

Eine solche Gewalt würde die Verwaltung unter Aufsicht der Gerichte stellen. Allein so weit zu gehen ist nicht nöthig und ist nicht den Gesetzen gemäß. — Die Bestimmung der Gränze zwischen richterlicher und Regierungsgewalt steht eben, wie früher dem Staatsrathe, jetzt dem C. C. Hofe zu und dieser Gerichtshof hat in strittigen Fällen darüber abzuurtheilen, ob die Verwaltung ihre Befugnisse überschritten habe.

Das nemliche Prinzip, welches oben gegen die Gerichte zur Geltung gebracht wurde, muß auch gegen die Verwaltung gelten; letztere darf ebensowenig selbst und ausschließlich über ihre Competenz entscheiden, als die Gerichte. — Auch hier fällt die rechtliche Begründung des Anspruchs und die Competenzfrage zusammen. Hat nach Maßgabe der vorgetragenen thatsächlichen Behauptungen die Verwaltung innerhalb ihrer Zuständigkeit gehandelt, so ist jede Einschreitung der Gerichte, geschehe sie direkt oder indirekt, eine unbefugte und unzuständige und der C. C. Hof muß dies aussprechen, falls die Frage vor ihn gelangt. — Erkennt jedoch dieser Gerichtshof, daß, bei Voraussetzung der Richtigkeit jener thatsächlichen Behauptungen, die Verwaltung die Gränzen ihrer Zuständigkeit überschritten und ungesetzlich gehandelt, so tritt hiermit die Zuständigkeit der Gerichte zum Schutze der verletzten Privatrechte ins Leben.

Es liegt wohl keine Gefahr für das öffentliche Wohl vor, wenn bei solchen Voraussetzungen den Gerichten die Befugniß eingeräumt wird, nicht bloß Geldentschädigungen zuzusprechen, sondern das verletzte Recht an und für sich zur Anerkennung zu bringen. — Wenn die Verfassungsurkunde (Tit. VIII § 5) sagt, es habe der Fiskus in allen streitigen Privatrechtsverhältnissen bei den Gerichten Recht zu nehmen, so spricht sie allgemein und es liegt daher, falls ein streitiges Privatrechtsverhältniß unzweifelhaft gegeben ist, kein Grund vor, dasselbe nur bezüglich der Geldinteresse, also nur in verkümmerter Weise zu schützen. Es würde ja, wollte man das entgegengesetzte Prinzip in seiner Schärfe zur Anwendung bringen, der Verwaltung allein das unbedingte Recht zustehen, über das Eigenthum der Unterthanen gegen Entschädigung zu verfügen! — Ein jus eminens dieser Art hat jetzt keine Berechtigung mehr.

Hier reihen sich Betrachtungen an, welche sich speziell auf das Verfassungsgesetz vom 17. Nov. 1837 über Zwangsabtretung beziehen und welche dahin führen möchten, daß jedenfalls in so fern, als es sich um zwangsweise Wegnahme des Eigenthums außerhalb der Fälle und Formen jenes Gesetzes handelt, die Zuständigkeit der Gerichte sich weiter erstrecken müsse, als auf die Beurtheilung der Höhe des Schadens.

Jenes Gesetz sagt, daß die Zwangsabtretung von

Eigenthum (Art. 1) und sonstigen dinglichen Rechten (Art. 2) für öffentliche Zwecke nur eintreten könne 1) in den bezeichneten Fällen, 2) nach vorgängiger Entscheidung des Staatsraths (in letzter Instanz) über die Nothwendigkeit der Abtretung, endlich 3) gegen vorausgängige volle Entschädigung, welche das Gericht festsetzt.

Was ist nun Rechtens, wenn diese Voraussetzungen nicht eintreffen, wenn also die Verwaltung etwa zu andern Zwecken, ohne administrativ-richterliche Entscheidung, ohne vorausgängige Entschädigung, eigenmächtig Privateigenthum in Besitz nimmt?

Man darf nicht sagen, es sei nicht zu erwarten, daß die Verwaltung sich ein solch ungesetzliches Verfahren erlaube, denn, wollte man voraussetzen, die Verwaltung thue immer nur das, was dem Gesetze gemäß ist, so wäre überhaupt jeder Schutz der Privatrechte durch die Gerichte unnöthig. — Dieser Schutz ist nicht sowohl gegen den bösen Willen, als vielmehr gegen die falsche, durch Privatinteresse getrübte Auffassung gerichtet und beruht auf dem Gedanken, daß die Gerichte die strengeren Prinzipien des Privatrechts richtiger zu beurtheilen im Stande seien, als die Verwaltungsbehörden. Es sind eben Fälle denkbar, wo die Verwaltung im besten Glauben handelt, in ihrem Rechte zu sein, z. B. wenn sie meint, mit dem wirklichen Eigenthümer eine gültige Uebereinkunft wegen Bewilligung der Zwangsabtretung abgeschlossen zu haben, wenn sie der Ansicht ist, der Staat selbst oder eine Gemeinde sei der wahre Eigenthümer, wenn sie glaubt, besondere gesetzliche Bestimmungen räumten ihr ausnahmsweise das Recht ein, außer den Fällen und Formen des Gesetzes von 1837 einzuschreiten, z. B. zu erklären, daß ein gewisses Stück Land ein öffentlicher Weg sei oder Theil eines solchen bilde.

Wären in solchen Fällen die Gerichte auf Zuspruch einer Geldentschädigung beschränkt, so würde dies dem Geiste des Zwangsabtretungsgesetzes wohl nicht entsprechen, denn eine Geldentschädigung, welche nachfolgt, versteht sich schon nach allgemeinen Grundsätzen von selbst und alle Garantieen, welche das Gesetz dem Eigenthümer gibt, wären demnach (wenigstens was den gerichtlichen Schutz betrifft) illusorisch. Da nun die Gerichte speziell zum Schutze des Privateigenthums berufen sind, da ferner die Verfassungsurkunde den Schutz der Privatrechte nicht auf den Geldwerth beschränkt, da endlich das öffentliche Interesse nicht darunter leiden kann, wenn in Fällen, wo die Verwaltung unzweifelhaft sich ungesetzliche Eingriffe erlaubte, sie angehalten würde, das angemaßte Recht zurückzugeben, so möchte die Zuständigkeit der Gerichte in fraglicher Richtung mit Grund nicht zu bestreiten sein. — Die Beschwerde beim Staatsrathe, welcher nur berathend einwirken könnte (Verordn. von 18. Nov. 1825) und die Beschwerde bei den Kammern, welche sich mit erschöpfender Instruktion der Sache und eingehender Prüfung der That- und Rechtsfragen nicht befassen können, geben denjenigen wirksamen Schutz nicht, wie ihn der Geist des Gesetzes erheischt und wie er der Natur der Sache nach nothwendig ist. — s. Erk. des C. C. H. vom 27. Juli 1863 (S. 1951). Bl. f. R. Bd. XXII S. 390. Seuff. Archiv Bd. IV Nr. 251 Z. 9 u. Bd. XIII Nr. 96. Pfeifer prakt. Erört. Bd. III Nr. X § 8 (S. 314).

Uebrigens ist bezüglich der Verordnung vom 18. Nov. 1825 zu bemerken, daß Verordnungen ohne Gesetzeskraft zur Grundlage für die Regulirung der Competenz, überhaupt nicht dienen können. Sie können bloß dienen zum Vollzuge von Gesetzen, sie können aber ein Gesetz weder ersetzen, noch ergänzen, noch sogar auf die Auslegung desselben maßgebend einwirken. — Befremdend ist es daher, daß hie und da bloß auf derartige Verordnungen, als Quellen zur Competenzbestimmung, Bezug genommen wird.

II. Was die Begründung des Klagebegehrens betrifft, so ist es wesentlich, zu wissen, ob der behauptete Anspruch aus einer privatrechtlichen Quelle sich herleitet, ob er sich auf einen Privatrechtstitel gründet, d. h. einen Titel, welcher im Sinne des Gesetzes ein gerichtlich einklagbares (erzwingbares) Recht begründet.

Privatrechtstitel sind oder können sein: 1) das Gesetz selbst, 2) Verträge und letzwillige Verfügungen, 3) Verjährung und Herkommen, 4) Verleihung durch Verwaltungsbeschlüsse und 5) widerrechtliche Handlungen. —

1) Gesetz.

Aus Wortlaut und Sinn der Gesetze ist zu ermessen, ob ein klagbares Recht verliehen werden sollte oder nicht. — Wo das Gesetz zur Regelung des Verhältnisses von Privaten zum Staate, zur Gemeinde 2c. aus Gründen des öffentlichen Wohls, Ansprüche auf Bezug von Unterstützungen oder Nutzungen verleiht, ist zu vermuthen, daß es die Einwirkung der Verwaltung nicht ausgeschlossen wissen wollte, so z. B. bei der Alimentation durch die Heimathsgemeinde, bei der Theilnahme an Gemeindenutzungen 2c. — Solche Rechte sind, was den gerichtlichen Schutz betrifft, bloß prekäre.

2) Verträge und letztwillige Verfügungen.

Verträge bilden in so fern immer Privatrechtstitel, als man darunter solche Verabredungen versteht, welche den Zweck haben, klagbare Rechte zu begründen. Ist nemlich der Zweck ein anderer, so liegt im Grunde kein Vertrag vor, sondern nur etwas, was einem Vertrage ähnlich ist, wie z. B. ein Gemeindebeschluß, der von allen Gemeindgliedern einstimmig gefaßt wurde (Bl. f. R. Bd. XX Anhang S. 1). — Ist die Absicht zwar auf Begründung klagbarer Rechte gerichtet, hat jedoch der Vertrag Verhältnisse des öffentlichen Lebens zum Gegenstande, über welche nicht disponirt werden kann, so ist derselbe unheilbar nichtig, kann also gleichfalls nicht zur Grundlage einer gerichtlichen Klage dienen. — s. Erk. des C. C. H. v. 25. Juli 1854 (S. 660) 29. Dez.

1856 (S. 69), 9. Dez. 1859 (S. 1345), 23. April 1861 (S. 422) und 3. Juni 1862 (S. 1967); Seuff. Archiv Bd. IV Nr. 251 Ziff. 1, Bd. XII Nr. 195.

Die Frage, ob eine Uebereinkunft in der Absicht abgeschlossen wurde, klagbare Rechte zu begründen, entscheiden die Gerichte ausschließlich; die Frage aber, ob durch die Uebereinkunft ein klagbares Recht entstehen konnte, gehört zur Competenz.

Bei Schenkungen, welche zu Gunsten von Stiftungen ꝛc. gemacht werden und gewisse Bestimmungen bezüglich der Verwaltung und Verwendung enthalten, entsteht häufig die Frage, ob beabsichtigt war, ein klagbares Recht zu geben, oder aber, ob nur eine leitende Norm für die Curatelbehörde, welche selbstverständlich dem Willen des Schenkgebers möglichst Rechnung zu tragen hat, gegeben werden wollte. Ist die Stiftung eine öffentliche, so spricht die Vermuthung wohl dafür, daß Letzteres gemeint war. — Bezüglich der letztwilligen Verfügungen gilt im Wesentlichen das Nemliche, wie bei Schenkungen.

Ein Vertrags-Verhältniß ist auch dasjenige, in welches der Staat als Unternehmer von Güter- und Personen-Transporten (der Post- und Eisenbahn-Fiscus) mit den Privaten tritt.

3) Verjährung und Herkommen.

Verjährung und Gewohnheitsrecht sind in gleicher Weise Quellen des öffentlichen, wie des Privatrechtes; wenn man ersteren Ausdruck nicht etwa in der engeren Bedeutung nimmt und bloß auf den Erwerb klagbarer Rechte anwendet. — Durch Fortdauer eines Besitzstandes, einer Uebung, können sowohl Rechte, welche unter dem Schutze der Gerichte stehen, als auch Ansprüche, welche die Verwaltung zu berücksichtigen hat, begründet werden. Ob das Eine oder das Andere der Fall sei, hängt von der Natur des Besitzstandes ab und diese von den thatsächlichen Verhältnissen, unter denen der Besitzstand sich gebildet. — Die Verjährung beruht nemlich auf der Annahme, daß die Duldung einer Rechts-Ausübung, wenn sie gewisse Zeit dauert, einer ausdrücklichen Verleihung des Rechts gleichstehe. Ist nun diese Duldung aus dem öffentlichen Rechte, z. B. aus dem Staats- oder Gemeinde-Verbande zu erklären, so können natürlich auch nur Ansprüche, welche dem öffentlichen Rechte angehören, daraus erwachsen. — Im Zweifel wird gegen denjenigen zu entscheiden sein, welcher ein klagbares Recht erworben haben will; vgl. Bl. f. R. Bd. XX S. 303 u. 327.

4) Verleihung.

Von den Concessionen, welche die Verwaltung innerhalb ihrer Zuständigkeit gibt, ist im Zweifel zu vermuthen, daß das Recht fortwährender amtlicher Einwirkung vorbehalten wurde, also auch das Recht der Rücknahme. Erk. des C. C. H. vom 23. März 1863 (S. 523), 9. Dez. 1859 (S. 1345). Anders ist es, wenn das Gesetz das Gegentheil verfügt. Wassergesetz vom 28. Mai 1852 Art. 13.

Auch das Verhältniß des Staats zu seinen Beamten kann, abgesehen von den pragmatischen Rechten, aus dem Gesichtspunkte der Verleihung, nicht aber des Vertragsverhältnisses aufgefaßt werden. — Man kann die Verleihung der amtlichen Gewalt und Funktion als das Wesentliche ansehen und den Umstand, daß ein Gehalt zugesichert wurde, als Nebensache betrachten.

5) Widerrechtliche Handlungen.

Ein Privatrechtstitel liegt endlich in jeder widerrechtlichen Handlung, welche einen Schaden am Vermögen zufügt. — Es ist Grundsatz, daß die Gerichte unbedingt über Klagen auf Schadensersatz erkennen dürfen und namentlich auch der Regierungsgewalt gegenüber, falls feststeht, daß dieselbe widerrechtlich gehandelt habe. — s. Erk. des C. C. H. vom 26. April 1853 (S. 610), 30. März 1857 (S. 741), 23. März 1863 (S. 569), 18. Sept. 1865 (S. 1073) u. 25. Juni 1866 (S. 973). Bl. f. R. Bd. I S. 207, VIII S. 126, XI S. 329, XVIII S. 15 Anhang, XX S. 81 und XXII S. 390. Seuff. Archiv Bd. V Nr. 281.

Dieses unbedingte Klagrecht besteht übrigens nur dem Staate selbst gegenüber, nicht aber auch gegen diejenigen Beamten, welchen die beschädigende Handlung zur Last fällt.

Es ist eine weitere Folgerung, welche sich aus der Unabhängigkeit der Regierungsgewalt herleitet, daß Verwaltungsbeamte wegen ihrer Amtshandlungen nicht vor Gericht gestellt werden können, wenn nicht der Sachverhalt vorher auf dem Verwaltungswege untersucht und durch die Staatsregierung die Ermächtigung zur Klagerhebung gegeben ist. — In der französischen Gesetzgebung ist durch Art. 75 der Constitution vom 13. Frim. VIII dieses Prinzip sanktionirt, im rechtsrheinischen Bayern wird es aus der Natur der Sache und aus der Disciplinargewalt gefolgert. Es würde die Energie der Verwaltung in fühlbarer Weise lähmen, wenn der Verwaltungsbeamte bei jedem Schritte, den er, sei es nach eigener Ueberzeugung, sei es nach den Weisungen der Oberbehörde, pflichtgemäß macht, fürchten müßte, wegen Schadensersatz belangt zu werden. s. Erk. des C. C. H. vom 3. Juli 1852 (S. 811 u. 825), 26. April 1853 (S. 610), 11. Juli 1853 (S. 910), 26. Juni 1858 (S. 969), 20. Juli 1858 (S. 1036), 18. Sept. 1865 (S. 1073), 18. Sept. 1866 (S. 1527) und 22. Dez. 1868 (S. 82).

§ 4.

Verhältniß des Staats zu seinen Beamten.

Der C. C. H. hat mehrfach den Satz ausgesprochen, daß das Verhältniß der Staatsdiener zum Staate seiner Natur nach kein Privatrechts-Verhältniß sei, daß es demgemäß nur in Folge besonderer gesetzlicher Verfügungen Klage vor den Gerichten begründe. — Hiernach wäre also nicht der Gesichtspunkt des Vertrages (der Dienstmiethe, des Mandats) maßgebend, sondern der Gesichtspunkt der Verleihung amtlicher Funktionen mit dem Vorbehalt, daß sich der Beamte allen Beschränkungen und Verfügungen unterwerfe, welche das Aufsichtsrecht und die Disziplinargewalt der Regierung mit sich bringt. — s. Erk. vom 20. Juni und 11. Juli 1853 (S. 877 und 910), 23. Nov. 1859 (S. 1322), 25. Juni 1863 (S. 1241) und 29. Februar 1864 (S. 305).

Diese Prinzipien finden ihre Anwendung auf alle Beamte, welche im öffentlichen Dienste stehen, also auch auf solche, welche bloß Gemeinde- oder Kirchenämter verwalten, sofern jene Seite ihrer Thätigkeit, welche sie unter Oberaufsicht der Staatsregierung stellt, in Betracht kommt. s. Erk. vom 3. Okt. 1854 (S. 929), 23. Nov. 1859 (S. 1322), 27. Dez. 1860 (S. 116), 29. April 1861 (S. 437), 23. März 1863 (S. 530). Nach diesen Anschauungen wurde z. B. die Verwaltung für zuständig erklärt, einen Landgerichtsdiener zur Zahlung des vorschriftsmäßigen Gehalts an seinen Gehülfen zu verurtheilen; (Erk. vom 10. März 1856 (S. 217) und 25. Okt. 1859 (S. 1080); Magistratsräthe wegen Unvorsichtigkeit im Dienste zur Schadloshaltung anzuhalten; Erk. vom 3. Okt. 1854 (S. 929); die Bezüge von Pfarrern und Lehrern im Conflikte mit den Amtsnachfolgern zu regeln. (Erk. vom 23. Nov. 1859 (S. 1322), 27. Dez. 1860 (S. 116), 23. April 1861 (S. 483), 23. März 1863 (S. 530) und 19. Sept. 1865 (S. 1089). Vgl. auch Erk. v. 11. Juli 1853 (S. 910) und (für die Pfalz) v. 27. April 1861 (S. 437); ferner G. O. v. 29. April 1869 Art. 158.

In Betreff der besonderen Verhältnisse der rechnungspflichtigen Beamten s. Erk. v. 3. Juli 1852 (S. 811 u. 825), 11. Juli 1853 (S. 910), 26. April 1853 (S. 655), 24. Dez. 1857 (S. 33), 3. Juni 1862 (S. 1974) und 23. März 1863 (S. 569), sowie Seuff. Archiv Bd. XI Nr. 297.

Es ist dabei selbstverständlich, daß sich die Verwaltung blos auf das Disziplinäre, Amtliche, d. h. auf Lösung der Frage zu beschränken hat, ob und wie weit der Beamte pflichtwidrig gehandelt habe und deßhalb haftbar sei. Ergeben sich weitere Fragen privatrechtlicher Natur, z. B. Berufung auf Zahlung, Compensation, Verantwortlichkeit eines Dritten, Cession &c., so ist die gerichtliche Competenz unbestritten. — Erk. des C. C. H. vom 3. Juli 1852 (S. 811 u. 825), vom 11. Juli 1853 (S. 910), 10. März 1856 (S. 217), 15. Dez. 1856 (S. 5) und 23. März 1863 (S. 569).

Es läßt sich nicht verkennen, daß bei strenger Durchführung dieser Prinzipien die amtliche Gewalt einerseits ihre natürlichen Gränzen überschreitet, zufolge deren sie nur zu solchen Maßnahmen berechtigt sein sollte, welche aus der prekären Natur des Dienstes sich herleiten, d. h. zur Entziehung dienstlicher Befugnisse und Bezüge mit Ausschluß jeder weitergreifenden Wirkung; daß ferner andererseits die pragmatischen Rechte gewisser Beamten gefährdet erscheinen, indem diese Rechte zwar nicht direkt durch Entziehung der Dienstbezüge selbst, wohl aber indirekt durch Auflage von Leistungen, welche die Gehaltsbezüge gegenstandslos machen, geschädigt werden können.

Zu wesentlich anderen Resultaten gelangt man, wenn man das Vertragsverhältniß in den Vordergrund stellt und mit Seuff. Comment. zur G. O. Bd. I S. 211 Note 207 von der Anschauung ausgeht, daß der § 29 des Staatsdiener-Ediktes, indem er für alle Verfügungen dieses Edikts den gerichtlichen Schutz gewährt, nur die Anwendung und Ausdehnung eines bestehenden Prinzipes enthalte; daß also die Zuständigkeit der Gerichte bei Klagen aus einem Dienstverhältnisse selbstverständlich sei. Hiernach hätten die Beamten ohne pragmatische Rechte nicht bloß für die bereits geleisteten Dienste den nemlichen Rechtsschutz wie andere, sondern es müßte überhaupt die Amtsgewalt der Verwaltung überall dort ihre natürlichen Gränzen finden, wo deren Eigenschaft als vertragschließender Theil in Betracht käme.

Wie dem auch sei, jedenfalls ist anerkannt, daß alle dem Staatsdiener-Edikte zuwiderlaufenden Verfügungen der Staatsgewalt, ohne Ausnahme, eine Privatrechtsverletzung enthalten. s. Erk. des C. C. H. vom 9. Dez. 1859 (S. 1338). Umzugsgebühren betr.

§ 5.

Entschädigungsklagen gegen den Staat und Verwaltungsbeamte.

Wie schon gesagt, ist nicht blos in jenen Fällen, wo bei berechtigten Amtshandlungen die Verpflichtung zur Schadenersatz-Leistung vorausgesetzt wird, sondern auch in jenen Fällen, wo die Verwaltung widerrechtlich gehandelt, ihre Amtsbefugnisse überschritten hat, Entschädigungsklage vor den Gerichten gegeben. — Diese Klage steht auch letzteren Falls dem Staate selbst (dem Fiskus) gegenüber unbedingt zu, ohne daß eine Entscheidung der Verwaltung selbst über Gesetzwidrigkeit oder Gesetzmäßigkeit der Amtshandlungen vorauszugehen hätte. — Behauptet die Verwaltung, sie habe in ihren Rechten gehandelt, so hat sie nöthigenfalls Competenz-Conflikt zu erheben und es ist Sache des C. C. Hofs, zu entscheiden, ob im gegebenen Falle von einem damnum injuria datum die Rede sein könne.

In diesem Sinne entschied ein Erkenntniß des C. C. H. v. 26. April 1853 (S. 610). Im entgegengesetzten Sinne ist entschieden im Erk. des C. C. H. vom 2. Juli 1867 (S. 881) und Seuff. Comment. zur G. O. Bd. I S. 209 und 210.

Mit letzterer Ansicht kann ich mich nicht befreunden, sie scheint mir vielmehr die Aufgabe des C. C. Hofs viel zu eng aufzufassen, welche, wie oben dargethan, sowohl den Gerichten als der Verwaltung gegenüber weiter geht, als man früher annahm. Dieser Ansicht gemäß wäre die Verwaltung selbst ausschließlicher Richter über ihre Competenz, d. h. über die Frage, wie weit sie gehen dürfe, ohne zivilrechtlich haftbar zu sein, oder unter welchen Voraussetzungen sie wegen culpa oder dolus einzustehen habe. Die Zuständigkeit der Gerichte träte nur ein, wenn die Verwaltung zugestehen würde, in

Verschuldung zu sein und der gerichtliche Schutz beschränkte sich auf einen sehr untergeordneten Punkt, nemlich die Ausmittlung des Schadens.

Die nemlichen Prinzipien müßten im Grunde auch maßgebend erachtet werden im Falle, wo durch Nachlässigkeit von Bediensteten der Staatsbahn ein Brand oder sonstiger Schaden verursacht wird, denn auch hier kann die Verwaltung sich darauf berufen, daß sie die Disziplin über ihre Beamten habe, und daß sie am besten zu beurtheilen wisse, ob dieselben durch Nichtbeobachtung der Dienstesvorschriften rc. gefehlt und der Gesichtspunkt des Vertrags fällt hier hinweg. Alle diese Erwägungen sind richtig, wenn sich der Anspruch gegen bestimmte Beamten richtet, nicht aber wenn der Verwaltung im Allgemeinen der Vorwurf gemacht wird, daß sie einen widerrechtlichen Schaden zugefügt.

Gleichgültig ist, ob die Beschädigung aus einer direkten Anordnung der Staatsregierung entstanden, oder aber ob sie nur Folge der Amtsthätigkeit ihrer Beamten ist. — Letzterer Satz findet seine Rechtfertigung schon in den allgemeinen Rechtsprinzipien, kraft deren der Mandant für die Handlungen seines Mandatars einzustehen hat. — Aus dem eigenthümlichen Verhältnisse der Unterthanen zum Staate, kraft dessen sie gezwungen sind, mit dem vom Staate zu seiner Vertretung aufgestellten Organen zu verkehren, leitet sich aber noch die weitergehende Folgerung, daß der Staat seine Beamten unbedingt zu vertreten hat, ohne daß zu untersuchen wäre, ob diese die Gränzen ihrer Amtsbefugnisse überschritten haben oder nicht. — Die Thatsache, daß der Beamte als solcher, nicht aber als Privatperson gehandelt, ist hier allein maßgebend. s. Seuff. Archiv Bd. V Nr. 281 (Erk. des O. A. G. vom 8. Juli 1851) vgl. auch Pfeifer prakt. Erört. Bd. III Nr. X § 13 (S. 374.)

Auch auf schuldhafte Unterlassungen kann sich die Haftbarkeit des Staates erstrecken. s. Erk. des C. C. H. v. 26. April 1853 (S. 610), welches sehr weit geht.

Im inneren Zusammenhange mit der unbedingten Vertretung der Beamten durch den Staat und mit dem diesem zustehenden Rechte der Aufsicht und Disziplin steht es und ist außerdem durch die Selbständigkeit der Verwaltung bedingt, daß Verwaltungsbeamte wegen amtlichen Handlungen oder Unterlassungen nur vor Gericht gezogen werden dürfen, wenn die vorgesetzte Behörde die Sachlage geprüft und die Verschuldung des Beamten ausgesprochen hat. — Mit diesem Ausspruche gibt die Staatsregierung kund, daß sie die fraglichen Handlungen als gesetzwidrig und als Ueberschreitung des amtlichen Mandats betrachte und nicht in der Lage sei, den Beamten mit ihrer Verantwortlichkeit zu decken. — Die Verweigerung der Ermächtigung zur Klage beseitigt die eigene Verantwortlichkeit nicht.

Selbstverständlich ist schließlich, daß Beschädigungen und Rechtsverletzungen, welche der Beamte nicht als solcher und in Ausübung seiner Amtsthätigkeit, sondern nur bei Gelegenheit derselben, verursacht hat, z. B. Injurien, ebenso zu betrachten sind, als seien sie von Privaten verübt. Erk. des C. C. H. v. 2. Juli 1852 (S. 803) und 18. Sept. 1865 (S. 1073).

§. 6.

Polizeigewalt nach Maßgabe des Polizeistrafgesetzes.

Nach den Grundsätzen des P. St. G. ist den Gerichten nicht bloß die Bestrafung der Polizeiübertretungen zugewiesen, sondern es hängt von ihrer Entscheidung auch die Wiederherstellung des ordnungsmäßigen Zustandes ab, in der Art, daß die Polizeigewalt zu den bezüglichen Maßregeln entweder der Ermächtigung, oder wenn sie vorläufig eingeschritten ist, der Genehmigung durch richterliches Urtheil bedarf. (Art. 28 und 30.) Es hat diese Befugniß der Gerichte eine um so größere Tragweite, als sie nach Art. 44 über die gesetzliche Giltigkeit der Polizeivorschriften abzuurtheilen haben.

Hieraus folgt, daß in Fällen fraglicher Art den Gerichten allein und ausschließlich die Entscheidung darüber zusteht, ob eine polizeiliche Maßregel gesetzwidrig sei und Grund zu Entschädigungs-Ansprüchen gebe oder nicht. — Es liegt hierin eine durch die Wichtigkeit der Materie sich rechtfertigende Abweichung von den vorstehend entwickelten allgemeinen Prinzipien, welche Abweichung einschränkend zu erklären ist, und nur auf jene Verhältnisse Anwendung findet, wo die Verwaltung ihre Befugnisse bloß in den Bestimmungen des P. St. G. findet. — Dieses Gesetz ist nemlich nicht bestimmt, die Zuständigkeit der Verwaltung in umfassender Weise zu regeln und zu begränzen, läßt vielmehr, soweit es nicht ändert, die allgemeinen Prinzipien bestehen.

Selbstverständlich kann die Verwaltung diese gerichtliche Controle nicht dadurch umgehen, daß sie etwa Polizeiverordnungen ohne Strafandrohung erläßt oder eine strafrechtliche Einschreitung und Prüfung nicht veranlaßt.

Als eine Lücke des Gesetzes ist hervorzuheben, daß die Prüfung der Gesetzmäßigkeit polizeilicher Maßregeln, sowie die dadurch bedingte Ermächtigung oder Genehmigung nur einen Nebenpunkt (eine Vorfrage) für die strafrichterliche Aburtheilung bildet und kein Weg vorgezeichnet ist für jene Fälle, wo eine solche Aburtheilung, sei es wegen Sterbfalles, sei es wegen Verjährung, sei es aus sonstigen Gründen, unmöglich ist. — Man hat übersehen, daß fragliche Ermächtigung oder Genehmigung selbständige Bedeutung hat und das Bedürfniß derselben bestehen bleibt, auch nachdem die Strafbarkeit der schuldigen Person weggefallen ist oder besteht, auch wenn eine solche nie vorhanden war. — Um diese Lücke im Geiste des Gesetzes auszufüllen, wird nichts erübrigen, als der Polizeigewalt die vorläufige Einschreitung (welche zu verwehren wer rückgängig zu machen ja gleichfalls kein gesetzlicher Weg gegeben ist) zu gestatten und im Falle, wo Jemand über gesetzwidrige Beschädigung sich beschwert, es dem Civilrichter zu überlassen, die Frage der Gesetzwidrigkeit zu prüfen. — Es wird keinem Anstande unterliegen, dem Civilrichter hier die nemliche Zuständigkeit einzuräumen, welche der Strafrichter hätte beanspruchen können, falls die Frage vor ihn gebracht worden wäre.

§ 7.

Vollzug von Verwaltungs-Beschlüssen.

Der C. C. H. hat in einer Reihe von Erkenntnissen als Regel anerkannt, daß diejenige Behörde, welche zuständig ist zur Entscheidung, auch zuständig ist zum Vollzuge. s. Erk. v. 26. April 1853 (S. 655), 20. Juni 1853 (S. 877), 3. Okt. 1854 (S. 929), 15. Dez. 1856 (S. 5) u. 7. Mai 1866 (S. 557).

Eine Modifikation dieser Regel trat ein bei Gemeindeumlagen, insofern den Gemeinden nur eine beschränkte Exekutions-Befugniß zustand. — Erk. vom 26. März 1860 22. und 23. Juni 1863, 26. Juli u. 14. Nov. 1864 u. 22. Mai 1865. s. jetzt Art. 48 der Gemeindeordnung vom 29. April 1869.

Eine Ausnahme wurde auch anerkannt bezüglich jener Vollzugsmaßregeln, welche ihrer Natur nach der Verwaltung fremd sind, z. B. Immobiliar-Exekution. s. Erk. v. 9. Juni 1857 (S. 727) u. 26. März 1860 (S. 377).

Bezüglich der Feststellung und Einklagung von Anwaltsgebühren in Administrativsachen s. Erk. v. 23. März 1857 (S. 318), 29. Febr. 1864 (S. 316) u. 13. Aug. 1866 (S. 1237).

In wie fern diese Prinzipien durch die Bestimmungen der neuen Proceßordnung (Hptst. XXXI) eine Aenderung erleiden, wird an entsprechender Stelle geprüft werden.

§ 8.

Abgaben und Umlagen.

Es ist unbestrittenes Prinzip, daß die Besteuerung der Unterthanen, d. h. die Sorge für Beischaffung der Mittel zur sachgemäßen Führung des öffentlichen Dienstes, eine Verwaltungssache sei. Dieses Prinzip geht, insofern es auf Entscheidungen über Steuerpflicht Anwendung findet, nicht gerade aus der inneren Natur des Gegenstandes hervor, weil die Steuern in der Regel nicht nach Ermessen der Regierung auferlegt werden, sondern durch Gesetze geregelt sind und es sich also um die Beurtheilung handelt, ob gegebenen Falls das Gesetz eine Steuer gestatte oder nicht. Die Gründe der Zuständigkeit liegen in der Wichtigkeit eines schnellen und sicheren Eingangs der Steuern und theilweise in der Mischung richterlicher und administrativer Erwägungen. — Etwas Abnormes und Ungehöriges könnte jedoch in der Zuweisung von Steuerfragen an die Gerichte nicht erblickt werden, wie denn z. B. dieselben in der Pfalz über Einregistrirungs-, Oktroi- und Stempel-Gebühren erkennen.

Die Zuständigkeit der Verwaltung erstreckt sich, wie wohl zu beachten, nicht bloß auf eine vorläufige, die Rückforderung vorbehaltende Entscheidung, sondern es steht derselben das endgültige Urtheil zu. Sie erkennt ausschließlich, ob und in welchem Betrage eine bestimmte Person steuerpflichtig sei.

Selbstverständlich liegt hierin auch die Würdigung aller Umstände, von denen gegebenen Falls die Steuerpflicht abhängt. Eine Rückforderung der auf Festsetzung der Verwaltung hin gezahlten Steuern kann daher dem Staate selbst gegenüber nur unter der Voraussetzung vor den Gerichten erhoben werden, daß die administrative Entscheidung unangefochten bleibt, z. B. auf Grund der Behauptung doppelter Zahlung. — Weitergehende Ausnahmen wären inkonsequent.

Da nun aber die Beschlüsse der Verwaltung nur dem Staate gegenüber die Steuerpflicht festsetzen, so steht es Demjenigen, welcher die Steuer gezahlt hat, frei, seinen Rückgriff gegen Andere zu nehmen, falls diese kraft Vertrages, vermöge Erbverhältnisse oder aus sonstigen civilrechtlichen Gründen zur Tragung der somit nur vorschußweise gezahlten Steuer verpflichtet sind. s. Seuff. Archiv Bd. I Nr. 105, Bd. IV Nr. 251, Bd. XI Nr. 95, Bd. XII Nr. 195. Etwas abweichend Bl. f. R. Bd. I S. 151.

Diese Prinzipien erstrecken sich auf alle öffentliche Abgaben, welcher Art sie auch seien, insbesondere auch auf Gemeinde- und Cultus-Umlagen, sowie überhaupt auf alle Leistungen, deren Natur oder deren geschichtliche Entstehung sie als zu öffentlichen Zwecken bestimmt erscheinen läßt. — Es ist dabei auch gleichgültig, ob die Abgabe in eine öffentliche Kasse fließt oder ob sie Theil des Gehaltes eines öffentlichen Beamten bildet, d. h. ob sie indirekt oder direkt zu öffentlichen Zwecken verwendet wird. s. im Allg. Erk. des C. C. H. v. 24. Juli 1854 (S. 622) u. 29. Dez. 1856 (S. 69); bez. der Beisteuer für die Armenpflege Erk. v. 16. Nov. 1858 (S. 1559), 23. Nov. 1859 (S. 1319) u. 27. Nov. 1860 (S. 1148); bez. der Cultusbedürfnisse der Juden Erk. v. 4. März 1856 (S. 193) und 3. Juni 1862 (S. 1967); bez. der Reichnisse: a) an Pfarrer Erk. v. 19. Juni 1855 (S. 823), 9. Juni 1857 (S. 776), 11. Nov. 1861 (S. 915), 4. Jan. u. 30. Dez. 1861 (S. 165 u. 81), 15. Dez. 1862 (S. 2648) u. 25. Juni 1866 (S. 941); b) an Lehrer und Küster Erk. v. 25. Juli 1854 (S. 660) u. 14. Nov. 1859 (S. 1129); c) an Mitgl. des Feldgerichts Erk. v. 19. Sept. 1865 (S. 1043); d) an öffentl. Güterbestätter Erk. v. 20. Juni 1853 (S. 877); bez. des örtl. Malzaufschlags Erk. v. 25. Okt. 1859 (S. 1072); bez. des Taxwesens Erk. v. 18. Jan. 1853 (S. 138) u. 18. Dez. 1865 (S. 67); bez. Erhebung von Wegzöllen Erk. v. 23. April 1861 (S. 422); bez. Erhebung von Wasserzins Erk. v. 6. Mai 1861 (S. 467); bez. der Haltung eines Zuchtstiers Erk. v. 20. März 1864 (S. 865). (In beiden letzteren Fällen wurden die Gerichte zuständig erklärt.)

§ 9.

Wegpolizei.

Es ist außer Frage, daß der Regierungsgewalt die unbeschränkte Verwaltung der öffentlichen Wege zusteht. Selbst die freie Verfügung darüber ist ihr nicht bestritten; sie kann daher Wege beliebig verlegen, ganz eingehen lassen, zu andern Zwecken verwenden, ohne daß sich Jemand deßhalb vor Gericht beschweren dürfte. s. Erk. des C. C. H. v. 20. Juni 1854 (S. 504 und 512) und 22. April 1861 (S. 409); Bl. f. R. Bd. I S. 332.

Da es die Bestimmung öffentlicher Wege ist, von Jedermann benützt zu werden, so kann aus deren Benützung, so lange sie auch gedauert haben möge, nie ein klagbares Recht entstehen, es müßte denn geradezu unmöglich sein, die besondere Art der Benützung aus der öffentlichen Bestimmung herzuleiten.

So selbstverständlich dieser Satz ist, so führt er doch in seiner unbeschränkten Anwendung zu großer Härte.

Die französische Jurisprudenz ist, im Gefühle dieser Härte, zu dem Auswege gekommen, daß sie solche Verfügungen der Verwaltung, welche die Benützung der an den Weg grenzenden Grundstücke, insbes. Bauten, wesentlich beeinträchtigen, welche also den Werth dieser Grundstücke wesentlich mindern, als Ueberschreitungen der Zuständigkeit betrachtet und gerichtliche Klage zuläßt. Sie geht von der Anschauung aus, daß die Angrenzer, so weit ihnen der Weg nothwendig ist, eine Servitut auf dessen Fortbestand haben, daß insbesondere derjenige, welcher mit ausdrücklicher oder stillschweigender Genehmigung der Verwaltung neben einem öffentlichen Wege gebaut hat, durch diese Thatsache allein schon das Recht erlangt, daß ihm die bestimmungsgemäße Benützung des Weges zum Ausgehen, Ausfahren 2c. nicht genommen oder dem Wesen nach verkümmert werden dürfe. — Es ist dies ein Recht, jenem vergleichbar, welches eine Conzession zur Errichtung eines Triebwerkes an einem öffentlichen Flusse verleiht.

Dieses Prinzip wird am klarsten aus einigen praktischen Fällen hervortreten. Auf Anordnung der Gemeinde-Verwaltung war auf einem öffentlichen Weg ein öffentliches Waschhaus erbaut worden, welches einem Hausbesitzer Ausgang und Aussicht wegnahm. Auf erhobene Klage erging folgendes Urtheil:

„Considérant, que les rues sont destinées à „donner aux édifices les jours, les vues et les „issues, qui leur sont necessaires et à servir à „l'ecoulement des eaux menagères et pluviales; „que tout édifice élevé a, par le seul fait de cette „situation un droit acquis à la jouissance du „passage“ etc.

Auf Cassationsrekurs entschied der Cassationshof durch Urtheil vom 10. Nov. 1841 (Sirey 1842 p. 178) in folgender Weise:

„Attendu, que l'arrêt attaqué, en condamnant „la commune de B. à détruire le lavoir qu'elle „avait fait construire dans la rue du Pont — comme „portant atteinte à la dite propriété, a, par cela „même statué sur une question, qui etait de sa „competence“ etc.

In einem 2. Falle war durch Erhöhung einer Straße ein an derselben liegendes Haus bedeutend entwerthet worden. Durch Urtheil vom 11. Dez. 1827 (Sir. 1829 I. 85) sprach sich der Cassationshof dahin aus:

„Attendu, que les lois etc. obligent bien les „habitans à supporter sans indemnité toutes „les charges et sujétions, que comportent le bon „ordre; mais qu'il n'en peut être de même toutes „les fois, que l'effet immédiat de travaux faits sur „la voie publique, est de ruiner ou de détériorer „notablement un immeuble; que dans ce dernier „cas, le dommage imposé à un ou plusieurs habitans, „dans l'interêt de tous, doit être l'objet d'une „indemnité“ etc.

Gleiches Urtheil erging am 18. Jan. 1826 (Sir. 1826 p. 269).

Ich glaubte diese beachtenswerthe Jurisprudenz, welche sich übrigens in neuerer Zeit dahin geändert hat, daß in solchen Fällen die Entscheidung den Organen der Verwaltungs-Justiz zustehe, hier anführen zu müssen, weil sie sich nur auf Grundlagen allgemeiner Rechtsprinzipien entwickelt hat und ihre Gründe daher, soweit sie stichhaltig erscheinen, allgemeine Anwendung zu finden geeignet sind.

In gleicher Weise, wie durch Benützung eines öffentlichen Weges Privatrechte nicht erworben werden, kann andererseits auch durch fortdauernde Unterhaltung des Wegs, resp. Bestreitung der Kosten derselben, keine Privat-Verpflichtung entstehen. — s. Erk. des C. C. H. vom 28. März 1867 (S. 465), Bl. f. R. Bd. XIX Anhang S. 106.

Was vorstehend von öffentlichen Wegen gesagt ist, gilt auch von öffentlichen Plätzen, sowie von allem Zubehör, wie Brunnen, Wasserleitungen, Bäumen, Brücken 2c. s. Erk. des C. C. H. v. 27. Dez. 1860 (S. 129), 6. Mai 1861 (S. 467), 7. Juni 1862 (S. 1983), 26. März 1867 (S. 409). Vgl. jedoch Erk. v. 23. März 1863 (S. 523).

Schwierigkeiten ergeben sich, wenn Streit entsteht, ob es sich überhaupt um einen öffentlichen Weg handle oder aber um Privateigenthum.

Daß diese Frage an und für sich vor die Gerichte gehöre, kann zwar nicht bezweifelt werden, allein strittig ist, wie weit hier der gerichtliche Schutz wirksam sei und ob nicht die Erklärung der Verwaltung, daß sie ein gewisses Stück Land als öffentlichen Weg erkläre und beanspruche, zur Folge habe, daß das vom Gerichte anzuerkennende Eigenthum sich in Entschädigung auflöse. Um diese Frage noch schärfer zu begrenzen, ist hervorzuheben, daß sie sich nur auf's petitorium bezieht.

Die einfachste und den Rechtsprinzipien am meisten entsprechende Lösung wäre wohl die, daß, nachdem die Gerichte entschieden haben, es sei irgend ein Stück Land, welches die Verwaltung als öffentlichen Weg beansprucht, freies Privateigenthum, die Verwaltung entweder dasselbe räumen oder aber die Zwangsabtretung nach dem Gesetze von 1837 herbeiführen müsse, falls die Voraussetzungen einer solchen gegeben wären. Diese streng juristische Lösung entspricht dem Geiste der neueren Gesetzgebung. So hat z. B. das Wasserbenützungsgesetz von 1852 die Befugniß der Verwaltung, einen Fluß als öffentlichen zu erklären, in ähnlicher Weise geregelt (Art. 3 und 5), obgleich Privatflüsse schon ihrer Natur nach in gewissem Grade der öffentlichen Benützung gewidmet sind und nicht in dem Grade Privateigenthum sein können, wie der Grund und Boden, welcher als Weg benützt wird.

Die bestehende Jurisprudenz scheint übrigens der Verwaltung weitergehende Befugnisse zuzugestehen. Im Erk. des C. C. H. vom 15. Februar 1864 (S. 223) wird von dem Satze ausgegangen, daß über die Frage, ob ein Weg ein öffentlicher sei, blos die Verwaltung entscheide; in Erk. vom 10. April und 24. April 1865 (S. 451 und 492) erscheint dieser Satz dahin gemildert, daß durch die Entscheidung der Verwaltung bloß das Bestehen des öffentl. Wegs an sich, als Servitut, festgestellt werde, daß jedoch die Frage, wem Grund und Boden eigenthümlich gehöre, frei bleibe. Durch Erk. vom 28. Dez. 1864 (S. 105) ist ausgesprochen, daß für die Frage, welche Behörde zur Entscheidung zuständig sei, lediglich die gegenwärtige Eigenschaft des Weges von Belang sei, durch Erk. vom 10. April 1865 (S. 443) aber, daß es ohne Belang sei, ob eine gewisse Fläche bereits zur Benützung der öffentlichen Straße gezogen worden sei.

Sucht man sich aus diesen Entscheidungen ein Gesammtbild zu machen, so möchte etwa die Jurisprudenz des obersten Gerichtshofs dahin sich zusammenfassen lassen: 1) Hat eine Fläche noch nicht als öffentlicher Weg gedient und handelt es sich also darum, einen solchen Weg neu zu gründen oder auszudehnen, so ist bloß das Gesetz über Zwangsabtretung maßgebend; 2) Ist jedoch eine Fläche bereits als öffentlicher Weg dauernd benützt worden, kommt ihr also faktisch die Eigenschaft eines öffentlichen Weges zu, so ist die Entscheidung der Verwaltung maßgebend für das Fortbestehen des Weges, und der Eigenthümer kann vor Gericht nur Schadensersatz verlangen.

Hiermit wäre allerdings ausgesprochen, daß in diesem Ausnahmsfalle die Verwaltung allein und ohne Einhaltung der Formen und Bedingungen des Gesetzes v. 1837, die Zwangsabtretung herbeiführen könne, denn ob das abzutretende Eigenthum in Streit ist oder nicht, ist im Grunde gleich und ebenso, ob die Abtretung dadurch erfolgt, daß mir der Schutz gegen Wegnahme versagt oder dadurch, daß ich positiv zur Hingabe genöthigt werde.

§ 10.

Wasserpolizei.

Diese Materie, welche am meisten Stoff zu Conflikten zu bieten scheint, ist durch das Ges. v. 28. Mai 1852 in einer Weise geregelt, daß seitdem ein nennenswerther Competenz-Conflikt nicht zu entscheiden war.

§ 11.

Zwangsabtretung zum öffentlichen Nutzen.

In dieser Beziehung ist das Ges. v. 17. Nov. 1837 maßgebend.

Der C. C. Hof hat entschieden:

1) Daß die Frage, ob der Expropriirende das Ganze nehmen müsse, oder sich auf den ihm nöthigen Theil eines Grundstückes beschränken dürfe, zur Entschädigungsfrage und daher vor die Gerichte gehöre. Erk. vom 18. Nov. u. 23. Dez. 1861 (S. 957 u. 29).

2) Daß ebenso die Gerichte zu erkennen haben, ob die Verwaltung von dem eingeleiteten Zwangsabtretungs-Verfahren zurücktreten dürfe. Erk. v. 30. Dez. 1861 (S. 90) und 1. März 1864 (S. 359).

§ 12.

Armenwesen.

Die Unterstützungen aus öffentl. Mitteln für Arme und Hülfsbedürftige, insbesondere die Alimentations-Ansprüche an die Heimathsgemeinde beruhen auf keinem privatrechtlichen Titel. s. Erk. vom 3. April 1852, 23. März 1857, 23. Dez. 1858, 25. Okt. und 4. Nov. 1859, 20. März 1864, 13. Nov. 1865 u. 8. Mai 1866. Heimathsgesetz vom 16. April 1868 Art. 23 u. 24.

§ 13.

Forstwesen.

Die Zuständigkeit in Forstsachen ist im Forstgesetze vom 28. März 1852 geregelt. — Hiernach haben die Gerichte zu erkennen über den Bestand und den Umfang von Forstberechtigungen; die Frage aber, ob nach den Regeln einer vernünftigen Forstwirthschaft die zuerkannte Berechtigung im gegebenen Falle ausgeübt werden könne, gehört zur Zuständigkeit der Forstverwaltung, welche nach Anrufen des belasteten Waldeigenthümers die zeitweise Beschränkung der Berechtigung verfügen kann. Bezüglich der hierbei sich ergebenden Anstände s. Erk. des C. C. H. vom 16. Nov. 1858 (S. 1585), 21. Okt. 1859 (S. 1049), 29. Dez. 1859 (S. 74) und 30. März 1863 (S. 596).

§ 14.

Gemeinde-Verwaltung.

Die Verwaltung der Gemeinde ist ein Zweig der öffentlichen Verwaltung; es sind daher im Wesentlichen die allgemeinen Prinzipien maßgebend.

Da nun bei der Entwicklung der jetzigen politischen Gemeinde vielfach privatrechtliche Verhältnisse (die Markgenossenschaft) einwirkten, so entsteht häufig Zweifel, ob gewisse gemeinschaftlich benützte Ländereien Eigenthum der politischen Gemeinde oder aber Privateigenthum der Nutzen ziehenden Gemeindeglieder seien; noch öfter aber, ob gewisse Nutzrechte an ungetheilten Gemeindegründen als Privatrechte (Servituten) zu betrachten seien, oder aber bloß als öffentlich-rechtliche Ansprüche.

In der Regel fehlen Titel, welche über die Natur der Ansprüche klaren Aufschluß geben und es bildet also die herkömmliche Art der Benützung die einzige Quelle, aus welcher Schlüsse gezogen werden können. — Ist nun die Benützung derartig gewesen, daß sie sich naturgemäß aus dem Gemeindeleben entwickelt haben kann, daß die Annahme statthaft ist, sie leite sich aus Verfügungen der Gemeindeverwaltung, aus dem, sei es ausdrücklich, sei es durch Duldung, kund gegebenen Willen der politischen Gemeinde her, so sind die privatrechtlichen Ansprüche zurückzuweisen. Im Zweifel wird für das Recht der Gemeinde zu entscheiden, d. h. den öffentlichen Interessen vor den Privatinteressen der Vorzug zu geben sein.

Aus dem Umstande, daß nur die Besitzer von Anwesen als nutzberechtigt galten, oder daß sich die Nutzungen nach der Größe der Anwesen vertheilten und eine feststehende Norm der Vertheilung hergebracht war, geht an und für sich die privatrechtliche Natur nicht hervor, denn auch diese Art der Vertheilung kann sich aus dem Gemeindeleben selbst entwickelt haben, indem es billig und sachgemäß erscheinen konnte, diejenigen Ortsangehörigen, welche vorzugsweise thätig ins Gemeindeleben eingriffen oder welche vorzugsweise an den Gemeindelasten betheiligt waren, auch einen Vorzug in den Nutzungen zu gestatten.

Daß die Art und Weise der herkömmlichen Vertheilung von derjenigen abweicht, welche durch das Gemeinde-Edikt normirt wurde, kann an und für sich gleichfalls kein Grund sein, anzunehmen, daß das Herkommen nicht im Gemeindeverbande wurzele. Andere Zeiten bedingen andere Ansichten. Es ist auf diesen Gesichtspunkt um so mehr Gewicht zu legen, als die meisten Streitigkeiten aus dem Bestreben der Gemeinde-Angehörigen, namentlich der reicheren, einflußreicheren (der Großbegüterten) entspringen, ihr Gemeindevermögen den Einflüssen des Gemeinde-Edikts und der durch dasselbe bedingten Curatel zu entziehen. — s. Erk. des C. C. H. vom 14. Dez. 1857 (S. 1717), 25. Juni 1858 (S. 837), 24. Jan., 14. März und 14. Okt. 1859 (S. 174, 291 und 989), 23. Dez. 1861 (S. 67) und 18. Sept. 1865 (S. 1115).

Es ist selbstverständlich, daß über die Frage, ob ein Ortsangehöriger als solcher Rechte auf die Gemeinde-Nutzungen habe, nur die Verwaltung zu entscheiden hat, wie überhaupt über die Beziehungen zwischen den Gemeinden und ihren Angehörigen, über die Rechte und Pflichten, welche aus dem Gemeindeverbande entspringen, nie die Gerichte entscheiden. — s. Erk. des C. C. H. vom 29. Dez. 1856 (S. 97), 15. Nov. 1858 (S. 1461) und 9. Dez. 1859 (S. 1333). Seuff. Archiv Bd. XIII Nr. 63. Art. 36 der Gemeindeordnung v. 29. April 1869.

Die Bestimmung der Flurgränze zwischen zwei Gemeinden ist eine Verwaltungssache, vorbehaltlich der Regulirung der privatrechtlichen Folgen, wenn solche entstehen, durch die Gerichte. s. Erk. des C. C. H. vom 11. April 1860 (S. 411). Seuff. Archiv Bd. IV Nr. 251 und Bd. V Nr. 282.

§ 15.

Cultus.

Auf anerkannte Religionsgesellschaften finden, da ihre Zwecke öffentliche sind, bezüglich ihrer äußeren Verhältnisse die allgemeinen Prinzipien Anwendung.

Auch die israelitischen Cultusgemeinden sind nicht als Privatgesellschaften zu betrachten. S. Erk. des C. C. H. vom 19. Juni 1855 (S. 823), 4. März 1856 (S. 193) und 3. Juni 1862 (S. 1967).

Die Regulirung der Bezüge der Geistlichen und die Streitigkeiten, welche sich bezüglich des Genusses der Pfründen erheben, gehören zur Zuständigkeit der Verwaltung. s. Erk. v. 9. Juni 1857 (S. 776), 23. Nov. 1859 (S. 1322), 11. Nov. und 30. Dez. 1861 (S. 915 und 81), 15. Dez. 1862 (S. 2645), 19. Sept. 1865 (S. 1089), endlich v. 25. Juni 1866 (S. 941).

Streitigkeiten über Kirchenbaulast sind, der Regel nach, privatrechtliche. s. Erk. des C. C. H. vom 17. und 25. Okt. 1859 (S. 1040 und 1080). Uebrigens steht die provisorische Verfügung unbestritten der Verwaltung zu. Erk. v. 26. Okt. 1857 (S. 1413).

§ 16.

Besonderheiten der Pfalz.

In Frankreich, wo die vollständige Trennung von Justiz und Verwaltung schon sehr lange Zeit besteht, haben sich unter dem Einflusse der Größe des Landes und eines sehr regsamen juristischen Lebens, sämmtliche die Grenzen der Verwaltung und Justiz betreffenden Streitfragen entweder ganz bereinigt oder es sind wenigstens die Gründe für und wider erschöpfend erörtert.

Es sollen daher hier nur einige Punkte hervorgehoben werden, in welchen neuere Gesetze, insbesondere unsere Verfassungsurkunde, eingreifende Aenderungen für die Pfalz bedingen.

Dareste, einer der besten neueren Schriftsteller im Verwaltungsfache, welcher insbesondere auch die ausländischen Gesetzgebungen gründlich kennt, findet sich in seinem Werke: „la justice administrative de la France“ zum Ausspruche veranlaßt:

„En France, la part de l’administration est plus „large que partout ailleurs.“

Dies ist vollkommen richtig, jedoch zu bemerken, daß das Uebergewicht der Verwaltung in etwas gemildert wird durch den Umstand, daß eine eigene Verwaltungs-Justiz besteht, welche von eigenen Behörden, nach eigenem Verfahren, geübt wird und alle Fälle umfaßt, wo die Verwaltung nicht rein nach Rücksichten der Zweckmäßigkeit verfügen darf, sondern über Ansprüche, die sich auf bestehende Gesetze und Verordnungen gründen, zu erkennen hat.

Vivien (études administratives) sagt: „le contentieux administratif se compose de toutes les réclamations fondées sur la violation des obligations imposées à l'administration par les lois et règlements, qui la regissent ou par les contrats, qu'elle sousorit."

Schon hieraus erhellt, daß der Grundsatz, es habe der Fiskus in streitigen Privatrechtsverhältnissen vor den gewöhnlichen Gerichten Recht zu nehmen, im Sinne, wie ihn unsere Verfassungsurkunde aufstellt, in Frankreich nicht gilt. Man kann eher umgekehrt sagen: Der Fiskus nimmt in Frankreich der Regel nach nur vor den Verwaltungs-Gerichten Recht."

In der Pfalz wurde durch Verordnung vom 6. Nov. 1817 das einzige damals dort bestehende besondere Organ für die Verwaltungs-Justiz aufgehoben und dessen Competenz unter Gerichte und Kreisregierung vertheilt. — Hiermit wurden jedoch nicht alle Streitigkeiten, welche ihrer privatrechtlichen Natur nach sich vor die Gerichte eignen, diesen zugewiesen und erfolgte um so weniger eine in dieser Richtung erschöpfende Competenz-Regulirung, als jene Verordnung nur über die Competenz der Präfekturräthe Verfügung trifft, während das französische Recht noch verschiedene andere Organe der Administrativ-Justiz kennt.

Uebrigens hat man nie bezweifelt, daß die ganze Administrativ-Justiz ihrem Wesen nach aufgehoben sei und hieraus, sowie aus den Prinzipien, welche unsere Verfassungsurkunde aufstellt, ergeben sich für die Zuständigkeit der Verwaltung mehrfache sehr wesentliche Folgerungen, insbesondere folgende:

I. Beschlüsse der Verwaltung erwachsen nicht in Rechtskraft.

Im französischen Rechte ist unbestritten, daß Beschlüsse der Verwaltungs-Justiz ganz in der nemlichen Weise rechtskräftig werden wie Urtheile der Gerichte.

Nachdem bei uns die Verwaltungs-Justiz mit ihren eigenthümlichen Organen und Formen dem Wesen nach beseitigt ist, sind alle Entscheidungen der Verwaltung nur noch als reine Verwaltungs-Beschlüsse zu behandeln; da nun aber unsere Verfassung die Privatrechte unter speziellen Schutz der Gerichte stellt und dieser Schutz sogar der Regierungsgewalt gegenüber eintreten soll, so treten alle jene Erwägungen in Kraft, gemäß deren es diesseits als ausgemacht gilt, daß Verfügungen der Verwaltung auf die Zuständigkeit der Gerichte einen maßgebenden Einfluß nicht äußern können.

Was oben in dieser Beziehung gesagt ist, gilt daher vollständig auch für die Pfalz, wie dies, wenigstens stillschweigend anerkannt ist in einem Erkenntnisse des Cassationshofes für die Pfalz vom 20. Juni 1868. (s. Zeitschrift für Gesetzgebung und Rechtspflege, neue Folge Bd. II S. 305.)

II. Ueberall, wo ein rein privatrechtliches Verhältniß vorliegt, haben bloß die Gerichte zu erkennen, ohne alle Rücksicht auf französische Spezialgesetze.

Nachdem in Titel XV § 8 der Verf.-Urk. jedem Unterthan Sicherheit seines Eigenthums und seiner Rechte gewährt ist, erklärt Tit. VIII § 5: „Der Fiskus wird in allen streitigen Privatrechtsverhältnissen bei den kgl. Gerichtshöfen Recht nehmen."

Ein solcher Grundsatz, in einem Staatsgrundgesetze ausgesprochen, muß nach seiner vollen Tragweite Anwendung finden und es können neben ihm die Ausnahmen früherer Spezialgesetze unmöglich fortbestehen; Die Regel: „lex posterior generalis non derogat priori speciali" gilt hier nicht, denn dieselbe ist nur ein Behelf, um den vermuthbaren Willen des Gesetzgebers herzustellen; wo aber dieser Willen klar ist und kein Zweifel besteht, daß der Gesetzgeber alle und jede Ausnahmsbestimmung beseitigen wollte, da kann von deren Anwendung keine Rede sein.

Es ist nun schon durch die Natur eines Verfassungs-Gesetzes, als des wichtigsten Gesetzes im Staate, bedingt, daß in Fällen, wo ein Grundsatz klar und bestimmt ausgesprochen ist, derselbe auch rein und unverfälscht durchgeführt werden muß und nicht aus gewöhnlichen, auf viel untergeordneteren Erwägungen beruhenden Gesetzen, Sonderbestimmungen beigezogen werden dürfen, um diesen Grundsatz zu verkümmern.

Besagte Stelle der Verfassung hat offenbar nicht den nichtssagenden Sinn, daß der Fiskus vor den Gerichten Recht nehmen müsse, soweit nicht nach den bestehenden Gesetzen etwas Anderes gelte, vielmehr ist sie gerade so aufzufassen, als wenn ausdrücklich beigefügt wäre, „es seien alle entgegenstehenden Bestimmungen ohne Ausnahme aufgehoben."

Ferner ist klar, daß, wenn von Privatrechtsverhältnissen die Rede ist, dieses Wort in demjenigen Sinne zu nehmen ist, welchen die Prinzipien des deutschen Rechtes damit verbinden, daß aber nicht gemeint war, es solle dasselbe in der Pfalz etwas Anders bedeuten, als diesseits.

Diese Prinzipien finden insbesondere bei Entschädigungsklagen gegen den Fiskus eine sehr wichtige praktische Anwendung.

In Frankreich unterscheidet man:

1) die Zwangsenteignung im engeren Sinne;

2) sonstige Eingriffe in Privat-Eigenthum, zu welchen die Verwaltung zwar befugt ist, jedoch nur gegen Entschädigung des Verletzten;

3) widerrechtliche Handlungen von Agenten der Verwaltung und zwar:

a. insofern diese Agenten selbst oder

b. insofern der Staat als civilverantwortlich für dieselben in Anspruch genommen wird.

Im Falle Nr. 1 sind die Gerichte zuständig. Was im französischen Rechte unter Zwangsenteignung gemeint sei, ergibt sich aus folgenden Worten von **Dareste** (l. c. S. 456):

„Le changement de propriétaire est le signe de „l'expropriation. Il ne suffit pas, que le droit de „l'ancien propriétaire soit atteint, il faut encore, „que l'Etat ou ses représentants acquièrent ce droit. „Autrement il n'y a plus expropriation, mais simple „dommage." Als Beispiel eines solchen dommage wird das Begründen einer Servitut bezeichnet.

Im Falle Nr. 2 unterschied der Cassationshof bis zum Jahre 1852 zwischen dommage permanent und dommage temporaire, indem er den ersten (z. B. das Begründen einer Servitut) als eine Art Expropriation betrachtete; nachdem aber der Staatsrath als Competenz-Conflikts-Hof immer das Gegegentheil entschied, fügte sich endlich der Cassationshof in seinem Erkenntnisse vom 29. März 1852 dieser Ansicht, so daß es jetzt als ausgemacht gilt, daß in allen Fällen ohne Ausnahme bloß die Verwaltung entscheide. s. auch Paris 17. Jan. 1857.

Bezüglich der Competenz in den Fällen Nr. 3 (a u. b) will ich der Kürze wegen die Worte von Dareste anführen. Er sagt l. c. S. 525:

„Lorsqu'il s'agit des délits ou quasi-délits com- „mis dans l'exécution des travaux publics, l'action „en responsabilité, soit contre l'agent du gouverne- „ment, si les travaux sont en regie, soit contre „l'entrepreneur, doit être portée devant les Conseils „de préfecture, sauf recours au Conseil d'Etat." (Handelt es sich nicht um travaux publics, so sind hier die Gerichte zuständig, jedoch nur nach Einholung der Ermächtigung des Staatsraths.)

Er sagt ferner S. 533:

„Il faut donc reconnaître, que la question est „jugée et que toute action en responsabilité „civile, dirigée contre l'Etat, doit être portée d'abord „devant le ministre compétent, puis devant le Con- „seil d'Etat, à moins qu'une loi expresse et formelle „n'indique une autre juridiction." Er bemerkt dabei: cette jurisprudence est d'autant plus remarquable qu'elle s'est formée toute entière sur les demandes en responsabilité civile formées contre l'administration des postes.

Von allen diesen Fällen der ausschließlichen Zuständigkeit der Verwaltung ist nun durch besagte Verordnung von 1817 (Z. III lit. d) nur der einzige, wo es sich um öffentliche Arbeiten handelt und zugleich die Beschädigung nur aus persönlichen Handlungen des Unternehmers (der sein Mandat überschritten), nicht aber aus Anordnungen der Verwaltung herrührt, den Gerichten zugewiesen; in allen anderen Fällen müßte also, wenn nicht Art. VIII § 5 der V. U. Maaß gäbe, die Verwaltung auch jetzt noch zuständig sein. — Wirklich haben sich auch mehrfach Urtheile pfälzischer Gerichte und zwar (meines Erinnerns) ursprünglich gegen die Meinung der Kreisregierung selbst, dahin ausgesprochen, daß bei Schäden, welche durch öffentliche Arbeiten verursacht sind und nicht unter die Ausnahme des Ziff. III lit. d cit. fallen, die Gerichte nicht zuständig seien. — Diese Ansicht, in deren Consequenz übrigens auch alle übrigen obbezeichneten Fälle der Zuständigkeit der Gerichte entzogen wären, halte ich nicht für richtig. — Wenn Jemand sich beschwert, daß durch Aenderung des natürlichen Wasserabflusses seine Wiese versumpft sei, daß ihm durch Anlagen irgend einer Art der Zugang zu seinem Eigenthum oder Licht und Luft genommen sei, daß Ausgrabungen neben seinem Hause dasselbe dem Einsturze nahe gebracht, daß man ihm willkürlich seine Erndte zerstört, so sind dies doch wohl reine Privatrechtsverhältnisse im Sinne der Verfassungs-Urkunde, mögen nun die Beschädigungen von Privaten oder vom Staate und seinen Beamten ausgegangen sein.

Ich glaube also, daß bezüglich aller Entschädigungsforderungen an den Fiskus oder an Verwaltungsbeamte für die Pfalz ganz die nemlichen Prinzipien gelten müssen, wie diesseits.

III. Bezüglich der Fragen, ob faktisch eine Zwangsabtretung stattgefunden habe, ob dieselbe rechtlich zulässig sei und welches die Folgen widerrechtlicher Aneignung von Privateigenthum seien, gelten in der Pfalz, **auch dem Staate gegenüber,** ganz die nemlichen Grundsätze, wie diesseits.

Welch beschränkten Begriff man in Frankreich mit der „Zwangsenteignung" verbindet, ist oben schon angedeutet.

Hierzu kommt, daß nach den Prinzipien des öffentlichen Rechtes daselbst einfache Erklärungen der Verwaltung genügen, um irgend ein Stück Land zu einem Theile der „domaine public", d. h. eines Weges, eines Flusses rc. zu machen und das Privateigenthum in Entschädigung aufzulösen. — Dareste l. c. sagt S. 258:

„La déclaration de domanialité a pour effet „d'incorporer au domaine public les biens, qu'elle „frappe et de les livrer immédiatement a l'usage „de tous." Und S. 259:

„Quant à l'action pétitoire, elle se ressout tou- „jours en réclamation d'indemnité. Le demandeur „devra prouver non pas qu'il est, mais qu'il a „été propriétaire, anterieurement à la déclaration „de domanialité."

Dieses Prinzip hat von jeher allgemein gegolten und das Gesetz vom 21. Mai 1836, welches entsprechende Bestimmungen bezüglich der „chemins vicinaux" enthält, bringt keine Neuerung, sondern gibt nur die spezielle Anwendung eines bestehenden Prinzipes.

Mit den Bestimmungen unserer Verfassungsgesetze möchte dasselbe sich nicht vereinigen lassen. — In Tit. IV § 8 der V. U. ist gesagt:

„Niemand darf gezwungen werden, sein Privateigen- „thum, selbst für öffentliche Zwecke, abzutreten, als nach „einer förmlichen Entscheidung des versammelten Staats- „rathes und nach vorgängiger Entschädigung."

Das Gesetz vom 17. Nov. 1837, gleichfalls ein Grundgesetz des Reichs, bestimmt die Fälle, in welchen allein eine Abtretung des Eigenthums oder eine Beschwerung mit einer Dienstbarkeit für öffentliche Zwecke verlangt werden könne. Wortlaut und Zweck dieses Gesetzes, insbesondere auch der besondere Vorbehalt in Art. 22, lassen keinen Zweifel, daß durch dasselbe die in Frage stehende Materie vollständig und ohne Vorbehalt geregelt werden sollte.

Steht daher eine Expropriation im Sinne dieses Gesetzes in Frage, so muß der Fall unbedingt nach den Verfügungen desselben beurtheilt werden und es ist nicht statthaft, besondere Expropriationsfälle aus Spezialgesetzen zu konstruiren. — Auch was die Frage betrifft, ob die Regierungsgewalt verpflichtet werden könne, eine außer den Fällen und Formen des Gesetzes vollzogene Enteignung wieder rückgängig zu machen, das in Besitz genommene Land zurückzugeben, sind die nemlichen Prinzipien anwendbar, wie diesseits.

Der C. C. Hof für die Pfalz hat sich in 4 Erkenntnissen, vom 26. Juli 1852 (S. 867), vom 12. Juli 1853 (S. 1075), vom 31. Juli 1854 (S. 673) und vom 5. Aug. 1867 (S. 929) über die Frage ausgesprochen. Soweit in diesen Erkenntnissen entschieden ist, daß Verwaltungsakte nicht mittelst Besitzklagen rückgängig gemacht werden können, finde ich sie vollkommen gerechtfertigt, insofern aber auch die petitorische Klage versagt und der Erklärung der Verwaltung, daß ein gewisses Stück Land ein öffentlicher Weg oder Theil eines solchen sei, die Wirkung einer vollständigen Expropriation beigelegt wird, halte ich sie mit den Grundsätzen unserer Verfassungsgesetze nicht vereinbarlich.

(Bezirksgerichte.)

Art. 2. — Vor die Bezirksgerichte gehören im ersten Rechtszuge alle vor den bürgerlichen Gerichten zu verhandelnden Rechtsstreitigkeiten, welche nicht andern Gerichten zugewiesen sind.

G. A. der K. der A. I S. 33. 34. 79. IV S. 4. — der K. der R. I S. 11—18.

1) Der hier ausgesprochene Grundsatz ist nicht ohne Wichtigkeit.

Die Bezirksgerichte bieten vermöge ihrer Organisation und des für sie geltenden Verfahrens alle Garantien für eine rasche und gründliche Rechtsprechung, — die Instruktion durch rechtskundige, geschäftserfahrene Anwälte, ein sich den Bedürfnissen anschmiegendes, ebenso zur Raschheit als zur Gründlichkeit geeignetes Verfahren, endlich kollegiale Berathung und Entscheidung. Sie sollen daher die ordentlichen Gerichte erster Instanz sein und nur aus besonderen Gründen soll die Zuständigkeit anderer Gerichte eintreten, welchen also hiermit dem Wesen nach die Eigenschaft von Ausnahmsgerichten gegeben ist. Abg. I 43 (v. Weiß).

2) Ein Ausfluß dieses Grundsatzes ist es, daß die bezirksgerichtliche Zuständigkeit in vielen Fällen die den Ausnahmsgerichten (Handelsgerichten, Landgerichten) zugewiesenen Sachen an sich zieht (Art. 10. 11. 31. 38).

In Frankreich besteht nur ein allgemeines Prinzip, welchem, da nähere Bestimmungen über dessen Anwendung fehlen, die neuere Jurisprudenz eine möglichst unbedingte Geltung zu verschaffen sucht, insbesondere auch dahin, daß Connexität und Vereinbarung immer hinreichen, um Sachen, welche an sich vor den Friedensrichter oder vor das Handelsgericht gehören, an das Bezirksgericht zu ziehen. — Dalloz repert. (exceptions) No. 197 u. (comp. civile des trib. d'arr.) No. 264. 268. 269.

Unsere Prozeßordnung zählt die Fälle, wo sich das Ueberwiegen der bezirksgerichtlichen Zuständigkeit in besagter Weise geltend macht, einzeln auf; es ist daher nicht gestattet, das Prinzip noch weiter auszudehnen.

3) Ein weiterer Ausfluß jenes Grundsatzes ist die wichtige Regel, daß überall, wo Zweifel obwalten, zu Gunsten der bezirksgerichtlichen Zuständigkeit zu entscheiden ist.

(Stadt- u. Landgerichte.)

Art. 3. — Vor die Einzelngerichte gehören, soweit das Gesetz nicht anders bestimmt, Klagen, welche in der Hauptsache an Geld oder Geldeswerth nicht über 150 Gulden, ohne Einrechnung der Zinsen, Kosten und Nutzungen betreffen.

Wird eine Klage von mehreren Klägern erhoben oder gegen mehrere Beklagte gerichtet, oder werden gegen denselben Beklagten mehrere Ansprüche in einer Klage verfolgt, so entscheidet für die Zuständigkeit der Gesammtwerth aller geltend gemachten Ansprüche.

G. A. der K. der A. I S. 33—41. 78. 79. 250. IV S. 4. 5. — der K. der R. I S. 18—32. IV S. 2.

1) Die Zuständigkeit der Landgerichte ist durch die neue Prozeßordnung (Art. 3 — 6. 953 und 965) im Vergleiche zur bisherigen Zuständigkeit der Landgerichte im diesseitigen Bayern etwas verengert, im Vergleiche zur bisherigen Zuständigkeit der Landgerichte der Pfalz nicht unerheblich erweitert.

2) Die Einschränkung der einzelrichterlichen Zuständigkeit rechtfertigt sich durch die Natur des neuen Verfahrens, welches viele jener besonderen

Vortheile, welche man früher nur vom Verfahren vor Einzelrichtern erwarten konnte, auch bei den Bezirksgerichten zu erreichen möglich macht. Was nemlich den Gesichtspunkt der Raschheit anbelangt, so wird in der Regel eine Entscheidung des Bezirksgerichts ebenso schnell zu erlangen sein, als eine Entscheidung des Landrichters, und erstere hat, abgesehen von größerer Zuverlässigkeit, noch das voraus, daß sie vielfach in letzter Instanz ergeht, wo die landrichterliche Entscheidung noch durch Berufung anfechtbar ist.

Die Vorzüge des landgerichtlichen Verfahrens bestehen hauptsächlich in seiner Wohlfeilheit, in größerer Nähe des Gerichtes, in dem Umstande, daß Personal- und Lokal-Kenntnisse des Richters in manchen Sachen die Rechtsprechung erleichtern und fördern, endlich darin, daß ein einzelner Richter mehr Beweglichkeit hat als ein Collegium, und daher manche Feststellungen und Ermittlungen leichter von ihm bethätigt werden können.

3) Das Gesetz weist den Landgerichten daher zu:

1) Bagatellsachen, in welchen die Kosten des bezirksgerichtlichen Verfahrens außer Verhältniß zur Sache stehen;

2) einfache Sachen, welche mehr arbitrio boni viri, als nach Rechtsgrundsätzen zu entscheiden sind, z. B. Schadenklagen;

3) gewisse Sachen, bei welchen es wünschenswerth ist, daß der Richter an Ort und Stelle sei, um schnell und persönlich einschreiten zu können, z. B. Miethstreite, Streit zwischen Reisenden und Wirthen ꝛc.

4) In den einzelnen Bestimmungen des Gesetzes haben diesseitige Gesetze als Muster gedient, namentlich § 1 der Novelle vom 17. Nov. 1837, wo die Fälle des beschleunigten Verfahrens mit mündlichem Verhöre bezeichnet sind, dann die sich hieran anschließenden Verfügungen der Gerichtsverfassungsgesetze von 1856 und 1861. — Auf die pfälzischen Einrichtungen hat man hier nur insofern Rücksicht genommen, als sie in einzelnen, allerdings nicht unwichtigen Punkten, mildernd und modifizirend einwirkten.

5) Der erste Absatz des Art. 3 enthält für die Pfalz drei wesentliche Veränderungen, nemlich:

1) daß die Competenzsumme auf 150 fl. erhöht ist;

2) daß auch der Geldeswerth entscheidet und

3) daß Zinsen, Nutzungen und Kosten nicht eingerechnet werden.

6) Was Z. 2 und 3 betrifft, so gelten im französischen Prozesse die praktischen und Competenzfragen abschneidenden Regeln, daß 1) überall, wo nicht eine bestimmte Geldsumme begehrt ist (valeur indeterminée), die Zuständigkeit des Bezirksgerichts Platz greift, und daß 2) bei Festsetzung des Streitgegenstandes die ganze Forderung, wie sie im Augenbicke der Zustellung der Ladung besteht — Haupt- und Nebensache zusammengerechnet — in Betracht kommt. — In ersterer Beziehung möchte ich die getroffene Aenderung nicht tadeln, in letzterer Beziehung bedauere ich jedoch, daß man durch Vorliebe für das einmal Bestehende sich hat bestimmen lassen, vor den Vorzügen des französischen Prinzipes die Augen zu verschließen. Letzteres hat für sich a) größere Einfachheit, indem alle Streitfragen, was Haupt- und Neben-Sache sei, wegfallen, und b) größere Wahrheit, da gewiß 100 fl. Zinsen so schwer wiegen, wie 100 fl. Kapital. Soll doch einmal das Viel oder Wenig des Geforderten den Ausschlag geben, so besteht kein Grund, zu unterscheiden, ob es Hauptsache oder Nebensache geheißen werde. Alle Gründe, welche man in Hannover und hier vorgebracht hat, gehen darauf hinaus, daß es eben von jeher so war — nemlich bei der Berufungssumme.

„Es schleppen sich Gesetz und Rechte
„Gleich einer ewigen Krankheit fort."

7) Was sind Zinsen, Kosten und Nutzungen?

Zinsen und Nutzungen erscheinen als Nebensache, sei es, daß sie zufolge Uebereinkunft, sei es, daß sie kraft Gesetzes geschuldet werden, z. B. weil der Beklagte das Kapital oder die Sache selbst benützt hat oder weil er im Verzuge gewesen ist (Bl. f. R. V 263).

Wesentlich ist, daß sie deßhalb verlangt werden, weil der Beklagte selbst das Kapital schuldig geblieben ist oder die Sache widerrechtlich in Besitz gehalten hat. Fordert jedoch A Kapital und Zins, welche B für ihn vereinnahmt oder welche er selbst zur Entlastung des B gezahlt hat, oder hat B sich Grundstücke des A sammt darauf befindlichen Früchten angeeignet und wird Herausgabe des Ganzen verlangt, so sind Zinsen und Nutzungen gleichfalls Hauptsache und es kommt nicht in Betracht, daß sie andern Personen gegenüber und in einem andern Schuldverhältnisse Nebensache gebildet hatten.

Fordert ein Mandatar oder Geschäftsführer Zinsen von Baarauslagen, so werden diese Zinsen als Nebensache anzusehen sein; es besteht kein genügender Grund, sie deshalb, weil sie kraft Gesetzes laufen, anders zu behandeln, als wenn sie bedungen gewesen wären. (Vgl. jedoch Seuff. Comm. IV S. 44). Anders ist es vielleicht, wenn ein Verwalter wegen Versäumung von Geldanlagen gesetzlich so behandelt würde, als hätte er die Gelder rechtzeitig angelegt und die Zinsen vereinnahmt. (Seuff. a. a. O.)

8) Werden Zinsen, Kosten und Nutzungen gleichzeitig mit der Hauptsache, zu welcher sie gehören, eingeklagt, so bleiben sie ganz außer Betracht; werden sie aber besonders eingeklagt, so sind sie selbst Hauptsache. (Abg. I S. 41). Es kann in dieser Weise, insbesondere bei der Unbeschränktheit des Zinsfußes, vorkommen, daß Zinsen, Kosten 2c., für sich eingeklagt, vor's Bezirksgericht gehören, mit der Hauptsache eingeklagt jedoch vor's Landgericht. Ein Prinzip, welches auf willkürlicher Grundlage ruht, muß eben hie und da zu sonderbaren Folgerungen führen.

9) Soweit Zinsen 2c. nicht zu derjenigen Hauptsache gehören, welche zugleich eingeklagt wird, sind sie selbst Hauptsache, z. B. wenn Zinsen eines bereits gezahlten oder noch nicht fälligen Kapitaltheiles verlangt werden. Edel Comm. z. G. B. Ges. von 1861 S. 48. Bl. f. R. XXV. 462. (Gegebenen Falls waren 140 fl. Kaufpreis und 320 fl. Zinsrückstände eingeklagt).

10) Wenn Nebensachen durch Novation oder überhaupt durch ein Schuldversprechen, welches einen selbständigen Klagegrund bildet, mit der Hauptsache verschmolzen sind, so ist eine Ausscheidung nicht mehr statthaft; das Ganze ist Hauptsache.

11) Unter Nutzungen sind auch Rückstände an Renten 2c. begriffen. Seuff. Comm. IV S. 46 Note 115. Edel Comm. S. 47 u. 48. Bl. f. R. XXV 458.

12) Unter Kosten sind vorzugsweise die vor Zustellung der Ladung entstandenen zu verstehen, denn bezüglich der Prozeßkosten war hier eine Bestimmung unnöthig. Man hat dabei an Kosten zu denken, welche direkt in Geltendmachung des eingeklagten Anspruches entstanden sind und zwar dem Beklagten gegenüber, z. B. Kosten von Mahnungen und sonstigen Zustellungen, Ladungen an's Vermittlungsamt u. s. w. — Wenn Jemand neben einer Hauptsumme auch Ersatz von Kosten verlangt, welche er an Andere hat zahlen müssen, z. B. im Fall einer Gewährschaftsklage, so ist diese Kostenforderung keine Nebensache.

13) Das Gesetz spricht nicht von „Schäden", wie die Novelle von 1837 § 1. Ger.O. Cap. XV § 3 und hannov. Entwurf § 6. — Wenn daher neben einer Hauptsache, außer Nutzungen und Zinsen, noch eine besondere Entschädigung wegen Entzug des Genusses verlangt wird, so ist diese bei Berechnung des Streitgegenstandes zu berücksichtigen. Vgl. Seuff. Comm. IV S. 45.

14) Gesammtwerth aller Ansprüche. Was bezüglich der Zusammenrechnung der Werthe hier bestimmt ist, gilt selbstverständlich nur bezüglich jener Ansprüche, bei welchen sich die Zuständigkeit nach dem Werthe des Streitgegenstandes richtet. Es ist dies durch die Natur der Sache bedingt, geht übrigens aus der Fassung des Gesetzes klar hervor.

Werden daher zugleich Ansprüche anderer Art, bei welchen das Landgericht unbedingt (Art. 6) oder gar nicht (Art. 5) zuständig ist, eingeklagt, so ist nach Art. 178 jedem einzelnen Anspruche gegenüber die Zuständigkeit zu prüfen. Wer z. B. mehrere Darlehen im Gesammtbetrage von 200 fl. und einen Miethzins von 200 fl. einklagt, muß wegen der ersten Forderung vor dem Bezirksgerichte, wegen der letzteren vor dem Landgerichte klagen. Betragen die Darlehen bloß 150 fl., so gehört das Ganze vor's Landgericht.

15) Ohne Zweifel finden die Grundsätze wegen Zusammenrechnung auch auf jene Fälle Anwendung, von welchen in Art. 7 Abs. 2 Z. 1 und in Art. 953 die Sprache ist.

Die ausschließliche Zuständigkeit der Handelsgerichte in Handelssachen und der Bezirksgerichte bei Vollstreckungs-Streitigkeiten ist Ausnahme von der Regel, und indem von dieser Ausnahme wieder Ausnahmen gemacht werden, wird die Regel zurückgeführt, d. h. es bleibt bei der Bestimmung des Art. 3.

Uebrigens führt doch die Natur der Handelssachen zu eigenthümlichen Folgen, welche es nöthig ist anzudeuten. Wird ein Civilanspruch von 100 fl. mit einem handelsrechtlichen Anspruche von 100 fl. zusammen eingeklagt, so gehören beide vor's Bezirkgericht, weil einerseits die Gesammtsumme die landgerichtliche Zuständigkeit überschreitet und weil anderseits das Handelsgericht nicht zuständig ist, über Civilsachen zu entscheiden, während das Bezirksgericht in so fern auch bezüglich der Handelssache zuständig erscheint, als es bei gesonderter Einklagung berufen war, in zweiter Instanz darüber zu entscheiden.

16) In Fällen, wo mehrere Personen gemeinschaftlich klagen oder belangt werden, entsteht die Frage, ob auf die Zulässigkeit der Streitgenossenschaft (Art. 63) Rücksicht zu nehmen sei oder nicht.

Man kann sagen: der Landrichter hat sich nur an die Thatsache zu halten, daß mehrere Personen als Kläger oder Beklagte erscheinen; prüft er, weitergehend, ob die Vereinigung dieser Personen berechtigt sei oder nicht, so überschreitet er das Gebiet der Competenzfrage und untersucht den Grund der Sache, was ihm nicht zusteht. Es scheint diese Auffassung um so berechtigter, da in Art. 3 der Beisatz: „in gesetzlich zulässiger Weise," welcher in Art. 20 vorkommt und auf welchen man dort besonderes Gewicht legte, fehlt. Vgl. auch Bl. f. R. XXV S. 462.

Nichts desto weniger halte ich die entgegengesetzte Ansicht für richtiger.

Es kann nicht erlaubt sein, willkürlich durch gesetzwidrige Häufung nicht zusammengehöriger Klagen die Zuständigkeit zu verrücken; die Frage, ob eine Klaghäufung statthaft sei oder nicht, ist daher Vorfrage zur Entscheidung der Zuständigkeit.

Alle Fragen, von denen die Zuständigkeit abhängt, hat, falls nicht ausdrückliches Verbot entgegensteht, der Richter zu prüfen, mögen sie nun formeller oder materieller Natur sein, wie denn z. B. die Fragen, ob ein Handelsgeschäft vorliege, ob Connexität gegeben sei, oft tief in's Materielle eingreifen, ja sich mit dem Grund der Sache identifiziren.

Wenn eine unstatthafte Streitgenossenschaft vor dem Bezirksgerichte erscheint, so hat dieses ohne allen Zweifel die Pflicht, auszusprechen, daß gesondert zu betrachtende Klagen vorliegen, und dem entsprechend über die Zuständigkeit zu entscheiden. Eignen sich die einzelnen Ansprüche vor's Landgericht, so hat es dorthin zu verweisen.

Offenbar ist es nun der Wille des Gesetzes nicht, daß, falls die Sache sofort vor's Landgericht gebracht wurde, dieses zuerst ans Bezirksgericht verweise, damit dieses ausspreche, es sei der Fall einer Streitgenossenschaft nicht gegeben und zurückverweise. Falls daher klar und zweifellos ist, daß eine gesetzlich zulässige Streitgenossenschaft nicht vorliege, hat der Landrichter die Vereinigung der verschiedenen Ansprüche in derselben Ladung als eine willkürliche und zufällige nicht zu beachten und ganz so zu verfahren, als seien verschiedene Klagen gestellt.

Man setze den Fall, A belange zwei im nemlichen Landgerichtsbezirke wohnhafte Personen, jede wegen eines Darlehens von 100 fl. vor dem Landgerichte und zwar der Kostensparung wegen in der nemlichen Ladung. Unbedenklich kann der Landrichter urtheilen. Wenn er will, kann er, dem Mangel der Zusammengehörigkeit Ausdruck gebend, zwei verschiedene Urtheile fällen; allein es ist dies nicht einmal nöthig und er kann recht gut sagen: „verurtheilt jeden der Beklagten, dem „Kläger 100 fl. mit Zins vom Tage der Klage, „sowie die Hälfte der Kosten zu zahlen." An der Sache wird hierdurch nichts geändert.

Schließlich sei erwähnt, daß Abs. 2 des Art. 3 seiner Entstehung nach sich an die Verfügungen über Streitgenossenschaft anschließt, indem sich erst bei der bezüglichen Diskussion das Bedürfniß ergab, ihn dem hannover. Entwurfe zu entlehnen. (Abg. I 78 u. 79.)

17) Ein Zusammenrechnen des Klagsanspruches mit Gegenansprüchen, welche auf dem Wege der Einrede (Art. 9) oder Widerklage (Art. 31) verfolgt werden, ist nicht statthaft.

Der Wortlaut des Art. 3 Abs. 2 schließt diesen Fall nicht ein; das frühere Recht verbot ein solches Zusammenrechnen (s. Novelle von 1837 § 62 — Ges. vom 4. Februar 1854 Art. 3); endlich deutet die Fassung von Art. 9 u. 11, sowie Art. 31 Abs. 4 klar an, daß das Gesetz die Gegenansprüche für sich allein ins Auge faßt.

18) Kann der Kläger durch Beschränkung des in der Ladung gestellten Begehrens die Unzuständigkeit beseitigen?

Ohne allen Zweifel kann dies geschehen durch rechtzeitige Zustellung einer neuen Ladung; allein kann es auch noch geschehen bei der öffentlichen Verhandlung?

Diese Frage ist zu verneinen, wenn der Beklagte nicht erschienen ist, denn insofern die Beschränkung des Begehrens die Zuständigkeit verrückt, enthält sie eine die Rechte des Beklagten berührende Klagsänderung, von welcher dieser in gesetzlicher Weise Kenntniß erhalten muß (Abg. II 268); sie ist aber zu bejahen, wenn der Beklagte erschienen ist, denn nach Art. 180 u. 506 sind Klagsänderungen an den Einzelgerichten unbedingt gestattet bis zum Schlusse der ersten Verhandlung. Anders verfügt der hannov. Entwurf (§ 7 Abs. 2), laut dessen mit Zustellung der Ladung die Zuständigkeit unabänderlich fixirt ist. (Verh. S. 378 u. 379.)

Art. 4. — **Bei der Werthsberechnung des Streitgegenstands sind jährliche Renten oder Leistungen, wenn die Zahl der Jahre bestimmt ist, für den ganzen Zeitraum zusammenzurechnen. Ist die Zahl der Jahre nicht bestimmt, so sind vier Gulden jährlicher Rente einer Summe von hundert Gulden gleichzuachten, es sei denn, daß ein Ablösungskapital besteht, in welchem Falle dieses der Berechnung zu Grund zu legen ist.**

Die Berechnung der Naturalleistungen richtet sich nach dem Jahresdurchschnitte der Preise an dem dem Lieferungsorte zunächst gelegenen Markte, wenn aber solche Preise nicht zu erheben sind, nach dem Jahresdurchschnitte der laufenden Preise am Lieferungsorte. Hat der Kläger alternativ eine bestimmte Geldforderung erhoben, so ist diese bei Beurtheilung der Zuständigkeit zu Grund zu legen.

G. A. der K. der A. III S. 12–14. 87. IV S. 4. — K. der R. I S. 32. 33.

1) Ueber Voraussetzung und Form der Werthserhebungen zur Festsetzung der Zuständigkeit enthalten die Art. 188 und 189 nähere Bestimmungen. Hier sind Anhaltspunkte bezüglich der Berechnung für einige besondere Fälle gegeben.

2) Jährliche Renten und Leistungen. Das Gesetz hat hier nicht Rückstände im Auge, denn sie sind entweder nur Nebensache, falls das Recht zur Rente selbst im Streite ist, und kommen dann gar nicht in Betracht, oder sie sind Hauptsache und dann gilt selbstverständlich die Gesammtforderung. Zweck des Gesetzes ist es vielmehr, jene Fälle zu regeln, wo das Recht auf periodische Leistungen strittig ist und es sich darum handelt, den Werth dieses Rechtes festzusetzen.

Die Zeitdauer der Leistungen kann genau bestimmt sein, z. B. wenn Jemand eine Rente auf 30 Jahre beansprucht, oder sie kann mehr oder minder unbestimmt sein, z. B. wenn die Rente für immer, oder lebenslänglich, oder bis zum Eintritte sonstiger ungewisser Ereignisse fortdauern soll. — Das Gesetz verfügt nun, daß für Leibrenten rc. ganz die nämliche Schätzung stattfinde, wie für ewige Renten, was den praktischen Vortheil hat, schwierige Berechnungen unnöthig zu machen.

Daß bei bestimmter Zeitdauer die Leistungen immer zusammenzurechnen sind, führt zu Widersprüchen, denn eine Rente, welche 50 Jahre dauert, ist hiernach gerade doppelt so viel werth, als eine solche, welche ewig dauert. Richtiger wäre es gewesen, beizusetzen: „jedoch darf hiedurch der Werth einer ewigen Rente nicht überschritten werden.“ Hannov. Entwurf § 6 Z. 3. — Seuff. Comm. Bd. IV S. 55 Note 139.

3) Ablösungskapital. Ob dieses Kapital kraft Gesetzes oder zufolge Uebereinkunft besteht, ist gleichgültig. Abg. III 13 (v. Weiß) Code civ. Art. 529 und 530.

4) Marktpreise. Man sollte meinen, irgend ein zunächst gelegener Markt müsse überall bestehen und sei also die für den entgegengesetzten Fall getroffene Vorsorge unnöthig. — Offenbar soll hier dem richterlichen Ermessen überlassen sein, zu würdigen, ob der Markt nahe genug gelegen sei, um dessen Preise als maßgebend zu betrachten.

Ueber den Sinn des Ausdrucks: „Jahresdurchschnitt“ wird in den Verhandlungen (Abg. III 87) bemerkt, es brauche der Richter nicht genau auf den Tag zu berechnen, sondern es sei ihm auch hier ein gewisser Spielraum gestattet.

5) Alternative Begehren. Die Bestimmung, es solle bei alternativem Begehren die Geldforderung entscheiden, ist unbedingt und gilt also auch, wo behauptet wird, es habe die Hauptleistung einen viel geringeren Werth als die alternative Geldforderung. Allerdings ist richtig, daß es so in der Macht des Klägers steht, indem er alternativ eine recht hohe Geldsumme verlangt, die unbedeutendste Sache vor's Bezirksgericht zu bringen; allein dieser Mißstand erscheint von geringer praktischer Bedeutung und ist nicht in Anschlag zu bringen gegenüber dem Vortheile der Sicherstellung der Zuständigkeit. — In Betracht dessen wurde denn auch bereits unter Herrschaft des G. V. G. von 1861 im nemlichen Sinne entschieden. Bl. f. R. XXVI 475.

6) Die Fassung des Gesetzes könnte auf den Gedanken bringen, als gelte die bezügliche Bestimmung nur, falls Naturalleistungen alternativ eingeklagt werden, nicht aber bei Vindikation von Mobilien; dies wäre nach der ursprünglichen Fassung (Entwurf Art. 652) und dem Gange der Diskussion vollständig unrichtig. (Abg. I 13 und 14, sowie 87. — Bl. f. R. a. a. O.)

Art. 5. — **Der Zuständigkeit der Einzelngerichte sind ohne Rücksicht auf den Werth des Streitgegenstands entzogen:**

1) **Klagen aus Ansprüchen, welche keine bestimmte Schätzung zulassen;**
2) **dingliche, Besitz-, Grenzscheidungs- und Theilungsklagen, welche ausschließlich oder auch nur zum Theile unbewegliche Sachen oder diesen gleichgeachtete Rechte zum Gegenstande haben;**
3) **Klagen auf verfallene Jahresrenten, auf sonstige periodisch wiederkehrende Bezüge oder auf Theilzahlungen, wenn das Hauptrecht selbst bestritten ist und den Werth von hundertfünfzig Gulden übersteigt;**
4) **Entschädigungsklagen gegen Richter, Staatsanwälte, Gerichtsschreiber, Notare, Anwälte oder Gerichtsvollzieher wegen Dienstwidrigkeiten.**

Die Bestimmung der Ziffer 2 findet keine Anwendung auf Klagen über Pfandrechte, bei welchen nur der Betrag der Forderung, für welche sie geltend gemacht werden, maßgebend ist.

G. A. K. der A. I S. 34—42. 44. 59. 60. 80. III S. 51. IV S. 5. 301 u. 302. — K. d. R. I S. 34. 35. IV S. 2—5.

1) Unmöglichkeit der Schätzung. Seuff. Com. Bd. IV S. 54 sagt: Die Unmöglichkeit einer bestimmten Schätzung kann in sehr verschiedenen Beziehungen des Gegenstandes ihren Grund haben, z. B. in der Ungewißheit über den Umfang der Geltendmachung eines Rechtes, oder über die Wiederkehr der Anwendungsfälle; in der Ungewißheit über die Dauer der Ausübung, wenn deren Endpunkt noch von einem ungewissen Ereignisse abhängt oder in der Ungewißheit über die Grundlage oder den Maßstab einer Werthbestimmung für das streitige Recht u. s. w.

Einer Schätzung entziehen sich Klagen, welche Familienrechte, Standes- und Ehrenrechte betreffen, oder die persönliche Freiheit oder Rechtsfähigkeit, ferner Rechnungsklagen 2c. Von Servituten ist hier Umgang zu nehmen, da alle dinglichen Klagen, als solche, der Zuständigkeit des L. G. entzogen sind.

2) Entschieden wurde:

1) Klagen auf Entschädigung, vorbehaltlich Liquidation, unterliegen keiner Schätzung. (Bl. f. R. VI 15.)

2) Ebenso Klagen wegen außerehelicher Vaterschaft (O. A. G. 8. März 1842). Anders ist es jedoch, wenn es sich nicht mehr um Anerkennung der Vaterschaft handelt, sondern blos Schadloshaltung, Alimente, verlangt werden. — (Bl. f. R. XIII 11 und 331, XXII 33.)

3) Bei Klagen auf Herausgabe von Urkunden fragt sich, ob die Urkunden blos Beweismittel für eine bestimmte Summe bilden oder ob ihre Tragweite unbestimmt ist. (Bl. f. R. XXVI 477.)

3) Dingliche Klagen. Eine dingliche Klage ist jede Klage, deren Rechtsgrund ein dingliches Recht und deren Zweck die Anerkennung und Geltendmachung dieses Rechts ist.

4) Das Gesetz will nur rein dingliche Klagen der Zuständigkeit des Landrichters entziehen, also nicht persönliche Immobiliarklagen. Abg. I 41. (v. Weiß).

Zu diesen gehören insbesondere auch die actiones in rem. scriptae, welche gegen den Besitzer einer Sache als solchen gehen, jedoch persönlicher Natur sind (§ 31 Inst. [4, 6] Windscheid Pand. § 45 Note 6), wie z. B. die actio quod metus causa, actio Pauliana, sofern der redliche Drittbesitzer wegen Bereicherung haftet, die actio ad exhibendum u. s. w. Ein auf sie bezüglicher Beisatz war bei der zweiten Lesung aufgenommen, wurde aber zuletzt wieder beseitigt. (Vgl. Bemerk. zu Art. 21.)

5) Wer einfach Schadenersatz wegen widerrechtlicher Handlungen begehrt, erhebt keine dingliche Klage, auch wenn er seinen Anspruch durch Hinweisung auf sein Eigenthums- oder sonstiges dingliches Recht, welches verletzt sein soll, begründet.

Auch der Umstand, daß zur Würdigung einer Entschädigungsklage (z. B. wegen Benachtheiligung durch eine Eisenbahnanlage) die Frage zu entscheiden ist, ob ein bestrittenes dingliches Recht früher bestanden habe, macht die Klage nicht zur dinglichen.

6) Die Thatsache, daß der Kläger Eigenthümer der Sache ist, deren Herausgabe er verlangt, genügt für sich allein nicht, um die Klage als eine dingliche erscheinen zu lassen, wenn nicht das dingliche Recht selbst, sondern ein Vertrag, oder eine sonstige persönliche Verpflichtung den Klagegrund bildet. — In der Pfalz z. B., wo es zum Uebertrage des Eigenthums einer Tradition nicht bedarf, vielmehr der Wille der Contrahenten genügt, müßte sonst die Klage des Käufers auf Lieferung der gekauften Sache immer eine dingliche Klage sein und es ist dies wirklich schon behauptet worden. (Troplong vente Nr. 262.) Allerdings sagt der Kläger, indem er den Kauf behauptet, ebendamit auch, daß er Eigenthümer sei, allein sein Eigenthum beruht ja nach der Klage nur auf dem Kaufvertrage und er macht daher nichts Anderes geltend, als die aus diesem Vertrage entspringende persönliche Verpflichtung.

Aehnlich verhält es sich mit der Klage auf Auflösung oder Vernichtung eines Kaufes. Sie ist persönlicher Natur und wenn dabei Rückgabe einer Sache verlangt wird, so geschieht dies auf Grund persönlicher Verpflichtung, zufolge deren der Käufer, ganz abgesehen von der Frage des Eigenthums, zu dieser Rückgabe verbunden ist.

7) Das Gesetz spricht nur von dinglichen Klagen im Gegensatze zu persönlichen, erkennt also gemischte Klagen nicht an.

Sowohl im römischen, als im französischen Rechte spricht man von solchen Klagen, wenn auch in verschiedenem Sinne.

Dort nennt man gemischte Klagen solche, bei denen jeder Theil Kläger und Beklagter sein kann; also die Theilungs- und Grenzberichtigungsklagen. — Dieselben sind durch besondere Bestimmung den dinglichen gleichgestellt und ist daher die betreffende Unterscheidung gegenstandslos.

In Frankreich waren die angesehensten Rechtsgelehrten von jeher der Ansicht, daß die einzelne Klage im Grunde nur dinglich oder persönlich sein könne und daß man wohl von einer Häufung von Klagen beider Art, nicht aber von gemischten

Klagen sprechen könne (so z. B. Chauveau sur Carré zu Art. 59, Einleitung); da nun aber das Gesetz (Art. 59 Cod. de proc.) ausdrücklich von gemischten Klagen spricht, so suchte man sich Fälle solcher Mischung zu konstruiren und es entstand ein unabsehbares Gewirr verschiedener Ansichten. (Das Nähere im Journal du Pal. v. action [dr. franc.] Nr. 165—235.)

Da übrigens die Friedensrichter über Immobiliarklagen, auch wenn sie persönlich sind, nie erkennen, da ferner die Unzuständigkeit des angegangenen Bezirksgerichts sich leicht heilen läßt (Art. 169 C. de pr.), da endlich die französ. Anwälte es sich zur Regel machen, unfruchtbare Inkompetenzeinreden, welche der Sache nichts nützen, ihnen aber schaden, zu unterlassen, so machten sich Mißstände nicht fühlbar.

Die bezügliche (jetzt müssige) Streitfrage hatte namentlich auch die Resolutionsklagen zum Gegenstande. Dieselben sind, wie erwähnt, rein persönlich, wenn sie gegen den Contrahenten gerichtet sind; sie sind aber dinglich, wenn sie sich gegen den dritten Besitzer richten, von welchem auf Grund der Vertragsauflösung die Sache vindizirt wird.

8) Allerdings kann man immerhin noch von gemischten Klagen in dem Sinne sprechen, daß der Fall der Häufung persönlicher und dinglicher Klaggründe eintreten kann. — So kann Jemand ein Grundstück verlangen, theils weil es sein Eigenthum ist, theils weil der Beklagte sich persönlich verpflichtet hat, es herauszugeben; so kann ferner die Resolutions- oder Nichtigkeits-Klage gegen den Kontrahenten und gegen den dritten Besitzer gleichzeitig erhoben werden.

Ohne Zweifel ist jede Klage, wenn auch nur ein Theil derselben einen dinglichen Charakter trägt, der Zuständigkeit des Landrichters im Ganzen entgegen; wobei jedoch zu beachten ist, daß es nicht gestattet ist, persönliche Ansprüche mit dinglichen beliebig zu verbinden, um die Zuständigkeit des Landrichters auszuschließen, daß vielmehr ein innerer Zusammenhang im Sinne des Art. 33 bestehen muß. (Art. 178.)

9) Die Grenzscheidungsklagen sind ausnahmslos der landgerichtlichen Zuständigkeit entzogen, ohne daß, wie aus der Aeußerung von Weiß (K. d. R. IV S. 4) vielleicht gefolgert werden könnte, aus der Klage schon hervorgehen müßte, daß und in wie fern das Eigenthum strittig sei. In der Regel stellt sich erst bei Gelegenheit der Ortsbesichtigung näher fest, in welcher Weise zwischen den Parteien Uneinigkeit wegen des Laufes der Gränze besteht. — Jene Aeußerung wollte nur andeuten, daß nicht wegen jeder Steinsetzung das Bezirksgericht angegangen werden müsse, weil das Vermarkungsgesetz bestehe.

10) Unter den Rechten, welche den unbeweglichen Sachen gleichstehen, sind vor Allem die Realrechte (Grundrenten, Zehnten, Handlöhne) zu verstehen. — (Abg. III 97 [Barth.])

Beschränkt sich die Klage auf Einforderung rückständigen Leistungen, so ist sie eine persönliche. — Seuff. Comm. Bd. I S. 92 und 93. Bayer. L. R. Thl. II cap. 10 § 4 Z. 7.

In der Pfalz gibt es keine deutsch-rechtlichen Reallasten mehr; die dort noch vorkommenden Grundrenten haben die Natur gewöhnlicher Forderungen.

11) Besitzklagen sind den Landgerichten ohne Ausnahme entzogen, also auch der Schutz im jüngsten Besitze, welchen ihnen die Gerichtsverfassungsgesetze zugewiesen hatten.

In der Pfalz gehören umgekehrt alle Besitzklagen zur Zuständigkeit des Landrichters, indem die bezüglichen Bestimmungen der franz. Gesetze durch das Einführungsgesetz (Art. 67) aufrecht erhalten worden sind.

12) Die Bestimmung, daß Pfandrechte hier, wo es sich bloß um Wichtigkeit und Werth des strittigen Rechts handelt, nicht wie andere dingliche Rechte behandelt werden, ist praktisch und beruht auf richtiger Würdigung der Natur jener Rechte.

Pfandrechte bilden nur Zubehör von Forderungen; letztere sind daher die Hauptsache und zwar nicht bloß dem Gläubiger, sondern auch dem Schuldner und dritten Besitzer gegenüber, welche jeden Augenblick durch Zahlung das dingliche Recht beseitigen können. — Der eventuelle Angriff auf die Sache kann nicht den Ausschlag geben, da jede persönliche Klage eventuell, d. h. für den Fall, als Beklagter verurtheilt wird und nicht zahlt, einen Angriff auf dessen ganzes Vermögen enthält.

13) Das Gesetz verfügt in doppelter Richtung, nemlich:

1. indem es die Pfandrechte ausnimmt, und
2. indem es erklärt, daß der Betrag der Forderung entscheide.

14) Da die Verfügung allgemein ist, so findet sie überall Anwendung, wo ein Pfandrecht Gegenstand des Streites ist, sei es nun, daß dasselbe zur Geltung gebracht, sei es, daß dasselbe beseitigt werden soll.

Was ersteren Gesichtspunkt betrifft, so wird nicht leicht mehr der Fall vorkommen, daß der Landrichter berufen wird, über ein Pfandrecht an unbeweglichen Sachen zu erkennen, denn nach Art. 822 und 1040, sowie nach Art. 2169

Code civ. bedarf der Gläubiger in allen Fällen, wo ihm eine vollstreckbare Urkunde zu Gebote steht, der Hypothekenklage gegen den Besitzer verpfändeter Liegenschaften nicht, kann vielmehr sofort im Wege der Vollstreckung vorschreiten und dann tritt nach Art. 840 die Zuständigkeit des Bezirksgerichts ein. — Praktische Bedeutung erhält also nur der zweite Gesichtspunkt, insofern er bei allen Klagen auf Löschung von Hypotheken und hypothekarischen Vormerkungen Anwendung findet. (Abg. IV S. 172—174.)

15) Hat man unter „Betrag der Forderung" die Gesammtforderung, für welche das Pfandrecht besteht, oder geltend gemacht wird, zu verstehen, oder nur das Kapital?

Ohne Zweifel soll hier kein neues Prinzip aufgestellt, sondern nur auf Art. 3 verwiesen sein. Es wird sogar dann nur die Hauptsache entscheiden, wenn die Forderung nicht behauptet, sondern verneint wird, wie bei der Löschungsklage, und zwar aus ähnlichen Gründen, wie bei der Provokationsklage. — Jedenfalls läßt sich nicht annehmen, daß der Gesetzgeber unter „Betrag der Forderung" etwas Anderes verstanden habe, wenn der Gläubiger Kläger, als wenn er Beklagter ist.

16) Die Bestimmung wegen Jahresrenten (Ziff. 3) ist im Grunde überflüssig, denn ist das Recht bestritten und über 150 fl. werth oder ein dingliches Recht, so genügen die Art. 4, 10 u. 11. In den Verhandlungen (Abg. I. S. 59 u. 60) herrscht etwas Verwirrung der Begriffe, jedoch scheint so viel hervorzugehen, daß man den Fall im Auge hatte, wo schon vor der Klage das Recht bestritten ist. Ist in solchem Falle nach civilrechtlichen Grundsätzen eine Klage auf Anerkennung des Rechtes, z. B. einer Gilte, einer Leibrente, zulässig, so erscheint fragliche Bestimmung wiederum überflüssig. Es bleibt also bloß der Fall, wo das Civilrecht eine derartige Präjudizialklage nicht zuläßt, und für diesen Fall muß, wenn Z. 3 nicht ganz zwecklos sein soll, angenommen werden, daß auf außergerichtliche Bestreitung des Hauptrechtes hin die verfallenen Leistungen vor dem Bezirksgerichte einzuklagen seien. Nimmt man dieses an, so bleibt die Zuständigkeit dieses Gerichts bestehen, auch wenn gerichtlich das Hauptrecht nicht bestritten wird; die Thatsache der Bestreitung (Berühmung) bildet eine Vorfrage für die Competenz. Jedenfalls war aber dieser Punkt nicht wichtig genug für eine besondere Bestimmung.

17) Bezüglich der Syndikatsklage hatte der Entwurf besondere Verfügungen (Art. 702 bis 711), welche man als unnöthig beseitigte, da, was die Frage der Haftbarkeit anbelangt, die allgemeinen Grundsätze (G. O. Cap. XVI § 3, Code civ. Art. 1382 u. 1383) ausreichten und, was die Zuständigkeit betrifft, es genüge, die Zuständigkeit des Landrichters auszuschließen (Abg. III 49—51).

18) Was Anwälte, Notare und Gerichtsvollzieher anbelangt, so verfügte der Entwurf (Art. 19 Abs. 2 u. 22 Z. 4), daß in Fällen, wo die Haftung derselben im Laufe des die Veranlassung zur Dienstwidrigkeit bietenden Rechtstreites beansprucht werde, das betreffende Gericht, also möglicherweise auch das Landgericht oder Handelsgericht zuständig sei; allein jene Verfügung fand lebhaften Widerspruch und wurde gestrichen (Abg. I 33).

19) Vorliegende Ausnahmsbestimmung gilt nur für dienstliche Handlungen und Unterlassungen. Offenbar ist hiermit nicht jeder Vorfall gemeint, welcher Anlaß zur disciplinären Einschreitung geben kann, denn bei dieser Voraussetzung wäre, da Richter, Notare u. s. w. auch wegen Privathandlungen, welche der Würde des Standes zuwider sind, disciplinirt werden können, keine Gränze gegeben und müßte in jeder Anschuldigung einer widerrechtlichen Handlung, auch die Anschuldigung einer Dienstwidrigkeit erblickt werden. Wenn daher ein Notar, Advokat wegen Besorgung von Darlehen, wegen Geschäftsführung u. dgl. in Anspruch genommen wird, ist Ziff. 4 nie anwendbar.

20) Fraglich ist, ob Ziff. 4 sich auch auf Advokaten-Funktionen im engeren Sinne bezieht, insbesondere auf Fälle, wo ein Advokat Parteien vor Landgerichten oder Handelsgerichten vertritt.

Man kann sagen: 1) Das Gesetz hält in Art. 78 — 82 die Funktionen der Advokaten und Anwälte scharf auseinander; Dienstwidrigkeiten der Anwälte heißt also so viel, wie D. in Anwalts-Funktionen. 2) Nur soweit Anwaltszwang besteht, haben die Advoken den Charakter öffentlicher Bediensteten, bei sonstigen Vertretungen sind sie nur gewöhnliche Prozeß-Bevollmächtigte. 3) In Art. 28 hat man absichtlich den Ausdruck „Anwälte" in „Advokaten" umgewandelt und qui dicit de uno, negat de altero.

Dem entgegen läßt sich geltend machen:

1) daß bei den Verhandlungen, zur Bezeichnung der Person, die Ausdrücke „Anwälte" und „Advokaten" als ganz gleichbedeutend gebraucht wurden, wie denn die nemliche Person immer beide Eigenschaften vereinigt (Abg. I. 115);

2) daß das Gesetz, wenn es von „Anwälten" spricht, nicht auch nothwendig „Anwalts-Funktionen" im Auge haben muß;

3) daß allerseits anerkannt wurde, es gelange bei Advokaten, auch wenn sie an Landgerichten oder Handelsgerichten auftreten, immerhin in gewissen Beziehungen, namentlich was Disciplin betrifft, ihre dienstliche Eigenschaft zur Geltung (Abg. I 94—97);

4) daß im Allgemeinen die Vertretung oder Verbeistandung von Parteien zur Amtssphäre des Advokaten gehört und es dem Geiste des Gesetzes widerstrebt, denselben wegen seines dienstlichen Verhaltens in solchen, nicht zu seiner ausschließlichen Zuständigkeit gehörigen Funktionen vor einem Einzelrichter Rede stehen zu lassen.

Ich halte letztere Gründe für überwiegend.

21) Wegen Verurtheilung von Anwälten ꝛc. zu den Kosten siehe die Bemerkungen zu Art. 110.

Die Hypothekenbeamten der Pfalz sind hier vergessen; sie unterliegen daher der gewöhnlichen Regel.

Art. 6. — **Ohne Rücksicht auf den Werth des Streitgegenstands gehören, vorbehaltlich der Bestimmungen des Art. 7, vor die Einzelngerichte:**

1) **Rechtsstreitigkeiten zwischen Vermiethern und Miethern von Wohnungs- und andern Räumen in Betreff des Miethverhältnisses, solange dasselbe noch besteht, und Rechtsstreitigkeiten, welche sich nach Auflösung des Miethverhältnisses wegen Forderungen für das letzte Jahr, wegen Räumung der Miethgegenstände oder wegen Geltendmachung der dem Vermiether im Betreffe der Mobilien des Miethers zustehenden Rechte ergeben;**

2) **Rechtsstreitigkeiten zwischen Handwerksmeistern und Gesellen oder Lehrjungen, zwischen Dienstherren und Dienstboten oder Taglöhnern, zwischen Fabrik-, Gewerbs- oder sonstigen Unternehmern und ihren Lohnarbeitern hinsichtlich des gegenseitigen dienstlichen oder gewerblichen Verhältnisses;**

3) **Rechtsstreitigkeiten zwischen Reisenden und Wirthen, Fuhrleuten, Schiffern oder Flößern wegen Wirthszechen, Fuhrlohn, Verlust oder Beschädigung der Habe des Reisenden oder wegen Verzögerung des Transports, desgleichen Rechtsstreitigkeiten zwischen Reisenden und Handwerkern wegen Forderungen, welche aus Anlaß der Reise entstanden sind;**

4) **Rechtsstreitigkeiten über Gegenstände des Handels und Wandels auf Messen und und Märkten, soferne sie während der Dauer der Messe oder des Marktes bei Gericht angebracht werden;**

5) **Klagen wegen Wildschadens, sowie Klagen wegen anderer Beschädigungen von Bodenerzeugnissen auf dem Felde, insbesondere wegen Beschädigung durch Ueberackern, Ueberfahren, Viehweiden, Grasen, Mähen, Ernten oder Einherbsten;**

6) **Klagen wegen Beschädigung von Einfriedungen, Wasserleitungen, Abflüssen, Wässerungsanlagen, Pfaden oder Wegen;**

7) **Klagen auf Anerkennung der Vaterschaft außerehelicher Kinder und Klagen auf Ernährung solcher Kinder, sowie Klagen auf Entschädigung einer außerehelich Geschwächten;**

8) **Klagen wegen Ehrenverletzungen, soferne sie bei den Civilgerichten noch zulässig und nicht auf Ersatz eines in Folge der Ehrenkränkung erlittenen Vermögensnachtheils oder auf Bezahlung eines Schmerzensgeldes gerichtet sind.**

G. A. der K. d. A. I S. 44—50. 60. 61. 80. 298. IV S. 5. 6. — der K. d. R. I. S. 35—44. IV S. 4. 5.

1) Die Bestimmungen dieses Artikels sind im Wesentlichen aus der Novelle von 1837 § 1 in die Ger.-Verf.-Gesetze von 1850, 1856 und 1861 und von da endlich in die neue Prozeß-Ordnung übergegangen. In Folge hiervon sind auch verschiedene Redaktionsmängel und Unklarheiten, welche Anlaß zu Controversen gegeben hatten und welche Seuffert (Comm. zur G. O. II S. 17 und 18) dadurch hervorhob, daß er mit markirter Schrift die dem künftigen Gesetzgeber zu empfehlenden Zusätze in den Text aufnahm, beibehalten worden.

Hervorzuheben ist, daß Art. 6 keine Anwendung findet, wenn Handelsgeschäfte in Frage sind.

Miethstreite. (Ziff. 1.)

2) Der Ausdruck „Miethe“ umfaßt zwar im weitesten Sinne auch den Pacht (Windscheid Pand. § 399), allein hier ist dieser ohne Zweifel ausgeschlossen (Vhdl. d. K. d. A. zur Nov. v. 1837 Bd. VIII S. 218), wie sich übrigens aus den Worten: „Wohnungs- und anderen Räumen“ von selbst ergibt.

Für den Begriff von Pacht entscheidet nicht sowohl der Zweck der Benützung — ob derselbe ein spekulativer, kaufmännischer ist — als vielmehr die Art der Benützung. Besteht diese ausschließlich oder doch vorzugsweise im Bezuge von Früchten (natürlichen oder industriellen) so liegt Pacht vor, sonst Miethe. Der Unterschied ist der von ususfructus und usus. Weiske Rechtslexikon B. VII S. 736, Windscheid Pand. § 399 Nr. 4, Bluntschli Privatr. § 124, preuß. L. R. Thl. I Tit. 21 § 259 und 260.

Das französische Recht unterscheidet bloß zwischen Gebäuden und Grundstücken, welche natürliche Früchte bringen (bail à loyer und bail à ferme). Troplong, louage, No. 527 u. 632. Journ. du Pal. (bail) No. 1079.

3) Wohnungs- und andere Räume. Der Ausdruck: „andere Räume", ganz allgemein genommen, fände Anwendung auf alle Immobilien, denn überall, wo es sich um Benützung von solchen handelt, handelt es sich auch um Benützung von Räumen.

Offenbar ist dies nicht der Sinn des Gesetzes, welches sonst sich begnügt haben würde, von der Miethe von Immobilien zu sprechen, im Gegensatze zum Pachte. Spezielle Ausdrücke bedingen auch einen speziellen Sinn.

Auch die geschichtliche Entstehung führt zu dieser Auslegung. In der Novelle von 1837 ist nur von „Wohnungen" die Sprache; die Jurisprudenz jedoch hatte, bei Gleichheit des Grundes, jene Bestimmung auch angewendet auf Räume, welche in ganz gleicher Weise wie Wohnungen benützt werden, als: Läden, Magazine u. s. w. (Seuff. Comm. B. II S. 18) und offenbar sollte durch fraglichen Zusatz dieser Ansicht in etwas erweiterter Weise Ausdruck gegeben werden. Schließlich läßt auch die Wortfassung selbst deutlich erkennen, daß man die Wohnungsräume als Hauptsache im Auge hatte und neben denselben noch solche Räume bezeichnen wollte, welche in ähnlicher Weise benützt werden, also Läden, Magazine, Speicher, Keller, Scheunen, Ställe u. s. w.

4) Ausgeschlossen erscheinen jene Miethverträge, bei denen die industrielle Ausnützung eines Erwerbsgeschäftes, die Benützung der im Gebäude vorhandenen Einrichtungen und Maschinen, der Wasserkräfte, der Kundschaft ꝛc., nicht aber bloß die Benützung eines Raumes, als Hauptsache erscheint, wie z. B. bei Mühlwerken, Brauereien, Fabriken u. s. w. Solche Verträge, bei welchen nicht sowohl das Gebäude, als das Geschäft, dessen Sitz es ist, vermiethet wird, nennt man im Leben und theilweise auch im Rechte, nicht Miethen, sondern Pächte; sollte aber Letzteres auch nicht der Fall sein, so erscheinen sie jedenfalls im Sinne vorliegender Bestimmung ausgeschlossen.

Obgleich daher das französische Recht auf Mühlpächte ꝛc. die Vorschriften des Code civ. über die Miethe (bail à loyer) anwendet, so wird dennoch vorliegende Bestimmung nicht anwendbar sein. (Vgl. übrigens Abg. I 45 [Völk]).

5) Eine weitere Frage ist es, ob auch Flächenräume gemeint seien, wenn sie für sich vermiethet werden, z. B. Gärten, Holzhöfe, Turnplätze, überhaupt gewöhnliche Grundstücke, welche nicht verpachtet, sondern vermiethet sind. Nach obigen Erörterungen und da Ausnahmsbestimmungen nicht auszudehnen sind, müssen sie als ausgeschlossen gelten. Dabei ist es ohne wesentliche Bedeutung, ob der Platz ein eingefriedigter oder ein offener ist.

6) Es kann die Frage entstehen, was Rechtens sei, wenn der nemliche Vertrag eine Miethe im Sinne vorliegender Bestimmung und eine Miethe oder einen Pacht sonstiger Gegenstände enthält. — Die französische Jurisprudenz frägt in solchen Fällen, was Hauptsache, was Nebensache sei, und bezweifelt nicht, es sei, falls z. B. mit einem Hause nebenbei noch einige Grundstücke in Genuß gegeben werden, das Ganze nach den Grundsätzen der Miethe zu behandeln. Troplong, louage, No. 127. Journal du Pal. (bail) No. 1079—1082.

Diese Jurisprudenz möchte sich zur Nachahmung empfehlen. Wenn daher beim Pachte eines Anwesens auch Wohngebäude zur Benützung gegeben sind, so ist die Zuständigkeit des Landrichters unbedingt ausgeschlossen, auch für Streitfälle, wo es sich nur um diese Gebäude handelt, z. B. wegen Baureparaturen an denselben.

7) „So lange dasselbe noch besteht." Wenn dem Landrichter während Bestands der Miethe eine so weit gehende Zuständigkeit eingeräumt ist, so geschieht dies in der Erwägung, daß von der Schlichtung der bezüglichen Streitigkeiten das friedliche Fortbestehen des Miethverhältnisses abhängt. Dieser Grundsatz fällt allerdings weg, wenn der Streit etwa kurz vor Ablauf der Miethzeit sich entspinnt, so daß die endliche Entscheidung oder auch nur die Anordnung vorsorglicher Maßregeln vor Auflösung der Miethe nicht zu erwarten ist; allein eine Ausnahme für solche Fälle zu machen war unthunlich und mußte die Hauptrücksicht, für die Kompetenz eine kennbare sichere Gränze zu geben, überwiegen. Es entscheidet daher unbedingt der Zeitpunkt der Entstehung des Streits, d. h. der Zustellung der Ladung.

8) Es fragt sich nun: „was hat man sich unter dem Bestehen des Miethverhältnisses zu

denken, das faktische oder das rechtliche Bestehen? — Offenbar das rechtliche!

Nach dem natürlichen Wortsinne sowie nach dem Geiste des Gesetzes bedeutet „Miethverhältniß" das „Vertrags-Verhältniß zwischen Miether und Vermiether, nicht aber einen gewissen faktischen Zustand. Vgl. Bl. f. R. IV 165 ff. Wenn daher der Vermiether den Miether faktisch ausgetrieben hat und Letzterer verlangt wieder in Besitz zu kommen, oder wenn umgekehrt der Miether die Miethe faktisch aufgegeben hat und der Vermiether verlangt, daß er seinen Vertragspflichten nachkomme, so ist der Landrichter zuständig, falls er findet, daß der Miethvertrag rechtlich noch in Kraft ist. Bl. f. R. XXVI 446.

9) Ohne Zweifel liegt auch die Frage des rechtlichen Bestehens in der Zuständigkeit des Landrichters, denn Regel ist, daß jeder Richter seine Zuständigkeit prüfen und feststellen dürfe, mag dieselbe auch von Thatsachen abhängen, welche ihn nöthigen, auf den Grund der Sache einzugehen. So gut das Handelsgericht entscheiden darf, ob ein Handelsgeschäft vorliege, so gut darf der Landrichter entscheiden, ob ein Miethvertrag bestehe.

Von anderer Anschauung gehen allerdings aus Umbscheiden (K. d. A. I 45) und v. Weiß (K. d. R. I 26) allein offenbar unter dem Einflusse der im französischen Rechte geltenden Bestimmungen. (Code de proc. Art. 3 Ziff. 4.) Daß die bezüglichen Aeußerungen ohne Erwiederung geblieben sind, kann nicht ins Gewicht fallen, weil 1) es sich nicht darum handelt, etwas Neues einzuführen, sondern die Bestimmungen des G.V.G. von 1861 beizubehalten, weil 2) anderseits auch Niemand zustimmte, vielmehr der beantragte Zusatz: „vorausgesetzt, daß die Existenz eines Miethvertrags nicht bestritten ist oder der Vollzug begonnen hat" abgelehnt wurde, und weil endlich 3) gerade die Streitigkeiten über Einzug und Auszug zu den dringlichsten gehören und von jeher als hierher gehörig betrachtet wurden. Seuff. Comm. B. II S. 18 Note 9. — Es tritt daher mit voller Kraft die Rechtsregel ein: ubi lex non distinguit, nec judicis est distinguere.

Auch die Frage, ob überhaupt ein Miethverhältniß entstanden sei, gehört zur Zuständigkeit des Landrichters; sie betrifft einen Streit zwischen Miether und Vermiether. Wollte man diese Frage ausscheiden, so müßten folgerichtig auch die Fragen, wie der Vertrag abgeschlossen worden, auf welche Sachen er sich erstrecke und ähnliche mitausgeschieden werden.

10) Als fortbestehend ist ein Miethverhältniß zu betrachten, wenn es nach Ablauf der ursprünglichen Miethzeit durch ausdrückliche oder stillschweigende Uebereinkunft in der Weise fortgesetzt wird, daß die Stipulationen des früheren Vertrages im Wesentlichen noch Geltung behalten.

Ist der frühere Miethvertrag ganz oder dem Wesen nach aufgehoben und durch einen neuen Vertrag ersetzt, so beginnt mit letzterem auch ein neues Miethverhältniß. Bl. f. R. IV 165 ff. — Seuff. Comm. B. II S. 18. — Edel Comm. z. G.V.G. S. 32.

Ob Eines oder das Andere der Fall sei, wird der Richter nach den Umständen des Falls würdigen, im Zweifel aber gegen die Zuständigkeit des Landrichters entscheiden.

11) Steht das Miethverhältniß fest, so erstreckt sich die Zuständigkeit des Landrichters über alle Streitigkeiten, welche die durch den Vertrag begründeten Rechte und Pflichten betreffen, insbesondere auch über Erfüllung übernommener Vertragspflichten, Entschädigungsansprüche, Auflösung der Miethe u. s. w. Bl. f. R. IV 165 ff.

12) Forderungen für das letzte Jahr. Die Allgemeinheit des Ausdruckes deutet an, daß der Gesetzgeber nicht etwa bloß den Miethzins für's letzte Jahr im Auge hatte, sondern auch alle sonstigen gegenseitigen Ansprüche, insofern sie sich auf Thatsachen gründen, welche ins letzte Jahr fallen.

13) Wegen Räumung der Miethgegenstände ist zu beachten Art. 69 des Polizei-Straf-Gesetzes.

14) Die Schlußbestimmung bezüglich der Mobilien ist nicht bloß mit Rücksicht auf das vom Vermiether beanspruchte Retentionsrecht, sondern auch auf Pfandrechte 2c. gegeben; jedoch wird immer vorausgesetzt, daß es sich um einen Rechtsstreit zwischen Vermiether und Miether handle, also ist z. B. die Geltendmachung von Rechten gegen dritte Besitzer. (Code civ. Art. 2102 Ziff. 1) nicht darunter begriffen. (Abg. I 60.)

Dienstverhältnisse. (Ziff. 2.)

15) Diese Ziffer ist ziemlich wörtlich der Novelle von 1837 entnommen, nur daß den Dienstboten noch die Taglöhner und den Gewerbsunternehmern noch sonstige Unternehmer beigefügt und statt „Arbeiter" — „Lohnarbeiter" gesetzt wurde.

16) Eine Streitfrage, welche leicht hätte beseitigt werden können, hat man stillschweigend mit herübergenommen, nemlich die Frage, ob das Bestehen des Dienstverhältnisses vorausgesetzt werde oder nicht.

Eine Reihe von Autoritäten hat sich für das Erstere ausgesprochen. Bl. f. R. II 415 ff. IV 165 ff. XXVI 446. Stenglein Zeitschr. B. III S. 132. Seuff. Comm. B. II S. 17.

Für das Letztere erklärt sich Edel Comm. S. 31. Die dem Erkenntnisse in Bl. f. R. XXVI 446 beigefügten Bemerkungen von Steppes lassen diese Frage unentschieden.

Die Ansicht von Edel möchte nach Wortlaut und Geist des Gesetzes die richtige sein.

Das Gesetz spricht allgemein und es tritt die Regel, daß der Richter nicht willkürlich unterscheiden dürfe, mit um so größerem Gewichte ein, als in der unmittelbar vorhergehenden Ziff. 1 ausdrücklich beigefügt ist: „so lange das Verhältniß noch besteht." — Es ist gewagt, bloß aus den Worten „Dienstherren" und „Dienstboten" zu folgern, daß bei Entstehung des Streites diese Eigenschaften noch vorhanden sein müßten.

Wenn daher der Geist des Gesetzes nicht entschieden auf eine andere Absicht schließen läßt, so wird eine Unterscheidung nicht zu machen sein. Dies ist nun nicht der Fall.

Die vorliegende Bestimmung wurzelt in verschiedenartigen Erwägungen. Man berücksichtigte:

1) die Dringlichkeit der Einschreitung, um die Hindernisse eines friedlichen Fortbestandes des Verhältnisses zu beseitigen;
2) die Dringlichkeit der Einschreitung auch deßhalb, um armen Leuten, welche aus dem Arbeitsverdienst ihren Lebensunterhalt ziehen, schnell zum Rechte zu verhelfen;
3) die Einfachheit der Rechtsverhältnisse;
4) die Nothwendigkeit eines wohlfeilen Verfahrens;
5) den Einfluß von Lokal- und Personal-Kenntnissen des Richters.

Von allen diesen Gründen fällt mit Auflösung des Dienstverhältnisses nur der erstere weg, alle andern dauern fort und gerade diese erscheinen als die wichtigsten, da, was Schnelligkeit betrifft, jetzt kein großer Unterschied mehr besteht zwischen landgerichtlichem und bezirksgerichtlichem Verfahren. — Hierzu kommt, daß jetzt, abweichend von der Novelle, auch die Taglöhner genannt sind, bei welchen vom Fortbestehen des Verhältnisses gar nicht die Rede sein kann.

Endlich ist als ein dem neuen Gesetze eigenthümlicher Grund anzuführen, daß derjenige Schriftsteller, welcher fragliche Ansicht aufgestellt hat, bei der Berathung mitwirkte, daß also wenigstens ein Gesetzgebungsfaktor stillschweigend diese Meinung vertreten hat. — Sollte man dieselbe nicht theilen, so wäre jedenfalls nicht das faktische, sondern das rechtliche Bestehen entscheidend.

17) Unter „Dienstverhältniß" ist hier das Nemliche zu verstehen, was Ziff. 1 unter „Miethverhältniß" versteht, d. h. alle aus der Eingehung, dem Vollzuge und der Auflösung des Dienstvertrages entstehenden Ansprüche. (Bl. f. R. XXVI 446. — Abg. I 46.)

Die Ansicht in Bl. f. R. IV. 165, daß Entschädigungsklagen wegen schlechter Arbeit oder Dienstversäumniß auszunehmen seien, ist gesetzlich nicht gerechtfertigt. Entschädigungen wegen Nichterfüllung der Vertragspflichten, sei es auf Seite des Herrn, sei es auf Seite des Dieners, betreffen offenbar den Vollzug des Dienstvertrages und gehören daher im Sinne des Gesetzes zur Zuständigkeit des Landrichters. Anders ist es, wenn es sich nicht um Verletzung besonderer Vertragspflichten, sondern um ein gewöhnliches damnum injuria datum handelt.

18) Selbstverständlich ist Ziff. 2 nicht anwendbar, wenn kein wirkliches Dienstverhältniß vorliegt, sondern nur etwas, was demselben ähnlich ist, wobei jedoch ein „Dingen" nicht stattgefunden hat, z. B. wenn Jemand als negotiorum gestor Dienste für einen Anderen verrichtet, wenn ein Sohn dem Vater die Dienste eines Knechtes leistet.

19) Das Wort: „Lohnarbeiter" ist gleich dem Worte: „Dienstboten" im Sinne des gewöhnlichen Lebens zu nehmen, wornach es nur bei Dienstleistungen niederer Art Anwendung findet. (Abg. I 46.) Gleichgültig ist, ob der Lohn nach der Stückzahl gereicht wird, jedoch fällt die Eigenschaft eines Lohnarbeiters hinweg, wenn der Arbeiter selbst wieder als Unternehmer erscheint, indem er die Arbeit auf eigene Wag und Gefahr fertigt.

20) Bei Arbeitern ꝛc. in kaufmännischen Geschäften (Art. 63 Ziff. 4 des Einf.-G. zum H. G. B.) findet Art. 7 Anwendung.

Reisende und Wirthe. (Ziff. 3.)

21) Man war von jeher einig, diese Bestimmung nur anzuwenden, wenn der eine Theil noch auf der Reise begriffen ist und zwar gerade auf derjenigen Reise, welche den Rechtsstreit veranlaßt hat. Für Klagen, welche erst erhoben werden, nachdem die Reise beendet, der Reisende zu Hause angelangt ist, gelten die gewöhnlichen Competenzregeln.

Das Gesetz setzt übrigens nicht voraus daß der Rechtsstreit gerade am Orte, wo die Veranlassung entsteht, anhängig werde, oder daß er zur Zeit, wo sich der Reisende noch im dortigen Gerichtsbezirke befindet, erhoben werde, vielmehr findet es auch seine Anwendung in Fällen, wo z. B. der Wirth dem Reisenden nachreist, ihn irgendwo auf der Reise erreicht und belangt.

Ferner wurde nie bezweifelt, daß unter Reisenden auch Kutscher, Schiffer Eisenbahnbedienstete u. s. w. zu verstehen seien, wenn sie mit Wirthen in Streit gerathen. Indem sie Reisende von Ort zu Ort bringen, werden sie selbst Reisende. Spies Erläut. zur Nov. v. 1837. — Seuff. Comm. B. II S. 18 Edel Comm. S. 33 — Bl. f. R. IV. 165 ff.

22) Diese der Fassung und dem Geiste des Gesetzes entsprechende Auslegung wird auch jetzt noch zu gelten haben und zwar um so mehr, als anzunehmen ist, daß der Gesetzgeber die bestehende Auslegung kannte und billigte.

Die isolirt stehende Ansicht von Spies, daß „Wirthe" blos „Gastwirthe" seien, erscheint nicht gerechtfertigt.

23) Zweifel kann der Fall erregen, wenn ein Fremder sich einige Zeit an einem Orte aufhält. Ein Aufenthalt von einigen Tagen kann natürlich nichts ändern; wer aber Monate oder Jahre sich an einem Orte außer seiner Heimath aufhält, kann offenbar nicht mehr als Reisender behandelt werden. Der Richter wird nach den Umständen des Falls und im Geiste des Gesetzes urtheilen.

24) Die Frage des Gerichtstandes wird durch vorliegende Bestimmung nicht berührt und doch war es geeignet, auch hierüber etwas zu verfügen. Ausländern gegenüber reicht zwar Art. 19 aus, allein bei Inländern bleibt nur Art. 23, welcher Schwierigkeiten bietet, da eine ausdrückliche Verabredung dahin, es solle die Zeche an Ort und Stelle bezahlt werden, nicht vorzukommen pflegt. Vorsichtsverfügungen können übrigens nach Art. 618 auch vom Landrichter des Ortes getroffen werden, und liegt eine solche vor, so wird es der Reisende in seinem eigenen Interesse geboten finden, durch Vereinbarung vor dem nemlichen Richter Recht zu nehmen.

25) Da Wirthe Kaufleute sind, so wird in vielen Fällen Art. 7 maßgebend sein und zwar selbst dem Reisenden gegenüber, wenn dieser Kaufmann ist. Bloße Handlungsreisende sind keine Kaufleute.

Messen und Märkte. (Ziff. 4.)

26) Der Streit muß sich auf jenen Handelsverkehr beziehen, zu dessen Erleichterung der in Frage stehende Markt bestimmt ist.

Keinen Unterschied macht es, ob gegen Einwohner oder gegen Fremde geklagt wird; auch beschränkt sich die Zuständigkeit nicht auf Streitigkeiten zwischen Verkäufern und Käufern, sondern sie geht auch auf civilrechtliche Streitigkeiten dieser Personen mit Mäklern oder sonstigen zur Vermittlung des Marktverkehres thätigen Personen. Bl. f. R. IV. 165 ff. — Edel Comm. S. 33.

27) Die Worte: „bei Gericht angebracht werden" deuteten unter dem alten Prozesse an, daß die Abgabe der Klagschrift genügte und Zustellung derselben nicht erforderlich war. Jetzt ist selbstverständlich nur die Zustellung der Ladung oder das freiwillige Erscheinen (Art. 504) entscheidend.

Die ganze Bestimmung hat übrigens keine besondere praktische Wichtigkeit, da Handelssachen unter Art. 7 fallen; Bedeutung hat sie nur für jene Fälle, wo gegen Nichtkaufleute geklagt wird.

Auch hier gilt das Nr. 24 bezüglich des Gerichtstandes Gesagte.

Entschädigungsklagen. (Ziff. 5 u. 6.)

28) Das Gesetz weist hier eine Reihe von Entschädigungsklagen der landgerichtlichen Zuständigkeit ohne Rücksicht auf die Summe zu. Da es die Fälle specialisirt, so ist klar, daß eine Ausdehnung auf andere ähnliche Fälle nicht zulässig, vielmehr die gegebene Schranke einzuhalten ist.

29) Bodenerzeugnisse ist nicht identisch mit Früchten, obgleich es in Art. 284 des St. G. B. in diesem Sinne gebraucht zu sein scheint; also werden auch Bäume und zwar selbst fruchttragende darunter begriffen sein. — Die Novelle von 1837 führte sie ausdrücklich an und die späteren Gesetze hatten nicht die Absicht zu ändern.

Ob die Bodenerzeugnisse auf freiem Felde oder in umfriedigten Räumen und Gärten sich befinden, wird keinen Unterschied begründen. Auch hier wollte man die Novelle, welche ausdrücklich der Gärten erwähnt, nicht ändern, da der Ausdruck „Feld" allgemein ist und man auch von „Gartenfeld" spricht.

Das Ges. v. 16/24 Aug. 1790 Tit. III. Art. 10 spricht von „dommages faits aux champs, fruits et recoltes", und auch diese Ausdrücke wurden allgemein ausgelegt. Insbesondere wurden auch „taillis" (Baumschläge) darunter begriffen (Toulouse 31. Jan. 1831).

30) Der Ausdruck „Einfriedigungen" in Ziff. 6 ist allgemein; es sind daher auch Garten- und Hof-Mauern darunter begriffen; überhaupt liegt im Geiste des Gesetzes kein Grund, die gebrauchten Ausdrücke in beschränkterem Sinne zu nehmen, als sie der Gesetzgeber gegeben hat.

31) Vorliegende Bestimmungen wollten die unbeschränkte Zuständigkeit blos einräumen:

1) bezüglich der Frage, ob nach allgemeinen Rechtsprinzipien eine Haftung eintrete, ob ein damnum injuria datum gegeben sei, und
2) bezüglich der Frage, wie hoch der Schaden sei.

Diese Zuständigkeit fällt daher hinweg, wenn der Beklagte auf Grund eines bestimmten dinglichen oder Besitz-Rechtes oder auf Grund eines Vertragsverhältnisses seine Entschädigungspflicht bestreitet. (Art. 9. — Abg. I 49. — Bl. f. R. IV 165.)

32) Bestreitet der Beklagte bloß, daß Kläger Eigenthümer sei, ohne selbst ein Recht in Anspruch zu nehmen, so ist dies eine einfache Bestreitung der Aktivlegitimation, welche keine weitere Folge hat, als wenn etwa die Eigenschaft als Cessionar oder die Erbqualität bestritten wird. — In vielen Fällen wird durch eine vom Kläger zu veranlassende Intervention des angeblich Berechtigten der Einwand beseitigt werden; der Landrichter wird wohlthun, den Kläger hierauf aufmerksam zu machen und auf Verlangen die nöthige Frist zu bewilligen.

33) Betrifft die nemliche beschädigende Handlung Gegenstände, welche in Ziff. 5 u. 6 benannt sind, und sonstige Gegenstände, so wird selbst wenn der Kläger die Ansprüche ausscheidet, nach Art. 33 seine Zuständigkeit wegfallen, falls nicht jeder Anspruch, für sich betrachtet, vor ihn gehört. (Vgl. Bemerk. zu Art. 3 Nr. 14.)

34) Das Gesetz unterscheidet nicht, ob die Beschädigung absichtlich oder ob sie aus Fahrlässigkeit verursacht worden sei. Auch Beschädigungen durch Unterlassungen, z. B. eines Angrenzers, werden nicht auszunehmen sein, falls dabei nicht etwa die Feststellung von Rechtsverhältnissen, welche der einzelrichterlichen Zuständigkeit entrückt sind, in Frage kommt. — Bl. f. R. XXV 442. — Journal du Pal. (justice de p.) Nr. 388. 389.

35) Bei der Allgemeinheit des Ausdrucks wird der Landrichter nicht bloß bezüglich der Beschädiger selbst zuständig sein, sondern auch bezüglich anderer Personen, welche für sie haftbar (civilverantwortlich) sind.

Ebenso wird er zuständig sein wegen der Schäden, welche durch Thiere oder Sachen verursacht sind.

In beiden Fällen liegt zudem immer die Vermuthung einer eigenen Verschuldung der Haftung zu Grunde.

Vaterschafts- und Alimentations-Klagen.

(Ziff. 7.)

36) Die bezeichneten Klagen sind dem Landrichter zugewiesen, weil sie der Natur der in Frage stehenden Verhältnisse wegen sich für ihn zu eignen schienen. Maßgebend war hierbei nicht bloß die Dringlichkeit der Aburtheilung — (welche bezüglich der Entschädigung der Geschwächten nicht einmal anzunehmen wäre) — sondern hauptsächlich die Einfachheit der Verhältnisse und Kostenersparung. — Ueberhaupt ist wiederholt zu betonen, daß für Bestimmung der landgerichtlichen Competenz der Gesichtspunkt der Dringlichkeit weit nicht mehr die große Bedeutung wie früher hat. Hieraus folgt, daß es einerlei ist, ob die ursprünglich Betheiligten selbst oder aber Rechtsnachfolger für sie im Streite sind und die Entscheidung in Stengl. Zeitschr. B. I S. 327 nicht gebilligt werden kann.

37) Ebenso ist es ohne Belang, ob die Alimente, welche für das uneheliche Kind verlangt werden, gegenwärtige und zukünftige, oder ob sie rückständige sind, denn es handelt sich in allen diesen Fällen um Leistungen für Ernährung des Kindes. — Wenn unter der Novelle von 1837 das Gegentheil angenommen wurde, so geschah es auf Grund der Motive des Gesetzes (S. 28) und der Ständeverhandlungen. — Unter den Gerichtsverfassungsgesetzen hat sich die entgegengesetzte Ansicht Bahn gebrochen und wurde ziemlich einhellig als richtig anerkannt, so daß über den Sinn des jetzigen Gesetzes kein Zweifel obwalten darf. Edel Comm. S. 34. — Stengl. Zeitschr. B. I S. 339. — Bl. f. R. XXVI 470. — Abg. I 47 (Franz).

38) Die Klagen auf Ernährung des Kindes und Entschädigung der Geschwächten fallen auch dann unter diese Bestimmungen, wenn über die Entschädigung durch Vertrag und Vergleich ein Abkommen getroffen wurde, auf dessen Erfüllung geklagt wird, oder wenn es sich um Auflösung eines Ernährungsvertrages oder um Erhöhung und Minderung vertragsmäßig festgesetzter Alimente handelt. — Der Anspruch erhält seinen rechtlichen Charakter aus der Thatsache, worin er seine ursprüngliche Entstehung (seine causa) findet.

So wurde früher entschieden und es ist anzunehmen, daß nichts geändert werden sollte. Edel Comm. S. 34. — Bl. f. R. XXV 428 XXVI 459. — Erk. des O. A. G. v. 27. März 1861. Reg. Nro. 758 60/61.

39) Auch in der Pfalz kommen diese Bestimmungen zur Anwendung, so weit dort Klage statthaft ist.

Durch Art. 86 des Einf. Ges. ist der Landrichter insbesondere auch ermächtigt, die in Art. 210 und 211 des Code civ. bezeichneten Entscheidungen zu geben.

Ehrenverletzungen. (Ziff. 8.)

40) Es ist hier die Klage auf Zuspruch einer als Strafe geltenden Geldsumme und auf Ehrenerklärung gemeint, welche laut Art. 64 des Einf.-Ges. zum St. G. B. vom 10. Nov. 1861 solchen Militärpersonen gegenüber noch besteht, welche nicht vor's Civilstrafgericht gestellt werden können.

Indem das Gesetz nur diese Klagen dem Landrichter zuweist und die Klagen auf Entschädigung und Schmerzensgeld (bei Realinjurien) den gewöhnlichen Regeln unterwirft, sind die früheren Streitfragen weggefallen.

In der Pfalz gibt es eine Klage wegen Ehrenkränkung, wie sie hier unterstellt ist, nicht.

41) **Für die Pfalz** bestehen noch zwei weitere Fälle, in welchen der Landrichter ausschließlich zuständig ist, nemlich:

1) die Besitzklagen (Ges. v. 16./24. August 1790 Tit. III Art. 10 Ziff. 2. — Einf. Ges. Art. 67) und

2) die Streitigkeiten wegen Oktroi-Gebühren (Ges. v. 2 Vend. VIII Art. 1 und 3. Einf. Ges. Art. 112).

Art. 3 des besagten Gesetzes sagt, daß Klage nur zulässig sei, wenn die Gebühr bezahlt ist und die Quittung dem Landrichter vorgelegt wird.

(Handelsgerichte.)

Art. 7. — Klagen in Handelssachen und Klagen aus Wechseln oder kaufmännischen Anweisungen gehören vor die Handelsgerichte.

Hievon sind ausgenommen:

1) Klagen aus den in Art. 63 Ziff. 1, 4, 6, 8, 9 und 10 des Einführungsgesetzes zum Handelsgesetzbuche erwähnten Handelssachen, sowie die wegen solcher Sachen bei Gericht zu stellenden Anträge, wenn der Anspruch in der Hauptsache an Geld oder Geldeswerth nicht über hundertfünfzig Gulden ohne Einrechnung der Zinsen, Kosten und Nutzungen betrifft;

2) Klagen gegen Nichtkaufleute aus Handelsgeschäften (Art. 271—276 des Handelsgesetzbuchs), wenn das Geschäft, aus welchem geklagt wird, auf Seiten des Beklagten kein Handelsgeschäft war.

G. A. der K. d. A. I S. 50. 51. 65. 72. 80. IV S. 6—10. — K. der R. I. S. 44—49.

1) Auf die Frage, was Handelssachen seien, ist die Antwort in Art. 63 des Einführungsgesetzes zum deutschen Handelsgesetzbuche vom 10. Nov. 1861 zu suchen. — Es ist dabei hervorzuheben, daß die Aufzählung der Handelssachen in Art. 63 eine erschöpfende sein soll, nicht eine bloß beispielsweise. Letzteres beabsichtigte der Entwurf, allein auf Antrag des Referenten Lauk wurde Ersteres beschlossen und das Wörtchen „insbesondere“ im Eingange gestrichen. (K. Verh. II. S. 58. 94. 131.) Diese Thatsache wurde mißachtet in Erk. des H. A. G. vom 4. Dez. 1865. (Zeitschr. XII 167.) Jener Artikel sagt:

Handelssachen sind:

1) die Rechtsverhältnisse, welche aus Handelsgeschäften (Art. 271—277 des allgemeinen deutschen Handelsgesetzbuches) zwischen den Betheiligten entstehen.

2) Die Handelsgeschäfte sind entweder Grundgeschäfte, d. h. solche, aus deren gewerblichem Betriebe die Eigenschaft eines Kaufmannes hervorgeht, oder Hülfsgeschäfte, d. h. solche, bei welchen vorausgesetzt wird, daß sie von einem Kaufmanne abgeschlossen worden seien.

Die Grundgeschäfte sind wiederum entweder 1) solche, bei denen das einzelne Geschäft ein Handelsgeschäft bildet (objektive Handelsgeschäfte), oder 2) solche, wo erst der Gewerbsbetrieb den Charakter bestimmt (subjektive Handelsgeschäfte — Gewerbs-Unternehmungen — entreprises im Sinne des Code de comm. Art. 632.)

I. Selbständige Handelsgeschäfte.

3) Das H. G. B. erkennt 4 Arten von Geschäften als solche an, welche für sich allein Handelsgeschäfte bilden, nemlich a) den Kauf zum Verkaufe, b) das Lieferungsgeschäft, c) die Versicherung auf Prämie und d) gewisse Geschäfte des Seehandels.

a. Kauf zum Verkaufe.

4) Handelsgeschäft ist der Kauf oder die anderweite Anschaffung von beweglichen Sachen, um sie in Natur oder nach einer Bearbeitung oder Verarbeitung weiter zu veräußern. Art. 271 Ziff. 1.

5) **Anderweite Anschaffung.** — Es ist hier jede kaufmännische Anschaffung gemeint, d. h. diejenige, welche darauf spekulirt, billig zu erwerben und um Gewinn wieder loszuschlagen. Schenkung ist keine solche Anschaffung, denn geschenkte Sachen schafft man nicht an, man erhält sie, sie fließen zu. — Wohl aber Tausch, Erwerb an Zahlungsstatt, Bezug anstatt Lohnes, kurz jede Anschaffung gegen Entgelt, bei welcher die Voraussetzung zutrifft, daß die Waare bei Anderen gesucht wurde, um Handel damit zu treiben. — Goldschmidt Handb. des Handelsrechts § 47. — Hahn Commentar zum H. G. B. Art. 271 § 9 u. 14. — Erk. des H. A. G. zu Nürnberg vom 3. Mai u. 18. Okt. 1867 (Zeitschr. für Gesetzgebung und Rechtspflege, neue Folge Bd. I S. 134 u. 274).

6) Die Gewinnung von Produkten durch Betrieb der Landwirthschaft oder durch sonstige wirthschaftliche Ausbeutung des Bodens kann selbstverständlich nie als Anschaffung gelten, mögen auch die Bodenerzeugnisse nur zum Zwecke des Verkaufes gewonnen werden, wie

beim Handelsgärtner, Ziegelbrenner u. s. w. Erk. des H. A. G. vom 3. Febr. 1863 (Zeitschr. XI 13), vom 31. März 1864 (Stenglein Zeitschr. IV 272), 5. März 1866 (Zeitschr. XIII 27), 2. März 1868 (Zeitschr., neue Folge, II 13). — Erk. des O. G. H. v. 5. Febr. 1864 (Bl. f. R. XXX 385) und 7. April 1866 (Bl. f. R. Erg. Bd. zu XXXI und XXXII S. 62). — vgl. Stengl. Zeitschr. IV 304.

7) **Bewegliche Sachen.** Ob die Sache im Augenblicke des Geschäfts schon beweglich war, oder erst in Folge desselben beweglich werden soll, ist gleichgültig. Auch Theile und Zubehör von Immobilien können in diesem Sinne bewegliche Sachen sein. Wer z. B. ein Haus auf den Abriß kauft, um die Baumaterialien zu verwerthen, einen Holzschlag, um das zu fällende Holz zu veräußern, ein Mühlwerk, um es vom Gebäude zu trennen und zu verwerthen, — schließt Handelsgeschäfte. Ebenso wer werthvolle Erde, Steine im Bruche kauft, um sie vom Boden zu trennen und Handel damit zu treiben. — Goldschm. § 58. — Hahn Art. 275 § 2. — Erk. des H. A. G. vom 14. April und 8. Sept. 1864 (Stengl. IV S. 272 u. 319).

Bei Kauf von Bodenerzeugnissen oder Bodenbestandtheilen (Holz, Torf, Steinen) ist übrigens wohl zu unterscheiden, ob es sich bloß um Erwerbung bestimmter Sachen handelt, oder aber um wirthschaftliche Benützung des Bodens; ob civilrechtlich ein Kauf oder ein Pacht vorliegt. Letzteren Falls ist Art. 275 des H. G. B. anwendbar. Erk. des O. G. H. v. 4. März 1865 (Bl. f. R. XXXI 253).

8) **Nach einer Bearbeitung rc.** Dies bietet Schwierigkeiten. Jeder Handwerker pflegt Sachen zu kaufen, um sie bei seiner Arbeit zu verwenden oder zu verbrauchen und um sie in Verbindung mit der Arbeit an die Kunden zu verkaufen. — So kauft der Schuster Leder, der Schneider Zwirn, Knöpfe, der Tüncher Farben, der Glaser Glas, der Schmied Kohlen u. s. w.

Unmöglich will das Gesetz, daß in allen diesen Fällen, auch bei noch so unbedeutenden Gegenständen, Handelsgeschäfte vorliegen. Es ist daher eine Gränze zu ziehen im Geiste des Handelsgesetzes.

9) Vorerst können solche Sachen nicht in Betracht kommen, welche bei der Arbeit verbraucht oder bloß gebraucht werden, ohne daß sie im Produkte, sei es mechanisch, sei es chemisch verbunden, vorhanden sind; Sachen, welche also nicht im Produkte selbst, sondern nur im Verkaufswerthe desselben (berechnungsweise) vertreten sind, z. B. Brennstoffe, Maschinenöl, Handwerkszeug u. s. w. — Goldschm. § 47. — Hahn Art. 271 § 15.

Es können aber ferner solche Sachen nicht in Betracht kommen, welche zwar dem Stoffe nach ins Produkt übergehen, jedoch nur unbedeutende Zuthaten, Nebensachen, im Vergleiche zu dem nicht handelsmäßig angeschafften Stoffe oder zum Arbeitsverdienste bilden, wie Knöpfe, Zwirn, welche der Schneider, Kleister, Pappendeckel, welche der Buchbinder, Farbstoffe, Lab, welche Färber, Tüncher, Lakirer verbrauchen. — Solche Sachen schafft der Handwerker nur an, damit sie ihm bei der Arbeit Dienste leisten.

Dabei muß es gleichgültig sein, ob die Nebensachen als Auslagen besonders in der Rechnung angeführt sind oder nicht, insofern eine solche Anführung nicht bezweckt, die einzelnen Sachen getrennt zu veräußern, sondern nur die Ueberzeugung von der Richtigkeit der Rechnung zu geben. — Goldschm. § 47. — Hahn Art. 271 § 15. — Erk. des H. A. G. vom 14. und 22. Febr., sowie 1. März 1867 (Zeitschr. neue F. I 25, 27 Note 6 u. 28). Erk. des O. G. H. v. 11. April 1865, 24. Mai und 30. Dez. 1867 und 28. Febr. 1868 (Bl. f. R. XXXI 270, XXXII 222, XXXIII 50 u. 121).

Gleiche Bewandtniß hat es mit dem Falle, wo für Bewirthschaftung des Bodens Hülfsstoffe angeschafft werden, z. B. wenn der Gärtner Samen, Dung kauft, der Ziegelbrenner Holz. Erk. des H. A. G. v. 2. März 1868 (Zeitschr. neue F. II S. 13. — Erk. des O. G. H. v. 5. Febr. 1864 (Bl. f. R. XXX 388).

10) Folgende Handwerker haben die Gerichte als Kaufleute anerkannt:

Apotheker — H. A. G. 23. April 1863 (Zeitschr. X 524).

Bäcker — H. A. G. 30. Juli 1863 (Stengl. IV 351).

Bräuer — H. A. G. 16. Juli 1863, 16. März 1866 u. 23. Aug. 1867. (Zeitschr. X 720, XIII 33 u. I [neue F.] 406.)

Flaschner (Blechschmiede) — H. A. G. 19. Aug. 1867 (Zeitschr. neue F. I 262).

Gerber — H. A. G. 1. Sept. 1864 (Stengl. IV 288). O. G. H. 25. Sept. 1863 (Bl. f. R. XXX 393).

Kürschner — H. A. G. 5 Febr. 1863 (Stengl. IV 16).

Müller — H. A. G. 9. Febr. 1862, 11. Juli 1864 u. 12. Nov. 1868. (Zeitschr. X 213, XI 108 u. neue F. I 132.)

Schäffler (Küfer) — H. A. G. 10. März 1864 (Stengl. IV 272).

Schmiede — H. A. G. 31. Aug. 1866 (Bl. f. R. XXXI Erg. Bd. 113) (?).

Schuster — H. A. G. 24. Okt. 1866 (Zeitschr. XIII 219).

Zimmerleute (!) — H. A. G. 2. Nov. 1864 (Zeitschr. XII 38); vgl. jedoch O. G. H. 18. Aug. 1865 (Bl. f. R. XXXI 302).

11) **Weiterveräußerung.** Dieselbe ist nicht für sich ein Handelsgeschäft, sondern sie gibt nur, sofern sie bei der Anschaffung bezweckt ist, dieser den kaufmännischen Charakter. — Das Wort: „Weiterveräußerung“ hat einen ähnlichen Sinn wie das Wort: „Anschaffung“, es ist also ein wirkliches Veräußern gemeint, kein bloßes Vermiethen (anders verfügte Art. 632 Code de c.); ferner ein Veräußern gegen Entgelt, keine reine Schenkung. Ebenso ist irgend eine kaufmännische (spekulative)

Absicht nöthig. — Diese Absicht muß nicht gerade auf Gewinn aus dem besonderen Kaufsgeschäfte gerichtet sein; der Gewinn kann auch mittelbar sein; es kann z. B. ein Kaufmann, mit der Gewißheit für die Waare nicht so viel zu erhalten, als er dafür auslegt, sie ankaufen, nur um sein Geschäft in Gang zu erhalten. — Auch die Absicht, einem Handelsgehülfen, Geschäftsfreunde als Aneiferung zu Dienstleistungen die Sache zu schenken, ist eine spekulative. — Wer jedoch Kartoffeln ankauft, um sie armen Leuten zum Ankaufspreise oder unter demselben abzulassen, macht kein Handelsgeschäft. Ebenso ist die Veräußerung von Lebensmitteln an die Mitglieder eines Consum-Vereines keine Wiederveräußerung im Sinne des Gesetzes. Erk. d. H. A. G. vom 9. Sept. 1867 (Zeitschr. n. F. I 270).

12) Die Wiederveräußerung muß **Hauptzweck** sein; wenn also ein Gutspächter Schaafe kauft, um sie zur Wollproduktion zu benützen und endlich wieder zu verkaufen, so ist dies kein H. G. Erk. des H. A. G. v. 5. März 1866 (Zeitschr. XIII 27); vgl. Erk. des H. A. G. v. 16. April 1866 (Zeitschr. XIII 221).

Der Ankauf von Thieren, z. B. Schweinen, um sie aufzuziehen, zu mästen und dann zu verkaufen, wurde von den französ. Gerichten nicht als Handelsgeschäft betrachtet, weil der Hauptzweck die Förderung der Landwirthschaft sei (cass. 16. April 1849, Dijon 15. Febr. 1847); es ist dies auch nach dem H. G. B. richtig.

13) Die Absicht muß darauf gerichtet sein, die Sache **als bewegliche** wieder zu veräußern.

Soll, dem Zwecke der Anschaffung gemäß, die Sache zu einer unbeweglichen umgewandelt oder zum Zubehör einer unbeweglichen Sache gemacht werden, und erst in diesem neuen Zustande ins Eigenthum des Erwerbers übergehen, so liegt ein H. G. nicht vor. Die Absicht der Immobilisirung hat hier die nemliche Wirkung, wie umgekehrt die Absicht der Mobilisirung und mit Recht, denn ebenso wie diese die Sache zur Handelswaare macht, bringt sie jene aus dem Handel.

Dieser Grundsatz findet Anwendung auf Unternehmung von Häuserbauten, Pflanzungen, Eisenbahn-Anlagen; ferner auf alle jene Handwerker, deren Geschäft darin besteht, das Zubehör von Bauten zu liefern, z. B. Dachdecker, Glaser, Maurer, Zimmerleute, Schreiner, Schlosser, Tüncher. Goldschm. § 58. — Hahn Art. 275 § 3. — Erk. d. H. A. G. v. 3. Jan. 1866 (Zeitschr. XIII 29) u. 1. Mai 1868 (Zeitschr. n. F. II 14). — Erk. des O. G. H. vom 29. Okt. 1864 und 18. Aug. 1865 (Bl. f. R. XXXI 239 u. 302; ferner Zeitschr. XII 40 u. Stengl. Zeitschr. S. 272 u. 288.)

14) In Frankreich bestehen in dieser Beziehung andere Grundsätze. Man nimmt an, daß Bau-Unternehmungen, bei welchen der Unternehmer das Material liefert oder eine größere Zahl Arbeiter in Thätigkeit setzt, als H. G. zu betrachten seien. Merlin. quest. (commerce) § 6 No. 2 u. 3. Pardessus (dr. comm.) Bd. I Nr. 36.

Diese Jurisprudenz beruht aber 1) darauf, daß das französische Handelsrecht weit weniger Gewicht auf den Umstand legt, daß der Vertrag eine unbewegliche Sache betrifft, wie es denn z. B. lange streitig war, ob Handel mit Immobilien H. G. begründe. Paris 5. Aug. 1847, 21. April u. 21. Mai 1849 und 8. Okt. 1851; und 2) darauf, daß auch die Miethe (von Arbeitern) — pour sous-louer — als H. G. gilt. Sie ist daher für die Auslegung unseres H. G. B. ohne Belang, mag jedoch von Einfluß auf manche Entscheidungen des Appell. Ger. zu Köln gewesen sein. — Uebrigens ging auch ein Erk. des H. A. G. v. 2. Nov. 1864 (Zeitschrift XII 38) von gleicher Ansicht aus.

15) In Fällen solcher Art ist es von Wesenheit, ob sich die Unternehmungen von den Lieferungen trennen lassen und letztere selbständige Geschäfte darstellen. vgl. Erk. d. H. A. G. v. 4. Febr. 1867 (Zeitschr. n. F. I 11) u. 18. Mai 1868 (Zeitschr. n. F. II 160).

Hat z. B. der Schreiner oder Zimmermann die Bretter für Fußböden, das Holz zum Gebälke käuflich überlassen, ehe er sein Werk beginnt, so bilden die Veräußerungen eigene Geschäfte und kommen die Sachen bloß als bewegliche in Betracht. Ob in der Rechnung die Material-Lieferungen besonders aufgeführt sind, ist nur in so fern von Bedeutung, als etwa daraus ein Schluß auf selbständigen Verkauf gezogen werden kann. Deßhalb ist denn auch die Entscheidung im Erk. des H. A. G. v. 1. März 1867 (Zeitschr. n. F. I 25) nicht ganz richtig; eben so gut wäre der Umstand, daß der Schneider Knöpfe, Seide, Futter neben seinem Arbeitsverdienste berechnet, von wesentlicher Bedeutung. (Hahn Art. 271 § 15).

16) Endlich muß die Absicht wieder zu veräußern beim Kaufe **erkennbar** sein, sei es aus den Erklärungen des Kaufenden, sei es aus den Umständen, insbesondere im Hinblicke auf das Erwerbsgeschäft des Käufers und die gewöhnliche Art des Betriebs desselben. — Geheime, nicht wenigstens zu vermuthende Absicht kann nie in Betracht kommen. Goldschm. § 47 Ziff. III. — Hahn Art. 271 §. 11. — (Zeitschr. n. F. II 140).

Andrerseits ist Aufgeben der ursprünglichen Absicht ohne Belang. Erk. des H. A. G. v. 25. Okt. 1867 (Zeitschr. n. F. I 407).

b. Lieferungs-Geschäfte.

17) H. G. ist die Uebernahme einer Lieferung beweglicher Sachen, welche der Uebernehmer zu diesem Zwecke anschafft (Art. 271 Z. 2).

Hier ist umgekehrt das Uebernehmen der Lieferung, d. h. der **Verkauf**, das Handelsgeschäft und die Absicht der Anschaffung (des Kaufs) bestimmt den Charakter des Geschäftes.

Der Lieferungsvertrag muß der Anschaffung voraus gehen; sind die zu liefernden Waaren bereits angeschafft, gekauft, so bildet die Lieferung das Realisationsgeschäft zu jenem Kaufe. Hahn Art. 271 § 17. Goldsch. § 48.

18) Bezüglich der Frage, was als bewegliche Sache zu betrachten sei, bezüglich der Absicht der Spekulation und überhaupt in allen sonstigen Beziehungen gelten die Grundsätze, wie sie oben erörtert sind.

Die Uebernahme der Lieferung von Produkten der Landwirthschaft, einer Ziegelei, welche mit eignem Stoffe betrieben wird, von Holz aus eignen oder gepachteten Waldungen — bildet daher ebensowenig ein H. G., als die Lieferung von Baumaterialien Seitens der Bau-Unternehmer, falls der Lieferungsvertrag sich nicht absondern läßt.

Auch ist es einerlei, ob die Sachen zwischen Anschaffung und Lieferung noch verarbeitet werden sollen. — Erk. d. H. A. G. v. 31. März u. 24. Okt. 1864 (Stengl. IV 272 u. 304), v. 3. Jan. 1866 (Zeitschr. XIII 29), v. 9. Febr. 1867 (Zeitschr. n. F. I 4) u. v. 1. Mai 1868 (Zeitschr. n. F. II 14). — Erk. d. O. G. H. v. 4. März 1865 (Bl. f. R. XXXI 253).

c. Versicherung auf Prämie.

19) Auch Versicherungen von Immobilien sind hierunter begriffen, insbes. alle Brandversicherungen, da hier ein Vertrag im Sinne des Art. 275 nicht vorliegt.

Versicherungen auf Gegenseitigkeit sind, da ihnen die kaufmännische Absicht fehlt, ausgeschlossen. — Goldschm. § 49. — Hahn Art. 271 § 19.

II. Gewerbs-Geschäfte.

20) Das H. G. B. kennt 5 Arten von Geschäften, welche die Eigenschaft von Handelsgeschäften gewinnen, sobald sie gewerbmäßig betrieben werden.

a. Fabrikmäßige Bearbeitung.

21) Die Bearbeitung fremder Stoffe ist nur Handelsgeschäft, wenn der Gewerbsbetrieb über den Umfang des Handwerks hinausgeht, d. h. wenn eine größere Zahl fremder Arbeitskräfte beschäftigt wird, größere Kapitalien in Umtrieb sind, überhaupt von einer Gewerbs-Unternehmung die Rede sein kann.

Es wurde entschieden, daß ein handwerkmäßiger Betrieb nicht vorliege:

bei einer Dampfwaschanstalt. H. A. G. 21. Aug. 1867 (Zeitschr. n. F. I 266). O. G. H. 31. Okt. 1868 (Bl. f. R. XXXIII 369);

bei einer größeren photographischen Anstalt. H. A. G. 1. Mai 1866 (Stengl. VII 95);

bei einer Dampfmühle. H. A. G. 12. Nov. 1866 (Zeitschr. n. F. I 132);

bei einem Glasschleifwerke. H. A. G. 8. Febr. 1867 (Bl. f. R. XXXII 28).

Liefert der Uebernehmer, der Hauptsache nach, den Stoff selbst, so ist Art. 271 anwendbar, jedoch nicht, wenn der Besteller zur Anschaffung auf seine Rechnung Auftrag gegeben hatte. — Goldschm. §. 52.

22) Bearbeitung eigener Sachen, z. B. Ziegelei mit eigenem Materiale, gehört nicht hierher; ebensowenig das Schaffen von Kunstwerken. Ueberhaupt setzt das Gewerbe die Absicht zu erwerben voraus.

b. Bankier-Geschäfte.

23) Der Bankier ist Vermittler des Geld- und Credit-Umlaufs.

Es gehört zu seinem Geschäfte natürlich auch die Vermittlung des Wechselverkehrs, das Diskontiren von W., das Ziehen von W. an fremde Plätze u. s. w. — Zu weit würde es gehen, wollte man aufstellen, jede Empfangnahme, Ausstellung oder Begebung eines Wechsels, sei zugleich ein Bankgeschäft. — vgl. Erk. des H. A. G. v. 13. Jan. u. 18. Okt. 1865 (Zeitschr. XII 3 u. 170).

Wer z. B. bei Darlehen mit eigenen Kapitalien sich in der Regel Wechsel ausstellen läßt, wird hierdurch nicht Bankier.

In gleicher Weise kann die auf reine Civilrechts-Verhältnisse — Richtigkeit eines Gutskaufs, einer Theilung — sich gründende Rückforderung einer gezahlten Wechselsumme nicht etwa deßhalb vor's Handelsgericht gebracht werden, weil der W. einem Kaufmanne ausgestellt gewesen sei und dieser hiermit (nach Art. 272 Abs. 4) ein Bankgeschäft gemacht habe. — Goldschm. § 53. Erk. des O. G. H. v. 14. Mai 1866 (Bl. f. R. XXXI 393) u. v. 22. März 1867 (Bl. f. R. XXXII 109).

24) Fraglich ist, ob und in wie weit Sparkassen, Hülfskassen, Vorschußvereine, Volksbanken u. s. w. als kaufmännische Bankgeschäfte zu betrachten seien.

Es wird darauf ankommen, ob das Geschäft an und für sich kaufmännisch, d. h. um zu erwerben, Gewinn zu machen, betrieben wird; was mit dem Gewinne geschieht, ob er zu wohlthätigen Zwecken verwendet, unter die Mitglieder des Vereins vertheilt wird, ist vollkommen gleichgültig. Erk. d. H. A. G. v. 30. Dez. 1867 (Zeitschr. n. F. I 409). Irgend eine Absicht des Gewinnes beim Geschäfte selbst muß aber offenbar vorliegen, denn „gewerbsmäßig" heißt nicht „gewohnheitsmäßig", deutet vielmehr auf die Absicht des Erwerbes. Eine Anstalt, welche Kapitalien zu 5 % annehmen würde, um sie zu 5% wieder auszuleihen, könnte daher kein Bankgeschäft genannt werden; ebensowenig treibt ein Verein Bankgeschäfte, dessen Zweck bloß ist, das von Vereinsmitgliedern aufgenommene Geld an Vereinsmitglieder wieder auszuleihen. Goldschm. § 53. A. M. Hahn Art. 272 § 10. — vgl. übrigens das Ges. über Genossenschaften vom 29. April. 1869. Art. 1 u. 11.

c. Commissionäre, Spediteure, Frachtführer.

25) Was zum Geschäfte eines Comm., Sped., Frachtf. gehöre, sagen die Art. 360, 379 u. 390 des H. G. B.

Zu den Transport-Anstalten im Sinne der Bestimmung des Art. 272 Z. 3 gehören auch die Verwaltungen der Staats-Posten und Staats-Eisenbahnen, sowohl was Güter- als was Personen-Verkehr betrifft.

— H. G. B. Art. 421. Erk. d. H. A. G. v. 23. Nov. 1866 (Zeitschr. XIII 210) und v. 26. Juni 1868 (Zeitschr. n. F. II 163).

Selbstverständlich ist der Staat nicht Kaufmann im Sinne des Art. 4 des H. G. B. (Goldschm. § 54).

Der Personen-Transport ist nur beim Großbetriebe (bei Anstalten) ein Handelsgewerbe. Lohnkutscher sind demnach keine Kaufleute. Erk. d. H. A. G. v. 16. Dez. 1864 (Stengl. IV 304) — Erk. d. O. G. H. v. 28. Dez. 1866 (Bl. f. R. Erg. Bd. zu XXXI 177).

d. Makler-Geschäfte.

26) Die Vermittlung muß sich auf Handelsgeschäfte beziehen. Auswanderungsagenten betreiben also nur in so fern H. G., als sie den Transport von Auswanderer vermitteln, Dienst-Vermittlungs-Anstalten nur in so fern, als sie sich mit Unterbringung von Geschäftsgehilfen, Fabrikarbeitern befassen.

Die Geschäfte der amtlichen Mäkler sind nicht Handelsgeschäfte, jedoch Handelssachen nach Art. 63 Z. 6 u. 9 das Einf. Ges. zum H. G. B.

e. Verlagsgeschäfte und Druckereien.

27) Der Zeitungsverleger ist Kaufmann Erk. d. H. A. G. v. 31. Jan. 1867 (Zeitschr. n. F. I 19).

Der Betrieb einer photographischen Anstalt, welche Verlagsverträge abschließt, wurde als H. G. erklärt. H. A. G. 1. Mai 1866 (Stengl. VII 95).

Hingegen wurde erkannt, daß der Betrieb einer lithographischen Druckerei seiner Natur nach handwerksmäßig sei. O. G. H. 20. Dez. 1867 (Bl. f. R. XXXIII 50).

f. Allgemeines.

28) Die in Art. 272 aufgezählten Gewerbsgeschäfte bilden nach der Schlußbestimmung jenes Art. auch als einzelne Geschäfte H. G., wenn sie von einem Kaufmanne vorgenommen werden.

Wenn es dort heißt: „von einem Kaufmann, im Betriebe seines Handelsgewerbes“, so soll damit nicht angedeutet sein, daß das Geschäft mit dem Handelsgewerbe in Verbindung stehen müsse, daß es als Ausfluß desselben zu betrachten sei, denn in dieser Beziehung ist Art. 273 maßgebend. Es soll vielmehr nur gesagt sein, daß der Kaufmann als solcher handeln müsse, d. h., daß ein kaufmännischer Zweck, der Zweck des Erwerbes, vorliegen müsse. Hahn, Art. 272 § 23.

Durch Ges. v. 29. April 1869 Art. 11 sind gewisse Genossenschaften als Kaufleute erklärt, folglich sind ihre Geschäfte Handelsgeschäfte.

III. Hülfsgeschäfte.

29) Alle einzelnen Geschäfte eines Kaufmanns, welche zum Betriebe seines Handelsgewerbes gehören, sind als H. G. anzusehen (Art. 273 Abs. 1).

Die Geschäfte, welche unter diesen Gesichtspunkte als H. G. erscheinen können, sind so vielfältig, als die Bedürfnisse des Handels und finden ihre Gränze nur in den Bestimmungen des Art. 275, gemäß dessen Verträge über unbewegliche Sachen nie Handelsgeschäfte sein können.

Es gehören hierher z B. Verträge mit Lehrlingen, Handwerksgesellen, Fabrikarbeitern überhaupt Gewerbsgehilfen, welche nicht zu den gewöhnlichen Taglöhnern oder dem Hausgesinde zu rechnen sind, ferner Aufnahmen von Darlehen, [H. A. G. 12. Nov. 1863 (Zeitsch. XI 7)] Bürgschaften im Interesse des Geschäfts z. B. gegen Provision, gegenseitige Versicherung, Rechtsgeschäfte, welche der Kaufmann mit Gläubigern oder Schuldnern auf Grundlage von Handelsgeschäften abschließt, z. B. Vergleiche, Novationen u. s. w.

Auch Miethe von beweglichen Sachen kann Hilfsgeschäft sein. Bezüglich der Miethe von Wirthschaften mit Inventar s. Erk. d. H. A. G. v. 18. Dez. 1865 (Zeitschrift XII 173) sowie Zeitschr. XIII S. 209.

Die Geschäfte der oben (Nr. 28) bezeichneten Genossenschaften sind Handels-Hülfsgeschäfte.

IV. Präsumtionen.

30) Art. 274 des H. G. B. enthält zwei für Bestimmung der Competenz sehr wichtige Verfügungen nemlich: 1) daß Verträge des Kaufmannes im Zweifel als zum Handelsbetriebe gehörig gelten und 2) daß Schuldscheine des Kaufmanns als im Betriebe des Handelsgewerbes gezeichnet gelten, sofern sich nicht aus ihnen selbst das Gegentheil ergibt.

31) Die Tragweite der 1. Verfügung besteht insbes. auch darin, daß ein Geschäft, für welches nach den beim Abschlusse erkennbaren Umständen ein zivilrechtlicher Grund nicht anzunehmen ist, unbedingt als H. G. zu gelten hat; daß es daher dem Kaufmanne nicht gestattet ist zu beweisen, daß nach den geheim gebliebenen Umständen kein H. G. vorläge, z. B. das Darlehen nicht zum Handel bestimmt gewesen und verwendet worden sei.

32) Was die 2. Verfügung anbelangt, so frägt sich: Gilt die aufgestellte Vermuthung nur für den Schuldschein als solchen, oder gilt sie auch für das ihm zu Grunde liegende Rechtsgeschäft?

Man kann sagen, daß die Wortfassung, namentlich der Gegensatz zu der unmittelbar vorausgehenden Verfügung, den Willen des Gesetzes unzweideutig erkennen lasse, hier eine praesumptio juris et de jure aufzustellen dafür, daß dem Schuldversprechen ein H. G. zu Grunde liege. — Folge würde sein, daß überall, wo ein solcher Schuldschein vorläge, auch selbstverständlich ein Handelsgeschäft gegeben und das Handelsgericht unbedingt zuständig wäre. Goldschm. § 58 — Erk. d. H. A. G. v. 10. Aug. 1866 (Stengl. VII 416), v. 24. Okt. 1866 (Zeitschr. XIII 219) und v. 10. Febr. 1868 (Zeitschr. n. F. II 8.) vgl. auch Bl. f. R. XXX 393.

33) Dennoch möchten die Gründe für die gegentheilige Ansicht überwiegen.

Das Gesetz will offenbar nicht sagen, daß ein derartiger Schuldschein ganz vom Schuldgrunde, von der Geschichte seiner Entstehung losgelöst sein, daß er als Formalakt gelten und als solcher ein selbständiges Handelsgeschäft bilden solle.

Sowohl nach deutschem als nach französischem Rechte ist bei einem Schuldscheine mit causa indiscreta (der lautet: „ich bekenne schuldig zu sein und verspreche zu zahlen") ein Zurückgehen auf den Schuldgrund nöthig und selbst wenn man annimmt, es habe der Gläubiger einen weiteren Beweis der causa nicht zu liefern, so kann es jedenfalls dem Schuldner nicht verwehrt sein, die wahre causa zur Geltung zu bringen. Dieser Schuldgrund allein bestimmt aber die innere Natur des Rechtsverhältnisses und ist maßgebend für die Frage, ob ein Handelsgeschäft oder ein civilrechtlicher Anspruch gegeben sei.

Unmöglich kann es Absicht des Gesetzes sein, daß ein Schuldschein, welcher ausgestellt ist für einen Gutskaufpreis, eine Theilungsherausgabe, eine Spielschuld, ein Heirathsgut u. s. w., bei welchem man aber vergessen hat den Schuldgrund zu bezeichnen oder bei welchem man einen falschen Schuldgrund (z. B. ein Darlehen) angeführt hat, deßhalb zu einem Handelsakte gestempelt und die rein zivilrechtlichen Verhältnisse vom Handelsgerichte abgeurtheilt werden sollen.

Ebensowenig ist statthaft, daß in solchen Fällen das Handelsgericht auf Grund von Art. 9 der P. O. den Inzidentpunkt d. h. hier die ganze Aburtheilung vor den Civilrichter verweise um sich auf den formellen Spruch des Endurtheils zu beschränken.

Ist dies nun richtig, so ist es nöthig, fragliche Gesetzesstelle (welche ausnahmsweise etwas übereilt redigirt ist), einschränkend zu erklären und zwar nach der Absicht des Gesetzgebers, wie sie in den Berathungen (Cons. Prot. S. 1296 u. 1297) zu Tage getreten ist, in der Art, daß die Rechtsvermuthung nur auf den Schuldschein an sich zu beziehen ist, welcher als kaufmännischer Schuldschein zu betrachten und allen für Beweiskraft, Uebertrag und Wirkung solcher Schuldscheine gegebenen besonderen Vorschriften (Art. 295, 300, 301, 305 des H. G. B.) unterworfen sein sollte. Das Gesetz hatte hauptsächlich den Schutz dritter Personen, welche in Besitz solcher Scheine gelangen, im Auge und wollte an deren äußere Erscheinung gewisse Folgen knüpfen, welche deren Werth als Verkehrsmittel erhöhen und ihnen annähernd die Wirkungen des Wechsels geben sollte.

34) Diese Ansicht findet eine gewichtige Unterstützung in der Auslegung, welche Art. 638 Code de comm. erfahren hat.

Dort ist nemlich bestimmt:

„Les billets souscrits par un commerçant seront „censés faits pour son commerce, lorsqu'une „autre cause n'y sera point énoncée;"

also genau das Nemliche, wie in unserem Artikel; trotzdessen hat sich die Jurisprudenz, nicht ohne lebhaften Widerspruch, dahin festgestellt, daß Gegenbeweis zuläßig sei und zwar selbst dann, wenn es sich um billets à ordre handelt und es ein Indossatar ist, welcher klagt. Merlin rep. (billets) §. 11 Nr. 11 bis — Pardessus No. 52 u. 1505 — Massé dr. comm. Bd. III No. 19 Nougier Bd. I S. 333 u. 336 — Cass. 20. Jan. 1836 — Bordeaux 19. Nov. 1836 — Metz 22. März 1839.

Man ist um so mehr berechtigt, aus dieser französ. Jurisprudenz Folgerungen zu ziehen, als, wie bekannt, die Ansichten rheinländischer Juristen großen Einfluß auf die Gestaltung des deutschen H. G. B. hatten und sich die Vermuthung aufdrängt, man habe fragliche Verfügung hauptsächlich im Hinblicke auf die gleiche Verfügung des Code de comm. aufgenommen und für unschädlich gehalten.

35) Für die aufgestellte Ansicht spricht sich im Wesentlichen aus Hahn Art. 274 § 3 und ein Erk. des O. A. G. vom 20. April 1868 Reg. Nr. 174. — Das oberwähnte Erkenntniß (Bl. f. R. XXX S. 393) läßt sie wenigstens frei.

Was die obenerwähnten Erk. des H. A. G. vom Jahre 1866 betrifft, so hätten sie sich durch Berufen auf Art. 272 Abs. 1 rechtfertigen lassen, da es sich von Darlehen handelte, bei welchen die geheim gebliebene Absicht des Empfängers und die wirkliche Verwendung des Geldes ohne allen Belang ist. Bezüglich des Falles, wo auch Nicht-Kaufleute im Schuldscheine unterzeichnet sind s. unten Nr. 48.

V. Unbewegliche Sachen.

36) Die Bestimmung des Art. 275: „Verträge über unbewegliche Sachen sind keine Handelsgeschäfte", ist allgemein und bildet eine alle vorausgehenden Bestimmungen treffende Ausnahme. — Aus solchen Verträgen können daher weder Handels-Grundgeschäfte, noch Handels-Hilfsgeschäfte hervorgehen.

Es gehören hierher:

1) alle Verträge, welche die Begründung, den Uebertrag oder die Aufhebung dinglicher oder persönlicher Rechte auf unbewegliche Sachen zum Gegenstande haben, also ebensowohl Kauf, Hypothekenbestellung als Pacht, Miethe Erk. d. H. A. G. v. 3. Febr. 1863 (Zeitschr. XI 13) — v. 18. Dez. 1865 (Zeitschr. XII 173) — Erk. des O. G. H. v. 8. Febr. 1867 (Bl. f. R. XXXII 28) vgl. jedoch Erk. des H. A. G. v. 1. Sept. 1866 (Zeitschr. XIII 209);

2) alle Verträge über Herstellung einer unbeweglichen Sache.

37) Man könnte behaupten daß Art. 275 Verträge letzterer Art nicht im Auge gehabt habe und daß dieselben, wenn auch nicht als H. Grundgeschäfte, doch als H. Hülfsgeschäfte betrachtet werden könnten,

wofür sich die französ. Jurisprudenz als Beleg anführen ließe; allein es erscheint richtiger und den Grundsätzen entsprechender obige Ansicht anzunehmen.

Man darf voraussetzen, daß das Gesetz klare, ineinandergreifende Prinzipien anerkennen wollte, daß aber nicht in der einen Richtung andere Begriffe gelten sollen, als in der anderen.

Sowie nun bei Auslegung des Art. 271 anzuerkennen war, daß Mobilien, welche angeschafft wurden, um zur Herstellung von Bauten verwendet und als Theile derselben weiterveräußert zu werden, als unbewegliche Sachen zu gelten haben', so muß hier das Nemliche gelten und so wie ferner beim Kaufe von Häusern zum Abbruche die Absicht zu mobilisiren entscheidet, so muß hier die Absicht zu immobilisiren entscheiden.

Ein Kaufmann welcher also zur Herrichtung irgend eines für sein Geschäft nöthigen Baues Verträge mit Unternehmern oder Handwerkern in der Art abschließt, daß ihm das fertige Werk übergeben wird, schließt hiermit ebensowenig ein H. G., als der Unternehmer oder Handwerker selbst. Anders ist es, wenn er wegen Lieferung der Stoffe besondere Verträge abschließt, wenn er die Stoffe kauft, um sie sodann in Baue zu verwenden. Dies wären ohne Zweifel H. Hülfsgeschäfte. Goldschm. § 59 — Hahn Art. 275 § 3 u. 4 — Erk. d. H. A. G. v. 4. Febr. 1867 (Zeitschr. n. F. I 11) u. v. 1. Mai 1868 (Zeitschr. n. F. II 14) ferner Zeitschr. XI 162. — Anders entschied der Appellhof zu Köln. s. oben Nr. 14.

38) Was die Verwendung beweglicher Sachen zur Herstellung oder Einrichtung von unbeweglichen Sachen betrifft, so wird zu unterscheiden sein zwischen solchen, welche sich mit letzteren so verbinden, daß sie natürliche Bestandtheile derselben werden und solchen, welche nur der Bestimmung des Eigenthümers gemäß Zubehör derselben bilden sollen.

Nur bei ersterer Art der Verwendung kann im Sinne des Art. 275 (d. h. im kaufmännischen Sinne) von einer unbeweglichen Sache die Rede sein. — Letztere Gegenstände, wie Ladeneinrichtungen, Maschinen, die bloß aufgestellt werden, Fässer u. s. w. bleiben in diesem Sinne beweglich und es wird auch ohne Belang sein, wenn sie in leichter Weise befestigt werden.

39) Eine Forderung erscheint als bewegliche Sache, mag sie mit einer Hypotheke verbunden sein oder nicht. Goldschm. § 58 — Hahn Art. 275 § 1.

VI. Einseitige Handelsgeschäfte.

40) Wenn Art. 277 des H. G. B. von Rechtsgeschäften spricht, welche nur auf Seite eines der Contrahenten Handelsgeschäfte sind, so hat er offenbar die beiden Vertragstheile (als Gegner) im Auge, nicht aber solche Personen, welche neben einander einem Dritten gegenüber sich verpflichten z. B. Mitschuldner, Bürgen u. s. w. vgl. Art. 280 u. 281 des H. G. B. — Die Ansicht in Erk. des H. A. G. vom 10. Febr. 1868 (Zeitschr. n. F. II 8) ist daher nicht gegründet.

VII. Allgemeine Grundsätze.

41) Wenn Geschäfte handelsrechtlicher und Geschäfte zivilrechtlicher Natur sich mischen, so ist zu untersuchen, welcher Theil als Hauptsache zu betrachten und geeignet ist, Natur und Charakter des Geschäftes zu bestimmen — dieser entscheidet. — Es wäre nicht dem Geiste des H. G. B. gemäß, als Regel anzuerkennen, daß die geringste Beimischung zivilrechtlichen Stoffes das Geschäft zum Civilgeschäfte mache; noch viel weniger das Umgekehrte. Soweit Trennung möglich, hat sie natürlich zu geschehen.

Wenn z. B. der Kaufmann, welcher eine Dampfmaschine um bestimmten Preis ankauft, dabei auch einen weiteren Vertrag dahin schließt, daß der Verfertiger der Maschine auch das Maschinen-Gebäude herstelle und die Maschine dort einrichte, so liegen zwei gesonderte Geschäfte vor, von denen das erste ein Handelsgeschäft ist, das zweite nicht. — Goldschm. § 47 Z. III — Erk. des O. G. H. v. 4. März 1865 (Bl. f. R. XXXI 253) — Journal du Pal. (acte de c.) No. 127 Paris 5. März 1846 -- Bordeaux 12. Juli 1848.

---

42) Handelssachen sind die Rechtsverhältnisse, welche aus Handelsgeschäften zwischen den Betheiligten entstehen. (s. oben Nr. 1). Handelsgeschäfte sind den Handelsgerichten zugewiesen, weil sie an sich, ihrer innern Natur nach, sich zur Beurtheilung durch diese Gerichte eigenen; es ist daher in der Regel gleichgültig, zwischen welchen Personen der Rechtstreit auszutragen ist. — Es ist dies hier ausdrücklich durch den Ausdruck „Betheiligte" angedeutet, welchem Ausdrucke im Geiste des Einf.-Ges. eine möglichst allgemeine Bedeutung zu geben ist. — Es erscheinen demnach als Betheiligte:

1) diejenigen, in deren Vertretung das Geschäft abgeschlossen worden ist;
2) die Erben und sonstigen Rechtsnachfolger;
3) die Bürgen.

43) Zu 1. Hieraus leitet sich z. B. ab, daß die Reklamation der Ehefrau gegen eine Handels-Bürgschaft des Mannes vors Handelsgericht zu bringen ist. Erk. des H. A. G. vom 14. Febr. 1868 (Zeitschr. n. F. II 4); daß ebenso die Ehefrau, wenn sie der Gütergemeinschaft wegen haftbar sein soll, vor dem Handelsgerichte zu belangen ist. Erk. des H. A. G. v. 13. April 1863 (Zeitschr. X 510) und vom

27. März 1868 (Zeitschr. n. F. II 9 und Note); vgl. im Allg. noch Erk. d. H. A. G. v. 3. Okt. 1866 (Zeitschr. VIII 207), sowie vom 1. Mai und 5. Juni 1868 (Zeitschr. n. F. II 162).

44) Zu 2. Was die Erben betrifft s. Bl. f. R. XVI 212 und XXVII 362, ferner XXXI 33 ff. Erk. des H. A. G. v. 16. Juli 1863 (Zeitschr. X 720).

45) Zu 3. Strittig ist, ob und in wie weit Bürgen einer Handelsschuld, wenn die Bürgschaft nicht an sich ein Handelsgeschäft ist (Art. 281 Abs. 2) vor's Handelsgericht gehören.

Die Bürgschaft ist nemlich in der Regel bloß Freundschaftsdienst und als solcher kein kaufmännisches Geschäft; sie wird das Letztere nur, wenn sich damit irgend eine Gegenleistung, irgend eine Spekulation verbindet, welche sie mehr als Akt der Klugheit als des Wohlwollens erscheinen läßt.

Hat nun aber der Bürge für eine Handelsschuld nicht selbst ein Handelsgeschäft abgeschlossen, so hat er sich doch jedenfalls bei einem solchen betheiligt, was z. B. Art. 281 dadurch anerkennt, daß ein solcher Bürge die civilrechtlichen Einreden verliert. Endemann (deutsches H. R. S. 711) sagt: „Eine solche Bürgschaft ist immer Handelssache, wenn auch nicht Handelsgeschäft!"

Die Frage, ob die Hauptschuld bestehe, muß dem Bürgen gegenüber ganz ebenso, wie gegenüber dem Hauptschuldner selbst, nach Grundsätzen des Handelsrechts beurtheilt und entschieden werden und es ist daher anzunehmen, daß der Gesetzgeber sie dem Handelsgerichte zuweisen wollte.

Zieht man in fernere Erwägung die Mißstände, welche es mit sich führen würde, wenn Bürger und Schuldner an zwei verschiedenen Gerichten Recht nehmen müßten; erwägt man endlich, daß jedem Gesetze im Zweifel diejenige Auslegung zu geben ist, gemäß welcher es am vernünftigsten und zweckentsprechendsten ist, so muß man zur Annahme gelangen, daß unter den Betheiligten auch die Bürgen begriffen sein sollten.

46) Es kann sich nun fragen:

hat der Bürge nur so weit, als es sich um Erörterung des Schuldverhältnisses handelt vor dem Handelsgerichte Rede zu stehen, so daß also, wenn sich Streit über die Verbürgung erhebt, dieser als civilrechtlicher Incidentpunkt in Betracht käme?

oder:

erkennt das H. G. zugleich über das Bürgschafts-Verhältniß?

Ich halte Letzteres für richtig.

Wenn alle Betheiligte vor's H. G. verwiesen sind, so gehört die Vorfrage, ob Jemand betheiligt sei, vor das nemliche Gericht. Uebrigens ist hier das Bürgschaftsverhältniß nur Nebenpunkt, die Schuldfrage die Hauptsache.

Der Einwand, daß das H. G. nicht berufen sei, über manche rein civilrechtliche Fragen z. B. Certioration der Ehefrau, zu entscheiden, ist ohne Belang, denn so wie die Civilgerichte häufig nach Handelsgesetzen und Handelsgrundsätzen erkennen müssen, so kommen auch die H. G. in die Lage, Grundsätze des Civilrechts in Anwendung zu bringen. Die Scheidung der Competenzen beider Gerichte tritt bloß ein nach Haupt-Gesichtspunkten und die Fiktion, als ob das eine Gericht unfähig sei, die der Regel nach in das Gebiet des anderen gehörigen Fragen zu beurtheilen, ist bei der Organisation fraglicher Gerichte unstatthaft, vorausgesetzt, daß es sich nicht um einen selbständigen Streitpunkt im Sinne des Art. 9 der P. O. handelt.

Am wenigsten kann dann ein Zweifel bestehen, wenn der Bürge ein persönliches Interesse hatte, den Credit des Hauptschuldners zu heben, wie z. B. der stille Gesellschafter oder die Ehefrau.

Das H. A. G. zu Nürnberg hat ständig nach vorstehender Ansicht geurtheilt. Erk. v. 13. April 1863 (Zeitschr. X 510), 11. Juli 1864 (Zeitschr. XI 108), 5. Februar und 16. April 1866 (Zeitschr. XIII 31 und 218), 5. Juli 1867 (Zeitschr. n. F. I 127) und 24. Jan. 1868 (Zeitschr. n. F. II 11).

Der oberste G. H. sprach sich ähnlich, jedoch weniger entschieden aus in Erk. des O. A. G. v. 17. Mai 1864 (Bl. f. R. XXXII 230) und Erk. d. O. G. H. v. 6. Dez. 1866 (Bl. f. R. [E. B.] XXXI 118).

Die Urtheile der Gerichte in andern deutschen Staaten sind, da es sich um den Sinn des Einführungsgesetzes handelt, nicht von Belang; noch weniger die Ansichten der französischen Gerichte. Uebrigens sind überall die Stimmen getheilt. Vgl. Journ. du Pal. (acte de c.) No. 490—495 und die in Goldschm. Zeitschr. Bd. VIII S. 25 und 27 angeführten Urtheile von Köln und Hamburg.

47) Eine Bürgschaft liegt auch vor, wenn Jemand im Schuldscheine als Solidarschuldner bezeichnet ist, in Wirklichkeit aber sich bloß verbürgt hat, was bei Ehefrauen zu vermuthen ist.

48) Wie verhält es sich nun aber, wenn mehrere Personen, von welchen keine bloß als Bürge erscheint, sich als Solidarschuldner verpflichtet haben und einigen gegenüber die Schuld als Handelsschuld, den anderen gegenüber als Civilschuld erscheint oder zu präsumiren ist?

Der Umstand, daß ein Kaufmann A und ein Bauer B das Darlehen gemeinschaftlich empfingen, gibt offenbar ebensowenig ein Recht zur Vermuthung, daß A sein Geld nicht zu Handelszwecken, als daß B sein Geld nicht für seine Landwirthschaft aufgenommen; im Gegentheile, es ist anzunehmen, daß Jeder seinen Theil zu den seinem Erwerbsgeschäfte entsprechenden Zwecken entlehnt und für den Theil des Anderen zugleich gebürgt habe. Man kann hier ebensogut sagen, A habe sich bei einem Civilgeschäfte, als B habe sich bei einem Handelsgeschäfte betheiligt und die Ansicht des H. A. G. in Erk. vom 5. Febr. 1866 (Zeitschr. XIII 31) und 10. Febr. 1868 (Zeitschrift n. F. II 8), daß die Präsumtion für die Handelssache sei, ist entschieden falsch. Im Gegentheile müßte im Zweifel die Zuständigkeit der ordentlichen Gerichte überwiegen.

Zur Lösung der Frage wird es geeignet sein, sich einen grellen Fall zu vergegenwärtigen. Man nehme an, es schulde der nemlichen Person Müller A aus einem Fruchthandel 500 fl. und Bauer B als Gutskaufschilling 500 fl. und Beide verpflichten sich solidarisch zur Zahlung von 1000 fl., sei es mit, sei es ohne Angabe des Schuldgrundes.

In diesem Falle wird ohne Zweifel jeder Anspruch von 500 fl. vor das für ihn zuständige Gericht zu bringen sein, wobei selbstverständlich beide Schuldner — der Eine als Hauptschuldner, der Andere als Bürge — zu belangen sind, den Gläubiger also der einzige Nachtheil trifft, daß er zwei Klagen statt einer zu erheben hat.

Gleiches muß folgerichtig auch für den Fall gelten, wo es sich um Rechtsgeschäfte gleicher Art handelt, wenn z. B. A und B jeder ein Darlehen in gewissem Betrage aufnimmt und Beide sich solidarisch für's Ganze verpflichten.

Für den besonderen Fall nun aber, wo das Darlehen gemeinschaftlich aufgenommen wurde in der Art, daß der Gläubiger nicht weiß, für welche Beträge der Eine Hauptschuldner, der Andere Bürge sei, läßt sich vielleicht die Ansicht rechtfertigen, daß es dem Gläubiger, kraft der Wirkungen der Solidarität, freistehe, jeden der Schuldner als Hauptschuldner für's Ganze zu behandeln, d. h., das Gericht zu wählen. Vgl. Urth. des Appellh. zu Köln v. 3. Mai 1864 (Archiv für Civil- und Criminal-R. der Rheinprovinz Bd. 58 S. 126).

49) Unter den Betheiligten entscheidet das Handelsgericht über alle aus dem Abschluße der Handelsgeschäfte sich herleitenden Ansprüche, also über Klagen auf Erfüllung, auf Entschädigung wegen Nichterfüllung und auf Auflösung handelsrechtlicher Verpflichtungen.

Auch Klagen wegen Bereicherung aus einem H. G. gehören daher vor's Handelsgericht. Erk. des H. A. G. v. 27. Juli 1863 (Zeitschr. X 740), Stengl. V S. 328.

Ebenso die Frage, ob ein Rechtstreit über eine Handelssache durch Vergleich erledigt sei. Erk. des H. A. G. v. 1. Mai 1866 (Stengl. VII 95).

50) Gründet sich eine Entschädigungsklage nicht auf das Handelsgeschäft, sondern auf die allgemeinen Prinzipien über Haftung für widerrechtliche Handlungen, so ist die Zuständigkeit des Handelsgerichts nicht gegeben. Erk. d. H. A. G. v. 26. Nov. 1866 u. 18. Okt. 1867 (Zeitschr. n. F. I 3 u. 274).

51) Der Umstand, daß Jemand (als Kaufmann) in's Handelsregister eingetragen ist, stellt zwar seine Absicht, das fragliche Geschäft zu treiben, außer Zweifel, kann jedoch nicht bewirken, daß dasselbe ein Handelsgeschäft werde, wenn es dies seiner Natur nach nicht ist. Das Handelsregister allein kann Niemanden zum Kaufmanne machen.

Entgegengesetzt wurde trotzdem entschieden in Erk. d. H. A. G. v. 26. Sept. 1866 (Zeitschr. XIII 204) u. v. 21. Jan. 1867 (Zeitschr. n. F. I 15).

Handelssachen sind ferner:

2) die Rechtsverhältnisse, welche das Recht zum Gebrauche einer bestimmten Firma oder die Entschädigung wegen widerrechtlichen Gebrauches einer Firma zum Gegenstande haben;

3) das Rechtsverhältniß, welches aus der Veräußerung eines bestehenden Handelsgeschäftes zwischen dem Veräußerer und dem Erwerber entsteht.

52) Die Uebernahme eines Handelsgeschäftes wird von der Jurisprudenz als Handels-Hülfsgeschäft anerkannt und zwar nicht bloß, wenn sie im Wege des Kaufes, sondern auch, wenn sie durch Pacht u. s. w. geschieht. Goldschm. § 57 II.

Vorstehende Verfügung in Ziff. 3 beseitigt jeden Zweifel, daß das ganze aus einer solchen Veräußerung entstehende Rechtsverhältniß, beiden Theilen gegenüber, zur Zuständigkeit des Handelsgerichts gehöre.

53) Es ist dabei ohne Belang, wenn unbewegliche Sachen mitveräußert werden, jedoch wird vorausgesetzt, daß das Handelsgeschäft die Hauptsache bilde, denn wird z. B. beim Verkaufe eines großen Anwesens zugleich die darauf ruhende Wirthsgerechtsame mitveräußert, so ist die Zuständigkeit des H. G. selbstverständlich nicht gegeben.

Nach einem Erkenntnisse des H. A. G. vom 18. Dez. 1865 (Zeitschr. XII 173) muß es sich um das Geschäft eines Voll-Kaufmannes (Art. 10 des H. G. B.) handeln.

4) die Rechtsverhältnisse zwischen den Kaufleuten und ihren Procuristen, Handlungsbevollmächtigten und Handlungsgehilfen, sowie den in ihren Gewerben angestellten Beamten und sonstigen Bediensteten, ferner die Rechtsverhältnisse dieser Personen aus Handlungen, durch welche sie sich im Gewerbe des Prinzipals dritten verantwortlich gemacht haben.

54) Die Verträge des Kaufmanns mit seinen Gewerbs-Bediensteten bilden Handels-Hülfsgeschäfte, gehören also ihm gegenüber schon nach Ziff. 1 zur Zuständigkeit des H.-Gerichts. Nach Ziff. 4 müssen auch die Bediensteten vor diesem Gerichte Recht nehmen. Als solche sind nur Personen anzusehen, welche speziell dem Geschäfte dienen, nicht aber gewöhnliche Taglöhner oder das Hausgesinde.

55) Die Jurisprudenz gibt der Zuständigkeit der H. G. in dieser Beziehung die größtmögliche Ausdehnung in der Art, daß auch Ansprüche, welche nicht gerade aus dem Dienstvertrage, sondern nur aus dem Dienstverhältnisse überhaupt sich herleiten, z. B. sogar widerrechtliche Handlungen, vor's H. G. gehören und daß dieses auch zuständig ist, wenn dritte Personen (z. B. der Vater eines Lehrlings) betheiligt erscheinen. — Erk. d. H. A. G. v. 12. Sept. 1864 (Stengl. IV 343), v. 21. Dez. 1864 (Stengl. V 343), v. 17. April u. 30. Juni 1868 (Zeitschr. n. F. II 157 u. 169), Erk. des O. G. G. v. 5. Febr. 1864 (Bl. f. R. XXX 385) u. 31. Aug. 1866 (Bl. f. R. Erg. Bd. zu XXXI 100).

Ein Erkenntniß des H. A. G. vom 26. Juni 1868 (Zeitschr. n. F. II 163) geht so weit, diese Bestimmung sogar auf das Verhältniß zwischen Eisenbahn- und Post-Verwaltung und ihren Beamten (einen Cassier) anzuwenden.

56) Was die Verantwortlichkeit der Handels-Bevollmächtigten 2c. dritten Personen gegenüber betrifft, so ist die betreffende Verfügung im Hinblicke auf Art. 55 des H. G. B. gegeben.

Auf gewöhnliche Bevollmächtigte erstreckt sie sich nicht, jedoch wird derjenige, welcher ohne Vollmacht oder mit Ueberschreitung der Vollmacht ein H. G. abgeschlossen hat, sich so behandeln lassen müssen, als habe er das Geschäft für eigene Rechnung abgeschlossen. Art. 298 des H. G. B.; vgl. jedoch Erk. des O. G. H. v. 22. Okt. 1864 (Bl. f. R. XXX 401).

5) die Rechtsverhältnisse der Handelsgesellschaften rücksichtlich des Vollzugs des Gesellschaftsvertrages und aus diesem während des Bestehens und nach der Auflösung der Gesellschaft;

ferner die Rechtsverhältnisse zwischen den Gesellschaftern und den Vorstehern und Liquidatoren der Gesellschaft, sowie die Rechtsverhältnisse dieser Personen untereinander;

ingleichen die Rechtsverhältnisse zwischen den stillen Gesellschaftern und dem Inhaber des Handelsgewerbes oder zwischen den Theilnehmern an einer Vereinigung zu einzelnen Handelsgeschäften für gemeinschaftliche Rechnung oder an einer Vereinigung zu gemeinschaftlichem Handelsbetriebe (Art. 10 Abs. 2 des allgemeinen deutschen Handelsgesetzbuches) aus dem gesellschaftlichen Verbande oder in Bezug auf die Liquidation oder die Auseinandersetzung.

57) Auch nach Auflösung einer Handelsgesellschaft und erfolgten Abrechnung sind die Handelsgerichte zuständig für Klagen, welche sich aus dem Gesellschafts-Vertrage herleiten. Erk. des H. A. G. v. 30. Dez. 1863 (Stengl. V 344).

6) die Rechtsverhältnisse, welche aus den Berufsgeschäften der Handelsmäkler, Dispacheurs, Güterbestätter, Wäger, Messer oder anderer Personen, welche die Menge oder die Güte der Waaren oder deren Verpackung für den Handelsverkehr öffentlich zu beglaubigen haben, zwischen ihnen und anderen Personen entstehen;

7) die Aufsicht über die Handelsmäkler, Dispacheurs und Güterbestätter in Bezug auf ihre Berufsgeschäfte, sowie deren Bestrafung wegen der von ihnen im Berufe begangenen Pflichtverletzungen.

58) Diese Bestimmung zieht auch die Geschäfte der amtlichen Handelsmäkler, welche keine Handelsgeschäfte sind, zur Zuständigkeit der Handelsgerichte.

8) die Rechtsverhältnisse des Seerechts; ferner jene, welche im Verkehr zu Land, auf Flüssen und Binnengewässern zwischen Frachtführern und den Absendern, Empfängern und anderen betheiligten Personen entstehen.

59) Offenbar sollen hiermit nicht alle Rechtsverhältnisse, welche aus Anlaß des Verkehrs entstanden sind, den Handelsgerichten zugewiesen werden, denn sonst würden ja alle Streitigkeiten mit Wirthen, alle Streitigkeiten wegen Beschädigung fremden Eigenthums durch Nachlässigkeit beim Fahren, Abladen u. s. w. der Zuständigkeit der gewöhnlichen Gerichte entzogen sein.

Man meinte sicher nur Verhältnisse, welche aus dem Frachtvertrage entspringen und mit demselben in Verbindung stehen.

So kommen z. B. Streitigkeiten mit Leuten, welche sich am Frachtgeschäfte betheiligen, auch ohne Frachtführer, Empfänger oder Absender zu sein, z. B. Packern, Abladern, Leuten, welche das Ueberführen der Waaren von Schiffen auf Eisenbahnen oder Wägen besorgen u. s. w., vor's Handelsgericht und es hat der Ausdruck: „andere betheiligte Personen“ allerdings seine Bedeutung. Auch dritte Personen, welche aus irgend einem Grunde mithaften, können darunter verstanden werden.

Die Entscheidung des H. G. A. vom 21. Dez. 1866 (Zeitschr. n. F. I 1) möchte daher zu weit gehen; ebenso diejenige vom 26. Sept. 1866 (Zeitschr. XIII 215), letztere wenigstens in den Gründen. — Vom Seerechte auf's Flußrecht zu schließen, ist bedenklich.

60) Auch Streitigkeiten mit dem Post- und Eisenbahn-Fiskus, welche den Frachtverkehr betreffen, gehören vor die Handelsgerichte. Erk. des H. A G. v. 26. Sept. u. 23. Nov. 1866 (Zeitschr. XIII 210 u. 215).

9) die Rechtsverhältnisse aus der Bestellung, Zurückforderung oder Geltendmachung von Faustpfändern für Forderungen aus Handelsgeschäften, aus dem Bestande oder der Ausübung des Retentionsrechtes wegen solcher Forderungen, sowie aus dem Bestande oder der Geltendmachung von gesetzlichen Pfandrechten an beweglichen Sachen für Forderungen aus Handelsgeschäften.

61) Das Gesetz hat hier vorzugsweise jene Retentions- und Pfand-Rechte im Auge, welche auf die Bestimmungen des H. G. B. sich gründen, z. B. in Art. 313 – 315. 374. 382. 409—412.

Bei der Allgemeinheit des Ausdruckes sind aber auch sonstige gesetzliche Pfandrechte oder Retentionsrechte, wenn sie nur an Forderungen aus Handelsgeschäften sich knüpfen, darunter begriffen, so z. B. das Recht des Verkäufers nach Art. 2102 Ziff. 4 des Code civil.

10) die Veräußerung von beweglichen Sachen und Werthpapieren in allen Fällen, in welchen dieselbe nach den Bestimmungen des allgemeinen deutschen Handelsgesetzbuches von dem Gerichte auch ohne vorgängige Klagestellung auf einseitigen Antrag eines der Betheiligten verfügt wird;

11) die Führung der Handelsregister und alle übrigen Rechtsangelegenheiten und Handlungen, welche durch sonstige Bestimmungen des allgemeinen deutschen Handelsgesetzbuches den Handelsgerichten überwiesen sind.

62) Die Bestimmungen in Ziff. 10 gelten nur für Fälle, wo das Gericht zu verfügen hat, nicht aber z. B. für den Fall des Art. 343 des H. G. B., wo der Verkäufer eigenmächtig verkaufen darf. Erk. des H. A. G. v. 20. Okt. 1864 (Stengl. V 344).

Wechselsachen.

63) Wenn das Gesetz Klagen aus Wechseln oder kaufmännischen Anweisungen unbedingt den H. G. zuweist, so meint es die Geltendmachung wechselrechtlicher Verpflichtungen nach Maßgabe der deutschen Wechselordnung und des Gesetzes vom 29. Juni 1851 über kaufmännische Anweisungen.

Wird nicht aus dem Wechsel selbst geklagt, sondern aus dem ihm zu Grunde liegenden Rechtsgeschäfte, so entscheidet die Natur dieses Geschäftes und treten überhaupt die gewöhnlichen Competenzregeln ein.

Dies gilt insbesondere für die bei einer Wechsel-Verurtheilung vorbehaltene Nachklage. Erk. des H. A. G. v. 27. Juli 1863 (Zeitschr. X 740), 13. Jan. u. 18. Okt. 1865 (Zeitschr. XII 3 u. 170), Erk. des O. G. H. v. 13. März 1865 (Bl. f. R. XXIX 375), 14. Mai 1866 (Bl. f. R. XXXI 393), 22. März 1867 (Bl. f. R. XXXII 109).

Ebenso wenn der Preis eines girirten Wechsels eingeklagt wird — Erk. des O. G. H. v. 20. April 1868 (Bl. f. R. XXXIII 161) —, oder wenn ein Aussteller, welcher gezahlt hat, seinen Rückgriff gegen diejenigen nimmt, welche als Mitschuldner mit ihm den Wechsel ausgestellt. Erk. des H. A. G. v. 1. März 1867 (Zeitschr. n. F. I 261).

In gleicher Weise liegt eine Wechselsache nicht vor, wenn Hypothek für eine Wechselschuld bestellt ist und die dingliche Hypothekenklage erhoben wird. Erk. des H. A. G. v. 4. Jan. 1867 (Zeitschr. n. F. I 5).

64) Es könnte sich fragen, ob die Amortisirung eines abhanden gekommenen Wechsels (Art. 73 der W. O.) vor's Handelsgericht gehöre, weil die Worte: „Klagen aus Wechseln“ hierauf nicht zu passen scheinen. — Unter der Herrschaft von Art. 67 des Einf. Ges. zum H. G. B. konnte darüber kein Zweifel obwalten, da es dort heißt, es erstrecke sich die Zuständigkeit der H. Ger. „auf alle Wechselsachen“. Erk. des H. A. G. v. 24. Dez. 1863 (Zeitschr. XI 4) Stengl. V 360.

Offenbar wollte nun aber das neue Gesetz nichts ändern und glaubte das Nemliche zu sagen.

Daß derselbe Grundsatz auch für die Werthpapiere, von welchen Art. 301 des H. G. B. spricht, zu gelten habe, möchte nicht zu bezweifeln sein, da Art. 305 die Amortisirung offenbar dem nämlichen Gerichte zuweisen wollte, welches der von ihm angeführte Art. 73 der W. O. im Auge hatte, und somit Art. 63 Ziff. 11 des Einf. Ges. Anwendung findet. — Die Motivirung in Erk. des H. A. G. v. 4. Dez. 1865 (Zeitschr. XII 167) ist allerdings nicht haltbar.

65) Zweifelhaft möchte sein, ob auch die Vindikation eines Wechsels oder sonstigen Handelspapieres auf Grund von Art. 74 der W. O. und 305 des H. G. B. vor's Handelsgericht gehöre, insofern dieselbe sich auf die Behauptung gründet, es finde im besonderen Falle das Wechselrecht keine Anwendung, vielmehr müsse sich der Besitzer seines bösen Glaubens wegen nach Civilrecht behandeln lassen. — Uebrigens muß doch immer im Geiste des Wechselrechts beurtheilt werden, ob Art. 74 der W. O. Anwendung findet. Die Zuständigkeit der H. G. wurde angenommen im Erk. des H. A. G. vom 4. Dez. 1865 (Zeitschr. XII 167) und zwar bezüglich eines verlorenen Bankscheines.

66) Die Stadt- und Landgerichte sind mit Ausnahme der Wechselsachen, der Klagen aus kaufmännischen Anweisungen und einiger Fälle von geringer praktischer Bedeutung in Art. 63 Ziff. 2. 3. 5. 7 u. 10 des Einf. Ges. zum H. G. B. in allen Handelssachen unter 150 fl. Werth zuständig und zwar ausschließlich. Sie erkennen über diese Sachen zwar nach Handelsrecht, jedoch selbstverständlich im gewöhnlichen Verfahren, wie es für die Landgerichte gilt, und die Berufung gegen ihre Urtheile geht an's Bezirksgericht (Art. 696).

67) Klagen gegen Kaufleute aus Handelsgeschäften gehören immer vor's Handelsgericht, selbst wenn die Handelsgeschäfte nur einseitige sind und ihnen gegenüber nicht als solche erscheinen (Art. 277 des H. G. B.). Der Kaufmann, welcher z. B. von einem andern Kaufmanne Waaren zum Verbrauche in seiner Haushaltung gekauft hat, muß sich zur Zahlung des Preises vor dem Handelsgerichte belangen lassen. Es geht dies aus der Fassung des Art. 7 Abs. 2 Ziff. 2 klar hervor und wurde auch dem Art. 64 des Einf. Ges. zum H. G. B. gegenüber anerkannt. Die Weglassung der Bezugnahme auf Art. 277 bei zweiter Lesung bezweckte keine Aenderung. Erk. des H. A. G. v. 8. Febr. 1865 (Stengl. IV 352) u. 27. März 1866 (Zeitschr. XIII 197).

(Ehegerichte.)

Art. 8. — In den Landestheilen diesseits des Rheins sind für Ehesachen der Katholiken die katholischen, für Ehesachen der Protestanten die protestantischen und für Ehesachen der Dissidenten die nach Art. 17 des Gesetzes vom 2. Mai 1868, die Schließung und Trennung von Ehen der keiner anerkannten Religionsgenossenschaft angehörigen Personen betr., durch k. Verordnung bezeichneten Ehegerichte ausschließend zuständig. Bei gemischten Ehen ist das erwähnte Gesetz vom 2. Mai 1868 Art. 18, sowie die Verordnung vom 28. Juli 1818 maßgebend.

G. A. der K. d. A. I S. 51. 52. 80. IV S. 10. 302. — K. d. R. I S. 49. IV S. 5. 6.

1) Unter Ehesachen sind hier nur zu verstehen Rechtsstreite über Gültigkeit und Trennung von Ehen oder über Scheidung von Tisch und Bett. Entwurf Art. 25. — Abg. I 52. — Seuff. Comm. Bd. I S. 140 Note 3.

Prozesse, welche die Schließung einer Ehe betreffen, z. B. Ergänzung der elterlichen Einwilligung, falls dieselbe nach Maßgabe der einschlägigen civilrechtlichen Prinzipien zur streitigen Rechtspflege gehört, sind keine Ehesachen im Sinne dieses Artikels. Bl. f. R. XXVIII S. 1 ff. — vgl. Verordnung v. 22. April 1811 Ziff. 2 (Rgbl. S. 817).

Auch Prozesse über Vollzug von Eheversprechen gehören vor die ordentlichen Gerichte. Verordn. v. 20. Juni 1807 (Rgbl. S. 1082).

2) Die Zuständigkeit der Ehegerichte erstreckt sich nicht bloß über die Hauptfrage der Trennung des ehelichen Bandes, sondern auch über das, was unzertrennbar damit zusammenhängt, nemlich die Fragen, wer der schuldige Theil sei, ob dem einen oder dem andern Theile die Wiederverehelichung, vorbehaltlich königlichen Dispenses, zu untersagen, ob und in welchem Grade die Ehescheidungsstrafen verwirkt seien. Seuff. Comm. Bd. I S. 142. Bl. f. R. VII 414.

Auch die Gestattung vorläufiger Absonderung während des Rechtsstreites gehört selbstverständlich und der Natur der zu treffenden Verfügung gemäß, zur Zuständigkeit des Ehegerichts. Gesetz v. 2. Mai 1868 Art. 20 Abs. 2. — Abg. I 33 (v. Weiß).

3) Alles, was sich auf die civilrechtlichen Folgen der Auflösung der Ehe bezieht, auf Auseinandersetzung des Vermögens, auf Erziehung der Kinder gehört nicht zur Zuständigkeit der Ehegerichte, welche überhaupt möglichst einschränkend zu bestimmen ist.

Deßhalb gehören auch Anträge auf Vermögenssicherung, insbesondere Beschränkung des Dispositionsrechts des Ehemannes, im Laufe des Ehescheidungsprozesses erhoben, vor die ordentlichen Gerichte. (Bl. f. R. XXI S. 209).

4) Auch Alimentations-Begehren sind den katholischen Ehegerichten unbedingt entzogen; den protestantischen Ehegerichten erkannte jedoch eine feststehende Jurisprudenz die Zuständigkeit zur Regelung der Alimentation für die Dauer des

Scheidungsprozesses sowie für Dauer der auf bestimmte Zeit bewilligten Scheidung von Tisch und Bett zu. Bl. f. R XVI S. 154 u. XXI 209.

Es ist anzunehmen, daß die neue P. O. den Begriff von „Ehesachen", wie ihn die Jurisprudenz gestaltet hatte, festhalten wollte und wird daher auch jetzt noch die nemliche Unterscheidung zu machen sein.

5) Ehegerichte sind für die Katholiken, in erster Instanz das bischöfliche oder erzbischöfliche Consistorium, in zweiter Instanz das bei jedem Erzbisthum bestehende Metropoliticum; jedoch ist Passau ausnahmsweise auch Ehegericht zweiter Instanz. s. Ver. v. 27. Mai 1826 Ziff. 3, 4 und 5.

Nach Ver. v. 27. Juni 1857 ist die zweite Instanz für München in Augsburg, für Bamberg in Würzburg. Die dritte Instanz bilden beide Erzbisthümer gegenseitig, kraft päpstlicher Delegation.

6) Ehegerichte der Protestanten sind in erster Instanz — für das Consistorium Ansbach und das Dekanat München, das k. Bezirksgericht Ansbach — für das Consistorium Bayreuth das dortige Bezirksgericht; in zweiter Instanz das Appell.-Gericht in Bamberg. Ver. v. 24. Febr. 1862 § 8.

7) Besondere Ehegerichte bestehen überhaupt nur für Katholiken, für die evangelisch-lutherische und für die evangelisch-reformirte Kirche. — Bei allen anderen anerkannten Kirchengesellschaften, also für die Bekenner der griechischen Kirche, die Mennoniten, Israeliten sind auch in Ehesachen die gewöhnlichen Gerichte zuständig. Bl. f. R. XVII 245. Minist. Reskr. v. 31. März 1821. Döllinger VI S. 193.

Für die Dissidenten, d. h. diejenigen Personen, welche keiner im Staate anerkannten (öffentlichen oder Privat-) Religionsgesellschaft angehören — (Deutschkatholiken, Mitglieder der freien Gemeinde 2c.) — sind durch Ges. v. 2. Mai 1868 Art. 17 gleichfalls eigene (durch Verordnung zu bestimmende) Gerichte bezeichnet, so daß also in dieser Richtung die Dissidenten bevorzugt sind vor den anerkannten Religionsgesellschaften. — vgl. Ver. v. 2. Nov. 1851. Rgbl. S. 1185.

8) Die Verordnung v. 28. Juli 1818 (Ges. Bl. v. 1818 S. 474) bestimmt in Ziff. I, daß der Gerichtsstand in Ehesachen unter Personen, welche verschiedenen Religionen zugethan sind, sich nach der Person des Beklagten richte. In Ziff. II und III ist dann weiter verfügt, wie die Entscheidung des hiernach zuständigen Gerichts in Einklang zu bringen sei mit den für den andern (klagenden) Ehetheil geltenden eherechtlichen Bestimmungen.

Auf Ansuchen dieses Ehetheils hat das für denselben in Ehesachen zuständige Gericht das Geeignete zu verfügen; amtliche Mittheilung des Erkenntnisses und amtliche Entschließung verlangt das Gericht nicht. Bl. f. R. XXI 396. Jetzt wäre dies schon durch die Natur des Verfahrens ausgeschlossen.

Wegen der besonderen Verhältnisse der Dissidenten vgl. Ges. v. 2. Mai 1868 Art. 18.

9) Die Bestimmungen jener Verordnung haben zwar zunächst nur das Verhältniß zwischen Katholiken und Protestanten im Auge, gelten aber der Allgemeinheit der in Ziff. I gebrauchten Worte wegen, sowie nach dem Geiste des Gesetzes für alle gemischten Ehen ohne Ausnahme, wie sie denn jetzt sogar für Dissidenten anwendbar erklärt worden sind. — Bl. f. R. XVII 241 ff.

10) Für die Frage, ob ein gewisses Ehegericht zuständig sei, ist bloß der Zeitpunkt der Klagestellung entscheidend. Bl. f. R. XVII 247 und 265. Erk. d. O. A. G. v. 10. Mai 1852.

Dabei genügen zur Feststellung der Zugehörigkeit zu einer bestimmten Religionsgesellschaft die nach Religionsedikt § 5—10 abgegebenen Erklärungen; die Aufnahme oder Entlassung ist in dieser Beziehung nicht erforderlich und selbst, wenn behauptet wird, es sei der Uebertritt mit List oder Gewalt bewirkt worden, behauptet vorerst die Vermuthung, daß die Wahl eine freie gewesen, ihre Geltung. Minist. Reskr. v. 28. Sept. 1833. — Bl. f. R. XXIII 129.

11) In der Pfalz gibt es keine Ehegerichte, sondern nur ein besonderes Verfahren für Ehesachen, welches durch Art. 69 des Einf. Gesetzes mit unwesentlichen Abänderungen aufrecht erhalten worden ist. — Bezüglich der freiwilligen Ehescheidungen ist, da sie nicht zur streitigen Rechtspflege gehören, ohnedem nichts geändert.

(Gemeinsame Bestimmungen.)

Art. 9. — **Die Zuständigkeit des mit einem Rechtsstreite befaßten Gerichts wird vorbehaltlich der Bestimmungen der Art. 10 und 31 auf Streitpunkte, welche nach Art. 2—8 zur Zuständigkeit eines andern Gerichts gehören, dadurch nicht erstreckt, daß ein solcher Streitpunkt im Laufe des bei dem Gerichte anhängigen Rechtsstreits in Folge gesetzlich zulässigen Vorbringens einer Partei Gegenstand der unmittelbaren oder mittelbaren Entscheidung wird.**

Art. 10. — **Ist im Falle des Art. 9 der Rechtsstreit bei einem Bezirksgerichte anhängig und handelt**

es sich um einen Streitpunkt, der nach Art. 3—6 oder Art. 7 Abs. 2 zur Zuständigkeit der Einzelngerichte gehören würde, so hat das Bezirksgericht auch über diesen Streitpunkt zu entscheiden.

Ist der Rechtsstreit bei einem Handelsgerichte anhängig und bildet eine Handelssache, die nur in Folge der Bestimmung des Art. 7 Abs. 2 nicht zur Zuständigkeit der Handelsgerichte gehört, den nach Art. 9 zu entscheidenden Streitpunkt, so hat das Handelsgericht auch über letztern zu entscheiden.

Art. 11. — Wird bei einem Einzelngerichte in der in Art. 9 bezeichneten Weise ein zur Zuständigkeit des Bezirksgerichts gehöriger Streitpunkt Gegenstand der Entscheidung, so wird das Bezirksgericht auch für die Entscheidung des anhängigen Rechtsstreits zuständig, wenn diese Entscheidung von der vorgängigen Erledigung des fraglichen Streitpunkts abhängt.

Unter derselben Voraussetzung wird, wenn bei einem Bezirks- oder Einzelngerichte in der in Art. 9 bezeichneten Weise ein zur Zuständigkeit der Handelsgerichte gehöriger Streitpunkt Gegenstand der Entscheidung wird, das Handelsgericht auch für den anhängigen Rechtsstreit in dem Falle zuständig, daß dieser eine dem Handelsgerichte nur durch Art. 7 Abs. 2 entzogene Handelssache bildet.

Die nach Abs. 1 oder 2 begründete Zuständigkeit der Bezirks- oder Handelsgerichte wird dadurch nicht aufgehoben, daß die eine oder andere Partei ihre Ansprüche ermäßigt oder nicht verfolgt, oder daß das Gericht die Trennung des Verfahrens anordnet.

G. A. der K. d. A. I S. 42—44. 53—59. 81 94. IV S. 10—12. 38. 302 — K. d. R. S. 52—66 IV S. 6.

1) Diese drei Artikel haben jene Fälle im Auge, wo durch die Vertheidigung auf die Klage, durch Einreden oder Repliken, Fragen strittig werden, deren Tragweite über den Klaganspruch hinausgeht.

Sie setzen voraus, daß über diese Zwischenfragen erkannt werden muß, um zur Entscheidung über den Klaganspruch zu gelangen. Sie setzen ferner voraus, daß diese Zwischenfragen für sich vor ein Gericht anderer Art gehören würden; denn ist dies nicht der Fall, so ist selbstverständlich das Gericht der Klage auch über alle Vorfragen zu erkennen zuständig.

2) Wenige Bestimmungen der P. O. hatten bei ihrer Geburt mit so vielen Schwierigkeiten zu kämpfen, als die vorliegenden und man muß dies natürlich finden, wenn man erwägt, daß hier ein Punkt gesetzgeberisch geregelt werden sollte, welcher seither ganz der Wissenschaft überlassen war, daß ferner die zu entscheidenden Fragen neu sind, wenigstens erst seit der Zeit praktische Bedeutung gewonnen haben, als in den Handels- und Landgerichten, Ausnahmsgerichte für ganze Gattungen von Rechtstreiten entstanden sind. Die Regel nemlich, daß der Richter der Hauptsache auch über alle Vor- und Zwischenfragen zu entscheiden habe, ist zwar natürlich und selbstverständlich, so lange es nur persönliche oder territoriale Rücksichten sind, welche die Gerichtszuständigkeit abgränzen; allein sie wird bedenklich, wenn sie zur Folge haben soll, Streitpunkte an ein Gericht zu ziehen, welchem sie ihrer Natur nach entzogen sein sollen.

3) Bei Lösung der vorliegenden Schwierigkeiten hatten zwei Gesichtspunkte in Betracht zu kommen; es war zu prüfen:

1) wie weit sich die Rechtskraft bei Entscheidung solcher Vor- und Zwischenfragen erstrecke und sodann

2) wie weit es rathsam sei, die Zuständigkeit der Gerichte auf Streitpunkte, welche ihrer Natur nach denselben fremd sind, auszudehnen.

4) Was ersteren Gesichtspunkt anbelangt, so sind zwei Hauptmeinungen möglich. Man kann sagen:

a) jede Zwischenfrage wird nur für den einzelnen Fall entschieden, oder aber

b) wenn irgend ein Punkt strittig wird und der Richter sich darüber ausspricht, so ist derselbe endgültig unter den Parteien entschieden, also nicht bloß für den einzelnen Klags- oder Wiederklags-Anspruch, sondern für alle sonstigen Rechtsverhältnisse.

Beide Meinungen haben ihre Vertheidiger gefunden, sowohl im deutschen als im französischen Rechte.

5) In Deutschland hat Savigny (Syst. des heut. röm. R. Bd. VI S. 361) letztere Ansicht vertreten und dieselbe ist seitdem herrschend geworden. Nichts desto weniger findet immer noch die entgegenstehende Ansicht ihre Anhänger und wird z. B. von Pfeifer in Archiv f. civil. Pr. Bd. 37 S. 258 — 261 mit großer Einsicht vertheidigt.

6) Die französ. Jurisprudenz ist hier von besonderer Bedeutung, da sie sich speziell bezüglich der von Ausnahmsgerichten zu entscheidenden Zwischenfragen (Inzidentpunkte) gebildet hat. Fragen, welche diesseits neu sind und erst in jüngster Zeit größere Wichtigkeit erlangten, wurden dort seit mehr als 60 Jahren geprüft, erörtert und zu lösen versucht.

Es haben sich vier verschiedene Ansichten entwickelt, nemlich:

a) Der Inzidentpunkt wird immer nur für den einzelnen Prozeß entschieden (Jousse — Carré compet. II S. 281).

b) Inzidentpunkte sind nur dann endgiltig entschieden, wenn besonderer Antrag deßhalb gestellt war, d. h. wenn sie Gegenstand eines Inzidentbegehrens bildeten und darüber im Urtheilssatze entschieden ist (die annotateurs von Curasson, traité de la comp. des juges de paix, Note a zu Nr. 178).

c) Alle Inzidentpunkte sind endgültig entschieden, falls Streit darüber entstanden war (Curasson a. a. O.)

d) Alle Inzidentpunkte sind endgültig entschieden, sogar wenn sie nicht Gegenstand eines förmlichen Streites waren. (Carrou u. Dalloz).

7) Von diesen Ansichten ist diejenige unter c die gangbarste und wird von Curasson in derselben Weise entwickelt, wie sie von Umbscheiden in seinem Antrage (Abg. I 42) geltend gemacht worden ist.

Curasson sagt: »le principe, que le juge de »l'action l'est aussi de l'exception doit être »restreint au cas, ou le jugement de l'exception »ne serait d'aucune influence sur d'autres »difficultés, qui pourraient se présenter entre »les mêmes parties.«

8) Die Ansicht unter d führt zu dem unpraktischen Resultate, daß sich z. B. der Landrichter in contumaciam unzuständig erklären muß, wenn Jemand Zinsen eines Kapitals, welches die landrichterliche Zuständigkeit überschreitet, einklagt. Dalloz (comp. civ. des trib. de p.) Nr. 39.

9) Am richtigsten erscheint mir die Ansicht unter b, weil sie die einfachste, gerechteste und praktischste ist, namentlich aber den leidigen Streit darüber beseitigt, was als stillschweigend entschieden zu betrachten sei.

Mit Recht sagt Pfeiffer a. a. O., daß es häufig nicht übersehen werden könne, welche Tragweite ein Inzidentpunkt für spätere Streitfälle haben möge, für Streitfälle, deren Entstehung noch gar nicht vorauszusehen sei; daß ferner es oft sehr unbillig sei, die Parteien zu zwingen, bei einer ganz unbedeutenden Sache die wichtigsten Präjudizialfragen, die ihnen augenblicklich gleichgiltig sind, für alle Zukunft endgültig aburtheilen zu lassen.

Den gewöhnlichen Einwand, daß widersprechende Urtheile verhütet werden müßten, würde ich nicht hoch anschlagen, denn 1) kann jede Partei durch Inzidentbegehren die endgültige Aburtheilung herbeiführen, 2) werden die Fälle, wo ein späteres Urtheil sich in offenen Widerspruch setzt mit einem früheren, nicht leicht vorkommen, geschieht es aber doch, so müssen so gewichtige Gründe vorliegen, daß es ein Gewinn für's materielle Recht ist, endlich 3) sind widersprechende Urtheile nie ganz zu vermeiden, wie es sich z. B. ereignen kann, daß im nemlichen Urtheile eine Partei dem einen Betheiligten gegenüber, gegen welchen sie durch Eideszuschiebung Beweis führt, obsiegt, während sie dem anderen Betheiligten gegenüber, weil Eideszuschiebung unstatthaft ist, oder der Eid geschworen wird, unterliegt. Art. 64 und 468.

10) Diese Ansicht, welcher in der französ. Praxis in so ferne Rechnung getragen wird, als die Anwälte bezüglich derjenigen Inzidentpunkte, deren endgültige Erledigung sie wünschen, förmliche Inzidentklage zu erheben pflegen, hat die Billigung des Gesetzgebers nicht erhalten. Derselbe hat im Wesentlichen die Ansicht von Curasson sich angeeignet, jedoch gewinnt dieselbe nach Maßgabe der Verhandlungen im G. G. A. und unter dem Einflusse diesseitiger Rechtsanschauungen nicht ganz die Tragweite, welche sie im französischen Prozesse hat.

11) Vor Allem ist hervorzuheben, daß die Frage der Zuständigkeit in untrennbarem Zusammenhange steht mit der Frage der Rechtskraft; daß beide Fragen nur zusammen gelöst werden können. Ist daher hergestellt, daß über eine gewisse Zwischenfrage rechtskräftig unter den Parteien entschieden wird, so ist zugleich ausgesprochen, daß sie bezüglich der Zuständigkeit als selbständiger Streitpunkt in Betracht kommt.

12) Nach dem klaren Wortlaute des Gesetzes kann die Entscheidung der Zwischenfrage unmittelbar oder mittelbar, d. h. ausdrücklich oder stillschweigend (implicite) erfolgen. Abg. I 58 (v. Weiß). Wie diese Bestimmung mit Art. 295 in Einklang zu bringen sei, wird bei jenem Artikel erörtert werden.

13) Die Worte: „in Folge gesetzlich zulässigen Vorbringens" hätten wohl als selbstverständlich wegbleiben können.

Man hatte Fälle im Auge, wo Jemand Einreden vorbringt, welche in der betr. Prozeßart (z. B. im Wechselprozesse) unzulässig sind, oder welche civilrechtlich unstatthaft sind, wie im possessorischen Rechtsstreite petitorische Rechtsgründe.

14) Nach den Verhandlungen ist sicher, daß man die Rechtskraft solcher Zwischen-Entscheidungen möglichst einschränken wollte. Abg. IV 11 (v. Weiß).

Sie tritt daher nur ein, wo wirklich Streit entsteht, in Folge der Entscheidung dieses Streites. Wenn z. B. 50 fl. als Zins oder als Theil eines Kapitales von 300 fl. eingeklagt werden, so kann sich der Landrichter nicht etwa sofort unzuständig erklären, sondern er wird erst unzuständig, falls der Beklagte erscheint und das Bestehen der Hauptschuld bestreitet. Zwar macht Barth (S. 59 und 60) bei Art. 4 eine Aeußerung, laut welcher er damals die oben (Nr. 8) als unpraktisch bezeichnete Ansicht theilte, allein nach dem Gange der Verhandlung ist nicht anzunehmen, daß dies die Ansicht des G. G. A. bei Art. 9 gewesen, wie denn auch die Fassung des Gesetzes zu erkennen gibt, daß die Unzuständigkeit erst durch die Erhebung des Inzidentstreites im Laufe des Rechtstreites herbeigeführt werden soll.

Selbstverständlich ist auch zuzugestehen, daß falls ein solcher Streit nicht entsteht, bezüglich des betreffenden Punkts, z. B. im obigen Falle der Kapitalforderung, auch keine Rechtskraft erwächst und es sich in künftigen Prozessen nur um Benützung von Zugeständnissen, nicht aber um rechtskräftige Entscheidung handeln kann. Sirey-Gilbert. Art. 1351 Nr. 64 — cass. 25 Aug. 1829.

15) Unter „Streitpunkten“ sind nur solche Zwischenfragen zu verstehen, welche Gegenstand eines selbständigen Rechtsstreites bieten können d. h., welche ein unter den Parteien festzustellendes besonderes Rechtsverhältniß betreffen. Abg. IV 11 (v. Weiß). Es ist hierbei nicht erforderlich, daß, auch abgesehen von dem durch die Klage gegebenen besonderen Anlasse, selbständige Klage hätte erhoben werden können, wie es denn z. B. civilrechtlich kein Klagrecht gibt zur Feststellung nicht fälliger oder bedingter Forderungen.

16) Als selbständige Streitpunkte sind nicht zu betrachten:

1) alle bloß das Verfahren betreffende Fragen, z. B. über Competenz, Nichtigkeit von Procedurakten u. s. w.;

2) alle Beweisfragen insbesondere die Entscheidung über Giltigkeit oder Zuläßigkeit von Beweismitteln. (Der einzige Punkt, welcher hätte Zweifel erregen können, nemlich das Erkennen über Aechtheit von Beweis-Urkunden, ist durch Art. 528 besonders geregelt);

3) die Feststellung früherer Rechtsverhältnisse, insofern daraus keine anderen Folgen, als diejenigen, welche Gegenstand der Klage bilden, entstehen können;

4) die bloßen Legitimationsfragen.

17) Zu 3. Wenn wegen Vertragsbruches eine Entschädigung von 100 fl. verlangt wird und der Beklagte wendet ein, es sei der Vertrag gar nicht zu Stande gekommen, so muß zwar darüber erkannt werden, ob jener Vertrag (welcher vielleicht hohe Werthe zum Gegenstande hatte) abgeschlossen worden sei, allein die Zuständigkeit des Landgerichts wird hierdurch nicht in Frage gestellt, denn es handelt sich immerhin nur um 100 fl. und jener Vertragsabschluß hat blos historischen Werth.

Die nemliche Bewandtniß hat es mit dem Falle, wo der Rest einer im Uebrigen bereits getilgten Forderung eingeklagt wird. Gleiches gilt, falls behufs Begründung der Berechnung einer Entschädigung bei einer Zwangsabtretung die Thatsache, ob ein gewisses dingliches Recht früher bestanden habe, Gegenstand des Streites wird.

18) Zu 4. Bei der Verhandlung wurden diese Fragen ausdrücklich und wiederholt als solche bezeichnet, welche selbständige Streitpunkte nicht bildeten und dabei namentlich hervorgehoben, daß sie nicht in Rechtskraft erwüchsen. Abg. I 55 (v. Neumayr.)

Dabei wird jedoch vorausgesetzt, daß es sich nur um den Legitimationspunkt handele. Wenn z. B. der Beklagte die Erbqualität des Klägers in Abrede stellt, oder seine eigene Erbqualität bestreitet, so liegen einfache Legitimationsfragen vor, behauptet er aber selbst Erbrechte, so entsteht ein selbständiger Streitpunkt. Aehnlich wie hier verhält es sich bei allen anderen Legitimationsfragen, z. B. wenn es sich fragt, ob Jemand Singularsuccessor sei, ob eine Ehefrau als gütergemein hafte, ob Jemand als Eigenthümer oder Besitzer einer Sache befugt sei, Entschädigung zu fordern. (Bl. f. R. XVIII 27).

19) Für die Pfalz ist hervorzuheben, daß diese Auffassung eine nicht unbedeutende Erweiterung der Zuständigkeit der Ausnahmsgerichte, namentlich der Handelsgerichte enthält.

Der französische Prozeß geht von der Fiction aus, als ob über rein civilrechtliche Fragen die Handelsgerichte nicht fähig seien zu entscheiden, und man ging z. B. so weit, auszusprechen, daß die H. Ger. nicht erkennen dürften, ob die Einrede des Betrugs oder Wuchers begründet sei, ob ein authentischer Akt über Handelsgeschäfte der Form nach gültig sei. Journ. du Pal. (comp. commerc.) Nr. 671—681. Ein Ausfluß derselben Idee ist die Bestimmung in Art. 426 C. de pr. wornach, falls die Erbqualität bestritten wird, die Entscheidung vor's Bezirksgericht zu verweisen ist.

Diesseits wurden seit Einführung der Handelsgerichte, wie mir scheint mit Recht, diesen Gerichten ausgedehntere Befugnisse eingeräumt und man nahm als selbstverständlich an, daß sie über alle Zwischenfragen, der Regel nach, urtheilen dürfen, mögen auch civilrechtliche Grundsätze anzuwenden sein. Bl. f. R. XXXI 50 und 109 — vgl. oben Art. 7 Nr. 46.

Diese Ansicht erscheint als diejenige des Gesetzgebers und muß daher in Zukunft auch in der Pfalz gelten. Was insbesondere die Erbqualität betrifft, so sind auch die Bestimmungen des Art. 800 Code civ. hier nicht von Einfluß, um so weniger, da die neuere Jurisprudenz das Urtheil, welches als Erbe verurtheilt, nicht über den einzelnen Fall wirken läßt. Demolombe zu Art. 800 Nr. 152.

20) Was den zweiten oben (Nr. 3) angeregten Gesichtspunkt betrifft, so suchte der Gesetzgeber eine Zersplitterung der Aburtheilung, sowie unnützes Hin- und Herweisen zu vermeiden, hätte es aber vielleicht in noch höherem Grade thun können.

Im französischen Prozesse hat sich in neuester Zeit, nach langem Kampfe, die praktische Ansicht Bahn gebrochen, daß die Bezirksgerichte als ordentliche Gerichte (par suite du principe de la plenitude de juridiction) die den Landgerichten und Handelsgerichten zugewiesenen Sachen auf Grund der Connexität an sich ziehe, also um so mehr bei Präjudizialfragen. Dalloz (exception) Nr. 197 (comp. civ. des trib.), Nr. 264—268 Journ. du Pal. (comp. commerc.), Nr. 709 Rodière saisie-arrêt I S. 131 und III S. 303.

Unsere P. O. bekennt sich bezüglich der Landgerichte zur nemlichen Ansicht, bezüglich der Handelsgerichte aber, abgesehen von den Ausnahmsfällen des Art. 7 Abs. 2 und 31, Abs. 3, nicht. Wenn daher Conflikt entsteht zwischen Bezirksgerichten und Landgerichten, so ist durch die klaren Vorschriften der Art. 10 und 11 sowie Art. 511 dafür gesorgt, daß das nemliche Gericht über Haupt- und Zwischen-Streit zuständig sei und bleibe. Man hielt dies übrigens schon früher so. s. Arnold prakt. Erörterung S. 285, u. Bl. f. R. IV 166.

Art. 11 Abs. 1 fügt in Folge einer erst bei zweiter Lesung gebrachten Aenderung beschränkend hinzu: „wenn diese Entscheidung von der vorgängigen Erledigung des Streitpunktes abhängt." Der Landrichter hat sich demnach einfach zu fragen, ob Grund vorliegen würde, die Entscheidung des Hauptstücks bis zur Erledigung des Incidentpunkts zu suspendiren. Ist dies der Fall, so wird das Bezirksgericht auch über den Hauptstreit zuständig.

21) Wenn Conflikt entsteht zwischen Handelsgerichten einerseits und Bezirks- oder Landgerichten andererseits, so muß (abgesehen vom Falle des Art. 7 Abs. 2) getrennte Aburtheilung stattfinden und zwar in der Weise, daß das mit der Hauptsache befaßte Gericht, nachdem es so weit nöthig oder zweckmäßig darüber verhandelt und geurtheilt hat, die endliche Entscheidung aufschiebt, bis über den vor den zuständigen Richter verwiesenen Zwischenstreit rechtskräftig erkannt ist.

22) Schwierigkeiten bietet solchen Falls die Compensationseinrede, insofern sich bei derselben civilrechtliche und prozessuale Grundsätze mischen.

Die natürlichste Theorie wäre wohl folgende:

a) Jede Gegenforderung, welche (die sonstigen Bedingungen der Compensation vorausgesetzt) dem Betrage nach (ziffermäßig) feststeht, ist als Zahlungseinrede zu behandeln, muß also immer zur Compensation zugelassen werden, mag sie auch bestritten und der Beweis schwierig sein, denn man nimmt ja im gewöhnlichen Prozesse nie Rücksicht auf die Schwierigkeit des Beweises von Einreden und denkt nicht daran, diese als »multis ambagibus innodatae« zum gesonderten Austrag zu verweisen. vgl. Seuff. Pand. B. III § 287.

b) Gegenforderungen, welche dem Betrage nach ungewiß sind, wie z. B. Schadenklagen, können nie die Compensations-Einrede begründen, sondern nur wiederklagsweise geltend gemacht werden, und es ist eine bloße Prozeßfrage, ob sie zuzulassen seien.

23) Das bestehende Recht, insbesondere in Deutschland, erkennt jedoch diesen Unterschied nicht an, behandelt vielmehr die Illiquidität, welche bloß im Beweise, und die Illiquidität, welche in der Forderung selbst liegt, ziemlich gleich und zwar in der Art, daß es, nach neuester Praxis, im Wesentlichen dem Ermessen des Richters überlassen bleibt, ob genügende Liquidität vorhanden sei. Const. 14. Cod. (4. 31). — Cod. Max. Th. IV. Cap. 15 § 1 Ziff. 11. — Preuß. L. R. Th. I Tit. 16 § 300—377. — Code civ. Art. 1291. — Bl. f. R. XXIV.

Offenbar sind diese Prinzipien nicht bloß prozessualer, sondern auch civilrechtlicher Natur, wie sie denn durch Civilrechtsgesetze ausgesprochen werden; sie sind daher durch die neue Prozeßordnung nicht aufgehoben.

24) Es fragt sich nun, ob jede Gegenforderung, welche nicht zur Zuständigkeit des betreffenden Richters gehört, als illiquide Gegenforderung zu behandeln und zum besonderen Austrag zu verweisen sei, oder aber, ob die Hauptsache bis zur Erledigung des Incidentpunktes zu suspendiren sei.

Das Erstere wäre das Einfachste, ist aber nicht unbedingt richtig. Es würden wohlerworbene Rechte des Beklagten empfindlich geschädigt, wenn Compensations-Einreden, welche zulässig wären, falls der Richter der Klage für sie zuständig sein würde, bloß deßhalb, weil dies nicht der Fall, ganz unbeachtet bleiben müßten. — Der Vorbehalt besonderer Austragung ist kein genügender

Ersatz, weil a) möglicherweise der Schaden, welcher dem Beklagten durch Verurtheilung und Urtheilsvollzug erwächst, nicht wieder gut zu machen ist, und weil b) die Gegenforderung vielleicht gar nicht mehr selbständig einklagbar ist, indem sie verjährt erscheint.

25) Um den Prinzipien zu genügen, werden daher folgende Regeln einzuhalten sein:

a) falls die Gegenforderung sich nach den Prinzipien des Civilrechts zur Compensation eignet, hat der Richter, nachdem er über das Bestehen der Hauptforderung erkannt, die Verurtheilung, soweit sie durch die Compensations-Einrede in Frage gestellt ist, zu vertagen, bis der zuständige Richter über das Bestehen der Gegenforderung erkannt hat;

b) falls sich jedoch nach jenen Prinzipien die Gegenforderung nicht zur Compensation eignet, hat der Richter sie einfach zur gesonderten Austragung abzuweisen.

26) Das französische Recht läßt in Fällen, wo eine Forderung dem Betrage nach illiquid ist, nie die Compensations-Einrede, sondern nur Wiederklage zum Zwecke gleichzeitiger Liquidirung und späterer Compensirung zu. In der Pfalz ist daher jede derartige Gegenforderung, für welche der Richter der Hauptsache nicht zuständig ist, abzuweisen.

27) Tritt nach Art. 11 Abs. 1 u. 2 die Zuständigkeit des Bezirks- oder Handelsgerichts ein, so hat sich der Landrichter unzuständig zu erklären und der Kläger kann seinen Anspruch ganz in der nemlichen Weise, wie er ihn vor's Einzelgericht gebracht hatte, vor das zuständige höhere Gericht bringen, abwartend, ob dort die Zwischenfrage wieder vorgebracht werde. Falls Letzteres nicht geschieht, bleibt nach Abs. 3 dennoch die Zuständigkeit des höheren Gerichts bestehen.

28) Welches höhere Gericht ist das zuständige, dasjenige, zu dessen Sprengel das Landgericht, oder dasjenige, vor welches der Incidentpunkt an und für sich gehört? — Letzteres wird z. B. verfügt in Art. 31 Abs. 4.

Der Grundgedanke des Gesetzes, daß der Incidentstreit für die Zuständigkeit maßgebend sein solle, wird auch für jene Fälle den Ausschlag geben, wo für diesen Streitpunkt ein besonderer Gerichtsstand, z. B. der Lage der Sache, besteht; besteht jedoch ein solcher nicht, so wird vor das dem Beklagten gegenüber zuständige höhere Gericht zu laden sein, denn eine Gleichstellung mit dem Falle förmlicher Wiederklage wäre nicht berechtigt.

29) Es könnte sich fragen, was für den Fall zu gelten habe, wenn der höhere Richter der Ansicht ist, es habe der Einzelrichter mit Unrecht seine Zuständigkeit bezüglich des Incidentstreites abgelehnt. — Auch in diesem Falle wird nach dem Willen des Gesetzes die Zuständigkeit des höheren Richters begründet bleiben, weil nach Art. 511 gegen die fragliche Entscheidung kein Rechtsmittel zugelassen ist, dieselbe also rechtskräftig wird, weil ferner die Schlußworte des Art. 11 ausdrücklich den Fall vorsehen, wenn eine gemeinschaftliche Verhandlung unnöthig sei. Abg. II 263 (Barth).

Indem der Landrichter die Sache abweist, erkennt er nicht an, von Anfang an unzuständig gewesen, sondern nur durch den Zwischenstreit unzuständig geworden zu sein; er überträgt daher die Sache, wie sie ist, an das höhere Gericht und könnte von einer Nichtigkeit der früheren Verhandlungen keine Rede sein.

Schließlich möge den Richtern der Rath ertheilt werden, sich, ehe sie sich bezüglich eines Zwischenstreits unzuständig erklären, zu vergewissern, ob die Unzuständigkeit nicht durch Vereinbarung beseitigt werden könne. Art. 39.

(Allgemeiner Gerichtsstand.)

Art. 12. — **Der allgemeine Gerichtsstand wird durch den Wohnsitz des Beklagten und, wenn der Beklagte seinen Wohnsitz an mehreren Orten hat, an jedem dieser Orte begründet.**

Für Personen, welche keinen Wohnsitz im Inlande haben, vertritt der Aufenthalt dessen Stelle. G. A. d. K. d. A. I S. 14. 16—18. 80. 81. IV S. 12 — K. d. R. I S. 66—71.

1) Wie die vorausgehenden Artikel sich mit Scheidung der Zuständigkeit unter Gerichten verschiedener Art beschäftigen, so machen es sich dieser und die folgenden Artikel zur Aufgabe, die Vertheilung der Rechtsstreite unter Gerichte der nemlichen Art zu regeln.

Ueber den allgemeinen Gerichtsstand, d. h. den G. für alle Streitsachen, welche nicht ihrer Natur wegen besonderen Gerichten zugewiesen sind, enthalten die Art. 12—20 die näheren Bestimmungen.

2) Physische Personen haben ihren allgemeinen Gerichtsstand bei den Gerichten, in deren Sprengel sie ihren Wohnsitz oder, in dessen Ermangelung, ihren Aufenthalt haben.

An den Wohnsitz knüpfen sich nicht bloß für den Gerichtsstand, sondern auch für die Civilrechte sehr wichtige Folgen; der Gesetzgeber hat es daher geeignet gefunden, den Begriff von „Wohnsitz“ für die P. O. nicht besonders aufzustellen, vielmehr die Grundsätze der Civilrechte als maßgebend vorauszusetzen. Vortrag v. Neum. zu Art. 2 des Entwurfs — Abg. I 7. — Es ist daher, falls Zweifel zu lösen sind, das am betreffenden Orte geltende Civilrecht zu Rathe zu ziehen.

3) Was den natürlichen (wirklichen) Wohnsitz anbelangt, so stimmen alle Rechte darin überein, daß Jemand seinen Wohnsitz am Orte habe, wo er sich in der Absicht niedergelassen, fortdauernd dort zu bleiben; welchen er zum Mittelpunkte seines gesellschaftlichen und Geschäftsverkehres macht, wie Seuffert (Comm. I S. 52) sagt. — l. 7 Cod. (10. 39) — G. O. Cap. I § 3 — Code civ. Art. 102.

Ebenso allgemein ist anerkannt, daß dieser Wohnsitz rein nur auf der Thatsache des Aufenthaltes, verbunden mit der Absicht, sich bleibend niederzulassen, beruht und unabhängig ist von Bürgerrecht, Heimat und Ansässigmachung. — Seuff. Comm. B. I S. 54 Note 8 — v. Nar Erl. z. Ges. v. 16. April 1868 Art. 43 Z. 5 Bl. f. R. VIII 270.

Der Richter wird im einzelnen Falle, unter Abwägung aller Umstände, die Frage des Wohnsitzes zu lösen und dabei im Auge zu behalten haben, daß, wenn der Wohnsitz einmal begründet war, im Zweifel dessen Beibehaltung anzunehmen und bloßes Entfernen, ohne klar erkennbare Absicht des Aufgebens, des Nichtwiederkehrens, nicht in Betracht kommt. Preuß. L. R. Einleitg. § 24. — Kreitmayer zur G. O. Cap. I § 3 lit. c.

Dabei ist zu beachten, daß zur Begründung eines neuen Wohnsitzes Willensfähigkeit und Willensfreiheit gehört. Seuff. Archiv X Nr. 12 Bl. f. R. XXIII 93.

4) Das Civilrecht kennt jedoch nicht bloß einen thatsächlichen, sondern auch einen vom Gesetze bestimmten Wohnsitz (domicilium necessarium), welcher, so lange die Bedingungen dazu bestehen jenen ausschließt und auch von diesem gesetzlichen Wohnsitze spricht, wie die Verhandlungen nicht im Mindesten zweifelhaft lassen, der Art. 12.

Einen gesetzlichen Wohnsitz haben Staats-, Gemeinde- und Kirchendiener. Seuff. Comm. I S. 55. — l. 8. Cod. (10. 39). Bezüglich der besonderen Grundsätze des französischen Rechts s. Code civ. Art. 106 u. 107.

5) Für Offiziere und im Offiziersrange stehende Militärbeamte hat, nach dem Willen des Gesetzgebers, das Ges. v. 16. Aug. 1828 § 3 Abs. 1, soweit es den Garnisonsort als Wohnsitz bezeichnet, fortdauernde Geltung. Es geht dies theils daraus hervor, daß im Einführungsgesetze Art. 3 Z. 14 bloß Abs. 2 jenes Artikels aufgehoben wird, theils daraus, daß ein Vorschlag des Minist.-Comm. (Abg. I 11), für Offiziere einen jenen Abs. 1 erläuternde und ergänzende Verfügung zu treffen, als unnöthig abgelehnt wurde. Richtiger wäre es gewesen, besonders zu verfügen, denn im Grunde enthielt jene Gesetzesbestimmung keine Festsetzung des bürgerlichen Wohnsitzes im Allgemeinen, sondern nur des Gerichtsstandes, wäre daher streng genommen durch Art. 2 des Einf. Ges. aufgehoben.

Als überflüssig kann sie nicht angesehen werden, schon deßhalb weil nach französischem Rechte (Code civ. Art. 106) Offiziere durch ihre Anstellung keinen gesetzlichen Wohnsitz erlangen.

Detachirte Offiziere haben ihren G. nicht dort, wo der Stab des Regimentes liegt, sondern dort, wo ihnen selbst die Garnison angewiesen ist. Bl. f. R. II 46 III 304.

6) Einen gesetzlichen Wohnsitz haben ferner Bevormundete. Seuff. Comm. I 56 — Code civ. Art. 108 — Von Kindern ist hier nicht zu sprechen, ebensowenig von Ehefrauen, da für diese der Gerichtsstand (Art. 11) eigens geregelt ist.

7) Zu erwähnen ist ferner der gesetzliche Wohnsitz, welchen Dienstboten unter gewissen Voraussetzungen bei der Herrschaft haben. — Seuff. Comm. I 56. — Bayer Civilproz. S. 184 — Seuff. Archiv IV Nr. 254. Code civ. Art. 109. — Die Bestimmung in Art. 18 macht diesen Wohnsitz nicht gegenstandslos.

8) Endlich gibt das römische Recht dem Exilirten einen gesetzlichen Wohnsitz und das neuere Recht wendet diese Bestimmung auf Sträflinge an.

Dieser Wohnsitz schließt jedoch den wirklichen nicht aus. L. 27 § 3 D. (50. 1.) Jedenfalls lag es in der Absicht des G. G. A. den letzteren Wohnsitz hier nicht auszuschließen. Abg. I. 14 (v. Neum.)

In der Pfalz besteht ein solcher Wohnsitz nicht, jedoch wird auf Sträflinge, welche nach Art. 32 des St. G. B. unter Curatel resp. Tutel stehen, Art. 108 Cod. civ., anwendbar sein. — Zach. I S. 302.

9) Das Gesetz erkennt an, daß Jemand mehrere Wohnsitze haben könne und hat hierbei die Fälle im Auge, wo eine Person sich abwechselnd an verschiedenen Orten, an jedem mit der Absicht bleibender Niederlassung, aufzuhalten pflegt. — Auch in vorstehender Nr. 8 ist ein Fall doppelten Wohnsitzes angedeutet. — Nach französischem Rechte kann fraglicher Fall nicht leicht vorkommen, da Art. 102 vom »principal établissement« spricht; nichts destoweniger ist er möglich. Weiß Handb. für Huissiers S. 159.

Ein Wohnsitz im Auslande wird nie beachtet, sei es bei Ausländern, sei es bei Inländern.

10) Nur im Falle, wo Jemand keinen (natürlichen oder gesetzlichen) Wohnsitz im Inlande hat, vertritt der Aufenthalt dessen Stelle.

Unter „Aufenthalt" hat man nicht etwa einen Ort zu verstehen, wo der Beklagte von der Ladung erreicht werden kann, vielmehr deutet der natürliche Sinn des Wortes schon die Absicht an, längere Zeit zu verweilen. Ein kurzer Aufenthalt, wie er beim Durchreisen vorkommt, ist nicht gemeint und daher der Sinn, welchen die hannover. Commission dem Worte gegeben, nicht gebilligt. Verhl. der h. Comm. S. 419 u. 420. — Abg. I 80 (Barth u. v. Weiß) R. R. I 66 (v. Heinz u. v. Schrenk).

Die Frage, ob ein Aufenthalt lange genug gedauert, um im Sinne des Gesetzes einen allgemeinen Gerichtsstand zu begründen, ist dem Ermessen des Richters überlassen, welcher in Fällen, wo Streitgenossen vor das Gericht des Aufenthalts gezogen werden sollen, streng prüfen wird.

11) Art. 12 gilt sowohl für Inländer als für Ausländer. Nähere Erörterungen bezüglich letzterer siehe bei Art. 19.

Art. 13. — **Bayerische Staatsangehörige, welche in einem andern Staate das Recht der Exterritorialität genießen oder mit ständiger dienstlicher Stellung verwendet sind, haben ihren allgemeinen Gerichtsstand vor den Gerichten der Hauptstadt.**

Ist die Hauptstadt in mehrere Gerichtsbezirke getheilt, so wird das Nähere durch Verordnung bestimmt. G. A. d. K. d. A. I S. 7—14. 81. IV S. 12. — K. d. R. I S. 71. 72. —

1) Man hat die allgemeine Fassung: „das Recht der Exterritorialität genießen" gewählt, und einen, größere Präzisirung bezweckenden, Antrag verworfen, um den völkerrechtlichen Grundsätzen nicht vorzugreifen. — Das jetzige Völkerrecht erkennt fragliches Recht zu: den Gesandten mit Gemahlin, Kindern und sonstigen, bei ihnen wohnenden, Familienmitgliedern, dann den Gesandtschafts-Sekretären, sonstigen Nebenbeamten und Bediensteten der Gesandtschaft, selbst Geistlichen und Aerzten, endlich auch den Dienstboten. Heffter, Völkerrecht § 221.

Agenten und Commissäre, welche in Staatsangelegenheiten an eine fremde Macht abgesendet werden, sind, falls die Sendung keine geheime ist, zwar von der ausländischen Gerichtsbarkeit befreit, genießen jedoch keiner völligen Exterritorialität (§ 222). Sie haben offenbar den Gerichtsstand des Art. 13 nur, wenn sie mit ständiger dienstlicher Stellung im Auslande verwendet sind, ist aber ihre Mission bloß vorübergehend, so sind sie am wirklichen Wohnsitze zu belangen.

Consule haben in der Regel keine Exterritorialität (Heffter a. a. O. § 226).

2) Was den Sinn der Worte: „mit ständiger dienstlicher Stellung" betrifft, so wurde vom Referenten (v. Neumayr) erklärt, daß dahin solche Fälle nicht gehören, wo ein Beamter unter Beibehaltung seines bisherigen Amtes, nur zu einer, wenn auch länger andauernden Funktion im Auslande in der Art berufen werde, daß er mit dem Aufhören dieser Funktion eo ipso wieder in seine frühere Stellung zurücktrete. Als Beispiel eines ständigen Dienstes wurde der Dienst der Zollvereins-Controleure angeführt. Gegen diese Auffassung erhob sich kein Einwand und wurde ferner als Ansicht des G. G. A. anerkannt, daß unter dienstlicher Stellung nur die Verwendung im bayrischen Staatsdienste zu verstehen sei.

3) Neben dem Gerichtsstande des Art. 13 besteht der G. des Art. 12 (ruhend) fort und tritt in Wirksamkeit, sobald die Voraussetzungen der Ausnahme wegfallen. — Es ist daher von Belang genau zu wissen, wann der Ausnahmszustand beginnt und wann er aufhört, da in Competenzfragen Klarheit und Bestimmtheit vor Allem nöthig ist.

Nach Völkerrecht beginnt der völkerrechtliche Charakter des Gesandten dem fremden Staate gegenüber, also das Recht der Exterritorialität, im Augenblicke, wo dieser Staat offizielle Kenntniß von Mission und Person des Gesandten erhält. Er endigt erst im Augenblicke, wo der Gesandte den betreffenden Staat wieder verläßt oder seinen Charakter durch förmliche Erklärung aufgibt oder die hiefür gesetzte Frist umlaufen ist. Gleiches gilt nach dessen Tode von seinen Angehörigen und Begleitern. Heffter a. a. O. § 228—230.

Art. 14. — **Ehefrauen haben den Gerichtsstand ihrer Ehemänner. Dieser Gerichtsstand bleibt ihnen auch nach der Auflösung der Ehe, sowie nach der Trennung von Tisch und Bett bis zur Eingehung einer andern Ehe oder Verlegung des Wohnsitzes in einen andern Gerichtsbezirk.**

Eheliche und diesen gleichgeachtete Kinder folgen dem Gerichtsstande des Vaters, uneheliche dem der Mutter. Sie behalten diesen allgemeinen Gerichtsstand, solange sie nicht einen andern erworben haben. G. A. d. K. d. A. I S. 7—14. 81. IV S. 12. — K. d. R. I S. 72.

1) Dieser Artikel wäre unnöthig und es würden die Grundsätze wegen des (gesetzlichen) Wohnsitzes genügen, wenn nicht Fälle vorkämen, wo Wohnsitz und Gerichtsstand verschieden sind, z. B. Art. 13 und 19. Vortrag von Neumayr zu Art. 3 des Entwurfs. — Auch für diese Fälle war es geeignet, den Gerichtsstand des Ehemannes resp. Vaters entscheiden zu lassen.

2) Daß der hier bezeichnete Gerichtsstand accessorisch sei zu demjenigen allgemeinen Gerichtsstande von welchem die Art. 12 und 13 sprechen, ist außer Zweifel; allein ist er es auch zu den Gerichtsständen der Art. 18 und 19?

Vorerst ist hervorzuheben, daß diese beiden Gerichtsstände unter die allgemeinen eingereiht sind, daß im Vortrage von Neumayr zu Art. 3 des Entwurfs beide ausdrücklich als solche bezeichnet werden, bei denen der accessorische Gerichtsstand der Ehefrauen und Kinder Anwendung finde und daß bei den Verhandlungen nirgends das Gegentheil gesagt wurde.

Daß die Art. 18 und 19 dem Art. 14 nachfolgen, erscheint (trotz der Bemerkungen Abg. I 81) ohne Belang, da dies offenbar nur auf äußeren Gründen beruht, weil man nemlich bezüglich ihrer die Verfügung des Art. 20 ausschließen wollte. Ebensowenig möchte auf die Abweichung in der Ausdrucksweise Gewicht zu legen sein; es mochte z. B. ungeeignet erscheinen, zu sagen, daß die in Art. 19 genannten Personen den allgemeinen Gerichtsstand an jedem Gerichte des Landes hätten.

3) Faßt man nun zuerst den Art. 19 in's Auge, so ist klar, daß die aufgeworfene Frage bejaht werden muß, denn sonst gäbe es ja für Ehefrauen und Kinder der betreffenden Personen gar keinen allgemeinen Gerichtsstand.

4) Größere Schwierigkeiten bietet Art. 18. Ohne Zweifel sollte er nach der ursprünglichen Ansicht des G. G. A. der K. d. Abg. das forum accessorium begründen. Es deutet darauf hin nicht bloß obenerwähnte Aeußerung des Referenten, sondern auch die Aeußerung von Barth (I 19), „daß zwei elektiv concurrirende Gerichtsstände des Wohnsitzes und des Aufenthaltes geschaffen werden sollten.“

Bedenken könnten jedoch erregt werden dadurch, daß später Art. 18 auf persönliche Verbindlichkeiten eingeschränkt wurde, und so in gewissem Grade ein besonderer Gerichtsstand entstanden ist.

Nichtsdestoweniger glaube ich, daß die ursprüngliche Ansicht, als den Charakter des fraglichen Gerichtsstandes bestimmend, Geltung behaupten muß.

Selbstverständlich ist es, daß der accessorische Gerichtsstand in jeder Beziehung die Natur des Hauptgerichtsstandes theilt und also nur für die Zeit des Aufenthalts und für persönliche Verbindlichkeiten Platz greift.

Will man vorstehende Ansicht nicht theilen, so wird sich für die gewöhnlichen Fälle, wo die Frau beim Manne, die Kinder beim Vater sich aufhalten, dennoch praktisch nichts ändern, weil für dieselben der Gerichtsstand des Art. 18 selbständig begründet wäre und zwar um so mehr, als jener Artikel von „ähnlichen Verhältnissen“ spricht.

5) Wohnsitz-Aenderungen, welche der Mann während des Scheidungs-Prozeßes vornimmt, bedingen allerdings den Gerichtsstand der Frau, jedoch kann daraus für dieselbe kein besonderer Nachtheil erwachsen, da sie sofort nach eingetretener Scheidung sich einen eigenen Wohnsitz gründen kann und dafür zu sorgen hat, daß hierüber keine Ungewißheit bleibe. Es kann sogar unter Umständen schon mit dem Augenblicke der Scheidung der wirkliche Wohnsitz in's Leben treten, wenn die Voraussetzungen dazu schon vorher bestanden.

6) Was die Frage betrifft, in welcher Weise die Ehefrau oder die Kinder einen neuen Gerichtsstand erwerben, so ist zu unterscheiden, ob mit Auflösung der Ehe oder mit dem Tode der Eltern das forum access. an sich weggefallen ist, oder ob die Kinder bei Lebzeiten der Eltern einen eigenen Gerichtsstand erwerben wollen.

Ersteren Falls ist von der (gesetzlichen) Vermuthung auszugehen, daß Frau und Kinder den Wohnsitz oder Aufenthalt des Gatten oder Vaters beibehalten wollen; es steht ihnen jedoch frei, in der nemlichen Weise, wie es dieser selbst hätte thun können, Beides zu ändern. Beruht daher der Gerichtsstand auf dem Wohnsitze, so kann auch nur die Aenderung des Wohnsitzes einen Wechsel bewirken; beruht er aber bloß auf dem Aufenthalte, so bewirkt die Aenderung des Aufenthalts auch die Aenderung des Gerichtsstandes.

Es muß dies, nach dem Geiste des Gesetzes, insbesondere auch von der Ehefrau gelten, und die Worte: „durch Verlegung des Wohnsitzes“ können um so weniger von Gewicht sein, als unmöglich ein Wohnsitz verlegt werden kann, wo keiner bestanden hat.

Im zweiten Falle werden strengere Anforderungen zu stellen sein, und wird, wenigstens diesseits des Rheins, eine Aenderung des Gerichtsstandes nur eintreten, wenn das Kind seinen eigenen Heerd gegründet und seine Absicht, den elterlichen Wohnsitz oder Aufenthalt aufzugeben, ganz unzweideutig an den Tag gelegt hat.

Art. 15. — **Der allgemeine Gerichtsstand des k. Fiskus richtet sich nach dem Sitze der Behörde, welcher im Verwaltungswege die Bescheidung des betreffenden Anspruchs in erster Instanz zusteht.**

Die Civilliste des Königs hat ihren allgemeinen Gerichtsstand vor den Gerichten der Hauptstadt.

Die Bestimmung des Art. 13 Abs. 2 findet auch hier Anwendung.

Art. 16. — **Der allgemeine Gerichtsstand der Gemeinden, Stiftungen und Körperschaften wird, soweit er nicht vom Gesetze besonders geregelt ist, durch den Sitz ihrer Verwaltung und in Ermangelung eines solchen durch den regelmäßigen Versammlungsort ihrer Vertreter bestimmt.**

Gleiches ist bei den Genossenschaften und bei den in ihren Privatrechtsverhältnissen nicht nach dem Handelsgesetzbuche zu beurtheilenden Gesellschaften und Vereinen der Fall.

Klagen von Mitgliedern einer Körperschaft oder einer der in Abs. 2 bezeichneten Vereinigungen unter sich, welche die Verhältnisse der Körperschaft oder Vereinigung betreffen, können, soweit das Gesetz nicht anders bestimmt, bei den nämlichen Gerichten angestellt werden.

Art. 17. — **Für den Gerichtsstand der Handelsgesellschaften und ihrer Mitglieder, sowie der Gesellschafts-Liquidatoren sind die Bestimmungen der Art. 111, 144, 164, 213 und 247 des Handelsgesetzbuches maßgebend.**

Klagen der Handelsgesellschafter und der Liquidatoren gegen einander in Gesellschaftsangelegenheiten können, solange die Liquidation nicht beendigt ist, bei den Gerichten des Orts angebracht werden, wo die Gesellschaft ihren Sitz hatt.

G. A. d. K. d. A. I S. 14—18. 81. 165. 298. IV S. 12. 13. — K. d. R. I S. 72—79 IV S. 6.

1) Diese drei Artikel regeln den allgemeinen Gerichtsstand von anderen als physischen Personen, von Körperschaften, Gesellschaften, Anstalten und Vermögensmassen mit eigener Persönlichkeit.

2) Durch die Bestimmungen über den Gerichtsstand des Fiskus, welche sämmtliche in dieser Beziehung seither bestandene Grundsätze und Spezialgesetze aufhebt, ist große Einfachheit in diese Materie gebracht worden.

Allerdings entsteht nun die Schwierigkeit, herauszufinden, welche Verwaltungsbehörde in erster Instanz zu entscheiden habe; allein in der Praxis wird sich diese Frage leicht erledigen, denn es muß ja, bevor eine persönliche Klage gegen den Fiskus erhoben werden kann, immer vorher der Anspruch bei der Verwaltung zur Geltung gebracht werden, und der Kläger erfährt daher, mit Bescheidung seiner Beschwerde, an welches Gericht er sich zu wenden habe.

Hat sich eine Verwaltungsbehörde zuständig erklärt und Bescheid erlassen, so wird eine Kritik, ob diese Zuständigkeit in der That begründet sei, nicht weiter statthaft sein. — Von einer näheren Erörterung, welche Behörde in jedem Falle zuständig sei, kann füglich Umgang genommen werden; sie würde auch, sollte sie erschöpfend sein, zu weit führen.

3) Da Art. 16 alle Genossenschaften, Gesellschaften und Vereine ganz denselben Bestimmungen unterwirft, wie Gemeinden und sonstige juristische Personen, so wäre es müßig, hier zu prüfen, ob zur Erzeugung einer juristischen Person förmliche Anerkennung durch die Staatsgewalt nöthig sei. s. hierüber Bluntschli Priv. R. § 34. — Windscheid Pand. § 60.

Hervorzuheben ist nur, daß der eigene Gerichtsstand eines Vereins, einer Gesellschaft nur dann als begründet erscheinen kann, wenn dieselben in der Eigenschaft von Personen in die Oeffentlichkeit getreten sind, sich als solche geltend gemacht haben. Besteht Ungewißheit darüber, an welchem von verschiedenen Orten ein Verein ꝛc. den Sitz seiner Verwaltung habe, oder wo der regelmäßige Versammlungsort seiner Vertreter sei, so hat ebenso wie bei mehrfachen Wohnsitzen (Art. 12) der Kläger die Wahl.

Selbstverständlich ist, daß durch die bloß den Gerichtsstand betreffenden Verfügungen des Art. 16 die civilrechtlichen Fragen, ob eine Stiftung, ein Verein u. s. w. als Rechtssubjekt anzuerkennen sei, Vermögen erwerben, vor Gericht belangt werden könne, nicht berührt werden.

4) Abs. 3 des Art. 16 gehört seiner Natur nach unter die Bestimmungen über die besonderen Gerichtsstände, sofern er gewisse Streitsachen unter Mitgliedern von Vereinen u. s. w. dem Gerichte, in dessen Sprengel der Verein seinen Sitz hat, zuweist (Abg. I 81). Er hat insbesondere auch solche Fälle im Auge, wo vom Vereine gegen einzelne Mitglieder auf Erfüllung ihrer Vereinspflichten geklagt wird.

5) Fraglich wird es sein, ob auch Klagen unter Vereinsmitgliedern, welche nach Auflösung des Vereines bei Liquidirung des Vermögens entstehen, gemeint sind? Man kann darauf hin-

weisen, daß 1) das Gesetz von den „nemlichen Gerichten" spreche, mit der Auflösung aber der allgemeine Gerichtsstand des Art. 16 weggefallen sei, daß 2) Art. 17 Abs. 2 für Handelsgesellschaften das Fortbestehen des Gerichtsstandes ausdrücklich verfüge.

Trotz dieser gewichtigen Gründe möchte obige Frage zu bejahen sein, und zwar hauptsächlich deßhalb, weil Abs. 3 einen besonderen (sachlichen) Gerichtsstand gründen will, für alle Streitsachen, welche die Vereinsverhältnisse betreffen, und kein innerer Grund besteht, zu unterscheiden, ob der Streit vor oder nach Auflösung des Vereins entstanden sei, wie denn gerade das Letztere in der Regel der Fall sein wird. — Die Worte: „nemliche Gerichte" sollen daher in Art. 16 Abs. 3 nur bedeuten: „Gerichte, wo der Sitz der Verwaltung ist." Die Verschiedenheit der Redaktion ist, wie die Verhandlungen zeigen, nur zufällig, denn es war die Absicht, Handels-Gesellschaften und Genossenschaften 2c. hier gleich zu behandeln. Abg. I 15 (v. Weiß).

Die Worte: „falls das Gesetz nicht anders bestimmt" sollen sich auf den Inhalt einzelner genehmigter Statuten oder einzeln zu erlassender Spezialgesetze beziehen. Abg. IV 12. 13 (v. Neumayr und v. Weiß).

6) Von den in Art. 17 angezogenen Artikeln des H. G. B. bestimmen Art. 111. 164 u. 213, daß der ordentliche Gerichtsstand der offenen Handelsgesellschaften, Commandit- und Aktien-Gesellschaften bei dem Gerichte sei, in dessen Bezirke sie ihren Sitz haben, und Art. 144 sowie Art. 247 verfügen, daß dieser Gerichtsstand auch nach Auflösung der Gesellschaften fortdauere. Auch Art. 172 und 244 des H. G. B. sind zu berücksichtigen.

Wo der Sitz einer Handelsgesellschaft sei, ist aus den Handelsregistern zu ersehen. Art. 86. 151 u. 210 des H. G. B.

Art. 18. — Personen, welche zum Behufe ihrer theoretischen oder praktischen Ausbildung in Wissenschaften, Künsten oder Gewerben oder als Pächter oder als Gehilfen, Schreiber, Gesellen, Fabrikarbeiter, Dienstboten oder in ähnlichen Verhältnissen außerhalb des Gerichtsbezirks ihres Wohnorts sich aufhalten, desgleichen Soldaten, Unteroffiziere und andere Militärpersonen dieses Rangs, welche im Inlande in Garnison oder an den ihnen angewiesenen ständigen Stationsorten sich befinden, können während ihres Aufenthalts bei den Gerichten des Aufenthaltsorts wegen persönlicher Verbindlichkeiten belangt werden.

G. A. d. K. d. A. I S. 7—14. 18. 19. IV S. 13. — K. d. R. I S. 79—82.

1) Dieser Gerichtsstand ist zwar insofern ein allgemeiner, als die Streitsachen, auf welche er sich erstreckt, nicht speziell bezeichnet sind; allein er hat den in Art. 12. 13 u. 14 bestimmten allgemeinen Gerichtsständen gegenüber immerhin auch die Natur eines Ausnahms-Gerichtsstandes und kann sogar, seitdem die Beschränkung auf persönliche Verbindlichkeiten beigefügt ist, in gewissem Sinne als besonderer Gerichtsstand bezeichnet werden.

2) Er tritt in allen Fällen ein, wo das bezeichnete Verhältniß sich bei irgend einer Person vorfindet, ohne alle Rücksicht auf deren sonstigen allgemeinen Gerichtsstand. Möglicherweise kann er sogar für Ehefrauen, wenn sie (getrennt vom Manne) in Verhältnissen fraglicher Weise, z. B. als Fabrikarbeiterinnen leben, begründet sein, vorausgesetzt, daß civilrechtlich ein selbständiges Klagerecht gegen die Ehefrau gegeben ist. — Anderseits ist selbstverständlich, daß die accessorischen allgemeinen Gerichtsstände der Ehefrauen, Kinder, Bevormundeten, Dienstboten auch neben Art. 18 Geltung behaupten.

3) Der Gerichtsstand dieses Artikels dauert nur so lange, als der Aufenthalt, welcher dazu Anlaß gibt.

Entsteht die Frage, ob er als beseitigt anzusehen sei, so ist vor Allem die Thatsache des Aufenthaltes in Betracht zu ziehen, in die Erörterung der Frage aber, ob etwa das veranlassende Vertragsverhältniß — der Pacht- oder Dienst-Vertrag — noch bestehe oder nicht, wird in der Regel nicht einzugehen sein. Auch dann nemlich, wenn der Aufenthalt nach Beendigung des Vertragsverhältnisses, jedoch aus Anlaß desselben, noch einige Zeit fortdauert, bleibt dem Geiste des Gesetzes gemäß, der Gerichtsstand begründet, denn sein Hauptgrund liegt in der längeren Dauer des Aufenthaltes, und das Vertrags-Verhältniß, welches diesen Aufenthalt veranlaßt hat, kommt nur insofern in Betracht, als durch dasselbe sich die Absicht des längeren Aufenthalts bekundet hat. Schon der Umstand, daß der Gesetzgeber jene Verhältnisse nur beispielsweise bezeichnet, deutet an, daß dem richterlichen Ermessen Raum gestattet sein soll.

4) Unter den „ähnlichen Verhältnissen", von welchen der Artikel spricht, sind solche zu verstehen, bei welchen in gleicher Weise, wie bei den angeführten Beispielen die Absicht längeren Aufenthalts vorauszusetzen ist. Es wurde zwar der Zusatz: „einen auf längere Dauer bemessenen

Aufenthalt", auf Vorschlag von Barth (I 12) beseitigt, allein nicht, weil man den Gesichtspunkt verwerflich fand, sondern, um nicht Anlaß zur Chicane zu geben.

5) Die Schlußworte: „wegen persönlicher Verbindlichkeiten" geben zu Zweifeln Veranlassung. — Die Kammer der Reichsräthe hat sie stillschweigend eingesetzt und die Kammer der Abgeordneten hat sie bei zweiter Lesung stillschweigend gebilligt.

Sollen sie bloß die dinglichen Mobiliarklagen ausschließen, oder aber hat der Ausdruck: „persönlich" eine weitergehende Bedeutung? Art. 18 ist dem Wesen nach dem Gesetzentwurfe der Nürnberger Commission über Rechtshülfe (§ 4) entnommen, welcher auch bei den Berathungen in Hannover als § 17 in Vorschlag gebracht worden ist (Verhdl. S. 433). Man hatte dort diesen Gerichtsstand, welchen man als besonderen bezeichnete, eingeschränkt auf Verbindlichkeiten, welche durch Verträge, Handlungen oder Unterlassungen der betreffenden Personen entstanden sind, und glaubte mit dieser Fassung namentlich alle Ansprüche aus Erbrechten ausgeschlossen zu haben. Schon damals wurde jedoch bemerkt, daß der Erbschaftsantritt, welcher fragliche Ansprüche begründe, eben auch eine persönliche Handlung sei. (Vhdl. S. 524.) Der Referent der Kammer der Reichsräthe (I 80) legte gleichfalls auf Ausschluß von Erbschaftsschulden besonderes Gewicht, jedoch geschah dies nicht zur Motivirung des fraglichen Zusatzes.

Außer Zweifel ist nun, daß unter persönlichen Verbindlichkeiten alle diejenigen zu verstehen sind, welche aus persönlich abgeschlossenen Verträgen oder aus widerrechtlichen Handlungen entstehen.

Wie verhält es sich nun aber 1) mit Verträgen, welche andere Personen abgeschlossen haben, Bevollmächtigte, Gesellschafter, der Mann für die Frau? 2) mit der Haftung aus Quasi-Contrakten oder für widerrechtliche Handlungen Anderer? 3) mit den persönlichen Verbindlichkeiten, welche sich bloß an den Besitz einer Sache knüpfen? 4) mit dem Eintritte in das ganze Schuldverhältniß einer anderen Person durch Erbschaft, Ehe?

Faßt man in's Auge, daß von Anfang an Art. 18 ganz allgemein sein sollte (Abg. I 18 und 19), daß ferner im Zweifel der natürliche Wortsinn entscheiden muß, hiernach aber persönliche Verbindlichkeiten solche sind, welche persönliche Klagen begründen, daß endlich der Richter nicht unterscheiden darf, wo das Gesetz nicht unterscheidet, so gelangt man zum Schlusse, daß durch fragliche Beschränkung bloß die dinglichen (Mobiliar-) Klagen betroffen werden und zwar trotzdem, daß eine bezügliche Absicht nirgends erklärt ist, im Gegentheile der Vortrag von Neumayr zu Art. 3 des Entwurfs gerade diese Klagen als solche bezeichnet, auf welche sich fraglicher Gerichtsstand zu erstrecken habe.

Will man weiter gehen, so darf man, mit Rücksicht auf oberwähnte Aeußerungen, die Beschränkung höchstens noch auf solche Fälle ausdehnen, wo die Verbindlichkeiten weder der Person des Beklagten gegenüber ursprünglich entstanden, noch von demselben speziell (durch Bürgschaft 2c.) übernommen worden sind. Dahin würden gehören Erbschaftsschulden und, der Gleichheit des Grundes wegen, Schulden, welche Mann oder Frau durch Eingehung der Ehe übernehmen.

6) Was Militärpersonen betrifft, so wurde in der Kammer der Reichsräthe die Ansicht konstatirt, daß Orte, wo sich dieselben vorübergehend auf Commando aufhalten, ohne Bedeutung seien, was übrigens sich aus der Fassung des Gesetzes von selbst ergibt.

Art. 19. — Personen, welche im Inlande weder einen Wohnsitz noch einen bekannten Aufenthalt haben, können vor den Gerichten eines jeden Orts in Bayern belangt werden, Ausländer von Ausländern jedoch vorbehaltlich besonderer gesetzlicher Bestimmung nur wegen solcher Verbindlichkeiten, die in Bayern entstanden sind.

Soweit Staatsverträge besondere Bestimmungen enthalten, finden diese Anwendung.

G. A. d. K. d. A. I S. 19—22. 80. 81. IV S. 13. 14. 36. 302. — K. d. R. I S. 82. IV 6.

1) Diese Verfügungen haben eine größere Tragweite, als es beim ersten Anblicke scheint. Sie regeln nicht blos den Gerichtsstand, sondern sie entscheiden nebenbei auch noch die sehr wichtige Frage, ob und unter welchen Voraussetzungen bayrische Gerichte berechtigt und verpflichtet seien, Rechtstreite unter Ausländern zu schlichten, eine Frage, welche vielleicht eine gesonderte Behandlung an einer anderen Stelle, verdient hätte.

2) Insofern verfügt wird, es solle, falls der Ausländer in Bayern weder Wohnsitz noch Aufenthalt habe, Klage von Ausländern gegen ihn nur unter gewissen Voraussetzungen statthaft sein, während Art. 12 eine derartige Beschränkung nicht enthält, erscheint als stillschweigend anerkannt, daß falls Ausländer Wohnsitz oder Aufenthalt in Bayern haben, sie gleich Inländern zu behandeln seien.

Es ist dies zwar der Absicht des Entwurfs (Art. 7) entgegen, wurde jedoch ausdrücklich als Ansicht der mit der Redaktion beauftragten Subcommission kundgegeben (Abg. I 81) und nicht wiedersprochen.

3) In Frage könnte gestellt werden, ob die Beschränkung des Klagerechts von Ausländern gegen Ausländer auch dann wegfalle, wenn ein besonderer Gerichtsstand gegeben ist, z. B., wenn der Vertrag zwar nicht in Bayern abgeschlossen wurde, jedoch nach ausdrücklicher Verabredung dort vollzogen werden soll (Art. 23).

In dieser Beziehung wird überall als selbstverständlich bezeichnet, daß die besonderen Gerichtsstände auch für Ausländer gelten (v. Neumayr Vortrag zu Art. 7 des Entwurfs), Abg. I 19 (v. Weiß) 20 und 21 (Vorschläge v. Umbscheiden u. Edel); allein es kann dies auch nur heißen, daß, falls ein Klagerecht bestehe, die besonderen Gerichtsstände zur Anwendung kommen. Im Entwurfe und im Vorschlage von Edel ist es offenbar so gemeint.

Die Subcommission (I 81) ging jedoch ohne Zweifel von einer wesentlich anderen Anschauung aus, nemlich davon, daß überall, wo nicht (wie in Art. 19) eine Beschränkung des Klagerechts unter Ausländern ausgesprochen sei, diese den Inländern gleich stehen. — Bei zweiter Lesung ist dies anerkannt im Vortrage zu Art. 33 (v. Neumayr).

Aus diesem Grunde hat man denn z. B. bei Art. 31 die Bestimmung des Art. 7 Abs. 3 des Entwurfes, daß im Falle der Connexität Wiederklagen auch unter Ausländern zulässig seien, als überflüssig beseitigt. Im nemlichen Sinne wurde, als man den Ausländern das Recht, gegen Ausländer Arrest anzulegen, einräumte, bemerkt, daß diese nunmehr auch die Hauptklage in foro arresti anstellen könnten. Abg. IV 13 in f. (Barth).

Der Sinn des Art. 19 ist also der:

„Insofern der Gerichtsstand sich blos auf „Art. 19 gründet, können Ausländer gegen Aus„länder nur klagen, wenn die Verbindlichkeit in „Bayern entstanden ist; in allen sonstigen Fällen „ist ihr Klagerecht nicht beschränkt.“

4) Soweit dem Ausländer ein Klagrecht versagt ist, ist der Richter nicht bloß berechtigt, sondern verpflichtet, die Klage zurückzuweisen und es kann nur fraglich sein, ob er dies auch von Amtswegen zu thun habe, oder aber, ob etwa durch Vereinbarung seine Unzuständigkeit beseitigt werden könne. Dürfte man im Mangel jener Voraussetzung nur den Grund zu einer gewöhnlichen Incompetenz-Einrede erblicken, so wäre Letzteres allerdings zu bejahen, allein dem ist nicht so.

Die bayerischen Gerichte haben zunächst die Aufgabe, für Inländer Recht zu sprechen und die Ausdehnung ihrer Zuständigkeit auf Prozesse unter Ausländern, so sehr sie auch den Forderungen des Zeitgeistes entspricht, erscheint immerhin nur als Ausnahme von dieser Grundregel. — Hat nun für einen gewissen Fall der Gesetzgeber seinen Willen kund gegeben, daß Klagen von Ausländern gegen Ausländer unstatthaft sein sollen, so liegt hierin nicht sowohl eine Competenzverfügung, als vielmehr die Versagung des Klagerechts aus Gründen der öffentlichen Ordnung. Es soll nicht ein bestimmtes Gericht, sondern es sollen alle bayrischen Gerichte unzuständig sein und hat daher jeder Richter die Klage zurückzuweisen, ohne Rücksicht auf den Willen der Parteien. Ausländer dürfen nicht nach Willkühr, für beliebige Rechtstreite, Zeit und Amtsthätigkeit des bayrischen Richters in Anspruch nehmen! vgl. Vortrag zu Art. 33 zweite Lesung (v. Neumayr).

5) Die Wortfassung: „welche im Inlande entstanden sind“ wurde absichtlich gewählt um auch andere als Vertragsverbindlichkeiten zu begreifen.

Es entstehen nun Verbindlichkeiten, welche sich aus Verträgen herleiten am Orte des Vertragsabschlusses; solche, welche sich aus Quasicontrakten herleiten, am Orte, wo die Handlung, aus welcher die Forderung entsteht (die Zahlung der Nichtschuld, die Geschäftsführung) stattfindet, solche welche sich aus dem Besitze einer Sache herleiten dort, wo der Beklagte die Sache in Besitz genommen hat, solche endlich, welche sich aus der Annahme einer Erbschaft herleiten, an jenem Orte, wo die Erbschaft sich eröffnet hat.

6) Es muß gleichgültig erscheinen, ob die Verbindlichkeit den Parteien selbst, oder aber ihren Rechtsvorgängern gegenüber in Bayern entstanden ist. Das Gesetz legt ausschließlich auf den Ort der Entstehung der Schuld an sich Gewicht und weder Wortlaut noch Geist desselben bedingen eine Unterscheidung.

7) Staatsverträge können (bezüglich der Klagen gegen Ausländer) besondere Bestimmungen treffen, also sowohl wegen der Zulässigkeit der Klage an sich, als auch bezüglich des zuständigen Gerichts. Es können die Verfügungen des Art. 19 eingeschränkt oder erweitert werden, jedoch liegt es im Geiste des Gesetzes, daß Ausländer nie besser gestellt werden können, als Inländer in gleicher Lage.

8) Der Gesetzgeber setzt voraus, daß der

Wohnsitz einer Person zu erforschen sein müsse, daß aber der Aufenthalt möglicherweise unbekannt bleiben könne. Der Richter wird eintretenden Falls zu prüfen haben, ob der Kläger die ihm obliegende Verpflichtung bezüglich Ermittlung des Aufenthaltes, genügend erfüllt habe oder nicht.

Art. 20. — Wird die Klage in gesetzlich zulässiger Weise gegen mehrere Personen gerichtet, so kann der Kläger sie bei den Gerichten eines jeden Orts erheben, an welchem der Gerichtsstand für einen der Beklagten nach Art. 12—17 begründet ist.

G. A. d. K. d. A. I S. 6. 7. 18. 19. 80. 81. IV S. 14. — K. d. R. I S. 83.

1) Hiermit ist zur Regelung der Zuständigkeit bei Belangung von Streitgenossen eine Einrichtung getroffen, welche in Frankreich von jeher bestanden und nie Mißstände ergeben hat.

2) Ist nach Lage der Sache Grund zu einer Streitgenossenschaft nicht gegeben (Art. 63), so hat der Richter bezüglich der nicht vor ihn gehörigen Personen seine Unzuständigkeit auszusprechen, falls diese nicht durch Vereinbarung beseitigt wird (Art. 39).

(Besondere Gerichtsstände.)

Art. 21. — Dingliche, Besitz-, Grenzscheidungs- und Theilungsklagen, welche ausschießlich oder auch nur zum Theile unbewegliche Sachen oder diesen gleichgeachtete Rechte zum Gegenstande haben, desgleichen alle gegen den Besitzer einer unbeweglichen Sache als solchen gerichteten Klagen sind bei den Gerichten des Orts anzubringen, wo die Sache liegt.

Bei den eine Grunddienstbarkeit oder Reallast betreffenden Klagen bestimmt sich der Gerichtsstand nach der Lage des dienenden oder belasteten Grundstücks.

Treffen mehrere Gerichtsstände dieser Art zusammen, so hat der Kläger unter denselben die Wahl.

G. A. d. K. d. A. I S. 22. 81. IV S. 14. 302. — K. d. R. I S. 83. IV S. 7.

1) Dieser Gerichtsstand schließt bezüglich der Streitsachen, für welche er gegeben ist, jeden anderen Gerichtsstand aus und kann sogar durch Vereinbarung nicht beseitigt werden (Art. 38 Ziff. 6), so daß, nach den Grundsätzen, welche unsere Prozeßordnung über die Wirkung der Unzuständigkeit aufstellt (Art. 265), diese sogar noch in der Kassationsinstanz (Art. 792) geltend gemacht werden kann.

Im Hinblicke auf diese *Folgen* ist es Pflicht des Richters, die Fälle, welche Art. 21 im Auge hat, genau zu sichten, mit Strenge alles nicht Hergehörige auszuscheiden und im Zweifel derjenigen Meinung den Vorzug zu geben, welche seine Tragweite beschränkt. Dieser Rath gilt dem Richter, für den klagenden Theil aber wird es umgekehrt rathsam sein, im Zweifel das Gericht der gelegenen Sache zu wählen, weil dieses wenigstens durch Vereinbarung zuständig werden kann, das andere nicht.

2) Weiter ist hervorzuheben, daß die beiden Art. 21 u. 22 fast wörtlich aus dem hannoveran. Entwurfe (§ 18 u. 19) entnommen worden sind, in welchen sie dem Wesen nach aus dem in Nürnberg beschlossenen Entwurfe eines deutschen Rechtshülfegesetzes übergegangen waren. Man wollte, in der Hoffnung, daß fragliche Bestimmungen auch im übrigen Deutschland Geltung erlangen würden, dieselben möglichst unverändert annehmen und hieraus leitet sich für die Gesetzesauslegung die Folgerung ab, daß den Ansichten, welche bei den Verhandlungen in Hannover sich geltend machten, Rechnung getragen werden muß.

3) Was den Begriff der dinglichen Klage anbelangt, ist auf die Bemerkung zu Art. 5 zu verweisen. — Die Pfandrechte, welche dort ausgenommen sind, erheischen hier eine nähere Besprechung.

Die Hypothekenklage in früherer Form ist durch die neue P. O. ziemlich gegenstandslos geworden. Der Gläubiger schreitet auf Grund seiner Notariatsurkunde oder seines Urtheiles sofort im Vollzugswege ein (Art. 822. 1040) und überläßt es dem Schuldner oder dritten Besitzer, durch Einspruch ihre Rechte geltend zu machen.

Bezüglich der Klagen auf Löschung von Hypotheken hat sich ein lebhafter Streit entsponnen, welcher auch jetzt noch gleiche Bedeutung hat. Es finden sich in den Blättern für R. verschiedenartige Erkenntnisse des Oberappell.-Gerichts (XVIII Erg. Bd. 13 u. XXIII 266) sowie Abhandlungen in verschiedenem Sinne (XXIV 4 ff. u. XXV 193 ff.).

Die nemliche Streitfrage besteht im französischen Rechte. (Journ. du Pal. [action dr. franç.] Nr. 136—140.) Für die Reduktionsklage ist in Art. 2159 u. 2161 Code civ. eine besondere Bestimmung gegeben, welche fortbesteht. Einf. Ges. Art. 110.

Der Eigenthümer, welcher auf Löschung einer Hypothek klagt, beansprucht allerdings die Freiheit seines Eigenthums von einer dinglichen Last, allein deßhalb allein ist seine Klage nicht nothwendig eine dingliche.

Gründet er nemlich seine Klage nur auf eine persönliche Verpflichtung, welche dem Beklagten ihm gegenüber obliegt z. B. auf die aus dem Hypothekenbestellungs-Vertrage entspringende Pflicht des Gläubigers, nach Tilgung der Schuld, die Hypothek zu löschen, so ist diese Klage rein persönlich, ganz ebenso, als wenn er etwa auf Vollzug eines besonderen Vertrages klagen würde, durch welchen sich der Gläubiger zur Löschung innerhalb bestimmter Frist verpflichtet hätte. Mit Wegfall der Forderung fällt von selbst auch die Hypothek als Zubehör und das Begehren der Löschung bildet ein bloßes Accessorium im Rechtsstreite über das Bestehen der Forderung. vgl. Bl. f. R. XI 34. XXV 191.

Gleiches wird wohl gelten müssen, falls der Schuldner gegen den Gläubiger Klage erhebt auf Vernichtung oder Auflösung des die Forderung und Hypothek-Bestellung bedingenden Vertrags und in Folge hiervon die Löschung beansprucht.

Anders ist es jedoch, wenn nicht auf Grund persönlicher Verpflichtung geklagt wird, wenn z. B. der dritte Besitzer auf Löschung klagt, denn in diesem Falle hat die Klage vollkommen die Natur einer Negatorienklage.

5) Daß der Gerichtsstand der gelegenen Sache den Charakter der Ausschließlichkeit nicht verliert durch Nebenforderungen, welche, als von der dinglichen Klage abhängend (als Nebensache im Sinne des Art. 33 Abs. 3), geltend gemacht werden, z. B. mit der Vindikation Ersatz der mala fide gezogenen Früchte, mit der Klage auf Anerkennung einer Reallast, Einforderung rückständiger Leistungen, ist selbstverständlich, obgleich auch hier das Gegentheil schon behauptet worden ist. Carré quest. 259.

Jeder Zweifel ist übrigens jetzt beseitigt durch die Bestimmung, daß Art. 21 anwendbar sei, wenn auch die Klage nur theilweise unbewegliche Sachen zum Gegenstande habe, womit zugleich gesagt ist, daß, wenn theilweise unbewegliche, theilweise bewegliche Sachen vindizirt werden, die bezüglich der Ersteren begründete Zuständigkeit überwiegt.

6) Wie ist es nun aber, wenn dingliche und persönliche Klagen gehäuft werden, wenn z. B. zugleich aus dinglichen und aus persönlichen Rechtsgründen geklagt wird, oder wenn die Resolutionsklage zugleich gegen den Schuldner und gegen den dritten Besitzer angestellt wird? Kann hier der Kläger seinen persönlichen Anspruch bei dem Gerichte des Wohnortes anbrigen und auf Grund des Art. 33 Abs. 1 den connexen dinglichen Anspruch damit verbinden?

Im Allgemeinen ist zwar nicht zu bestreiten, daß Art. 33 Abs. 1 auch auf den Gerichtsstand des Art. 21 Anwendung findet, allein bei der Ausschließlichkeit, welche der Gesetzgeber diesem Gerichtsstande gegeben hat, wird anzunehmen sein, daß der Kläger in Fällen solcher Art verpflichtet sei, das Gericht der gelegenen Sache zu wählen; jedenfalls wird dies sehr rathsam sein.

7) Art. 21 spricht nur von „Klagen", hat also nicht jene Fälle im Auge, wo durch das Vorbringen einer Partei im Laufe eines Rechtsstreites (durch Einreden, Repliken) Streit über ein dingliches Recht entsteht. Ohne Zweifel liegt es nicht in der Absicht des Gesetzes, daß bei solchen Zwischenfragen dinglicher Art vom angegangenen Bezirksgerichte an ein anderes Bezirksgericht verwiesen werden müsse, wie es nach Art. 3—11 bei Conflikten verschiedenartiger Gerichte vorgeschrieben ist. Art. 33 muß hier Maß geben, denn daß in solchen Fällen Connexität vorliege, ist wohl nicht zu bezweifeln.

8) Was die Besitzklagen betrifft, so ist nur zu erwähnen, daß diese Bestimmung auch in der Pfalz Anwendung findet, denn es ist zwar Art. 3 Ziff. 2 Code de proc., nicht aber auch der den Gerichtsstand bestimmende Eingang jenes Artikels aufrecht erhalten (Einf. Ges. Art. 67). Man könnte diese Thatsache für belanglos halten, da hier wie dort vom Gerichte des Orts der gelegenen Sache die Rede ist; allein sie ist in so fern nicht ohne Bedeutung, als die besondere Auslegung, welche die französische Jurisprudenz dem Ausdrucke: »objet litigieux« gegeben hat, z. B. bezüglich der Servituten, des Wasserlaufes 2c., jetzt keinen Werth mehr hat.

9) Welche Klagen richten sich gegen den Besitzer einer Sache als solchen?

Der erste Gedanke ist wohl, daß die actiones in rem scriptae gemeint seien, allein liest man das Referat zweiter Lesung zu Hauptst. 26 Art. 12 und die Aeußerungen des Ministerial-Commissärs (Abg. III 12), so wird man irre. Gehört die Ersatzklage desjenigen, welcher statt eines Besitzers Grundsteuern zahlt, hierher, so gehören alle Fälle hierher, wo Jemand als negotiorum gestor Auslagen, welche sich auf eine Sache beziehen, gemacht hat, wo also aus Anlaß eines Besitzes ein Anspruch entstanden ist, gleichviel, ob der Besitz zur Zeit der Klagserhebung noch fortdauert oder nicht. Man darf billig fragen, ob Grund vorgelegen hätte, für Fälle dieser Art einen ausschließlichen Gerichtsstand der Lage der Sache zu schaffen.

10) Offenbar ist aber auch der Sinn der fraglichen Bestimmung ein ganz anderer, und um das Richtige zu finden, muß auf die Verhand-

lungen in Hannover zurückgegangen werden, aus welchen dieselbe genau in der Fassung, wie sie vorliegt, hervorgegangen ist.

Dort hatte Niemand den mindesten Zweifel, daß ausschließlich nur die actiones in rem scriptae gemeint seien, d. h. jene persönlichen Klagen, welche gleich den dinglichen Klagen den Besitzer als solchen angreifen. Es wurde dies ausdrücklich als einstimmige Ansicht kundgegeben und ein Vorschlag, die Worte: »actiones in rem scriptae« eingeschaltet beizufügen, nur deßhalb verworfen, weil dies selbstverständlich sei und lateinische Worte in einem deutschen Gesetze vermieden werden müßten.

Hierzu kommt, daß ein Antrag, dahin gehend, auch rein persönliche Klagen, wenn dieselben aus dem Besitze des Grundstückes oder aus Handlungen fließen, welche der Beklagte als Besitzer vorgenommen hat, sowie alle Klagen auf Einräumung und Wiedererlangung eines Grundstückes, dem Gerichte der gelegenen Sache zuzuweisen, als ungeeignet und prinzipwidrig verworfen worden ist. Verhdl. S. 439 u. 440.

11) Ist nun klar, was man in Hannover wollte, so ist auch sicher, was man bei uns wollte, denn fragliche Worte wurden, wie der ganze Artikel 21, ohne eingehende Diskussion angenommen, weil man eben nichts Anderes verfügen wollte, die erwähnten Aeußerungen aber haben nur den Charakter und Werth gelegentlicher Bemerkungen.

Diese Auslegung entspricht übrigens auch dem natürlichen Wortsinne, da Klagen nur dann gegen den Besitzer als solchen sich richten, wenn sie sich an den Besitz des Beklagten knüpfen, nicht aber auch, wenn sie unabhängig davon fortbestehen.

Sie ist um so mehr die richtige, als sie sich an das bestehende Recht anschließt, denn die bayer. G. O. Cap. I § 9 hat, wenn sie von Klagen spricht, „welche mehr auf die Sache selbst, als auf die Person gehen," hauptsächlich die actiones in rem scriptae im Auge (weil sie naturam et indolem realium actionum an sich haben), wie dies aus den Anmerkungen zu jener Stelle, sowie zum bayer. L. R. Thl. II Cap. I § 11 Ziff. 3 in f. klar hervorgeht.

12) Als Klagen, welche sich gegen den Besitzer als solchen richten, sind daher z. B. zu betrachten die actio quod metus causa und die actio Pauliana, insofern mittelst derselben Grundstücke vom redlichen dritten Besitzer zurückverlangt werden.

13) In der Pfalz kennt man actiones in rem scriptae dem Namen nach nicht, wohl aber der Sache nach, denn es gibt allerdings Klagen, zufolge deren Jemand nur deßhalb, weil er eine Sache sine causa im Besitze hat und durch deren Besitz bereichert ist, in Anspruch genommen werden kann.

Man wird sich gegebenen Falles fragen müssen, ob das Klagerecht am Besitze der Sache haftet oder aber, ob es auch gegeben wäre (als Entschädigungsklage), wenn Beklagter nicht mehr im Besitze wäre. — Will man z. B. die Resolutions- oder Nichtigkeits-Klage gegen den redlichen dritten Besitzer nicht als dinglich gelten lassen, so ist sie jedenfalls eine solche, welche sich gegen den Besitzer als solchen richtet.

Die Klagen, welche aus Art. 1384 u. 1386 Code civ. für denjenigen entstehen, welcher durch die unbewegliche Sache eines Anderen beschädigt worden ist, gehören nicht hierher.

14) Bei Klagen, welche den Wasserlauf eines Flusses betreffen, kommt jene Stelle des Flusses in Betracht, wo die in Frage stehenden Vorrichtungen zum Wässern u. s. w. beansprucht werden, nicht aber etwa jene, wo ein mehrere Stunden abwärts liegendes Mühlwerk Schaden erleidet.

15) Der Umstand, daß in Fällen, wo Grundstücke in verschiedenen Gerichtsbezirken liegen, dem Kläger ein unbedingtes Klagerecht gegeben wird, möchte andeuten, daß man auf die Ausschließlichkeit des betr. Gerichtsstandes einen besonders großen Werth nicht legte, denn es kann z. B. die Klage auf Theilung einer großen Masse von Immobilien in einen fremden Gerichtsbezirk gezogen werden, wenn auch nur die kleinste Parzelle dort gelegen ist.

16) Ueber die Frage ob unter „Theilungsklagen" auch Klagen auf Erbtheilung gemeint seien, siehe den folgenden Art. Nr. 4.

Art. 22. — **In Verlassenschaftssachen können:**

1) Klagen, welche das Erbrecht, den Besitz der Erbschaft, die Geltendmachung von Ansprüchen aus Vermächtnissen oder sonstigen Verfügungen auf den Todesfall oder die Theilung der Erbschaft betreffen,

2) Klagen der Erbschaftsgläubiger

vor den Gerichten, bei welchen der Erblasser zur Zeit seines Ablebens nach Art. 12—14 seinen allgemeinen Gerichtsstand gehabt hat, erhoben werden, die unter Ziff. 2 bezeichneten jedoch nur, so lange der Nachlaß als solcher ganz oder theilweise noch im Gerichtsbezirke vorhanden oder, wenn der Erben mehrere sind, noch nicht getheilt ist.

G. A. d. K. d. A. I S. 22. 81. IV S. 14. 15. — K. d. R. S. 84. 85.

1) Ziff. 1 trifft alle Klagen, vermittelst welcher Ansprüche auf eine Erbschaft oder auf Theile derselben verfolgt oder bereinigt werden und zwar können sie ohne Beschränkung auf eine gewisse Zeit oder auf gewisse Umstände, unbedingt immer am Gerichte der Erbschaft erhoben werden.

2) Die erste sich darbietende Frage ist, in welchem Verhältnisse Art. 22 zu Art. 21 steht, ob er die Ausschließlichkeit des Gerichtsstandes der gelegenen Sache beschränkt, oder aber, ob in Fällen, wo Art. 21 anwendbar ist, die Anwendnng des Art. 22 wegfällt.

Nach den natürlichen Regeln der Auslegung, nach der bestimmten Aeußerung des Referenten v. Neumayr, endlich nach den Verhandlungen in Hannover kann nicht bezweifelt werden, daß Letzteres der Sinn des Gesetzes sei. — Mit Einführung der neuen P. O. ist daher der ausschließliche Gerichtsstand der Erbschaft, wie ihn der französische Prozeß unbedingt bis zur Theilung, der bayerische Prozeß wenigstens bis zur förmlichen Besitzeinweisung (Anshändigung) anerkannt hat, aufgehoben.

3) Dies gilt selbstverständlich nur für die streitige Rechtspflege, für die Verlassenschafts-Behandlung aber ist am bestehenden Rechte nichts geändert.

Ebenso gilt in der Pfalz für die nicht streitige Rechtspflege, wozu z. B. Theilungs-Ermächtigungen und Theilungs-Homologationen gehören, bei welchen das Gericht bloß die Zustimmung Rechtsunfähiger zu ergänzen hat, auch in Zukunft noch der Artikel 59 Code de proc. — (Vgl. ferner Einf. Ges. Art. 94 und 95).

Bezüglich Eröffnung des erbschaftlichen Liquidations-Prozesses nach preuß. L. R. gilt Art. 54 des Einf. Ges.

4) Es entsteht nun die weitere Frage, ob auch für die Erbtheilungsklage sowie für die hereditatis petitio, falls diese die Masse im Ganzen betrifft, der Gerichtsstand der gelegenen Sache entscheide, falls Immobilien in der Masse sind.

Die Tragweite dieser Fragen wird sich am besten ermessen lassen, wenn ein greller Fall in's Licht gezogen wird.

Man setze den Fall, daß eine in Bamberg wohnhafte Person mit Hinterlassung eines bedeutenden Mobiliar-Vermögens stirbt und zum Nachlasse auch ein Stück Land gehört, welches der Erblasser, sei es aus Veranlassung eines früheren Aufenthalts, sei es auf Grund einer Erbschaft, in Zweibrücken besaß.

Soll nun das Gericht in Zweibrücken ausschließlich zuständig sein für die Erbtheilung, obgleich der ganze Nachlaß sich in Bamberg befindet, obgleich alle Erben dort wohnen und die Theilung nach Bamberger Landrecht (dessen Geist so schwer zu ermitteln ist) vorgenommen werden muß? Man erwäge dabei noch, daß diese Unzuständigkeit nicht durch Vereinbarung gedeckt werden könnte, daß sie von Amtswegen berücksichtigt werden müßte, daß endlich aus der Klage wahrscheinlich gar nicht ersichtlich ist, ob und welche Liegenschaften zur Masse gehören, dies sich vielmehr erst bei den Theilungsverhandlungen ergeben wird!

5) Unmöglich ist dem Gesetzgeber die Absicht zuzutrauen, etwas derartiges einzuführen und es erscheint daher die Annahme berechtigt, daß der Art. 21 jene Fälle, wo eine Erbmasse im Ganzen (mit allen ihren Aktiven und Passiven) Gegenstand des Rechtsstreites ist, gar nicht treffen will.

Vorerst ist zu bemerken, daß die Worte: „ausschließlich oder auch nur zum Theile ꝛc.“ in Art. 21 nicht etwa dahin gedeutet werden dürfen, als hätten sie vorzugsweise den Fall einer Erbmasse im Auge. Jene Worte wurden im Reichsrathe stillschweigend eingesetzt und ohne weitere Erörterung, als daß sie eigentlich selbstverständlich seien, belassen.

Die Quelle zur richtigen Auslegung des Gesetzes bilden auch hier wiederum die Verhandlungen in Hannover, indem man im Bestreben, das dort sowie in Nürnberg Vereinbarte möglichst unverändert anzunehmen, auf tieferes Eingehen in die Sache verzichtete. K. d. R. I 84 (v. Bayer.)

In dem den erbschaftlichen Gerichtsstand bestimmenden § 19 des hannoveran. Entwurfs ist zum Schlusse ausdrücklich ausgesprochen, es solle hierdurch der Gerichtsstand der belegenen Sache (§ 17) nicht berührt werden. Nichtsdestoweniger und trotzdem, daß § 17 gleichfalls die Theilungsklagen benennt, sprach nach längerer Debatte die Commission ihre Ansicht dahin aus, daß jener Vorbehalt sich auf Universalklagen, nemlich die hereditatis petitio und die actio familiae erciscundae, nicht beziehe, weil diese Klagen gar nicht Gegenstand des § 17 bildeten. — Es ist zu bemerken, daß jener § 17 allerdings etwas anders gefaßt war, als unser Art. 21, indem es dort hieß: „Für dingliche Klagen, mit Inbegriff der Theilungsklagen“; allein offenbar sollte durch die veränderte Redaktion in der Sache nichts geändert werden. — Verhdl. S. 499—501 u. 519—521.

6) Diese Auslegung des Gesetzes, welche dem Geiste desselben entschieden entspricht, läßt sich auch mit dem Wortlaute recht gut in Einklang bringen.

Wenn Art. 21 von Klagen spricht, welche unbewegliche Sachen zum Gegenstande haben, so meint er Sachen, welche für sich allein in Betracht kommen, auf welche sich die Klage direkt richtet und welche ebendeßhalb in der Ladung zu bezeichnen sind.

Eine Erbschaft im Ganzen, ein Vermögen, bildet aber eine Sache für sich, bei der die einzelnen Bestandtheile in den Hintergrund treten. vgl. Weiske Rechtslexikon Bd. XV S. 678.

Es mag davon abgesehen werden, daß die Erbschaft, so lange sie nicht angetreten ist, sogar als juristische Person behandelt wird, jedenfalls macht sich deren Rechtseinheit in sehr bedeutender Weise auch sonst geltend, wie denn z. B. aus derselben sich der Grundsatz herleitet, daß für alle das Erbrecht betreffenden Fragen nur die Gesetze des Ortes, wo die Erbschaft ihren Wohnsitz hat, maßgebend sind, gleichviel, wo die einzelnen Masse-Bestandtheile sich befinden.

7) Demgemäß geschieht dem Texte des Gesetzes keine Gewalt, wenn man Klagen, welche die Erbmasse im Ganzen betreffen, d. h. Klagen auf Anerkennung des Erbrechts oder auf Aushändigung der Erbschaft im Ganzen oder auf Erbtheilung nicht darunter begriffen erklärt.

Unter Theilungsklagen würde daher Art. 21 nur die actio communi dividundo verstehen, wohin allerdings auch die Klage auf Theilung von Erbmassegegenständen, welche unvertheilt geblieben waren, gehört.

Schließlich möge erwähnt sein, daß offenbar auch Reichsrath v. Bayer (I 84) das Verhältniß beider Artikel in diesem Sinne aufgefaßt hat.

8) Läßt sich nun auch in dieser Weise ein Mißstand glücklich beseitigen, so ist ein anderer Mißstand leider nicht zu beseitigen, nemlich der, daß der Gerichtsstand des Art. 22 in jeder Beziehung bloß fakultativ ist und also z. B. Erbtheilungsklagen am Wohnorte eines beliebigen Miterben angebracht werden können.

Es lagen offenbar viel gewichtigere Gründe (z. B. daß fast in jedem Gerichtsbezirke ein anderes Erbrecht gilt) dafür vor, für Erbtheilungen einen ausschließlichen Gerichtsstand zu schaffen, als für Vindikationen und sonstige dingliche Klagen und es ist wirklich auffallend, daß dieses praktische Bedürfniß nicht einmal in Anregung gebracht worden ist, obgleich in der Pfalz ein derartiger Gerichtsstand besteht, obgleich ferner er auch diesseits, sogar im Kampfe gegen die Gerichtsordnung, aus der Praxis sich bis zu gewissem Grade herausgebildet hatte (Bl. f. R. XVII 281. XIX 65 ff. Stürzer Ger. Verf. S. 193), obgleich endlich auch das Rechtshülfegesetz (§ 9) ihn anerkannte.

Uebrigens wird der eigene Vortheil die Erben dazu führen, den erbschaftlichen Gerichtsstand zu wählen.

9) Klagen der Erbschafts-Gläubiger können nur eine bestimmte Zeit lang vor dem Gerichte der Erbschaft angebracht werden und zwar ist zu unterscheiden zwischen dem Falle, wo nur ein Erbe vorhanden ist und dem Falle, wo der Erben mehrere sind. — In letzterem Falle hört jener Gerichtsstand mit Abschluß der Erbtheilung auf, d. h. mit demjenigen Rechtsakte, durch welchen die Erbschaft im Ganzen bereinigt wird, mögen auch noch einzelne Massegegenstände ungetheilt beiben.

10) Die Theilung, welche hier das Gesetz im Auge hat, ist keine bloß faktische, sondern eine rechtliche und es wird daher nicht bloß erforderlich sein, daß sie der Form nach gültig sei, sondern auch, daß die etwa erforderlichen Genehmigungen und gerichtlichen Bestätigungen erfolgt seien, wenn die Klage der Erbschafts-Gläubiger unzulässig werden soll. Verhdl. in Hannover. S. 457. — Uebrigens werden diese im Zweifel den allgem. Gerichtsstand eines der Erben wählen.

11) Ist nur ein Erbe vorhanden, so sollte, nach dem Entwurfe, der Gerichtsstand dauern bis zur gerichtlichen Besitzeinweisung resp. Aushändigung des Nachlasses; allein in Erwägung, daß man in der Pfalz, bei gewöhnlichen Erben, keine solche Besitzeinweisung kennt, nahm man die durch gleiche Erwägungen veranlaßte Fassung des hannoveran. Entwurfes an, welche man jedoch dahin vervollständigte, daß der Nachlaß „als solcher" noch im Gerichtsbezirke vorhanden sein müsse.

12) Wie man sich einen Fall zu denken habe, wo der Nachlaß, welchen ein einziger Erbe in Besitz genommen, noch als solcher im Gerichtsbezirke vorhanden sei, ist schwer zu bestimmen.

Am besten kommt man in's Klare, wenn man sich die Idee, welche den Gesetzgeber geleitet hat, vergegenwärtigt. — Es sollte für den Fall Vorsorge getroffen werden, wo ein Auswärtiger Erbe wird, welcher auswärts wohnen bleibt.

Derselbe wird natürlich die Masse theils an seinen Wohnort verbringen, theils versilbern und nach kurzer Frist am Orte der Erbschaft nichts weiter mehr besitzen, als etwa einige Immobilien, welche er für zweckmäßig fand, nicht zu veräußern.

So lange nun diese, die Verschmelzung des Nachlasses mit dem Vermögen des Erben bezweckende, faktische Vereinigung noch nicht vollendet ist, macht sich der Nachlaß als solcher geltend; später erscheint er mit dem Vermögen des Erben vermischt. — Das Meiste wird hier immer dem richterlichen Ermessen überlassen bleiben.

Diesseits fällt der Gerichtsstand der Erbschaft für die Erbschafts-Gläubiger jedenfalls nie vor der Besitzeinweisung weg.

Art. 23. — **Ist die Erfüllung eines Vertrags nur an einem bestimmten Orte möglich oder der Ort derselben in dem Vertrage ausdrücklich bezeichnet, so können bei den Gerichten dieses Orts sowohl die Klagen auf Erfüllung oder Aufhebung des Vertrages, als die auf Entschädigung wegen Nichterfüllung oder nicht gehöriger Erfüllung erhoben werden.**

G. A. d. K. d. A. I S. 23. 82. — K. d. R. I S. 85.

1) Dieser Gerichtsstand beruht auf der Idee einer freiwilligen Unterwerfung, und hauptsächlich hierauf gründet sich die Bedingung, daß der Ort der Erfüllung im Vertrage ausdrücklich bezeichnet sein müsse. Dieses Wort ist streng zu nehmen, und können Umstände des Falles oder gesetzliche Bestimmungen, mag sich aus denselben auch noch so sicher der Erfüllungsort folgern lassen, nicht genügen.

Auch bei den Verhandlungen in Hannover nahm man das Wort in diesem Sinne und wurde deßhalb, weil man anders beschloß, gesagt: „nach ausdrücklicher oder stillschweigender Uebereinkunft, nach der Natur der Sache, oder nach gesetzlicher Bestimmung.“ Auch die gleiche Verfügung in G. O. Cap. I § 6 in f. wurde so ausgelegt.

2) Spricht man vom Orte der Erfüllung, so denkt man nur an eine bestimmte Leistung; bei zweiseitigen Verträgen kommen aber Leistungen auf beiden Seiten in Betracht.

Es kann nun vorkommen, daß diese Leistungen an verschiedenen Orten stattfinden sollen, oder daß für die eine Leistung der Ort der Erfüllung ausdrücklich bestimmt ist, für die andere aber nicht. Es kann auch vorkommen, daß für jede Leistung ausdrücklich ein anderer Erfüllungsort festgesetzt ist, z. B. wenn bedungen ist, es solle der Verkäufer am Orte A liefern, und der Käufer, nach bestimmter Frist, am Orte B den Kaufpreis zahlen. Wo ist in solchen Fällen der Erfüllungsort?

3) Man könnte sagen, daß dem Wortlaute des Gesetzes gemäß der Gerichtsstand des Erfüllungsortes nur dann gegeben sei, wenn der ganze Vertrag, d. h. die beiderseitigen Leistungen an einem bestimmten Orte zu erfüllen seien; allein dies ist offenbar nicht der Sinn des Gesetzes und würde auch den Grundsätzen, wie sie bis jetzt gelten, widerstreiten.

4) Faßt man nun vorbezeichnete Fälle in's Auge, so eignen sich Klagen auf Erfüllung, sowie auf Entschädigung wegen Nichterfüllung ausschließlich nur für den Ort, wo der Beklagte zu erfüllen hatte. — Gerade hieraus folgt aber, daß das Gesetz nicht meint, es solle die Festsetzung des Erfüllungsortes bezüglich einer der beiderseitigen Leistungen beiden Theilen gegenüber den Gerichtsstand bestimmen; daß also auch, was die Klage auf Aufhebung des Vertrages betrifft, bloß der Ort in's Auge zu fassen ist, wo für den Beklagten die Erfüllung ausdrücklich bedungen war.

So hat es der hannov. Entwurf (§ 20) ausdrücklich verfügt, nachdem es vorher (Verhdl. S. 466 u. 469) als selbstverständlich bezeichnet worden war.

Es entspricht dies im Grunde auch dem vermuthbaren Willen der Contrahenten; denn wenn auch die Annahme erlaubt ist, es verpflichte sich derjenige, welcher sich verbindlich macht, einen Vertrag an einem bestimmten Orte zu erfüllen, hiemit auch, am nemlichen Orte Recht zu nehmen, so gilt doch nicht Gleiches von demjenigen, welcher dort bloß zum Empfange berechtigt erscheint.

5) Auch wenn nur für einen Theil der Leistung ein Erfüllungsort ausdrücklich bestimmt ist, kann die Erfüllung dieses Theiles, sowie alle sich daran knüpfenden Folgen, ja sogar die Aufhebung des Vertrages wegen Nichtigkeit dort geltend gemacht werden.

6) Die Unmöglichkeit der Erfüllung an einem andern Orte ist z. B. gegeben, wenn Jemand ein Grundstück zu überliefern, eine Reparatur an Gebäulichkeiten zu machen hat u. s. w.

Für die Pfalz gelten, laut Einf. Ges. Art. 64, die Wirkungen, welche sich an die Erwählung eines Wohnsitzes für die Vertragserfüllung bezüglich des Gerichtsstandes knüpfen (Art. 111 Cod. civ.), fort.

Art. 24. — **Kaufleute, welche ihre Hauptniederlassung außerhalb ihres Wohnsitzes haben, können wegen aller Ansprüche aus Handelssachen, desgleichen aus Wechseln oder kaufmännischen Anweisungen auch bei den Gerichten des Orts belangt werden, wo sich diese Niederlassung befindet.**

Art. 25. — **Kaufleute, Handels- und sonstige Gesellschaften, sowie Genossenschaften, welche an einem andern Orte als dem ihrer Hauptniederlassung beziehungsweise ihres Sitzes Zweigniederlassungen oder Agenturen haben, von denen aus Geschäfte geschlossen oder vermittelt werden,**

können wegen aller Ansprüche an die Zweigniederlassung oder aus den von ihren Agenturen abgeschlossenen oder vermittelten Geschäften auch bei den Gerichten des Orts belangt werden, wo sich die Zweigniederlassung beziehungsweise die Agentur befindet.

G. A. d. K. d. A. I S. 18. 81. 298 IV S. 15. — K. d. R. I S. 85.

1) Diese beiden Artikel enthalten eine Ausdehnung und Verbesserung von Art. 65 des Einf. Ges. zum H. G. B., unter Herbeiziehen der Bestimmungen von § 16 Abs. 1 des hannoveranischen Entwurfes.

Durch Art. 24 ist für Kaufleute, welche den Sitz ihres Handelsgeschäftes außerhalb ihres Wohnortes haben, ein zweiter allgemeiner Gerichtsstand, jedoch nur für Handelssachen, gegründet.

2) In Art. 25 mußten, da es sich um Gründung eines Gerichtsstandes für Zweig-Niederlassungen und Agenturen handelte, auch die Handels-Gesellschaften berücksichtigt werden, und dabei wurden die bezüglichen Bestimmungen, im Einklange mit Art. 16, auch auf gewöhnliche Gesellschaften und Genossenschaften ausgedehnt. — Das zu Art. 16 Gesagte gilt auch hier.

3) Hervorzuheben ist, daß Art. 25 sich nicht beschränkt, von Ansprüchen aus Handelssachen zu sprechen, was übrigens schon wegen des Hereinziehens gewöhnlicher Gesellschaften nicht der Fall sein konnte. Hieraus scheint sich der Widerspruch zu ergeben, daß Klagen, welche keine Handelssachen betreffen, falls sie aus Rechtsgeschäften der Zweig-Niederlassung hervorgehen, einen gesonderten Gerichtsstand der Niederlassung haben, falls sie aber aus Rechtsgeschäften der Haupt-Niederlassung hervorgehen, nicht. — Diese Anomalie erklärt sich dadurch, daß Art. 24 dem § 65 des besagten Einf. Ges., Art. 25 aber dem § 16 Abs. 1 des hannov. Entwurfes entstammt.

Selbstverständlich erscheint jedoch, daß der Gerichtsstand des Art. 25 auch für die Haupt-Niederlassung zu gelten hat. Uebrigens werden nicht leicht Fälle vorkommen, wo Geschäfte, welche Handels-Niederlassungen, ihrer Bestimmung gemäß, abschließen, keine Handelsgeschäfte sind.

Art. 26. — Personen, welche außerhalb ihres Wohnsitzes ein mit Wohn- und Wirthschaftsgebäuden versehenes Gut als Eigenthümer, Nutznießer oder Pächter bewirthschaften oder bewirthschaften lassen, können wegen aller auf die Bewirthschaftung des Guts sich beziehenden Rechtsverhältnisse auch bei den Gerichten belangt werden, in deren Bezirk das Gut gelegen ist.

G. A. d. K. d. A. I S. 18. 19. 81 IV S. 15. — K. d. R. I S. 85.

1) Dieser Artikel ist fast wörtlich dem hannov. Entwurfe (§ 16 Abs. 2) entlehnt. Dort wird der betreffende Gerichtsstand, als G. der Niederlassung bezeichnet und dem G. der Handelsniederlassung (§ 16 Abs. 1) zur Seite gestellt.

Offenbar beruht er, ebenso wie der vorhergehende Artikel (25) auf der Annahme, es unterwerfe sich derjenige, welcher an einem Orte außerhalb seines Wohnsitzes ein selbständiges Erwerbsgeschäft gründet, für alle darauf bezüglichen Rechtsgeschäfte, stillschweigend der Gerichtsbarkeit dieses Ortes.

2) Hieraus wäre eigentlich zu folgern, daß dieser Gerichtsstand, gleich demjenigen des Art. 23 fortdauere, so lange ein in der Periode der Bewirthschaftung entstandenes Rechtsverhältniß zu bereinigen sei, ohne Rücksicht, ob die Bewirthschaftung selbst fortdauere; allein dies würde nicht dem Willen des Gesetzgebers entsprechen, da Referent sowohl als Ministerial-Commissär auf Anfrage übereinstimmend erklärt haben, es erlösche der Gerichtsstand einem Pächter gegenüber mit Aufhören des Pachtverhältnisses (Abg. I 19), und diese Erklärung nirgends Widerspruch gefunden hat.

Demgemäß dauert der in Frage stehende Gerichtsstand nur so lange, als die Bewirthschaftung des Gutes für Rechnung der betreffenden Person, — in gleicher Weise, wie der Gerichtsstand des Art. 18 so lange dauert, als der Aufenthalt. — Allerdings dürfte Art. 26, um diesen Sinn auszudrücken, besser redigirt sein.

3) Das Gut muß sich durch eigene Wohn- und Wirthschafts-Gebäude, als ein selbständiges, für sich bestehendes Wirthschaftsgut ankündigen.

Ebenso ist erforderlich, daß es sich um ein wirkliches Wirthschaftsgut handele, zu dessen Dienste die Gebäulichkeiten bestimmt sind, nicht aber umgekehrt um ein Landhaus, zu dem etliche Grundstücke gehören.

4) Was die Rechtsverhältnisse anbelangt, welche sich auf die Bewirthschaftung beziehen, so hat man zunächst an Anschaffungen von Werkzeugen, Stoffen u. s. w. zu Wirthschaftszwecken, an Herstellung und Einrichtung von Wirthschaftsgebäuden, endlich an den Absatz der Produkte zu denken — kurz an alles das, was, falls die Bewirthschaftung eines Gutes ein Handelsgewerbe sein könnte, als Handelsgeschäft zu betrachten sein würde.

Selbstverständlich muß aber die Beziehung zur Bewirthschaftung vollkommen klar und sicher sein; wenn daher auch Darlehen, welche ausdrücklich zu Wirthschaftszwecken gemacht worden sind, als hierher gehörig erscheinen können, insbesondere, wenn die wirkliche Verwendung feststeht, so kann doch von Vermuthungen, wie sie Art. 274 des H. G. B. aufstellt, selbstverständlich die Rede nicht sein.

5) Was insbesondere die Pächter betrifft, so kommt hier zunächst nicht ihr Verhältniß zu den Verpächtern (der Pachtvertrag) in Betracht, wie im Falle des Art. 6 Ziff. 1, sondern ihr Verhältniß zu dritten Personen, aus Anlaß der Bewirthschaftung.

Uebrigens ist zu bemerken, daß bezüglich des Pachtes der Art. 18 fast immer den Art. 26 überflüssig machen wird, da der Fall, wo Aufenthalt und Bewirthschaftung nicht gleichzeitig endigen, ein sehr seltener ist.

Art. 27. — Klagen aus einer geführten Verwaltung können bei den Gerichten des Orts angestellt werden, wo die Verwaltung geführt wurde.

Diese Gerichte sind ausschließend zuständig, wenn die Obrigkeit des Orts die Verwaltung angeordnet hat.

G. A. d. K. d. A. I S. 23. 82. IV 15. — K. d. R. I S. 85.

1) Der Gerichtsstand der Verwaltung wurde nach den Grundsätzen des gemeinen Rechts (l. 54 § 1 Dig. [3. 3], l. 19 § 1 Dig. (5. 1), l. 1 und 2 Cod. [3. 21]) durch den Ort der Geschäftsführung bestimmt.

Die bayer. G. O. hatte für gerichtlich bestellte Verwalter (worunter auch die Vormünder) den Ort der Bestellung maßgebend erklärt.

Der Code de proc. endlich hatte (Art. 527) 1) für gerichtlich bestellte Verwalter den Ort ihrer Bestellung, 2) für Vormünder, den Ort des Anfalls der Vormundschaft und 3) für sonstige Verwalter den Wohnort als ausschließlichen Gerichtsstand bezeichnet.

Die neue Bestimmung ist vielleicht sachlich richtiger, allein die früheren haben den Vorzug der Einfachheit und Sicherheit, welcher in Competenz-Bestimmungen sehr schwer wiegt.

2) Welches ist der Ort, wo die Verwaltung geführt wurde?

In gewissem Sinne läßt sich sagen, es sei dies immer der Wohnort des Verwalters, Vormunds 2c., denn so wie dieser seine eigenen Geschäfte von dort aus besorgt, so wird er auch die anvertraute Verwaltung von dort aus besorgen, wenigstens was die Oberleitung betrifft. Hiernach würde das Gesetz bloß den Fall treffen, wo während der Verwaltung oder nach derselben der Wohnsitz verlegt worden ist.

Allein dies ist nicht der Sinn des Gesetzes; dasselbe setzt voraus, daß an dem einen Ort der Verwalter seinen Wohnsitz haben und an einem anderen Orte die Verwaltung von ihm geführt werden könne. vgl. l. 19 § 1 Dig. (5. 1).

3) Die Frage, wo die Verwaltung geführt worden sei, löst sich daher in die Frage auf, wo die Verwaltungs-Handlungen stattgefunden haben, wo das zu verwaltende Vermögen sich befand und hierbei wird die Gesammtheit aller Verwaltungs-Handlungen, die ganze Geschäftsführung in's Auge zu fassen sein.

Das Gesetz betrachtet offenbar einen bestimmten Ort als Sitz der Verwaltung und will nicht sagen, daß in allen Gerichtsbezirken, wo einzelne Verwaltungshandlungen vorgenommen wurden, wo einzelne Masseschuldner wohnen und zahlen, wo einzelne Grundstücke liegen, der Gerichtsstand der geführten Verwaltung begründet sei. Es wäre dies ebenso dem Wortlaute als dem Geiste des Gesetzes zuwider. Das Beste wird in Zweifelsfällen das richterliche Ermessen thun müssen, den Klägern aber ist anzurathen, falls sie ihrer Sache nicht ganz sicher sind, das Gericht des Wohnortes zu wählen.

4) Wichtiger wird die Sache, wenn die Verwaltung von der Obrigkeit bestellt war, denn in diesem Falle ist der Gerichtsstand ein ausschließlicher und sogar die Vereinbarung nicht gestattet. Voraussetzung des Gerichtsstandes ist auch hier die Geschäftsführung innerhalb des Gerichtsbezirkes, womit sich der weitere Umstand verbindet, daß die obrigkeitliche Anordnung der Verwaltung im nemlichen Gerichtsbezirke stattgefunden habe.

5) Was ist nun eine von der Obrigkeit angeordnete Verwaltung?

Die bayer. G. O. Cap. I § 7 spricht von „Bestellung“ durch die Obrigkeit und obgleich dieser Ausdruck noch bestimmter auf eine obrigkeitliche Ernennung hinzudeuten scheint, als der Ausdruck „Anordnung“, so zweifelte man doch nicht, daß auch die B e s t ä t i g u n g durch die Obrigkeit, wie sie diesseits bezüglich der testamentarischen und gesetzlichen Vormünder stattzufinden hat, darunter begriffen sei.

Wer bestätigen darf, darf auch die Bestätigung versagen und folgerichtig hier selbst ernennen; die Uebertragung der Vormundschaft beruht daher immerhin auf obrigkeitlicher Verfügung. Seuff. Comm. Bd. I S. 72 Note 1.

Auch unter der neuen P. O. ist dies als richtig anzuerkennen.

6) Wie verhält es sich nun aber mit den Vormündern der Pfalz? — Ist ihre Verwaltung als von der Obrigkeit angeordnet zu betrachten oder nicht?

Die Vormundschaft wird in der Pfalz übertragen durch Verfügung der Eltern, durch das Gesetz und durch Wahl des Familienraths. Die Gerichte haben weder zu ernennen, noch zu bestätigen.

Dennoch aber findet eine gewisse obervormundschaftliche Einwirkung der Gerichte statt, indem bei Berufung, Zusammensetzung und Beschlüssen des Familienraths der Landrichter eine wichtige Rolle spielt und die Entsetzung unwürdiger oder unfähiger Vormünder Sache der Gerichte ist. Die Thätigkeit des diesseitigen Richters ist mehr präventiv, diejenige des pfälzischen Richters mehr repressiv.

Ist nun jene obervormundschaftliche Einwirkung einer Anordnung der Verwaltung im Sinne unseres Artikels gleich zu achten?

7) Ich glaube dies nicht und zwar aus folgenden Gründen:

1) es wäre sprachwidrig und sachwidrig, den Familienrath als Obrigkeit und dessen sich in der Regel bloß auf die Wahl beschränkende Thätigkeit als obrigkeitliche Anordnung einer Verwaltung zu bezeichnen; die Mitwirkung des Landrichters aber erscheint ohne Belang, da sie sich im Wesen auf Leitung des Verfahrens beschränkt;

2) jedenfalls würden die nicht vom Familienrathe gewählten Vormünder nicht als obrigkeitlich bestellt zu erachten sein, würde also ein Unterschied entstehen, welcher keine innere Berechtigung hat;

3) der französische Gesetzgeber hat in Art. 527 Code de proc. die Vormünder den gerichtlich bestellten Verwaltern entgegengesetzt;

4) im Zweifel ist für Freiheit der Wahl zu entscheiden und zwar um so mehr, als die praktischen Vortheile auf dieser Seite sind.

Die Vormundschaft in der Pfalz wäre demnach allerdings als eine im öffentlichen Interesse bestehende, vom Gesetze angeordnete Verwaltung zu betrachten, jedoch nicht als eine von der Obrigkeit eines bestimmten Ortes angeordnete.

8) Gleiches gilt selbstverständlich auch von den für Interdizirte (Art. 505 Code civ.) oder für Sträflinge (Art. 31 des St. G. B.) bestellten Vormündern. Daß die Gerichte in den Interdiktions-Urtheilen überflüssiger Weise anzuordnen pflegen, es sei dem Interdizirten ein Vormund zu ernennen, ist natürlich ohne Belang.

Art. 28. — Ansprüche der Advokaten, Prozeßbevollmächtigten und Beistände wegen ihrer Gebühren und Auslagen, desgleichen Ansprüche gegen solche Personen wegen zu viel erhaltenen Vorschusses müssen bei dem Gerichte geltend gemacht werden, wo die betreffende Streitsache anhängig war oder ist. G. A. d. K. d. A. I S. 66. 82. IV S. 15—18. — K. d. R. I. S. 38. 89.

1) Es handelt sich hier um Ansprüche wegen Auslagen und Gebühren, welche in einem Rechtsstreite erwachsen sind, gegen die eigene Partei und wird bestimmt, daß solche Ansprüche immer die Natur der Hauptsache theilen und immer vor demjenigen Gerichte geltend zu machen sind, wo sie entstanden. (vgl. Art. 38 Ziff. 6.)

2) Diese Zutheilung der Competenz erstreckt sich selbst auf höhere Gerichte, und ist also hier ein ausschließlicher Gerichtsstand höchsten Grades geschaffen. Insbesondere ist auch die Streitfrage beseitigt, ob Gebühren in Handelssachen vor den Handelsgerichten eingeklagt werden können. Bl. f. R. XXXIII 53. Ursprünglich bildete dieser Artikel einen Theil des Art. 33 und reihte sich der Bestimmung an, daß der Richter der Hauptsache auch für die Nebensache zuständig sei.

3) Zu erwähnen ist, daß Anwälte ihre Gebühren und Auslagen nicht immer auf dem Wege der Klage beitreiben müssen. (Art. 118.)

Art. 29. — Klagen aus unerlaubten Handlungen können bei den Gerichten des Orts angebracht werden, wo die Handlung begangen worden ist.

Hat die Verübung der unerlaubten Handlung auf mehrere Orte sich erstreckt oder ist die Handlung an einem Orte begonnen, an einem andern fortgesetzt oder vollendet worden, so steht dem Kläger zwischen den Gerichten dieser Orte die Wahl zu.

Art. 30. — Klagen gegen den k. Fiskus wegen Verletzung der den Staatsdienern und ihren Hinterlassenen nach der IX. Verfassungsbeilage zustehenden Rechte können bei den Gerichten des Orts, wo der betreffende Staatsdiener bei Erlassung der Verfügung angestellt war oder, falls er sich damals nicht mehr in Dienstesactivität befunden hat, seinen Wohnsitz hatte, von Hinterlassenen eines Staatsdieners aber bei den Gerichten des letzten Wohnsitzes des Staatsdieners erhoben werden. G. A. d. K. d. A. I S. 23. 82. IV S. 16. 28. — K. d. R. I S. 90.

1) Eine unerlaubte Handlung im Sinne des Art. 29 ist jede Handlung, welche, abgesehen von Verletzung besonderer Vertragspflichten, nach allgemeinen Prinzipien des Rechts, als widerrechtlich erscheint, ob sie nun strafbar sei oder nur Entschädigungsansprüche begründe.

2) Nach Wortlaut und Geist des Gesetzes ist dieser Gerichtsstand nicht bloß demjenigen gegenüber gegeben, welchem die unerlaubte Handlung persönlich zur Last fällt, sondern auch demjenigen, welcher (als civilverantwortlich) für ihn haftet. Auf die bloß durch das Gesetz, nicht aber durch vorliegendes Verschulden begründete Haftung für Thiere und Sachen läßt sich allerdings der Gerichtsstand nicht ausdehnen.

3) Art. 30 wurde bei erster Lesung in der Kammer der Reichsräthe eingestellt, weil man der Ansicht war, es enthalte die Anwendung des Art. 15 auf vorliegende Fälle eine zu große Härte.

Art. 31. — **Gegenansprüche, die mit dem Klaganspruche in rechtlichem Zusammenhange stehen oder zugleich den Gegenstand einer Einrede bilden, können bei dem Gerichte, bei welchem die Klage im ersten Rechtszuge anhängig ist, durch Widerklage verfolgt werden.**

Diese Bestimmung findet keine Anwendung auf Ansprüche, welche selbst durch Vereinbarung nicht an das angerufene Gericht gebracht werden können.

Ansprüche aus Handelssachen, welche nicht unter Art. 7 Abs. 2 fallen, können im Wege der Widerklage vor den Bezirks- und Einzelngerichten nur durch Vereinbarung geltend gemacht werden, ausgenommen wenn bei einem Bezirks- oder Einzelngerichte in statthafter Weise aus einer Handelssache Klage gestellt worden ist, in welchem Falle daselbst auch wegen anderer Handelssachen, ohne daß eine Vereinbarung erforderlich ist, Widerklage erhoben werden kann.

Ueberschreitet der durch gesetzlich zulässige Widerklage bei einem Einzelngerichte erhobene Anspruch die Grenzen der einzelngerichtlichen Zuständigkeit, so hat, wenn beide Klagen Handelssachen betreffen, das bezüglich des durch die Widerklage geltend gemachten Anspruchs an sich zuständige Handelsgericht, in allen andern Fällen das bezüglich dieses Anspruchs an sich zuständige Bezirksgericht über beide zu entscheiden. Die Bestimmung des Art. 11 Abs. 3 findet auch hier Anwendung.

Widerklage gegen Widerklage findet nicht statt.

Die Entscheidung darüber, ob der mittels Widerklage verfolgte Gegenanspruch mit der Hauptklage in rechtlichem Zusammenhange stehe, kann durch Rechtsmittel nicht angefochten werden. G. A. d. K. d. A. I S. 23—30. 82. 83. 86. 87. 288. IV S. 16. 17. — K. d. R. I S. 90—98. 120—131. IV S. 7.

1) Während die Art. 9—11 sich mit den im Laufe eines Rechtsstreites zu entscheidenden Vor- und Zwischenfragen im Allgemeinen befassen, hat Art. 31 nur den Fall einer *selbständigen förmlichen Widerklage* im Auge. Für solche Widerklagen kommt ausschließlich letzterer Artikel zur Anwendung, wie dies der Vorbehalt in Art. 9 ausdrücklich anerkennt. — K. d. R. I 65 (v. Bayer).

Der Unterschied zwischen einer Widerklage und einem Zwischenstreite liegt darin:

1) daß jene selbständig neben der Hauptklage besteht und über sie erkannt werden *muß*, wenn auch die Hauptklage, sei es durch Abstand, sei es durch Abweisung, wegfällt, während dieser gegenstandslos wird, falls nach Lage der Sache es *unnöthig* ist, darüber zu entscheiden;

2) daß über die Widerklage *förmlich* zu erkennen ist, während über Zwischenstreite auch mittelbare Entscheidung erfolgen *kann*.

Es ist wichtig diesen Unterschied festzuhalten, da er in Fällen, wo Widerklage nicht statthaft ist (z. B. Abs. 4), Bedeutung gewinnt.

2) Art. 31 ist bestimmt, die Grundsätze der Widerklage im Allgemeinen zu regeln; wenn er daher auch zunächst nur vom Falle spricht, wo ein eigener Gerichtsstand begründet werden soll, so gilt er doch auch für den Fall, wo das Gericht der Hauptklage bereits das zuständige Gericht für die Widerklage ist. Abg. I 29 (Wiedenh.) 82 (v. Weiß). In Hannover wurde ein bezüglicher Zusatz als selbstverständlich beseitigt.

Es hat nemlich die Widerklage zweifache Wirkungen; sie bewirkt nicht bloß die Prorogirung des Gerichtsstandes, sondern auch den Anschluß an den Hauptprozeß in Form einfachen Antrages, sowie (in der Regel) gleichzeitige Verhandlung.

3) Die Widerklage ist vom Beklagten gegen den *Kläger* zu richten, d. h. gegen diejenige Person, welche ihn mittelst selbständiger Klage angegriffen hat; es liegt ihr der Gedanke der Abwehr zu Grunde. Gegen Personen, welche in anderer Eigenschaft im Prozesse sind, z. B. als Mitbeklagte, Neben-Intervenienten, ist sie nicht statthaft. Wohl aber ist der Haupt-Intervenient (Art. 67) als Kläger zu betrachten; ebenso

der Gewährschaftskläger (Art. 69). Ferner kann, falls mehrere Personen klagen, gegen jede derselben Widerklage erhoben werden, vorausgesetzt, daß ihrem Anspruche gegenüber Connexität besteht.

4) Widerklage ist auch unter Ausländern statthaft und zwar ohne Unterschied, ob die Gegenforderung in Bayern entstanden ist oder nicht. Bei Verhandlung über Art. 16 des Entwurfs wurde dies ausdrücklich anerkannt. Abg. I 30 (v. Neumayr und v. Weiß). Die bezügliche Bestimmung (Art. 7 Abs. 3 des Entw.) ließ man als überflüssig weg, nachdem auch für Widerklagen unter Inländern Connexität beschlossen war. Vgl. oben Art. 19 Nr. 3.

5) Das Erforderniß des „rechtlichen Zusammenhanges" kam erst nach längerem Kampfe in's Gesetz. Es soll damit gesagt sein, die Streitpunkte müßten in einem solchen (sachlichen) Zusammenhange stehen, daß aus der Beurtheilung des einen sich rechtliche Folgen für Beurtheilung des anderen ergeben.

Daß man der „Einreden" noch besonders erwähnt, erscheint beim ersten Anblicke überflüssig, denn eine Einrede als solche steht ja im engsten rechtlichen Zusammenhange mit der Klage, wie dies auch bei Verhandlungen zu Hannover anerkannt worden ist und zwar selbst für die Compensations-Einrede, falls sie klar ist.

Dennoch aber machte man in Hannover den in Frage stehenden Beisatz und zwar im Hinblicke auf jene Compensations-Einreden, bei deren Zulassung neben civilrechtlichen auch prozessuale Erwägungen einwirken, welche je nach Ermessen des Richters zugelassen werden können oder nicht. vgl. oben Art. 9—11 Nr. 22—26.

6) Falls eine solche Einrede wegen Illiquidität der Forderung zurückgewiesen wird, muß die mit ihr verbundene Widerklage das nemliche Schicksal theilen.

Nach dem Wortlaute des Gesetzes könnte man allerdings sagen, es genüge die Erhebung der Einrede, allein ohne Zweifel wird vorausgesetzt, es müsse sich der Gegenanspruch auch zur Einrede eignen, wie dies der hannover. Entwurf bestimmte. Indem man diesen Ausdruck verbesserte, verfiel man in einen anderen Fehler; die richtige Fassung wäre eigentlich: „welche Gegenstand einer Einrede bilden und sich zur solchen eignen."

7) Der Rechtsstreit muß in erster Instanz noch anhängig sein — mehr wird nicht gefordert; also kann die Widerklage in jeder Lage der Sache, so lange das Endurtheil erster Instanz noch nicht gefällt ist, dort angebracht werden. Wird sie der Klagbeantwortung nachgängig erhoben, so ist durch Art. 157 getrennte Verhandlung zur Regel gemacht.

8) Widerklage ist, der Regel nach, zulässig, wo Vereinbarung zulässig ist; es geht also das Gesetz von der Fiktion aus, als ob in der Klagserhebung die Einwilligung zum Vorbringen connexer Widerklagen gegeben wäre.

Durch Widerklage kann daher eine Civilsache nie vor ein Handelsgericht und eine dingliche Klage nie vor ein anderes Gericht, als das der Lage der Sache gebracht werden. Andere Anschauungen gelten für bloße Zwischenstreite (vgl. oben Art. 21 Nr. 7).

9) Von der Regel, daß Vereinbarung zu präsumiren sei, ist für Handelssachen in so fern eine Ausnahme gemacht, als wirkliche Vereinbarung gefordert wird.

Diese Ausnahme erleidet aber wiederum eine Ausnahme, d. h. die Regel bleibt bestehen, wenn eine Handelssache in statthafter Weise an Civilgerichte gebracht war, nemlich entweder durch Vereinbarung oder auf Grund des Art. 7 Abs. 2. Liegt dieser Fall vor, so soll in connexen Handelssachen jeder Art (selbstverständlich mit Ausnahme der Wechselsachen Art. 38 Ziff. 10) Widerklage zulässig sein; bei den Einzelngerichten jedoch mit Vorbehalt der Sonderbestimmungen in Abs. 4.

10) In Abs. 4 sind bezüglich der bei Einzelngerichten angebrachten, ihre Zuständigkeit überschreitenden Widerklagen besondere Vorschriften gegeben, ähnlich denen des Art. 11 Abs. 1 bei Zwischenstreiten.

Der Landrichter prüft, ob die gesetzlichen Erfordernisse einer Widerklage vorliegen. Ist dies nicht der Fall, so weist er die Widerklage ab und entscheidet in der Hauptsache, was Rechtens; ist es aber der Fall, so erklärt er sich unzuständig. Auf Grund dieses Urtheils bringt der Kläger seine Klage vor das für die Widerklage zuständige höhere Gericht, es dem Beklagten überlassend, ob er seine Widerklage dort wieder vorbringen wolle. vgl. Art. 511.

11) Widerklage gegen Widerklage findet nicht statt.

Dieser Satz, ein Axiom des alten Prozesses, kommt in Conflikt mit den Prinzipien des Art. 9.

Der Grundsatz, daß alle Entscheidungen über selbständige Zwischenstreite in Rechtskraft erwachsen, gilt nemlich für Repliken und Dupliken so gut wie für Einreden, und da man einmal die unmittelbare und mittelbare Aburtheilung solcher Zwischenstreite sanktionirt hat, lag kein Grund vor, den Parteien das Recht zu versagen, sie auch zum Gegenstande förmlicher Incidentklage zu machen. Die Fälle solcher Incidentklagen kommen im französischen Prozeß nicht bloß manchmal, sondern häufig vor. Ich erinnere z. B. an folgenden Fall: Eine Gegenforderung wird zur Compensation und Widerklage benützt; Widerbeklagter wendet ein, der Vertrag oder Akt, auf welchen sich die Gegenforderung gründet, sei nichtig und erhebt Incidentklage auf Nichtigerklärung (Art. 1304 Code civ.).

Die bestimmte Vorschrift unseres Artikels schließt (höchst unpraktischer Weise) diese Incidentklage, welche sich nicht etwa unter die Art. 181 und 182 bringen läßt, aus, sofern sie Anspruch macht, als förmliche selbständige Klage zu gelten.

12) Folgt hieraus, daß Incidentklagen fraglicher Art fortan gar nicht mehr statthaft seien?

Es wird zu unterscheiden sein. Art. 9 spricht aus, daß Zwischenstreite mittelbar oder unmittelbar abgeurtheilt werden können. Es erscheint nun natürlich, daß der Richter, wenn er einen solchen Streit entscheidet, offen und geradezu erklären darf, daß er darüber entscheide; daß ihn also nichts hindert, sich im Urtheilssatze über Punkte auszusprechen, welche nicht Gegenstand förmlicher Klage oder Widerklage waren.

Man hat dies im französischen Verfahren von jeher so gehalten und z. B. keinen Anstand genommen, in Fällen, wie der oben angeführte, zu sagen:

„indem das Gericht erkennt, daß der Vertrag „(Akt) nichtig sei, weist es die Gegenforderung „als unbegründet ab,"

d. h. den entscheidenden Theil der Gründe in's Urtheil aufzunehmen.

War förmliche Incidentklage erhoben, so wählte man die direkte Form, z. B.: über die Incidentklage erkennend, erklärt das Gericht den Vertrag (Akt) für nichtig, weist sofort ꝛc.

Es steht nun offenbar nichts im Wege, daß die replizirende Partei beantrage, es möge, falls fraglicher Zwischenstreit zur Entscheidung komme, darüber ausdrückliches Erkenntniß erfolgen.

Der Unterschied zwischen förmlicher Incidentklage und einem solchen Antrage läge darin, daß über erstere nothwendig erkannt werden müßte, während letzterer möglicherweise gegenstandslos werden könnte.

13) Der Sinn des Abs. 5 ist wohl der, daß die Frage, ob Connexität bestehe oder nicht, durch die erste richterliche Entscheidung endgültig erledigt sein solle. Wäre es bloß Absicht des Gesetzes gewesen, die selbständige Berufung auszuschließen, die Berufung mit dem Endurtheile aber vorzubehalten, so hätte es sich anders ausgedrückt.

Der Sinn des Gesetzes muß sofort klar werden, wenn man erwägt, daß dasselbe zwei Fälle trifft, nemlich den Fall, wo der Richter die Widerklage für zulässig erklärt, und den Fall, wo er sie als unzulässig abweist. Im letzteren Falle liegt doch ohne Zweifel ein Endurtheil vor, dennoch aber soll ein Rechtsmittel nicht zulässig sein!

Sollte nun der Gesetzgeber für den ersteren Fall allein eine andere Absicht gehabt haben? sollte er so unpraktisch gewesen sein, daß er, nachdem die ganze Verhandlung durchgeführt ist, die Beweise erhoben sind und die Sache zur endlichen Entscheidung reif ist, in der Berufungsinstanz noch eine Untersuchung bezüglich der Connexität zuließe, d. h. eines Punktes, welchen er selbst ursprünglich gar nicht als Vorbedingung der Widerklage gelten lassen wollte?

Die Aeußerungen im Reichsrathe (I 130) beruhen offenbar auf falscher Auffassung der Tragweite und des Sinnes fraglicher Verfügung; überhaupt muß man sich hüten, derartigen, oft nur polemischen, Gelegenheits-Aeußerungen allzuviel Werth beizulegen.

14) Im Falle, wo sich der Landrichter auf Grund von Abs. 4 für unzuständig erklärt, ist gemäß Art. 511 seine Entscheidung nicht bloß bezüglich der Frage der Connexität, sondern im Ganzen endgültig, jedoch nur so weit es sich um seine eigene Unzuständigkeit handelt, da er natürlich die Sache nicht rechtsgültig einem bestimmten Gerichte (Bezirksgerichte oder Handelsgerichte) zuweisen kann. Abg. II 262 (v. Weiß), 263 (Barth).

Art. 32. — **Ist gegen einen Inländer, der im Inlande keinen Wohnsitz hat, oder gegen einen Ausländer Arrest verfügt worden, so kann die Klage in der Hauptsache bei den Gerichten des Orts der Arrestverfügung erhoben werden.**

G. A. d. K. d. A. I S. 30 in f., 31, IV S. 17. — K. d. R. I S. 98, 99.

Was unter Arrest zu verstehen sei, ist aus Art. 607 zu entnehmen.

Dort ist zugleich bestimmt, daß die Arrestverfügung unbedingt auch unter Ausländern zulässig sei. Eine solche Verfügung hat den Gerichtsstand des Art. 32 zur Folge, auch wenn die Verbindlichkeit nicht in Bayern entstanden ist. Abg. I 31 (Umbsch.), IV 13 in f. (Barth), Vortrag zur zweiten Lesung Hauptst. 23 Art. 3 (v. Neumayr).

Art. 33. — **Rechtsstreitigkeiten derselben Parteien, welche in solcher Verbindung stehen, daß die Verhandlung und Entscheidung durch verschiedene Gerichte nicht ohne Nachtheil erfolgen kann,**

sind, wenn eine Partei es beantragt, bei einem und demselben Gerichte zu verhandeln und zu entscheiden.

Die vorstehende Bestimmung findet keine Anwendung, wenn die eine Sache vor ein Bezirks- oder Einzelngericht, die andere dagegen vor ein Handels- oder Ehegericht gehört, es sei denn, daß die bezirks- oder einzelngerichtliche Zuständigkeit in den Bestimmungen des Art. 7 Abs. 2 begründet ist, in welchem Falle beide Sachen beim Handelsgerichte zu verhandeln und zu entscheiden sind.

Das Gericht der Hauptsache ist auch für die Nebensachen zuständig. Als solche sind insbesondere Streitigkeiten über die in einem Prozesse veranlaßten Kosten und über den Ersatz des durch den Prozeß weiter verursachten Schadens anzusehen.

G. A. d. K. d. A. I S. 31—33. 66. 83. 298. IV S. 17. — K. d. R. I S. 99. 131. 132. IV S. 7.

1) Hier sind zwei verschiedene Gerichtsstände geregelt. In Abs. 1 und 2 des Artikels wird von der Connexität überhaupt, in Abs. 3 aber von dem besonderen Verhältnisse zwischen Haupt- und Neben-Sache gesprochen.

2) Was zuerst das letztere Verhältniß betrifft, so ist der Ausdruck „Nebensache" in der engeren Bedeutung zu nehmen und sind damit jene Ansprüche und Begehren gemeint, welche Zubehör des Hauptanspruches bilden und von dessen Entscheidung abhängen. Es muß die Annahme berechtigt sein, der Gesetzgeber habe, indem er einen Gerichtsstand für die Hauptsache festsetzte, hiermit auch selbstverständlich die Nebensache treffen wollen.

Nebensache in diesem Sinne ist z. B. die Entschädigung wegen Besitzentziehung gegenüber der Klage auf Schutz im Besitze, der Ersatz von Früchten bei der Vindikation, die Einforderung verfallener Leistungen und Zinsen bei Geltendmachung eines Realrechtes oder Einklagung eines Kapitals u. s. w. Als Nebensachen erscheinen ferner alle jene Begehren, welche nur den Zweck verfolgen, die Geltendmachung des Haupt-Anspruches zu ermöglichen und zu befördern, wie z. B. Erwirkung des Armenrechts, Editionsbegehren, Vorsichtsverfügungen im Laufe eines Rechtsstreites, in welchen Beziehungen übrigens überall durch besondere Bestimmungen vorgesorgt ist.

3) Daß man solche besondere Bestimmungen für nöthig hielt, daß man der Kosten ausdrücklich als Nebensache erwähnte, endlich die Beispiele, welche bezüglich solcher Fälle, welche nicht Nebensache seien, gegeben werden Abg. I 33 (Barth), 66 (v. Weiß), — alles dies deutet an, daß dem Begriffe der „Nebensache" enge Grenzen gezogen werden sollten. Zwischenstreite im Sinne des Art. 9 gehören jedenfalls nicht darunter.

4) Eine Nebensache in diesem Sinne theilt immer die Natur der Hauptsache und in Folge hiervon auch deren Gerichtsstand. Im Grunde wird hier kein neuer Gerichtsstand geschaffen, sondern nur der Umfang bezeichnet, in welchem der für eine bestimmte Rechtssache begründete Gerichtsstand wirksam sei.

In Hannover war man deßhalb der Ansicht, daß eine Bestimmung der Art, wie sie in Abs. 3 gegeben ist, nichtssagend sei und daß es genüge, bezüglich der Rechtshängigkeit zu verfügen, (wie dies in Art. 179 geschieht), daß die Streitsache, sammt allem, was dazu gehört, der Gerichtsbarkeit des angerufenen Gerichts unterworfen bleibe. (Verhandl. S. 518).

5) Von größerer Tragweite ist die Bestimmung in Abs. 1, durch welche ein besonderer Gerichtsstand der Zusammengehörigkeit (forum connexitatis) begründet wird.

6) Die Ausdrücke, mit welchen das Gesetz hier den Begriff der Connexität bestimmt, sind höchst allgemein und lassen dem richterlichen Ermessen den weitesten Spielraum.

Da nicht bloß von „rechtlichen Naththeilen" gesprochen wird, so hat man nicht nur an solche Fälle zu denken, wo die Entscheidung der einen Sache von rechtlichem Einflusse auf die Entscheidung der anderen ist, sondern auch an solche, wo durch gleichzeitige Verhandlung Ersperniß an Kosten und schnellere oder gründlichere Erledigung herbeigeführt werden kann.

Man darf sich nicht wundern, daß eine so weit gehende Befugniß des Richters lebhaften Widerspruch erfuhr, wie sie denn auch in Hannover, als zur Willkür führend, abgelehnt wurde; allein ich halte vom praktischen Standpunkte die getroffene Bestimmung für gut und fürchte nichts von der Willkür, weil 1) vorauszusetzen ist, daß die Gerichte im Geiste des Gesetzes urthälen und eine Verweisung aus bloßen Zweckmäßigkeitsgründen nur verfügen werden, wo ernstliche und wichtige Gründe vorliegen, weil 2) es bei jetzigen Zuständen in der Regel ganz gleichgültig ist, welches von mehreren gleichartigen Gerichten entscheide und weil 3) das Interesse der Anwälte dabei betheiligt ist, nicht ohne Noth Verweisungen herbeizuführen.

7) Die Worte: „dieselben Parteien" kamen auf Anregung von Edel in den Text, um Fälle auszuschließen, wo in den verchiedenen Rechtsstreiten ganz andere Parteien sein. Es wird

nicht erforderlich sein, daß alle Parteien die nemlichen sein müssen und möchte es der Anwendung des Gesetzes, nach dessen Geiste, nicht im Wege stehen, wenn in einem Prozesse etwa noch ein Streitgenosse ist, welcher im anderen nicht vorkommt.

8) Nach französischem Prozesse entsteht aus der Connexität, ebenso wie aus der Litispendenz die Einrede der Incompetenz und zwar in demjenigen Rechtsstreite, welcher zuletzt anhängig geworden ist. (Art. 171 Code de proc.)

Nach dem Wortlaute des Abs. 1 könnte man annehmen, daß die verschiedenen Gerichte gleichheitlich unzuständig seien und erst durch die nach Maßgabe des Art. 34 erfolgende Regulirung, dasjenige derselben zuständig werde, welches vom Obergerichte bezeichnet sei.

Man kann dies jedoch nicht als Sinn des Gesetzes betrachten und zwar, abgesehen vom Vorbilde des französischen Prozesses, 1) im Hinblicke auf Art. 179, 2) weil für Fälle, wo die Gerichte im Unterordnungs-Verhältnisse stehen, der Weg des Art. 34 verschlossen ist und 3) im Hinblicke auf die Verhandlungen. Abg. I 61 (v. Neumayr und v. Weiß), 66 (v. Weiß).

Es ist vielmehr anzunehmen, daß der Gesetzgeber, dem französischen Rechte folgend, zwei Wege eröffnen wollte, um die Verbindung zusammengehöriger Sachen zu bewirken, die Einrede der Connexität und die Regulirung des Gerichtsstandes durch das Obergericht.

9) Wird angenommen, es sei eine Einrede gegeben, so folgt hieraus, daß das Verlangen der Verweisung resp. Competenz-Regulirung nicht mehr gestellt werden kann, wenn sich diejenige Partei, welche die Einrede hätte vorschützen können, auf den Streit eingelassen hat. Der besondere Gerichtsstand der Connexität ist dann durch Vereinbarung beseitigt (Art. 39. — Abg. I 66 und 83).

Die Worte: „wenn eine Partei es beantragt“, drücken dies zwar nicht bestimmt aus, indem sie nur eine Verfügung von Amtswegen ausschließen; allein offenbar lag es in der Absicht des Gesetzgebers, die Grundsätze über Vereinbarung hier anwendbar zu erklären. Er wollte nicht billigen, daß Prozesse, welche ganz oder großen Theils durchgeführt sind, auf Verlangen einer Partei noch vor andere Gerichte verwiesen werden müßten.

10) Die einzige Gränze, welche der Regulirung des Gerichtsstandes aus dem Grunde der Connexität gesetzt ist, besteht darin, daß nach Abs. 2 Sachen, welche vor Bezirks- oder Einzel-Gerichte gehören, nicht vor Handels- oder Ehe-Gerichte gebracht werden dürfen, und umgekehrt. In allen übrigen Beziehungen besteht also volle Freiheit.

Es kann somit die Regulirung stattfinden:

1) bei Sachen, wovon die eine am Landgerichte, die andere am Bezirksgerichte anhängig ist;
2) bei dinglichen Rechtsstreiten und überhaupt in Fällen, wo Vereinbarung ausgeschlossen ist.

Nur der in Art. 28 geschaffene Gerichtsstand wird unangetastet bleiben müssen.

11) Es kann demzufolge der Fall sich ereignen, daß eine Sache, welche auf Grund von Art. 31 Abs. 2 oder 5 als Widerklage nicht angebracht werden könnte, auf Grund der Connexität an das nemliche Gericht verwiesen werden darf. Anomalien dieser Art sind die Folge kasuistischer Gesetze, welche, statt leitende Grundsätze zu geben, für jeden besonderen Fall auch zugleich die Folgen ziehen und die Anwendung regeln. — Wo jeder Artikel seinen besonderen Geist hat, läßt sich ein Geist des Gesetzes schwer ermitteln.

12) Die Fassung des Abs. 2 drückt übrigens offenbar den Gedanken des Gesetzgebers nicht ganz richtig aus.

Dem bloßen Wortlaute nachgehend, würde man dazu gelangen, daß Handelssachen vor Ehegerichte gebracht werden könnten, und umgekehrt. Fälle der Connexität ließen sich bei bestehender Gütersonderung wohl konstruiren. Ebenso lag es sicher nicht im Willen des Gesetzgebers, daß eine bezirksgerichtliche Sache auf Grund der Connexität vor ein Landgericht gebracht werden könnte.

Der Sinn des Gesetzes läßt sich vielmehr dahin formuliren:

„Auf Grund vorstehender Bestimmung darf „nie die Verweisung an ein Gericht anderer „Art erfolgen, jedoch können die vor Einzel„gerichte gehörigen Sachen den Bezirksgerichten „und müssen die in Art. 7 Abs. 2 bezeichneten „Handelssachen den Handelsgerichten zugewiesen „werden.“

13) Offenbar ist es Wille des Gesetzes, daß bei Handelssachen, insbesondere auch den einseitigen Handelsgeschäften (Art. 7 Abs. 2 Ziff. 2) die Zuweisung immer nur an das Handelsgericht zu geschehen habe, so daß also die Prioriät der Klagestellung am Bezirksgerichte, wenigstens hier, ohne allen Einfluß ist.

Dies steht nun nicht recht im Einklange mit den Bestimmungen bezüglich der Widerklage. — Widerklagen aus Handelssachen können nemlich laut Art. 31 Abs. 3 unbedingt an's Bezirksgericht gebracht werden, falls die Hauptklage eine Handelssache betrifft. Man sollte nun denken, in Fällen letzterer Art könne man vom Beklagten verlangen, er solle seinen connexen Anspruch als Widerklage beim Bezirksgerichte geltend machen; es wäre dies ebenso billig als praktisch. — Statt dessen erlaubt ihm das Gesetz, den connexen Anspruch beim Handelsgerichte anzubringen und die bereits beim Bezirksgerichte anhängig gewordene auch Sache dorthin zu ziehen!

Es ist dies wiederum eine Folge der Casuistik, welche sich nicht hinwegdeuten läßt, die aber zum Glücke ohne praktische Bedeutung sein wird, da Pflichtgefühl und Interesse die Anwälte abhalten werden, derartige Kunststücke zu versuchen.

14) In gleicher Weise, wie im ebenbesprochenen Falle, kann, wenn die eine Sache vor einem Landgerichte, die andere vor einem Bezirksgerichte anhängig ist, die Verweisung immer nur an's Bezirksgericht geschehen, mag auch die Klage am Landgerichte die frühere sein.

Eine nothwendige Folge hieraus ist, daß in beiden Fällen (Nr. 13 u. 14) die Einrede der Unzuständigkeit auch in derjenigen Streitsache entstehen kann, welche zuerst anhängig geworden ist; daß also der Richter, welcher ursprünglich der zuständige war, auf Grund einer bei einem anderen Gerichte angebrachten connexen Sache unzuständig werden kann, in gleicher Weise, wie dies in Art. 11 u. 31 Abs. 4 bestimmt ist. Man darf nicht sagen, es entstehe in solchen Fällen keine Incompetenz-Einrede, sondern könne nur die in Art. 34 vorgesehene Regulirung stattfinden, denn für Festsetzung der Zuständigkeit zwischen Bezirksgerichten und den ihnen untergeordneten Landgerichten gibt es keine Regulirung.

15) In den Fällen, wo Verweisung wegen Connexität nicht statthaft ist, oder wo sie nicht begehrt wird, müssen Parteien und Gerichte die Nachtheile, welche durch Trennung der Verhandlung entstehen können, in anderer Weise abzuwenden suchen und zwar am einfachsten durch Vertagung der Verhandlung in der einen Sache, bis die andere in den einschlägigen Punkten abgeurtheilt ist, oder bis die Prozeßakten derselben vorgelegt werden können.

16) Schließlich bemerke ich, daß Verweisungen wegen Connexität in der Pfalz zu den Seltenheiten gehören, und daß es auch diesseits voraussichtlich so werden wird.

Festsetzung der Zuständigkeit.

Art. 34. — **Ist die Zuständigkeit mehrerer nicht im Unterordnungsverhältnisse stehender Gerichte in derselben Sache streitig oder sind Rechtsstreitigkeiten der in Art. 33 Abs. 1 bezeichneten Art vor verschiedenen nicht im Unterordnungsverhältnisse stehenden Gerichten anhängig geworden, so ist jede Partei befugt, die Festsetzung der Zuständigkeit bei dem nächsten den verschiedenen Gerichten gemeinsamen Obergerichte und beim Mangel eines solchen bei dem obersten Gerichtshofe mittels einfacher Vorstellung nachzusuchen.**

G. A. d. K. d. A. I S. 61—63. 233. IV S. 17. — K. r. R. I S. 99—101.

1) Die Art. 34—37 geben ein sehr einfaches und zweckmäßiges Verfahren, um in gewissen Fällen die Zuständigkeit endgültig zu regeln; dasselbe soll die bezüglichen Vorschriften des Gesetzes über Competenz-Conflikte vom 28. Mai 1850, sowie das Ges. vom 27. Vent. VIII Art. 76, endlich die Verfügungen der Art. 363 bis 367 Code de proc. über das réglement de juges ersetzen.

Die dem hannov. Entwurfe entnommene Fassung des Gesetzes ist nicht ganz scharf, wie dies auch schon in Hannover gerügt wurde (Verhdl. S. 550); das Ges. von 28. Mai 1850 sagte richtiger: „zwischen mehreren Gerichten."

2) Art. 34 hat zwei verschiedene Fälle im Auge, welche getrennt zu halten sind, nemlich 1) den Fall, wo zwischen mehreren Gerichten Streit über die Zuständigkeit entsteht (Competenz-Conflikt) und 2) den Fall, wo Rechtsstreite, welche an verschiedenen Gerichten anhängig sind, zusammengehören (Regulirung der Competenz, réglement de juges im engeren Sinne).

Competenz-Conflikte.

3) Der Competenz-Conflikt setzt voraus, daß verschiedene Gerichte, in der nemlichen Sache, sich über ihre Zuständigkeit ausgesprochen haben und diese Aussprüche im Widerspruche stehen.

Der Conflikt ist ein verneinender, wenn jedes Gericht seine Zuständigkeit ablehnt; er ist ein bejahender, wenn jedes Gericht die Zuständigkeit in Anspruch nimmt.

4) Sobald ein zweites Gericht sein widersprechendes Urtheil erlassen hat, ist der Conflikt gegeben mag immerhin das Urtheil noch anfechtbar sein; jedoch ist es den Parteien nicht verwehrt, vorerst die Rechtsmittel zu versuchen. Bl. f. R. XVI 143, XVII 172, XVIII 281 Note.

Falls das zweite Gericht gleich den ersten die Zuständigkeit ablehnt, jedoch die Zuständigkeit eines dritten Gerichts gegeben erachtet, besteht ein Conflikt erst, wenn auch dieses dritte Gericht ablehnt. vgl. Bl. f. R. XX 389.

5) Falls die nemliche Sache gleichzeitig bei verschiedenen Gerichten anhängig ist, wird es

jeder Partei gestattet sein, sofort, ohne die Einrede der Litispendenz zu versuchen, oder die einen Conflikt begründenden Urtheile abzuwarten, die Regulirung der Competenz zu betreiben, denn es sind hier offenbar die Grundsätze über Connexität arg. a majori anwendbar.

6) Das Gesetz erkennt einen Competenz-Conflikt nicht an, wenn die Gerichte im Unterordnungs-Verhältnisse stehen, d. h. wenn ein niederes Gericht demjenigen höheren Gerichte, zu dessen Bezirke es gehört, gegenübersteht. Es geht also von der Ansicht aus, daß in solchen Fällen ein Conflikt nicht vorkommen, oder daß er jedenfalls in anderer Weise einfacher erledigt werden könne.

Faßt man zuerst den Fall in's Auge, daß das höhere Gericht zuerst entscheidet, so soll offenbar, im Sinne des Gesetzes, dessen Urtheil maßgebend sein und falls es daher seine Zuständigkeit ablehnt, so entscheidet es hiemit nicht bloß (negativ) über seine eigene Unzuständigkeit, sondern auch (positiv) über die Zuständigkeit des untergebenen Gerichts; sein Urtheil ist zugleich zuweisend.

7) Für den Fall, wo der niedere Richter zuerst entscheidet, ist die Lösung nicht so leicht. Wenn gegen das betreffende Urtheil Berufung ergriffen werden kann und ergriffen wird, macht sich die Sache allerdings ebenfalls einfach; ist aber dieser Fall nicht gegeben, wird also das Urtheil des niederen Gerichts rechtskräftig, so entstehen Schwierigkeiten.

Spricht das höhere Gericht, welches selbstverständlich an die Ansicht des unteren Gerichts nicht gebunden ist, gleichfalls seine Unzuständigkeit aus, so stehen zwei gleich berechtigte rechtskräftige Erkenntnisse einander gegenüber; denn zu behaupten, daß die Rechtskraft der Urtheile geringer sei, wenn sie von niederen, als wenn sie von höheren Richtern ausgegangen sind, wäre höchst unjuristisch.

Da nun aber das Gesetz hier einen Conflikt nicht annimmt, und ein Ausweg nothwendig bestehen muß, so folgt, daß nach dem Willen des Gesetzes, auch in diesem Falle, ausnahmsweise, der Ausspruch des höheren Richters maßgebend sein soll, daß derselbe also zugleich die Regulirung enthält. vgl. Bl. f. R. III 175 Note 7.

8) Indem das Einf. Gesetz (Art. 4) die betreffenden Verfügungen des Ges. v. 28. Mai 1850 aufhebt, verfügt es zugleich, daß die Bestimmungen der Art. 34—37 auch für Gegenstände der nichtstreitigen Rechtspflege zu gelten haben. Hierbei kann der Antrag auf Festsetzung der Zuständigkeit auch vom Staatsanwalte des zur Entscheidung berufenen Obergerichts gestellt werden. — Dieser Staatsanwalt wird in der Regel auf Anregung einer Partei, des Staatsanwalts am betr. Untergerichte oder des Untergerichts selbst, seinen Antrag stellen; das Gesetz erlaubt ihm jedoch, verpflichtet ihn also auch, in Fällen, wo das öffentliche Interesse berührt ist, von Amtswegen zu handeln.

Regulirung der Zuständigkeit.

9) Die Regulirung der Zuständigkeit im engeren Sinne setzt voraus, daß zusammengehörige Sachen an verschiedenen Gerichten anhängig werden, ohne Rücksicht darauf, ob diese Gerichte oder eines derselben sich bereits über die Zuständigkeit ausgesprochen haben oder nicht.

10) In diesem Falle ist, wie oben erwähnt, in der Regel die Wahl gegeben zwischen der Einrede der Connexität nnd dem Antrage auf Regulirung der Zuständigkeit.

Jene Einrede steht selbstverständlich nur einer der Parteien zu, kann ferner nur bei einem der Gerichte geltend gemacht werden und ihre Wirkung kann nur die sein, die Zuständigkeit dieses Gerichtes zu beseitigen, um sodann den Anspruch als Zwischenstreit oder Widerklage vor das andere Gericht zu bringen. Bei diesem anderen Gerichte können aber neue Anstände und am Ende ein Competenz-Conflikt entstehen.

Der Weg der Regulirung hingegen steht jeder Partei offen, und geht direkt auf's Ziel los, die Zuständigkeit endgültig festzustellen. Da er zugleich sehr einfach ist und wenig Kosten verursacht, so wird er in der Regel, wenn nicht immer, vorzuziehen sein.

11) Kann das Obergericht unter den in Frage stehenden Gerichten, vorausgesetzt, daß deren Zuständigkeit an sich gegeben ist, beliebig wählen? oder aber muß es auf die Priorität der Anhängigkeit Rücksicht nehmen?

Die Allgemeinheit des Ausdrucks in Art. 33 und 34; der Umstand, daß nach Art. 33 Abs. 2 Handelssachen immer an's Handelsgericht und landgerichtliche Sachen immer an's Bezirksgericht zu verweisen sind; der fernere Umstand, daß viele Ansprüche, welche im Sinne des Art. 33 connex sind, gar nicht im Wege der Klage oder Widerklage vor das zuerst angegangene Gericht gebracht werden dürfen; endlich der Geist des Gesetzes, welcher die Zuweisung an dasjenige Gericht verlangt, wo die Gründe der Zweckmäßigkeit überwiegen, möchte dahin führen, daß in Fällen, wo nur die Connexität, nicht aber die Litispendenz (Art. 179) in Betracht kommt, das Obergericht freie Wahl habe. — Es läßt sich jedoch nicht läugnen, daß auch Gründe für die gegentheilige Ansicht bestehen.

12) Nicht unnütz möchte es sein, anzuführen, daß die französische Jurisprudenz, trotz des Art. 171 Code de proc., welcher die Einreden der Litispendenz und Connexität auf gleiche Linie stellt, im Falle eines réglement de juges auf Grund bloßer Connexität, dem Oberrichter gestattet, das zuletzt angegangene Gericht zu wählen, falls die dort anhängige Sache von stark überwiegender Bedeutung ist. Dalloz rep. (régl. de j.) Nr. 134. — Schlink § 306 Ziff. 8. — Von dieser Ausnahme zur freien Wahl ist nur ein kleiner Schritt.

13) Stehen die Gerichte im Verhältnisse der Unterordnung, so ist auch hier (wie mir scheint, ohne genügenden Grund) der Weg der Regulirung versagt, bleibt also bloß die Einrede und finden die oben Nr. 6 und 7 gemachten Bemerkungen Anwendung.

14) Hat eine Partei die Einrede der Connexität geltend gemacht, so ist sie deßhalb nicht gezwungen, dieselbe durch alle Instanzen zu verfolgen; es wird ihr vielmehr immer freistehen, die Zuständigkeit regeln zu lassen. Journ. du Pal. (régl. de j.) Nr. 75.

15) Was die Wirkung der Entscheidung des Obergerichtes auf die anhängigen Rechtsstreite betrifft, so hat man bei den Verhandlungen (Abg. I 63) die Begriffe etwas vermengt, indem man bald den Fall des Competenzconfliktes, bald den Fall der Connexität im Auge hatte.

Liegt in der Entscheidung der Ausspruch, daß eines der Gerichte von Anfang an unzuständig gewesen sei, wie es bei Competenzconflikten der Fall ist, so ist selbstverständlich alles nichtig, was vor dem unzuständigen Richter geschehen ist; weist aber das Obergericht nur aus Gründen der Zweckmäßigkeit eine Sache, für welche das angerufene Gericht sonst zuständig war, einem andern Gerichte zu, so findet eine einfache Uebertragung dieser Sache an dieses letztere Gericht statt. — Es wird letzteren Falls nicht entschieden, es sei das bezeichnete Gericht das allein zuständige, sondern dasselbe nur bevollmächtigt, über beide Streitsachen zu verhandeln und zu entscheiden, wie dies besonders scharf hervortritt, wenn die Zuweisung an das zuletzt angegangene Gericht erfolgt.

16) Um Einheit in die Prinzipien zu bringen, möchte ich diese Anschauung auch auf die Einrede der Connexität anwenden, dieselbe natürlich im engeren Sinne genommen, wo sie bloß eine Verweisung aus Gründen der Zweckmäßigkeit (nicht der Litispendenz 2c.) bezweckt. In der Natur derselben scheint es mir zu liegen, daß sie nicht eine schon von Anfang an bestandene, sondern nur eine mit dem Vorbringen der Einrede, d. h. dem Verlangen der Verweisung, entstehende Unzuständigkeit bezeichne.

Art. 35. — **Die Vorstellung ist dem Gegentheile zuzustellen und sammt der Zustellungsurkunde und den zur Begründung des Gesuchs erforderlichen Belegen auf der Gerichtsschreiberei des Obergerichts einzureichen.**

Die Gegenpartei kann innerhalb fünfzehn Tagen nach der Zustellung ihre Bemerkungen mit den erforderlichen Belegen daselbst einreichen.

Nach Ablauf dieser Frist entscheidet das Obergericht nach Vernehmung des Staatsanwalts, wenn ein solcher an dem Gerichte aufgestellt ist.

Das die Zuständigkeit festsetzende Erkenntniß wird durch den Staatsanwalt — falls ein solcher am Gerichte nicht aufgestellt ist, durch den Gerichtsvorstand — den betreffenden Untergerichten mitgetheilt. Den Betheiligten ist durch den Gerichtsschreiber des als zuständig erkannten Gerichts Kenntniß zu geben.

Gegen das Erkenntniß, welches die Zuständigkeit festsetzt, finden keine Rechtsmittel statt.

Art. 36. — **Das Obergericht kann auf Antrag des Gesuchstellers sofort nach Einreichung der Vorstellung vorbehaltlich der etwa gebotenen Vorsichtsverfügungen die Einstellung des Verfahrens bei den mit der Sache befaßten Gerichten anordnen.**

Art. 37. — **Wird das Gesuch auf Festsetzung der Zuständigkeit verworfen, so hat das Obergericht zugleich über die dadurch veranlaßten Kosten zu entscheiden. Im entgegengesetzten Falle bleibt die Entscheidung über sämmtliche bisher erwachsene Kosten dem Endurtheile vorbehalten.**

Alle auf die Festsetzung der Zuständigkeit bezüglichen Eingaben, Verhandlungen, Entscheidungen und Ausfertigungen sind tax- und stempelfrei.

G. A. d. K. d. A. I S. 61—63. 233. 294. 298—300. IV S. 17. — K. d. R. I S. 102—107. IV S. 7.

1) Das hier vorgezeichnete Verfahren, einfach und wohlfeil, ist weit praktischer als dasjenige, welches die Art. 363 ff. Code de proc. geben, von welchen ebendeßhalb fast nie Gebrauch gemacht wurde.

Die Entscheidung soll auf einfache Vorstellung

hin erfolgen d. h. also nach den Vorschriften der Art. 647—654, von welchen namentlich auch Art. 650 Anwendung findet Abg. l 62 (v. Neum.)

2) Die Frist von 15 Tagen wird eintretenden Falls nach Vorschrift des Art. 209 verlängert.

3) Was die Mittheilung des Erkenntnisses an die Untergerichte und Parteien betrifft, so merkt man dem Art. 35 an, daß er redigirt wurde, ehe man an die Bestimmungen des Hauptst. XXV dachte.

Er geht offenbar von der Voraussetzung aus, daß die Urschrift des Erkenntnisses im Verwahre des Gerichtsschreibers am Obergerichte verbleibe, dieser aber auf Begehren des Staatsanwaltes oder Gerichtsvorstandes Abschriften davon fertige, welche den Untergerichten mitgetheilt werden. Durch den Gerichtsschreiber desjenigen Gerichts, welchem die Sache zugewiesen wurde, sollen sodann beide Parteien vom Urtheile Kenntniß erhalten, d. h. Einsicht der bei ihm verwahrten Ausfertigung des Verweisungs-Erkenntnisses.

Hiermit läßt sich nun die Bestimmung des Art. 651 nicht vereinigen, welcher vorschreibt, daß — falls das Gesetz nicht anders verfügt — die Entscheidungen auf einfache Vorstellungen dem Gesuchsteller in Urschrift auszuhändigen seien.

Bei diesem Conflikte glaube ich, daß Zweck und Sinn des Art. 35 die Anwendung des Art. 651 ausschließen und bezüglich der Mittheilung des Urtheils nur die Sonderbestimmungen jenes Artikels gelten. Insbesondere aber wird es als Wille des Gesetzes zu betrachten sein, daß so wichtige Erkenntnisse, wie diejenigen über Competenzconflikte, nicht, gleich einer Entscheidung über ein Arrestgesuch &c., in Urschrift abzugeben seien.

4) Gegen das die Zuständigkeit regelnde Erkenntniß ist kein Rechtsmittel zulässig, also auch nicht die Nichtigkeitsbeschwerde!

5) Die nach Art. 36 getroffene Verfügung wird selbstverständlich in der nemlichen Weise zur Kenntniß der Untergerichte und der Parteien gebracht, wie das Enderkenntniß.

6) Nachdem die Verweisung einer Streitsache vor ein bestimmtes Gericht ausgesprochen worden, ist es Aufgabe der Parteien, dieselbe dort anhängig zu machen. Im Falle der Connexität ist die zugewiesene Sache im Wege einfachen motivirten Antrages (Art. 483. vgl. Art. 510) mit der anhängigen Sache in Verbindung zu bringen. Die in Art. 37 verfügte Taxfreiheit begreift alle in die Staatskasse fließenden Gefälle. Ges. v. 28. Mai 1850, Art. 24.

Vereinbarter Gerichtsstand.

Art. 38. — **Im ersten Rechtszuge können die Parteien eine Streitsache durch ausdrückliche oder stillschweigende Vereinbarung auch an ein nicht zuständiges Gericht bringen.**

Diese Vereinbarung ist unstatthaft:

1) **bei Streitigkeiten über Gültigkeit oder Trennung von Ehen;**

2) **bei Klagen auf Aufhebung der ehelichen Gütergemeinschaft oder Aenderung der ehelichen Güterverhältnisse, wenn das betreffende Civilrecht den Eheleuten nicht gestattet, diese Aufhebung oder Aenderung durch Vertrag vorzunehmen;**

3) **bei Streitigkeiten über den Personenstand mit Ausnahme der Klagen auf Anerkennung der Vaterschaft außerehelicher Kinder;**

4) **bei Streitigkeiten über die Bestellung oder Enthebung von Vormündern, gerichtlichen Beiständen und Pflegern;**

5) **bei Entschädigungsklagen gegen Richter, Staatsanwälte, Gerichtsschreiber, Notare, Anwälte oder Gerichtsvollzieher wegen Dienstwidrigkeiten;**

6) **bei den in Art. 21, Art. 27 Abs. 2, Art. 28, 590 und 604 bezeichneten Klagen;**

7) **bei Anständen und Streitigkeiten im Vollstreckungs- und Gantverfahren;**

8) **wenn durch die Vereinbarung die Zuständigkeit eines Appellations- oder Handels-Appellationsgerichts oder des obersten Gerichtshofs begründet werden soll;**

9) **wenn durch die Vereinbarung die Zuständigkeit eines Handels- oder Ehegerichts auf Streitsachen, welche nicht zur Zuständigkeit dieser Gerichte gehören, ausgedehnt werden will — unbeschadet jedoch der Vereinbarung auf ein Handelsgericht in den in Art. 7 Abs. 2 bezeichneten Handelssachen;**

10) **wenn für die Klagen aus Wechseln oder kaufmännischen Anweisungen ein Bezirks- oder Einzelngericht zuständig werden soll.**

G. A. d. K. d. A. I S. 63, 64, 66—71, 83, 84, 299 IV S. 18. — K. d. R. I S. 107—117, IV S. 7.

1) Allzustrenge Competenzregeln, welche in jedem Ueberschreiten der dem einzelnen Richter gesetzten Schranken eine schwere, mit unheilbarer Nichtigkeit zu ahndende, Versündigung erblicken,

eignen sich nicht mehr für die jetzigen Zustände und den Geist der jetzigen Gesetze; sie mögen sehr schön sein in der „grauen Theorie“, allein sie taugen nichts im praktischen Leben. Dies ist insbesondere auch anerkannt in Frankreich. Jene schönklingenden, aber unpraktischen Worte von Carré, welche Edel Comm. zum G. V. G. v. 1861 Art. 9 anführt, haben, wie so viele Ansichten von Carré, schon längst ihre Geltung verloren; im Gegentheile ist in neuerer Zeit das Streben der Jurisprudenz entschieden dahin gerichtet, bezüglich der Competenz, insbesondere bezüglich der Prorogation, möglichst liberale Grundsätze zur Geltung zu bringen (vgl. oben Art. 9—11 Nr. 19).

Unsere neue Prozeßordnung hat, wie nicht zu verkennen, durch Beseitigung der unheilbaren Nichtigkeit in ihrer seitherigen Ausdehnung und durch Erweiterung des Rechts der Vereinbarung einen großen Schritt vorwärts gethan; um so mehr ist zu beklagen, daß sie in einem Punkte rückwärts geschritten ist.

2) Es gibt zwei Hauptarten der Unzuständigkeit, nemlich 1) eine sachliche, wenn die Streitsache einem Gerichte anderer Art, und 2) eine örtliche, wenn sie dem gleichartigen Gerichte eines andern Ortes zugewiesen ist.

Letztere Unzuständigkeit ist bei jetzigen Zuständen, wo alle Gerichte vom Staate bestellt sind und gleiche Garantieen bieten, von sehr untergeordneter Bedeutung. Ob es geeignet sei, daß das Bezirksgericht A oder daß das Bezirksgericht B entscheide, ist eine Frage, welche, seltene Ausnahmen abgerechnet, kein öffentliches Interesse berührt, bei deren Lösung vielmehr nur gewöhnliche Rücksichten der Zweckmäßigkeit, der Kostenersparung ꝛc. den Ausschlag geben; es stand daher nichts im Wege, hier der Vereinbarung vollen Spielraum zu gestatten, wie dies seither in der Pfalz unbedingt, diesseits wenigstens bei Einwilligung des prorogirten Richters der Fall gewesen ist.

3) Nichtsdestoweniger hat Art. 38 in einer Reihe von Fällen (Ziff. 1—7) die Vereinbarung über ein anderes Gericht der nemlichen Art völlig ausgeschlossen.

Man dachte, wie die Verhandlungen zeigen, an den Fall, wo die Parteien eine wichtige Sache, z. B. eine Ehesache, willkürlich vor ein Gericht ziehen wollen, welches offenbar das zuständige nicht ist; allein, abgesehen davon, daß kein besonderes Unglück darin erblickt werden kann, wenn statt des Ehegerichts A das Ehegericht B entscheidet, ist dieser Fall unpraktisch, d. h. er wird nicht leicht vorkommen.

Hätte man sich mehr die praktischen Fälle vergegenwärtigt, z. B. jene Fälle, wo es zweifelhaft ist, ob eine Klage dinglich, ob sie persönlich sei, ob der Beklagte seinen Wohnsitz oder Aufenthalt hier oder dort, oder ob er gar keinen Wohnsitz und Aufenthalt habe u. s. w., so würde die Sache vielleicht in anderem Lichte erschienen sein. Was insbesondere die Ehesachen in der Pfalz anbelangt, so könnte ich Fälle namhaft machen, in denen es höchst erwünscht war, daß durch Vereinbarung die Frage, welches Bezirksgericht das zuständige sei, beseitigt wurde.

Ferner ist nicht zu übersehen, daß es Fälle gibt, wo jene Zweckmäßigkeitsgründe, welche für Austheilung der Prozesse unter die Gerichte gleicher Art maßgebend waren, ausnahmsweise wegfallen, und daß das Vorhandensein eines solchen Ausnahmszustandes ohne Gefahr für die öffentliche Ordnung wohl vermuthet werden darf, wenn beide Parteien einig sind, bei einem andern Gerichte Recht zu nehmen.

4) Andrerseits sind aber noch weiter die schlimmen Folgen nicht außer Acht zu lassen, welche aus einer derartigen Steigerung der Ausschließlichkeit der Gerichtsstände sich ergeben und welche im grellen Mißverhältnisse stehen zu den Vortheilen, welche man sich davon verspricht.

Der Kläger kann in zweifelhaften Fällen, bei größter Vorsicht, doch nur dasjenige Gericht wählen, welches er selbst für das zuständige hält. Erzeigt ihm nun der Beklagte nicht den Gefallen, eine Incompetenz-Einrede vorzubringen und hierdurch eine der Rechtskraft fähige Entscheidung herbeizuführen, so hängt über seinem Prozesse so lange, bis alle Rechtsmittel erschöpft sind, das Damoklesschwert der unheilbaren Nichtigkeit. In jedem Augenblicke, in der Berufungs- und Cassations-Instanz, kann, sei es auf Anregung des Beklagten, sei es von Amtswegen, die Unzuständigkeit ausgesprochen werden, falls das betreffende Gericht bezüglich der vorliegenden Rechtsverhältnisse oder Thatsachen die Ansicht des Klägers nicht theilt, oder neue Thatsachen vorgebracht werden. (Art. 707.)

Man darf nicht sagen, wenn der Beklagte erst in der Berufungsinstanz geltend mache, das angegangene Gericht sei nicht dasjenige seines Wohnsitzes ꝛc., so sei dies Chikane, und das Gericht müsse Chikanen zurückweisen; denn es ist der Richter nicht berufen, das Gesetz zu verbessern, und (wie Grant sagt) der beste Weg, um Mängel des Gesetzes bald zu beseitigen, ist, es streng zu vollziehen.

5) Schließlich ist seltsam, daß man von den Vorschlägen, der Gerichtsstand der gelegenen Sache solle nur ein fakultativer sein, zum entgegen-

gesetzten Extreme überspringen konnte, ihn zu einem nothwendigen zu machen, d. h. mit dessen Nichtbeachtung eine, bis zur Erschöpfung aller Rechtsmittel unheilbare, Nichtigkeit zu verbinden!

Befürchtete man etwa, die Anwälte würden ohne alle praktischen Vortheile für die Parteien, bloß ihres Interesse halber, Prozesse vor falsche Gerichte ziehen — eine Furcht, welche ich nach meinen Erfahrungen nicht theile — so hätte man höchstens noch die Zustimmung des angegangenen Gerichts verlangen, d. h. man hätte diesem Gerichte die Befugniß einräumen dürfen, in seinem ersten Erkenntnisse von Amtswegen die Sache zurückzuweisen.

6) Vorstehende Erörterung bezweckt hauptsächlich, die wichtigen Folgen der die Vereinbarung ausschließenden Bestimmungen des Art. 38 grell vor Augen zu führen, um diejenigen, welche Klagen einzuleiten haben, zu veranlassen, bei Wahl des Gerichtes mit größter Vorsicht zu Werke zu gehen.

Sind mehrere Gerichte in Frage, so ist es im Zweifel rathsam, dasjenige zu wählen, welches nöthigenfalls durch Vereinbarung zuständig werden kann.

Ferner wird in Fällen, wo Vereinbarung ausgeschlossen ist, dem Beklagten anzurathen sein, überall, wo auch nur entfernt ein Anlaß dazu gegeben erscheint, die Einrede der Unzuständigkeit (natürlich nur mit eventueller Einlassung auf die Sache) vorzuschützen, weil dies der einzige Weg ist, um Sicherheit zu schaffen, und es sonst geschehen könnte, daß, falls etwa in erster Instanz zum Nachtheile des Klägers entschieden wäre, dieser selbst in zweiter Instanz die Unzuständigkeit anregen würde.

7) Sämmtliche Verfügungen in Ziff. 1—7 wirken in beiden obenbezeichneten Richtungen, verbieten nemlich a) daß die angeführten Streitsachen an ein Gericht anderer Art und b) daß sie an das Gericht eines anderen Ortes gebracht werden.

Es können also nach Ziff. 7 Streitigkeiten im Vollstreckungsverfahren, sofern sie dem Bezirksgerichte zugewiesen sind, nicht an's Landgericht und umgekehrt die dem Landgerichte zugewiesenen nicht an's Bezirksgericht gebracht werden. Abgesehen von der Spezialbestimmung in Art. 28 ist dies wohl der einzige Fall, wo das Bezirksgericht eine landgerichtliche Sache von Amtswegen zurückweisen muß, — eine Anomalie, welche zwar wahrscheinlich nur daher rührt, daß die Fassung des Art. 38 schon in zweiter Lesung festgestellt war, als Art. 953 in's Gesetz kam, welche sich jedoch, da der Wortlaut klar ist, nicht wegstreiten läßt.

8) Bei Ehesachen fällt jetzt selbstverständlich auch jene Prorogation weg, welche durch Art. 4 der Verordnung vom 12. Dez. 1822 gestattet war.

9) Was die Streitigkeiten über Bestellung und Enthebung von Vormündern betrifft, so ist auf Art. 88 des Einf. Ges. hinzuweisen, wornach in der Pfalz Klagen auf Aufhebung von Familienraths-Beschlüssen beim Bezirksgerichte angestellt werden, in dessen Sprengel der Beschluß gefaßt worden ist.

10) In allen Fällen, welche Art. 38 nicht ausdrücklich ausnimmt, ist Vereinbarung unbedingt gestattet. Es kann also der Regel nach durch Vereinbarung zuständig werden:

a) das Bezirksgericht für Sachen, welche an die Handelsgerichte oder Landgerichte gehören, z. B. in der Pfalz für Besitzklagen;

b) das Landgericht für Sachen, welche an die Bezirksgerichte oder Handelsgerichte gehören.

Für die Wechselsachen besteht in so fern eine Ausnahme, als für sie zwar ein anderes Gericht als ein Handelsgericht nie zuständig werden kann, jedoch die Vereinbarung über das Handelsgericht eines andern Ortes nicht ausgeschlossen ist.

11) Daß Vereinbarung auch unter Ausländern unbedingt zulässig sei, falls für dieselben ein Klagrecht im Inlande besteht, ist selbstverständlich, wurde übrigens bei den Verhandlungen ausdrücklich anerkannt.

Art. 39. — **Stillschweigende Vereinbarung wird angenommen, wenn der Beklagte sich vor dem nicht zuständigen Gerichte auf den Streit eingelassen hat, ohne die Einrede der Unzuständigkeit vorzuschützen.**

Zur Erweiterung der Zuständigkeit eines Einzelngerichts wird jedoch erfordert, daß die Parteien sich hierüber ausdrücklich zu Protokoll erklären, nachdem der Richter sie über seine Unzuständigkeit belehrt hat.

In Versäumungsfällen gilt die Vereinbarung als abgelehnt.

G. A. d. K. d. A. I S. 71. 72. 209. IV S. 18. — K. d. R. I S. 117. 118.

1) Die Annahme, daß der Beklagte, welcher sich auf den Streit einläßt, ohne die Einrede der Unzuständigkeit vorzuschützen, sich freiwillig dem angegangenen Gerichte unterwerfe, enthält eine Rechtsvermuthung, gegen welche kein Beweis zulässig ist und wäre demnach der Beklagte nicht

etwa später mit dem Einwande zu hören, er habe die Absicht nicht gehabt zu vereinbaren oder er sei über rechtliche oder thatsächliche Gesichtspunkte im Irrthum gewesen. Sie wirkt ebenso wie der Ausschluß mit einer Einrede.

2) Ebensowenig wird besondere Vollmacht oder Rechtsfähigkeit Seitens des Vertreters verlangt werden können. Wer überhaupt die Fähigkeit vor Gericht zu stehen oder Jemanden dort zu vertreten, besitzt (Art. 58 und 59), hat auch die Fähigkeit, eine Vereinbarung über den Gerichtsstand zu treffen, mag sie stillschweigend oder ausdrücklich geschehen (Art. 60 und 92).

Vereinbarung ist kein Vergleich und es ist offenbar auch nicht die Absicht der P. O. dieselbe gleich einem Vergleiche zu behandeln, wie Letzteres die französische Jurisprudenz bezüglich der die sachliche Zuständigkeit ändernden Prorogation angenommen hat. Insbesondere kann auch aus Art. 1321 für vorliegenden Fall nichts gefolgert werden, denn die Bestellung eines Schiedsgerichts und die Uebertragung einer Streitsache an ein vom Staate bestelltes Gericht, mit Einhaltung der für die Vereinbarung vom Gesetze gezogenen Gränzen, sind zwei grundverschiedene Dinge.

3) Streiteinlassung. Die Ablehnung des Richters (Art. 44) sowie die in Art. 185 u. 186 bezeichneten Einwände und Einreden können vorgebracht werden, ohne die Einrede der Unzuständigkeit zu gefährden; hat sich jedoch der Beklagte, etwa zugleich mit denselben auf den Streit eingelassen, ohne diese Einrede vorzubringen, so ist sie verwirkt, d. h. es ist Vereinbarung anzunehmen. Abg. I 71 (v. Weiß).

4) Es kann keinem Zweifel unterliegen, daß die Bestimmung in Absatz 1 auch das schriftliche Vorverfahren im Auge hat (vgl. Art. 184 Abs. 3). Hat jedoch der Beklagte in seinem ersten Antrage die Einrede der Unzuständigkeit nur überhaupt geltend gemacht, so genügt dies, sollte es auch erst nach der Einlassung geschehen sein. Eine Prozeßschrift ist als Ganzes zu betrachten und die Reihenfolge des Vorbringens kann eine Rechtsverlustigung nicht zur Folge haben.

5) Bei den Einzelngerichten ist die Vereinbarung nur wirksam, wenn, nach Belehrung durch den Richter, die Parteien sich darüber zu Protokoll erklärt haben.

Es ist eigen, daß verlangt wird, beide Parteien seien zu belehren und hätten ihre Einwilligung zu Protokoll zu erklären; man sollte meinen, im Falle, wo der Kläger eine Ladung hat zustellen lassen, wie es Regel ist, sei sein Wille hinlänglich bekundet und wenn nun der Beklagte erscheint und zufrieden ist, vor dem vom Kläger gewählten Richter sein Recht zu nehmen, so dürfte es nicht mehr in der Macht des Klägers stehen, durch Verweigerung seiner Zustimmung die Zuständigkeit in Frage zu stellen!

Die betreffende Bestimmung ist dem Art. 7 Code de proc. entnommen, hatte jedoch dort einen etwas anderen Sinn. Sie hatte nemlich dort zunächst nur den Fall im Auge, wo die Parteien ohne Ladung, freiwillig, vor dem Friedensrichter erscheinen, in welchem Falle die Protokollirung auch die Ladung ersetzen muß und sich von selbst versteht, daß auch der Kläger zu hören ist. Für den Fall, wo durch Zustellung einer Ladung das Verfahren regelmäßig eingeleitet war, wendete man die Regel des Art. 170 Code de proc. an, gemäß welcher jede Unzuständigkeit, welche nicht sachlicher Natur ist, durch Nichtvorschützen der bezüglichen Einrede beseitigt wird und es stand nur noch in Frage, ob dieser Grundsatz auch bei der die friedensgerichtliche Competenzsumme überschreitenden Prorogation zu gelten habe, wie z. B. Chauveau sur Carré quest. 26 und cass. 12. März 1832 annehmen, oder aber nicht.

7) Der bestimmte klare Wortlaut unserer Bestimmung erlaubt nun aber offenbar nicht, auf jene französische Jurisprudenz Rücksicht zu nehmen, vielmehr erscheint außer Zweifel, daß das Erforderniß der Belehrung und Protokollar-Erklärung sowohl 1) im Falle gilt, wo eine Ladung ergangen ist, als 2) im Falle, wo es sich nur um eine örtliche Unzuständigkeit, d. h. die Frage handelt, ob das Landgericht A oder das Landgericht B erkennen solle.

Der erstere Fall ist nun allerdings ohne praktische Bedeutung, denn der Kläger wird wohl seine Zustimmung nie versagen, da ihn im Falle der Klagsabweisung die Kosten treffen und zudem der Richter veranlaßt sein könnte, eine der Frivolität entsprechende besondere Entschädigung auszusprechen. Art. 33 Abs. 3.

Was aber letzteren Fall betrifft, so treten hier alle Mißstände ein, wie sie oben (zu Art. 38 Nr. 4) erörtert worden sind. Dem Landrichter ist daher anzurathen, überall, wo irgend ein Zweifel an seiner Zuständigkeit möglich ist, die Parteien zur ausdrücklichen Vereinbarung zu bestimmen. Er mag dabei allerdings in die Lage kommen, den Beklagten auf die Möglichkeit chikanöser Einwände aufmerksam machen zu müssen; allein es erscheint dies als das kleinere Uebel und noch schlimmer wäre es, wenn der Prozeß auf die Gefahr hin zu Ende geführt würde, daß später alles vernichtet werden könnte.

8) Bei der protokollarischen Erklärung sind diejenigen Formen zu beobachten, welche Art. 166

und 167 vorschreiben. Sie ist so abzufassen, daß die Streitsache oder der Zwischenstreit (Art. 9) bezüglich deren die Zuständigkeit des Landrichters begründet werden soll, in ihren wesentlichen Theilen (Art. 225) klar bezeichnet wird.

Liegt eine Ladung vor, so wird Bezugnahme auf dieselbe genügen, und zwar um so mehr, da der Sachverhalt doch wieder in's Urtheil selbst aufgenommen werden muß. (Art. 515).

In Frankreich ist durch Dekret vom 16. Febr. 1811 (Tarif) § 11 verfügt, daß die Prorogations-Erklärungen mit den Urtheilen zu verbinden seien. Eine gleiche Verfügung hat unsere P. O. nicht und es steht daher nichts im Wege, daß das Urtheil sich beschränke, bei Darstellung des Sachverhaltes die in gesondertem Akte beurkundete Erklärung über die Vereinbarung anzuführen, wie man eine Vorladung anführt. Es scheint auch der Gesetzgeber ein anderes Verfahren nicht im Auge gehabt zu haben, weil er unter den in das Urtheilsbuch einzutragenden Bestandtheilen des Urtheiles (Art. 515) der in Frage stehenden Erklärung nicht erwähnt.

Einer Ausfertigung dieser Erklärung bedarf es nur im Falle der Ergreifung von Rechtsmitteln; für den Vollzug ist sie nicht nöthig, wie denn überhaupt das Urtheil, auch wenn es ganz unzuständig erlassen wurde, durch Ablauf der zur Erhebung von Rechtsmitteln gegebenen Fristen in Rechtskraft erwächst.

Anderseits möchte jedoch auch nichts im Wege stehen, die Prorogations-Erklärung mit dem Urtheile zu verbinden, was in manchen Fällen in so fern zweckmäßig erscheint, als die Geschichtserzählung des Urtheils durch Bezugnahme auf jene Erklärung sehr abgekürzt werden kann.

9) Erscheint der Beklagte nicht, so hat nach Art. 39 Abs. 3 jeder Richter seine Zuständigkeit, möge sie von sachlichen oder örtlichen Rücksichten abhängen, von Amtswegen zu prüfen, und, falls er sie nicht gegeben erachtet, die Klage abzuweisen. (Vgl. Art. 189).

Behinderung und Ablehnung der Richter, Staatsanwälte und Gerichtsschreiber.

Art. 40. — **Behinderung des Richters findet statt:**

1) in Sachen, in welchen er Partei oder regreßpflichtig ist;

2) in Sachen seiner wirklichen oder gewesenen Ehegattin;

3) in Sachen von Personen, welche mit ihm in gerader Linie oder in der Seitenlinie bis einschlüssig zum dritten Grade nach bürgerlicher Berechnung verwandt oder verschwägert sind;

4) in Sachen seiner Pflegbefohlenen;

5) in Sachen, in welchen er als Anwalt, Bevollmächtigter oder Beistand bestellt oder als gesetzlicher Vertreter einer der Parteien aufzutreten berechtigt ist oder war;

6) in Sachen, in welchen es sich um die Anfechtung oder Auslegung eines von ihm aufgenommenen oder bestätigten Akts der nichtstreitigen Rechtspflege oder in einem höheren Rechtszuge um Anfechtung einer Entscheidung handelt, bei deren Erlassung er als Richter mitgewirkt oder als Staatsanwalt Antrag gestellt hat.

Art. 41. — **Der Richter ist im Falle der Behinderung verpflichtet, sich jeder Thätigkeit in dem Rechtsstreite zu enthalten und sofort dem Gerichtsvorstande Kenntniß zu geben.**

Ist der Gerichtsvorstand selbst verhindert, so hat er dies seinem Stellvertreter und in Ermangelung eines solchen demjenigen Gerichte mitzutheilen, welches über eine ihn betreffende Ablehnung zu entscheiden haben würde.

Die von einem behinderten Richter nach Eintritt des Behinderungsgrundes vorgenommenen Prozeßhandlungen sind nichtig.

G. A. d. K. d. A. I S. 74. 233. 291. 299. IV S. 18. 19. — K. d. R. I S. 132—141.

1) Das Gesetz unterscheidet nach dem Vorbilde des hannoveranischen Entwurfes zwischen Behinderung des Richters, welche von selbst eintritt und wirkt und zwischen Ablehnung des Richters, welche das Gesuch einer Partei voraussetzt und erst von Mittheilung dieses Gesuches an den Richter, dessen Amtsthätigkeit lähmt. Die Fälle der Behinderung sind genau bestimmt, die Fälle der Ablehnung sind dem richterlichen Ermessen überlassen.

2) Diese Theorie, insbesondere der Satz, daß alles was der behinderte Richter gethan, aus Gründen der öffentlichen Ordnung nichtig sei, ist an sich schön und richtig, aber ein bischen unpraktisch. Um für Fälle, welche nie vorkommen, recht gut zu sorgen, hat man in Fällen, welche oft vorkommen, viel geschadet, sollte auch nur die große Aengstlichkeit in Anschlag gebracht werden, welche sich so wichtigen Folgen gegenüber nothwendig ergeben muß.

Eben diese wichtigen Folgen sind eine Mahnung, die Fälle der Behinderung einer genauen Prüfung und Sichtung zu unterwerfen, wobei nach der Natur der in Frage stehenden Bestimmungen und nach dem ausgesprochenen Willen des Gesetzgebers eine möglichst einschränkende Auslegung geboten erscheint.

3) Art. 40 Ziff. 1 erklärt den Richter behindert, welcher Partei ist.

Ist im Prozesse einer Aktiengesellschaft derjenige Richter Partei, welcher Aktien besitzt?

Man kann sagen, es seien im Prozesse einer Gesellschaft nur die Mitglieder der Gesellschaft als Parteien zu betrachten, denn die Verwaltungsräthe oder Direktoren, welche letztere möglicherweise ein eignes Interesse gar nicht haben, seien keine Parteien, sondern nur Vertreter oder Bevollmächtigte. Bei einer Aktiengesellschaft wäre demnach jeder Aktienbesitzer als Partei zu betrachten und auf den Werth der einzelnen Aktie im Verhältnisse zum ganzen Kapitale könnte es offenbar nicht ankommen, da, was vom Besitzer einer einzigen Aktie gälte, rechtlich auch vom Besitzer von hundert oder tausend Aktien gelten müßte.

Die Folgen dieser strengen Ansicht wären sehr weitgehend. In der Pfalz z. B. besitzen viele Richter Aktien der pfälzischen Bahnen, und diesseits viele Richter Aktien der Ostbahnen; diese alle würden also in den Prozessen der betreffenden Bahngesellschaften behindert sein und ihre Mitwirkung würde alle Verhandlungen und Entscheidungen nichtig machen. Wenn also die Ostbahngesellschaft einen Prozeß im Werthe von 1000 fl. führt, so wäre der Richter, welcher eine einzige Ostbahn-Aktie besitzt, obgleich nicht einmal zu einem Pfennig betheiligt, unfähig zu urtheilen!

Dies kann offenbar die Absicht des Gesetzes nicht sein. Dasselbe hatte sicher nur den Fall im Auge, wo der Richter förmlich die Stelle einer Partei im Rechtsstreite hat, wo er in demselben persönlich aufgeführt ist oder (wie bei einer offenen Handelsgesellschaft) wenigstens persönlich zu Prozeßhandlungen (Eiden 2c.) beigezogen werden kann. Ein Aktienbesitzer ist wohl betheiligt, jedoch nicht Partei, wie bei den Verhandlungen in Hannover (S. 615) ausdrücklich anerkannt worden ist.

Für die Richtigkeit dieser Auffassung spricht der Umstand, daß der Beisatz: „Mitberechtigter oder Mitverpflichteter" weggelassen wurde, weil in solchen Fällen nur Grund zur Ablehnung gegeben sei. Abg. IV 18 (v. Weiß). Wenn nemlich der Umstand, daß der Richter aktenmäßig solidarischer Mitberechtigter oder Mitverpflichteter einer Partei ist, nicht als Behinderung gilt, so kann auch der Aktienbesitz nicht von Belang sein.

Das Nemliche wird vom stillen Gesellschafter zu gelten haben

Ebenso ist der Richter nicht als Partei zu betrachten in Prozessen der Gemeinden, welcher er angehört, mag es sich auch um Nutzungen handeln, an denen jeder Gemeindebürger betheiligt ist

Als Ansicht des Ausschusses wurde erklärt (IV 18), daß auch Intervenienten, Litisconsorten, Adcitaten als Parteien zu betrachten seien. Was die Adcitaten betrifft, ist jedoch zu bemerken, daß sie nur als Parteien betrachtet werden können, wenn sie als solche förmlich beigeladen sind, daß aber eine bloße Benachrichtigung vom Prozesse, z. B. eine Streitverkündigung, Niemanden zur Partei macht.

4) Der Eigenschaft einer Partei wird gleichgestellt die Regreßpflicht.

Es ist dies im Grunde eine Inconsequenz, denn die Regreßpflicht enthält keine stärkere Betheiligung als die Mitberechtigung und Mitverpflichtung. Die Folge ist übrigens, daß wenn ein solidarischer Mitschuldner oder Bürge des Richters belangt wird, dieser als behindert erscheint, weil hier zugleich eine Regreßpflicht eintritt, daß, wenn aber ein Hauptschuldner belangt wird, für welchen der Richter solidarisch gebürgt hat, keine Behinderung vorliegt.

Abgesehen hiervon ist diese Bestimmung etwas unpraktisch, da das Vorliegen einer Regreßpflicht nicht immer klar und greifbar ist, von sehr schwierigen Rechts- oder That-Fragen abhängen, ja unter Umständen dem Richter selbst unbekannt sein kann.

Es kann nemlich, nach der Fassung des Gesetzes, kein Zweifel bestehen, daß nicht erfordert wird, es müsse der Richter schon als regreßpflichtig belangt oder ihm wenigstens der Streit verkündet worden sein, daß es vielmehr genügt, wenn eine Regreßpflicht überhaupt vorliege.

Der Fall, wo deßhalb Anstände hervorgerufen werden, wird übrigens nicht leicht vorkommen, denn selbstverständlich wird hier, wie in allen Fällen, wo auch nur die entfernteste Möglichkeit einer Behinderung gegeben ist, der Richter selbst seine Amtsthätigkeit ablehnen.

5) Die Worte: „gewesene Ehegatten" wurden gesetzt, um auch den Fall der Nichtigerklärung einer Ehe zu begreifen.

6) Unter Verwandten, im Sinne der Ziff. 3, sind alle Blutsverwandten zu verstehen ohne Unterschied, ob die Verwandtschaft durch eheliche oder uneheliche Zeugung entstanden ist. Die Grund-

sätze des französischen Rechts, daß uneheliche Kinder mit den Verwandten ihrer Eltern in keinem Verhältnisse der Verwandtschaft stehen, gelten hier nicht.

Verwandtschaft durch Adoption ist nur Grund zur Ablehnung. Abg. I 291 (Barth).

Wenn in den oben Nr. 3 angeführten Fällen die Betheiligung des Richters selbst keine Behinderung begründet, so kann um so weniger die Betheiligung von Verwandten 2c. Grund einer Behinderung sein. vgl. Zink z. Not. Ges. Art. 47 Ziff. 2.

7) Die Pflegbefohlenen wurden eingesetzt, um Einklang mit den Bestimmungen des Art. 201 herbeizuführen. Abg. I 291. Zufolge dieser Bestimmung ist der Richter auch dann in den Prozessen seiner Mündel und Curanden behindert, wenn er im einzelnen Falle ihr Vertreter nicht ist und nicht sein kann.

8) Der Beisatz der zwei Worte: „und war“ gibt der Ziff. 5 eine große, vielleicht zu große Tragweite.

Was die Bestellung zum Anwalte oder Beistande betrifft, so setzt dieselbe nothwendig einen anhängigen oder beabsichtigten Prozeß voraus, für welchen der förmliche Auftrag, als Anwalt oder Beistand in der fraglichen Sache aufzutreten erfolgt ist. — Bloße Rathsertheilungen genügen nicht (R. R. I 134). Wer jedoch z. B. ein Gesuch um Ermächtigung zu einer Theilung oder um Homologation einer solchen eingereicht hat, ist behindert in Fällen, wo es sich um Anfechtung oder Auslegung dieser Theilung handelt. Einem Richter, welcher früher Anwalt war, wird daher große Vorsicht anzurathen sein.

Als Bevollmächtigter kann Jemand bestellt sein, auch ohne alle Rücksicht auf einen Prozeß, und dies auszudrücken, ist der Zweck des Wortes. Abg. I 74 (v. Weiß). Wer also bezüglich eines Rechtsgeschäftes oder Rechtsverhältnisses irgend einmal Bevollmächtigter war, darf nie mehr Richter sein in Prozessen, welche dasselbe zum Gegenstande haben oder wesentlich berühren.

9) An gleicher Allgemeinheit leidet die Bestimmung, daß Niemand Richter sein dürfe in Sachen, worin er einmal als Vertreter einer der Parteien aufzutreten berechtigt war.

Man wird prüfen, müssen, ob das Rechtsverhältniß, welches Gegenstand des Prozesses bildet, zur Zeit, als der Richter gesetzlicher Vertreter der Partei war, bereits vorhanden war, so daß Prozeß darüber hätte entstehen können, wenn sich Anlaß dazu ergeben hätte. Den früheren Vormund berühren z. B. die Rechtsgeschäfte, welche der spätere Vormund abgeschlossen hat, nicht, wohl aber seine eigenen, sowie diejenigen seines Vorgängers.

10) Was die frühere Antragstellung als Staatsanwalt betrifft, so ist nicht ganz klar, was gemeint sei. Wirkliche Anträge stellt der Staatsanwalt nur, wo er Partei (partie principale) ist, sonst gibt er eigentlich nur Gutachten ab, welche man jedoch auch Anträge zu nennen pflegt. Es ist nun allerdings anzunehmen, daß hier das Wort im weiteren Sinne gemeint sei, allein es entsteht die Frage, ob nur jene Fälle getroffen werden wollen, wo das Gesetz verfügt, daß die Staatsbehörde zu hören sei (was bis jetzt in der Pfalz in sehr vielen Fällen Vorschrift war), oder auch jene, wo sie für gut fand, aus freiem Antriebe gutachtliche Bemerkungen zu machen.

Es kann sein, daß die Staatsbehörde in Sachen, welche nicht communicabel waren, einen großen auf das Detail der Sache eingehenden Vortrag gehalten hat, von welchem im Urtheile nichts erwähnt ist, während sie in einer communicablen Sache, wo im Urtheile steht: „nach Anhörung der Staatsbehörde“, nur den unschuldigen Antrag gestellt hat, es bleibe die Entscheidung der Weisheit des Gerichts überlassen.

Den Richtern, welche früher Staatsanwälte waren, wird anzurathen sein, ohne Unterschied in allen Sachen, wo sie als in der Sitzung anwesend im Urtheile bezeichnet sind, ihr Amt abzulehnen.

11) Die Nichtigkeit, welche Art. 41 Abs. 3 ausspricht, ist selbstverständlich keine völlig unheilbare, denn unsere P. O. kennt solche Nichtigkeiten nicht mehr. Sie muß durch die gewöhnlichen Rechtsmittel geltend gemacht werden. Insbesondere ist die Nichtigkeitsbeschwerde (Art. 788 Ziff. 6) und in Ausnahmsfällen die Wiederaufnahme des Verfahrens (Art. 761 Ziff. 7) zulässig.

Art. 42. — **Ein Richter kann wegen Behinderung oder wegen Besorgniß der Befangenheit abgelehnt werden.**

Im letztern Falle findet die Ablehnung aus allen Gründen statt, welche geeignet sind, Mißtrauen gegen die Unparteilichkeit des Richters zu rechtfertigen.

Art. 43. — **Die Ablehnungsgründe können von jeder Partei geltend gemacht werden, ohne Rücksicht darauf, ob nach Beschaffenheit dieser Gründe die ablehnende Partei selbst oder die Gegenpartei als gefährdet erscheint.**

Mehrere gleichzeitig vorhandene Ablehnungsgründe gegen denselben Richter oder gegen verschiedene Mitglieder des nämlichen Gerichts sind zusammen vorzubringen.

Art. 44. — **Das Recht, einen Richter wegen Besorgniß der Befangenheit abzulehnen, kann nur solange ausgeübt werden, als die Partei sich nicht vor dem abzulehnenden Richter in Verhandlungen eingelassen oder ein Gesuch an denselben gestellt hat.**

Im weitern Laufe des Verfahrens ist eine solche Ablehnung nur dann gestattet, wenn die Thatsachen, welche sie begründen, erst später eingetreten oder zur Kenntniß der Partei gelangt sind, was von dieser in Ermangelung anderweitiger genügender Bescheinigung eidlich zu erhärten ist.

G. A. d. K. d. A I S. 74. 75. 123. IV S. 19. 20. — K. d. R. I S. 141—143 IV S. 7. 8.

1) Die Ablehnung soll wegen aller Gründe stattfinden können, welche geeignet sind, Mißtrauen gegen die Unparteilichkeit des Richters zu rechtfertigen. — Rechtsansichten, welche der Richter in veröffentlichten Werken oder gesprächsweise kundgegeben hat, vermögen nie seine Unparteilichkeit in Frage zu stellen; ebensowenig Ansichten, welche er pflichtgemäß in früheren Erkenntnissen oder sonst in dienstlicher Eigenschaft an den Tag gelegt hat, mag es auch in der nemlichen Sache gewesen sein, den Fall des Art. 40 Ziff. 6 ausgenommen.

Hat sich jedoch der Richter außerdienstlich über eine bestimmte Streitsache geäußert, so ist dies allerdings ein Grund der Ablehnung; ebenso wenn er Rath in der Sache ertheilt hat.

2) Das Recht der Ablehnung, wenn es nicht auf Behinderung sich gründet, ist erloschen, wenn die Partei sich vor dem betreffenden Richter in Verhandlungen irgend einer Art eingelassen oder irgend ein Gesuch an ihn gestellt hat. — Wenn daher auch nur die Einrede der Unzuständigkeit vorgebracht oder ein Vertagungsbegehren gestellt worden ist, so liegt darin ein Verzicht auf die Ablehnung, falls die Partei nicht in der Art. 44 Abs. 2 bezeichneten Weise darthun kann, daß sie vom Ablehnungsgrunde keine Kenntniß hatte.

Art. 45. — **Die Ablehnung eines Richters ist bei dem Gerichte, bei welchem der Abgelehnte angestellt ist, mittels einfacher Vorstellung anzubringen, welche auch vor dem Gerichtsschreiber zu Protokoll gegeben werden kann.**

Die Vorstellung muß die Thatsachen enthalten, welche die Ablehnung begründen. Zugleich sind die zu deren Bescheinigung dienenden Belege zu übergeben und die etwaigen weitern Bescheinigungsmittel, deren Erhebung die Partei beantragt, anzuführen. Die Bescheinigung durch Eid ist unzulässig.

Wird die Ablehnung in einer bereits anhängigen Sache angebracht, so hat der Gesuchsteller der Gegenpartei von dem Gesuche Kenntniß zu geben.

Art. 46. — **Wird ein Mitglied eines Collegialgerichts abgelehnt, so ist die Erklärung des Abgelehnten durch den Gerichtsvorstand einzuholen, welcher, soferne er die Sache nicht selbst durch geeignete Anordnung zu erledigen vermag, die Entscheidung des Gerichts zu veranlassen und, wenn dieses beschlußunfähig ist, die Sache dem vorgesetzten Gerichte zur Entscheidung vorzulegen hat.**

Art. 47. — **Die Vorstellung, mittels deren ein Mitglied eines Einzelngerichts abgelehnt wird, ist von diesem Gerichte mit der Erklärung des Abgelehnten an das vorgesetzte Bezirksgericht zur Entscheidung einzusenden.**

Dieser Einsendung bedarf es nicht, wenn der abgelehnte Richter das Gesuch für begründet erachtet und ein Stellvertreter desselben vorhanden ist.

Art. 48. — **Die in Art. 46 und 47 erwähnte Entscheidung erfolgt nach Vernehmung des Staatsanwalts, wenn ein solcher an dem Gerichte angestellt ist.**

Bezüglich der Eröffnung an das Untergericht und an die Betheiligten findet die Bestimmung des Art. 35 Abs. 4 Anwendung.

Art. 49. — **Gegen die Entscheidung, welche der Ablehnung stattgibt, ist kein Rechtsmittel zulässig. Gegen die Verwerfung des Gesuchs kann innerhalb acht Tagen nach Eröffnung des Erkenntnisses Beschwerde erhoben werden.**

Auch hier gilt die Bestimmung des Art. 45 Abs. 3.

Art. 50. — **Das Verfahren ist, wenn dem Gesuche stattgegeben wird, tax- und stempelfrei. Im Falle der Zurückweisung des Gesuchs hat der Gesuchsteller die Kosten zu tragen.**

Liegt dem Gesuche böse Absicht oder Leichtfertigkeit zu Grunde, so ist der Gesuchsteller, nach Umständen dessen Gewalthaber, in eine Geldstrafe bis zu fünfzig Gulden zu verfällen.

Art. 51. — **Von der Zeit an, wo der Richter von der Ablehnung amtliche Kenntniß erhält, hat er sich der weitern Thätigkeit in dem Rechtsstreite zu enthalten.**

Handelt er dieser Vorschrift entgegen, so ist, wenn dem Gesuche stattgegeben wird, das Verfahren nichtig.

Ist der abgelehnte Richter als Commissär mit der Vornahme eines Geschäfts beauftragt, welches als dringlich erscheint, so ist von dem Gerichtsvorstande ein anderer Commissär zur Aushilfe zu ernennen.

G. A. d. K. d. A. I. S. 74 75. 84. 233. 294. 299. IV S. 19. 20. 302. — K. d. R. I S. 143—146. IV S. 8. 9.

1) Mit der Verfügung des Art. 45, daß die Ablehnung mittelst einfacher Vorstellung anzubringen sei, sind die Bestimmungen des Hauptstücks XXV anwendbar erklärt, soweit nicht eine Ausnahme von denselben anzunehmen ist.

2) Indem das Gesetz in Art. 45 Abs. 2 nur von Bescheinigungen spricht, welche beizubringen oder zu beantragen seien, deutet es hinlänglich an, daß strenge Beweisführung nicht verlangt wird.

3) Die Kenntnißgabe, von welcher Art. 45, Abs. 3 spricht, erfolgt im Wege abschriftlicher Zustellung des Gesuchs durch einen Gerichtsboten (Art. 101). Das Gesetz verlangt, daß die Gegenpartei vom Gesuche, also nicht bloß von der Eingabe des Gesuches, Kenntniß erhalte.

4) Bezüglich der Eröffnungen an das Untergericht und an die Betheiligten, wovon Art. 48 spricht, gilt das zu Art. 35 Nr. 3 Gesagte.

Die Erhebung der Beschwerde, von welcher in Art. 49 die Rede ist, richtet sich nach den Vorschriften des Hauptstücks XXVIII. vgl. Abg. I 194 (v. Neumayr).

5) Die amtliche Kenntniß, welche nach Art. 51 die Amtsthätigkeit des Richters hemmt, erfolgt entweder durch Eingabe des Gesuchs, wenn der Richter, an welchen es gerichtet, selbst abgelehnt ist, oder durch die Aufforderung zur Erklärung nach Art. 46.

Durch die Vorschrift, daß die Nichtigkeit der Amtshandlungen vom Schicksale der Ablehnung abhängig sei, soll offenbar ganz frivolen, rein nur auf Chikane berechneten Ablehnungsgesuchen entgegengetreten werden. In solchen Ausnahmsfällen wird der Richter im Interesse des Rechts und zur Abwendung der etwa beabsichtigten Beschädigungen der Gegenpartei, soweit nöthig, weiter handeln können, ohne eine Pflichtverletzung zu begehen. Es könnte ja sonst ein böswilliger Schuldner durch beliebige Ablehnungsgesuche die Thätigkeit der Gerichte ihm gegenüber für einige Zeit ganz lahm legen.

Art. 52. — **Die Art. 40—51 sind auch auf Gerichtsschreiber anzuwenden, jedoch tritt die in Art. 41 Abs. 3 und Art. 51 Abs. 2 angedrohte Nichtigkeit der Prozeßhandlung nicht ein, wenn der Gerichtsschreiber als Protokollführer unter Leitung eines Richters gehandelt hat.**

Der Gerichtsschreiber kann auch abgelehnt werden, wenn er mit dem die Verhandlung leitenden Richter in gerader Linie oder bis einschlüssig zu dritten Grade in der Seitenlinie nach bürgerlicher Berechnung verwandt oder verschwägert ist.

Wird ein Gerichtsschreiber eines Einzelngerichts abgelehnt, so erfolgt die etwa erforderliche Entscheidung durch den Vorstand dieses Gerichts oder dessen Stellvertreter, im Falle der Behinderung derselben durch das vorgesetzte Bezirksgericht.

Die Beschwerdeführung gegen Entscheidungen des Vorstands eines Einzelngerichts oder seines Stellvertreters geht an das vorgesetzte Bezirksgericht.

Art. 53. — **Ablehnung staatsanwaltschaftlicher Beamten ist unstatthaft; doch können die Parteien in den hiezu geeigneten Fällen die Abordnung eines andern Mitglieds der Staatsanwaltschaft bei dieser selbst oder bei der unmittelbar vorgesetzten Behörde nachsuchen.**

G. A. d. K. d. A. I S. 75 76. 84. 233. 291. 299. IV. S. 20. — K. d. R. I. S. 146—148.

1) Die Bestimmung, daß die Behinderung oder Ablehnung eines Gerichtschreibers nur dann Nichtigkeit begründen könne, wenn er selbständig gehandelt hat, z. B. im Falle des Art. 45, nicht aber, wenn er bloß Protokollführer war, wie z. B. in der Sitzung, ist höchst sachgemäß. Die Folge der Nichtbeachtung des Willens des Gesetzes ist letzteren Falles bloß disciplinäre Ahndung.

2) Der Antrag auf Abordnung eines anderen Mitgliedes der Staatsanwaltschaft hat nicht die Wirkung einer Ablehnung, und es wird, da das Gesetz etwas Bezügliches nicht verfügt, durch denselben das gerichtliche Verfahren in keiner Weise gehemmt oder verzögert.

Es wird übrigens dem Staatsanwalte freistehen, geeigneten Falles Antrag auf Vertagung zu stellen und dem Gerichte, einen solchen Antrag zu berücksichtigen oder nicht. Jedenfalls wird aber der Staatsanwalt auf das Gesuch Bescheid erlassen müssen, denn da die Parteien das Recht des Gesuchs haben, so sind sie auch berechtigt, förmlichen Bescheid zu verlangen.

Uebertragung der Gerichtsbarkeit.

Art. 54. — Die Verweisung einer Sache von dem an sich zuständigen Gerichte an ein anderes von gleicher Ordnung ist durch das vorgesetzte Gericht auf Antrag einer Partei oder des Staatsanwalts oder auch von Amtswegen zu verfügen, wenn bei dem an sich zuständigen Gerichte die zur Ausübung des Richteramts erforderlichen Personen nicht vorhanden oder an dieser Ausübung gehindert sind oder die Verhandlung der Sache durch andere Umstände unmöglich gemacht ist.

Die Anordnung erfolgt nach Vernehmung des Staatsanwalts, wenn ein solcher bei dem Gerichte aufgestellt ist. Ein Rechtsmittel findet hiegegen nicht statt.

Bezüglich der Eröffnung an die Untergerichte und an die Betheiligten gilt die Bestimmung des Art. 35 Abs. 4.

Dringliche Verfügungen können unmittelbar von dem vorgesetzten Gerichte getroffen werden.

Im Uebrigen richtet sich das Verfahren nach den Bestimmungen des XXV. Hauptstücks.

G. A. d. K. d. A. I S. 73. 84. 233. 299. IV S. 20. — K. d. R. I S. 149.

1) Der Mangel der nöthigen Richter kann eintreten aus rechtlichen Gründen, in Folge von Behinderung und Ablehnung, oder aus thatsächlichen Gründen, wegen Todesfall, Krankheit, Kriegsereignisse ꝛc.; immer aber müssen die Umstände der Art sein, daß eine Unmöglichkeit angenommen werden kann. Die Abordnung eines anderen Gerichtes wegen Gefährdung der öffentlichen Ordnung und Sicherheit wurde, als zu weit gehend, nicht zugelassen.

2) Die Verfügungen des Ger. V. G. v. 1861 Art. 37, wornach im Falle, wo an einem Collegialgerichte die zur Beschlußfassung erforderliche Zahl von Richtern nicht vorhanden ist, Mitglieder der nächstgelegenen Bezirks-, Stadt- oder Land-Gerichte zugezogen werden sollen, werden durch Art. 54 nicht beseitigt. Nur wenn dieses Mittel nicht ausreicht, soll die Abordnung erfolgen. Abg. I 73 (v. Neumayr u. v. Weiß).

3) Was die Mittheilungen an Untergerichte und Betheiligte betrifft s. Art. 35 Nr. 3.

Dienstliche Ersuchen und Aufträge.

Art. 55. — Uebertragung von richteramtlichen Handlungen durch Ersuchen an gleichgestellte oder durch Auftrag an untergeordnete Gerichte findet nur in den durch das Gesetz bezeichneten Fällen statt.

Auch den von einem ausländischen Gerichte im Laufe eines bei demselben anhängigen Streits gestellten Ersuchen ist vorbehaltlich besonderer Staatsverträge und der allenfalls durch Verordnung bestimmten Retorsionsmaßregeln zu entsprechen, wenn die Verfassung und die Gesetze des Königreichs nicht entgegenstehen, dem ersuchenden Gerichte in der Sache kein Eingriff in die Zuständigkeit der bayerischen Gerichte zur Last fällt und die Kosten gedeckt sind.

Was das gegenwärtige Gesetzbuch von dem beauftragten Richter sagt, ist auch von dem ersuchten zu verstehen.

G. A. d. K. d. A. I S. 72. 73. 84. 294 295. 299. IV S. 20. — K. d. R. I S. 150—152.

1) Das Gesetz stellt für die streitige Rechtspflege als Grundsatz auf, daß richteramtliche Handlungen nur in den durch das Gesetz bezeichneten Fällen an andere Gerichte, seien es gleichgestellte oder untergeordnete, übertragen werden können. Diese Fälle betreffen insbesondere die Beweisaufnahmen. Art. 334 u. 335.

Auch für die Ersuchen ausländischer Gerichte wird dieser Grundsatz, dem Wesen nach, Anwendung finden müssen. Die Worte in Abs. 2: „im Laufe eines — Streites“ wurden beigefügt in der Erwägung, daß für die Ersuchen um Anordnung von Vollstreckungen gesonderte Bestimmungen gegeben sind. Art. 823 und 824.

2) In der Natur des jetzigen Verfahrens ist es begründet, daß keine besonderen Ersuchschreiben mehr abgefaßt werden, welche sich direkt und amtlich an andere Gerichte richten. Der Richter spricht am Schlusse seines Urtheiles oder sonstigen Bescheides das Ersuchen oder den Auftrag an das zu bezeichnende Gericht aus und überläßt es den Parteien, den Vollzug herbeizuführen.

Auch beim Ersuchen an ausländische Gerichte hat dies zu gelten und kann in diesem Falle das Ersuchen auch allgemein an das zuständige Gericht des betreffenden Ortes gerichtet werden.

3) Wann fällt einem ausländischen Gerichte

ein Eingriff in die Zuständigkeit der bayerischen Gerichte zur Last?

Es wird dies der Fall sein, wenn in der Unterstellung, daß jenes Gericht zu Bayern gehörte, dennoch nicht es, sondern ein anderes bayerisches Gericht zuständig wäre. Die Thatsache, daß überhaupt Klage vor den bayerischen Gerichten möglich gewesen wäre, kann offenbar nicht maßgebend sein, denn bei der großen Ausdehnung, welche unsere P. O. der Zuständigkeit bei Klagen gegen Ausländer, ja unter Ausländern, gibt, würde bei dieser Auffassung nahezu in allen Streitsachen ein Eingriff in die Zuständigkeit bayerischer Gerichte anzunehmen sein.

Wenn daher ein Inländer im Auslande seinen Wohnsitz hat, so wird es nicht als Beeinträchtigung der bayerischen Gerichte erscheinen, falls er dort belangt wird.

Was die Vereinbarung betrifft, so wird sie allerdings wirksam sein, wenn sie ganz freiwillig und in Fällen, welche sich dazu eignen, stattgefunden hat. Aus dem Umstande aber, daß ein Inländer, einer ihm Auslande gegen ihn erhobenen Klage, die Einrede der Unzuständigkeit nicht entgegengesetzt hat, wird eine stillschweigende Vereinbarung nicht zu folgern sein, da Niemanden zuzumuthen ist, eine Einrede vorzuschützen, welche nach den Gesetzen des betr. Landes offenbar unbegründet erschiene und abgewiesen werden müßte.

Schließlich ist zu bemerken, daß, wenn die Gerichte allzustreng sein wollten in Wahrung ihrer Zuständigkeit durch Abweisung von Requisitionen, sie in der Regel nur den Interessen der bayerischen Unterthanen schaden würden. Ich hätte es aus diesem Gesichtspunkte sogar für zweckmäßig gehalten, die fragliche Beschränkung ganz wegzulassen, wenigstens nur für den Fall zu geben, wo ein bayerischer Unterthan Abweisung des Gesuches verlangt.

4) Was die Art der Erledigung ausländischer Requisitionen anbelangt, so möchte es kein Gewinn sein, daß der frühere Absatz 3, welcher eine Offizialerledigung zuließ, beseitigt worden ist.

In der Pfalz wurde es seither verschieden gehalten. Einige Gerichte ließen, gestützt auf vereinzelte französische Autoritäten, die einfache Offizial-Erledigung zu; andere Gerichte fanden sie, nach den bestehenden Prinzipien, nicht statthaft, dabei jedoch lebhaft beklagend, daß dieser einfachere Weg gesetzlich nicht geboten sei.

Da nemlich die ausländischen Gerichte ihre Requisitionsschreiben immer an das Gericht selbst oder die Staatsanwaltschaft bei demselben richteten, so war zuerst jedesmal eine umständliche Correspondenz nöthig, um das requirirende Gericht über den Gang und die Forderungen des pfälzischen Verfahrens gehörig zu unterrichten. — War dies glücklich erreicht, so übernahm es gewöhnlich der Staatsanwalt, nachdem entsprechender Kostenvorschuß erhoben war, für die ausländische Partei einen Anwalt zu wählen, und durch diesen die Sache, sowie es die Form verlangte, besorgen zu lassen. Es fand also, dem Wesen nach, dennoch ein Offizial-Verfahren statt, nur mit dem Unterschiede, daß viele Schreibereien, große Verzögerungen und um etwa 20 bis 30 Gulden mehr Kosten entstanden. Es lohnte sich wahrhaftig der Mühe nicht, dieses Verfahren aus der Pfalz zu importiren!

Uebrigens ist zu bemerken, daß es immerhin nöthig gewesen wäre, die betreffende Bestimmung nur fakultativ zu fassen, da eine Offizial-Erledigung allerdings jenen Ländern gegenüber, wo das französische Verfahren gilt, nicht paßt.

5) Ersuchen ausländischer Gerichte um Beweisaufnahmen werden selbstverständlich immer durch Beauftragung eines Commissärs erledigt. Es steht nichts im Wege, daß die ausländischen Gerichte ihr Ersuchen sofort an den betreffenden Einzelrichter richten, wo sie mit geringeren Kosten erledigt werden, denn auf Prüfung der Frage, ob der Einzelrichter zur Entscheidung des betreffenden Rechtsstreites zuständig sein würde, wird es hier nicht ankommen.

Abhülfe gegen Verzögerung der Rechtspflege.

Art. 56. — **Beschwerden wegen Verzögerung der streitigen oder freiwilligen Rechtspflege können bei dem Vorstande des unmittelbar vorgesetzten Gerichts und, wenn sie gegen ein Mitglied eines Collegialgerichts gerichtet sind, auch bei dem Vorstande dieses Gerichts angebracht werden.**

Der angerufene Gerichtsvorstand hat die Beschwerde, wenn er sie nicht augenscheinlich ungegründet findet, dem betreffenden Gerichte oder Richter gegen Empfangsbestätigung unter Beifügung der Aufforderung mitzutheilen, binnen bestimmter Frist die Beschwerde zu heben und darüber, daß dies geschehen, Anzeige zu erstatten oder die bestehenden Hindernisse bekannt zu geben.

Mit der Aufforderung kann nach Umständen die Androhung einer Ungehorsamsstrafe

bis zu fünfundzwanzig Gulden verbunden werden, deren Verhängung, wenn der Aufforderung nicht Folge geleistet wird, sofort von dem angerufenen Gerichtsvorstande auszusprechen ist.

Gegen diese Strafverfügung findet binnen fünfzehn Tagen von der Mittheilung das Rechtsmittel der Beschwerde statt. Weitere Rechtsmittel sind nicht zuläßig.

Art. 57. — Verzögerungsbeschwerden gegen Appellationsgerichte, Handels-Appellationsgerichte oder den obersten Gerichtshof, sowie gegen die Präsidenten dieser Gerichte sind bei dem Staatsministerium der Justiz einzubringen, von welchem in diesem Falle die in Art. 56 Abs. 2 u. 3 bezeichneten Verfügungen auszugehen haben, ohne daß dagegen ein Rechtsmittel Platz greift. G. A. d. K. d. A. III S. 48. 49. 128. 129. IV S. 20. 302. — K. d. R. I S. 152—154.

Diese beiden Artikel behandeln im Grunde disciplinäre Maßregeln und die Fälle, von welchen sie sprechen, werden, wie zu hoffen, nicht vorkommen. Sollte dennoch ein solcher Fall sich ereignen, so sind die gegebenen Bestimmungen klar und bedürfen keiner Erläuterung.

II. Hauptstück.

Parteien.

Befugniß vor Gericht zu handeln.

Art. 58. — Die persönliche Fähigkeit der Parteien, vor Gericht zu handeln, die Vertretung derjenigen Personen, welchen diese Fähigkeit mangelt, und die Nothwendigkeit besonderer Ermächtigung einer Partei oder ihres gesetzlichen Vertreters zur Prozeßführung ist nach den Bestimmungen der einschlägigen Gesetze zu beurtheilen.

G. A. d. K. d. A. I S. 76. 77. 84. 85. IV S. 20. — K. d. R. I S. 155—158.

1) In einem Rechtsstreite sind zu unterscheiden: 1) die Parteien, 2) die gesetzlichen Vertreter von Parteien und 3) die Anwälte und sonstigen Bevollmächtigten.

Parteien im Rechtsstreite sind diejenigen physischen oder juristischen Personen, um deren Rechte es sich handelt; für deren Rechnung der Streit geführt wird.

In einem erweiterten, jedoch uneigentlichen, Sinne wird das Wort im Hauptstücke III gebraucht, wo es bloß den Gegensatz zu Anwälten und Bevollmächtigten bildet, also auch die gesetzlichen Vertreter begreift.

Gesetzliche Vertreter sind diejenigen Personen, welche berufen sind, an Stelle solcher Parteien Prozeß zu erheben oder zu führen, welchen die persönliche Fähigkeit, vor Gericht zu handeln, fehlt, sei es aus thatsächlichen Gründen (bei juristischen Personen), sei es aus rechtlichen Gründen (wegen Mangels der Rechtsfähigkeit). Ob der Vertreter durch das Gesetz selbst oder durch die Obrigkeit oder endlich durch Vertrag (Statuten) bestellt ist, erscheint ohne Belang. s. hannov. Entw. Art. 48 und Verhdl. S. 1306 u. 1307.

Der Vertreter führt den Prozeß nur für fremde Rechnung; die Rechtskraft des Urtheils, sowie alle sonstigen Vortheile und Nachtheile treffen bloß die Partei. Die Personen der Parteien und der gesetzlichen Vertreter sind daher streng auseinander zu halten und ist dieser Trennung nach dem Willen des Gesetzes in den Prozeßakten ein entsprechender Ausdruck zu geben. Unklare Formen führen leicht zu unklaren Begriffen.

Deßhalb verlangen die Art. 165 und 515 in den Anträgen und Urtheilen nur die Angabe der Parteien, weil es hier darauf ankommt, sofort zu ersehen, welche Personen der Rechtsstreit betreffe. Es würde diesen Vorschriften nicht entsprechen, wenn etwa, statt der Gemeinde der Magistrat, statt des Mündels der Vormund, statt des Fiskus die Kreisregierung, Kammer der Finanzen, angeführt wäre, wie Letzteres in der Pfalz Uebung ist. Anders ist es bei den Zustellungen der Gerichtsboten (Art. 202), wo der Auftrag gebende Vertreter in den Vordergrund tritt.

In manchen Fällen sind die Eigenschaften von Vertreter und Partei vereinigt, z. B. wenn der Mann für die Frau, der Pfarrer für die Pfründe klagt und beide zugleich als Nutznießer betheiligt sind.

2) Die Parteien sowohl als die gesetzlichen Vertreter können zur Prozeßführung noch besonderer Ermächtigung oder Verbeistandung bedürfen.

Ueber die Fragen nun, wer gesetzlicher Vertreter sei, wann und wie Ermächtigung einzutreten habe, gibt die P. O. keinen Aufschluß, verweist vielmehr auf die bestehenden Gesetze, unter welchen natürlich auch die bayer. G. Ord, sofern aus ihr bezügliche Grundsätze abzuleiten sind, begriffen ist.

3) Was zuerst den kgl. Fiskus in seinen verschiedenen Richtungen betrifft, so sind die bestehenden organisatorischen Verordnungen maßgebend. s. Seuff. Comm. Bd. II. S. 121. — Uebrigens ist zu bemerken, daß die Fiskale nicht als gesetzliche Vertreter im Sinne unserer P. O. anzusehen sind, sondern nur als Anwälte des Fiskus. Art. 79 Abs. 3. — Vortrag des Ref. v. Neumayr zu den Art. 47, sowie 419—422 des Entwurfs.

4) Was die Gemeinden betrifft, so sind jetzt durch die zwei Gemeindeordnungen vom 29. April 1869 ziemlich gleichförmige Bestimmungen für das ganze Reich gegeben. Die Prozeßführung ist den Gemeinden allein übertragen und der Curatelconsens beseitigt. (Diesseit. G. O. Art. 206 Ziff. 5. — Pfälz. G. O. Art. 130 a. E.)

Gesetzliche Vertreter der Gemeinden sind in Städten und Märkten mit städtischer Verfassung die Magistrate, in sonstigen Gemeinden die Gemeindeausschüsse. (Diess. G. O. Art. 84 u. 130.) Einer weiteren Ermächtigung bedürfen diese Vertreter nur bei Vergleichen und Streitabständen. (Art. 112 Ziff. 12 u. Art. 147.) In der Pfalz ist der Gemeinderath gesetzlicher Vertreter der Gemeinde und dessen Vollzugsorgan der Bürgermeister. (Art. 54.)

Erhebt sich zwischen Gemeindegliedern Streit, ob gewisse Gegenstände Eigenthum der Gemeinde oder Privateigenthum seien, oder ob Einzelne klagbare Nutzrechte am Gemeindeeigenthum zu beanspruchen haben, so stellt, falls nöthig, die vorgesetzte Verwaltungsbehörde (das Bezirksamt, die Kreisregierung) einen Anwalt für die Gemeinde auf. (Diess. G. O. Art. 37 — pfälz. G. O. Art. 28.) Die Curatelbehörde ist in solchen Ausnahmsfällen, wo die Interessen der Gemeinden und die Interessen ihrer gewöhnlichen Vertreter (in der Regel der Großbegüterten) in Widerspruch stehen, die gesetzliche Vertreterin der Gemeinde und von ihr hat daher auch der aufgestellte Anwalt seine Weisungen zu empfangen.

Was von den Prozessen der Gemeinden gesagt ist, gilt auch von den Prozessen der in Verwaltung der politischen Gemeinde stehenden Stiftungen. — (Diess. G. O. Art. 206 Ziff. 5 — pfälz. G. O. Art. 130.)

5) Die Verwaltung des Kirchenvermögens wird durch die neuen Gemeindeordnungen nicht berührt. (Diess. G. O. Art. 206 a. E. — pfälz. G. O. Art. 129.)

Es bleibt also in dieser Richtung die Nothwendigkeit des Curatelconsenses in der nemlichen Weise, wie seither, bestehen. Derselbe ist diesseits nöthig sowohl für die Rechtsstreite der durch die Kirchenverwaltungen vertretenen Kirchenstiftungen, als für die Rechtsstreite, welche Nutznießer von Pfründen (Pfarrer und Benefiziaten) für dieselben führen. Revid. G. Edikt § 59 Abs. 3—5 und § 94 Abs. 5—8. Ver. v. 6. Dez. 1808 Art. 15 (R. Bl. S. 2817).

Geistliche Genossenschaften, insbesondere Klöster bedürfen desselben nicht. Bl. f. R. XXI S. 494.

Ebenso besteht in der Pfalz die Nothwendigkeit der Ermächtigung durch die Curatelbehörde für die Prozesse der katholischen Kirchenfabriken (Dekret v. 30. Dez. 1809 Art. 77), der protestantischen Presbyterien (Ver. v. 18. Jan. 1819) und der Pfründen (Dekret v. 6. Nov. 1813 Art. 14, 29 u. 51). Die gerichtliche Vertretung steht in der Pfalz den Rechnern zu, wie denn überhaupt bei Corporationen und Stiftungen dieselbe nach französischem Rechte nicht Collegien übertragen ist, wie diesseits, sondern einzelnen Personen.

Ueber die Bedeutung von Art. 4 des Concordates s. Erk. des Cass. Hofes der Pfalz vom 16. Dez. 1861. Bl. f. R. XXVII S. 24 ff.

6) Das Nemliche, wie vom Kirchenvermögen, gilt von allen öffentlichen Stiftungen, welche nicht von den Gemeinden verwaltet werden, insbesondere auch den Spitälern. Ver. v. 17. Dez. 1825 § 69. Ver. v. 6. März 1817 Art. 9 (R. Bl. S. 157) — arrêté v. 7. Mess. IX Art. 13 und arrêté v. 19. Vend. XII.

Universitäten bedürfen des Curatelconsenses nicht; der Verwaltungsausschuß beschließt selbständig über Erhebung von Prozessen. Ver. vom 20. Dez. 1815 Art. 9 (R. Bl. v. 1816 S. 133) u. Ver. v. 30. Sept. 1819 (R. Bl. S. 942).

7) Handelsgesellschaften, sowie Genossenschaften und Vereine, welche den durch die bezüglichen Gesetze vom 29. April 1869 gestellten Erfordernissen genügen, treten als eigene Personen im Rechtsstreite auf und werden durch die statutenmäßig bestellten Vorstände oder Geschäftsführer gesetzlich vertreten. — H. G. B. Art. 111, 117, 164, 167, 196, 213 und 227. — Gesetz über Genossenschaften v. 29. April 1869 Art. 11—17 und 72. — Gesetz über Vereine vom nemlichen Tage Art. 10 und 16.

Was Aktiengesellschaften, welche nicht als Handelsgesellschaften zu betrachten sind, z. B. zur Ausbeutung von Bergwerken, betrifft, so bringt es die Natur der Sache mit sich, daß sie nur durch Vertreter Rechtsstreite führen können (Bluntschli d. Privatr. § 39 Ziff. 8); es ist dies jetzt durch das solche Gesellschaften betreffende Gesetz vom 29. April 1869 außer Zweifel gestellt.

Bei gewöhnlichen, auf einzelne bestimmte Mitglieder sich beschränkenden Civilgesellschaften und Vereinen müssen die einzelnen Mitglieder auftreten.

8) Bezüglich der Vertretung von Rechtsunfähigen gelten diesseits im Allgemeinen folgende Grundsätze:

a) Minderjährige und kuratelmäßige Personen sind vertreten durch ihre Vormünder und Curatoren. Die Zustimmung der obervormundschaftlichen Behörde zur Prozeßführung ist kein allgemeines Erforderniß. Erk. d. O. A. G. v. 13. Jan. 1868 Reg.=Nr. 1349 66/67.

b) Hauskinder, auch wenn sie volljährig sind, bedürfen, wenn es sich nicht um Sondergüter handelt, über welche sie frei verfügen dürfen, der Verbeistandung oder Ermächtigung durch den Vater. Wer daher ein Hauskind belangt, hat den Vater mitvorzuladen. Erscheint derselbe nicht, so gilt dies als Ermächtigung zur selbständigen Verhandlung. Selbst wenn der Vater erscheint, kann er die Wirksamkeit nachtheiliger gerichtlicher Erklärungen des Hauskindes nicht hindern, sondern sie nur durch Nachweis ihrer Unrichtigkeit entkräften.

Zu bemerken ist, daß der Beistand des Vaters nicht sowohl in dessen Interesse, als vielmehr im Interesse des Hauskindes selbst vorgeschrieben ist, woraus folgt, daß die Nichtigkeit der Verhandlung auch von Letzterem angeregt werden kann und von Amtswegen zu berücksichtigen ist. Bl. f. R. III 200, XII 299. — Seuff. Comm. Bd. II S. 112. Uebrigens möchte es wohl an der Zeit sein, die zu unseren Verhältnissen nicht mehr passenden Bestimmungen über Hauskinder ganz zu beseitigen.

c) Ehefrauen bedürfen, falls es sich nicht um Rezeptizgüter handelt, zum Auftreten vor Gericht, der Einwilligung des Ehemannes. Derselbe ist daher, wenn die Ehefrau verklagt wird, zum Zwecke der Ertheilung seiner Einwilligung mitvorzuladen. Seine Weigerung jedoch ist, falls diese Vorladung geschehen, ohne Wirkung. Bl. f. R. XXIII 369.

d) Was die Rechtsfähigkeit des in Gant Gerathenen betrifft, s. P. O. Art. 1208. 1210. 1219 und 1221.

e) Zuchthaussträflinge stehen nach Art. 32 des St. G. B. den Minderjährigen gleich und werden durch ihre Curatoren vor Gericht vertreten.

9) Was die besonderen Rechte der Pfalz betrifft, so sind bezüglich der Minderjährigen und Interdizirten maßgebend die Art. 464. 465 und 509 Code civil; bezüglich der emanzipirten Minderjährigen Art. 482 allda; bezüglich der Personen, welchen ein Beistand gegeben ist, Art. 513 allda; bezüglich der Ehefrauen die Art 215 und 218 allda.

Aus dem Einf. Ges. sind als hierher bezüglich anzuführen die Art. 87 (Ermächtigung von Ehefrauen), Art. 89 (Theilungsgesuche von Vormündern) und Art. 92 (Interdiktion.) — Diese Artikel bestimmen jedoch, abgesehen von kleinen Aenderungen im Verfahren, nichts Neues; insbesondere gilt dies auch von Art. 89, welcher die Vereinigung einer seit 20 Jahren nicht mehr strittigen Rechtsfrage bezweckt und in dieser Beziehung fast mehr verdirbt als gut macht, da gefolgert werden könnte, falls nur Minderjährige, z. B. Kinder zweier Ehen, betheiligt seien, genüge es nicht, wenn die Ermächtigung des Einen der Vormünder vorliege. — Eine Abänderung des Art. 465 l. c. in diesem Sinne war aber nicht beabsichtigt; man wollte diesen Artikel ausdehnen, nicht einschränken.

Die Befugnisse der Curatoren für Abwesende richten sich nach dem Mandate, welches ihnen das Ernennungs=Urtheil gegeben hat. Im Zweifel haben sie bloß das Recht, reine Verwaltungshandlungen vorzunehmen und bedürfen zu allen weitergehenden Schritten besonderer gerichtlichen Ermächtigung.

Eine besondere Rechtsunfähigkeit wird begründet durch die Ordonnanz, welche gemäß Art. 465 Code d'instr. crim. der Präsident des Schwurgerichts gegen einen abwesenden Angeklagten erläßt. Ueber die rechtlichen Folgen dieser Rechtsunfähigkeit bestehen verschiedene Ansichten, jedoch ist darüber kein Streit, daß das Recht, vor Gericht zu stehen, durch sie verloren geht. Jene Ordonnanz und ihre Folgen bleiben auch bestehen, wenn der flüchtige Verbrecher sich gestellt hat oder verhaftet worden ist. (Art. 476 Code d'instr.)

Art. 59. — **Bei Gefahr auf Verzug können auch Personen, die unter väterlicher Gewalt, Vormundschaft oder Pflegschaft stehen, oder über die betreffenden Vermögensrechte nicht frei zu verfügen haben oder als Vertreter eines Andern mit der etwa erforderlichen besondern Ermächtigung nicht versehen sind, zum selbständigen Handeln vor Gericht gelassen werden.**

G. A. der K. d. A. I. S. 76. 77. 84. 85. 170. IV S. 20. — K. d. R. I S. 161. 162.

1) Dieser Artikel enthält eine Neuerung, welche berechtigt ist; allein bei der Unbestimmtheit der Fassung liegt die Gefahr nahe, daß sie eine über den Willen des Gesetzgebers hinausgehende

Tragweite erhalte. — Zu verhüten, daß dieses geschehe, ist Aufgabe des Richters, dessen Ermessen hier fast alles überlassen bleibt.

2) Der Richter hat zwei Fragen zu prüfen, nemlich 1) ob Gefahr auf dem Verzuge stehe und 2) ob nicht sonstige Gründe es ungeeignet erscheinen lassen, das selbständige Handeln zuzulassen. — In letzterer Beziehung ist ihm vollkommen freie Hand gegeben. — Wenn auch bei den Verhandlungen jene Fälle besonders angedeutet wurden, wo Kinder oder Geisteskranke aufzutreten versuchen würden, so schließt doch die allgemeine Fassung des Gesetzes auch andere Rücksichten nicht aus und werden dieselben insbesondere dem Interesse des Rechtsunfähigen zu entnehmen sein.

3) Die Erklärung des Richters, er lasse im Hinblicke auf die Dringlichkeit des Falles den Rechtsunfähigen zum selbständigen Handeln zu, wirkt als Ermächtigung zu den fraglichen Prozeßhandlungen und beseitigt für dieselben die Wirkungen der Rechtsunfähigkeit. — Es ist dies die natürliche Auslegung des Art. 59; bei den Verhandlungen wurde übrigens auch ausdrücklich erklärt, daß Art. 62 hier keine Anwendung finde, sowie daß eine spätere Genehmigung, wie sie der hannover. Entwurf (§ 50) vorbehält, nicht nöthig sei. Abg. I 85 (v. Neum.)

Jene Wirkung erstreckt sich natürlich nur auf gewöhnliche Prozeßhandlungen, nicht aber auf Rechtsverzichte und ähnliche Rechtshandlungen.

4) Das Gesetz verlangt offenbar keine vorausgehende Ermächtigung des Richters, sondern setzt voraus, daß derselbe erst, nachdem Anträge an ihn gebracht sind, sich über die Fragen der Dringlichkeit und der Zulassung ausspreche. — Da nun die Gültigkeit der Prozeßhandlungen davon abhängt, daß sich der Richter über beide Fragen schlüssig gemacht und sie entschieden habe, so ist es nöthig, daß diesen Entscheidungen ein formeller Ausdruck gegeben werde. Es wird zwar hinreichen, wenn die Entscheidungsgründe sich bestimmt deßhalb aussprechen; allein richtiger und dem Geiste des neuen Verfahrens entsprechender erscheint es jedenfalls, wenn im Urtheilssatze selbst eine bezügliche Erklärung erfolgt, ähnlich etwa, wie es in der Pfalz bei Ermächtigung beklagter Ehefrauen geschieht, daß gesagt wird: „ermächtigt, wegen Gefahr auf Verzug, den A selbständig vor Gericht zu handeln — die bezeichneten Anträge zu stellen."

5) Man sollte glauben, die Zulassung Rechtsunfähiger könne nur nothwendig sein, wenn Vorsichtsverfügungen in Frage sind, und es scheint allerdings, daß man diese Maßregeln besonders im Auge gehabt habe (R.R. I S. 162 [v. Weiß]); allein hätte man nichts weiter gewollt, so würde wohl eine entsprechende Bemerkung in Hauptstück XXIV, etwa in Art. 637, genügt haben.

Da nun die Fassung des Gesetzes allgemein ist, so erleidet es keinen Anstand, daß Rechtsunfähige auch in sonstigen Fällen zugelassen werden dürfen; jedoch wird es allerdings — abgesehen vom Falle, wo eine Erscheinungsfrist zu wahren ist — nicht leicht vorkommen, daß gesagt werden kann, die Gefahr auf dem Verzuge bedinge weitergreifende Maßregeln.

6) Das selbständige Handeln ist nur zuzulassen, so weit es nöthig ist, um Gefahr zu beseitigen. — Sowohl in Hannover als hier wurde dies für selbstverständlich erklärt (s. Verhdl. in Hannov. S. 687. — Abg. I 77 [Barth]); überhaupt hatte man nur ein vorübergehendes, gewöhnlich im Anfange des Prozesses stattfindendes Handeln im Auge. Abg. I. 85 (v. Neumayr).

Die fragliche Ermächtigung ist daher ihrer Natur nach keine allgemeine, sich auf einen ganzen Rechtstreit beziehende, sondern sie hat einzelne Prozeßhandlungen zum Gegenstande.

Es kann deßhalb vorkommen, daß, falls verschiedene Anträge gestellt sind, der Richter bezüglich des einen dieser Anträge das selbständige Handeln zuläßt, die übrigen aber, sei es wegen Mangels der Dringlichkeit, sei es aus sonstigen Erwägungen, zurückweist.

Es ist sogar der Fall möglich, daß der Richter im Laufe eines Verfahrens die Ermächtigung zum weiteren Handeln verweigert, wo dann die Grundsätze über Aufhören der Rechtsfähigkeit (Art. 691) Maß zu geben hätten. Zweifellos ist, daß die Befugniß selbständig zu handeln im Augenblicke erlischt, wo der gesetzliche Vertreter selbst auftritt.

7) Was die in Art. 59 bezeichneten Personen betrifft, ist zu bemerken:

In Pflegschaft stehen Personen, denen Vormünder oder Curatoren bestellt sind.

Unter den Personen, welche über die betreffenden, d. h. ihre eigenen in Frage stehenden, Vermögensrechte, nicht frei zu verfügen haben, sind insbesondere auch zu rechnen Ehefrauen, emanzipirte Minderjährige und Personen, denen in der Pfalz ein Beistand gegeben ist.

Vertreter von Andern sollen in Fällen zugelassen werden können, wo die erforderliche besondere Ermächtigung fehlt, — ihre Eigenschaft als Vertreter darf daher nicht zweifelhaft sein.

Art. 60. — **Soweit das Gesetz nicht anders bestimmt, sind die gesetzlichen Vertreter der Parteien den selbständigen Parteien gleichgestellt und wie diese zu allen Prozeßhandlungen befugt.**

Art. 61. — **Wer als gesetzlicher Vertreter einer Partei auftritt, hat sich über seine Befugniß hiezu, wenn sie nicht gerichtskundig ist, sowie über den Besitz der etwa erforderlichen besondern Ermächtigung zur Prozeßführung auszuweisen.**

Ebenso haben andere Personen, welche eine besondere Bewilligung zur Prozeßführung bedürfen, die Ertheilung dieser Bewilligung darzuthun.

G. A. der K. d. A. I S. 76. 77. 84. 85. 170. IV S. 20. — K. d. R. I S. 158—163.

1) Die Prozeßordnung gibt ein einheitliches Verfahren für alle Streitsachen, und unterscheidet in der Regel nicht, ob die Parteien vollkommen oder unvollkommen rechtsfähig sind, und ob sie selbst oder ihre gesetzlichen Vertreter den Rechtsstreit führen. Wer daher den gesetzlichen Anforderungen genügt, um in einer Streitsache vor Gericht zu stehen, der ist, soweit nicht besondere gesetzliche Verfügungen entgegenstehen, auch befugt, alles vorzunehmen, was Natur und Zweck des gerichtlichen Verfahrens mit sich bringen, und ebenso treffen ihn alle Nachtheile, welche das Gesetz an Versäumung von Fristen oder sonstige Unterlassungen knüpft. Es gilt dies sowohl von den Parteien selbst, als von ihren Vertretern.

2) Dieses in der Natur der Sache begründete und von jeher geltende Prinzip hat durch Art. 60 eine bestimmte Anerkennung und Anwendung gefunden.

Derselbe spricht zwar nur von den gesetzlichen Vertretern, wohl deßhalb, weil hier die Möglichkeit eines Zweifels näher lag; allein offenbar muß der nemliche Grundsatz anwendbar sein, wenn die Parteien selbst besonderer Ermächtigung bedurften (z. B. Ehefrauen, Hauskinder) und diese Ermächtigung vorliegt. Ebenso ist (nach Art. 62) selbstverständlich, daß die Prozeßhandlungen der Vertreter nur dann gültig sein können, wenn sie mit der erforderlichen besonderen Ermächtigung versehen sind. Es stand dies im Entwurfe und wurde stillschweigend weggelassen, wie anzunehmen, als unnöthig. s. Abg. I 85 (v. Weiß).

Die Fassung des Gesetzes, welcher Referent v. Heintz (R. R. I S. 158) Geltung zu verschaffen suchte, war demgemäß eine ganz berechtigte.

3) Fragliche Grundsätze gelten für alle Prozeßhandlungen im engeren Sinne, also für Geständnisse, Gebrauch von Beweismitteln, insbesondere Eideszuschiebung, Eideserklärung u. s. w. — Vergleiche und Verzichte auf Rechte gehören nicht dahin.

4) Die Bestimmung in Art. 62, daß der Richter von Amtswegen den Mangel der Handelnsfähigkeit zu berücksichtigen habe, legt ihm die Pflicht auf, überall, wo das betreffende Verhältniß nicht gerichtskundig ist, auch von Amtswegen die Vorlage der nöthigen Nachweise zu verlangen. — In welchen Fällen Gerichtskundigkeit anzunehmen sei, ist völlig dem richterlichen Ermessen überlassen. Wenn die Gegenpartei auf Befragen keinen Anstand erhebt, die gemachten Angaben vielmehr als richtig bestätigt, so wird der Richter in der Regel keine Veranlassung haben, weitere Nachweise zu verlangen; jedenfalls nicht in der Weise, daß das Verfahren dadurch verzögert werde.

Ist die Vertretung gesetzlich geordnet, wie bei Gemeinden, Kirchenstiftungen rc., so ist sie immer gerichtskundig.

Art. 62. — **Der Mangel der in Art. 58 bezeichneten Erfordernisse der Prozeßführung ist in jeder Lage der Sache sowohl von Amtswegen als auf Anregung einer Partei zu beachten und hat, wenn er nicht im Laufe des Verfahrens innerhalb einer vom Gerichte zu bestimmenden Frist gehoben wird, Nichtigkeit des Verhandelten zur Folge.**

Ist in der Sache das Endurtheil im letzten ordentlichen Rechtszuge erfolgt, so kann die Nichtigkeit nur mehr von den Parteien, und zwar von derjenigen Partei, auf deren Seite der Mangel bestanden, nur so lange, als das Verfahren nicht von ihr nach Hebung des Mangels ausdrücklich oder stillschweigend anerkannt worden ist, von der Gegenpartei aber nur dann geltend gemacht werden, wenn sie bei der Verhandlung zum angefochtenen Urtheile den Mangel angeregt hat.

G. A. der K. d. A. I S. 76. 77. 84. 85. 170. IV S. 20. — K. d. R. I S. 163—166.

1) Das Gesetz hat die Absicht, die Folgen, welche aus dem Mangel der in Art. 58 bezeichneten Erfordernisse der Prozeßführung (der Handelnsfähigkeit, gesetzlichen Vertretung und Ermächtigung) hervorgehen, in erschöpfender Weise zu regeln.

Es unterscheidet zwei Zeitabschnitte, nemlich 1) die Zeit vor Erlaß des Endurtheiles im letzten ordentlichen Rechtszuge d. h. eines Endurtheiles, welches nicht mehr durch Einspruch oder Berufung angefochten werden kann und 2) die Zeit nach Erlaß eines solchen Endurtheiles.

2) Für ersteren Zeitabschnitt stellt es zwei Hauptgrundsätze auf, nemlich:

a) Fragliche Mängel begründen (für den Prozeß) absolute Nichtigkeit des Verhandelten und

b) diese Nichtigkeit ist jedoch heilbar durch Hebung des Mangels und Genehmigung.

3) Der Gesetzgeber hielt es für ordnungswidrig, einen Rechtsstreit auf die Gefahr hin fortzuführen, daß das Verfahren nach dem Belieben einer Partei später für nichtig erklärt werden müßte und in dieser prozessualen Erwägung ist der Grund zu suchen, warum bei jeder Nichtigkeit wegen Mangels eines Erfordernisses zur Prozeßführung der Richter verpflichtet ist, sie von Amtswegen zu berücksichtigen. Es ist daher nicht zu untersuchen, zu Gunsten welcher Personen etwa gewisse Ermächtigungen ꝛc. vom Gerichte vorgeschrieben seien; sobald die Vorschrift der Art ist, daß von irgend einer Seite eine Nichtigkeit darauf gegründet werden kann, ist diese von Amtswegen zu beachten.

4) Indem gesagt wird, es solle Nichtigkeit eintreten, wenn der Mangel nicht gehoben werde, ist ausgesprochen, daß diese Nichtigkeit ihrer Natur nach eine heilbare sein solle.

Da das Gesetz allgemein spricht, so wird diese Heilbarkeit nicht bloß anzunehmen sein in Fällen, wo besondere Ermächtigung, Streitconsens, Verbeistandung nöthig war, sondern auch in sonstigen Fällen, z. B. wenn der Rechtsunfähige selbst statt seines gesetzlichen Vertreters aufgetreten ist, oder umgekehrt Letzterer, nachdem seine Eigenschaft erloschen war.

Wenn nach Art. 59 die bloße Zustimmung des Gerichts genügen kann, um die Prozeßhandlungen eines Rechtsunfähigen gültig zu machen, so konnte der Gesetzgeber um so weniger Anstand nehmen, der Genehmigung des gesetzlichen Vertreters diese heilende Kraft zu verleihen. Weder auf Seite des Rechtsunfähigen noch auf Seite des Gegners ist ein Grund zu finden, um nach dieser Genehmigung noch eine Nichtigkeit anzunehmen.

5) Selbstverständlich erscheint, daß zur Heilung der Nichtigkeit nicht bloß erfordert wird, daß die Vertretung, Ermächtigung ꝛc. nach Vorschrift des Gesetzes geordnet, sondern daß auch dasjenige, was in nichtiger Weise verhandelt ist, gutgeheißen werde. Abg. I 85 (v. Neumayr).

Diese Genehmigung kann ausdrücklich oder stillschweigend geschehen und wird Letzteres in Fällen, wo die Prozeßführung in den Händen der nemlichen Person bleibt, welche nur besonderer Ermächtigung ꝛc. bedurft hatte, leicht anzunehmen sein. s. hannov. Verhdl. S. 686.

6) Höchst zweckmäßig erscheint es, daß dem Richter zur Pflicht gemacht ist, bevor er die Nichtigkeit ausspricht, den Versuch zu machen, ob etwa durch Gestattung einer angemessenen Frist der Mangel gehoben werden könne. Die nöthigen Schritte hierzu, insbesondere die zur Ersetzung von Streitconsensen und Ermächtigungen etwa nöthigen Beiladungen sind natürlich ganz den Parteien überlassen.

7) Ist die Frist verstrichen, ohne daß die Nichtigkeit beseitigt ist, so hat der Richter sachgemäß zu entscheiden und zwar nicht bloß über die Zwischenfrage der Nichtigkeit, sondern in der Streitsache selbst.

Besteht der Mangel auf Seite des Klägers, so ist die Klage als unstatthaft abzuweisen.

Besteht der Mangel auf Seite des Beklagten, so sind die Anträge, welche in der Ladung genommen sind, sofern sie nicht seitdem eine Aenderung erfahren haben, nach Maßgabe des Art. 297 zuzusprechen. Vgl. hannov. Verhdl. S. 685.

Beides gilt natürlich nur in der Voraussetzung, daß es sich um einen von Anfang an bestandenen Mangel handelt. Gleichgültig ist es, ob die Sache noch im ersten Rechtszuge begriffen, oder bereits vor dem Berufungsgerichte anhängig ist; nur darf selbstverständlich die Rechtskraft einer erstrichterlichen Entscheidung nicht im Wege stehen.

8) Will der richtige Vertreter des Beklagten die mangelhafte Prozeßführung nicht genehmigen, so ist nicht nöthig, daß er zuerst Abweisung der Klage aussprechen lasse, um dann Einspruch zu erheben, vielmehr kann er sofort den Rechtsstreit selbst aufnehmen, gleich als wäre noch nichts darin geschehen, d. h. also durch Anwaltsbestellung und Zustellung seines motivirten Antrages. Im ersten Urtheile spricht dann das Gericht die Nichtigkeit der betreffenden Prozeßführung aus, verfügt, so weit nöthig, wegen der Kosten und entscheidet in der Hauptsache, was Rechtens.

9) Schließlich sei bemerkt, daß bei einiger Vorsicht der Anwälte und Gerichte, Fälle, wo wegen Mangels der Handelnsfähigkeit ein Verfahren zu vernichten ist, nicht leicht vorkommen werden.

10) Sobald ein nicht mehr durch Einspruch oder Berufung anfechtbares Endurtheil ergangen ist, erleidet die Sachlage eine wesentliche Aenderung. Nunmehr überwiegen die Rücksichten für Aufrechthaltung der ergangenen Entscheidung und es kann die vorhandene Nichtigkeit von Amtswegen gar nicht mehr berücksichtigt, von der Gegenpartei aber nur unter der Voraussetzung geltend gemacht werden, daß sie bei der Verhandlung zum angefochtenen Urtheile

den Mangel angeregt, d. h. zu ihren Gunsten geltend gemacht hat. Es liegt hierin eine Ausnahme von dem allgemeinen Grundsatze des Art. 792.

Der Regel nach kann daher von nun an die Nichtigkeit nur noch von der Partei, auf deren Seite sie stattgefunden hat, geltend gemacht werden; sie ist zu einer bloßen Anfechtbarkeit geworden. Das nemliche Recht wie die Partei hat übrigens auch der Dritte, welcher für sie Nichtigkeitsbeschwerde erheben darf. Art. 789.

11) Wenn das Gesetz von „dem Endurtheile“ spricht, so begreift es auch das Endurtheil über einen Theil des Streitgegenstandes. Selbstverständlich ist jedoch die Nichtigkeit nur so weit beseitigt, als dieses Urtheil fähig ist, unanfechtbar zu werden und bleibt also für den noch nicht rechtskräftig entschiedenen Streitpunkt bestehen.

Streitgenossenschaft.

Art. 63. — Personen, die in Ansehung des Streitgegenstands in Rechtsgemeinschaft stehen oder aus demselben thatsächlichen und rechtlichen Grunde berechtigt oder verpflichtet sind, können als Streitgenossen gemeinschaftlich klagen oder belangt werden.

Gemeinschaftliche Rechtsverfolgung und Vertheidigung findet auch statt, wenn gleichartige Ansprüche oder Verpflichtungen auf einem im Wesentlichen gleichartigen thatsächlichen und rechtlichen Grunde beruhen.

G. A. der K. d. A. I S. 77, 78, 170, IV S. 20 — K. d. R. I. S. 156 - 168.

1) Art. 63 gibt die Bestimmungen von § 52 und § 53 des hannov. Entwurfs dem Wesen nach wörtlich wieder. Die sehr weitgehenden Grundsätze, welche die Rechtslehrer in neuerer Zeit bezüglich der subjektiven Klagenhäufung aufstellen, zufolge deren so ziemlich alles dem richterlichen Ermessen überlassen bleibt, wurden zwar nicht angenommen, allein dennoch ist durch Abs. 2 des Artikels der Rahmen für den Begriff der Streitgenossenschaft sehr weit gespannt und der richterlichen Würdigung genügender Spielraum gegeben.

2) Die Fälle, in welchen mehrere Personen gemeinschaftlich als Kläger oder als Beklagte vor Gericht zu stellen sind, können unter vier verschiedene Gesichtspunkte gebracht werden. Man kann unterscheiden:

a) Fälle, wo gleichzeitige Verhandlung mit einer Mehrzahl von Personen zivilrechtlich nothwendig ist, z. B. bei Theilungen;

b) Fälle, wo mehrere Personen in Rechtsgemeinschaft stehen, d. h. wo sie an den nemlichen Rechten oder Pflichten betheiligt sind, wie z. B. Miteigenthümer, Solidarschuldner rc.;

c) Fälle, wo Rechte und Pflichten zwar gesondert neben einander stehen, jedoch thatsächlich und rechtlich den nemlichen Ursprung haben, z. B. wenn Miterben klagen oder verklagt werden und der Streitgegenstand theilbar ist;

d) Fälle, wo sonstige Gründe der Zweckmäßigkeit (Kostenersparung, Aufklärung des Sachverhalts, Verhütung widersprechender Entscheidungen u. dgl.) für eine gemeinschaftlich Verhandlung sprechen.

Unsere Prozeßordnung hat nicht bloß die drei ersten Fälle, in welchen die Nothwendigkeit oder Nützlichkeit der Streitgenossenschaft klar zu Tage liegt und nie bezweifelt wurde, anerkannt, sondern sie hat, gleichmäßig dem praktischen Bedürfnisse sowie dem Standpunkte der Wissenschaft Rechnung tragend, auch den letzten Fall berücksichtigt, jedoch dabei leitende Gesichtspunkte gegeben, um der Willkür Schranken zu setzen.

3) Es wird nemlich verlangt, daß die Rechte und Pflichten, um welche es sich handelt, gleichartig seien und auf einem wesentlichen gleichartigen thatsächlichen und rechtlichen Grunde beruhen.

Diese Voraussetzungen hielt der Gesetzgeber für genügend, um die Vermuthung der Zweckmäßigkeit einer gemeinschaftlichen Verhandlung zu rechtfertigen.

Allerdings eröffnen die Fragen, was gleichartig, insbesondere was wesentlich gleichartig sei, dem richterlichen Ermessen noch ein großes Feld; allein es ist wenigstens ein fester Haltpunkt gegeben und in den meisten Fällen wird sich sofort mit Sicherheit bestimmen lassen, ob Gleichartigkeit im Sinne des Gesetzes gegeben sei oder aber nicht.

4) An die Frage, ob der Fall einer Streitgenossenschaft vorliege, knüpfen sich unter Umständen wichtige Folgen, z. B. bezüglich des Gerichtsstandes (Art. 20) und bezüglich der Zuständigkeit der Landgerichte (Art. 3 Abs. 2). In Fällen solcher Art ist es Pflicht des Richters, streng darüber zu wachen, daß den Forderungen des Gesetzes genügt sei; handelt es sich jedoch um Fälle, wo er sowohl der Sache als dem Orte nach der zuständige Richter ist, so liegt kein Grund vor, Strenge walten zu lassen, vielmehr werden bloß Erwägungen der Zweckmäßigkeit darüber bestimmen, ob nach Maßgabe des Art. 157 gemeinschaftliche oder getrennte Verhandlung einzutreten habe.

Es ist hier zu bemerken, daß im jetzigen Verfahren eine gleichzeitige Verhandlung verschiedener Streitsachen jene Mißstände nicht mehr im Gefolge hat, wie früher und zwar hauptsächlich deßhalb, weil das Beweisinterlokut im früheren Sinne weggefallen und das ganze Beweisverfahren ein anderes geworden ist.

Einen großen Unterschied macht es natürlich auch, ob die Mehreren, welche zusammen sprechen, jeder seinen eigenen, oft eigensinnigen, schriftlichen Weg geht und der Richter das, was jeder vorbringt, so nehmen muß, wie er es gibt oder aber, ob die Sprechenden sich einander in öffentlicher Sitzung gegenüber stehen und der Richter fragen kann, wenn er Widersprüche findet.

Aus meiner langjährigen Praxis in der Pfalz ist mir kein Fall erinnerlich, wo aus der Vereinigung von Streitsachen oder prozeßführenden Personen Unklarheit oder Unordnung im Prozesse entstanden wäre, obgleich in manchen Prozessen eine Reihe von Garantiebeklagten, Intervenienten, Beigeladenen mit verschiedenartigen Interessen vorkamen und oft vier und mehr Anwälte zugleich thätig waren. Im Gegentheile erschien es immer als ein großer Gewinn für das materielle Recht und trug namentlich zur Klärung des Sachverhalts wesentlich bei, wenn alle irgendwie betheiligten Personen zusammen auftraten, um ihre Behauptungen und ihre Rechte zur Geltung zu bringen. Ich erinnere mich deßhalb wohl einer Reihe von Fällen, wo Prozesse vereinigt, aber keines einzigen, wo solche getrennt wurden; höchstens, daß seltener Weise eine Widerklage zur gesonderten Austragung verwiesen wurde, was aber aus andern Gründen, nicht aus Furcht vor Unordnung im Prozesse, geschah.

5) Als Fälle, welche unter Abs. 2 zu bringen seien, wurden angeführt, wenn eine größere Zahl von Giltpflichtigen oder Forstberechtigten, wobei gleichmäßig Verjährung oder Herkommen als Gründe der Entstehung der Rechte geltend gemacht werden, zusammen belangt sind oder auftreten.

Kein Zweifel kann bestehen, daß auch dort, wo der Fall einer Streitgenossenschaft gegeben ist, das Gericht die Befugniß habe, auf Grund des Art. 157 die Verhandlungen zu trennen; jedoch wird meines Erachtens eine Veranlassung dazu nie vorliegen.

Art. 64. — **Streitgenossen stehen, soweit das Gesetz nicht anders verfügt, der Gegenpartei dergestalt als Einzelne gegenüber, daß die Angriffs- und Vertheidigungsmittel des einen Streitgenossen den andern ebensowenig nützen, als die Handlungen und Unterlassungen desselben den andern zum Nachtheile gereichen.**

Für die Prozeßführung haben Streitgenossen, soweit für sie kein gesondertes Interesse besteht, einen gemeinschaftlichen Vertreter zu bestellen.

Ist dies bei Beginn der Verhandlung noch nicht geschehen, so hat das Gericht auf Verlangen der Gegenpartei die Vertretung zu regeln.

In allen Fällen kann das Gericht die unterliegende Partei von den Mehrkosten entbinden, welche dadurch entstanden sind, daß die obsiegende Partei der Vorschrift des Abs. 2 nicht nachgekommen ist. G. A. d. K. d. A. I S. 77. 78. 170. IV S. 20. — K. d. R. I S. 166—168.

1) Es wird hier der prozessuale Grundsatz aufgestellt, daß Prozeßhandlungen des einen Streitgenossen dem andern weder nützen noch schaden werden, jedoch jene Fälle ausgenommen, wo das Gesetz anders verfügt.

Unter „dem Gesetze“ ist nicht etwa die P. O. zu verstehen, sondern alle Gesetze, vorzugsweise die civilrechtlichen (Abg. I 78); auch wollte der Gesetzgeber nicht bloß von ausdrücklichen gesetzlichen Verfügungen sprechen, meinte vielmehr auch anerkannte Prinzipien, welche sich aus dem Geiste des Gesetzes herleiten. Der hannov. Entwurf sagte: „sofern sich nicht aus civilrechtlichen Grundsätzen etwas Anderes ergibt“, und dies ist wohl auch der Sinn unseres Gesetzes.

2) In eine genaue Erörterung darüber, was in den verschiedenen Gesetzgebungen Rechtens sei, kann hier nicht eingegangen werden; jedoch pflegen sich die Ausnahmsfälle, wo Handlungen des einen Mitberechtigten oder Mitverpflichteten auch dem anderen gegenüber wirken, auf die Solidarität und die Untheilbarkeit des Streitgegenstandes zu beschränken und selbst hier in der Regel nur eintreten, wenn es sich um Gewinn, nicht aber, wenn es sich um Verlust handelt. vgl. bayer. L. R. Thl. IV Cap. I § 22 Ziff. 3. — Preuß. L. R. Thl. I Tit. V § 435—438. — Code civ. Art. 1199 u. 1365. — Seuffert Archiv Bd. XII. Nr. 12. — Windscheid Pand. § 295—299.

3) Die Interessen der Streitgenossen können sich vereinigen oder können widersprechend sein, denn es ist nicht das Verhältniß, in welchem sie unter sich stehen, sondern die Art und Weise, wie sie zusammen der Gegenpartei gegenüberstehen, was die Streitgenossenschaft begründet. So sind z. B. zwei als Mitschuldner belangte Personen Streitgenossen, obgleich Jeder behauptet, der Andere sei ausschließlich der Schuldner. So hat ferner derjenige Mitschuldner, welcher behauptet, bloß Bürge zu sein, und deßhalb seinen Rückgriff gegen

den andern Mitschuldner nimmt, offenbar ein gesondertes, widersprechendes Interesse.

In Fällen nun, wo solche widerstreitende Interessen vorliegen, kann selbstverständlich der nemliche Vertreter nicht für beide Streitgenossen auftreten; er müßte sich ja selbst bekämpfen; besteht jedoch ein derartiger Widerstreit nicht, so verpflichtet das Gesetz zur Bestellung eines gemeinschaftlichen Vertreters.

Der Umstand, daß ein Streitgenosse außer den gemeinschaftlichen Mitteln des Angriffs und der Vertheidigung noch besondere geltend zu machen hat, begründet kein „gesondertes Interesse" im Sinne des Gesetzes und gibt daher auch kein Recht auf gesonderte Vertretung. Das Gesetz verlangt vielmehr einen Widerstreit der Interessen, wie nach den Gründen, aus welchen ein weitergehender Zusatz des Entwurfes gestrichen wurde, nicht zu bezweifeln ist. (R. R. I 167. — Vortrag des Refer. v. Neumayr zur 2. Lesung Hauptst. II Art. 7.)

4) Es werden dem Richter zwei verschiedene Mittel an die Hand gegeben, um Streitgenossen zur Bestellung eines gemeinschaftlichen Vertreters zu zwingen, nemlich:

1) ein direktes, durch Regelung der Vertretung, und
2) ein indirektes, durch Belastung mit den Mehrkosten.

5) Die Regelung der Vertretung durch das Gericht findet nur statt auf Antrag der Gegenpartei, und erst dann, wenn die Sache zur Verhandlung gekommen ist. Durch die Verhandlung wird nemlich der Richter in den Stand gesetzt, sicher zu beurtheilen, ob widerstreitendes Interesse vorliege oder nicht, und hat in seinem Urtheile entsprechend zu verfügen.

Es frägt sich nun, ob diese Verfügung dem betreffenden Anwalte sofort Mandat gebe, für diejenigen Streitgenossen, welche er seither nicht vertrat, zu handeln. Das Gesetz sagt dies nicht und nach dem Geiste des neuen Verfahrens wird es nicht anzunehmen, vielmehr die richterliche Regelung bloß als eine Weisung zu betrachten sein, einen bestimmten Vertreter zu nehmen, mit der Folge, daß alle Kosten ohne Unterschied, welche durch Beibehaltung des seitherigen Vertreters erwachsen, unbedingt der ungehorsamen Partei zur Last bleiben, sowie vorbehaltlich disciplinärer Ahndung, falls ein Anwalt Schuld trägt. Will eine Partei ihren besonderen Vertreter auf ihre Kosten beibehalten oder will sie sich in Fällen, wo kein Anwaltszwang besteht, selbst vertreten, so steht nichts im Wege, denn die Verfügungen wegen gemeinschaftlicher Vertretung sind bloß im Interesse der Gegenpartei gegeben.

6) Was die Belastung mit den Mehrkosten betrifft, so ist es dem Ermessen des Richters überlassen, ob und in welcher Weise dieselbe einzutreten habe. Er hat dabei die Verschuldung zur Richtschnur zu nehmen.

Hat ein Streitgenosse einen eignen Vertreter bestellt, obgleich er wußte, daß die anderen Streitgenossen bereits einen Vertreter hatten (bei der Lokalisirung der Anwälte ist dies in der Regel leicht zu ermitteln), sowie daß ein widerstreitendes Interesse nicht vorliege, so hat ihn allein die Strafe zu treffen, unter Umständen auch den Vertreter selbst. Art. 110. Trifft jedoch nach vorliegenden Umständen die Streitgenossen gleiche Verschuldung, so ist auch die Strafe zu theilen.

7) Da das Gesetz von Vertretern im Allgemeinen spricht, so sind seine Bestimmungen nicht blos anwendbar im Anwaltsprozesse (Art. 79), sondern auch im Parteiprozesse (Art. 78), falls Vertreter bestellt sind. Selbstverständlich kann im Parteiprozesse eine Partei nie gezwungen werden, sich des Vertreters der Streitgenossen zu bedienen, falls sie vorzieht, ihre Sache persönlich zu führen.

Art. 65. — Ist die Führung des Rechtsstreits oder der Vollzug des Urtheils durch gemeinschaftliche Verhandlung mit mehreren Genossen bedingt, so kann der klagende Theil die Mitberechtigten zur Theilnahme an dem Streite beiladen. Der beklagte Theil kann verlangen, daß der Kläger die übrigen Rechts- oder Verbindlichkeitsgenossen beilade, oder er kann deren Beiladung auch selbst bewirken.

Die Beigeladenen treten in das Verhältniß von Parteien und das Urthäl erhält gegen sie, auch wenn sie nicht erschienen sind, die den allgemein gesetzlichen Bestimmungen entsprechende Wirksamkeit. Erfolgt die Beiladung erst im Laufe des Prozesses, so können sie ihre Rechte ohne Rücksicht auf die Prozeßlage geltend machen.

G. A. der K. d. A. I S. 78. 79. 170. 171. II S. 295. IV S. 20. 303. — K. d. R. I S. 168. IV. S. 9—11.

1) Dieser Artikel bringt eine Neuerung, welche jedoch vollkommen berechtigt ist; es wäre sogar zu wünschen, daß der Gesetzgeber in der Gestattung von Beiladungen noch etwas weiter gegangen wäre, wenn auch nicht grade, was Streitgenossen betrifft, doch in anderen Richtungen.

a) Fälle der Beiladung.

2) Die Bezeichnung der Fälle der Beilad-

ung, wie sie Abs. 1 des Artikels gibt, ist etwas unbestimmt und, wie v. Neumayr in seinem Vortrage richtig bemerkt, man kann alles und nichts darin finden. Zieht man jedoch den Geist des Gesetzes zu Rath und faßt man dasjenige in's Auge, was bei den Verhandlungen (Abg. I 79) geäußert worden ist, so lassen sich dennoch die Fälle, welche das Gesetz treffen will, ziemlich bestimmt hervorheben wenn auch allerdings eine erschöpfende Aufzählung nicht möglich ist.

3) Für's Erste ist zu beachten, daß das Gesetz hier nur von solchen Beiladungen spricht, wo Streitgenossen im Sinne des Art. 63 vor Gericht zu ziehen sind. Er ist also z. B. nicht anwendbar, wenn es sich fragt, ob der einen oder der andern Person ein gewisses Recht zustehe, denn Personen, welche sich gegenseitig ihr Recht bestreiten, könnten nicht als Streitgenossen klagen. Der Schuldner, welcher behauptet, es seien mehrere Prätendenten (Cessionare) der Forderung vorhanden, und wünscht, sie möchten sämmtlich in den Rechtsstreit gezogen werden, damit er sicher wisse, an wen er zu zahlen habe, findet daher in Art. 65 keine Berechtigung, dies zu erzwingen.

Andrerseits ist auch sicher, daß nicht in einem jeden Falle von Streitgenossenschaft auch die Beiladung statthaft ist; es müssen vielmehr besondere Umstände vorliegen, nemlich, die Beiladung muß entweder zur Führung des Rechtsstreites oder zur Sicherung des Vollzuges nöthig sein.

4) Der erstere Gesichtspunkt (Nothwendigkeit zur Führung des Rechtsstreites) tritt, im Sinne des Gesetzes, ein, wenn eine civilrechtliche Bestimmung vorschreibt, es solle gemeinschaftlich mit sonstigen Betheiligten verhandelt werden, oder wenigstens das Recht gibt, deren Beiladung zu verlangen. Die Verhandlungen lassen keinen Zweifel, daß solche Bestimmungen der Civilgesetze wirksam bleiben sollten.

Hierher gehören, abgesehen von Theilungsklagen, z. B. die Bestimmungen des preuß. L. R. Thl. I. Tit. V § 450 u. Tit. XVII § 151; dann des Code civil Art. 99, 1225 u. 1760.

Dieser Gesichtspunkt tritt ferner ein bei Gränzberichtigungsstreiten, wenn die Ermittlung der richtigen Gränze nur durch Beiziehung verschiedener Grundeigenthümer möglich ist; dann in dem Falle des Art. 645 Code civ., wenn der Richter die Rechte auf Wasserbenützung zu regeln berufen wird.

Das Recht einer Gewährschaftsklage, welches Art. 69 der P. O. gibt und welches auch Platz greifen kann bei Streitgenossen, z. B. Solidarschuldnern, Bürgen, sofern diese ihren Rückgriff nehmen, ist nach den bezüglichen besonderen Grundsätzen zu beurtheilen.

5) Der zweite Gesichtspunkt (Sicherung des Vollzuges) tritt ein in Fällen, wo der Streitgegenstand untheilbar ist. In solchen Fällen kann nämlich das Urtheil, falls es zum Nachtheile eines der Mitberechtigten oder Mitverpflichteten lautet, seinen Genossen gegenüber nicht vollzogen werden, bevor nicht auch gegen diese ein obsiegliches Urtheil erwirkt ist. Handelt es sich daher z. B. um Geltendmachen einer Servitut auf ein im Miteigenthume befindliches Grundstück oder um Freiheit des Eigenthums von irgend einer dinglichen Last (z. B. einem Wässerungsrechte), bei welcher eine Mehrzahl von Personen bethätigt ist, so kann Beiladung stattfinden.

Was die bloße Solidarität betrifft, so kann nicht gesagt werden, daß der Vollzug bedingt sei durch gemeinschaftliche Verhandlung.

b) Verfahren und Wirkungen.

6) Was das Verfahren anbelangt, so ist zu beachten, daß es sich nicht um eine Art Streitverkündigung handelt, welche nur einen oder den andern Rechtsnachtheil zur Folge haben soll, sondern, daß der Beigeladene Partei im Rechtsstreite werden und ein der Rechtskraft fähiges Urtheil gegen ihn ergehen soll. f. Art. 487. Es sind daher alle jene Vorschriften, dem Wesen nach, zu erfüllen, wie sie das Gesetz zur Erwirkung einer Verurtheilung vorschreibt.

Hieraus leitet sich ab, daß in der Beiladung der Sachverhalt und die zum Grunde der Sache zu stellenden Anträge im Sinne von Art. 225 der P. O. kundgegeben werden müssen; daß ferner im Falle des Nichterscheinens nur bezüglich solcher Anträge, welche aus der Beiladung ersichtlich sind, das Urtheil gemeinschaftlich erklärt werden kann. Ebendeßhalb sind die Beigeladenen als Parteien in den Anträgen und Urtheilen aufzuführen.

7) Was zuerst den Kläger betrifft, so gibt ihm das Gesetz das Recht, seine Mitberechtigten beizuladen; zur Beiladung derjenigen Personen, welche ihm mitverpflichtet sind, bedurfte es selbstverständlich einer besonderen Ermächtigung nicht.

Dem Beklagten hingegen sind zwei Wege eröffnet, um sowohl die Streitgenossen des Klägers als seine eigenen in den Rechtsstreit zu ziehen; er kann nemlich 1) verlangen, daß der Kläger beilade und kann 2) selbst beiladen.

Indem er jenes Verlangen stellt, macht er die exceptio plurium litis consortium geltend, welche Einrede jedoch zunächst nur eine dilatorische Wirkung hat, indem dem Kläger, falls er nicht sofort freiwillig beiladet, vom Gerichte eine Frist zur Beiladung gesetzt wird. Ist diese Frist unbenützt verstrichen, so muß die Klage auf Verlangen des Beklagten als unstatthaft zurückgewiesen werden.

8) Inhalt der Ladung und Anträge richten sich natürlich nach dem Rechtsverhältnisse, in welchem der Beiladende und der Beigeladene unter einander stehen.

Wenn der Kläger seinen Mitberechtigten beiladet, so hat er daher genau den Inhalt der Hauptladung (am besten durch Zustellung einer Abschrift derselben) mitzutheilen und hiermit die Aufforderung zu verbinden, am Rechtsstreite Theil zu nehmen, widrigenfalls der Antrag bei Gericht gestellt werden würde, das ergehende Urtheil auch gegen ihn wirksam zu erklären.

Betrifft die Beiladung eine Person, welche dem Kläger mitverpflichtet ist, so hat natürlich die Ladung in derselben Weise zu geschehen, als wenn diese Person ursprünglich mitvorgeladen worden wäre.

9) Erscheint der Beigeladene und nimmt Theil am Rechtsstreite, so ist die Sache einfach; nur möchte zu bemerken sein, daß zum Eintritte in den Rechtsstreit die Zustellung eines Anwaltsaktes an sämmtliche Anwälte, wie sie (Art. 488) für Nebeninterventionen vorgeschrieben ist, genügend erscheint.

Der Fall des Nichterscheinens bedarf jedoch einer näheren Erörterung.

Da es sich um Herbeiführung eines der Rechtskraft fähigen Urtheils handelt, so kann kein Zweifel bestehen, daß die Vorschriften des Hauptst. VIII über Versäumungsurtheile ihre Anwendung finden. Die Worte: „die den allgemeinen gesetzlichen Bestimmungen entsprechende Wirksamkeit“ dürfen nicht irre leiten und etwa auf den Gedanken führen, es solle hiermit die Art oder der Grad der Wirksamkeit der Urtheile gegen die Beigeladenen von civilrechtlichen Grundsätzen abhängig gemacht werden. Jene Worte wurden beigefügt, um die im Entwurfe vorkommenden Worte: „unter den gesetzlichen Voraussetzungen für Versäumungsurtheile“ zu ersetzen, weil diese, in Berücksichtigung, daß auch Verbindungsurtheile vorkommen können, nicht ganz correkt erschienen. s. Abg. IV S. 303 (v. Neumayr).

10) Vielleicht wäre bei den Beiladungen, welche Art. 65 gestattet, ein Verfahren am zweckmäßigsten, welches von vornherein zu verfügen erlaubte, daß wegen Nichterscheinens des Beigeladenen das zukünftige Verfahren gemeinschaftlich sein solle, so daß also das Endurtheil contradiktorisch gegen beide Streitgenossen erginge, allein ein solches Ausnahmsverfahren gestattet unsere Prozeßordnung nur in jenen Fällen, welche sich nach Art. 316 zum Erlasse eines Verbindungsurtheiles eignen.

Der Fall eines solchen Verbindungsurtheiles ist nun wohl gegeben, wenn der Kläger einen Streitgenossen des Beklagten vorladet und dieser nicht erscheint, nicht aber, wenn er seinen Mitberechtigten vorladet. In letzterem Falle hat daher ein gewöhnliches Versäumungsurtheil zu ergehen, und zwar in der Art, daß im Endurtheile als jenem Urtheile, welches gemeinschaftlich werden soll, ausgesprochen wird, es sei dasselbe auch gegen den Beigeladenen wirksam. Ich halte es nemlich nach der Natur der Beiladung und im Geiste des Verfahrens für nöthig, daß ein förmlicher Ausspruch in dieser Richtung erfolge.

Das Nichterscheinen des Beigeladenen ist selbstverständlich schon in der ersten Verhandlung bei welcher er zu erscheinen hatte, zu beurkunden, was insbesondere im Parteiprozesse von Wesenheit ist.

11) Gegen dieses Versäumungsurtheil kann der Beigeladene, wie gegen jedes andere Urtheil dieser Art, Einspruch erheben, sei es um geltend zu machen, daß die gesetzlichen Voraussetzungen einer Beiladung mangelten, sei es, um in der Sache selbst seine Rechte zur Geltung zu bringen.

Intervention.

Art. 66. — **Ein Dritter ist berechtigt, in einem anhängigen Rechtsstreite in jeder Lage desselben zu interveniren:**

1) **wenn ihm ein selbständiges, eine oder beide Parteien ganz oder theilweise ausschließendes Recht auf den Streitgegenstand zusteht (Hauptintervention);**

2) **wenn ein ihm zustehendes Recht durch den Sieg einer der Parteien bedingt ist oder ihm aus dem Unterliegen derselben ein rechtlicher Nachtheil erwachsen würde (Nebenintervention).**

Art. 67. — **Der Hauptintervenient hat seinen Anspruch bei demjenigen Gerichte anzubringen, bei welchem zur Zeit der Intervention der Hauptstreit anhängig ist.**

Die Hauptintervention ist als Klage zu betrachten und soweit das Gesetz nicht anders verfügt, nach den über Klagen geltenden Grundsätzen zu beurtheilen.

Ist das Urtheil in der Hauptsache von der Entscheidung der Intervention abhängig und ist gleichzeitige Verhandlung nicht möglich, so hat die erstere bis zur rechtskräftigen Entscheidung der letztern zu beruhen.

Art. 68. — Der Nebenintervenient tritt einer der Parteien zu ihrer Unterstützung bei. Er muß die Sache in dem Stande nehmen, in welchem sie sich zur Zeit der Intervention befindet.

Im Fortgange des Rechtsstreits ist er befugt, für die von ihm verbeistandete Partei alles Sachdienliche, namentlich die Einlegung von Rechtsmitteln, mit Wirksamkeit vorzunehmen.

G. A. d. K. d. A. I S. 93. 171. 172. 288. 289. 299. IV S. 20. — K. d. R. I S. 168 u. 169.

1) Das französische Prozeßgesetz ist bezüglich der Intervention sehr lakonisch; von den Fällen, in denen sie statthaft sei, spricht es gar nicht, sondern regelt bloß das Verfahren. Art. 339—341. Dabei wird ein Unterschied zwischen Haupt- und Nebenintervention, zwischen Geltendmachung eigner Rechte und bloßer Hülfeleistung, nicht gemacht, vielmehr vorausgesetzt, daß sich die Rolle des Intervenienten im Rechtsstreite von selbst durch sein Interesse und die auf Grund desselben zu nehmenden Anträge ergeben müsse. Die Jurisprudenz hatte daher freien Spielraum und ließ Intervention überall zu, wo bezüglich eines bestehenden Rechtes irgend ein Interesse, sei es ein thatsächliches, sei es ein rechtliches zu wahren war — eine Freiheit, welche nur günstig gewirkt hat.

In ähnlicher allgemeiner Weise verfügt übrigens auch die bayer. Ger. O. cap. VIII § 4, indem sie Intervention zuläßt, „wo ein Dritter Schaden oder Nutzen zu gewarten hat.“

Unsere Prozeßordnung gestattet zwei Arten von Interventionen nemlich eine Hauptintervention und eine Nebenintervention. Beide sind sowohl nach ihren Voraussetzungen als auch dem Verfahren nach unterschieden und es wird daher geeignet sein, sie getrennt zu besprechen.

a) Hauptintervention.

2) Die Hauptintervention bildete sich im deutschen Prozesse bloß durch die Praxis und es ist dies der sicherste Beweis, daß sie prozessuales Bedürfniß ist.

In Hannover hat man mit ebensoviel Gelehrsamkeit als Scharfsinn darzuthun versucht, es sei das ganze Institut der Hauptintervention verwerflich und empfehle sich der österreichische und nassauische Prozeß, welche sie verbieten, zur Nachahmung; von allen vorgebrachten Gründen erscheint jedoch für das mündliche Verfahren, nur derjenige praktisch, welcher betont, daß, falls die Hauptintervention wirklich einem Bedürfnisse entspräche, man auch den Zwang zulassen müßte.

Allerdings glaube ich und zwar auf Grund eigener Erfahrungen, daß die in den Ländern, wo der französische Prozeß gilt, bestehende Uebung, gemäß deren der Richter befugt ist, bei Vorlage wichtiger Gründe, die Beiladung dritter Prätendenten zu gestatten, sehr wohlthätig wirke und zur Aufklärung des Sachverhalts, Minderung der Prozesse und Verhütung widersprechender Urtheile wesentlich beitrage.

Wie schon oben (Art. 63 Nr. 4) bemerkt, macht sich überhaupt im mündlichen Verfahren das Bedürfniß geltend, alles Zusammengehörige möglichst zu vereinigen und alle Personen, welche betheiligt sind, zugleich zu hören. Hieraus erklärt sich, wie, ohne irgend einen Anhalt im Texte des Gesetzes das besagte System der Beiladung (intervention passive ou forcée — déclaration de jugement commun) eine so große Ausdehnung gewinnen konnte.

Im seitherigen schriftlichen Verfahren lag allerdings die Sache anders, und wer dasselbe kennt, findet es sehr wohl erklärlich, daß sich die Idee festsetzen mußte, es seien Beiladungen an sich etwas Schlimmes, zur Verwirrung Führendes, was möglichst verhütet werden müsse.

3) Zur Hauptintervention berechtigt ist derjenige, welcher ein die Rechte einer der beiden Parteien ganz oder theilweise ausschließendes Recht am Streitgegenstande behauptet.

Die Rechte beider Parteien sind z. B. ausgeschlossen, wenn der Intervenient das Grundstück oder die Erbschaft, um welche sich zwei Personen streiten, für sich in Anspruch nimmt; die Rechte einer Partei sind z. B. ausgeschlossen, wenn der Intervenient behauptet, eine Forderung, welche eingeklagt wird, stehe ihm zu.

Zu bemerken ist, daß hier nur von Interventionen im Laufe eines Rechtsstreites die Rede ist, nicht aber von solchen im Vollstreckungsverfahren, indem z. B. ein Dritter Eigenthumsansprüche auf gepfändete Sachen erhebt. Hierüber bestehen eigene Vorschriften (Art. 870).

4) Die Hauptintervention ist in jeder Lage der Sache statthaft und ist immer bei demjenigen Gerichte anzubringen, wo die Hauptsache anhängig ist, mag der Gerichtstand auch nur durch Vereinbarung begründet sein. (Vortrag v. Neumayr zur 2. Lesung Hauptst. II Art. 10 u. 11.)

Es gilt dies nicht nur vom ersten Rechtszuge, ohne Rücksicht auf das Stadium, in welchem sich das Verfahren befindet, sondern auch von der Berufungsinstanz, so daß also hier der Ausnahmsfall gegeben ist, daß eine selbständige Klage, mit Ueberspringung der ersten Instanz, unmittelbar bei dem Appellationsgerichte angebracht werden darf. Da nach dem neuen Verfahren die

Instruktion in beiden Instanzen in gleicher Weise (durch motivirte Anträge) geschieht, so macht sich die Sache formell sehr einfach; materiell aber sind große Vortheile damit verbunden.

Obgleich es heißt: „in jeder Lage der Sache", so wird doch eine Hauptintervention beim obersten Gerichtshofe nicht zulässig sein, weil sie ihrer Natur nach nur vor einem solchen Gerichte und in einem solchen Stadium des Verfahrens angebracht werden kann, wo ein Eingehen auf den Grund der Sache statthaft ist. Findet jedoch, nach Vernichtung eines Urtheils, neues Verfahren über den Grund der Sache statt, so ist auch die Hauptintervention wiederum zulässig.

5) Diese Intervention wird immer erhoben durch förmliche Klage, welche sämmtlichen Parteien des anhängigen Rechtsstreites zuzustellen ist. Da nun aber nach Art. 488 fragliche Zustellung in Fällen, wo die Parteien durch Anwälte vertreten sind, an letztere erfolgt, auch jedem Anwalte nur eine einzige Abschrift gegeben wird, so unterscheidet sich diese Klage der Form nach nicht viel von einem Anwaltsakte, welcher zudem, wenn er gut abgefaßt ist, auch alles dasjenige enthalten wird, was zu einer Klage nöthig ist.

Die Bestimmung in Art. 67 Abs. 3 enthält im Wesentlichen eine Anwendung der Art. 170 ausgesprochenen Prinzipien; da hier übrigens speziell verfügt ist, so wird eine Suspendirung der Hauptsache in vorliegendem Fall nur statthaft sein, wenn gleichzeitige Verhandlung nicht möglich, d. h. wohl mit allzugroßen Mißständen verbunden sein würde.

Bei Handels- und Einzeln-Gerichten kann der Hauptintervenient, ohne Zustellung einer Ladung, sofort in der Sitzung auftreten (Art. 510); ein Verfahren, welches übrigens in der Regel nicht rathsam ist, da es Vertagungen nöthig macht und überhaupt die Sache verzögert, statt beschleunigt.

b) Nebenintervention.

6) Das Wesen der Nebenintervention liegt darin, daß hier der Intervenient nur in den Rechtsstreit eintritt, um eine oder die andere Partei in ihrem Angriffe oder in ihrer Vertheidigung zu unterstützen. Sobald er neue Ansprüche für sich selbst geltend macht, tritt er aus seiner Rolle heraus.

Das Recht zur Nebenintervention ist einem Dritten gegeben:

1) wen ein ihm zustehendes Recht durch den Sieg einer der Parteien bedingt ist, oder
2) wenn ihm aus dem Unterliegen derselben ein rechtlicher Nachtheil erwachsen würde.

In beiden Fällen setzt das Gesetz voraus, daß der Intervenirende ein bereits entstandenes Recht besitzen müsse, auf welches der Ausgang des Rechtsstreites von Einfluß sei. Ein Interesse, welches bloß in Gefährdung mehr oder minder sicherer Hoffnungen, in freundschaftlicher Theilnahme, im Ehrenpunkte bestünde, also sich nicht auf klagbare Rechte stützte, könnte das Recht zur Nebenintervention nie begründen. Dieses eigene Recht bildet zwar die Legitimation des Nebenintervenienten, darf aber nicht direkt Gegenstand des Rechtsstreits werden.

8) Was nun die erste der obbezeichneten gesetzlichen Voraussetzungen anbelangt, so wird sie überall gegeben sein, wo nach den Grundsätzen des Civilrechtes der Sieg einer Partei auch demjenigen, welcher interveniren will, zum Vortheile gereicht. — So nützt z. B. in der Regel der Sieg des Testamentserben dem Legatare, der Sieg des Eigenthümers eines Grundstückes allen denjenigen, welche dingliche Rechte (Nutzrechte, Pfandrechte) an demselben haben, überhaupt bei untheilbarem Streitgegenstande oder bei Solidarverhältnissen der Sieg des einen Mitberechtigten oder Mitverpflichteten dem andern.

Allerdings ist in diesen Fällen nicht immer das Recht des Intervenienten vollständig vom Siege der Hauptpartei abhängig, so zwar, daß je nachdem der Rechtsstreit endigte, das Recht gewonnen oder verloren wäre; allein dies erfordern weder Wortlaut noch Sinn des Gesetzes, vielmehr wird es genügen, wenn auch nur der Vortheil des Rechtsstreites dem Intervenienten zu gut kommt.

Vollständig ist jedoch z. B. das Recht des Intervenienten durch den Sieg der Hauptpartei bedingt, wenn es sich um Wahrung von Rechten am Streitgegenstande handelt, welche erst während des Rechtsstreites erworben wurden (Seuff. Archiv Bd. XV Nr. 161 a. E.), oder wenn ein Gläubiger auf Grund des Art. 1166 Code civ. die Rechte des Schuldners ausübt.

9) Was die zweite Voraussetzung betrifft, so erscheint sie weitergreifend.

Ursprünglich war bloß von „Nachtheil" die Rede; die nähere Bezeichnung „rechtlicher Nachtheil" fügte man nur bei im Hinblicke auf Fälle, wo etwa Jemand am Rechtsstreite einer Person, welche er später zu beerben gedenkt, sich betheiligen wollte, also, wo nicht ein bereits entstandenes Recht zu wahren ist. (R. R. I 169.) Es soll also das Wörtchen „rechtlich" nicht den Gedanken ausdrücken, als ob die Entscheidung gegen die Hauptpartei ganz oder theilweise ihre Rechtskraft auch auf den Intervenienten erstrecken müsse, sondern es soll nur andeuten, daß es sich um Beschädigung eines wirklich bestehenden Rechtes handeln müsse. Beides ist sehr verschieden. — Wenn z. B. ein Schuldner die Mittel zur Befriedigung seiner Gläubiger betrügerisch beseitigt, so wird das Recht des Gläubigers an und für sich nicht verkürzt — er kann es vor Gericht nach wie vor geltend machen; allein Niemand wird bestreiten können, daß dennoch der Gläubiger in seinen Rechten beschädigt sei. Renaud (Lehrb. des gem. deutschen Civ. Proz. § 47) sagt deßhalb: „es müsse entweder ein Recht oder die wirksame Geltendmachung desselben durch den Sieg der Hauptpartei bedingt sein.“ Aehnlich sagt von Neumayr (Abg. I 93): „es müsse das Recht beschädigt sein,“ und im hannov. Entwurfe heißt es: „wenn ein ihm zustehendes Recht gefährdet wird.“

10) Der Hauptfall, welcher hierher gehört, ist wohl der, wenn Jemand im Falle des Unterliegens einer Partei einer Regreßklage Seitens derselben ausgesetzt wäre. Hat eine Streitverkündigung stattgefunden, so ist das Recht zur Intervention klar (Art. 70 Abs. 4); allein dasselbe muß auch gegeben sein, wenn die Streitverkündigung unterlassen worden ist. Abgesehen davon, daß in der Intervention zugleich ein Verzicht auf die Streitverkündigung zu erblicken sein wird (Art. 70 Abs. 3), hat der mit Regreßklage Bedrohte ein lebhaftes Interesse, den Anspruch sofort abweisen zu machen, um nicht später einem Prozesse darüber, ob das Recht bestreitbar gewesen, oder nicht, ausgesetzt zu sein.

Ueberhaupt wird es im Geiste des Gesetzes liegen, die Bestimmungen über Intervention nicht allzu beschränkend auszulegen, sondern vorzugsweise den praktischen Erwägungen Rechnung zu tragen.

11) Es entsteht nun die Frage: Welche rechtliche Stellung hat der Nebenintervenient vom Augenblicke an, wo er in den Rechtsstreit eingetreten ist?

Ist die Sachlage etwa so zu betrachten, als wenn zwei Streitgenossen das nemliche untheilbare Recht geltend machen, so daß also der Nebenintervenient gleichberechtigt wäre mit der Hauptpartei und keiner dem Andern etwas zum Schaden thun könnte, oder aber ist der Nebenintervenient nur eine Art Geschäftsführer, welcher dort eingreift, wo die Hauptpartei etwas versäumt oder übersieht, ohne jedoch benachtheiligende Geständnisse, Verzichte 2c. verhüten zu können?

Diese sehr schwierige Frage hat die Mitglieder der hannov. Commission lange beschäftigt und es wurden die verschiedenartigsten Ansichten zu Tage gefördert. (Verh. S. 754—790). Schließlich sprach sich die Mehrheit für die letztere Ansicht aus und man nahm deßhalb in § 60 des Entwurfes die ausdrückliche Bestimmung auf: „Der Nebenintervenient kann alle Prozeßhandlungen mit Wirksamkeit vornehmen, insoweit dieselben nicht mit Erklärungen und Handlungen der Hauptpartei im Widerspruche stehen.“

Unsere Prozeßordnung sagt bloß das Erstere ohne letzteren Zusatz, und es möchte hieraus zu folgern sein, daß sie die Ansicht der hannov. Commission nicht theilte, jedenfalls in ihrer Allgemeinheit für gewagt hielt und es gerathen fand, diesen heiklen Punkt der Wissenschaft zu überlassen.

12) Als wirkliche Streitgenossen sind nun offenbar, wenigstens der Regel nach, die Nebenintervenienten nicht zu betrachten, denn ihre Anträge sind nicht dahin gerichtet, daß ihnen selbst, sondern, daß der Hauptpartei etwas zugesprochen werden solle, wobei es gleichgültig ist, wenn zufällig dieses Recht identisch ist mit ihrem eigenen. Nur im Hinblicke hierauf konnte das Gesetz die Nebenintervention in jeder Lage der Sache, d. h. selbst in den höheren Instanzen noch zulassen.

Anderseits ist wiederum zu beachten, daß die Nebenintervention wesentlich auch zur Wahrung und Sicherung eines eigenen Rechtes des Intervenienten bestimmt ist und daß sie in der Regel nicht bloß den Zweck hat, die Nachtheile abzuwenden, welche durch Nachlässigkeit oder Mangel an Einsicht der Hauptpartei entstehen können, sondern auch zu verhüten, daß durch Collusion derselben mit der Gegenpartei das Recht des Nebenintervenienten beschädigt werde. (Renaud a. a. O. Note 10.) Mit der Nebenintervention erhebt der Intervenient Einspruch dagegen, daß fortan etwas zum Schaden seines Rechtes geschehe und soll nicht dieser Einspruch völlig illusorisch werden, so muß er zur Folge haben, daß das unbeschränkte Verfügungsrecht der Hauptpartei einige Beschränkung erleide und dem Nebenintervenienten das Recht zustehe, sich Prozeßhandlungen, welche seinen Schaden bezwecken, zu widersetzen und sie, soweit es die Wahrung seines Rechtes erheischt, für wirkungslos erklären zu lassen. Vgl. die Aeußerungen, welche Abg. I 171, Spalte 1, über die Rechte des Nebenintervenienten und dessen Befugniß, sich gegen Collusion zu sichern, im Namen der Subkommission gemacht wurden.

13) Der Umfang der bezüglichen Wirkungen der Nebenintervention wird sich nach der Natur der zu wahrenden Rechte richten.

Handelt es sich z. B. bloß um Sicherung vor irgend einer Regreßpflicht, so genügt es, wenn die Hauptpartei zur Strafe ihrer schuldvollen Handlungen das Recht auf Schadloshaltung verliert. (Seuff. Comm. Bd. II S. 418 Note 11 b.) Handelt es sich jedoch um ein Recht, bei welchem der Intervenient mitbetheiligt ist, oder um Sicherung der Rechte eines Gläubigers durch Intervention (Art. 882. 1166 Code civ.), so müssen offenbar dem Intervenienten größere Befugnisse zustehen. Wollte man dieses nicht zugeben, so müßte man, wie es in Hannover geschah, als Grundsatz anerkennen, daß die Rechtskraft der ergehenden Entscheidungen dem Nebenintervenienten als solchem nicht entgegengehalten werden könne.

14) Schließlich ergibt sich Anlaß zu einer allgemeinen Bemerkung.

Die Fälle, von welchen Art. 66 spricht, sind ohne Zweifel die einzigen, in welchen das Eintreten eines Dritten in einen Rechtsstreit *in jeder Lage der Sache* geschehen kann; allein sind sie auch die einzigen, in welchen ein *freiwilliges* Eintreten dritter Personen überhaupt statthaft ist?

Für die Verneinung dieser Frage läßt sich anführen, daß das Gesetz zwar die *Beiladung* Dritter, also den *Zwang* zur Einmischung, außer den besonders vorgesehenen Fällen verbietet, daß jedoch ein gleiches Verbot bezüglich der *freiwilligen* Einmischung nicht besteht.

Faßt man nun z. B. Fälle in's Auge, wo Jemand in einem Rechtsstreite auftreten soll, nicht gerade, um daran Theil zu nehmen, sondern um Erklärungen zu geben (Art. 75 u. 371 Abs. 3), so wäre es sicher dem Geiste des Gesetzes zuwider, hier ein freiwilliges Erscheinen nicht zu gestatten, vielmehr auf einer Beiladung zu bestehen, obgleich für solche Fälle das Recht der Intervention nicht ausdrücklich gegeben und das freiwillige Erscheinen vor Gericht nur im Verfahren von Handels- und Einzelngerichten allgemein gestattet ist.

Es möchte sich daher die Ansicht vertreten lassen, daß ein freiwilliges Auftreten in einem *bereits anhängigen* Rechtsstreite, d. h. eine Intervention im weitesten Sinne dieses Wortes, nicht immer einer *ausdrücklichen* Billigung des Gesetzes bedarf, um zugelassen werden zu können.

Streitverkündung und Gewährschaftsklage.

Art. 69. — **Glaubt eine Partei, daß sie im Falle des Unterliegens im Rechtsstreite wegen des Streitgegenstands Gewährleistung oder Schadloshaltung von einem Dritten fordern könne, so kann sie diesem den Streit verkünden. Sie kann damit die Klage auf Gewährleistung oder Schadloshaltung (Gewährschaftsklage) verbinden.**

Das nämliche Recht steht unter den gleichen Voraussetzungen auch demjenigen zu, welchem der Streit verkündet wurde.

Art. 70. — **Die Streitverkündung und Erhebung der Gewährschaftsklage kann geschehen, solange dem Aufgeforderten nach der Lage des Rechtsstreits noch möglich ist, seine Angriffs- und Vertheidigungsmittel vollständig zu gebrauchen.**

Die Partei, welche die ihr nach bürgerlichem Rechte obliegende Streitverkündung unterlassen oder den Streit nicht rechtzeitig verkündet hat, verliert ihr Recht auf Gewährleistung oder Entschädigung, ausgenommen wenn auf Streitverkündung Verzicht geleistet wurde oder nachgewiesen wird, daß das Recht des Entwährenden unanfechtbar war.

Nimmt der rechtzeitig Aufgeforderte an dem Streite nicht Theil, so kann er den Einwand nicht geltend machen, daß der Rechtsstreit von Seiten des Auffordernden fehlerhaft geführt worden ist.

Betheiligt er sich am Streite, so erscheint er als Nebenintervenient.

Seine Betheiligung gilt nicht als Anerkennung, daß der, welcher den Streit verkündet hat, einen Rückgriff gegen ihn habe.

Art. 71. — **Wer unter Streitverkündung mit der Gewährschaftsklage belangt wird, ist verbunden, darüber bei dem Gerichte, wo die Hauptsache anhängig ist, zu verhandeln, auch wenn er die Verpflichtung zur Gewährschaft oder Schadloshaltung in Abrede stellt. Ergibt sich jedoch aus den Umständen, daß die Hauptklage nur erhoben wurde, um ihn vor einem andern als seinem ordentlichen Gerichte belangen zu können, oder ist das Gericht der Hauptklage nur durch Vereinbarung zuständig geworden, so kann er die Verweisung vor sein ordentliches Gericht verlangen.**

Erfolgte die Streitverkündung erst im Rechtszuge der Berufung, so kann der Aufgeforderte die Verweisung der Gewährschaftsklage in die Vorinstanz oder auch vor sein ordentliches Gericht beanspruchen.

Gehört die Gewährschaftsklage nach Art. 2—7 vor ein anderes Gericht, so ist sie auf Antrag und, wenn das Gericht der Hauptsache auch nicht durch Vereinbarung zuständig werden kann, von Amtswegen an das zuständige Gericht zu verweisen, ausgenommen wenn die Hauptsache bei einem Bezirks- oder Handelsgerichte anhängig ist und die Gewährschaftsklage im ersten Falle vor ein Einzelngericht, im zweiten Falle nach Art. 7 Abs. 2 vor ein Bezirks- oder Einzelngericht gehören würde.

Art. 72. — **Ueber die Gewährschaftsklage ist gleichzeitig mit der Hauptklage zu entscheiden, wenn dies nach der Lage der beiden Rechtsstreite möglich ist.**

Die Entscheidung über die Hauptklage darf, abgesehen von den zur Streitverkündung und Gewährschaftsklage eingeräumten Fristen, durch die Gewährschaftsklage nicht aufgehalten werden und letztere ist in allen Fällen, welche eine Verzögerung mit sich bringen oder besorgen lassen, auf Antrag oder von Amtswegen zur gesonderten Verhandlung zu verweisen. G. A. d. K. d. A. I S. 87—91. 171. 299. IV S. 20. — K. d. R. I S. 169—175.

1) Unsere Prozeßordnung hat den Unterschied zwischen dem Anspruche auf Gewährleistung und dem Rückgriffe aus andern Gründen, wie ihn die bayer. Ger.-Ord. Cap. VIII § 2 und theilweise auch der Code de proc. Art. 182 u. 183 anerkennen, vollständig beseitigt. Wer immer im Falle des Unterliegens im Rechtsstreite Schadloshaltung von anderen Personen verlangen darf, unterliegt allen Bestimmungen, wie sie die Art. 69 bis 72 über Streitverkündung und Gewährschaftsklage gegeben haben. Dieselben gelten daher ebensowohl für die Eviktionsfälle, als für Fälle, wo ein Solidarschuldner vom anderen Ersatz dessen verlangt, was er mehr als seinen Theil gezahlt, wo ein Bürge, ein Civilverantwortlicher Ersatz vom Hauptschuldner verlangt, wo der cedirte Schuldner wegen Zahlungen an den Cedenten, welche er dem Cessionare gegenüber nicht zur Geltung bringen kann, seinen Rückgriff gegen jenen nimmt u. s. w.

In allen diesen Fällen gibt das Gesetz die Wahl, bloß den Streit zu verkünden oder sofort Gewährschaftsklage zu erheben.

a) Streitverkündung.

2) Die Streitverkündung ist die Benachrichtigung vom Entstehen des Rechtsstreites, verbunden mit der Ankündigung der Absicht, im Falle des Unterliegens Schadloshaltung zu verlangen. Zugleich wird es geeignet sein, die Aufforderung ergehen zu lassen, zur Bekämpfung der erhobenen Ansprüche am Rechtsstreite Theil zu nehmen, widrigenfalls der Einwand, daß der Rechtsstreit fehlerhaft geführt worden sei, nicht mehr geltend gemacht werden könnte.

3) Der Zweck einer Streitverkündung bedingt es, daß dem Regreßpflichtigen klarer Aufschluß darüber zu geben ist, zwischen welchen Parteien der Sreit sich entsponnen habe; auf welche Thatsachen sich der Anspruch, welcher Anlaß zum Rückgriffe geben soll, stütze; in welcher Richtung und Ausdehnung endlich Schadloshaltung begehrt werde. Die nähere Begründung der Regreßpflicht gehört zur Gewährschaftsklage.

4) Die Streitverkündung erfolgt im Anwaltsprozesse durch einen Anwaltsakt (Art. 487), d. h. es fertigt der Anwalt des Streitverkündenden einen Akt, welcher die nöthigen Mittheilungen und Erklärungen enthält (Art. 165), und diesen Akt läßt er durch einen Gerichtsboten zustellen (Art. 202) Daß Abschrift der die Streitverkündung veranlassenden Prozeßakte — der Klageschrift, des Antrags — mitgetheilt werde, schreibt das Gesetz nicht vor, jedoch wird es sehr zweckmäßig sein, dies zu thun, weil auf diese Weise der beste Aufschluß über die Sachlage gegeben wird und die Streitverkündung selbst durch Bezugnahme auf den betreffenden Prozeßakt sehr abgekürzt werden kann.

Im Parteiprozesse erfolgt die Streitverkündung bloß durch Gerichtsbotenakt, und wird es besonders hier anzurathen sein, die Zustellung der Klageschrift oder, falls der Anlaß zur Streitverkündung erst im Laufe des Rechtsstreites sich ergab, des die bezüglichen Behauptungen und Anträge bekundenden Urtheiles nie zu unterlassen, indem so am sichersten dem Einwande, daß die Streitverkündung ungenügend sei, vorgebeugt wird.

5) Die Streitverkündung hat in der Regel sofort zu geschehen, nachdem der Anlaß dazu entstanden ist, sei dies durch Erhebung der Klage, sei es durch Einreden oder Repliken, z. B. wenn dem Cessionare das Bestehen der eingeklagten Forderung bestritten wird. Das Gesetz gibt zu diesem Zwecke kurze Fristen (Art. 233).

Es kann dieselbe übrigens auch noch später geschehen, jedoch muß dann derjenige, welcher den Streit verkündet, dem Einwande mit Erfolg begegnen können, daß es dem Regreßpflichtigen nicht mehr möglich gewesen sei, seine Angriffs- und Vertheidigungsmittel vollständig zu gebrauchen. Selbst in der Berufungsinstanz wird sie sehr häufig noch mit Erfolg geschehen können, weil nach dem neuen Verfahren auch dort noch alle Angriffs- und Vertheidigungsmittel, soweit nicht Verzicht, Rechtskraft oder besondere Vorschrift des Gesetzes im Wege stehen, frei benützt werden dürfen. Art. 707. Vgl. R. R. IV 12.

Liegen Rechtsverlustigungen durch Versäumung von Prozeßhandlungen, von Beweisführungen, welche in der Berufungsinstanz nicht ergänzt werden können (Art. 707 Abs. 4), Verzichte, Geständnisse in Mitte, so hat die Streitverkündung nur in so fern noch Wirkung, als vollständiger Nachweis erbracht werden kann, daß diese Thatsachen für das in Frage stehende Recht belanglos waren.

Mit einer späteren Streitverkündung ist zugleich Aufschluß über die Lage des Rechtsstreites, so weit es für den Regreßpflichtigen von wesentlichem Belang ist, zu geben, jedenfalls aber die Bezeichnung des Gerichtes, an welchem der Streit zur Zeit anhängig ist, nie zu unterlassen. Eine abschriftliche Mittheilung von Aktenstücken ist auch hier nicht geboten, kann jedoch sachgemäß sein.

6) Derjenige, welchem der Streit verkündet worden, ist nicht verpflichtet, irgend eine Erklärung abzugeben; er hat die Wahl, sich ganz ruhig zu verhalten, oder als Nebenintervenient in den Rechtsstreit einzutreten.

Ein Ungehorsamsverfahren irgend einer Art findet gegen ihn nicht statt; wenn also die Streitverkündung, ihrem Inhalte oder der Art und Weise ihrer Zustellung nach, nicht zu bemängeln ist, so bringt sie sofort die Wirkungen hervor, welche Art. 70 Abs. 3 festsetzt.

7) Man könnte es vielleicht als eine Lücke des Gesetzes bezeichnen, daß, namentlich in den Fällen, von welchen Art. 233 spricht, dem Aufgeforderten nicht eine bestimmte Frist frei gegeben sei, um als Nebenintervenient eintreten zu können. Ohne Zweifel war es die Meinung des Gesetzgebers, daß sich eine nach Maßgabe der Umstände, insbesondere der Entfernungen, zu bemessende Frist von selbst verstehe und daß die Streitverkündung als rechtzeitig geschehen nicht zu erachten sei, wenn diese Frist nicht gegönnt und hiedurch der Aufgeforderte in seinen Rechten verkürzt werde.

8) Der Aufgeforderte kann seinen Vormännern in gleicher Weise und gleicher Frist den Streit verkünden. Nimmt er nicht als Nebenintervenient Theil am Rechtsstreite, so ist er nicht etwa verpflichtet, einen Anwalt aufzustellen, bloß um den Worten des Art. 487 Abs. 2 zu genügen, welche besagen, es habe die Streitverkündung durch Zustellung eines Anwaltsaktes zu geschehen. Jene Worte haben nur den gewöhnlichen Fall im Auge, wo ein Anwalt bestellt ist, in sonstigen Fällen hat die Streitverkündung ebenso wie im handelsgerichtlichen und landgerichtlichen Verfahren bloß durch Gerichtsvollzieherakt zu geschehen.

Selbstverständlich ist, daß die Unthätigkeit der Erstaufgeforderten die Nachfolgenden nicht hindert, ihre eventuellen Rechte durch Nebenintervention zu wahren.

b) Gewährschaftsklage.

9) Die Gewährschaftsklage konnte seither diesseits nur erhoben werden, nachdem der Gewährschaftskläger im Vorprozesse unterlegen war und wenn er etwa Ersatz wegen einer Zahlung, zu welcher er verurtheilt war, verlangte, diese Zahlung geleistet hatte. Erst dann war für ihn actio nata. Die Prozeßordnung erlaubt es nun, diese Klage sofort mit der Streitverkündung zu verbinden.

Diese Neuerung brach sich nur mit großen Schwierigkeiten Bahn, in Hannover aber vermochte sie gar nicht durchzudringen; trotzdem ist sie eine nicht genug zu schätzende Wohlthat für die Rechtspflege und entspricht einem großen praktischen Bedürfnisse.

10) Ein Fall aus der Praxis wird dies anschaulich machen.

Am 28. August 1855 verkaufte B an A um den Preis von 77 fl. einen mageren Ochsen, welcher Anfangs September an Lungenfäule verendete.

A klagte gegen B auf Rückzahlung des erlegten Kaufpreises. Da der Ochse innerhalb der gesetzlichen Garantiefrist durch sechs Hände gegangen war, so verkündete B dem C, C dem D, D dem E, E dem F und F dem G den Streit.

Der Prozeß wurde in gewohnter Weise geführt, mit obligaten Widersprüchen und Beweisen und endete mit verurtheilendem Erkenntnisse vom 17. Oktober 1857.

Am 16. März 1858 erhob B Gewährschaftsklage gegen C auf Zahlung von 319 fl. Endurtheil am 9. April 1861.

Am 26. August 1861 erhob C Klage gegen D auf Zahlung von 561 fl. Endurtheil am 12. Nov. 1863.

Am 27. Juli 1864 erhob D Klage gegen E auf Zahlung von 963 fl.

In allen diesen Rechtsstreiten wurden der Verkauf sowie die Identität des Ochsen bestritten und mußten Beweise geführt werden, welche natürlich im Verlaufe der Zeit immer schwieriger wurden, obgleich man durch kunstvolle Aufbewahrung der Ochsenhaut zu helfen versucht hatte.

Im letzten Rechtsstreite erging am 17. Mai 1868 Erkenntniß des Oberappellationsgerichtes (Reg. Nr. 297), welches dem Kläger D den Erfüllungseid über die Identität des Ochsen auferlegte.

Ist nun dieser Rechtsstreit geendet, so stehen zwei weitere in Aussicht mit entsprechenden Mehrungen der Summen und die Verkäufer F und G, einfache Bauersleute, welche vermuthlich keine Ahnung haben von der Größe der Gefahr, welche über ihrem Haupte schwebt, sehen sich plötzlich wegen jenes vor 15 oder 20 Jahren verkauften Ochsen mit Entschädigungsklagen von weit über 1000 fl. überfallen. Ob sie diesen Stoß aushalten oder darüber zu Grunde gehen, ist natürlich dem prinzipiellen Juristen gleichgültig.

Betrachten wir, zum Gegensatze, wie sich der Fall in der Pfalz gestaltet haben würde, und zwar, indem wir von der ungünstigsten Voraussetzung ausgehen, es hätte sich die Sache vor's Bezirksgericht geeignet.

Dort würde B mit abgekürzter Frist sofort in eine bestimmte Sitzung geladen worden sein, und C — G wären auf Gewährschaft beigeladen worden.

Es wäre nun zwischen allen Betheiligten der Fall verhandelt worden; falls nöthig, hätte man 4 — 6 Wochen später in einer weitern Sitzung Zeugen und Sachverständige vernommen, und nach Verlauf von etwa acht Wochen, von der ersten Ladung gerechnet, würde Endurtheil in letzter Instanz ergangen sein, welches dem G die Zahlung des von A verlangten Kaufpreises und der Prozeßkosten auferlegt haben würde.

Man vergleiche nun: dort zwanzigjähriger Prozeß — Schwierigkeit der Herstellung des Thatbestandes — Kosten, welche zwanzigmal so viel betragen, als die Hauptsache, aber das Prinzip in blendender Reinheit; hier Prozeß von acht Wochen — schnelle und sichere Aufklärung des Thatbestands — geringe Kosten, aber leider das Prinzip etwas getrübt!

11) Zur Begründung der Gewährschaftsklage ist natürlich, und zwar aus noch stärkeren Gründen als bei der Streitverkündung, genauer Aufschluß über den Gegenstand der Hauptklage und die dort gestellten Anträge zu geben, und wird es, wenn auch nicht unbedingt nothwendig, doch höchst zweckmäßig sein, die Hauptklage selbst oder den Antrag, welcher Anlaß zur Gewährschaftsklage gegeben, in Abschrift zuzustellen. Abg. II. 294. 295. (Barth, Umbsch., Schmitt). Außerdem sind auch noch die bezüglich der Schadloshaltung zu stellenden Anträge zu begründen.

Das Begehren richtet sich zunächst auf die Gewährschaftspflicht im Allgemeinen, d. h. die Pflicht, den gegen den Gewährschaftskläger erhobenen Anspruch oder Einwand zu beseitigen, und, falls dies nicht möglich sei, diesen schadlos zu stellen. Hieran schließen sich die im Falle des Unterliegens entstehenden Entschädigungsansprüche selbst.

In letzterer Beziehung ist natürlich das Begehren, je nach der Natur des Falles, ein verschiedenes.

Handelt es sich um einen Rückgriff wegen einer vom Gewährschaftskläger zu leistenden Zahlung, so pflegt der Antrag dahin gefaßt zu werden:

„es möge Gewährschaftsbeklagter verpflichtet er-
„klärt werden, dem Gewährschaftskläger das-
„jenige zu ersetzen, wozu er dem Hauptkläger
„gegenüber in Haupt- und Neben-Sache ver-
„urtheilt werden würde."

Handelt es sich um Eviktion, so sind die Entschädigungsansprüche in der nemlichen Weise bedingt geltend zu machen, wie sie im Falle, wo im Hauptprozesse bereits rechtskräftig entschieden wäre, unbedingt geltend zu machen sein würden. Es steht übrigens nichts im Wege, vorerst nur Antrag zu stellen auf Ausspruch der Pflicht zum Schadensersatze, die Festsetzung des Schadens aber einem späteren Verfahren vorzubehalten, was hie und da sogar nöthig sein wird, da es ja der im Augenblicke der thatsächlichen Entwährung entstehende Schaden ist, auf welchen es ankommt.

12) Die Erhebung der Gewährschaftsklage kann, gleich der Streitverkündung, in jeder Lage der Sache, in erster oder zweiter Instanz, geschehen, falls sie nur der Prozeßlage nach als rechtzeitig erscheint. Art. 70 Abs. 1.

Nur unter dieser Voraussetzung genießt sie der besonderen gesetzlichen Begünstigungen, nemlich a) daß Klage auf Schadloshaltung schon erhoben werden kann, obgleich ein Schaden noch nicht entstanden ist, sondern nur droht, und b) daß der Gewährschaftsbeklagte vor dem Gerichte der Hauptklage Rede stehen muß.

13) Falls aber auch diese allgemeine Voraussetzung vorliegt, so ist dennoch die Verbindung der Gewährschaftsklage mit der Hauptklage ausgeschlossen, oder kann dieselbe wenigstens bestritten werden:

1) wenn das Gericht der Hauptklage seiner Art nach nicht zuständig ist für die Gewährschaftsklage;
2) wenn das Gericht der Hauptklage nur durch Vereinbarung begründet ist;
3) wenn die Hauptklage nur in der Absicht erhoben wurde, den Gerichtsstand für die Gewährschaftsklage zu verrücken, und

4) wenn die Gewährschaftsklage erst im Laufe der Berufungsinstanz erhoben worden ist.

Zu 1. Was den ersten Fall anbelangt, so wiederholt Art. 71 Abs. 3 im Grunde nur, was Art. 33 bereits verfügt hat, nemlich, daß bei Connexität das Bezirksgericht die einzelrichterlichen und das Handelsgericht die in Art. 7 Abs. 2 bezeichneten Sachen an sich ziehe, im Uebrigen aber, soweit nicht Vereinbarung eintreten kann und eingetreten ist, die Connexität nicht hinreiche, um die Zuständigkeit eines Gerichtes anderer Art zu bewirken.

Praktisch wäre es gewesen, die Wirkungen der Connexität hier in so weit zu erweitern, daß das Bezirksgericht auch über handelsgerichtliche Gewährschaftsklagen erkennen dürfte, denn es kommt, namentlich bei redhibitorischen Klagen, sehr häufig vor, daß von einer Reihe Gewährschaftspflichtiger der eine Theil vor's Bezirksgericht gehört, der andere aber vor's Handelsgericht.

Zu 2. Was den zweiten Fall betrifft, so ist dessen Tragweite ziemlich bedeutend, weil das Gesetz auch das Versäumen der Einrede der Unzuständigkeit unter dem Gesichtspunkte der Vereinbarung auffaßt und daher alle Fälle hieher gehören, wo Zweifel irgend einer Art über die Zuständigkeit, sei es die sachliche oder die örtliche, erhoben werden können. Wenn daher der Gewährschaftsbeklagte beigeladen wird, nachdem über die Zuständigkeit bereits entschieden oder die bezügliche Einrede durch Stillschweigen verwirkt ist, sei es auch nur, weil der Anlaß zur Gewährschaftsklage erst später sich ergeben, so kann er die Frage der Zuständigkeit dennoch anregen, um die Abweisung der Gewährschaftsklage darauf zu gründen.

Meiner Meinung nach wäre dieser Ausnahmsfall besser weggeblieben, da der einzige beachtenswerthe Gesichtspunkt, daß sich die Hauptparteien in der bösen Absicht, den Gewährschaftsbeklagten vor ein fremdes Gericht zu ziehen, vereinbaren könnten, schon durch Ziffer 3 gedeckt erscheint.

Das Beste ist übrigens, daß, wenn der Gewährschaftsbeklagte schweigt, die Unzuständigkeit durch seine eigene Vereinbarung beseitigt erscheint, und in der Regel wird er Interesse haben, zu schweigen.

Zu 3. Der hier vorgesehene Fall wird wohl in der Praxis nicht leicht vorkommen; mir ist wenigstens kein Fall bekannt, wo die gleiche Bestimmung des Cod. de proc. Art. 181 praktisch geworden wäre. Es würde ein Einverständniß zwischen Hauptkläger und Hauptbeklagten vorauszusetzen sein, in der Art z. B., daß jener einen am nemlichen Orte mit ihm wohnenden guten Freund als Bürgen für einen entfernt wohnenden Schuldner vorladen würde, um diesen Schuldner auf dem Wege der Garantieklage vor sein (des Klägers) Gericht ziehen zu lassen.

Zu 4. Der Gesetzgeber hatte hier nur von der Berufung zu sprechen, denn in der Cassationsinstanz ist selbstverständlich eine Gewährschaftsklage nicht statthaft. R. R. IV 12.

Eigenthümlich erscheint, daß dem Gewährschaftsbeklagten die Wahl gegeben ist, zwischen dem Gerichte, wo die Hauptsache früher im ersten Rechtszuge verhandelt worden ist, und seinem eigenen Gerichte. Man dachte wohl, er könne selbst ein Interesse haben, seine Sachen vor ein Gericht zu bringen, welches bereits Kenntniß vom Sachverhalte habe und die entscheidenden Gesichtspunkte sofort zu würdigen wisse.

In Folge der Verweisung vor ein anderes Gericht tritt der Gewährschaftsbeklagte ganz aus dem Hauptprozesse, falls er nicht ausdrücklich auch als Nebenintervenient aufgetreten war; die Streitverkündung, welche in Anstellung der Gewährschaftsklage liegt, behält aber jedenfalls ihre volle Wirkung.

14) Erscheint der Gewährschaftsbeklagte nicht, so ergeht gegen ihn ein gewöhnliches Versäumungsurtheil; ein Verbindungsurtheil (Art. 316) aber nur in so fern, als der nemliche Gewährschaftskläger mehrere Personen belangt hat. Abg. II 102. (Umbsch.)

Da die Gewährschaftsklage nur einen eventuellen Ausspruch bezweckt und das Urtheil über dieselbe nie vor dem Urtheile in der Hauptsache gesprochen werden kann, so bringt es die Natur der Sache mit sich, daß auch das Versäumungsurtheil erst mit dem Urtheile in der Hauptsache zu sprechen sei.

Wird durch den Sieg des Gewährschaftsklägers in der Hauptsache die Gewährschaftsklage gegenstandslos, so erübrigt nur, dies zu erklären und dem unterliegenden Theile, in der Regel dem Hauptkläger, auch die Kosten der Streitverkündung nebst Gewährschaftsklage zur Last zu legen.

Gegen das Versäumungsurtheil kann Einspruch erhoben werden, welcher die gewöhnlichen gesetzlichen Wirkungen hat, jedoch keinen Falls die an die Streitverkündung sich knüpfenden gesetzlichen Fragen zu beseitigen vermag.

15) Wer mit Gewährschaftsklage belangt ist, kann in gleicher Weise und in gleicher Frist seinerseits Gewährschaftsklage erheben und es gilt bezüglich des Gerichtsstandes für diese Untergewährschaftsklage ganz das Nemliche, wie bezüglich der Hauptgewährschaftsklage.

Wenn nun aber der ersten Person nur der Streit verkündet worden ist, muß sich diese ihrem

Vormanne gegenüber gleichfalls auf eine Streitverkündung beschränken, oder aber darf sie, als Nebenintervenientin in den Rechtsstreit eintretend, mittelst Gewährschaftsklage denselben belangen?

Die Allgemeinheit der Ausdrucksweise in Art. 69 Abs. 2 spricht dafür, und es möchte daher für den Fall, als dieser Nebenintervenient ausdrücklich erklärt, daß er seine in der Streitverkündung behauptete Verpflichtung zur Gewährleistung oder Schadloshaltung anerkenne, kein gegründeter Einwand dagegen erhoben werden können; behält er sich jedoch das Recht vor, die später gegen ihn zu erhebende Gewährschaftsklage zu bestreiten, so ist es offenbar nicht statthaft, daß er jetzt schon, wegen einer nur möglichen, aber noch nicht erhobenen Gewährschaftsklage seinen Rückgriff nehme.

16) Aus dem Umstande, daß das Gesetz überall von einer mit der Streitverkündung zu verbindenden Gewährschaftsklage spricht, darf nicht gefolgert werden, daß derjenige, welcher zuerst bloß den Streit verkündet, hiermit auf nachträgliche Erhebung der Gewährschaftsklage im Laufe des Hauptrechtsstreites, verzichte — vorbehaltlich natürlich, ihn mit den Mehrkosten zu belasten. Es wird ja in der Regel dem Regreßpflichtigen selbst nur erwünscht sein, wenn die Sache auf einmal abgemacht wird, während er andern Falls einen doppelten Prozeß, zuerst als Nebenintervenient und später als Beklagter, durchmachen müßte.

17) Falls sich der Anlaß zur Gewährschaftsklage einer Person gegenüber ergibt, welche bereits am Rechtsstreite in irgend einer Weise betheiligt ist, wird diese Klage immer durch Anwaltsakt zu erheben sein.

Dieses Verfahren hat nemlich, nach dem Geiste des Verfahrens und im Sinne der Verfügung des Art. 483 überall Platz zu greifen, wo irgend eine zum Rechtsstreite gehörige und in ihm zu verhandelnde Streitfrage unter den Parteien entsteht. Ist dasselbe ja sogar bei der Hauptintervention, dem Wesen nach, statthaft.

Wenn daher Solidarschuldner oder Bürgen, welche zugleich mit dem Mit- oder Hauptschuldner vorgeladen sind, ihren Rückgriff nehmen, so haben sie, vorausgesetzt, daß für die zu Belangenden Anwälte aufgestellt sind, ihre Gewährschaftsklage nicht auf dem Wege selbständiger, der Partei selbst zuzustellender Klage, sondern durch Zustellung eines motivirten Antrages zu erheben. Das Nemliche wird gelten müssen, wenn der mit der Gewährschaftsklage zu Belangende bereits als Nebenintervenient im Rechtsstreite aufgetreten ist.

18) Zu Behandlung der Gewährschaftsklage gibt das Gesetz dem Richter nur die allgemeine Weisung, zu verhüten, daß durch dieselbe die Entscheidung der Hauptklage verzögert werde, — sonst alle mögliche Freiheit.

In der Praxis macht sich die Sache leicht, insbesondere ergeben sich im Laufe der Verhandlung fast immer genügende Anhaltspunkte, um die etwa zuzuerkennende Entschädigung zu würdigen und in dieser Richtung Beweiserhebung unnöthig zu machen.

Man darf auch nicht befürchten, es möchte, bei einer größeren Reihe von Gewährschaftspflichtigen, Verwirrung in den Anträgen entstehen, denn Jeder verlangt nur Ersatz dessen, was er an den Vormann zahlen mußte, und es handelt sich daher überall um dieselbe Summe, nemlich um dasjenige, was der Hauptbeklagte oder (bei Eviktionsfällen) der erste Gewährschaftsbeklagte zu zahlen verurtheilt würde, sowie um die Prozeßkosten.

Beiladung.

Art. 73. — Beiladung eines Dritten zu einem Rechtsstreite findet nur in den durch das Gesetz vorgesehenen Fällen statt. G. A. d. K. d. A. I S. 91. 92. 171. IV S. 20. 35. 36. — K. d. R. I S. 176.

Wegen der Beiladungen verweise ich auf das, was oben zu Art. 63 in Nr. 4 und zu Art. 66 bis 68 in Nr. 2 bereits bemerkt ist.

Wenn Art. 73 sagt: „durch das Gesetz", nicht aber: „durch dieses Gesetz, so ist hiermit ausgesprochen, daß alle auf civilrechtliche Bestimmungen sich gründenden Beiladungen aufrecht erhalten sind. Ueber den Sinn des bezüglichen Ausdrucks s. Abg. I S. 78 Spalte 2. Vgl. Abg. IV 36 (v. Weiß).

Die Adcitationen von Amtswegen, welche die G. O. Cap. VIII § 4 Z. 5 vorschreibt, welche übrigens keine Beiladungen im Sinne der neuen Prozeßordnung wären, sind schon durch die Natur des neuen Verfahrens beseitigt, welches kein derartiges amtliches Eingreifen kennt.

Wo eine Beiladung zu bethätigen ist, hat sie selbstverständlich immer auf Betreiben der betreffenden Partei zu geschehen.

Benennung des rechten Besitzers.

Art. 74. — Der mit einer dinglichen oder dieser gleichzuachtenden Klage als Besitzer einer Sache in Anspruch genommene Beklagte kann, wenn er die Sache im Namen eines Andern besitzt, diesen dem Kläger benennen.

Erfolgt die Benennung erst nach Ablauf der zur Beantwortung der Klage gegebenen Frist, so hat der Beklagte die durch diese Verzögerung verursachten Kosten zu ersetzen.

Art. 75. — Bestreitet der Kläger die Behauptung des Beklagten, so ist auf Antrag des letztern die Beiladung des Benannten zur Abgabe seiner Erklärung anzuordnen. Hiebei hat das Gericht die Frist für die Beiladung und für die Abgabe der Erklärung des Benannten zu bestimmen. Die Beiladung ist von dem Beklagten unter abschriftlicher Mittheilung der Klage zu bewirken.

Die Benennung wird als nicht geschehen betrachtet, wenn der Beklagte den Antrag auf Beiladung nicht stellt oder den Benannten in der vorgesetzten Frist nicht beiladet.

Art. 76. — Gibt der Benannte die Behauptung des Beklagten als richtig zu, so kann der Kläger demungeachtet den Rechtsstreit gegen den Beklagten fortsetzen, hat aber dann zu beweisen, daß dieser im eigenen Namen besitze.

Widerspricht der Benannte die Behauptung des Beklagten oder gibt er keine Erklärung ab, so kann der Beklagte den Streit allein fortsetzen oder sich durch Ueberlassung des Besitzes an den Kläger von der Klage befreien.

Ein Ungehorsamsverfahren findet gegen den Benannten nicht statt.

Art. 77. — Erkennt der Kläger die Behauptung des Beklagten gleich Anfangs oder nach erfolgter Erklärung des Benannten als richtig an, so ist der Beklagte von der Klage zu entbinden.

G. A. d. K. d. A. I S. 92. 93. 171. 299. IV S. 20. 21. — K. d. R. I S. 176. 177.

1) Die Lehre von der nominatio oder laudatio auctoris gehört fast mehr dem Civilrechte als dem Prozesse an; sie berührt nemlich 1) die Frage, in wie weit derjenige, welcher in fremdem Namen besitzt, Störungen im Besitze durch Rechtsansprüche Dritter, seinem Auktor sogleich anzuzeigen habe, und 2) die Frage, gegen welche Personen dingliche oder Besitzklagen gültig erhoben werden können, ob bloß gegen den Besitzer in eigenem oder auch gegen den Besitzer in fremdem Namen.

Nach der bekannten Ansicht Ulpians (l. 9. Dig. [6. 1.]), kann die rei vindicatio nicht bloß gegen denjenigen, welcher als Eigenthümer besitzt, sondern gegen jeden, welcher die Sache inne hat (qui tenet et habet restituendi facultatem) erhoben werden. Eine Aenderung brachte jedoch die Const. 2 Cod. (3. 19), insofern dieselbe dem Besitzer in fremdem Namen das Recht gab, sich durch Nennung des rechten Besitzers aus dem Streite zu ziehen und somit jenen ulpianischen Grundsatz in seinen Wirkungen nahezu aufhob. Versäumte der Beklagte den Einwand, daß er der wirkliche Besitzer nicht sei, so war er eine Person, qui liti se obtulit und wurde als fictus possessor behandelt.

Was das französische Recht betrifft, so gilt der allgemeine Grundsatz, daß dingliche Klagen nur gegen denjenigen erhoben werden können, welcher selbst irgend ein dingliches Recht auf die Sache beansprucht und dies durch seine Besitzhandlungen bekundet. Dieser Grundsatz findet in Art. 1727 Code civ. eine besondere Anwendung auf Miethverhältnisse, bei welchen Zweifel möglich war, indem nach französischem Rechte das Recht des Miethers einem dinglichen Rechte sehr nahe steht, so zwar, daß Troplong geradezu behaupten zu dürfen glaubt, die Miethe sei ein dingliches Recht.

Eine prozessuale Bestimmung, wie es in Fällen, wo der unrichtige Besitzer geladen ist, zu halten sei, fand der französische Gesetzgeber nicht nöthig; die allgemeinen Grundsätze des Prozesses erschienen ihm ausreichend, und in der That ist in der Praxis auch nie eine Lücke des Gesetzes empfunden worden.

2) Aus Vorstehendem möchte folgern, daß die bezüglichen Verfügungen unserer P. O. für die Pfalz vollkommen entbehrlich waren; für diesseits mochte es räthlich sein, um irrige Deutungen zu verhüten, das Bestehende nicht zu beseitigen, ohne etwas Entsprechendes an die Stelle zu setzen.

Uebrigens werden, wie auch bei den Verhandlungen anerkannt wurde, die Fälle der Anwendung fraglicher Verfügungen höchst selten sein, weil natürlich jeder, welcher eine dingliche Klage anstellt, darauf bedacht sein wird, den rechten Beklagten zu wählen, nicht aber eine Person, in deren Belieben es gestellt ist, die Klage als unstatthaft abweisen zu lassen, abgesehen davon, daß ein gegen diese Person erfochtener Sieg nichts nützen würde.

3) Hat der als Besitzer geladene Beklagte gar kein Recht auf die Sache, auch nicht einmal ein persönliches, wie z. B. derjenige, welcher nur auf Ruf und Widerruf besitzt, oder ein Verwalter, so hat er natürlich kein Interesse und folglich auch kein Recht, mehr zu verlangen, als daß die Klage als unstatthaft abgewiesen werde; hat er aber zugleich ein selbständiges persönliches

Recht, wie z. B. der Pächter, so kann für ihn ein Interesse bestehen, daß der Rechtsstreit unter Beiziehung des Eigenthumsbesitzers endgültig zum Austrage gebracht werde, und es entsteht die Frage, ob und welcher gesetzliche Weg ihm hiezu offen stehe.

Man kann sagen, es sei die Klage entweder gegen den rechten Beklagten gestellt, oder nicht; letzteren Falles mache entweder der Beklagte den Einwand der mangelnden Passivlegitimation nicht geltend und werde als fictus possessor behandelt, oder aber er mache diesen Einwand geltend, und dann sei die Klage abzuweisen — ein Drittes gebe es nicht; man könne nicht zugleich die Klage als unstatthaft bekämpfen und verlangen, daß über sie verhandelt werde; dies sei ein innerer Widerspruch.

Dagegen möchte sich mit Recht erwiedern lassen:

1) Es ist Regel, daß dingliche Klagen gegen jeden Inhaber erhoben werden können, und diese Regel erleidet eine Einschränkung nur, so weit der Beklagte vom Rechtsmittel der Benennung des Auktors Gebrauch macht.

2) Das Gesetz spricht nur von „können", räumt also bloß eine Befugniß ein, und entzieht das Recht nicht, sich auch in sonstiger Weise zu vertheidigen.

3) Wer von einem Pächter vindizirt, greift hiermit auch das persönliche Recht desselben an, will seinen Pacht aufgehoben wissen. Wäre die Klage gegen den Eigenthumsbesitzer erhoben worden, so hätte ohne Zweifel der Pächter als Nebenintervenient sich am Rechtsstreite betheiligen dürfen, um sein eigenes, vielleicht sehr werthvolles Recht zu wahren; sollte er nun, nachdem er bereits in Prozeß gezogen ist und lebhaftes Interesse hat, schnell aus der Ungewißheit gezogen zu werden, genöthigt sein, die Klage erst abweisen zu lassen, um sich später an dem neuen Rechtsstreite zu betheiligen?

Ich nehme daher an, daß der Pächter allerdings befugt ist, auf Grund von Art. 65 der P. O. die Beiladung des Auktors zu verlangen oder selbst beizuladen, in dieser Weise den der Einleitung des Prozesses anklebenden Mangel zu beseitigen und zu bewirken, daß endgiltig über die erhobene Klage entschieden werden könne. Seuff. Archiv Bd. X Nr. 118. In diesen Fällen wird der Beklagte zugleich Veranlassung haben, Gewährschaftsklage anzustellen. Abg. IV 21 (v. Neumayr).

Hiermit stimmt auch das französische Recht überein, indem Art. 1727 Code civ. sagt: »Il doit appeller le bailleur en garantie, et doit être mis hors d'instance, s'il l'exige.«

4) Das Gesetz spricht von „dinglichen oder diesen gleichzuachtenden Klagen."

Unter letzteren Klagen sind im Sinne dieser Bestimmung alle jene zu verstehen, welche, gegen den Besitzer als solchen gehend, sich nicht auf persönliche und vom Besitze unabhängige Verpflichtungen gründen, also die Grenzberichtigungs- und Theilungsklagen, wenn man sie nicht als dingliche gelten lassen will, dann die actiones in rem scriptae und die Besitzklagen, insofern letztere einen juristischen Besitz voraussetzen, also die remedia adipiscendae et retinendae possessionis.

Es galt dies schon unter der Gerichtsordnung, indem Kreitmayer in den Anmerk. zu Cap. VIII § 3 sagt, unter den Realklagen seien hier auch die actiones in rem scriptae und mixtae begriffen, ebenso, wie die possessoriae, sofern sie nicht ex delicto possessoris herrühren, wie das interdictum unde vi. Seuff. Comm. Bd. II. S. 140, Note 1 b. Offenbar ist für die Auslegung unserer Prozeßordnung diese bestehende Ansicht von entscheidendem Gewichte. Vgl. jedoch für den gemeinen Prozeß Seuff. Archiv Bd. XII Nr. 85.

Bei Klagen, welche persönliche Verpflichtungen zum Gegenstande haben, bei welchen also die Frage, ob der Beklagte sich im rechtlichen Besitze befinde, ohne entscheidenden Einfluß ist, sind die Art. 74—77 nicht anwendbar. Wenn daher der Pächter zugleich persönlich in Anspruch genommen wird, weil er z. B. in bösem Glauben, wissend, daß er von einem Nichteigenthümer gepachtet, die Früchte bezogen habe und zur Entschädigung deßhalb verpflichtet sei, kann er sich durch Nennung des Auktors nicht von der Klage befreien. Abg. I 92 (v. Weiß).

5) Als Besitzer einer Sache. Unter Besitzer ist hier nicht bloß derjenige zu verstehen, welcher im Namen des Eigenthümers die Sache inne hat, sondern auch derjenige, welcher dingliche Nutzrechte (Weiderechte, Forstrechte, Fischereirechte u. dgl.) als Pächter oder sonst im Namen eines Dritten (eines Quasibesitzers) ausübt. Alle Gründe des Gesetzes treffen auch hier zu, weßhalb man es in Hannover im Hinblicke auf die bestehende Gerichtspraxis als selbstverständlich betrachtete. Verhdl. S. 849—851. Seuff. Archiv Bd. IV Nr. 265.

6) Im Namen eines Anderen besitzt nur derjenige, welcher entweder gar kein Recht oder bloß ein persönliches abgeleitetes Recht an der Sache beansprucht; behauptet er selbst ein dingliches Recht irgend einer Art, z. B. einen Nießbrauch, ein Pfandrecht, so kann er durch Benennung des Eigenthümers sich nicht aus dem Rechtsstreite ziehen; es müßte denn sein eigenes Recht durch die Klage gar nicht in Frage gestellt sein. Seuff. Comm. Bd. II S. 411.

7) Die Benennung des Auktors hat vollständig die Wirkung des Einwandes der mangelnden Passivlegitimation. Der Kläger muß also beweisen, daß der Beklagte in eigenem Namen besessen habe und wenn ihm dies nicht gelingt, oder er die Behauptung des Beklagten als richtig anerkennen muß, so wird die Klage als unstatthaft abgewiesen. Art. 77. Selbstverständlich ist in diesem Falle der Kläger auch in die Kosten zu verurtheilen, mit Ausnahme derjenigen, welche etwa gemäß Art. 74 Abs. 2 dem Beklagten zu Last zu legen sind.

Der Benannte selbst kann nur auf Grund einer selbständigen Klage vor Gericht gezogen werden; eine bezügliche Bestimmung wurde als selbstverständlich gestrichen.

8) Was das Verfahren betrifft, so kann sich der Beklagte auf die Benennung beschränken, ohne zugleich auf die Hauptsache sich einzulassen. Art. 186 Ziff. 3. Auf die Erklärung des Klägers hin kann er die Sache in die Sitzung bringen, um, je nachdem die Erklärung lautet, entweder die Abweisung der Klage aussprechen oder die Beiladung verfügen zu lassen. Diese besondere Verfügung des Gerichtes, zu welcher es vielleicht keiner förmlichen kontradiktorischen Verhandlung bedurft hätte, ist unentbehrlich, da durch dieselbe die Fristen zur Beiladung und Erklärung bestimmt werden müssen. Hiermit ist übrigens nicht gesagt, daß der Benannte nicht freiwillig erscheinen dürfe, um seine Erklärung abzugeben.

9) Die Beiladung hat hier nicht die Bedeutung wie sonst eine Beiladung im Sinne der Prozeßordnung, nemlich daß der Beigeladene Partei im Rechtsstreite werden solle, vielmehr erfolgt sie nur zum Zwecke der Abgabe seiner Erklärung ob er das in Frage stehende dingliche Recht für sich in Anspruch nehme oder nicht. Leistet er dieser Aufforderung innerhalb bestimmter Frist nicht Folge, so trifft ihn, ähnlich wie bei der Streitverkündung, nur der Nachtheil, daß er nunmehr dem Beklagten keinen Vorwurf machen kann, wenn dieser sich durch Ueberlassung des Besitzes von der Klage frei macht.

Deßhalb war ebensowenig, wie bei der Streitverkündung, Veranlassung gegeben, ein Ungehorsamsverfahren Platz greifen zu lassen.

10) Nimmt der Benannte ein dingliches Recht nicht in Anspruch, so kann er einfach schweigen, bestätigt er aber die Behauptung des Beklagten, so wird er gut thun, seine bezügliche Erklärung durch dessen Anwalt abgeben zu lassen. Die Kosten dieser Erklärung hat Kläger im Falle seines Unterliegens zu ersetzen.

III. Hauptstück.

Bevollmächtigte, Beistände, Anwälte und Gerichtsvollzieher.

Vertreter vor Gericht.

Art. 78. — **Vor den Handels- und Einzelngerichten können die Parteien allein oder mit einem Beistand auftreten oder sich durch Bevollmächtigte vertreten lassen (Parteiprozeß).**

Bevollmächtigter oder Beistand kann Jeder sein, der die Fähigkeit hat, vor Gericht zu handeln.

Art. 79. — **Im Verfahren vor den Bezirks- Appellations- und Handelsappellations-Gerichten, dann bei dem obersten Gerichtshofe müssen die Parteien, soweit nicht das Gesetz eine Ausnahme gestattet, sich durch Anwälte vertreten lassen (Anwaltsprozeß).**

Diese Vertretung kann bei dem obersten Gerichtshofe durch jeden bayerischen Advokaten, bei den übrigen in Abs. 1 genannten Gerichten nur durch die am Sitze des Prozeßgerichts wohnenden und zur anwaltschaftlichen Vertretung zugelassenen Advokaten geschehen.

In eigener Sache können Advokaten ihre Prozesse selbst führen. Die Prozesse des k. Fiskus können durch Fiskale geführt werden. Beides ist jedoch bei den Bezirks-, Appellations- und Handels-Appellationsgerichten nur dann zulässig, wenn der Advokat oder Fiskal am Sitze des betreffenden Gerichts seinen Wohnsitz hat.

Was das Gesetz über Prozeßhandlungen der Partei-Anwälte bestimmt, ist in den in Abs. 3 bezeichneten Fällen von den Prozeßhandlungen der Fiskale und der in eigener Sache handelnden Advokaten zu verstehen.

G. A. d. K. d. A. I S. 94—101. 112. 113. 124. 132. 138. 172. III S. 65. IV S. 21. — K. d. R. I S. 177—184. IV S. 12.

1) Die Parteien oder deren gesetzliche Vertreter müssen sich zur Prozeßführung entweder rechtsverständiger Vertreter bedienen, oder aber sie dürfen ihre Sache selbst vertreten. Das erstere

Verfahren, der Anwaltsprozeß, ist Regel, das letztere Verfahren, der Parteiprozeß, ist nur ausnahmsweise gestattet, insbesondere bei Einzelngerichten und Handelsgerichten erster Instanz.

I. Parteiprozeß.

2) Im Parteiprozesse haben die Parteien oder deren gesetzliche Vertreter die Wahl, entweder selbst (sei es allein, sei es mit einem Beistande) vor Gericht aufzutreten, oder aber sich durch einen Prozeßbevollmächtigten vertreten zu lassen.

Der Gebrauch von Bevollmächtigten und Beiständen wird von der Prozeßordnung als Recht anerkannt und es kommt dieser Gesichtspunkt auch den Gegenparteien gegenüber in so fern zur Geltung, als gemäß Art. 106 Abs. 3 dieselben sich die Gebühren solcher Hilfspersonen, wenn es Advokaten oder Rechtspraktikanten sind, aufrechnen lassen müssen.

Sind andere Personen, als die bezeichneten, gewählt worden, so darf sie zwar das Gericht nicht zurückweisen, allein es steht ihm frei zu würdigen, ob die hierdurch veranlaßten Kosten, was deren Ersatz durch die Gegenpartei betrifft, als unnütz zu betrachten seien.

3) Mit dieser letzteren Verfügung ist den Landrichtern eine Waffe in die Hand gegeben, um dem Treiben gemeinschädlicher Winkeladvokaten entgegenzuwirken, von welcher Waffe sie nicht unterlassen werden, einen weisen Gebrauch zu machen.

Ein weiteres Mittel zu demselben Zwecke liegt in der Befugniß, welche Art. 155 der P. O. dem Richter gibt, jeder Zeit von Amtswegen das persönliche Erscheinen der Parteien zu verordnen.

Es wäre übrigens ein Mißgriff, wenn die Landrichter meinten, es sei ihre Aufgabe, auf gänzliche Beseitigung solcher Hülfspersonen, welche eine regelrechte juristische Ausbildung nicht besitzen, hinzuwirken.

In der Pfalz befinden sich fast an jedem Landgerichtssitze, selbst dort, wo Advokaten in großer Zahl sind, sogenannte Geschäftsleute, welche in Rechtsangelegenheiten gewisse niedrigere, dem wahren Berufe des Advokaten ferne liegende und sich für denselben nicht eignende Dienste leisten, und welche insbesondere auch Parteien, die auswärts wohnen oder aus sonstigen Gründen verhindert sind, persönlich vor Gericht zu erscheinen, vor den Landgerichten vertreten, da Advokaten, ja selbst Rechtspraktikanten nur höchst ausnahmsweise dort aufzutreten pflegen. Solche Leute werden in der Regel auch von den Bezirksgerichten mit Verwaltung von Vakantmassen, Gantmassen, sowie mit sonstigen Geschäften, welche Erfahrung in Rechtsgeschäften voraussetzen, beauftragt und indem die Gerichte hierbei besorgt sind nur Personen, welche sich durch rechtlichen Sinn und Charakter auszeichnen, zu wählen und zu begünstigen, wecken sie den Eifer, durch gutes Verhalten das Vertrauen der Gerichte sich zu erwerben und zu erhalten. Daß aus solchen Zuständen nichts Schlimmes hervorgehe, möchte wohl daraus sich ergeben, daß die Zahl der Prozesse in der Pfalz, im Vergleiche zu diesseits, verschwindend klein ist.

Diesseits werden gleiche Ursachen gleiche, jedenfalls ähnliche, Wirkungen erzeugen, und da nun das Bestehen von Geschäftsleuten besagter Art an vielen Orten Bedürfniß ist, so wird das Streben der Gerichte sich nicht darauf richten dürfen, sie zu unterdrücken, sondern ihre Thätigkeit in die rechte Bahn zu leiten.

4) Prozeßbevollmächtigter kann Jeder sein, welcher die Fähigkeit hat vor Gericht zu handeln.

Dies wird wohl bedeuten, daß der Bevollmächtigte fähig sein müßte, in Rechtsstreiten, welche ihn selbst angehen, vor Gericht zu stehen; daß es aber in allen eignen Angelegenheiten der Fall sein müßte, ist nicht gesagt und deßhalb wird es z. B. keinen Zweifel erleiden, daß volljährige Hauskinder als Prozeßbevollmächtigte verwendet werden können. Es liegt hier eine Abweichung vor, von der allgemeinen Rechtsregel, daß bei Handlungen des Bevollmächtigten nicht auf seine eigene, sondern auf des Vollmachtgebers Rechtsfähigkeit Rücksicht zu nehmen sei und also auch Minderjährige, falls sie willensfähig sind, als Bevollmächtigte benützt werden können.

Weitere Forderungen außer der Fähigkeit vor Gericht zu handeln, werden nicht gestellt; es dürfen daher auch Frauenspersonen, falls ihnen diese Fähigkeit zukommt, Prozeßbevollmächtigte sein. Abg. I 112 (v. Weiß).

Sonstige Vorschriften, welche gewissen Personen, z. B. Staatsbeamten, Geistlichen ꝛc. verbieten, als Bevollmächtigte vor Gericht aufzutreten, sind nicht prozessualer Natur und vermögen die Giltigkeit der bezüglichen Prozeßhandlungen nicht in Frage zu stellen.

II. Anwaltsprozeß.

a) Advokaten und Anwälte.

5) Das Gesetz macht einen Unterschied zwischen Advokaten und Anwälten, welcher jedoch bis jetzt wenigstens, nicht die Personen betrifft, da beide Eigenschaften immer bei den nemlichen Personen vereinigt sind, wohl aber die Funktionen.

Advokaten sind Personen, welche obrigkeitlich bestellt sind, um rechtsunkundigen Leuten in Rechtsangelegenheiten Rath und Beistand zu leisten; Anwälte, im Sinne der Prozeßordnung, sind diejenigen Advokaten, welche ausschließlich berufen sind, vor gewissen Gerichten die Prozesse an Stelle der Parteien zu führen. Jenes ist der weitere, dieses der engere Begriff.

Gemäß der Bestimmungen der Prozeßordnung könnte es daher wohl geschehen, daß die Staatsregierung Jemanden die Eigenschaft eines Advokaten verliehe, ohne ihm zugleich die Eigenschaft eines Anwaltes an Bezirksgerichten ꝛc. zu verleihen, allein nicht umgekehrt könnte sie Jemanden zum Anwalte machen, welcher nicht Advokat wäre.

6) Jeder Advokat als solcher hat das Recht:

1) am obersten Gerichtshofe die anwaltschaftlichen Funktionen auszuüben. Art. 79 Abs. 2;

2) die Parteien bei verschiedenen einzelnen Prozeßhandlungen zu vertreten z. B. bei Beweisaufnahmen von einem Richterkommissäre (Art. 341), bei Vorsichtsverfügungen (Art. 637) und zwar überall ohne besonderer Vollmacht zu bedürfen;

3) in jeder Streitsache, vor allen Gerichten ohne Unterschied, die Rechte der Parteien im mündlichen Vortrage geltend zu machen — zu plädiren. Art. 80.

Vor Handelsgerichten und Landgerichten können die Parteien zwar auch andere Personen beiziehen, allein Advokaten genießen des Vorzuges, daß ihre Dienstleistungen, was Aufrechnung der Kosten betrifft, nie als unnütz betrachtet werden können.

b) Anwaltszwang.

7) Die Vorschrift, daß in allen wichtigeren Rechtshändeln die Parteien nicht selbst vor Gericht auftreten dürfen, sondern sich rechtsgelehrter in gerichtlichen Geschäften erfahrener Vertreter bedienen müssen, enthält zwar eine Bevormundung, allein eine solche, welche bei vollkommneren Rechtszuständen nicht entbehrt werden kann und ohne welche eine geordnete Rechtspflege nicht möglich ist.

Es ist diese Wahrheit von jeher anerkannt worden und wenn man in Zeiten der Ueberstürzung z. B. bei der ersten französischen Revolution, volle Freiheit einführte, so war man sehr bald durch die massenhaft zu Tage tretenden Uebelstände gezwungen, zur Beschränkung zurückzukehren.

8) Das Bedürfniß des Anwaltszwanges besteht im mündlichen Verfahren, wie es unsere Prozeßordnung durchführt, in noch viel höherem Grade, als im früheren schriftlichen Verfahren, wie dies der Gesetzgeber durch strengere und schärfere Durchführung des Prinzipes denn auch anerkannt hat.

Wer nemlich auch nur einen oberflächlichen Blick auf das neue Verfahren und die Art und Weise, wie die Anwälte in dasselbe eingreifen, wirft, muß sofort erkennen, daß deren Stellung wesentlich verschieden ist von derjenigen, welchen ihnen, beziehungsweise den Advokaten, der alte Prozeß zugewiesen hatte.

Der Anwalt ist nicht mehr einfacher Bevollmächtigter oder Beistand mit der Aufgabe, dem Richter die Sache klarer und sachgemäßer vorzutragen, als es die Partei selbst im Stande gewesen wäre, sondern es ist ein großer Theil der früheren richterlichen Thätigkeit auf ihn übergegangen. Das Gericht kümmert sich weder um die Vorbereitung des Rechtsstreites zur Verhandlung durch Schriftenwechsel, noch um den Vollzug seiner Interlokute durch Ladung von Zeugen, Sachverständigen ꝛc. noch endlich um Zustellung und Vollzug seiner Endurtheile; in allen diesen Beziehungen liegt die Prozeßleitung in den Händen der Anwälte. Ihr Wirkungskreis ist daher ein viel größerer, ihre Stellung eine höhere, mehr amtliche geworden, und eben hieraus leitet sich die Folgerung ab, daß sie noch weniger als früher entbehrt werden können und daß es unmöglich ist, das was ihnen anvertraut ist, in die Hände der Parteien selbst oder freigewählter Bevollmächtigten zu legen.

9) Die Vortheile des Anwaltszwanges machen sich in zwei Hauptrichtungen geltend.

a) Indem dem Richter die Streitsache nach ihren thatsächlichen und rechtlichen Gesichtspunkten geklärt und geordnet vorgetragen wird, indem ferner die Anwälte die ganze äußere Prozeßleitung sowie den Vollzug der richterlichen Bescheide auf sich nehmen, wird dem Richter sehr viel Zeit und Mühe erspart, welche er seinem eigentlichen Berufe, der richterlichen Beurtheilung zuwenden kann. Ein in Anschlag zu bringender Gewinn ist dabei auch der Einfluß, welchen es im Allgemeinen auf den Geist der Rechtsprechung übt, wenn der Richter nicht mehr genöthigt ist, einen Haupttheil seiner Aufmerksamkeit jenen geistlosen, die ordnungsmäßige Beschaffenheit der Akten und den äußern Gang des Prozesses betreffenden Arbeiten zuzuwenden, Arbeiten, welche die Anwälte ihren ersten Schreibern zu überlassen pflegen. Fortdauernde Beschäftigung mit solchen kleinlichen Dingen nährt den Hang zur Pedanterie und erzeugt bei weniger Begabten jenen kleinlichen Sinn, welcher seinen Stolz hineinsetzt, in Nebendingen Großes zu leisten, um das Wesentliche zu übersehen.

b) Wenn der Richter rechtsunkundige Personen vor sich hat, so ist er genöthigt, sie über die Tragweite ihrer Erklärungen, über die Folgen, welche aus Zugeständnissen entstehen können, zu belehren, sie auf etwa zu erhebende Einreden aufmerksam zu machen — kurz ihnen direkt oder indirekt Rath zu ertheilen, und tritt hiermit, sei es auch nur scheinbar, aus der passiven und unpartheiischen Stellung heraus, welche so nothwendig ist, um ihm das volle Vertrauen der Parteien zu sichern.

Diese schiefe Stellung macht sich in der Pfalz hie und da in Handelssachen sehr fühlbar und geschieht es nicht selten, daß der Richter sich veranlaßt findet, einer Partei anzurathen, sie möge sich im weiteren Verlaufe des Rechtsstreites eines rechtskundigen Beistandes bedienen.

10) Wie schon erwähnt, ist der Anwaltszwang durch die neue Prozeßordnung viel strenger durchgeführt, als es im seitherigen schriftlichen Verfahren der Fall gewesen ist, in welchem nur vorgeschrieben war, sich zu gewissen Prozeßhandlungen des Beistandes eines Advokaten zu bedienen.

Es gilt jetzt für streitige Rechtssachen unbedingt als Grundsatz, daß vor den in Art. 79 bezeichneten Gerichten die Parteien oder deren gesetzliche Vertreter sich eines Anwaltes, welcher nicht neben ihnen, sondern an ihrer Stelle auftritt, bedienen müssen und zwar für das ganze gerichtliche Verfahren d. h. für alle an das Gericht zu stellenden Anträge, für das Auftreten bei der öffentlichen Verhandlung und für sonstige Prozeßhandlungen jeder Art. Dieser Anwalt ist dominus litis für die ganze Prozeßführung und selbst, wenn ein besonderer Advokat die mündliche Rechtsvertheidigung führt, ist er allein es, welcher die maßgebenden Anträge zu stellen hat. Abg. I 118 (v. Weiß).

Eine Ausnahme besteht nur für jene Fälle, wo das Gesetz ausdrücklich das persönliche Auftreten der Partei erlaubt, z. B. im Beweisverfahren (Art. 341), bei Vorsichtsverfügungen (Art. 637), im Vollzugsverfahren (Art. 952, 1033, 1116), im Gantverfahren (Art. 1253), sowie ferner dort, wo es in der Natur der Sache begründet ist, z. B. wenn das persönliche Erscheinen verfügt ist (Art. 155), bei Eidesleistungen rc.

Weggefallen ist daher jetzt das Vorrecht der Siegelmäßigen, ihre Eingaben selbst zu machen, und hiermit der letzte Rest der Siegelmäßigkeit (Einf. Ges. Art. 3 Ziff. 16); ferner die Befugniß der Parteien, ihre Erklärungen persönlich vor Gericht zu Protokoll zu geben. Ebenso entspricht es dem Willen des Gesetzes nicht mehr, daß ein Anwalt durch einfaches Beisetzen seiner Unterschrift die von anderen Personen verfaßten Schriften billige, vielmehr muß die Schrift von ihm selbst ausgehen, und nur umgekehrt kommt es vor, daß die Partei, zur Ersetzung einer Spezialvollmacht Prozeßschriften mit unterzeichnet. Art. 92 Abs. 3.

Auch die Bestimmung über die anwaltschaftliche Vertretung gewisser juristischen Personen durch andere Personen als die gewöhnlichen Anwälte z. B. der Universitäten durch ihre Syndiken, der Städte durch rechtskundige Magistratsräthe fällt weg. Nur der Fiskus macht eine Ausnahme, insofern er durch seinen Fiskal vertreten werden kann.

Um sich in dieser Beziehung ganz bestimmt auszudrücken, hatte man in Art. 79 Abs. 1 gesagt: „soweit nicht das gegenwärtige Gesetzbuch eine Ausnahme gestattet.“ Abg. I 112 (Barth). Dies änderte man später ohne besonderen Grund und sagte: „das Gesetz.“ Abg. IV 65 (v. Weiß). Offenbar sollte hierdurch an den Grundsätzen, wie sie früher anerkannt worden waren, nichts geändert werden, und man hatte wohl nur zukünftige Spezialgesetze im Auge, wenn man auf gesetzliche Bestimmungen außer der Prozeßordnung hinwies.

c) Lokalisirung der Anwälte.

11) Nach französischer Organisation hat jedes Gericht, sowie es seine Richter, seine Staatsanwälte und seine Gerichtsschreiber hat, auch seine eigenen, ihm allein zugehörigen, Anwälte, welche ausschließlich befugt sind, die Anwaltsgeschäfte bei demselben zu verrichten. Unsere Prozeßordnung hat den Grundsatz der Lokalisirung nicht in dieser Strenge durchgeführt und läßt zu den Anwaltsgeschäften jeden Advokaten zu, welcher am Gerichtssitze wohnt und zur anwaltschaftlichen Vertretung zugelassen ist.

12) Obgleich demnach das Prinzip der Lokalisirung in viel milderer Form auftritt, so steht es doch an sich zu sehr im Widerspruche mit den diesseits bestehenden Einrichtungen und Gewohnheiten, als daß man sich darüber wundern dürfte, wenn großes Widerstreben gegen dasselbe sich kund gab und es nur nach einigem Kampfe zur Anerkennung gelangte.

Wer immer jedoch sich mit dem Gange des neuen Verfahrens näher vertraut gemacht hat, mußte zur Ueberzeugung gelangen, daß es rein unmöglich sei, dasselbe ohne Lokalisirung der Anwälte durchzuführen.

Das neue Verfahren setzt nemlich einen beständigen unmittelbaren Verkehr der Anwälte unter sich, sowie mit den Gerichtschreibern und dem Gerichte selbst voraus, und findet darin seine wesentlichsten Vortheile. Noch ehe eine Sache in die Sitzung gelangt, wechseln die Anwälte unter sich die motivirten Anträge, theilen sich die Urkunden, sowie es gerade erwünscht ist, zur Einsicht mit, verschaffen sich Gewißheit darüber, ob ihre Parteien dieselben anerkennen oder bestreiten, besprechen sich hie und da persönlich zur Beseitigung von Anständen im Verfahren, Ersparung unnützer Formen, Kürzung von Fristen, was alles mit den größten Schwierigkeiten verknüpft wäre, wenn die Anwälte nicht am nemlichen Orte wohnten. Ist die Sache zur öffentlichen Verhandlung gelangt, so kann allerdings auch ein auswärtiger Anwalt erscheinen, um sie zu vertreten; allein, dürfte jeder Anwalt an jedem Gerichte des Königreichs Prozesse führen, so wäre es in vielen Fällen ein Ding der Unmöglichkeit, die Sitzung so zu bestimmen, daß alle betheiligten Anwälte zugleich erscheinen könnten. Wäre es aber auch gelungen, die Anwälte zusammenzubringen, so könnten Hindernisse eintreten, welche Vertagung nöthig machten; es könnte sich z. B. ergeben, daß weitere Urkunden beizubringen, neue Ermittlungen, geeignet, den Sachverhalt aufzuklären oder ein Interlokut zu ersparen, vorzunehmen seien; es könnte eine Partei, deren Gegenwart nöthig oder sachdienlich wäre, am Erscheinen verhindert sein — alles Zwischenfälle, wie sie in einem Verfahren, welches weniger auf formale als auf materielle Erledigung gerichtet ist, so häufig vorkommen. Eine Unzahl von Vertagungen wäre die Folge; ein ewiges Hin- und Herreisen der Anwälte wäre unvermeidlich; die Prozeßkosten würden sich im Uebermaße häufen!

Wollte man einwenden, es könne sich ja der auswärtige Anwalt vertreten lassen, so würde man zeigen, daß man von dem öffentlich mündlichen Verfahren den rechten Begriff nicht habe, daß man sich vorstelle, es könne bei der öffentlichen Verhandlung eine Vertretung so leicht stattfinden, wie etwa bei einem Zeugenverhöre, einer Eidesabnahme, einer Urkundenproduktion, wo ein College dem anderen wohl den Gefallen erzeigt, statt seiner der Prozeßhandlung beizuwohnen und nach gegebenen Weisungen das Interesse der Partei zu wahren; allein dem ist nicht so. In der öffentlichen Verhandlung concentrirt sich der ganze Prozeß und es kann Niemand eine Sache dort vertreten, welcher mit derselben nicht vollständig vertraut ist, welcher nicht nur im Stande ist, alle thatsächlichen und rechtlichen Gesichtspunkte gründlich zu erörtern, sondern auch geeignet zu handeln, wenn die Sache im Laufe der Verhandlung, durch neuvorgebrachte Thatsachen, neue Urkunden, neue Rechtsbegründung eine ganz andere Gestalt erhält und demgemäß die genommenen Anträge abzuändern, oder neue Anträge zu nehmen sind. Insbesondere muß er, da die Artikulirung der Beweise mit Angabe der Art der Beweismittel sofort in der Sitzung zu erfolgen hat, durch Verkehr mit der Partei selbst, in den Stand gesetzt sein, zu ermessen, über welche Thatsachen es derselben möglich sei, Beweise zu erbringen, und ob es nicht angemessen sei, durch Eideszuschiebung unnöthige Kosten zu ersparen. Es ist somit klar, daß die Partei, welche einen auswärts wohnenden Anwalt hätte, sehr häufig, ja wohl in der Regel, gezwungen sein würde, neben demselben noch einen zweiten, am Gerichtssitze wohnhaften Anwalt zu nehmen und zu bezahlen.

Kommt es nun zur Vollziehung eines Zwischenbescheides oder eines Endurtheiles, so ist es wiederum vom größten Vortheile, wenn die Anwälte oder deren Gehülfen persönlich mit dem Gerichtschreiber verkehren, bei welchem Einsicht der ergangenen Urtheile zu nehmen ist, welcher auf Begehren Ausfertigung der Urtheile, Zeugenverhöre ꝛc. gibt, mit welchen man sich wegen der Gebühren und Auslagen berechnet.

Ebenso wäre es schlimm, wenn wegen der vielfachen Zustellungen im Laufe des Prozesses immer Correspondenz und Berechnung mit entfernt wohnenden Gerichtsboten nöthig wäre.

Ein scheinbar unbedeutender, aber praktisch hoch anschlagender Gewinn ist es endlich, daß die Verlegungen von Tagfahrten wegen Verhinderung der Anwälte, wie sie diesseits so häufig vorkommen, in Folge der Lokalisirung nahezu ganz wegfallen, indem das Gericht oder der Richterkommissär aus dem Geschäftskalender des Gerichtschreibers genau entnehmen können, an welchen Tagen die betreffenden Anwälte geschäftlich verhindert seien.

Beim neuen Verfahren kämen übrigens noch die öffentlichen Verhandlungen als neue Behinderungsursachen zu den früheren, und es würde, ohne Lokalisirung, wohl selten ein Anwalt persönlich einer Tagfahrt beiwohnen können.

13) Aus vorstehenden Erörterungen möchte erhellen, daß es vollkommen sachgemäß ist, wenn in Art. 79 Abs. 3 verfügt wird, es dürften Advokaten auch ihre eignen Prozesse, sowie ferner Fiskale die Prozesse des Fiskus nur unter der Voraussetzung selbst führen, daß sie am Sitze des Gerichtes wohnten.

Hat daher der Fiskus an einem sonstigen Orte einen Prozeß zu führen, so muß er, wie jede andere Partei, sich durch einen gewöhnlichen Anwalt vertreten lassen. Es gilt dies insbesondere auch für Rechtsstreite über Einregistrirungs- und Stempel-Gebühren in der Pfalz, wenn in dieser Beziehung bei Einführung der Prozeßordnung ein abänderndes Gesetz nicht erlassen sein sollte, denn die das bezügliche Verfahren betreffenden Sonderbestimmungen sind durch Art. 2 des Einf.-Ges. aufgehoben.

14) Sowie der Gesetzgeber dem Grundsatze der Lokalisirung die volle gebührende Anerkennung zu Theil hat werden lassen, so war er anderseits bestrebt, ihn möglichst auf das durch das Bedürfniß vorgezeichnete Gebiet zu beschränken.

So verfügte er, daß am obersten Gerichtshofe, wo das Verfahren dem Wesen nach ein schriftliches ist und es sich bloß um Würdigung festgestellter Thatsachen handelt, jeder Advokat des Reichs als solcher die anwaltschaftliche Vertretung übernehmen dürfe.

So erlaubt er ferner bei manchen einzelnen Prozeßhandlungen, insbesondere solchen, welche dringlicher Natur sind, daß sie auch von auswärtigen Advokaten vorgenommen werden dürfen. Art. 341. 367.

Schließlich erlaubt er den an einem Orte wohnhaften Anwälten, an allen Gerichten dieses Ortes aufzutreten. Diese, eine sehr wichtige Abweichung von den französischen Prinzipien enthaltende Neuerung, ist wohl im Allgemeinen zu billigen, allein für Orte, wo Gerichte und Senate von Gerichten in größerer Zahl bestehen, insbesondere für München, möchten daraus wesentliche Mißstände sich ergeben. Einigermaßen, wenn auch nicht ganz, könnte dadurch vorgebeugt werden, daß die Gerichte ihre regelmäßigen Sitzungen auf verschiedene Tage verlegten, allein wahrscheinlich wird sich bald das Bedürfniß ergeben, durch eine gesetzliche Verfügung nachzuhelfen.

d) Anstellung der Anwälte.

15) Die Frage der Freigabe der Advokatur war gerade zur Zeit, als die neue Prozeßordnung in die Kammer gelangte, plötzlich zu einer sehr brennenden geworden, und dieser Umstand gab Veranlassung, daß man im Gesetze die Worte: „angestellten Advokaten“ in die Worte: „wohnenden und zur anwaltschaftlichen Vertretung zugelassenen Advokaten“ umwandelte, um so die Entscheidung darüber, ob der jetzige gesetzliche Zustand, gemäß dessen die Staatsregierung den Wohnsitz der Advokaten und Anwälte bezeichnet, zu ändern sei, einem späteren Gesetze vorzubehalten. Vgl. Vortrag des Referenten v. Bomhard zur 2. Lesung S. 34—36.

Da der Streit wegen Freigabe der Advokatur hierdurch als schwebend bezeichnet ist, übrigens auch die Frage an sich sehr wichtig und folgenreich erscheint, so kann eine umständlichere Besprechung hier nicht umgangen werden.

16) Vor Allem ist hervorzuheben, daß es sich selbstverständlich nicht um eine Beseitigung des Instituts der Advokaten handelt, d. h. davon, daß Jedermann, wer gerade Lust und Beruf dazu spürt und etwa eine bezügliche Steuer zahlt, sich mit dem Gewerbe der Vertretung vor Gericht befassen dürfe, sondern daß Garantieen für eine gründliche juristische Bildung und für Zuverlässigkeit des Charakters auch von denjenigen verlangt werden, welche der Freigabe der Advokatur das Wort reden, wie denn auch weiter nicht verkannt wird, daß zur Hebung des Ansehens des Standes und zur Ausscheidung unlauterer Elemente eine strenge Disciplin erforderlich sei.

Es fragt sich also nur, ob Jeder, welcher die vorgeschriebenen Prüfungen bestanden und etwaige sonstige Bedingungen erfüllt hat, befugt sein solle, sich an jedem beliebigen Orte als Advokat oder Anwalt niederzulassen, in der Weise, wie jetzt die ärztliche Praxis freigegeben ist.

17) Meiner Meinung nach ist zu unterscheiden zwischen den Funktionen des Advokaten und den Funktionen des Anwaltes.

Was die ersteren betrifft, so halte ich deren Freigabe für unschädlich, und scheinen mir genügende Gründe zu einer Beschränkung hier nicht vorzuliegen; was aber letztere betrifft, so bin ich der Ansicht, daß das Begehren der Freigabe nicht gerechtfertigt sei, mit selbstverständlicher Ausnahme jener Anwaltsfunktionen, zu welchen die Prozeßordnung jeden Advokaten zuläßt.

Die Gründe für diese Ansicht liegen theils im Prinzipe der Lokalisirung, theils in der besonderen amtlichen Stellung, welche die neue Prozeßordnung den Anwälten gegeben hat.

18) Wenn das Gesetz die Parteien zwingt, ihre Anwälte aus der Zahl der am Sitze des Gerichtes wohnenden Advokaten zu wählen, so muß es auch dafür sorgen, daß geschäftstüchtige, begabte und zuverlässige Advokaten in genügender Zahl dort zu finden seien.

Erfahrungsgemäß sind mindestens 5—6 Anwälte an jedem Bezirksgerichte nöthig, wenn für die Rechtspflege gut gesorgt sein soll, und zwar theils deßhalb, weil in manchen Rechtsstreiten mehrere Anwälte, oft vier und fünf, gleichzeitig auftreten müssen, theils im Hinblicke auf das den Parteien in gewissem Umfange nothwendig zu gestattende Wahlrecht.

Die freie Concurrenz wirkt nun allerdings in manchen Beziehungen Wunder, so z. B. auf nationalökonomischem Gebiete; allein, wie es keine Universalmedizin gibt, so gibt es auch, mit Ausnahme der mathematischen Lehrsätze, nicht leicht ein Prinzip, welches überall anwendbar wäre, und so möchte insbesondere die freie Concurrenz nicht genügen, um zu bewirken, daß sich an den unbedeutenderen Bezirksgerichten immer die nöthige Zahl tüchtiger Anwälte vorfinde. Vgl. Abg. 199 (Barth).

Nimmt man aber auch an, es werde diese Zahl an sich nicht fehlen, so werden wenigstens alle besseren Elemente sich den reicheren Bezirken zuwenden, insbesondere jenen Städten, wo eine Mehrzahl von Gerichten besteht, wo ein größerer Wirkungskreis offen steht, wo das Leben angenehmer ist; die Nebenorte aber werden mit den geringen Kräften vorlieb nehmen müssen.

Auch auf ökonomischem Gebiete bringt die Freiheit der Concurrenz ähnliche Wirkungen hervor, allein dort sind sie nicht schädlich. Wenn sich nämlich die intelligenteren, strebsameren, mit größeren Kapitalien arbeitenden Gewerbsleute den großen Städten zuwenden, so hat dies keine Mißstände im Gefolge, denn auf dem Lande und an kleinen Orten hat man eben kein Bedürfniß nach feinerer Arbeit, und soweit es dennoch bei Einzelnen besteht, können diese in die Städte gehen, wo sie zu finden ist.

Es ist nun aber offenbar nicht statthaft, auch das Recht gleich einer Waare zu behandeln und etwa zu sagen: „Die Leute an Nebenorten brauchen keine gute Justiz; sie haben kein Bedürfniß darnach und können daher auch mit geringen Richtern und geringen Anwälten vorlieb nehmen."

Ebensowenig als aus der Gewerbsfreiheit darf man aus der Freiheit der ärztlichen Praxis Schlüsse ziehen, denn einmal findet sich an jedem Landgerichtssitze ein Gerichtsarzt, und sodann steht es Jedermann frei, sich an einen auswärtigen Arzt zu wenden.

Ein Mißgriff wäre es auch, wollte man folgern: falls sich die nöthige Zahl tüchtiger Anwälte an einem Gerichte nicht von selbst ergebe, so sei dies eben ein Beweis, daß der betreffende Ort sich zu einem Gerichtssitze nicht eigne. Diese Anschauung würde eine sehr falsche Auffassung der Pflichten des Staates gegen seine Unterthanen bekunden; sie würde die Rechtspflege vom gewerblichen Standpunkte auffassen und etwa auf den Satz hinausgehen: „Eine Gegend, welche ein Gericht nicht vollständig ernähren kann, braucht auch keins."

Offenbar ist dies keine Erwägung, welche bei einer weisen Regierung maßgebend sein darf; man darf nicht Leute, welche in armer, wenig bevölkerter Gegend wohnen, und welche gerade wegen ihrer Armuth und wegen des Mangels guter Verkehrsmittel besondere Berücksichtigung verdienen, zwingen, 30 bis 40 Stunden weit zu reisen, um Rechtsrath und Rechtshülfe zu finden, und als Beschuldigte, Zeugen, Parteien, vor Gericht zu erscheinen und zwar alles dies bloß deßhalb, weil sich an näheren Orten die erforderlichen Anwälte nicht ansäßig machen würden!

19) Ein weiterer Grund gegen Freigabe der anwaltschaftlichen Funktionen liegt in der Stellung, welche die neue Prozeßordnung den Anwälten gibt, in der Wichtigkeit und großen Ausdehnung ihrer Befugnisse, wodurch ihnen, gleich den Notären, annähernd ein amtlicher Charakter verliehen ist. Je größere Gewalt in die Hände des Anwaltes gelegt ist, je mehr die Parteien gezwungen sind, ihm anzuvertrauen, desto größer müssen anderseits die Schutzmittel sein gegen Mißbrauch dieses Vertrauens.

In dieser Beziehung entsteht nun umgekehrt daraus Gefahr, daß sich an manchen Orten eine Ueberzahl von Anwälten ansammeln würde.

Ist nemlich die Konkurrenz zu stark, reiben sich die Bestrebungen, Praxis zu gewinnen oder eine gewonnene zu erhalten, zu oft und zu heftig an einander, handelt es sich gar um Sicherung der Existenz, so kann sich unmöglich — die menschliche Natur müßte sich denn verläugnen — jener Geist der Uneigennützigkeit, jener Stolz, welcher alle niedrigeren Mittel zur Gewinnung von Clientel verachtet, kurz das Gefühl der Advokatenehre bei den Einzelnen und beim ganzen Stande in dem Grade ausbilden, wie es für eine vollkommen gute Rechtspflege unerläßlich ist. Man wird nichts Ungehöriges darin finden, sich mit Winkelagenten in ständigen Verkehr zu setzen, um sich aus den Landgerichtsbezirken Clienten zuweisen zu lassen; man wird jedenfalls nicht verschmähen, sich mit Geschäften zu befaßen, welche dem wirklichen Berufe des Anwaltes fern liegen und welche dem Ansehen des Advokatenstandes im Publikum schaden.

20) Ziehe ich die Summe aller Erwägungen, so erscheint klar, daß das Interesse des rechtsuchenden Publikums — und dieses allein wird entscheidend sein, nicht aber dasjenige der erwerbsuchenden Adspiranten — bei einer Freigabe der Anwaltschaft Schaden leiden würde.

Will man zum Schlusse noch die Erfahrung zu Rathe ziehen — da es denn doch einmal herkömmlich ist, diese zuletzt zu fragen — so möchte darauf hinzuweisen sein, daß sich dort, wo das öffentlich mündliche Verfahren schon seit Jahrzehnten besteht, ein Bedürfniß zur Freigabe der anwaltschaftlichen Funktionen nirgends gezeigt hat.

Art. 80. — Die mündliche Rechtsvertheidigung kann vor den Bezirks-, Appellations- und Handels-Appellationsgerichten unter dem Beistande des aufgestellten Anwalts auch von andern bayerischen Advokaten geführt werden.

Außerdem sind zur mündlichen Rechtsvertheidigung unter Beistand des aufgestellten Anwalts die Parteien und nach Maßgabe der einschlägigen Verordnungen und allgemeinen Ministerialverfügungen die geprüften Rechtspraktikanten zuzulassen. Das Gericht kann diesen Personen jedoch das Wort entziehen, wenn sie sich nicht fähig zeigen, die Sache in der angemessenen Art vorzutragen, oder in ihren Vorträgen die erforderliche Ruhe und Haltung nicht bewahren.

G. A. d. K. d. A. I S. 94—111. 117—119. 132. IV S. 21. — K. d. R. I S. 184—188.

1) Die mündliche Rechtsvertheidigung, d. h. die Begründung der genommenen Anträge in thatsächlicher und rechtlicher Beziehung, durch mündlichen Vortrag, ist die besondere Aufgabe des Advokaten, wenn man sich diesen vom Anwalte getrennt denkt.

Nach unseren Einrichtungen wird allerdings von dieser Trennung in der Praxis wenig zu bemerken sein, denn fast ausnahmslos werden die Anwälte auch zugleich die mündlichen Vorträge halten und zwar schon deßhalb, weil, außerordentliche Fälle abgerechnet, kein Anwalt sich wird nachsagen lassen, er bedürfe noch eines Fürsprechers, um dem Gerichte die Sache klar und bündig vorzutragen. Im Civilprozesse kommt es zudem nicht auf besondere Beredsamkeit an, welche allerdings nicht Jedermann zu besitzen braucht, sondern auf Rechtskenntnisse sowie auf die Fähigkeit die wesentlichen Punkte zu fassen und hervorzuheben, und wer gestehen müßte, diese Fähigkeit nicht zu besitzen, der würde seinem Ansehen als Anwalt in sehr bedenklicher Weise schaden. Endlich wird schon der Umstand, daß für etwa beigezogene Advokaten keine Reisekosten in Anwendung gebracht werden dürfen (Art. 106 Abs. 4) verhüten, daß dies häufig geschehe.

Der Fall, wo eine andere Person, als der bestellte Anwalt oder die Partei selbst, den mündlichen Vortrag hält, wird daher nur eintreten, wenn etwa in einer besonders wichtigen und schwierigen Sache eine auswärtige Berühmtheit beigezogen wird, oder wenn der Anwalt hie und da einen bei ihm praktizirenden Rechtskandidaten sich im öffentlichen Vortrage üben läßt oder endlich, wenn er bei eigener Verhinderung sich der Hülfe eines Collegen oder eines Rechtspraktikanten bedient. Was letzteren Fall betrifft, so pflegten in der Pfalz, wo eine Substituirung durch Ministerialentschließung nicht besteht, die Anwälte, welche durch Krankheit, durch ihre Funktion als Abgeordnete rc. auf längere Zeit verhindert waren, sich in der Weise zu helfen, daß sie durch fähige Rechtspraktikanten ihre Sachen plädiren ließen, wobei ein oder der andere gerade in der Sitzung anwesende College ihnen den Gefallen erzeigte, anwaltschaftlichen Beistand zu leisten, d. h. die zu stellenden Anträge zu verlesen.

2) Die Verbeistandung des sprechenden Advokaten durch einen am Sitze des Gerichtes wohnenden Anwalt ist deßhalb nöthig, weil der letztere allein als Stellvertreter der Partei zu betrachten ist und Anträge nur von ihm gültig genommen werden können. Es ist ein solcher daher auch nöthig, wenn die Partei selbst zugegen ist.

Uebrigens steht nichts im Wege, daß der Anwalt, wenn er seine Anträge gestellt hat und sicher ist, es werde seine Thätigkeit nicht weiter in Anspruch genommen werden, sich entferne, und der Advokat außer seiner Gegenwart den mündlichen Vortrag halte.

3) Zur mündlichen Rechtsvertheidigung sind außer den Advokaten auch noch berechtigt, die Parteien selbst und Rechtspraktikanten, nachdem sie die Staatsprüfung bestanden haben, sofern das Gericht nicht besondere Gründe findet sie zurückzuweisen und, soweit es die Rechtspraktikanten betrifft, falls nicht Verordnungen oder allgemeine Ministerialverfügungen im Wege stehen.

Dasselbe Recht wie die Parteien haben auch deren gesetzliche Vertreter. Art. 60. Abg. I 118 (Wiedenh.).

Als gesetzlicher Vertreter ist der Fiskal nicht zu betrachten, er ist bloß Anwalt. (s. Bemerk. zu Art. 58 Nr. 3). Die Ansicht, welche R. R. I 184 kund gegeben wird, ist daher in dieser Beziehung nicht richtig; übrigens wird der Fiskal, nachdem ihm das Gesetz die Eigenschaft eines Anwaltes, also a fortiori auch eines Advokaten des Fiskus gibt, auch in Prozessen, welche der Fiskus an auswärtigen Gerichten führt, zur mündlichen Rechtsvertheidigung für denselben auftreten dürfen.

4) Für die mündlichen Vorträge der Parteien, deren gesetzlicher Vertreter, sowie der Rechtspraktikanten, können im Anwaltsprozesse besondere Gebühren der Gegenpartei nicht aufgerechnet werden, wie das Gesetz dadurch andeutet, daß es nirgends davon spricht.

Art. 81. — **Die Verhältnisse der Advokaten in Bezug auf dienstliche Stellung und Disciplin regelt, soweit nicht das gegenwärtige Gesetzbuch hierüber Bestimmungen enthält, die im Gesetzeswege zu erlassende Advokatenordnung.**

Art. 82. — **Die Gebühren der Advokaten für die in Art. 80 Abs. 1 bezeichneten Rechtsvertheidigungen, sowie für ihre Dienstleistungen als Anwälte, dann als Bevollmächtigte oder Beistände bei Handels- oder Einzelngerichten werden durch Verordnung bestimmt.**

Gleiches gilt von den Gebühren der als Bevollmächtigte oder Beistände bei Handels- oder Einzelngerichten beigezogenen Rechtspraktikanten.

G. A. d. K. d. A. I S. 94—101. 113—116. 129—132. 172. IV S. 21. 22. K. d. R. I S. 190—203.

1) Wenn hier bestimmt ist, daß die dienstliche Stellung und Disziplin der Advokaten auf dem Wege des Gesetzes, die Gebühren aber auf dem Wege der Verordnung geregelt werden sollen, so erscheint beides gleich sachgemäß.

Advokaten und Anwälte sind, als Hülfsorgane der Gerichte, für die Rechtspflege so wichtig, sie bilden einen so wesentlichen Bestandtheil der gerichtlichen Organisation, daß es geboten erscheint, für ihre dienstliche Stellung, für das Maß ihrer Rechte und Pflichten, eine festere, dauerndere Grundlage zu schaffen, als dies durch eine Regulirung im Verordnungswege geschehen würde.

Die Verleihung einer selbständigen gesicherten Stellung trägt dazu bei, das Ansehen des Advokatenstandes zu heben und den guten Geist in demselben zu fördern; beides allerdings nur unter der Voraussetzung, daß eine strenge, alle schlechten Elemente schnell und sicher ausscheidende Disziplin eingeführt wird. Statt der vielen kleinen, bloß ärgernden, aber nicht bessernden Ordnungsstrafen, wird man sich gewöhnen müssen, nur selten und bei wichtigen Anlässen, dann aber mit Ernst einzuschreiten; statt polizeilich zu maßregeln, wird man strafen müssen und es wird nicht etwa vorkommen dürfen, daß Leute, welche die gröbsten wucherischen Uebervortheilungen und gemeine Gaunereien verübt, mit einigen Wochen Disziplinararrest abgewandelt werden, um nach dessen Erstehung die Ehre, Advokaten zu sein, nach wie vor zu genießen.

Soll es mit dem Ansehen des Advokatenstandes gut bestellt sein, so wird sich die Disziplinargewalt namentlich auch auf das außerdienstliche Verhalten des Advokaten erstrecken müssen, und überhaupt als Grundsatz festzuhalten sein, daß der Advokat mit Annahme seiner bevorzugten Stellung, seines öffentlichen Dienstes, gleich jedem anderen Beamten, die Pflicht übernimmt, sich in jeder Beziehung so zu benehmen, daß er dem Amte Ehre mache, und nichts thue, was das Ansehen des Standes und das Vertrauen auf die Rechtlichkeit und Ehrenhaftigkeit derjenigen, welche demselben angehören, zu erschüttern geeignet sei.

Aufgabe der Gesetzgebung und der Gerichte wird es sein, zu verhüten, daß nicht die Disziplinargewalt auf Gebiete sich verirre, wo ein mit dem öffentlichen Dienste zusammenhängendes Interesse nicht gefährdet ist.

Die Natur der Disziplinarstrafen bedingt es ferner, daß sie nicht den Beamten als Privatperson, sondern seine bevorzugte Stellung, seine amtliche Eigenschaft treffen und als geeignete Disziplinarstrafen sind daher nicht gewöhnliche Polizeistrafen wie Geldstrafen und Arrest zu betrachten, sondern Verweis, zeitliche Entsetzung vom Amte und Absetzung.

2) Aufgabe der Advokatenordnung wird es insbesondere auch sein, zu bestimmen, in wie fern die Anwälte verpflichtet seien, ihr Amt zu leihen, und in welcher Weise von Amtswegen für Vertretung von Parteien zu sorgen sei, welche keinen Anwalt finden.

3) Was die Festsetzung der Gebühren anbelangt, so handelt es sich nicht bloß um diejenigen Gebühren, welche der Gegenpartei aufgerechnet werden dürfen, sondern auch um diejenigen, welche der eigenen Partei gegenüber beansprucht werden.

In letzterer Beziehung wird in Art. 117 Abs. 2 der Vorbehalt gemacht, daß in der gesetzlichen Advokatenordnung näher bestimmt werde, in wie fern es statthaft sei, höhere Gebühren, als die vorschriftsmäßigen durch besonderes Uebereinkommen sich zu sichern.

Erwägt man einerseits, daß das Publikum gezwungen ist, sich eines am Gerichtssitze wohnhaften Anwaltes zu bedienen und diesem die ganze Prozeßleitung zu überlassen; erwägt man anderseits, wie schädlich es auf den Charakter des Standes einwirken und wie sehr das Ansehen desselben darunter leiden müßte, wenn auch nur bei einem kleinen Theile der Anwälte es Uebung werden sollte, vor Uebernahme der Prozesse wegen des Honorares zu handeln, oder den Diensteifer nach dem Maße der versprochenen Belohnung zu richten, so erscheint es ebensowohl unbillig als gemeinschädlich, für bloße Anwaltsdienste solche Uebereinkommen zu gestatten.

Ist die Gebührenordnung der Art, daß der fähige und thätige Anwalt im Durchschnitte sein reichliches Einkommen findet, so kann er der besonderen Gratifikationen entbehren; daß sie aber nöthig seien, um den gehörigen Diensteifer zu erzeugen, dürfte zur Ehre des Standes nicht anzunehmen sein. Vgl. die Bemerkungen von Barth. Abg. I 172.

Bevollmächtigung der Gewalthaber.

Art. 83. — Wer im Parteiprozesse als Gewalthaber eines Andern auftritt, ist, soweit das Gesetz nicht anders verfügt, zu keiner Prozeßhandlung zuzulassen, ehe er sich über seinen Auftrag durch Vorlage einer Vollmacht ausgewiesen hat.

Art. 84. — Vertagung der Verhandlung findet zum Zwecke der Berichtigung des Vollmachtspunktes mit Zustimmung der Gegenpartei statt.

Auch ohne solche Zustimmung kann sie bewilligt werden:

1) wenn der als Gewalthaber Auftretende seinen Auftrag und zugleich ein Hinderniß der rechtzeitigen Bereinigung des Vollmachtspunktes wahrscheinlich macht;

2) wenn die beigebrachte Vollmacht an einem Mangel leidet, welcher nachträglich verbessert werden kann.

Art. 85. — Vollmachten können durch Notariatsakt oder durch Privaturkunde mit obrigkeitlich oder notariell beglaubigter Unterschrift des Vollmachtgebers ausgestellt werden.

Vollmachten, welche von einer Stelle oder Behörde oder von der Verwaltung einer Körperschaft oder Stiftung ertheilt und in gehöriger Form gefertigt sind, bedürfen keiner weitern Beglaubigung.

Art. 86. — Bei Vollmachten, welche im Auslande mittels Privaturkunde ausgestellt werden, genügt die Beglaubigung durch die bayerische Gesandtschaft oder ein bayerisches Consulat.

Ergeben sich Bedenken über die Aechtheit einer Vollmacht, welche von einem ausländischen Notar oder einer ausländischen Behörde aufgenommen oder beglaubigt, oder welche von einer ausländischen Stelle oder Behörde oder von der Verwaltung einer ausländischen Körperschaft oder Stiftung ertheilt ist, so kann das Prozeßgericht auf Antrag der Gegenpartei die Einholung der Bestätigung der höheren ausländischen Landesstellen, nach Umständen der einschlägigen bayerischen Gesandtschaft oder eines bayerischen Consulats verfügen.

Art. 87. — Vollmachten sind in Urschrift oder in einfacher Abschrift, auf welcher der Gerichtsschreiber den befundenen Gleichlaut mit der vorgelegten Urschrift zu bestätigen hat, zu übergeben.

Ist eine Vollmacht, welche sich auf alle Rechtsstreitigkeiten des Vollmachtgebers oder doch über den einzelnen Rechtsstreit hinaus erstreckt, bei demselben Gerichte in einer andern Sache bereits hinterlegt worden, so genügt die Bezugnahme darauf.

Der Widerruf einer bei Gericht hinterlegten Vollmacht ist auf Begehren der Partei von dem Gerichtsschreiber auf der Urkunde selbst vorzumerken.

Art. 88. — Wird der Auftrag bei einer Verhandlung ertheilt, so genügt die Beurkundung im Urtheilsbuche oder Protokolle.

G. A. d. K. d. A. I S. 124—126. 132—135. 172. 299. II S. 454. 455. IV S. 22.
K. d. R. I S. 203—215.

1) Die Art. 83—88 sprechen von Vollmachten zu Prozeßhandlungen für Andere im Allgemeinen, finden jedoch, der Verfügung des Art. 89 gegenüber, ihre Anwendung nur im Parteiprozesse, sowie in den Fällen des Art. 92. In den Art. 89 bis 91 schließen sich die Bestimmungen über die Prozeßvollmacht im engern Sinne, d. h. die Vollmacht zur Prozeßführung überhaupt, an; endlich werden in Art. 92 die Ausnahmsfälle aufgezählt, für welche besondere Vollmacht nöthig ist.

2) Die Verpflichtung, sich durch Vollmacht auszuweisen, gilt für Jeden ohne Unterschied, welcher als Bevollmächtigter der Parteien oder deren gesetzlicher Vertreter im Parteiprozesse auftritt, also auch für Advokaten und Anwälte. Nur jene Fälle sind ausgenommen, wo das Gesetz anders bestimmt, z. B. bei Abkürzung von Fristen (Art. 502), Vorsichtsverfügungen (Art. 637).

a) Inhalt der Vollmachten.

3) Art. 83 spricht ganz allgemein von einem Auftrage zu Prozeßhandlungen, ohne näher anzugeben, welches der Inhalt der Vollmacht sein müsse.

Kann nun Jemand vor einem Einzelngerichte oder Handelsgerichte als Bevollmächtigter auftreten, mit einer Vollmacht in der Hand, welche, ohne etwas von Prozeßführungen zu sagen, bloß dahin lautet, daß er zur Vermögensverwaltung ermächtigt sei, oder daß er beauftragt sei, alle Rechtsgeschäfte zu besorgen?

Man kann sagen:

1) Ob eine Vollmacht gewisse Rechtshandlungen umfasse oder nicht, ist eine civilrechtliche Frage, und der Gesetzgeber deutet durch die Allgemeinheit der Fassung an, daß er die bezüglichen Grundsätze des Civilrechts walten lassen, insbesondere der freien Würdigung des Willens des Vollmachtgebers nicht vorgreifen wolle;

2) In Art. 90 ist zwar bestimmt, welches die Tragweite einer Prozeßvollmacht sei, nirgends aber ausgesprochen, daß eine solche besondere Prozeßvollmacht immer nöthig sei, wie dies der Entwurf (Art. 66 und 71) verfügt hatte.

3) Bei den Verhandlungen hat der Ministerialkommissär betont, es müßten bei den Landgerichten auch allgemeine Vollmachten zur Geschäftsbesorgung genügen, und auf Veranlassung dieser Bemerkung wurde damals das Wort „Prozeßvollmacht" in „Vollmacht" umgewandelt. Abg. I 124.

Dem läßt sich entgegnen:

1) Das Recht der Vertretung vor Gericht ist ein höchst wichtiges, denn insofern aus dem gerichtlichen Verfahren ein rechtskräftiges Urtheil hervorgeht, können einfache Nachlässigkeiten und Unterlassungen hier gleiche Wirkung äußern, wie sonst Rechtsverzichte. Man hat dies von jeher anerkannt und deßhalb Spezialvollmacht zur Prozeßführung verlangt; insbesondere schrieb dies das französische Recht für Handelssachen vor (Code de proc. Art. 421) und selbst für friedensgerichtliche Sachen nahm die Jurisprudenz, obgleich der Text des Gesetzes (Art. 9) Spezialvollmacht nicht verlangt, die Nothwendigkeit einer solchen an. Chauveau sur Carré quest. 43. — Schlink Comm. § 504 Ziff. 2.

2) Bei Redaktion der bezüglichen Beschlüsse des G. G. A. wurde der Vorschlag, eine Prozeßvollmacht zu verlangen, von Neuem gemacht und diesmal nur in der Erwägung beseitigt, daß auch Vertretungen bei einzelnen Prozeßhandlungen (bei Zeugenverhören 2c.) vorkommen könnten. Abg. I 133 (Barth).

3) Aus der Fassung des Art. 87 Abs. 3 und aus den bezüglichen Verhandlungen (Vortrag zu Art. 71 des Entwurfs — Abg. I 133 [Barth] u. 134 a. E.) geht hervor, daß man nur drei Arten von Vollmachten im Auge hatte, nemlich a) Prozeßvollmachten für Rechtsstreite überhaupt, b) Prozeßvollmachten für bestimmte Rechtsstreite und c) Vollmachten für einzelne Prozeßhandlungen, sei es, weil für dieselben Spezialvollmacht vorgeschrieben sei, sei es, weil die Partei ihre Vollmacht auf dieselben beschränken wolle.

Ich glaube, daß letztere Gründe überwiegen und die Ansicht des Gesetzgebers darstellen. Dabei ist jedoch selbstverständlich, daß es nicht gerade auf besondere Ausdrücke ankomme, vielmehr genüge, wenn die Absicht, zur Prozeßführung zu ermächtigen, klar und bestimmt sich erkennen läßt. Ebenso ist ausdrückliche Vollmacht zur Prozeßführung nicht nöthig, wo sie kraft gesetzlicher Vermuthung besteht, wie z. B. beim Prokuristen (Art. 40 des H. G. B.).

4) Der Entwurf (Art. 71), welcher nur Prozeßvollmacht für bestimmte Rechtsstreite zuließ, enthielt außerdem noch verschiedene Weisungen über die Abfassung dieser Vollmacht, welche im Wesentlichen auch in den hannoveranischen Entwurf aufgenommen wurden (§ 96).

Mit Recht hat man diese Vorschriften beseitigt, denn daß eine Vollmacht die Personen des Vollmachtgebers und des Bevollmächtigten, sowie den Gegenstand der Vollmacht klar bezeichnen müsse, versteht sich wohl von selbst.

b) Form der Vollmachten.

5) Die Vollmacht zu Prozeßhandlungen muß entweder schriftlich abgefaßt sein und dem Gerichte vorgelegt werden, oder es muß die Bevollmächtigung bei einer gerichtlichen Verhandlung, sei es in der Sitzung, sei es vor dem Richterkommissäre, mündlich erklärt werden.

Im ersteren Falle muß die vorzulegende Urkunde entweder ein Notariatsakt sein, oder eine Privaturkunde, welche obrigkeitlich oder notariell beglaubigt ist.

6) Die obrigkeitliche Beglaubigung setzt nicht etwa voraus, daß die Behörde eine gerichtliche, oder daß sie durch Verordnung zu solchen Beglaubigungen ermächtigt sei, vielmehr soll nach dem Willen des Gesetzgebers jede obrigkeitliche Beglaubigung genügen, insbesondere diejenige eines Gemeindevorstehers, eines Bürgermeisteramtes. Abg. I 126 (v. Weiß). — R. R. I 210 (v. Weiß).

Eine notarielle Beglaubigung hat die Erklärung zu enthalten, entweder, daß die Unterschrift im Beisein des Notars beigesetzt, oder daß sie vor ihm als ächt anerkannt worden sei (Geschäftsordnung für die Notare vom 1. Juni 1862 § 92).

Geringere Anforderungen werden wohl auch an sonstige Beglaubigungen nicht zu stellen sein, und möchte es daher nicht genügen, wenn der Gemeindevorsteher auf seine vermeintliche Kenntniß der Unterschrift hin, ohne den Vollmachtgeber zu hören, die Aechtheit der Unterschrift bescheinigen würde.

Ferner ist den Beglaubigungen die dienstliche Form zu geben und das Dienstsiegel beizudrücken.

7) Dem Bestreben, die Formen möglichst zu vereinfachen, entspringt weiter die Verfügung, daß nicht bloß Vollmachten, welche von Behörden selbst, sondern auch solche, welche von Verwaltungen der Stiftungen und Körperschaften in gehöriger Form ausgestellt sind, keiner Beglaubigung bedürfen, sowie die Bestimmung des Einführungsgesetzes Art. 3 Ziff. 6, welche den Art. 97 des Notariatsgesetzes, soweit es sich um notariell aufgenommene oder beglaubigte Vollmachten (d. h. Prozeßvollmachten) und damit in Verbindung stehende Genehmigungen handelt, aufhebt.

8) Was die Bestätigung betrifft, welche nach Art. 86 das Gericht, auf Antrag der Gegenpartei, bei Vollmachten oder Beglaubigungen ausländischer Behörden anordnen kann, so erstreckt sich dieselbe sowohl auf die amtlichen Befugnisse der betreffenden Behörden, als auf die Thatsache, daß die Urkunde von ihnen herrühre.

9) Wird die Vollmacht mündlich in der Sitzung ertheilt, so ist sie im Urtheilsbuche, wird sie vor einem Richterkommissäre ertheilt, so ist sie im betreffenden Protokolle zu beurkunden.

Die Beurkundung im Urtheilsbuche geschieht nicht etwa durch einen besonderen Eintrag, sondern dergestalt, daß in dem betreffenden Urtheile, sei es auch nur ein Vertagungsurtheil, vom Gerichte zugleich Urkunde über die Bevollmächtigung ertheilt wird. In diesem Falle genügen selbstverständlich die Formen des Urtheilseintrages und ist es nicht nöthig, daß der Eintrag dem Vollmachtgeber vorgelesen und von ihm unterzeichnet werde.

c) Hinterlegung der Vollmachten.

10) Die Vollmachten im Prozesse sind bei Gericht zu hinterlegen und aufzubewahren; letzteres sowohl zum Zwecke des Gebrauches bei späteren Verhandlungen, als auch zur Führung des Beweises der Bevollmächtigung, wenn diese etwa später bestritten werden sollte.

11) Die Hinterlegung, über welche selbstverständlich ein Akt nicht aufzunehmen ist (Abg. I 126 [v. Weiß]), kann sowohl in Urschrift, als in einer vom Gerichtsschreiber als richtig zu bestätigenden Abschrift geschehen.

Letztere Verfügung war vom Referenten v. Heintz beanstandet worden und zwar, wie ich glaube, nicht ohne Grund, da, wenn später die Aechtheit der Urkunde in Frage kommt, aus der Abschrift ein Aufschluß nicht zu erholen ist.

Es mag dieser Gesichtspunkt ohne besondere Bedeutung sein, wenn Notariatsurkunden in Frage stehen, da wegen deren Bestehens und Inhalts aus den betreffenden Urschriften oder Registern Aufschluß zu erholen sein wird; allein er erscheint allerdings von Belang bei gewöhnlichen Privaturkunden, welche vom Gemeindevorsteher beglaubigt sind.

Nach Verlauf längerer Zeit werden sich solche obrigkeitliche Personen nicht mehr erinnern, ob und wann sie eine Urkunde fraglichen Inhalts beglaubigt haben, ganz abgesehen davon, daß sie verstorben sein können, sowie daß die Unterschrift ächt, der Inhalt aber gefälscht sein kann.

Ich muß gestehen, daß ich in der Hinterlegung unbeglaubigter Privaturkunden in Urschrift, wie sie bei den Landgerichten der Pfalz nach bestehender Anordnung erfolgt, größere Sicherheit finden würde, als in der Hinterlegung beglaubigter Privaturkunden in Abschrift. Es wird nicht leicht Jemand wagen, mit einer falschen Urkunde aufzutreten, wenn er weiß, daß das corpus delicti hinterlegt bleibt. Wenn man bedenkt, welch verschiedenartige Personen vor den Landgerichten aufzutreten pflegen, und daß die Parteien dort auch ohne Ladung erscheinen können, so erscheint die Sache nicht ohne praktische Bedeutung.

12) Sehr zweckmäßig erscheint die Vorschrift, daß der Widerruf einer hinterlegten Vollmacht vom Gerichtsschreiber vorzumerken sei. Für diese Vormerkung ist eine Form nicht vorgeschrieben; es genügt daher einfache Notiz, welcher jedoch selbstverständlich Datum und Unterschrift beizufügen sind.

d) Verfahren bei Mangel der Vollmacht.

13) Das Gericht darf einen Gewalthaber zur Verhandlung nur zulassen, wenn er gehörige Vollmacht besitzt; dasselbe hat daher den Vollmachtspunkt vor Beginn der Verhandlung von Amtswegen zu prüfen und je nach Befund bezüglich desselben zu entscheiden.

Regel ist, daß die Partei, für welche eine nicht gehörig bevollmächtigte Person auftritt, als nichterschienen behandelt und demgemäß Versäumungsurtheil erlassen werde.

Ausnahmsweise ist jedoch Vertagung zu bewilligen, wenn die Gegenpartei einwilligt, und kann dieselbe bewilligt werden, wenn einer der sonstigen in Art. 84 näher bezeichneten Fälle gegeben ist.

Eine vorläufige Verhandlung der Sache auf Grund vermutheter Vollmacht und mit Vorbehalt nachträglicher Genehmigung in einer späteren Sitzung ist nach dem Geiste des Verfahrens und nach dem ausgesprochenen Willen des Gesetzgebers nicht statthaft. Vortrag des Referenten v. Neumayr zu Art. 69 des Entwurfs — Abg. I 133 (v. Neumayr u. Barth). Selbstverständlich steht jedoch nichts im Wege, einstweilen in die Verhandlung der Sache einzugehen, wenn der Bevollmächtigte glaubhaft versichert, er werde im Laufe der Verhandlung selbst die Vollmacht oder deren Berichtigung beibringen.

Was den Fall betrifft, wenn der Mangel erst später entdeckt wird, so behandelt diesen Art. 100.

Art. 89. — Im Anwaltsprozesse bedarf der für eine Partei auftretende Advokat keines besondern Nachweises der Bevollmächtigung.

Fiskale sind bei allen Gerichten durch ihr Amt bevollmächtigt.

G. A. der K. d. A. I S. 108—111. 119—125. 132. 135. 172—175. IV S. 22. K. d. R. I S. 215—218.

1) Es mag vielleicht keine von den Neuerungen, welche die Prozeßordnung bringt, so überraschend und so gewagt erschienen sein, als der Satz, daß die Anwälte keine Prozeßvollmacht vorzulegen brauchen. Wer sich vergegenwärtigt, welche große Sorgfalt von jeher der Berichtigung des Vollmachtspunktes zugewendet worden ist, muß sicher denken, ein Rechtsstreit, in welchem dieser hochwichtige Punkt ganz unbeachtet bleibe, werde rein auf Sand gebaut, und jeder Windstoß müsse hinreichen, das leichtfertige Gebäude umzuwerfen.

Es geht jedoch hier, wie so häufig, daß etwas, was vom theoretischen Standpunkte sich höchst bedenklich ausnimmt, in der Praxis sich ganz leicht macht, während umgekehrt manches theoretisch Richtige äußerst unpraktisch ist. Prozeßgesetze sind nun aber, was leider lange Zeit verkannt wurde, hauptsächlich berufen, die praktischen Gesichtspunkte zu berücksichtigen; sie sollen nicht auf polizeilichem Wege, durch eine Menge schützender Formen, durch Rechtsverlustigungen und Strafandrohungen ihren Zweck zu erreichen suchen, sondern dadurch, daß sie ein organisches Leben schaffen, welches die schädlichen Stoffe nicht aufkommen läßt, oder sie von selbst ausscheidet.

Mit den Vollmachtsberichtigungen verhält es sich ähnlich, wie mit den Paßvorschriften. Welcher Polizeimann hätte vor einigen Jahrzehnten es für möglich gehalten, daß die öffentliche Sicherheit ganz ohne Pässe bestehen könne? Und doch besteht sie, und zwar trotz des ungeheuer gesteigerten Verkehres, und vielleicht in höherem Grade als früher.

2) Der fragliche Grundsatz hat, eben weil er so sehr vom Hergebrachten abweicht, seine Anerkennung nur der einstimmigen Versicherung aller pfälzischen Juristen zu verdanken, daß seit mehr als 50 Jahren ein Fall der Vernichtung, ja auch nur der ernstlichen Anfechtung einer Verhandlung wegen Mangels der Prozeßvollmacht nicht vorgekommen sei, sowie ferner einer gewissen, die neue Prozeßordnung durchdringenden, Neigung, die Befugnisse der Advokaten auszudehnen, welche hier wenigstens nur Gutes gewirkt hat.

Bemerkenswerth ist übrigens, wie richtig man sofort das Wesen dieses Grundsatzes erfaßt hat, so zwar, daß man in mancher Beziehung, z. B. was die Legitimirung durch Besitz der Prozeßakten betrifft, die von pfälzischer Seite ausgegangenen Vorschläge verbesserte.

3) Um den Sinn des Gesetzes möglichst klar hervortreten zu lassen, wird es geeignet sein, zuerst das französische Recht ins Auge zu fassen, und dann die Abweichungen unserer Prozeßordnung zu bezeichnen.

Nach französischem Rechte hat jeder ministerielle Beamte (Anwalt, Gerichtsbote), welcher in seiner amtlichen Eigenschaft für eine Partei handelt, die Rechtsvermuthung für sich, beauftragt zu sein. Dalloz repert. (désaveu) No. 25.

Der Anwalt legitimirt sich also durch seine Erklärung, er sei Vertreter, und es kann von ihm weder Seitens des Gerichtes noch Seitens der Gegenpartei irgend ein Vollmachtsnachweis, sei es durch Besitz der Akten, sei es durch Besitz einer Spezialvollmacht, wo eine solche nöthig ist, verlangt werden.

Der Besitz der Akten ist somit nicht nöthig zur Legitimation, sondern nur, weil er den Beweis des Auftrages der eigenen Partei gegenüber gibt, und daß er diesen Beweis bilden könne, erscheint als eine wichtige Ausnahme von den gewöhnlichen Beweisregeln, zufolge deren bei Werthen über 70 fl. das Mandat bloß durch Urkunden bewiesen werden kann.

Daß ferner auch in den Fällen des Art. 352 C. de pr. Vorlage der Spezialvollmacht nicht verlangt werden könne, wird zwar von Chauveau sur Carré (quest. 1300) bestritten, ist jedoch in der Praxis allgemein anerkannt. Dalloz repert. (désaveu) No. 74.

Gegen Handlungen des Anwaltes, welche er ohne jedes Mandat oder ohne die erforderliche Spezialvollmacht vorgenommen, ist der Partei die Nichtigkeitsklage, der désaveu, gestattet, welcher sich also nicht auf die Fälle des Art. 352 beschränkt, wie man nach dessen Fassung annehmen könnte. Chauveau sur Carré (quest. 1301).

4) Unsere Prozeßordnung hat, mit richtigem Takte, gleichfalls die einfache Erklärung des Anwaltes zur Legitimation als genügend erachtet, und die ursprüngliche Vorschrift, daß sich derselbe durch Aktenbesitz legitimiren müsse, beseitigt — eine Vorschrift, welche, den Charakter einer halben Maßregel an sich tragend, in Fällen, wo noch keine Akten bestehen, oder wo sie der Anwalt augenblicklich nicht zur Hand hat, oder bei Vorlage von Privatschriften, deren Aechtheit nicht zugegeben wird, sehr störend wirken müßte.

Was die Tragweite der dem Anwalte ertheilten Prozeßvollmacht betrifft, so ist die Prozeßordnung (Art. 90 u. 91) weiter gegangen, als der Code de proc. in Art. 352, und war diese Erweiterung dadurch geboten, daß man, abweichend vom französischen Rechte, in den Fällen, für welche Spezialvollmacht vorgeschrieben ist, die Vorlage dieser Vollmacht und überhaupt die vorausgängige Bereinigung des Vollmachtspunktes vorschrieb. Man fühlte, daß Art. 89 werthlos sein würde, wenn man nicht die Nothwendigkeit der Spezialvollmacht sehr einschränkte.

Bezüglich der Nichtigkeitsklagen hat man im Wesentlichen die Grundsätze des französischen Rechtes beibehalten, sie jedoch auf den Parteiprozeß ausgedehnt. Die Befugniß des Widerrufs, welche der Entwurf in Art. 77—80 der Partei einräumen wollte, wurde beseitigt.

5) Wie schon angedeutet, steht der Grundsatz, daß Anwälte ohne förmliche Prozeßvollmacht auftreten dürfen, mit dem durch das neue Verfahren begründeten, jedenfalls wesentlich gesteigerten, amtlichen Charakter der Anwälte im Zusammenhange, und hieraus erklärt sich, warum derselbe nur für den Anwaltsprozeß Geltung hat, d. h. für diejenigen Fälle, in welchen der Anwalt als gesetzlich nothwendiger amtlicher Vertreter der Partei erscheint.

Es läßt sich allerdings nicht verkennen, daß ein Hauptgrund für Annahme jenes Grundsatzes, nemlich das den Advokaten vermöge ihrer Stellung gebührende Vertrauen, für eine allgemeine Anwendung desselben spricht, und zwar um so mehr, als jede Vertretung von Parteien im Allgemeinen zu den Dienstgeschäften des Advokaten gehört; allein man legte besonderes Gewicht auf das eine strengere, unmittelbarere und ständigere Ueberwachung der Anwälte bedingende Prinzip der Lokalisirung, und hielt es deßhalb für bedenklich, das Gebiet des Anwaltsprozesses zu überschreiten. Abg. I 172 a. E. (Barth).

Die Vorschrift des Art. 89 gilt übrigens so allgemein, als sie lautet, also auch dort, wo das Prinzip der Lokalisirung eine Ausnahme erleidet, z. B. im Verfahren beim obersten Gerichtshofe oder im Falle des Art. 341 der P. O.

Soweit ausnahmsweise ein Anwaltszwang nicht besteht, z. B. beim Rangordnungsverfahren, bei der Gant, fand der Gesetzgeber es geeignet, durch besondere Bestimmungen Vorsorge zu treffen. Art. 1116 u. 1184. Auch Art. 637 kann hieher gezogen werden, obgleich wohl die natürliche Auslegung darauf geführt haben würde, daß, wo im Anwaltsprozesse Vorsichtsmaßregeln beantragt werden, der prozeßführende Anwalt ohne Vorlage einer Vollmacht befugt sei, den Antrag zu stellen.

6) Art. 89 betrifft nur die Anwaltsfunktionen; der Advokat, welcher bloß die mündliche Rechtsvertheidigung führt (Art. 80), bedarf einer Vollmacht nicht, da er ja nur unter Beistand des Anwaltes auftritt und seine Erklärungen, Zugeständnisse 2c. nur Werth haben, insofern sie der Anwalt ausdrücklich oder stillschweigend billigt. Deßhalb entschieden denn auch die französischen Gerichte, daß gegen den Advokaten der désaveu nicht Platz greife. Chauveau sur Carré, quest. 1225. — Journal du Pal. (désaveu) No. 31—33.

7) Der Anwalt soll des besonderen Nachweises der Bevollmächtigung enthoben sein, d. h. seine eigene Erklärung soll, sowohl dem Gerichte als der Gegenpartei, als genügender Nachweis gelten.

Hiermit ist natürlich nicht gesagt, daß der Anwalt auch der eigenen Partei gegenüber eines solchen Nachweises nicht bedürfe, vielmehr sind in dieser Richtung, mit geringer Abweichung, ganz die civilrechtlichen Grundsätze maßgebend, wie bei Art. 95 ff. näher erörtert werden wird.

8) Der Grundsatz des Art. 89 gilt nicht nur für den Hauptanwalt, welchen die Partei selbst aufgestellt hat, sondern auch für denjenigen Anwalt, welcher für einzelne Prozeßhandlungen als dessen Stellvertreter auftritt. Art. 91. Es kömmt in der Praxis häufig vor, daß bei Verhinderung des bestellten Anwaltes ein anderer für ihn auftritt, indem er einfach erklärt, er handele zur Entlastung seines Collegen. Abg. I 127 (v. Weiß).

9) Fiskale bedürfen auch im Parteiprozesse keiner Prozeßvollmacht, wohl aber der Spezialvollmacht in den Fällen des Art. 92.

Art. 90. — **Die Prozeßvollmacht gilt, soweit das Gesetz nicht specielle Ermächtigung fordert, für alle im Laufe des Rechtsstreits mit Einschluß der Nebenstreitigkeiten vorkommenden Prozeßhandlungen, insbesondere auch für alle thatsächlichen Erklärungen und Geständnisse.**

Thatsächliche Erklärungen und Geständnisse des Gewalthabers können von der mitanwohnenden Partei widerrufen oder berichtigt werden, soferne dies auf der Stelle geschieht.

Art. 91. — **Durch die Prozeßvollmacht ist der Gewalthaber zugleich ermächtigt, zur Vornahme einzelner Prozeßhandlungen unter seiner Verantwortlichkeit einen Stellvertreter zu bezeichnen.**

G. A. d. K. d. A. I. S. 126. 127. 133—136. IV S. 22. — K. d. R. I S. 218—222.

1) Diese beiden Artikel bestimmen die Befugnisse desjenigen, welchem im Allgemeinen Auftrag zur Prozeßführung gegeben ist, sei es durch eine Vollmachtsurkunde im Parteiprozesse, sei es zufolge der Rechtsvermuthung, welche Art. 89 mit den Erklärungen der Anwälte und Fiskale verbindet.

Dem Prozeßbevollmächtigten räumt das Gesetz die Befugniß ein, alles dasjenige für die Partei zu thun, was der Zweck des Prozesses *in der Regel* mit sich bringt. Hierzu gehören insbesondere auch thatsächliche Erklärungen und Zugeständnisse, da es in jedem Rechtsstreite nöthig ist, festzustellen, was unter den Parteien bestritten, was unbestritten sei; ebenso gehört dazu der Gebrauch von Beweismitteln und die Erklärung über solche, namentlich also Zuschiebung und Annahme von Eiden, Anerkennung von Urkunden u. s. w.

Ausgenommen sind nur jene Prozeßhandlungen, für welche das Gesetz besondere Ermächtigung verlangt, insbesondere die Fälle des Art. 92.

2) Der Anwalt, welcher im *Anwaltsprozesse* als Vertreter einer Partei auftritt, hat alle Befugnisse, welche die Prozeßvollmacht nach dem Gesetze gibt, und es erscheint der Gegenpartei gegenüber, d. h. *für den Prozeß*, ohne Belang, wenn ihm etwa besondere einschränkende Weisungen gegeben sind. Es geht nicht an, daß eine Partei nur theilweise, nur in gewisser Richtung, durch Anwalt erscheine, und wenn selbst der förmliche Widerruf der Prozeßvollmacht, nach Art. 94, für den Gegner nur Geltung hat, falls er mit neuer Anwaltsbestellung verbunden ist, so kann noch weniger eine Begränzung der Vollmacht ihm gegenüber eine Wirkung äußern. Vgl. hannov. Entw. § 100.

3) „*im Laufe des Rechtsstreits.*“

Ein Rechtsstreit im Allgemeinen währt so lange, bis ein nicht mehr anfechtbares, ein den Streit vollständig bereinigendes Endurtheil ergangen ist; so weit er aber an einem bestimmten Gerichte hängt, bis die Aufgabe dieses Gerichtes erschöpft ist.

Ebensolang dauert jedenfalls auch die Verpflichtung des bestellten Anwaltes oder sonstigen Gewalthabers und wirkt die ertheilte Prozeßvollmacht. Außerdem aber hat derselbe selbstverständlich noch alles dasjenige zu besorgen, was nöthig ist, um das ergangene Urtheil rechtskräftig und zum Vollzuge geeignet zu machen, z. B. die Festsetzung der Kosten, die Ausfertigung und Zustellung des Urtheiles.

Was den *Vollzug der Endurtheile* anbelangt, so war beabsichtigt, auch diesen in das Gebiet der Prozeßvollmacht zu bringen, allein bei zweiter Lesung (Abg. IV 22 Sp. 2) wurde die betreffende Bestimmung beseitigt. Zum Vollstreckungsverfahren ist daher neue Bevollmächtigung nöthig.

4) Gilt die Prozeßvollmacht nur für die einzelne Instanz, oder gilt sie für alle Instanzen? Ermächtigt sie insbesondere zur Einlegung von Rechtsmitteln?

Diese Frage ist nicht ohne Bedeutung, weil nach der Prozeßordnung nicht selten Fälle vorkommen, wo der nemliche Anwalt die Sache in verschiedenen Instanzen vertreten darf, ganz abgesehen davon, daß die Art. 90 u. 91 auch für den Parteiprozeß gelten.

Die Verhandlungen bieten Stoff zu Zweifeln.

Referent v. Neumayr (Vortrag zu Art. 74 des Entwurfs) hält die Befugniß, Rechtsmittel zu ergreifen, für selbstverständlich, und will nur der Vollständigkeit wegen sie anführen, gleich der Widerklage, Anerkennung von Urkunden 2c. Bei den Verhandlungen sprachen jedoch Barth und Umbscheiden sich im entgegengesetzten Sinne aus (Abg. I 126 u. 127), indem sie zur Vertretung in der Berufungsinstanz *neues* Mandat nöthig finden, und diesen Aeußerungen nachgängig wurde, ohne weitere Anregung dieses Punktes, es bei dem Entwurfe belassen.

Im französischen Prozesse ist die Frage, soweit sie die *Vertretung* vor höheren Gerichten betrifft, natürlich gegenstandslos; was jedoch die *Einlegung* der Berufung anbelangt, sind die Stimmen getheilt. Merlin hält den Anwalt erster Instanz befugt, während Chauveau sur Carré (quest. 382 bis) der Ansicht ist, daß die Prozeßführung dem Anwalte nur für das Gericht anvertraut sei, *bei welchem er angestellt ist*, daß er also zur Berufung keine Mission habe, mit Ausnahme der Fälle, wo die Berufungsfrist von der Zustellung an den Anwalt laufe.

Trotz des großen Gewichtes, welches obigen Aeußerungen im G. G. A. zukommt, möchte ich dennoch annehmen, daß sich in denselben die Ansicht aller Gesetzgebungsfaktoren nicht ausdrücke, und zwar aus folgenden Gründen:

1) Der Wortlaut des Gesetzes ist entschieden dagegen, denn ein Rechtsstreit ist offenbar so lange im Laufe, als nicht Enderkenntniß in letzter Instanz ergangen ist, wie dies bei Erörterung der Frage, ob die Prozeßvollmacht auch auf die Zwangsvollstreckung auszudehnen sei, ausdrücklich hervorgehoben wurde. Abg. IV 22 (v. Weiß).

2) Hätte das Gesetz die Wirkung der Prozeßvollmacht auf ein bestimmtes Gericht, einen bestimmten Rechtszug, beschränken wollen, so hätte es sich ausdrücken müssen, wie in Art 852.

3) Das diesseitige Recht, welchem die Bestimmungen über den Umfang der Generalvollmacht im Wesentlichen nachgebildet sind, läßt dieselbe für alle Instanzen wirken. Seuff. Comm. Bd. II S. 386 u. 387.

4) Das Ergreifen von Rechtsmitteln ist seiner Natur nach konservatorisch, kein Rechtsverzicht.

5) Art. 92 findet nöthig, für Verzichte auf Rechtsmittel Spezialvollmacht vorzuschreiben.

6) Wenn bei Berufungen ꝛc. immer angegeben werden muß, welcher Anwalt die Vertretung in der höheren Instanz habe, so folgt daraus nicht, daß derselbe der Partei gegenüber immer neue Vollmacht nöthig habe.

Diese Ansicht läßt übrigens die Verpflichtung des Anwalts, sich vorher mit seiner Partei zu benehmen, ehe er ein Rechtsmittel ergreift, unberührt, wie ihm denn diese Verpflichtung auch bei Geständnissen ꝛc. unzweifelhaft obliegt.

Rathsam bleibt es, den bestehenden Zweifeln gegenüber, immerhin, daß sich die Anwälte zur Vertretung in höheren Instanzen neue Vollmacht geben lassen, und zwar schriftliche, da der Besitz der Akten den Beweis einer neuen Vollmacht wohl nicht liefern könnte.

5) „mit Einschluß der Nebenstreitigkeiten."

Daß mit diesen Worten nicht bloß die gewöhnlichen Zwischenstreite gemeint, sondern dieselben in sehr weitem Sinne zu nehmen seien, geht daraus hervor, daß man die Anführung der Widerklage als selbstverständlich beseitigt hat.

Es gehören alle Streitigkeiten hierher, welche wegen Zusammenhangs mit der Hauptsache zugleich mit ihr verhandelt werden. Vgl. R. R. I 220. — v. Neumayr Vortrag zur 2. Lesung, Hptst. III Art. 13.

6) Thatsächliche Erklärungen und Geständnisse des Gewalthabers sollen nach Art. 90 Abs. 2 von der Partei, welche in der Sitzung oder bei der Verhandlung vor einem Richterkommissäre zugegen ist, sofort widerrufen oder berichtigt werden können. So vollständig daher auch im Anwaltsprozesse die Parteien durch ihre Anwälte vertreten sind, so hat doch überall, wo die Partei oder deren gesetzlicher Vertreter selbst spricht, nur dasjenige Geltung, was sie selbst erklärt, und der Anwalt ist in solchen Fällen der Partei gegenüber in ähnlicher Lage, wie der Advokat dem ihn verbeistandenden Anwalte. Abg. I 118 (v. Weiß).

Die Berichtigung der Erklärungen des Anwaltes muß sofort geschehen, d. h. jedenfalls noch vor Schluß der betreffenden Verhandlung; sie wird jedoch schon früher ausgeschlossen erscheinen, wenn, den Umständen nach, stillschweigende Zustimmung anzunehmen ist. Die Würdigung der Verhältnisse ist ganz den Gerichten überlassen.

7) Indem der Gesetzgeber dieses Berichtigungsrecht ausdrücklich anerkennt, obgleich es sich, wie v. Neumayr zu Art. 77 des Entwurfs richtig bemerkt, eigentlich von selbst versteht, verrückt er nichts an den Grundsätzen, welche bezüglich des Verhältnisses des schriftlichen Vorverfahrens zur Verhandlung in der Sitzung bestehen, und hat überhaupt nicht die Absicht, das Recht des Widerrufes, wie es der Entwurf gegeben hatte, auf einem Umwege wieder einzuführen.

Das schriftliche Vorverfahren ist, nach Art. 251 der P. O, allerdings bloß vorbereitend, d. h. es bringt in der Regel keine Verlustigungen mit sich, und die Parteien können alles nachtragen, was sie an Mitteln des Angriffes und der Vertheidigung etwa versäumt haben, sowie ihre Anträge ändern. Hieraus folgt nun aber nicht, daß alle Erklärungen im Vorverfahren nur auf Ruf und Widerruf gemacht werden, und daß rechtsverbindliche Verzichte und Zugeständnisse darin nicht gegeben werden könnten. Unsere P. O. geht nicht so weit, wie § 131 des hannov. Entwurfs.

Würde man, dem Wortlaute einer Aeußerung bei den Verhandlungen (Abg. I 135) gemäß, die Partei für befugt erachten, alles, was ihr Anwalt in Anträgen oder in sonstigen Zustellungen erklärt hat, in der Sitzung zu widerrufen, so müßte man auch dem Anwalte selbst diese Befugniß zugestehen, da die Rechte der Partei nicht darunter leiden könnten, daß sie verhindert wäre, in der Sitzung zu erscheinen.

Allerdings ist es richtig, daß jedes Geständniß wegen Irrthums widerrufen werden kann, und daß bezüglich der Erklärungen in den Anträgen ein Irrthum des Anwaltes unter Umständen leicht angenommen werden kann.

Näheres hierüber bei Art. 251.

8) Zur Substituirung wird, abweichend von der Gerichtsordnung, eine Spezialvollmacht nicht verlangt, jedoch nur insofern, als Vornahme einzelner Prozeßhandlungen in Frage ist.

Als einzelne Prozeßhandlungen in diesem Sinne sind auch die Vertretung der Sache in der Sitzung, sowie die Fertigung der motivirten Anträge zu betrachten; überhaupt liegt die Würdigung, ob es sich bloß um Uebertragung einzelner Prozeßhandlungen oder des Prozesses selbst handelt — zu welch letzterer Spezialvollmacht nöthig wäre — ganz im Ermessen des Gerichtes. Dieses wird nicht allzustreng sein, da ja die Verantwortlichkeit immer auf dem Substituenten lastet. Vgl. Abg. I 127 (v. Weiß).

Art. 92. — **Specielle Ermächtigung ist außer den in besondern Bestimmungen des Gesetzes vorgesehenen Fällen erforderlich:**

1) zur Abschließung von Vergleichen, Schieds- und Nachlaßverträgen;

2) zum Verzicht auf Ableistung eines von der Gegenpartei zu schwörenden Eids;

3) zur ausdrücklichen Verzichtleistung auf ein Rechtsmittel;

4) zum gänzlichen Abstand vom Prozesse;

5) zum Empfange von Geld oder Geldeswerth mit Ausnahme jedoch der von dem Gegner zu bezahlenden Prozeßkosten.

Die Bestimmungen des Art. 89 finden keine Anwendung auf Fälle, in welchen nach dem Gesetze specielle Ermächtigung erforderlich ist.

Der Vorlage einer Vollmachtsurkunde zum Nachweise der speciellen Ermächtigung bedarf es nicht, wenn die Partei bei der betreffenden Prozeßhandlung mit anwesend ist oder die bezügliche Prozeßschrift — falls diese der Gegenpartei zugestellt wird, die der letztern einzuhändigende Abschrift — mit unterzeichnet hat.

G. A. d. K. d. A. I S. 123. 124. 127. 136. 175. II S. 289. 377. IV. S. 22. 23.
K. d. R. I S. 222. 223.

1) Indem das Gesetz hier die Fälle aufzählt, in welchen Spezialvollmacht nöthig sein soll, gibt es negativ eine noch schärfere Begränzung des Umfangs der allgemeinen Prozeßvollmacht.

In allen diesen Fällen gelten, da Art. 89 keine Anwendung findet, die Bestimmungen der Artikel 83. 84 u. ff. auch für den Anwaltsprozeß. Es muß daher der Vollmachtspunkt berichtigt sein, bevor der Anwalt zugelassen werden darf, die betreffenden Rechtshandlungen vorzunehmen.

2) Unter Spezialvollmacht ist nicht eine Vollmacht für den speziellen Fall, sondern eine solche zu verstehen, welche für die betreffende Art von Rechtshandlungen ausdrücklich gegeben ist.

3) Wenn die Partei oder deren gesetzlicher Vertreter bei einer Prozeßhandlung, zu welcher Spezialvollmacht nöthig, anwesend ist und schweigt, so wird diese Vollmacht als gegeben erachtet. Selbstverständlich ist die Gegenwart aller Personen nöthig, deren Rechte durch die betreffende Handlung in Frage gestellt sind.

Die Thatsache der Anwesenheit ist urkundlich festzustellen, und es wird dies sachgemäß in der Weise zu geschehen haben, daß das Gericht, ähnlich wie in den Fällen des Art. 281 Abs. 2, im Urtheile Urkunde über diese Anwesenheit gibt. Am besten ist es, die Partei selbst zur Erklärung zu veranlassen und diese zu beurkunden.

4) Falls die Bevollmächtigung in einer Prozeßschrift — einem Antrage oder sonstigen Anwaltsakte — ertheilt wird, genügt die Unterschrift der Partei oder des gesetzlichen Vertreters auf der dem Gegner einzuhändigenden Abschrift; jedoch wird es rathsam sein, daß der Anwalt auch das Original unterzeichnen lasse. Abg. IV 289 (v. Weiß), 377 (Barth).

Im Parteiprozesse ist Art. 102 maßgebend.

5) Was die einzelnen Fälle anbelangt, für welche Art. 92 Spezialvollmacht verlangt, so ist zu Ziff. 1 zu bemerken, daß, gemäß unserer Prozeßordnung, der Haupteid nicht unter dem Gesichtspunkte eines Vergleiches, sondern eines Beweismittels zu betrachten ist. Auch nach französischem Rechte ist dies, der neueren Jurisprudenz und Praxis nach, richtig; jedenfalls aber wollte Art. 92 die Zuschiebung und Annahme eines Haupteides nicht von einer Spezialvollmacht abhängig machen.

6) Ziff. 3 spricht von „ausdrücklichem Verzichte“ auf ein Rechtsmittel; zum still-

schweigenden Verzichte bedarf es also einer speziellen Ermächtigung nicht.

Ein stillschweigender Verzicht kann nun in zweifacher Weise stattfinden, nemlich 1) durch Versäumen der Frist zur Einlegung von Rechtsmitteln, und 2) durch Vollzug des Urtheiles im Sinne der Artikel 695, 766 u. 795 der P. O., z. B. durch Einlassung auf den Grund der Sache nach Abweisung der Einrede der Unzuständigkeit, durch Betreiben der Ableistung eines auferlegten Eides ꝛc.

Da das Gesetz nicht unterscheidet, so ist auch in letzterem Falle der Verzicht ohne spezielle Ermächtigung wirksam, und möchte sogar anzunehmen sein, daß ihn das Gesetz vorzugsweise im Auge hatte, da die Versäumung der Nothfristen in der Regel nicht als Verzicht bezeichnet wird. Uebrigens enspricht dies auch dem früher geltenden Rechte.

7) Nach Ziff. 4 soll nur zum gänzlichen Abstande vom Prozesse, nicht zum theilweisen, eine Spezialvollmacht nöthig sein; es wurde ein den theilweisen Abstand betreffender Beisatz gestrichen, weil man nicht wollte, daß das Aufgeben einzelner Ansprüche an Vorlage spezieller Vollmacht gebunden sein solle. Abg. I 124 (Barth).

Der Abstand von eingelegten Berufungen und Nichtigkeitsbeschwerden wird in der Regel unter den Gesichtspunkt des Verzichtes auf Rechtsmittel fallen.

8) Unter „Abstand“ versteht unsere Prozeßordnung, nach Art. 496, die Erklärung des Klägers, daß er den Rechtsstreit aufgebe, d. h. daß er seine Ansprüche im anhängigen Rechtsstreite nicht weiter verfolge, ohne Verzicht auf die Ansprüche selbst.

Es entsteht nun die Frage, wie es sich mit einem Verzichte auf die Klagsansprüche selbst oder umgekehrt mit freiwilliger Unterwerfung unter dieselbe verhalte?

Daß der Anwalt einzelne Ansprüche fallen lassen dürfe, sie nicht weiter zu verfolgen brauche, wenn er sie für unhaltbar erkennt, daß er ferner unnütze Einreden, bezüglich deren er selbst einsieht, daß er sie besser nicht vorgebracht hätte, wieder aufgeben dürfe, bringt der Zweck eines guten Prozesses mit sich, und es würde höchst unpraktisch sein, bei Prozeßhandlungen dieser Art immer Vorlage von Spezialvollmachten zu verlangen.

Ebenso hat es keinen Anstand, daß der Anwalt indirekt, durch thatsächliche Erklärungen und Zugeständnisse, Rechte einräumen oder aufgeben könne, denn es folgt dies aus Art. 90 Abs. 1. Handelt es sich jedoch um direkte Verzichte auf Rechte, so wird anzunehmen sein, daß solche keine Prozeßhandlungen im engeren Sinne bilden, daß sie also in der Prozeßvollmacht nicht enthalten und überhaupt bloß nach den Grundsätzen des Civilrechtes zu beurtheilen seien, und dies zwar nicht nur dem Bevollmächtigten, sondern auch dem Vollmachtgeber gegenüber, falls dieser der gesetzliche Vertreter einer Partei ist. Vgl. Abg. II 286 (v. Neumayr) — hannover. Verhdl. S. 1277 — Chauveau sur Carré quest. 382 bis und quest. 1451 bis im Eingange.

In Frankreich pflegen die Anwälte, wenn sie bei Aufgeben von Ansprüchen, Einreden ꝛc. nicht sicher sind, ob ihre Parteien zustimmen, die Entscheidung darüber dem Ermessen des Gerichts zu überlassen, ein Ausweg, welcher sich in Fällen, wo Zweifel bestehen, ob Spezialvollmacht erforderlich sei, sehr empfehlen dürfte.

Art. 93. — Die Vollmacht bleibt für die Erben und Rechtsnachfolger des Vollmachtgebers, auch wenn sie nicht ausdrücklich auf diese gestellt ist, soweit in Wirksamkeit, als es sich um anhängige Rechtsstreite handelt.

G. A. d. K. d. A. I S. 127. 136. 137. 175. IV S. 23. — K. d. R. I S. 223. 224.

1) Die Bestimmung, daß die Vollmacht im Prozesse auf die Erben und Rechtsnachfolger übergehe, ursprünglich nur für allgemeine Prozeßvollmachten gegeben, später aber auch auf Spezialvollmachten ausgedehnt, ist der bayer. Gerichtsordnung Cap. VII Ziff. 2 entnommen.

Das Gesetz setzt hierbei solche Erben und Rechtsnachfolger voraus, auf welche der Rechtsstreit selbst übergeht, und hat daher den Fall nicht im Auge, wo die Vollmacht vom gesetzlichen Vertreter ausgegangen ist. Vgl. Abg. IV 102 (v. Weiß).

2) Unter „Rechtsnachfolger“ sind, dem natürlichen Sinne dieses Wortes gemäß, nur die Nachfolger im strittigen Rechte selbst, nicht aber die Nachfolger in der Vertretung dieses Rechtes gemeint.

Auf die Fälle, wo eine Aenderung in der Handelnsfähigkeit der Partei, oder in der Person ihres gesetzlichen Vertreters, vorgeht, ist demnach Art. 93 nicht anzuwenden, mag auch die ratio legis dafür sprechen. Vgl. hannover. Entwurf § 104. Zwar wurde dieser Artikel anfänglich von Barth (Abg. I 137) in diesem Sinne aufgefaßt, allein bei den Verhandlungen über die Unterbrechung der Instanz wurde wiederholt und entschieden die entgegengesetzte Ansicht ausgesprochen. Abg. II 282 (v. Weiß und v. Neumayr), 283 (Schmitt). IV 102 (v. Weiß), 105 (Barth).

Für Fälle dieser Art ist daher nur Art. 492 Abs. 2 maßgebend, gemäß dessen der Prozeßbevollmächtigte zwar verpflichtet ist, sofort Anzeige von der Aenderung zu machen, jedoch bis dahin, sowohl der Gegenpartei als der eigenen Partei gegenüber, zur Vertretung befugt ist. Mit der Anzeige erlischt seine Vollmacht. Abg. I 105 (Barth).

3) Stirbt der Vollmachtsgeber, ehe der Rechtsstreit anhängig, d. h. Ladung ergangen ist, so fällt die Ausnahmsbestimmung des Art. 93 hinweg.

Die Frage, was zum anhängigen Rechtsstreite gehöre, beantwortet sich nach Art. 90.

Art. 94. — **Die Vollmacht kann von dem Vollmachtgeber jederzeit, von dem Gewalthaber aber nur in der Art aufgekündigt werden, daß der Vollmachtgeber im Stande ist, für seine anderweitige Vertretung noch rechtzeitig zu sorgen.**

Die Aufkündigung der Vollmacht, von welcher Seite sie geschehen mag, wird der Gegenpartei gegenüber erst mit der Anzeige der Aufkündigung, im Anwaltsprozesse aber erst mit der Anzeige der Bestellung eines neuen Anwalts wirksam.

G. A. d. K. d. A. I S. 127. 137. 289. IV S. 23. — K. d. R. I S. 223. 224.

1) Die Verfügungen, welche die Aufkündigung der Vollmacht betreffen, haben für den Prozeß nur Bedeutung, insofern es sich um deren Wirkung der Gegenpartei gegenüber handelt.

Das Gesetz stellt in dieser Beziehung den allgemeinen, auch für Zustellungsbevollmächtigte (Art. 192 Abs. 3) anerkannten, Grundsatz auf, daß Aufkündigungen erst im Augenblicke der Anzeige an die Gegenpartei für diese wirksam werden, daß also bis dahin alle Prozeßhandlungen von den Bevollmächtigten giltig vorgenommen, Urtheile gegen sie giltig erwirkt werden können.

Diese Anzeige hat durch Zustellung einer Erklärung zu geschehen; übrigens wurde als Ansicht der Subkommission ausgesprochen und vom Ausschusse anerkannt, daß in Fällen, wo die Gegenpartei in sonstiger Weise sichere Kenntniß von Zurücknahme der Vollmacht erhalten habe, sie aus dem Mangel förmlicher Anzeige keine Vortheile werde ableiten können. Abg. I 289.

2) Für den Anwaltsprozeß gilt die besondere Regel, daß die Zurücknahme der Prozeßvollmacht nur Wirkung äußert vom Zeitpunkte an, wo ein neuer Anwalt bestellt ist.

So lange diese Ersetzung nicht geschehen, bleibt die Partei von ihrem früheren Anwalte vertreten, und kann dasjenige, was durch ihn oder gegen ihn im Rechtsstreite geschehen ist, nicht wegen Mangels der Bevollmächtigung angefochten werden. Selbst die Kenntniß, welche die Gegenpartei von der Thatsache der Aufkündigung hat, ist in diesem Falle ohne allen Belang.

Der zurücktretende Anwalt wird übrigens, eintretenden Falles, als verpflichtet zu erachten sein, für die Partei um Gestattung einer Frist nachzusuchen.

Nichtigkeit wegen Mangels der Vollmacht.

Art. 95. — **Die Partei, für welche ohne Auftrag zur Prozeßführung oder ohne die erforderliche spezielle Ermächtigung Prozeßhandlungen vorgenommen wurden, kann auf Nichtigerklärung dieser Handlungen, sowie der daraufhin ergangenen Entscheidungen Klage erheben.**

Die Klage ist gegen denjenigen, der als Gewalthaber aufgetreten ist, und gegen die in der Hauptsache betheiligte Gegenpartei zu richten.

Der beklagte Theil hat den Beweis des von der Klagspartei ertheilten Auftrags zu führen. Ist nachgewiesen oder aus den Umständen zu entnehmen, daß die Partei dem als Gewalthaber für sie aufgetretenen Advokaten die Prozeßschriften selbst übergeben oder übersendet hat oder hat übergeben oder übersenden lassen, so liegt ihr der Gegenbeweis ob, daß dies nicht zum Zwecke der Prozeßführung geschehen sei.

Art. 96. — **Die Nichtigkeitsklage findet nicht statt, wenn die Partei die betreffende Prozeßhandlung nachträglich genehmigt, desgleichen, wenn sie die Entscheidung ausdrücklich anerkannt oder freiwillig vollzogen hat.**

Ist in der Sache das Endurtheil im letzten ordentlichen Rechtszuge erfolgt, so kann die Nichtigkeitsklage nur so lange erhoben werden, als nicht ein Vollstreckungsmittel am Vermögen oder an der Person der Partei verwirklicht worden und das betreffende Verfahren zum Schlusse gediehen ist.

Art. 97. — **Ueber die Nichtigkeitsklage hat das Gericht zu entscheiden, bei welchem die angefochtene Handlung vorgenommen oder von welchem die beschwerende Entscheidung erlassen wurde.**

Das Verfahren in der Hauptsache wird durch Anstellung der Nichtigkeitsklage unterbrochen, falls der Nichtigkeitskläger dies beantragt. Dem Gerichte steht jedoch die Befugniß zu, für die Verfolgung der Nichtigkeitsklage unter dem Rechtsnachtheile der Annahme des Verzichts auf diese Klage und der Verurtheilung zum Schadensersatze angemessene Fristen festzusetzen.

Art. 98. — **Wird die Nichtigkeitsklage als gegründet erklärt, so ist die angefochtene Handlung, sowie die etwa daraufhin ergangene Entscheidung zu vernichten.**

In Folge davon treten alle auf die vernichtete Handlung oder Entscheidung gestützten weitern Verhandlungen und Entscheidungen außer Wirkung.

Der unbefugt als Gewalthaber Aufgetretene ist in alle Prozeßkosten und zum Ersatze des den Hauptparteien verursachten Schadens zu verurtheilen.

Art. 99. — **Im Falle der Verwerfung der Nichtigkeitsklage hat der Kläger die dadurch verursachten Kosten zu tragen und der Gegenpartei im Hauptprozesse Schadensersatz zu leisten.**

Ueberdies kann er in eine Geldstrafe bis zu hundert Gulden, sowie zur Bezahlung einer Genugthuungssumme an den Gewalthaber verurtheilt werden. Der Betrag dieser Summe wird von dem Gerichte nach freiem Ermessen unter Berücksichtigung der Umstände und persönlichen Verhältnisse festgesetzt.

G. A. d. K. d. A. I S. 123. 127. 128. 137. 138. 175. 299. IV S. 23. 303.
K. d. R. I S. 226—229.

1) Die Klage auf Nichtigerklärung von Prozeßhandlungen und richterlichen Entscheidungen wegen Mangels der Bevollmächtigung ist der désaveu des französischen Prozesses, ein Verfahren, über welches der Code de proc. eine Reihe von Artikeln (352—362) enthält, welches aber in der Pfalz bis jetzt gegenstandslos geblieben ist. Hoffentlich wird Aehnliches auch diesseits eintreten.

Fragliche Klage findet nach der P. O. nicht bloß dem Anwalte, sondern jedem Prozeßbevollmächtigten gegenüber statt, was als eine Abweichung vom französischen Prozesse zu betrachten ist, obgleich einzelne Schriftsteller (Chauveau quest. 1296) in der Natur der Prozeßvollmacht den Grund zum désaveu finden und ihn daher auch zulassen bei Vertretungen vor Friedensgerichten und Handelsgerichten.

Uebrigens ist darauf hinzuweisen, daß die Nichtigkeitsklage wohl nur Bedeutung haben kann für jene Fälle, wo ein Anwalt kraft seines gesetzlich vermutheten Mandats handelt; denn in allen sonstigen Fällen findet ja Bereinigung des Vollmachtspunktes von Amtswegen statt, und müßte daher Verschuldung des Vertreters, der Gegenpartei und des Gerichts zusammentreffen, wenn Veranlassung zu einer solchen Klage gegeben sein sollte.

2) Die Nichtigkeitsklage ist statthaft, wenn die zur Prozeßhandlung *erforderliche* Vollmacht mangelt, also im Anwaltsprozesse nur dann, wenn der Anwalt entweder zur Führung des Prozesses überhaupt keinen Auftrag hatte, oder aber wenn er in Fällen, wo spezielle Ermächtigung vorgeschrieben ist, mit dieser nicht versehen war.

Soweit sich der Anwalt innerhalb der Schranken hält, welche die Art. 90 u. 91 für die Prozeßvollmacht geben, können daher seine Handlungen nie Anlaß zu einer Nichtigkeitsklage geben, mag er auch das Interesse des Klienten noch so schwer verletzt und mag er selbst den ausdrücklichen Weisungen desselben entgegengehandelt haben. Verschuldungen dieser Art begründen nur eine *Entschädigungsklage*, welche jedoch den Rechtsbestand des Prozesses nicht berührt.

3) Ist Nichtigkeitsklage erhoben, so ist es Sache des Gewalthabers, sowie der etwa bei Aufrechthaltung des Prozeßaktes betheiligten Gegenpartei, den Nachweis des Auftrages zu führen, welcher Nachweis sich sowohl für den Anwaltsprozeß als für den Parteiprozeß ganz nach *civilrechtlichen* Grundsätzen richtet, und zwar insbesondere auch, was die Form der Ertheilung des Auftrages anbelangt. Es ist also auf die Vorschriften der Art. 85 ff. hier, wo die Vernichtung einer *bereits geschehenen* Prozeßhandlung in Frage steht, keine Rücksicht zu nehmen.

Der Beweis des Auftrages erhält für Advokaten eine besondere Erleichterung dadurch, daß das Gesetz für den Fall, wo *ein Advokat* die Prozeßschriften mit Wissen und Willen der Partei erhalten hat, die Rechtsvermuthung aufstellt, daß er zur Prozeßführung bevollmächtigt worden sei, eine Bestimmung, welche natürlich auch für den Parteiprozeß gilt.

Diese Rechtsvermuthung ist von besonderer Wichtigkeit für die Pfalz, da hiermit die bezügliche, auf dem Herkommen beruhende Ausnahme von den Verfügungen des Art. 1341 Code civ. aufrecht erhalten ist.

4) Nach Art. 96 wird durch nachträgliche Genehmigung die Nichtigkeit geheilt, und es kann nun die Frage entstehen, ob eine nachträglich ertheilte Vollmacht von selbst die Genehmigung enthalte.

Es wurden in dieser Beziehung zwei entgegengesetzte Meinungen geltend gemacht, welchen die vermittelnde, vom Ausschusse als richtig anerkannte, Ansicht von Barth entgegentrat, daß die Umstände entscheiden müßten, ob eine derartige Vollmacht zugleich als Genehmigung zu gelten habe oder nicht. Aus diesem Grunde wurde ein bezüglich gemachter Zusatz wieder gestrichen. Abg. IV 23.

5) Die Bestimmung in Art. 96 Abs. 2, daß die Nichtigkeitsklage ausgeschlossen sei, falls auf Grund eines Endurtheiles letzter Instanz irgend ein Vollstreckungsverfahren am Vermögen oder an der Person durchgeführt worden sei, ist den Art. 157, 159 u. 362 des Code de proc. nachgebildet. Man sieht nemlich das Endurtheil als gegen eine Person ergangen an, welche in Unkenntniß dessen ist, was vorgegangen, und man verlangt, um deren Einspruch auszuschließen, eine Thatsache, aus welcher sich mit Sicherheit folgern läßt, daß sie entweder Kenntniß erlangt haben müsse, oder daß es nur großem Leichtsinne zuzuschreiben sei, wenn dies nicht geschehen.

Wie im Falle des Art. 159 cit. ein acte de carence als ungenügend zum Ausschlusse des Einspruches erkannt wurde, so wird aus gleichem Grunde es auch hier zur Verwirklichung eines Vollstreckungsmittels am Vermögen nicht genügen, bloß festzustellen, daß nichts Pfändbares vorhanden sei.

6) Wenn Art. 97 von Unterbrechung des Verfahrens in der Hauptsache spricht, so ist nur der Rechtsstreit selbst gemeint; bezüglich des Vollstreckungsverfahrens aber gilt bloß Art. 877, gemäß dessen es dem Ermessen des Gerichts, bei welchem die Nichtigkeitsklage anhängig ist, überlassen bleibt, die Einstellung zu verordnen.

7) Das Klagsbegehren ist auf Nichtigerklärung der betreffenden Prozeßhandlung, sowie der zunächst auf Grund derselben ergangenen Entscheidung zu richten, eintretenden Falls auch auf Ersatz des Schadens.

Die Nichtigkeit der auf die vernichteten Prozeßhandlungen und Entscheidungen sich stützenden weiteren Verhandlungen und Entscheidungen soll zwar nach Art. 98 Abs. 2 eine von selbst eintretende Folge sein; allein es wird mindestens sehr rathsam sein, auch bezüglich ihrer die Vernichtung zu begehren, und zwar schon deßhalb, um einen, jeden Zweifel beseitigenden, förmlichen Ausspruch darüber zu erhalten, daß sie bloß Ausfluß der vernichteten Akte seien.

Art. 100. — **Auch ohne Klage der Partei, für welche gehandelt wurde, sind die unbefugt vorgenommenen Handlungen und die etwa daraufhin ergangenen Entscheidungen sowohl auf Antrag der Gegenpartei als von Amtswegen zu vernichten, wenn der Mangel des erforderlichen Nachweises der Bevollmächtigung im Laufe des Verfahrens wahrgenommen und die Vollmacht oder doch die Genehmigung der vorgenommenen Handlungen innerhalb einer vom Gerichte zu bestimmenden Frist nicht nachgetragen wird.**

Der unbefugt als Gewalthaber Aufgetretene ist auch in diesem Falle der Gegenpartei zum Ersatze der Kosten und Schäden verpflichtet.

G. A. d. K. d. A. I S. 124. 125. 137. 138. IV S. 23. — K. d. R. I S. 229.

1) Der nachträglich eingefügte Art. 100 trifft Vorsorge für den Fall, wo übersehen worden, daß der erforderliche Nachweis der Bevollmächtigung nicht vorliege, und dieses Uebersehen im Laufe des Verfahrens noch entdeckt wurde.

Er beruht auf dem richtigen Gedanken, daß es nicht geeignet sei, Prozeßhandlungen, welche nicht hätten zugelassen werden sollen und welche vermuthbar der Vernichtung ausgesetzt sind, zur Grundlage weiterer gerichtlichen Entscheidungen zu machen. Mit der Regel, auf welcher die Artikel 95—99 beruhen, daß das bereits Geschehene giltig bleibe, bis die eigene Partei es anficht, steht er allerdings nicht im Einklange, bildet vielmehr eine Ausnahme derselben.

2) Indem Art. 100 verfügt, daß in allen Fällen, wo binnen einer zu setzenden Frist Vollmacht oder Genehmigung nicht beigebracht werde, nicht bloß Prozeßhandlungen, sondern auch Urtheile von Amtswegen zu vernichten seien, scheint er etwas über das Ziel hinauszuschießen und die Rechte, welche Art. 95 Abs. 3 gibt, wieder zu entziehen. Dort ist nemlich gestattet, den wirklich ertheilten Auftrag in jeder civilrechtlich zulässigen Weise darzuthun, sogar durch die im Besitze der Prozeßschriften liegende Rechtsvermuthung, wäh-

rend hier die einfache Weigerung der Partei, ihren Auftrag zuzugestehen und das Geschehene durch Genehmigung anzuerkennen, hinzureichen scheint, um ergangene Urtheile zu vernichten.

Diesem Widerspruche ließe sich nur dadurch begegnen, daß man, als Gegensatz zur Nichtigkeitsklage, eine Klage des Gewalthabers oder der Gegenpartei auf Anerkennung der Vollmacht zuließe und zu deren Durchführung geeignete Frist bewilligte.

3) „im Laufe des Verfahrens."

Diese Worte können wohl nur von dem in Frage stehenden Rechtsstreite selbst, d. h. dem Verfahren bis zum Endurtheile, zu verstehen sein, nicht aber vom Vollstreckungsverfahren, welches nach dem Geiste der Prozeßordnung davon getrennt zu halten ist.

Auch in der Berufungs- oder Kassations-Instanz kann übrigens die Nichtigkeit berücksichtigt und ausgesprochen werden.

4) Der Umstand, daß eine Entscheidung rechtskräftig sein würde, wenn die Partei richtig vertreten gewesen wäre, kann an und für sich kein Grund sein, die Vernichtung auszuschließen, jedoch liegt es im Geiste der Bestimmungen des Art. 100, daß nur dasjenige vernichtet werden könne, was noch Einfluß im Rechtsstreite hat, was noch zur Grundlage künftiger Entscheidungen dienen soll. Ist der Streitpunkt, auf welchen sich die fehlerhafte Prozeßordnung bezieht, nicht mehr Gegenstand des Prozesses, sei es im ersten, sei es im höheren Rechtszuge, so ist Art. 100 offenbar nicht anwendbar.

5) Bei Bewilligung der Frist zur Beibringung der Vollmacht oder Genehmigung werden die Gerichte möglichst Nachsicht üben und beachten, daß die Verschuldung nicht bloß dem Gewalthaber, welcher glauben mochte, seine Vollmacht genüge, sondern auch der Gegenpartei und dem Gerichte selbst zur Last fällt.

6) Schließlich möchte zu erwähnen sein, daß der Gesetzgeber offenbar voraussetzt, der nemliche Gewalthaber, von welchem die fehlerhafte Prozeßhandlung ausgegangen, sei noch im Rechtsstreite als solcher thätig; allein es ist möglich, daß er seitdem ersetzt oder gestorben ist, und für diese Fälle paßt Art. 100 nicht recht.

Jedenfalls könnten die Folgen, welche Abs. 2 ausspricht, nur eintreten, nachdem der Gewalthaber oder seine Erben beigeladen oder wenigstens fömlich in Verzug gesetzt worden wären.

Gerichtsvollzieher.

Art. 101. — Die Zustellung der im Prozesse von einer Partei an die andere ergehenden Vorladungen, Bekanntmachungen, Aufforderungen und sonstigen Mittheilungen, dann der richterlichen Entscheidungen gehört, soweit das Gesetz nicht anders bestimmt, zum Dienste der Gerichtsvollzieher, deren sich die Parteien nach Maßgabe der hierüber im Gesetze getroffenen nähern Bestimmungen zu bedienen haben.

Das Gleiche gilt von der Zwangsvollstreckung und der Gant.

Auch außerhalb des Prozesses sind die Parteien befugt, durch die Gerichtsvollzieher alle diejenigen Zustellungen von Erklärungen, Anerbietungen etc. an andere machen zu lassen, welche sie zur Wahrung ihrer Rechte als dienlich erachten.

G. A. d. K. d. A. I S. 128. 131. 138. 292. 293. IV S. 23. — K. d. R. I S. 229. 230.

1) Das Institut der Gerichtsvollzieher ist dem französischen Prozesse entnommen und beruht, gleich dem Institute der Anwälte, wie dieses die Prozeßordnung so zu sagen neu geschaffen hat, auf der das ganze neue Verfahren beherrschenden Idee, daß das Richteramt streng auf das ihm eigene Gebiet der Rechtsprechung zu beschränken und von Nebengeschäften so viel möglich zu entlasten sei.

Die Amtsthätigkeit des Gerichtsvollziehers kann daher als ein abgetrennter Theil der richterlichen Gewalt betrachtet werden, und es läßt sich sagen, der Gerichtsvollzieher handle an Stelle des Gerichts, wenn er auf Begehren der Parteien selbständig Rechtshandlungen vornimmt, welche früher unmittelbar vom Gerichte ausgingen oder wenigstens nur auf besondere Weisung desselben erfolgten.

So leitet er im Parteiprozesse den Rechtsstreit ein durch Fertigen und Zustellen der Ladung; besorgt ferner alle in und außer dem Prozesse nöthigen Zustellungen selbständig im Auftrage der Parteien oder Anwälte; ist endlich der Regel nach mit selbständiger Durchführung der Zwangsvollstreckungen beauftragt.

Der amtliche Charakter der Gerichtsvollzieher bringt es mit sich, daß sie ihre Dienste leisten müssen, wenn ein gesetzlicher Grund zur Ablehnung nicht besteht; jedoch sind sie deßhalb nicht gerade mechanische Organe der Parteien, so wenig als die Notare und Anwälte.

Sie sind unter Umständen sogar berufen, den

Parteien Rath zu ertheilen, sie über die Folgen gewisser Rechtshandlungen aufzuklären, für sie den Weg zu ermitteln, auf welchem sie z. B. bei Zwangsvollstreckungen am besten zum Ziele gelangen, und können verantwortlich gemacht werden, wenn sie durch falsche Einleitung von Klagen, durch unnütze Executionen rc. das Interesse ihrer Mandanten verletzen. Im praktischen Leben pflegen die Gerichtsvollzieher eine nicht unwichtige Rolle als Berather der Parteien zu spielen und tragen wesentlich bei, den Mangel von Anwälten an den Landgerichtssitzen nicht fühlbar zu machen.

Das Nähere über die dienstliche Stellung der Gerichtsvollzieher, über das Maß ihrer Pflichten, über die Art und Weise, wie sie ihre Geschäfte zu versehen haben, ist der in Aussicht stehenden Gerichtsbotenordnung vorbehalten, und genügen daher, da etwas Erschöpfendes und Zuverlässiges doch nicht gesagt werden könnte, diese allgemeinen Bemerkungen.

2) Ueberblickt man das Gebiet der amtlichen Thätigkeit der Gerichtsvollzieher, wie es sich nach den Bestimmungen der Prozeßordnung abgränzt, so findet man, daß diese Thätigkeit hauptsächlich zwei Arten von Geschäften begreift, nemlich: 1) in amtlicher Weise Kenntniß von Willenserklärungen oder Urkunden zu geben (Art. 101) und 2) die Urtheile im Zwangswege zu vollstrecken (Art. 837).

In ersterer Beziehung ist die Zuständigkeit des Gerichtsvollziehers Regel, und Ausnahmen treten nur ein, wo sie das Gesetz besonders bezeichnet, z. B. in Art. 205.

Der Gerichtsvollzieher ist entweder unmittelbares Organ der Mittheilungen, indem er selbst, im Namen der ihn beauftragenden Personen, Erklärungen abgibt, oder aber er stellt nur Schriftstücke (Urkunden, Anwaltsakte) zu, welche solche Erklärungen enthalten. Zu erwähnen ist, daß Art. 101 Abs. 3 sich nicht ganz genau ausdrückt, da man dem Wortlaute nach glauben könnte, es seien bloß Mittheilungen erster Art gemeint, also außergerichtliche Zustellungen von Cessionen oder sonstigen Urkunden nicht darin begriffen.

Was die Hilfeleistung der Gerichtsvollzieher in den Sitzungen betrifft, so wird hierüber die Gerichtsvollzieherordnung das Geeignete verfügen.

Art. 102. — Die durch den Gerichtsvollzieher im Namen einer Partei gemachten Erklärungen, welche Zugeständnisse, Anerbietungen, Einwilligungen oder Verzichte zum Gegenstande haben, sind rechtlich nur wirksam, wenn der Gerichtsvollzieher mit dem Nachweise spezieller Ermächtigung versehen oder die der Gegenpartei eingehändigte Abschrift der Zustellungsurkunde von der Partei, welche die Erklärung machen läßt, unterzeichnet ist.

Für die Aechtheit der Unterschrift der Partei ist im letztern Falle der Gerichtsvollzieher verantwortlich, im erstern Falle hat er eine Abschrift der Vollmachtsurkunde mit der betreffenden Erklärung der Gegenpartei zuzustellen.

G. A. d. K. d. A. I S. 131. 175. IV. S. 23. — K. d. R. I S. 230. 231.

1) Nach französischem Rechte hat der Gerichtsbote die nemliche Rechtsvermuthung für sich, zu allen von ihm abgegebenen Erklärungen und vorgenommenen Rechtshandlungen, soweit sie innerhalb seiner Amtssphäre liegen, beauftragt zu sein, wie der Anwalt, und es ist in der nemlichen Weise, wie bei diesem, immer die »demande en désaveu« nöthig, um seine Akte zu vernichten. In der Pfalz wurde dieser Zustand nie als ein rechtsgefährdender betrachtet, und es ist mir nur ein einziger Fall bekannt, wo ein Gerichtsbote desavouirt wurde, ohne daß jedoch die Sache zur gerichtlichen Verhandlung gelangt wäre.

Unsere Prozeßordnung behandelt die Gerichtsvollzieher weniger günstig, indem sie für viele Erklärungen, welche der Anwalt auf Grund seines vermutheten Mandates abgeben darf, den Nachweis spezieller Ermächtigung verlangt. Es mag dies diesseits, wo die Gerichtsvollzieher in erster Zeit nicht sehr zuverlässig sein werden, seine Berechtigung haben; übrigens glaube ich, daß man später sich veranlaßt sehen dürfte, zum französischen Rechte zurückzukehren, und auch hier, wie in so vielen Dingen, die repressiven Maßregeln den präventiven vorzuziehen.

2) Was die gewöhnlichen Akte betrifft, so erkennt auch unsere Prozeßordnung als Grundsatz an, daß der Gerichtsvollzieher, kraft seiner eignen amtlichen Erklärung, als beauftragt zu erachten sei, und es wurde hier ebenso, wie bei den Anwälten, die Bestimmung, daß er sich durch den Besitz der Akten zu legitimiren habe, als werthlos gestrichen. Abg. I 175 (Barth).

Alle Erklärungen jedoch, welche Zugeständnisse, Anerbietungen, Einwilligungen oder Verzichte zum Gegenstande haben, sollen nur unter der Voraussetzung rechtlich wirksam sein, daß der Nachweis spezieller Ermächtigung in vorgeschriebener Weise gegeben sei.

Es ist hier ein Unterschied hervorzuheben, welcher bezüglich des Nachweises der Spezialvollmacht zwischen Anwälten und Gerichtsvollziehern besteht und welcher sehr wesentlich und folgenreich erscheint. Der Anwalt nemlich soll, nach Art. 83 und 92 Abs. 2, zu keiner Prozeßhandlung zugelassen werden, bevor jener Nachweis vorliegt; die Akte des Gerichtsvollziehers jedoch sollen rechtsunwirksam sein, wenn fraglicher Nachweis mangelt. Für die Nothwendigkeit der Nichtigkeitsklage möchten hieraus Folgerungen abzuleiten sein.

3) Die Worte: „welche Zugeständnisse, Verzichte ꝛc. zum Gegenstande haben,“ bedeuten wohl nicht soviel, als wenn es hieße: „zur Folge haben“. Es möchte angedeutet sein, daß die Erklärung direkt auf solche Zugeständnisse ꝛc. gerichtet sein müsse, so daß also Erklärungen, aus welchen, sei es für sich, sei es in Verbindung mit andern Umständen, ein Verzicht oder ein Zugeständniß bloß gefolgert werden könnte, nicht gemeint seien.

Ferner hat das Gesetz nur solche Erklärungen im Auge, welche durch den Gerichtsvollzieher selbst Namens der Partei abgegeben werden, nicht aber solche, wo er bloß einen Akt der Partei oder ihres Vertreters zustellt und also nichts weiter beurkundet, als diese Zustellung und den Auftrag dazu. Es wurde dies ausdrücklich anerkannt und sogar, um dieser Anschauung Ausdruck zu geben, am Schlusse von Abs. 1 statt: „die Erklärung zustellen läßt“ gesetzt: „die Erklärung machen läßt.“ Abg. I 131 a. E. und 132.

Allerdings liegt auch in Fällen dieser Art die rechtserzeugende Handlung der Regel nach nicht im Akte selbst, sondern in der Zustellung; allein es kommt in Betracht, daß beim Vorliegen urkundlicher Erklärungen die Vermuthung dafür spricht, es sei auch die Zustellung derselben beabsichtigt gewesen.

4) Hat der Gerichtsvollzieher seinen Auftrag von dem Bevollmächtigten der Partei oder des gesetzlichen Vertreters derselben empfangen, so hat er selbstverständlich, um dem Willen des Gesetzes zu genügen, auch noch die erste Vollmacht zuzustellen.

5) Was die Form der Vollmacht anbelangt, so enthält in dieser Beziehung das Gesetz keine Vorschriften; es genügt also jede Privaturkunde auch ohne Beglaubigung. Für die Aechtheit derselben ist der Gerichtsvollzieher, abgesehen von besonderer Verschuldung, nicht verantwortlich.

Die Vollmachtsurkunde wird, auch wenn die Gerichtsvollzieherordnung hierüber nichts bestimmen sollte, vom Gerichtsvollzieher selbst, schon seiner Sicherheit wegen, aufzubewahren sein.

Art. 103. — **Die Bestimmungen über die Nichtigkeitsklage gegen Gewalthaber (Art. 95 bis 100) finden bei Diensteshandlungen der Gerichtsvollzieher analoge Anwendung.**

Ist der angefochtene Gerichtsvollzieherakt nicht in einem Rechtsstreite vorgekommen, so ist die Nichtigkeitsklage bei dem Bezirksgerichte des Orts zu erheben, wo der Akt errichtet wurde. G. A. der K. d. A. I S. 132. 175. IV S. 23. — K. d. R. I S. 231.

1) Die Bestimmungen über die Nichtigkeitsklagen gegen Gewalthaber sollen bei allen Diensteshandlungen der Gerichtsvollzieher, also sowohl in der streitigen, als in der unstreitigen Rechtspflege Anwendung finden und zwar in analoger Weise. Dieser letztere Beisatz erscheint sehr gerechtfertigt, denn in der That wollen in manchen Beziehungen jene Bestimmungen nicht passen.

2) Handelt es sich um gewöhnliche Akte, welche der Gerichtsvollzieher kraft des gesetzlich vermutheten Mandates vornehmen darf, so ist die Nichtigkeitsklage ebenso wie bei Anwälten nur statthaft, wenn er ganz ohne Auftrag gehandelt hat, und in diesem Falle findet auch die vollständige Anwendung der in Art. 95 — 100 enthaltenen Bestimmungen nicht die geringste Schwierigkeit. Der Akt bleibt giltig, so lange er nicht durch die Partei selbst als nichtig angefochten wird.

3) Handelt es sich jedoch um Akte, für welche Art. 102 den Nachweis spezieller Ermächtigung verlangt, so ergeben sich erhebliche Anstände, welche um so unangenehmer erscheinen, als gerade hier klare Grundsätze wünschenswerth gewesen wären, denn die Fälle von Nichtigkeitsklagen werden bei Gerichtsvollziehern jedenfalls häufiger vorkommen als bei Anwälten, theils weil bei jenen keine gerichtliche Controle vorausgeht, theils weil von ihnen Mißgriffe eher zu befürchten sind.

Nach Art. 102 Abs. 1 sind Erklärungen, welche ohne den erforderlichen Nachweis der Bevollmächtigung stattfanden, rechtsunwirksam. Hieraus folgt wohl, daß wenn solche Erklärungen irgendwo geltend gemacht werden wollen, Jeder, wer immer Interesse hat, deren Nichtigkeit vorschützen könne, d. h. vorschützen könne, die Erklärung gehe gar nicht von der Person, in deren Namen sie geschehen, aus; in gleicher Weise, wie in jedem anderen Falle, wo für einen Dritten etwas ohne Auftrag geschehen ist. Vgl. I 175 (v. Weiß). Während also, nach den Prinzipien der Art. 95—99, die Vollmacht als bestehend, die Handlung als giltig und wirksam vorausgesetzt wird, bis die Partei selbst Nichtigkeitsklage erhebt, gilt hier umgekehrt als Grundsatz, daß die Handlung als unwirksam anzusehen ist, bis sie etwa durch Nachbringung der Vollmacht oder Genehmigung giltig wird.

Eine Nichtigkeitsklage erscheint daher hier überhaupt nicht nöthig, selbst wenn der Fall des Art. 100 nicht gegeben ist.

4) Von diesem Gesichtspunkte ausgehend, gelangt man zu folgenden Resultaten:

Ohne Zweifel kann die Partei selbständige Nichtigkeitsklage erheben, und es ist diesen Falls alles anwendbar, was die Art. 95—99 bestimmen; bezüglich des Gerichtsstandes aber gilt Art. 103 Abs. 2.

Eine solche Klage ist jedoch, wie gesagt, nicht nöthig.

Wird der betreffende Akt derjenigen Person, in deren Namen die Erklärung abgegeben wurde, selbst entgegengehalten, so kann diese sich auf die Bemerkung beschränken, es sei ihr die Erklärung fremd, dieselbe sei gesetzlich nicht wirksam. Es ist dann Sache desjenigen, welcher aus fraglichem Akte Rechte für sich herleiten will, im Sinne des Art. 95 Abs. 3 nachzuweisen, daß Bevollmächtigung vorgelegen habe. In dieser Beziehung stehen ihm dieselben Rechte zu, wie dem Gerichtsvollzieher selbst, welcher letztere ohne Zweifel als Nebenintervenient auftreten kann, übrigens schon des Regresses wegen beizuladen sein wird.

Wird der betreffende Akt irgendeinem Dritten entgegengehalten, so ist offenbar dieser gleichfalls berechtigt, ihn als rechtlich unwirksam zurückzuweisen, und es ist Sache des Betheiligten, entweder den Auftrag nachzuweisen, oder aber die Genehmigung binnen einer vom Gerichte festzusetzenden Frist beizubringen.

5) In Vorstehendem darf man nicht etwa eine bloße Anwendung von Art. 100 der P. O. erblicken wollen, denn, streng genommen, läßt sich jener Artikel hier fast gar nicht anwenden, weil nicht zu ermessen ist, was die Worte „im Laufe des Verfahrens" hier bedeuten sollen, wo es sich in der Regel nicht um Erklärungen in einem Rechtsstreite handelt; ganz abgesehen davon, daß der Gerichtsbote nicht in der Weise, wie der Prozeßbevollmächtigte Theil am Rechtsstreite nimmt, also immer förmliche Beiladung nöthig wäre.

Seinem Geiste nach hat jedoch Art. 100 allerdings zur Anwendung zu kommen, und es wird daher nie die Vernichtung eines Aktes, welchen die Partei selbst nicht angreift, ausgesprochen werden dürfen, bevor, nach Vorschrift jenes Artikels, der Versuch, die Nichtigkeit zu heilen, gemacht worden ist.

6) Schließlich ist darauf hinzuweisen, daß die aus Art. 102 sich ergebende Nichtigkeit nicht nothwendig den ganzen Akt trifft, sondern zunächst nur die betreffende Erklärung, das Uebrige aber nur, insofern es davon abhängt. Es hat dann der Gesichtspunkt der Ueberschreitung des gesetzlich vermutheten Mandats Maß zu geben.

Art. 104. — **Die Verhältnisse der Gerichtsvollzieher in Bezug auf dienstliche Stellung und Disciplin regelt, soweit nicht das gegenwärtige Gesetzbuch hierüber Bestimmungen enthält, die im Verordnungswege zu erlassende Gerichtsvollzieherordnung. Nach Ablauf von fünf Jahren von Einführung des gegenwärtigen Gesetzes an gerechnet können Aenderungen in der dann bestehenden Gerichtsvollzieherordnung nur mehr im Gesetzeswege getroffen werden und ist längstens bis dahin eine revidirte Gerichtsvollzieherordnung den Kammern des Landtags zur Berathung und Zustimmung vorzulegen.**

Die Gebühren der Gerichtsvollzieher werden durch Verordnung bestimmt.

G. A. d. K. d. A. I S. 128—131. IV S. 23. 303—307. — K. d. R. I S. 231. 232.

Durch die Gerichtsvollzieherordnung soll das im diesseitigen Bayern bis jetzt fremde Institut der Gerichtsvollzieher organisirt und ins Leben eingeführt werden.

Soll dieses Institut jene Vortheile bringen, welche man sich davon verspricht und, nach den Erfahrungen anderer Länder davon versprechen darf, so wird hauptsächlich Zweierlei zu beachten sein, nemlich 1) den Gerichtsvollziehern ein genügendes Einkommen zu sichern, und 2) sie unter strenge Disciplin zu stellen.

Zur wirksamen Handhabung dieser Disciplin wird die Hilfe der Staatsanwaltschaft nicht entbehrt werden können.

Zum Schlusse dieses Hauptstückes sei bemerkt, daß auf Seite 117 Ziff. 7 die Einschaltung: „(d. h. Prozeßvollmachten)" wegzubleiben hat. Abg. IV 386.

IV. Hauptstück.

Kosten, Entschädigungen, Sicherheitsleistung, gerichtliche Hinterlegung, Armenrecht und Strafen.

Prozeßkosten.

Art. 105. — **Während des Prozesses hat jede Partei die durch ihre Handlungen und Anträge veranlaßten Kosten vorläufig auszulegen.**

Kosten, welche durch gemeinschaftliche Anträge der Parteien oder für beide Parteien durch eine von Amtswegen erlassene Verfügung veranlaßt werden, sind einstweilen gemeinschaftlich zu bestreiten.

G. A. d. K. d. A. I S. 138. 176. IV S. 23. — K. d. R. I S. 232—234.

1) Für ein Verfahren, in welchem die Prozeßleitung und der Betrieb des Prozesses, selbst in solchen Fällen, wo der Richter von Amtswegen verfügt hat, ganz der Thätigkeit der Parteien überlassen ist, wo selbst die Verhandlung in der Sitzung und Urtheilsfällung nur auf Betrieb einer Partei stattfindet, eignet sich am besten der Grundsatz des französischen Rechts, zufolge dessen alle Auslagen, welche einer Partei durch ihre Prozeßhandlungen und ihren Prozeßbetrieb erwachsen, vorläufig ihr zur Last bleiben, bis im Endurtheile darüber Entscheidung ergeht.

Es ist dies ein einfaches, alle Schwierigkeiten beseitigendes System, und entspricht dasselbe zugleich der Billigkeit. Verlangt nemlich das Interesse einer Partei die Betreibung, so mag sie auch die Kosten vorlegen; unbillig aber möchte es erscheinen, die Gegenpartei beizuziehen, welche vielleicht das entgegengesetzte Interesse hat, den Prozeß beruhen zu lassen.

Allerdings geschieht es auf diese Weise häufig, daß die eine Partei — in der Regel der Kläger — viel mehr Kosten auslegt als die andere, allein mit Unrecht würde man hieraus Nachtheile für die endliche Kostenvertheilung folgern. Das Gericht ersieht ja aus den Akten, in welchem Maße jede Partei den Rechtsstreit betrieben habe, zudem unterläßt der Anwalt der überlasteten Partei nie, im Vortrage darauf aufmerksam zu machen, und es ist wohl selbstverständlich, daß eine einfache Kostenvergleichung nicht ausgesprochen wird, wenn sie der Sachlage nicht entspricht.

2) Unsere Prozeßordnung hat zwar im Allgemeinen besagtes Prinzip sich angeeignet, jedoch davon in Art. 105 Abs. 2 die Ausnahme gemacht, daß Kosten, welche durch gemeinschaftliche Anträge der Parteien oder für beide Parteien durch eine von Amtswegen erlassene Verfügung veranlaßt werden, gemeinschaftlich zu bestreiten seien, eine Ausnahme, welche aus dem alten Verfahren übertragen, nicht mehr so recht paßt und in der Anwendung sich der Natur des neuen Verfahrens wird anfügen müssen

Wie die Verhandlungen außer Zweifel setzen, handelt es sich hier nicht etwa bloß um die richterlichen Bescheide selbst (also Taxen und Stempelgebühren der Urschrift), sondern hauptsächlich auch um den Vollzug derselben. Da nun dieser Vollzug nur auf Betreiben einer Partei eintritt, da ferner das Aerar, der Gerichtschreiber, der Gerichtsbote, die Experten sich bezüglich ihrer Gebühren doch wohl nur an diejenige Person, auf deren Anstehen gehandelt wird, halten können, so wird der betreibende Theil, ohnerachtet fraglicher Bestimmung, für die erwachsenden Auslagen einstehen müssen.

Demnach würde sich die Wirkung jener Bestimmung darauf beschränken, das Verhältniß unter den Parteien zu regeln und den betreibenden Theil zu berechtigen, sofort, schon im Laufe des Verfahrens, Ersatz seiner Mehrauslagen zu verlangen, in derselben Art, wie dies in G. O. Cap. VI § 11 a. E. bestimmt ist. Das Ergebniß, wenn auch auf anderem Wege erreicht, ist dasselbe.

3) Wenn das Gesetz von „beiden Parteien" spricht, so hat es den gewöhnlichen Fall im Auge und deutet zugleich an, daß es für die Vertheilung ohne Belang sei, wenn auf der einen Seite sich mehrere Streitgenossen, Nebenintervenienten ꝛc. befinden. Uebrigens können auch mehr als zwei Parteien in Betracht kommen, z. B. wenn ein Kläger, ein Beklagter und ein Hauptintervenient sich um das Eigenthum eines Grundstücks streiten, und nun im gemeinschaftlichen Interesse ein Augenschein angeordnet wird. In diesem Falle würde ohne Zweifel jeder ein Drittel der Kosten vorzulegen haben.

4) Fragliche Ausnahme trifft bloß den Fall, wo die nemliche Maßregel von beiden Parteien beantragt oder im Interesse beider Theile von Amtswegen verfügt wird. Abg. I 176 (Edel und v. Neumayr). Sie wird sich daher, wie dies auch nach früherem Rechte der Fall war, so ziemlich beschränken auf den Augenschein und die Zuziehung von Sachverstän-

digen zur Aufklärung des Sachverhaltes. G.O. Cap. XII § 3 Nr. 2 u. 5 — Bl. f. R. I 97 — hannov. Verhdl. S. 859 u. 860.

Zwischenbescheide, welche zu Beweisen zulassen, fallen nicht unter die Ausnahme, sondern unter die Regel, und es hat daher jede Partei diejenigen Kosten, welche durch ihre Beweisführung, d. h. durch ihren Betrieb der Sache erwachsen, selbst zu bestreiten. Bl. f. R. I 97, Anm. 2.

Zu den Kosten, welche gemeinschaftlich zu bestreiten sind, gehören nur Baarauslagen, welche ihrer Natur nach sofort zu entrichten sind, also nicht die Gebühren der Anwälte oder Reiseentschädigungen der Parteien.

5) Es ist nicht nöthig, daß der Richter in seinem Zwischenbescheide ausdrücklich anordne, es habe der Vollzug auf gemeinschaftliche Kosten zu geschehen, oder ausdrücklich erkläre, der Bescheid sei im Interesse beider Parteien erlassen; allein ich würde es geeignet finden, dies zu thun, um jede Ungewißheit zu beseitigen.

6) Besondere Bedeutung hat die Vorschrift des Abs. 2 bei Rechtsstreiten, in welchen eine Partei im Armenrechte streitet, insofern bezüglich des auf die arme Partei treffenden Kostenantheiles das Armenrecht wirkt, insbesondere auch Tagegelder und Reisekosten der Gerichtspersonen theilweise von der Staatskasse vorzuschießen sind. Art. 134.

Art. 106. — **Der unterliegende Theil ist schuldig, der Gegenpartei alle durch den Rechtsstreit verursachten gerichtlichen und außergerichtlichen Kosten zu ersetzen.**

Vom Ersatze ausgeschlossen sind die Kosten, welche durch Verschulden oder durch überflüssige Handlungen der obsiegenden Partei oder ihres Gewalthabers entstanden sind. Welche Kosten als solche zu betrachten sind, ist ohne Zulassung eines Beweisverfahrens nach richterlichem Ermessen zu entscheiden.

Ist ein Advokat oder Rechtspraktikant bei einem Handels- oder Einzelngerichte als Beistand oder Bevollmächtigter beigezogen worden, so kann der Richter nach Umständen die dadurch verursachten Reisekosten ganz oder theilweise vom Ersatze ausschließen, nicht aber die Gebühren für die Verhandlung selbst.

Reisekosten, welche im Verfahren vor den Bezirks-, Appellations- und Handels-Appellationsgerichten durch Beiziehung eines auswärtigen Advokaten zur mündlichen Rechtsvertheidigung erwachsen sind, kommen nicht zum Ersatze.

Der Kostenersatz für Reisen der Parteien, welche der Richter nicht als überflüssig erkannt hat, richtet sich nach dem im Verordnungswege zu erlassenden Tarife.

Art. 107. — **Für die Thätigkeit des Fiskals oder des in eigener Sache aufgetretenen Advokaten hat die in die Kosten verurtheilte Gegenpartei im Anwaltsprozesse die für Anwaltsgeschäfte bestimmten Gebühren zu vergüten.**

Die in eigener Sache bei Handels- oder Einzelngerichten aufgetretenen Advokaten können von der in die Kosten verurtheilten Gegenpartei jene Gebühren in Anspruch nehmen, welche ihnen vor denselben Gerichten als Bevollmächtigten zukommen.

Art. 108. — **Besteht die unterliegende Partei aus mehreren Personen, so sind die Kosten auf sie nach Verhältniß ihrer Betheiligung am Streitgegenstande oder, wenn in dieser Beziehung keine wesentliche Verschiedenheit obwaltet, nach Köpfen zu vertheilen.**

Unterliegen jene Personen auf Grund einer solidarischen Verbindlichkeit, so sind sie solidarisch zum Kostenersatze zu verurtheilen.

Die solidarische Verpflichtung zum Kostenersatze kann auch ausgesprochen werden, wenn den Verurtheilten Streitmuthwille zur Last fällt.

Art. 109. — **Wenn die Parteien wechselseitig theils obsiegen, theils unterliegen, sind die Kosten zu vergleichen oder verhältnißmäßig zu theilen.**

Das Gericht kann jedoch auch in einem solchen Falle den vollen Kostenersatz auflegen, wenn die Zuvielforderung eine verhältnißmäßig geringfügige war und keine besondern Kosten veranlaßt hat, ferner wenn der Betrag der Forderung von der Festsetzung durch richterliches Ermessen, von der Ausmittelung durch Sachverständige oder von einer gegenseitigen Berechnung abhängig war.

Im Falle der Vergleichung der Kosten hat jede Partei ihre Kosten allein zu tragen.

G. A. d. K. d. A. I S. 138—150. 176. 234. IV S. 23. — K. d. A. I S. 234—240.

1) Das Gesetz regelt hier die endliche Vertheilung der Prozeßkosten unter den streitenden Theilen, indem es bestimmt 1) welche Kosten zu ersetzen seien und 2) wer sie zu ersetzen habe.

Unter den Kosten eines Rechtsstreites sind nur die Baarauslagen zu verstehen, welche für die Partei durch Führung desselben erwachsen; sonstiger Schaden, z. B. wegen Zeitversäumniß der Parteien, gehört nicht hierher, fällt vielmehr unter den Gesichtspunkt des Art. 119 der P. O.

Die Kosten der Ausfertigung und Zustellung von Endurtheilen werden, selbst wenn eine Verurtheilung ausgesprochen ist, nicht als zum Vollstreckungsverfahren, sondern als zum Rechtsstreite gehörig zu betrachten sein.

a) Welche Kosten eignen sich zum Ersatze?

2) Nur diejenigen Kosten dürfen in Ansatz kommen, welche zur Geltendmachung der Rechte der Partei nothwendig oder zweckdienlich erscheinen; ausgeschlossen sind die durch überflüssige, unnütze Handlungen, oder durch Verschulden erwachsenen.

Ob Kosten, welche durch Nichterscheinen verursacht wurden, als verschuldet anzusehen seien, wird von den Umständen abhängen. Wegen der Versäumungsurtheile s. Art. 297 u. ff.

Die Ausscheidung ist, falls nicht etwa im Urtheile selbst bereits verfügt wurde, dem taxirenden Richter überlassen.

3) Kosten, welche durch Beiziehen von Advokaten oder Rechtspraktikanten bei Handels- oder Einzelgerichten erwachsen, dürfen nach Art. 106 nie als unnütz betrachtet werden, mit Ausnahme jedoch der Reisekosten, bezüglich deren das richterliche Ermessen entscheidet. Hieraus folgt, daß bei anderen Bevollmächtigten das Ermessen des Richters vollkommen freien Spielraum hat.

Auch in sonstigen Fällen, wo bei gerichtlichen Verhandlungen ein Anwaltszwang nicht besteht, z. B. beim Rangordnungs- und Gant-Verfahren (Art. 1116 u. 1184), werden im Geiste des Gesetzes die nämlichen Grundsätze Maß zu geben haben.

Für das Verfahren an den Gerichten, wo Anwaltszwang besteht, bestimmt Art. 106 Abs. 4, daß Reisekosten auswärtiger Advokaten nicht zu ersetzen seien; aus noch stärkeren Gründen gilt dies für Rechtspraktikanten im Falle des Art. 80 Abs. 2.

Daß für die mündliche Rechtsvertheidigung nur ein einziger Ansatz zu gestatten sei, auch wenn der verbeistandende Anwalt selbst aufklärende Bemerkungen beigefügt hat, erscheint wohl selbstverständlich; jedoch bezieht der Anwalt eine besondere Gebühr für Beistand. Abg. I 143 (v. Weiß).

Was die Reisen der Parteien und ihrer gesetzlichen Vertreter betrifft, so gehören nur Baarauslagen hierher und wird ferner vorausgesetzt, daß die Reisen durch den Rechtsstreit veranlaßt und nach richterlichem Ermessen nicht überflüssig waren. Abg. I 176 (Barth).

b) Wer hat die Kosten zu ersetzen?

4) Das Gesetz beantwortet diese Frage in doppelter Richtung, nemlich 1) was das Verhältniß der unterliegenden Parteien oder Personen unter sich und 2) was deren Verhältniß zur obsiegenden Partei betrifft.

5) Zu 1. In ersterer Beziehung ist es der Wille des Gesetzes, daß sich der Richter in seinem Urtheile bestimmt darüber ausspreche, in welchem Verhältnisse die unterliegenden Personen verpflichtet seien, der obsiegenden Partei die Kosten zu ersetzen.

Der Regel nach hat er hierbei das Verhältniß der Betheiligung am Streitgegenstande zu Grunde zu legen, z. B. nach Verhältniß der Erbtheile, der Miteigenthumsansprüche 2c. Besteht in dieser Beziehung kein wesentlicher Unterschied, so soll nach Köpfen getheilt werden, und es wird wohl zu vermuthen sein, daß der Richter eine solche gleichheitliche Kostenauflage beabsichtigt habe, wenn er nicht anders verfügt hat.

Die nemlichen Grundsätze gelten auch, wenn mehrere selbständige Parteien einer andern gegenüber gemeinschaftlich unterliegen, z. B. Beklagter und Hauptintervenient dem Kläger gegenüber bezüglich derjenigen Kosten, welche während gemeinschaftlicher Führung des Rechtsstreites entstanden sind.

6) Bei solidarischen Verurtheilungen ist auch der Kostenersatz, als Zubehör, unter solidarischer Haftung auszusprechen, jedoch selbstverständlich nur soweit die Solidarität reicht. Wenn z. B. für einen der Solidarschuldner dessen Erben im Rechtsstreite sind, so ist ausdrücklich zu erklären, daß diese unter sich nach Verhältniß ihrer Erbtheile haften.

Untheilbare Verbindlichkeiten stehen den solidarischen nicht gleich, denn die Kosten sind theilbar. Der Referent der Kammer der R. R. hatte Gleichstellung vorgeschlagen, diesen Vorschlag aber wieder fallen lassen.

7) Zu 2. Was das Verhältniß zur obsiegenden Partei anbelangt, so spricht Art. 106 Abs. 1 als Grundsatz aus, daß der unterliegende Theil alle Kosten zu tragen habe. Eine Rücksichtnahme darauf, daß eine Partei „redliche Ursache zum Streite gehabt," findet daher nicht mehr statt; nur umgekehrt wird nach Art. 108 Abs. 3

Streitmuthwille mit solidarischer Verurtheilung beahndet.

Nach Art. 109 Abs. 2 darf der Richter in zwei Fällen ein vollständiges Unterliegen selbst dann annehmen, wenn die Anträge des obsiegenden Theils nicht ganz zugesprochen worden sind, nemlich 1) im Falle, wo die Zuvielforderung nur geringfügig ist und keine besonderen Kosten verursacht hat, und 2) im Falle, wo die genaue Bestimmung einer Forderung von Schätzung oder Berechnung abhängt.

Hat der Kläger im letztgedachten Falle eine offenbar übertriebene Forderung aufgestellt, so daß anzunehmen, das Maßlose seiner Ansprüche möge die Entstehung des Rechtsstreites veranlaßt oder einen Vergleich verhindert haben, oder ist er etwa gar Schuld, daß die Sache in kostspieligerer Weise vor dem Bezirksgerichte oder Handelsgerichte verhandelt werden mußte, während sie sich vor den Einzelrichter geeignet hätte, so wird der Richter sich nicht veranlaßt sehen, von der Regel abzuweichen.

8) Eine natürliche Folge des obigen Grundsatzes ist die Bestimmung in Art. 109 Abs. 1, daß bei wechselseitigem Unterliegen der Parteien die Kosten zu vergleichen oder verhältnißmäßig zu theilen seien. Vielleicht hätte es genügt, das Letztere zu sagen, denn eine ganze oder theilweise Vergleichung ist im Grunde nichts weiter, als eine verhältnißmäßige Austheilung; nur daß die Theilungsziffer nicht ausgedrückt ist.

Die Allgemeinheit dieser Bestimmung gibt dem Richter vollkommen freie Hand. Derselbe ist nicht mehr gebunden, in der eintönigen unbehilflichen Weise, wie es bis jetzt Uebung war, nur zwischen gänzlicher Verurtheilung und gänzlicher Vergleichung zu wählen; vielmehr hindert ihn nichts, bei der Kostenzutheilung den verschiedenartigen Gestaltungen der Sachlage Rechnung zu tragen und sich diejenige Form auszuwählen, welche den Umständen am besten zu entsprechen scheint.

Maßgebende Erwägungen bei Vertheilung der Kosten werden insbesondere sein: a) das Maß des gegenseitigen Unterliegens, wobei auch Zwischenstreite im Sinne des Art. 9 in Betracht kommen, und b) der Anlaß zur Entstehung der Kosten, indem kleine Nebenpunkte oft große Kosten verursachen. Uebrigens sind Erwägungen anderer Art nicht ausgeschlossen.

Mit Unrecht würde man etwa aus Art. 108 Abs. 1 eine Pflicht für den Richter herleiten wollen, auf das Verhältniß des Werthes der Streitpunkte, bezüglich deren das wechselseitige Unterliegen stattfindet, das entscheidende Gewicht zu legen. Die Gründe, welche für das Verhältniß unter Genossen bestimmend waren, lassen sich auf das Verhältniß unter Gegnern, welche verschiedene Rechte in verschiedener Weise verfolgen, nicht anwenden.

9) Die Frage, welches der geeignetste Weg zur Vertheilung der Kosten sei, wird nach den Bedürfnissen des Falles zu entscheiden sein.

In der Pfalz verfährt man hauptsächlich auf dreierlei Art, nemlich:

1) indem man aus sämmtlichen Prozeßkosten eine Masse bildet und davon jeder Partei einen Bruchtheil zur Last legt;
2) indem man eine Partei verurtheilt, der andern einen gewissen Theil ihrer Kosten zu ersetzen, die übrigen beiderseitigen Kosten aber vergleicht;
3) indem man einfach Kostenvergleichung ausspricht.

Bei der ersten Art der Vertheilung müssen beide Parteien ihre Kosten liquidiren (Art. 113 Abs. 2), und es ergibt sich dann erst durch Berechnung, ob und was eine der anderen zu ersetzen hat. Dieselbe bietet den Vortheil, daß ein Eingehen auf die Frage, wieviel Kosten jede Partei ausgelegt habe, unnöthig ist, und wird daher bei größeren und verwickelteren Prozessen als sachgemäß betrachtet.

Die ganze oder theilweise Vergleichung der Kosten pflegt man in einfachen Sachen zu wählen, wo die Umstände es gestatten, sofort die Tragweite derselben mit Rücksicht auf die beiderseitigen Kostenvorlagen zu ermessen.

10) In Fällen, wo über verschiedene Klagen, sei es unter zwei, sei es unter mehr Parteien, im nemlichen Rechtsstreite verhandelt und erkannt wird, z. B. bei Widerklagen, bei Hauptinterventionen, bei Streitigkeiten im Theilungs- oder Rangordnungs-Verfahren, ist der Richter gesetzlich zwar nicht gehindert, wegen der Kosten der einzelnen Klagen oder Streitpunkte gesondert zu verfügen, allein es wird dies in der Regel sehr unzweckmäßig sein. Auch hier wird das Zusammenfassen und Austheilen aller Kosten in den meisten Fällen vorzuziehen sein; es ist nicht bloß das einfachere Verfahren, sondern auch das gerechtere, indem der Richter bei Bestimmung der Bruchtheile allen besonderen Umständen jeder Art Rechnung zu tragen vermag.

Ebenso können unter Umständen die Kosten mehrerer Instanzen in eine Masse vereinigt werden, um nach Maßgabe des Unterliegens darüber zu verfügen.

11) Was die Gewährschaftsklagen betrifft, so erfordert das Eventualverhältniß, in welchem sie unter sich, sowie zur Hauptsache stehen, eine besondere Berücksichtigung.

Es wäre z. B. nicht richtig, wollte man im Falle, wo Hauptklage und sämmtliche Gewährschaftsklagen für begründet erklärt werden, den letzten Gewährschaftsbeklagten direkt in alle Kosten verurtheilen; vielmehr ist die Sache gerade so zu behandeln, als wären die verschiedenen Rechtsstreite wirklich nacheinander durchgeführt worden.

Im gegebenen Falle müßte man also den Hauptbeklagten dem Hauptkläger gegenüber in die Kosten der Hauptklage verurtheilen, sofort weiter den ersten Gewährschaftsbeklagten verurtheilen, dem Hauptbeklagten diejenigen Kosten zu ersetzen, welche er dem Hauptkläger gegenüber zu tragen hat, und ihm zugleich die Kosten der Gewährschaftsklage zur Last legen u. s. w. Zweckmäßiger würde es übrigens sein, nicht von Kosten der Hauptklage ꝛc. zu sprechen, was bei der Ausscheidung Schwierigkeiten veranlassen könnte, sondern kurzweg den Hauptbeklagten zu verurtheilen, dem Hauptkläger seine sämmtlichen Kosten zu ersetzen, sofort weiter den ersten Gewährschaftsbeklagten, dem Hauptbeklagten diejenigen Kosten, welche er dem Hauptkläger gegenüber zu tragen hat, und seine eigenen zu ersetzen u. s. w.

Erwägt man, daß möglicherweise der letzte Gewährschaftsbeklagte nicht zahlfähig oder ein Ausländer sein kann, so fühlt man sofort, daß es unrecht wäre, den Hauptkläger wegen des Kostenersatzes, statt an seinen unmittelbaren Gegner, an eine Person zu verweisen, welche ihm fremd ist.

12) Bei der Allgemeinheit der Verfügungen des Gesetzes müssen die Grundsätze wegen des Ersatzes der Kosten auch in jenen Fällen zur Anwendung kommen, wo der Staatsanwalt als selbständige Partei im Rechtsstreite auftritt, also in den Fällen der Art. 184. 191. 491 Code civil, sowie des preuß. Landrechts Thl. I Tit. 38 § 1 — 8 (Einführ.-Ges. Art. 35). Der Ersatz ist in solchen Fällen natürlich vom Fiskus zu leisten. Abg. I 140 (Franz, v. Weiß).

Auch die Beschränkung des Kostenersatzes, welche in der Pfalz, bei Prozessen über Registrir-Gebühren, dem Staate gegenüber eintrat, erscheint aufgehoben.

Was schließlich den Art. 21 des Zwangsabtretungsgesetzes betrifft, laut dessen die Kosten des Verfahrens in erster Instanz immer dem Expropriirenden zur Last fallen, so bleibt er — ich möchte fast sagen: leider — bestehen, da Art. 6 des Einführungsgesetzes ihn unberührt läßt, übrigens auch fragliche Bestimmung keine rein prozessuale ist, sondern eher gesagt werden kann, daß sie eine Bedingung des Zwangs zur Abtretung festsetze und den Umfang der Entschädigungspflicht regle.

Art. 110. — **Gesetzliche Vertreter, Anwälte, sonstige Prozeßbevollmächtigte und Gerichtsvollzieher können persönlich zur Tragung der Kosten verurtheilt werden, welche sie durch grobes Verschulden oder Verletzung bestimmter Dienstesvorschriften veranlaßt haben.**

In solchen Fällen ist den betreffenden Personen vorher Gelegenheit zu ihrer Verantwortung zu geben. Zu diesem Zwecke sind sie nach Bedürfniß selbst von Amtswegen beizuladen. G. A. b. K. d. A. I S. 145. 176. 177. IV S. 24. — K. d. R. I S. 240. 241.

1) Die Bestimmungen dieses Artikels, deren Vorbild sich in Art. 132 Code de proc. findet, bezwecken den Schutz der Parteien gegen leichtsinnige Handlungen ihrer Vertreter; sie erstrecken sich jedoch nur auf Prozeßkosten, nicht auf sonstigen Schaden.

Voraussetzung der persönlichen Verurtheilung zu den Kosten ist ein grobes Verschulden oder die Verletzung bestimmter Dienstesvorschriften. Anwälte und Gerichtsvollzieher, welche bestimmte Dienstesvorschriften verletzen, sind daher von Gesetzeswegen in grobem Verschulden.

2) Der Umstand, daß ein gesetzlicher Vertreter zugleich in eigenem Namen betheiligt ist, kann offenbar der Anwendung des Art. 110 nicht im Wege stehen; in diesem Falle besteht die Folge der persönlichen Verurtheilung zu den Kosten eben darin, daß der Vertreter sie nun ausschließlich zu tragen hat.

3) Das Gesetz spricht allgemein von allen Kosten, welche durch Verschuldung veranlaßt sind, und unterscheidet nicht, auf welcher Seite sie erwachsen seien. Seine Verfügung wirkt also nicht bloß der Gegenpartei gegenüber, in der Art, daß nicht die Partei selbst, sondern der Vertreter ꝛc. persönlich verurtheilt wird, ihr die Kosten zu ersetzen, sondern sie wirkt auch der eigenen Partei gegenüber, indem sie das Recht nimmt, derselben die Kosten in Anrechnung zu bringen.

Das Gesetz gibt also hier dem Richter eine ziemlich scharfe Waffe in die Hand, welche mit Vorsicht zu gebrauchen sein wird.

4) Selbstverständlich erscheint, daß jede derartige Verurtheilung bestimmt im Urtheilssatze auszusprechen und mit Entscheidungsgründen zu versehen ist; ferner daß sie die Kosten, um welche es sich handelt, genau zu bezeichnen hat.

In Frankreich entstand Streit darüber, ob sie von Amtswegen ausgesprochen werden dürfe; nach unserer Prozeßordnung kann in dieser Beziehung ein Zweifel nicht bestehen, denn schon aus der Fassung des Gesetzes geht klar hervor, daß ein amtliches Einschreiten statthaft sein solle, abgesehen davon, daß der Geist des Gesetzes, welches der abwesenden Partei Schutz gegen Verschuldungen ihres Vertreters gewähren will, entschieden dafür spricht.

5) Indem das Gesetz als Grundsatz ausspricht, daß eine solche Verurtheilung nicht erfolgen könne, bevor nicht den betreffenden Personen Gelegenheit zur Verantwortung gegeben sei, hat es den Art. 132 Code de pr. wesentlich verbessert.

Ueber die Tragweite dieses Grundsatzes, insbesondere sein Verhältniß zu dem die Beiladung betreffenden Zusatze, sind nähere Erläuterungen nöthig.

Die im Art. 110 genannten Personen sind nicht Parteien im Rechtsstreite, und es frägt sich nun, ob es der Wille des Gesetzes sei, daß trotzdessen eine Verurtheilung gegen sie soll ergehen dürfen, so daß also (wie im Art. 132 C. de pr.) die allgemeinen Grundsätze hier eine Ausnahme erleiden würden; oder aber, ob das Gesetz voraussetze, daß in allen Fällen vorher eine Beiladung stattfinde, um die betreffenden Personen förmlich zu Parteien zu machen?

Faßt man den Beschluß des G. A. der K. der R. (I 240) in's Auge und erwägt man, daß die K. der Abg. diesem Beschlusse im Allgemeinen beitrat und den die Beiladung betreffenden Satz nur deßhalb beifügte, damit das Verbot des Art. 73 einer etwa nöthigen Beiladung nicht im Wege stehe, so erscheint es richtig, das Erstere als Ansicht des Gesetzgebers zu betrachten. Die Worte „nach Bedürfniß", würden also, wie die jetzige Interpunktion es zuläßt, auf die Beiladungen überhaupt, nicht aber bloß auf den Fall, wo sie von Amtswegen geschehen, zu beziehen sein.

Offenbar ist diese Lösung auch die sachgemäßeste, denn es wäre ein zweckloser Formalismus, zu verlangen, daß ein Vertreter, welcher als solcher bei der Verhandlung thätig und in der Sitzung anwesend ist, noch förmlich geladen werde, um ihn im Sinne des Art. 110 als Partei zu behandeln.

Der Sinn des Gesetzes ist daher folgender:

Ist einer Person, welche bereits als Vertreter einer Partei im Prozesse sich befindet, genügende Gelegenheit zur Verantwortung geboten worden, sei es durch Zustellung eines Antrags, sei es durch Aufforderung des Richters in der Sitzung, so reicht dies hin, um sie — ausnahmsweise — als Partei zu behandeln, und die persönliche Verurtheilung zu den Kosten gegen sie auszusprechen; ist dies jedoch nicht der Fall, so ist förmliche Beiladung nöthig.

Die Aufforderung zur Verantwortung muß selbstverständlich aus dem Urtheile zu ersehen sein, sei es aus den genommenen Anträgen, sei es durch Beurkundung in der Darstellung des Sachverhalts oder im Urtheilssatze.

6) Die Verfügung, daß das Gericht von Amtswegen beizuladen habe, gehört dem Geiste des alten Prozesses an, denn offenbar ist gemeint, daß das Gericht nicht bloß die Beiladung anordne, den Parteien aber den Vollzug überlasse, sondern daß es direkten Auftrag ergehen lasse. Abg. I 145 (v. Weiß). Um dies nun mit dem neuen Verfahren in Einklang zu bringen, wird die Sachlage so aufzufassen sein, als habe das Gericht seine Weisung an Stelle der Parteien gegeben, als handle der Gerichtsbote rc. auf Anstehen beider Parteien, so daß also die erwachsenden Kosten von diesen gleichheitlich zu beziehen sind.

7) Es ist klar, daß nur dasjenige Gericht die in Frage stehende Verurtheilung aussprechen dürfe, welches mit der Sache befaßt ist, also möglicherweise auch ein Handelsgericht oder ein Landgericht, und in so fern enthält Art. 110 eine Ausnahme von der allgemeinen Bestimmung des Art. 5 Ziff. 4.

8) Der persönlich zu den Kosten verurtheilte Vertreter rc. hat die gewöhnlichen Rechtsmittel des Einspruchs, der Berufung rc. Abg. I 177 (v. Weiß).

Art. 111. — **Das Endurtheil in der Hauptsache hat zugleich die Entscheidung im Kostenpunkte zu enthalten, soweit nicht hierüber bezüglich einzelner Prozeßhandlungen oder Zwischenstreitigkeiten bereits erkannt worden ist.**

Mit der Verwerfung eines Rechtsmittels ist in allen Fällen die Entscheidung über die dadurch verursachten Kosten zu verbinden.

G. A. d. K. d. A. I S. 145. 176. IV S. 24. — K. d. R. I S. 241.

1) Das Gesetz gibt hier dem Richter zwei Vorschriften, nemlich, daß er 1) beim Endurtheile in der Hauptsache, und 2) bei Verwerfung von Rechtsmitteln immer zugleich über

die Kosten zu entscheiden habe; in allen sonstigen Beziehungen läßt es ihm völlig freie Hand, den geeigneten Zeitpunkt für diese Entscheidung zu wählen, und die Kosten der Zwischenstreite mit der Hauptsache zu verbinden oder davon zu trennen.

2) Unter Endurtheil ist hier das die Sache vollständig bereinigende Urtheil gemeint; es will also das Gesetz den Richter nicht zwingen, jedesmal, wenn er über einen Theil des Hauptbegehrens endlich entscheidet, zugleich die denselben betreffenden Kosten auszuscheiden und darüber zu erkennen.

Wenn zufolge eines Urtheils eine Partei aus dem Rechtsstreite scheidet, so ist selbstverständlich ihr gegenüber immer über die Kosten zu erkennen; dabei kann es jedoch vorkommen, daß das Gericht, indem es eine der im Rechtsstreite verbleibenden Parteien verurtheilt, dem Austretenden die Kosten zu ersetzen, den Vorbehalt macht, unter den verbleibenden Parteien weiter bezüglich derselben zu verfügen.

Hat der Richter versäumt, im Endurtheile wegen der Kosten zu verfügen, so ist sein Urtheil mangelhaft und bedarf der Ergänzung, welche nach Maßgabe des Art. 283 erfolgt. Der Grundsatz, daß in Fällen, wo das Urtheil schweigt, die Kostenvergleichung zu vermuthen sei (Ger. O. Cap. XVII § 4 Ziff. 4), gilt daher nicht mehr.

3) Der Richter kann veranlaßt sein, schon im Laufe des Rechtsstreites bezüglich der Kosten zu erkennen, wenn er über Theile des Hauptbegehrens oder aber über Zwischenstreite endlich entscheidet, sowie ferner, wenn er gewisse Prozeßhandlungen für nichtig oder nutzlos erklärt.

Die Zwischenstreite können verschiedener Art sein, nemlich entweder selbständige Streitpunkte, deren Wirkungen sich über den anhängigen Rechtsstreit hinaus erstrecken (Art. 9), oder Zwischenstreite, welche sich auf diesen Rechtsstreit beschränken, d. h. nur für das den Gegenstand der Klage oder Widerklage bildende Begehren von Werth sind.

Letztere können wiederum auf das Recht selbst sich beziehen, wie z. B. Legitimationsfragen, oder aber nur auf das Verfahren, wie die Frage der Zuständigkeit, der Nichtigkeit von Prozeßakten ꝛc.

In allen diesen Richtungen ist es dem Richter gestattet, über die durch den Zwischenstreit veranlaßten Kosten zu erkennen, jedoch wird er schon deßhalb nicht häufig in die Lage kommen, es zu thun, weil nach den Grundsätzen unserer Prozeßordnung die Zwischenentscheidungen der Regel nach nur auf Widerruf erlassen werden. (Art. 296. 682 und 683.)

4) In der Regel wird es übrigens nicht sachentsprechend sein, über Kosten von Zwischenstreiten, selbst wenn sie als Präjudizialsachen (Art. 100) behandelt werden, gesondert zu verfügen, theils weil denn doch diejenige Person, welche in der Hauptsache am Ende unterliegt, auch die Zwischenstreite verschuldet hat, theils weil nach völlig durchverhandelter und aufgeklärter Sache die Kostenvertheilung in gerechterer und leichterer Weise wird geschehen können.

In der Praxis pflegt man daher soviel möglich den Kostenpunkt dem Endurtheile vorzubehalten und nur dann eine Ausnahme zu machen, wenn durch offenbar muthwillige und leichtfertige Anträge Kosten verursacht worden sind.

5) Die nemliche Regel gilt auch, wenn über einen unbedeutenden Theil der Hauptsache endlich entschieden wird; betrifft jedoch die Entscheidung einen wichtigeren Punkt, so erscheint es geeignet und dem Willen des Gesetzes entsprechend, auch über den bezüglichen Theil der Kosten zu verfügen. Insbesondere wird dies nie zu unterlassen sein, falls die Kosten von Bedeutung sind, weil sonst der Kostenpunkt der Beilegung der noch übrigen Streitpunkte hindernd im Wege stehen könnte.

Ergeht ein Endurtheil, welches nur noch einen unbedeutenden Punkt zur Liquidirung und Entscheidung vorbehält, so kann sich der Richter veranlaßt finden, über sämmtliche erwachsene Kosten sofort zu erkennen.

In Fällen, wo das Gericht die Verpflichtung zum Schadensersatze, zur Rechnungsablage, zur Theilung ausspricht, wird es im Sinne des Gesetzes auch sofort über die Kosten zu erkennen haben. Vgl. Art. 887 und 896.

6) Was die durch Rechtsmittel verursachten Kosten betrifft, so gibt das Gesetz nur für den Fall der Verwerfung eine bindende Vorschrift, woraus folgt, daß für den Fall, wo die Rechtsmittel als begründet erklärt werden und abändernd erkannt wird, der Richter freie Hand habe und nicht behindert sei, sie dem künftigen Endurtheile vorzubehalten.

Was von einer gänzlichen Verwerfung gilt, findet auch entsprechende Anwendung auf eine theilweise Verwerfung.

Art. 112. — **Versichert der Anwalt der obsiegenden Partei vor oder unmittelbar nach Verkündung des Urtheils, daß er die Kosten ganz oder zum größten Theile aus eigenen Mitteln bestritten habe, so ist derselbe im Urtheile zu ermächtigen, die Verurtheilung im Kosten-**

punkte vorbehaltlich der Abrechnung mit seiner Partei allein und im eigenen Namen in Vollzug setzen zu lassen.

G. A. d. K. d. A. I S. 150. 177. IV S. 24. — K. d. R. I S. 241. 242. IV. S. 14.

1) Dieser Artikel entspricht dem Art. 133 Code de proc. und ist bestimmt, den Anwalt, welcher ohne genügenden Vorschuß einen Rechtsstreit geführt und gewonnen hat, der eigenen Partei gegenüber sicher zu stellen.

Das Gesetz sagt, der Anwalt müsse vor oder unmittelbar nach der Verkündung des Urtheils versichern, daß er die Kosten ganz oder zum größten Theile aus eigenen Mitteln bestritten habe.

Was das Erstere betrifft, so muß aus der Versicherung hervorgehen, daß der Anwalt zur Zeit der Verhandlung einen genügenden Vorschuß nicht habe; es wird also eine frühere, etwa im Schriftenwechsel abgegebene, Erklärung nicht genügen.

Die Zulassung einer Versicherung nach Verkündung des Urtheiles rechtfertigt sich deßhalb, weil erst durch diese Verkündung der Anwalt erfährt, daß seiner Partei der Kostenersatz zuerkannt worden sei. Sie muß spätestens in derjenigen Sitzung geschehen, in welcher der Urtheilsspruch erfolgt.

Ueber die Versicherung des Anwalts ist im Urtheilssatze Urkunde zu geben und sofort die Ermächtigung auszusprechen, die zugesprochenen Kosten in eigenem Namen von der Gegenpartei zu erheben.

2) Diese Ermächtigung wirkt als gerichtliche Anweisung und zwar vom Augenblicke des Anspruches an, und hebt sofort das Verfügungsrecht der Partei — welche jedoch immerhin Hauptschuldnerin des Anwalts bleibt — über die fragliche Kostenforderung auf. Abg. I 177 (zu Art. 96).

Selbstverständlich ist, daß die Rechte des Anwaltes keine besseren sind, als sie der Partei selbst zugestanden haben würden, daß also die Einlegung von Rechtsmitteln auch dessen Anweisung in Frage stellt und deren Vollzug hemmt.

Leistet die Gegenpartei Zahlung an den Anwalt, so ist diese als zur Entlastung der Partei geschehen zu betrachten, und Rückforderungen auf Grund etwa eintretender Vernichtung des Urtheils sind nicht gegen den Anwalt, sondern gegen die Partei zu richten. Vgl. Chauveau sur Carré quest. 570 ter.

3) Wird der Rechtsstreit im Armenrechte geführt, so bedarf es einer Versicherung des Anwaltes nicht und erfolgt die Einsetzung in die Rechte der Partei von Amtswegen. Art. 144.

Art. 113. — **Im Anwaltsprozesse hat vor Ausfertigung des Urtheils der Anwalt der obsiegenden Partei ein specifizirtes Kostenverzeichniß, soweit solches zum Zwecke der zum Vollzuge des Urtheils erforderlichen Liquidation der Prozeßkosten nothwendig ist, nebst Akten und Belegen auf der Gerichtsschreiberei einzureichen.**

Ist auf verhältnißmäßige Theilung der Kosten erkannt, so ist die Gegenpartei aufzufordern, binnen drei Tagen ein Gleiches zu thun.

Die Prüfung der Verzeichnisse und die Festsetzung des Kostenbetrags erfolgt durch den Vorsitzenden oder ein von ihm beauftragtes Gerichtsmitglied, welches zum Urtheile mitgewirkt hat. Ist der Vorsitzende verhindert, so tritt an seine Stelle der Gerichtsvorstand. Der die Kosten festsetzende Beschluß ist auf das Verzeichniß selbst zu setzen und bleibt auf der Gerichtsschreiberei hinterlegt, wo die Betheiligten Einsicht davon nehmen können.

Die mit dem Kostenverzeichnisse eingereichten Akten und Belege werden nach Festsetzung der Kosten zurückgegeben.

Der Betrag der liquidirten Kosten ist in den Urtheilssatz selbst aufzunehmen. Hat im Falle des Abs. 2 die Gegenpartei der an sie ergangenen Aufforderung nicht Genüge geleistet, so sind deren Kosten bei Ausfertigung des Urtheils nicht zu berücksichtigen.

War vor Ausfertigung des Urtheils ein Kostenverzeichniß nicht oder nicht von allen Betheiligten eingereicht worden, so kann die säumige Partei zwar ihre Kosten auch noch später festsetzen lassen und eine vollstreckbare Ausfertigung dieser Festsetzung verlangen, es können aber die dadurch erwachsenden besondern Kosten der Gegenpartei nicht aufgerechnet werden.

Art. 114. — **Die Kostenfestsetzung kann von den Parteien, soweit nicht über einzelne Ansätze contradictorisch verhandelt wurde, innerhalb einer unerstreckbaren Frist von acht Tagen von Zustellung des betreffenden Urtheils oder Beschlusses angefochten werden.**

Der Einspruch erfolgt durch Zustellung eines die Beschwerden bezeichnenden Anwaltsakts an den Anwalt der Gegenpartei oder an diese selbst, wenn für sie ein Anwalt nicht

aufgestellt ist. Ein schriftliches Vorverfahren findet in der Sache nicht statt und gegen die Entscheidung ist kein selbstständiges Rechtsmittel zulässig.

Art. 115. — Im Parteiprozesse sind die Kosten bei der Verhandlung zu liquidiren und im Urtheile festzusetzen. Die Festsetzung erfolgt, soweit nicht die betreffende Gebührenordnung Maß gibt, nach freiem Ermessen des Richters.

Gegen die Kostenfestsetzung findet kein selbständiges Rechtsmittel statt.

G. A. d. K. d. A. I S. 151—154. 177. 289. IV S. 24. — K. d. R. R. I S. 242—248. IV. S. 14. 15.

1) Diese drei Artikel regeln das Verfahren zur Festsetzung der laut des Urtheilsspruches zu ersetzenden Kosten; sie gelten also nur für das Verhältniß der Parteien unter sich, nicht aber für das Verhältniß der Anwälte und Prozeßbevollmächtigten der eignen Partei gegenüber, in welch letzterer Beziehung die Artikel 117 u. 118 maßgebend sind.

Die beiden ersten Artikel sprechen vom Anwaltsprozesse, der letztere spricht vom Parteiprozesse.

a) Anwaltsprozeß.

2) Im mündlichen Verfahren, wo kein Referent die Akten vorher in Händen hat und prüft, wo das Gericht erst in der Sitzung den Rechtsstreit kennen lernt, wo endlich häufig das Urtheil sofort nach der Verhandlung gesprochen wird, wäre es höchst ungeeignet, die Kosten schon im Laufe der Verhandlung zu liquidiren; denn wenn auch in gewöhnlichen Fällen die Kostenverzeichnisse in der Sitzung vorgelegt werden könnten, so wäre doch eine eingehende amtliche Prüfung derselben, wie sie im Interesse der Parteien verlangt wird, nicht wohl möglich. Es empfiehlt sich daher ein Ausweg, welcher gestattet, die Liquidation dem Spruche des Urtheiles nachgängig vorzunehmen und das Urtheil in dieser Beziehung zu ergänzen, was um so weniger einem Anstande unterliegen kann, als die Taxe im Wesentlichen doch bloß Sache des Richters ist und die Rechte der Parteien durch Gestattung eines Einspruches genügend gewahrt erscheinen.

Unsere Prozeßordnung hat für den Anwaltsprozeß diesem Gesichtspunkte volle Rechnung getragen und dem Wesen nach dasjenige Verfahren sich angeeignet, welches in Frankreich für den summarischen Prozeß gilt.

3) Als Regel ist aufgestellt, daß der Betrag der Kosten in den Urtheilsatz selbst aufzunehmen sei (Art. 113 Abs. 5), und zwar soll dies geschehen können bis zur Aussertigung des Urtheils. Da nun selbstverständlich die Abfassung des Urtheils und dessen Eintrag ins Urtheilsbuch nicht aufgeschoben werden können, bis es einer oder der andern Partei beliebt, ihre Kosten festsetzen und das Urtheil ausfertigen zu lassen, so ist klar, daß es statthaft ist, den Kostenbetrag nachträglich beizufügen.

Bei den französischen Gerichten besteht die Uebung, im Urtheilseintrage den Raum für Einsetzung der Summen freizulassen und später auf Grund der richterlichen Taxe auszufüllen. Dieses Verfahren wird als dasjenige zu betrachten sein, welches der Gesetzgeber im Auge hatte.

4) In Fällen, wo beide Parteien ihre Kosten zu liquidiren haben, weil aus denselben eine Masse gebildet worden ist, pflegt sich in der Praxis ein Anstand nicht zu ergeben; sollte jedoch der Gegenanwalt sich weigern oder säumig sein, so kann nach Verlauf der in Art. 113 bestimmten Frist von drei Tagen das Urtheil ausgefertigt werden, ohne die betreffenden Kosten zu enthalten. Die Folge ist, daß vorläufig die Sache so betrachtet wird, als seien der Gegenpartei zur Anrechnung geeignete Kosten nicht entstanden, und daß die Kosten, welche durch eine erst später stattfindende Liquidirung veranlaßt werden, ihr zur Last bleiben.

Als solche verschuldete Kosten dürften unter Umständen sogar diejenigen, welche durch Versuch des Vollzuges der Kostenverurtheilung entstehen, zu betrachten sein; denn es kann die fleißige Partei nicht darunter leiden, daß ihr Gegner sie im Unklaren läßt und seine Pflicht versäumt. Vgl. Abg. I 152 (v. Weiß).

5) Die Taxe nimmt ein einzelner Richter vor, mit Vorbehalt, auf dem Wege des Einspruchs eine Entscheidung des Gerichtes zu erwirken.

In der Pfalz war es seither Uebung, einem bestimmten Gerichtsmitgliede die ganze Taxe zu übertragen, was den Vortheil hatte, Einheit in deren Handhabung zu bringen, jedoch den Nachtheil, daß dem taxirenden Richter die Prozesse oft unbekannt waren.

Unsere Prozeßordnung bestimmt als Regel, daß nur ein Richter, welcher beim Urtheile mitgewirkt hat, taxiren dürfe. Die einzige Ausnahme besteht bezüglich des Gerichtsvorstandes, welcher bei Verhinderung des Vorsitzenden eintritt, und, nach Laut des Gesetzes, gleich diesem die Wahl hat, selbst zu taxiren, oder einen Beisitzer zu beauftragen. Für den Gerichtsvorstand tritt selbstverständlich im Verhinderungsfalle dasjenige Gerichtsmitglied ein, welches ihn ersetzt. R. R. IV 14 (v. Weiß).

Um den Zweck einer stätigen, gleichmäßigen Taxe zu erreichen und häufige Einsprüche zu verhüten, möchte es rathsam sein, daß man sich über die Art und Weise der Handhabung der Taxe in zweifelhaften Punkten möglichst verständige.

6) Aufgabe des taxirenden Richters ist es, die Gebührenansätze nach Maßgabe der Gebührenordnung zu prüfen und zu berichtigen, Gebühren und Auslagen, welche im Sinne des Art. 106 Abs. 2 als überflüssig erscheinen, zu streichen, und in Fällen, wo die Kosten verschiedener Klagen oder Streitpunkte, z. B. von Haupt- und Widerklage, Haupt- und Gewährschaftsklage rc., auszuscheiden sind, zu bestimmen, welche Kosten zu jeder Klage gehören.

7) Die Einspruchsfrist von acht Tagen (Art. 114) läuft für alle Parteien, also auch für diejenige, welche die Taxe erwirkt hat (Abg. I 177 [Barth zu Art. 100]), von Zustellung des den Kostenbetrag enthaltenden Urtheils, oder des die Kosten festsetzenden Beschlusses des taxirenden Richters, an den Anwalt oder an die Partei selbst, falls diese nicht durch Anwalt vertreten sein sollte. Es ist Sache der in Verzug gesetzten Parteien, sich durch Einsichtnahme des auf der Gerichtschreiberei hinterlegten taxirten Kostenverzeichnisses (Art. 113 Abs. 3) zu vergewissern, ob und welche Beschwerden sie gegen die Taxe zu erheben haben.

Die Verhandlung und Entscheidung über den Einspruch erfolgt in öffentlicher Gerichtssitzung. Abg. I 153 (v. Weiß). Schriftliches Vorverfahren ist dabei ausgeschlossen; es werden daher (wie nach Art. 260 Ziff. 2) in der Sitzung nur einfache Anträge abgegeben.

b) Parteiprozeß.

8) In Frankreich wird die Liquidation der Kosten im Parteiprozesse ähnlich behandelt, wie im summarischen Anwaltsprozesse. Man findet es unbedenklich, beim Urtheilsspruche bloß allgemein in die Kosten zu verurtheilen und den Betrag der Kosten auf nachfolgende Liquidirung des Richters hin ins Urtheil einzustellen. Art. 27 Abs. 2 Code de proc. deutet z. B. auf eine nachträgliche Liquidirung hin. In Handelssachen pflegen, in Fällen, wo Anwälte als Bevollmächtigte auftreten, sogar förmliche Kostenverzeichnisse eingereicht zu werden.

Anders verfügt unsere Prozeßordnung.

Art. 115 sagt, es seien die Kosten bei der Verhandlung zu liquidiren und im Urtheile festzusetzen. Dies ist wohl nur so zu verstehen, daß die Kostenverurtheilung gleich jeder andern Verurtheilung bestimmt und unter Angabe der Summen ins Urtheil aufzunehmen und mit dem Urtheilssatze zu verlesen sei. Art. 277.

Wie schon oben (Nr. 2) erörtert wurde, ist eine solche Art der Liquidirung für das mündliche Verfahren nicht zweckmäßig, wirkt vielmehr sehr hemmend und eignet sich dieselbe am wenigsten für Handelsgerichte und Landgerichte, denn gerade bei diesen Gerichten ist eine sofortige und schnelle Urtheilsfällung wünschenswerth und vom Gesetze sogar ausdrücklich zur Vorschrift gemacht. Art. 514. Offenbar ist es mißlich, wenn bloß der Kostenliquidirung wegen ein Urtheil zum Spruche vertagt werden muß, was in Sachen, wo Zwischenbescheide ergangen sind, sich meistens kaum wird vermeiden lassen.

9) Sollte die Praxis eine andere, der Uebung des französischen Prozesses entsprechendere, Auslegung für den Art. 115 finden, so wäre dies erwünscht. Vielleicht ließe sich annehmen, daß der Gesetzgeber bloß verlange, es sollten die Parteien ihre Kosten bei der Verhandlung liquidiren, etwa soweit nöthig Kostenverzeichnisse vorlegen und begründen, und es habe sodann der Richter, ähnlich wie in Art. 113 Abs. 5, beim Eintragen ins Urtheilsbuch den Kostenbetrag aufzunehmen?

Art. 116. — **Wo das Gesetz vorschreibt, daß die Erhebung einer neuen Klage oder die Fortsetzung eines Verfahrens nicht eher statthaft sei, als bis der Gegenpartei die ihr bisher verursachten Kosten ersetzt sind, hat, wenn dieser Ersatz dadurch gehindert wird, daß die zu dessen Empfang berechtigte Partei die Festsetzung der Kosten verzögert oder deren Angabe verweigert, das Gericht hiezu auf einfache Vorstellung des Betheiligten eine angemessene Frist zu bestimmen, nach deren Ablauf die Erhebung der neuen Klage beziehungsweise die Fortsetzung des Verfahrens gestattet wird.**

G. A. d. K. d. A. II S. 286. 289. IV S. 87. — K. d. R. IV S. 15.

Dieser erst bei zweiter Lesung eingefügte Artikel soll, ähnlich wie Art. 27 Code de proc., Aushilfe geben für Fälle, wo die Erhebung einer neuen Klage oder die Fortsetzung des Verfahrens von einem Kostenersatze abhängt und die forderungsberechtigte Partei säumig ist, die Kosten festsetzen zu lassen oder von der erfolgten Festsetzung Kenntniß zu geben.

Er unterstellt eine nachträgliche Festsetzung und kann also, wenn man voraussetzt, daß im Parteiprozesse das Urtheil selbst immer schon die Liquidirung enthalte, wohl nur im Anwaltsprozesse Anwendung finden.

Fälle, wie sie das Gesetz im Auge hat, bieten die Artikel 303, 498 u. 588.

Art. 117. — **Die Gebühren der Advokaten und Rechtspraktikanten richten sich in Ermangelung eines wirksamen anderweitigen Uebereinkommens auch der eigenen Partei gegenüber nach der Gebührenordnung.**

In wie weit ein solches Uebereinkommen zulässig und wirksam ist, bestimmt die Advokatenordnung.

Art. 118. — **Der eigenen Partei gegenüber haben Anwälte, Beistände und Bevollmächtigte ihre Forderung für Gebühren und Auslagen auf dem Wege der Klage geltend zu machen.**

Im Anwaltsprozesse können die Anwälte ihre Forderungen für Gebühren und Auslagen auch dadurch beitreiben, daß sie dieselben auf Grund der Gebührenordnung gerichtlich feststellen lassen und hiefür einen Vollstreckungsbeschluß gegen ihre eigene Partei erwirken.

In diesem Falle finden die Bestimmungen der Art. 113 und 114 unter nachstehenden Abweichungen Anwendung:

1) **auf dem Kostenverzeichnisse hat der Anwalt die erhaltenen Kostenvorschüsse anzugeben und zu beantragen, daß sein Guthaben auf Grund der Gebührenordnung festgestellt und hiefür ein Vollstreckungsbeschluß gegen seine Partei erlassen werde;**
2) **der Gerichtsvorstand oder ein von ihm beauftragtes Gerichtsmitglied hat das Kostenverzeichniß zu prüfen, das Guthaben des Anwalts festzustellen und hiefür den beantragten Vollstreckungsbeschluß zu erlassen;**
3) **der Einspruch kann auch durch Gerichtsvollzieherakt erfolgen und die Einspruch erhebende Partei braucht keinen Anwalt aufzustellen;**
4) **über den Einspruch wird ohne schriftliches Vorverfahren verhandelt und entschieden.**

G. A. d. K. d. A. I S. 152—154. 163—165. 177. 178. 299. IV S. 24. 307—309.
K. d. R. I S. 248—254. IV S. 15. 16.

1) Während die Artikel 113—115 nur das Verhältniß unter den Parteien im Auge haben, regeln diese beiden Artikel das Verhältniß der Prozeßbevollmächtigten zu ihren Parteien.

Beide Verhältnisse sind getrennt zu halten, und es läßt sich nicht sagen, eine Taxe, welche nach Art. 113 zum Zwecke des Kostenersatzes durch die Gegenpartei erwirkt worden ist, müsse auch geeignet sein, die Grundlage für die Kostenforderung des Anwaltes an die eigne Partei zu bilden.

Nach dem Texte des Gesetzes, sowie nach den Verhandlungen kann hierüber nicht der mindeste Zweifel obwalten (s. insbes. Abg. I 177), wie es denn auch in der Natur der Sache begründet ist, da der eignen Partei gegenüber manche Gebühren und Auslagen gerechtfertigt sein können, welche der Gegenpartei gegenüber als überflüssig zu streichen sind, z. B. solche, welche durch besondere Weisungen der Partei oder deren Verschulden veranlaßt sind. So pflegte man in der Pfalz die Kosten, welche durch freiwilligen Wechsel des Anwaltes veranlaßt wurden, wohl der Partei, nicht aber auch der Gegenpartei gegenüber zu taxiren, und Gleiches verfügte der Tarif bezüglich der Gebühren des Anwalts für Beistand bei einer Expertise.

2) Was das Maß der Gebühren betrifft, welche Advokaten oder Rechtspraktikanten, sei es im Anwaltsprozesse, sei es im Parteiprozesse, der eignen Partei gegenüber verlangen dürfen, so bestimmt dies, so weit nicht ein wirksames Uebereinkommen vorliegt, die Gebührenordnung. In wie weit solche Uebereinkommen wirksam seien, insbesondere bei Anwaltsgebühren, wird die Advokatenordnung bestimmen.

Hat ein Advokat ohne giltiges Uebereinkommen mehr von der Partei bezogen, als ihm zukommt, so kann das Zuvielgezahlte als Nichtschuld zurückgefordert werden und tritt unter Umständen disciplinäre Ahndung ein.

3) Anwälte, Beistände und Bevollmächtigte, welche ihre Dienste leisteten, ohne Vorschuß empfangen zu haben, machen ihre Gebühren und Auslagen auf dem Wege der Klage geltend (Art. 118 Abs. 1), wobei bezüglich des Gerichtsstandes Art. 28 maßgebend ist.

Den Anwälten ist ausnahmsweise wegen ihrer Dienste im Anwaltsprozesse durch Art. 118 Abs. 2 u. 3 noch ein zweiter Weg eröffnet, welcher sie schneller, einfacher und mit weniger Kosten zum Ziele führen soll. Es ist ihnen nemlich gestattet, ihre Kosten sofort gerichtlich festsetzen und diese Taxe vollziehbar erklären zu lassen.

Das Gesetz spricht hier mit Recht nicht von einer vollstreckbaren Ausfertigung des Beschlusses, wie im Art. 113, sondern von einem Vollstreckungsbeschlusse, weil dort ein Urtheil vorliegt, zu dessen Ergänzung der Beschluß dient, während hier der Beschluß ein Urtheil ersetzen soll.

Indem es heißt, die Taxe sei auf Grund der Gebührenordnung festzustellen, ist genügend angedeutet, daß für Ansätze, welche bloß auf Uebereinkunft beruhen, dieser besondere Weg nicht gegeben sei.

4) Das Verfahren, welches der Anwalt in fraglichem Falle einzuschlagen hat, soll dasjenige sein, welches die Art. 113 u. 114 für die Taxe unter den Parteien bestimmen, mit verschiedenen Abänderungen, wie sie in Art. 118 Abs. 3 näher bezeichnet sind.

Dasselbe gestaltet sich zufolge dieser Combination ganz eigenthümlich.

Hervorzuheben ist:

1) Der auf das Kostenverzeichniß zu setzende Vollstreckungsbeschluß, welcher natürlich die Partei, gegen welche, und den Betrag, für welchen die Taxe vollstreckbar erklärt wird, zu bezeichnen hat, bleibt nach Art. 113 Abs. 3 hinterlegt und der Gerichtschreiber ertheilt auf Verlangen Ausfertigung.

2) Während Art. 113 großes Gewicht darauf legt, die Taxe nur einem Richter, welcher beim Urtheile mitgewirkt hat, anzuvertrauen, ist hier der Gerichtsvorstand damit betraut, welcher jeden beliebigen Richter beauftragen kann.

3) Gegen den Beschluß haben beide Theile das Recht des Einspruchs und zwar innerhalb der Frist von acht Tagen, welche für beide Theile erst vom Tage der Urtheilszustellung läuft, und ferner erfolgt der Einspruch beiderseits durch Zustellung eines die Beschwerden enthaltenden Aktes an den Gegner (Art. 114). Der Anwalt ist also, kraft Gesetzes, hier der Partei gleichgestellt, obgleich das Einspruchsverfahren eigentlich nur für letztere paßt.

Für die Partei erweitert sich die Frist nach Maßgabe des Art. 209.

4) Erhebt der Anwalt Einspruch, so wird er jedenfalls zugleich den Vollstreckungsbeschluß zustellen lassen müssen, falls dieses nicht bereits geschehen.

5) Da bestimmt ist, daß die Partei keinen Anwalt aufzustellen brauche, so darf sie auch ihre Sache in der Sitzung persönlich vertreten und ist überhaupt ihr gegenüber nach den Grundsätzen des Parteiprozesses zu verfahren (s. ursprüngl. Fassung Abg. I 163).

6) Gegen die Entscheidung des Gerichts sind die gewöhnlichen Rechtsmittel zulässig, so daß also die Schlußworte von Art. 114 hier nicht gelten, wie sie denn schon deßhalb nicht passen, weil der Ausschluß selbständiger Rechtsmittel hier gleichbedeutend wäre mit dem Ausschlusse aller Rechtsmittel. Vgl. R. R. IV 308 (v. Bomhard).

Ueberblickt man dieses Verfahren, so möchte man denken, es sei auf diesem den Anwälten eröffneten Seitenwege mit seinen vielen Windungen und Unebenheiten nicht viel gewonnen; allein dennoch wird es sich wahrscheinlich praktisch bewähren, und zwar deßhalb, weil Einsprüche höchst selten vorkommen werden.

5) Obgleich, wie bemerkt, Taxe für die Gegenpartei und Taxe für die eigne Partei verschiedene Dinge sind, so steht doch nichts im Wege, beide zu vereinigen, wenn nur den beiderseitigen Vorschriften genügt ist. Es kann der Richter die Kosten der Partei gegenüber festsetzen und Vollstreckungsbeschluß erlassen, sodann aber erklären, ob alle oder welche dieser Kosten der Gegenpartei gegenüber in Anrechnung zu kommen haben.

Entschädigungen.

Art. 119. — Wird von einer Partei der Ersatz eines ihr außer den Prozeßkosten durch einen Rechtsstreit, eine Vollstreckung oder den Vollzug einer Vorsichtsverfügung verursachten weitern Schadens beansprucht, so hat das mit der Sache befaßte Gericht, beziehungsweise das Vollstreckungsgericht, auch hierüber zu erkennen.

Erhellt der Schaden aus den vorliegenden Umständen oder ist derselbe genugsam bescheinigt, so kann das Gericht den Betrag des zu leistenden Ersatzes sofort nach freiem Ermessen festsetzen.

Erforderlichen Falls ist der Entschädigungsanspruch zur nachträglichen besonderen Liquidation zu verweisen.

G. A. d. K. d. A. I S. 154. 169. 178. IV S. 24. — K. d. R. I S. 254 IV S. 16.

1) Das Gesetz spricht hier von dem außer den Prozeßkosten noch weiter entstandenen Schaden. Ein solcher Schaden muß wohl bestimmt und unmittelbar aus dem Prozesse 2c. hervorgehen, und die Fälle werden nicht häufig sein, wo aus diesem Grunde eine Entschädigung

zuzusprechen sein wird. Ich möchte behaupten, daß der ganze Artikel besser weggeblieben wäre, weil er nur zu derartigen Ansprüchen provozirt und im Grunde überflüssig ist. Das Recht selbst folgt aus den Grundsätzen des Civilrechts und Art. 33 Abs. 3, die Zuständigkeit gleichfalls aus diesem Artikel, das Verfahren endlich aus Art. 330 und 896, sowie den allgemeinen Prinzipien der Beweisführung.

2) Der Abs. 2 dieses Artikels gibt dem Richter volle Freiheit, nach den Umständen zu würdigen, ob und welcher Schaden anzunehmen sei. Es scheint zwar, als wolle das Gesetz nur die Schätzung eines gegebenen Schadens dem richterlichen Ermessen überlassen, allein wer ganz beliebig bestimmen darf, wie hoch der Schaden sei, darf offenbar auch erklären, daß ein Schaden gar nicht vorliege. Es liegt dies auch schon im Geiste des neuen Beweisverfahrens.

3) Bei Vorsichtsverfügungen ist als das „mit der Sache" befaßte Gericht nicht dasjenige zu betrachten, welches diese Verfügung erlassen hat, sondern dasjenige, welches im Falle eines Einwandes über deren Bestand zu erkennen hat. Abg. IV 24 (v. Weiß und v. Neumayr) — R. R. IV 16 (v. Bomhard).

Sicherheitsleistung.

Art. 120. — **Der als Kläger auftretende Ausländer muß vorbehaltlich besonderer Staatsverträge dem inländischen Beklagten auf dessen Verlangen für die Prozeßkosten Sicherheit leisten, ausgenommen:**

1) **wenn die Klage in Folge einer Aufforderungsklage gestellt wurde;**
2) **wenn die Klage die Aufhebung einer gegen den Kläger ergangenen Vorsichtsverfügung oder eines gegen ihn auf Grund einer vollstreckbaren Urkunde eingeleiteten Vollstreckungsverfahrens zum Gegenstande hat;**
3) **bei Klagen aus einem im Hypothekenbuche eingetragenen oder auf inländische öffentliche Urkunden gestützten Anspruche;**
4) **bei Widerklagen;**
5) **in Handels- und Wechselsachen, sowie bei Klagen aus kaufmännischen Anweisungen;**
6) **bei Liquidationen im Gantverfahren.**

Die Sicherheitsleistung kann im ersten Rechtszuge nur für die Kosten dieses Rechtszugs gefordert werden. In einem höhern Rechtszuge kann die Sicherheitsleistung für die Kosten desselben nur gefordert werden, wenn das Rechtsmittel von dem Kläger eingelegt worden ist, dann aber ohne Unterschied, ob sie in einem frühern Rechtszuge gefordert werden konnte und ob sie gefordert wurde oder nicht.

Art. 121. — **Zeigt sich im Laufe des Rechtszugs, daß die geleistete Sicherheit nicht hinreicht, oder verliert der Kläger erst im Laufe des Rechtszugs seine Eigenschaft als Inländer, so kann nachträglich die Ergänzung beziehungsweise Bestellung der Sicherheit verlangt werden.**

Art. 122. — **Der Antrag auf Sicherheitsleistung ist auf eine bestimmte Summe zu richten. Soweit sich die Parteien über den Betrag der zu leistenden Sicherheit und über die Frist zur Sicherheitsleistung nicht vereinigen, hat das Gericht Beides nach freiem Ermessen festzusetzen.**

Art. 123. — **Die Sicherheit muß in Ermangelung anderweitiger Uebereinkunft durch gerichtliche Hinterlegung des Betrags in baarem Gelde, in bayerischen Staatspapieren oder in sonstigen durch Verordnung für zulässig erklärten Werthpapieren geleistet werden. Der Werth der Papiere ist nach dem Tagskurse zu berechnen.**

Wird die Sicherheit geleistet, so ist der Gegenpartei die über die Hinterlegung ausgestellte Bescheinigung zustellen zu lassen.

Wird die Sicherheit in der dafür bestimmten Frist nicht geleistet, so ist auf Antrag des Beklagten der Kläger als von der Klage beziehungsweise dem Rechtsmittel abstehend zu erachten und zur Erstattung der verursachten Prozeßkosten zu verurtheilen.

Art. 124. — **Gegen die bezüglich der Sicherheitsleistung für die Prozeßkosten ergehenden Entscheidungen ist außer dem Falle des Art. 123 Abs. 3 ein selbständiges Rechtsmittel nicht zulässig.**

G. A. d. K. d. A. I S. 154—160. 165—169. 178. 179. 299. IV S. 25. 309.
K. d. R. I S. 254—259. IV S. 16. 17.

1) Die cautio pro expensis, von welcher diese fünf Artikel handeln, bestand in ähnlicher Weise sowohl diesseits, als in der Pfalz. Prozeß-Novelle von 1819 § 8 — Code de proc. Art. 166 — Code civil Art. 16.

Ihr Zweck ist, dem Inländer, welcher von

einem Ausländer mit Klage angegriffen ist, den Rückersatz der Prozeßkosten zu sichern. Sie hat einzig und allein diese Kosten zum Gegenstande, nicht aber einen sonstigen Schaden im Sinne des Art. 119.

a) Fälle der Kostencaution.

2) Der Kläger muß Ausländer, der Beklagte Inländer sein; für den Fall, wo Ausländer gegen Ausländer klagt, tritt daher die Cautionspflicht nicht ein, und wenn beklagte Streitgenossen theilweise Ausländer, theilweise Inländer sind, so besteht sie nur den letzteren gegenüber. Befinden sich umgekehrt unter klagenden Streitgenossen zum Theile Ausländer, so sind nur diese verpflichtet, Sicherheit zu leisten, und zwar in dem Maße, wie sie im Falle des Unterliegens nach Art. 108 zum Kostenersatze verpflichtet wären.

Wenn das Gesetz von Ausländern und Inländern spricht, so meint es bloß die Staatsangehörigkeit, und ist also weder auf Wohnsitz noch auf Güterbesitz Rücksicht zu nehmen.

Maßgebend ist ferner nur die Thatsache der Klagerhebung, und es kann sich daher der Beklagte nicht darauf berufen, daß das Klagrecht ursprünglich einem Ausländer zustand und erst durch Erbgang, Cession &c. auf den klagenden Inländer überging. Bl. f. R. XVII 12. Anderseits wird es auch ohne Belang sein, wenn im Laufe des Rechtsstreites der Ausländer durch Vertrag sein Recht an einen Inländer überträgt.

3) Verliert der Kläger im Laufe des Rechtsstreites die Eigenschaft eines Inländers, so kann nach Art. 121 nachträglich die Cautionsleistung begehrt werden. Das Nemliche wird, bei vollkommener Gleichheit des Grundes, auch der Fall sein, wenn an Stelle des Klägers ausländische Erben treten.

Es fragt sich, ob hieraus gefolgert werden könne, daß, wenn umgekehrt der Ausländer bayerischer Unterthan wird, oder ein Inländer ihn beerbt, die Cautionspflicht nachträglich wegfalle? Außer Zweifel möchte sein, daß das Recht, Sicherstellung zu erlangen, wegfällt; allein ich würde auch annehmen, daß die Freigabe einer bereits gestellten Caution begehrt werden könne.

4) Nur derjenige tritt im Sinne des Gesetzes als Kläger auf, welcher selbständig angreift, also ohne Zweifel der Hauptintervenient, der Dritte, welcher Widerspruch erhebt gegen eine Beschlagnahme (Art. 870), und der Gewährschaftskläger, nicht aber der Streitgenosse, welcher vom Beklagten selbst oder auf dessen Begehren beigeladen wird (Art. 65).

Was den Nebenintervenienten betrifft, so wurde der Vorschlag, ihn für kautionspflichtig zu erklären, abgewiesen, jedoch anderseits auch nicht bestimmt ausgesprochen, daß er es nicht sei. Dennoch möchte Letzteres als Ansicht des Gesetzgebers zu betrachten sein. Vgl. Vortrag des Referenten v. Neumayr zu Art. 104 des Entw. — Abg. I 155 (v. Neumayr).

Ueberhaupt ist, da es sich um eine Ausnahmsbestimmung handelt, sowie nach dem Willen des Gesetzgebers, möglichst einschränkende Auslegung geboten. Vortrag des Ref. v. Neumayr a. a. O.

5) Von der Regel, daß ausländische Kläger Sicherheit für Prozeßkosten zu leisten haben, macht das Gesetz verschiedene Ausnahmen und zwar nach vier Gesichtspunkten, nemlich 1) für Fälle, wo der Angriff des Beklagten selbst oder aber eine von ihm ausgegangene Aufforderung die Klage veranlaßt hat (Ziff. 1, 2 u. 4), 2) für Fälle, wo eine starke Vermuthung für die Richtigkeit des Klaganspruchs gegeben ist (Ziff. 3), 3) für Handelssachen (Ziff. 5), weil das Interesse des Handelsverkehres eine feindselige Behandlung der Ausländer nicht gestattet, und 4) für die Gant (Ziff. 6), weil hier das Gesetz selbst ein Auftreten aller Gläubiger verlangt.

6) Klagen aus einem im Hypothekenbuche eingetragenen Anspruche.

Was das diesseitige Recht betrifft, so ist außer Zweifel, daß die dingliche Hypothekenklage hierher gehört, mag sie gegen den Schuldner, mag sie gegen den dritten Besitzer gerichtet sein.

Ist aber auch die persönliche Klage gegen den Schuldner gemeint?

Für Bejahung dieser Frage sprechen gewichtige Gründe — vor Allem der Wortlaut des Gesetzes, dann aber der Umstand, daß Hypothekareinträge die Einwilligung oder Beiladung des Schuldners voraussetzen, also, wenn auch nicht immer Beweis, doch starke Vermuthung für das Bestehen der Schuld gegeben ist.

Dennoch möchte ich annehmen, es sei beim Hypothekareintrage ebenso zu halten, wie bei der öffentlichen Urkunde, es müsse sich also der Anspruch auf diesen Eintrag stützen, und habe der Gesetzgeber nicht die Absicht gehabt, eine bloß persönliche Klage, welche der Gläubiger gegen den nicht mehr im Besitze des Hypothekenobjektes befindlichen Schuldner oder dessen Erben anstellt und für welche der Eintrag im Hypothekenbuche gleichgiltig ist, von der Cautionspflicht auszunehmen. Fragliche Bestimmung wurde nemlich nur zur Hebung des Realkredits gegeben (Abg. I 156 [Barth], im Hinblicke auf die eigenthümlichen

Wirkungen eines Hypothekareintrages, und zwar namentlich auf die § 25 und § 26 des Hypothekengesetzes, welche den redlichen Erwerber gegen jede Anfechtung der Forderung sicherstellen.

Tritt man dieser Ansicht bei, so findet die Anwendung dieser Bestimmung auf die Pfalz keinen Anstand; sie ist gegenstandslos. Ist man jedoch anderer Meinung, so erheben sich große Schwierigkeiten.

In der Pfalz findet nemlich der Hypothekareintrag auf einseitiges Begehren des Gläubigers statt, und wenn auch in der Regel Vorlage eines Titels verlangt wird, so kann dieser doch in manchen Fällen, z. B. beim Kaufprivilege, nur eine gewöhnliche Privaturkunde sein; bei Legalhypotheken aber bedarf es nicht einmal der Vorlage eines Titels. Der Eintrag an sich ist hier offenbar nicht geeignet, eine Vermuthung für die Richtigkeit der Forderung zu begründen, und die Gründe des Gesetzes fallen also vollständig hinweg.

Nichtsdestoweniger wird es nicht angehen, zu trennen, und diesseits nach dem Wortlaute, jenseits aber nach dem Geiste des Gesetzes sich zu richten, denn das Gesetz spricht allgemein.

Nur was die Legalhypotheken betrifft, dürfte eine Ausnahme zu machen sein. Abgesehen davon, daß solche Hypotheken auch ohne Eintrag bestehen, läßt der Eintrag, wenn er stattfindet, den Anspruch völlig unbestimmt und sagt im Grunde nichts weiter, als daß, so weit Ansprüche der bezeichneten Art bestehen sollten, das Hypothekarrecht für dieselbe beansprucht werde. Hier verschwindet nicht nur der Geist des Gesetzes ganz spurlos, sondern paßt auch nicht mehr der Wortlaut.

Fälle, wo Ausländer Ansprüche, für welche Legalhypotheke besteht, geltend machen, können leicht vorkommen, z. B. wenn ein Mündel Ausländer wird, wenn ausländische Erben, Cessionare, subrogirte Gläubiger von Ehefrauen oder Mündeln auftreten.

7) Klagen aus einem auf öffentliche Urkunden gestützten Anspruche.

Es ist klar, daß, falls eine Urkunde vorgelegt wird, welche ihrer äußeren Erscheinung nach eine formgerechte inländische öffentliche Urkunde ist, und welche im Allgemeinen geeignet erscheint, den erhobenen Anspruch zu begründen, die Pflicht zur Cautionsleistung wegfällt und es ohne Belang erscheint, daß etwa der Anspruch aus Gründen, welche nicht aus der Urkunde zu ersehen sind, angefochten werde, z. B. wegen Irrthums, Betrugs ꝛc., oder wegen Tilgung der Forderung durch Zahlung, Verzicht ꝛc. Sogar wenn diese Einwände mit öffentlichen Urkunden belegt sind, wird keine Ausnahme zu machen sein, da es hiezu einer ausdrücklichen Verfügung des Gesetzes bedürfte.

Fraglich kann aber sein, ob der Richter sich mit der Erklärung des Klägers, er stütze seinen Anspruch auf die öffentliche Urkunde, begnügen müsse, oder ob er prüfen dürfe, in wie ferne deren Inhalt geeignet sei, diesen Anspruch zu begründen.

Dem Wortlaute nach möchte man Ersteres annehmen, dem Geiste nach aber dürfte Letzteres das Richtige sein. Eine Stütze, welche sich als morsch erweist und bei erster Berührung zusammenbricht, ist keine. Wenn daher z. B. nach Inhalt der Urkunde die Schuld noch nicht fällig ist, so kann sie für sich nicht zur Begründung der Klage dienen, es muß vielmehr das Wegfallen der Frist durch andere Umstände (Vermögensverfall, Verzicht ꝛc.) erwiesen werden. Ebenso würde eine Urkunde nicht geeignet sein, einen Anspruch zu begründen, wenn sie so offenbar unklar wäre, daß nur mit Hilfe eines Interpretationsbeweises die klägerische Auslegung angenommen werden könnte.

Uebrigens bedingt es die Natur des in Frage stehenden Zwischenstreits, daß das Gericht sich auf eine möglichst summarische Prüfung beschränke.

Es kann sich weiter fragen, ob nur der Anspruch für sich auf eine solche Urkunde sich stützen müsse, oder ob auch zur Sachlegitimation des Klägers eine solche erfordert werde. Erwägt man, daß selbst zur Einleitung eines Vollstreckungsverfahrens, für welche gleichfalls eine Cautionspflicht nicht besteht, derartige Urkunden nicht verlangt werden (Art. 821 Abs. 2 und Art. 835), so möchte diese Frage zu verneinen sein.

8) Da das Gesetz alle Handelssachen ausnimmt, so sind auch solche gemeint, welche nach Art. 7 Abs. 2 vor die Landgerichte oder Bezirksgerichte gehören, oder welche nach Art. 38 durch Vereinbarung vor diese Gerichte gebracht worden sind.

9) Im Falle der Häufung von Ansprüchen, welche unter die Regel, und von Ansprüchen, welche unter die Ausnahmen fallen, z B. wenn einzelne Forderungen durch inländische öffentliche Urkunden erwiesen sind, andere nicht, oder wenn Handelsforderungen mit gewöhnlichen Forderungen eingeklagt werden, hat der Richter bei Festsetzung der Cautionssumme geeignete Rücksicht zu nehmen.

10) Nach dem Systeme der Prozeßordnung sind die Kosten eines jeden Rechtszuges für sich allein ins Auge zu fassen, und gelten sogar, bezüglich der Voraussetzungen der Cautionspflicht,

in den höheren Rechtszügen ganz andere Grundsätze, als im ersten.

Auch dort beschränkt sich allerdings die Cautionspflicht auf den Kläger und trifft denselben, wenn er das Rechtsmittel eingelegt hat; allein der Umstand, daß bei dieser Sachlage der Beklagte bereits eine richterliche Entscheidung für sich hat, rechtfertigt es, daß nunmehr der Kläger unbedingt zur Cautionsleistung verpflichtet ist, ohne Rücksicht darauf, ob in den früheren Instanzen Caution verlangt war oder verlangt werden konnte. In den höheren Rechtszügen findet also auch in Handels- und Wechselsachen Cautionsleistung statt.

Es dürfte wohl anzunehmen sein, daß das Gesetz den Kläger nur in so fern dieser unbedingten Cautionspflicht unterwerfen wollte, als er es war, welcher die Sache in die höhere Instanz gebracht hat, daß also der bloße Anschluß an eine vorausgehende Berufung des Beklagten ohne Bedeutung ist. Jedenfalls müßte dies in Fällen anzunehmen sein, wo der Anschluß keine Selbständigkeit hat. Art. 703.

11) Bei den Worten: „In einem höheren Rechtszuge" hatte das Gesetz nur die Berufung und Nichtigkeitsbeschwerde im Auge, wie dies, abgesehen vom Wortlaute, auch aus den Verhandlungen hervorgeht. Abg. I 166, 167 (v. Neumayr).

Obgleich daher die Gründe des Gesetzes vollkommen auch auf das Rechtsmittel der Wiederaufnahme des Verfahrens passen, werden doch hier die gewöhnlichen Grundsätze zur Anwendung kommen müssen.

Bildet die Wiederaufnahme nur einen Zwischenstreit, so gehören ihre Kosten, gleich denjenigen des Einspruches, zum betreffenden Rechtsstreite; tritt sie aber als selbständige Klage auf, so ist sie gleich jeder andern Klage zu behandeln und kann daher unter Umständen auch der ursprüngliche Beklagte cautionspflichtig sein.

12) Schließlich ist zu erwähnen, daß die Grundsätze des französischen Rechts über die Cautionspflicht des ausländischen Civilklägers im Strafverfahren durch diese bloß den Civilprozeß betreffenden Verfügungen nicht berührt werden.

b) Verfahren.

13) Der Beklagte, welcher Caution begehrt, erhebt hiermit eine Einrede im Sinne des Art. 184, welche also, bei Strafe des Ausschlusses, im ersten motivirten Antrage beziehungsweise in der ersten Verhandlung vorzubringen ist. Sie kann mit der Hauptsache und andern Einreden verbunden, oder für sich allein vorgeschützt werden (Art. 185), Letzteres jedoch nur unter Erfüllung der Vorschrift des Art. 232.

Das Begehren ist auf eine bestimmte Summe zu richten (Art. 122).

Fügt sich der Kläger, so ist richterliche Entscheidung nicht nöthig (Art. 122), vielmehr genügt es, daß derselbe dies dem Gegner erkläre, sofort oder binnen etwa verabredeter Frist die Cautionssumme nach Art. 123 hinterlege und den Hinterlegungsschein zustellen lasse.

Bestreitet der Kläger seine Verpflichtung oder die Höhe der Summe, so ist der Zwischenpunkt in die Sitzung zu bringen, und zwar, wenn nicht abgekürztes Verfahren eintritt (Art. 259, 260), auf gewöhnlichem Wege, wobei jedoch der Regel nach die Verhandlung sofort nach Hinterlegung der Anträge stattfindet (Art. 241 Abs. 7). Zweckmäßig wäre es gewesen, hier immer abgekürztes Verfahren eintreten zu lassen.

14) Bestreitet der Kläger, Ausländer zu sein, so muß Beklagter Beweis führen, jedoch liegt es im Geiste des Gesetzes, bei solch untergeordneten, den Grund der Sache nicht berührenden Vorfragen strenge Beweise nicht zu verlangen, wie denn schon die Ger.-O. Cap. VIII § 5 vorschreibt: „man solle das punctum cautionis allezeit nur summarie instruiren." Mir sind in der Praxis viele Fälle vorgekommen, wo sich Streit erhob, ob Kläger als Ausländer zu behandeln seien, oder genügende Garantie durch Immobiliarbesitz böten (Art. 167 C. de pr.), allein nie wurde Beweis auferlegt, vielmehr immer nach Bescheinigungen oder sonstigen aus der Verhandlung sich ergebenden Anhaltspunkten entschieden.

15) Die Cautionssumme wird vom Richter nach freiem Ermessen bestimmt; derselbe hat hiebei den muthmaßlichen Umfang des Rechtsstreites, insbesondere die in Aussicht stehenden Beweise in Erwägung zu ziehen, jedenfalls aber nur denjenigen Theil der Kosten zu berücksichtigen, für welchen der Ausländer ersatzpflichtig werden kann.

Im Zweifel wird er die Summe nicht zu hoch greifen, da ja Ergänzung stattfinden kann (Art. 121). Eine solche wird z. B. beanzeigt sein, wenn der Kläger, welcher ursprünglich nur als Streitgenosse in Betracht kam, später den Rechtsstreit allein fortführt.

Indem der Richter die Cautionsleistung auferlegt, setzt er für dieselbe zugleich eine Frist fest, welche nach Maßgabe der Verhältnisse, in der Regel mit Rücksicht auf die Entfernung des Wohnsitzes der Partei zu bestimmen ist.

16) Die gesetzliche Art der Cautionsleistung ist bloß die Hinterlegung von Geld oder Werthpapieren (Art. 123 Abs. 1), jedoch kann

sie zufolge Uebereinkunft auch in sonstiger Weise stattfinden. In der Pfalz pflegen die Anwälte die Sache in der Art abzumachen, daß der Anwalt der cautionspflichtigen Partei, nachdem er selbst sich durch Vorschuß oder in sonstiger Weise gesichert, die Selbsthaftung übernimmt.

Der Hinterlegungsschein ist dem Gegner zuzustellen, jedoch sagt das Gesetz nicht, es müsse dies innerhalb der zur Cautionsleistung gesetzten Frist geschehen; es kann daher aus einer Versäumung der Zustellung nicht die Verwirkung der Frist, sondern nur die Haftung für verursachte Kosten gefolgert werden.

17) Leistet der Kläger die Sicherheit nicht, so hat der Beklagte die Wahl, 1) den Rechtsstreit dennoch fortzusetzen mit Verzicht auf die Caution, oder 2) sich unthätig zu verhalten und jeden Versuch des Klägers zur Fortsetzung des Rechtsstreits zurückzuweisen, oder endlich 3) zu beantragen, daß der Kläger als von der Klage oder dem Rechtsmittel abstehend erklärt und in die Kosten verurtheilt werde.

So lange ein solcher Antrag nicht zugestellt ist, darf der Kläger, trotz Ablaufs der Frist, das Versäumte nachholen; ist jedoch die Zustellung erfolgt, so hat der Beklagte ein erworbenes Recht, den Abstand erklären zu lassen (Art. 215 Abs. 2), auf welches er selbstverständlich auch wieder verzichten kann. Abg. I 275.

Die Fiktion des Abstandes, wie sie als Folge einer Versäumung eintritt, hat vollständig die Wirkungen, welche dem freiwillig erklärten Abstande nach Art. 498 zukommen.

14) In Art. 124 ist verfügt, daß selbständige Rechtsmittel gegen die Entscheidungen über Cautionsleistung nicht zulässig seien; hieraus folgt, daß nichts im Wege stehe, ein verworfenes Cautionsbegehren bei Gelegenheit der Berufung gegen das Endurtheil, zur Geltung zu bringen.

Ein solches im Berufungswege vorgebrachtes Cautionsbegehren ist ein ganz anderes, als dasjenige, von welchem Art. 120 Abs. 2 spricht.

Dort handelt es sich um einen Einwand, welcher, die Klage unberührt lassend, sich bloß gegen das Rechtsmittel richtet, und wird begehrt, es solle die Verfolgung der Berufung verwehrt sein, bis Sicherheit wegen der Kosten der zweiten Instanz geleistet sei; hier dagegen wird begehrt, es möge das Appellationsgericht erkennen, wie der erste Richter hätte erkennen sollen, d. h. daß Caution wegen der Kosten erster Instanz zu leisten sei, widrigenfalls Kläger als von der Klage abstehend betrachtet werde. In diesem Falle kann daher das Cautionsbegehren auch vorkommen, wenn Beklagter die Berufung ergriffen hat.

Uebrigens ist zu bemerken, daß es gegenstandslos wird, über die Cautionsleistung wegen der Kosten erster Instanz zu erkennen, falls sofort endgiltig über die Kosten entschieden werden kann.

Art. 125. — **Wird im Falle der Anstellung einer Widerklage über die Hauptklage früher als über die Widerklage entschieden oder erfolgt eine Verurtheilung unter Vorbehalt einer Nachklage, so kann das Gericht bei vorliegender genügender Bescheinigung der Wider- oder Nachklage zugleich verfügen, daß der Vollzug des Urtheils nur gegen Leistung einer Sicherheit stattfinden dürfe. Das Gericht bestimmt in diesem Falle den Betrag der zu leistenden Sicherheit, welcher jedoch den zuerkannten Werth nicht übersteigen darf.**

Handelt es sich um eine Nachklage, so ist zugleich eine Frist für die Verfolgung derselben unter dem Rechtsnachtheile der Annahme des Verzichts auf die Sicherheitsleistung festzusetzen.

Art. 126. — **Die in Art. 125 bezeichnete Sicherheitsleistung kann geschehen:**

1) durch Hinterlegung der festgesetzten Summe in der in Art. 123 Abs. 1 bezeichneten Weise;

2) durch Hinterlegung eines sonstigen angemessenen Faustpfands;

3) durch Hypothekstellung auf inländische Liegenschaften;

4) durch Stellung eines vermöglichen, leicht zu belangenden Bürgen;

5) dadurch, daß die obsiegende Partei dem Wider- oder Nachkläger gestattet, den hiezu erforderlichen Theil seiner im Haupt- oder Vorprozesse festgestellten Schuld gerichtlich zu hinterlegen.

Art. 127. — **Macht der zur Sicherheitsleistung Verpflichtete von der Bestimmung des Art. 126 Ziff. 5 Gebrauch, so hat er seine desfallsige Erklärung, soferne sie nicht sofort bei Verkündung des betreffenden Urtheils abgegeben und im Urtheilsbuche beurkundet worden ist, der Gegenpartei zustellen zu lassen.**

Wird die Sicherheit durch Hinterlegung der erforderlichen Summe (Art. 123 Abs. 1)

geleistet, so ist der Gegenpartei die über die Hinterlegung ausgefertigte Bescheinigung zustellen zu lassen, worauf ein weiteres Verfahren nicht stattfindet.

In jedem andern Falle hat der zur Sicherheitsleistung Verpflichtete der Gegenpartei seine Erklärung darüber, wie er die Sicherheit leisten wolle, unter dem Anerbieten der Mittheilung der Nachweise über die Zulänglichkeit der angebotenen Sicherheitsmittel zustellen zu lassen.

Mit dieser Erklärung ist die Vorladung in eine Sitzung, welche erforderlichen Falls durch den Gerichts- beziehungsweise den Senatsvorstand auf Ersuchen bestimmt wird, zu verbinden, damit in dieser, falls die Gegenpartei sich nicht vorher mit dem Anerbieten zufrieden erklärt, ohne weiteres Vorverfahren über die Zulänglichkeit der angebotenen Sicherheitsmittel entschieden werde.

Das Gericht kann die Beibringung weiterer Nachweise anordnen.

Art. 128. — Wird die Stellung eines Bürgen zugelassen, so hat sich dieser in einer Notariatsurkunde über die einzugehende Verpflichtung zu erklären.

Einem solchen Bürgen steht weder die Rechtswohlthat der Vorausklagung noch beim Vorhandensein mehrerer Bürgen die Rechtswohlthat der Theilung zu.

Art. 129. — Gegen die gemäß Art. 125 und 127 über den Anspruch auf Sicherheitsleistung und über Zulänglichkeit der angebotenen Mittel ergangenen Urtheile sind selbständige Rechtsmittel zulässig.

Ist die als zulänglich erkannte Sicherheit geleistet, so wird durch Einspruch oder Berufung gegen die betreffende Entscheidung die einstweilige Vollstreckung des auf die Haupt- oder Vorklage erfolgten Urtheils nicht ausgeschlossen.

Art. 130. — Die Bestimmungen der Art. 125 — 129 finden auch auf andere Fälle Anwendung, in welchen wegen Wiedererstattung eines Streit- oder Exekutions-Gegenstands oder für den durch eine Vollstreckung oder den Vollzug einer Vorsichtsverfügung verursachten Schaden Sicherheit zu leisten ist.

G. A. der K. d. A. I S. 158—160. 166—169. 179. 180. 209. IV S. 25.
K. d. R. I S. 259—265. IV S. 16.

1) Nachdem die vorausgehenden Bestimmungen sich bloß mit der Kostenkaution beschäftigten, haben diese sechs Artikel die übrigen im Civilprozesse vorkommenden Sicherheitsleistungen zum Gegenstande. Zunächst spricht das Gesetz zwar nur von zwei besonderen, die Nachklage und die Widerklage betreffenden, Fällen; allein die für diese beiden Fälle gegebenen Bestimmungen werden zuletzt durch Art. 130 auf sonstige Sicherheitsleistungen ausgedehnt, und gerade diese letzteren sind es, welche ihnen einen größere praktische Bedeutung geben.

a) Fälle der Sicherheitsleistung.

2) Unter „Nachklagen" verstand man bis jetzt nur solche Klagen, vermittelst deren Punkte, über welche in der Vorklage, nach der Natur der besonderen Prozeßart, nicht entschieden werden konnte, zum Austrage gebracht wurden. Sie konnten also im ordentlichen Verfahren nicht vorkommen, sondern nur im Exekutiv- und Wechsel-Prozesse. Insbesondere konnte in Fällen, wo das Gericht, unter Abweisung unstatthafter Compensationseinreden oder Widerklagen, Gegenansprüche zum besonderen Austrag verwiesen hatte, die spätere Einklagung solcher Ansprüche nicht unter den Gesichtspunkt einer Nachklage gebracht werden. Siehe hierüber Seuff. Comm. Bd. II S. 403 — Bl. f. R. Bd. I S. 252.

Die Erklärung, welche Abg. I S. 158 gegeben wird, leidet daher an Unbestimmtheit, und es läßt sich nicht bezweifeln, daß der Gesetzgeber, wenn er in Art. 125 vom „Vorbehalte einer Nachklage" spricht, nur eine Nachklage im Sinne des früheren Rechtes meinte. Mag auch jetzt eine Nachklage dieser Art keine besondere Bedeutung mehr haben, weil der Executivprozeß glücklich beseitigt und der Wechselprozeß wesentlich geändert worden ist, so lag die Sache doch anders nach dem Entwurfe, aus welchem diese Bestimmung herrührt, indem dort der Executivprozeß in alter Weise beibehalten war (Art. 620 ff.) und im Wechselprozesse Einreden, welche nicht mit Urkunden belegt waren, keine Beachtung finden sollten.

3) Was die Widerklagen betrifft, so genügt es, daß sie den Anforderungen des Art. 31 entsprechen, d. h. daß gleichzeitige Verhandlung am nemlichen Gerichte statthaft sei; ob sie wirklich stattfinde oder ob das Gericht aus Gründen der Zweckmäßigkeit getrennte Verhandlung verfügt (Art. 157), erscheint gleichgiltig. Hannov. Verhdl. S. 958.

4) Die „vorliegende genügende Be-

scheinigung" des Art. 125 bezieht sich auf die thatsächliche und rechtliche Begründung des Anspruchs, welcher mit Widerklage oder Nachklage verfolgt wird, nicht etwa auf die Thatsache der Klagserhebung, denn diese wäre bei der ersten Klage selbstverständlich, bei der letzten aber nicht möglich.

Zur Bescheinigung ist nicht gerade ein Schriftstück nothwendig, vielmehr genügen alle Umstände, welche Wahrscheinlichkeit begründen (Abg. II 168 [Barth]). Das Gesetz gibt also dem Richter hier die Weisung, vorsichtig zu verfahren, und nur dann eine Auflage zu machen, wenn er guten Grund hat, anzunehmen, es möchten die Gegenansprüche oder Einreden auch begründet sein.

Obgleich übrigens solche Bescheinigung gegeben ist, kann dennoch der Richter von Auflage einer Sicherheitsleistüng Umgang nehmen, wenn sonstige Gründe ihn dazu bestimmen.

5) Daß diese Auflage von Amtswegen gemacht werden dürfe, kann um so weniger zweifelhaft sein, als der Vorschlag, einen Parteiantrag zu verlangen, gerade auf Grund der Erwägung, daß in manchen Fällen amtliche Verfügung zweckmäßig sein möge, verworfen worden ist. Abg. I 169 (v. Weiß).

Sie ist im verurtheilenden Erkenntnisse selbst auszusprechen, und zugleich ist der Betrag zu bestimmen, welcher den zuerkannten Werth nicht übersteigen soll, sich also nicht etwa auf Entschädigungen wegen des Vollzugs erstrecken darf.

6) Nach Art. 130 finden die Art. 125—129 auch Anwendung in sonstigen Fällen, wo wegen Wiedererstattung eines Streit- oder Exekutions-Gegenstandes oder für den durch Vollstreckungen oder Vorsichtsverfügungen verursachten Schaden Sicherheit zu leisten ist, d. h. in allen Fällen, wo die Prozeßordnung Sicherheitsleistung anordnet oder dem Richter anzuordnen gestattet.

Für Fälle dieser Art, welche sich z. B. in den Art. 268, 549, 587, 609, 615, 631, 777, 799, 876 und 1118 finden, gilt alles das, was nachstehend über die Art der Sicherheitsleistung und das Verfahren gesagt wird.

7) Bezüglich derjenigen Sicherheitsleistung, welche nach Art. 6 Abs. 5 des Einführungsgesetzes bei Zwangsabtretungen eintritt, ist dort eine besondere Vorschrift gegeben, gemäß welcher die Sicherheitsleistung nur in der Weise, wie die Kostencaution zu erfolgen hat und zugleich der Gerichtsstand geregelt wird, falls sich über Höhe der Summe oder die Zulänglichkeit der Mittel Streit erhebt.

b) Art der Sicherheitsleistung.

8) Die Sicherheitsleistungen im Allgemeinen können in vierfacher Weise geschehen, nemlich 1) durch baare Hinterlegung, 2) durch Faustpfand, 3) durch Hypotheke, 4) durch Bürgen. Für Nachklagen und Widerklagen ist noch eine besondere Art von Sicherheitsleistung dadurch geschaffen, daß der Verurtheilte den zu seiner Sicherung nöthigen Betrag nicht in die Hände des Gläubigers zahlt, sondern bei Gericht hinterlegt.

Was nun die Hinterlegung von Faustpfändern anbelangt, so ist wohl selbstverständlich, daß sie eine gerichtliche sein müsse, obgleich dies hier nicht ausdrücklich gesagt ist.

Was die Bürgen betrifft, so sollen sie vermöglich und leicht zu belangen sein.

In beiden Richtungen bleibt die nähere Würdigung natürlich dem Richter überlassen, welcher freiesten Spielraum hat und sogar nicht gehindert ist, Ausländer zuzulassen, falls diese durch Ansässigkeit und Vermögensbesitz im Inlande genügende Garantie bieten. Vgl. übrigens Vortrag zu Art. 108 des Entwurfs.

Die Worte: „leicht zu belangen" gelten natürlich auch dem Vollzuge; denn Ausländer sind z. B. immer sehr leicht zu belangen, allein nicht immer auch leicht zu fassen.

Als ungeeignete Bürgen werden demnach, der Regel nach, zu betrachten sein: Ausländer, dann Inländer, welche im Auslande wohnen oder ihr Vermögen dort haben; endlich Inländer, welche zwar im Inlande, jedoch so entfernt wohnen, daß Ausklagung und Vollstreckung mit großen Unbequemlichkeiten verbunden sein würden.

c) Verfahren.

9) Die Vorschrift, daß der Richter, indem er eine Sicherheitsleistung anordnet, auch zugleich den Betrag derselben zu bestimmen habe, gilt nicht nur für die Fälle des Art. 125, sondern für alle Fälle, auf welche Art. 130 Anwendung findet. Es kann dies um so weniger Zweifel erleiden, da die Bestimmung des Art. 130 ursprünglich einen Bestandtheil des Art. 125 bildete (Abg. I 166), übrigens auch Art. 126 Ziff. 1 die Festsetzung der Cautionssumme voraussetzt.

10) Das Verfahren zum Vollzuge des die Sicherheitsleistung auflegenden Urtheiles oder Beschlusses ist, je nach der gewählten Art der Sicherheitsleistung, ein verschiedenes.

Will der Hauptkläger den Widerkläger oder Nachkläger ermächtigen, sich durch Hinterlegung der betreffenden Summe die Sicherheit selbst zu stellen, so kann er dies sofort bei Verkündung des Urtheils erklären. Ueber diese Erklärung wird, ebenso wie im Falle des Art. 112, im Urtheile selbst Urkunde ertheilt, und hiermit ist dieser Punkt beendet. Erfolgt die Erklärung erst später, so ist sie dem Gegner zuzustellen.

Im Falle der Hinterlegung von baarem Gelde oder von Werthpapieren genügt, wie schon Art. 123 verfügt, Zustellung des Hinterlegungsscheines.

11) Was nun aber die weiteren Sicherheitsmittel — Faustpfand, Hypotheke und Bürgen — betrifft, so machen dieselben ein etwas umständlicheres Verfahren nöthig.

Zuerst hat der Verpflichtete dem Gegner eine Erklärung darüber zustellen zu lassen, wie er Sicherheit leisten wolle. Er hat darin die Sicherheitsmittel nicht bloß allgemein, sondern auch im Einzelnen genau zu bezeichnen, also anzugeben, welche beweglichen Sachen er zum Faustpfand, welche Grundstücke zur Hypotheke geben wolle oder welche Personen sich verbürgen sollen.

Hiermit hat er das Anerbieten zu verbinden, Nachweise über die Tauglichkeit dieser Sicherheitsmittel mitzutheilen, d. h. dem Gegner, sobald er es verlangt, Einsicht davon zu gestatten. Im Anwaltsprozesse erfolgt diese Mittheilung in der durch Art. 172 ff. vorgeschriebenen Weise — in der Praxis einfach so, daß der betreffende Anwalt sich die Aktenstücke zur Einsicht holen läßt; im Parteiprozesse wird es geeignet sein, im Zustellungsakte zu erklären, wo die Einsichtnahme stattfinden könne, ob bei der Partei selbst oder einer Vertrauensperson, z. B. dem Gerichtsvollzieher.

Endlich soll mit fraglicher Erklärung Vorladung in eine bestimmte Sitzung verbunden werden, also ohne Rücksicht, ob Streit in Aussicht stehe oder nicht. Zur Vereinfachung und Beschleunigung des Verfahrens mag dies sachgemäß sein, jedoch wird in den meisten Fällen die Vorladung gegenstandslos werden, weil der Gegner zufrieden ist. Um übrigens eine gütliche Vereinigung zu ermöglichen, wird es geeignet sein, die Sitzung nicht allzunahe zu setzen, was auch schon deßhalb sich empfiehlt, damit Raum gelassen werde zur Einsicht der Nachweise, sowie zu etwaigen Erkundigungen, und die Sache nicht unreif zur Verhandlung komme.

In der Sitzung soll ohne Vorverfahren, d. h. ohne Zustellung motivirter Anträge, über die Zulänglichkeit der Sicherheitsmittel verhandelt werden, wobei es dem Richter freisteht, weitere Nachweise von Amtswegen anzuordnen.

Das Wort: „Zulänglichkeit" ist im weiteren Sinne zu nehmen und begreift auch die Zulässigkeit, z. B. wenn Hypotheke auf ausländische Liegenschaften angeboten würde.

12) Ist das Sicherheitsmittel vom Gegner angenommen oder vom Gerichte zugelassen, so erfolgt die Sicherheitsleistung in geeigneter Weise, wobei immer zu beachten, daß Nachweis darüber dem Gegner zuzustellen ist, also je nach Umständen Hinterlegungsschein, Hypothekenauszug oder Bürgschaftsurkunde.

Verbürgungen sind in Notariatsurkunden zu erklären, und es steht kraft Gesetzes den Bürgen die Einrede der Vorausklage und der Theilung nicht zu.

13) Gegen alle Urtheile über die Pflicht zur Sicherstellung oder über die Tauglichkeit der Sicherheitsmittel sind selbständige Rechtsmittel zulässig (Art. 129), d. h. die Rechtsmittel sind nicht deßhalb ausgeschlossen, weil diese Urtheile keine Endurtheile oder denselben gleichgestellt sind. Art. 682, 683, 788.

Die anderen Voraussetzungen der Zulässigkeit von Rechtsmitteln: Berufungssumme ꝛc., müssen natürlich gegeben sein. Abg. IV 25 (zu Art. 24).

Im Falle der Sicherheitsleistung wegen einer Widerklage oder Nachklage wird der Urtheilsvollzug durch Einspruch oder Berufung gegen Entscheidungen über Zulänglichkeit der Sicherheitsmittel nicht gehemmt (Art. 129 Abs. 2).

14) Für die Pfalz ist zu bemerken, daß durch Einführungsgesetz Art. 105 die Bestimmungen über Sicherheitsleistung auch auf den Fall des Art. 2185 Ziff. 5 Code civil anwendbar erklärt worden sind.

Ferner ist darauf hinzuweisen, daß bei allen Verbürgungen, auf welche die Art. 125 — 130 Anwendung finden, die auf die gerichtlichen Bürgen sich beziehenden Artikel 2040 — 2042 Code civ. keine Geltung mehr haben. Die Spezialität vorliegender Bestimmungen und ihre prozessuale Natur bedingen dies im Geiste von Art. 2 des Einf.-Gesetzes.

Art. 131. — **Legen die Gesetze eines auswärtigen Staats den vor den dortigen Gerichten klagenden bayerischen Staatsangehörigen eine ausgedehntere Verpflichtung zur Sicherheitsleistung auf, als in den Art. 120 — 130 bestimmt ist, so unterliegen Angehörige dieses Staats, wenn sie vor bayerischen Gerichten klagend auftreten, der gleichen Verpflichtung.**

S. A. d. K. d. A. I S. 158—160. 165. 166. 178. 180. — K. d. R. I S. 265. 266.

1) Um diesen Artikel richtig zu würdigen, muß man wissen, daß derselbe ursprünglich einen Bestandtheil von Art. 120 bildete, also sich nur auf die cautio pro expensis bezog, daß er aber

später durch die Subkommission, ohne Aenderung der Fassung, an's Ende des Abschnittes gesetzt und auf alle Fälle der Sicherheitsleistung ausgedehnt wurde. Vortrag des Ref. v. Neumayr zu Art. 104 des Entwurfs und Abg. I 165 — Abg. I 178 (zu Art. 104).

So kommt es, daß derselbe nach Fassung und Inhalt bloß zu Art. 120 paßt, in der Anwendung auf die übrigen in ihm angezogenen Artikel aber erhebliche Schwierigkeiten bietet.

Es ist in letzterer Beziehung hervorzuheben:

1) Daß die Worte: „klagend auftreten" sich für sämmtliche Fälle der Art. 125—130 nicht eignen; denn selbst bei Widerklage und Nachklage kann man nicht sagen, es müsse der Hauptkläger deßhalb Caution leisten, weil er klagend auftrete — ganz abgesehen davon, daß bei manchen Sicherheitsleistungen auch der Beklagte der Verpflichtete sein kann und daß in andern Fällen, z. B. bei Vollstreckung ꝛc. weder vom Kläger noch vom Beklagten die Rede sein kann;

2) daß die Fälle der Art. 125—130 ausnahmslos solche sind, wo Inländer die nemliche Verpflichtung der Cautionsleistung haben, wie Ausländer;

3) daß Art. 131 von Verpflichtungen spricht, welche in den Art. 120—130 bestimmt seien, während in Art. 130 eine Verpflichtung zur Sicherheitsleistung gar nicht ausgesprochen, sondern nur für Fälle, in denen die Cautionspflicht an sonstigen Stellen des Gesetzes bestimmt ist, das Verfahren geregelt wird;

4) daß von den angezogenen Artikeln 120—130 die meisten sich rein nur auf das Verfahren beziehen.

Wenn irgendwo, so wird es daher hier nothwendig sein, die Worte des Gesetzes an zweite Stelle zu verweisen, und den Geist desselben vorwalten zu lassen.

2) Vor Allem wird außer Zweifel sein, daß das Gesetz nicht die Absicht hatte, den natürlichen Begriff der Retorsion zu ändern.

Die Retorsion ist nur die Abwehr einer Feindseligkeit, das Schutzmittel zur Verhütung ungleichartiger Behandlung von Ausländern und Inländern; allein man spricht nicht von einer Retorsion in Fällen, wo der ausländische Staat keinen Unterschied macht zwischen seinen eigenen Unterthanen und Fremden. Es ist noch keinem Staate eingefallen, deßhalb, weil in einem anderen Staate gewisse Beweise nicht zugelassen werden, nun auch bei Prozessen der Unterthanen jenes Staates diese Beweise retorsionsweise auszuschließen.

Der Umstand also, daß ein ausländisches Gesetz bei Widerklagen, provisorischem Vollzuge von Urtheilen, Vorsichtsverfügungen ꝛc. Sicherheitsleistungen auferlegt, welche unsere Prozeßordnung nicht kennt, reicht nicht hin, um den Art. 131 anwendbar zu machen, wohl aber wird er dann wirksam, wenn in irgend einer dieser Beziehungen der Bayer schlimmer gestellt sein sollte, als der Angehörige des betreffenden Staates.

3) Nachdem die Retorsion in dieser Weise auf das ihr eigenthümliche Gebiet verwiesen ist, wird es nicht nöthig sein, auf die Worte: „klagend auftreten" ein besonderes Gewicht zu legen. In der Anwendung auf die Fälle der Art. 125 und 130 sollen diese Worte offenbar nur bedeuten: „vor Gericht auftreten", oder noch richtiger: „ihre Rechte auf gerichtlichem Wege verfolgen".

4) Kein Zweifel kann darüber obwalten, daß das Gesetz die Retorsion nur bezüglich der Verpflichtung selbst einführen wollte, d. h. bezüglich der Bestimmung der Fälle der Sicherheitsleistung und bezüglich des Umfangs derselben in diesen Fällen, nicht aber auch bezüglich der zulässigen Sicherheitsmittel oder gar bezüglich des Verfahrens. Abg. I 180 (Edel, Barth).

5) Demgemäß würde sich der Sinn des Art. 131 etwa dahin zusammenfassen lassen:

„Legen die Gesetze eines auswärtigen Staates „bayerischen Staatsangehörigen, welche ihre „Rechte dort verfolgen, als solchen eine aus„gedehntere Verpflichtung zur Sicherheitsleistung „auf, als dies für die Fälle der Art. 120, „125 und 130 bestimmt ist, so unterliegen „Angehörige dieses Staates, wenn sie in „Bayern ihre Rechte verfolgen, den gleichen „Bestimmungen."

Gerichtliche Hinterlegung.

Art. 132. — **Die Bestimmungen darüber, wie in den Fällen, für welche die gerichtliche Hinterlegung von Geld oder andern Sachen gesetzlich angeordnet oder gestattet ist, diese Hinterlegung stattzufinden hat, sowie über die Aufbewahrung und die Wiederaushändigung der hinterlegten Gelder und Sachen werden, soweit das Gesetz eine Vorschrift nicht enthält, im Verordnungswege erlassen.**

Insbesondere kann durch Verordnung bestimmt werden, daß die Betheiligten die von ihnen zu hinterlegenden Gelder bei den in der Verordnung bezeichneten öffentlichen Kassen,

Banken oder ähnlichen Anstalten einzuzahlen und bei Gericht nur die ihnen hierüber ertheilte Bescheinigung zu hinterlegen haben. G. A. d. K. d. A. IV S. 25. — K. d. R. IV S. 16.

Dieser Artikel wurde erst bei zweiter Lesung eingefügt, um eine gesetzliche Grundlage für die Regulirung der gerichtlichen Hinterlegungen, welche das Gesetz anordnet oder zuläßt, zu gewinnen.

Die näheren Bestimmungen sind hiernach einer kgl. Verordnung vorbehalten, welche wohl nicht bloß die Fälle der streitigen, sondern auch der unstreitigen Rechtspflege (z. B. Art. 1257 Code civ.) umfassen wird.

Armenrecht.

Art. 133. — **Wer ohne Beeinträchtigung des nothwendigen Unterhalts für sich und seine Familie nicht im Stande ist, die Kosten eines zu beginnenden oder bereits anhängigen Rechtsstreits oder einer Vollstreckung zu bestreiten, kann die Bewilligung des Armenrechts verlangen, wenn sein Anspruch oder seine Rechtsvertheidigung nicht als muthwillig erscheint.**

Auch Ausländern kann das Armenrecht ertheilt werden, wenn die bayerischen Staatsangehörigen in dem Staate, welchem der Ausländer angehört, gleiche Vergünstigung genießen. G. A. d. K. d. A. I. S. 161. 180. IV S. 25. 26. — K. d. R. I S. 268—275. — IV S. 16.

1) Das Armenrecht ist gewiß eine sehr wohlthätige Einrichtung, ohne welche der Arme oft rechtlos gestellt wäre; allein diese wohlthätige Einrichtung kann zu einer schädlichen werden, wenn Mißbrauch damit getrieben wird. Wird das Armenrecht allzu leicht gewährt, so leistet es der Prozeßsucht und Chikane Vorschub; es ermöglicht, ohne irgend ein Risiko, durch nichtige Einwände die Geltendmachung wohlbegründeter Rechte zu erschweren, ja dieselben durch Verursachen von Kosten, für die es keinen Ersatz gibt, geradezu werthlos zu machen.

Diesseits hat man in dieser Beziehung Erfahrungen gemacht, und deßhalb hielt es unsere Prozeßordnung, der in der Pfalz geltenden Verordnung vom 19. Nov. 1814 folgend, für gut, die Bewilligung des Armenrechts nicht bloß davon abhängig zu machen, daß die Partei vermögenslos sei, sondern auch davon, daß sie nicht muthwillig sich in Prozeß einlasse, daß sie, um mit der Gerichtsordnung zu sprechen, „redliche Ursache zum Streiten habe".

2) Art. 133 gibt das Armenrecht sowohl für Rechtsstreite als für Vollstreckungen, also für das ganze Gebiet der streitigen Rechtspflege. Für die nichtstreitige Rechtspflege findet sich keine Bestimmung, es behalten hier also die bestehenden Grundsätze Geltung.

3) Was das Erforderniß der Armuth betrifft, so wird verlangt, daß Jemand, ohne Beeinträchtigung des nothwendigen Lebensunterhalts für sich und seine Familie, nicht im Stande sei, die in Aussicht stehenden Prozeßkosten zu bestreiten. Auf ein standesmäßiges Auskommen ist daher keine Rücksicht zu nehmen.

Ob die Partei von ihrem Capitalvermögen oder von dessen Rente, oder von ihrem Erwerbe zugleich Unterhalt und Kosten bestreiten könne, ist gleichgiltig. Seuff. Comm. Bd. II S. 135 — Art. 138 Abs. 1.

Selbstverständlich sind bloß die Vermögensverhältnisse der Partei selbst, nicht aber des gesetzlichen Vertreters entscheidend; wenn jedoch der letztere zugleich verpflichtet ist, die Kosten aus eignen Mitteln zu bestreiten, z. B. der Vater für die Kinder, deren Vermögen er in Nutznießung hat, der Mann für die Frau, so werden allerdings auch dessen Vermögensverhältnisse in Betracht kommen. Seuff. a. a. O.

Ob etwa dritte Personen verpflichtet seien, die Kosten vorzuschießen, ist nicht zu prüfen; die bezügliche Verfügung des Entwurfs wurde gerade beseitigt, um solche Prüfungen nicht nöthig zu machen. R. R. I 274 (v. Bayer). In der Alimentationspflicht an sich würde jedenfalls eine solche Verpflichtung nicht begründet sein. Seuff. a. a. O.

Als vermögenslos im Sinne des Art. 133 kann auch Jemand betrachtet werden, wenn er rechtlich Vermögen besitzt, welches aber nicht greifbar ist, welches z. B. gerade durch den Rechtsstreit oder die Vollstreckung, für welche das Armenrecht begehrt wird, flüssig gemacht werden soll. Die Worte: „im Stande sein" lassen diesen weiteren Sinn zu. Vgl. Abg. IV 310 (v. Weiß).

4) Die Bestimmungen des Art. 133 haben nur physische Personen im Auge, wie schon aus dem Wortlaute zu folgern, wie aber auch vom Ministerialkommissär förmlich erklärt worden ist, ohne daß sich Widerspruch erhoben hätte. Abg. I 161.

In Art. 8 des Ges. vom 22. Mai 1869 ist übrigens bestimmt: „Die Armenpflegen sind für Rechtsstreitigkeiten kraft des Gesetzes zum Armenrechte zugelassen", und diese Bestimmung hat der Prozeßordnung gegenüber volle Geltung. Abg. I 161 und 181 (Barth, v. Neumayr). Da in dieser

Ausnahmsbestimmung nur von „Rechtsstreitigkeiten" die Rede ist, so werden Vollstreckungen nicht darunter begriffen sein. In dieser Beziehung, sowie in Fällen der nichtstreitigen Rechtspflege werden die Armenpflegen nur die Freiheit von Taxe und Stempel gemäß Art. 8 Abs. 1 a. a. O. anzusprechen haben.

5) Bei Ausländern ist die Zulassung nicht von Staatsverträgen, sondern nur von Reziprozität abhängig gemacht.

Solche Reziprozität besteht mit dem Großherzogthume Hessen (laut Vertrags v. 24. Dez. 1820), mit Nassau (laut Vertrags v. 10. Sept. 1823), mit Kurhessen (laut Vertrags vom 16. März 1827), mit Württemberg (laut Minist.-Entschl. vom 16. April 1852 [Döllinger Bd. XXXIII S. 14]) und mit Koburg-Gotha (laut Vertrags v. 4. Jan. 1855). Mit Preußen besteht eine Uebereinkunft wegen Erledigung von Requisitionen in Armensachen vom Jahre 1834 (Reg.-Bl. S. 811).

Art. 134. — **Die Zulassung zum Armenrechte bewirkt die einstweilige Befreiung:**

1) von der Entrichtung der von diesem Zeitpunkte an erlaufenden Gerichtskosten, Taxen, Stempel- und Portogebühren, sowie der betreffenden Gebühren der Anwälte, Notare und Gerichtsvollzieher;

2) von Zahlung der Tagegelder und Reisekosten der Gerichtspersonen.

Die unter Ziff. 1 bezeichneten Kosten und Gebühren sind vorzumerken, die unter Ziff. 2 bezeichneten werden einstweilen von der Staatskassa vorgeschossen.

G. A. d. K. d. A. 1 S. 161. 180. IV S. 26. 37. — K. d. R. I. S. 275.

1) Das Armenrecht bewirkt, vorbehaltlich der Nachzahlung unter den Voraussetzungen des Art. 143, die Befreiung:

1) von allen Bezügen der Staatskasse an Taxen, Stempel und Porto;
2) von den Gebühren der Anwälte, Notare und Gerichtsvollzieher;
3) von Tagegeldern und Reisekosten der Gerichtspersonen.

Außerdem erwähnt das Gesetz noch im Allgemeinen der Gerichtskosten, und es ist anzunehmen, daß hierunter die Gebühren der Gerichtschreiber begriffen sein sollten, weil derselben nicht besonders erwähnt ist. Dies gilt insbesondere auch von den Gebühren, welche Art. 170 denselben zuweist.

Die Befreiung tritt ein vom Augenblicke der Bewilligung an, erstreckt sich also nicht auf Rückstände. Abg. IV 26 (zu Art. 28).

2) Für alle sonstigen Kosten wirkt das Armenrecht nicht, insbesondere nicht für Gebühren von Sachverständigen und Zeugen, für Reisekosten der Anwälte und für Baarauslagen jeder Art.

Wenn die arme Partei solche Auslagen nicht zu bestreiten im Stande ist, so kann sie eben den Prozeß nicht betreiben. Ein Beiziehen der Armenkasse, wie es seither geschah, könnte, nach der Natur des jetzigen Verfahrens, jedenfalls nicht von Amtswegen erfolgen, sondern wäre Sache der Partei.

Die Gerichte werden übrigens bedacht sein, Baarauslagen möglichst zu verhüten, indem sie z. B. die Zeugen durch den Landrichter verhören lassen.

3) Die Tagegelder und Reisekosten der Gerichtspersonen, unter welchen ohne Zweifel auch die Gerichtschreiber, sowie eintretenden Falls die Staatsanwälte begriffen sind, werden nicht vorgemerkt, sondern vorschußweise durch die Staatskasse bestritten — dies natürlich nur in so fern, als sie nach Maßgabe des Art. 105 von der armen Partei vorläufig auszulegen wären.

4) Das Armenrecht befreit den Ausländer, welchem es bewilligt wird, nicht von der Kostencaution, wenn nicht etwa in Staatsverträgen anders verfügt ist. Sowohl diesseits als in der Pfalz war man von jeher dieser Ansicht, und ihre Richtigkeit kann jetzt um so weniger mehr in Zweifel gezogen werden, als ein Vorbehalt, welcher in Art. 111 des Entwurfs bezüglich der Kostenkaution gemacht war, als selbstverständlich gestrichen wurde. Abg. I 180 (zu Art. 111).

Uebrigens werden in solchen Fällen die Gerichte mit besonderer Vorsicht darauf achten, daß die Caution nicht zu hoch gegriffen und die nöthige Frist gegeben werde.

Art. 135. — **Das Armenrecht wird von dem Gerichte, bei welchem der Rechtsstreit anhängig gemacht werden soll oder schon anhängig ist, und zwar vorbehaltlich der Bestimmung des Art. 141, für jeden Rechtszug besonders ertheilt.**

Bei Vollstreckungen wird das Armenrecht von dem Vollstreckungsgerichte ertheilt.

Art. 136. — **Ist bei dem Gerichte, welches das Armenrecht zu ertheilen hat, ein Staatsanwalt aufgestellt, so ist das Gesuch um Ertheilung des Armenrechts unter Vorlage aller auf den**

Gegenstand bezüglichen Aktenstücke und sonstigen Behelfe schriftlich oder mündlich bei dem Staatsanwalte anzubringen.

Art. 137. — Erachtet der Staatsanwalt den behaupteten Anspruch oder die beabsichtigte Vertheidigung in Würdigung der Thatsachen und Beweisbehelfe oder des Rechtspunkts für muthwillig, so hat er dies dem Nachsuchenden zu eröffnen.

Ist der Staatsanwalt der Ansicht, daß der Anspruch oder die beabsichtige Vertheidigung als muthwillig nicht betrachtet werden könne, so hat er das Gesuch nebst den Erhebungen über die Vermögensverhältnisse des Nachsuchenden an das Gericht abzugeben und zugleich die schriftliche Erklärung beizufügen, daß der Ertheilung des Armenrechts aus der Prüfung des behaupteten Anspruchs oder der beabsichtigten Vertheidigung kein Hinderniß entgegenstehe.

Art. 138. — Das Gericht erkennt über die Ertheilung des Armenrechts in geheimer Sitzung und bewilligt dasselbe, wenn die Vermögenslosigkeit nachgewiesen ist. Hiebei ist der muthmaßliche Kostenaufwand in Anschlag zu bringen und die Fähigkeit zur Bestreitung dieses Aufwands nach dem vorhandenen Vermögen und dem möglichen Erwerbe ohne Rücksicht auf den Schuldenstand zu bemessen.

Sind Ergänzungen in dieser Beziehung nothwendig, so werden die desfallsigen Anordnungen des Gerichts von dem Staatsanwalte vollzogen.

Von dem gefaßten Beschlusse hat der Staatsanwalt dem Nachsuchenden Kenntniß zu geben.

Gegen den Beschluß finden Rechtsmittel nicht statt.

Art. 139. — Wird nach Ertheilung des Armenrechts die Sache nicht von einem am Sitze des Prozeßgerichts wohnenden und zur anwaltschaftlichen Vertretung zugelassenen Advokaten freiwillig übernommen, so hat der Gerichtsvorstand sofort zur Vertretung einen dieser Advokaten zu bezeichnen. Diese Bezeichnung vertritt für den Anwalt die Stelle der Prozeßvollmacht.

Für die Zustellungen und etwa nöthigen Notariatsgeschäfte werden die Gerichtsvollzieher und Notare, wenn die betreffenden Geschäfte innerhalb des Bezirks des Gerichts, bei dem die Sache anhängig ist oder anhängig werden soll, vorzunehmen sind, von dem Vorstande dieses Gerichts, andernfalls von dem Vorstande desjenigen Bezirksgerichts, in dessen Sprengel sie ihren Wohnsitz haben, bezeichnet.

Art. 140. — In den zur Zuständigkeit eines Gerichts, bei welchem ein Staatsanwalt nicht aufgestellt ist, gehörigen Sachen ist das Gesuch um Zulassung zum Armenrechte bei dem Gerichte selbst anzubringen und steht diesem die Instruktion und Entscheidung zu. Die Bestimmungen des Art. 139 Abs. 1 finden im Anwaltsprozesse, die Bestimmungen des Art. 138 Abs. 4 und Art. 139 Abs. 2 sowohl in diesem als im Parteiprozesse Anwendung.

Art. 141. — Die Ertheilung des Armenrechts gilt auch für die höhere Instanz, wenn die Sache in Folge eines von der Gegenpartei ergriffenen Rechtsmittels dahin gelangt. Dem Vorstande des Obergerichts stehen bezüglich der Bezeichnung eines Anwalts, der Gerichtsvollzieher und Notare dieselben Befugnisse zu, als wenn das Armenrecht von diesem Gerichte ertheilt worden wäre.

G. A. d. K. d. A. I S. 161. 162. 180. 299. IV S. 26. 27. 37. 309. 310.
K. d. R. I S. 275—283. IV S. 17. 18.

1) In diesen sieben Artikeln wird das Verfahren bei Armenrechtssachen geregelt.

Nach dem Systeme unserer Prozeßordnung muß das Armenrecht für jeden Rechtszug, also auch für die Berufungs- und Cassations-Instanz, besonders begehrt und bewilligt werden, und zwar ohne Ausnahme von demjenigen Gerichte, bei welchem der Rechtsstreit anhängig ist oder werden soll.

Die Bewilligung wirkt bloß für dieses Gericht; würde daher Jemand eine Klage, für welche er das Armenrecht bei einem Gerichte erwirkt hätte, an einem andern Gerichte anbringen wollen, so müßte er dort neuerdings um Bewilligung nachsuchen; die erste Bewilligung wäre unzuständig ertheilt.

Nur in einem einzigen Falle wirkt die Ertheilung des Armenrechts auch für die höheren Instanzen, nemlich, wenn die Sache in Folge eines vom Gegner ergriffenen Rechtsmittels dahin gelangt ist (Art. 141). Die Partie behält dann das Armenrecht zwar zunächst nur zur Vertheidigung gegen das ergriffene Rechtsmittel; allein dasselbe wirkt auch für die von ihm selbst anschlußweise eingelegten Rechtsmittel. Abg. I 161 (v. Weiß).

Was die Vollstreckungen anbelangt, so wird das Armenrecht vom Vollstreckungsgerichte ertheilt, welches in der Regel das Bezirksgericht ist (Art. 840), jedoch, wenn der Werth von gepfändeten Mobilien 150 Gulden nicht übersteigt, ausnahmsweise auch das Landgericht sein kann. Bis zum Augenblicke der Pfändung ist auch in letzterem Falle immer das Bezirksgericht zuständig. Abg. IV 309, 310.

2) Was die Prüfung und Bescheidung der Armenrechtsgesuche betrifft, so unterscheidet das Gesetz zwischen der Frage der Vertretbarkeit der Sache und der Frage der Vermögenslosigkeit; die erstere gehört zur Zuständigkeit des Staatsanwaltes, falls ein solcher bei dem betreffenden Gerichte angestellt ist. Gerichte dieser letzteren Art sind die Bezirksgerichte, Appellationsgerichte und der oberste Gerichtshof; die Zuständigkeit des Staatsanwaltes ist aber ausgeschlossen bei Landgerichten, Handelsgerichten, Handelsappellationsgerichten.

Der Umstand, daß ein Bezirksgericht zugleich Handelsgericht ist (im Sinne, wie dies nach Art. 56—60 des Einf.-Ges. zum H. G. B. möglich ist), gibt also dem bei demselben angestellten Staatsanwalte nicht die Befugniß, Armenrechtsgesuche in Handelssachen zu behandeln — welche übrigens sehr selten vorkommen.

3) In der Pfalz wurden die Armenrechtsgesuche von jeher durch die Staatsprokuratoren instruirt, welche sich dabei der Hilfe der Landrichter bedienten, als derjenigen Organe, welche sich hiefür in jedem Betrachte am besten eigneten. Der Landrichter vernahm beide Theile und machte, wenn es ihm nicht etwa gelang, die Sache gütlich beizulegen, diejenigen Ermittlungen und Erhebungen, welche nöthig erschienen, um das Für und Wider vollkommen klar zu stellen. Ueber das Ergebniß berichtete er dem Staatsanwalte. Diese gründlichen Instruktionen hatten, außer der Verhütung muthwilliger Armenrechtsprozesse, noch den weiteren Vortheil, daß der Pflichtanwalt sofort gut und richtig instruirt wurde.

Unsere Prozeßordnung sagt zwar nicht ausdrücklich, daß der Staatsanwalt eine amtliche Instruktion vorzunehmen habe, allein es versteht sich das von selbst und ist auch durch die Worte: „aus der Prüfung des behaupteten Anspruchs“, sowie durch Art. 145 genügend angedeutet.

Durch die Erklärung des Staatsanwaltes über die Vertretbarkeit der Sache, sei sie nun bejahend oder verneinend, ist dieser Punkt erledigt; jedoch steht es dem Gesuchsteller, welcher abgewiesen wurde, frei, sich beim Oberstaatsanwalte und Justizminister zu beschweren um Aenderung des Beschlusses zu erwirken. Vortrag des Ref. v. Neumayr zur 2. Lesung, Hptst. IV Art. 31 — Abg. IV 27 — R. R. IV 18.

4) Da die Erklärung des Staatsanwaltes bestimmt ist, die Grundlage für die richterliche Entschließung zu bilden, so hat derselbe möglichst genau sich darüber auszusprechen, in welcher Richtung und in welchem Umfange das Armenrecht bewilligt werden könne.

In der Regel ist es allerdings rathsam, den Rahmen nicht zu eng zu spannen und, falls nur der Hauptsache nach ein Streitmuthwille nicht vorliegt, dem zu ernennenden Pflichtanwalte die möglichste Freiheit der Bewegung vorzubehalten. Andrerseits aber erleidet es auch keinen Zweifel, daß der Staatsanwalt nicht der Art beengt ist, um das Gesuch entweder ganz abweisen oder ganz zulassen zu müssen, daß es ihm vielmehr freisteht, das Gesuch nur in einer bestimmten Richtung, bezüglich eines Theils der Ansprüche, für muthwillig zu erklären, im Uebrigen aber zuzulassen. Es kann nicht in der Macht einer Partei stehen, dadurch, daß sie ihrem großen Unrechte einige Körnlein Recht beimischt, sich das Armenrecht für's Ganze zu erzwingen.

Der Staatsanwalt kann auch ein Gesuch als muthwillig abweisen, wenn zwar der Anspruch im Allgemeinen begründet scheint, jedoch Klage beim Bezirksgerichte erhoben werden will, während sich die Sache, falls keine übertriebene Forderung gestellt würde, vor's Landgericht eignen würde — ein Gesichtspunkt, welcher bei Schadenklagen sehr oft praktisch wird.

Die Zulässig-Erklärung des Staatsanwaltes und die hierauf sich gründende Bewilligung des Gerichtes wirken für die ganze bezügliche Streitsache mit allen dazu gehörigen Nebenstreitigkeiten. Vgl. Art. 90.

5) Das Gericht beschränkt sich einzig und allein auf Prüfung und Entscheidung der Frage der Vermögenslosigkeit. Nähere Vorschriften über den Nachweis der Vermögenslosigkeit sollen durch Verordnungen gegeben werden, welche jedoch selbstverständlich nur das Verfahren zu regeln haben und nicht so weit gehen dürfen, den Gerichten indirekt die Entscheidung zu entziehen.

6) Die Geschäftsbehandlung bei Gericht soll nach Art. 145 und 169 durch Verordnung näher bestimmt werden. Ohne Zweifel wird angeordnet werden, daß alle Gerichtsbeschlüsse über Armenrechtsgesuche in ein besonderes Register einzutragen und zum Zwecke der Mittheilung an den Pflichtanwalt — beziehungsweise an den Staatsanwalt — vom Gerichtschreiber auszufertigen seien.

Sowohl bei Abweisung als bei Zulassung des

Gesuches hat der Staatsanwalt sofort den Gesuchsteller, sei dieser die Partei selbst oder ihr Vertreter, von dem gerichtlichen Beschlusse auf geeignetem Wege in Kenntniß zu setzen.

Die Bezeichnung des Pflichtanwaltes erfolgt nicht, wie seither in der Pfalz, durch den Staatsanwalt, sondern durch den Gerichtsvorstand, welcher auf die dem Anwalte einzuhändigende Ausfertigung seine Verfügung setzt.

Auch bezüglich der Aufträge an Notare und Gerichtsvollzieher, soweit sie im Bezirke wohnen, ist es sachgemäß, sofort zu verfügen.

7) Nach Art. 139 soll nur dann ein Pflichtanwalt bezeichnet werden, wenn nicht einer der Anwälte freiwillig die Sache übernimmt; allein falls nicht schon ein Anwalt das Gesuch eingereicht oder die Partei einen solchen bezeichnet hat, wird es nicht nöthig sein, Umfrage zu halten, ob etwa Jemand die Vertretung übernehmen wolle. Es ist ja kein Anwalt berechtigt, die Vertretung ohne Mandat der Partei oder Bezeichnung des Gerichtsvorstandes zu übernehmen.

Die Bezeichnung des Gerichtsvorstandes gibt Prozeßvollmacht im Sinne der Art. 90 und 91. Es kann also die Partei nicht mehr geltend machen, der Anwalt habe von ihr keinen Auftrag; jedoch steht es ihr jederzeit frei, mit Beobachtung der Vorschrift in Art. 94 Abs. 2 das in ihrem Namen gegebene Mandat zu kündigen. Abg. IV 26 (zu Art. 33).

8) An den Gerichten, bei welchen ein Staatsanwalt nicht aufgestellt ist, fällt dessen Amtsthätigkeit in Armensachen den Gerichten selbst zu. Es erscheint dieß sehr geeignet für die Landgerichte, wo ein einzelner Richter ist und es sich um einfache oder geringfügige Sachen handelt; allein was die Handelsgerichte und Handelsappellationsgerichte anbelangt, so wäre es recht gut einzurichten gewesen, daß die Staatsanwälte an den entsprechenden Bezirksgerichten oder Appellationsgerichten die Instruktion besorgt hätten.

Auch bei den Beschlüssen dieser Gerichte sind Rechtsmittel unbedingt ausgeschlossen.

Art. 142. — **Das Armenrecht kann jederzeit von dem mit dem Rechtsstreite befaßten Gerichte wieder entzogen werden, wenn das Gericht die Ueberzeugung gewinnt, daß die bei der Ertheilung angenommenen Voraussetzungen nicht vorhanden waren oder weggefallen sind.**

In allen Fällen erlischt das Armenrecht mit dem Tode desjenigen, dem es ertheilt wurde. (G. A. d. K. d. A. I S. 162. 181. IV S. 27. — K. d. R. I S. 283.

1) Der Richter, bei welchem der Rechtsstreit anhängig ist, hat immer das Recht, das für denselben gewährte Armenrecht von Amtswegen wieder zu entziehen, sobald er findet, daß die Voraussetzungen zu dessen Verleihung nicht gegeben seien.

Die Befugnisse des Richters beschränken sich in dieser Beziehung nicht auf Prüfung der Vermögensverhältnisse, sondern erstrecken sich auch auf die Frage, ob Streitmuthwille vorliege, und dieß mit vollem Rechte, da nunmehr beiden Theilen Gelegenheit geboten war, ihre Rechte geltend zu machen, also der Richter ganz innerhalb seiner Aufgabe handelt, wenn er sich über Grund oder Ungrund der Behauptungen einer Partei ausspricht.

Auch das für Betrieb einer Vollstreckung gewährte Armenrecht kann wieder entzogen werden, wenn sich bei Gelegenheit der Verhandlung über einen erhobenen Widerspruch ergibt, daß die Voraussetzungen dazu nicht vorliegen; jedoch wird der Einzelrichter nie befugt sein, einen die Vollstreckung an sich betreffenden Beschluß des Bezirksgerichts aufzuheben.

2) Das Armenrecht erlischt immer mit dem Tode derjenigen Person, welcher es ertheilt worden ist.

Obgleich die Gründe dieser Bestimmung für die Fälle, wo eine Vakantmasse an Stelle des Verstorbenen tritt, oder wo die Erben nur mit der Rechtswohlthat des Inventars annehmen — Fälle, welche wohl die Regel bilden werden — nicht recht passen, so wird doch, den klaren Worten des Gesetzes gegenüber, eine Ausnahme nicht zu machen sein.

Falls der Verstorbene von Streitgenossen, welche gleichfalls zum Armenrechte zugelassen sind, beerbt wird, möchte übrigens anzunehmen sein, daß diese auch für den ererbten Anspruch ihr Armenrecht geltend machen dürfen.

Art. 143. — **Kommt die Partei später in Vermögensverhältnisse, bei deren Vorhandensein ihr das Armenrecht nicht würde bewilligt worden sein, so tritt die Verpflichtung zur Nachzahlung aller vorgemerkten und vom Staate vorgeschossenen Beträge ein.**

Gleiches gilt, wenn eine zahlungsfähige Partei die Ertheilung des Armenrechts durch unwahre Angaben über ihre Vermögensverhältnisse erschlichen hat.

Ueber das Vorhandensein der in Abs. 1 und 2 bezeichneten Voraussetzungen und die daraus sich ergebende Verpflichtung erkennt das Gericht, bei welchem die Sache noch an-

hängig ist, falls aber der Rechtsstreit beendigt ist, das Gericht, bei welchem das Armenrecht zuerst ertheilt wurde. Die Entscheidung erfolgt in geheimer Sitzung auf Anregung der Betheiligten oder des Staatsanwalts oder selbst von Amtswegen.

G. A. d. K. d. A. I S. 162. 181. 290. IV S. 27. — K. d. R. I S. 283. 284. IV S. 18.

1) Es liegt in der Natur des Armenrechts, daß die Kosten nicht geschenkt, sondern nur, so lange die Armuth dauert, kreditirt sind. Sobald daher sich ergibt, daß die Partei, welche die Vortheile des Armenrechts gezogen hat, Vermögen besitze, sei es nun, daß sie dasselbe ursprünglich besaß und zu verheimlichen wußte, sei es, daß sie es erst später erwarb, so können die Kosten nachträglich von ihr verlangt werden.

Versteht die Partei sich nicht etwa freiwillig zu dieser Nachzahlung, so soll das Gericht dieselbe anordnen, und zwar durch eine in geheimer Sitzung zu erlassende Entscheidung, welche nicht bloß auf Anregung der Betheiligten (des Aerars, der Anwälte, Notare, Gerichtsvollzieher), sondern auch auf Antrag des Staatsanwaltes und sogar von Amtswegen erfolgt.

2) Diese Entscheidung ist offenbar keine solche, auf Grund deren sofort ein Vollstreckungsverfahren eingeleitet werden könnte. Während Art. 118 verfügt, daß der eigenen Partei gegenüber die Kosten auf dem Wege der Klage einzutreiben seien, und sogar für Advokaten im Anwaltsprozesse einen Weg vorschreibt, welcher etwaigen Einwänden der Partei Raum läßt, kann hier nicht eine Verurtheilung von Amtswegen, ohne Gehör der Partei, beabsichtigt sein!

Die in Frage stehende Entscheidung enthält daher nichts weiter, als die Erklärung, daß das früher bewilligte Armenrecht nicht mehr im Wege stehe, die von der Partei geschuldeten Gebühren und Auslagen zu fordern, vorbehaltlich der Liquidirung auf gesetzlichem Wege. Es handelt sich einfach um Aufhebung der Wirkungen des Armenrechts, ähnlich wie in Art. 142, nur mit dem Unterschiede, daß dort die noch zu machenden, hier die bereits gemachten Kosten in Frage sind.

3) Indem das Gesetz hier eine Entscheidung von Amtswegen zuläßt, hat es offenbar nur jene Fälle im Auge, wo die Sache noch anhängig ist; denn die Gerichte haben keinen Beruf, nachzuforschen, ob Personen, welchen sie früher, in bereits erledigten Prozessen, das Armenrecht bewilligt hatten, etwa seitdem zu Vermögen gekommen seien.

Ist nun die Sache noch anhängig, so wird der Richter zugleich mit Entziehung des Armenrechts für die Zukunft auch die Verpflichtung zur Nachzahlung der früheren Kosten auszusprechen haben, und es fragt sich, ob Beides nicht im nemlichen Urtheile geschehen dürfe, oder ob die letztere Entscheidung nothwendig in geheimer Sitzung zu erfolgen habe?

Da der Gesetzgeber offenbar hier eine Geheimhaltung nicht bezweckte, sondern die Entscheidung in geheimer Sitzung nur gestattete, der Vereinfachung wegen, so steht wohl nichts im Wege, den in Frage stehenden Ausspruch gegebenen Falles in ein gewöhnliches, in öffentlicher Sitzung gesprochenes, Urtheil aufzunehmen.

4) Bei den Verhandlungen wurde angeregt, wie es sich mit der Verjährung der Ansprüche der Anwälte gegenüber den Bestimmungen des Ges. vom 26. März 1859 und des Art. 2273 Cod. civ. verhalte, und mit Recht bemerkt, daß selbstverständlich eine Verjährung erst laufe vom Augenblicke an, wo die Voraussetzungen zur Einforderung gegeben seien, d. h. wo die Partei zu Vermögen gelange, oder der Anwalt erfahre, daß sie dasselbe früher verheimlicht habe. Abg. I 181. Da übrigens eine Vorbedingung zur Einklagung der Kosten die gerichtliche Aufhebung des Armenrechts nach Art. 143 Abs. 3 bildet, so ist klar, daß eine Verjährung nicht laufen könne, so lange diese Aufhebung verweigert wird.

Art. 144. — **Im Falle des Obsiegens der zum Armenrechte zugelassenen Partei sind der k. Fiskus, die Anwälte, Gerichtsvollzieher und Notare durch einen Beisatz im Urtheile zu ermächtigen, die Verurtheilung im Kostenpunkte bezüglich der ihnen zukommenden Beträge für sich gegen den unterliegenden Theil in Vollzug setzen zu lassen.**

Art. 145. — **Nähere Bestimmungen über die Behandlung der Armenrechtsgesuche und Armensachen, namentlich über den Nachweis der Vermögenslosigkeit, die Instruktion der Armenrechtsgesuche, die Vormerkung und den Vorschuß der Kosten u. s. w., bleiben dem Verordnungswege vorbehalten.** G. A. d. K. d. A. I S. 150. 162. 163. 181. IV S. 27. — K. d. R. I S. 284.

1) Das Armenrecht wird nur gewährt zu Gunsten der armen Partei, um ihr die Verfolgung ihrer Rechte möglich zu machen, und hieraus leitet sich die natürliche Folge ab, daß die Gegenpartei, wenn sie unterliegt, alle Kosten, von deren Bestreitung die arme Partei einstweilen

befreit war, ersetzen muß. Da nun aber in diesem Falle nicht die Partei selbst forderungsberechtigt ist, sondern der Fiskus, der Anwalt ꝛc., so entspricht es der Natur der Sache, daß das Gericht hier ebenso, wie im Falle des Art. 112 (zu welchem Art. 144 ursprünglich gehörte), die Berechtigten zur direkten Erhebung ermächtige, und zwar von Amtswegen.

Diese Ermächtigung wird jedem Berechtigten nur ertheilt für den ihm zukommenden Betrag, für welchen er sofort in alle Rechte der Partei bezüglich der Liquidirung und Verfolgung des Kostenanspruchs eintritt. Art. 113 ff. Wurde der Kostenersatz nur theilweise zugesprochen, so erfolgt selbstverständlich die Einsetzung in die Rechte der Partei für alle Berechtigte nur verhältnißmäßig.

2) Das Gesetz schreibt als Regel vor, daß die Liquidirung der Kosten vor Ausfertigung des Urtheils erfolge und der liquidirte Betrag in den Urtheilssatz aufzunehmen sei (Art. 113); sein Wille ist es also, daß aus dem Urtheile selbst zu ersehen sei, wie viel Kosten und an wen sie der Verurtheilte schulde.

Hieraus leitet sich die Verpflichtung für den Anwalt der obsiegenden Partei ab, bei der von ihm einzureichenden Kostenliquidation die Forderungen der verschiedenen Berechtigten einzusetzen und auszuscheiden, damit sie in dieser Weise in's Urtheil aufgenommen werden.

3) In Frage könnte gezogen werden, ob die Ermächtigung zum Vollzuge, von welcher Art. 144 spricht, auch gegeben werden könne, wenn die Gegenpartei selbst im Genusse des Armenrechts ist? Zwar wird es immerhin nöthig sein, die Einsetzung in die Rechte der Partei für den Fall auszusprechen, als die Gegenpartei zu Vermögen kommen sollte; allein hat sich der Richter auf eine solche bedingte Verfügung zu beschränken?

Es lägen manche Gründe vor, diese Frage zu bejahen, und es könnte selbst die Praxis des früheren Rechtes dafür angerufen werden (Seuff. Comm. Bd. II S. 138 Note 14); allein ich finde es bedenklich, der allgemeinen Fassung des Art. 114 gegenüber für diesen Fall eine Ausnahme zu schaffen. Um dies thun zu können, müßte man dem Art. 134 den Sinn unterlegen, daß das Armenrecht auch Befreiung von den bezüglichen Kosten der Gegenpartei bewirken solle — einen Sinn, welchen er offenbar nicht hat und welcher dahin führen würde, auch denjenigen Anwalt, welcher wegen Mangels an Vorschuß sich in die Kostenforderung will einweisen lassen (Art. 112), zurückzuweisen.

Strafen.

Art. 146. — **Die auf Grund des gegenwärtigen Gesetzbuchs oder der Advokatenordnung gegen Advokaten verhängten Geldstrafen fallen dem Pensionsfond für die Hinterlassenen der Advokaten des Königreichs zu.**

Die auf Grund des gegenwärtigen Gesetzbuchs oder der Gerichtsvollzieherordnung gegen Gerichtsvollzieher verhängten Geldstrafen sind zur Unterstützung der Gerichtsvollzieher oder ihrer Hinterlassenen zu verwenden.

Alle übrigen auf Grund des gegenwärtigen Gesetzbuchs verhängten Geldstrafen sind vorbehaltlich der Bestimmung des Art. 864 Abs. 5 durch Verordnung für die Advokaten, die Gerichtsvollzieher oder die bei den Gerichten angestellten niedern Bediensteten oder deren Hinterbliebene zu verwenden.

Art. 147. — **Die auf Grund des gegenwärtigen Gesetzbuchs verhängten Geldstrafen sind in gleicher Weise wie die von den Strafgerichten ausgesprochenen Geldstrafen beizutreiben.**

Sie sind in Arreststrafen umzuwandeln, wenn ihre gänzliche oder theilweise Uneinbringlichkeit durch ein Zeugniß des Erhebungsbeamten dargethan ist.

Die Umwandlung erfolgt auf Antrag des Staatsanwalts durch das Gericht, welches die Strafe ausgesprochen hat, unter Anwendung des im Polizeistrafgesetzbuche festgesetzten Maßstabs. Der Arrest wird als Civilstrafe auf Betreiben des Staatsanwalts vollzogen.

Bei den Gerichten, an welchen ein Staatsanwalt nicht angestellt ist, hat die Umwandlung von Amtswegen, der Vollzug des Arrests aber auf Betreiben des Gerichtsvorstands zu geschehen.

In wie ferne bezüglich derjenigen Geldstrafen, welche als Vollstreckungsmittel in Anwendung kommen, eine Abweichung von diesen Vorschriften einzutreten hat, ist in Art. 864 bestimmt.

Der Verurtheilte ist jederzeit befugt, sich durch Erlegung des Strafbetrags, soweit derselbe durch den erstandenen Arrest noch nicht getilgt ist, von dem letztern frei zu machen.

G. A. d. K. d. A. III S. 609. 610. 616. 617. IV S. 27. — K. d. R. IV S. 18. 19.

Die Bestimmungen dieser beiden Artikel sind so einfach und klar, daß erläuternde Bemerkungen unnöthig erscheinen.

Indem Art. 147 die Eintreibung der Geldstrafen regelt, spricht er ausschließlich von denjenigen, welche in der Prozeßordnung selbst angedroht sind. Solche finden sich in den Artikeln 50, 56, 99, 174, 381, 385, 389, 427, 432, 614, 785, 813.

V. Hauptstück.

Allgemeine Vorschriften über das Verfahren.

Oeffentlichkeit der Verhandlung.

Art. 148. — **Die Verhandlungen vor den Gerichten sind öffentlich, soweit das Gesetz keine Ausnahme macht.**

Kinder und solche Personen, welche in einer der Würde des Gerichts nicht entsprechenden Weise erscheinen, haben keinen Zutritt.

Art. 149. — **Die Oeffentlichkeit der Verhandlung kann beschränkt werden, wenn Aergerniß oder Gefährdung des öffentlichen Friedens zu besorgen ist.**

Das Gericht beschließt hierüber auf Antrag oder von Amtswegen, ohne daß gegen den Beschluß ein Rechtsmittel stattfindet.

Wenn die Oeffentlichkeit beschränkt ist, kann jede Partei außer ihrem Gewalthaber drei Personen ihres Vertrauens zur Seite behalten. Andere Personen sind ausgeschlossen.

G. A. d. K. d. A. I S. 190—192. 233. 279. IV S. 27. — K. d. R. I S. 284. 285.

1) Oeffentlichkeit und Mündlichkeit bilden die Grundlagen des neuen Verfahrens.

Unverkennbar ist von beiden Prinzipien das letztere von weit überwiegender Bedeutung. Dieses Prinzip allein bestimmt das Wesen des neuen Verfahrens und setzt dasselbe in so schroffen Gegensatz zum früheren; es bildet zugleich die Hauptquelle der großen Vortheile, welche das neue Verfahren bietet. Eine Oeffentlichkeit in gewissem Grade liegt zudem im Prinzipe der Mündlichkeit an sich, insofern dasselbe die Anwesenheit der Anwälte und Parteien bei der gerichtlichen Verhandlung bedingt.

Die Oeffentlichkeit in weiterem Sinne, wie sie Art. 148 zur Regel macht, dient nur dazu, das mündliche Verfahren in seiner Wirksamkeit zu unterstützen und diese zu steigern. In dieser Richtung sind jedoch die Vortheile desselben sehr hoch anzuschlagen.

2) Allerdings wirkt die Oeffentlichkeit im Civilprozesse in etwas anderer Weise als im Strafprozesse, wie denn auch das Publikum, welches in Betracht kommt, ein anderes ist.

Vor den Strafgerichten werden in der Regel Gegenstände verhandelt, über welche sich Jeder, der die Verhandlungen mit Aufmerksamkeit verfolgt und gesunden Menschenverstand besitzt, ein Urtheil zu bilden vermag; in den Civilsitzungen aber handelt es sich fast immer um Fragen, zu deren richtiger Auffassung und Beurtheilung juristische Kenntnisse und Erfahrungen erforderlich sind. Wer solche nicht besitzt, hat weder Beruf noch Lust, den Verhandlungen zu folgen.

So kommt es, daß das Publikum in Civilsitzungen sich gewöhnlich bloß bildet aus den Parteien der verschiedenen zur Verhandlung anberaumten Sachen, aus den Advokaten, welche in diesen Sachen auftreten, und aus Rechtspraktikanten, welche zu ihrer Belehrung den Sitzungen beiwohnen. Hierzu sind noch die Beamten zu zählen, welche gemäß ihrer Dienstpflicht in den Sitzungen anwesend sind, nemlich der Staatsanwalt, der Gerichtsschreiber und der Gerichtsvollzieher.

Es erscheint nun aber durchaus nicht nöthig, daß Personen in größerer Zahl in der Sitzung anwesend seien, um die Vortheile, welche das Gesetz im Civilprozesse von der Oeffentlichkeit verlangt, zu bewirken; denn es kommt hier nicht sowohl auf die Quantität, als auf die Qualität der Personen an. Die rechtsverständigen Zuhörer allein sind es, welche zu beurtheilen im Stande sind, ob und wie Richter und Advokaten ihre Pflichten erfüllen, und ihr Urtheil ist natürlich auch in den Kreisen des größeren Publikums maßgebend. Ihre Anwesenheit allein vermag anderseits auch einen bestimmenden Einfluß auf die Verhandlungen zu üben.

Faßt man nun zuerst die Thätigkeit des Richters in's Auge, so ist die Oeffentlichkeit der Verhandlung für ihn ein sehr wirksamer Sporn, alles dasjenige zu thun, was Sachkundige von einem gewissenhaften und fähigen Richter verlangen, d. h. die Verhandlung in vollkommen unparteilicher Weise zu leiten, alles anzuregen, was zur Aufklärung der Sache nöthig ist, nie ein Urtheil zu fällen, bevor der Sachverhalt völlig klargestellt ist, unnütze Verhandlungen abzuschneiden und natürlich schließlich den Nagel auf den Kopf zu treffen.

So wenig das Publikum der Oberflächlichkeit geneigt ist, so wenig liebt es anderseits auch ein pedantisches, in werthlosen Nebendingen sich abmühendes, Verfahren; es schätzt denjenigen Richter am meisten, welcher rasch das Wesentliche der Sache herauszugreifen versteht und, indem er demselben die vollste Beachtung zuwendet, das Unwesentliche zur Seite schiebt. Es ist ein Hauptvorzug der Oeffentlichkeit und Mündlichkeit, diese Fähigkeit des Richters zu wecken und zu entwickeln.

Ebenso günstig, wie auf die Amtsthätigkeit des Richters, wirkt die Oeffentlichkeit auch auf die Amtsthätigkeit der Advokaten, deren Thun und Lassen nicht bloß unter der Controle der eignen Parteien, sondern auch aller Mitglieder des Gerichtes, des Staatsanwaltes, sowie ihrer eignen Collegen und des sonstigen Publikums steht.

Bezüglich der segensreichen Folgen, welche von der Oeffentlichkeit für den Geist des Advokatenstandes überhaupt zu erwarten sind, genügt es, auf das vortreffliche Werk von Zink (die Ermittlung des Sachverhalts im französischen Civilprozesse) zu verweisen.

3) Unsere Prozeßordnung erklärt die Oeffentlichkeit der gerichtlichen Verhandlungen als Regel und will, daß sie bei Strafe der Nichtigkeit überall eintrete, wo nicht eine ausdrückliche Ausnahme im Gesetze gemacht ist. Art. 788 Ziff. 5.

Aus der Thatsache, daß die öffentliche Verhandlung in den Augen des Gesetzes als die vollkommnere, stärkere Garantieen für die Rechtsprechung bietende erscheint, folgt, daß es nicht verwehrt sein könne, in Punkten, wo das Gesetz die Entscheidung in geheimer Sitzung anordnet, ausnahmsweise auch in öffentlicher Sitzung zu entscheiden, wenn *alle* Voraussetzungen dazu gegeben sind und der Gesetzgeber nicht gerade zum Zwecke der Geheimhaltung die Verhandlung in öffentlicher Sitzung ausgeschlossen hat. Vgl. oben zu Art. 143 Nr. 3.

4) Indem Art. 148 verfügt, daß Kinder, sowie Personen, welche in einer der Würde des Gerichts nicht entsprechenden Weise erscheinen, keinen Zutritt haben sollen, läßt es dem Ermessen des Vorsitzenden, welchem hier ohne Zweifel die Verfügung zusteht, ziemlichen Spielraum.

Unter letztgedachten Personen sind wohl hauptsächlich solche begriffen, welche betrunken oder in unanständiger Kleidung vor Gericht erscheinen.

5) Beschränkung der Oeffentlichkeit darf nur verfügt werden, wenn *Aergerniß* oder *Gefährdung des öffentlichen Friedens* zu besorgen ist.

Der Ausdruck „*Aergerniß*" ist an sich etwas unbestimmt und großer Ausdehnung fähig; es wird jedoch anzunehmen sein, der Gesetzgeber habe ihn nur in beschränkterem Sinne gemeint und hauptsächlich Fälle, wo das Sittlichkeitsgefühl verletzt würde, im Auge gehabt. Bei den Verhandlungen sprach man wenigstens nur von Fällen solcher Art. Uebrigens dürfte hieraus doch wiederum nicht zu folgern sein, daß der Gesetzgeber ausschließlich bloß unsittliche Vorgänge gemeint habe, weil man sonst vorgezogen haben würde, die Worte des hannov. Entwurfs (§ 116) zu wählen, welcher von „Gefahr für die Sittlichkeit" spricht.

Mit dem Ausdrucke „*Gefährdung des öffentlichen Friedens*" sind zunächst Fälle gemeint, wo Störungen im *Sitzungssaale* durch eine aufgeregte Menge zu besorgen sind (Abg. I 192 [Völk]); allein er erstreckt sich offenbar auch auf derartige Störungen, welche außerhalb des Sitzungssaales als unmittelbare Folge einer Verhandlung eintreten können.

Um das Herbeiziehen rein politischer Motive zu verhüten, wurde die ursprüngliche Fassung: „Gefährdung der öffentlichen *Ordnung*" geändert.

6) Bei Beschränkung der Oeffentlichkeit kann jede Partei drei Personen ihres Vertrauens zur Seite behalten.

Unter „Partei" sind wohl die sämmtlichen vom *nemlichen Anwalte* vertretenen Streitgenossen begriffen.

Advokaten und selbst Gerichtspersonen erscheinen ausgeschlossen — eigentlich ohne genügenden Grund, da es sich ja nicht um Geheimhaltung handelt und nicht zu besorgen sein dürfte, es möchte solchen Personen ein sie beschädigendes Aergerniß gegeben werden, oder es möchte von ihnen die Veranlassung zu einer Störung des öffentlichen Friedens ausgehen.

Uebrigens kann die Rede nicht davon sein, daß die Anwesenheit solcher Personen eine Nichtigkeit begründe, und überhaupt wird es, da hier der Ausschluß der Oeffentlichkeit nicht auf dem Gesetze beruht, sondern auf dem Ermessen des Richters, keinem Anstande unterliegen, daß das nemliche richterliche Ermessen auch beliebigen anderen Personen die Beiwohnung gestatte.

Leitung der Verhandlung.

Art. 150. — Der Vorsitzende oder Einzelnrichter leitet die Verhandlung.

Er eröffnet und schließt die Sitzung, ertheilt das Wort, vernimmt die Parteien, die Zeugen und die Sachverständigen und spricht das Urtheil aus.

G. A. d. K. d. A. I S. 192. 193. 197. 198. 233. 234. 280 IV S. 27. K. d. R. I S. 285. 286.

1) Dieser Artikel gibt in wenigen einfachen Zügen ein klares Bild von der Thätigkeit des Richters bei Leitung der öffentlichen Verhandlungen. Es genügen diese allgemeinen Sätze vollständig für den einsichtsvollen Richter; mangelt es aber an Einsicht, so möchte auch mit den ausführlichsten, pedantischsten Vorschriften nicht gedient sein — sie würden mehr verwirren, als aufklären.

2) Die Aufgabe des Vorsitzenden im Civilverfahren, namentlich an Gerichten erster Instanz, wo die Klarstellung der Sache oft erst in der Sitzung unter Mithilfe des Richters erfolgt, ist eine sehr wichtige, und man darf wohl sagen, daß von der Art und Weise, wie er dieselbe löst, es wesentlich abhänge, ob die Rechtspflege eine gute oder mangelhafte zu nennen sei.

Fehlt es dem Vorsitzenden an schneller Auffassung, an der Gabe, die Sache in ihren thatsächlichen und rechtlichen Gesichtspunkten zu durchdringen, weiß er das Wesentliche vom Unwesentlichen nicht sofort zu trennen, so wird die Verhandlung unklar, verwirrt und schleppt sich in unerquicklicher Lahmheit und Breite dahin. Jede Partei glaubt natürlich nicht auf das Wort verzichten zu dürfen, so lange sie wahrnimmt, daß der Richter nicht klar sei, und zudem reizt dessen Unbehilflichkeit oft zu Versuchen, im Trüben zu fischen, welche sich klaren Augen gegenüber gar nicht an's Licht gewagt hätten.

Sitzungspolizei.

Art. 151. — Der Vorsitzende oder Einzelnrichter handhabt die Sitzungspolizei.

Er trifft die geeigneten Maßregeln, um Störungen der Verhandlungen und Ordnungswidrigkeiten abzuwenden und zu unterdrücken.

Er ist befugt, Zuhörer, welche den Gang der Verhandlung durch Zeichen des Beifalls oder Mißfallens oder auf andere Weise stören, aus dem Sitzungssaale entfernen und bei besonders erschwerenden Umständen bis auf vier und zwanzig Stunden zur Haft bringen zu lassen.

Parteien, Beistände und Gewalthaber, welche sich ungebührlich betragen, werden vom Vorsitzenden oder Einzelnrichter zur Ordnung verwiesen. Fügen sie sich seiner Mahnung nicht, so kann das Gericht die Verhandlung auf ihre Kosten vertagen oder ihre Entfernung aus dem Sitzungssaale anordnen, auch eine sofort vollstreckbare Arreststrafe bis zu vier und zwanzig Stunden gegen sie erkennen. In den beiden letztern Fällen wird in der Sache selbst in gleicher Weise verfahren, als wenn sie sich freiwillig während der Verhandlung entfernt hätten.

Macht sich ein als Beistand oder Gewalthaber oder zur Ausführung der mündlichen Rechtsvertheidigung zugezogener Advokat solcher Ungebühr schuldig, so kann er vom Vorsitzenden oder Einzelnrichter zur Ordnung gemahnt werden. Fügt er sich dieser Mahnung nicht, so kann die Vertagung der Verhandlung auf seine Kosten erfolgen.

Die Bestrafung des Schuldigen und das dabei zu beobachtende Verfahren richtet sich in den Fällen des Abs. 5 nach den Bestimmungen der Advokatenordnung.

Gegen die in Abs. 3—5 bezeichneten Verfügungen finden Rechtsmittel nicht statt.

In allen Fällen bleibt die etwa veranlaßte strafrechtliche Einschreitung vorbehalten.

Art. 152. — Wurde in der öffentlichen Sitzung eine Handlung, wegen welcher strafrechtliche Einschreitung angezeigt ist, begangen, so hat das Gericht dieselbe durch Protokoll festzustellen und dieses dem Staatsanwalte zu übersenden. In Fällen, in welchen nach den bestehenden Gesetzen der Thäter in Untersuchungshaft genommen werden kann oder provisorische Festnahme durch die Polizeibehörde gestattet ist, kann das Gericht zugleich die provisorische Festnahme verfügen. Der Festgenommene muß ohne Verzug dem zuständigen Staatsanwalte, Untersuchungsrichter oder Einzelnrichter vorgeführt werden.

Art. 153. — Die in Art. 150—152 bezeichneten Befugnisse und Obliegenheiten haben auch Gerichtsmitglieder, von welchen außerhalb der Sitzung Amtshandlungen vorgenommen werden.

Was in den angeführten Artikeln bezüglich der Sitzung und des Sitzungssaales be-

stimmt ist, gilt in diesem Falle von den durch das Gerichtsmitglied vorzunehmenden Amtshandlungen und dem Orte, wo sie vorgenommen werden.

G. A. d. K. d. A. I S. 193. 194. 197. 198. 233. 234. 280. IV S. 27. 310—312.
K. d. R. I S. 286—292. IV S. 20—23.

1) Während Art. 150 die Leitung der Verhandlung in die Hände des Vorsitzenden legt, überträgt ihm Art. 151 noch weiter die Handhabung der Sitzungspolizei.

Er soll zu diesem Zwecke im Allgemeinen befugt sein, alle Maßregeln nach freiem Ermessen zu treffen, welche zur Aufrechthaltung der Ordnung nöthig sind. An diese allgemeine Befugniß reiht das Gesetz Vorschriften an für den besonderen Fall, wo gegen einzelne Personen wegen ordnungswidrigen Verhaltens einzuschreiten ist, und unterscheidet dabei mit Rücksicht auf die Art der Theilnahme an den Verhandlungen: 1) gewöhnliche Zuhörer, 2) gewöhnliche Betheiligte und 3) betheiligte Advokaten.

2) Zu 1. Zuhörer können sofort, ohne vorausgehenden Ordnungsruf, aus dem Sitzungssaale entfernt, ja bei besonders erschwerenden Umständen sogar zur Haft gebracht werden.

Unter den Begriff von „Zuhörern" fallen alle Personen, welche nicht bei der in Verhandlung begriffenen Sache betheiligt sind, oder deren Betheiligung dabei ihr Ende erreicht hat. An der Verhandlung nicht mehr betheiligt sind z. B. Rechtspraktikanten, nachdem ihnen auf Grund von Art. 80 das Wort entzogen ist (Abg. I 234 [v. Neumayr]), oder Zeugen und Sachverständige, nachdem sie vernommen sind (Abg. I 194 [v. Weiß]).

Personen, welche bei einer späteren Verhandlung betheiligt sind, kann der Vorsitzende zwar entfernen, er muß ihnen aber den Zeitpunkt angeben, wann sie zur Verhandlung ihrer Sache wieder im Sitzungssaale erscheinen dürfen. Jedenfalls könnte die Entfernung eines solchen Betheiligten für die ganze Sitzung nie vom Vorsitzenden allein und ohne vorausgegangenen Ordnungsruf erfolgen.

Zu 2. Bei Betheiligten — Parteien, Gewalthabern und Beiständen — muß ein Ordnungsruf vorausgehen, und erst wenn sich dieser erfolglos zeigt, dürfen die weiteren Maßnahmen eintreten, welche zudem nur vom Gerichte verfügt werden können.

Was Zeugen und Sachverständige betrifft, welche in der Sitzung zu vernehmen sind, so ist es klar, daß Fälle vorkommen können, wo die Aufrechthaltung der Ordnung es nothwendig macht, sie zu entfernen, und die Aeußerung (Abg. I 194), daß Einschreiten gegen Zeugen nicht statthaft sei, geht zu weit. Offenbar sind dieselben jedoch als Betheiligte und nicht als bloße Zuhörer zu behandeln. Die Verurtheilung in die Kosten würde sich bei ihnen schon auf die Bestimmungen der Art. 427 und 432 gründen lassen.

Zu 3. Gegen Advokaten, welche im Anwaltsprozesse oder im Parteiprozesse als solche auftreten, kann, wenn der Ordnungsruf ohne Erfolg geblieben, bloß die Vertagung auf ihre Kosten verfügt werden.

Weitere disciplinäre Einschreitung, welche veranlaßt sein könnte, richtet sich nach der Advokatenordnung. Auch in diesem Falle erleidet der Grundsatz des Art. 5 Ziff. 4 eine Ausnahme.

3) Die vom Gerichte getroffenen Maßregeln, welche Verurtheilung zu Kosten enthalten, oder welche eine Verhaftung anordnen, oder endlich aus welchen rechtliche Folgen für den Rechtsstreit entstehen, bedürfen natürlich einer urkundlichen Feststellung.

Was zuerst die Vertagung auf Kosten des Ruhestörers betrifft, so versteht sich von selbst, daß eine förmliche Verurtheilung in die betreffenden Kosten im Vertagungsurtheile auszusprechen ist.

Was die Ausweisung der Parteien oder ihrer Gewalthaber anbelangt, so erhält diese Maßregel durch die Verfügung, daß in der Sache gerade so zu verfahren sei, als sei die Entfernung eine freiwillige, eine sehr große Tragweite.

Erfolgt nemlich die Ausweisung vor Stellung der Anträge, so ist der Ausgewiesene als nicht erschienen zu behandeln; erfolgt sie aber später, so wird gegen ihn kontradiktorisch verfahren, ohne Rücksicht darauf, daß er nicht mehr im Stande ist, seine Anträge zu begründen oder nach Bedürfniß zu ändern (Art. 254). Es kann sogar der Fall eintreten, daß die Partei in Folge ihrer Ausweisung als den Eid verweigernd zu betrachten ist (Art. 465).

Diese Folgen erscheinen um so gewichtiger, als gegen die Ausweisungsbeschlüsse Rechtsmittel nicht zuläßig sind (Art. 151 Abs. 7).

Angesichts dieser Wirkungen und da das Gericht selbst es ist, welches verfügt, wird es geeignet sein, besonderen Beschluß in's Urtheilsbuch aufzunehmen (Art. 281 Abs. 2), welcher dann in der Geschichtserzählung des ergehenden Urtheils angeführt werden kann.

Zu erwähnen möchte hier sein, daß ursprünglich ein Zusatz gemacht war, welcher das Gericht ermächtigte, Verfügungen dieser Art jederzeit wieder zurückzunehmen, und dieser Zusatz als selbstverständlich beseitigt worden ist. Abg. I 234 (Barth).

Was die Verhängung der Haft anbelangt, welche keine eigentliche Strafe ist (Art. 151 Abs. 8), sondern welche nur die Fortsetzung oder Wiederholung ungehöriger Auftritte, durch Wiedereindringen in den Sitzungssaal ꝛc., verhindern soll (R. R. I 288 [v. Weiß]), so verlangte der Gesetzgeber ursprünglich nur eine Erwähnung im Sitzungsprotokolle (Abg. I 234); als jedoch später dieses Protokoll beseitigt worden war, wurde bemerkt, es habe eine Constatirung anderer Art an die Stelle zu treten. Abg. I 280 (Barth). Hiernach möchte es, um den Willen des Gesetzes zu erfüllen, genügen, daß je nach Umständen das Gericht selbst oder der Vorsitzende auf Grund vorliegender Bestimmung einen Haftbefehl erläßt, auf welchen hin die Aufnahme ins Gefängniß erfolgt.

Die Ausweisung von Zuhörern und der Ordnungsruf bedürfen einer Constatirung nicht.

4) Alle Befugnisse, welche Art. 151 dem Vorsitzenden und dem Gerichte gibt, stehen auch den Richterkommissären zu (Art. 153). Diese dürfen daher, ohne daß Rechtsmittel zulässig wären, auf Kosten der Parteien, Anwälte ꝛc. die Verhandlung vertagen! Vgl. Art. 420 Abs. 3.

5) Nachdem hier der Gesetzgeber sowohl die Maßregeln zur Handhabung der Sitzungspolizei, als auch das Verfahren in Fällen, wo strafbare Handlungen in der Sitzung begangen werden, in erschöpfender Weise behandelt hat, fällt die Anwendung der Art. 504 ff. Code d'instr. crim. für das Gebiet des Civilprozesses hinweg. Namentlich kann von einer Zuständigkeit der Civilgerichte zur sofortigen Aburtheilung einer strafbaren Handlung, soweit sie den Bestimmungen des Art. 31 des Einführungsgesetzes zum St. G. B. gegenüber noch Geltung hat, nicht mehr die Rede sein.

Fragerecht.

Art. 154. — **Der Vorsitzende oder Einzelnrichter hat durch sachgemäße Fragen von den Parteien und ihren Gewalthabern alle Aufklärungen zu erholen, welche zum Verständnisse der geltend gemachten Thatsachen und der gestellten Anträge, zur Ergänzung und Erläuterung unvollständiger, unbestimmter oder undeutlicher Erklärungen oder sonst zur Feststellung des Sachverhalts erforderlich scheinen. Mit seiner Erlaubniß können auch die übrigen Gerichtsmitglieder, sowie die Parteien und deren Gewalthaber oder Beistände unmittelbar Fragen stellen.**

Zweifel über die Zulässigkeit einer Frage entscheidet das Gericht.

Persönliches Erscheinen der Parteien.

Art. 155. — **Erachtet das Gericht zur Aufklärung der Sache für angemessen, die Parteien selbst zu vernehmen, so kann ihr persönliches Erscheinen in einer festzusetzenden Sitzung verfügt werden.**

Ist eine Partei durch Krankheit oder Gebrechen verhindert, persönlich in der Sitzung zu erscheinen, so kann das Gericht die Vernehmung derselben über bestimmte, in das Urtheil aufzunehmende Fragen durch ein Gerichtsmitglied oder durch den Richter des Wohnorts der Partei anordnen. Die Gegenpartei ist in diesem Falle von Zeit und Ort der Vernehmung durch den Gerichtsschreiber in Kenntniß zu setzen. Sie kann bei der Vernehmung sich vertreten lassen und auch persönlich mit oder ohne Vertreter oder Beistand erscheinen.

G. A. d. K. d. A. I S. 194—198. 280. 281. IV S. 27. 37.
K. d. R. I S. 292. 293. IV S. 23.

1) Die Aufklärung des Sachverhalts durch Fragestellung an die Anwälte und an die Parteien ist so sehr in der Natur des mündlichen Verfahrens begründet, daß es eigenthümlich klingt, wenn das Gesetz ein Fragerecht des Richters förmlich anerkennt, gleich als könnte dieses Recht in Zweifel gezogen werden, wenn eine ausdrückliche Verleihung nicht bestünde. Uebrigens mag im Hinblicke darauf, daß das ganze Verfahren ein neues ist, diese Anerkennung nicht ganz ohne Nutzen sein.

In den höheren Instanzen, wo in der Regel der Stoff schon gelichtet und gesichtet ist, erscheint das Eingreifen des Richters in die Verhandlung von weniger Bedeutung; allein für die erste Instanz ist es von höchster Wichtigkeit. Es begreift sich dies leicht, wenn in's Auge gefaßt wird, daß in dringlichen Sachen, dann vor den Handelsgerichten und Landgerichten ein schriftliches Vorverfahren der öffentlichen Verhandlung nicht vorausgeht; daß oft die Anwälte und Prozeßbevollmächtigten nicht einmal im Stande sind, sich durch ihre eignen Parteien genügend informiren zu lassen, geschweige denn die Aufstellungen des

Gegners in Betracht zu ziehen; daß endlich, ganz abgesehen hievon, durch Vorbringen neuer Thatsachen oder Urkunden, sowie durch die mündlichen Erklärungen der Parteien die Sachlage sich inmitten der Verhandlung ganz anders gestalten kann.

Wenn es sich daher in höheren Instanzen mehr um ruhige geordnete Entwicklung und Beleuchtung gegebener Verhältnisse handelt, so tritt in erster Instanz die Entwirrung des Sachverhalts, das Auffinden und Feststellen der maßgebenden Gesichtspunkte in den Vordergrund. Dort herrscht in der Regel epische Ruhe und Breite, hier dramatische Lebendigkeit und Kürze.

2) Beim Parteiprozesse, wo Leute, welche mehr oder weniger rechtsunkundig sind, vor Gericht zu erscheinen pflegen, springt es wohl sofort in die Augen, daß vom klaren Blicke und richtigen Takte des die Verhandlung leitenden Richters außerordentlich viel abhänge, daß, je nachdem dieser seiner Aufgabe gewachsen ist oder nicht, die Instruktion eine rasche oder langsame, eine gründliche oder oberflächliche, ja daß oft das ganze Schicksal des Prozesses davon bedingt sei.

Allein auch für den Anwaltsprozeß ist dies annähernd richtig.

Es kommt auch bei den tüchtigsten und gewandtesten Anwälten hie und da vor, daß sie im Eifer der Diskussion, in Verfolgung eines sie beherrschenden Ideengangs, Umstände übersehen oder nicht gehörig beleuchten, welche für die richterliche Beurtheilung wichtig sind, und daß der Richter, welchen seine Stellung befähigt, mit größerer Ruhe und Unbefangenheit das Ganze zu überschauen, sich veranlaßt findet, durch sachgemäße Fragen die Lücken zu ergänzen und Zweifel aufzuklären. Hat der Richter aber Advokaten vor sich, denen es an der nöthigen Einsicht oder Gewandtheit fehlt, so wird seine Wirksamkeit noch in viel höherem Maße in Anspruch genommen, wenn nicht das gute Recht der Parteien Schaden leiden soll.

Allerdings würde er seine Pflichten sehr verkennen, wollte er Rath ertheilen, oder irgendwie seine Meinung kundgeben; allein soweit er ohne Gefährdung seiner unparteiischen Stellung durch Anregungen und Fragestellungen zur Aufklärung oder richtigen Behandlung der Sache beitragen kann, ist es seine Pflicht, dies zu thun. Eine Anwendung dieses Grundsatzes findet sich in Art. 328 Abs. 4.

3) In dieser Einwirkung des Richters bei der Instruktion der Sache liegt einer der wesentlichsten Vorzüge des neuen Verfahrens. Sie trägt dazu bei, daß gleich vom Beginne des Prozesses an die materielle Wahrheit zur Geltung gelange und der Formalismus keinen Boden gewinne.

Es wird z. B. in Zukunft der Fall nicht vorkommen können, daß eine Klage, eine Einrede 2c. als nicht genügend substantiirt erklärt wird, im Sinne wie dies im alten Prozesse geschah. Der Richter, welcher so etwas ausspräche, müßte sich selbst ein Armuthszeugniß geben, d. h. er müßte zugestehen, daß er entweder seine Pflichten nicht gehörig erfüllt habe, oder daß er nicht fähig gewesen sei, einzusehen, worauf es ankomme. War die Klage oder Einrede nicht genügend substantiirt, so war es an ihm, zu veranlassen, daß sie substantiirt werde, oder an's Licht zu bringen, daß sie nicht substantiirt werden könne, daß sie grundlos sei. Er hat kein stummes Papier mehr vor sich, sondern lebende Personen, welche gefragt werden und welche Antwort geben können.

Der Richter kommt daher nur in die Lage, entweder eine Klage zuzusprechen, oder Beweis aufzulegen, oder ganz abzuweisen; ein Abweisen in angebrachter Art, mit der Folge, daß später die nemliche Klage, mit neuen Behauptungen ausgerüstet, wieder erscheinen könnte, gibt es nicht mehr, ebensowenig als im Strafverfahren eine absolutio ab instantia.

Ich muß gestehen, daß, als ich in die diesseitige Praxis trat, nichts mir so auffallend vorkam, als die so häufig auftretenden Erklärungen, daß Klagen, Einreden oder Repliken nicht genügend substantiirt seien. Erscheint dies schon als großer Mißstand bei Klagsansprüchen, insofern der nemliche Prozeß zwei-, dreimal, ja öfter vor Gericht erscheint und durchverhandelt wird, so ist die Sache noch viel schlimmer bei Einreden und Repliken, wo der Schaden in der Regel nicht mehr gut zu machen ist.

In der Pfalz scheute sich der Richter, gestützt auf Rechte, welche ihm das Gesetz gab, gewiß nicht, seiner Ueberzeugung von der materiellen Wahrheit Ausdruck zu geben — abzuschneiden und durchzuschneiden, wie man zu sagen pflegt; allein es geschah dies erst instructa causa, nachdem die wichtigen, durch die Verhandlung gebotenen Mittel der Aufklärung — Fragen an die Parteien, Prüfung der Urkunden 2c. — erschöpft waren und er sich überzeugt hielt, daß ein Beweisverfahren zu keinem Ziele führen werde. Diesseits jedoch wurden oft unter dem Titel des Mangels der Substantiirung, prima vista, die wichtigsten Einreden 2c. auf die Seite geschoben und in einem Prozesse, welcher sonst an der pedantischsten Aengstlichkeit, an einem krankhaften Streben nach Gründlichkeit litt, herrschte hier auf einmal eine Kühnheit, welche oft an reine Willkür grenzte.

Allerdings lag die Schuld bloß im Prozesse, namentlich in der Schwierigkeit, welche die Fassung der Beweisinterlokute machte; es war ein Nothweg, welchen sich der Richter zu bahnen gezwungen war, um das Verfahren einigermaßen praktisch zu machen.

4) Von großem Gewichte ist die Befugniß, welche Art. 155 dem Richter gibt, in allen Fällen, wo er es zur Aufklärung der Sache als nöthig erachtet, das persönliche Erscheinen der Parteien zu verordnen.

In der Pfalz ist es Regel, daß die Parteien auch ohne besondere Anordnung des Gerichts den Verhandlungen beiwohnen. Sie selbst haben begreiflich Interesse, zu hören, wie ihr Prozeß plädirt werde; für die Anwälte aber ist es von großem Vortheile, die Parteien zur Seite zu haben. Diese können ihnen Aufschlüsse geben über neu vorgebrachte Thatsachen, können auftauchende Zweifel aufklären, über Urkunden, welche vorgelegt werden, sich erklären, und können endlich eintretenden Falls die nöthigen Spezialvollmachten sofort ertheilen.

Bei Bestimmung des Tages zur mündlichen Verhandlung (Art. 241 Abs. 6) pflegt man daher auch auf das Erscheinen der Parteien Rücksicht zu nehmen. Die Anwälte geben diesen von der Festsetzung des Sitzungstages Nachricht, sowie Aufschluß darüber, ob ihr Erscheinen gewünscht werde.

Erscheinen die Parteien nicht von selbst und zeigt sich deren Anwesenheit als sachgemäß, so genügt es in der Regel, die Verhandlung einfach in eine spätere Sitzung zu vertagen und die Anwälte vom Wunsche des Gerichts in Kenntniß zu setzen. Ein förmliches Urtheil wird gewöhnlich nur erlassen, wenn nicht zu erwarten ist, daß die Parteien ohne gerichtliche Nöthigung erscheinen werden, oder wenn sonst besondere Gründe vorliegen.

Zu einer Anordnung des persönlichen Erscheinens wird sich der Richter namentlich dann veranlaßt finden, wenn verwirrte thatsächliche Verhältnisse vorliegen, wenn zu erwarten steht, es möchten sich durch Gegenüberstellen der Parteien selbst manche Streitpunkte bereinigen, wenn vorauszusehen, daß es auf Eidesleistungen ankommen werde, wo dann die Erklärung über Annahme oder Zurückschiebung, in der Regel selbst die Eidesleistung sofort erfolgen kann, endlich wenn ein Vergleich zu hoffen steht.

In der Regel wird das Erscheinen beider Parteien verordnet; es steht jedoch nichts im Wege, daß der Richter ausnahmsweise nur das Erscheinen einer Partei anordne, z. B. wenn die andre Partei sehr weit entfernt wohnt, oder nicht die geringste Kenntniß vom Sachverhalte hat.

5) Zur Vernehmung der Parteien wird im Anwaltsprozesse der Richter erst schreiten, nachdem beide Anwälte so weit nöthig den Sachverhalt dargelegt haben, und er vollkommen im Stande ist, zu ermessen, welches die maßgebenden faktischen und rechtlichen Gesichtspunkte seien.

Was die Parteien dem Richter erklären, hat natürlich unbedingt Geltung, ohne Rücksicht auf etwa abweichende Aufstellungen der Anwälte; es ist ja gerade einer der Hauptzwecke ihrer Vernehmung, Thatsachen, welche die Anwälte unrichtig aufgefaßt oder vorgetragen haben, in's rechte Licht zu setzen.

Allerdings hat nun in dieser Beziehung der Richter diesseits nicht ganz die günstige Stellung, wie der Richter in der Pfalz.

Er kann der Partei nicht sagen, daß ihrer Sache, wenn sie rechtlich sei, durch wahrheitsgetreue Erzählung des Sachverhalts am besten gedient werde, daß er Geständnisse, welche sie mache, nicht theilen werde; es wird vielmehr der Richter für die Partei, welche er ausfrägt, manchmal im Lichte eines Mannes dastehen, welcher sie zu schädlichen Geständnissen zu verleiten, um ihr gutes Recht zu bringen sucht. Statt dem Vertrauen, wie es der pfälzische Richter findet, wird ihm Argwohn begegnen.

Auch der Vorhalt, daß es schließlich auf Eideserklärung ankommen werde, wird in der Regel nicht wirksam sein; denn abgesehen davon, daß es Fälle gibt, wo Eidesleistung nicht statthaft ist, wird die Partei auch wohl erwägen und durch ihren Anwalt erfahren haben, daß, sowie sie den Klagegrund zugesteht, ihr Prozeß verloren ist, während so lange sie läugnet, die Gegenpartei immerhin nicht sicher ist, ob geschworen werde oder nicht, und vielleicht zum Vergleiche sich herbeilassen wird. Endlich zeigt leider die Erfahrung, daß es den Leuten, wenn sie von ihrem guten Rechte überzeugt sind, wenig Skrupel zu machen pflegt, wie der Eid gefaßt sei, ob sie der Richter über alle Vorgänge oder nur über einen Theil derselben schwören lasse — wenn sie nur schwören dürfen. Was ihnen der Formalismus des Prozesses versagt, das geben sie sich selber, nemlich die Untheilbarkeit ihrer Angaben.

Ich glaube daher zuversichtlich, daß die Mündlichkeit des Verfahrens sehr bald dahin führen wird, die Theorie von der Theilung des Geständnisses als ein dem freien Geiste des neuen

Prozesses widerstrebendes Ueberbleibsel der alten Zeit zu betrachten, das man bei nächster Gelegenheit abschneidet.

6) Ein Hauptvortheil der persönlichen Anwesenheit der Parteien ist auch die Herbeiführung von Vergleichen.

Wenn der Richter nach durchverhandelter Sache die Parteien vortreten läßt, findet er sie gewöhnlich in versöhnlicher Stimmung. Während beim Beginne der Verhandlung jede Partei, voll Siegesgewißheit, Vergleichsvorschläge schroff abgewiesen hätte, sind jetzt, nachdem jede den Advokaten des Gegners gehört, die Ueberzeugungen etwas wankend geworden und Vorschläge zur Güte finden williges Gehör.

Versteht es der Richter, welchem nunmehr die Sache in allen Einzelnheiten klar vor Augen liegt, in einer Vertrauen einflößenden Weise den Parteien den Weg zum Vergleiche zu ebnen, so werden oft ganz überraschende Resultate erzielt.

Kommt es auf Erwägungen an, welche anzuregen sich für den Richter seiner Stellung wegen nicht ziemt, z. B. daß die Sache sich für eine Partei schlimm gestaltet habe 2c., so ist es sachgemäß, die Sache kurze Zeit auszusetzen, um den Parteien Gelegenheit zu geben, sich mit ihren Anwälten zu benehmen.

In der Pfalz pflegen die Anwälte dem Gerichte und dem Publikum gegenüber einen Stolz hineinzusetzen, in dieser Weise zur Beilegung von Rechtsstreiten beizutragen, und ich bin überzeugt, daß im nemlichen Geiste auch die Advokaten diesseits handeln werden.

Art. 156. — **Welche Folgen in Bezug auf die Feststellung des Sachverhalts die Verweigerung der Antwort auf gestellte Fragen und im Falle des Art. 155 das Nichterscheinen nach sich ziehe, bleibt dem richterlichen Ermessen anheimgegeben.**

G. A. d. K. d. A. I S. 194—198. IV S. 27. — K. d. R. I S. 293.

1) Wenn auf die Fragen, welche der Richter in den Fällen der Art. 154 und 155 an die Partei selbst oder an deren Gewalthaber stellt, keine genügende Antwort erfolgt, oder wenn, nachdem das persönliche Erscheinen verordnet worden war, die Partei nicht erscheint, so soll es dem richterlichen Ermessen überlassen bleiben, welche Folgen hieraus für die Feststellung des Sachverhalts zu ziehen seien. Vgl. Art. 164 Abs. 3.

Diese Verfügung hat eine große Tragweite.

2) Die französische Jurisprudenz, welche nicht auf bestimmtem Gesetzestexte beruht, sondern sich nur aus allgemeinen Prinzipien entwickelt hat, nimmt gleichfalls an, daß es dem Richter freistehe, aus dem Nichterscheinen einer Partei, deren persönliches Erscheinen verordnet war, die sachgemäßen Folgerungen zu ziehen; allein sie geht dabei nur vom Gesichtspunkte eines gewöhnlichen Vermuthungsbeweises aus, nicht aber von demjenigen eines Geständnisses. Die Folge ist, daß der französische Richter in Fällen, wo der Beweis durch Vermuthungen ausgeschlossen ist, d. h. in allen Fällen, wo Zeugenbeweis nicht zugelassen wird, nicht befugt ist, aus dem Nichterscheinen einen Beweis zu folgern. Chauveau sur Carré quest. 502 bis.

Es frägt sich nun, ob die Bestimmungen des Art. 156 auch nur in diesem beschränkten Sinne zu nehmen seien?

Die ganz allgemeine Fassung des Gesetzes möchte eine solche Unterscheidung nicht gestatten. Wenn der Gesetzgeber sagt, der Richter dürfe die ihm gutdünkenden Folgen für Feststellung des Sachverhalts ziehen, so dachte er wohl vorzugsweise an Annahme von Zugeständnissen, und es erscheint dies um so weniger zu bezweifeln, als er den Fall des Nichterscheinens und den Fall der Verweigerung der Antwort auf bestimmte Fragen ganz gleichstellt, im letzteren Falle aber offenbar die Annahme eines Zugeständnisses das Naturgemäße ist und, wie Art. 164 Abs. 3 zeigt, beabsichtigt war.

Man dürfte schließlich auch nicht sagen, es sei für die Pfalz eine Ausnahme zu machen, weil der Gesetzgeber nur das diesseitige, den Zeugen- und Vermuthungs-Beweis fast ausnahmslos gestattende Verfahren vor Augen gehabt; denn die Verfügung des Art. 156 fand sich genau in der nämlichen Fassung schon in Art. 130 des Entwurfs, welcher bekanntlich fragliche Beweise sehr einschränkte.

3) Erkennt man diese Ansicht als die richtige, so ist allerdings zuzugestehen, daß die Gewalt, wie sie im Falle des Nichterscheinens dem Richter in die Hand gegeben wird, eine außerordentliche, von den gewöhnlichen Grundsätzen abweichende ist.

Zwar ist es richtig, daß auch im Falle, wo der Beklagte auf Ladung nicht erscheint (Art. 297), Geständniß angenommen wird, allein dort ist wenigstens das Rechtsmittel des Einspruchs unbedingt zugelassen, ohne daß es einer Restitution bedürfte. Ebenso wäre die Verweisung auf die Folgen des Nichterscheinens bei Eidesleistungen (Art. 465) nicht zutreffend, da hier der Geladene wenigstens genau weiß, um welche

Thatsachen es sich handle, und genau zu ermessen vermag, welche Folgen sein Ausbleiben haben werde, während derjenige, welcher einfach zum Erscheinen aufgefordert ist, oft vollständig im Unklaren ist, über welche Thatsachen er vernommen werden soll.

So unbeschränkt übrigens das Ermessen des Richters in fraglicher Beziehung auch sein mag, so findet es dennoch in zweifacher Richtung seine in der Natur der Sache begründete Schranke.

Es erscheint nemlich selbstverständlich, daß der Richter aus dem Nichterscheinen oder Nichtantworten Beweise nicht ableiten dürfe, wenn selbst das ausdrückliche Geständniß einen Beweis nicht zu liefern vermöchte.

Ebenso versteht es sich von selbst, daß nur für die Feststellung solcher Thatsachen Folgen abgeleitet werden dürfen, welche zur Zeit, als das persönliche Erscheinen verordnet wurde, bereits Gegenstand der Verhandlung gewesen waren, nicht aber für solche, welche etwa erst in der zum persönlichen Erscheinen anberaumten Sitzung neu vorgebracht werden.

4) Die wichtigen Folgen, welche sich an das Nichterscheinen knüpfen, sind eine Mahnung für die Anwälte, dafür zu sorgen, daß ihre Parteien schnell und sicher von der gerichtlichen Anordnung in Kenntniß gesetzt werden, sowie ferner, daß sie bei eintretenden Verhinderungen rechtzeitig Kenntniß und Bescheinigung erhalten, um das Ausbleiben vor Gericht entschuldigen zu können.

Pflicht des Richters ist es anderseits, die Gewalt, welche ihm das Gesetz verleiht, nur mit größter Vorsicht zu gebrauchen, sowohl was die Annahme eines verschuldeten Ausbleibens, als was die aus demselben zu ziehenden Folgerungen anbelangt. Liegt einige Wahrscheinlichkeit vor, daß die Partei von der Aufforderung nicht erreicht worden, oder daß sie am Erscheinen verhindert gewesen sei, so genügt es, das Ausbleiben zu beurkunden und die Verhandlung in eine spätere Sitzung zu vertagen, in welcher dann, falls die Partei wiederholt ausbleibt oder eine genügende Entschuldigung nicht beigebracht wird, die sachgemäßen Folgerungen gezogen werden können.

5) Es versteht sich wohl von selbst, daß das Gericht nur dann befugt ist, aus dem Nichterscheinen Folgen abzuleiten, wenn förmliches Urtheil erlassen und dieses in der Weise zugestellt worden ist, daß eine rechtzeitige Benachrichtigung der Partei erfolgen konnte. Dabei sind jedenfalls die Fristbestimmungen des Art. 209 zu beobachten.

6) Hat das Gericht mit Unrecht Folgerungen aus dem Ausbleiben einer Partei gezogen, so gibt es, falls auf Grund derselben ein Endurtheil ergangen ist, kein Mittel, um durch nachträgliches Erscheinen das Geschehene wieder rückgängig zu machen, außer dem Wege der Wiedereinsetzung in den vorigen Stand unter den in Art. 216 bestimmten Voraussetzungen, und dem Wege der Berufung, falls derselbe an sich zulässig ist.

Verbindung und Trennung der Verhandlungen.

Art. 157. — Die Verbindung mehrerer bei einem Gerichte anhängigen Rechtsstreitigkeiten, welche in sachlichem und rechtlichem Zusammenhange stehen oder zwischen denselben Parteien obschweben, kann auf Antrag und selbst von Amtswegen angeordnet werden, so oft dies im Interesse der Parteien gelegen oder der Ordnung des Verfahrens angemessen erscheint.

Ebenso kann in einem Rechtsstreite die Trennung der Verhandlung über einzelne Streitpunkte oder einzelnen Parteien gegenüber verfügt werden, wenn hiedurch eine zweckmäßige Vereinfachung des Verfahrens zu erwarten ist.

Eine Widerklage, die nicht schon mit der Vernehmlassung auf die Hauptklage verbunden wurde, darf nur dann gleichzeitig mit dieser verhandelt werden, wenn dadurch die Verhandlung der Hauptklage keine Verzögerung erleidet.

In allen Fällen steht es dem Gerichte zu, die Reihenfolge zu bestimmen, in welcher die Verhandlung über mehrere Streitpunkte einzutreten hat.

Rechtsmittel finden gegen die gemäß Abs. 1—4 erlassenen Verfügungen nicht statt.

G. A. d. K. d. A. I S. 199. 280. 281. II S. 293. IV S. 27. 28. — K. d. R. I S. 293. 294.

1) Den Gerichten ist so ziemlich volle Freiheit gegeben, Rechtsstreite, welche bei ihnen anhängig sind, zu verbinden oder zu trennen, wenn das Eine oder das Andere zur leichteren Verhandlung, zur bessern Aufklärung oder zur Ersparung von Kosten als zweckdienlich sich darstellt.

Beides kann sowohl auf Antrag als von Amtswegen geschehen.

Bezirksgerichte und Handelsgerichte sind als verschiedene Gerichte zu betrachten, auch wenn die nemlichen Richter bei beiden angestellt sind; ihre Rechtsstreite könnten daher höchstens auf Grund des Art. 33 verbunden werden. Ich führe dies an, weil das Appellationsgericht der Pfalz früher der Ansicht huldigte, daß in solchen Fällen die einfache Verbindung verordnet werden dürfe; jetzt könnte hiervon um so weniger die Rede sein, als bei den Handelsgerichten sich auch noch Beisitzer aus dem Kaufmannsstande befinden.

2) Was insbesondere die Verbindung betrifft, so sollte nach dem Entwurfe dieselbe nur verfügt werden dürfen bei Prozessen unter den nemlichen Parteien; allein mit Recht hat der Ausschuß der K. d. R. diese Befugniß ausgedehnt.

Wie schon oben (zu Art. 63 Nr. 4 und zu Art. 66 — 68 Nr. 2) bemerkt worden ist, erträgt das mündliche Verfahren eine Vereinigung verschiedener Prozesse viel leichter als das frühere schriftliche, und es macht sich sogar ein Bedürfniß zur Verbindung konnexer Sachen geltend. Dieselbe ist insbesondere auch dann sehr ersprießlich und räthlich, wenn es zu Beweisaufnahmen (Augenschein, Expertise, Zeugenverhör) kommt, welche ganz oder der Hauptsache nach für mehrere Rechtsstreite von Belang sind. Es kann unter Umständen die Verbindung bloß für solche Beweisaufnahmen ausgesprochen werden.

Die Verbindung erfolgt in der Weise, daß man die betreffenden Sachen in die nemliche Sitzung zur Verhandlung bringt, im nemlichen Urtheile über sie erkennt und unter Anführung der Nummern des Hauptverzeichnisses die Verbindung verfügt.

3) Zu einer Trennung von Streitsachen wird nur selten Veranlassung gegeben sein, und selbst in Fällen, wo eine Widerklage verspätet angebracht ist (Art. 157 Abs. 3), wird in der Regel kein Grund dazu vorliegen.

Schluß der Verhandlung.

Art. 158. — Das Gericht kann den Schluß der Verhandlung verfügen, wenn es die Sache für hinlänglich aufgeklärt erachtet; doch darf einer Partei, gegen welche, seitdem sie zuletzt das Wort hatte, neue Thatsachen oder neue Rechtsgründe vorgebracht worden sind, das Wort zur Erwiderung nicht versagt werden.

G. A. d. K. d. A. I S. 199 200 281. IV S. 28. — K. d. R. I S. 295 296.

1) Zweck der Verhandlung ist die Aufklärung des Gerichtes. Sobald dieses über alle Punkte, welche für Schöpfung des Urtheils von Belang sind, genügend unterrichtet ist, erscheint weitere Verhandlung zwecklos und ist dieselbe zu schließen.

Da nun aber die Anwälte oder Parteien nicht wissen können, auf welche Gesichtspunkte das Gericht Gewicht lege und wie es entscheiden werde; da sie, wenn es bloß von ihnen abhinge, alle erdenklichen Eventualitäten, mögen sie für das Gericht noch so werthlos sein, berücksichtigen und besprechen müßten; da sie endlich nicht wissen können, *wann* das Gericht über alle Punkte aufgeklärt sei, so ergibt sich die Nothwendigkeit von selbst, daß das Gericht zur geeigneten Zeit eingreife und den Schluß der Verhandlungen verfüge. Ein solches Eingreifen des Gerichtes muß begreiflicherweise in erster Instanz, wo die Sachen sich mehr drängen, wo meist die Zeit knapp zugemessen ist, wo endlich viel zu sichten ist und viele unwesentliche und unerhebliche Gesichtspunkte auszuscheiden sind, in weit stärkerem Maße stattfinden, als in den höheren Instanzen.

Hervorzuheben ist, daß der *Schluß* der Verhandlung vom *Gerichte* ausgesprochen wird, die *Leitung* derselben und die Ertheilung des Worts aber Sache des *Vorsitzenden* ist. Beides steht nun in Wechselwirkung, denn der Vorsitzende muß wissen, in welcher Richtung das Gericht weitere Aufklärung verlange, welche Punkte es für werthlos oder für gewichtig halte, um die Verhandlung sachgemäß leiten zu können.

2) Die Befugniß des Gerichtes, den Schluß der Verhandlungen zu verfügen, macht sich in zwei Richtungen geltend, nemlich:

1) darin, daß es Verhandlungen über Punkte, welche für sein Urtheil werthlos sind, nicht zuläßt, und
2) darin, daß es den Verhandlungen über erhebliche Punkte Einhalt gebietet, sobald es genügend aufgeklärt ist.

In ersterer Richtung sind besondere Erläuterungen nöthig.

Eine der wichtigsten Pflichten des Richters ist es, nie *gegen* eine Partei zu erkennen, bevor ihr Gelegenheit geboten war, ihre Gründe vollständig geltend zu machen. Es wäre Leichtsinn, ja Gewissenlosigkeit, wollte der Richter einer Partei, welche noch *neue* Gründe vorzubringen hat, das Wort abschneiden und *gegen sie* entscheiden. Mag der Richter auch noch so scharfsinnig sein, so kann er nie im Voraus wissen, ob nicht etwas vorgebracht werde, was dennoch geeignet wäre, auf seine Ueberzeugung bestimmend einzuwirken.

Anders verhält sich jedoch die Sache, wenn die Entscheidung *zu Gunsten* derjenigen Partei ergeht, welcher das Wort entzogen wird. Schöpft der Richter schon aus dem Vortrage des Gegners die Ueberzeugung, daß eine Partei Recht habe, zu welchem Zwecke soll er diese noch einen langen Vortrag halten lassen? Umgekehrt kann es geschehen, daß der Richter, nachdem er sich vom Rechte einer Partei überzeugt zu haben glaubt, deren Vortrag unterbricht, um vorerst den Gegner zu hören. Aendert sich nach Anhörung der Gegengründe seine Ueberzeugung nicht, so kann er sofort sprechen; ändert sich dieselbe aber, so gibt er eben das Wort zur Ergänzung des unterbrochenen Vortrages.

In gleicher Weise verhält es sich, wenn eine Reihe eventueller Gesichtspunkte geltend zu machen sind. Hält nemlich das Gericht schon den ersten Gesichtspunkt für entscheidend, z. B. die Einrede der Unzuständigkeit, der Verjährung &c., so ist es offenbar sachgemäß, die Verhandlung vorerst auf diesen Punkt zu beschränken, und sobald derselbe völlig aufgeklärt, die Verhandlungen zu schließen.

3) Das Gesetz verpflichtet den Richter durch ausdrückliche Vorschrift, einer Partei nie das Wort zu entziehen zur Entgegnung auf neue Thatsachen oder Rechtsgründe, und spricht hiermit nur nachdrücklich aus, was sich nach obigen Erörterungen von selbst versteht, wenn der Richter seine Pflicht nicht gröblich verletzen will. Auch diese Vorschrift sagt jedoch nur, daß der Richter, wenn er den neu vorgebrachten Thatsachen oder Rechtsgründen Beachtung schenken will, die Entgegnung hören müsse, hindert ihn jedoch nicht, sofort zu Gunsten der angegriffenen Partei zu erkennen.

4) Allerdings haben vorstehende Unterscheidungen nur für den Fall Geltung, als das Gericht in der Lage ist, sofort zu entscheiden, wie es in allen einfachen Sachen Regel ist. Bietet die Sache Schwierigkeiten und wird zum Spruche vertagt, so ist es im Gegentheil sachgemäß, alle Punkte gleichmäßig und vollständig verhandeln zu lassen, weil nicht zu ermessen ist, wie sich in Folge der Berathung die Ansicht des Gerichts gestalten werde, und dieses genöthigt wäre, die Verhandlungen neu zu eröffnen, falls es Punkte berücksichtigen wollte, welche nicht erschöpfend erörtert wären.

5) Wenn auch das Gericht den Schluß der Verhandlung ausgesprochen hat, so steht doch nichts im Wege, in jedem Augenblicke, so lange bis das Urtheil gesprochen ist, die Wiederaufnahme der Verhandlungen zu verfügen (Art. 274). Dieser Wiederaufnahme steht insbesondere die Bestimmung im Art. 160, daß nach dem Vortrage des Staatsanwaltes die Partei nur noch zu Berichtigungen das Wort erhalten könne, nicht entgegen. In Folge der Wiederaufnahme tritt eben eine neue Verhandlung ein, nach welcher auch der Staatsanwalt von Neuem das Wort ergreifen darf. In Frankreich besteht das noch strengere Verbot des Dekrets vom 30. März 1808 Art. 84, allein es wird ebenso gehalten.

6) Auf besondere Anregung (Abg. I 199 [Umbscheiden]) sollte auch eine Bestimmung in's Gesetz aufgenommen werden dahin, daß eine Berathung des Gerichtes über den Schluß der Verhandlung erst eintreten dürfe, nachdem der Vorsitzende den im Vortrage begriffenen Anwalt aufgefordert, seinen Vortrag zu unterbrechen.

Mit Recht hat der gesunde Sinn der Gesetzgebungsausschüsse eine ebenso unnütze als pedantische Vorschrift, zu welcher in gleichem Geiste auch noch hätte hinzugefügt werden dürfen, daß der Richter während des Vortrages eines Anwaltes nicht schlafen solle, abgewiesen. Hat ein Vorsitzender wirklich seine Pflicht verletzt, so ist der Fall gegeben, ihn zu discipliniren, nicht aber ziemt es sich, für jede mögliche Ungehörigkeit, für jedes Gericht und jeden Advokaten, ein Gesetz zu erlassen.

Mitwirkung des Staatsanwalts.

Art. 159. — **In wie weit die Staatsanwaltschaft bei dem Verfahren in bürgerlichen Rechtsstreitigkeiten mitzuwirken hat, bestimmt das Gesetz.**

Art. 160. — **In dem Verfahren vor den Bezirks- und Appellationsgerichten ist der Staatsanwalt in folgenden Fällen befugt, den öffentlichen Sitzungen beizuwohnen und, wenn er es im öffentlichen Interesse oder zur Aufrechthaltung der Gesetze für dienlich erachtet, nach dem Schlusse der Verhandlung dem Gerichte seine Ansicht vorzutragen:**

1) bei Streitigkeiten über den Personenstand;

2) bei Streitigkeiten über die Bestellung oder Enthebung von Vormündern, gerichtlichen Beiständen und Pflegern;

3) bei Streitigkeiten der unter Vormundschaft oder Vermögenscuratel stehenden physischen Personen, dann wenn die Curatel einer vacanten Erbschaft betheiligt ist;

4) bei Verhandlungen, welche Abwesende betreffen;

5) bei Entschädigungsklagen gegen Richter, Staatsanwälte, Gerichtsschreiber, Notare,

Anwälte oder Gerichtsvollzieher wegen Entschädigungsansprüchen aus Amtshandlungen dieser Personen;

6) bei Streitigkeiten über Giltigkeit oder Trennung von Ehen;

7) bei Klagen auf Aufhebung der ehelichen Gütergemeinschaft oder Aenderung der ehelichen Güterverhältnisse, wenn das betreffende Civilrecht den Eheleuten nicht gestattet, diese Aufhebung oder Aenderung durch Vertrag vorzunehmen;

8) bei Verhandlungen über die Vollstreckbarkeitserklärung einer im Auslande ergangenen gerichtlichen Entscheidung;

9) bei den in Art. 590 und 604 bezeichneten Klagen;

10) in Vollstreckungs- und Gantsachen.

Nachdem der Staatsanwalt gesprochen hat, darf den Parteien das Wort nur gegeben werden, um Thatsachen zu berichtigen oder auf neue Rechtsgründe zu antworten.

G. A. d. K. d. A. I S. 200—233. 281. 282. IV S. 28—35. 312—318.
K. d. R. R. I S. 296—319. IV. S. 23—25.

1) Ueber die Stellung, welche die Staatsanwaltschaft im neuen Verfahren einzunehmen habe, namentlich über ihre Theilnahme an den öffentlichen Verhandlungen ist sehr viel gesprochen worden.

Wie so häufig in Sachen, wo extreme Ansichten sich begegnen, blieb es schließlich bei der Wahl eines Mittelweges, und zwar desjenigen, welcher bereits bei Beginn der Verhandlungen angebahnt worden war. Es gibt nun verschiedene Mittelwege — solche, bei denen man von einer „goldenen Mittelstraße" spricht, und wieder solche, bei denen man sagt: „halbe Maßregeln taugen nichts." Der vorliegende möchte zur letzteren Art hinneigen.

2) Ich muß gestehen, daß ich von jeher die Wirksamkeit der Staatsbehörde auf dem Gebiete der Civilrechtspflege, und zwar in dem Umfange, wie sie seither in der Pfalz bestand, für sehr zweckentsprechend und nutzbringend gehalten habe und auch jetzt noch halte. Diese Ansicht ist zwar in Deutschland jetzt eine Ketzerei, welche einer theilweise fanatischen Orthodoxie gegenübersteht, und es wäre wohl ein viel dankbareres Geschäft, mit dem Strome zu schwimmen; allein da denn doch die Ketzer nicht mehr verbrannt werden, so will ich es immerhin wagen, meine Meinung kund zu geben, für welche sich wenigstens das anführen läßt, daß sie nicht auf Glauben beruht, sondern auf eigenem Wahrnehmen.

3) Spürt man den Ursachen nach, warum irgend ein Organismus gesund und lebenskräftig sei, so zeigt sich sehr häufig, daß es solche sind, welche leise und unscheinbar, aber nachhaltig wirken. Als eine solche im Stillen wirkende, aber nachhaltige Ursache erscheint mir nun auch die Thätigkeit der Staatsanwaltschaft auf dem Gebiete der Civilrechtspflege.

Es läßt sich für Jemanden, der nicht völlig sachkundig und sacherfahren ist, nicht recht klar machen, wie und wo eigentlich die Thätigkeit der Staatsanwälte Nutzen stifte. Was darüber gesagt werden kann und so vielfach gesagt worden ist, läßt sich fast alles im Einzelnen widerlegen oder mit Gegengründen aufwägen, so wie man einen Indizienbeweis leicht widerlegen kann, wenn man jedes Indizium für sich unter die Lupe bringt.

Nur zwei Punkte will ich hervorheben, weil hier die Wahrheit in die Augen springt, daß nemlich 1) die Ueberwachung der Civilrechtspflege im Ganzen und Einzelnen eine ganz andere, eine zugleich wirksamere und vorurtheilslosere sein muß, wenn sie eigenen Beamten zum besonderen Berufe übertragen ist, als wenn sie bloß von den Gerichten geübt wird, für die sie nur ein nicht gerade angenehmes Nebengeschäft bildet, und daß 2) das Bewußtsein einer immer rührigen, unausgesetzten Ueberwachung an sich allein schon hinreicht, Vieles zu verhüten.

4) Uebrigens scheint es mir, daß überhaupt hier der Fall nicht gegeben sei, sich die Wahrheit so a priori zu konstruiren, und ich selbst schöpfte meine Ueberzeugung hauptsächlich nur aus Erfahrungen.

Werfe ich nemlich einen Blick auf die großen Mißstände, welche sich in der pfälzischen Rechtspflege zur Zeit, als die Pfalz mit Bayern vereinigt wurde, und noch lange nachher darboten, — fasse ich anderseits die geordneten Zustände der jetzigen Zeit in's Auge, sowie das große Vertrauen, welches nicht bloß die Gerichte selbst, sondern auch die sonstigen Organe der Rechtspflege, die Anwälte, Notare, Gerichtsvollzieher heim Volke genießen, und frage ich nun, welchen Ursachen diese Verbesserungen zuzuschreiben seien, so muß ich mir antworten, daß ein guter, ja der beste Theil davon auf Rechnung des Einflusses der Staatsbehörde zu setzen sei.

Die wesentlichsten Fortschritte und Verbesserungen finden ihre Quelle in Anregungen, welche von Beamten der Staatsbehörde ausgegangen sind. Das Gute ist jetzt da; wer aber nicht etwa zufällig die alten Correspondenzregister durchliest, erfährt kaum mehr, wie es entstanden und wem es zu danken ist.

Hat nun dieser Einfluß der Staatsbehörde vielleicht die richterliche Unabhängigkeit gefährdet?

Versteht man unter Unabhängigkeit die Freiheit, seine Pflichten zu vernachlässigen, so mag es sein; in einem anderen Sinne gewiß nicht! Es gab Zeiten in der Pfalz, wo die Denuntiationssucht sehr bereit war, alles hervorzuziehen, was einen schlimmen Schein auf das Wirken der Staatsanwaltschaft oder einzelner Organe derselben zu werfen geeignet war; nie aber wagte man zu behaupten, es sei jemals auf dem Gebiete der Civilrechtspflege die Unabhängigkeit der Gerichte gefährdet, oder es seien auch nur entfernte Versuche dazu gemacht worden.

5) Wer nun die Ueberwachung der gesammten Civilrechtspflege durch die Staatsanwaltschaft als eine Wohlthat, als im öffentlichen Interesse begründet ansieht, der muß offenbar eine wesentliche Verkümmerung ihrer Wirksamkeit darin finden, daß man sie fernhält von den öffentlichen Sitzungen, d. h. demjenigen Orte, wo sich nicht bloß die Thätigkeit der Gerichte und Anwälte konzentrirt, sondern wo auch über die Thätigkeit der Landrichter, deren Urtheile angefochten werden, der Notare, deren Akte man angreift, der Gerichtsvollzieher, welche sich etwa bei Zustellungen, Pfändungen 2c. Ordnungswidrigkeiten zu Schulden kommen ließen, manche Aufschlüsse zu erheben sind. Man verspricht sich so große Vortheile von der Controle, welche das Publikum beim Lichte der Oeffentlichkeit übt, — warum will man die Controle der Staatsanwaltschaft dabei ausschließen?

Was nun insbesondere das Recht der Conclusionen betrifft, so lege ich, namentlich in erster Instanz, wo die Staatsanwälte in der Regel keine Gelegenheit haben, sich vorzubereiten, für die Rechtsprechung darauf kein großes Gewicht. Immerhin ist aber das Gutachten des Staatsanwalts nur nützlich, nie schädlich, kann hie und da dem Rechte sogar wesentliche Dienste leisten, und mit Recht bemerkte Völk (Abg. IV S. 318), welcher die Mitwirkung der Staatsanwaltschaft überhaupt ausgeschlossen wissen wollte, daß man entweder den Staatsanwalt gar nicht als solchen in der Sitzung zulassen, oder ihm auch das Wort gönnen solle.

Von besonderem Werthe erscheint mir aber die Theilnahme der Staatsanwaltschaft in den Civilsitzungen namentlich für sie selbst zu sein. Sie verliert hierdurch ihre Einseitigkeit, ihren bloß polizeilichen Charakter; sie gewöhnt sich mehr unparteilich, mit den Augen eines Richters die Sachen zu betrachten; erhält endlich Gelegenheit, sich auch in der Pflege des Civilrechts, diesem wichtigsten und schwierigsten Gebiete des Rechts, wissenschaftlich und praktisch fortzubilden. Mögen diese letzteren Vortheile Manchem auch nur als Nebensachen erscheinen, so sind es immer Vortheile.

6) Diesen kurzen Nachruf glaubte ich einem guten alten Bekannten, welchem ich Vieles schulde, widmen zu müssen, und wende mich nun zu den Bestimmungen des Art. 160.

Dieselben sind der Art, daß ich überzeugt bin, sie werden ein todter Buchstabe bleiben, und es werden sich die Staatsanwälte, nachdem sie in keiner Sache (ganz seltene Ausnahmen abgerechnet) mehr gehört werden müssen, in den meisten Sachen aber nicht sprechen, ja nicht einmal in amtlicher Eigenschaft anwesend sein dürfen, gewöhnen, aus den Sitzungen ganz wegzubleiben. Meiner Ansicht nach hätte Art. 160 ebensogut gestrichen, als so wie er lautet beibehalten werden können.

7) Das Gesetz erklärt den Staatsanwalt „befugt", in den von ihm bezeichneten Sachen den Sitzungen beizuwohnen, spricht aber nicht aus, daß ihm jedesmal, wenn eine solche Sache zur Verhandlung komme, Nachricht zu geben und er aufzufordern sei, in der Sitzung zu erscheinen.

Ein solches Verfahren würde zu großen Störungen und Verzögerungen führen. Wenn z. B. eine Reihe von Contumazialsachen oder sonstigen kleinen Sachen (Theilungsbegehren, Cautionsbegehren 2c.) zum Aufrufe kämen, in welchen der Staatsanwalt theils berechtigt wäre, theils nicht, so müßte in jedem Falle, wo eine Sache erster Art an die Reihe käme, zum Staatsanwalte gesendet und zugewartet werden, bis dieser erscheint oder erklärt, nicht erscheinen zu wollen. Es ist auch nicht möglich, vorher zu wissen, welche Sachen zur Verhandlung kommen, da das Gericht oft selbst erst in der Sitzung davon Kenntniß erhält oder sich Anlaß gibt, zu verhandeln. (Art. 241 Abs. 7).

Es genügt daher, wenn der Staatsanwalt Nachricht erhält, daß und wann Sitzung sei. Bezüglich der Sachen, welche zur Verhandlung kommen, kann er sich Aufschluß aus dem Sitzungsverzeichnisse (Art. 244) in Verbindung mit dem Hauptverzeichnisse (Art. 235) erholen. In Fällen, wo ein besonderes öffentliches Interesse betheiligt erscheint, z. B. im Falle des Art. 384, wird der Vorsitzende dem Staatsanwalte Mittheilung zugehen lassen.

8) Es frägt sich weiter: Darf der Staatsanwalt sitzen bleiben, wenn Sachen verhandelt

werden, in welchem ihm die Befugniß beizuwohnen nicht zusteht?

Es ist die gegentheilige Ansicht vielfach bei den Verhandlungen kundgegeben worden; ich glaube aber, daß sie weder nach dem Texte noch nach dem Geiste des Gesetzes die richtige ist. Sie würde in erster Instanz den Art. 160 geradezu unausführbar machen.

In der Regel läßt sich nemlich die Reihenfolge der zu verhandelnden Sachen, selbst wenn sie dem Richter vorher bekannt sind, nicht im Voraus bestimmen. Es hängt viel davon ab, ob die Anwälte schon bereit, die Parteien schon anwesend sind, und gar häufig kommt es vor, daß Verhandlungen ausgesetzt oder zurückgestellt werden müssen, weil sich Vergleichsunterhandlungen entsponnen haben, weil Jemand, der schwören soll, sich besinnen will, weil der Anwalt mit seiner Partei wegen neu vorgebrachten Thatsachen sich benehmen, neue Urkunden ꝛc. beiholen lassen will ꝛc. Zudem besteht keine Verpflichtung für das Gericht, auf die Wünsche des Staatsanwalts Rücksicht zu nehmen, und hie und da würde man sich nicht sehr beeifern, dem Staatsanwalte gefällig zu sein.

Man stelle sich nun vor, in welch angenehmer und würdiger Lage der Staatsanwalt wäre! Er müßte zuerst ausspähen, wann gerade eine Verhandlung, welche seine Anwesenheit erlaubt, beginne, denn käme er einen Augenblick zu früh, so würde er sich der Gefahr aussetzen, von seinem Stuhle wieder fortgewiesen zu werden. Säße er nun einige Minuten an seinem Platze, so würde vielleicht das Gericht auf eine andere Sache überspringen und er müßte wieder verschwinden, um nach gleich kurzer Zeit wieder aufzutauchen.

Unmöglich kann etwas Derartiges vom Gesetzgeber beabsichtigt gewesen sein! Der Wortlaut des Art. 160 macht diese Auslegung aber auch keineswegs nöthig, und sie hat außer den allgemeinen Prinzipien insbesondere den Grundsatz gegen sich, daß von Gesetzen immer anzunehmen sei, daß sie etwas Vernünftiges gewollt haben.

Das Prinzip der Oeffentlichkeit besteht ohne Zweifel auch für den Staatsanwalt, da er nicht zu denjenigen Personen gehört, welche Art. 148 Abs. 1 ausschließt. Er kann daher ohne Zweifel als Zuhörer zugegen sein. Sollte er nun verpflichtet sein, sich in den für gewöhnliche Zuhörer bestimmten Raum zu begeben, und sollte es ihm verwehrt sein, sich auch, wenn er nur zuhören will, auf seinen gewohnten Stuhl zu setzen, welcher eigens für ihn dasteht? Ebensogut könnte man verlangen, daß ein Anwalt für die Zeit, wo eine ihm fremde Sache verhandelt wird, das barreau verlasse und sich unter das Publikum mische, damit das Gericht nicht durch seine kritischen Amtsblicke beängstigt werde.

Der Sinn des Gesetzes ist daher der, daß der Staatsanwalt nur in den bezeichneten Fällen als Beamter der Verhandlung beiwohnen dürfe, daß er aber in allen sonstigen Fällen nicht mehr und nicht weniger sei als ein Zuhörer, welcher sich in die Verhandlung nicht einmischen darf, welcher der Disciplin des Vorsitzenden unterworfen ist (Art. 151 Abs. 3), welcher endlich sich entfernen muß, falls die Oeffentlichkeit beschränkt wird (Art. 149). Vgl. Abg. IV 317 (Völk).

9) Faßt man nun die einzelnen Fälle in's Auge, wo dem Staatsanwalte das Recht, seine gutachtliche Ansicht zu äußern, verliehen ist, so ist Ziff. 5 nur bei Entschädigungsklagen anwendbar, trifft also nicht Fälle, wo nach Art. 110 oder Art. 151 gelegentlich eine Kostenverurtheilung gegen Anwälte ausgesprochen wird.

Unter den Trennungen von Ehen in Ziff. 6 sind wohl auch die Trennungen von Tisch und Bett begriffen.

Unter Vollstreckungssachen (Ziff. 10) sind alle Streitigkeiten zu verstehen, welche durch Vollstreckungen veranlaßt werden, also insbesondere auch Rangordnungsstreite.

Sollten Zweifel entstehen, ob der Staatsanwalt befugt sei, das Wort zu ergreifen, so sind dieselben im Geiste des Gesetzes gegen ihn zu lösen. Jedenfalls aber könnte, auch wenn er irrthümlich gehört worden wäre, wo kein Recht bestand, hieraus eine Nichtigkeit der Verhandlung nicht gefolgert werden.

Nachdem der Staatsanwalt gesprochen, darf den Anwälten nur noch das Wort zu Berichtigungen gegeben werden; allein dies steht nicht im Wege, die Verhandlungen wieder neu aufzunehmen (s. oben zu Art. 158 Nr. 3).

10) So bestimmt auch Art. 160 jede Verpflichtung des Staatsanwalts zur Antragstellung in der Sitzung auszuschließen scheint, so gibt es doch einzelne Fälle, wo sie besteht.

Eine solche Ausnahme verfügt die Prozeßordnung selbst für das Verfahren vor den protestantischen Ehegerichten. Art. 672 u. 679.

Solche Ausnahmen bestehen ferner für die Pfalz in allen jenen Fällen, wo die bezüglichen Bestimmungen der pfälzischen Gesetzgebung, insofern diese die Mitwirkung des Staatsprokurators ausdrücklich vorschreiben, aufrecht erhalten worden sind, insbesondere:

1) bei Ehescheidungen und Trennungen von Tisch und Bett. Art. 69 des Einf.-Ges.;
2) bei Interdiktionen. Art. 92 des Einf.-Ges. und Art. 892 Code de proc.;
3) in jenen Fällen der nichtstreitigen Rechtspflege, wo in der Sitzung auf Antrag des Staatsprokurators zu entscheiden war, z. B. bei Rektifikationen von Civilstandsakten (Art. 83 des Einf.-Ges.), bei Bestellung von Curatoren für Abwesende und bei Besitzeinweisungen (Art. 84 des Einf.-Ges.) rc.

In wie weit solche Fälle noch jetzt in die öffentliche Sitzung gehören, ist zu erörtern bei Art. 642 der P. O.

11) Art. 160 spricht ausschließlich nur von der Berechtigung der Staatsanwälte, den öffentlichen Sitzungen der Bezirks- und Appellations-Gerichte beizuwohnen und seine Ansicht vorzutragen, d. h. von dem Rechte derselben als »partie jointe« im Sinne des französischen Prozesses, läßt aber in allen übrigen Beziehungen die gesetzliche Wirksamkeit der Staatsanwaltschaft auf dem Gebiete der Civilrechtspflege unberührt. Um dies klar auszudrücken, wurde Art. 159 gebildet.

Vor Allem ist hervorzuheben, daß alle jene Befugnisse, welche der Staatsanwaltschaft als »partie principale« zur Verfolgung oder Vertretung gewisser Rechte aus Gründen des öffentlichen Wohls zustehen, unverändert bleiben. Der Staatsanwalt handelt hier als gesetzlicher Vertreter, also nach Grundsätzen, welche nicht dem Prozesse, sondern dem Civilrechte angehören.

Die Fälle, in denen der Staatsanwalt als Partei erscheint, sind folgende:

I. Im diesseitigen Bayern ist der Staatsanwalt befugt, vor den protestantischen Ehegerichten bei Klagen auf Vernichtung oder Scheidung von Ehen, sowie auf Trennung von Tisch und Bett nach Maßgabe der Art. 672, 674, 678, 679 und 680 als Partei aufzutreten.

II. In der Pfalz besteht fort:
1) das Recht, die gesetzliche Vertretung von Abwesenden zu beantragen (Art. 114 Code civil — Art. 84 des Einf.-Ges.);
2) die Bestimmung in Art. 116 Code civil, daß das Zeugenverhör zur Feststellung der Abwesenheit contradiktorisch mit der Staatsbehörde abzuhalten sei, sowie die Verpflichtung, welche Art. 118 Code civil auferlegt (Art. 84 des Einf.-Ges.);
3) das Recht, welches die Art. 184, 190, 191 und 200 Code civil bezüglich Vernichtung oder Aufrechthaltung einer Ehe geben;
4) das Recht, im Falle des Art. 491 Code civil die Interdiktion zu betreiben (Art. 92 des Einf.-Ges.);
5) das Recht, Curatoren für Vakantmassen bestellen zu lassen (Art. 812 Code civil);
6) das Recht, welches Art. 1057 Code civil für den Fall einer Substitution gibt;
7) die Bestimmung in Art. 2145 Code civil, gemäß welcher bei Klagen auf Beschränkung von Legalhypotheken contradiktorisch mit der Staatsbehörde verhandelt werden soll;
8) das Recht zur Verfolgung von Kirchenrechnern nach Art. 90 des Dekrets vom 30. Dezbr. 1809;
9) diejenigen Bestimmungen, kraft deren die Staatsprokuratoren befugt sind, Civilstandsbeamte, Notare rc. vor die Civilgerichte zu stellen, um Disciplinarstrafen gegen sie aussprechen zu lassen.

III. Im Gebiete des preußischen Landrechts hat der Staatsanwalt das Recht:
1) nach Thl. I Tit. 38 § 1—8 der preuß. Gerichtsordnung zu beantragen, daß Jemand für wahn- oder blödsinnig erklärt werde (Einf.-Ges. Art. 35).
2) den Antrag zu stellen, daß Jemand als Verschwender erklärt werde (Einf.-Ges. Art. 36).

12) Weitere im Gesetze begründete Berechtigungen der Staatsanwälte sind:
1) Der Staatsanwalt am obersten Gerichtshofe hat bei allen Nichtigkeitsbeschwerden ohne Ausnahme seine Anträge in der Sitzung zu nehmen. Art. 806 und 807.
2) Die Verweisung einer Sache vor ein anderes Gericht im Falle des Art. 54 der P. O. kann vom Staatsanwalt beantragt werden.
3) Bei Entscheidungen auf einfache Vorstellungen hat der Staatsanwalt immer Antrag zu stellen. Art. 645—649.
4) Er entscheidet über die Erheblichkeit von Armenrechtsgesuchen. Art. 136 u. 137.
5) Es werden ihm die Zustellungen für Ausländer und Personen ohne bekannten Aufenthalt gemacht. Art. 193 u. 194.
6) Außerdem ist in einer Reihe besonderer Fälle die Mitwirkung der Staatsanwälte vorgesehen, z. B. in der P. O. Art. 35, 48, 384, 595, 747, 1186 u. 1192, im Einf.-Ges. Art. 30, 31, 33, 35, 36, 39, 83 (C. civ. Art. 99 — C. de proc. Art. 856, 858), 87 (C. de proc. Art. 862, 863), 88 (C. civ. Art. 496 — C. de proc. Art. 891, 892, 896), 93, 95, 97, 102 (C. civ. Art. 2194) und 136.

Selbstverständlich bestehen auch alle gesetzlichen Bestimmungen fort, zufolge deren die Staatsprokuratoren der Pfalz in der nichtstreitigen Rechtspflege zu wirken berufen sind, z. B. bei Homologationen von Familienrathsbeschlüssen, Theilungen ꝛc.

13) Die Anwaltsdienste, welche die Staatsprokuratoren der Pfalz in Domanialsachen seither dem Fiskus leisteten, erscheinen beseitigt, da der Fiskus entweder durch einen Anwalt oder durch den Fiskal erscheinen muß. Art. 79.

Gerichtssprache.

Art. 161. — **Alle Eingaben an die Gerichte, ferner die bei Gericht aufgenommenen und die von Anwälten oder Gerichtsvollziehern gefertigten Urkunden und Schriften müssen bei Strafe der Nichtbeachtung in deutscher Sprache verfaßt sein.**

Werden Urkunden vorgelegt oder zugestellt, welche in einer fremden Sprache verfaßt sind, und liegt eine von einem verpflichteten Uebersetzer herrührende Uebertragung nicht vor, so kann das Gericht die Herstellung einer solchen auf Antrag oder von Amtswegen verfügen.

Bei den Verhandlungen darf nur deutsch gesprochen werden. Für Personen, welche der deutschen Sprache nicht kundig sind, ist ein verpflichteter Dolmetscher beizuziehen.

Art. 162. — **Mit Taubstummen, welche lesen und schreiben können, ist mittels der Schrift zu verhandeln; auf demselben Wege sind an Taube, welche lesen können, die Fragen zu stellen und von Stummen, welche des Schreibens kundig sind, die Antworten zu erholen.**

In Ermangelung dieser Voraussetzungen findet auch bei den in Abs. 1 bezeichneten Personen die Beiziehung eines verpflichteten Dolmetschers statt.

Art. 163. — **Die Ernennung und Verpflichtung der Uebersetzer und Dolmetscher geschieht, soweit solche bei dem Gerichte nicht ständig aufgestellt, die ständig aufgestellten verhindert oder Ablehnungsgründe, welche der Gerichtsvorstand erheblich findet, gegen sie vorgebracht sind, durch diesen oder ein von ihm beauftragtes Gerichtsmitglied.**

Uebersetzer und Dolmetscher, deren Verwendung bei einem durch einen beauftragten Richter vorzunehmenden Geschäfte nothwendig wird, hat dieser zu ernennen und zu verpflichten. G. A. d. K. d. A. I S. 235. 282. II S. 220. IV S. 37. — K. d. R. I S. 319. 320. IV S. 25. 26.

1) Daß Verhandlungen vor Gericht nur in deutscher Sprache stattfinden dürfen, ist selbstverständlich.

Was das Beiziehen verpflichteter Uebersetzer und Dolmetscher anbelangt, so können solche entweder für vorkommende Fälle im Voraus bestellt sein, oder es kann die Bestellung im einzelnen Falle, wo es sich gerade als nöthig ergibt, stattfinden. Letzteren Falls ist es der Gerichtsvorstand, welchem der Vereinfachung wegen die Ernennung und Verpflichtung übertragen ist. Aus gleichem Grunde haben auch Richterkommissäre diese Befugniß.

Was ersteren Fall betrifft, so galt bisher in Frankreich, sowie in der Pfalz die Uebung, daß für alle häufiger vorkommenden Fälle das Gericht zum Voraus einen Uebersetzer oder Dolmetscher bezeichnete und eidlich verpflichtete. Jetzt besteht hierfür eine ausdrückliche Gesetzesbestimmung, und da nirgends vorgeschrieben ist, von wem solche ständige Uebersetzer und Dolmetscher zu ernennen und zu verpflichten seien, so erscheint selbstverständlich, daß nur das Gericht selbst dazu befugt ist. Eine Ausdehnung der Zuständigkeit des Gerichtsvorstandes auf allgemeine Bestellungen erscheint nicht statthaft.

2) Unter „Verpflichtung" ist eine Beeidigung zu verstehen, obgleich man daraus, daß letzterer Ausdruck, welchen der Entwurf hatte, geändert wurde, versucht wäre, auf eine andere Bedeutung zu schließen, etwa anzunehmen, daß ein Handgelöbniß genüge. Ein Dolmetscher ist übrigens im Grunde ein Sachverständiger und mußte als solcher auch nach früherem Rechte beeidigt werden. Vgl. Art. 443. In Art. 447 ließ man das Wort „beeidigen" stehen.

3) Die Ernennung und Verpflichtung ist selbstverständlich zu beurkunden und zwar durch Aufnahme eines Protokolls. Eintretenden Falls wird auch eine Beurkundung im Urtheile genügen.

Parteivorträge.

Art. 164. — **Die Parteien sind verbunden, die Thatsachen der Wahrheit gemäß vollständig und bestimmt anzugeben.**

Jede Partei kann die vom Gegner behaupteten Thatsachen allgemein zugeben. Geschieht dies nicht, so muß sie sich über die einzelnen Thatsachen genau erklären.

Hat eine Partei Thatsachen in der Beantwortung übergangen oder ungenügend beantwortet und hat die Aufforderung des Richters zu einer bestimmten und erschöpfenden

Erklärung keinen Erfolg gehabt, so können jene Thatsachen nach Umständen vom Richter als zugestanden angenommen werden.

G. A. d. K. d. A. I S. 235. 236. 282. IV S. 87. — K. d. R. I S. 320.

1) In diesen Sätzen spricht sich der Grundcharakter des neuen Prozesses aus. Er soll auf Wahrheit gebaut werden, während sich vom alten Prozesse mit Fug und Recht behaupten ließ, er sei auf die Lüge gebaut.

2) Das Gesetz verlangt zum Ersten, daß jede Partei eine vollständige wahrheitsgetreue Geschichtserzählung gebe.

Diese Verpflichtung ist, wie begreiflich, eine verschiedene, je nachdem es sich um Thatsachen handelt, welche die Partei aus eigener Wahrnehmung kennt, oder aber um Thatsachen, welche ihr nur aus Mittheilungen Anderer oder gar nicht bekannt sind.

Thatsachen, welche sie selbst wahrgenommen hat, muß sie genau der Wahrheit gemäß erzählen, und da nun die Wahrheit keine mehrfache sein kann, so dürfen sich in ihrer Erzählung keine unlösbaren Widerspüche finden. Was würde man von einem Zeugen halten, welcher etwa erklärte: „Ich habe den X damals nicht im Wirthshause gesehen; sollte ich ihn aber dennoch gesehen haben, so weiß ich, daß er betrunken war und hinter dem Tische neben der Einschenke saß"? Offenbar hieße es mit Recht: „der Zeuge hat gelogen!" Das Nemliche wird der Richter im neuen Verfahren von einer Partei annehmen, welche etwa erklärt: „Ich habe das Geld nicht empfangen; sollte ich es aber dennoch empfangen haben, so habe ich es wieder zurückgezahlt." Da nun aber die Partei zur Angabe der Wahrheit verpflichtet war, so wird der Richter aus noch stärkeren Gründen, als bei bloßer Verweigerung der Antwort, das Geständniß annehmen, daß die Partei wirklich Geld empfangen habe. Man kann also in gewissem Sinne jetzt sagen: »qui excipit, fatetur.«

Allerdings können Fälle vorkommen, wo sich auch solche scheinbar widersprechende Angaben mit der Wahrheitsliebe vereinigen lassen, z. B. wenn Jemand sagt: „Ich habe das Geld nicht von A empfangen, war jedoch durch die und die Umstände verleitet, zu glauben, daß ich es von ihm empfangen hätte, und habe es deßhalb zurückgezahlt."

3) Handelt es sich um Thatsachen, welche die Partei nicht aus eigener Wahrnehmung kennt, so können natürlich derartige Widersprüche vorkommen, ohne daß der Richter zur Annahme berechtigt wäre, die Partei wolle die Wahrheit nicht sagen. Wenn z. B. ein Erbe erklärt: „Ich weiß nicht, ob mein Erblasser besagtes Darlehen empfangen hat; sollte es aber der Fall sein, so hat er es ganz gewiß wieder zurückgezahlt", so ist dies eine Erklärung, welche im vollkommensten guten Glauben gemacht sein kann.

In gleicher Weise verhält es sich mit Thatsachen, deren Erinnerung der Partei nicht zugemuthet werden kann, welche ihr wegen Länge der Zeit fremd geworden sind. Vgl. Art. 455 Abs. 2.

4) Das Gesetz verlangt zum Zweiten, daß jede Partei bestimmte Antworten gebe auf die Behauptungen des Gegners, und verfügt, daß, falls sie auf Aufforderung des Richters hin eine genügende Antwort nicht gebe, Geständniß angenommen werden dürfe.

Die Parteien genügen der Anforderung, welche in dieser Beziehung das Gesetz an sie stellt, offenbar nicht, wenn sie, wie dies bis jetzt geschah, die einzelnen Sätze der Geschichtserzählung des Gegners herausnehmen und erklären: „Widersprochen wird rc.", sondern es wird von ihnen eine zusammenhängende Geschichtserzählung verlangt, eine Geschichtserzählung, welche sich über alle angeregten erheblichen Punkte verbreitet und aus welcher sich zugleich entnehmen läßt, was von den Behauptungen des Gegners wahr und was falsch sein soll.

Die Theorie des speziellen Widerspruchs, von welcher sich die Novelle von 1837 Wunder versprach, ist völlig aufgegeben, und zwar der Art, daß der Gesetzgeber, um ja sicher zu sein, daß ein Rückfall in die früheren Anschauungen nicht stattfinde, sich möglichst verklausuliren zu müssen glaubte. Er verlangt, daß die Partei über einzelne Thatsachen vom Richter zu einer bestimmten und erschöpfenden Erklärung aufgefordert sein müsse, und daß dann erst in's Ermessen des Richters gestellt sei, nach Umständen ein Geständniß anzunehmen.

Jene Theorie war, ähnlich wie die Präklusionsfrist für Einreden, Repliken rc., dann die bindende Kraft des Beweis-Interlokutes und Anderes der Art (auch Art. 14 des Notariatsgesetzes könnte hierher gerechnet werden), ein Ausfluß des alten Systems, welches alle Schäden mit künstlichen drastischen Mitteln heilen zu können glaubte und im Prozesse nichts Besseres kannte, als Präklusionen und Fiktionen. Und doch lag das Gute so nahe, da einfache Hausmittel — gute Diät, frische Luft, Bewegung im Freien — völlig genügten.

5) Als ein solches einfaches Hausmittel möchte auch die Untheilbarkeit des Geständnisses anzusehen

sein. Man gestatte mir dieses »Caeterum censeo« in Berücksichtigung, daß gerade hier besondere Veranlassung vorliegt, von der Sache zu sprechen.

Wie so viele gute Sachen wurde auch diese Theorie nicht durch die Wissenschaft entdeckt, welche in Frankreich lange Zeit andere Wege ging, sondern auf empirischem Wege durch die Praxis. Der Richter fühlte, daß er die Wahrheit nicht hören würde, wenn Anwälte und Parteien fürchten müßten, daß er ihre Geschichtserzählung zerlege, und nach der Theorie über Theilung der Beweislast das Eine glaube, das Andere nicht. Er fand, daß dem Zwecke des Prozesses nur gedient sei, wenn er entweder alles als wahr annehme oder nichts, und so bürgerte sich allmälig das Prinzip der Untheilbarkeit des Geständnisses, wie es im französischen Prozesse verstanden wird, ein.

Ist nun dieses Prinzip gut und brauchbar, ist es nützlich für den Prozeß, — was schadet es, daß es sich theoretisch nicht so gut ausnimmt, daß es nicht so kunstvoll aussieht, wie das andere? Ich meine, wir haben mit den schönen Theorien schlimme Erfahrungen genug gemacht, und erinnere nur an obige Erörterungen bezüglich der Gewährschaftsklage (S. 100).

Schriftsätze.

Art. 165. — **Die Schriftsätze der Anwälte (Anwaltsakte) haben zu enthalten:**

1) die Bezeichnung des Schriftsatzes als Klage, motivirter Antrag u. s. w.;

2) die Anführung der Parteien nach Vor- und Familiennamen, Stand oder Gewerbe, Wohnort und Parteistellung;

3) die allgemeine Bezeichnung des Streitgegenstands;

4) die Benennung des Gerichts, vor welchem die Sache verhandelt werden soll;

5) das Gesuch der Partei und dessen Begründung;

6) die Unterschrift des Anwalts.

Besteht eine Partei aus mehreren Personen, so bedarf es einer Wiederholung der einmal geschehenen Aufzählung in den folgenden Schriftsätzen nicht.

Das Gesuch muß sowohl hinsichtlich der Beschaffenheit als der Größe des Verlangten in der Haupt- und so viel möglich auch in der Nebensache genau bestimmt sein.

Die thatsächliche und, wo eine solche überhaupt nöthig, auch die rechtliche Begründung ist in den Schriftsätzen nur in bündiger Kürze vorzutragen.

G. A. d. K. d. A. I S. 236—238. 241. 282. IV S. 37. — K. d. R. I. S. 320.

1) Nach der Mündlichkeit der Verhandlungen ist die Instruktion der Prozesse durch die Anwälte diejenige Eigenthümlichkeit des neuen Verfahrens, durch welche sich dasselbe seiner äußeren Erscheinung nach vom früheren am meisten unterscheidet.

Der Anwalt wendet sich nun nicht mehr an's Gericht, um ein prozeßleitendes Dekret zu erwirken, sondern verkehrt direkt mit seinen Collegen ohne anderen Vermittler als den Gerichtsvollzieher, und auch dieser ist nicht unumgänglich nothwendig. Art. 205.

Der Verkehr unter den Anwälten erfolgt durch Zustellung von Anwaltsakten, d. h. die Anwälte fertigen Schriften (Akte), in welchen die für Aufklärung des Sachverhalts oder für den Betrieb des Prozesses nöthigen Anträge, Erklärungen, Kundgebungen und Aufforderungen enthalten sind, und diese Akte lassen sie sofort durch den Gerichtsvollzieher dem Gegner zustellen. Allerdings kommt es auch noch vor, daß Gesuche direkt an das Gericht oder an einen Richterkommissär gerichtet werden, allein nur in Fällen, wo auf *einseitiges* Ansuchen eine Entschließung erfolgen soll.

2) Alle vom Anwalte zu Zwecken des Prozesses gefertigten Schriften bezeichnete man in den Ländern des französischen Prozesses als Anwaltsakte (actes d'avoué).

Man unterschied mit Rücksicht auf Inhalt und Taxe ganz einfache Anwaltsakte (simples actes), z. B. Anwaltsbestellungen, Aufforderungen zum Erscheinen in der Sitzung; dann wichtigere Akte, wie Klagabstand, Wiederaufnahme des Verfahrens; endlich die Haupt-Prozeßschriften (requêtes, conclusions motivées, qualités) — alles dies umfaßte der allgemeine Begriff von actes d'avoué. — Dalloz repert. (exploit) No. 642.

Unsere Prozeßordnung verbindet mit dem Ausdrucke „Anwaltsakte" offenbar gleichfalls diesen allgemeinen Sinn, welcher nicht allein in der geschichtlichen Entstehung, sowie in der Natur der Sache seine Begründung findet, sondern sich auch durch die Stellung des Art. 165 im allgemeinen Theile von selbst ergibt. Es war nöthig, dies hervorzuheben, weil die Bestimmungen des Art 165 zunächst nur die wichtigsten Anwaltsakte — Klagschriften und motivirte Anträge — vor Augen hatten und nur für diese ganz passen, so daß man versucht sein könnte, anzunehmen, sie bezögen sich,, geich den auch von Schriftsätzen der Anwälte sprechenden Vorschriften in § 120 des hannoveranischen Entwurfs nur auf den Schriftenwechsel.

3) Um insbesondere den pfälzischen Juristen einen klaren Einblick in den wahren Sinn des Art. 165 zu geben, ist es nöthig, auf dessen Entstehung zurückzugehen.

Der Entwurf (Art. 138 Abs. 1) verlangte, daß die Schriftsätze der Anwälte, welche bei Gericht eingereicht oder dem Gegner zugestellt werden, auf der ersten Seite bezeichnen sollten: den Zweck, die Parteien, den Streitgegenstand, das Gericht und die Beilagen.

Es erhell hieraus einestheils, daß man alle Schriftsätze der Anwälte im Auge hatte, anderntheils aber, daß man diejenigen Formen vorzuschreiben bezweckte, welche im alten schriftlichen Verfahren beibachtet wurden. Dort trugen nemlich die Eingaben der Advokaten auf der ersten Seite nur eine Ueberschrift, z. B. in folgender Weise:

Zum kgl. Bezirksgerichte N. N.
Replik
in Sachen des A — Klägers gegen B — Beklagten
wegen Vertragsauflösung
(mit 2 Beilagen).

Man meinte also einen Betreff, ein rubrum, d. h. eine Form, wie sie das schriftliche Verfahren zur Erhaltung der Ordnung im Registraturwesen erfordert.

Vorschriften über sonstige Formen der Akten selbst, sowie über den Inhalt der Akten folgten in Art. 138 Abs. 2 und Art. 139 des Entwurfes.

Die Gesetzgebungsausschüsse haben nun, ohne die Absicht einer Aenderung kundzugeben, all dieses verschmolzen, und der jetzige Art. 165 trägt stark die Spuren davon, daß zwei verschiedenartige Elemente gewaltsam vereinigt worden sind.

So kommt es, daß dessen Vorschriften nur für gewisse Arten von Anwaltsakten (die requêtes und conclusions motivées des französischen Prozesses) vollständig passen, in der Anwendung auf sonstige Anwaltsakte sich jedoch Schwierigkeiten ergeben. Wie kann man z. B. sagen, es habe jeder Anwaltsakt das Gesuch der Partei und dessen Begründung zu enthalten, da es doch eine Menge solcher Akte gibt, z. B. Anwaltsbestellungen, Aufforderungen zum Erscheinen in der Sitzung, zur Aktenmittheilung, Abstehungen, Wiederaufnahme der Instanz rc., wo von einem Gesuche nicht die Rede sein kann? Selbst bei der Streitverkündung (Art. 487 Abs. 2) hat diejenige Partei, welche den Streit verkündet, kein Gesuch zu stellen und zu begründen.

4) Die Idee des Entwurfes, daß es im mündlichen Verfahren nöthig sei, für jeden Anwaltsakt die Bezeichnung des Gerichts, sowie die Angabe des Betreffs vorzuschreiben, erscheint als eine verfehlte, im alten Verfahren wurzelnde. Im mündlichen Verfahren, wo es keine Gerichtsakten im bisherigen Sinne gibt, wo immer die nemlichen Anwälte mit einander verkehren, wo die Anwälte zudem keine Fabrikgeschäfte mehr haben, sondern jeder nur so viel Prozesse führt, als er persönlich übersehen und bewältigen kann, ergibt sich kein Bedürfniß, Formen vorzuschreiben, deren Zweck bloß ist, die Ordnung in den Akten zu erhalten. Das Wenige, was hierzu nöthig ist, ergibt sich von selbst.

In der Pfalz z. B. pflegen die Anwälte einem jeden Aktenhefte ein besonderes Blatt Papier unterzulegen, auf welches sie die Urkunden, sowie die einzelnen Aktenstücke in der Reihenfolge, wie sie der Prozeß ergibt, in einfachster Weise aufheften. Auf jener Unterlage notirt man den Namen des Anwaltes, und in höchst summarischer Weise (z. B. Schmidt gegen Müller) den Betreff des Prozesses. Manche Anwälte setzen noch die Nummer des Hauptverzeichnisses (der Rolle) bei. Was man im schriftlichen Verfahren den „Betreff" nennt, kommt in den einzelnen Anwaltsakten, soweit es nicht aus dem Inhalte der Akten sich von selbst ergibt, nicht mehr vor. Auch die Bezeichnung des Gerichts ist unnöthig. Welches Bezirksgericht soll denn z. B. gemeint sein, als dasjenige, an welchem die Anwälte fungiren?

Ein Antrag lautete seither in der Pfalz, wie folgt:

Antrag
für B — Beklagten und Widerkläger, vertreten
durch Anwalt X,
gegen A — Kläger und Widerbeklagten, vertreten
durch Anwalt Y.

Für den Beklagten trage ich an:
In Betracht, daß rc.
aus diesen Gründen
gefalle es dem kgl. Bezirksgerichte, in der Hauptklage erkennend rc.

Eine Anwaltbestellung lautete etwa:

Anwaltsbestellung.
Unterzeichneter Anwalt erklärt seinem Collegen B, als Anwalt von C — Kläger, daß er auf Ladung des Gerichtsboten X vom 6. Januar 1869 als Anwalt bestellt sei für — (folgen die Namen).

Soll nun ein Antrag ganz im Sinne, wie es Art. 165 meint, abgefaßt sein, so hat er etwa wie folgt zu lauten:

Motivirter Antrag.

In Sachen des A — Klägers und Widerbeklagten (vertreten durch Anwalt Y)

gegen

B — Beklagten und Widerkläger (vertreten durch Anwalt X)

Forderung betreffend,

trage ich für den Beklagten dahin an:

In Betracht, daß ꝛc.

aus diesen Gründen

gefalle es dem kgl. Bezirksgerichte München l/J. ꝛc.

Aehnlich würde auch in allen sonstigen Anwaltsakten Betreff und Gericht zu bezeichnen sein. Zur Bezeichnung des Gerichts möchte es übrigens genügen, oben an den Rand zu setzen: „Kgl. Bezirksgericht N. N.“

5) Was die Anführung der Parteien betrifft, so ist dieses Wort hier im Sinne des Art. 58 zu nehmen; es sollen demnach diejenigen Personen benannt sein, für deren Rechnung der Rechtsstreit geführt wird, also nicht bloß die gesetzlichen Vertreter. Letztere sind zwar überall inbegriffen, wenn das Gesetz von den Handlungen der Parteien spricht (Art. 60), in der Regel jedoch nicht, wenn von Bezeichnung der Parteien die Rede ist. Uebrigens wird ihre Anführung in allen wichtigeren Akten (Anträgen, Qualitäten ꝛc.) selbstverständlich sein.

Die Angabe der Anwälte ist nicht vorgeschrieben, jedoch erscheint es sachgemäß, sie bei den Anträgen nie zu unterlassen, damit sofort ersehen werden könne, ob und von wem eine Partei vertreten sei.

Außer Bezeichnung der Parteien ist auch noch die Bezeichnung ihrer Parteistellungen vorgeschrieben. Hiermit ist nicht bloß die Haupt-Parteirolle, sondern auch die Parteistellung in zugleich verhandelten Nebenstreiten, z. B. in Widerklagen, Gewährschaftsklagen, Interventionen zu verstehen. In der Pfalz wenigstens pflegt man nie zu unterlassen, in den Anträgen die Stellung der Parteien in allen diesen Beziehungen genau zu bezeichnen. Das Gericht erhält hierdurch sofort einen allgemeinen Ueberblick.

6) In Abs. 2 des Art. 165 ist verfügt, daß die Anführung aller zur nemlichen Partei gehörigen Personen nur im ersten Schriftsatze enthalten sein müsse. Diese an sich sehr zweckmäßige Vorschrift möchte mangelhaft darin sein, daß sie vom ersten Schriftsatze spricht, während sie nur von der Klagschrift und dem ersten Antrage hätte sprechen sollen. Es erscheint z. B. nicht geeignet, in der Anwaltsbestellung, welche der erste Anwaltsakt des Beklagten ist, alle Parteien, auch solche Beklagte, für welche der Anwalt nicht auftritt, zu bezeichnen und sodann im Antrage, wo Jedermann eine vollständige Bezeichnung sucht, die Parteien nur summarisch anzuführen. Zudem sind oft bei der Anwaltsbestellung alle Parteien gar nicht bekannt, z. B. im Falle der Gewährschaftsklage, der Beiladung ꝛc.

Da übrigens der ganze Artikel 165 die Anträge vorzugsweise im Auge hat, so möchte anzunehmen sein, daß der Gesetzgeber für den ersten Antrag immer vollständige Bezeichnung der Parteien verlangt.

Es erscheint selbstverständlich, daß die bezügliche Vorschrift nur gilt 1) bezüglich des ersten Schriftsatzes eines jeden Anwaltes und 2) bezüglich des ersten Schriftsatzes, welcher einem bestimmten Gegner zugestellt wird.

Ebenso sind Aenderungen, welche sich in den Personen ergeben, immer sofort nachzutragen, damit sich nicht unrichtige Bezeichnungen den ganzen Prozeß hindurch fortschleppen.

7) Was das Gesuch der Partei und seine Begründung anbelangt, so ist, wie gesagt, die bezügliche Vorschrift für einen großen Theil der Anwaltsakten gegenstandslos. Für die Klagschrift und die motivirten Anträge bestehen außerdem besondere Vorschriften in den Art. 225 und 230.

Die Nebensachen betreffend, wurden die Worte: „so viel als möglich“ beigefügt, um anzudeuten, daß die Liquidation in der Nebensache nicht immer schon bei der Klage mit absoluter Bestimmtheit, wie dies hinsichtlich der Hauptsache möglich, geschehen könne und müsse. Abg. I 282 (zu Art. 138). Uebrigens ist im Art. 225, wo speziell von der Klage die Rede ist, ein solcher Unterschied nicht gemacht.

8) Schließlich ist darauf hinzuweisen, daß nach Art. 218 Prozeßhandlungen nur dann für nichtig erklärt werden können, wenn ihnen dasjenige fehlt, was nach der Natur und dem Zwecke der Handlung zum Wesen derselben gehört, daß also eine Abweichung von den durch Art. 165 vorgeschriebenen Formen ganz unschädlich ist, sofern nur der Akt selbst alles enthält, was er seinem Zwecke nach zu enthalten hat.

Die Anwälte brauchen daher sich bei ihren Akten nicht allzu ängstlich an die Form zu halten, wenn nur am Inhalte nichts Wesentliches fehlt. In diesem Betracht erscheinen die Formen, wie sie bis jetzt bei den Anwaltsakten der Pfalz beobachtet wurden, vollkommen genügend.

Protokolle.

Art. 166. — Protokolle sind so einzurichten, daß sie Zeit und Ort der Handlung und die Namen der dabei mitwirkenden oder als betheiligt anwesenden Personen enthalten.

Das Protokoll ist in Gegenwart der erwähnten Personen, wo möglich bei der Handlung selbst aufzunehmen und sowohl von den Betheiligten als von dem Richter und dem Gerichtsschreiber zu unterschreiben.

Vor der Unterschrift ist das Protokoll zu verlesen und hievon, sowie von der erfolgten Genehmigung darin ausdrücklich Erwähnung zu thun.

Verweigert ein Betheiligter die Genehmigung oder die Unterschrift, bedient er sich eines Handzeichens oder hat die Aufnahme des Protokolles nicht bei der Handlung selbst geschehen können, so ist dies gleichfalls anzugeben.

Das abgeschlossene Protokoll ist mit dem Gerichtssiegel zu versehen und, wenn es aus mehreren Bogen besteht, der diese verbindende Faden durch das Siegel zu befestigen.

Ausnahmen von vorstehenden Vorschriften bestimmt das Gesetz.

Art. 167. — In Protokollen darf nichts überschrieben, zwischen den Zeilen eingeschaltet oder radirt werden.

Sind Worte zu durchstreichen, so muß das Durchstrichene leserlich bleiben. Die Zahl der durchstrichenen Worte ist am Rande oder Schlusse zu bemerken.

Randbemerkungen, sowie jene Abänderungen oder Zusätze, welche erst nach der Unterschrift gemacht werden, sind besonders zu unterzeichnen.

Art. 168. — In wie ferne Protokolle wegen Zuwiderhandlung gegen die Vorschriften der Art. 166 und 167 ganz oder theilweise als ungiltig oder nicht beweiskräftig zu betrachten sind, bleibt dem richterlichen Ermessen nach Beschaffenheit des einzelnen Falls überlassen.

G. A. d. K. d. A. I. S. 238. 239. 282. 283. IV S. 37. — K. d. R. I S. 320. 321. IV S. 26.

1) Gerichtliche Protokolle sind Urkunden, in denen der Richter Thatsachen, welche er in amtlicher Eigenschaft wahrgenommen, bezeugt.

Diese Thatsachen können Erklärungen von Personen sein, z. B. bei Zeugenverhören, Eidesabnahmen, Vereinbarungen über den Gerichtsstand, oder sie können sonstige Vorgänge bilden, wie z. B. der Befund von Oertlichkeiten, von Urkunden, das Nichterscheinen einer Partei 2c. Ueberall handelt hier der Richter bloß als Zeuge und seine Aufgabe beschränkt sich darauf, dasjenige, was er wahrgenommen, der Wahrheit getreu wiederzugeben.

2) Das Gesetz gibt ziemlich umständliche Vorschriften über die Formen der gerichtlichen Protokolle. Sind diese Vorschriften sämmtlich beobachtet, so hat das Protokoll den vollen Charakter einer öffentlichen Urkunde und muß ihm die hierauf zukommende Beweiskraft beigelegt werden; jedoch ist nach Art. 372 der Beweis der Falschheit nicht ausgeschlossen.

Sind besagte Vorschriften nicht sämmtlich beobachtet, so soll es nach Art. 168 in's Ermessen des urtheilenden Richters gestellt sein, ob die Mängel wesentlich genug seien, um in seinen Augen die Beweiskraft ganz oder theilweise aufzuheben.

Die Gewalt, welche hier das Gesetz dem Richter einräumt, ist eine sehr große, mag man nun die Verwerfung oder die Zulassung solcher mangelhafter Urkunden in's Auge fassen. In letzterer Beziehung ist z. B. der Richter nicht gehindert, gerichtliche Protokolle als solche zuzulassen, welche mit der Unterschrift des Richters oder Gerichtsschreibers nicht versehen sind. Seuff. Commt. Bd. II S. 219. Die Thatsache, daß ein Protokoll als eine vom Richter ausgegangene öffentliche Urkunde unter den Akten des Gerichts aufbewahrt wird, bürgt eben schon in gewissem Grade dafür, daß es in Richtigkeit sei.

3) Die Beurkundungen von Thatsachen, welche der Richter bei der öffentlichen Verhandlung wahrnimmt, sind, soweit nicht die Aufnahme eines besonderen Protokolls vorgeschrieben ist, wie in Art. 39 und 419, nicht an die Vorschriften für die gerichtlichen Protokolle gebunden; es genügen vielmehr die Formen, wie sie für den Eintrag der Urtheile ins Urtheilsbuch vorgeschrieben sind. Art. 248, 280 und 281.

Der Grund dieser Ausnahme, welche man im französischen Prozesse als sich von selbst verstehend betrachtete, liegt in den besonderen Garantien, welche die Oeffentlichkeit der Verhandlungen gegen unrichtige Beurkundung der fraglichen, zudem meist sehr einfachen Vorgänge bietet.

In den Artikeln 248 und 281 sind zwar nur bestimmte Arten von Erklärungen, z. B. Geständnisse 2c., angeführt; allein es läßt sich nicht bezweifeln, daß nach dem Geiste des Gesetzes das Nemliche auch für alle sonstigen Beurkundungen zu gelten habe, wie denn z. B. das Beurkunden des Nichterscheinens von Parteien, der

Eideserklärungen oder Eidesabnahmen in der Sitzung ohne Zweifel im Urtheilsbuche zu erfolgen hat. In der Pfalz nahm man nicht den mindesten Anstand, auch in Fällen, wo der Befund von Urschriften, welche die Notare auf Anordnen des Gerichts vorlegten, der Inhalt von Handelsbüchern oder von sonstigen Urkunden, welche nicht bei den Akten bleiben konnten, aktenmäßig festzustellen war, im Urtheile selbst das Nöthige zu beurkunden. Das Gericht nahm alle Wahrnehmungen von Erheblichkeit in die Gründe seines Urtheils auf, und erklärte dann im Urtheilssatze, daß es Urkunde ertheile über den Befund in der vorbezeichneten Weise.

4) Die Protokolle sind das Werk des Richters, jedoch handelt derselbe immer unter Beistand des Gerichtschreibers, welcher seiner Weisung gemäß die Protokolle niederschreibt und mit ihm unterzeichnet.

Auch die Betheiligten, d. h. diejenigen Personen, deren Erklärungen zu Protokoll genommen werden, sowie die Parteien und deren Vertreter, falls diese anwesend sind, haben zu unterzeichnen, und zwar nachdem das Protokoll ihnen vorgelesen und von ihnen genehmigt worden ist.

Die Verweigerung der Genehmigung oder Unterschrift Seitens dieser Personen kann übrigens dasjenige, was der Richter als seine Wahrnehmung im Protokoll erklärt hat, nicht in Frage stellen oder die Glaubwürdigkeit des Protokolles schwächen. Selbst Geständnisse, welche bekundet sind, werden durch bloße Weigerung des Gestehenden, das Protokoll zu genehmigen, nicht wirkungslos, wenn auch allerdings unter Umständen eine Vermuthung sich daraus herleiten mag, daß sie auf Irrthum beruhen möchten. Seuff. Comm. Bd. II S. 222 Note 8.

Hat ein Protokoll den Zweck, die Willenserklärung einer Partei zu beurkunden, wie z. B. bei der Vereinbarung über den Gerichtsstand (Art. 39), so sind die nemlichen Grundsätze maßgebend wie bei Notariatsakten, d. h. der Wille ist als nicht vorhanden anzunehmen, wenn die betreffende Person nach der Vorlesung ihre Genehmigung und Unterschrift verweigert.

5) Die Protokolle sind, wo möglich, bei der Handlung selbst aufzunehmen. In den meisten Fällen, z. B. bei Zeugenverhören, Beeidigungen 2c., liegt die sofortige Aufnahme in der Natur der Sache und wird es gar nie oder doch nur höchst selten vorkommen, daß eine Verschiebung stattfindet.

Nur bei Augenscheinsprotokollen wird der Fall häufig eintreten. In der Regel kann dieses Protokoll nicht sofort am Orte der Wahrnehmungen errichtet werden und findet dessen Aufnahme entweder in einer nahe gelegenen Behausung oder am Gerichtssitze statt. Es kann nun leicht geschehen, daß die Betheiligten hierbei nicht erscheinen, und da sie nach dem Willen des Gesetzes ein Recht darauf haben, bei Aufnahme des Protokolles zugegen zu sein, insbesondere wenn Erklärungen von ihnen beurkundet werden sollen, so ist es nothwendig, festzustellen, daß sie beigerufen worden seien. Es wird zu diesem Zwecke genügen, daß der Richter ihnen bei Schluß der Ortsbesichtigung Zeit und Ort der Aufnahme des Protokolles kundgebe und dies später im Protokolle erwähne. Erscheinen sie dann nicht, so ist die Sachlage dieselbe, als hätten sie sich bei Vornahme des Augenscheins selbst entfernt, ohne die Aufnahme des Protokolles abzuwarten.

6) Die Vorschriften über die Formen der gerichtlichen Protokolle gelten zukünftig in der Pfalz auch für das Ehescheidungs- und Interdiktions-Verfahren, überhaupt in allen Fällen, wo besondere Einrichtungen der Pfalz aufrecht erhalten sind und soweit die bezüglichen pfälzischen Gesetze keine besonderen Vorschriften über die Formen geben.

7) Der Entwurf hatte in seinen Artikeln 142 und 143 noch besondere Sitzungsprotokolle vorgeschrieben; diese Vorschriften wurden jedoch in richtiger Würdigung des Geistes des neuen Verfahrens beseitigt. Es wird daher in der Sitzung kein besonderes Protokoll geführt, sondern der Gerichtschreiber macht sich, soweit nöthig, Notizen, welche ihm bei Fertigung der Einträge ins Urtheilsbuch zur Grundlage dienen.

Gerichtsakten.

Art. 169. — **Die Vorschriften über Anlegung und Führung der Gerichtsakten werden, soweit hierüber nicht das Gesetz bestimmt, im Verordnungswege erlassen.**

Art. 170. — **Von den Gerichtsakten hat der Gerichtsschreiber unter Beaufsichtigung Einsicht zu gestatten und gegen Bezahlung der Gebühren die verlangten Abschriften und Auszüge zu ertheilen. Doch ist dritten Personen, soweit das Gesetz nicht anders bestimmt, von Protokollen, welche in geheimer Sitzung oder bei beschränkter Oeffentlichkeit aufgenommen wurden, von den in solchen Sitzungen erlassenen Entscheidungen und von den auf der Gerichts-**

schreiberei geführten Registern nur mit Ermächtigung des Gerichtsvorstands Einsicht zu gestatten oder Auszug zu geben. Die Ermächtigung ist nur dann zu ertheilen, wenn ein rechtliches Interesse bescheinigt wird.

Die Gutachten der Gerichtsmitglieder, die Entwürfe zu Entscheidungen, die Berichte an höhere Stellen, sowie Aktenstücke, welche Straf- oder Disciplinarverfügungen gegen Beamte oder den innern Dienst betreffen, dürfen weder Parteien noch dritten Personen mitgetheilt werden. G. A. d. K. d. A. I S. 242. 243. 283. IV S. 37. — K. d. R. I S. 321. 322. IV S. 26.

1) Die Gerichtsakten bestehen aus den Urtheilsbüchern, aus richterlichen Verfügungen und Entscheidungen, welche nicht in's Urtheilsbuch eingetragen, jedoch auch nicht in Urschrift abgegeben werden, aus den Protokollen, welche der Richter und ausnahmsweise auch der Gerichtschreiber allein aufnimmt, und aus den auf der Gerichtschreiberei geführten Registern.

Alle diese Akten werden vom Gerichtschreiber aufbewahrt (Einf.-Ges. Art. 130), welcher davon Einsicht gestattet und Abschriften ertheilt.

Das mündliche Verfahren bedingt es, daß die Gerichtsakten sich auf ein sehr bescheidenes Maß beschränken. Die Akten, welche z. B. an einem Bezirksgerichte der Pfalz im Verlaufe von 50 Jahren erwachsen sind, nehmen nicht so viel Raum ein, als die Aktenstöße, welche sich an einem diesseitigen stark beschäftigten Bezirksgerichte im Laufe eines einzigen Jahres anhäufen.

Hieraus ergibt sich, daß das Registraturwesen sehr einfach ist, ich möchte fast sagen, ganz verschwindet. Die Urtheile werden nach der Reihenfolge zusammengelegt und am Schlusse des Jahrs gebunden; die Protokolle legt man in besondere Fächer und zwar der Zeitfolge nach, ohne Ausscheidung, welches Inhalts sie seien oder zu welchem Rechtsstreite sie gehören. Die Vormerkung der Nummer des Hauptverzeichnisses genügt, um sofort zu ersehen, wohin sie gehören, und das Urtheil zu finden, auf welches sie Bezug haben. In gleicher Weise werden die hinterlegten Anträge, die Qualitäten und die sonstigen Akten nach Bedürfniß in besonderen Fächern der Zeitfolge nach aufbewahrt. Complizirte Vorschriften zur Handhabung der Ordnung sind daher nicht nöthig; es genügen wenige gut geführte Register.

2) Es ist Regel, daß der Gerichtschreiber von allen Gerichtsakten Jedermann, der es verlangt, Einsicht gestatten dürfe; das Prinzip der Oeffentlichkeit gilt daher auch für die Akten.

Ausnahmsweise darf dritten Personen, d. h. solchen, welche weder Parteien im Rechtsstreite noch deren Bevollmächtigte oder Rechtsnachfolger sind, von den Protokollen und Entscheidungen in geheimer Sitzung oder bei beschränkter Oeffentlichkeit, sowie von den auf der Gerichtschreiberei geführten Registern nur mit Ermächtigung des Gerichtsvorstandes Kenntniß gegeben werden. Dieser darf die Ermächtigung nur ertheilen, wenn rechtliches Interesse bescheinigt ist. Es wird daher, wenigstens für den Fall, wo es sich um Abschrift-Ertheilung handelt, nöthig sein, daß er eine Verfügung erlasse, welche der Gerichtschreiber aufbewahrt. Der Staatsanwalt, welchem sein Dienst eine gewisse Ueberwachung zur Pflicht macht (Einf.-Ges. Art. 130 und 131), wird als Dritter im Sinne dieser Bestimmung nicht anzusehen sein.

Die Oeffentlichkeit der Gerichtsakten bringt es mit sich, daß Anwälte und Parteien von den betreffenden Akten sich selbst Abschrift nehmen oder nehmen lassen dürfen, welche Abschriften selbstverständlich nur den Werth von Privatnotizen haben. Abg. I 243 (v. Weiß).

3) Von Gutachten der Gerichtsmitglieder, Entwürfen zu Entscheidungen (welche übrigens zu den Gerichtsakten gar nicht gezählt werden können, sondern Privateigenthum des betreffenden Richters sind), von Berichten an höhere Stellen, sowie von Aktenstücken, welche Straf- oder Disciplinarverfügungen gegen Beamte oder den innern Dienst betreffen, darf weder den Parteien noch dritten Personen Mittheilung gemacht werden.

Unter Parteien sind den Straf- und Disciplinarverfügungen gegenüber nur diejenigen Personen zu verstehen, in deren Rechtsstreite etwa gelegentlich die Verurtheilung eines Beamten stattgefunden hat; denn diese Beamten selbst oder der Staatsanwalt werden allerdings berechtigt sein, Mittheilung der Urtheile zu verlangen.

Da das Gesetz nicht unterscheidet, so sind hier auch solche Disciplinarverfügungen unter dem Verbote begriffen, welche auf Verhandlung in öffentlicher Sitzung hin ergangen sind, wie z. B. die Disciplinarurtheile gegen Civilstandsbeamte und Notare.

Parteiakten.

Art. 171. — **Die Parteiakten, welche sich aus den wechselseitig mitgetheilten Aktenstücken und aus den Urkunden bilden, von denen die Partei Gebrauch gemacht hat oder nach Inhalt ihrer Schriftsätze Gebrauch machen will, sind stets vollständig und geordnet zu erhalten und sind**

beiden Theilen insofern gemeinschaftlich, als jede Partei nicht nur auf deren Inhalt zur Begründung ihrer Anträge vor Gericht Bezug nehmen, sondern auch von den wechselseitig zugestellten Aktenstücken im Falle des Verlustes der eigenen Aktenstücke Abschriften gegen die Schreibgebühr verlangen kann.

G. A. d. K. d. A. I S. 243. 244. 283. IV. S. 37. 318. — K. d. R. I S. 322—324 IV. S. 26.

1) An Stelle der Gerichtsakten des seitherigen schriftlichen Verfahrens treten jetzt der Hauptsache nach die Parteiakten, welche etwas ganz Anderes bedeuten, als das, was man bis jetzt unter Manualakten des Anwalts verstand.

Sie bilden sich 1) aus sämmtlichen Prozeßakten — Anwaltsakten, Ausfertigungen von Urtheilen und gerichtlichen Protokollen, Urschriften richterlicher Beschlüsse auf einfache Vorstellung &c. — und 2) aus den Urkunden, von welchen die Parteien in dieser oder einer früheren Instanz bereits Gebrauch gemacht haben oder nach Inhalt ihrer Schriftsätze Gebrauch machen wollen. Sie sind Eigenthum der Parteien, denen sie nach geendigtem Rechtsstreite oder nach Rücknahme des Mandats vom Anwalte auszuhändigen sind.

Wegen ihrer Ordnung siehe oben die Bemerkungen zu Art. 165 Nr. 4. Die Correspondenz der Anwälte mit ihren Parteien gehört nicht zu den Parteiakten, falls nicht der Anwalt besonderen Grund hat, sie beizufügen.

2) Die Parteiakten sind im Laufe des ganzen Rechtsstreites Gemeingut der Parteien in der Art, daß jede Partei das Recht hat, auf die Akten der anderen Bezug zu nehmen und sich, falls nöthig, Abschrift davon fertigen zu lassen. Hieraus ergibt sich, daß Urkunden, welche einmal den Akten einverleibt und in dieser Weise der Gegenpartei mitgetheilt worden sind, nicht mehr entfernt werden dürfen.

3) Daß die Parteiakten dem Gerichte vollständig vorzulegen seien, wenn dieses auf Grund derselben irgend eine Entscheidung geben soll, versteht sich von selbst. Sie bleiben nach Verhandlung der Sache so lange in Händen des Gerichts, bis das Urtheil gesprochen ist.

In sonstigen Fällen darf der Richter die Vorlage der Parteiakten nur verlangen, wenn das Gesetz ihn dazu ermächtigt, z. B. im Falle des Art. 341. Abg. I 243 (Völk).

Mittheilung von Urkunden.

Art. 172. — **Im Anwaltsprozesse können die Parteien gegenseitig die Mittheilung ihrer Parteiakten verlangen.**

Gleiches gilt von den in der Sache ergangenen Entscheidungen, aufgenommenen Protokollen und sonstigen gerichtlichen Akten, die sich in Urschrift, Ausfertigung oder Abschrift im Besitze einer Partei befinden, dem Gegentheile aber nicht zugestellt sind.

So lange dem Begehren auf Mittheilung der in Abs. 1 und 2 erwähnten Urkunden nicht entsprochen ist, besteht keine Verpflichtung, auf die Verhandlung einzugehen. Auch hat das Gericht auf Antrag der Partei, welche die Mittheilung vergeblich begehrte, dem Anwalte der Gegenpartei und zwar, wenn der Antrag nicht in der Sitzung bei der Verhandlung oder sofort nach dem Aufrufe der Sache gestellt wurde, durch einen in geheimer Sitzung zu fassenden Beschluß zur Mittheilung eine kurze Frist vorzusetzen. Erfolgt die Mittheilung innerhalb dieser Frist nicht oder nicht vollständig, so darf von den noch nicht mitgetheilten Urkunden bei der Verhandlung nur mit Zustimmung der Partei, an welche die Mittheilung zu geschehen hatte, Gebrauch gemacht werden; auch ist letztere befugt, sich von den betreffenden Urkunden auf Kosten des Gegners Ausfertigungen oder Abschriften, soweit dies ausführbar, geben zu lassen.

Will eine Partei von einer in ihrem Besitze befindlichen Urkunde, worauf sie in ihren Schriftsätzen keinen Bezug genommen hat, bei einer Verhandlung Gebrauch machen, so hat sie diese Urkunde vor der Verhandlung der Gegenpartei auch ohne Aufforderung mitzutheilen, widrigenfalls auf Antrag der letztern die Vertagung der Sache, nach Umständen auf Kosten des Säumigen, und selbst die Ausschließung der Urkunde von der betreffenden Verhandlung verfügt werden kann.

Art. 173. — **Die Mittheilung der Urkunden kann von Hand zu Hand gegen Empfangsbescheinigung oder durch Hinterlegung auf der Gerichtsschreiberei geschehen. Jedem Aktenhefte ist ein Verzeichniß der in demselben enthaltenen Urkunden beizufügen.**

Ist die Frist zur Einsichtnahme nicht bei der Mittheilung durch den Inhaber der Urkunden oder durch gerichtliche Anordnung erweitert worden, so beträgt sie drei Tage vom

Tage der Ausstellung der Bescheinigung oder der Kundmachung der geschehenen Hinterlegung. Findet die Verhandlung noch vor Ablauf der Frist statt, so muß die Rückgabe jedenfalls vor der Verhandlung erfolgen.

Art. 174. — Erfolgt die Rückgabe der von Hand zu Hand mitgetheilten Urkunden nicht rechtzeitig, so ist der säumige Anwalt auf schriftlichen Antrag der Gegenpartei und Vorlage der Empfangsbescheinigung ohne weitere Verhandlung von dem Gerichte in geheimer Sitzung zur sofortigen Rückgabe der Urkunden und in die Kosten zu verurtheilen.

Der Verurtheilte kann das Erkenntniß innerhalb einer unerstreckbaren Frist von vier und zwanzig Stunden von der Zustellung an mit Einspruch anfechten, über welchen in einer sofort anzuberaumenden Sitzung ohne weiteres Vorverfahren zu verhandeln ist. Unterliegt der Verurtheilte hiebei, so kann ihn das Gericht außerdem noch in eine Geldbuße bis zu fünfzig Gulden verfällen.

Soweit das Erkenntniß die Rückgabe der Urkunden betrifft, ist es mittels Personalhaft vollstreckbar.

Art. 175. — Durch die Vorschriften der Art. 172—174 werden die Bestimmungen des Handelsgesetzbuchs über Vorlegung der Handelsbücher und der Tagebücher der Mäkler nicht berührt.

G. A. d. K. d. A. I S. 244—249. 283. 284. III S. 16. 27. IV S. 37. 38. 318.
K. d. R. I S. 324—327 IV. S. 26.

1) Die Mittheilung der Parteiakten vor der öffentlichen Verhandlung ist sehr wichtig; sie trägt wesentlich dazu bei, die Verhandlung selbst zu vereinfachen und eine rasche Erledigung herbeizuführen.

Die Vorschriften, welche unser Gesetz in dieser Beziehung gibt, erscheinen im Allgemeinen und Besonderen sehr sachgemäß.

a) Pflicht zur Aktenmittheilung.

2) Die Pflicht zur Aktenmittheilung trifft nicht bloß die eigentlichen Prozeßakten, sondern vorzugsweise auch die Urkunden, von welchen die Parteien bei der Verhandlung Gebrauch zu machen beabsichtigen. Ursprünglich wollte man sie sogar auf diese Urkunden beschränken, allein mit Recht hat man später die Ausscheidung der Prozeßakten wieder beseitigt. Dieselbe mußte schon deßhalb unpraktisch erscheinen, weil Urkunden und Prozeßakten in der Regel im nemlichen Aktenhefte vereinigt sind; übrigens besteht hie und da ein Interesse, auch die Prozeßakten des Gegners einzusehen, weil sie die Originalien eines Theils der Akten enthalten. Schon der Grundsatz der Gemeinschaftlichkeit aller Parteiakten bedingt es, daß sie auf Begehren sämmtlich mitzutheilen sind.

3) Kommt der Inhalt von Handelsbüchern in Betracht, so pflegen die Parteien Auszüge aus denselben, häufig mit einer Beglaubigung versehen (Art. 83 des Notar.-Ges.), ihren Akten beizufügen. Genügt dies nicht, so kann das Gericht nach Maßgabe des Handelsgesetzbuches Art. 37 — 40 die Vorlage der Handelsbücher anordnen; ebenso der Tagebücher der Handelsmäkler (Art. 79).

In der Praxis geschieht es häufig, daß die Anwälte, wenn sie voraussehen, daß es auf Einsicht der Handelsbücher ankomme, ihre Parteien veranlassen, dieselben freiwillig zur öffentlichen Verhandlung mitzubringen. Nachdem vor der Verhandlung, oft noch in der Sitzung, der Gegenanwalt Einsicht genommen, werden sie dann dem Gerichte vorgelegt. In gleicher Weise wird es mit sonstigen Urkunden (Katasterplänen, Lagerbüchern, Registern ꝛc.) gehalten, welche nicht auf längere Zeit entbehrt werden können.

4) Was die Prozeßakten betrifft, sowie jene Urkunden, auf welche die Parteien in ihren Schriftsätzen Bezug genommen haben, so hat die Mittheilung nur zu erfolgen auf Begehren des Gegners, indem vorauszusetzen ist, daß dieser die Einsichtnahme nicht nöthig habe, wenn er sie nicht begehrt.

Handelt es sich jedoch um Urkunden, welche in den Schriftsätzen nicht erwähnt sind, so muß auch ohne Aufforderung die Mittheilung derselben erfolgen. Ist dies nicht geschehen, so kann das Gericht auf Antrag der betheiligten Parteien die Verhandlung vertagen, unter Umständen sogar auf Kosten des Säumigen; ja es kann selbst die Ausschließung der Urkunden von der betreffenden Verhandlung verfügen. Diese Vorschriften haben den Zweck, von Ueberraschungen des Gegners abzuschrecken.

5) Falls die Partei die Mittheilung der Akten vor der Verhandlung begehrt hat — was nöthigenfalls durch Zustellung eines Anwaltsakts geschieht — steht ihr ein Recht zu, das Eingehen auf die Verhandlung zu verweigern, so lange, bis ihrem Begehren entsprochen ist. Im Falle jedoch, wo die Partei eine Urkunde,

auf welche sie sich früher nicht bezogen hat, erst in der Sitzung vorlegt, heißt es bloß, daß das Gericht die Vertagung verfügen könne.

Dies erscheint beim ersten Anblicke als eine Inkonsequenz, ist jedoch ganz gerechtfertigt, da es in letzterem Falle möglich ist, daß der Verspätung der Vorlage ein Verschulden des Anwaltes oder der Partei gar nicht zu Grunde liege. Es wäre nun aber offenbar zwecklos, ohne solches Verschulden die Verhandlung zu vertagen, wenn klar ist, daß der Gegner vollkommen im Stande sei, die vorgelegte einfache Urkunde zu prüfen und sich darüber zu erklären. Im Parteiprozesse werden ja die Urkunden immer erst in der Sitzung mitgetheilt.

6) Falls eine Partei dem Begehren um Mittheilung von Urkunden nicht entspricht, kann das Gericht in der durch Art. 172 Abs. 3 bezeichneten Weise dieselbe anordnen, und bei fortgesetzter Weigerung erwächst für die Gegenpartei das Recht, die Urkunden von der Verhandlung auszuschließen.

Diese Ausschließung hat übrigens gleich der nach Art. 172 Abs. 4 durch das Gericht zu verfügenden Ausschließung weniger Bedeutung, als es den Anschein hat. Sie wirkt nemlich nur für die betreffende Verhandlung, entzieht also der Partei das Recht nicht, die nemliche Urkunde bei einer späteren Verhandlung oder in der Berufungsinstanz (Art. 707) wieder geltend zu machen, so daß also der Ausschluß nur dann Werth hat, wenn etwa sofort Endurtheil in letzter Instanz ergeht. In allen andern Fällen wird die Gegenpartei selbst Interesse haben die Ausschließung nicht zu verlangen und entweder sich auf Prüfung der Urkunde einlassen oder Vertagung begehren.

Von Ausschließung der Prozeßakten, von denen der Gegner Abschrift in seinen eigenen Akten besitzt, kann ohnedem keine Rede sein.

7) Das Gesetz enthält keine Bestimmung darüber, wie lange vor der Verhandlung die Aktenmittheilung zu erfolgen habe. Ist dem Gegner eine sorgfältige Prüfung der mitgetheilten Urkunden nicht mehr möglich gewesen, so steht ihm selbstverständlich das Recht zu, Vertagung zu verlangen.

8) Die Verpflichtung zur Aktenmittheilung gilt nur für den Anwaltsprozeß, hier jedoch ohne Unterschied, ob das gewöhnliche oder das abgekürzte Verfahren stattfindet.

Im Parteiprozesse werden die Urkunden erst in der Sitzung vorgelegt und dem Gegner mitgetheilt (Art. 506).

b) Verfahren.

9) Für die Aktenmittheilung gibt das Gesetz einen zweifachen Weg, nemlich 1) von Hand zu Hand gegen Empfangsbescheinigung, und 2) durch Hinterlegung auf der Gerichtschreiberei.

Ganz das Nemliche verordnete Art. 189 Code de proc., nichtsdestoweniger wurde in der Regel viel einfacher verfahren.

In der Pfalz kam es meines Wissens nie vor, daß die Akten auf dem Wege der Hinterlegung mitgetheilt wurden, und selbst die Mittheilung von Hand zu Hand pflegte immer ohne Empfangsbescheinigung zu geschehen. Der Anwalt ließ, so wie er es gerade nöthig hatte, sich durch seinen Schreiber die Akten vom Gegenanwalte holen, prüfte dieselben, vergewisserte sich insbesondere, ob seine Partei die Urkunden des Gegners anerkenne und sendete sofort die Akten in gleich formloser Weise wieder zurück. Selbst ein Aktenverzeichniß, wie es Art. 173 vorschreibt und welches allerdings sachgemäß ist, pflegte nicht gefertigt zu werden. Aus dieser einfachen Art der Geschäftsbehandlung haben sich nie Anstände ergeben.

10) Was schließlich die Bestimmungen des Art. 174 betrifft, welche den Fall vorsehen, wo ein Anwalt sich weigert, die Akten zurückzugeben, so setze ich voraus, daß sie nie zur Anwendung kommen.

Klagen gegen den k. Fiskus.

Art. 176. — **Ansprüche gegen den k. Fiskus können erst dann gerichtlich verfolgt werden, wenn der Betheiligte sich an die zunächst zuständige höhere Verwaltungsstelle um Abhilfe gewendet und entweder eine abschlägige oder innerhalb sechs Wochen gar keine Entschließung erhalten hat, unbeschadet jedoch der Anträge auf Erlassung von Vorsichtsverfügungen.**

Die betreffenden Verwaltungsstellen haben über derlei Gesuche den Betheiligten die Empfangsscheine ungesäumt und unentgeltlich auszufertigen.

G. A. d. K. d. A. I S. 249. 250. 284. IV S. 38. — K. d. R. I S. 328—330.

1) In der Pfalz durfte nach Gesetz vom 5. Nov. 1790 Tit. III Art. 15 keine Klage gegen den Fiskus erhoben werden, bevor nicht bei der Departementalverwaltung (der Kreisregierung K. des J.) ein bezügliches Gesuch eingereicht war, auf welches innerhalb Monatsfrist Antwort erfolgen sollte.

Diesseits bestand eine ähnliche Bestimmung

in der Prozeßnovelle von 1819 § 9, welche zur Erläuterung und Erweiterung einer am 2. Febr. 1809 an die Appellationsgerichte erlassenen Verfügung auf Wunsch der Stände ins Gesetz aufgenommen worden war.

Unsere Prozeßordnung hat diese Bestimmung der Novelle zum Muster genommen und sie fast wörtlich in Art. 176 wiedergegeben, woraus folgt, daß bezüglich der Auslegung dieses Artikels die diesseits bestehende Jurisprudenz maßgebend ist. Seuff. Comm. Bd. II S. 129—133.

2) Art. 176 setzt voraus, daß Jemand, welcher durch Handlungen oder Verfügungen einer Verwaltungsbehörde in seinen Rechten gekränkt zu sein behauptet, bei der vorgesetzten Verwaltungsstelle Abhilfe gesucht und nicht gefunden habe. Gönner Commentar zur Novelle von 1819 S. 125. Er bezweckt, unnütze und voreilige Prozesse zu verhüten, und es liegt ihm die Erwägung zu Grunde, daß gegen rechtsverletzende Akte und Bescheide der niederen Behörden sehr oft ohne Betretung des Rechtsweges Abhilfe erlangt werden könne, wenn der Verletzte sich beschwerend an die höhere Behörde wende.

Einen derartigen Versuch, außergerichtlich sein Recht zu erlangen, macht das Gesetz jedem Kläger gegen den Fiskus zur Pflicht; um jedoch keine allzugroßen Verzögerungen herbeizuführen, fügt es beschränkend bei, daß 1) bloß die zunächst zuständige höhere Stelle anzugehen, also nicht der ganze administrative Instanzenzug durchzumachen sei, und daß 2) das Recht zur Klage nur sechs Wochen lang behindert werden könne.

Erfolgte die rechtsverletzende Verfügung durch die höchste Verwaltungsstelle, so kann natürlich sofort der Rechtsweg betreten werden. Seuff. a. a. O. S. 131.

3) Soll Art. 176 anwendbar sein, so muß ein Anspruch gegen den Fiskus verfolgt, d. h. es muß von ihm Anerkennung irgend eines dinglichen oder persönlichen Rechtes verlangt werden.

Aufforderungsklagen (Art. 569 ff.) gehören nicht hieher. Bl. f. R. Bd. II S. 152.

Auch auf Widerklagen wendete man den § 9 der Novelle nicht an, und zwar theils mit Rücksicht auf das Erforderniß der Connexität, theils weil der Widerkläger ein Recht auf gleichzeitige Verhandlung habe. Seuff. a. a. O. S. 130. Da die nemlichen Gründe auch jetzt noch bestehen, so wird in gleichem Sinne zu entscheiden sein.

4) Die Nichteinhaltung der Vorschrift des Art. 176 begründet eine dilatorische Einrede, welche jedoch nicht von der Einlassung in die Hauptsache befreit. Art. 184—186.

Dieselbe wird als gegenstandslos geworden zu betrachten sein, wenn zur Zeit der öffentlichen Verhandlung ein abweisender Bescheid auf die erhobene Beschwerde erfolgt oder die sechswöchentliche Frist abgelaufen ist.

Doppelklagen.

Art. 177. — Haben, wo dies nach der Natur der Klage zulässig ist, beide Theile dieselbe Klage gegenseitig gestellt, so ist diejenige Partei als Kläger zu betrachten, deren Klage zuerst zugestellt wurde.

Ist dies ungewiß und treffen die Parteien keine Uebereinkunft, so entscheidet das Loos.

G. A. d. K. d. A. I S. 250. 284. 285. IV S. 38. — K. d. R. I S. 330. IV S. 26.

1) Wie schon die Ueberschrift „Doppelklagen" andeutet, handelt es sich hier um die sogenannten judicia duplicia, die Theilungs- und Grenzscheidungsklagen, und werden bei ihnen die Rollen des Klägers und des Beklagten in gleicher Weise bestimmt, wie es schon im römischen Prozesse geschah. l. 13 u. 14 Dig. (5, 1). Besondere praktische Folgen entspringen aus dieser Rollenvertheilung nicht, jedoch kann unter Umständen die Kostenkaution dadurch bedingt sein.

2) Es versteht sich von selbst, daß durch die Bestimmung des Art. 177 die Klage derjenigen Partei, welcher die Rolle des Beklagten zufällt, ihre Wirkungen nicht vollständig verliert. Wenn die Klage des Gegners wegfällt, sei es wegen Mängel in der Einleitung, sei es durch Abstand, so behauptet jene Klage gleich einer Widerklage ihre selbständige Geltung. Vgl. Abg. I 284 (v. Weiß).

Für den Fall, wo die Klagen an verschiedenen Gerichten angebracht sind, ist Art. 179 maßgebend.

Klagenhäufung.

Art. 178. — Mehrere Ansprüche gegen den nämlichen Beklagten können, auch wenn sie auf verschiedenen Thatsachen oder Rechtsgründen beruhen, in einer Klage verbunden werden, soferne für sämmtliche Ansprüche das Gericht zuständig und die vom Kläger gewählte Prozeßart zulässig ist.

G. A. der K. d. A. I S. 250. 285. IV S. 38. — K. d. R. I S. 330.

1) Das Gesetz gestattet unbedingt die Vereinigung verschiedener Ansprüche desselben Klägers gegen den nemlichen Beklagten, ohne Rücksicht auf Zusammenhang oder Verwandtschaft dieser Ansprüche. Die einzige Bedingung, welche es stellt, ist, daß das angegangene Gericht für sämmtliche Ansprüche zuständig sei und die gewählte Prozeßart sich für sie sämmtlich eigne. Dabei kommt auch diejenige Zuständigkeit in Betracht, welche durch Vereinbarung begründet wird.

2) Die Verschiedenheit der Prozeßarten, welche die Klagsvereinigung hindern soll, muß offenbar im Verfahren selbst begründet sein. Jene besonderen Bestimmungen z. B., welche die Hauptstücke XX und XXII über Zulässigkeit von Besitz- und Provokationsklagen, sowie über die Wirkungen der betreffenden Urtheile geben, bilden keine besondere Prozeßarten.

Sollte ein Kläger Ansprüche vereinigen, welche, obgleich vor das nemliche Gericht gehörig, sich doch zur Verhandlung im nemlichen Verfahren nicht eignen, so würde das Gericht nach Art. 157 die Trennung zu verfügen und jeden Anspruch auf denjenigen Weg zu weisen haben, welcher für ihn der geeignete ist.

Wirkung der Klagzustellung.

Art. 179. — **Die Zustellung der Klage hat folgende Wirkungen:**

1) die Streitsache sammt Allem, was dazu gehört, wird der Gerichtsbarkeit des angerufenen Gerichts mit Ausschluß anderer gleich zuständiger Gerichte, vor welche etwa eine spätere Ladung ergeht, unterworfen, doch erlischt diese Wirkung der Prävention wieder, wenn die Partei, welche die daraus entspringende Einrede geltend machen konnte, sich bei einem andern Gerichte einläßt;

2) die Zuständigkeit des Gerichts für die Sache dauert fort bis zu deren Beendigung;

3) der Beklagte hat die Befugniß, eine Widerklage zu erheben.

Ueberdies treten alle nach bürgerlichen Gesetzen an die Klaganmeldung, die Vorladung oder Einlassung geknüpften Wirkungen bezüglich des Rechtsverhältnisses selbst, wie die Versetzung des Beklagten in Verzug oder bösen Glauben, das Verbot einseitiger Neuerung u. s. w., mit der Zustellung der Klage ein.

Die Wirkungen der Klagzustellung werden durch die endliche Entscheidung der Sache im ersten Rechtszuge, so lange diese Entscheidung die Rechtskraft nicht beschritten hat, nicht unterbrochen.

G. A. d. K. d. A. I S. 250. 285. III S. 92. 102. 103. IV S. 38. K. d. R. I S. 330—332.

1) Für die Wirkungen, welche sich an die Anhängigkeit eines Rechtsstreites knüpfen, war im ältern römischen Rechte bloß der Zeitpunkt der litis contestatio maßgebend, später jedoch traten die meisten derselben schon ein mit der Zustellung der Klagschrift, und einige derselben, z. B. die Unterbrechung der Verjährung, schon mit der Eingabe der Klagschrift beim Richter.

Diese drei Zeitpunkte vereinigen sich jetzt zu einem einzigen, nemlich dem Zeitpunkte der Klagzustellung oder richtiger der Vorladung, denn eine bloße Zustellung der Klagschrift ohne Ladung vor ein bestimmtes Gericht wäre ohne Bedeutung. Im Augenblicke der Klagszustellung mit Vorladung wird der Rechtsstreit anhängig und treten nicht bloß für den Prozeß, sondern auch in civilrechtlicher Beziehung jene Folgen ein, welche früher das Gesetz an die Streiteinlassung, Vorladung und Klagsanmeldung knüpfte.

2) Die Wirkungen der Klagszustellung dauern fort, so lange der Rechtsstreit an sich anhängig ist, also bis derselbe durch Endurtheil oder Abstand vollständig erledigt ist. So lange noch über die Klage zu erkennen ist, so lange muß sie auch wirken, und es wäre sonderbar, wollte man deren Wirkungen von Erledigung einer gewissen Instanz abhängig machen.

Eine Anwendung dieses Grundsatzes findet sich in der Schlußbestimmung des Art. 169, jedoch gefährdet gerade diese Anwendung den Grundsatz selbst, indem gefolgert werden könnte, in allen sonstigen Fällen fielen während der Zeit, wo eine Instanz nicht anhängig ist, alle Wirkungen der Klage hinweg. Wenn z. B. auf Nichtigkeitsbeschwerde hin oder in Folge einer Wiederaufnahme des Verfahrens ein Urtheil, welches die Klage abwies, vernichtet worden ist und nun über den Grund der Sache neu erkannt werden muß, so müßte man annehmen, daß vom Spruche des früheren Urtheils an bis zum Augenblicke, wo das vernichtende Urtheil zugestellt wird, sämmtliche Wirkungen der Klage — mala fides, Zinsenlauf, Unterbrechung der Verjährung — aufgehoben seien.

Ich würde dies nicht für richtig halten, bin vielmehr der Ansicht, es habe als durchgreifendes Prinzip zu gelten, daß die Wirkungen einer Klage fortdauern, so lange noch über dieselbe zu erkennen ist.

a) Prozessuale Wirkungen.

3) Unsere Prozeßordnung knüpft drei prozessuale Folgen an die Vorladung, nemlich 1) die Prävention, 2) die Fortdauer der Gerichtsbarkeit und 3) das Recht zur Widerklage.

Was die Prävention betrifft, so wird durch die Vorladung die Streitsache mit Allem, was dazu gehört, d. h. was als Nebensache im Sinne des Art. 33 Abs. 3 erscheint, der Gerichtsbarkeit des zuerst befaßten Gerichtes unterworfen, mit Ausschluß anderer gleich zuständiger Gerichte, für welche eine spätere Ladung ergeht.

Für den Fall, wo das zuerst angegangene Gericht nicht zuständig ist, kann natürlich von einer Prävention nicht die Rede sein, und für den Fall, wo das später angegangene Gericht unzuständig ist, bedarf es derselben nicht, jedoch kann sie letzteren Falls nützlich sein, um jeden Zweifel über die Zuständigkeit sofort zu beseitigen.

Ein ausländisches Gericht kann einem inländischen Gerichte gegenüber als zuständig nicht betrachtet werden, jedoch wird die Prävention auch hier wirksam sein, wenn es sich um Prozesse unter Ausländern handelt, da ja in solchen Fällen das ausländische Urtheil auch im Inlande wirkt. Ark. 824 Abs. 3.

Die Prävention begründet die Einrede der Litispendenz, welche in allen Fällen vorgeschützt werden kann, wo irgend ein Streitpunkt, welcher bei einem Gerichte angebracht wird, bereits an einem andern Gerichte in zuständiger Weise anhängig ist. Diese Einrede ist das Abbild der Einrede der res judicata und tritt unter den nemlichen Voraussetzungen ein für die noch zu entscheidenden, wie letztere für die schon entschiedenen Streitpunkte.

Liegt Identität der Streitsachen vor, so wird die ganze Klage wegen Unzuständigkeit des Gerichts abgewiesen.

Besteht die Litispendenz nur bezüglich eines oder des andern Streitpunktes, so ist entweder das Erkenntniß zu suspendiren, bis über den bereits anhängigen (präjudiziellen) Punkt rechtskräftig entschieden ist, oder es sind die beiden Rechtsstreite im Wege der Competenzregulirung zu vereinigen.

Die Einrede der Litispendenz wird beseitigt, wenn die Partei, welcher sie zusteht, sich auf die Hauptsache einläßt, ohne sie vorzuschützen, und zwar gilt dies auch schon für das schriftliche Vorverfahren (Art. 184). In diesem Falle erlischt die ausschließliche Zuständigkeit des Gerichts, welches die Prävention für sich hatte.

4) Eine zweite prozessuale Folge ist die Fortdauer der Gerichtsbarkeit. Alle Thatsachen, von welchen die Zuständigkeit des Gerichtes abhängt, bemessen sich daher bloß nach dem Zeitpunkte der Vorladung, und später eintretende Veränderungen, welcher Art sie auch sein mögen, können das Recht und die Verpflichtung des einmal giltig befaßten Gerichtes, den Rechtsstreit bis zu Ende durchzuführen und abzuurtheilen, nicht mehr aufheben. Mag daher eine Partei ihren Wohnort ändern, ja selbst Ausländer werden, oder mag der Streitgegenstand an Werth steigen oder sinken, so kann dies die einmal begründete Zuständigkeit nicht mehr verrücken.

Eine weitere Folge der Ladung ist endlich das Recht zur Erhebung von Widerklagen, bezüglich deren zu Art. 31 das Nöthige gesagt ist.

b) Civilrechtliche Wirkungen.

5) Das Gesetz verfügt, daß alle durch die Civilgesetze an Klaganmeldung, Vorladung oder Einlassung geknüpften Wirkungen nunmehr mit der Klagszustellung eintreten sollen.

So allgemein diese Worte lauten, so ist doch für diejenigen Folgen der Litiskontestation eine Ausnahme zu machen, welche eine mitwirkende Willensthätigkeit des Beklagten voraussetzen, wie z. B. die Behandlung desselben als fictus possessor, qui liti se obtulit. R. R. I 332 (v. Bayer).

6) Als civilrechtliche Folgen der Klagszustellung kommen insbesondere in Betracht 1) die Unterbrechung der Verjährung, 2) die Versetzung des Beklagten in bösen Glauben, 3) der Eintritt des Verzugs und 4) das Verbot einseitiger Neuerung.

Was zuerst die Verjährung anbelangt, so galt im gemeinen Rechte der Grundsatz, daß die Litiskontestation die Temporalklagen perpetuire, d. h. daß Ansprüche, wegen deren ein Rechtsstreit anhängig ist, erst in 40 Jahren vom Augenblicke an, wo der Prozeß liegen bleibt, verjähren. Das Nemliche ist bestimmt in Cap. III § 9 Ziff. 5 der Gerichtsordnung, und da diese Bestimmung keine bloß prozessuale, die Erlöschung des Rechtsstreites allein betreffende ist, sondern sich auf das Klagrecht selbst erstreckt, so muß sie als fortbestehend gelten. Vgl. Seuff. Comm. Bd. II S. 145.

Im französischen Rechte gilt der Grundsatz, daß so lange der Rechtsstreit anhängig ist, eine Verjährung überhaupt nicht laufe, also auch dann nicht, wenn das Verfahren liegen bleibt. Troplong préscription No. 683.

Ein Gegengewicht gegen dieses sehr weitgehende Prinzip fand sich in den Bestimmungen der Art. 397 — 401 Code de proc., gemäß deren bei Unterbrechung des Verfahrens während dreier Jahre jede Partei berechtigt war, die Peremption der Instanz aussprechen zu lassen, in welchem Falle nach Art. 2247 Code civil die durch die Ladung eingetretene Unterbrechung der Verjährung als nicht geschehen zu betrachten war.

Das Gegengewicht ist nunmehr weggefallen — folgt hieraus, daß besagtes Prinzip nicht mehr bestehe? — Ich hielte es für gewagt, diese Folgerung zu ziehen.

Bei den Verhandlungen über das Einführungsgesetz (Abg. IV S. 391) wurde anerkannt, daß die Klagszustellung insbesondere auch in jenen Fällen für die Unterbrechung der Verjährung oder für den Lauf von Fristen entscheidend sei, wo die Klage ausnahmsweise **vor** der Zustellung bei Gericht eingereicht und von demselben einer Prüfung unterworfen wird, wie z. B. in Ehescheidungssachen.

7) Eine zweite civilrechtliche Folge der Klagszustellung besteht darin, daß derjenige, welcher auf Herausgabe einer Sache belangt ist, durch dieselbe in bösen Glauben versetzt wird. Er wird für den Fall seines späteren Unterliegens **kraft Gesetzes** so behandelt, als sei er vom Augenblicke an, wo er vor Gericht geladen wurde, in bösem Glauben gewesen.

Dieser im römischen Civilrechte begründete Satz (l. 25 § 7 Dig. [5. 3]) hat in der Gerichtsordnung ausdrückliche Anerkennung gefunden (Cap. V § 9 Ziff. 2), und diese civilrechtliche Bestimmung ist als fortbestehend zu erachten.

Auch das französische Recht erkennt als Grundsatz an, daß vom Augenblicke der Ladung der Beklagte nicht mehr als in gutem Glauben befindlich betrachtet werde. Code civ. Art. 549, 550 — Chauveau sur Carré. Einleitung zu Art. 59 Ziff. 7.

Mit der Annahme des bösen Glaubens hängt die Verpflichtung zusammen, die Sache cum omni causa herauszugeben, d. h. mit allem, was in der Voraussetzung, es hätte der Beklagte schon im Augenblicke der Ladung die Sache herausgegeben, als Zubehör derselben zu betrachten sein würde.

8) In gleicher Weise wird durch die Ladung der **Verzug** des Beklagten begründet, und muß sich derselbe alle Folgen gefallen lassen, welche sich hieran knüpfen, insbesondere auch von den eingeklagten Forderungen Verzugszinsen zahlen. Kreitmayer zur G. O. Cap. VI § 1 lit. g — Bayer Civilprozeß S. 564 — Seuff. Comm. Bd. II S. 277 — Code civil Art. 1153, 1155, 1207, 1479, 1682 und 1904.

9) Als eine weitere civilrechtliche Folge führt das Gesetz das Verbot einseitiger Neuerung an.

Es versteht sich wohl von selbst, daß eine Partei nach Beginn des Rechtsstreites am Streitgegenstande keine die **eventuellen Rechte des Gegners gefährdenden** Aenderungen vornehmen dürfe. Obgleich daher unsere Prozeßordnung eine besondere Attentatenbeschwerde nicht kennt, so steht doch ohne Zweifel dem gefährdeten Theile das Recht zu, eine Vorsichtsverfügung zu beantragen, welche ihn in einfacherer Weise zum nemlichen Ziele führt.

Klagänderung.

Art. 180. — **Der Beklagte kann sich Aenderungen widersetzen, welche nach der Vernehmunglassung in dem Gegenstande der Klage, in ihrer thatsächlichen Begründung oder durch Erweiterung des Gesuchs vorgenommen werden.**

Art. 181. — **Nachträge, welche nur die Erläuterung undeutlicher oder die Ergänzung unvollständiger Anführungen oder die Berichtigung offenbarer Irrthümer in einzelnen Ausdrücken, Bezeichnungen, Namen oder Zahlen zum Gegenstande haben, sind als Aenderung der Klage nicht zu betrachten.**

Gleiches gilt, wenn die Erhöhung der Forderung sich nur als eine richtigere Berechnung aus den Ansätzen der Klage darstellt.

Art. 182. — **Die Bestimmung des Art. 180 findet keine Anwendung, wenn die Forderung eines Mehrbetrags keinen Anlaß zu einer neuen, von dem Inhalte der Klagbeantwortung wesentlich abweichenden Vertheidigung enthält oder statt der ursprünglich geforderten Sache wegen der Veräußerung oder wegen des Untergangs derselben die Leistung der Entschädigung gefordert wird.**

Ebenso kann in jedem Stande der Sache die Klage durch Zusätze vervollständigt werden, welche Punkte betreffen, die mit dem Gegenstande der Klage zusammenhängen und von der Entscheidung über dieselbe abhängig sind, wie Nebenansprüche an Früchten, Zinsen

und Entschädigungen, oder weitere Ansprüche, welche seit Anstellung der Klage aus dem nämlichen Klaggrunde erwachsen sind.

Art. 183. — **Unter allen Verhältnissen kann der Kläger die Klage beschränken, doch hat er die durch die frühere Ausdehnung etwa veranlaßten Kosten zu tragen.**

G. A. d. K. d. A. I S. 250—252. 285. 286. IV S. 38. — K. d. R. I S. 332.

1) Es gibt wenig Materien, wo sich in allgemeinen Sätzen so leicht das Richtige sagen läßt und wo sich so viele Schwierigkeiten bieten, wenn man versucht, theoretisch mehr ins Einzelne zu gehen, als in der Lehre von der Klagsänderung, der mutatio libelli. Es ist gewiß ebenso einfach als richtig, wenn die Gerichtsordnung sagt, die Aenderung müsse im „Hauptwerke" geschehen, und die Anmerkungen von Kreitmayer hinzufügen, bloße Emendationen schadeten nichts, oder wenn man sagt, es dürfe kein neuer Klaggrund unterschoben und im Hauptgegenstande der Klage nichts verändert werden. Sucht man nun aber diese Sätze mehr in's Conkrete aufzulösen, sie greifbar zu machen, so findet man — wenigstens ich — daß dies nicht leicht möglich sei und daß das Beste dabei im besonderen Falle das Ermessen des Richters thun müsse. Zu meinem Troste ersehe ich, daß es auch der hannoveranischen Commission (Verhdl. S. 1565—1590) nicht besser ergangen ist und daß selbst Seuffert, welcher in seinem Commentare Bd. II S. 206—214 mit gewohnter Gründlichkeit und Schärfe den Stoff behandelt, auch nur zu mehr oder minder allgemeinen Gesichtspunkten und zur Hervorhebung einzelner Fälle gelangt.

Im neuen Verfahren wird übrigens die Frage der Klagsänderung bei Weitem keine so große Rolle spielen, wie im früheren Verfahren. Zwei wichtige Umstände wirken dagegen, nemlich 1) daß die Advokaten nicht mehr fabrikmäßig arbeiten, sondern persönlich die Prozesse einleiten und gut einleiten müssen, wenn sie dieselben mit Ehren vertreten wollen, und 2) daß die öffentliche Verhandlung Gelegenheit und Mittel bietet, Mängel der Klagen zu heben, ohne daß das Recht der Vertheidigung Noth leidet.

Es ist daher in der Pfalz ein sehr seltener Fall, daß eine mutatio libelli behauptet, und ein noch viel seltenerer, daß sie mit Grund behauptet wird.

Die Tendenz des neuen Verfahrens geht übrigens noch viel entschiedener als diejenige des früheren dahin, jede Klage, wenn immer möglich, aufrecht zu erhalten.

2) Um soviel als möglich Licht in der Sache zu erhalten, wird es geeignet sein, zuerst die Prinzipien des französischen Rechtes in's Auge zu fassen, dann diejenigen der Gerichtsordnung und endlich die an letztere sich anschließenden, jedoch in manchen Beziehungen vermittelnden Prinzipien der neuen Prozeßordnung.

Der Code de procedure spricht nirgends aus, daß Klagsänderungen nicht erlaubt seien, allein die französische Jurisprudenz und Doktrin erkannte es immer als einen aus der Natur der Sache und aus dem Geiste des Verfahrens sich herleitenden Grundsatz an.

Da das Gesetz im gewöhnlichen Verfahren freiwilliges Erscheinen der Parteien vor Gericht nicht erlaubt, sondern aus Gründen der öffentlichen Ordnung verlangt, daß förmliche Ladung vorausgehe, da es ferner verlangt, daß die Partei selbst (nicht bloß der Anwalt) durch diese Ladung von den Klagsansprüchen in Kenntniß gesetzt werde und ihr zugleich zur Sorge für ihre Vertretung und Vertheidigung die gesetzlichen Erscheinungsfristen zu belassen seien, so erklärte man es für unstatthaft, im Wege bloßer Zustellungen von Anwalt zu Anwalt Aenderungen oder Zusätze der Art zu machen, daß die Klage als ganz oder theilweise ohne Ladung vor den Richter gebracht erscheinen müßte.

In Dalloz repert. (v. incident) No. 21 wird in dieser Beziehung gesagt:

»C'est principe, 1) que toute demande judiciaire doit être libellée, c'est à dire, que l'exploit introductif de l'instance doit contenir et les moyens et les conclusions; 2) que le defendeur doit jouir d'un delai etc.«

Und weiter:

»Un defendeur ne peut être tenu de répondre, qu'a la demande et a ce qui en est la suite.«

Allerdings konnten nach Art. 337 Code de proc. auch durch einfachen Anwaltsakt Incidentklagen erhoben werden, welche im Falle, wo sie vom Kläger ausgingen, demandes additionelles genannt wurden; allein dieselben waren nur statthaft:

1) wegen Incidentbegehren, welche durch Einreden des Beklagten veranlaßt wurden, z. B. wenn Nichtigerklärung eines von demselben geltend gemachten Vertrags verlangt wurde, und
2) wegen Ansprüchen, welche aus der Klage sich herleiteten und erst nach derselben entstanden, als welche z. B. Chauveau sur Carré (Einleitung zu Art. 337) anführt: »demandes en

provision, en payement des loyers échus ou de dommages causés depuis l'action principale.«

Nach französischem Rechte war also von der Ladung an jede eigentliche Klagsänderung ausgeschlossen.

Handelte es sich darum, eine neue Klage an Stelle einer früheren fehlerhaften zu setzen, so mußte zuerst Klagsabstand erfolgen und dann neue Klage erhoben werden; handelte es sich nur darum, Klagspunkte oder Klagsgründe nachzutragen, so gab man nachträgliche Ladung und vereinigte nach Ablauf der Fristen die beiden Rechtsstreite.

3) Was nun die Prinzipien der Gerichtsordnung betrifft, so verfügte dieselbe in Cap. IV § 13, daß der Kläger nach der Kriegsbefestigung, d. h. nach der Litiskontestation, am „Hauptwerke" der Klage nichts mehr ändern dürfe. Vorher durfte er also, auch wenn die Klage bereits zugestellt und Einreden ohne Streiteinlassung vorgebracht waren, ohne Erklärung eines Abstandes, beliebige Aenderungen an der Klage vornehmen, welche natürlich neue Fristen zur Vernehmlassung eröffneten.

Ueber den Sinn und die Tragweite der fraglichen Bestimmung der G. O. haben sich in der Praxis bestimmte Prinzipien entwickelt, welche bei Seuffert a. a. O. näher erörtert sind.

4) Was schließlich die Prozeßordnung betrifft, so hat dieselbe bezüglich des Begriffs einer Klagsänderung so ziemlich die diesseits geltenden Grundsätze sich angeeignet, zum Theile sogar der nemlichen Worte sich bedient, mit denen Seuffert den Sinn der Gerichtsordnung zu erläutern sucht. Es ist dies als wichtig für die Auslegung des Gesetzes zu beachten.

Im Allgemeinen ist darauf hinzuweisen, daß das Gesetz durch die Worte: „der Beklagte kann sich Aenderungen widersetzen," andeutet, daß die Thatsache der Klagsänderung nicht von Amtswegen berücksichtigt werden dürfe, sondern nur, wenn der Beklagte eine Einrede darauf gründet.

Es frägt sich nun weiter:

a) Was ist Klagsänderung?

5) Die Frage der Klagsänderung steht mit der Frage, was Gegenstand des Rechtsstreites bilde und in Rechtskraft erwachse, in nothwendigem innerem Zusammenhange.

Jede Klage verlangt vom Richter, er möge erkennen, daß einer bestimmten Person, einer bestimmten andern Person gegenüber, aus einem bestimmten Grunde ein bestimmtes Recht zustehe. Ueber diese Punkte soll rechtskräftig erkannt werden; sie bestimmen die Identität eines Rechtsstreites; sie allein kommen daher auch bei der Frage, ob der Rechtsstreit geändert werde, in Betracht.

Eine Klagsänderung ist daher eine Aenderung in den Parteien oder im Klaggrunde oder im Klaggesuche, welches letztere zugleich den Gegenstand der Klage begreift.

6) Eine unstatthafte Aenderung in den Parteien liegt nicht bloß dann vor, wenn ganz andere Personen auftreten, sondern auch, wenn die Personen in anderer Eigenschaft auftreten, z. B. derjenige, welcher ursprünglich in eignem Namen klagte, später als gesetzlicher Vertreter eines Andern den Rechtsstreit weiterführen will.

7) Aenderungen im Klaggrunde, d. h. in der Geschichtserzählung, durch welche das Klagbegehren begründet werden soll, bilden nur dann eine Aenderung der Klage selbst, wenn ein wesentlich anderer Klaggrund unterschoben werden will, d. h. ein solcher, welchem, falls er später mit neuer Klage verfolgt würde, die Einrede der res judicata nicht entgegengehalten werden könnte. Neue Thatsachen zur Begründung der nemlichen Klage können immer, sogar noch in der Berufungsinstanz vorgebracht werden. Abg. IV 38 (v. Neum.).

Liegt eine wesentliche, die Identität des Rechtsstreits aufhebende Aenderung der Klagsbegründung nicht vor, so können Unvollständigkeiten in Darstellung des Sachverhalts (in der Klagssubstantiirung) oder Unklarheiten und Irrthümer ohne allen Anstand berichtigt werden, wie dies Art. 181 ausdrücklich anerkennt.

Die nemliche Abänderung kann oft je nach Umständen als bloße Berichtigung oder als Klagsänderung erscheinen. Wenn z. B. ein Darlehen von 100 fl. eingeklagt wird, welches am 1. Mai gegeben worden sei, so kann unbedenklich im Antrage berichtigt werden, das Darlehen habe am 1. Juni stattgefunden, falls es sich nur um ein einziges Darlehen handelt. Stehen aber zwei Darlehen in Frage, das eine vom 1. Mai, welches eingeklagt wurde, und ein zweites vom 1. Juni, dessen Einklagung vorbehalten bleibt, so geht es offenbar nicht an, später statt des ersteren das letztere unterzuschieben.

Ebenso wie im Strafverfahren kommt es zur Erkennung der Identität des Rechtsstreites nur auf die Thatsachen selbst an, nicht aber auf deren rechtliche Qualifikation, ja sogar nicht auf Nebenumstände, aus denen sich etwa andere rechtliche Gesichtspunkte ergeben. Wenn z. B. auf Grund der Hingabe einer bestimmten Geldsumme eine Klage auf Rückzahlung erhoben wird, steht der Umstand, daß in der Klage diese Hingabe als depositum bezeichnet wird, nicht im Wege, in den Anträgen und bei der öffentlichen Verhandlung ein Darlehen geltend zu machen, und zwar selbst dann, wenn erst aus neu vorgebrachten Thatsachen sich ergibt, daß ein Darlehen vorgelegen habe.

Es dürfte der Natur des neuen Verfahrens angemessen sein, in ähnlichen Fällen möglichst Nachsicht zu üben.

8) Was das Klaggesuch anbelangt, so ist zu unterscheiden der Gegenstand, auf welchen sich dasselbe richtet, und das Gesuch an sich, seine Art und sein Umfang.

Es ist selbstverständlich, daß es nicht angehe, einen ganz anderen Gegenstand unterzuschieben, z. B. eine Klage, welche auf das Grundstück A gerichtet war, später auf das Grundstück B zu richten. Nicht als Klagsänderung erscheint es jedoch, wenn bloß eine irrige Bezeichnung des Grundstückes A verbessert wird.

Daß das Gesuch an sich immer eingeschränkt werden könne, ist durch eine ausdrückliche Verfügung in Art. 183 anerkannt, wäre aber auch ohnedies selbstverständlich gewesen. Wer das Mehr begehrt, begehrt auch das Weniger, und es kann daher nie eine unstatthafte Aenderung der Klage darin liegen, daß Jemand sein Begehren beschränkt.

Eine Erweiterung des Gesuches ist allerdings eine wirkliche Klagsänderung; allein auch hier hielt es der Gesetzgeber mit Recht für geeignet, Nachsicht zu üben, weil in der Regel, sofern an Klaggrund und Klaggegenstand sich nichts ändert, die Ausdehnung des Gesuches allein den Beklagten in seiner Vertheidigung nicht verkürzt, und es bei dieser Voraussetzung reiner Formalismus wäre, den Kläger zum Klagsabstande und zur Erhebung neuer Klage zu nöthigen. Der hannoveranische Entwurf (§ 237) erklärte sogar jede Erweiterung des Gesuches zulässig, unsere Prozeßordnung hat jedoch in Art. 182 Abs. 2 dem Ermessen des Rechts Raum gelassen.

In gleicher Weise ist es gestattet, statt der ursprünglich geforderten Sache wegen der Veräußerung oder wegen des Untergangs derselben die Leistung der Entschädigung zu fordern.

Schließlich erlaubt das Gesetz, in jedem Stande der Sache die Klage zu vervollständigen durch Begehren von Nebenansprüchen, die von Entscheidung der Hauptsache abhängen, wie Früchte, Zinsen, Entschädigungen, mögen sie vor oder nach Anstellung der Klage entstanden sein; ferner von Ansprüchen, welche seit Anstellung der Klage aus dem nemlichen Klaggrunde erwachsen sind, z. B. Theile der nemlichen Forderung, welche erst im Laufe des Rechtsstreites fällig geworden sind.

b) Wie lange findet die Klagsänderung statt?

9) Im Parteiprozesse ist Klagsänderung statthaft bis zum Schlusse der ersten Verhandlung (Art. 506 Abs. 3).

Im Anwaltsprozesse findet sie statt bis zur Vernehmlassung.

Es bildet letztere Bestimmung eine Abweichung vom französischen Prozesse, welcher Aenderung der Klage nach der Ladung ausschloß. Bildet sie nun auch eine Abweichung vom seitherigen schriftlichen Verfahren, welches sie bis zur Litiskontestation zuließ?

Man könnte sagen, es sei nirgends die Absicht einer Abweichung vom bestehenden Rechte kundgegeben, also anzunehmen, daß man die Vernehmlassung auf die Hauptsache, d. h. die Streiteinlassung, gemeint habe, und dies zwar um so mehr, als bis dahin der Beklagte sich noch gar nicht über den Grund der Sache ausgesprochen habe, also auch nicht gesagt werden könne, er sei in seiner Vertheidigung beirrt und behindert.

Dagegen läßt sich jedoch einwenden, und zwar wie mir scheint mit Recht, daß man unter Vernehmlassung die Antwort auf die Klage im Allgemeinen versteht, von welcher die Streiteinlassung nur einen Theil bildet (Seuff. Comm. Bd. II S. 303 Note 1), und daß der Gesetzgeber, welcher auf richtige Wahl der Ausdrücke Gewicht legte, sicher nicht von der Vernehmlassung, sondern, wie in den nahestehenden Art. 179 und 186, von der Einlassung auf die Klage gesprochen haben würde, wenn er diese gemeint hätte. Vgl. auch Abg. I 251 (v. Weiß). Ferner ist zu bemerken, daß die Klagsänderung auch für das Schicksal von Einwänden und Einreden, welche von der Streiteinlassung befreien, maßgebend sein kann. Endlich lag es in der Absicht des Gesetzgebers, den Zeitraum für Klagsänderungen möglichst zu beschränken. Es wäre sogar prinzipiell richtiger gewesen, gleich dem französischen Prozesse und dem ihm beitretenden hannov. Entwurfe (§ 237), den Zeitpunkt der Klagszustellung auch in dieser Beziehung allein Maß geben zu lassen.

Mit Zustellung eines motivirten Antrages Seitens des Beklagten, in welchem er in irgend einer Weise die Klage bekämpft, fällt daher das Recht zur Klagsänderung hinweg.

c) Wie erfolgt die Klagsänderung?

10) Es frägt sich nun, wie hat die Aenderung der Klage vor der Vernehmlassung zu geschehen — auf dem Wege eines gewöhnlichen Antrags, also durch Anwaltsakt, oder auf dem Wege der Ladung?

Zweck und Wirkung einer Klagsänderung besteht darin, entweder eine neue Klage an Stelle der früheren zu setzen, oder die letztere durch Zusätze zu ergänzen, sei es durch Beifügen neuer Klaggründe oder durch Beifügen neuer Gesuche oder durch Ausdehnung des Rechtsstreits auf neue Streitpunkte. Dies kann nun aber nach der Natur des jetzigen Verfahrens im gewöhnlichen Prozesse nur durch Zustellung einer Klage an die Partei selbst geschehen, und sind hier alle Gründe anwendbar, welche oben Nr. 2 angeführt worden sind.

Allerdings kennt das Gesetz Fälle, wo selbständige Klagen durch Zustellung von Anwaltsakten erhoben werden, wie z. B. im Falle der Widerklage, der Hauptintervention; allein es sind dies immer nur Ausnahmen, welche auf besonderen Gründen beruhen; Regel aber ist es, daß ein Rechtsstreit nur im Wege förmlicher Klagzustellung mit Vorladung der Partei anhängig werden könne, und am allerwenigsten wäre Grund gegeben, zu Gunsten eines nachlässigen Klägers hiervon eine Ausnahme zu machen.

Aus der Zulassung von Klagsänderungen bis zur Vernehmlassung zieht daher der Kläger nur folgende Vortheile:

1) daß im Falle der Ergänzung der Klage er ein Recht darauf hat, den Klagsnachtrag zugleich mit der ersten Klage verhandeln zu lassen, daß also die Verhandlung über diese Klage suspendirt bleiben muß, bis der Nachtrag zur Verhandlung reif ist, und

2) daß im Falle der Ersetzung der früheren Klage durch eine neue ein förmlicher Klagsabstand nicht nöthig ist.

Was den Parteiprozeß betrifft, wo die Ladung keine nothwendige Voraussetzung ist (Art. 504) und wo der Gesetzgeber besonders verfügt, es könne die Aenderung der Klage noch im Laufe der ersten Verhandlung stattfinden, so möchte anzunehmen sein, daß mündliche Erklärungen in der Sitzung genügen. Jedoch wird dies nur unter der Voraussetzung geschehen können, daß die Klage in ihrer neuen Gestaltung sich an die durch die Ladung gegebene wenigstens anschließe, unter den Begriff einer bloßen Aenderung falle; denn es könnte ohne Zustimmung des Beklagten, der vielleicht bloß durch Bevollmächtigten vertreten ist, nimmermehr gestattet sein, mit einer vollständig neuen Klage aufzutreten.

Einreden.

Art. 184. — **Soweit das Gesetz nicht anders bestimmt, sind Einreden, welche, ohne die Sache selbst zu berühren, nur auf Grund von Prozeßvorschriften die einstweilige Abwendung oder den Aufschub des Prozesses bezwecken, mit einander vorzubringen und ist damit die Einlassung in der Hauptsache zu verbinden.**

Werden solche Einreden später vorgebracht, so dürfen sie nur dann berücksichtigt werden, wenn sie erst im Verlaufe des Verfahrens zur Entstehung gelangt oder auch von Amtswegen zu berücksichtigen sind.

Vorstehende Bestimmungen kommen auch schon bei dem schriftlichen Vorverfahren, wo ein solches stattfindet, zur Anwendung.

G. A. d. K. d. A. I S. 254. 286. IV S. 38. 318. — K. d. R. I S. 332. IV S. 26. 27.

1) So heilsam und für das materielle Recht förderlich es erscheint, wenn die Prozeßordnung das Vorbringen von Einreden, welche die Sache selbst betreffen, nicht in den engen Raum von Präclusivfristen einzwängt, so gerechtfertigt erscheint es andererseits, daß für Einreden, welche nur die formelle Seite des Prozesses betreffen, eine Ausnahme gemacht und vorgeschrieben werde, daß sie bei Beginn des Verfahrens vorzubringen seien. Es wäre höchst ungeeignet und würde nicht das Recht selbst, sondern nur die Chikane begünstigen, wenn man nach durchverhandelter Sache, nach Führung kostspieliger Beweise den Beklagten noch mit Einwänden hören würde, welche sich bloß auf die Form beziehen und welche er in der Lage war, sofort bei Beginn des Rechtsstreites geltend zu machen.

2) Das Gesetz verfügt deßhalb, daß Einreden, welche, ohne die Sache selbst zu berühren, nur auf Grund von Prozeßvorschriften die einstweilige Abwendung oder den Aufschub des Prozesses bezwecken, d. h. die sogenannten Prozeßeinreden 1) zugleich mit der Einlassung in der Hauptsache und 2) miteinander vorzubringen seien, widrigenfalls sie nicht zu berücksichtigen seien.

Es erblickt in dem Nichtvorschützen dieser Einreden einen Verzicht auf dieselben und macht daher eine Ausnahme für die eigentlich selbstverständlichen Fälle, wo die Einrede erst im Laufe des Verfahrens entstanden, oder von Amtswegen zu berücksichtigen ist (Art. 264 Abs. 3).

3) Die Prozeßeinreden des Art. 184 sind weder die prozeßhindernden noch die dilatorischen Einreden des gemeinen Prozesses. Prozeßhindernd nennt man dort gewisse peremtorische Einreden, welche von der Einlassung befreien, wie z. B. die Einrede der Rechtskraft, des Vergleichs ꝛc.; unter dilatorischen Einreden aber begreift man alle diejenigen, deren Wirkung sich darauf beschränkt, den Klaganspruch oder Prozeß zur Zeit zu beseitigen, also auch Einreden, welche das Recht selbst berühren, wie die Einrede der Fristgestattung, die exceptio divisionis, excussionis etc., während Art. 184 Einreden dieser letzteren Art nicht trifft.

Damit eine Einrede als Prozeßeinrede erscheine, ist nicht nöthig, daß sie ausschließlich aus Prozeßschriften sich herleite, wie denn z. B. die Einrede des Mangels der Fähigkeit vor Gericht zu stehen, oder als gesetzlicher Vertreter aufzutreten, ohne Zweifel als eine solche Einrede zu betrachten ist, obgleich Art. 58 auf die bezüglichen civilrechtlichen Grundsätze verweist. Das Hauptgewicht ist auf die Wirkung zu legen.

Prozeßeinreden im Sinne des Art. 184 sind daher z. B. die Einrede der Kostenkaution, der Unzuständigkeit des Gerichts, der Unstatthaftigkeit einer Widerklage, des Mangels der Fähigkeit vor Gericht zu stehen, des Mangels der Prozeßvollmacht oder der vorausgängigen Beschwerde bei der Verwaltungsbehörde in Fiscalsachen.

4) Das Gesetz macht für Prozeßeinreden eine Ausnahme von dem in Art. 251 ausgesprochenen Prinzipe, daß das schriftliche Vorverfahren nur vorbereitend sei und einen Ausschluß von Prozeßhandlungen nicht begründe.

Der Ausschluß tritt hier mit Zustellung desjenigen Schriftsatzes ein, in welchem die Einrede nach Vorschrift des Art. 184 hätte geltend gemacht werden sollen. Es wäre unstatthaft, sie in einem späteren Schriftsatze nachzutragen, auch wenn dieser Nachtrag noch innerhalb der Frist für die Vernehmlassung (Art. 231) zugestellt würde, denn der Sinn des Art. 184 ist in dieser Beziehung ein anderer, als derjenige von Cap. VI § 2 der Gerichtsordnung.

Ohne Bedeutung erscheint es jedoch, ob eine solche Einrede zu Anfang oder zu Ende eines Antrages vorgebracht wird, denn jedes Schriftstück hat nur als Ganzes Geltung. Eine strengere Auslegung würde ich für nutzlose Pedanterie und im Geiste des Gesetzes, welches nur rechtzeitiges Anbringen erzwingen will, nicht begründet halten.

Ebenso ist es im Parteiprozesse ohne Belang, in welcher Reihenfolge die Einwände des Beklagten vorgetragen werden; ja es sind dort die Prozeßeinreden sogar nach der Replik des Klägers und bis zum Schlusse der ersten Verhandlung zulässig (Art. 506), was als Aenderung der früheren Prinzipien im entgegengesetzten Sinne erscheint. Kommt jedoch im Anwaltsprozesse die Sache ohne Schriftenwechsel in die Sitzung, so können Prozeßeinreden nach der Replik nicht mehr nachgetragen werden.

5) Prozeßeinreden, welche erst im Verlaufe des Prozesses entstanden sind, erscheinen im Geiste der Bestimmungen des Art. 184 verwirkt, wenn sie nicht im nächsten, die Hauptsache oder andere Einreden betreffenden Antrage geltend gemacht werden. Es besteht für sie eine Ausnahme nur so weit, als der Grund wirkt, welcher die Ausnahme veranlaßt hat. Sofern mittelst derselben Nichtigkeiten von Prozeßhandlungen geltend gemacht werden, gilt die besondere Vorschrift des Art. 219.

6) Alle sonstigen Einreden sind, soweit nicht besondere gesetzliche Verfügungen Maß geben, z. B. bei Ablehnung des Richters (Art. 44), bei der Verweigerung der Aktenmittheilung, sofern man hierin eine Einrede erblickt (Art. 172), an keine Zeit gebunden und können nach den Grundsätzen des neuen Prozesses in jeder Lage der Sache, selbst nach durchgeführtem Beweisverfahren, ja sogar in der Berufungsinstanz, falls nicht Verzicht anzunehmen ist (Art. 707), zur Geltung gebracht werden.

Art. 185. — Der Beklagte kann bis zur Beseitigung des Grundes seiner Einrede jede weitere Antwort verweigern:

1) **wenn er die Einrede der mangelnden Sicherheitsleistung für die Prozeßkosten vorschützt;**
2) **wenn er als Erbe oder wegen bestandener Gütergemeinschaft belangt wird und sich darauf beruft, daß die ihm nach bürgerlichen Gesetzen eingeräumte Bedenkzeit sich noch im Laufe befindet;**
3) **wenn er die Zulässigkeit der Klage aus dem Grunde bestreitet, weil der Kläger dem in einem frühern Verfahren gegen ihn ergangenen Urtheile noch nicht Genüge geleistet hat, ungeachtet hiedurch die Zulässigkeit der gegenwärtigen Klage bedingt ist.**

Art. 186. — **Zur Einlassung in der Hauptsache ist der Beklagte nicht verpflichtet:**
1) wenn er die Zuständigkeit des Gerichts bestreitet oder die Verweisung an ein anderes Gericht verlangt;
2) wenn er die Einrede der nicht ordnungsmäßig erfolgten Ladung oder eine Einrede vorbringt, welche die Befähigung zur Prozeßführung betrifft;
3) wenn er die Nothwendigkeit der Beiladung weiterer Personen behauptet.

G. A. d. K. d. A. I S. 255—257. 286. IV S. 38. — K. d. R. I S. 332. 333.

1) Diese beiden Artikel zählen diejenigen bevorzugten Prozeßeinreden auf, bezüglich welcher die Vorschriften des Art. 184, es seien Prozeßeinreden mit einander vorzubringen und mit denselben zugleich die Einlassung in die Hauptsache zu verbinden, eine Ausnahme erleiden. Im Hinblicke auf letzteren Umstand kann man sie als prozeßhindernde Einreden bezeichnen, jedoch erscheint es, da man hiermit seither einen andern Sinn verband und da auch die Präjudizialeinreden (falls man solche annimmt) von der Einlassung befreien, einfacher und klarer, bloß von bevorzugten Prozeßeinreden zu sprechen.

Es werden zwei Arten solcher Prozeßeinreden unterschieden, nemlich in Art. 185 besonders bevorzugte, welche von jeder weiteren Antwort befreien, und in Art. 186 einfach bevorzugte, welche bloß von der Einlassung in die Hauptsache befreien.

2) Was den gesetzgeberischen Werth dieser Verfügungen betrifft, welche eine bedeutende Lücke in die auch im neuen Prozesse giltige Eventualmaxime bringen, so möchte derselbe sehr problematisch sein. In den Fällen des Art. 185 läßt sich das Abweichen von dieser Maxime wohl rechtfertigen, denn die zu würdigenden Verhältnisse sind in der Regel sehr einfach, und es liegen besondere Gründe vor, die Beklagten hier vorerst mit Eingehen auf die Sache nicht zu behelligen. Auch wird sich Art. 185 nur wenig fühlbar machen. Was jedoch die Verfügungen des Art. 186 anbelangt, welche eine sehr häufige Anwendung zu finden geeignet sind, so betrachte ich sie den seitherigen Zuständen diesseits sowohl als in der Pfalz gegenüber als Rückschritt.

Man gab zu, daß in der Pfalz von der Befugniß, die Einrede der Incompetenz, Nichtigkeit der Ladung 2c. getrennt von der Hauptsache vorzubringen, nie Gebrauch gemacht werde, — es ist mir kein Fall erinnerlich, wo es geschehen wäre — daß also die strenge Durchführung der Eventualmaxime sich als praktisches Bedürfniß geltend machte. (Abg. I 255) Man hätte hinzufügen dürfen, daß die französische Jurisprudenz jene Befugniß auch rechtlich möglichst einzuengen suchte, und z. B. dem Richter gestattete, zu verfügen, daß unmittelbar nach Abweisung solcher Prozeßeinreden über den Grund der Sache verhandelt werde. Cass. 5. Juli 1809. Toulouse 19. April 1844. Douai 30. Juli 1845. Chauveau sur Carré quest. 735 (Note).

Angesichts dieser praktischen Erfahrungen hätte man eigentlich zur Ueberzeugung gelangen müssen, daß derartige Ausnahmen keine innere Berechtigung haben, daß sie nur als Aufforderungen zur Chikane wirken und geeignet sind, die Uebung leichtfertiger Anwälte zu begünstigen, welche, um des erschöpfenden Studiums ihres Prozesses einstweilen sich entschlagen zu können, irgend eine Prozeßeinrede vorschieben. Der einsichtsvolle und gewissenhafte Anwalt wird nicht eher Anträge stellen, bevor er den ganzen Prozeß gründlich inne hat, denn nur alsdann vermag er zu ermessen, ob es im Interesse seiner Partei liege, Prozeßeinreden zu erheben, ob und in welcher Weise etwa ein Vergleich rathsam sei. Einen völlig klaren Einblick in den Prozeß gewinnt er aber nur dadurch, daß er sich auf die Sache einläßt und hierdurch den Gegner veranlaßt, seine Angriffs- und Vertheidigungsmittel vollständig zu entwickeln.

In der Pfalz ist es Uebung geworden, daß die Anwälte Prozeßeinreden nur selten und nur dann vorschützen, wenn ein loyales materielles Interesse dafür vorliegt, und sie pflegen nie zu unterlassen, gewissermaßen zur Entschuldigung, dieses Interesse hervorzuheben. Es kommt häufig vor, daß noch in der Sitzung, wenn sich ergibt, daß dieses Interesse wegfalle, erhobene Prozeßeinreden zurückgenommen werden. Alles dies, sowie der eigene Vortheil des Anwaltes, für welchen es eine Erleichterung ist, den Prozeß von vornherein nach allen Richtungen zu bearbeiten, endlich die Erwägung, daß es in der Regel nicht möglich ist, Vergleiche anzubahnen, so lange die Hauptsache noch unklar bleibt, bewirkten, daß die eventuelle Einlassung zur durchgreifenden Regel geworden ist. Man darf nicht denken, es seien hierdurch unnütze Vorträge bei der öffentlichen Verhandlung veranlaßt worden, denn, wenn eine Prozeßeinrede dem Gerichte beachtenswerth erschien, wurde eben der Vortrag auf dieselbe beschränkt. In der Pfalz wird es hoffentlich, trotz der provozirenden Bestimmungen des Art. 186 bei der seitherigen Uebung bleiben; ob sich aber diesseits eine gleiche Uebung bilden werde, möchte man fast bezweifeln, wenn man erwägt, wie häufig von dem Rechte der Verweigerung der Streiteinlassung in den seltenen Fällen, wo es bis jetzt bestand, Gebrauch gemacht wurde.

Uebrigens ist anzuerkennen, daß der Gesetzgeber die schlimmen Wirkungen fraglicher Bestimmungen dadurch mindert, daß er in Art. 232 eine kurze Frist setzt und das Recht der Berufung nur für die Einrede der Unzuständigkeit gibt. Weitere Nachhilfe ließe sich in der Taxe treffen.

3) Für die Auslegung der Art. 185 und 186 ist im Allgemeinen der Grundsatz leitend, daß überall, wo nicht eine Abweichung von den Vorschriften des Art. 184 klar ausgesprochen ist, diese Vorschriften Maß geben. Es erleidet daher keinen Zweifel, daß auch die bevorzugten Prozeßeinreden verwirkt sind, wenn sie nicht rechtzeitig vorgeschützt werden.

a) Besonders bevorzugte Prozeßeinreden.

4) Die drei Einreden des Art. 185 sind nicht bloß von gleichzeitiger Einlassung in die Hauptsache, sondern auch von jeder weiteren Antwort befreit, d. h. es brauchen auch sonstige Prozeßeinreden, insbesondere jene des Art. 186 nicht damit verbunden zu werden.

Natürliche Folge ist, daß diese letzteren Einreden nicht ausgeschlossen werden, und zwar selbst dann nicht, wenn etwa der Beklagte freiwillig die eine oder die andere derselben mit einer jener drei Einreden verbunden haben sollte. Hat jedoch der Beklagte, was ihm zu thun freisteht, sich gleichzeitig in die Hauptsache eingelassen, so werden alle Prozeßeinreden, welche nicht mit vorgebracht wurden, als verwirkt zu betrachten sein.

5) Es frägt sich, ob die drei Einreden auch unter sich gesondert geltend gemacht werden dürfen. Wenn ein Ausländer, nach Abstehung von einem früheren Prozesse, gegen Erben klagt, kann Grund zu allen drei Einreden gegeben sein. Kann nun der Beklagte, mit einer beliebigen dieser Einreden beginnend, sie eine nach der andern vorschützen, oder muß er sie vereinigen?

Man kann sagen, es müsse der Grundsatz durchgreifen, daß, wo nicht ausdrücklich anders bestimmt ist, Art. 184 seine Anwendung finde; allein beachtet man den Wortlaut, welcher für jede Einrede verfügt, es dürfe weitere Antwort verweigert werden, bis der Grund dieser Einrede beseitigt sei, faßt man ferner den Redaktionsvorschlag des kgl. Ministerial-Commissärs (Abg. I 255) ins Auge, welcher nur deshalb eine andere Fassung erhielt, um anzudeuten, daß es auf die Reihenfolge nicht ankomme (Abg. I 257 [Edel]), erwägt man endlich, daß der entgegenstehende Vorschlag des Referenten (Abg. I 257) keine Beachtung fand, so muß Ersteres als Wille des Gesetzgebers betrachtet werden.

Uebrigens bringt es die Natur der Einrede der Prozeßkostenkaution mit sich, daß, falls sie auch mit anderen Einreden vereinigt auftritt, über sie zuerst zu erkennen ist. Es könnte nicht angehen, über die Frage, ob Erbschaftsannahme stattgefunden, ob ein Besitzurtheil vollzogen sei, Beweise aufzulegen, während der Beklagte bezüglich seiner Kosten nicht gesichert wäre.

6) Indem gesagt wird, es könne die weitere Antwort verweigert werden bis zur Beseitigung des Grundes der Einrede, ist angedeutet, daß diese drei Einreden zunächst die Klage an sich nicht angreifen, daß vielmehr die Unstatthaftigkeit der Klage durch nachträgliche Beseitigung des Mangels geheilt werden könne. Es gilt dieser Grundsatz übrigens auch für sonstige prozessuale Einreden, deren Grund sich beseitigen läßt, z. B. die Einrede des Mangels der Ermächtigung, des Mangels der Beschwerdeführung bei der Verwaltung in Fiskalsachen. Selbstverständlich fallen etwaige frustratorische Kosten dem Kläger, der sie verschuldet hat, zur Last.

7) Was die Einrede des Erben oder der Ehefrau wegen Laufes der Bedenkzeit betrifft, so ist sie ihrer Natur nach eine, das Recht selbst nicht berührende, Prozeßeinrede, obgleich sie sich auf Vorschriften der Civilgesetze gründet. Da der Zweck derselben nur darauf gerichtet ist, die gesetzliche Bedenkzeit wegen Annahme oder Verzicht zu sichern, so hat das Urtheil, welches sie für begründet erklärt, nicht auszusprechen, es sei die Klage als unstatthaft abzuweisen, sondern nur, es habe das Verfahren bis nach Ablauf der (kurzen) Bedenkfrist zu beruhen. Insbesondere steht hier auch Art. 797 Code civil nicht im Wege. Chauveau sur Carré quest. 756. Im Augenblicke, wo, sei es durch Annahme der Erbschaft, sei es durch Ablauf der Bedenkzeit, der Grund der Einrede wegfällt, erscheint sie selbst beseitigt, so daß also in der Regel die einfache Vertagung genügen wird.

Behauptet der Kläger, es habe der Erbe oder die Ehefrau bereits rechtswirksam angenommen, so kann sich diese Prozeßeinrede zu einem Präjudizialpunkte im Sinne des Art. 190 gestalten.

8) Die Fälle, welche Ziff. 3 im Auge hat, sind: die Abweisung einer Klage wegen Unzuständigkeit mit Rücksicht auf den Werth des Streitgegenstands (Art. 188), der Abstand von einem früheren Prozesse (Art. 498) und das Unterliegen

in einem Besitzstreite (Art. 588). Hat in diesen Fällen der Kläger nicht spätestens zur Zeit der Verhandlung die Bedingung der Zulässigkeit der Klage erfüllt, so ist dieselbe als unstatthaft abzuweisen.

b) Einfach bevorzugte Prozeßeinreden.

9) Die Einreden des Art. 186 sind nur von der Einlassung in die Hauptsache befreit, also bleibt die durch Art. 184 ausgesprochene Verpflichtung, alle Prozeßeinreden vereinigt vorzubringen, ihnen gegenüber bestehen. Es sind somit nicht bloß die Einreden des Art. 186 selbst zu vereinigen, sondern es sind auch alle sonstigen Prozeßeinreden bei Strafe des Ausschlusses damit zu verbinden.

Wurden Einreden des Art. 186 ohne Einlassung auf die Hauptsache vorgebracht und findet sie das Gericht grundlos, so spricht es deren Verwerfung aus und verfügt, daß in der Sache weiter verhandelt werde. Das weitere Verfahren richtet sich nach Art. 256.

10) Wenn das Gesetz in Ziff. 2 von der Einrede der nicht ordnungsmäßigen Ladung spricht, so meint es, wie auch der hannover. Entwurf (§ 243), welchem diese Fassung entlehnt ist (Abg. I 257), nicht bloß die Ladung im engeren Sinne, d. h. den Gerichtsvollzieherakt, durch welchen die Zustellung der Klagschrift beurkundet wird, sondern auch den Inhalt der Klagschrift, wie denn im Parteiprozesse Beides zusammenfällt.

Es gehören also alle Einreden hierher, welche sich darauf gründen, daß die mit der Ladung gestellte Klage, ihrer Form nach, denjenigen Forderungen nicht entspreche, welche das Gesetz (Art. 225 und 501) an sie stellt, daß z. B. in der Darstellung des Sachverhaltes, in Bezeichnung des Streitgegenstandes etwas Wesentliches mangele. (Art. 218 Abs. 2.) Allerdings eröffnet sich hierdurch ein ergiebiges Feld für Chikanen, denen jedoch der Richter dadurch begegnen kann, daß er sofort nach Abweisung der Einrede auf Grund von Art. 259 Abs. 4 eine der nächsten Sitzungen zur Verhandlung in der Hauptsache anberaumt.

11) Einreden, welche die Befähigung zur Prozeßführung betreffen, sind zunächst solche, welche sich aus den Bestimmungen der Art. 58 bis 61 über die Fähigkeit vor Gericht zu stehen und die Befugniß als gesetzlicher Vertreter zu handeln, herleiten.

Ursprünglich hieß es: „Befähigung der Partei zur Prozeßführung“. Die Worte „der Partei“ wurden von der Subkommission (Abg. I 286) ohne Angabe des Grundes beseitigt, offenbar um anzudeuten, daß nicht bloß die Partei, sondern auch alle Personen, welche für sie auftreten, gemeint seien. Deshalb ist denn auch der Ausdruck „Befähigung“ im weiteren Sinne zu nehmen, so daß er auch die „Befugniß“ Prozeß zu führen umfaßt. Vgl. hannover. Entwurf § 243.

Es könnte sich fragen, ob auch die Befugniß als Prozeßbevollmächtigter aufzutreten, hierher gehöre, allein da die nemlichen Gründe obwalten, auch der Bevollmächtigte als prozeßführend bezeichnet werden kann und vom Gesetze vielfach so bezeichnet wird (Art. 79, 95), so möchte die Frage zu bejahen sein. Zudem wird die Frage der Prozeßvollmacht nie Verzögerungen veranlassen, da sie nur im Parteiprozesse aufgeworfen werden, dort aber der Richter immer sofortige Verhandlung über die Sache anordnen kann.

12) Eine Nothwendigkeit der Beiladung ist überall anzunehmen, wo der Beklagte kraft Gesetzes das Recht hat, eine Beiladung selbst vorzunehmen, oder zu verlangen, daß Kläger sie vornehme. Im ersten Falle, welcher auch die Gewährschaftsklage begreift, handelt es sich bloß um Aufschub des Verfahrens, im zweiten Falle jedoch um Auflage an den Kläger und Abweisung seiner Klage als unstatthaft, falls er der Auflage nicht nachkommt.

Art. 187. — **Gegen die Verwerfung einer gerichtsablehnenden Einrede findet, soweit das Gesetz nicht anders bestimmt, selbständige Berufung statt, welche innerhalb fünfzehn Tagen, von Zustellung des Urtheils an die Partei, im Anwaltsprozesse von Zustellung des Urtheils an den Anwalt gerechnet, erhoben werden muß.**

In solchem Falle beruht die weitere Verhandlung bis zur Entscheidung des Obergerichts.

G. A. d. K. d. A. I S. 257. 258. 286. III S. 86. IV. S. 38.
K. d. R. I S. 333. IV S. 27.

1) Urtheile, welche Prozeßeinreden verwerfen, sind, sofern nicht etwa zugleich Endurtheil in der Hauptsache erfolgt, bloße Zwischenurtheile, gegen welche selbständige Rechtsmittel nach Art. 682 und 788 nicht ergriffen werden können. Es gilt dies insbesondere auch für Fälle, wo eine bevorzugte Prozeßeinrede nach Art. 232 zur gesonderten Verhandlung und Entscheidung gebracht

worden ist, denn Prozeßeinreden als solche sind keine Präjudizialsachen im Sinne der Art. 190 und 682 Abs. 2. Abg. I 256 (v. Weiß).

2) Nur für die gerichtsablehnende Einrede glaubte der Gesetzgeber eine Ausnahme machen zu müssen und läßt das Rechtsmittel der **Berufung** gegen Urtheile, welche dieselbe verwerfen, allgemein zu, also ohne Unterschied, ob über dieselbe gesondert entschieden wurde, oder ob zugleich Erkenntniß in der Hauptsache erging.

Um Prozeßverzögerungen zu verhüten, knüpft er diese Berufung an die kurze Frist von 15 Tagen, welche zudem von Zustellung an den Anwalt läuft, falls ein solcher bestellt ist, eine Sonderbestimmung, welche natürlich nur maßgebend ist, wenn das Recht der Berufung sich bloß auf die Entscheidung über diese Prozeßeinrede gründet. Unterliegt das Urtheil auch noch aus andern Gründen der Berufung, so gelten die gewöhnlichen Grundsätze.

3) Selbstverständlich ist die Berufung auch in diesem Falle nur statthaft, wenn für den in Frage gestellten Anspruch die **Berufungssumme** gegeben, oder seiner Natur nach nicht erforderlich ist. Art. 549 des Entwurfs, aus welchem das Gegentheil zu folgern war, wurde gestrichen.

Ebenso versteht sich von selbst, daß der Anwalt Mandat hat, diese Berufung zu ergreifen, auch wenn er die Partei in der Berufungsinstanz nicht vertritt oder vertreten kann.

Die Schlußbestimmung, daß bis zur Entscheidung über die Berufung, oder richtiger bis zur **Zustellung** dieser Entscheidung das Verfahren beruhe, enthält nur eine Anwendung der Bestimmungen von Art. 490 Abs. 1 und 699.

4) Da Art. 187 nur von der Berufung, nicht aber auch von der Nichtigkeitsbeschwerde spricht, so gelten in dieser Beziehung die allgemeinen Grundsätze des Art. 788.

Art. 188. — **Will der Beklagte die Zuständigkeit des Gerichts aus dem Grunde bestreiten, weil die Sache nach dem Geldwerthe des Streitgegenstands vor ein anderes Gericht gehöre, so hat er dies vor jeder andern Aeußerung in der Sache, die in Art. 185 bezeichneten Einreden ausgenommen, geltend zu machen.**

Die Parteien haben in solchen Fällen die zur Ermittelung des Werths dienlichen, ihnen verfügbaren Behelfe in der Verhandlung vorzulegen.

Findet sich das Gericht weder hiedurch noch sonst in der Lage, über den Werth des Streitgegenstands die erforderliche Entscheidung zu treffen, so ist der Werth in Ermangelung eines Uebereinkommens durch Vernehmung von Sachverständigen zu erheben.

Wegen behaupteter Unrichtigkeit des Gutachtens der Sachverständigen ist ein weiteres Gutachten nicht zu erheben.

Erweist sich die Einrede als grundlos, so hat der Beklagte die dadurch veranlaßten Kosten zu tragen.

Gegen die Verwerfung der Einrede findet kein Rechtsmittel statt und die Zuständigkeit des Gerichts kann wegen des angeblich höhern Werths des Streitgegenstands vor dem höhern Gerichte auch dann nicht angefochten werden, wenn die Sache in Folge eines aus einem andern Grunde eingelegten Rechtsmittels dahin gelangt.

Wird die Unzuständigkeit des Gerichts ausgesprochen, so wird durch das rechtskräftige Urtheil des Collegialgerichts die Zuständigkeit des Einzelngerichts, durch das rechtskräftige Urtheil des Einzelngerichts die Zuständigkeit des Collegialgerichts dergestalt begründet, daß eine Anfechtung oder Prüfung der Zuständigkeit, soweit diese durch den Werth des Streitgegenstands bedingt erscheint, nicht mehr zulässig ist.

Die neue Klage kann nicht erhoben werden, ehe die durch die frühere verursachten Kosten ersetzt sind.

Art. 189. — **Von Amtswegen ist die Klage abzuweisen, wenn im Verfahren von Einzelngerichten der Werth des Streitgegenstands, soweit die Feststellung der Zuständigkeit davon abhängt, aus der Klage nicht zu ersehen und der Beklagte bei der Verhandlung nicht erschienen ist.**

G. A. d. K. d. A. I S. 258. 259. 286—288. III. S. 12—14. IV S. 38. 318.
K. d. R. I S. 336—338. IV S. 27. 28.

1) Die Fälle, wo die Zuständigkeit der Gerichte von Schätzung des Streitgegenstandes abhängt, haben sich zwar durch Ausscheidung der dinglichen Immobiliarklagen und Besitzklagen erheblich vermindert, werden jedoch immerhin nicht selten sein.

Der Gesetzgeber war, und gewiß mit Recht, bemüht, gerichtliche Schätzungen dieser Art möglichst zu vermeiden, und sofern sie nicht zu vermeiden sind, zu vereinfachen und zu beschleunigen. Er nöthigt den Kläger zur Angabe des Werths in der Ladung (Art. 189), verlangt vom Beklagten Geltendmachung der Einrede vor jeder anderen Aeußerung, erlaubt dem Richter selbst zu schätzen, wo immer er sich dazu fähig hält, gibt endlich seiner Entscheidung sofort Rechtskraft und unbedingte Wirkung, sogar zur Feststellung der Berufungssumme (Art. 689).

Demnach darf es sicher auch als Wille des Gesetzes anzusehen sein, daß der Richter nur dann zu solchen Schätzungen schreite, wenn er Grund hat, anzunehmen, daß eine sichere, das ganze Interesse umfassende Abschätzung möglich sei, mit andern Worten, daß er im Zweifel den Fall des Art. 5 Ziff. 1 als gegeben zu erachten habe. Offenbar sind hier ganz andere Erwägungen maßgebend, als in Fällen, wo die Abschätzung nothwendig ist, z. B. wenn die Geldentschädigung zu ermitteln ist, welche im Falle der Nichterfüllung, schuldhaften Zerstörung 2c. zu leisten sei. Abschätzungen dieser Art müssen möglich sein, und wenn sichere Anhaltspunkte fehlen, so greift der Richter durch und setzt nach bestem Ermessen die Summe fest. Anders verhält es sich, wenn die Abschätzung nur geschehen soll, sofern sie sicher geschehen kann. Vgl. die Bemerkung des Referenten zum Antrage von K. Barth. Abg. I 259.

2) Der Geldwerth des Streitgegenstandes ist der gemeine Werth desselben im Verkehre, unter Beachtung aller Umstände, welche den Werth des Gegenstandes selbst im besonderen Falle bestimmen. Der subjektive Werth für eine der Parteien mit Rücksicht auf beabsichtigte Unternehmungen oder ähnliche Umstände, oder gar der Affektionswerth kommt nicht in Betracht.

In dieser Weise wurde § 61 der Novelle von 1837 ausgelegt. (Seuff. Comm. Bd. IV S. 61).

Stehen Leistungen in Frage, welche durch Andere besorgt werden können, so wird zu prüfen sein, welchen Kostenaufwand diese Erfüllung veranlassen würde.

Wegen einiger besonderen Fälle der Schätzung siehe Art. 4.

3) Die Unzuständigkeit wegen des Werths des Streitgegenstandes ist der Regel nach nur zu berücksichtigen, wo sie einredeweise geltend gemacht wird.

Im Falle des Nichterscheinens des Beklagten ist entweder der Werth aus der Klage ersichtlich oder nicht.

Bei erster Unterstellung wird gemäß Art. 297 und 520 die Angabe des Klägers als zugestanden betrachtet und auf Grund derselben über die Zuständigkeit, welche hier allerdings von Amtswegen zu berücksichtigen ist, entschieden. (Abg. I 287, v. Neumayr u. Barth).

Bei letzter Unterstellung ist, falls die Sache vor's Landgericht gebracht war, der Art. 189 maßgebend, falls sie aber vor's Bezirksgericht gebracht war, ist nach dem Willen des Gesetzgebers (Abg. I 287) anzunehmen, daß der Kläger behaupten wollte, es falle die Klage dem Werthe nach in die Zuständigkeit dieses Gerichtes als des ordentlichen. Auch für die Handelsgerichte muß, den Landgerichten gegenüber, das Nemliche gelten. Der Gesetzgeber wollte also in diesen Fällen keine Prüfung von Amtswegen.

Im Falle des Erscheinens des Beklagten bieten sich Zweifel dar. Gilt auch für diesen Fall die Regel des Art. 265, daß der Richter seine Zuständigkeit in jeder Lage der Sache von Amtswegen zu prüfen habe, oder ist sie aufgehoben?

Die praktischen Folgen dieser Frage werden durch die Prinzipien über Vereinbarung nicht beseitigt, weil im landgerichtlichen Verfahren eine Vereinbarung nur wirkt, wenn sie nach Belehrung zu Protokoll genommen ist, und weil sie auch sonst nur eintritt in Folge der Streiteinlassung.

Für die erstere Ansicht läßt sich sagen, daß der Laut des Gesetzes nur das Recht des Beklagten, fragliche Einrede vorzuschützen, beschränke, keineswegs aber auch das Recht des Richters, die Unzuständigkeit von Amtswegen zu berücksichtigen, falls genügende Gründe dazu vorliegen.

Für die letztere Ansicht, welche ich für die richtige halte, ist anzuführen, daß die Bestimmung, es müsse die Einrede vor jeder sonstigen Aeußerung vorgeschützt werden, keinen Sinn und keine Bedeutung hätte, wenn dieselbe gemäß Art. 184 Abs. 2 und Art. 265 dennoch zu jeder Zeit berücksichtigt werden müßte. Daß sie in geeigneten Fällen durch Vereinbarung beseitigt werden könne, verstand sich von selbst.

Für diese Auslegung sprechen auch die Aeußerungen des Ministerial-Commissärs (Abg. I 258) und der Subcommission zu Art. 165 (Abg. I 287), sowie die ganze Tendenz des Art. 188, welchem offenbar der Gedanke fern lag, es dürfe bei Mangel protokollarischer Erklärung über die Vereinbarung die fragliche Unzuständigkeit in jeder Lage der Sache angeregt und berücksichtigt werden.

4) Die in Frage stehende Einrede ist vor jeder anderen Aeußerung in der Sache, die Prozeßeinreden des Art. 185 ausgenommen, geltend zu machen.

Diese Vorschrift besteht nur für den Anwaltsprozeß, denn für den Parteiprozeß gilt Art. 506 Abs. 2, gemäß dessen auch diese Einrede bis zum Schlusse der ersten Verhandlung vorgebracht werden darf. Der Vorschlag des Referenten, für sie eine Ausnahme zu machen, wurde verworfen. (Abg. II S. 258).

Was den Anwaltsprozeß betrifft, so will Art. 188 Abs. 1 nicht sagen, es sei fragliche Einrede getrennt von sonstigen Prozeßeinreden oder von der Einlassung in die Hauptsache vorzubringen, enthält also keine Ausnahme von der Bestimmung des Art. 184, daß alle Prozeßeinreden zu vereinigen seien, und von der Bestimmung des Art. 186, welche gleichzeitige Einlassung in die Hauptsache gestattet. Die Ausnahmsstellung dieser Einrede besteht also nur darin, daß sie verwirkt ist, sobald der Beklagte irgend eine andere Prozeßeinrede, außer denen des Art. 185, vorgebracht oder sich in die Hauptsache eingelassen hat, daß also die Reihenfolge des Vorbringens hier unbedingt entscheidet.

5) Behelfe zur Ermittelung des Werthes sind alle Umstände, welche geeignet sind, auf die Ueberzeugung des Richters einzuwirken, also selbst außergerichtliche Schätzungen, sofern es sicher ist, daß sie von Leuten ausgehen, welche der Richter für zulässig hält.

Auch wenn die Parteien keine Behelfe vorlegen, kann der Richter aus sonstigen, den Vorträgen zu entnehmenden oder ihm bekannten Umständen seine Ueberzeugung bilden.

Kommt es zur Erhebung eines Gutachtens von Sachverständigen, so sind die Vorschriften von Hauptstück XIII maßgebend. Der Richter wird jedoch so einfach verfahren, als es das Gesetz nur immer erlaubt, also in der Regel bloß einen Sachverständigen ernennen (Art. 434) und diesen in der Sitzung vernehmen (Art. 447), was den Vortheil hat, daß bei Verwerfung der Einrede ein Protokoll nicht nöthig ist (Art. 419 Abs. 5). Wenn das Gesetz verbietet, wegen Unrichtigkeit des Gutachtens ein weiteres zu erheben (vgl. Art. 448), so schließt dies die Befugniß nicht aus, nach Art. 446 die Sachverständigen zur Erläuterung eines unklaren oder unvollkommenen Gutachtens in die Sitzung zu laden.

6) Aus dem Streben des Gesetzgebers, Streit wegen des Werthes möglichst zu verhüten, leiten sich zwei Strafbestimmungen her, nemlich 1) daß im Falle der Unzuständigkeit der Kläger keine neue Klage erheben dürfe, bevor er die Kosten der früheren ersetzt, und 2) daß im Falle der Zuständigkeit Beklagter immer in die Kosten des Incidentpunkts zu verurtheilen sei.

7) Die Verfügungen in Abs. 7 enthalten eine Abweichung von den allgemeinen Prinzipien, welche um so greller hervortritt, als sie auch jede Rücksichtsnahme auf Werthsänderungen beseitigt und in Fällen, wo die neue Klagstellung erst nach längerer Zeit erfolgt, der Werth ein wesentlich anderer geworden sein kann. Es mindert sich das Auffallende jedoch, wenn erwogen wird, daß auch im Laufe eines länger dauernden Rechtsstreites der Werth des Streitgegenstands sich wesentlich ändern kann und das Gesetz eben in fraglicher Richtung den neuen Rechtsstreit als Fortsetzung des früheren betrachtet wissen will. Geeignet wäre es vielleicht gewesen, eine Frist für Anstellung der neuen Klage zu bestimmen.

Die bezügliche Ausnahmsbestimmung begreift jedoch offenbar nicht jene Fälle, wo der Streitgegenstand selbst eine wesentliche Aenderung erlitten hat. Wer z. B. ein Anlehensloos im Werthe von 150 fl. vindizirt hat, klagt nicht wegen des nemlichen Streitgegenstandes, wenn dieses Loos mittlerweile 50,000 fl. gewonnen hat, ebensowenig als behauptet werden könnte, die frühere Schätzung dieses Looses sei maßgebend für die Zulässigkeit der Berufung (Art. 689).

Schließlich ist hervorzuheben, daß nur darüber Rechtskraft entsteht, ob die Sache sich des Werthes wegen vor ein Collegialgericht oder vor das Einzelgericht eigne, nicht aber darüber, welches Gericht, ob z. B. das Bezirksgericht oder das Handelsgericht zuständig sei, oder ob nicht nach andern Gesichtspunkten, z. B. auf Grund von Art. 5 oder 6, die Zuständigkeit des ersten Gerichts dennoch gegeben sei.

8) Die Abweisung der Klage im Falle des Art. 189 hat ihren Grund bloß in der Unregelmäßigkeit des Verfahrens, in der Ordnungswidrigkeit der Ladung im Sinne von Art. 186 Ziff. 2; sie enthält jedoch keine Entscheidung über die Zuständigkeit und steht nicht im Wege, die nemliche Klage beim nemlichen Richter wiederholt anzubringen. Abg. I 287 (zu Art. 166a).

Die Fassung: „aus der Klage nicht zu ersehen" wurde gewählt, um anzuzeigen, daß eine ausdrückliche Angabe des Werthes nicht gemeint sei. Abg. I 288 (zu Art. 166).

Präjudicialsachen.

Art. 190. — **Hängt die Entscheidung eines Rechtsstreits von der Verhandlung und Entscheidung über einen vorher zu erledigenden, durch das nämliche Gericht zu entscheidenden Streitpunkt ab, so kann die Verhandlung vorerst auf diesen Präjudicialpunkt beschränkt werden. Das Gericht ist jedoch, wenn die Entscheidung des Präjudicialpunktes eine Beweisführung**

oder sonstige weitere Verhandlung zu veranlassen geeignet scheint, befugt, die Parteien zu gleichzeitiger Geltendmachung ihrer übrigen Rechtsbehelfe anzuhalten; auch kann es, wenn mehrere bei ihm anhängige Rechtsstreite mit dem zu entscheidenden Präjudicialpunkte in sachlichem und rechtlichem Zusammenhange stehen, deren Verbindung, soweit ihm dieselbe angemessen erscheint, anordnen.

Ist der Präjudicialpunkt bei einem andern Gerichte als dem für die Entscheidung des Rechtsstreits zuständigen oder bei einer Verwaltungsbehörde zu entscheiden, so hat das Gericht auf Antrag oder von Amtswegen die Verhandlung des bei ihm anhängigen Rechtsstreits ganz oder theilweise bis nach rechtskräftiger Erledigung des Präjudicialpunktes auszusetzen. Es kann aber zugleich vorsorgliche Verfügungen erlassen und der betreffenden Partei zur Betreibung der Sache geeignete Fristen setzen.

Art. 191. — **Wenn aus Veranlassung eines Rechtsstreits ein zur Einleitung strafrechtlichen Verfahrens hinreichender Verdacht der Verübung einer strafbaren That sich ergibt, deren Ermittelung auf die Entscheidung des Rechtsstreits Einfluß zu äußern vermag, so kann die Verhandlung und Entscheidung des letztern bis nach Beendigung des Strafverfahrens ausgesetzt werden. Zugleich kann das Gericht vorsorgliche Verfügungen erlassen.**

G. A. d. K. d. A. I S. 23. 259. 260. 288. 289. III S. 85. 86. IV S. 38.
K. d. R. I S. 338. 339. IV S. 28.

1) Das Gesetz behandelt hier die Präjudicialpunkte, und zwar in dreifacher Richtung, nemlich 1) den Fall, wo die Vorfrage vom nemlichen Gerichte zu entscheiden ist, 2) den Fall, wo ein anderes Gericht oder die Verwaltung darüber zu entscheiden hat, und 3) den Fall, wo die Entscheidung des Rechtsstreites von einem Strafverfahren abhängt.

a) Präjudicialpunkte, welche das nemliche Gericht entscheidet.

2) Meiner Ansicht nach war es ein Mißgriff, besondere Vorschriften wegen Präjudicialsachen dieser Art zu geben, insbesondere so, wie geschehen. Der Vorschlag des Referenten, diese Bestimmungen zu streichen und sich mit Art. 157 zu begnügen, war dem Geiste des neuen Verfahrens weit entsprechender und empfahl sich um so mehr zur Annahme, als er mit den Principien und der Praxis, wie sie in der Pfalz sich bewährt haben, vollkommen übereinstimmte.

3) Was sind Präjudicialsachen?

Unter Präjudicialsachen verstand man bis jetzt selbständige Streitpunkte, welche mit der anhängigen Streitsache der Art connex sind, daß sie die Vorbedingung für deren Entscheidung bilden. Seuffert (Comm. Bd. II S. 322) definirt die Präjudicialeinreden dahin: „daß sie den Stoff eines selbständigen Rechtsstreites darbieten müssen."

Der Begriff, welchen unsere Prozeßordnung mit dem Ausdrucke verbindet, ist offenbar auf diese Grundlage zurückzuführen, jedoch ist nach der Allgemeinheit der Wortfassung und nach den Verhandlungen über Art. 682 Abs. 2 (Abg. III S. 82—85) anzunehmen, daß nicht gerade erfordert werde, es müsse der Stoff eines selbständigen Rechtsstreites vorliegen, daß vielmehr als Präjudicialpunkte alle Streitpunkte ohne Ausnahme behandelt werden können, durch welche die Entscheidung der Hauptsache bedingt ist.

Ausgeschlossen erscheinen daher die Prozeßeinreden, und es wäre unrichtig, die gesonderte Aburtheilung einer bevorzugten Prozeßeinrede der gesonderten Aburtheilung eines Präjudicialpunktes gleichzustellen. Für die Frage der Zulässigkeit der Berufung ist dies von großer Bedeutung; ebenso für das Verfahren (Art. 232 u. 237).

4) „so kann die Verhandlung beschränkt werden."

Da unter „Verhandlung" in der Regel nur das Verfahren in öffentlicher Sitzung zu verstehen ist, nicht aber das schriftliche Vorverfahren, so sollte man aus dem Wortlaute des Art. 190 schließen, es werde der Beklagte durch Vorschieben eines Präjudicialpunktes nicht von der Verpflichtung befreit, sich in seiner Vernehmlassung auf die ganze Hauptsache einzulassen.

Es wäre dies offenbar auch sachgemäß, da erst in Folge einer eingehenden Besprechung des ganzen Sachverhalts der Richter zu beurtheilen vermag, ob es geeignet sei, einen Präjudicialpunkt gesondert zu verhandeln, ob insbesondere nicht die Entscheidung desselben gegenstandslos werde. Was nützt z. B. die Verhandlung und Entscheidung schwieriger Legitimationspunkte (Statusfragen, Erbfragen), wenn der Richter den Anspruch sofort in letzter Instanz als gegen die öffentliche Ordnung verstoßend, als verjährt, als noch nicht fällig zurückweisen kann?

Der Inhalt des Art. 256, sowie die Gründe, mit welchen der kgl. Ministerial-Commissär ihn empfahl (Abg. II 123), lassen jedoch annehmen, daß dem Beklagten, welcher einen Präjudicialpunkt zur gesonderten Verhandlung bringen will, gestattet sein solle, sich vorerst auf die Hauptsache nicht weiter einzulassen. Der Gesetzgeber ist, wenn man diese Schlußfolgerung richtig findet, auf den Standpunkt der Ger.=O. Cap. VI § 3 Ziff. 3 zurückgeschritten und hat die von der Streiteinlassung befreienden Präjudicialeinreden wieder eingeführt.

Diese prozeßhindernde Einrede steht zu denjenigen der Art. 185 und 186 in Unterordnung, insofern sie schon als Anfang der Einlassung in die Hauptsache, nemlich als Aeußerung über die Begründung des Klagsanspruchs, zu betrachten ist. Die Prozeßeinreden sind daher mit den Präjudicialpunkten immer zu verbinden, wenn sie nicht verwirkt sein sollen.

5) Auch wenn der Beklagte sich im Vorverfahren auf die Hauptsache vollständig eingelassen hat — und es ist zu wünschen, daß dies immer geschehe — können Präjudicialpunkte zur besonderen Verhandlung gebracht werden, und zwar von beiden Theilen. Abg. I 259 (v. Weiß). Es geschieht dies, indem die Partei, welche diese Sonderung verlangt, oder beide Parteien diejenigen Anträge, welche sie in der Sitzung nehmen, auf den Präjudicialpunkt beschränken und gesonderte Verhandlung begehren.

Im Parteiprozesse und in Sachen, wo der Dringlichkeit wegen direkt zur Verhandlung geladen wird (Art. 259), wirft sich selbstverständlich die Frage der Sonderung immer erst in der Sitzung auf.

6) Das Gericht ist, wenn die Entscheidung des Präjudicialpunktes eine Beweisführung oder sonstige weitere Verhandlung zu veranlassen scheint, befugt, die Parteien zur gleichzeitigen Geltendmachung ihrer übrigen Rechtsbehelfe anzuhalten.

Die Ausdrücke, deren sich hier das Gesetz bedient, sind der Art, daß das Gericht ziemlich volle Freiheit hat, die gesonderte Verhandlung überall zurückzuweisen, wo sie nicht sachgemäß, d. h. wo sie geeignet ist, die Erledigung des Prozesses zu verzögern, die Gewinnung übersichtlicher Klarheit zu hindern, die Kosten zu mehren.

Hat das Vorverfahren in der Hauptsache bereits stattgefunden, so steht nichts im Wege, die sofortige Verhandlung der Hauptsache anzuordnen. Jeder Anwalt muß auf eine Verfügung dieser Art im Voraus gerüstet sein und sich deßhalb gefallen lassen, im Weigerungsfalle als nicht erscheinend behandelt zu werden. Ebenso ist es im Parteiprozesse und bei direkter Ladung in die Sitzung.

Hat das Vorverfahren in der Hauptsache noch nicht stattgefunden, so kann das Gericht allerdings nichts weiter thun, als die gleichzeitige Verhandlung anzuordnen, und muß es den Parteien überlassen, nach Maßgabe des Art. 256 die Sache wieder in die Sitzung zu bringen, falls nicht etwa aus Gründen der Dringlichkeit sofort der Tag zur Verhandlung bestimmt werden kann (Art. 259 Abs. 4).

b) Präjudicialpunkte, welche nicht vom nemlichen Gerichte entschieden werden.

7) Der Abs. 2 des Art. 190 hat sowohl jene Fälle im Auge, wo ein Streitpunkt, welcher die Vorfrage für die Entscheidung eines Rechtsstreites bietet, bei der Verwaltung oder bei einem andern Gerichte bereits anhängig ist, eine Verbindung der konnexen Rechtsstreite aber letzteren Falles nicht statthaft oder nicht beantragt ist (Art. 33), als auch jene Fälle, wo sich im Laufe des Verfahrens ein Zwischenstreit ergibt, welcher nach Art. 9 — 11 vor ein anderes Gericht zur gesonderten Austragung verwiesen werden muß. R. N. I 339.

Daß in solchen Fällen das Verfahren auszusetzen sei, ist selbstverständlich. Natürlich ist jedoch die Verhandlung und Entscheidung nur in so weit auszusetzen, als für dieselben die Entscheidung des Präjudicialpunktes maßgebend sein wird, im Uebrigen aber ist, soweit möglich, der anhängige Rechtsstreit fortzuführen. Handelt es sich z. B. um eine Compensationsforderung, so steht nichts im Wege, daß das Gericht über das Bestehen der Hauptforderung endgiltig entscheide, und nur die Frage, ob dieselbe durch die Gegenforderung ganz oder theilweise getilgt sei, späterer Entscheidung vorbehalte

8) Die Frage, welche Folgen einzutreten hätten, wenn die etwa zur Betreibung des Präjudicialstreits gesetzte Frist unbenützt bleibe, ließ man offen, weil es bei der Verschiedenheit der Fälle gewagt sei, ein allgemeines Präjudiz zu setzen. Abg. IV 38 (v. Weiß).

Ist das Verfahren bereits anhängig, so steht es jeder Partei frei, die Sache zu betreiben, und es liegt daher kein Grund vor, durch Vorsetzen einer Frist einen Zwang auszuüben.

Auch bei Zwischenstreiten, deren Austrag bei anderen Gerichten erst veranlaßt werden soll, erscheint dies nicht unbedingt nothwendig. Ich bin nemlich der Ansicht, der Ausspruch des Gerichts, daß die Erledigung dieses Zwischenstreites zur Entscheidung der Hauptsache nöthig sei, begründe ein Recht für jede der Parteien, den Rechtsstreit darüber anhängig zu machen, ganz abgesehen davon, ob nach allgemeinen Grundsätzen ein Klagrecht bestehen würde, und unbeschadet der Frage der Beweislast, — eine Ansicht, auf welcher z. B. auch die Bestimmung des Art. 528 beruht.

Uebrigens wird immerhin nur diejenige Partei als vorzugsweise verpflichtet zur Klagerhebung zu betrachten sein, welche den fraglichen Punkt für sich geltend gemacht hat. Ist nun dieser eine Frist gesetzt, und wird die auferlegte Klagerhebung schuldhaft unterlassen, so wird anzunehmen sein, es sei der fragliche Einwand aufgegeben worden, er werde nicht mehr geltend gemacht. Ein Ausspruch über die Begründung des Zwischenpunktes dürfte jedenfalls nicht erfolgen.

c) Präjudicielle Wirkung des Strafverfahrens.

9) Durch Art. 323 ist verfügt, daß Thatsachen, wegen deren Jemand durch ein inländisches Strafgericht für schuldig erkannt wurde, bei den Civilgerichten als erwiesen zu betrachten seien. Hieraus folgt, daß freisprechende Urtheile der Strafgerichte den Civilrichter nicht binden. Verhdl. zu Art. 323. Abg. II. S. 157 bis 160.

Mit Rücksicht auf jene Folge der strafrechtlichen Verurtheilung verfügt das Gesetz hier, daß bei hinreichendem Verdachte einer strafbaren Handlung, welche für Entscheidung eines Rechtsstreites von Belang sei, die Verhandlung und Entscheidung dieses Rechtsstreites ausgesetzt werden könne.

Man wählte diese Fassung, welche das Ermessen des Gerichts entscheiden läßt, in der Erwägung, daß es sich hier weder von einer sachlichen Unzuständigkeit, noch von einer eigentlichen Litispendenz handle, vielmehr um einen Vortheil für diejenige Partei, welche durch Vorlage eines etwa ergehenden Strafurtheils sich die Beweislast ersparen kann. (Abg. I 260.) Uebrigens ist doch auch ein öffentliches Interesse im Spiele, da es immerhin als ein Mißstand zu betrachten ist, wenn zuerst der Civilrichter erklärt, eine That sei nicht erwiesen, später aber der Strafrichter, sie sei erwiesen. Deshalb überläßt das Gesetz es nicht den Parteien, sondern dem Gerichte, die Aussetzung des Rechtsstreites zu verfügen, und es kann nach der Fassung des Gesetzes und nach der Natur der in Frage stehenden Verfügung nicht im Zweifel sein, daß das Gericht dieselbe auch ohne Parteiantrag erlassen dürfe. Vgl. in letzterer Beziehung die Verhdl. zu Art. 109 des Entwurfs (jetzt Art. 125) Abg. I S. 168 und 169.

Es wird namentlich dann Grund vorliegen, den Civilpunkt sofort abzuurtheilen, wenn die Thatsachen, soweit sie für denselben von Belang erscheinen, zugestanden sind, oder sofort als erwiesen angenommen werden können. Setzt das Gericht das Verfahren aus, so ist gegen diese Verfügung selbständige Berufung zulässig Art. 683 Ziff. 3.

10) In der Regel ist es eine strafbare Handlung des Beklagten, welche in Frage steht, und bei der Diskussion hatte man vorzugsweise solche Handlungen im Auge. Es kann aber auch der Fall sein, daß die strafbare Handlung dem Kläger oder gar einem Dritten zur Last fällt, z. B. wenn Verdacht vorhanden ist, es seien Urkunden, auf welche Kläger seine Legitimation stützt, gefälscht. Die Worte des Gesetzes unterscheiden nicht, weder hier noch in Art. 323.

Ebensowenig unterscheiden beide Artikel, welcher Art das strafrechtliche Verfahren sei und sie gelten daher auch für Polizeiübertretungen. Abg. II 159.

11) Für die Pfalz ergibt sich die Frage, ob Art. 3 Code d'instr., insofern er vorschreibt, es müsse das Verfahren über die Civilklage suspendirt werden, falls das Strafverfahren vor Beginn oder während des Civilverfahrens wirklich eingeleitet worden sei, noch fortgelte?

Offenbar handelt es sich hier nicht um die civilrechtliche Frage, ob ein Klagrecht gegeben sei, sondern um eine Bestimmung, welche dem Prozesse angehört. Dieselbe erscheint daher durch Art. 2 des Einführungsgesetzes aufgehoben.

Nur für das Ehescheidungsverfahren bleibt die betreffende Vorschrift in Art. 235 Code civil bestehen. Einf.-Ges. Art. 69.

Zustellungen.

Art. 192. — **Soweit nicht ausdrücklich etwas anderes bestimmt ist, haben im gerichtlichen Verfahren die Zustellungen auf Betreiben der Partei an die Gegenpartei selbst oder an einen von ihr aufgestellten, am Sitze des Gerichts, bei dem die Sache anhängig ist, wohnhaften Zustellungsbevollmächtigten zu geschehen; im Anwaltsprozesse, wenn beide Theile durch Anwälte vertreten sind, auf Betreiben des Anwalts an den Gegenanwalt.**

Die in Art. 682 und 683 bezeichneten Urtheile sind im Anwaltsprozesse außer dem Anwalte auch der Partei selbst oder ihrem Zustellungsbevollmächtigten zuzustellen. Die Zustellung an den Anwalt hat vorauszugehen. Ist der Anwalt nicht mehr in Funktion, so genügt die Zustellung an die Partei oder ihren Zustellungsbevollmächtigten. In der Zustellung an die Partei oder ihren Zustellungsbevollmächtigten ist jene an den Anwalt unter Anführung des Datums derselben zu erwähnen oder der Grund der Unterlassung anzugeben.

Die Aufkündigung der Vollmacht wird auch bei Zustellungsbevollmächtigten der Gegenpartei gegenüber erst mit der Anzeige der Aufkündigung wirksam.

G. A. d. K. d. A. I S. 262. 263. 289. II S. 377. III S. 89. 92. 93. IV S. 38. 199. 200.
K. d. R. I S. 339. IV S. 28. 29.

1) Eine tiefgreifende Eigenheit des neuen Verfahrens ist der Grundsatz des Parteibetriebes, wie er hier Ausdruck findet, der Grundsatz nemlich, daß 1) in der Regel der Prozeß nur fortschreitet, wenn eine Partei ihn betreibt, und daß 2) Mittheilungen und Ladungen, welche der Betrieb des Prozesses nöthig macht, ohne Vermittlung des Gerichtes, bloß auf Grund der von den Parteien den Gerichtsvollziehern gegebenen Aufträge erfolgen.

a) Vom Parteibetriebe überhaupt.

2) Es ist ein allgemeiner Grundsatz des französischen und unseres neuen Prozesses, daß die Zustellungen jeder Art nur auf Betreiben der dabei interessirten Parteien stattfinden.

Dieser Grundsatz findet hier Anerkennung, jedoch nicht in so klarer und vollständiger Weise, wie es zu wünschen wäre. Es gibt nemlich außer den Zustellungen, welche Art. 192 im Auge hat, noch ferner 1) Zustellungen an dritte Personen, wie Zeugen, Sachverständige u. s. w., und 2) außergerichtliche Zustellungen im Sinne von Art. 101 Abs. 1 u. 2, und kann kein Zweifel darüber obwalten, daß der nemliche Grundsatz auch für diese Geltung habe.

3) Das Gericht selbst hat sich daher nicht mehr mit Zustellungen zu beschäftigen, und spricht sich in der Regel nicht einmal darüber aus, ob und welche Zustellungen vorzunehmen seien; die Partei muß selbst wissen, was das Gesetz von ihr verlangt. Geschieht es aber ausnahmsweise, daß eine Vorladung oder Zustellung gerichtlich verfügt wird, wie in den Fällen der Art. 508 u. 525, wenn die Beiladung eines Dritten angeordnet wird, so geht doch der Vollzug solcher Verfügungen nicht vom Gerichte, sondern von dem betreibenden Theile aus, welcher dem Gerichtsvollzieher entsprechenden Auftrag gibt.

b) Wer ist betreibender Theil?

4) Regel ist, daß die Zustellungen auf Betreiben der Partei selbst oder aber ihres gesetzlichen Vertreters (Art. 60) geschehen. Hiermit ist gesagt, daß der Auftrag an den Gerichtsvollzieher von diesen ausgehen muß und selbstverständlich auch diese als Auftraggeber im Akte zu bezeichnen sind.

Dies schließt jedoch nicht aus, daß dem Gerichtsvollzieher der Auftrag auch durch Mittelspersonen zugekommen sein könne, wie z. B. der Auftrag des Magistrats durch den Bürgermeister, der Auftrag einer abwesenden Partei durch ihren Bevollmächtigten, in gleicher Weise, wie ja auch der Anwalt seinen Auftrag durch Mittelspersonen erhalten haben kann; allein diese Personen sind bloß die Organe zur Uebermittlung und erscheinen im Akte nicht als betreibende Theile. Der Gerichtsvollzieher ist verantwortlich dafür, daß diese Mittelspersonen befugt waren, ihm den Auftrag zu geben, und es treffen ihn zunächst die Folgen der Nichtigkeitsklage (Art. 99 u. 103), vorbehaltlich seines Rückgriffes an die falschen Mandanten.

5) Eine Ausnahme besteht für den Verkehr unter den Anwälten im Anwaltsprozesse, d. h. für die Zustellungen von Anwalt zu Anwalt, mögen sie nun Anwaltsakte oder sonstige Urkunden (Protokolle, Urtheile ꝛc.) zum Gegenstande haben.

Sie erfolgen in formloser Weise bloß auf Betreiben des Anwaltes, als Herrn des Prozesses, an den Gegenanwalt und bedürfen nach Art. 205 nicht einmal der Vermittlung des Gerichtsvollziehers.

Diese Ausnahme erstreckt sich nicht auf Zustellungen an die Partei selbst, z. B. von Ladungen oder von Urtheilen, gegen welche selbständige Rechtsmittel zuläßig sind, oder auf Zustellungen an dritte Personen: Zeugen, Experten ꝛc., selbst wenn sie im Anwaltsprozesse im Auftrage des Anwaltes erfolgen, denn sie sind keine Mittheilungen von Anwalt zu Anwalt. Es erscheint bei ihnen sachgemäß und im Interesse des Gegners begründet, daß die Bezeichnung der Partei selbst nicht unterlassen werde, und wurden daher solche Zustellungen von jeher auf Betreiben der Partei, jedoch unter Bezeichnung des beauftragenden Anwalts, gemacht.

Aus der Stellung, welche der Anwalt im Anwaltsprozesse einnimmt, ergibt sich übrigens die Folgerung, daß der Gerichtsvollzieher, welcher aus Auftrag des Anwaltes handelt, durch dessen Verantwortlichkeit gedeckt ist, und die Nichtigkeitsklage sich nur gegen den Anwalt, nicht aber gegen den Gerichtsvollzieher richtet. So wurde auch im französischen Prozesse entschieden. Chauveau sur Carré quest. 1297 Ziff. 2. Journal du Palais (désaveu) No. 26 — (huissiers) No. 120.

Man könnte mit Rücksicht hierauf sagen, daß solche Zustellungen thatsächlich auf Betreiben des Anwaltes, der Form nach auf Betreiben der Partei geschehen.

c) An wen geschieht die Zustellung?

6) Die Zustellung geschieht an die Gegenpartei oder an den Gegenanwalt. Der Zustellung an die Gegenpartei steht diejenige an den von ihr am Sitze des Prozeßgerichts bestellten Zustellungs-Bevollmächtigten vollkommen gleich; die Zustellung an den Anwalt kann sie jedoch nicht ersetzen.

Zustellungs-Bevollmächtigter ist nur derjenige, welcher besonders zu diesem Zwecke beauftragt ist. Ein Zwang dazu besteht der Regel nach nicht, sogar nicht beim Verfahren vor Handelsgerichten und Landgerichten. In der Prozeßvollmacht an sich ist die Vollmacht Zustellungen in Empfang zu nehmen nicht begriffen, jedoch steht nichts im Wege, den Prozeß-Bevollmächtigten zugleich als Zustellungs-Bevollmächtigten zu bezeichnen, und es wird dies im Parteiprozesse, namentlich im handelsgerichtlichen Verfahren, sehr rathsam sein. Vgl. Code de proc. Art. 422.

Nach den Worten des Gesetzes hat der betreibende Theil die Wahl, ob er die Zustellung der Gegenpartei selbst oder dem Zustellungs-Bevollmächtigten machen will. Es galt dies auch im französischen Prozesse und hat die Erwägung für sich, daß eine Zustellung, welche der Partei selbst geschieht, in der Regel für sie das Vortheilhaftere sei. Uebrigens könnte man auch sagen, daß eine Partei, welche, ohne dazu genöthigt zu sein, einen Zustellungs-Bevollmächtigten aufstellt, hierdurch zu erkennen gebe, daß sie die Zustellungen nur bei diesem gemacht wünsche.

Was die Aufkündigung dieser Vollmacht betrifft, s. Bemerkungen zu Art. 94.

7) Die in Art. 682 und 683 bezeichneten Urtheile sollen auch im Anwaltsprozesse den Parteien oder deren Zustellungs-Bevollmächtigten zugestellt werden, jedoch nur, nachdem die Zustellung an den Anwalt vorausgegangen ist. Diese Vorschrift findet ihren Grund darin, daß nach dem Willen des Gesetzgebers die Frist zur Berufung und Nichtigkeitsbeschwerde (besondere Ausnahmen, wie z. B. in Art. 187, abgerechnet) nur von der Zustellung an die Partei an laufen soll, wie dies der Entwurf (Art. 658, 660 u. 740) ausdrücklich und allgemein bestimmt hatte.

Insofern nun aber hier, sowie in dem sich anschließenden Art. 210, nur von den in Art. 682 und 683 bezeichneten Urtheilen die Sprache ist, erscheint der Gedanke des Gesetzgebers nicht erschöpfend ausgesprochen, denn es gibt außer jenen Urtheilen noch manche andere (z. B. in Art. 129), wo kraft besonderer Bestimmung selbständige Rechtsmittel zulässig sind. Der Gesetzgeber hätte wohl sagen sollen: „Urtheile, gegen welche das Gesetz selbständige Rechtsmittel zuläßt, sind, soweit nicht bestimmt ist, daß die Frist von Zustellung an den Anwalt laufe, außer dem Anwalte 2c." Ob dem Wortlaute des Gesetzes gegenüber diese Auslegung zulässig sei, wird bei Art. 697 näher besprochen werden.

Erwähnt mag sein, daß es vielleicht rathsam gewesen wäre, die Zustellung fraglicher Urtheile an die Partei nicht zu einer allgemeinen Vorschrift zu machen, vielmehr es bei den Bestimmungen des französischen Prozesses, welchen der Entwurf folgte, zu belassen, gemäß deren diese Zustellung nur nöthig war, wenn es galt, die Berufungsfrist in Lauf zu bringen, so daß sie bei Zwischenurtheilen in der Regel unterblieb.

8) Bei der Zustellung an die Partei ist die Zustellung an den Anwalt anzuführen, weil die Partei oder der Dritte, gegen welche etwa das Urtheil vollzogen werden soll, wissen müssen, ob die gesetzlichen Vorschriften beobachtet worden seien. S. Vortrag des Referenten v. Bomhard zu Hauptst. XXX Art. 11.

d) Welche Urkunden sind zuzustellen?

9) Die französischen Rechtslehrer stellten für alle Prozeßakten ohne Unterschied (Urtheile, Protokolle, Anwaltsakte) als in der Natur der Sache begründet, den Satz auf: »un acte non signifié est consideré comme n'existant pas.« Auch für unsere Prozeßordnung wird dies im Allgemeinen richtig sein.

Daß Prozeßschriften der Parteien keine Wirkung äußern können, so lange sie nicht zugestellt sind, begreift sich leicht; ebenso, daß gerichtliche Verfügungen derjenigen Partei, welche bei deren Erlaß nicht zugegen war, mitgetheilt werden müssen, bevor sie gegen sie in Vollzug gesetzt werden können.

Allein auch für richterliche Verfügungen, bei deren Erlaß die Parteien zugegen waren, gilt als Regel, daß deren Zustellung nöthig ist, um sie wirksam zu machen und die dadurch bedingten Fristen in Lauf zu setzen. Die Bestimmung in Art. 192 Abs. 2 ist nur ein Anwendung dieser Regel.

Erst durch abschriftliche Zustellung solcher Verfügungen erhält der Gegner diejenige genaue Kenntniß des Inhalts, welche das Gesetz verlangt, und wird zugleich der Wille, sie in Wirksamkeit und den Gegner in Verzug zu setzen, bekundet. Zudem besteht für jede Partei ein Interesse, alle prozessualen Aktenstücke entweder in Urschrift oder in Abschrift bei ihren Parteiakten zu besitzen, ein Interesse, welches durch das Recht,

Aktenmittheilung zu verlangen, nur zum Theil beseitigt wird.

Es wird daher als Grundsatz anzuerkennen sein, daß alle prozessualen Aktenstücke, von welchen eine Partei Gebrauch machen will, der anderen Partei zuzustellen seien, falls nicht nach dem ausgesprochenen oder klar erkennbaren Willen des Gesetzes die im Verwahr des Gerichtschreibers befindliche Urschrift benützt werden soll. Dies gilt im Allgemeinen auch von gerichtlichen Protokollen. Ausnahmen macht das Gesetz z. B. in Art. 281 für unbedeutende Urtheile und in Art. 344 für Protokolle über Beweisaufnahme.

Art. 193. — **In Fällen, in welchen die Zustellung an die Partei selbst zu geschehen hat, erfolgt dieselbe vorbehaltlich besonderer gesetzlicher Bestimmung:**

1) **für Personen, welchen die Befugniß, selbständig vor Gericht zu handeln, fehlt, an ihre gesetzlichen Vertreter;**
2) **für den k. Fiskus, die Civilliste des Königs, Gemeinden, Stiftungen und andere öffentliche Anstalten oder Körperschaften an deren gesetzliche Vertreter oder Vorstände;**
3) **für Handelsgesellschaften an die in den Art. 117, 144, 167, 196 und 235 des Handelsgesetzbuchs bezeichneten Personen;**
4) **für andere Gesellschaften, Vereine oder Genossenschaften an deren Vorstände oder die mit der Vertretung der betreffenden Vereinigung beauftragten Mitglieder oder Beamten;**
5) **für Gantmassen an den Massaverwalter oder in dessen Ermangelung an den Commissär;**
6) **für Personen, welche nur im Auslande einen bestimmten Wohnsitz haben (vorbehaltlich bestimmter Staatsverträge und vorbehaltlich der Befugniß, solchen Personen die Zustellung im Inlande persönlich oder in ihrer Wohnung zu machen), ferner für Personen, deren Aufenthalt unbekannt ist, an den Staatsanwalt des Prozeßgerichts oder, wenn bei diesem ein Staatsanwalt nicht aufgestellt ist, an den Staatsanwalt des Bezirksgerichts, in dessen Sprengel das Prozeßgericht seinen Sitz hat;**
7) **für die in § 4 des Gesetzes vom 15. August 1828, die Militärgerichtsbarkeit in bürgerlichen Rechtssachen betreffend, genannten Militärpersonen an die daselbst bezeichneten Commandanten, welche die Behändigung der empfangenen Aktenstücke an denjenigen, für welchen die Zustellung bestimmt ist, zu bewerkstelligen und Bescheinigung hierüber an den Gerichtsvollzieher gelangen zu lassen haben.**

Zustellungen, welche an Handelsgesellschaften oder an Kaufleute in Handelssachen zu bewirken sind, können auch an deren Prokuristen oder, sofern die Zustellung eine mit einer Zweigniederlassung im Zusammenhange stehende Angelegenheit betrifft, an den zum Betriebe der Zweigniederlassung bestellten Handlungsbevollmächtigten gemacht werden.

Art. 194. — **Die Staatsanwaltschaft hat bei Zustellungen an Personen, welche im Auslande ihren Wohnsitz haben, die Weiterbeförderung der empfangenen Aktenstücke auf diplomatischem Wege zu veranlassen, soweit nicht durch Staatsverträge ein anderer Weg vorgezeichnet ist.**

Betrifft die Zustellung eine Person, deren Aufenthaltsort unbekannt ist, so hat der Staatsanwalt die entsprechende Bekanntmachung in einem oder mehreren öffentlichen Blättern nach den hierüber im Verordnungswege zu erlassenden Vorschriften zu bewerkstelligen.

Ist in andern Fällen eine Zustellung an die Staatsanwaltschaft für eine Partei in gesetzlich zulässiger Weise geschehen, so hat der Staatsanwalt für die Behändigung an die Partei in der den Verhältnissen entsprechenden Weise zu sorgen.

G. A. d. K. d. A. I. S. 264—267. 289. III S. 438. IV S. 38. 39.
K. d. R. I S. 339—342. IV S. 29.

1) Bei jeder Zustellung kommen zwei Personen in Frage: diejenige, welche zustellen läßt, und diejenige, an welche die Zustellung sich richtet. In der Pfalz pflegt man sie Requirent und Requisit zu nennen. Statt des ersteren Ausdrucks ist es wohl geeigneter, mit dem Gesetze vom „betreibenden Theile“ zu sprechen; für den zweiten Ausdruck läßt sich aber eine kurze deutsche Bezeichnung nicht finden, wenn man nicht etwa einfach vom „Gegner“ sprechen will.

Zustellungen von Partei zu Partei richten sich an die Gegenpartei selbst oder deren gesetzliche

Vertreter; da es jedoch nicht immer möglich ist, die Zustellung an diese selbst zu machen, insofern der Gerichtsvollzieher bestimmte physische Personen braucht, mit denen er sprechen und denen er die Abschriften behändigen könne, so war es nöthig, für gewisse Fälle besondere Organe als Vermittler der Zustellung zu bezeichnen.

Das Gesetz sorgt hier in doppelter Richtung.

In Art. 193 trifft es Fürsorge für Fälle, wo eine Zustellung an den Gegner selbst im Sinne des Gesetzes nicht möglich ist oder nicht rathsam erscheint, und bestimmt, an welche Personen in solchen Fällen die Zustellung geschehen müsse. Diese Personen kann man als gesetzliche Vertreter zum Zwecke der Zustellung bezeichnen.

In Art. 196—198 gibt es Vorschriften für Fälle, wo diejenigen Personen, an welche die Zustellung zunächst zu geschehen hat, zur Zeit nicht zu treffen sind oder die Annahme verweigern, und wird bestimmt, an welche Mittelspersonen alsdann die Zustellung geschehen dürfe.

2) Die Bestimmung in Art. 193 Ziff. 1 erscheint im Grunde überflüssig, da es sich nach allgemeinen Grundsätzen von selbst versteht, daß an Personen, welche unfähig sind, vor Gericht zu handeln (an Minderjährige, Interdicirte ꝛc.), auch Zustellungen nicht rechtswirksam gemacht werden können, vielmehr hier, wie überall, die gesetzlichen Vertreter an ihre Stelle treten.

3) Zustellungen an den Fiskus, an Gemeinden ꝛc.

Auch bei juristischen Personen ist im Sinne des Gesetzes nur eine einzige, der Gesammtheit geltende Zustellung zu machen.

In Ziff. 2 ist gesagt, es solle für den Fiscus, die Civilliste, für Gemeinden, Stiftungen und andere öffentliche Anstalten oder Körperschaften die Zustellung an die gesetzlichen Vertreter oder die Vorstände erfolgen.

Da die gesetzliche Vertretung in der Regel einem Collegium zusteht, z. B. für den Staat den Kreisregierungen Kammer der Finanzen, für die Gemeinden den Magistraten oder Gemeindeausschüssen, und es weder angeht, daß der Gerichtsvollzieher jedem einzelnen Mitgliede eine besondere Zustellung mache, noch auch, daß er das Collegium sich versammeln lasse, um ihm im Ganzen seinen Akt zuzustellen, so kann im Sinne des Gesetzes die Zustellnng nur an die Vorstände dieser Collegien geschehen. Hierin ist wohl der Grund zu suchen, warum auf Vorschlag des Referenten v. Neumayr die Worte: „oder Vorstände" beigefügt wurden. Es soll damit gesagt sein, daß in Fällen, wo entweder die gesetzliche Vertretung zur Prozeßführung nicht bestimmt geregelt ist, oder wo eine Zustellung an die bestehende Vertretung deren Natur nach unthunlich erscheint, die Vorstände als gesetzliche Vertreter zum Empfange der Zustellungen zu betrachten seien.

Zustellungen an die Kreisregierungen erfolgen daher an den Regierungspräsidenten, und Zustellungen an Magistrate oder Gemeindeausschüsse an den Bürgermeister der Gemeinde. Wird die Vorstandschaft durch einen Stellvertreter ausgeübt, so erfolgt die Zustellung an diesen.

Ist einer einzelnen Person die gesetzliche Vertretung im Prozesse übertragen, wie z. B. in der Pfalz den Rechnern von Kirchenfabriken, so ist, nach dem Geiste des Gesetzes, ihnen allein die Zustellung zu machen.

4) Was insbesondere den kgl. Fiscus betrifft, so haben die Zustellungen an die Vorstände derjenigen Amtsstellen zu erfolgen, welchen nach den in Kraft befindlichen Vorschriften die Vertretung des Fiscus im Prozesse übertragen ist.

Soweit nicht Ausnahmen bestehen, steht den kgl. Kreisregierungen K. d. F. diese Vertretung zu. (Verordnung v. 17. Dez. 1825 § 87 u. 120.) Ausnahmen bestehen jedoch für verschiedene Zweige der Verwaltung, z. B. das Zollwesen, Militärwesen, Postwesen, Bergwesen. Ausführlichere Erörterungen s. in Seuff. Comm. Bd. II S. 121 ff. — Weiß Handb. für Huissiers S. 204—208 und Dr. G. Schmitt, der Gerichtsvollzieherdienst S. 46 bis 53.

Es wäre nicht richtig, wollte man die Vertreter des Fiscus mit jenen Behörden, deren Sitz nach Art. 15 den allgemeinen Gerichtsstand des Fiscus bestimmt, identificiren. In der Regel werden allerdings diejenigen Behörden, welche in erster Instanz über einen Antrag zu entscheiden haben, auch die gesetzlichen Vertreter des Fiscus in bezüglichen Prozessen sein; allein nothwendig ist dies nicht, und es kann recht gut der Fall sein oder verfügt werden, daß der einen Behörde die Entscheidung in erster Instanz, einer anderen aber die Vertretung im Prozesse zugewiesen sei. Die Zustellung hat aber immer bei der letzteren zu geschehen, mag ihr Sitz auch außerhalb des Gerichtssitzes sein, wie dies ja bei den besonderen Gerichtsständen in der Regel der Fall ist.

5) Zustellungen an Gesellschaften und Vereine.

Für Handelsgesellschaften sind die Art. 117, 167, 196 und 235 des Handelsgesetzbuches anwendbar erklärt, wornach Zustellungen an einen zur Vertretung befugten Gesellschafter, bei Aktiengesellschaften an ein Mitglied des Vorstandes, welches zu zeichnen oder mitzuzeichnen befugt ist, oder an einen Beamten der

Gesellschaft, welcher dieselbe vor Gericht zu vertreten berechtigt ist, zu geschehen haben.

Ebenso ist Art. 144 und sind mit demselben auch die Art. 172 und 244 aufrecht erhalten, wornach Zustellungen auch nach Auflösung der Gesellschaft an einen der Liquidatoren geschehen können. Abg. I 265 (v. Weiß).

Was sonstige Gesellschaften, Vereine und Genossenschaften anbelangt, so hat der Gerichtsvollzieher, ähnlich wie im Falle des Art. 235 des H. G. B., die Wahl, die Zustellung an deren Vorstand oder an Mitglieder und Beamte, welche mit der Vertretung beauftragt sind, zu machen. Selbstverständlich hat das Gesetz hier nur Vereinigungen im Auge, welchen nach civilrechtlichen Grundsätzen Persönlichkeit zukömmt, welche als juristische Personen auftreten können (Referat zu Art. 175 Ziff. 8 des Entwurfs); es beschränkt sich also die Anwendbarkeit dieser Bestimmung auf jene Vereine, Genossenschaften und Gesellschaften, von welchen die drei bezüglichen Gesetze vom 29. April 1869 sprechen.

Bei gewöhnlichen Civilgesellschaften, sowie bei Vereinigungen zu Handelszwecken, welche nicht unter den Begriff von Handelsgesellschaften fallen (Art. 10 Abs. 2 und Art. 266 des H. G. B.), hat die Zustellung an die einzelnen Gesellschafter zu erfolgen. (Referat zu Art. 175 Ziff. 7 des Entw.)

6) Hat eine Handelsgesellschaft oder ein Kaufmann einen Prokuristen aufgestellt, so kann die Zustellung auch an diesen geschehen, jedoch nur in Handelssachen, was wohl so viel heißt, als bezüglich aller Angelegenheiten, in welchen nach Art. 42 des H. G. B. ein Prokurist zu handeln ermächtigt ist.

Auch an Handelsbevollmächtigte (Art. 47 des H. G. B.) kann ausnahmsweise die Zustellung erfolgen, wenn sie für den Betrieb einer Zweigniederlassung bestellt sind und es sich um Angelegenheiten dieser Niederlassung handelt.

7) Zustellungen für das Ausland.

Zustellungen an Personen, welche im Auslande wohnen, können, sofern nicht Staatsverträge ausnahmsweise auch den Zustellungsakten ausländischer Beamten rechtliche Wirkung verleihen, nur an einen im Inlande wohnenden Stellvertreter erfolgen, und als solchen bezeichnet das Gesetz den Staatsanwalt.

Die bezügliche Bestimmung scheint nicht recht im Einklange zu stehen, mit jener des Art. 12 über den allgemeinen Gerichtsstand. Dort ist gesagt, daß bei Personen, welche keinen Wohnsitz im Inlande haben, der Ort des Aufenthalts entscheide, und man sollte daher meinen, es dürfe nur dann die Vermittlung des Staatsanwalts Platz greifen, wenn weder Wohnsitz noch Aufenthalt im Inlande gegeben sei. Es läßt sich jedoch immerhin behaupten, daß bezüglich der Frage der Zustellung andere Erwägungen maßgebend seien, als bezüglich der Frage der Zuständigkeit, und ist daher auf diesen Widerspruch kein Gewicht zu legen.

In allen Fällen, wo der Gegner, mag er Ausländer oder Inländer sein, einen bestimmten Wohnsitz nur im Auslande hat, tritt daher die Zustellung an den Staatsanwalt ein, jedoch ist es immer auch gestattet, die Zustellung an die Person oder in der Wohnung (nicht zu verwechseln mit Wohnsitz) zu machen, so daß also der Aufenthalt doch in so fern zur Geltung gelangt, als es von dem Belieben des betreibenden Theils abhängt, ihn zu berücksichtigen.

Zu erwähnen ist, daß dem Wortlaute des Gesetzes gemäß hier, abweichend von Art. 195 Abs. 3, die Zustellung an die Person auch zulässig ist, wenn eine Wohnung besteht.

8) Von der Zustellung an den Staatsanwalt an laufen die Fristen, wie sie nach Art. 209 durch Verordnung bestimmt werden.

Der Staatsanwalt hat deßhalb nach Art. 194 die Pflicht, ohne Verzug die Uebermittlung der Zustellung an die Person, für welche sie bestimmt ist, zu veranlassen, und zwar auf diplomatischem Wege, wenn nicht durch Staatsverträge ein kürzerer angeordnet ist. Solche Verträge sind höchst wünschenswerth, denn der diplomatische Weg ist, wie bekannt, umständlich und zeitraubend. Obgleich z. B. der französische Prozeß den Ausländern lange Fristen gibt, sind mir doch Fälle vorgekommen, wo Zustellungen, welche in Frankreich für bayerische Unterthanen erfolgten, erst in die Hände des bayerischen Staatsanwaltes gelangten, nachdem die Fristen bereits abgelaufen waren.

Ob der Staatsanwalt und die sonstigen Behörden, durch deren Hände die Zustellung befördert wird, ihre Pflicht erfüllen oder versäumen, ist für die Rechtsgiltigkeit der Zustellung und den Lauf der Fristen gleichgiltig, kann jedoch für Restitutionsgesuche (Art. 217) von Belang sein, weßhalb denn auch der Staatsanwalt nicht unterlassen wird, Bescheinigung über die erfolgte Aushändigung zu erheben und dem betreffenden Anwalte oder Gerichtsvollzieher mitzutheilen.

9) Staatsverträge über direkte Uebermittlung wurden abgeschlossen mit dem Großherzogthum Hessen (Regsbl. v. 1818 S. 192 und Minist.-Rescr. vom 18. Sept. 1837) — mit Hannover und Baden vom 12. Juli 1818 (Regsbl. S. 757) — mit Preußen wegen der

beiderseitigen Rheinprovinzen vom 4. Okt. 1819 (Intellig.-Bl. der Pfalz S. 625) — mit Oldenburg (wegen Birkenfeld) laut Minist.-Erkl. vom 3. Mai 1837 (Amtsbl. der Pfalz S. 368) und mit Frankfurt laut Minist.-Rescr. v. 20. Juni 1847 (Regsbl. S. 773).

Nach Justizminist.-Rescr. vom 30. Sept. 1829 (Seuff. Comm. II S. 261) sind die Untergerichte ermächtigt, Requisitionsschreiben an auswärtige Gerichte in deutschen Bundesstaaten, welchen die requirirende Behörde nahe gelegen ist, unmittelbar zu erlassen. Es möchte diese zweckmäßige Verfügung auch jetzt noch analog, d. h. für die Uebermittlung der Staatsanwälte und für die Staaten, welche früher zum deutschen Bunde gehörten, anzuwenden sein. Daß das Gesetz von „Staatsverträgen" spricht, möchte nicht von Belang sein, da die Giltigkeit der Zustellung von der Art und Weise der Uebermittlung nicht abhängt. Läßt die Staatsregierung direkten Verkehr zu, und lassen sich die auswärtigen Behörden darauf ein, — wer könnte sich beschweren?

Staatsverträge, welche sich auf die Kosten beziehen, wurden abgeschlossen mit Württemberg (Minist.-Rescr. vom 16. April 1826 und 12. Januar 1854 [Kreisamtsblätter]) — mit Preußen vom Jahre 1834 (Regsbl. S. 812) — mit Oesterreich vom Jahre 1852 (Regsbl. S. 107). Uebrigens verfügt eine Minist.-Entschl. vom 2. Mai 1833 (Kreisamtsblätter), daß alle Insinuationen von Urkunden auswärtiger Gerichte an bayerische Unterthanen tax-, stempel- und portofrei seien, was selbstverständlich auch von Zustellungen auswärtiger Gerichtsvollzieher gilt.

10) Zustellungen an Leute ohne bekannten Aufenthalt.

Auch hier erfolgen die Zustellungen an den Staatsanwalt. Art. 69 Ziff. 8 Code de proc. hatte die nemliche Vorschrift, jedoch blieb dieselbe ein todter Buchstabe, da das Gesetz den Staatsanwälten nirgends eine Thätigkeit vorschrieb und diese daher auch nichts zu thun pflegten, obgleich der Gesetzgeber wohl die Bestimmungen von Art. 112 Code civil, gemäß deren der Staatsanwalt verpflichtet ist, für die Vertretung von Abwesenden zu sorgen, im Auge gehabt hatte, — Bestimmungen, welche auch jetzt noch gelten.

Unsere Prozeßordnung verfügt höchst sachgemäß, daß der Staatsanwalt eine entsprechende Bekanntmachung in öffentlichen Blättern — eine Art Ediktalladung — zu bewerkstelligen habe.

Man wählte den Ausdruck: „entsprechende Bekanntmachung", um anzudeuten, daß nicht der ganze Inhalt der Zustellungsurkunde veröffentlicht werden müsse. — Es wird also genügen, wenn der Gegenstand der Zustellung kurz bezeichnet, und die betreffende Person aufgefordert wird, die für sie bestimmte Abschrift auf dem Amtszimmer des Staatsanwalts in Empfang zu nehmen.

Man wählte ferner die allgemeine Bezeichnung: „öffentliche Blätter", um anzudeuten, daß auch ausländische Blätter gewählt werden dürfen. — Die Anheftung am Gerichtsbrette wurde als bedeutungslos mit Recht beseitigt.

11) Zur Bestimmung in Abs. 3 des Art. 194 fand man sich veranlaßt, im Hinblicke auf Art. 851, wornach der Staatsanwalt unter gewissen Voraussetzungen an die Stelle eines Zustellungsbevollmächtigten im Vollstreckungsverfahren tritt. — Wohnt in solchen Fällen die Partei, welcher die Zustellung gilt, im Inlande, so wird der Staatsanwalt ihr die Abschrift direkt zusenden oder einhändigen lassen, selbstverständlich auch hier unter Erhebung einer Empfangsbescheinigung.

12) Zustellung an Militärpersonen.

Das Gesetz bezieht sich auf § 4 des Ges. vom 15. Aug. 1828, welcher lautet:

„An alle aktive Offiziere oder im Offiziersrange stehende aktive Militärbeamten, „ferner an die bei den Corps befindlichen Unteroffiziere und Soldaten zu machenden „Insinuationen werden von den Gerichten den „Commandanten der Regimenter selbständiger Bataillone oder Corps hinsichtlich der „diesen untergebenen, in Bezug auf andere „Personen aber, welche zu solchen Regimentern, Bataillonen oder Corps nicht gehören, „den Commandantschaften zugesendet rc."

Ebenso wie bei den Staatsanwälten sind auch hier die Zustellungen wirksam vom Augenblicke an, wo sie den Commandanten gemacht werden.

Daß hier ausdrücklich die Erhebung einer Bescheinigung über stattgefundene Behändigung und Abgabe derselben an den Gerichtsvollzieher vorgeschrieben ist, während man eine solche Vorschrift beim Staatsanwalte nicht nöthig fand, erscheint ohne wesentlichen Belang und hat nur Bezug auf Restitutionsfragen. R. R. I 341 (v. Heintz). Vgl. Art. 209 Abs. 3. Uebrigens mag sich diese Abweichung theilweise auch daraus herleiten, daß nach dem Entwurfe (Art. 175 Ziff. 11 und Art. 176) diese Zustellung wirklich erst vom Augenblicke der Aushändigung als geschehen erachtet werden sollte.

Art. 195. — **Die Zustellung hat in der Wohnung oder dem Geschäftslokale Desjenigen zu geschehen, an welchen sie zu bewirken ist.**

Die Annahme von Zustellungen außerhalb der Wohnung oder des Geschäftslokals kann verweigert werden.

Hat Derjenige, an welchen die Zustellung zu bewirken ist, im Inlande weder eine Wohnung noch ein Geschäftslokal, so kann ihm die Zustellung an jedem Orte, wo er getroffen wird, gemacht werden.

Art. 196. — **Wird Derjenige, an welchen die Zustellung zu bewirken ist, in seiner Wohnung oder in seinem Geschäftslokale nicht getroffen, so kann die Zustellung daselbst an einen in derselben Familiengemeinschaft lebenden erwachsenen Angehörigen oder an einen Bediensteten gemacht werden.**

Art. 197. — **Wird, abgesehen von den Bestimmungen des Art. 195 Abs. 2 und Art. 199 Abs. 3, die Annahme der Zustellung verweigert oder ist in der Wohnung Desjenigen, dem zugestellt werden soll, weder er selbst noch eine der in Art. 196 bezeichneten Personen angetroffen worden, so kann die Zustellung an den Vorsteher der betreffenden Gemeinde- oder Ortsabtheilung (Viertel, Distrikt) oder an dessen Stellvertreter geschehen und hat dieser die Behändigung zu besorgen.**

G. A. d. K. d. A. I S. 261. 264—266. 289. 290. IV S. 39.
K. d. R. I S. 342.

1) Die einfachste und sicherste Art der Zustellung ist es, wenn der Gerichtsvollzieher mit derjenigen Person, an welche sie zu bewirken ist — d. h. je nach Umständen mit der Partei selbst, deren gesetzlichem Vertreter, dem besonderen in Art. 193 Ziff. 2—7 bezeichneten Vertreter für Zustellungen, dem Zustellungsbevollmächtigten oder dem Anwalte — selbst spricht und ihr die Abschrift einhändigt. — Da jedoch die Zustellung nicht vom Zufalle abhängen darf, ob jene Personen getroffen werden, oder sich treffen lassen, so werden in Art. 195—198 Vorschriften über den Ort, wo, und über die Personen, durch deren Vermittlung, falls nöthig, die Zustellung geschehen soll, gegeben.

a) Ort der Zustellung.

2) Die Zustellung soll entweder in der Wohnung oder im Geschäftslokale geschehen und kann sogar, wenn sie anderswo versucht wird, zurückgewiesen werden.

Vielleicht wäre es praktischer gewesen, mit dem französischen Prozesse das Hauptgewicht auf die Zustellung an die Person zu legen, und ein so weit gehendes Recht der Verweigerung der Annahme nicht einzuräumen. Durch die Furcht, es möchte die Freiheit vom Gerichtsvollzieher zur Chikane benützt werden, hat man sich zu einer Beschränkung bestimmen lassen, welche die Thüre zu einer viel gefährlicheren Chikane der Partei öffnet.

In der Pfalz haben sich aus der vollen Freiheit, welche dem Gerichtsvollzieher gestattet war, nie die geringsten Mißstände ergeben, wohl aber half sie über manche Anstände hinweg, welche die Frage, was als Wohnung anzusehen, wer als Bediensteter zu betrachten sei, bieten. Wenn z. B. beim Verkehre auf Messen und Märkten, bei Streit zwischen Wirthen und Reisenden (Art. 6 Ziff. 3 u. 4), oder bei Vorsichtsverfügungen (Art. 621) Zustellungen schnell an fremden Orten gemacht werden sollen, so wird der Gerichtsvollzieher oft in Verlegenheit kommen, wenn ihm der Betreffende sagt: „Ich lasse mir in München nichts zustellen, ich wohne in Wunsiedel". — Ebenso verhält es sich, wenn einem Anwalte im Sitzungssaale eine dringliche Zustellung zu machen ist.

3) Das Wort „Wohnung" ist nicht mit „Wohnsitz" zu verwechseln, denn eine Wohnung kann auch derjenige haben, welcher beabsichtigt, sich nur einige Zeit lang an einem Orte aufzuhalten.

Man darf einerseits den Begriff dieses Wortes nicht zu eng nehmen, weil die Verweigerung der Annahme sich daran knüpft und der Chikane Thür und Thor geöffnet wäre, wollte man die Absicht eines lange dauernden, bleibenden Aufenthalts verlangen. Abg. I 266 (v. Neumayr). Andererseits geht es auch nicht an, jedes vorübergehende Verweilen in einem Gasthofe, auf Besuch bei Verwandten, eine Wohnung begründen zu lassen, weil die Art. 196 u. 197, welche im Falle der Nichtanwesenheit die Zustellung an Mittelspersonen gestatten, offenbar mehr voraussetzen, als ein solch flüchtiges Verweilen.

Der eine Gesichtspunkt drängt zur Ausdehnung, der andere zur Beschränkung des Begriffes.

Man erkennt, daß es schwer hält, den Begriff so zu bestimmen, daß er den praktischen Anforderungen nach allen Seiten genüge. Bei dieser Sachlage wird dem richterlichen Ermessen großer Spielraum zu gestatten und namentlich anzuerkennen sein, daß im Sinne des Art. 193 Ziff. 6, sowie in Fällen, wo nach dem Willen des Gesetzes an Ort und Stelle zuzustellen ist, wo Dringlichkeit vorliegt, auch ein vorübergehendes Verweilen als Wohnung betrachtet werden darf, jedenfalls in dem Sinne, daß die dort an die Person selbst gemachte Zustellung nicht als unstatthaft zurückgewiesen werden kann. — Wer persönlich getroffen wird, kann mindestens den Einwand nicht erheben, er habe die Absicht regelmäßigen Wiederkehrens, welche überall die Grundbedingung einer Wohnung ist, nicht gehabt.

Eine Wohnung gilt für alle Personen, welche dort als Familienangehörige, Bedienstete 2c. mitwohnen, und umfaßt selbstverständlich nicht blos die besonderen Wohngemächer, sondern alle sonstigen dazu gehörigen Räume.

4) Das Geschäftslokal einer Person ist derjenige Ort, wo sie für Leute, welche mit ihr geschäftlich verkehren wollen, regelmäßig zu treffen ist. Geschäftslokal ist daher das Comptoir des Kaufmannes, die Amtsstube des Anwaltes, des Notars. In der Regel ist es mit der Wohnung verbunden, kann aber auch davon getrennt sein.

Das Gesetz gibt die Wahl zwischen Wohnung und Geschäftslokal, jedoch ist ihm der erstere Ort der wichtigere, an welchem die Zustellung immer versucht werden muß. Für Fälle, wo die Zustellung gerade in Geschäftssachen erfolgt, wie z. B. von Anwalt zu Anwalt, liegt es in der Natur der Sache, vorzugsweise das Geschäftslokal zu wählen.

5) Im Falle, wo Jemand weder Wohnung noch Geschäftslokal im Inlande hat, ist der Gerichtsvollzieher befugt, die Zustellung ihm persönlich an jedem Orte zu machen, jedoch versteht sich von selbst, daß ihn sein Dienst verpflichtet, die durch die Umstände gebotenen Rücksichten zu nehmen und weder einen Gottesdienst noch eine Gerichtsverhandlung zu stören.

6) In der Pfalz besteht die Eigenthümlichkeit der Zustellung im erwählten Wohnsitze nach Art. 65 des Einführungsgesetzes fort. Es kann daher in der bezeichneten Wohnung zugestellt werden, auch wenn die Person, bei welcher ursprünglich Wohnsitz erwählt war, mittlerweile ihren Wohnsitz geändert hat oder gestorben ist, vorausgesetzt, daß nicht die Wohnsitzerwählung ausdrücklich in der Weise geschehen war, daß die jeweilige Wohnung einer Person maßgebend sein solle.

Die Zustellung selbst richtet sich natürlich nach den Bestimmungen der Art. 195—197.

b) Mittelspersonen für die Zustellung.

7) Wenn der Gerichtsvollzieher, welcher in der Wohnung oder im Geschäftslokale eine Zustellung machen will, die Person, welcher sie gilt, nicht selbst dort antrifft, so darf er die Zustellung daselbst an einen in derselben Familiengemeinschaft lebenden erwachsenen Angehörigen oder an einen Bediensteten machen.

Art. 68 Code de proc. sprach in ähnlicher Weise von »ses parens ou serviteurs«, welchen Worten man eine den Zwecken des Gesetzes entsprechende, sehr freie Auslegung gab. Eine ähnliche freie Auslegung wird auch hier geboten und in's Auge zu fassen sein, daß das Gesetz alle jene Personen begreifen wollte, welche in ständigem Verkehre mit dem Requisiten und in solchen Beziehungen zu ihm stehen, daß zu erwarten ist, es werde ihm durch dieselben die Zustellung sicher und schnell behändigt werden.

8) Das Gesetz erlaubt die Zustellung an Angehörige und Bedienstete nur, wenn sie in der Wohnung oder im Geschäftslokale geschieht; es dürfte also der Gerichtsvollzieher nicht etwa, nachdem er sich von der Abwesenheit des Requisiten überzeugt, jenen Personen an einem anderen Orte die Zustellung machen; jedoch steht nichts im Wege, daß er sich mit ihnen an den Ort, wo die Zustellung giltig geschehen kann, begebe.

9) Angehörige der Familie.

Schon die Ausdrucksweise gibt kund, daß das Gesetz nicht bloß Verwandte und Verschwägerte im streng juristischen Sinne meint, oder gar nur solche, welche noch in der Gewalt des Hauptes der Familie stehen, sondern daß er auch sonstige Personen, welche das Familienleben theilen und gleich Angehörigen der Familie behandelt werden, z. B. Pflegekinder, Mündel u. s. w., bezeichnen will. Das Hauptgewicht ist auf die Thatsache des Zusammenwohnens und auf die Zustellung in der Wohnung zu legen.

Die französische Jurisprudenz kam zu gleichem Resultate, obgleich ihr die Worte des Gesetzes »ses parens« viel mehr Schwierigkeiten bereiteten. Carré (quest. 360 Note 2) beantwortet die Frage, ob die Zustellung an eine Person geschehen könne, welche beim Requisiten wohnt, ohne mit ihm verwandt zu sein, in Uebereinstimmung mit der Jurisprudenz, dahin:

»Nous croirions, qu'on devrait suivre plu-
»tôt l'esprit de la loi, que la rigueur du texte.
»La loi veut assurer, que l'exploit sera remis
»à l'assigné. Or, cette certitude n'est-elle pas
»suffisamment acquise, lorsqu'il est laissé à
»une personne liée avec l'assigné par tous

»les rapports d'intérêt, de bienveillance et »d'amitié, que suppose la cohabitation?«

Leute, welche ihren eigenen Haushalt führen, können allerdings nicht als zur Familiengemeinschaft gehörig betrachtet werden, auch wenn sie verwandt sind.

10) Unter „erwachsenen Personen" sind nicht gerade Großjährige zu verstehen (Bl. f. R. Bd. XV S. 192), sondern Personen, welche fähig sind, die Wichtigkeit des Dienstes, welcher von ihnen verlangt wird, zu begreifen. Der Zeitpunkt der Mündigkeit (Stürzer C.R.V. S. 508), oder noch besser das vom Strafgesetzbuche (Art. 76) als Zeitpunkt voller Zurechnungsfähigkeit festgesetzte 16. Lebensjahr, werden im Zweifel als Anhaltspunkte zu dienen haben. Jedenfalls ist nicht entscheidend, ob die betreffende Person auch physisch schon vollkommen ausgebildet ist.

11) Bedienstete.

Es erscheint außer Zweifel, daß dieser Ausdruck im weiteren Sinne zu nehmen sei und alle Personen umfasse, welche auf irgend eine Weise in ständigem Dienstverhältnisse zum Requisiten stehen, also nicht bloß die Dienstboten, sondern auch die Bediensteten höherer Art — Verwalter, Geschäftsführer, Hauslehrer, Buchhalter, Geschäftsgehilfen, Schreiber u. s. w. So wurde der Ausdruck »serviteur« im französischen Prozesse ausgelegt und sogar der Ausdruck „Domestiken", dessen sich die Gerichtsordnung Cap. V § 8 Ziff. 2 bedient, wurde so verstanden. Seuff. Comm. Bd. II S. 263.

Es ist nicht erforderlich, daß der Bedienstete beim Requisiten wohne, oder von ihm verköstigt werde, was z. B. bei Schreibern von Advokaten nicht der Fall zu sein pflegt, vielmehr genügt das Dienstverhältniß an und für sich, zufolge dessen der Bedienstete ständig im Verkehre mit dem Requisiten steht und regelmäßig in dessen Wohnung oder Geschäftslokal kommt.

Personen, welche nicht in festem Dienste stehen, sondern nur häufig bei dem Requisiten arbeiten, wie Taglöhner, Näherinnen rc., können nicht als dessen Bedienstete betrachtet werden.

12) Das Gesetz setzt allerdings Jemanden voraus, welcher im Dienste Desjenigen stehe, welchem die Zustellung gilt (Abg. I 290 [Barth]), allein auch in dieser Richtung ist es möglichst frei auszulegen.

Die Dienstboten einer Person werden z. B. auch als Bedienstete ihrer Familienangehörigen zu betrachten und zur Empfangnahme von Zustellungen für dieselben geeignet sein. Wohnt Jemand in einem Gasthause, so werden der Wirth und seine Diener als Bedienstete im Sinne des Gesetzes gelten. (Weiß, Handb. f. Huissiers S. 174.) Die französische Jurisprudenz nahm ferner an, daß der Portier eines Hauses zum Dienste aller Bewohner desselben bestellt sei.

Es ist eine freiere Auslegung um so mehr erlaubt, als die Worte des Gesetzes allgemein lauten, und wäre es doch sonderbar, wenn wir dieser Fassung gegenüber zur Beschränkung kämen, während die französische Jurisprudenz der beschränkteren Fassung des Gesetzes (ses serviteurs) gegenüber zur freieren Auffassung gelangt ist.

13) Bei Bediensteten heißt es nicht, daß sie erwachsen sein müßten, es versteht sich jedoch von selbst, daß eine Person, welcher die Fähigkeit der Beurtheilung fehlt, z. B. einem kleinen Kindsmädchen, eine Zustellung nicht gemacht werden könne. Es wird daher ziemlich das Nemliche gelten, wie bei Angehörigen.

14) Es wirft sich die Frage auf, wie den Bediensteten selbst die Zustellung zu machen sei. Können andere, dem nemlichen Hausstande angehörige Bedienstete, oder können der Dienstherr und dessen Angehörige Zustellungen für sie in Empfang nehmen?

Offenbar bietet diese Art der Uebermittlung mehr Garantie, als diejenige durch den Ortsvorsteher, und deßhalb machte sich im französischen Prozesse die Ansicht geltend, daß sie dem Willen des bezeichneten Gesetzes genüge, daß überhaupt grundsätzlich die Zustellung an jede Person giltig geschehen könne, welche mit dem Requisiten zum nemlichen Hauswesen gehöre. Weiß a. a. O. S. 176.

Soweit noch von einem Dienstverhältnisse die Rede sein kann, wenn auch nur einem abgeleiteten, z. B. beim Verhältnisse des Hauslehrers zu den gewöhnlichen Dienstboten, möchte diese Auslegung unter den Text des Gesetzes zu bringen sein; im Uebrigen erscheint sie gewagt, wenn auch nicht verkannt werden kann, daß sie den praktischen Bedürfnissen entspreche, und zu wünschen ist, sie möchte vom Gesetzgeber berücksichtigt worden sein.

15) Distriktsvorsteher.

Wird die Annahme ohne Grund verweigert, oder ist in der Wohnung Niemand, an den eine Zustellung giltig gemacht werden könnte, so geschieht dieselbe an den Vorsteher des Gemeindedistrikts oder dessen Stellvertreter, welche die Behändigung zu besorgen verpflichtet sind. Wo die Gemeinde in Distrikte getheilt ist, darf daher die Zustellung nicht an den Ortsvorstand (Bürgermeister) als solchen erfolgen, selbstverständlich aber dann, wenn eine solche Abtheilung nicht besteht.

Wie der Distriktsvorsteher die Behändigung zu besorgen habe, ist nicht gesagt, es ist dies also seinem Ermessen überlassen. Uebrigens wird er verpflichtet sein, dafür zu sorgen, daß sie wo möglich an die Person selbst erfolge und Bescheinigung erhoben werde, welche zu seiner eignen Rechtfertigung, sowie zur Abschneidung frivoler Restitutionsgesuche dienlich sein kann.

Der Umstand, daß im Geschäftslokale Niemand zu treffen ist, berechtigt den Gerichtsvollzieher noch nicht, die Zustellung beim Distriktsvorsteher zu machen, vielmehr muß er sich zuerst in die Wohnung begeben. Im umgekehrten Falle ist er aber nicht verpflichtet, die Zustellung im Geschäftslokale zu versuchen.

16) Allgemeines.

Der Gerichtsvollzieher hat in seinem Akte alle Umstände anzugeben, durch welche im einzelnen Falle die Giltigkeit der Zustellung bedingt ist, also gegebenen Falls zu erwähnen, daß er den Requisiten in seiner Wohnung, in seinem Geschäftslokale nicht getroffen, daß derselbe die Annahme verweigert habe, von welcher Art das Verhältniß der Familienangehörigkeit und des Dienstes der Mittelspersonen sei u. s. w.

Es wäre z. B. ungenügend, einfach zu sagen: „sprechend mit der Dienstmagd A B“, oder: „sprechend mit seinem Sohne X“, wie Letzteres seither genügte; vielmehr muß es etwa heißen:

„sprechend in seiner (des Requisiten) Wohnung, da „ich ihn daselbst nicht antraf, mit seiner Dienst„magd A B“, oder: „mit seinem bei ihm woh„nenden erwachsenen Sohne X.“

Art. 198. — **Zustellungen an die Staatsanwälte und Militär-Commandanten (Art. 193 Ziff. 6 u. 7) haben, dringende Fälle ausgenommen, in deren Dienstlokalitäten zu geschehen.**

Ist der Staatsanwalt oder Commandant daselbst nicht anwesend, so kann die Zustellung an seinen Stellvertreter oder an jede andere dort befindliche, zum Dienste der Staatsanwaltschaft beziehungsweise Commandantschaft gehörige Person gemacht werden.

G. A. d. K. d. A. I S. 264—266. 290. IV S. 39. — K. d. R. I S. 342. 343.

1) Zustellungen an Staatsanwälte oder Commandanten in den Fällen des Art. 193 Ziff. 6 u. 7 haben, dringliche Fälle ausgenommen, in welchen also die Zustellung in der Wohnung geschehen darf, nur in den Dienstlokalitäten stattzufinden. Für Fälle anderer Art, in denen Zustellungen an die Staatsanwälte in dienstlicher Eigenschaft gemacht werden, z. B. im Falle des Art. 851, oder wenn der Staatsanwalt als Partei erscheint, gilt der Wortlaut des Gesetzes nicht, wohl aber der Geist desselben.

2) Im Falle der Abwesenheit soll die Zustellung daselbst an die Stellvertreter, oder sonstige zum Dienste gehörige Personen geschehen. Für die Möglichkeit, daß auch diese Personen nicht getroffen werden, ist hier nicht Fürsorge getroffen, weil das Gesetz voraussetzt, es müsse der Gerichtsvollzieher die bestimmten Dienststunden wählen, an welchen immer Jemand zu treffen sein werde. Liegt Dringlichkeit vor, welche die Einhaltung dieser Stunden nicht gestattet, so darf ja die Zustellung in der Wohnung stattfinden.

Art. 199. — **An Sonn- und gebotenen Feiertagen, ferner vor sechs Uhr Morgens und nach acht Uhr Abends dürfen Zustellungen nur mit richterlicher Erlaubniß gemacht werden.**

Diese Erlaubniß kann nur in dringenden Fällen, in solchen aber sowohl von dem Vorstande des Gerichts, bei welchem die Sache anhängig ist oder anhängig gemacht werden soll, als auch von dem Einzelnrichter des Orts, wo die Zustellung zu machen ist oder der Gerichtsvollzieher seinen Wohnsitz hat, ertheilt werden. Die bezügliche Verfügung ist in der Zustellungsurkunde anzuführen und mit derselben abschriftlich mitzutheilen.

Die Annahme von Zustellungen, welche gegen diese Vorschriften verstoßen, kann verweigert werden.

G. A. d. K. d. A. I S. 268. 291. IV S. 39. 40. — K. d. R. I S. 343. 344. IV S. 29.

1) Dieser Artikel bestimmt die Zeit der Zustellungen, deren Nichteinhaltung jedoch keine Nichtigkeit, sondern nur das Recht der Verweigerung der Annahme begründet.

Im französischen Prozesse war die Tageszeit, während welcher Zustellungen geschehen durften, für den Winter und für den Sommer verschieden bestimmt und waren ferner Ausnahmen selbst im Falle der Dringlichkeit nicht gestattet. Die Bestimmungen unserer Prozeßordnung, welche auch für das Vollstreckungsverfahren gelten (Art. 846), sind offenbar einfacher und zweckmäßiger.

2) Unter den „gebotenen Feiertagen“ sind nach Erklärung des G. A. der K. d. Abg., welche stillschweigend Billigung gefunden hat, nur solche zu verstehen, welche durch Verordnung, sei es für das ganze Reich, sei es für einzelne Theile, als solche bestimmt sind. Abg. IV 40. In der Pfalz kannte man bis jetzt nur gesetzliche Feiertage.

3) Durch richterliche Erlaubniß kann der Gerichtsvollzieher nicht bloß ermächtigt werden, an Sonn- und Feiertagen, sondern sogar zur Nachtzeit zuzustellen, woraus sich natürlich auch ein Recht herleitet, zu dieser Zeit Eintritt in die Wohnung zu verlangen.

Art. 200. — Wer eine Zustellung machen läßt, hat hiefür unter den Gerichtsvollziehern des Gerichtssprengels, in welchem sie gemacht werden soll, die Wahl, doch fallen Mehrkosten, welche durch Verwendung eines außerhalb des einzelngerichtlichen Bezirks, wo die Zustellung zu geschehen hat, wohnenden Gerichtsvollziehers entstehen, dem veranlassenden Theile zur Last, ausgenommen wenn die Verwendung der in diesem Bezirke wohnenden Gerichtsvollzieher wegen deren Behinderung (Art. 201) oder aus andern Gründen unmöglich war.

Art. 201. — Der Gerichtsvollzieher darf bei Strafe der Nichtigkeit keine Zustellung in einer Sache machen, bei welcher er selbst, seine wirkliche oder gewesene Ehefrau, seine Verwandten oder Verschwägerten in gerader Linie oder in der Seitenlinie einschlüssig bis zum dritten Grade nach bürgerlicher Berechnung oder seine Pflegbefohlenen betheiligt sind.

G. A. d. K. d. A. I S. 267. 268. 291. IV S. 40. 318. — K. d. R. I S. 344. IV S. 29.

1) Das Gesetz beantwortet hier die Frage, welcher Gerichtsvollzieher im gegebenen Falle befugt sei, zu handeln, indem es 1) das Gebiet seiner Zuständigkeit, und 2) die Gründe der Behinderung bestimmt.

a) Amtsgebiet des Gerichtsvollziehers.

2) Jeder Gerichtsvollzieher ohne Unterschied darf im ganzen Gebiete des Bezirksgerichts, wo er wohnt, Zustellungen machen, überhaupt sein Amt ausüben, denn was die Art. 200 u. 201 verfügen, ist durch Art. 206 auch auf sonstige Zustellungen, und durch Art. 839 auf die Zwangsvollstreckung überhaupt ausgedehnt.

Die Wahl steht dem betreibenden Theile frei, jedoch fallen ihm etwaige Mehrkosten, d. h. höhere Reisekosten, welche durch Verwendung eines außerhalb des Landgerichtsbezirkes wohnenden Gerichtsvollziehers erwachsen, zur Last. Eine Ausnahme hiervon besteht bei vorhandener Unmöglichkeit, welche auch dann gegeben erscheint, wenn es in dringlichen Fällen nicht möglich ist, durch einen auswärtigen Gerichtsvollzieher einen Auftrag schnell und sicher besorgen zu lassen.

b) Behinderung des Gerichtsvollziehers.

3) Art. 201 wurde, was die Fälle der Behinderung betrifft, absichtlich, um Gleichförmigkeit zu erzielen, dem Art. 47 des Notariatsgesetzes nachgebildet (Abg. I 268 u. 291), ein Umstand, welcher für dessen Auslegung nicht ohne Bedeutung ist.

4) Was sind Verwandte und Verschwägerte?

Das Gesetz versteht hierunter wohl alle diejenigen Personen, welchen diese Eigenschaft nach den Grundsätzen des bürgerlichen Rechtes zukommt.

Dieses Recht kennt nun Blutsverwandte und Verwandte durch Adoption. Die erstere Verwandtschaft beruht entweder auf ehelicher oder auf unehelicher Geburt. Nach der Allgemeinheit des Ausdrucks, sowie nach dem Grunde des Gesetzes sind alle diese Verwandten gemeint.

Was insbesondere die Adoption betrifft, so ist dieselbe ebensowenig hier, als im Sinne des Art. 47 des Notariatsgesetzes (v. Zink Comm. S. 203) auszunehmen, und die besonderen Bedenken, welche die Aeußerung im Namen der Subcommission (Abg. I 291) für Auslegung des Art. 40 ergibt, finden hier keine Anwendung. Adoption und uneheliche Geburt begründen übrigens in der Regel nur ein auf wenige Personen begränztes Verwandtschaftsverhältniß; nach den einzelnen Gesetzgebungen in verschiedener Weise.

Die Verwandtschaft in der Seitenlinie bildet nur bis zum dritten Grade (dem Verhältnisse von Onkel und Neffen) einen Behinderungsgrund, und in derselben Weise die Schwägerschaft. Unter Verschwägerung versteht man das Verhältniß zwischen dem einen Ehegatten und den Verwandten (nicht auch Verschwägerten) des andern Ehegatten.

Das Nähere in diesen Beziehungen ist zu ersehen bei Dr. Schmitt, der Gerichtsvollzieherdienst S. 17—24. Dem dort Gesagten ist für die Pfalz nur noch beizufügen, daß, um die Eigenschaft eines natürlichen Kindes der Mutter gegenüber anzunehmen, es nicht grade nöthig ist, daß förmliche Anerkennung oder Urtheil vorliege, indem die neuere Jurisprudenz, milderen Ansichten huldigend, die possession d'état auch bei unehelichen Kindern als zum Beweise der Mutterschaft dienlich erachtet und die Thatsache der Mutterschaft wirksam ist (z. B. bezüglich der Erbberechtigung), auch bevor ein Urtheil sie anerkannt hat. Demolombe t. XIV No. 15.

5) Was sind Pflegbefohlene?

Pflegbefohlene sind alle jene Personen, welche unter Vormundschaft oder Curatel stehen, welche vom Gesetze, vom Gerichte oder von irgend einem sonstigen zur Fürsorge für Rechtsunfähige berufenen Organe der Pflege einer andern Person anvertraut sind. Eine Ausdehnung auf Personen, welche nur thatsächlich in Pflege stehen (alumni), möchte nicht im Willen des Gesetzes liegen. Es läßt sich nicht annehmen, daß ein solch loses Verhältniß einen Behinderungsgrund für Akte des Gerichtsvollziehers bilden solle, während es bei den viel wichtigeren Akten des Notars ohne Belang ist. Zudem würde dies zu sehr ins Unbestimmte führen und die Erwägung entgegenstehen, daß Ausnahmsbestimmungen einschränkend zu erklären sind. Art. 212 des Strafgesetzb. beruht auf ganz anderen Erwägungen.

6) Was ist Betheiligung?

Die Frage, wer als betheiligt zu erachten sei, ist nicht ohne Schwierigkeiten.

Was zuerst die Betheiligung des Gerichtsvollziehers selbst betrifft, so ist offenbar nicht erforderlich, daß er selbst Partei in der Sache sei, vielmehr genügt es, daß er Interesse dabei habe. Es werden im Allgemeinen die Grundsätze, welche seither bezüglich der Untüchtigkeit von Zeugen in eigner Sache galten, hier Maß geben, wobei jedoch zu beachten, daß dort (nach den Anmerkungen von Kreitmayer) ein direktes Interesse verlangt wurde, während hier das Gesetz allgemein spricht.

7) Der Gerichtsvollzieher ist daher betheiligt, wenn ihm ein unmittelbarer Vortheil oder Nachtheil aus dem Ausgange des Rechtsstreites erwachsen kann, z. B. wenn er Bürge, Mitschuldner oder Miteigenthümer ist, ein von dem in Streite befangenen sich ableitendes Recht beansprucht, regreßpflichtig erscheint. Gleiches Interesse liegt vor bei stillen Gesellschaftern oder bei Gemeindegliedern in Prozessen der Gemeinde, welche sie unmittelbar betreffen. Seuffert Archiv Bd. I Nr. 372 Bd. VI Nr. 70 Bd. IX Nr. 91.

Die zu erwartenden Vortheile oder Nachtheile müssen natürlich ernstliche sein; nicht jedes auch noch so geringfügige Interesse kann die Unparteilichkeit des Gerichtsvollziehers in Frage stellen. Seuff. Archiv Bd. III Nr. 393. Der Besitz einzelner Aktien bei größeren Unternehmungen kann in der Regel ein ernstliches Interesse nicht begründen; allein es wäre offenbar irrig, den Satz aufzustellen, daß Aktienbesitz nie als Betheiligung gelten könne, denn wenn Jemand bei kleinen Unternehmungen einen namhaften Theil des Aktienkapitals vertritt oder wenn ein Rechtsstreit das ganze Schicksal des Unternehmens in Frage stellt, so ist allerdings ein sehr ernstliches und naheliegendes Interesse gegeben.

8) Endlich erscheint es auch als Betheiligung, wenn der Gerichtsvollzieher gesetzlicher Vertreter, Prozeßbevollmächtigter oder Beistand einer Partei ist. Abg. I S. 268 (v. Neumayr). Er hat hier zwar kein unmittelbares Vermögensinteresse und dasjenige Interesse, welches darin liegt, daß er wegen etwaiger Verschuldungen oder Mandatsüberschreitungen haftbar sein würde, möchte zu fern liegen, um ins Gewicht zu fallen (Seuff. Archiv Bd. II Nr. 105 Bd. III Nr. 287 a. E. Bd. VI Nr. 275); allein es geht offenbar nicht an, daß der Gerichtsvollzieher in einem Prozesse, welchen er selbst führt oder führen hilft, sich selbst das Mandat gebe, und dies erscheint hier als der Grund, warum ihn der Gesetzgeber als betheiligt erachten und ihm Zustellungen untersagen will Vgl. Seuff. Archiv Bd. VI Nr. 71. Abg. I 268 (v. Neumayr, v. Weiß).

9) Offenbar wird auch erfordert, daß der Gerichtsvollzieher von seiner Betheiligung Kenntniß gehabt habe. In der Regel wird dies zwar bei seiner eignen Betheiligung keinem Zweifel unterliegen, allein es können dennoch Fälle vorkommen, wo die Kenntniß mangelt, z. B. wenn es sich um eine Entschädigungsklage wegen Schlägerei handelt und sich später herausstellt, daß ein Sohn des Gerichtsvollziehers, für den er haftbar ist, mitschuldig war, oder wenn die Betheiligung aus einem Erbanfalle sich ergibt, welcher dem Gerichtsvollzieher im Augenblicke der Zustellung noch unbekannt war.

10) Gilt das Nemliche auch bezüglich der Betheiligung von Verwandten ꝛc.?

Im französischen Prozesse war die Betheiligung von Verwandten eine Behinderung sowohl für den Notar (Ges. v. 25 Vent. XI Art. 8), als für den Gerichtsboten (Code de proc. Art. 66), jedoch gelangte man im Hinblicke auf die Verschiedenheit der Natur und Wichtigkeit der bezüglichen Akte zu verschiedenartiger Auffassung. Bei Notariatsakten nahm man z. B. an (wie dies in Zink Comm. S. 203 auch für das diesseitige Notariatsgesetz als maßgebend angenommen wurde), daß ein Notar keinen Akt aufnehmen dürfe, bei welchem seine Verwandten in der Eigenschaft als Vormünder, Curatoren oder Bevollmächtigte handelten; bei Gerichtsbotenakten aber kam man zur entgegengesetzten Ansicht. Chauveau sur Carré quest. 343 ter.

Da unser Art. 201 absichtlich dem Art. 47 des Not.-Ges. nachgebildet wurde, und da derselbe von der Betheiligung des Gerichtsboten selbst und seiner Verwandten in ganz gleicher Weise spricht, so wird im Allgemeinen ein Unterschied nicht zu machen sein, obgleich es vielleicht im Hinblicke auf die gedrohte Nichtigkeit und die Natur der Gerichtsvollzieherakte zweckmäßig gewesen wäre, zu sagen: „bei welcher er selbst betheiligt oder seine Verwandte 2c. Parteien sind.“

Dennoch möchte ich annehmen, daß die Gleichheit nur besteht, so weit sich die Betheiligung auf ein Vermögensinteresse gründet, nicht aber insofern sie auf der besonderen Erwägung beruht, daß der Gerichtsvollzieher sich nicht selbst beauftragen dürfe. Ich würde daher mit der französischen Jurisprudenz annehmen, daß der Gerichtsvollzieher Zustellungen machen dürfe in Sachen, in welchen Verwandte 2c. nur als gesetzliche Vertreter, Anwälte, Prozeßbevollmächtigte oder Beistände betheiligt sind.

Das Erforderniß, daß der Gerichtsvollzieher Kenntniß von der Betheiligung gehabt haben müsse, ist bei dritten Personen natürlich von weit größerer praktischer Bedeutung, als bei ihm selbst.

11) Schließlich wird im Allgemeinen als Grundsatz anzuerkennen sein, daß ein ernstliches, nahe liegendes, dem Gerichtsvollzieher bekanntes Interesse vorliegen müsse, und daß eintretenden Falls das richterliche Ermessen zu entscheiden habe.

12) Wann tritt Nichtigkeit ein?

Es frägt sich, ob die Nichtigkeit, welche Art. 201 verfügt, von jeder Partei und ob sie von Amtswegen geltend gemacht werden könne?

Die französische Jurisprudenz nahm, aus der besonderen Natur der Gerichtsvollzieherakte folgernd, an, daß diejenige Partei, welche den Gerichtsvollzieher beauftragt hat, kein Recht der Anfechtung habe. Chauveau sur Carré quest. 339. Diese Ansicht möchte auch dem Art. 201 gegenüber, in welchen die Androhung der Nichtigkeit aus Art. 66 des Code de proc. übergegangen ist, die richtige und dem Willen des Gesetzgebers entsprechende sein, und zwar um so mehr, als Art. 219 für Prozeßhandlungen die allgemeine Vorsicht gibt, daß Niemand befugt sei, seine eigenen Handlungen anzufechten.

Eine Berücksichtigung von Amtswegen liegt wohl ebenfalls nicht im Willen des Gesetzgebers, denn es wäre offenbar den Zwecken des Gesetzes entgegen, wenn prozessuale Akten solcher Art, gegen welche die Parteien selbst nichts einzuwenden haben, in jeder Lage der Sache für nichtig erklärt werden könnten. Durch Nichtvorschützen der Nichtigkeit im Falle des Art. 219 Abs. 2 erscheint dieselbe daher beseitigt.

Art. 202. — **Ueber jede Zustellung hat der Gerichtsvollzieher eine Zustellungsurkunde zu errichten, deren Urschrift dem Auftraggeber einzuhändigen ist.**

Die Zustellungsurkunde hat zu enthalten:

1) **Jahr, Monat und Tag der Zustellung, wobei die Zahlen mit Buchstaben zu schreiben sind;**
2) **Vor- und Familiennamen, Stand oder Gewerbe und Wohnort Desjenigen, auf dessen Betreiben, sowie Desjenigen, an welchen die Zustellung gemacht wird — bei Handlungshäusern, Gesellschaften, Genossenschaften und Vereinen die Firma oder den Namen, sowie den Ort, wo sie ihren Sitz haben;**
3) **den Ort der Zustellung und die Bezeichnung der Person, an welche der Gerichtsvollzieher behändigt hat;**
4) **Namen, Wohnort und dienstliche Eigenschaft des Gerichtsvollziehers;**
5) **Unterschrift des letztern.**

Bei Zustellungen, welche auf Betreiben des gesetzlichen Vertreters einer Partei oder an einen solchen gemacht werden, ist diese Eigenschaft anzugeben und zugleich die Partei selbst in der in Abs. 2 Ziff. 2 erwähnten Weise zu bezeichnen.

Geschieht die Zustellung auf Betreiben mehrerer Personen oder wird sie für eine Streitgenossenschaft an einen Zustellungsbevollmächtigten gemacht und wird zugleich ein Schriftstück mitgetheilt, in welchem die einzelnen Betheiligten genügend bezeichnet sind, so kann in der Zustellungsurkunde hierauf Bezug genommen werden.

Bei Zustellungen unter Anwälten wird der Vorschrift des Abs. 2 Ziff. 2 durch Angabe ihrer Namen genügt.

Art. 203. — **Besteht die Partei, an welche eine Zustellung zu machen ist, aus mehreren Personen, so hat die Zustellung, soweit das Gesetz nicht anders bestimmt, an jede derselben zu geschehen.**

Jeder Person, welcher eine Zustellung gemacht wird, ist Abschrift sowohl der Zustellungsurkunde, als der mitgetheilten Schrift zu behändigen. Daß dies geschehen, ist in der Zustellungsurkunde anzuführen.

Bei Zustellungen an den Zustellungsbevollmächtigten einer Streitgenossenschaft bedarf

es nur der Behändigung einer einzigen Abschrift. Dasselbe gilt bei Zustellungen unter Anwälten, wenn auch der Anwalt verschiedene Parteien vertritt oder die von ihm vertretene Partei aus mehreren Personen besteht.

Die Abschriften der mitzutheilenden Schriften müssen, wenn die Zustellung auf Betreiben eines Anwalts gemacht oder ein Anwaltsakt zugestellt wird, von dem Anwalte, in den übrigen Fällen von dem Gerichtsvollzieher beglaubigt werden.

Art. 204. — Die von den Gerichtsvollziehern in gesetzlicher Form errichteten Zustellungsurkunden sind öffentliche Urkunden.

Stimmen Ur- und Abschrift der Zustellungsurkunde nicht überein, so ist für die Partei, an welche die Zustellung geschah, nur der Inhalt der ihr eingehändigten Abschrift maßgebend.

Art. 205. — Anwälte können Zustellungen an den Gegenanwalt ohne Vermittelung eines Gerichtsvollziehers bewirken. Die in diesem Falle erforderliche Empfangsbescheinigung ist mit Angabe des Datums auf die Urschrift der zugestellten Urkunde oder der besondern Zustellungsurkunde zu setzen und von dem Gegenanwalte zu unterzeichnen.

G. A. d. K. d. A. I S. 263. 264. 267. 268. 291. 292. IV S. 40. 69. 75.
K. d. R. I S. 344—347. IV. S. 30.

1) In diesen Artikeln gibt das Gesetz Vorschriften über die Art der Zustellung, über den Inhalt der Zustellungsurkunden und über deren Beweiskraft.

a) Art der Zustellung.

2) Die Zustellungen im gerichtlichen Verfahren geschehen nach Art. 101 Abs. 1 durch den Gerichtsvollzieher, jedoch dürfen solche von Anwalt zu Anwalt, gemäß Art. 205, ausnahmsweise auch unmittelbar gegen einfache Empfangsbescheinigung erfolgen, ein Verfahren, welches zweckmäßig ist und bei manchen Anwaltsakten, z. B. den Qualitäten, hie und da auch bis jetzt schon geübt wurde.

3) Unter Zustellung versteht man, wie schon zu Art. 101 bemerkt, nicht bloß die abschriftliche Mittheilung von Urkunden, sondern auch Mittheilungen, deren Organ der Gerichtsvollzieher selbst ist, z. B. Ladungen im Parteiprozesse, Aufforderungen, Anerbieten 2c.

Die Amtsthätigkeit des Gerichtsvollziehers beschränkt sich nun selbstverständlich nicht darauf, daß er der betreffenden Person eine Abschrift der von ihm errichteten Urkunde einhändige, sondern er hat ihr auch mündlich, in klarer und bündiger Weise, diejenigen Erklärungen zu machen, welche er beurkundet, und unter Umständen, z. B. bei Zahlungsanerbieten, auch die Erwiderung jener Person in seine Urkunde aufzunehmen.

Auf Grund dieser Erklärungen und zur sichereren Verständigung, insbesondere Uebermittlung, händigt er, mit Abschrift der etwa zuzustellenden Urkunde, sofort Abschrift seiner Zustellungsurkunde ein, und diese Behändigung ist allerdings so wichtig, daß ohne sie eine giltige Zustellung nicht besteht, und daß die Verweigerung der Annahme die Zustellung auf anderem Wege (Art. 197) nöthig macht.

4) Der Regel nach ist einer jeden Person (physischen oder juristischen) eine besondere Zustellung zu machen, und folgegemäß für jede Person eine besondere Abschrift zu fertigen und zu behändigen. Es muß daher z. B. jedem Ehegatten eine Abschrift behändigt werden, sollte auch der Ehemann nur der Ermächtigung oder des Streitconsenses wegen in Betracht kommen.

Diese Regel gilt auch, wenn Zustellungen an mehrere Personen bei dem nemlichen Zustellungsvertreter, z. B. dem Staatsanwalte, erfolgen, selbst wenn sie im nemlichen Akte beurkundet sind; denn der Staatsanwalt vertritt hier jede Person einzeln und muß jeder besonders die für sie bestimmte Abschrift übermitteln.

Nur für Zustellungen an den Zustellungs-Bevollmächtigten einer Streitgenossenschaft genügt ausnahmsweise eine einzige Abschrift. Dasselbe gilt bei allen Zustellungen von Anwalt zu Anwalt.

5) Der Gerichtsvollzieher hat die Richtigkeit der Abschriften von Urkunden zu beglaubigen und natürlich auch diese Abschriften anzufertigen. Handelt es sich jedoch von Anwaltsakten oder von Urkunden (Urtheilen, Protokollen), welche auf Betreiben eines Anwaltes zuzustellen sind, so obliegt die Fertigung und Beglaubigung dem Anwalte.

Letztere Ausnahme gilt nur für den Anwaltsprozeß, soweit der Anwalt als solcher handelt. Wenn übrigens behauptet wird (Abg. I 267), es sei mit Erlassung des Endurtheils die eigentliche anwaltschaftliche Thätigkeit beendet, so ist dies nicht völlig richtig, denn die Festsetzung der Kosten, die Darstellung des Sachverhalts (Art. 285), die Zustellung des Urtheils an den Gegenanwalt (Art. 192 Abs. 2) sind allerdings eigentliche Anwaltsgeschäfte und überhaupt gehört zur Funktion des Anwaltes noch alles, was nöthig ist, um die Endurtheile zum Vollzuge fähig oder rechtskräftig zu machen.

Es ist zu erwähnen, daß die seitherigen Befugnisse der Anwälte der Pfalz zur Fertigung von Abschriften eine Einschränkung erleiden, und zwar ist dies mit Absicht geschehen (Abg. I 267). Aus den Worten des kgl. Ministerial-Commissärs geht zugleich hervor, daß man unter den Zustellungen auf Betreiben des Anwalts auch hier nur die Zustellungen von Anwalt zu Anwalt zu verstehen habe, nicht auch Zustellungen, welche aus Auftrag des Anwaltes an die Partei selbst oder an dritte Personen geschehen.

b) Inhalt und Form der Zustellungs-Urkunden.

6) In Art. 202 ist angegeben, was das Gesetz bei jeder Zustellungsurkunde verlange. Die Nichtbeobachtung dieser Vorschriften begründet jedenfalls eine Pflichtverletzung von Seiten des Gerichtsvollziehers, macht jedoch die Urkunde nur nichtig oder beweisuntüchtig, wenn der Mangel das Wesentliche betrifft (Art. 218). Außerdem kann auch Berichtigung verfügt werden (Art. 220).

7) Was unter „betreibendem Theile" zu verstehen sei, wurde bereits zu Art. 192 Nr. 4 näher erörtert. Ist derselbe eine physische Person, so sind Vor- und Familiennamen, Stand oder Gewerbe und Wohnort anzugeben; eine Ausnahme besteht jedoch für Handelshäuser, insofern hier auch der einzelne Kaufmann, falls er eine Firma führt, mit dieser bezeichnet werden kann. Die Gesellschaften, Genossenschaften und Vereine, von denen hier das Gesetz noch weiter spricht, sind offenbar nur solche, welchen Persönlichkeit zukömmt, und von welchen in Art. 193 Ziff. 3 u. 4 die Rede ist.

Ist der betreibende Theil ein Collegium, so versteht sich von selbst, daß die Vorschriften wegen Angaben der Namen &c. wegfallen, soweit sie gegenstandslos sind. Es genügt also, zu sagen: „Auf Betreiben des Magistrats der Stadt X, als gesetzlichen Vertreters dieser Stadt," oder: „Auf Betreiben der kgl. Kreisregierung der Pfalz K. der F., als gesetzlichen Vertreterin des kgl. Fiskus."

Tritt der gesetzliche Vertreter als betreibender Theil auf, so ist auch noch die Partei selbst in gleicher Weise zu bezeichnen (Art. 202 Abs. 2).

Ist dem Gerichtsvollzieher der Auftrag durch Vermittlung eines einfachen Bevollmächtigten, als welcher außer dem Bereiche des Anwaltsprozesses auch der Anwalt zu betrachten ist, zugegangen, so ist es nicht nöthig, dies anzuführen, jedoch steht auch kein Verbot entgegen und gereicht es häufig dem Gegner selbst zum Vortheile, wenn er erfährt, an wen er sich zu wenden habe (Weiß Handb. für Huissiers S. 138 u. 139). Es steht also nichts im Wege, etwa zu sagen: „Auf Betreiben von A B, Kaufmann in Leipzig, welcher laut Vollmacht vom — den Geschäftsmann C in X mit Führung dieses Prozesses beauftragt hat."

8) Was die Personen betrifft, an welche die Zustellungen zu machen sind, so sind dies, wie zu Art. 193 bemerkt, nur physische Personen und gehören dazu auch die Zustellungsvertreter (Art. 193 Ziff. 2—7), etwaige Zustellungsbevollmächtigte und Personen, in deren Wohnung Domizil erwählt ist (Einf.-Ges. Art. 65). Auch hier genügt die Bezeichnung derjenigen Person, an welche die Zustellung gemacht wird, nicht, sondern ist nöthig, anzugeben, in welcher Eigenschaft sie ihr gemacht werde, und erscheint diese Angabe wesentlich, wenn die Urkunde ihren Zweck erfüllen soll.

Es liegt daher im Sinne des Art. 203 Abs. 3, daß alle Personen genau zu bezeichnen seien, in deren Vertretung die Zustellung in Empfang genommen worden ist.

Es wäre z. B. zu sagen:

„habe ich — dem A B, Kaufmann in X, in seiner
„Eigenschaft als Zustellungsbevollmächtigter für C —
„B — D &c., klägerische Streitgenossen &c."

oder:

„habe ich — dem Magistrate der Stadt München,
„als deren gesetzlichem Vertreter, und zwar für den-
„selben dem ersten Bürgermeister X allda, sprechend
„in dessen Wohnung mit &c."

9) Sehr sachgemäß erscheint es, wenn das Gesetz zur Bezeichnung der Parteien eine einfache Hinweisung auf die zuzustellenden Schriftstücke gestattet; es wird dies zur Verhütung unnöthiger Vielschreiberei viel beitragen. Es ist dabei klar, daß das, was der Gerichtsvollzieher thun kann, er im gegebenen Falle pflichtgemäß thun muß und etwaige unnütze Kosten ihm zur Last zu legen wären.

10) Die Angabe des Ortes der Zustellung ist nöthig, um festzustellen, daß der Gerichtsvollzieher innerhalb seines Amtsbezirkes gehandelt, sowie ferner, daß er die Zustellung vorschriftsmäßig in der Wohnung, im Geschäfts- oder Dienstlokale bethätigt habe. Die Mittelsperson, mit welcher er spricht, und welcher er

die Abschrift behändigt, soll er „bezeichnen", d. h. in der Art bezeichnen, daß ein Zweifel über die Person nicht möglich ist, und daß aus der Bezeichnung entnommen werden kann, ob die Zustellung giltig an diese Person geschehen konnte.

Wie bereits oben (Art. 195—197 Nr. 16) bemerkt, genügt auch dies noch nicht, sondern es sind auch alle jene Umstände zu beurkunden, welche die Behändigung an diese besondere Person statthaft machen.

Es muß z. B. gesagt sein:

„habe ich dem A B, Schuster in X, da ich in dessen „Wohnung allda weder ihn selbst, noch erwachsene „Familienangehörige oder Bedienstete desselben an„traf, sprechend mit dem Bürgermeister des Orts C ꝛc."

11) Bei Zustellungen von Anwalt zu Anwalt genügt es, die Namen der Anwälte anzugeben, und es gestalten sich daher diese Urkunden höchst einfach, etwa dahin:

„Heute den — — —

„Auf Betreiben des Anwaltes A habe ich — dem „Anwalte B, sprechend auf seiner Schreibstube mit „seinem Geschäftsgehilfen X, Abschrift von vorstehen„der Anwaltsbestellung (Antrage, Urtheilsausfertig„ung) und von dieser meiner Urkunde zugestellt."

c) Beweiskraft der Zustellungs-Urkunden.

12) Alle Zustellungsurkunden der Gerichtsvollzieher sind öffentliche Urkunden und haben bezüglich dessen, was diese Beamten aus eigner Wahrnehmung beurkunden, diejenige Beweiskraft, welche die Art. 354, 368 und 372 solchen Urkunden beimessen.

Urschriften und Abschriften derselben sind im Grunde nur mehrfache Exemplare der nemlichen Urkunde, deren jede Partei eines als Beweismittel eingehändigt erhält, weßhalb die französischen Rechtsgelehrten sagen: »En matière »d'exploit la copie tient lieu d'original à l'as»signé.« Hieraus folgerte man, daß die Nichtigkeit eines der beiden Exemplare den Akt im Ganzen nichtig mache. Chauveau sur Carré quest. 227.

Unsere Prozeßordnung verfügt, daß für die Partei, an welche die Zustellung geschah, nur die eingehändigte Abschrift maßgebend sei, woraus zu folgern sein dürfte, daß sie sich auf Mängel der Urschrift nicht berufen könne, falls ihr eignes Exemplar in Richtigkeit ist — eine Ansicht, welche auch in Frankreich schon ihre Vertreter hatte. Carré a. a. O.

Art. 206. — **Die Bestimmungen der Art. 193—202, Art. 203 Abs. 1 und 2 und Art. 204 finden auch auf die in Art. 101 Abs. 2 und 3 erwähnten Zustellungen Anwendung.**

Für die in Art. 193 Ziff. 6 bezeichneten Personen sind solche Zustellungen an den Staatsanwalt des Bezirksgerichts zu machen, in dessen Sprengel derjenige, auf dessen Betreiben die Zustellung stattfindet, oder, wenn letztere auf Betreiben mehrerer Personen erfolgt, eine derselben ihren Wohnsitz hat.

G. A. d. K. d. A. I S. 292. IV S. 40. 41. — K. d. R. I S. 347.

Durch diesen Artikel werden die Vorschriften über die Zustellungen im gerichtlichen Verfahren mit wenig Ausnahmen auf alle außergerichtlichen Zustellungen, sowie auf Zustellungen im Vollstreckungsverfahren und in der Gant ausgedehnt. Manche dieser Vorschriften haben übrigens nicht bloß für Zustellungen, sondern für Gerichtsbotenakte im Allgemeinen zu gelten, z. B. die Vorschrift wegen der Beweiskraft (Art. 204 Abs. 1).

Hervorzuheben ist, daß die Verfügung in Art. 203 Abs. 3, laut welcher bei Zustellungs-Bevollmächtigten eine einzige Abschrift genügt, nicht zu denjenigen gehört, welche auf sonstige Zustellungen ausgedehnt sind, was für das Vollstreckungsverfahren wichtig ist.

Tagfahrten und Fristen.

Art. 207. — **Soferne die Ladung nicht auf eine bestimmte Stunde gestellt ist, gilt die auf einen Vormittag angesetzte Tagfahrt Mittags um zwölf Uhr, die auf einen ganzen Tag oder einen Nachmittag angesetzte Abends um sechs Uhr als abgelaufen.**

Im Falle der Ladung auf eine bestimmte Stunde ist die Tagfahrt von der Partei versäumt, wenn diese weder bei dem Aufrufe der Sache noch vor dem Schlusse der Verhandlung sich meldet.

Art. 208. — **Der Fristenlauf richtet sich bei vereinbarten Fristen nach dem vereinbarten Tage, bei gesetzlichen oder vom Gerichte bestimmten mit Rücksicht auf die einschlägigen Bestimmungen des Gesetzes nach dem Tage der Zustellung oder der mündlichen Eröffnung der richterlichen Verfügung in der Art, daß der folgende Tag als der erste der Frist gerechnet wird.**

Ist die Frist nach Monaten bestimmt, so wird der Monat zu dreißig Tagen gerechnet.

Die Frist endigt mit dem letzten Tage und, wenn dieser ein Sonn- oder gebotener Feiertag ist, mit dem nächstfolgenden Werktage.

Bei Fristverlängerungen wird die bewilligte neue Frist, soweit nicht anders bestimmt ist, vom Ablauf der vorigen an gerechnet.

G. A. d. K. d. A. I S. 269. 270. 293. IV S. 40. 41. — K. d. R. I S. 347. IV S. 30.

1) Tagfahrten.

Unter Tagfahrt versteht man den Tag, welcher zur Vornahme irgend einer prozessualen Handlung bestimmt ist. In der Regel wird sie vom Richter für den Prozeß festgesetzt, jedoch kommt es auch vor, daß die Parteien sich selbst den Tag bestimmen, wie z. B. bei Ladungen vor's Handelsgericht oder Landgericht oder beim freiwilligen Erscheinen vor diesen Gerichten.

Die Ladung zur Tagfahrt, von welcher Art. 207 spricht, begreift natürlich auch den Fall, wo eine Zustellung durch den Gerichtsvollzieher nicht nöthig ist, sondern mündliche Eröffnung genügt, z. B. Art. 525.

2) In Art. 207 Abs. 2 hat der Gesetzgeber zunächst den Fall im Auge, wo auf eine bestimmte Stunde in die Sitzung geladen ist (Art. 259, 501), und verfügt, daß sofort ein Versäumungsurtheil begehrt und erlassen werden dürfe, sobald diese Stunde verstrichen sei, daß aber die Partei noch rechtzeitig erscheine, wenn sie vor Schluß der Verhandlung über die betreffende Sache, also vor Ausspruch des Versäumungsurtheiles sich anmelde. Vgl. Art. 250 Abs. 4.

Der nemliche Grundsatz gilt jedoch auch für sonstige gerichtliche Verhandlungen gegen die Partei, und wird sogar dritten Personen, z. B. Zeugen, gegenüber Anwendung finden, und dieß zwar schon deßhalb, weil er eigentlich selbstverständlich ist.

3) Fristen.

Die Fristen sind entweder von den Parteien, oder vom Richter, oder vom Gesetze bestimmt. In allen diesen Fällen können sie entweder von einem gewissen Tage vorwärts, oder von einem gewissen Tage rückwärts gerechnet werden. Letzteres ist z. B. der Fall, wenn das Gesetz in Art. 231 und 242 die Frist für die motivirten Anträge vom Sitzungstage rückwärts bestimmt, oder wenn der Richter im Falle des Art. 323 Abs. 2 etwa verfügen würde, es habe binnen einer gewissen Frist vor der neuen Verhandlung die Mittheilung der Urkunden stattzufinden. Für beide Arten von Fristen gilt der Grundsatz, daß sie voll sein müssen, daß also der Tag, von welchem an sie berechnet werden, nicht zähle. Für die erstere Art ist ferner verfügt, daß, wenn der letzte Tag der Frist ein Sonntag oder gebotener Feiertag (s. Art. 199 Nr. 2) sei, der nächstfolgende Werktag an dessen Stelle trete, eine Verfügung, welche dem diesseitigen Prozesse entlehnt ist.

Die besondere Gattung von Fristen, welche das französische Recht unter der Bezeichnung »délais francs« kennt, ist für den Civilprozeß beseitigt.

4) Die vereinbarten und die richterlichen Fristen können auch so bezeichnet werden, daß sofort der Tag, an welchem sie zu Ende gehen, angegeben wird. Laufen jedoch die richterlichen Fristen nicht von der Eröffnung durch den Richter, sondern von der Zustellung an, wie dies als Regel zu gelten hat, so lassen sie sich in dieser Weise nicht füglich festsetzen.

5) Fristverlängerungen werden vom Ablaufe der vorigen Frist an gerechnet. Ist der letzte Tag der vorigen Frist ein Feiertag, so sollte man denken, es seien die beiden Fristen als ein Ganzes zu betrachten und dürfe daher dieser Feiertag nicht berücksichtigt werden. Nichtsdestoweniger wird dem Wortlaute des Gesetzes und dem bestehenden Gerichtsgebrauche nach (Bl. f. R. I S. 246) das Gegentheil anzunehmen sein.

Noch weniger Zweifel besteht für die Fälle, wo sich sonst zwei Fristen aneinander reihen, z. B. nach Art. 232 und 233.

6) In der Pfalz kennt man eine besondere Art von richterlichen Fristen, die délais de grâce, d. h. Gnadenfristen, welche der Richter nach seinem Ermessen für den Vollzug seiner Urtheile bewilligen kann. Das Recht, solche Fristen zu geben, welches mehr dem Civilrechte als dem Prozesse angehört, sich übrigens auch auf das Civilgesetz (Art. 1244 Code civ.) gründet, besteht ohne Zweifel unversehrt fort (Abg. III 155), die Bestimmungen der Art. 122—125 Code de proc. jedoch erscheinen, soweit sie prozessualisch sind (Einf.-Ges. Art. 3 Ziff. 1), aufgehoben.

Daß diese Frist nicht in einem späteren Urtheile bewilligt werden könne (Art. 122 Code de proc.), etwa im Vollstreckungsverfahren, erscheint auch jetzt noch selbstverständlich, da es ja nicht statthaft sein kann, ein gesprochenes Urtheil wieder theilweise aufzuheben. Chauveau sur Carré quest. 525.

Die Fristbewilligung geschieht in der Regel der Art, daß die Zeitpunkte der Fälligkeit bezeichnet werden, und es erscheint dies auch jetzt noch zulässig, mag nun das Urtheil ein contradiktorisches oder ein Versäumungsurtheil sein.

Bei Versäumungsurtheilen ist übrigens jetzt das Recht des Richters in der Art beschränkt, daß er die aufgestellten Thatsachen als wahr annehmen muß (Art. 297). Ist nur ein gewisser Zeitraum bezeichnet, der Tag aber, von welchem er zu berechnen sei, nicht angegeben, so beginnt nach den Grundsätzen der Prozeßordnung die Frist nur von der Zustellung; die abweichende Bestimmung in Art. 123 erscheint aufgehoben.

Für die Frage, unter welchen Umständen die Gnadenfrist bewilligt werden könne, ist Art. 124 Code de proc., welcher übrigens hier nur eine Anwendung des Art. 1188 Code civ. bildet, auch jetzt noch maßgebend, denn er erscheint in dieser Richtung nur als Ergänzung der civilrechtlichen Bestimmungen des Art. 1244 Code civil. Für die Frage jedoch, unter welchen Umständen die bewilligte Frist verwirkt sei, gilt jetzt Art. 830.

Schließlich ist zu erwähnen, daß Art. 157 Code de commerce für Wechsel eine Ausnahme von den Bestimmungen des Art. 1244 Code civ. enthielt, und jener Artikel seiner Zeit aus Unvorsichtigkeit mit den übrigen Bestimmungen des Code de comm. aufgehoben wurde. Nichtsdestoweniger wird im Geiste der Verfügungen der Art. 548 und 549 die Bewilligung von Fristen in Wechselsachen nicht gestattet sein.

Art. 209. — **Vorbehaltlich besonderer gesetzlicher Bestimmungen werden bei Zustellungen, in Folge deren die betreffende Person an einem andern Orte, als dem, wo sie wohnt oder sich aufhält, zu erscheinen oder eine Handlung vorzunehmen hat, die gesetzlichen Fristen, selbst wenn sie für unerstreckbar erklärt sind, sowie auch die Zeiträume, welche nach gesetzlicher Bestimmung zwischen einer Tagfahrt und der Ladung zu derselben in Mitte liegen müssen, erweitert:**

1) **für Personen, die im Sprengel eines andern, jedoch zu demselben Appellationsgerichte gehörigen Bezirksgerichts wohnen oder sich aufhalten, um vier Tage;**
2) **für Personen, die im Inlande, jedoch in einem andern Appellationsgerichtssprengel wohnen oder sich aufhalten, um acht Tage;**
3) **für Personen, die im Auslande wohnen oder sich aufhalten, um die durch Verordnung bestimmte Zeit.**

Geht die Zustellung eine Person an, deren Aufenthaltsort unbekannt ist, so wird die gesetzliche Frist um einen Monat erweitert.

Bei Militärpersonen ist nicht der Wohnort, sondern der Ort der Zustellung für die Fristerweiterung maßgebend.

Auf die Erweiterung der Frist ist es ohne Einfluß, wenn die Zustellung statt an die Partei selbst an einen Zustellungsbevollmächtigten stattfindet.

Wird einem Ausländer die Zustellung im Inlande persönlich oder in seiner Wohnung gemacht, so hat er nur diejenige Frist, welche dem Inländer zukommt, der an dem Orte wohnt, wo die Zustellung gemacht worden ist.

G. A. d. K. d. A. I S. 270. 271. 293. IV S. 40. 41. — K. d. R. I S. 347. IV S. 30.

1) Die Fristen, welche das Gesetz selbst bestimmt, sind natürlich für die gewöhnlichen Fälle berechnet und können unter Umständen ungenügend sein. Für solche Ausnahmsfälle waren daher Fristerweiterungen nöthig, welche Art. 209 in ebenso einfacher als zweckmäßiger Weise bestimmt.

Die Bestimmung in Art. 1033 Code de proc., zufolge welcher für jeden einzelnen Fall die Entfernung genau berechnet werden mußte, war, streng genommen, richtiger, denn es können allerdings jetzt grelle Ungleichheiten vorkommen. Ein Einwohner von München l/J., welcher vor's Bezirksgericht München r/J. geladen wird, erfreut sich z. B. einer Zusatzfrist von vier Tagen, während dem Einwohner von Tegernsee oder Bad Kreuth, welcher vor das nemliche Gericht geladen wird, gar keine Zusatzfrist gegönnt ist. Allein die Bestimmung unserer Prozeßordnung ist praktischer; sie bietet den Vortheil größerer Einfachheit und Sicherheit, welcher hier schwerer wiegt, als der Vortheil völliger Gleichheit.

2) Die Erweiterungen des Art. 209 gelten für alle Fristen ohne Unterschied, und gerade deßhalb, weil die Regel eine durchgreifende ist, hat der Gesetzgeber die Bezugnahme auf diesen Artikel, wie sie der Entwurf für eine Reihe einzelner Fälle enthält, überall beseitigt. Wo eine Ausnahme bestehen soll, z. B. in Art. 338, ist es ausdrücklich gesagt.

Nur für das Vollstreckungsverfahren ist in Art. 853 die umgekehrte Regel aufgestellt.

3) Wirft sich die Frage auf, ob eine Frist zu erweitern sei, so sind zwei Orte in's Auge zu fassen, derjenige, wo die Person, gegen welche die Frist läuft, wohnt oder sich aufhält, und derjenige, wo sie selbst, oder der von ihr beauf-

tragte Beamte (Anwalt oder Gerichtsvollzieher) erscheinen oder handeln soll.

Unter dem Orte, „wo eine Person wohnt“, kann wohl nur der Ort, wo sie ihren Wohnort, d. h. ihren bürgerlichen Wohnsitz, hat, verstanden werden (Seuff. Comm. Bd. 1 S. 52). Es gibt dies schon der Beisatz: „oder sich aufhält“ zu erkennen, denn es soll hier offenbar Bezug genommen werden auf die Unterscheidung in Art. 12 und gesagt werden, daß, wenn kein Wohnsitz besteht, der Aufenthalt an die Stelle trete.

Der Grund, warum der Gesetzgeber die Fristen immer nur nach dem Wohnorte oder Aufenthaltsorte berechnen läßt, liegt darin, daß vorauszusetzen ist, es finde die Partei bloß dort die Mittel zur wirksamen Geltendmachung ihrer Rechte — thatsächliche Aufklärungen, Urkunden, Rechtsrath. Deßhalb wurden denn auch im französischen Prozesse, wo Zustellungen an die Person unbedingt gestattet, ja sogar Regel waren, die Fristen immer nur nach dem Wohnsitze berechnet, mochte selbst die Ladung am Gerichtssitze gegeben worden sein. In dringlichen Fällen half man eben durch Ladung mit kurzer Frist, ein Auskunftsmittel, welches sich auch jetzt noch (Art. 259) bietet.

Es erschiene daher gegen den Geist des Gesetzes, wollte man den Begriff von „Wohnung“ im Sinne des Art. 195 als maßgebend erachten, denn jener Begriff ist, wie erörtert, ein sehr weitgehender und dehnbarer, und schon der Umstand, daß in Art. 209 Abs. 5 die Zustellung in der Wohnung als Ausnahme angeführt ist, zeigt, daß man etwas Anderes gemeint habe. Deßhalb ist denn auch, falls die Zustellung im Geschäftslokale gemacht wurde, für die Fristberechnung doch nur der Wohnort entscheidend, was in manchen Fällen, z. B. wenn ein Kaufmann in der Vorstadt Au wohnt, in der Stadt München aber sein Geschäftslokal hat, praktisch werden kann.

Hat Jemand weder Wohnsitz noch Aufenthalt, so muß derjenige Ort maßgebend sein, wo ihm die Zustellung persönlich gemacht wird.

Im Zweifel wird der Gerichtsvollzieher natürlich immer die längere Frist in seiner Ladung anführen (Art. 226 Abs. 3, Art. 698 Abs. 3).

4) Wenn das Gesetz besondere, durch Verordnung zu bestimmende Fristen für Leute vorsieht, welche im Auslande wohnen oder sich aufhalten, so hat es offenbar zunächst jene Fälle im Auge, wo die Zustellung an den Staatsanwalt geschieht und durch diesen übermittelt werden muß; jedoch darf hieraus nicht gefolgert werden, daß in Fällen, wo diese Vermittlung des Staatsanwaltes nicht eintritt, fragliche Bestimmung keine Anwendung finde. Schon die Ausnahme in Art. 209 Abs. 5 spricht gegen eine solche Auslegung, und aus den Verhandlungen (Abg. I 271) geht hervor, daß sogar dann, wenn die Zustellung an den Zustellungsbevollmächtigten des Ausländers geschah, für diesen die längeren Fristen laufen. Uebrigens hatte Referent v. Neumayr (Vortrag zu Art. 185) die entgegenstehende Ansicht vertreten, fand jedoch keine Zustimmung.

5) Bei Militärpersonen ist nicht deren Wohnort, sondern der Ort der Zustellung maßgebend. Es sind hierbei jene Militärpersonen und jene Zustellung gemeint, von welchen in Art. 193 Ziff. 7 die Sprache ist.

6) Die Verfügung, daß es gleichgiltig sei, ob die Zustellung an die Partei selbst oder an deren Zustellungsbevollmächtigten stattfinde, will besagen, daß auch bei der letzteren Zustellung die Fristen so zu berechnen seien, als sei sie der Partei selbst an ihrem Wohnorte gemacht worden. Es gilt dies, wie gesagt, sogar für den Fall, wo die Partei im Auslande wohnt (Abg. I 271).

Der hier ausgesprochene Grundsatz findet seine gute Begründung darin, daß der Zustellungsbevollmächtigte die Urkunde erst der Partei selbst zusenden und diese sodann von ihrem Wohnsitze aus handeln muß, weßhalb denn auch die französische Jurisprudenz für den Fall der Ladung am gewählten Wohnsitze das Nemliche als richtig anerkannte. Chauveau sur Carré quest. 379. Allerdings ist dies noch kein Grund, die langen, nur für den diplomatischen Weg berechneten Fristen zu gestatten, und es wird Aufgabe der zu erlassenden Verordnung sein, auch diesen Fall vorauszusehen und etwa den Fällen des direkten Verkehres gleichzustellen.

7) Der Schlußsatz von Art. 209 macht eine Ausnahme für den Fall, wo einem Ausländer die Zustellung persönlich oder in seiner Wohnung im Inlande gemacht wird. Gilt dieselbe im gleichen Falle auch für Inländer, welche nur im Auslande einen bestimmten Wohnsitz haben (Art. 193 Ziff. 6)? — Offenbar nicht!

Das Gesetz, welches ja den Art. 193 vor sich hatte und theilweise wiederholt, spricht ausdrücklich nur von Ausländern und es handelt sich hier um eine Ausnahmsbestimmung, welche nicht ohne Härte ist, z. B. im Falle, wo einer Person, welche auf einer Reise begriffen ist, zugemuthet wird, in kurzer Frist irgendwo wegen wichtiger Rechtsangelegenheiten Rede zu stehen.

Zudem gibt es Inländer, deren Dienstpflicht ihnen den Wohnsitz im Auslande anweist.

Auch für diesen Fall möchte es übrigens geeignet sein, die Fristen des diplomatischen Weges abzukürzen.

8) Eine Frage ist schließlich, ob Art. 209 auch für Zustellungen von Anwalt zu Anwalt gelte?

Auf Anfrage äußerte sich der königl. Ministerialkommissär verneinend, fügte jedoch hinzu, daß es sich übrigens hier in der Regel auch nur von richterlichen Fristen handele (I 271). — Nichtsdestoweniger möchte ich das Gegentheil annehmen.

Jene Aeußerung gibt nur die Ansicht des französischen Rechts wieder, welches allerdings nur von Zustellungen an die Partei spricht, und erscheint aufgewogen durch die späteren Aeußerungen des kgl. Ministerialkommissärs zu Art. 291 des Entwurfs, welcher Erweiterungsfristen berechnen wollte und zwar vom Wohnorte des Anwaltes an (Abg. II 164).

Unsere Prozeßordnung spricht nun aber allgemein von Fällen, wo eine Person an einem entfernten Orte zu handeln habe und diese Person kann ebensogut der Anwalt, als die Partei, als ein Zeuge sein. Es erscheint mir daher z. B. zweifellos, daß die im Art. 187 festgesetzte von der Zustellung an den Anwalt laufende Berufungsfrist eintretenden Falls erweitert werden müsse und zwar je nachdem man den Anwalt zur Einlegung der Berufung für befugt erachtet oder ein persönliches Handeln der Partei verlangt, entweder mit Rücksicht auf den Wohnort des Anwalts oder mit Rücksicht auf den Wohnort der Partei.

Dabei will ich nicht unterlassen, anzuführen, daß selbst die französische Jurisprudenz das Bedürfniß fühlte, manche von Zustellung an den Anwalt als solchen laufenden Fristen zu erweitern, z. B. die Berufungsfrist des Art. 669 Code de proc. Chauveau sur Carré quest. 2193 und 3410.

Art. 210. — Haben mehrere Personen wegen des nämlichen, wenn auch theilbaren Gegenstands zu handeln oder zu erscheinen, so gilt für alle die längste Frist.

Durch die Zustellung wird der Fristenlauf auch gegen die Partei begründet, welche die Zustellung veranlaßt hat.

Bei Endurtheilen, sowie bei Urtheilen, welche hinsichtlich der Berufung den Endurtheilen gleichgestellt sind (Art. 682 und 683), beginnt der Fristenlauf, soweit das Gesetz nicht anders bestimmt, erst mit der Zustellung an die Partei oder ihren Zustellungsbevollmächtigten.

G. A. d. K. d. A. I S. 271. 293. III S. 92. 93. IV S. 41. 87. 200. K. d. R. I S. 347. IV S. 30.

1) Nach Art. 151 Code de proc. kann, falls mehrere Personen wegen des nemlichen Gegenstandes vor Gericht geladen sind, kein Versäumungsurtheil genommen werden, bevor die längste Erscheinungsfrist verstrichen ist. Jene spezielle Verfügung ist nun hier zu einem allgemeinen Grundsatze erweitert.

Dieser Grundsatz beruht auf der nemlichen Erwägung, wie die Bestimmung in Art. 316 wegen der Verbindungsurtheile. Das Gesetz will widersprechende Entscheidungen in connexen Streitpunkten verhüten und deßhalb gibt er seine Vorschrift ebenso für die Fälle der Theilbarkeit als der Untheilbarkeit des Streitgegenstandes. Ist der Gegenstand ein ganz anderer, so laufen natürlich die Fristen getrennt und es ist ohne Belang, daß die Begehren etwa in der nemlichen Ladung vereinigt sind.

2) Durch die Bestimmung, daß die Zustellung den Lauf der Fristen auch für den zustellenden Theil begründe, ist der Satz des französischen Prozesses: »nul ne se forclot soi-même« beseitigt — und wohl mit Recht.

Wenn für beide Theile die Verpflichtung zum Handeln von Zustellung einer Urkunde abhängt, z. B. bei Einlegung von Rechtsmitteln, Beweisantritt, so ist es wohl ebenso billig als vernünftig, daß derjenige, welcher den Anderen in Verzug setzt, also zeigt, daß er den Inhalt der Urkunde genau kenne und deren Vollzug wolle, vom nemlichen Augenblicke an auch sich selbst als in Verzug befindlich betrachte. Ebenso ist selbstverständlich, daß derjenige, welcher einen Anderen vor Gericht ladet, hiermit auch sich selbst verpflichtet, vor Gericht zu erscheinen (Abg. IV 87).

3) Der Schlußabsatz von Art. 210 bringt, wie bereits bei Art. 192 Nr. 7 erörtert, eine Neuerung in so fern, als die Zustellung der in Art. 682 u. 683 bezeichneten Urtheile an die Partei allgemein vorgeschrieben ist, wenn Fristen auf Grund derselben laufen sollen, während sie in der Pfalz bis jetzt nur nöthig war für die Berufungsfrist. Wenn auch der Gesetzgeber, wie aus den Verhandlungen (Abg. III 92, 93) hervorgeht, hauptsächlich die Berufungsfrist im Auge hatte, so spricht er doch allgemein, und dieser Umstand hat um so größeres Gewicht, als

er fragliche Bestimmung, den Entwurf abändernd, in den allgemeinen Theil verwies.

Die bezügliche Vorschrift ist natürlich strenge auszulegen, und trifft bloß diejenigen Theile der Urtheile, welche unter die Gesichtspunkte der Art. 682 u. 683 fallen. (Art. 490 Abs. 2. — Art. 708 möchte nicht im Wege stehen.)

Daß der Zustellung an die Partei diejenige an den Anwalt immer vorauszugehen habe, ergibt sich aus Art. 192.

Näheres in dieser Beziehung wird bei einzelnen Gelegenheiten, wo die praktischen Folgen sich fühlbar machen, z. B. bei der Eidesauflage (Art. 460) und der Berufung, gesagt werden.

Art. 211. — **Fristen zu persönlichem Erscheinen oder Handeln werden durch den Tod der Partei oder ihres gesetzlichen Vertreters, sowie durch jede Veränderung in der Eigenschaft, durch welche die Befugniß dieser Personen zur Prozeßführung bedingt ist, dergestalt unterbrochen, daß erst mit der Zustellung an die Person, welche nunmehr den Prozeß zu führen hat, eine neue volle Frist zu laufen beginnt.**

Diese Zustellung kann den Erben insgesammt und ohne Bezeichnung der einzelnen in der letzten Wohnung des Erblassers und, wenn daselbst weder ein Familienglied noch ein Bediensteter desselben zu treffen ist, durch Zustellung an den Gerichtsschreiber des Einzelngerichts gemacht werden, in dessen Bezirke der Erblasser zur Zeit seines Todes nach Art. 12—14 seinen allgemeinen Gerichtsstand hatte.

Erfolgt die Zustellung während der zur Inventarserrichtung oder zur Erklärung über Annahme oder Ausschlagung der Erbschaft oder Gütergemeinschaft nach bürgerlichem Rechte durch das Gesetz oder von dem zuständigen Gerichte eingeräumten Zeit, so beginnt erst mit dem Ablaufe dieser Zeit die in Abs. 1 bestimmte neue Frist, es sei denn, daß für die liegende Erbschaft ein zur Prozeßführung befugter Curator bestellt und an diesen die Zustellung erfolgt ist.

G. A. d. K. d. A. I S. 271—273. 293. 294. III S. 19. IV S. 41. K. d. R. I S. 347. 348. IV S. 30.

1) Der Lauf aller Fristen steht natürlich still, wenn das ganze gerichtliche Verfahren eine Unterbrechung erleidet (Art. 490 u. 491). Ein ähnlicher Stillstand tritt für gewöhnliche Prozesse ein während der Gerichtsferien (Art. 139 u. 142 des Einführungsges.). In Art. 211 behandelt das Gesetz nur eine besondere Art der Unterbrechung bei Fristen, welche ein persönliches Handeln der Partei voraussetzen.

2) Ist eine Partei durch Anwalt oder Prozeßbevollmächtigten mit genügender Vollmacht vertreten, so kann der Prozeß in der Regel ungehindert fortschreiten, ohne daß auf Sterbfall, Verlust der Rechtsfähigkeit oder Wechsel der Vertretung Rücksicht zu nehmen wäre, da ja nach Art. 93 die Prozeßvollmacht auch nach dem Tode des Vollmachtgebers fortdauert und da ferner nach Art. 491 Abs. 2 sonstige Aenderungen erst wirksam werden durch förmliche Anzeige. Stehen jedoch Handlungen in Frage, welche von der Partei oder deren gesetzliche Vertreter persönlich auszugehen haben, so müssen Aenderungen der bezeichneten Art billiger Weise berücksichtigt werden und zwar durch wiederholte Aufforderung der neu auftretenden Personen, von denen zu vermuthen ist, daß sie von der früheren Aufforderung nichts wissen.

Der bezügliche Grundsatz war auch anerkannt im französischen Prozesse, jedoch nur für bestimmte Fälle, z. B. für Ladungen in Art. 345 Code de proc., für Berufungen in Art. 447; im Uebrigen galten die Grundsätze über Unterbrechung der Instanz.

Unsere Prozeßordnung spricht ein allgemeines Prinzip aus.

a) Persönliches Handeln.

3) Fristen zum persönlichen Erscheinen oder Handeln sind gegeben, wo die Partei, unter welcher hier überall auch der gesetzliche Vertreter begriffen ist, persönlich auftreten oder handeln muß, oder wo es bestimmter Wille des Gesetzes ist, daß sie in die Lage versetzt werde, ihre Rechte persönlich zu vertreten.

Die Nothwendigkeit des persönlichen Handelns liegt vor, wenn ein Prozeßbevollmächtigter nicht aufgestellt ist, oder wenn der bestellte Anwalt oder sonstige Prozeßbevollmächtigte mit der zur Vornahme der betreffenden Handlung nöthigen Vollmacht nicht versehen ist, oder wenn eine Vertretung der Natur der Handlung gemäß nicht möglich ist.

In allen diesen Fällen ergeben sich keine Zweifel; schwieriger aber gestaltet sich die Sache, wenn das persönliche Auftreten der Partei nicht nöthig, sondern nur gestattet ist, z. B. bei Beweisaufnahmen (Art. 341). In dieser Beziehung wird an den betreffenden Orten das Nähere bemerkt werden.

4) Von den verschiedenen Fristen, welche

hierher gehören, sollen hier nur zwei Arten als besonders wichtig näher besprochen werden, nemlich die Ladungsfristen und die Fristen zur Ergreifung von Rechtsmitteln.

Was die ersteren betrifft, so ist klar, daß die Partei persönlich für ihre gerichtliche Vertretung sorgen muß. Wenn sie daher im Laufe der Erscheinungsfrist stirbt oder rechtsunfähig wird, ohne vorher Anwalt oder Prozeßbevollmächtigten bestellt zu haben, so tritt eine Unterbrechung auf Grund von Art. 211 ein und es ist die Ladung wiederholt zuzustellen; natürlich unbeschadet der sonstigen rechtlichen Wirksamkeit der bereits gegebenen.

5) Was die Fristen zur Ergreifung von Rechtsmitteln betrifft, so ist kein Zweifel, daß sie hierher gehören.

Indem der Gesetzgeber vorschreibt, daß die in Art. 682 u. 683 bezeichneten Urtheile nicht bloß den Anwälten, sondern auch den Parteien selbst zuzustellen seien, gibt er bestimmt zu erkennen, daß er diese in die Lage versetzen will, persönlich zu handeln. Wenn man daher auch der in den Bemerkungen zu Art. 90 Nr. 4 vertretenen Ansicht beipflichtet, daß in manchen Fällen der Anwalt als solcher Mandat habe, Berufung zu ergreifen, nemlich falls er entweder 1) auch in zweiter Instanz aufzutreten befugt ist, oder 2) es sich um Zwischenurtheile handelt, so ist doch klar, daß das Gesetz ein persönliches Handeln der Partei erwartet und möglich machen will. Uebrigens hat sich der Gesetzgeber auch bestimmt ausgesprochen. Verhdl. zu Art. 661, 720 u. 740 des Entwurfs. Abg. III S. 19, 58, 64, 65.

Nur für den einen Fall, wenn die Berufungsfrist von der Zustellung an den Anwalt läuft, möchte der Geist des Gesetzes eine Ausnahme erheischen. Es ist zu erwägen, 1) daß die wiederholte Zustellung doch nur wiederum an den Anwalt geschehen müßte und 2) daß durch Berufen auf das Absterben, die Heirath ꝛc. irgend einer entfernt wohnenden Partei der Vorwand zur maßlosen Erweiterung der Fristen und zu Restitutionsgesuchen gegeben wäre, welche sicher nicht in der Absicht des Gesetzes lagen. Dasselbe wollte für bloße Prozeßfragen rasche Erledigung.

Was den Einspruch betrifft, so wird geeigneten Orts das Nähere bemerkt werden.

b) Unterbrechung.

6) Die Unterbrechung fraglicher Fristen dürfte man eigentlich eher eine Aufhebung, Vereitelung derselben nennen, denn es beginnt von der neuen Zustellung an wieder eine volle Frist. Der Gesetzgeber geht von der Rechtsvermuthung aus, daß die neu aufgeforderte Person ganz in Unkenntniß sich befinde, und ihr diejenige Frist, auf welche sie nach Maßgabe ihres Wohn- oder Aufenthaltsortes Anspruch hat, vollständig gegönnt werden müsse. Die neue Frist kann daher länger oder kürzer sein, als die frühere.

Ferner ist zu beachten, daß die Unterbrechung mit der Thatsache, an welche sie sich knüpft, von Rechtswegen eintritt, ohne daß eine Anzeige nöthig wäre.

7) Der Fall der Unterbrechung ist gegeben, wenn diejenige Person, welche handeln soll, stirbt oder zu handeln unfähig wird.

Letzteres ist der Fall, wenn sie ihre Rechtsfähigkeit zum Handeln vor Gericht ganz oder theilweise verliert, oder wenn diejenige Eigenschaft, auf Grund deren sie zur Prozeßführung berufen war, aufhört.

Ein theilweiser Verlust der Rechtsfähigkeit liegt z. B. vor, wenn eine Frauensperson heirathet oder Jemand zum Verschwender erklärt wird. Der Ehemann oder Beistand, welche zur Mitvertretung berufen sind, müssen durch eine ihnen zu machende Zustellung in Verzug gesetzt werden.

Ein bloßer Verlust der Eigenschaft zur Vertretung liegt vor, wenn ein Vormund, Curator entsetzt wird. Auf Wechsel der Mitglieder eines Collegiums, z. B. eines Gemeinderaths, dürfte die bezügliche Vorschrift keine Anwendung finden.

8) Besteht die Aenderung darin, daß eine Person, welche bereits im Prozesse ist, ihre volle Rechtsfähigkeit wieder erlangt, daß z. B. eine Ehefrau Wittwe wird, ein Haussohn aus der väterlichen Gewalt tritt, so kann dies selbstverständlich keinen Grund der Unterbrechung bilden, mag auch der Wortlaut des Gesetzes Fälle dieser Art nicht ausscheiden. Ueberhaupt findet fragliche Vorschrift keine Anwendung, wenn eine Person, welcher die Zustellung bereits gemacht wurde, auch nach der eingetretenen Aenderung zur vollen Vertretung befugt ist.

Zu erwähnen ist schließlich, daß Art. 211, abweichend von Art. 491 Ziff. 3 den Fall, wo die Partei selbst handelsfähig wird, nicht ausscheidet; wohl mit Recht, denn was der Vormund wußte, weiß nicht nothwendig auch der volljährig gewordene Mündel.

c) Ladung.

9) Das Gesetz verlangt eine wiederholte, an die nunmehr zum Handeln berufene Person gerichtete Zustellung, nimmt jedoch auf die That-

sache, daß bereits eine Zustellung vorausging, mit Art. 447 Code de proc. in so fern Rücksicht, als es für Ladungen von Erben die Form sehr vereinfacht.

Es darf sich diese Ladung an die Erben im Allgemeinen, ohne nähere Bezeichnung, richten und ist zudem die Art der Zustellung noch besonders geregelt. Diese geschieht nemlich in der letzten Wohnung des Erblassers an Jemand, welcher zu dessen Lebzeiten mit ihm in Familiengemeinschaft lebte oder in dessen Diensten stand (Art. 195). Ist eine solche Person dort nicht zu treffen, so ist die Zustellung nicht dem Ortsvorsteher (Art. 197) zu machen, sondern dem Gerichtsschreiber des Einzelngerichtes, wo der Erblasser seinen Gerichtsstand hatte, d. h. welches diesseits mit Behandlung der Verlassenschaft beauftragt ist.

Was der Gerichtsschreiber zu thun habe, ist nicht gesagt, jedoch versteht sich wohl von selbst, daß er nicht bloß berufen sei, die behändigte Abschrift aufzubewahren und etwa den Interessenten, welche darnach fragen, vorzuzeigen, denn bei dieser Voraussetzung wäre der Anschlag am Gerichtsbrette oder die Zustellung an den Ortsvorsteher vorzuziehen gewesen. Er wird daher verpflichtet sein, dem Landrichter Mittheilung zu machen, damit dieser bei der Verlassenschaftsbehandlung geeignete Fürsorge treffe, oder in der Pfalz unter Umständen die Vertretung von Vakantmassen, von Abwesenden oder Minderjährigen veranlasse.

Was die neue Frist betrifft, so richtet sie sich bloß nach dem letzten Wohnorte des Erblassers, denn der Wohnort der Erben selbst kann nicht in Betracht kommen.

10) Die Bestimmung, daß die Fristen während der für Inventarserrichtung ꝛc. eingeräumten Zeit beruhen, kann diesseits, wo diese Zeit sehr lang ist, wo sie vom Richter bestimmt wird, oder, wie nach preußischem Landrechte, von Kenntniß des Erbanfalles und Entfernung der Erben abhängt, große Verzögerung herbeiführen. Deßhalb ist hinzugefügt, daß, falls für die liegende Erbschaft ein, zur Prozeßführung befugter Curator bestellt sei, die Zustellung an diesen die Frist sofort in Lauf bringe. Es wird dies ein Antrieb sein, auf Bestellung solcher Curatoren hinzuwirken. In der Pfalz, wo jeder Erbe von Rechtswegen an Stelle des Erblassers tritt, entsteht eine liegende Erbschaft erst vom Augenblicke an, wo das Gericht das Vorhandensein einer Vakantmasse ausspricht. Auf Curatoren solcher Vakantmassen, welche immer zur Prozeßführung befugt sind, ist das Gesetz anwendbar.

Art. 212. — **Durch Uebereinkunft der Parteien können Tagfahrten verschoben und Fristen abgekürzt oder verlängert werden, soweit es sich nicht um die von dem Gesetze für die Einlegung von Rechtsmitteln vorgeschriebenen oder um sonstige vom Gesetze als unerstreckbar bezeichnete Fristen handelt.**

Bezüglich der Wiederanberaumung einer verschobenen Tagfahrt finden die allgemeinen Bestimmungen Anwendung.

Gewalthaber bleiben für den Mißbrauch bei Bewilligung von Fristverlängerungen und Vertagungen den Parteien verantwortlich.

Art. 213. — **Durch das Gericht können gesetzliche Fristen nur in den vom Gesetze besonders bestimmten Fällen abgekürzt oder verlängert werden.**

Die Verlegung von Tagfahrten und die Verlängerung richterlich festgesetzter Fristen kann sowohl das Gericht als der beauftragte Richter aus erheblichen Gründen verfügen.

Soll dies auf Antrag geschehen, so ist nöthigenfalls Bescheinigung der Gründe zu verlangen und, wenn wiederholte Verlegung einer Tagfahrt oder wiederholte Fristverlängerung auf Ansuchen derselben Partei stattfinden soll, der Gegner vorher zu hören.

Art. 214. — **Soweit über Handlungen vom Gerichte oder von einem beauftragten Richter Protokolle errichtet werden, ist die Einhaltung der Tagfahrt oder Frist nach dem Inhalte dieser Protokolle zu bemessen.**

Ist bei vereitelten Tagfahrten kein Protokoll zu errichten, so hat der Gerichsschreiber die Anwesenheit der erschienenen Partei vorzumerken und auf Verlangen Bescheinigung darüber auszustellen.

Bei Uebergabe einer Schrift, sowie bei Hinterlegung von Akten ist die Zeit der Uebergabe auf der Schrift oder dem Akte durch den Gerichtsschreiber unter Beifügung des Handzugs anzuführen. Solche Bescheinigungen sind maßgebend bis zum Beweise des Gegentheils.

Die Uebergabe von Schriften und die Hinterlegung von Akten auf der Gerichtsschreiberei kann nur während der Gerichtszeit stattfinden.

G. A. d. K. d. A. I S. 273. 274. 294. 295. II S. 281. 282. IV S. 41. — K. d. R. I S. 348.

1) Das System der Prozeßordnung bezüglich der Verlängerung von Fristen wird Abg. I S. 294 kurz dahin zusammengefaßt:

„Richterliche Fristen können sowohl vom „Richter, als von den Parteien beliebig „verlängert werden.

„Gesetzliche Fristen können, soweit sie nicht „unerstreckbar sind, wohl von den Parteien, „nicht aber vom Richter (besondere Ausnahmen abgerechnet) verlängert werden."

Das Nemliche gilt von Verlegung der Tagfahrten und theilweise von Verkürzung der Fristen.

2) Die den Parteien eingeräumte Befugniß, welche übrigens doch hie und da eine Ausnahme erleidet (z. B. Art. 249), geht sehr weit, fast zu weit, wenn erwogen wird, daß das Interesse der Parteien nicht immer identisch ist mit dem Interesse ihrer Vertreter, und es für Letztere selbst oft erwünscht ist, wenn das Ermessen des Richters ihnen über die Alternative weghilft, entweder ungefällig gegen einen Collegen zu sein und eintretenden Falls Retorsion befürchten zu müssen, oder das Interesse ihrer Klienten außer Acht zu lassen. Der französische Prozeß kennt eine so weit gehende Freiheit nicht, läßt vielmehr, sobald einmal das Gericht selbst mit der Sache befaßt ist, dessen Ermessen entscheiden und droht kleine Strafen für den betreibenden Anwalt, wenn etwa beide Theile sich der Anordnung des Gerichts nicht fügen sollten.

Den Nachtheilen, welche aus der größeren Freiheit für das Interesse der Parteien erwachsen können, wird dadurch zu begegnen sein, daß mit größerer Strenge die Haftbarkeit der Vertreter wegen Mißbrauch in Anspruch genommen wird und dürfte in dieser Beziehung insbesondere die Bestimmung des Art. 110 zu beachten sein.

Es versteht sich von selbst, ist übrigens auch im Gesetze angedeutet, daß die Parteien sich bloß wegen Verlegung einer Tagfahrt einigen, dieselbe aber nicht selbst festsetzen dürfen.

3) Das Gericht kann aus erheblichen Gründen die Verlängerung von Fristen oder die Verlegung von Tagfahrten von Amtswegen anordnen, falls es nach allgemeinen prozessualen Prinzipien veranlaßt ist, eine solche Anordnung zu erlassen, z. B. eine Verhandlung zu vertagen, ein Zeugenverhör zu verlegen. In Fällen, wo es nur auf Grund einer Antragstellung mit der Frage befaßt wird, kann es sich über die Vorschriften des Art. 213 Abs. 3, welcher Bescheinigung bezw. Hören des Gegners verlangt, nicht hinwegsetzen.

Das nemliche Recht, wie das Gericht selbst, hat auch der beauftragte oder ersuchte Richter innerhalb der Gränzen seines Auftrages.

4) Es frägt sich, in welcher Form die Fristverlängerungsgesuche zu erheben und zu erledigen seien?

Nach allgemeinen Grundsätzen muß die Antwort lauten: „Die nemliche Form, in welcher „die Frist gegeben wurde, muß auch maßgebend „sein für die Abänderung, denn es handelt sich „um theilweise Aufhebung einer richterlichen Verfügung." Wäre daher die Frist vom Gerichte in der Sitzung gegeben worden, z. B. bei Anordnen eines Zeugenverhörs (Art. 406), einer Eidesauflage (Art. 460), so müßte auch die Frage der Verlängerung wieder in die Sitzung gebracht werden. Dies stünde zudem in Einklang mit dem Grundsatze, daß Oeffentlichkeit und Mündlichkeit nur beseitigt werden dürfen, wo das Gesetz dies ausdrücklich erlaubt.

Offenbar wäre es nun aber viel sachentsprechender, hier den Weg der einfachen Vorstellung zu wählen, und es frägt sich, ob derselbe der Fassung von Art. 642 gegenüber zulässig sei.

Außer Zweifel möchte sein, daß der Gesetzgeber diesen Weg im Auge gehabt habe. Es wurde dies bestimmt ausgesprochen (Abg. II 211 [v. Weiß]) und möchte es einem bloßen Uebersehen zuzuschreiben sein, daß man in Art. 213 nicht ebenso wie an anderen Orten, dem Verlangen des Art. 642 gemäß, eine ausdrückliche Verfügung aufnahm.

Was nun den ersten Antrag auf Fristverlängerung betrifft, so kann demselben auf einseitiges Ansuchen und bloße Bescheinigung hin, ohne Vernehmung des Gegners, willfahrt werden. Hier erscheinen alle Bedingungen vereint, welche das Gesetz für den Weg der einfachen Vorstellung voraussetzt, und da die Absicht des Gesetzgebers außer Zweifel steht, eine öffentliche Verhandlung aber rein zwecklos wäre, so möchte ich diesen Weg für statthaft erachten.

Was jedoch das wiederholte Gesuch anbelangt, so ist hier vorgeschrieben, daß der Gegner zu hören sei, und da weder in Art. 213 noch in Hauptst. XXV Bestimmungen darüber enthalten sind, wie die Vernehmung des Gegners stattfinden solle, so wird es nöthig sein, den fraglichen Zwischenpunkt nach den gewöhnlichen Regeln in die Sitzung zu bringen.

Diese Lösung stimmt auch überein mit den Gesichtspunkten, welche bei den Verhandlungen über Art. 892 (Abg. III 384 (v. Weiß)) geltend gemacht worden sind.

5) Unerstreckbar sind alle Fristen für Einlegung von Rechtsmitteln (Buch III), also insbesondere auch in den Fällen, wo das Gesetz Beschwerde zuläßt (Art. 738), sowie ferner jene Fristen, welche ausdrücklich vom Gesetze als unerstreckbar erklärt sind. Unter letztere gehört insbesondere die Frist zum Einspruche gegen Versäumungsurtheile (Art. 309, 368), welcher Einspruch übrigens seiner Natur nach ebenfalls ein Rechtsmittel ist.

6) Die Verfügungen in Art. 314 bedürfen näherer Erläuterung nicht. Die Vorschrift, daß der Gerichtschreiber auf die bei ihm eingereichten Akten und Schriften sein praesentatum zu setzen habe, beruht hauptsächlich auf Gründen der Zweckmäßigkeit, denn im neuen Verfahren ist der Zeitpunkt des Einlaufs bei Gericht nur selten von Erheblichkeit. Bei Anträgen, welche in der Sitzung hinterlegt werden, erfüllt der Vorsitzende diese Förmlichkeit (Art. 241 u. 247).

Art. 215. — **Die Nichtvornahme einer Handlung in der dazu anberaumten Tagfahrt oder innerhalb der dazu bestimmten Frist hat, soferne das Gesetz nicht anders bestimmt, den Ausschluß der säumigen Partei mit der vorzunehmenden Handlung zur Folge.**

Die Nachtheile versäumter Tagfahrten und Fristen treten ohne Androhung ein. Sie sind mit Ablauf der festgesetzten Zeit verwirkt, wenn nicht das Gesetz einen auf Verwirklichung des Rechtsnachtheils gerichteten Antrag des Gegners verlangt. Ist letzteres der Fall, so kann die versäumte Handlung, so lange der Antrag nicht gestellt ist, nachgeholt werden.

Kosten- und Schadensersatz aus Versäumnissen ist nur auf Verlangen der Gegenpartei zuzuerkennen. G. A. d. K. d. A. I S. 275. 295. IV S. 41. — K. d. R. I S. 348.

1) Die Prinzipien des französischen Prozesses sind, was die Wirkung der Fristen betrifft, so ziemlich das Widerspiel von denen, welche im diesseitigen Prozesse seither galten.

Dort ist Freiheit der Bewegung Regel und nur ausnahmsweise sind Verlustigungen gedroht, welche dann aber streng und unerbittlich vollzogen werden. Hier war umgekehrt Beschränkung Regel und bewegte sich alles in starren Formen, allein überall waren Hinterthüren geöffnet; man übte Nachsicht und drückte selbst hie und da die Augen zu.

So sind denn im französischen Prozesse alle Fristen im Zweifel nur comminatorisch, d. h. das Gesetz sagt bloß, es sei ein gewisser Zeitraum vergönnt zur Ueberlegung, nach dessen Verlauf aber sei der Gegner befugt, die Sache zu betreiben und eine Verlustigung aussprechen zu lassen. Bis zu diesem Ausspruche kann das Versäumte immer noch nachgeholt werden, vorbehaltlich etwaiger Haftung wegen verschuldeter Kosten. Nur jene Fristen sind präklusiv, bei welchen es das Gesetz besonders bestimmt, z. B. in den Art. 157, 160, 257, 278, 444, 756 Code de proc. Sie sind, wenige Fälle abgerechnet, zugleich unerstrecklich, und selbst eine Restitution kennt das französische Recht nicht. Art. 1029 Code de proc.

Im diesseitigen Prozesse waren umgekehrt alle Fristen, mit Ausnahme einer einzigen, peremtorisch, jedoch waren sie anderseits nichts weniger als unerstrecklich und außerdem wurde Restitution bewilligt.

Unsere Prozeßordnung hat die Grundsätze des diesseitigen Prozesses der Form nach beibehalten, jedoch so viele durch die Natur des neuen Verfahrens bedingte Abweichungen zugelassen, daß man sagen kann, es überwiege materiell der französische Prozeß. Immerhin aber wird der pfälzische Jurist nie außer Acht lassen dürfen, daß das, was früher bei ihm Ausnahme war, jetzt zur Regel geworden ist.

2) Art. 215 stellt als Grundsatz auf, daß, wenn eine Frist oder Tagfahrt zur Vornahme einer Handlung gegeben sei, diese Handlung mit Umlauf der bestimmten Zeit ausgeschlossen werde und dies zwar von Rechtswegen, falls nicht das Gesetz einen Antrag des Gegners verlange. Letzteren Falls verlängert sich die Frist von selbst bis zur Stellung bezw. Zustellung dieses Antrages.

Dieser Grundsatz lautet sehr streng, verliert jedoch schon durch die einzige Verfügung des Art. 251 einen großen, ja den größten Theil seiner Bedeutung. Er erleidet ferner Ausnahmen überall, wo das Gesetz es anders bestimmt, und man hat hierbei nicht gerade nur an ausdrückliche Bestimmungen zu denken, vielmehr wird es genügen, daß der Wille des Gesetzes, es solle die Folge eine andere als der Ausschluß sein, klar ersichtlich sei.

Auch die Verfügung, daß die versäumte Handlung nur so lange nachgeholt werden dürfe, als der Antrag nicht gestellt sei, daß also die Antragstellung ein erworbenes Recht gebe, erleidet in ihrer Anwendung manche Ausnahmen. So ist in Art. 207 Abs. 2 verfügt, daß bei Tagfahrten die Versäumungen erst eintreten am Schlusse der Verhandlung, woraus folgt, daß die Antragstellung für sich hier einen Ausschluß nicht begründe.

3) Bei Fristen, welche zwar präklusiv sind, jedoch erstreckt werden können, muß die Verlängerung begehrt werden, bevor die Frist verlaufen ist.

Das Begehren an sich genügt, den Ausschluß zu verhindern, falls es begründet erscheint, und es ist offenbar nicht nöthig, daß die Verlängerung schon innerhalb der Frist ausgesprochen werde. Vgl. Art. 216 a. E. Wird jedoch das Begehren für grundlos erklärt, so liegt hierin zugleich der Ausspruch, daß die Frist schuldhaft versäumt worden sei, und es tritt also sofort die Wirkung des Ausschlusses ein, wie sie nach der Novelle von 1837 § 33 erst bei Abweisung des zweiten Gesuches zu erfolgen hatte.

Art. 216. — Wiedereinsetzung in den vorigen Stand gegen die Versäumung von Tagfahrten oder Fristen darf, abgesehen von besondern Bestimmungen des Gesetzes, nur dann bewilligt werden, wenn die Partei durch Abwesenheit, schwere Krankheit oder andere unabwendbare Verhinderungen, wohin jedoch bloße Nachlässigkeit der Gewalthaber oder Gerichtsvollzieher nicht zu rechnen ist, in die Lage gesetzt war,] weder die versäumte Handlung vornehmen, noch geeigneten Falls die Verlegung der Tagfahrt oder Verlängerung der Frist nachsuchen zu können.

Art. 217. — Das Gesuch um Wiedereinsetzung ist unter genauer Angabe der Verhinderungsursache binnen einer unerstreckbaren Frist von fünfzehn Tagen von dem Tage an, an welchem die Verhinderungsursache aufgehört hat, mittels Zustellung an die Gegenpartei anzubringen. In derselben Frist ist die versäumte Handlung, soweit dies geschehen kann, vorzunehmen oder der geeignete Antrag auf Bestimmung einer neuen Frist oder Tagfahrt zu stellen.

Dem um Wiedereinsetzung Nachsuchenden liegt bei erhobenem Widerspruche der Beweis der Verhinderung und ihrer Dauer ob.

Durch das Gesuch um Wiedereinsetzung gegen den Ablauf der Berufungsfrist wird die eingeleitete Vollstreckung des Urtheils solange nicht aufgehalten, als nicht vom Obergerichte die Einstellung verfügt wird. G. A. d. K. d. A. I S. 275. 276. 295, 296. II. S. 105. IV S. 41. 97. K. d. R. I S. 348. IV S. 30. 31.

1) Der seitherige Prozeß kannte zwei verschiedene Restitutionen, nemlich die restitutio contra sententiam und die restitutio contra lapsum termini. Statt der ersteren hat unsere Prozeßordnung das Rechtsmittel der Wiederaufnahme des Verfahrens (Hptst. XXIX); die letztere ist Gegenstand der vorstehenden beiden Artikel.

2) Wie bereits erwähnt, ist dem französischen Prozesse die Restitution gegen Fristversäumnisse fremd. Allerdings müßte wohl in Fällen völliger Unmöglichkeit, z. B. der Hemmung jeden Verkehrs, des faktischen Aufhörens der Funktion gewisser Beamten, der Grundsatz gelten: »impossibilium non datur obligatio«; allein Hindernisse solcher Art sind höchst selten, und ich erinnere mich keines Falles, wo auch nur versucht worden wäre, gegen eine eingetretene Präklusion aus diesem Grunde anzukämpfen.

Diesseits ließ das Gesetz Restitution gegen Versäumniß von Fristen oder Ablauf derselben allgemein zu, und wenn auch die Novelle von 1837 den Weg dazu bedeutend erschwerte, so blieben doch die Restitutionsgesuche eine sehr gewöhnliche Erscheinung.

Die neue Prozeßordnung läßt zwar die Restitution zu und zwar etwa unter den nemlichen Voraussetzungen, wie der § 38 der Novelle von 1837, jedoch wird sie thatsächlich viel seltener werden, theils weil durch Art. 251 die Ursachen größtentheils beseitigt sind, theils weil die Anwälte sich jetzt persönlich mit allen ihren Prozessen befassen müssen.

a) Fälle der Wiedereinsetzung i. d. v. St.

3) Wiedereinsetzung in den vorigen Stand soll gewährt werden, wenn die Partei durch Abwesenheit, Krankheit oder andere unabwendbare Verhinderungen in die Lage gesetzt war, weder die Handlung vorzunehmen, noch Fristverlängerung, wo sie statthaft ist, nachzusuchen.

Der Ausdruck „unabwendbar" deutet an, daß die Partei völlig frei von jeder Verschuldung sein müsse. Es kann daher auch die Abwesenheit nur angerufen werden, insofern daraus der Mangel eines Verschuldens hervorgeht, und würde z. B. eine Person, welche nach empfangener Zustellung verreist wäre, ohne für Vornahme der betreffenden Handlung Sorge zu tragen, sich mit ihrer Abwesenheit nicht entschuldigen können.

Eine Verschuldung liegt ohne Zweifel auch vor, wenn die Partei die Handlung durch einen Bevollmächtigten hätte vornehmen lassen können, jedoch dies zu thun versäumt hat. Novelle von 1837 § 35.

4) Tritt das Hinderniß in derjenigen Person ein, welche aus Auftrag der Partei die in Frage stehende Handlung vorzunehmen hatte (beim Anwalte, Gerichtsvollzieher, Prozeß- oder Zustellungsbevollmächtigten), so begründet dies ebensogut einen Grund der Wiedereinsetzung, als wenn es bei der Partei selbst eingetreten wäre; umgekehrt wirkt auch deren Verschuldung gleich der Verschuldung der Partei.

Personen, welche das Gesetz als Stellvertreter oder Mittelspersonen zur Empfangnahme von Zustellungen bezeichnet, können nicht als Gewalthaber der Partei betrachtet werden, und es schließt daher ihre Verschuldung die Wiedereinsetzung nicht aus.

Es muß vielmehr die Thatsache, daß eine Zustellung nicht übermittelt worden ist, daß diejenige Person, welcher sie galt, gar nichts davon erfahren hat, gerade als die stärkste Verhinderungsursache betrachtet werden, welche sich denken läßt, und muß dieselbe immer zur Restitution genügen. Die Restitution erscheint in diesem Falle zugleich als nothwendige Ergänzung der Vorschriften wegen des Einspruchs gegen Versäumungsurtheile, denn während der französische Prozeß, von der Vermuthung ausgehend, es habe Ladung und Urtheilungszustellung den Beklagten nicht erreicht, den Einspruch desselben so lange zuläßt, bis das Urtheil vollständig vollzogen ist (Art. 158 u. 159 Code de proc.), gibt unsere Prozeßordnung nur eine Frist von 15 Tagen. Ohne jene Restitution läge hierin eine höchst ungerechtfertigte Härte.

5) Bei Lösung der Frage, ob im einzelnen Falle ein unabwendbares Hinderniß im Sinne des Gesetzes vorliege, hat natürlich das richterliche Ermessen großen Spielraum. Die Gerichte werden übrigens im Auge behalten, daß der Gesetzgeber die Wiedereinsetzung in den vorigen Stand möglichst einschränken wollte, und daß es ihnen nicht zusteht, Rechte, welche wohl erworben sind, durch übelangebrachte Nachsicht in Frage zu stellen.

b) Verfahren.

6) Falls die Folgen der Versäumung bereits in einem Urtheile Ausdruck gefunden haben und dieses rechtskräftig geworden ist, kann von einer Wiedereinsetzung in den vorigen Stand keine Rede mehr sein; es kann sich dann nur noch fragen, ob die Voraussetzungen zur Wiederaufnahme des Verfahrens gegeben seien. Natürlich ist der Fall nicht hierher zu zählen, wo die Wiedereinsetzung gerade gegen Versäumniß der Frist zur Anfechtung des Urtheils nachgesucht wird, also die Rechtskraft des Urtheiles vom Erfolge des Gesuches abhängt.

Ist zwar ein Urtheil ergangen, dasselbe aber noch nicht rechtskräftig geworden, so muß das Gesuch um Wiedereinsetzung mit den gegen das Urtheil zu ergreifenden Rechtsmitteln verbunden und mittelst derselben geltend gemacht werden.

7) Die Wiedereinsetzung wird in einem an das Gericht sich wendenden Gesuche verlangt, welches dem Gegner zuzustellen ist. Die unerstreckbare Frist zur Zustellung dieses Gesuches beträgt 15 Tage vom Wegfallen der Verhinderungsursache an.

Liegt diese Ursache in Unkenntniß der Thatsache der Zustellung, so läuft die Frist vom Augenblicke der Kenntniß an, sonst vom Zeitpunkte an, wo die Fähigkeit zu handeln oder durch Andere handeln zu lassen, wieder eingetreten ist. Auch hier fällt selbstverständlich dem richterlichen Ermessen eine wichtige Rolle zu, und auch hier ergibt sich für den Richter die Mahnung, nicht allzu nachsichtig zu sein.

In der nemlichen Frist von 15 Tagen ist die Handlung selbst vorzunehmen, oder, sofern dies nicht möglich oder zur Zeit zwecklos wäre, wenigstens Antrag auf neue Fristgestattung oder Tagfahrt zu stellen. Wer daher z. B. Restitution gegen Versäumung der Berufungsfrist anstrebt, muß innerhalb besagter Frist die Berufung ergreifen und mit derselben ein förmliches Gesuch um Wiedereinsetzung in den vorigen Stand verbinden.

8) Das Gesuch richtet sich an dasjenige Gericht, bei welchem zur Zeit der Rechtsstreit anhängig ist. Ist es während des Laufs der Berufungsfrist anzubringen, so richtet es sich an das Appellationsgericht und ist mit demselben die Berufung zu verbinden, welche nöthig ist, um es zur Geltung bringen zu können.

9) Ueber dasselbe ist in öffentlicher Sitzung zu verhandeln und zu entscheiden, in welche dieser Zwischenpunkt sei es für sich allein, sei es zugleich mit der Hauptsache auf gewöhnlichem Wege gebracht wird (Art. 483—485). Werden die im Gesuche angegebenen Verhinderungsgründe nicht widersprochen, so erkennt das Gericht über deren Werth, werden sie widersprochen, so hat

der Gesuchsteller Beweis der Verhinderung selbst, sowie ihrer Dauer zu erbringen. Das Gesetz verlangt also vollen Beweis, bloße Bescheinigung genügt nicht.

Nichtigkeit von Prozeßhandlungen.

Art. 218. — **Prozeßhandlungen, welche einem ausdrücklichen gesetzlichen Verbote zuwiderlaufen, sind nichtig, es sei denn, daß das Gesetz, ohne die Nichtigkeit anzudrohen, einen andern Nachtheil oder eine Strafe auf die Uebertretung gesetzt hat.**

Nichtig sind ferner Handlungen, soweit ihnen die Erfordernisse fehlen, die das Gesetz unter Androhung der Nichtigkeit vorschreibt oder die nach der Natur und dem Zwecke der Handlung zum Wesen derselben gehören.

Mit der nichtigen Handlung unterliegt Alles, was im Zusammenhange mit ihr auf sie gefolgt ist, ebenfalls der Nichtigkeit.

Art. 219. — **Eigene Handlungen darf Niemand als nichtig anfechten, außer soweit die Nichtigkeit auch von Amtswegen zu berücksichtigen ist.**

Die Gegenpartei kann Nichtigkeiten, welche weder von Amtswegen zu berücksichtigen sind, noch kraft besonderer gesetzlicher Bestimmung in jeder Lage der Sache eingewendet werden dürfen, nur bei der nächsten eigenen Prozeßhandlung oder, wenn keine solche dazwischen liegt, bei der nächsten gerichtlichen Verhandlung geltend machen; doch wird die Geltendmachung der Nichtigkeit durch vorläufige Ablehnung des Gerichtsstands oder einer Gerichtsperson und durch das Vorbringen einer der in Art. 185 erwähnten Einreden nicht ausgeschlossen.

Art. 220. — **Wird die Nichtigkeit einer Prozeßhandlung geltend gemacht, so ist darüber vor allem Andern zu entscheiden. Handelt es sich um eine Zustellung und findet der Richter, daß aus der nichtigen Handlung kein Nachtheil erwachsen ist, oder daß ohne Nachtheil für die Gegenpartei eine Berichtigung oder Ergänzung der fehlerhaften Zustellung oder die Wiederholung derselben stattfinden kann, so hat er auf Kosten der fehlenden Partei oder des schuldigen Gerichtsvollziehers das Eine oder Andere zu verfügen oder die sonst zur Abhilfe geeigneten Anordnungen zu treffen.**

G. A. d. K. d. A. I S. 276. 277. 296. 300. IV S. 41. — K. d. R. I S. 348. IV S. 31.

1) Prozeßhandlungen sind Handlungen, welche auf Grund von Prozeßvorschriften vorgenommen werden, um das gerichtliche Verfahren zu betreiben und dessen Erledigung herbeizuführen.

Sie können von der Partei selbst oder denjenigen Personen, welche in deren Namen handeln (Anwälten, Bevollmächtigten, Gerichtsvollziehern), ausgehen, oder endlich vom Gerichte. Jedoch ist anzunehmen, daß das Gesetz hier ebensowenig als der Code de procédure, wenn er von »actes de procédure« spricht (Art. 173, 1030), richterliche Entscheidungen im Auge gehabt habe und zwar schon deßhalb, weil bezüglich der Anfechtung solcher Entscheidungen, insbesondere auf Grund von Nichtigkeiten, gesonderte Vorschriften bestehen.

2) Die Nichtigkeit von Prozeßhandlungen kann auf verschiedenartigen Gründen beruhen; sie kann darin begründet sein, daß Personen gehandelt haben, welchen die Befugniß dazu mangelte, oder darin, daß der Inhalt, oder endlich darin, daß die Form der Handlung den Forderungen des Gesetzes nicht entspricht. Auf alle diese Fälle finden die Vorschriften der Art. 218 bis 220 Anwendung.

3) Diese Vorschriften erstrecken sich ferner auf den Civilprozeß im weitesten Sinne (Commentar Seite 1), also nicht bloß auf das Verfahren von den Gerichten selbst, sondern auch auf das Vollstreckungsverfahren, wie dies mehrfach anerkannt worden ist. S. Vortrag des Referenten v. Neumayr zu Art. 797 u. 946 des Entwurfs und bezügliche Verhandlungen der G. G. A. Abg. III S. 175 u. 276.

a) Fälle der Nichtigkeit.

4) Das Gesetz unterscheidet zwischen Prozeßvorschriften, welche verbieten, und solchen, welche gebieten.

Ist eine Handlung ausdrücklich verboten, so besteht die Rechtsvermuthung, daß an die Zuwiderhandlung gegen das Verbot sich die Nichtigkeit dieser Handlung knüpfen solle, eine Vermuthung, welche jedoch wegfällt, wenn bloß Nachtheile sonstiger Art gedroht sind.

Sind aber bloß Vorschriften darüber gegeben, wie eine Prozeßhandlung beschaffen sein solle, was von derselben verlangt werde so hat die Nichtbeobachtung dieser Vorschriften eine Nichtigkeit nur dann zur Folge, wenn entweder dies ausdrücklich angedroht ist, oder wenn der Mangel nach Zweck und Natur der Prozeßhandlung ein wesentlicher ist.

Dieses System, welches die Würdigung der Verhältnisse im einzelnen Falle dem richterlichen Ermessen überläßt, ist offenbar ein richtiges, wie schon aus dem Umstande hervorgeht, daß in Frankreich Jurisprudenz und Doktrin bestrebt waren, dasselbe den casuistischen Bestimmungen des Code de procédure gegenüber so viel nur immer möglich zur Geltung zu bringen.

Die Ausdrucksweise: „soweit ihnen ꝛc." wurde absichtlich gewählt, um anzudeuten, daß eine Prozeßhandlung auch theilweise nichtig und theilweise giltig sein könne. Abg. I 296.

Die Nichtigkeit einer Handlung hat selbstverständlich auch die Nichtigkeit alles dessen zur Folge, was sich darauf stützt, was ohne dieselbe nicht zu Recht bestehen kann.

b) Geltendmachung der Nichtigkeit.

5) Die Nichtigkeiten sind entweder von Amtswegen zu berücksichtigen, oder nur unter der Voraussetzung, daß sie von den Parteien geltend gemacht werden.

Es gibt eine Reihe von Fällen, in denen das Gesetz ausdrücklich erklärt, daß der Richter gewisse Nichtigkeiten von Amtswegen berücksichtigen solle, insbesondere geschieht dies bezüglich der Mängel in der Befugniß zu handeln (Art. 62, 83, 100). Es wäre jedoch irrig, wollte man hieraus folgern, es müsse immer eine besondere Ermächtigung des Gesetzes vorliegen, um eine Nichtigkeit von Amtswegen berücksichtigen zu dürfen, denn nirgends hat der Gesetzgeber dies ausgesprochen, vielmehr ergibt sich aus Art. 264, daß alle Nichtigkeiten, auf welche nach dem Willen des Gesetzes die Parteien nicht verzichten können, welche auf Gründen der öffentlichen Ordnung beruhen, von Amtswegen zu beachten seien.

Man wird daher im einzelnen Falle auf die innere Natur der übertretenen Vorschrift, auf Grund und Zweck derselben, Rücksicht zu nehmen und zu fragen haben, ob dieselbe nur im Interesse der Parteien gegeben sei, oder ob ihr ein der Willkür der Parteien entzogenes öffentliches Interesse zu Grunde liege. Der Umstand, daß das Gesetz eine Nichtigkeit ausdrücklich androht, ist an sich noch kein Kennzeichen, daß es dieselbe von Amtswegen berücksichtigt haben wolle. Vgl. Art. 201 Nr. 9.

6) Eine von Amtswegen zu beachtende Nichtigkeit besteht so lange fort, bis ein Urtheil ergangen ist, gegen welches das Rechtsmittel der Nichtigkeitsbeschwerde (Art. 788 Ziff. 6), unter Umständen auch dasjenige der Wiederaufnahme des Verfahrens (Art. 761 Ziff. 8), nicht mehr zulässig ist. Unheilbare Nichtigkeiten im Sinne des früheren Prozesses sind der Prozeßordnung unbekannt.

7) Für Nichtigkeiten, welche nicht von Amtswegen zu berücksichtigen sind, schreibt das Gesetz vor:

1) daß Niemand seine eigenen Handlungen anfechten dürfe und
2) daß auch von Seiten des Gegners die Anfechtung nur bei der nächsten eignen Prozeßhandlung oder gerichtlichen Verhandlung erfolgen könne, falls nicht etwa ausdrücklich gestattet sei, eine Nichtigkeit in jeder Lage der Sache einzuwenden.

Was zuerst die eignen Prozeßhandlungen einer Partei betrifft, so sind zu denselben ohne Zweifel auch solche zu zählen, welche von Personen, welche in deren Auftrage handelten, für sie vorgenommen worden sind.

Die weitere Vorschrift, daß die Nichtigkeiten bei der nächsten Prozeßhandlung vorzubringen seien, ist dem Art. 173 Code de proc. entnommen, welcher Artikel nach Stellung und Wortlaut zwar nur das erste Vorverfahren im Auge zu haben scheint, jedoch zufolge einstimmiger Jurisprudenz auf das ganze gerichtliche Verfahren in allen seinen Stadien entsprechende Anwendung gefunden hat. Es ist diese Vorschrift als eine sachgemäße Erweiterung der Prinzipien des Art. 186 zu betrachten, insofern dort nur von einer einzelnen, vom Beklagten im ersten Schriftenwechsel vorzuschützenden Nichtigkeit (der Ladung) die Sprache ist, während hier die Nichtigkeiten von Prozeßhandlungen überhaupt behandelt werden, ohne Rücksicht darauf, wann und von wem sie vorgeschützt werden.

8) Die Worte: „bei der nächsten eignen Prozeßhandlung" sind aus dem Entwurfe in das Gesetzbuch übergegangen, ohne daß sich irgendwo eine Erläuterung oder Andeutung fände, was man darunter zu verstehen habe.

Ließe man den Wortlaut allein entscheiden, so wäre jedes thätige Auftreten im Prozesse gemeint; es müßten also mit jeder Anwaltsbestellung, mit jedem Begehren einer Aktenmittheilung oder Vertagung ꝛc. auch die Anträge auf Nichtigerklärung vorausgängiger Prozeßhandlungen bei Strafe des Ausschlusses verbunden werden.

Offenbar wäre es nun aber ganz sachwidrig, aus Prozeßhandlungen dieser Art einen Verzicht auf Geltendmachung von Nichtigkeiten zu folgern, denn es läßt sich von denselben weder sagen, sie seien bestimmt zur Geltendmachung von Nichtigkeiten, noch auch, sie setzten die Giltigkeit der früheren Prozeßhandlung voraus; im Gegentheile ist ihr Zweck oft gerade darauf gerichtet, Gewißheit zu erlangen, ob Nichtigkeiten bestehen und ob es rathsam sei, dieselben zur Geltung zu bringen.

Es wird daher anzunehmen sein, daß die Absicht des Gesetzes so weit nicht gehe und zwar um so sicherer, als die vorbezeichneten einleitenden Prozeßhandlungen ja nicht einmal die Einreden des Art. 185 auszuschließen im Stande sind, welchen Einreden doch der Vorrang vor den Nichtigkeiten eingeräumt ist! Auch scheinen die Worte „geltend machen" anzudeuten, daß eine Prozeßhandlung in Frage sein müsse, welche sich einigermaßen dazu eigne eine Nichtigkeit zur Geltung zu bringen, was von einer Anwaltbestellung ꝛc. nicht wohl gesagt werden kann.

Frägt man nun, wo die Grenze zu ziehen und welches der wahre Sinn des Gesetzes sei, so sieht man sich veranlaßt, die französische Jurisprudenz zu Rathe zu ziehen, in gleicher Weise, wie man bei Prinzipien, welche dem diesseitigen Prozesse entlehnt sind, sich in der diesseitigen Jurisprudenz umsieht. — Man wird annehmen dürfen, daß der Entwurf jene Grundsätze, welche sich in Auslegung des Art, 173 Code de pr. gebildet haben, anerkennen wollte; daß er das Prinzip nicht ohne seinen Geist einführen wollte.

9) Die fragliche Lehre und namentlich der Stand der Jurisprudenz findet sich ausführlich behandelt bei Chauveau sur Carré quest. 639 bis. Als Prozeßhandlungen, welche einen Verzicht auf Nichtigkeiten von Prozeduraken begründen, sieht man an:

1) solche, deren Bestimmung es ist, zur Geltendmachung von Rechtsbehelfen zu dienen, also vorzugsweise die motivirten Anträge;
2) solche, welche sich an die nichtige Prozeßhandlung anschließen, dieselbe als giltig voraussetzen z. B. die Mitwirkung bei einem Zeugenverhöre gegenüber der Nichtigkeit der Beiladung oder Zeugen-Denunziation.

Man erachtet Prozeßhandlungen für unschädlich, bei welchen die Vermuthung eines Verzichts auf die Nichtigkeii durch Natur und Zweck der Handlung ausgeschlossen ist. Boncenne, théorie de la proc. civ. t. I. No. 146, geht noch weiter, indem er sagt:

»Tous les préliminaires, qui ne sont »point en desaccord absolu avec l'in»tention de proposer une nullité, ne peuvent »pas faire supposer qu'on y ait renoncé.«

So nahm man an, daß eine Anwaltsbestellung, ein Vertagungsbegehren, eine Aufforderung zum Erscheinen in der Sitzung, die Beiladung eines Gewährschaftspflichtigen und die Anzeige davon, keine Handlungen seien, aus welchen Verzichte auf Nichtigkeiten gefolgert werden könnten. Ferner wurde erkannt, daß ein Beklagter, welcher bei Nichterscheinen des Klägers bloß verlangt, es möge die Klage als nicht angebracht erklärt werden (was jetzt gemäß Art. 303 immer geschieht), des Rechtes nicht verlustig werde, später, wenn auf erhobenen Einspruch hin kontradiktorisch verhandelt wird, Nichtigkeiten der Ladung geltend zu machen. So wurde endlich entschieden, daß derjenige, welcher nach Ablauf der, von einem nichtigen Zustellungsakte an, sich berechnenden Frist, Berufung ergreift, nicht gehalten sei, schon mit der Berufung jene Nichtigkeit geltend zu machen, daß es ihm vielmehr freistehe, fraglichen Zustellungsakt, welcher ihm möglicherweise unbekannt ist, ganz zu ignoriren, bis er ihm vom Gegner entgegengehalten wird. Andererseits wurde erkannt, daß, wer einem Zeugenverhöre, sei es persönlich, sei es durch einen Anwalt beiwohne, ohne die Nichtigkeit seiner Beiladung oder der Zeugendenunziation bestimmt anzumelden, des Rechts, dieselbe geltend zu machen, verlustig werde, und zwar auf Grund von Art. 173 Code de proc. — Chauveau sur Carré quest. 1022.

10) Vielleicht genügt man dem Geiste des Gesetzes und zugleich seinem Wortlaute am besten, wenn man folgenden Satz aufstellt:

„Das Gesetz meint jede Prozeßhandlung, „welche nicht ihrer Natur und ihrem Zwecke „nach, die Absicht des Verzichts auf eine Nich„tigkeit ausschließt."

11) Der Entwurf (Art. 199) hatte die Kenntniß der nichtigen Handlung gefordert, die Subkommission ließ jedoch unter dem Titel einer Redaktionsänderung diesen Zusatz weg. Wie der oben (Nr. 9) erwähnte Fall zeigt, kann es allerdings vorkommen, daß der Handelnde von dem nichtigen Akte nichts weiß, oder seine Bedeutung nicht kennt, Beides vielleicht gerade in Folge seiner Mangelhaftigkeit, und es ist wohl kein Zweifel, daß alsdann eine Verlustigung nicht eintrete.

Als weiteres Erforderniß dürfte anzusehen sein, daß derjenigen Partei gegenüber gehandelt worden sein müsse, gegen welche die Nichtigkeit geltend gemacht werden könnte. Wer z. B. einen Gewährschaftspflichtigen oder Streitgenossen beiladet, ist sicher nicht gehalten, diesen Personen gegenüber Nichtigkeiten des Verfahrens geltend zu machen, in welches sie erst eintreten sollen; vielmehr soll gerade die Beiladung den Beigeladenen selbst die Geltendmachung solcher Nichtigkeiten ermöglichen.

12) Endlich ist zu erwähnen, daß es zur Wahrung des Rechts zwar genügt, eine Nichtigkeit bei einem Zeugenverhöre oder sonstigem Akte außer der Sitzung anzumelden, daß jedoch diese Anmeldung wirkungslos ist, wenn die Nichtigkeit nicht bei der Verhandlung in der Sitzung geltend gemacht und Gegenstand der dort gestellten Anträge wird.

c) Entscheidung über Nichtigkeiten.

13) Wenn gesagt ist, es sei über die Nichtigkeit von Prozeßhandlungen vor allem Anderen zu entscheiden, so heißt dies nicht, daß gesondert darüber entschieden werden solle, noch weniger aber, daß es gestattet sei, den Einwand der Nichtigkeit gesondert vorzubringen. Das Gesetz will vielmehr nur verfügen, daß das Gericht die vorgeschützte Nichtigkeit zuerst seiner Prüfung zu unterwerfen habe, daß es also nicht wegen einer Inkompetenzeinrede Beweise auflegen dürfe, ohne vorher die Einrede der Nichtigkeit der Ladung oder sonstiger Prozedurakten gewürdigt zu haben.

In dieser Beziehung wirkt demnach Art. 220 modifizirend auf Art. 186 zurück, insofern er die Reihenfolge, in welcher die dort erwähnten drei Einreden vom Richter zu behandeln seien, bestimmt. Inkompetenzeinrede und Nichtigkeitseinrede kommen demzufolge in das umgekehrte Verhältniß, wie im französischen Prozesse.

Natürlich hat die Verhandlung über die Einreden des Art. 185 auch hier vorzugehen.

14) Die Bestimmung, daß bei Zustellungen der Richter, falls kein Nachtheil erwachsen oder zu besorgen sei, über die Nichtigkeit hinweggehen und Berichtigung anordnen dürfe, ist aus dem Entwurfe ohne weitere Bemerkung in das Gesetz übertragen worden, gleich als verstünde sie sich von selbst und sei nicht daran zu denken, daß sie Schwierigkeiten bereite.

Liest man, daß Berichtigung oder Wiederholung der Zustellung anzuordnen sei, so denkt man sofort an den Fall, wo der Geladene nicht erschienen ist, allein gerade diesen Fall hat der Gesetzgeber zunächst nicht im Auge.

Im Entwurfe (Art. 198) war nur vom Falle die Rede, wo eine Nichtigkeit von der Gegenpartei geltend gemacht wird, woraus gefolgert werden könnte, man habe den Fall des Nichterscheinens sogar ausschließen wollen, denn es kann wohl keinem Zweifel unterliegen, daß auch in diesem letzteren Falle eine Prüfung der Zustellung einzutreten habe. Die Subkommission hat nun zwar fraglichen Beisatz weggelassen, jedoch dabei nur die Absicht einer Redaktionsänderung ausgesprochen, und einen anderen Satz vorgeschoben, welcher gleichfalls von einer Geltendmachung durch die Partei spricht.

Hierzu kommt, daß auch die Entstehung von Art. 198 des Entwurfs für eine Beschränkung auf den Fall des Erscheinens zu sprechen scheint. Es waren nemlich einzelne französische Juristen (Carré, Boncenne) der Meinung, durch das Erscheinen einer Partei sei klar gestellt, daß die Zustellung ihren Zweck erfüllt habe, daß ein Nachtheil nicht erwachsen sei, und es könne im Hinblicke hierauf von Ausspruch der Nichtigkeit Umgang genommen werden. (Chauveau sur C. quest. 739 bis.) Dem wurde entgegnet, daß man nicht das Erscheinen bestrafen dürfe, indem man ihm die Wirkung beilege, Nichtigkeiten der Zustellung zu beseitigen, daß ferner die Zulassung solcher Billigkeitsrücksichten dahin führen würde, die Vorschriften selbst nicht mehr zu beachten. Dieser Ansicht huldigte die Praxis; wahrscheinlich aber ist in jener ersteren Ansicht die Veranlassung von Art. 198 des Entwurfs und somit auch des jetzigen Art. 220 zu suchen.

Trotz dieser gewichtigen Gründe möchte ich annehmen, daß der Gesetzgeber nicht daran dachte, zwischen dem Erscheinen und Nichterscheinen einen Unterschied zu machen, und daß der Entwurf, wenn er von Geltendmachung der Nichtigkeit sprach, nur hervorzuheben gedachte, daß ohne diese Geltendmachung die Nichtigkeit gedeckt sei. Es wäre schlimm, wenn das Erscheinen gestraft und eine Belohnung auf das Ausbleiben gesetzt sein sollte!

Wenn daher die Umstände der Art sind, daß der Richter annehmen kann, durch eine wiederholte richtige Zustellung falle jeder Grund zur Beschwerde weg, so wird er auch im Falle des Nichterscheinens vom Ausspruche der Nichtigkeit Umgang nehmen dürfen. Der betreffenden Partei bleibt es jedoch unbenommen, später darzuthun, daß ihr ein Nachtheil erwachsen sei.

15) Forscht man nun näher nach Sinn und Tragweite vorliegender Bestimmung, so erscheint klar, daß sie nicht bloß unwesentliche, eine Nichtigkeit nicht begründende Mängel im Auge habe, wie dies nach Aeußerungen des kgl. Ministerial-Commissärs (Abg. I 276 und II 5) angenommen werden könnte, sondern sich auch auf Berichtigungen solcher Zustellungen erstrecke, welche nach Art. 218 als nichtig zu erachten sein würden. Die Worte: „daß aus der nichtigen Handlung kein Nachtheil erwachsen ist“ lassen keinen Zweifel.

Hiermit ist nun dem Richter eine große Gewalt in die Hand gegeben, und zwar zu derjenigen, welche ihm bereits Art. 218 Abs. 2 verliehen hat, — eine Gewalt, welche, wenn sie nicht mit großer Umsicht geübt wird, ins Prinziplose führen muß.

16) Schwierigkeiten bietet die Frage, was als Nachtheil zu betrachten sei. Steht nicht die Einhaltung von Präklusivfristen oder der Eintritt sonstiger Rechtsverlustigungen in Frage, sondern handelt es sich nur um Maßregeln, welche kurze Verzögerungen im Gange des Prozesses veranlassen, so wird eine Benachtheiligung der Gegenpartei nicht leicht anzunehmen sein.

Wie ist es nun aber, wenn von der Giltigkeit einer Zustellung (eines Appellaktes, einer Vorladung) die Einhaltung einer Präklusivfrist oder die Verjährung des Klaganspruches abhängt?

Man kann sagen, daß solchen Falls die Gegenpartei ein wohlerworbenes Recht erlangt habe und schon in der Restitution gegen den Ablauf der Frist, welche in einem derartigen Ausspruche läge, eine Benachtheiligung gefunden werden müßte, daß ferner die Androhung mancher Nichtigkeiten z. B. derjenigen des Art. 201, rein gegenstandslos würde, wenn es gestattet wäre, wegen Nichtvorhandenseins eines Nachtheils davon Umgang zu nehmen; denn welcher Nachtheil könnte daraus hergeleitet werden, daß ein Gerichtsvollzieher in Sachen seiner Angehörigen gehandelt hätte, vorausgesetzt, daß sein Akt im Uebrigen vollkommen in Richtigkeit wäre? Man kann beifügen, daß offenbar der Gesetzgeber nur an jene Fälle gedacht habe, wo kein ernstliches Interesse zur Geltendmachung der Nichtigkeit vorliege, wo nichts Weiteres damit zu erreichen sei, als eine Prozeßverzögerung oder als ein Zwang zur Erhebung einer neuen Klage, — kurz, wo nur die Absicht einer Chikane zu Grunde liege.

Dagegen läßt sich aber geltend machen, daß unverkennbar die erste Alternative der fraglichen Bestimmung ihre Anwendung finden müsse, da hier ja das Gesetz nicht davon spreche: „daß durch die Beseitigung der Nichtigkeit ein Nachtheil nicht entstehe", sondern: „daß aus der nichtigen Handlung selbst ein Nachtheil nicht erwachsen sei." Ferner läßt sich geltend machen, daß das Gesetz nicht unterscheide und daß es jenen Nachtheil, welcher in der Nichtbeachtung der Nichtigkeit an und für sich liegt, nicht gemeint haben könne, da ja dieser immer eintreten würde; daß es wohl nur Nachtheile sonstiger Art im Auge gehabt habe z. B. wenn die Gegenpartei in Unkenntniß der Zustellung oder in Irrthum bezüglich dessen, was sie bezweckt, über den Prozeßgegenstand verfügt oder sonstige Rechtshandlungen vorgenommen hätte, welche in Frage gestellt wären, wenn die Zustellung für giltig betrachtet würde.

So sehr ich geneigt wäre, die erstere Ansicht vorzuziehen, so glaube ich doch, daß in der Hauptsache die letztere dem Texte und dem Willen des Gesetzes entspricht.

Pflichtet man dieser Ansicht bei, so wird zu beachten sein, daß der Fall, wo von der Giltigkeit der Zustellung Rechtsverlustigungen bedingt sind, ausschließlich bloß unter die erste Alternative fällt, indem offenbar eine Berichtigung oder Wiederholung der Zustellung ohne Benachtheiligung nicht stattfinden könnte. Hieraus wäre zu folgern, daß die Zustellung so beschaffen sein müsse, um unter den gegebenen Verhältnissen ihrem Zweke vollkommen zu genügen, und daß eine Ergänzung nicht rückwirken dürfe.

17) Die Wiederholung oder Berichtigung der Zustellung möchte beim Erscheinen der betreffenden Partei in der Regel gegenstandslos sein, denn schon die Verhandlung über die Nichtigkeit gibt ja genaue Kenntniß alles dessen, was durch die Zustellung mitgetheilt werden soll. Uebrigens möchte es schon deßhalb geeignet sein, hie und da solche neue Zustellungen anzuordnen, weil hierin zugleich eine sehr sachgemäße Strafe für den nachlässigen Theil liegt.

Sühneversuch.

Art. 221. — **Das Prozeßgericht kann in jeder Lage der Sache einen Sühneversuch vornehmen oder auch die Vornahme eines solchen durch ein Gerichtsmitglied oder Einzelngericht anordnen.**

Auch einem Richter, welcher nur mit Vornahme einzelner Prozeßhandlungen beauftragt ist, steht das Recht zu, Vergleichsverhandlungen vorzunehmen.

Zwang zu persönlichem Erscheinen der Parteien behufs Sühneversuchs findet nicht statt.

Art. 222. — **Das Vermittlungsamt der Gemeinden, Militärbehörden und Universitätsrektorate richtet sich nach den hierüber bestehenden besondern Bestimmungen.**

Vor Anstellung einer Klage bei dem Bezirks- oder Handelsgerichte kann der Kläger, wenn beide Theile selbständig und über den Gegenstand der Klage frei zu verfügen befugt sind, den zu Belangenden unter summarischer Bezeichnung des Klagegegenstands zum Versuche der Sühne auch vor das Einzelngericht vorfordern lassen, vor welchem dieser oder, falls mehrere Personen zusammen zu belangen sind, eine derselben nach Art. 12 — 17 den allgemeinen Gerichtsstand hat.

Für den Kläger besteht keine Verbindlichkeit zur Anrufung eines der in Abs. 1 und 2 bezeichneten Vermittlungsämter, und der zu Belangende unterliegt im Falle des Nichterscheinens keiner Strafe.

G. A. d. K. d. A. I S. 277. 278. 296—298. IV S. 41. K. d. R. I S. 348. 349. IV S. 31.

1) Die Prozeßordnung hat jeden Zwang zum Vermittlungsversuche vor Anstellung der Klage beseitigt, und wohl mit Recht, denn, wie die Erfahrung lehrt, haben solche Versuche wenig Werth.

In der Regel lassen sich Vergleiche, welche ohne Gefahr der Schädigung des materiellen Rechtes, allen Gesichtspunkten Rechnung tragen und zum wahren Vortheile beider Theile gereichen, erst vermitteln, nachdem die Sache gründlich instruirt und verhandelt worden ist. Dann erst befindet sich der Richter in der Lage, richtige Vergleichsvorschläge machen zu können und wissen die Parteien und deren Rathgeber zu ermessen, was ihr wahrer Vortheil sei.

Vergleiche, welche nach völliger Aufklärung des Sachverhaltes zu Stande kommen, befriedigen daher in der Regel beide Theile und stiften Frieden, während übereilte oder halb aufgezwungene Vergleiche meist nur die Erbitterung verschärfen und Schuld tragen, daß in diesem oder in einem anderen Punkte der Streit wieder von Neuem zum Ausbruche kommt.

2) Das Gesetz gibt sowohl dem Richter als dem Kläger das Recht, Vermittlungsversuche zu veranlassen; jedoch in beiden Fällen besteht keine Verpflichtung, der bezüglichen Einladung Folge zu leisten und bei der etwa festgesetzten Tagfahrt zu erscheinen.

Der Richter wird in der Regel seine Vermittlungsversuche gelegentlich vornehmen, wenn die Parteien bei Verhandlung ihrer Sache, bei Ortsbesichtigungen, Zeugenverhören &c. vor ihm erscheinen. Ordnet das Gericht die Vornahme eines Sühneversuches durch ein Gerichtsmitglied oder durch einen Landrichter an, so liegt offenbar eine förmliche Vorladung der Parteien nicht in der Absicht des Gesetzes, vielmehr werden dieselben durch Vermittlung der Anwälte oder in sonst geeigneter Weise einzuladen sein.

3) Die Befugniß, welche dem Kläger gegeben ist, unter gewissen Voraussetzungen den Beklagten vor eines der in Art. 222 Abs. 1 und 2 bezeichneten Vermittlungsämter zu laden, hat nur die Wirkung, daß 1) die betreffende Behörde verpflichtet ist, den Sühneversuch vorzunehmen, und daß 2) die hierdurch verursachten Kosten, insbesondere der Ladung, als Prozeßkosten in Betracht kommen, vorausgesetzt, daß der Kläger selbst erschienen ist.

Aller Wahrscheinlichkeit nach wird jedoch von dieser Befugniß nur selten Gebrauch gemacht werden, um so gewisser, da die Bestimmung des Entwurfs, welche im Einklange mit Art. 57 Code de proc. der Ladung vor's Vermittlungsamt rechtliche Wirkungen gab, beseitigt worden ist, dieselbe also für Unterbrechung der Verjährung, Zinsenlauf &c. ohne besondere Bedeutung ist.

4) Das Vermittlungsamt der Gemeinde besteht nur diesseits und richtet sich jetzt nach Art. 100 und 144 der neuen Gemeindeordnung, welche besagen:

„Die Ausübung des Vermittlungsamtes bei „Rechtsstreitigkeiten unter Gemeindeange„hörigen steht dem Bürgermeister zu: „Derselbe ist jedoch befugt, hiermit ein anderes „Magistratsmitglied oder einen höheren Ge„meindebediensteten (bei Landgemeinden ein „anderes Gemeindeausschußmitglied) zu beauf„tragen. Den Betheiligten ist es unbenommen „Männer ihres Vertrauens zu benennen, welche „zum Sühneversuch beizuziehen sind. Die „Zulassung von Advokaten ist ausgeschlossen."

„Wenn auf gehörige Ladung nicht beide „Parteien erscheinen, so ist der Vermittlungs„versuch als vereitelt zu erachten. Ist der „Kläger nicht erschienen, so verwirkt er eine „Geldbuße von 30 kr. zum Besten der Ge„meindekasse.

„Die Verhandlungen und Ausfertigungen „des Vermittlungsamtes sind tax- und stem„pelfrei."

Unter Gemeindeangehörigen sind alle Personen verstanden, welche ihren Wohnsitz in der Gemeinde haben; das Bürgerrecht wird nicht erfordert.

5) Das Vermittlungsamt der Militärbehörden ist geregelt durch §. 5 des Ges. vom 15. August 1828. Es erstreckt sich jetzt, da ein befreiter Gerichtsstand nicht mehr besteht, auf alle im aktiven Dienste befindlichen Militärpersonen.

Das Vermittlungsamt der Universitätsrektorate für Klagen gegen Studirende ist geregelt durch die Satzungen für die Studierenden an den k. bayer. Universitäten vom 1. Okt. 1849 Tit. III §. 38 lit. g.

6) Erscheint bei einem vom Kläger veranlaßten Vermittlungsversuche dieser selbst nicht, so fallen die verursachten Kosten ihm zur Last. Abg. I. 297 (Barth). Wenn dort weiter bemerkt ist, es sei der Kläger erst nach Zahlung

seiner Geldstrafe von 30 kr. befugt, Klage zu erheben, so möchte dies unrichtig sein, denn, abgesehen davon daß die neue Gemeindeordnung die bezügliche frühere Verfügung nicht wiederholt und selbst früher das Bestehen einer dilatorischen Einrede nicht angenommen wurde (Seuff. Com. Bd. II S. 126 Note 4), so wäre jene Verfügung durch Art. 2 des Einführungsgesetzes aufgehoben.

Vergleich.

Art. 223. — **Ist ein Vergleich oder eine sonstige auf den Rechtsstreit bezügliche Uebereinkunft vor einem Vermittlungsamte, dem Prozeßgerichte oder einem beauftragten Richter zu Stande gekommen, so soll darüber ein Protokoll aufgenommen werden.**

Die vor dem Prozeßgerichte, vor einem beauftragten Richter oder vor dem Vermittlungsamte der Einzelngerichte geschlossene Uebereinkunft, zu welcher die Theile rechtlich befähigt sind, unterliegt der Vollstreckung gleich einem rechtskräftigen Urtheile. Jeder Betheiligte, der den Vollzug der Verhandlung zu beantragen berechtigt ist, kann eine vollstreckbare Ausfertigung verlangen.

Die von den übrigen Vermittlungsämtern in vorgeschriebener Form errichteten Protokolle haben die Wirksamkeit öffentlicher Urkunden. Durch dieselben werden jedoch in den Fällen, wo das Gesetz Notariatsurkunden verlangt, letztere nicht ersetzt.

G. A. d. K. d. A. I S. 278. 279. 297. 298. III S. 430. 431. IV S. 41.
K. d. R. I S. 350—352. IV S. 31.

1) Ueber Vergleiche, welche vor dem Richter oder vor einem Vermittlungsamte zu Stande kommen, ist Protokoll zu errichten.

Das Nemliche gilt von jeder sonstigen auf den Rechtsstreit bezüglichen, d. h. die ganze oder theilweise Erledigung desselben betreffenden Uebereinkunft, z. B. von Schenkungen, Verzichten, welche eine Partei zu Gunsten einer anderen erklärt. Eine Uebereinkunft, durch welche zu Gunsten von dritten nicht im Prozesse befindlichen Personen über den Prozeßgegenstand verfügt wird, kann nicht hierher gezogen werden und überhaupt ist der Begriff einer auf den Rechtsstreit bezüglichen Uebereinkunft nur im Hinblicke auf den Zweck des Gesetzes und möglichst einschränkend zu bestimmen.

2) Daß die Gerichte hier mit Beurkundung von Verträgen betraut werden, bildet eine Ausnahme von der Regel, welche solche Akte der freiwilligen Gerichtsbarkeit der Geschäftssphäre der Notare zuweist. Der französische Prozeß kannte diese Ausnahme nicht; man hielt es jedoch für zweckmäßig, sie einzuführen, in der Erwägung, daß bloß mündlich abgeschlossene Verträge oft wieder strittig oder rückgängig würden, wenn nicht sofort eine urkundliche Feststellung stattfände.

Für die betreffenden Protokolle sind die Vorschriften der Art. 166—168 zu beobachten.

Es kommt nicht selten vor, daß die Parteien über einzelne Streitpunkte z. B. über den Betrag eines einzelnen Entschädigungspostens, sich in der Sitzung einigen. In solchen Fällen pflegte man seither den Weg der Beurkundung im Urtheile zu wählen, und ich glaube, daß derselbe auch jetzt noch gestattet und vorzuziehen sei. — Die eine Partei erklärt, daß sie ihre Forderung auf eine gewisse Summe beschränke, die andere aber, daß sie die Richtigkeit dieser Forderung zugestehe und Beides sind Erklärungen, wie sie nach Art. 248 sich zur Beurkundung im Urtheile eignen. Die Form der Protokollirung ist bei dieser Beurkundung nicht nöthig, wie denn überhaupt als Grundsatz zu gelten hat, daß überall, wo der Richter im Urtheile selbst irgend eine Thatsache beurkundet, die Form des Urtheils genügt. Es kann sogar der Fall sein, daß in Folge derartiger Beurkundungen der ganze Streitgegenstand beseitigt wird, allein ein eigentlicher Vergleich entsteht hieraus doch nicht, da dem Richter immerhin die Aufgabe bleibt, wegen der Kosten zu entscheiden was Rechtens.

3) Bezüglich der protokollirten Verträge gelten die allgemeinen Grundsätze.

Es kann daher vorkommen, daß nicht alle betheiligten Personen anwesend oder vollständig rechtsfähig sind, indem z. B. die Genehmigung der betreffenden Behörden oder Personen vorbehalten wird oder Einer der Anwesenden sich für den Beitritt eines Abwesenden stark macht. Allerdings ist in solchen Fällen der Vertrag vorerst nicht vollgiltig und namentlich kann die Vollstreckung nur eintreten, wenn die Urkunde jenen Bedingungen genügt, welche für die Vollstreckbarkeit von Urkunden gestellt sind. Gelingt es nicht, die Vervollständigung herbeizuführen, so nimmt eben der Rechtsstreit seinen Fortgang. Uebrigens möchte es in solchen Fällen meist rathsam sein, eine Protokollirung gar nicht vorzunehmen, sondern die Parteien auf den Weg außergerichtlicher Regelung zu verweisen und hierzu geeignete Frist zu setzen.

4) Alle von Richtern in zuständiger Weise abgeschlossenen Vergleiche haben die zivilrechtliche Wirkung, wie sie nach Ger. O. cap. XVII §. 1 Ziff. 12—14 den gerichtlichen Vergleichen und nach Notariatsgesetz Art. 21 notarischen Vergleichen zukommt. Auch sind sie, falls die Bedingungen gegeben erscheinen, in gleicher Weise vollstreckbar wie rechtskräftige Urtheile oder Notariatsakte.

Die am Vermittlungsamte der Gemeinden, Militärbehörden oder Universitätsrektorate aufgenommenen Protokolle haben, falls sie in vorschriftsmäßiger Form errichtet sind, die Wirksamkeit öffentlicher Urkunden d. h. sie bilden Beweis gleich diesen und erzeugen einen rechtsverbindlichen Vertrag im Sinne, wie es das Gerichtsverfassungsgesetz vom 1 Juli 1856 Art. 12 bestimmte, auch ohne daß eine theilweise Erfüllung stattgefunden hat.

Die besonderen zivilrechtlichen Wirkungen gerichtlicher Vergleiche, was Anfechtbarkeit u. dgl. betrifft, können sie jedoch nur dann beanspruchen, wenn ein ganzer oder theilweiser Vollzug, und zwar ein solcher, welcher einigermaßen von Erheblichkeit ist (Bl. f. R. XXX S. 350), hinzugetreten ist. Edel Comm. zum Gesetze vom 1 Juli 1856 S. 114. — Seuffert Comm. Bd. IV S. 241. — Abg. I 298 (Barth).

Vergleiche, welche bloß mündlich vor einem Vermittlungsamte abgeschlossen wurden, können überhaupt nur durch theilweisen Vollzug rechtsverbindlich werden.

Was die Pfalz betrifft, so kennt man dort keinen Unterschied zwischen gerichtlichen und außergerichtlichen Vergleichen und es sind überall die nemlichen civilrechtlichen Grundsätze maßgebend, selbst wenn der Vergleich mündlich abgeschlossen und in dieser Form wirksam ist. Art. 2044 ff. Code civil.

Erscheint der Vergleich als Handelsgeschäft, so ist Art. 317 des Handelsgesetzbuches maßgebend.

5) Aus der Bestimmung, daß die Protokolle der nichtrichterlichen Vermittlungsämter Notariatsurkunden in Fällen, wo solche nöthig sind, also namentlich auch bei Art. 14 des N. G., nicht ersetzen, ist zu folgern, daß umgekehrt die richterlichen Vergleiche den Notariatsurkunden gleichstehen. Es wurde dies auch ausdrücklich anerkannt (Abg. I 297), und mit der Bemerkung begründet, daß solche Vergleiche den Urtheilen gleichstünden, was allerdings nicht wörtlich zu nehmen ist.

6) Es kommt manchmal vor, daß beiderseits ein mündlicher Vergleich behauptet wird, von jedem Theile jedoch in anderer Gestalt und keine derselben im Stande ist, ihren Beweis anders als durch Eideszuschiebung zu erbringen.

Wollte man hier dem Kläger entgegenhalten, es stehe fest, daß die Sache durch Vergleich erledigt sei, und er könne nach seiner eignen Behauptung nur noch auf Erfüllung des Vergleiches klagen, so wäre er sehr schlimm gestellt; sein ursprüngliches Klagrecht hätte er verloren und den Beweis des Vergleichs könnte er nicht erbringen. Seine Aufrichtigkeit und Loyalität, den wahren Sachverhalt anzugeben, statt einfach vom Vergleiche zu schweigen, würden bestraft.

Offenbar darf hier der Kläger, dem Widerspruche des Beklagten gegenüber, vom Vergleiche Umgang nehmen und es dem Letzteren überlassen, auf dem Wege der Einrede seinen Vergleich darzuthun. Jedenfalls unterliegt dies in der Pfalz keinem Anstande.

7) Für die Pfalz ist schließlich zu erwähnen, daß durch Art. 91 des Einführungsgesetzes der Art. 467 Code civ. geändert worden ist, und jetzt bei Vergleichen von Minderjährigen ein vom Bezirksgerichte genehmigter Familienrathsbeschluß genügt.

II. Buch.

Verfahren im ersten Rechtszuge.

Erster Abschnitt.

Ordentliches Verfahren vor den Bezirksgerichten.

VI. Hauptstück.

Verfahren im Allgemeinen.

Einleitung.

1) Der Code de proc. unterscheidet beim Verfahren vor den Bezirksgerichten zwischen gewöhnlichen und summarischen Sachen (matières ordinaires et matières sommaires). Für Erstere bestimmt er einen Schriftenwechsel in der Form von Bittschriften (requêtes); für letztere gibt er gar kein Vorverfahren (Art. 405). Durch Dekret vom 30 März 1808 Art. 33 und 70 wurde jedoch später bei allen Sachen die Zustellung von Anträgen mit Gründen (conclusions motivées) mindestens 3 Tage vor der Sitzung vorgeschrieben.

Weitere Unterschiede bestehen bezüglich des Zeugenbeweises, indem bei gewöhnlichen Sachen die Zeugen von einem beauftragten Richter, bei summarischen Sachen in der Sitzung verhört werden; ferner darin, daß Letztere auch in den Ferien vorgebracht werden dürfen und eine einfachere Taxe für sie gegeben ist.

Außerdem gestattet der Code de proc. (Art. 93—115 für besonders verwickelte Prozesse ein rein schriftliches Verfahren mit mündlichen Vorträgen.

2) Unser Entwurf hatte die Unterscheidung zwischen gewöhnlichem und beschleunigtem Verfahren beibehalten, und in Art. 230 eine Reihe von Rechtsstreiten bezeichnet, in welchen das letztere stattfinden sollte.

Die Gesetzgebungsausschüsse fanden es jedoch geeignet, diese Unterscheidung zu beseitigen und ein einheitliches Verfahren zu schaffen, welches sich im Wesen das summarische Verfahren des französischen Prozesses zum Muster genommen hat.

Meiner Meinung nach war dies ein glücklicher Gedanke.

3) Die Eintheilung der Sachen in ordinäre und summarische hat auch im französischen Prozesse wenig praktischen Werth. Die requêtes und die conclusions motivées weichen nur in Form und Fristenbestimmung unbedeutend von einander ab; in der Praxis verschwand der Unterschied ganz und man pflegt nur motivirte Anträge zu wechseln.

Da es nun ferner keine Nichtigkeit begründet, wenn eine summarische Sache ordinär behandelt wird, und da jede ordinäre Sache dadurch, daß man sie für dringlich erklärt, zur summarischen gemacht werden kann (Art. 404 Code de proc.), so hat die ganze Unterscheidung wenig innere Berechtigung; sie stört mehr, als sie nützt, und gibt namentlich bei der Taxe zu vielen Streitfragen Anlaß.

Es ist immer ein Uebelstand, wenn vielerlei Verfahren bestehen, weil es verwirrt und eine Reihe besonderer Streitfragen erzeugt; für unsere Prozeßordnung lag aber um so weniger Grund zu solcher Vervielfältigung vor, als das gewöhnliche Verfahren so schmiegsam und elastisch ist, daß allen Bedürfnissen des Falles, sowohl was Gründlichkeit, als was Raschheit betrifft, volle Rechnung getragen werden kann.

Namentlich ist nach meinen Erfahrungen nicht zu besorgen, daß bei Prozessen, welche ein umfangreiches Material bieten, oder in welchen eine Menge verschiedenartiger Ansprüche und Anträge sich kreuzen und stoßen, Verwirrung entstehen möge, welche die mündliche Verhandlung nicht im Stande wäre zu bewältigen. — Gerade die mündliche Verhandlung führt weit leichter, sicherer und schneller zur Klarheit, vorausgesetzt, daß die Anwälte ihr Faktum im Kopfe und die Richter die Augen offen haben. Der beste Beweis liegt in der Thatsache, daß das schriftliche Verfahren meines Wissens in der Pfalz noch nie zur Anwendung gekommen ist.

Verfahren vor der Sitzung.

Art. 224. — **Die Klage wird dadurch erhoben, daß der Kläger die Klageschrift dem Beklagten zustellen läßt.**

Art. 225. — **Die Klageschrift muß von dem zur Vertretung des Klägers bestellten Anwalte gefertigt sein. Sie soll unter genauer Bezeichnung des Streitgegenstands eine gedrängte aber vollständige und deutliche Darstellung der den Klaganspruch begründenden Thatsachen, den Rechtsgrund, aus welchem der Anspruch abgeleitet wird, und ein bestimmtes Gesuch in der Hauptsache sowohl als in den Nebenpunkten enthalten.**

G. A. d. K. d. A. II S. 4—6. 114. 115. 450. IV S. 69. 75.
K. d. R. II S. 8—21. IV S. 34.

1) Wer einen Rechtsstreit beginnen will, muß sich vor Allem fragen, ob er berechtigt sei, klagend aufzutreten.

Diese Frage ist zwar eine civilrechtliche, allein sie hängt so innig mit dem Prozesse zusammen, daß sie nicht umgangen werden kann, wie denn der Gesetzgeber selbst in vielfacher Beziehung z. B. in den Art. 569, 570, 579, 585, 630, 1217 sich mit ihrer Lösung beschäftigt hat.

a) Wer kann klagen?

2) Der Besitz eines Rechtes, welches unter dem Schutze der Gerichte steht, gibt an und für sich noch kein Recht zu klagen, selbst nicht, wenn das Recht bestritten wird.

Nur wenn eine ernstliche Störung oder Kränkung des Rechtes stattgefunden hat, ist es der Regel nach gestattet, die Gerichte um Schutz und Hilfe anzugehen. Es muß actio nata sein; es muß ein interêt né et actuel vorliegen.

Die Voraussetzungen sind verschieden, je nachdem es sich um dingliche oder um persönliche Klagen handelt.

3) Bei einer dinglichen Klage ist das Hauptbegehren auf Anerkennung des dinglichen Rechtes gerichtet und hieran schließen sich die Ansprüche auf gewisse Leistungen, auf Besitzeinräumung, Schadenersatz ꝛc. an.

Soll die Klage auf Anerkennung eines dinglichen Rechtes gegeben sein, so muß dasselbe im Ernste und thatsächlich strittig gemacht sein; es muß sich Jemand ein Recht anmaßen, welches das Recht des Klägers aufheben oder beschränken würde und diese Anmaßung muß durch Handlungen sich geäußert haben. Der richtige Beklagte ist nur derjenige, welcher das entgegenstehende Recht für sich in Anspruch nimmt.

Eine Anmaßung ohne Handlungen, d. h. eine Berühmung in Schrift oder Rede wird zwar von manchen französischen Juristen, gewissermaßen zum Ersatze der Provokationsklage, als trouble de droit, zur Begründung dinglicher Klagen zugelassen, allein jetzt, wo für sie ein eigener Rechtsweg gegeben ist, dürfte sie allein nicht mehr genügen. Ebensowenig genügen anderseits Handlungen ohne Anmaßung. Wer aus Bequemlichkeit über ein fremdes Stück Land geht, wer aus Muthwille oder Bosheit fremdes Eigenthum beschädigt, gibt keinen Anlaß zu einer dinglichen Klage.

Natürlich können auch rechtswidrige Handlungen allein schon sich als Rechtsanmaßungen charakterisiren und im Zweifel werden sie sogar als solche gelten dürfen. Auch das Bestehenlassen eines gefahrdrohenden oder beschädigenden Zustandes kann als Rechtsanmaßung betrachtet werden und eine dingliche Klage auf Anerkennung der Rechtswidrigkeit jenes Zustandes und dessen Beseitigung begründen.

Handelt es sich um Reallasten (Grundrenten, Baulast ꝛc.), so begründet die Weigerung, eine fällige Leistung zu erfüllen, die Rechtsstörung und somit das Recht, die dingliche Klage zu erheben. — Vgl. übrigens Seuff. Archiv. Bd. XV Nr. 80 Note 1.

4) Bei einer persönlichen Klage ist das Hauptbegehren auf Verurtheilung zu einer Leistung gerichtet und das Begehren auf Anerkennung des zu Grunde liegenden Rechtsverhältnisses bildet nur eine Vorfrage oder schließt sich jenem Hauptbegehren an.

Soll Klage auf Verurtheilung zu einer persönlichen Leistung gegeben sein, so muß der Beklagte mit dieser Leistung im Verzuge sein (dieses Wort im weitesten Sinne genommen) und die freiwillige Erfüllung verweigern.

Uebrigens ist Weigerung anzunehmen, wenn der Schuldner trotz der Fälligkeit der Leistung dieselbe nicht erfüllt oder den Gläubiger in Verzug des Empfanges versetzt hat. — Jedenfalls wird aus dem Mangel vorgängiger Weigerung kein Einwand hergeleitet werden können, wenn vor Gericht die Verpflichtung zur Leistung in der That bestritten wird. Windscheid Bd. I S. 296 Note 4.

5) Klagen, welche bloß die Anerkennung persönlicher Rechte zum Gegenstande haben, welche z. B. bloß darauf gerichtet sind, daß zukünftige oder bedingte Verpflichtungen festgestellt werden

möchten, daß über die Giltigkeit oder die Auslegung von Verträgen das Gericht ein Urtheil abgebe, sind nicht statthaft, selbst wenn bereits Widerspruch sich bekundet haben sollte; es müßte denn das Gesetz ausdrücklich eine Ausnahme machen.

Als Regel ist dies allgemein anerkannt, jedoch lassen manche Gerichte, insbesondere die obersten Gerichtshöfe von Stuttgart und Dresden Ausnahmen für Fälle zu, wo ein entschiedenes Interesse dargethan werden kann. Vgl. einerseits Seuff. Archiv Bd. VI Nr. 319. VII Nr. 298. VIII Nr. 247. X Nr. 108. XV Nr. 144; andererseits Bd. II Nr. 249. III Nr. 305, 306, 307. IV Nr. 19. Für das französ. Recht s. Dalloz repert. (v. action), Journal du Palais (v. action), Chauveau sur Carré, introduction tit. V chap. II.

Für die strengere Einhaltung der Regel möchte die besondere Erwägung sprechen, daß unsere Prozeßordnung diejenigen Ausnahmen, welche sie nöthig fand, speziell bezeichnet hat. Art. 569, 570, 579, 630, 836, 1217.

6) Anders gestaltet sich die Sachlage, wenn ein Theil derjenigen Leistungen, welche sich aus einem Rechtsverhältnisse ergeben, bereits fällig ist, denn bei dieser Voraussetzung können auch die noch nicht fälligen Leistungen Gegenstand der Aburtheilung werden und zwar nicht bloß indirekt, auf Grund der Entscheidung über einen, Bestand und Tragweite des Rechtsverhältnisses betreffenden Zwischenstreit, sondern, wenn es sich um Feststellung eines fortdauernden Verhältnisses handelt, sogar direkt. So kann mit Einklagung fälliger Alimente zugleich die Feststellung der Alimentationspflicht für die Zukunft begehrt werden. Seuff. Archiv XIV Nr. 5 und 145.

Ueberhaupt sind weniger strenge Anforderungen zu stellen, wenn ein Rechtsstreit doch einmal besteht oder nicht zu umgehen ist; es wird dann die Erwägung Einfluß üben dürfen, daß es zweckmäßig sei, alle konnexen Streitpunkte gleichzeitig und sofort zu bereinigen. In diesem Geiste verfügt z. B. das Gesetz, daß alle Vorfragen und Zwischenfragen, welche ein Rechtsstreit ergibt, in ihrer ganzen Tragweite, mag diese auch unfällige oder ungewisse Verpflichtungen umfassen, entschieden werden; im nemlichen Geiste verbindet das Gesetz die Gewährschaftsklage mit der Hauptklage.

7) Eine Frage ist es, ob der Mangel, welcher darin liegt, daß ein Anspruch zur Zeit seiner Erhebung noch nicht fällig ist (die plus petitio ratione temporis), dadurch gehoben werden könne, daß dieser Anspruch im Laufe des Prozesses und vor Spruch des Urtheiles fällig wird.

Im französischen Prozesse wird dieselbe unbedingt verneint, im deutschen Prozesse jedoch sind die Stimmen getheilt. Manche Gerichte verneinen gleichfalls (Seuff. Archiv Bd. VII Nr. 298); der Gerichtsgebrauch aber ist entschieden für die Bejahung und zwar namentlich in Bayern. Bl. f. R. Bd. I S. 413. IV S. 80. XI S. 341.

So wie die Frage, ob im Augenblicke der Ladung ein Klagrecht bestehe, eine zivilrechtliche ist, so ist die Frage, ob eine unbefugt erhobene Klage durch spätere Ereignisse zulässig werden könne, ohne Zweifel eine Prozeßfrage. Dieselbe ist also nur nach den Grundsätzen und im Geiste des neuen Verfahrens zu entscheiden und dürfte man sich insbesondere auf fr. 16 Dig. (5. 3) nicht mehr berufen.

Meiner Meinung nach ist es das Beste, fest an den Prinzipien zu halten, gemäß deren der Richter, um zu erkennen, ob eine Klage mit Recht oder mit Unrecht erhoben worden sei, nur auf den Zeitpunkt der Klagzustellung zu achten hat. Billigkeitsrücksichten, welche sich nicht auf das Gesetz selbst gründen, schädigen das Recht und setzen an dessen Stelle Gunst und Willkühr. Sie nützen manchmal im Kleinen und Einzelnen, schaden aber immer im Großen und Ganzen, indem sie Rechtsunsicherheit erzeugen und Prozesse provoziren.

8) Eine andere Frage möchte sein, ob es statthaft sei, in Fällen wo der Klagsanspruch eine Versetzung in Verzug voraussetzt, diese mit der Klage zu verbinden, in der Weise nemlich, daß Vorladung für den Fall ergeht, daß der Aufforderung innerhalb der gesteckten Frist nicht entsprochen würde. Es handelt sich hier um Cumulirung zweier Fristen, einer kürzeren zur Erfüllung, einer längeren zum Erscheinen vor Gericht. Die französische Praxis nahm an, daß dieser einfachere, Kosten und Zeit ersparende Weg prinzipiell zulässig sei, und ich finde keinen Grund anderer Ansicht zu sein.

9) Als eine bloß auf Anerkennung gerichtete Klage ist es nicht zu betrachten, wenn Jemand in Fällen, wo es das Gesetz gestattet, auf Verbriefung eines Vertrages oder auf Nichtigerklärung eines solchen klagt. Solchen Klagen liegt die Verpflichtung zu Grunde, das Bestehen oder aber die Nichtigkeit eines Vertrages urkundlich anzuerkennen, und wegen Nichterfüllung dieser Verpflichtung wird geklagt, so daß ein Klagerecht selbst dann bleibt, wenn etwa ein Streit über das Rechtsverhältniß selbst gar nicht besteht. Seuff. Archiv Bd. III Nr. 307. VI Nr. 319.

10) Eine eigene Art von Klagen bilden die Präjudizialklagen des römischen Rechtes, Klagen, welche ebenso wie die dinglichen auf Anerkennung eines Rechtsverhältnisses gerichtet sind und in

den Quellen geradezu als dingliche bezeichnet werden. §. 13 Inst. (4. 6.)

Es sind dies vorzugsweise Klagen auf Anerkennung von Familienverhältnissen, welche gleich den dinglichen nur voraussetzen, daß die Absicht, das Verhältniß zu bestreiten durch rechtswidrige Handlungen an den Tag gelegt wurde, oder sonst ein ernstliches Interesse dafür besteht; jedoch nimmt man an, daß die Präjudizialklagen sich nicht auf Statusfragen beschränken. Windscheid Pand. Bd. I S. 96.

b) Wie ist zu klagen.

11) Die Zustellung einer Klagschrift an den Beklagten (die Vorladung) bildet die nothwendige Grundlage des Prozesses beim bezirksgerichtlichen Verfahren.

Ein freiwilliges Erscheinen, wie es das Gesetz bei Handelsgerichten und Landgerichten zuläßt, ist hier nicht gestattet und es müßte daher das Gericht ein Verfahren zurückweisen, welches sich nicht durch Vorlage einer Ladung legitimiren könnte. Liegt eine Ladung vor, so können allerdings Ordnungswidrigkeiten und Nichtigkeiten derselben geheilt werden.

12) Wie bekannt, gehört in Frankreich die Fertigung der Ladung auch im Anwaltsprozesse zum Dienste des Gerichtsboten. Unsere Prozeßordnung läßt schon hier, vor Beginn des Rechtsstreits, den Anwalt als solchen handelnd auftreten und überträgt demselben die Fertigung der Klagschrift, dem Gerichtsvollzieher aber deren Zustellung.

Diese Lösung bot sich durch die Natur der Verhältnisse von selbst dar. Da nemlich der Kläger einen Anwalt haben muß, so ist nichts natürlicher, als daß er sich schon vor Erhebung der Klage um einen solchen umsehe, sich mit ihm berathe, und durch ihn den Prozeß einleiten lasse. Es leuchtet auch ein, daß derjenige, welcher berufen ist den Prozeß zu führen, am besten zu beurtheilen vermöge, wie er am besten einzuleiten sei, ganz abgesehen davon, daß beim Anwalte größere Rechtskenntniß zu vermuthen ist, als beim Gerichtsvollzieher.

So bildete sich denn in der Pfalz die Uebung von selbst, daß in allen schwierigen Prozessen der Anwalt das Libell zur Ladung entwarf und den Gerichtsboten beauftragte. Dies ist nunmehr zur allgemeinen Vorschrift geworden, eine Neuerung, welche um so sachgemäßer erscheint, als noch weitere Vortheile für die Stellung der Anwälte im Allgemeinen damit verbunden sind, daß sich die Parteien zuerst an sie und nicht zuerst an die Gerichtsvollzieher zu wenden haben.

13) Der Anwalt fertigt die Klagschrift als Anwaltsakt nach Maßgabe der Vorschriften des Art. 165 und gibt dem Gerichtsvollzieher Auftrag zur Zustellung, welche jedoch, da sie nicht von Anwalt zu Anwalt geschieht, nicht auf Betreiben des Anwaltes, sondern auf Betreiben der Partei stattfindet, wie dies durch Aenderung der ursprünglichen Redaktion auch Ausdruck gefunden hat. Vgl. Bemerk. zu Art. 192 Nr. 5.

14) Was den Inhalt der Klagschrift betrifft, so hat der Gesetzgeber eine glückliche Fassung gewählt, welche gerade nicht mehr und nicht weniger sagt, als zu sagen war. Vorschriften, welche in's Einzelne gehen, wie sie der Code de proc. gibt, sind offenbar hier nicht am Platze, besonders, wenn sie, wie dort, Nichtigkeit zur Folge haben; es muß dem Ermessen des Richters überlassen bleiben, ob nach den Bedürfnissen des Falles dem Wesen genügt sei oder nicht.

Die Forderungen, welche das Gesetz an eine vollkommene Klagschrift stellt, betreffen den Streitgegenstand, den Klaggrund, den Rechtsgrund und das Gesuch.

15) Streitgegenstand.

Die Bezeichnung des Streitgegenstandes wird wohl immer entweder zur Klagbegründung oder zum Gesuche gehören, wenn Erstere vollständig und Letzteres bestimmt sein soll. Das Gesetz hat deßhalb eine Fassung gewählt, welche andeutet, daß es zwar wichtig ist, den Streitgegenstand zu bezeichnen, jedoch nicht nöthig, dies gesondert zu thun.

Bei persönlichen Klagen ergibt sich der Streitgegenstand aus der Klagbegründung, denn wer die Entstehung eines persönlichen Anspruchs darlegt, bezeichnet hiemit auch den Streitgegenstand.

Bei dinglichen Klagen ist die genaue Bezeichnung des Streitgegenstandes schon deßhalb unentbehrlich, weil ohne sie das Gesuch unbestimmt bleibt. Das Nächste, was man nemlich von Demjenigen, welcher Anerkennung eines dinglichen Rechts anstrebt, verlangt, ist, daß er angebe, an welcher Sache, unter Umständen auch für welche Sache er sein Recht anerkannt wissen wolle, und es müssen diese Sachen der Art genau gekennzeichnet sein, daß ein Irrthum des Beklagten nicht möglich ist. Wie dies am besten zu geschehen habe, hat der Kläger zu ermessen, welcher hier eher zu viel, als zu wenig thun wird.

Bei gewöhnlichen Grundstücken genügt es, die Markung, die Flurabtheilung, die Plannummer des Katasters und die Art der Benützung (ob Ackerfeld, Wiese, Weinberg, Wald, Oedung) anzugeben. Auch Angabe des Flächeninhalts und der Nebenläger wird meist sachgemäß sein.

Bei Gebäulichkeiten wird es nöthig sein, Bestimmung des Hauptgebäudes und des Zubehörs, Straße und Hausnummer anzugeben.

Handelt es sich um größere geschlossene Complexe von Grundstücken, so genügt in der Regel die ortsübliche Bezeichnung nebst Angabe der Markung.

Bilden nur einzelne Theile von Grundstücken Gegenstand des Rechtsstreites, so sind auch diese soviel möglich zu bezeichnen, namentlich aber wird man bei Servitutstreiten bestrebt sein müssen, die Oertlichkeiten, auf welche sich die Ausübung der Servitut erstrecken soll, kenntlich zu machen.

Uebrigens bringt es die Natur der Sache mit sich, daß in manchen Fällen eine erschöpfende Bezeichnung ohne Beigabe eines Planes nicht möglich ist, und es darf dann füglich der Verhandlung oder der Ortsbesichtigung überlassen bleiben, was an Schärfe der Bezeichnung noch fehlt, zu ergänzen. Bei Grenzstreiten ergibt sich sogar in der Regel erst bei Gelegenheit der Ortsbesichtigung genau, ob und welche Grenztheile streitig seien.

16) Klaggrund.

Die Angabe des Klaggrundes ist ein sehr wesentlicher Theil der Klagschrift, und es können dessen Erfordernisse nicht wohl richtiger und schöner hervorgehoben werden, als wenn gesagt wird, es solle die Darstellung gedrängt und doch vollständig und dabei klar sein.

Da jedes Klagbegehren dahin gerichtet ist, es möge der Richter erkennen, daß dem Kläger zur Zeit ein klagbarer Anspruch gegen den Beklagten zustehe, so muß die Klagschrift alle Thatsachen anführen, welche dazu dienen, das Begehren in diesen Richtungen zu begründen. Es muß also nicht bloß die Entstehung des Rechtes an sich, sondern müssen auch die Sachlegitimation, die Fälligkeit des Anspruches und die sonstigen, die Klagbarkeit begründenden Umstände aus der Klagschrift zu ersehen sein. Ist die Statthaftigkeit der Klage von einem Anerbieten des Klägers abhängig, z. B. Zug um Zug zu erfüllen, so soll auch dieses in der Klagschrift enthalten sein.

Eine genaue in's Einzelne gehende Substantiirung der Thatsachen, wie sie etwa später bei einem Beweiserbieten nöthig ist und wie sie seither der Fassung des Beweisinterlokutes wegen gefordert wurde, verlangt das Gesetz nicht; es will keine weitschweifige, umständliche, sondern eine gedrängte Darstellung. Vgl. Bemerk. zu Art. 154, 155 Nr. 3.

17) Die Unterscheidung, welche die Gerichtsordnung zwischen persönlichen und dinglichen Klagen machte, indem sie bei letzteren die Angabe der causa proxima seu generalis, d. h. die Behauptung, Eigenthümer, Servitutberechtigter zu sein, genügend erklärte, erscheint jetzt beseitigt und ist auch bei dinglichen Klagen die Art der Erwerbung des Rechtes anzugeben.

Die näheren Aufschlüsse darüber, was zur Klagbegründung gehöre, d. h. was der Kläger zu behaupten habe, um im Falle des Nichterscheinens des Zuspruchs seiner Klage sicher zu sein, sind dem einschlägigen Civilrechte zu entnehmen.

In der Regel fällt dasjenige, was zu behaupten, mit dem, was später im Falle des Widerspruchs zu beweisen ist, zusammen, jedoch nicht immer, indem manche zum Klaggrunde gehörigen Thatsachen bis zur Bestreitung als selbstverständlich vorausgesetzt werden, wie denn z. B. es diesseits anerkannt ist, daß bei einem zweiseitigen Vertrage der Kläger die Erfüllung seiner Verpflichtung nicht zu behaupten, jedoch im Falle der Bestreitung zu beweisen habe.

18) Rechtsgrund.

Die Geschichtserzählung wird mit dem Gesuche in Verbindung gesetzt durch Bezeichnen der rechtlichen Grundsätze, vermittelst deren sich das letztere aus dem ersteren herleitet. Hierdurch tritt scharf hervor, ob ein dinglicher oder persönlicher Anspruch erhoben, ob aus einem Vertrage oder aus einer rechtswidrigen Handlung geklagt, ob das Recht oder der Besitz beansprucht werde.

Wenn das Gesetz Angabe des Rechtsgrundes fordert, so ist dies nicht so zu verstehen, als ob auf die technische Bezeichnung der Klage oder gar auf die Anführung der zur Anwendung kommenden gesetzlichen Bestimmungen etwas ankomme. Was Rechtens sei, hat der Richter von Amtswegen zu ermitteln (Art. 264), und die Benennung der Klage hat nach dem Geiste des neuen Verfahrens noch weniger Bedeutung, als nach dem Geiste der Gerichtsordnung, zu welcher Kreitmayer (Cap. IV § 8) bemerkt, der Richter dürfe das, was als depositum verlangt worden, als mutuum zusprechen, weil nicht sowohl in petito als in medio concludendi (d. h. im Rechtsgrunde) gefehlt sei.

Die Angabe des Rechtsgrundes ist daher mehr aus Gründen der Zweckmäßigkeit, als der Nothwendigkeit vorgeschrieben.

19) Gesuch.

Den wichtigsten, unentbehrlichsten und die größte Sorgfalt des Anwaltes beanspruchenden Theil der Klagschrift bildet das Gesuch.

Bezüglich der Fragen, welche Gesuche statthaft und wie dieselben einzurichten seien, sind die einschlägigen Civilgesetze maßgebend.

Aus dem Umstande, daß ein „bestimmtes" Gesuch verlangt ist, darf nicht etwa gefolgert werden, es müsse jedes Gesuch auf eine bestimmte Sache oder Summe gerichtet sein, denn bei Universalklagen könnte dies z. B. nicht gefordert werden. Es soll nur gesagt sein, daß das Gesuch der Natur der Klage entsprechend, möglichst bestimmt sein müsse.

Was insbesondere die Nebenpunkte anbelangt, so ist es oft nicht möglich, jedenfalls nicht sachgemäß, dieselben schon bei der Klagestellung der Summe nach zu bestimmen, z. B. wenn Ersatz von Nutzungen oder von Schaden begehrt wird. Verlangt der Kläger z. B. Erfüllung einer Verpflichtung und für den Fall der Nichterfüllung binnen einer vom Gerichte zu setzenden Frist zugleich Entschädigung, oder verlangt ein Gewährschaftskläger Entschädigung für den Fall der Entwährung, so ist offenbar eine genaue Bezeichnung des Schadens, welcher sich nach den Umständen zur Zeit des Eintritts der Entschädigungspflicht bemißt, gar nicht möglich.

Es genügt in solchen Fällen die Verpflichtung an sich, also bei Nutzungen Sache und Zeit, für welche sie verlangt werden, bei Schadenersatz die denselben veranlassenden Handlungen und Umstände bestimmt zu bezeichnen; die Liquidirung kann später erfolgen. Art. 896 ff. Es wurde dies auch bei den Verhandlungen anerkannt. S. Bemerkungen zu Art. 165 Nr. 7 und Abg. IV S. 73 und 74.

Indem das Gesetz vorschreibt, daß auch in den Nebenpunkten ein bestimmtes Gesuch zu stellen sei, hat es den Standpunkt der Gerichtsordnung (Cap. IV § 7 Ziff. 6), welche dem Richter gestattete, über Nebensachen auch ohne Gesuch zu erkennen, verlassen. Nur bezüglich der Prozeßkosten darf der Richter auch jetzt noch von Amtswegen erkennen (Art. 262). Vgl. Art. 182 Abs. 2.

20) Die Hauptforderung, welche an ein Gesuch zu stellen ist, besteht darin, daß es mit der Geschichtserzählung im Einklange stehe; es muß so beschaffen sein, daß im Falle des Nichterscheinens auf Grund desselben die Verurtheilung ausgesprochen werden kann. Hiemit ist jedoch nicht gesagt, daß nicht später neue Thatsachen nachgetragen werden könnten, um das Gesuch noch besser und in anderer Weise zu begründen. Solche Thatsachen sind vielmehr immer zulässig, selbst in der Berufungsinstanz (Art. 707), vorausgesetzt, daß nicht die Klage selbst in ihrer Grundlage geändert wird.

Hat der Kläger zu wenig, oder etwas Anderes, als er sollte, begehrt (Art. 262), so läßt sich nur durch Klagänderung (Art. 180) oder Klagabstand (Art. 296) abhelfen, so lange diese Wege noch offen stehen; hat er zuviel verlangt, so wird das Mehrbegehren abgewiesen (Art. 263). Die plus petitio re bildet daher keine Prozeßeinrede mehr.

21) Entspricht der Inhalt der Klagschrift den Anforderungen des Art. 225 im Wesentlichen nicht, so kann die Ladung nach Art. 186 Ziff. 2 als ordnungswidrig und nichtig angefochten werden.

Art. 220, welcher bestimmt, daß bei Zustellungen von der Nichtigkeit abgesehen werden dürfe, falls ein Nachtheil nicht vorliege, ist zwar nicht anwendbar, weil er nur von Mängeln der Zustellung selbst, nicht aber der zugestellten Urkunden spricht; allein schon der Art. 218 gibt dem Richter genügenden Spielraum, um allen Umständen Rechnung zu tragen, und wird er, dem Geiste des Verfahrens entsprechend, Erläuterungen in den motivirten Anträgen oder bei der Verhandlung überall zulassen, wo dies ohne Benachtheiligung des Gegners geschehen kann.

Art. 226. — **Mit der Zustellung der Klageschrift an den Beklagten ist die Aufforderung zu verbinden, innerhalb der gesetzlichen Frist aus den am Sitze des Prozeßgerichts wohnenden und zur anwaltschaftlichen Vertretung zugelassenen Advokaten einen Anwalt zu bestellen und durch ihn dem Gegenanwalte von der erfolgten Bestellung Anzeige machen zu lassen.**

Die Frist, in welcher der Beklagte der Aufforderung zu genügen hat (Erscheinungsfrist), beträgt acht Tage vom Tage der Klagestellung.

Die Dauer der Erscheinungsfrist muß unter Berücksichtigung der Bestimmung des Art. 209 in der Zustellungsurkunde angegeben sein.

Art. 227. — **In den Fällen des Art. 79 Abs. 3 wahrt der Beklagte die Erscheinungsfrist durch die dem Gegenanwalte zugestellte Bezeichnung des mit der Prozeßführung beauftragten Fiskals, beziehungsweise durch die Erklärung, daß er als Advokat seine Sache selbst führen wolle.** G. A. d. K. d. A. II S. 4–6. 115. IV S. 69. — K. d. R. II S. 8–21.

1) Die Zustellung der Klagschrift bezeichnet den Beginn des Prozesses; mit ihr wird derselbe anhängig und treten alle Folgen ein, welche das Gesetz an diese Thatsache knüpft. Art. 179,

Sie erfolgt durch den Gerichtsvollzieher nach Maßgabe der allgemeinen Vorschriften über Zustellungen, also gemäß Art. 203 Abs. 1 an jede zu ladende Person besonders. Die nöthigen Abschriften der Klagschrift fertigt nach Art. 203 Abs. 4 der Anwalt.

2) Die Klagschrift enthält (nach Art. 165) die genaue Bezeichnung der Parteien, falls daher der Kläger mehrere sind, hat der Gerichtsvollzieher nach Art. 202 Abs. 4 einfach auf die Klagschrift zu verweisen; was jedoch die zu ladenden Beklagten betrifft, so sind dieselben in dem sie betreffenden Zustellungsakte wiederholt zu bezeichnen, und ist es hiebei Pflicht des Gerichtsvollziehers, zu ermitteln, ob die Bezeichnung der Klagschrift eine richtige sei. Unbedeutende und klare Irrungen wird er in seinem Akte berichtigen, bei wichtigeren aber wird er den Anwalt zum Zwecke einer Verbesserung der Klagschrift benachrichtigen. Es könnte nemlich eine Ladung nicht als ordnungsmäßig gelten, wenn die geladene Person in der Klagschrift nicht bezeichnet wäre.

3) Außer der Zustellung selbst überträgt das Gesetz auch noch die Aufforderung zum Erscheinen und die Bezeichnung der Erscheinungsfrist dem Gerichtsvollzieher, während nach dem Entwurfe die Klagschrift selbst diese Angaben enthalten sollte.

In der Pfalz lautete die Ladung bisher nur dahin, daß der Beklagte aufgefordert wurde, in der bezeichneten Frist durch Anwalt oder mittelst Anwaltsbestellung zu erscheinen, und dies genügte, da Jedermann wußte, daß nur einer der Anwälte am Prozeßgerichte gewählt werden könne, der bestellte Anwalt aber nicht im Zweifel war, was er zu thun hatte. Jetzt ist vorgeschrieben, es solle die Aufforderung ausdrücklich dahin lauten: „aus den am Sitze des Prozeßgerichtes „wohnenden und zur anwaltschaftlichen Vertretung zugelassenen Advokaten einen Anwalt zu „bestellen und durch ihn der Gegenpartei von „der erfolgten Bestellung Anzeige machen zu „lassen,“ und es wird rathsam sein, sich genau an diese Vorschrift zu halten.

4) Von Wichtigkeit ist die Erscheinungsfrist, welche im Zustellungsakte unter Berücksichtigung der durch Art. 209 bestimmten Zusatzfristen zu bezeichnen ist. Es genügt nicht, zu sagen: „inner„halb der nach Art. 209 erweiterten Frist von „acht Tagen,“ vielmehr will das Gesetz offenbar, daß die Zeitdauer der Frist im Ganzen genau angegeben, daß also gesagt werde: „innerhalb acht, zwölf, sechzehn Tagen 2c.“ Im Zweifel ist die längere Frist zu wählen, denn das Zuviel schadet hier nichts, wohl aber das Zuwenig.

5) Ist der Fiskus oder ist ein Anwalt in eigner Sache zu laden, so ist wohl kein Mangel der Ladung darin zu erblicken, wenn nicht ausdrücklich aufmerksam gemacht ist, es dürfe der Erstere auch durch den Fiskal und der Letztere auch selbst erscheinen.

Art. 228. — **Ist für den Beklagten kein Anwalt bestellt worden, so kann der Anwalt des Klägers nach Ablauf der Erscheinungsfrist die Sache für die Sitzung anmelden.**

G. A. d. K. d. A. II S. 21. 26. 27. 104. 110. 112. 115. 450. — K. d. R. II S. 21.

1) Wird innerhalb der Erscheinungsfrist eine Anwaltsbestellung für den Beklagten nicht zugestellt, so darf dieser als nicht erschienen behandelt werden. Persönliches Erscheinen vor Gericht kann die Anwaltsbestellung nie ersetzen, selbst wenn auf kurze Frist unmittelbar in die Sitzung geladen ist; es könnte höchstens Anlaß geben, gemäß Art. 305 die Verhandlung auszusetzen.

2) Die Erscheinungsfrist ist übrigens nicht präclusiv, vielmehr geht aus Art. 250 Abs. 4 hervor, daß noch in der Sitzung und bis zum Ausspruche des Versäumungsurtheiles ein Anwalt für den Beklagten giltig auftreten kann. Die Wirkung dieser Frist besteht daher nur darin, daß nach Ablauf derselben der Kläger befugt ist, die Sache zur Sitzung anzumelden (Art. 235).

Art. 229. — **Ist ein Anwalt für den Beklagten bestellt, so haben sich die Anwälte, soweit das Gesetz nicht anders bestimmt, wechselseitig ihre motivirten Anträge zustellen zu lassen.**

Art. 230. — **Die motivirten Anträge dienen als Grundlage für die Verhandlung.**

Sie haben das bestimmte Gesuch der Partei bezüglich der zu erlassenden Entscheidung und davon gesondert in gedrängter Darstellung die zur Begründung des Gesuchs nach der Sachlage erforderlichen thatsächlichen Anführungen in Verbindung mit den wesentlichen rechtlichen Gesichtspunkten zu enthalten.

Eventuelle Bitten sind dem Gesuche beizufügen, auch ist anzugeben, welche Thatsachen die Partei zu beweisen erbötig ist und welcher Arten von Beweismitteln sie sich dazu bedienen will.

Soweit die Behauptungen und die Rechtsvertheidigung des Klägers in der Klageschrift niedergelegt sind, ist in dessen motivirtem Antrage hierauf lediglich Bezug zu nehmen.

Art. 231. — **Der Anwalt des Beklagten hat seinen motivirten Antrag innerhalb fünfzehn Tagen nach Ablauf der Erscheinungsfrist zustellen zu lassen, der Anwalt des Klägers den seinigen spätestens drei Tage vor der Sitzung, in welcher die Sache zum Aufrufe kommt.**

G. A. d. K. d. A. II S. 6—10. 12. 13. 28. 29. 57—60. 103. 104. 107—111. 115. 450. IV S. 69. 70. K. d. R. II S. 21. 22. IV S. 34.

1) Hat der Beklagte einen Anwalt aufgestellt, so besteht dessen erste Amtshandlung darin, dem Anwalte des Klägers einen Anwaltsakt zustellen zu lassen, in welchem er einfach seine Bestellung anzeigt. (Vgl. Bemerk. zu Art. 165 Nr. 4 a. E.) Mit dieser Zustellung wird die Sache vorerst contradiktorisch, und es beginnt nunmehr zur Vorbereitung der mündlichen Verhandlung eine Art Schriftenwechsel durch Zustellung motivirter Anträge.

a) Inhalt der Anträge.

2) Die motivirten Anträge sollen den Parteien Gelegenheit bieten, ihre Angriffs- und Vertheidigungsmittel vollständig zu entwickeln; sie sollen ein vorläufiges Bild des Kampfes geben, welcher später in der Sitzung ausgestritten wird.

Ihr Zweck bringt es daher mit sich, daß sie dem Wesen nach all' das enthalten, was die im schriftlichen Verfahren gewechselten Schriften enthielten; außerdem aber soll noch aus ihnen zu ersehen sein, welche Thatsachen jede Partei beweisen könne, welche Art von Beweismittel ihr dabei zu Gebot stehen und was sie gegen Beweiserbieten und Beweismittel des Gegners einzuwenden habe.

Das ihnen zugewiesene Material ist daher ein sehr reiches; um so mehr aber müssen die Anwälte im Auge behalten, daß eine „gedrängte Darstellung“ von ihnen verlangt werde und daß den Weitschweifigkeiten der seitherigen Prozeßschriften durch Streichung der Gebühren entgegengetreten werden müßte. Namentlich wären lange Rechtsbetrachtungen nicht am Platze. Rechtliche Erwägungen gehören im Grunde nur in die mündlichen Vorträge und wurden vom Gesetzgeber im Vorverfahren nur deßhalb zugelassen, weil sie oft des Zusammenhangs und der Klarheit wegen nicht zu umgehen sind.

3) Der Antrag des Beklagten hat zuerst die Prozeßeinreden geltend zu machen, sodann auf das thatsächliche Vorbringen des Klägers zu antworten und zugleich die Einreden zum Grunde der Sache vorzuschützen, endlich etwaige Widerklagen zu erheben. Einreden und Widerklagen sind sachgemäß zu begründen.

Schließlich sind die entsprechenden Haupt- und eventuellen Gesuche zu stellen, und zwar in der Gestalt, wie der Beklagte wünscht, daß das Gericht eintretenden Falls erkennen möge.

Beim Geltendmachen von Prozeßeinreden, mögen sie prozeßhindernd sein oder nicht, braucht der Beklagte nicht förmlich zu erklären, daß er die Streiteinlassung verweigere oder daß er sich nur eventuell auf den Streit einlasse, ebensowenig, als jetzt noch die Gerichte erkennen werden, es sei die bedingte Streiteinlassung als unbedingt zu erachten. Es wären dies unnütze Redensarten.

Bei der Antwort auf die thatsächlichen Behauptungen der Klage ist zu beachten, daß das Gesetz einen speziellen Widerspruch im Sinne der Novelle von 1837 nicht verlangt, sondern nur eine eingehende Antwort auf das Vorbringen des Gegners (Art. 164), eine gedrängte Darstellung der thatsächlichen Anführungen (Art. 230). Der Beklagte entspricht dem Willen des Gesetzes, indem er der Geschichtserzählung des Klägers einfach diejenige Darstellung des Sachverhalts entgegengesetzt, welche er für die richtige erklärt. Der ganze erste Theil der seitherigen Prozeßschriften, soweit er lautete: „Widersprochen wird &c.“ ist daher entbehrlich und es werden sich die Anwälte gewöhnen müssen, mit dem zweiten Theile, wo gesagt wurde: „Der Sachverhalt war vielmehr folgender &c.“ zu beginnen. Aus dieser zusammenhängenden Geschichtserzählung ergibt sich schon von selbst, was widersprochen sei, und in der Regel wird auch das Material der Einreden aus derselben hervorgehen.

Da die Parteien dem Gerichte volle Wahrheit schuldig sind (Art. 164), so dürfen sich in den thatsächlichen Behauptungen, soweit davon der Beklagte eigene Kenntniß hat, keine unlösbaren Widersprüche finden. Vgl. übrigens Bemerk. zu Art. 155 Nr. 5 und Art. 164 Nr. 5.

Die verschiedenen Gesuche sind vereinigt am Schlusse des Antrages vorzubringen, selbst die auf die Widerklage bezüglichen nicht ausgenommen. Es ist diese Methode die einzig praktische, welche sofort ein übersichtliches Bild von dem gibt, was die Partei erstrebt. Die Gesuche selbst sind möglichst klar und einfach zu fassen. Es genügt z. B. zu begehren, daß die Klage als unzulässig (zur Zeit) oder unbegründet abgewiesen werde; warum dies geschehen solle, ergibt sich aus den Motiven des Antrags.

4) Was den Antrag des Klägers betrifft, so bildet derselbe die Replik des früheren Verfahrens und gilt bezüglich der Antwort auf Einreden, Zwischenbegehren und Widerklagen das

Nemliche, was soeben bezüglich der Antwort auf die Klage gesagt worden ist. Eine Wiederholung dessen, was schon in der Klagschrift steht, ist durch Art. 230 Abs. 4 untersagt; die hierdurch verursachten Kosten müßten daher als frustratorisch erscheinen.

Bringt der Kläger Repliken vor, so darf natürlich der Beklagte in einem nachträglichen Antrage darauf antworten.

5) Das Gesetz bestimmt, daß die Parteien in den Anträgen schon ihre Beweise zu erbieten und die Art ihrer Beweismittel zu bezeichnen haben.

Es findet diese Bestimmung ihre Erklärung darin, daß schon bei der ersten Verhandlung eine Beweisführung und Beweisprüfung stattfindet, und nur in Fällen, wo das Gericht nicht im Stande ist, sich aus den vorliegenden Urkunden und Vermuthungen volle Ueberzeugung zu verschaffen, Beweise anzuordnen sind; daß ferner die Beweisauflage selbst in der Regel nur nach Maßgabe der besonderen Parteianträge stattfindet und in denselben sofort die Art der Beweismittel zu bezeichnen ist. Das Gesetz will nun schon im Vorverfahren Gelegenheit geben, die Beweisfragen zu erörtern, Beweise als unerheblich, Beweismittel (Zeugen, Eide) als unstatthaft zu bestreiten.

Unter den zu bezeichnenden Beweismitteln sind alle diejenigen zu verstehen, welche das Gesetz als solche zuläßt, also Urkunden, Augenschein, Zeugen, Sachverständige und Eide (Art. 325). Bei Urkunden kommt es allerdings nur ausnahmsweise zu einem Beweiserbieten (Art. 329), da jede Partei verpflichtet ist, alle Urkunden, welche sie im Besitze hat, schon im Vorverfahren mitzutheilen, und diese Mittheilung (Art. 172) selbstverständlich das Beweiserbieten unnöthig macht. Allerdings kann sich jedoch Anlaß zu Beweiserbieten im Falle der Bestreitung der Urkunden ergeben, sei es, um deren Aechtheit darzuthun, sei es, um dieselben wegen Betrugs, Irrthums ꝛc. anzufechten (Art. 373 und 376).

Die Beweiserbieten reihen sich eventuell den Hauptgesuchen an, z. B. indem begehrt wird: „eventuell den Beklagten zum Zeugenbeweise darüber zuzulassen: 1) daß ꝛc.", oder: „zu verfügen, daß sich Sachverständige gutachtlich über folgende Punkte aussprechen, nemlich ꝛc.", oder: „Urkunde zu ertheilen, daß der Beklagte dem Kläger den Eid darüber zuschiebt ꝛc."

Die durch Zeugen zu erweisenden Thatsachen sind genau zu artikuliren und die den Sachverständigen vorzulegenden Fragen oder die Eidessätze genau zu bezeichnen. Eventuelle Eidesanträge werden übrigens in der Regel der Verhandlung vorbehalten.

Beim Antrage auf Augenschein ist es in der Regel nicht nöthig, die Thatsache zu bezeichnen, welche durch denselben erwiesen werden sollen. Er dient zur Aufklärung des Sachverhalts im Allgemeinen und kann deßhalb immer von Amtswegen angeordnet werden (Art. 396).

6) Nach dem klaren Wortlaute des Gesetzes soll zugleich mit der Behauptung der Thatsachen der Beweis über dieselben erboten werden.

Es stimmt dies nicht ganz überein mit der in der Pfalz bestehenden Praxis. Man pflegte nemlich, bevor man Beweise erbot, abzuwarten, ob und wie der Gegner die Thatsachen bestreite, so daß also der Beklagte in der Regel erst dann seine Beweise formulirte, nachdem ihm der Antrag des Klägers zugestellt war, und zwar in einem ergänzenden Antrage. Oft wurden die Beweise sogar erst in der Sitzung erboten.

Offenbar ist es in manchen Fällen nicht sachgemäß, sofort umständliche, die Anträge unmäßig vergrößernde Beweiserbieten zu machen, ehe man weiß, was der Gegner antworten werde. Dieselben erweisen sich häufig als nutzloser Ballast, und selbst im Falle der Bestreitung werden im Hinblicke auf die Art und Weise der gegnerischen Darstellung des Sachverhalts meist Aenderungen und Zusätze nöthig. Anderseits bietet das sofortige Beweiserbieten den Vortheil, daß der Gegner sich auch sofort über die Beweise erklären kann.

Je nach Umständen wird das Eine oder das Andere als das Sachgemäßere erscheinen.

Die Bestimmungen unserer Prozeßordnung stehen meiner Meinung nach nicht im Wege, den praktischen Erwägungen nach jeder Richtung Rechnung zu tragen, und es könnte daher nicht als gesetzwidrig gelten, die Beweiserbieten erst in einem nachträglichen Antrage zu bringen. Allerdings jedoch würde der Gegner die genommenen Anträge im Sinne des Art. 242 als ungenügend bezeichnen können, wenn ein Beweiserbieten überhaupt nicht vorläge, dasselbe vielmehr für die Verhandlung vorbehalten werden wollte.

b) Fristen für die Anträge.

7) Für den Antrag des Beklagten, welcher als erste Aeußerung desselben der wichtigste ist, gibt das Gesetz eine Frist von 15 Tagen, vom Ablaufe der Erscheinungsfrist gerechnet, wobei, wenn mehrere Beklagte mit verschiedenen Fristen geladen sind, Art. 210 Abs. 1 zur Anwendung kommt.

Bezüglich des klägerischen Antrags ist nur bestimmt, daß er mindestens drei Tage vor Hinterlegung der Anträge (Art. 240) zugestellt sein müsse. Das Gleiche gilt bezüglich etwaiger nachträglicher Anträge beider Theile (Art. 242 Abs. 2).

Durch die Bestimmung, daß jede Sache wenigstens 15 Tage lang auf der Wochentabelle stehen müsse (Art. 237 Abs. 5), bevor sie zum Aufrufe gelangen könne, ist hinreichende Zeit gegeben, um diesen Verpflichtungen zu genügen. Wenn nöthig, kann Vertagung bewilligt werden (Art. 242).

8) Die Fristen zur Zustellung der Anträge haben, dem vorbereitenden Charakter des Vorverfahrens entsprechend, nichts Präclusives (Art. 251). Der Ablauf der Frist für den Antrag des Beklagten hat nur zur Folge, daß nach Art. 234 die Sache zur Sitzung angemeldet werden kann. Die Fristen des Art. 242 Abs. 2 können nur Anlaß geben, daß der Gegner die Einlassung in die Verhandlung zur Zeit verweigert.

Ferner sind den Parteien (Art. 251 Abs. 2), unter Umständen auch den Anwälten (Art. 110), die Kosten, welche sie durch Vernachlässigung der bezüglichen Vorschrift verschuldet haben, zur Last zu legen.

c) Allgemeine Bemerkungen.

9) Ueberblickt man die Vorschriften über das Vorverfahren, so fällt auf, daß unter allen Umständen von jeder Partei nur ein einziger Antrag verlangt wird und nicht einmal für Einhaltung der natürlichen Reihenfolge gesorgt ist, indem es z. B. nach Art. 242 Abs. 2 recht gut der Fall sein kann, daß der Kläger, welcher Interesse hat, das Verfahren zu beschleunigen, seinen Antrag vor demjenigen des Beklagten zustellen läßt. Man sollte meinen, es müsse hieraus Unordnung entstehen, und könne der Zweck des Gesetzes, mittelst des Vorverfahrens die Sache nach allen Richtungen vollständig aufzuklären, nicht erreicht werden.

Diese Befürchtung wäre jedoch, wie die Erfahrung zeigt, grundlos, und es zeigt sich auch hier wieder, daß sich in einem gesunden Organismus Vieles von selbst macht, was in einem kranken durch künstliche Mitttel bewirkt werden muß.

Uebrigens ist im Auge zu behalten, daß selbst ein Abweichen von der Regel keine wesentlichen Nachtheile bringt, indem das ganze Vorverfahren ja nur vorbereitend ist und nur auf Gründen der Zweckmäßigkeit, nicht aber der Nothwendigkeit beruht. Es ist zu erwägen, daß im Parteiprozesse oder bei Ladung mit abgekürzter Frist, beide Parteien erst in der Sitzung erfahren, was sie gegenseitig vorzubringen haben, dennoch aber von ihnen verlangt wird, daß sie zur sofortigen Entgegnung gerüstet seien. Dabei ist darauf hinzuweisen, daß Aenderungen und Zusätze zu den Anträgen immer gestattet sind, sowohl bei Hinterlegung der Anträge (Art. 241 Abs. 3 u. 4), als selbst noch bei der Verhandlung (Art. 245 Abs. 2 u. Art. 247).

10) In Erwägung aller dieser Verhältnisse hielt das Gesetz einen Zwang nur in so fern für nöthig, als es vorschreibt:

1) daß jede Partei verpflichtet sei, drei Tage vor der Sitzung, jedenfalls einen motivirten Antrag zuzustellen, welcher Alles zu enthalten habe, was den Umständen nach, d. h. mit Rücksicht auf die zu stellenden Gesuche und auf die vorausgängigen Aeußerungen des Gegners von einem solchen Antrage verlangt werden könne, und

2) daß, falls diese Verpflichtung versäumt ist, dem Gegner das Recht zustehe, die Einlassung in die Verhandlung zu verweigern.

Im Uebrigen überläßt es Alles der Einsicht und dem Pflichtgefühle der Anwälte, welche schon deßhalb sich beeifern werden, zu thun, was sachgemäß und vernünftig ist, weil sie hievon Lob und Anerkennung, vom Gegentheile aber Tadel zu erwarten haben, was Beides schwer wiegt im Lichte der Oeffentlichkeit.

Art. 232. — **Will der Beklagte vorläufig nur eine oder mehrere der in Art. 185 und 186 bezeichneten Einreden vorbringen, so muß er seinen auf diese Einreden beschränkten motivirten Antrag innerhalb acht Tagen nach Ablauf der Erscheinungsfrist zustellen lassen, widrigenfalls er des Rechts, solche Einreden ohne gleichzeitige Einlassung in der Hauptsache vorzubringen, verlustig wird.**

Dem Ermessen des Klägers bleibt in solchen Fällen anheimgegeben, ob er einen motivirten Antrag zustellen lassen will.

G. A. d. K. d. A. II S. 60. 104. 110—112. 116. 117. — K. d. R. II. S. 22.

1) Das Gesetz hat hier nicht die Absicht, an den Vorschriften der Art. 184—186 irgend etwas zu ändern, sondern es will nur das Vorverfahren regeln für Fälle, wo von dem Rechte der gesonderten Austragung bevorzugter Prozeßeinreden, wie es dort verliehen ist, Gebrauch gemacht wird.

Es bleibt daher insbesondere auch der Grundsatz bestehen, daß die Prozeßeinreden des Art. 186 vereinigt vorzubringen und selbst gewöhnliche Prozeßeinreden mit demselben zu verbinden sind. S. Bemerk. zu Art. 186 Nr. 9.

Zwar scheinen die Worte: „auf diese Einreden

beschränkten Antrag“ anzudeuten, es dürften die bevorzugten Einreden nur für sich allein vorgebracht werden; allein schon die späteren Worte: „ohne gleichzeitige Einlassung in die Hauptsache“ lassen erkennen, daß die Absicht nicht vorlag, gewöhnliche Prozeßeinreden auszuschließen. Ursprünglich wollte man in solchem Falle gar keine motivirten Anträge zulassen, entschloß sich aber doch dazu und fügte die fraglichen Worte zu dem Zwecke bei, um Erörterungen über den Grund der Sache auszuschließen und zu sagen, daß die Anträge sich auf die zur gesonderten Entscheidung kommenden Vorfragen zu beschränken haben. Abg. II 112.

2) Durch Zustellung eines auf diese Vorfragen beschränkten Antrages gibt der Beklagte seinen Willen genügend zu erkennen, dieselben zur gesonderten Aburtheilung zu bringen, und es bedarf keiner weiteren Erklärung.

Wenn derselbe nun aber zwar die achttägige Frist gewahrt, jedoch sich gleichzeitig auf die Hauptsache eingelassen hat, verliert er hierdurch das Recht der gesonderten Aburtheilung, oder handelt es sich bloß um Streichung der unnützen Kosten?

Der Wortlaut des Art. 232, welcher die Wahrung des Rechtes ebensowohl an die Beschränkung des Antrages, als an de Einhaltung der achttägigen Frist knüpft, ist für erstere Meinung und, wie ich meine, auch der Geist, denn, sobald einmal die ganze Sache zur Verhandlung reif geworden ist, hat nach Art. 157 nur der Richter zu verfügen, ob einzelne Streitpunkte gesondert zu verhandeln seien oder nicht.

3) Der Beklagte hat die fraglichen Prozeßeinreden in einem Antrage zu begründen und entsprechenden Beweis zu erbieten, dem Kläger jedoch steht es frei, einen motivirten Antrag zuzustellen oder nicht. In vielen Fällen wird es erwünscht sein, auch die Entgegnung des Klägers zu kennen und zwar um so mehr, als über Einreden fraglicher Art höchst summarisch, auf die bei der Verhandlung vorgelegten Urkunden und Bescheinigungen hin, entschieden zu werden pflegt, und der klägerische Antrag dem Beklagten zur Richtschnur dient, ob und welche Beweismittel er beizuschaffen habe.

4) Mit Versäumung der achttägigen Frist ist das Recht auf gesonderte Aburtheilung unbedingt verwirkt. Außerdem sorgt der Gesetzgeber für Beschleunigung dieser Aburtheilung durch die Verfügungen der Art. 237 Abs. 5 und Art. 241 Abs. 7.

Art. 233. — **Will der Beklagte einen Dritten als Gewährschaftsbeklagten in den Streit ziehen oder ohne Gewährschaftsklage eine Streitverkündung vornehmen, so hat er dies innerhalb fünfzehn Tagen nach Ablauf der Erscheinungsfrist, in den Fällen des Art. 185 innerhalb fünfzehn Tagen nach Beseitigung des Grundes der betreffenden Einrede zu bewerkstelligen. Innerhalb der nämlichen Frist hat er dem Anwalte des Klägers unter genauer Bezeichnung der betreffenden Umstände von dem Geschehenen Anzeige zu machen.**

Die Frist für Zustellung des motivirten Antrags des Beklagten beginnt im Falle einer Gewährschaftsklage mit Ablauf der von dem Gewährschaftsbeklagten gestatteten Erscheinungsfrist, im Falle dagegen nur der Streit verkündet wurde, mit Ablauf der Frist für die Streitverkündung.

Macht derjenige, welchem der Streit verkündet wurde, auch seinerseits wieder von der Befugniß des Art. 69 Gebrauch, so finden die Bestimmungen der Abs. 1 und 2 analoge Anwendung.

Ergibt sich erst im weitern Verlaufe des Prozesses Anlaß zur Streitverkündung, beziehungsweise zur Erhebung einer Gewährschaftsklage, so kann die betreffende Partei hiezu erforderlichen Falls in der zur Hinterlegung der Anträge oder zur Verhandlung festgesetzten Sitzung angemessene Frist begehren.

G. A. d. K. d. A. II S. 11—13. 104. 110. 111. 116. 117. 450. IV S. 70. — K. d. R. II S. 23. 24.

a) Frist für die Gewährschaftsklage.

1) Zur Vornahme der Streitverkündung und Erhebung der Gewährschaftsklage (Art. 69) gibt das Gesetz hier dem Beklagten eine bestimmte Frist.

Diese Frist ist nicht präclusiv in dem Sinne, daß nach Ablauf derselben eine Streitverkündung nicht mehr wirksam geschehen könnte, die Verbindung der Gewährschaftsklage mit der Hauptklage nicht mehr statthaft wäre, denn Art. 70 sagt das Gegentheil (s. Bemerk. zu Art. 70 Nr. 5 u. 12). Ihre Versäumung hat vielmehr nur zur Folge, daß 1) der Prozeß durch Rücksichten auf Streitverkündung und Gewährschaftsklage nicht mehr aufgehalten wird, und daß 2) der Beklagte sich auf Erörterung der Frage einlassen muß, ob es dem Gewährschaftspflichtigen noch möglich gewesen sei, seine Angriffs- und Vertheidigungsmittel vollständig zu gebrauchen (Art. 70 Abs. 1).

2) Die Frist beträgt 15 Tage von Ablauf

der Erscheinungsfrist an und erweitert sich nach Maßgabe des Art. 209.

Der Wortlaut dieses Artikels, welcher voraussetzt, daß die Frist zum Handeln in Folge einer Zustellung laufe, paßt in so fern hierher, als die Zustellung der Klagschrift auch den Lauf der Frist für die Streitverkündung bedingt; übrigens wurde die Anwendbarkeit von Art. 209 ausdrücklich anerkannt (Abg. II 11 [Barth]).

Die Erweiterung berechnete sich nach dem Code de proc. mit Rücksicht auf den Wohnort des Beklagten selbst, weil die Frist zur Beiladung dort vom Tage der Ladung lief und ein Handeln der Partei verlangt wurde; im Geiste unserer Prozeßordnung wird sie mit Rücksicht auf die Entfernung zwischen dem Sitze des Prozeßgerichts, wo der zum Handeln verpflichtete Anwalt wohnt, und dem Orte, wo die betreffende Zustellung (bei mehreren die entfernteste) zu machen ist, zu berechnen sein (Abg. II 11 [Barth]).

Es folgt hieraus, daß die Frist zur Streitverkündung nicht immer mit der Frist zur Klagbeantwortung zusammenfällt, wie man beim ersten Anblicke meinen sollte.

3) Innerhalb dieser Frist ist nicht nur die fragliche Handlung selbst vorzunehmen, sondern ist auch davon, daß dies geschehen sei, dem Kläger Anzeige zu machen, und zwar durch Anwaltsakt, welcher dem Anwalte des Klägers zuzustellen ist und eine genaue Bezeichnung der betreffenden Umstände zu enthalten hat.

Was das letztere Erforderniß anbelangt, so wird die Bezeichnung, wenn auch genau, doch kurz zu fassen sein. Da das Gesetz nicht vorschreibt, daß Abschrift der Streitverkündung oder Gewährschaftsklage zuzustellen sei, so setzt es offenbar nur ein Hervorheben der wesentlichen Umstände voraus und erwartet, daß nähere Aufschlüsse auf dem Wege der Aktenmittheilung (Art. 172) erholt werden. Als solche wesentliche Umstände erscheinen: die Bezeichnung der Person des Gewährschaftspflichtigen und des Grundes der Gewährschaftspflicht, sowie Angabe des Datums der Zustellung und der Erscheinungsfrist für den Gewährschaftsbeklagten.

Die Erheblichkeit der beiden letzteren Angaben liegt darin, daß durch dieselben der Kläger erfährt: 1) ob die Frist zur Streitverkündung und Gewährschaftsklage eingehalten worden sei, und 2) wann die Frist zur Zustellung der motivirten Anträge beginne.

Anders ist es im französischen Prozesse, welcher überhaupt von wesentlich verschiedenen Grundsätzen ausgeht. Dort beträgt die Frist zur Garantieklage nur acht Tage und läuft von der Ladung an. Bei dieser Kürze der Frist wird es erklärlich, daß Art. 179 Code de proc. vorerst nur eine einfache Anzeige, d. h. die Mittheilung, daß Auftrag zur Garantieklage gegeben sei, verlangt. Eine ähnliche Anzeige schrieb auch Art. 210 des Entwurfes vor, welcher später eine zweite Anzeige über geschehene Zustellung folgen sollte. Man hielt es jedoch geeignet, nur eine einzige Anzeige zu verlangen, und die Worte des Gesetzes: „von dem Geschehenen Anzeige zu machen" lassen es nicht im Zweifel, daß Nachricht davon zu geben sei, daß und wie die Zustellung wirklich stattgefunden habe. Die Frist, welche vergönnt ist — 23 Tage von der Ladung an, ohne die Zusatzfristen — reicht hierzu vollkommen aus; allerdings darf der Beklagte mit der Zustellung nicht bis zu Ende der Frist warten, sondern muß sie der Art vornehmen, daß ihm der Nachweis darüber zeitig genug zukommt, um die Anzeige zu machen.

4) Ist die Streitverkündung rechtzeitig erfolgt, jedoch die Anzeige davon nicht rechtzeitig oder mangelhaft geschehen, so ist ohne Zweifel der Kläger befugt, die Sache sofort zur Sitzung anzumelden. Es frägt sich aber, ob der Beklagte nicht durch nachträgliche Anzeige, sei es vor, sei es nach der Anmeldung, seine Rechte wahren und nach Art. 242 Vertagung verlangen könne.

Allerdings scheint die strenge Vorschrift des Art. 215 entgegenzustehen, allein dieselbe ist durch Art. 251 für das Vorverfahren aufgehoben und es tritt die Erwägung ein, daß, die Rechtzeitigkeit der Zustellung vorausgesetzt, der Kläger nicht den mindesten Nachtheil hat, daß ferner kein Grund vorliegt, hier strenger zu sein, als bei einer verspäteten Anwaltsbestellung. Ich glaube daher, daß allerdings ein Recht auf Vertagung bestehe, vorbehaltlich der Ueberbürdung der verursachten Mehrkosten; jedenfalls aber würde das Gericht sich veranlaßt finden, die Vertagung zu bewilligen, wie denn die Praxis die gleichzeitige Verhandlung von Haupt- und Gewährschaftsklage, als im Interesse der Sache begründet, möglichst zu begünstigen pflegt.

Es ist hier darauf aufmerksam zu machen, daß es auch bei rechtzeitiger Anzeige leicht vorkommen kann, daß der Kläger in Unkenntniß der Streitverkündung oder Gewährschaftsklage die Sache anmeldet, weil die fragliche Frist sich nach Maßgabe des Art. 209 erweitert, während die Frist zur Klagbeantwortung unveränderlich 15 Tage beträgt.

5) Wird eine der Einreden des Art. 185 vorgeschützt, so beginnt die Frist erst mit Beseitig-

ung des Grundes der Einrede. Diese Beseitigung tritt ein bei der Kostenkaution mit Zustellung des Hinterlegungsscheines, bei der Bedenkzeit des Erben oder der Ehefrau mit Ablauf derselben, endlich im Falle der Ziff. 3 des Art. 185 mit Erfüllung der bezüglichen Verpflichtung.

In letzterem Falle wird der Zeitpunkt, von welchem an die Frist zu laufen beginnt, oft unbestimmt sein, da, abgesehen davon, daß es strittig sein kann, ob völlige Erfüllung, z. B. der Auflage eines Besitzurtheiles, anzunehmen sei, auch nöthig sein möchte, daß die Partei oder vielmehr der zu handeln berufene Anwalt Kenntniß davon habe.

6) Außer dem Falle der Beseitigung des Grundes der Einrede, ist auch noch der weitere Fall ins Auge zu fassen, wo die Einrede bestritten wird und das Gericht sie für grundlos erklärt.

Es wäre wohl nicht dem Willen des Gesetzes entsprechend, wollte man den Beklagten deßhalb, weil er irriger Weise die Einrede für begründet hielt, der gesetzlichen Fristen für die Streitverkündung für verlustig erklären. Da nun in Art. 256 für Fälle, wo erst nach Entscheidung einer Vorfrage die Einlassung in die Hauptsache zu erfolgen hat, die Regelung der Fristen dem Gerichte übertragen ist, so wird das Gericht bei dieser Regelung zugleich die in Aussicht gestellten Streitverkündungen oder Gewährschaftsklagen zu beachten haben.

7) Man könnte fragen, ob fragliche Ausnahmsbestimmung des Art. 233 Abs. 1 nur Anwendung finde, wenn die Einrede Gegenstand gesonderter Aburtheilung sei, oder auch, wenn sich etwa der Beklagte zugleich auf die Hauptsache eingelassen habe? Allerdings wird der Beklagte, welcher im Sinne hat, seinen Rückgriff zu nehmen, so unvorsichtig nicht sein, Letzteres zu thun; allein möglich ist es immerhin.

Wird in diesem Falle die Einrede für begründet erklärt, so fällt entweder die Hauptklage ganz hinweg, oder sie bleibt beruhen bis zur Beseitigung des Grundes der Einrede, und bei letzterer Voraussetzung wird Art. 233 allerdings Anwendung finden.

Wird die Einrede verworfen, so ist das Gericht nicht gehindert, sofort über den Grund der Klage zu erkennen.

8) Offenbar ist es bloß ein Recht, jedoch keine Pflicht des Beklagten, bei Vorhandensein der bezeichneten Einreden die Streitverkündung oder Gewährschaftsklage zu verschieben; es steht ihm also frei, auf Gewährschaft zu laden und später doch solche Einreden vorzuschützen.

Es wäre ebenso unrichtig, in Erhebung der Gewährschaftsklage einen Verzicht auf fragliche Einreden zu erblicken, als zu sagen, daß Kläger jene Klage als verfrüht bekämpfen und deren Kosten als frustratorisch bezeichnen dürfte. Die Anstellung der Hauptklage an und für sich ist genügender Grund zur Klage auf Gewährschaft.

b) Erweiterung der Fristen für die Anträge.

9) Streitverkündung und Gewährschaftsklage haben wesentlichen Einfluß auf die Bestimmung der Fristen zur Zustellung der motivirten Anträge.

Wenn der Beklagte eine Person, gegen welche er im Falle des Unterliegens seinen Rückgriff nehmen will, auf Gewährschaft beiladet oder ihr den Streit verkündet, so erwartet er natürlich von derselben Unterstützung bei Bekämpfung der Klage, insbesondere Mittheilung erheblicher Urkunden und Aufklärungen über den Sachverhalt, bezüglich dessen in der Regel der Gewährschaftspflichtige besser unterrichtet ist, als er selbst. Außerdem liegt für ihn schon deßhalb Veranlassung vor, mit der Antwort auf die Klage zurückzuhalten, bis der Gewährschaftspflichtige sich am Streite betheiligen kann, weil er bei seiner Vertheidigung dessen Wünsche berücksichtigen muß, um sich nicht dem Vorwurfe auszusetzen, daß er den Verlust des Prozesses verschuldet habe.

Hieraus erklärt sich, daß das Gesetz die Frist für den motivirten Antrag des Beklagten im Falle der Streitverkündung erst beginnen läßt vom Zeitpunkte an, wo die zur Vornahme derselben gegebene Frist, und im Falle der Gewährschaftsklage vom Zeitpunkte an, wo die Erscheinungsfrist für den Gewährschaftsbeklagten (und wenn deren mehrere sind, die längste) verstrichen ist.

10) Bei der Gewährschaftsklage war diese Erweiterung der Frist um so selbstverständlicher, als das Gesetz deren gleichzeitige Verhandlung mit der Hauptklage will, also die letztere doch erst zur Verhandlung kommen kann, wenn die erstere auch dazu reif ist.

Was die Streitverkündung betrifft, so setzt das Gesetz voraus, die fünfzehntägige Frist des Art. 233 Abs. 2, mit ihrer etwaigen Erweiterung, sowie in Verbindung mit derjenigen Zeit, welche nöthig ist, um die Sache in die Sitzung zu bringen, werde dem Gewährschaftspflichtigen immer genügen, wenn er als Nebenintervenient sich am Streite zu betheiligen wünsche. In der Regel ist dies richtig, allein nicht immer, namentlich z. B. nicht, wenn die Streitverkündung einem Ausländer oder einer Person ohne bekannten Wohn- und Aufenthaltsort geschehen ist. Es wurde deßhalb schon zu Art. 69 Nr. 5 bemerkt, daß es sachgemäß gewesen wäre, bestimmte, den Erscheinungsfristen ähnliche Fristen für die Streitverkündung zu geben.

In Fällen nun, wo die gewöhnliche Zeit nicht ausreicht, wird es Pflicht des Beklagten sein, dafür zu sorgen, daß dem Gewährschaftspflichtigen genügende Zeit geboten sei. Er wird daher 1) die Streitverkündung so früh als möglich vornehmen, wird 2) soweit es von ihm abhängt, die Sache nicht zu bald, namentlich nicht mit abgekürzter Frist, in die Sitzung bringen, wird endlich 3) falls nöthig, beantragen, daß das Gericht durch Vertagung oder durch geeignete Fixirung der mündlichen Verhandlung Raum gebe für Eintritt des Gewährschaftspflichtigen in den Streit.

c) Untergewährschaftsklagen.

11) Wenn der erste Gewährschaftspflichtige seinerseits wieder seinen Rückgriff nehmen will, so sollen die nemlichen Bestimmungen analoge Anwendung finden.

Der Gewährschaftsbeklagte hat daher eine Frist von 15 Tagen von Ablauf der ihm zustehenden Erscheinungsfrist an, erweitert nach Art. 209, um seine Untergewährschaftsklage anzustellen. Bringt er Einreden des Art. 185 gesondert vor, so ist er gleich dem Hauptbeklagten berechtigt, bis zur Bereinigung dieses zwischen ihm und diesem auszutragenden Streitpunkts, seinen Rückgriff zu verschieben.

Schwieriger macht sich die Analogie für die Streitverkündung, welche überhaupt nirgends recht in das neue Verfahren passen will.

Offenbar soll der Aufgeforderte die nemliche Frist von 15 Tagen haben, wie sie der Auffordernde gehabt hatte. Nun berechnete sich aber diese letztere Frist von Ablauf der Erscheinungsfrist an, während für Denjenigen, welchem bloß der Streit verkündet worden ist, eine Erscheinungsfrist nicht besteht. Hieraus wäre zu folgern, daß sich bei ihm die Frist von Zustellung der Streitverkündung an berechne; allein dies ist nur sachgemäß für die gewöhnlichen Fälle, nicht aber dort, wo das Gesetz eine Fristerweiterung deßhalb gibt, weil es annimmt, es komme die Zustellung nicht vor Ablauf einer gewissen Zeit dem Requisiten zu, z. B. bei Zustellungen an Ausländer. Läßt man z. B. bei Ausländern die Frist von Zustellung der Streitverkündung an laufen, so wird sie meist verstrichen sein, bevor die aufgeforderte Person Kenntniß von der Streitverkündung erhalten hat.

Nichtsdestoweniger wird nichts Anderes übrig bleiben, als in allen Fällen die fragliche Frist von Zustellung der Streitverkündung an laufen zu lassen. Erscheint sie im einzelnen Falle nicht zureichend, so wird eben Vertagung zu bewilligen sein.

12) Eine weitere Frage ist, wie sich die Fristerweiterung bei den weiteren Streitverkündigungen berechne.

Es ist schon zu Art. 69 Nr. 8 bemerkt worden, daß derjenige, welchem der Streit verkündet worden ist, welcher jedoch am Streite sich nicht betheiligen will, nicht verpflichtet sei, bloß zum Zwecke der Zustellung seiner Streitverkündung einen Anwalt aufzustellen, daß es vielmehr genüge, einen Gerichtsvollzieher zu beauftragen. In diesem Falle berechnet sich die Erweiterung offenbar nach dem Wohnorte der streitverkündenden Partei selbst. Wohnt dieselbe im Auslande, so werden jene Fristen analog maßgebend sein, welche für den direkten Verkehr mit dem Auslande durch Verordnung festgesetzt werden.

In der Praxis werden sich übrigens, da die Gerichte überall durch entsprechende Vertagungen (Art. 243), geeigneten Falls durch Bewilligung der Beiladung mit abgekürzter Frist nachhelfen können, viel weniger Schwierigkeiten ergeben, als man vermuthen sollte.

13) Von den weiteren Streitverkündungen und Gewährschaftsklagen muß natürlich innerhalb der Frist jedesmal Anzeige gemacht werden.

Dieselbe erfolgt bei Untergewährschaftsklagen durch Anwaltsakt, welcher sämmtlichen im Rechtsstreite aufgestellten Anwälten zuzustellen ist (Art. 489). Bei Streitverkündungen ist das Gleiche der Fall, wenn der Verkündende durch Anwalt vertreten ist, sonst durch Gerichtsvollzieherakte, welche den betreffenden Anwälten zuzustellen sind.

d) Spätere Gewährschaftsklagen.

14) Der letzte Absatz des Art. 233 spricht von Fällen, wo der Anlaß zur Streitverkündung nicht schon durch die Klage gegeben ist, sondern erst später sich ergibt, was z. B. vorkommt, wenn der klagende Cessionar auf Widerspruch des Beklagten seinen Rückgriff gegen den Cedenten nimmt.

In diesem Falle **kann**, wie das Gesetz sich ausdrückt, die Partei Frist **begehren**. Die Worte: „man kann begehren" bedeuten in der Regel: „man hat das **Recht** zu begehren", welchen Sinn sie z. B. ausgesprochenermaßen in Art. 69 haben, wie denn auch die Worte: »pourront être reprochés« in Art. 283 Code de proc. nicht anders verstanden wurden. Man hätte um so mehr Grund, sich für diese Auslegung zu entscheiden, als die Art. 69 ff. ein Recht zur Beiladung geben. Endlich erscheint es auch recht und billig, den Regreßberechtigten nicht darunter leiden zu lassen, daß der Gegner ihm zu spät Anlaß gegeben, seinen Regreß zu suchen.

Wenn nichtsdestoweniger bei den Verhandlungen (Abg. I 116, 117) erklärt wurde, daß es dem Ermessen des Gerichts anheimgestellt sein solle, ob eine Frist zu bewilligen sei und welche, so ist dies doch nur in dem Sinne aufzufassen, daß das Gericht prüfen dürfe, ob ernstlicher Anlaß zu einem Rückgriffe vorliege und ob nicht bereits genügende Frist für denselben gegeben gewesen und versäumt worden sei. In ihrem gesetzlichen Rechte auf Beiladung darf das Gericht eine Partei nie verkürzen.

e) Allgemeine Bemerkungen.

15) Die Fristen, welche unsere Prozeßordnung in Art. 233 gibt, sind, wie bereits erwähnt, bedeutend länger, als diejenigen des französischen Prozesses, und es kann, wenn, wie dies in Eviktionsfällen nicht selten ist, eine lange Reihe von Gewährschaftspflichtigen in Frage steht, eine unmäßige Verzögerung des Verfahrens sich ergeben.

Erträgt die Hauptsache eine solche Verzögerung nicht, so steht der Ausweg frei, das abgekürzte Verfahren zu wählen. Ist die Hauptsache dringlich, so erhalten hiermit auch alle Gewährschaftsklagen den Charakter der Dringlichkeit, und das Gericht kann die Beiladung der Gewährschaftspflichtigen in die bestimmte Sitzung nicht versagen. Reicht die Zeit nicht aus, so genügt Vertagung in eine andere Sitzung.

Art. 234. — **Nach Zustellung des motivirten Antrags des Beklagten oder Ablauf der dafür bestimmten Frist ist jede Partei berechtigt, die Sache für die Sitzung anzumelden.**

Art. 235. — **Die Anmeldung der Sache für die Sitzung (Art. 228 und 234) geschieht schriftlich oder mündlich bei dem Gerichtsschreiber.**

Hiebei sind Vor- und Familiennamen, Wohnort, Stand oder Gewerbe der Parteien, der Streitgegenstand, die aufgestellten Anwälte und der Tag der Klagzustellung anzugeben.

Beim Vorhandensein mehrerer Kläger oder Beklagter genügt die Bezeichnung je eines von ihnen.

Geschah die Klagzustellung an mehrere Beklagte an verschiedenen Tagen, so ist der Tag der letzten Zustellung anzugeben.

Ist der Fall des Art. 232 gegeben, so ist dies besonders zu bemerken.

Art. 236. — **Alle gemäß Art. 235 angemeldeten Sachen sind unverzüglich nach der Reihenfolge der Anmeldung in ein von dem Gerichtsschreiber zu führendes Verzeichniß (Hauptverzeichniß) einzutragen.**

Art. 237. — **Die im Laufe einer Woche in das Hauptverzeichniß eingetragenen Sachen, in welchen für den Beklagten ein Anwalt bestellt ist, hat der Gerichtsschreiber am letzten Wochentage in eine Tabelle (Wochentabelle) zu bringen.**

In diese Tabelle sind auch ältere Sachen, deren Lauf durch ein Zwischenurtheil oder in sonstiger Weise unterbrochen war, aufzunehmen, wenn eine Partei dem Gerichtsschreiber die Absicht, sie wieder zu betreiben, erklärt.

Die Tabelle ist am Tage ihrer Anfertigung in dem Sitzungssaale und auf der Gerichtsschreiberei auf solange anzuheften, bis die darin vorgetragenen Sachen zum Aufrufe in der Sitzung gekommen sind.

Für diesen Aufruf bestimmt der Gerichtsvorstand durch eine im Sitzungssaale anzuheftende Anordnung ein für allemal einen Tag in der Woche.

Der Aufruf hat zu erfolgen, sobald an dem bestimmten Wochentage in den Fällen des Art. 232 sechs, in den übrigen Fällen fünfzehn Tage seit Anheftung der Tabelle abgelaufen sind.

Der Tag, an welchem die Sache hienach zum Aufrufe zu kommen hat, muß in der Tabelle angegeben sein. Sie muß außerdem die Namen der Parteien und Anwälte, dann die Ordnungszahl enthalten, unter der die Sache in das Hauptverzeichniß eingetragen ist.

Auch hat der Gerichtsschreiber den Tag der Anheftung der Tabelle auf dieser unter Beifügung seiner Unterschrift zu bemerken.

Art. 238. — **Befinden sich an einem Gerichte mehrere Senate, die Civilrechtsstreitigkeiten zu entscheiden haben, so theilt der Gerichtsvorstand die in das Hauptverzeichniß eingetragenen Sachen, in welchen ein Anwalt für den Beklagten aufgestellt ist, sofort nach dem Eintrage den einzelnen Senaten zu.**

In diesem Falle werden bei den Senaten über die ihnen zugetheilten Sachen besondere Verzeichnisse geführt, in welche sie von dem Gerichtsschreiber sofort nach der Zutheilung einzutragen sind. Die Wochentabelle wird für die verschiedenen Senate getrennt gefertigt und angeheftet. Der Wochentag zum Aufrufe ist für jeden Senat besonders zu bestimmen.

Art. 239. — Spätestens drei Tage, nachdem durch Anheftung der Wochentabelle der Sitzungstag bestimmt ist, hat in den darin vorgetragenen Sachen der Anwalt des betreibenden Theils dem Gegenanwalte die Aufforderung zum Erscheinen in der Sitzung zustellen zu lassen.

G. A. d. K. d. A. II S. 14—28. 32. 33. 104. 110. 112. 117. 118. 450. IV S. 70. 98. K. d. R. II S. 24. IV S. 34.

1) Sobald der motivirte Antrag des Beklagten zugestellt, oder die für diese Zustellung gegebene Frist verstrichen ist, steht es jeder Partei frei, auf dem durch die Art. 235—243 vorgezeichneten Wege die Sache in die Sitzung und zur Verhandlung zu bringen.

Dieser Weg erscheint beim ersten Anblicke etwas umständlich und zeitraubend, allein bei näherer Betrachtung wird man erkennen, daß er sachentsprechend ist, wie er denn auch die praktischen Erfahrungen für sich hat.

Die bezüglichen Vorschriften sind dem zum Vollzuge des Code de procedure erlassenen Dekrete vom 30. März 1808 entnommen und haben den doppelten Zweck: 1) in den Geschäftsgang Ordnung zu bringen, und 2) eine erschöpfende Instruktion der Prozesse zu ermöglichen.

In ersterer Beziehung sollen sie bewirken, daß jede Sache in der ihr gebührenden Reihenfolge vorkomme, daß das Gericht sowohl als die Anwälte im Voraus Kenntniß davon erhalten, was verhandelt werde, daß endlich die Sitzungen nicht überladen werden und jede Sache an dem für sie bestimmten Tage auch wirklich zur Verhandlung komme.

In letzterer Beziehung soll der Zeitraum, welcher zwischen der Anmeldung einer Sache und dem Tage der Verhandlung in Mitte liegt, die allgemeine gesetzliche Frist für alle diejenigen Prozeßhandlungen und Maßnahmen bilden, bezüglich deren das Gesetz besondere Fristen zu setzen nicht nöthig hielt, welche jedoch erforderlich sind, damit die Sache vollkommen aufgeklärt und reif zur Verhandlung gelange, wohin, außer dem motivirten Antrage des Klägers, etwaige nachträgliche Anträge beider Parteien, dann die Erhebungen von Beweismitteln und von thatsächlichen Aufklärungen zu rechnen sind. Deßhalb trifft denn auch das Gesetz Vorkehrung, daß die Absicht, eine Sache zur Sitzung zu bringen, gehörig veröffentlicht werde.

2) Der erste Schritt, um zur Verhandlung zu gelangen, besteht darin, daß diejenige Partei, welche die Sache betreiben will — der fleißige Theil — die Sache beim Gerichtschreiber zur Sitzung anmelde.

Erst mit dieser Anmeldung und dem auf Grund derselben sofort im Hauptverzeichnisse zu machenden Eintrage ist der Rechtsstreit, welcher bis dahin nur unter den Anwälten verhandelt wurde, für das Gericht vorhanden, kommt als Geschäftslast desselben in Betracht und ist für den Richter die Möglichkeit gegeben, auf dessen Erledigung hinzuwirken.

Die Anmeldung ist an keine Form gebunden. Es ist weder, wenn sie schriftlich geschieht, ein Anwaltsakt, noch, wenn sie mündlich geschieht, ein Protokoll nöthig, vielmehr genügt es, dem Gerichtsschreiber in einer schriftlichen Notiz oder mündlich Dasjenige mitzutheilen, was nach Art. 235 zum vorschriftsmäßigen Eintrage erfordert wird.

3) Das Hauptverzeichniß ist bestimmt, alle am Gerichte anhängigen Prozesse aufzunehmen, die gewöhnlichen sowohl als die im abgekürzten Verfahren zu erledigenden (Art. 260 Ziff. 1), jedoch auch nur Prozesse, so daß also Sachen, welche auf einfache Vorstellung zu erledigen sind, nicht in dieses Verzeichniß aufgenommen werden (Art. 652).

Theilt sich das Gericht in mehrere Senate, so ist für jeden Senat noch ein besonderes Verzeichniß zu führen (Art. 238 Abs. 2).

Der Prozeß bleibt aufgetragen, bis er vom betreffenden Gerichte vollständig erledigt ist, oder in den vom Gesetze vorgesehenen Fällen das Gericht die Streichung verfügt. Wenn daher eine Sache nach Durchführung eines Beweisverfahrens, nach Abweisung einer Berufung oder aus einer sonstigen Veranlassung zur weiteren Aburtheilung in die Sitzung gebracht wird, bedarf es keinen neuen Eintrags ins Hauptverzeichniß, vielmehr behält sie hier ihre frühere Nummer und wird nur zur Wochentabelle angemeldet. Selbst wenn durch Versäumungsurtheil endliche Entscheidung erging, jedoch in Folge erhobenen Einspruchs die wiederholte Aburtheilung stattzufinden hat, bleibt der alte Eintrag in Geltung, oder, wenn man will, lebt er wieder auf (Art. 313).

Nach förmlicher Streichung ist jedoch neuer Eintrag nöthig (Art. 255).

4) Was Form und Inhalt des Hauptverzeichnisses anbelangt, so werden, soweit das Gesetz

selbst nicht schon Vorschriften gibt (Art. 235), zur Herbeiführung gleichförmiger Geschäftsbehandlung allgemeine Anordnungen erlassen und Formularien mitgetheilt werden (Art. 258). Selbstverständlich erscheint, daß die Einträge möglichst übersichtlich, nach Abtheilungen gesondert, zu geschehen haben und namentlich erscheint es sachgemäß, in einer besonderen Abtheilung die gerichtlichen Verfügungen in jeder Sache bis zum Endurtheile oder zur Streichung vorzumerken. Die Einsicht des Hauptverzeichnisses soll sofort einen Ueberblick über den Stand des Prozesses geben.

5) Am letzten Tage jeder Woche fertigt der Gerichtschreiber über alle contradiktorischen Sachen, welche im gewöhnlichen Verfahren zur Sitzung gebracht werden sollen, und zu diesem Zwecke im Laufe der Woche angemeldet wurden, die Wochentabelle. In derselben ist namentlich auch der nach Art. 237 Abs. 4 u. 5 sich von selbst bestimmende Tag zu bezeichnen, an welchem die Sache zur Hinterlegung der Anträge aufgerufen wird.

Von dieser Tabelle ist sofort ein Exemplar im Sitzungssaale und ein zweites auf der Gerichtskanzlei zum Zwecke der Kundmachung anzuheften und so lange angeheftet zu lassen, bis die eingetragenen Sachen zum Aufrufe gelangt sind.

Erfolgt Vertagung zur Hinterlegung, so möchte es der Ordnung wegen geeignet sein, die Sache sofort auf die nächste Wochentabelle zu übertragen.

6) Spätestens drei Tage nach der Anheftung, oder, besser gesagt, innerhalb der drei auf die Anheftung folgenden Tage, hat der betreibende Anwalt den Gegenanwalt zum Erscheinen in der Sitzung durch Anwaltsakt auffordern zu lassen. Diese Aufforderung, welche dem Gegner mindestens 12 Tage sichert, um seine Anträge für die Sitzung vorzubereiten, ist in so fern von Wichtigkeit, als ohne dieselbe ein Versäumungsurtheil gegen den Anwalt nicht erwirkt werden kann (Art. 301).

Verfahren in der Sitzung:
1) wenn ein Anwalt für den Beklagten bestellt ist:
a) zur Hinterlegung der Anträge.

Art. 240. — **In der Sitzung ist, wenn ein Anwalt für den Beklagten bestellt ist, zunächst zur Hinterlegung der Anträge zu schreiten.**

Die in Gemäßheit der Bestimmungen der Art. 237 und 238 oder in Folge einer Vertagung zu diesem Zwecke aufzurufenden Sachen sind nach der Reihenfolge des Hauptverzeichnisses, aber vor jenen, in welchen in der Sitzung die Verhandlung stattfinden soll, durch den diensthabenden Gerichtsvollzieher zum Aufrufe zu bringen.

Art. 241. — **Ist bei dem Aufrufe zur Hinterlegung der Anträge keiner der Anwälte erschienen und dem Gerichte auch kein Verhältniß bekannt geworden, wegen dessen es sich veranlaßt findet, die Sache zu vertagen, so ist die Streichung vom Hauptverzeichnisse zu verfügen.**

Ist nur ein Anwalt oder von mehreren aufgestellten Anwälten nur ein Theil erschienen, so ist, wenn nicht besondere Verhältnisse entgegenstehen, sofort nach Hauptstück VIII Antrag zu stellen. Wird dies unterlassen, so ist auch in diesem Falle die Streichung der Sache anzuordnen.

Sind bei dem Aufrufe alle in der Sache aufgestellten Anwälte erschienen, so hat jeder von ihnen seine Gesuche, wie sie sich nach dem motivirten Antrage und den etwa nöthig befundenen Abänderungen und Zusätzen gestalten, zu verlesen und Abschrift dieses Antrags dem Vorsitzenden zu übergeben. Letzterer hat auf der übergebenen Abschrift den Tag der Hinterlegung unter Beifügung seines Namenszugs zu bemerken.

Sind hinsichtlich der Gesuche Aenderungen oder Zusätze gemacht worden, so bedarf es einer besonderen Motivirung derselben nicht. Es ist aber in diesem Falle dem Gegenanwalte Abschrift des nunmehrigen Gesuches spätestens bei der Hinterlegung von kurzer Hand mitzutheilen.

Die bei Gericht zu hinterlegenden Anträge haben zugleich das vollständige Verzeichniß der im Prozesse befindlichen Parteien nach Vor- und Familiennamen, Stand, Wohnort und Parteistellung zu enthalten.

Das Gericht bestimmt, nachdem es die Anwälte über die bei der Fixirung zu berücksichtigenden Umstände vernommen hat, eine spätere Sitzung zur Verhandlung.

In den in Art. 232 bezeichneten, sowie in Sachen, bei denen sich aus den verlesenen Gesuchen ergibt, daß im Wesentlichen ein Streit unter den Parteien nicht obwaltet, kann das Gericht anordnen, daß die Verhandlung noch in der nämlichen Sitzung stattzufinden habe.

Art. 242. — **Wird Vertagung zur Hinterlegung der Anträge nachgesucht, so ist sie sogleich nach dem Aufrufe und zwar, wenn nicht eine weitere Entscheidung des Gerichts verlangt wird, mündlich zu beantragen.**

Dem Vertagungsbegehren muß entsprochen werden, wenn der Gegenanwalt seinen Verpflichtungen bezüglich der Mittheilung oder bezüglich der Rückgabe der Urkunden (Art. 172 — 174) nicht nachgekommen ist, oder den vorschriftsmäßig mitzutheilenden motivirten Antrag überhaupt nicht oder nicht spätestens drei Tage vor der Sitzung hat zustellen lassen, oder endlich durch verfrühte Anmeldung der Sache die Gegenpartei in den ihr gesetzlich gegebenen Fristen verkürzt hat.

In andern Fällen ist eine Vertagung, in welche der Gegenanwalt nicht einwilligt, nur dann zu bewilligen, wenn erhebliche Gründe glaubhaft dargelegt werden.

Art. 243. — **Wird dem Vertagungsbegehren entsprochen, so hat das Gericht zugleich eine andere Sitzung zur Hinterlegung der Anträge zu bestimmen.**

Findet die Vertagung statt, weil die Sache wegen Verwickelung des Falls, Unzulänglichkeit der gesetzlichen Fristen oder sonstiger Hindernisse im bisherigen Vorverfahren nicht genügend vorbereitet werden konnte, so kann das Gericht auf Antrag einer Partei angemessene Fristen zu weiterem Vorverfahren festsetzen. In diesem Falle kommt die Sache erst dann wieder zum Aufrufe, wenn sie vom Gerichtsschreiber in Gemäßheit der Bestimmungen des Art. 237 Abs. 2 neuerdings in die Wochentabelle eingetragen worden ist.

G. A. d. K. d. A. II S. 14—23. 29—32. 104. 112. 113. 118. 119. 450. IV S. 70. 71. 75. 76.
K. d. R. II S. 24—31. IV S. 34.

1) Im gewöhnlichen Verfahren findet zuerst bloß die Hinterlegung der Anträge statt und wird dann erst der Tag der Verhandlung bestimmt.

Es gewährt diese Einrichtung große Vortheile, theils, indem sie verhütet, daß die Prozesse übereilt und unreif zur Verhandlung kommen, theils, indem sie dem Richter Gelegenheit geben, sich schon vorher mit den zu verhandelnden Sachen bekannt zu machen, theils endlich, indem sie eine sachgemäße Vertheilung der Prozesse auf die verschiedenen Sitzungstage möglich macht. Namentlich vom letzteren Gesichtspunkte aus erscheint sie bei größerem Drange der Geschäfte unentbehrlich.

a) Hinterlegung der Anträge.

2) Die Hinterlegung der Anträge findet an einem besonders hierzu bestimmten Wochentage statt (Art. 237 Abs. 4) und zwar beim Beginne der Sitzung (Art. 240 Abs. 1). Letzteres ist vorgeschrieben, um die Zeit derjenigen Anwälte, welche bloß zur Hinterlegung der Anträge in der Sitzung erscheinen, nicht mehr als nöthig in Anspruch zu nehmen.

Sie erfolgt in der Weise, daß jeder Anwalt das Gesuch seines motivirten Antrages verliest und den Antrag selbst abschriftlich zu Gerichtshänden gibt. Es ist also nicht etwa bloß das Gesuch, sondern es ist der ganze motivirte Antrag zu hinterlegen, und sind die Motive namentlich deßhalb von Belang, weil sie den Richter in den Stand setzen, schon vor der Verhandlung einen Ueberblick über die strittigen That- und Rechtsfragen zu gewinnen.

Gesuche, welche neu hinzugefügt werden, bedürfen einer besonderen Motivirung nicht, sind jedoch dem Gegner abschriftlich mitzutheilen, und zwar kann dies noch in der Sitzung selbst, durch Einhändigung einer vom Anwalte unterzeichneten Abschrift geschehen.

Zu beachten ist, daß das Gesetz in den hinterlegten Anträgen immer eine vollständige und genaue Bezeichnung aller Personen verlangt, die nemliche, welche später in das Urtheil aufzunehmen ist (Art. 285 Ziff. 1). Werden mehrere Anträge der nemlichen Partei hinterlegt, so ist diese Bezeichnung nicht in jedem Antrage zu wiederholen.

3) Ist einer der Anwälte nicht erschienen oder nach Art. 253 als nicht erschienen zu betrachten, so sind, wenn nicht besondere Umstände entgegenstehen, die Erschienenen verpflichtet, auf Erlaß eines Versäumungs- oder Verbindungsurtheiles nach Maßgabe der Bestimmungen in Hauptst. VIII anzutragen; im Weigerungsfalle erfolgt die Streichung vom Hauptverzeichnisse.

Es steht dies nicht ganz im Einklange mit dem Prinzipe des Art. 242 Abs. 3, gemäß dessen die Anwälte es in der Gewalt haben, sich gegenseitig Vertagungen zur Hinterlegung der Anträge zu bewilligen, was vielleicht daher rührt, daß man hier die Prinzipien des französischen Prozesses, dort diejenigen des deutschen Prozesses walten ließ.

Zu erwähnen ist, daß möglicherweise nur dem einen Anwalte gegenüber Versäumungsurtheil ergeht, dem anderen gegenüber aber der Tag zur Verhandlung festzusetzen ist.

4) Erscheinen sämmtliche Anwälte nicht und findet das Gericht keinen besonderen Grund zur Vertagung, so verfügt es die Streichung der Sache vom Hauptverzeichnisse. Es bedarf dann einer neuen Anmeldung und eines neuen Eintrags, um sie wieder vor Gericht zu bringen.

b) Festsetzung des Tags der Verhandlung.

5) Sind die Anträge hinterlegt, so bestimmt das Gericht eine spätere Sitzung zur Verhandlung. Es wird hierbei geleitet einerseits durch die Aufschlüsse, welche ihm die Anwälte über Dringlichkeit, Umfang und Zusammengehörigkeit der Sachen geben, sowie durch die Wünsche, welche mit Rücksicht auf weitere Erhebungen, auf Verhinderungen oder auf das persönliche Erscheinen der Parteien geäußert werden; anderseits durch die Zeit, welche an den verschiedenen Sitzungstagen zu Gebot steht. Im Zweifel haben die älteren Nummern vor den jüngeren den Vorzug.

Bei einiger Sorgfalt läßt sich immer der Tag für die Verhandlung so festsetzen, daß diese auch sicher zur bestimmten Zeit stattfinden und erledigt werden kann, was wegen des persönlichen Erscheinens der Parteien von großer Wichtigkeit ist.

6) Das Dekret vom 30. März 1808 sagte bloß, es solle nach Hinterlegung der Anträge ein Tag zum Plädiren fixirt werden und hieraus folgerte man, daß die Anwälte gerüstet sein müßten, sofort zu plädiren, wenn das Gericht es anordne. Unsere Prozeßordnung schreibt jedoch eine spätere Sitzung vor, so daß also nicht der nemliche Tag, wohl aber der nächstfolgende bestimmt werden kann.

Eine Ausnahme besteht 1) für Einreden des Art. 185, wenn sie zur gesonderten Aburtheilung gebracht werden, und 2) für Sachen, von denen sich aus dem Gesuche ergibt, daß im Wesentlichen ein Streit nicht obwalte. In diesen beiden Fällen soll das Gericht die sofortige Verhandlung anordnen dürfen.

Was den zweiten Fall betrifft, so ist dem richterlichen Ermessen ziemlicher Spielraum gelassen, indem bloß erfordert wird, daß im Wesentlichen ein Streit nicht bestehe. Es sind alle ganz einfachen, schnell und leicht zu erledigenden Sachen gemeint, z. B. Theilungsklagen, wenn bloß das Theilungsverfahren anzuordnen ist, Fälle, wo die Schuld zugestanden und Frist begehrt wird, wo sofort klar ist, daß vorerst nur auf Ortsbesichtigung zu erkennen sei, wo der Betrag einer Prozeßkaution festzusetzen ist 2c.

c) Vertagung zur Hinterlegung.

7) Die Hinterlegung der Anträge kann auf Begehren in eine andere Sitzung vertagt werden, und zwar muß dem bezüglichen Begehren entsprochen werden:

1) wenn die vorschriftsmäßige Aktenmittheilung verweigert wurde;
2) wenn der Gegner seinen motivirten Antrag nicht wenigstens drei Tage vor der Sitzung hat zustellen lassen;
3) wenn der Gegner die Sache zu früh angemeldet hat und hierdurch der Antragsteller in den ihm gesetzlich zustehenden Fristen verkürzt wurde;
4) wenn der Gegner einwilligt.

8) Was die Verweigerung der Aktenmittheilung betrifft, so ist auf die Bemerkungen zu Art. 172 Nr. 4, 5 u. 7 zu verweisen. Der Fall, daß eine Urkunde erst in der Sitzung vorgelegt wird, kommt selbstverständlich bei der Hinterlegung der Anträge nicht vor.

Was die Zustellung der motivirten Anträge betrifft, so war es nöthig, auch für den Beklagten eine Frist rückwärts vom Tage der Sitzung festzusetzen, weil die Frist des Art. 231 hier nicht genügen würde (s. v. Bomhard Correferat zu Hauptst. VI Art. 19). Hat jede Partei drei Tage zuvor einen, den Forderungen des Art. 230 entsprechenden, Antrag zustellen lassen, so fällt das Recht auf Vertagung hinweg.

Was die verfrühte Anmeldung betrifft, so erwog man, daß der Gerichtsschreiber eine Controle darüber, ob die Anmeldung schon statthaft sei, weder üben dürfe noch könne, Letzteres schon deßhalb nicht, weil er nicht weiß, ob Streitverkündung, Gewährschaftsklage 2c. stattgefunden habe. Es war daher nöthig, für den Fall der Verkürzung des Gegners, diesem ein Recht auf Vertagung zu geben, wobei es gleichgiltig erscheint, ob die Anmeldung mit oder ohne Wissen zu früh geschah. (S. Bemerk. zu Art. 233 Nr. 4.)

Was schließlich die Vereinbarung der Vertagung anbelangt, so gestattet, wie bereits bemerkt, der französische Prozeß eine solche nicht, indem er zwar die Parteien völlig frei gewähren läßt, so lange das Gericht mit der Sache noch nicht befaßt ist, dann aber diesem allein die Verfügung in die Hand gibt.

9) In allen sonstigen Fällen hängt die Vertagung vom Ermessen des Gerichts ab, welches sie nur aus erheblichen Gründen bewilligen soll.

Dies gilt also selbst dann, wenn die in Art. 239 vorgeschriebene Aufforderung zum Erscheinen versäumt wurde, oder wenn bezüglich der Anheftung auf der Wochentabelle eine Ordnungswidrigkeit unterlaufen ist. Der kgl. Ministerial-

Commissär macht zwar Abg. II S. 119 eine abweichende Aeußerung, allein im Gesetze steht hiervon nichts.

10) Zeigt sich, daß wegen besonderer Umstände die Fristen des Vorverfahrens zur erschöpfenden Vorbereitung der Sache nicht ausreichten, so kann das Gericht nach Art. 243 neue Fristen für dieses Verfahren festsetzen und auf unbestimmte Zeit vertagen. Man nannte dies seither die Streichung von der Wochentabelle. Zu dieser Maßregel wird insbesondere bei Gewährschaftsklagen oder sonstigen Beiladungen hie und da Anlaß gegeben sein. Vgl. Bemerk. zu Art. 233 Nr. 4 u. 11.

11) Bloße Vertagungsbegehren sind mündlich zu stellen, und das Urtheil, welches die Vertagung bewilligt, bedarf keiner Gründe (Art. 275). Bei Abweisungen wird es sachgemäß sein, das Begehren im Urtheilssatze selbst zu beurkunden und z. B. zu sagen: „A. d. Gr. ertheilt das Gericht Urkunde, daß Beklagter bloß Vertagung begehrt, aber weitere Anträge nicht stellt, verurtheilt ihn sofort, ohne Beachtung jenes Begehrens 2c. 2c."

b) zur Verhandlung.

Art. 244. — Ueber die zur Verhandlung aufzurufenden Sachen hat der Gerichtsschreiber für jede Sitzung ein Verzeichniß (Sitzungsverzeichniß) herzustellen und dabei, soweit nicht der Senatsvorstand aus dringenden Gründen anders bestimmt, die Reihenfolge des Hauptverzeichnisses einzuhalten.

Der Aufruf erfolgt durch den dienstthuenden Gerichtsvollzieher nach der Ordnung des Sitzungsverzeichnisses. Eine Abweichung hievon ist nur auf Verfügung des Vorsitzenden und, wenn die betheiligten Anwälte nicht zustimmen, nur wegen besonderer Umstände zulässig. In keinem Falle darf eine Sache außer der Reihenfolge des Sitzungsverzeichnisses aufgerufen werden, wenn nicht alle in der Sache aufgestellten Anwälte nebst den etwa mit der mündlichen Rechtsvertheidigung beauftragten Personen anwesend sind.

Art. 245. — Ist beim Aufrufe der Sache zur Verhandlung keiner der Anwälte erschienen und dem Gerichte auch kein Verhältniß bekannt geworden, wegen dessen es sich veranlaßt findet, die Sache zu vertagen, so ist die Streichung vom Hauptverzeichnisse zu verfügen.

Ist nur ein Anwalt oder von mehreren aufgestellten Anwälten nur ein Theil erschienen, so ist gleichwohl in die Verhandlung einzutreten. Das in diesem Falle in der Sache ergehende Urtheil ist, wenn die Anträge vorher hinterlegt worden sind, auch gegenüber der bei der Verhandlung nicht vertretenen Partei als ein contradiktorisches zu betrachten. Es dürfen aber alsdann weder die in den hinterlegten Anträgen enthaltenen Gesuche zum Nachtheile der nicht vertretenen Partei abgeändert, noch zu deren Begründung neue Thatsachen vorgebracht werden, ohne daß dem nicht erschienenen Anwalte durch einen spätestens am Tage vor der Verhandlung zugestellten Schriftsatz davon unter Mittheilung der betreffenden Urkunden Kenntniß gegeben worden ist. Ist dies nicht geschehen, so kann der erschienene Anwalt behufs der nachträglichen Mittheilung an den Gegenanwalt Vertagung begehren.

Art. 246. — Die Verhandlung wird, soferne die besondere Natur des Streitverhältnisses nicht eine Abweichung bedingt, mit dem Vortrage des klägerischen Anwalts begonnen.

Derselbe verliest das Gesuch aus seinem hinterlegten Antrage, der ihm zu diesem Behufe zu übergeben ist, und trägt sodann unter Ablesung des erheblichen Inhalts der benützten Urkunden die weitere Ausführung in thatsächlicher und rechtlicher Beziehung vor, wobei schriftliche Notizen benützt werden dürfen.

In gleicher Weise folgt hierauf der Vortrag der Anwälte der Streitgenossen des Klägers, des Anwalts des Beklagten, der Anwälte seiner Verbindlichkeitsgenossen und Gewährsmänner.

Der weitere Gang der Verhandlung richtet sich nach den allgemeinen Bestimmungen des V. Hauptstücks.

Art. 247. — Werden im Verlaufe der Verhandlung neue Gesuche gestellt oder an den gestellten Gesuchen Aenderungen vorgenommen, so sind diese nach geschehener Verlesung dem Vorsitzenden schriftlich zu übergeben und hat letzterer den Tag der Uebergabe unter Beifügung seines Namenszugs darauf zu bemerken.

Art. 248. — Hat eine Partei im Laufe der Verhandlung Klagegründe oder Einreden zurückgezogen, solche zugestanden oder sonst Anerkenntnisse gemacht, so kann die Gegenpartei

darüber Urkunde von dem Gerichte verlangen. Der Antrag ist schriftlich zu übergeben und vor der Beurkundung die andere Partei darüber zu hören.

Art. 249. — Vertagung der Verhandlung darf, wenn die Hinterlegung der Anträge in einer frühern Sitzung erfolgt ist, auch mit Einwilligung der Gegenpartei nur aus erheblichen Gründen bewilligt werden. Mit der Bewilligung ist die neuerliche Festsetzung des Sitzungstags zu verbinden. G. A. d. K. d. A. II S. 14—23. 33—39. 119—121. 450. IV S. 71—73. K. d. R. II S. 31. IV. S. 34. 35. 320. 340.

1) Den weitaus wichtigsten Theil des neuen Verfahrens bildet die Verhandlung in der Sitzung. Alles, was sonst im Prozesse geschieht, dient in der Regel nur zur Vorbereitung der öffentlich mündlichen Verhandlung und ist bestimmt, das Material für dieselbe zu sammeln und zu sichten.

Vorschriften für dieselbe geben vorstehende sechs Artikel und zwar zunächst für den gewöhnlichen Fall, wo die Hinterlegung der Anträge vorausgegangen ist.

a) Sitzungsverzeichniß.

2) Für jede Sitzung fertigt der Gerichtsschreiber ein Verzeichniß, in welches die Sachen nach der Reihenfolge des Hauptverzeichnisses einzutragen sind, und nach dieser Reihenfolge soll sodann auch der Aufruf in der Sitzung und die Verhandlung erfolgen.

In der Pfalz pflegt man ein für's ganze Jahr berechnetes Sitzungsregister zu halten, in welches der Vorsitzende oder ein Richter die bei Hinterlegung der Anträge bestimmten Sitzungstage sofort einträgt und der Gerichtsschreiber jene Sachen, für welche Ladung auf kurze Frist bewilligt wird oder welche sonst direkt in die Sitzung gebracht werden, nachträgt. Zugleich wird die muthmaßliche Dauer jeder Verhandlung vorgemerkt.

Ein solches Register wird auch jetzt nicht zu entbehren sein, weil das Gericht nicht im Stande ist, richtig zu fixiren, wenn ihm nicht eine Uebersicht über alle bereits erfolgten Fixationen vor Augen liegt, und weil unter Umständen, z. B. bei Verbindungsurtheilen, auf weite Zeit hinaus fixirt werden muß. Da in dessen Einträgen begreiflicher Weise nicht immer die Reihenfolge, in welcher die Sachen aufzurufen sind, eingehalten ist, so kann dasselbe als Ersatz des in Art. 244 vorgeschriebenen Sitzungsverzeichnisses nicht dienen, vielmehr wird aus demselben für jede Sitzung ein besonderes, dem Gerichtsvollzieher zum Zwecke des Aufrufes einzuhändigendes Verzeichniß herzustellen sein, von welchem die Anwälte jeder Zeit Einsicht nehmen können.

3) Der Senatsvorstand kann aus dringenden Gründen gestatten, daß im Sitzungsverzeichnisse von der Reihe des Hauptverzeichnisses abgewichen werde, in welchem Falle er dasselbe mitunterzeichnen wird.

Der Vorsitzende kann wegen besonderer Umstände auch noch die Reihenfolge des Sitzungsverzeichnisses ändern. Nie jedoch soll es erlaubt sein, eine Sache außer Ordnung des Sitzungsverzeichnisses aufzurufen, wenn nicht die betheiligten Anwälte und Rechtsvertheidiger sämmtlich anwesend sind.

Durch letztere Verfügung soll, scheint es, den Anwälten es möglich gemacht werden, sich zu entfernen, bis ihre Sache an die Reihe komme; allein es möchte gefährlich sein, sich auf derartige Berechnungen zu verlassen, denn Sachen, welche zeitraubend zu sein scheinen, können in Folge unvorhergesehener Umstände wegfallen oder sich vereinfachen. Der einzig sichere Weg bleibt daher immer der, daß der Anwalt beim Vorsitzenden anfrage, ob und auf wie lange Zeit es thunlich sei, daß er sich entferne; übrigens wird in geeigneten Fällen der Vorsitzende von selbst sich verpflichtet erachten, den Anwälten die Zeit zu bezeichnen, wann sie zur Verhandlung einer späteren Sache zu erscheinen haben.

b) Verfahren in der Sitzung im Allg.

4) Die Vorschriften, welche Art. 246 darüber gibt, was die Anwälte bei der Verhandlung zu thun und in welcher Reihenfolge sie zu sprechen haben, bedürfen keiner Erläuterung. Es versteht sich von selbst, daß Dasjenige zu geschehen habe, was sachgemäß und was vernünftig ist.

5) Neue Gesuche oder Aenderungen der Gesuche sind auch bei der Verhandlung noch zulässig, sofern sie keine wirkliche Klagänderung enthalten. Diese Gesuche, welche in der Regel nur Beweiserbieten zum Gegenstande haben, sind schriftlich einzureichen, natürlich ohne Motivirung.

Nach bestehender Uebung nahmen die Anwälte an den hinterlegten Anträgen die nöthigen Aenderungen vor, strichen gestellte Anträge durch, änderten andere ab oder setzten weitere eventuelle Anträge bei. Es ist dies das einfachste und zweckmäßigste Verfahren, da es jede Unklarheit darüber beseitigt, was an den früheren Anträgen geändert werden wolle und was als das endgiltige Gesuch in die Urtheilsausfertigung aufzunehmen sei (Art. 289 Abs. 2); obgleich daher Art. 247 dasselbe nicht gerade im Auge hat, so möchte doch nichts im Wege stehen, es auch ferner zu beobachten. Allerdings wäre auf den Anträgen der Tag der Aenderung vorzumerken.

6) Es ist, wie schon bemerkt, Prinzip des neuen Verfahrens, daß über Vorgänge in der Sitzung keine Protokolle errichtet werden müssen, es vielmehr genügt, wenn das Urtheil darüber Urkunde ertheilt. Das Licht der Oeffentlichkeit, die Controle, welche in der Anwesenheit des ganzen Gerichts und aller Betheiligten liegt, lassen hier weitere Formen als die für das Urtheil selbst vorgeschriebenen, unnöthig erscheinen.

Um jedoch bei Zugeständnissen und Verzichten jeden Einwand des Mißverständnisses und der Ueberraschung zu beseitigen, gibt Art. 248 der Gegenpartei das Recht, zu verlangen, daß nicht etwa erst in dem später ergehenden Urtheile, sondern sofort Urkunde ertheilt und in dieser Weise die betreffende Thatsache sicher gestellt werde.

Dieses Begehren ist schriftlich zu stellen und vor der Beurkundung diejenige Partei, von welcher die Erklärung ausgegangen ist, zu hören. Die Beurkundung selbst erfolgt nach Art. 281 Abs. 3, also ohne Gründe, jedoch wird es dem Willen des Gesetzes entsprechen, von der Thatsache, daß der Gegner gehört worden sei, Erwähnung zu machen und z. B. zu sagen: „Das Gericht gibt auf Antrag des Beklagten und nach Vernehmung des Klägers Urkunde darüber, daß 2c."

7) Indem Art. 248 besagtes Recht gibt, ändert er sonst nichts an den Prinzipien, sagt insbesondere nicht, daß Zugeständnisse 2c. nur auf diesem Wege festgestellt werden könnten, und wenn derselbe nicht eingehalten sei, nicht beachtet werden dürften, was denn auch dem Geiste des Verfahrens wenig entsprechen, und dieses namentlich in Fällen, wo die Sache ohne Vorverfahren direkt in die Sitzung kommt, sehr ungelenk machen würde. Vgl. Abg. II 39 (v. Weiß, Völk).

Wenn daher z. B. der Beklagte die Entstehung der Schuld zugibt und bloß Einreden vorschützt, oder wenn er bei dieser Voraussetzung in der Pfalz dem Kläger den Beweis des Klaggrundes erläßt, so ist das Gericht nicht gehindert, diese Erklärungen im Urtheilssatze zu beurkunden, auch wenn schriftliche Anträge deßhalb nicht gestellt sind. Selbstverständlich hat dasselbe die Pflicht, auf bestimmte, jedes Mißverständniß ausschließende Erklärungen zu dringen, im Parteiprozesse unter Umständen die Parteien über die Tragweite ihrer Erklärungen zu belehren.

Häufig werden sich übrigens aus den Gesuchen die Zugeständnisse von selbst ergeben.

8) Vertagungen hängen, sobald die Sache bis zur Verhandlung gediehen ist, nicht mehr vom Willen der Parteien, sondern nur vom Ermessen des Gerichtes ab.

Allerdings steht es den Parteien frei, nicht zu erscheinen, und hierdurch die Streichung der Sache herbeizuführen; allein dann müssen sie die hieran sich knüpfenden Verzögerungen und Kosten sich gefallen lassen und ihren Parteien gegenüber verantworten. Ist die Sache verhandelt und zum Spruche vertagt, so fällt auch dieser indirekte Einfluß der Parteien weg. S. Verhdl. zu Art. 451 des Entwurfes. Abg. II S. 281 u. 282.

c) Nichterscheinen der Anwälte.

9) Wenn zur Verhandlung kein Anwalt erscheint, so ist, wenn nicht etwa besondere Umstände, z. B. die Kenntniß von Verhinderungsursachen, das Gericht zu einer Vertagung bestimmen, die Streichung vom Hauptverzeichnisse zu verfügen.

Die Hinterlegung der Anträge verliert also in diesem Falle ihre Wirkung; es muß die Sache von Neuem angemeldet, eingetragen und auf die Wochentabelle gesetzt und es müssen die Anträge nochmals hinterlegt werden. Was die bereits hinterlegten Anträge betrifft, so sind sie, als vorerst zwecklos, zurückzugeben und können später neuerdings hinterlegt werden.

10) Wenn auch nur Einer der Anwälte erscheint, so findet die Verhandlung statt und zwar als eine contradiktorische. Im französischen Prozesse besteht Streit, ob die Hinterlegung der Anträge eine Sache contradiktorisch mache; unsere Prozeßordnung hat sich für die gewöhnliche, auch in der Pfalz geltende, Ansicht entschieden.

Aus der Thatsache, daß die Verhandlung eine contradiktorische ist, ergibt sich die Folge, daß hier nicht die Behauptungen der erscheinenden Partei als zugestanden betrachtet werden, sondern daß auf die Gesuche, welche die nichterschienene Partei in ihren hinterlegten Anträgen stellte, und auf die Thatsachen, mit welchen sie diese Gesuche begründete, Rücksicht zu nehmen ist. Der Nichterschienene wird durch seine motivirten Anträge vertreten und es ist selbstverständlich, daß der Richter von diesen, sowie überhaupt von den Parteiakten, Kenntniß nehmen darf (Art. 269 Abs. 3). Vgl. die Verhandl. zu Art. 270 des Entwurfs, Abg. II S. 100, 101 u. 122.

Insofern hierbei das Prinzip der Mündlichkeit etwas beeinträchtigt wird, wie dies auch bei den Verhandlungen hervorgehoben wurde (Abg. II 36 [v. Neumayr]), beruht dies im Willen des Gesetzes, welches die praktischere Lösung der konsequenteren vorzog, übrigens hierin nur den

Prinzipien des französischen Prozesses folgte (vgl. die Bemerk. zu Art. 252—255 Nr. 9 a. E.). Uebrigens wird, meinen Erfahrungen nach, der Fall, wo nach Hinterlegung der Anträge ein Anwalt nicht erscheint, ein höchst seltener sein.

11) Die Entscheidung, daß die Hinterlegung der Anträge eine Sache contradiktorisch mache, steht mit dem Satze, daß Aenderungen der Gesuche, neue Thatsachen und Urkunden noch bei der Verhandlung nachgetragen werden können, nicht recht im Einklange, und es ergab sich daher das Bedürfniß, für diese Fälle Vorsorge zu treffen, was im Art. 245 Abs. 2 geschieht.

Es wird hier der Ort sein, zugleich die Frage der Klagänderung überhaupt einer wiederholten Prüfung zu unterziehen.

12) Aenderung des Gesuchs und der Begründung.

Zu Art. 180—182 Nr. 10 ist die Ansicht ausgesprochen, daß bei wirklichen Klagänderungen eine Zustellung an die Partei nöthig sei. Diese Ansicht, welche sich aus den Prinzipien des französischen Prozesses und der Natur der Sache herleitete, entspricht, wie sich bei genauerer Prüfung der verschiedenen hier einschlägigen Gesetzesbestimmungen ergibt, dem Willen unserer Prozeßordnung nicht, vielmehr setzt letztere voraus, daß Klagänderungen durch einfachen Anwaltsakt eingeführt werden können.

Nur in so fern ist jene Ansicht festzuhalten, als nicht unter dem Namen einer Klagsabänderung eine ganz neue, mit der früheren nicht in Verbindung stehende, Klage unterschoben werden dürfe. Zwar steht hier Art. 180 nicht entgegen, wohl aber widersetzen sich die allgemeinen Prinzipien, gemäß deren es im Anwaltsprozesse nicht gestattet ist, ohne Ladung vor Gericht zu erscheinen, und der Anwalt des Beklagten nur Mandat hat für den durch die Klagschrift eingeleiteten Prozeß und was sich daraus herleitet (Art. 90).

13) Da nun aber jede wirkliche Klagabänderung in einer oder der anderen Richtung zugleich eine neue Klage darstellt, so wäre eigentlich, wie dies auch hervorgehoben wurde (Abg. II 37 [v. Neumayer]) und auch im seitherigen Prozesse galt, Veranlassung gewesen, neue Frist zur Klagbeantwortung zu eröffnen, und zwar um so mehr, als die Erscheinungsfrist für diesen Fall gar nicht in Anschlag zu bringen ist und der Anwalt des Beklagten sich neue Information von der Partei holen muß.

Ferner sind Streitverkündung, Gewährschafts- und Untergewährschaftsklagen auch nur für die ursprüngliche Klage berechnet, und es werden also diese Akte, unter Mittheilung der Klagnachträge, häufig neu vorzunehmen sein. Kurz, das ganze Gebäude des Prozesses verschiebt sich und bedarf nach allen Richtungen einer gründlichen Reparatur.

Da nun in diesen Beziehungen keine Vorsorge getroffen ist, so erübrigt nur, einen ausgiebigen Gebrauch von der Bestimmung des Art. 243 Abs. 2 zu machen, welcher überhaupt als Universalmittel zur Heilung aller Gebrechen betrachtet werden kann.

14) Es frägt sich nun, welche Art von Aenderung die hier zunächst zu besprechende Verfügung des Art. 245 Abs. 2 im Auge habe?

Dieselbe wurde veranlaßt durch die Bemerkung von Umbscheiden (Abg. II 36), daß Klagänderungen, welche an sich bei der Verhandlung noch zulässig sind (Art. 181 u. 182), auch noch dann stattfinden dürften, wenn einer der Anwälte nicht erschienen sei. Man hielt dies für bedenklich und war der Ansicht, daß, wenn eine contradiktorische Verhandlung angenommen werden solle, keine Partei, weder der Kläger noch der Beklagte, befugt sein dürfe, nach Hinterlegung der Anträge an ihren Gesuchen und deren thatsächlicher Begründung einseitig etwas zu ändern, d. h. man war der Ansicht, daß diejenigen Aenderungen, welche im Falle des Erscheinens erlaubt sind, im Falle des Nichterscheinens an vorausgehende Mittheilung zu knüpfen seien.

Hiernach erleidet es keinen Zweifel, daß man vorzugsweise solche Aenderungen im Auge hatte, welche keine wirklichen Klagänderungen bilden, und daß der Gesetzgeber vom Gedanken geleitet war, es dürfe die Verhandlung einem nicht erschienenen Anwalte gegenüber nur zur Erläuterung und Geltendmachung desjenigen Materials benützt werden, welches die hinterlegten Anträge bieten.

Fraglich könnte nur sein, ob neue Beweiserbieten ohne die vorgeschriebene Mittheilung gestellt werden dürfen, ob z. B. derjenige, welcher im hinterlegten Antrage bloß den Eid zuschiebt, bei der Verhandlung Zeugenbeweis erbieten könne. Solche Beweiserbieten sind im weiteren Sinne auch als Gesuche zu bezeichnen, wie sie denn in der Gesuchsform aufzutreten pflegen; jedoch faßt sie das Gesetz selbst (Art. 230) nicht als eventuelle Gesuche auf und die Aeußerung des Ministerial-Commissärs (Abg. II 37) hat in dieser Richtung keine Entgegnung gefunden. Ich würde sie daher für zulässig erachten.

Selbstverständlich ist auch das Erbieten zum Urkundenbeweise statthaft, während das Vorlegen neuer, in den zugestellten Anträgen nicht geltend gemachter Urkunden (Art. 172 Abs. 4) nicht gestattet, vielmehr dem Vorbringen neuer Thatsachen gleich zu achten ist.

15) Bezieht sich jedoch die Verfügung des Art. 245 Abs. 2 auch auf wirkliche Klagänderungen?

Man kann sagen, daß das Gesetz nicht unterscheide, daß ferner auch bei den Verhandlungen häufig von Klagänderungen im Allgemeinen gesprochen werde und der, zur Zeit angenommene, Vorschlag von Völk (Abg. II 38) ziemlich entschieden auf wirkliche Klagänderungen hindeute, daß ferner Klagänderungen überhaupt nur unerlaubt seien, sofern sich der Beklagte widersetze. Endlich scheint auch Barth Commentar S. 477 Nr. IV dieser Ansicht zu sein.

Anderseits läßt sich sagen, daß die Veranlassung zu fraglicher Bestimmung und die ersten Vorschläge des Minist.-Commissärs (Abg. II 37) darauf hindeuten, daß man wirkliche Klagänderungen nicht im Auge hatte, daß ferner der Vorschlag von Völk später stillschweigend beseitigt wurde, daß endlich, wenn Klagänderungen zulässig sind, denen sich der Beklagte nicht widersetzt, dies nur unter dem Gesichtspunkte einer Einwilligung gilt, die kurze Frist aber, welche hier für die Mittheilung gegeben ist, unmöglich genügen kann, eine solche Einwilligung zu präsumiren.

Letztere Ansicht erscheint mir als die richtige, und ich halte geradezu für unmöglich, daß es Wille des Gesetzgebers sei, es solle aus einer Abends zuvor gemachten Mittheilung eine contradiktorische, im Falle, wo keine Berufung zulässig ist, unanfechtbare, Verurtheilung auf Grund einer in vielen Beziehungen ganz neuen Klage hervorgehen. Auf diesem Wege könnte höchstens ein Versäumungsurtheil erwirkt werden, und auch für dieses wäre, bei wirklichen Klagänderungen, die eintägige Frist zu kurz (Art. 302). Wollte man auf die Wiedereinsetzung in den vorigen Stand hinweisen, so wäre zu erwidern, daß diese nicht benutzt werden kann, um rechtskräftige Urtheile anzufechten, daß sie überhaupt ein Rechtsmittel nicht ist, wie dies zu Art. 551 noch näher erörtert werden wird.

Die Folge ist, daß der Anwalt, welcher auf Grund der Hinterlegung der Anträge ein contradiktorisches Urtheil erwirken will, mit wirklichen Klageänderungen von Amtswegen zurückzuweisen ist.

2) wenn für den Beklagten ein Anwalt nicht bestellt ist.

Art. 250. — Hat der Beklagte keinen Anwalt bestellt, so kann der Anwalt des Klägers, sobald der Eintrag in das Hauptverzeichniß erfolgt ist, ohne vorgängige Festsetzung einer Tagfahrt in jeder ihm beliebigen Sitzung und in jedem ihm beliebigen Senate, welcher Civilrechtsstreitigkeiten zu entscheiden hat, den Antrag auf Erlassung eines Versäumungsurtheils stellen. Die Absicht, dies zu thun, kann noch in der Sitzung selbst erklärt werden.

Solche Sachen sind bezüglich des Aufrufs an die Reihenfolge des Sitzungsverzeichnisses nicht gebunden.

Der Antrag ist zu verlesen, mündlich kurz zu begründen und schriftlich zu übergeben. Er darf nur das Gesuch des Klägers in der Hauptsache und in den Nebenpunkten enthalten.

Tritt, ehe das Versäumungsurtheil verkündet ist, für den Beklagten ein Anwalt in der Sitzung auf, so wird die Sache zur wechselseitigen Zustellung der motivirten Anträge ausgesetzt und das Gericht bestimmt zugleich die Fristen hiefür. Die Sache kommt in diesem Falle erst wieder zum Aufrufe, wenn sie von dem Gerichtsschreiber in Gemäßheit des Art. 237 Abs. 2 neuerdings in die Wochentabelle eingetragen worden ist.

G. A. d. K. d. A. II S. 14—22. 26. 27. 32—34. 39. 104. 121. IV S. 71. 72.
K. d. R. II S. 31. 32. IV S. 35.

1) Im Falle, wo für den Beklagten ein Anwalt nicht aufgestellt ist, kann der Anwalt des Klägers, sofort nach Ablauf der Erscheinungsfrist und nachdem er die Sache ins Hauptverzeichniß hat eintragen lassen, in jeder Civilsitzung, welcher Senat sie auch halten möge, Antrag auf Erlassung eines Versäumungsurtheiles stellen.

Die Reihenfolge des Sitzungsverzeichnisses ist dabei nicht einzuhalten, weil vorausgesetzt wird, daß sich Contumazialsachen, deren Verhandlung in der Regel nur einige Minuten beansprucht, zwischen die fixirten Sachen ohne Störung einschieben lassen.

Uebrigens trifft diese Voraussetzung doch nicht immer zu, indem in Fällen, wo das strittige Recht der Verfügung der Parteien entrückt ist und wo das Nichterscheinen den Beweis nicht ersetzt (Art. 297 und 324 Abs. 2) die Verhandlung oft längere Zeit in Anspruch nimmt. Es sind mir Fälle erinnerlich, wo Contumazialverhandlungen bei Interdiktionen, Gütertrennungsklagen, Klagen auf Trennung von Tisch und Bett &c.

mehrere Stunden dauerten. In Fällen dieser Art kann natürlich die Erledigung der fixirten Verhandlungen durch das plötzliche Auftreten von Anträgen auf Versäumungsurtheile nicht in Frage gestellt werden, vielmehr müssen sich die Antragsteller gefallen lassen, wenn ihre Sachen in spätere Sitzungen vertagt werden. Am geeignetsten wird es sein, solche Sachen bei Gelegenheit der Hinterlegung der Anträge zur Fixation anzumelden.

2) Tritt, ehe das Versäumungsurtheil verkündet ist, ein Anwalt für den Beklagten in der Sitzung auf, so verliert die Sache sofort die Natur einer Contumazialsache und tritt, wie in sonstigen Sachen, das Vorverfahren durch Zustellung motivirter Anträge ein, für welche jedoch das Gericht die Fristen bestimmt. In der Regel wird es sich bloß um eine Frist zur Zustellung des Antrags des Beklagten handeln, welche als vom Tage der Verkündung an laufend zu bezeichnen ist; allein es kann auch auf Gewährschaftsklagen Rücksicht zu nehmen sein, und möchte es dann geeignet sein, einfach zu sagen, daß sich jene Frist nach Maßgabe des Art. 233 erweitere.

Um die Sache später in die Sitzung zu bringen, bedarf es natürlich nicht des Eintrages ins Hauptverzeichniß, welche bereits erfolgt ist, sondern nur der Anmeldung zur Wochentabelle, wie bei älteren Sachen, die wiederholt zur Sitzung kommen. Wenn das Gesetz sagt: „neuerdings in die Wochentabelle eintragen," so ist diese Ausdrucksweise in so fern nicht richtig, als ein solcher Eintrag noch gar nicht stattgefunden hatte.

Ueber die Anwaltsbestellung ertheilt das Gericht Urkunde (Art. 281 Abs. 2).

3) Es versteht sich von selbst, daß eine Anwaltsbestellung, welche vor der Sitzung erfolgt, gleichfalls die Wirkung hat, die Erwirkung eines Versäumungsurtheils zu verhindern. Die Bemerkung des Minist.-Commissärs (Abg. II 27), daß in solchen Fällen die Frist zur Klagbeantwortung von der Anwaltsbestellung an laufe, ist bei Aenderung der bezüglichen Bestimmungen nicht mehr anwendbar, und es hat der Anwalt nur auf den etwa noch übrigen Theil der Frist des Art. 231 ein Recht. Reicht die Zeit nicht aus, so kann Vertagung bewilligt werden.

Gemeinsame Bestimmungen.

Art. 251. — **Unbeschadet der besonders verhängten Nachtheile und soweit das Gesetz nicht anders bestimmt, werden durch den Ablauf der für das Vorverfahren festgesetzten Fristen die betreffenden Handlungen nicht ausgeschlossen, sondern können die Parteien diese Handlungen noch nachträglich vornehmen oder ergänzen und selbst bei der Verhandlung noch weitere Gesuche stellen.**

Die Partei, welche eine Verzögerung des Prozesses durch verspätete oder unvollständige Anträge verschuldete, hat jedoch für die hieraus entspringenden Nachtheile einzustehen. Insbesondere sind, wenn in einem solchen Falle eine Vertagung nothwendig wird, der säumigen Partei die Kosten zu überbürden.

G. A. d. K. d. A. II S. 39. 40. 104. 113. 121. 450. IV S. 72.
K. d. R. II S. 32—34. IV S. 35.

1) In Art. 251 ist eben so klar als richtig das Verhältniß des Vorverfahrens zur öffentlich mündlichen Verhandlung gekennzeichnet.

Der Schwerpunkt des ganzen Verfahrens soll in dieser Verhandlung liegen, und alles was vorausgeht, soll nur vorbereitend sein, d. h. es soll darauf hinwirken, daß eine erschöpfende, den Sachverhalt nach allen Richtungen aufklärende Verhandlung möglich sei, und daß das materielle Recht voll zur Geltung gelange.

Deßhalb sind die Fristen des Vorverfahrens in Allem, was den Grund der Sache berührt, keine Ausschlußfristen, und ist jeder Partei verstattet, noch bei der Verhandlung selbst alles zum Angriffe oder zur Vertheidigung Dienliche an thatsächlichen Aufklärungen (Substantiirung), Einreden, Repliken, Beweismaterial rc. geltend zu machen, auch wenn sie es vorher versäumt hat. Die einzigen Nachtheile schuldhafter Verspätung bestehen in Aufbürdung etwa verursachter Kosten und in dem Tadel, welcher den nachläßigen oder ungeschickten Anwalt trifft, und sie genügen.

2) Allerdings liegen im neuen Verfahren an und für sich gewichtige Ursachen, welche Nachlässigkeiten in der Prozeßeinleitung und Mißgriffe in der Behandlung des Sachverhalts, wie sie früher hie und da sich zeigten, nicht aufkommen lassen.

Solche Ursachen sind insbesondere, daß 1) die Verpflichtung, sofort Beweise zu artikuliren, dazu nöthigt, sich von vorn herein mit allen Einzelnheiten des Sachverhalts bekannt zu machen, und daß 2) die Anwälte selbst handeln, und zwar im Bewußtsein handeln, die Sache in der Sitzung vertreten und dem Gegner auf seine Einwände, dem Richter auf seine Fragen sofort Antwort geben zu müssen. Es entwickelt sich so von selbst und aus dem eignen Interesse der Anwälte heraus die Gewohnheit, den Sachverhalt gleich im Beginne des Prozesses nach allen Richtungen hin gründlich zu studiren und zu bearbeiten.

3) Wenn nun auch das Vorverfahren nur vorbereitend sein soll, so würde man doch den Sinn des Art. 251 verkennen und ihm eine allzugroße Tragweite geben, wollte man annehmen, er habe nicht bloß Versäumungen, sondern auch positive Handlungen im Auge, und es lasse sich aus ihm der Satz folgern, daß Verzichte und Zugeständnisse, welche die Schriftsätze des Vorverfahrens enthalten, nur auf Ruf und Widerruf gemacht seien und nach Belieben zurückgenommen werden könnten.

Dieser Punkt, welcher von großer prinzipieller Wichtigkeit ist, erheischt eine eingehendere Erörterung.

4) Es wird geeignet sein, zuerst die Prinzipien des französischen Prozesses, aus denen die Bestimmungen des Art. 251 geschöpft sind, klar zu legen.

Der französische Prozeß kennt nur Präclusionen für formelle Fragen (Prozeßeinreden), nicht aber für Fragen, welche das Recht selbst berühren, und erkennt als Prinzip an, daß, so lange der Richter nicht endgiltig über einen Streitpunkt erkannt habe, nichts ausgeschlossen werden dürfe, was zur Herstellung der materiellen Wahrheit dient. Der Weg zu dieser Wahrheit darf dem Richter durch bloße Formen nie versperrt sein.

Hieraus leitet sich eine Reihe von Grundsätzen ab, welche, obgleich größtentheils nirgends bestimmt ausgesprochen, doch von jeher unbestritten galten. Hierher gehört z. B. der Grundsatz, daß das Beweisinterlokut den Richter nicht binde, sowie ferner der Grundsatz, daß Mittel zur Geltendmachung eines Rechtes oder zur Abwehr von Angriffen auf dasselbe, insbesondere Einreden zum Grunde der Sache, nie wegen bloßer Versäumung ausgeschlossen werden, so lange nicht die Rechtskraft eines Urtheils entgegensteht. Dies gilt nicht bloß für das Vorverfahren, sondern auch für die Verhandlung selbst, insofern sie kein Endurtheil zur Folge hat, und selbst für letzteren Fall, soweit Einspruch oder Berufung zulässig ist.

Soweit jedoch dieses Prinzip nicht im Wege steht, haben Prozeßhandlungen des Vorverfahrens die nemliche rechtliche Wirkung, wie solche bei der mündlichen Verhandlung, und so hat man denn nie bezweifelt, daß Geständnisse und Verzichte, welche ein Anwalt innerhalb der Grenzen seines Mandats in den Anträgen erklärt, in gleicher Weise rechtswirksam seien, wie diejenigen, welche er in der Sitzung macht. Duranton droit civil. Bd. VII Nr. 545 sagt: »L'aveu judiciaire peut »avoir lieu ou par des actes de procédure, »signifiés dans le cours de l'instance, ou à »l'audience.« Das Nemliche sagen Toullier und Marcadé zu Art. 1356 Code civil.

5) Es erscheint dies auch vollkommen in der Natur der Sache begründet.

Wenn Erklärungen, welche die Partei durch einen Gerichtsvollzieher zustellen läßt, oder welche sie sonst, im Laufe des Prozesses oder vorher, irgendwie abgibt oder durch einen Bevollmächtigten abgeben läßt, rechtlich wirksam sind und als Beweismittel benützt werden; warum soll nur dasjenige, was die Partei durch ihren Anwalt sagen läßt, gar nichts gelten und nicht einmal die Kraft außergerichtlichen Geständnisses haben? Ist es doch Grundsatz, daß, was der Anwalt als dominus litis spricht und thut, gerade so zu betrachten sei, als habe es die Partei selbst gesprochen und gethan, und ist doch gerade der Anwalt diejenige Person, welche am besten das Gewicht ihrer Erklärungen und die Tragweite, welche sie für den in Frage stehenden Prozeß haben, zu beurtheilen vermag. Daß die Erklärungen schriftlich geschahen, ist sicher ebenfalls kein Grund, anzunehmen, daß sie weniger überlegt seien, als wenn sie mündlich abgegeben wurden.

6) Um nun auf die Bestimmungen der Prozeßordnung überzugehen, so gibt Art. 251 den Art. 209 des Entwurfs mit wenigen, nur die Fassung betreffenden, Aenderungen wieder.

Wie in den Motiven zum Entwurfe (S. 549) ausdrücklich bemerkt ist, so wollte man in diesem Punkte die Prinzipien des französischen Prozesses, nicht mehr und nicht weniger, zur Geltung bringen, und der Widerruf, von welchem Art. 77 des Entwurfs sprach, war nur eine besondere Art von désaveu und erforderte den Nachweis einer Mandatsüberschreitung. Hiemit stimmt auch vollkommen der Wortlaut des Art. 251 überein, denn in demselben läßt sich offenbar, bei einer natürlichen Auslegung, nur derjenige Sinn finden, wie er eben als Prinzip des französischen Prozesses dargelegt worden ist, und man müßte ihm Gewalt anthun, wollte man daraus den Satz ableiten, daß Geständnisse und Verzichte bei der Verhandlung beliebig widerrufen werden könnten.

Nichtsdestoweniger lassen sich ernstliche Zweifel erheben, ob nicht dennoch der Gesetzgeber die Absicht gehabt habe, Letzteres zu bestimmen, — Zweifel, welche durch verschiedene Aeußerungen bei den Verhandlungen veranlaßt sind.

Dahin gehört insbesondere die Aeußerung des k. Minist.-Commissärs zu Art. 93 (Abg. I 135 a. E.), eine weitere zu Art. 459 des Entwurfs (Abg. II 288), wo gesagt wird, der prozessuale Nexus unter den Parteien entstehe erst durch die mündliche Verhandlung, und die Erklärung von Umbscheiden an letzterer Stelle, welcher geradezu ausspricht, es dürften die in den gewechselten Schriften enthaltenen Erklärungen und Geständnisse unbedingt zurückgenommen werden!

7) Die Quelle dieser Anschauungen möchte im hannoverischen Entwurfe zu finden sein, welcher in § 131 sagt:

„Die mündliche Verhandlung bildet, soferne „dieses Gesetz nicht etwas Anderes bestimmt, „die ausschließliche Grundlage für die richterliche Entscheidung."

Nach den Verhandlungen (S. 94—121) soll hiermit gesagt sein, daß neben den mündlichen Erklärungen in der Sitzung, die in den Schriftsätzen niedergelegten schriftlichen Erklärungen völlig werthlos seien. Demnach wäre also der Schriftenwechsel nichts als ein leerer Tausch von Worten, eine Art Vorbesprechung unter der stillschweigenden Bedingung, daß alles, was gesprochen werde, nichts gelte, wenn es nicht später von Neuem vorgebracht werde! Ich glaube schwerlich, daß dem neuen Verfahren ein Dienst erwiesen wäre, wenn man in dieser Weise den Inhalt der Schriftsätze rein auf Nichts reduzirte; man würde vielleicht bald die Erfahrung machen, daß sie auch wie etwas, was nichts bedeutet, behandelt würden.

Die ganze Idee erscheint mir als Ausfluß jener in Zeiten des Uebergangs vorwaltenden Neigung, von einem Extreme ins andere überzuspringen, — von größter Gebundenheit und Einzwängung zur größten Ungebundenheit und Willkür, und anzunehmen, weil das Bestehende schlecht sei, müsse das gerade Gegentheil davon gut sein.

8) Ich glaube nun behaupten zu dürfen, daß jene Idee dem Texte und dem Geiste unserer Prozeßordnung gegenüber keine Berechtigung habe, vielmehr diejenigen Grundsätze maßgebend seien, welche im französischen Prozesse seither galten und sich bewährt haben.

Die Gründe fasse ich kurz dahin zusammen:

1) Es wäre etwas Abnormes, wenn positive Erklärungen in den Schriftsätzen keine Bedeutung haben sollten, und es könnte dies nur angenommen werden, wenn das Gesetz sich bestimmt in diesem Sinne ausspräche;

2) ein solcher Ausspruch liegt jedoch nicht vor, im Gegentheile läßt Art. 251, in welchem er hätte erfolgen müssen, auf die gegentheilige Absicht schließen;

3) die Unterstellung, daß man dem hannoverischen Entwurfe habe folgen wollen, ist positiv ausgeschlossen, weil Art. 251 nur den Inhalt des § 132 jenes Entwurfes wiedergibt, während eine ähnliche Bestimmung, wie diejenige des § 131, sich nirgends findet;

4) einzelne Aeußerungen in den Gesezgebungs-Ausschüssen, mögen sie noch so bestimmt lauten, vermögen weder eine gesetzliche Bestimmung, welche nicht vorliegt, zu schaffen, noch den klaren Sinn einer gegebenen Bestimmung zu ändern. Es läßt sich insbesondere nicht voraussetzen, daß alle Faktoren der Gesetzgebung die oberwähnten Aeußerungen vor Augen hatten, als sie dem Art. 251, bei welchem man nichts Derartiges geäußert hatte, ihre Zustimmung gaben, und daß diese Zustimmung erfolgt sein würde, wenn der Wortlaut des Artikels jenen Aeußerungen entspräche.

9) Das Ergebniß vorstehender Erörterungen ist demnach:

daß Erklärungen der Anwälte in den motivirten Anträgen oder in sonstigen zugestellten Schriften ebenso wirksam sind, als wenn sie in der Sitzung erfolgen;

daß es daher nicht angeht, Geständnisse oder Verzichte, welche der Anwalt in den Grenzen seines Mandates gegeben, einfach in der Sitzung zu widerrufen und für nicht geschehen zu erklären, vielmehr solcher Widerruf nur statthaft ist, wenn Irrthum dargethan werden kann;

daß jedoch, was die Frage des Irrthums betrifft, das Gericht volle Freiheit hat, die Umstände zu würdigen;

daß endlich hiermit die erst später zu erörternde Frage nicht berührt wird, ob Geständnisse schon durch die Zustellung oder erst mit der Annahme bindend werden.

Art. 252. — **Ist die Tagfahrt zur Hinterlegung der Anträge oder zur Verhandlung in Abwesenheit eines der betheiligten Anwälte in der Sitzung bestimmt worden, so muß der betreibende Theil jenem Anwalte spätestens am Tage vor der anberaumten Sitzung eine Aufforderung zum Erscheinen in derselben zustellen lassen. Diese Verbindlichkeit fällt jedoch weg, wenn die Verhandlung wegen Mangels an Zeit verlegt worden ist.**

Art. 253. — **Als nicht erschienen ist auch der Anwalt zu betrachten, welcher in der Sitzung zwar gegenwärtig ist, aber, sei es überhaupt oder nach Verwerfung eines Vertagungsbegehrens, keinen Antrag hinterlegt, beziehungsweise in die Verhandlung nicht eintritt.**

Art. 254. — **Haben die Anwälte Anträge hinterlegt, so ist die Sache als contradiktorisch zu be-**

trachten, ohne Rücksicht darauf, ob der Antrag alle Punkte, welche er nach der Lage der Sache und gesetzlicher Vorschrift zu berühren hat, wirklich berührt und ob der Anwalt bei der ganzen Verhandlung zugegen war oder nicht.

Art. 255. — Sachen, welche von dem Hauptverzeichnisse gestrichen wurden, können jederzeit zur Eintragung wieder angemeldet werden. Sie sind wie neueingetragene zu behandeln, doch bedarf es keiner wiederholten Zustellung motivirter Anträge.

G. A. d. K. d. A. II S. 22. 23. 29. 30. 39. 121. 122. 167 a. E. 450. IV S. 72. 73. 76.
K. d. R. II S. 34—37. IV S. 35.

1) Das Gesetz gibt hier verschiedene allgemeine Bestimmungen, hauptsächlich zur Erläuterung des Sinnes und der Tragweite der vorausgängigen Vorschriften.

a) Auffordern zum Erscheinen (Art. 252).

Ist in Gegenwart der betheiligten Anwälte ein Sitzungstag bestimmt worden, so macht die Verkündung dieser Verfügung jede weitere Aufforderung unnöthig (vgl. Art. 208 Abs. 1), und dieser Fall erscheint auch dann gegeben, wenn etwa der Anwalt nicht persönlich anwesend war, sondern sich durch einen Collegen vertreten ließ.

War jedoch einer der Anwälte bei der Tagfahrt, welche zur Hinterlegung der Anträge oder zur Verhandlung festgesetzt wurde, nicht zugegen, so muß er durch eine, spätestens am Tage vor der anberaumten Sitzung zuzustellende Aufforderung zum Erscheinen, in Verzug gesetzt werden, wenn aus der Versäumung der Tagfahrt Nachtheile für ihn hervorgehen sollen. Der Grund, warum hier eine kürzere Frist gesetzt ist, als im Falle der Fixirung durch die Wochentabelle (Art. 239), liegt darin, daß eine wiederholte Versäumung vorausgesetzt wird.

Die fragliche Bestimmung findet auch Anwendung auf Vertagungen, mit einziger Ausnahme des Falles, wo die Verhandlung wegen Mangels an Zeit verlegt werden mußte, d. h. wenn sie wegen anderer die Sitzung ausfüllender Verhandlungen verschoben wurde, oder wenn sie selbst mehrere Sitzungstage in Anspruch nimmt. Da übrigens Vertagungsurtheile nicht motivirt werden, so wird oft nicht zu ermessen sein, ob das Gericht gerade wegen Mangels an Zeit vertagt habe, wenn dieß im Urtheilsbuche nicht erwähnt ist.

2) Ist die vorgeschriebene Aufforderung unterblieben, so kann kein Versäumungsurtheil erwirkt werden (Art. 301 Abs. 2). Aber auch in Fällen, wo ein solches Urtheil nicht in Frage steht, z. B. wenn nach Hinterlegung der Anträge zur Verhandlung vertagt worden ist, wie dies nach Art. 245 Abs. 1 und Art. 249 auch beim Ausbleiben der Anwälte geschehen kann, wird die Verhandlung nicht stattfinden dürfen. Es wird in solchen Fällen entweder neue Vertagung erfolgen müssen, oder die Streichung vom Hauptverzeichnisse zu verfügen sein, denn der Anwalt, welcher wegen fraglicher Unterlassung nicht zur Verhandlung zugelassen wird, ist gerade so zu behandeln, wie derjenige, welcher nicht erschienen ist.

3) Ist eine Sache als Contumazialsache vertagt worden, was z. B. stattfinden kann, wenn in Fällen, wo aus dem Nichterscheinen des Beklagten ein Zugeständniß nicht folgt, der Kläger zur Erholung weiterer Aufschlüsse eine Vertagung nachsucht, oder wenn das Versäumungsurtheil gegen einen Gewährschaftsbeklagten bis zur Entscheidung über die Hauptklage ausgesetzt wird, so möchte eine weitere Aufforderung an den nicht erschienenen Anwalt nicht geboten sein. Es wird in solchen Fällen das Nichterscheinen beurkundet und die Verhandlung über die Contumazialsache vertagt oder suspendirt. Erscheint der Gegenanwalt nicht freiwillig bei der späteren Verhandlung (in welchem Falle die Analogie des Art. 240 Abs. 4 Platz greifen wird), so werden die Folgen der früheren Versäumung ausgesprochen.

Uebrigens möchte es dem Wortlaute des Gesetzes gegenüber doch gerathen sein, auch in solchen Fällen eine Aufforderung nicht zu unterlassen.

b) Nichterscheinen (Art. 253).

4) Das Nichterscheinen des Anwaltes im Sinne der Prozeßordnung liegt nicht in der persönlichen Abwesenheit, sondern im Unterlassen der Antragstellung. Es ist daher auch der in der Sitzung anwesende Anwalt als nicht erschienen zu betrachten, wenn er keinen Antrag stellt oder blos um Vertagung nachsucht, wie es denn häufig geschieht, daß die Anwälte selbst erklären, daß sie nicht erscheinen.

Um den Sinn des Art. 253 nicht mißzuverstehen, ist im Auge zu behalten, daß er bloß sagt, es stehe die persönliche Anwesenheit des Anwaltes oder ein Vertagungsbegehren nicht im Wege, ihn als nicht erscheinend zu behandeln; ob ein Versäumungsurtheil oder ein contradiktorisches Urtheil ergehe, bestimmt sich nach den allgemeinen Prinzipien. Vgl. Abg. IV 72. 73.

c) Wirkung der Hinterlegung der Anträge (Art. 254).

5) Die Hinterlegung der Anträge, mag sie

nun in der besonders hierzu bestimmten Sitzung (Art. 240) oder bei der Verhandlung (Art. 260, 344 Abs. 1) erfolgen, hat die Wirkung, die Sache bezüglich aller Punkte, welche die Anträge nach Lage der Sache zu berühren haben, contradiktorisch zu machen.

Es ist demnach nicht statthaft, eine Verhandlung zu spalten und sie in einer Hinsicht als contradiktorisch, in anderer als contumaziell zu behandeln. Allerdings kann es jedoch vorkommen, daß in der nemlichen Sitzung, in der nemlichen Sache, auf Grund einer gesonderten Verhandlung, contradiktorisches und Versäumungs-Urtheil ergeht, z. B. wenn nach contradiktorischer Verhandlung und Entscheidung über einen Präjudizialpunkt oder über eine bevorzugte Prozeßeinrede das Gericht in Fällen, welche sich dazu eignen (im abgekürzten Verfahren, im Parteiprozesse), die sofortige Verhandlung in der Hauptsache angeordnet hat und nun ein Anwalt erklärt, weitere Anträge nicht zu nehmen.

6) Aus dem Prinzipe des Art. 254 folgt, daß wegen Unvollständigkeit der hinterlegten Anträge die Fiktion von Zugeständnissen auf Grund des Art. 301 nie statthaft ist, sondern nur die allgemeinen Bestimmungen des Art. 164 Maß geben.

Sind alle Anwälte bei der Verhandlung zugegen, so macht natürlich der Vorsitzende auf die vorhandenen Mängel aufmerksam und veranlaßt, daß sie gehoben werden. Weigert sich ein Anwalt, weitere Anträge zu stellen, etwa weil er meint, die Sachlage erfordere dies nicht und er habe ein Recht, sich nicht weiter einzulassen, so hat er die Folgen zu tragen, wenn das Gericht, ohne Rücksicht auf seine grundlos befundene Weigerung, in der Sache spricht und diese Entscheidung als contradiktorisch gilt.

Ist einer der Anwälte bei der Verhandlung nicht zugegen und ist es der von diesem hinterlegte Antrag, welcher mangelhaft ist, so tritt die nemliche Folge ein, wie in dem soeben erörterten Falle der Weigerung. Ist es aber der Antrag des erscheinenden Anwalts, welcher die Mängel trägt, so muß er von den nöthigen Aenderungen und Zusätzen, nach Maßgabe des Art. 245 Abs. 2, dem Gegenanwalte Mittheilung machen.

7) Eine wichtige Frage ist, welche Punkte gegebenen Falls ein Antrag zu berühren habe.

Was zunächst die erste Verhandlung anbelangt, so setzt das Gesetz voraus, daß jede Partei sich auf alle strittigen Punkte, welche die Sache sowohl bezüglich der Haupt- und Widerklage, als bezüglich der etwa beigeladenen oder intervenirenden Parteien bietet, erschöpfend einlasse und ihre entsprechenden Haupt- und Subsidiaranträge stelle. Ausnahmen von dieser Regel treten nur ein, wo das Gesetz die gesonderte Verhandlung eines Streitpunktes ausdrücklich gestattet, nemlich für bevorzugte Prozeßeinreden (Art. 232), für Präjudizialpunkte (Art. 256) und für Zwischenpunkte, welche vor der Hauptsache zu erledigen sind (Art. 485). Bezüglich der Präjudizialpunkte wird zu Art. 256 Näheres bemerkt werden.

Was die späteren Verhandlungen betrifft, so gelten die nemlichen Grundsätze in analoger Weise (Art. 257). Wenn daher bei Beweisaufnahmen sich Incidentpunkte ergeben, welche vor der Hauptsache zu entscheiden sind, z. B. die Frage, ob ein Zeuge verwerflich, ob eine Eidesannahme genügend sei, so haben die Anträge sich auf diese Punkte zu beschränken, und wenn nach Entscheidung über dieselben, nach Abhör der Zeugen oder Abnahme des Eides, sodann die Verhandlung über die Hauptsache erfolgt und hierbei einer der Anwälte keinen Antrag nimmt, so ist das Urtheil in der Hauptsache ein Versäumungsurtheil.

8) Was schließlich die Frage betrifft, in wie weit die einmal erfolgte Hinterlegung der Anträge nicht bloß für die nächste, sondern auch für eine spätere Verhandlung wirke, so wird bei Art. 307 das Nöthige gesagt werden.

d) Streichung vom Hauptverzeichnisse (Art. 255).

9) Indem das Gesetz verfügt, daß gestrichene Sachen, wenn sie wieder angemeldet werden, wie neu eingetragene zu behandeln seien und nur die Beschränkung beifügt, daß die wiederholte Zustellung motivirter Anträge nicht nöthig sei, spricht es, meiner Ansicht nach, aus, daß im Falle, wo die Streichung auf Grund von Art. 245 Abs. 1 erfolgt, die Hinterlegung der Anträge ihre Wirkung verliere, daß das bezügliche Verfahren zur Strafe der Parteien als vereitelt anzusehen und die Anträge als zurückgenommen zu betrachten seien.

Wäre dies nicht der Wille des Gesetzgebers, so hätte er nicht blos sagen dürfen, daß es keiner wiederholten Zustellung, sondern auch, daß es keiner wiederholten Hinterlegung der Anträge mehr bedürfe, und zwar um so mehr, da er bei seiner Verfügung den Fall des Art. 245 Abs. 1 besonders im Auge hatte. Abg. II 39 (v. Weiß). Offenbar wären, wenn die Hinterlegung der Anträge fortwirken würde, die sämmtlichen Vorschriften über Eintrag auf die Wochentabelle, über Auffordern zur Hinterlegung der Anträge und über diese Hinterlegung selbst rein überflüssig; es hätte nur der wiederholten Festsetzung eines Tags zur Verhandlung bedurft. Ist aber die wiederholte Hinterlegung der Anträge nöthig, so treten auch für den Fall, wo sie nicht erfolgt, die Folgen ein, welche Art. 241 dafür vorsieht.

Auch im französischen Prozesse betrachtet man die Sachlage von diesem Gesichtspunkte. Ein Urtheil des Kassationshofes vom 3. August 1844 (Dalloz, jugement, No. 166) erkennt an, daß der Richter im Falle, wo nach Hinterlegung der Anträge beide Anwälte nicht erscheinen, berechtigt sei, entweder Verzicht auf die hinterlegten Anträge anzunehmen und zu streichen, oder die Einreichung der Parteiakten zu verlangen und auf Grund derselben contradiktorisch zu entscheiden.

10) Die Streichung einer Sache vom Hauptverzeichnisse erfolgt nur, wo sie gesetzlich angeordnet ist. Findet die Sache durch Endurtheil ihre Erledigung, so wird sie nicht gestrichen, sondern es genügt, daß aus der betreffenden Vormerkung die Erledigung sich ergebe. Kommt sie aus besonderer Veranlassung, z. B. in Folge der Einlegung eines Einspruchs, in Folge einer Reformation und Rückverweisung zur ersten Instanz, auf's Neue vor Gericht, so erscheint sie unter der früheren Nummer.

11) Es kann nun aber die Erledigung einer Sache auch erfolgen, ohne daß das Gericht Kenntniß davon erhält, z. B. durch Abstand, Vergleich ꝛc.

In solchen Fällen pflegte man, und zwar gewöhnlich am Schlusse des Jahres, durch Anfrage bei den Anwälten zu ermitteln, was erledigt sei, und wenn die betheiligten Anwälte erklärten, es werde eine Sache nicht mehr betrieben, so pflegte das Gericht ebenso, wie in Fällen, wo die Anwälte nicht erscheinen, die Streichung zu verordnen. Man nannte dies die Bereinigung des Hauptverzeichnisses. Ich glaube, daß bei Einwilligung der Anwälte auch jetzt noch solche Streichungen stattfinden können, jedenfalls wird es sachgemäß sein, Erledigungen der bezeichneten Art zu ermitteln und vorzumerken, damit nicht Sachen als Rückstand erscheinen, welche längst beendet sind.

Art. 256. — **Hat das Vorverfahren in der Hauptsache erst nach Erledigung eines Präjudicial- oder Zwischenpunktes stattzufinden, so kann die Anmeldung zur Wochentabelle (Art. 237 Abs. 2) erst geschehen, nachdem der Beklagte seinen motivirten Antrag hat zustellen lassen oder von der ihm auf Betreiben des Klägers zugestellten Aufforderung, diese Zustellung zu bewerkstelligen, fünfzehn Tage verstrichen sind.**

G. A. d. K. d. A. II S. 123. 450. IV S. 73. — K. d. R. I S. 37. 38.

1) Dieser Artikel hat Fälle im Auge, wo Vorfragen zur Entscheidung gelangen, ohne daß noch das Vorverfahren in der Hauptsache stattgefunden hat und bezeichnet als Fälle dieser Art die Erledigung von Präjudizial- und Zwischenpunkten.

Was Präjudizialpunkte seien, sagt Art. 190 und unter Zwischenpunkten versteht man Zwischenstreite im Sinne von Art. 483 ff., z. B. das Begehren der Herausgabe einer wichtigen Urkunde ꝛc. Man darf nun wohl mit Recht fragen, warum der Fall der gesonderten Aburtheilung einer bevorzugten Prozeßeinrede nicht besonders bezeichnet sei, denn es besteht kein Zweifel, daß er hierher gehöre, ja daß er vorzugsweise Anlaß zur Entstehung des Art. 256 gegeben habe. Abg. II 123 (v. Weiß).

In der ursprünglichen Fassung war beigesetzt: „aus sonstigen Gründen", die Subcommission ließ jedoch diesen Beisatz weg und es sind daher die Prozeßeinreden nothwendig entweder unter den Begriff von „Präjudizialpunkten" oder unter den Begriff von „Zwischenpunkten" zu bringen. Keine dieser Bezeichnungen will nun passen, insbesondere auch nicht diejenige als „Präjudizialpunkte," denn der Art. 190 berechtigt, mit diesem Ausdrucke einen bestimmten Sinn zu verbinden, und darunter Streitpunkte zu verstehen, welche den Grund der Sache berühren, deren gesonderte Aburtheilung nur vom Ermessen des Gerichts abhängt, jedoch immer selbständige Berufung zulässig macht, was Alles bei Prozeßeinreden nicht der Fall ist. Nichtsdestoweniger wurde zu Art. 269 des Entwurfs bemerkt, der Einreden sei dort nicht zu erwähnen, weil sie unter den Präjudizialpunkten begriffen seien (Abg. II 137).

Meines Erachtens gerieth man in dieser Weise in eine Vermengung der Prinzipien und Begriffe und es wird nöthig sein, daß man, um wieder festen Boden zu gewinnen, Präjudizialpunkte im weiteren Sinne (Vorfragen) und Präjudizialpunkte im engeren Sinne (Präjudizialsachen) unterscheide. Wie dem auch sei, so viel steht außer Frage, daß die gesonderte Entscheidung bevorzugter Prozeßeinreden hierher gehöre.

2) Es ist schon bei Art. 190 aus Art. 256 die Folgerung gezogen worden, daß das Gesetz dem Beklagten erlaube, Präjudizialsachen gesondert und ohne weitere Einlassung in die Hauptsache vorzubringen. Die Aeußerungen des Minist.-

Commissärs (Abg. II 123), sowie die Verhandlungen zu Art. 269 des Entwurfs (Abg. II 97 und 100) lassen hierüber keinen Zweifel, namentlich da dort Präjudizialpunkte und prozeßhindernde Einreden neben einander angeführt werden. Ueber die Tragweite jener Befugniß des Beklagten können jedoch Zweifel entstehen.

Frägt man nemlich, was Präjudizialpunkt sei, so gibt der Art. 190 zur Antwort: „ein Streitpunkt, welchen das Gericht zur gesonderten Aburtheilung geeignet findet.“ Es läßt sich nun schwer vereinigen, daß einerseits der Beklagte befugt sein solle, unter Vorschieben eines Präjudizialpunktes die weitere Einlassung zu verweigern und daß anderseits es immer vom Ermessen des Gerichts abhänge, ob ein Präjudizialpunkt gegeben sei.

Obgleich diese Frage schon bei Art. 190 erörtert worden ist, so glaube ich doch darauf zurückkommen zu müssen, um einen neuen Gesichtspunkt anzuregen, wie ich denn der Ansicht bin, daß es bei Kommentaren über neue Gesetze, welche einer erst sich bildenden Jurisprudenz den Weg bahnen oder ebenen sollen, eine Hauptaufgabe sei, die verschiedenen sich als möglich darbietenden Gesichtspunkte anzuregen, zu beleuchten und in ihren praktischen Wirkungen klar zu legen. Solche Erörterungen können selbst dann noch nützlich sein, wenn das Richtige verfehlt wird.

3) Es läßt sich sagen:

Da das Gesetz den Begriff einer Präjudizialsache völlig unbestimmt läßt, so kann es nicht in der Willkühr des Anwaltes liegen, einen beliebigen Streitpunkt als Präjudizialsache zu bezeichnen und vorerst die weitere Einlassung zu verweigern.

Er kann Letzteres nur insofern thun, als nach der Natur des Streitpunkts, die Genehmigung der gesonderten Aburtheilung Seitens des Gerichts mit Sicherheit vorauszusetzen ist. Erkennt später das Gericht, es liege kein Grund zur gesonderten Verhandlung vor, so erklärt es hiermit zugleich, daß die Verweigerung der Einlassung ungerechtfertigt gewesen sei, und kann sodann entweder die sofortige gleichzeitige Verhandlung in der Hauptsache anordnen oder die ganze Verhandlung in eine andere Sitzung vertagen, je nachdem es Frivolität annimmt oder nicht.

Nur im Falle, wo das Gericht den Präjudizialpunkt wirklich zur gesonderten Verhandlung zuläßt, wäre Art. 256 anwendbar; es würde also die Verweigerung der Einlassung auf Wag und Gefahr des Beklagten geschehen, allerdings mit minder strengen Folgen, als früher.

Ich glaube, daß vorstehende Lösung große praktische Vorzüge bietet.

4) Art. 256 findet nur Anwendung, wenn das Vorverfahren in der Hauptsache noch nicht stattgefunden hat, fällt also weg, wenn das Vorverfahren sich auch über die Hauptsache ausdehnte und nur gesonderte Verhandlung und Aburtheilung verfügt worden ist, sei es auf Grund von Art. 190 oder von Art. 157 Abs. 2. In letzterem Falle kann die Anmeldung zur Wochentabelle sofort erfolgen, und kann sogar das Gericht sich veranlaßt finden, sofort die Sitzung zur Hinterlegung der Anträge in der Hauptsache, oder falls diese Anträge schon hinterlegt sind, zur Verhandlung zu bestimmen.

5) Erscheint der Fall des Art. 256 gegeben, so ist es Sache der Parteien, die Verhandlung der Hauptsache zu betreiben, jedoch darf die Anmeldung zur Wochentabelle nur stattfinden, nachdem der Antrag des Beklagten zugestellt oder die hierzu eröffnete 15tägige Frist verstrichen ist.

Seither pflegte in Fällen dieser Art sofort bei Spruch des Urtheils eine weitere Sitzung zur Hinterlegung der Anträge und Verhandlung fixirt zu werden, ein Verfahren, welches jetzt nur noch statthaft ist, wenn Gefahr auf dem Verzuge im Sinne des Art. 259 vorliegt.

Wird Berufung ergriffen, so wird das Verfahren unterbrochen (Art. 490) und ist nöthigenfalls die Vertagung auf unbestimmte Zeit, d. h. die Streichung von der Wochentabelle zu verfügen (Art. 243 Abs. 2).

Art. 257. — **Die Vorschriften über das Vorverfahren gelten für alle im Prozesse aufgetretenen Haupt- und Nebenparteien. Sie finden, soweit das Gesetz nicht besondere Bestimmungen enthält, auf alle im Laufe des Prozesses vorkommenden Verhandlungen analoge Anwendung.**

Art. 258. — **Die näheren Vorschriften über Anlage und Führung des Hauptverzeichnisses und der für die einzelnen Senate bestimmten besonderen Verzeichnisse werden, soweit nicht das Gesetz hierüber verfügt, im Verordnungswege erlassen.**

G. A. d. K. d. A. II S. 22. 33. 40. 123. 167. a. E. 450. IV S. 73. — K. d. R. II S. 38. IV S. 35.

1) Die Vorschriften über das Vorverfahren gelten für alle auftretenden Haupt- und Nebenparteien, wie denn Art. 489 noch besonders verfügt, daß alle Zustellungen an sämmtliche Parteien zu geschehen haben und jede Partei zur Betreibung des Rechtsstreites berechtigt sei.

Wenn ein Hauptintervenient auftritt, so erscheinen ihm gegenüber die bereits in Streite befindlichen Parteien als Beklagte (Art. 67 und 488) und hieraus ließe sich folgern, daß sie die Frist des Art. 231 zur Klagebeantwortung beanspruchen dürften, wobei, da die Hauptinterventionsklage durch Zustellung an die Anwälte erhoben wird, somit die Parteien schon als erschienen zu gelten haben, jene Frist von der Zustellung an laufen würde. Eintretenden Falls wird das Gericht durch das Universalmittel der Vertagung nachhelfen. Vgl. die Verhdl. zu Art. 450b des Entwurfs (Abg. II 295).

2) Die Vorschriften für das Vorverfahren sollen ferner auf alle im späteren Verlaufe des Prozesses vorkommende Verhandlungen analoge Anwendung finden. Wer daher eine Sache von Neuem in die Sitzung bringen will, muß in der Regel alle Formen und Fristen beobachten, wie sie für die erste Verhandlung vorgeschrieben sind.

Diese Anwendung fällt jedoch hinweg, wenn das Gesetz anders verfügt, indem z. B. bei Anordnen des persönlichen Erscheinens (Art. 155) oder bei Beweisaufnahmen (Art. 334), sofort eine Sitzung zur Vornahme der betreffenden Handlungen und damit zugleich zur weiteren Verhandlung (Art. 344) bestimmt wird oder werden kann.

Sie fällt ferner weg, soweit die Analogie nicht Platz greift, wie denn, z. B. in Fällen, wo die Hinterlegung der Anträge bereits erfolgt ist und fortwirkt, neue Zustellung und Hinterlegung von Anträgen nicht nothwendig ist.

Abgekürztes Verfahren bei Gefahr auf Verzug.

Art. 259. — **Sowohl in den bereits anhängigen als auch in den erst anhängig zu machenden Sachen kann der Gerichts- oder, wenn die Sache schon einem Senate zugetheilt ist, der Senatsvorstand bei Gefahr auf Verzug auf Ansuchen der gefährdeten Partei einen Tag und eintretenden Falls eine Stunde zur sofortigen Verhandlung ohne Rücksicht auf die gewöhnlichen Fristen festsetzen.**

Die Verfügung, welche ohne weitere Förmlichkeit, wenn das Ansuchen vor Zustellung der Klageschrift gestellt wurde, auf die Klageschrift, sonst auf das Gesuch zu setzen ist und gegebenen Falls auch den Senat, in welchem die Sache verhandelt werden soll, zu bezeichnen hat, muß, wenn die Klageschrift noch nicht zugestellt ist, mit dieser, andernfalls durch besondern Akt der Gegenpartei unverzüglich zugestellt werden.

Mit der Zustellung ist, wenn sie an den Anwalt der Gegenpartei geschieht, die Aufforderung zum Erscheinen in der festgesetzten Sitzung, im Falle aber, daß sie an die Partei selbst zu geschehen hat, die Aufforderung zu verbinden, ungesäumt einen Anwalt aufzustellen, der für sie in der anberaumten Sitzung zu erscheinen hat.

In bereits anhängigen Sachen kann die in Abs. 1 bezeichnete Verfügung auch von dem Gerichte erlassen werden, wenn sie bei einer auf die Sache bezüglichen Verhandlung Anlaß dazu ergeben und eine Partei es beantragt hat.

Art. 260. — **Ist die Sitzung zur Verhandlung nach Art. 259 festgesetzt worden, so kommen folgende besondere Bestimmungen zur Anwendung:**

1) **Die Anmeldung der Sache zum Eintrage in das Hauptverzeichniß kann noch während der Sitzung geschehen. Der Aufruf erfolgt auf Anordnung des Vorsitzenden ohne Rücksicht auf die Reihenfolge.**

2) **Die Hinterlegung von Anträgen findet nur bei der Verhandlung statt. Die vorgängige Zustellung motivirter Anträge ist nicht geboten.**

3) **Besteht Anlaß zur Streitverkündung beziehungsweise zur Erhebung einer Gewährschaftsklage, so hat das Gericht hiefür in der Sitzung auf Antrag der betreffenden Partei unter Vertagung der Hauptsache angemessene Frist zu gewähren. Mit der Verhandlung der Hauptsache ist, vorbehaltlich der Bestimmungen des Art. 72, jene der Gewährschaftsklage, ohne daß es der vorgängigen Zustellung motivirter Anträge bedarf, zu verbinden und der Gewährschaftsbeklagte bei Zustellung der Klageschrift deshalb aufzufordern, ungesäumt einen Anwalt aufzustellen, der für ihn in der zur Verhandlung der Sache festgesetzten Sitzung zu erscheinen hat.**

4) **Widerklagen sind, wenn deren gleichzeitige Entscheidung eine nachtheilige Verzögerung besorgen läßt, zur besondern Verhandlung zu verweisen.**

Art. 261. — **Ergibt sich, daß eine Sache mit Unrecht zu dem in Art. 259 und 260 bezeichneten abgekürzten Verfahren gebracht ist oder daß sie darin nach Beschaffenheit des Falls nicht**

erledigt werden kann, so hat das Gericht, soweit es erforderlich erscheint, die dem regelmäßigen Verfahren entsprechenden Verhandlungen unter Festsetzung angemessener Fristen anzuordnen.

Gleiches hat bezüglich einer etwa erhobenen Gewährschaftsklage unter Verweisung derselben zur gesonderten Verhandlung zu geschehen, wenn sich ergibt, daß sie nach Beschaffenheit des Falls im abgekürzten Verfahren nicht erledigt werden kann.

Weder gegen diese noch gegen sonstige Anordnungen des Gerichts oder des Gerichts- oder Senatsvorstands in Betreff der Zulassung oder Verweisung des abgekürzten Verfahrens findet ein Rechtsmittel statt.

G. A. d. K. d. A. II S. 49—58. 104. 107—109. 113. 114. 123.—127. 450. III S. 92. 103. IV S. 73.
K. d. R. II S. 38—40. IV S. 35.

1) Die Vorschriften über das abgekürzte Verfahren geben dem Prozeßgange bei den Bezirksgerichten eine Beweglichkeit und Geschmeidigkeit, welche ihn fähig macht, allen Bedürfnissen der Praxis zu genügen und namentlich, was Raschheit der Aburtheilung betrifft, das Nemliche zu leisten, wie das handelsgerichtliche und landgerichtliche Verfahren, ja noch Besseres, weil der Vortheil der Instruktion durch Anwälte hinzutritt. Vgl. Bemerk. zu Art. 2 Nr. 1, zu Art. 3 Nr. 2 und zu Art. 78, 79 Nr. 9.

2) Die Abkürzung des Verfahrens besteht darin, daß mit Beiseiteschieben aller vorbereitenden Formen und Fristen sofort zur Verhandlung in der Sitzung (Art. 246) geschritten wird. Im Uebrigen, namentlich bezüglich des Beweisverfahrens, besteht zwischen gewöhnlichen und dringlichen Sachen kein Unterschied, jedoch versteht es sich wohl von selbst, daß bei Festsetzung von Fristen und Tagfahrten überall besondere Rücksicht auf die Dringlichkeit der Sache zu nehmen sei und werden, z. B. in dringlichen Sachen die Beweisaufnahmen, wo immer thunlich, in die Sitzung selbst zu verlegen sein.

3) Das abgekürzte Verfahren soll gestattet werden, wenn Gefahr auf Verzug ist.

Eine solche Gefahr besteht für diejenige Partei, welcher aus der Verzögerung der Entscheidung erhebliche Nachtheile zu erwachsen drohen, sei es, daß das strittige Recht selbst, was Beweisführung oder Urtheilsvollzug betrifft, gefährdet wäre, sei es, daß das Fortbestehen des Zustandes der Ungewißheit oder die Weigerung, rechtlichen Verpflichtungen nachzukommen, sonst bedeutenden Schaden verursachen würde.

Natürlich hat das richterliche Ermessen hier den größten Spielraum und darf insbesondere auch die Erwägung Einfluß äußern, ob eine Sache, ihrer Natur nach, sich zu einem einfachen und summarischen Verfahren eigne oder nicht, wie dies der Gesetzgeber selbst andeutet in Art. 261 Abs. 1. Bei sehr einfachen Streitpunkten, wie z. B. Prozeßeinreden, wird auch ein geringerer Grad der Dringlichkeit genügen.

Der Weg des abgekürzten Verfahrens kann sowohl bei Beginn des Prozesses, als im Laufe desselben betreten werden. Der erstere Fall ist der gewöhnliche, praktisch wichtigste und daher zunächst zu besprechen.

a) Ladung auf kurze Frist.

4) Die Ladung auf kurze Frist wird vom Gerichtsvorstande bewilligt, welcher seine Verfügung, einfach lautend, daß zur Verhandlung der betreffenden Streitsache die zu bezeichnende Sitzung bestimmt werde, auf die ihm vorzulegende Klagschrift setzt. Dem Gerichtsvorstande sind die Thatsachen, auf welche sich die Gefahr auf dem Verzuge gründet, vorzutragen und ist hiermit ein bezügliches Gesuch zu verbinden.

Man pflegte seither immer ein besonderes Gesuch einzureichen, nach dem Willen der Prozeßordnung soll jedoch die Klagschrift dasselbe ersetzen, so daß also am Schlusse der Klagschrift die Gründe der Dringlichkeit, so weit nöthig, darzulegen und das Gesuch um Gestattung der Ladung auf kurze Frist zu stellen sein wird.

5) Da das Gesetz ganz allgemein spricht, so können alle Ladungsfristen ohne Unterschied gekürzt werden, also auch bei Ladungen von Ausländern und Leuten ohne bekannten Aufenthalt, wie dies ausdrücklich anerkannt wurde (Abg. II 124).

Diese letzteren Fristen haben allerdings das Besondere, daß sie nur theilweise zum Handeln, theilweise aber deßhalb gegeben sind, weil vorausgesetzt wird, daß vor Ablauf eines gewissen Zeitraums die Ladung diejenige Person, welcher sie gilt, gar nicht erreiche, und es ist klar, daß dieser letztere Theil ohne die größte Ungerechtigkeit nicht entzogen werden dürfte. Allein diese Erwägung hat nur thatsächlichen Werth, insofern sie für den Gerichtsvorstand bei Festsetzung der Tagfahrt und für das Gericht im Falle des Art. 300 bestimmend sein wird, steht jedoch rechtlich der Ladung auf kurze Frist nicht im Wege, wie Letzteres im französischen Prozesse der Fall ist.

Ueberhaupt ist bezüglich der Frage, welche Frist dem Beklagten zum Erscheinen zu gönnen sei, dem Gerichtsvorstande die vollste Freiheit gegeben, und konnte dies auch nicht anders sein, da die Umstände des Falles entscheiden müssen — der Grad der Dringlichkeit, die Natur des Rechtsverhältnisses, vor Allem aber die besonderen Gründe, um anzunehmen, daß die zu ladende Person am bestimmten Tage erscheinen und ihre Vertheidigung vorbringen könne.

6) Das Gesetz sagt nur, daß der Tag zur Verhandlung zu bestimmen, nicht aber, daß auch die Frist zwischen der Ladung und diesem Tage zu bezeichnen sei. Es entspricht dies der in der Pfalz bestehenden Uebung und ist auch eine solche Bezeichnung nicht nöthig, da das Gesetz vorschreibt, daß die Ladung unverzüglich zu geschehen habe und der Anwalt oder Gerichtsvollzieher für schuldhafte Verzögerungen einzustehen hätte (Art. 300). Uebrigens mag erwähnt sein, daß man in der Pfalz doch hie und da noch die Auflage beifügte, binnen einer gewissen Frist nach der Bewilligung oder vor der Sitzung zu laden und, wie ich glaube, könnte dies auch jetzt noch geschehen.

7) Die Verfügung des Gerichtsvorstandes ist mit der Klagschrift zuzustellen, und bei der Ladung der Beklagte aufzufordern, einen Anwalt aufzustellen, welcher für ihn in der bezeichneten Sitzung zu erscheinen habe. Diese besondere Aufforderung, welche verhüten soll, daß rechtsunkundige Personen meinen, es genüge, wenn sie persönlich in der Sitzung erscheinen, darf der Gerichtsvollzieher nie unterlassen.

8) Verhandlung in der Sitzung.

Die Verhandlung in der Sitzung bietet in Fällen, wo direkte Ladung ergangen ist, so ziemlich das nemliche Bild, wie die Verhandlung im Parteiprozesse.

Nichtsdestoweniger erscheint es nicht statthaft, die Vorschriften, welche für den letzteren Prozeß gegeben sind, ohne Weiteres analog anzuwenden, denn dieselben beruhen größtentheils auf der besonderen Erwägung, daß rechtsunkundige Personen vor Gericht stehen, von welchen man strenge Einhaltung der Formen nicht wohl verlangen könne. Dies gilt namentlich von der Bestimmung in Art. 506 Abs. 2, daß Klagänderungen und Prozeßeinreden bis zum Schlusse der ersten Verhandlung, also der Streiteinlassung, Replik nachgängig, vorgebracht werden dürfen, und es würde den Regeln der Auslegung geradezu widerstreiten, diese Ausnahme in den Anwaltsprozeß herüberzuziehen. Abg. II 258 (v. Weiß). Uebrigens ist es auch nicht Schade darum, wenn solche Nachschleppungen zurückgewiesen werden, denn weder Klagänderungen noch Prozeßeinreden verdienen besondere Begünstigung.

9) Wenn mit abgekürzter Frist direkt in die Sitzung geladen ist, so müssen beide Theile darauf gerüstet sein, falls nöthig, über alle Streitpunkte, welche die Sache bietet, sofort zu verhandeln, also über Prozeßeinreden, mögen sie bevorzugt sein oder nicht, über Präjudizial- und Incidentpunkte, sowie endlich über den Grund der Sache und sogar über Widerklagen. Was im Vorverfahren gemessenen Ganges hintereinander herschreitet, tritt hier auf einmal auf.

Allerdings werden durch Einleitung des abgekürzten Verfahrens die allgemeinen Prinzipien, welche gewisse Prozeßeinreden von der Einlassung befreien oder welche dem Gerichte gestatten, einzelne Streitpunkte, namentlich Präjudizialpunkte, getrennt zu verhandeln und abzuurtheilen, nicht aufgehoben, jedoch kann das Gericht sofort nach Aburtheilung solcher Vorfragen über den Grund der Sache weiter verhandeln lassen.

10) Die Anmeldung zum Hauptverzeichnisse kann noch während der Sitzung geschehen und der Aufruf erfolgt ohne Rücksicht auf die Reihenfolge des Sitzungsverzeichnisses. Selbstverständlich wird jedoch schon bei Anberaumung des Sitzungstages Rücksicht darauf genommen, daß die nöthige Zeit frei sei.

Die Zustellung motivirter Anträge ist nicht geboten, jedoch steht auch nichts im Wege, daß sie dennoch stattfinde, wenn die Zeit dazu ausreicht und die Sache es erheischt. In Fällen, wo der Beklagte Einwände vorzubringen hat, welche eingehendere Erörterung und Beweisführung beanspruchen, ist es oft sehr wünschenswerth und der Verhandlung selbst höchst förderlich, wenn wenigstens der Antrag des Beklagten vorher zugestellt wird, und Mittheilung der Akten erfolgt; jedenfalls dürften die hierdurch verursachten Kosten nicht als frustratorisch erachtet werden. Verhdl. zu Art. 234 des Entw. Abg. II 113 u. 114.

11) Was die Gewährschaftsklage betrifft, so hat, insofern das Gesetz ein Recht auf gleichzeitige Verhandlung gibt, die Dringlichkeit der Hauptklage auch die Dringlichkeit der Gewährschaftsklage zur Folge, nnd falls daher zur Verhandlung einer Sache Ladung auf kurze Frist bewilligt worden ist, so kann der Gerichtsvorstand die Beiladung des Gewährschaftspflichtigen in die nemliche Sitzung nicht versagen, sofern er die Zeit dazu ausreichend findet.

Sehr häufig wird daher in der anberaumten Sitzung sofort unter allen Betheiligten verhandelt werden können.

Auch die Streitverkündung kann sofort nach der Ladung erfolgen, und genügt es, zur Wahrung der Regreßansprüche, wenn dem Gewährschaftspflichtigen bis zu dem ihm mitzutheilenden Tage der Verhandlung ein genügender Zeitraum bleibt, um in der Sitzung zu interveniren.

12) Hat die Gewährschaftsklage oder Streitverkündung nicht schon vorher stattgefunden und ergibt sich in der Sitzung, daß Grund dazu vorliege, sei es nun auf Seiten des Klägers, sei es auf Seiten des Beklagten, so trifft Art. 260 Ziff. 3 dahin Vorsorge, daß das Gericht die Verhandlung in eine andere, den Umständen entsprechend zu bestimmende, Sitzung vertage und für den Fall der Gewährschaftsklage, gemäß Art. 259 Abs. 4 die Beiladung auf kurze Frist bewillige. Dies ist der Sinn besagter Bestimmung, welche wohl klarer und einfacher gefaßt sein könnte.

Die bezügliche Verfügung des Gerichts wird mit der Klagschrift zuzustellen sein (Art. 259 Abs. 2).

13) Was in Nr. 11 und 12 bezüglich der Beiladung von Gewährschaftspflichtigen bemerkt ist, wird wohl in analoger Weise auch für sonstige Beiladungen, z. B. von Streitgenossen, zu gelten haben.

14) Wenn in Art. 260 Ziff. 4 verfügt ist, daß Widerklagen zur gesonderten Verhandlung verwiesen werden können, so gilt dies nicht von solchen Widerklagen, welche zugleich den Stoff vorgeschützter Einreden bilden, denn, was als Einrede zugelassen werden muß, darf als Widerklage nicht zurückgewiesen werden.

b) Abkürzung des Verfahrens im Laufe des Prozesses.

15) Auch in Rechtsstreiten, welche schon anhängig sind, kann zu jeder Zeit, sobald sich die Dringlichkeit ergibt, vom gewöhnlichen ins abgekürzte Verfahren übergegangen werden, und zwar auf Begehren der gefährdeten Partei, mag diese nun der Kläger oder der Beklagte, eine Haupt- oder eine Nebenpartei sein. In der Regel hat allerdings nur der Kläger Interesse daran, daß eine rasche Entscheidung erfolge; allein es gibt doch auch viele Fälle, wo dieses Interesse auf Seite des Beklagten besteht, so z. B. bei Einwänden, welche vom Schuldner oder von Dritten gegen begonnene Vollstreckungen erhoben werden (Art. 869 u. 870).

Die Abkürzung des Verfahrens besteht auch hier nur darin, daß sofort, ohne Beachtung sonstiger Formen und Fristen, ein Tag zur Verhandlung festgesetzt wird, und zwar entweder nur für einzelne Streitpunkte (Incidentpunkte, Prozeßeinreden), falls nur bezüglich dieser die Dringlichkeit anzunehmen ist, oder Antrag gestellt ist, oder aber für die ganze Streitsache.

16) Der Anwalt, welcher in diesem Falle die Verhandlung außer der Ordnung herbeizuführen wünscht, hat ein Gesuch an den Gerichtsvorstand oder, wenn die Sache bereits einem Senate zugetheilt war, an den Senatsvorstand zu richten, in welchem er die Gründe der Dringlichkeit darlegt und, eintretenden Falls, die Streitpunkte, über welche verhandelt werden soll, bezeichnet. Auf dieses Gesuch setzt der Vorstand seine Verfügung und Beides ist unverzüglich dem Gegenanwalte mit Aufforderung zum Erscheinen in der Sitzung zuzustellen.

Ergibt sich der Anlaß zur Verhandlung mit abgekürzter Frist in der Sitzung, so bedarf es eines Gesuches an den Gerichtsvorstand nicht, vielmehr erläßt das Gericht selbst die bezügliche Verfügung (Art. 259 Abs. 4).

17) Für die Verhandlung selbst gilt, nach Lage der Sache, das Nemliche, wie im Falle, wo von vornherein auf kurze Frist geladen ist, und auch Streitverkündung, Gewährschaftsklagen und sonstige Beiladungen können noch berücksichtigt werden, wenn sie nicht verspätet erscheinen (Art. 233 Abs. 4).

c) Allgemeine Bemerkungen.

18) Die Verfügungen des Art. 259 beziehen sich zunächst nur auf eine einzige Verhandlung. Ergibt dieselbe kein Endurtheil, so frägt es sich, ob die Gefahr auf dem Verzuge noch fortdauere oder nicht.

Letzteren Falls tritt von selbst und ohne daß es nöthig wäre, dies besonders zu verfügen, das gewöhnliche Verfahren ein; denn es ist wohl zu beachten, daß es keine summarischen Sachen mehr gibt, sondern nur einzelne summarische Verhandlungen.

Ersteren Falls ist Anlaß gegeben, auch für die nachfolgenden Verhandlungen das abgekürzte Verfahren zuzulassen und es gestaltet sich in dieser Weise faktisch das ganze Verfahren zu einem summarischen. Das Gericht wird in der Regel sofort, nachdem es Vorfragen abgeurtheilt oder auf Beweis erkannt hat, vorausgesetzt, daß es nicht in der Lage ist, in der nemlichen Sitzung weiter zu verhandeln, eine spätere Sitzung zur Verhandlung anberaumen (Art. 259 Abs. 4). Es kann dies sogar dann geschehen, wenn die Beweisaufnahme nicht, oder nicht vollständig in der Sitzung stattfindet, wenn z. B. weit entfernt wohnende oder kranke Personen zeugschaftlich zu vernehmen sind oder Eide zu schwören haben. Man nahm in Fällen dieser Art in der Pfalz nie Anstand, unter Berücksichtigung der Zeit, welche muthmaßlich zur Beweisaufnahme erforderlich ist, sofort den Tag der Verhandlung festzusetzen, ein Verfahren welches ebenso einfach als praktisch ist.

19) Sowie zu jeder Zeit der Weg des abgekürzten Verfahrens betreten werden kann, so kann er auch zu jeder Zeit wieder verlassen werden, insbesondere kann in Fällen, wo dieses Verfahren bereits bewilligt und die Verhandlung begonnen ist, die Sache sofort zum ordentlichen Verfahren verwiesen werden, wenn sich zeigt, entweder 1) daß die Vorbedingungen desselben fehlen, insbesondere daß die Bewilligung durch unwahre Behauptungen erschlichen worden sei, oder 2) daß die Sache ihrer Beschaffenheit nach, sich nicht im abgekürzten Verfahren erledigen lasse, daß sie eine summarische Behandlung nicht ertrage.

In Fällen solcher Art ist das Gericht nicht genöthigt, immer die ganze Verhandlung als vereitelt zu erklären, vielmehr wird es, so weit die Sache völlig reif ist, entscheiden, z. B. Prozeßeinreden und dergleichen Vorfragen erledigen, im Uebrigen aber die Sache zum Vorverfahren verweisen, unter Bestimmung der erforderlichen Fristen. (Vgl. Bemerk. zu Art. 250 Nr. 2).

20) Der Fall, daß eine Sache, welche dringlich ist, bloß ihrer sonstigen Beschaffenheit wegen nicht im abgekürzten Verfahren erledigt werden kann, wird, meinen Erfahrungen gemäß, nicht leicht vorkommen. Allerdings ist zuzugestehen, daß eine erschöpfende, völlig aufklärende Verhandlung oft ohne großen Zeitverlust nicht möglich ist, wenn nicht vorher motivirte Anträge gewechselt und die Akten mitgetheilt worden sind, allein dem läßt sich leicht abhelfen, ohne daß es nöthig ist, die ganze Sache auf den langsamen Weg des gewöhnlichen Vorverfahrens zu verweisen.

Es entspricht offenbar dem Sinne des Art. 260 Abs. 1, daß das Gericht auch nur theilweise, so weit es gerade nöthig erscheint, zum gewöhnlichen Verfahren zurückkehren dürfe, daß es ihm also gestattet sei, nur einzelne Vorbereitungshandlungen (Zustellung von Anträgen, Mittheilung der Akten) anzuordnen, dafür Frist zu setzen und zugleich die Sitzung zur weiteren Verhandlung anzuberaumen.

Auch bei Gewährschaftsklagen wird es nur höchst selten nöthig sein, sie aus dem abgekürzten Verfahren wegzuweisen, wohl aber wird es öfter geschehen, daß nach Aburtheilung einer dringlichen Hauptklage, eine an sich nicht dringliche Gewährschaftsklage anhängig bleibt und im gewöhnlichen Verfahren weiter verhandelt wird.

21) Schließlich ist zu erwähnen, daß gegen die Verfügungen, welche die Zulassung oder Verweigerung des abgekürzten Verfahrens betreffen, Rechtsmittel irgend einer Art nicht zulässig sind.

VII. Hauptstück.

Urtheil.

Allgemeine Bestimmungen.

Art. 262. — **Das Gericht darf, abgesehen von der Verbesserung bloßer Rechnungsfehler, der Partei ein Anderes oder Mehreres, als um was sie gebeten hat, nicht zuerkennen.**

Der Ausspruch über den Ersatz der Prozeßkosten ergeht von Amtswegen.

Art. 263. — **Hat eine Partei nach Größe oder Beschaffenheit ihres Anspruchs zu viel verlangt, so hat die Zuerkennung in dem Maße zu erfolgen, in welchem das Gericht sie begründet findet.**

Art. 264. — **In der rechtlichen Würdigung des Falls ist das Gericht von dem Vorbringen der Parteien unabhängig.**

Es ist an den Antrag auf Einleitung eines Vor- oder Zwischenverfahrens, das es für überflüssig erachtet, nicht gebunden.

Unbegründete und unstatthafte Ansprüche und Anträge, namentlich solche, denen eine Einrede entgegensteht, auf welche die Parteien nach den bestehenden Gesetzen rechtsgiltig nicht verzichten können, sowie unerhebliche oder gesetzlich nicht zulässige Angriffs-, Vertheidigungs- und Beweismittel unterliegen der Zurückweisung auch ohne Antrag der Gegenpartei.

Einreden, Repliken und sonstige selbständige Rechtsbehelfe, deren thatsächliche Unterlage sich aus der Verhandlung ergibt, dürfen auch ohne desfallsigen Parteiantrag vom Gerichte berücksichtigt werden, soferne weder aus der Verhandlung hervorgeht, daß sie als solche nicht geltend gemacht werden wollten, noch eine besondere gesetzliche Bestimmung entgegensteht.

Art. 265. — **Die Unzuständigkeit des Gerichts ist, soferne sie nicht durch eine zulässige Vereinbarung beseitigt erscheint, in jeder Lage des Rechtsstreits auf Antrag oder von Amtswegen auszusprechen.**

G. A. d. K. d. A. I S. 70. 72. II S. 60—63. 128. IV S. 73. 74. 76.
K. d. R. II S. 41—54. IV S. 35. 36.

1) Das Gesetz gibt hier Vorschriften über den Umfang der richterlichen Gewalt; es sucht auszuscheiden, in welchen Beziehungen der Richter von Amtswegen erkennen dürfe und in welchen Beziehungen er an die Anträge und Vorträge der Parteien gebunden sei.

a) Rechtliche Würdigung.

2) Die rechtliche Würdigung des Falls ist ausschließlich Sache des Richters, welcher in dieser Beziehung vom Vorbringen der Parteien ganz unabhängig ist. Sie begreift die Lösung der Fragen, welches Recht zur Anwendung zu kommen habe und wie dasselbe auszulegen und auf die gegebenen Thatsachen anzuwenden sei.

Gegenstand der ersteren Frage bildet zunächst die schwierige Lehre von der Collision der Statuten, eine Lehre, welche diesseits durch die noch fortgeltenden Bestimmungen der Ger.-Ordn. Cap. XIV § 7 Nr. 8, so wie die erläuternde Verfügung vom 11. Juni 1816, in der Pfalz aber durch Art. 3 Code civil geregelt wird; hier wie dort jedoch nur in den Hauptrichtungen und nicht der Art, daß nicht die besonderen Civilgesetze (preuß. Landr. Einleitg. §. 23 — 35; bayer. L. R. Thl. I cap. II § 17), namentlich aber die allgemeinen Rechtsprinzipien ergänzend aushelfen müßten. — Vgl. für das diesseitige Recht: Seuffert Comment. Bd. I S. 303—339 und für die Pfalz: Demolombe, cours de Code civ. Bd. I Nr. 68—108 und Foelix, droit international.

Ist ermittelt, welcher Ort maßgebend sei, so entsteht die weitere Frage, welche Gesetzgebung dort Geltung habe, ein Punkt, welcher diesseits, wo sehr oft die einzelnen Häuser der nemlichen Ortschaft unter Herrschaft verschiedener Gesetze stehen, manche Schwierigkeiten bietet. Die erschöpfendste und annähernd richtigste Zusammenstellung in dieser Beziehung bietet die Civilgesetzstatistik von J. Peißl.

3) Zu den Rechten, welche der Richter von Amtswegen zu ermitteln und zu berücksichtigen hat, gehört nicht bloß das geschriebene Recht im weitesten Umfange, (sowohl des Inlandes als des Auslandes, sowohl die Gesetzgebungen, welche große Gebiete umfassen, als die Partikularstatuten einzelner Gemeinden), sondern auch das Gewohnheitsrecht.

Diese letztere Rechtsquelle wird vom französischen Rechte nicht anerkannt, und wenn auch einzelne Stimmen älterer Rechtslehrer anderer Ansicht sind, so ist doch die Jurisprudenz entschieden dagegen. Demolombe Bd. I Nr. 35.

Das preußische Landrecht schließt das Gewohnheitsrecht aus, soweit eine Abänderung der bestehenden Gesetzgebung in Frage ist, läßt dasselbe aber zu als ergänzende Rechtsquelle.

Die übrigen geltenden Rechte, insbesondere das bayer. Landrecht sowie das gemeine Recht erkennen das Gewohnheitsrecht als selbständige Rechtsquelle unbedingt an.

Ueber die Frage, was als Gewohnheitsrecht oder Herkommen (welche Ausdrücke in der Regel als gleichbedeutend gebraucht werden) zu gelten habe, gehen die Ansichten auseinander.

Manche behaupten, daß man von einem Gewohnheitsrechte oder Herkommen nur sprechen dürfe, wenn die Uebung einer Rechtsregel, eines Rechtssatzes innerhalb eines gewissen Gebietes behauptet werde, nie aber, wenn es sich nur um Ausübung und Erwerb bestimmter Rechte handele, in welchem Falle nur die Grundsätze über Verjährung zu gelten hätten. Seuff. Archiv Bd. I Nr. 3, IX Nr. 116, X Nr. 190, XI Nr. 2 XIII Nr. 1 und 204.

Andere lassen im Gegentheile das Herkommen ganz allgemein auch bei bestimmten Rechtsverhältnissen zu. Vgl. Seuff. Archiv. Bd. III Nr. 256 u. Bd. XIV Nr. 93, wo das Prinzip scharf ausgesprochen ist, und Bd. III Nr. 291, 292, 293 VII Nr. 279 IX Nr. 243 sowie Bl. f. R. Bd. XX S. 367, 380 und Bd. XXII S. 298, wo es wenigstens Anwendung gefunden hat.

Am richtigsten ist wohl diejenige Ansicht, welche ein zweifaches Herkommen unterscheidet, 1) ein Herkommen als Gewohnheitsrecht, für Bildung von Rechtsregeln und Rechtssätzen und 2) ein Herkommen als besonderer Entstehungsgrund für bestimmte Rechtsverhältnisse. Nur das Herkommen ersterer Art läßt sich als eine durch den Richter von Amtswegen zu erforschende und zu berücksichtigende Rechtsquelle betrachten, beim letzteren aber hängt die Berücksichtigung vom Vorbringen der Partei und von Beweisführung ab, ebenso wie bei der unvordenklichen Verjährung.

Diese Ansicht hat insbesondere auch in einer Reihe von Erkenntnissen des obersten Gerichtshofes Ausdruck gefunden. Bl. f. R. Bd. VII S. 142 und 33* VIII S. 117 XIX S. 285 XXI S. 491 XXV S. 49 (XXXI u. XXXII) Erg.-Bd. S. 305.

Hierbei bleibt die Frage unberührt, ob auch ein einzelnes Rechtsverhältniß auf dem Wege des Herkommens begründet werden könne, oder ob eine Mehrzahl ähnlicher Rechtsverhältnisse, namentlich Wechselbeziehungen zwischen einer größeren Zahl von Personen, dazu erforderlich seien. Bl. f. R. XIV S. 351.

Bezüglich der Art und Weise der Ermittlung von Gewohnheitsrechten Näheres bei Art. 321.

4) Als eine besondere Quelle des Rechtes waren bis jetzt die Plenarbeschlüsse des obersten Gerichtshofes gemäß Ges. vom 17. November 1837 zu betrachten, insofern sie auch für künftige völlig gleichartige Fälle wirkten und, wenn auch nicht die Kraft eines Gesetzes, doch die Kraft eines für Zweifelsfälle maßgebenden Präjudizes (Gerichtsgebrauchs) im Sinne von Theil I Cap. II § 14 Nr. 3 des bayr. Landrechtes hatten. Jenes Gesetz ist nun zwar durch das Einführungsgesetz Art. 3 Ziff. 12 aufgehoben, allein die bereits ergangenen Plenarbeschlüsse behaupten nichts destoweniger bezüglich der entschiedenen Streitfragen die frühere Wirkung und müssen vom Richter beachtet werden.

b) Parteianträge.

5) Der Richter darf, so weit es sich um Zuspruch eines Rechtes handelt, nie über das Begehren der Partei (des Klägers) hinausgehen, und etwas Anderes oder mehr als verlangt wird, zuerkennen; jedoch steht nichts im Wege, daß er das Begehrte aus anderen Gründen zuspreche, namentlich auch thatsächliche Erwägungen, welchen die Partei kein Gewicht beilegte, für erheblich erachte, vorausgesetzt, daß die Thatsachen sich aus der Verhandlung ergeben und keine unzulässige Aenderung des Klaggrundes damit verbunden ist.

Eine Ausnahme von diesem Verbote besteht für bloße Rechnungsfehler, sowie für die Prozeßkosten.

Wegen der Prozeßkosten darf der Richter sowohl bei Zwischenurtheilen als bei Endurtheilen immer erkennen, wie es ihm geeignet erscheint, auch wenn Anträge deßhalb nicht gestellt sind. Der Entwurf wollte, im Einklange mit dem diesseits bestehenden Rechte, das Gleiche auch für sonstige Entschädigungen, sowie für Früchte und Zinsen verfügen, allein man hielt dies für zu weit gehend und zwar mit Recht, da Art. 182 Gelegenheit bietet, solche Nebensachen in jedem Stande der Sache bis zum Endurtheile geltend zu machen.

6) Größere Freiheit ist dem Richter gegönnt, wenn es sich nicht um Zuspruch, sondern um Abweisung von Ansprüchen handelt.

Daß es nicht verwehrt sein könne, weniger zuzusprechen, bloß deßhalb, weil mehr begehrt ist, versteht sich so sehr von selbst, daß Art. 263 wohl nicht entstanden wäre, hätte man nicht hervorheben wollen, daß die plus petitio re als dilatorische Einrede ein für allemal beseitigt sei.

Hat der Beklagte Antrag auf Abweisung des Klaganspruches gestellt, so ist der Richter an die Rechtsgründe und Thatsachen, worauf sich dieser Antrag stützt, nicht gebunden, vielmehr steht es ihm frei, auch aus anderen Gesichtspunkten, welche ihm die richtigen scheinen, demselben stattzugeben; er kann z. B., wenn die Klage bloß mit einer peremtorischen Einrede bekämpft wird, sie wegen Mangelhaftigkeit des Klaggrundes zurückweisen und umgekehrt, letzteren Falles jedoch mit Berücksichtigung der Vorschriften in Art. 264 Abs. 4.

7) Das Gesetz gibt dem Richter aber auch die Befugniß, selbst ohne Antrag des Beklagten ungegründete oder unstatthafte Ansprüche zurückzuweisen.

Die bezügliche Bestimmung ist eine fast wörtliche Wiederholung dessen, was Seuffert in seinem Commentare Bd. I S. 391 ausspricht und es läßt sich hieraus folgern, daß auch das Nemliche gemeint sei. Allerdings hat Seuffert an jener Stelle nur die Abweisung a limine im Auge und sagte, es seien Ansprüche und Anträge, welche ex ipsis narratis als grundlos oder unstatthaft erscheinen, ohne Gehör des Gegners zurückzuweisen; allein unsere Prozeßordnung kennt eine Abweisung a limine nicht, und dies mußte dem Gesetzgeber gegenwärtig sein. Auch ist klar, daß Art. 263 Abs. 3 nicht vom Falle spricht, wo Versäumnungsurtheil ergeht, welcher Fall durch die Art. 297 u. 301 geregelt ist, sondern voraussetzt, daß beide Anwälte Anträge genommen haben.

Der Sinn des Gesetzes möchte daher sein, daß Ansprüche, welche nach dem eigenen Vorbringen des Klägers als unstatthaft oder ungegründet erscheinen, unbedingt zurückzuweisen seien, trotzdem daß der Beklagte dies in seinem Antrage nicht begehrte; ganz in derselben Weise, wie es früher bei der Abweisung a limine der Fall war. Abg. II S. 62 (v. Neumayr).

Unzweifelhaft ist insbesondere die Befugniß des Richters, von Amtswegen einzugreifen, wenn es sich um Interessen handelt, welche der Verfügung der Parteien entzogen sind, oder wenn Gründe des öffentlichen Interesse ihn verpflichten, gewisse Ansprüche abzuweisen, z. B. die Ein=

klagung des Preises für Verübung eines Deliktes. Hieher gehört auch der vom Gesetze vorgesehene Fall, daß Einreden entgegenstehen, auf welche nicht rechtsgiltig verzichtet werden kann. Er darf solche Gesichtspunkte berücksichtigen, wenn sie sich irgendwie aus der Verhandlung ergeben. Vgl. Referat 2. Lesung Hptst. XXIX Art. 5 (v. Neumayr).

8) Was die den Prozeßgang und die Beweisführung betreffenden Anträge anbelangt, so hat der Richter völlig freie Hand, alle Maßregeln, welche er für überflüssig oder unerheblich hält, zurückzuweisen und sofort in der Hauptsache zu erkennen; aus noch viel stärkeren Gründen natürlich solche, welche gesetzlich unstatthaft sind.

Umgekehrt steht es ihm jedoch nicht in gleicher Weise frei, Beweiserhebungen jeder Art von Amtswegen anzuordnen; vielmehr darf dies nur dort geschehen, wo das Gesetz es ausdrücklich gestattet, wie z. B. beim Anordnen des persönlichen Erscheinens (Art. 155), einer Expertise (Art. 433), eines Augenscheines (Art. 396). Vgl. Art. 328.

c. Partei-Vorbringen.

9) Der Richter darf in der Regel nur diejenigen Thatsachen berücksichtigen, welche ihm die Partei bei der Verhandlung vorträgt, und darf auf die in den motivirten Anträgen enthaltene Darstellung nur in so weit Rücksicht nehmen, als sie mit dem Vortrage in der Sitzung übereinstimmt, oder die Partei selbst darauf Bezug nimmt. Dies hindert denselben jedoch nicht, den Inhalt der motivirten Anträge unter Umständen als Beweismaterial zu benützen.

10) Alle Thatsachen, welche die Verhandlung ergibt, darf der Richter berücksichtigen und die ihm sachgemäß erscheinenden Rechtsfolgen daraus ziehen, vorausgesetzt, daß sie nicht ultra petita führen.

Es gilt dies insbesondere auch von Thatsachen, welche geeignet sind, den Grund von Einreden oder Repliken zu bilden, selbst wenn sie als solche nicht ausdrücklich geltend gemacht werden; es müßte denn sein 1) daß aus der Verhandlung die Gewißheit sich ergäbe, daß sie nicht geltend gemacht werden wollen oder 2) daß eine besondere gesetzliche, d. h. civilrechtliche Bestimmung entgegensteht.

Was den ersten Ausnahmsfall betrifft, so erleidet er wiederum eine Ausnahme, wenn Einreden in Frage sind, auf welche giltig nicht verzichtet werden kann. Besteht Zweifel ob eine Einrede geltend gemacht werden wolle oder nicht, so ist es Pflicht des Vorsitzenden, durch geeignete Fragen Aufklärung zu verschaffen. Art. 274 Abs. 2.

Was den zweiten Ausnahmsfall betrifft, so wurde er veranlaßt durch den Hinblick auf Art. 2223 Code civ., welcher dem Richter verbietet, die Einrede der Verjährung von Amtswegen zu berücksichtigen, während bekanntlich die Ger.-Ordnung gerade hier das Entgegengesetzte bestimmt. Jene Vorschrift des Art. 2223 Code civ. besteht also fort; sie erscheint zivilrechtlicher Natur, insofern sie die Wirkung der Verjährung dahin bestimmt, daß das Klagrecht als unversehrt fortbestehend gedacht wird, so lange es nicht durch ausdrückliches Vorschützen der Verjährung angefochten wird.

Derselbe Grundsatz wird auch auf sonstige Einreden Anwendung finden, insofern deren Wirksamkeit nach den Prinzipien des Civilrechts von ausdrücklicher Geltendmachung abhängt, z. B. auf die Einrede der Compensation. Windscheid Pand. § 349 Nr. 3 Note 3 und Nr. 5.

d) Frage der Zuständigkeit.

11) Der Satz, daß die Unzuständigkeit des Gerichts in jeder Lage des Rechtsstreits, und zwar von Amtswegen, zu berücksichtigen sei, so weit sie nicht durch Vereinbarung beseitigt erscheint, möchte in dieser Ausdehnung sehr unpraktisch sein und dem Geiste der jetzigen Rechtspflege widerstreben.

Derselbe ist berechtigt, wo das Gericht der Natur des Rechtsstreites wegen unzuständig ist, wo seine Fähigkeit, über den gegebenen Fall mit vollkommener Sachkunde zu entscheiden, in Zweifel gezogen werden kann, allein nicht, wo es sich nur um die territoriale Abgränzung der Gebiete gleichartiger Gerichte handelt. Der Unterschied, ob das Bezirksgericht in A oder das Bezirksgericht in B entscheide, erscheint bei jetzigen Zuständen so geringfügig, daß er gar nicht in Anschlag zu bringen ist gegenüber den großen Uebelständen, welche damit verbunden sind, daß völlig durchgeführte Prozesse, noch in höchster Instanz, gegen den Willen beider Parteien, von Amtswegen, vernichtet werden dürfen und müssen, weil der Kläger in der Wahl zwischen A und B sich geirrt und z. B. eine Klage für rein persönlich gehalten hat, welche eigentlich dinglich oder in rem scripta ist. Man muß Jurist sein, um nur überhaupt so etwas für möglich zu halten.

Ferner möchte es verfehlt sein, daß der Gesetzgeber die Beseitigung der Unzuständigkeitseinrede immer nur unter dem Gesichtspunkte einer stillschweigenden Vereinbarung auffaßt, welche Auffassung sehr häufig reine Fiktion ist; es wäre richtiger und zugleich praktischer gewesen, wenn nicht überall, doch jedenfalls bei der örtlichen Unzuständigkeit, nur den Gesichtspunkt der Versäumung einer Prozeßeinrede walten zu lassen.

Ich glaube daher, daß man Unrecht gethan, die Vorschläge des Correferenten v. Bomhard (R. R. II S. 49—54) nicht zu beachten.

Vgl. noch weiter die Bemerkungen zu Art. 38 Nr. 2—6 und zu Art. 39 Nr. 7.

Art. 266. — **Ist von mehreren in derselben Klage begriffenen Forderungen oder im Falle der Klagenhäufung von den zusammen angebrachten Klagen die eine zum Endurtheile, die andere nur zu einem Zwischenbescheide reif, so ist gleichwohl über beide in demselben Urtheile das Erforderliche zu erkennen.**

Art. 267. — **Ist ein Theil des Klaganspruchs nicht mehr streitig, so darf die Verurtheilung des Beklagten bezüglich dieses Theils durch die Entscheidung über den noch streitigen nicht aufgehalten werden.** G. A. d. K. d. A. II S. 63. 128. IV S. 74. — K. d. R. II S. 54. IV S. 36.

1) Es wird hier dem Richter untersagt, die Entscheidung über liquide Ansprüche bloß deßhalb aufzuschieben, weil andere Ansprüche noch illiquid seien, und zwar sowohl für den Fall, wo von mehreren gleichzeitig verfolgten Ansprüchen nur ein Theil zur endlichen Entscheidung reif ist (Art. 266), als für den Fall, wo der nemliche Anspruch zum Theile liquid, zum Theile aber illiquid ist.

Auch ist es gleichgiltig, ob Antrag auf sofortige Entscheidung gestellt war, oder nicht. Abg. II 128 (zu Hauptst. VII Art. 6) im Gegensatze zu Abg. II 63 (v. Neumayr).

2) Ohnerachtet dieser Vorschrift kann es dem Richter nicht verwehrt sein, in Fällen, wo die Parteien selbst die Entscheidung eines liquiden Punkts vertagt wünschen, wozu sie der Unwichtigkeit dieses Punktes wegen oder im Hinblicke auf das Recht der Berufung ein Interesse haben können, diese Vertagung auszusprechen.

Art. 268. — **Urtheile, welche auf ausdrückliches, im Prozesse gemachtes Anerkenntniß der Verbindlichkeit ergehen, unterliegen ohne Zulassung einer Berufung der sofortigen Vollstreckung.**

Wird im Urtheile die Pflicht des Beklagten zur Erfüllung einer in einer Urkunde übernommenen Verbindlichkeit ausgesprochen und ist die Urkunde eine öffentliche oder im Prozesse von dem erschienenen Schuldner anerkannt, so kann die obsiegende Partei verlangen, daß das Urtheil als ohne Rücksicht auf Einspruch oder Berufung vorläufig vollstreckbar erklärt werde.

Das Urtheil kann in gleicher Weise für vorläufig vollstreckbar erklärt werden, wenn die Verzögerung der Vollstreckung dem Gläubiger einen unersetzlichen oder unverhältnißmäßigen Nachtheil zu bringen droht.

In den Fällen des Abs. 3 darf die Vollstreckung nur nach erfolgter Sicherheitsleistung stattfinden. Das Gleiche kann das Gericht auch in den Fällen des Abs. 2 verordnen.

G. A. d. K. d. A. II S. 63—66. 128. 129. IV S. 74. — K. d. R. II S. 54—58. IV S. 36.

1) Dieser Artikel behandelt zwei verschiedene Sachen, nemlich 1) den Ausschluß der Berufung bei Urtheilen, welche auf Anerkenntniß ergehen, und 2) die vorläufige Vollstreckbarkeit mancher Urtheile.

a) Urtheile auf Anerkenntniß.

2) Die Verfügung, daß Urtheile, welche auf ausdrückliches, im Prozesse gemachtes Anerkenntniß der Verbindlichkeit ergehen, ohne Zulassung einer Berufung der sofortigen Vollstreckung unterliegen, ist eine Anwendung des Satzes: »confessus pro judicato habetur«, möchte jedoch mit den Prinzipien des neuen Verfahrens nicht ganz im Einklange stehen.

Nach früherem Verfahren verlor mit dem unumwundenen Zugeständnisse des Klagsanspruches die Sache den Charakter einer Streitsache; es bedurfte keines Urtheils mehr und wurde auf Grund des Anerkenntnisses die Exekution eingeleitet. Das Zugeständniß selbst jedoch konnte, wenn neue Thatsachen vorgebracht wurden, welche es als irrthümlich erscheinen ließen, durch das Rechtsmittel der restitutio in integrum contra sententiam entkräftet werden.

Nach jetzigem Verfahren ist trotz des Anerkenntnisses eine Verurtheilung auszusprechen, und daselbe bildet daher nur die thatsächliche Grundlage eines Urtheiles, welches rechtskräftig erscheint, soweit nicht Rechtsmittel zulässig sind. Der Irrthum der zugestehenden Partei könnte nun die Wiederaufnahme des Verfahrens nur begründen, wenn er aus den Prozeßakten selbst hervorginge (Art. 761 Ziff. 1), was wohl nie der Fall sein wird, und da das Gesetz auch den Weg der Berufung abschneidet, so ist jede Möglichkeit genommen, irrthümliche Zugeständnisse anzufechten, was insbesondere bei Anwendung des Art. 268 auf den Parteiprozeß, wo die Geständnisse ohne Beistand von Rechtskundigen erfolgen, unter Umständen sehr schlimm sein kann.

Mit Recht galt daher, meiner Meinung nach, im französischen Prozesse als Grundsatz, daß Anerkenntnisse für die Frage der Zulässigkeit der Berufung ohne Bedeutung seien, und daß alles, worüber der Richter spreche, auch als Streitpunkt in Betracht komme.

3) Aus Vorstehendem möchte hervorgehen, daß Anlaß gegeben sei, fragliche Verfügung in möglichst enge Gränzen einzuschränken, was denn auch ihre Natur als Ausnahmsbestimmung schon nöthig macht.

Zum Ersten ist hervorzuheben, daß dieselbe den Richter der ihm durch Art. 264 Abs. 3 auferlegten Verpflichtung nicht enthebt, auch im Falle ausdrücklichen Zugeständnisses der vorgetragenen Thatsachen zu prüfen, ob durch dieselben der in Frage stehende Anspruch auch begründet werden könne, und daß, falls er in dieser Beziehung unrichtig geurtheilt hat, dieses Urtheil, wie jedes andere, den gewöhnlichen Rechtsmitteln unterworfen sei. Seuff. Comm. Bd. I S. 391 Note 36. Namentlich gilt dies, wenn Rechtsverhältnisse in Frage sind, über welche die Parteien nicht verfügen können, wo also das Geständniß höchstens als Beweisbehelf Geltung haben, nie aber den Beweis ersetzen kann.

4) Ferner ist hervorzuheben, daß in jenen Fällen, wo der Richter ein Zugeständniß mit Unrecht angenommen hat, sei es, daß er im Irrthum war bezüglich der Erklärungen der Partei, sei es, daß er die gesetzlichen Bedingungen eines Geständnisses verkannte, z. B. die Prinzipien über die Untheilbarkeit des Geständnisses verletzte, die gewöhnlichen Rechtsmittel nicht ausgeschlossen sind. Abg. II 128 (zu Hptst. VII Art. 7) und R. R. II 56 (v. Weiß).

b) Vorläufige Vollstreckung.

5) Die obsiegende Partei hat ein Recht, die vorläufige Vollstreckbarkeit zu verlangen, wenn die Pflicht zur Erfüllung einer in einer Urkunde übernommenen Verbindlichkeit ausgesprochen wird und diese Urkunde eine öffentliche oder im Prozesse vom Schuldner anerkannte Privaturkunde ist. Dem Ermessen des Gerichts ist es jedoch anheimgegeben, vorausgehende Sicherheitsleistung anzuordnen (Abs. 4).

Was eine öffentliche Urkunde oder dieser gleich zu achten sei, bemißt sich nach den Bestimmungen in Hauptstück X, und ist insbesondere hervorzuheben, daß das Gesetz keinen Unterschied macht, ob eine inländische oder ausländische öffentliche Urkunde in Frage stehe. Abg. II 65, 66 (v. Weiß, Barth). Bezüglich der letzteren sind übrigens die Bestimmungen in Art. 372 Abs. 2 zu beachten.

6) Wenn das Gesetz von einer in einer Urkunde übernommenen Verbindlichkeit spricht, so ist hiermit jede persönliche Verpflichtung gemeint, gleichviel, ob sie auf eine Leistung, oder auf Anerkennung eines Rechtes gerichtet, ob das Versprechen ein einseitiges sei oder ihm eine Gegenleistung gegenüberstehe. Abg. II 65 (Schmitt).

Die vorläufige Vollstreckbarkeit kann nun Jedem gegenüber begehrt werden, welcher aus der Uebernahme der Verbindlichkeit haftet, also nicht bloß gegen den ursprünglichen Contrahenten, sondern auch gegen dessen Erben, nicht aber gegen dritte Personen. Abg. II 65 (Umbscheiden). Anders wäre möglicherweise zu erkennen gewesen nach Art. 244 des Entwurfs, welcher davon sprach: „daß der Anspruch auf einer öffentlichen Urkunde &c. beruhe."

7) Ein Recht auf vorläufige Vollstreckung besteht nur insofern, als die Verurtheilung sich ausschließlich auf Urkunden der bezeichneten Art oder auf Geständniß gründet, nicht aber wenn Thatsachen beizuziehen sind, welche in anderer Weise bewiesen werden müssen. Ein solcher Fall kann z. B. vorliegen, wenn die Thatsache einer Aufkündigung oder des Verzichts auf eine in der Urkunde bedungene Frist festzustellen, oder wenn bei Klagen gegen Erben die Erbqualität streitig ist.

Ohne Belang erscheint es jedoch, daß die fragliche Urkunde als gefälscht bestritten, oder behauptet wird, sie sei durch Zwang, Betrug, Irrthum zu Stande gekommen oder simulirt. Abg. II 65 u. 66 (Umbscheiden, v. Neumayr). Noch weniger erheblich ist es, daß die aus der Urkunde sich ergebende Verpflichtung aus irgend einem Grunde bestritten wird, oder daß der Inhalt unklar ist und das Gericht nur auf dem Wege der Auslegung zum verurtheilenden Erkenntnisse gelangt. Endlich ist es auch unerheblich, daß sonstige öffentliche oder Privaturkunden entgegengehalten werden.

Einwände und Bedenken dieser Art verlieren allen Einfluß, sobald das Gericht sie für grundlos erklärt.

8) Die vorläufige Vollstreckung ist zuzulassen ohne Rücksicht auf Einspruch oder Berufung, woraus erhellt, daß der Gesetzgeber auch den Fall eines Versäumungsurtheiles im Auge hat.

Von der Wiederaufnahme des Verfahrens und der Nichtigkeitsbeschwerde ist nicht die Rede, obgleich nach den Bestimmungen der Art. 777 und 799 auch dort die Frage nicht vollkommen gegenstandslos ist. Es wird am entsprechenden Orte erörtert werden, ob in Fällen, welche unter Art. 268 Abs. 2 fallen, Einstellung der Vollstreckung verfügt werden dürfe.

Da die Verfügung nur auf Verlangen des obsiegenden Theils erfolgt, so hat sie sich nach dem Maaße dieses Verlangens zu richten, also nicht auf die Berufung auszudehnen, wenn bloß bezüglich des Einspruchs Antrag gestellt ist.

9) Das Gericht kann die vorläufige Vollstreckung gestatten, wenn die Verzögerung dem Gläubiger einen unersetzlichen oder unverhältnißmäßigen Nachtheil zu bringen droht, d. h. einen Nachtheil, welcher außer Verhältniß steht zum Schaden, welcher dem Schuldner durch den Vollzug entstehen kann.

In diesem Falle hat dem Vollzuge immer Sicherheitsleistung vorauszugehen. Es wird geeignet sein, dies im Urtheile auszusprechen; da jedoch das Gesetz einen solchen Ausspruch nicht vorschreibt, so wird die Sicherheitsleistung als selbstverständlich zu betrachten sein, wenn aus dem Urtheile sich ergibt, daß die Verfügung bloß auf Grund der Dringlichkeit erfolgte.

Ueberhaupt wird es sowohl im Falle von Abs. 2 als von Abs. 3 geeignet sein, immer auszusprechen, ob die vorläufige Vollstreckung mit oder ohne Sicherheitsleistung zugelassen werde, damit die Gerichtsvollzieher nicht im Zweifel sein können, was zu geschehen habe.

Da in dem Mehr auch das Minder enthalten ist, so wird dem Gerichte auch gestattet sein, die vorläufige Vollstreckbarkeit auf den Fall der Berufung zu beschränken.

10) Ueber die Art und Weise, wie im Falle der Berufung die vorläufige Vollstreckbarkeit oder deren Aufhebung erwirkt werden könne, enthalten die Art. 700 und 701 besondere Bestimmungen. Im Falle des Einspruches kann das Gericht sofort bei der ersten Verhandlung seine Verfügung zurücknehmen (Art. 314).

Wegen weiterer Fälle vorläufiger Vollstreckung s. Art. 513, 549, 587 u. 639.

Fällung und Verkündung des Urtheils.

Art. 269. — **Die Fällung und Verkündung des Urtheils hat, wenn die Sache zur Entscheidung reif ist, sofort nach dem Schlusse der Verhandlung zu geschehen.**

Erachtet das Gericht umfassendere Berathung für erforderlich, so ist eine spätere Sitzung zur Urtheilsverkündung zu bestimmen.

Zum Zwecke der Benützung bei der Urtheilsfällung sind nach beendigter Verhandlung die Parteiakten dem Gerichte zu übergeben.

Art. 270. — **An der Urtheilsfällung können nur jene Richter theilnehmen, vor welchen die Verhandlung stattgefunden hat.**

Art. 271. — **Die Berathung und Abstimmung ist geheim. Ein Protokoll wird hierüber nicht geführt.**

Der Vorsitzende leitet und schließt die Berathung. Hält ein Gerichtsmitglied die Sache nicht für hinreichend erörtert, so kann die Fortsetzung der Berathung von dem Gerichte beschlossen werden.

Ist umfassendere Berathung nöthig erachtet worden, so kann der Vorsitzende einen Berichterstatter ernennen, welcher die entscheidenden thatsächlichen und rechtlichen Punkte mündlich zu erörtern, die erforderlichen Nachweise aus den Akten zu geben und seine Ansicht über die zu erlassende Entscheidung auszusprechen hat. Der Vorsitzende kann die Berichterstattung auch selbst übernehmen.

Art. 272. — **Ergibt sich aus der Berathung keine Einmüthigkeit der Ansichten, so ist zur Abstimmung zu schreiten.**

Die Richter stimmen nach der Reihe, der dem Range nach letzte zuerst, der Vorsitzende zuletzt, jedoch hat in allen Fällen der Berichterstatter seine Stimme zuerst abzugeben. Bei der Abstimmung darf keine neue Entwickelung der Gründe zugelassen werden.

Kein Richter darf die Abstimmung verweigern, wenn er auch bezüglich einer vorhergegangenen Frage in der Minderheit geblieben ist.

Der Vorsitzende stellt die Fragen, sammelt die Stimmen und berechnet das Stimmverhältniß. Streitigkeiten, die sich hiebei ergeben, entscheidet das Gericht.

Art. 273. — **Ergibt die Abstimmung keine absolute Mehrheit, so ist zu wiederholter Berathung und Abstimmung zu schreiten. Bleibt auch diese fruchtlos und bezieht sich die Meinungsverschiedenheit nur auf Größen oder Summen, so sind die Stimmen, welche sich für das**

Meiste aussprechen, mit denen für die nächstfolgend geringere Summe oder Größe solange zusammenzuzählen, bis sich eine Summe oder Größe ergibt, in welcher die absolute Mehrheit zusammentrifft. In allen andern Fällen entscheidet die relative Mehrheit; haben sich aber die Meinungen vereinzelt oder ist auf verschiedene Meinungen die gleiche relative Mehrheit gefallen, so hat der Vorsitzende für eine dieser Meinungen den Ausschlag zu geben.

Art. 274. — Findet das Gericht die Sache nicht genugsam aufgeklärt, so kann es Wiederaufnahme der Verhandlung in einer sofort anzuberaumenden Sitzung verfügen.

Dies hat insbesondere zu geschehen, wenn Zweifel bestehen, ob es die Absicht der Partei gewesen sei, einen bestimmten Rechtsbehelf geltend zu machen. (Art. 264 Abs. 4.)

G. A. d. K. d. A. II S. 60. 67—71. 129. 130. 451. IV S. 74.
K. d. R. II. S. 58. IV S. 36.

1) Der Weg, auf welchem der Richter im neuen Verfahren zur Kenntniß des Sachverhalts und zur Bildung seines Urtheils gelangt, ist wesentlich verschieden von dem bisherigen; an Stelle der Referate ist die unmittelbare Anschauung getreten.

Die Entscheidung auf Grund von Referaten hat, namentlich in erster Instanz, wo die Geschäfte sich drängen, wo viel zu entwirren und zu sichten ist und die Referenten nicht immer genügende Erfahrung und Ueberblick besitzen, erhebliche Nachtheile. Von der Gewissenhaftigkeit und Einsicht des Referenten, welcher allein mit dem Prozesse völlig vertraut und allein in der Lage ist, ihn nach seinen thatsächlichen und rechtlichen Schwierigkeiten gründlich kennen zu lernen, hängt natürlich ungemein viel ab und das schriftlich ausgearbeitete Gutachten, welches er zur Sitzung mitbringt und welches zugleich seinen Urtheilsentwurf — ich möchte sagen: „sein Vorurtheil" — bildet, hat sehr häufig einen überwiegenden Einfluß.

Anders ist es im mündlichen Verfahren.

Hier wird der ganze Prozeß vor sämmtlichen Mitgliedern des Gerichts verhandelt, und jedes Mitglied gewinnt die nemliche vollständige Einsicht in alle Einzelnheiten, wie sie früher nur der Referent hatte. Bietet die Sache Schwierigkeiten, welche genauere Einsicht und Prüfung der Akten, oder gründlichere Ueberlegung nöthig erscheinen lassen, so muß allerdings Vertagung zum Spruche eintreten, weil kein Referent da ist, welcher die nöthigen Nachforschungen schon besorgt hat; allein gerade hierin liegt ein großer Vortheil, weil nunmehr jedes einzelne Gerichtsmitglied in der Lage ist, selbst zu forschen und die Sache in ruhiger Erwägung bei sich auszutragen. Auch das ist Gewinn, daß sich die Richter nicht mehr aushelfen lassen können von Accessisten und Rechtspraktikanten.

2) Die einzelnen, etwas umständlichen Vorschriften, welche das Gesetz über die Art und Weise der Berathung und Beschlußfassung gibt, bedürfen keiner sehr eingehenden Erläuterung; sie sind ziemlich klar und selbstverständlich.

Es war seither in der Pfalz Uebung, alle Urtheile, wegen welcher das Gericht sich sofort zu einigen vermochte, auch sofort zu sprechen. Man machte an den Vorsitzenden die Anforderung, daß er genügende Gewandtheit besitze, um in allen Fällen die Entscheidungsgründe sofort klar und erschöpfend mündlich zu entwickeln.

In jenen Fällen, wo das Gericht nicht sofort schlüssig wurde, pflegte man, um die Sitzung nicht unnöthigerweise durch Berathungen aufzuhalten, zum Urtheilsspruche zu vertagen, und zwar, falls nicht besondere Dringlichkeit eine Ausnahme nöthig machte, in der Weise, daß sämmtliche in der nemlichen Woche vertagten Urtheile in der nächsten Woche, an dem zur Hinterlegung der Anträge bestimmten Tage, welcher alle Anwälte in der Sitzung zu vereinigen pflegt, gesprochen wurden.

Zu Ende jeder Woche wurde ein Tag für die Berathung sämmtlicher vertagter Urtheile freigelassen.

3) Alle vertagten Sachen wurden in der Regel, zum Zwecke besonderer Prüfung und Berichterstattung an dem zur Berathung bestimmten Tage, unter die Gerichtsmitglieder vertheilt, wobei auch der Vorsitzende seinen Theil, und zwar nicht den unwichtigsten, sich zuwies.

Diese Berichterstattung erfolgte, wie dies auch Art. 271 Abs. 3 vorschreibt, nur mündlich und namentlich war es auch nie Sitte, daß der berichterstattende Richter einen Urtheilsentwurf fertigte und zur Berathung mitbrachte. Letzteres wurde nicht blos nicht verlangt, sondern prinzipiell nicht geduldet, und zwar in der, wie mir scheint richtigen Erwägung, daß eine Redaktion nach der Berathung und Beschlußfassung viel gründlicher und der Ansicht des Gerichts entsprechender auszufallen pflegt, als eine solche, welche nach einseitiger Auffassung im Voraus vorbereitet ist; ganz abgesehen davon, daß ein schon im Voraus vollständig ausgearbeitetes Urtheil oft zum Vorurtheile wird, welches den Verfasser hindert, so unbefangen in die Besprechung einzugehen, als es sonst der Fall wäre.

4) Findet das Gericht, daß die Verhandlung nicht erschöpfend gewesen sei, so kann es deren Wiederaufnahme verfügen.

Gewöhnlich sind es nur einzelne Punkte, welche näherer Aufklärung bedürfen — Anfragen, ob eine gewisse Einrede geltend gemacht werde (Art. 264 Abs. 4), ob gewisse Beweise erboten werden wollen (Art. 328 Abs. 4) 2c. — und genügt es, in der zum Spruche des Urtheils anberaumten Sitzung, die Anwälte, falls beide zugegen sind, zu befragen.

Wird die Aufklärung gegeben, so läßt sich in der Regel sofort das Urtheil sprechen, und sind die Gründe etwa noch nicht abgefaßt, so steht nichts im Wege, sie mündlich zu entwickeln, da die Verhandlung immerhin als wiederaufgenommen erscheint und demnach die Urtheilsverkündung als zum Spruche vertagt nicht mehr zu betrachten ist.

Kann das Urtheil nicht sofort gesprochen werden, oder erscheint weitere Verhandlung in einer späteren Sitzung nöthig, so vertagt das Gericht die Sache zum Urtheilsspruche oder zur weiteren Verhandlung, in welch' letzterem Falle Art. 252 anwendbar sein kann.

5) Wenn das Gesetz sagt, es dürften bei Fällung des Urtheils nur Richter theilnehmen, vor welchen die Verhandlung stattgefunden habe, so meint es nur die mündliche Verhandlung, von welcher die Art. 244—249 sprechen, also nicht etwa die Hinterlegung der Anträge.

Aus der Vorschrift, daß Berathung und Abstimmung geheim sein sollen, ist nicht zu folgern, daß die Anwesenheit anderer Richter, als derjenigen, welche an dem einzelnen gerade in Berathung gezogenen Falle theilnehmen, oder selbst des Gerichtsschreibers verboten sei, daß hierin etwas Disziplinwidriges liege. Abg. II S. 68 (v. Weiß). Von sonstigen Folgen könnte ohnedem keine Rede sein.

6) Wie die Beschlußfassung stattzufinden habe, ist in den Art. 272 u. 273 eingehend erörtert.

Während der französische Prozeß absolute Mehrheit verlangt und besondere Vorschriften gibt, um dieselbe herbeizuführen, begnügt sich unsere Prozeßordnung, den Prinzipien der bayr. Ger.-O. im Wesentlichen folgend, mit relativer Mehrheit; dies jedoch, wie wohl zu beachten, nur dann, wenn eine nochmalige Berathung und Abstimmung gezeigt hat, daß absolute Mehrheit nicht zu erzielen sei.

Der Vorsitzende stimmt nicht, wie früher, nur in solchen Fällen, wo Stimmengleichheit sich ergibt, sondern immer, und seine Stimme gibt, wenn nicht einmal eine relative Mehrheit zu erzielen ist, den Ausschlag. Abg. II 68 u. 70.

Bestehen über Summen oder Größen verschiedene Meinungen, so ist diejenige Summe oder Größe maßgebend, für welche sich eine absolute Mehrheit ergibt. Erklären sich z. B. 5 Stimmen je für 1000, 900, 300, 200 und 100 fl., so sind drei Stimmen, d. h. die absolute Mehrheit dafür, daß wenigstens 300 fl. zuzusprechen seien.

Art. 275. — **Jedes Urtheil, mit Ausnahme jener, welche nur eine Vertagung, die Anordnung einer Ergänzung oder eine ähnliche vorbereitende Verfügung zum Gegenstande haben, ist mit Entscheidungsgründen zu versehen, die in bündiger Kürze die thatsächliche und rechtliche Begründung des Ausspruchs enthalten.**

Art. 276. — **Nach der Abstimmung ist der Urtheilssatz niederzuschreiben, der Genehmigung des Gerichts zu unterstellen und, wenn das Urtheil nicht sogleich verkündet wird, von sämmtlichen Richtern zu unterzeichnen.**

Art. 277. — **Die Verkündung des Urtheils erfolgt in der Sitzung durch wörtliche Verlesung des Urtheilssatzes und der Entscheidungsgründe.**

Sind die Entscheidungsgründe bei der Verkündung des Urtheils noch nicht schriftlich abgefaßt, so genügt die Verlesung des Urtheilssatzes und die mündliche Entwickelung der Entscheidungsgründe.

Bei der Verkündung des Urtheils haben alle Richter gegenwärtig zu sein, welche zu dem Urtheile mitgewirkt haben. Ist dies wegen Todes oder Erkrankung einzelner Richter nicht möglich, so kann die Verkündung dennoch rechtswirksam geschehen.

Art. 278. — **Die Entscheidungsgründe müssen, wenn die Urtheilsverkündung vertagt worden ist, vor der Verkündung, andernfalls spätestens drei Tage nach der Verkündung durch den Vorsitzenden oder einen von ihm beauftragten, mit dem Urtheile im Wesentlichen einverstandenen Richter abgefaßt werden.**

Die Entscheidungsgründe sind in einem Zusammentritte sämmtlicher Richter, welche zu dem Urtheile mitgewirkt haben, abzulesen und der Genehmigung zu unterstellen.

Ist ein Richter hiebei zu erscheinen gehindert, so kann, wenn über die Entscheidungsgründe unter den übrigen betheiligten Richtern keine Meinungsverschiedenheit besteht, seine Zustimmung in geeigneter Weise erholt werden.

G. A. d. K. d. A. II S. 63. 71—75. 87. 88. 129. 130. IV S. 74. 75.
K. d. R. II S. 58—65. IV S. 36—38.

1) Das Urtheil, soweit es der Richter zu fertigen und zu verkünden hat, besteht aus dem Urtheilssatze und den Entscheidungsgründen; es frägt sich daher, wie diese Theile des Urtheils abzufassen seien.

a) Urtheilssatz.

2) Im Gesetze selbst findet sich über die Frage, wie der Urtheilssatz zu fassen sei, kein Aufschluß und, wie mir scheint, mit Recht.

Der einsichtsvolle Richter wird wissen, wie er zu sprechen habe, und der richtige Gedanke wird die richtige Form schon finden. Stehende Formeln bringen in der Regel mehr Schaden als Nutzen, weil sie an Stelle des eigenen Denkens die Schablone setzen.

3) Was zunächst den Inhalt betrifft, so hat der Richter zu entscheiden, wie es dem Rechte und den Parteianträgen gemäß ist, und zwar in allen vor ihn gebrachten Streitpunkten, sowohl in Haupt- als Nebensache.

Ueber diejenigen Streitpunkte, welche selbstständige, rechtskräftig festzustellende Rechtsverhältnisse betreffen, muß der Urtheilssatz in bestimmter Weise erkennen, sei es zusprechend, sei es abweisend. Es wäre daher ungehörig, die richterliche Entscheidung theilweise in die Entscheidungsgründe zu verweisen, und z. B. im Urtheilssatze einen Theil der Forderung zuzusprechen, die Mehrforderung aber bloß in den Entscheidungsgründen abzuerkennen.

Selbstverständlich erscheint, daß alles, was der Richter im Laufe des Rechtsstreites verfügt (Beweisauflagen, Sicherheitsleistungen 2c.) im Urtheilssatze seine Stelle zu finden habe.

Was die Abweisung von Einreden und abweisende Zwischenbescheide ähnlicher Art betrifft, so ist es, falls der Zwischenpunkt nicht etwa Gegenstand gesonderter Aburtheilung ist, in der Regel nicht nothwendig, förmlich im Urtheilssatze zu erkennen.

Nur bei solchen abweisenden Bescheiden, gegen welche selbständige Rechtsmittel zulässig sind, wie z. B. bei Abweisung der Einrede der Unzuständigkeit, wird ein Ausspruch im Urtheilssatze nicht unterlassen werden dürfen. Ueberhaupt läßt sich als leitender Grundsatz aufstellen, daß jede Entscheidung, welche selbständiger Rechtskraft fähig ist, ihren Ausdruck im Urtheilssatze zu finden habe, während in Fällen, wo der Richter an seine Verfügung nicht gebunden ist (Art. 296) bloße Zurückweisungen auch in den Entscheidungsgründen Platz finden dürfen, wie sie denn auch nur den Werth von solchen haben.

4) Eine andere Frage ist, ob es nicht zweckmäßig sei, auch in Fällen letzterer Art förmlich zu entscheiden.

In der Pfalz war es bis jetzt üblich, den Urtheilssatz so zu fassen, daß er ein übersichtliches Bild aller, bezüglich der Haupt- und Subsidiäranträge der Parteien ergangenen Entscheidungen bot, und man nahm der Vollständigkeit halber auch solche Verfügungen auf, welche einer Rechtskraft nicht fähig sind, wie z. B. die Zurückweisung eines unerheblichen Beweiserbietens. Man sagte z. B.:

aus diesen Gründen

über die Hauptklage erkennend:

weist das kgl. Bez.-Gericht die Einreden der Unzuständigkeit und der Nichtigkeit der Ladung als ungegründet ab;

gibt Urkunde, daß Beklagter den vom Kläger vorgelegten Schuldschein vom — als ächt anerkennt;

verurtheilt sofort den Beklagten, ohne Beachtung des von ihm erbotenen Zeugenbeweises, der für unerheblich, sowie der Eideszuschiebung, welche für unstatthaft erklärt wird, an den Kläger die Summe von — nebst Zins zu 5% vom — zu zahlen;

weist jedoch das Mehrbegehren als unbegründet ab;

über die Widerklage erkennend:

läßt es, ohne Beachtung der Einrede der Unzulässigkeit, den Widerkläger zum Beweise durch Zeugen darüber zu: 1) 2c.

schließlich über die Kosten erkennend, legt es die Hälfte aller bis jetzt erwachsenen Kosten dem Beklagten zur Last und behält die übrigen vor für die Widerklage.

Man wird hieraus erkennen, daß in der Pfalz die Urtheilssätze viel umständlicher und wortreicher sind, als diesseits, wo man im Gegensatze allzu lakonisch zu sprechen pflegt.

Ich glaube, daß die pfälzische Uebung praktische Vortheile hat, namentlich für das neue Verfahren, bemerke übrigens, daß es ziemlich gleichgiltig ist, wie man es halte, wenn nur im Wesentlichen nichts versäumt wird. In solchen Dingen pflegt man sich durch das Herkommen bestimmen zu lassen und so wird man denn, da das Gesetz freie Hand läßt, vermuthlich in der Pfalz sowie diesseits dasjenige beibehalten, was man gewohnt ist. Zu erwähnen möchte sein, daß die Gründe, welche für die pfälzische Uebung sprechen, dadurch etwas abgeschwächt worden sind, daß die Entscheidungen über Zwischenfragen (Einreden, Zulässigkeit von Beweisarten und Beweismitteln 2c.) nach Art. 296 keiner Rechtskraft mehr fähig sind.

5) Form.

Was die Form der richterlichen Entscheidung betrifft, so ist sie so zu wählen, daß sie am klarsten, einfachsten und sprachrichtigsten den Gedanken ausdrückt.

In dieser Beziehung möchten nun die diesseits üblichen Formen nicht geeignet sein, als Muster zu dienen. Wenn man, statt eine Prozeßeinrede abzuweisen, sagt: „man erachte die bedingte Streiteinlassung als unbedingt geschehen", oder wenn man in verschiedenartiger Weise „entbindet", oder wenn man erklärt, „es sei der Beklagte schuldig das Recht des Klägers anzuerkennen", oder wenn man „die Abweisung bedeutet", oder es „bei einem Erkenntnisse beläßt", so sind dies zum Theile unbehilfliche, zum Theile veraltete Redeweisen, welche füglich mit dem alten Prozesse zu Grabe getragen werden können.

6) Ein Urtheil enthält entweder einen Zuspruch oder eine Abweisung.

Im ersteren Falle ist es Sache des Richters, geradezu und bestimmt zu verfügen.

Handelt es sich um Feststellung streitiger Rechtsverhältnisse, wie bei dinglichen Klagen, Präjudizialklagen, so soll das Urtheil geradezu erklären: „es stehe dem Kläger das streitige Recht (Eigenthum, Servitut 2c.) zu".

Handelt es sich um Leistungen, so ist der geeignetste Ausdruck die Verurtheilung. Im Urtheile liegt der doppelte Ausspruch, daß eine Verpflichtung bestehe und daß ihr Vollzug erzwungen werden dürfe, und Beides findet sich durch das Wort „verurtheilen" ausgedrückt.

7) Im Falle der Abweisung der Klage sind nur zwei Fälle möglich, nemlich:

1) daß der Richter auf den Grund der Sache eingeht und den Klagsanspruch zurückweist, oder
2) daß er, ohne den Grund der Sache zu berühren, nur die Klage an sich zurückweist, das Band der Klage löst.

Im ersteren Falle ist die Klage als ungegründet, im zweiten als unzulässig abzuweisen.

Diese beiden Redeweisen genügen streng genommen, denn aus den Entscheidungsgründen ist zu ersehen, warum die Klage als ungegründet, oder warum sie als unzulässig abgewiesen werde, ob Ersteres geschehe, weil es am Klagegrunde fehlte oder weil Einreden entgegenstanden und ob Letzteres geschehe auf Grund der einen oder der anderen Prozeßeinrede. Nichts destoweniger möchte es geeignet sein, auch im Urtheilssatze die besondere Veranlassung noch näher anzugeben, wie dies denn auch in der Praxis zu geschehen pflegt.

Was die Begründung des Klagsanspruches anbelangt, so gehören zu derselben ohne Zweifel auch die Fragen der Legitimation zur Sache und der Fälligkeit, denn das Begehren richtet sich dahin: „daß dem Kläger gegen den Beklagten ein zur Zeit verfolgbares Recht zustehe", und erscheint also unbegründet, wenn eines dieser Erfordernisse fehlt. Diese Fälle haben jedoch das Eigene, daß ein Urtheil über den Bestand des Anspruches an und für sich nicht erfolgt, was für die Wirkungen der Rechtskraft von Bedeutung ist. Im Hinblicke hierauf möchte es nicht unpassend sein, beizufügen: „weist die Klage „zur Zeit" oder „wegen Mangels der Legitimation" als unbegründet ab."

Noch stärkere Gründe sprechen bei Abweisungen wegen Unzulässigkeit dafür, die besondere Veranlassung beizufügen, indem man etwa sagt:

weist die Klage wegen Unzuständigkeit des Gerichts, wegen Nichtigkeit der Ladung, wegen mangelnder Fähigkeit des Klägers vor Gericht zu stehen, wegen Nichtstellung der Prozeßkaution 2c. als unzulässig ab.

8) Schließlich möchte ich empfehlen, den Ausdruck: „von der Klage entbinden" ganz aus der Gerichtssprache zu beseitigen.

Abgesehen davon, daß er ungewöhnlich ist und es einem gebildeten Nichtjuristen wohl nie in den Sinn kommen würde, sich so auszudrücken, ist seine Anwendung auch sprachlich unrichtig, da „von der Klage entbinden" eigentlich nur bedeutet: „das Band der Klage lösen, die Rechtshängigkeit beseitigen", also nur etwa die Klagabweisung auf Grund einer Prozeßeinrede in dieser Weise bezeichnet werden könnte. Frägt man einen Kläger, wie sein Prozeß ausgegangen sei, so wird er gewiß nicht antworten, der Gegner sei entbunden worden, sondern wird sagen, er selbst sei mit seiner Klage abgewiesen worden, und ich meine, die Gerichtssprache solle sich ohne Noth nicht von der gewöhnlichen Sprache entfernen.

b) Entscheidungsgründe.

9) Die Verfassungsurkunde Tit. VIII § 2 sagt: „Alle Gerichtsstellen sind verbunden, ihren

Urtheilen Entscheidungsgründe beizufügen und die Prozeßordnung läßt in Art. 788 Ziff. 4 Nichtigkeitsbeschwerde gegen Endentscheidungen zu, welche nicht mit Gründen versehen sind. Die Entscheidungsgründe bilden daher einen höchst wesentlichen Bestandtheil des Urtheils und es ist wichtig, sich klar zu machen, wo und wie sie verlangt werden.

10) Wie das Wort schon andeutet, sind nur für Entscheidungen Gründe zu geben, also sind sie für bloße Beurkundungen nicht nothwendig. Insofern jedoch die beurkundeten Thatsachen (Geständnisse, Verzichte, Befund von Urkunden) die Grundlage der Entscheidung bilden, läßt sich deren Erwähnung in den Gründen nicht umgehen und so hat sich denn die Uebung gebildet, auch die Beurkundungen kurz zu motiviren, z. B. indem man sagt:

In Erw., daß Beklagter in der Sitzung zugestanden hat, das in Frage stehende Darlehen von 700 fl. empfangen zu haben, worüber Urkunde zu ertheilen ist, 2c.

Vgl. Bemerk. zu Art. 166—168 Nr. 3.

11) Die Verpflichtung, Entscheidungsgründe beizufügen, erstreckt sich auf alle Urtheile, mit einziger Ausnahme derjenigen, welche nur eine Vertagung, die Anordnung einer Ergänzung oder eine ähnliche vorbereitende Verfügung zum Gegenstande haben. Die angeführten Beispiele deuten an, daß man nur die allereinfachsten Verfügungen ausnehmen wollte, solche, bei denen die Gründe selbstverständlich oder völlig gleichgiltig sind. Auch hier kann sich jedoch hie und da die Angabe von Gründen als nöthig erweisen, weil das Gesetz besondere Folgen an dieselben knüpft, wie z. B. bei der Vertagung im Falle von Art. 252 a. E. — Anordnungen des persönlichen Erscheinens oder eines Augenscheines, obgleich ganz allgemeine und vorbereitende Maßregeln, dürfen doch nicht einer Vertagung gleichgestellt zu werden und sind zu begründen, natürlich in der Regel nur so allgemein, als es die Maßregel selbst ist, z. B.:

In Erw., daß es zur Aufklärung des Sachverhalts nöthig erscheint, vor Allem die Parteien selbst zu hören, — eine Besichtigung der strittigen Oertlichkeiten vorzunehmen 2c.

12) Eine Begründung ist zweifellos nöthig bei Anordnen von Beweisen, bei Entscheidung über Beweismittel, bei Verwerfung von Prozeßeinreden und bei Erledigung von Zwischenfragen jeder Art, auch wenn die Entscheidung nach Maßgabe des Art. 296 der Rechtskraft nicht fähig ist und den Richter nicht bindet. Da es jedoch im Wesen derartiger Entscheidungen liegt, daß sie nur vorbereitend seien und daß alles, was darin fehlerhaft ist, im Endurtheile wieder gut gemacht werden könne, so dürfen auch Mängel in der Begründung ergänzt und berichtigt werden und begründen dieselben insofern nur eine Ordnungswidrigkeit, jedoch keine Nichtigkeit.

Wenn es auch nicht erlaubt ist, Zwischenbescheide besagter Art, ohne Gründe zu lassen, so ist es doch natürlich, daß diese Gründe nicht so vollständig und erschöpfend zu sein brauchen, als es bei Entscheidungen gefordert wird, welche der Rechtskraft fähig sind. Es genügt daher, in wenigen Sätzen die Hauptgesichtspunkte hervorzuheben, und gestalten sich solche Urtheile oft außerordentlich einfach, z. B. wie folgt:

In Erw., daß Beklagter in Abrede stellt, das behauptete Darlehen empfangen zu haben, und Kläger Beweis durch Zeugen erbietet, welcher zulässig und erheblich ist;

a. d. Gr.

läßt das k. Bez.-G. den Kläger zum Beweise durch Zeugen darüber zu 2c.; bestimmt zur Vernehmung der Zeugen und Gegenzeugen, sowie zur weiteren Verhandlung die Sitzung vom —.

Diese kurze Begründung der Zwischenurtheile hat den großen praktischen Vortheil, daß dieselben in der Regel sofort und ohne Aufenthalt in der Sitzung gesprochen werden können.

13) Von größerer Wichtigkeit sind die Entscheidungsgründe bei denjenigen Urtheilen, welche der Rechtskraft fähig sind (Art. 682 und 683), denn auf sie findet Art. 788 Ziff. 4 seine Anwendung und der Mangel der vom Gesetze verlangten Gründe hat Nichtigkeit der Entscheidung zur Folge.

Die Entscheidungsgründe sollen nach Art. 275 in bündiger Kürze, die thatsächliche und rechtliche Begründung des Ausspruches enthalten. Sie müssen so beschaffen sein, daß sich die Entscheidung in logischer Gedankenfolge aus ihnen ergibt und ihre besondere Aufgabe ist es, alle Einwände, welche die unterliegende Partei vorgebracht hat, eingehend zu widerlegen, damit sich die Entscheidung als das Werk gründlicher und unparteiischer Erwägung bekunde.

Die Vorschrift bündiger Kürze schließt nicht aus, daß die Entscheidungsgründe eingehend und erschöpfend sein müssen und zwar je nach dem Bedürfnisse des Falles in höherem oder minderem Grade. Es genügt daher nicht, bloß der Form nach Entscheidungsgründe beizufügen, in welcher man, die Entscheidung selbst nur etwas umschreibend, idem per idem begründet, und Gründe, welche lauten: „In Erw., daß nach den Ergebnissen der Verhandlung sich der Klaganspruch als unbegründet darstellt, a. d. Gr. weist das B. G. die Klage als unbegründet ab," könnten die Entscheidung vor der Vernichtung nicht schützen.

14) Die Entscheidungsgründe haben sich zwar über sämmtliche Haupt- und Nebenpunkte zu erstrecken, jedoch bedürfen solche Anordnungen des Richters keiner gesonderten Begründung, welche nur die selbstverständliche Folge einer getroffenen Entscheidung bilden, oder welche bloß den Vollzug derselben betreffen, wie z. B. die Regelung eines Vorverfahrens, einer Beweisaufnahme, eines Vollzuges in den Fällen der Art. 860 und 862.

Der Richter könnte nur sagen: „In Erw., daß es geeignet ist, zu verfügen" ꝛc. oder „daß nach dem Gesetze zu verfügen ist" ꝛc., und dies verlangt das Gesetz so wenig, als es Gründe für Vertagungen ꝛc. verlangt. Zudem spricht Art. 788 Ziff. 4 nur von einer Entscheidung.

Was die Entscheidung über die Kosten betrifft, so ist sie in der Regel auch keiner eingehenderen Begründung fähig, denn die Sätze: „In Erw., daß der unterliegende Theil die Kosten zu tragen hat" oder: „In Erw., daß die Kosten nach dem Maße des Unterliegens zu vertheilen sind", sagen im Grunde nur, was selbstverständlich ist; dennoch möchte es rathsam sein, eine Begründung nie zu unterlassen.

15) Form.

Was die äußere Form und Stellung der Entscheidungsgründe anbelangt, so bestehen zwischen der Uebung in der Pfalz und diesseits sehr augenfällige Unterschiede.

Dort setzt man die Gründe vor die Entscheidung und beobachtet ohne Ausnahme die Form der „Erwägungen"; hier folgen umgekehrt die Gründe der Entscheidung nach und werden in Form gewöhnlicher „Erörterung" vorgetragen.

Was zuerst die Reihenfolge anbelangt, so ist es Sitte, erst zu überlegen und dann zu beschließen, und so meine ich denn, die Natur der Sache führe dahin, auch im Urtheile zuerst die Gründe und zuletzt die Entscheidung zu bringen. Ich finde es daher ungerechtfertigt, daß diese natürliche Reihenfolge, welche Art. 253 des Entwurfs anerkannt hatte, im Art. 280 geändert worden ist.

16) Was nun die Frage betrifft, ob die Form der Erwägung oder die Form der Erörterung die bessere sei, so hat jede derselben ihre Vortheile, jedoch bin ich der Ansicht, daß im Allgemeinen die erstere Form für das mündliche Verfahren die geeignetere sei.

Wer in mündlicher Entwicklung der Entscheidungsgründe den Versuch mit beiden Formen macht, wird finden, daß die Form der Erörterung eintönig, trocken und schwierig ist, während die Form der Erwägung schwungvoll und energisch lautet und die Gedanken sich gleichsam von selbst in die Form einfügen. Jeder neue Gesichtspunkt kennzeichnet sich durch die Einleitungsworte: „In Erwägung" und es tritt so dem Sprechenden ebenso wie dem Hörenden die Gliederung der Schlußfolgerungen lebendig vor Augen.

Schließlich hat die Erwägungsform noch einen großen Vorzug darin, daß sie zwingt, sich kurz zu fassen, ein Vorzug, welcher bei uns, wo man gern in's Breite sich verliert, nicht zu unterschätzen ist.

17) Wenn nun auch die Form der Erwägung für den mündlichen Spruch ohne vorausgängige schriftliche Redaktion, sowie für alle einfacheren Urtheile wesentliche Vorzüge bietet, so läßt sich anderseits nicht in Abrede stellen, daß für weitläufige und komplizirte Begründungen die gewöhnliche Redeweise sich besser eignet, um klar die Gedanken zu entwickeln.

In der Pfalz wird man, schon der Gewohnheit wegen, überall bei der Erwägungsform bleiben, diesseits aber wird man aus gleichem Grunde die hergebrachte Form nicht ganz aufgeben, jedoch wird wahrscheinlich das praktische Bedürfniß dahin führen, bei allen einfachen Urtheilen namentlich den sofort in der Sitzung gesprochenen, die Form der Erwägung zu wählen.

18) Was die innere Form der Erwägungsgründe betrifft, so erscheint als die beste Methode die, welche vom Allgemeinen ins Besondere gehend, für jeden Punkt zuerst die einschlägigen rechtlichen Prinzipien erörtert und feststellt und sodann dieselben auf den gegebenen Fall anwendet.

Es ist dabei im Auge zu behalten, daß ein Theil des Stoffes, welchen man seither, namentlich in erster Instanz, den Entscheidungsgründen einzuverleiben pflegte, schon in den Gesuchen und in der Darstellung des Sachverhaltes (Art. 285) welche vorausgehen, enthalten ist und daß die Gründe hieran anknüpfen können und sollen.

Es wäre irrig, wollte man annehmen, der Richter habe auf Sachverhalt und Gesuch, weil sie erst später ins Urtheil kommen und das Werk der Anwälte sind, keine Rücksicht zu nehmen. Das Urtheil bildet in der Form, wie es bestimmt ist, ausgefertigt zu werden, ein geschlossenes Ganze, mit einem darstellenden, einem erwägenden und einem entscheidenden Theile, und diese 3 Theile schließen sich an einander an und stehen in inniger Verbindung mit einander. Man hielt es in der Pfalz daher immer für fehlerhaft, wenn die Gründe ohne Noth d. h. ohne durch Rücksicht auf Deutlichkeit dazu veranlaßt zu sein, sich über das verbreiten, was Gegenstand der Qualitäten ist.

c) Abfassung und Verkündung des Urtheils.

19) Es ist zu unterscheiden, ob das Urtheil sofort nach Schluß der Verhandlung gesprochen oder ob es zum Spruche vertagt wird.

Im ersteren Falle ist der Urtheilssatz niederzuschreiben und diese schriftliche Notiz zu verlesen.

Die Entscheidungsgründe dürfen auch mündlich entwickelt werden, jedoch sind sie binnen 3 Tagen abzufassen und vom Gerichte zu genehmigen (Art. 278 Abs. 1 u. 2). Sie werden in dieser Form ins Urtheil eingesetzt, und der Vorsitzende, welcher den Eintrag im Urtheilsbuche unterzeichnet, ist verantwortlich dafür, daß die Genehmigung aller mitwirkenden Richter erfolgt sei.

Die Vorschrift, daß in allen Fällen, also bei den einfachsten Zwischenbescheiden, sowie bei Versäumungsurtheilen der Urtheilssatz niederzuschreiben und wörtlich abzulesen sei, wird in der Pfalz, wo man freiere Bewegung gewöhnt ist und sich wohl dabei befunden hat, als eine nutzlose zeitraubende Form empfunden werden.

Uebrigens ist darauf hinzuweisen, daß das Gesetz bloß etwas Geschriebenes verlangt, was abgelesen werden könne, daß also, wenn es sich bloß darum handelt, den von einer Partei genommenen Antrag ganz oder theilweise zuzusprechen, nichts im Wege steht, diesen Antrag zu benützen, da wohl das Gesetz auf ein besonderes Blatt Papier keinen Werth legt. Die Vernachlässigung fraglicher Vorschrift begründet jedenfalls nur eine Ordnungswidrigkeit, nie eine Nichtigkeit, da es sich nicht um Zuwiderhandlung gegen ein Verbot (Art. 218) handelt.

Urtheile, welche keiner Erwägungsgründe bedürfen (Art. 275), bedürfen im Sinne des Gesetzes auch keiner Niederschreibung.

20) Im Falle der Vertagung zum Spruche soll nach der Abstimmung der Urtheilssatz niedergeschrieben und von sämmtlichen Richtern unterzeichnet werden; die Entscheidungsgründe aber sind vor der Verkündung abzufassen und mit dem Urtheilssatze zu verlesen.

Das Gesetz sagt es zwar nicht ausdrücklich, setzt es jedoch offenbar voraus, daß die Abfassung und Unterzeichnung des Urtheilssatzes sofort nach der Abstimmung geschehe. Da nun aber die Abstimmung recht gut auch eine vorläufige sein kann, da sie ferner bis zur Verkündung des Urtheils jeder Zeit geändert werden kann, so steht nichts im Wege, die Redaktion und Genehmigung des ganzen Urtheiles abzuwarten, um dann erst die fragliche Förmlichkeit zu erfüllen. Dabei erscheint selbstverständlich, daß geeigneten Falls auch auf die Anträge Bezug genommen werden darf und es insbesondere nicht nöthig ist, Beweisanträge, welche oft mehrere Bogen umfassen, aus denselben bloß abzuschreiben.

21) Die Unterzeichnung der Richter hat hauptsächlich zum Zwecke, für den Fall der Urtheilsverkündung außer Anwesenheit eines Richters (Art. 277 Abs. 3) eine besondere Garantie zu geben (Abg. II 74 u. R. R. II 58). Es ist nun zwar nirgends gesagt, daß in diesem Falle die Verkündung nur dann giltig geschehen könne, wenn die Unterzeichnung des nicht anwesenden Richters vorliege, jedoch möchte es dem Willen des Gesetzes entsprechen, anzunehmen, daß dieser Richter, wenn er noch nicht unterzeichnet hat, auch seine Meinung noch nicht bindend ausgesprochen habe, und zu einer wiederholten Verhandlung zu schreiten.

Der von den Richtern unterzeichnete Aufsatz ist kein Protokoll, sondern nur eine durch die Unterschriften gebilligte Notiz, welche den Zweck hat, bei Verkündung und Eintrag des Urtheils zur Grundlage zu dienen. Sie verliert mit diesem Eintrage ihren Werth, da das Urtheil den Beweis in sich selbst trägt, daß es in gesetzlicher Weise zu Stande gekommen sei.

22) Die Urtheilsverkündung hat bei Strafe der Nichtigkeit (Art. 788 Ziff. 5) in öffentlicher Sitzung zu geschehen und zwar in Gegenwart aller Richter, welche zum Urtheile mitwirkten. Das Urtheil entsteht erst mit der Verkündung und nur wenn es in besagter Weise verkündet worden ist, erscheint es als das Werk aller Richter. Die Nichtanwesenheit eines derselben würde daher Nichtigkeit begründen. Vgl. R. R. II 60 (v. Weiß).

Eine Ausnahme ist jedoch gemacht für zwei Fälle, nemlich den Fall des Todes und den Fall der Erkrankung einzelner Richter, worunter auch mehrere Richter, jedoch nicht alle zu verstehen sind. Die Verhinderungsursache muß ausdrücklich im Urtheile erwähnt sein (Art. 280) und diese Erwähnung genügt, um die Verkündung giltig zu machen. Für sonstige Verhinderungen (Abwesenheit, Dienstgeschäfte, Versetzung rc.) bleibt die Regel bestehen.

Hat irgend eine, wenn auch unbedeutende Ergänzung der Verhandlung stattzufinden, so ist fragliche Ausnahme nicht gegeben, vielmehr muß, wenn nicht mit Vertagung zu helfen ist, die ganze Verhandlung von Neuem erfolgen.

Urtheilsbuch.

Art. 279. — Bei jedem Senate, in welchem Civilrechtsstreitigkeiten zu entscheiden sind, wird ein Urtheilsbuch geführt. In dieses Urtheilsbuch werden alle Urtheile, welche der Senat in Civilrechtsstreitigkeiten erläßt, fortlaufend nach der Zeit der Verkündung durch den Gerichtsschreiber eingetragen.

Art. 280. — Der in Art. 279 erwähnte Eintrag hat zu umfassen:

1) den Tag der Urtheilsverkündung;
2) die Namen der Richter, des Staatsanwalts und des Gerichtsschreibers, welche bei der Verkündung anwesend waren; wenn die Anwesenheit aller Richter, die zu dem Urtheile mitgewirkt haben, nicht möglich war, auch die Namen der abwesenden und den Grund der Verhinderung;
3) die Bezeichnung der Parteien nach Vor- und Familiennamen, Stand oder Gewerbe, Wohnort und Parteistellung nebst der Angabe, ob und durch welche Anwälte die Parteien vertreten und ob die Anwälte bei der Verhandlung erschienen sind oder nicht;
4) den Urtheilssatz und die Entscheidungsgründe und zwar letztere unter Anfügung an den Urtheilssatz auch dann, wenn sie erst nach der Urtheilsverkündung schriftlich abgefaßt worden sind.

Der Tag der Urtheilsverkündung ist als Ueberschrift an die Spitze des Eintrags zu setzen.

Der in Ziff. 2 bezeichnete Theil des Eintrags geschieht durch Vormerkung am Rande. Hiebei genügt, wenn mehrere Einträge aus der nämlichen Sitzung auf einander folgen, bei welchen dieselben Gerichtspersonen und Verhältnisse vorzumerken wären, die Hinweisung auf die frühere Vormerkung.

Zur Bezeichnung einer Partei, die aus mehreren Personen besteht, genügt, wenn in der betreffenden Sache ein Eintrag bereits stattgefunden und seitdem eine Veränderung sich nicht ergeben hat, die Hinweisung auf den früheren Eintrag.

Der Eintrag ist von dem Vorsitzenden und von jenem Gerichtsschreiber, welcher bei der Verkündung anwesend war, am Schlusse zu unterzeichnen.

Bei Verhinderung des Vorsitzenden unterzeichnet statt seiner der im Range nächstfolgende, bei Verhinderung des Gerichtsschreibers der im Range letzte derjenigen Richter, welche zum Urtheile mitgewirkt haben. Der Verhinderung ist bei der Unterschrift Erwähnung zu thun.

Art. 281. — In das Urtheilsbuch müssen auch die Verlagungsurtheile, die Verfügungen, daß eine Sache vom Hauptverzeichnisse zu streichen sei, die Beurkundungen über Hinterlegung der Anträge und hierauf erfolgte Festsetzung einer Sitzung zur Verhandlung, sowie jene Beurkundungen eingetragen werden, welche nach Art. 248 stattzufinden haben.

Gleiches gilt von der in der Sitzung erklärten Anwaltsbestellung, der einem Gewalthaber bei der Verhandlung ertheilten Vollmacht und in ähnlichen Fällen.

Bei solchen Einträgen genügt außer der bezüglichen Beurkundung oder der Angabe des Gerichtsbeschlusses die Bezeichnung der Parteien, ihrer Vertreter und des Streitgegenstands. Insbesondere ist der Inhalt der hinterlegten Anträge nicht anzugeben. Die Bestimmungen des Art. 280 Abs. 2—6 finden analoge Anwendung.

G. A. d. K. d. A. II S. 72. 73. 75—91. 95. 130. 131. 451. IV S. 80. 81.
K. d. R. II S. 85—88. IV S. 38.

1) Gerichtsakten im Sinn wie bisher gibt es in Zukunft nicht mehr, und das Einzige, was nach Erledigung eines Rechtsstreites bei Gericht zurück bleibt, sind etwaige Protokolle (Zeugenvernehmungen, Augenschein), das Urtheil, wie es ins Urtheilsbuch eingetragen ist, der Sachverhalt (Art. 285) und die hinterlegten Anträge.

Die schriftlichen Aufsätze, welche beim Eintrage des Urtheiles zur Grundlage dienten, haben mit diesem ihren Zweck erfüllt und sind werthlos, wie der Entwurf zu einem Protokolle, nachdem das Protokoll aufgenommen ist. Man bewahrt hie und da die wichtigeren Urtheilsentwürfe auf zur Sammlung von Präjudizien.

2) Für jeden Senat eines Gerichts besteht ein Urtheilsbuch, in welches alle Urtheile dieses Senats, so wie die Beurkundungen, von denen Art. 281 spricht, der Zeitfolge nach vom Gerichtsschreiber eingetragen werden. Unter Urtheilen sind bloß solche Entscheidungen zu ver-

stehen, welche nach in öffentlicher Sitzung gepflogenen Verhandlung erlassen werden (Abg. II 80), jedoch sind ohne Zweifel auch Entscheidungen ins Urtheilsbuch aufzunehmen, welche bei beschränkter Oeffentlichkeit (Art. 149) ergangen sind (Art. 288).

Der vom Gesetze gebrauchte Ausdruck „Urtheilsbuch" deutet schon an, daß die Urtheilshefte nach passenden Zeitabschnitten gebunden werden sollen.

3) Bei jedem Eintrage sind am Rande die Namen der bei der Verkündung anwesenden bezw. betheiligten Gerichtspersonen (Art. 280 Ziff. 2) zu bezeichnen, was den Vortheil bietet, daß bei der nemlichen Zusammensetzung des Gerichts, einfach auf den ersten Eintrag Bezug genommen werden kann (Art. 280 Abs. 3).

Der Eintrag selbst enthält als Ueberschrift das Datum und sodann folgt die Bezeichnung der sämmtlichen Parteien und ihrer Anwälte mit Angabe der Parteistellungen der Ersteren, so wie ob die Letzteren bei der Verhandlung erschienen waren oder nicht.

Die Parteien sind nach dem letzten, in der Regel aus den hinterlegten Anträgen (Art. 241 Abs. 5) zu entnehmenden, Stande des Prozesses zu bezeichnen, und zwar beim ersten Eintrage im betreffenden Prozesse vollständig, bei den späteren, sofern nicht Aenderungen stattfanden, bloß summarisch durch die Bezeichnung: „X und Genossen", jedoch mit Hinweisung auf den früheren Eintrag (Art. 280 Abs. 4).

Obgleich die vollständige Bezeichnung der Parteien in das Urtheilsbuch selbst eingetragen wird, so kommt dennoch in die Urtheilsausfertigung nicht dieser Eintrag, sondern die in Gemäßheit des Art. 285 durch die Parteien festgestellte Bezeichnung (Art. 289 Abs. 2). Man könnte fragen, ob nicht die eine oder die andere Bezeichnung entbehrlich gewesen wäre.

4) Zuletzt folgen Urtheilssatz und Entscheidungsgründe, zwischen welche jedoch in der Ausfertigung später der Sachverhalt und die Gesuche eingeschoben werden sollen (Art. 289).

Meiner Meinung nach (Bemerk. zu Art. 275 bis 279 Nr. 15), wäre es natürlicher gewesen, die Entscheidungsgründe voranzustellen, so daß also Sachverhalt, Gründe und Entscheidung auf einander folgen würden.

Wenn übrigens auch der Gesetzgeber hier die entgegenstehende Regel gibt und sie in Art. 289 wiederholt, so wurde doch bei den Verhandlungen ausdrücklich anerkannt, daß die Reihenfolge auch eine andere sein dürfe (Abg. II 87 a. E.) Es ist daher der Richter nicht gehindert, diejenige Form für sein Urtheil zu wählen, welche ihm den Umständen nach die entsprechendste erscheint.

5) Der Eintrag wird nur vom Vorsitzenden und vom Gerichtsschreiber unterzeichnet und zwar selbstverständlich von demjenigen Gerichtsschreiber, welcher bei der Verkündung zugegen gewesen ist.

Die Randbemerkung zur Bezeichnung der Gerichtspersonen bedarf keiner besonderen Unterzeichnung und wurde eine entgegenstehende Bestimmung gestrichen (Abg. IV 81), wohl nicht mit Recht, da ja Randbemerkungen in der Regel besonders zu genehmigen sind (Art. 167) und gerade die hier in Frage stehende von hoher Wichtigkeit ist, indem von ihrer Richtigkeit die Giltigkeit des Urtheiles abhängen kann.

Für den Fall der Verhinderung trifft Art. 280 Abs. 6 Vorsorge.

6) Bei Vertagungs- und Streichungsurtheilen — man darf wohl sagen, bei allen jenen Urtheilen, welche keiner Entscheidungsgründe bedürfen (Art. 275) — sowie bei allen Beurkundungen, welche das Gericht gesondert, d. h. nicht bei Gelegenheit eines mit Entscheidungsgründen versehenen Urtheiles gibt, gestaltet sich der Eintrag viel einfacher. Die Entscheidungsgründe fallen weg und an Stelle des Urtheilssatzes tritt der Beschluß oder die Beurkundung, welche z. B. lautet: „Das Gericht vertagt die Sache zur Hinterlegung der Anträge — zur Verhandlung — in die Sitzung vom rc.", oder: „Das Gericht ertheilt Urkunde, daß sämmtliche Anwälte Anträge genommen und hinterlegt haben und bestimmt zur Verhandlung die Sitzung vom rc."

In allem Uebrigen richten sich diese Einträge nach den für die gewöhnlichen Urtheile gegebenen Vorschriften, denn wenn auch Art. 281 Abs. 3 vom Tage der Verkündung oder von der Bezeichnung der Gerichtspersonen nichts erwähnt, so ist doch durch die Bezugnahme auf Art. 280 Abs. 2—6 genügend angedeutet und liegt es in der Natur der Sache, daß Beides nicht fehlen dürfe.

Wenn das Gesetz hier noch besonders die Bezeichnung des Streitgegenstandes verlangt, so meint es jene kurze Bezeichnung, von welcher auch Art. 165 spricht.

Einträge fraglicher Art werden in der Regel nicht ausgefertigt (Art. 243), machen aber besondere Umstände dennoch eine Ausfertigung nöthig, so erfolgt sie in der Form, wie der Eintrag lautet; Qualitäten gibt es nur bei den gewöhnlichen Urtheilen.

Abänderung des Urtheils.

Art. 282. — Schreibfehler, sichtliche Versehen in einzelnen Worten und Zahlen, sowie bloße Rechnungsfehler können von dem Gerichte, welches das Urtheil erlassen hat, selbst verbessert werden.

Die Verbesserung darf, wenn der Irrthum im Urtheilssatze sich findet, nach der Verkündung, außerdem nach der Unterzeichnung des in das Urtheilsbuch eingetragenen Urtheils nur noch auf Begehren einer Partei und nur durch nachträgliches Urtheil erfolgen.

Das Begehren muß durch motivirten Antrag gestellt werden. Letzterer ist dem Senatsvorstande vorzulegen und, nachdem dieser darauf die Sitzung zur Verhandlung bestimmt hat, dem Gegner mit der Aufforderung zum Erscheinen in der bestimmten Sitzung zustellen zu lassen.

Hat die Gegenpartei keinen Anwalt, so ist der Antrag ihr selbst mit der Aufforderung zuzustellen, sofort einen Anwalt zu bestellen, der für sie in der festgesetzten Sitzung zu erscheinen hat.

Zwischen der Zustellung und dem Sitzungstage muß im einen wie im andern Falle eine Frist von drei Tagen in Mitte liegen.

Die Gegenpartei braucht keinen motivirten Antrag zustellen zu lassen. Die Hinterlegung der Anträge findet nur bei der Verhandlung statt.

Wird auf Verbesserung des Urtheils erkannt, so sind die Kosten des Zwischenverfahrens in derselben Weise wie jene der Hauptsache zu tragen; im andern Falle ist der Antragsteller in die dadurch veranlaßten Kosten zu verurtheilen.

Art. 283. — Ist in einem bereits verkündeten Urtheil ein Streitpunkt aus Versehen übergangen oder über den Ersatz der Prozeßkosten nicht erkannt worden, oder enthält ein solches Urtheil einen Widerspruch in seinen Verfügungen oder eine durchaus unverständliche Stelle, so kann die erforderliche Urtheilsabänderung durch das Gericht, welches das Urtheil erlassen hat, in dem durch Art. 282 Abs. 2—7 vorgezeichneten Verfahren getroffen werden, wenn der Antrag darauf innerhalb dreißig Tagen von Zustellung des Urtheils an gestellt wird.

Art. 284. — Von den nach Art. 282 oder 283 erlassenen nachträglichen Urtheilen ist am Rande des ersten Urtheils Vormerkung zu machen und muß allen Ausfertigungen, welche nach diesem Zeitpunkte erfolgen, am Schlusse zugleich eine solche des nachträglichen Urtheils beigefügt werden.

G. A. d. K. d. A. II S. 72. 91. 92. 131. 132. 451. III S. 52. 53. IV S. 81.
K. d. R. II S. 88—90. IV S. 38. 39.

1) Das Gesetz regelt hier die Berichtigung von Irrthümern, Uebersehen und Unklarheiten, welche sich in den Urtheilen und zwar in demjenigen Theile derselben vorfinden, welcher das Werk des Richters ist und ins Urtheilsbuch eingetragen wird, während für Berichtigungen des Schriftsatzes, von welchem Art. 285 spricht, der Art. 286 maßgebend ist.

Es unterscheidet: 1) einfache und klare Versehen, (Schreibfehler, sichtliche Versehen in einzelnen Worten oder Zahlen, Rechnungsirrthümer), bei welchen die Berichtigung nur formeller Natur ist und 2) wichtigere Unregelmäßigkeiten (Uebergehen von Streitpunkten, insbesondere auch des Kostenpunkts, Widersprüche und Unklarheiten in der Entscheidung), bei welchen richterliche Würdigung und Entscheidung nöthig ist.

gehend, weil unter dem Namen einer Berichtigung auch wirkliche Aenderungen der Entscheidung vorgenommen werden könnten, und man hielt es deßhalb für rathsam, dem Rechte der Berichtigung von Amtswegen möglichst enge Gränzen zu ziehen und selbst den ursprünglichen Beschluß, bei Berichtigungen weder Einspruch noch selbständige Rechtsmittel zuzulassen, wieder zu beseitigen.

Es ist zu unterscheiden, ob die Berichtigung im Urtheilssatze oder in einem sonstigen Theile des Urtheils, z. B. in den Entscheidungsgründen, vorzunehmen ist. Im ersteren Falle kann sie bis zur Verkündung des Urtheils, im zweiten aber bis zur Unterzeichnung des Eintrages im Urtheilsbuche, unbedingt und ohne Form geschehen; jedoch versteht es sich von selbst, daß auch bei Aenderungen dieser Art der Vorsitzende nicht eigenmächtig verfügen dürfe, sondern sich der Zu-

3) Das Begehren ist durch motivirten Antrag anzubringen, welcher dem Gegenanwalte zuzustellen ist, und zwar sind in diesem Falle die Anwälte auch nach Erlaß des Endurtheils noch als die gesetzlichen Vertreter der Parteien zu betrachten. Abg. II 132 (v. Weiß).

Hat die Gegenpartei keinen Anwalt, sei es weil ein Versäumungsurtheil in Frage ist (v. Neumayr Referat, 2. Lesung zu Hptst. VII Art. 22), oder weil der bestellt gewesene Anwalt nicht mehr am Gerichte fungirt, so ist ihr selbst der Antrag zuzustellen.

Mit der Zustellung ist sofort in die vom Senatsvorstande bezeichnete Sitzung zu laden, und zwar mit einer Erscheinungsfrist von drei Tagen, welche im Falle der Ladung der Partei sich nach Art. 209 erweitert. Bei der Fixation hat selbstverständlich der Senatsvorstand auf diese Frist Rücksicht zu nehmen, übrigens wird bei Gefahr auf Verzug auch mit abgekürzter Frist geladen werden können.

4) Die Berichtigung kann verlangt werden sowohl bei Urtheilen, welche der Rechtskraft fähig sind, als auch bei solchen, welche dies nicht sind (Art. 296); jedoch wird bei letzteren, da sie den Richter überhaupt nicht binden, wohl selten oder nie Anlaß zu einem solchen Verlangen gegeben sein.

Gegen das berichtigende Urtheil sind die gewöhnlichen Rechtsmittel zulässig.

b) Ergänzungen und Interpretationen.

5) Wenn der Richter vergessen hat, über einen Streitpunkt zu erkennen, oder wenn seine Entscheidung nicht klar ist, so hat er seine Aufgabe noch nicht erfüllt, welche darin besteht, daß er bestimmtes Urtheil über alle Streitpunkte abgebe.

Man könnte nun meinen, es verstehe sich von selbst, daß der Richter veranlaßt werden könne, nachträglich zu thun, was noch nicht geschehen ist, und es bedürfe einerseits hierzu keiner besonderen gesetzlichen Erlaubniß, noch sei es andererseits sachgemäß, eine Ausschlußfrist zu setzen, nach deren Verlauf eine Erledigung des Rechtsstreits fingirt werde, welche im Grunde nicht bestehe. Nichtsdestoweniger nimmt der Ausspruch des Richters, daß er die Sache als erledigt betrachte, mag er auch irrthümlich sein, soviel Geltung in Anspruch, daß das Gesetz eine Reaktion dagegen für nöthig erachtet. Es sieht daher den Antrag auf Vervollständigung des Urtheils als eine Art Rechtsmittel an, und macht dessen Zulässigkeit von Einhaltung einer bestimmten Frist abhängig.

Der Entwurf hatte für Fälle dieser Art geradezu das Rechtsmittel der Wiederaufnahme des Verfahrens gegeben und eine Ausnahme nur gemacht für Reklamationen, die sofort bei Spruch des Urtheils erfolgen (Art. 257); man hielt es jedoch geeigneter, das Berichtigungsverfahren, wie es für einfache Versehen gegeben ist, auch hier vorzuschreiben und nur eine Ausschlußfrist beizufügen. Für das Verfahren selbst gelten daher vorstehende Bemerkungen Nr. 3 und 4.

6) Indem der Gesetzgeber an Stelle der Wiederaufnahme des Verfahrens eine einfache Berichtigung setzte, hat sich die Sachlage in sofern wesentlich geändert, daß nun die Berichtigung auch herbeigeführt werden kann, wenn das Urtheil der Rechtskraft nicht fähig oder wenn die Rechtskraft noch nicht eingetreten ist.

Es steht letzteren Falls in der Wahl der Partei, die Berichtigung im Wege der Berufung oder im Wege des Art. 283 zu veranlassen, und hat sie das Letztere gewählt, so frägt sich, ob und wie weit hiedurch die Frist zur Berufung gegen das ergangene Urtheil suspendirt sei.

Wird der Antrag auf Berichtigung zurückgewiesen, so ist zwar gegen diese Abweisung als solche Berufung zulässig, allein das zu berichtigende Urtheil ist trotz der Einleitung des Berichtigungsverfahrens fähig, in Rechtskraft überzugehen, da das Gesetz nicht sagt, daß dieses Verfahren den Lauf der Berufungsfrist hemme.

Wird dem besagten Antrage stattgegeben, so möchte es dem Geiste des Gesetzes entsprechen, daß das abgeänderte Urtheil ganz an die Stelle des früheren trete, daß also der Gesammtinhalt des neuen Urtheils maßgebend sei für die Zulässigkeit der Berufung, und daß ferner die Berufungsfrist erst von Zustellung desselben laufe. S. unten Nr. 16. Uebrigens lassen sich auch Gründe für's Gegentheil geltend machen, insbesondere wenn das erste Urtheil an und für sich, ohne Beiziehung der übergangenen oder unklar entschiedenen Punkte, der Berufung unterlag; es möchte daher rathsam sein, im Zweifel sofort Berufung zu ergreifen.

Schließlich fragt sich, ob es statthaft sei, eine Berufung eventuell mit dem Berichtigungsverfahren zu verbinden. Dagegen spricht die Analogie von Art. 310; dafür, daß das Gesetz es hier nicht verbietet und daß die Wahrung von Rechten zu begünstigen ist.

7) Die Frist zur Beantragung der Berichtigung beträgt 30 Tage von Zustellung des Urtheils, und zwar an die Partei. Ursprünglich war gesagt: „innerhalb der Berufungsfrist" und die neue Fassung wurde nur gewählt, um auch

die Fälle zu begreifen, wo eine Berufung nicht statthaft sei.

Diese Frist hat überhaupt ganz die Natur der zur Einlegung von Rechtsmitteln gegebenen Fristen; sie erweitert sich daher nach Maßgabe des Art. 209 und wird, da offenbar der Gesetzgeber die Partei selbst in die Lage versetzen will, zu handeln, unterbrochen nach Maßgabe des Art. 211.

8) Die Versäumung der Frist hat, soweit nicht sonstige Rechtsmittel zulässig sind und ergriffen werden, zur Folge, daß der Rechtsstreit als solcher für erledigt gilt, daß also die Wirkungen der Rechtshängigkeit wegfallen. Hiermit ist jedoch nicht gesagt, daß die übergangenen Streitpunkte als abgewiesen gelten, oder daß eine Interpretation nicht mehr statthaft sei, wie dies in beiden Richtungen noch näher erörtert werden wird.

9) Uebergangene Streitpunkte.

Das Gesetz meint hier selbständige Streitpunkte, welche Gegenstand bestimmter Anträge bilden und über welche im Urtheilssatze ausdrücklich zu erkennen wäre.

Hat der Richter etwa solche Punkte übersehen, welche einer getroffenen Entscheidung gegenüber nur als Motive in Betracht kommen, wie z. B. wenn er, eine vorgeschützte Einrede nicht beachtend, die Klage zugesprochen hat, so mag sein Urtheil zwar nichtig sein wegen Mangels von Entscheidungsgründen, der Fall des Art. 283 ist jedoch nicht gegeben. Vgl. Chauv. sur C. quest. 1748.

Das Gesetz hat bloß eine Ergänzung des Urtheils im Auge, hier aber würde es sich um Aufhebung einer getroffenen Entscheidung handeln. Zu einer Aenderung des Urtheils im letzteren Sinne dürfte der Richter nur im Kostenpunkte berechtigt sein, insoweit die Entscheidung des übergangenen Punktes eine andere Vertheilung der Kosten nöthig machen sollte. Nur in diesem Sinne läßt sich auch die Verfügung in Art. 282 Abs. 7 hier anwenden.

10) Der Richter muß den Streitpunkt aus Versehen übergangen haben. Dieser Fall ist aber nicht gegeben, wenn ein Streitpunkt zur späteren Entscheidung vorbehalten wurde, obgleich nach dem Willen des Gesetzes (Art. 266 und 267) über denselben sofort hätte entschieden werden sollen. Wenn der Richter interloquirt oder sonst einen Zwischenbescheid erläßt, ohne gewisse Streitpunkte, auf welche sich dieser Bescheid nicht erstreckt, zu berühren, so wird im Zweifel anzunehmen sein, daß er sie der in Aussicht stehenden späteren Entscheidung vorbehalten habe.

11) Hat der Richter bloß mit einer allgemeinen Verfügung, z. B. mit den Worten: „weist im Uebrigen die Anträge der Parteien ab", über den Streit im Ganzen erkannt, jedoch diese Verfügung bezüglich einzelner Streitpunkte nicht mit Gründen versehen, obgleich solche im Sinne des Art. 275 nöthig waren, so ist die Annahme gerechtfertigt, daß diese Streitpunkte übersehen worden seien, da Sinn und Tragweite einer solchen Verfügung sich nur im Zusammenhalte mit den Gründen erkennen läßt. Es wird also in Fällen dieser Art der Weg des Art. 283 gestattet sein, wie dies auch die französische Jurisprudenz annimmt (Chauv. sur Carré quest. 1748), und ist es jedenfalls nicht nothwendig, auf Grund von Art. 788 Ziff. 4 Nichtigkeitsbeschwerde zu ergreifen.

12) Was die Entscheidung wegen der Kosten betrifft, so macht Art. 111 dem Richter nur bei Endurtheilen in der Hauptsache und bei Verwerfung eines Rechtsmittels zur Pflicht, zugleich über die Kosten zu erkennen; in allen anderen Fällen kann er den Kostenpunkt vorbehalten, und dieser Vorbehalt wird, wenn er schweigt, als selbstverständlich gelten.

Der Kostenpunkt wurde hier besonders erwähnt, um keinen Zweifel zu lassen, daß eine stillschweigende Vergleichung der Kosten, wie sie die Ger.-Ordnung kennt, nicht mehr bestehe.

13) Ist die Präclusivfrist des Art. 283 versäumt, so ist der übergangene Streitpunkt als erledigt zu betrachten; es frägt sich nun aber, ob die Folgen einer Klagabweisung oder nur die Folgen eines Klagabstandes eintreten.

Für Ersteres läßt sich sagen:

Da das Gesetz verlangt, daß gegen das Urtheil durch Ergreifung eines Rechtsmittels reagirt werde, so nimmt es offenbar an, daß entschieden worden sei, wenn auch nur in unvollkommener Weise. Ist dieser Rechtsweg versäumt, so wird die unvollkommene Entscheidung zu einer vollkommenen, d. h. es gilt der Anspruch als abgewiesen. Hätte man voraussetzen dürfen, daß der übergangene Streitpunkt Anlaß zu einem neuen Prozesse geben könne, so hätte man wahrscheinlich vorgezogen, eine Präclusivfrist nicht zu setzen, denn mag der Antrag auf nachträgliche Aburtheilung auch noch so spät kommen, immerhin ist es zweckmäßiger, daß dieselbe auf Grund des schon gepflogenen Vorverfahrens durch den bereits instruirten Richter erfolge, als daß ein neuer Prozeß begonnen werde.

Erwägungen dieser Art bestimmten die französische Jurisprudenz, bei Versäumung der für Fälle solcher Art gegebenen requête civile die

Erlöschung des Klagerechts anzunehmen. Chauv. sur Carré quest. 1749 ter.

Anderseits läßt sich geltend machen, daß bei Verlustigungen eher das Mindere als das Mehr anzunehmen sei; daß ferner die Gleichstellung des Falls der Uebergehung eines Streitpunktes mit dem Falle einer unklaren Entscheidung darauf hindeute, man habe an etwas Definitives nicht gedacht, indem es selbstverständlich für die Unklarheit keine Rechtskraft gibt.

Ich halte letztere Gründe für überwiegend und nehme an, daß bei Streitpunkten, die völlig übergangen wurden, das Klagrecht fortbestehe. Was den Kostenpunkt betrifft, so läßt sich derselbe allerdings vom Rechtsstreite nicht loslösen, und es tritt daher faktisch eine Kostenvergleichung ein, indem jeder Theil seine Kosten behält.

14) Unklare Entscheidungen.

Wenn das Urtheil Widersprüche in seinen Verfügungen enthält oder sein Sinn zweideutig ist, so handelt es sich um Interpretation desselben und diese erfolgt sachgemäß durch das nemliche Gericht. Diese Befugniß der Gerichte, den Sinn ihrer Entscheidungen aufzuklären, muß sich streng innerhalb ihrer Grenzen halten; es müssen also wirkliche Widersprüche zu lösen, wirkliche Zweifel zu klären sein, und wäre es eine offene Gesetzesverletzung, wenn unter dem Vorwande der Interpretation ergangene Entscheidungen abgeändert würden.

15) Der Ablauf der Präclusivfrist des Art. 283 hat ohne Zweifel zur Folge, daß die ausschließliche Zuständigkeit des erkennenden Gerichts zur Interpretation seines Urtheils wegfällt, jedoch erscheint es klar und hätte es sich auch ohne die wiederholte ausdrückliche Anerkennung der Gesetzgebungsausschüsse (Abg. III 113, IV 81) wohl von selbst verstanden, daß eine Interpretation dessen, was unklar ist, immer verlangt werden könne, sei es im Vollstreckungsverfahren, sei es im besonderen Klagwege, sofern die Bedingungen zur Anstellung einer Klage gegeben sind.

c) Gemeinschaftliches.

16) Von den Berichtigungsurtheilen, welche auf Grund der Art. 282 und 283 ergehen, ist am Rande der berichtigten Urtheile Vormerkung zu machen, welche den Ausfertigungen beizufügen ist.

Auch hieraus möchte hervorgehen, daß das Gesetz immer, also auch bei Ergänzungen, beide Entscheidungen als ein Ganzes betrachtet wissen will. S. oben Nr. 6.

Darstellung des Sachverhaltes.

Art. 285. — **Nach der Verkündung des Urtheils hat der Anwalt der in der Hauptsache obsiegenden Partei dem Anwalte der Gegenpartei und, wenn in der Sache mehrere Anwälte aufgestellt sind, jedem derselben einen Schriftsatz zustellen zu lassen, der enthalten muß:**

1) **die Bezeichnung der Parteien nach Vor- und Familiennamen, Stand oder Gewerbe, Wohnort und Parteistellung, nebst der Angabe, ob und durch welche Anwälte die Parteien vertreten und ob die Anwälte bei der Verhandlung erschienen sind oder nicht;**
2) **eine gedrängte Darstellung des Sachverhalts, nämlich der dem Rechtsstreite zu Grunde liegenden Sachverhältnisse und des Prozeßgangs, insbesondere der thatsächlichen Behauptungen der Parteien, der daraus abgeleiteten Rechtsbehelfe und der gemachten Geständnisse;**
3) **den Wortlaut der bei der Verhandlung gestellten Gesuche.**

Hat der Anwalt der obsiegenden Partei diesen Schriftsatz nicht innerhalb acht Tagen nach Verkündung des Urtheils zustellen lassen, so ist jeder andere in der Sache aufgestellte Anwalt befugt, denselben zu fertigen und zustellen zu lassen.

Art. 286. — **Verlangt einer der Anwälte eine Abänderung der in dem ihm zugestellten Schriftsatze enthaltenen Personenangabe (Art. 285 Ziff. 1) oder der darin enthaltenen Darstellung (Art. 285 Ziff. 2 und 3), so hat er dies spätestens am Tage nach der Zustellung dem zustellenden Gerichtsvollzieher mündlich zu erklären. Eine nähere Angabe der zu beantragenden Abänderung ist damit nicht zu verbinden. Der Gerichtsvollzieher ist verpflichtet, die ihm gemachte Erklärung auf der Urschrift der Zustellungsurkunde, welche er zu diesem Behufe an dem auf die Zustellung folgenden Tage in Händen zu behalten hat, vorzumerken.**

Ist Abänderung verlangt worden, so bestimmt der Vorsitzende, in dessen Verhinderung der älteste der bei der Urtheilsfällung thätig gewesenen Richter, auf die mündlichen Bemerkungen der ohne Förmlichkeit vorbeschiedenen Parteien, ob und welche Abänderung

vorzunehmen sei. Bejahenden Falls nimmt der Richter die erforderliche Aenderung auf dem Schriftsatze von kurzer Hand selbst vor. Andernfalls ist der Zustellungsurkunde die Bemerkung beizusetzen, daß dem erhobenen Verlangen keine Folge gegeben worden sei. Diese Bemerkung beziehungsweise die etwa vorgenommenen Aenderungen werden von dem Richter unterzeichnet. Rechtsmittel gegen die getroffene Bestimmung finden nicht statt.

Art. 287. — Der in Art. 285 bezeichnete Schriftsatz ist, wenn ein Verlangen auf Abänderung desselben nicht erhoben worden oder das erhobene erledigt ist, sofort auf der Gerichtsschreiberei zu hinterlegen. G. A. d. K. d. A. II S. 72. 75—91. 92—94. 130. IV S. 76—80. 82. 104. 320. 340. 496. K. d. R. II S. 67—79. 90—94 IV S. 39.

1) Der Wegfall besonderer Gerichtsakten macht es erklärlich, daß das Urtheil Manches enthalten müsse, was seither aus den Akten ergänzt werden konnte. Alles, was dazu dient, um die Tragweite der Rechtskraft zu bemessen, muß jetzt aus dem Urtheile selbst hervorgehen, welches daher außer der Entscheidung selbst und ihren Gründen noch zu enthalten hat: 1) eine genaue Bezeichnung der Parteien und ihrer Eigenschaften, 2) die wörtliche Anführung der bei der Verhandlung gestellten Gesuche und 3) eine besondere Darstellung des Sachverhalts.

Ueber die Frage, wer diesen letzteren Theil des Urtheils zu fertigen habe, ob das Gericht oder die Anwälte, ist sehr lebhaft verhandelt und gestritten worden.

Im älteren französischen Prozesse geschah die Redaktion des ganzen mündlich gesprochenen Urtheils durch den Gerichtschreiber, unter Aufsicht und Leitung des Vorsitzenden. Während der Revolutionszeit hatte sich der Mißstand eingebürgert, daß an manchen Gerichten der Anwalt der obsiegenden Partei das ganze Urtheil redigirte, selbstverständlich mit nachfolgender Billigung des Vorsitzenden. Der Code de procedure hat etwas Neues eingeführt, indem er theilt und die Redaktion der Entscheidung mit Gründen dem Vorsitzenden, die Fertigung der Qualitäten aber den Anwälten, unter Vorbehalt richterlicher Regelung im Falle des Streites, übertrug, — eine Einrichtung, deren Werth in Frankreich sehr bestritten ist. Vgl. Carré, proc. civ. zu Art. 142 und Abg. II 76.

2) Meiner Meinung nach hat die Uebertragung des fraglichen Geschäftes an die Anwälte eine besondere prinzipielle Bedeutung nicht, und erscheint es ebenso grundlos, wenn man einerseits besorgt, es werde der Sachverhalt häufig in Conflikt kommen mit Urtheilssatz und Entscheidungsgründen, als wenn man anderseits befürchtet, der Richter werde das Faktum willkürlich behandeln.

In letzterer Beziehung genügt es, auf den Parteiprozeß zu verweisen.

Im Parteiprozesse ist die Darstellung des Sachverhaltes von weit größerer Wichtigkeit als im Anwaltsprozesse, weil sie dort in Protokollirung von mündlichen Erklärungen der Parteien in der Sitzung besteht, während sie hier in der Regel nichts weiter ist, als ein Auszug aus den motivirten Anträgen. Nichtsdestoweniger wird sie jetzt (Art. 515) und wurde sie in der Pfalz von jeher ohne Anstand durch den Richter, bezw. durch den Gerichtsschreiber als Organ desselben, gefertigt. Wenn Letzterer, wie Umbscheiden (IV 76) anführt, hie und da dieses Geschäft auf die Bevollmächtigten der Parteien überträgt, so ist dies ein Mißstand, ähnlich demjenigen, daß manche Richter sich früher aus Bequemlichkeit von den Anwälten die Vertheilungsentwürfe beim Rangordnungsverfahren fertigen ließen; die Manifestation eines praktischen Bedürfnisses darin zu finden, möchte gewagt sein.

Ein anderer Gesichtspunkt ist jedoch derjenige der Zweckmäßigkeit, und in dieser Richtung bietet allerdings die fragliche Einrichtung Vortheile, welche bedeutend genug sind, um die entgegenstehenden Nachtheile zu überwiegen. Es wird durch dieselbe dem Richter ein großes Stück Arbeit abgenommen, und zwar eine Arbeit, welche keine besondere geistige Thätigkeit in Anspruch nimmt und auch von den Anwälten nicht selbst besorgt, sondern den Gehilfen überlassen zu werden pflegt. Diese Geschäftserleichterung für die Gerichte ist nicht gering anzuschlagen und möchte ich annehmen, daß an jedem Bezirksgerichte durchschnittlich ein Richter mehr erforderlich wäre, wenn der Sachverhalt durch die Richter gefertigt werden müßte.

a) Inhalt des Schriftsatzes.

3) Den Schriftsatz, von welchem Art. 285 spricht, nennt man in der französischen Rechtssprache: „die Qualitäten", weil einen Bestandtheil desselben die Bezeichnung der Personen und ihrer Eigenschaften bildet; unsere Prozeßordnung bezeichnet ihn mit gleichem oder noch besserem Rechte als: „Darstellung des Sachverhalts". Vielleicht ist es das Geeignetste, kurzweg vom „Sachverhalte" zu sprechen.

Er besteht aus drei Theilen: Bezeichnung der Parteien, Sachverhalt und Gesuchen.

Die Bezeichnung der Parteien erfolgt ganz so, wie in den hinterlegten Anträgen (Art. 241) und beim Urtheilseintrage (Art. 280), und sind hier unter „Parteien“ zunächst diejenigen Personen zu verstehen, auf deren Rechnung der Prozeß geführt wird. Jedoch ist auch die Angabe der gesetzlichen Vertreter, welche den Prozeß führen, nicht zu unterlassen.

Die Gesuche, zu welchen hier insbesondere auch die Beweiserbieten gehören, sind den hinterlegten Anträgen zu entnehmen, welche, sofern nöthig, zu diesem Zwecke dem betreffenden Anwalte einzuhändigen sind. Gesuche, welche bloß mündlich in der Sitzung gestellt werden (Art. 242), pflegt man in der Geschichtserzählung zu berühren.

4) Was nun die Darstellung des Sachverhalts betrifft, so soll dieselbe in gedrängter Kürze ein treues Bild dessen geben, was von den Parteien bei der Verhandlung vorgebracht worden ist, um die gestellten Gesuche durch Thatsachen zu begründen. Dabei ist selbstverständlich nur das, was auf den in Frage stehenden Rechtsstreit Bezug hat, aufzunehmen; was aber diesem fremd ist, muß auch der Darstellung des Sachverhaltes fremd bleiben.

In der Regel läßt sich der Stoff zum Sachverhalte aus den motivirten Anträgen entnehmen, und gestaltet sich daher thatsächlich die Darstellung des Sachverhalts als eine Zusammenstellung des Inhalts dieser Anträge.

Man pflegt mit den unstrittigen, die Grundlage des Rechtsstreites bildenden Thatsachen zu beginnen, und die weiteren zum Klaggrunde gehörigen Behauptungen anzureihen, unter Bezeichnung der Ansprüche, welche daraus hergeleitet werden sollen. Sodann folgen die Gegenbehauptungen des Beklagten, die Entwicklung der verschiedenen Einreden, die Erwiderungen hierauf, Repliken rc. — Widerklagen, Interventionen rc. sind natürlich selbständig zu entwickeln.

5) Mit dem Sachverhalte verbindet sich, soweit nöthig, die Darlegung des Prozeßganges.

In dieser Beziehung ist möglichste Beschränkung anzurathen und eignet sich nur dasjenige zur Aufnahme, was zum Verständnisse der Prozeßlage nicht entbehrt werden kann, oder was Anlaß zu Zwischenstreiten gegeben hat.

Beim Sachverhalte des ersten Urtheils ist z. B. in der Regel von allen vorausgehenden Prozeßhandlungen nichts weiter zu besprechen, als die dem Rechtsstreite zu Grunde liegende Klagschrift; Anwaltsbestellung, Aktenmittheilung, Schriftenwechsel, Hinterlegung der Anträge, Vertagungen vor der Verhandlung und sonstige vorbereitende Handlungen brauchen nicht erwähnt zu werden, falls nicht etwa die Entscheidung besonderen Anlaß dazu gibt. Ebenso bedingt es der bloß vorbereitende Charakter des Vorverfahrens, daß Aenderungen der Gesuche, Aufgeben von Einreden und Vorkommnisse ähnlicher Art nicht anzuführen sind, denn der Sachverhalt hat nur dasjenige zu enthalten, was in der Sitzung geltend gemacht wird, und soll über Dinge weggehen, die bloß Projekt geblieben sind. Klagänderungen sind allerdings hervorzuheben.

In den späteren Urtheilen ist der Zwischenbescheide und zwar auch solcher, welche keiner Rechtskraft fähig sind, zu erwähnen und die Art ihrer Erledigung zu bezeichnen, z. B. durch Anführung der Protokolle über Zeugenverhöre, Augenschein rc. Eine nähere Entwicklung der Ergebnisse der Beweiserhebungen, z. B. Angabe der Namen der Zeugen oder gar deren Aussagen, wäre nicht am Orte; vielmehr gehören die Erörterungen über die Beweisführung nur in die Entscheidungsgründe. Nur in so fern, als etwa die Beweiserhebung Anlaß zu Zwischenstreiten gegeben hat, ist die thatsächliche Grundlage dieser Zwischenstreite im Sachverhalte zu geben. In gleicher Weise ist auch der Inhalt von Urkunden nur soweit anzuführen, als er die Grundlage von Klagbegehren oder Einreden bildet, nicht aber soweit er bloß als Beweismaterial in Betracht kommt.

6) Es wäre irrig, wollte man annehmen, der Sachverhalt habe sich nur über diejenigen Punkte zu erstrecken, welche wirklich entschieden worden sind, vielmehr muß er alle Punkte umfassen, deren Entscheidung beantragt war, welche Gegenstand der Haupt- und eventuellen Gesuche gewesen sind. Abg. II 89.

Insbesondere darf man nicht glauben, weil die Zwischenbescheide mit wenig Ausnahmen nur vorbereitend seien, so sei es unnöthig, den ganzen Sachverhalt in dieselben aufzunehmen, und genüge es, dies im späteren Endurtheile zu thun. Es mag unerörtert bleiben, ob nicht der Gesetzgeber etwas Derartiges hätte bestimmen können, soviel erscheint sicher, daß er es nicht bestimmen wollte, und daß daher, wie es übrigens im französischen Prozesse immer galt, für Zwischenbescheide jeder Art (natürlich Vertagungen und ähnliche Verfügungen [Art. 275 u. 281] ausgenommen), selbst wenn es sich nur um allgemeine Maßregeln, wie persönliches Erscheinen, Augenschein rc., handelt, der Sachverhalt der Vorschrift des Art. 285 gemäß gefertigt werden muß.

7) Um nun zu vermeiden, daß in einer Reihe von Urtheilen des nemlichen Gerichts, in der nemlichen Sache, dieselbe Geschichtserzählung

sich wiederhole, war es seither Gebrauch, in den späteren Urtheilen auf die frühere Darstellung zu verweisen und an diese anknüpfend nur das beizufügen, was sich etwa geändert, oder was sich im Prozeßgange Neues ergeben hatte. Man sagte z. B.: „Durch Zwischenbescheid vom —, in welchem der Sachverhalt im Uebrigen dargestellt ist, wurden beide Parteien zu Zeugenbeweisen zugelassen 2c."

Offenbar steht nichts im Wege, dieses Verfahren auch jetzt noch zu beobachten, und es erscheint dasselbe sogar dem Willen des Gesetzgebers entsprechend, da es im Entwurfe erster Lesung (Hauptst. VII Art. 18 Abs. 3) ausdrücklich gestattet war und bei der Umwandlung, welche fragliche Bestimmung später erfuhr, die Absicht einer Aenderung in dieser Richtung nicht kundgegeben worden ist. Allerdings ist es ein Mißstand, wenn der Sachverhalt, welcher dem Endurtheile zu Grunde liegt, erst aus früheren Zwischenbescheiden beigeholt werden muß; allein ein noch größerer Mißstand würde es sein, wenn in jedem Urtheile das Nemliche wiederholt werden müßte. Zum Mindesten dürfte eine solche Wiederholung nicht in späteren Zwischenbescheiden stattfinden. In den Urtheilen höherer Instanzen pflegte man eine Bezugnahme auf den Sachverhalt im Urtheile der niederen Instanz zu vermeiden.

8) Eine weitere Abkürzung, welche ebenso zulässig als sachgemäß ist, besteht darin, daß man vielfach in der Lage ist, auf die nachfolgenden Beweiserbieten, welche häufig ein vollständiges Bild der Parteibehauptungen geben, zu verweisen. Es wäre ungeeignet, im nemlichen Schriftsatze das Nemliche zweimal zu sagen.

b) Beweiskraft des Sachverhalts.

9) Ueber die Bedeutung, welche der ins Urtheil aufzunehmende Sachverhalt habe, ist bei den Verhandlungen vielerlei Widersprechendes geäußert worden, und wenn auch als sicher gelten darf, daß man im Allgemeinen die Grundsätze des französischen Prozesses sich anzueignen gedachte, so sind doch auch hierüber wiederum verschiedene Ansichten laut geworden, was wohl dadurch sich erklärt, daß sich in der Praxis fast nie Anstände ergeben. Vgl. die Aeußerungen Abg. II 90 (v. Weiß und Umbscheiden).

10) Um Klarheit zu gewinnen, ist es nöthig, Natur und Zweck fraglicher Einrichtung ins Auge zu fassen und dabei zunächst vom Parteiprozesse auszugehen, in welchem das ganze Urtheil das Werk des Richters ist, wie es eigentlich naturgemäß erscheint.

Es ist begreiflich, daß im Parteiprozesse auf irgend eine Weise beurkundet werden müsse, was die Parteien mündlich in der Sitzung vorgebracht haben. Geschieht dies nicht in einem besonderen Sitzungsprotokolle, welches mit Recht als höchst unpraktisch beseitigt wurde, so muß es im Urtheile selbst geschehen, entweder im Urtheilssatze, oder in den Gründen, oder in einem besonderen Abschnitte.

Der Urtheilssatz eignet sich wohl dazu, einzelne wichtige Erklärungen zu beurkunden, nicht aber, eine ganze Geschichtserzählung aufzunehmen, und ebensowenig sind die Entscheidungsgründe der passende Ort, da sie bestimmt sind, zu prüfen und festzustellen, was strittig ist, nicht aber einfach zu beurkunden. So ergibt sich denn von selbst das Bedürfniß einer besonderen Darstellung des Sachverhalts, deren Zweck bloß ist, zu beurkunden, was verhandelt wurde; dieselbe hat daher alle Wirkungen einer Beurkundung, allein auch nur diese.

Hieraus folgt einerseits, daß von einer Rechtskraft dessen, was im Sachverhalte als Thatsache vorgetragen ist, nie die Rede sein könne, da wohl Entscheidungen über strittige Thatsachen in Rechtskraft übergehen, nicht aber Beurkundungen. Um dies besser hervorzuheben, sagte man in der Ueberschrift nicht „Feststellung", sondern „Darstellung des Sachverhalts" (Abg. IV 82).

Hieraus folgt anderseits, daß die Darstellung des Sachverhalts die volle Wirkung einer richterlichen Beurkundung hat, die nemliche Wirkung, als hätte der Richter ein Protokoll im Sinne des Art. 166 oder der Novelle von 1837 § 9 aufgenommen. Daß die Protokollarform nicht eingehalten worden, erscheint ohne Bedeutung, da es Grundsatz des mündlichen Verfahrens ist, daß das, was der Richter im Urtheile beurkundet, jener Form nicht bedürfe. Vgl. Bemerk. zu Art. 166 Nr. 3 und 248 Nr. 6 u. 7.

11) Der Sachverhalt bildet daher Beweis der darin beurkundeten, auf den Prozeß bezüglichen Vorgänge, jedoch nur vorbehaltlich des Nachweises der Unrichtigkeit, insbesondere des Irrthums, welcher hier ebenso zulässig ist, wie bei jeder andern öffentlichen Urkunde (Art. 372).

Zur Beurkundung von Thatsachen, welche nicht zum Prozesse gehören, ist der Richter nicht berufen, und seine Beurkundungen haben daher zunächst nur Geltung für den in Frage stehenden Prozeß; jedoch ist bei dem Prinzipe der freien Beweiswürdigung natürlich, daß sie möglicherweise auch über den Prozeß hinaus auf andere Rechtsverhältnisse wirken können.

12) Was nun im Parteiprozesse durch den Richter beurkundet wird, das soll nach dem von

unserer Prozeßordnung angenommenen Systeme im Anwaltsprozesse durch die Parteien selbst beurkundet werden.

Die übereinstimmende Erklärung der Parteien, welche das Gesetz bei Mangel eines Einwandes innerhalb der durch Art. 286 gesetzten Frist annimmt, vertritt eine Beurkundung und bildet vollen Beweis für den Prozeß in allen Instanzen, vorbehaltlich des Nachweises, daß ein Irrthum vorliege. Man hat dies in Frankreich nie bezweifelt. Chauveau sur Carré quest. 601.

Hierdurch ist natürlich das Recht und die Pflicht des Richters nicht beseitigt, wichtigere Vorkommnisse selbst und zwar im Urtheilssatze zu beurkunden. Derartige Beurkundungen sind oft von großer praktischer Bedeutung, weil im Falle, wo später die Parteien sich nicht einigen, es für den Vorsitzenden höchst schwierig, ja unmöglich ist, den Laut mündlicher Erklärungen festzustellen, ganz abgesehen von dem rechtlichen Werthe dieser Feststellung.

13) Wenn im Falle der Uneinigkeit der Parteien der Vorsitzende den Sachverhalt bestimmt, so könnte man denken, es müsse nun dessen Entscheidung die nemliche Kraft haben, wie die Beurkundung des Richters im Parteiprozesse.

Dies wäre jedoch nicht richtig.

Es ist hier vorerst nicht das Gericht selbst, sondern ein einzelnes Mitglied des Gerichts, welches Zeugschaft gibt, sodann aber begründet es einen großen Unterschied, ob Richter und Gerichtsschreiber sofort nach der Sitzung die Vorgänge in derselben beurkunden, nachdem sie im Voraus wußten, daß ihnen diese Pflicht obliege, oder ob erst in späterer Zeit ein Richter als Zeuge über Vorgänge aufgerufen wird, welche er keine besondere Veranlassung hatte, seinem Gedächtnisse einzuprägen oder sich vorzumerken. Solchen Entscheidungen des Präsidenten legt daher die französische Jurisprudenz die volle Wirkung einer richterlichen Beurkundung nicht bei, und auch für unsere Prozeßordnung wird dies anzunehmen sein. Chauv. sur Carré quest. 603. Abg. II 90 (v. Weiß).

14) Es kann geschehen, daß der von den Parteien gefertigte Sachverhalt mit dem sonstigen Urtheile in Widerspruch geräth, obgleich dieser Fall sehr selten sein wird und mir nicht bekannt ist, daß er jemals in der Pfalz vorgekommen sei.

Sollte sich ein solcher Widerspruch ergeben, so darf man im Zweifel annehmen, daß dasjenige, was der Richter im Urtheilssatze beurkundet, richtig sei, die abweichende Darstellung des Sachverhalts aber auf Irrthum beruhe.

Steht nun aber fest, daß die Parteien sich nicht geirrt, vielmehr wissentlich gehandelt, so ist umgekehrt deren Erklärung allein maßgebend, weil in derselben die Anerkennung liegt, es sei die Beurkundung des Richters eine irrige gewesen.

15) Was die Entscheidungsgründe anbelangt, so dürfen sie dem vereinbarten Sachverhalte gegenüber eine Geltung nicht beanspruchen.

Indem der Richter seine Entscheidungsgründe fertigt, handelt er nicht in der Absicht, etwas zu beurkunden, sondern eine getroffene Entscheidung zu rechtfertigen, und schon deßhalb können seine Erklärungen und Voraussetzungen das Gewicht richterlicher Beurkundungen nicht beanspruchen, abgesehen davon, daß es meist im Zweifel bleibt, ob man es mit einer bloßen Folgerung, also einer subjektiven Ansicht, oder ob man es mit einer objektiven Bezeugung zu thun habe. Die Bemerkung des Minist.-Commissärs (Abg. IV 79) ist daher nur so zu verstehen, daß die Entscheidungsgründe auf ihrem Gebiete, d. h. insofern sie strittige Thatsachen feststellen, durch den Sachverhalt der Parteien nicht geändert werden könnten.

c) Verfahren.

16) Es ist als ein Mißstand des französischen Verfahrens zu betrachten, daß die Qualitäten erst bei Ausfertigung des Urtheils, also oft sehr spät, nach Monaten, ja Jahren, abgefaßt werden müssen und es, da zudem an manchen Gerichten die hinterlegten Anträge nicht aufbewahrt, sondern den Anwälten zurückgegeben werden, dann sehr schwierig ist, den Thatbestand richtig aufzustellen.

Der Gesetzgeber fühlte diesen Mißstand und sucht ihm dadurch zu begegnen, daß er dem Anwalte der in der Hauptsache obsiegenden Partei eine Frist von acht Tagen von Verkündung des Urtheils an gibt, nach Verlauf welcher Frist jeder andere im Rechtsstreite aufgestellte Anwalt das Recht habe, den Sachverhalt zu fertigen und die dafür bestimmten Gebühren zu beziehen. Außerdem sind Vorschriften in der Advokatenordnung in Aussicht gestellt.

Bestehen Zweifel, welcher Anwalt als in der Hauptsache obsiegend zu betrachten sei, so hat derjenige den Vorzug, welcher die Verhandlung betrieben hat.

Die Zustellung hat an sämmtliche Anwälte der Sache zu geschehen, auch an solche, gegen welche die Ausfertigung nicht benützt werden soll, und es ist dies wohl selbstverständlich, da ja der Sachverhalt eine Ergänzung des Urtheils bildet.

Manche Anwälte der Pfalz haben die Uebung eingeführt, die Qualitäten nicht zustellen zu lassen, sondern sich zur Durchsicht und Billigung zuzusenden, ein Verfahren, welches als sachgemäß empfohlen werden kann.

17) Gegen Personenangabe und Darstellung des Sachverhalts — die Gesuche werden wörtlich abgeschrieben — kann jeder Gegenanwalt binnen einem Tage durch mündliche Erklärung beim Gerichtsvollzieher Einwand erheben, über welchen vom Vorsitzenden, oder bei dessen Verhinderung vom ältesten der bei der Urtheilsfällung thätig gewesenen Richter, in der formlosen Weise, wie Art. 286 es bestimmt, entschieden wird.

Diese Frist läuft ausnahmsweise auch während der Gerichtsferien (Einf.-Ges. Art. 139).

Die Bestimmung des Zeitpunkts der Verhandlung vor dem Vorsitzenden und die Einladung der Gegenanwälte zum Erscheinen, geschehen mündlich und formlos

18) Ist der Sachverhalt fertig, so wird er auf der Gerichtsschreiberei hinterlegt und aufbewahrt, um als ein wesentlicher Bestandtheil des Urtheils jeder Zeit, so oft eine Ausfertigung nöthig ist, benützt zu werden.

Ausfertigung des Urtheils.

Art. 288. — **Von den bei unbeschränkter Oeffentlichkeit der Verhandlung erlassenen Urtheilen unter Aufsicht des Gerichtsschreibers Einsicht zu nehmen und einfache Ausfertigungen davon gegen Entrichtung der Gebühren zu verlangen, steht Jedermann frei.**

Außerdem kann jede Partei, zu deren Gunsten Verurtheilung erfolgt ist, behufs der Zwangsvollstreckung gegen Entrichtung der Gebühren eine vollstreckbare Ausfertigung des Urtheils erholen.

Art. 289. — **Die Urtheilsausfertigungen werden vom Gerichtsschreiber ertheilt. Sie führen die Ueberschrift: „Im Namen Seiner Majestät des Königs von Bayern“ und müssen enthalten:**

1) die Bezeichnung des Gerichts;

2) die Bezeichnung der Parteien und ihrer Vertreter;

3) den Urtheilssatz;

4) den Sachverhalt und die gestellten Gesuche;

5) die Entscheidungsgründe;

6) den Tag der Verkündung die Bezeichnung der hiebei anwesenden Gerichtspersonen und, falls nicht alle Richter, welche zu dem Urtheile mitgewirkt haben, bei der Verkündung anwesend waren, auch die Namen der abwesenden und den Grund der Abwesenheit.

Die Bezeichnung der Parteien und ihrer Vertreter, der Sachverhalt und die gestellten Gesuche sind nach dem in Gemäßheit des Art. 285 gefertigten Schriftsatze, der Tag der Verkündung, der Urtheilssatz und die Entscheidungsgründe nach dem Eintrage im Urtheilsbuche, die Bezeichnung der Gerichtspersonen nach den im Urtheilsbuche enthaltenen bezüglichen Vormerkungen einzurücken.

Am Schlusse hat der Gerichtsschreiber die auf der Urschrift befindlichen Unterschriften anzugeben, den Gleichlaut durch seine Unterschrift unter Beifügung des Datums zu bescheinigen und das Gerichtssiegel beizudrücken.

Art. 290. — **Vollstreckbare Ausfertigungen tragen unter den Worten: „Im Namen Seiner Majestät des Königs von Bayern“ die weitere Ueberschrift: „Vollstreckbare Ausfertigung“ und am Schlusse nach der Angabe der auf der Urschrift befindlichen Unterschriften die Worte: „Vorstehende dem N. N. (Bezeichnung der Partei nach Namen oder Parteistellung) ertheilte Ausfertigung wird hiemit als vollstreckbar erklärt.“**

Wird eine vollstreckbare Ausfertigung ertheilt, so hat der Gerichtsschreiber davon unter Angabe der Partei, an welche sie erfolgt ist, und des Tags der Ertheilung im Urtheilsbuche auf der Urschrift Vormerkung zu machen und der Vormerkung seinen Namenszug beizufügen.

Art. 291. — **Eine zweite vollstreckbare Ausfertigung darf derselben Partei nicht ertheilt werden, außer auf schriftliches Gesuch und auf Grund eines vom Gerichtsvorstande nach Vorladung der Gegenpartei erlassenen Beschlusses.**

Von diesem auf der Gerichtsschreiberei aufzubewahrenden Beschlusse wird auf der Urschrift des Urtheils Vormerkung gemacht. Er ist auf der neuen, als zweite zu bezeichnenden, Ausfertigung anzuführen.

Ergibt sich aus dem Vorbringen der Parteien, daß nur ein Theil der im Urtheile festgesetzten Schuld noch im Rückstande sich befindet, so ist dies im Beschlusse zu bemerken und die Ausfertigung nur für den rückständigen Schuldbetrag vollstreckbar zu erklären.

Gegen den Beschluß, wodurch eine neue Ausfertigung bewilligt wurde, findet weder Einspruch noch Beschwerde statt.

Art. 292. — **Wird die Ertheilung einer Ausfertigung von dem Gerichtsschreiber oder von dem Gerichts-Vorstande verweigert, so kann die Partei, welche dieselbe verlangt hat, sich dagegen mittels einfacher Vorstellung an das Gericht wenden.**

Wird die verlangte Ausfertigung auch von dem Gerichte verweigert, so steht der Partei gegen den betreffenden Beschluß das Rechtsmittel der Beschwerde zu.

Gegen den Gerichtsbeschluß, durch welchen die verlangte Ausfertigung bewilligt wird, findet kein Rechtsmittel statt, und es kommen bezüglich desselben, wenn es sich um eine zweite vollstreckbare Ausfertigung handelt, die Bestimmungen des Art. 291 Abs. 2 zur Anwendung.

Art. 293. — **Die in Art. 281 angeführten Beschlüsse und Beurkundungen sind, wenn nicht besondere Verhältnisse eine Ausnahme veranlassen, nicht auszufertigen.**

G. A. d. K. d. A. II S. 72. 94. 95. 132. 133. 451. IV S. 82. 83. K. d. R. II S. 94. 95. IV S. 39—41.

1) Alles, was zum Urtheile gehört, also Urtheilseintrag und Sachverhalt, ist öffentlich, wie die Gerichtsverhandlung und Urtheilsverkündung selbst es waren.

Von den in öffentlicher Sitzung erlassenen Urtheilen kann daher Jedermann, auch wenn er ganz unbetheiligt ist, unter Aufsicht des Gerichtsschreibers Einsicht nehmen und einfache Ausfertigung verlangen, selbstverständlich gegen Entrichtung der festgesetzten Gebühren.

Ist das Urtheil jedoch in geheimer Sitzung oder bei beschränkter Oeffentlichkeit (Art. 149) gesprochen worden, so ist dritten Personen diese Kenntnißnahme nur gestattet, wenn sie auf Grund eines rechtlichen Interesse die Ermächtigung des Gerichtsvorstandes erwirken. Vgl. Bemerk. zu Art. 170 Nr. 2.

Vollstreckbare Ausfertigungen kann zudem nur eine Partei, welche Verurtheilung erwirkt hat, verlangen.

a) Ausfertigung im Allgemeinen.

2) Bei der Urtheilsausfertigung vereinigt der Gerichtsschreiber die getrennten Bestandtheile des Urtheils und gibt ihnen eine einheitliche Form, und zwar in der Art, wie dies in Art. 289 näher bezeichnet ist. Erst in der Ausfertigung stellt sich daher das Urtheil auch seiner äußeren Erscheinung nach als vollständig dar.

Das Gesetz unterscheidet einfache Ausfertigungen, welche nur die Stelle gewöhnlicher beglaubigter Abschriften vertreten, und vollstreckbare Ausfertigungen zum Zwecke des Vollzuges.

3) Die Form, welche Art. 289 für das vollständige Urtheil gibt, weicht von derjenigen, wie sie bis jetzt in den Ländern des französischen Rechts üblich war, erheblich ab und ist insbesondere die Anordnung der verschiedenen Theile eine ganz andere.

Der wichtigste Unterschied besteht darin, daß der Urtheilssatz vorausgestellt wird, die Entscheidungsgründe aber, durch Sachverhalt und Gesuche davon getrennt, an's Ende. Bereits früher (Bemerk. zu Art. 275 Nr. 15 und zu Art. 280 Nr. 4) sprach ich meine Ansicht aus, daß diese Aenderung nicht logisch sei, und die richtige Reihenfolge sein müsse: Sachverhalt, Gesuche, Gründe und Entscheidung. Die dort gemachte Bemerkung, daß nach dem Willen des Gesetzgebers nichts im Wege stehe, auch eine andere Reihenfolge zu beobachten, gilt auch hier, und namentlich dürfte der Gerichtsschreiber nicht eigenmächtig, bloß um den Worten des Art. 289 zu genügen, die Entscheidungsgründe dem Urtheilssatze nachstellen, wenn der Richter das Urtheil in der Erwägungsform gesprochen und, wie es diesen Falles selbstverständlich ist, dieselben vorangestellt hätte. In diesem Falle ist nothwendig der Urtheilssatz an's Ende zu stellen, da Sachverhalt und Gesuche den Entscheidungsgründen immer vorausgehen müssen.

Besonders hervorzuheben ist, daß die Bezeichnung der Parteien aus dem Sachverhalte (Art. 285 Ziff. 1) zu entnehmen, d. h. wörtlich aus demselben abzuschreiben ist, nicht aber aus dem Urtheilseintrage.

Hervorzuheben ist ferner, daß nicht bloß das Datum der Urtheilsverkündung, welches natürlich einen wesentlichen Bestandtheil des Urtheils selbst bildet, sondern auch das Datum der Ausfertigung anzugeben ist.

4) Ein ausgefertigtes Urtheil, in diejenige Form gefaßt, wie sie Art. 289 voraussetzt,

lautet seinen allgemeinen Umrissen nach etwa wie folgt:

Im Namen Sr. Maj. des Königs von Bayern.

Das kgl. Bezirksgericht München l/J. hat in Sachen von

A— Hauptkläger, vertreten durch Anwalt X;

gegen

B— Hauptbeklagten und Gewährschaftskläger, vertreten durch Anwalt Y;

gegen

C— Gewährschaftsbeklagten, vertreten durch Anwalt Z;

folgendes Urtheil erlassen:

Das Gericht

1) über die Hauptklage erkennend:

weist die Einrede der Unzuständigkeit des Gerichtes ab;

erklärt, daß dem Hauptkläger A, als Eigenthümer der Grundstücke — —, das Recht zustehe, 2c. 2c.

verurtheilt den Hauptbeklagten B, unter Abweisung des Mehrbegehrens als unbegründet, an den Hauptkläger als Entschädigung wegen Störung dieses Rechtes die Summe von 20 fl. zu zahlen;

verurtheilt ihn schließlich dem Hauptkläger gegenüber zu den Kosten;

2) über die Gewährschaftsklage erkennend:

gibt Urkunde, daß der Gewährschaftsbeklagte seine Pflicht der Gewährleistung anerkennt;

verurtheilt denselben, sofort, unter Abweisung des Mehrbegehrens als unbegründet (und ohne Beachtung der erbotenen Beweise), an den Gewährschaftskläger, als Entschädigung wegen Minderwerths seines Hauses, die Summe von 200 fl. mit Zins von heute an zu zahlen, und ihm ferner obige Beträge, in welche er dem Hauptkläger gegenüber verurtheilt worden ist, zu ersetzen;

verurtheilt ihn schließlich in die Kosten der Gewährschaftsklage.

Sachverhalt.

Laut Akt vor Notar X— vom — erwarb B— von C— das Wohnhaus — um den Preis von 5000 fl. In diesem Akte ist angegeben, 2c. 2c.

Bei der öffentlichen Verhandlung vom — nahmen die Anwälte der Parteien folgende Anträge:

Anwalt X trug an für den Hauptkläger:

es gefalle dem kgl. Bezirksgerichte, 2c.

Anwalt Y trug an für den Hauptbeklagten und Gewährschaftskläger:

es gefalle dem kgl. Bezirksgerichte:

a) zur Hauptklage 2c.,

b) zur Gewährschaftsklage 2c.

Anwalt Z trug an für den Gewährschaftsbeklagten 2c.

Nach Schluß der Verhandlung wurde der Spruch des Urtheils in die heutige Sitzung vertagt, in welcher obiger Urtheilssatz verkündet wurde nebst folgenden Gründen:

Entscheidungsgründe.

Was zuerst die Hauptklage und zwar die derselben entgegengesetzte Einrede der Unzuständigkeit betrifft, so erscheint diese Einrede unbegründet, denn 2c.

Was die Begründung der Hauptklage anbelangt, 2c.

Was die Gewährschaftsklage anbelangt, 2c.

Die Kosten betreffend, 2c.

So verkündet in öffentlicher Sitzung des Gerichts vom —, wo zugegen waren — —

Auf der Urschrift sind unterzeichnet 2c.

Für richtige Ausfertigung

München, den — —

Der k. Bezirksgerichtsschreiber

5) Die in Art. 281 angeführten Beschlüsse und Beurkundungen, welche keiner Entscheidungsgründe bedürfen, werden in der Regel auch nicht ausgefertigt (Art. 293). Sollte aus besonderer Veranlassnng dennoch eine Ausfertigung nöthig sein, so würde dieselbe in einfacher Abschrift des Eintrages im Urtheilsbuche bestehen. Von Fertigung eines Sachverhaltes kann bei dergleichen Verfügungen nicht die Rede sein.

b) Vollstreckbare Ausfertigung.

6) Nach seitherigem Verfahren hatte der Richter, in dessen Händen der Urtheilsvollzug lag, die einzelnen Vollzugsmaßregeln anzuordnen. An Stelle dieser einzelnen Verfügungen tritt nun die vom Gerichtsschreiber, als dem Organe des Gerichts, dem Urtheile beigefügte allgemeine Vollstreckbarkeitserklärung, deren Wirkung nach Art. 822 darin besteht, daß nunmehr das Urtheil auf Betreiben des obsiegenden Theils in jeder nach den Bestimmungen von Buch IV zulässigen Weise zum Vollzuge gebracht werden kann.

Die Form, welche zu beobachten ist, damit eine Ausfertigung als vollstreckbar gelte, ist durch Art. 290 genau vorgezeichnet. Es ist insbesondere darin die Partei, für welche sie zu gelten hat, nach Namen oder Parteistellung zu bezeichnen, so daß es also z. B. genügt, zu sagen: „Vorstehende, den Klägern ertheilte Ausfertigung 2c. Die Namen ergeben sich aus dem Urtheile selbst.

7) In der Regel ist jede Partei nur berechtigt, eine einzige vollstreckbare Ausfertigung zu verlangen, weshalb der Gerichtsschreiber verpflichtet ist, im Urtheilsbuche vorzumerken, für welche Partei er sie ertheilt habe.

Will die nemliche Partei eine zweite

vollstreckbare Ausfertigung, etwa weil ihr die erste zu Verlust gegangen ist, so muß sie bezw. ihr Anwalt, ein schriftliches Gesuch an den Gerichtsvorstand richten, aus welchem natürlich erhellen muß: 1) daß die Forderung ganz oder theilweise noch bestehe, und 2) aus welchen Gründen die erste Ausfertigung nicht mehr benützt werden könne. Der Gerichtsvorstand bestimmt einen Tag, um die Gegenpartei, d. h. diejenige Partei, gegen welche der Vollzug stattfinden soll, zur Verhandlung vor ihm zu laden, welche Tagfahrtbestimmung, wie im Falle des Art. 259, auf das Gesuch selbst zu setzen und mit diesem zuzustellen sein wird.

8) Der Grund, warum das Gesetz diese Beiladung anordnet, ist augenfällig. Der Gläubiger, welcher die ihm ertheilte vollstreckbare Ausfertigung nicht mehr besitzt, muß vorerst die Vermuthung gegen sich gelten lassen, daß die Schuld getilgt sei (Vgl. Art. 1283 Code civ. und bayer. Landr. Thl. IV Cap. XIV § 13 Ziff. 1), und darf sich nicht beschweren, wenn ihm eine zweite Vollstreckungsurkunde nicht gegeben wird, bevor der Schuldner gehört oder doch wenigstens in die Lage versetzt ist, sei es durch Vorzeigen der in seinem Besitze befindlichen ersten vollstreckbaren Ausfertigung, sei es durch Quittungen oder sonstige Urkunden, darzuthun, daß die Schuld nicht mehr bestehe.

Das Gewicht der etwa vom Schuldner vorgebrachten Einwände zu würdigen, ist dem freien Ermessen des Richters überlassen.

Die Entscheidung des Gerichtsvorstandes ist endgiltig, falls er bewilligt, und zwar gleichviel, ob der Schuldner erschienen war oder nicht; sie ist jedoch anfechtbar im Falle der Verweigerung. Dieser Unterschied ist leicht erklärlich, da die Bewilligung nur zur Folge hat, daß der Gläubiger zum Vollzuge schreiten kann, im Uebrigen aber die Rechte des Schuldners völlig unberührt bleiben und im Wege des Einspruchs gegen die Vollstreckung zur Geltung gebracht werden können; während hingegen die Verweigerung tiefgreifende Wirkungen hat. Hieraus leitet sich zugleich die Folge, daß der Richter im Zweifel zu bewilligen hat, und daß er nur dann verweigern soll, wenn sehr dringende Gründe dazu vorliegen.

9) Gegen die Verweigerung des Gerichtsvorstandes kann der Gläubiger sich an das Gericht selbst wenden, und falls auch dieses verweigert, die Entscheidung des höheren Gerichts veranlassen.

Ersteres geschieht auf dem Wege einfacher Vorstellung (Hauptst. XXV), d. h. es wird auf einseitiges Verlangen des Gläubigers ohne weitere Beiziehung des Schuldners entschieden. In der nemlichen Weise wird folgegemäß auch die Beschwerde an das Obergericht zu erledigen sein.

Es erscheint dies als eine Anomalie, nachdem einmal eine contradiktorische Verhandlung vor dem Gerichtsvorstande vorausgegangen.

10) Der Beschluß, durch welchen der Gerichtsvorstand oder das Gericht selbst der Partei eine zweite vollstreckbare Ausfertigung bewilligt, ist auf der Gerichtsschreiberei aufzubewahren. Da für Verweigerungsbeschlüsse dies nicht bestimmt ist, auch die nemlichen Gründe nicht vorliegen, so werden dieselben nach Art. 651 in Urschrift hinauszugeben sein.

Eine Motivirung des vom Gerichtsvorstande ausgehenden Beschlusses ist nicht vorgeschrieben, jedoch erscheint sie im Falle der Verweigerung schon deßhalb nothwendig, weil außerdem die Gerichte, welche auf einseitige Vorstellung oder Beschwerde zu erkennen haben, gar nicht erfahren, was vom Schuldner eingewendet worden war. Es wird sogar sachgemäß sein, daß der Gerichtsvorstand mit seinem Beschlusse eine kurze Darstellung des Sachverhalts verbinde.

11) Schließlich wirft sich die Frage auf: „Welches sind die Folgen der Verweigerung?“

Will der Gläubiger eine Klage auf Verurtheilung erheben, so steht ihm die Einrede der abgeurtheilten Sache entgegen; will er aber das erwirkte Urtheil vollstrecken, so ist ihm durch fraglichen Beschluß der einzige Weg versperrt, auf welchem er zur Vollstreckung gelangen kann! — Somit sollte man meinen, es sei der Gläubiger rechtlos gestellt, falls ihm nicht etwa aus besonderen Gründen ein Klagrecht zustehe, z. B. eine Klage auf Herausgabe der ersten Ausfertigung, welche in Folge Zwangs, Betrugs, Irrthums in die Hände des Schuldners gelangt ist, eine Klage auf Vernichtung einer erschlichenen Quittung rc. Offenbar kann nun aber der Verlust des Rechtes die Folge eines so formlosen Verfahrens, wie des hier in Frage stehenden, nicht sein, und es muß angenommen werden, daß in allen Fällen ohne Ausnahme der Gläubiger befugt sei, seine Rechte auf dem Wege gewöhnlicher Klage zu verfolgen.

Diese Klage hat das Fortbestehen der betreffenden Schuld zum Gegenstande, und die Thatsache, welche das Recht zur Klage begründet, ist die Verweigerung einer zweiten vollstreckbaren Ausfertigung.

Wirksamkeit des Urtheils.

Art. 294. — **Die Wirkung des Urtheils ist beschränkt einerseits auf den Gegenstand des Rechtsstreits und die in diesem entschiedenen Streitpunkte, anderseits auf die in dem Streite aufgetretenen oder in denselben beigeladenen Personen, Diejenigen, deren Rechte nach civilrechtlichen Grundsätzen durch eine der prozeßführenden Parteien im Rechtsstreite vertreten wurden, und die Erben der vorbezeichneten Personen. Doch müssen auch solche Dritte, welche erst nach Erhebung des Streits ein Recht an der streitigen Sache von einer der Parteien erworben haben, das Urtheil gegen sich gelten lassen, soweit nicht eine Ausnahme zu Gunsten der Besitzer beweglicher Sachen im Civilrechte begründet ist.**

Art. 295. — **Nur die in dem Urtheile enthaltene Entscheidung ist der Rechtskraft fähig, doch kann der übrige Inhalt des Urtheils zur Bemessung der Absicht des Gerichts in Betreff des Sinnes und Umfangs der Entscheidung benützt werden.**

Art. 296. — **Richterliche Verfügungen, welche weder Endurtheile noch bezüglich der Zulassung der Berufung diesen gleichgestellt sind, können, soweit das Gesetz nicht anders bestimmt, von den Parteien im nämlichen Rechtszuge sowohl vor als nach stattgehabtem Vollzuge, und selbst wenn sie freiwillig vollzogen wurden, noch angefochten und von dem Richter, der sie erlassen hat, noch zurückgenommen oder abgeändert werden, so lange nicht ein appellables Urtheil, zu dessen Unterlagen sie gehören, ergangen oder über das gegen die Verfügung eingelegte Rechtsmittel der Beschwerde von dem Beschwerdegerichte entschieden ist. Durch die Anfechtung wird der Vollzug der angefochtenen Verfügung nicht gehemmt.**

G. A. d. K. d. A. II S. 66. 67. 71. 133. 134. 451. III S. 129. IV S. 83.
K. d. R. II S. 96. IV S. 41.

1) Das richterliche Urtheil ist bestimmt: 1) Rechte, über welche Streit besteht, festzustellen, und 2) die Erfüllung von Verbindlichkeiten im Zwangswege herbeizuführen.

Indem der Richter strittige Rechte feststellt, schafft er formelles Recht, und seine Entscheidung gilt nach Erschöpfung der gegebenen Rechtsmittel unbedingt als Recht, mag sie auch in Wahrheit dies nicht sein. Das römische Recht sagt daher: »res judicata pro veritate habetur,« und: »sententia jus facit« (l. 207 Dig. [50. 17], l. 50 § 1 Dig. [30]); das französische Recht aber reiht die Rechtskraft der Urtheile unter die gesetzlichen Präsumtionen ein (Art. 1350 Code civ.).

Eben diese tiefeingreifende Wirkung der Urtheile, welche immer die Möglichkeit nahe legt, daß das gefundene Recht auch Unrecht sein könne, macht es nöthig, die Rechtskraft derselben möglichst eng zu begrenzen und sie auf dasjenige Gebiet zu beschränken, welches nach dem Zwecke des Prozesses ihr nothwendig eigen sein muß.

Es bieten sich in dieser Beziehung verschiedene Fragen dar, nemlich: 1) wie weit die Rechtskraft gegebener Endentscheidungen wirke, 2) unter welchen Voraussetzungen eine solche Entscheidung anzunehmen sei, und 3) inwiefern auch Zwischenbescheide der Rechtskraft fähig seien.

2) Die Rechtskraft eines Urtheils erstreckt sich nur auf den Gegenstand des Rechtsstreits und die in ihm entschiedenen Streitpunkte, so ist hiermit dem Wesen nach nur die Regel des römischen Rechts ausgesprochen: »quoties eadem quaestio inter easdem personas revocatur.« L. 3 Dig. (44. 2). Offenbar sollten durch diese allgemeinen Sätze nur die bestehenden Prinzipien aufrecht erhalten werden, und ist daher auf diese näher einzugehen.

3) Der Richter, bei welchem eine Klage angebracht wird, ist berufen, zu entscheiden, ob aus dem bestimmten Klaggrunde dem Kläger gegen den Beklagten das bestimmte Recht, welches zur Zeit einklagbar ist, zustehe. Die Rechtskraft seines Urtheils erstreckt sich daher über Alles, was er in diesen Beziehungen entscheidet, jedoch in der Regel nicht weiter.

Hat der Richter bloß ausgesprochen, es bestehe das Recht zur Zeit nicht, so bleibt die Frage frei, ob es nach Eintritt der Fälligkeit sich als begründet erweise.

Hat er bloß ausgesprochen, es sei der Kläger nicht diejenige Person, welche das Recht geltend machen könne, oder es sei der Beklagte nicht diejenige Person, gegen welche es bestehe, so bleibt die Frage frei, ob es nicht einer anderen Person, oder gegen eine solche zustehe, und wenn später der Kläger bezw. Beklagte selbst an die Stelle dieser anderen Person tritt, so kann später unter den nemlichen Parteien ein verurtheilendes Er-

dasselbe Recht aus einem anderen Klaggrunde verfolgt werden.

Endlich steht der Umstand, daß das verlangte Recht aberkannt worden ist, nicht im Wege, ein Recht auf eine andere Sache, oder ein Recht ganz anderer Art aus dem nemlichen Klaggrunde zu verfolgen.

α. Gleichheit des Klaggrundes.

4) Sowohl nach römischem als nach französischem Rechte wurde nie bezweifelt, daß als Gegenstand eines Rechtsstreites nicht die Frage, ob das beanspruchte Recht überhaupt bestehe, sondern ob es aus dem namhaft gemachten besonderen Grunde geltend gemacht werden könne, anzusehen sei.

Nur bei dinglichen Klagen gestaltete sich die Sachlage in so fern anders, als bei denselben die Angabe des besonderen Entstehungsgrundes (der causa remota) nicht nöthig war, vielmehr das Recht an sich als Klaggrund genügte. In Folge hiervon mußte auch das ergehende Urtheil unbedingt über Bestehen oder Nichtbestehen des Rechtes entscheiden. Selbst nach römischem Rechte fiel jedoch diese Ausnahme hinweg, wenn der Kläger sich bloß auf einen bestimmten Entstehungsgrund gestützt hatte (l. 11 § 2 und l. 13 § 2 Dig. [44. 2]), und wenn auch in neuerer Zeit durch Anregung von Puchta Zweifel entstanden, so müssen diese jedenfalls jetzt schwinden, nachdem unsere Prozeßordnung bei allen, also auch bei dinglichen Klagen, eine genaue Bezeichnung des Entstehungsgrundes vorschreibt (Art. 225).

Es darf daher jetzt als durchgreifender Grundsatz gelten, daß die Abweisung einer Klage nicht im Wege stehe, das nemliche Recht aus einem selbständigen neuen Klaggrunde geltend zu machen.

5) Es frägt sich nun aber: „Was ist ein selbständiger Klaggrund?" — eine Frage, welche in dreifacher Richtung von großer Bedeutung ist, nemlich für die Klagänderung, für die Rechtskraft der Urtheile und für das Vorbringen neuer Thatsachen im Laufe des Rechtsstreites.

Thatsachen nemlich, welche zur Vervollständigung, Bestärkung oder zum Beweise des nemlichen Klaggrundes dienen, bedingen keine Klagänderung, sondern sind nur Behelfe (moyens in der französischen Rechtssprache), welche geltend gemacht werden dürfen, so lange über den Grund der Klage noch nicht rechtskräftig erkannt ist; liegt jedoch ein solches Erkenntniß vor, so sind sie werthlos. Anderseits bleibt Alles, was zu einem anderen Klaggrunde gehört, von der Rechtskraft des Urtheils unberührt, kann aber ebendeßhalb, wenn es vorgebracht wird, den Fall zulässiger Klagänderung ausgenommen, nichts nützen.

6) Unter dem „Klaggrunde" versteht man nun den Inbegriff aller Thatsachen, welche nach civilrechtlichen Grundsätzen dazu gehören, um das geltend gemachte Recht zu erzeugen. Da nun das nemliche Recht auf verschiedenen Wegen erzeugt werden kann, so bildet jede selbständige Art der Entstehung auch einen selbständigen Klaggrund.

Dabei kommt es nur darauf an, daß die thatsächliche Grundlage im Wesen dieselbe sei; die rechtliche Qualifikation ist nicht von Bedeutung, sofern sie nicht etwa dahin führt, daß das Recht selbst, welches geltend gemacht wird, sich wesentlich ändert, z. B. aus einem dinglichen Rechte ein persönlicher Anspruch wird. Wenn A behauptet, daß er dem B zur bestimmten Zeit eine bestimmte Summe Geldes gegeben, damit er sie nach bestimmter Zeit zurückerstatte, so ist es ganz gleichgiltig, ob er ein Darlehen oder ein Depositum einklagt, und es wäre reinste Pedanterie, wenn z. B. der Richter, welcher sich durch die Beweisführung überzeugt, es liege nicht das eingeklagte Depositum, sondern ein Darlehen vor, die Klage zurückweisen und dem Kläger zumuthen würde, neue Klage wegen Darlehens zu erheben. Anders wäre es wohl, wenn es sich darum handelte, ob Darlehen oder Zahlung einer Nichtschuld vorliege. Ebenso verhält es sich, wenn eine bestimmte Sache zurückverlangt wird, weil sie auf bestimmte Zeit in Genuß gegeben war; ob die Hingabe als Miethe, als Commodat oder als Prekarium aufgefaßt werde, ist gleich.

Nachdem der Gesetzgeber in Zulassung wirklicher Klagänderungen in so hohem Grade (ich möchte fast sagen: bis ins Prinziplose) nachsichtig gewesen ist, erschiene es um so weniger gerechtfertigt, Klagänderungen künstlich zu schaffen.

7) Zu einem gegebenen Klaggrunde gehört alles, was sich seiner besonderen Natur nach an ihn anschließt, und es erscheint im Zwecke und Geiste des Prozesses begründet, hier die Grenzen so weit als möglich zu ziehen, um einerseits das Nachbringen von Thatsachen im nemlichen Prozesse zu erleichtern, und um anderseits der Vervielfältigung der Prozesse vorzubeugen. Wer z. B. auf Grund des Besitzes ein Recht beansprucht, darf im Laufe des Rechtsstreites sowohl den Erwerb durch zehn- oder dreißigjährigen als durch unvordenklichen Besitz und durch Herkommen geltend machen, ohne die Klage zu ändern; anderseits ist es ihm aber auch nicht gestattet, auf einen nicht hervorgehobenen Gesichtspunkt dieser Art eine neue Klage zu gründen.

8) Auch im Falle, wo der neu vorgebrachte Klaggrund im Allgemeinen als ein selbständiger erscheint, kann durch die frühere Entscheiduug demselben die rechtliche Grundlage entzogen sein. So hat die Entscheidung, daß ein Uebereinkommen auf gesetzwidriger causa beruhe, zur Folge, daß ein auf dieselbe sich gründendes selbständiges Schuldversprechen (constitutum debiti proprii) nicht mehr einklagbar ist.

β. Gleichheit des verfolgten Rechts.

9) Eine Verschiedenheit des geltend gemachten Rechts liegt vor:

1) wenn das nemliche Recht an einer anderen Sache geltend gemacht wird, und

2) wenn ein Recht ganz anderer Art, sei es auch an der nemlichen Sache, beansprucht wird.

10) Was ersteren Fall betrifft, so ist begreiflich, daß die Erklärung des Richters, es stehe mir ein Recht auf das Grundstück A nicht zu, nicht maßgebend sein könne für die Frage, ob mir das nemliche Recht aus dem nemlichen Klaggrunde auf das Grundstück B zustehe. Dabei ist natürlich davon abzusehen, daß der Richter zugleich Vorfragen entschieden haben könne, welche auch für das Recht am Grundstücke B von Belang sind, z. B. bezüglich der Giltigkeit eines Vertrages, des Vorhandenseins einer Erbqualität ꝛc.

Läßt sich der neue Anspruch nur als einen Theil des früheren Anspruchs betrachten, so zwar daß nach der Vorschrift des Art. 263 der Richter ihn hätte zuerkennen müssen, wenn er ihn als begründet erachtet hätte, so ist er natürlich in der Rechtskraft begriffen. Es kann Niemand eine kleinere Summe oder einen Theil eines Grundstückes verlangen, nachdem er mit seinem Anspruch auf's Ganze abgewiesen ist.

Wer umgekehrt mit einem Theile abgewiesen ist, wird zwar hiedurch allein nicht behindert, die übrigen Theile zu verlangen, allein jedenfalls nicht das Ganze einschlüssig jenes Theils.

11) Was den zweiten Fall betrifft, so ist ebenfalls klar, daß Demjenigen, welcher in einer neuen Klage ein seiner Natur nach ganz verschiedenes Recht beansprucht, die Einrede der Rechtskraft nicht im Wege stehen könne, z. B. wenn er statt des Besitzes das Eigenthum, statt des Eigenthums ein Pfandrecht oder eine Grunddienstbarkeit, statt eines dinglichen Rechtes ein persönliches in Anspruch nimmt.

Auch hier greift jedoch obige Regel Platz, daß, wenn es sich bloß um ein Zuvielbegehren im Sinne des Art. 263 (nach der Beschaffenheit des Anspruchs) handelt, die Rechtskraft wirke. So z. B. kann Demjenigen, welcher das Eigenthum beansprucht, die Nutznießung zugesprochen werden (l. 21 § 3 Dig. [44. 2]); so liegt ferner in der servitus viae auch die servitus itineris.

γ. Gleichheit der Parteien.

12) Wenn es im Art. 294 heißt, die Rechtskraft beschränke sich auf die aufgetretenen oder beigeladenen Personen, so sind hiermit jene Personen gemeint, auf deren Rechnung der Streit geführt wird, die Parteien im engeren Sinne (Art. 58); man dürfte daher nicht folgern, daß Dasjenige, was dem gesetzlichen Vertreter einer Partei gegenüber entschieden sei, diesem Vertreter später, wenn er für sich persönlich klagt, unbedingt als res judicata entgegengehalten werden könnte, und umgekehrt. Auch die Eigenschaft, in welcher eine Person in einem Rechtsstreite auftritt, ist von Wesenheit für dessen Identität und zwar ebensowohl für die Frage der Klagänderung, als für die Frage der Rechtskraft.

Dies schließt jedoch nicht aus, daß die Betheiligung des Vertreters am Rechtsstreite und seine Kenntniß desselben, unter Umständen Wirkungen äußern könne. Bl. f. R. Bd. XXIX S. 63.

13) Es ist in der Natur der Sache begründet, daß ein Urtheil die Rechte von Personen nicht beeinträchtigen könne, welche im Rechtsstreite nicht aufgetreten oder wenigstens zu demselben beigeladen waren. Selbst wenn der Richter im Civilprozesse, ebenso wie im Strafprozesse, von Amtswegen einschreiten und das materielle Recht ergründen dürfte, müßte dieser Grundsatz gelten, da Niemand verurtheilt werden darf, der nicht gehört worden ist; um so mehr muß dies der besonderen Natur des Civilprozesses gegenüber der Fall sein, in welchem Verzichte, Geständnisse, Versäumungen von Prozeßhandlungen den wesentlichsten Einfluß auf das Schicksal der Sache üben.

Uebrigens ist es gleichfalls selbstverständlich, daß wer verpflichtet ist, die Rechtshandlungen einer Person anzuerkennen, auch die gegen dieselben ergangenen Urtheile gegen sich gelten lassen müsse.

14) Als dritte, im Rechtsstreite nicht vertretene, Personen können daher nicht betrachtet werden die Erben und überhaupt die Rechtsnachfolger der Parteien, insofern ihnen der Grundsatz entgegensteht, daß sie nur soviel Rechte erwerben konnten, als die Letzteren selbst besaßen.

Es gilt dies von jedem Erwerber des strittigen Rechtes, unter der Voraussetzung, daß der Erwerb erst nach Erhebung des Streites, d. h. nach Zustellung der Ladung (Art. 179) stattgefunden habe. Ist diese Voraussetzung gegeben, so gilt das ergehende Urtheil auch gegen den neuen Erwerber und tritt selbst eine Unterbrechung des Verfahrens nicht ein, wenn die Abtretung des Rechts zur Kenntniß der Gegenpartei gebracht wird (Art. 493).

Gegen Collusion ist der Erwerber geschützt durch das Rechtsmittel der Wiederaufnahme des Verfahrens (Art. 765 Abs. 2) und außerdem steht es ihm frei, zu interveniren.

15) Um übrigens den Sinn fraglicher Verfügung richtig zu verstehen, ist im Auge zu behalten, daß sie nichts weiter sagen will, als daß der Erwerber eines strittigen Rechts es gegen sich gelten lassen müsse, wenn erkannt wird, es habe dieses Recht zur Zeit der Klagstellung, also auch seines Erwerbs, nicht bestanden. Es treffen ihn nur die Folgen, welche aus dieser Thatsache sich herleiten, keine weiteren.

Es wäre daher falsch, wollte man den Dritten so ansehen, als sei er selbst verurtheilt, und wollte man ihn demzufolge des strittigen Rechtes auch in jenen Fällen verlustig erachten, wo die Thatsache, daß das Recht zur Zeit des Uebertrags nicht bestanden, aus besonderen Gründen für ihn ganz gleichgiltig ist.

Der Gesetzgeber hat, die Richtigkeit dieser Ansicht fühlend, im Hinblicke auf die Bestimmungen des Handelsgesetzes und des pfälzischen Civilgesetzes eine Beschränkung für bewegliche Sachen beigefügt; allein es wäre besser gewesen, er hätte dies unterlassen, denn es könnte nunmehr gefolgert werden, daß in allen anderen Fällen das Urtheil unbedingt wirke. Hiermit wäre z. B. der Grundsatz des Hypothekengesetzes aufgehoben, daß Derjenige, welcher im Vertrauen auf das Hypothekenbuch eine Hypotheke erworben hat, vollkommen sicher sei; es würden nemlich die später ergehenden Urtheile bereits anhängiger Prozesse gegen ihn wirken, auch wenn eine Vormerkung nicht eingetragen wäre.

Offenbar lag etwas Derartiges nicht im Willen des Gesetzgebers, und es muß daher das Prinzip, so wie es oben aufgestellt wurde, allgemein gelten.

16) Schließlich ist zu bemerken, daß das, was in dieser Beziehung unsere Prozeßordnung verfügt, sowohl diesseits als in der Pfalz von jeher für Recht gehalten wurde, und auch in Frankreich sprechen sich, abweichenden Ansichten gegenüber, die bewährtesten Rechtsgelehrten, insbesondere Chauveau sur Carré (quest. 1710 ter), dafür aus. Es erscheint auch so vernünftig und den Prinzipien über die Wirkungen der Klagzustellung entsprechend, daß nicht zu begreifen ist, wie man glauben konnte, es sei der Pfalz ein Dienst erwiesen, wenn die bezügliche Controverse fortbestehe. Abg. II S. 66, 67, 71, 134. Uebrigens war zu beachten, daß selbst die Gegner von Chauveau dem Urtheile nur die unbedingte Rechtskraft absprachen, indem sie die tierce opposition zuließen, daß aber dieses Rechtsmittel nicht mehr besteht und Art. 765 Abs. 2 nur den Fall der Collusion deckt.

17) Als dritte Personen dürfen ferner nicht betrachtet werden die Gläubiger einer Partei als solche. Diese müssen vielmehr alle Urtheile gegen sich gelten lassen, wenn sie nicht etwa darzuthun vermögen, daß sie das Werk einer gespielten Gefährde seien (Art. 765 Abs. 2).

18) Was sonstige Personen betrifft, welche ihre Rechte nicht von einer der Parteien herleiten, oder welche sie wenigstens zur Zeit, als der Rechtsstreit anhängig wurde, bereits erworben hatten, so gilt als Regel, daß ihnen die ergangenen Urtheile weder schaden noch nützen. Die Civilgesetze lassen jedoch Ausnahmen von dieser Regel zu, und unsere Prozeßordnung erhält dieselben in Art. 294 aufrecht, indem sie die Rechtskraft auch gegen Personen wirken läßt, „deren Rechte nach civilrechtlichen Grundsätzen durch eine der prozeßführenden Parteien im Rechtsstreite vertreten wurden."

19) Was nun zuerst das diesseitige Recht betrifft, so bezeichnet die Gerichtsordnung Cap. XIV § 11 zwei Ausnahmsfälle, in denen die res judicata auch gegen Dritte wirken solle, nemlich:

1) „wann er zwar selbst ein gemeinschaftlich- und „vorzügliches Recht bei der strittigen Sache, „und annebens von dem Streite gutes Wissen „gehabt, gleichwohl aber sich desselben nicht „angenommen hat;

2) „wann die Sache mit dem rechtmäßigen contra„dictore einmal ausgestritten worden ist, und „anbei in Ansehen des Dritten die nemlichen, „oder noch stärkeren Ursachen obwalten."

Diesen Ausnahmen liegt der Gedanke zu Grunde, daß unter den gegebenen Voraussetzungen die Rechte dritter Personen als durch die im Streite befindlichen Parteien vertreten zu erachten seien; es wird also eine Art gesetzlicher Vertretung angenommen, welche sich von derjenigen des Art. 60 darin unterscheidet, daß sie nicht, gleich jener, offen auftritt und im Prozesse Ausdruck findet. Fragliche Bestimmungen enthalten somit civilrechtliche Grundsätze im Sinne des erwähnten Vorbehaltes und bestehen fort. Uebrigens geben sie im Wesen nur die Prinzipien des gemeinen Rechtes wieder.

20) Was den ersten Ausnahmsfall betrifft, welcher seine Quelle in l. 63 Dig. (42. 1) findet, so setzt er voraus, daß der Dritte ein gemeinschaftliches und vorzügliches Recht habe, und daß er wissentlich die Durchführung des Prozesses einem entfernteren Interessenten (welcher ihm weichen müßte) überlassen habe.

Unter „Gemeinschaftlichkeit" ist nur irgend eine gemeinschaftliche Betheiligung (causa communis) zu verstehen, z. B. wenn der Pfandgläubiger einem Prozesse unthätig zusieht, welchen der Pfandschuldner wegen des Eigenthums führt, ebenso der Käufer der Prozeßführung des Verkäufers, der Ehemann der Prozeßführung der Ehefrau oder des Schwiegervaters wegen des Heirathsgutes. Seuff. Comm. Bd. III S. 477.

21) Was den zweiten Ausnahmsfall betrifft, so ist erforderlich: 1) daß die Sache mit dem »legitimus contradictor« ausgestritten worden sei, und 2) daß »eadem vel major vincendi ratio« obwalte.

Durch letzteres Erforderniß werden die Fälle ausgeschlossen: a) wo der legitimus contradictor bloß durch persönliches Verschulden, in Folge Nichterscheinens, Versäumung von Prozeßhandlungen, Verzichts ꝛc. unterlegen ist, und b) wo er nur auf Grund eines persönlichen Versprechens verurtheilt worden ist. Vgl. Anmerk. von Kreitmayer zu fraglicher Stelle.

22) Die Frage, wer als legitimus contradictor — nicht zu verwechseln mit dem gesetzlichen Vertreter des Art. 59 — zu gelten habe, ist nach den betreffenden Civilrechten zu beurtheilen.

Das gemeine Recht erkennt z. B. an, daß das Urtheil, welches dem Vater gegenüber die Abstammung ausspricht, auch für die übrigen Familien-Angehörigen Geltung habe. L. 1 § 16 u. l. 3 pr. Dig. (25—3). Ferner gilt die Entscheidung zwischen Testamentserben und Intestaterben über die Giltigkeit des Testaments auch für die Legatare. L. 50 § 1 Dig. (30); l. 14 Dig. (49—1); l. 3 pr. Dig. (20—1). Aehnliche Fälle kennt das preußische Landrecht. Abg. II S. 134 (Franz).

Auf Streitgenossen, wie Miterben, Mitschuldner ꝛc. erstreckt sich diese Ausnahme nicht, vielmehr ist jeder derselben nur legit. contradictor pro sua parte. Art. 64. Kreitmayer Anmerk. a. a. O. § 11 lit. g a. E.

sonders insofern es sich um eine vortheilhafte Entscheidung handelt. Vgl. l. 4 § 3 Dig. (8—5); l. 11 § 1 u. 2 Dig. (39—3); bayr. Landr. Thl. IV § 22 Ziff. 3 u. § 23 Ziff. 3; Glück Pand. Bd. X S. 236; Seuff. Archiv Bd. XII Nr. 12; Windscheid Pand. Bd. II § 295 Note 8 u. § 299 Note 11.

23) Die französische Gesetzgebung bietet nur wenig spezielle Vorschriften über die Wirkung der Rechtskraft gegen dritte Personen und die bezügliche Jurisprudenz findet ihre Grundlage wesentlich im römischen Rechte, jedoch in der Art, daß sich aus dessen einzelnen Bestimmungen allgemeine Prinzipien herausgebildet haben.

Art. 1351 Code civ. sagt allgemein: »Il faut, que la demande soit entre les mêmes parties, et formée par elles et contre elles en la même qualité.« Dieser Grundsatz erleidet durch die bloße Thatsache, daß ein Dritter das gleiche Interesse hat, oder daß die nemlichen sachlichen und rechtlichen Gründe auch für ihn gelten, keine Aenderung. Die Jurisprudenz unterscheidet jedoch, ob das Recht, um welches gestritten wurde, ganz oder theilweise das nemliche sei, oder ob ein Betheiligter nur sein besonderes Recht verfolge.

Bei gewöhnlichen Mitberechtigten und Mitverpflichteten ist Letzteres der Fall. Wenn daher Einer von mehreren Miterben seinen Theil an einer Forderung des Nachlasses einklagt, oder seinen Erbtheil geltend macht, so entsteht aus diesem Rechtsstreite, mag er ausgehen, wie er wolle, keine Rechtskraft für die übrigen Miterben. Das Nemliche gilt von Miteigenthümern.

24) Anders ist es, wenn das nemliche Recht in Frage steht. Bei dieser Voraussetzung nimmt man an, daß jeder Betheiligte stillschweigendes Mandat habe, zum Vortheile aller Betheiligten zu handeln, und läßt die Rechtskraft wirken, so weit die Entscheidung vortheilhaft ist, während man sie auch hier ausschließt, sofern die Rechte des Mitbetheiligten geschädigt werden sollen. Es ist dieses Prinzip, welches, wie oben angedeutet, von manchen Rechtsgelehrten (z. B. Glück) auch für das gemeine Recht anerkannt wird, ebenso rationell als praktisch, denn es erscheint durch dasselbe einerseits das Grundprinzip des Prozesses, daß nie gegen Jemanden erkannt werden dürfe, ohne daß er gehört worden sei, vollkommen gewahrt, und werden doch anderseits Vervielfältigungen der Prozesse und widersprechende Ent-

Prozeß mit einem Dritten führt, das ergehende Urtheil bei Eintritt der Bedingung für den Erwerber gelte, soweit es günstig, nicht aber, soweit es ungünstig sei. Das Nemliche gilt umgekehrt, falls derjenige, welcher unter einer Resolutiv-Bedingung erworben hat, den Prozeß durchführt, und später durch Eintritt der Bedingung der Uebertrag aufgehoben wird.

Denselben Grundsatz wendete man an auf das Verhältniß zwischen Eigenthümer und Nutznießer, auf Miteigenthümer der Geltendmachung einer Servitut gegenüber, auf Solidarschuldner und Schuldner bei untheilbaren Verbindlichkeiten ꝛc.

In allen diesen Fällen gilt der Mitbetheiligte als legitimus contradictor, um zum Vortheile seiner Genossen zu handeln. Auch dem »heritier apparent,« insofern ihm die Verwaltung im weitesten Umfange zusteht, wird diese Eigenschaft zuerkannt.

Jedoch erstreckt sich auch in der bezeichneten Richtung die Rechtskraft immerhin nur so weit, als die nemliche causa, dieselbe ratio vincendi vorhanden ist.

Eine besondere Anwendung dieser Grundsätze findet sich in den Bestimmungen der Art. 1224 und 1305 Code civil.

25) Allerdings gehen in mancher Beziehung die Ansichten auch weiter und dehnen die Rechtskraft auf Entscheidungen aus, welche nachtheilig sind. In dieser Hinsicht möchte nun darauf aufmerksam zu machen sein, daß sich durch Einführung der Prozeßordnung die Sachlage in einem wesentlichen Punkte verändert hat.

Das französische Recht kennt nemlich einen Mittelzustand, in welchem eine Entscheidung bis zu gewissem Grade Rechtskraft ausübt, jedoch keine vollständige, so zwar, daß es dem Dritten gestattet ist, durch ein besonderes Rechtsmittel, die tierce opposition, die ergangene Entscheidung umzustoßen. Art. 474 C. de proc. verlangt für dieses Rechtsmittel: »un jugement, qui préjudicie à ses droits, et lors duquel ni elle, ni ceux, qu'elle répresente n'ont été appelés.«

Die Frage, in welchen Fällen tierce opposition zuläßig oder nöthig sei, ist eine der bestrittensten und hängt natürlich mit der Frage der Rechtskraft auf's innigste zusammen. Es ist selbstverständlich, daß Niemand den schwierigen, im Falle des Unterliegens mit bedeutender Geldstrafe bedrohten Weg der tierce opposition wählen wird, wenn er einfach sagen darf, das Urtheil sei für ihn res inter alios. Ebenso steht anderseits dieses Rechtsmittel Niemanden zu, welcher im Rechtsstreite vertreten war.

Manche Juristen glaubten nun der Rechtskraft eine weitere Ausdehnung geben zu dürfen, weil sie in den betreffenden Fällen tierce opposition zuließen und hierdurch die Rechte des Dritten genügend gewahrt erachteten. Unsere Prozeßordnung kennt besagtes Rechtsmittel nicht und hat nur einen demselben unterworfenen Fall — allerdings den gewöhnlichsten — im Art. 765 Abs. 2 als Wiederaufnahme des Verfahrens aufrecht erhalten. Die Folge hiervon wird sein, daß man die Prinzipien über die Rechtskraft schärfer fassen muß, weil nur die Wahl freisteht, dieselbe gar nicht oder voll walten zu lassen. S. über die ganze Lehre Dalloz repert. (chose jugée) Nr. 252 ff.

26) Schließlich ist zu erwähnen, daß die Regel des römischen Rechtes, daß Statusfragen, mit dem legit. contradictor durchgestritten, auch für die übrigen Verwandten entschieden seien, von manchen Schriftstellern (Toullier, Duranton) auch für das französische Recht anerkannt wird, während Andere sie bestreiten. Dalloz a. a. O. Nr. 271.

b) Was ist entschieden? (Art. 295.)

27) Wenn Art. 295 sagt: „Nur die im Urtheile enthaltene Entscheidung ist der Rechtskraft fähig," so spricht er einen Grundsatz aus, welcher von jeher in allen Gesetzgebungen Anerkennung gefunden hat. Fraglich kann nur sein, was man als Entscheidung zu betrachten habe.

Ebenso ist ferner selbstverständlich, daß zur Bemessung des Sinnes einer richterlichen Entscheidung die Entscheidungsgründe benützt werden dürfen, da es wohl eine sicherere Quelle zur Auslegung nicht gibt, als die erläuternden Worte, welche der Erklärende selbst sofort beigefügt hat.

Die ursprüngliche Fassung (Abg. II 147) wies geradezu auf die Entscheidungsgründe hin; man änderte sie jedoch, um die Deutung auszuschließen, als ob der Sachverhalt der Rechtskraft fähig sei (Abg. IV 83). Man möchte hiermit fast aus der Scylla in die Charybdis gerathen sein, denn die neue Fassung läßt die Deutung zu, als ob der von den Anwälten gefertigte Sachverhalt zur Ergründung der Absicht des Richters maßgebend sei; dies könnte aber nur in höchst beschränkter Weise gelten, nemlich insofern im Zweifel anzunehmen ist, daß der Richter nur über das, was Streitgegenstand, nicht aber ultra petita habe erkennen wollen.

28) Das Gesetz spricht nur allgemein von der „im Urtheile enthaltenen Entscheidung", und erklärt sich nicht darüber, ob es darunter nur Entscheidungen im Urtheilssatze verstehe, oder ob es auch Entscheidungen in den Gründen zulasse.

Es ist nun bekanntlich sowohl im deutschen als im französischen Prozesse eine vielbestrittene Frage, ob und in wie weit Entscheidungen, welche der Rechtskraft fähig sind, auch in den Gründen des Urtheils gegeben werden können.

Meiner Ansicht nach wäre es das Richtige gewesen, zu bestimmen, daß unbedingt nur dasjenige, was der Richter im Urtheilssatze ausspricht, der Rechtskraft fähig sei, die Gründe aber immer nur zur Auslegung beigezogen werden dürfen. Auch Vorfragen und Zwischenpunkte würden demgemäß nur insofern als rechtskräftig entschieden gelten, als die Parteien förmlichen Antrag (Incidentklage) auf Entscheidung gestellt hätten und diese im Urtheilssatze selbst gegeben worden wäre.

Sowohl im deutschen als im französischen Prozesse hat sich jedoch, wenn auch nicht ohne starken Widerspruch, eine laxere Ansicht Bahn gebrochen, wornach zwar eine des Vollzugs fähige Entscheidung nur im Urtheilssatze, jedoch die Feststellung eines Rechtsverhältnisses auch bloß in den Gründen erfolgen kann, und es erscheint nach den Bestimmungen der Art. 9—11 der P. O. und den bezüglichen Verhandlungen außer Zweifel, daß unsere Prozeßordnung sich dieser Ansicht anschließen wollte. Wenn nemlich in Art. 9 von einer „mittelbaren“, d. h. stillschweigenden Entscheidung von Incidentpunkten die Rede ist, so kann hiermit nur eine solche Entscheidung gemeint sein, welche nicht ausdrücklich im Urtheilssatze gegeben ist, sondern nur aus den Gründen hervorgeht. S. Bemerk. zu Art. 9 bis 11, Nr. 6—12. Vgl. Seuff. Comm. Bd. III S. 473 u. 474, womit jedoch die Bemerkung in Bd. IV S. 42 Note 107 nicht im Einklange steht. Bayer. Civilpr. S. 138.

29) Wie schon früher (zu Art. 275—278 Nr. 3) bemerkt wurde, ist über die von den Parteien förmlich gestellten Begehren immer auch förmlich im Urtheilssatze zu entscheiden; es kann daher oder soll wenigstens eine Entscheidung in den Gründen nur bezüglich solcher Vor- und Zwischenfragen erfolgen, welche nicht Gegenstand besonderer Incidentbegehren bilden, sondern nur als Grundlage für die Hauptentscheidung in Betracht kommen, z. B. die Feststellung des Bestandes, der rechtlichen Giltigkeit oder Ungiltigkeit des Vertrages, auf welchen sich eine eingeklagte Forderung gründet, die Feststellung einer Erbqualität 2c.

Derartige Entscheidungen, welche nur deßhalb erfolgen, weil sie die Vorbedingungen zur Hauptentscheidung bilden, erlangen zudem, zufolge des in Art. 296 ausgesprochenen Prinzipes, in Sachen, welche der Berufung unterliegen, nur Rechtskraft mit und in der nächsten appellablen Entscheidung, deren Grundlage sie bilden. Bis dahin kommt ihnen nur der Werth einer vorläufig ausgesprochenen Ansicht zu.

30) Wenn nun aber auch Entscheidungen, welche bloß in den Gründen liegen, in der Weise wie besagt, rechtskräftig werden können, so ist doch strenge am Grundsatze festzuhalten, daß nichts als entschieden betrachtet werden könne, was nicht Gegenstand eines Streites unter den Parteien gewesen ist. Nur wo Streit vorlag, kann vernünftigerweise von einer Entscheidung gesprochen werden.

Die Thatsache, daß irgend ein Rechtsverhältniß die Grundlage einer ergangenen Entscheidung bildet, genügt für sich allein noch nicht, um anzunehmen, daß dasselbe rechtskräftig festgestellt sei.

Wenn daher der Beklagte nicht erschienen ist und deßhalb die Behauptungen des Klägers als wahr angenommen werden, so ergibt sich aus dem ergehenden Versäumungsurtheile nur Rechtskraft bezüglich dessen, was unmittelbar Gegenstand der Klage war und im Urtheilssatze zugesprochen wurde, nicht aber auch bezüglich sonstiger Rechtsverhältnisse, mögen sie auch mit dem zugesprochenen Rechte in noch so inniger Verbindung stehen. Das Nemliche gilt auch, wenn der Beklagte erschienen war und die betreffenden Thatsachen oder Rechtsverhältnisse nicht in Abrede gestellt, ja förmlich zugestanden hat. Ein solches Geständniß kann allerdings und wird in der Regel auch für sonstige Rechtsverhältnisse, welche sich daraus folgern lassen, maßgebend sein; allein es ist ein großer Unterschied, ob bloßes Geständniß vorliegt, welches jeder Zeit wegen Irrthums wieder aufgehoben werden kann, oder aber eine rechtskräftige richterliche Feststellung, welche nach Erschöpfung der Rechtsmittel unanfechtbar ist. (Vgl. Bemerk. zu Art. 9—11 Nr. 14.)

In gleicher Weise ist es anderseits auch ohne Belang, wenn der Richter etwa von Amtswegen und ohne durch einen Streit unter den Parteien veranlaßt zu sein, seine Ansicht über einen Punkt, z. B. über seine Zuständigkeit, ausgesprochen. Eine solche Aeußerung könnte nicht rechtskräftig werden (Art. 187), wie sie denn auch früher der Geltendmachung der unheilbaren Nichtigkeit nicht im Wege stand.

31) Allerdings ist die Folge dieses Prinzipes, daß möglicherweise widersprechende Entscheidungen über die nemlichen Rechtsverhältnisse unter den nemlichen Parteien erfolgen, allein dies erscheint jedenfalls als das mindere Uebel.

Man muß sich im Civilprozesse immer vergegenwärtigen, daß das gefundene Recht möglicherweise nur ein formelles ist. Entspricht nun eine Entscheidung nicht dem materiellen Rechte, sei es aus Verschulden der Partei, sei es aus Verschulden des Richters, so möchte es ein Glück, nicht aber ein Unglück zu nennen sein, wenn die Entscheidung in möglichst engen Grenzen gehalten und die Möglichkeit offen gelassen wird, wenigstens für diejenigen Punkte, welche nicht Gegenstand der Entscheidung bilden, das materielle Recht zu retten.

Ich würde aus dieser Erwägung sogar noch weiter gehen und, wie oben (Nr. 28) bemerkt, auch wirkliche Entscheidungen ausnehmen, wenn sie nicht direkt, sondern nur *nebenbei* erfolgen.

c) Rechtskraft von Zwischenbescheiden. (Art. 296.)

32) Durch Art. 296 ist dem Richter, was Aenderung von Zwischenverfügungen jeder Art betrifft, eine Freiheit der Bewegung gegeben, wie sie weder der diesseitige noch der französische Prozeß bis jetzt kannte.

In letzterem gilt wohl als Grundsatz, daß Beweisinterlokute den Richter bezüglich der Fragen der Beweislast und der Erheblichkeit des Beweises nicht binden; allein, was Entscheidungen über Vorfragen und Zwischenstreite betrifft, so sind sie ebensogut der Rechtskraft fähig und der Berufung unterworfen, wie die Endentscheidungen.

Die Bestimmungen des Art. 296 sind übrigens nur die Consequenz der Grundsätze, welche die Prozeßordnung über Zulassung der *Berufung* gegen Zwischenbescheide aufstellt. Die große Beschränkung dort mußte eine entsprechend große Freiheit hier zur Folge haben.

Ob der Gesetzgeber in Beidem Recht gethan, wird die Erfahrung lehren.

33) Besagte Bestimmungen haben ihren Ursprung in Art. 647 des Entwurfes, welcher aussprach, daß richterliche Verfügungen, welche einer *selbständigen* Berufung nicht unterliegen, auch noch „*im nemlichen Rechtszuge*“ angefochten werden könnten. Abg. III 9 (Barth). Man fand es sachgemäß, diesem Ausspruche, an welchem man etwas zu ändern nicht beabsichtigte, seine Stelle unter den vom Verfahren im ersten Rechtszuge handelnden Bestimmungen anzuweisen und ihm zugleich eine entsprechendere Fassung zu geben.

Der Zweck des Gesetzgebers war also lediglich darauf gerichtet, die Härte, welche in der außergewöhnlichen Beschränkung der selbständigen Berufung liegt, dadurch zu mildern, daß man dem ersten Richter erlaubte, *sich selbst zu reformiren*. Zugleich dehnte man diese Erlaubniß auch auf den Fall, wo Beschwerde zulässig ist, aus.

34) Es folgt schon hieraus, daß in jenen Fällen, wo eine Berufung oder Beschwerde überhaupt nicht zulässig ist, die Bestimmungen des Art. 296 keine Anwendung finden, vielmehr der natürliche Grundsatz seine Geltung behauptet, daß das, was der Richter einmal gesprochen hat, von ihm selbst nicht mehr abgeändert werden könne.

Man könnte zwar einwenden, weil fragliche Bestimmungen jetzt hier und nicht mehr bei der Berufung vorgetragen seien, seien sie auch allgemein zu nehmen und sei vorauszusetzen, der Gesetzgeber habe beabsichtigt, im Interesse des *materiellen Rechts* das Abgehen von einer irrigen Verfügung zu gestatten, so lange nicht ein Endurtheil oder wenigstens ein demselben gleichstehendes Urtheil ergangen sei; in ähnlicher Weise, wie in Art. 345 bezüglich der Wirkung des Beweisinterlokutes verfügt ist. Man könnte dabei darauf hinweisen, daß Art. 647 des Entwurfs beide Fälle gleichstellte.

Allein es ist zu bemerken, daß offenbar die *nächste* Absicht des Gesetzgebers *hier* nicht auf die Wahrung des materiellen Rechtes gerichtet war, welchem Rechte z. B. wenig damit gedient wäre, wenn eine früher verworfene Prozeßeinrede später für begründet erklärt würde, sondern daß er einen Ausweg gestatten wollte, um ein Angehen des höheren Richters unnöthig zu machen. Auch der Wortlaut des Artikels spricht dafür, obgleich die Fassung als eine gelungene nicht bezeichnet werden kann, denn die Worte allein würden dahin führen, daß in Sachen, in welchen wegen Mangels der Berufungssumme eine Berufung nicht zuläßig wäre, Zwischenentscheidungen *gar nie* rechtskräftig werden könnten.

35) Der Ausdruck „Endurtheile“ ist selbstverständlich ganz im Sinne des Art. 682 zu nehmen, unter den Urtheilen aber, welchen bezüglich der Zulassung der Berufung den Endurtheilen gleichstehen, hat man nicht blos diejenigen zu verstehen, welche Art. 683 anführt, sondern auch sonstige Zwischenurtheile, gegen welche kraft besonderer gesetzlicher Bestimmung selbständige Berufung zuläßig ist.

Als bloß vorläufige widerrufliche Entscheidungen erscheinen daher z. B. die Abweisungen von Einreden, seien es Prozeßeinreden oder solche zum Grunde der Sache, dann Entscheidungen, welche über den Werth von Beweismitteln erkennen, welche Urkunden, Rechtsgeschäfte für giltig oder ungiltig erklären, kurz alle Entscheidungen und Verfügungen jeder Art, welche zwar auf dem

Wege der Berufung oder Beschwerde angefochten werden können, gegen welche aber selbständige Berufung nicht statthaft ist.

Was die Beweisurtheile anbelangt, so besteht für sie der besondere Grundsatz, daß sie zwar formell erledigt werden müssen (Art. 332), das Gericht aber materiell an dieselben nicht gebunden ist (Art. 345).

36) Die vorläufige Entscheidung wird zur endgiltigen, sobald ein der selbständigen Berufung fähiges Urtheil ergangen ist, dessen Unterlage sie bildet, mag auch nur über einen Theil der Sache in dieser Weise entschieden und mögen also aus jener vorläufigen Entscheidung noch nicht alle zulässigen Folgerungen gezogen sein. Jedes Endurtheil oder sonstige einer selbständigen Rechtskraft fähige Urtheil enthält daher stillschweigend die Endentscheidung über alle Vorfragen, auf welche es sich stützt.

Was insbesondere den Fall betrifft, wo Beschwerde zulässig ist, so ist natürlich eine Rücknahme der betreffenden Verfügung nicht gestattet, wenn die Beschwerde selbst, wegen Ablaufs der dafür gesetzten Frist nicht mehr statthaft ist. Ist über eine Beschwerde vom höheren Richter bereits entschieden, so kann selbstverständlich der niedere Richter diese Entscheidung nicht mehr abändern.

VIII. Hauptstück.

Versäumungsurtheil.

Versäumungsurtheil gegen den Beklagten.

Art. 297. — Ist für den Beklagten kein Anwalt bestellt, die Klage aber nach den gesetzlichen Vorschriften erhoben und die Erscheinungsfrist abgelaufen, so soll das Gericht vorbehaltlich der Bestimmung des Art. 324 Abs. 2 auf Antrag des klägerischen Anwalts die zur Begründung des Klaganspruchs in der Klageschrift geltend gemachten Thatsachen als zugestanden betrachten und dem daselbst gestellten Gesuche, soweit es nach jenen Thatsachen rechtlich begründet ist, entsprechen. Soweit das Gesuch rechtlich nicht begründet erscheint, ist die Abweisung der Klage auszusprechen.

Ist die Klage nicht nach den gesetzlichen Vorschriften erhoben oder die Erscheinungsfrist nicht abgelaufen, so ist der klägerische Antrag zur Zeit zurückzuweisen.

Art. 298. — Ist seit dem Ablaufe der Erscheinungsfrist ein Jahr verstrichen, ohne daß für den Beklagten ein Anwalt bestellt wurde, so kann der Kläger ein Versäumungsurtheil erst erwirken, wenn er den Beklagten unter Bezugnahme auf die frühere Klage, deren sonstige rechtliche Folgen bestehen bleiben, wiederholt zur Bestellung eines Anwalts hat auffordern lassen und seit dieser Aufforderung die Erscheinungsfrist abgelaufen ist.

Art. 299. — Will der Kläger in einer Sache, in welcher für den Beklagten kein Anwalt bestellt ist, die Klage in ihrem Gegenstande, in ihrer thatsächlichen Begründung oder durch Erweiterung des Gesuchs ändern, so muß er dies durch Zustellung eines von seinem Anwalte gefertigten Schriftsatzes unter Anführung der betreffenden Urkunden dem Beklagten mittheilen. In einem solchen Falle kann ein Versäumungsurtheil erst erwirkt werden, wenn seit der Zustellung ein der Erscheinungsfrist gleichkommender Zeitraum verstrichen ist.

Art. 300. — Die Vertagung der Sache und die neuerliche Vorladung des Beklagten kann verfügt werden, wenn im Falle des Art. 259 die dem Beklagten zur Bestellung eines Anwalts vergönnt gewesene Frist dem Gerichte nicht ausreichend erscheint. Das Gericht bestimmt alsdann den Tag, bis zu welchem die neuerliche Vorladung des Beklagten zu geschehen hat.

G. A. d. K. d. A. II S. 95—99. 103. 106. 107. 135. 138. 139. 171. 268. 269. 451. IV S. 83.
K. d. R. II S. 96. IV. S. 41.

1) Das Contumazialverfahren unserer Prozeßordnung ist dem Wesen nach dem französischen Prozesse entlehnt, bietet jedoch, namentlich was den Einspruch anbelangt, einige erhebliche Neuerungen.

Es findet sowohl dem Beklagten als dem Kläger gegenüber statt und ist dem Ersteren gegenüber sogar ein zweifaches, indem es entweder eintritt, weil der Beklagte keinen Anwalt aufgestellt hat, oder deßhalb, weil der aufgestellte Anwalt nicht erscheint. Ersteren Falls spricht man im französischen Prozesse von einem »défaut contre partie« oder »défaut faute de comparaître«, letzteren Falls aber von einem »défaut contre avoué« oder »défaut faute de conclure.«

Die Art. 297—300 haben ersteren Fall zum Gegenstande.

2) Da das Gesetz gegen jedes Versäumungs-

Urtheil das besondere Rechtsmittel des Einspruchs zuläßt, so durfte es bezüglich der Folgen der Versäumung sehr streng sein; es konnte Umgang nehmen von einer wiederholten Ladung mit Androhung der Präclusion (Nov. von 1837 § 29) und durfte das Prinzip der affirmativen Litiscontestation in voller Strenge durchführen. In dieser Weise ist ein sehr praktischer Weg gewonnen, um überall, wo Einreden gegen einen Anspruch nicht erhoben werden, schnell ein vollziehbares Urtheil zu erlangen.

Was die gesetzliche Vermuthung eines Zugeständnisses betrifft, ist man weiter gegangen, als der französische Prozeß, welcher in Art. 150 C. de proc. verlangt, daß das Begehren »juste et bien verifiée« sei, womit im Wesentlichen gesagt ist, es sei in's Ermessen des Richters gestellt, Beweis zu verlangen, oder ein stillschweigendes Zugeständniß anzunehmen. In der That wird auch in Fällen, wo das Geständniß beweisgebend ist, ein Beweis fast nie verlangt, und gilt daher thatsächlich das Prinzip der affirmativen Litiscontestation, obgleich es anderseits zu weit geht, zu behaupten, es sei eine Ausnahme nie vorgekommen, denn mir selbst sind mehrere Fälle der Art erinnerlich. Vgl. Art. 316 Nr. 3.

3) Der Richter hat, wenn der Kläger Versäumungsurtheil begehrt, zuerst zu prüfen, ob die Klage nach den gesetzlichen Vorschriften erhoben und die Erscheinungsfrist abgelaufen sei.

Im Entwurfe (Art. 265) hieß es: „wenn die Zustellung der Klage gehörig nachgewiesen ist;“ diese Fassung erschien jedoch zu eng und wurde nach und nach (Abg. II S. 95, 135, 269 u. 451) immer mehr erweitert, bis sie die jetzige Gestalt erhielt. Es soll gesagt sein, daß sowohl die Klagschrift als die Zustellung den Anforderungen der Art. 225 und 226 entsprechen müssen, vorausgesetzt, daß diese im Sinne von Art. 218 als wesentlich erscheinen.

Nichtigkeiten der Ladung sind daher hier durch den Richter von Amtswegen zu beachten, und der Kläger findet sich in Versäumungsfällen insofern schlimmer gestellt, als die Nichtigkeiten nicht durch das Stillschweigen des Beklagten geheilt werden können. Es galt dies übrigens auch schon im französischen Prozesse, obgleich das Gesetz es nicht ausdrücklich verfügte. Chauveau sur Carré quest. 616 ter.

Findet der Richter, daß die Ladung nichtig sei, so weist er die Klage als ordnungswidrig angebracht, d h. als unzulässig, ab. Falls die Nichtigkeit in der Zustellung liegt, wird es ihm freistehen, nach Art. 220 Abhilfe anzuordnen. Im Entwurfe (Art. 266) war ihm dies sogar zur Pflicht gemacht und diese Bestimmung bei erster Berathung (Abg. II 99) nicht geändert; die Subcommission brachte jedoch stillschweigend die jetzige Fassung, vielleicht im Hinblicke auf Art. 220. Jedenfalls möchte hierin ein neuer Beleg für die Richtigkeit der zu Art. 220 Nr. 14 geäußerten Ansicht zu finden sein.

Findet der Richter, daß die Erscheinungsfrist nicht abgelaufen sei, so weist er den Antrag als verfrüht zurück, und es steht dem Kläger frei, nach Ablauf der Frist von Neuem Antrag zu stellen. Abg. II 267 (v. Weiß). Ein Urtheil letzterer Art wird übrigens nicht leicht vorkommen, da der Anwalt, vom Richter auf seinen Irrthum aufmerksam gemacht, es vorziehen wird, seinen Antrag vorerst zurückzuziehen.

4) Selbstverständlich hat der Richter außer Ladung und Erscheinungsfrist auch noch alle sonstigen von Amtswegen zu berücksichtigenden Umstände zu prüfen, von denen die Zulässigkeit der Klage abhängt, so namentlich die Handelnsfähigkeit (Art. 62), im Parteiprozesse die Prozeßvollmacht, die Zuständigkeit (Art. 39 Abs. 3). Auch was die Zuständigkeit betrifft, ist daher der Kläger schlimmer gestellt beim Ausbleiben, als beim Erscheinen des Beklagten.

5) Folge des Nichterscheinens ist, daß alle in der Klagschrift geltend gemachten Thatsachen als zugestanden gelten.

Diese Folge trifft alle Thatsachen ohne Unterschied, mögen sie nun für die Zulässigkeit der Klage — die Fähigkeit zu handeln, die Zuständigkeit ꝛc. — von Belang sein, oder für deren Begründung. Der Ausdruck „zur Begründung des Klaganspruches“ ist daher im weiteren Sinne zu nehmen, und bedeutet so viel als: „zur Durchführung der Klage“. Es kann keinen Zweifel erleiden, daß der Richter auch die Behauptung, daß der Vertrag an einem gewissen Orte abgeschlossen sei, daß der Beklagte seinen Wohnsitz irgendwo habe, daß eine Waare zum Zwecke des Wiederverkaufes erworben worden sei, zur Bemessung seiner Zuständigkeit als wahr anzunehmen habe.

6) Diese gesetzliche Vermuthung eines Geständnisses hat, soweit es sich um Erlaß eines Versäumungsurtheils handelt, vollkommen die Wirkung eines wirklichen Geständnisses, jedoch auch nicht mehr.

Wo daher das Geständniß nicht genügt, einen Beweis zu erbringen, wie in manchen Sachen, wo das öffentliche Interesse betheiligt ist, z. B. bei Ehescheidungen, Interdiktionen, Gütertrennungen in der Pfalz, kann um so weniger das fingirte

Geständniß diese Kraft haben (Art. 324 Abs. 2). In Fällen dieser Art muß der Kläger ebenso wie nach dem Systeme der negativen Litiskontestation sonstigen Beweis erbringen.

Auch dort, wo das Gesetz ausdrücklich urkundlichen Nachweis verlangt, wie z. B. bezüglich der Prozeßvollmacht (Art. 82), vermag das Nichterscheinen diesen nicht zu ersetzen.

7) Daß das Gesuch zuzusprechen sei, soweit es rechtlich begründet, und abzuweisen, soweit es dies nicht ist, hätte sich auch ohne besondere Verfügung von selbst verstanden. Ebenso versteht sich von selbst, was bezüglich der Kosten zu erkennen sei (R. K. II S. 97).

Die Entscheidungsgründe des Versäumungsurtheils sind so einfach als möglich zu fassen.

In der Pfalz lauteten sie seither in gewöhnlichen Sachen etwa, wie folgt:

In Erw., daß Beklagter auf gehörige Ladung keinen Anwalt aufgestellt hat (daß der Anwalt des Bekl., obgleich gehörig aufgefordert, in heutiger Sitzung keinen Antrag genommen hat);

In Erw., daß die Anträge des Klägers nach Maßgabe seiner thatsächlichen Behauptungen rechtlich begründet erscheinen;

A. d. Gr.

gibt das kgl. Bezirksgericht Urkunde rc.

Allerdings sagen solche Gründe sehr wenig, allein da die Thatsachen im Sachverhalte (Art. 308) vorgetragen und Einwände nicht zu widerlegen sind, so möchten sie zur Noth genügen.

8) Ist auf kurze Frist geladen, so kann das Versäumungsurtheil nur in derjenigen Sitzung genommen werden, in welche vorgeladen worden ist. Hat der Kläger diese Sitzung versäumt, so kann er in einer späteren Sitzung ein Versäumungsurtheil nicht begehren, denn es ist für dieselbe nicht geladen und die Thatsache des Nichterscheinens am bestimmten Tage ist nicht gerichtlich festgestellt. Es ist in solchen Fällen, ebenso wie beim Verfahren im Parteiprozesse (Abg. II 267 [v. Weiß]) mit Bezug auf die frühere Zustellung neu vorzuladen.

9) Läßt der Kläger von Ablauf der Erscheinungsfrist an ein ganzes Jahr verstreichen, ohne ein Versäumungsurtheil zu erwirken, so spricht eine so starke Vermuthung dafür, daß ein Abkommen getroffen, die Sache erledigt sei, daß das Gesetz dem Kläger zur Pflicht macht, neu vorzuladen und den Ablauf einer neuen Erscheinungsfrist abzuwarten. Art. 298. Abg. II S. 103 u. 106.

In der neuen Ladung wird einfach Bezug genommen auf die selbstverständlich genau zu bezeichnende frühere Klage, deren Wirkungen ungeschmälert fortdauern und auf Grund deren das Urtheil genommen wird.

10) Es ist selbstverständlich, daß ein Versäumungsurtheil nur auf Grund des Inhalts der Klagschrift, wie sie dem Beklagten zugestellt wurde, ergehen könne. Thatsachen, welche dort nicht erwähnt sind, können als zugestanden nicht gelten, auf Gesuche, welche dort nicht gestellt sind, darf sich eine Verurtheilung nicht gründen, wenn nicht die Grundregel des Prozesses: »audiatur et altera pars« grell verletzt werden soll.

Um nun dennoch Klagänderungen zu ermöglichen, schreibt Art. 299 vor, daß dieselben auf dem Wege der Zustellung eines Anwaltsaktes zu geschehen haben und Versäumungsurtheil erst dann erwirkt werden könne, wenn von dieser Zustellung an eine neue Erscheinungsfrist verstrichen sei, m. a. W.: das Gesetz spricht aus, daß der Partei ein Klagsnachtrag zuzustellen sei, wie dies auch das einzig Richtige ist und meiner Ansicht nach bei jeder wirklichen Klagänderung hätte vorgeschrieben werden sollen.

11) Da das Gesetz in Art. 299 genau die nemlichen Ausdrücke gebraucht, wie in Art. 180, so ist klar, daß hier unter Klagänderung das Nemliche zu verstehen ist, wie dort. Hieraus möchte zu folgern sein, daß auch Art. 181 seine Anwendung finde, insofern er den Begriff einer wirklichen Klagänderung näher bestimmt, obgleich nicht zu läugnen ist, daß der Grundsatz des rechtlichen Gehörs einigermaßen gefährdet erscheint, wenn alle Aenderungen, von welchen jener Artikel spricht, insbesondere Erläuterungen undeutlicher oder die Ergänzungen unvollständiger Anführungen, einseitig, ohne daß der Gegner in der Lage ist, zu antworten, vorgenommen werden können. Jedenfalls würden die Gerichte sehr streng bei Anwendung des Art. 181 zu Werk gehen müssen; den Anwälten aber ist zu rathen, in allen Fällen, wo der Irrthum nicht ganz offen und erkennbar zu Tage liegt, einen Klagsnachtrag zuzustellen.

Was den Art. 182 betrifft, so enthält er nicht bloß eine nähere Bestimmung des Begriffs, sondern wirkliche Ausnahmen, welche die Möglichkeit einer Erwiderung voraussetzen, und können daher seine Bestimmungen hier keine Anwendung finden.

Man könnte vielleicht fragen, ob nicht vergessene Nebensachen, als: Zinsen, Früchte rc., ohne Klagsnachtrag gefordert werden dürften; allein offenbar ist dies nicht statthaft, denn das Verlangen solcher Nebensachen versteht sich nicht von selbst, und es hatte vielleicht der Beklagte keinen Anlaß, sich zu vertheidigen gegen Ein=

klagung eines unverzinslichen Kapitals, während er sich allerdings vertheidigt haben würde, wenn ein verzinsliches Kapital eingeklagt worden wäre. Anders ist es natürlich bezüglich der Prozeßkosten (Art. 262).

12) Ist mit kurzer Frist geladen (Art. 259) und hält das Gericht die zufolge der Verfügung des Gerichts- oder Senats-Vorstandes gegebene Frist bei vorliegenden Umständen für ungenügend, so kann es einstweilen von Erlaß eines Versäumungsurtheils Umgang nehmen und wiederholte Vorladung in eine sofort zu bestimmende andere Sitzung verfügen.

Bei dieser wiederholten Ladung bleibt es nicht, wie bei der ersten, dem Kläger überlassen, unverzüglich zu laden, sondern das Gericht bestimmt zugleich den Tag, bis zu welchem die Ladung gegeben sein muß, d. h. es setzt zugleich die Erscheinungsfrist fest. Abg. II 99 (v. Weiß).

Fragliche Bestimmung gilt auch für den Fall, wo das Gericht selbst die Ladung auf kurze Frist, z. B. zur Beiladung eines Gewährschaftsbeklagten, bewilligt hat, obgleich Abs. 4 des Art. 159 erst später beigefügt wurde; denn ihr Zweck ist nicht bloß darauf gerichtet, daß das Gericht die Verfügung des Vorstandes berichtigen solle, sondern auch, daß Vorsorge getroffen werde, wenn die Partei nicht schnell genug geladen hat, oder wenn sich neue Umstände ergeben, welche die Frist als unzureichend erscheinen lassen.

Art. 301. — **Ist für den Beklagten ein Anwalt bestellt, derselbe aber in der zur Hinterlegung der Anträge oder unmittelbar zur Verhandlung bestimmten Sitzung nicht erschienen, so kann der klägerische Anwalt, wenn er seinen motivirten Antrag und die Aufforderung zum Erscheinen in der Sitzung, wo solche erforderlich sind, rechtzeitig hat zustellen lassen, die Erlassung eines Versäumungsurtheils beantragen. Das Gericht hat hierauf vorbehaltlich der Bestimmung des Art. 324 Abs. 2 die zur Begründung des Klaganspruchs in der Klageschrift und den weiter zugestellten Schriftsätzen geltend gemachten Thatsachen als zugestanden zu betrachten und dem daselbst gestellten Gesuche, soweit es nach jenen Thatsachen rechtlich begründet ist, zu entsprechen, und zwar auch dann, wenn für den Beklagten ein motivirter Antrag zugestellt ist und darin die klägerischen Behauptungen widersprochen sind. Soweit das Gesuch des Klägers rechtlich nicht begründet erscheint, ist die Abweisung der Klage auszusprechen.**

Hat der Anwalt des Klägers den vorgeschriebenen motivirten Antrag oder die erforderliche Aufforderung zum Erscheinen in der Sitzung nicht oder nicht rechtzeitig zustellen lassen, so hat das Gericht den klägerischen Antrag zur Zeit zurückzuweisen.

Art. 302. — **Will im Falle des Art. 301 der Kläger eine dem Beklagten noch nicht mitgetheilte Aenderung seines Anspruchs im Gegenstande oder in der thatsächlichen Begründung oder durch Erweiterung desselben vornehmen, so muß er Vertagung der Sache begehren und in der Zwischenzeit dem Gegenanwalte durch einen Schriftsatz von der beabsichtigten Aenderung unter Mittheilung der betreffenden Urkunden Kenntniß geben.**

G. A. d. K. d. A. II S. 95—99. 135. 136. 171. 451. IV S. 83.
K. d. R. II S. 96—98. IV S. 41.

1) Im Falle des Nichterscheinens des für den Beklagten bestellten Anwaltes gelten im Allgemeinen die nemlichen Grundsätze, wie im Falle des Nichterscheinens des Beklagten selbst. Die Anwaltsbestellung an sich bedingt nur insofern eine Aenderung, als der bestellte Anwalt durch rechtzeitige Zustellung eines motivirten Antrags (Art. 231) und Aufforderung zum Erscheinen (Art. 239 u. 252) in Verzug gesetzt sein muß, bevor Versäumungsurtheil erwirkt werden kann.

Als nicht erschienen ist derjenige Anwalt zu betrachten, welcher in der zu diesem Zwecke bestimmten Sitzung keinen Antrag nimmt (Art. 253 u. 254); Nichterscheinen oder Nichtbetheiligung bei der Verhandlung allein begründet kein Versäumungsurtheil. Anders verfügte der Entwurf (Art. 265). Bemerk. zu Art. 245 Nr. 10.

2) Die in der Klagschrift, sowie in den weiter zugestellten Schriftsätzen geltend gemachten Thatsachen werden ebenso wie im Falle des Art. 297 als zugestanden betrachtet, und gelten in dieser Beziehung die dortigen Bemerkungen.

Der Gesetzgeber setzt hinzu, daß dieses Zugeständniß auch dann angenommen werde, wenn der Beklagte im zugestellten Antrage die klägerischen Behauptungen bereits bestritten hatte, und befindet sich bei diesem Ausspruche ganz im Einklange mit den Prinzipien, zufolge deren das Vorverfahren nur vorbereitend ist und was im Schriftenwechsel geltend gemacht wurde, als aufgegeben gilt, wenn es nicht in der Sitzung aufrecht erhalten wird. (S. Bemerk. zu Art. 264 Nr. 9.) Auch im französischen Prozesse ist der Richter nicht gezwungen, im Falle des Nichterscheinens des Anwalts, auf die bloß in den Akten liegenden Bestreitungen von Thatsachen Rücksicht zu nehmen, jedoch darf er es thun, weil es ihm zusteht zu prüfen, ob das Begehren »bien verifiée« sei.

3) Aus der Thatsache, daß dasjenige, was Beklagter im Vorverfahren sich zu Gunsten geltend gemacht, nur gilt, insofern es in der Sitzung aufrecht erhalten wird, folgt natürlich nicht, daß dasjenige, was sich aus dem Vorverfahren zu Gunsten des Klägers ergibt, durch das Nichterscheinen des Anwalts des Beklagten seine Wirkung verliere. Man kann wohl auf eigene, nicht aber auf fremde Rechte verzichten.

Zum Berufen auf Verzichte und Geständnisse wird allerdings kein Anlaß gegeben sein, da ja ein allgemeines Geständniß präsumirt wird; allein Rechtsverlustigungen, z. B. Präclusionen von Prozeßeinreden, können wirksam geltend gemacht werden.

4) Es ist hier die Frage zu prüfen, inwiefern Prozeßeinreden, namentlich die Einrede der Nichtigkeit der Ladung, auch bei dem gegen den Anwalt erwirkten Versäumungsurtheile von Amtswegen berücksichtigt werden dürfen.

Im Entwurfe (Art. 265) waren auch in dieser Hinsicht das Nichterscheinen der Partei und des Anwalts ganz gleich gestellt; nachdem man aber die beiden Arten von Versäumungsurtheilen in verschiedene Artikel gebracht, ließ man im letzteren Falle die Bestimmung, daß der Richter zu prüfen habe, ob die Klage nach den gesetzlichen Vorschriften erhoben sei, hinweg.

Folgt nun, daß diese Prüfung immer einzutreten, oder daß sie immer zu unterbleiben habe? Wohl keines von Beiden!

Wie schon bemerkt, beruht fragliche Prüfung auf einem allgemeinen Prinzipe, zufolge dessen der Richter verpflichtet ist, zu untersuchen, ob nach den vorgetragenen Thatsachen die Klage zulässig und begründet sei. Art. 264 Abs. 3.

Ergibt sich daher eine Prozeßeinrede aus dem eigenen Vorbringen des Klägers oder aus den von ihm vorgelegten Akten, so muß sie der Richter berücksichtigen, falls sie nicht präcludirt erscheint, d. h. falls sie entweder rechtzeitig geltend gemacht wurde (Art. 184) oder wenigstens noch geltend gemacht werden dürfte.

Erscheint jedoch die Einrede präcludirt, so fällt sie selbstverständlich weg. Es gilt dies insbesondere auch von der Einrede der Unzuständigkeit, denn Art. 39 Abs. 3 hat den Fall, wo im Vorverfahren bereits stillschweigende Vereinbarung erfolgt ist, nicht im Auge.

5) Was Klaganderungen betrifft, so hat, wie schon bemerkt (Art. 245 Nr. 12, 13), die Prozeßordnung das Prinzip angenommen, daß die wichtigsten Klagänderungen durch bloße Zustellung an den Anwalt, ohne Benachrichtigung der Partei selbst, ohne Einhaltung weiterer Fristen als derjenigen, welche für Zustellung der motivirten Anträge gegeben sind (Art. 231), geschehen können.

Die Bestimmmung des Art. 302 ist nur die einfache Consequenz dieses Prinzipes.

Hat nemlich der klägerische Anwalt vergessen, seine Klagänderung rechtzeitig zuzustellen, so soll er in der zur Hinterlegung der Anträge oder unmittelbar zur Verhandlung bestimmten Sitzung Vertagung begehren und in der Zwischenzeit die betreffende Zustellung machen. Eine Frist ist weiter nicht bestimmt.

Wie aus den Verhandlungen (Abg. II 135) hervorgeht, betrachtete man diesen Fall als gleichartig mit demjenigen des Art. 245 Abs. 2, allein ganz mit Unrecht, denn dort handelt es sich vom Falle, wo die Hinterlegung der Anträge bereits stattgefunden hat und Aenderungen, welche keine wirklichen Klagänderungen sind, vorgenommen werden sollen; hier aber handelt es sich darum, für wirkliche Klagänderungen ein Urtheil zu erwirken. (Vgl. Bemerk. zu Art. 245 Nr. 14 u. 15.) Auch in diesem Falle eine Tags zuvor gemachte Zustellung für genügend zu erklären, möchte etwas zu summarisch sein. Uebrigens kann das Gericht unter Umständen nochmals vertagen (Art. 305). Was den Begriff der Klagänderung betrifft, so gilt das zu Art. 299 Nr. 11 Gesagte.

Versäumungsurtheil gegen den Kläger.

Art. 303. — Erscheint in der zur Hinterlegung der Anträge oder unmittelbar zur Verhandlung bestimmten Sitzung, obgleich die erforderliche Aufforderung zum Erscheinen in der Sitzung ergangen ist, der Anwalt des Klägers nicht, so ist auf Begehren des Gegenanwalts die Klage für nicht angebracht zu erklären und die Verurtheilung des Klägers in die Kosten ohne weitere Prüfung der Sache auszusprechen.

Dieser Ausspruch hat die Folge, daß der Kläger, ehe er dem Beklagten die Kosten ersetzt hat, weder durch Einspruch gegen das Versäumungsurtheil die bisherige Verhandlung fortsetzen, noch über denselben Gegenstand eine neue Klage gegen den früheren Beklagten erheben kann. G. A. d. K. d. A. II S. 95—97. 136. 451. IV S. 83—86. — K. d. R. II S. 98—103. IV S. 41.

1) Da der Kläger in der Klagschrift nothwendig einen Anwalt bestellen muß (Art. 225), so war hier nur vom Falle des Nichterscheinens seines Anwaltes zu sprechen.

Im französischen Prozesse ist es bestritten, welche Folgen dieses Nichterscheinen habe, jedoch nimmt die neuere Jurisprudenz, im Anschlusse an die Ansicht von Chauveau (quest. 617) an, daß es darauf ankomme, was der Beklagte begehre. Verlangt er, daß die Klage als nicht angebracht erklärt werde, so liegt kein Grund vor, weiter zu gehen; verlangt er aber, daß auf die Sache selbst eingegangen werde, so liegt ebenfalls kein Grund vor, warum der Richter nicht über einen Rechtsstreit erkennen solle, welchen der Kläger anhängig gemacht und bezüglich dessen er eine Absicht abzustehen nicht kundgegeben hat. Nur darüber besteht Zweifel, ob der Richter sich zu beschränken habe, denjenigen Theil der Klage, welcher nach dem Vorbringen des Beklagten grundlos erscheint, abzuweisen, während er im Uebrigen die Klage für nicht angebracht erklärt, oder ob er auch ohne Schädigung des Prinzipes der Mündlichkeit zusprechen dürfe, was zugestanden ist? — Letzteres ist wohl das Richtige, denn man darf die Prinzipien nicht zu Tode hetzen.

2) Unsere Prozeßordnung hätte vielleicht wohl gethan, diese Jurisprudenz zu Grunde zu legen, um so mehr, da sie die Provocationsklage zuläßt welche dem französischen Rechte unbekannt ist.

Eine Klagerhebung ist doch jedenfalls eine Berühmung.

Ist es nun praktisch, den Beklagten, welcher Erledigung wünscht, zu nöthigen, daß er zuerst die Klage abweisen lasse, dann Provocationsklage erhebe, um ewiges Stillschweigen zu gebieten und, falls die provocirte Klage erhoben wird, einen neuen Prozeß durchzuführen, d. h. daß er drei Prozesse führen muß, um zu erreichen, was so leicht in einem einzigen hätte erreicht werden können? Vgl. R. R. II S. 95 (v. Bomhard).

Der Gesetzgeber glaubte jedoch diesen Gesichtspunkten keine Beachtung schenken zu dürfen, und legte die gesetzliche Vermuthung eines Klagabstandes zu Grunde, so daß also der Beklagte keinen andern Antrag stellen kann, als den, daß die Klage ohne Prüfung ihrer Begründung für nicht angebracht erklärt werde. Er bestimmte ferner im Einklange mit Art. 498, daß vor Ersatz der Kosten weder neue Klage noch Einspruch zugelassen werde.

Mit dieser Abweisung der Klage, falls sie nicht auf dem Wege des Einspruchs wieder beseitigt wird, fallen, wie die Worte schon ausdrücken, übrigens auch in den Verhandlungen (Abg. II 97), sowie in Art. 498 anerkannt ist, alle civilrechtlichen Wirkungen der Klage als solcher hinweg.

Stellt der Anwalt des Beklagten keinen Antrag auf Abweisung, so wird entweder gestrichen oder vertagt.

Versäumungsurtheil im Falle einer Widerklage.

Art. 304. — **Für die Widerklage kommen, wenn der Anwalt des Widerklägers in der zur Hinterlegung der motivirten Anträge oder unmittelbar zur Verhandlung bestimmten Sitzung nicht erschienen ist, die Bestimmungen des Art. 303, wenn aber der Widerbeklagte in der erwähnten Sitzung ohne Vertretung bleibt, die Vorschriften der Art. 301 und 302 zur analogen Anwendung.** G. A. d. K. d. A. II S. 96. 97. 136. 451. — K. d. R. II. S. 103.

1) Für die Widerklagen gelten, sowohl auf Seite des Widerklägers als des Widerbeklagten, ganz die nemlichen Grundsätze, wie bei Hauptklagen; jedoch kann natürlich nur vom Nichterscheinen des Anwalts die Rede sein.

2) Die Grundsätze der Art. 297—303 gelten überhaupt in allen Fällen, wo zwei Parteien als Kläger und Beklagter sich gegenüberstehen, also insbesondere auch bei Hauptinterventionen und Gewährschaftsklagen.

Bei Hauptinterventionen möchte sich recht augenfällig zeigen, daß die Bestimmungen in Art. 303 nicht praktisch sind, denn, während die im Prozesse befindlichen Parteien das größte Interesse haben, daß dem intervenirenden Prätendenten gegenüber die Sache bereinigt werde und die französische Praxis gerade deßhalb eine »intervention forcée,« d. h. die Beiladung gestattet, können jetzt die beklagten Parteien nichts weiter thun, als den Hauptintervenienten wieder aus dem Rechtsstreite hinauszuweisen!

3) Was die Gewährschaftsklage betrifft, so bedingt es deren eventuelle Natur, daß im Falle Nichterscheinens des Gewährschaftsbeklagten vorerst nur Urkunde darüber gegeben, das Versäumungsurtheil auf Grund jenes Nichterscheinens aber erst ausgesprochen werde, nachdem in der Hauptsache erkannt ist.

Weitere Ladungen oder Aufforderungen brauchen, sofern nicht Klagänderungen unterlaufen, an den Gewährschaftsbeklagten oder seinen Anwalt nicht zu ergehen, da es sich im Grunde nur um Fortsetzung einer bereits begonnenen Contumazial-Verhandlung, um Vertagung des Versäumungs-

Urtheiles zum Spruche handelt; jedoch wird es im Hinblick auf die Fassung des Art. 252 rathsam sein, in Fällen, wo Anwalt bestellt ist, diesen zum Erscheinen wiederholt aufzufordern. Vgl. auch Art. 489 Abs. 2.

Erscheint der Anwalt des Gewährschaftsklägers nicht und bestreitet der Gewährschaftsbeklagte die Hauptklage, so wird er es gleichfalls in seinem Interesse begründet finden, vorerst einen Antrag auf Zurückweisung der Gewährschaftsklage nicht zu stellen.

Gemeinsame Bestimmungen.

Art. 305. — **Sind dem Gerichte Umstände bekannt, welche den Beklagten in die Unmöglichkeit einen Anwalt zu bestellen oder einen der bestellten Anwälte in die Unmöglichkeit zu erscheinen versetzt haben, so ist die Verhandlung auszusetzen und geeigneten Falls die Wiedervorladung anzuordnen.**

Art. 306. — **Gegen alle in derselben Streitsache vorgeladenen, aber nicht erschienenen Parteien ist durch ein und dasselbe Urtheil zu erkennen.**

Laufen gegen mehrere vorgeladene aber nicht erschienene Parteien verschiedene Fristen, so kann ein Versäumungsurtheil erst nach Ablauf der längsten Frist erlassen werden.

Art. 307. — **Ist über einen Präjudicial- oder Incidentpunkt Urtheil ergangen, so finden bezüglich des weiteren Verfahrens die Bestimmungen der Art. 297 — 306 analoge Anwendung.**

Art. 308. — **Auch bei Versäumungsurtheilen hat der Anwalt, welcher das Urtheil erwirkt hat, alsbald nach dessen Verkündung den in Art. 285 bezeichneten Schriftsatz zu fertigen und auf der Gerichtsschreiberei zu hinterlegen. Eine Zustellung an die Gegenpartei findet nicht statt, gleichviel ob ein Anwalt für dieselbe aufgestellt ist oder nicht.**

G. A. d. K. d. A. II S. 96—100. 136. 137. IV S. 87. — K. d. R. II S. 103. 298. 299. IV S. 41.

1) Für das Verfahren bei Versäumungen ist im Allgemeinen zu bemerken, daß diejenige Partei, welche zum Erscheinen in einer bestimmten Sitzung auffordert, hiermit auch sich selbst verpflichtet, in dieser Sitzung zu erscheinen. Art. 210 Abs. 2.

2) Eine allgemeine Frage ist ferner, ob ein vom Richter ausgesprochenes Versäumungsurtheil sofort zurückgenommen werden könne, wenn die säumige Partei noch in der nemlichen Sitzung erscheint.

In Frankreich war es durch Art. 5 Tit. 14 der Ordonnanz von 1667 dem Richter gestattet, ein Versäumungsurtheil in der nemlichen Sitzung zurückzunehmen (rabattre le défaut), und einige Rechtslehrer halten dies auch jetzt noch zulässig, obgleich der Code de proc. jene Bestimmung nicht wiederholt hat.

Im Gesetzgebungsausschusse der K. d. A. (I 275, II 138, 139, IV 87) wurde die Frage angeregt, jedoch der Vorschlag, dem Richter unter gewissen Voraussetzungen die Rücknahme seines Urtheils zu gestatten, verworfen, so daß also jeder Zweifel beseitigt erscheint. Uebrigens ist doch zu beachten, daß es mißlich ist, wenn derjenige, welcher einige Minuten zu spät erscheint, gezwungen wird, den Weg förmlichen Einspruches einzuschlagen, während es so einfach und förderlich wäre, die Sache so zu behandeln, als sei der Einspruch bereits erfolgt und zugelassen.

Um dem praktischen Bedürfnisse Rechnung zu tragen, namentlich für den Fall der Ladung mit kurzer Frist oder im Parteiprozesse, möchte ich mit Chauveau (quest. 621) dem Richter rathen, die Versäumungssachen möglichst an's Ende der Sitzung zu stellen, jedenfalls nicht zu früh vorzunehmen. Es genügt übrigens, wenn auch nur die Verkündung des Urtheils bis zum Schlusse der Sitzung verschoben wird. Art. 250 Abs. 4.

a) Vertagung und Wiedervorladung (Art. 305).

3) Falls das Gericht Umstände kennt, welche die Partei bezw. den Anwalt in die Unmöglichkeit versetzt haben, zu erscheinen, so soll es die Verhandlung aussetzen und geeigneten Falls die Wiedervorladung anordnen. Handelt es sich vom Nichterscheinen des Anwalts, so wird sich die wiederholte Aufforderung desselben nach Art. 252 von selbst verstehen.

Das Anordnen der Wiedervorladung steht im Einklange mit den Prinzipien, wie sie zu Art. 220 Nr. 14 und zu Art. 297 Nr. 3 entwickelt sind.

Das Aussetzen der Verhandlung wird, abgesehen vom Falle der Wiedervorladung, in der Vertagung derselben in eine andere Sitzung bestehen. Zu gleichem Zwecke führt es jedoch, wenn das Versäumungsurtheil zum Spruche vertagt wird. Bemerk. zu Art. 250 Nr. 2 u. 3.

4) Das Gesetz verlangt eine Unmöglichkeit des Erscheinens, will also nicht, daß das Gericht aus Gründen anderer Art, namentlich nicht aus bloßen Billigkeitsrücksichten, ein Versäumungsurtheil verweigere. In Betreff der Würdigung der Umstände,

aus denen diese Unmöglichkeit sich folgert, ist ihm volle Freiheit gegeben, ebenso bezüglich der Frage, ob es sachgemäß sei, eine Wiedervorladung anzuordnen. Letzteres darf natürlich nur geschehen, falls anzunehmen ist, es sei die Partei von der Ladung nicht erreicht worden. Durch die neue Ladung werden selbstverständlich die Wirkungen der früheren nicht beseitigt.

b) Mehrheit der nichterschienenen Parteien (Art. 306).

5) Art. 306 wurde aus dem Entwurfe (Art. 267) ohne weitere Bemerkung aufgenommen und gibt die Bestimmungen der Art. 151 und 152 Code de proc.

Er enthält eine Anwendung des Prinzipes, welches bereits den Fristbestimmungen der Art. 210 und 233 zu Grunde liegt und aus welchem in Art. 316 weitere Folgen gezogen werden, daß es nemlich zur bestmöglichen Aufklärung der Sache und zur Verhütung widersprechender Urtheile sachgemäß ist, unter allen Personen, welche bei einer Streitsache betheiligt sind, gleichzeitig zu verhandeln und zu entscheiden.

6) Zunächst hat er wohl den Fall im Auge, wo mehrere Personen als Streitgenossen belangt worden sind; allein nach seiner Fassung und nach dem Zwecke des Gesetzes ist er möglichst allgemein anzuwenden.

Vorausgesetzt wird jedoch, daß „dieselbe Streitsache“ vorliege, d. h. daß die Entscheidungen gegen die vorgeladenen Parteien im inneren Zusammenhange stehen und Widerspruch der Urtheile zu befürchten sei. In Fällen, wo etwa ein Kläger ganz verschiedene Ansprüche gegen verschiedene Personen in der nemlichen Klage willkürlich vereinigt hätte, stünde nichts im Wege, gegen jeden Beklagten gesondert vorzugehen.

c) Präjudizialpunkte (Art. 307).

7) Präjudizial- und Incidentpunkte setzen eine Anregung des Gegners voraus, und es ist daher nicht wohl begreiflich, wie die Art. 297—300, auf welche sich Art. 307 gleichfalls beruft, zur Anwendung kommen können; man müßte denn gerade an eine Unterbrechung des Verfahrens (Art. 491 u. 495) denken.

Unter Präjudizialpunkten sind hier alle zur gesonderten Verhandlung gebrachten Vorfragen, also auch bevorzugte Prozeßeinreden, zu verstehen, Abg. II 137 (zu Art. 11 Hptst. IX) und fällt daher der Begriff nicht mit jenem der Präjudizialsachen in Art. 190 und Art. 682 Abs. 2 zusammen. Vgl. Bemerk. zu Art. 190 Nr. 3 und zu Art. 256 Nr. 2 u. 3.

8) Das Gesetz hat offenbar zunächst nur den Fall im Auge, wo die betreffende Vor- oder Zwischenfrage zur gesonderten Verhandlung gebracht wurde und die genommenen Anträge sich auf diese Frage beschränkten. Es erklärt, daß in diesem Falle die Sache nur contradiktorisch sei bezüglich Entscheidung der betreffenden Frage, daß aber, wenn später zur Verhandlung in der Hauptsache von einer oder von der andern Partei keine Anträge genommen werden, Versäumungsurtheil in der Hauptsache ergehe.

Die Folgen der Versäumung sind die nemlichen, wie im Falle, wo die Hauptsache sofort zur Verhandlung gekommen ist, namentlich tritt auch im Falle des Nichterscheinens des Klägers die Folge ein, daß die Klage für nicht angebracht erklärt wird.

9) Es möchte übrigens zu bezweifeln sein, ob auch dann, wenn irgend eine zum Grunde der Sache gehörige Vorfrage, z. B. die Frage der Erbqualität, als Präjudizialpunkt gesondert erledigt worden ist, der Beklagte sich mit der Fiktion des Klagabstandes abfertigen lassen müsse. Dieser Fall kann sich allerdings nur ergeben, wenn man annimmt, es sei das Vorbringen eines solchen Präjudizialpunktes ohne Einlassung in die Hauptsache zulässig (Bemerk. zu Art. 256 Nr. 2), und auch dann wird er nicht leicht vorkommen; übrigens ist er immerhin möglich und wird nach den Prinzipien über Klagabstand zu entscheiden sein.

Ist nemlich der Kläger nach Erlaß eines solchen präjudiziellen Urtheils nicht mehr befugt, von der Klage abzustehen, so kann er offenbar einen solchen Abstand auch nicht durch sein bloßes Nichterscheinen herbeiführen.

Ich halte nun dafür, daß Art. 496 hier einen Abstand nicht mehr gestattet und daß daher, da zudem Art. 307 selbst nur von einer analogen Anwendung spricht, die Folgen des Nichterscheinens des Klägers darin bestehen, daß sein Begehren, soweit es nach den Behauptungen des Beklagten unbegründet erscheint, abzuweisen sei. Insoweit es begründet erscheint, müßte, da unsere Prozeßordnung einen Klagszuspruch ohne einen in der Sitzung gestellten Antrag nicht gestattet, die Klage für nicht angebracht erklärt werden. Vgl. Entwurf Art. 269 Abs. 2.

10) Die allgemeine Fassung des Art. 307 könnte Zweifel darüber erregen, ob er nicht auch in solchen Fällen zur Anwendung komme, wo bereits Anträge zur Hauptsache in der Sitzung genommen waren und nur die Verhandlung über den Präjudizial- oder Incidentpunkt gesondert erfolgte, was nach Art. 190 bei Präjudizialsachen und nach Art. 157 bei allen Streitpunkten, also

sogar bei gewöhnlichen Prozeßeinreden, angeordnet werden kann. Es könnten diese Zweifel um so begründeter erscheinen, da die bestimmtere Fassung des Art. 256 gegenübersteht.

Diese Frage entscheidet sich nach den Grundsätzen über die Wirkung der Hinterlegung der Anträge, welche es demnach geeignet ist, hier näher zu erörtern.

11) Im französischen Prozesse gilt im Allgemeinen als Grundsatz, daß mit jedem Vorbescheide die Sache in ein neues Stadium trete, und bei der nächsten Verhandlung die Frage, ob Versäumungsurtheil ergehe oder nicht, allein von der Thatsache abhänge, ob bei derselben die Anwälte erscheinen bezw. Antrag nehmen oder nicht. Die im früheren Stadium erfolgte Antragstellung wirkt in dieser Richtung nicht fort.

Der Entwurf unserer P. O. hatte diesem Grundsatze in Art. 269 einen bestimmten und ganz allgemeinen Ausdruck gegeben und mußte dies wohl auch thun, da er in Art. 268 Ziff. 2 das bloße Nichterscheinen bei der Verhandlung ein Versäumungsurtheil bewirken läßt, also unmöglich die Hinterlegung der Anträge auf spätere Urtheile fortwirken lassen konnte, nachdem er ihr die Wirkung sogar für das erste Urtheil, für welches sie genommen waren, versagt hatte.

Unsere Prozeßordnung geht jedoch von wesentlich verschiedener Anschauung aus.

Sie erkennt als Grundsatz an, daß, sobald die Anträge gegenseitig in der Sitzung genommen sind, die Sache contradiktorisch werde, und zwar für alles, was Gegenstand dieser Anträge ist oder der Sachlage nach sein soll, ohne Rücksicht darauf, ob die Anwälte bei der späteren Verhandlung erscheinen oder nicht.

Die einfache Consequenz dieses Grundsatzes führt dahin, daß die Sache contradiktorisch bleibe, bis über die gestellten Anträge endgiltig entschieden ist; ob eine einzige Verhandlung dazu hinreiche, oder ob mehrere Verhandlungen nöthig seien, kann als unwesentlich erachtet werden, und zwar um so mehr, da ja auch bei der ersten Verhandlung Aenderungen der Gesichtspunkte, ja sogar der Anträge und Thatsachen (Art. 245) stattfinden konnten, ohne der contradiktorischen Natur des Urtheils im Wege zu stehen.

Wirklich wurde auch bei den Verhandlungen (zu Art. 269 Abg. II 99, 100; zu Art. 295 Abg. II 166, 167) der Hinterlegung der Anträge diese Tragweite vindizirt, jedoch schließlich für das nach durchgeführtem Beweisverfahren erfolgende Urtheil in Art. 346 eine Ausnahme gemacht und Einspruch zugelassen. Es geschah dies in der Erwägung, daß in Folge des Ergebnisses der Beweisführung die Sache präsumtiv eine ganz andere Gestalt gewonnen habe. In sonstigen Beziehungen bleibt es also beim aufgestellten Grundsatze.

12) Hieraus folgt nun, daß, sobald einmal Anträge zum Grunde der Sache genommen sind, es ohne Belang ist, wenn über irgend eine Vorfrage gesondert entschieden und die weitere Entscheidung einem späteren Urtheile vorbehalten wird; auch dieses spätere Urtheil wird auf Grund der bereits genommenen Anträge ein contradiktorisches. Abg. II 99 (v. Weiß).

Weiter ist aber zu folgern, daß auch in allen sonstigen Fällen, wo irgend ein Vorbescheid, welcher kein Beweisurtheil im Sinne des Gesetzes ist, ergeht, z. B. beim Verordnen des persönlichen Erscheinens, die hinterlegten Anträge fortwirken.

Alle Urtheile jedoch, welche auf einen der in Art. 325 bezeichneten Beweise erkennen, fallen unter den Gesichtspunkt des Art. 346, also auch Urtheile, welche Augenschein anordnen oder einen Eid auferlegen. Wenn daher der Eid in der nemlichen Sitzung geleistet wird und der Anwalt der Gegenpartei keine weiteren Anträge nimmt, so ist das ergehende Urtheil ein Versäumungsurtheil im Sinne des Art. 346, obgleich in derselben Sitzung von beiden Parteien bereits Anträge zum Grunde der Sache genommen wurden.

d) Sachverhalt (Art. 308).

13) Da der Sachverhalt zur Vollständigkeit des Urtheils gehört, so darf er auch beim Versäumungsurtheile nicht fehlen, und da er einmal den Anwälten zugewiesen ist, so war es natürlich, auch hier keine Ausnahme zu machen. Die Zustellung an die Gegenpartei fällt hinweg, selbst wenn das Versäumungsurtheil gegen Anwalt erwirkt war.

Einspruch gegen das Versäumungsurtheil.

Art. 309. — Die Partei, gegen welche ein Versäumungs-Urtheil erlassen worden ist, kann die Zurücknahme dieses Urtheils und die neuerliche Aburtheilung der Sache durch dasselbe Gericht veranlassen, indem sie innerhalb einer unerstreckbaren Frist von acht Tagen nach Zustellung des Urtheils Einspruch dagegen erhebt.

Art. 310. — Wer gegen ein Versäumungsurtheil Berufung ergriffen hat, kann von dem Rechte des Einspruchs gegen dieses Urtheil keinen Gebrauch mehr machen. Auch die Verbindung des Einspruchs mit der Berufung ist unstatthaft.

Art. 311. — Der Einspruch wird dadurch erhoben, daß der von der Partei bestellte Anwalt der Gegenpartei einen Anwaltsakt zustellen läßt, der die Erklärung enthält, daß gegen das Versäumungsurtheil Einspruch erhoben werde.

Art. 312. — Zugleich mit der Anmeldung des Einspruchs oder innerhalb der darauf folgenden acht Tage hat der Anwalt des Einspruchklägers einen motivirten Antrag zustellen zu lassen, aus dem zu entnehmen ist, in welchen Punkten, dann aus welchen sachlichen oder rechtlichen Gründen der Einspruch erhoben wird.

Auf den Grund, aus welchem die Partei in der betreffenden Sitzung nicht vertreten war, hat es nicht anzukommen.

Hat die Partei ihre Rechtsvertheidigung bereits früher der andern zustellen lassen, so kann hierauf Bezug genommen werden.

Art. 313. — Drei Tage nach Zustellung des in Art. 312 bezeichneten Antrags oder Ablauf der hiefür gestatteten Frist steht es jeder Partei frei, die Sache zum Eintrage in die Wochen-Tabelle anzumelden.

Wenigstens drei Tage vor der Sitzung, in welcher die Sache zum Aufrufe kommt, hat die Gegenpartei ihren motivirten Antrag zustellen zu lassen, soferne dies nicht bereits früher geschehen ist.

Art. 314. — Das Gericht ist durch das Versäumungsurtheil, soweit sich ihm der Verurtheilte nicht unterworfen hat, bei der neuerlichen Aburtheilung der Sache nicht gebunden; es kann das frühere Urtheil sowohl bestätigen, als ganz oder theilweise abändern und zwar auch zum Nachtheile des Einspruchklägers.

Von der Entscheidung ist am Rande des Versäumungsurtheils Vormerkung zu machen.

Art. 315. — Bleibt der Einspruchkläger bei der Verhandlung über den Einspruch abermals unvertreten, so ist dieser ohne weitere Prüfung zu verwerfen und findet gegen dieses Urtheil kein Einspruch mehr statt.

G. A. d. K. d. A. II S. 96. 102. 103. 105. 106. 137. 138. III S. 20. 129. 130. IV S. 87. 88.
K. d. R. II S. 105. IV S. 41.

1) Ein Versäumungsurtheil unterscheidet sich von einem contradiktorischen nur dadurch, daß es durch Einspruch angefochten werden kann; im Uebrigen hat es ganz dieselbe Natur und äußert, wenn es rechtskräftig geworden, dieselben Wirkungen.

Spricht es eine Klage ganz oder theilweise zu, so ist es ebensogut ein Endurtheil, als wenn contradiktorisch entschieden worden wäre, und findet daher Art. 192 Abs. 2, insofern er verfügt, daß Endurtheile und Urtheile, welche diesen nach Art. 682 und 683 gleichstehen, immer auch der Partei selbst zuzustellen seien, auch auf Versäumungsurtheile Anwendung. Abg. II 102 (v. Weiß).

2) Der Einspruch ist ein Rechtsmittel, welches dem diesseitigen Verfahren bis jetzt unbekannt war, denn die Remonstration war nur statthaft, wenn einseitig, ohne Aufforderung zur Vertheidigung, gesprochen worden war.

Es bildet dieses Rechtsmittel das nothwendige Gegengewicht gegen die weitgehenden Wirkungen, welche das Gesetz an das Nichterscheinen vor Gericht knüpft, insofern es zur Folge hat, daß diese Wirkungen nur bedingt eintreten, d. h. für den Fall, als nicht der Betroffene innerhalb der gegebenen kurzen Frist erklärt, daß er sich vertheidigen wolle. Sowie diese Erklärung erfolgt, fallen auch alle Folgen der Versäumung (abgesehen vom Kostenpunkte) hinweg, und die contradiktorische Aburtheilung findet in gleicher Weise statt, als hätte die Versäumung gar nie stattgefunden. Chauveau sur C. (quest. 657) sagt: »L'opposition opère de plein droit le rabattement du défaut.«

Ich nenne den Einspruch ein Rechtsmittel, obgleich ihn das Gesetz nicht in dem von den Rechtsmitteln handelnden dritten Buche aufführt, weil er seiner inneren Natur nach als ein solches erscheinen muß. Auch bei den Verhandlungen (Abg. II 270 a. E. und 294) wurde er mehrfach so bezeichnet, und die französischen Rechtslehrer zählen zu den ordentlichen Rechtsmitteln die Berufung und den Einspruch, obgleich der Code de proc. ebenfalls nur beim Versäumungsurtheile, nicht aber bei den Rechtsmitteln von letzterem spricht.

3) Der Einspruch ist gegen alle Versäumungsurtheile ohne Ausnahme zulässig; es kommt daher nicht auf den Werth des Streitgegenstandes an und ebensowenig ist nöthig, daß ein Endurtheil oder ein diesem gleichstehendes Urtheil vorliege, wie dies bei Berufung und Nichtigkeitsbeschwerde verlangt wird.

Allerdings werden thatsächlich die Versäumungsurtheile fast immer Endurtheile sein. Nur in

Fällen, wo das Geständniß nicht beweisgebend ist (Art. 324), wird es hie und da vorkommen, daß Zwischenbescheide ergehen; ebenso bei Versäumungsurtheilen gegen den Anwalt, wenn derjenige Anwalt, welcher eine Prozeßeinrede zur gesonderten Verhandluug bringt, ausbleibt und die Einrede verworfen wird, sowie bei Urtheilen auf Grund einer Beweisführung (Art. 345):

Selbst in den seltenen Fällen, wo solche Zwischenentscheidungen erfolgen, ist es in der Regel nicht nöthig, Einspruch zu erheben, da sie in Sachen, welche der Berufung unterliegen, nicht rechtskräftig werden und vom nemlichen Richter wieder zurückgenommen werden können (Art. 296).

Bei Urtheilen, welche auf Beweis erkennen, kann jedoch der Einspruch insofern von Nutzen sein, als er die Wirkung des Art. 332 aufhebt, denn trotz der etwas zu allgemeinen Fassung dieses Artikels kann kein Zweifel bestehen, daß auf diesem Wege der nemliche Richter sein Beweisurtheil wieder zurücknehmen kann.

a) Frist zum Einspruche.

4) Die Frist zur Erhebung des Einspruchs beträgt acht Tage von Zustellung des Urtheils an und ist unerstreckbar.

Insofern das Versäumungsurtheil ein Endurtheil im Sinne der Art. 682 und 683 ist, läuft diese Frist zufolge der Verfügung des Art. 192 Abs. 2 erst von der Zustellung an die Partei an, ohne Unterschied, ob das Versäumungsurtheil gegen die Partei oder gegen den Anwalt ergangen ist.

Mit dieser Bestimmuug weicht die Prozeßordnung in höchst greller Weise vom französischen Prozesse ab, und zwar in doppelter Richtung, da dieser Prozeß einerseits beim défaut contre partie eine viel ausgedehntere Frist gibt, nemlich bis zum Vollzuge des Urtheils (C. de pr. Art. 158), anderseits aber beim défaut contre avoué die Frist schon von Zustellung an den Anwalt laufen läßt (C. de pr. Art. 157).

Die erste Abweichung wäre höchst ungerechtfertigt, wenn nicht die Prozeßordnung in Art. 216 den Ausweg der Wiedereinsetzung in den vorigen Stand eröffnete, falls die Partei darthun kann, daß sie durch Abwesenheit, schwere Krankheit oder andere unabwendbare Verhinderungen, wozu insbesondere auch die Thatsache, daß ihr die Zustellung nicht zugekommen, zu rechnen ist, außer Stand gewesen sei, rechtzeitig Einspruch zu erheben.

Allerdings bleibt immerhin noch der bedeutende Unterschied, daß der Nichterschienene jetzt den Beweis von Ursache und Dauer der Verhinderung führen muß, eine Bestimmung, welche große Härten zur Folge hätte, wenn die Richter strenge Anforderungen an diesen Beweis stellen würden. Der Entwurf (Art. 273) hatte im Gefühl dieser Härten eine Präsumtion für den Nichterschienenen sprechen lassen, und falls ein genügender Verhinderungsgrund bezeichnet war, dem Gegner den Gegenbeweis auferlegt.

5) Ist das Versäumungsurtheil kein Endurtheil (s. oben Nr. 3), so läuft nach Maßgabe des Art. 192 Abs. 1 die Frist zum Einspruche von Zustellung an den Anwalt an, sofern ein solcher aufgestellt ist. Der Entwurf (Art. 272) wollte allerdings diese Frist ohne Ausnahme von Zustellung an die Partei laufen lassen, und bei den Verhandlungen wurde die Absicht einer Aenderung nicht kundgegeben, vielmehr das Nemliche gesagt (Abg. II 102); allein man dachte offenbar nicht an den seltenen Fall, wo das Versäumungsurtheil kein Endurtheil sei. Nachdem die allgemeinen Prinzipien einmal für maßgebend erklärt sind, muß man sie auch in allen ihren Folgen walten lassen. Uebrigens entspricht dies auch dem Geiste des Gesetzes.

6) Es steht außer Zweifel, daß die Einspruchfrist nach Maßgabe des Art. 209 sich erweitert, und zwar in allen Fällen, wo sie von Zustellung an die Partei läuft, mit Rücksicht auf deren eigenen Wohnort, da das Gesetz auch dann, wenn das Versäumungsurtheil gegen den Anwalt erging, ein Handeln der Partei selbst erwartet.

Aus dem nemlichen Grunde findet auch die Unterbrechung der Frist nach Maßgabe des Art. 211 statt.

7) Die Fristen zum Einspruch und zur Berufung, vorausgesetzt daß letztere statthaft ist, laufen nebeneinander (Art. 694 u. 697 Abs. 2), und es hat der Nichterschienene die Wahl, ob er das eine oder andere Rechtsmittel gebrauchen wolle. Wählt er die Berufung, so verzichtet er hiermit auf den Einspruch, während, wenn er zum Letzteren greift, gegen das neu ergehende Urtheil später immer noch Berufung statthaft ist.

Wird sofort Berufung ergriffen, so ist vor dem höheren Richter die Sache ebenso abzuurtheilen, wie sie im Falle des Einspruches vor dem nemlichen Richter abzuurtheilen gewesen sein würde; bezüglich einer Abänderung zum Nachtheile des Appellanten ist jedoch nicht Art. 314, sondern Art. 729 maßgebend.

8) Wenn das Versäumungsurtheil gegen mehrere Personen erging und die eine Einspruch erhebt, während die andere Berufung ergreift, so soll nach Art. 722 die Verhandlung über die

Berufung bis zur Erledigung des Einspruchs ausgesetzt bleiben.

Es kann nun aber auch der Fall sein, daß Derjenige, welcher das Versäumungsurtheil erwirkt hat, Berufung ergreift, während der Gegner Einspruch erhebt. Auch auf diesen Fall wird Art. 722 bei der Allgemeinheit seiner Fassung Anwendung finden, und zwar um so mehr, da nach Art. 314 bei Erledigung des Einspruchs auch die Berufungsbeschwerde beseitigt werden kann.

b) Verfahren.

9) Die einfache, in einem Anwaltsakte abgegebene Erklärung, daß gegen das zu bezeichnende Versäumungsurtheil Einspruch erhoben werde, genügt, um dieses Rechtsmittel zu sichern. Der Gesetzgeber fand es geeignet, die Einhaltung der bezüglichen Präclusivfrist so wenig als möglich an Formen zu binden, und hatte hierzu um so mehr Grund, da er diese Frist so kurz machte.

10) Sobald die Einspruchserklärung erfolgt ist, tritt die Sache in's Stadium des Vorverfahrens, und wird nach dem Stande unmittelbar vor Erlaß des Versäumungsurtheiles darin verhandelt.

Wenn auch das Versäumungsurtheil für den Fall späterer Bestätigung, oder wiederholten Ausbleibens, bedingte Wirkung behält, so fallen doch die Folgen der Versäumung sofort hinweg, und die Parteien können alle Rechtsbehelfe gerade so geltend machen, als sei jenes Urtheil nicht ergangen.

11) Für die Begründung des Einspruches, welche nach französischem Rechte mit dessen Erhebung verbunden sein mußte, gibt unsere Prozeßordnung eine weitere Frist von acht Tagen von der Erhebung an, welche Frist jedoch weder unerstreckbar noch präclusiv ist, da kein Zweifel bestehen kann, daß hier Art. 251, welcher für das Vorverfahren keine Präclusion zuläßt, anwendbar sei.

Unter Begründung des Einspruchs ist nicht die Rechtfertigung des Nichterscheinens zu verstehen, denn hierzu besteht keine Verpflichtung, und nur für den Kostenpunkt kann es von Belang sein, zu prüfen, ob die Versäumung verschuldet sei oder nicht. Man versteht darunter vielmehr nur die Darlegung der Gründe für Aenderung des ergangenen Spruches.

12) Dieselbe erfolgt durch Zustellung eines motivirten Antrags, welcher alles das enthalten muß, was die Sachlage erfordert.

Ist es der Kläger, welcher Einspruch erhebt, so muß derselbe sofort auf den bereits früher zugestellten Antrag des Beklagten sachgemäß antworten.

Ist der Beklagte der Einspruchskläger und hat derselbe, was der gewöhnliche Fall ist, noch keinen Antrag zugestellt, so gelten für das Vorbringen und den Ausschluß von Prozeßeinreden (Art. 39, 184, 188 Abs. 1 2c.), für die Pflicht zur Einlassung (Art. 184) 2c., die allgemeinen Vorschriften. Die Einspruchserklärung **für sich allein** bewirkt einen Ausschluß vom Prozeßeinreden nicht; sie wirkt in dieser Beziehung nicht mehr, wie eine Anwaltsbestellung.

Hatte der Einspruchskläger einen Antrag bereits früher zugestellt, so ist es ihm gestattet, auf denselben Bezug zu nehmen.

13) Man könnte fragen, ob der Beklagte, welcher verurtheilt ist, noch das Recht habe, **ohne Einlassung** auf die Hauptsache bevorzugte Prozeßeinreden oder Präjudizialpunkte vorzubringen, oder ob er nicht vielmehr, der allgemeinen Fassung des Art. 311 gegenüber, sich **sofort** über **alle** Punkte eventuell verbreiten müsse.

Meiner Ansicht nach besteht kein rechtlicher Grund, warum der Beklagte, von welchem vermuthet wird, daß ihn die Ladung nicht erreicht habe, bloß wegen seines Nichterscheinens des fraglichen Rechtes (welches allerdings sonst nicht zu begünstigen ist) verlustig werden sollte, und es erscheint mir außer Zweifel, daß er auch in dieser Richtung so verfahren dürfe, als sei ein Versäumungsurtheil nicht ergangen.

Allerdings kann es so vorkommen, daß über den Werth des erhobenen Einspruchs in verschiedenen Urtheilen erkannt werden muß, daß z. B. in einem ersten Urtheile eine Prozeßeinrede verworfen, in einem zweiten Urtheile aber in der Hauptsache gesprochen wird, in welchem Falle die besonderen Bestimmungen der Art. 314 und 315 auf diese **beiden** Urtheile Anwendung finden.

14) Ohne Zweifel ist anderseits auch diejenige Partei, welche das Versäumungsurtheil erwirkt hat, befugt, nicht bloß neue Thatsachen und Rechtsbehelfe zur Bekämpfung des Einspruches geltend zu machen, sondern auch ihr Begehren zu berichtigen. Ja sogar wirkliche Klagänderungen sind ihr nicht verwehrt, falls sonst die Voraussetzungen dazu gegeben sind. Abg. II 106 (v. Weiß).

15) Sobald der zur Begründung des Einspruchs dienende Antrag zugestellt, oder die Frist dazu umlaufen ist, kann jede Partei die Sache zur **Wochentabelle** anmelden. Eine Anmeldung zum Hauptverzeichnisse ist nicht mehr nöthig, da die Sache nach Art. 250 dort schon eingetragen sein muß.

Nach Art. 313 muß die Gegenpartei drei Tage vor der Sitzung ihren motivirten Antrag zustellen lassen, sofern dies nicht bereits früher geschehen sein sollte. Eigentlich hätte gesagt werden sollen, daß für jede Partei diese Frist gelte, denn es wird wohl Art. 242 Abs. 2 auch hier seine Anwendung finden müssen. Die abweichende Fassung rührt daher, daß nach Feststellung des jetzigen Art. 313 (Abg. III 129) der jetzige Art. 242 (Hptst. VIII Art. 19) geändert wurde (R. R. II 26 u. 27).

16) Die Bestimmungen der Art. 312 u. 313 gelten auch für den Fall, wo das Versäumungsurtheil im abgekürzten Verfahren (Art. 259) erwirkt worden ist, und es ist der Einspruchskläger nicht etwa verpflichtet, die Sache sofort in die Sitzung zu bringen.

Dem Gegner ist es jedoch unbenommen, auch für die Verhandlung über den Einspruch das abgekürzte Verfahren zu veranlassen. In diesem Falle kann, sofern das Versäumungsurtheil in der Hauptsache erkannt hat, sofort zur Verhandlung der ganzen Sache Sitzung anberaumt werden, mag auch der Beklagte sich auf Vorschützen einer bevorzugten Prozeßeinrede beschränkt haben. Die Folge ist, daß sofort, nach Aburtheilung der Prozeßeinrede, zur Verhandlung in der Hauptsache geschritten werden kann.

c) Urtheil.

17) Der Einspruch hat vor anderen Rechtsmitteln das Eigene, daß er, was die neuerliche Aburtheilung betrifft, die Wirkungen des angefochtenen Urtheils vollständig aufhebt, so daß dieses Urtheil auch zum Vortheile der Gegenpartei geändert werden darf, ohne daß diese verpflichtet wäre, ein Rechtsmittel zu ergreifen.

Natürlich darf hieraus nicht gefolgert werden, daß der rechtzeitig erhobene Einspruch das Versäumungsurtheil in allen Richtungen vernichte, als ob es nie gesprochen worden wäre; vielmehr behält dasselbe, soweit es recht gesprochen ist und bestätigt wird, allerdings seine Wirksamkeit als Urtheil, was in mancher Beziehung, z. B. für den Vorrang eines Arrestklägers (Art. 985), in der Pfalz für Hypothekar-Einschreibungen, von wesentlichem Belange ist.

In dem ergehenden Urtheile wird daher das Versäumungsurtheil nicht etwa ignorirt und in den Sachverhalt verwiesen, sondern der Urtheilssatz lautet: „das Gericht nimmt den Einspruch als begründet an,“ oder: „weist ihn als unbegründet ab.“

18) Die Wirkungen des Einspruchs treffen natürlich nur diejenigen Entscheidungen, welche er angreift; für unangefochtene Streitpunkte bleibt das Versäumungsurtheil in Kraft.

Für den angefochtenen Theil der Entscheidung bleibt der Einspruch so lange wirksam, bis der nemliche Richter endlich darüber erkannt hat, ob das Versäumungsurtheil zu bestätigen sei oder nicht. Selbst in Fällen, wo Interlokute oder sonstige Zwischenbescheide ergehen, erfolgt doch erst im Endurtheile Ausspruch darüber, ob der Einspruch begründet oder unbegründet sei.

19) Wird der Einspruch für vollständig begründet erklärt, so kann sich fragen, was bezüglich der Kosten des Versäumungsurtheiles zu verfügen sei?

In der Pfalz war es bis jetzt Uebung, in dieser Richtung von der Präsumtion einer Verschuldung auszugehen und dem Einspruchskläger die durch sein früheres Nichterscheinen veranlaßten Kosten zur Last zu legen. Nach den allgemeinen Bestimmungen des Art. 106 Abs. 2 ist dies auch jetzt noch gerechtfertigt, wie übrigens bei den Verhandlungen (Abg. II 105, 106) ausdrücklich anerkannt wurde.

Gewinnt übrigens der Richter die Ueberzeugung, es liege eine Verschuldung nicht vor, so wird es sachgemäß sein, auch die Kosten des Versäumungsurtheiles gleich sonstigen Prozeßkosten dem unterliegenden Theile zur Last zu legen.

20) Von der endlichen Entscheidung über den Einspruch ist am Rande des Versäumungsurtheiles Vormerkung zu machen (Art. 314), und da das Gesetz nicht unterscheidet, hat dies sowohl von Bestätigungen als Abänderungen zu gelten, was als Abweichung von den Vorschriften der Art. 737, 786 und 818 hervorzuheben ist.

Die Vormerkung wird in derselben Weise und im nemlichen Umfange, wie in den durch besagte drei Artikel vorgesehenen Fällen zu machen sein, — durch einfache Notiz, welche der Gerichtsschreiber unterzeichnet.

Daß diese Vormerkung jeder Ausfertigung oder Abschrift des Urtheils beizufügen sei, wird hier nicht gesagt; jedoch möchte es selbstverständlich erscheinen; jedenfalls ist es sachgemäß.

21) Bleibt der Einspruchskläger bei der Verhandlung über den Einspruch aus, so ist die Folge: 1) daß der Einspruch ohne weitere Prüfung zu verwerfen ist, und 2) daß gegen dieses Urtheil kein Einspruch mehr erhoben werden kann.

Es frägt sich, welche Verhandlung das Gesetz hier im Auge habe?

Der Grundsatz, daß ein zweiter Einspruch Seitens der nemlichen Partei nicht statthaft sei, ist dem französischen Prozesse entlehnt (Art. 165

C. de pr.), erscheint übrigens selbstverständlich, da es sonst in das Belieben einer Partei gestellt wäre, durch fortgesetztes Nichterscheinen die Erwirkung eines rechtskräftigen Urtheils unmöglich zu machen.

In der französischen Jurisprudenz ist nun strittig, ob der Satz: »opposition sur opposition ne vaut« nur für das erste ergehende Urtheil gelte, oder ob er auch Anwendung finde, wenn contradiktorisch auf Beweis erkannt wird, beim späteren Endurtheile aber der Oppositionskläger ausbleibt. Carré und Thomine lassen gegen dieses Endurtheil Opposition zu, Chauveau aber nicht, weil erst durch dieses Urtheil über den Werth der Opposition endlich entschieden werde (Chauv. sur C. quest. 694).

22) Unsere Prozeßordnung hat offenbar nur die erste Verhandlung, oder richtiger: die erste Sitzung im Auge, in welcher nach Erhebung des Einspruchs die Anträge über dessen Begründung genommen worden. Wird in diesem Stadium die Sache dadurch contradiktorisch, daß beide Theile Anträge nehmen, so fällt die fernere Anwendung des Art. 315 hinweg und gelten die besonderen Bestimmungen des Art. 346.

Daß dies der Gedanke des Gesetzgebers gewesen sei, geht schon daraus hervor, daß er für den Fall, welchen er unterstellt, die Abweisung des Einspruchs ohne nähere Prüfung vorschreibt.

23) Andere Gesichtspunkte haben für den Fall zu gelten, wo in Folge gesonderter Verhandlung über Prozeßeinreden 2c. das Gericht in die Lage versetzt wird, in verschiedenen Urtheilen über den Einspruch zu erkennen (s. oben Nr. 13). In diesem Falle werden bei der ersten Verhandlung die Anträge nicht erschöpfend genommen und muß also auch für die spätere Verhandlung Art. 315 maßgebend sein.

Wenn daher nach contradiktorischer Verwerfung der Prozeßeinrede die Anträge in der Hauptsache hinterlegt werden sollen, und hierbei der Anwalt des Einspruchsklägers nicht erscheint, so ist sein Einspruch ohne weitere Prüfung zu verwerfen, und ist gegen dieses Urtheil weiterer Einspruch nicht statthaft. Es ist dieser Fall ganz demjenigen gleich, der zu Art. 307 Nr. 6 u. 7 besprochen wurde.

24) Wenn das Gesetz sagt, daß bei wiederholtem Nichterscheinen der Einspruch ohne weitere Prüfung zu verwerfen sei, so liegt dieser Verfügung der nemliche Gedanke zu Grunde, wie der Verfügung des Art. 303, nemlich die Vermuthung des Abstandes vom eingelegten Rechtsmittel.

Die sonstigen Rechtsmittel — Berufung, Nichtigkeitsbeschwerde — sind hiermit nicht ausgeschlossen; eine Wiedereinsetzung in den vorigen Stand könnte jedoch nach Ausspruch der Abweisung nicht mehr stattfinden.

Hat das Gericht Gründe, um anzunehmen, daß der Einspruchskläger ohne Schuld verhindert gewesen sei zu erscheinen, so wird Art. 305, unter Umständen auch Art. 300, anzuwenden sein.

25) Offenbar geht der Sinn des Gesetzes dahin, daß nur die Verwerfung des Einspruchs begehrt werden könne, gerade so, wie nach Art. 303 nur das Begehren der Zurückweisung der Klage als nicht angebracht gestellt werden kann.

Es ist dies für den Fall von Klagänderungen irgend einer Art von Wichtigkeit.

Bei den Verhandlungen (Abg. II 106) berücksichtigte man anfänglich den Fall der Klagänderung und gab, von der Ansicht ausgehend, daß das neue Urtheil nur soweit keinem weiteren Einspruche unterliege, als es das angefochtene Versäumungsurtheil bestätige, dem jetzigen Art. 315 eine entsprechende Fassung. Die Subcommission war jedoch der Meinung, es sei besser, in Uebereinstimmung mit dem Strafprozesse zu verfügen, daß der Richter lediglich das frühere Urtheil zu bestätigen habe (Abg. II 138).

Es ist somit klar, daß Klagänderungen nur bedingt zur Geltung gelangen können, d. h. für den Fall, daß der Einspruchkläger erscheint und contradiktorisch mit ihm verhandelt wird. Ebenso wie in Art. 303 der Hauptkläger, hat es hier der Hauptbeklagte und Einspruchskläger in der Hand, durch sein Nichterscheinen das Eingehen auf den Grund der Sache zu verhindern.

26) Die Ausnahmsbestimmungen des Art. 315 gelten nur für den Einspruchskläger, nicht aber für die Gegenpartei, welche das Versäumungsurtheil erwirkt hat. Es frägt sich nun, wie die Sache sich gestalte, wenn bei Verhandlung über den Einspruch die letztere Partei ausbleibt?

Manche französische Juristen meinen, es seien hier beide Parteien gehört und hätten Anträge genommen, wenn auch zu verschiedenen Zeitpunkten, das Urtheil sei daher contradiktorisch. Die Mehrzahl, worunter Chauveau (quest. 695 bis) ist jedoch anderer Ansicht und macht geltend, 1) daß Anträge, welche nicht gleichzeitig, sondern zu verschiedener Zeit und unter verschiedenen Umständen genommen seien, eine Sache nicht contradictorisch machen könnten, und 2) daß das entgegengesetzte Prinzip sich im Parteiprozesse nicht anwenden lasse, weil dort Ladung der Partei nöthig sei, beim Nichterscheinen aber die Vermuthung Platz greife, es sei die Ladung der Partei gar nicht zugekommen.

Ich würde die letztere Ansicht theilen und daher in Versäumungsfällen dieser Art die allgemeinen Regeln anwenden. Es wäre sicher nicht gerechtfertigt, den Beklagten deßhalb, weil er früher einmal die Zurückweisung der Klage auf Grund von Art. 303 beantragte, beim späteren Nichterscheinen so zu behandeln, als hätte er sich auf die Klage vertheidigt. Ebenso verhält es sich mit dem Kläger den im Einspruchsverfahren vorgebrachten Einreden gegenüber.

Verbindungsurtheil.

Art. 316. — **Ist in der zur Hinterlegung der Anträge oder unmittelbar zur Verhandlung bestimmten Sitzung von mehreren Beklagten nur ein Theil vertreten, so hat, wenn dies von dem Kläger und, im Falle der Kläger mehrere sind, von sämmtlichen Klägern beantragt wird, auch gegen die Erschienenen die Verhandlung vorläufig nicht stattzufinden, sondern ist, nachdem die erschienenen Anwälte ihre Anträge gestellt und hinterlegt haben, eine spätere Sitzung zur Verhandlung festzusetzen.**

Dabei macht es keinen Unterschied, ob die in der Sitzung nicht vertretenen Beklagten keinen Anwalt aufgestellt haben oder die von ihnen aufgestellten Anwälte nicht erschienen sind.

Die Nichterschienenen sind aufzufordern, in der neuerlichen Sitzung zur Verhandlung zu erscheinen beziehungsweise einen Anwalt aufzustellen, der sie in jener Sitzung zu vertreten hat.

Das Gericht bestimmt die Frist, innerhalb welcher diese Aufforderung zugestellt werden muß.

Die vorstehenden Verfügungen sind in der in Art. 281 bestimmten Weise in das Urtheilsbuch einzutragen.

Art. 317. — **Erscheinen in der durch Verbindungsurtheil zur Verhandlung festgesetzten Sitzung abermals nicht alle Beklagten, so wird — und zwar ohne Unterschied, welche Beklagte ausgeblieben sind — auf die mit den Erschienenen gepflogene Verhandlung gegen alle Betheiligten durch das nämliche Urtheil entschieden, wobei die von jenen vorgebrachten Einreden und ihre sonstige Vertheidigung ebenso zu betrachten sind, als wenn auch die Nichterschienenen sie vorgebracht hätten.**

Das Urtheil hat zum Vortheile wie zum Nachtheile der Nichterschienenen die Wirksamkeit eines contradiktorischen.

Die Vorschriften der Abs. 1 und 2 finden auch auf alle späteren Verhandlungen, welche in dem betreffenden Rechtsstreite in der nämlichen Instanz gepflogen werden, Anwendung, ohne daß es einer Wiederholung der in Art. 316 Abs. 3 bezeichneten Aufforderung bedarf. Auch sind, wenn die Verhandlung weiter vertagt oder ein Vorbescheid erlassen wird, desgleichen wenn ein Beweis- oder sonstiges Zwischenverfahren stattfindet, jenen Beklagten, welche keinen Anwalt aufgestellt haben, Zustellungen nicht zu machen.

Bei der nach Art. 316 Abs. 3 den Nichterschienenen zuzustellenden Aufforderung sind dieselben auf die in Abs. 1—3 bezeichneten Folgen des abermaligen Nichterscheinens aufmerksam zu machen.

Art. 318. — **Sind die nicht erschienenen Beklagten bei der nach Lage der Sache zu erlassenden Entscheidung unbetheiligt, so finden die Bestimmungen der Art. 316 und 317 keine Anwendung.**

G. A. d. K. d. A. II S. 96. 101. 102. 137. 269. 270. 451. IV S. 87. 88. 107. 113—115.
K. d. R. II S. 103—105. IV S. 41.

1) Das Verbindungsurtheil (le défaut joint — le jugement de jonction) ist eine Erfindung des Code de procedure. Es soll verhüten, daß über die nemlichen Streitpunkte im nemlichen Rechtsstreite verschiedenartig erkannt werde, und die Idee, auf welcher es beruht, ist ähnlich derjenigen, welche den Bestimmungen der l. 63 Dig. (42—1) und der Ger. O. Cap. XIV § 11 Ziff. 4 zu Grunde liegt, gemäß deren der Betheiligte, welcher unthätig zusieht, wie ein Mitbetheiligter die Sache ausstreitet, durch diesen vertreten erachtet wird. Der Gesetzgeber stellt nemlich für den Fall, als ein Streitgenosse trotz wiederholter Aufforderung ausbleibt, die Vermuthung auf, daß er den erschienenen Streitgenossen seine Vertheidigung überlassen habe.

Ohne Zweifel hat der Code de proc. hier etwas geschaffen, was an sich gut und praktisch ist, allein in der Art und Weise, wie er es einführte, treten erhebliche Gebrechen zu Tage, so daß sich Chauveau quest. 632 veranlaßt findet, zu bemerken: »Les innovations ne sont pas toujours complètes et des lacunes qu'elles offrent naissent de graves et sérieuses difficultés.«

Es wurde in der Praxis als großer Mißstand empfunden, daß förmliches Urtheil erlassen und ausgefertigt, daß ferner die gewöhnlichen Ladungsfristen eingehalten werden mußten, was oft bedeutende Kostenmehrung und Zeitverschwendung zur Folge hatte.

Als ein weiterer Mangel erscheint es, daß das Gesetz zu allgemein verfügt und Fälle trifft, auf welche es seinem Geiste nach nicht paßt. Es wäre nemlich sachgemäß gewesen, die Verbindung nur so weit auszusprechen, als eine causa communis vorliegt, als »eadem ratio vincendi« vorhanden ist; denn einerseits liegt kein Bedürfniß vor, im Interesse der Einheit der Rechtsprechung weiter zu gehen, und anderseits ist die Fiktion unstatthaft, es sei der Nichterschienene vom Erschienenen auch in solchen Punkten vertreten, welche dieser geltend zu machen weder Recht noch Interesse hatte.

Wenn z. B. Hauptschuldner und Bürge zusammen vorgeladen sind und Letzterer nicht erscheint, so rechtfertigt es sich wohl, daß die Entscheidung bezüglich des Bestehens der Hauptschuld auch für den Bürgen gelte; allein daß auch über die Bürgschaftsleistung an sich contradiktorisch entschieden werde, geht doch zu weit. Man sollte denken, bezüglich aller Einwände, welche der Streitgenosse geltend zu machen kein Recht und kein Interesse hatte, müßte das Recht auf dem Wege des Einspruchs noch geltend gemacht werden dürfen. Nichtsdestoweniger bestand der kategorischen Vorschrift des Art. 153 Code de proc. gegenüber nie ein Zweifel, daß im unterstellten Falle das gegen den Bürgen ergehende Urtheil in jeder Richtung contradiktorisch sei. Gleiches ist der Fall, wenn der nichterschienene Miterbe einzuwenden hat, daß er für seine Person auf den Nachlaß verzichtet habe, überhaupt bei allen persönlichen Einwänden.

2) Unsere Prozeßordnung hat von den gerügten Mängeln die beiden ersten völlig beseitigt, indem sie das Verfahren so einrichtete, daß es wenig Zeitaufwand und wenig Kosten verursacht; allein dem Gedanken, daß die Verbindung nur so weit einzutreten habe, als das Interesse gemeinschaftlich sei, wurde keine Rechnung getragen, vielmehr einfach die allgemeine Fassung des Art. 153 Code de proc. beibehalten.

a) Fälle der Verbindung.

3) Die Verbindung ist nach Art. 316 auszusprechen, wenn in derjenigen Sitzung, in welcher die Anträge genommen werden, also die Sache contradiktorisch wird, von mehreren Beklagten ein Theil erscheint, ein Theil aber nicht erscheint und sämmtliche Kläger es beantragen.

Während der französische Prozeß den Richter verpflichtet, überall, wo Grund zum Erlasse eines Verbindungsurtheils vorliegt, dieses von Amtswegen zu sprechen, und auch der Entwurf (Art. 271) dies bestimmte, verlangt die Prozeßordnung, ins entgegengesetzte Extrem übergehend, es müßten sämmtliche Kläger Antrag stellen.

Ursprünglich erlaubte man es wenigstens dem Richter, auch von Amtswegen zu verfügen (Abg. II 149), und gerade mit Rücksicht hierauf fand man es unbedenklich, den Antrag sämmtlicher Kläger zu verlangen (Abg. II 137). Später (R. R. II 104) strich man die betreffende Bestimmung und zwar aus Gründen, welche durch die spätere Aenderung der Fassung des Art. 317 Abs. 3 (Abg. IV 114) völlig beseitigt worden sind; nichtsdestoweniger blieb jene Streichung und blieb die Beschränkung auf den Antrag sämmtlicher Kläger.

Meiner Meinung nach ist sehr zu wünschen, daß fragliche Bestimmung geblieben wäre, denn das Verbindungsurtheil ist nicht bloß eingeführt im Interesse der Kläger, sondern auch im Interesse der Beklagten, überhaupt im Interesse geordneter Rechtspflege, und die Vereinfachung des Verfahrens mußte alle früher (Abg. II 101 [Umbsch.]) erhobenen Bedenken beseitigen. — Man denke sich folgenden Fall: A und B werden als Miterben wegen einer Schuld des Nachlasses belangt. A erscheint und weist sofort nach, daß die Schuld gar nie bestanden habe oder daß sie getilgt worden sei; B aber erscheint nicht. Begehrt nun der Kläger gegen B Versäumungsurtheil, so ist der Richter gezwungen, die Behauptungen des Klägers diesem Beklagten gegenüber als wahr anzunehmen, obgleich ihm der Beweis vor Augen liegt, daß sie unwahr seien! Im französischen Prozesse hilft man sich in dergleichen Fällen, bei Sachen, wo défaut joint nicht statthaft ist, z. B. bei Handelssachen, mit der gesetzlichen Bestimmung, daß der Richter auch in Versäumungsfällen prüfen dürfe, ob der Anspruch »juste et bien verifiée« sei. Wenn nöthig, vertagt man den Spruch des défaut, bis gegen den Mitbeklagten contradiktorische Endentscheidung ergehen kann. Die Fiktion des Geständnisses läßt aber diesen Ausweg nicht mehr zu, und zeigt sich also auch hier wieder, wie vorsichtig der Gesetzgeber mit Fiktionen sein soll.

4) Es ist selbstverständlich und in der Natur des Verbindungsurtheils begründet, daß die That-

sache gleichzeitiger Klagerhebung gegen mehrere Beklagte nicht genüge, vielmehr eine gemeinschaftliche Betheiligung vorliegen, Grund zu einer Streitgenossenschaft gegeben sein müsse. Die zufällige Vereinigung verschiedenartiger Ansprüche gegen verschiedene Personen in der nemlichen Klage kann daher nicht Anlaß zu einem Verbindungsurtheile geben.

Sogar im Falle, wo gemeinschaftliche Betheiligung am Streitgegenstande vorliegt, kann nach Art. 318 ein Verbindungsurtheil nicht begehrt werden, wenn nach Lage der Sache die Nichterschienenen an der zu erlassenden Entscheidung nicht betheiligt sind.

Der Gesetzgeber hatte bei dieser letzteren Bestimmung Fälle im Auge, wo der erscheinende Beklagte Vorfragen zur Entscheidung bringt, welche ihn allein angehen, z. B. die Einrede der Nichtigkeit seiner Ladung, des Verzichts auf die Erbschaft 2c. Außer Zweifel erscheint deren Anwendung, wenn die betreffende Vorfrage Gegenstand gesonderter Aburtheilung wird, jedoch wird sie nach dem Wortlaute des Art. 318 auch dann nicht ausgeschlossen sein, wenn zugleich die Einlassung in der Hauptsache stattgefunden hat, das Gericht jedoch in der Lage ist, auf Grund der Entscheidung über die Vorfrage die Klage sofort abzuweisen.

Bei gesonderter Aburtheilung von Vorfragen bleibt dem Kläger immerhin das Recht, später, wenn es zur Einlassung in die Hauptsache kommt, die Verbindung noch zu erwirken.

5) Offenbar verlangt das Gesetz nicht, daß die Interessen der Erschienenen und der Nichterschienenen in jeder Beziehung identisch sein müßten, vielmehr genügt es, wenn ein gemeinschaftliches Interesse auch nur in gewisser Richtung besteht.

Ein auffälliges Beispiel letzterer Art bietet das Arrestverfahren.

Nach Art. 980 und 981 sollen die Klagen gegen den Arrestbeklagten und gegen den Drittschuldner vereinigt werden und zwar deßhalb, weil zu erkennen ist, ob der Drittschuldner zur Entlastung des Arrestbeklagten Zahlung leisten dürfe und müsse, bei diesem Ausspruche aber beide Parteien betheiligt sind. Die Gemeinschaftlichkeit des Interesse in dieser Richtung erschien nun der französischen Jurisprudenz genügender Grund, ein Verbindungsurtheil für nöthig zu erklären, obgleich nicht zu verkennen ist, daß in anderen Beziehungen die Interessen wesentlich auseinandergehen. Vgl. Chauv. sur C. quest. 621 quinties No. 3.

Es wirft sich hier die Frage auf, ob nicht in Fällen, wo das Interesse nur theilweise gemeinschaftlich ist, die Verbindung gleichfalls nur theilweise zu verfügen sei; und zwar ist der Fall zu unterscheiden, wo das Interesse bezüglich ganzer Streitpunkte wegfällt, und derjenige, wo nur bezüglich einzelner den nemlichen Streitpunkt betreffender Fragen gesondertes Interesse besteht.

Der erstere Fall ist z. B. gegeben, wenn zwei verschiedene Forderungen eingeklagt werden, von denen die eine gemeinschaftlich ist, die andere aber ausschließlich gegen den Nichterschienenen geltend gemacht wird. Ich möchte annehmen, daß der Kläger hier Verbindungsurtheil wegen der ersteren und Versäumungsurtheil wegen der letzteren Forderung begehren dürfe, obgleich, wie nicht zu verkennen, eine Anomalie darin liegt, daß theilweise contradiktorisch, theilweise contumaziell entschieden werde. Das Verbindungsurtheil ist eben an und für sich eine Anomalie.

Was den zweiten Fall anbelangt, siehe unten Nr. 17.

6) Der französische Prozeß läßt das Verbindungsurtheil nur beim Nichterscheinen der Partei zu, unsere Prozeßordnung hat es aber auch auf das Nichterscheinen des Anwaltes ausgedehnt. In Folge hievon kann sich der Fall eines Verbindungsurtheiles auch in späteren Stadien des Verfahrens, nach Aburtheilung von Vorfragen, nach Beweiserhebungen 2c. ergeben, und consequent wäre es eigentlich gewesen, nunmehr auch den Fall beizuziehen, wo von mehreren Klägern ein Theil erscheint, ein anderer nicht.

Das Gesetz beschränkt jedoch die Verbindung ausdrücklich auf die Beklagten.

7) Es hat dabei solche Personen im Auge, welche dem nemlichen Kläger gegenüber als Beklagte erscheinen; die Verbindung findet daher nicht statt zwischen Beklagten und beigeladenen Streitgenossen des Klägers (Abg. II 101), und ebensowenig zwischen Hauptbeklagten und Gewährschaftsbeklagten (Abg. II 102), mögen sie auch dem Hauptkläger gegenüber gleiches Interesse haben.

Ob die Beklagten zu gleicher Zeit oder gar in der nemlichen Ladung vorgeladen seien, ist ohne Belang; weder Wortlaut noch Zweck des Gesetzes bedingen einen Unterschied.

b) Verfahren.

8) Das Verfahren wird von unserer Prozeßordnung in höchst zweckmäßiger Weise geregelt.

Dieselbe stellt den Ausspruch der Verbindung einer Vertagung gleich, so daß der Eintrag des Urtheils nach Maßgabe von Art. 281 erfolgt, und zu demselben weder Entscheidungsgründe noch Sachverhalt gefertigt werden (Abg. IV 114).

Die Verbindung kann erst verfügt werden, nachdem die erschienenen Anwälte ihre Anträge genommen und hinterlegt haben, wobei der klägerische Antrag das Begehren um Ausspruch der Verbindung zu enthalten hat.

Das Gericht beurkundet die Hinterlegung der Anträge, sowie das Nichterscheinen, und fügt dann einfach bei, daß es auf Antrag sämmtlicher Kläger die Verbindung der Sachen der Beklagten verfüge und eine Sitzung zur Verhandlung festsetze, in welche die Nichterschienenen zu laden seien.

Zugleich bestimmt es die Frist, innerhalb welcher die neue Aufforderung zum Erscheinen zuzustellen ist, und hiermit auch für den Fall wo die Partei selbst aufzufordern ist, die neue Erscheinungsfrist, in welcher Beziehung ihm die gleiche Freiheit gegeben ist, wie im abgekürzten Verfahren (Art. 259), so daß gesagt werden kann, das Gesetz präsumire hier die Dringlichkeit.

9) Es war bis jetzt herkömmlich, den Nichterschienenen in die durch sein Nichterscheinen veranlaßten Kosten zu verurtheilen; allein da die Verbindung bloß als Vertagung behandelt wird und nur die Kosten einer einfachen Aufforderung erwachsen, da die Verbindung auch nur auf Wunsch des Klägers erfolgt, möchte kein Anlaß mehr bestehen, wegen der Kosten besondere Verfügung zu treffen, wenigstens nicht im Verbindungs-Urtheile.

10) Nach französischem Prozesse muß das in gewöhnlicher Form gefertigte, durch Einrücken der Anträge und des Sachverhalts oft sehr umfangreiche Urtheil ausgefertigt und allen Nichterschienenen mit Ladung in der gewöhnlichen Frist zugestellt werden; unsere Prozeßordnung jedoch verlangt weder Ausfertigung noch Zustellung, sondern begnügt sich mit der Vorschrift, daß man die Nichterschienenen auffordere, in der zur Verhandlung festgesetzten Sitzung zu erscheinen, wobei sie selbstverständlich zugleich von der Verfügung des Gerichts in Kenntniß zu setzen sind.

Vielleicht wäre es sachgemäß gewesen, für den Fall des Nichterscheinens der Partei, eine abschriftliche Zustellung oder eine Wiederholung der früheren Ladung anzuordnen, da ja im Zweifel anzunehmen ist, es habe jene Ladung sie nicht erreicht; jedenfalls aber wird es nöthig sein, auf die frühere Ladung Bezug zu nehmen und sie bestimmt zu bezeichnen, um jeden Zweifel bezüglich der Identität des Rechtsstreites zu beseitigen.

In Art. 317 Abs. 4 ist vorgeschrieben, daß mit der Aufforderung eine Hinweisung auf die durch Art. 317 Abs. 1—3 bestimmten Folgen des abermaligen Nichterscheinens zu verbinden sei. Ergeht die Aufforderung an die Partei selbst, so dürfte es dem Willen des Gesetzes nicht genügen, einfach auf Art. 317 zu verweisen, vielmehr wird es nöthig sein, die verschiedenen Folgen namhaft zu machen, was am sichersten durch abschriftliche Mittheilung der Bestimmungen des Art. 317 Abs. 1—3 geschieht.

11) Auch für Klagänderungen im Sinne der Art. 180 und 182 kann die Verbindung erwirkt werden; jedoch würde es nicht etwa genügen, mit der Aufforderung zum Erscheinen in der zur Verhandlung anberaumten Sitzung einen Klagsnachtrag zu verbinden, denn diese erste Ladung könnte nach Art. 299 und 302 nur zu einem Versäumungsurtheile führen; vielmehr müßte die Verbindung in derjenigen Sitzung, welche zur Stellung der Anträge bezüglich des Klagsnachtrages bestimmt ist, begehrt und erwirkt werden.

12) Wurde eine Verbindung verfügt, obgleich sie bei obwaltenden Umständen unstatthaft war, und ist in Folge dessen zum Nachtheile des Nichterschienenen erkannt worden, so steht diesem ohne Zweifel das Recht zu, diese Entscheidung anzufechten, und zwar mittelst Einspruchs da er befugt ist, die Nichtigkeit der Verbindung geltend zu machen. Das Verbindungsurtheil für sich kann, da es nicht zugestellt wird, keine Rechtskraft erlangen.

c) Wirkung der Verbindung.

13) Das Verbindungsurtheil hat die ganz eigenthümliche Wirkung, daß für alle Beklagten, also nicht bloß für diejenigen, welche durch ihr Nichterscheinen Anlaß zur Verbindung gegeben haben, und für die ganze Dauer der Instanz, die Vertretung der Nichterscheinenden durch die Erscheinenden eintritt, und so lange noch irgend Einer der Beklagten erscheint, ein Versäumungsurtheil nicht möglich ist.

Wenn daher die ursprünglich Nichterschienenen später erscheinen, hingegen die ursprünglich Erschienenen später ausbleiben, so kehrt sich das Verhältniß um und Erstere vertreten die Letzteren. Ebenso wird dadurch, daß sämmtliche Beklagte in der zur Verhandlung anberaumten Sitzung erscheinen, die Wirkung des Verbindungsurtheiles nicht völlig beseitigt; denn wenn Einer derselben in einem späteren Stadium, z. B. nach der Beweiserhebung, ausbleibt, so tritt sie wieder ein.

14) Die Verbindung wirkt immer für den Rechtsstreit im Ganzen, sollten auch in der Sitzung, in welcher sie verfügt wurde, die Anträge nur bezüglich einer Vorfrage genommen worden sein. Man darf nicht etwa glauben, daß in letz-

terem Falle die Verbindung nur bis zur Erledigung der betreffenden Anträge gelte; denn diese Anträge werden ja dem Nichterschienenen bei der Aufforderung gar nicht mitgetheilt.

Sie wirkt übrigens selbstverständlich nur vom Augenblicke des Ausspruchs an, und für dasjenige, was bei damaligem Stande der Sache Gegenstand des Streites gewesen ist. Spätere Aenderungen oder Zusätze zur Klage fallen nicht ins Bereich ihrer Wirkung, ebensowenig als Begehren, welche dem Nichterschienenen gegenüber bereits aufgegeben waren.

15) Die natürliche Folge der Fiktion der Vertretung ist, daß alles, was die Erschienenen zur Bestreitung des Klaggrundes oder an Einreden vorbringen, auch für die Nichterschienenen gilt. Selbstverständlich sind Einwände auszunehmen, welche bloß die Person betreffen, wie z. B. wenn der erscheinende Miterbe behauptet, daß er verzichtet habe, daß ihm persönlich die Schuld erlassen worden sei.

Es kann vorkommen, daß von mehreren erschienenen Beklagten ein jeder seinen besonderen Weg der Vertheidigung einschlägt, daß der Eine zugesteht, was der Andere in Abrede stellt, der Eine Einreden aufrecht erhält, welche der Andere aufgibt, und es frägt sich nun: „Welcher dieser Beklagten ist als Vertreter der Nichterschienenen zu betrachten?" Offenbar derjenige, dessen Vertheidigung diesen am günstigsten ist.

16) Die dem Ausspruche des Verbindungsurtheils nachgängig in der nemlichen Instanz ergehenden Urtheile sind sämmtlich contradiktorisch, so lange Einer der Beklagten erscheint, und zwar ohne daß an die Nichterschienenen, wenn sie keinen Anwalt haben, irgend eine weitere Aufforderung zu richten wäre.

Wie ist es nun aber, wenn alle Beklagte ausbleiben, oder wenn der Kläger nicht erscheint?

Im Wortlaute des Art. 317 Abs. 2 ist die Lösung dieser Fragen nicht zu suchen, da derselbe nur von demjenigen Urtheile spricht, welches in der nächsten zur Verhandlung anberaumten Sitzung ergeht, in dieser Sitzung aber, da durch Hinterlegung der Anträge die Sache contradiktorisch wird, von einem Versäumungsurtheil gegen früher Erschienene nicht die Rede sein kann. Die unterstellten Fälle können vielmehr nur bei solchen Verhandlungen eintreten, welche nach Aburtheilung einer Vorfrage oder nach einer Beweiserhebung erfolgen.

Man muß daher nach dem Geiste des Gesetzes fragen.

Das Gesetz will verhüten, daß dem Einen gegenüber contradiktorisch, dem Anderen gegenüber contumaziell entschieden werde; ist aber das Urtheil im Ganzen ein Versäumungsurtheil, wie in den beiden unterstellten Fällen, so liegt kein Grund vor, von der Regel abzugehen. Es läßt sich die Fiktion einer Vertretung unmöglich aufrecht erhalten, wenn Niemand erscheint, wie dies namentlich sehr grell in die Augen fällt, wenn man sich den Fall vergegenwärtigt, es seien nach Aburtheilung einer Vorfrage erst Anträge in der Hauptsache zu nehmen und nun sämmtliche Beklagte nicht erschienen!

Ich glaubte diesen Punkt um so mehr hervorheben zu müssen, da die französische Jurisprudenz auf Grund der kategorischen Verfügung des Art. 153 Code de pr. eine abweichende Ansicht hat. Chauveau sur C. quest. 632.

17) Die nach Ausspruch der Verbindung in derselben Instanz ergehenden Urtheile sind nicht bloß contradiktorisch für diejenigen Fragen, in welchen Gemeinschaftlichkeit des Interesse (eadem ratio vincendi) besteht, sondern im Ganzen.

Es ist dies, wie bereits oben Nr. 1 bemerkt, eine Anomalie, die sich jedoch nicht beseitigen läßt, weil eine Unterscheidung durch die allgemeine Fassung des Gesetzes und durch die Herleitung der fraglichen Bestimmung aus dem französischen Rechte ausgeschlossen ist. Hätte der Gesetzgeber eine Beschränkung einführen wollen, so hätte er in Art. 317 Abs. 2 sagen müssen: „soweit Gemeinschaftlichkeit des Interesse besteht," oder: „soweit es sich um Vertheidigungsbehelfe handelt, welche der Erscheinende Recht oder Interesse gehabt hätte vorzubringen."

Auch aus Art. 318 läßt sich eine derartige Beschränkung nicht folgern. Schon der Wortlaut würde nicht passen, da jener Artikel nur von Fällen spricht, wo der Erschienene unbetheiligt ist. Uebrigens geht aus der ursprünglichen Fassung dieser Verfügung (Entwurf Art. 271 Abs. 4 und Abg. II 96), sowie den Worten, mit welchen der k. Ministerial-Commissär sie einführte (Abg. II 101) hervor, daß man nur die besonderen Fälle im Auge hatte, wo bei Vorfragen die Nichterschienenen unbetheiligt seien, Fälle, für welche auch die französische Jurisprudenz eine Ausnahme zuließ (Schlink Comm. § 407 Nr. 10), daß man jedoch nicht entfernt daran dachte, zu verfügen, daß ein Urtheil bezüglich des nemlichen Streitpunktes theils contradiktorisch, theils contumaziell sein könne, so richtig es auch vielleicht gewesen wäre, dies hier zu thun. Vgl. oben Nr. 5.

IX. Hauptstück.

Beweis.

Einleitung.

1) Ist der Richter durch die Verhandlung darüber aufgeklärt, welche Thatsachen gegenseitig behauptet werden und was davon für seine Entscheidung von Belang sei, so tritt die Frage an ihn heran, ob diese Thatsachen auch bewiesen seien, oder ob sie noch des Beweises bedürfen.

Die Beweise werden im Civilprozesse nicht von Amtswegen erhoben, sondern es ist Aufgabe jeder Partei, dem Richter diejenigen Thatsachen zu erweisen, bezüglich welcher ihr die Beweislast obliegt, und was sie nicht zu erweisen vermag, das besteht nicht.

2) Der Beweis setzt Ueberzeugung voraus, bei manchen Beweismitteln (Urkunden, Eid) allerdings nur eine solche, welche formell, auf juridischem Wege sich bildet; das Gesetz kennt aber auch bloße Bescheinigungen, bei welchen Wahrscheinlichkeit genügt. (S. Entw. Art. 282. Abg. II 157 u. 168).

Die Prozeßordnung spricht an vielen Stellen von bloßen Bescheinigungen (Art. 44, 45, 119, 125, 188, 213, 347, 608), erklärt sich jedoch nicht darüber, in welcher Weise dieselben zu erbringen seien, und was als Bescheinigungsmittel zu gelten habe. Sie hat sogar den Art. 282 Abs. 3 des Entwurfs, welcher den Begriff festzustellen strebte und von Beweisen und Behelfen sprach, die nach dem Ermessen des Richters Wahrscheinlichkeit begründen, als unnöthig beseitigt.

Aus diesem Stillschweigen des Gesetzes wird zu folgern sein, daß es ganz dem Richter überlassen bleiben solle, zu ermessen, ob die vorgebrachten Beweisbehelfe geeignet seien, den nach Lage der Sache erforderlichen Grad von Wahrscheinlichkeit zu begründen.

Offenbar ist dies auch das Richtige. Es wäre ein großer Mißgriff gewesen, hier beengende Vorschriften zu geben, und in den unterstellten Fällen, welche das Gesetz selbst für unwichtig ansieht, oder bei welchen es nur eine vorsorgliche Verfügung im Auge hat, dem Richter nicht zuzutrauen, daß er richtig zu beurtheilen wisse, ob Wahrscheinlichkeit vorliege oder nicht. Auch im früheren Verfahren war es annähernd so, und wurden z. B. auch unbeeidigte Zeugen, Urkunden, welche nicht anerkannt waren, und Vermuthungen jeder Art als Mittel zur Bescheinigung zugelassen. Seuff. Comm. Bd. III S. 17 Note 3.

3) Es dürfte ferner als dem Geiste des Gesetzes entsprechend zu erachten sein, daß der Richter bezüglich der Beweiserhebung nicht unbedingt an die Vorschriften, welche für die eigentliche Beweisführung gegeben sind, gebunden sei.

Offenbar setzt die Prozeßordnung in den Fällen, wo sie Bescheinigung verlangt, zunächst nicht voraus, daß ein Beweisurtheil ergehe und sodann nach den für das Beweisverfahren geltenden Regeln verfahren werde. Ausnahmsweise mag sich wohl Anlaß hiezu ergeben, allein die Regel, wie sie dem Gesetzgeber vor Augen schwebte, wird sein, daß urkundliche Bescheinigungen vorgelegt werden.

Oeffentliche und Privaturkunden, gegen welche kein besonderer Verdacht besteht, sowie amtliche Zeugnisse, sind geeignete Bescheinigungsmittel; aber auch Zeugnisse und Gutachten von Privatpersonen (z. B. Aerzten, Bauverständigen) können dazu dienen, falls das Gericht keine Veranlassung hat, an der Aechtheit der Erklärung und an der Zuverlässigkeit der Erklärenden zu zweifeln.

Beweispflicht.

Art. 319. — **Welche Thatsachen zur Begründung eines Rechtsanspruchs und der dagegen erhobenen Vertheidigung gehören und welche Beweislast hienach die Parteien trifft, ist nach den bürgerlichen Gesetzen zu beurtheilen.** G. A. d. K. d. A. II S. 157. 324. 325. — K. d. R. II S. 105.

1) Die Frage, wen die Beweislast treffe, entscheidet sich nach den Grundsätzen des Civilrechts.

Wenn sie auch immerhin noch eine sehr wichtige ist, so hat sie doch durch den Grundsatz, daß das Beweisinterlokut nicht binde, einen großen Theil ihrer früheren Bedeutung verloren. Der Richter wird sich zwar auch jetzt noch bei jeder Beweisauflage klar machen müssen, auf welcher Seite die Beweislast sei, allein sollte er sich auch ganz oder theilweise irren, so brächte dies der Sache selbst keinen besonderen Nachtheil, denn die Folge wäre bloß, daß der auferlegte Hauptbeweis am Ende als Gegenbeweis, und der Gegenbeweis als Hauptbeweis zu gelten hätte. Allerdings muß beim Endurtheile oder bei einer Eidesauflage die Frage der Beweislast falls nöthig endgiltig entschieden werden, allein in weitaus den meisten Fällen wird jene Frage durch die Beweiserhebung gegenstandslos.

2) Nach den Grundsätzen des Civilrechts hat

der Kläger (von einzelnen Ausnahmen abgesehen) Klaggrund und Repliken, der Beklagte aber Einreden und Dupliken zu erweisen. Diese Sätze sind sehr einfach, fördern aber nicht viel weiter, da sie zur weiteren Frage führen, was zum Klaggrunde, was zu den Einreden rc. gehöre.

Als Grundsatz läßt sich aufstellen, daß der Kläger alle diejenigen Thatsachen zu erweisen habe, welche zunächst und wesentlich nöthig sind, um das in Frage stehende Klagrecht zu erzeugen; welches aber diese Thatsachen seien, ist aus der besonderen Natur eines jeden Rechtsverhältnisses zu beurtheilen.

Hält nun der Beklagte entgegen, daß wegen besonderer thatsächlicher Verhältnisse das fragliche Recht dennoch nicht, oder wenigstens nicht in der Art, wie behauptet, zur Entstehung gelangt sei, so macht er einen Ausnahmsfall geltend, bewegt sich also auf dem Gebiete der Einrede und ist beweispflichtig. So braucht derjenige, welcher seine Klage auf ein Rechtsgeschäft stützt, bloß zu beweisen, daß dieses giltig verabredet worden sei, nicht aber auch, daß der Gegner mit Zurechnungsfähigkeit gehandelt, daß derselbe nicht durch Irrthum, List oder Zwang dazu verleitet worden sei; vielmehr ist es Sache des Gegners, welcher das Vorhandensein dieser besonderen Mängel behauptet, sie auch nachzuweisen. Ebenso verhält es sich, wenn geltend gemacht wird, es sei eine Verpflichtung nur unter einer Bedingung oder mit einer Fristbestimmung eingegangen worden; denn Bedingungslosigkeit und sofortige Fälligkeit sind im Zweifel zu vermuthen. Es erleidet z. B. keinen Zweifel, daß auf Grund eines Schuldscheines geklagt werden kann, auch wenn nicht ausdrücklich darin steht, die Schuld sei unbedingt und müsse auf erstes Begehren gezahlt werden, und daß ferner, falls der Beklagte einwendet, es sei eine Bedingung oder Frist verabredet worden, von welcher im Schuldscheine nichts gesagt ist, er selbst, nicht aber der Kläger, beweispflichtig ist.

Hält der Beklagte entgegen, es sei das entstandene Recht durch spätere Thatsachen wieder aufgehoben oder geändert worden, so ist es noch viel klarer, daß ihm der Beweis obliege.

3) Was von der Einrede gegenüber dem Klaggrunde gilt, gilt ebenso von der Replik gegenüber der Einrede rc.

Näheres Eingehen auf die einzelnen sich bezüglich der Beweislast darbietenden Fragen würde zu weit führen. Ich verweise auf Seuff. Comm. Bd. III S. 51 ff. und Bayer Civilpr. § 227.

Art. 320. — Thatsachen, welche gemein-, gerichts- oder ortskundig sind, bedürfen keines Beweises.

Art. 321. — Partikularrechte, welche nicht gemeinkundig sind, bedürfen des Beweises, gleichviel ob sie auf Gesetzen und Statuten oder auf Gewohnheit und Herkommen beruhen. Doch soll das Gericht auch von Amtswegen die ihm zu Gebote stehenden Mittel anwenden, um sich von nicht gemeinkundigen Partikularrechten Kenntniß zu verschaffen.

Ueber ausländische Gesetze und Statuten kann das Gericht Beweis verlangen, wenn sie ihm nicht zuverlässig bekannt sind.

G. A. d. K. d. A. II S. 157. 160. 324. 325. IV S. 88. — K. d. R. II S. 105. IV S. 41.

1) In der Regel sind alle strittigen Thatsachen zu beweisen, allein auch nur Thatsachen, nicht aber das Recht, welches der Richter kennen oder von Amtswegen erforschen muß. Von dieser Regel enthalten vorstehende beide Artikel Ausnahmen.

a) Partikularrechte.

2) Die Verfügung, daß Partikularrechte, welche nicht gemeinkundig sind, des Beweises bedürfen, ist eine Wiederholung der Bestimmung in Ger.-Ord. Cap. IX § 3 Ziff. 2, und der Zusatz: „daß die Gerichte nichtsdestoweniger solche Rechte auch von Amtswegen erforschen sollen,“ steht ebenso im Einklange mit der bestehenden Jurisprudenz. Vgl. Seuff. Comm. Bd. III S. 20—23.

Seuffert sagt an bezeichneter Stelle: der Richter solle aus den Generalakten des Gerichts, durch Correspondenz mit höheren Behörden, mit früheren Beamten, mit dem Landesarchive oder dem historischen Vereine der Provinz, ferner durch Vernehmung kundiger Personen und durch Nachforschung in älteren Prozeßakten erforschen, ob das behauptete Partikularrecht gemeinkundig sei, und erst wenn diese Nachforschung ohne Erfolg bleibe, habe er Beweis aufzulegen.

Wenn auch, was das Eingreifen von Amtswegen anbelangt, die Stellung der Gerichte im neuen Prozesse eine wesentlich andere geworden ist, indem dieselben sich in der Regel passiv verhalten und sich darauf beschränken, zu entscheiden oder anzuordnen, es den Parteien überlassend, die Anordnungen zu vollziehen, indem sie insbesondere mit amtlichen Correspondenzen sich nicht mehr befassen, so möchte ich doch annehmen, daß hier nach dem Willen des Gesetzgebers eine Ausnahme eintrete und den Gerichten eine wenn auch nicht gleiche doch ähnliche Rolle zugedacht sei, wie die seitherige. Etwaige Correspondenzen würden jedoch nicht vom Gerichte selbst, sondern vom Gerichtsvorstande zu führen sein.

3) Auch wenn das Gericht Beweis auferlegt hat, erscheint die Beweisführung der Partei immerhin nur als Beihilfe zu der von Amtswegen zu pflegenden Nachforschung. Seuff. a. a. O. S. 21.

Diese Nachforschungen des Gerichts erfolgen nicht ausschließlich für den besonderen Rechtsfall, sondern im Interesse der Rechtspflege überhaupt, um ein Recht, das verborgen ist, gemeinkundig zu machen und in zukünftigen Fällen anwenden zu können.

4) Das Gesetz macht keinen Unterschied, ob das zu ermittelnde Partikularrecht auf Gesetz und Statuten oder Gewohnheit und Herkommen beruhe.

Bei Gesetzen wird wohl die Gemeinkundigkeit nie mangeln, bei Statuten höchst selten; besondere Bedeutung hat daher nur das Gewohnheitsrecht. Zu diesem werden auch Handelsgebräuche, in so weit sie Rechtsquelle sein können (Art. 1 des H.G.B.), zu rechnen sein.

Was Gewohnheit und Herkommen betrifft, s. Bemerk. zu Art. 264 Nr. 3.

5) Gemeinkundig ist ein Recht nur dann, wenn es unter denjenigen Personen, welche sich mit der Rechtspflege befassen, allgemein bekannt ist. Daß es unter denjenigen Personen, bei welchen es zur Anwendung kommt, z. B. bei Kaufleuten, gemeinkundig sei, erscheint nicht maßgebend.

Ein Recht, welches gemeinkundig im Gebiete ist, für welches es gilt, ist gemeinkundig für das ganze Reich und soll nicht Gegenstand einer Beweisauflage, sondern amtlicher Ermittlung sein.

b) Ausländisches Recht.

6) Ueber ausländische Gesetze und Statuten kann der Richter Beweis verlangen, wenn sie ihm nicht zuverlässig bekannt sind. Die Beweise, welche hier von den Parteien erbracht werden können, sind, außer veröffentlichten Gesetzbüchern, Lehrbüchern rc., die amtlichen Erklärungen von Gerichten oder sonstigen Justizbehörden, zeugschaftliche Vernehmung angesehener Rechtsgelehrten rc.

Selbstverständlich darf und soll auch hier, wie überhaupt überall, wo es sich um Ergründung des Rechts handelt, der Richter von Amtswegen nachforschen.

c) Notorietät von Thatsachen.

7) Auch reine Thatsachen bedürfen keines Beweises, wenn sie gemein-, gerichts- oder ortskundig sind.

Von der Gerichtskundigkeit sprach der Entwurf (Art. 285) nicht, und sie wurde mit der Bemerkung beigefügt, es sei die Bedeutung als allgemein verständlich vorauszusetzen. Referat zu Art. 285 (v. Neumayr). Hieraus möchte zu folgern sein, daß der Begriff, welchen man bisher nach G.O. Cap. XII § 5 damit verband, zu Grunde zu legen sei, soweit nicht etwa die Natur des neuen Verfahrens entgegensteht.

8) Gerichtskundig ist das, was ein Gericht aus den früheren gerichtlichen Verhandlungen oder aus den in gerichtlichem Verwahr befindlichen Akten weiß oder erfahren kann.

Ein Adhibiren fremder Akten möchte der Natur des neuen Verfahrens widerstreben, da dieses Gerichtsakten nicht kennt und den Gerichten eine vorwiegend passive Rolle zuweist, aus welcher sie der Regel nach nicht heraustretten sollen. Namentlich kennt das neue Verfahren keine Correspondenz der Gerichte mit anderen Gerichten und Behörden, und selbst in Fällen, wo sie in Urtheilen oder Beschlüssen bezügliche Ansuchen stellen, ist es Sache der Parteien, den Volzug zu veranlassen. Vgl. Bemerk. zu Art. 55 Nr. 4. Es ist daher anzunehmen, daß man nicht daran dachte, unter den Begriff der Gerichtskundigkeit auch dasjenige zu bringen, was der Richter erst in Folge von Erhebungen bei anderen Behörden erfahren könnte. Vgl. Abg. II 156 u. 157 (zu Art. 282).

Ein Fall, wo in der Pfalz häufig von der Gerichtskundigkeit Vortheil gezogen wurde, ist der, wo bezüglich des den Gegenstand des Civilrechtsstreites bildenden Vorfalles ein Strafverfahren stattgefunden hatte. Man nahm keinen Anstand, bei Aburtheilung der Civilsache die Untersuchungsakten zu benützen, soweit es die Grundsätze des Civilprozesses erlauben, welche z. B. die Benützung von Zeugenverhören ausschließen. Waren die Strafakten nicht zur Hand, so pflegte der Staatsanwalt dafür zu sorgen, daß sie beigeschafft wurden.

9) Wie sich von selbst versteht, ist eine Thatsache nicht bloß deßhalb, weil sie in einem früheren Prozesse als wahr galt, auch in einem späteren als erwiesen zu betrachten; es wird vielmehr nur die Thatsache, daß etwas vor dem Richter vorgegangen, etwas von ihm beobachtet oder durch ihn entschieden worden sei, festgestellt, die Frage aber, ob und wie weit hieraus Folgerungen für den anhängigen Rechtsstreit zu ziehen seien, bleibt vollkommen frei.

10) Gemein- und ortskundig (notorisch) ist, was, sei es im ganzen Lande, sei es am Sitze des Gerichts, so allgemein bekannt ist, daß es in Abrede zu stellen Chikane wäre. Seuff. Comm. Bd. III S. 342. Was Jedermann weiß, darf und muß auch der Richter wissen, jedoch wird es nöthig sein, dieser Wissenschaft in den Gründen des Urtheils bestimmten Ausdruck zu geben, da Thatsachen für das Gericht erster Instanz

notorisch sein können, ohne es auch für das höhere Gericht zu sein.

Was der Richter nur persönlich und als Privatperson weiß, darf er bei der Urtheilsfällung nicht berücksichtigen; er kann nicht zugleich Zeuge und Richter sein.

11) Sehr zu unterscheiden von der Notorietät ist der „gemeine Ruf", d. h. die übereinstimmende Meinung, welche im Publikum wegen eines Sachverhaltes besteht, insofern er kein Wissen, sondern ein bloßes Meinen voraussetzt. G. O. Cap. XII § 6. Die Prozeßordnung kennt ihn als besondere Beweisart nicht.

12) Schließlich ist hervorzuheben, daß die Art. 320 und 321, ebenso wie Art. 319 laut Art. 66 des Einf.-Ges. in der Pfalz nicht gelten. Es lag eigentlich kein Anlaß vor, sie auszuschließen, da in der Pfalz ziemlich die gleichen Grundsätze bestehen und selbst die Bestimmungen bezüglich der Partikularrechte nicht ganz gegenstandslos erscheinen, da die Anwendung von Rechten des diesseitigen Bayerns in Frage kommen kann.

Art. 322. — **Der Beweis der Thatsache, auf welche es unmittelbar ankommt, wird durch den Beweis einer andern ersetzt, wenn die erwiesene Thatsache mit der zu erweisenden in solcher Verbindung steht, daß von jener auf diese mit Nothwendigkeit geschlossen werden muß, oder wenn die eine Thatsache die Voraussetzung enthält, unter welcher die andere nach gesetzlicher Bestimmung als wahr anzunehmen ist.**

Wahrscheinlichkeitsgründe, welchen das Gesetz eine solche Wirkung nicht beilegt (gemeine Vermuthungen), können zwar, wenn die Thatsachen, worauf sie beruhen, vollständig erwiesen sind, nach richterlichem Ermessen als Beweisbehelfe dienen, niemals aber den Beweis völlig ersetzen, es sei denn, daß es sich um die Beschaffenheit eines innern Willensakts handelt, worüber eine unmittelbare Beweisführung nicht geschehen kann, oder daß mehrere solche Vermuthungen zusammentreffen, von denen jede vollständig erwiesen ist und die nicht nur unter sich übereinstimmen, sondern auch in so enger Beziehung mit der zu erweisenden Thatsache stehen, daß letztere dem Gerichte als unzweifelhaft sich darstellt.

Wo das Gesetz den Zeugenbeweis ausschließt, kommen auch gemeine Vermuthungen nicht in Betracht.

Art. 323. — **Thatsachen, wegen deren Jemand durch rechtskräftiges Urtheil eines inländischen Strafgerichts für schuldig erkannt wurde, haben auch vor den bürgerlichen Gerichten als erwiesen zu gelten und ist hiegegen keine Beweisführung weiter zulässig.**

G. A. d. K. d. A. I S. 23. 259—261. II S. 157—160. 319—323. 325. IV S. 88.
K. d. R. II S. 105. IV S. 41.

1) Wird der Beweis einer Thatsache in der Art geführt, daß man statt derselben eine andere Thatsache nachweist, aus welcher auf jene geschlossen werden kann, so spricht man von künstlichem Beweise.

Ist die Schlußfolgerung eine nothwendige, wie z. B. daß ich an einem gewissen Orte etwas nicht gethan haben kann, wenn ich genau zur nemlichen Zeit an einem andern Orte gewesen bin, so ersetzt die eine Thatsache die andere vollständig und wird mit der einen auch die andere erweisen. Von einem Vermuthungsbeweise kann in diesem Falle die Rede nicht sein.

Ist die Schlußfolgerung keine nothwendige, muß vielmehr der Richter seine Ueberzeugung mehr oder weniger nur aus Gründen der Wahrscheinlichkeit bilden, so spricht man von einem Vermuthungsbeweise.

In vielen Fällen hat das Gesetz ausgesprochen, daß bei Vorhandensein einer gewissen Thatsache eine andere als erwiesen zu betrachten sei. Die Schlußfolgerung ist dann ebenfalls eine nothwendige; da sie es jedoch nur kraft Verfügung des Gesetzes, nicht aber kraft innerer Nothwendigkeit ist, so spricht man auch hier von Vermuthung.

Es ist daher zu unterscheiden zwischen gesetzlichen und gemeinen Vermuthungen (praesumtiones juris und praesumtiones hominis).

a) Gesetzliche Vermuthungen.

2) Die gesetzlichen Vermuthungen sind entweder 1) solche, gegen welche das Gesetz einen Gegenbeweis nicht zuläßt (praesumtiones juris et de jure) und welche man daher berechtigt ist Fiktionen zu nennen, oder 2) solche, welche bloß die Beweislast verrücken, gegen welche also Gegenbeweis zulässig ist (praesumtiones juris schlechtweg). Endlich gibt es gesetzliche Vermuthungen, welche zwischen Beiden die Mitte halten, indem der Gegenbeweis nur in mehr oder minder beschränkter Weise zugelassen wird.

S. nähere Erörterungen in Seuff. Commentar Bd. III S. 282 ff.

b) Gemeine Vermuthungen.

3) Bei dem Beweise durch gemeine Vermuthungen ist die Prozeßordnung wieder in die alte Beweistheorie verfallen. Vermuthungen sollen den Beweis nie völlig ersetzen, ausgenommen 1) wenn es sich um einen inneren Willensakt handelt, oder 2) wenn mehrere Vermuthungen von vorschriftsmäßiger Güte zusammentreffen; außerdem sollen die als Vermuthung dienenden Thatsachen selbst vollständig erwiesen sein.

Meiner Meinung nach haben diese Vorschriften wenig praktischen Werth und wenig praktische Wirkung. Im Grunde wird jeder Richter sich doch nur die einfache Frage vorlegen, ob er genügende Ueberzeugung gewonnen habe oder nicht, wie er es ja selbst in Strafsachen, wo höhere Interessen im Spiele sind, zu thun gewöhnt ist.

So weit besagte Vorschriften aber wirken, wirken sie schlimm und verkehrt. Wenn z. B. A zwei beliebige Vermuthungen für sich hat, daß B von ihm ein gewisses Darlehen empfangen, so ist der Richter rechtlich nicht gehindert, Beweis anzunehmen, denn die Frage der Uebereinstimmung und der Schlüssigkeit hat er bloß mit seinem Gewissen abzumachen, ebenso wie die Frage, ob er die Vermuthungen selbst als vollständig bewiesen erachte. Wenn jedoch A nachweist, daß B in unzweifelhafter Absicht zu gestehen, mit den kleinsten Umständen vor einer Menge von Zeugen erzählt hat, wo und wie er das Darlehen von A erhalten, so ist dies bloß eine einzige Vermuthung, welche einen vollen Beweis nie zu geben vermag. Die Folge ist, daß A seinen Prozeß verliert, wenn zufällig der Erfüllungseid nicht statthaft ist!

4) Man darf wohl mit Recht fragen, ob denn unsere Richter weniger fähig oder weniger gewissenhaft seien, als die Richter in den Ländern, wo französisches Recht gilt und wo man nie etwas Bedenkliches darin fand, daß das Gesetz den Richter nicht unter Vormundschaft stellt, sondern ihm volle Freiheit gibt, selbst zu würdigen, ob er überzeugt sei.

Der Code civil Art. 1353 sagt einfach: »Les présomptions sont abandonnées aux lumières et à la prudence du magistrat, qui ne doit admettre que des présomptions graves, précises et concordantes,« und diese Worte drücken alles aus, was nach meiner Meinung in dieser Beziehung gesagt werden kann und soll.

In der Pfalz ist Art. 1353 auch jetzt noch maßgebend, da Art. 322 dort nicht gilt (Einf.-Ges. Art. 66); allein ich glaube, man könnte seine Worte im Grunde auch diesseits zur Richtschnur nehmen; denn, so gewunden sich das Gesetz im Art. 322 ausdrückt, am Ende sagt es doch weiter nichts, als daß der Richter nicht auf Vermuthung hin sprechen solle, wenn er nicht vollständig überzeugt sei. Was die verlangte Mehrheit der Vermuthungen anbelangt, so wird es in den meisten Fällen nicht schwer sein, zu einer ersten Vermuthung auch noch eine zweite zu finden.

5) Erscheinen einzelne Vermuthungen nicht vollständig erwiesen, so kann der Richter zur Ergänzung einen Erfüllungseid beifügen (Art. 469). Wahrscheinlich wird jedoch von dieser Befugniß nicht häufig Gebrauch gemacht werden, denn das Ausflicken der Beweise mit Notheiden widerstrebt überhaupt dem Geiste des neuen Verfahrens. Der französische Prozeß kennt die Notheide gleichfalls (Art. 1366 C. civ.), nichtsdestoweniger ist mir aus meiner Praxis nur ein einziger Fall erinnerlich, wo auf einen solchen Eid erkannt wurde.

6) Schließlich ist hervorzuheben, daß Beweis durch Vermuthungen nur in Fällen geführt werden darf, wo Zeugenbeweis statthaft ist, also z. B. nicht gegen den Inhalt einer vollbeweisenden Urkunde (Art. 399). Das Nemliche bestimmt Art. 1353 Code civil.

c) Beweiskraft der Strafurtheile.

7) Unter dem Gesichtspunkte einer gesetzlichen Vermuthung und zwar einer praesumtio juris et de jure betrachtet der Gesetzgeber auch die Beweiskraft der Strafurtheile.

Thatsachen, welche im Civilprozesse festgestellt sind, gelten für andere Rechtsstreite nur insofern, als es die Prinzipien über die Wirkungen der Rechtskraft mit sich bringen, und zwar mit vollem Rechte, da der Civilprozeß mehr oder minder nur formelle Wahrheit gibt.

Anders ist es im Strafprozesse, dessen Streben bloß auf Ermittlung der materiellen Wahrheit gerichtet ist und wo zudem als Grundsatz gilt, daß beim geringsten Zweifel Freisprechung zu erfolgen habe. Hat daher der Strafrichter eine Thatsache als erwiesen erklärt und auf dieselbe einen Strafausspruch gegründet, so soll nach Art. 323 diese Thatsache auch vor den bürgerlichen Gerichten als erwiesen gelten und jede Gegenbeweisführung ausgeschlossen sein.

Das Nemliche galt auch schon früher, sowohl diesseits als in der Pfalz.

8) Eine Streitfrage war es von jeher, ob auch freisprechende Urtheile, wenn sie über das Nichtbestehen einer Thatsache sich aussprechen,

oder wenn sie nach Maßgabe der Umstände sich nur auf dieses Nichtbestehen gründen können, für den Civilrechtspunkt wirksam seien.

In Deutschland und in Frankreich erklärte sich die Jurisprudenz dagegen, weil 1) der Civilkläger nicht gehört worden sei, und weil 2) der Strafrichter seine Gründe nur abfasse, um darzuthun, warum er nicht zur Verurtheilung gelangt sei, nicht aber um irgend etwas positiv festzustellen.

Bei den Verhandlungen wurde ein entgegenstehender Antrag verworfen (Abg. II 159—160), so daß also jetzt kein Zweifel mehr darüber besteht, daß freisprechende Urtheile ohne allen rechtlichen Einfluß für den Civilpunkt sind.

9) Man könnte fragen, ob nicht eine Ausnahme zu machen sei für Urtheile, welche das Vorhandensein der strafbaren That aussprechen, jedoch aus irgend einem besondern Grunde — wegen Verjährung, Mangels der Antragstellung &c., dennoch zur Freisprechung gelangen? — Hier wäre derjenige, gegen welchen das Urtheil gelten soll, allerdings gehört; allein offenbar kann ein Urtheil, welches am Ende doch freispricht, für seine gravirenden Erwägungen nicht denjenigen Werth beanspruchen, wie ein verurtheilendes; es ist nur zufällig, wenn es auf Würdigung der Thatsache eingeht, denn eigentlich hätte es erklären können und sollen, daß es darauf gar nicht ankomme. Es kann daher kein Zweifel obwalten, daß Art. 323, welcher verlangt, daß Jemand für schuldig erkannt worden sei, in der Regel einen Strafausspruch voraussetzt.

Nur für das schwurgerichtliche Verfahren wird eine Ausnahme zu machen sein, indem Ausspruch der Schuld und Ausspruch der Strafe getrennt sind und offenbar kein Grund besteht, anzunehmen, es sei ein Wahrspruch, welcher das „schuldig" ausspricht, weniger das Werk reifer und gewissenhafter Ueberlegung, wenn das Gericht später erklärt, es sei rechtlich eine strafbare That nicht gegeben, als wenn es eine Strafe verfügt. Auch der Wortlaut des Art. 323 begreift diesen Fall, da nicht gesagt ist, es müsse Jemand einer strafbaren Thatsache schuldig erklärt worden sein.

10) Art. 323 gilt für alle Strafurtheile inländischer Gerichte ohne Ausnahme, also insbesondere auch für Urtheile der Polizeistrafgerichte, ja selbst für die auf Grund des Art. 75 des Einf.-Ges. zum Strafgesetze ergehenden Strafverfügungen, wenn sie durch Versäumung des Einspruchs rechtskräftig geworden sind. Abg. II 159 (v. Neumayr und v. Weiß).

Beweisanerbieten und Beweismittel.

Art. 324. — **Bleiben am Schlusse einer Verhandlung erhebliche Thatsachen zwischen den Parteien streitig und unerwiesen, so hat jede Partei in ihren schriftlichen Anträgen die Sätze aufzustellen, die sie in Bezug auf diese Thatsachen zu beweisen sich erbietet, und die Beweismittel, deren sie sich dazu bedienen will, ihrer Art nach anzugeben.**

Diese Vorschrift findet auch dann Anwendung, wenn erhebliche Thatsachen, die vom Gegner anerkannt oder nach gesetzlicher Vorschrift als anerkannt zu betrachten sind, im gegebenen Falle durch das bloße Anerkenntniß nicht in volle rechtliche Gewißheit gesetzt werden. In wie weit dies der Fall und in wie weit ein von einer Partei gemachtes Geständniß gegen dieselbe theilbar ist, richtet sich nach den Bestimmungen des einschlägigen Rechts. G. A. d. K. d. A. II S. 151—153. 168—176. 325. 326. IV S. 88. 89. 320—326. 340. K. d. R. II S. 105—113. IV S. 41—43.

1) Ob ein Beweis anzuordnen sei, und welcher, ergibt sich erst am Schlusse der mündlichen Verhandlung, denn es sind natürlich nur solche Thatsachen zu erweisen, welche durch die bei der Verhandlung zu Gebot stehenden Mittel (Geständniß, Notorietät, Urkunden und Vermuthungen) nicht völlig klargestellt werden konnten.

2) Die Parteien sind verpflichtet, die Beweise, welche sie zu führen bereit sind, in ihren Anträgen anzubieten, und zwar indem sie die einzelnen Beweissätze aufstellen und die Beweismittel der Art nach bezeichnen.

Nach dem Laute des Art. 324 Abs. 1 könnte man glauben, es seien diese Beweisanträge immer erst bei Schluß der Verhandlung zu nehmen; allein dies wäre nicht richtig, da aus Art. 230 Abs. 3 zu entnehmen ist, daß schon im Vorverfahren jede Partei ihre Beweise eventuell anzubieten habe. Es will daher das Gesetz nur sagen, daß am Schlusse der Verhandlung die endgiltigen Beweisanträge zu stellen seien, mit Abstreichung dessen, was etwa durch die Verhandlung unnöthig geworden ist, und mit Beifügung dessen, was sich erst im Laufe der Verhandlung als erheblich ergeben hat.

3) Die Beweissätze, deren Aufstellung den Parteien zur Pflicht gemacht wird, ersetzen im Grunde die Beweisartikel des alten Prozesses, und es ist nicht ganz richtig, wenn man behauptet hat, das neue Verfahren verlange eine solche Artikulirung

nicht. S. Abg. II 152 (v. Weiß), jedoch auch R. R. II 111 (v. Weiß).

Der Code de proc. (Art. 252) schrieb sogar vor, daß die Artikulirung für den Zeugenbeweis in einem besonderen Akte geschehe, allein die Praxis brachte, diese Form bei Seite schiebend, dieselbe sofort in den Anträgen, und dieser Praxis folgte unsere Prozeßordnung.

Die Beweissätze der Anträge unterscheiden sich freilich in der äußeren Erscheinung bedeutend von den früheren Beweisartikeln. Letztere waren die Fragen, welche an die einzelnen Zeugen gestellt werden sollten, und es ist erklärlich, daß man in der Besorgniß, es möchte ein Punkt übersehen oder es möchten die Zeugen nicht genügend ausgefragt werden, den Thatbestand sehr breitschlug und Vieles wiederholte. Die Beweissätze hingegen sind bloß bestimmt, dem Zeugen, der Gegenpartei und dem Gerichte in kurzer bündiger Weise ein klares übersichtliches Bild der zu erweisenden einzelnen Thatsachen zu geben, damit der Zeuge wisse, worüber er auszusagen habe, die Gegenpartei, gegen was sie ihre Vertheidigung zu richten habe, das Gericht endlich, ob das Beweisanerbieten erheblich sei.

4) Die Form der Beweissätze und der Beweisanerbieten selbst richtet sich nach der Art der Beweismittel.

Beim Zeugenbeweise beantragt die Partei, das Gericht möge sie zum Beweise durch Zeugen darüber zulassen, daß 1) 2c., und sind nun die einzelnen Thatsachen kurz zu artikuliren.

Beim Beweise durch Sachverständige beantragt die Partei, das Gericht möge anordnen, daß Sachverständige sich gutachtlich über die zu bezeichnenden Fragen aussprechen.

Beim Augenscheine bedarf es keiner Beweissätze, sondern wird nur verlangt, das Gericht wolle vor weiterer Entscheidung Augenschein anordnen.

Beim Eide endlich lautet der Antrag: das Gericht möge Urkunde ertheilen, daß die Partei dem Gegner den Eid über die zu bezeichnenden Thatsachen zuschiebe, oder: es möge ihm diesen Eid auferlegen.

5) Man pflegt bei der ersten Verhandlung zur Hauptsache alle Beweise zu erbieten, welche man zu führen im Stande ist, natürlich manche nur eventuell. Eideszuschiebungen kann man jedoch in Fällen, wo sicher ist, daß das Gericht nicht endlich erkennen werde, füglich einer späteren Verhandlung vorbehalten.

Eine Verpflichtung, alle Beweise bei der ersten Verhandlung zur Hauptsache anzubieten, besteht nicht, da das Gericht auch noch in späteren Verhandlungen Beweise, welche übersehen worden waren oder deren Erheblichkeit sich erst nachträglich ergab, auflegen kann. Es wurde deßhalb absichtlich gesagt: „eine Verhandlung“, um nicht zur Meinung zu verleiten, es sei nur die erste Verhandlung gemeint. Abg. II 325.

Allerdings dürfen solche nachträgliche Beweisauflagen nur als Ausnahmen vorkommen (mir ist aus meiner Praxis kein Fall erinnerlich) und die Gerichte werden gegen nachgeschleppte Beweisanerbieten streng sein müssen.

Vom Geständnisse.

6) Man unterscheidet gerichtliche und außergerichtliche Geständnisse.

Wenn in Art. 324 Abs. 1 gesagt ist, daß nur über Thatsachen, welche streitig bleiben, Beweis anzubieten sei, so ist hiemit anerkannt, daß das gerichtliche Geständniß vollen Beweis gebe oder, wenn man will, diesen ersetze. Abg. II 176 (zu Art. 306 des Entw.).

a) Gerichtliches Geständniß.

7) Als ein gerichtliches Geständniß läßt sich nur dasjenige ansehen, welches im gerichtlichen Verfahren über den in Frage stehenden Rechtsstreit abgegeben wird, denn nur für diesen Fall läßt sich sagen, daß die Thatsache nicht streitig sei. Geständnisse in anderen Prozessen, mögen diese auch mit dem betreffenden in Verbindung stehen, sind für diesen keine gerichtlichen.

Ob das Geständniß bei der Verhandlung in der Sitzung erfolgt, oder bei Gelegenheit eines Beweisverfahrens vor dem damit beauftragten Richter, oder in zugestellten Prozeßschriften, ist gleichgiltig, — in allen diesen Fällen liegt das Bewußtsein und die Absicht vor, eine für Entscheidung der Streitsache erhebliche Erklärung abzugeben. Die französische Jurisprudenz erkennt sogar Geständnisse als gerichtliche an, welche vor dem durch das Gericht mit einer Theilung beauftragten Notare erfolgen.

Geständnisse vor dem Vermittlungsamte, obgleich vor Beginn des eigentlichen Prozesses gemacht, wurden in Frankreich, wenn auch nicht ohne Widerspruch, als gerichtliche anerkannt. Bei der untergeordneten Rolle, welche der Vermittlungsversuch im neuen Verfahren spielt, bei dem losen, zufälligen Zusammenhange, in welchem er zum Rechtsstreite steht, auf welchen er nicht die geringste rechtliche Wirkung äußert (Bemerk. zu Art. 221 Nr. 3), endlich da das Vermittlungsamt auch nichtrichterlichen Behörden übertragen ist, möchte dies dem Geiste der Prozeßordnung nicht entsprechen.

8) Fähigkeit zu Geständnissen.

Daß das Geständniß auf Freiheit des Willens beruhen müsse, d. h. daß es nichtig sei, wenn Zwang, Betrug oder Irrthum vorliegt, versteht sich von selbst.

Was nun aber die Rechtsfähigkeit zur Abgabe eines gerichtlichen Geständnisses anbelangt, so darf man dieses weder einem Vergleiche, noch einer Veräußerung oder einem Verzichte gleichstellen, denn alle diese Akte stehen im Belieben der Parteien und treten im Rechtsstreite nur zufällig auf; die wahrheitsgetreue Darstellung der Thatsachen aber ist Pflicht der Parteien, und ist bedingt durch den Zweck des Verfahrens. Wer daher zur gesetzlichen Vertretung im Prozesse berechtigt ist, der muß auch befugt sein, Thatsachen zuzugestehen, und nie kann eine Partei rechtlich gezwungen sein, etwas zu bestreiten, was ihrer Ueberzeugung nach wahr ist.

Aus den Bestimmungen der Art. 60 und 90 Abs. 1 geht hervor, daß diese Anschauung dem Willen des Gesetzes entspricht. Vgl. Abg. II 171 (zu Art. 303 des Entw.).

9) Wenn in Art. 324 Abs. 2 von Fällen die Sprache ist, wo Thatsachen durch bloßes Anerkenntniß nicht in volle Gewißheit gesetzt werden können, so hatte man hier nur Rechtsverhältnisse im Auge, welche überhaupt der Privatwillkür entzogen sind, wie z. B. Ehescheidungen (Art. 667), Interdiktionen 2c. Solche Thatsachen gelten auch im Falle des Ausbleibens nie als zugestanden (Art. 297 und 301).

10) Annahme des Geständnisses.

Das gerichtliche Geständniß ist seinem Wesen nach ein Beweismittel, ebensogut wie die Eidesauflage, welche nur den Weg bildet, um ein Zugeständniß zu erzwingen. Man muß entweder mit Zachariä (franz. Civilrecht § 749 Note 5) Geständniß und Eid von den Beweismitteln ausschließen, oder beide darunter begreifen. Letzteres erscheint richtiger und entspricht den bestehenden Gesetzgebungen, denn sowohl die Gerichtsordnung (Cap. XII § 1) als der Code civ. (Art. 1356) erklären, daß das Geständniß vollen Beweis gebe, und der Entwurf (Art. 306) stellte dasselbe als regina probationum an die Spitze der Beweismittel.

Die Frage könnte als eine müßige erscheinen, wenn nicht die weitere Frage damit in Verbindung stünde, ob ein gerichtliches Geständniß zurückgenommen werden dürfe, so lange es nicht förmlich angenommen ist. Erblickt man nemlich mit Zachariä im Geständnisse bloß einen Verzicht auf das Recht, Beweis zu verlangen, so ist, wie bei jedem Verzichte, die Rücknahme unbedingt gestattet, so lange nicht die Annahme erklärt ist; sieht man jedoch im Geständnisse ein Mittel zum Beweise, so übt es seine Wirkung, sobald es im Verfahren aufgetreten ist, und kann durch einfachen Widerruf nicht ungeschehen gemacht werden.

11) Im deutschen Prozesse nimmt die neuere Jurisprudenz an, es sei eine Annahme des Geständnisses nicht nöthig (Bayer Civilpr. § 223 Ziff. 6) und der Entwurf (Art. 307) hatte dies ausdrücklich bestimmt. Die Ger.-Ordn. (a. a. O. Ziff. 9) erklärt wenigstens, daß die Annahme präsumirt werde, bis das Gegentheil erwiesen sei.

Im französischen Rechte galt früher ziemlich allgemein die Ansicht, daß Geständnisse nur durch Annahme unwiderruflich werden; neuere Schriftsteller jedoch erklären diese Ansicht, welche jedenfalls im Wortlaute des Art. 1356 keinen Halt hat, für verwerflich (Journ. du Pal. [aveu] No. 185). Selbst die Schriftsteller der ersteren Ansicht (Merlin, Toullier) räumen doch ein, daß in manchen Fällen, z. B. wenn das persönliche Erscheinen verordnet war, eine Annahme im Voraus präsumirt werden müsse. Es möchte billig zu fragen sein, ob nicht, da jede Partei von vornherein aufgefordert und verpflichtet erscheint, den wahren Sachverhalt anzugeben, in allen Fällen eine Annahme im Voraus zu präsumiren sei.

Unsere Prozeßordnung spricht sich über die Frage nicht aus, jedoch erleidet es nach den Verhandlungen keinen Zweifel, daß man eine Annahme des gerichtlichen Geständnisses nicht für nothwendig hielt; denn es wurde Art. 302 Abs. 2 des Entwurfs nur deßhalb gestrichen, weil seine Bestimmung nach dermaligem Stande der Jurisprudenz selbstverständlich sei. Abg. II 171.

Es erscheint dies auch der Natur und dem Zwecke des Prozesses ganz entsprechend, denn das Geständniß wird nicht bloß dem Gegner, sondern in gewissem Sinne auch dem Gerichte gemacht, wie denn z. B. Niemand behaupten wird, das Gericht müsse auch über zugestandene Thatsachen Beweis auferlegen, wenn die Annahme des Geständnisses noch nicht erklärt sei. Uebrigens würde es, wenn man die Annahme verlangte, zu nichts weiter führen, als daß diese zur stehenden Redensart würde.

12) Widerruf des Geständnisses.

Geständnisse, welche vor Gericht abgegeben wurden oder in zugestellten Prozeßschriften enthalten sind, können nur widerrufen werden, wenn sie nicht das Ergebniß freien Willens sind, namentlich wenn sie auf Irrthum beruhen.

In dieser Beziehung ist nun, da es sich von einem inneren Willensakte handelt, also Vermuthungen unbedingt statthaft sind, dem richterlichen Ermessen der weiteste Spielraum gegeben, und es wird der Richter namentlich in solchen Fällen keine strengen Anforderungen stellen, wo der Erklärende kein eigenes Wissen hat, wenn z. B. Anwälte, Bevollmächtigte, gesetzliche Vertreter Thatsachen zugestehen, welche ihnen fremd sind, und wahrscheinlich gemacht wird, daß sie durch ungenaue Information irre geführt worden seien.

Was Art. 90 Abs. 2 verfügt, ist im Grunde keine Ausnahme von vorstehender Regel, sondern nur Anerkennung des Grundsatzes, daß bei Anwesenheit der Partei deren persönliche Erklärungen mehr gelten, als diejenigen des Anwalts. Vgl. Bemerk. zu Art. 90 Nr. 6 u. 7 und zu Art. 251 Nr. 3—9.

13) Untheilbarkeit des Geständnisses. Eine sehr wichtige Frage, in welcher das deutsche und das französische Recht sehr weit auseinandergehen und in welcher die abweichenden Prinzipien des letzteren Rechts in der Pfalz noch fortbestehen, ist die Frage der Untheilbarkeit des Geständnisses.

In Deutschland hält man auch den Parteierklärungen gegenüber Klaggrund und Einrede scharf getrennt und frägt bloß: was hat Beklagter zum Klaggrunde geantwortet? ohne in Anschlag zu bringen, was er auf Einreden Bezügliches beigefügt hat.

In Frankreich hingegen läßt man die Geschichtserzählung der Partei als ein Ganzes gelten und fragt: was hat Beklagter zur Sache erklärt? — geht aus seinen Erklärungen hervor, daß das Recht bestehe, oder nicht? Die Aufforderung, sich über die Sache, sei es eidlich, sei es unbeeidigt, zu erklären, betrachtet man als Aufforderung, Zeuge in eigener Sache zu sein, und wie man einen Zeugen, selbst wenn er betheiligt ist, über alles hören muß, was er zur Sache Gehöriges weiß, so hört man auch die Partei über den ganzen Sachverhalt und läßt ihre Erklärungen entweder im Ganzen oder gar nicht gelten. Handelt es sich z. B. um ein Darlehen, welches der Beklagte zurückgezahlt haben will, und ist der Kläger bei Mangel sonstigen Beweises auf die Wahrheitsliebe des Beklagten angewiesen, so kann ja dieser, wenn er lügen oder seinen Eid brechen will, sofort behaupten, er habe das Geld nicht empfangen; nimmt man aber an, er spreche die Wahrheit, warum ihm nur einen Theil glauben, den andern nicht?

14) Das ist es, was man im französischen Rechte unter dem Prinzipe der Untheilbarkeit des Geständnisses versteht. Dasselbe beruht nicht etwa auf einem Gesetzestexte, sondern hat sich rein aus den Bedürfnissen des praktischen Lebens und zwar nach langem Kampfe herausgebildet, indem man sich überzeugte, daß das mündliche Verfahren seine heilsamen Wirkungen nicht vollständig geben könne, wenn die Parteien immer vor dem Richter auf der Hut sein müßten, fürchtend, daß er das, was sie ihm ehrlich und aufrichtig sagen, zu ihrem Nachtheile theile, daß Verschmitztheit, Lüge und Meineid siegen und die Ehrlichkeit zu kurz komme.

Es läßt sich, was die prozessuale Behandlung des Geständnisses betrifft, eine gewisse Aehnlichkeit finden zwischen Civilprozeß und Strafprozeß. Wie hier früher alle Hilfsmittel der Untersuchung darauf gerichtet waren, Geständnisse zu erlangen, so suchte man auch dort sich Geständnisse dadurch zu verschaffen, daß man den Angegriffenen nöthigte, sich bloß über denjenigen Theil des Thatbestandes zu erklären, welcher nach den Kunstregeln über Vertheilung der Beweislast zum Beweise des Gegners gehört. Die Unbehilflichkeit des Verfahrens machte hier wie dort solche Auswege nöthig.

Das französische Recht verlangt nun auch im Civilprozesse vom Angegriffenen nur die Erklärung, ob er sich schuldig bekenne oder nicht, natürlich mit der Verpflichtung, in ausführlicher Geschichtserzählung das „Nichtschuldig“ zu begründen.

15) Meiner Ansicht nach entsprechen die Anschauungen des französischen Rechtes allein dem Geiste des neuen Verfahrens, welches auf Loyalität gebaut sein muß, und ich hege keinen Zweifel, daß sie sich später durch alle Vorurtheile hindurch ebenso Bahn brechen werden, wie so Vieles sich Bahn gebrochen hat, was vor 30 oder 40 Jahren noch als unbedingt verwerflich galt.

Ich bin sogar überzeugt, daß nur das seitherige schriftliche Verfahren mit seinen beengenden gekünstelten Formen Schuld trägt, daß sie nicht schon längst Eingang gefunden haben, wie denn der Satz der G. O. Cap. XII § 1 Ziff. 10: „Was nur bedingungsweise eingestanden wird, kann auch nur bedingungsweise auf- und angenommen werden“, hierfür eine noch geeignetere Grundlage geboten hätte, als der allgemeine Satz in Art. 1356 C. civ., daß das Geständniß nicht getheilt werden dürfe.

Ein augenfälliges Beispiel, wie sich auch jetzt schon die Theilung des Geständnisses als Mißstand geltend macht, bieten die Ansichten über die Beweislast bei Bedingungen.

Der Beklagte, welcher behauptet, es sei eine Bedingung oder eine Frist verabredet worden, befindet sich offenbar auf dem Boden der Einrede. Wenn er nun aber, einen Vertrag im Uebrigen vollständig zugestehend, beifügt, es sei derselbe unter einer Suspensivbedingung abgeschlossen worden, so fühlt man unwillkürlich, wie hart und ungerecht es sei, bei solcher Sachlage ein Zugeständniß anzunehmen, und es haben sich daher sehr bewährte Rechtslehrer dafür ausgesprochen, daß eine solche Erklärung als negative Litiscontestation zu betrachten und Kläger mit dem Beweise zu belasten sei, gleich als wäre ein Geständniß nicht erfolgt. Seuff. Comm. Bd. III S. 52. Offenbar ist diese Ansicht, man mag sie wenden wie man will, nur auf die Idee der Untheilbarkeit des Geständnisses zurückzuführen, und wenn sich die neuere Jurisprudenz der entgegengesetzten Ansicht zugewendet hat, so ist sie zwar insofern vollkommen im Rechte, als sie das Prinzip der Theilung streng durchführt, allein jeder Unbefangene wird auch hier wieder gestehen müssen, daß man Jurist sein müsse, um zu begreifen, daß dies recht sei!

16) Wenn auch nach französischem Rechte das Geständniß grundsätzlich untheilbar ist, so steht doch anderseits nichts im Wege, daß der Richter aus den Erklärungen einer Partei, namentlich solchen, die unklar sind oder Widersprüche zeigen, Vermuthungen ziehe, und falls diese Vermuthungen stark genug sind, um seine Ueberzeugung zu begründen, den Beweis der gegnerischen Behauptungen annehme.

Man wird jedoch zugestehen, daß es einen großen Unterschied mache, ob eine Thatsache als streitig betrachtet, jedoch aus der Art und Weise der Erklärungen in Verbindung mit sonstigen Umständen der Beweis gefolgert werde, oder ob man annehme, es sei die Thatsache zugestanden und es komme auf Beweis nicht weiter an.

17) Nach Art. 66 des Einf.-Ges. hat in der Pfalz der Art. 1356 Code civ. noch fernerhin Geltung, jedoch ist dies mit Vorbehalt der Ausnahmen zu verstehen, welche durch entgegenstehende Vorschriften und Prinzipien der auch für die Pfalz giltigen Theile der Prozeßordnung bedingt sind. So z. B. kann offenbar die dem Art. 352 Code de proc. entsprechende Bestimmung, daß ein gerichtliches Geständniß Spezialvollmacht voraussetze, den Verfügungen des Art. 90 über die Tragweite der Prozeßvollmacht gegenüber keine Geltung beanspruchen.

Im Wesentlichen ist es bloß der Grundsatz der Untheilbarkeit des Geständnisses, für welchen Art. 1356 fortwirkt.

b) Außergerichtliches Geständniß.

18) Das außergerichtliche mündliche Geständniß ist nur eine Vermuthung im Sinne von Art. 322 Abs. 2 und kann daher, besondere Ausnahmen (Art. 355) abgerechnet, für sich allein nie einen Beweis bilden, es müßte sich denn um einen inneren Willensakt handeln.

Hiermit hat die P. O. den Standpunkt der G. O. (a. a. O. Ziff. 6) beibehalten, ob mit Recht, sei dahingestellt; jedoch darf sich die Pfalz Glück wünschen, daß für sie die Art. 1353 und 1355 Code civ. fortbestehen (Art. 66 des Einf.-Ges.)

Art. 325. — Die zulässigen Arten von Beweismitteln sind Urkunden, Augenschein, Zeugen, Sachverständige und Eid.

Art. 326. — Will eine Partei durch Schlüsse oder Vermuthungen Beweis führen, so hat sie ihr Beweisanerbieten auf jene Thatsachen, aus welchen der Schluß gezogen oder die Vermuthung abgeleitet werden soll, zu richten, es schließt aber ein solches Anerbieten nicht aus, daß gleichzeitig auch unmittelbarer Beweis angeboten werde.

Art. 327. — Die Parteien können sich zum Nachweise einer und derselben Thatsache gleichzeitig verschiedener Arten von Beweismitteln bedienen.

Wird d e Eideszuschiebung mit andern Beweismitteln verbunden, so gilt der Eid als nur für den Fall zugeschoben, daß der mittels der andern Beweismittel versuchte Beweis mißlingen sollte.

G. A. d. K. d. A. II S. 155. 156. 325. 326. IV S. 89.
K. d. R. II S. 113 IV S. 43.

1) Art. 325 zählt die zulässigen Arten der Beweismittel auf und hatte dabei nur Veranlassung, von solchen zu sprechen, wegen deren eine Beweisauflage erfolgen kann. Solche Beweismittel sind Urkunden, Augenschein, Zeugen, Sachverständige und Eid.

2) Soll der Beweis durch Schlüsse (Art. 322 Abs. 1) oder durch Vermuthungen (Art. 322 Abs. 2) geführt werden, so hat sich das Beweisanerbieten auf diejenigen Thatsachen zu richten, aus welchen die Schlüsse oden Vermuthungen abgeleitet werden sollen. Es versteht sich dies nach dem Zwecke der Beweisanerbieten von selbst; ebenso, daß gleichzeitig unmittelbarer Beweis erbeten werden dürfe.

3) In gleicher Weise erscheint es selbstverständlich, daß zum Nachweise der nemlichen That-

sache auch verschiedene Beweismittel angeboten werden können, und daß die Eideszuschiebung, wenn sie mit anderen Beweismitteln auftritt, immer nur eventuell erfolgt.

Wie schon bemerkt, wird häufig der Eid bei der ersten Verhandlung noch gar nicht zugeschoben, sondern man wartet das Ergebniß der anderen Beweisführungen ab. Auch sonstige Beweismittel, wie Zeugen, Sachverständige, können unter Umständen vorbehalten bleiben, z. B. wenn es klar ist, daß vorerst ein Augenschein stattfinden müsse.

Beweisurtheil

Art. 328. — **Das Gericht hat die Erheblichkeit der Beweissätze, sowie die Zulässigkeit der vorgeschlagenen Arten von Beweismitteln zu prüfen und hienach das Beweisurtheil zu erlassen.**

In dem Beweisurtheile sind die Thatsachen, welche eine Partei zu beweisen hat, und die zugelassenen Arten von Beweismitteln bestimmt zu bezeichnen.

Das Gericht ist hiebei an die Wortfassung der von den Parteien aufgestellten Beweissätze nicht gebunden, kann aber in dem Beweisurtheile weder eine Partei über Thatsachen zum Beweise lassen, für welche sie solchen nicht bei der Verhandlung angeboten hat, noch ihr andere Arten von Beweismitteln als die angebotenen gestatten.

Hält das Gericht einen nicht angebotenen Beweis für nöthig, ohne daß die betreffende Partei auf den Mangel des Anerbietens in der Verhandlung von dem Vorsitzenden aufmerksam gemacht worden ist, so ist die Wiederaufnahme der Verhandlung (Art. 274) zu verfügen. G. A. d. K. d. A. II S. 151 153—155. 326. — K. d. R. II S. 113.

1) Eine der wichtigsten und zugleich segensreichsten Neuerungen, welche die Prozeßordnung gebracht hat, ist die Beseitigung des Beweisinterlokutes im Sinne des alten Verfahrens, jener Schranke, welche das Verfahren in zwei streng gesonderte Theile zerlegte und dem materiellen Rechte den Weg versperrte.

Das Beweisurtheil unserer Prozeßordnung ist etwas ganz Anderes, steht damit nur in entfernter Verwandtschaft und es ist nothwendig, dies nie aus den Augen zu verlieren, wenn man nicht Gefahr laufen will, den rechten Weg zu verfehlen.

2) Das alte Beweisinterlokut stellte sich die schwierige, oft nahezu unmögliche Aufgabe, auf Grund der Erklärungen im Schriftenwechsel sofort ein bedingtes Endurtheil über den Rechtsstreit zu fällen, und für alle Eventualitäten der Beweisergebnisse im Voraus die Entscheidung zu geben.

Es entsprangen hieraus schlimme Folgen in Masse.

Welch großer Aufwand von Gelehrsamkeit und Scharfsinn, von Zeit und Mühe wurde z. B. jahraus jahrein auf Eventualitäten verschwendet, welche schließlich gegenstandslos waren!

Wie oft wurden Ansprüche und Einwände nur deßhalb als nicht substantiirt abgewiesen, weil der Richter nicht im Stande war, ein Beweisinterlokut, so wie es die Regeln der Kunst verlangten, aufzubauen! Konnten doch Entschädigungs-Begehren fast nie substantiirt werden!

Wie schlimm wirkte ferner die Sucht, günstige Beweisintelokute zu erringen, theils indem sie zu Entstllungen des Sachverhalts verleitete, theils indem sie die Geschäftslast der höheren Gerichte vermehrte!

Wie häufig endlich kam es vor, daß das Beweisergebniß in den durch das Interlokut gezogenen unabänderlichen Rahmen gar nicht paßte, und man sich nur durch gewaltsame Behandlung der vorliegenden Beweise oder gar nicht helfen konnte!

3) Alle diese Mißstände sind mit einem Schlage dadurch beseitigt, daß das Beweisurtheil kein bedingtes Endurtheil mehr ist, sondern nur eine Instruktionsmaßregel.

Der Richter, welcher jetzt Beweis auferlegt, spricht bloß aus: „Ich bin durch die Verhandlung noch nicht vollständig aufgeklärt und verlange, daß mir in der und der Richtung noch Beweis erbracht werde, bevor ich mein Urtheil gebe." Das Beweisurtheil hat daher (abgesehen von Eidesauflagen) rechtlich keine weitere Bedeutung, als etwa der Beschluß, durch welchen früher der Richter vor Erlaß seines Interlokutes einen Augenschein anordnete oder die Adhibirung von Akten verfügte.

Allerdings wird der Richter auch jetz noch prüfen, ob Beweis nöthig sei und wen die Beweislast treffe, und er würde sich dem Vorwurfe des Leichtsinns oder der Ungeschicklichkeit aussetzen, wenn er überflüssige oder verkehrte Beweisauflagen machen würde; allein er braucht wenigstens nicht mehr so ängstlich zu sein, braucht nicht jedes Wort auf die Wagschale zu legen, und es genügt, wenn die erbotenen Beweise im Ganzen und dem Wesen nach nöthig und erheblich sind. Läßt sich doch einmal eine Beweiserhebung nicht umgehen, so erscheint es sogar sehr rathsam, an den einzelnen Beweissätzen nicht zu mäkeln, sondern alles zuzulassen, was nicht offenbar zwecklos ist, und so den Sachverhalt nach allen möglicherweise erheblichen Richtungen völlig klar zu stellen. Es gilt dies namentlich für Fälle, wo Berufung ergriffen werden kann.

4) Der Unterschied zwischen früher und jetzt läßt sich vielleicht am lebendigsten durch ein Gleichniß vor Augen führen.

Der Richter im alten Verfahren war ein Scharfschütze, welcher auf 300 Schritte Entfernung, vorsichtig zielend, alle Kunst aufbietend, den Wind und das Licht und alle sonstige Eventualitäten in Berechnung bringend, das Ziel zu treffen suchte; der Richter im neuen Verfahren geht, vielleicht nur ein gutes Reiterpistol in der Hand haltend, ruhig vorwärts, bis er hart am Ziele ist, und dann schießt er los.

Die erste Methode bietet ohne allen Zweifel Gelegenheit, größere Kunst zu zeigen, allein die letzte gibt größere Sicherheit; den Parteien aber liegt weniger an fein ausgemeiselten Interlokuten, als an ihrem Rechte.

a) Fälle der Beweisauflage.

5) Findet sich das Gericht nach Schluß der mündlichen Verhandlung in einer oder der anderen Richtung noch nicht völlig aufgeklärt, so prüft es die Beweisanerbieten der Parteien und läßt diejenige Partei, welche es beweispflichtig erachtet, zu den von ihr erbotenen Beweisen zu, falls diese zuläßig und erheblich sind.

Wo das Gesetz nicht eine Ausnahme macht, wie z. B. beim Augenscheine (Art. 396) und bei der Expertise (Art. 433), dürfen nur solche Beweise angeordnet werden, zu welchen sich die Parteien erboten haben. Der Vorsitzende ist jedoch verpflichtet, die Parteien auf Beweise aufmerksam zu machen, welche sie anzubieten versäumt haben, und falls er dies unterlassen hat, das Gericht aber bei der Berathung findet, daß ein nicht angebotener Beweis nöthig sei, so ist die Wiederaufnahme des Verfahrens zu verfügen, natürlich nur, um klar zu stellen, ob der fragliche Beweis erboten werde und was die Gegenpartei etwa gegen ihn einzuwenden habe.

Wurde ein Beweis über eine gewisse Thatsache zwar angeboten, allein in mangelhafter Weise, so wird der Vorsitzende sich zwar gleichfalls verpflichtet fühlen, die Partei zur Hebung des Mangels aufzufordern, und das Gericht wird geeigneten Falls die Wiederaufnahme des Verfahrens anordnen, allein die zwingende Vorschrift des Art. 328 Abs. 4 mit ihren rechtlichen Folgen läßt sich auf diesen Fall nicht anwenden.

6) Erbietet eine Partei trotz erfolgter Aufforderung über eine Thatsache, welche sie zu erweisen hat und welche nach Ansicht des Gerichts noch des Beweises bedarf, einen zuläßigen und erheblichen Beweis nicht, so ist diese Thatsache als unerweislich zu betrachten; würde jedoch das Gericht ohne eine solche Aufforderung Letzteres annehmen, so wäre dies eine Rechtsverletzung. Abg. II 154 (Barth).

Es folgt hieraus, daß es sehr wichtig, ja nothwendig ist, besagte Aufforderung urkundlich festzustellen, und wird dies am besten durch eine Beurkundung im Urtheilssatze geschehen, wobei auf die nähere Auseinandersetzung der Entscheidungsgründe Bezug genommen werden kann.

7) Indem das Gesetz sagt, das Gericht solle nur Beweis auferlegen, wenn es die Thatsache für unerwiesen erachte (Art. 324), und ferner, es habe die Erheblichkeit der Beweissätze zu prüfen (Art. 328), eröffnet es dem richterlichen Ermessen ein weites Feld.

Zuerst steht fest, daß, wenn die Ueberzeugung des Richters durch die Verhandlung in der Sitzung, auf Grund der gebotenen Beweise (Notorietät, Urkunden, Vermuthungen), oder auf Grund vorausgegangener Beweiserhebungen irgend einer Art (z. B. Augenschein), vollständig begründet ist, derselbe nicht nöthig hat, weitere Beweisanerbieten zu berücksichtigen, sollten sie auch in noch so entschiedener Weise auftreten. Vgl. Verhdl. zu Art. 278 des Entw. Abg. II 149, 150.

Es gilt dies nach der Prozeßordnung (Art. 457 Ziff. 4) sogar von der Eideszuschiebung, während nach französischem Rechte, welches in diesem Punkte für die Pfalz noch gilt, früher die Ansicht bestand, der Haupteid dürfe, falls er an sich zuläßig ist, nie zurückgewiesen werden, und erst die neuere Jurisprudenz dem Richter gestattet, eventuelle Eideszuschiebungen, wenn sie offenbar frivol erscheinen, unbeachtet zu lassen.

8) Insbesondere wird es dem Richter auch zustehen, in Fällen, wo er völlig überzeugt ist, es könne durch die Beweiserhebungen kein sichereres Ergebniß gewonnen werden, als dasjenige, welches er aus den durch die Verhandlung gebotenen Elementen zu ziehen vermag, von Beweisauflagen Umgang zu nehmen.

Die Bestimmung des Art. 330 ist, in dieser Richtung betrachtet, nicht als eine Ausnahme aufzufassen, sondern als der Ausfluß einer allgemeineren Regel, wie denn z. B. die französischen Gerichte, obgleich ihnen das Gesetz keine derartige ausdrückliche Bestimmung bot, nie den geringsten Anstand genommen haben, Schadenersatz-

Ansprüche selbst zu würdigen. Die Prinzipien über Vermuthungsbeweis führen zu dieser Regel, deren Fortbestand in der Pfalz, wo die Art. 1352 und 1355 Code civ. noch gelten, keinem Anstande unterliegen kann.

Demnach dürfte anzunehmen sein, daß auch in Fällen, wo es sich um Schätzung eines Früchtegenusses unter gewöhnlichen Umständen, oder um Schätzung gewöhnlicher Dienstleistungen handelt, der Richter nicht gewungen sei, Beweis aufzulegen, wenn er durch die Verhandlung eine genügende Ueberzeugung gewonnen hat. Allerdings steht ihm hier nicht ganz die Gewalt zu, wie im Falle des Art. 330, und er dürfte bloße Wahrscheinlichkeit nicht als Ueberzeugung gelten lassen. Abg. II 179 (v. Weiß).

9) Findet der Richter weitere Aufklärung nöthig, so hat er die Erheblichkeit der erbotenen Beweise zu prüfen.

Ein Beweisanerbieten ist unerheblich, wenn der Richter, selbst die Wahrheit der aufgestellten Beweissätze vorausgesetzt, nicht in der Lage wäre, die Anträge der Parteien zuzusprechen, sei es, weil die Thatsachen keinen genügenden Schluß auf das geltend gemachte Recht zulassen, sei es, weil die angeführten Vermuthungen nicht im Stande wären, seine Ueberzeugung von der Thatsache, auf welche es ankommt, zu begründen, oder wenigstens zur Auflage eines Erfüllungseides zu führen.

10) Es könnte sich fragen, ob der Richter Beweisanerbieten auch dann als unerheblich beseitigen dürfe, wenn er der Ansicht ist, es sei die Führung des Beweises unmöglich, oder es seien die behaupteten Thatsachen selbst in hohem Grade unwahrscheinlich. Die französische Jurisprudenz gibt bezüglich des Zeugenbeweises, welcher hier hauptsächlich in Betracht kommt, dem Richter diese Befugniß und zwar mit Rücksicht auf die Worte des Art. 253 Code de proc.: »pourra être ordonnée.«

Man könnte geltend machen, daß das Wort: „Erheblichkeit" in seinem weiteren Sinne auch solche Rücksichten nicht ausschließe.

Ich möchte jedoch annehmen, daß im Sinne unserer Prozeßordnung die Befugniß des Richters nicht so weit gehe, Zeugenbeweis über genau und bestimmt bezeichnete Thatsachen, welche als wahr angenommen erheblich wären, bloß deßhalb zurückzuweisen, weil er der Ansicht ist, sie seien nicht wahr, oder es könne die Partei den Beweis nicht erbringen.

Anders ist es natürlich, wenn der Richter den Gegenbeweis als bereits erbracht annimmt. Anders ist es ferner, wenn das Beweisanerbieten zu unbestimmt und unklar ist, um den Anforderungen des Art. 324 zu entsprechen. In solchen Fällen kann allerdings der Richter das Beweisanerbieten als ungenügend und die Thatsachen als unerweislich betrachten, in gleicher Weise, wie er jetzt ein Vorbringen für ungenügend substantiirt erklärt.

11) Es versteht sich wohl von selbst, daß die Beweissätze, welche der Richter zuläßt, nicht immer das ganze Beweisthema erschöpfen müssen, wie beim seitherigen Interlokute, sondern daß sich der Richter nur zu fragen hat, ob die Thatsachen, wegen deren er Beweis zuläßt, in Verbindung mit dem sonstigen Beweismateriale seine Ueberzeugung zu begründen im Stande seien.

b) Fassung des Beweisurtheils.

12) Das Beweisurtheil bezeichnet die zu erweisenden Thatsachen, die Art der Beweismittel und die Partei, welche zum Beweise zugelassen wird.

Wenn Art. 328 Abs. 2 diese Vorschrift gibt, so will er nur sagen: „so weit es nach der Natur der Beweismittel nöthig ist," denn beim Augenscheine sind weder die zu beweisenden Thatsachen, noch ist in der Regel die Partei, welche Beweis zu führen hat, zu bezeichnen, vielmehr genügt es, daß das Gericht die Vornahme desselben anordne. Was sollte es nützen, hier Beweissätze aufzustellen?

Auch beim Beweise durch Sachverständige pflegt man in Fällen, wo das Gericht Veranlassung gehabt hätte, denselben von Amtswegen anzuordnen, in dieser Weise zu erkennen, indem man den Sachverständigen die Auflage macht, sich über die von beiden Theilen vorgeschlagenen und als erheblich befundenen Fragen, sowie über diejenigen weiteren Fragen, welche etwa das Gericht sich veranlaßt sieht, von Amtswegen beizufügen, zu erklären.

Im Uebrigen hat die Fassung der Beweisauflage der oben (zu Art. 324 Nr. 4) bezeichneten Fassung der Beweisanerbieten zu entsprechen.

13) Bezüglich der Frage, ob Beweise, welche verschiedene im Eventualverhältnisse stehende Streitpunkte betreffen, sowie verschiedene Beweismittel für die nemliche Thatsache, im nemlichen Beweisurtheile zu vereinigen, oder ob sie zu trennen und einzelne Beweise oder Beweismittel späteren Urtheilen vorzubehalten seien, ist den Gerichten keine bestimmte Vorschrift gegeben; es haben sich dieselben daher durch die Natur der Streitpunkte und Beweismittel, sowie durch Gründe der Zweckmäßigkeit bestimmen zu lassen.

14) Was zuerst die Häufung von Beweismitteln anbelangt, so macht hier der Eid insofern eine Ausnahme, als er immer nur eventuell

in Betracht kommt und die Eidesauflage erst erfolgen kann, wenn sich nach Erhebung und Würdigung der sonstigen Beweise Anlaß dazu ergibt. Der Eid wird daher vom Richter nie mit andern Beweismitteln kumulirt; bedingte Eidesauflagen gibt es nicht.

Kommt es in der Sache auf Augenschein an, so werden in der Regel andere Beweismittel damit nicht verbunden, sei es, weil der Augenschein geeignet ist, sie unnöthig zu machen, sei es, weil sich erst durch denselben die Sachlage soweit klärt, um die Punkte, in welchen noch weiterer Beweis nöthig ist, hervortreten zu lassen. Nicht selten findet man es jedoch auch zweckmäßig, Expertise oder Zeugenbeweis mit dem Augenscheine zu verbinden. Es kann wünschenswerth sein, daß die Sachverständigen den Richter beim Augenschein unterstützen, oder daß die Zeugen an Ort und Stelle vernommen werden; es kann auch die Rücksicht auf Kostenersparung oder auf Beschleunigung der Entscheidung solche Verbindungen veranlassen.

Zeugenverhör und Expertise werden gewöhnlich kumulirt, jedoch kann es der Fall sein, daß erst durch die Zeugen die Grundlage für die an die Sachverständigen zu richtenden Fragen gewonnen werden muß.

15) Was die Häufung der Beweise über verschiedene Streitpunkte anbelangt, so hängt hier alles von Gründen der Zweckmäßigkeit, namentlich von der Rücksicht auf Kostenersparung und Vereinfachung des Verfahrens ab.

Wie der Richter bei der Verhandlung einzelne Streitpunkte lostrennen kann, so kann er dies auch im Beweisurtheile. Es kann z. B. im Falle, wo eine Urkunde als unächt angefochten, eventuell aber behauptet wird, sie sei durch Betrug zu Stande gekommen, sachgemäß sein, vorerst nur Beweis bezüglich der Aechtheit anzuordnen, die voraussichtlich umfangreichen und kostspieligen weiteren Beweise aber einem späteren Urtheile vorzubehalten; es kann ferner geeignet sein, Beweise, welche in weiter Ferne, mit großen Kosten und Zeitverlust zu führen wären, einstweilen nicht aufzulegen, und abzuwarten, ob nicht durch andere Beweiserhebungen dieselben gegenstandslos werden.

Anderseits hat der Richter dieselbe Freiheit in Vereinigung der Beweise und steht sogar nichts im Wege, zugleich wegen einer Prozeßeinrede und wegen der Hauptsache Beweis aufzulegen, wie es denn manchmal (z. B. bei der Frage, ob ein Handelsgeschäft vorliege) sehr unzweckmäßig wäre, Competenz und Grund der Sache zu trennen, während Beides im nemlichen Beweisverfahren und mit den nemlichen Beweismitteln aufgeklärt werden kann.

16) Legt das Gericht Beweise auf, welche unter sich im Eventualverhältnisse stehen, so ist es durchaus nicht nöthig, dies im Urtheilssatze auszusprechen, oder anzugeben, was die Folge sei, wenn der eine oder andere Beweis geführt oder nicht geführt würde. Eine solche Kundgabe wäre ohne Zweck, da der Richter doch nicht daran gebunden wäre.

Es genügt also, die Beweissätze einfach nebeneinander zu stellen.

Art. 329. — **Ein Urtheil auf Beweisführung durch Urkunden darf nur erlassen werden, wenn besondere Verhältnisse es der Sachlage angemessen erscheinen lassen.**

In Ermangelung solcher Verhältnisse ist, wenn eine Partei die zur Begründung ihrer Anträge erforderlichen Urkunden bei der Verhandlung nicht besitzt und sich angewendeten Fleißes ungeachtet bis dahin nicht verschaffen konnte, oder wenn sich die Nothwendigkeit ihrer Geltendmachung erst aus der Verhandlung ergibt, Vertagung zu bewilligen und zugleich die Frist zur Mittheilung der Urkunden festzusetzen.

Auch ohne solche Vertagung ist die Benützung bisher nicht gebrauchter Urkunden bei einer späteren Verhandlung nicht ausgeschlossen. Dies gilt auch von Urkunden, welche wegen unterlassener Mittheilung an die Gegenpartei von einer früheren Verhandlung ausgeschlossen waren (Art. 172), soferne die Mittheilung inzwischen erfolgt ist.

Art. 330. — **Ist bei feststehender Verpflichtung zur Erstattung eines Schadens die Ermittlung des Betrags durch Beweisführung voraussichtlich nicht zu erzielen oder mit unverhältnißmäßigen Schwierigkeiten verbunden, so hat das Gericht eine solche Beweisführung nicht zuzulassen, sondern die Größe der Entschädigung nach dem Ergebnisse der Verhandlung und allenfalls auf Grund eines vorher von Amtswegen zu erholenden Gutachtens von Sachverständigen der Billigkeit gemäß festzusetzen.**

G. A. d. K. d. A. II S. 149—151. 178. 179. 326. 327. IV S. 89.
K. d. R. II S. 113. IV S. 43.

1) Der Gesetzgeber bezeichnet hier zwei Fälle, in denen er will, daß in der Regel ein Beweisurtheil nicht erlassen werde, nemlich 1) beim Beweise durch Urkunden und 2) bei Feststellung von Schadenersatzansprüchen.

a) Urkundenbeweis (Art. 329).

2) Wie aus den Bestimmungen der Art. 172, 242 und 246 hervorgeht, setzt das neue Verfahren voraus, daß soweit möglich schon bei der ersten Verhandlung alle zur Sache gehörigen Urkunden in Urschrift (Art. 366, 367) vorgelegt werden, und zwar nachdem sie vorher bereits dem Gegner mitgetheilt waren.

Es erklärt sich hieraus, wie bestimmt werden konnte, es solle auf Beweisführung durch Urkunden nur höchst ausnahmsweise, falls ganz besondere Verhältnisse es der Sachlage angemessen erscheinen lassen, erkannt werden. Ein solcher Fall kann z. B. gegeben sein, wenn die Herbeischaffung der Urkunden große Kosten machen oder Schwierigkeiten bieten würde und es zweckmäßig ist, zuvor über deren Erheblichkeit zu entscheiden. In der Regel soll durch einfache Vertagung geholfen und auch diese soll nur bewilligt werden, wenn die Partei wahrscheinlich macht, daß ihr eine Verschuldung nicht zur Last falle.

3) Die Benützung von Urkunden ist nie ausgeschlossen, so lange es noch auf eine Beweisführung ankommt, und liegt hierin ein weiterer Grund für die Entbehrlichkeit besonderer Beweisauflage. Ist Endurtheil gefällt oder die Entscheidung von einer Eidesleistung abhängig gemacht, so kann natürlich, abgesehen vom Falle der Berufung (Art. 707) oder der Wiederaufnahme des Verfahrens (Art. 761 Ziff. 2) auch die Vorlage von Urkunden nichts mehr nützen.

Wichtig ist, daß selbst Urkunden, welche wegen unterlassener Mittheilung von einer Verhandlung ausgeschlossen waren, dennoch später noch benützt werden dürfen. Vgl. Bemerk. zu Art. 172 Nr. 6.

Gleiches wird selbst dann gelten, wenn der Urkundenbeweis förmlich zugelassen, jedoch zu führen versäumt worden war, unbeschadet der Haftung für die verschuldeten Kosten.

b) Schadenersatz (Art. 330).

4) Die Bestimmung, daß das Gericht den Betrag eines zu ersetzenden Schadens unter Umständen frei würdigen dürfe, ist eine höchst praktische und hilft einem diesseits sehr fühlbaren Bedürfnisse ab.

In der Pfalz hatte man, auf Grund der Prinzipien über Vermuthungsbeweis, von jeher dem Richter diese Befugniß zugestanden, und es war ein seltener Fall, wenn Beweis über den Betrag eines Schadens zugelassen wurde.

Natürlich erstreckte sich diese Befugniß des pfälzischen Richters nicht bloß auf Würdigung von Schäden, sondern auch auf Verhältnisse ähnlicher Art, überhaupt auf alle Fälle, wo der Richter sich sagen mußte, daß ihm ein Beweisverfahren keine bessere Aufklärung verschaffen könne, oder daß wenigstens der mögliche Gewinn ganz außer Verhältniß stehe zu den Kosten und zu der Prozeßverzögerung, welche die Beweiserhebung verursachen würde. Wer aus Erfahrung weiß, wie unzuverlässig in der Regel die Gutachten von Sachverständigen sind und wie häufig diese von ganz anderen Rücksichten sich leiten lassen, als denjenigen, welche der Richter als maßgebend zu erachten hat, der kann darin nur einen Gewinn für das materielle Recht erblicken, ganz abgesehen von den sonstigen Vortheilen. Ist es mir doch vorgekommen, daß drei Experten es für unmöglich erklärten, dreißig Grundstücke von ziemlich gleicher Größe in zwei Loose zu bringen, weil sie, natürlich ohne es offen zu sagen, der Ansicht waren, es sei die Versteigerung zweckmäßig, um dem Vater und Vormunde baares Geld zu verschaffen!

5) In der Pfalz besteht diese Gewalt des Richters, da sie nur Ausfluß der allgemeinen Grundsätze über den Beweis durch Vermuthungen ist, ungeschmälert fort;. diesseits aber ist ein Unterschied zu machen zwischen der Würdigung von Schäden und der Würdigung von thatsächlichen Verhältnissen anderer Art. Bloß in ersterer Beziehung ist dem Richter volle Freiheit gegeben, im Uebrigen ist er an die etwas beengenden Vorschriften des Art. 322 Abs. 2 gebunden. Vgl. Bemerk. zu Art. 328 Nr. 8 und Abg. II 179 (v. Weiß).

Art. 331. — **Das Beweisurtheil hat der betreibende Theil ausfertigen und dem Gegner zustellen zu lassen.**

Ist im Urtheile die Tagfahrt zur Beweisaufnahme bestimmt, so muß die Zustellung wenigstens acht Tage vor der Tagfahrt geschehen.

Die Vorschrift des Art. 209 findet hiebei keine Anwendung, dagegen ist das Prozeßgericht befugt, die Zeit, welche zwischen der Zustellung und der Tagfahrt in Mitte zu liegen hat, nach Bedürfniß der Sache mit Rücksicht auf die Wohnorte und die sonstigen Verhältnisse der Parteien zu erweitern.

Art. 332. — Das Beweisurtheil kann von dem Gerichte, welches dasselbe erlassen hat, vor der Beweisaufnahme nicht wieder zurückgenommen werden.

G. A. d. K. d. A. II S. 162—164. 326. 327. III S. 129. IV S. 89. 93.
K. d. R. II S. 113. IV S. 43.

1) Die Vorschrift, daß der betreibende Theil das Beweisurtheil ausfertigen und dem Gegner (d. h. dem Anwalte der Gegenpartei oder, falls ein solcher nicht aufgestellt ist, dieser selbst) zustellen lassen müsse, ist nicht so allgemein zu nehmen als sie lautet, denn es gibt einzelne Fälle, wo weder Ausfertigung noch Zustellung nöthig ist, z. B. wenn ein zugeschobener oder zurückgeschobener Eid sofort in der Sitzung geleistet wird (Art. 462)

Betreibender Theil ist derjenige, welcher das Beweisurtheil zum Vollzuge bringt. In der Regel betreibt die zum Hauptbeweise zugelassene Partei, welche auch, als die im Sinne des Art. 285 obsiegende Partei, den Sachverhalt zu fertigen hat, den Vollzug des Beweisurtheils; ist dieselbe jedoch säumig, so kann auch der Gegner die Betreibung in die Hand nehmen, geschehe es auch nur zum Zwecke, den zugelassenen Beweis auszuschließen (Art. 406).

2) Wurde die Tagfahrt zur Beweisaufnahme im Urtheile nicht bestimmt, so versteht sich eigentlich die Zustellung von selbst, denn erst von dieser Zustellung an laufen in der Regel die Fristen zur Antretung der Beweise (Art. 406), und der mit der Beweisaufnahme beauftragte Richter setzt keine Tagfahrt fest, wenn ihm nicht Urtheilsausfertigung und Zustellungsakt vorgelegt werden.

Wurde jedoch im Urtheile sofort auch der Tag der Beweisaufnahme bezeichnet, so verfügt Art. 331 Abs. 2, daß das Beweisurtheil wenigstens acht Tage zuvor zugestellt werden müsse.

Diese Zustellung, welche nach Art. 339 zugleich als Vorladung der Gegenpartei gilt, muß geschehen, gleichviel ob die Anwälte oder Parteien bei Spruch des Beweisurtheiles zugegen waren oder nicht, und zwar deßhalb, weil es sich hier nicht bloß um Kundgabe des Tags der weiteren Verhandlung, sondern auch um genaue Kenntniß vom Inhalte des Urtheils, der einzelnen Beweissätze und der in den Entscheidungsgründen entwickelten richterlichen Auffassung der Sachlage handelt.

Ist fragliche Zustellung gar nicht oder nicht mit Einhaltung der gesetzlichen Frist erfolgt, so ist der Gegner nicht verpflichtet, sich auf die Beweisaufnahme einzulassen, und kann sie, falls sie dennoch stattfindet, als nichtig anfechten.

3) Die vom Gesetze bestimmte Frist möchte für den Zweck, welchen sie erreichen will, etwas zu kurz sein, wie es denn z. B. dem Gegner nicht möglich ist, nach einer erst zu Ende der Frist erfolgten Zustellung des Urtheils neue Zeugen zu benennen; allein es wird sich dieser Mißstand in der Praxis nicht fühlbar machen, um so weniger, da dem Gerichte das Recht der Erweiterung zusteht.

4) Fragliche Frist unterliegt der gesetzlichen Erweiterung auf Grund der Bestimmungen des Art. 209 nicht, und zwar weder mit Rücksicht auf den Wohnort der Partei noch mit Rücksicht auf den Wohnort des Anwalts. Es gilt dies, da das Gesetz nicht unterscheidet, auch im Falle, wo die Partei, gegen welche die Beweisführung betrieben wird, nicht durch Anwalt vertreten ist, z. B. wenn der Beweis durch Versäumungsurtheil auferlegt wurde.

Mit dieser Verfügung hat die Prozeßordnung einen fühlbaren Mißstand des französischen Prozesses beseitigt, zugleich aber hat sie weise vorgesorgt, daß nicht ein Mißstand entgegengesetzter Art eintrete und die Parteien in ihren Rechten verkürzt werden, indem sie dem Richter die Befugniß einräumte, nach Bedürfniß der Sache die Frist zu erweitern.

Die Hauptrücksicht, welche den Richter hierbei zu leiten hat, besteht in den gewöhnlichen Fällen darin, daß er den sämmtlichen Parteien und deren Gewalthabern das Erscheinen bei der Beweisaufnahme möglich mache, und er wird daher so viel Zeit frei zu lassen haben, als nach obwaltenden Verhältnissen hierzu nöthig ist.

Ausnahmsweise kann er jedoch auch veranlaßt sein, das Erscheinen einer Partei, namentlich einzelner Streitgenossen, ganz außer Berücksichtigung zu lassen, wenn genügender Grund vorliegt, anzunehmen, daß dieselben wegen großer Entfernung oder sonstiger Hindernisse nicht persönlich erscheinen können, oder daß ihre Anwesenheit zwecklos wäre. Die Rücksicht auf die Anwesenheit der Partei erschien dem Gesetzgeber nicht so wichtig, um sie nicht ausnahmsweise durch andere Rücksichten überwiegen zu lassen.

Ein Recht, die Beweisaufnahme deßhalb anzufechten, weil wegen Kürze der vom Richter bestimmten Frist das persönliche Erscheinen unmöglich gewesen sei, oder Wiedereinsetzung in den vorigen Stand deßhalb zu verlangen, besteht, den Fall ausgenommen, wo das persönliche Erscheinen zur Beweisaufnahme nothwendig ist, wie bei der Eidesleistung, nicht. Ein solches Recht würde die Vortheile der gesetzlichen Verfügung geradezu wieder aufheben.

5) Es könnte sich fragen, ob die Frist, welche der Partei zum Erscheinen bei einer Beweisaufnahme gegeben ist, als eine Frist zum persönlichen Handeln oder Erscheinen im Sinne des Art. 211 anzusehen sei.

Einerseits ist zu beachten, daß die Parteien nicht bloß befugt sind, bei der Beweisnahme persönlich zu erscheinen und ihre Rechte zu wahren, sondern daß der Gesetzgeber auch durch besondere Vorschriften (Art. 331 Abs. 3, Art. 339) dafür Vorsorge getroffen hat, ihnen das Erscheinen zu ermöglichen und zu erleichtern; anderseits ist jedoch die Anwesenheit der Partei, sofern es sich nicht darum handelt, daß sie einen Eid zu leisten hat, nicht nöthig (Art. 340), und der Umstand, daß die Zustellung bloß an den Anwalt erfolgt und es in's freie Ermessen des Richters gestellt ist, ob und in wie weit er bei seiner Fristbestimmung Rücksicht auf das Erscheinen der Partei nehmen wolle, deutet an, daß ein besonderer Werth auf jene Anwesenheit nicht gelegt werde.

Ich finde letztere Rücksichten überwiegend und nehme an, daß Art. 211 auf die Fristen, welche für das Erscheinen der Parteien bei Beweisaufnahmen, die auch in ihrer Abwesenheit stattfinden können, gegeben sind, nicht anwendbar seien, und zwar um so mehr, als weiter in Betracht kommt, daß der Gesetzgeber den Art. 209, welcher in der Regel mit Art. 211 Hand in Hand geht, ausgeschlossen hat, und als der Entwurf (Art. 291) sogar den Wohnort der Partei bei der Fristerweiterung ganz außer Betracht gelassen und nur den Wohnort des Anwalts berücksichtigt hatte.

Diese Lösung hat auch die gewichtigsten praktischen Erwägungen für sich, indem es zu den größten Ungereimtheiten führen würde, wenn die Thatsache, daß irgend ein in Nordamerika oder sonstwo in der Ferne sich aufhaltender Streitgenosse kurz vor der Beweisaufnahme gestorben wäre oder seinen Stand verändert hätte, eine Unterbrechung von Rechtswegen und die Nichtigkeit des Verfahrens zur Folge haben würde! Etwas Derartiges kann der Gesetzgeber nicht gewollt haben.

6) Hat der Richter ein Beweisurtheil erlassen, so darf er selbst es nicht zurücknehmen, sondern muß es vollziehen, selbst wenn er mittlerweile seine Ansicht geändert hat und obgleich ihn nichts hindert, dieser neuen Ansicht in seinem Endurtheile Ausdruck zu geben.

Uebrigens versteht sich von selbst, daß Art. 332 nicht für den Fall gilt, wo die Beweisaufnahme gegenstandslos wird, sei es weil der Beweisführer darauf verzichtet, sei es weil der Gegner die zu erweisenden Thatsachen zugibt.

Ebenso kann das Beweisurtheil auf dem Wege des Einspruchs vom nemlichen Richter zurückgenommen werden.

Gegenbeweis.

Art. 333. — **Die Führung des Gegenbeweises, soweit er nicht gesetzlich ausgeschlossen oder beschränkt ist, steht jeder Partei von Rechtswegen frei.**

Will eine Partei die gegen sie streitende gesetzliche Vermuthung oder den gegen sie in der Verhandlung gelieferten Beweis durch den Nachweis des Gegentheils zerstören, so ist ein solcher Beweis bei der Verhandlung anzubieten und bleibt dagegen der andern Partei der Gegenbeweis offen.

Gleiches gilt von dem Falle, wenn eine Partei nicht das gerade Gegentheil dessen, was ihr Gegner zu beweisen hat, sondern andere Thatsachen, wodurch die Thatsache des Hauptbeweises ausgeschlossen werden soll, zu erproben beabsichtigt. Ergibt sich das Bedürfniß eines derartigen Gegenbeweises erst im Laufe des Beweisverfahrens, so kann die betreffende Partei sich bei der auf das durchgeführte Beweisverfahren folgenden Verhandlung nachträglich dazu erbieten.

G. A. d. K. d. A. II S. 151—153. 157. 160. 236. 237. 320—323. 327. IV S. 89. K. d. R. II S. 113. IV. S. 43.

1) Wer angegriffen wird, hat das Recht, sich zu vertheidigen, und so ist es selbstverständlich, daß die Führung des Gegenbeweises von Rechtswegen zustehe.

Die Frage, ob ein auferlegter Beweis seiner inneren Natur nach als Hauptbeweis oder als Gegenbeweis anzusehen sei, macht dem französischen Richter wenig Sorge, denn beide Arten von Beweis werden in der nemlichen Weise geführt, und wenn Art. 1341 Code civ. sagt, daß gegen den Inhalt von Urkunden ein Zeugenbeweis nicht zulässig sei, so gilt dies ebenso für den Fall, wo der Gegenbeweis durch eine Urkunde geführt wird, als für den Fall, wo der Hauptbeweisführer eine Urkunde für sich hat. Jeder Beweis, welcher im Urtheile auferlegt wird, gilt ihm ebendeßhalb als Hauptbeweis, als ein Angriff, gegen welchen der Gegenbeweis von Rechtswegen stattfindet.

Anders war es im deutschen Prozesse, wo für den direkten Gegenbeweis der Haupteid ausgeschlossen war und außerdem der Satz galt: »reprobatio reprobationis non datur.«

In der Pfalz hat sich im Wesentlichen nichts geändert, da Art. 457 Ziff. 4 daselbst nicht gilt und die Bestimmungen des Art. 333, namentlich im Hinblicke auf Art. 345 a. E., nicht tief eingreifen; allein für diesseits behauptet die Unterscheidung zwischen Hauptbeweis und Gegenbeweis größere praktische Bedeutung.

2) Wer über diejenigen Thatsachen, welche er nach den allgemeinen Regeln über die Beweislast zu erweisen hat, Beweis führt, führt einen Hauptbeweis, und jeder Beweis, welcher bezweckt, diese Beweisführung direkt oder indirekt zu zerstören, erscheint als Gegenbeweis. Demnach wäre auch der Beweis, welcher gegen eine Rechtsvermuthung geführt wird, als Hauptbeweis zu betrachten, obgleich man ihn, von anderer Anschauung ausgehend, auch füglich einen Gegenbeweis nennen könnte.

Es ist zu unterscheiden:

I. Gegenbeweis, welcher gegen die zu erweisenden Thatsachen selbst gerichtet ist und zwar:

1) direkter Gegenbeweis, welcher das gerade Gegentheil von Dem darthut, was der Gegner behauptet, und
2) indirekter oder künstlicher Gegenbeweis, welcher andere Thatsachen nachweist, aus denen durch Schlußfolgerung die Unwahrheit der Behauptungen des Gegners dargethan werden soll.

II. Gegenbeweis, welcher nur die Beweismittel des Gegners zu entkräften sucht.

Den letztern Beweis (die sog. Beweiseinreden) betrachtete die Jurisprudenz von jeher als einen indirekten Gegenbeweis (Seuff. Comm. Bd. III. S. 46), auch der Entwurf (Art. 279) faßte ihn so auf, und die Prozeßordnung geht, wie die Verhandlungen (Abg. II 236 [Barth], 237 [v. Weiß], 327) zeigen, von einer anderen Anschauung nicht aus, wenn auch der Wortlaut des Gesetzes (Art. 333 Abs. 3) dies nicht klar erkennen läßt.

Der Beweis von Einreden kann, dem Beweise des Klaggrundes gegenüber, nie als Gegenbeweis gelten, da er nicht darauf abzielt, diesen Beweis selbst zu zerstören, sondern nur dessen rechtliche Folgen zu beseitigen. Er richtet sich gegen das Recht, nicht gegen die Beweisführung.

3) Art. 333 Abs. 1 bestimmt, daß der Gegenbeweis von Rechtswegen zustehe, soweit er nicht gesetzlich ausgeschlossen oder beschränkt sei.

Ausgeschlossen ist derselbe bei einer praesumtio juris et de jure, welche also hier vom Gesetzgeber als Hauptbeweis betrachtet wird.

Beschränkt ist er, wo das Gesetz einen höheren Grad des Gegenbeweises verlangt, wie dies früher bei Schuldurkunden und Quittungen nach Verlauf der Frist zur Erhebung der querela non numeratae pecuniae der Fall war, oder wo einzelne Beweismittel ausgeschlossen sind, wie z. B. der Zeugenbeweis gegen den Inhalt einer Urkunde (Art. 399).

4) Art. 333 Abs. 2 bestimmt, daß diejenige Partei, welche eine Rechtsvermuthung oder einen bei der Verhandlung bereits erbrachten Beweis entkräften wolle, bezüglichen Beweis anzubieten habe, gegen welchen der Gegenbeweis offen stehe. Hiermit ist gesagt, daß solche Beweise, was Führung des Gegenbeweises anbelangt, als Hauptbeweise zu behandeln seien, eine Bestimmung, welche, sofern sie den in der Verhandlung geführten Beweis betrifft, offenbar eine Ausnahme schafft und den Satz: »reprobatio reprobationis non datur« umstößt, wie er denn überhaupt keinen Werth mehr hat.

Wenn das Gesetz von dem bei der Verhandlung geführten Beweise spricht, so hat es wohl hauptsächlich einen Beweis durch Urkunden im Auge; allein da es bezüglich der Art des Beweises nicht unterscheidet, so wird auch der Richter nicht unterscheiden dürfen, und wenn ihm daher die Verhandlung irgend einen Beweis der Art liefert, daß er das betreffende Recht zusprechen muß, falls es der Gegenbeweisführung nicht gelingt, seine Ueberzeugung zu erschüttern, so darf und soll er den Gegenbeweis als Hauptbeweis auferlegen. Vgl. Seuff. Comm. Bd. III S. 46 Note 2a.

5) Art. 333 Abs. 3 verfügt, daß auch der Gegenbeweis dann gesondert anzubieten und aufzuerlegen sei, wenn er ein künstlicher sei, d. h. wenn er sich auf andere Thatsachen, als diejenigen, welche Gegenstand des Hauptbeweises sind, erstrecke.

Es ist dies in der Pfalz von jeher so geübt worden, obgleich das Gesetz dazu nicht verpflichtete, und zwar weil man es für natürlich und sachentsprechend hielt, im Urtheile alle besonderen Thatumstände, über welche sich die Beweisführung zu erstrecken hat, anzuführen. (S. Bemerk. zu Art. 324 Nr. 4). Man ließ sich überhaupt hier von Gründen der Zweckmäßigkeit leiten und machte hie und da selbst beim direkten Gegenbeweise, z. B. wenn zwei verschiedene Versionen des Lautes eines mündlich abgeschlossenen Vertrages in Betracht kommen, die abweichenden Angaben der Gegenpartei zum Gegenstande einer Beweisauflage, weil dies zur Auffrischung des

Gedächtnisses der Zeugen und zum Anhaltspunkte für den Richter beim Verhöre sachgemäß erschien. Das Beweisurtheil bindet ja nicht und es hindert daher nichts, das zu thun, was der Sache am förderlichsten ist.

Sollten einzelne Thatsachen, welche zum künstlichen Gegenbeweise gehören, nicht ausdrücklich zum Beweise auferlegt werden, so ist dies insofern kein wesentlicher Nachtheil, als nach Art. 345 der Beweis nichtsdestoweniger gelegentlich erhoben und berücksichtigt werden darf.

Gegen den künstlichen Gegenbeweis ist selbstverständlich wiederum Gegenbeweis zulässig.

6) Die Schlußworte des Art. 333 treffen Vorsorge für Fälle, wo sich das Bedürfniß, einen indirekten Gegenbeweis, namentlich aber einen solchen, der die gebrauchten Beweismittel zu entkräften, z. B. die Unglaubwürdigkeit von Zeugen darzuthun sucht, erst im Laufe des Beweisverfahrens ergibt, indem verfügt wird, daß in diesem Falle nachträglicher Beweis erboten und zugelassen werden könne.

Natürlich wird, so weit möglich, der Richter bestrebt sein müssen, sofort bei der Beweisaufnahme die betreffenden Thatsachen klar zu stellen, wozu Art. 345 die Möglichkeit bietet. An der Hand der so gewonnenen Anhaltspunkte wird in der Regel die Sachlage sich würdigen lassen, und werden nachträgliche Beweisauflagen, welche die Prozesse verzögern und vertheuern, vermieden werden können.

Beweisaufnahme

Art. 334. — **Gestatten Gegenstand und Art der Beweisführung die Aufnahme des Beweises in der Sitzung, so hat das Beweisurtheil zugleich die Sitzung zu bestimmen, in welcher die Beweisaufnahme vorgenommen werden soll. Andernfalls beauftragt das Gericht damit eines seiner Mitglieder oder ein Einzelngericht des Königreichs. Kann das bezeichnete Gerichtsmitglied wegen eingetretener Verhinderung die aufgetragene Handlung nicht vornehmen, so ernennt der Senatsvorstand ein anderes Mitglied an dessen Stelle und läßt die Anwälte davon durch die Gerichtsschreiberei in Kenntniß setzen.**

Art. 335. — **Um Beweisaufnahmen, welche im Auslande vorgenommen werden sollen, ist die betreffende ausländische Gerichtsbehörde, falls aber hiegegen besondere Bedenken bestehen, die betreffende bayerische Gesandtschaft oder ein bayerisches Consulat zu ersuchen.**

Zur Giltigkeit solcher Beweishandlungen ist es vorbehaltlich besonderer Bestimmungen des Gesetzes genügend, wenn die Handlung den am Orte geltenden Vorschriften oder der bayerischen Prozeßordnung entspricht.

G. A. d. K. d. A. II S. 160–162. 327. 328. — K. d. R. II S. 113. 114.

1) Die Beweisaufnahmen sollen in der Sitzung geschehen. Ist dies jedoch nicht thunlich, sei es wegen der Natur des Beweises, wie beim Augenscheine, in der Regel auch beim Gutachten Sachverständiger, sei es aus gewichtigen Gründen anderer Art, wegen Krankheit oder großer Entfernung der Zeugen, Schwierigkeit und Umständlichkeit der Beweisaufnahme, Ueberhäufung des Gerichts mit Geschäften, so findet die Beweisaufnahme durch einen beauftragten Richter statt. In diesen Fällen beauftragt das Gericht entweder eines seiner Mitglieder oder ein Einzelgericht des Königreichs.

Es versteht sich wohl von selbst, daß in der Regel einer der Richter, welche das Beweisurtheil erlassen haben, zu bezeichnen sei, da dieser die Sache bereits kennt und weiß, in welchem Sinne die Beweisaufnahme stattfinden solle, auf welche Gesichtspunkte besonderer Werth zu legen sei; allein nach dem Laute des Gesetzes steht nichts entgegen, ausnahmsweise auch ein anderes Gerichtsmitglied zu bezeichnen.

Hat die Beweisaufnahme in einem anderen Gerichtsbezirke stattzufinden, oder sind alle Mitglieder des Gerichts als verhindert zu betrachten, oder lassen Rücksichten auf Kostenersparung (Art. 404) es rathsam erscheinen, so ist ein Einzelgericht des Reiches zu beauftragen. Demgemäß wäre es nicht statthaft, das Ersuchen an ein anderes Bezirksgericht des Reiches zu richten, und ist es ferner gleichgiltig, ob das Einzelgericht dem beauftragenden Gerichte untergeordnet ist oder nicht.

2) Bei Verhinderung des bezeichneten Gerichtsmitgliedes wird ein anderes Mitglied durch den Senatsvorstand bezeichnet, welcher jedoch selbstverständlich nur über die seinem Senate zugetheilten Gerichtsmitglieder verfügen darf. Abg. II 161.

Diese Vorschrift gilt für alle Fälle der Verhinderung im weitesten Sinne dieses Wortes, also auch für den Fall, wenn der Richter gestorben, entsetzt oder versetzt worden ist.

Sie erscheint höchst sachgemäß; daß insbesondere

die Bedenken, welche bei den Verhandlungen (Abg. II 161) erhoben wurden, rein aus der Luft gegriffen waren, ergibt sich daraus, daß die französische Praxis es ganz unbedenklich findet, in Fällen, wo der Richter noch in Funktion am Gerichte und nur wegen Krankheit ꝛc. verhindert ist, ohne Weiteres irgend einen Collegen zu dessen Entlastung handeln zu lassen. Sie schafft sich hiermit gewissermaßen einen Nothweg.

3) Sind Beweisaufnahmen im Auslande vorzunehmen, so richtet das Gericht am Schlusse seines Urtheils ein bezügliches Ersuchen an die betreffende ausländische Gerichtsbehörde; im Falle aber hiegegen besondere Bedenken bestehen, an eine bayer. Gesandtschaft oder an ein bayer. Consulat. Den Vollzug zu veranlassen, ist Sache der Parteien.

Die betreffende Gerichtsbehörde ist diejenige, welche für den Ort, wo die Beweisaufnahme stattfinden soll, zuständig ist, gerichtliche Akte dieser Art vorzunehmen. Auf die Frage, ob sie etwa in vorliegendem Rechtsstreite zuständig sein würde, ist kein Werth zu legen. Vgl. Bemerk. zu Art. 55 Nr. 5.

Es erscheint nicht unumgänglich nöthig, daß die Gerichtsbehörde im Urtheile benannt oder bestimmt bezeichnet sei; denn in Fällen, wo im fernen Auslande Beweise zu erheben sind, ist dies oft unmöglich. In solchen Ausnahmsfällen muß es daher genügen, daß das Ersuchen allgemein an die für den zu bezeichnenden Ort zuständige Gerichtsbehörde gerichtet werde und sich später aus der Beweisaufnahme die Zuständigkeit der handelnden Behörde ergebe.

4) Zur Giltigkeit solcher im Auslande vorgenommenen Beweishandlungen genügt es, wenn sie entweder den am Orte geltenden Vorschriften oder den Vorschriften der bayer. Prozeßordnung entsprechen.

Der Entwurf (Art. 288) wollte das ausländische Recht bloß für die Formen der Beweisaufnahmen gelten lassen; allein man hielt es nöthig, weiter zu gehen und die jetzige Fassung zu wählen, ohne sich zu verhehlen, daß Schwierigkeiten entstehen könnten. Abg. II 328 (zu Art. 16).

Offenbar ist es die Meinung des Gesetzes nicht, daß das ganze Beweisverfahren nach der ausländischen Gesetzgebung sich regeln dürfe, vielmehr spricht dasselbe nur von der Giltigkeit von Beweishandlungen, d. h. solchen Handlungen, welche sich direkt auf die Beweisaufnahme beziehen und im Auslande bethätigt werden müssen. Zu diesen Handlungen gehört z. B. auch das Vorladen der im Auslande wohnhaften Zeugen. Vorschriften der Prozeßordnung, welche nicht die Beweishandlungen selbst, sondern das vorbereitende Verfahren zum Gegenstande haben, und welche ebensogut beobachtet werden können, als wenn die Beweisaufnahme im Inlande geschähe, dürfen nicht versäumt werden.

So hat der Beweisaufnahme nicht allein die Zustellung des Beweisurtheils vorauszugehen, sondern muß auch die Zustellung des Beschlusses, welcher Tagfahrt zur Beweisaufnahme festsetzt (Art. 338), innerhalb der gesetzlichen Frist stattfinden. Es wäre schlimm, wenn deßhalb, weil der Beweis in Württemberg oder Baden aufgenommen wird, diese Zustellung unterlassen und so der Gegenpartei die Möglichkeit entzogen werden könnte, dabei zugegen zu sein oder sich vertreten zu lassen. Auch bezüglich der Einhaltung der Fristen zum Antritte des Zeugenbeweises und zur Mittheilung des Verzeichnisses der Zeugen (Art. 406 u. 412) kommen nur die Vorschriften der Prozeßordnung zur Anwendung. Vgl. Art. 407.

Eine vom zuständigen Gerichte des Auslandes erfolgte Beweisaufnahme hat selbstverständlich die Vermuthung für sich, den Gesetzen des Auslandes zu entsprechen, und bedarf es in dieser Beziehung keines Nachweises.

Art. 336. — **Hat eine Partei von verschiedenen Arten von Beweismitteln Gebrauch gemacht, so sind diese, soweit es ihre Natur gestattet, bei der Beweisaufnahme zu verbinden.**

Art. 337. — **Jeder Partei steht das Recht zu, von ihr vorgeschlagene Beweis- oder Gegenbeweismittel wieder fallen zu lassen; sind aber Urkunden mitgetheilt, sind Zeugen oder Sachverständige als solche der Gegenpartei bereits bekannt gegeben, oder ist ein Augenschein bereits begonnen, so kann auf diese Beweismittel einseitig nicht mehr verzichtet werden.**

G. A. d. K. d. A. II S. 155. 156. 328. IV S. 89. — K. d. R. II S. 114. IV. S. 43.

1) Die Vorschrift des Art. 336 bezielt Vereinfachung des Verfahrens und Minderung der Kosten, und gilt als Weisung sowohl für die Parteien bei ihren Anträgen auf Beweisaufnahme, als für das Gericht oder den beauftragten Richter bei Festsetzung der Tagfahrt.

Mit dem Augenscheine kann häufig Expertise oder Zeugenverhör vereinigt werden; auch Zeugenverhör und Expertise lassen sich manchmal verbinden.

2) In Art. 337 ist der Zeitpunkt bestimmt, welcher die Beweismittel gemeinschaftlich macht, so daß sie einseitig nicht mehr zurückgenommen werden können. Bei Urkunden ist die Mit-

theilung derselben entscheidend, sei es, daß dieselbe im Vorverfahren nach Vorschrift von Art. 172 und 173 geschehe, sei es daß sie geschehe durch Vorlage und Geltendmachung der Urkunden in der Sitzung. Auch das französische Recht erkennt diesen Grundsatz an und Art. 409 Code penal droht eine Strafe für diejenigen, welche eine Urkunde absichtlich beseitigen, nachdem sie einmal im Prozesse geltend gemacht war.

Sollte eine bereits mitgetheilte Urkunde später nicht mehr vorgelegt werden, so würde zu vermuthen sein, daß sie durch Schuld der Partei, welche verpflichtet war, sie im gemeinschaftlichen Interesse zu verwahren, bezw. ihres Anwaltes zu Verlust gegangen sei, und müßte der Nachweis des Mangels einer Verschuldung geführt werden. Das Gericht würde, ähnlich wie im Falle des Art. 156, die sachgemäßen Folgerungen ziehen dürfen. S. Art. 393 Abs. 2.

Zeugen und Sachverständige werden gemeinschaftlich, sobald sie der Gegenpartei bekannt gegeben sind, also Zeugen durch die in Gemäßheit des Art. 412 erfolgende Zustellung, Sachverständige dadurch, daß sie in der Sitzung oder in gesonderter Zustellung vorgeschlagen werden. Offenbar läßt der natürliche Sinn der gesetzlichen Bestimmung keine andere Auslegung zu, als daß die Gegenpartei das Recht habe, einen Sachverständigen, der vorgeschlagen ist, durch ihre Zustimmung zu einem gewählten zu machen. Auf Sachverständige, welche das Gericht ernannt hat, kann selbstverständlich nie einseitig verzichtet werden.

Der Augenschein soll gemeinschaftlich werden, sobald er begonnen ist.

3) Ist ein Beweis von Amtswegen angeordnet, wie dies beim Augenscheine Regel ist, so kann selbstverständlich von einem Verzichte auf die Beweisaufnahme überhaupt keine Rede sein.

Art. 338. — **Ist die Tagfahrt zur Beweisaufnahme nicht im Beweisurtheile bestimmt, so muß der dieselbe festsetzende Beschluß dem Gegner wenigstens acht Tage vor der Tagfahrt zugestellt werden. Die Vorschrift des Art. 209 findet hiebei keine Anwendung, dagegen ist der beauftragte Richter befugt, die Zeit, welche zwischen der Zustellung und der Tagfahrt in Mitte zu liegen hat, nach Bedürfniß der Sache mit Rücksicht auf die Wohnorte und die sonstigen Verhältnisse der Parteien zu erweitern.**

Art. 339. — **Die Zustellung des die Tagfahrt zur Beweisaufnahme festsetzenden Urtheils oder Beschlusses (Art. 331 und 338) gilt als Vorladung der Gegenpartei.**

Art. 340. — **Erscheinen bei der Tagfahrt die Parteien weder persönlich noch durch Gewalthaber, so ist gleichwohl, soweit es geschehen kann, zur Beweisaufnahme zu schreiten. Gegen die Nichterschienenen tritt der Ausschluß der Handlungen ein, welche ihnen dabei zugestanden wären.** G. A. d. K. d. A. II S. 162—164. 328. IV S. 89. 98. — K. d. R. II S. 114. IV S. 43.

1) Hat das Beweisurtheil die Tagfahrt zur Beweisaufnahme nicht bestimmt, so muß diese Bestimmung durch Beschluß des beauftragten oder ersuchten Richters geschehen.

Der Anwalt des betreibenden Theils richtet, unter Vorlage der Ausfertigung des Beweisurtheils oder der zugestellten Abschrift desselben, an den Richter ein bezügliches Gesuch, auf welches dieser seinen Beschluß setzt, der in Urschrift hinausgegeben wird. Dieser Beschluß ist dem Gegenanwalte zuzustellen und zwar nebst dem Urtheile, zu dessen Vollzug er erging, falls letztere Zustellung, wie es Regel ist, nicht bereits geschehen sein sollte.

2) Das Gesetz bestimmt, wie in Art. 331, daß die Zustellung besagten Beschlusses mindestens acht Tage vor der Beweisaufnahme stattzufinden habe und daß auf dieselbe Art. 209 nicht anwendbar sei.

Es bestimmt ferner, daß der beauftragte Richter befugt sei, diese Frist zu erweitern. Vielleicht wäre es geeigneter gewesen, dieses unter Umständen sehr wichtige und folgenreiche Recht dem Gerichte selbst vorzubehalten, welches bei Spruch seines Beweisurtheiles recht gut in der Lage ist, zu beurtheilen, ob die Frist von acht Tagen ungenügend sei und welche Erweiterung nach Maßgabe der Wohnorte und der sonstigen Verhältnisse der Parteien nöthig sei. Dem beauftragten Richter hätte man vielleicht gestatten können, bei besonderen Umständen die Frist noch weiter auszudehnen.

Im Uebrigen gilt alles, was oben zu Art. 331 Nr. 2—5 bemerkt worden ist, insbesondere auch bezüglich der Anwendbarkeit des Art. 211.

3) Die auf Grund von Art. 331 oder 338 erfolgte Mittheilung der Tagfahrt an den Anwalt der Gegenpartei gilt als Vorladung für diese selbst; es ist daher Sache des Anwaltes, seine Partei zeitig von Festsetzung der Tagfahrt in Kenntniß und in die Lage zu versetzen, zu erscheinen.

Die Pflicht der Vertretung oder der Sorge für die Vertretung obliegt zunächst ihm selbst.

4) Die Beweisaufnahme findet statt, ob die Parteien dabei erscheinen oder sich vertreten lassen,

oder nicht; letzteren Falls ist anzunehmen, daß sie es nicht für nöthig halten, zugegen zu sein. Selbstverständlich erleidet dies eine Ausnahme, soweit die Beweisaufnahme durch die Anwesenheit der Partei bedingt ist, z. B. bei einer Eidesleistung.

Durch das Nichterscheinen entgehen der Partei diejenigen Vortheile, welche die Anwesenheit ihr hätte verschaffen können, sei es durch Aufklärungen, welche sie dem Richter oder den Sachverständigen zu geben im Stande gewesen wäre, sei es durch Fragen, welche sie an die Zeugen gestellt, sei es durch Vorhalt, welchen sie dem zum Eide zugelassenen Gegner gemacht hätte. Vgl. Verhdl. Abg. II 331 (zu Art. 27).

Setzt die Beweisaufnahme ein Handeln der Partei voraus, wie bei der Eidesauflage, so wird sie damit ausgeschlossen, sofern sie nicht Verlegung der Tagfahrt (Art. 464) oder Wiedereinsetzung in den vorigen Stand erwirkt.

Art. 341. — **Das Verfahren bei der Beweisaufnahme durch einen beauftragten Richter ist nicht öffentlich. Die Parteien können sich dabei durch ihren aufgestellten Anwalt oder durch einen andern bayerischen Advokaten vertreten lassen und auch persönlich mit oder ohne Vertreter oder Beistand erscheinen.**

Der beauftragte Richter kann veranlassen, daß ihm die Parteiakten zur Einsicht vorgelegt werden. Die Akten über die gepflogenen Verhandlungen sind an die Gerichtsschreiberei des Prozeßgerichts abzugeben.

Art. 342. — **Die Befugniß des beauftragten Richters erstreckt sich vorbehaltlich besonderer gesetzlicher Bestimmung nicht auf Anwendung von Zwangsmaßregeln.**

Ergeben sich vor dem beauftragten Richter Anstände oder Streitigkeiten, zu deren Entscheidung ihm nicht durch besondere Verfügung des Gesetzes die Ermächtigung ertheilt ist, so hat er mit der Erhebung des Beweises, soweit es die Umstände gestatten und ein wesentlicher Nachtheil dadurch nicht entstehen kann, fortzufahren, die Anstände oder Streitigkeiten und die darüber abgegebenen Erklärungen der Parteien aber zu Protokoll zu nehmen und zur Verhandlung an das Prozeßgericht zu verweisen.

Kann diese Verhandlung nicht bis zur nächsten Verhandlung in der Hauptsache ausgesetzt bleiben, so ist die Sitzung dafür auf schriftliches Ansuchen einer Partei durch den Senatsvorstand festzusetzen und seine Verfügung der Gegenpartei unverzüglich mit der Aufforderung zum Erscheinen in der festgesetzten Sitzung zustellen zu lassen. Zustellung motivirter Anträge ist nicht geboten. Gegen das Urtheil steht einer Partei, welche sich über die erhobenen Anstände oder Streitigkeiten vor dem beauftragten Richter erklärt hat oder hätte erklären können, kein Einspruch zu.

G. A. d. K. d. A. II S. 161. 162. 164. 165. 182. 183. 328. 329. 336. 451. IV S. 89. 90.
K. d. R. II S. 114. IV S. 43.

1) In diesen beiden Artikeln regelt das Gesetz das Verfahren vor dem beauftragten Richter, bestimmt dessen Befugnisse und gibt Vorschriften, wie es zu halten sei, wenn sich bei der Beweisaufnahme vor demselben Streitigkeiten ergeben.

a) Verfahren.

2) Bei Beweisaufnahmen, welche nicht in der Sitzung, sondern durch einen beauftragten Richter geschehen, glaubte der Gesetzgeber, aus naheliegenden Gründen der Zweckmäßigkeit, den Anwaltszwang nicht streng durchführen zu müssen.

Die Parteien dürfen nicht nur persönlich erscheinen und ihre Rechte wahren, sondern es ist ihnen auch gestattet, wenn sie sich vertreten lassen wollen, ihre Vertretung einem beliebigen Advokaten des Inlandes zu übertragen, ohne Rücksicht, ob er zu Anwaltsfunktionen am Orte, wo das Beweisverfahren stattfindet, berechtigt sei oder nicht. Endlich können sie, falls sie persönlich erscheinen, eine beliebige Person als Rechtsbeistand beiziehen.

Der Advokat, durch welchen sich die Partei vertreten läßt oder welchen, was Regel ist, ihr Anwalt für sie substituirt, bedarf keines besonderen Nachweises der Bevollmächtigung, ist vielmehr kraft seiner Erklärung, mit der Vertretung beauftragt zu sein, befugt, alle Handlungen vorzunehmen, welche der Zweck der in Frage stehenden gerichtlichen Verhandlung mit sich bringt. Es wäre dem Geiste des Gesetzes zuwider, hier eine Ausnahme zu machen. Vgl. Bemerk. zu Art. 89 Nr. 5.

Er hat auch dann den Charakter eines Vertreters, wenn die Partei persönlich anwesend ist. Abg. II 336 (Behringer).

Die Oeffentlichkeit ist bei Beweisaufnahmen durch einen beauftragten Richter ausgeschlossen.

3) Findet die Beweisaufnahme in der Sitzung statt, so gelten die Ausnahmsbestimmungen

des Art. 341 nicht und bleibt es bei den gewöhnlichen Grundsätzen. Das Verfahren ist daher öffentlich, in derselben Weise, wie überhaupt die Verhandlungen in der Sitzung in Gemäßheit der Grundsätze der Art. 148 und 149.

Auch in diesem Falle wird zwar der Beweis, soweit möglich, auch dann aufgenommen, wenn die Parteien nicht erscheinen, denn Art. 340 spricht allgemein; allein da nach Art. 344 Abs. 1 sofort nach Beendigung der Beweisaufnahme die Verhandlung stattfinden soll, so werden die Anwälte zugegen sein müssen, wenn sie nicht wollen, daß Versäumungsurtheil ergehe.

Was die Geltendmachung der Rechte der Parteien bei der Beweisaufnahme — das Erheben von Einwänden, das Stellen von Anträgen — betrifft, so gelten hier die allgemeinen Grundsätze, vermöge deren im Anwaltsprozesse die Partei nicht befugt ist, persönlich zu handeln, sondern durch einen Anwalt des Prozeßgerichtes vertreten sein muß. Abg. II 161 a. E. (v. Neumayr).

4) Dem beauftragten Richter werden einige Zeit vor der Beweisaufnahme die Parteiakten zur Einsicht mitgetheilt, was wohl in allen Fällen sachgemäß ist und geschehen soll. Auch im Falle, wo ein Einzelrichter beauftragt ist, erscheint es in der Regel rathsam, daß ihm wenigstens eine der Parteien ihre Akten zusende.

Ist diese Mittheilung nicht geschehen, so kann der Richter anordnen, daß ihm die Akten vorgelegt werden. Selbstverständlich ist weder für diese Anordnung noch für die Vorlage irgend eine Förmlichkeit nöthig, und um dies anzudeuten, wurde der Ausdruck: „veranlassen" gewählt. Abg. IV 89 a. E.

Hat eine Beweisaufnahme im fernen Auslande stattzufinden, so kann nicht verlangt werden, daß die Akten versendet werden sollen, auf die Gefahr hin, daß sie verloren gehen oder wenigstens Monate lang ausbleiben. In solchen Fällen muß das Urtheil genügen, welches ja alle wesentlichen Punkte enthält und für den besonderen Zweck mit besonderer Sorgfalt abgefaßt zu werden pflegt. Ueberhaupt sind die Vorschriften, welche bezüglich des beauftragten Richters gegeben sind, nicht unbedingt, sondern nur analog auf ausländische Behörden, welche ersucht werden, anzuwenden.

Bei Beweisaufnahmen in der Sitzung bedarf es einer vorausgängigen Mittheilung der Prozeßakten nicht. Die Anwälte tragen, soweit nöthig, den Sachverhalt vor und händigen sofort dem Gerichte ihre Akten zur Benützung ein.

5) Da der beauftragte Richter seine Funktion nur als Stellvertreter ausübt, so ist es natürlich, daß die Protokolle, welche er aufnimmt, Eigenthum des beauftragenden Gerichtes seien und daher dem Gerichtsschreiber dieses Gerichtes zur vorschriftsmäßigen Aufbewahrung in Urschrift zugesendet werden müssen. Art. 341 Abs. 2.

b) Anstände und Streitigkeiten.

6) Der beauftragte oder ersuchte Richter hat nur ein begrenztes Mandat und darf in der Regel nur beurkunden, was zum Zwecke der Beweisaufnahme geschieht, jedoch keine Entscheidung treffen, es sei denn daß ihn eine ausdrückliche Bestimmung des Gesetzes dazu ermächtigte (vgl. Art. 430).

Die gleiche Regel gilt für Anwendung von Zwangsmaßregeln (vgl. Art. 427).

7) Ergeben sich Anstände, welche der Richter von Amtswegen zu erheben sich veranlaßt findet, oder entstehen Streitigkeiten unter den Parteien, so hat der Richter diese Anstände und Steitigkeiten, sowie die darüber abgegebenen Erklärungen der Parteien, eintretenden Falls auch die Thatsache, daß eine oder die andere Partei nichts erwidert hat, urkundlich festzustellen, die Verhandlung aber an's Prozeßgericht zu verweisen.

Mit der Erhebung des Beweises hat er nichtsdestoweniger in der Regel fortzufahren. Das Gesetz sagt hier: „soweit es die Umstände gestatten und ein wesentlicher Nachtheil daraus nicht entstehen kann," hätte aber auch beifügen dürfen: „soweit das Gesetz nicht anders verfügt," denn in einer Reihe von Fällen ist ausdrücklich vorgeschrieben, daß die Beweisaufnahme ausgesetzt werden solle, bis das Prozeßgericht über den Zwischenstreit entschieden habe, z. B. wenn es sich um Untüchtigkeit von Zeugen (Art. 425 Abs. 1) oder eine Eidesleistung (Art. 450) handelt. Ueberhaupt hat der Gesetzgeber für alle wichtigeren Fälle bei den einzelnen Beweismitteln Vorsorge getroffen.

8) Die Verhandlung über Zwischenstreite bei der Beweisaufnahme erfolgt in Fällen, wo diese trotz des Zwischenstreites vollständig stattgefunden hat, gewöhnlich in der nemlichen Sitzung, in welcher auch die Hauptsache verhandelt wird, obgleich nicht immer in der nemlichen Verhandlung, wie denn z. B. über die Verwerfung von Zeugen gesondert zu verhandeln und zu entscheiden ist, ehe in die Verhandlung der Hauptsache eingegangen werden kann. Art. 426 Abs. 3.

9) Liegt Grund vor, über solche Zwischenstreite in einer besonderen Sitzung zu verhandeln, ein Fall, der überall gegeben ist, wo die Beweisaufnahme erst nach deren Entscheidung stattfinden oder beendigt werden kann, so ist dafür ein möglichst summarisches Verfahren vorgeschrieben und

zwar so ziemlich das nemliche, wie es die Art. 259 und 485 bestimmen.

Der Senatsvorstand setzt auf Gesuch des Anwaltes einer Partei in der zu Art. 338 Nr. 1 bezeichneten Weise eine Sitzung fest und diese Fixation ist unverzüglich dem Gegner mit Aufforderung zum Erscheinen zuzustellen.

Zustellung motivirter Anträge ist nicht geboten, d. h. es findet kein Vorverfahren statt, jedoch sind allerdings den allgemeinen Grundsätzen des Verfahrens gemäß einfache Anträge in der Sitzung zu nehmen und zu hinterlegen.

10) Eine Eigenheit dieses Verfahrens ist es, daß derjenigen Partei, welche bei der Beweisaufnahme oder vielmehr bei Protokollirung der bezüglichen Anstände und Streitigkeiten zugegen oder vertreten war, das Recht des Einspruches unbedingt versagt ist, so daß also hier nicht die Antragstellung in der Sitzung, sondern die bloße Anwesenheit bei der Beweisaufnahme, die Möglichkeit, sich dort zu vertheidigen, die Sache contradiktorisch macht.

Als eine selbstverständliche, im Geiste des Gesetzes begründete Folge dieser Ausnahmsbestimmung erscheint es, daß die Erklärungen, welche die Partcien selbst oder deren Vertreter vor dem beauftragten Richter abgegeben haben, Berücksichtigung finden müssen; es gilt also in gewissem Sinne hier schriftliches Verfahren.

11) Die Ausnahmsbestimmung bezüglich des Einspruches gilt nur für den Fall der gesonderten Verhandlung von Zwischenstreiten. Findet die Verhandlung gleichzeitig mit der Verhandlung der Hauptsache statt, so daß weder die Beweisaufnahme noch die Verhandlung der Hauptsache durch Zulassung des Einspruches verzögert wird, so fällt der Grund der Ausnahme und diese selbst weg. Abg. II 165 (v. Weiß). Es gelten in diesem Falle überhaupt nur die allgemeinen Grundsätze.

Art. 343. — **Den Zeugen und Sachverständigen ist die in der Gebührenordnung begründete Entschädigung für Reisekosten und Zeitversäumniß, sowie nach Umständen für die Erstattung des Gutachtens auf Begehren anzuweisen.**

Zur Bestreitung der Vergütungen für die Zeugen und Sachverständigen, der Tagegelder und Reisekosten für Gerichtspersonen, welche eine Beweishandlung außerhalb des Gerichtssitzes aufzunehmen haben, und der durch Aufnahme eines Beweises im Auslande sich ergebenden Kosten hat der Beweisführer eine von dem Vorsitzenden oder dem mit der Beweisaufnahme beauftragten Richter festzusetzende Summe auf der Gerichtsschreiberei zu hinterlegen.

Die Zeugen und Sachverständigen werden durch den Gerichtsschreiber aus den hinterlegten Beträgen befriedigt.

Personen, welche vom Gerichtssitze entfernt wohnen, sind nicht verpflichtet, der Ladung Folge zu leisten, wenn sie Bescheinigung darüber verlangt haben, daß die in Abs. 2 vorschriebene Hinterlegung stattgefunden habe, und ihnen diese Bescheinigung nicht geliefert worden ist.

Die näheren Bestimmungen, insbesondere über die Art, wie die erwähnte Bescheinigung zu verlangen und zu liefern ist, sowie die Gebührenordnung werden im Verordnungswege erlassen.

G. A. d. K. d. A. II S. 164. 216. 329. 330. 451. IV S. 90. 93. K. d. R. II S. 114. IV S. 43.

1) Diesseits sorgte bis jetzt das Gericht selbst für Bestreitung der Kosten, in der Pfalz aber war diese Sorge ausschließlich den Parteien in die Hand gegeben.

Wer in der Pfalz irgend ein gerichtliches Verfahren betreiben wollte, konnte dies nur thun, indem er die damit verbundenen Kosten bestritt und die betreffenden ministeriellen Beamten im Voraus wegen derselben sicherstellte; für Ansprüche von Zeugen und Experten bestand zwar keine derartige Sicherstellung, allein das Gesetz gab einen sehr einfachen Weg, um sie nöthigenfalls einzutreiben, indem es die Taxe des Richters vollziehbar erklärte. Die Anwälte pflegten dafür zu sorgen, daß vor den Beweisaufnahmen die dazu nöthigen Geldmittel vorschußweise in ihre Hände kamen und es ergaben sich so nie Schwierigkeiten, insbesondere erinnere ich mich keines Falles, wo Experten oder Zeugen ihre Gebühren hätten eintreiben müssen.

Unsere Prozeßordnung schlägt einen Mittelweg ein, indem sie vorschreibt, daß zur Bestreitung bestimmter in Art. 343 Abs. 2 bezeichneter Kosten eine entsprechende Summe zum Voraus auf der Gerichtsschreiberei hinterlegt werde.

Im Uebrigen bleibt es bei der allgemeinen Regel des Art. 105, daß jede Partei die Kosten, welche sie veranlaßt, bestreiten müsse, und besteht keine Vorschrift darüber, wie dies geschehe. In der Praxis gestaltet sich die Sache einfach so, daß der aufgestellte Anwalt, von welchem ja auch die Aufträge auszugehen pflegen, alle Auslagen an Gerichtschreiber, Gerichtsvollzieher rc. bestreitet, nachdem er sich durch Vorschuß oder sonstwie seiner Partei gegenüber sichergestellt hat.

2) Eine vorausgängige Hinterlegung der Kosten auf der Gerichtschreiberei ist zunächst vorgeschrieben für die Vergütungen, welche Zeugen und Sachverständige nach Maßgabe der Gebührenordnung zu beanspruchen haben.

Die Bestimmung der Summe erfolgt, je nachdem die Beweisaufnahme in der Sitzung erfolgt oder nicht, entweder durch den Vorsitzenden, oder durch den beauftragten Richter. Aus den hinterlegten Geldern werden später Zeugen und Sachverständige durch den Gerichtsschreiber befriedigt.

Die praktische Durchführung dieser Verfügungen könnte manche Schwierigkeiten bieten.

Zum Ersten ist es schwer, die nöthige Summe im Voraus mit einiger Sicherheit zu bestimmen, da bei Festsetzung der Tagfahrt sich meist nicht ermessen läßt, wie viele Zeugen und aus welchen Entfernungen zu vernehmen seien, wie viel Zeit die Verrichtungen der Experten in Anspruch nehmen werden. Bestimmt der Richter zu viel, so beschwert er die Partei; bestimmt er zu wenig, so schädigt er die Zeugen und Experten, welchen er jetzt keine vollziehbare Taxe mehr geben kann, welche er vielmehr auf den gewöhnlichen Klagweg verweisen muß. Zudem hat, was die Zeugen betrifft, der Richter keine weiteren Anhaltspunkte, als die eignen Angaben der Partei.

Zum Weiteren gibt es kein Mittel, die Parteien anzuhalten, daß sie eine Verfügung des Richters veranlassen, daß sie demselben richtige Angaben machen und daß sie dessen Anordnung vollziehen. Es wurde dieser Mangel bei den Verhandlungen angedeutet (Abg. II 164), allein später nichts gethan oder geäußert, was ihn beseitigen könnte.

3) Da übrigens vorauszusetzen ist, daß die Anwälte den guten Willen haben, zum Vollzuge des Gesetzes mitzuwirken, es auch eine Pflichtverletzung wäre, wenn sie dies unterließen, so möchte in den gewöhnlichen Fällen die Sache sich von selbst machen, wie sie auf anderem Wege sich bis jetzt auch in der Pfalz gemacht hat, und es scheint, daß dies der Gedanke des Gesetzgebers gewesen sei.

Bei Festsetzung der Tagfahrt wird sich der Richter angeben lassen, wieviel Zeugen und aus welcher Entfernung vernommen werden sollen, und hiernach sofort die zu hinterlegende Summe bestimmen. Bei der Expertise sind ihm noch sicherere Anhaltspunkte gegeben. Ergibt sich später, daß mehr Zeugen oder andere zu vernehmen sind, oder kommen die Parteien über andere Sachverständige überein, so ist der Anwalt verpflichtet, weitere Verfügung zu veranlassen und der Richter wird selbst von Amtswegen verfügen dürfen, wenn er aus den mitgetheilten Parteiakten entnimmt, daß die bezeichnete Summe nicht reiche.

Leistet die Partei keine Folge, so gibt es allerdings in der Regel kein Zwangsmittel, namentlich aber wäre es unstatthaft, die Beweisaufnahme deßhalb zu verweigern, weil die Hinterlegung nicht stattgefunden habe. Für diesen Fall, sowie für den Fall, wo die hinterlegte Summe nicht ausreicht, wäre es sachgemäß gewesen, die Bestimmung des französischen Prozesses beizubehalten, daß der Richter eine sofort vollziehbare Taxe geben dürfe.

Nur für einen einzigen Fall besteht ein indirekter Zwang, nemlich, wenn ein Zeuge oder Experte, welcher vom Gerichtssitze entfernt wohnt, Bescheinigung darüber verlangt, daß die ihm gebührende Vergütung hinterlegt sei, und diese Bescheinigung nicht geliefert wird. Art. 343 Abs. 4.

4) Das Gesetz sagt, die bestimmte Summe solle auf der Gerichtsschreiberei hinterlegt werden.

Ich halte es für selbstverständlich, daß nur die Gerichtsschreiberei desjenigen Gerichts gemeint sein könne, bei welchem die Beweisaufnahme stattfindet, also eintretenden Falls diejenige des beauftragten Einzelgerichts. Nur der Gerichtsschreiber dieses Gerichts kann auch mit Auszahlung der Gebühren beauftragt sein.

Es erscheint mir ferner selbstverständlich, daß die Gebühren sofort auszuzahlen seien, nachdem der Richter Anweisung gegeben, was bei Zeugen unmittelbar nach deren Vernehmung zu geschehen hat. Es darf offenbar dem Zeugen, welcher entfernt vom Gerichtssitze vernommen wird, nicht zugemuthet werden, sich bloß der Erhebung seiner Gebühren wegen auf die Gerichtsschreiberei zu begeben, d. h. von Neuem Zeit und Mühe zu verwenden, für die er neue Gebühren beanspruchen könnte.

5) Die Hinterlegung ist ferner vorgeschrieben für die Taggelder und Reisekosten der Gerichtspersonen.

Diese Bestimmung bietet keine Schwierigkeiten, denn einerseits ist klar, daß hier die Festsetzung der Summe immer mit Sicherheit geschehen könne, anderseits aber wird nicht zu bestreiten sein, daß die Gerichtspersonen ihre Dienstleistungen verweigern dürfen, wenn ihnen nicht Bürgschaft für Ersatz der damit verbundenen Kosten geboten ist.

Unter den Gerichtspersonen ist der Gerichtsschreiber begriffen, und ebenso der Staatsanwalt, wo dessen Anwesenheit nöthig ist, wie in der Pfalz bei Interdiktionen, Abwesenheitserklärungen 2c.

6) Die Hinterlegung ist endlich vorgeschrieben für Kosten, welche sich durch Aufnahme eines Beweises im Auslande ergeben.

Ich muß gestehen, daß ich Sinn und Werth dieser Bestimmung nicht recht begreife.

Sie wurde aus dem Entwurfe (Art. 292) herübergenommen, wo sie insofern Bedeutung hatte, als, wie sich aus Art. 33 Abs. 3 folgern läßt, der Entwurf die Requisitionen ausländischer Behörden nicht auf Betreiben der Partei, sondern durch direktes Eingreifen des Gerichts erledigt haben wollte. Wo das Gericht direkt requirirt, muß es, bezw. der Staat, natürlich auch für die Kosten einstehen und folgerichtig Deckung verlangen.

Nachdem es nun aber Prinzip unserer Prozeßordnung ist, daß überall, möge die Requisition vom Inlande ins Ausland oder vom Auslande ins Inland gerichtet sein, Parteibetrieb nöthig sei, ist nicht einzusehen, wozu der Regel nach eine Hinterlegung dienen solle.

Stellt irgend ein Anwalt bei einer ausländischen Gerichtsbehörde das Ansuchen um Erledigung einer Requisition, so wird jene Behörde diesem Ansuchen nur dann entsprechen, wenn nach Maßgabe der bei ihr geltenden Gesetze für Bestreitung der Kosten gesorgt ist, und es erscheint unnöthig, daß unsere Prozeßordnung für sie den Vormund mache. Wo französisches Verfahren gilt, wird sich z. B. das Gericht um die Kosten gar nicht kümmern, sondern dem betreibenden Anwalte die Sorge überlassen. Wo deutsches Verfahren gilt, wird das Gericht sich zwar darum kümmern, jedoch sich an den beantragenden Anwalt halten.

In allen Fällen wird daher der inländische Anwalt durch Vermittlung eines ausländischen Collegen, möglichen Falles auch direkt, die im Auslande erwachsenden Kosten bestreiten müssen, wenn er die Sache erledigt haben will.

Soll er nun trotzdessen das Geld auch noch auf der Gerichtsschreiberei hinterlegen? Und was soll der Gerichtsschreiber mit dem Gelde anfangen? Es ist hier zu bemerken, daß das Gesetz ohne Zweifel hier den Gerichtsschreiber des Prozeßgerichtes meint, denn über die Funktionen ausländischer Gerichtsschreiber kann es nicht verfügen, auch gibt es bei Gesandtschaften und Consulaten keine Gerichtsschreiber.

Soll der Gerichtsschreiber etwa mit seinen auswärtigen Collegen correspondiren und auf Liquidation hin die Kosten einsenden? Französische oder rheinländische Gerichtsschreiber würden ihm einfach antworten, daß dies ihr Geschäft nicht sei.

Soll er etwa mit dem ausländischen Advokaten, welchem die Betreibung der Sache obliegt, sich ins Benehmen setzen?

7) Offenbar liegt all das nicht im Willen des Gesetzes.

Der Zweck fraglicher Bestimmung ist ohne Zweifel nur der, dem bayerischen Staate für Fälle, wo er auf Grund der Requisitionen seiner Behörden haftbar gemacht werden könnte, Garantie zu leisten. Praktisch wird sie daher nur in solchen Fällen werden, wo entweder Seitens der ausländischen Behörde die Uebernahme einer Haftung, oder Seitens der Partei die diplomatische Vermittlung begehrt und das Eine oder das Andere von vorausgängiger Hinterlegung der nöthigen Geldsumme abhängig gemacht wird. Für diese Fälle ist die Gerichtsschreiberei der Ort, wo die Hinterlegung stattfindet.

Wird hingegen die Requisition ohne Anstand auf bloßen Parteibetrieb erledigt, so besteht kein Anlaß, Geld zu hinterlegen, und würde die Hinterlegung auch verfügt, so bestünde keine Verpflichtung, Folge zu leisten.

Eine besondere Bedeutung hat schließlich fragliche Vorschrift für den Ausnahmsfall des Art. 407, für welchen sie allerdings vollkommen paßt.

Verfahren und Urtheil nach der Beweisaufnahme.

Art. 344. — Hat die Beweisaufnahme in der Sitzung stattgefunden, so ist in der Regel unmittelbar darauf über die Hauptsache zu verhandeln. Vertagt das Gericht die Verhandlung in eine folgende Sitzung, so ist Zustellung motivirter Anträge gleichwohl nicht erforderlich. Im einen wie im andern Falle sind jedoch die Anträge der Parteien dem Vorsitzenden bei der Verhandlung schriftlich zu übergeben.

Hat die Beweisaufnahme nicht in der Sitzung stattgefunden, so kann jede Partei nach dem Schlusse des Beweisverfahrens die Sache zur Eintragung in die Wochentabelle anmelden und haben sodann die Anwälte wenigstens drei Tage vor der zur Hinterlegung bestimmten Sitzung sich wechselseitig motivirte Anträge zustellen zu lassen. In diesen sind die Ergebnisse der Beweisführung, soweit sie die Partei für sich benützen will, und die zu verhandelnden Streitpunkte kurz zusammenzustellen.

Die über die Beweisaufnahme geführten Protokolle werden bei der Verhandlung durch den Gerichtsschreiber in Urschrift vorgelegt. Die Anwälte können von der Gerichtsschreiberei einfache Abschriften dieser Protokolle erholen, für welche lediglich die Schreibgebühr zu entrichten ist.

Art. 345. — **Bei Fällung des nach durchgeführtem Beweisverfahren zu erlassenden Urtheils hat das Gericht, wo das Gesetz nicht anders bestimmt, das Ergebniß der Beweisführung nach freier Ueberzeugung zu würdigen. Der Inhalt des Beweisurtheils ist hiebei nur soweit bindend, als in diesem etwa auf Eidesleistung erkannt ist. Hat sich durch das Beweisverfahren Beweis über mittelbar erhebliche Thatsachen (Art. 322) ergeben, so kann das Gericht diese berücksichtigen, auch wenn das Beweisanerbieten nicht darauf gerichtet war.**

Art. 346. — **Sind für die in Art. 344 bezeichnete Verhandlung von einer Partei Anträge nicht hinterlegt worden, so hat das Gericht nach Lage der Sache zu erkennen. Gegen dieses Urtheil steht jedoch der nicht erschienenen Partei das Recht des Einspruchs zu.**

G. A. d. K. d. A. II S. 153—157. 165—167. 330. 331. IV S. 90. 326. 340.
K. d. R. II S. 114—116. IV S. 43.

1) Diese drei Artikel regeln das Verfahren nach Aufnahme des Beweises, den Standpunkt des Richters bei dem erfolgenden Urtheile, endlich den Fall, wo eine der Parteien nicht weiter erscheint.

a) Verfahren nach der Beweisaufnahme (Art. 344).

2) Das auf die Beweisaufnahme folgende Verfahren ist ein verschiedenes, je nachdem die Beweisaufnahme in der Sitzung stattgefunden hat oder außer derselben.

Im ersteren Falle soll die Verhandlung der Hauptsache — worunter jedoch, falls etwa die Beweisaufnahme bloß bezüglich einer Vorfrage stattfand, auch diese zu verstehen ist — in der Regel unmittelbar auf die Beweisaufnahme folgen, was mehrfache Vortheile bietet, indem die gewonnenen Aufklärungen noch frisch in der Erinnerung der Richter sind, von einer Protokollirung Umgang genommen werden kann, die Verhandlung selbst kürzer ist und Kosten erspart werden. In Sachen, welche der Berufung nicht unterliegen und wo deßhalb die Protokollirung unterlassen werden kann (Art. 419 Abs. 5), ist eine sofortige Verhandlung, wenigstens eine solche, welche nur durch einen kurzen Zeitraum von der Beweisaufnahme getrennt ist, geradezu nothwendig, wenn nicht der Eindruck derselben theilweise verwischt werden soll, ganz abgesehen davon, daß möglicherweise einer der Richter oder Anwälte später verhindert sein könnte, was eine Wiederholung der Beweisaufnahme nöthig machen würde.

Die sofortige Verhandlung hat den weiteren Vortheil, welcher in der Praxis verwerthet zu werden pflegt, daß man, falls sich Lücken in der Beweisaufnahme ergeben oder es überhaupt wünschenswerth ist, weitere Aufklärungen zu erhalten, die Zeugen oder Sachverständigen wieder vorrufen und befragen kann. Das Gesetz steht einem solchen Verfahren durchaus nicht im Wege, wie denn im Zweifel nie verwehrt ist, das zu thun, was zur Ermittlung der Wahrheit dient.

3) Die Verhandlung stellt sich, falls die Beweisaufnahme in der Sitzung erfolgt, nur als eine Fortsetzung des Verfahrens dar, und findet sie daher nicht sofort statt, so tritt nur einfache Vertagung ein. Abg. II 165 (v. Weiß).

Motivirte Anträge sind hier nie erforderlich, also auch nicht im Falle einer Vertagung, jedoch schließt sie der Wortlaut des Gesetzes auch nicht aus, und wird daher zu gelten haben, was zu Art. 260 Nr. 10 gesagt ist, vielleicht mit der für den Kostenpunkt wichtigen Beschränkung, daß im vorliegenden Falle das Wechseln von Anträgen weniger Nutzen zu bieten pflegt, als im Falle des abgekürzten Verfahrens, wo die Sache neu in die Sitzung kommt.

Daß einfache Anträge zu nehmen seien, wäre eigentlich selbstverständlich gewesen, denn die Natur des Verfahrens bringt es mit sich, daß diejenigen Anträge genommen und hinterlegt werden müssen, welche bestimmt sind, in den Sachverhalt und mit diesem ins Urtheil aufgenommen zu werden.

4) Ergeben sich Zwischenstreite über Verwerfung von Zeugen ꝛc., so werden dieselben vom Gerichte sofort entschieden und die Zwischenurtheile vollzogen. Beweisaufnahme und Verhandlung können ohne Anstand stattfinden, da solche Urtheile für sich nicht rechtskräftig werden und einer selbständigen Berufung nicht unterliegen. Eine Ausnahme bildet jedoch der Fall, wo es sich um eine Eidesleistung handelt.

5) Im Falle, wo die Beweisaufnahme nicht in der Sitzung stattgefunden hat, ist das Verfahren etwas umständlicher.

Es wird dann die Sache vom fleißigsten Theile in gewöhnlicher Weise zur Verhandlung gebracht, d. h. durch Anmeldung zur Wochentabelle und Wechseln motivirter Anträge, unter Einhaltung der dreitägigen Frist, wie sie auch Art. 242 Abs. 2 bestimmt.

Der Stoff dieser Anträge ist reichhaltiger, als derjenige der früheren Beweisdeduktionen, da es nicht bloß darauf ankommt, darzuthun, daß der Beweis so wie er auferlegt war geführt oder nicht geführt sei, sondern das ganze Material des Prozesses unter Benützung der neugewonnenen Aufklärungen neu und selbständig zu verarbeiten. Daß hiebei die Anwälte sich größter Kürze zu befleißigen und unter Umständen auf die Entwicklungen früherer Anträge zu verweisen haben, versteht sich nach der Natur des mündlichen Verfahrens von selbst.

6) Es kann sich ereignen, daß die Beweisaufnahmen theilweise in der Sitzung, theilweise außer derselben stattzufinden haben, z. B. wenn einzelne Zeugen wegen Krankheit, großer Entfernung 2c. durch einen beauftragten oder ersuchten Richter verhört werden müssen, oder wenn Expertise und Zeugenverhör zugleich angeordnet wurden und erstere außer der Sitzung, letzteres in derselben stattfindet.

In solchen Fällen pflegte man in der Pfalz immer in der Art zu verfahren, wie es Art. 408 vorschreibt, daß nemlich im Beweisurtheile sofort Tagfahrt zur Beweisaufnahme in der Sitzung anberaumt und diese so gewählt wurde, daß in der nemlichen Sitzung voraussichtlich auch die sonst erhobenen Beweise benützt werden konnten und einer sofortigen Verhandlung nichts im Wege stand. Dieses Verfahren erschien namentlich dann nöthig, wenn die Beweisaufnahme in der Sitzung nicht protokollirt wurde, und pflegte man, wenn sich später ergab, daß die Tagfahrt zu kurz fixirt war, dieselbe zu verlegen.

7) Es frägt sich nun, ob in gemischten Fällen dieser Art nach dem Willen unserer Prozeßordnung das Verfahren des Art. 344 Abs. 1 oder dasjenige des Art. 344 Abs. 2 einzutreten habe?

Man wird unterscheiden müssen, ob die Beweisaufnahme in der Sitzung den Schluß des Beweisverfahrens bildet oder nicht.

Für ersteren Fall, welcher nach dem Willen des Gesetzes (Art. 408) Regel sein soll, sind offenbar die Bestimmungen des Art. 344 Abs. 2 ganz unpassend. Wozu die Anmeldung zur Wochentabelle, wenn schon im Beweisurtheile eine Sitzung bestimmt ist, und was soll die vorausgängige Zustellung motivirter Anträge nützen, wenn ein Haupttheil des Beweises erst in der Sitzung selbst aufgenommen wird?

Sollen etwa über die Aussagen einzelner Zeugen Anträge gewechselt werden?

Auch die Annahme, daß erst nach Erledigung der Beweisaufnahme eine besondere Sitzung zur Verhandlung bestimmt und für diese motivirte Anträge gewechselt werden sollen, erscheint unstatthaft; denn es würden durch ein solches Verfahren die mit jener Beweisaufnahme bezweckten Vortheile wieder verloren gehen, und wäre es bei dieser Unterstellung immer zweckmäßig, die ganze Beweisaufnahme außerhalb der Sitzung vorzunehmen. Die Bestimmung des Art. 408 wäre offenbar nicht gegeben worden, hätte der Gesetzgeber nicht vorausgesetzt, es könnte sofort nach der Beweisaufnahme auch die Verhandlung stattfinden und könnten bei dieser die vorliegenden Protokolle benützt werden.

Es erscheint mir demnach zweifellos, daß in Fällen, wo die Protokolle über sonstige Beweisaufnahmen zur Zeit der Beweisaufnahme in der Sitzung bereits vorliegen, wie dies nach dem Willen des Gesetzes wo möglich immer der Fall sein soll, bloß die Vorschriften des Art. 344 Abs. 1 Maß geben. Praktische Bedenken stehen durchaus nicht entgegen. Jede Partei weiß ja, daß im Beweisurtheile bezeichnete Sitzung zur Beweisaufnahme und Verhandlung bestimmt ist, es pflegt dies auch im Urtheile ausdrücklich ausgesprochen zu werden; sie weiß ferner durch die ihr gemachten Zustellungen, daß und wann die Beweisaufnahme außer der Sitzung geschehen sei, ist also vollkommen in der Lage, vor der Sitzung die betreffenden Protokolle einzusehen oder sich Abschriften geben zu lassen. Sollte dies nicht geschehen sein, so kann das Gericht auf Grund von Art. 344 Abs. 1 kurze Vertagung bewilligen.

Hat das Gericht Veranlassung, Dringlichkeit anzunehmen, so steht ohnedem außer Frage, daß es im Beweisurtheile die sofortige Verhandlung verfügen dürfe (Art. 259).

Anders gestaltet sich die Sache, wenn ausnahmsweise das Beweisverfahren in der Sitzung demjenigen außer der Sitzung vorausgeht. In diesem Falle muß auch in der Sitzung immer protokollirt werden und die Vorschrift des Art. 344 Abs. 1, daß sofort verhandelt werde, läßt sich nicht anwenden; auch die Folgerungen aus dem Art. 408 fallen hinweg; endlich ist es nöthig, die Sache durch Anmeldung zur Wochentabelle in die Sitzung zu bringen. Hier wird also nach dem Willen des Gesetzes Art. 344 Abs. 2 zur Anwendung zu kommen haben.

Schließlich sei bemerkt, daß es in der Pfalz immer so, wie vorstehend erörtert, gehalten worden ist.

8) Die Protokolle über Beweisaufnahme werden, auch wenn diese außer der Sitzung stattgefunden hat, weder ausgefertigt noch zugestellt, sondern vom Gerichtsschreiber in Urschrift vorgelegt. Wird Berufung ergriffen, so werden die Urschriften an die Gerichtsschreiberei des Berufungsgerichtes eingesendet (Art. 711).

Den Anwälten ist gestattet, sich zu ihrem Gebrauche einfache Abschriften, für welche nur die Schreibgebühren des Gerichtsschreibers zu entrichten sind, welche also weder dem Stempel noch einer Taxe unterliegen, geben zu lassen. Die bezüglichen Kosten gehören zum Prozesse.

b) Urtheil nach der Beweisaufnahme (Art. 345).

9) Aus der Natur des Beweisurtheiles (s. Bemerk. zu Art. 328 Nr. 3) folgt von selbst, daß der Richter durch die frühere Verhandlung und das auf Grund derselben gefällte Urtheil in der Freiheit seiner Bewegung nicht im mindesten gehemmt ist. Jene frühere Verhandlung führte zu keinem Ergebnisse, weil der Richter über Manches noch im Unklaren war; die gewünschten Aufklärungen sind beigebracht und es findet nun die Verhandlung von Neuem statt.

Der Richter darf daher nicht bloß neue Behelfe zum Angriffe oder zur Vertheidigung, insbesondere Einreden oder Repliken, sofern sie nicht durch besondere Verfügung des Gesetzes ausgeschlossen erscheinen (Art. 184), berücksichtigen (Art. 251), sondern er darf auch die Frage der Beweislast und der Erheblichkeit der Beweise unabhängig von seiner im Beweisurtheile geäußerten Ansicht frei würdigen, namentlich aber auch die Beweisführung.

In letzterer Beziehung läßt er das ganze Beweismaterial, sowohl dasjenige, welches schon bei der früheren Verhandlung vorlag, als dasjenige, welches die Beweisaufnahmen ergeben haben, als endlich sonstige Beweismomente, welche aus nachträglich vorgelegten Urkunden (Art. 329 Abs. 3), aus Erklärungen der Parteien oder neu hervortretenden Vermuthungen sich ergeben, auf seine Ueberzeugung wirken und bildet sich aus dem Gesammtergebnisse sein Urtheil.

10) Was insbesondere den Vermuthungsbeweis anbelangt, so enthält Art. 345 die sehr zweckmäßige Vorschrift, daß auch solche Vermuthungen berücksichtigt werden dürfen, wegen deren nicht ausdrücklich Beweis auferlegt war, welche aber das Beweisverfahren gelegentlich zu Tage gefördert hat.

Es ist dies zugleich eine Weisung für den Richter, auch Vermuthungen dieser Art bei der Beweisaufnahme zu berücksichtigen und sich nicht allzu ängstlich an den Wortlaut der Beweisauflage zu halten. Das Gesetz ist bestrebt, überall der materiellen Wahrheit den Weg zu bahnen, und in diesem Bestreben will es vom Richter unterstützt sein.

11) Eine Ausnahme von dem Grundsatze, daß der Richter völlig freie Hand habe, bildet der Fall, wo das Beweisurtheil auf Eidesleistung erkannt hatte. Für diesen Ausnahmsfall gilt als Regel, daß das Beweisurtheil den Richter binde, daß er also von der Ansicht, welche er dort bezüglich der Beweislast und der Erheblichkeit der Eidesauflage ausgesprochen, nicht abgehen könne, eine Regel, welche durch die Wichtigkeit der in Frage stehenden Handlung bedingt ist und in Verbindung steht mit der Verfügung des Art. 683 Ziff. 1, daß gegen solche Urtheile selbständige Berufung zulässig sei.

Uebrigens erleidet auch dieser Satz wieder einige Einschränkung durch die besonderen Bestimmungen in Art. 460 Abs. 2.

12) Es geht aus den vorentwickelten Prinzipien von selbst hervor, daß das auf die Beweisaufnahme folgende Urtheil nicht nothwendig ein Endurtheil sein müsse, daß vielmehr auch weitere Beweise angeordnet werden können. Abg. II. 153 Sp. 2.

Eidesauflagen erfolgen in Fällen, wo auch sonstiger Beweis erboten war und zugelassen wurde, immer erst in demjenigen Urtheile, welches über das Ergebniß der sonstigen Beweisführung erkennt.

In Fällen, wo das Gericht von Amtswegen verfügen darf, wie bei der Expertise (Art. 448) und beim Augenscheine (Art. 396), ist es, falls es die Beweisaufnahme ungenügend findet, unbehindert, in der nemlichen Richtung neue Erhebungen anzuordnen.

Wiederholung eines Zeugenbeweises über die nemlichen Thatsachen ist nur statthaft, wenn die Beweisaufnahme sich als nichtig erweist, jedoch darf die nachträgliche Vernehmung neuentdeckter Zeugen zugelassen werden (Art. 415).

c) Versäumungsurtheil (Art. 346).

13) Die Frage, ob die beim Beweisurtheile genommenen Anträge auch für die spätere, nach erhobenen Beweisen eintretende Verhandlung in der Art nachwirke, daß die Sache immer noch contradiktorisch bleibe, war Gegenstand langer Erörterungen.

Anfänglich bejahte man sie, schließlich aber vereinigte man sich zur entgegenstehenden Ansicht, indem die Erwägung durchschlug, daß in den meisten Fällen sich in Folge der Beweiserhebungen die Sachlage wesentlich ändere. Man gelangte, den Prinzipien des französischen Prozesses folgend, zu einem Mittelwege, indem man zwar einerseits den Gerichten vorschrieb, nach Lage der Sache zu erkennen, anderseits aber der nichterschienenen Partei das Recht des Einspruches wahrte. Die Folge ist, daß auch die Grundsätze wegen Erlasses eines Verbindungsurtheils eintretenden Falls zur Anwendung kommen. Vgl. Bemerk. zu Art. 316 bis 318 Nr. 6.

14) Wenn das Gesetz sagt: „nach Lage der Sache," so heißt dies: unter Berücksichtigung der aus dem Sachverhalte des früheren Urtheils zu ersehenden Anträge, Angriffs- und Vertheidigungsmittel der nichterschienenen Partei, sowie des gesammten Beweismaterials.

Es hat also hier der Richter den Stand der Sache im Interesse der nichterschienenen Partei von Amtswegen zu prüfen, eine Prüfung, welche übrigens in der Regel kein schwieriges Geschäft ist, da das Nichterscheinen einer früher erschienenen Partei nach durchgeführtem Beweisverfahren gewöhnlich nur vorkommt nach Leistung eines Eides und fast immer das Zeichen ist, daß der Anwalt die Sache als verloren aufgibt. Allerdings können auch Fälle vorkommen, wo der Anwalt wegen Mangels an Vorschuß oder aus sonstigen Gründen die Sache nicht mehr vertritt, oder wo er die Sachlage irrig beurtheilt hat, und es sind mir solche Fälle erinnerlich, wo das Gericht veranlaßt war, ganz oder theilweise zu Gunsten des Nichterschienenen zu sprechen.

15) Schließlich ist zu beachten, daß Art. 346 nur den Fall im Auge hat, wo ein Beweisverfahren durchgeführt worden ist, wo Beweisaufnahmen irgend einer Art stattgefunden haben, also nicht angerufen werden kann, wenn etwa das Beweisurtheil unvollzogen geblieben ist.

Beweis zum ewigen Gedächtniß.

Art. 347. — Bescheinigt eine Partei, daß die Vornahme eines Augenscheins oder die Vernehmung von Zeugen oder Sachverständigen bei Gefahr des Verlustes dieser Beweismittel oder wesentlicher Erschwerung ihrer Benützung keinen Aufschub duldet, so kann sie, ehe im Prozesse zur Beweisführung geschritten wird und selbst vor Einleitung des Prozesses, die vorsorgliche Erhebung mittels einfacher Vorstellung verlangen.

Art. 348. — Das Gesuch um Beweisaufnahme zum ewigen Gedächtniß ist bei dem Gerichte anzubringen, bei welchem der betreffende Rechtsstreit anhängig ist oder anhängig werden soll.

Bei besonders dringender Gefahr kann das Gesuch an jedes Bezirks- oder Einzelngericht gebracht werden, das den Beweis ohne Verzögerung zu erheben vermag.

In der Vorstellung sollen die veranlassenden Umstände, die Thatsachen, worüber Beweisaufnahme beantragt wird, und die zu vernehmenden Zeugen oder Sachverständigen genau bezeichnet sein.

Die zur Bescheinigung der Gefahr dienenden Behelfe sind der Vorstellung beizufügen.

Art. 349. — Erscheint das Gesuch um Beweisaufnahme zum ewigen Gedächtniß als zulässig, so ist sofort die Beweisaufnahme zu verfügen.

Gegen die Abweisung findet, falls sie durch ein Gericht erster Instanz erfolgt ist, das Rechtsmittel der Beschwerde statt.

Art. 350. — Die Beweisaufnahme zum ewigen Gedächtniß geschieht, wenn das Gericht, welches sie zugelassen hat, ein Collegialrecht ist, durch einen beauftragten Richter.

Zu der für die Beweisaufnahme festgesetzten Tagfahrt hat der Beweisführer seinen Gegner unter abschriftlicher Zustellung der Vorstellung und der vom Gerichte darauf ergangenen Verfügung rechtzeitig vorladen zu lassen.

Vorstellung und Verfügung, sowie die Vorladung des Gegners sind dem über die Beweisaufnahme zu errichtenden Protokolle beizufügen. Letzteres bleibt bei dem Gerichte, welches den Beweis aufgenommen hat, hinterlegt, ist aber in Urschrift an das Prozeßgericht abzugeben, wenn dieses auf Antrag einer Partei die Ablieferung veranlaßt.

Art. 351. — Wird ein zum ewigen Gedächtniß aufgenommener Beweis im Rechtsstreite benützt, so sind dem Gegner alle Einreden gegen die Zulässigkeit, wie gegen Form und Inhalt der Beweisaufnahme vorbehalten, ohne Unterschied, ob er bei dieser anwesend war oder nicht.

Jede Partei ist berechtigt, im Prozesse die nochmalige Erhebung oder die Ergänzung des zum ewigen Gedächtniß aufgenommenen Beweises, soweit sie noch möglich ist, zu beantragen.

Art. 352. — Im Uebrigen finden die allgemeinen Vorschriften über das Beweisverfahren und die

besondern über Aufnahme der in Art. 347 angeführten Beweisarten auch auf den Beweis zum ewigen Gedächtniß analoge Anwendung.

G. A. d. K. d. A. II S. 168. 331. 332. 452. IV S. 90. — K. d. R. II S. 116. IV S. 43.

1) Der Beweis zum ewigen Gedächtnisse war bis jetzt in der Pfalz nicht bekannt, wenn man nicht etwa Fälle, wo der Zustand von Waaren festgestellt wurde (Art. 106 Code de comm.), oder wo der Präsident im Refereeverfahren einen Augenschein vornahm (Art. 806 Code de proc.), hierher ziehen will. Ohne Zweifel darf diese Neuerung als ein Gewinn betrachtet werden.

a) Fälle dieser Beweisaufnahme.

2) Der Beweis zum ewigen Gedächtnisse setzt voraus, daß entweder ein Prozeß bereits begonnen habe, oder daß ein solcher wenigstens in Aussicht stehe, wie dies daraus hervorgeht, daß das Gesetz Zustellung an den Gegner verlangt und dasjenige Gericht für zuständig erklärt, bei welchem der Rechtsstreit anhängig ist oder werden soll.

Der Entwurf (Art. 301) hatte diesen Beweis auch zugelassen, wenn ein bestimmter Prozeßgegner nicht bezeichnet werden könne; allein man hielt dafür, daß es nicht geeignet sei, in Fällen dieser Art die richterliche Thätigkeit in Anspruch zu nehmen. Referat zu Art. 301 des Entw. (v. Neumayr.) Es wird hieraus zu folgern sein, daß ein Gesuch zurückzuweisen sei, welches einen in Aussicht stehenden Prozeß und einen bestimmten Prozeßgegner nicht zu bezeichnen vermag.

3) Das Recht, eine solche Beweisaufnahme zu verlangen, steht sowohl dem Kläger als dem Beklagten zu. Dem Ersteren hatte die Gerichtsordnung zur Pflicht gemacht, binnen Jahresfrist Klage zu erheben, wenn diese nicht bereits erhoben sei, und es wäre vielleicht rathsam gewesen, diese Bestimmung beizubehalten.

Was den Beklagten betrifft, so ist nicht erforderlich, daß bereits eine Berühmung im Sinne des Art. 569 stattgefunden habe, sondern genügt es, wenn aus seiner Aufstellung hervorgeht, daß eine bestimmte Person Klage gegen ihn erheben könne. Daß ihm die Kosten zur Last bleiben, wenn es nicht zum Prozesse kommt, ist genügender Schutz gegen frivole Gesuche.

4) Der Beweis zum ewigen Gedächtnisse ist nur gestattet für drei Beweismittel, nemlich für den Augenschein, für Zeugen und Sachverständige.

Bezüglich der Urkunden ist im Hauptstücke XXI Vorsorge getroffen; übrigens ist nicht zu bezweifeln, daß, soweit die Anfechtung von Urkunden durch Vernehmung von Zeugen oder Sachverständigen bedingt ist, auch in dieser Richtung eine Beweisaufnahme zum ewigen Gedächtnisse statthaft sei. Art. 347 unterscheidet nicht, ob dieser Beweis für die dem Rechtsstreite zu Grunde liegenden Thatsachen selbst, oder für Beweismittel, welche die Entscheidung des Rechtsstreites bedingen, von Belang sei.

5) Voraussetzung ist Gefahr des Verlustes bezeichneter Beweismittel oder Gefahr wesentlicher Erschwerung ihrer Benützung, und zwar muß diese der Art sein, daß nicht bis zur Beweisaufnahme im ordentlichen Verfahren zugewartet werden kann.

Welche Umstände eine solche Gefahr bedingen, ist der freien Würdigung des Richters überlassen. Hohes Alter oder bedenkliche Krankheit von Zeugen, Veränderlichkeit der für den Rechtsstreit wichtigen Oertlichkeiten oder Sachen, sind die gewöhnlichen Anlässe.

b) Verfahren.

6) Zuständig sind diejenigen Gerichte, bei welchen der Rechtsstreit anhängig ist oder anhängig werden soll, also nicht bloß die gewöhnlichen, sondern auch die Ausnahmsgerichte, unter Umständen die Gerichte, welche über die Berufung zu entscheiden haben.

Bei besonderer Dringlichkeit soll dasjenige Bezirksgericht oder Einzelgericht zuständig sein, durch welches die Beweisaufnahme am schnellsten geschehen kann.

Der oberste Gerichtshof wird als ein Gericht, bei welchem der Rechtsstreit im Sinne des Art. 348 anhängig ist, nie betrachtet werden dürfen, da er nicht über den Grund der Sache erkennt und Funktionen dieser Art überhaupt außer seiner Geschäftssphäre liegen. Es war auch im Entwurfe (Art. 298), wo die Mitwirkung des Staatsanwaltes verlangt wurde, nur von Bezirks- und Appellationsgerichten die Rede. Allerdings entsteht nun die Frage, welches Gericht in Fällen zuständig sei, wo nur noch Nichtigkeitsbeschwerde zuläßig ist, da selbstverständlich dasjenige Gericht, an welches im Falle der Vernichtung die Sache verwiesen wird, nicht bekannt ist. Es wird in diesem Falle Art. 348 Abs. 2 Maß geben müssen, d. h. wenn die Beweisaufnahme nicht bis zur Entscheidung des obersten Gerichtshofes warten kann, ist dasjenige Bezirksgericht oder Einzelgericht zuständig, welches die Beweisaufnahme am besten bethätigen kann.

Während des Laufes der Berufungsfrist ist das Gericht, welches über die Berufung zu erkennen hat, als dasjenige zu betrachten, bei welchem der Rechtsstreit anhängig gemacht werden soll, wenn auch das Gesetz diesen Fall nicht gerade im Auge gehabt haben mag.

Ebenso verhält es sich, wenn Wiederaufnahme des Verfahrens in Aussicht steht.

7) Das Verfahren wird eingeleitet durch eine einfache Vorst llung (Art. 642), in welcher die veranlassenden Umstände, die Thatsachen, worüber Beweisaufnahme verlangt wird, endlich die Zeugen und Sachverständigen, welche vernommen werden sollen, zu bezeichnen sind. Wie schon bemerkt, ist unter den „veranlassenden Umständen" eintretenden Falls auch die Darlegung, daß ein Prozeß in Aussicht stehe, sowie die Bezeichnung des Prozeßgegners zu begreifen.

Dieser Vorstellung sind die zur Bescheinigung der Gefahr dienenden Behelfe beizufügen (s. Einleitung zu Hauptst. IX Nr. 2); in sonstiger Richtung wird eine Bescheinigung nicht verlangt.

8) Auf die eingereichte Vorstellung hin wird nach Maßgabe der Vorschriften des Hauptstückes XXV verfahren und entschieden.

Gegen den Beschluß, welchen der Beweis zuläßt, gibt es kein Rechtsmittel; wird jedoch das Gesuch abgewiesen, so ist Beschwerde (Hptst. XXVIII) gestattet, falls die Abweisung durch ein Gericht erster Instanz erfolgt ist. Das Gesetz spricht hier von Gerichten erster Instanz im Gegensatze zu solchen, bei denen der Rechtsstreit auf eingelegte Berufung hin anhängig wird, so daß also das Bezirksgericht je nach Umständen als Gericht erster oder zweiter Instanz in Betracht kommen kann.

Man könnte fragen, ob nicht auch in solchen Fällen das Recht der Beschwerde ausgeschlossen sei, wo der in erster Instanz anhängige Rechtsstreit einer Berufung nicht unterliegt; allein offenbar ist dies nicht der Wille des Gesetzgebers und konnte es auch nicht sein, weil nach den Prinzipien unserer Prozeßordnung erst bei Erlaß eines der selbständigen Berufung unterliegenden Urtheiles sich bestimmt, ob Berufung zulässig sei oder nicht, und selbst in Sachen, wo die Möglichkeit von Berufungen anscheinend völlig ausgeschlossen ist, durch spätere Klagänderungen, Häufung von Zinsen und Kosten (Art. 686) ꝛc. solche zulässig werden können.

9) Da bei einer Beweisaufnahme zum ewigen Gedächtnisse von einer sofortigen Verhandlung die Rede nicht sein kann, so wäre es zwecklos, dieselbe in der Sitzung vorzunehmen, und verfügt daher das Gesetz, daß Collegialgerichte immer einen Richter zu beauftragen bezw. zu ersuchen haben. Auch der Einzelrichter wird natürlich den Beweis nicht in der Sitzung erheben.

Nachdem die Tagfahrt festgesetzt ist, läßt der Beweisführer dem Prozeßgegner die Vorstellung nebst der Verfügung des Gerichts zustellen und zugleich denselben rechtzeitig vorladen.

Von einer Zustellung des besonderen Beschlusses, welcher die Tagfahrt festsetzt, spricht das Gesetz nicht, jedoch möchte sie im Hinblicke auf Art. 352 bezw. 338 nicht zu unterlassen sein.

10) Es frägt sich, was unter „rechtzeitiger Vorladung" zu verstehen sei, einem Ausdrucke, welcher aus dem Entwurfe (Art. 299) ohne Bemerkung in das Gesetz überging. Soll gesagt sein, daß blos das Ermessen entscheide, oder aber wollte man auf die allgemeinen Vorschriften der Art. 331 und 338 verweisen?

Offenbar wäre es völlig unstatthaft, der Gegenpartei hier größere Rechte zuzugestehen als im gewöhnlichen Verfahren, und anzunehmen, dieselbe habe unter allen Umständen ein Recht auf diejenige Frist, welche nöthig ist, damit sie persönlich erscheinen könne. In Fällen, wo der Gegner oder ein Theil der Gegner weit entfernt, z. B. in Nordamerika, wohnt, würde eine rechtzeitige Vorladung in diesem Sinne das ganze Verfahren zwecklos machen.

Es erscheint daher so viel außer Zweifel, daß wenn die nöthigenfalls durch den Richter zu erweiternde Frist von 8 Tagen, wie sie obbesagte Artikel bestimmen, eingehalten wurde, die Zustellung als rechtzeitig geschehen betrachtet werden müsse.

Schwieriger möchte die Frage sein, ob nicht unter Umständen eine kürzere Frist genüge.

Nach dem Entwurfe ergaben sich keine Schwierigkeiten, da derselbe in Art. 291 dem Prozeßgerichte eine jede Aenderung, also auch eine Kürzung der Frist erlaubte; unsere Prozeßordnung erlaubt jedoch blos eine Erweiterung. Obgleich nun nicht zu läugnen ist, daß bei großer Dringlichkeit eine Kürzung besagter Frist sehr wünschenswerth erscheinen kann, so wird doch nichts übrig bleiben, als sich an die Bestimmungen der Art. 331 und 338 zu halten, und zwar um so mehr, als auch die Einhaltung der achttägigen Frist zur Zeugendenunciation (Art. 412) nicht umgangen werden kann. In Hannover hatte man in § 315 und 316 dadurch Vorsorge getroffen, daß man die Ladung nur vorschrieb, sofern sie nach Lage der Sache geschehen könne, und auch die seitherige Praxis in Bayern ließ für sehr dringliche Fälle den Ausweg der Offizialvertretung zu.

Schließlich ist zu bemerken, daß von Anwendung des Art. 525 Abs. 2 nicht die Rede sein kann, weil die Tagfahrt nicht auf Grund einer Verhandlung in der Sitzung bestimmt wird und überhaupt eine Vorladung hier nie umgangen werden darf.

11) Art. 352 verfügt, daß im Uebrigen die allgemeinen Vorschriften über das Beweisverfahren analoge Anwendung finden sollen.

Zu diesen allgemeinen Vorschriften sind, dem Geiste des Gesetzes gemäß, auch die Bestimmungen des Art. 412 über die Frist für Zustellung eines Verzeichnisses der Zeugen zu rechnen; jedoch ist eine besondere Zustellung nicht nöthig, weil in der Vorstellung selbst die Zeugen genau bezeichnet sein müssen.

Ebenso gelten die Vorschriften der Art. 409 bis 411 über Ladung der Zeugen.

Verfügt der Einzelrichter einen Zeugenbeweis zum ewigen Gedächtnisse in Sachen, für welche er zuständig ist, so wird Art. 530 Maß geben. In diesem Falle möchte die dreitägige Frist zur Bezeichnung der Zeugen zugleich als Frist zur Vorladung der Gegenpartei zu gelten haben.

12) Auch beim Beweise zum ewigen Gedächtnisse können sich Anstände ergeben, welche eine sofortige Entscheidung nöthig machen, insofern davon die Beweisaufnahme selbst abhängt, z. B. die Frage, ob ein Zeuge als untüchtig anzusehen sei. Es muß dabei nach Analogie der allgemeinen Vorschriften verfahren werden, so daß also der beauftragte Richter nicht befugt erscheint, solche Anstände selbst zu beseitigen, sondern verpflichtet ist, sie an das Gericht, welches ihn beauftragt hat, zu verweisen.

Anderseits wird es jedoch keinem Anstande unterliegen, daß der Richter, welcher auf Grund von Art. 348 Abs. 2 in einer Sache, für deren Entscheidung er nicht zuständig gewesen wäre, einen Beweis zum ewigen Gedächtnisse verfügt hatte, auch sich ergebende Anstände selbst beseitige. Die ergehenden Entscheidungen sind übrigens nur vorläufige, bestimmt, die der Beweisaufnahme entgegenstehenden Hindernisse zu beseitigen. Art. 351 Abs. 1.

c) Wirkungen der Beweisaufnahme.

13) Der Beweis zum ewigen Gedächtnisse ist bestimmt, Beweise zu fixiren, deren Erhebung später unmöglich werden könnte; so weit diese Voraussetzung nicht eintritt, muß es immer gestattet sein, zum ordentlichen Verfahren zurückzukehren und eine Wiederholung oder Ergänzung der Beweisaufnahme zu verlangen.

Die Worte des Gesetzes: „Jede Partei ist berechtigt zu beantragen", könnten der Ansicht Raum geben, als solle blos gesagt sein, es dürfe das Gericht auf Antrag einer Partei die Wiederholung der Beweisaufnahme verfügen, allein offenbar ist gemeint, daß jede Partei ein Recht auf Wiederholung haben solle. Der Entwurf sagte entschiedener: „ist berechtigt zu verlangen." Es war dies auch früher so und erscheint natürlich, da die fragliche Beweisaufnahme immerhin nur ein Nothbehelf und es leicht möglich ist, daß man bei derselben die Tragweite gewisser Thatsachen, die Erheblichkeit gewisser Punkte noch nicht recht zu würdigen wußte, was um so mehr in's Gewicht fällt, als häufig die Parteien noch nicht durch Anwälte vertreten sind.

Trotz der Wiederholung der Beweisaufnahme wird dennoch auch die frühere noch berücksichtigt werden dürfen.

14) Das Gesetz verfügt ausdrücklich, daß dem Gegner alle Einreden gegen die Zulässigkeit, wie gegen Form und Inhalt der fraglichen Beweisaufnahme vorbehalten seien und zwar ohne Unterschied, ob er dabei anwesend war oder nicht.

Gilt dies auch vom Falle des Art. 412 Abs. 2?

Für die Verneinung läßt sich anführen, daß jene Vorschrift höchst speziell sei und auch beim landgerichtlichen Verfahren, wo doch den Parteien präsumtiv Rechtsbeistände nicht zur Seite stehen, gelte; anderseits aber läßt sich geltend machen, daß das Gesetz ganz allgemein verfüge und gerade solche Fälle im Auge zu haben scheine, wo nach gewöhnlichem Verfahren Präclusion eintreten würde, und ist zu beachten, daß es sich hier um sehr wichtige Rechtsangelegenheiten handeln kann, wo Rechtsverlustigungen nie eintreten dürfen, wenn nicht die Vertretung und Rechtsvertheidigung eine vollständige war.

Ich halte letztere Gründe für überwiegend.

15) Geht im Falle des Art. 348 Abs. 2 aus dem Beschlusse des Richters nicht hervor, daß besondere Dringlichkeit vorliege, oder ist dies in der That nicht der Fall, oder hat sich der Gesuchsteller oder das Gericht selbst bezüglich der Zuständigkeit geirrt, so kann die Frage entstehen, welche Wirkungen einem vom unzuständigen Richter aufgenommenen Beweise zum ewigen Gedächtnisse zukommen.

Da es sich hier nicht um eine Entscheidung, sondern um eine Beurkundung, man möchte sagen, um einen Akt der freiwilligen Gerichtsbarkeit, handelt, so liegt es nicht im Geiste des Gesetzes, strenge Anforderungen zu stellen, und wird daher im Zweifel anzunehmen sein, daß derjenige Grad der Dringlichkeit vorliege, welcher bei Bezirksgerichten oder Einzelgerichten die Frage der Zuständigkeit für den Rechtsstreit selbst als müßig erscheinen läßt. Gefahr und Dringlichkeit sind auch ziemlich ungreifbare Thatsachen, bei denen das Ermessen des Richters einen weiten Spielraum haben muß. Zudem kommt zu erwägen, daß in Fällen, wo sich später zeigt, daß eine

Beweiserhebung nicht mehr möglich ist, weil der Zeuge starb, der Thatbestand sich änderte, hierin allein in der Regel auch schon der Beweis liegt, daß die Beweisaufnahme besonders dringlich gewesen sei; ist aber dieselbe noch möglich, so hat ja jeder Theil ohnedies das Recht, eine Wiederholung zu verlangen.

Abgesehen hiervon muß jedoch als Prinzip zugestanden werden, daß ein Beweis zum ewigen Gedächtniß, welcher vom unzuständigen Richter aufgenommen wurde, einen gerichtlichen Beweis nicht ersetzen könne, sondern nur zur Bescheinigung dienlich sei. Vgl. Seuffert Comm. Bd. III S. 70. Es liegt hierin eine Mahnung, sich bei Zweifel, ob eine Handelssache vorliege oder nicht, immer ans Bezirksgericht zu wenden, da für dieses im Nothfalle Art. 348 Abs. 2 angerufen werden kann.

16) Was die Kosten der fraglichen Beweisaufnahme betrifft, so wurde anerkannt, daß es von den Umständen abhänge, ob dieselben später als Prozeßkosten zuzulassen seien oder nicht. Ist die Beweisaufnahme irgendwie nützlich, so wird die Zulassung nicht verweigert werden dürfen. Abg. II S. 168.

X. Hauptstück.

Urkunden.

Vorbemerkung für die Pfalz.

G. A. d. K. d. A. IV S. 429—435. 436. 450—452. — K. d. R. IV S. 46.

Laut Art. 66 des Einführungsgesetzes haben für die Pfalz die Art. 353—369, dann Art. 394 u. 395 dieses Hauptstückes keine Geltung, dagegen bleiben dort die Bestimmungen der Art. 1317—1340 Code civil in Kraft.

In diesen aufrecht erhaltenen Artikeln des Code civil kommen nun Vorschriften vor, welche mit den auch für die Pfalz geltenden Vorschriften der Prozeßordnung concurriren, z. B. Art. 1323 Code civ. mit Art. 370 u. 371 der P.O., ferner Art. 1319 Abs. 2 Code civ. mit Art. 868 Ziff. 2 der P.O. 2c. Sollten sich in dieser Beziehung Konflikte ergeben, welche übrigens für die Bestimmungen über den Urkundenbeweis nicht zu befürchten sind, so würden die besonderen Vorschriften der Prozeßordnung Geltung behaupten. Ein Fall dieser Art wurde berührt in den Bemerk. zu Art. 324 Nr. 19.

Es ist in dieser Beziehung hervorzuheben, daß die von pfälzischer Seite ursprünglich vorgeschlagene Fassung des besagten Art. 66 (Abg. IV 436) lautete: „Die übrigen Bestimmungen der Hauptstücke IX—XIV, welche das Beweisverfahren regeln, treten neben den Art. 1315—1369 Code civ. in Kraft“, daß dann Umbscheiden vorschlug, den Zwischensatz: „welche — regeln“ zu streichen (Abg. IV 450), und daß schließlich als selbstverständlich anerkannt wurde, daß alle Bestimmungen der Prozeßordnung, welche nicht ausdrücklich ausgenommen seien, zu gelten haben. Abg. IV 451 (Umbscheiden — Schmitt).

Arten der Urkunden und deren Beweiskraft.

Art. 353. — **Urkunden, welche von einer öffentlichen Behörde innerhalb der Grenzen ihrer Amtsbefugnisse oder von einer mit öffentlichem Glauben versehenen Person innerhalb des ihr zugewiesenen Geschäftskreises in der vorgeschriebenen Form errichtet sind, gelten als öffentliche Urkunden. Alle übrigen Schriften sind Privaturkunden.**

Kann eine Urkunde wegen eines wesentlichen Mangels nicht als öffentliche gelten, so wird dadurch nicht ausgeschlossen, daß sie als Privaturkunde in Betracht komme.

Art. 354. — **Oeffentliche Urkunden bilden vollständigen Beweis gegen wen immer über die von dem Beamten aufgenommenen Verhandlungen und Erklärungen, sowie über seine thatsächlichen Wahrnehmungen und Handlungen.**

Art. 355. — **Privaturkunden dienen als Beweismittel für den Aussteller nur soweit, als das Gesetz dies ausnahmsweise zuläßt.**

Im Uebrigen haben die in Privaturkunden, welche von dem Aussteller unterschrieben sind, enthaltenen Erklärungen und Anerkenntnisse in Betreff der damit zusammenhängenden Rechtsverhältnisse dieselbe Beweiskraft wie öffentliche Urkunden. Dem sonstigen Inhalte solcher Urkunden kann gegen den Aussteller, seine Rechtsnachfolger und jene Personen, welche er durch seine Handlungen verpflichten kann, volle Beweiskraft beigemessen werden.

Art. 356. — **Gegenscheine gegen öffentliche oder Privaturkunden sind nur unter den contrahirenden Theilen, ihren Rechtsnachfolgern und jenen Personen, welche sie durch ihre Handlungen verpflichten können, nicht aber gegen Dritte wirksam.**

Art. 357. — **Privaturkunden, welche von dem Aussteller nicht unterschrieben sind, wohin auch die nur mit einem Handzeichen versehenen gehören, machen, soweit das Gesetz nicht anders bestimmt, für sich allein niemals vollen Beweis.**

G. A. d. K. d. A. II S. 186—188. 194—200. 202. 203. 297. 301—305. 332. 333. IV S. 90.
K. d. R. II S. 117—149. IV S. 43.

1) Nachdem der Gesetzgeber erkannt, daß bei der Bedeutung, welche die Urkunden im Rechtsverkehre haben, es nöthig sei, ihnen gegenüber die Freiheit der Beweiswürdigung etwas zu beschränken und eine formelle Beweiskraft zu schaffen, war er bemüht, die Grundsätze über diese Beweiskraft bestimmt und erschöpfend zu geben.

Meiner Ansicht nach sind jedoch die bezüglichen Vorschriften, sowohl nach Fassung als nach Inhalt, als gelungen nicht zu betrachten, und wäre es rathsam gewesen, die an den hannov. Entwurf sich anlehnenden Vorschläge des Correferenten von Bomhard (R.R. II 118—149) zu beachten. Jedenfalls darf sich die Pfalz Glück wünschen, daß die dort geltenden Grundsätze, welchen zwar gleichfalls ein mangelhafter Gesetzestext zu Grunde liegt, welche sich aber im Verlaufe der Zeit klar und praktisch herausgebildet haben, ihr erhalten geblieben sind.

2) Das Gesetz unterscheidet nur zwischen öffentlichen Urkunden und Privaturkunden.

Die Wissenschaft erkennt noch zwei weitere Unterscheidungen als wesentlich an, welche es nöthig ist hervorzuheben.

Man unterscheidet 1) Schriften, welche in der Absicht abgefaßt werden, eine Willenserklärung, eine Thatsache festzustellen (Urkunden im engeren Sinne), und 2) Schriften, welche bloß gelegentlich von Umständen sprechen, welche beweiserheblich sind. Bei ersteren ist die Absicht, sich rechtlich zu verpflichten, klar, bei letzteren ist sie fraglich.

Der Gesetzgeber hatte die Wahl, nur die Schriften erster Art zum Gegenstande besonderer Vorschriften zu machen, sonstige Schriften aber dem Vermuthungsbeweise zu überlassen, wie dies das französische Gesetz gethan hat (Zach. f. C. Bd. IV § 750) und der Entwurf beabsichtigte, oder aber alle Schriften zu umfassen, wie es in der Ger.=O. (Cap. XI § 3) geschieht. Er hat das Letztere gewählt; wie mir scheint, ohne genügenden Grund und nicht zum Vortheile seiner Bestimmungen, in welche durch die Rücksichtsnahme auf alle möglichen Schriften viel Unklares gekommen ist.

3) Man unterscheidet ferner 1) Urkunden, welche nur sich selbst beweisen sollen, d. h. beweisen sollen, daß gewisse schriftliche Willenserklärungen von gewissen Personen abgegeben worden seien (dispositive Urkunden), und 2) Urkunden, welche bestimmt sind, zum Beweise anderer Thatsachen zu dienen (Beweisurkunden im engeren Sinne — Anerkennungen).

Urkunden erster Art liegen vor, wenn nach dem Willen des Gesetzes bloß schriftliche Erklärungen Werth haben, oder wenn nach dem Willen der Contrahenten nur die schriftliche Abfassung Geltung haben soll, oder endlich, wenn die rechtserzeugenden Erklärungen überhaupt nur schriftlich erfolgen, wie z. B. beim Vertragsabschlusse durch Correspondenz.

Urkunden letzter Art liegen vor, wenn ein bereits vorher endgiltig abgeschlossener Vertrag nur zur Sicherung des Beweises verbrieft wird, wenn der Empfang eines Darlehens, einer Zahlung bescheinigt wird 2c.

Die nemliche Urkunde kann in einer Richtung als dispositiv, in anderer als einfache Beweisurkunde in Betracht kommen.

Die praktische Bedeutung dieser Unterscheidung liegt darin, daß eine Urkunde, so weit sie keinen Anspruch macht, zurückzuwirken, vielmehr sich begnügt, ihren eigenen Inhalt zu erweisen, unbedingt für Jeden und gegen Jeden beweist, während eine Urkunde, welche frühere Thatsachen anerkennt, zu der wichtigen Frage Anlaß gibt, wie weit durch Anerkennungen auch Beweis gegen dritte Personen geliefert werden könne.

Auch in dieser Richtung hält das Gesetz die Begriffe nicht immer genügend auseinander.

a) Oeffentliche Urkunden.

4) Eine öffentliche Urkunde ist diejenige, welche von einer öffentlichen Behörde, innerhalb der Grenzen ihrer Amtsbefugnisse, oder vor einer mit öffentlichem Glauben versehenen Person, innerhalb des ihr zugewiesenen Geschäftskreises, in der vorgeschriebenen Form errichtet worden ist.

Unter den mit öffentlichem Glauben versehenen Personen sind solche zu verstehen, denen die Feststellung gewisser Thatsachen im öffentlichen Interesse anvertraut ist, und es gehören hierher z. B. Notäre, Gerichtsvollzieher, Pfarrer in ihrer Eigenschaft als Civilstandsbeamte 2c.

Jede Ueberschreitung der Amts- oder Dienstsphäre nimmt der Urkunde, insoweit sie sich auf unzuständigen Gebiete bewegt, den Charakter einer öffentlichen.

Von Einhaltung der vorgeschriebenen Formen ist jedoch die Giltigkeit der Urkunde als einer öffentlichen nur in sofern bedingt, als die Form eine wesentliche ist.

Fehlt eines der drei bezeichneten Erfordernisse, so gilt zwar die Urkunde nicht als eine öffentliche, kann jedoch als Privaturkunde Geltung haben. Ob und in wie weit Letzteres der Fall sei, hängt davon ab, ob sie den Anforderungen, welche gesetzlich an diese gemacht werden, genügen. Ist z. B. die Urkunde von derjenigen Person, gegen welche sie gelten soll, nicht unterzeichnet, so wird sie in der Regel auch als Privaturkunde werthlos sein; sie erscheint nur als schriftliches Zeugniß einer Privatperson.

5) Eine öffentliche Urkunde hat volle Beweiskraft gegen Jedermann, bezüglich dessen, was der Beamte aus eigner Wahrnehmung bezeugt. Auf diesen einfachen Satz lassen sich die verschiedenen Ausdrücke zurückführen, mit denen Art. 354 die Sache bezeichnet, denn wenn der Beamte bezeugt, was er selbst thut, geschieht dies sicher auch aus eigner Wahrnehmung.

Uebrigens ist das Beiwort: „thatsächliche Wahrnehmungen" nicht glücklich gewählt, denn soweit rechtliche Wahrnehmungen ausgeschlossen werden sollen, ist es völlig unnöthig, im Uebrigen aber sagt es zu viel. Die Wahrnehmungen nemlich, welche der Beamte bezüglich der Zurechnungsfähigkeit einer Person, deren Erklärungen er beurkundet, macht und wiedergibt, sind ohne Zweifel ebenfalls thatsächliche, denn die Zurechnungsfähigkeit ist überall eine Thatfrage, nichtsdestoweniger bildet in dieser Beziehung der Akt keinen vollständigen Beweis, gegen welchen nach Art. 399 Beweis durch Zeugen oder Vermuthungen nicht statthaft wäre. Abg. II 304 (Umbsch.).

Es hätte sollen gesagt werden: „sinnliche Wahrnehmungen" im Gegensatze zu Wahrnehmungen durch Schlußfolgerung, zu Beurtheilungen.

6) Das Gesetz bestimmt nur, daß dasjenige, was der Beamte bezeugt, als wahr zu gelten habe, läßt aber die civilrechtlichen Fragen über die Wirksamkeit der abgegebenen Willenserklärungen und Anerkennungen völlig unberührt. R.R. II 120—124.

Die hierher gehörigen Fragen, z. B. ob Erklärungen für den Erklärenden wirken, ob Anerkennungen früherer Thatsachen gegen Dritte wirken, in wie fern Erklärungen, welche nicht direkt Gegenstand der Beurkundung waren, sondern nur gelegentlich erfolgten, beweiskräftig seien, ob der animus confitendi anzunehmen sei — sind in gleicher Weise erheblich für öffentliche wie für Privaturkunden. Der hannoveranische Entwurf hat dies richtig erkannt und (§ 372) berücksichtigt, allein unsere Prozeßordnung hat fragliche Wirkungen sonderbarer Weise als Eigenthümlichkeiten der Privaturkunden behandelt, wie denn sogar die Bestimmungen über Gegenscheine ursprünglich nur für Privaturkunden gegeben wurden.

Aus dem Stillschweigen des Gesetzes folgt übrigens, daß in allen angedeuteten Richtungen die bestehenden civilrechtlichen Grundsätze fortgelten.

7) Was zuerst die Frage betrifft, ob Erklärungen einer Person auch für sie selbst Rechte erzeugen oder beweisen können, so versteht sich von selbst, daß man in der Regel durch eigene Erklärungen keine Rechte erwerben, Niemanden verpflichten und nichts beweisen könne, mag die Erklärung so feierlich geschehen und so stark erwiesen sein, als sie wolle. Es gilt dies in gleicher Weise, mag die Erklärung in einer öffentlichen Urkunde, in einer Privaturkunde oder mündlich geschehen sein.

Dennoch aber kommen Fälle vor, wo aus der Thatsache, daß eine Person eine gewisse Erklärung abgegeben, auch für sie Rechte sich herleiten oder Beweisbehelfe für sie gezogen werden können. So kann z. B. die Thatsache, daß Jemand eine Protestation (etwa im Hypothekenbuche), die Kündigung einer Miethe, eines Darlehns, das Offert zu einem Vertrage erklärt hat, theils direkt, theils indirekt Rechte für den Erklärenden erzeugen. So kann ferner die Thatsache, daß Jemand zu gewisser Zeit, unter gewissen Umständen ein Recht behauptet hat, möglicherweise eine Vermuthung für ihn begründen.

Insofern nun eine Urkunde den Beweis solcher Kundgaben und Behauptungen liefert, beweist sie offenbar für den Aussteller und ist es deßhalb von der Wissenschaft anerkannt, daß der Satz: „scriptura pro scribente non probat", keine unbedingte Geltung habe, und wie die meisten allgemeinen Sätze dieser Art cum grano salis anzuwenden sei. Vgl. Bayer C.P. § 252. Seuff. Comm. Bd. III S. 166 Note 3, S. 169 und 170.

8) Was die weitere Frage betrifft, in wie fern Anerkennungen gegen dritte Personen wirken, so ist diese gleichfalls die nemliche, mag die Anerkennung in einer öffentlichen oder Privaturkunde oder mündlich geschehen sein.

Nur derjenige kann in der Regel rechtsgiltig anerkennen, welcher zur Zeit seiner Erklärung über das in Frage stehende Recht verfügen kann. Anerkennungen wirken daher gegen den Erklärenden selbst, gegen seine Erben, gegen jene Personen, welche das Recht später von ihm erwerben, und gegen jene Personen, welche er zur Zeit der Anerkennung (als Vormund, Mandatar ꝛc.) durch seine Handlungen verpflichten konnte. Gläubiger, welche noch kein Recht auf bestimmte Sachen (durch Hypothek, Arrest ꝛc.) erworben haben, müssen Anerkennungen gegen sich gelten lassen, sofern sie nicht nachweisen, daß ein Betrug gegen sie geübt worden sei.

Anerkennungen wirken dagegen nicht gegen Dritte, d. h. gegen Personen, über deren Rechte der Anerkennende nicht verfügen darf, sollte ihm auch früher, zur Zeit als die anerkannte Thatsache sich ereignete, ein solches Verfügungsrecht zugestanden haben. Seuff. Archiv Bd. IV Nr. 261.

In diesem letzteren Falle lassen jedoch die Civilgesetze hie und da Ausnahmen zu, beruhend auf Rücksichten der Billigkeit und des präsumtiven Willens der Betheiligten. So z. B. gilt das Schuldbekenntniß des Hauptschuldners in der Regel auch gegen den Bürgen. Vgl. Bl. f. R. Bd. IX S. 323. Seuff. Archiv Bd. III Nr. 216; dagegen Seuff. Archiv Bd. II Nr. 185 IV Nr. 224, XV Nr. 23. Auf gleichen Gründen beruht es, wenn im Prozesse Geständnisse des früheren Mandatars gegen den Mandanten oder des Cedenten gegen den Cessionar als beweisgebend erachtet werden. Vgl. Seuff. Archiv Bd. IV Nr. 262 VIII Nr. 331 u. XI Nr. 310; dagegen Bd. III Nr. 128, XVI Nr. 165, XVIII Nr. 64. G. O. Cap. XIII § 1 Ziff. 3.

Endlich kann auch die Bestimmung, daß Privaturkunden gewissen Personen gegenüber ihr Datum selbst beweisen, als eine hierher gehörige Ausnahme gelten.

9) Was schließlich die Frage betrifft, in wie weit Erklärungen, welche nicht direkt Gegenstand der Beurkundung sind, oder wenigstens mit dem beurkundeten Rechtsgeschäfte in engem Zusammenhange stehen, welche vielmehr nur gelegentlich erfolgen oder erwähnt werden, Beweiskraft haben, so können sie in sofern nicht vollbeweisend sein, auch nicht gegen den Erklärenden selbst, als etwa die Absicht, ein Geständniß zu machen, nicht außer Zweifel steht.

b) Privaturkunden.

10) Privaturkunden unterscheiden sich von öffentlichen nur in sofern, als sie 1) ihre Aechtheit nicht selbst beweisen, und als 2) nicht sicher ist, zu welcher Zeit sie entstanden seien.

Setzt man diese beiden Umstände als feststehend voraus, so besteht zwischen beiden Arten von Urkunden ein rechtlicher Unterschied nicht, wenn auch faktisch oft ins Gewicht fällt, daß bei öffentlichen Urkunden reiflichere Ueberlegung und Belehrung durch den Beamten vorauszusetzen ist.

11) In Art. 355 Abs. 1 ist gesagt: „Privaturkunden dienen als Beweismittel für den Aussteller nur so weit, als das Gesetz dies ausnahmsweise zuläßt."

Unter den Ausnahmen des Gesetzes können wohl nur solche verstanden werden, welche sich auf bestimmte gesetzliche Vorschriften gründen, insbesondere auf Art. 34 des Handelsgesetzbuches und auf Art. 364 sowie 365 der Prozeßordnung, welche an Stelle der entsprechenden Bestimmungen der Ger.-O. Cap. XI § 3 Ziff. 2 getreten sind.

Uebrigens müssen noch weitere Ausnahmen zugelassen werden, als solche, welche in Gesetzen ausdrücklich gegeben sind.

12) Wie schon oben (Nr. 7) bemerkt, ist der Satz, daß Urkunden nicht gegen den Aussteller beweisen, theils unnöthig, theils unrichtig. Solche Sätze, die nichts nützen und nur schaden können, sollte der Gesetzgeber vermeiden; sie werfen nur Steine in den Weg, welche die Auslegung Mühe hat wieder wegzuräumen.

So weit das Dasein einer Erklärung an sich rechtliche Folgen hat, beweisen auch Privaturkunden ebensogut für als gegen den Aussteller. Es erleidet z. B. keinen Zweifel, daß im Falle, wo ein Vertrag auf dem Wege der Correspondenz zu Stande gekommen ist, jede Partei auch ihre eigenen Briefe als Beweismaterial benützen dürfe, sei es, daß sie dieselben zufällig in Händen hat, sei es, daß sie auf Grund des Art. 386 Abs. 3 die Herausgabe erwirkt. Ferner ist nicht zu bezweifeln, daß wenn eine Urkunde theils Erklärungen zum Nachtheile, theils solche zum Vortheile des Erklärenden enthält, dieselben nicht willkührlich getrennt werden dürfen und nicht gesagt werden darf: „soweit die Urkunde gegen den Aussteller lautet, gilt sie, so weit sie für ihn lautet, gilt sie nicht." Vgl. Seuff. Comm. Bd. III S. 169 Note 9. Jedoch auch Bayer C. P. § 254, wo der Grundsatz der Theilbarkeit auch hier mit Strenge durchgeführt wird.

Aus den eigenen Erklärungen eines Berechtigten können unter besonderen Umständen sogar Beweisbehelfe zur Bildung und Unterstützung eines Vermuthungsbeweises gezogen werden. Seuff. Comm. Bd. III S. 169 Note 8, 9, 10. Man setze den Fall, es lege der klagende Erbe einen Brief vor, welchen der Erblasser Angesichts des Todes geschrieben und worin er erklärt, daß Jemand zu gewisser Zeit, unter gewissen Umständen ein bestimmtes Darlehen von ihm erhalten. Falls nun hiezu noch ein außergerichtliches mündliches Geständniß des Schuldners kommt, welches genau mit diesen Angaben übereinstimmt, welcher Richter wird bezweifeln, daß diese zwei Vermuthungen zum vollen Beweise genügen? Die erste Vermuthung ist nun aber durch die eigene Schrift des Gläubigers, im Sinne des Art. 322 Abs. 2, vollständig erwiesen.

Ebenso wird man im Falle, wo ein Mann nach dem Tode der Frau eine Schuld der Gütergemeinschaft bezahlt hat und nun den Erben der Frau gegenüber, durch Vorlage seines eigenen, mit sicherem Datum versehenen Schuldscheines, darzuthun versucht, daß die Schuld während der Ehe entstanden sei, ihn nicht einfach mit der Bemerkung zurückweisen dürfen: „eine Urkunde beweise nichts für den Aussteller."

13) In Art. 355 Abs. 2 ist gesagt: „Im Uebrigen haben die in Privaturkunden, welche von dem Aussteller unterschrieben sind, enthaltenen Erklärungen und Anerkenntnisse in Betreff der damit zusammenhängenden Rechtsverhältnisse, dieselbe Beweiskraft wie öffentliche Urkunden."

Beim ersten Anblicke macht diese Bestimmung in Verbindung mit dem, was vorausgeht und nachfolgt, den Eindruck, als wolle der Gesetzgeber hier die Beweiskraft der in Privaturkunden enthaltenen Erklärungen und Anerkennungen überhaupt, also auch Dritten gegenüber regeln. Dies ist nun aber offenbar nicht der Sinn des Gesetzes, denn es konnte dasselbe unmöglich bestimmen, es seien Anerkennungen unbedingt, gegen wen immer, beweisgebend, also auch gegen Personen, welche zur Zeit der Anerkennung bereits Rechte erworben hatten, über welche der Aussteller der Urkunde nicht mehr verfügen konnte. Man konnte der Beweiskraft von Privaturkunden keine größere Tragweite geben wollen, als derjenigen von öffentlichen Urkunden.

Der Gesetzgeber wollte vielmehr nur sagen: „Wenn eine unterzeichnete Privaturkunde vorliegt, so haben die in derselben enthaltenen Erklärungen über Rechtsverhältnisse sowie die Anerkennungen von solchen, als das Werk des Ausstellers zu gelten, so wird rechtlich vermuthet, daß sie mit Wissen und Willen von ihm abgegeben worden seien, in gleicher Weise, als seien sie in einer öffentlichen Urkunde konstatirt. Sie beweisen daher in dieser Richtung gegen Jedermann und — darf man beifügen — für Jedermann, also auch für den Aussteller selbst. Ohne Zweifel wollte auch v. Neumayer (Referat 2. Lesung) nichts anderes ausdrücken, wenn er bemerkte, es sei Zweck dieser Bestimmung, die Beweiskraft von Privaturkunden Dritten gegenüber zu bestimmen.

Welche Wirkungen die Anerkennungen dritten Personen gegenüber äußern, bestimmt sich ebenso wie bei den öffentlichen Urkunden nach den Grundsätzen des Civilrechts, und gelten also die oben (Nr. 8) angedeuteten Prinzipien. Es wurde dies bei den Verhandlungen, unter Ablehnung der Anträge von Franz und Schmitt, welche die Wirkungen von Anerkennungen dritten Personen gegenüber geregelt wissen wollten, klar ausgesprochen. Abg. II 198 und 200 (v. Weiß).

14) Auch bei dieser beschränkteren Deutung geht übrigens der Wortlaut des Gesetzes zu weit, indem er von Privaturkunden überhaupt spricht, während er nur Urkunden im engeren Sinne, d. h. solche, deren Zweck die Feststellung von Rechtsverhältnissen ist, im Auge hatte.

Nicht überall, wo ein unterschriebenes Schriftstück vorliegt, welches Anerkennungen enthält, kann die Absicht sich zu verpflichten, der animus confitendi, angenommen werden. Wer z. B. in einem Briefe um Unterstützung nachsucht, und um seine Bedürftigkeit in recht helles Licht zu stellen, anführt, daß er die und die Beträge an die und die Personen schulde, hat offenbar nicht die Absicht, dem angeblichen Gläubiger ein Geständniß zu machen. Ebenso war man seither nicht geneigt, Schulderklärungen, welche Eltern oder Verwandte zur Erwerbung der Ansässigmachungsbewilligung abgaben, als Schuldbriefe gelten zu lassen.

Daß man hier nur Urkunden im engeren Sinne im Auge hatte ist zwar nicht bestimmt ausgesprochen, erscheint aber angedeutet durch die Worte: „in Betreff der damit zusammenhängenden Rechtsverhältnisse," denn man konnte dabei wohl nur an Rechtsverhältnisse denken, welche festzustellen Zweck der Urkunde ist. Auch die Verhandlungen geben es zu erkennen. Abg. II 302 (Barth), 303 a. E., 304 Sp. 2.

15) Die Schlußworte: „Dem sonstigen Inhalte solcher Urkunden kann gegen den Aussteller, seine Rechtsnachfolger und jene Personen, welche er durch seine Handlungen verpflichten kann, volle Beweiskraft beigemessen werden," erregen fast Bedenken, ob die oben (Nr. 13) entwickelte Ansicht die richtige sei.

Im Einklange mit jener Ansicht würde nemlich der Sinn dieser Schlußworte sich dahin bestimmen: „Bei Erklärungen und Angaben, welche nicht mit dem durch die Urkunden festzustellenden Rechtsverhältnisse zusammenhängen, fällt die rechtliche Vermuthung, daß sie mit Wissen und Willen des Ausstellers in die Urkunde gekommen seien oder daß dieser die Absicht gehabt sich zu verpflichten oder zu gestehen, hinweg, und es hat der Richter nach Lage der Umstände zu ermessen, ob er Beides als vollbewiesen annehmen wolle."

Nun ist aber nicht einzusehen, warum der Gesetzgeber hier ausnahmsweise bestimmte Personen bezeichnete, gegen welche solche Erklärungen beweisen dürfen, denn die Existenz der Erklärungen wird ebensogut gegen Jedermann erwiesen, als wären sie einem öffentlichen Akte beurkundet, oder als hätten sie direkt auf festzustellende Rechtsverhältnisse Bezug, die beweisende Kraft aber würdigt der Richter und die Wirkungen endlich bestimmen sich nach den Grundsätzen des Civilrechts. Auch bei öffentlichen Urkunden kann, wie oben (Nr. 9) bemerkt, sich die Frage ergeben, welche Beweiskraft gelegentlichen Aeußerungen zukomme, dort aber fand man nicht für nöthig, Beschränkungen auf gewisse Personen beizufügen. Ich muß daher gestehen, daß ich den Werth und Sinn dieser beschränkenden Bestimmungen nicht recht einsehe.

Nach einer früheren Fassung (Abg. II 304) hatten fragliche Schlußworte zum Zwecke, die Beweiskraft von Anerkennungen früherer Thatsachen dritten Personen gegenüber zu regeln und bildeten einen Gegensatz zum vorausgehenden Satze, welcher nur von „Willenserklärungen" sprach, allein dieser Standpunkt wurde bei der Schlußredaktion, welche auch für Anerkennungen volle Beweiskraft gegen Jedermann gibt, verlassen.

Für die Frage, wer Rechtsnachfolger ꝛc. sei, ist jedenfalls nur der Zeitpunkt der Ausstellung der Urkunde maßgebend.

16) Privaturkunden, welche vom Aussteller nicht unterzeichnet sind, wozu auch die mit Handzeichen versehenen zählen, sollen für sich allein nie vollen Beweis machen. Sie sind also bloße Beweisbehelfe, welche durch sonstige Vermuthungen zum vollen Beweise verstärkt werden können, und steht die Bestimmung des Art. 357 in Verbindung mit der Beweistheorie des Art. 322, welche eine einzige Vermuthung nie vollen Beweis liefern läßt.

Ohne Zweifel hatte der Gesetzgeber zunächst nur Schriften im Auge, welche von der Hand desjenigen herrühren, gegen welchen sie gelten sollen, Notizen desselben ꝛc.; allein, was die mit Handzeichen versehenen Schriftstücke betrifft, so läßt sich wohl nicht voraussetzen, daß diese vom Aussteller geschrieben seien. Man wird daher an Fälle zu denken haben, wo zugestanden oder erwiesen ist, daß Jemand sein Handzeichen unter eine Schrift gesetzt habe.

17) Liegt eine unterzeichnete Urkunde vor, so sind Randschriften und selbst Nachschriften, welche nicht besonders unterzeichnet sind, als in der Unterschrift begriffen zu betrachten, wenigstens insofern, als es nach Art. 368 dem Ermessen des Richters anheimgegeben ist, sie als Bestandtheile der unterzeichneten Urkunde gelten zu lassen. R.R. II 147, 148.

c) Gegenscheine.

18) Die Bestimmung, das Gegenscheine nicht gegen Dritte gelten, ist dem Art. 1321 Code civil entlehnt. Sie war dort ebenso, wie die Bestimmung über Beweiskraft gelegentlicher Bemerkungen (Art. 1320), zunächst für öffentliche Urkunden gegeben, wurde jedoch durch die allgemeine Verfügung des Art. 1322 auf Privaturkunden übertragen.

Bei den Verhandlungen (Abg. II 332) stellte man sich auf den falschen Standpunkt, fragliche Bestimmungen als Besonderheiten der Privaturkunden zu behandeln, hat jedoch später bezüglich der Gegenscheine diesen Irrthum berichtigt. R.R. II 145 (v. Bomhard). Trotzdem erscheint mir Art. 356 in der Fassung, welche er schließlich erhielt, verfehlt.

19) Die Bestimmung des Code civil: »Les contre-lettres ne peuvent avoir leur effet qu'entre les parties contractantes; elles n'ont point d'effet contre les tiers,« will den Urkunden, und zwar vorzugsweise den öffentlichen, eine besondere Bedeutung dadurch verleihen, daß sie Jeden, der auf Grund einer Urkunde bestimmte Rechte erwirbt, unbedingt gegen den Einwand schützt, als sei dieselbe nur ein Scheinakt. Die Einrede der Simulation ist also einer Urkunde gegenüber rein persönlich, und kann Dritten, welche im Vertrauen auf die Urkunde Rechte erwerben, nicht entgegengehalten werden, ähnlich wie dem Erwerber eines Wechsels gegenüber alle Einreden, welche sich aus der Person des früheren Besitzers herleiten, ausgeschlossen sind.

Dieser civilrechtliche Grundsatz beruht auf ganz richtigen Erwägungen, denn Scheinakte sind im Interesse des Verkehrs nicht zu begünstigen, und wer über einen solchen Akt eine Urkunde errichtet, muß sich bewußt sein, daß durch dieselbe Dritte in Irrthum verleitet werden können; es erscheint daher vollkommen gerechtfertigt, daß man in Fällen, wo Schaden zu leiden ist, diesen derjenigen Person zuweise, welche den Scheinakt errichtet hat, nicht aber derjenigen, welche durch diesen Akt getäuscht worden ist.

Es ergeben sich hieraus zwei wesentliche Folgerungen, nemlich:

1) daß Art. 1321 Code civ. nur der gelegentliche Ausdruck eines allgemeinen civilrechtlichen Grundsatzes ist, welcher dahin zu bestimmen ist: „die Einrede des Scheines ist einer Urkunde gegenüber auf die Contrahenten beschränkt," und

2) daß dieser Artikel zunächst und hauptsächlich den Schutz besonderer Rechtsnachfolger bezweckt.

20) Was die erste Folgerung betrifft, so gibt sich dieselbe von selbst, denn wenn sogar urkundlicher Nachweis der Simulation nichts gilt, so kann noch viel weniger Nachweis durch Zeugen oder Vermuthungen statthaft sein. Mündliche Gegenabreden können nicht wirken, wenn sogar schriftlichen die Wirkung versagt ist.

Es ist dies in der französischen Jurisprudenz unbestritten. Wenn der französische Gesetzgeber nur von »contre-lettres« spricht, so läßt sich dies einigermaßen dadurch entschuldigen, daß er für den Beweis der Simulation, einer Urkunde gegenüber Zeugenbeweis nicht zuläßt; anders ist es bei unserer Prozeßordnung, welche hier abweichend bestimmt (Art. 399 Abs. 2).

Was nun den Sinn des Art. 356 in dieser Richtung betrifft, so müßte man, einfach dem Wortlaute dieses Artikels, sowie des Art. 399 Abs. 2 folgend, annehmen, daß die Simulation eines Aktes zwar nicht durch Urkunden, selbst nicht durch öffentliche, erwiesen werden könne, wohl aber immer durch Zeugen und Vermuthungen! Offenbar ist es nicht statthaft, diese Consequenz zu ziehen, und wird man daher zum Schlusse gelangen müssen, daß ebenso wie im französischen Rechte, aus welchem er herstammt, der Satz, daß Gegenscheine gegen Dritte nicht wirken, die Bedeutung habe, daß Dritten gegenüber, welche in gutem Glauben sind, die Scheinnatur einer Urkunde überhaupt nicht geltend gemacht werden dürfe.

Die Scheinnatur von Geschäften, für welche eine vollbeweisende Urkunde nicht vorliegt, kann natürlich auf jede Weise bewiesen werden; ebenso ist der Beweis nicht beschränkt Personen gegenüber, welche keine Dritte im Sinne von Art. 356 sind.

21) Was nun die zweite Folgerung betrifft, so hielt es die französische Jurisprudenz für selbstverständlich, daß Art. 1321 C. c. vorzugsweise die Rechtsnachfolger im Auge habe.

Bei den Verhandlungen sprach man ursprünglich, sich an den Wortlaut des französischen Gesetzes haltend, nur von „Dritten," bei 2. Lesung jedoch (Abg. IV 90) machte man den Zusatz: „ihren Rechtsnachfolgern rc.," welcher eine Verbesserung bezweckte, jedoch meiner Ansicht nach den Gedanken, welcher der ganzen Ausnahmsbestimmung zu Grunde liegt, fälscht und dieser ihre Bedeutung nimmt.

Offenbar sind nemlich nach dem natürlichen Sinne des Wortes und im Hinblicke auf die im Art. 358 Abs. 1 gemachte Unterscheidung unter den Rechtsnachfolgern hier auch die besonderen Rechtsnachfolger begriffen, d. h. gerade diejenigen Personen, zu deren Schutze fragliche Ausnahmsbestimmung geschaffen wurde. Schließt z. B. A im Vertrauen auf eine ihm vorgelegte Urkunde, laut deren B ein Grundstück von C angekauft hat, mit B einen Vertrag ab, sei es, daß er sich das Grundstück weiter verkaufen oder verpachten läßt, sei es, daß er den Kaufpreis durch Cession erwirbt, so ist er nicht dagegen gesichert, daß C selbst oder ein Rechtsnachfolger desselben mit einem Gegenscheine auftrete und den verbrieften Kauf als Scheingeschäft vernichten lasse. Eben so verhält es sich, wenn etwa C dem B fingirte Quittungen wegen Zahlung des Kaufpreises ausgestellt hätte, und A im Vertrauen auf die Ernstlichkeit dieser Quittungen seinen Kaufpreis an B auszahlt. C könnte auf Grund von Gegenscheinen später seinen Kaufpreis nebst dem sich etwa daran knüpfenden Eigenthumsvorbehalte und sonstigen Rechten geltend machen.

22) Gegenscheine sind öffentliche oder Privaturkunden, durch welche eine in einer Urkunde enthaltene Uebereinkunft unter den Parteien insgeheim aufgehoben oder geändert wird. (Zach. fr. C. Bd. IV S. 437.)

Urkunden durch welche eine ernstliche Uebereinkunft später wieder rückgängig gemacht oder geändert wird, fallen nicht unter den Begriff von Gegenscheinen; jedoch ist es gleichgültig, ob der Gegenschein vor, bei oder nach der Urkunde, welche er als scheinbar erklären soll, zu Stande gekommen ist und kann natürlich der Umstand, daß er nur die Form eines neuen Vertrages annimmt, die Bestimmung des Gesetzes nicht beseitigen.

Gleichgiltig erscheint es, welchen Inhaltes die Urkunde ist, welche entkräftet werden soll, ob durch dieselbe ein Rechtsverhältniß neu begründet oder ein früheres anerkannt werden soll. Abg. IV. 90.

23) Die Worte: „jenen Personen, welche sie durch ihre Handlungen verpflichten können," haben den nemlichen Sinn wie im Art. 358. Es werden wohl nur diejenigen Rechte in Betracht kommen, über welche durch Ausstellung des Gegenscheines verfügt wird. Im Falle, von welchen

Abg. II. 332 die Sprache ist, kann z. B. der Gutsverwalter beauftragt sein Zahlungen zu leisten, nicht aber auch geleistete Zahlungen rückgängig zu machen, Geld aufzunehmen.

Art. 358. — **Das Datum von Privaturkunden wird, soweit das Gesetz nicht anders bestimmt, durch die Urkunde nur bewiesen gegen den Aussteller, gegen jene Personen, welche er durch seine Handlungen verpflichten kann, und gegen seine Rechtsnachfolger, gegen besondere Rechtsnachfolger jedoch nur soweit, als diese die ihrem Vorfahrer zugestandenen Rechte gegen Dritte geltend machen.**

Andern Personen gegenüber hat die Privaturkunde ein sicheres Datum nur von dem Tage, an welchem sie entweder

1) **bei einem Einzelngerichte oder Notar behufs der Feststellung ihres Datums vorgelegt und eingetragen, oder**
2) **das Dasein der Urkunde und ihr wesentlicher Inhalt in einem Obsignations-Protokolle, einem Inventar oder sonstwie durch öffentliche Beurkundung festgestellt worden, oder**
3) **eine der Personen, welche die Urkunde unterzeichnet haben, mit Tod abgegangen ist.**

Ergibt sich jedoch aus der besonderen Beschaffenheit der Urkunde oder aus sonstigen feststehenden Umständen, daß die Urkunde schon an einem frühern als dem in Abs. 2 bezeichneten Tage ausgestellt war, so ist dieser frühere Tag als Datum der Urkunde anzunehmen.

Eine weitere Beweisführung, daß die Urkunde schon vor dem nach Abs. 2 oder 3 als Datum derselben anzunehmenden Tage ausgestellt war, ist nicht zulässig.

Art. 359. — **Werden Privaturkunden auf der Gerichtsschreiberei eines Einzelngerichts oder bei einem Notar zum Zwecke der Feststellung ihres Datums vorgelegt, so sind sie von dem Gerichtsschreiber oder Notar sofort ihrem wesentlichen Inhalte nach in ein dazu bestimmtes, für den Gerichtsschreiber von dem Gerichtsvorstande, für den Notar von dem Vorstande des Bezirksgerichts mit Seitenzahl und Handzug versehenes Buch einzutragen.**

Bei der Eintragung sind zugleich alle Auffallenheiten, welche die Urkunde darbietet, kurz vorzumerken, insbesondere Ausstreichungen, Radirungen, Ueberschreibungen, Correcturen, Nachträge und Randbemerkungen, welche nicht durch die sämmtlichen auf der Urkunde befindlichen Unterschriften besonders genehmigt sind.

Ueber die Vorlage ist eine den Tag derselben bezeichnende Bescheinigung auf der vorgelegten Urkunde auszustellen. Sind bei dem Eintrage Auffallenheiten vorgemerkt worden, so hat die Bescheinigung auch hievon Erwähnung zu thun.

Abschrift der Einträge ist jedem Betheiligten auf Verlangen gegen Erlag der Kosten zu ertheilen.

Weitere Vorschriften über die Einrichtung und Führung der betreffenden Bücher, sowie über die Form der auszustellenden Bescheinigungen bleiben dem Verordnungswege vorbehalten. G. A. d. K. d. A. II S. 194—202. 297. 304. 305. 332. 333. III S. 358. 359. IV S. 90—94. 98. 107—109. 326. 340. — K. d. R. II S. 149—168. IV S. 43.

1) Die Rechtshandlungen einer Person können in einem gewissen Zeitraume für eine andere Person verpflichtend sein, in einem anderen aber nicht. Entsteht nun die Frage, in welche Zeit die Rechtshandlung falle, so gibt hierüber offenbar das Datum, welches der bezüglichen Privaturkunde gegeben ist, keinen zuverlässigen Aufschluß; dasselbe kann ebensogut falsch als richtig sein. Allerdings sind Fälschung und Betrug nicht zu präsumiren, allein anderseits erheischt es auch die Rechtssicherheit, dafür zu sorgen, daß wohlerworbene Rechte nicht ewig unsicher und gefährdet bleiben und durch Vordatiren später verfertigter Privaturkunden willkürlich aufgehoben werden können.

Auf diesen Erwägungen beruhen die Bestimmungen des Art. 1328 Code civil, daß Privaturkunden ihr Datum nicht gegen Dritte erweisen, ein Prinzip, welches auch in Deutschland in neuerer Zeit ziemlich allgemein Anerkennung gefunden hat (Bl. f. R. Bd. XVIII S. 161 ff. Bd. XX S. 65. — Seuffert's Archiv Bd. XII Nr. 97 und Bd. XIII Nr. 193), und welchem im Wesentlichen unsere Prozeßordnung gefolgt ist.

2) Was Art. 1328 Code civ. unter „Dritten" verstehe, das war Gegenstand langjähriger heftiger Controversen, welche sich jedoch in letzter Zeit ziemlich geklärt haben, so zwar, daß die meisten Punkte als feststehend zu betrachten sind. Die Jurisprudenz hat sich denjenigen Weg ge-

bahnt, welcher dem Zwecke des Gesetzes und den Bedürfnissen des Verkehrs am angemessensten erschien, und unpraktische Ansichten, wie z. B. diejenige von Toullier, konnten nie festen Boden gewinnen und sind längst allgemein aufgegeben.

Man kam zu folgenden Resultaten:

I. Gegen Universalsuccessoren des Ausstellers beweist die Privaturkunde ihr Datum unbedingt, weil Jemand, der eine ganze Vermögensmasse unausgeschieden übernimmt, denjenigen Rechtsschutz nicht beanspruchen darf, wie derjenige, welchem ein Recht auf einen bestimmten Gegenstand abgetreten wird.

II. Gegen Singularsuccessoren beweist die Privaturkunde ihr Datum nie, falls es sich um die Frage handelt, wem unter verschiedenen Erwerbern des nemlichen Rechts der Vorzug gebühre.

Man erwog:

1) Wer zwei verschiedenen Personen Rechte überträgt, die sich ausschließen, übt jedenfalls einen Betrug; es handelt sich also nicht davon, ob Ehrlichkeit oder Betrug zu präsumiren sei, sondern nur, wer der Betrogene sei. In diesem Zweifel ist es nun gewiß gerechtfertigt, demjenigen Prätendenten den Vorzug zu geben, dessen Urkunde irgend ein sicheres Datum trägt, oder der im Besitze ist, nicht aber demjenigen, dessen Urkunde möglicherweise einen Augenblick zuvor zum Zwecke des Betrugs gefertigt sein kann.

2) Wer ein Recht erwirbt, ist in culpa, wenn er nicht für ein sicheres Beweismittel sorgt, und verdient keinen Schutz demjenigen gegenüber, welcher sorgsam gewesen ist. Der Saumselige kann füglich auf den Regreß an seinen Autor verwiesen werden, auf dessen Ehrlichkeit er sich leichtsinniger Weise verlassen hat.

3) Es ist im öffentlichen Interesse begründet, daß der Erwerber eines Rechts gegen Willkür und Betrug des Rechtsvorgängers sichergestellt werde, daß das erworbene Recht nicht, so lange dieser lebt, von dessen Ehrlichkeit und gutem Willen abhängig sei.

III. Insoferne jedoch ein Singularsuccessor nur dem seitherigen Schuldner seines Rechtsvorgängers gegenübertritt, wie der Cessionar dem cedirten Schuldner, wäre es schlimm und für den Verkehr störend, wenn alle Privaturkunden, z. B. Quittungen, welche dem Rechtsvorgänger gegenüber Geltung hatten, durch das Auftreten eines neuen Gläubigers ihre Geltung verlieren sollten. In diesem Falle ist es nicht ein zur Zeit des Uebertrags unbekannter und ungewisser Dritter, sondern es ist eine bekannte Person, der Schuldner, welchem der Rechtsnachfolger gegenübersteht, und es erscheint billig, hier den Schuldner mehr zu schützen, als den neuen Gläubiger, welcher so unbesonnen war, das Recht zu erwerben, ohne sich zu überzeugen, ob und in welchem Umfange die Verpflichtung noch bestand.

Die Jurisprudenz nahm daher an, daß in der Regel die Urkunde ihr Datum auch dem neuen Gläubiger gegenüber beweise, daß es jedoch dem Richter gestattet sei, wenn die Umstände einen Betrug nahe legen oder eine besondere Berücksichtigung des Schuldners nicht rechtfertigen, auch die Anerkennung des Datums zu versagen. So pflegte man bei Vorauszahlungen Strenge walten zu lassen.

IV. Gläubiger, welche, um zu ihrer Befriedigung zu gelangen, auf gewisse Gegenstände oder Rechte des Schuldners die Hand legen, sind offenbar, insofern sie eine zwangsweise Ueberlassung dieser Vermögenstheile erstreben und erwirken, als besondere Rechtsnachfolger zu betrachten. Insofern sie daher dem Schuldner des Schuldners gegenüberstehen, wendete man die Grundsätze unter Nr. III, insofern sie aber andern Gläubigern oder Rechtsnachfolgern gegenüberstehen, die Grundsätze unter Nr. II an.

V. Ist die Urkunde von einer Person ausgestellt, welche zur Zeit der Ausstellung eine andere Person giltig vertreten konnte (vom Vormunde, Ehemanne, Mandatare rc.), so beweist sie ihr Datum gegen letztere und zwar aus naheliegenden Gründen, 1) weil es sich nicht fragt wer, sondern ob betrogen sei, Betrug aber nicht vermuthet wird, und 2) weil die Geschäftsführung des Vertreters zum größten Nachtheile des Vertretenen selbst sehr gehemmt sein würde, wenn die Personen, mit welchen er verkehrt, genöthigt wären, sich immer sicheres Datum zu verschaffen.

VI. In allen sonstigen Fällen, z. B. wenn die Privaturkunde als Besitztitel zur Begründung einer Ersitzung geltend gemacht wird rc., gibt die Privaturkunde selbst kein sicheres Datum.

Unser Art. 358 hat, wie sein Inhalt zeigt, sich diese Anschauungen im Wesentlichen zum Muster genommen, und kann daher zu dessen Erklärung auf dieselben Bezug genommen werden.

a) Fälle, in welchen die Privaturkunde ihr Datum selbst beweist.

3) Privaturkunden beweisen ihr Datum zunächst gegen den Aussteller.

Diese Bestimmung gewinnt besondere praktische Bedeutung in Fällen, wo der Aussteller zu einer gewissen Zeit rechtsfähig war, zu einer andern Zeit aber nicht. Die Möglichkeit, daß durch Vordatiren oder Rückdatiren der Urkunde diese fälschlicherweise in die Zeit der Rechtsfähigkeit verlegt worden sein könne, steht also der beweisenden Kraft derselben nicht im Wege.

4) Sie beweisen ferner gegen Personen, welche der Aussteller durch seine Handlungen verpflichten kann.

Das Gesetz meint hier Fälle, wo der Aussteller zur Zeit, welche die Urkunde angibt, berechtigt war, über das in Frage stehende einer andern Person zugehörige Recht in deren Namen zu verfügen, als deren Vormund, Curator, Mandatar 2c.

Gläubiger sind zwar auch verpflichtet, die Handlungen, welche ihr Schuldner zur Zeit, wo sie noch keine besonderen Rechte durch Beschlagnahme 2c. erlangt hatten, ohne Gefährde vorgenommen hat, anzuerkennen; allein der Schuldner kann nicht über ihre Rechte verfügen, kann sie nicht förmlich verpflichten. Abg. II 305 Sp. 1.

5) Sie beweisen endlich gegen Rechtsnachfolger.

Bei allgemeinen Rechtsnachfolgern gilt dies unbedingt, bei besonderen aber nur, soweit diese die ihrem Vorfahrer zugestandenen Rechte gegen Dritte geltend machen.

Aus den Verhandlungen (Abg. IV 91, 92) geht hervor, daß man hier diejenige Unterscheidung machen wollte, welche oben Nr. 2 (II u. III) näher bezeichnet ist.

Wollte man die Worte des Gesetzes ganz allgemein nehmen, so würde die Ausnahme die Regel aufheben, denn auch der Käufer, welcher einem concurrirenden Käufer entgegentritt, macht im Grunde die seinem Rechtsvorfahrer zugestandenen Rechte gegen diesen geltend. So meint es aber das Gesetz nicht, hat vielmehr den Fall im Auge, wo ein Schuldner einem neuen Gläubiger, welcher das ihm übertragene Recht gegen ihn verfolgt, zu seiner Vertheidigung Urkunden entgegenhält, welche vom früheren Gläubiger herrühren.

Wo der Dritte dem besonderen Rechtsnachfolger als Prätendent entgegentritt, sei es bezüglich des ganzen Rechtes, sei es bezüglich eines Theils, indem er Servitutrechte, Pfandrechte 2c. geltend macht, beweist seine Privaturkunde ihr Datum nicht.

6) Als Rechtsnachfolger im weiteren Sinne werden auch Gläubiger zu betrachten sein, welche mit gerichtlicher Hilfe bestimmte Gegenstände oder Rechte ihres Schuldners in Beschlag nehmen.

Sie unbedingt als Dritte zu betrachten, so daß also für den Schuldner, bei welchem Arrest angelegt wird, alle Privatquittungen 2c. werthlos wären, geht offenbar nicht an und lag auch nicht in der Absicht des Gesetzgebers (Abg. IV 91). Zwar wurden besondere Bestimmungen bezüglich der Gläubiger in Aussicht gestellt (a. a. O. v. Weiß), allein es erfolgten solche nur für die Gant (Art. 1277).

Es bleibt demnach nur die Analogie des Rechtsnachfolgers. Wird daher einem Gläubiger, welcher im Besitze seines Schuldners befindliche Mobilien gepfändet hat, eine Privaturkunde entgegengehalten, laut deren diese Mobilien vorher bereits verkauft gewesen sein sollen, so wird er einfach geltend machen dürfen, daß diese Urkunde kein sicheres Datum gegen ihn habe; legt aber ein Gläubiger Beschlag auf eine Forderung seines Schuldners, und werden ihm Privatquittungen entgegengehalten, so werden diese ihr Datum gegen ihn beweisen.

7) Allen sonstigen Personen gegenüber wird das Datum von Privaturkunden durch sie selbst nicht bewiesen.

Auch in Fällen, wo solche Urkunden ihr Datum erweisen, ist es natürlich nicht verwehrt, dessen Unrichtigkeit nachzuweisen. Soll die falsche Angabe des Datums eine betrügerische sein, so versteht sich von selbst, daß der Beweis durch alle Beweismittel ohne Unterschied, namentlich auch durch Vermuthungen, geführt werden könne, aber auch wenn bloß Simulation vorliegt, wird nach Art. 399 Abs. 2 die Beweisführung nicht beschränkt sein.

b) Feststellung des Datums.

8) In Frankreich ist das Hauptmittel, um den Beweis zu sichern, die Registrirung (Art. 1328 Code civ.); unsere Prozeßordnung schafft ein ganz analoges Auskunftsmittel dadurch, daß Privaturkunden bloß zum Zwecke der Sicherung ihres Datums bei einem Einzelgerichte oder Notare vorgelegt werden können.

Sie werden vom betr. Gerichtsschreiber oder Notare ihrem wesentlichen Inhalte nach in ein besonderes Register eingetragen und es wird über die Vorlage eine den Tag derselben bezeichnende Bescheinigung auf der Urkunde selbst ausgestellt.

Diese Register, von deren Einträgen jeder Betheiligte Abschrift verlangen kann, werden insbesondere auch für Fälle von Bedeutung sein, wo die Privaturkunde zu Verlust gegangen ist.

Die Art und Weise der Einträge und Bescheinigungen wird in Art. 359 näher bestimmt und ist weitere Regelung auf dem Wege der Verordnung vorbehalten.

9) Das Datum ist ferner gesichert, 1) wenn eine der Personen, welche die Urkunde unterzeichnet, gestorben ist, oder 2) wenn das Dasein der Urkunde und ihr wesentlicher Inhalt in einem Versiegelungsprotokolle, Inventare oder sonstwie in einer öffentlichen Urkunde festgestellt ist.

Mit den Worten „wesentlicher Inhalt" soll dem Zwecke des Gesetzes gemäß nur gesagt sein, es müsse die Urkunde der Art gekennzeichnet sein, daß kein Zweifel bleibe, sie habe in der Weise, wie sie lautet, damals schon bestanden.

10) Schließlich sagt das Gesetz, es dürfe auch aus der besonderen Beschaffenheit der Urkunde oder aus sonstigen feststehenden Umständen der Beweis geschöpft werden, daß die Urkunde zu einer gewissen Zeit bereits bestanden habe.

Man dachte dabei an Fälle, wo durch den Poststempel eines Briefes, durch den Umstand, daß eine der unterzeichneten Personen in einer gewissen Zeit durch Lähmung &c. unfähig geworden sei, überhaupt oder so wie geschehen zu unterzeichnen, und in ähnlicher Weise die Ueberzeugung eines früheren Bestehens begründet werde. An die Vorschriften des Art. 322 Abs. 2 ist der Richter bei diesem Vermuthungsbeweise nicht gebunden.

Eine förmliche Beweisauflage wollte man ausschließen, wie dies der Ausdruck „feststehende Umstände" andeutet. Abg. IV 92 (v. Weiß, Barth). Uebrigens steht nichts im Wege, daß der Richter aus einem in anderer Richtung, z. B. über den Abschluß des Geschäftes auferlegten Beweise, Präsumtionen ziehe (Abg. IV 92), und es kann daher indirekt auch eine Beweiserhebung stattfinden.

11) Im Schlußsatze des Art. 358 ist bestimmt, daß eine weitere Beweisführung über das Datum der Urkunde nicht zulässig sei.

Man sollte meinen, es sei hiermit eine praesumtio juris et de jure dafür geschaffen, daß die Urkunde nicht früher, als am Tage, wo sie registrirt &c. worden sei, bestanden habe; allein es ist dem nicht so und ist jener Schlußsatz weniger schlimm, als er scheint.

Es leuchtet ein, daß in einem Gesetze, welches wie unsere Prozeßordnung den Zeugenbeweis über das Rechtsgeschäft selbst unbedingt zuläßt, ein Verbot dieser Art nicht die Tragweite haben könne, wie in einem Gesetze, welches in der Regel den Zeugenbeweis ausschließt, wie der Code civil. Man kann Jemanden, welcher eine Privaturkunde ohne sicheres Datum besitzt, nicht sagen: „Es ist schlimm, daß du eine Urkunde hast; wäre dies nicht der Fall, so dürftest du Zeugenbeweis führen!"

Wenn daher ein erheblicher Beweis durch Zeugen oder Vermuthungen dahin erboten wird, daß zu einer gewissen Zeit ein Rechtsgeschäft abgeschlossen worden sei, so darf und soll der Richter diesen Beweis zulassen und bei Führung desselben darf die Urkunde als Beweisbehelf in Betracht kommen, also namentlich zum Nachweise des Inhaltes der Verabredung dienen. R.R. II 167, 168 (v. Bomhard, v. Weiß). — Abg. IV 92 (Barth), 109 (v. Weiß). Auf einem Umwege gelangt man also hier doch dazu, das Datum in anderer Art zu beweisen.

12) Schließlich ist zu bemerken, daß die Bestimmungen wegen des sicheren Datums und der Art des Nachweises desselben auch für Handelssachen gelten; der Vorschlag, für dieselben eine Ausnahme zu machen, wurde abgelehnt. Abg. IV 107—109.

Art. 360. — **Die Beweiskraft öffentlicher Urkunden haben auch die Saal-, Grund- und Lagerbücher und andere Aufzeichnungen ähnlicher Art, wenn sie ordnungsmäßig und mit Zuziehung der Betheiligten unter deren allseitiger Anerkennung errichtet sind.**

Auch beim Mangel dieser Erfordernisse kann das Gericht den fraglichen Urkunden gleichwohl dieselbe Beweiskraft beimessen, wenn sie ihrer Beschaffenheit nach zu keinem Bedenken Anlaß geben und durch ihr Alter oder andere Beweisbehelfe unterstützt sind.

Art. 361. — **Die Beweiskraft öffentlicher Urkunden kann der Richter nach Ermessen aller Umstände auch solchen Privaturkunden beilegen, welche seit langer Zeit in öffentlichen Archiven oder Registraturen aufbewahrt sind.**

Das Gleiche gilt von den seit langer Zeit in gemeinschaftlichen Familienarchiven aufbewahrten Privaturkunden, soweit es sich um Streitigkeiten unter Mitgliedern der Familie handelt.

Art. 362. — **In wie weit in Ermangelung öffentlicher Urkunden durch die Aufschreibungen von Ascendenten über die Geburt und den Tod ihrer Abkömmlinge Beweis geliefert wird, ist vom Gerichte nach den Umständen zu bemessen.**

Art. 363. — **Die von der Hand des Gläubigers auf eine von ihm vorgelegte Schuldurkunde geschriebenen Bemerkungen, welche die gänzliche oder theilweise Tilgung der Schuld zum**

Gegenstande haben, können gegen den Gläubiger auch ohne Unterschrift als vollbeweisend angenommen werden.

Art. 364. — Bezüglich der Beweiskraft der Tagebücher und Schlußnoten der Handelsmäkler (Sensale) und für die Beweisführung durch Handelsbücher bei Streitigkeiten unter Kaufleuten sind die Bestimmungen des Handelsgesetzbuchs maßgebend.

Ordnungsmäßig geführte Handelsbücher haben bei Streitigkeiten über Handelssachen auch gegen Nichtkaufleute die nämliche Beweiskraft, wie bei Streitigkeiten unter Kaufleuten. Bei Streitigkeiten anderer Art liefern sie, soweit es sich um eine Forderung wegen Waarenlieferung handelt, gegen Nichtkaufleute über die Größe der Forderung wie bei Streitigkeiten unter Kaufleuten Beweis, wenn die Ablieferung der Waaren oder die Thatsache, daß der Schuldner in der Zeit, aus welcher die Forderung herrührt, Waaren ähnlicher Art von dem Gläubiger auf Borg zu empfangen pflegte, zugestanden oder anderweit nachgewiesen ist.

Art. 365. — Die Bücher der in Art. 10 des Handelsgesetzbuchs genannten Gewerbtreibenden, der sonstigen Gewerbsleute, der Apotheker, Aerzte, Wundärzte, Hebammen, Notare, Advokaten und Gerichtsvollzieher können, wenn sie regelmäßig fortlaufend, ohne Ausstreichungen, Radirungen, Einschaltungen und Correcturen geführt, gebunden und mit Blätterzahlen versehen sind, in Betreff der stattgehabten einzelnen Leistungen als beweiskräftig angenommen werden, falls zugestanden oder erwiesen ist, daß der angebliche Schuldner in der Zeit, aus welcher die Forderung herrührt, ein Kunde Gast, Patient oder Client des Beweisführers war.

Das Gleiche gilt den Gehilfen und Arbeitern der Fabrikanten, Gewerbsleute und Handwerker gegenüber von den Handbüchern der letztern hinsichtlich der den erstern zur Bearbeitung übergebenen Stoffe und der zurückempfangenen Fabrikate, ferner Gehilfen, Dienstboten und Taglöhnern gegenüber hinsichtlich des bedungenen oder bezahlten Lohns von den Büchern der Kaufleute, Apotheker, Notare, Advokaten, Gerichtsvollzieher und Sensale, sowie auch von den Haushaltungsbüchern der Dienstherrschaften.

Die Gegenpartei kann, wenn das Buch als beweiskräftig angenommen wird, die eidliche Erhärtung des in Frage stehenden Inhalts desselben verlangen.

G. A. d. K. d. A. II S. 188—194. 202. 203. 300. 308. 310. 312. 313. 333. IV S. 94. 326. 340.
K. d. R. II S. 168—172. IV S. 43.

1) Man stellte sich die Frage, ob es nicht sachgemäß sei, eine formelle Beweiskraft nur für öffentliche Urkunden und unterzeichnete Privaturkunden festzusetzen, die Würdigung aller sonstigen Urkunden aber, welche nur als mehr oder minder starke Vermuthungen in Betracht kämen, dem richterlichen Ermessen zu überlassen.

Für diese freiere Anschauung, welche allerdings volle Freigebung des Vermuthungsbeweises voraussetzte, sprachen sich v. Neumayr und Völk aus; nachdem man aber den Vermuthungsbeweis durch eine Beweistheorie eingeengt hatte, war ihr der Boden entzogen und erschien es nöthig, für gewisse Arten von Schriftstücken besondere Vorschriften zu geben, um für sie die Folgen jener Beweistheorie zu beseitigen. Solche Vorschriften geben die Art. 360—365.

a) Saal- und Lagerbücher (Art. 360).

2) Saal- und Lagerbücher sind Bücher, wie sie seit dem 15. Jahrhunderte in Deutschland ziemlich allgemein eingeführt wurden, um die bäuerlichen Güter gewisser Bezirke mit Angabe der Eigenthumsverhältnisse, insbesondere der auf dem Eigenthume ruhenden Reallasten zu verzeichnen. Mochte auch der nächste Zweck bloß auf sichere Erhebung gutsherrlicher Gefälle gerichtet sein, so galten solche Bücher, sofern sie unter öffentlicher Autorität mit Beiziehung der Betheiligten errichtet waren, doch allgemein als beweisgebend. Seuff. Archiv Bd. V Nr. 77.

Was den Ausdruck „Grundbücher" betrifft, so ist er hier gleichbedeutend mit Saal- und Lagerbüchern; im engeren Sinne bezeichnet man sonst damit Bücher, von deren Einträgen das Eigenthum bedingt ist.

Wenn das Gesetz von „andern Aufzeichnungen ähnlicher Art" spricht, so hat es Register über besondere Gefälle (Zehnten, Gilten ꝛc.) im Auge.

Im Entwurfe waren auch die Steuerbücher besonders erwähnt, allein man hielt diesen Ausdruck für zu weitgehend, namentlich im Hinblicke auf den zufolge Edikts vom 13. Mai 1808 angelegten provisorischen Steuerkataster, dessen Einträgen eine Beweiskraft nicht zukam (Verordnung vom 24. August 1813).

3) Was den auf Grund des Gesetzes v. 15. August 1828 hergestellten definitiven Grundsteuer-

kataster anbelangt, so ist in § 95 jenes Gesetzes eine dreijährige Frist gesetzt zur Anmeldung von Beschwerden wegen irriger Liquidation der Dominikalien, Zehnten und anderer nutzbaren Rechte jeder Art, und wird dann weiter bestimmt:

„Nach dem Ablaufe dieser Fristen sind alle „nicht angemeldeten Ansprüche und Reklama„tionen ausgeschlossen und der Grundsteuer„kataster, sowie das mit demselben in Ver„bindung stehende Umschreibkataster, inso„ferne sie die gesetzlichen Erfordernisse haben, „gelten als Saal- und Lagerbuch mit „Beweiskraft, nicht nur in Ansehung der „Steuerverhältnisse, sondern auch über die „Rechte und Verbindlichkeiten der Be„theiligten für die Zukunft."

Zur Auslegung dieser Bestimmung ist Folgendes zu bemerken:

Zweck des Grundsteuerkatasters ist zunächst, eine sichere Grundlage zur Steuererhebung zu gewinnen, und es erscheint nur als ein gelegentlich sich anschließender Nebenzweck, wenn ihm auch die Eigenschaft eines Saal- und Lagerbuches beigelegt wird.

Hieraus folgt, daß der Kataster diese letztere Eigenschaft nur bezüglich solcher dinglicher Rechte haben kann, welche Gegenstand der Besteuerung sind, wie die Dominikalien, Holz-, Fisch- und Jagdrechte, Alpenweide ꝛc., bezüglich aller sonstiger Rechte aber, z. B. Baulast, reale Gewerbrechte, gewöhnliche Weiderechte, Servituten ꝛc. von einer besonderen Beweiskraft des Katasters nicht die Rede sein kann. Bl. f. R. Bd. XIX S. 143.

Was die besteuerten Rechte betrifft, so ist zu unterscheiden zwischen dem Eigenthume und den besteuerten Nutzrechten.

Nur für diese letzteren Rechte gibt § 95 die dreijährige Reklamationsfrist und bestimmt, daß nach deren Ablauf der Kataster vollbeweisend sei für Rechte und Verbindlichkeiten. Nach der Jurisprudenz des k. O.-A.-Gerichts begründet jedoch auch in dieser Richtung der Kataster keine neuen Rechte; er ist nur Mittel zum Beweise des Klaggrundes, nicht aber Mittel zu dessen Ersetzung, und der Gegenbeweis, sowie der Nachweis, daß Rechte, deren Eintrag versäumt wurde, dennoch bestehen, ist nicht ausgeschlossen. Bl. f. R. Bd. XIV S. 224, XXI S. 174, XXII S. 38, XXVIII S. 54. A. M. Kumpf (§ 95 des G. St. G.) S. 17.

Die formelle Beweiskraft, welche § 95 an die Versäumung besagter Reklamationsfrist knüpft, besteht ohne allen Zweifel fort und dürfte man nicht etwa daraus, daß Art. 360 von „allseitiger Anerkennung" spricht, das Gegentheil folgern. Die stillschweigende Anerkennung, welche das Gesetz präsumirt, müßte jedenfalls einer ausdrücklichen gleichstehen.

Was den Nachweis des Eigenthums betrifft, so kann der Grundsteuerkataster in dieser Beziehung nur als Beweisbehelf, sowie als Mittel zur Bescheinigung dienen. Seuff. Comm. Bd. III S. 154 Note 16.

4) Die Voraussetzungen, unter welchen das Gesetz die Saal- und Lagerbücher als öffentliche Urkunden gelten läßt, sind, daß sie ordnungsmäßig, mit Zuziehung der Betheiligten, unter deren allseitiger Anerkennung errichtet seien. Zur ordnungsmäßigen Einrichtung gehörte bis jetzt auch, daß sie überhaupt die Merkmale einer amtlichen Errichtung an sich tragen. Seuff. Archiv Bd. I Nr. 136, Bd. V Nr. 77. Nach der Aeußerung des Minist.-Commissärs (Abg. II 307) und im Hinblicke auf Art. 374 möchte jedoch anzunehmen sein, daß, was die älteren Saal- und Lagerbücher betrifft, hierauf ein entscheidendes Gewicht nicht mehr zu legen sei.

Bei besagten Voraussetzungen haben sie die Beweiskraft öffentlicher Urkunden im Sinne von Art. 354, d. h. sie geben vollen Beweis dafür, daß das darin Aufgezeichnete von den dabei mitwirkenden Betheiligten erklärt und anerkannt worden sei und zwar in der Absicht rechtlicher Verpflichtung. Die Tragweite und die rechtlichen Folgen dieser Erklärungen und Anerkennungen bestimmen sich nach den Grundsätzen des Civilrechts. Abg. II 188 (v. Neumayr), 189 (v. Weiß), 191 (Schmitt).

5) Auch wenn besagte Voraussetzungen fehlen, kann das Gericht gleichwohl die Saal- und Lagerbücher als öffentliche Urkunden gelten lassen, wenn sie ihrer Beschaffenheit nach zu keinem Bedenken Anlaß geben und durch ihr Alter oder andere Beweisbehelfe unterstützt sind.

Was die Auslegung dieser zweiten Bestimmung betrifft, welche praktisch wichtiger ist als die erste, so erscheinen hier die Grundsätze wegen Geltung der Urkunde als einer öffentlichen und wegen ihrer Tauglichkeit, gewisse Rechtsverhältnisse nachzuweisen, vermengt, wie dies auch schon im Entwurfe der Fall war.

Ein altes Saalbuch z. B., welches die Zuziehung der Betheiligten nicht constatirt, ist offenbar eine bloße Zusammenstellung, welche von irgend einer vermuthbar amtlichen Person, auf Grund gepflogener Nachforschungen und Prüfungen, nach bestem Wissen und Gewissen gefertigt worden ist. Offenbar ist nun das, was jene Person als das Ergebniß ihrer Ermittlungen niedergeschrieben, keine eigene Wahrnehmung im Sinne des Art. 354, und gäbe man daher einem solchen Saalbuche nur diejenige Beweiskraft, wie sie aus Art. 354 zu folgern ist, so würde es weiter nichts beweisen, als daß es ächt sei und daß die Aufzeichnungen überhaupt stattgefunden haben. Diese Aufzeichnungen selbst hätten jedoch nur den Werth einer vollbewiesenen Vermuthung (Art. 322 Abs. 2), und könnten deßhalb nur Beweis bilden, insofern noch andere vollbewiesene Vermuthungen hinzutreten würden. Es ist nun aber gerade Zweck des Gesetzes, hier die Erfordernisse des gewöhnlichen Vermuthungsbeweises zu beseitigen, und den in Frage stehenden Urkunden eine formelle Beweiskraft bezüglich gewisser Rechtsverhältnisse zu sichern. Hieraus folgt, daß das Gesetz nicht bloß sagen will, es sollen Saalbücher fraglicher Art als öffentliche Urkunden gelten dürfen, sondern auch noch weiter, es dürfe der Richter auf Grund solcher Bücher den Beweis der darin verzeichneten Rechtsverhältnisse annehmen, falls sie alt oder durch andere Beweisbehelfe irgend einer Art unterstützt seien.

Die Bezugnahme auf sonstige Beweisbehelfe deutet bestimmt darauf hin, daß dies der Wille des Gesetzes sei; denn was hätte es für einen Sinn, zu sagen, eine Urkunde gelte deßhalb als eine öffentliche, weil sie durch andere Beweisbehelfe unterstützt sei? Auch die Aeußerung des k. Minist.-Commissärs (Abg. II 189), daß im Falle, wo das Alter 2c. für die Saalbücher spreche, die Verhandlungen und Erklärungen der Betheiligten als festgestellt (soll wohl heißen: „ersetzt") erscheinen sollen, deutet darauf hin. Allerdings ist dann anzunehmen, daß die Aeußerungen des Referenten (Abg. II 188 a. E.) den Sinn des Gesetzes nicht erschöpfen.

Die nemlichen Grundsätze galten übrigens auch früher. Seuff. Comm. Bd. III S. 155 lit. c.

b) Archivalische Urkunden (Art. 361).

6) Sind Privaturkunden seit langer Zeit in öffentlichen Archiven oder Registraturen aufbewahrt, so streiten so gewichtige Vermuthungen für ihre Aechtheit, daß das Gesetz dem Richter erlaubt, nach Ermessen aller Umstände ihnen die Beweiskraft öffentlicher Urkunden beizulegen. Welche rechtliche Wirksamkeit sie sonst haben, hängt von ihrem Inhalte ab.

Ebenso verhält es sich mit Privaturkunden, welche seit langer Zeit in gemeinschaftlichen Familien-Archiven aufbewahrt sind, jedoch nur für Streitigkeiten unter Familiengliedern.

In beiden Fällen wird vorausgesetzt, daß die lange Zeit dauernde Aufbewahrung in fraglichen Archiven feststehe. Wie lang die Zeit sein müsse, hat der Richter nach dem Geiste des Gesetzes zu würdigen und dabei zu beachten, daß das Gesetz solche Fälle im Auge hat; wo der Nachweis der Aechtheit wegen Länge der Zeit nicht mehr leicht zu erbringen wäre.

c) Aufschreibungen von Ascendenten (Art. 362).

7) Der Entwurf (Art. 324) hatte dem Richter gestattet, den Aufzeichnungen der Eltern über Geburt und Tod von Kindern, in Ermanglung öffentlicher Urkunden, die Beweiskraft öffentlicher Urkunden zu geben. Offenbar war dies eine Vermengung der Begriffe von Beweiskraft und Beweistauglichkeit im Sinne, wie oben (Nr. 5) erwähnt.

Die Prozeßordnung hat, diesen Fehler vermeidend, geradezu gesagt, daß der Richter in Ermangelung öffentlicher Urkunden in den bezüglichen Aufzeichnungen der Ascendenten, den Beweis finden könne. Hiermit ist also bloß die Beweistauglichkeit ausgesprochen und die Eigenschaft der Urkunden als Privaturkunden nicht geändert.

d) Notizen des Gläubigers (Art. 363).

8) Die Bestimmung, daß Bemerkungen von der Hand des Gläubigers auf einer von ihm vorgelegten Schuldurkunde, welche die Tilgung der Schuld zum Gegenstande haben, gegen ihn als vollbeweisend angenommen werden können, erschien nöthig im Hinblicke auf Art. 322, welcher eine Vermuthung zum vollen Beweise nicht genügen läßt, und auf Art. 357, welcher sagt, daß nichtunterzeichnete Privaturkunden nie vollen Beweis machen.

Der Vorschlag, auch den Einträgen in Hausbüchern diese besondere Beweiskraft zu geben, wurde verworfen (Abg. II 310) und bei dieser Gelegenheit hervorgehoben, daß für die Wirksamkeit solcher Einträge die civilrechtlichen Bestimmungen maßgebend sein müßten. Allerdings wird nicht zu bezweifeln sein, daß z. B. die Verfügung im bayer. Landrecht Thl. III Cap. I § 15 Ziff. 22, laut welcher die Aufzeichnungen des Erblassers Beweis bezüglich der Conferenden geben, fortgelte, theils im Hinblicke auf Art. 357, welcher auf gesetzliche Ausnahmen verweist, theils weil bezüglich der Frage, ob urkundliche Feststellungen auch gegen Dritte wirken, überall die civilrechtlichen Prinzipien Maß geben.

Auch nach gemeinem Rechte wird die Tauglichkeit solcher Aufzeichnungen als Beweismittel angenommen. Seuffert Archiv Bd. X Nr. 272.

e) Handelsbücher (Art. 364).

9) Nach Art. 364 Abs. 1 gelten für die Beweiskraft der Tagebücher und Schlußnoten der

Handelsmäkler (Sensale) die Art. 77 u. 78 des Handelsgesetzbuches und für die Beweiskraft der Handelsbücher bei Streitigkeiten über Handelssachen unter Kaufleuten der Art. 34 daselbst.

Was diesen Art. 34 betrifft, welcher für die Pfalz die einzige maßgebende Norm bildet, so stellt er zwar als Regel auf, daß die Handelsbücher nur unvollständigen Beweis bilden, welcher durch Eid oder sonstige Beweismittel zu ergänzen sei, überläßt es aber in seinen nachfolgenden Verfügungen dennoch dem richterlichen Ermessen, nach Umständen vollen oder gar keinen Beweis anzunehmen, Letzteres namentlich dann, wenn die Handelsbücher beider Streitstheile nicht übereinstimmen. Bezüglich der Auslegung seiner Bestimmungen ist Folgendes zu bemerken.

10) Die Präsumtion der Richtigkeit, welche eine ordnungsmäßige kaufmännische Buchführung begründet, wirkt unbedingt, also zum Beweise für und zum Beweise gegen den Kaufmann, sowie gegen Dritte, auch wenn diese bei fraglichem Geschäfte nicht direkt betheiligt waren.

Sie erstreckt sich nicht bloß auf das, was eingetragen ist, sondern auch auf den Mangel eines Eintrages. S. Anschütz Comment. z. H. G. B. Bd. I S. 258.

Sie erstreckt sich ferner auch auf die Handelsbücher ausländischer Kaufleute. S. Urtheile des Obertribunals in Berlin vom 3. Mai 1845, 11. Febr. 1851 und 18. Juni 1863. Nach diesen Urtheilen wären solchen Falls die Gesetze des Orts, wo die Handelsbücher geführt wurden, maßgebend.

Unter „Handelssachen" sind vorzugsweise Handelsgeschäfte, für deren Eintrag nach Art. 28 die Handelsbücher bestimmt sind, zu verstehen, und es ist dabei gleichgiltig, welcher Art dieselben seien, ob Grundgeschäfte oder Hilfsgeschäfte, ob zweiseitige oder einseitige Handelsgeschäfte. Daß auch die letzteren gemeint seien, ergibt sich aus Art. 277 des H. G. B. und kann bei uns um so weniger bezweifelt werden, als sowohl Art. 64 des Einf.-Ges. zum H. G. B., als Art. 7 der P. O. sie als Handelssachen bezeichnet und nur ausnahmsweise den Civilgerichten zuweist. Anschütz a. a. O. Bd. I S. 256. Es ist hier hervorzuheben, daß es für die Beweiskraft der Handelsbücher ganz gleichgiltig ist, ob das Handelsgericht oder ob das Civilgericht in der Sache zuständig sei, wie denn Art. 40 des H. G. B. von Fällen spricht, wo es sich um Auseinandersetzung von Erbschaften und Gütergemeinschaften handelt.

Unter „Kaufleuten" versteht Art. 34 nur die **Vollkaufleute**, nicht aber jene Handelsleute mit geringem Gewerbbetriebe, bei welchen nach Art. 10 des H. G. B. die Bestimmungen über Handelsbücher keine Anwendung finden. Handelsleute dieser letzteren Art gelten daher hier als Nichtkaufleute.

Was schließlich den Notheid betrifft, welchen der Richter auferlegen kann, so spricht sich das H. G. B. selbst über die Natur desselben nicht näher aus, und es werden daher die bestehenden gesetzlichen Bestimmungen zur Anwendung zu kommen haben — diesseits die Art. 454—456 und 458 der P. O., in der Pfalz die Art. 1367, 1369 u. 2275 Code civil. Einen besonderen Buch-Eid gibt es nicht mehr.

11) In Art. 364 Abs. 2 sind zwei weitere Bestimmungen getroffen, welche die Grundsätze des Art. 34 ausdehnen, nemlich:

1) daß ordnungsmäßig geführte Handelsbücher bei Streitigkeiten über Handelssachen auch gegen Nichtkaufleute die in Art. 34 des H. G. B. normirte Beweiskraft haben und
2) daß bei Streitigkeiten anderer Art, sofern es sich um Waarenlieferungen handelt, die Handelsbücher unter gewissen Voraussetzungen bezüglich der Größe der Forderung in nemlicher Weise Beweis geben sollen.

Was erstere Bestimmung betrifft, so muß für den Ausdruck „Handelssachen" hier ganz der nemliche Sinn beansprucht werden, wie in Art. 34 des H. G. B., so daß also auch einseitige Handelsgeschäfte darunter begriffen sind.

Die zweite Bestimmung wäre demnach überflüssig, wenn man bei „Waarenlieferungen" an solche Waaren denken würde, mit denen der Kaufmann Handel treibt. Wirklich wurde auch der Sinn des entsprechenden Art. 335 des Entwurfs im Archiv für Handelsrecht Bd. II S. 355 in dieser Weise aufgefaßt, indem dort bemerkt ist, der Art. 73 des Einführungsgesetzes zum H. G. B. gehe weiter, als jene Bestimmung des Entwurfes. Allein im Sinne der Prozeßordnung, wie er vom Minist.-Commissär (Abg. II 305 und R. R. II 170) scharf hervorgehoben wurde, soll umgekehrt die fragliche Bestimmung weiter gehen, als jener Art. 73 des Einf.-Ges. und zur Anwendung kommen, wenn gewöhnliche Civilrechtsgeschäfte in Frage sind.

Man wird daher an Fälle zu denken haben, wo die Waarenlieferung auf Seite des Kaufmannes kein Handelsgeschäft ist, wie z. B. wenn ein Kaufmann, der zugleich eine Ziegelei betreibt, Ziegelwaaren geliefert hat. Auch in diesen Fällen hat jedoch nur das Handelsbuch eines Vollkaufmannes diese bevorzugte Beweiskraft; jeder andere Gewerbtreibende, auch wenn er ganz ordnungsgemäße Handelsbücher führt, fällt unter die Bestimmungen des Art 365.

f) Bücher von Gewerbtreibenden (Art. 365).

12) Die Bestimmungen in Art. 365 enthalten eine Ausdehnung der ähnlichen Bestimmungen in Gerichtsordnung Cap. XI § 3 Ziff. 2. Sie beruhen auf einem Bedürfnisse des praktischen Lebens, indem Leistungen der fraglichen Art in anderer Weise schwer zu beweisen sind, und finden ihre Rechtfertigung ebenso wie die Beweiskraft der Handelsbücher, in der starken Präsumtion, welche aus der Ordnung und Regelmäßigkeit der Aufzeichnungen entsteht. Sie haben ihr Gegengewicht in den kurzen Verjährungsfristen, welche für dergleichen Leistungen bestehen; wie diese den Schuldner schützen, so schützen sie den Gläubiger.

Vorbedingung der Beweiskraft solcher Aufzeichnungen ist vor Allem die Ordnungsmäßigkeit derselben, für welche der Gesetzgeber besorgt war, noch besondere Merkmale zu geben. Die bezüglichen Vorschriften werden nicht bloß von den in Abs. 1 bezeichneten Büchern von Gewerbtreibenden, sondern auch von den Handbüchern und Haushaltungsbüchern zu gelten haben, von welchen in Abs. 2 die Sprache ist. Die Natur der Sache, sowie die Worte: „das Gleiche gilt" bedingen dies.

Bei den Büchern der Gewerbtreibenden 2c. ist fernere Voraussetzung der Beweiskraft, daß in der Zeit, aus welcher die Forderung herrührt, der angebliche Schuldner ein Kunde, Gast, Patient oder Klient des Beweisführers war. In den Fällen, welche Abs. 2 aufzählt, tritt an Stelle dieser Voraussetzung das vom Gesetz als bestehend vorausgesetzte Dienstverhältniß.

Was den Eid anbelangt, welchen die Gegenpartei verlangen kann, so richtet er sich nach den Vorschriften der Art. 454—456 und ist kein bloßer Bucheid im Sinne des früheren Rechts.

Art. 366. — Soweit das Gesetz nicht anders bestimmt, haben nur Urschriften Beweiskraft.

Als Urschrift gilt nicht nur die zuerst errichtete Urkunde, sondern auch jede spätere, bei deren Abfassung der Errichtungsakt wiederholt wurde.

Art. 367. — Der Urschrift gelten gleich:

1) die von einer öffentlichen Behörde oder einer mit öffentlichem Glauben versehenen Person gefertigten und beglaubigten Ausfertigungen, Abschriften und Auszüge der von ihr amtlich verwahrten öffentlichen Urkunden;

2) Abschriften, welche in Gegenwart oder bei gehöriger Ladung der Betheiligten, nach genauer Untersuchung der Urschrift und mit Beifügung einer Beschreibung der dabei gefundenen erheblichen Umstände, gerichtlich oder von einer vom Gerichte beauftragten oder vermöge gesetzlicher Vorschrift dazu berechtigten öffentlichen Behörde oder Person als mit dieser Urschrift gleichlautend beglaubigt worden sind;

3) Abschriften, welche in gleicher Weise von einer solchen Abschrift gefertigt wurden.

In allen diesen Fällen kann die Vorlage der Urschrift, wenn sie zu erlangen steht, vom Gerichte auf Antrag der Gegenpartei oder auch von Amtswegen angeordnet werden.

Alte Abschriften, welche auch in öffentlichen Archiven oder Registraturen aufbewahrt sind oder wenigstens von einer bekannten Kanzleihand herrühren, kann das Gericht nach den Umständen der Urschrift gleichstellen. Das Gleiche gilt von alten Abschriften, welche in gemeinschaftlichen Familien-Archiven aufbewahrt sind, soweit es sich um Streitigkeiten unter Mitgliedern der Familie handelt.

G. A. d. K. d. A. II S. 204. 297. 298 305. 308. 333. IV S. 94. — K. d. R. II S. 172. IV S. 44.

1) In der Regel hat nur die Urschrift einer Urkunde Beweiskraft, und wenn das Gesetz Mittheilung von Urkunden (Art. 172) oder Vorlage derselben (Art. 246, 370) vorschreibt, versteht es darunter nur Urschriften oder Abschriften, welche gesetzlich der Urschrift gleich stehen.

Die Begriffsbestimmung ist aus Bayer's Civilprozeß § 251 entnommen, wo gesagt wird:

„Unter Originalien versteht man nicht bloß „das erste in vollkommener Form vollzogene „Exemplar einer Urkunde, sondern jedes Exemplar, bei dessen Abfassung der ursprüngliche „Errichtungsakt von denselben Hauptpersonen „wiederholt worden ist. Es können daher von „der nemlichen Urkunde mehrere Originalien „vorhanden sein."

Die Errichtung einer zweiten Urschrift kann übrigens nicht bloß nachträglich, sondern auch gleichzeitig geschehen, wie es denn üblich, in der Pfalz sogar bei Strafe der Nichtigkeit vorgeschrieben ist, bei zweiseitigen Verträgen für jeden Contrahenten sofort eine besondere Urschrift zu fertigen.

2) Nach Art. 367 sollen der Urschrift gleich gelten:

I. Ausfertigungen, Abschriften und Auszüge, welche ein Beamter von öffentlichen Urkunden gibt, welche von ihm selbst aufgenommen oder bei ihm amtlich verwahrt sind.

Das Gesetz spricht hier nur von öffentlichen Urkunden im Sinne des Art. 353 und meint nur Ausfertigungen rc. von Urschriften solcher Urkunden. Abschriften von Ausfertigungen öffentlicher Urkunden oder von Privaturkunden, welche ein Notar oder Gerichtsschreiber (Art. 87) in Verwahr hat, fallen daher nicht unter diese Bestimmung, noch weniger Abschriften, welche ein Notar gemäß Art. 84 des Not.-Gesetzes von Urkunden gibt, welche ihm bloß zu diesem Zwecke vorgelegt wurden.

Wo durch besondere Verfügung des Gesetzes einer Ausfertigung die volle Wirkung einer Urschrift beigelegt ist, z. B. in Art. 90 u. 92 des Not.-Ges., wird dieselbe auch hier als solche zu behandeln sein. Privaturkunden, welche beim Notare hinterlegt werden, um die Eigenschaft von Notariatsurkunden zu erlangen (Art. 22 des Not.-Ges.), bilden in Verbindung mit dem Hinterlegungsakte eine Urschrift.

3) Indem das Gesetz hier Ausfertigungen und Abschriften gleichstellt, ist die Unterscheidung, welche Art. 87 des Not.-Ges. zwischen Hauptausfertigungen und einfachen Abschriften macht, soweit es die Beweiskraft betrifft, aufgehoben.

Die bezügliche Unterscheidung war dem Art. 1335 Code civ. entlehnt, welcher seine Bestimmungen nicht bloß für Notariatsurkunden, sondern allgemein für alle öffentlichen Akte gibt. Indem nun die Prozeßordnung, jenen Grundsatz des Code civ. verlassend, alle von einer zuständigen Behörde ausgehenden Ausfertigungen und Abschriften bezüglich der Beweiskraft gleichstellt, beseitigt sie offenbar auch dasjenige, was von den Verfügungen jenes Art. 1335 ins Not.-Ges. übergegangen war. Einf.-Ges. Art. 2 Abs. 2.

Uebrigens führt schon der Wortlaut des Art. 87 des Not.-Ges. zum nemlichen Ergebnisse, da dort gesagt ist, daß spätere Ausfertigungen bloß die Wirksamkeit von Abschriften haben, Abschriften aber jetzt der Urschrift gleich gelten.

4) Der Urschrift gelten ferner gleich:

II. Abschriften, welche unter Beiziehung der Betheiligten gerichtlich oder von einer vom Gerichte beauftragten oder vermöge gesetzlicher Vorschrift dazu berechtigten öffentlichen Behörde oder Person, beglaubigt sind.

Hier wird nicht unterschieden, ob die Abschrift von einer öffentlichen Urkunde genommen sei, oder von einer Urkunde, welche bezüglich der Beweiskraft einer öffentlichen gleichgeachtet wird, oder endlich von einer Privaturkunde. Selbstverständlich kann jedoch bei Privaturkunden eine Abschrift nur dann die Urschrift ersetzen, wenn die Aechtheit unbestritten ist, denn es ist Niemand verpflichtet, sich zu erklären, ob er eine Unterschrift als ächt anerkenne, wenn ihm bloß eine Abschrift, möge sie auch noch so authentisch sein, vorgelegt wird.

5) Da die Art. 391 u. 392 sehr praktische Auswege eröffnen, um die Urschriften selbst dem Gerichte zugänglich zu machen, so wird es nur selten nöthig sein, gerichtliche Abschriften zu erheben.

Hie und da wird sich Anlaß dazu ergeben bei Urkunden, welche wegen ihres Umfanges, wegen der Nothwendigkeit fortwährender Benützung oder aus sonstigen Gründen nicht eingesendet werden können, oder deren Einsendung (z. B. von ausländischen Behörden) verweigert wird; vorausgesetzt, daß der Beamte, welcher die Urkunde in Verwahr hat, nicht befugt ist, beweiskräftige Abschriften oder Auszüge im Sinne von Ziff. I zu geben, oder daß die Auszüge von Jemanden erhoben werden müssen, welcher genau zu beurtheilen vermag, was für den Rechtsstreit erheblich sei. Besondere Vorschriften sind in dieser Beziehung für Handelsbücher gegeben durch Art. 38 u. 39 des Handelsgesetzbuches.

In Fällen solcher Art läßt das Gericht die Partei zum Urkundenbeweise zu und beauftragt ein Mitglied des Gerichts oder einen Einzelrichter mit Erhebung der Abschriften oder Auszüge. Das Verfahren richtet sich nach den Bestimmungen über Augenschein.

Auch in Fällen, wo dem Gerichte die Urschrift zur Einsicht vorgelegt wird, oder dasselbe, weil die Ausfertigung nicht genügt, diese Vorlage angeordnet hat, kommt es manchmal in die Lage, die Beschaffenheit und den Inhalt der Urschrift, welche nicht bei den Akten bleiben kann, festzustellen. Man pflegt in den Entscheidungsgründen das Nöthige zu sagen und sodann im Urtheilssatze, darauf Bezug nehmend, Urkunde zu ertheilen.

6) Voraussetzung der Ausnahme in Ziff. II ist in allen Fällen, daß die Abschriftnahme in Gegenwart oder bei gehöriger Ladung der Betheiligten, als welche, da solche Abschriften gewöhnlich nur aus Anlaß eines Rechtsstreites erhoben werden, die Parteien zu betrachten sind, geschehe.

Ohne Zweifel ist auch ein Notar zuständig, Abschriften im Sinne vorliegender Bestimmung zu fertigen, wenn die Betheiligten freiwillig vor ihm erscheinen. Art. 84 des Not.-Gesetzes.

7) Der Urschrift gelten ferner gleich:

III. Abschriften, welche in gleicher Weise, von einer solchen Abschrift gefertigt werden.

Es ist hier dasjenige wiederholt, was die Gerichts-Ordnung Cap. XI § 4 Ziff. 4, bezw.

Seuffert im Commentare zu dieser Stelle (Bd. III S. 185 und 186) sagt.

Dem Wortlaute nach müßte man annehmen, daß das Gesetz Fälle im Auge habe, wo die Vorschriften der Ziff. 2, also insbesondere die Beiziehung der Betheiligten, sowohl bei der ersten als bei der zweiten Abschrift beobachtet worden seien, wie dies auch wirklich der Sinn fraglicher Stelle der Ger.-Ordnung ursprünglich war. Da jedoch eine unter Zuziehung der Betheiligten gefertigte gerichtliche Abschrift offenbar diejenige Urkunde, von welcher sie genommen wird, mag sie nun Urschrift oder Ausfertigung sein, geradezu ersetzt, so muß es im Geiste des Gesetzes wohl gleichgiltig sein, ob die erste Abschrift nach Ziff. 1 oder nach Ziff. 2 errichtet worden ist. Vgl. Seuff. Comm. Bd. III S. 185.

8) Endlich können, nach Ermessen des Richters, der Urschrift gleichgestellt werden:

IV. Alte Abschriften, welche in öffentlichen Archiven oder Registraturen aufbewahrt sind, oder wenigstens von einer bekannten Kanzleihand herrühren.

Auch diese Ausnahme ist fast wörtlich der Ger.-Ordnung Cap. XI § 4 Ziff. 1 entnommen.

Die erste und wichtigste Voraussetzung ist das Alter der Abschrift, außerdem aber muß entweder die eine oder die andere der beiden übrigen Voraussetzungen gegeben sein. Rührt die Urkunde von einer bekannten Kanzleihand her, so läßt sich aus den Schriftzügen ein Schluß auf ihre Aechtheit ziehen, wurde sie aber in einem öffentlichen Archive aufbewahrt, so ergibt sich aus der Thatsache, daß man ihr diese Wichtigkeit beilegte in Verbindung mit der langen Dauer dieser Aufbewahrung, die Vermuthung der Aechtheit und Richtigkeit.

Wie solche Abschriften beschaffen, ob sie insbesondere vom Verfertiger unterzeichnet sein müssen, läßt das Gesetz unentschieden.

Die gleiche Ausnahme wurde, im Einklange mit den Bestimmungen des Art. 361 Abs. 2 für alte Abschriften, die in Familienarchiven aufbewahrt sind, gegeben, jedoch dort nur für Streitigkeiten unter Familienmitgliedern.

9) Es liegt in der Natur der Sache, daß Abschriften nur so weit gelten, als sie mit der Urschrift übereinstimmen, und daß nur die Präsumtion dieser Uebereinstimmung Grund ist, wenn gewisse Abschriften der Urschrift gleich gestellt sind. Besteht nun die Urschrift selbst nicht mehr, ist sie verloren oder überhaupt nicht zu erlangen, so bleibt nichts übrig, als sich an die Abschrift zu halten, ist aber die Urschrift vorhanden und zugänglich, so muß, wo Anlaß dazu gegeben ist, auf sie zurückgegriffen werden.

Der französische Gesetzgeber (Art. 1334 Code civ.) gab der Gegenpartei unbedingt bei jeder Abschrift, sogar bei Hauptausfertigungen, das Recht zu verlangen, daß Einsicht der Urschrift genommen werde. Die Oeffentlichkeit und Mündlichkeit des Verfahrens, welche den Geist der Chikane nicht aufkommen läßt, bewirkte jedoch, daß thatsächlich nie eine von einem öffentlichen Beamten gefertigte Abschrift in Zweifel gezogen wurde, wenn nicht sehr triftige Gründe dazu vorlagen, selbst nicht in Fällen, wo die Abschrift nach den strengen Bestimmungen des Art. 1335 Code civ. nur als Beweisbehelf (commencement de preuve par écrit) dienlich gewesen wäre. Mir kam nur ein einziger Fall vor, wo auf die Urschrift zurückgegriffen wurde und zwar aus ganz besonderen durch die Beschaffenheit dieser Urschrift bedingten Gründen.

Auch der Entwurf wollte der Gegenpartei dieses Recht einräumen, allein man fand es im Hinblicke auf den Mißbrauch welcher diesseits mit Nichtanerkennen von Urkunden getrieben wurde und in Erwägung, daß Gewohnheiten sich nicht so schnell ablegen, rathsam, dem Gerichte allein die Verfügung in die Hand zu geben.

Dieses wird die Vorlage oder Einsicht der Urkunde nur anordnen, wenn wichtige Gründe dafür vorliegen (Abg. II 204 Sp. 1) insbesondere auf Antrag des Gegners nur dann, wenn derselbe bestimmte Thatsachen anführen und glaubhaft machen kann, welche diese Maßregel rechtfertigen.

Handelt es sich blos darum, daß in der Abschrift aus Versehen etwas ausgelassen oder unrichtig wiedergegeben sein soll, so läßt sich durch Erholung einer berichtigten Abschrift, zu welcher Vertagung zu bewilligen ist, abhelfen.

Art. 368. — Inwieferne Durchstreichungen, Radirungen, Zusätze, Einschaltungen oder sonstige äußere Mängel einer Urkunde ihre Beweiskraft im Ganzen oder theilweise aufheben oder mindern, bleibt, soferne nicht die Gesetze hierüber besondere Bestimmungen enthalten, der richterlichen Beurtheilung überlassen.

G. A. d. K. d. A. II S. 298. 306. 333. IV S. 94. — K. d. R. II S. 172. IV S. 44.

1) Die Frage, in wie fern äußere Mängel einer Urkunde (Durchstreichungen, Radirungen, Zusätze, Einschaltungen 2c.), ihre Beweiskraft ganz oder theilweise aufheben oder

mindern, überläßt das Gesetz dem richterlichen Ermessen, sofern nicht besondere gesetzliche Vorschriften bestehen, wie dies z. B. bezüglich der Notariatsurkunden der Fall ist.

Diese Bestimmung, welche im Einklange mit dem die gerichtlichen Protokolle betreffenden Art. 187 steht, findet ihre Anwendung hauptsächlich bei Privaturkunden und überhaupt allen jenen Urkunden (z. B. Saal- und Lagerbücher), für welche eine besondere Form nicht vorgeschrieben ist oder die Folgen der Nichtbeachtung nicht geregelt sind.

Namentlich ist es auch Sache des Richters, zu würdigen, in wie fern Randbemerkungen oder Nachschriften in Privaturkunden, wenn sie nicht besonders unterzeichnet sind, als Bestandtheile der Urkunden selbst zu gelten haben oder nicht. R. R. II 147—149. Abg. IV. 94 (zu Art. 15).

2) In Correkturen, welche offenbar unwesentlich sind, dürfte der Richter nie einen Grund finden, einer Urkunde den Glauben zu versagen. Es wäre nicht Anwendung, sondern Mißbrauch der Bestimmungen des Art. 368, es wäre Gesetzesverletzung, wollte er willkürlich eine Privaturkunde als nicht beweisgebend erklären, weil irgend ein völlig bedeutungsloses Wort durchstrichen, korrigirt oder beigefügt wäre.

Art. 369. — **Das Gericht ist auch da, wo einer Urkunde nach gesetzlicher Bestimmung volle Beweiskraft zukommen würde, nicht gehalten, ihr diese beizumessen, wenn die Urkunde auf eine andere nicht mit vorgelegte sich bezieht oder nicht vollständig vorgelegt wurde.**

Doch genügt bei Urkunden von größerem Umfange, wovon nur einzelne Theile mit dem Streitgegenstande in Verbindung stehen, die Vorlage dieser Theile, sofern nicht das Gericht auf Verlangen der Gegenpartei die Vorlage der ganzen Urkunde angeordnet hat.

G. A. d. K. d. A. II S. 204. 298. 305. 306. 333. IV S. 94. 98. — K. d. R. II S. 172. IV S. 44

1) Urkunden, welche auf andere Urkunden Bezug nehmen, beweisen in der Regel für sich allein nichts, nach dem Grundsatze: »referens sine relato non probat.«

Es ist diese in Nov. 119 Cap. 3 ausgesprochene Regel durch die Ger.-O. (Cap. XI § 5 Ziff. 7) mit den Worten anerkannt:

„Wenn sich das produzirte Dokument auf „ein anderes bezieht, so muß dieses zugleich „mit produzirt werden, es sei denn offenbar, „daß der Gegentheil solches zu seiner Defension nicht bedarf."

Seuffert bemerkt in seinem Commentare (Bd. III S. 197):

„Eine solche Bezugnahme ist vorhanden, „wenn das eine Dokument (referens) auf „das andere (relatum) als den Träger der „näheren Bestimmungen, oder zum Zwecke der „Auslegung, Ergänzung oder Vervollständigung verweist, nicht aber schon dann, wenn „in der produzirten Urkunde des Daseins einer „andern nur beiläufig Erwähnung geschieht; „ebenso nicht dann, wenn das produzirte Dokument laut seines Inhaltes an die Stelle „des darin erwähnten treten sollte, und wenn „bei Abfassung des produzirten Dokumentes „die Absicht zu Grunde lag, das andere „außer Kraft zu setzen oder überflüssig zu „machen."

Diese Bemerkungen können auch jetzt noch zur Richtschnur dienen, um zu erkennen, was man unter einer „Bezugnahme" im Sinne des Art. 369 zu verstehen habe, und unter welcher Voraussetzung das richterliche Ermessen Platz greifen dürfe. Vgl. auch Bayer. Civilpr. § 255 II.

Was die Ausübung dieses Ermessens in Fällen, wo es statthaft ist, betrifft, so kann ich auch in dieser Beziehung nichts Besseres thun, als die Worte Seuffert's zu wiederholen, welcher S. 198 die Vorlage der in Bezug genommenen Urkunde für nicht geboten hält:

„Wenn die produzirte Urkunde allein oder „in Verbindung mit anderen Behelfen, von „allem, was auf das fragliche Rechtsverhältniß Einfluß haben könnte, nichts ungewiß „läßt, oder wenn über den Inhalt und die „Beschaffenheit des documentum relatum nach „allen wesentlichen Merkmalen volle Gewißheit vorliegt."

2) Wurde eine Urkunde nicht vollständig, sondern nur auszugsweise oder stückweise vorgelegt, so hat auch hier der Richter zu ermessen, ob diese Mangelhaftigkeit der Vorlage ihn hindere, eine Ueberzeugung zu gewinnen oder nicht; jedoch ist beschränkend beigefügt, daß bei Urkunden von größerem Umfange, wenn nur einzelne Theile mit dem Streitgegenstande in Verbindung stehen, der Richter nur dann befugt sei, aus der Unvollständigkeit der Vorlage nachtheilige Schlüsse zu ziehen, wenn der Gegner die Vorlage verlangt und das Gericht sie angeordnet hatte, trotzdessen aber die Ergänzung nicht erfolgt ist.

Handelt es sich von Urkunden, deren einzelne Bestimmungen ein geschlossenes Ganze bilden, z. B. Vertragsurkunden, Testamenten ꝛc. (documentis connexis im Sinne der Ger.-O.), so ist, da bei solchen Urkunden zudem von einem größeren Umfange gewöhnlich die Rede nicht sein kann, der Richter durch die Vorschrift in Art. 369 Abs. 2 nicht gehindert, auch ohne Antrag auf Ergänzung, der Urkunde die Beweiskraft zu versagen, jedoch wird er sich, dem Geiste des Verfahrens gemäß (Art. 328 Abs. 4) verpflichtet fühlen, die Partei, welche die Urkunde vorlegt, zur Erklärung zu veranlassen, ob sie die für sachgemäß befundene Ergänzung bethätigen wolle und könne oder nicht.

Verfahren bei der Vorlage.

Art. 370. — **Die Vorlage der Urkunden erfolgt in der Sitzung.**

Die Parteien haben sich spätestens in der Sitzung, in welcher die Urkunde gegen sie vorgelegt wird, über deren Aechtheit zu erklären und ihre Einreden gegen die Urkunde vorzutragen.

Erfolgt auf die Aufforderung der vorlegenden Partei oder des Vorsitzenden keine bestimmte Erklärung, so ist die Urkunde als anerkannt zu betrachten.

Einwendungen gegen die Erheblichkeit oder Zulässigkeit der vorgelegten Beweisurkunden befreien an sich nicht von der Verbindlichkeit zur Erklärung über deren Aechtheit, das Gericht kann aber die Partei auf Antrag ermächtigen, die Erklärung erst nach erfolgter Entscheidung über die erhobenen Einwendungen abzugeben.

Art. 371. — **Derjenige, gegen welchen eine Privaturkunde geltend gemacht wird, die nicht von ihm, sondern von einem Dritten ausgestellt sein soll, kann sich auf die Erklärung beschränken, daß er nicht wisse, ob die Urkunde von dem Dritten herrühre. Er hat damit, wenn die Urkunde von seinem Rechtsvorfahrer oder sonst von einer Person, für deren Handlung er haftbar ist, herrühren soll, noch die weitere Erklärung zu verbinden, daß er nach sorgfältiger Benützung der ihm zu Gebote stehenden Ueberzeugungsmittel die Urkunde als ächt anzuerkennen nicht vermöge. Diese Erklärungen haben die nämliche Wirkung wie die Abläugnung.**

Ist die Urkunde von einem Dritten ausgestellt, von welchem der Beweisführer sein Recht im Verhältnisse zu der Gegenpartei ableitet oder welcher bei Ausstellung der Urkunde im Namen der Gegenpartei gehandelt hat, so kann der Beweisführer diesen Dritten zur Anerkennung der Urkunde beiladen lassen. Welche Wirkung dem Ungehorsame beziehungsweise der Erklärung des Dritten beizumessen sei und inwieferne namentlich die Anerkennung der Urkunde gegen die Gegenpartei beweise, hat das Gericht nach der Stellung und dem Rechtsverhältnisse der Parteien zu beurtheilen.

G. A. d. K. d. A. II S. 205 298. 314 334. IV S. 94. — K. d. R. II S. 172 IV S. 44.

1) Wie bei Art. 172 bemerkt, will das Gesetz, daß schon vor der Verhandlung die Urkunden, welche bei derselben benützt werden sollen, gegenseitig mitgetheilt werden, und kann, falls dies nicht geschehen, unter Umständen die Zurückweisung der Urkunden von der Verhandlung verlangt oder verfügt werden.

Es ergibt sich ferner aus dem Zwecke der motivirten Anträge (Bemerk. zu Art. 230 Nr. 2, 5 und 6), daß die Erklärung über die Aechtheit der mitgetheilten Urkunden und die Formulirung von Beweiseinreden schon in den Anträgen erfolge.

An diesen Prinzipien soll, wie zudem ausdrücklich anerkannt wurde (Abg. II 205 Sp. 1 u. 314 Sp. 1), durch Art. 370 nichts geändert, vielmehr nur gesagt werden: 1) daß die Urkunden in derjenigen Sitzung, in welcher sie geltend gemacht werden (Art. 329 Abs. 2), dem Gerichte vorzulegen seien, und 2) daß die Erklärung über deren Aechtheit und das Vorbringen von Beweiseinreden, falls Beides nicht bereits geschehen, spätestens in dieser Sitzung erfolgen müsse.

2) Für das abgekürzte Verfahren ist, falls mittelst desselben der Prozeß eingeleitet wird, die Sachlage in so fern eine besondere, als hier nur der Beklagte in der Lage ist, vorher seine Urkunden mitzutheilen und auch dieser hierzu nicht immer Zeit hat, während der Kläger in der Regel, d. h. wenn nicht ausnahmsweise der Anwalt des Beklagten sich veranlaßt findet, vorher einen Antrag zuzustellen (Bemerk. zu Art. 259 Nr. 10), erst in der Sitzung erfährt, welcher Anwalt ihm gegenüberstehe. Die Natur der Sache bedingt es, daß die Aktenmittheilung in solchen Fällen gewöhnlich erst in der Sitzung stattfindet.

3) Ist die Mittheilung der Urkunden rechtzeitig erfolgt (Art. 172 Nr. 7), so ist der Gegner verpflichtet, sich sofort über die Aechtheit zu erklären und seine Beweiseinreden vorzubringen. Nur aus besonderen Gründen wird der Anwalt

mit dem Einwande zu hören sein, daß er nicht wisse, ob seine Partei die Urkunde anerkenne, in welchem Falle Vertagung zu bewilligen, unter Umständen auch das persönliche Erscheinen anzuordnen ist.

Außerdem kann das Gericht aus besonderen Gründen, auf Antrag gestatten, einstweilen die Erklärnng über die Aechtheit zu unterlassen, bis über die gegen Erheblichkeit und Zulässigkeit der Urkunde erhobenen Einwände abweisend erkannt sei, eine Ausnahme, welche beigefügt wurde, um zwecklose Beweiserbieten über die Aechtheit zu vermeiden, also im Hinblicke auf Fälle, wo offenbar die Urkunde belanglos ist. Findet übrigens das Gericht am Schlusse seiner Berathung, daß dennoch auf die Urkunde Werth zu legen sei, so kann es die Verhandlung wieder aufnehmen. Art 274 u. 328.

4) Erfolgt auf Aufforderung hin keine bestimmte Erklärung und findet sich das Gericht auch nicht veranlaßt, eine etwa begehrte Vertagung zu bewilligen, so ist die Urkunde als anerkannt zu betrachten. Das bloße Stillschweigen dem Vortrage des Gegners gegenüber, darf daher nicht als Anerkennung gelten, vielmehr ist eine förmliche, in der Sitzung erfolgte Aufforderung von Seiten der Gegenpartei oder des Gerichts nöthig, woraus denn die Nothwendigkeit folgt, diese Aufforderung auch zu beurkunden und zwar am sachgemäßesten im Urtheilssatze.

Wird eine Urkunde anerkannt, so ist es nicht nöthig, dies besonders zu beurkunden, vielmehr genügt es, wenn sie als unbestritten im Sachverhalte angeführt wird; jedoch pflegt man, wenn Privaturkunden von besonderer Wichtigkeit in Frage sind, über die erfolgte Anerkennung im Urtheilssatze Urkunde zu ertheilen.

5) Das Gesetz unterscheidet bezüglich der Art der Erklärung in Art. 371 Abs. 1 drei Fälle. Es ist hervorzuheben, daß hier nicht, wie in Art. 355 Abs. 2 oder Art. 358 Abs. 1 gesagt ist: „welche er durch seine Handlungen verpflichten kann", vielmehr absichtlich (Abg. II 314 [v. Weiß]) eine weitere Fassung gewählt wurde, um auch die Gläubiger und sonstige Personen zu begreifen, welche geschehene Handlungen eines Dritten anerkennen müssen, ohne daß dieser sie förmlich verpflichten, d. h. über ihre Rechte verfügen könnte.

Beiladung des Ausstellers.

6) Die Bestimmung in Art. 371 Abs. 2 stand ursprünglich im Zusammenhange mit Art. 419 des Entwurfs, welcher verfügte, daß man gewisse dritte Personen beiladen dürfe, um ihnen Eide zuzuschieben.

Gegen jenen Artikel wurde eingewendet, eine solche Beiladung führe im Grunde nur zu einer Zeugschaft, es sei aber ungehörig, Dritte, welche nicht wirklich Parteien seien und werden sollen, in einen Prozeß zu ziehen, namentlich aber sei es ungehörig, wenn gesagt werde, das Gericht habe nach der Stellung und dem Rechtsverhältnisse der Parteien zu beurtheilen, welches die Folgen des Ungehorsams oder der abgegebenen Erklärungen seien. Auf Grund dieser Erwägungen wurde jener Artikel gestrichen. Referat zu Art. 419 und Verh. Abg. II 247.

Offenbar hätten dieselben Erwägungen aber auch zur Streichung der vorliegenden Bestimmung führen müssen und diese stehet nun da als das übriggebliebene Bruchstück einer aufgegebenen Idee, als eine Vorschrift, welche durch Wegfallen jenes Art. 419 theilweise ihren Halt verloren hat und überhaupt zum Verfahren nicht recht passen will. Ihre Auslegung bietet um so mehr Schwierigkeit, als sie fast ohne Diskussion, sowie sie lautete, aus dem Entwurfe ins Gesetz übergegangen ist.

7) Das Gesetz hat hier offenbar keine Beiladung zum Zwecke einer förmlichen Theilnahme am Rechtsstreite im Auge, eine solche bei welcher Anträge auf Verurtheilung gegen den Beigeladenen zu nehmen seien, sondern eine Beiladung, welche nichts weiter bezweckt, als die Erklärung über die Urkunde, welche so zu sagen Beweismittel ist. Vgl. Abg. II 247 (v. Weiß) und Referat zu Art. 56 des Entwurfs.

Deßhalb kann denn auch, ähnlich wie bei einer Zeugenladung, nur der Aussteller persönlich beigeladen werden, es können aber nicht dessen Erben geladen werden, wie dies der Entwurf (Art. 246) durch den als überflüssig beseitigten Beisatz: „noch lebenden" hervorgehoben hatte. Ebenso nicht seine Vertreter, falls er etwa rechtsunfähig geworden ist.

Wie regelt sich nun das Verfahren und welches sind die Folgen des Ungehorsams und der Erklärungen?

8) In der Regel wird Anlaß zu einer Gewährschaftsklage gegeben sein, und es ergibt sich dann das Verfahren von selbst (Abg. II 247); kann oder will jedoch eine solche Klage nicht erhoben werden, so ergeben sich Zweifel.

Genügt es, den Aussteller gleich einem Zeugen in die Sitzung zu laden, wie im Falle des Art. 381, oder aber ist es nöthig, ihn gleich einer Partei zu laden, damit er durch einen Anwalt seine Erklärung mache, bei welcher Voraussetzung dann je nach Umständen das gewöhnliche oder das abgekürzte Verfahren Platz greifen würde?

Nach dem Sinne, welchen das Gesetz mit dem Ausdrucke „Beiladung" verbindet, im Hinblicke auf die Ausnahmsbestimmung des Art. 381 und in Erwägung, daß die Art. 359 und 419 des Entwurfs die Zuschiebung des Haupteides an den Beigeladenen zulassen wollten, möchte Letzteres als der Wille des Gesetzgebers anzusehen sein. Vgl. Art. 56 des Entwurfs und Bemerkungen des Referenten zu demselben, ferner Bemerk. des Minist.-Comm. (Abg. II 247).

9) Da sich der Anlaß zur Beiladung erst durch Bestreitung der Aechtheit ergibt, so wird der Beweisführer beantragen, daß ihm die zur Beiladung nöthige Frist bewilligt werde, welche, falls die Urkunde erheblich erscheint, nicht verweigert werden darf.

Die Ladung wird der Art zu fassen sein, daß der Beigeladene aufgefordert wird, vor Gericht zu erscheinen, um sich über die Aechtheit der (genau zu bezeichnenden) Urkunde zu erklären, widrigenfalls angenommen würde, daß er dieselbe als ächt anerkenne.

Erscheint der Beigeladene nicht, so wird Versäumungsurtheil zu erlassen sein, welches die Urkunde für anerkannt erklärt und den Nichterschienenen in die Kosten verurtheilt.

Erscheint der Beigeladene und gibt seine Erklärung ab, so ist der Zweck der Beiladung erreicht. Der Beiladende wird verurtheilt, ihm die Kosten zu ersetzen, vorbehaltlich über dieselben im Hauptprozesse, je nach dessen Ausgange, weiter zu entscheiden (Bemerk. zu Art. 111 Nr. 2).

Eine Eideszuschiebung an den Beigeladenen, um die Aechtheit festzustellen, d. h. ein Geständniß von ihm zu erzwingen, ist nach den Grundsätzen, welche man bezüglich der Verhandlungen über Art. 419 des Entwurfs als maßgebend angenommen hat, nicht statthaft (vgl. auch Art. 381), wie überhaupt, da es sich nur um eine Beweisführung unter den Hauptparteien handelt, jedes weitere Verfahren gegen den Beigeladenen wegfällt. Uebrigens wird dieser häufig selbst Interesse haben, als Nebenintervenient im Prozesse zu bleiben.

10) Die Frage, welches die Folgen des Ungehorsams oder der abgegebenen Erklärungen seien, bietet gleichfalls Schwierigkeiten.

Vor Allem sind die Grundsätze bezüglich des Beweises des Datums und des Beweises der Aechtheit auseinander zu halten. (Abg. II 314). Daraus, daß eine Urkunde unter Voraussetzung ihrer Aechtheit, ihr Datum auch gegen einen Dritten beweist, folgt nicht, daß auch die Aechtheit selbst durch das Geständniß einer Person festgestellt werden könne, welche zur Zeit, wo sie es abgibt, diesen Dritten nicht mehr verpflichten kann.

Will nun das Gesetz blos sagen, es sollen diejenigen Folgen eintreten, welche sich aus den civilrechtlichen Grundsätzen über die Wirksamkeit von Urtheilen oder Geständnissen gegen Dritte ergeben, oder soll es dem Richter überlassen sein, nach freiem Ermessen Folgerungen für den Beweis der Aechtheit zu ziehen?

Ich möchte folgende Wirkungen annehmen:

1) daß die Erklärungen des Beigeladenen oder die Entscheidung gegen denselben maßgebend sei in Fällen, wo dies ausnahmsweise die Grundsätze des Civilrechts bedingen;

2) daß in sonstigen Fällen daraus Beweisbehelfe (Vermuthungen) gezogen werden dürfen, welche sehr gewichtig sein können, falls der Beigeladene gegen sein eigenes Interesse Geständnisse macht;

3) daß der Beigeladene selbst seine Erklärungen und dasjenige, was gegen ihn als erwiesen betrachtet wird, später, wenn etwa rechtliche Folgerungen gegen ihn selbst Seitens der Hauptparteien daraus gezogen werden sollen, gegen sich gelten lassen muß.

11) Schließlich die Bemerkung, daß es in der Regel sachgemäß sein wird, entweder den Aussteller als Gewährschaftsbeklagten in den Prozeß zu ziehen, oder aber ihn als Zeuge zu benutzen, was ja, da das Gesetz keine Verwerfungsgründe kennt und Zeugenbeweis über die Aechtheit immer statthaft ist, freisteht.

Beweis der Aechtheit oder Fälschung.

Art. 372. — **Ist eine öffentliche Urkunde in gehöriger Form vorgelegt, so hat derjenige, der sie als falsch angreift, den Beweis darüber zu führen.**

Ausländische öffentliche Urkunden, welchen die Beglaubigung der betreffenden bayerischen Gesandtschaft oder eines bayerischen Consulats fehlt, desgleichen inländische Notariatsurkunden, welchen die durch das Notariatsgesetz vorgeschriebene gerichtliche Beglaubigung mangelt, sind bezüglich des Aechtheitsbeweises wie Privaturkunden zu behandeln, soferne das Gericht nicht nach den Umständen des Falls erkennt, daß die Urkunde die Vermuthung der Aechtheit für sich habe. Hat sich im entgegengesetzten Falle die beweisführende Partei vorsorglich zur nachträglichen Beibringung der mangelnden Beglaubigung erboten, so ist ihr hiezu Gelegenheit durch Vertagung zu geben.

Art. 373. — Wird die Aechtheit einer Privaturkunde bestritten, so muß die Partei, welche die Urkunde geltend macht, ihre Aechtheit erproben.

Will der Unterzeichner einer Privaturkunde behaupten, daß die Unterzeichnung der Urkunde auf Zwang, Betrug oder Irrthum beruhe, daß der Text der Urkunde gefälscht oder daß ein Blanquet mißbraucht worden sei, so ist es an ihm, dies zu beweisen.

Art. 374. — Urkunden, die so alt sind, daß Niemand mehr die Aechtheit der Schrift oder Unterschrift zu erkennen vermag, kann das Gericht nach Ermessen des Falls als ächt gelten lassen, wenn es sich um ein Grund-, Saal- oder Lagerbuch oder eine ähnliche Aufschreibung handelt, oder wenn die Urkunden seit langer Zeit in öffentlichen Archiven oder Registraturen oder in einem unter den Streitstheilen gemeinschaftlichen Familienarchive aufbewahrt wurden.

Art. 375. — Wer eine Urkunde zum Beweise für sich auch nur in Abschrift oder im Auszuge vorlegt, erkennt damit die Aechtheit der ganzen Urkunde an. Behauptet er, daß ein Theil derselben unächt sei, so liegt ihm der Beweis hierüber ob.

G. A. d. K. d. A. II S. 187. 188. 204. 205. 298. 299. 314. 315. 334. 335. IV S. 94.
K. d. R. II S. 172 IV S. 44.

1) Unter Aechtheit einer Urkunde versteht man, daß sie von derjenigen Person herrühre, welche nach ihrem Inhalte als Urheber erscheint. Eine öffentliche Urkunde ist ächt, wenn sie von dem bezeichneten Beamten aufgenommen ist, eine Privaturkunde, wenn die Unterschrift oder (bei nicht unterschriebenen Urkunden, olographischen Testamenten in der Pfalz 2c.) die Schrift vom Aussteller herrührt. Vgl. Bayer. Civilpr. §. 255.

Wer eine Urkunde für sich selbst vorlegt, sei es auch nur in Abschrift oder im Auszuge, erkennt deren Aechtheit an (Art. 375) vorbehaltlich des Nachweises, daß Theile, welche er nicht geltend macht, dennoch unächt oder gefälscht seien.

Natürlich tritt diese Folge nur ein, sofern es sich um die nemliche Urkunde handelt, also nicht, wenn mehrere selbstständige Urkunden, mögen sie auch in innerem Zusammenhange stehen, auf demselben Blatte Papier zufällig vereinigt sind. Ferner ist hervorzuheben, daß fragliche Folge nur an die Vorlage der Urkunden (Art. 370 Abs. 1) geknüpft ist, also nicht an die Mittheilung, obgleich diese die Urkunde gemeinschaftlich macht (Art. 337).

2) Oeffentliche Urkunden unterscheiden sich von Privaturkunden wesentlich dadurch, daß für erstere die gesetzliche Vermuthung der Aechtheit besteht, für letztere nicht.

Kündigt sich eine Urkunde ihrer äußeren Erscheinung nach als eine öffentliche Urkunde an, d. h. als eine solche, die von einer zuständigen Behörde in vorgeschriebener Form errichtet ist (Art. 353), und wird sie in gehöriger Form in Vorlage gebracht, d. h. in Urschrift oder einer dieser gleichgeltenden Abschrift (Art. 367), so muß derjenige, welcher behauptet, daß sie falsch sei, den Beweis darüber führen.

Fehlt bei ausländischen öffentlichen Urkunden die gesandtschaftliche oder bei inländischen Notariatsurkunden die gerichtliche Beglaubigung, wo diese nöthig (Not.=Ges. Art. 97 — Ges. vom 25. Vent. XI Art. 28), so ist es in's Ermessen des Gerichtes gestellt, die Aechtheit anzunehmen oder Beweis zu verlangen. Letzteren Falls wird es genügen, die fehlende Beglaubigung beizubringen und wird hierzu Frist zu bewilligen sein, auch wenn nur nachsorglich darum gebeten wird.

Für sonstige öffentliche Urkunden des Inlandes gilt diese Bestimmung nicht, und darf auch nicht auf die Civilstandsakten der Pfalz (Code civ. Art. 45) ausgedehnt werden, so nahe die Analogie liegen mag.

3) Was jene Urkunden betrifft, von welchen gesagt ist, daß sie die Beweiskraft öffentlicher Urkunden haben sollen oder können (Art. 360 u. 361), so sollte man meinen, diese Beweiskraft bestehe vorzugsweise darin, daß sie die Vermuthung der Aechtheit für sich haben, allein es wurde bei den Verhandlungen (Abg. II. 314) ausdrücklich erklärt und auch Art. 374 deutet es an, daß solche Urkunden bezüglich der Aechtheit den Privaturkunden gleichstehen sollen.

Man darf billig fragen: „Was bleibt denn von der besonderen Beweiskraft des Art. 354 für derartige Urkunden noch übrig? Ihre Aechtheit sollen sie nicht erweisen, die Wahrheit der betreffenden Aufzeichnungen können sie nicht erweisen, da sinnliche Wahrnehmungen nicht in Frage sind, das Datum endlich brauchen sie in der Regel nicht zu erweisen!

Es möchte dies ein neuer Beleg dafür sein, daß der Begriff von „Beweiskraft", wie ihn Art. 354 auffaßt, allmälig sich verschoben hat und daß man in den Art. 360 und 361 nicht sowohl sagen wollte, es hätten fragliche Urkunden die Beweiskraft öffentlicher Urkunden, als vielmehr, es dürfe aus ihnen allein der Beweis gewisser Thatsachen geschöpft werden. Vgl. Bemerk. zu Art. 360 ff. Nr. 1, 5 u. 7.

Erst die Bestimmungen des Art. 374 verleihen eigentlich jenen Urkunden theilweise die Beweiskraft öffentlicher Urkunden, indem verfügt wird, daß wenn dieselben sehr alt seien, unter Hinzutreten gewisser sonstiger Voraussetzungen, der Richter die Aechtheit präsumiren dürfe.

4) Die einfache Bestreitung der Aechtheit einer Privaturkunde entzieht derselben ihre beweisende Kraft und verpflichtet die Partei, welche sie geltend macht, die Aechtheit zu erproben, d. h. zu beweisen.

Ist die Urkunde ächt, so muß derjenige, welcher ihre Beweiskraft aus sonstigen Gründen — wegen Fälschung, Zwangs, Irrthums 2c. — anficht, Beweis deßhalb erbringen. Das Gesetz hat hier die Beweiseinreden im Auge, d. h. Einwände, welche sich bloß gegen die Urkunde als Beweismittel richten, und welche mit den Einwänden gegen das Rechtsgeschäft selbst in der Regel nicht zusammenfallen. So kann z. B. die Unterzeichnung einer Urkunde durch Zwang, List erwirkt oder das Ergebniß eines Irrthums sein, während das Rechtsgeschäft in Wahrheit so abgeschlossen wurde, wie es die Urkunde bezeugt, anderseits aber kann das Rechtsgeschäft Ergebniß eines Betrugs oder eines Irrthums sein, während die Urkunde an diesen Mängeln nicht leidet.

Art. 376. — Als unächt oder falsch angefochtene Urkunden sind von dem Producenten und dem Vorsitzenden mit Handzug zu versehen und zu Gerichtshanden zu nehmen.

Die Beweise über Aechtheit oder Fälschung der Urkunde sind sofort anzubieten, außer wenn die Erklärung über die Urkunde erst in der Sitzung erfolgt ist, welchen Falls auf Antrag die Verhandlung in eine spätere Sitzung zu vertagen ist.

Das weitere Verfahren richtet sich vorbehaltlich der Bestimmungen der Art. 377—385 nach den allgemeinen Vorschriften.

Art. 377. — Wird der Aechtheitsbeweis durch Schriftenvergleichung geführt, so kann das Gericht diese entweder in einer festzusetzenden spätern Sitzung selbst vornehmen oder die Zuziehung von Sachverständigen anordnen. Letztern Falls finden die Vorschriften über den Beweis durch Sachverständige Anwendung.

Art. 378. — In der zur Schriftenvergleichung bestimmten Sitzung, falls aber Sachverständige beigezogen sind, bei der Einweisungstagfahrt sind von dem Beweisführer die Vergleichungsschriften vorzulegen.

Erscheint hiebei die Gegenpartei nicht, so gelten die beigebrachten Vergleichungsschriften als anerkannt.

Nicht nur das Gericht, sondern auch der beauftragte Richter kann verfügen, daß die Gegenpartei in der zur Vorlage der Vergleichungsschriften bestimmten Tagfahrt persönlich erscheine.

Art. 379. — Als zur Schriftenvergleichung tauglich dürfen, wenn die Parteien sich nicht anders einigen, und unbeschadet der Bestimmung des Art. 378 Abs. 2 nur von der Hand des angeblichen Ausstellers der bestrittenen Urkunde herrührende Schriften oder Unterschriften angenommen werden, welche sich entweder in fehlerfreien öffentlichen Urkunden befinden oder deren Aechtheit von der betreffenden Partei im Prozesse oder bei einer andern Gelegenheit ausdrücklich anerkannt wurde.

Ist nur ein Theil der angefochtenen Urkunde bestritten, der übrige aber anerkannt, so kann letzterer zur Schriftenvergleichung benützt werden.

Art. 380. — In Ermangelung hinlänglicher Vergleichungsschriften kann der Beweisführer verlangen, daß die Partei, deren Schrift oder Unterschrift zu prüfen ist, einen ihr zu dictirenden Aufsatz zur Vergleichung niederschreibe.

Der Beweisführer muß in diesem Falle die Partei zum persönlichen Erscheinen bei der in Art. 388 Abs. 1 bezeichneten Sitzung oder Einweisungstagfahrt vorladen lassen.

Bleibt die Partei ohne genügende Entschuldigung aus, so wird die Urkunde als anerkannt betrachtet, wenn in der Vorladung auf diese Bestimmung aufmerksam gemacht ist.

Ist die Partei durch Krankheit, weite Entfernung vom Gerichtssitze oder andere Umstände verhindert, sich vor dem Prozeßgerichte einzufinden, so kann dieses anordnen, daß die Verhandlung bei dem Gerichte ihres Wohnorts beziehungsweise in ihrer Wohnung vor einem beauftragten Richter stattfinde.

Art. 381. — Auch der Dritte, welcher die zu prüfende Urkunde geschrieben oder unterschrieben haben soll, kann zur Erklärung über die Vergleichungsurkunden und zum Niederschreiben eines Aufsatzes behufs der Schriftenvergleichung vorgeladen werden, wobei gegebenen Falls die Bestimmung des Art. 380 Abs. 4 Anwendung findet.

Im Ungehorsamsfalle kommen die gegen ungehorsame Zeugen gegebenen Vorschriften zur analogen Anwendung.

Art. 382. — Rücksichtlich des Gutachtens der Sachverständigen gelten die Vorschriften des XIII. Hauptstücks, doch darf vollständiger Beweis der Aechtheit einer Privaturkunde auf Grund der Schriftenvergleichung nur dann angenommen werden, wenn deren Ergebniß durch andere Umstände dergestalt unterstützt ist, daß das Gericht aus dem Zusammenhange die Ueberzeugung von der Aechtheit der Urkunde gewinnt.

Art. 383. — Soll die Aechtheit einer Privaturkunde durch Zuschiebung des Haupteids erwiesen werden und ist ein Dritter als Urheber der Schrift bezeichnet, so hat die Partei, welcher der Eid zugeschoben wurde, die Wahrheit der in Art. 371 Abs. 1 bezeichneten Erklärungen zu beschwören.

G. A. d. K. d. A. II S. 205. 206. 299. 315. 334. 335. IV S. 94. 98. 326. 340.
K. d. R. II S. 172. IV. S. 44—46.

1) Der französische Prozeß kennt ein besonderes Verfahren zum Nachweise der Aechtheit von Privaturkunden (la vérification des écritures) und ein besonderes Verfahren zum Nachweise der Falschheit von Urkunden überhaupt (l'inscription en faux).

Der Begriff der Falschheit (le faux incident civil) ist ein rein civilrechtlicher und erscheint es für die Fälschungsklage gleichgültig, ob strafrechtlich die Merkmale einer Fälschung vorliegen oder nicht. Eine öffentliche Urkunde ist in diesem Sinne falsch, wenn sie aus irgend einem Grunde, sei es in Folge absichtlicher Fälschung, sei es in Folge eines Versehens oder gar aus Zufall, dasjenige nicht bezeugt, was sie der Wahrheit gemäß bezeugen sollte. Eine Privaturkunde ist falsch, nicht bloß wenn sie wissentlich falsch gefertigt oder nachträglich gefälscht worden ist, sondern auch wenn durch Betrug oder Irrthum etwas in sie gekommen, was derjenige, welcher sie unterzeichnete, nicht die Absicht hatte zu erklären oder zu bescheinigen. Selbst wenn eine wahrheitswidrige Beurkundung durch Zwang herbeigeführt worden ist, hält man den Weg der Fälschungsklage für entsprechend. (Zachar. fr. Civilr. Bd. IV S. 462 Note 6).

Der »erreur involontaire du redacteur« gilt hier gleichviel wie die absichtliche Fälschung: »car le procès est fait a la pièce seule, sans aucunement inculper la personne,« Chauveau quest. 1867 bis — Dalloz repert. (faux incident) No. 72 ff.

2) Unsere Prozeßordnung gibt für den Beweis der Aechtheit und der Falschheit ein gemeinschaftliches Verfahren, was sachgemäß erscheint; nicht in gleicher Weise möchte es jedoch zu billigen sein, daß sie bezüglich der falschen Urkunden den strafrechtlichen und den civilrechtlichen Gesichtspunkt — Fälschung und Falschheit — nicht auseinanderhält, wie dies bei Art 399 näher erörtert werden wird.

a) Verfahren im Allgemeinen.

3) Ist eine Urkunde als unächt oder als falsch angefochten, so wird sie sofort zu Gerichtshänden genommen und vorschriftsmäßig paraphirt.

Die Beweise sind in der Regel sofort anzubieten, und, wenn die Urkunde als erheblich befunden wird, auch sofort aufzulegen; falls jedoch die Erklärung über die Urkunde erst in der Sitzung erfolgt, muß auf Antrag des Beweisführers die Verhandlung vertagt werden. In der Regel wird auch in solchen Fällen eine Vertagung nicht nöthig sein, wenigstens nicht bezüglich des Aechtheitsbeweises, indem hier das Beweiserbieten gewöhnlich nur dahin geht: „die Partei zum Beweise durch Zeugen und Sachverständige (durch Schriftvergleichung) darüber zuzulassen, daß die Unterschrift bezw. Schrift vom Aussteller herrühre."

b) Schriftvergleichung.

4) Beim Beweise durch Schriftvergleichung hat das Gericht die Wahl, diese Vergleichung *selbst vorzunehmen*, d. h. auf dem Wege des Augenscheins die Sache aufzuklären, oder sie durch *Sachverständige* vornehmen zu lassen.

Ersteren Falls wird die betreffende Partei zum bezüglichen Beweise durch Schriftvergleichung zugelassen und sofort eine Sitzung bestimmt, in welcher diese durch das Gericht selbst zu geschehen habe.

Letzteren Falls läßt das Gericht zum Beweise durch Sachverständige zu oder ordnet ein Gutachten von Sachverständigen an und richtet sich das weitere Verfahren nach den Vorschriften in Hauptstück XIII.

5) In der zur Vornahme der Schriftvergleichung bestimmten Sitzung oder Tagfahrt sind natürlich die Vergleichsschriften vorzulegen.

Als Vergleichsschriften läßt das Gesetz nur solche Schriften oder Unterschriften zu, welche 1) in fehlerfreien öffentlichen Urkunden sich befinden, oder 2) deren Aechtheit im Prozesse selbst oder bei einer anderen Gelegenheit ausdrücklich anerkannt wurde. Auch die Urkunde selbst kann als Vergleichsschrift dienen, wenn sie theilweise anerkannt ist.

Unter fehlerfreien öffentlichen Urkunden sind solche zu verstehen, welche nach Maßgabe von Art. 368 in ihrer Beweiskraft, namentlich was die fragliche Unterschrift betrifft, nicht beeinträchtigt erscheinen.

Die Worte; „bei einer anderen Gelegenheit" sind bei ihrer Allgemeinheit dahin zu deuten, daß jede ausdrückliche Anerkennung, wenn sie feststeht, genüge, auch wenn sie anderen Personen gegenüber abgegeben wurde.

Durch das Beiwort „ausdrückliche" sind Fälle ausgeschlossen, wo eine Urkunde vom Gerichte für ächt erklärt wurde oder die Anerkennung nur aus den Umständen gefolgert werden soll. (Abg. II 206.)

Eine neue Beweisführung über die Aechtheit von Vergleichsschriften ist daher gesetzlich ausgeschlossen und ebenso will das Gesetz nicht, daß über die Thatsache der Anerkennung erst Beweise geführt werden sollen. Frivole Einwände sind selbstverständlich zurückzuweisen.

6) Erscheint bei der zur Schriftvergleichung bestimmten Sitzung oder Tagfahrt die Gegenpartei nicht, so gelten die Vergleichsschriften als anerkannt (Art. 378 Abs. 2). Es bedarf, um diese Folge herbeizuführen, weder einer besonderen Aufforderung noch Androhung, wie im Falle des Art. 380 Abs. 3, jedoch wird es im Parteiprozesse geeignet sein, daß der Richter den Gegner auf die besonderen Folgen des Nichterscheinens aufmerksam mache.

Wird das persönliche Erscheinen der Gegenpartei verordnet (Art. 378 Abs. 3), so ist diese durch ihren Anwalt, welchem das Urtheil oder der Beschluß zugestellt wurde, in Kenntniß zu setzen. Eine solche Anordnung erscheint nur veranlaßt, wenn die vorzulegenden Vergleichsschriften von der Gegenpartei selbst oder einer ihr nahestehenden Person herrühren sollen.

Welches sind nun die Folgen, wenn das persönliche Erscheinen angeordnet war, jedoch nur der Anwalt erscheint? Haben die Vergleichsschriften als anerkannt zu gelten und ist der Anwalt oder Bevollmächtigte nicht zu hören, wenn er Einwände gegen sie erhebt, oder treten nur jene Folgen ein, welche Art. 156 bezeichnet?

Man würde vielleicht zur ersteren Annahme kommen, namentlich da die Art. 155 u. 156 nur das Erscheinen bei der Verhandlung im Auge haben, wenn nicht das Gegentheil ausdrücklich ausgesprochen worden wäre. Abg. II 206 (zu Art. 354).

Ist das persönliche Erscheinen durch einen beauftragten Richter angeordnet worden, so steht es offenbar diesem nicht zu, aus dem Nichterscheinen Folgerungen irgend einer Art zu ziehen, und werden überhaupt alle Anstände, welche sich bezüglich der Vergleichsschriften ergeben, sofort vor das beauftragende Gericht zu verweisen sein, da sich vor Vereinigung derselben eine Schriftenvergleichung nicht wohl vornehmen läßt.

Die Anerkennung der Vergleichsschriften, welche als Folge des Nichterscheinens präsumirt wird, kann, da hier das Erscheinen bei einer Beweisaufnahme, nicht aber bei der Verhandlung in Frage ist, nicht etwa auf dem Wege des Einspruchs beseitigt werden, sondern nur durch Wiedereinsetzung in den vorigen Stand, falls eine solche rechtzeitig begehrt wird. Vgl. Abg. II 206 (v. Weiß).

7) Das Gesetz eröffnet einen besonderen Weg, um sich eine Vergleichsschrift zu verschaffen, dadurch, daß es gestattet, diejenige Person, von welcher die angefochtene Schrift herrühren soll, zum Zwecke der Niederschreibung eines zur Vergleichung dienenden Aufsatzes vorladen zu lassen. Diese Vorladung steht dem Beweisführer frei, ohne daß sie das Gericht besonders zu gestatten oder anzuordnen hätte.

Ist auf diese Vorladung der Grundsatz des Art. 192 anwendbar, gemäß dessen im Anwaltsprozesse die Zustellungen nur an den Anwalt zu geschehen haben, welchem die Sorge obliegt, die Partei zu benachrichtigen, oder setzt das Gesetz eine Vorladung der Partei selbst voraus?

Nach dem Entwurfe (Art. 356), dessen Worte ziemlich unverändert beibehalten wurden, war ohne Zweifel eine persönliche Vorladung gemeint, wie aus Art. 172 des Entwurfs sich ergibt, welcher verfügte, daß alle persönlichen Vorladungen an die Partei selbst zu geschehen haben. Hierin ist auch der Grund der Bestimmung zu suchen, daß in der Vorladung auf die Folgen des Nichterscheinens besonders aufmerksam zu machen sei.

Man kann noch ferner darauf hinweisen, daß der Ausdruck „vorladen" auf eine der Zeugenladung ähnliche Ladung deute und daß der Gesetzgeber wohl nicht gewollt habe, es solle die Vorladung des Art. 380 anders erfolgen, als die Vorladung des Art. 381.

Trotz diesen gewichtigen Gründen halte ich die entgegengesetzte Ansicht für richtig, weil sie die nothwendige Folge der Aenderung des im besagten Art. 172 aufgestellten Prinzipes ist und bei Gelegenheit dieser Aenderung ausdrücklich erklärt wurde, daß auch Ladungen der Partei durch Vermittlung des Anwaltes als Zustellungsbevollmächtigten erfolgen. Referat zu Art. 172 und Abg. I 262. Vgl. auch Art. 339.

Die fragliche Frist erweitert sich jedenfalls nach Maßgabe von Art. 209 und wird unterbrochen nach Maßgabe des Art. 211.

8) Das Nichterscheinen der Partei ohne genügende Entschuldigung hat zur Folge, daß die Urkunde als anerkannt betrachtet wird, jedoch nur, wenn in der Vorladung hierauf aufmerksam gemacht worden war. Es wird beizufügen sein, daß die Vorladung auch ihren Zweck, nemlich daß der Geladene eine Vergleichsschrift niederschreiben solle, kund geben müsse, denn nur hierdurch unterscheidet sie sich von der nach Art. 378 Abs. 3 zu gebenden Ladung.

Die Folgen des Nichterscheinens können, ebenso wie in dem oben Nr. 6 a. E. besprochenen Falle, nicht durch bloßen Einspruch beseitigt werden, jedoch kann der Nichterschienene bei der Verhandlung der Sache seine Entschuldigungsgründe vorbringen, und falls Versäumungsurtheil erging, auf dem Wege des Einspruchs dieselben zur Geltung bringen.

Das Gesetz sagt nicht, daß die Entschuldigung sofort bei der Tagfahrt vorzubringen sei, und will offenbar auch nicht, daß als Entschuldigungsgründe nur solche gelten dürfen, welche nach Art. 216 die Wiedereinsetzung in den vorigen Stand begründen würden, indem es bei dieser Unterstellung überhaupt nicht nöthig gewesen wäre, hier besonders von einer Entschuldigung zu sprechen. Folge ist, daß auch die Frist des Art. 217 hier nicht maßgebend sein kann.

9) Ist die Partei verhindert, vor dem Prozeßgerichte persönlich zu erscheinen, so kann dieses anordnen, daß die Aufnahme der Vergleichsschrift in der Wohnung bezw. am Wohnorte stattfinde. Gilt dies auch, wenn die Schriftvergleichung vor einem beauftragten Richter erfolgt oder kann hier der Richter, ebenso wie in Art. 378 Abs. 3 oder in Art. 407 die bezügliche Anordnung treffen?

Der Entwurf kannte eine Schriftvergleichung in der Sitzung nicht, nichtsdestoweniger sprach Art. 356 vom Falle, wo „die Partei verhindert sei, sich vor Gericht einzufinden," offenbar im Hinblicke darauf, daß die Expertise zum Zwecke der Schriftvergleichung immer am Sitze des Gerichtes stattfinde. Wenn später statt „Gericht" der Ausdruck „Prozeßgericht" gesetzt wurde, so wollte hiemit nichts geändert werden.

Bis zur zweiten Lesung in der Kammer der Reichsräthe sagte nun das Gesetz nicht, daß gerade das Prozeßgericht die bezügliche Anordnung zu treffen habe und, wäre es so geblieben, so würde man wohl keinen Anstand genommen haben, dem beauftragten Richter fragliche Anordnung zu gestatten, wie dies im Entwurfe ausdrücklich geschah.

Die Verbesserung, welche man schließlich in der Redaktion vornahm, hat jedoch diesen sachgemäßen Weg verschlossen und bleibt den klaren Worten des Gesetzes und der Bestimmung des Art. 342 Abs. 2 gegenüber nichts übrig, als eintretenden Falls den Zwischenpunkt in die Sitzung zu bringen und durch das Prozeßgericht die Anordnung treffen zu lassen.

Uebrigens ist zu beachten, daß das Gesetz nicht verlangt, es müsse eine Vorladung der Partei vorausgehen, und daher nichts im Wege steht, sofort bei Fällung des Beweisurtheils die fragliche Anordnung zu erlassen. Abg. IV 326.

10) Auch dritte Personen können zu fraglichem Zwecke vorgeladen werden und zwar ebenfalls ohne besondere gerichtliche Ermächtigung. Bei Verhinderungen gilt das soeben Nr. 9 Gesagte.

Diese Vorladung, welche wesentlich verschieden ist von der Beiladung des Art. 371 Abs. 2, wird gleich einer Zeugenladung behandelt und im Falle des Ungehorsams kommen die bezüglichen Vorschriften der Art. 427—430 zur Anwendung.

11) Schließlich glaubte der Gesetzgeber für die Beweisführung durch Schriftvergleichung eine Beweistheorie im Geiste der Gerichtsordnung Cap. XI § 8 Ziff. 3 dahin aufstellen zu müssen, daß ein voller Beweis nur angenommen werden dürfe, wenn noch andere Umstände unterstützend hinzutreten. Naturam furca expellas — —

Denkt man an Fälle, wo auf den ersten Blick sich aus der Schriftvergleichung die Aechtheit ergibt, z. B. wo ein Brief, ein selbstgeschriebenes Testament mit anerkannten Briefen oder größeren Schriftstücken verglichen wird, wo ferner ohne Schriftvergleichung ein Beweis unmöglich wäre, weil Eideszuschiebung unstatthaft ist 2c., so wird man in dieser Verfügung einen Gewinn für das materielle Recht nicht erblicken können. Man hätte wohl vom Gedanken ausgehen dürfen, daß eine Bevormundung, wie sie den Richtern zur Zeit von Kreitmayer gegenüber und unter dem alten Verfahren vielleicht sachgemäß war, jetzt füglich entbehrt werden könne.

c) Eideszuschiebung.

12) Nach der Fassung, welche Art. 383 im Entwurfe hatte (Art. 359), sollte gesagt sein, daß auch dem nach Art. 371 beigeladenen Dritten der Eid zugeschoben werden könne, aus der Aenderung in Verbindung mit der Streichung von Art. 419 des Entwurfs folgt jedoch, daß dies nicht statthaft sein soll.

Wie Art. 383 jetzt lautet, bestimmt er nur die Eidesformel für die Hauptpartei.

Art. 384. — **Der Staatsanwalt kann an allen Verhandlungen über den Beweis der Aechtheit oder Fälschung einer Urkunde in der Sitzung sich betheiligen.**

Ergibt das Verfahren Anzeichen einer strafbaren Fälschung, so ist die Sache zur strafrechtlichen Untersuchung zu verweisen. Das Verfahren ist in solchen Fällen bis nach Erledigung der Untersuchung einzustellen, soferne nicht der Beweisführer auf die Benützung der Urkunde verzichtet oder das Gericht sich überzeugt, daß es deren zur Erweisung des Anspruchs des Beweisführers nicht bedarf, oder daß die Urkunde jedenfalls nicht würde beachtet werden können.

G. A. d. K. d. A. II S. 208. 209. 299. 316. 335. 452. IV S. 94.
K. d. R. II S. 172. IV S. 46.

1) Der Grund, warum dem Staatsanwalte erlaubt ist, sich bei allen Verhandlungen über den Beweis der Aechtheit oder Fälschung von Urkunden in der Sitzung zu betheiligen, liegt nahe, und es wäre nur zu wünschen, der Gesetzgeber hätte auch Sorge dafür getragen, daß der Staatsanwalt, der ja in der Regel den Sitzungen nicht beiwohnen soll, Kenntniß von jedem Falle dieser Art erhalte. Wo das öffentliche Interesse betheiligt ist, sind doch wohl andere Rücksichten maßgebend, als diejenigen, welche für die Intervention eines beliebigen Privatinteressenten gelten.

Im Geiste des Gesetzes wird übrigens der Vorsitzende verpflichtet sein, dem Staatsanwalte Kenntniß geben zu lassen. (Vgl. Abg. II 208 a. E.)

2) Die Bestimmung, daß bei Verdacht einer strafbaren Fälschung das Verfahren von Amtswegen einzustellen sei, steht im Einklange mit den Bestimmungen des Art. 191, und ist das, was dort in's Ermessen des Gerichtes gestellt ist, hier zur bindenden Vorschrift gemacht.

Natürlich ist diese Einstellung des Verfahrens nur nöthig, soweit die Entscheidung des Civilrechtsstreites von der Frage der Fälschung bedingt, soweit diese präjudiziell ist, wie dies Art. 384 Abs. 2 näher bestimmt.

Art. 385. — **Eine Partei, welche muthwilligerweise die Aechtheit einer Privaturkunde abgeläugnet oder eine öffentliche Urkunde als falsch angefochten hat, kann durch das Urtheil, welches die Aechtheit der Urkunde in Folge der darüber stattgehabten Beweisführung ausspricht, in eine Geldstrafe bis zu hundert Gulden verurtheilt werden.**

G. A. d. K. d. A. II S. 208. 299. 316. 335. IV S. 94. — K. d. R. II S. 172. IV S. 46.

1) Der französische Gesetzgeber (Art. 213 und 246 Code de proc.) droht weit strengere Strafen, welche immer ausgesprochen werden müssen, ohne Prüfung, ob Muthwille vorliege oder nicht. Sie sind verwirkt mit Erhebung des Zwischenstreits und können selbst durch Abstand oder Zugeständniß nicht mehr beseitigt werden.

Die Strafverfügung des Art. 385 erscheint im Gegensatze hierzu als eine höchst milde, ich möchte sagen: matte und kraftlose, welche ihren Zweck, abschreckend zu wirken, wohl schwerlich erreichen wird.

2) Die Strafe ist nur für Fälle gedroht, wo die Aechtheit einer Urkunde, sei es durch Nichtanerkennung (bei Privaturkunden), sei es durch Anfechtung (bei öffentlichen Urkunden) muthwilliger Weise in Frage gestellt worden ist, und es soll das Urtheil, welches die Aechtheit ausspricht, auch die gedrohte Geldstrafe verhängen.

Hieraus folgt, daß eine Strafe nicht eintreten kann, wenn zwar die Aechtheit einer Privaturkunde zugegeben, diese Urkunde jedoch als verfälscht (Art. 373 Abs. 2) angefochten wird, mag die Anfechtung auch noch so muthwillig sein. Ich will nicht behaupten, daß dies sachentsprechend sei, allein der Sinn des Gesetzes muß es wohl sein.

Man könnte nun meinen, es müsse das Gleiche auch der Fall sein bei öffentlichen Urkunden, d. h. es dürfe die Strafe nur ausgesprochen werden, wenn es sich darum handle, daß die Urkunde falsch angefertigt, nicht aber, daß sie, ursprünglich ächt, erst später gefälscht worden sei; allein dies ist der Wille des Gesetzes nicht, wie sich schlagend daraus ergibt, daß es ursprünglich hieß: „unächt oder verfälscht“, und diese beiden Worte stillschweigend in das Wort „falsch“ zusammengefaßt wurden. (Abg. II 316). Unter dem Ausspruche der „Aechtheit“ versteht also das Gesetz hier einen Ausspruch dahin, daß die Urkunde als öffentliche ursprünglich gefertigt und später auch nicht gefälscht worden sei.

Auf intellektuelle Fälschungen, d. h. auf wahrheitswidrige Beurkundungen, läßt sich jedoch auch bei öffentlichen Urkunden die Strafbestimmung nicht ausdehnen. Vgl. Abg. II 337 (zu Hauptst. XII Art. 1).

Noch weniger läßt sie sich anwenden auf Fälle, wo bloß aus Versehen etwas unrichtig beurkundet worden sein soll, d. h. wenn die Falschheit eine rein civilrechtliche ist im Sinne, wie oben zu Art. 376—383 Nr. 1 erörtert wurde.

3) Die Bestreitung muß eine muthwillige sein.

Eine solche ist immer gegeben, wenn die Partei persönlich weiß, daß die Urkunde ächt sei, wenn sie bei der Aufnahme einer öffentlichen Urkunde selbst mitgewirkt, eine Privaturkunde selbst unterzeichnet hat, es müßten denn außerordentliche Umstände, wie Gedächtnißschwäche, Unzurechnungsfähigkeit zur Zeit der Handlung ꝛc., zur Entschuldigung dienen.

Sie kann aber auch gegeben sein, wenn die Partei keine persönliche Kenntniß hatte, ihr jedoch die Beweise so klar vorlagen, daß sie selbst den Ungrund ihrer Einwände einsehen mußte. Insbesondere unterscheidet das Gesetz bei Abläugnen von Unterschriften nicht, ob es sich von eigenen oder fremden Unterschriften handle.

Sogar für den Fall, als der Muthwille erwiesen ist, steht es übrigens noch im Ermessen des Gerichtes, eine Geldstrafe zu verhängen oder nicht.

4) Geht die Anfechtung von mehreren Parteien aus oder besteht eine Partei aus mehreren Personen, so ist die Geldstrafe gegen jede Person, deren Anfechtung als muthwillig befunden wird, gesondert auszusprechen. Der persönliche Charakter der Geldstrafen unserer Prozeßordnung, wie er namentlich in den Bestimmungen des Art. 147 scharf hervortritt, bedingt dies. Anders war es im französischen Prozesse.

Es frägt sich, ob und gegen wen die Strafe auszusprechen sei, wenn ein gesetzlicher Vertreter muthwilliger Weise eine Unterschrift — vielleicht seine eigene — abgeläugnet hat.

Einerseits läßt sich sagen: Es handelt sich hier von einer Strafe, unter Umständen (Art. 147) sogar von einer Arreststrafe, und kann diese nicht gegen eine Partei ausgesprochen werden, welche nicht selbst muthwillig gehandelt hat; ebensowenig aber auch gegen den gesetzlichen Vertreter, der nicht Partei ist und der nach Art. 110 zwar zum Ersatze von Kosten, nicht aber zu einer Geldstrafe verurtheilt werden kann.

Hiergegen läßt sich einwenden, daß diese Lösung eine fühlbare Lücke im Gesetze ließe, daß überall, wo die Anfechtung eine muthwillige ist, das Gericht auch befugt sein müsse, die Strafe auszusprechen und die Handlungen des gesetzlichen Vertreters auch Handlungen der Partei seien (Art. 60); daß übrigens der Partei freistehe, ihren Rückgriff gegen den Vertreter zu nehmen, und dieser nach Art. 110 sogar sofort zum Ersatze verurtheilt werden könne, da alle Ausgaben, welche der Prozeß für die Partei veranlaßt, im weiteren Sinne als Prozeßkosten betrachtet werden könnten. Es läßt sich beifügen, daß fragliche Geldstrafe civilrechtlicher Natur sei, wie denn selbst die an ihre Stelle tretende Arreststrafe in Art. 147 ausdrücklich als Civilstrafe bezeichnet wird, und daß nicht anzunehmen sei, das Gesetz wolle bei Gemeinden, Corporationen, Aktiengesellschaften ꝛc. die Geldstrafe unbedingt ausschließen, auch wenn die Anfechtung noch so muthwillig sei.

Nicht verkennend, daß eine vollkommen befriedigende Lösung nicht möglich sei, möchte ich mich dieser letzteren Ansicht als der praktischeren anschließen und zwar hauptsächlich deßhalb, weil ja das Gericht auch dann, wenn der Muthwille bewiesen ist, es immer noch in der Gewalt hat, vom Ausspruch einer Strafe Umgang zu nehmen, und diese Befugniß gerade für Fälle, wie vorliegender, gegeben zu sein scheint, da sie sonst keinen Sinn hätte. Wäre den Umständen nach anzunehmen, daß es zu einer Verwandlung der Geldstrafe in Arreststrafe kommen müßte, so würde dies Veranlassung sein, eine Strafe nicht auszusprechen.

5) Da das Gesetz die Verurtheilung zur Geldstrafe nur in demjenigen Urtheile gestattet, welches in Folge der bezüglich der Aechtheit stattgefundenen Beweisführung die Aechtheit der Urkunde ausspricht, so ist klar, daß wenn es aus irgend einem Grunde nicht zu diesem Spruche kommt, auch die Geldstrafe nicht verhängt werden kann.

Durch diese Bestimmung büßt die Strafdrohung den geringen Werth, welchen sie als Abschreckungsmittel hat, noch vollends ein, da es der betreffenden Partei freisteht, wenn sie sieht, daß klare Beweise gegen sie vorliegen, oder daß sie ihren Zweck, den Prozeß zu verzögern, erreicht hat, die Urkunde anzuerkennen und so eine Entscheidung unnöthig zu machen. In den Fällen, wo die Frivolität am klarsten ist, fällt also die Strafe hinweg.

Herausgabe von Urkunden.

Art. 386. — **Hat eine Partei eine Urkunde als Beweismittel bezeichnet und der Gegenpartei mitgetheilt, ohne sie in der Sitzung zur Vorlage zu bringen, so kann die Gegenpartei, welche diese Urkunde als Beweismittel für sich benützen will, von ihr deren Herausgabe verlangen.**

Außerdem kann jede Partei die Herausgabe einer zum Beweise oder zur Schriftenvergleichung erforderlichen Urkunde von der Gegenpartei, wie auch von dem dritten Besitzer verlangen, wenn ihr das Eigenthum oder Miteigenthum an der Urkunde zusteht oder die Urkunde ihrem Inhalte nach eine gemeinschaftliche ist.

Als dem Inhalte nach gemeinschaftlich gelten Urkunden für die Personen, in deren Interesse sie errichtet oder deren gegenseitige Rechtsverhältnisse darin beurkundet sind. In diesem Sinne sind namentlich die über ein Rechtsgeschäft gepflogenen schriftlichen Verhandlungen unter den Betheiligten gemeinschaftliche Urkunden.

Der Pflicht zur Herausgabe kann für den Prozeß auch durch Hinterlegung der Urkunde auf der Gerichtsschreiberei des Prozeßgerichts genügt werden.

G. A. d. K. d. A. II S. 207. 300. 316. 335. 336. 452. — K. d. R. II S. 172.

1) Die Gerichtsordnung dehnte die Editionspflicht sehr weit aus, indem sie 1) zum Zwecke der bloßen Vertheidigung eine unbedingte Verpflichtung anerkannte, und 2) sogar zu Gunsten des angreifenden Theils dem Richter gestattete, die Edition überall anzuordnen, wo er es billig erachtete.

Im Gegensatze hierzu schränkt das französische Recht die Editionspflicht zu sehr ein und läßt sie eigentlich bloß dort zu, wo ein Eigenthum oder Miteigenthum geltend gemacht werden kann.

Unsere Prozeßordnung geht einen Mittelweg. Sie beseitigt den Unterschied zwischen Kläger und Beklagten, sowie das freie Ermessen des Richters, spricht jedoch eine Verpflichtung zur Herausgabe einer Urkunde zu Gunsten jeder Partei aus, für welche dieselbe ihrem Inhalte nach eine gemeinschaftliche ist.

Wenn ferner gesagt wird, daß die Herausgabe jeder Urkunde verlangt werden könne, welche bereits als Beweismittel bezeichnet und der Gegenpartei mitgetheilt worden sei (Art. 172), so ist dies nur die selbstverständliche Anwendung des in Art. 337 ausgesprochenen Prinzipes.

2) Vor Allem ist hervorzuheben, daß das Gesetz hier nur die Pflicht zur Herausgabe von Urkunden zum Zwecke der Benützung in einem bestimmten Rechtsstreite, und so weit es für diesen erforderlich ist, regelt, und daher weder die civilrechtlichen Grundsätze bezüglich des Rechtes, die Auslieferung einer Urkunde auf dem Wege der Klage zu verlangen, noch die gesetzlichen Bestimmungen bezüglich der Berechtigung, sich Abschriften öffentlicher Urkunden von den betreffenden Beamten ertheilen zu lassen, berührt werden. (Abg. II 207 Sp. 2.) Will daher eine Partei ein selbstständiges Begehren auf Auslieferung einer Urkunde, sei es im Wege der Klage, sei es im Wege der Widerklage erheben, so steht ihr dies frei, und muß dann über dieses Begehren nach Maßgabe der allgemeinen prozessualen Grundsätze verhandelt und entschieden werden.

3) Unter „Herausgabe“ versteht somit die Prozeßordnung das Nemliche, was das frühere Recht unter „Edition“ verstanden hatte, nemlich die bloße Mittheilung der Urkunde, so weit es zur Benützung im Rechtsstreite nöthig ist.

Sie erfolget durch Einhändigung an die Partei bezw. deren Anwalt gegen Empfangsbescheinigung, oder durch Hinterlegung auf der Gerichtschreiberei des Prozeßgerichtes, unter Umständen auch durch Aufnahme einer gerichtlichen Abschrift im Sinne von Art. 367 Ziff. 2.

Befindet sich die Urkunde bei den Akten des Gegners, so ist das Begehren der Herausgabe insofern gegenstandslos, als die Aktenmittheilung nicht verweigert wird.

4) Die erste Voraussetzung des Gesetzes ist, daß die Urkunde zum Beweise oder zur Schriftvergleichung erforderlich sei, denn ist weder das Eine noch das Andere der Fall, so kann zwar immerhin ein Recht bestehen, auf Auslieferung der Urkunde zu klagen, allein es handelt sich nicht mehr um einen Zwischenstreit im Prozesse, wovon hier allein die Rede ist.

Steht die Benützung der Urkunde zum Zwecke der Beweisführung in Frage, so kann das Verlangen auf Herausgabe gestellt werden, sobald und solange die Urkunde als Beweismittel geltend gemacht werden kann (Art. 329, 707). Daß eine Beweisauflage vorausgehe, ist durchaus nicht nöthig.

5) Weitere Voraussetzung ist, daß entweder ein Eigenthumsrecht der Urkunde geltend gemacht werden könne, oder dieselbe ihrem Inhalte nach eine gemeinschaftliche sei. Der Begriff der Gemeinschaftlichkeit ist gesetzlich dahin bestimmt, daß sie für Personen bestehe, in deren Interesse die Urkunde errichtet oder deren gegenseitige Rechtsverhältnisse darin beurkundet seien und

werden beispielsweise die über ein Rechtsgeschäft gepflogenen schriftlichen Verhandlungen angeführt.

Im Interesse einer Person ist eine Urkunde errichtet, wenn Rechte oder Verpflichtungen derselben darin beurkundet sind. So sind z. B. Testamente im Interesse aller Personen errichtet, welchen darin eine Zuwendung oder eine Auflage gemacht wird, ferner Verträge im Interesse derjenigen Personen, von welchen oder für welche sie abgeschlossen worden sind. In der Regel ist übrigens in solchen Fällen ein Eigenthum oder Miteigenthum gegeben.

Die gegenseitigen Rechtsverhältnisse erscheinen z. B. beurkundet, wenn es sich um Schriften handelt, die nicht gerade zum Zwecke einer Beurkundung abgefaßt, dennoch aber zum Nachweise der gegenseitigen Rechtsverhältnisse tauglich sind, oder wenn urkundliche Feststellungen unter Rechtsvorgängern in Frage sind.

Unter letzteren Gesichtspunkt fallen insbesondere Saal- und Lagerbücher, sowie andere Aufzeichnungen ähnlicher Art, indem bei Urkunden dieser Art angenommen wird, daß sie im gegenseitig-gemeinschaftlichen Interesse errichtet worden seien (Seuff. Comm. Bd. III S. 206 u. 207); unter den ersteren Gesichtspunkt fallen schriftliche Mittheilungen behufs Abschluß oder Vollzug von Rechtsgeschäften. (Seuffert a. a. O. S. 205 Note 19.) Die Aeußerung des Referenten der K. d. R. (Verhdl. Bd. II S. 144) beruht daher offenbar auf Irrthum und ist den Grundsätzen des französischen Rechts, nicht aber denjenigen der Prozeßordnung entsprechend.

6) Ueberhaupt ist zu beachten, daß die Prinzipien des französischen Rechtes hier sehr wesentliche Aenderungen erleiden. Es wird z. B. jetzt in Fällen, wo ein Vertrag in mehreren Exemplaren errichtet ist, vom Gegner die Herausgabe des für ihn errichteten und ihm eigenthümlich zugehörigen Exemplares verlangt werden können; ebenso kann der Aussteller einer Quittung verlangen, daß diese, als sein Interesse berührend, ihm zur Benützung mitgetheilt werde, falls er aus dem Bestehen dieser Quittung Dritten gegenüber oder zum Beweise einer Anerkennung, einer Unterbrechung der Verjährung 2c. rechtliche Folgerungen ableiten kann. (Seuff. Comm. Bd. III S. 205 Note 16.)

7) Schließlich ist hervorzuheben, daß das Gesetz von „gegenseitigen Rechtsverhältnissen" spricht, also der Umstand, daß Rechtsverhältnisse von Dritten auf eine Urkunde gegründet werden können, eine Pflicht zur Herausgabe nicht begründet. So können dritte Personen nicht die Herausgabe von Rechnungen und Inventaren, in denen ihre Zahlungen erwähnt oder ihre Ansprüche anerkannt sind, verlangen.

Art. 387. — **Richtet sich das Begehren auf Herausgabe einer Urkunde an die Gegenpartei, so ist es mittels motivirten Antrags zu erheben, welcher eine möglichst genaue Bezeichnung der Urkunde zu enthalten hat.**

Art. 388. — **Befindet sich die Urkunde im Besitze eines im Prozesse nicht betheiligten Dritten und versteht sich dieser zu ihrer Herausgabe nicht, so ist er vor dem für seine Person zuständigen Gerichte zu belangen.**

Das Prozeßgericht kann auf Antrag die Einstellung des Verfahrens in der Hauptsache verfügen und bestimmt in diesem Falle zugleich eine angemessene Frist zur Beibringung der Urkunde. Ist die Partei bei Ablauf dieser Frist noch nicht im Besitze der Urkunde, so kann sie Verlängerung beanspruchen, wenn sie bescheinigt, daß sie in Betreibung der Klage auf Herausgabe den erforderlichen Fleiß aufgewendet habe.

Art. 389. — **Verweigert die Gegenpartei auf ergangenes Urtheil die Herausgabe der Urkunde ohne hinreichenden Grund, so ist der angegebene Inhalt als wahr, falls aber die Herausgabe lediglich zum Behufe der Schriftenvergleichung verlangt wurde, der Aechtheitsbeweis als erbracht anzunehmen.**

Gegen den dritten Besitzer der Urkunde ist im Falle der Weigerung auf Geldstrafe bis zu fünfzig Gulden und geeigneten Falls auf eine angemessene Entschädigung zu erkennen.

Art. 390. — **Läugnet der angebliche Besitzer der Urkunde den Besitz, so hat er auf Verlangen des Antragstellers zu schwören, daß er die Urkunde weder besitze, noch sich des Besitzes zu dem Zwecke, um den Rechtsstand des Antragstellers zu erschweren, entäußert habe, auch nicht wisse, wo die Urkunde sich befinde.**

Die Eidesweigerung zieht, je nachdem es sich um die Gegenpartei oder um einen dritten Besitzer handelt, die in Abs. 1 oder die in Abs. 2 des Art. 389 bezeichneten Folgen nach sich.

G. A. d. K. d. A. II S. 208. 300. 316. 335. 336. IV S. 94.
K. d. R. II S. 172. IV S. 46.

1) Das Verfahren, um die Herausgabe einer Urkunde zu erzwingen, ist ein verschiedenes, je nachdem diese im Besitze einer Partei oder eines Dritten sich befindet.

Im ersteren Falle liegt ein Zwischenstreit im Sinne des Art. 483 vor und wird daher das Begehren durch einen motivirten Antrag gestellt, gewöhnlich in demjenigen Antrage, welcher zur Hauptsache genommen wird. Die Urkunde ist möglichst genau zu bezeichnen, insbesondere auch ihr Inhalt im Wesentlichen anzugeben; Letzteres deßhalb, weil die Herausgabe nur verlangt werden kann, wenn die Urkunde ihrem Inhalte nach gemeinschaftlich ist, weil ferner die Verweigerung der Herausgabe durch Annahme der Wahrheit des angegebenen Inhalts bestraft werden soll.

2) Dritte Personen sind vor dem für sie zuständigen Gerichte (Art. 12—20) mit besonderer Klage zu belangen, und auch hier ist möglichst genaue Bezeichnung der Urkunde durch die allgemeine Vorschrift des Art. 225 geboten. Das Klagbegehren richtet sich dahin, daß der Dritte verurtheilt werde, die bezeichnete Urkunde zur Benützung in dem zu bezeichnenden Rechtsstreite herauszugeben.

Auch in diesem Falle hat der entstehende Streit dem Hauptprozesse gegenüber die Natur eines Zwischen- oder Nebenstreites, insofern es sich blos darum handelt, ein Beweismittel für jenen Prozeß zu gewinnen.

Das Recht der Klagestellung leitet sich daraus her, daß die Urkunde als Beweismittel dienlich ist. In der Regel wird die Klage erst erhoben werden, nachdem das Prozeßgericht auf Begehren Frist zur Beibringung der Urkunde, d. h. zur Anstellung und Durchführung der nöthigen Klage gegeben und mit dieser gerichtlichen Verfügung ist dann zugleich das Recht zur Klagestellung begründet. Uebrigens schreibt das Gesetz nicht vor, daß vorerst über die Vorfrage der Beweiserheblichkeit vom Prozeßgerichte erkannt sein müsse, obgleich eine solche Vorschrift vielleicht sachgemäß gewesen wäre, und es steht daher nichts im Wege, sofort, ohne irgend eine Ermächtigung den Dritten auf Herausgabe einer Beweisurkunde zu belangen. Wird in diesem Falle eingewendet, es sei die Urkunde gar nicht als Beweismittel dienlich, es sei also nicht actio nata, so wird der angegangene Richter sich auch auf die Prüfung dieser Frage einlassen müssen.

3) Wer von Jemanden die Herausgabe einer Urkunde auf Grund von Art. 386 verlangt, muß nachweisen, daß derselbe sich in deren Besitze befinde, und daß sie gemeinschaftlich sei.

Zum Nachweise des Besitzes können die gewöhnlichen Beweismittel (Urkunden, Zeugen, Vermuthungen) benützt werden, und es wäre irrig, wollte man etwa aus Art. 390 folgern, das einzige Beweismittel sei der Editionseid. Jener Artikel bestimmt nur, wie in Fällen, wo es auf Eid ankommt, derselbe auferlegt werden solle; er hält den besonderen Editionseid mit seiner stehenden Formel, wie ihn das frühere Verfahren (G. O. Cap. XI § 6 Ziff. 5) festsetzte, aufrecht — ob mit Recht, möchte allerdings zu bezweifeln sein.

Bezüglich dieses Eides ist im gemeinen Prozesse bestritten, ob er als ein gewöhnlicher nur besonders gefaßter Eid zu betrachten sei, oder ob es ein ganz eigenthümlicher Eid sei, bei welchem die für andere Eide, insbesondere den Haupteid geltenden Grundsätze keine Anwendung finden. (Bayer Civilpr. § 295.) Im bayer. Prozesse nahm man letzteres an (Seuff. Comm. Bd. III S. 215) und ist dies auch als die Ansicht der Prozeßordnung vorauszusetzen, weßhalb z. B. die Zurückschiebung ausgeschlossen erscheint.

Uebrigens wurde schon im früheren Rechte anerkannt, daß der Fall des eigenthümlichen Editionseides nur dann gegeben sei, wenn es sich darum handele, abgesehen vom Grunde des Editionsanspruches den Besitz der Urkunde darzuthun, daß also wenn bestimmte Thatsachen z. B. Hinterlegung der Urkunde, Einhändigung zum Vollzuge eines Mandates 2c. behauptet werden, bezüglich derselben der Haupteid zugeschoben werden könne. (Seuff. Comm. Bd. III S. 215 Note 48.)

4) Die Frage, ob der Eid einem gesetzlichen Vertreter auferlegt werden könne, löst sich nach allgemeinen Prinzipien, also diesseits nach den Bestimmungen in Hauptst. XIV, in der Pfalz nach dem dort geltenden Rechte.

Könnte gegebenen Falles der Eid einem gesetzlichen Vertreter als solchem nicht auferlegt werden, so dürfte er ihm nichtsdestoweniger als einem Dritten auferlegt werden und würden die Folgen, welche Art. 289 Abs. 2 bestimmt, eintreten.

5) Indem die Eidesformel auch dahin lautet, daß der angebliche Besitzer 1) sich des Besitzes zum Zwecke, um den Rechtsstand des Antragstellers zu erschweren, nicht entäußert habe, und daß er 2) nicht wisse, wo die Urkunde sich befinde, entfernt sie sich vom Gebiete, auf welchem sich Antrag bezw. Klage bewegen, indem diese nur gegen den Besitzer gerichtet sind und Herausgabe der Urkunde verlangen.

Die erstere Abweichung hängt mit dem Grundsatze des römischen Rechtes zusammen, daß derjenige, qui dolo desiit possidere, als Besitzer behandelt und belangt werden dürfe. Es möchte sich hieraus folgern lassen, daß der Nachweis einer böswilligen Entäußerng auch in anderer Weise als durch den Editionseid geführt werden dürfe, wie dies die Ger. Ord. Cap. XI. § 6 Ziff. 4 ausdrücklich bestimmte. Ob die Entäußerung vor oder nach dem Begehren der Herausgabe stattgefunden, erscheint gleichgültig, da die Worte des Gesetzes nicht unterscheiden und auch nach dem Geiste desselben nicht zu unterscheiden ist.

6) Folge der Verweigerung der durch Urtheil angeordneten Herausgabe ist der Gegenpartei gegenüber die Annahme, daß der angegebene Inhalt wahr, bezw. die Unterschrift ächt sei, dem Dritten gegenüber Verurtheilung zu einer Geldstrafe bis zu 50 Gulden und unter Umständen zur Entschädigung.

Setzt man voraus, eine Partei, welche die Urkunde in der Hand hat und sie jeden Augenblick herausgeben kann, wenn sie nur will, weigere sich der richterlichen Anordnung Folge zu leisten, so erscheint die besagte gesetzliche Präsumtion als Strafe vollständig gerechtfertigt, denkt man aber an Fälle, wo der Beweis mehr oder weniger nur formell ist, oder wo angenommen wird, es sei der Besitz böswillig aufgegeben worden, so kann unter Umständen die Präsumtion der Wahrheit dessen, was es dem Gegner beliebt hat, als Inhalt der Urkunde anzugeben, eine viel zu weit greifende Folge sein.

Die Gerichtsordnung ging nicht so weit, alle Angaben des Gegners ohne Weiteres für wahr zu erklären, sondern ließ diesen wenigstens noch schwören.

7) Vielleicht sind die Worte „ohne hinreichenden Grund" bestimmt und geeignet, Mißstände in fraglicher Richtung zu beseitigen.

Sie lassen sich offenbar nicht anders erklären, als daß nach ergangenem Urtheile noch Gründe zur Würdigung kommen können, im Hinblicke auf welche die Unterlassung der Herausgabe als entschuldigt betrachtet und von der gesetzlichen Strafe Umgang genommen werden dürfe. Allerdings muß dahin gestellt bleiben, ob man bei der ursprünglichen Fassung (Entwurf Art. 365 und Abg. II 300) nicht etwas Anderes meinte, allein jetzt, nachdem die Worte „auf ergangenes Urtheil" eingeschoben sind, läßt sich unmöglich annehmen, man habe nichts weiter bezweckt, als völlig unnützer Weise darauf aufmerksam zu machen, daß der Richter die Herausgabe nur anzuordnen habe, falls dieselbe ohne hinreichenden Grund verweigert werde.

Daraus, daß das Gericht aus besonderen Gründen die gesetzliche Präsumtion nicht eintreten ließe, würde keineswegs folgen, daß nun das Urtheil keine Wirkung äußerte, vielmehr wäre das Gericht berechtigt, aus der Vorenthaltung oder Beseitigung der Urkunde, theils unter dem Gesichtspunkte der Entschädigungspflicht, theils nach den Prinzipien des Vermuthungsbeweises die sachgemäßen Folgerungen zu ziehen.

Der Unterschied bestünde nur darin, daß es frei würdigen würde und nicht mehr gezwungen wäre, der Präsumtion gemäß zu sprechen.

Sollte z. B. die Urkunde nur als Vergleichsschrift in einem Aechtheitsbeweise dienen, so wird kein Grund vorliegen, irgend eine nachtheilige Folge eintreten zu lassen, falls der Richter aus sonstigen Vergleichsschriften, Zeugenaussagen oder Vermuthungen die volle Ueberzeugung der Unächtheit gewinnt. Auch in Fällen, wo die Partei, indem sie die Herausgabe verlangte, den Inhalt der Urkunde zwar im Allgemeinen jedoch nicht so genau angeben konnte, als es für die Entscheidung nöthig ist, muß das richterliche Ermessen Maß geben.

8) Das Urtheil, welches zur Herausgabe verpflichtet erklärt, setzt zugleich eine Frist für dieselbe und falls diese Frist versäumt wird, sind nach Maßgabe des Art. 389 die sachgemäßen Folgen auszusprechen.

Was die Entschädigung anbelangt, zu welcher Dritte nach Ermessen des Gerichts verurtheilt werden können, so steht nichts im Wege, dieselbe sofort bei Zustellung der Klage eventuell geltend zu machen, und ebenso kann das Gericht, indem es die Pflicht zur Herausgabe ausspricht, sofort für den Fall als in der gegebenen Frist dem Urtheile nicht Genüge geleistet würde, zur Entschädigung verurtheilen. Vgl. Bemerk. zu Art. 225 Nr. 19. Eine Geldstrafe läßt sich allerdings nicht eventuell aussprechen.

9) Die Weigerung den Editionseid zu schwören, soll nach Art. 390 Abs. 2 die nemlichen Folgen nach sich ziehen, wie die Weigerung die Urkunde auf Urtheil hin herauszugeben.

Man sollte zwar glauben, es müsse auf die Eidesverweigerung hin erst Verurtheilung zur Herausgabe eintreten und wenn diesem Urtheile nicht entsprochen werde, dann erst sei der Fall gegeben, fragliche Folgen auszusprechen, allein das Gesetz hat offenbar nicht diesen Sinn, will vielmehr, von der Ansicht ausgehend, daß mit der Eidesverweigerung auch die Verweigerung der Herausgabe genügend festgestellt sei, es solle sofort nach Maßgabe von Art. 389 Abs. 1 oder Abs. 2 erkannt werden. Durch nachträgliche Vorlage der Urkunden kann übrigens der Ausspruch fraglicher Folgen jeder Zeit verhindert werden.

10) Die gedrohten Folgen treten ein, auch wenn der angebliche Besitzer nur in einer oder der anderen der in Art. 390 Abs. 1 bezeichneten Richtungen den Editionseid nicht leistet, insbesondere auch, wenn er anzugeben sich weigert, wo die Urkunde sich befinde.

Für manche Fälle, z. B. wenn der Dritte zugestehen muß, sich der Urkunde schon früher arglistig entäußert zu haben, und klar ist, daß es nicht mehr in seiner Macht stehe sie beizuschaffen, ist offenbar eine Geldstrafe ganz unpassend, dennoch aber müßte sie, da das Gesetz nicht unterscheidet, ausgesprochen werden.

Art. 391. — Von Urkunden, welche sich bei einer öffentlichen Behörde finden, hat diese vorbehaltlich besonderer gesetzlicher Bestimmung Vorlage und Einsicht zu gewähren und beglaubigte Abschrift zu ertheilen, wenn die Zustimmung desjenigen, auf dessen Antrag oder in dessen Interesse die Urkunde bei der Behörde errichtet oder hinterlegt wurde, beigebracht oder seine Verpflichtung hiezu rechtskräftig ausgesprochen ist.

Art. 392. — Will eine Partei Akten eines andern Gerichts oder in den Händen einer sonstigen öffentlichen Behörde befindliche Urkunden zu ihrer Beweisführung benützen, so hat sie an das mit dem Rechtsstreite befaßte Gericht unter möglichst genauer Bezeichnung der betreffenden Aktenstücke und Urkunden das Ansuchen um deren Herbeischaffung zu richten.

Das Ansuchen kann mittels einfacher Vorstellung oder bei Gelegenheit einer in der Sache stattfindenden Verhandlung mittels Antrags gestellt werden.

Das Gericht hat, wenn es den Gesuchsteller zur Benützung der bezeichneten Aktenstücke und Urkunden berechtigt erachtet, dem Gesuche durch Anordnung der geeigneten Requisition zu entsprechen. Letztere wird durch den Staatsanwalt vollzogen und die eingekommenen Akten werden auf der Gerichtsschreiberei zur Benützung hinterlegt.

G. A. d. K. d. A. II S. 207. 208. 300. 316. 317. 336. 452. IV S. 94. 95. — K. d. R. II S. 172. IV S. 46.

1) Die Art 391 und 392 treffen Vorsorge für Fälle, wo die Urkunden, welche zur Beweisführung benutzt werden sollen (öffentliche oder Privaturkunden), bei einer öffentlichen Behörde verwahrt sind, in welchen also nur das Recht zur Benützung streitig sein kann.

Es versteht sich von selbst, daß hierdurch die gesetzlichen Bestimmungen über das Recht, Einsicht und Abschrift von öffentlichen Urkunden zu verlangen, keine Aenderung erleiden. Art. 170. 288. 359 Abs. 4. — Not.=Ges. Art. 93.

2) Wenn Art. 291 die Behörden verpflichtet, Einsicht oder Abschrift zu gestatten, falls die Zustimmung desjenigen, auf dessen Antrag oder in dessen Interesse die Urkunde errichtet oder hinterlegt wurde, beigebracht oder durch gerichtlichen Spruch ergänzt sei, so spricht es hiermit einen allgemeinen Grundsatz aus, welcher überall Anwendung findet, wo nicht besondere gesetzliche Vorschriften Maß geben.

Bei Notariatsakten muß die Zustimmung von einer Person ausgehen, welche berechtigt ist, Einsicht oder Abschrift derselben zu verlangen, und dürfte aus dem Wortlaute des Art. 291 nicht gefolgert werden, daß Personen, welche in einem Testamente bedacht sind, sich zu Lebzeiten des Testators Abschrift ertheilen lassen könnten. Art. 94 des Not.=Ges. — Abg. II 316.

Ist durch Urtheil die Verpflichtung einer Partei ausgesprochen, die Benützung einer Urkunde zu gestatten, so ersetzt dieses Urtheil die Zustimmung, und die betreffende Behörde ist, falls ihr in der durch Art. 828 bezeichneten Weise die Rechtskraft des Urtheils nachgewiesen wird, verpflichtet, die Einsicht oder Erhebung einer Abschrift ebenso zu gestatten, als hätte jene Partei es verlangt.

3) In Art. 392 ist ein sehr praktischer Weg eröffnet, um die Urschriften von Urkunden oder Akten, welche bei öffentlichen Behörden verwahrt sind, dem Gerichte zugänglich zu machen.

Auf Vorstellung (Hptst. XXV) oder Antrag erläßt das Gericht eine bezügliche Requisition. Diese wird in Urschrift (Art. 651) oder Ausfertigung dem Staatsanwalte vorgelegt, welcher ohne weitere Förmlichkeit die Akten oder Urkunden amtlich erhebt und auf der Gerichtsschreiberei zur Benützung durch die Parteien und das Gericht hinterlegt. Ein Hinterlegungsakt ist ebensowenig als im Falle des Art. 173 zu errichten. Sobald der beabsichtigte Zweck erreicht ist, wird die Urkunde auf dem nemlichen Wege wieder zurückbefördert.

4) Der Ausdruck „öffentliche Behörde" möchte hier und in Art. 391 im weiteren Sinne zu nehmen sein und alle Amtspersonen begreifen, welche Urkunden im öffentlichen Interesse aufzubewahren haben. Daß die Civilstandsbeamten

darunter begriffen seien, wurde bei den Verhandlungen anerkannt (Abg. II 316 a. E.).

Bezüglich der Notare möchten Zweifel bestehen, jedenfalls steht der in der Pfalz seither eingehaltene Weg offen, daß das Gericht anordnet, es solle der Notar in einer zu bestimmenden Sitzung die Urschrift vorlegen. Bei diesem Verfahren bereitet auch Art. 92 des Not.-Ges. keine Schwierigkeiten.

Verfahren bei zu Verlust gegangenen Urkunden.

Art. 393. — **Ist eine auf den Prozeß bezügliche Urkunde erwiesenermaßen vorhanden gewesen, aber verloren gegangen, unleserlich oder sonst unbrauchbar geworden und hat der Beweisführer dies nicht arglistiger Weise selbst veranlaßt, so darf er Beschaffenheit und Inhalt der Urkunde mit allen gesetzlich zulässigen Arten von Beweismitteln bewahrheiten und zwar selbst bei Rechtsgeschäften, zu deren Wesenheit oder Beweis eine Urkunde gehört.**

Hat der Prozeßgegner verschuldet, daß die Urkunde verloren gegangen oder unbrauchbar geworden ist, so kann nach Erwägung aller Umstände die Angabe des Beweisführers über die Beschaffenheit und den Inhalt der Urkunde entweder sofort oder nach vorgängiger eidlicher Erhärtung als wahr angenommen werden.

G. A. d. K. d. A. II S. 300. 317. 336. IV S. 98. 99. — K. d. R. II S. 172. IV S. 46.

1) Daß das Dasein einer Urkunde, welche durch Zufall verloren ging oder unbrauchbar wurde, mit Beweismitteln jeder Art nachgewiesen werden dürfe, und dieser Nachweis die Urkunde ersetze, ist ein Satz, welcher von jeher in allen Gesetzgebungen anerkannt wurde und nur bezüglich der Wechsel in Art. 73 der D. W. O. einige Einschränkung erleidet.

Nicht in gleicher Weise verhält es sich, wenn der Verlust durch Verschulden desjenigen, welcher die Urkunde geltend machen will, herbeigeführt worden ist; denn für diesen Fall ließ sowohl die Gerichtsordnung (Cap. XI § 12) als der Code civil (Art. 1348 Ziff. 4) eine Ersetzung der Urkunde durch sonstigen Beweis nicht zu. Auch der Entwurf (Art. 345) stellte diesen Grundsatz auf, unsere Prozeßordnung jedoch hat, ohne daß eine Motivirung dieser Abweichung stattgefunden hätte, die Ausnahme auf den Fall der Arglist beschränkt, so daß also die einfache Verschuldung kein Hinderniß bildet, die Urkunde durch sonstigen Beweis zu ersetzen.

Es gilt dies nach der diesem Hauptstücke vorausgeschickten Vorbemerkung auch für die Pfalz und erleidet daher Art. 1348 Ziff. 3 Code civil in diesem Sinne eine Aenderung.

2) Die Beweisführung hat sich sowohl auf die giltige Errichtung als auf den Inhalt der Urkunde zu erstrecken.

Auch die Thatsache des Verlustes ist darzuthun, denn es kann nicht genügen, daß man bloß behaupte, sie verloren zu haben und sich so der Vorlage derselben, von welcher man vielleicht Nachtheil befürchtet, entziehe. Daß der Verlust arglistig veranlaßt sei, ist vom Gegner zu erweisen.

3) Hat der Prozeßgegner den Verlust der Urkunde verschuldet, so kann nach Erwägung aller Umstände die Angabe des Beweisführers über Beschaffenheit und Inhalt der Urkunde, entweder sofort oder nach Leistung eines Eides, als wahr angenommen werden.

Es ist dies eine sehr weitgehende Befugniß, von welcher mit größter Vorsicht Gebrauch zu machen ist, namentlich wenn es sich nicht um Arglist handelt, sondern einfache Verschuldung vorliegt. Dieselbe leitet sich aus dem Gesichtspunkte der Entschädigung her, welche hier sachgemäß dadurch geleistet wird, daß man das Beweismittel, dessen Verlust verschuldet wurde, als bestehend betrachtet. Vgl. Bemerk. zu Art. 387 bis 390 Nr. 7.

4) Nothwendige Voraussetzung, um diese Folge eintreten zu lassen, ist selbstverständlich, daß der Beweisführer ein Recht auf die Urkunde habe, im Sinne wie dies Art. 386 bestimmt.

Da es sich um eine Frage der Entschädigung handelt, so wird dem Beweise der Verschuldung gegenüber dem Prozeßgegner auch der Nachweis gestattet sein, daß Beschaffenheit und Inhalt der Urkunde ein anderer gewesen sei, als behauptet wird, und das Ergebniß dieses Beweises ist bei der richterlichen Entscheidung zu berücksichtigen. Ueberhaupt ist das Gericht nach der Fassung des Gesetzes nicht gehindert, in jeder Richtung seiner Ueberzeugung gemäß zu erkennen, und so gut es die Angaben des Beweisführers ganz als Wahrheit annehmen kann, kann es ihnen auch nur theilweise Glauben schenken.

Kerbhölzer.

Art. 394. — **Wenn feststeht, daß die Parteien für ihren Verkehr Kerb- oder Spanhölzer gebraucht haben, so beweisen solche, falls sie unverfälscht erscheinen und unter sich übereinstimmen.**

Weigert sich eine Partei ohne genügenden Grund, ihr Holz vorzulegen, so gilt das vorgelegte der andern Partei.

Denkmäler und ähnliche Zeichen.

Art. 395. — **In wie weit durch Denkmäler, Grenzzeichen, Marksteine, Aichpfähle und ähnliche Zeichen Beweis geliefert werde, bleibt, soweit nicht die Gesetze hierüber besondere Bestimmungen enthalten, der richterlichen Beurtheilung überlassen.**

G. A. d. K. d. A. II S. 202. 203. 300. 317. 336. — K. d. R. II. S. 172.

1) Wenn Kerbhölzer Beweis bilden sollen, so ist nöthig: 1) daß die bezügliche Verabredung der Parteien feststehe, 2) daß sie dem Gerichte als unverfälscht erscheinen, endlich 3) daß sie übereinstimmen.

Die Weigerung einer Partei, ihr Kerbholz vorzulegen, ist begründet, wenn sie nachweist, daß sie es ohne Verschulden nicht mehr besitzt.

2) Die Verfügung bezüglich der Denkmäler ꝛc. hat insofern Bedeutnng, als durch dieselbe die Verfügung, daß eine einzige Vermuthung keinen Beweis bilden dürfe, eine Ausnahme erleidet.

XI. Hauptstück.

Augenschein.

Zulässigkeit.

Art. 396. — **Das Gericht kann in jeder Lage des Rechtsstreits auf Antrag einer Partei oder von Amtswegen einen gerichtlichen Augenschein anordnen.**

Verfahren.

Art. 397. — **Ist der Augenschein am Gerichtssitze oder in dessen Nähe vorzunehmen, so kann die Vornahme durch das ganze Gericht geschehen. In diesem Falle ist Ort und Zeit des Augenscheins im Urtheile festzusetzen.**

Ist dagegen der Ort so weit entfernt, daß Reisekosten verursacht würden, oder ist eine ausgedehnte Zeugenvernehmung mit dem Augenscheine zu verbinden, so ist ein Gerichtsmitglied oder ein Einzelngericht mit der Vornahme zu beauftragen. In diesem Falle wird Ort und Zeit des Augenscheins auf das Gesuch der betreibenden Partei von dem beauftragten Richter bestimmt.

Art. 398. — **Der Vorsitzende oder beauftragte Richter hat über die streitigen Punkte die Parteien soweit nöthig zu vernehmen, die von ihnen vorgelegten Grundrisse und Zeichnungen mit dem Gegenstande des Augenscheins zu vergleichen und sie gegebenen Falls hienach zu berichtigen.**

Ist keine brauchbare Zeichnung vorgelegt, eine solche aber zum Verständnisse nöthig, so hat der Vorsitzende oder beauftragte Richter, falls Sachverständige zugezogen sind, durch diese eine Zeichnung anfertigen zu lassen, andernfalls eine solche selbst zu fertigen oder damit einen zu ernennenden Sachverständigen zu beauftragen.

Werden Sachverständige zu dem Augenscheine beigezogen oder ist mit diesem ein Zeugenverhör zu verbinden, so hat der Vorsitzende oder beauftragte Richter die Sachverständigen und Zeugen auf die Gegenstände der Untersuchung und Vernehmung aufmerksam zu machen.

In das über den Befund zu errichtende Protokoll sind die von den Parteien bei dem Augenscheine abgegebenen Erklärungen und gestellten Anträge aufzunehmen.

G. A. d. K. d. A. II S. 177. 178. 336. 337. IV S. 95. 98. — K. d. R. II S. 172—176. IV S. 46.

1) Unter richterlichem Augenscheine versteht man in weiterem Sinne die persönliche Einsicht, welche der Richter von den für den Rechtsstreit erheblichen Oertlichkeiten, Sachen, Urkunden (Art. 377) nimmt, in welchem Sinne derselbe auch in der Sitzung selbst stattfinden kann. Unsere Prozeßordnung hat jedoch in vorstehenden Artikeln zunächst nur die Besichtigung von Oertlichkeiten — die Ortsbesichtigung — im Auge, bei welcher selbstverständlich eine Beweisaufnahme in der Sitzung nicht wohl vorkommen kann.

2) Der Augenschein wirkt unmittelbar auf die Ueberzeugung des Richters, und ist mehr als jedes andere Beweismittel geeignet, diesen aufzuklären, und die Wahrheit zu Tage zu fördern, weßhalb er denn auch des Vorzuges genießt, in jeder Lage der Sache von Amtswegen angeordnet werden zu dürfen. Die Worte: „in jeder Lage des Rechtsstreites“ haben übrigens nicht ganz die Tragweite wie in Art. 276, denn ein Augenschein kann nur angeordnet werden, so lange es auf Beweisführung noch ankommt, also

z. B. nicht durch den obersten Gerichtshof und ebensowenig, wenn die Endentscheidung nur noch von einer Eidesleistung abhängt.

3) In der Regel wird der Augenschein nicht durch das ganze Gericht, sondern durch einen einzelnen Richter vorgenommen und es ist rathsam, einen Richter zu wählen, welcher beim Beweisurtheile mitgewirkt hat und auch bei der weiteren Verhandlung voraussichtlich mitwirken kann.

Das Verfahren richtet sich nach den allgemeinen Vorschriften des Hauptst. IX.

Es läßt also der betreibende Theil das Urtheil ausfertigen und zustellen (Art. 331); der beauftragte Richter setzt Tagfahrt fest, welche mit Einhaltung der in Art. 338 bestimmten Frist gleichfalls zuzustellen ist. Nach beendigtem Augenscheine wird die Sache in der durch Art. 344 Abs. 2 bezeichneten Weise (Auftrag auf die Wochentabelle, Wechseln motivirter Anträge in der bestimmten Frist) in die Sitzung gebracht.

4) Was den Augenschein selbst betrifft, so hat der Richter die Aufgabe, alle Punkte, welche für die Entscheidung der Sache von Erheblichkeit sein können, und welche sich oft erst durch Befragen der Parteien an Ort und Stelle klar herausstellen, soweit möglich festzustellen. Ortsbesichtigungen, welche mit Einsicht und Sorgfalt aufgenommen sind, tragen unter Umständen außerordentlich viel bei zur Herbeiführung einer schnellen und richtigen Entscheidung und zur Ersparung fernerer Beweiserhebungen.

Im Uebrigen ist auf die besonderen Vorschriften, welche Art. 398 gibt, hinzuweisen.

Das Protokoll ist nach Maßgabe der Art. 166 und 167 abzufassen.

5) Die Bestimmung, daß dem Gerichte gestattet sei, in Fällen wo keine Reisekosten (d. h. solche des Gerichts) verursacht werden, den Augenschein selbst vorzunehmen, ist eine sehr praktische Neuerung, welche jedoch nicht ganz so verwerthet ist, wie es hätte geschehen können.

Wie einfach und sachgemäß wäre es, wenn in solchen Fällen das Gericht mit der Tagfahrt zum Augenscheine zugleich den Tag der weiteren Verhandlung festsetzen würde und bestimmt wäre, daß der Spruch dieses Urtheils in Gegenwart der Parteien ebenso wie in Art. 252 als Zustellung und Vorladung gelte, daß endlich für die weitere Verhandlung Abs. 1 nicht aber Abs. 2 des Art. 344 maßgebend sei! Welchen Zweck hat z. B. die Ausfertigung und Zustellung des Beweisurtheiles hier, wo im Urtheile nichts weiter steht, als daß das Gericht es sachgemäß befunden habe, vor weiterer Entscheidung einen Augenschein anzuordnen?

Zwar wurde vom k. Minist.-Comm. (R. R. II 175) erwidert, ein solches Verfahren erscheine nicht ausgeschlossen, wenn beide Anwälte damit einverstanden seien, allein wollte man von der Voraussetzung ausgehen, es seien die Anwälte immer einverstanden zu thun und zu gestatten was sachgemäß sei, so wären die meisten Prozeßvorschriften füglich zu entbehren.

6) Die Leitung des Verfahrens beim Augenscheine und die Aufnahme desselben ist nach Art. 398 dem Vorsitzenden übertragen, welcher insbesondere auch allein den Sachverständigen zur Fertigung des etwa nöthigen Planes ernennt und beauftragt.

Folgerichtig ist auch die Abfassung des Protokolles Sache des Vorsitzenden. Natürlich sind aber die übrigen Gerichtsmitglieder nicht blos berechtigt, sondern auch verpflichtet, sachgemäß zur Aufklärung der Sache beizutragen (Art. 154), und haben dieselben, da hier nicht Art. 280, sondern Art. 166 Maß gibt, das Protokoll mitzuunterzeichnen. Bezüglich des Protokollsabschlusses vgl. die Bemerk. zu Art. 166—168 Nr. 5.

XII. Hauptstück.

Zeugen.

Allgemeine Bestimmungen.

Art. 399. — Zeugenbeweis ist nicht zulässig gegen den Inhalt einer Urkunde, welcher kraft gesetzlicher Bestimmung volle Beweiskraft beigemessen werden muß, und über Verabredungen, welche bei oder vor der Errichtung einer solchen Urkunde stattgefunden haben sollen.

Diese Bestimmung findet keine Anwendung auf die Anfechtung der Rechtsgeschäfte wegen Zwang, Betrug, Irrthum oder Simulation. Auch kann über die Behauptung, daß in einer öffentlichen Urkunde in Folge einer strafbaren Handlung des beurkundenden Beamten oder eines Dritten unrichtige Beurkundungen stattgefunden haben, Beweis durch Zeugen geführt werden.

G. A. d. K. d. A. II S. 317—319. 337. IV S. 95. 326—330.
K. d. R. II S. 177—205. IV S. 47—57.

1) Die Bestimmungen des Art. 399 sind das Einzige, was von den Bestrebungen, im Anschlusse an die Prinzipien des französischen Rechts den Zeugenbeweis zu beschränken, übrig geblieben

ist; übrigens würde man irren, wollte man annehmen, das, was dieser Artikel jetzt sagt, sei französisches Recht.

Letzteres Recht besteht für die Pfalz, wo Art. 399 nicht gilt (Einf.-Ges. Art. 66) noch fort, und ich halte es geeignet, zuerst einen Blick auf dasselbe zu werfen und dann die Erklärung von Art. 399 anzureihen.

Pfälzisches Recht.

2) In Art. 1341 Code civil ist bestimmt, daß gegen den Laut einer Urkunde Zeugenbeweis nicht statthaft sei, jedoch erleidet dieser Grundsatz Ausnahmen: 1) für Handelsachen (wenigstens nach der überwiegenden Meinung), 2) für Fälle, wo ein commencement de preuve par écrit vorliegt (Art. 1347), und 3) für Fälle, wo es unmöglich war, sich einen Urkundenbeweis zu verschaffen.

Die letztere Ausnahme wendet man an auf den Nachweis von Zwang, Betrug oder Irrthum, weil vernünftiger Weise nicht verlangt werden kann, es solle Jemand über einen Betrug oder Irrthum zum Voraus sich eine Urkunde verschaffen. Sie findet ferner Anwendung auf Fälle, wo die Urkunde im Sinne, wie zu Art. 376—383 Nr. 1 bemerkt, civilrechtlich falsch sein soll, d. h. wo bewiesen werden will, es sei etwas ohne Wissen und Willen eines Contrahenten in dieselbe gekommen. (Vgl. Art. 232 Code de proc.)

Die Simulation kann jedoch einer Urkunde gegenüber nie durch Zeugen erwiesen werden, denn wer freiwillig etwas Wahrheitswidriges verbrieft, kann nicht behaupten, es sei ihm unmöglich gewesen, sich einen Urkundenbeweis zu verschaffen.

3) Es ergibt sich hieraus, daß auch nach französischem Rechte der Nachweis, es sei eine Urkunde wahrheitswidrig aufgenommen, prinzipiell betrachtet, ziemlich frei und unbehindert ist.

Eine sehr wirksame thatsächliche Beschränkung liegt jedoch darin, daß derjenige, welcher eine Urkunde als falsch angreift, sich dem umständlichen formenreichen Verfahren unterwerfen muß, wie es die Art. 214—251 Code de proc. vorschreiben, namentlich aber, daß jeder Angriff, welcher nicht durchdringt, mit einer Geldstrafe von mindestens 300 Franken geahndet wird.

Das Fälschungsverfahren des Code de proc. ist nun für die Pfalz beseitigt und das neue Verfahren, wie es die Art. 376—385 der P. O. regeln, hat wenig Abschreckendes mehr; dennoch bestehen die Prinzipien, nach welchen sich die Zulässigkeit des Zeugenbeweises zum Nachweise der Falschheit einer Urkunde bestimmt, im Sinne des französischen Rechtes unverändert fort!

4) Was den Zeugenbeweis in Handelssachen betrifft, so möchte es sachgemäß sein, eine allgemeine Erörterung hier anzufügen.

Für dessen Zulässigkeit ist jetzt Art. 80 des Einf.-Ges. zum Handelsgesetzbuche maßgebend. Im Hinblicke auf Art. 63 und 64 jenes Gesetzes wird nun kein Zweifel bestehen dürfen, daß auch Rechtsgeschäfte, welche nur einem der Contrahenten gegenüber Handelsgeschäfte sind (Art. 277 des H. G. B.), als Handelssachen im Sinne des Art. 80 cit. zu betrachten seien, daß es also bezüglich der Zulässigkeit des Zeugenbeweises keinen Unterschied begründe, ob gegen den Kaufmann oder gegen den Nichtkaufmann geklagt, ob der Streit vor dem Handelsgerichte oder vor dem Civilgerichte geführt werde.

Eine Unterscheidung, gemäß deren das nemliche Geschäft, je nach der Art und Weise, wie es zur Beurtheilung der Gerichte gebracht wird, durch Zeugen erwiesen werden könnte oder nicht, wäre entschieden gegen Willen und Geist des Gesetzes. Vgl. Bemerk. zu Art. 360. 365 Nr. 10.

Diesseitiges Recht.

5) Art. 399 weicht vom französischen Rechte in doppelter Richtung ab. Er dehnt einerseits die Zulässigkeit des Zeugenbeweises aus, indem er ihn zuläßt 1) bei Verabredungen, welche nach der Errichtung der Urkunden stattgefunden haben sollen, 2) bezüglich der Simulation; er schränkt ihn jedoch anderseits ein, indem keine Ausnahme mehr besteht 1) für den Anfang eines Schriftbeweises, 2) für Handelssachen, 3) für den Nachweis der Unrichtigkeit einer öffentlichen Urkunde, wenn sie nicht Folge einer strafbaren Handlung ist.

6) Vor Allem ist hervorzuheben, daß der bevorzugte Schutz nur solchen Urkunden gegeben ist, welchen volle Beweiskraft beigemessen werden muß, nicht aber solchen, bei denen es im Ermessen des Richters liegt, sie vollbeweisend gelten zu lassen. Gegen letztere ist der Zeugenbeweis unbeschränkt gestattet.

Ferner ist zu beachten, daß beim Nachweise der Aufhebung oder Abänderung eines beurkundeten Rechtsgeschäftes der Zeugenbeweis nicht beschränkt ist.

Selbst bei Nebenabreden, welche vor oder bei Errichtung einer Urkunde stattfinden, ist der Zeugenbeweis nur in so fern ausgeschlossen, als sie im Widerspruch mit derselben stehen, als dargethan werden will, es sei etwas Anderes verabredet als verbrieft. Ist der Sinn einer Urkunde zweideutig, so muß, so weit es zur Hebung dieser Zweideutigkeit nöthig ist, Beweis durch Vermuthungen und Zeugen gestattet sein;

denn es läßt sich nicht behaupten, ein solcher Beweis sei gegen den Inhalt der Urkunde gerichtet. Die französische Jurisprudenz hat nie bezweifelt, daß der Interpretationsbeweis zur Ermittlung des Sinnes einer unklaren Urkunde durch Zeugen und Vermuthungen geführt werden dürfe, selbst in Fällen, wo das Rechtsgeschäft selbst gar nicht durch Zeugen bewiesen werden könnte.

7) Die Ausnahme, welche das Gesetz für die Anfechtung von Rechtsgeschäften wegen Zwang, Betrug, Irrthum und Simulation macht, bedarf einer eingehenderen Besprechung.

Wie schon zu Art. 373 Nr. 4 angeführt, ist es nicht gleichbedeutend, ob von Anfechtung von Rechtsgeschäften oder von Anfechtung von Urkunden die Rede ist, ob bewiesen werden soll, daß ein Rechtsgeschäft als auf Betrug oder Irrthum beruhend der Rescission unterliege, oder aber, daß die Ausstellung einer Urkunde durch Betrug erwirkt, unter dem Einflusse eines Irrthums erfolgt sei.

Man könnte nun behaupten, daß vorliegende Bestimmung streng auf die Anfechtung der Rechtsgeschäfte zu beschränken sei, und ließe sich für diese Ansicht anführen: 1) der Wortlaut des Gesetzes, 2) der Gegensatz in der Fassung des Art. 373 und 3) der Umstand, daß die Schlußworte von Abs. 2 für die Anfechtung von Urkunden wegen unrichtiger Beurkundung besondere Bestimmungen geben.

Diese Auffassung würde jedoch zu einem so verkehrten Resultate führen, daß nicht angenommen werden darf, es entspreche dieselbe dem Willen des Gesetzgebers. Würde nemlich Jemand behaupten, es sei eine Urkunde mit seinem Wissen und Willen wahrheitswidrig gefertigt, d. h. sie sei simulirt, so dürfte er den Beweis durch Zeugen führen, würde er aber behaupten, es sei der wahrheitswidrige Inhalt ohne sein Wissen und seinen Willen in die Urkunde gekommen, so wäre der Zeugenbeweis ausgeschlossen! — Je größer die eigene Verschuldung, desto leichter der Beweis!

8) Verfolgt man die Geschichte der Entstehung des Art. 399, so wird klar, daß in der That der Gesetzgeber von einer anderen Anschauung ausgegangen ist.

In Art. 374 des Entwurfes war, ganz im Einklange mit den Prinzipien des französischen Rechtes, eine allgemeine, alle Beschränkungen des Zeugenbeweises umfassende Ausnahme gemacht für den Fall, wo es unmöglich ist, sich schriftlichen Beweis zu verschaffen, und wurde zur näheren Erläuterung des Sinnes, welchen das Gesetz hier mit „Unmöglichkeit" verbinde, unter Ziff. 4 auch die Anfechtung von Rechtsgeschäften wegen Zwang, Betrug und Irrthum, Simulation und Fälschung aufgeführt. Es ist klar, daß man hier das Wort „Rechtsgeschäfte" in sehr weitem Sinne nahm und darunter auch die über die Rechtsgeschäfte abgefaßten Urkunden begriff, denn sonst hätte man unmöglich von einer Anfechtung wegen Fälschung sprechen können.

Nachdem von den beabsichtigten Beschränkungen des Zeugenbeweises nur die einzige, den Beweis gegen den Inhalt von Urkunden betreffende aufrecht erhalten wurde, fügte man derselben die Ausnahme der Ziff. 4 in unveränderter Fassung bei, strich jedoch die Fälschung und machte bezüglich derselben später einen besonderen Zusatz.

Es erscheint mir nun außer Zweifel, daß am Sinne fraglicher Ausnahme sich hierdurch nichts Wesentliches geändert hat.

Nach wie vor wird für die Erklärung des Gesetzes maßgebend sein, daß fragliche Ausnahme nur der Ausfluß eines allgemeinen Grundsatzes ist, wonach Zeugenbeweis nicht versagt werden darf, wenn es nicht möglich war, sich einen Urkundenbeweis zu verschaffen. Eine solche Unmöglichkeit ist aber überall gegeben, wo es sich um Zwang, Betrug oder Irrthum handelt, mögen diese Anfechtungsgründe auftreten wo und wie sie wollen.

Ferner ist von Belang, daß die Anfechtung wegen Simulation, welche stehen blieb, sich ihrer Natur nach direkt gegen die Urkunde richtet, denn die Simulation besteht ja gerade darin, daß über ein Rechtsgeschäft, welches gar nicht besteht, also auch nicht angefochten zu werden braucht, eine Urkunde errichtet wurde, welche ihm den Schein des Bestehens gibt.

Der Umstand, daß die Fälschung beseitigt wurde, erscheint näher betrachtet ohne Belang, denn die an die Stelle getretene Verfügung sieht nur den Fall der Anfechtung einer öffentlichen Urkunde vor, und gerade hieraus läßt sich folgern, daß bei Privaturkunden ein Unterschied zwischen Anfechtung der Rechtsgeschäfte und der Urkunden nicht gemacht werden wollte. Bei diesen letzteren Urkunden läßt sich die Anfechtung der Urkunde, im weiteren Sinne auch als eine Anfechtung des Rechtsgeschäftes selbst, in der Art wie es von den Contrahenten beurkundet worden ist, auffassen.

9) Daß das Gesetz, im Widerspruche mit dem französischen Rechte, auch den Fall der Simulation ausnimmt, erscheint im Grunde als eine Inconsequenz, denn wer einen Scheinakt

errichtet, kann offenbar nicht vorschützen, er habe sich keinen Schriftenbeweis verschaffen können. Es lag bloß an ihm, den Scheinakt nicht zu machen oder sich einen Gegenschein ausstellen zu lassen. Zudem ist nicht einzusehen, warum Scheinakte, welchen immer der Zweck einer Täuschung, sei es auch nur des Aerars, zu Grunde liegt, besonders begünstigt werden sollen. Vgl. die Bemerk. R. R. II 202. 203 (v. Bomhard).

Simulation ist gegeben, so oft absichtlich etwas beurkundet wird, was dem Willen der Contrahenten nicht entspricht.

Sie kann sich auf den Inhalt der Urkunde im Ganzen erstrecken oder nur auf Theile derselben, in welch letzterem Falle als Grundsatz gilt: »plus valet quod agitur, quam quod simulate concipitur.« Die abweichende Ansicht, welche der k. Minist.-Commissär (R. R. II 203) ausgesprochen hat, kann wohl nicht Anspruch darauf machen, maßgebend zu sein.

10) Die Schlußbestimmung, daß unrichtige Beurkundungen in öffentlichen Urkunden nur dann durch Zeugen erwiesen werden dürfen, wenn eine strafbare Handlung vorliegt, enthält, wie oben Nr. 1 u. 2 bemerkt, eine Beschränkung der Prinzipien des französischen Rechts, zu deren Rechtfertigung sich darauf hinweisen läßt, daß die Prozeßordnung die Fälschungsklage, was Formen und Strafe anbelangt, in so hohem Maße erleichtert hat.

Der Ausdruck „strafbare Handlung" ist jedenfalls in möglichst weitem Sinne zu nehmen, und sind namentlich auch disziplinäre Maßnahmen darunter begriffen, dies um so zweifelloser, als bei Einführung der fraglichen Schlußbestimmung ihr Sinn in dieser Weise näher erläutert worden ist. (Abg. II 337 Sp. 2). Da nicht leicht eine wahrheitswidrige Beurkundung in einer öffentlichen Urkunde vorkommen kann, ohne daß den Beamten eine disziplinär zu ahndende Verschuldung trifft, so wird allerdings hiermit die Ausnahme zur Regel gemacht.

11) Ohne Zweifel verlangt das Gesetz auch nicht, daß vorher vom Strafgerichte oder der Disziplinarbehörde die Strafbarkeit anerkannt worden sei, was in Fällen, wo Verjährung, Todesfall ꝛc. der Einschreitung im Wege stehen, gar nicht möglich sein würde, vielmehr ist das Prozeßgericht befugt, diese Vorfrage selbst zu prüfen und zu entscheiden.

Am besten wäre es wohl gewesen, der Wahrheit in keinem Falle den Weg zu verschließen, jedoch durch strengere Strafen vor frivolen Anfechtungen abzuschrecken.

12) Was schließlich die Handelssachen betrifft, so macht das Gesetz für dieselben keine Ausnahme und es muß also wohl Art. 399 maßgebend sein (Art. 524). Vgl. Bemerk. zu Art. 358 Nr. 12. — Art. 317 des H. G. B. steht hier nicht im Wege.

Art. 400. — **Untüchtige Zeugen und als solche von Amtswegen zu verwerfen sind:**

1) **Geistliche in Ansehung dessen, was ihnen in der Beichte oder bei Ausübung der Seelsorge im Vertrauen auf die ihnen obliegende Pflicht zur Verschwiegenheit mitgetheilt wurde;**

2) **öffentliche Beamte, welche durch ihre Aussage eine amtliche Verpflichtung zur Verschwiegenheit verletzen würden, soferne sie nicht von der betreffenden Behörde nach Maßgabe der hierüber im Verordnungswege zu erlassenden Bestimmungen zur Vernehmlassung ermächtigt sind;**

3) **Personen, welchen in Folge ihres Amts, Stands oder Gewerbs Geheimnisse anvertraut sind, deren Offenbarung ihnen durch die Strafgesetze verboten ist, in Ansehung der Thatsachen, auf welche diese Verpflichtung sich bezieht, und soferne nicht die Enthebung von der Pflicht zur Verschwiegenheit durch die Betheiligten erfolgt ist.**

Art. 401. — **Das Zeugniß darf verweigert werden:**

1) **wenn der Zeuge nach Art. 400 wegen Untüchtigkeit von der Zeugschaft befreit ist;**

2) **wenn der Zeuge der wirkliche oder gewesene Ehegatte eines der Streitstheile ist oder zu einem derselben in gerader Linie oder in der Seitenlinie bis einschlüssig zum dritten Grade nach bürgerlicher Berechnung verwandt oder verschwägert ist oder zu einem der Streitstheile im Pflegschaftsverhältnisse steht;**

3) **über Fragen, deren bejahende oder verneinende Beantwortung dem Zeugen oder einem seiner in Ziff. 2 bezeichneten Angehörigen Schande oder erheblichen Nachtheil bringen würde.**

G. A. d. K. d. A. II S. 215. 216. 221. 224. 228—232. 337 338. IV S. 96.
K. d. R. II S. 205—208. 210. 211. IV S. 57.

1) Nach dem Entwurfe und nach den Verhandlungen erster Lesung sollten unterschieden werden: 1) Fälle, in welchen der Zeuge aus Gründen der öffentlichen Ordnung zurückzuweisen

ist (Untüchtigkeit), 2) Fälle, in welchen er auf Verlangen des Gegners verworfen werden muß (Verwerflichkeit), und 3) Fälle, wo er selbst seine Zeugschaft ablehnen kann (Verweigerungsrecht).

Bei zweiter Lesung hielt man es geeignet, die Fälle zweiter Art ganz zu beseitigen und dem Richter die freie Würdigung zu überlassen, ob und wie viel Glauben er dem verdächtigen Zeugen schenken wolle.

Für die Pfalz ist dies ein Sprung von einem Extreme ins andere und es möchte sehr fraglich sein, ob es gut gewesen, so weit zu gehen. Aus der dem Richter gelassenen Freiheit fürchte ich nichts, im Gegentheile, ich hätte gewünscht, es wäre demselben consequenter Weise auch sonst mehr Vertrauen geschenkt worden (Bemerk. zu Art. 322 und 382 Nr. 11); allein ich fürchte, daß die Zulassung der nächsten Verwandten, der Ehegatten, der unmittelbaren Mitbetheiligten zur Zeugschaft zu Meineiden verleiten, daß sie der Moral viel mehr schaden, als der Rechtsprechung nützen werde.

Das durch Art. 401 gegebene Recht der Zeugschaftsverweigerung erscheint ungenügend, denn wie natürlich, denkt jeder derartige Zeuge, aus seiner Weigerung werde man folgern, daß er nur Schlimmes, nichts Günstiges für den Beweisführer auszusagen habe und schon dieser Gedanke, mag er richtig sein oder nicht, wird Viele bestimmen, ihr Zeugniß nicht zu verweigern, sondern zur Verdeckung der Wahrheit und Trübung des Sachverhaltes ihr Schärflein beizutragen.

a) Untüchtigkeit.

2) Untüchtige Zeugen dürfen vom Richter nicht vernommen werden, auch wenn sie selbst keinen Einwand erheben und keine der Parteien sich der Vernehmung widersetzt. Rücksichten der öffentlichen Ordnung sind es, welche hier eine Verwerfung von Amtswegen geboten erscheinen lassen.

Uebrigens versteht sich von selbst, daß der Richter von diesem Rechte der Zurückweisung nur mit größter Vorsicht Gebrauch machen und es bloß dann üben dürfe, wenn klar vor Augen liegt, daß einer der Fälle des Art. 400 vorliege, daß er durch die Vernehmung des Zeugen einer pflichtwidrigen oder strafbaren Handlung Vorschub leisten würde.

3) Untüchtig sind 1) Geistliche bezüglich dessen was ihnen in der Beichte oder bei Ausübung der Seelsorge, im Vertrauen auf ihre Pflicht zur Verschwiegenheit mitgetheilt wurde. Nicht jede vertrauliche Mittheilung an einen Geistlichen steht unter dem Schutze dieser Bestimmung, sondern nur diejenige, bei welcher der Geistliche in Ausübung der Seelsorge begriffen war, d. h. welche geschah, um von ihm geistlichen Trost und Beruhigung des Gewissens zu erlangen.

Man sollte denken, die Pflicht der Geheimhaltung und mit derselben auch die Verwerfung von Amtswegen falle hinweg, wenn diejenige Person, welche das Geheimniß mittheilte, selbst den Geistlichen ermächtigt, als Zeuge auszusagen; allein es ist zu bemerken, daß Völk den Antrag gestellt hatte, in dieser Beziehung zwischen den unter dem Siegel der Beichte und den sonst anvertrauten Geheimnissen zu unterscheiden, dieser Antrag jedoch verworfen worden ist. Abg. II 228—230.

4) Untüchtig sind 2) öffentliche Beamte, welche die Pflicht der Amtsverschwiegenheit verletzen würden (Art. 365 u. 396 des St. G. B.), jedoch nur, falls sie nicht von der zuständigen vorgesetzten Behörde von dieser Pflicht entbunden worden sind. (Vgl. Art. 411 u. 429.)

Der Umstand, daß das Gesetz eine Ermächtigung der vorgesetzten Behörde für genügend erklärt, um die Untüchtigkeit zu beseitigen, deutet schon an, daß es sich hier nur um solche Amtsgeheimnisse handelt, bei deren Verletzung öffentliche Interessen betheiligt sind und deßhalb ist auch der Ausdruck „Beamte“ im engeren Sinne zu nehmen. Namentlich können Notare nicht darunter begriffen werden, obgleich Art. 46 des Not.-Ges. sie ausdrücklich zum Amtsgeheimnisse verpflichtet; sie fallen vielmehr, wie die Geschichte der Entstehung des Art. 400 außer Zweifel setzt, unter die Bestimmungen von Ziff. 3. Vgl. Abg. II 231 a. E. und II 338.

5) Untüchtig sind 3) alle Personen, welche durch Mittheilung von Thatsachen, deren Geheimhaltung ihnen im Interesse von Privatpersonen geboten ist, sich einer strafbaren Handlung schuldig machen würden.

Es sind in dieser Beziehung die Art. 338, 339, 365 u. 396 des St.G.B. und das Ges. v. 28. Mai 1870 maßgebend. Art. 338 erklärt Jeden strafbar, welcher unbefugt fremde Handels-, Fabrik- oder Gewerbs-Geheimnisse, deren Kenntniß er vermöge seines Berufes oder durch rechtswidrige Mittel erlangte, mittheilt; Art. 339 droht Strafe für Anwälte, Vertheidiger in Strafsachen, Aerzte, Hebammen, Apotheker und deren Gehülfen, sowie die zu niederen ärztlichen Dienstleistungen berufenen Personen, welche Geheimnisse, zu deren Kenntniß sie vermöge ihres Berufes oder Gewerbes gelangten, verrathen; die übrigen Gesetzesstellen endlich finden Anwendung auf Notare und Gerichtsvollzieher, welche mit Verletzung ihrer Amtspflicht Thatsachen mittheilen.

6) Die Untüchtigkeit ist auch hier keine absolute, fällt vielmehr weg, wenn die Betheiligten einwilligen.

Betheiligte sind diejenigen Personen, welchen das Geheimniß angehört, wer diese aber seien, beurtheilt sich nach den besonderen Verhältnissen des Falles.

Nicht immer ist derjenige der Betheiligte, welcher das Geheimniß anvertraut hat, denn was z. B. der Vormund im Prozesse des Mündels dem Anwalte anvertraute, ist nicht sein, sondern seines Mündels Geheimniß, und er selbst könnte nach beendigter Vormundschaft nicht darüber verfügen, noch weniger seine Erben.

Es kann ein Geheimniß auch mehreren Personen angehören und dann ist in der Regel die Einwilligung aller Betheiligten nöthig.

Was die Notare und Gerichtsvollzieher betrifft, so sind für sie die Bestimmungen des Notariatsgesetzes und der Gerichtsvollzieherordnung insofern maßgebend, als dort nähere Vorschriften darüber gegeben sind, welche Mittheilungen eine Verletzung der Amtspflicht enthalten. Ueber einen vollständig abgeschlossenen Notariatsakt z. B., so wie über alles, was unmittelbar damit zusammenhängt, darf der Notar auf Ermächtigung eines einzelnen, wenn auch noch so gering Betheiligten Mittheilungen machen (Art. 93). Vgl. im Uebrigen Zink's Comment. zum N.G. S. 191 (Note 52) u. S. 376 (Nr. 24).

7) Im früheren Rechte gab es noch manche andere Untüchtigkeitsgründe, welche unbeachtet geblieben sind.

Zunächst fällt es auf, daß der Gesetzgeber die eigene Betheiligung des Zeugen, mag sie noch so stark und unmittelbar sein, ganz unberücksichtigt läßt. Es kann daher vorkommen, daß der belangte Schuldner einen solidarischen Mitschuldner oder Bürgen als Zeugen für die erfolgte Zahlung der Schuld beeidigen und verhören läßt. Uebrigens wird dennoch eine durch das Wesen der Zeugschaft bedingte natürliche Gränze zu ziehen sein und wird man sich auf die Freiheit, welche das Gesetz gibt, nicht berufen dürfen, um Personen, welche förmlich Partei im Rechtsstreite sind, als Zeugen zu benützen.

Die Rolle einer Partei und eines Zeugen sind unvereinbar, wenn sie bei dem nemlichen Streitpunkte zusammentreffen. Partei ist Jeder, der als solche zum Rechtsstreite beigeladen ist und dessen Erklärungen als Parteierklärungen maßgebend sind, insbesondere Jeder, welcher in die Lage kommen kann, im nemlichen Rechtsstreite wegen der betreffenden Thatsachen einen Parteieid zu leisten.

Deßhalb kann eine Person, welche als gesetzlicher Vertreter einer Partei im Prozesse auftritt, nicht für oder gegen sie als Zeuge benützt werden. In gleicher Weise werden Streitgenossen oder Beigeladene, bezüglich derjenigen Thatsachen, welche ihnen selbst gegenüber sahentscheidend sind, nicht als Zeugen benützt werden dürfen.

Uebrigens ist der Umstand, daß Jemand als Partei in einen Prozeß gezogen wurde, für sich allein kein Grund, ihn als Zeugen unmöglich zu machen, denn es können Thatsachen zum Beweise kommen, welche ihm ganz fremd sind, bei denen er wenigstens nicht in die Lage kommen kann, sich zum Vortheile etwas zu bezeugen. Falls z. B. mehrere Miterben belangt sind und der eine behauptet, er habe seinen Theil bezahlt, so kann über diese Thatsache der Streitgenosse füglich als Zeuge vernommen werden, nicht aber wenn es sich darum handelt, ob die Forderung überhaupt bestehe. So kann ferner, wenn Mehrere als mithaftbar wegen eines zugefügten Schadens belangt werden, ein Streitgenosse vom anderen als Zeuge darüber benützt werden, daß er nicht betheiligt gewesen sei. Seuffert Archiv Bd. XVII Nr. 168; vgl. Bd. III. Nr. 212. Noch weniger kann es Anstand finden, Jemanden als Zeugen zu laden, welcher zwar früher im Prozesse gewesen, jedoch an demselben nicht mehr betheiligt ist.

8) Als untüchtig wollte man ursprünglich auch Personen erklären, welche körperlich oder geistig unfähig waren, Wahrnehmungen zu machen oder unfähig sind, sie mitzutheilen; allein die Subkommission meinte, daß für dergleichen Fälle eine besondere Vorschrift nicht nöthig sei.

Was die Unfähigkeit zur Zeit der Wahrnehmung selbst betrifft, so ist es sonderbar, hieraus einen Grund zur Untüchtigkeit zu machen; ebensogut könnte man sagen, ein Zeuge sei untüchtig, wenn er von der Sache nichts wisse.

Was die Unfähigkeit zur Zeit der Vernehmung betrifft, so ist es selbstverständlich und liegt dem Gesagten gemäß im Willen des Gesetzes, daß der Richter einen Zeugen zurückweisen müsse, welcher im Augenblicke, wo er vernommen werden soll, nicht zurechnungsfähig ist. Ist dies Folge einer Verschuldung des Zeugen, z. B. der Betrunkenheit, so wird er als nichterschienener Zeuge zu behandeln sein (Art. 427).

b) Zeugschaftsverweigerung.

9) Daß untüchtige Zeugen ihre Zeugschaft verweigern dürfen, ist selbstverständlich, dennoch

mag die betreffende Bestimmung in so fern nicht ganz überflüssig sein, als in Art. 431 für die Fälle, wo die Zeugschaft verweigert wird, der Beweis der Untüchtigkeit besonders geregelt wird.

Was die Fälle von Art. 401 Ziff. 2 betrifft, so hat man die Fassung absichtlich den Bestimmungen der Art. 40 und 201 angepaßt und gelten daher die dort gegebenen Erläuterungen auch hier.

Wenn hier von Pflegschaftsverhältnissen überhaupt, nicht aber blos von Pflegbefohlenen die Sprache ist, wie in Art. 40 und 201, so liegt der Grund darin, daß man dachte, es habe auch derjenige, welchem die Pflege anvertraut ist, in Betracht zu kommen. Jedenfalls ist sicher, daß unter Pflegschaft hier nichts anderes verstanden wird als in jenen Artikeln, denn im Entwurfe und Referate war dieses Verhältniß gar nicht berührt und kam später nur deßhalb ins Gesetz, um den Einklang mit besagten beiden Artikeln herzustellen.

10) Schließlich gibt das Gesetz dem Zeugen das Recht, über einzelne Fragen die Antwort zu verweigern, wenn deren Bejahung oder Verneinung ihm oder seinen in Ziff. 2 bezeichneten Angehörigen Schande oder erheblichen Nachtheil bringen würde.

Es muß sich um eine wirkliche Schande, nicht aber um bloße Unannehmlichkeit handeln und die Vermögensnachtheile müssen erheblich sein, wenn die Verweigerung begründet sein soll. Ob diese Voraussetzungen gegeben, ob insbesondere der Nachtheil im Sinne des Gesetzes als ein erheblicher zu betrachten sei, hat das Gericht zu würdigen. Vgl. die Bemerk. zu Art. 431 Nr. 1.

Anordnung des Zeugenverhörs.

Art. 402. — **Soweit das Gesetz nicht anders bestimmt, hat die Vernehmung der Zeugen in der Sitzung stattzufinden. In diesem Falle ist in dem Urtheile, welches den Zeugenbeweis anordnet, zugleich der Sitzungstag festzusetzen.**

Art. 403. — **Die Vernehmung der Mitglieder des königlichen Hauses richtet sich nach den Bestimmungen des Familienstatuts.**

Art. 404. — **Zeugen, die wegen Krankheit oder Gebrechlichkeit bei Gericht nicht erscheinen können, sind durch einen beauftragten Richter in ihrer Wohnung zu vernehmen.**

Zeugen, welche eine zum Armenrechte gelassene Partei vernehmen lassen will, sind in der Regel durch das Einzelngericht ihres Wohnorts zu vernehmen, wenn der Sitz desselben diesem näher ist, als der des Prozeßgerichts.

Der mit einem Augenscheine beauftragte Richter hat auch die damit verbundenen Zeugenverhöre vorzunehmen.

Art. 405. — **Das Gericht kann die Vernehmung aller oder einzelner Zeugen einem beauftragten Richter ausnahmsweise auch deshalb übertragen, weil nach der Beschaffenheit der zu beweisenden Thatsachen und den Erklärungen der Parteien anzunehmen ist, daß die Vernehmung der Zeugen durch das Gericht mehrere Sitzungstage in Anspruch nehmen würde, oder weil sonst besondere Hindernisse ihr entgegenstehen.**

G. A. d. K. d. A. II S. 209—211. 338. 339. IV S. 96. — K. d. R. II S. 212. 213. IV S. 57.

1) Diese Artikel enthalten nur die besondere Anwendung der in Art. 334 gegebenen allgemeinen Vorschriften.

Regel soll sein die Vernehmung der Zeugen in der Sitzung, ausnahmsweise jedoch darf auch ein Richter beauftragt werden, wenn die Vernehmung voraussichtlich mehr als einen Sitzungstag in Anspruch nehmen würde oder wenn sonstige besondere Hindernisse im Wege stehen (Art. 405).

Ob zu befürchten sei, daß mehr als ein Sitzungstag beansprucht werde, wie lang ein Sitzungstag sei, welche Hindernisse genügen, um von der Regel abzuweichen — all dies ist dem richterlichen Ermessen überlassen, so daß es sich also nicht sowohl um eine bindende Vorschrift, als um einen, allerdings entschieden ausgesprochenen, Wunsch des Gesetzgebers handelt.

Trügt meine Ahnung nicht, so werden die Gerichte sehr geneigt sein, die Ausnahme zur Regel zu machen und in allen der Berufung unterliegenden Streitsachen einen Richter zu beauftragen, denn bei der Unbeschränktheit des Zeugenbeweises, wie sie diesseits besteht, müßte die Geschäftslast der Gerichte erster Instanz eine erdrückende werden, wenn alle Zeugenverhöre in der Sitzung abgehalten und protokollirt werden müßten. Sogar in der Pfalz, wo seither nur 10—20 ordinäre Zeugenverhöre an jedem Bezirksgerichte jährlich vorkamen, würde dies nicht thunlich sein. Zudem würde die Zeit der Anwälte in ungewöhnlicher und für ihre sonstigen Dienstgeschäfte nachtheiliger

Weise in Anspruch genommen, da sie bei Zeugenverhören in der Sitzung persönlich zugegen sein müssen, während bei Zeugenverhören außer der Sitzung die Parteien durch einen Anwaltsgehilfen verbeistandet werden können.

2) Wenn in Art. 404 und 405 vom „beauftragten Richter" die Rede ist, so darf man hieraus im Zusammenhalte mit Art. 407 nicht etwa folgern, daß bei Zeugenverhören immer zunächst ein Mitglied des Prozeßgerichtes zu beauftragen sei, von welchem dann die weiteren Aufträge an Einzelrichter und die Ersuchen an auswärtige Gerichte auszugehen hätten, vielmehr sind auch hier die allgemeinen Prinzipien (Art. 334) maßgebend. Vgl. Art. 341, 342.

3) Für Zeugenverhöre, welche sachentsprechend nur stattfinden können, nachdem der Richter selbst, sowie die Zeugen vorher die Oertlichkeiten besichtigt haben, und von den Parteien auf die erheblichen Punkte aufmerksam gemacht worden sind, ergibt sich die Zweckmäßigkeit, ja Nothwendigkeit der Beauftragung eines Richters von selbst, sofern nicht ausnahmsweise das ganze Gericht den Augenschein vornimmt. Deßhalb verfügt denn auch Art. 404 Abs. 3, daß überall, wo die Zeugenvernehmung mit einem Augenscheine verbunden sei, dieselbe durch einen beauftragten Richter und zwar den nemlichen, welcher auch den Augenschein vornimmt, zu geschehen habe.

Weitere Ausnahmen macht Art. 404 für Kranke oder Gebrechliche, welche in ihrer Wohnung zu vernehmen sind (was übrigens nach Art. 405 selbstverständlich gewesen wäre), sowie für Zeugen, welche eine zum Armenrechte zugelassene Partei vernehmen läßt. Bei Letzterer ist bloß die Rücksicht der Kostenersparung maßgebend, und falls diese nicht eintritt oder andere Rücksichten überwiegen, bleibt es daher bei der Regel.

4) Die Vernehmung der Mitglieder des königlichen Hauses richtet sich nach den Bestimmungen des jeweils geltenden Familienstatuts. Das jetzt giltige Familienstatut vom 5. August 1819 schreibt in Tit. X § 3 vor, daß die Vernehmung durch einen Präsidenten des Oberappellationsgerichts, also jetzt des obersten Gerichtshofes, zu erfolgen habe und dem einschlägigen Gerichte mitzutheilen sei.

Eine Beiziehung der Parteien ist im Sinne fraglicher Bestimmung ausgeschlossen. Referat zu Art. 378 (v. Neumayr).

Art. 406. — **Soll das Zeugenverhör nicht in der Sitzung geschehen, so ist im Urtheile zugleich die Frist festzusetzen, innerhalb welcher die beweisführende Partei den beauftragten Richter um Festsetzung der Tagfahrt zur Vernehmung der Zeugen zu ersuchen hat. Die Frist läuft von der Zustellung des Urtheils an und gilt, soferne das Gericht nicht anders verfügt, auch für die Gegenpartei bezüglich des ihr gesetzlich zustehenden Gegenbeweises.**

Dem schriftlich zu stellenden Gesuche ist die Ausfertigung oder zugestellte Abschrift des Urtheils beizufügen und sind in dem Gesuche, soweit thunlich, die Zeugen nach Namen, Stand oder Gewerbe und Wohnort anzugeben.

Der beauftragte Richter hat auch ein nach Ablauf der Frist gestelltes Gesuch dann zu berücksichtigen, wenn die Einwilligung der Gegenpartei beigebracht ist.

Alle von einem beauftragten Richter in derselben Sache vorzunehmenden Zeugenverhöre sind möglichst zu der nämlichen Tagfahrt zu verweisen.

Art. 407. — **Der beauftragte Richter kann, wenn besondere Gründe es angemessen erscheinen lassen, die Vernehmung entfernt wohnender oder am Erscheinen verhinderter Zeugen weiter dem betreffenden Einzelngerichte übertragen, sowie gegebenen Falls die Beweisaufnahme im Auslande (Art. 335) beschließen.**

Im einen wie im andern Falle hat er die Festsetzung der Tagfahrt zu veranlassen und von letzterer dem betreibenden Anwalte behufs der Kundmachung an die Gegenpartei und der Zeugenvorladung Kenntniß zu geben.

Art. 408. — **Sind theils in der Sitzung, theils außerhalb derselben Zeugen zu vernehmen, so haben soviel als möglich die außerhalb stattfindenden Vernehmungen den übrigen dergestalt vorauszugehen, daß bei letztern die betreffenden Protokolle benützt werden können.**

G. A. d. K. d. A. II S. 209—212. 339. 452. IV S. 96. — K. d. R. II S. 213. IV S. 57.

1) Die Vorschrift, daß binnen bestimmter Frist von Zustellung des Urtheils an, bei Strafe des Ausschlusses, das Gesuch um Festsetzung der Tagfahrt zur Zeugenvernehmung eingereicht sein müsse, ist dem französischen Prozesse (Code de proc. Art. 256—259) entlehnt.

Es wäre unrichtig, wollte man sagen, es sei diese Frist zur Antretung des Beweises gegeben, denn die Beweisantretung erfolgt erst mit der Benennung der Zeugen gemäß Art. 412; es läßt sich dieselbe daher nur als eine Frist zum Beginne des Beweisverfahrens bezeichnen.

Zweck derselben ist, den Beweisführer zur raschen Betreibung zu nöthigen, wie denn alle Verfügungen des französischen Gesetzgebers darauf zielen, eine möglichst rasche Beendigung der Beweisaufnahme beim Zeugenbeweise herbeizuführen, um Einwirkungen auf die Zeugen und künstliche Vorbereitung von Beweisen zu verhüten — »pour écarter des témoins toute influence de suggestion étrangère, toutes tentations de subornation« (rapport au corps legisl.).

2) Das Gericht hat bei Festsetzung der Frist zunächst den Ort, wo das Gesuch einzureichen ist, zu berücksichtigen, denn handelt es sich um Beweisaufnahme bei einem entfernten Landgerichte oder gar im Auslande, so ist natürlich eine viel längere Frist nöthig, als wenn ein Richter des Prozeßgerichtes die Tagfahrt festzusetzen hat. In letzterem Falle wird eine Frist von 8—14 Tagen der Regel nach genügen.

Ferner wird das Gericht Rücksicht nehmen auf den Wohnsitz derjenigen Person, von welcher der Anwalt seine Aufschlüsse bezüglich der vorzuschlagenden Zeugen erwartet, weil ja diese Zeugen dem beauftragten Richter, zum Zwecke richtiger Festsetzung der Tagfahrt, bezeichnet werden sollen.

Wird mehreren Parteien Beweis auferlegt, so ist für jede die Frist zu bestimmen, was in der Regel durch eine gemeinschaftliche Verfügung geschehen wird, etwa dahin: „setzt zur Einreichung der Gesuche um Tagfahrt eine Frist von 8 Tagen fest.“

3) Die Frist läuft von Zustellung des Urtheils an den Anwalt, falls ein solcher bestellt ist (Art 192), und kann nach Art. 212 u. 213 erweitert werden.

Sie läuft auch gegen diejenige Person, von welcher die Zustellung ausgeht, und gilt sowohl für den Hauptbeweis, als für den gesetzlich zustehenden Gegenbeweis, falls in letzterer Beziehung das Gericht nicht ausdrücklich eine Ausnahme macht. Bezüglich des im Urtheile förmlich auferlegten Gegenbeweises bedurfte es keiner besonderen Bestimmung.

4) Was den seltenen Fall betrifft, wo der Zeugenbeweis durch ein Versäumungsurtheil angeordnet wurde, so wird einerseits anzunehmen sein, daß die Frist auch während der Einspruchsfrist laufe, ohne daß Art. 826 entgegensteht und anderseits, daß sie durch Erhebung des Einspruchs unterbrochen werde.

Weil die Frist zum Einspruche sich nach Art. 209 erweitert, so kann es allerdings vorkommen, daß derselbe erst erhoben wird, nachdem die Frist zum Beginne des Beweisverfahrens längst verstrichen ist. In Frankreich tritt der nemliche Fall bei der Berufung (welche dort gegen Interlokute gestattet ist) nicht selten ein und auch bei uns ist dies möglich, wenn theilweise endgültig, theilweise auf Zeugenbeweis erkannt wird (Art. 708). Gelingt es in derartigen Fällen dem säumigen Beweisführer nicht, eine Abänderung des Urtheils zu erlangen (Art. 314), so ist er des Rechts Zeugenbeweis zu führen verlustig, womit natürlich nicht gesagt ist, daß er überhaupt beweisfällig oder gar sachfällig sei.

5) Jede Partei wahrt ihre Frist dadurch, daß sie ein Gesuch um Festsetzung der Tagfahrt an den Richter stellt.

Ist dieser ein inländischer, so wird das Gesuch beim Gerichtschreiber, als dem Vermittler zwischen Gericht und Anwälten, übergeben, welcher nach Art. 214 die Zeit der Uebergabe vormerkt und dasselbe sofort dem Richter vorlegt. Vgl. Art. 644 und 654. Selbstverständlich ist auch die Eingabe, welche beim Richter unmittelbar stattfindet, keine ungültige.

Mit dem Gesuche ist Ausfertigung des Urtheils vorzulegen. In der Regel wird der Richter auch Nachweis der Zustellung verlangen dürfen, denn ohne diese weiß er ja nicht, ob die Frist noch laufe oder bereits verstrichen sei, letzteren Falls aber soll er, wie aus Art. 406 Abs. 3 hervorgeht, die Tagfahrtsbestimmung verweigern, wenn nicht die Einwilligung der Gegenpartei beigebracht wird.

Der Richter setzt seinen Beschluß auf das Gesuch selbst, beides aber wird in Urschrift durch Vermittlung des Gerichtsschreibers dem betreffenden Anwalte ausgehändigt, welcher die Zustellung nach Maßgabe von Art. 338 und 339 bethätigt.

6) Wird die besagte Frist versäumt, so ist das Recht, den betreffenden Zeugenbeweis zu führen, verwirkt, falls nicht Wiedereinsetzung in den vorigen Stand verlangt werden kann. Im Wege des Einspruchs oder der Berufung läßt sich nicht abhelfen.

Uebrigens wird diese Verwirkung sowie die Nichtigkeit des etwa doch abgehaltenen Zeugenverhörs beseitigt durch die Einwilligung der Gegenpartei, welche sich auch durch konkludente Handlungen kundgeben kann (Art. 406 Abs. 3). Bezüglich der Nichtigkeit gilt Art. 219.

7) Die Bestimmung im Art. 407 hat Fälle im Auge, wo sich erst nach Erlaß des Beweisurtheils die Nothwendigkeit oder Zweckmäßigkeit der Uebertragung von Zeugenvernehmungen an bestimmte Richter ergibt.

Diese Fälle werden nicht selten sein, weil beim Urtheilsspruche die Parteien in der Regel noch nicht genau angeben können, welche Zeugen sie abhören lassen werden, übrigens auch Krankheit, Wechsel des Aufenthalts 2c. die Sachlage ändern. Das Auskunftsmittel, welches vom Gesetze hier gegeben wird, ist sehr praktisch und selbst die Vorschrift, daß der vom Gericht beauftragte Richter sich direkt mit dem betreffenden Gerichte des Inlandes oder Auslandes ins Benehmen setze, die Festsetzung der Tagfahrt auf dem Amtswege erwirke und von derselben dem betreibenden Anwalte amtlich Kenntniß gebe, halte ich für vollkommen gerechtfertigt, mag sie immerhin den Prinzipien des Parteibetriebes etwas widerstreben. Man darf die Prinzipien nicht todt hetzen, am wenigsten im Rechtsleben.

Hervorzuheben ist, daß die Befugniß der Ueberweisung (Subdelegation) nur für zwei Voraussetzungen besteht, nämlich daß der Zeuge entfernt wohne, d. h. sich aufhalte, oder daß er am Erscheinen verhindert sei.

8) Fragliche Befugniß der Ueberweisung steht jedem beauftragten Richter zu, mag er nun Mitglied des Prozeßgerichts oder Einzelrichter sein. Selbst ausländische Gerichte sind im Ausdrucke „beauftragte Richter" inbegriffen, und es ist auch für sie von Belang, daß in jedem Auftrage oder Ersuchen die stillschweigende Ermächtigung zur weiteren Beauftragung liegt.

Dieses Recht übt der Richter von Amtswegen, sowie der Anlaß dazu sich ihm darbietet.

Das Gesetz sagt nicht, es solle die erwirkte Festsetzung der Tagfahrt dem betreibenden Anwalte ausgehändigt, sondern nur, es solle ihm von der Tagfahrt Kenntniß gegeben werden. Offenbar will das Gesetz, daß diese Mittheilung gleich einer Tagfahrtsbestimmung gelte, woraus folgt, daß sie in einem schriftlichen Erlaß zu erfolgen hat, welcher dem betreibenden Anwalte einzuhändigen und von diesem nach Art. 338 und 339 zuzustellen ist.

9) Die Bestimmung des Art 408 entspricht dem Verfahren, wie es bisher in der Pfalz geübt worden ist und sich auf den ersten Blick als sachgemäß empfiehlt.

In der Regel läßt sich ziemlich sicher berechnen, wie viel Zeit erforderlich sei, um die Beweisaufnahme außerhalb der Sitzung zu bethätigen und demgemäß die Sitzung zur weiteren Beweisaufnahme und Verhandlung festzusetzen. Sollten unvorhergesehene Hindernisse es nöthig machen, so wäre von den Anwälten rechtzeitig Vertagung in eine andere Sitzung zu veranlassen.

Zweck dieser Bestimmung ist es offenbar, zu bewirken, daß mit der Beweisaufnahme in der Sitzung die Instruktion geschlossen sei und auf dieselbe sofort die Verhandlung folgen könne; es sollen die Protokolle bei der Verhandlung benützt werden. Die ursprüngliche Fassung (Referat zu Art. 378 d und Abg. II 211) drückte sich in dieser Beziehung viel richtiger aus. Vgl. die Bemerk. zu Art. 344 Nr. 6 u. 7.

Vorladung der Zeugen.

Art. 409. — **Die Vorladung der Zeugen zur Vernehmungstagfahrt zu bewerkstelligen, liegt der Partei ob, welche sie vorführen will.**

In der Vorladung sind die Parteien, das Gericht oder der beauftragte Richter, Ort und Zeit der Vernehmung und die nach dem Beweisurtheile zu beweisenden Thatsachen, letztere soweit sie den Gegenstand der Vernehmung bilden, anzuführen.

Art. 410. — **Zwischen der Zustellung der Vorladung an den Zeugen und der Vernehmungstagfahrt müssen wenigstens drei Tage in Mitte liegen.**

Bei öffentlichen Beamten oder Bediensteten kann Art und Zeit der Ladungszustellung im Interesse des Dienstes durch Verordnung anders bestimmt werden.

Art. 411. — **Ist zur Vernehmlassung eines öffentlichen Beamten die Ermächtigung der vorgesetzten Stelle erforderlich, so hat der Beweisführer diese nach den hierüber im Verordnungswege zu erlassenden Vorschriften zu erholen und dem Zeugen mit der Vorladung abschriftlich zustellen zu lassen.**

Hat der Beweisführer die nachgesuchte Ermächtigung nicht rechtzeitig erhalten, so kann er Vertagung der betreffenden Vernehmung beantragen, wenn er bescheinigt, daß er den erforderlichen Fleiß angewendet habe.

G. A. d. K. d. A. II S. 213. 214. 216. 226—229. 339. 340. IV S. 96. 98. 99.
K. d. R. II S. 213. IV S. 57.

1) Jede Partei hat diejenigen Zeugen, welche sie vernehmen lassen will, durch den Gerichtsvollzieher vorladen zu lassen.

Diese Vorladung ist jedoch nicht, wie im französischen Prozesse bei Strafe der Nichtigkeit vorgeschrieben, und es möchte eine Nichtigkeit auch nicht auf Grund von Art. 218 gegeben sein; es kann daher ein Zeuge giltig vernommen werden, auch wenn er ohne Ladung freiwillig erscheint, vorausgesetzt, daß er nach Art. 412 gehörig kundgegeben ist. Noch weniger steht seiner Vernehmung entgegen, daß die Vorladung nicht in vorgeschriebener Frist und Form erfolgt ist. Abg. II 216 (v. Weiß).

2) Obgleich mit Kundmachung der Zeugen (Art. 412) dieselben gemeinschaftlich werden (Art. 337), so ist der Beweisführer nicht verpflichtet die benannten Zeugen auch vorladen zu lassen und ebensowenig gehindert, eine gegebene Vorladung wieder zurückzunehmen.

Legt daher eine Partei Werth auf die Vernehmung eines Zeugen, so darf sie sich nicht dabei beruhigen, daß derselbe vom Gegner benannt wurde, sondern muß, um sicher zu gehen, ihn auch ihrerseits vorladen lassen. Eine neue Kundgabe von ihrer Seite ist, da ihr bereits ein Recht auf den Zeugen zusteht, nicht nöthig.

3) Die Vorladung hat, unbeschadet der Vorschriften des Art. 202, alles das anzuführen, was dem Zeugen zu wissen nöthig ist, wie dies Art. 409 Abs. 2 näher bestimmt.

Von Wichtigkeit erscheint insbesondere auch, daß der Zeuge von den Thatsachen, über welche er vernommen werden soll, Kenntniß erhalte, damit er vorher darüber nachdenke, sein Gedächtniß auffrische und sich völlig darüber klar werde, was er mit gutem Gewissen behaupten könne, was nicht. Man wird dieser Form am besten genügen, indem man, wie es seither in der Pfalz geschah, jedem Zeugen denjenigen Theil des Urtheilssatzes, welcher die betreffende Beweisauflage enthält, mit der Vorladung abschriftlich zustellen läßt. Die Ausscheidung einzelner Beweissätze ist nicht nöthig, da jeder Zeuge über das ganze Beweisthema vernommen wird. Diese Abschrift fertigt der Gerichtsvollzieher (Art. 203) nach Weisung des Anwaltes.

4) Die Ladungsfrist beträgt 3 Tage und erweitert sich nach Maßgabe des Art. 209 mit Rücksicht auf den Aufenthaltsort des Zeugen und den Ort des Zeugenverhörs.

Vorladung öffentlicher Beamter.

5) Oeffentliche Beamte oder Bedienstete werden gleich gewöhnlichen Zeugen geladen, soweit nicht durch Verordnung bezüglich der Art und Form der Ladungszustellung etwas Abweichendes bestimmt wird.

Der Grund dieser Ausnahme liegt in der Rücksicht auf den öffentlichen Dienst, welcher dadurch, daß ein Beamter oder Bediensteter von einer Partei als Zeuge beansprucht wird, nicht Noth leiden darf. Es ist theils dafür zu sorgen, daß dem Bediensteten selbst die nöthige Zeit geboten sei, um seine Dienstgeschäfte einzurichten, theils dafür, daß die vorgesetzte Behörde in Kenntniß gesetzt werde, um sachgemäße Anordnungen für den Dienst zu treffen, wie dies z. B. bei Ladungen von Zollbediensteten von großer Wichtigkeit ist.

Bei Militärpersonen ist schon durch Art. 193 Vorsorge getroffen.

6) Ist im Falle des Art. 400 Ziff. 2 zur Vernehmung eines Beamten die Ermächtigung der vorgesetzten Stelle nöthig, so ist diese vom Beweisführer zu erholen und mit der Vorladung abschriftlich zuzustellen. Wird dies unterlassen und hatte der Beamte dem Gerichte angezeigt, daß er jene Ermächtigung nöthig finde, so ist er nicht verpflichtet, der Vorladung Folge zu leisten (Art. 429).

Kundmachung an die Gegenpartei.

Art. 412. — Spätestens acht Tage vor der Vernehmungstagfahrt hat jede Partei, welche Zeugen vorführen will, ein Verzeichniß derselben nach Vor- und Familiennamen, Stand oder Gewerbe und Wohnort der Gegenpartei zustellen zu lassen.

Ist die Zustellung des Verzeichnisses nicht rechtzeitig erfolgt oder läßt dieses die Identität der Personen nicht entnehmen, so kann die Gegenpartei verlangen, daß die betreffenden Zeugen nicht vernommen beziehungsweise ihre Aussagen nicht berücksichtigt werden. Dieses Verlangen ist ausgeschlossen, wenn die Partei oder ihr Gewalthaber der Vernehmung beigewohnt und den betreffenden Antrag nicht spätestens nach der Erklärung des Zeugen über die allgemeinen Fragen gestellt hat.

G. A. d. K. d. A. II S. 212. 213. 340. 341. IV S. 96. — K. d. R. II S. 216—218. IV. S. 57.

1) Jede Partei hat dem Gegner die Zeugen, welche sie vernehmen lassen will, genau zu bezeichnen, und zwar spätestens acht Tage vor der Vernehmungstagfahrt, also in der nemlichen Frist, wie sie in der Regel auch für die Vorladung des Gegners gilt (Art. 331, 338, 339).

Diese Kundgabe ist von großer Wichtigkeit; sie soll Ueberraschungen verhüten und den Gegner in die Lage setzen, über die Person des Zeugen, über alle jene Thatsachen, welche dessen Tüchtigkeit oder Glaubwürdigkeit bedingen, Erkundigungen einzuziehen, und durch Antragstellung, Befragen der Zeugen, Beibringen von Urkunden, sowie in jeder sonst geeigneten Weise sein Interesse zu wahren.

Zur Vorladung von Gegenzeugen, um die Glaubwürdigkeit kundgegebener Zeugen zu schwächen,

z. B. darzuthun, daß sie zur Zeit der Handlung an einem anderen Orte sich befanden, wird allerdings in der Regel, d. h. falls der Beweisführer nicht etwa freiwillig seine Kundgabe frühzeitig genug gemacht oder falls der beauftragte Richter nicht etwa für den Gegenbeweis eine spätere Tagfahrt festgesetzt hat, keine Zeit gegönnt sein. Es wäre vielleicht geeignet gewesen, den Gegenbeweis mit einer kürzeren Frist zu begünstigen und so die Betretung des umständlichen Wegs, wie ihn Art. 414 bietet, unnöthig zu machen.

2) Die Kundgabe der Zeugen hat nach Art. 337 die Wirkung, sie gemeinschaftlich zu machen, und hieraus folgt, daß der Gegner sie verhören lassen kann, ohne seinerseits den Willen, sie als Gegenzeugen zu benützen, kundzugeben. Allerdings ist es dann Sache des Gegners, zu sorgen, daß der Zeuge geladen werde oder freiwillig erscheine.

Eine weitere Folge der Kundgabe spricht Art. 413 aus.

3) Der französische Gesetzgeber legte der Zeugendenunziation eine so hohe Wichtigkeit bei, daß der geringste Mangel in der Bezeichnung des Zeugen mit Nichtigkeit bedroht war (Art. 261 Code de proc.), eine Strenge, welche die Praxis durchaus nicht billigte und der sie nach Möglichkeit entgegenzuwirken suchte. Unsere Prozeßordnung verlangt zwar ebenfalls eine genaue Bezeichnung, läßt jedoch dem richterlichen Ermessen weisen Spielraum und verfügt, daß ein Zeuge nur dann auf Grund ungenügender Bezeichnung verworfen werden dürfe, wenn die Identität der Person in Frage stehe.

Es ist nun möglich, daß bei Bezeichnung eines Zeugen den besonderen Vorschriften des Art. 412 Abs. 1 vollkommen genügt sei, dennoch aber Zweifel bezüglich der Identität bestehen, weil mehrere Personen, auf welche die nemliche Bezeichnung paßt, an demselben Orte wohnen. Bei dieser Voraussetzung ist es rathsam, noch besondere Kennzeichen beizufügen, etwa das Alter, die Hausnummer anzugeben; allein ein Grund zur Verwerfung möchte, auch wenn dies nicht geschehen sollte, trotz der allgemeinen Fassung des Art. 412 Abs. 2 nicht gegeben sein. In solchen jedenfalls seltenen Fällen hat der Gegner seine Erkundigungen auf alle Personen, für welche die Bezeichnung paßt, auszudehnen.

4) Ist die Kundgabe verspätet oder leidet sie an wesentlichen Mängeln, so ist der Zeuge auf Antrag des Gegners zu verwerfen (Art. 424). Das Recht auf diesen Zeugen ist verwirkt, sobald der Gegner den Verwerfungsgrund geltend macht, und kann der Richter nicht etwa durch Vertagung der Beweisaufnahme nachhelfen. Man glaubte, und mit Recht, es müsse hier Strenge walten. Abg. II 213.

Von einer Erstreckung der Frist durch den Richter, sei es in direkter Weise, sei es durch Verlegung der Tagfahrt, kann, da es sich von einer gesetzlichen Frist handelt, überhaupt nicht die Rede sein.

Selbstverständlich finden auch Art. 209 und 211 keine Anwendung.

5) Stillschweigender Verzicht auf Verwerfung eines Zeugen wird angenommen, wenn die Gegenpartei beim Zeugenverhöre zugegen oder vertreten war und nicht spätestens nach Vernehmung des Zeugen über die allgemeinen Fragen Antrag gestellt wird. Diese Verfügung ist sehr natürlich, denn es kann offenbar nicht gestattet sein, daß der Gegner abwarte, was der Zeuge aussage, ob er günstig, ob er ungünstig für ihn spreche, um sich dann erst zu erklären, ob er ihn als gehörig kundgemacht betrachten wolle oder nicht. Verhdl. R. R. II 216 (v. Bomhard).

Ist die Gegenpartei beim Zeugenverhöre nicht vertreten, so darf der Richter nicht etwa von Amtswegen die Vernehmung des Zeugen ablehnen, denn das Gesetz verlangt Antrag der Gegenpartei. Dieser Antrag kann in diesem Falle bei der Verhandlung gestellt werden und bedarf es zur Ausübung dieses Rechtes selbstverständlich keiner Restitution.

Uebrigens sind meiner Meinung nach die Bestimmungen des Art. 219 hier anwendbar, da, wenn das Gesetz auch nur von einer Verwerfung spricht (Art. 424), im Grunde es sich doch darum handelt, die stattgefundene Zeugenvernehmung als nichtig anzufechten. Die französische Jurisprudenz, welche immerhin als Quelle der Auslegung benützt werden darf, erachtete hauptsächlich den Fall der mangelhaften Denunziation als einen solchen, wo das Prinzip des Art. 173 analog zur Anwendung komme. Bemerk. zu Art. 219 Nr. 9.

Art. 413. — **An Stelle eines der Gegenpartei rechtzeitig kundgegebenen Zeugen, dessen Vernehmung ohne Verschulden des Beweisführers unmöglich geworden ist, darf dieser in einer von dem Gerichte oder von dem beauftragten Richter festzusetzenden Frist andere Zeugen in Vorschlag bringen.**

Art. 414. — **Die Beweisführung gegen die Glaubwürdigkeit eines Zeugen ist vom Gerichte nach-**

träglich zu gestatten, wenn ein dahin zielendes Begehren bei der auf das Zeugenverhör folgenden Verhandlung gestellt wird.

Gleiches gilt von dem Gegenbeweise, wenn nach dem Ermessen des Gerichts die Veranlassung dazu erst durch die Zeugenaussage gegeben wurde.

Art. 415. — **Das Gericht kann Zeugen, von welchen der Beweisführer erklärt, daß er sie trotz angewandten Fleißes vor Ablauf der in Art. 412 bezeichneten Frist nicht aufgefunden habe, auch nach Ablauf derselben und bis zum Schlusse der nach Beweisaufnahme in der Hauptsache folgenden Verhandlung zulassen, wenn sich das Vorbringen des Beweisführers nicht als unglaubwürdig darstellt und auch das Gericht nicht die Sache für bereits genügend aufgeklärt erachtet.**

Ergibt sich aus der Vernehmung des Zeugen, daß mit der nachträglichen Bezeichnung desselben nur eine muthwillige Verzögerung bezielt wurde, so ist der Beweisführer in eine Geldstrafe bis zu hundert Gulden zu verurtheilen.

G. A. d. K. d. A. II S. 235—238. 340. 341. IV S. 96. 97. 330. 341.
K. d. R. II S. 218—221. IV S. 57.

1) Ist ein Zeugenbeweis (Haupt- oder Gegenbeweis) nicht angetreten, oder sind die Zeugen nicht vorschriftsmäßig kundgegeben, so ist in der Regel das Recht auf Führung des betreffenden Zeugenbeweises verloren und die Benützung der betreffenden Zeugen verwirkt, und zwar nicht bloß für die erste, sondern auch für die Berufungs-Instanz (Art. 707).

Von dieser Regel gestatten jedoch Art. 413 bis 415 Ausnahmen im Interesse des materiellen Rechtes, welche, wenn der Richter sie nicht durch übelangebrachte Nachsicht zur Regel werden läßt, sehr zweckmäßig und völlig gerechtfertigt sind.

a) Ersetzung weggefallener Zeugen (Art. 413).

2) Ist ein Zeuge rechtzeitig kundgegeben, wird jedoch dessen Vernehmung aus irgend einem Grunde — weil er stirbt, unzurechnungsfähig wird, sein Aufenthalt nicht ermittelt werden kann — ohne Verschulden des Beweisführers unmöglich, so dürfen an dessen Stelle andere Zeugen in Vorschlag gebracht werden.

Es kann sich fragen, ob das Hinderniß der Vernehmung nothwendig der Kundgabe nachgängig eingetreten sein müsse, wie die Worte: „unmöglich geworden sind“ anzudeuten scheinen, oder ob unter Umständen auch ein Hinderniß Beachtung finden könne, welches zur Zeit der Kundgabe schon eingetreten, jedoch dem Beweisführer unbekannt geblieben war.

In der Regel wird bei Fällen dieser Art eine Verschuldung anzunehmen sein; allein es ist immerhin möglich, daß eine solche nicht vorliege, z. B. wenn kurz vor der Kundgabe der entfernt wohnende Zeuge gestorben, flüchtig gegangen, eine Geistesstörung bei ihm zum Ausbruche gekommen ist, und es wäre offenbar dem Geiste des Gesetzes zuwider, hier die Ersetzung auszuschließen. Das Wesentliche liegt wohl in dem Erforderniſſe der Verschuldung. Der Richter wird nach den Umständen, nach den Erklärungen anderer Zeugen (Art. 345 a. E.), nach vorgelegten Bescheinigungen sich seine Ueberzeugung bilden, im Zweifel aber berücksichtigen, daß die Zulassung einer Ersetzung die Ausnahme bildet.

3) Indem das Gesetz sagt: „an Stelle“ des weggefallenen Zeugen dürften andere Zeugen benannt werden, so scheint es vorauszusetzen, daß die neuen Zeugen nur über solche Thatsachen vorzuschlagen seien, bezüglich deren die weggefallenen hätten aussagen können und sollen; allein offenbar läßt sich, da die Zeugen nicht für einzelne Beweisartikel, sondern für das ganze Beweisthema vorgeschlagen werden, eine solche Ausscheidung nicht machen.

Das Recht der Benennung von Ersatzzeugen hat daher jetzt eine viel größere Tragweite, als es im alten Prozesse hatte, und bietet einen Weg, um alle bezüglich der Kundgabe von Zeugen begangenen Versäumnisse wieder gut zu machen. Um so vorsichtiger müssen die Gerichte prüfen, ob Grund zu einer Ersetzung gegeben sei.

Erheben sich in dieser Beziehung Anstände, so verweist der beauftragte Richter dieselben zur Entscheidung vor das Prozeßgericht, wird jedoch die Zeugen vorläufig vernehmen, falls nicht klar ist, daß der Fall der Ersetzung nicht vorliege (Art. 342).

4) Wenn das Gesetz nur von rechtzeitig kundgegebenen, nicht auch von vorschriftsmäßig bezeichneten Zeugen spricht, so findet dies seine natürliche Erklärung darin, daß von einem Zeugen, dessen Identität zweifelhaft ist, auch nicht gesagt werden kann, ob dessen Vernehmung möglich oder unmöglich gewesen sei.

b) Zulassung ergänzender Beweise (Art. 414).

5) Oft ergibt sich erst durch Benennung und Vernehmung der Zeugen, daß Umstände für die

Beweisführung erheblich sind, welche nicht Gegenstand der Beweisauflage waren und sein konnten, und es wäre ungerecht, wollte man eine Partei mit Beweisen ausschließen, welche anzutreten ihr nicht möglich gewesen ist. Der Gesetzgeber gibt daher ein **Recht**, nachträglich zum Beweise zugelassen zu werden: 1) um die Glaubwürdigkeit eines Zeugen anzugreifen, und 2) um Gegenbeweise zu führen, deren Erheblichkeit sich erst durch Zeugenaussagen ergeben hat.

6) Unter ersteren Gesichtspunkt fallen alle Umstände, welche geeignet sind, die Glaubwürdigkeit eines Zeugen in anderer Weise, als durch Nachweis der Wahrheit oder Unwahrheit der zum Beweise ausgesetzten Thatsachen, zu schwächen, also Verhältnisse, wie sie bisher die Exceptionsmäßigkeit oder Verwerflichkeit begründeten, schlechter Ruf des Zeugen, Aeußerungen im entgegengesetzten Sinne, Nichtanwesenheit am Orte der Handlung &c. Ebenso wie früher die Verwerfungsgründe Gegenstand einer besonderen Beweisauflage sein konnten, so mußte dies jetzt, nachdem ein Recht der Verwerfung nicht mehr anerkannt ist, bezüglich der die Glaubwürdigkeit betreffenden Thatsachen der Fall sein.

Unter letzteren Gesichtspunkt fällt der Gegenbeweis gegen Thatsachen, welche nicht Gegenstand ausdrücklicher Beweisauflagen waren, sich vielmehr erst gelegentlich bei der Beweisaufnahme ergeben (Art. 345 a. E.), und zwar hat der Gesetzgeber hier vorzugsweise den **direkten** Gegenbeweis im Auge, da bezüglich des indirekten Gegenbeweises durch die noch allgemeinere Verfügung des Art. 333 Abs. 3 bereits Vorsorge getroffen ist.

7) In beiden Fällen erfolgt eine neue Beweisauflage, bei welcher selbstverständlich die Frage der Erheblichkeit zu prüfen und ein Beweis nicht zugelassen ist, wenn die richterliche Ueberzeugung durch das gebotene Beweismaterial genügend festgestellt erscheint.

Nach meinen Erfahrungen wird es zu derartigen Beweisauflagen nur höchst selten kommen; in der Regel wird sich durch Befragen der Zeugen, durch Vorlage von Urkunden, durch Vermuthungen der Beweis, soweit nöthig, ergeben. Es ist mir nur ein einziger Fall erinnerlich, wo wegen einer Zeugenreproche Beweis auferlegt wurde. Zu beachten ist schließlich, daß das Gesetz von **Beweisführung** überhaupt spricht, nicht blos vom Beweise durch Zeugen.

c) **Neuentdeckte Zeugen** (Art. 415).

8) Art. 415 gibt eine eigentümliche Restitution, welche sowohl was die Restitutionsgründe, als was den Beweis, als was schließlich die Frist betrifft, an weniger strenge Voraussetzungen geknüpft ist, als diejenigen des Art 216.

Die betreffende Bestimmung erscheint im Interesse des materiellen Rechtes vollkommen gerechtfertigt, auch wurde sehr mit Unrecht bei den Verhandlungen geltend gemacht, sie bedinge eine große Neuerung für die Pfalz, dem die neuere Jurisprudenz in der Pfalz und in Frankreich läßt, in Anerkennung des praktischen Bedürfnisses, eine Prorogation der Zeugenverhöre auch zum Zwecke der Vernehmung **neuentdeckter Zeugen** zu.

Die Art und Weise, wie das Gesetz verfügt, ist ebenso geeignet, dem praktischen Bedürfnisse zu genügen, als Mißbrauch zu verhüten; denn 1) ist es ganz ins Ermessen des Gerichts gestellt, in Berücksichtigung der näheren thatsächlichen Auseinandersetzungen der Parteien, unter Beiziehung aller sonst gebotenen Beweise und Vermuthungen, solche angeblich neuentdeckte Zeugen zuzulassen oder nicht, und 2) ist für den Fall, wo nur muthwillige Verzögerung bezweckt wird, eine Geldstrafe gedroht.

Was diese Strafe betrifft s. Bemerk. zu Art. 385 Nr. 4.

9) Neuentdeckte Zeugen können zugelassen werden, solange die Verhandlung in der **Hauptsache** nicht geschlossen ist, d. h. jene Verhandlung, in welcher die Zeugenaussage noch verwerthet werden kann.

Es gilt dies auch für die Verhandlung in der Berufungsinstanz — überhaupt überall, wo die Thatsache, auf welche die Beweisführung sich bezieht, noch nicht rechtskräftig festgestellt ist. Abg. II 237 u. 238.

Gang der Vernehmung.

Art. 416. — **Bei der Zeugenvernehmung ermahnt der Vorsitzende oder beauftragte Richter die Zeugen zu wahrheitsgetreuer Aussage mit der Eröffnung, daß sie diese zu beschwören haben werden, belehrt sie auf eine ihrer Persönlichkeit angemessene Art über die Bedeutung des Eids und die Folgen des Meineids und ordnet hierauf an, daß sich die Zeugen zurückziehen, bis sie zur Vernehmung vorgerufen werden.**

Art. 417. — **Die Zeugen werden einzeln vorgerufen und vernommen.**

Jeder Zeuge hat vor seiner Vernehmung den Eid zu leisten, daß er über den Gegenstand, worüber er vernommen wird, seine volle Wissenschaft angeben und wissentlich weder

etwas Wahres verschweigen noch etwas Unwahres einmischen werde. Diese Eidesformel ist dem Zeugen vorzulesen und von ihm mit den Worten zu beschwören: „Dieses schwöre ich, so wahr mir Gott helfe."

Gehört der Zeuge einem religiösen Bekenntnisse an, welches die förmliche Eidesleistung nicht gestattet, so tritt an deren Stelle eine dem Bekenntnisse des Zeugen entsprechende Betheuerung. Eine solche Betheuerung steht dem Eide gleich.

Art. 418. — Personen unter sechzehn Jahren, Taubstumme und Solche, welchen nach den Strafgesetzen die Fähigkeit zur Ableistung eines Zeugeneids entzogen ist, werden unbeeidigt vernommen.

Art. 419. — Die Vernehmung beginnt mit den allgemeinen Fragen über des Zeugen Vor- und Familiennamen, Alter, Stand oder Gewerbe und Wohnort, seine allenfallsigen Verwandtschafts-, Schwägerschafts- oder sonstigen Verhältnisse zu den Parteien und seine etwaige Betheiligung bei dem Ausgange der Sache.

Hierauf sind dem Zeugen die zu beweisenden Thatsachen zu eröffnen und, soweit es für den Zweck nothwendig erscheint, zu erläutern, und ist er sodann zu zusammenhängender Erzählung dessen, was ihm darüber bekannt ist, zu veranlassen.

Nach Beendigung der Erzählung hat der Richter die zur Aufklärung und Vervollständigung der Aussage oder zur Erforschung des Grundes der Wissenschaft des Zeugen etwa noch erforderlichen Fragen an denselben zu stellen.

Die Aussage ist ihrem Inhalte nach zu Protokoll zu nehmen und können die Parteien und ihre Gewalthaber geeigneten Falls die Aufnahme der eigenen Worte des Zeugen in das Protokoll verlangen.

Von der Aufnahme eines Protokolles kann durch Gerichtsbeschluß abgesehen werden, wenn die Beweisaufnahme in der Sitzung erfolgt, die Verhandlung über das Beweisergebniß in der nämlichen oder in einer der nächstfolgenden Sitzungen stattfinden kann, das zu erlassende Urtheil der Berufung nicht unterliegt und auch sonst keine Bedenken bestehen.

Art. 420. — Die Parteien, ihre Beistände und Gewalthaber dürfen den Zeugen nicht unterbrechen, sie können aber den Richter ersuchen, ihm diejenigen Fragen vorzulegen, welche sie zur Aufklärung der Sache für dienlich erachten. Auch können die Gerichtsmitglieder, die Parteien, deren Beistände und Gewalthaber mit Erlaubniß des Vorsitzenden beziehungsweise des beauftragten Richters unmittelbare Fragen an die Zeugen stellen.

Zweifel über die Zulässigkeit einer Frage entscheidet, wenn die Vernehmung in der Sitzung stattfindet, das Gericht. Hat ein beauftragter Richter die Zulassung einer Frage verweigert, so muß dies auf Begehren unter wörtlicher Anführung der Frage im Protokolle bemerkt werden. Erklärt später das Gericht die Weigerung für unstatthaft, so ist die weitere Vernehmung der Zeugen anzuordnen.

Erlauben sich Parteien, Beistände oder Gewalthaber Unterbrechungen, Beleidigungen oder ohne erhaltene Bewilligung unmittelbare Fragen an die Zeugen, so finden die Vorschriften des Art. 151 Abs. 4—8 Anwendung.

Art. 421. — Will eine Partei bei dem Zeugenverhöre vor dem beauftragten Richter nicht erscheinen, so kann sie sowohl den Antrag auf Verwerfung bestimmter Zeugen, als die Fragen, welche sie den Zeugen vorgelegt wünscht, schriftlich einreichen.

Der Richter hat von solchen Eingaben der erschienenen Gegenpartei Kenntniß zu geben, auf die eingereichten Fragen aber in der Vernehmung nur soweit Rücksicht zu nehmen, als er es für angemessen erachtet.

Art. 422. — Die abgehörten Zeugen haben bei der Vernehmung der folgenden gegenwärtig zu bleiben, soweit nicht das Gericht oder der beauftragte Richter ihre weitere Anwesenheit für entbehrlich erachtet oder die einstweilige Entfernung eines Zeugen auf dessen Antrag aus erheblichen Gründen gestattet.

Die Vernehmung eines Zeugen kann wieder aufgenommen werden, so oft die inzwischen weiter gepflogenen Vernehmungen es angemessen erscheinen lassen. Zeugen, welche sich widersprechen, sind einander gegenüber zu stellen und wiederholt zu befragen.

Weigert sich der beauftragte Richter, auf die weitere Vernehmung oder Gegenüberstellung einzugehen, so ist über Begehren und Weigerung im Protokolle Urkunde zu ertheilen und das Gericht kann auf Antrag nachträglich das Geeignete verordnen.

G. A. d. K. d. A. II S. 212. 216—221. 341. 342. IV S. 97. 99. — K. d. R. II S. 221—224. IV S. 57.

1) Die Vorschriften, welche hier über Art und Weise der Vernehmung der Zeugen gegeben werden, sind umständlich genug, um zugleich eine Instruktion zu ersetzen, so daß das, was zur Erklärung weiter beizufügen ist, sich auf Weniges beschränken kann.

Ein höchst wesentlicher Unterschied zwischen der Zeugenvernehmung des neuen und des alten Prozesses tritt darin hervor, daß keine Zerstückelung der Thatsachen in Beweisartikel mehr stattfindet und die stückweise Aufnahme der Zeugenaussagen wegfällt. Der Zeuge wird jetzt aufgefordert, alles, was er bezüglich des Beweisthemas weiß, auszusagen, und seine Erklärungen werden in fortlaufender geschlossener Erzählung zu Protokoll genommen.

Es leuchtet ein, daß in dieser Weise dem urtheilenden Richter ein viel klareres, wahrheitsgetreueres Bild von dem geboten wird, was die Zeugen aussagen wollen und können. Er ist sicher, reine Thatsachen, so wie sie der Zeuge aus seiner Erinnerung schöpft und wiedergibt, zu erhalten, nicht aber Schlußfolgerungen, welche der Zeuge, veranlaßt durch ungeschickte oder allzu geschickte Beweisartikel einmengt, oder gar Schlußfolgerungen des vernehmenden Richters selbst, wenn er bloß sagen läßt: „diesen Artikel muß ich bestätigen.“ Ferner ist der Richter viel besser im Stande, aus der Art und Weise der Darstellung, aus dem Gange und Zusammenhange der Geschichtserzählung die *innere* Glaubwürdigkeit einer Aussage zu beurtheilen.

Er verfährt daher am richtigsten, wenn er den Zeugen ganz aussprechen läßt und selbst auf Unrichtigkeiten und Widersprüche, wenn sie nicht offene Versehen sind, vorerst nicht aufmerksam macht, vielmehr alles, so wie es der Zeuge vorbringt, anhört und aufnimmt, sich vorbehaltend, durch spätere Fragestellung Unrichtiges zu berichtigen und Widersprüche aufzuklären. Alle Schwankungen in der Aussage, alle Unsicherheiten und Widersprüche müssen sich treu im Protokolle abspiegeln, und es ist von größtem Gewichte, zu wissen, was ein Zeuge zuerst gesagt habe und wie er dazu gelangt sei, seine ursprüngliche Angabe zu ändern.

2) *Beeidigung.*

Indem Art. 417 sagt, daß jeder Zeuge den Eid zu leisten habe und die Eidesformel bestimmt, sind alle früheren Ausnahmen beseitigt, namentlich die durch das Edikt über die Siegelmäßigkeit § 13 vorgesehene besondere Art der Beeidigung (Einf.-Ges. Art. 3 Ziff. 16) und der *Judeneid.*

Auch die Erinnerung der Beamten an ihren Diensteid, sowie die besondere Eidesformel für fürstliche Personen ist weggefallen.

Nur für Fälle, wo das *religiöse Bekenntniß* den Eidschwur nicht gestattet, wie bei Mennoniten, darf an dessen Stelle die einfache Betheuerung treten.

Weitere Formen, als sie Art. 417 gibt, sind *gesetzlich* nicht geboten.

Schließlich ist hervorzuheben, daß die Beeidigung im öffentlichen Interesse vorgeschrieben ist und durch Einverständniß der Parteien nicht beseitigt werden kann; die entgegenstehende Verfügung des Entwurfes wurde gestrichen. Sie erscheint offenbar als eine nach der Natur und dem Zwecke der Zeugenvernehmung zum Wesen derselbe gehörige Handlung.

3) Was die Vernehmung von *Taubstummen* betrifft, so sind die Vorschriften der Art. 162 u. 163 maßgebend. Ebenso ist bei Zeugen, welche der deutschen Sprache nicht mächtig sind, die Beiziehung von Dollmetschern nach Art. 161 u. 163 geboten.

Die Fähigkeit zur Ableistung eines Zeugeneides ist nach dem Strafgesetzbuche allen Personen entzogen, welche zur Todes- oder Zuchthausstrafe verurtheilt sind, und zwar vom Augenblicke der Rechtskraft des Urtheils an, so lange die Strafzeit dauert (Art. 31 des St.G.B.); ferner ohne Beschränkung der Dauer denjenigen Personen, welche wegen Meineides (Art. 192) bestraft sind. Eine Eidesunfähigkeit bestimmt auch Art. 258, jedoch nur für Strafsachen; sie wirkt übrigens auch für civilrechtliche Ansprüche, die *zugleich* geltend gemacht werden.

Durch Begnadigung kann jedoch die Eidesfähigkeit wieder hergestellt werden (Ges. über Aufhebung der Straffolgen vom 10. Juli 1861).

4) *Verfahren im Allgemeinen.*

Bei Stellung der *allgemeinen Fragen* hat der Richter von Amtswegen alle Verhältnisse zu erheben, welche für die Glaubwürdigkeit des Zeugen von Einfluß sein können, insbesondere auch Verhältnisse, welche eine Abhängigkeit des Zeugen vom Beweisführer begründen, wie das Dienstverhältniß. Fragen dieser Art können nie dem Antrage auf Verwerfung des Zeugen nach Art. 412 Abs. 2 im Wege stehen.

Eine Erläuterung der zu beweisenden Thatsachen ist in der Regel nicht nöthig, weil ja jeder Zeuge bei seiner Vorladung Kenntniß davon erhält. Gewöhnlich genügt es, den Zeugen zu fragen, ob er seine Vorladung gelesen habe und wisse, vorüber er auszusagen habe.

5) Die Leitung des Verfahrens ist durch das Gesetz sachgemäß ganz in die Hand des Vorsitzenden bezw. beauftragten Richters gelegt, ohne dessen Erlaubniß keine Frage an den Zeugen gestellt werden darf, selbst nicht von Seiten der übrigen Gerichtsmitglieder. Der Gefahr, daß durch diese dem einzelnen Richter eingeräumte Gewalt die Rechte der Parteien geschädigt werden, ist dadurch vorgebeugt, daß überall, wo Zweifel über die Zulässigkeit einer Frage entsteht, d. h. wo sich die fragende Person bei der Zurückweisung der Frage nicht beruhigt, die Entscheidung des Gerichts einzutreten hat.

Findet das Zeugenverhör in der Sitzung statt und ist das Gericht der Ansicht, es sei die Frage zu stellen, so bedarf es förmlicher Entscheidung und Eintrags ins Urtheilsbuch nicht. Der Vorsitzende stellt die Frage, und hiermit ist die Sache erledigt.

Wird die Frage als unstatthaft erklärt, so ist in möglichst kurzer und einfacher Form zu entscheiden.

6) Die Bestimmung in Art. 421, daß die Parteien ihre Anträge auf Verwerfung von Zeugen auch schriftlich einreichen dürfen, hatte ursprünglich wenn nicht ausschließlich doch vorzugsweise die Verwerfung wegen Verwandtschaft &c. im Auge, welche das Gesetz damals noch zuließ und welche unter Strafe des Ausschlusses bei der Beweisaufnahme selbst vorgebracht werden mußte. Jetzt kann sie nur noch Anwendung finden auf die Fälle der Untüchtigkeit und des Mangels der Kundgabe, in welcher Beziehung es jedoch nicht nöthig ist, seine Rechte zu wahren, indem die Anfechtung auch noch bei der Verhandlung stattfinden kann.

Die schriftlich eingereichten Anträge haben übrigens die nemliche Wirkung, wie die bei der Beweisaufnahme mündlich gestellten.

7) Wenn Art. 422 sagt, daß die abgehörten Zeugen bei der Vernehmung der folgenden gegenwärtig zu bleiben haben, so soll kein besonderer Werth darauf gelegt werden, daß die Aussage der folgenden Zeugen in Gegenwart der abgehörten erfolge, vielmehr will einfach erklärt werden, daß die Zeugen sich zur nachträglichen Vernehmung bereit halten müssen.

Daß die Vernehmung eines Zeugen wieder aufgenommen und durch Gegenüberstellen von Zeugen oder wiederholtes Befragen Widersprüche beseitigt, Dunkelheiten aufgeklärt werden dürfen, erscheint sehr sachgemäß und wurde auch in der Pfalz in Fällen, wo das Zeugenverhör ohne Protokollirung in der Sitzung abgehalten wurde, in vollem Maße geübt.

Diese Befugniß dauert bis zum Schlusse der Zeugenvernehmung.

8) Protokollirung.

In der Regel ist über die Zeugenaussagen Protokoll nach Art. 166 ff. aufzunehmen; findet jedoch das Zeugenverhör in der Sitzung statt und unterliegt das zu erlassende Urtheil der Berufung nicht, so kann das Gericht beschließen, daß von einer Protokollirung Umgang genommen werden solle.

Die Hauptfrage ist hier die Appellabilität, und dieselbe ist nicht so einfach, wie unter Herrschaft des französischen Rechtes, wo mit Zustellung der Ladung der Charakter der Sache als einer appellablen oder nicht appellablen fixirt war. Jetzt ist die Zulässigkeit der Berufung durch die Beschwerdesumme bedingt, diese aber ergibt sich erst durch das Urtheil. Es ergibt sich hieraus, daß nur in jenen Fällen die Unstatthaftigkeit der Berufung schon bei Beginn des Zeugenverhörs sichersteht, wo der ganze Streitgegenstand die Berufungssumme, also im bezirksgerichtlichen Verfahren die Summe von 300 Gulden nicht erreicht.

Nichtsdestoweniger darf auch in Fällen, wo der Streitgegenstand höher ist, unter Umständen von der Protokollirung Umgang genommen werden, wenn das Gericht sich sofort in der Sitzung überzeugt, daß das ergehende Urtheil der Berufung nicht unterliegen werde. Erstreckt sich z. B. der Zeugenbeweis nur auf gewisse Streitpunkte, während bezüglich der übrigen Streitpunkte, welche vom Beweise durch Urkunden, Vermuthungen abhängen, das Gericht bereits schlüssig ist, so kann es hierauf bei Lösung der Frage der Appellabilität Rücksicht nehmen. Aehnlich verhält es sich, wenn nur ein einziger Zeuge zu vernehmen ist; denn es wäre zwecklos, ein Protokoll aufzunehmen, wenn das Gericht, nachdem es den Zeugen gehört, in der Lage ist, ein Urtheil zu sprechen, gegen welches Berufung nicht zulässig ist.

Allein auch für den Fall, wo mehrere Zeugen zu vernehmen sind, könnte es meiner Meinung nach nicht als ein ungesetzliches Verfahren bezeichnet werden, wenn das Gericht einen Zeugen um den andern abhören und sich erst, nachdem sämmtliche Zeugen gehört sind, über die Protokollirung schlüssig machen würde. Allerdings wäre es in diesem Falle nöthig, bei Vernehmung eines jeden Zeugen die bereits vernommenen vorläufig wieder abtreten zu lassen, um für den Fall, als es zur Protokollirung zu kommen hätte, der Vorschrift des Art. 417 Abs. 1 genügen zu können.

Jedenfalls darf die Protokollirung nur dann unterlassen werden, wenn die Unstatthaftigkeit einer Berufung ganz zweifellos erscheint. Abg. II 218 (v. Weiß). Der Umstand, daß über den betreffenden Streitpunkt eine selbständige Berufung nicht statthaft ist, kann diese Unterlassung nicht rechtfertigen.

9) Auch wenn die Sache der Berufung nicht unterliegt, kann die Aufnahme eines Protokolles veranlaßt sein, und zwar 1) wenn noch weitere Zeugenvernehmungen oder Instruktionshandlungen zu bethätigen sind und zu befürchten steht, es würden zur Zeit der Verhandlung die Aussagen der Zeugen nicht mehr frisch im Gedächtnisse der Richter sein (Abg. II 218), ferner 2) wenn sich Anlaß zu neuen Beweisauflagen ergibt (Art. 414). Uebrigens ist durch Art. 408 Vorsorge getroffen, daß der erstere Fall nicht häufig vorkomme.

10) Nach Laut des Gesetzes setzt die Abweichung von der Regel der Protokollirung einen Gerichtsbeschluß voraus.

Dieser Beschluß hat keine weitere Bedeutung, als daß er die Ansicht des Gerichts constatirt. Zeigt sich, daß das Gericht geirrt, so muß eben später eine wiederholte Zeugenvernehmung stattfinden; eine Anfechtung jenes Beschlusses ist nicht nöthig. Ich nehme daher an, daß der Eintrag nach der Vorschrift des Art. 281 stattzufinden habe. Jedenfalls genügt es, wenn das ergehende Urtheil zugleich den Beschluß enthält.

Art. 423. — **Sind die Zeugen nicht gesetzlicher Ordnung gemäß oder nicht vollständig vernommen worden, finden sich in ihren Aussagen Unbestimmtheiten oder Zweideutigkeiten, oder wünschen sie selbst ihre Aussagen zu ergänzen oder zu berichtigen, so kann das Gericht auch nach Beendigung des Zeugenverhörs, solange die Aburtheilung nicht erfolgt ist, auf Antrag oder von Amtswegen die wiederholte Vernehmung anordnen.**

G. A. d. K. d. A. II S. 233–235. 342. IV S. 97. — K. d. R. II S. 224.

1) Daß das Gericht unter gewissen Voraussetzungen eine wiederholte Vernehmung von Zeugen anordnen dürfe, erscheint im Interesse der Wahrheit geboten, und das Bedürfniß einer solchen Bestimmung wurde auch in der Pfalz von jeher lebhaft gefühlt und anerkannt, namentlich für den Fall, wo aus Schuld des Richters das Zeugenverhör unklar oder unvollständig geworden ist. Nur wer blind für alles einsteht, was im Code de procedure steht, kann dies verkennen.

Nach der Bestimmung des Art. 423 hat das Gericht frei zu würdigen, ob es die nachträgliche Vernehmung zulassen wolle oder nicht, und ist sogar in Fällen, wo der Zeuge selbst erklärt, seine Aussage sei falsch oder ungenau, zur Zulassung gesetzlich nicht verpflichtet.

2) Die fragliche Anordnung kann erfolgen, wenn der Zeuge nicht gesetzlicher Ordnung gemäß oder nicht vollständig vernommen worden ist.

Das Gesetz hat hier solche Ordnungswidrigkeiten im Auge, welche wesentliche Formen betreffen oder wenigstens geeignet sind, die Glaubwürdigkeit der Zeugen oder die Zuverlässigkeit der Beweisaufnahme zu schwächen, z. B. wenn Zeugen nicht beeidigt wurden, unter Umständen auch, wenn sie nicht abgesondert vernommen, nicht wegen ihrer Betheiligung am Rechtsstreite befragt wurden.

Fragliche Anordnung kann ferner erfolgen, wenn sich in den Aussagen der Zeugen Unbestimmtheiten oder Zweideutigkeiten zeigen, sei es durch Schuld des Richters, sei es durch Schuld des Zeugen; endlich wenn die Zeugen selbst ihre Aussagen zu ergänzen oder zu berichtigen wünschen. Die Anordnung erläßt das Gericht, falls nöthig, von Amtswegen.

Als eine weitere Ausnahme, die sich von selbst versteht, läßt sich anführen, daß in Fällen, wo die Protokollirung unterlassen wurde, sich aber später dennoch als nöthig ergibt, weil andere Richter oder die nemlichen Richter zu einer Zeit, wo sie sich der Aussage nicht mehr genau erinnern, auf Grund der Beweisaufnahme urtheilen sollen, eine wiederholte Vernehmung der Zeugen stattfinden muß. Es kann auch ohne Schuld des Gerichts, durch plötzlichen Tod eines Gerichtsmitgliedes und ähnliche Ursachen, sich hierzu leicht Veranlassung ergeben.

3) Die Worte: „so lange die Aburtheilung nicht erfolgt ist,“ erscheinen nicht ganz genau, denn sie lassen die Deutung zu, als ob der Berufungsrichter nicht mehr befugt sei, die Wiederholung eines Zeugenverhörs anzuordnen, was nicht beabsichtigt ist. Es soll gesagt sein: „so lange über die betreffende Thatsache noch nicht rechtskräftig abgeurtheilt ist.“

Indem das Gericht eine wiederholte Vernehmung anordnet, ordnet es ein neues Zeugenverhör an, bei welchem alle Förmlichkeiten, soweit sie nicht, wie z. B. die Kundgabe, gegenstandslos geworden sind, beobachtet werden müssen.

Verfahren in Verwerfungsfällen.

Art. 424. — Handelt es sich um Verwerfung eines Zeugen (Art. 400 und Art. 412 Abs. 2) und wird ein Verwerfungsantrag in der Sitzung gestellt, so ist darüber, nöthigen Falls nach Vernehmung des Zeugen über die Verwerfungsgründe, sofort zu entscheiden und darf, wenn der Antrag für begründet erkannt wird, der Zeuge nicht weiter gehört werden.

Art. 425. — Ergeben sich vor dem beauftragten Richter Zweifel darüber, ob ein Zeuge nicht als untüchtig (Art. 400) zu verwerfen sei, so ist die Vernehmung dieses Zeugen bis zur Entscheidung des Gerichts auszusetzen.

Wird vor dem beauftragten Richter die Verwerfung eines Zeugen auf Grund des Art. 412 Abs. 2 beantragt, so hat der beauftragte Richter, wenn der Beweisführer auf der Vernehmung besteht, die Bemerkungen und Anträge der Parteien, sowie die über den Verwerfungsgrund vom Zeugen etwa abgegebene Erklärung zu Protokoll zu nehmen und hierauf zur Abhör des Zeugen zu schreiten.

Art. 426. — Jede Partei ist befugt, die Entscheidung des Gerichts über die vor dem beauftragten Richter geltend gemachten Verwerfungsgründe zu veranlassen.

Bedarf es darüber eines Zeugenbeweises, so ist er bei der Verhandlung sogleich mittels Bezeichnung der Zeugen anzubieten. Die Aufnahme dieses Beweises hat, soferne nicht besondere Hindernisse entgegenstehen, durch das Gericht selbst zu geschehen und die Sitzung hiezu, sowie, wenn thunlich, auch zur Verhandlung in der Hauptsache ist sogleich zu bestimmen.

Wird der Zeuge verworfen, so darf die von dem beauftragten Richter aufgenommene Aussage des Zeugen nicht berücksichtigt werden.

G. A. d. K. d. A. II S. 226—228. 232. 233. 342. 343. 452. IV S. 97. 98.
K. d. R. II S. 224—229. IV S. 57.

1) Das Verfahren in Fällen, wo die Verwerfung eines Zeugen, sei es wegen Untüchtigkeit (Art. 400), sei es wegen Mangels vorschriftsmäßiger Kundgabe, in Frage steht, ist ein verschiedenes, je nachdem das Zeugenverhör in der Sitzung oder vor einem beauftragten Richter stattfindet.

a) Zeugenverhör in der Sitzung.

2) Wird in der Sitzung Antrag auf Verwerfung eines Zeugen gestellt, so ist darüber sofort zu entscheiden, und das Urtheil wird sofort vollzogen, sei es durch Vernehmung der Zeugen, sei es durch Zurückweisung desselben. Der Möglichkeit, daß in Fällen, wo Berufung zuläßig ist, der höhere Richter eine andere Ansicht habe, wurde keine Rechnung getragen, selbstverständlich kann jedoch in der Berufungsinstanz die nachträgliche Vernehmung eines verworfenen Zeugen angeordnet werden und umgekehrt (Abg. II 242, 243).

Den erforderlichen Beweis schöpft das Gericht aus den Erklärungen des Zeugen, welcher, sofern nöthig, über die Verwerfungsgründe zu vernehmen ist.

Daß in den Fällen des Art. 400 die eidliche Erklärung des Zeugen, wenigstens der Regel nach, genügen müsse, geht aus Art. 431 Abs. 2 u. 3 hervor, und auch was den Fall des Art. 412 betrifft, werden weitere Aufklärungen in der Regel nicht nöthig sein. Uebrigens steht nichts im Wege, daß das Gericht, um sich zu vergewissern, ob die Mangelhaftigkeit der Kundgabe Zweifel über die Identität begründen könne, Urkunden, welche die Gegenpartei beibringt, zu Rathe ziehe, oder andere Zeugen (Art. 345 a. E.) befrage.

Eine Beweisauflage setzt das Gesetz hier nicht voraus, jedoch müßte sie ebensogut, wie im Falle des Art. 426 Abs. 2 statthaft sein, wenn Anlaß gegeben wäre.

3) Selbstverständlich erscheint es, daß wenn das Gericht von Amtswegen eine Untüchtigkeit annimmt, es gleichfalls sofort zu entscheiden habe, und der Zeuge nicht vernommen werden dürfe.

Für die Fälle, wo der Zeuge selbst seine Untüchtigkeit geltend macht und die Zeugschaft verweigert, trifft Art. 431 Vorsorge.

b) Zeugenverhör außer der Sitzung.

4) Dem beauftragten Richter steht die Entscheidung darüber, ob ein Zeuge zu verwerfen sei, nicht zu, und es kann sich nur fragen, ob er die Vernehmung bis zur Entscheidung des Prozeßgerichtes aussetzen, oder sie vorläufig bethätigen solle. In dieser Beziehung enthält nun Art. 425 der allgemeinen Regel des Art. 342 gegenüber besondere Vorschriften.

Handelt es sich um Untüchtigkeit (Art. 400), so soll die Vernehmung des Zeugen ausgesetzt bleiben und zwar aus dem sehr natürlichen Grunde, weil hier kein bloßes Partei-Interesse in Frage, sondern die öffentliche Ordnung dabei betheiligt ist, daß unter den Voraussetzungen des Art. 400 eine Zeugenaussage nicht stattfinde.

5) Das Gesetz sagt: „ergeben sich Zweifel darüber", und dieser Fall ist offenbar gegeben, wenn der Zeuge selbst oder wenn der Richter der Ansicht ist, daß Untüchtigkeit vorliege; allein fraglich ist es, ob er auch gegeben sei, wenn es bloß die Gegenpartei ist, welche eine derartige Behauptung aufstellt.

Wenn der Zeuge selbst seine Zeugschaft nicht verweigert und wenn auch der Richter keinen Grund findet, ihn als untüchtig zu betrachten, so ist sicher die öffentliche Ordnung nicht besonders betheiligt, und falls nun die Gegenpartei allein geltend macht, es sei der Zeuge untüchtig, so tritt offenbar ein Partei-Interesse in den Vordergrund und es liegt ebensowenig Grund vor, die Vernehmung des Zeugen bis zur Entscheidung über den Verwerfungsantrag zu verzögern, als im Falle des Art. 412. Nahm doch der Gesetzgeber keinen Anstoß daran, daß das Urtheil des ersten Richters, welches den Einwand der Untüchtigkeit verwirft, sofort vollzogen werde, obgleich der höhere Richter ihn später für begründet erklären kann.

Meiner Meinung nach hätten die Erwägungen, welche Correferent v. Bomhard (R. R. II 225) vortrug, Beachtung verdient. Die Entgegnung, welche der kgl. Minist.-Commissär damals gab, erscheint nichts weniger als schlagend, übrigens ist sie, da sie die Ansicht beider Ausschüsse darstellt, für die Auslegung maßgebend, und es ist daher zu prüfen, was man unter jenem „objektiven Zweifel", von welchem gesprochen wird, zu verstehen habe.

Man kann sagen, es entstehe immer Zweifel, wenn irgend ein Betheiligter, sei es der Zeuge selbst, sei es der Richter oder die Gegenpartei, denselben anrege, und das Gesetz habe also den nemlichen Sinn, als wenn es hieße: „Ergibt sich — — die Frage, ob ꝛc."

Mit dieser Erklärung käme man jedoch dahin, daß der frivolste, rein auf Prozeßverzögerung gerichtete, auf den nahen Tod des Zeugen speculirende Einwand die Aussetzung der Zeugenvernehmung zur Folge haben müßte. Ich nehme an, daß das Gesetz soweit nicht gehen wolle, daß vielmehr, wie es auch der Wortsinn mit sich bringt, ernstliche Zweifel entstehen müssen und der beauftragte Richter prüfen dürfe, ob der Zweifel ein ernstlicher sei. Hiernach ist allerdings nicht die subjektive Ansicht des Richters maßgebend, sondern derselbe hat weiter zu fragen, ob Zweifel möglich seien, ob andere Rechtsverständige anderer Ansicht sein könnten. Ist völlig klar, daß nur Chikane vorliege, so darf der Richter nach Art. 342 zur vorläufigen Vernehmung schreiten. Vgl. die Bemerk. zu Art. 431 Nr. 3.

6) Soll der Zeuge deßhalb verworfen werden, weil er nicht vorschriftsmäßig kundgegeben wurde, so hat ihn der Richter unter Protokollirung der Anträge und Erklärungen einstweilen zu vernehmen, falls nicht der Beweisführer, die Begründung der Verwerfung anerkennend, auf Vernehmung verzichtet.

7) Wurde die Zeugenaussage vorläufig zu Protokoll genommen, so findet die Verhandlung über die Verwerfung zugleich mit der Verhandlung der Hauptsache, d. h. in der nemlichen Sitzung statt.

Die allgemeinen Prinzipien des Verfahrens (Art. 342, 484) bedingen dies, und es liegt um so weniger Grund vor, den fraglichen Zwischenpunkt zum Gegenstande einer besonderen Aburtheilung zu machen, als gegen das ergehende Urtheil eine selbständige Berufung nicht zulässig ist und es nicht den mindesten Anstand finden kann, unmittelbar nach demselben zur weiteren Verhandlung in der Hauptsache zu schreiten.

Sogar im französischen Prozesse, wo selbständige Berufung gegen dergleichen Incident-Urtheile statthaft ist, gilt es als selbstverständlich, als eine durch die Natur der Sache gebotene und gegen den Wortlaut des Gesetzes zu gestattende Ausnahme, daß Urtheile über Verwerfungsgründe sofort vollzogen werden können. Man pflegte in der Pfalz von jeher und fast ausnahmslos mit den Anträgen wegen Zeugen-Reprochen eventuell die Anträge in der Hauptsache zu verbinden und die ganze Verhandlung in die nemliche Sitzung zu bringen. Aus meiner Erfahrung ist mir nur ein einziger Fall bekannt, wo Zeugenreprochen Gegenstand gesonderter Aburtheilung waren, und dies zwar deßhalb, weil fast sämmtliche Zeugen angefochten waren, und die Parteien vor Eingehen in die Hauptsache die betreffenden Vorfragen endgiltig durch alle Instanzen wollten entscheiden lassen.

Zugleich ist zu beachten, daß es zu einer Beweisauflage nie kommen wird, wie schon oben Nr. 2 erörtert worden ist. Wenn Art. 426 Abs. 2 eine solche Beweisauflage vorsieht und bei den Verhandlungen (Abg. II 229) geäußert wurde, es könne die Nothwendigkeit gesonderter Aburtheilung des Zwischenpunktes leicht vorkommen, so erklärt sich dies daraus, daß man das Recht der Verwerfung im engeren Sinne (wegen Verwandtschaft ꝛc.) im Auge hatte, welches bei zweiter Lesung beseitigt wurde.

Die Art. 424 und 426 tragen überhaupt die Spuren davon, daß sie unter dem Einflusse anderer Anschauungen entstanden sind, als derjenigen, welche zuletzt maßgebend wurden, wie denn der letztere Artikel eine besondere Beweisauflage voraussetzt der erstere nicht, obgleich kein Grund vorliegt, einen Unterschied zu machen.

8) Wurde die Vernehmung des Zeugen bis zur Entscheidung über die Verwerfung ausgesetzt, so bringt der fleißigste Theil den Zwischenpunkt in die Sitzung und gilt für die Aburtheilung und das Verfahren, was in Art. 342 Abs. 2 bestimmt ist.

Verfahren gegen nicht erschienene Zeugen.

Art. 427. — Zeugen, welche einer rechtsförmlichen Vorladung keine Folge geleistet haben, sind, soferne das Gesetz nicht anders bestimmt, zu einer neuerlichen Tagfahrt vorzuladen und auf Antrag des Beweisführers von dem Gerichte oder beauftragten Richter durch einen vollstreckbaren Beschluß in die durch die Vereitelung der Tagfahrt und durch die Wiedervorladung verursachten Kosten zu verurtheilen.

Im Falle wiederholten Nichterscheinens ist überdies auf Geldstrafe bis zu fünfzig Gulden gegen sie zu erkennen und kann das Gericht oder der beauftragte Richter die zwangsweise Vorführung verordnen.

Zur Anwendung der Bestimmungen des Abs. 1 oder 2 wird deren ausdrückliche Bekanntgabe in der Vorladung vorausgesetzt.

G. A. d. K. d. A. II S. 214. 226. 343. 344. 452. IV S. 98. — K. d. R. II S. 230. IV. S. 57.

1) Wer rechtsförmlich als Zeuge geladen wurde, ist der Regel nach verpflichtet, zu erscheinen, auch wenn er von der Sache nicht das Mindeste weiß, oder wenn er wegen Untüchtigkeit oder aus sonstigen Gründen das Recht hat, seine Zeugschaft zu verweigern.

Er ist verpflichtet, so zu erscheinen, daß er im Stande ist, auf die an ihn gerichteten Fragen vernünftig zu antworten, und wenn er sich durch eigene Schuld, z. B. durch Betrunkenheit, in die Lage versetzt hat, als Zeuge nicht vernommen werden zu können, wird er als nicht erschienen zu betrachten sein.

Rechtsförmlich ist die Vorladung, wenn sie durch den Gerichtsvollzieher, mit Einhaltung der wesentlichen Formen von Zustellungen, geschehen ist, wenn namentlich auch die besonderen Vorschriften der Art. 409 u. 410 über Formen und Fristen der Zeugenladung beobachtet worden sind.

2) Erscheint der Zeuge nicht, so ist er von Neuem vorzuladen und auf Antrag des Beweisführers vom Gerichte oder vom beauftragten Richter in die durch Vereitelung der Tagfahrt und durch die Wiedervorladung verursachten Kosten zu verurtheilen.

Beides hat zu unterbleiben, wenn die Parteien auf den Zeugen verzichten; verlangt aber auch nur eine Partei, daß der Zeuge gehört werde, oder sind nicht alle Parteien zugegen, so ist die Wiedervorladung zu verfügen, und falls sofort ein bezügliches Ansuchen gestellt wird, die Tagfahrt festzusetzen.

Daß die Verurtheilung zu den Kosten vom Antrage des Beweisführers abhänge, erscheint nicht ganz sachgemäß. Richtiger wäre es wohl gewesen zu sagen: „auf Antrag einer Partei,“ denn der Zeuge ist gemeinschaftlich und es kann auch die Gegenpartei die Wiedervorladung beabsichtigen; ferner fallen die Kosten dem unterliegenden Theile zur Last, und hat also jede Partei Interesse, daß sie vom schuldigen Zeugen getragen werden. Vgl. Bemerk. des Ministerial-Commiss. Abg. III 106 a. E. und Abg. II 452 (zu Art. 34). Die ausgesprochene Verurtheilung gereicht jedenfalls beiden Parteien zum Vortheile, so daß auch die Gegenpartei Ersatz der ihr durch die vereitelte Tagfahrt erwachsenen Kosten beanspruchen kann.

Als Beweisführer ist hier diejenige Partei zu betrachten, welche den Zeugen vorgeladen hat, und ist zu beachten, daß der von der einen Partei kundgegebene Zeuge auch von der Gegenpartei vorgeladen werden kann. Haben beide Parteien vorgeladen, so sind sie beide Beweisführer. Vgl. Bemerk. zu Art. 412 Nr. 2 und Abg. II 452 (zu Art. 34).

3) Bei wiederholtem Nichterscheinen ist Geldstrafe zu verhängen und kann sogar die zwangsweise Vorführung verfügt werden.

Es fragt sich, ob diese Folgen auch dann eintreten, wenn bei der ersten Tagfahrt eine Verurtheilung nicht ausgesprochen wurde, sei es weil der Beweisführer es nicht beantragt hatte, sei es weil die Verhinderung des Zeugen hinreichend bescheinigt war (Art. 428), oder ob das Gesetz eine erste Bestrafung voraussetze, auf welche dann eine zweite als Rückfallsstrafe folge? Nach den Worten des Gesetzes ist Ersteres anzunehmen, und erscheint es auch als das Praktischere, da der Zeuge durch die Wiedervorladung erfährt, daß bereits eine Tagfahrt vereitelt ist.

Eine zwangsweise Vorführung wird der Richter natürlich nur anordnen, wenn das erste Nichterscheinen verschuldet war. War dies nicht der Fall, so wird er diese Maßregel erst bei nochmaligem Nichterscheinen verfügen, wenn er sie überhaupt für angemessen erachtet. Bei der Verhaftung müssen die Bestimmungen über Ausübung der Personalhaft, namentlich Art. 1147, maßgebend sein.

4) Wenn schließlich gesagt wird, daß zur Anordnung der fraglichen Bestimmungen die ausdrückliche Bekanntgabe in der Vorladung vorausgesetzt werde, so sind hiermit nur die Strafbestimmungen gemeint, denn zur Festsetzung einer neuen Tagfahrt und zur Wiedervorladung bedarf es keiner vorausgehenden Drohung.

5) Der Beschluß des Richters ist sofort vollstreckbar, und hat daher der Gerichtsschreiber auf Verlangen vollstreckbare Ausfertigung zu geben.

Art. 428. — **Von der in Art. 427 vorgesehenen Verurtheilung ist Umgang zu nehmen, wenn mit oder ohne Zuthun des Zeugen bereits ausreichend bescheinigt ist, daß der Zeuge zu erscheinen verhindert oder im gegebenen Falle der Vorladung Folge zu leisten nicht verpflichtet war. Hat der Zeuge einen gesetzlichen Grund, sich der Zeugschaft zu entschlagen, und hat er dem Gerichte oder beauftragten Richter angezeigt, daß er davon Gebrauch machen wolle, so hat, wenn jener Grund bereits erwiesen vorliegt, sowohl die Verurtheilung als die Anberaumung einer neuen Vernehmungstagfahrt zu unterbleiben.**

Art. 429. — **Hat ein als Zeuge vorgeschlagener öffentlicher Beamter dem Gerichte oder beauftragten Richter rechtzeitig unter Bezugnahme auf seine Dienstpflicht angezeigt, daß er die Vernehmlassung von der Ermächtigung der vorgesetzten Behörde abhängig machen zu müssen glaube, und ist die Einhaltung der Vorschriften des Art. 411 nicht nachgewiesen, so ist er von der Verpflichtung zum persönlichen Erscheinen bei der Vernehmungstagfahrt befreit und kann seine Wiedervorladung nur stattfinden, nachdem die Ermächtigung der vorgesetzten Behörde zur Vernehmlassung beigebracht ist.**

G. A. d. K. d. A. II S. 226. 227. 233. 343. 344. IV S. 98. — K. d. R. II S. 236. IV S. 57.

1) Diese beiden Artikel geben die Ausnahmen von der Regel des Art. 427.

Es soll eine Verurtheilung des Zeugen nicht erfolgen, wenn bereits ausreichend bescheinigt ist, daß der Zeuge verhindert oder der Vorladung Folge zu leisten nicht verpflichtet sei.

Was die Bescheinigung anbelangt, welche, wenn sie nicht bereits aus den Akten, insbesondere der Ladung, entnommen werden kann, vom Zeugen beizubringen ist, s. die Einleitung zu Hauptstück IX Nr. 2 und 3.

Der Fall, wo der Zeuge zu erscheinen nicht verpflichtet ist, erscheint, abgesehen von Mängeln der Vorladung, gegeben, wenn die verlangte Hinterlegung der Zeugengebühren nicht erfolgt ist (Art. 343 Abs. 4), sowie im Falle des Art. 429.

2) Nicht bloß von der Verurtheilung, sondern auch von Anberaumung einer neuen Tagfahrt ist Umgang zu nehmen, wenn der Zeuge dem Gerichte oder beauftragten Richter angezeigt hat, daß er die Zeugschaft verweigere, und bereits der Nachweis vorliegt, daß die Weigerung gesetzlich begründet sei. Diese Anzeige hat jedenfalls in sicherer Weise zu geschehen, also schriftlich oder durch eine gehörig bevollmächtigte Person, und werden die Beweise (eine bloße Bescheinigung genügt hier nicht), sofern sie nicht schon in den Akten liegen, wie dies bei Verwandtschaft, Betheiligung am Rechtsstreite rc. häufig der Fall ist, oder aus der Natur der verlangten Zeugenaussage sich ergeben, mit derselben vorzulegen sein.

Hat der beauftragte Richter mit Unrecht angenommen, daß ein Grund zur Weigerung vorliege oder bewiesen sei, so kann jede Partei bei der Verhandlung verlangen, daß die Vernehmung des Zeugen angeordnet werde, und kann selbst schon vorher auf dem Wege der Beschwerde (Art. 738 Ziff. 1) Abhilfe erlangen.

3) Für öffentliche Beamte ist die besondere Ausnahme gemacht, daß die rechtzeitige Anzeige, sie könnten ihrer Ueberzeugung nach ohne Ermächtigung der vorgesetzten Behörde nicht aussagen, sie der Verpflichtung zum Erscheinen enthebt. Es wird in diesem Falle zwar neue Tagfahrt anberaumt, allein die Wiedervorladung kann wirksam nur geschehen, nachdem die erforderliche Ermächtigung gemäß Art. 411 beigebracht ist.

Die Anzeige ist an den Vorstand des Gerichts bezw. den beauftragten Richter zu richten und ist rechtzeitig, wenn sie eintrifft, bevor die Folgen der Versäumung ausgesprochen sind.

Art. 430. — **Die Verurtheilung nach Art. 427 ist zurückzunehmen, wenn der Verurtheilte Einspruch erhebt und nachweist, daß die Vorladung nicht in gesetzlicher Weise erfolgte oder daß er nicht verpflichtet oder nicht im Stande war, derselben Folge zu leisten.**

Wird der Verurtheilte später vernommen, so kann er den Einspruch bei der Vernehmung mündlich erheben und hat das Gericht oder der beauftragte Richter darüber sofort Verhandlung zu pflegen und Entscheidung zu treffen.

Findet eine spätere Vernehmung nicht statt, so ist der Einspruch bis zur Vollstreckung zulässig. Er wird dadurch erhoben, daß der Verurtheilte dem Anwalte des Beweisführers eine Urkunde zustellen läßt, welche außer der Erklärung des Einspruchs und Angabe der Gründe Vorladung in eine vom Senatsvorstande zur Verhandlung festgesetzte Sitzung enthalten muß.

Hat im Falle des Abs. 2 ein beauftragter Richter über den Einspruch erkannt, so kann sich dagegen sowohl der verurtheilte Zeuge als auch der Beweisführer an das Prozeßgericht wenden. Er hat zu diesem Behufe dem Gegner innerhalb fünfzehn Tagen vom Erkenntnisse an eine bezügliche Zustellung machen zu lassen, welche zugleich Vorladung in eine vom Senatsvorstande zur Verhandlung festgesetzte Sitzung zu enthalten hat.

In den Fällen der Abs. 3 und 4 findet ein schriftliches Vorverfahren nicht statt und der verurtheilte Zeuge kann auch ohne Anwalt in der Sitzung erscheinen und verhandeln.

Gegen die vom Gerichte in Gemäßheit der Abs. 2—4 erlassenen Urtheile sind Einspruch und Rechtsmittel nicht zulässig.

G. A. d. K. d. A. II S. 214. 344. 452. IV S. 98. 330. 331. 341. — K. d. R. II S. 230. IV S. 57.

1) Die Verurtheilung ist zurückzunehmen, falls der Zeuge nachweist, daß die Vorladung nicht in gesetzlicher Weise erfolgt sei (Bemerk. zu Art. 427 Nr. 1), oder daß er nicht verpflichtet war, derselben Folge zu leisten (Art. 343 Abs. 4 und Art. 429), oder endlich, daß er nicht im Stande gewesen zu erscheinen. Die Ursachen der Verhinderung können der verschiedensten Art sein, und es ist ganz dem Ermessen des Richters überlassen, ob sie zur Entschuldigung genügen.

Da das Gesetz bloß von einer Zurücknahme der Verurtheilnng im Ganzen spricht, zudem auch die angeführten Fälle nur solche sind, in welchen völlige Aufhebung gerechtfertigt erscheint, so sollte man meinen, es sei eine theilweise Zurücknahme, z. B. eine Herabsetzung der ausgesprochenen Geldstrafe, nicht statthaft; allein offenbar muß auch hier der Grundsatz gelten, daß im Mehr das Mindere enthalten sei. Man setze den Fall, es sei eine sehr hohe Strafe verhängt worden, weil der Richter böswilliges Ausbleiben annahm oder voraussetzte, der Zeuge sei sehr vermögend, bei der Verhandlung über den Einspruch zeigt sich aber, daß das Ausbleiben zwar nicht völlig entschuldigt war, jedoch mildernde Umstände vorliegen oder der Zeuge arm sei. Ohne Zweifel liegt es im Geiste des Gesetzes, in Fällen dieser Art eine Minderung der Strafe zu gestatten.

2) Das Mittel zur Erwirkung der Zurücknahme ist der Einspruch, welcher entweder bei der späteren Vernehmung vom Zeugen mündlich vorgebracht (Abs. 2) oder durch Zustellung eines Einspruchsaktes mit Ladung in eine bestimmte Sitzung des Prozeßgerichts erhoben wird (Abs. 3).

Findet eine spätere Vernehmung nicht statt, sei es weil auf den Zeugen verzichtet wird, oder der Rechtsstreit sich durch Vergleich, Abstand 2c. erledigt, sei es weil bei der neuen Tagfahrt der Zeuge wiederholt ausbleibt, so ist der Einspruch zulässig bis zur Vollstreckung.

Aus dieser Bestimmung folgt: 1) daß das Stillschweigen des Zeugen bei seiner späteren Vernehmung oder vielmehr bei seinem späteren Erscheinen als ein Verzicht auf diesen Einspruch betrachtet wird, und 2) daß auf vorliegenden Einspruch Art. 826 keine Anwendung findet.

Die Worte: „bis zur Vollstreckung" können sowohl bedeuten: „bis die Vollstreckung begonnen hat," oder: „bis sie vollendet ist." Sie sind schon im Entwurfe enthalten, und es möchte vorauszusetzen sein, daß sie dort den nemlichen Sinn haben sollten, wie die Worte: »jusqu'à l'exécution« in Art. 158 Code de proc., nemlich: „bis die Verurtheilung vollstreckt ist."

3) Wird der Einspruch bei Gelegenheit der späteren Vernehmung erhoben, so entscheidet das Gericht oder der beauftragte Richter darüber, mögen die Parteien zugegen sein, um ihre Rechte zu wahren, oder nicht; sie erscheinen mit etwaigen Einwänden ausgeschlossen (Art. 340).

In allen sonstigen Fällen ist der Einspruch immer vor's Prozeßgericht zu bringen, selbst wenn es ein beauftragter Richter war, von welchem die Verurtheilung ausgegangen ist. Es ist dann der Anwalt des Beweisführers unter Erhebung des Einspruchs und Angabe der Gründe desselben in eine bestimmte Sitzung zu laden. Daß hier nur vom Beweisführer die Sprache, erscheint nicht ganz richtig, da der Zeuge gemeinschaftlich ist und die strittige Frage alle Parteien berührt. Allerdings ist es die Consequenz von Art. 427 (s. Bemerk. allda Nr. 2).

Die Verhandlung erfolgt ohne schriftliches

Vorverfahren und es kann der Zeuge ohne Anwalt erscheinen und verhandeln.

4) In Fällen, wo der beauftragte Richter über den Einspruch erkannt hat, steht sowohl dem Zeugen als dem Beweisführer das Recht zu, sich an das Prozeßgericht zu wenden. Es ist innerhalb 15 Tagen vom Erkenntnisse (nicht von dessen Zustellung) bezügliche Vorladung in eine bestimmte Sitzung zu geben, in welcher ebenso wie im vorbesprochenen Falle verhandelt wird.

5) Art. 430 soll offenbar das Verfahren für Fälle, wo Zeugen die auf Grund von Art. 427 gegen sie ergangenen Verurtheilungen anfechten wollen, sowie für die weiteren Entscheidungen, welche durch diese Anfechtungen veranlaßt werden, erschöpfend regeln; es ist deßhalb neben dem Einspruche nicht etwa Beschwerde auf Grund von Art. 738 Ziff. 2 u. 3 statthaft.

Es frägt sich jedoch, ob dieses Rechtsmittel nicht der Partei zu Gebot stehe, wenn ihr Antrag auf Verurtheilung des Zeugen zum Kostenersatze abgewiesen worden ist, und allerdings möchte dies anzunehmen sein, selbst dann, wenn die Entscheidung in der Sitzung erging, da es sich nicht um eine Entscheidung unter den Parteien, sondern zwischen den Parteien einerseits und dem Zeugen andererseits handelt.

Verfahren bei Verweigerung des Zeugnisses oder Eids.

Art. 431. — **Verweigert ein Zeuge wegen angeblichen Vorhandenseins eines der in Art. 401 Ziff. 2 und 3 bezeichneten Verhältnisse die Vernehmlassung und ist die Grundlosigkeit seiner Weigerung weder von dem Beweisführer dargethan noch sonst ersichtlich, so genügt zum Nachweise die auf Verlangen des Beweisführers eidlich zu bekräftigende Erklärung des Zeugen über das behauptete Verhältniß.**

Geschieht die Verweigerung aus einem der in Art. 400 Ziff. 1 und 3 bezeichneten Gründe, so ist der Zeuge von der Pflicht zur Zeugnißleistung frei, wenn er erklärt und auf Verlangen einer Partei eidlich bekräftigt, daß er die Thatsache, worüber er aussagen soll, in dem betreffenden Berufsverhältnisse erfahren habe und daß er durch ihre Offenbarung die ihm vermöge jenes Verhältnisses obliegende Pflicht zur Verschwiegenheit zu verletzen glaube.

In dem Falle des Art. 400 Ziff. 2 vertritt die unter Bezugnahme auf seine Dienstpflicht abgebene Erklärung des Beamten, daß er die Vernehmlassung von der Ermächtigung seiner vorgesetzten Behörde abhängig machen zu müssen glaube, die Stelle des in Abs. 2 bezeichneten Eids.

G. A. d. K. d. A. II S. 215. 226. 227. 232. 233. 344. IV S. 99. — K. d. R. II S. 230. IV S. 57.

1) Das Gesetz regelt hier das Verfahren bei Verweigerung der Zeugschaft für die verschiedenen Fälle, in welchen diese statthaft ist.

Erfolgt die Weigerung auf Grund von Art. 401 Ziff. 2 u. 3, also in Fällen, wo es sich nicht um Untüchtigkeit des Zeugen handelt, so soll das Gericht prüfen, ob nicht die Grundlosigkeit der Weigerung dargethan oder ersichtlich sei. Die Natur der Sache bedingt es, daß nöthigenfalls zur Beibringung solcher Beweise Frist zu gestatten sei.

Liegt dieser Beweis nicht vor, so genügt die eidliche Erklärung des Zeugen über das behauptete Verhältniß. Handelt es sich übrigens davon, daß die Beantwortung einer Frage dem Zeugen oder seinen Angehörigen Schande oder erheblichen Nachtheil bringen würde (Art. 401 Ziff. 3), so wird die eidliche Erklärung des Zeugen nicht leicht den Ausschlag geben. Der Richter wird sich aus der Fragestellung selbst, in Verbindung mit den Umständen des Falls, seine Ueberzeugung zu bilden haben, denn es handelt sich hier im Wesentlichen nur um Schlußfolgerungen und Beurtheilungen.

Erfolgt die Weigerung im Falle einer behaupteten Untüchtigkeit (Art. 400), so entscheidet unbedingt die eidliche Erklärung, welche der Zeuge nach Maßgabe der näheren Vorschriften in Abs. 2 und 3 des Art. 431 abgibt.

Eigenthümlich erscheint, daß der letztere Eid auf Verlangen einer Partei, der erstere auf Verlangen des Beweisführers zu leisten sein soll.

2) Findet das Zeugenverhör in der Sitzung statt, so entscheidet das Gericht falls nöthig sofort, ob die Weigerung begründet sei, und der Zeuge ist verpflichtet, sich diesem Spruche zu fügen, wenn er nicht nach Art. 432 verurtheilt werden will.

Zwar steht ihm das Rechtsmittel der Beschwerde zu (Abg. III 105, 106), allein dasselbe hat keine aufschiebende Wirkung (Art. 742), und es bleibt ihm daher, wenn er mit seiner Weigerung vor dem höheren Richter durchzudringen hofft, nichts übrig, als sich wegen fortgesetzter Weigerung verurtheilen zu lassen und gegen beide Entscheidungen Beschwerde zu erheben.

3) Findet das Zeugenverhör vor einem beauftragten Richter statt, so entsteht die Frage, ob dieser befugt sei, über Grund oder Ungrund der Weigerung zu entscheiden.

Aus Art. 431 ergibt sich, daß der beauftragte Richter einen Zeugen zu Geldstrafe verurtheilen dürfe, wenn derselbe seine Vernehmlassung ohne gesetzlichen Grund verweigere, und es möchte sich hieraus folgern lassen, daß die Frage, ob eine Weigerung gesetzlich begründet sei, dem Zeugen gegenüber auch vom beauftragten Richter gewürdigt werden dürfe. Hiermit stehen auch die Bestimmungen des Art. 428 im Einklange, und offenbar wäre es nicht sachgemäß, bei jeder noch so grundlosen und frivolen Weigerung die Vorfrage der Begründung vor's Prozeßgericht zu bringen.

Eine Ausnahme ist natürlich zu machen für Fälle, wo die Weigerung Zweifel wegen des Bestehens einer Untüchtigkeit im Sinne von Art. 425 (s. Bemerk. allda Nr. 5) erregt, d. h. wo der Ungrund der Weigerung nicht offen und klar zu Tage liegt.

Den Parteien gegenüber bildet die Weigerung immer einen Anstand im Sinne des Art. 342, und steht es daher dem beauftragten Richter nicht zu, bezügliche Parteianträge selbst abzuweisen, vielmehr muß er die Frage, ob der Zeuge zu vernehmen sei oder nicht, vor's Prozeßgericht verweisen.

Die Erledigung des Zwischenpunkts erfolgt nach Art. 342 Abs. 2, und ist es nicht nöthig, den Zeugen in die Sitzung beizuladen, da das Gesetz es nicht vorschreibt. Es genügt, daß der Richter die Begründung der Weigerung umständlich zu Protokoll nimmt und etwaige Belege beifügt. Gegen die Entscheidung des Prozeßgerichts steht dem Zeugen selbstverständlich das Rechtsmittel der Beschwerde zu.

4) Eine weitere Frage ist es, ob das Gesetz verlange, daß der Zeuge zuerst unbeeidigt mit seinen Einwänden gehört und dann die Sache vor's Prozeßgericht verwiesen werde, damit dieses entscheide, ob die in Art. 431 bezeichneten Eide zu leisten seien oder nicht?

Ein solches Verfahren wäre höchst schleppend und unpraktisch; ich glaube daher nicht, daß es im Sinne des Gesetzes sei.

Setzt man voraus, daß beide Parteien zugeben, es sei bei Vorliegen der behaupteten Thatsachen die Weigerung begründet, und sich darauf beschränken, die eidliche Bekräftigung zu verlangen, so ist klar, daß der beauftragte Richter diese Eide sofort abzunehmen habe.

Allein auch in Fällen, wo Anstände erhoben werden, z. B. behauptet wird, der Zeuge sei kein öffentlicher Beamte im Sinne des Art. 400 oder es handle sich nicht um Berufsverhältnisse der Art, wie sie dort in Ziff. 1 und 3 vorgesehen sind, steht nichts im Wege, daß der beauftragte Richter die eidlichen Erklärungen über die Weigerungsgründe auf Antrag vorläufig erhebe, so daß dem Prozeßgerichte nur die Aufgabe bleibt, zu entscheiden, ob diese Erklärungen erheblich seien oder nicht, ebenso wie es auch sonst bei bereits aufgenommenen eidlichen Zeugenaussagen sich nachträglich erst über die Erheblichkeit ausspricht (Art. 342 Abs. 2). Art. 425 ist kein Hinderniß, da er nur die Vernehmung über das Beweisthema, d. h. über Thatsachen, bei deren Kundgabe öffentliche Interessen in Frage sind, zum Gegenstande hat, während es sich hier nur von Vorfragen handelt.

Art. 432. — **Zeugen, welche die Eidesleistung beziehungsweise die an deren Stelle tretende Betheuerung oder die Vernehmlassung, es sei im Allgemeinen oder über einzelne Punkte, ohne gesetzlichen Grund verweigern, werden der Partei für die verursachten Kosten verantwortlich und verfallen in Geldstrafe bis zu fünfzig Gulden.**

Erfolgt die Verurtheilung gegen sie durch einen beauftragten Richter, so kann innerhalb acht Tagen Beschwerde dagegen bei dem Prozeßgerichte in der in Art. 430 Abs. 4 bezeichneten Weise erhoben werden. Die ausgesprochene Strafe ist wieder aufzuheben, wenn der Zeuge sofort in der Sitznng, in welcher die Verurtheilung erfolgt oder die gegen den Ausspruch des beauftragten Richters erhobene Beschwerde abgewiesen worden ist, seiner Zeugenpflicht genügt. G. A. d K. d. A. II S. 214. 215. 344. IV S. 98. 99. — K. d. R. II S. 230. IV. S. 57.

1) Die Folge unbefugter Weigerung soll Verurtheilung des Zeugen zu Geldstrafe und Kosten sein. Nach den Worten des Gesetzes könnte die Verurtheilung sofort mit der Erklärung des Ungrunds der Weigerung erfolgen, allein offenbar liegt es im Geiste des Gesetzes, daß in Fällen, wo die Weigerung nicht offenbar frivol ist, sondern ernstliche Gründe dafür vorgebracht werden, der Richter vorerst nur die Verpflichtung zur Zeugschaft und erst bei fortgesetzter Weigerung die Verurtheilung wegen Widerspenstigkeit ausspreche.

2) Auch in sonstiger Beziehung erscheint die Fassung dieses Artikels unklar und unvollständig.

Es ist nicht gesagt, ob sofort die Verurtheilung zu den Kosten zu erfolgen habe, ob der beauftragte Richter dazu befugt sei, ob der Beschluß vollstreckbar sei, und selbst die nach Art. 342 Abs. 1 nöthige Ermächtigung für den beauftragten Richter, die Geldstrafe zu verhängen, muß erst aus Abs. 2 des Artikels gefolgert werden.

Richtiger lautete der Entwurf. Derselbe sprach von Verantwortlichkeit für Kosten und Schäden und setzte in dieser Beziehung eine Entschädigungsklage voraus, wie sie auch die französische Jurisprudenz zuließ (Chauveau quest. 1036); zum Ausspruche der Strafverfügungen ermächtigte er ausdrücklich auch den beauftragten Richter. Es entsteht nun die Frage, ob trotzdem daß die Haftung jetzt auf die Kosten beschränkt ist, nur eine gewöhnliche Entschädigungsklage stattfinde, welche allerdings als Gewährschaftsklage mit dem Hauptstreite verbunden werden dürfte, oder ob Art. 427 analoge Anwendung finde.

Aus der Allgemeinheit der Worte: „Erfolgt die Verurtheilung ꝛc." wäre ich geneigt zu folgern, daß beide Verurtheilungen (zu Kosten und zu Geldstrafe) auch vom beauftragten Richter ausgesprochen werden dürfen, woraus sich denn von selbst ergibt, daß die Verurtheilung sofort, ohne weiteres Verfahren, eintreten kann. Die Kosten, welche hier in Frage stehen, sind diejenigen der Vorladung des Zeugen und der etwaigen Vereitelung der Tagfahrt.

3) Gegen die Verurtheilung durch den beauftragten Richter darf der Zeuge binnen acht Tagen vom Erkenntnisse an das Recht der Beschwerde in der durch Art. 430 Abs. 4 bestimmten Weise ausüben. Ob auch Abs. 5 und 6 allda anwendbar seien, ist nicht gesagt — gleichfalls eine offenbare Unvollständigkeit, denn Abs. 5 soll jedenfalls Anwendung finden!

Ist die Verurtheilung vom Gerichte ausgegangen, so steht dem Zeugen das Rechtsmittel der Beschwerde nach Hauptst. XXVIII zu. Vgl. Abg. III 105 und 106.

4) Die Androhung der Geldstrafe soll nur das Mittel sein, um eine Zeugenaussage zu erzwingen; es war daher sachgemäß, auch nach Ausspruch derselben, diesen Zweck nicht aus den Augen zu verlieren, und für den Fall, wo der Zeuge sich dazu versteht, seiner Pflicht zu genügen, die Aufhebung der Strafe in Aussicht zu stellen.

Das Gesetz schreibt diese Aufhebung vor, wenn der Zeuge in der nemlichen Sitzung, in welcher die Strafbarkeit seiner Weigerung ausgesprochen wird, seiner Zeugenpflicht genüge, setzt aber dabei als selbstverständlich voraus, daß das Erbieten zu einer Zeit geschehen müsse, wo die Aussage noch für die Sache verwerthet werden kann. Ein Zeuge kann seiner Zeugenpflicht nicht mehr genügen, wenn in Folge seiner Säumigkeit die ganze Aussage gegenstandslos geworden ist.

Daß hier von „Strafe", nicht aber von „Verurtheilung", wie im vorhergehenden Satze, gesprochen wird, möchte ein weiterer Grund sein, mit letzterem Ausdrucke auch die Kostenverurtheilung zu begreifen.

XIII. Hauptstück.

Sachverständige.

Allgemeine Bestimmungen.

Art. 433. — **Die Begutachtung durch Sachverständige ist auf Antrag oder von Amtswegen anzuordnen, wenn eine besondere Vorschrift des Gesetzes es erfordert oder das Gericht zur Ermittelung oder Beurtheilung streitiger Thatsachen oder Zustände ein solches Gutachten für nöthig oder dienlich erachtet. Diese Anordnung kann in jeder Lage der Sache getroffen werden.**

Art. 434. — **Die Parteien können durch Uebereinkunft bestimmen, wie viele und welche Sachverständige beigezogen werden sollen. In Ermangelung einer solchen Uebereinkunft werden die Sachverständigen vom Gerichte oder einem beauftragten Richter ernannt. In diesem Falle sind in der Regel drei Sachverständige zu bestellen, in einfachen und geringfügigen Sachen genügt einer. Den Parteien ist jederzeit unbenommen, noch über eine andere Zahl oder andere Personen sich zu vereinbaren.**

Art. 435. — **Die vom Gerichte oder dem beauftragten Richter ernannten Sachverständigen können aus gleichen Gründen wie die Richter abgelehnt werden. Die von den Parteien erwählten Sachverständigen können nur aus Gründen abgelehnt werden, welche erst nach der Wahl eingetreten oder bekannt geworden sind.**

Art. 436. — **Sachverständige, welche zur Abgabe von Gutachten der verlangten Art öffentlich bestellt**

sind, können sich ohne erhebliche Gründe einem ihnen gemachten Auftrage nicht entziehen. Andere Personen sind nicht verpflichtet, die Wahl oder Ernennung als Sachverständige anzunehmen. G. A. d. K. d. A. II S. 178—181. 344. 345. IV S. 98. — K. d. R. II S. 230.

1) Sachverständige sollen den Richter bei Feststellung und Beurtheilung von thatsächlichen Verhältnissen unterstützen; sie sollen dessen Gehilfen und Rathgeber sein in Fällen, wo er selbst die besonderen wissenschaftlichen, technischen, lokalen Kenntnisse nicht in dem Maße besitzt, um den Sachverhalt mit der nöthigen Gründlichkeit aufzufassen und zu beurtheilen.

Man pflegt zu unterscheiden zwischen wahrnehmenden oder darstellenden und beurtheilenden Sachverständigen, je nachdem es sich bloß darum handelt, daß der Sachverständige bei Feststellung des Thatbestands Hilfe leiste, z. B. bei einem Augenscheine die sachgemäßen Untersuchungen, Messungen vornehme, die Pläne fertige 2c., oder aber darum, daß er sein gutachtliches Urtheil abgebe.

Aus der Natur und dem Zwecke der Begutachtung durch Sachverständige ergibt sich von selbst, daß sie von Amtswegen und in jeder Lage der Sache, so lange es für die richterliche Entscheidung von Nutzen sein kann, angeordnet werden dürfe.

a) Ernennung der Sachverständigen (Art. 434).

2) Sind sämmtliche Parteien einig, so ist deren Willen maßgebend, sowohl bezüglich der Zahl der Sachverständigen, als bezüglich der Personen.

Dieses Recht können die Parteien zu jeder Zeit ausüben, selbst dann, wenn die ursprünglich bezeichneten Sachverständigen bereits vorgeladen waren, ja sogar ihre Verrichtungen begonnen hatten, und ohne Rücksicht darauf, ob die Anordnung des Gutachtens auf Parteiantrag oder von Amtswegen erfolgt ist. Nur für den Fall eines Obergutachtens besteht eine Ausnahme (Art. 448).

3) In Ermangelung einer Uebereinkunft wird der Sachverständige vom Gerichte oder beauftragten Richter ernannt. Natürlich hat das Gericht, wenn es selbst ernennen will, nicht abzuwarten, ob etwa eine Uebereinkunft erfolge, um dann in einem ergänzenden Urtheile die Sachverständigen zu ernennen, vielmehr ist sofort im Beweisurtheile für den Fall, als die Parteien sich nicht in anderer Weise einigen, die Ernennung auszusprechen (Art. 438 Abs. 1), wie dies in der Pfalz (nach Vorschrift von Art. 305 Code de proc.) bisher geschah.

Soweit die Parteien sich in der Sitzung über die Sachverständigen einigen, ertheilt das Gericht darüber Urkunde und fällt die eventuelle Ernennung durch das Gericht oder den beauftragten Richter als gegenstandslos hinweg. Schließlich unterliegt es keinem Anstande, daß die Parteien bloß den einen oder den anderen der gerichtlich ernannten Experten durch eine andere Person ersetzen können.

4) Soll die Ernennung durch den beauftragten Richter erfolgen, so erscheint es sachgemäß, ihm diese Befugniß im Urtheile zu übertragen, jedoch ist eine ausdrückliche Uebertragung nicht nothwendig, vielmehr erfolgt sie stillschweigend dadurch, daß das Gericht nicht selbst ernannt hat.

So war es im Entwurfe (Art. 313), im Vorschlage des Referenten und in der ursprünglichen Fassung (Abg. II 180) bestimmt, und die Aenderungen der Subcommission (Abg. II 345) sollten keine materielle sein. Mit dieser Auffassung stimmt auch Art. 434 vollkommen überein und Art. 438 Abs. 2 läßt sie wenigstens zu; schließlich ist sie entschieden praktisch, indem sie ein ergänzendes Urtheil unnöthig macht.

5) Was die Zahl der Sachverständigen betrifft, so läßt zwar die Fassung des Gesetzes Zweifel zu, ob nicht auch dieser Punkt dem beauftragten Richter überlassen werden könne; allein ich möchte annehmen, daß immer das Gericht selbst zu entscheiden habe, ob die Begutachtung durch drei Sachverständige erfolge solle, oder ob einer genüge.

b) Recht der Ablehnung (Art. 435).

6) Da die Sachverständigen in gewissem Sinne Richterfunktionen ausüben, so ist es natürlich, wenn das Gesetz sie aus gleichen Gründen wie Richter (Art. 42) ablehnen läßt. In den Fällen, wo der Richter behindert wäre, tritt bei Sachverständigen nur die Ablehnung ein; es könnte also, falls diese nicht stattfindet, von einer Nichtigkeit nicht die Rede sein.

Daß Sachverständige, welche aus freier Wahl der Parteien hervorgegangen sind, nur abgelehnt werden dürfen, wenn der Grund erst nach der Wahl eingetreten oder bekannt geworden ist, erscheint selbstverständlich. Die Wahl einer Partei erfolgt mit Zustellung des Anwaltsaktes, in welchem sie ihren bezüglichen Willen kundgeben, denn hiermit erlangt die Gegenpartei ein Recht (Art. 337).

c) Recht der Weigerung (Art. 436).

7) Personen, welche als Sachverständige gewählt oder ernannt werden, sind in der Regel nicht

verpflichtet, ihre Dienste zu leihen, und es begreift sich leicht, daß hier, wo die Wahl freisteht, andere Grundsätze gelten müssen, als bei der Zeugschaft.

Eine Ausnahme macht das Gesetz nur für solche Personen, welche zur Abgabe von Gutachten der verlangten Art öffentlich bestellt sind, wenn sie nicht erhebliche Gründe für ihre Weigerung vorbringen können. Ueber die Folgen der Nichterfüllung dieser Pflicht s. Bemerk. zu Art. 441 Nr. 10.

Art. 437. — **Das Gericht ist nicht gezwungen, unbedingt nach der Mehrheit der Stimmen der Sachverständigen zu entscheiden; es hat vielmehr die verschiedenen Meinungen nach den hiefür entwickelten Gründen und dem darin bekundeten Grade der Kunst- und Sachkenntnisse zu würdigen. Selbst einem einstimmigen Gutachten braucht es nicht gegen seine Ueberzeugung zu folgen.**

G. A. d. K. d. A. II S. 183. 185. 186. 345. IV S. 98. — K. d. R. II S. 230. IV 57—59.

1) Die Bestimmungen dieses Artikels sind von höchster Wichtigkeit; sie bezeichnen klar und scharf die Stellung, welche das Gutachten der Sachverständigen im neuen Verfahren einnimmt, sowie den Gegensatz der jetzigen Prinzipien zu den früheren.

Der Richter ist, dem Gutachten der Sachverständigen gegenüber, nicht mehr bloß die Maschine, welche deren Ausspruch constatirt und aus demselben die Folgerungen für den Rechtsstreit zieht; er bleibt vielmehr, wie es der Würde seines Amts entspricht und zur Ermittlung der Wahrheit nothwendig ist, Herr der Sache, die Sachverständigen aber sind bloß seine Rathgeber. Nur die Ueberzeugung des Richters entscheidet und die Ansicht der Sachverständigen hat nur insofern Werth, als sie auf die richterliche Ueberzeugung bestimmend einzuwirken vermag.

Es läßt sich daher nicht mehr sagen, es sei dem Richter nicht erlaubt, sich selbst die Funktion eines Sachverständigen anzumaßen, vielmehr ist es sein Recht und seine Pflicht, sich selbst seine Ansicht zu bilden und dieser gemäß zu erkennen, wie dies unzweideutig und energisch ausgesprochen ist in dem Satze, daß er selbst dem einstimmigen Gutachten der Sachverständigen gegen seine Ueberzeugung zu folgen nicht verpflichtet sei.

Erwägt man, wie unzuverlässig häufig die Aussprüche der Sachverständigen sind, wie diese oft, gleich den Geschwornen in Strafsachen, mehr die Folgen ihres Gutachtens als dieses selbst in Betracht ziehen und sich mittelbar die Funktionen des Richters anmaßen, so kann man diese dem französischen Prozesse entlehnten Bestimmungen nur als einen sehr werthvollen Fortschritt begrüßen.

2) Gewinnt der Richter, welcher sich mit dem Ausspruche der Sachverständigen nicht einverstanden erklären kann, aus den Aufschlüssen, welche ihm die Gründe der Sachverständigen an die Hand geben, in Verbindung mit den sonst durch die Verhandlung gebotenen Anhaltspunkten eine genügende Ueberzeugung, so entscheidet er sofort; vermag er jedoch eine solche Ueberzeugung sich nicht zu verschaffen, so macht er von den ihm durch die Art. 446 u. 448 gebotenen Auskunftsmitteln Gebrauch.

Unter Umständen werden die Erwägungen, wie sie zu Art. 328 Nr. 8 und Art. 330 Nr. 4 u. 5 gegeben wurden, maßgebend sein.

Verfahren.

Art. 438. — **In dem Urtheile, welches eine Begutachtung anordnet, hat das Gericht zugleich deren Gegenstand, die zu beantwortenden Fragen und die Sachverständigen zu bezeichnen.**

Erfordert das Gutachten eine vorgängige Untersuchung oder Besichtigung des Gegenstands und kann diese nicht in der Sitzung vorgenommen werden, oder steht ein umfassenderes Gutachten zu erwarten, so hat das Gericht mit dem Vollzuge des Urtheils einen in diesem zu bestimmenden Richter zu beauftragen. Dem beauftragten Richter kann alsdann auch die Ernennung der Sachverständigen überlassen werden und steht es jeder Partei zu, bei ihm die Festsetzung der Tagfahrt zur Einweisung der Sachverständigen in das übertragene Geschäft, sowie gegebenen Falls deren Ernennung zu beantragen.

G. A. d. K. d. A. II S. 179. 180. 182. 345. IV S. 98. — K. d. R. II S. 230. IV S. 59.

1) Das Beweisurtheil hat den Gegenstand der Begutachtung, die von den Sachverständigen zu beantwortenden Fragen und die Personen der Sachverständigen zu bezeichnen.

Was die Bezeichnung der Personen betrifft, s. Bemerk. zu Art. 434 Nr. 3.

Was den Gegenstand betrifft, so ist natürlich, daß die Sachverständigen genau wissen müssen, über was sie ihr Gutachten abgeben sollen; allein in der Regel bezeichnen die zu stellenden Fragen auch den Gegenstand der Begutachtung in erschöpfender Weise und ist daher eine gesonderte Bezeichnung desselben nicht nöthig.

Was die Fragen betrifft, so ist das Gericht an die Anträge der Parteien nicht gebunden und wird eine Fassung wählen, welche möglichst objektiv gehalten ist. Handelt es sich z. B. um Abschätzung eines Grundstückes, so wird nicht zu fragen sein: „ob dasselbe den behaupteten Werth von 500 fl. oder wieviel weniger habe," sondern: „welches der gemeine Werth des fraglichen Grundstückes sei."

2) Was die Fassung des Urtheilssatzes anbelangt, so erbieten sich in der Regel die Parteien zum Beweise durch Sachverständige und jede Partei bringt diejenigen Fragen in Vorschlag, welche sie beantwortet zu haben wünscht. Es steht nun nichts im Wege, das Urtheil so zu fassen, daß man die beweispflichtige Partei zum Beweise durch Sachverständige zuläßt und die verschiedenen Fragen anreiht; allein richtiger erscheint es, wenn das Gericht ausspricht, daß es ein Gutachten von Sachverständigen anordne und sofort den Sachverständigen die Auflage macht, über die von den beiden Parteien vorgeschlagenen Fragen, soweit sie erheblich sind, sowie über die etwa von Amtswegen beizufügenden Fragen ihr Gutachten abzugeben. So war seither die Uebung in der Pfalz und es erscheint diese Form auch durch die Worte des Art. 433 angedeutet. Allerdings erscheint es im Hinblick auf Art. 440 sachgemäß, auszusprechen, ob die Anordnung von Amtswegen geschehe, oder aber ob bloß auf Parteiantrag, d. h. auf Antrag derjenigen Partei, welche das Gericht als beweispflichtig erachtet.

Das Urtheil würde also z. B. lauten: „A. d. Gr. „verordnet das Gericht von Amtswegen (auf An„trag des Klägers, des Beklagten, beider Par„teien), daß vor weiterer Entscheidung Sach„verständige sich gutachtlich darüber aussprechen, „1) 2c.;

„ernennt als Sachverständige, falls die Par„teien sich nicht in anderer Weise einigen, 2c."

oder:

„verfügt, daß drei Sachverständige zu er„nennen seien, und überträgt deren Ernennung, „sowie den weiteren Vollzug des Urtheils dem „Bezirksgerichtsrathe X."

3) Das Gesetz gestattet dem Gerichte, je nach Bedürfniß des Falles, anzuordnen, daß die Begutachtung in der Sitzung stattfinde, oder den Vollzug des Urtheils einem beauftragten Richter zu übertragen. Das Verfahren richtet sich in beiden Fällen nach den allgemeinen Prinzipien; es hat aber nach Vorschrift des Art. 331 der betreibende Theil das Beweisurtheil ausfertigen und zustellen zu lassen. Im ersteren Falle wird vorausgesetzt, daß eine vorausgehende Besichtigung und Untersuchung nicht nöthig ist, oder diese, wie bei kleineren Mobiliargegenständen, in der Sitzung vorgenommen werden kann, zugleich aber die zu beantwortenden Fragen so einfach erscheinen, daß eine sofortige Abgabe des Gutachtens erwartet werden kann.

Den Fall, wo nur das Gutachten in der Sitzung abzugeben ist, sieht Art. 447 vor.

4) Ist der Vollzug des Urtheils einem beauftragten Richter übertragen und diesem zugleich die Ernennung der Sachverständigen überlassen, wie dies im Zweifel anzunehmen ist (Bemerk. zu Art. 433 Nr. 4), so erfolgt zuerst diese Ernennung und sodann die Anberaumung einer Tagfahrt zur Einweisung der Sachverständigen in das übertragene Geschäft (Art. 444).

Es läßt sich nun die Frage aufwerfen, ob zur Ernennung der Sachverständigen nicht besondere Tagfahrt festzusetzen und der Gegner dazu beizuziehen sei, da die Parteien in allen Fällen, mag die Ernennung in der Sitzung oder durch einen beauftragten Richter geschehen, ein lebhaftes Interesse haben, dem Richter ihre Wünsche kundzugeben und ihre Einwände gegen gewisse Persönlichkeiten vorzutragen, ja es in der Regel dem Richter selbst sehr erwünscht ist, bevor er seine Wahl trifft, die Parteien zu hören; allein es scheint dies nicht der Wille des Gesetzes zu sein.

Aus Art. 442 geht klar hervor, daß auf ein contradiktorisches Verfahren bei der Ernennung kein Werth gelegt wird und die Fassung von Art. 438 Abs. 2 läßt erkennen, daß bloß zur Einweisung der Sachverständigen Tagfahrt festzusetzen ist, die Ernennung aber auf einseitigen Antrag erfolgt.

Die Partei, welche die Sache zu betreiben, die Erledigung des Interlokuts herbeizuführen wünscht, reicht daher ein Gesuch um Ernennung der Sachverständigen und sofortige Festsetzung der Tagfahrt zur Einweisung ein, und diesem Gesuche entsprechend erfolgt die richterliche Verfügung, welche nach Art. 338 zuzustellen ist.

Es möchte geeignet sein, hier darauf hinzuweisen, daß in dergleichen Fällen, wo der fleißigere Theil aufgefordert ist, zu handeln, die Anwälte gewisse collegiale Regeln einzuhalten pflegen, indem derjenige Anwalt, welcher die Sache im Ganzen betreibt oder welchem eine bestimmte Beweisauflage gemacht ist, als vorzugsweise berechtigt gilt, die betreffenden Akte vorzunehmen, und der Gegenanwalt erst dann handelt, wenn er den Collegen ohne Erfolg gemahnt hat.

Art. 439. — **Die Ablehnung eines Sachverständigen muß der Gegenpartei binnen acht Tagen von der Zustellung des Urtheils oder Beschlusses, wodurch die Sachverständigen ernannt worden sind, und wenn der Ablehnungsgrund erst nach der Wahl oder Ernennung eingetreten oder bekannt geworden ist, binnen acht Tagen nach erlangter Kunde davon unter Angabe der Gründe erklärt werden.**

Willigt die Gegenpartei nicht in die Wahl oder Ernennung eines andern Sachverständigen, so ist der Streit zur Entscheidung des Gerichts zu bringen.

Gegen die Entscheidung findet keine selbständige Berufung statt. Wird die Ablehnung begründet gefunden, so kann das Gericht zugleich einen andern Sachverständigen an die Stelle des abgelehnten ernennen oder die Ernennung dem beauftragten Richter, wenn ein solcher aufgestellt ist, überlassen.

Art. 440. — **Für die Vorladung der Sachverständigen hat die Partei, welche die Begutachtung beantragt hat, falls aber letztere von Amtswegen angeordnet wurde, der betreibende Theil zu sorgen.**

Art. 441. — **Als Sachverständige gewählte oder ernannte Personen, welche die Wahl oder Ernennung nicht annehmen wollen, müssen dies nach erhaltener Vorladung zeitig auf der Gerichtsschreiberei mündlich oder schriftlich anzeigen, widrigenfalls sie in die veranlaßten Kosten und selbst zum Ersatze des Schadens verurtheilt werden können, welcher durch die in Folge ihrer verspäteten Anzeige eingetretene Verzögerung entstanden ist. Solche Verurtheilung findet auch statt, wenn der Sachverständige die Wahl oder Ernennung angenommen hat, aber den in Folge hievon ihm obliegenden Verpflichtungen ohne genügende Entschuldigung nicht nachkommt. Der Einspruch gegen eine Verurtheilung richtet sich nach Art. 430.**

Art. 442. — **Von der ihm angezeigten Nichtannahme eines Sachverständigen muß der Gerichtsschreiber den Anwälten der Parteien sofort Kenntniß geben. Vereinigen sich letztere nicht über die Wahl eines andern Sachverständigen, so hat der beauftragte Richter oder, wenn ein solcher nicht aufgestellt ist, der Senatsvorstand auf schriftliches Gesuch einen andern Sachverständigen zu ernennen; er kann damit erforderlichen Falls die Verlegung der Tagfahrt verbinden. Den betreffenden Beschluß hat die Partei, welche ihn erwirkt hat, sofort der Gegenpartei zustellen zu lassen.**

G. A. d. K. d. A. II S. 180—182. 345. 453. IV S. 98. — K. d. R. II S. 230. 231. IV S. 59.

1) Diese Artikel regeln das Verfahren, welches der Beeidigung und Einweisung der Sachverständigen vorausgeht, und sprechen von der Ablehnung der Sachverständigen, von der Vorladung derselben und von ihrer Weigerung, die Wahl anzunehmen.

a) Ablehnung.

2) Die Partei, welche einen Sachverständigen ablehnen will, muß binnen acht Tagen von Zustellung des Urtheils oder Beschlusses, welcher den Sachverständigen ernennt, bezw. von erlangter Kenntniß des Ablehnungsgrundes an, der Gegenpartei diese Ablehnung unter Angabe der Gründe durch Anwaltsakt erklären. Sachgemäß wird es sein, zugleich einen neuen Sachverständigen vorzuschlagen.

Hat der Gegner keinen Einwand zu erheben, so theilt er dies durch eine Erklärung mit und ist sodann, je nach Umständen, entweder ein neuer Sachverständiger zu ernennen oder der gewählte sofort vorzuladen. Reicht die Zeit nicht mehr aus, so ist eine neue Tagfahrt festzusetzen. Werden Einwände erhoben oder gibt die Gegenpartei eine Erklärung nicht ab, so wird der Zwischenstreit in die Sitzung gebracht und nach Art. 485 entschieden.

Das Gericht kann, falls es die Ablehnung für begründet erachtet, sofort den neuen Sachverständigen ernennen, sogar in Fällen, wo es die Ernennung einem beauftragten Richter übertragen hatte.

3) Wenn verfügt ist, es sei gegen die Entscheidung wegen der Ablehnung selbständige Berufung nicht statthaft — eine Verfügung, welche aus dem Entwurfe ohne Bemerkung beibehalten worden ist — so drängt sich die Frage auf, ob denn außerdem Berufung zulässig gewesen wäre, und diese Frage muß offenbar verneint werden.

b) Vorladung der Sachverständigen.

4) Der Entwurf (Art. 317 Abs. 1) verfügte, es seien die Sachverständigen durch den betreibenden Theil vorzuladen; auf Vorschlag des Referenten wurde jedoch ohne jede Bemerkung die jetzige Fassung gewählt, welche, zwei Fälle unterscheidend, die Bestimmung des Entwurfs nur für den Fall beibehält, wo das Gutachten von Amtswegen angeordnet wurde, für den Fall aber,

wo die Anordnung auf Antrag einer Partei erfolgt ist, dieser Partei die **Verpflichtung** auferlegt, für die Vorladung zu sorgen. Diese Verpflichtung lastet auf dieser Partei unbedingt, also selbst dann, wenn etwa die Gegenpartei die Festsetzung der Tagfahrt erwirkt hat. Die Zustellung des bezüglichen Beschlusses erscheint dann nur als das Mittel, um die beweispflichtige Partei in Verzug zu setzen.

Es frägt sich nun, welches die Folgen seien, wenn fragliche Verpflichtung nicht erfüllt wird?

Ist das Gutachten **bloß** auf Antrag einer Partei angeordnet worden und erscheint diese folglich nach Ansicht des Richters beweispflichtig, so wird aus der Thatsache, daß sie nicht für Vorladung der Sachverständigen sorgt, und auch eine Verlegung der Tagfahrt nicht rechtzeig erwirkt, zu folgern sein, daß sie ihren Beweis nicht liefern könne, und ihre Behauptungen dürfen, soweit sie von fraglichem Gutachten abhängen, als unerweislich betrachtet werden.

5) Will die Gegenpartei selbst für Vorladung der Sachverständigen sorgen, so ist ihr dies meiner Ansicht nach unverwehrt, denn es kann auch in ihrem Interesse liegen, daß das Gutachten erhoben werde, und falls die Sache zur Verhandlung kommt, könnte das Gericht sich veranlaßt finden, behufs Aufklärung des Sachverhalts von Amtswegen die Begutachtung anzuordnen, was ihm um so mehr freistünde, als es an seine frühere Ansicht bezüglich der Beweispflicht nicht gebunden ist. Es liegt hierin zugleich eine Mahnung für die Gerichte, in Fällen, wo irgendwie Grund vorliegt, eine Begutachtung von Amtswegen anzuordnen, dies auszusprechen, auch wenn Parteianträge vorliegen; es liegt hierin der Ausspruch, daß **beide** Parteien verpflichtet sind, für die Beweiserhebung zu sorgen.

6) Die Vorladung hat die Aufforderung zu enthalten, am betreffenden Tage zum Zwecke der Beeidigung und Einweisung in das übertragene Geschäft, eintretenden Falls, wenn nemlich die Begutachtung sofort in der Sitzung geschehen soll, zur Abgabe ihres Gutachtens zu erscheinen.

Für den letzteren Fall wäre es sehr geeignet gewesen, den Sachverständigen mit der Vorladung Kenntniß der zu beantwortenden Fragen geben zu lassen. Wenn es sich bloß um ein technisches Gutachten handelt und vorausgängige Prüfung und Untersuchung eines Gegenstandes nicht nöthig ist, liegt die Zweckmäßigkeit solcher vorausgängiger Mittheilungen auf flacher Hand; allein auch in anderen Fällen ist es in der Regel für die Sachverständigen sehr erwünscht, wenn sie vorher über den Gegenstand im **Allgemeinen** sich klar machen können und die Prüfung und Begutachtung sie nicht unvorbereitet überrascht. Es wird sachgemäß und im Interesse der Parteien selbst begründet sein, freiwillig diese Mittheilungen zu machen, deren Kosten jedenfalls nicht als frustratorisch betrachtet werden könnten.

c) Weigerung der Sachverständigen.

7) Abgesehen von dem in Art. 436 bezeichneten Falle können Personen, welche als Sachverständige gewählt oder vom Gerichte ernannt sind, ihre Dienste zwar verweigern, allein sie sind verpflichtet, von dieser Weigerung nach Empfang ihrer Vorladung **zeitig** Anzeige zu machen und zwar entweder mündlich oder schriftlich auf der Gerichtsschreiberei des Prozeßgerichts. Im Falle der Versäumung dieser Pflicht können sie zum Ersatze der hierdurch veranlaßten Kosten und Schäden verurtheilt werden. Abweichend von Art. 427 ist hier die Verurtheilung ins Ermessen des Gerichts gestellt.

Was als eine **zeitige** Anzeige zu betrachten sei, hat der Richter zu würdigen. Offenbar besteht die Pflicht zur Anzeige **sofort** nach Zustellung der Vorladung und ist der Sachverständige für jede Verzögerung verantwortlich, wenn durch dieselbe Kosten oder Schäden entstanden sind und nicht etwa die obwaltenden Umstände, z. B. daß der Sachverständige bei der Zustellung abwesend oder krank war, zur Entschuldigung dienen.

Im Hinblicke auf fragliche Strafandrohung wird den Sachverständigen zu rathen sein, mit der Anzeige ihrer Weigerung zugleich die Kundgabe und Bescheinigung etwaiger Verhinderungsgründe zu verbinden.

Die Kosten, welche in Betracht kommen, sind insbesondere diejenigen, welche durch Vereitlung einer Tagfahrt an Gebühren der anderen Sachverständigen, Gerichtskosten rc. entstehen.

Unter Schäden sind solche zu verstehen, welche den Parteien außer den Kosten noch weiter im Prozesse entstehen (Art. 119), z. B. die Fütterungskosten für Vieh. Abg. II 180 (v. Weiß).

8) Ueber die Fragen, wer diese Verurtheilung auszusprechen habe, ob auch der beauftragte Richter dazu berechtigt sei, ob sie sofort, ohne den Sachverständigen zu hören, ausgesprochen werden könne, sagt das Gesetz nichts, so wenig als in Art. 332.

Der Entwurf (Art. 314 Abs. 2) sprach aus, daß die fragliche Verurtheilung durch das Prozeßgericht auszusprechen sei, und eine Aenderung dieser Bestimmung war laut der Verhandlungen nicht beabsichtigt. Da diese Lösung auch dem Prinzipe des Art. 342 entspricht, so ist nicht zu bezweifeln, daß dem beauftragten Richter in diesem Falle das Recht zum Ausspruche einer Verurtheilung nicht zustehe. Der Gegengrund, welchen man daraus, daß das Gesetz für den Einspruch ganz allgemein den Art. 430 anwendbar erklärt, ableiten könnte, möchte zu schwach sein, um in Betracht zu kommen.

Ist daher der Vollzug des Beweisurtheils einem beauftragten Richter übertragen, so ist zuzuwarten, bis die Sache zur Verhandlung kommt, und dann die Verurtheilung zu beantragen.

9) Daß die Verurtheilung ohne weitere Vorladung des Sachverständigen auszusprechen sei, läßt sich aus der Analogie der Bestimmungen wegen der Zeugen, aus der Allgemeinheit der Worte des Gesetzes, insbesondere aber aus dem Umstande entnehmen, daß schließlich gesagt ist: „Der Einspruch richtet sich nach Art. 430."

Aus der Anwendbarkeit des Art. 430 folgt weiter, daß die ergehende Verurtheilung vollstreckbar sein müsse; denn wenn der Einspruch bis zur Vollstreckung zulässig sein soll, so muß wohl auch die Möglichkeit einer Vollstreckung angenommen werden.

10) Was den Fall betrifft, wo eine zur Abgabe von Gutachten öffentlich bestellte Person sich weigert, entsteht die Frage, wer darüber zu entscheiden habe, ob erhebliche Gründe zur Weigerung vorliegen.

Der kgl. Minist.-Commissär äußerte (Abg. II 180), es habe hier nicht das Prozeßgericht, sondern die vorgesetzte Aufsichtsbehörde zu entscheiden, und da diese Ansicht keinen Widerspruch erfahren hat, so wird sie als diejenige des Gesetzgebers anzusehen sein. Wenn der Sachverständige mit seiner Anzeige eine bezügliche Billigung dieser Aufsichtsbehörde vorlegt, hat er als entschuldigt zu gelten.

11) Der Gerichtsschreiber hat die Pflicht, den Anwälten der Parteien sofort Kenntniß von der Weigerung zu geben, welche einen neuen Sachverständigen wählen oder ihn ernennen lassen.

Die Ernennung erfolgt durch den beauftragten Richter, selbst wenn der weggefallene Sachverständige durch das Gericht selbst ernannt war, eine Unregelmäßigkeit, welche bei wichtigen Sachen ihr Bedenkliches hat und leicht Anlaß zur Erhebung neuer Gutachten geben kann, wenn der Richter eine Person wählt, welche das Vertrauen des Gerichts nicht hat.

In Fällen, wo ein beauftragter Richter nicht aufgestellt ist, erfolgt die Ernennung durch den Senatsvorstand, was wohl für alle Fälle, in denen die Ernennung vom Gerichte selbst ausging, das Sachentsprechende gewesen wäre. Die Ernennung erfolgt auf einseitiges schriftliches Ansuchen.

12) Die oben besprochene Verurtheilung findet auch statt, wenn der Sachverständige, nach Annahme der Wahl, ohne genügende Entschuldigung, seinen Verpflichtungen nicht nachkommt. Nach der Fassung des Gesetzes tritt auch hier das Ermessen des Gerichts ein, obwohl es geeigneter gewesen, zu verfügen wie in Art. 427.

Art. 443. — Sachverständige, welche nicht schon im Allgemeinen für Begutachtungen der betreffenden Art in Pflicht genommen sind, sind darauf zu beeidigen, daß sie das von ihnen geforderte Gutachten gewissenhaft und nach bestem Wissen abgeben wollen.

Im Uebrigen richtet sich die Vernehmung, abgesehen von den Fällen des Art. 438 Abs. 2, soweit nicht die Natur der Sache eine Abweichung bedingt, nach den über die Vernehmung der Zeugen bestehenden Vorschriften.

Art. 444. — In den Fällen des Art. 438 Abs. 2 hat der Richter in der Einweisungstagfahrt, mit welcher der gerichtliche Augenschein, wo ein solcher nöthig, zu verbinden ist, die Sachverständigen unter Behändigung des Urtheils und der nöthigen Aktenstücke über den Gegenstand ihrer Untersuchung und Begutachtung zu belehren, sie gegebenen Falls zu beeidigen und die Frist zur Einreichung des Gutachtens zu bestimmen.

Die Sachverständigen können unmittelbar nach dieser Einweisung zur Untersuchung und Begutachtung schreiten oder Ort und Zeit zu deren Vornahme festsetzen und zwar auch dann, wenn die eine oder andere Partei in der Einweisungstagfahrt nicht erschienen ist. Der betreffenden Partei ist in solchem Falle keine besondere Zustellung zu machen.

Bei der Untersuchung können die Parteien alle zur Aufklärung der Sache dienlichen Erklärungen abgeben und Anträge stellen. Die Anwesenheit des Richters hiebei ist nicht erforderlich. G. A. d. K. d. A. II S. 182. 345. 453. IV S. 98. — K. d. R. II S. 231. IV S. 59.

1) Der Entwurf (Art. 318) wollte die Beeidigung der Sachverständigen vom Verlangen der Parteien abhängig machen, allein mit Recht wurde diese Bestimmung beseitigt und die Beeidigung vorgeschrieben.

Die Formel des Eides gibt Art. 443 Abs. 1.

2) Falls die Begutachtung in der Sitzung erfolgt (Art. 438 Abs. 1), gibt der Vorsitzende, nachdem die Anwälte soweit nöthig den Sachverhalt kurz vorgetragen haben und die Beeidigung stattgefunden hat, den Sachverständigen Kenntniß vom Gegenstande ihres Gutachtens, legt ihnen die Fragen, welche sie zu beantworten haben, vor, und belehrt sie soweit nöthig. Nachdem die etwa erforderlichen Untersuchungen und Prüfungen stattgefunden haben, zu deren Vornahme nöthigenfalls die Verhandlung der Sache (mit Einschiebung einer anderen Verhandlung) ausgesetzt werden kann, werden die Sachverständigen nach den Vorschriften vernommen, wie sie für die Zeugenvernehmungen gegeben sind. Je nach Umständen sind daher ihre Erklärungen zu Protokoll zu nehmen oder nicht (Art. 419).

Auch in den Fällen des Art. 438 Abs. 2 wird diese Bestimmung maßgebend sein, wenn ausnahmsweise die Vernehmung der Sachverständigen in der Sitzung erfolgt. Art. 446 u. 447.

3) Erfolgt die Beweisaufnahme außer der Sitzung (Art. 438 Abs. 2), so hat der beauftragte Richter die Sachverständigen zu beeidigen und in ihr Geschäft einzuweisen. Diese Einweisung erfolgt dadurch, daß er ihnen das Urtheil, aus welchem der Gegenstand des Gutachtens und die zu beantwortenden Fragen zu ersehen sind, sowie die sonst nöthigen Aktenstücke (z. B. Zeugenverhöre über den Geisteszustand einer Person, über Krankheitserscheinungen, Fundberichte rc.) einhändigt, sie auf die Gesichtspunkte, auf welche vom rechtlichen Standpunkte aus besonderes Gewicht zu legen ist, aufmerksam macht und sie überhaupt über die Art und Weise, wie sie ihr Gutachten abzufassen haben, um den Vorschriften des Gesetzes und den Wünschen des Gerichts zu genügen, soweit nöthig belehrt.

Zugleich bestimmt der Richter die Frist zur Einreichung des Gutachtens, wobei er selbstverständlich die Bemerkungen und Wünsche der Sachverständigen hören und berücksichtigen wird. Diese Fristbestimmung ist von Belang, wenn es sich um Haftung der Sachverständigen wegen schuldhafter Verzögerungen handelt (Art. 441).

4) Untersuchung sowie Begutachtung erfolgen am Orte und zur Zeit, wie dies die Sachverständigen bei der Einweisung bestimmen, unter Umständen sofort, und braucht der Richter bei den Verrichtungen der Sachverständigen nicht anwesend zu sein.

Die Parteien sind durch die Vorladung zur Einweisungstagfahrt (Art. 339) stillschweigend zur ganzen Beweisaufnahme, also auch zu den Verrichtungen der Sachverständigen, vorgeladen und es bedarf keiner weiteren Zustellungen, wenn die Sachverständigen zu ihren Untersuchungen in Abwesenheit einer Partei Tagfahrten festsetzen oder verlegen.

Uebrigens ist zu beachten, daß sie berechtigt sind, bei den Untersuchungen der Sachverständigen anwesend zu sein und durch Erklärungen oder Antragstellung ihre Rechte zu wahren (Art. 338 und 444 Abs. 3). Die Sachverständigen sind daher verpflichtet, ihre bezüglichen Tagfahrts-Bestimmungen den anwesenden Parteien oder deren Vertretern kundzugeben, und daß dies geschehen, in ihrem Gutachten anzuführen.

Zur Berathung und zur Abfassung des Gutachtens sind die Parteien nicht beizuziehen.

Art. 445. — **Das nach Art. 444 einzureichende Gutachten hat eine kurze Darstellung der vorgenommenen Untersuchung, die Erklärungen und Anträge der Parteien und eine bestimmte und klare Beantwortung der aufgestellten Fragen nebst der Entwickelung der Gründe zu enthalten.**

Stimmen die Sachverständigen in ihrem Gutachten nicht überein, so muß dasselbe die verschiedenen Meinungen und deren Begründung angeben und zugleich entnehmen lassen, welcher dieser Meinungen jeder einzelne Sachverständige war. Auch kann jeder Sachverständige verlangen, daß seine Meinung wörtlich in das Gutachten aufgenommen werde.

Das Gutachten muß datirt und von allen Sachverständigen unterzeichnet sein. Es wird von ihnen an die Gerichtsschreiberei übersendet oder von einem aus ihrer Mitte persönlich übergeben.

Sollte einer der Sachverständigen des Schreibens nicht erfahren sein oder können sie sich über die Abfassung ihres Gutachtens nicht einigen, so haben sie das Gutachten gemeinschaftlich dem beauftragten Richter zu Protokoll zu geben. In solchen Fällen liegt dem Richter ob, durch geeignete Fragen und Anordnungen für die vollständige und erschöpfende Abfassung des Gutachtens Sorge zu tragen.

Wird in einfachen Sachen mit der Einweisung ein gerichtlicher Augenschein verbunden, so können die Sachverständigen ihr Gutachten sogleich bei diesem und zwar auch dann dem beauftragten Richter zu Protokoll geben, wenn die Voraussetzungen des Abs. 4 nicht vorhanden sind.

Art. 446. — Das Gericht kann, wenn es dies zur Aufklärung der Sache dienlich erachtet, verordnen, daß die Sachverständigen zur Erläuterung ihres nach Art. 445 abgegebenen Gutachtens in eine festgesetzte Gerichtssitzung vorgeladen werden.

Art. 447. — Das Gericht kann auch in dem Urtheile, wodurch die Begutachtung angeordnet und ein beauftragter Richter bestellt wird, verfügen, daß dieser nur die Einweisung der Sachverständigen vorzunehmen, die letzteren aber Befundbericht und Gutachten in einer im Urtheile festzusetzenden Sitzung mündlich abzugeben haben.

G. A. d. K. d. A. II S. 179. 183—185. 345. IV S. 98. 99. — K. d. R. II S. 231. IV S. 59.

1) Das Gutachten ist in der Regel schriftlich abzufassen unter Beobachtung der Vorschriften, wie sie Art. 445 Abs. 1—3 gibt, wobei hervorzuheben, daß im Gegensatze zum französischen Rechte die Kundgabe der persönlichen Ansichten der einzelnen Sachverständigen nicht bloß erlaubt, sondern sogar geboten ist.

Einer der Sachverständigen besorgt die Abfassung nach Maßgabe der gefaßten Beschlüsse und kundgegebenen besonderen Gründe und Meinungen, die übrigen aber unterzeichnen, wenn sie nach Durchlesung den Inhalt als richtig erkennen.

Das Gutachten wird auf der Gerichtsschreiberei hinterlegt. Da diese Hinterlegung keine vorübergehende ist, es sich auch nicht um eine Urkunde handelt, welche vom Gericht selbst oder für dasselbe aufgenommen wurde, sondern um eine Privaturkunde, welche erst durch die Hinterlegung ein Bestandtheil der Gerichtsakten werden soll, so erscheint es sachgemäß, wenigstens rathsam, daß der Gerichtsschreiber einen Hinterlegungsakt anfertige. Es möchte hier die Vormerkung, von welcher Art. 214 spricht, nicht genügen.

2) Ist einer der Sachverständigen des Schreibens nicht kundig (es sollte eigentlich heißen: „des Lesens und Unterschreibens"), oder können sich dieselben nicht einigen über die Abfassung, so haben sie ihr Gutachten dem beauftragten Richter gemeinschaftlich zu Protokoll zu geben. Dieses Protokoll ist so abzufassen, wie es die Sachverständigen selbst gemeinschaftlich abfassen sollen; es setzt also das Gesetz nicht etwa voraus, daß der Richter die Sachverständigen gesondert, gleich Zeugen, vernehme.

Auch in sonstigen Fällen ist die Protokollirung durch den Richter statthaft, wenn die Sache einfach ist und zugleich ein gerichtlicher Augenschein stattfindet.

3) Sehr zweckmäßig erscheinen die Bestimmungen der Artikel 446 und 447.

Ersterer bestimmt, daß durch Anordnung des Gerichts die Sachverständigen zur Erläuterung ihres Gutachtens in die Sitzung vorgeladen werden können. Hierdurch wird in den meisten Fällen die Einholung eines neuen Gutachtens unnöthig gemacht.

Die Vernehmung wird unter Erinnerung an den bereits geleisteten Eid nach Art. 443 Abs. 2 zu geschehen haben und wird über die Erklärungen in der Regel (Art. 419) Protokoll aufzunehmen sein.

4) Art. 447 stellt es den Gerichten frei, zu verfügen, daß der beauftragte Richter bloß die Einweisung vorzunehmen habe, die Sachverständigen aber Befundbericht und Gutachten in einer schon im Beweisurtheile festzusetzenden Sitzung eidlich abzugeben haben.

Offenbar will das Gesetz nicht bloß die Einweisung, sondern auch die zur Begutachtung nöthigen Untersuchungen außer der Sitzung vorgenommen wissen, so daß also die Sachverständigen in der Sitzung erscheinen, um gleich Zeugen über Verhältnisse auszusagen, welche ihnen bereits völlig bekannt sind.

Bezüglich des Rechts der Parteien, bei der Einweisung, sowie bei den Untersuchungen zugegen zu sein, gelten die allgemeinen Grundsätze.

Von einer Beeidigung durch den beauftragten Richter brauchte das Gesetz nicht zu sprechen, weil dieselbe nachträglich in der Sitzung erfolgt.

Da auch von einer Ernennung durch den beauftragten Richter nicht die Rede ist, so scheint es, als ob das Gesetz voraussetze, daß im gegebenen Falle das Gericht immer selbst die Sachverständigen erinnere, allein offenbar ist dies nicht nöthig.

5) Indem verfügt ist, daß sofort im Beweisurtheile die Sitzung zur Abgabe des Gutachtens und selbstverständlich zur Verhandlung (Art. 344) bestimmt werde, wird das Verfahren sehr vereinfacht. Das Gericht bestimmt die Sitzung so, daß voraussichtlich die Zeit ausreicht; sollte dies nicht der Fall sein, so hat Vertagung einzutreten.

Anordnung wiederholter Begutachtung.

Art. 448. — Ist das Gericht durch das abgegebene Gutachten nicht vollständig aufgeklärt, so kann es zur Abgabe eines neuen Gutachtens andere, wo möglich technisch und wissenschaftlich höher gestellte Sachverständige ernennen, welche befugt sind, von ihren Vorgängern die

geeigneten Aufschlüsse zu verlangen. Das Gericht ist in solchen Fällen nicht gehindert, auch das erste Gutachten bei seiner Entscheidung zu berücksichtigen.

G. A. d. K. d. A. II S. 183—186. 345. — K. d. R. II S. 231.

1) Das Gericht kann überall, wo es dies nöthig findet, von Amtswegen die Abgabe eines Obergutachtens durch andere Sachverständige anordnen, und in diesem Falle steht die Bezeichnung der Sachverständigen ihm ausschließlich zu; das Wahlrecht der Parteien fällt hinweg (Abg. II 345).

Das neue Gutachten kann selbstverständlich auch bloß bezüglich gewisser Theile des ersten Gutachtens angeordnet werden, z. B. bloß bezüglich des eigentlich begutachtenden, nicht aber bezüglich des feststellenden Theils.

2) In allen Fällen sind die neuen Sachverständigen befugt, von ihren Vorgängern die geeigneten Aufschlüsse zu verlangen, und hieraus folgt, daß diese verpflichtet sind, solche Aufschlüsse auf Verlangen zu geben, und daß sie ihre Pflicht im Sinne des Art. 441 a. E. verletzen, wenn sie sich dessen weigern.

Wie diese Aufschlüsse zu erheben und zu ertheilen seien, ist nicht bestimmt. In vielen Fällen möchte es sachgemäß sein, die früheren Sachverständigen zu den Verrichtungen der neuen beizuladen, damit sie mündlich die geeigneten Aufschlüsse geben; übrigens werden auch schriftliche Mittheilungen, als Erläuterungen und Ergänzungen des früheren Gutachtens, erhoben werden können.

3) Veranlassung zur Anordnung eines neuen Gutachtens liegt auch dann vor, wenn die Expertise nichtig ist, jedoch sind in solchen Fällen die besonderen Vorschriften des Art. 448 nicht maßgebend und es kann das Gericht veranlaßt sein, die nemlichen Sachverständigen mit Abgabe eines neuen Gutachtens zu beauftragen. Nichtigkeit könnte, da das Gesetz an keine seiner Vorschriften diese Folge ausdrücklich knüpft, nur angenommen werden, wenn dasjenige fehlt, was zum Wesen der Handlung gehört (Art. 218), wie z. B. wenn die Unterschrift eines Sachverständigen fehlt, wenn das Recht der Parteien, der Einweisung und Untersuchung der Sachverständigen beizuwohnen, verletzt ist.

Unter Umständen, z. B. wenn die Beeidigung unterlassen wurde, kann wohl nach Analogie der Art. 446 und 447 dadurch nachgeholfen werden, daß das Gericht die Vorladung und Vernehmung der Sachverständigen in der Sitzung anordnet.

XIV. Hauptstück.

Eid.

Vorbemerkung für die Pfalz.

1) Nach Art. 66 des Einf.-Gesetzes treten von diesem Hauptstücke die Art. 449—459, 465, 469—472 in der Pfalz nicht in Wirksamkeit; dagegen bleiben die Bestimmungen der Art. 1357 bis 1369 Code civil in Kraft.

Bezüglich etwaiger Collisionen dieser letzteren Artikel mit sonstigen auch für die Pfalz geltenden Bestimmungen der Prozeßordnung, ist zu verweisen auf die Vorbemerkung zu Hauptstück X.

2) Was die Natur des Haupteides nach französischem Rechte betrifft, so gehen die Ansichten der Rechtsgelehrten auseinander, indem manche, namentlich die Civilisten (Zachariä, Demolombe) den Gesichtspunkt des Vergleiches für maßgebend erachten, während andere in der Eideszuschiebung ein Beweismittel erblicken.

Der letzteren Ansicht, welche wohl die richtigere und practischere ist, folgt die Praxis, namentlich in den Rheinlanden (Schlink Comm. Bd. II § 333), und findet es ganz unbedenklich, daß gesetzliche Vertreter von der Eideszuschiebung Gebrauch machen, wenn sonstige Beweismittel fehlen oder sich als unzureichend erweisen.

Was die weitere Frage betrifft, wem der Eid zugeschoben werden könne, macht sich allerdings der Gesichtspunkt, daß in der Wahl, den Eid zu leisten oder zu verweigern, im Grunde das Recht der Veräußerung enthalten sei, in der Praxis entschieden geltend, und man nimmt an, daß in der Regel nur der Partei selbst der Eid zugeschoben werden könne, einem gesetzlichen Vertreter aber nur dann, wenn das in Frage stehende Recht seiner Verfügung unterliegt und durch Verweigerung des Eides seine eigene Verantwortlichkeit ins Leben tritt. So kann z. B. dem Vormunde unbedenklich der Eid zugeschoben werden, ob er nicht eine gewisse Zahlung empfangen habe, weil in der Eidesverweigerung das Zugeständniß des Empfangs liegt und hieraus die Pflicht folgt, das empfangene Geld dem Mündel zu verrechnen. Chauveau (quest. 514 u. 515) geht sogar so weit, zu behaupten, daß dem gesetzlichen Vertreter der Eid **nie** zugeschoben werden könne, weil der **Parteieneid**, seiner Natur und dem Willen des Gesetzes nach, immer nur der Partei selbst auferlegt werden dürfe, jeder Andere aber als Zeuge erscheine.

Der Umstand, daß unsere Prozeßordnung den Eid als **Beweismittel** behandelt, namentlich aber in dem auch für die Pfalz geltenden Art. 325 als solches ausdrücklich bezeichnet, möchte dazu beitragen, die fragliche Controverse des französischen Rechts, was das Recht der **Zuschiebung** des Eides betrifft, ein für allemal zu beseitigen und im Sinne der in der Praxis bereits herrschenden Ansicht zu entscheiden.

Zugeschobener Eid.

Art. 449. — **Soweit das Gesetz nicht anders bestimmt, kann jede Partei der andern über erhebliche Thatsachen den Eid zuschieben und zwar in jedem Stande der Sache und ohne Unterschied, ob sie andere Beweismittel hat oder nicht.**

G. A. d. K. d. A. II S. 238. 239. 345. 346. — K. d. R. II S. 231.

1) Im alten Prozesse spielte der Eid eine ungemein wichtige Rolle.

Wo immer die Unbehilflichkeit des Verfahrens keinen anderen Ausweg ließ, mußten Eide aushelfen, deren man etwa zehn verschiedene Sorten hatte. Mit Eiden füllte man alle Lücken der künstlichen Beweise aus, und Eide gebrauchte man als Brücken, um über die Schwierigkeiten hinüberzukommen, welche durch die Unnatur des Prozesses entstanden; kurz Eide waren das Universalmittel für alle Mängel und Gebrechen.

Das mündliche, auf freier Beweiswürdigung beruhende Verfahren fühlt im Gegentheile nicht das geringste Bedürfniß nach Eiden, und die Praxis ist bestrebt, sie zu beseitigen oder zu beschränken, wo sie nur kann, wie denn z. B. von der Befugniß des Art. 1367 Code civ., Notheide aufzulegen, so gut wie nie Gebrauch gemacht wird.

Unsere Prozeßordnung kränkelt hier noch etwas an den Anschauungen des alten Prozesses; sie betrachtet den Eid noch zu sehr als etwas Unentbehrliches und meint, es müsse in jeder Sache Jemand da sein, den man schwören lassen könne, während es besser gewesen wäre, den Eid nur als etwas Zufälliges zu behandeln, als ein Auskunftsmittel, welches man zuläßt, wenn gerade die Vorbedingungen dazu gegeben sind.

2) Was die Natur des Eides, insbesondere des zugeschobenen oder Haupteides, von welchem in Art. 449 die Rede ist, betrifft, so kann kein Zweifel obwalten, daß er nach dem Systeme unserer Prozeßordnung bloß als Beweismittel zu betrachten ist.

Es folgt hieraus, daß Jeder, der zur Prozeßführung befugt ist, auch die Befugniß hat, zum Beweise bestrittener Thatsachen Eide zuzuschieben, daß also diese Befugniß nicht bloß jedem gesetzlichen Vertreter zusteht, sondern auch in der Prozeßvollmacht, namentlich auch in derjenigen, welche beim Anwalte gesetzlich vermuthet wird, enthalten ist. **Vgl. Bemerk. zu Art. 90 Nr. 1.**

3) Dem Schwurpflichtigen gegenüber erscheint die Eideszuschiebung als ein Mittel, um ein Geständniß, nemlich das stillschweigende, welches in der Eidesverweigerung liegt, zu erzwingen.

Ob hieraus mit Recht gefolgert werden dürfe, daß jeder Person, welche fähig ist, ein gerichtliches Geständniß zu machen, auch der Eid zugeschoben werden könne, wird bei Art. 451—453 besprochen werden.

Jedenfalls hat umgekehrt als Prinzip zu gelten, daß in Fällen, wo eine Thatsache selbst durch förmliches gerichtliches Geständniß nicht in rechtliche **Gewißheit** gesetzt werden kann, d. h. in jenen Fällen, welche Art. 324 Abs. 2 im Auge hat, auch das Beweismittel der Eideszuschiebung nicht mit demselben Erfolge wie in andern Fällen benützt werden könne. Ist nemlich ein Recht der Verfügung den Parteien entzogen, verbietet das Civilgesetz (Abg. II 170 [v. Weiß]) aus Gründen der öffentlichen Ordnung, auf bloße Willensäußerungen derselben Rücksicht zu nehmen, so kann offenbar das fingirte Geständniß, welches in der Verweigerung der Antwort auf gestellte Fragen (Art. 176) oder in der Eidesverweigerung (Art. 465 Abs. 3) liegt, keine stärkere rechtliche Wirkung äußern, als das ausdrückliche Geständniß; es kann nicht erlaubt sein, durch das Spiel einer Eideszuschiebung und Eidesverweigerung das gesetzliche Verbot illusorisch zu machen.

Die Eideszuschiebung ist in solchen Fällen nicht ausgeschlossen, wohl aber die sachentscheidende Wirkung der Eidesverweigerung. Abg. II 242, Sp. 1 a. E. und 347 (zu Art. 9).

4) Die Eideszuschiebung kann im jedem Stande der Sache geschehen, d. h. so lange es überhaupt noch auf Beweisführung über die betreffende Thatsache ankommt.

Es geschieht zwar nicht selten, daß man auch die **eventuellen** Eideszuschiebungen schon den motivirten Anträgen beifügt, allein in der Regel wartet man damit bis zur Verhandlung und zwar wenn klar ist, daß vorerst nur auf sonstigen Beweis zu erkennen sei, bis zur Verhandlung über die Beweisführung. Hie und da kündigt der Anwalt seine Absicht, äußersten Falls den Eid zuzuschieben, einstweilen nur mündlich an, und das Gericht fordert ihn, wenn sich Anlaß dazu ergibt, auf, den Antrag zu formuliren.

Die praktischen Gründe für diese Uebung liegen einestheils darin, daß zur Zeit, wo der Gegner sein Angriffs- und Vertheidigungssystem vollständig entwickelt hat und der Sachverhalt möglichst aufgeklärt ist, sich besser ermessen läßt, ob, wie und wem der Eid zuzuschieben sei; anderntheils darin, daß es unzweckmäßig erscheint, eventuelle Eideszuschiebungen welche oft sehr umfangreich sind, als überflüssigen Ballast durch alle Anträge und alle Zwischenurtheile mitzuschleppen.

Ganz abgesehen hievon ergibt sich der Anlaß zu Eideszuschiebungen oft plötzlich im Laufe der Verhandlung, wie dies leicht erklärlich ist bei einem Verfahren, welches erlaubt, alles Versäumte noch bei der Verhandlung nachzuholen und das System des Angriffs oder der Vertheidigung hier noch zu ändern.

5) Ueberhaupt ist es die Eigenheit des neuen Verfahrens, daß bei der Verhandlung sich jeden Augenblick neue Gesichtspunkte, neue Wendungen der Sachlage darbieten können, welche neue Anträge, neue thatsächliche Erörterungen und Feststellungen bedingen.

Da nun der Anwalt allein die Partei vertritt, dem Advokaten aber, welcher etwa die Rechtsvertheidigung übernommen, als solchem das Recht der Vertretung nicht zusteht, so ist es klar, warum der Gesetzgeber in Art. 80 sagt, die mündliche Rechtsvertheidigung könne durch einen Advokaten unter Beistand des Anwalts übernommen werden, denn der Advokat wäre bei derartigen Aenderungen der Sachlage rein hilflos und die Rechte der Partei wären in hohem Grade gefährdet.

Ich nehme hier Veranlassung, auf eine Bemerkung zurückzukommen, welche ich zu jenem Artikel Nr 2 dahin gemacht, daß der Anwalt sich entfernen könne, wenn er sicher sei, seine Anwesenheit sei nicht weiter nöthig, indem ich aufmerksam gemacht wurde, es könne diese Bemerkung diesseits, wo das Verfahren neu ist, zu Mißverständnissen und Mißbräuchen führen.

Es solle nur gesagt sein, daß die Anwesenheit des Anwaltes nicht unbedingt nöthig sei, daß dem Advokaten nicht deßhalb das Wort versagt werden müsse, weil der Anwalt nicht neben ihm stehe.

Allerdings wird jedoch der unterstellte Fall nur selten eintreten, etwa dort, wo es sich um Beleuchtung reiner Rechtsfragen handelt und durch Benehmen mit dem Gegenanwalte feststeht, daß sich am thatsächlichen Materiale nichts ändern wird.

Zudem ist es nöthig, die Erlaubniß des Gerichts einzuholen, theils weil dieses veranlaßt sein könnte, von Amtswegen weitere Aufschlüsse zu verlangen, theils weil dadurch, daß das Gericht sein Urtheil nicht vertagt, sondern sofort spricht, die weitere Thätigkeit des Anwalts nöthig sein könnte, theils endlich weil äußersten Falles der Anwalt wieder herbeigerufen werden müßte. So hielt man es seither in der Pfalz und gestattete dem Anwalt, sich zu entfernen, um nicht in Fällen, wo er bloß als Figurant anwesend sein könnte, seine Zeit unnöthiger Weise in Anspruch zu nehmen.

6) Von dem Antrage, durch welchen der Anwalt bei der Verhandlung einen Eid zuschiebt, wird dem Gegner keine Abschrift mitgetheilt, derselbe wird vielmehr nach Art. 247 einfach dem Vorsitzenden übergeben, um einen Bestandtheil der hinterlegten Anträge zu bilden.

Die Frage, ob diese Anträge beim Gerichte aufbewahrt zu bleiben haben oder nach dem Spruche des Urtheils den Parteien zurückzugeben seien, ist nicht ohne praktische Bedeutung; und auf erfolgte Anregung finde ich mich veranlaßt, sie nachträglich näher, als bis jetzt geschehen, zu erörtern.

Weder der Code de proc. noch die Prozeßordnung enthalten hierüber eine klare Vorschrift, in der Pfalz aber wurde es seither verschieden gehalten, indem manche Gerichte die hinterlegten Anträge aufbewahrten, andere nicht.

Was zuerst den Wortlaut des Gesetzes anbelangt, so ist in derselben Weise, wie bezüglich des Sachverhalts (Art. 287) einfach die Hinterlegung verfügt, über deren Dauer aber nichts bestimmt. Wenn Art. 246 Abs. 2 sagt, die hinterlegten Anträge seien dem Anwalte bei der Verhandlung zu übergeben, so fügt er bei: „zum Behufe der Verlesung," d. h. zum vorübergehenden Gebrauche, und es läßt sich hieraus offenbar mehr für als gegen die Aufbewahrung folgern. Ob die hinterlegten Anträge zu den Parteiakten gehören, welche nach Spruch des Urtheils zurückzugeben sind, ist eine petitio principii; ihrer Natur nach wäre eher das Gegentheil anzunehmen und auch der Wortlaut des Art. 171 umfaßt sie nicht.

Was den Geist des Gesetzes betrifft, so ist ins Auge zu fassen, daß die hinterlegten Anträge bestimmt sind, die bei der Verhandlung gestellten Parteibegehren zu fixiren und später durch wörtliche Einrückung dieser Begehren in den Sachverhalt einen wesentlichen Bestandtheil des Urtheils zu bilden; sie gehören also zum Urtheile und es liegt im öffentlichen Interesse, daß sie zu diesem verwahrt werden.

Allerdings verliert dieser Gesichtspunkt seine Bedeutung, wenn der Sachverhalt gefertigt und hinterlegt ist; allein es ist wohl zu beachten, daß kein Zwang zur Fertigung des Sachverhaltes besteht und daß möglicherweise Wochen, Monate, ja Jahre vergehen können, bis sich eine Partei dazu veranlaßt findet. Unter Umständen, z. B. wenn die unterliegende Partei, um die Kosten der Ausfertigung zu ersparen, sich fügt, erfolgt sie gar nie, dennoch aber kann später das Urtheil für andere Verhältnisse von Wichtigkeit sein.

Es möchte nun nicht dem Willen des Gesetzes entsprechen, daß in der Zwischenzeit die bei Gericht hinterlegten Anträge, welche, wie z. B. bei gelegentlichen Eideszuschiebungen, oft nur in einem einzigen Exemplare vorliegen, der Verfügung der Parteien und den damit verbundenen Zufällen überlassen bleiben.

Auf Grund vorstehender Erwägungen möchte sich folgende vermittelnde Ansicht empfehlen:

Die hinterlegten Anträge haben auch nach dem Spruche und Eintrage des Urtheils bei Gericht zu bleiben, bis der Sachverhalt hinterlegt ist. Zum Behufe der Fertigung des Sachverhalts händigt sie der Gerichtsschreiber, analog wie im Falle des Art. 246 Abs. 2, dem betreffenden Anwalte auf kurze Zeit ein. Ist der Sachverhalt vorschriftsmäßig gefertigt und hinterlegt, so steht nichts im Wege, die Anträge den Parteien zurückzugeben; sie haben ihren Zweck vollständig erfüllt.

Art. 450. — **Personen, welchen nach den Strafgesetzen die Fähigkeit zur Ableistung eines Parteieids entzogen ist, kann der Eid nicht zugeschoben werden.**

Gleiches gilt von Personen, welche ihrer Vernunft nicht mächtig oder so schwachen Verstandes sind, daß ihnen die erforderliche Einsicht über Wesen und Zweck des Eids mangelt, oder welche nicht fähig sind, sich in Worten mündlich oder schriftlich auszudrücken.

In den Fällen der Abs. 1 und 2 dürfen statt der Eideszuschiebung, soferne sie an sich zulässig wäre, alle andern Beweismittel, auch die sonst nach der Beschaffenheit des Falls ausgeschlossenen, benützt werden.

G. A. d. K. d. A. II S. 245. 246. 345. 346. IV S. 99. — K. d. R. II S. 231. 232. IV S. 59.

1) Nach den jetzt bestehenden Strafgesetzen tritt die Unfähigkeit, einen Parteieneid zu leisten, nur in einem einzigen Falle ein, nemlich in Folge einer Verurtheilung zu Todes- oder Zuchthausstrafe, für die Dauer der Strafzeit (Art. 31 des St. G. B.). Für den nemlichen Zeitraum ist aber der Zuchthaussträfling unter Curatel gestellt (Art. 32 des St. G. B.), kann also nach Art. 451 der Eid bloß dem Curator zugeschoben werden.

Offenbar ist daher Abs. 1 der jetzigen Strafgesetzgebung gegenüber gegenstandslos, wenn man nicht etwa an einen Fall denkt, wo auf dem Wege der Gnade die Rechtsunfähigkeit aufgehoben wird, während die Zuchthausstrafe und mit ihr die Eidesunfähigkeit fortdauert.

2) Aus gleichem Grunde ist auch die Bestimmung in Abs. 2 meist gegenstandslos, denn die Personen, von welchen er spricht, werden in der Regel unter Vormundschaft oder Curatel stehen.

Uebrigens sind doch Fälle möglich, wo diese Voraussetzung nicht eintrifft, und es hat dann das Gericht nach freiem Ermessen zu entscheiden, ob die genügende Einsicht über Zweck und Wesen des Eides vorhanden sei oder nicht.

Besondere Bedeutung hat Abs. 2 bezüglich der Stummen und Tauben, insofern er die Eidesleistung ausschließt bei Personen, welche weder mündlich noch schriftlich in Worten sich auszudrücken vermögen. Es wäre daher unstatthaft, einen Eid auf dem Wege bloßer Geberdensprache abzunehmen, möchte dieselbe auch noch so verständlich sein. Vgl. Art. 476.

3) Die Bestimmung in Abs. 3 erscheint vollkommen berechtigt, insofern sie die verschuldete Eidesunfähigkeit des Abs. 1 betrifft, weniger jedoch, soweit es sich um die unverschuldete Eidesunfähigkeit des Abs. 2 handelt.

Wer durch Verübung eines Verbrechens sich eidesunfähig macht und hierdurch dem Gegner ein Beweismittel, auf welches er sich Rechnung machen durfte, entzieht, darf sich nicht beschwert finden, wenn diesem zum Ersatze seines Verlustes sonstige Beweismittel eingeräumt werden.

Anders verhält es sich, wenn die Eidesunfähigkeit eine unverschuldete, zufällige ist. Eine Pflicht zur Ersatzleistung liegt hier nicht vor; wollte man aber die Idee verfolgen, daß derjenige, welcher zur Zeit der Entstehung seines Rechts in der Lage war, einen Eid zuschieben zu können, diesen Vortheil ohne seine Schuld nicht verlieren dürfe, so mußte man viel weiter gehen und anders verfügen. Es war nemlich den Fällen, wo eine eidesfähige Person später, durch Geistesstörung, Verstümmelung ꝛc., diese Fähigkeit verliert, der Fall ganz gleichzustellen, wo durch Todesfall oder überhaupt durch Zufall irgend einer Art die Möglichkeit der Eideszuschiebung wegfällt. Anderseits mußte man den Fall weglassen, wo schon zur Zeit der Entstehung des Rechts die Eidesunfähigkeit vorhanden war; denn wer einem Taubstummen ohne Zeugen Geld leiht, darf sich später nicht beklagen, wenn er diesem den Eid nicht zuschieben kann.

4) Uebrigens haben diese Erwägungen insofern wenig praktische Bedeutung, als der Abs. 3 nur für die Fälle gilt, welche in Abs. 1 und 2 vorgesehen sind, also mit diesen gegenstandslos wird.

Allerdings könnten in dieser Beziehung auch Zweifel bestehen. Dürfte man nemlich bloß den Geist des Gesetzes walten lassen, so wäre das Gewicht nur auf die Thatsache zu legen, daß Jemand durch seine Schuld dem Gegner das Beweismittel der Eideszuschiebung entzogen hat, und wäre es gleichgiltig, ob diese Folge durch Verlust der Rechtsfähigkeit (Art. 451) oder durch Verlust der Eidesfähigkeit (Art. 450 Abs. 1) herbeigeführt worden wäre; allein nach den Worten des Gesetzes möchte diese Auslegung ausgeschlossen sein und zwar hauptsächlich auch deßhalb, weil es nicht angehen möchte, die Fälle des Abs. 2 anders zu behandeln, als diejenigen des Abs. 1.

Art. 451. — **Steht derjenige, gegen welchen durch Eideszuschiebung Beweis erbracht werden soll, unter Vormundschaft oder Curatel, so hat die Eideszuschiebung an den Vormund oder Curator zu geschehen, doch kann bei Minderjährigen, wenn der Eid über eigene Handlungen oder Wahrnehmungen derselben gefordert wird, der Minderjährige das sechzehnte Lebensjahr bereits zurückgelegt hat und keiner der in Art. 450 erwähnten Fälle gegeben ist, das Gericht auf Antrag der Partei, welche den Eid zuschiebt, anordnen, daß letzterer durch den Minderjährigen selbst geleistet werde.**

Art. 452. — **Für juristische Personen sind ihre Vertreter, für den k. Fiskus und die Civilliste des Königs die betreffenden Beamten, für Genossenschaften, Vereine und Gesellschaften, deren Vertretung nicht durch das Gesetz geregelt ist, die Vorstände oder die sonstigen nach den Satzungen bestellten Vertreter schwurpflichtig.**

Art. 453. — **Besteht im Falle des Art. 451 oder 452 die Vertretung aus mehreren Personen, so ist der Eid, wenn er nur die eigene Handlung oder Wahrnehmung einzelner aus ihrer Mitte betrifft, von diesen, auf keinen Fall aber von mehr als drei Vertretern, zu leisten.**

Sind mehr als drei Vertreter, von welchen der Eid gefordert werden könnte, vorhanden oder ergibt sich sonst Zweifel, wer als Vertreter einer Partei den Eid zu leisten habe, so entscheidet beim Mangel einer Vereinbarung der Parteien das Gericht.

Dem Gerichte steht auch zu, statt der Vorstände einer Genossenschaft, eines Vereines oder einer Gesellschaft einzelne Mitglieder als schwurpflichtig zu erklären.

G. A. d. K. d. A. II S. 245—250. 345. 346. IV S. 99. — K. d. R. II S. 232—235. IV S. 59.

1) Die Eideszuschiebung läßt dem Gegner nur die Wahl, entweder zu schwören oder zu gestehen; sie erscheint daher als ein Mittel, um Geständnisse zu erzwingen. Art. 465 Abs. 3.

Von diesem Standpunkte aus läßt sich geltend machen, es könne jeder Partei, welche ein rechtsgiltiges gerichtliches Geständniß machen kann, auch der Eid zugeschoben werden, also nicht bloß der Partei im engeren Sinne, sondern auch jedem gesetzlichen Vertreter. Vgl. Bemerk. zu Art. 324 Nr. 8. Diese Ansicht ist auch wirklich diejenige, von welcher unsere Prozeßordnung ausgeht; allein daß sie völlig richtig sei, möchte ich nicht zugeben.

Der gesetzliche Vertreter, welcher aus freien Stücken oder auf einfaches Befragen etwas zugesteht, handelt ohne Nöthigung und kann in vollem Maße dafür verantwortlich gemacht werden, wenn er durch diese Handlung die Partei beschädigt, wenn er in wahrheitswidriger leichtsinniger Weise etwas zugestanden hat. Etwas anders ist die Sachlage, wenn der gesetzliche Vertreter vor die Alternative gestellt wird, zu schwören oder zuzugestehen. Es wird nicht leicht Jemand deßhalb verantwortlich gemacht werden können, weil er sich weigert zu schwören, weil er übertrieben gewissenhaft ist, weil er z. B. sagt: „Ich glaube meiner Sache ganz sicher zu sein, allein schwören will ich doch nicht.“ Gibt es doch Leute, welche den Eid überhaupt scheuen und in ihren eigenen Angelegenheiten lieber offenbares Unrecht leiden, als schwören. Abg. IV 100 (Barth).

Indem man daher die Eideszuschiebung an gesetzliche Vertreter unbedingt gestattet, gibt man diesen mittelbar die freie Verfügung über das strittige Recht, und das möchte denn doch zu weit gehen. Noch schärfer tritt dieser Mißstand hervor, wenn Eideszuschiebung sogar an Personen gestattet wird, denen nicht einmal die gesetzliche Vertretung zusteht und die ein giltiges Geständniß nicht machen könnten, z. B. an einzelne Mitglieder einer Vertretung oder an beliebige Mitglieder eines Vereines oder einer Gesellschaft. Allerdings hat das Gesetz im Wesentlichen nur beibehalten, was im alten Verfahren bestand, allein meiner Ansicht nach wäre Anlaß gegeben gewesen, zu neuen Ideen überzugehen und die Parteieneide, welche in der Regel mehr zur Chikane als zur Ermittlung der Wahrheit dienen, möglichst zu beschränken.

a) Vormünder und Curatoren.

2) Steht eine Partei unter Vormundschaft oder Curatel, so ist der Eid nicht ihr selbst, sondern nur dem Vormunde oder Curator zuzuschieben, fällt also hinweg, wenn er unter obwaltenden Umständen, z. B. weil die Wissenschaft von der Sache fehlt, diesen nicht zugeschoben werden kann. Abg. II 345 (zu Art. 3).

Die Tragweite dieses Grundsatzes ergibt sich aus den Bestimmungen des Art. 454. Bemerk. zu Art. 454 Nr. 4.

3) Von diesem Grundsatze macht das Gesetz nur eine einzige Ausnahme für Minderjährige über 16 Jahre, indem diese über eigene Handlungen und Wahrnehmungen zum Eide zugelassen werden können.

Ursprünglich sollte diese Zuschiebung der Partei in die Hand gegeben werden, später jedoch fand man sich durch die gewichtigen Bedenken, welche dagegen geltend gemacht wurden (R. R. II 232 bis 234) bewogen, das Ermessen des Gerichts walten zu lassen.

Die Gerichte werden mit größter Vorsicht von dieser Gewalt Gebrauch machen und erwägen, daß sie mit dem Urtheile, welches dem Minderjährigen den Eid auferlegt, das Schicksal des Rechtsstreites unwiderruflich von dessen Willen abhängig machen und ihm möglicherweise die Macht geben, den Schutz, welchen die Civilgesetze dem Minderjährigen gegen eigenen Leichtsinn und Unverstand geben, illusorisch zu machen. Die Persönlichkeit des Minderjährigen wird dabei von entscheidendem Einflusse sein.

Ueber die Art und Weise, wie der Minderjährige zur Eidesleistung beizuziehen sei, war nichts zu bestimmen, denn derselbe ist bereits im Prozesse, wenn auch durch den Vormund vertreten, und es genügt daher die Zustellung des betreffenden Urtheils oder Beschlusses an den Vormund, welcher dafür Sorge zu tragen hat, daß der Minderjährige Kenntniß erlange und bei der Tagfahrt erscheine.

b) Vertreter juristischer Personen.

4) Was die Eidesleistung für juristische Personen, für Gesellschaften, Vereine ꝛc. betrifft, so wurden im Wesentlichen die Grundsätze beibehalten, wie sie im alten Verfahren galten.

In der Regel sind für juristische Personen deren gesetzliche Vertreter (Bemerk. zu Art. 58 Nr. 4—7) schwurpflichtig.

5) Eine Abweichung von dieser Regel tritt für den Fiskus ein, insofern für ihn die betreffenden Beamten schwurpflichtig sein sollen. Es kann nemlich keinem Zweifel unterliegen, daß hiermit nicht etwa bloß diejenigen Beamten gemeint seien, welchen die gesetzliche Vertretung zusteht, z. B. die Mitglieder der Kreisregierungen K. d. F. (Bemerk. zu Art. 193 Nr. 4) oder gar nur die Fiskale, welche als solche nur Anwälte des Fiskus sind.

Um klar zu stellen, welchen Sinn das Gesetz mit diesen Worten verbinde, möchte es geeignet sein, die Worte anzuführen, mit welchen Referent v. Neumayr seinen mit unwesentlichen Aenderungen angenommenen Vorschlag begründete (Referat zu Art. 419—422). Er sagt:

„Es wird die Schwurpflicht eben denjenigen „Verwaltungsbeamten (welcher übrigens auch „ein Fiskalbeamter sein kann) zu treffen haben, „welcher nach Beschaffenheit des conkreten Falles „von den zu beschwörenden Handlungen oder Thatsachen persönliche Kenntniß hat oder sich die „nöthige Kenntniß gemäß Art. 411 Ziff. 4 (welchem jetzt die Schlußbestimmung von Art. 454 „entspricht) am leichtesten verschaffen kann.

„Die einschlägige Stelle wird durch den fiskalischen Prozeßbevollmächtigten jedesmal diesen Verwaltungsbeamten zu bezeichnen und wenn von „der Gegenpartei Anstände erhoben werden, wird „das Gericht zu entscheiden haben."

Schwurpflichtig wären also z. B. Rentbeamte bezüglich der an sie gemachten Zahlungen, Beamte, welche Verträge im Namen des Fiskus abgeschlossen haben, bezüglich dieser Verträge, Forstbeamte bezüglich der Wahrnehmungen bei Ausübung der Forstrechte ꝛc.

Zu bemerken ist jedoch, daß die Schwurpflicht nur Beamte im engeren Sinne, solche, welche in ihrer Sphäre den Staat selbständig zu vertreten haben, trifft, nie aber auf niedere Bedienstete ausgedehnt werden kann.

6) Was die Gesellschaften, Vereine und Genossenschaften betrifft, deren Vertretung nicht durch das Gesetz geregelt ist, so sind die satzungsmäßig bestimmten Vorstände oder Vertreter schwurpflichtig (Bemerk. zu Art. 58 Nr. 7).

Für Gesellschaften ohne Persönlichkeit, bei denen die einzelnen Mitglieder im Rechtsstreite auftreten, sind die Grundsätze über Streitgenossenschaft maßgebend.

7) Falls die Vertretung eines Rechtsunfähigen oder einer juristischen Person aus mehreren

Personen besteht, trifft Art. 453 Vorsorge dahin, daß 1) wenn es sich nur um eigene Handlungen oder Wahrnehmungen einzelner aus ihrer Mitte handelt, auch nur diese schwurpflichtig seien, und daß 2) der Eid nie von mehr als drei Vertretern zu leisten sei.

Letztere Beschränkung hat einzutreten, wenn mehr als drei Vertreter eigene Kenntniß von der Sache haben, oder wenn es sich um einen Wissenseid handelt im Sinne von Art. 454 a. E. und Art. 456.

Die Auswahl dieser drei Vertreter, sowie überhaupt die Bestimmung der Schwurpflichtigen in allen Fällen, wo deßhalb Streit unter den Parteien entsteht, insbesondere auch der Beamten, welche für den Fiskus zu schwören haben, steht dem Gerichte zu. Muthmaßliche Kenntniß vom Sachverhalte, Gewissenhaftigkeit, Einsicht haben bei der Wahl zu leiten.

8) Schließlich ist den Gerichten gestattet, statt der Vorstände von Gesellschaften, Vereinen oder Genossenschaften einzelne Mitglieder für schwurpflichtig zu erklären.

Die Tragweite dieser Bestimmung ist eine außerordentliche, denn es darf an die Eidesverweigerung von Personen, welche civilrechtlich nicht entfernt befugt wären, über das strittige Recht zu verfügen, welche nur ein höchst unbedeutendes Interesse an der Sache haben, das Schicksal des Prozesses geknüpft werden. Nach dem Laute des Gesetzes stünde sogar nichts im Wege, irgend einem Mitglied einer Aktiengesellschaft den Parteieneid aufzulegen! Es ist zu erwarten, daß die Gerichte von der ihnen eingeräumten Gewalt einen weisen Gebrauch machen und sie so wenig als möglich anwenden werden.

Obgleich nicht gesagt ist, daß eine solche Eidesauflage nur auf Parteiantrag geschehen könne, wie dies Art. 451 ausspricht, so möchte dies doch nach allgemeinen Prinzipien als selbstverständlich zu erachten sein.

9) Nach den Bestimmungen der Art. 452 und 453 kann der Parteieneid Personen auferlegt werden, welche nach allgemeinen Prinzipien nur die Eigenschaft von Zeugen, wenn auch betheiligter Zeugen, hätten. Es gilt dies nicht bloß von Beamten, welche für den Fiskus, und von einzelnen Gesellschaftern, welche für die Gesellschaft zu schwören haben, sondern auch von einzelnen Mitgliedern einer collegialen Vertretung, z. B. eines Magistrates, eines Gemeinderaths; denn nicht die einzelnen Personen bilden die Vertretung, sondern das nach Stimmenmehrheit beschließende Collegium.

Solche schwurpflichtige Personen werden kraft dieser Spezialbestimmungen nur für den besonderen Anlaß der Eidesleistung zum Range gesetzlicher Vertreter erhoben.

Es frägt sich nun: 1) in welcher Art sind solche Personen zur Eidesleistung beizuziehen, und 2) können sie auch als Zeugen vernommen werden?

Was die erste Frage betrifft, so erscheint es beim Stillschweigen des Gesetzes zweifellos, daß die der Partei gemachte Zustellung des Urtheils oder Beschlusses, wodurch Tagfahrt zur Eidesleistung bestimmt wird, genüge und es Sache der Partei bezw. des Anwaltes sei, zu sorgen, daß der Schwurpflichtige Kenntniß erhalte und erscheine.

Was die zweite Frage betrifft, so ist es zwar im Allgemeinen richtig, daß Personen, welchen der Parteieneid zugeschoben werden kann, nicht im nemlichen Rechtsstreite als Zeugen dienen können (Bemerk. zu Art. 400 Nr. 8), allein, wie in der Regel kein Prinzip auf die Spitze getrieben werden darf, so möchte auch das fragliche Prinzip hier, wo die schwurpflichtige Person nicht der gesetzliche Vertreter im Rechtsstreite an sich ist, sondern nur ausnahmsweise gleich diesem behandelt wird, eine Ausnahme erleiden. Würde man anders entscheiden, so wäre die Folge, daß alle Beamten dem Fiskus gegenüber und alle Mitglieder von Gesellschaften, Vereinen rc. diesen gegenüber nicht als Zeugen dienen könnten, denn insofern sie etwas von der Sache wüßten, also ihre Zeugschaft Werth hätte, könnte ihnen auch der Parteieneid auferlegt werden.

In der Regel wird es für die Partei vortheilhafter sein, solche Personen als Zeugen zu benützen, und es erscheint selbstverständlich, daß sie hiermit auf das Recht verzichte, sie den Parteieneid schwören zu lassen.

c) Eidesleistung durch Dritte.

10) Der Entwurf (Art. 419) wollte auch die Beiladung dritter Personen — Cedenten, Mandatare früherer Vormünder rc. — bloß zum Zwecke der Eideszuschiebung gestatten, auf Vorschlag des Referenten v. Neumayr wurde jedoch diese Bestimmung gestrichen, weil solche Personen nur als Zeugen betrachtet werden könnten. Ursprünglich beschloß man (als Art. 319 Abs. 1) ein ausdrückliches Verbot der Eideszuschiebung an dritte Personen auszusprechen (Abg. II 247), allein die Subcommission ließ diesen Satz ohne irgend eine Andeutung des Grundes weg, offenbar jedoch nicht deßhalb, weil man ihn für unrichtig, sondern weil man ihn bei Stillschweigen des Gesetzes für selbstverständlich hielt.

Hiernach steht außer Zweifel, daß auch die Eideszuschiebung an den Cedenten, wie sie von der Ger.=O. Cap. XIII § 1 Nr. 3 zugelassen wurde, jetzt nicht mehr statthaft ist.

Art. 454. — Die Eideszuschiebung findet statt über eigene Handlungen des Schwurpflichtigen, über Thatsachen, welche er unmittelbar wahrgenommen haben soll, über Handlungen dritter Personen, für welche er haftet, und in den Fällen der Art. 451 und 452 über Thatsachen, wovon er vermöge seiner einschlägigen Dienstes- oder Geschäftsführung Kenntniß erlangt haben oder sich verschaffen kann.

Art. 455. — Ist der Eid über eigene Handlungen oder Wahrnehmungen des Schwurpflichtigen zugeschoben, so hat dieser nach genauer und vollständiger Angabe des Sachverhältnisses, soweit eine solche möglich, zu schwören, daß er nichts oder nichts Weiteres als das Angeführte gethan oder wahrgenommen habe.

Kann demjenigen, welchem der Eid über eigene Handlungen oder Wahrnehmungen zugeschoben ist, nach den Umständen des Falls die Ableistung des Eids über die Thatsachen selbst nicht wohl zugemuthet werden, so hat das Gericht auf seinen Antrag anzuordnen, daß der Eid nur über das Nichtwissen oder Nichterinnern zu leisten sei.

Art. 456. — Ist der Eid nicht über eigene Handlungen oder Wahrnehmungen des Schwurpflichtigen zugeschoben, so hat dieser die ihm zu Gebote stehenden Mittel zur Erforschung der Wahrheit anzuwenden und nach genauer und vollständiger Angabe des etwa Erforschten zu schwören, daß ihm ungeachtet gewissenhafter Nachforschung von den Thatsachen, welche Gegenstand der Eideszuschiebung sind, nichts oder nichts Weiteres als das Angegebene bekannt sei.

G. A. d. K. d. A. II S. 239. 240. 247—249. 346—348. IV S. 99.
K. d. R. II. S. 235. IV S. 59.

Art. 454 bezeichnet die Thatsachen, über welche denjenigen Personen, welche nach Maßgabe der vorausgehenden Artikel 449, 451—453 schwurpflichtig sind, der Eid zugeschoben werden könne.

Vor Allem ist nach dem Wesen des Parteieneides, welchem die Idee einer Zeugschaft in eigener Sache zu Grunde liegt, selbstverständlich, daß der Eid nur über reine Thatsachen zugeschoben werden kann, nicht aber über Rechtsbegriffe, und selbst was die Thatsachen betrifft, enthält Art. 457 Nr. 2 eine sachgemäße Beschränkung.

2) Eigene Handlungen, sowie Thatsachen, welche unmittelbar durch die Sinne wahrgenommen wurden, sind natürlich zunächst und vorzugsweise Gegenstand der Eideszuschiebung. Man könnte sagen, sie allein eigneten sich dazu, da in der Regel nur ihnen gegenüber der Nachweis eines Meineids geführt werden kann, wie denn die Ger.=O. den Haupteid auf Thatsachen dieser Art beschränkte.

Unsere Prozeßordnung geht jedoch weiter und läßt die Eideszuschiebung auch zu: 1) über fremde Handlungen, welche man zu vertreten hat, und 2) über Thatsachen, von welchen ein gesetzlicher Vertreter vermöge seiner Dienstes= oder Geschäftsführung Kenntniß erlangt haben oder sich verschaffen kann.

3) Was fremde Handlungen betrifft, so versteht sich wohl von selbst, daß nicht der Fall gemeint sei, wo eine fremde Handlung in Gegenwart des Schwurpflichtigen vorfiel, denn bei dieser Voraussetzung wäre eine unmittelbare Wahrnehmung gegeben, sondern der Fall, wo der Schwurpflichtige eigenes Wissen davon nicht hat.

Der Eid soll, wie aus Art. 456 hervorgeht, dahin geleistet werden, daß der Schwörende alle Mittel, die Wahrheit zu erforschen, angewendet, dessenungeachtet aber nichts Weiteres, als was er angibt, erfahren habe, d. h. es handelt sich um einen Wisseneid, welcher in der Erwägung zugelassen wurde, daß Interesse und Pflicht bestehe, sich auch um fremde Handlungen zu kümmern, wenn diese das eigene Recht berühren.

Hervorzuheben ist, daß der Eid nicht bloß auf jenes Wissen sich richtet, welches der Schwörende zur Zeit der Eideszuschiebung oder Eidesleistung zufällig hat, sondern daß dieser für verpflichtet erklärt ist, in der Zwischenzeit bis zur Eidesleistung alle ihm zu Gebote stehenden Mittel zur Erforschung der Wahrheit anzuwenden.

4) Was die Eidesleistung der gesetzlichen Vertreter anbelangt, so könnte man aus den Schlußworten des Art. 454 in Verbindung mit einer Aeußerung des Referenten (Abg. II 346 Sp. 1) folgern, es hätten dieselben ausschließlich nur über solche Thatsachen zu schwören, von denen sie vermöge ihrer Dienstes= oder Geschäftsführung Kenntniß erlangten; allein dies ist offenbar der Sinn des Gesetzes nicht.

Was ein gesetzlicher Vertreter mit eigenen Sinnen wahrgenommen, mag die Wahrnehmung erfolgt sein wie und wo sie wolle, das darf er nicht wegläugnen, muß es vielmehr zugestehen, und kann nach den Prinzipien, von welchen unsere P. O. ausgeht, durch Eideszuschiebung zu diesem Geständnisse gezwungen werden. In dieser unbedingten Weise wurde die Schwurpflicht der gesetzlichen Vertreter bei den Verhandlungen anerkannt (Referat zu Art. 419—422 Ziff. 3 — Abg. II 247—249) und entgegenstehenden Ansichten (v. Weiß, Barth) gegenüber aufrecht erhalten. Es kann somit der Vormund auch bezüglich eines Deliktes des Mündels schwurpflichtig sein, wenn er zufällig Zeuge desselben gewesen ist.

Die Schlußbestimmung von Art. 454 ist daher nicht beschränkend, sondern ausdehnend, und besagt, es solle bei gesetzlichen Vertretern auch noch der Wissenseid zugeschoben werden können bezüglich dessen, was sie aus ihrer Geschäftsführung erfahren haben, z. B. über Verwaltungshandlungen eines früheren Vertreters. Es handelt sich um Kundgabe von Umständen, aus denen der Richter im Stande ist, seine Ueberzeugung bezüglich der zu beweisenden Thatsache zu schöpfen.

Die Formel dieser Eidesleistung ist in Art. 456 bestimmt.

5) Es frägt sich, ob das eben Gesagte auch von jenen Schwurpflichtigen zu gelten habe, welchen die volle Eigenschaft gesetzlicher Vertreter nicht zukommt (Bemerk. zu Art. 451—453 Nr. 9), namentlich von Beamten, welche für den Fiskus schwören.

Die allgemeinen, aus der Stellung der gesetzlichen Vertreter im Prozesse sich herleitenden Gründe finden hier keine Anwendung, jedoch unterscheidet anderseits der Wortlaut des Art. 454 nicht.

Trotz dieses letzteren Umstandes nehme ich an, daß das Gesetz, indem es sagt, daß die „betreffenden Beamten" zu schwören haben, nur solche Beamte meint, welche die Kenntniß der betreffenden Thatsachen aus ihrer Dienstführung schöpfen, nicht aber Beamte, welche zufällig Zeuge von Vorfällen, welche ihren Dienst gar nicht berühren, gewesen sind.

Gleiches wird auch von sonstigen Schwurpflichtigen dieser Art gelten.

6) Ueber die Art und Weise, wie die eidliche Erklärung zu erfolgen habe, enthalten die Art. 455 u. 456 nähere Vorschriften, aus denen hervorgeht, daß der Schwurpflichtige alles, was er von der Sache weiß, genau und vollständig anzugeben und sodann je nach Umständen beizufügen hat, entweder: daß er nichts weiter wisse, oder: daß er trotz sorgfältiger Nachforschungen nichts weiter habe erfahren können.

Der Schwörende darf sich daher nicht darauf beschränken, einfach zu erklären, daß er verneine was der Gegner behaupte, um dann sofort den Eid mit „Nein und nicht wahr &c." auszuschwören, sondern er wird gleich einem Zeugen aufgefordert, eine zusammenhängende Erklärung über den Sachverhalt, soweit er Gegenstand der Eideszuschiebung ist, zu geben. Abg. II 239, 240 (v. Weiß). Vgl. auch die Verhdl. über Art. 415 des Entwurfs (Abg. II 240 u. 241), sowie über Art. 424—427 (Abg. II 250—252). Allerdings ist dabei vorausgesetzt, daß es sich um die verschiedenartige Darstellung eines gewissen Vorfalles handle, denn wenn das, was der Gegner behauptet, gar nicht vorgefallen ist, läßt sich freilich auch nichts weiter erzählen.

Finden sich Lücken in der Erzählung, oder sind Punkte, auf welche nach der Eidesauflage Werth zu legen ist, nicht beachtet, oder werden unbestimmte, ausweichende Erklärungen gemacht, so ist der Schwurpflichtige durch geeignete Fragestellung zu bestimmten Antworten anzuhalten.

Wie hieraus erhellt, ist kein Gewicht darauf zu legen, daß die Eideserklärung sich in ihrer Fassung genau an die Sätze der Eidesauflage anschließe, vielmehr kann sie, falls eine abweichende Geschichtserzählung gemacht wird, eine ganz andere Form annehmen, wie denn z. B. in der Pfalz, in Folge des Prinzipes der Untheilbarkeit des Geständnisses, alle Umstände, welche für das Bestehen des strittigen Rechts erheblich sind, sogar rechtszerstörliche Einreden, hereingezogen werden können.

Das Wesen liegt darin, daß der Gesammtinhalt der Erklärungen des Schwurpflichtigen die Verneinung dessen enthalte, was die Eideszuschiebung bejaht.

7) In Fällen, wo der Eid sofort in der Sitzung geleistet wird, wie dies in einfachen und unwichtigen Sachen Regel ist, wo also eine schriftliche Eidesabnahme nicht vorausgeht, erfolgt daher die Abnahme des Eides in ähnlicher Weise, wie die Vernehmung eines Zeugen. Die schwurpflichtige Person, über den Gegenstand der Eidesleistung gehörig belehrt, erzählt den Sachverhalt, wie sie ihn zu beschwören bereit ist, und ergibt sich diese Erzählung als sachentscheidend, so wird sie gleich einer Zeugenaussage protokollirt, d. h. im Urtheile beurkundet, natürlich weniger ausführlich und nur in gedrängtester Kürze.

Ist eine förmliche schriftliche Eidesannahme vorausgegangen, so dient diese als Anhaltspunkt zur Eidesabnahme und Beurkundung; allein auch in diesem Falle ist es nach Art. 455 nöthig, eine freie Erzählung zu verlangen, um sicher zu sein, daß die schriftliche Fassung richtig und vollständig das enthalte, was beschworen werden will und kann.

8) Ueber **eigene** Wahrnehmungen muß der Schwurpflichtige **bestimmte** Erklärungen abgeben und ist er nicht mit der Ausrede zu hören, daß er sich nicht mehr erinnere; jedoch sind Fälle möglich, wo ein genaues Erinnern dem Schwurpflichtigen nicht zugemuthet werden kann, z. B. bei Thatsachen, welche in sehr ferner Zeit liegen, oder welche, wie z. B. Rechnungsverhältnisse, unbedeutende Lieferungen und Zahlungen, auch nach Verlauf kürzerer Zeit sich aus dem Gedächtnisse leicht verlieren, oder welche endlich zu einer Zeit vorfielen, als der Schwörende seiner Sinne nicht ganz mächtig war.

Für solche Fälle ließ man von jeher eine Ausnahme zu, und ich bemerke dies namentlich auch für die **Pfalz** (quia impossibilium non datur obligatio). Durch Art. 455 Abs. 2 ist diese Ausnahme nunmehr ausdrücklich anerkannt.

Art. 457. — **Die Eideszuschiebung findet nicht statt:**

1) über unerlaubte Handlungen, welche mit Verbrechens- oder Vergehensstrafe bedroht sind;

2) über Thatsachen, welche durch Augenschein oder Beiziehung von Sachverständigen außer Zweifel gesetzt werden können;

3) zur Führung des Gegenbeweises, soferne Beweis und Gegenbeweis unmittelbar die nämlichen Thatsachen zum Gegenstande haben;

4) wenn das Gegentheil der zu beschwörenden Thatsache vollständig bewiesen oder offenkundig ist;

5) zum Beweise der Unächtheit einer öffentlichen Urkunde.

Eideszuschiebung gegen eine gesetzliche Vermuthung ist nur soweit ausgeschlossen, als das Gesetz überhaupt den Gegenbeweis ausschließt.

Gegen den Inhalt einer vollbeweisenden Urkunde ist Eideszuschiebung soweit gestattet, als dadurch das beurkundete Geschäft wegen Zwang, Betrug, Irrthum oder Simulation angefochten wird.

Art. 458. — **Darüber, was die Partei, welcher der Eid zugeschoben werden will, von einer Sache glaube oder nicht glaube, oder welche Ueberzeugung sie davon habe, findet die Eideszuschiebung nur in den vom Gesetze bestimmten Fällen statt.**

G. A. d. K. d. A. II S. 239. 241—245. 317. 348. IV S. 99. 331—333. 367.
K. d. R. II S. 235. IV S. 59.

1) In diesen Artikeln werden die Ausnahmen und Einschränkungen, welche die in Art. 454 gegebene Regel erleidet, bestimmt.

a) Strafbare Handlungen.

2) Die erste Ausnahme betrifft Handlungen, welche mit **Verbrechens-** oder **Vergehensstrafe** bedroht sind.

Sie beruht auf der nemlichen Erwägung, aus welcher im Art. 195 Ziff. 6 des St.G.B. eine strafrechtliche Verfolgung wegen Meineids ausgeschlossen ist, wenn Jemand Thatsachen fälschlich beschworen hat, deren wahre Angabe **gegen ihn selbst** eine strafrechtliche Verfolgung wegen Verbrechens oder Vergehens nach sich ziehen konnte. Liegt in der einen Wagschale das Geldinteresse und zugleich die Furcht vor einer drohenden Strafverfolgung, in der andern aber nichts als ein strafloser Meineid, so ist offenbar die Versuchung, diesen Meineid zu leisten, zu groß, und mit Recht hat man die Eideszuschiebung hier nicht zugelassen.

Droht bloß eine Uebertretungsstrafe oder eine Disciplinareinschreitung, so ist die Eideszuschiebung statthaft.

3) Die Frage, ob eine Handlung mit Verbrechens- oder Vergehensstrafe bedroht sei, ist vom Richter nach Maßgabe der Eideszuschiebung in Verbindung mit den sonst gegebenen Anhaltspunkten zu prüfen und zu entscheiden. Ist, wie dies gewöhnlich der Fall sein wird, eine Strafuntersuchung vorausgegangen, so werden für die Frage, ob Vergehen oder Uebertretung vorliege, dort Aufschlüsse zu finden sein, z. B. bezüglich des Werthes des Entwendeten, der Dauer der Arbeitsunfähigkeit. Abg. IV 333 Sp. 1 (v. Neumayr). Im Zweifel ist die Eideszuschiebung zuzulassen.

Selbstverständlich kommt es nur darauf an, ob die in Frage stehenden Strafen **gedroht** seien, ist es also ohne Belang, wenn etwa der Strafrichter nach verhandelter Sache eine Uebertretungsstrafe aussprechen dürfte. Auf die Frage, ob ein leichterer Fall gegeben sei, darf sich der Civilrichter nicht einlassen.

4) Fraglich könnte sein, ob Eideszuschiebung statthaft sei, wenn die Handlung zwar an sich mit Strafen besagter Art bedroht ist, jedoch wegen Verjährung, wegen Ablaufs der Frist zur Stellung eines Strafantrags (St.G.B. Art. 88), wegen

rechtskräftiger Freisprechung (Art. 90 allda) oder aus ähnlichen Gründen eine Strafe nicht ausgesprochen werden kann. In Fällen dieser Art war allerdings die That zur Zeit der Verübung mit Strafe bedroht, ist es aber zur Zeit der Eideszuschiebung nicht mehr, erscheint vielmehr straflos; hieraus möchte folgen, das letztere statthaft sei. Es entspricht diese Lösung auch dem Geiste des Gesetzes, wie er aus den Verhandlungen hervortritt, denn der Grund, warum man fragliche Ausnahme nach langem Kampfe einführte, lag nicht in dem Entehrenden der That, sondern in der drohenden Strafe.

5) Das Gesetz sagt allgemein: „Eideszuschiebung findet nicht statt über unerlaubte Handlungen," ohne anzudeuten, wessen Handlungen gemeint seien, ob nur diejenigen des Schwörenden oder auch fremde.

Daß Handlungen eines beliebigen Dritten nicht in Betracht kommen, ist wohl klar, allein Zweifel könnten entstehen, wenn ein gesetzlicher Vertreter die Partei, welche er vertritt (der Vormund seinen Mündel, der Mann seine Frau), einer strafbaren Handlung anschuldigen soll. Es kann dieser Fall eintreten, wenn der Vertreter zufällig Zeuge gewesen ist, oder wenn er aus seiner Geschäftsführung Thatsachen erfahren hat, aus welchen die Schuld sich folgert.

Ich nehme an, daß das Gesetz ausschließlich nur eigene Handlungen des Schwörenden im Auge hatte, und daß es in dieser Beziehung von der nemlichen Anschauung ausging, wie Art. 195 des St. G. B.

b) Begutachtungen.

6) Eidliche Parteierklärungen sind Zeugschaften in eigener Sache und sollen daher in der Regel nur ein bestimmtes, auf sinnlicher Wahrnehmung beruhendes Wissen zum Gegenstande haben. Handelt es sich um Beurtheilungen, um Schlußfolgerungen, kurz um Beweise, wie sie durch Gutachten Sachverständiger erbracht werden, so schließt unsere Prozeßordnung die Eideszuschiebung aus — eine Ausnahme, welche schon durch die Erwägung gerechtfertigt erscheint, daß bei Beschwören von Meinungen und Ansichten der Nachweis eines Meineids nie möglich ist. Ob das Gericht ein Gutachten Sachverständiger wirklich anordnet oder selbst im Stande ist, den Sachverhalt zu würdigen (Art. 330), erscheint gleichgiltig.

Eine Ausnahme von besagter Regel bildet die Zulassung des Schätzungseides (Art. 470).

7) Wenn ferner bestimmt ist, es solle eine Eideszuschiebung nicht stattfinden über Thatsachen, welche durch Augenschein außer Zweifel gestellt werden können, so beruht dies theils auf der nemlichen Erwägung, theils auf der weiteren, daß Eide möglichst zu vermeiden, also zurückzuweisen seien, wenn der Richter auf anderem Wege sich eine untrügliche Ueberzeugung verschaffen könne.

In diesem Falle ist deßhalb die Eideszuschiebung auch dann ausgeschlossen, wenn es sich um sinnlich wahrnehmbare Thatsachen handelt.

c) Gegenbeweis.

8) Der Satz, daß der Gegenbeweis nicht durch Eideszuschiebung erbracht werden dürfe, ist in der Pfalz etwas ganz Fremdes; man hat dort keine Idee davon, daß eine derartige Bestimmung sachgemäß oder daß sie gar Bedürfniß sein könne. Ich muß gestehen, daß ich ihm in der Allgemeinheit, wie er gilt, keine Berechtigung zugestehen kann, namentlich im neuen Verfahren.

Man sagt: „Entweder ist kein, oder nur theilweiser oder voller Beweis geliefert; im ersten Falle ist Eideszuschiebung zwecklos, im zweiten haben Notheide einzutreten, im dritten aber darf man zum vollen Beweise nicht auch noch einen Eid verlangen!" Diese Gründe scheinen richtig, sind es aber nicht.

Im ersten Falle ist der Eid allerdings zwecklos, insofern er nur eventuell zugeschoben ist und erst nach durchgeführtem Beweisverfahren in Frage kommt; allein er ist im neuen Verfahren ein praktisches Bedürfniß für Fälle, wo der Gegenbeweispflichtige, um die Sache rasch bei der ersten Verhandlung zu erledigen, die Entscheidung vom Eide des Gegners abhängig machen will.

Im letzten Falle wäre der vorgebrachte Grund richtig und die Eideszuschiebung frivol, wenn es nur solche Beweise gäbe, welche eine die Möglichkeit des Gegentheils ausschließende richterliche Ueberzeugung begründeten; allein es gibt auch Beweise, welche sich bloß aus Vermuthungen bilden, und gibt insbesondere formelle Beweise, welche der Richter gezwungen ist anzunehmen, auch ohne überzeugt zu sein, wie z. B. die Beweise durch Urkunden. Ich sehe nun nicht ein, warum es in Fällen dieser Art verwehrt sein soll, an's Gewissen des vom Sachverhalte genau unterrichteten Gegners zu appelliren, und warum man einen Menschen, welcher wissentlich Lügen vorbringt und auf dieselben einen ungerechten Prozeß gründet, durch Verbot der Eideszuschiebung begünstigt.

Nach vorstehenden Bemerkungen wird man es natürlich finden, wenn ich geneigt bin, die Tragweite der Ziff. 3 des Art. 457 nach Möglichkeit zu beschränken; ob mit Recht, möge die Praxis würdigen.

9) Wie aus den Bemerkungen zu Art. 333 hervorgeht, ist es oft schwer zu entscheiden, ob ein Hauptbeweis oder ein Gegenbeweis vorliege. Nicht bloß die Frage der Beweispflicht birgt solche Schwierigkeiten, sondern auch die Bestimmungen des Art. 333 Abs. 2 geben zu Zweifeln Anlaß, insofern sie von Beweisen sprechen, welche eigentlich Gegenbeweise wären, jedoch gleich Hauptbeweisen behandelt werden.

Was die Frage der Beweispflicht anbelangt, so ergeben sich in der Praxis, namentlich vor den Handelsgerichten, sehr häufig Fälle, wo der Beklagte erklärt: „Ich will es nicht auf kostspielige Beweise ankommen lassen — ich will keinen großen Prozeß — wenn der Kläger, der hier anwesend ist, beschwört, daß das wahr sei, was er vorträgt, so will ich den Prozeß verloren haben!"

Soll nun der Richter entgegnen: „Das geht nicht an; der Kläger ist eigentlich beweispflichtig, also trifft dich der Gegenbeweis und du darfst den Eid nicht zuschieben; es muß also auf Zeugenbeweis erkannt werden"?

Ich glaube nicht, daß dies vernünftig wäre, und nehme daher auch nicht an, daß es dem Willen des Gesetzes entspreche.

Ist der Kläger einverstanden, so werden sich ohnedem keine Schwierigkeiten ergeben, allein selbst wenn der Kläger die Eideszuschiebung bestreitet und auf Zulassung eines erbotenen Zeugenbeweises besteht, wird er, da die Prozeßordnung eine Gewissensvertretung nicht kennt, mit diesem Verlangen zurückzuweisen sein. Nimmt nemlich der Beklagte freiwillig die Beweispflicht auf sich, so fällt jedes Interesse für den Kläger hinweg, darauf zu bestehen, daß er beweispflichtig sei, und es könnte dies bloß als eine auf Kostenmehrung zum Schaden des Gegners abzielende Chikane betrachtet werden. Ueberhaupt hat die Bestimmung in Ziff. 3 zunächst nur die Fälle des alten Verfahrens im Auge, d. h. Fälle, wo über die Beweispflicht bereits erkannt ist und der Gegenbeweis durch eventuelle Eideszuschiebung geführt werden will.

10) Was die Gegenbeweise betrifft, welche nach Art. 333 Abs. 2 gleich Hauptbeweisen behandelt werden, so ist bezüglich der gesetzlichen Vermuthung ausdrücklich bestimmt, daß der Beweis gegen sie durch Eideszuschiebung geführt werden dürfe (Art. 457 Abs. 2). Der Beweis, welcher dem Nichtbeweispflichtigen in Fällen auferlegt wird, wo der Richter aus der Verhandlung bereits den Hauptbeweis schöpft, würde demnach, zufolge des Grundsatzes: »qui dicit de uno, negat de altero,« hier als Gegenbeweis zu betrachten sein. Hieraus würde jedoch folgen, daß der Gegenbeweis, welchen Art. 333 gegen einen solchen Beweis ausdrücklich zuläßt, hier die Natur eines Hauptbeweises hätte und also durch Eideszuschiebung erbracht werden könnte.

Uebrigens erscheint diese Frage, welche an sich schwierig wäre, gegenstandslos, da in Fällen, wo das Gericht vollen Beweis annimmt, Ziff. 4 Maß gibt.

11) Die Eideszuschiebung ist nur für denjenigen Gegenbeweis ausgeschlossen, welcher unmittelbar die nemlichen Thatsachen zum Gegenstande hat, wie der Hauptbeweis, also nicht bei indirekten Gegenbeweisen (Bemerk. zu Art. 333 Nr. 2), noch weniger bei Beweiseinreden.

Falls der Gegenbeweisführer eine Thatsache erweisen will, aus welcher ein nothwendiger Schluß auf die Unwahrheit der vom Hauptbeweisführer aufgestellten Thatsachen zu ziehen ist, z. B. ein Alibi (Bemerk. zu Art. 322 Nr. 1), könnte man zweifeln. Ich würde vorziehen, dem Wortlaute der gesetzlichen Bestimmung gemäß den Eid zuzulassen, soweit nicht Ziff. 4 im Wege steht.

d) Vollbewiesene Thatsachen.

12) Die Eideszuschiebung soll ferner ausgeschlossen sein, wenn das Gegentheil der zu beschwörenden Thatsachen vollständig erwiesen oder offenkundig ist.

Diese Bestimmung entspricht jenem Satze des kanonischen Rechtes: »actor qui plene probavit, non debet compelli jurare,« aus welchem man die Unzulässigkeit der Eideszuschiebung beim Gegenbeweise hergeleitet hat. Sie beruht daher so ziemlich auf dem nemlichen Gedanken, wie die Bestimmung in Ziff. 3, und aus den Gründen, wie sie oben (Nr. 8) erörtert sind, erscheint sie mir so wenig gerechtfertigt, wie diese letztere, insoferne sie den Eid nicht bloß dort ausschließt, wo die Zuschiebung frivol erscheint, weil die richterliche Ueberzeugung bereits vollständig feststeht, sondern auch dort, wo der Beweis nur ein formeller ist, insbesondere gegen den Laut vollbeweisender Urkunden. Es ist schon sehr fraglich, ob es rathsam sei, die Eideszuschiebung gegen den Inhalt einer öffentlichen Urkunde auszuschließen (die Praxis der Pfalz, so sehr sie sonst dem Eide feindlich ist, läßt sie unbedenklich zu und findet darin einen Gewinn für das materielle Recht); jedenfalls aber möchte es zu weit gehen, auch Privaturkunden in dieses Verbot zu ziehen.

Wenn in Privaturkunden etwas unrichtig beurkundet ist, so vermögen in der Regel bloß die vertragsschließenden Theile darüber Aufschluß zu geben; verweigert man nun dem einen Theile die

Berufung an das Gewissen des andern Theils, so nimmt man ihm jede Möglichkeit des Beweises und unterstützt geradezu Lüge und Unredlichkeit. Man setze den Fall, es sei ein Schuldschein ausgestellt und dem Gläubiger ausgehändigt worden in der Voraussetzung, daß dieser sofort das Geld gebe; das Geld wird nicht gegeben, der Schuldschein aber trotzdem eingeklagt. Muß sich nicht das Rechtsgefühl des Richters empören, wenn er im Bewußtsein, daß der Schuldner im Rechte sei, diesem das einzige Beweismittel, welches er haben kann, verweigern muß? (Vgl. Bl. f. R. Erg.-Bd. zu 31 u. 32 S. 170.) Man erwäge dabei, daß Art. 399 Abs. 1 jeden Beweis durch Zeugen und Vermuthungen ausschließt; was für Beweise bleiben denn überhaupt übrig?

Nach vorstehenden Bemerkungen ist auch hier Grund gegeben, die Ausnahme möglichst einzuschränken.

13) Das Gesetz schließt die Eideszuschiebung nur für den Fall aus, wo der Beweis bereits vollständig geführt ist; es hat Fälle im Auge, wo dem Richter durch die Verhandlung oder durch ein Beweisverfahren ein vollständiger Beweis bereits geboten ist, und sagt, es solle, nachdem ein solcher Beweis vorliegt, die Eideszuschiebung nicht mehr zugelassen werden.

Beweise, welche erst angeboten werden, erst geführt werden sollen, kommen nicht in Betracht, denn es handelt sich hier nicht um eine Gewissensvertretung.

Letztere Bemerkung gilt auch für den Fall, wo der Beweis durch Urkunden bloß angeboten wird, die Urkunden aber nicht sofort vorgelegt werden; jedoch kann hier der Richter durch Vertagung die Sachlage ändern, auch kommt die Schlußbestimmung von Art. 460 in Betracht.

Werden Urkunden sofort vorgelegt, die erheblich scheinen, so wird der Gegner nicht durch bloße Bestreitung der Aechtheit die Anwendung des Gesetzes beseitigen können.

14) Als Ausnahme von dieser Ausnahme, d. h. als Rückkehr zu der Regel erscheint es, wenn im Schlußsatze des Art. 457 die Eideszuschiebung gegen den Inhalt einer vollbeweisenden Urkunde gestattet ist, soweit dadurch das beurkundete Geschäft wegen Zwang, Betrug, Irrthum oder Simulation angefochten wird.

Es ist dieser Bestimmung die weiteste Auslegung zu geben, insbesondere ist in der Anfechtung wegen Simulation nicht bloß die Simulation des ganzen Geschäfts, sondern auch einzelner Theile desselben begriffen.

15) Das Gesetz spricht nur von Anfechtung des beurkundeten Geschäfts, nicht auch vom Falle, wo eine Privaturkunde an sich angefochten wird (Art. 373 Abs. 2); allein, wie das Gesetz überhaupt in dieser Beziehung nicht scharf unterscheidet (Bemerk. zu Art. 399 Nr. 7), die Anfechtung einer Privaturkunde und die Anfechtung des darin beurkundeten Geschäfts auch in der Regel zusammenfallen, so wird auch der letztere Fall als inbegriffen zu erachten sein.

e) Unächtheit öffentlicher Urkunden.

16) Eine Eideszuschiebung ist schließlich unstatthaft zum Beweise der Unächtheit einer öffentlichen Urkunde.

Nach der Begriffsbestimmung des Gesetzes ist mit diesen Worten nicht bloß der Fall begriffen, wo die ganze Urkunde das Machwerk eines Fälschers ist, sondern auch der Fall, wo nur einzelne Theile gefälscht sein sollen (Bemerk. zu Art. 385 Nr. 2).

Intellektuelle Fälschungen, sowie überhaupt der Nachweis, es sei eine öffentliche Urkunde mit oder ohne Abschrift falsch aufgenommen, fallen unter die Ausnahme der Ziff. 4.

f) Glaubenseid.

17) Mit Recht schließt das Gesetz Eide aus, welche nur allgemein auf das Glauben, auf die Ansicht oder selbst Ueberzeugung, welche sich Jemand bezüglich einer Thatsache gebildet habe, gerichtet sind. Die Gründe hiefür sind treffend hervorgehoben im Referate zu Art. 411 bis 415 des Entwurfs.

Der Eid bezüglich einer Ueberzeugung ist nicht mit dem Wissenseid zu vermengen, von welchem das Gesetz in Art. 456 spricht. Es ist in Art. 458 nur von Fällen die Rede, wo Jemand seine aus Schlußfolgerungen gebildete Ueberzeugung von Thatsachen, die er nicht selbst wahrgenommen, beschwören soll.

Art. 459. — Die Partei, welcher der Eid zugeschoben ist, hat die Wahl, ob sie ihn annehmen oder der Gegenpartei zurückschieben will.

Die Zurückschiebung ist ausgeschlossen, wenn auf Seiten der Partei, welche den zurückgeschobenen Eid zu schwören hätte, die Bedingungen nicht vorhanden sind, unter welchen er ihr hätte zugeschoben werden können.

Die Zuschiebung oder Zurückschiebung des Eids kann nicht mehr zurückgenommen werden, sobald die Partei, welche den Eid schwören soll, sich zur Annahme bereit erklärt hat.

G. A. d. K. d. A. II S. 250. 347. 348. — K. d. R. II S. 235.

1) Die Partei, welcher ein Eid zugeschoben wurde, hat die Wahl, diesen Eid zu schwören, zurückzuschieben oder zu verweigern.

Die Zurückschiebung eines Eides ist zwar eine sehr wichtige folgenschwere Handlung, von welcher eher als von der Zuschiebung gesagt werden könnte, sie sei species transactionis, allein es ist klar, daß demjenigen, welcher frei wählen darf zwischen Ausschwören und Verweigern, auch der Mittelweg der Zurückschiebung offen stehen müsse. Zweifel kann nur entstehen bezüglich jener Schwurpflichtigen, welche weder Parteien noch gesetzliche Vertreter sind, z. B. Beamte, welche für den Staat, Mitglieder einer Gesellschaft, welche für diese schwören sollen.

Da es immer der Anwalt ist, von welchem die betreffende Erklärung ausgeht, so wird diese Frage im Anwaltsprozesse nicht leicht hervortreten, und es kann hier nur für den Anwalt die Frage entstehen, von wem er die bezügliche Weisung zu empfangen habe. Meiner Ansicht nach ist die gesetzliche Vertretung allein berechtigt, einen Eid zurückzuschieben, die schwurpflichtige Person aber hat bloß zu erklären, ob sie schwöre oder nicht. Sie vermag nicht einmal durch ihre Erklärungen die Zurückschiebung unzulässig zu machen.

2) Die Zurückschiebung hat die nemlichen Thatsachen zum Gegenstande, wie die Zuschiebung; sie enthält die Aufforderung an die beweispflichtige Partei, nunmehr selbst dasjenige eidlich zu bekräftigen, was sie durch Zuschiebung des Eides erweisen wollte. Hiermit ist jedoch nicht gesagt, daß die Zurückschiebung immer an die Fassung der Zuschiebung gebunden sei, vielmehr kann die zurückschiebende Partei ihre abweichende Geschichtserzählung zu Grunde legen, was die Folge hat, daß sich der Gegner nicht begnügen darf, dasjenige eidlich zu bekräftigen, was er selbst behauptet hat, sondern genöthigt ist, sich auf die positiven Behauptungen des Gegners in seiner Eideserklärung einzulassen.

3) Im Uebrigen sind für die Zurückschiebung die nemlichen allgemeinen Grundsätze maßgebend, wie für die Zuschiebung, finden also die Bestimmungen der Art. 450 — 458 auch auf den zurückgeschobenen Eid ihre Anwendung.

Insbesondere können unter Umständen auch der Minderjährige selbst oder einzelne Vertreter oder einzelne Gesellschaftsmitglieder für schwurpflichtig erklärt werden, kann ferner der zurückgeschobene Eid ein bloßer Wissenseid sein, selbst wenn die Eideszuschiebung eigene Handlungen oder Wahrnehmungen zum Gegenstande hatte. Es ist dies die Consequenz der Bestimmung in Art. 459 Abs. 2, obgleich es wohl besser gewesen wäre, im letztberegten Falle eine Zurückschiebung nicht zu gestatten, wie es der Entwurf (Art. 423) bestimmte.

Die Ausnahme, welche Art. 457 Ziff. 3 für den Gegenbeweis macht, ist natürlich durch das Wesen der Zurückschiebung ausgeschlossen.

4) Zuschiebung sowie Zurückschiebung des Eides können nicht mehr zurückgenommen werden, wenn die Partei, welche den Eid schwören soll, sich zur Annahme bereit erklärt hat.

Ist bereits Urtheil ergangen, welches die Entscheidung vom Eide abhängig macht, so ist klar, daß der Eid nicht mehr zurückgenommen werden könne, falls entweder vor dem Urtheile die Annahme, sei es auch nur eventuell, erfolgt war, oder falls nach dem Urtheile die Annahme des zugeschobenen oder zurückgeschobenen Eides erklärt wird.

Es frägt sich nun aber, wie es sich im Falle verhalte, wo der Eid zwar durch Urtheil auferlegt, die Annahmserklärung aber noch nicht erfolgt ist.

Ohne Zweifel kann die Zurücknahme auf dem Wege der Berufung, falls diese statthaft ist, wirksam gemacht werden; allein die französische Jurisprudenz hält diesen Weg nicht für nothwendig, gestattet vielmehr die einfache Rücknahme, deren Folge natürlich ist, daß das Beweisurtheil gegenstandslos und neue Entscheidung nöthig wird. Paris, 25. März 1854 (Dalloz 55 [2. 142]). Diese Ansicht hängt mit der Anschauung zusammen, daß die Eideszuschiebung ein bloßes Vergleichsanerbieten sei, über welches das Gericht Urkunde ertheile; da nun aber nach unserer Prozeßordnung dieselbe als Beweismittel erscheint, da das Gericht also keinen Vergleichsvorschlag beurkundet, sondern einen Beweis auferlegt, da ferner Beweisurtheile vom nemlichen Richter nicht zurückgenommen werden dürfen (Art. 332) und, falls sie auf Eid erkennen, den Richter binden (Art. 345), so möchte ich annehmen, daß der durch Urtheil auferlegte Eid nicht mehr willkürlich zurückgenommen werden könne.

Uebrigens lassen sich auch Gründe für das Gegentheil anführen, insbesondere die Tendenz des Gesetzgebers, Eide möglichst zu verhüten, welche ihn sogar bestimmt, falls neue Behelfe vorgelegt werden (Art. 460 Abs. 2), die Aufhebung der Eidesauflage zu verfügen (Art. 460 Abs. 2).

5) Eidesannahmen in den Anträgen werden nicht im Wege stehen, bei der Verhandlung noch sonstige Beweismittel anzubieten, selbst wenn die Partei sich auf Eideszuschiebung beschränkt hatte. Hier wird das Prinzip des Art. 251 maßgebend sein, in Verbindung mit dem Umstande, daß die Eideszuschiebung nur ein Beweismittel

ist, nicht aber ein Vergleichsvorschlag oder ein Verzicht.

6) Das Gesetz spricht hier bloß davon, daß sich der Gegner zur Annahme bereit erkläre, legt also keinen Werth darauf, daß hiermit zugleich eine vollständige, den Forderungen der Art. 455 und 456 entsprechende Eideserklärung verbunden sei, obwohl dies in der Regel der Fall sein wird. Ist jene Erklärung — sei es bei der Verhandlung, sei es durch Zustellung — erfolgt, so besteht ein wohlerworbenes Recht für die betreffende Partei, den Eid mit den Folgen, welche sich nach der Sachlage daran knüpfen, auszuschwören, vorbehaltlich der Ausnahme, welche Art. 460 Abs. 2 bedingt.

Art. 460. — Das Gericht entscheidet über die bei der Verhandlung gegen den Eidessatz und die Zulässigkeit der Zuschiebung oder Zurückschiebung erhobenen Einwendungen, setzt jenen vorläufig fest und bestimmt die Sitzung für die Eidesleistung.

Ist die Erklärung über Annahme oder Zurückschiebung des Eids bei Erlassung des Urtheils noch nicht erfolgt, so ist in diesem eine von seiner Zustellung laufende Frist zu bestimmen, in welcher die bezeichnete Erklärung bei Vermeidung der Annahme der Eidesverweigerung zugestellt werden muß, und eine weitere Frist für die Zustellung der etwa nöthig werdenden Antwort. Streitigkeiten, die aus den Erklärungen der Parteien sich ergeben, werden in der zur Eidesleistung anberaumten Sitzung entschieden. Hiebei wird auch der Eidessatz endgiltig festgesetzt. Macht jedoch der Schwurpflichtige neue thatsächliche Angaben oder werden weitere Behelfe vorgelegt, so hat das Gericht diese Angaben und Behelfe im Zusammenhalte mit dem bereits vorliegenden Beweismaterial zu prüfen und, wenn die geänderte Sachlage es erfordert, eine neue Entscheidung zu erlassen, wobei nach Umständen auch weiterer Beweis angeordnet werden kann.

Art. 461. — Der Schwurpflichtige kann selbst nach der definitiven Festsetzung des Eidessatzes frühere Behauptungen zurücknehmen oder Zugeständnisse machen und sich zu einer hienach beschränkten Eidesleistung erbieten.

G. A. d. K. d. A. II S. 240. 241. 250—253 348. 349. IV S. 101 102. 334. 367. K. d. R. II S. 235. IV S. 61.

1) Im betreffenden Verfahren sind drei Abschnitte ins Auge zu fassen, nemlich: 1) die Eideszuschiebung nebst Verhandlung über deren Erheblichkeit, 2) die Eideserklärung nebst entsprechender Verhandlung, und 3) die Eidesabnahme. Diese Akte können unmittelbar nacheinander in der nemlichen Sitzung stattfinden; sie können auch ganz gesondert auftreten.

In der Pfalz erfolgte seither die Erklärung über die Eidesannahme immer erst nach dem auf Eid erkennenden Urtheile, und das Verfahren gestaltete sich, da das Gesetz vollkommen freie Hand ließ, nach Bedürfniß der Fälle in verschiedener Weise.

Waren die Parteien in der Sitzung anwesend und standen auch sonst keine Bedenken entgegen, so wurde im Urtheile, welches den Eid auferlegte, angeordnet, daß sich der Schwurpflichtige sofort über Annahme des Eides erkläre und im Falle relevanter Annahme ihn ausschwöre. Der Vorsitzende ließ denselben vortreten, belehrte ihn über die Wichtigkeit des Eides und den Gegenstand der Eidesleistung und forderte ihn auf, den Sachverhalt so zu erzählen, wie er ihn eidlich zu beschwören im Stande und Willens sei. Nachdem die Gegenpartei ihre persönlichen Gegenbemerkungen vorgebracht, nachdem ferner der Richter die geeigneten besonderen Fragen gestellt und überhaupt alles gethan hatte, was ihm die Pflicht zur Ermittelung der Wahrheit und zur Verhütung eines Meineides gebot, wurde der Eid, falls die Annahme sich als erheblich ergab, abgenommen und sofort, unter Beurkundung der Eidesleistung, das Endurtheil gefällt.

Konnte den Umständen nach der Eid nicht sofort in der Sitzung geleistet werden, so setzte das Gericht in der Regel Fristen zur Eideserklärung und deren Bestreitung und verordnete, daß im Falle relevanter Annahme der Eid in einer bestimmten Sitzung oder vor einem Richtercommissär ausgeschworen werde. Beide Fristen waren nicht präclusiv, und konnte das etwa Versäumte nachgeholt werden, so lange der Eid nicht geleistet, bezw. ein Urtheil, welches ihn für verweigert erklärte, nicht ergangen war.

War die Sache einfach oder sehr dringlich, so wurde ausnahmsweise verfügt, daß der Schwurpflichtige in der anberaumten Sitzung sich über den Eid erkläre und ihn ausschwöre.

2) Unsere Prozeßordnung bringt in dieses Verfahren verschiedene Aenderungen.

Zum Ersten setzt sie voraus, daß die Eideserklärung auch schon vor Erlassung des Urtheils, also eventuell, erfolgen könne und, wie aus den Verhandlungen hervorgeht, soll dies sogar die Regel sein. Diese eventuelle Eidesannahme erfolgt entweder schon in den zugestellten und hinterlegten Anträgen (Art. 230) oder bei der Verhandlung. Das Verfahren kürzt sich hierdurch in der Art ab, daß das Gericht im nemlichen Urtheile, welches den Eid auferlegt, zugleich über die bezüglich der Eidesannahme etwa erhobenen Anstände entscheidet, daß es darin diese Annahme beurkundet und den Eidessatz endgiltig feststellt. In Fällen, wo der Eid sofort in der Sitzung geleistet werden soll, insbesondere im Parteiprozesse (Art. 531), ist es, meinen Erfahrungen nach, sachgemäßer, die Eideserklärung erst nach Auflage des Eides machen zu lassen.

Ebenso wie die Eideserklärung, soll auch die Zurückschiebung des Eides in der Regel eventuell geschehen, und hat dies zur Folge, daß sofort nur der zurückgeschobene Eid auferlegt wird.

3) Weitere Aenderungen bestehen darin, daß jetzt in allen Fällen, wo die Erklärung über Annahme und Zurückschiebung des Eides nicht bereits vor dem Urtheile erfolgt ist, Fristen zur Annahme und zur Antwort auf dieselbe zu setzen sind, von denen die erstere eine Ausschlußfrist ist. Es wäre also im Anwaltsprozesse nicht mehr gestattet, anzuordnen, daß die Eideserklärung in der zur Eidesabnahme bestimmten Sitzung erfolge.

Ist in der ersten Frist, welche für Annahme oder Zurückschiebung gegeben ist, eine Erklärung nicht erfolgt, so gilt der Eid als verweigert, und es kann diese Folge nur auf dem Wege der Wiedereinsetzung in den vorigen Stand (Art. 216) beseitigt werden.

Um diese Frist zu wahren, genügt es übrigens nicht, innerhalb derselben einfach zu erklären, daß man den Eid annehme, vielmehr muß die Eideserklärung eine auf die Thatsache eingehende sein, im Sinne, wie es die Art. 455 und 456 verlangen, und schließlich muß sie erheblich sein. Entspricht sie diesen Anforderungen dem Wesen nach nicht, will z. B. der Schwurpflichtige bloß beschwören, daß er sich nicht mehr erinnere, und findet das Gericht keinen Anlaß, den Eid auch in dieser Weise zuzulassen (Art. 455 Abs. 2), oder schiebt er den Eid in unzulässiger Weise zurück, so muß der Eid als verweigert gelten.

Uebrigens kommt es nur darauf an, daß die Erklärung im Wesentlichen erheblich und genügend sei; Erläuterungen, unwesentliche Zusätze, bestimmtere Fassung können auch noch bei Gelegenheit der Eidesabnahme erfolgen.

4) Daß das Gesetz fragliche Frist ausdrücklich für eine Ausschlußfrist erklärt, möchte im Hinblick auf Art. 215 überflüssig erscheinen. Es ergibt sich nun aber die Frage, ob nicht kraft jenes Art. 215 auch die Frist für die Antwort als Ausschlußfrist zu betrachten sei, so daß also deren Versäumung zur Folge hätte, daß die Eidesannahme nicht mehr bestritten werden könnte und der Eidessatz durch dieselbe endgiltig bestimmt wäre.

Es ist zu beachten, daß diese zweite Frist auf Antrag von Dingler (Abg. II 253), um sich dem bis jetzt in der Pfalz bestehenden Verfahren anzuschließen, ins Gesetz aufgenommen wurde. Nach diesem Zwecke und bei dem Gegensatze, welchen das Hervorheben der präklusiven Wirkung bei der ersten Frist bildet, dürfte außer Zweifel sein, daß man nicht daran dachte, eine zweite Ausschlußfrist zu geben. Da nun auch der Wortlaut des Gesetzes dieser Auslegung einigermaßen günstig ist, indem nur gesagt ist, es solle eine Frist für die „Antwort" bestimmt werden, und es später heißt, in der Sitzung werde der Eidessatz endgiltig festgesetzt, so möchte ich annehmen, daß diese Frist nur die Wirkung der Fristen des Vorverfahrens (Art. 251), welchen sie ihrem Zwecke nach vollkommen ähnlich ist, habe, und Einwände gegen die Eidesannahme noch vorgebracht werden können, bis der Eid geleistet ist. So wurde es seither in der Pfalz gehalten, ohne daß Mißstände sich ergaben, selbst nicht, wenn der Eid durch einen beauftragten Richter abzunehmen war, indem dieser entstehende Anstände protokollirte und zur gerichtlichen Entscheidung verwies.

5) Die Frist zur Erklärung über Annahme oder Zurückschiebung des Eides läuft nicht von Zustellung des Urtheils an den Anwalt, sondern gemäß der Bestimmung des Art. 210 von Zustellung an die Partei.

Daß hier die Zustellung an die Partei maßgebend ist, hat übrigens seinen Grund nicht etwa darin, daß ein persönliches Handeln der Partei vorausgesetzt würde und diese deßhalb persönlich aufgefordert werden müßte, sondern in der Erwägung, daß der Vollzug eines der Berufung unterworfenen Urtheils nicht erzwungen werden dürfe, bevor nicht auch die Frist zur Einlegung der Berufung in Lauf gesetzt sei. Hieraus folgt, daß die Zustellung an die Partei immer genügt, und jenen Personen, welche sonst schwurpflichtig sind (dem Mündel, einzelnen Vertretern rc.) besondere Zustellungen nicht zu machen sind. Es ist Sache der Partei, bezw. des Anwaltes, sie in Kenntniß zu setzen.

Die Zustellung an die Partei ist übrigens nicht bloß nöthig, um die Frist zur Eidesabnahme in Lauf, sondern überhaupt, um das Beweisurtheil, welches auf Eid erkennt, zum Vollzuge zu bringen, also auch für die durch Art. 331 vorgeschriebene Zustellung; es ist daher ohne Belang, wenn etwa die Eidesabnahme bereits im Urtheile beurkundet ist und nur Tagfahrt zur Eidesleistung festgesetzt wird.

Ob es praktisch sei, hier immer eine Zustellung an die Partei zu verlangen, möchte ich nach meinen Erfahrungen bezweifeln; es werden unter Umständen ganz unnützer Weise sehr große Kosten verursacht. Uebrigens können die Anwälte durch gegenseitiges Benehmen die Zustellung an die Parteien in der Regel unnöthig machen, und sie werden sich verpflichtet fühlen, dies, wo immer möglich, zu thun.

6) Was die Anwendung des Art. 209 betrifft, so betrachtet unser Gesetz die Eidesleistung als eine Beweisaufnahme und findet also nach Maßgabe von Art. 331 Abs. 3 eine Fristenerweiterung hier nicht statt. Durch die Vorschriften der Art. 464 und 468 ist Vorsorge getroffen, daß die schwurpflichtige Partei keinen Schaden leide.

Ebensowenig findet Art. 209 auf die Frist zur Eideserklärung Anwendung. Man könnte zwar sagen, der Umstand, daß der Anwalt von der schwurpflichtigen Person sich Instruktionen bezüglich der Art und Weise der Abgabe der Erklärung erholen müsse, genüge, um ein persönliches Handeln im Sinne des Art. 209 anzunehmen; allein dieser Gesichtspunkt ist nicht entscheidend, da ja auch bei sonstigen Beweismitteln, z. B. beim Zeugenbeweis, der Anwalt mit der Partei sich benehmen muß. Abgesehen davon, daß der Anwalt verpflichtet ist, sich schon vorher die nöthigen Aufklärungen zu verschaffen, ist dies auch nur eine Rücksicht, welche der Richter bei Ausmessung der Frist zu beachten hat. Vgl. die Bemerkungen des Referenten zu Art. 173 des Entw., welche bei den Verhandlungen als richtig anerkannt wurden (Abg. II 262). Art. 210 Abs. 3 kommt hier nicht in Betracht, da er Vorsorge treffen will, daß Fristen dieser Art immer gleichzeitig mit der Berufungsfrist beginnen, hieraus aber nichts folgt für die Dauer der Frist. Aus gleichen Gründen findet hier auch Art. 211 keine Anwendung.

Was die Frist zur Antwort auf die Eideserklärung betrifft, so ist selbstverständlich auf dieselbe weder Art. 209 noch Art. 211 anwendbar.

Neue Aburtheilung.

7) Die Schlußbestimmung von Art. 460, daß in Fällen, wo der Schwurpflichtige neue thatsächliche Angaben macht oder weitere Belege vorgelegt werden, eine neue Entscheidung erfolgen könne, ist eine Neuerung, nicht bloß für diesseits, sondern auch für die Pfalz. Es ist nemlich nach französischem Prozesse nur zweierlei möglich, daß der Eid sachentscheidend ausgeschworen werde, oder nicht, weßhalb an manchen Gerichten die, jetzt unzweifelhaft ausgeschlossene, Uebung bestand, mit Auflage des Eides sofort ein bedingtes Endurtheil zu sprechen.

Die eingeführte Neuerung hat gewichtige Gründe für sich, und ich möchte sie vorerst — und vorausgesetzt, daß nicht die Praxis Mißstände aufdeckt — als einen das materielle Recht fördernden Fortschritt begrüßen.

8) Es fällt in die Augen, daß fragliche Bestimmung mit dem Prinzipe, daß Urtheile, welche auf Eid erkennen, den Richter binden (Art. 345) und selbständig in Rechtskraft übergehen (Art. 683), nicht ganz im Einklange stehe, und es frägt sich, wie weit sie demselben Abbruch thue.

Im Allgemeinen darf als feststehend angenommen werden, daß das Gesetz nur eine Entscheidung bezüglich der Beweismittel im Auge hat. Vermuthungen, welche sich aus neu vorgebrachten Thatsachen herleiten, Urkunden und sonstige Beweiserhebungen sollen unter Umständen benützt werden dürfen, um, mit Umgehung des Eides, diejenigen Thatsachen, welche als erheblich und sachentscheidend im Urtheile bezeichnet sind, zu erweisen.

Was im Urtheile bezüglich der Beweispflicht ausgesprochen ist, kann auf diesem Wege nicht geändert werden, und bleibt die in dieser Richtung ergangene Entscheidung maßgebend, auch wenn das Gericht vorerst noch weitere Beweisauflagen machen sollte. Vgl. Abg. II 347 (zu Art. 12). Würde man der Ansicht sein, daß in solchen Fällen der Richter die volle Freiheit der Bewegung, wie sie Art. 345 als Regel aufstellt, zurückerwerbe, so würde die Vorlage irgend eines neuen Beleges, das Auftauchen irgend eines neuen Umstandes in der Eideserklärung genügen, die ganze Rechtskraft des auf Eid erkennenden Interlokutes aufzuheben.

9) Was die Frage betrifft, wann und wie eine derartige Aenderung des Beweisurtheils erwirkt werden könne, so setzen die Worte des Gesetzes zunächst voraus, daß dieselbe bei Gelegenheit des Zwischenstreites beantragt werde, welcher sich über die Erheblichkeit der Eidesannahme und die Festsetzung des Eidessatzes ergibt. Eine Beschränkung auf diesen Fall würde jedoch offenbar dem Geiste des Gesetzes nicht entsprechen, denn die Folge wäre, daß neue Urkunden nicht berücksichtigt werden könnten, wenn ein solcher Zwischenstreit nicht erhoben wäre, und ebenso-

wenig in Fällen, wo auf Grund einer eventuellen Eidesannahme der Eidessatz bereits im Urtheile endgiltig festgestellt wäre. Der wahre Sinn des Gesetzes scheint mir vielmehr der zu sein, daß solche Behelfe, welche die Sachlage ändern, in Betracht kommen dürfen, so lange der Eid noch nicht wirklich ausgeschworen ist, so lange der Zweck des Gesetzes, unnöthige Eide zu verhüten, erreicht werden kann. Abg. IV S. 101 Sp. 2 (Barth, v. Weiß).

Was die neue Entscheidung auf Grund neuer Thatsachen betrifft, so bin ich jedoch der Ansicht, daß dieselbe ausgeschlossen sei, sobald der Eidessatz endgiltig festgestellt ist. Es wäre also eine Partei nicht zu hören, wenn sie erst nach Verwerfung ihrer Einwände gegen die Eideserklärung mit einem Antrage auf Aenderung des Urtheils auftreten wollte.

10) Frägt man, was unter neuen thatsächlichen Aufstellungen zu verstehen sei, so ist vorerst ins Auge zu fassen, daß nur von neuen Thatsachen in der Eideserklärung die Rede ist; also wäre es ohne Belang, wenn etwa der Beweispflichtige neue Behauptungen aufstellen und zu erweisen sich erbieten würde.

Ferner erscheint klar, daß nur solche Thatsachen gemeint seien, welche bei der früheren Verhandlung nicht geltend gemacht wurden, und deßhalb nicht berücksichtigt werden konnten, nicht aber solche, welche nur in der Eideszuschiebung nicht enthalten sind. Es ist dies von besonderer Wichtigkeit für die Pfalz, wo zufolge der dort geltenden Prinzipien über die Untheilbarkeit des Geständnisses auch Thatsachen, welche nur Einreden begründen, in die Eideserklärung aufgenommen werden dürfen.

Der Gedanke des Gesetzgebers ist folgender: Wenn die schwurpflichtige Partei zugestehen muß, früher die Thatsachen nicht richtig oder nicht vollständig vorgetragen zu haben, und die hieraus sich ergebende Sachlage der Art ist, daß, wenn sie früher vorgelegen hätte, das Gericht nicht auf Eid erkannt, sondern eine andere Entscheidung gegeben hätte, so soll dasselbe nicht gehindert sein, diese Entscheidung auch noch nachträglich zu erlassen.

11) Diese neue Entscheidung wird wohl nur zu Gunsten des Beweispflichtigen ausfallen können, indem nemlich das Gericht aus den neuen Thatsachen Vermuthungen zieht, sei es, um einen vollen Beweis anzunehmen, sei es, um den Erfüllungseid aufzulegen, sei es endlich um sonstige Beweise zuzulassen, welche es früher unberücksichtigt gelassen hatte. Die Fälle, in denen diese Befugniß des Richters praktische Bedeutung gewinnt, sind namentlich jene, wo Jemand über das schwören muß, was er von fremden Handlungen in Erfahrung gebracht (Art. 456), und ist es bemerkenswerth, daß fragliche Bestimmung ursprünglich (Art. 415 des Entw.) den Fall, wo Jemand über eigene Handlungen zu schwören hatte, gar nicht begriff.

Daß die Aenderung der Entscheidung auch zu Gunsten des Schwurpflichtigen ausfallen könne, ist zwar durch die Worte des Gesetzes nicht ausgeschlossen, allein ich wüßte mir einen praktischen Fall dieser Art nicht zu denken. Bringt nemlich der Schwurpflichtige neue Umstände vor, welche ihm günstig sind, so darf er nicht etwa zum Beweise derselben zugelassen werden, denn unsere Prozeßordnung kennt keine Gewissensvertretung und schließt die Eideszuschiebung nur da aus, wo vollständiger Beweis bereits vorliegt. Es kann sich daher für ihn nur darum handeln, ob seine Eideserklärung im Ganzen der Eidesauflage gegenüber erheblich sei oder nicht.

12) Unter „neuen Behelfen" sind Urkunden jeder Art zu verstehen, seien sie vollbeweisend oder nicht.

Sie müssen sofort vorgelegt werden, wenn sie Beachtung finden sollen; bloßes Beweiserbieten würde also nicht zu berücksichtigen sein, und auch auf Vertagung zum Zwecke der Vorlage wird in diesem Falle das Gericht nicht leicht eingehen.

Der Wortlaut des Gesetzes unterscheidet nicht, ob die Behelfe von der einen oder von der anderen Partei vorgelegt werden, ob die Aenderung der Entscheidung zu Gunsten des Schwurpflichtigen oder des Beweispflichtigen erfolge, und erscheint es auch als Wille des Gesetzgebers, solche Unterscheidungen auszuschließen. Der Entwurf (Art. 415) sprach nur davon, daß der Schwurpflichtige neue Behelfe vorlege, und hatte Fälle im Auge, wo Jemand, der nach Art. 456 verpflichtet ist, anzugeben, was er auf Nachforschung von den betreffenden Thatsachen ermittelt habe, neue Beweisurkunden vorbringt, die er auf Nachsuchen noch aufgefunden. Auch die erste Redaktion bei den Verhandlungen (Abg. II 252) behielt diese Fassung bei, die Subcommission jedoch (Abg. II 347) brachte die neue Fassung, welche unter dem Gewande einer bloßen Redaktionsänderung an Stelle einer Ausnahmsbestimmung ein allgemeines Prinzip setzt. Nach dem jetzigen Wortlaute, der gerade durch die vorgenommene Aenderung besondere Bedeutung erhält, und nach den Erläuterungen, welche der kgl. Minist.-Commissär (Abg. IV 101) gibt, erscheint der Sinn des Gesetzes klar.

Auf Seite des Beweispflichtigen ist daher das nachträgliche Beibringen von Behelfen ein Mittel, um den Eid, trotzdem, daß derselbe bereits angenommen ist, wieder zu beseitigen, und andern Beweis an die Stelle zu setzen; für den Schwurpflichtigen ist es ein Mittel, die Eideszuschiebung nachträglich unstatthaft zu machen, falls die Urkunde für sich allein oder in Verbindung mit dem sonstigen Beweismaterial einen vollständigen Beweis zu seinen Gunsten ergibt (Art. 457 Ziff. 4). Im letzteren Falle — der jedoch für die Pfalz wegfällt — findet also Gewissensvertretung statt. Vgl. Abg. II 347 (zu Art. 12).

Die frühere Bemerkung (zu Art. 457 Nr. 13), daß die einfache Bestreitung der Aechtheit der Urkunde ohne Belang sei, gilt auch hier.

13) Es läßt sich nicht verkennen, daß diese Freiheit im Nachbringen von Behelfen zu großer Willkür im Verfahren, zu Prozeßverzögerung und Kostenmehrung zu führen geeignet ist, wenn die Gerichte nicht gegen hervortretenden Mißbrauch streng einschreiten.

In dieser Beziehung ist darauf aufmerksam zu machen, daß auch für diese Behelfe die Bestimmungen des Art. 172 gelten, wornach sie bei Unterlassung vorausgängiger Mittheilung von der Verhandlung zurückzuweisen sind, was hier gleich einer definitiven Verwerfung wirkt, und daß jedenfalls der Partei oder dem Anwalte die Mehrkosten zur Last zu legen sind, welche durch die Unterlassung rechtzeitiger Vorlage, wenn sie verschuldet erscheint, entstanden sind.

Die Frage, ob wegen Vorlage neuer Urkunden eine Aenderung der Entscheidung einzutreten habe, ist auf dem Wege eines Zwischenstreites in die Sitzung zu bringen.

Aenderung des Eidessatzes (Art. 461).

14) Art. 461 enthält eigentlich nur eine Verwahrung gegen die Annahme, als müsse der Eid Wort für Wort so geleistet werden, wie er nach der endgiltigen Festsetzung des Eidessatzes lautet; denn es erscheint selbstverständlich, daß der Schwurpflichtige frühere Behauptungen oder Bestreitungen zurücknehmen und die entgegenstehenden Angaben des Gegners als richtig zugeben dürfe. Geständnisse — ganze oder theilweise — zu erzwingen, ist ja gerade Zweck der Eidesauflage. Wenn z. B. der Beweispflichtige, dem der Eid zurückgeschoben wurde, erklärt, er könne seine frühere Behauptung, 200 fl. darlehensweise gegeben zu haben, nicht beschwören, wohl aber, daß es 180 fl. gewesen seien, oder wenn umgekehrt der Gegner auf die Eideszuschiebung erklärt, er könne den Empfang von 180 fl. nicht abschwören, wohl aber, daß es mehr gewesen sei, so liegt auf flacher Hand, daß diese Aenderungen der Abnahme des Eides nicht im Wege stehen können.

15) Unter Umständen kann sich die Frage aufwerfen, ob das Zugeständniß einzelner früher abgeläugneter Umstände den Eid ganz oder theilweise unerheblich mache, und es kann nöthig sein, daß das Gericht hierüber entscheide (Abg. II 241 Sp. 1 a. E.).

Diese Entscheidung hat sich jedoch meiner Ansicht nach bloß auf die beregte Frage zu beschränken, und kann von einer neuen Entscheidung, welche den Eid beseitigt, nicht mehr die Rede sein. Aus der Fassung des Art. 461, aus seiner gesonderten Stellung dem Art. 460 gegenüber, endlich aus dem Umstande, daß hier nicht von neuen Thatsachen, sondern nur vom Zugeständniß dessen, was früher bereits bestritten war, die Rede ist, scheint mir dies mit Nothwendigkeit zu folgen. Vgl. jedoch Abg. IV 101 (v. Weiß).

Art. 462. — In der Sitzung, in welcher das in Art. 460 Abs. 1 erwähnte Urtheil verkündet wird, darf der zugeschobene Eid nicht geschworen werden, ausgenommen wenn beide Theile es beantragen.

In der zur Leistung des zugeschobenen Eids bestimmten Sitzung kann, falls der Eid zurückgeschoben wurde, sofort zur Eidesabnahme geschritten werden, wenn der Schwurpflichtige anwesend und zur Leistung erbötig ist. Andernfalls bestimmt das Gericht dafür eine weitere Sitzung.

G. A. d. K. d. A. II S. 250—252. 348. 349. 453. IV S. 102 105. K. d. R. II S. 235. IV S. 61.

1) Um übereilte Eidesabnahmen zu verhüten und dem Schwurpflichtigen Zeit zur reiflichen Ueberlegung zu sichern, ist verfügt, daß der Eid nicht in der nemlichen Sitzung, in welcher er auferlegt wird, ausgeschworen werden dürfe, falls nicht beide Theile die sofortige Eidesleistung beantragen.

Das Nemliche muß auch vom zurückgeschobenen Eide gelten, falls sofort auf diesen erkannt worden ist (Bemerk. zu Art. 460 Nr. 2); wurde jedoch der Eid erst zurückgeschoben, nachdem er bereits auferlegt und die Sitzung zu dessen Leistung bestimmt war, so kann in dieser Sitzung auch der zurückgeschobene Eid sofort geschworen werden, wenn der Schwurpflichtige anwesend und zum Schwure bereit ist. Im letzteren Falle wird also nicht die Zustimmung beider Theile verlangt, sondern genügt es, daß die schwurpflichtige Person keinen Einwand erhebe.

2) Damit eine sofortige Eidesleistung stattfinden könne, ist nöthig, daß beide Theile Antrag stellen; ein bloßes Dulden würde also nicht genügen.

In dieser Antragstellung liegt zugleich der Verzicht auf die Fristen und Formen, welche für Beweisaufnahmen überhaupt und für den Eid insbesondere vorgeschrieben sind (Art. 331, 338, 460); namentlich ist das Gericht ermächtigt, sofort nach Spruch des Urtheils die Erklärung über die Eidesannahme zu erheben, den Gegner mit seinen Erinnerungen zu hören und über etwaige Zwischenstreite zu entscheiden. Ferner liegt in dieser Antragstellung ein stillschweigender Verzicht auf die Berufung gegen das auf Eid erkennende Urtheil (Art. 463 Abs. 2). Bemerk. zu Art. 90 Nr. 6.

3) Uebrigens ist das Gericht nicht verpflichtet, den Eid sofort abzunehmen, auch wenn beide Theile es verlangen; namentlich ist auf die Zustimmung des Schwurpflichtigen in der Regel wenig Gewicht zu legen, da gerade Personen, die ein böses Gewissen haben, sich am bereitwilligsten zu zeigen pflegen.

Bestehen daher Bedenken, ob der Eid mit gutem Gewissen geschworen werden könne, so hat das Gericht von Amtswegen zu vertagen. In solchen Fällen genügt es gewöhnlich, die Verhandlung auf kurze Zeit — etwa mit Einschiebung anderer Verhandlungen — auszusetzen; wenn nicht, so bestimmt das Gericht eine spätere Sitzung zur Fortsetzung der bereits begonnenen Eidesverhandlung, und bedarf es keiner weiteren Ladung oder Aufforderung. Vgl. Art. 252.

4) Werden die Anträge auf sofortige Abnahme des Eides nicht gestellt, so hat das Gericht nach Art. 460 Abs. 1 oder Abs. 2 zu verfügen.

Im Falle des Abs. 2 gilt die Sitzung, welche zur Eidesleistung bestimmt ist, zugleich zur Verhandlung über etwaige Zwischenstreite. Ebenso gilt sie zugleich für die weitere Verhandlung nach der Eidesleistung (Art. 344 Abs. 1).

Es ist zwar nicht nöthig, jedoch vielleicht sachgemäß, dies im Urtheile auszudrücken und etwa zu sagen:

„gibt Urkunde, daß Kläger dem Beklagten den „Eid dahin zuschiebt, 2c. 2c."

„gibt dem Beklagten eine Frist von — Tagen, „um sich über diesen Eid zu erklären, dem Kläger „eine Frist von — Tagen, um auf diese Erklärung „zu antworten;

„setzt zur Entscheidung über etwaige Zwischen„streite, zur Eidesleistung und weiteren Verhandlung „die Sitzung vom — fest."

Die Formel: „gibt Urkunde", welche sich in der Pfalz eingebürgert hat, beruht auf der Erwägung, daß der Eidessatz nicht durch die Eidesauflage, sondern durch die Eideserklärung oder das in Folge derselben etwa ergehende Zwischenurtheil festgestellt werde. Man findet darin die Erklärung des Gerichts, daß die Eideszuschiebung in der Weise, wie sie beurkundet wird, erheblich sei. Allerdings übte auf die Bildung dieser Formel auch die Ansicht, wornach die Eideszuschiebung bloß als ein Vergleichsvorschlag erscheint, welchen der Richter beurkundet, Einfluß.

Richtiger wäre es vielleicht, zu sagen:

„erkennt, daß Beklagter den Haupteid zu schwören „habe, welcher ihm darüber zugeschoben ist 2c."

5) Das gewöhnliche Verfahren, welches Zustellung des Beweisurtheiles an die Partei und Einhaltung langer Fristen bedingt, ist zeitraubend und kostspielig; es wird daher unter Umständen sachgemäß sein, dasselbe mit Zustimmung der Parteien zu umgehen.

Wenn z. B. die Anwälte auf Befragen erklären, sie würden, falls das Gericht auf Eid erkenne, veranlassen, daß ihre Parteien oder wenigstens die schwurpflichtigen Personen in einer der nächsten Sitzungen erscheinen, damit der Eid sofort geschworen werden könne, so kann das Gericht einfach den Spruch des Urtheils in die betreffende Sitzung vertagen, in welcher sodann nach Art. 462 Abs. 1 der Eid sofort abgenommen werden und Endentscheidung erfolgen kann. Auch die Vertagung der Verhandlung führt zu diesem Ziele.

Erscheint allerdings der Schwurpflichtige in der bezeichneten Sitzung nicht, so muß nach der Regel verfahren werden.

6) Wird für Ausschwörung des zurückgeschobenen Eides eine weitere Sitzung bestimmt (Art. 462 a. E.), so ist nicht etwa nach Vorschrift des Art. 460 Abs. 2 zu verfahren, in der Art, daß Fristen für Eideserklärung und Antwort darauf gegeben würden.

In der Regel wird die Annahme des zurückgeschobenen Eides innerhalb der in Art. 460 Abs. 2 vorgesehenen zweiten Frist bereits erfolgt sein; sollte dies aber nicht geschehen sein, so wäre, wenn die oben (zu Art. 460 Nr. 4) ausgesprochene Ansicht richtig ist, eine Eidesverweigerung nicht anzunehmen und könnten Eideserklärung und Bestreitung derselben noch in der zur Eidesleistung bestimmten Sitzung erfolgen. Es tritt also für den zurückgeschobenen Eid, falls die Zurückschiebung erst nach der Auflage erfolgt, das Verfahren ein, wie es Art. 531 für den Parteiprozeß vorschreibt und wie es seither in der Pfalz auch für den zugeschobenen Eid galt.

Man darf hierin keine Anomalie finden, denn die Erklärung auf den zurückgeschobenen Eid, welche in der Zuschiebung eigentlich schon antizipirt ist, hat offenbar viel geringere Bedeutung, als die Erklärung auf den zugeschobenen Eid.

Art. 463. — **Erklärt eine Partei, daß sie Berufung ergreifen wolle, so darf zur Abnahme des Eids vorläufig nicht geschritten werden.**

Hat die Gegenpartei die Abnahme des Eids ohne Erklärung, daß sie Berufung ergreife, geschehen lassen, so wird angenommen, daß sie auf die Berufung in dem betreffenden Punkte verzichte.

G. A. d. K. d. A. II S. 252. 255. 348. 349. — K. d. R. II S. 235.

1) Nach dem Systeme unserer Prozeßordnung bildet der Lauf der Berufungsfrist kein Hemmniß für den Vollzug, sondern nur die Einlegung der Berufung (Art. 827), so daß also nach allgemeinen Prinzipien jede Partei berechtigt wäre, die Eidesleistung zu veranlassen, ohne Rücksicht darauf, daß im Wege der Berufung später der Eid für unerheblich oder unnöthig erklärt werden könnte.

Es ist klar, daß hierin ein Mißstand läge, indem gewichtige Rücksichten der Moral dafür sprechen, nicht ohne Noth Meineide zu provoziren oder den Fall herbeizuführen, daß über die nemliche Thatsache beide Parteien im entgegengesetzten Sinne zum Schwure kommen. Im Bestreben, diesem Mißstande so viel wie möglich zu begegnen, verfügt Art. 463: 1) daß in Fällen, wo eine Partei erklärt, Berufung ergreifen zu wollen, die Eidesleistung vorläufig zu unterbleiben habe, und 2) daß die Partei, welche die Eidesleistung geschehen läßt, hierdurch auf die Berufung verzichte. Gleichen Zweck verfolgen die Art. 777 und 799.

2) Offenbar werden durch diese Bestimmungen irrelevante Eidesleistungen nicht vollständig beseitigt, denn abgesehen vom Falle der Aufhebung eines Urtheils im Wege der Nichtigkeitsbeschwerde, ist auch im Falle, wo die Gegenpartei bei der Eidesleistung nicht anwesend war, die Möglichkeit einer Aenderung des Urtheils im Wege der Berufung gegeben. Der Gesetzgeber war sich dessen auch wohl bewußt (Abg. II 252) und es ist für die Auslegung des Gesetzes nicht ohne Bedeutung, daß nicht beabsichtigt war, Eidesleistungen vor eingetretener Rechtskraft des Urtheils ganz zu beseitigen, sondern nur, sie möglichst zu beschränken.

3) Erklärt eine Partei, Berufung ergreifen zu wollen, so soll die Eidesleistung vorläufig unterbleiben.

Es ist zu beachten, daß das Gesetz beide Parteien im Auge hat, während der Entwurf (Art. 429) nur von der Partei, gegen welche der Eid geleistet werden soll, sprach, was eigentlich prinzipiell richtiger war.

Die Aenderung wurde auf Antrag des Abgeordneten Dingler beschlossen (Abg. II 255 a. E.). Als selbstverständlich hätte sie nicht betrachtet werden können, denn dem Schwurpflichtigen gegenüber läßt sich nicht sagen, es wäre möglich, daß ein irrelevanter Eid geleistet würde. Für ihn handelt es sich bloß darum, die Bedenkzeit zu erweitern und die Präsumtion der Eidesverweigerung (Art. 465) abzuwenden.

4) Die bloße Kundgabe der Absicht, Berufung zu ergreifen, genügt, und nach den Worten des Gesetzes hätte das Gericht nicht einmal zu prüfen, ob die Berufung auch statthaft sei. Nichtsdestoweniger glaube ich im Hinblicke auf Art. 699 und 827, daß das Gericht auf Prüfung dieser letzteren Frage eingehen dürfe, denn es kann doch wohl die Absicht, etwas zu thun, nicht mehr Wirkung äußern, als die That selbst.

Allerdings wird es jedoch Pflicht des Gerichts sein, im Zweifel die Eidesabnahme zu vertagen und nur dann die Erklärung einer beabsichtigten Berufung unberücksichtigt zu lassen, wenn vollkommen klar zu Tage liegt, daß es bloß auf Chikane abgesehen sei. Vgl. Abg. III 91 u. 92 (v. Weiß).

Durch eine vorsorgliche Vollstreckbarkeitserklärung (Art. 268), welche nur auf Endurtheile anwendbar ist, könnte Art. 463 nicht beseitigt werden.

5) Wird in der zur Eidesleistung festgesetzten Sitzung ein Appellakt vorgelegt, so wird das Verfahren auf unbestimmte Zeit, d. h. bis zur Erledigung der Berufung, suspendirt, bezw. die Streichung von der Wochentabelle verfügt (Bemerk. zu Art. 240—243 Nr. 10); es frägt sich, ob das Gleiche zu gelten habe, wenn bloß die Absicht, Berufung zu ergreifen erklärt wird.

Der Entwurf bestimmte dies; auf erhobenen Einwand beschloß man, vorläufig es dabei zu belassen (Abg. II 252); später jedoch brachte die Subcommission ohne weitere Begründung die jetzige Fassung (Abg. II 348). Ich möchte aus dieser

Fassung auf eine Aenderung der ursprünglichen Anschauung schließen und annehmen, daß im gegebenen Falle zur Eidesleistung eine weitere Tagfahrt festzusetzen sei, bis zu welcher die betreffende Partei Zeit habe, ihre Absicht zu verwirklichen. Wird in der späteren Tagfahrt der Nachweis der wirklichen Ergreifung der Berufung nicht vorgelegt, so wird es nicht gestattet sein, wiederholt zu erklären, daß man Berufung beabsichtige, und so die Eidesleistung während der ganzen Berufungsfrist unmöglich zu machen.

Ich folgere dies aus dem Worte „vorläufig", ferner aus dem Umstande, daß Art. 463 Abs. 2 die Möglichkeit einer Eidesabnahme trotz solcher Erklärung voraussetzt, endlich aus dem Geiste des Gesetzes, welches, wie gesagt, die Eidesleistungen vor eingetretener Rechtskraft nur beschränken, nicht beseitigen will. Hätte das Gesetz gewollt, daß in solchen Fällen vor Ablauf der Berufungsfrist die Eidesabnahme nicht stattfinden dürfe, so hätte es dies ja einfach sagen können!

Allerdings kann und soll das Gericht, wenn annehmbare Entschuldigungen vorgebracht werden, weiter vertagen.

6) Die Anwesenheit der Gegenpartei bei der Eidesleistung begründet einen stillschweigenden Verzicht auf die Berufung, wenn nicht die Erklärung, dieses Rechtsmittel zu ergreifen, erfolgt ist (Art. 463 Abs. 2). Daß hier gesagt ist: „Berufung ergreifen", in Abs. 1 aber: „Berufung ergreifen wollen", ist eine kleine Nachlässigkeit der Redaktion; offenbar ist das Nemliche gemeint.

Der stillschweigende Verzicht auf Rechtsmittel liegt in den Befugnissen des Anwalts (Bemerk. zu Art. 92 Nr. 6), und es ist daher nicht zu bezweifeln, daß die Anwesenheit desselben bei der Eidesleistung einen Verzicht auf die Berufung bewirke. Dabei ist jedoch zu beachten, daß es nicht auf die physische Gegenwart, sondern auf die Betheiligung bei der Verhandlung ankommt. Es ist daher nicht nöthig, daß der Anwalt für die Dauer der Eidesleistung sich aus der Sitzung entferne, vielmehr genügt es, daß er erkläre, sich nicht zu betheiligen, d. h. als nicht anwesend betrachtet werden zu wollen. Vgl. Art. 253 und Abg. II 252.

7) Wenn eine Partei, wie ihr dies nach Art. 341 zusteht, bei der Eidesabnahme sich in anderer Weise als durch ihren Anwalt vertreten läßt, so enthält auch die Gegenwart dieses Bevollmächtigten einen stillschweigenden Verzicht auf die Berufung, denn in fraglicher Vollmacht liegt die Ermächtigung, alles vorzunehmen, was die Beweisaufnahme mit sich bringt, sowie die Unterwerfung unter die Folgen, welche das Thun oder Unterlassen des Bevollmächtigten bedingt.

Von selbst versteht es sich, daß, wenn nur ein Theil der Parteien anwesend oder vertreten war, auch nur für diesen der Verzicht eintritt.

8) Da Art. 463 nur vom Rechtsmittel der Berufung spricht, so ist klar, daß er auf sonstige Rechtsmittel, namentlich die Nichtigkeitsbeschwerde, keine Anwendung findet.

Art. 464. — **Wird vor oder in der zur Eidesleistung festgesetzten Sitzung Bescheinigung darüber beigebracht, daß der Schwurpflichtige zu erscheinen außer Stande ist, so ist eine weitere Tagfahrt zur Eidesleistung anzuordnen.**

G. A. d. K. d. A. II S. 252. 348. 349. IV S. 102. — K. d. R. II S 235. IV S. 61.

1) Nach den strengen Prinzipien, wie sie Art. 215 aufstellt, hätte das Ausbleiben des Schwurpflichtigen in der bestimmten Tagfahrt zur Folge, daß das Recht den Eid zu leisten verwirkt wäre, und könnte diese Folge nur durch Wiedereinsetzung in den vorigen Stand (Art. 216) wieder beseitigt werden.

Im Gefühle, daß diese Strenge hier nicht am Platze wäre, bestimmt Art. 464, es solle auf bloße Bescheinigung einer Verhinderung (Vorbemerk. zu Hptst. IX) die Eidesleistung in eine andere Sitzung vertagt werden. Diese Bescheinigung soll nicht bloß in, sondern auch vor der Sitzung beigebracht werden können, das Gesetz hat also auch eine schriftliche Benachrichtigung, welche an den Gerichtsvorstand oder an den beauftragten Richter zu richten wäre, im Auge. Vgl. Art. 421 und 429.

Ob sie im Sinne des Gesetzes genüge, hat der Richter frei zu würdigen.

2) Es handelt sich hier nicht um einfache Vertagung der Tagfahrt im Sinne von Art. 213 Abs. 2 (vgl. Bemerk. zu Art. 215 Nr. 3), sondern um Entscheidung darüber, ob eine bereits eingetretene Versäumung der Tagfahrt die Rechtsverlustigung zur Folge habe oder nicht.

Ohne Vorlage einer Bescheinigung darf (abgesehen vom Falle des Art. 463 Abs. 2) das Gericht eine neue Tagfahrt nicht festsetzen, muß vielmehr die Folgen, welche Art. 465 Abs. 3 bestimmt, aussprechen, und bleibt dem Schwurpflichtigen nur der Weg des Art. 468. Der Zusammenhalt von Art. 215 und 464 führt zu dieser Ansicht.

Art. 465. — Die Leistung des Eides bildet vollkommenen Beweis der beschworenen Thatsache zwischen den Parteien.

Der dem Gegner erlassene Eid ist dem geleisteten gleichzuachten.

Die ungerechtfertigte Nichtannahme oder Verweigerung des Eids, sowie das unentschuldigte Nichterscheinen des Schwurpflichtigen in der zur Eidesleistung anberaumten Sitzung gilt als Zugeständniß des Gegentheils der zu beschwörenden Thatsache.

G. A. d. K. d. A. II S. 252. 348. 349. — K. d. R. II S. 235.

1) Die Bestimmungen dieses Artikels (welcher für die Pfalz nicht gilt) beruhen auf der Anschauung, daß die Eideszuschiebung ein Beweismittel sei und daß sie dazu diene, Geständnisse zu erzwingen.

Wenn gesagt ist, es bilde die Leistung des Eides vollkommenen Beweis der beschworenen Thatsache, so ist dieser Satz in der Allgemeinheit, wie er lautet, nicht richtig, vielmehr ist beizufügen, daß es sich um Thatsachen handeln müsse, welche durch Geständniß in volle Gewißheit gesetzt werden können. Handelt es sich um andere Thatsachen (Art. 324 Abs. 2), so muß entweder die Eideszuschiebung für unstatthaft erklärt werden, oder es kann vom Eide allein die Entscheidung nicht abhängen. Ersteres wäre prinzipiell richtiger und gilt in der Pfalz, Letzteres aber entspricht dem Willen des Gesetzgebers. Vgl. Bemerk. zu Art. 449 Nr. 3.

Auch der Satz, daß die Eidesverweigerung so viel wirke, wie ein Geständniß der schwurpflichtigen Person, darf nicht wörtlich genommen werden, denn insofern der Eid auch Personen zugeschoben werden kann, welche ein rechtswirksames Geständniß nicht machen könnten, wirkt sie mehr; sie bewirkt die Fiktion eines Geständnisses der Partei selbst.

2) Der Schwurpflichtige erwirbt mit der Auflage und Annahme des Eides das Recht, durch Ausschwören desselben vollen Beweis zu führen; wenn daher der Gegner den Eid erläßt, so verzichtet er hierdurch auf Führung dieses Beweises. Zur Erlassung eines auferlegten Eides bedarf der Anwalt einer Spezialvollmacht (Art. 92 Ziff. 2).

3) Wenn das Gesetz von einer gerechtfertigten Nichtannahme des Eides spricht, so hat es Fälle im Auge, wo die Frist zur Annahme durch eingelegte Berufung unterbrochen war, oder wo gegen den Ablauf der Frist Wiedereinsetzung in den vorigen Stand erwirkt wird, oder wo die Zurückschiebung erfolgte, obgleich sie unstatthaft war.

Die Verweigerung des Eides ist ferner gerechtfertigt, wenn der Schwurpflichtige erklärt, Berufung ergreifen zu wollen (Art. 462 Abs. 1).

4) Das Nichterscheinen des Schwurpflichtigen in der Sitzung bezw. in der vom beauftragten Richter bestimmten Tagfahrt ist entschuldigt, wenn einer der im Gesetze vorgesehenen Entschuldigungsfälle vorliegt, also: wenn die Bescheinigung, von welcher Art. 464 spricht, beigebracht wird, oder wenn auf dem Wege, welchen Art. 468 bietet, die Verhinderung nachgewiesen wird, oder wenn die Ladung den Vorschriften des Gesetzes nicht entspricht, oder endlich, wenn Rechtsmittel eingelegt sind (Art. 699, 777, 799).

Art. 466. — Der Eid gilt als verweigert, wenn von mehreren schwurpflichtigen Vertretern auch nur einer ihn nicht leistet.

Art. 467. — Ein Streitgenosse wird durch die Eidesleistung der übrigen von der Schwurpflicht nur dann befreit, wenn das bürgerliche Recht oder ein Parteiübereinkommen dies mit sich bringt.

G. A. d. K. d. A. II S. 247—250. 349. — K. d. R. II S. 235.

1) Daß in Fällen, wo mehrere Vertreter für schwurpflichtig erklärt werden (Art. 453), alle schwören müssen, versteht sich wohl von selbst. Warum mehrere bezeichnen, wenn einer genügen würde?

Ist es ein Mißstand, daß durch die Eidesverweigerung eines einzigen Vertreters das Recht der Partei verloren gehe, obgleich die übrigen Vertreter den Eid geleistet haben, so liegt derselbe im Systeme.

2) Die Wirkung, welche die Eidesleistung eines Streitgenossen für die übrigen äußert, bestimmt sich nach den Grundsätzen des Civilrechts, und sind dies ziemlich die nemlichen, wie sie bezüglich der Rechtskraft der Urtheile gelten (Bemerk. zu Art. 294 Nr. 12—16).

In der Regel haben also alle Streitgenossen zu schwören und schwört jeder nur für sein Recht; auch ist es ohne Belang, wenn demzufolge in der nemlichen Sache widersprechende Entscheidungen ergehen müssen, wenn z. B. dem einen Erben gegenüber auf Grund seiner Eidesleistung das Recht zugesprochen, dem anderen gegenüber auf Grund seiner Eidesverweigerung dasselbe aberkannt wird.

Diese Regel erleidet jedoch Ausnahmen, von denen die gewöhnlichste die Untheilbarkeit des Rechtes ist, z. B. wenn das Bestehen einer Servitut mehreren Miteigenthümern gegenüber im Streite ist. Für die Pfalz ist Art. 1365 Code civ. zu beachten. Hat in solchen Ausnahmsfällen einer der Streitgenossen geschworen, so ist hiermit auch der Sieg des andern entschieden, und dessen Eidesleistung erscheint gegenstandslos.

4) Auch durch Parteiübereinkommen kann an die Eidesleistng eines der Streitgenossen der Sieg der anderen geknüpft werden. Ein derartiges Uebereinkommen, durch welches eine Partei ihr Recht von der Erklärung eines Dritten, welche außerdem ohne rechtliche Folgen wäre, abhängig macht, darf als eine gewöhnliche Prozeßhandlung, zu welcher die allgemeine Prozeßvollmacht genügt, nicht betrachtet werden, indem es je nach Umständen unter Ziff. 1 oder Ziff. 2 des Art. 92 fällt.

Art. 468. — Gegen das Urtheil, durch welches der Eid als verweigert erklärt wird, kann die schwurpflichtige Partei, wenn sie bei der Tagfahrt zur Eidesleistung nicht anwesend war, innerhalb einer unerstreckbaren Frist von acht Tagen nach Zustellung des Urtheils unter Anerbietung des Beweises der Verhinderung Einspruch erheben, und zwar auch dann, wenn ihr Anwalt gegenwärtig war, aber keinen Antrag auf Vertagung gestellt hat oder dieser wegen nicht genügender Bescheinigung der Verhinderung verworfen wurde.

G. A. d. K. d. A. II S. 252. 349. IV S. 102. 334. 367. — K. d. R. II S. 235. IV S. 61.

1) Art. 468 bildet die Ergänzung des Art. 464, mit welchem er auch im Entwurfe verbunden war, und eröffnet einen weiteren Weg, um der Strenge des Art. 215 zu entgehen.

Der Entwurf fand sich veranlaßt, dieses eigenthümliche Einspruchsverfahren, welches auch einem contradiktorischen Urtheile gegenüber eintritt, einzuführen, weil nach Erlaß eines Urtheiles die Wiedereinsetzung in den vorigen Stand nicht mehr statthaft ist, wie er denn überall streng am Grundsatze festhält, daß die Wiedereinsetzung in den vorigen Stand kein Rechtsmittel sei und nie benützt werden könne, ein Urtheil aufzuheben. Auch im Wege des gewöhnlichen Einspruchs und selbst der Berufung würde die eingetretene Präclusion nicht mehr ungeschehen gemacht werden können. Art. 707 Abs. 3.

2) Nach dem Willen des Gesetzgebers soll die Frist zum Einspruche ganz die nemliche sein, wie beim Versäumungsurtheile, welchem es, insofern man nur die Person des Schwurpflichtigen berücksichtigt, ähnlich ist. Ursprünglich hatte man einfach auf Art. 309 verwiesen, und wenn man später (Abg. IV 102) die Fassung änderte, so geschah dies bloß, um eine Verweisung zu vermeiden.

Was bezüglich jener Frist zu Art. 309 Nr. 4 bis 6 gesagt ist, gilt auch hier, und finden also insbesondere auch die Art. 209 und 211 Anwendung.

3) Es frägt sich: Wie ist dieser Einspruch zu erheben, und wie ist auf denselben zu verfahren?

Da es sich nicht um einen Zwischenstreit handelt, sondern um Anfechtung eines Urtheils, um Geltendmachen eines Rechtsmittels, und da das Gesetz dieses Rechtsmittel Einspruch nennt, so sind wohl die Vorschriften von Hauptstück VIII maßgebend, um so mehr, da sie der Natur der Sache entsprechen.

Uebrigens wird die spezielle Vorschrift, daß der vorliegende Einspruch unter Anerbietung des Beweises der Verhinderung zu erheben sei, eine Abweichung bedingen. Offenbar will nemlich das Gesetz, es solle sofort mit der Erklärung des Einspruchs (Art. 311) auch dieses Beweiserbieten erfolgen, und da dasselbe die ganze Begründung des Einspruchs enthält, so erscheint die Zustellung eines besonderen Antrags, welcher die Motive des Einspruchs zu enthalten hätte (Art. 312), überflüssig. Vorerst handelt es sich ja einzig und allein um die Frage, ob die Eidesleistung präcludirt oder noch zuzulassen sei.

4) Unter „Verhinderung“ versteht das Gesetz das Nemliche, wie in Art. 464, und sind also die Bestimmungen des Art. 216 nicht maßgebend, obgleich sie so ziemlich zum nemlichen Resultate führen.

Es genügt der Nachweis, daß der Schwurpflichtige außer Stand gewesen, zu erscheinen, und steht die nähere Würdigung dem Richter zu. Verhältnisse, welche die Wiedereinsetzung in den vorigen Stand begründen würden, müssen übrigens jedenfalls auch als Behinderungen im Sinne des Art. 468 gelten.

Hervorzuheben ist, daß einerseits Nachweis, nicht aber bloße Bescheinigung verlangt wird, während anderseits dieser Nachweis nur anzubieten, nicht sofort beizubringen ist. In der Regel wird das Gericht in den Umständen und vorgelegten Bescheinigungen genügende Anhaltspunkte finden, um seine Ueberzeugung zu bilden.

Gerichtlich auferlegter Eid.

Art. 469. — Ist eine erhebliche Thatsache zwar nicht vollständig erwiesen, aber in hohem Grade wahrscheinlich gemacht, so kann das Gericht die betreffende Partei auf Antrag oder von Amtswegen zum Erfüllungseide zulassen, soweit es sich um ihre eigenen Handlungen oder Wahrnehmungen handelt.

Der Erfüllungseid ist sowohl über die Thatsache, auf welche es unmittelbar ankommt, als über Thatsachen, die für den künstlichen Beweis (Art. 322) erheblich sind, zulässig, es darf aber zu letzterem Behufe nur dann auf den Erfüllungseid erkannt werden, wenn der künstliche Beweis dadurch dergestalt ergänzt wird, daß voller Beweis für die unmittelbar erhebliche Thatsache vorliegt.

Auf den Erfüllungseid über die Thatsache, auf welche es unmittelbar ankommt, kann auch dann erkannt werden, wenn das in Art. 322 Abs. 2 vorausgesetzte Zusammentreffen mehrerer vollständig erwiesener gemeiner Vermuthungen zwar vorhanden ist, der Richter aber gleichwohl volle Gewißheit nicht annehmen zu können glaubt.

Art. 470. — Wenn der zur Herausgabe einer Sache Verpflichtete die Erfüllung dieser Verpflichtung verweigert oder durch Arglist oder grobes Verschulden vereitelt, so ist die Gegenpartei auf ihr Verlangen zur eidlichen Erhärtung des Werths der Sache zuzulassen.

Dieser Schätzungseid darf über den gemeinen Werth hinaus auf denjenigen erstreckt werden, welchen die Sache nach den vorliegenden besondern Verhältnissen für den Schwörenden haben würde. Dagegen kommt der blos eingebildete Werth (Affectionswerth) nicht in Betracht.

In gleicher Weise ist bei Klagen wegen gewaltsamer Besitzentsetzung oder wegen Beschädigung durch Arglist oder grobes Verschulden der Beschädigte über die ihm abhanden gekommenen oder beschädigten Sachen und deren Werth beziehungsweise über die Höhe des erlittenen Schadens zum Schätzungseide zuzulassen.

Das Gericht hat in allen diesen Fällen die Summe zu bestimmen, bis zu welcher der Eid zugelassen wird.

Art. 471. — Wenn Jemand verbunden ist, einen Inbegriff von Sachen oder Rechten ganz oder zu einem bestimmten Antheile herauszugeben oder über ihren Bestand Auskunft zu ertheilen, so kann der Berechtigte von dem Verpflichteten den Eid verlangen, daß er Alles vollständig und getreulich angeben wolle, soferne aber der Verpflichtete eine Angabe gemacht hat, den Eid, daß er Alles vollständig und getreulich angegeben habe.

Von Ascendenten können weder ihre Abkömmlinge noch deren Vormünder oder Pfleger einen Offenbarungseid verlangen.

Bei ungerechtfertigter Verweigerung des Offenbarungseids kann der zur Forderung desselben Berechtigte nach Beschaffenheit des Falls verlangen, zum Schätzungseide zugelassen zu werden.

Art. 472. — Die Bestimmungen des Art. 450 Abs. 1 und 2, dann der Art. 451—453, 461 und 463—468 finden auch bei dem richterlich auferlegten Eide analoge Anwendung.

Wird der Schätzungseid nicht geleistet, so tritt der Verlust des Anspruchs ein, soweit dieser durch den auferlegten Eid bedingt ist.

G. A. d. K. d. A. II S. 252. 349. 350. 453. IV S. 102. — K. d. R. II S. 235—239. IV. S. 61.

1) Wenn das Gesetz die Eide, von denen hier die Rede ist, als gerichtlich auferlegte Eide im Gegensatze zum zugeschobenen Eide bezeichnet, so ist dies nicht ganz richtig, denn nach den Prinzipien unserer Prozeßordnung enthält das Urtheil, welches auf den Haupteid erkennt, nicht bloß die Beurkundung eines *Vergleichsvorschlages*, sondern eine *Beweisauflage*; es wird daher auch der Haupteid gerichtlich auferlegt, und besteht nur der Unterschied, daß dies geschieht aus *Anlaß* einer *Zuschiebung*, während beim Erfüllungseide, Schätzungseide und Offenbarungseide der Anlaß ein anderer ist.

a) *Erfüllungseid.*

2) Unsere Prozeßordnung sucht die Notheide zu beschränken und hat daher den Reinigungseid ganz beseitigt, den Erfüllungseid aber nur zugelassen, wenn eigene *Handlungen* oder *Wahrnehmungen* des Schwörenden in Frage stehen.

Wie schon bemerkt (zu Art. 322 Nr. 5), ist das mündliche Verfahren solchen Eiden nicht günstig, und es wird sich wohl auch diesseits die Uebung bilden, ganz selten vom Erfüllungseide Gebrauch zu machen. Nur insofern hat dieser Eid diesseits eine besondere Bedeutung, als er dazu dienen kann, die Fessel der Beweistheorie, welche dem Richter beim Vermuthungsbeweise angelegt ist, zu sprengen.

Eine größere Bedeutung hat er ferner im landgerichtlichen Verfahren, insofern er unter Umständen ein Mittel bietet, Bagatellsachen schnell und einfach zu erledigen, namentlich wenn dem Landrichter die nöthige Personalkenntniß zu Gebote steht.

3) Das Gesetz verfügt, es dürfe der Erfüllungseid auch über einzelne Thatsachen, welche Theile eines künstlichen Beweises bilden, auferlegt werden; um jedoch zu verhüten, daß nicht noch ein zweiter Erfüllungseid (über die Hauptsache) nöthig werde, setzt es hinzu, es müsse jener Erfüllungseid den Beweis vollständig machen, d. h. er müsse sachentscheidend sein.

Die Eidesauflage bezüglich solcher Nebenumstände, aus denen erst auf die zu beweisende Hauptsache geschlossen werden soll, wird vorzugsweise vorkommen in Fällen, wo der Beweispflichtige kein eigenes Wissen von dieser Hauptsache hat. Besteht eigenes Wissen in der einen sowohl als in der anderen Beziehung, so hat der Richter die Wahl, den Eid nur über die Nebenumstände oder über die Hauptsache aufzulegen; er wird jedoch nur bei besonderen Umständen veranlaßt sein, Ersteres zu wählen, z. B. falls er annimmt, es sei in diesem Falle ein Meineid weniger zu befürchten, als im anderen.

b) Schätzungseid (Art. 470).

4) Durch Art. 470 wird der Schätzungseid, das juramentum in litem des alten Prozesses, aufrecht erhalten und zwar, wie früher, unter dem Gesichtspunkte einer Strafe für Arglist, grobes Verschulden und Gewaltthat (Referat zu Art. 433 des Entw.).

Durch Zulassung dieses Eides hat man den Grundsatz des Art. 457 Ziff. 2 verlassen und zwar in dem Maße, daß man den Schätzungseid sogar in Fällen gestattet, wo es möglich ist, den Werth oder Schaden in anderer Weise (durch Zeugen und Sachverständige) zu ermitteln. Daß nemlich Letzteres Wille des Gesetzes sei, kann, nachdem man die bezügliche Einschränkung des Entwurfes beseitigt hat, keinen Zweifel erleiden (Referat a. a. O.).

Ob eine solche Ausdehnung des Schätzungseides sachgemäß, ob überhaupt dieser Eid den Bestimmungen des Art. 330 gegenüber Bedürfniß sei, möchte sehr in Frage sein; in der Pfalz wenigstens hat ein solches Bedürfniß sich nicht fühlbar gemacht, und selbst von der sehr beschränkten Verfügung in Art. 1669 Code civil wurde meines Wissens nie Gebrauch gemacht.

5) Der Schätzungseid ist zugelassen:

1) bei Nichterfüllung der Pflicht zur Herausgabe einer Sache;

2) bei gewaltsamer Besitzentsetzung und

3) bei Beschädigungen überhaupt, wenn Arglist oder grobes Verschulden vorliegt.

In allen diesen Fällen hat der Beschädigte ein Recht darauf, mit Umgehung anderer Beweise, zum Schätzungseide zugelassen zu werden, wenn die Voraussetzungen dazu gegeben sind.

Es liegt jedoch in der Natur der Sache, daß dieser Eid nicht aufzulegen ist, wenn das Gericht in irgend einer Weise, namentlich zufolge der ihm durch Art. 330 verliehenen Gewalt, seine Ueberzeugung über den Betrag des Schadens sich bereits gebildet hat. Es folgt dies mit Nothwendigkeit aus der Befugniß, im Voraus die Summe zu bestimmen, bis zu welcher der Eid zugelassen wird; denn erklärt das Gericht eine gewisse Summe als klar gestellt, so spricht es hiermit aus, daß es den Eid über diese Summe hinaus nicht zulasse, der Beschädigte aber hat sicher kein Interesse, zu verlangen, man möge ihn zum Schwure zulassen, daß der Werth nicht geringer gewesen.

Das Gesetz trifft also nur Fälle, wo eine Beweisauflage nöthig wäre, um Werth oder Schaden zu ermitteln, und gibt dem Beschädigten zur Strafe des Beschädigers das Recht, sofort durch Schätzungseid den Schaden feststellen zu lassen und so ein Beweisverfahren zu vermeiden (Referat a. a. O.).

6) Das Gesetz sagt ganz allgemein, es sei die Gegenpartei auf Verlangen zum Eide zuzulassen, unterscheidet also nicht, ob es der Beschädigte selbst, oder ein gesetzlicher Vertreter oder ein Rechtsnachfolger sei, welcher zu schwören sich erbietet, und ebensowenig, ob eigenes Wissen anzunehmen sei oder nicht. Es liegt um so weniger Grund vor, einen solchen Unterschied zu machen, als ihn auch das ältere Recht (G. O. Cap. XIII § 4 Ziff. 1 und Anmerk. von Kreitmayr — Seuff. Comm. Bd. III S. 413) nicht kennt, als ferner die Art. 454—456 hier keine Anwendung finden (Art. 472), und als endlich es sich hier nicht sowohl um eine Zeugschaft, als um ein Gutachten handelt.

7) Wird die Leistung des Schätzungseides verweigert, so ist die Folge, daß der betreffende Anspruch wegfällt, jedoch nur soweit er durch diesen Eid bedingt ist (Art. 472 Abs. 2). Es kann nemlich der Fall sein, daß das Gericht einen bestimmten Schaden als bereits erwiesen annimmt und nur bezüglich des Mehrbetrags sich veranlaßt findet, den Schätzungseid aufzulegen;

bei dieser Voraussetzung aber ist die Eidesverweigerung nur für diesen Mehrbetrag entscheidend.

Was die Bestimmung der Summe betrifft, bis zu welcher der Eid zugelassen wird (Art. 470 Abs. 4), so ist dem Gerichte vollste Freiheit gegeben, und es versteht sich von selbst, daß es hier rein nach Muthmaßungen handelt, denn wäre Ueberzeugung gegeben, sei es auch nur eine solche, wie sie Art. 330 voraussetzt, so fiele der Schätzungseid hinweg.

8) Herausgabe von Sachen.

Was insbesondere die Herausgabe von Sachen betrifft, so ist der Schätzungseid bloß gestattet, um den Werth der Sachen zu ermitteln, und zwar in zwei Fällen, nemlich 1) wenn die Herausgabe verweigert und 2) wenn sie durch Arglist oder grobes Verschulden vereitelt wird. Handelt es sich zugleich um einen Schaden anderer Art, so wäre unter diesem Gesichtspunkte der Eid unstatthaft, jedoch kann er unter dem Gesichtspunkte des Art. 470 Abs. 3 zulässig sein.

Unter „Sachen" sind offenbar bestimmte Sachen gemeint; denn handelt es sich nur unbestimmt um Lieferung vertretbarer Sachen, z. B. von Waaren in bestimmter Qualität, so kann nicht gesagt werden, es sei die Herausgabe von Sachen in Frage. Uebrigens ist eine bestimmte Sache gegeben, wenn auch nur ein Theil einer Sache herauszugeben, z. B. von einem bestimmten Waarenvorrathe nur ein Theil zu liefern ist, diese Lieferung aber verweigert oder durch Vernichtung oder Beseitigung der Waare unmöglich gemacht wird.

Ob die Herausgabe auf Grund einer dinglichen oder persönlichen Klage verlangt wird, erscheint gleichgiltig.

9) Obgleich die Unterscheidung der Gerichtsordnung zwischen Sachen, die einen bestimmten Preis haben, und anderen nicht wiederholt ist, so ist doch klar und selbstverständlich, daß der Schätzungseid wegfallen müsse, wo von einer Schätzung nicht die Rede sein kann, z. B. wenn Rückgabe einer in Verwahr gegebenen Summe Geldes verlangt wird.

Ebenso fällt dieser Eid weg, wenn der Preis bereits bekannt ist, so daß also ziemlich die nemlichen Grundsätze gelten, wie unter Herrschaft der G. O., und ebensowenig jetzt wie früher der Schätzungseid am Platze ist, wenn der Werth einer Staatsobligation, welche Börsenkurs hat, oder eines Buches, welches im Buchhandel zu kaufen ist, bestimmt werden soll.

10) Der Schätzungseid tritt selbstverständlich nur ein, wenn an Stelle der Hauptverpflichtung zur Herausgabe der Sache die Verpflichtung zum Ersatze des Werthes tritt, fällt also hinweg, wenn diese Herausgabe auf dem Wege des Zwanges sicher erlangt werden kann, also bei Immobilien überhaupt, und bei Mobilien, die bereits vorsorglich beschlagnahmt sind. Die bloße Möglichkeit, die Sache selbst auf dem Wege des Zwanges zu erlangen, beseitigt den Schätzungseid nicht, denn nach dem Gesetze begründet schon die Verweigerung der Herausgabe ein Recht auf diesen Eid und wird nicht verlangt, daß vorher der Versuch gemacht werde, die Herausgabe zu erzwingen. Ebenso ist unnöthig, daß ein Urtheil, welches die Pflicht zur Herausgabe ausspricht, vorausgehe, sofern nicht das Civilrecht dies bedingt.

Selbstverständlich muß, wenn die Verweigerung der Herausgabe in besagter Weise gestraft werden soll, die Möglichkeit derselben völlig erwiesen sein.

11) Gewaltsame Besitzentsetzung.

Es war Absicht des Gesetzgebers, die gemeinrechtlichen Grundsätze bezüglich des juramentum Zenonianum einzuführen, gemäß deren bei gewaltsamer Besitzentsetzung der Beschädigte zum Schwure darüber zugelassen wurde, daß er bei der Entsetzung bewegliche Sachen eingebüßt habe, und welches der Werth dieser Sachen sei. const. 9, C. (8. 4) — Bayer Civilpr. § 274 — Referat zu Art. 433 d. Entw.). Die Worte: „über die ihm abhanden gekommenen oder beschädigten Sachen und deren Werth" beziehen sich also offenbar bloß auf den Fall der gewaltsamen Besitzentsetzung.

12) Beschädigungen im Allgemeinen.

Wegen Beschädigungen im Allgemeinen läßt das Gesetz den Schätzungseid nur zu, wenn Arglist oder grobes Verschulden nachgewiesen ist.

Welcher Art die Beschädigung sei, ist gleichgiltig und ist fragliche Bestimmung insbesondere nicht auf Beschädigungen von Sachen zu beschränken (Referat a. a. O.). Den Schätzungseid wegen des Schmerzengeldes würde ich übrigens nicht mehr zulassen, theils weil das Schmerzengeld keine Entschädigung, sondern eine Strafe ist, theils weil das Gesetz den Eid über den Affektionswerth, dessen Formel allein hier passen würde, nicht mehr zuläßt.

c) Offenbarungseid (Art. 471).

13) Ist Jemand verpflichtet, einen Inbegriff von Sachen oder Rechten (Seuff. Archiv Bd. XV Nr. 261), d. h. eine Vermögensmasse, ganz oder theilweise herauszugeben oder über deren

Bestand Auskunft zu ertheilen, so kann von ihm der Offenbarungseid verlangt werden. Derselbe beruht, gleich der Pflicht zur Aufstellung eines Inventars oder zur Rechnungsablage, auf der Erwägung, daß vom Bestande einer Masse nur derjenige genaue Kenntniß haben könne, welcher in deren Besitze ist oder war, und daß es dessen nächste Pflicht sei, denjenigen, welche auf die Masse Rechte geltend zu machen haben, deren Bestand kundzugeben.

In allen Fällen, wo nach dem Civilrechte eine derartige Verpflichtung besteht und erwiesen ist, kann zur wirksameren Geltendmachung des entsprechenden Rechtes eidliche Angabe, d. h. der Offenbarungseid, verlangt werden.

14) Bezüglich der Frage, unter welchen Voraussetzungen eine Person verbunden sei, eine Masse herauszugeben oder deren Bestand kundzugeben, in welchem Verhältnisse sie zu derselben gestanden haben müsse, bestimmt unsere Prozeßordnung nichts; es ist also klar, daß das Bestehende fortgilt, und zwar selbst dasjenige, was aus den Bestimmungen der Gerichtsordnung Cap. XIII § 5 in dieser Beziehung gefolgert wird. Es muß also Jemand eine Masse als solche in Verwahr oder Verwaltung gehabt haben und könnte der Offenbarungseid nicht von Personen verlangt werden, welche zufällig sich in der Lage befunden haben, den Bestand einer Masse kennen zu lernen oder etwas davon zu entfremden, z. B. von Dienstboten oder Hausgenossen in der Wohnung des Verstorbenen. Seuff. Comm. Bd. III S. 421.

15) Daß der Offenbarungseid den Ascendenten gegenüber ausgeschlossen wird und zwar unbedingt, also selbst dann, wenn es sich von einer gewöhnlichen Geschäftsführung, einem Gesellschaftsverhältnisse ꝛc. handelt, möchte zu weit gehen. Seither bestand eine Ausnahme nur bezüglich der Auszeigung des Mutterguts, und auch hier war dem richterlichen Ermessen Spielraum gelassen. Hielt man es für ungehörig, daß Kinder die Eltern der Lüge bezichtigen und sie möglicherweise zum Meineide treiben, so durfte man auch die Eideszuschiebung nicht gestatten.

16) Die Verweigerung der Leistung dieses Eides hat für den Gegner das Recht zur Folge, zum Schätzungseide gelassen zu werden, welcher also auch hier den Charakter einer Strafverfügung behauptet.

Das Gesetz sagt: „nach Beschaffenheit des Falles," was wohl nur bedeutet: „wenn der Sachlage nach eine Entschädigung an Stelle der Verweigerung der Kundgabe treten kann." Es ist dies nicht immer der Fall, z. B. nicht beim Offenbarungseide, welchen ein Schuldner zu leisten hat. Seuff. Comm. Bd. III S. 423 Note 8.

Für das Verständniß jener aus dem Entwurfe beibehaltenen Worte ist erheblich, daß sich der Schlußsatz des Art. 1248 der P.O. im Entwurfe nicht fand.

d) Gemeinschaftliche Bestimmungen (Art. 472).

17) Was Eidesfähigkeit (Art. 450), Schwurpflichtigkeit (Art. 451—453), Folgen der Leistung und Verweigerung (Art. 465—467), endlich die Verfügungen über Berufung, Einspruch und Vertagung (Art. 463, 464, 468) betrifft, so gilt das, was für den zugeschobenen Eid verfügt ist, analog auch für den Erfüllungseid, Schätzungseid und Offenbarungseid, vorbehaltlich der Sonderbestimmungen über die Folgen der Eidesverweigerung in Art. 471 Abs. 3 und Art. 472 Abs. 2.

Das Gesetz mußte von einer analogen Anwendung sprechen, da manche Bestimmungen sich nicht direkt anwenden lassen, z. B. diejenigen des Art. 465 auf den Offenbarungseid. Vgl. bezüglich der Folgen der Leistung dieses Eides Seuff. Archiv Bd. VIII Nr. 190.

18) Aus Art. 472 folgt, daß die Gerichte rechtlich nicht gehindert sind, auch einem Minderjährigen den Erfüllungs- oder Schätzungseid aufzulegen. Daß in Art. 451 ein Antrag des Gegners gefordert wird, stünde dessen analoger Anwendung nicht im Wege, denn es hat jene Vorschrift nur Sinn für den zugeschobenen Eid. Beim Schätzungseide müßte analog der Vormund das bezügliche Verlangen stellen.

Ebenso können Verwaltungsbeamten oder einzelnen Gesellschaftern (Art. 452 und Art. 453 Abs. 3) solche Eide auferlegt werden.

Verfahren bei Abnahme des Eids.

Art. 473. — Der Eid muß von dem Schwurpflichtigen in Person geleistet werden. Er wird mit den Anfangsworten:

„Ich schwöre bei Gott dem Allmächtigen und Allwissenden"

und mit den Schlußworten:

„So wahr mir Gott helfe"

geleistet.

Gehört der Schwurpflichtige einem Religionsbekenntnisse an, welches die förmliche Eidesleistung nicht gestattet, so hat an deren Stelle eine dem Bekenntnisse des Schwur-

pflichtigen entsprechende Betheuerung zu treten. Diese Betheuerung steht dem förmlichen Eide gleich.

Art. 474. — **Der Schwörende hat in der Regel den ganzen Inhalt des Eids nachzusprechen. Ist dies nicht wohl thunlich, so kann der Eidessatz vorgelesen werden. Solchen Falls hat der Schwörende nur die Eidesformel nachzusprechen, in welche eine Hinweisung auf den vorgelesenen Eidessatz aufzunehmen ist.**

Art. 475. — **Der Eidesleistung hat eine der Persönlichkeit des Schwörenden angemessene Belehrung über die Bedeutung des Eids und die Folgen des Meineids und erforderlichen Falls über den Sinn des zu beschwörenden Satzes vorauszugehen.**

Art. 476. — **Taube, welche lesen können, haben, nachdem ihnen die in Art. 475 vorgeschriebene Belehrung und die schriftlich abgefaßte Eidesformel, in welche der festgestellte Eidessatz einzurücken ist, zum Durchlesen vorgelegt worden, die letztere laut abzulesen.**

Stumme und Taubstumme, welche lesen und schreiben können, haben sich nach Anhörung oder Durchlesung der Belehrung und der Eidesformel mit Eidessatz schriftlich zu erklären, ob sie den Eid leisten wollen. Sie leisten den Eid dadurch, daß sie die Eidesformel vor Gericht niederschreiben und unterzeichnen.

Art. 477. — **Ist der Schwörende der deutschen Sprache nicht mächtig, so muß die Belehrung und Eidesformel durch einen beeidigten Uebersetzer in eine ihm geläufige Sprache übersetzt und die Eidesformel in dieser Sprache von ihm nachgesprochen werden.**

G. A. d. K. d. A. II S. 252. 253 350. IV S. 102. 105. — K. d. R. II S. 239 IV S. 61.

1) Die Vorschriften, welche hier über die Form der Eidesabnahme gegeben werden, sind so umständlich, daß zur Erläuterung nur wenig beizufügen ist.

Daß der Eid persönlich zu leisten sei, versteht sich nach der Natur dieser Handlung von selbst und war eine ausdrückliche Bestimmung nur deßhalb veranlaßt, weil seither der Fall vorkommen konnte, daß der Anwalt in die Seele der Partei den Schwur leistete. Eine derartige abnorme Eidesleistung ist jetzt unbedingt ausgeschlossen.

Was jene Schwurpflichtigen betrifft, welchen ihre Religion den Schwur verbietet, so ist für den Parteieneid wiederholt, was in Art. 417 für den Zeugeneid bestimmt ist.

Wird der Eid nach der Formel, wie sie Art. 473 gibt, ausgeschworen, so ist dem Gesetze Genüge geleistet, und sind weitere Formen gesetzlich nicht geboten; jedoch erscheint es im Hinblicke auf den religiösen Charakter der Handlung sachgemäß, die Form des Aufhebens der rechten Hand, wie sie seither bei jedem Eide üblich war, nicht zu unterlassen.

Zu erwähnen ist, daß der Entwurf hier vorschrieb, es müsse der Schwurpflichtige persönlich geladen werden, diese Vorschrift jedoch in der Erwägung beseitigt wurde, daß die Zustellung an den Anwalt überall genügen müsse. Nachdem übrigens jetzt alle Urtheile, welche auf Eid erkennen, der Partei zugestellt werden müssen, erhält diese dennoch faktisch eine persönliche Ladung. Vgl. Bemerk. zu Art. 460 Nr. 5 u. 6.

2) Bezüglich der Frage, ob der Schwörende den ganzen Eidessatz wörtlich nachzusprechen habe, oder ob es genüge, wenn er nach Vorlesung desselben bloß die Eidesformel ausspreche, bestand in der Pfalz seither verschiedene Uebung. An manchen Gerichten hielt man das erstere, an manchen das letztere Verfahren ein.

Das erstere Verfahren mag prinzipiell richtiger sein, ist aber in vielen Fällen unpraktisch, indem beim stückweisen Vorsprechen und Nachsprechen einzelner Worte der Zusammenhang der Worte und Sätze verloren geht, und der Schwörende, im Vertrauen, man werde ihm das Richtige vorsagen, gedankenlos nur Worte nachspricht, ohne sich des Sinnes und der Tragweite derselben bewußt zu sein. Diesem Mißstande gegenüber empfahl sich das letztere Verfahren um so mehr, als der Schwurpflichtige immer veranlaßt wurde, sich umständlich über die zu beschwörenden Thatsachen auszusprechen, also eine Erklärung aus seinem Munde wirklich vorlag, wenn auch nicht gerade in der kurzen Fassung des Eidessatzes.

Unsere Prozeßordnung schlägt einen Mittelweg ein, insofern sie das Nachsprechen des ganzen Eidessatzes zwar zur Regel macht, jedoch überall, wo dies nicht wohl thunlich erscheint, das bloße eidliche Bestätigen des vorgelesenen Eidessatzes erlaubt.

Ob das Einhalten der Regel „wohl thunlich" sei, hat der Richter frei zu ermessen, und bedarf es deshalb keiner besonderen Entscheidung. Er wird insbesondere Rücksicht darauf nehmen, ob der Eidessatz einfach oder verwickelt sei, und ob der Schwörende mehr oder weniger Intelligenz besitze.

3) Daß ein bestimmt formulirter Eidessatz vorgelesen werde, ist nach Vorschrift unserer

Prozeßordnung unumgänglich; es wäre daher nicht statthaft, sofort, nachdem der Schwurpflichtige seine Erklärungen abgegeben, ihn dieselben mit der Formel: „Alles dies beschwöre ich 2c." eidlich bestätigen zu lassen.

Ist der Eidessatz nicht schriftlich formulirt, wie es im Parteiprozesse Regel ist, so fertigt ihn der Richter nach Maßgabe der mündlichen Eideserklärung notizweise in entsprechend kurzer Fassung und liest denselben vor Abnahme des Eides dem Schwurpflichtigen vor.

4) Ueber die Art und Weise, wie die Eidesleistung zu beurkunden sei, sagt das Gesetz nichts.

Nach dem Entwurfe konnte die Beurkundung im Sitzungsprotokolle geschehen; da dieses jedoch beseitigt, da auch nicht, wie bei der Vernehmung von Zeugen und Sachverständigen (Art. 419 und 443) Aufnahme eines besonderen Protokolles vorgeschrieben ist, so ist klar, daß die Beurkundung des in der Sitzung ausgeschworenen Eides im Urtheilsbuche zu geschehen hat.

Im Parteiprozesse kann dieselbe füglich in den Sachverhalt aufgenommen werden, im Anwaltsprozesse jedoch wird der Richter entweder eine besondere Beurkundung nach Maßgabe der Art. 248 und 281 ins Urtheilsbuch aufnehmen, oder, wie es Regel ist, im Urtheilssatze Urkunde ertheilen. Letzteres kann entweder in der Weise geschehen, daß er in den Entscheidungsgründen die Thatsachen anführt, im Urtheilssatze aber, darauf Bezug nehmend, Urkunde ertheilt, oder daß er die ganze Beurkundung sofort in den Urtheilssatz aufnimmt. Er sagt z. B.:

ertheilt Urkunde, daß Beklagter den ihm durch Vorbescheid vom — auferlegten Eid in heutiger Sitzung dahin ausgeschworen hat: „Ich schwöre bei Gott „dem Allmächtigen und Allwissenden, daß 2c. 2c. „So wahr mir Gott helfe;"

weist sofort die Klage als unbegründet ab 2c.

Es ist meiner Ansicht nach nicht nöthig, zu beurkunden, ob der Eid durch Nachsprechen oder aber durch Bestätigen des Vorgelesenen geleistet worden sei, denn beide Formen sind in gleicher Weise giltig und begründen eine gesetzliche Eidesleistung.

Hat die Eidesleistung schriflich (Art. 476 Abs. 2) oder in einer fremden Sprache (Art. 477) stattgefunden, so ist allerdings die Einhaltung der bezüglichen Form näher zu constatiren.

5) Daß der Eidesleistung eine sachgemäße Belehrung und Verwarnung vor Meineid vorauszugehen habe, erscheint selbstverständlich. Besondere Beurkundung, daß dies geschehen, ist nicht unbedingt nöthig.

Was den Schätzungseid und Offenbarungseid betrifft, so ist zu beachten, daß bei ihnen der Meineid nicht strafbar ist (Art. 195 des St. G. B.), was ein weiterer Grund sein möchte, den ersteren Eid möglichst zu beschränken. Beim Offenbarungseide kann übrigens die Eidesleistung wider besseres Wissen eine Bestrafung wegen Unterschlagung oder den Verlust von Erbrechten zur Folge haben.

6) Bei der Eidesleistung durch Taube und Stumme sind nur Fälle vorgesehen, wo diese durch Wort oder Schrift sich verständlich machen können. Eine Eidesleistung im Wege der Geberdensprache ist ausgeschlossen (vgl. Art. 450 Abs. 2).

7) Bei Eidesleistungen von Personen, welche der deutschen Sprache nicht mächtig sind, ist immer ein beeidigter Uebersetzer beizuziehen, und wurde die Ausnahme, welche der Entwurf für den Fall vorsah, wo der Richter selbst der fremden Sprache mächtig sei, beseitigt (vgl. Art. 163).

Art. 478. — **Stehen erhebliche Schwierigkeiten oder Hindernisse entgegen, daß der Eid in der Sitzung des Prozeßgerichts abgenommen werde, so kann die Abnahme des Eids einem Einzelngerichte, nach Umständen auch einem ausländischen Gerichte oder, wenn hiegegen besondere Bedenken bestehen, der betreffenden bayerischen Gesandtschaft oder einem bayerischen Consulate übertragen werden.**

In diesem Falle steht es jeder Partei frei, sobald die Sache dazu bereift ist, bei dem beauftragten Richter die Festsetzung des Orts und der Zeit der Eidesleistung nachzusuchen.

Dem Gesuche sind die einschlägigen Aktenstücke — die Urtheile in der Ausfertigung oder der zugestellten Abschrift — beizufügen.

Art. 479. — **Ist der Schwurpflichtige wegen Krankheit oder Gebrechlichkeit außer Stande, vor Gericht zu erscheinen, so hat die Eidesabnahme in der Wohnung stattzufinden und kann die desfallsige Anordnung sowohl von dem Prozeßgerichte als von dem beauftragten Richter getroffen werden.**

Das Prozeßgericht kann auch aus andern erheblichen Gründen die Eidesabnahme in der Wohnung verordnen. Ist die Eidesabnahme in der Wohnung vor dem Prozeßgerichte verordnet, so kann es damit auch eines seiner Mitglieder beauftragen

Art. 480. — **Hat die Eidesleistung vor einem beauftragten Richter stattzufinden, so ist bei sich ergebenden Streitigkeiten zu deren vorgängiger Entscheidung auf Betreiben der einen oder andern Partei eine besondere Sitzung des Gerichts festzusetzen.**

G. A. d. K. d. A. II S. 250—252. 254. 255. 350. — K. d. R. II S. 239.

1) Den Vorschriften, welche das Gesetz über Beweisaufnahmen durch einen beauftragten Richter gibt, läßt sich der Vorwurf zu großer Einfachheit nicht machen, denn zuerst werden allgemeine Prinzipien aufgestellt und sodann bei den einzelnen Beweisarten das Verfügte theils wiederholt, theils in verschiedener Weise geändert. So werden hier ziemlich erschöpfende Vorschriften bezüglich der Eidesabnahme gegeben.

Regel ist, wie schon Art. 460 Abs. 1 bestimmt, daß der Eid in der Sitzung des Prozeßgerichtes ausgeschworen werde; stehen jedoch erhebliche Schwierigkeiten entgegen (große Entfernung, Krankheit &c.), so kann die Abnahme des Eids einem beauftragten Richter übertragen werden.

Es wird unterschieden: 1) ob es sich bloß darum handelt, daß der Eid nicht in der Sitzung des Prozeßgerichts abgenommen werden könne, während kein Hinderniß besteht, daß der Schwurpflichtige vor dem beauftragten Richter erscheine, oder 2) ob der Eid in der Wohnung des Schwurpflichtigen abzunehmen sei. Im ersteren Falle (in der Regel der Fall großer Entfernung) ist es nicht gestattet, daß ein Mitglied des Gerichts beauftragt werde; im letzteren aber kann es geschehen.

Ist der Grund, welcher die Eidesabnahme in der Wohnung nöthig macht, Krankheit oder Gebrechlichkeit, so ist auch der beauftragte Richter befugt, dieselbe anzuordnen.

2) Das Verfahren ist das gewöhnliche.

Nachdem das Urtheil zugestellt ist (Art. 192, 331) und die betreffenden Erklärungen von Anwalt zu Anwalt abgegeben sind (Art. 460 Abs. 2), richtet der fleißigste Theil, unter Vorlage der betreffenden Aktenstücke, ein Gesuch an den Richter um Festsetzung der Tagfahrt. Was zu Art. 406 Nr. 5 gesagt ist, gilt auch hier.

In der Praxis pflegt der Anwalt dem Richter sofort seine sämmtlichen Parteiakten vorzulegen, da dies sachgemäß ist und der Richter ein Recht hat, deren Einsicht zu verlangen (Art. 341).

3) Bei der Wichtigkeit der in Frage stehenden Handlung ist es begreiflich, daß ein beauftragter Richter weder die sich ergebenden Streitigkeiten selbst entscheiden, noch auch mit Vorbehalt derselben zur Eidesabnahme schreiten dürfe. Er hat vielmehr immer die Erledigung seines Auftrages auszusetzen, bis vom Prozeßgerichte entschieden ist.

Uebrigens will offenbar das Gesetz nicht, daß die Frage, ob der Eid durch Nachsprechen des ganzen Eidessatzes oder durch Bestätigen desselben auf Vorlesung (Art. 474) zu schwören sei, zum Gegenstande eines Zwischenstreits gemacht werden könne, vielmehr ist es dem Ermessen des beauftragten Richters überlassen, die nach vorliegenden Umständen passende Form zu wählen.

Ueber die Eidesleistung ist ein umständliches, den ganzen Hergang, namentlich auch die Beobachtung der in den Art. 474—477 gegebenen Vorschriften, beurkundendes Protokoll aufzunehmen.

Art. 481. — **Sind im Schwurtermine beide Parteien vor dem beauftragten Richter erschienen und vereinigen sie sich über nachträgliche Zurückschiebung des Eids oder eine veränderte Fassung der Eidesformel, so ist der beauftragte Richter befugt, den Eid nach diesem Uebereinkommen abzunehmen.**

G. A. d. K. d. A. II S. 254. 255. 350. — K. d. R. II S. 239.

1) Wenn beide Parteien vor dem beauftragten Richter erscheinen und sich vereinigen, sei es über nachträgliche Zurückschiebung des Eides, sei es über eine veränderte Fassung der Eidesformel, so ist der Richter befugt, den Eid diesem Uebereinkommen gemäß abzunehmen (Art. 481).

In dieser Verfügung liegt, was den zurückgeschobenen Eid betrifft, eine Abweichung von der Regel, welche voraussetzen würde, daß der zurückgeschobene Eid durch neues Urtheil auferlegt und dessen Abnahme dem Richter aufgetragen würde. Ein solches Urtheil wird auf diesem Wege umgangen und wird die Abnahme des zurückgeschobenen Eides als eine Art der Erledigung des den zugeschobenen Eid auferlegenden Urtheils behandelt, was vielleicht nicht correkt, jedoch sehr praktisch ist.

Es wäre hieraus zu folgern, daß auch in Fällen, wo das Prozeßgericht selbst den Eid in der Sitzung abnimmt, diesem die gleiche Befugniß zustehe, den zurückgeschobenen Eid ohne weiteres Urtheil abzunehmen. Was dem beauftragten Richter gestattet ist, kann ihm nicht versagt sein; auch spricht Art. 462 Abs. 2 dafür.

Das Gesetz hat zunächst nur den Fall einer nachträglichen Zurückschiebung, d. h. den Fall im Auge, wo der Eid vorher angenommen war und erst vor dem beauftragten Richter die Zurückschiebung erklärt und vereinbart wird, jedoch ist selbstverständlich, daß auch für den Fall, wo der Eid sofort, d. h. in der Frist des Art. 460 Abs. 2 zurückgeschoben wurde, das Nemliche zu gelten hat.

2) Was den Fall einer Aenderung der Eidesformel betrifft, welches letztere Wort hier in einem Sinne gebraucht wird, welchen der Gesetzgeber sonst nicht damit verbindet (Art. 474), so frägt es sich: sind bloß Aenderungen an jenem Eidessatze gemeint, wie ihn das Beweisurtheil vorläufig feststellt (Art. 460 Abs. 1), oder Aenderungen derjenigen Fassung, wie sie durch die gewechselten Schriftsätze (Art. 460 Abs. 2) sich bestimmt, oder endlich an dem vom Gerichte endgiltig festgesetzten Eidessatze?

Um diese Fragen zu beantworten, ist auf Art. 460 Abs. 2 zurückzugreifen.

Wenn dort gesagt ist, in der Sitzung, welche zur Eidesleistung anberaumt ist, werde der Eidessatz endgiltig festgestellt, so liegt darin nicht die Vorschrift, daß jedesmal ein Urtheil ergehen müsse, welches etwaige Aenderungen gutheiße und zulasse. Ein solches Urtheil ist nur nöthig, wenn Einwände erhoben wurden; ist aber die Eidesannahme unbeanstandet geblieben und liegt auch kein Anlaß vor, sie von Amtswegen zu beanstanden, so kann der Eid sofort in der geänderten Fassung abgenommen werden und ist es nicht nöthig, durch ein besonderes Urtheil diese Eidesabnahme für statthaft zu erklären. Der Entwurf (Art. 425 Abs. 3) hatte dies angedeutet, indem er sagte: „setzt die Eidesformel erforderlichen Falls endgiltig fest", und hieran sollte nichts geändert werden (Abg. II 348, zu Art. 13).

Ist nun der Eid durch einen beauftragten Richter abzunehmen, so ist das natürliche, in der Pfalz bis jetzt geltende Verfahren dasjenige, welches Referent v. Neumayr (Abg. II 255 Sp. 1) vorgeschlagen hat, daß nemlich, falls sich kein Anstand erhebt, der Richter den Eid in der Fassung, wie sie sich durch die unbeanstandet gebliebene Eidesannahme feststellte, abnehme, ohne Rücksicht darauf, ob beide Parteien bei der Tagfahrt erschienen sind oder nicht.

Gegen diesen Vorschlag wurde von Barth geltend gemacht, es dürfte zweckmäßig sein, den Richter immer erst dann zu beauftragen, wenn feststehe, wer zu schwören habe und was zu beschwören sei, und es machte nun der kgl. Minist.-Commissär einen vermittelnden Vorschlag, welchem der jetzige Art. 481 sein Dasein verdankt und welchen er dahin erläuterte, daß eine weitere Sitzung (d. h. ein Urtheil) immer nöthig sei, wenn sich die Parteien im Termine vor dem beauftragten Richter nicht einigen.

Bei dieser Sachlage sollte man meinen, der Wille des Gesetzgebers sei ganz klar und gehe dahin, daß, abgesehen von den Ausnahmen des Art. 481, ein beauftragter Richter den Eid unbedingt nur in derjenigen Fassung abnehmen dürfe, wie er urtheilsmäßig festgestellt sei. Ich halte es für möglich, daß einzelne Faktoren der Gesetzgebung wirklich von dieser Anschauung ausgegangen seien, bin aber der Ansicht, daß sie dem wahren Sinne des Gesetzes nicht entspreche.

Offenbar ist kein vernünftiger Grund dafür zu finden, warum die in den zugestellten Erklärungen liegende Vereinbarung nicht gerade so viel wirken solle, wie die bei der Tagfahrt erklärte. Ferner leuchtet ein, daß es höchst unpraktisch wäre, zu verlangen, daß zuerst auf's Gerathewohl der Versuch gemacht würde, ob alle Parteien bei der Eidesleistung erscheinen und sich vereinbaren, im Falle aber, wo irgend ein Betheiligter ausbleibt, Urtheil des Prozeßgerichts erwirkt werden müsse, um zu constatiren, daß kein Streit vorliege!

Faßt man bloß den Text des Gesetzes ins Auge, so spricht dasselbe nur von den besonderen Fällen, wo erst vor dem beauftragten Richter eine Aenderung der Sachlage eintritt, indem der Eid nachträglich zurückgeschoben oder erst hier eine Aenderung der Fassung vereinbart wird. Trotz dieser neuen Gestaltung der Sachlage soll dennoch der Richter den Eid abnehmen dürfen, wenn ihn beide Parteien dazu ermächtigen.

Hiermit ist nun nicht gesagt, daß in allen sonstigen Fällen ein Urtheil nöthig sei, vielmehr sind solche Fälle nach den allgemeinen Prinzipien zu beurtheilen, gemäß deren der Richter Auftrag hat, den Eid in derjenigen Fassung abzunehmen, wie sie in dem zu diesem Zwecke vorgezeichneten Verfahren (Art. 460 Abs. 2) sich festgestellt hat. Hat der Gegner die Eidesannahme für genügend erklärt oder hat er sie unbestritten gelassen, so ist sie für den Richter maßgebend.

Die besagte Aeußerung des kgl. Minist.-Commissärs, welche Zweifel erregen könnte, hatte offenbar nur den Fall der Eideszurückschiebung im Auge, für welchen im französischen Prozesse neues Urtheil nöthig war, und auch nur auf diesen Fall bezog sich die Opposition von Umbscheiden. Der beste Beweis hiefür liegt darin, daß der kgl. Minist.-Commissär grade aus Anlaß der Bestimmungen des Art. 28. es für nöthig erklärte, auch die Vorlage der gewechselten Schriftsätze der Anwälte anzuordnen, was keinen Sinn hätte, wenn nur die Erklärungen bei der Tagfahrt von Bedeutung wären.

Wenn daher Art. 481 von „veränderter Fassung der Eidesformel" spricht, so meint er nur Fälle, wo die durch die Erklärungen in den Schriftsätzen festgestellte Fassung geändert werden soll, oder wo an der richterlichen Feststelluug zulässige Aenderungen vorgenommen werden sollen. Vgl. Abg. II 255 Sp. 1 (Barth) und Abg. II 251 Sp. 2 (v. Weiß).

Jene Aenderungen, von welchen Art. 462 spricht, werden nie der Eidesabnahme im Wege stehen, denn sie sind im Grunde keine Aenderungen.

3) Das Gesetz setzt voraus, daß beide Parteien erschienen sind und ihre Zustimmung geben, findet also keine Anwendung, wenn eine Partei aus verschiedenen Personen besteht und diese nur zum Theile erscheinen oder vertreten sind. Sind mehr als zwei Parteien im Prozesse, so müssen sämmtliche Parteien, die bei der Eidesleistung betheiligt sind, ihre Zustimmung erklären.

Die Anwälte der Parteien erscheinen, da keiner der Ausnahmsfälle des Art. 92 gegeben ist, insbesondere auch kein Vergleich vorliegt, auf Grund ihrer allgemeinen Prozeßvollmacht befugt, ein solches Uebereinkommen abzuschließen.

Ferner setzt das Gesetz eine ausdrückliche Erklärung voraus und würde also ein bloßes Dulden nicht genügen.

4) Obgleich man bei den Verhandlungen annahm, daß in Fällen, wie sie Art. 481 unterstellt, der Richter nicht in die Lage komme, zu urtheilen, so ist dies doch nicht unbedingt richtig, denn es kann die Frage entstehen, ob der Eid nicht von Amtswegen als unstatthaft zurückzuweisen sei (Art. 450).

Hat der beauftragte Richter in solchen Fällen Zweifel, ob der Eid statthaft sei (vgl. Art. 425 Abs. 1), so hat er die Eidesabnahme zu verweigern und die Parteien vor das Prozeßgericht zu verweisen, denn, wie wohl zu beachten, erklärt ihn das Gesetz nur befugt, nicht verpflichtet, den Eid abzunehmen.

5) Weiter ist zu beachten, daß der beauftragte Richter auf Grund eines solchen Uebereinkommens möglicherweise einen Eid abnimmt, welchen das Prozeßgericht zurückgewiesen hätte, welcher also später für unerheblich erklärt wird. Durch Rücksichtsnahme auf solche jedenfalls zu den höchst seltenen Ausnahmen gehörige Fälle ließ sich mit Recht der Gesetzgeber nicht beirren; denn die Möglichkeit, daß unerhebliche Eide geschworen werden, läßt sich, wie zu Art. 463 Nr. 2 gezeigt, nie ganz beseitigen.

Verfahren bei Eintritt von Tod oder Eidesunfähigkeit.

Art. 482. — **Wenn der Schwurpflichtige vor der Eidesleistung stirbt oder eidesunfähig wird, so darf bei zugeschobenen oder zurückgeschobenen Eiden die Gegenpartei alle Befugnisse hinsichtlich der Beweisführung noch geltend machen, welche ihr vor der Zuschiebung oder Zurückschiebung zustanden, bei andern Eiden aber ist nach Anhörung der Parteien so zu erkennen, als wenn der Schwurpflichtige schon zur Zeit der Auferlegung des Eids gestorben oder eidesunfähig gewesen wäre.**

War jedoch die gestorbene oder durch Krankheit unfähig gewordene Partei durch Arglist oder grobes Verschulden der Gegenpartei an der Ableistung des Eides verhindert, so gilt der Eid als geleistet, soferne sich der Schwurpflichtige persönlich oder durch seinen Anwalt zu dessen Ableistung erboten hatte.

G. A. d. K. d. A. II S. 255. 351. IV S. 102. — K. d. R. II S. 239—241. IV S. 61.

1) Der ganze Art. 482 ist mit wenigen Redaktionsänderungen wortgetreu dem hannoveranischen Entwurfe entnommen, wo er den § 426 bildet.

Nach Abs. 1 desselben soll im Falle, wo der Schwurpflichtige vor der Eidesleistung stirbt oder eidesunfähig wird, eine Wiedereinsetzung in den vorigen Stand eintreten und sollen Eideszuschiebung, Eideszurückschiebung und Eidesauflage als nicht geschehen betrachtet werden.

Diese Bestimmung ist ganz allgemein und kommt es weder darauf an, ob die Eidesunfähigkeit verschuldet oder unverschuldet, noch ob der Eid bereits angenommen ist oder nicht.

2) Es könnte die Frage aufgeworfen werden, ob nicht das Wort „eidesunfähig“ hier im weitesten Sinne zu nehmen und auch die Handelnsunfähigkeit darunter zu begreifen sei, so daß also in Fällen, wo der schwurpflichtige Vormund entsetzt wird oder die Partei in Gant geräth, die Bestimmungen des Art. 482 Anwendung fänden.

Offenbar lassen sich aus dem Geiste des Gesetzes gewichtige Gründe hiefür geltend machen, allein daß eine solche Ausdehnung des Begriffs, welche dem Wortlaute Zwang anthun würde, nicht im Willen des Gesetzgebers begründet sei, geht aus den hannoveranischen Verhandlungen (S. 2875 ff.) hervor, wo der Antrag, auch den Verlust der Handelnsfähigkeit zu berücksichtigen, als bedenklich zurückgewiesen wurde. Ist daher der Eid einer bestimmten Person einmal rechtskräftig auferlegt, so bleibt die Entscheidung von dessen Ableistung bedingt, mag auch die Handelnsfähigkeit sich ändern; für diese Handlung bleibt sie bestehen.

Inwiefern Art. 1277 Abs. 3 für die Gant eine Ausnahme bedinge, wird dort erörtert werden.

3) Die Kammer der Reichsräthe hatte die Bestimmungen des Art. 482 auch auf sonstige Fälle ausgedehnt, wo die Unmöglichkeit, einen Eid zu leisten, eintritt, und zwar, wie aus den Bemerkungen des Correferenten v. Bomhard hervorgeht, hauptsächlich im Hinblicke auf den Fall, wo die schwurpflichtige Person abwesend ist und man nicht zu ermitteln vermag, wo sie sich aufhalte und ob sie überhaupt noch am Leben sei.

Ist es unbedingt gestattet, solchen Personen Eide zuzuschieben oder die Fiktion der Eidesverweigerung auf sie anzuwenden, so sind sie rechtlos gestellt und die Chikane hat freien Paß. Meiner Ansicht nach hat man daher sehr Unrecht gethan, jenen sachgemäßen Zusatz wieder zu beseitigen; im Gegentheile wäre Anlaß gegeben gewesen, auch für die Eideszuschiebung einen entsprechenden Zusatz zu machen. Nahm man Anstoß an der Allgemeinheit der Verfügung, so lag es nahe, sie auf den besonders bezeichneten Fall zu beschränken.

Es ist mir in der Praxis ein Fall dieser Art vorgekommen, in welchem die Eideszuschiebung sofort als chikanös zurückgewiesen wurde und zwar auf Grund der in dieser Beziehung durch die neuere französische Jurisprudenz dem Richter eingeräumte Befugniß, Eideszuschiebungen, die offenbar frivol sind, unbeachtet zu lassen. In der Pfalz steht dieser Ausweg auch jetzt noch offen, allein für diesseits wüßte ich keine ausreichende Abhilfe, denn das allgemeine Prinzip, daß eine Verpflichtung für Unmögliches oder Unvernünftiges nicht bestehe, kann gegenüber der ausdrücklichen Zurückweisung der vorgeschlagenen Ausnahme nicht angerufen werden. Das Setzen langer Fristen, sowie die Wiedereinsetzung in den vorigen Stand sind Behelfe, die nicht genügen. Der beste Ausweg wird sein, rechtzeitig für gesetzliche Vertretung solcher Personen Sorge zu tragen.

Auch hier tritt wieder der Widerspruch hervor, daß man den Eid zuläßt, wo er verwerflich, und verwirft, wo er Bedürfniß ist.

4) In Abs. 2 wird eine Ausnahmsbestimmung gegeben für Fälle, wo durch Arglist oder grobes Verschulden der Gegenpartei die Eidesleistung verhindert worden ist.

Diese Ausnahme tritt nur ein, wenn die Unmöglichkeit der Eidesleistung durch Tod oder Krankheit (körperliche oder geistige) herbeigeführt worden ist, schließt also den Fall aus, wo die Eidesunfähigkeit verschuldet ist.

Sie tritt ferner nur ein, wenn sich der Schwurpflichtige zur Eidesleistung bereits erboten hatte. Dieses Erbieten ist im nemlichen Sinne zu nehmen, wie in Art. 459 Abs. 3. Es muß natürlich eine Prozeßhandlung bilden, d. h. entweder in einem vom Anwalte zugestellten Schriftsatze enthalten sein, oder mündlich in der Sitzung bezw. vor dem beauftragten Richter erfolgen. Außergerichtliche Aeußerungen wären ohne Belang.

Ob das Erbieten vor oder nach der Eidesauflage erfolgte, ist, da das Gesetz nicht unterscheidet, gleichgiltig und wurde dies bei den hannoveranischen Verhandlungen (S. 2875) ausdrücklich anerkannt.

Ebenso wurde anerkannt, daß im Einlegen von Rechtsmitteln zwar Arglist oder grobes Verschulden liegen könne, jedoch nicht liegen müsse.

XV. Hauptstück.

Zwischenstreite und Betheiligung dritter Personen.

Zwischenstreite.

Art. 483. — **Will während des Rechtsstreits eine Partei gegen die andere ein damit im Zusammenhange stehendes Begehren, welches nicht blos das Verfahren betrifft, erheben, so hat dies in einem der Gegenpartei zuzustellenden motivirten Antrage zu geschehen.**

Erfolgt die Zustellung an den Gegenanwalt, so kann das Begehren auch mit einem die Hauptsache betreffenden motivirten Antrage verbunden werden.

Art. 484. — **Ueber die unter den Parteien während eines Rechtsstreits entstehenden Zwischenstreite, sie mögen unter Art. 483 fallen oder nur das Verfahren betreffen, ist gleichzeitig mit der Hauptsache zu verhandeln und zu entscheiden, es sei denn, daß die weitere Verhandlung der Hauptsache die vorgängige Entscheidung des Zwischenstreits erfordert oder das Gericht nach Art. 157 Abs. 2 die Trennung der Verhandlung verfügt.**

Art. 485. — **Erfordert die weitere Verhandlung der Hauptsache die vorgängige Entscheidung des Zwischenstreites, so setzt der Senatsvorstand auf Ansuchen einer der Parteien eine Sitzung unmittelbar zur Verhandlung über den Zwischenstreit fest.**

Diese Verfügung muß dem Gegenanwalte unverzüglich mit der Aufforderung, in der anberaumten Sitzung zu erscheinen, zugestellt werden. Hat die Gegenpartei keinen Anwalt aufgestellt, so ist in den Fällen des Art. 483 Zustellung der Verfügung nur dann erforderlich, wenn die Verhandlung stattfinden soll, ehe seit der Zustellung des motivirten Antrags ein der Erscheinungsfrist gleichkommender Zeitraum verstrichen ist.

Zustellung weiterer motivirter Anträge ist nicht geboten.

Art. 486. — Ist in einem Zwischenstreite, von dessen Entscheidung die Verhandlung der Hauptsache abhängt, Berufung ergriffen, so kann das Gericht eine Frist festsetzen, nach deren Ablauf mit der Verhandlung der Sache ohne Rücksicht auf die noch unerledigte Berufung vorgefahren werden soll, wenn der Appellant nicht bescheinigt, daß er auf Betreibung der Sache den erforderlichen Fleiß gewendet habe.

G. A. d. K. d. A. II S. 291—294. 351. 453. IV S. 102. 105. — K. d. R. II S. 241. IV S. 61.

1) Zwischenstreit im weiteren Sinne ist jeder neben dem Hauptstreite unter den Parteien sich erhebende Streit, sei es, daß er sich an diesen bloß anschließt, sei es daß er Vorfragen betrifft, deren Entscheidung nöthig ist, um zur Endentscheidung zu gelangen. In diesem Sinne erscheinen auch die Widerklagen, sowie die nachträglichen Begehren, von welchen Art. 182 Abs. 2 spricht, als Zwischenstreite.

Unter Zwischenstreiten im engeren Sinne versteht man bloß besagte Vorfragen, während Streitpunkte, welche sich an den Hauptstreit bloß anschließen, noch als Hauptstreitpunkte in Betracht kommen.

Unsere Prozeßordnung nimmt das Wort im weiteren Sinne.

2) Bezüglich des Verfahrens unterscheidet das Gesetz zwei Arten von Zwischenstreiten, nemlich 1) solche, welche bloß das Verfahren betreffen, und 2) solche, welche weiter gehen.

Die Grenzlinie zwischen beiden Arten zu ziehen, bietet einige Schwierigkeit, da die Ausdrucksweise höchst allgemein ist, und die Worte: „welche bloß das Verfahren betreffen," offenbar nicht ganz sachentsprechend sind. Wenn z. B. Streitigkeiten im Beweisverfahren (wegen Verwerflichkeit, Untüchtigkeit von Zeugen, Erheblichkeit von Eidesannahmen) als solche bezeichnet werden, welche bloß das Verfahren betreffen (Abg. II 293 Sp. 1 [v. Weiß]), so ist dies sicher nicht richtig gesagt, denn Streitigkeiten dieser Art sind für Entscheidung der Sache selbst von großer Erheblichkeit.

Um den Gedanken des Gesetzgebers richtig zu erfassen, ist auf den französischen Prozeß zurückzugehen. Die Art. 337 u. 338 Code de proc. sprechen von »demandes incidentes« und bezeichnen hiemit selbständige connexe Streitpunkte, welche im Laufe des Prozesses geltend gemacht werden, um im Anschlusse an denselben verhandelt zu werden. Gehen sie vom Kläger aus, so bezeichnet man sie besonders als »demandes additionelles«, gehen sie vom Beklagten aus, als »demandes reconventionelles«. In der Pfalz nannte man sie allgemein „Incidentklagen". Im nemlichen Sinne sprach auch Art. 448 des Entwurfs von Zwischenstreiten. Der kgl. Minist.-Commissär schlug nun vor, auch die sonstigen Zwischenstreite, welche keine selbständigen Streitpunkte zum Gegenstande und nur für die Entscheidung des in Frage stehenden Prozesses Bedeutung haben, anzureihen, da auch bezüglich ihrer allgemeine Bestimmungen maßgebend seien (Abg. II 292 Sp. 1), und bezeichnete sie dabei als solche, welche bloß das Verfahren betreffen.

Die Zwischenstreite, von welchen Art. 483 spricht, sind also nur solche, welche selbständige Streitpunkte zum Gegenstande haben, und zwar entweder 1) solche, welche sich dem Hauptstreite bloß anschließen, wie Widerklagen oder nachträgliche Begehren des Klägers, oder 2) solche, welche zugleich Vorfragen für die Entscheidung der Hauptsache bilden im Sinne der Art. 9—11 der P.O. Vgl. Bemerk. zu Art. 9—11 Nr. 15 bis 18, zu Art. 31, Nr. 11 u. 12, zu Art. 295 Nr. 28 u. 29.

3) Die ganze Unterscheidung des Gesetzes hat übrigens nur insofern praktische Bedeutung, als bei Zwischenstreiten des Art. 483 (bei Incidentklagen), in Fällen, wo der Gegner nicht durch Anwalt vertreten ist, die Grundsätze über Versäumungsurtheile maßgeben und die Zustellung des motivirten Antrags an die Partei die Stelle der Ladung vertritt. Vgl. Art. 299.

Das Gesetz setzt dies in Art. 485 Abs. 2 als selbstverständlich voraus und regelt bloß die Anwendung für den Fall, wo zur Aburtheilung des Zwischenstreits eine besondere Sitzung fixirt wird, in der Art, daß je nachdem die Erscheinungsfrist umlaufen ist oder nicht, die Kundgabe der Fixation als überflüssig wegfällt oder als Ladung mit kurzer Frist (Art. 259) wirkt.

Die bezüglichen Prinzipien finden namentlich auch Anwendung, wenn Verbindungsurtheil erlassen ist und Incidentklagen erhoben werden, bei welchen der Nichterschienene betheiligt ist. Bemerk. zu Art. 316—318 Nr. 14.

4) Ein weiterer Unterschied soll nach dem Gesetze darin bestehen, daß Incidentklagen immer durch Zustellung eines motivirten Antrages anzubringen sind, während bei sonstigen Zwischenstreiten dies nicht vorgeschrieben ist; allein bei näherer Betrachtung zerfällt er so ziemlich in nichts.

Sieht man nemlich von jenen Fällen ab, wo der Streitpunkt bereits durch gerichtliches Protokoll fixirt ist und für welche das Gesetz besondere Vorschriften gibt (Art. 342), so ist selbstverständlich bei jedem Zwischenstreite eine Erklärung des Anwaltes nöthig, worin dieser unter Darlegung der Gründe sein Begehren stellt, d. h. ein motivirter Antrag. Man hätte daher füglich sagen können: „Soweit das Gesetz nicht anders bestimmt, werden Zwischenstreite durch Zustellung eines motivirten Antrags erhoben."

5) In der Regel lassen sich die Anträge für Zwischenstreite mit den gewöhnlichen motivirten Anträgen verbinden, und da der Anwalt alles meiden soll, was Kostenmehrung oder Prozeßverzögerung verursacht, so ist es seine Pflicht, nicht ohne dringenden Anlaß besonderen Antrag zu stellen.

Zum gleichen Zwecke der Vereinfachung des Verfahrens schreibt Art. 484 vor, daß über Zwischenstreite, wenn möglich, gleichzeitig mit der Hauptsache verhandelt und entschieden werden solle.

Endlich versteht es sich von selbst, daß alle Incidentklagen, wo möglich, gleichzeitig vorzubringen und die durch unnöthige Trennung veranlaßten Mehrkosten der Partei bezw. dem Anwalte zur Last zu legen sind. Man hatte dies ursprünglich in einem Zusatze zu Art. 483 ausdrücklich verfügt, hielt aber zuletzt dafür, daß es nach den allgemeinen Prinzipien selbstverständlich sei.

6) Erfordert die weitere Verhandlung der Hauptsache die vorgängige Entscheidung des Zwischenpunktes, läßt sich dieser also nicht eventuell mit der Hauptsache verhandeln, so soll nach Art. 485 sofort eine Sitzung zur Verhandlung über den Zwischenstreit festgesetzt werden, d. h. diese Verhandlung wird kraft Gesetzes als dringlich (Art. 259) betrachtet.

So allgemein, wie diese Bestimmung lautet, entspricht sie weder dem Bedürfnisse der Praxis, noch auch dem wahren Willen des Gesetzgebers. Es kommen nemlich Zwischenstreite vor, deren Entscheidung der Verhandlung der Hauptsache nothwendig vorausgehen muß, wie z. B. die Frage, ob ein Zeuge verwerflich, ob eine Eidesannahme giltig sei, welche man aber dennoch nicht in besonderer Sitzung zu verhandeln, sondern soweit möglich mit der Hauptsache zu verbinden pflegt. Man vereinigt in den Anträgen Zwischenstreit und Hauptsache und läßt für beide die nemliche Sitzung bestimmen, damit sofort nach Aburtheilung des Zwischenstreites in der Hauptsache verhandelt und entschieden werden könne. Bemerk. zu Art. 342 Nr. 8 u. 9 und zu Art. 344 Nr. 4. Um sich ganz richtig auszudrücken, hätte der Gesetzgeber beifügen müssen: „und ist dessen Aburtheilung in besonderer Sitzung nöthig oder sachgemäß."

Es hat das Gesetz hier jene Fälle im Auge, wo die Entscheidung des Zwischenstreits stattfinden muß, ehe ein Beweisverfahren vor dem beauftragten Richter beendet werden kann, oder wo Präjudizialpunkte (Art. 190, 256) zum gesonderten Austrag zu bringen sind, oder wo besonderer Anlaß vorliegt, eine gesonderte Aburtheilung zu gestatten.

Daß in solchen Fällen der gesonderten Aburtheilung eines Zwischenstreites weitere motivirte Anträge nicht geboten seien, steht im Einklange mit den besonderen Vorschriften, wie sie die Prozeßordnung in ähnlichen Fällen gibt, z. B. in Art. 232 Abs. 3 und Art. 260 Ziff. 2. Wie dort ist es auch hier nicht verwehrt, freiwillig solche Anträge zuzustellen, wenn dies sachgemäß erscheint.

7) Wenn Art. 486 verfügt, es dürfe im Falle der Berufung gegen Zwischenstreite besagter Art das Gericht eine Frist zur Erledigung dieser Berufung setzen, so ist diese Verfügung wohl im Geiste des Entwurfes gerechtfertigt, welcher (Art. 208) ein amtliches Eingreifen des Gerichts zur Betreibung der Prozesse gestattete, nicht aber auch im Geiste der Prozeßordnung, welche bloß Parteibetrieb kennt und es genügend findet, daß jeder Partei das Recht der Betreibung zustehe. Sie erscheint als ein Bruchstück, das von jenem Prinzipe des Entwurfes aus Versehen übrig geblieben ist.

Die Tragweite der Bestimmung des Art. 486 ist eine ziemlich große, denn es ist zu beachten, daß es sich um Zwischenfragen präjudizieller Natur handelt, also die gesetzlichen Grundsätze über den Suspensiveffekt der eingelegten Berufung eine Ausnahme erleiden und das Gericht auf die Gefahr hin weiter entscheidet, daß die Entscheidung des Präjudizialpunktes später geändert werde.

Das Gesetz spricht übrigens nur vom Falle, wo die Verhandlung der Hauptsache von Entscheidung des Zwischenstreites abhängt, wie dies bei Präjudizialsachen (Art. 190) der Fall ist, trifft also nicht Fälle, wo die Erledigung eines Beweisverfahrens, z. B. die Ausschwörung eines Eides, durch diese Entscheidung bedingt ist.

Die Gerichte werden in der Erwägung, daß das Gesetz im Allgemeinen einen Prozeßbetrieb von Amtswegen nicht will, daß er auch nicht nöthig ist, von der ihnen hier eingeräumten Befugniß einen sparsamen Gebrauch machen.

Betheiligung dritter Personen.

Art. 487. — **Beiladung Dritter findet in der für Erhebung von Klagen vorgeschriebenen Weise statt. Den Anwälten der übrigen Parteien ist davon durch Anwaltsakt Kenntniß zu geben.**

Streitverkündung ohne gleichzeitige Erhebung einer Gewährschaftsklage geschieht durch Zustellung eines Anwaltsakts.

Art. 488. — **Die Hauptintervention erfolgt mittelst einer gegen sämmtliche Hauptparteien gerichteten Klage. Die Zustellung der Klageschrift geschieht für Parteien, welche einen Anwalt bereits aufgestellt haben, an diesen und genügt für alle durch den nämlichen Anwalt Vertretenen eine einzige Abschrift.**

Die Nebenintervention erfolgt durch Anwaltsakt, welcher den sämmtlichen im Rechtsstreite aufgestellten Anwälten zugestellt werden muß.

Art. 489. — **Die Anwälte der Beigeladenen und der Intervenienten können von sämmtlichen im Prozesse aufgestellten Anwälten die Mittheilung sowohl der in ihrem Besitze befindlichen Urkunden, von welchen diese Gebrauch bereits gemacht haben oder nach Inhalt ihrer Schriftsätze noch zu machen beabsichtigen, als auch der bisher zugestellten Aktenstücke verlangen und finden im Uebrigen die Bestimmungen der Art. 172—174 Anwendung.**

Alle nach der Beiladung oder Intervention sich ergebenden Zustellungen sind in gleicher Weise, wie an die Anwälte der Hauptparteien, auch an die der Beigeladenen oder Intervenienten zu machen und ebenso müssen auch diese die Zustellungen an sämmtliche aufgestellte Anwälte machen lassen.

Die Anwälte der Beigeladenen oder Intervenienten sind unter denselben Voraussetzungen, wie die Anwälte der Hauptparteien, zur Betreibung der Sache berechtigt.

G. A. d. K. d. A. II S. 291. 292. 294—296. 351. IV S. 102. 105. — K. d. R. II. S. 241. IV S. 61.

1) Das Gesetz gibt hier Vorschriften für Fälle der Beiladung oder Intervention dritter Personen, welche ebenso einfach als sachgemäß sind.

Durch eine Beiladung im Sinne der Prozeßordnung soll der Beigeladene Partei im Prozesse werden; ihr Zweck ist, daß Urtheil gegen ihn ergehe oder die unter den übrigen Parteien ergehende Entscheidung auch Rechtskraft gegen ihn erlange, und so bringt es denn die Natur der Sache mit sich, daß die Formen der Klagstellung eingehalten werden müssen, wie dies Art. 487 vorschreibt.

Diese Vorschrift umfaßt alle Beiladungen, insbesondere auch Gewährschaftsklagen, findet jedoch selbstverständlich keine Anwendung auf Fälle, wo diejenige Person, gegen welche der Anspruch erhoben, z. B die Gewährschaftsklage gestellt wird, bereits im Prozesse sich befindet. In diesen Fällen handelt es sich um einen Zwischenstreit im Sinne des Art. 483, um eine Incidentklage. Vgl. Bemerk. zu Art. 69—72. Nr. 17.

2) Um der Vorschrift des Art. 225 wegen Darstellung der den Klaganspruch begründenden Thatsachen zu genügen, erscheint es sachgemäß, Abschrift des die Beiladung veranlassenden Prozeßaktes (der Ladung, des Antrags, des Urtheils) zuzustellen, und, auf dessen Inhalt Bezug nehmend, die weiteren zur Klagbegründung dienenden Thatsachen anzureihen. Es ist dieses Verfahren das einfachste und zugleich sicherste, und wurde es in der Praxis von jeher eingehalten. Vgl. Bemerk. zu Art. 65 Nr. 6 und 8, ferner zu Art. 69 bis 72 Nr. 11.

Wegen der Beiladung des rechten Besitzers s. Bemerk. zu Art. 74—77 Nr. 8 u. 9.

Auch bei Streitverkündungen ist es sachgemäß, den veranlassenden Prozeßakt zuzustellen. Bemerk. zu Art. 69—72 Nr. 4.

3) Von der erfolgten Beiladung ist den Anwälten der bereits im Streite befindlichen Parteien durch Anwaltsakt Kenntniß zu geben. Wie und wann diese Kundgabe zu bethätigen sei, ist nicht näher bestimmt.

Insofern es sich um Benachrichtigung von einer bereits geschehenen Beiladung handelt (Abg. II 291, 294) und der Nachweis derselben sich bei den Akten befindet, genügt eine möglichst einfache Erklärung unter Anerbieten der Aktenmittheilung. Bei Gewährschaftsklagen gelten die besonderen Vorschriften des Art. 233.

Die Kundgabe muß erfolgen, sobald der Nachweis der Beiladung dem Anwalte zugekommen ist, und Verzögerungen würden die Aufbürdung der durch dieselben veranlaßten Kosten zur Folge haben. Bemerk. zu Art. 233 Nr. 3.

4) Bei Interventionen befinden sich die Parteien, gegen welche Anträge genommen werden, bereits im Prozesse, und es ist daher natürlich, wenn das Gesetz hier aus der nemlichen Erwägung, wie bei Widerklagen und Incidentklagen überhaupt, die Zustellung an die Anwälte genügend findet.

Bei Hauptinterventionen ist eine gegen sämmtliche Hauptparteien zu richtende Klage vorgeschrieben, d. h. es muß der zuzustellende Anwaltsakt jenen Forderungen entsprechen, welche nach Art. 225 für Klagschriften gelten, und muß die Zustellung an alle Parteien erfolgen, ohne Unterschied, ob für sie ein Anwalt aufgestellt ist oder nicht.

Ist ein Anwalt aufgestellt, so erfolgt, wie bei der Incidentklage, die Zustellung nur an den Anwalt und genügt, wie überall, wo dem Anwalte als solchem eine Zustellung gemacht wird, eine einzige Abschrift für alle durch den nemlichen Anwalt Vertretenen.

Ist für eine Partei kein Anwalt aufgestellt, wohin insbesondere auch der Fall zu zählen, wenn gegen sie Verbindungsurtheil ergangen ist, so erfolgt die Zustellung der Klagschrift nach den gewöhnlichen Regeln, d. h. mittelst Vorladung unter Einhaltung der vorschriftsmäßigen Erscheinungsfrist.

Der Hauptintervenient hat Sorge zu tragen, daß er seine Sache mit dem bereits anhängigen Verfahren in passender Weise verbinde, also nöthigenfalls die Ermächtigung zur Ladung auf kurze Frist nachzusuchen oder Vertagungsanträge zu stellen. Vgl. Abg. II 295 (: Weiß).

5) Bei Nebeninterventionen, welche nur neue Personen, nicht aber neue Ansprüche in den Prozeß bringen, genügt die Zustellung eines sie erklärenden Anwaltsaktes an die aufgestellten Anwälte. Falls Jemand als Nebenintervenient eines Nichterschienenen in den Prozeß tritt — ein Fall, der nicht leicht vorkommen wird — erfolgt allerdings ihm gegenüber contradiktorische Verhandlung, das ergehende Urtheil aber ist der Hauptpartei gegenüber nur ein Versäumungsurtheil. Anlaß zu einem Verbindungsurtheile ist hier nicht gegeben. Abg. II 295 Sp. 2.

6) Wer in einen Prozeß als Partei sich einmischt oder beigezogen wird, tritt sofort in alle Rechte der ursprünglichen Parteien ein. Er ist daher 1) berechtigt, zu verlangen daß ihm alle bereits erwachsenen Prozeßaten mitgetheilt werden (Art. 172—175 Nr. 2 u 9), und wird 2) fortan, was Zustellung von Prozeßschriften und Prozeßbetrieb betrifft, den ursprünglichen Parteien vollkommen gleichgestellt.

7) Was namentlich die Zustellungen anbelangt, so ist es durchgreifender Grundsatz des Verfahrens, daß sie immer an sämmtliche Anwälte, welche bei dem in Frage stehenden Prozesse betheiligt sind, zu geschehen haben, mögen sie auch nicht für alle erheblich sein.

Die Betheiligung am Prozesse an und für sich gibt dem Anwalte ein Recht, von allem Kenntniß zu erhalten, was im Prozesse vorgeht.

XVI. Hauptstück.

Unterbrechung und Aufhebung der Verhandlungen.

Unterbrechung des Verfahrens.

Art. 490. — Das Verfahren und der Lauf der Fristen wird unterbrochen, wenn jenes wegen Ablehnung eines Gerichtsmitglieds nicht fortgesetzt werden kann oder ein Zwischenurtheil durch Berufung mit aufschiebender Wirkung angegriffen ist.

Beschränkt sich die Berufung auf einen Theil des Streits, so wird in Ermangelung entgegengesetzter Uebereinkunft oder Verfügung die Verhandlung der nicht angefochtenen Punkte fortgesetzt.

G. A. d. K. d. A. II S. 281. 282. 351. — K. d. R. II S. 241.

1) Was dieser Artikel bestimmt, folgt eigentlich aus sonstigen gesetzlichen Bestimmungen und allgemeinen Prinzipien von selbst.

Nach Art. 51 versteht sich von selbst, daß das Verfahren eine Unterbrechung erleiden müsse, soweit für dasselbe die Amtsthätigkeit eines abgelehnten Richters in Anspruch genommen wird, und aus Art. 699 folgt von selbst, daß die giltige Einlegung einer statthaften Berufung jedes weitere Verfahren hemme. Ebenso erscheint selbstverständlich, daß die Unterbrechung des Verfahrens auch den Fristenlauf unterbrechen müsse, denn wo giltige Prozeßhandlungen nicht vorgenommen werden können, können auch keine Fristen für dieselben laufen.

2) Wie Art. 490 nur ausdrücklich ausspricht, was eigentlich schon in den Art. 51 und 699 liegt, so bemißt sich auch seine Tragweite nach diesen Artikeln.

Es steht insbesondere nicht in der Macht einer

Partei, durch frivole Ablehnungen die Amtsthätigkeit eines Richters nach Belieben zu lähmen, oder sich nach Belieben die Fristen zu verlängern. Vgl. Bemerk. zu Art. 51 Nr. 5.

Was die Berufung gegen Zwischenurtheile betrifft, so ist deren Wirkung nach Art. 699 eine aufschiebende, wenn die Berufung in giltiger Weise erfolgt und wenn sie statthaft ist. Der Entwurf (Art. 452) führte als Fall, in welchem die Berufung keine aufschiebende Wirkung habe, denjenigen an, wo das Zwischenurtheil für vorläufig vollstreckbar erklärt worden sei, allein die Subcommission änderte die Redaction, und nach allgemeinen Prinzipien (Art. 268) gibt es keine vorläufige Vollstreckbarkeit für reine Zwischenurtheile. So kommt es, daß unter der Form einer Redaktionsänderung der Sinn des Gesetzes sich vollständig geändert hat.

Auch der Grundsatz, daß bei der Beschränkung der Berufung auf einen Theil des Streites nur für diesen Theil und was dazu gehört die Unterbrechung eintrete, folgt aus allgemeinen Principien; jedoch ist hervorzuheben, daß das Gesetz ausdrücklich den Richter befugt erklärt, nach freiem Ermessen das Verfahren auch bezüglich der nicht angefochtenen Punkte zu suspendiren.

3) Man würde irren, wollte man voraussetzen, der Gesetzgeber habe eine erschöpfende Aufzählung der Fälle, in denen das Verfahren oder der Fristenlauf eine Unterbrechung erleide, geben wollen.

Was z. B. den Vollzug von Zwischenurtheilen betrifft, so wird derselbe nicht bloß durch Berufung, sondern auch durch Einspruch (Art. 826), und wenn eine Eidesleistung in Frage steht, durch Wiederaufnahme des Verfahrens (Art. 777) und Nichtigkeitsbeschwerde (Art. 799) gehemmt.

Ferner tritt Unterbrechung des Verfahrens ein in Fällen, wo ein Zwischenstreit sich erhebt, von dessen Entscheidung die Verhandlung der Hauptsache abhängt (Art. 484), oder wenn ein Präjudizialverfahren vor einem anderen Gerichte auszutragen ist (Art. 9 u. 191).

Eine Unterbrechung des Laufs der Fristen tritt auch ein während der Gerichtsferien (Einf.-Ges. Art. 139) und des Laufs von Fristen zum persönlichen Handeln in den durch Art. 211 bezeichneten Fällen.

4) Auch durch Uebereinkommen der Parteien kann das Verfahren zeitweise unterbrochen werden. Es folgt dies aus Art. 212 und den allgemeinen Prinzipien und wurde die bezügliche Bestimmung des Entwurfs (Art. 451) als selbstverständlich gestrichen. Der Abschluß einer solchen Uebereinkunft liegt in den Befugnissen des Anwalts, welcher jedoch für Mißbrauch streng verantwortlich zu machen ist. Vgl. Art. 212 Abs. 3.

Auch ohne förmliche Uebereinkunft können die Parteien die Sache beruhen lassen, indem sie dieselbe nicht betreiben. War sie bereits in die Sitzung gebracht, so hat dieser Nichtbetrieb die Streichung vom Hauptverzeichnisse zur Folge. Bemerk. zu Art. 249 Nr. 8.

Art. 491. — **Unbeschadet der Bestimmung des Art. 211 wird das Verfahren und der Fristenlauf unterbrochen:**

1) durch den Tod einer Partei, soferne sie nicht durch einen Prozeßbevollmächtigten vertreten ist;

2) durch den Verlust der Fähigkeit einer Partei, vor Gericht zu handeln, oder ihrer Befugniß zur Prozeßführung über den Streitgegenstand;

3) durch den Tod ihres gesetzlichen Vertreters oder das Aufhören der seine Vertretungsbefugniß bedingenden Eigenschaft, soferne letzteres nicht Folge der eingetretenen Handlungsfähigkeit der Partei ist;

4) durch den Tod oder die Suspension des Anwalts und durch das Aufhören seiner Funktion als Advokat am Prozeßgerichte.

Hat in den Fällen der Ziffern 2 und 3 die Partei oder deren gesetzlicher Vertreter einen Prozeßbevollmächtigten, so tritt die Unterbrechung erst mit der Anzeige, welche der Prozeßbevollmächtigte von der stattgehabten Veränderung an die Gegenpartei zu machen hat, ein und bleibt der letztere bis dahin zur Ausführung seiner Vollmacht befugt.

Die eingetretene Unterbrechung verhindert den Antrag des Staatsanwalts und die Erlassung des Urtheils nicht, wenn die Parteivorträge bereits geschlossen sind.

G. A. d. K. d. A. II S. 282—284. 351. IV S. 102. 105. — K. d. R. II S. 242—244. IV S. 61.

1) Wenn diejenige Person, welcher gesetzlich die Führung des Prozesses obliegt (die Partei selbst, der gesetzliche Vertreter, der Anwalt), stirbt oder die Fähigkeit zu handeln verliert, so muß natürlich der betreffenden Partei gegenüber das Verfahren einstweilen beruhen, bis für eine neue Vertretung gesorgt oder dazu Gelegenheit geboten ist, und diese Unterbrechung muß ihre Wirkungen

auch auf sonstige Parteien erstrecken, insofern das Verfahren ein gemeinschaftliches ist. Es frägt sich jedoch:

1) ob und in wie weit Anlaß gegeben sei, eine ertheilte Prozeßvollmacht auch nach Eintritt des Todes oder der Rechtsunfähigkeit des Vollmachtgebers fortwirken zu lassen;

2) ob die Unterbrechung mit der veranlassenden Thatsache von Rechtswegen eintreten solle, oder erst mit der Anzeige davon;

3) ob beim Tode der Partei es nicht schon deshalb rathsam sei, eine Unterbrechung eintreten zu lassen, damit den neu in den Prozeß tretenden Erben gegenüber die Frage der Erbqualität und der Haftung sofort bereinigt werde.

Unsere Prozeßordnung weicht bei Lösung dieser Fragen bedeutend vom französischen Prozesse ab, verfügt in manchen Beziehungen sogar das gerade Gegentheil.

Nach französischem Prozesse unterbricht z. B. der Tod einer Partei das Verfahren immer, mag ein Prozeßbevollmächtigter bestellt sein oder nicht, jedoch nur vom Augenblicke der Notifikation an; hingegen bedingen Aenderungen der Rechtsfähigkeit oder Wechsel der gesetzlichen Vertretung keine Unterbrechung. Letzteres wird zwar von zwei vereinzelten Stimmen (Demiau und Schlink) bestritten, allein die Ansicht aller anderen Schriftsteller (Chauveau [quest. 1283], Pigeau, Thomine, Bioche), sowie die Praxis (Cass. 3. Juni 1818 und 11. Juni 1830 — Nîmes, 6. Nov. 1826) ist dafür.

Unsere Proceßordnung gibt umgekehrt den letzteren Thatsachen eine viel stärkere Wirkung, als der ersteren.

2) Im Allgemeinen ist hervorzuheben, daß nach Schluß der Parteivorträge (Art. 158) die Urtheilsfällung durch Aenderungen in der Person der Parteien oder ihrer Vertreter nicht mehr gehemmt werden kann; selbstverständlich nur unter der Voraussetzung, daß dieselbe ohne Wiederaufnahme der Verhandlung (Art. 274 u. 328 Abs. 4) erfolgen könne.

Ferner ist darauf hinzuweisen, daß die Bestimmungen des Art. 211 wegen Unterbrechung von Fristen zum persönlichen Handeln durch Art. 491 nicht berührt werden.

a) Tod der Partei.

3) Im Anschlusse an das im Art. 93 ausgesprochene Prinzip verfügt das Gesetz, daß in Fällen, wo die Partei durch einen Prozeßbevollmächtigten vertreten sei, ihr Tod eine Unterbrechung des Verfahrens nicht begründe, was für den Anwaltsprozeß, von welchem allein hier die Sprache ist, fast soviel bedeutet, als wenn gesagt wäre, der Tod der Partei begründe nie eine Unterbrechung.

Ob die Partei selbst oder ob ihr gesetzlicher Vertreter den Prozeßbevollmächtigten bestellt habe, erscheint gleichgiltig, und in diesem Betrachte geht Art. 491 weiter, als Art. 93.

4) Aus dem Satze, daß beim Vorhandensein eines Prozeßbevollmächtigten eine Unterbrechung nicht stattfindet, folgt, daß der Rechtsstreit ganz ohne Rücksicht auf den eingetretenen Todesfall, gewissermaßen mit dem Verstorbenen, fortgeführt werden kann.

Die Erben kommen nur insoweit in Betracht, als der für den Verstorbenen bestellte Anwalt verpflichtet ist, sich mit ihnen ins Benehmen zu setzen und seine weiteren Weisungen von ihnen zu erholen. Für die Gegenpartei ist es gleichgiltig, wer Erbe sei; die Namen der Erben erscheinen nicht in den Parteischriften und Urtheilen, noch weniger ist es statthaft, persönliche Anträge gegen sie zu nehmen.

Hieraus ergibt sich die natürliche Folge, daß das ergehende Urtheil nur in der Art gegen die Erben vollzogen werden kann, als wäre der Todesfall erst nach dem Urtheile eingetreten, daß also Streitigkeiten über die Erbqualität, über bedingte oder unbedingte Haftung im Vollstreckungsverfahren auszutragen sind. Art. 833.

5) Uebrigens gilt der Satz, daß auf die Personen der Erben keine Rücksicht zu nehmen sei, auch abgesehen von Art. 211, nur so weit, als die Wirkungen der Prozeßvollmacht reichen.

Handelt es sich um Zustellungen, welche an die Partei selbst zu geschehen haben, z. B. von Endurtheilen im Sinne der Art. 682 u. 683, so sind dieselben allerdings den Erben zu machen, und ist es Sache der Parteien, auf deren Anstehen die Zustellung erfolgt, bezw. ihres Anwaltes oder Gerichtsvollziehers, zu ermitteln, wer die rechten Erben seien. Für diesen Fall wäre es nicht statthaft, die Zustellung nach Art. 211 Abs. 2 zu machen, denn jene formlose Art der Benachrichtigung ist streng auf die Ausnahmsfälle zu beschränken, für welche sie das Gesetz gibt, nemlich 1) auf den Fall, wo eine Frist zum persönlichen Handeln bereits im Laufe war und unterbrochen wurde, und 2) auf den Fall, wo ein unterbrochenes Verfahren im Allgemeinen wieder in Gang zu bringen ist (Art. 495 Abs. 2).

Ebenso müssen Spezialvollmachten (Art. 92) von den einzelnen Erben erhoben werden.

6) Wenn auch das persönliche Auftreten der Erben im besagten Falle nicht nöthig ist, so steht doch anderseits nichts im Wege, daß es freiwillig

geschehe, und können die Erben durch ihr Interesse dazu veranlaßt sein. Im französischen Prozesse wird dies in Fällen von Aenderungen in der Person des gesetzlichen Vertreters, obgleich solche eine Unterbrechung dort nicht begründen, nicht bezweifelt. Chauveau sur Carré, zu Art. 346.

Wollte die Gegenpartei die Erben persönlich in den Rechtsstreit ziehen, um Anträge auf persönliche Verurtheilung gegen sie zu nehmen, so müßten dieselben, gleich als wären sie fremde Personen, förmlich beigeladen werden.

7) Ist die Partei nicht durch Prozeßbevollmächtigte vertreten, so tritt die Unterbrechung mit dem Tode der Partei von Rechtswegen ein, ebenso wie im Falle des Art. 211, und bedarf es also keiner Anzeige, wie nach französischem Verfahren.

Diese Verfügung, welche erst nachträglich (Abg. IV 105) in's Gesetz kam, ist für den Parteiprozeß von großer Bedeutung, doch ist ihre Tragweite nicht ganz so groß, als es beim ersten Anblicke erscheint, da in Fällen, wo die Parteien entfernt wohnen, dieselben sich immer vertreten lassen, und in Fällen, wo sie in der Nähe sind, der Eintritt von Todesfällen gemeinkundig oder leicht zu erfahren ist.

8) Als durch Prozeßbevollmächtigten vertreten ist auch diejenige Partei zu erachten, gegen welche Verbindungsurtheil ergangen war; sie wird von dem Anwalte des Mitbeklagten mitvertreten.

b) Aenderungen, welche die Rechtsfähigkeit der Partei oder die Person ihres gesetzlichen Vertreters betreffen.

9) Verliert eine Partei die Fähigkeit, im Prozesse zu handeln, indem sie mundtodt erklärt, unter Curatel gestellt wird, in Gant geräth, oder verliert sie ihren gesetzlichen Vertreter, sei es weil er stirbt, sei es weil er entsetzt wird oder sonst seine Befugnisse aufhören, so läßt unsere Prozeßordnung, abweichend vom französischen Rechte, gleichfalls die Unterbrechung des Verfahrens eintreten, und zwar in schärferer Weise, als beim Tode der Partei, indem hier die Prozeßvollmacht nur eine Zeit lang, nemlich bis zur Anzeige der Aenderung, den Eintritt der Unterbrechung hindert. Meiner Ansicht nach hätte man füglich auch hier die Prozeßvollmacht fortwirken lassen können, es dem Anwalte überlassend, sich mit dem neuen Vertreter ins Benehmen zu setzen und die etwa nöthigen Fristen zu erwirken.

10) Eine Unterbrechung tritt nicht ein, wenn mit dem Aufhören der Vertretungsbefugniß die Handelnsfähigkeit der Partei beginnt, z. B. wenn der Mündel volljährig wird.

Indem das Gesetz diese Ausnahme dem hannoveranischen Entwurfe entlehnte, zog es in Erwägung, daß hier sofort Jemand vorhanden sei, welcher die Befugniß im Prozesse zu handeln besitze; allein es möchte in Frage stehen, ob diese Erwägung durchschlägt, denn 1) ist zu beachten, daß die Partei präsumtiv ganz in Unkenntniß von der seitherigen Prozeßführung ist (Bemerk. zu Art. 211 Nr. 8), und 2) wäre folgerichtig die Ausnahme auf alle Fälle auszudehnen gewesen, wo die Vertretung keine Unterbrechung erleidet, z. B. auf jene Fälle, wo zugleich mit Entsetzung eines gesetzlichen Vertreters der Nachfolger ernannt wird.

11) Steht die Vertretung einer juristischen Person zu, z. B. einem Magistrate, so kann selbstverständlich das Ableben, der Austritt, die Entsetzung und Ersetzung einzelner Collegialmitglieder keine Unterbrechung begründen. Vertreter ist das Collegium im Ganzen, nicht aber das einzelne Mitglied.

Bedenklicher möchte die Frage sein, ob in Fällen, wo das ganze Collegium erneuert wird, die Unterbrechung eintrete. Da gesetzlicher Vertreter der Magistrat an sich ist, welcher seine Vertretungseigenschaft behält, so lang die Gesetzgebung sich nicht ändert, und da die Personen, aus denen er sich bildet, im Prozesse keine Bedeutung haben und nicht genannt werden, so nehme ich an, daß in solchen Fällen eine Unterbrechung nicht eintrete.

12) Die Unterbrechung tritt in den vorbezeichneten Fällen von Rechtswegen ein, wenn ein Prozeßbevollmächtigter nicht aufgestellt ist, sonst nur vom Augenblicke an, wo dieser von der Aenderung Anzeige macht. Bis zu diesem Augenblicke dauern die Wirkungen der Prozeßvollmacht der Gegenpartei gegenüber fort, und dürfen dieser die civilrechtlichen Grundsätze über Erlöschung des Mandats nicht entgegengehalten werden. Insbesondere könnte von Erhebung der Nichtigkeitsklage des Art. 95 nicht die Rede sein, so wenig als im Falle, wo eine Partei dem Anwalte das Mandat gekündigt hat, ohne neuen Anwalt zu bestellen. Art. 94 Abs. 2.

13) Der eigenen Partei gegenüber tritt die Verantwortlichkeit des Prozeßbevollmächtigten allerdings ein, wenn er den Prozeß fortführt, ohne sich vergewissert zu haben, daß das Mandat erneuert werde, und Art. 491 erklärt ihn daher verpflichtet, Anzeige von der Aenderung zu machen, und zwar, wie selbstverständlich, sofort, nachdem er selbst Nachricht davon erhält.

Der Hauptzweck dieser Anzeige ist allerdings, Kenntniß von der Erlöschung des Mandats zu geben, und man könnte daher meinen, es habe dieselbe zu unterbleiben, wenn der Prozeßbevollmächtigte bereits neues Mandat durch den derzeitigen Vertreter der Partei erhalten habe. Mag auch in diesem Falle der Prozeßbevollmächtigte sich keinem besonderen Nachtheile aussetzen, wenn er die Anzeige unterläßt, so handelt er doch richtiger und dem Gesetze entsprechend, wenn er sie macht und mit derselben zugleich die Erklärung der Wiederaufnahme, oder vielmehr Fortsetzung des Verfahrens verbindet.

c) Aenderungen in der Person des Anwalts.

14) Daß im Anwaltsprozesse eine Unterbrechung stattfinden müsse, wenn der bestellte Anwalt, d. h. diejenige Person, welcher kraft Gesetzes die ganze Leitung des Prozesses obliegt, stirbt, oder sonst in die Unmöglichkeit versetzt wird seinen Dienst zu versehen, ist klar.

Ebenso begreift sich leicht, daß diese Unterbrechung ohne Anzeige eintreten müsse, denn derartige Aenderungen können dem Gegenanwalte nicht unbekannt bleiben, auch wäre zu fragen, wer denn die Anzeige zu machen hätte.

15) Für den Fall, wo ein gewöhnlicher Prozeßbevollmächtigter aufgestellt ist, hat der Gesetzgeber eine ähnliche Verfügung nicht nöthig gefunden. Der Tod eines Prozeßbevollmächtigten im Parteiprozesse bedingt daher keine Unterbrechung, jedoch ist es natürlich Pflicht der Gerichte, durch sachgemäße Vertagung Vorsorge zu treffen, daß die Rechte entfernt wohnender Parteien nicht Schaden leiden.

Art. 492. — Alle nach dem Eintritte der Unterbrechung (Art. 490 und 491) vorgenommenen Prozeßhandlungen sind der Gegenpartei gegenüber wirkungslos, solange das Verfahren nicht ordnungsmäßig wieder aufgenommen worden ist.

Laufen in den Fällen des Art. 491 Fristen, so beginnt mit der Wiederaufnahme des Verfahrens eine neue volle Frist.

Prozeßhandlungen, welche nach eingetretener Unterbrechung vor dem Gerichte oder dem beauftragten Richter vorgenommen wurden, ehe diese von dem betreffenden Ereignisse Kenntniß erhielten, sind giltig, soferne nicht längstens bei der nächsten Verhandlung die Wiederholung der Handlung von einer der Parteien verlangt wird.

G. A. d. K. d. A. II S. 284. 351. IV S. 106. 115. — K. d. R. II S. 244. IV. S. 61.

1) Es ist die natürliche Folge jeder Unterbrechung des Verfahrens, daß Prozeßhandlungen, mögen sie von den Parteien oder mögen sie vom Richter ausgehen, nicht giltig vorgenommen werden können, so lange der Zustand der Unterbrechung dauert.

Die Nichtigkeit solcher Prozeßhandlungen ist jedoch nach dem Grunde ihrer Entstehung und ihrem Zwecke keine absolute, und das Gesetz erkennt dies ausdrücklich an, indem es sie nur „der Gegenpartei gegenüber“ ausspricht, was im Gegensatze zu derjenigen Partei gesagt ist, welche die Prozeßhandlung vornahm oder vornehmen ließ. Der Gedanke des Gesetzes läßt sich wohl richtiger negativ dahin ausdrücken, daß einer Partei das Recht der Anfechtung nicht zustehe, wenn die Prozeßhandlung von ihr selbst ausgegangen ist. Vgl. Art. 219 Abs. 1.

2) Sowie Abs. 1 vorzugsweise von den Handlungen der Parteien spricht, so spricht Abs. 3 von jenen Prozeßhandlungen, welche vom Richter ausgehen, und ist darauf aufmerksam zu machen, daß in Folge eines Druckfehlers in der amtlichen Ausgabe des Gesetzbuches gesagt ist: „vor dem Gerichte“, statt „von dem Gerichte“.

Hat der Richter in Unkenntniß der Unterbrechung Prozeßhandlungen vorgenommen, so sollen diese nichtig sein, falls eine der Parteien bei der nächsten Verhandlung die Wiederholung verlangt.

Der Entwurf hatte solche Handlungen für giltig erklärt, jedoch dem Gerichte die Befugniß eingeräumt, eine Wiederholung anzuordnen. Vielleicht wäre es besser gewesen, diese Verfügung, zu deren Aenderung (Abg. IV 106) genügende Gründe nicht vorlagen, zu belassen. Was jetzt verfügt ist, erscheint eigentlich nur als eine Anwendung der allgemeinen Prinzipien und könnte zu der irrigen Meinung Anlaß geben, als seien auf Prozeßhandlungen, welche von der Partei ausgehen, die Bestimmungen des Art. 219 Abs. 2 nicht anwendbar.

3) Was die Unterbrechung von Fristen anbelangt, so ist die natürliche Regel, daß nur der Lauf derselben gehemmt wird, also nach Aufhebung der Unterbrechung keine neue Frist beginnt, sondern nur die frühere Frist ihren Lauf fortsetzt. So geschieht es, wenn die Unterbrechung Folge der Einlegung von Rechtsmitteln, des Eintritts der Gerichtsferien rc. ist.

Für die Fälle des Art. 491 ist nun aber ausnahmsweise verfügt, daß mit Wiederaufnahme des Verfahrens eine neue volle Frist beginne, wie dies auch Art. 211 schon bestimmt hat. Der

Grund dieser Ausnahme liegt in dem Umstande, daß in jenen Fällen neue Personen auftreten, um die Leitung des Prozesses zu übernehmen, und das Gesetz die Rechtsvermuthung zu Grunde legt, es seien diese Personen völlig in Unkenntniß von der Lage des Prozesses und müsse ihnen daher die volle Frist gegönnt werden, welche das Gesetz für die in Frage stehende Rechtshandlung nöthig hält. Bemerk. zu Art. 211 Nr. 6.

Die neue Frist läuft vom Augenblicke an, wo das Verfahren nach Maßgabe der Art. 494 u. 495 als wiederaufgenommen zu betrachten ist.

Art. 493. — **Der Uebergang des streitigen Rechts oder der angeblich belasteten Sache durch besonderen Rechtstitel unterbricht den Lauf des Prozesses nicht.**

Der nunmehr Betheiligte kann in den Streit eintreten und ihn in der Lage, worin er sich befindet, fortsetzen.

Der Austritt des bisherigen Betheiligten setzt die Einwilligung der Gegenpartei oder die richterliche Entscheidung voraus, daß letztere an seinem Verbleiben im Prozesse kein Interesse habe.

Für die bisherigen Kosten haftet der in den Streit eingetretene Rechtsnachfolger neben der ursprünglichen Partei, vorbehaltlich seines Rückgriffs an diese.

Für die weiteren Kosten haftet die ursprüngliche Partei dem Gegner soweit, als sie von dem Rechtsnachfolger nicht zu erholen sind.

G. A. d. K. d. A. II S. 284. 351. — K. d. R. II S. 244.

1) Eine Unterbrechung des Verfahrens tritt nur ein, wo das Gesetz es ausdrücklich verfügt, oder wo sich eine solche aus gesetzlichen Bestimmungen mit Nothwendigkeit folgern läßt; es hätte daher des Ausspruches, daß die Abtretung strittiger Rechte eine Unterbrechung nicht begründe, eigentlich nicht beburft.

Wenn das Gesetz vom Uebergange des streitigen Rechts durch besondere Rechtstitel spricht, so meint es damit jeden Uebergang, welcher nicht unter die Bestimmungen des Art. 491 Ziff. 1 fällt, begreift also die Abtretung einer ganzen Vermögensmasse so gut als die Abtretung einzelner Gegenstände und erstreckt sich auf erzwungene Abtretungen so gut, wie auf freiwillige. Im Falle eines Legates ist hingegen Art. 491 Ziff. 1 maßgebend.

2) Wenn auch der Fortgang des Prozesses durch Veräußerung des Streitgegenstandes keine Störung erleidet, so steht es doch dem Rechtsnachfolger frei, in den Rechtsstreit einzutreten, um diesen in der Lage, worin er sich befindet, fortzusetzen.

Dieser Eintritt erfolgt in der Form einer Nebenintervention, jedoch ist die Rolle des eintretenden Rechtsnachfolgers eine bedeutendere, als diejenige eines Nebenintervenienten, denn es wird der Prozeß auf dessen Rechnung geführt, der Rechtsvorgänger aber tritt in die Rolle einer Nebenperson zurück, welche im Prozesse nicht nöthig ist und nur insofern in demselben bleibt, als bei ihr selbst oder aber bei der Gegenpartei ein besonderes Interesse dazu vorliegt.

3) Der Rechtsvorgänger kann aus dem Prozesse austreten und dessen Durchführung dem Rechtsnachfolger allein überlassen, 1) wenn der Gegner einwilligt, oder 2) wenn das Gericht findet, daß ein Interesse am Verbleiben im Prozesse für ihn nicht bestehe und deshalb den Austritt gestattet.

Besteht irgend ein rechtliches oder thatsächliches Interesse für die Gegenpartei, z. B. daß durch Eideszuschiebung Beweis geführt werden soll, daß durch Anordnen des persönlichen Erscheinens Beweisbehelfe gewonnen werden können ꝛc., so liegt Grund vor, den Austritt zu versagen. Der Kostenpunkt allein kann ein Hinderniß für den Austritt nicht bilden, da in dieser Beziehung das Interesse der Gegenpartei durch die Bestimmungen in Abs. 3 u. 4 des Art. 493 vollständig gewahrt erscheint.

4) Es kann auch umgekehrt die Frage entstehen, ob der Austritt des Rechtsvorgängers erzwungen werden könne.

Offenbar ist ein solcher Zwang nicht statthaft, sofern für ihn irgend ein Interesse besteht, im Prozesse zu bleiben, sei es wegen der Haftung für die Kosten, sei es wegen der drohenden Gewährleistung; sollte jedoch jedes Interesse wegfallen und wären die beiden anderen Parteien einig, den Rechtsstreit unter sich auszutragen, so dürfte das Gericht ihn mit demselben Rechte ausweisen, mit welchem es einen Nebenintervenienten ausweist, welcher ein Interesse nicht darthun kann.

5) Was die Haftung für die Kosten betrifft, so hatten die bezüglichen Bestimmungen (Abs. 4 u. 5) im Entwurfe wohl nur den Fall des Austrittes des Rechtsvorgängers (Abs. 3) im Auge, nach jetziger Fassung wird jedoch auch der Fall seines Verbleibens im Prozesse inbegriffen sein.

Das Gesetz bestimmt, daß beide Personen (Rechtsvorgänger und Rechtsnachfolger) für die

Prozeßkosten haften, jedoch verschieden, je nachdem die Kosten vor oder nach dem Eintritte des letzteren entstanden sind. Bei ersteren Kosten hat die Gegenpartei die Wahl, von wem sie dieselbe verlangen will, die Haftung ist also eine solidarische; die letzteren Kosten sind zunächst vom Rechtsnachfolger zu fordern und der Rechtsvorgänger haftet bloß als Bürge.

Ist der letztere im Prozesse verblieben, so ist natürlich das Gericht nicht gehindert, ihm auch persönlich und direkt Kosten zur Last zu legen.

Wiederaufnahme des unterbrochenen Verfahrens.

Art. 494. — **Das unterbrochene Verfahren wird wieder aufgenommen:**

1) in den Fällen des Art. 490 durch die Zustellung der betreffenden rechtskräftigen Entscheidung;

2) in den Fällen des Art. 491 Ziff. 1—3 durch die von Seiten des Neueintretenden an die Gegenpartei zugestellte Erklärung der Wiederaufnahme des Verfahrens;

3) im Falle des Art. 491 Ziff. 4 durch die Kundmachung von der Aufstellung eines neuen Anwalts an die Gegenpartei.

Art. 495. — **In den Fällen des Art. 491 kann die betreffende Partei zur Fortsetzung des Verfahrens durch eine Aufforderung angehalten werden, die den Vorschriften des Art. 226 entspricht und die Angabe der bisher aufgestellten Anwälte, sowie die Anträge enthält, welche, falls die Partei der Aufforderung nicht nachkommt, hinsichtlich der Hauptsache beabsichtigt sind.**

Den Erben kann diese Aufforderung in der in Art. 211 Abs. 2 bezeichneten Weise zugestellt werden.

Wird der Aufforderung in der in Art. 226 bezeichneten Frist nicht entsprochen, so ist das Verfahren als wieder aufgenommen zu betrachten und wird auf Begehren der Gegenpartei, ohne daß es eines Urtheils über die Zulassung der Wiederaufnahme bedarf, die Verhandlung der Hauptsache nach Maßgabe des Stands, in welchem sie sich befindet, fortgesetzt.

War bei Unterbrechung des Verfahrens eine Frist im Laufe, so beginnt die nach Art. 492 Abs. 2 eintretende neue Frist nach Ablauf jener, welche für Fortsetzung des Verfahrens durch die Aufforderung gegeben ist.

G. A. d. K. d. A. II S. 284. 285. 351. IV S. 102. 106. — K. d. R. II S. 244. 245. IV S. 61.

1) Sowie der Grund der Unterbrechung wegfällt, kann das Verfahren wieder aufgenommen werden, und zwar entweder freiwillig, oder, falls nöthig, auf dem Wege des Zwangs. Vom ersten Falle spricht Art. 494, vom letzten Art. 495.

a) Freiwillige Wiederaufnahme.

2) In den Fällen des Art. 490 kann, sobald das bestehende Hinderniß durch rechtskräftige Entscheidung (Art. 764) beseitigt ist, jede Partei das Verfahren wieder aufnehmen und zwar indem sie diese Entscheidung zustellen läßt. Die Zustellung genügt, und bedarf es der besonderen Erklärung, daß man das Verfahren fortsetzen oder wieder in Gang bringen wolle, nicht.

Im Falle, wo Berufung gegen ein Zwischenurtheil ergriffen war, ist es nicht jene Zustellung, welche nach Art. 192 an den Anwalt der Berufungsinstanz und die Partei selbst zu geschehen hat, durch welche das Verfahren wieder aufgenommen wird und die unterbrochenen Fristen wieder in Lauf gesetzt werden, sondern die Zustellung an den in der unterbrochenen Instanz bestellten Anwalt, denn dieser allein ist in der Lage, handeln zu können und handeln zu müssen, und jene Zustellungen, welche ihm unbekannt sind, jedenfalls verspätet zur Kenntniß kommen, können ihn nicht in Verzug setzen. Es folgert sich dies aus den allgemeinen Prinzipien; dem Art. 192 in seiner jetzigen Fassung gegenüber wäre es aber sachgemäß gewesen, besondere Bestimmung zu geben. Vgl. Bemerk. zu Art. 192 Nr. 9. Chauveau sur C. quest. 991. Schlink Comm. § 299.

Uebrigens ist zu erwähnen, daß bei Eidesauflagen auch die Zustellung des Berufungsurtheiles nicht immer genügt, obgleich es im Sinne des Gesetzes (Art. 764) rechtskräftig ist, vielmehr im Falle ergriffener Nichtigkeitsbeschwerde erst mit Zustellung des oberstrichterlichen Urtheiles die Fortsetzung des Verfahrens stattfinden kann.

3) Was für die beiden in Art. 490 bezeichneten Fälle bestimmt ist, findet entsprechende Anwendung auch auf sonstige Fälle, wo in ähnlicher Weise eine Unterbrechung des Verfahrens stattgefunden hat. Bemerk. zu Art. 490 Nr. 3.

4) In den Fällen, wo die Unterbrechung

durch Aenderungen in der Person der Partei oder des gesetzlichen Vertreters veranlaßt wurden (Art. 491 Ziff. 1—3), erfolgt die Wiederaufnahme durch Zustellung eines Aktes, in welchem der betreffende Anwalt erklärt: „er sei für die neu eingetretene Person als Anwalt bestellt und nehme für dieselbe das Verfahren wieder auf.“

Es kann der Fall sein, daß diese Erklärung erfolgt, bevor die Unterbrechung eingetreten ist, z. B. ehe die Gegenpartei von den eingetretenen Aenderungen in Kenntniß gesetzt ist (Art. 491 Abs. 2); sie bewirkt dann nicht sowohl eine Wiederaufnahme, als die ungestörte Fortsetzung des Verfahrens.

5) Hat die Unterbrechung ihren Grund in der Person des Anwalts (Art. 491 Ziff. 4), so wird das Verfahren wieder aufgenommen durch die Anzeige von der Bestellung eines neuen Anwaltes.

b) Erzwungene Wiederaufnahme.

6) Nimmt diejenige Partei, auf deren Seite in den Fällen des Art. 491 eine Unterbrechung veranlaßt wurde, nicht von freien Stücken das Verfahren auf, so muß es für die anderen Parteien Mittel geben, den Fortgang des Rechtsstreites zu erzwingen.

Das Gesetz schreibt vor, daß der betreffenden Partei eine Aufforderung zur Fortsetzung des Verfahrens zugestellt werden müsse, welche den Vorschriften des Art. 226 zu entsprechen habe, d. h. welche die Aufforderung enthalte, innerhalb der nach den Wohnorten der aufzufordernden Personen sich regelnden gesetzlichen Frist einen Anwalt zu bestellen und durch ihn dem Gegenanwalte von der erfolgten Bestellung Anzeige machen zu lassen.

Diese allgemeine Vorschrift erscheint für den Anwaltsprozeß vollkommen gerechtfertigt, da ja in allen Fällen des Art. 491 der Grund der Unterbrechung darin liegt, daß ein zur Vertretung fähiger Anwalt nicht mehr vorhanden ist, also ein neuer Anwalt zu bestellen oder dem früher bestellten neue Vollmacht zu geben ist. Im Parteiprozesse hat die Aufforderung der Natur des Verfahrens entsprechend anders zu lauten (Art. 534).

7) Außerdem sind in der Zustellung die bisher aufgestellten Anwälte aller Parteien, natürlich mit Bezeichnung der Parteien, für welche sie bestellt sind, anzugeben, sowie die Anträge, welche, falls die Partei der Aufforderung nicht nachkommen sollte, hinsichtlich der Hauptsache beabsichtigt sind.

Von „Hauptsache“ wird hier gesprochen im Gegensatze zum Zwischenpunkte der Wiederaufnahme des Verfahrens. Es sind jene Anträge gemeint, welche der Auffordernde bei der ersten Verhandlung der Sache nehmen wird, und welche je nach dem Stande des Prozesses oder nach der prozessualen Stellung des Auffordernden sehr verschieden sind. Nicht immer kann der Auffordernde genau wissen, welche Anträge er beim Nichterscheinen des Aufgeforderten nehmen werde, denn ist z. B. ein Beweisverfahren unterbrochen worden, so muß dasselbe vorher durchgeführt werden, ehe eine Verhandlung stattfinden kann, und die bei dieser Verhandlung zu stellenden Anträge richten sich natürlich nach den Ergebnissen des Beweisverfahrens (Art. 346). Die Forderung des Gesetzes beschränkt sich daher im Wesen darauf, daß die Anträge bezüglich der Endentscheidung, und zwar insbesondere die weitgehendsten, mitgetheilt worden sein müssen, wenn die Ladung als genügend (Art. 297) betrachtet werden soll.

Weitere Mittheilungen, als die hier ausdrücklich vorgeschriebenen, sind nicht nöthig, namentlich bedarf es keiner Begründung der Anträge. Alles Weitere erfährt der Aufgeforderte, wenn er in den Rechtsstreit eintritt.

8) Die Aufforderung hat sich an diejenigen Personen zu richten, welche als Parteien oder gesetzliche Vertreter den Prozeß zu führen, bzw. den Anwalt zu bestellen haben. Im Falle der Unterbrechung durch den Tod der Partei gestattet das Gesetz, daß die Zustellung an deren Erben in der durch Art. 211 bezeichneten Weise geschehe, d. h. an diese insgesammt, ohne nähere Bezeichnung, und zwar in der letzten Wohnung des Erblassers.

Eine in dieser formlosen Weise erfolgte Ladung kann offenbar keine weitergehende Wirkung haben, als daß der Rechtsstreit im Namen des Nachlasses, gewissermaßen dem Verstorbenen gegenüber, sich fortsetzt, ebenso wie im Falle, wo der Prozeß einem bestellten Prozeßbevollmächtigten gegenüber fortgeführt wird. Bemerk. zu Art. 491 Nr. 3 u. 4.

Persönliche Anträge gegen die Erben könnten auf Grund einer solchen Ladung nicht genommen werden und ebensowenig ließe sich aus dem ergehenden Urtheile etwas für die Erbqualität folgern (Code civ. Art. 800). Anderseits bildet aber auch das ergehende Urtheil Rechtskraft gegen jeden Vertreter des Nachlasses, wer es immer auch sei.

Zu bemerken ist, daß das Gesetz bloß sagt, die Aufforderung könne in besagter Weise den Erben zugestellt werden, also es gestattet, die Zustellung auch in gewöhnlicher Weise zu machen, was in manchen Fällen vorzuziehen sein wird.

Wird ein Anwalt wirklich bestellt, so kann dieser nicht für die Erben im Allgemeinen auftreten, sondern muß genau die Personen bezeichnen, für welche er auftritt, sowie die Qualität, in welcher diese das Verfahren aufnehmen.

9) Stellt der Aufgeforderte keinen Anwalt auf, so ist trotzdessen das Verfahren als wieder aufgenommen zu betrachten, und zwar vom Augenblicke an, wo die Erscheinungsfrist, d. h. die Frist zur Wiederaufnahme, umlaufen ist.

Es bedarf keines besondern Urtheils, welches das Verfahren für wiederaufgenommen erklärt, wie dies im französischen Prozesse unpraktischer Weise Vorschrift war, vielmehr setzt sich das Verfahren ohne Weiteres wieder in Gang, und zwar nach dem Stande der Sache im Augenblicke der Unterbrechung, jedoch unter Erneuerung der vereitelten Fristen (Art. 492 Abs. 2).

10) Dabei entsteht nun die Frage: Welcher Natur ist dieses weitere Verfahren? Sind die Urtheile, welche ergehen, Versäumungsurtheile, oder gelten sie als contradiktorische?

Es wäre nicht ganz unnöthig gewesen, wenn die Prozeßordnung diesen Punkt geregelt hätte, um so mehr, als die französischen Prinzipien sich nicht überall anwenden lassen, weil die Wirkung der Hinterlegung der Anträge sowohl im Allgemeinen, als namentlich für die Unterbrechung des Verfahrens dort eine andere ist, als nach der Prozeßordnung. Vgl. P. O. Art. 491 Abs. 3 und Code de proc. Art. 343.

An der Hand der allgemeinen Prinzipien ergibt sich folgende Lösung:

Vom Augenblicke der Unterbrechung an und so lange die betreffende Partei nicht vertreten ist oder erscheint, kann das Verfahren nur ein contumazielles sein, und es kann daher über Streitpunkte, welche bei Eintritt der Unterbrechung noch nicht contradiktorisch geworden waren (Art. 254) später nur Versäumungsurtheil ergehen. Waren also bei Eintritt der Unterbrechung die beiderseitigen Anträge noch nicht hinterlegt, oder wurde ein Beweisverfahren unterbrochen, so ist das ergehende Urtheil ohne Zweifel ein Versäumungsurtheil.

Folge hiervon ist, daß auch die Grundsätze über Verbindungsurtheile ihre Anwendung finden, falls die Vorbedingungen dazu gegeben sind, d. h. falls einer der Beklagten bei Hinterlegung der Anträge nicht erscheint. Bei der Wiedervorladung, die zufolge eines solchen Verbindungsurtheils stattzufinden hat, genügt offenbar die formlose Zustellung an die Erben (Art. 495 Abs. 2), wenn die Aufforderung selbst in dieser Form ergangen war.

11) Etwas zweifelhaft wird die Sache, wenn zur Zeit der Unterbrechung die beiderseitigen Anträge bereits hinterlegt waren.

Soweit diese Anträge nach allgemeinen Prinzipien fortwirken (Bemerk. zu Art. 307 Nr. 11 und 12), kann diese Wirkung weder durch die Unterbrechung des Verfahrens, noch durch das Nichterscheinen der zur Wiederaufnahme aufgeforderten Personen beseitigt werden. Es kann daher keinem Zweifel unterliegen, daß solche Anträge berücksichtigt werden müssen; allein es könnte sich fragen, ob nicht trotzdessen hier ebenso, wie in dem Falle des Art. 346, ein Versäumungsurtheil ergehe.

Gründe hierzu lägen allerdings vor, und zwar vielleicht noch stärkere, als bei Art. 346. Wenn nemlich im Falle vollständig geregelter Vertretung der Anwalt in späteren Sitzungen nicht erscheint, um seine Anträge zu vertheidigen, zu ändern oder zu ergänzen, so ist die Vermuthung gerechtfertigt, daß eine besondere Vertheidigung nicht nöthig, daß nichts zu ändern und hinzuzusetzen sei; allein im unterstellten Falle ist eben **kein Vertreter** vorhanden, welcher im **Stande** wäre, zu handeln, die Aufforderung zur Bestellung eines Vertreters hat vielleicht die Partei nicht erreicht!

So beachtenswerth auch diese Gründe erscheinen mögen, so halte ich sie dennoch nicht für wichtig genug, um die allgemeinen Prinzipien, welche durch den Ausspruch: „die Verhandlung sei nach Maßgabe ihres **Standes** fortzusetzen," für maßgebend erklärt sind, zu ändern, und nehme daher an, daß im unterstellten Falle contradiktorisches Urtheil ergehe.

Abstand vom Prozesse.

Art. 496. — **Der Kläger kann, ohne das angesprochene Recht selbst aufzugeben, von dem Prozesse abstehen.**

Ist der Schluß der ersten die Hauptsache betreffenden Verhandlung bereits erfolgt, so ist der Beklagte befugt, auf der gerichtlichen Entscheidung der Sache zu bestehen.

Art. 497. — **Die Erklärung des Abstandes ist der Gegenpartei zuzustellen. Ist sie nicht von der Partei selbst unterzeichnet, so muß zugleich die betreffende Specialvollmacht zugestellt werden, falls sie nicht schon früher zugestellt oder bei Gericht hinterlegt ist.**

Die Erklärung des Abstands kann auch mündlich in einer Gerichtssitzung, in welcher

beide Parteien erschienen sind, gemacht werden, wenn die Partei, für welche der Abstand erklärt werden will, persönlich gegenwärtig oder der Gewalthaber dazu mit Vollmacht versehen ist.

Die Gegenpartei ist gehalten, sich innerhalb acht Tagen bei Vermeidung der Annahme der Zustimmung über den Abstand zu erklären.

Art. 498. — **Der Abstand versetzt die Sache in die Lage vor Erhebung der Klage zurück und es fallen mit dem Abstande alle Wirkungen der Klage weg. Der Abstand verpflichtet außerdem den Kläger zum Ersatze sämmtlicher Kosten, soweit nicht darüber rechtskräftig erkannt ist. Erst nach geleistetem Ersatze darf neue Klage erhoben werden.**

G. A. d. K. d. A. II S. 286—289. 351. 453. IV S. 102. 103. 106.
K. d. R. II S. 245—248. IV S. 61.

1) De Abstand des Klägers ist entweder mit einem Aufgeben des geltend gemachten Anspruches verbunden, oder aber er betrifft nur den Prozeß, ohne das Recht selbst zu berühren.

Nur der letztere Abstand ist Gegenstand vorstehender drei Artikel, für den ersteren aber sind civilrechtliche Grundsätze maßgebend, weßhalb denn auch eine bezügliche Bestimmung des Entwurfs gestrichen wurde.

Uebrigens ist selbstverständlich, daß ein Abstand, in welchem der Kläger auf eine nach den Grundsätzen des Civilrechts bindende Weise sein Recht aufgibt, den Prozeß beende und zwar aus dem einfachen Grunde, weil nichts mehr zu entscheiden ist. Das Nemliche läßt sich sagen, wenn der Kläger auch nur den primären Antrag des Beklagten als begründet zugibt.

a) Zulässigkeit des Abstandes.

2) Weil der Abstand vom Prozesse das Recht nicht entzieht, sofort wegen des nemlichen Anspruchs neue Klage zu erheben, so ergibt sich von selbst, daß es nicht in der Willkür des Klägers stehen dürfe, zu jeder Zeit vom Prozesse abzustehen und auf diese Weise dem Beklagten die etwa erwachsenen Vortheile wieder zu entziehen oder ihn muthwillig von einem Prozesse in den anderen zu schleppen.

Nach französischem Prozesse darf der Kläger in jeder Lage der Sache abstehen, jedoch, falls Beklagter nicht einwilligt, nur auf Grund gerichtlicher Entscheidung, durch welche festgestellt wird, daß für letzteren kein Interesse bestehe, seine Einwilligung zu verweigern. Unsere Prozeßordnung wählte ein anderes System, indem sie den einseitigen Abstand bis zum Schlusse der ersten die Hauptsache betreffenden Verhandlung unbedingt gestattet nach diesem Zeitpunkte aber ebenso unbedingt ausschließt, wenn nicht die Einwilligung des Beklagten erfolgt.

Dieses System erscheint mir in doppelter Richtung verfehlt.

Was erstens die unbedingte Gestattung betrifft, so steht dieselbe im Widerspruche mit den Prinzipien der Provokationsklage. Eine Klagestellung ist gewiß eine Berühmung. Ist es nun praktisch und rationell, den Beklagten, welcher über den Grund der Sache erkannt, d. h. entschieden haben will, es stehe dem Kläger das beanspruchte Recht nicht zu, auf den Weg der Provokationsklage zu verweisen, also zu verlangen, er solle einen besonderen Prozeß führen, um das Vorhandensein einer Berühmung aussprechen und eine Frist zur Wiedererhebung der Klage setzen zu lassen? — Vgl. R. R. II 245, 246 (v. Bomhard).

Was zweitens die unbedingte Ausschließung betrifft, so geht auch in dieser Richtung das Gesetz zu weit, wenigstens seinem Wortlaute nach, denn offenbar besteht für den Beklagten kein Interesse, auf einer Aburtheilung zu bestehen, wenn er beantragt hatte, es sei die Klage als unstatthaft oder als verfrüht abzuweisen und Kläger mit Erklärung seines Abstandes die Begründetheit dieser Einwände zugibt.

Ich bin übrigens der Ansicht, daß das Gesetz diesen Fall nicht im Auge hatte, und daher in demselben die Einwilligung des Beklagten nicht nöthig wäre, vorausgesetzt 1) daß der Abstand alles einräumt, was mit fraglichen Einreden bezweckt wird, wie z. B. wenn die Nichtigkeit der Ladung zugegeben, die behauptete Fristgestattung eingeräumt wird ꝛc., und 2) daß Beklagter nicht fragliche Einreden fallen läßt, was in der Antwort auf den Abstand noch giltig geschehen könnte. Vgl. oben Nr. 1 a. E.

3) Während der Entwurf die Abgabe der Vernehmlassung als Endpunkt für den einseitigen Abstand bezeichnet, rückt die Prozeßordnung diesen Endpunkt weiter hinaus und zwar an den Schluß der ersten Verhandlung in der Hauptsache (Art. 246). Weder die Hinterlegung der Anträge noch die Parteivorträge schließen also diesen Abstand aus, sondern er wird erst unstatthaft, nachdem der Schluß der Verhandlung im Sinne der Art. 158 und 160 ausgesprochen ist.

Nur eine Verhandlung, welche die Hauptsache betrifft, ist erheblich, also nicht eine solche, in welcher bevorzugte Prozeßeinreden (Art. 185 und 186) zur gesonderten Aburtheilung gebracht werden (Art. 232), oder in welcher ein den Grund der Sache unberührt lassender Zwischenstreit, z. B. eine vorsorgliche Maßregel, erledigt werden soll.

Verhandlungen über Präjudizialsachen im Sinne des Art. 190, z. B. über die Erbqualität einer Partei, sind jedoch zur Hauptsache zu rechnen; sie enthalten eine Einlassung auf den Grund der Sache. Vgl. Bemerk. zu Art. 307 Nr. 9.

4) In vorstehenden Artikeln hat der Gesetzgeber, ebenso wie der Code de proc. in Art. 402 und 403 (Chauveau quest. 1455), zunächst nur den gänzlichen Abstand vom Prozesse im Auge, allein was sie bestimmen, gilt in analoger Weise auch von einem theilweisen Abstande.

Was ferner von der Klage gesagt ist, gilt unter gleichen Voraussetzungen auch für die Widerklage und ebenso ist selbstverständlich, daß Einreden, z. B. Compensationseinreden, aufgegeben werden können mit dem Vorbehalte, sie später auf dem Wege der Klage zu verfolgen. Abg. II 289 Sp. 1.

5) Das Gesetz spricht nur vom Falle, wo der Kläger von der Klage absteht, erstreckt sich also nicht auf die Zurücknahme von Rechtsmitteln, um so weniger als eine entsprechende Bestimmung des Entwurfes (Art. 461) beseitigt worden ist. Es wäre nicht statthaft, denjenigen, welcher Berufung oder Nichtigkeitsbeschwerde ergreift, Einspruch erhebt, als Kläger für die entsprechende Instanz zu behandeln; jedoch kann allerdings der Abstand von der Klage auch noch in höherer Instanz stattfinden. Vgl. hannov. Verhdl. S. 1265 bis 1272. Auf die Zurücknahme eines Rechtsmittels finden daher die besonderen Bestimmungen über den Abstand vom Prozesse keine Anwendung und es richten sich dieselben nach allgemeinen Prinzipien. Erfolgt sie nach Ablauf der Nothfrist, so enthält sie einen Verzicht auf das Rechtsmittel.

b) Verfahren.

6) Die Erklärung des Abstandes ist der Gegenpartei zuzustellen und diese hat innerhalb acht Tagen etwaige Einwände vorzubringen, widrigenfalls Zustimmung angenommen wird.

Die Zustellung erfolgt im Anwaltsprozesse durch Anwaltsakt, von welchem jedoch gefordert wird, entweder daß er in Original und Abschrift (Art. 92 Abs. 3) von der Partei selbst unterzeichnet, oder daß er von einer Zustellung der betreffenden Spezialvollmacht begleitet sei. Wie aus Art. 92 Ziff. 4 hervorgeht, bedarf es einer Spezialvollmacht nur für den gänzlichen Abstand vom Prozesse, und haben somit die Bestimmungen über Mitunterzeichnung der Partei und Zustellung der Spezialvollmacht auch nur diesen Fall im Auge.

7) Das Gesetz gestattet, daß der Abstand auch mündlich in der Sitzung erklärt werde, vorausgesetzt, daß in dieser Sitzung beide Parteien erscheinen, d. h. im Anwaltsprozesse durch Anwälte vertreten sind, und daß diejenige Partei, welche den Abstand erklärt, persönlich zugegen sei oder genügende Vollmacht von ihr vorliege.

Daß ein Theil der Beklagten nur in Folge Verbindungsurtheils (Art. 316) als vertreten betrachtet wird, steht der mündlichen Erklärung des Abstandes nicht im Wege.

Auch für diesen Fall steht dem Beklagten, wenn er nicht vorzieht, sich sofort zu erklären, die achttägige Frist zu, welche im Sinne des Art. 497 vom Tage der Sitzung an laufen wird.

Ueber die beiderseitigen Erklärungen ist Urkunde zu ertheilen.

8) Da der Abstand vom Prozesse nur eine Prozeßhandlung ist, so hat jeder gesetzliche Vertreter einer Partei Befugniß, die bezügliche Erklärung rechtswirksam abzugeben oder Vollmacht zur Abgabe derselben auszustellen. Anders ist es, wenn das Recht selbst aufgegeben werden soll, denn in diesem Falle sind die Grundsätze des Civilrechts maßgebend.

c) Wirkungen.

9) Mit dem Abstande fallen alle Wirkungen hinweg, welche die Klage als solche äußert (Art. 179), nicht aber jene, welche sich an dieselbe abgesehen vom Prozesse knüpfen, welche ihr in der Eigenschaft einer gewöhnlichen Willensäußerung schon zukommen, und ist es daher nicht ganz richtig, wenn das Gesetz sagt, der Abstand versetze die Sache in die Lage vor Erhebung der Klage zurück. Insofern z. B. die Verjährung durch eine einfache Aufforderung unterbrochen werden kann, behauptet die Klage als solche ihre Wirkung; ebenso kann sie wirksam sein, insofern sie einen Verzicht, die Ausübung eines Wahlrechts enthält. R.R. II 247, 248 (v. Weiß).

Geständnisse, welche etwa schon gemacht waren, verlieren zwar ihren Werth als gerichtliche Geständnisse, behalten aber im Uebrigen ihre Bedeutung.

Was insbesondere die Verjährung betrifft, so ist hervorzuheben, daß durch Art. 498 alle civilrechtlichen Bestimmungen beseitigt sind, welche die Wirkungen der Klagestellung oder Klageanmeldung auch nach dem Abstande fortdauern lassen.

10) Mit Erklärung des Abstandes verpflichtet sich der Kläger, die sämmtlichen Kosten zu ersetzen, soweit nicht rechtskräftig darüber erkannt ist.

Daß diese Kosten in der Weise, wie es die Art. 113 ff. bestimmen, festzusetzen seien, kann einem gegründeten Zweifel nicht unterliegen, ebenso, daß im Falle der Verzögerung Art. 116 zur Anwendung komme (Abg. II 286 u. 289); allein fraglich ist, welcher Weg einzuschlagen sei, um die Zahlung der festgesetzten Kosten durch Zwang zu erlangen, falls der abstehende Kläger nicht freiwillig zahlt. Art. 498 gibt zwar ein indirektes Zwangsmittel in der Vorschrift, daß eine neue Klage erst erhoben werden könne, nachdem die Kosten der ersten ersetzt seien, allein offenbar ist dieses Mittel ungenügend, und zwar schon deshalb, weil der Kläger vielleicht gar nicht daran denkt, neue Klage zu erheben.

Der französische Gesetzgeber hatte (Code de proc. Art. 402) ausdrücklich bestimmt, daß der Gerichtsvorstand eine vollziehbare Ordonnanz zu erlassen habe. Da nun unsere Prozeßordnung nichts bestimmt, da ferner die Beschlüsse, welche die Kosten festsetzen, nur insoferne vollstreckbar sind, als sie zur Ergänzung eines vollstreckbaren Urtheiles dienen und dies selbst von der vollstreckbaren Ausfertigung des Art. 113 Abs. 6 gilt, so wäre den Prinzipien nach zu entscheiden, daß auf Grund der Kostenfestsetzung erst Urtheil erwirkt werden müsse.

Ich bezweifle sehr, ob dies im Willen des Gesetzes gelegen, allein offenbar würde man sich von den Prinzipien in bedenklicher Weise entfernen, wollte man gestatten, auf die gewechselten Anwaltsakte hin ein Vollstreckungsverfahren einzuleiten.

10) Der Abstand eines einzelnen Streitgenossen ist ohne Zweifel statthaft, jedoch wirkt er nur für diesen. Ebensowenig kann der Streitabstand den besonderen Rechten von Rechtsnachfolgern, welche bereits in den Prozeß eingetreten sind (Art. 493), oder von Intervenienten Eintrag thun.

Zweiter Abschnitt.

XVII. Hauptstück.

Ordentliches Verfahren vor den Handels- und Einzelngerichten.

Einleitung.

Das Verfahren vor Handelsgerichten und Einzelngerichten (der Parteiprozeß) charakterisirt sich dadurch, daß die Prozeßführung nicht in die Hände von Anwälten gelegt ist, daß der Verhandlung in der Sitzung kein schriftliches Vorverfahren vorausgeht, daß überhaupt das Streben möglichst rascher und einfacher Erledigung in den Vordergrund tritt.

Der Gesetzgeber fand es sachgemäß, das Verfahren vor beiden Arten von Gerichten, welches der Entwurf getrennt hielt, zu verschmelzen, und hat ohne Zweifel Recht daran gethan, da im Wesentlichen die nemlichen Gesichtspunkte maßgebend sind.

Uebrigens ist doch zu beachten, daß bei Einzelngerichten, wo nur Bagatellsachen oder Sachen sehr einfacher Art vorkommen, in der Regel formloser verfahren werden kann, als bei Handelsgerichten, wo oft sehr wichtige und schwierige Prozesse zu verhandeln sind, wie dies denn auch der Gesetzgeber durch verschiedene Ausnahms-Bestimmungen anerkannt hat. Es zeigt sich daher in der Praxis das Bestreben, in allen wichtigeren Sachen das handelsgerichtliche Verfahren dem Verfahren vor den Bezirksgerichten thatsächlich anzunähern, indem die in der Regel als Prozeßbevollmächtigte bestellten Anwälte in ähnlich kunstgerechter Weise verfahren, wie sie es im Anwaltsprozesse gewohnt sind. So ist es z. B. an manchen Orten üblich, daß die Anwälte auch in Handelssachen kurze motivirte Anträge notizweise fertigen und mit den Akten dem Gerichte vorlegen, ein Verfahren, welches für die Anwälte sowohl als für die Gerichte große Vortheile bietet.

Gerichtssitzungen.

Art. 499. — **Bei den Handels- und Einzelngerichten sind je nach Bedürfniß einer odere mehrere Tage in der Woche zu bestimmen, an denen öffentliche Sitzungen stattfinden.**

Art. 500. — **Auf Ansuchen können Sitzungen auch auf andere als die ein für allemal festgesetzten Sitzungstage anberaumt werden. Dies geschieht bei den Handelsgerichten durch den Gerichtsvorstand.**

G. A. d. K. d. A. II S. 256. 257. 274. 275. 351. — K. d. R. II S. 246.

1) Im Parteiprozesse wird ebenso wie im abgekürzten Verfahren (Art. 259) der Beklagte sofort zur Verhandlung in die Sitzung geladen.

Die Sitzungstage und die Dauer der Sitzungszeit werden im Voraus bestimmt und veröffentlicht, dem Kläger aber steht es frei, in eine dieser Sitzungen beliebig zu laden.

Man könnte fragen, ob nicht in dieser Weise sich Mißstände ergeben, indem die Sachen sich unverhältnißmäßig auf die einzelnen Sitzungen vertheilen, und ob es nicht besser gewesen wäre, vorzuschreiben, daß der Kläger sich die Sitzung vom Richter bestimmen lasse; allein die Erfahrung zeigt, daß letztere Förmlichkeit, welche immerhin Zeitverlust, Mühe und Kosten bedingen würde, füglich entbehrt werden kann. Sollten sich ausnahmsweise die Sachen in einer Sitzung übermäßig anhäufen, so erledigt der Richter eben nur soviel er kann, mit Bevorzugung der Sachen, welche dringlich oder einfach, oder bei denen die Parteien persönlich zugegen sind, und vertagt die übrigen in eine nächste Sitzung.

2) Auf Ansuchen können Sitzungen auch auf andere Tage, als die im Voraus festgesetzten, anberaumt werden. Wie aus Art. 503 hervorgeht, ist zu diesem Zwecke eine Verfügung des Einzelnrichters bezw. Gerichtsvorstandes zu erwirken und mit der Klage zuzustellen — welche letztere Förmlichkeit füglich hätte erspart werden können.

Verfahren im Allgemeinen.

Art. 501. — **Die Klage wird bei den Handels- und Einzelngerichten dadurch erhoben, daß der Kläger dem Beklagten einen Gerichtsvollzieherakt zustellen läßt, welcher neben den allgemeinen Erfordernissen der Zustellungsurkunden enthalten muß:**

1) die Bezeichnung des Gerichts;

2) die Vorladung des Beklagten in die Sitzung des Gerichts — gegebenen Falls der zu bezeichnenden Gerichtsabtheilung — auf einen bestimmten Sitzungstag und auf eine bestimmte Sitzungsstunde;

3) die Bezeichnung des Klagegegenstands, die Angabe des Klagegrundes und ein bestimmtes Gesuch.

Einer vorgängigen Anmeldung der Klage bedarf es nicht.

Art. 502. — **Zwischen der Klagezustellung und dem Sitzungstage müssen wenigstens drei Tage in Mitte liegen.**

In dringenden Fällen kann der Gerichtsvorstand oder Einzelnrichter die Frist auf Ansuchen des Klägers abkürzen, jedoch nur so weit, daß die Zustellung an den Beklagten und dessen Erscheinen in der anberaumten Sitzung noch möglich ist.

Art. 503. — **Das Ansuchen um Anberaumung eines besondern Sitzungstags zur Verhandlung der Klage oder um Abkürzung der Vorladungsfrist kann Namens des Klägers auch von dem mit Zustellung der Klage beauftragten Gerichtsvollzieher und zwar ohne besondere Vollmacht gestellt werden. Die Verfügung ist dem Beklagten mit der Klage zuzustellen.**

Art. 504. — **Die Parteien können auch ohne vorgängige Ladung in der Sitzung erscheinen und den Rechtsstreit verhandeln.**

Art. 505. — **Außer der Klage findet kein schriftliches Vorverfahren statt.**

G. A. d. K. d. A. II S. 256—260. 274—276. 351. 453. IV S. 103. 106. — K. d. R. II S. 248. IV S. 61.

1) Das Verfahren im Parteiprozesse ist sehr einfach und nimmt einen natürlichen, alle künstlichen Formen möglichst vermeidenden Verlauf.

Der Kläger ruft den Beklagten unmittelbar vor den Richter und vor diesem wird sofort verhandelt, ohne Vorverfahren und ohne Vermittlung von Anwälten. Erscheinen beide Parteien freiwillig, so bedarf es nicht einmal einer Ladung.

a) Vorladung.

2) Der Regel nach wird die Klage durch eine Vorladung erhoben, welche Gericht und Sitzungszeit bezeichnet und zugleich die wesentlichen Theile einer Klageschrift enthält.

Die Fertigung dieser Vorladung ist ganz dem Gerichtsvollzieher übertragen, welchem also auch die Sorge für richtige Klagestellung obliegt, falls ihn der Kläger damit betraut hat. In wichtigeren Sachen, namentlich Handelssachen, pflegt der Auftrag zur Ladung dem Gerichtsvollzieher vom Prozeßbevollmächtigten des Klägers zuzugehen und dieser das Klaglibell zu entwerfen, und es ist selbstverständlich, daß sich der Gerichtsvollzieher nach diesem Entwurfe zu richten hat.

Die Worte, deren sich das Gesetz in Art. 501 Ziff. 3 bedient, deuten an, daß an die Klagschrift zwar dem Wesen nach die nemlichen

Anforderungen gestellt werden, wie im Anwaltsprozesse (Art. 225), daß es aber weniger streng damit genommen werden soll.

3) Wenn vorgeschrieben ist, es solle auf eine bestimmte Sitzungsstunde geladen werden, so beruht dies nicht auf der Voraussetzung, daß sich der Gerichtsvollzieher vorher mit dem Richter benehme, denn das Gesetz bestimmt ausdrücklich, es sei eine vorausgehende Anmeldung der Klage nicht nöthig, auch wäre eine geordnete Fixation im Voraus nicht wohl möglich.

Es steht daher dem Kläger frei, sich eine beliebige in die Sitzungszeit fallende Stunde zu wählen und auf dieselbe vorzuladen. Abg. II 256, 257. Hieraus geht zugleich hervor, daß der Richter nicht bloß den Beginn seiner Sitzungen, sondern auch die Dauer der Sitzungszeit im Voraus bestimmen und ankündigen müsse.

Meiner Ansicht nach wäre es sehr sachgemäß gewesen, alle Ladungen auf den Beginn der Sitzung geben zu lassen, natürlich vorbehaltlich besonderer Firirung des Richters.

Darf jeder Kläger nach Belieben seine Stunde wählen, so kann sich die Uebung bilden, daß die meisten oder alle Sachen in die Mitte oder zu Ende der Sitzung geladen werden, weil es für die Parteien oder ihre Prozeßbevollmächtigten so am bequemsten ist. Folge wäre, daß der Richter die halbe Zeit müßig säße. Abgesehen hiervon tritt jedenfalls der Mißstand ein, daß der Richter sich die ganze Sitzungszeit über zur Verhandlung bereit halten, daß er so zu sagen die Bureauzeit aushalten muß, denn er ist nie sicher, ob nicht eine oder die andere Sache nachkomme. Wird hingegen jede Sache zum Beginne der Sitzung geladen, so ist die Möglichkeit gegeben, mit Rücksicht auf Dringlichkeit der Sache, auf das Bedürfniß näherer Prüfung durch die Prozeßbevollmächtigten, auf Vergleichsunterhandlungen ꝛc., die sachgemäße Reihenfolge eintreten zu lassen.

Es wird gut sein, wenn die Gerichte den nachtheiligen Folgen der unpraktischen Bestimmung des Gesetzes möglichst entgegenzuwirken suchen. Es stehen ihnen hierzu Mittel zu Gebot, sei es, indem sie den Gerichtsvollziehern ihres Bezirkes, von welchen in der Regel die Ladungen ausgehen, ihre Wünsche zu erkennen geben (Abg. II 257 [v. Weiß]), sei es, indem sie die außer der Ordnung geladenen Sachen an's Ende der Sitzung stellen oder eintretenden Falles vertagen.

4) Die Ladungsfrist beträgt hier drei Tage, selbstverständlich mit der Erweiterung in Gemäßheit des Art. 209.

In dringenden Fällen kann diese Frist abgekürzt werden, und zwar auf schriftliches oder mündliches Ansuchen, welches zu stellen der Gerichtsvollzieher von Rechtswegen bevollmächtigt ist. Die richterliche Verfügung ist mit der Klage zuzustellen, natürlich unverzüglich (Art. 259 Abs. 2), widrigenfalls nach Art. 520 Abs. 2 nochmalige Vorladung verordnet werden kann.

b) Freiwilliges Erscheinen.

5) Daß die Parteien ohne vorgängige Ladung freiwillig in der Sitzung erscheinen können, um ihre Sache verhandeln zu lassen, ist eine Ausnahme von dem sonst geltenden und gerade durch diese Ausnahme bestätigten Grundsatze, daß ein Prozeß nur auf Grund der Zustellung einer Klagschrift vor den Richter gebracht werden könne, widrigenfalls dieser die an ihn gerichteten Anträge als unstatthaft zurückzuweisen habe.

Der französische Prozeß ließ diese Ausnahme bloß beim Einzelngerichte zu (Code de proc. Art. 7), unsere Prozeßordnung dehnt sie jedoch auf Handelsgerichte aus — man könnte bezweifeln, ob mit Recht, ob es nicht im Gegentheil rathsam gewesen wäre, die ganze Ausnahme zu beseitigen.

Praktisch ist das betreffende Verfahren nicht, wenigstens nicht in Fällen, wo ernstlicher Streit vorliegt, denn weit entfernt, den Gang der Sache zu vereinfachen oder zu beschleunigen, pflegt es vielmehr das Gegentheil zu bewirken. Erfahrungsgemäß wird denn auch von der Erlaubniß des freiwilligen Erscheinens nur Gebrauch gemacht, wo kein Streit besteht, in der Regel, wo es sich darum handelt, Wucher oder sonstige lichtscheue Geschäfte in das Gewand einer rechtskräftigen Entscheidung zu kleiden und so eines bevorzugten gesetzlichen Schutzes theilhaftig werden zu lassen.

6) Es frägt sich: Wie ist Art. 504 mit Art. 179, welcher die Rechtshängigkeit mit ihren verschiedenen Folgen an die Klagzustellung knüpft, zu vereinigen?

Offenbar läßt sich im Falle, wo das Verfahren mit dem freiwilligen Erscheinen der Parteien beginnt, Art. 179 nur in analoger Weise anwenden, und wird anzunehmen sein, daß die dem Beklagten gegenüber vor dem Richter erfolgende Entwicklung der Klage als Klagzustellung zu gelten habe.

Hieraus folgt zugleich, daß es unbedingt und in allen Fällen nöthig ist, sofort diese Klagerhebung zu beurkunden. Der Code de proc. (Art. 7) hatte ein besonderes Protokoll vorgeschrieben (Bemerk. zu Art. 39 Nr. 5), und der Entwurf (Art. 473) verlangte Beurkundung im Sitzungsprotokolle, unsere Prozeßordnung aber schweigt. Mit Beseitigung des Sitzungsprotokolles wurde auch vorliegende Frage stillschweigend beseitigt.

Ergeht ein förmliches Urtheil in der betreffenden Sitzung, so hat selbstverständlich der Sachverhalt dieses Urtheils die Klage vorzutragen, und genügt dies vollkommen, da besondere Protokollirung nicht vorgeschrieben ist. Wird jedoch bloß vertagt, so würde, falls der Eintrag nur nach Vorschrift des Art. 281 stattfände, jede Beurkundung fehlen. Es ergibt sich daher das Bedürfniß, hier eine Ausnahme zu machen und auch im Falle einer bloßen Vertagung das Klagvorbringen zu beurkunden, soweit dies nöthig ist, um den Mangel der Ladung zu decken.

7) Da die Parteien ein Recht haben, freiwillig in der Sitzung zu erscheinen, so darf der Richter sie nie zurückweisen, wenn sie sich innerhalb der zum Voraus bestimmten Sitzungszeit vor ihm einfinden und Urtheil begehren. Allerdings steht es ihm frei, zu vertagen.

Art. 506. — **Erscheinen beide Theile, so hat zunächst der Kläger seine Klage vorzutragen und zu begründen. Hierauf hat der Beklagte zu antworten und seine etwaigen Einreden vorzubringen, worauf weiter bis zum Schlusse zu verhandeln ist. Beide Theile haben die Urkunden, auf welche sie sich berufen, soweit möglich sogleich in Urschrift vorzulegen und sich zu erklären, ob sie die von der Gegenpartei vorgelegten Urkunden anerkennen oder bestreiten.**

Klagänderungen, sowie solche Einreden gegen die Klage, welche vor den Bezirksgerichten an einen bestimmten Abschnitt des Verfahrens gebunden sind, können vor den Handels- und Einzelngerichten bis zum Schlusse der ersten Verhandlung geltend gemacht werden.

Art. 507. — **Im Verfahren vor den Handelsgerichten ist vor oder während der Sitzung dem Gerichtsschreiber die Klagurkunde zur Eintragung in ein Verzeichniß vorzulegen, welches über die beim Gerichte anhängigen Sachen nach Maßgabe der auf dem Verordnungswege darüber zu erlassenden nähern Vorschriften zu führen ist. Bei Nichterscheinen des Klägers erfolgt die Eintragung auf Grund der vom Beklagten zu übergebenden Abschrift.**

Sind die Parteien ohne vorgängige Ladung in der Sitzung erschienen, so geschieht der Eintrag auf mündliches Anmelden des Klägers.

G. A. d. K. d. A. II S. 257—259. 275—277. 351. 352. IV S. 103. — K. d. R. II S. 248. IV S. 61.

1) Für die Verhandlung, d. h. für das Verfahren in der Sitzung, gelten, soweit nicht besondere Ausnahmen gemacht sind, die allgemeinen Grundsätze des Hauptst. V. Was also dort von der Pflicht zur eventuellen Streiteinlassung (Art. 184), vom Rechte, gewisse Prozeßeinreden (Art. 185 u. 186) gesondert vorzubringen oder Präjudizialsachen (Art. 190) gesondert verhandeln zu lassen, bestimmt ist, findet ebenso Anwendung im Parteiprozesse als im Anwaltsprozesse.

Nur in der äußeren Erscheinung gibt sich ein merklicher Unterschied kund, insofern im Parteiprozesse das methodische Vorgehen wegfällt und alles unvorbereitet und auf einmal in der Sitzung auftritt. Die Parteien müssen hier gerüstet sein, wegen aller auftauchenden Fragen sofort Rede zu stehen und nach Beseitigung etwaiger Zwischenstreite oder Vorfragen sofort weiter zu verhandeln.

2) Eine durch die Eigenheit des Parteiprozesses gebotene Ausnahme von den allgemeinen Vorschriften macht das Gesetz für Klagänderungen und solche Einreden, welche sonst an einen bestimmten Abschnitt des Verfahrens gebunden sind, insofern diese bis zum Schlusse der ersten Verhandlung giltig geschehen können. Da in der Sitzung alle Prozeßhandlungen sich unmittelbar aneinander reihen, da bei mündlichen Vorträgen, zumal unvorbereiteten, genaue Einhaltung von Formen nicht verlangt werden kann, namentlich aber da es in der Regel Rechtsunkundige sind, welche im Parteiprozesse handeln, so ging der Gesetzgeber mit vollstem Rechte von der Ansicht aus, daß es auf die Reihenfolge des Vorbringens nicht ankommen dürfe, vielmehr die Verhandlung nur als ein Ganzes in Betracht zu kommen habe.

Die erste Verhandlung endigt, wenn das Gericht zum Zwecke der Urtheilsfällung den Schluß derselben ausspricht, und kann daher auch mehrere Sitzungen dauern. Vertagungen der Sache zur Verhandlung oder Fortsetzung der bereits begonnenen Verhandlung in einer späteren Sitzung stehen daher einer Klagänderung oder dem Vorbringen einer Prozeßeinrede nicht im Wege. Abg. II 258 (v. Weiß).

Selbst mit vorstehender Begrenzung ist der Ausdruck: „erste Verhandlung“ nicht nach dem Wortlaute zu nehmen, denn es gibt Fälle, wo auch bei einer zweiten Verhandlung noch Prozeßeinreden vorgebracht werden können. Offenbar meint nemlich der Gesetzgeber nur jene erste Verhandlung, in welcher die fragliche Prozeßhandlung nach Maßgabe der allgemeinen Prinzipien hätte vorkommen müssen, und denkt nicht daran, im Parteiprozesse strengere Anforderungen zu stellen. Wenn daher z. B. eine bevorzugte Prozeßeinrede gesondert vorgebracht und wegen derselben interloquirt oder nach deren Abweisung die Sache zur weiteren Verhandlung vertagt wurde, so sind offenbar gewöhnliche Prozeßeinreden in der späteren Verhandlung noch zulässig.

Hat jedoch die Einlassung auf den Grund der Sache statgefunden und ist in Folge hiervon ein Urtheil ergangen, welches kein bloßes Vertagungsurtheil ist, so sind sowohl Klagänderungen als Prozeßeinreden ausgeschlossen.

3) Unter den Einreden, welche das Gesetz hier im Auge hat, sind nicht bloß die Prozeßeinreden der Art. 184—186, deren Geltendmachung sonst durch die Streiteinlassung beseitigt wird, begriffen, sondern auch sonstige Einreden, welche noch mehr beschränkt sind, z. B. diejenige des Art. 188. Bemerk. zu Art. 188 Nr. 4.

Die Ablehnung des Richters möchte jedoch unter den Gesichtspunkt einer solchen Einrede nicht zu bringen sein, selbst wenn sie vom Beklagten ausgeht; für sie ist bloß Art. 44 maßgebend.

Wegen Klagänderungen s. Bemerk. zu Art. 180—183, insbesondere Nr. 10 a. E.

4) Was den Gang der mündlichen Verhandlung betrifft, so ist er natürlich im Wesentlichen derselbe wie im Anwaltsprozesse, nur etwas lebhafter und wechselvoller, da die Klärung der Sache, welche dort dem Schriftenwechsel obliegt, hier in der Sitzung vor sich gehen muß und ein weit wirksameres Eingreifen des Richters bedingt ist, namentlich in Fällen, wo die Parteien nicht durch Rechtsverständige vertreten oder verbeiständet sind.

Der Richter gibt natürlich zuerst dem Kläger das Wort, um, anknüpfend an den Inhalt der Ladung, eine Klage zu stellen, und hört sodann den Beklagten mit seinen Einwänden und seiner abweichenden Geschichtserzählung. Etwaige Urkunden läßt er sich vorlegen und vergewissert sich, ob sie bestritten werden oder nicht.

Den sich aus den Vorträgen der Parteien und den Urkunden ergebenden Stoff sucht er durch Fragestellungen zu klären, aus demselben das Wesentliche auszuscheiden und die Wege zu erforschen, welche zur materiellen Wahrheit leiten.

Besondere Aufmerksamkeit wendet er der Frage zu, ob genügende Beweise bereits vorliegen und welche noch geführt werden können; denn ist sicher, daß Beweisauflagen oder Vertagungen zur Beibringung weiterer Aufklärungen nicht zu vermeiden sind, so ist es in der Regel sachgemäß, alle weiteren Erörterungen, auch über Punkte, welche möglicherweise gesondert abgeurtheilt werden könnten, der späteren Verhandlung vorzubehalten.

5) Es ist ebenso das Recht als die Pflicht des Richters, den Parteien die sachgemäße Geltendmachung der ihnen zu Gebot stehenden Mittel des Angriffs und der Vertheidigung zu erleichtern, sie auf Punkte, welche sie übersehen haben, aufmerksam zu machen und nöthige Ergänzungen zu veranlassen.

Diese Amtsthätigkeit des Richters, welche selbstverständlich nur im Dienste des materiellen Rechtes geübt werden darf, erfordert Umsicht und richtigen Takt. Es ist oft eine höchst schwierige, ja unmögliche Aufgabe für den Richter, einer Partei auf den richtigen Weg zu helfen, ohne seine unparteiische Stellung zu gefährden und in die Rolle eines Rathgebers zu fallen.

Im Hinblicke hierauf war vom Referenten vorgeschlagen, man möge die Gerichte befugt erklären, die Parteien zur Annahme eines rechtsverständigen Vertreters anzuhalten (Abg. II 276). Dieser Vorschlag wurde zwar bekämpft, jedoch nur insofern, als damit ein Zwang ausgeübt werden solle; daß der Richter veranlaßt sein könne, den Rath zur Beiziehung eines rechtskundigen Beistandes zu geben und deßhalb die Verhandlung zu vertagen, wurde allseitig anerkannt.

6) Ueber die Verhandlungen in der Sitzung wird auch im Parteiprozesse kein Protokoll geführt. Mit Hilfe einfacher Notizen, welche sich der Gerichtsschreiber und, soweit er es nöthig hält, auch der Vorsitzende macht, wird das Urtheil gefertigt, welches in Sachverhalt und Gesuchen alle erheblichen Beurkundungen enthalten muß.

Sind die Parteien durch Advokaten vertreten, so pflegen diese ihre Anträge zu Papier zu bringen (Art. 536), unter Umständen sogar durch kurze Geschichtserzählungen zu motiviren, ein Verfahren, welches in complizirteren Handelssachen sehr förderlich ist.

Was den wichtigsten Theil des Urtheils, den Urtheilssatz, betrifft, so ist durch Art. 277 Abs. 1 u. 2 dafür gesorgt, daß darüber schriftliche Aufzeichnung bestehe, also insbesondere auch über den Laut von Beweisauflagen, von Eidesauflagen und von Erklärungen, über welche das Gericht Urkunde ertheilt (was auch ohne Anwendung des Art. 248 statthaft ist).

7) Bei den Handelsgerichten ist, laut Art. 507, ähnlich wie bei den Bezirksgerichten (Art. 236) ein besonderes Verzeichniß der anhängig werdenden Prozesse zu führen, in welches

jede Sache eingetragen sein muß, bevor sie verhandelt werden darf.

Die besonderen, das Hauptverzeichniß bei den Bezirksgerichten betreffenden Bestimmungen über Einhaltung der Reihenfolge beim Aufrufe (Art. 244 Abs. 1), über Streichung vom Hauptverzeichnisse, falls beide Parteien nicht erscheinen (Art. 245 Abs. 1), über die Wiederanmeldung gestrichener Sachen (Art. 255) sind hier nicht anwendbar erklärt, gelten also nur soweit, als sie, wie z. B. die Bestimmung des Art. 244 Abs. 1, selbstverständlich sind.

Für die Einzelngerichte ist die Führung solcher Register gesetzlich nicht vorgeschrieben. Man glaubte hier die Regelung dem Verordnungswege überlassen zu müssen, was wohl ebensogut bezüglich der Handelsgerichte hätte der Fall sein können.

Art. 508. — Wird die Verhandlung der Sache in eine spätere Sitzung des Handels- oder Einzelngerichts vertagt, so ist die Vorladung des Beklagten, gleichviel ob er bei der Vertagung anwesend war oder nicht, nur dann erforderlich, wenn sie für den betreffenden Fall im Gesetze besonders vorgeschrieben oder vom Gerichte angeordnet ist.

G. A. d. K. d. A. II S. 352. — K. d. R. II S. 248.

1) Wenn in der Sitzung, auf welche der Beklagte vorgeladen ist, keine der Parteien erscheint, so hat die Ladung als solche ihren Werth verloren, und soll später die Sache dennoch zur Verhandlung kommen, so muß neue Ladung ergehen.

Soweit jedoch die erste Ladung zugleich die Zustellung der Klageschrift enthält und die Anhängigkeit der Sache (Art. 179) begründet, behält sie ihre Wirkung, und es hat also die neue Zustellung sich nur auf den Akt der Ladung, d. h. der Aufforderung zum Erscheinen zu beschränken, im Uebrigen aber auf die schon gegebene Vorladung zu beziehen. Sie ersetzt für den Parteiprozeß die Aufforderung des Art. 239.

Diese neue Ladung kann ebensogut vom Beklagten als vom Kläger ausgehen, denn auch der erstere kann, wenn er ein Versäumungsurtheil auf Grund von Art. 5 nehmen will, dies nur unter der Voraussetzung thun, daß der Kläger in die betreffende Sitzung geladen war.

2) In gleicher Weise hat neue Ladung zu ergehen in allen Fällen, wo die Verhandlung auf unbestimmte Zeit vertagt oder überhaupt ohne sofortige Festsetzung einer neuen Tagfahrt ausgesetzt wird.

Anders ist es jedoch, wenn das Gericht sofort Tagfahrt zur weiteren Verhandlung anberaumt; denn in diesem Fall gilt die Verkündigung des Richters, welche in Gegenwart der Parteien erfolgt, gleich einer Ladung.

Es läßt sich dies schon aus allgemeinen Prinzipien folgern, da nirgends bestimmt ist, es müsse eine Tagfahrt durch besonderen Zustellungsakt zur Kunde des Gegners gebracht werden, wenn sie Geltung haben solle. Selbst für den Fall, wo der Beklagte bei der Vertagung nicht zugegen war, folgt eigentlich aus den allgemeinen Prinzipien, daß eine Ladung desselben nicht nöthig sei, denn der Versäumungsfall, und hiermit die Zulässigkeit des Versäumungsurtheils ist durch das Ausbleiben bei der ersten Tagfahrt begründet, und die Sache wird bloß vertagt, um in der Eigenschaft einer Contumazialsache später verhandelt zu werden. Bemerk. zu Art. 252 Nr. 3.

Art. 508 verfügt daher im Grunde nur etwas was selbstverständlich ist, und es ist wichtig, dies hervorzuheben, da die getroffene Bestimmung in sofern unvollkommen erscheint, als sie bloß von der Vorladung des Beklagten spricht, obgleich für die Vorladung des Klägers das nemliche zu gelten hat. Auch der Kläger befindet sich nemlich im Versäumungsfalle, wenn er in der in seiner Gegenwart zur Verhandlung bestimmten Sitzung nicht erscheint.

3) Wenn Ladungen stattzufinden haben, was im Beweisverfahren nicht selten der Fall ist, so geschehen sie entweder an die Partei selbst oder an deren Zustellungsbevollmächtigten.

Vielleicht wäre es zweckmäßig gewesen anzuordnen, daß in Fällen, wo nicht sofort bei der ersten Verhandlung endlich entschieden werden kann, wo also ein Zwischenbescheid ergeht, die Parteien Zustellungsbevollmächtigte am Gerichtssitze zu wählen haben, widrigenfalls die Zustellungen an den Gerichtsschreiber des Prozeßgerichts zu geschehen hätten, wie dies der Code de proc. Art. 422 für Handelssachen verfügte und auch der Entwurf (Art. 472) bestimmte. Setzt man den Fall, daß die Partei aus einer größeren Zahl von Personen, z. B. Erben, besteht, welche an verschiedenen Orten in weiter Entfernung wohnen, so macht die persönliche Zustellung der Beweisurtheile (Art. 331), Tagfahrtsbestimmungen (Art. 338), Zeugenkundgaben (Art. 412) ꝛc. das Verfahren sehr umständlich und kostspielig, was sicher der Natur des Parteiprozesses keineswegs entspricht.

Obgleich das Gesetz es nicht nöthig gefunden hat, die Aufstellung von Zustellungsbevollmächtigten zur Zwangspflicht zu machen, so wird es doch den Parteien im eigenen Interesse anzurathen sein, daß sie, wo Anlaß dazu gegeben ist, freiwillig solche Bevollmächtigte bestellen. Sind die Parteien durch Prozeßbevollmächtigte vertreten, so ist es sachgemäß, daß diese sich zugleich die Eigenschaft von Zustellungsbevollmächtigten geben lassen, welche in der Prozeßvollmacht an sich nicht enthalten ist (Abg. I 262, 263). Auch der Richter wird es nicht unterlassen, bei Erlaß eines Zwischenbescheids den Parteien die Aufstellung von Zustellungsbevollmächtigten anzurathen. Erfolgt diese Bestellung vor ihm, so ertheilt er darüber Urkunde.

Daß der Prozeßbevollmächtigte kraft seiner Prozeßvollmacht einen Zustellungsbevollmächtigten bestelle — für die Partei Wohnsitz erwähle, um mit dem Code de proc. zu sprechen — möchte nicht mehr angehen, da nach der Prozeßordnung die Partei ein Recht hat auf persönliche Zustellung und der Verzicht auf dieses Recht die Grenzen der Prozeßvollmacht überschreitet.

Gut wäre es vielleicht gewesen, zu bestimmen, daß wo im Gerichtsbezirke wohnhafte Prozeßbevollmächtigte aufgestellt sind, alle Zustellungen, mit Ausnahme der Endurtheile, giltig an diese gemacht werden können.

4) Was die Vertagungen im Allgemeinen betrifft, so fand der Gesetzgeber nicht für nöthig, dem Richter besondere Weisungen zu geben, wie sie für den Anwaltsprozeß bestehen; er hielt die allgemeinen Grundsätze für ausreichend, welche durch die Art. 212 und 213 gegeben sind. Abg. II 260 (zu Art. 507 g). Hiernach hat der Richter im Parteiprozesse volle Freiheit, aus erheblichen Gründen eine Vertagung zu verfügen, und auch die Parteien sind befugt, sich Vertagung zu bewilligen, sogar ohne jede Beschränkung, da Art. 249 hier nicht gilt.

Die Festsetzung des Sitzungstages zur weiteren Verhandlung ist übrigens Sache des Richters.

Art. 509. — **Will der Beklagte einen Dritten in den Streit ziehen, so kann er ihn sofort nach Zustellung der Klage in die nämliche Sitzung, in welche er selbst geladen ist, beiladen lassen, soferne dies noch rechtzeitig (Art. 502) geschehen kann. Hat die Beiladung nicht in solcher Weise stattgefunden oder will der Kläger in Folge des Vorbringens des Beklagten einen Dritten in den Streit ziehen, so vertagt das Gericht, falls es die Beiladung nicht für augenscheinlich zwecklos erachtet, die Verhandlung der Sache in eine spätere Sitzung.**

Die Beiladung erfolgt in der in Art. 501 Abs. 1 angegebenen Weise unter Zustellung einer Abschrift der Klage.

Art. 510. — **Will während des Rechtsstreits eine Partei gegen die andere ein damit im Zusammenhange stehendes Begehren oder eine Widerklage erheben oder will ein Dritter in den Streit eintreten, so kann dies durch mündliche Erklärung bei der Verhandlung geschehen. Der Partei ist jedoch unbenommen, ihre Erklärung auch schon zuvor der Gegenpartei durch Gerichtsvollzieherakt zustellen zu lassen.**

Bei Zwischenstreiten kommen bezüglich der weitern Verhandlung die Bestimmungen der Art. 484—486 zur Anwendung.

Art. 511. — **Im Verfahren vor den Einzelngerichten hat im Falle des Art. 11 oder Art. 31 Abs. 4 das Gericht, wenn nicht seine Zuständigkeit durch Vereinbarung begründet wird, die Sache vor das Collegialgericht zu verweisen und diesem auch die Entscheidung über die bisher erlaufenen Kosten vorzubehalten. Gegen dieses Urtheil ist kein Rechtsmittel zulässig. Das Collegialgericht bleibt zuständig, auch wenn die Widerklage oder das Rechtsverhältniß, welches die Verweisung veranlaßte, nachher nicht mehr geltend gemacht wird.**

G. A. d. K. d. A. II S. 260—263. 277. 296. 352. IV S. 103. — K. d. R. II S. 252. IV S. 61.

1) Was die Berechtigung zur Beiladung dritter Personen in den Prozeß, sowie zur Intervention, zur Erhebung von Widerklagen und Zwischenstreiten betrifft, so gelten natürlich für den Parteiprozeß keine anderen Grundsätze, als für den Anwaltsprozeß; das Verfahren jedoch ist abweichend.

a) Beiladung.

2) Wenn im Parteiprozesse die Hauptladung sofort zur Verhandlung in der Sitzung gegeben wird, so muß auch die Beiladung in der nemlichen Weise erfolgen.

Ist es der Beklagte, welcher beizuladen hat, z. B. auf Gewährschaft, so läßt derselbe den Gewährschaftspflichtigen sofort in die nemliche Sitzung laden, in welche er selbst geladen ist. Reicht die ihm gegönnte Zeit dazu aus, so hält er die gewöhnliche Ladungsfrist (Art. 502) ein; wenn nicht, so erwirkt er sich die Erlaubniß, auf kurze Frist zu laden (Art. 503). In gleicher Weise verhält es sich mit etwaigen Untergewährschaftsklagen.

3) Hat die Beiladung nicht sofort stattgefunden, so erbittet sich der Beklagte bei der Verhandlung die entsprechende Frist durch Vertagung der Verhandlung, und der Richter ist verpflichtet, dem bezüglichen Ansuchen zu willfahren, falls er die Beiladung nicht für augenscheinlich zwecklos erachtet. Durch letztere Worte gibt das Gesetz dem Richter die Macht, frivole nur auf Prozeßverzögerung abzielende Vertagungsbegehren zurückzuweisen, was allerdings unter Umständen auch zu einer Beschränkung des durch Art. 70 gegebenen Rechts der Beiladung eines Gewährschaftspflichtigen führen kann.

Man könnte fragen, ob der Richter das Vertagungsbegehren nicht auch dann zurückweisen dürfe, wenn der Beklagte die zur Beiladung nöthige Frist gehabt hätte, diese Frist aber von ihm schuldhaft versäumt worden ist? — Die Fassung des Gesetzes möchte dies nicht erlauben, vielmehr zur Annahme führen, daß der Richter die nöthige Frist gestatten müsse, wenn sie bei der ersten Verhandlung begehrt wird und die Beiladung nicht augenscheinlich zwecklos ist.

4) Das Gleiche gilt, wenn der Kläger in Folge Vorbringens des Beklagten beiladen will, z. B. wenn der klagende Cessionar, auf Bestreitung der Forderung hin, den Cedenten als gewährschaftspflichtig belangt; überhaupt in allen Fällen, wo der Anlaß zur Beiladung sich erst später ergibt, was auch auf Seite des Beklagten der Fall sein kann. Vgl. Bemerk. zu Art. 233 Nr. 14. Das Gesetz drückt sich daher in Art. 509 etwas zu eng aus.

5) Die Beiladung erfolgt in der für gewöhnliche Ladungen (Art. 501) vorgeschriebenen Weise. Vgl. Art. 487.

Wenn das Gesetz vorschreibt: „unter Zustellung einer Abschrift der Klage", so erscheint eine solche bestimmte Vorschrift hier um so sachgemäßer, als die Beiladungen nicht, wie im Anwaltsprozesse, durch Anwälte besorgt werden müssen. Vgl. Bemerk. zu Art. 65 Nr. 8 und Art. 69—72 Nr. 11.

Will der auf Gewährschaft Beigeladene eine Untergewährschaftsklage erheben, so hat er, um der Vorschrift des Art. 509 zu genügen, nicht bloß die Gewährschaftsklage, sondern auch die Hauptklage abschriftlich zuzustellen, denn seine Beiladung ist durch diese beiden Klagen veranlaßt.

Ist die Beiladung nicht durch eine Klage, sondern durch ein Vorbringen bei der Verhandlung (durch Klagbestreitung, Einrede, Replik) veranlaßt worden, so findet vorliegende Bestimmung zwar keine Anwendung, jedoch ist selbstverständlich, daß dieser Anlaß als zur Klagebegründung gehörig kundzugeben ist. Es gilt für diesen Fall, was zu Art. 487 Nr. 2 bemerkt wurde.

b) Interventionen und Zwischenstreite.

6) Was im Anwaltsprozesse durch Zustellung eines Anwaltsaktes geschieht, das darf im Parteiprozesse durch mündliche Erklärung in der Sitzung geschehen, also ist es natürlich, daß alle Zwischenstreite, insbesondere auch Widerklagen, in dieser Weise erhoben werden können, und daß es selbst dritten Personen (Intervenienten, besonderen Rechtsnachfolgern [Art. 493]) freisteht, durch eine einfache mündliche Erklärung in den Rechtsstreit einzutreten. Nicht einmal die Hauptintervention macht eine Ausnahme, insbesondere steht hier die Vorschrift in Art. 67, daß diese Intervention als Klage zu behandeln sei, nicht im Wege.

Die Beurkundung erfolgt in solchen Fällen durch das Urtheil, und gilt in dieser Beziehung, was zu Art. 504 Nr. 6 gesagt ist.

Mit Recht fügt das Gesetz bei, daß es der Partei unbenommen sei, ihre Erklärung auch schon vorher durch Gerichtsvollzieherakt zustellen zu lassen. Die Erfahrung zeigt, daß wenn in Folge von Widerklagen, Zusätzen zur Klage, Hauptinterventionen ꝛc. neue Streitpunkte, auf welche der Gegner nicht vorbereitet ist, plötzlich in der Sitzung auftreten, dies fast immer Anlaß gibt zu weitläufigen Erörterungen, zur Vertagung und wiederholten Verhandlung, so daß statt der gehofften Beschleunigung des Verfahrens sich eine Verzögerung desselben ergibt. In der Pfalz war es daher in Handelssachen bis jetzt Uebung, solche Zwischenklagen vorher zuzustellen.

7) Für die fragliche Zustellung ist keine Form vorgeschrieben, und es bedarf einer solchen auch nicht, insofern es sich bloß um eine Vorbereitung der mündlichen Verhandlung, also um etwas, was zwar zweckmäßig jedoch nicht nothwendig ist, handelt; insofern die Zustellung jedoch die Anhängigkeit des betreffenden Streitpunktes mit ihren gesetzlichen Folgen (Art. 179) begründen soll, muß sie allerdings den Anforderungen einer Vorladung (Art. 501) genügen.

Ferner ist zu beachten, daß die mündliche Erklärung eine Zustellung nur ersetzen kann, wenn der Gegner in der Sitzung anwesend oder vertreten ist, daß aber im Falle des Nichterscheinens selbständige Begehren, z. B. bei Klagänderungen, Hauptinterventionen ꝛc., gegen ihn nur erhoben werden dürfen, wenn er deshalb förmlich geladen war und zwar mit Einhaltung der gesetzlichen Erscheinungsfrist. Art. 299 und Art. 485 Abs. 2.

8) Bei Zwischenstreiten (Bemerk. zu Art. 483 Nr. 1 u. 2) kommen bezüglich des weiteren Verfahrens die Bestimmungen der Art. 484 bis 486 zur Anwendung und ist auf das dort Gesagte zu verweisen.

9) Was in Art. 511 verfügt wird, erscheint nur als eine Wiederholung dessen, was schon im allgemeinen Theile bestimmt ist, und genügt es, auf die bezüglichen Bemerkungen zu Art. 11 Nr. 27 — 29 und Art. 31 Nr. 13 u. 14 zu verweisen.

Urtheil.

Art. 512. — **Auf das Urtheil finden bei den Einzelngerichten die Bestimmungen der Art. 262—268, 274, 275 und 277 Abs. 1 und 2, bei den Handelsgerichten außer diesen auch Art. 269—273, 276 und 277 Abs. 3 Anwendung.**

Art. 513. — **An den Handelsgerichten haben bei der Abstimmung vorbehaltlich dessen, was in Art. 272 Abs. 2 bezüglich des Berichterstatters vorgeschrieben ist, die Beisitzer aus dem Handelsstande, vom jüngsten angefangen, ihre Stimmen zuerst abzugeben.**

Ueber das Vorhandensein von Handelsgebräuchen können die Handelsgerichte auf Grund eigener Kenntniß entscheiden. Sie sind aber auch befugt, ein besonderes Beweisverfahren darüber anzuordnen.

Die Urtheile der Handelsgerichte müssen in allen Fällen, wenn die obsiegende Partei es verlangt, als ohne Rücksicht auf Einspruch oder Berufung vorläufig vollstreckbar erklärt werden, doch darf in andern als den in Art. 268 Abs. 1 und 2 bezeichneten Fällen die Vollstreckung nur nach erfolgter Sicherheitsleistung stattfinden.

In Rechnungssachen und sonst in verwickelten Fällen können die Handelsgerichte die Parteien vor Sachverständige verweisen, welche die Parteien zu vernehmen, die Vermittlung zu versuchen und, falls eine solche nicht zu Stande kommt, ein Gutachten abzugeben haben. Ueber die Vernehmung der Parteien müssen die Sachverständigen Protokoll errichten, welches von den Parteien zu unterzeichnen ist. Das Protokoll ist mit dem Gutachten auf der Gerichtsschreiberei zu hinterlegen.

G. A. d. K. d. A. II S. 263. 265. 277. 278. 352. IV S. 103. — K. d. R. II S. 252. IV S. 61.

1) Die Rechte und Pflichten des Richters bei Fällung des Urtheils sind im Parteiprozesse dieselben, wie im Anwaltsprozesse, und auch bezüglich der Form gilt in der Hauptsache dasselbe.

Art. 512 zählt diejenigen Bestimmungen von Hauptst. VII, welche auch im Parteiprozesse gelten, auf. Es gehören dahin insbesondere die Bestimmungen, gemäß deren es dem Richter von Amtswegen zusteht, über die Kosten zu erkennen (Art. 262), ungegründete und unstatthafte Anträge zurückzuweisen (Art. 264), seine Unzuständigkeit, falls sie nicht durch Vereinbarung beseitigt ist, auszusprechen (Art. 265); ferner die Bestimmungen über vorläufige Vollstreckbarkeit der Urtheile (Art. 268), über die Nothwendigkeit von Entscheidungsgründen (Art. 275) und über die Art der Urtheilsverkündung (Art. 277 Abs. 1 und 2).

Für die Anwendung jener allgemeinen Vorschriften ist die Thatsache nicht ohne Belang, daß der Richter in der Regel rechtsunkundige Personen vor sich hat, denen er, soweit es seine amtliche Stellung erlaubt, behilflich sein muß, den richtigen Weg zu finden — selbstverständlich soweit es zugleich der Weg des Rechts und der Wahrheit ist, denn Chikane zu befördern ist der Richter nie verpflichtet. Es wird z. B. der Richter solchen Personen gegenüber, ohne eine auf Befragen abgegebene ausdrückliche Erklärung, nicht annehmen dürfen, daß Einreden ꝛc., deren thatsächliche Grundlage sich aus der Verhandlung ergibt, nicht geltend gemacht werden wollen (Art. 264 Abs. 4), und er wird, in Fällen wo Vereinbarung möglich ist, seine Unzuständigkeit nie von Amtswegen aussprechen, bevor er den Versuch gemacht hat, eine Vereinbarung zu erwirken (Art. 39 u. 265). Auch wird er, falls der Fall zur Verfügung der vorläufigen Vollstreckbarkeit gegeben ist, die obsiegende Partei befragen, ob sie einen bezüglichen Antrag stellen wolle (Art. 268).

2) Für die Urtheile der Handelsgerichte fügt das Gesetz noch jene Vorschriften bei, welche durch deren Eigenschaft als Collegialgerichte bedingt sind, nemlich die Vorschriften in Art. 269 bis 273, 276 u. 277 Abs. 3, und gibt ferner in Art. 513 Ausnahmsbestimmungen mit Rücksicht auf die Zusammensetzung der Handelsgerichte und die Natur der Handelssachen.

Nach der ersten dieser Ausnahmsbestimmungen sollen die Beisitzer aus dem Handelsstande zuerst abstimmen, was, abgesehen von dem jetzt geltenden Prinzipe, diejenigen Richter, welche vermuthbar das selbständigste Urtheil haben, zuletzt stimmen zu lassen, seine Rechtfertigung namentlich darin findet, daß die beisitzenden Kaufleute mit ihrer Eigenschaft als stimmberechtigte Richter auch noch die Eigenschaft von Sachverständigen vereinigen.

3) Weiter ist bestimmt, daß über das Vorhandensein von Handelsgebräuchen die Handelsgerichte auf Grund eigener Kenntniß entscheiden dürfen.

Die Tragweite dieser Ausnahme ist nicht groß, denn soweit die Handelsgebräuche als Gewohnheitsrecht sich auffassen lassen, versteht es sich von selbst, daß der Richter nicht gehemmt sei, sie anzuwenden (Bemerk. zu Art. 321 Nr. 3); soweit es sich aber um Uebungen handelt, welche für die Auslegung von Verträgen, für die Annahme einer Verschuldung ꝛc. von Erheblichkeit sind, wird in der Regel die Bestimmung von Art. 320 Platz greifen, gemäß welcher dasjenige, was gemein-, gerichts- oder ortskundig ist, keines Beweises bedarf.

Insofern nun aber die fragliche Bestimmung wirklich eine Ausnahme enthält, beschränkt sich diese nach Wortlaut und Geist des Gesetzes auf die Handelsgerichte, läßt sich also nicht auf Fälle ausdehnen, wo Bezirksgerichte oder Einzelnrichter in die Lage kommen, über Handelssachen zu erkennen.

4) Eine dritte Ausnahmsbestimmung geht dahin, daß alle Urtheile der Handelsgerichte vorläufig vollstreckbar erklärt werden müssen, wenn der obsiegende Theil es verlangt. Die vorläufige Vollstreckung soll jedoch immer nur gegen Sicherheitsleistung stattfinden, mit Ausnahme der Fälle des Art. 268 Abs. 1 u. 2, nemlich bei Urtheilen, welche auf ausdrückliches Anerkenntniß oder welche auf Grund öffentlicher Urkunden oder anerkannter Privaturkunden erfolgen, und bei welchen eine Sicherheitsleistung entweder gar nicht eintritt oder deren Anordnung vom Ermessen des Richters abhängt.

Diese Bestimmung hat ebenso wie Art. 268 nur die Vollstreckung von Endurtheilen im Auge, jene Vollstreckung, welche sich der in Art. 856 bis 865 bezeichneten Mittel bedient, nicht aber den Vollzug von Zwischenbescheiden. Es dürfte daher aus derselben z. B. nicht gefolgert werden, daß auf ein handelsgerichtliches Urtheil, welches die Entscheidung von einer Eidesleistung abhängig macht, die Vorschriften der Art. 463 Abs. 1 und Art. 699 nicht anwendbar seien.

Auch die hier in Frage stehende Ausnahme beschränkt sich auf die Urtheile der Handelsgerichte und läßt sich nicht ausdehnen auf Urtheile anderer Gerichte in Handelssachen. Durch die Vereinbarung auf ein Bezirksgericht oder Landgericht verzichtet also der Kläger auf den betreffenden Vortheil.

Verweisung vor Sachverständige.

5) Durch eine vierte Ausnahmsbestimmung endlich wird den Handelsgerichten erlaubt, in verwickelten Fällen die Parteien vor Sachverständige zu verweisen, welche die Parteien zu vernehmen, die Vermittlung zu versuchen und, falls eine solche nicht zu Stande kommt, ein Gutachten abzugeben haben. Es ist dies fast wörtlich dasselbe, was der Code de proc. in Art. 429 verfügt, wo gesagt ist: »il sera nommé un ou trois arbitres, pour entendre les parties et les concilier, si faire se peut, sinon donner leur avis.«

Dieselben Personen, welche der Code de proc. unpassender Weise als »arbitres« (Schiedsrichter) bezeichnet, nennt unsere Prozeßordnung richtiger „Sachverständige", jedoch erscheint auch diese Bezeichnung nicht völlig entsprechend, insofern es sich hier nicht von Funktionen gewöhnlicher Sachverständigen im Sinne von Hauptst. XIII handelt.

6) Ueber die Frage, ob die Vorschriften dieses Hauptstückes auch hier zur Anwendung zu kommen haben, finden sich in den Verhandlungen zwei ganz entgegengesetzte Aussprüche. Während nemlich zuerst (Abg. II 278) als selbstverständlich erklärt wird, daß die allgemeinen Bestimmungen über Sachverständige auch hier Anwendung finden, wird später (Abg. IV 103 Sp. 2) gesagt, es verstehe sich von selbst, daß jene Bestimmungen nicht anzuwenden seien, und beigefügt, es sei übrigens unnöthig, etwas Näheres zu bestimmen, indem das einzuhaltende Verfahren aus der Natur der Sache sich ergebe.

Offenbar ist dieser letztere Ausspruch der maßgebende.

7) Nach Wortlaut und Zweck des Gesetzes werden die Sachverständigen durch das Handelsgericht zu ernennen sein und zwar in derjenigen Zahl, welche dem Gerichte sachgemäß erscheint. Die Wahl der Parteien, welche der Code de proc. entscheiden läßt, käme somit nur als Bestimmungsgrund für den Richter in Betracht.

Eine Beeidigung der Sachverständigen, sowie eine Einweisung derselben in ihr Geschäft findet nicht statt und ebensowenig wird ein Richter mit dem Vollzuge des Urtheils beauftragt. Abg. IV 103 Sp. 2 (v. Weiß).

Der fleißigere Theil läßt das Urtheil ausfertigen und setzt unter Vorlage desselben die Sachverständigen in Kenntniß von dem ihnen gewordenen Auftrage, veranlaßt sofort, daß eine Tagfahrt zur Verhandlung bestimmt werde und daß der Gegner bei derselben erscheine, Letzteres indem er sich gütlich mit ihm verständigt oder indem er ihm durch den Gerichtsvollzieher eine Aufforderung zustellen läßt.

Vor den Sachverständigen wird verfahren, wie diese es zur Aufklärung der Sache für dienlich erachten und anordnen.

Ihre Aufgabe besteht darin, durch Vernehmung der Parteien und Einsicht der von diesen vorzulegenden Bücher, Rechnungen und sonstiger urkundlichen Behelfe Klarheit in die Sachlage zu bringen, festzustellen, was strittig sei, was nicht, dabei dahin zu wirken, daß sich die Parteien soviel als möglich einigen, und schließlich über diejenigen Punkte, welche strittig bleiben, sich gutachtlich zu äußern.

Dieses Gutachten soll natürlich nur ein thatsächliches sein, und es wird den Sachverständigen nicht zugemuthet, Rechtsfragen zu erörtern. Sie sollen sich z. B. darüber aussprechen, ob nach Maßgabe ihrer Ermittlungen die Behauptungen der einen oder der andern Partei als wahr oder wahrscheinlich zu betrachten seien, ob in gewissen Vorgängen nach kaufmännischer Auffassung und nach der gegebenen Sachlage eine Verschuldung liege, welche Entschädigung unter gewissen Umständen sachentsprechend sei 2c. — alles unter Angabe der Gründe.

8) Ueber die Vernehmung der Parteien haben die Sachverständigen Protokoll zu errichten, welches von den Parteien zu unterzeichnen ist und welchem sodann das Gutachten angefügt wird.

Es frägt sich, welche Beweiskraft ein solches Protokoll habe.

Die französische Jurisprudenz (Chauv. sur C. quest. 1223 — cass. 14. Jan. 1836) nimmt allgemein an, daß den Berichten von Experten die Beweiskraft öffentlicher Urkunden zukomme bezüglich alles dessen, was die Experten in Vollzug der nach Gesetz und Urtheil ihnen obliegenden Mission beurkunden. Wenn das Gesetz — so folgert man — von den Sachverständigen Beurkundung gewisser Thatsachen verlangt, wenn es ihnen zugleich die Abfassung ihres Berichtes in ganz selbständiger Weise überläßt, so muß es auch sein Wille sein, ihnen im Umfange dieser Thätigkeit öffentlichen Glauben zu verleihen.

Diese Ansicht hat offenbar in gewisser Richtung ihre volle Berechtigung. Insofern es sich nemlich um den Nachweis handelt, daß bei einer Expertise die gesetzlichen Vorschriften beobachtet worden seien, muß das Protokoll der Sachverständigen zum vollen Beweis genügen, und es kann nicht noch ein ergänzender Beweis darüber verlangt werden, daß dies oder jenes, was die Sachverständigen bekunden, auch wirklich geschehen sei. Ebenso beweist das Protokoll der Experten seine Aechtheit selbst.

9) Stellt man nun die Frage, ob insbesondere dasjenige, was in einem nach Maßgabe des Art. 513 Abs. 4 aufgenommenen Protokolle über die Erklärungen der Parteien, über Geständnisse, Anerkennungen, Verzichte derselben angeführt ist, als vollbewiesen zu gelten habe, so ist man vorstehenden Erwägungen folgend geneigt, dies zu bejahen und zwar im Hinblicke darauf, daß solche Protokolle ja gerade die Beurkundung von Parteierklärungen zum Zwecke haben.

Beachtet man nun aber weiter, daß nach den Verhandlungen die Unterschrift der Parteien nur deßhalb vorgeschrieben wurde, weil man die Constatirung von Geständnissen den Sachverständigen nicht allein überlassen wollte (Abg. II 278 Sp. 1 [v. Weiß]), so möchte die Annahme sich rechtfertigen, daß nach dem Willen des Gesetzes nur solche Erklärungen als vollbewiesen zu gelten haben, welche die Unterschrift der erklärenden Partei tragen. Die Aechtheit dieser Unterschrift wird durch das Protokoll erwiesen.

Die Folge dieser Ansicht ist, daß in Fällen, wo die Partei nicht unterzeichnen kann oder will, das Protokoll ihr gegenüber nicht vollbeweisend ist, was jedoch nicht hindert, daß es als ein der richterlichen Würdigung überlassener Beweisbehelf gelte.

Geständnisse vor den Sachverständigen sind als gerichtliche zu betrachten, da sie während des Prozesses, in einem prozessualen Verfahren gemacht sind.

Was den Abschluß von Vergleichen betrifft, so sind hierüber die allgemeinen Bestimmungen maßgebend. S. die Aeußerungen des Minist.-Commissärs Abg. II 265 Sp. 1 u. II 278 Sp. 1.

10) Erscheint die eine Partei bei der zur Verhandlung anberaumten Tagfahrt trotz förmlicher Aufforderung nicht und wird es nicht für geeignet befunden, eine weitere Tagfahrt anzuberaumen, so errichten die Sachverständigen nichtsdestoweniger Protokoll, in welchem sie das Nichterscheinen beurkunden. Dem Gerichte steht es dann frei, aus dieser Thatsache die sachgemäßen Folgerungen zu ziehen. Abg. II 278 Sp. 2 (v. Weiß). Sind mehrere im Streite befangenen Parteien erschienen, so schreiten die Sachverständigen zur Verhandlung, mag auch eine weitere Partei ausge-

blieben sein; ihr Mandat erscheint durch dieses Ausbleiben nicht gegenstandslos geworden.

11) Die Verweisung vor Sachverständige ist erfahrungsgemäß eine Maßregel von großem praktischem Werthe. Wenn bei den Verhandlungen (Abg. II 278) geäußert wurde, in der Pfalz kämen solche Verweisungen nicht häufig vor, so mag dies für ein einzelnes Gericht richtig sein, nach meinen Erfahrungen aber wird davon sehr häufig Gebrauch gemacht und zwar mit bestem Erfolge.

Art. 514. — Das Urtheil soll bei den Handels- und Einzelngerichten in der Regel sogleich nach der Verhandlung erlassen und verkündet werden.

Bietet die Beurtheilung der Sache besondere Schwierigkeiten dar, so kann das Gericht die Verkündung des Urtheils auf eine spätere Stunde des nämlichen Tags oder in eine der nächsten Sitzungen verlagen. Die in Bezug genommenen Urkunden und die etwa vorhandenen sonstigen Parteiakten sind in solchen Fällen dem Richter zu übergeben.

Art. 515. — Die vollständige Abfassung des Urtheils hat bei den Handels- und Einzelngerichten, wenn die Verkündung auf einen späteren Sitzungstag verschoben wurde, vor der Verkündung, in andern Fällen spätestens drei Tage danach zu geschehen. Die Handelsgerichte haben hiebei dasjenige, was in Art. 278 Abs. 2 für die Abfassung der Entscheidungsgründe vorgeschrieben ist, bezüglich der Abfassung des ganzen Urtheils zu beobachten.

Das vollständig abgefaßte Urtheil muß enthalten:

1) die Bezeichnung des Gerichts, der Parteien, ihrer Bevollmächtigten oder Beistände und des Streitgegenstands;
2) den Urtheilssatz;
3) eine gedrängte Darstellung des Sachverhalts, sowie die Gesuche der Parteien;
4) die Entscheidungsgründe;
5) den Tag der Urtheilsverkündung;
6) bei den Handelsgerichten die Namen der Richter und des Gerichtsschreibers, welche bei der Verkündung anwesend waren, falls aber die Anwesenheit aller Richter, die zu dem Urtheile mitgewirkt haben, nicht möglich war, auch die Namen der abwesenden und den Grund der Abwesenheit, bei den Einzelngerichten den Namen des Richters und des Gerichtsschreibers.

Art. 516. — Das Urtheil wird in das bei jedem Handels- und Einzelngerichte und, wenn bei einem Gerichte mehrere Abtheilungen bestehen, bei jeder Abtheilung zu führende Urtheilsbuch durch den Gerichtsschreiber unter analoger Anwendung der Bestimmungen des Art. 280 Abs. 1—4 eingetragen.

Der Eintrag wird im Urtheilsbuche bei den Einzelngerichten von dem Einzelnrichter und dem bei der Verkündung anwesenden Gerichtsschreiber, bei den Handelsgerichten in der in Art. 280 Abs. 5 und 6 bestimmten Weise unterzeichnet.

Die Vorschriften des Art. 281 finden auch bei den Handels- und Einzelngerichten Anwendung.

Art. 517. — Hinsichtlich der Abänderung von Urtheilen kommen die Bestimmungen der Art. 282 bis 284 mit nachfolgenden Abweichungen zur Anwendung:

1) das Begehren auf Abänderung ist durch einen der Gegenpartei zuzustellenden Gerichtsvollzieherakt zu stellen, welcher die Punkte, bezüglich deren Abänderung verlangt wird, bezeichnen und Vorladung in eine bestimmte Sitzung unter Beobachtung der Bestimmungen des Art. 502 enthalten muß;
2) die Parteien können jedoch auch ohne Ladung in der Sitzung erscheinen und das Abänderungsbegehren mündlich stellen;
3) das Verfahren über das Abänderungsbegehren richtet sich nach den Bestimmungen des gegenwärtigen Hauptstücks.

Art. 518. — Hinsichtlich der Ausfertigung kommen bei den Handels- und Einzelngerichten die Art. 288—293 mit folgenden besondern Bestimmungen zur Anwendung:

1) auch die Bezeichnung der Parteien und ihrer Vertreter, der Sachverhalt und die gestellten Gesuche sind nach dem Eintrage im Urtheilsbuche in die Ausfertigung einzurücken, und zwar müssen, wenn bei Bezeichnung einer Partei in Gemäßheit des Art. 280 Abs. 4 eine Hinweisung auf einen frühern Eintrag stattgefunden

hat, in der Ausfertigung sämmtliche bei dem Rechtsstreite betheiligte Personen auf Grund des früheren Eintrags nach Vor- und Familiennamen, Stand oder Gewerbe, Wohnort und Parteistellung bezeichnet werden;

2) bei den Einzelngerichten steht im Falle des Art. 292 Abs. 1 der betreffenden Partei sofort das Rechtsmittel der Beschwerde zu.

Art. 519. — **Die Wirksamkeit der Urtheile richtet sich auch bei den Handels- und Einzelngerichten nach den Bestimmungen der Art. 294—296.**

G. A. d. K. d. A. II S. 263. 264. 277. 278. 352. 453. VI S. 103—107. K. d. R. II S. 252—254. IV S. 61.

1) Urtheilsspruch.

Während das Gesetz im Anwaltsprozesse es ganz dem richterlichen Ermessen anheimstellt, das Urtheil sofort zu sprechen, oder den Spruch zu vertagen, stellt es im Parteiprozesse, mit Rücksicht auf die zu vermuthende Dringlichkeit oder Einfachheit, Ersteres als Regel auf und bestimmt, daß Vertagung zum Spruche nur eintreten solle, wenn die Sache besondere Schwierigkeiten biete. Die Zweckmäßigkeit der Vertagung ergibt sich in Handelssachen besonders dann, wenn eine Correspondenz oder überhaupt eine größere Zahl von Urkunden zu würdigen ist, denn es macht einen großen Unterschied, ob man nach eigener Einsichtnahme Sinn und Zusammenhang der Urkunden ruhig und unbefangen erwägt, oder ob man bloß anhört, wie die Parteien, jede im Sinne ihres Interesse, den Inhalt drehen und deuten.

Wenn gesagt ist, es könne auch auf eine spätere Stunde vertagt werden, so hätte sich dies wohl von selbst verstanden, wie es sich denn auch für den Anwaltsprozeß von selbst versteht, obgleich Art. 269 nichts davon sagt.

Ebenso ist es selbstverständlich, daß alle Urkunden und Akten, auf welche sich die Parteien in ihren Vorträgen beziehen, dem Richter auf Verlangen vorzulegen sind und daß dieser sie nicht eher wieder aus der Hand zu geben braucht, als bis er sein Urtheil gesprochen hat. Es gilt dies daher nicht bloß für den Fall, wo förmlich zum Spruche vertagt wird, sondern auch für den Fall, wo das Gericht sich bloß in sein Berathungszimmer zurückzieht, um das Urtheil sofort zu schöpfen und zu sprechen.

2) Urtheilsabfassung.

Die vollständige Abfassung des Urtheils, namentlich auch der Entscheidungsgründe, erfolgt in Fällen, wo das Urtheil am nemlichen Tage gesprochen wird, nach dem Spruche und zwar innerhalb einer Frist von drei Tagen; in Fällen aber, wo der Urtheilsspruch an einem späteren Sitzungstage erfolgt, vor dem Spruche. Wird also nur auf eine andere Stunde des nemlichen Tages vertagt, so ist eine vorausgängige Abfassung nicht nöthig.

Im Parteiprozesse ist die Abfassung des ganzen Urtheils das Werk des Richters, wie es eigentlich naturgemäß ist; der Richter hat also nicht bloß für Abfassung von Urtheilsatz und Entscheidungsgründen zu sorgen, sondern auch für die richtige Bezeichnung der Parteien, für Sachverhalt und Gesuche. Dieser ganze Inhalt ist in der Art, wie es Art. 278 Abs. 2 vorschreibt, im handelsgerichtlichen Verfahren der Genehmigung sämmtlicher Richter, welche zum Urtheile mitgewirkt haben, zu unterstellen. Die Verkündigung erstreckt sich natürlich immer nur auf Urtheilssatz und Entscheidungsgründe.

3) Was die einzelnen Bestandtheile des Urtheils anbelangt, so wäre die Bezeichnung des Streitgegenstandes wohl nicht nöthig gewesen. Sie erscheint als Reminiscenz aus dem alten Prozesse, wo die Aufstellung und Festhaltung eines „Betreffs" der Registratur wegen nicht entbehrt werden konnte. Vgl. Bemerk. zu Art. 165 Nr. 3 u. 4. Für den Anwaltsprozeß ist diese Form nicht vorgeschrieben (Art. 285 u. 289) und auch bei der Ausfertigung von Urtheilen im Parteiprozesse (Art. 518) fand man nicht nöthig, ihrer zu erwähnen.

Auch die Bezeichnung des Gerichts bei jedem Urtheilseintrage erscheint unnöthig; sie gehört nur in die Urtheilsausfertigung.

Wie in Art. 285 wird eine gedrängte Darstellung des Sachverhalts verlangt, und was dort erläuternd beigefügt wird, läßt sich auch hier anwenden. Wegen des Inhaltes des Sachverhaltes s. Bemerk. zu Art. 285 Nr. 4—8. Die Anführung der gestellten Gesuche bildet eigentlich hier einen Theil des Sachverhaltes, und es geschah bloß, um die Wichtigkeit derselben hervorzuheben, daß man ihrer besonders erwähnte. Wegen der Beweiskraft des Sachverhaltes s. Bemerk. zu Art. 285 Nr. 9—11.

Wenn schließlich, im Einklange mit Art. 280 Abs. 2, der Fall vorgesehen ist, wo nicht alle Richter bei der Urtheilsverkündung anwesend seien, so geschieht dies im Hinblicke auf Art. 277 Abs. 3, wo für den Tod oder die Erkrankung einzelner Richter eine Ausnahme gemacht ist. Eine

Ersetzung des Einzelnrichters beim Urtheilsspruche ist nicht statthaft.

4) Urtheilseintrag.

Auch bei den Handelsgerichten und Einzelngerichten bestehen Urtheilsbücher, bestimmt, die in der Sitzung gesprochenen Urtheile aufzunehmen (Bemerk. zu Art. 280 Nr. 1 u. 2).

Für den Eintrag sollen die Vorschriften in Art. 280 Abs. 1—4 gelten, jedoch nur analog, weil im Parteiprozesse nicht bloß jene Theile des Urtheils einzutragen sind, welche in Art. 280 aufgezählt werden, sondern der Eintrag das ganze Urtheil umfaßt, allerdings nicht ganz in der Form, wie es in der Ausfertigung erscheint.

Die Bezeichnung der Gerichtsmitglieder erfolgt demnach bloß am Rande, und genügt es, bei späteren Einträgen darauf Bezug zu nehmen (Abs. 3).

Der Tag der Urtheilsverkündung bildet die Ueberschrift (Abs. 2).

Was die Bezeichnung des Gerichts betrifft, so liegt es wohl nicht im Willen des Gesetzes, daß dieselbe bei jedem Urtheilseintrage vollständig wiederholt werde.

Das eingetragene Urtheil wird bloß vom Vorsitzenden und vom Gerichtsschreiber unterzeichnet (Bemerk. zu Art. 280 Nr. 5).

Auch die Bestimmungen des Art. 281 über die Form des Eintrags von Vertagungs- und ähnlichen Urtheilen sind für den Parteiprozeß anwendbar erklärt (Bemerk. zu Art. 281 Nr. 6).

5) Urtheilsänderungen.

Was die Abänderung von Urtheilen wegen klarer Versehen, übergangener Streitpunkte und Unklarheit der Entscheidung betrifft, so gelten die nemlichen Grundsätze, wie sie in Art. 282—284 für den Anwaltsprozeß gegeben sind, und werden nur einige durch die Natur des Parteiprozesses bedingte Abweichungen beigefügt.

Demgemäß ist das Begehren, statt durch Anwaltsakt, durch Akt des Gerichtsvollziehers zu erheben und zwar unter Bezeichnung der zu ändernden Punkte und unter Vorladung mit Einhaltung der in Art. 502 bezeichneten Frist. Von einer Begründung des Gesuches spricht das Gesetz nicht, doch ist es rathsam, eine solche nicht zu unterlassen, namentlich dann nicht, wenn es sich um Interpretation eines unklaren Urtheils handelt.

Daß die Parteien auch ohne Ladung erscheinen können, liegt in der Natur des Parteiprozesses.

Als eine Eigenthümlichkeit ist hervorzuheben, daß im Parteiprozesse auch Irrthümer im Sachverhalte, wenn sie von der in Art. 282 Abs. 1 bezeichneten Art sind, auf dem in Frage stehenden Wege berichtigt werden, während im Anwaltsprozesse in dieser Beziehung Art. 286 maßgebend ist. Wegen Unrichtigkeit der Beurkundung kann der richterlich festgesetzte Sachverhalt auf diesem Wege nicht angefochten werden.

6) Urtheilsausfertigung.

Was die Ausfertigung der Urtheile im Parteiprozesse betrifft, so sind die Vorschriften der Art. 288—293 für maßgebend erklärt und gelten die Bemerkungen zu jenen Artikeln.

Die Zusätze, welche das Gesetz macht, sind durch die Natur des Parteiprozesses bedingt. Hervorzuheben ist, daß auch im Falle, wo die Beschwerde wegen Verweigerung einer Ausfertigung gegen den Gerichtsschreiber gerichtet ist, dieselbe sofort an das höhere Gericht sich wendet, also nicht verlangt wird, daß vorher der Einzelnrichter angegangen werde. Der kgl. Minist.-Commissär sprach dabei seine Ansicht aus, daß nichts im Wege stehe, freiwillig sich an den Landrichter um Abhilfe zu wenden, und daß dieser die Befugniß habe, dem Gerichtsschreiber entsprechenden Auftrag zu geben.

7) Wirkung der Urtheile.

Was die Wirksamkeit der Urtheile betrifft, so ist einfach Bezug zu nehmen auf die Bemerkungen zu Art. 294—296.

Versäumungsurtheil.

Art. 520. — **Erscheint im Verfahren vor den Handels- und Einzelngerichten in der Sitzung, in welche die Vorladung erfolgte, oder in welche die Sache zur Verhandlung vertagt wurde, der Beklagte nicht, so soll das Gericht auf Antrag des Klägers die in der Klage zur Begründung des klägerischen Anspruchs geltend gemachten Thatsachen als zugestanden betrachten und dem darin gestellten Gesuche unter Verurtheilung des Beklagten in die Kosten entsprechen, wenn die Klage nach den gesetzlichen Vorschriften erhoben, die nach Art. 502 vorgeschriebene Frist eingehalten und das klägerische Begehren nach den geltend gemachten Thatsachen rechtlich begründet ist. Andernfalls ist die Klage unter Verurtheilung des Klägers in die Kosten abzuweisen. Ist die Abweisung erfolgt, weil die Klage nicht nach den gesetzlichen Vorschriften erhoben oder die in Art. 502 vorgeschriebene Frist nicht eingehalten wurde, so ist es dem Kläger unbenommen, sofort neue Klage zu erheben.**

Wenn dem Gerichte Umstände bekannt sind, welche den Beklagten in die Unmöglichkeit, zu erscheinen oder einen Bevollmächtigten aufzustellen, versetzten, oder wenn die auf abgekürzte Frist stattgefundene Vorladung so spät erfolgt ist, daß dem Beklagten das Erscheinen nicht wohl mehr zugemuthet werden konnte, so kann das Gericht die Verhandlung aussetzen und die nochmalige Vorladung des Beklagten anordnen. Es bestimmt dann zugleich die Zeit, welche zwischen der Vorladung und der Sitzung in Mitte liegen muß.

Gegen alle vorgeladenen, aber nicht erschienenen Beklagten ist durch ein und dasselbe Urtheil zu erkennen. Kann das Urtheil wegen mangelhafter Ladung eines ausgebliebenen Beklagten nicht erlassen werden, so ist die Sitzung bezüglich der Erschienenen zu vertagen und dem Kläger die Vorladung des Nichterschienenen in die neue Sitzung aufzugeben.

Art. 521. — Erscheint der Kläger in der zur Verhandlung der Sache bestimmten Sitzung nicht, so ist auf Begehren der Gegenpartei die Abweisung der Klage und die Verurtheilung des Klägers in die Kosten ohne weitere Prüfung der Sache auszusprechen. Der Kläger kann in diesem Falle weder die bisherige Verhandlung durch Einspruch gegen das Versäumungsurtheil fortsetzen, noch über denselben Gegenstand gegen den Beklagten eine neue Klage erheben, ehe er diesem die ihm verursachten Kosten ersetzt hat.

Einspruch.

Art. 522. — Parteien, gegen welche von einem Handels- oder Einzelngerichte ein Versäumungsurtheil erlassen wurde, können innerhalb einer unerstreckbaren Frist von acht Tagen nach Zustellung dieses Urtheils Einspruch dagegen erheben.

Der Einspruch erfolgt mittels eines an die Partei, welche das Versäumungsurtheil erwirkt hat, zuzustellenden Gerichtsvollzieherakts, der neben den allgemeinen Erfordernissen der Zustellungsurkunden enthalten muß:

1) die Bezeichnung des Urtheils, gegen welches Einspruch erhoben wird;
2) die Gründe des Einspruchs und
3) die Vorladung der Gegenpartei in die nächste Gerichtssitzung, jedoch mit Beobachtung der in Art. 502 Abs. 1 bestimmten Frist.

Die Bestimmungen der Art. 310—312, 314 und 315 finden auch hier Anwendung.

G. A. d. K. d. A. II S. 265—270. 279. 352. 453. IV S. 107. 334.
K. d. R. II S. 254. 255. IV S. 61. 62.

1) Der Gesetzgeber fand es nicht sachgemäß, sich bezüglich der Versäumungsurtheile einfach auf das Verfahren im Anwaltsprozesse zu beziehen und auszusprechen, daß die dortigen Bestimmungen analoge Anwendung finden, hielt es vielmehr im Hinblicke auf die Eigenthümlichkeit des Parteiprozesses geeignet, gesonderte Verfügungen zu geben.

a) Versäumungsurtheil gegen den Beklagten (Art. 520).

2) Wenn der Beklagte in der durch die Vorladung bezeichneten Sitzung nicht persönlich oder durch gehörig bevollmächtigten Vertreter erscheint, so ist die Sachlage ganz die nemliche, als wenn im Anwaltsprozesse der Beklagte innerhalb der gesetzlichen Frist oder in derjenigen Sitzung, in welche er auf kurze Frist vorgeladen ist, nicht mittelst Aufstellung eines Anwaltes erscheint.

Ein Unterschied ergibt sich jedoch für den Fall, wo der Beklagte erschienen ist.

Im Anwaltsprozesse ist nemlich in diesem Falle das Stellen von Anträgen entscheidend für die Natur des Verfahrens. Selbst wenn der Anwalt in der Sitzung anwesend ist, jedoch keinen Antrag nimmt oder sich auf einen Vertagungsantrag beschränkt, ist das ergehende Urtheil ein Versäumungsurtheil, während umgekehrt das Stellen von Anträgen die Sache contradiktorisch macht und erhält bis zum Erlasse eines Beweisurtheiles.

Im Parteiprozesse hingegen ist nur das Erscheinen bei der Verhandlung maßgebend, und ist es für die Natur des ergehenden Urtheils ohne Belang, ob und welche Anträge genommen werden. Es geht dies aus der Fassung des Art. 520 klar hervor und ist es um so wichtiger, dies zu betonen, als die französische Jurisprudenz den Unterschied zwischen défaut faute de comparaître und défaut faute de conclure auch in den Parteiprozeß hineintrug (Chauveau sur C. quest. 1546).

Sollte daher der Beklagte, aufgefordert seine Erklärungen zu geben, sich darauf beschränken, die Vertagung zu beantragen, und selbst nach Zurückweisung dieses Antrages keine weiteren Anträge stellen, so wäre nichtsdestoweniger das ergehende Urtheil contradiktorisch.

3) Versäumungsurtheil ergeht, wenn der Beklagte in der Sitzung, in welche er geladen ist,

oder in welche die Sache zur Verhandlung vertagt ist, nicht erscheint.

Eine Vertagung kann eintreten, um eine bereits begonnene Verhandlung an einem späteren Tage fortzusetzen, oder aber um an einem späteren Tage die Verhandlung zu beginnen. Nach dem Willen des Gesetzes ist im ersten Falle das Urtheil contradiktorisch, und zwar aus demselben Grunde, weßhalb contradiktorisches Urtheil ergeht, wenn etwa der Beklagte sich mitten in der Verhandlung entfernt. Nur im letzten Falle ergeht Versäumungsurtheil, und um dies besser hervorzuheben, wurde die ursprüngliche Fassung, welche lautete: „in welche die Verhandlung der Sache vertagt wurde," abgeändert. Vgl. Abg. II 267 (v. Weiß) und R. R. II 254 (v. Bomhard).

Eine Sache ist bloß zur Fortsetzung der Verhandlung vertagt, falls sich beide Parteien bereits ausgesprochen haben, wenn auch noch nicht vollständig, und zur weiteren Verhandlung vor dem nemlichen Richter eine spätere Sitzung anberaumt wird. In diesem Falle bilden die verschiedenen Verhandlungen ein Ganzes (Abg. II 258 Sp. 2), und was die Parteien in denselben vorgebracht haben, wird zusammen im Sachverhalte des ergehenden Urtheils beurkundet.

Sachgemäß ist es, bei jeder Vertagung förmlich auszusprechen, ob sie bloß zur Fortsetzung der Verhandlung oder zur Verhandlung bestimmt werde; jedenfalls muß darüber der Sachverhalt vollkommen Aufschluß geben. Im Zweifel ist Letzteres anzunehmen.

4) Nach dem Wortlaute des Art. 520 Abs. 1 könnte man meinen, es müsse die ganze Sitzungszeit abgewartet werden, bevor ein Versäumungsurtheil gesprochen werden könne, allein dies ist nicht der Sinn des Gesetzes.

Sobald die Stunde, auf welche vorgeladen ist (Art. 501), gekommen, darf Versäumungsurtheil beantragt und gesprochen werden; jedoch wird die Sache contradiktorisch, falls der Beklagte vor der Verkündung des Urtheils erscheint. Was Art. 250 Abs. 4 für den Anwaltsprozeß ausdrücklich verfügt, das folgt für den Parteiprozeß aus Art. 207 Abs. 2, denn die Worte: „vor dem Schlusse der Verhandlung" stehen um so weniger entgegen, als ja das Gericht befugt ist, eine geschlossene Verhandlung wieder zu eröffnen. Jedenfalls ist es der Wille des Gesetzes nicht, daß die Erklärung des Richters, es sei die Verhandlung geschlossen, wie sie z. B. in einer Vertagung zum Spruche liegt, die Möglichkeit abschneide, das Verfahren contradiktorisch zu machen. Vgl. Bemerk. zu Art. 305—308 Nr. 2.

5) Es kann sich fragen, was zu gelten habe, wenn über einen Präjudizialpunkt im Sinne des Art. 256 Urtheil ergangen ist und nun das weitere Verfahren einzutreten hat. Von Seite des Referenten war vorgeschlagen (Abg. II 266), diesen Punkt zu regeln, auf die Bemerkung des k. Minist.-Commissärs jedoch, daß dies im Parteiprozesse nicht nöthig sei (Abg. II 268), unterblieb es.

Man wird unterscheiden müssen.

Wenn nach Abweisung einer bevorzugten Prozeßeinrede oder nach Erledigung einer sonstigen Vorfrage das Gericht anordnet, es solle sofort in der Hauptsache verhandelt werden, wie dies Regel ist, so ist das weiter ergehende Urtheil contradiktorisch, da in der betreffenden Sitzung der Beklagte erschienen war. Hat jedoch das Gericht nach Aburtheilung der Vorfrage eine spätere Sitzung zur Verhandlung der Hauptsache bestimmt und bleibt der Beklagte in dieser Sitzung aus, so ergeht Versäumungsurtheil.

6) Die Folgen des Nichterscheinens sind für den Parteiprozeß ganz die nemlichen, wie für den Anwaltsprozeß, und wenn in Art. 520 theilweise andere Worte gebraucht werden, als in Art. 297, so gehen sie doch auf das Nemliche hinaus. Es kann daher auf die Bemerkungen zu letzterem Artikel Nr. 3—8 verwiesen werden.

Was insbesondere in Art. 520 bezüglich der Kosten gesagt ist, wurde in Art. 297 als sich von selbst verstehend gestrichen. R. R. II 97 u. Abg. IV 83. Ebenso hielt man dort nicht für nöthig, ausdrücklich zu erklären, daß im Falle einer Abweisung der Klage, wegen Nichtigkeit der Ladung, neue Klage erhoben werden dürfe. Den Fall des Art. 324 Abs 2 berührte man nicht, weil man ihn im Parteiprozesse nicht für möglich hielt.

Die gesetzliche Vermuthung eines Geständnisses beschränkt sich selbstverständlich auf die Fälle, wo Versäumungsurtheil ergeht. Weigert sich der erschienene Beklagte, sich zur Sache auszusprechen oder Anträge zu nehmen, so gilt er als nicht geständig, jedoch kann der Richter aus seinem Verhalten die sachgemäßen Folgerungen für den Beweis der in Frage stehenden Thatsache ziehen. Bemerk. zu Art. 156.

7) In Art. 520 Abs. 2 ist, wenn auch mit anderen Worten, wiederholt, was die Art. 300 u. 305 verfügen, und gelten daher die Bemerk. zu jenen beiden Artikeln Nr. 12 bezw. Nr. 2—4.

Ein bloßes Aussetzen der Verhandlung ohne Wiedervorladung, wie es beim Nichterscheinen des Anwaltes meist zum Ziele führt, hielt man hier nicht zweckentsprechend; übrigens ist deßhalb das Gericht nicht gehindert, die Verhandlung oder den Spruch in eine andere Sitzung zu vertagen. Bemerk. zu Art. 508 und oben Nr. 4.

Im Falle, wo ein Vertreter auftritt, welcher keine genügende Vollmacht vorlegen kann, ist Art. 84 maßgebend.

Die betreffende Verfügung des Gerichts eignet sich zum Eintrage nach Art. 281.

Es wird genügen, zu sagen:

„Das Gericht verordnet, daß der Beklagte wieder„holt in die Sitzung vom — geladen und ihm die „Ladung vor dem — zugestellt werde."

In der neuen Ladung ist auf die frühere, welche giltig bleibt, Bezug zu nehmen. Liegt in der Fristbestimmung zugleich eine Kürzung der Erscheinungsfrist, so ist die Verfügung des Gerichts zuzustellen (Art. 503). Entspricht der Kläger der richterlichen Auflage nicht, so wird die Klage als nicht vorschriftsmäßig erhoben abzuweisen sein.

8) Die Bestimmung, daß gegen alle nichterschienenen Beklagten durch dasselbe Urtheil zu erkennen sei, entspricht der Bestimmung in Art. 306 Abs. 1, und kann daher auf die Bemerk. zu jenem Artikel Nr. 5 u. 6 Bezug genommen werden.

Die Folge derselben ist, daß wenn einem der nichterschienenen Beklagten gegenüber die Verhandlung ausgesetzt wird (oben Nr. 7), gleiche Vertagung auch den andern gegenüber ausgesprochen werden muß; jedoch ist es nicht nöthig, diejenigen Beklagten, deren Ausbleiben unentschuldigt ist, frisch zu laden. Art. 508 und unten Nr. 11.

9) Was die Anwendung dieser Bestimmung auf den Fall betrifft, wo eine der Ladungen an wesentlichen Mängeln leidet, so ist sie neu und völlig verschieden von der Verfügung des Art. 306 Abs. 2, obgleich sie aus derselben hervorgegangen ist.

Jene Verfügung war nemlich für den Parteiprozeß völlig gegenstandslos, da es sich hier von selbst versteht, daß alle Beklagten in die nemliche Sitzung geladen werden. Man glaubte jedoch den Fall berücksichtigen zu müssen, daß bei einem der Beklagten die Erscheinungsfrist nicht eingehalten sei, und dies gab Anlaß zur vorliegenden Verfügung, welche man auf alle Fälle ausdehnte, wo die Klage so mangelhaft ist, daß auf Grund derselben eine Verurtheilung nicht ergehen kann.

Es wurde demgemäß Vorsorge getroffen für den Fall, wo die Klage einem der Beklagten gegenüber wegen Nichtigkeit der Ladung abzuweisen ist und erst auf neue Vorladung hin ein Versäumungsurtheil erwirkt werden soll — einen Fall, welcher ebensogut auch im Anwaltsprozesse vorkommen kann, dort aber unberücksichtigt gelassen ist.

10) Die Frage, was der Richter auf Grund fraglicher Bestimmung zu erkennen habe, ist nicht so einfach als sie scheint.

Vor allem ist zu bemerken, daß das Gesetz sich nicht ganz genau ausdrückt, wenn es sagt: „kann das Urtheil 2c. — nicht erlassen werden," denn der Umstand, daß einem der Beklagten gegenüber die Ladung nichtig ist, steht nicht im Wege, sofort Urtheil zu erlassen; nur über den Grund der Sache kann ihm gegenüber nicht erkannt werden.

Ohne Zweifel hat der Beklagte, dessen Ladung nichtig ist, ein Recht darauf, daß diese Nichtigkeit ausgesprochen, daß der Schein der Anhängigkeit der Sache mit ihren Folgen (Art. 179) beseitigt und die Kosten dem Kläger zur Last gelegt werden, und dieses Recht muß der Richter trotz des Nichterscheinens wahren (Art. 520 Abs. 1). Die in Frage stehende Bestimmung will hieran nichts ändern, ihr Zweck ist vielmehr nur dahin gerichtet, den Kläger in die Lage zu versetzen, daß er eine neue giltige Ladung geben und ein gleichzeitiges Urtheil gegen alle Streitgenossen erwirken könne. Dabei ist zu beachten, daß ein Zwang zu dieser neuen Ladung nicht bestehen kann, denn sowie es dem Kläger freistund, den betreffenden Beklagten gar nicht zu laden, so steht es ihm auch frei, die Klage gegen ihn aufzugeben.

Auf Grund dieser Erwägungen bin ich der Ansicht, daß der Richter sofort die Nichtigkeit der Ladung auszusprechen und die Klage als unzulässig abzuweisen habe, daß er aber zugleich die Verhandlung im Uebrigen in eine bestimmte Sitzung vertagen und dem Kläger aufzugeben habe, in dieselbe den betreffenden Beklagten neu vorzuladen. Der Kläger ist natürlich zugleich in die Kosten zu verurtheilen, worunter insbesondere auch jene zu begreifen sind, welche die vereitelte Tagfahrt verursacht hat. Abg. II 268 (v. Neumayr).

11) Die Wiedervorladung hat nur bezüglich des betreffenden Beklagten zu erfolgen, nicht bezüglich der übrigen Nichterschienenen.

Das Gesetz spricht sich in dieser Beziehung ungenau aus, und man sollte wenn man es liest meinen, es handle sich vom Falle eines Verbindungsurtheiles, wo ein Theil der Beklagten erschienen ist, der andere nicht. Es wird aber hier der Fall unterstellt, wo mehrere Beklagte, möglicherweise alle, nicht erscheinen.

Nach den Verhandlungen (Abg. II 268) könnte man nun die Ansicht gewinnen, es seien alle Nichterschienenen wiedervorzuladen, allein der Laut des Gesetzes spräche nicht hiefür und auch nicht dessen Geist; denn wenn Jemand auf giltige Ladung nicht erscheint und dieses Nichterscheinen beurkundet ist, so ist der Fall der Versäumung gegeben und es bedarf keiner neuen Ladung, um die Folgen daraus in einer anderen Sitzung, in welche die Verhandlung oder der Spruch vertagt ist, zu ziehen. Vgl. Bemerk. zu Art. 316 Nr. 3 a. E. Uebrigens wird durch den (später beschlossenen) Art. 508 jeder Zweifel beseitigt.

12) Wie selbstverständlich können durch ein Versäumungsurtheil nur solche Begehren zugesprochen werden, wegen welcher geladen war; es dürfen also Klaganderungen und Zusätze zur Klage nur berücksichtigt werden, insofern wegen derselben nachträgliche Ladung mit Einhaltung der gesetzlichen Erscheinungsfrist gegeben worden ist. Bemerk. zu Art. 299 Nr. 10 u. 11 und Abg. II 268.

Ebenso versteht sich von selbst, daß bezüglich der Widerklage dasselbe gilt, wie bezüglich der Hauptklage. Wenn daher das Gericht nach Verhandlung und Aburtheilung der Hauptklage eine spätere Sitzung bestimmt zur Verhandlung der Widerklage, und der Widerbeklagte erscheint in dieser Sitzung nicht, so ergeht gegen ihn Versäumungsurtheil mit den Folgen, wie sie Art. 520 ausspricht.

b) Versäumungsurtheil gegen den Kläger (Art. 521).

13) Erscheint in der zur Verhandlung bestimmten Sitzung, d. h. in den Fällen, wie sie Art. 520 voraussetzt, der Kläger nicht, so treten die nemlichen Folgen ein, wie sie in Art. 303 für den Anwaltsprozeß bestimmt sind, und ist daher auf die Bemerkungen zu jenem Artikel zu verweisen.

Wenn nach Art. 303 die Klage für „nicht angebracht" erklärt, nach Art. 521 aber „abgewiesen" werden soll, so begründet dies keinen Unterschied. Die verschiedene Fassung rührt daher, daß man in Art. 521 die Ausdrucksweise von Art. 264 und 507° des Entwurfs beibehielt, während man sie in Art. 303, um den Willen des Gesetzes schärfer hervorzuheben, änderte (Abg. II 96 [Umbscheiden]). Daß eine Abweichung nicht entfernt beabsichtigt war, geht aus den Verhandlungen (Abg. II 266 — 269) hervor, laut deren man anfänglich einfach auf Art. 303 verweisen wollte, später aber, um Allegationen zu vermeiden, die jetzige Fassung wählte.

Ueber die Folgen des Nichterscheinens nach Erledigung von Vorfragen s. Bemerk. zu Art. 307.

c) Einspruch (Art. 522).

14) Für den Einspruch gelten im Parteiprozesse die nemlichen Grundsätze, wie im Anwaltsprozesse, mit dem Unterschiede, daß der Einspruch nicht durch Anwaltsakt, sondern durch Gerichtsvollzieherakt erhoben wird, daß ferner mit demselben zugleich die Gründe anzugeben sind, daß endlich Vorladung in die nächste sich eignende Sitzung zu geben ist.

Wenn das Gesetz sagt, der Einspruch müsse diesen Vorschriften entsprechen, so folgt hieraus nicht, daß, wenn das Eine oder das Andere fehlt, derselbe nichtig erklärt werden müsse, vielmehr ist Art. 218 Abs. 2 maßgebend, zufolge dessen nur solche Prozeßhandlungen für nichtig zu erklären sind, denen dasjenige fehlt, was nach Natur und Zweck der Handlung zum Wesen derselben gehört.

Insbesondere wäre eine Nichtigkeit nicht aus dem Umstande herzuleiten, daß die Vorladung nicht in die nächste, sondern in eine spätere Sitzung gegeben ist, denn es kann nie von wesentlicher Bedeutung sein, in welcher Sitzung verhandelt wird. Die Folge einer solchen Mißachtung der gesetzlichen Vorschrift wäre bloß, daß der Einspruchsbeklagte befugt wäre, sofort in eine frühere Sitzung laden zu lassen und die hierdurch verursachten Kosten dem Einspruchskläger zur Last fallen würden.

Im Uebrigen gelten die Bemerkungen zu Art. 309 — 315.

Verbindungsurtheil.

Art. 523. — Erscheint im Verfahren vor den Handels- und Einzelngerichten von mehreren Beklagten nur ein Theil, so hat, wenn dies vom Kläger, im Falle aber der Kläger mehrere sind, von sämmtlichen Klägern beantragt wird, auch gegen die Erschienenen die Verhandlung vorläufig nicht stattzufinden, sondern ist die Sache in eine spätere Sitzung zu vertagen, in welche die sämmtlichen Beklagten, soweit sie nicht bei Verkündung des Vertagungsurtheils gegenwärtig waren, neuerdings vorzuladen sind.

Bleiben in der neuerlich anberaumten Sitzung der Kläger oder sämmtliche Beklagte aus, so ergeht gegen sie das entsprechende Versäumungsurtheil.

Erscheint abermals nur ein Theil der Beklagten, so wird, und zwar ohne Unterschied, welche Beklagte ausgeblieben sind, auf die mit den Erschienenen gepflogene Verhandlung

gegen alle Betheiligten durch das nämliche Urtheil entschieden, wobei die von den Erschienenen vorgebrachten Einreden und ihre sonstige Vertheidigung ebenso zu betrachten sind, als wenn auch die Nichterschienenen sie vorgebracht hätten. Das Urtheil hat in diesem Falle zum Vortheile wie zum Nachtheile der Nichterschienenen die Wirksamkeit eines contradictorischen.

Die Vorschriften der Abs. 2 und 3 finden auch auf alle spätern Verhandlungen, welche in dem betreffenden Rechtsstreite in der nämlichen Instanz gepflogen werden, Anwendung, ohne daß es einer wiederholten Vorladung im Sinne des Abs. 1 bedarf. Auch sind, wenn die Verhandlung weiter vertagt oder ein Vorbescheid erlassen wird, desgleichen wenn ein Beweis- oder ein sonstiges Zwischenverfahren stattfindet, jenen Beklagten, welche auch auf die wiederholte Vorladung nicht erschienen sind, Zustellungen nicht zu machen.

Bei der nach Abs. 1 den Nichterschienenen zuzustellenden Vorladung sind dieselben auf die in Abs. 3 und 4 bezeichneten Folgen des abermaligen Nichterscheinens aufmerksam zu machen.

Sind die nicht erschienenen Beklagten bei der nach Lage der Sache zu erlassenden Entscheidung unbetheiligt, so finden die Bestimmungen des gegenwärtigen Artikels keine Anwendung. G. A. d. K. d. A. II S. 265—267. 269. 279. 352. 453. IV S. 107. 115. K. d. R. II. S. 255. IV S. 62.

1) Unsere Prozeßordnung hat das Verbindungsurtheil auch für den Parteiprozeß eingeführt, in welchem es nach französischem Prozesse keine Anwendung fand.

Art. 523 wiederholt im Wesentlichen die Bestimmungen der Art. 316 — 318 und fügt diejenigen Abweichungen bei, welche durch die Natur des Parteiprozesses bedingt erscheinen.

Die erste Abweichung betrifft die Bedingungen zum Erlasse eines Verbindungsurtheiles. Da nemlich eine Hinterlegung der Anträge im Parteiprozesse nicht stattfindet, so ist der Fall eines Verbindungsurtheiles nur gegeben, wenn in der Sitzung, in welche die Vorladung erfolgt oder in welche die Sache zur Verhandlung vertagt ist (Art. 520 Abs. 1) ein Theil der Beklagten erscheint, ein anderer nicht.

Einfacher und schärfer läßt sich der Wille des Gesetzes dahin ausdrücken, daß überall, wo gegen einen Theil der Beklagten Versäumungsurtheil ergehen müßte, gegen einen anderen Theil aber contradiktorisches Urtheil, im Interesse der Einheit der Rechtsprechung die Verbindung verlangt werden kann. Es gilt dies ebenso wie im Anwaltsprozesse nicht nur für die erste Verhandlung, sondern auch für die späteren Stadien des Verfahrens.

2) Eine zweite Abweichung ist bedingt durch den Umstand, daß im Parteiprozesse die Hinterlegung bezw. Stellung von Anträgen nicht maßgebend ist für die Natur des Verfahrens (Bemerk. zu Art. 520 Nr. 2 u. Abg. II 267 Sp. 1). Hieraus leitet sich die Folge, daß das nächste auf die Verbindung folgende Urtheil nicht nothwendig ein contradiktorisches sein muß, sondern daß, wenn alle Beklagten ausbleiben, oder wenn der Kläger nicht erscheint, ein Versäumungsurtheil ergeht. Im Anwaltsprozesse kann dieser Fall erst bei späteren Urtheilen eintreten (Bemerk. zu Art. 316 Nr. 16).

3) Auffallend ist es, daß die Bestimmungen in Art. 316 Abs. 4 u. 5 nicht wiederholt worden sind.

Die erste Bestimmung wäre allerdings nur erheblich für die seltenen Fälle, wo zugleich eine Abkürzung der Erscheinungsfrist bewilligt wird (z. B. bei Ausländern und Leuten ohne bekannten Aufenthalt), und auch in diesen Fällen ist es dem Richter nicht verwehrt, die Frist für die Zustellung der neuen Ladung zu bestimmen (Bemerk. zu Art. 259 Nr. 6), was gerade im Parteiprozesse besonders sachgemäß, ja natürlich ist.

Daß der Eintrag des Urtheils nach Art. 281 stattzufinden habe, versteht sich wohl von selbst, wie es denn überhaupt keinen Zweifel erleidet, daß auch im Parteiprozesse das Verbindungsurtheil gleich einer Vertagung zu behandeln ist.

Im Uebrigen ist auf die Bemerkungen zu den Art. 316—318 zu verweisen.

Beweisführung.

Art. 524. — **Die Beweisführung richtet sich im Verfahren vor den Handels- und Einzelngerichten, soweit im gegenwärtigen Hauptstücke nicht anders verfügt ist, nach der Analogie der in den Hauptst. IX — XIV gegebenen Bestimmungen.**

Art. 525. — **Ordnet das Gericht eine von ihm vorzunehmende Beweiserhebung an, so hat es zu-**

gleich Zeit und Ort der Aufnahme festzusetzen, desgleichen am Schlusse des Beweisverfahrens Tag und Stunde der weitern Verhandlung, falls letztere nicht sofort stattfinden kann.

Diese Festsetzungen gelten im Verfahren vor den Einzelngerichten als Kundmachung und Vorladung für die Parteien, dieselben mögen erschienen sein oder nicht, doch kann vorbehaltlich der Bestimmung des Art. 523 Abs. 4 das Gericht in einzelnen Fällen eine besondere Kundmachung oder Vorladung der Partei verfügen. Ausfertigung und Zustellung des Beweisurtheils findet im Verfahren vor den Einzelngerichten nicht statt.

Im Verfahren vor den Handelsgerichten finden die Bestimmungen der Art. 331 und 338 Anwendung.

Art. 526. — Wo im Verfahren vor den Handelsgerichten mit der Beweisaufnahme ein Gerichtsmitglied zu beauftragen ist, muß hiezu ein rechtskundiges gewählt werden.

Art. 527. — Die Parteien können im Verfahren vor den Handels- und Einzelngerichten der Beweisaufnahme persönlich oder durch Bevollmächtigte und im ersten Falle allein oder mit einem Beistande anwohnen.

Art. 528. — Wenn eine Urkunde nicht anerkannt oder wenn sie als falsch angegriffen wird, findet das Verfahren über die Aechtheit oder Fälschung vor dem Handels- oder Einzelngerichte statt, jedoch nur so weit, als die Urkunde einen Gegenstand betrifft, der zur Zuständigkeit des Handels- oder Einzelngerichts gehört.

Ist dies nicht der Fall, so soll der Richter die Urkunde mit seinem Namenszuge bezeichnen und die Parteien zur Einleitung des Verfahrens über die Aechtheit oder Fälschung der Urkunde vor das zuständige Bezirksgericht beziehungsweise Handelsgericht verweisen, welches eintretenden Falls in Anwendung der Bestimmungen des Art. 11 auch über die Hauptsache zu erkennen hat.

Art. 529. — Die in Art. 392 erwähnten Requisitionen werden bei den Handels- und Einzelngerichten durch den Gerichtsvorstand oder Einzelnrichter selbst vorgenommen.

Art. 530. — Beim Zeugenbeweise ist die in Art. 412 bestimmte Frist auf drei Tage beschränkt. Die Mittheilung des Beweissatzes an die Zeugen ist nicht erforderlich.

Art. 531. — Im Falle einer Eideszuschiebung haben die erforderlichen Parteierklärungen und die Entscheidung des Gerichts über den Eidessatz, sowie über die Zulässigkeit der Zuschiebung oder Zurückschiebung sogleich zu erfolgen und ist der Eid, wenn der Schwurpflichtige persönlich anwesend ist, in der Regel in der nämlichen Gerichtssitzung zu schwören oder abzulehnen. Nach richterlichem Ermessen kann jedoch zur Erklärung über Annahme oder Zurückschiebung des Eids sowie zur Eidesleistung eine besondere Sitzung festgesetzt werden.

Art. 532. — Im Verfahren vor den Einzelngerichten kann, wenn eine Beweisaufnahme außerhalb des Gerichtssitzes stattgefunden hat, zur weiteren Verhandlung und zur Verkündung des Urtheils sogleich an dem Orte, wo die Beweisaufnahme vor sich ging, geschritten werden.

G. A. d. K. d. A. II S. 270—273. 279. 352. IV S. 107—111. 334—336.
K. d. R. II S. 255—259. IV S. 62. 63.

1) Für das Beweisverfahren läßt das Gesetz im Allgemeinen die **Analogie** der Bestimmungen in Hauptstück IX—XIV gelten und fügt nur in Art. 525—532 einzelne Ausnahmen bei, theils für den Parteiprozeß überhaupt, theils für Handelsgerichte oder Einzelngerichte insbesondere.

Es ist hervorzuheben, daß ein Theil jener Bestimmungen in Hauptst. IX—XIV in der Pfalz nicht gilt, nemlich die Art. 319—322 über Beweispflicht, die Art. 353—369, 394 u. 395 über die Beweiskraft der verschiedenen Urkunden, Art. 399 über Zulässigkeit des Zeugenbeweises und die Art. 449—459, 465, 469—472 über die verschiedenen Arten von Eiden, deren Zulässigkeit und Wirkung. Vgl. Einleitung zu Hauptst. X.

a) Beweis im Allgemeinen.

2) Die Beweisführung im Allgeminen richtet sich nach den Grundsätzen, wie sie in Hauptst. IX aufgestellt sind. Namentlich gilt, was dort gesagt ist:

über die Beweispflicht (Art. 319—323);

über die Beweisprüfung sofort bei der ersten Verhandlung (Art. 324, 329, 330);

über die Pflicht der Parteien, ihre Beweise anzubieten (Art. 324), und der Gerichte, im Beweisurtheile die zu erweisenden Thatsachen, sowie die Art der Beweismittel zu bezeichnen (Art. 328);

über das Urtheil nach der Beweisaufnahme, insbesondere die Pflicht des Richters, das Beweisergebniß zu prüfen, auch wenn eine der

Parteien bei der Verhandlung nicht erscheint (Art. 346);
endlich über den Beweis zum ewigen Gedächtnisse (Art. 347—352).

3) Während im Anwaltsprozesse nur bei Beweisaufnahmen in der Sitzung oder beim Augenscheine, welchen das ganze Gericht vornimmt, die Tagfahrt sofort im Beweisurtheile festzusetzen ist, verfügt Art. 525 Abs. 1, daß dies in allen Fällen zu geschehen habe, wo eine Beweiserhebung vom Gerichte vorzunehmen sei.

Es hat diese Ausnahmsbestimmung, wenn auch ihrem Wortlaute nach allgemein, doch nur praktische Folgen für die Einzelngerichte; denn auf Fälle, wo das Handelsgericht eines seiner Mitglieder mit Aufnahme des Beweises beauftragt, dürfte sie nicht zu erstrecken sein. Die Schlußbestimmung, daß nach der Beweisaufnahme sofort der Tag zur Verhandlung festzusetzen sei, sowie die in Abs. 3 enthaltene Hinweisung auf Art. 338, endlich der Wortlaut des Gesetzes möchten dies andeuten.

Für die Fälle, wo ein anderer als der urtheilende Richter den Beweis aufzunehmen hat, gelten die allgemeinen Regeln der Art. 334 ff.

4) Wenn Art. 525 Abs. 1 weiter verfügt, es habe das Gericht, falls es selbst die Beweisaufnahme vornimmt, sofort nach derselben Tag und Stunde der weiteren Verhandlung festzusetzen, so wird hiermit die Vorschrift des Art. 344 Abs. 1 auf jene Fälle ausgedehnt, wo der Einzelnrichter die Beweisaufnahme außer der Sitzung vorgenommen hat. Die Gründe für eine sofortige Verhandlung sind im Parteiprozesse, wo alles auf schnelle und einfache Erledigung drängt, noch weit stärker, als im Anwaltsprozesse. Vgl. Bemerk. zu Art. 344 Nr. 2.

Uebrigens darf man aus der in Frage stehenden Verfügung nicht folgern, daß das Gericht mit Festsetzung der Tagfahrt zur Verhandlung immer zuwarten müsse, bis die Beweisaufnahme beendet sei. Es gilt jene Verfügung nur für den Fall, wo die Festsetzung nicht bereits vorher stattgefunden hat.

In der Pfalz pflegt man auch in solchen Fällen, wo eine Beweisaufnahme außer der Sitzung, ja selbst im Auslande, angeordnet wird, immer so zu verfahren, daß man im Beweisurtheile sofort den Tag zur Verhandlung nach der Beweiserhebung festsetzt. Können am bestimmten Tage die betreffenden Protokolle noch nicht vorgelegt werden, was nur ausnahmsweise vorkommt, so erfolgt Vertagung. Dieses Verfahren hat große praktische Vortheile. Einestheils ist sicher, an welchem Tage die Sache verhandelt werden soll, und das Gericht kann sich bezüglich seiner sonstigen Fixationen, die Parteien aber bezüglich des persönlichen Erscheinens darnach richten, anderntheils ist eine neue Vorladung mit Einhaltung genügender Frist erspart, welche in Fällen, wo die Beweisaufnahme durch einen beauftragten Richter geschieht, nicht umgangen werden könnte.

5) Für die Einzelngerichte hat das Gesetz in Art. 525 Abs. 2 das Beweisverfahren sehr vereinfacht, indem es erklärt, daß Ausfertigung und Zustellung des Beweisurtheiles nicht stattfinden, und daß jene Festsetzungen, von welchen Abs. 1 spricht, zugleich als Kundmachung und Vorladung zu gelten haben, selbst wenn die Parteien dabei nicht zugegen waren.

Der Gesetzgeber hatte bei dieser Bestimmung nur den gewöhnlichen Fall im Auge, wo der Einzelnrichter im Beweisurtheile selbst die Tagfahrt zur Beweisaufnahme festsetzt; hat jedoch die Beweisaufnahme durch einen anderen Einzelnrichter oder durch einen ausländischen Richter zu geschehen, so läßt sich dieselbe nicht anwenden, und es muß, soweit es die Natur der Sache erfordert, zur Regel zurückgegriffen werden.

Zum Ersten läßt sich in Fällen dieser Art eine Ausfertigung des Beweisurtheiles nicht umgehen, da sie dem beauftragten Richter in Vorlage zu bringen ist.

Zum Weiteren ist es nöthig, die Tagfahrtsbestimmung des beauftragten Richters zuzustellen, weil die Gegenpartei in die Lage versetzt werden muß, ihre Beweismittel anzukündigen (Art. 530) und zu benützen und bei der Beweisaufnahme zugegen zu sein (Art. 527).

Es wird in diesem Falle auch die achttägige Frist des Art. 338 einzuhalten sein; denn 1) ist die Ausnahmsbestimmung, daß in der Festsetzung der Tagfahrt auch die Vorladung liege, nur für den Fall gegeben, wo diese Festsetzung im Beweisurtheile erfolgt, und 2) darf die Zeit der Zustellung nicht der Willkür der Parteien überlassen bleiben.

Für das handelsgerichtliche Verfahren gelten die Ausnahmsbestimmungen in Abs. 2 nicht; es wäre also selbstverständlich, daß es hier bei der Regel bleibt, auch wenn es in Abs. 3 nicht ausdrücklich erklärt wäre. Ebendeßhalb finden nicht bloß die Art. 331 u. 338, sondern auch Art. 339 und die sonstigen allgemeinen Vorschriften Anwendung.

6) Eine weitere bloß die Einzelngerichte berührende Ausnahme gibt Art. 532, indem er verfügt, daß der Einzelnrichter in Fällen, wo die

Beweisaufnahme außerhalb der Sitzung erfolgt, sofort am Orte derselben zur Verhandlung und Verkündung des Urtheils schreiten könne.

Da nicht vorgeschrieben ist, es solle diese Verhandlung schon vorher angekündigt werden, da ferner nicht gesagt ist, es müßten alle Parteien zugegen sein, so gelten die nemlichen Grundsätze, wie bei Beweisaufnahmen in der Sitzung. Die Parteien müssen wissen, daß möglicherweise sofort nach der Beweisaufnahme zur Verhandlung geschritten werde.

Uebrigens wird der Richter in Fällen, wo er eine derartige Aburtheilung an Ort und Stelle beabsichtigt, nie unterlassen, dies anzukündigen, und es wird sogar gut sein, im Urtheile auszusprechen, daß die Tagfahrt eintretenden Falls auch zur sofortigen Verhandlung an Ort und Stelle bestimmt werde.

Das Urtheil wird ebenso eingetragen, wie die in der Sitzung gesprochenen Urtheile.

7) Was die Sonderbestimmungen der Art. 526 und 527 betrifft, so bedürfen dieselben keiner Erläuterung; nur ist hervorzuheben, daß Bevollmächtigte, sich durch Vollmacht ausweisen müssen und selbst für Advokaten hier keine Ausnahme gilt. Bemerk. zu Art. 89 Nr. 5.

b) Urkundenbeweis.

8) Bei den Verhandlungen zweiter Lesung (Abg. IV 107—111) war vorgeschlagen worden, die Bestimmungen über sicheres Datum (Art. 358, 359), sowie jene über die Unzulässigkeit des Zeugenbeweises gegen vollbeweisende Urkunden (Art. 399), für Handelssachen zu beseitigen, allein dieser Vorschlag fand keine Annahme. Für die Pfalz bleibt nach Art. 66 des Einf.-G. das dortige Recht in Geltung.

9) Die Vorschriften der Art. 172 ff. über vorausgängige Mittheilung der Urkunden finden im Parteiprozesse keine Anwendung, jedoch ist jede Partei verpflichtet, die Urkunden, welche sie als Beweismittel benützen will, in die Sitzung mitzubringen und vorzulegen (Art. 506).

Die Vorschrift, daß ein Urtheil auf Beweisführung durch Urkunden nur höchst ausnahmsweise erlassen werden dürfe (Art. 329), gilt auch im Parteiprozesse und wird gerade hier mit besonderer Strenge einzuhalten sein. Eintretenden Falls ist kurze Vertagung zur Beibringung der fehlenden Urkunden zu bewilligen.

10) Wird eine Urkunde als unächt oder falsch angegriffen, so sind die Handelsgerichte und Einzelngerichte befugt, auch über diesen Zwischenstreit zu erkennen, jedoch nur soweit, als die Urkunde einen Gegenstand betrifft, der zur Zuständigkeit dieser Gerichte gehört (Art. 528). Hat die Urkunde im Ganzen oder auch nur theilweise einen nicht zur Zuständigkeit dieser Ausnahmsgerichte gehörigen Gegenstand, so ist der Zwischenstreit vor das zuständige Gericht zu verweisen, nemlich in der Regel vor das Bezirksgericht als das ordentliche Gericht (Art. 2), in den Fällen des Art. 7 Abs. 2 auch vor's Handelsgericht. Dieses Gericht soll eintretenden Falls in Anwendung der Bestimmungen des Art. 11 auch über die Hauptsache erkennen.

Selbstverständlich ist auch hier der Richter nicht befugt, die Aburtheilung einem bestimmten Gerichte zuzuweisen, vielmehr spricht derselbe nur seine eigene Unzuständigkeit aus. Bemerk. zu Art. 31 Nr. 14.

11) In der Regel haben Zwischenstreite, welche sich über die Tauglichkeit und Erheblichkeit von Beweismitteln ergeben, keine selbständige Bedeutung, werden vielmehr nur für den in Frage stehenden Rechtsstreit entschieden. Wenn der Gesetzgeber für die Urkunden vorberegte Ausnahme machte, so geschah es im Hinblicke auf die ihnen zustehende formelle Beweiskraft, welche sie mit den beurkundeten Rechtshandlungen und Rechtsgeschäften mehr oder weniger identifizirt. Man fand es unpassend, daß die Frage, ob eine Urkunde ächt sei oder nicht, unter den nemlichen Parteien mehrmals Gegenstand der Aburtheilung werden könne, je nachdem der eine oder der andere Anspruch darauf gegründet wird. Sobald man aber annahm, daß die Zwischenfrage für den ganzen Inhalt der Urkunde rechtskräftig entschieden werde, befand man sich auf dem Boden eines selbständigen Zwischenstreites im Sinne der Art. 9—11 und mußte die Natur dieses Zwischenstreites für die Zuständigkeit maßgebend sein.

12) Die Frage, unter welchen Voraussetzungen eine Urkunde ihrem Inhalte nach vor's Handelsgericht bezw. Einzelngericht gehöre oder vor's Bezirksgericht, ist nicht ganz einfach.

Die Zuständigkeit des Handelsgerichts erscheint überschritten, wenn eine Schuldanerkennung, eine Cession rc. außer Handelsgeschäften auch reine Civilgeschäfte zum Gegenstande hat. Abg. IV 110 Sp. 2. Der Umstand, daß eine Cession an sich kein Handelsgeschäft ist, steht übrigens der Zuständigkeit des Handelsgerichtes nicht im Wege, falls sie bloß den Uebertrag einer Handelsforderung beurkundet und nur der Legitimation wegen in Frage steht. Bemerk. zu Art. 7 Nr. 46 und zu Art. 9 Nr. 18 u. 19.

Die einzelnrichterliche Zuständigkeit erscheint, abgesehen von den Fällen des Art. 5, überschritten, wenn die in der Urkunde übernommenen Leistungen bezw. Gegenleistungen oder die durch dieselbe bewirkten Entlastungen die Summe dieser Zuständigkeit übersteigen. Auf die möglichen Folgen, welche aus der Nichtvollziehung eines Vertrages entstehen können, darf selbstverständlich keine Rücksicht genommen werden, denn diese wären immer unbestimmbar.

Uebrigens kommen auch die übernommenen Leistungen nicht unbedingt in Betracht, sondern nur insofern sie noch rechtlichen Werth haben und Anlaß zur Klage geben können. Wird z. B. nur der Rest eines Darlehens eingeklagt, so ist es ohne Belang, daß die Urkunde eine die einzelnrichterliche Zuständigkeit übersteigende Verpflichtung enthält; es genügt, daß der noch geschuldete Rest unter diese Zuständigkeit fällt.

13) Wenn Art. 528 Abs. 2 sagt, das Gericht, vor welches der Zwischenstreit gewiesen werde, habe eintretenden Falls auch über die Hauptsache zu erkennen, so sind hiermit jene Fälle gemeint, wo nach Art. 11 eine solche Ueberweisung der Zuständigkeit eintritt.

Eine Ueberweisung vom Handelsgerichte an's Bezirksgericht findet hiernach nicht statt, und es muß also in Fällen, wo das Handelsgericht sich unzuständig erklärt, über die Aechtheit oder Fälschung einer Urkunde zu erkennen, das Bezirksgericht sich auf die Aburtheilung dieses Zwischenpunktes beschränken, das spätere Erkenntniß in der Hauptsache aber dem Handelsgerichte überlassen, wie dies in der Pfalz bis jetzt in allen Fällen geschah. Bemerk. zu Art. 11 Nr. 21. Was Abg. IV 110 Sp. 2 gesagt ist, beruht offenbar auf unrichtiger Auffassung.

Eine Ueberweisung findet ferner nur statt, soweit die Entscheidung der Hauptsache von der Entscheidung des Zwischenpunktes abhängt; soweit jedoch der mit der Sache befaßte Richter im Stande ist, auch ohne Benützung der angefochtenen Urkunde zu entscheiden, hat er dies zu thun. Art. 266.

Wird eine Urkunde als durch Fälschung verändert angefochten, so ist nicht der Inhalt der ganzen Urkunde maßgebend, sondern nur der angeblich gefälschte Theil.

14) Die Art und Weise, wie die Sache bei dem Gerichte, welches für den Zwischenstreit zuständig erscheint, anzubringen ist, hängt davon ab, ob dieses Gericht auch über die Hauptsache zu entscheiden habe oder nicht.

In letzterem Falle wird der Zwischenstreit unmittelbar vor dieses Gericht gebracht und beantragt, es möge dasselbe erkennen, daß die Urkunde ächt oder daß sie unächt, daß sie in der behaupteten Weise gefälscht sei oder nicht, je nachdem die eine oder die andere Partei die Sache anbringt. Meiner Ansicht nach sind nemlich beide Parteien berechtigt, mit dem betreffenden Antrage vor Gericht zu treten, und das Recht dazu schöpfen sie aus der erfolgten Ueberweisung. Bemerk. zu Art. 190 Nr. 7 u. 8.

In ersterem Falle bringt der Kläger seinen Anspruch in der nemlichen Weise, wie er ihn vor's Einzelngericht gebracht hatte, nunmehr vor den höheren Richter, welcher nach Art. 11 Abs. 3 zuständig bleibt, auch wenn die Urkunde gar nicht mehr bestritten wird. Bemerk. zu Art. 11 Nr. 27.

Sollte sich in diesem Falle ergeben, daß die Anfechtung bloß muthwilliger Weise, um die Zuständigkeit zu verrücken, stattgefunden habe, so wären der betreffenden Partei auch im Falle ihres Obsiegens die Mehrkosten, welche durch die Verhandlung vor dem höheren Gerichte und die Ueberweisung selbst entstanden sind, zur Last zu legen.

c) Zeugenbeweis.

15) Das Verfahren beim Zeugenbeweise ist für die Handelsgerichte das nemliche, wie im Anwaltsprozesse, mit der einzigen Ausnahme, daß die Frist zur Kundmachung der Zeugen nicht acht, sondern drei Tage beträgt, und daß die Mittheilung des Beweissatzes an die Zeugen nicht nöthig ist. Letztere Förmlichkeit ist übrigens so sachgemäß und macht, wenn Vorladung erfolgt, so wenig Mühe und Kosten, daß es in vielen Fällen rathsam sein möchte, sie dennoch zu beobachten.

Mit Rücksicht auf die verschiedenen Formen und Fristen, welche bei Durchführung eines Zeugenbeweises zu wahren sind und deren Nichtbeachtung große Rechtsverlustigungen zur Folge hat, pflegt man in Fällen, wo Parteien, welche persönlich auftreten, zu diesem Beweise zugelassen werden, denselben das Benehmen mit einem Rechtsverständigen anzurathen. Jedenfalls ist es sachgemäß, daß der Vorsitzende auf die wichtigsten Punkte — die Einhaltung der Fristen zum Beginne des Verfahrens (Art. 406) und zur Kundmachung der Zeugen (Art. 530) — besonders aufmerksam mache.

16) Bei den Einzelngerichten wird zwar durch die Bestimmung in Art. 525 Abs. 1 u. 2 eine große Vereinfachung des Verfahrens erzielt, allein es bleiben immerhin noch mehr Formen zu beobachten, als sie der französische Prozeß kannte.

Die Frist zum Beginne des Verfahrens (Art. 406) fällt zwar in der Regel hinweg, weil der Einzelnrichter auch bei Zeugenverhören außerhalb der Sitzung sofort die Tagfahrt festsetzt; allein falls ein anderer Richter um Vornahme des Zeugenverhörs ersucht wird, muß, kraft der allgemeinen Verfügung des Art. 524, auch Art. 406 mit seinen Folgen zur Anwendung kommen, wobei jedoch, im Geiste von Art. 525 Abs. 2, die vom Richter bestimmte Frist vom Spruche des Urtheils an laufen wird.

Als die wichtigste Form erscheint die Kundmachung der Zeugen innerhalb der gesetzlichen Frist, und ist es daher sachgemäß, daß der Einzelnrichter die Parteien darauf aufmerksam mache, daß sie nur solche Zeugen abhören lassen dürfen, welche mindestens drei Tage zuvor dem Gegner durch Gerichtsvollzieherakt unter genauer Bezeichnung kundgegeben worden seien.

d) Sachverständige.

17) Bei einfachen Sachen wird man für Einholung des Gutachtens von Sachverständigen im Parteiprozesse immer den kürzeren und wohlfeileren Weg wählen, wie er durch Art. 447 geboten ist, nemlich daß die Sachverständigen, nachdem sie ihre Prüfung vorgenommen, in der Sitzung gleich Zeugen vernommen werden.

Ordnet der Einzelnrichter eine Expertise an, so setzt er sofort die Tagfahrt zur Einweisung der Sachverständigen fest, welche als Vorladung für die Parteien gilt (Art. 525). Auch die Sitzung zur weiteren Verhandlung wird in der Regel im Beweisurtheile zu bestimmen sein (s. oben Nr. 4).

Schließlich ist zu bemerken, daß Sachverständige nicht nothwendig vorgeladen werden müssen, sondern auch ohne Ladung vor Gericht erscheinen können (Abg. II 271 Sp. 2). Es gilt dies im Parteiprozesse, wo die Mittheilung des Beweissatzes nicht verlangt wird, auch von Zeugen.

e) Eid.

18) Das Verfahren im Falle einer Eideszuschiebung ist für den Parteiprozeß sehr vereinfacht. Die Erklärung über Annahme oder Zurückschiebung des Eides, die Antwort hierauf, die Entscheidung über erhobene Anstände nebst endgiltiger Feststellung des Eidesatzes, endlich der Regel nach die Ausschwörung des Eides erfolgen in der nemlichen Sitzung, in welcher der Eid auferlegt worden ist.

Wegen der gerichtlich auferlegten Eide brauchte nichts gesagt zu werden, da die bezüglichen Förmlichkeiten (Art. 460, 462) nur für den zugeschobenen Eid gegeben sind.

Selbstverständlich behaupten alle sonstigen Bestimmungen in Hauptst. XIV auch im Parteiprozesse ihre Geltung, insbesondere was in Art. 460 über die Eideserklärung auf einen zugeschobenen Eid und die Befugniß des Richters, auf Grund derselben neue Entscheidung zu erlassen, gesagt ist, ferner die Bestimmungen in Art. 463, wornach die Erklärung einer Partei, Berufung ergreifen zu wollen, die Abnahme des Eides hindert und die Anwesenheit bei der Eidesleistung als Verzicht auf die Berufung betrachtet wird. Sind die Parteien nicht durch Rechtsverständige vertreten oder verbeistandet, so erscheint es sachgemäß, daß der Richter sie auf diese Folgen aufmerksam mache.

19) Wenn Art. 531 beifügt, nach Ermessen des Richters könne zur Erklärung über Annahme und Zurückschiebung des Eides sowie zur Eidesleistung eine besondere Sitzung festgesetzt werden, so hätte sich dies wohl von selbst verstanden, denn es kann dem Richter nie verwehrt sein zu vertagen, wenn eine Vertagung durch die Sachlage bedingt ist. Verlangt das Gesetz sofortige Verhandlung, wie hier, so heißt dies nur: falls es der Sachlage nach geschehen kann. Bemerk. zu Art. 508.

Unterbrechung und Aufhebung der Verhandlungen.

Art. 533. — **Bezüglich der Unterbrechung des Verfahrens und des Abstands vom Prozesse finden im Verfahren vor den Handels- und Einzelngerichten die Bestimmungen des Hptst. XVI, mit Ausnahme der in Art. 491 Ziff. 4, Art. 494 Ziff. 3 und Art. 495 enthaltenen, Anwendung.**

Bei den Einzelngerichten tritt eine Unterbrechung des Verfahrens auch ein, wenn wegen Behinderung des Richters gemäß Art. 41 Abs. 2 Mittheilung an das Obergericht nothwendig wird. Das unterbrochene Verfahren wird in diesem Falle wieder aufgenommen durch die Zustellung der nach Art. 54 erfolgten obergerichtlichen Anordnung.

Art. 534. — **In den Fällen des Art. 491 Ziff. 1—3 kann im Verfahren vor den Handels- und Einzelngerichten die betreffende Partei zur Fortsetzung des unterbrochenen Verfahrens durch Zustellung einer Aufforderung angehalten werden, welche gegebenen Falls zugleich Vorladung in eine Gerichtssitzung zu dem Zwecke enthält, damit die Verhandlung der Hauptsache nach Maßgabe des Stands, in welchem sie sich befindet, fortgesetzt werde.**

An Erben kann die Zustellung dieser Aufforderung in der in Art. 211 Abs. 2 bezeichneten Weise geschehen.

Art. 535. — Die nach Art. 491 Abs. 2 erforderliche Anzeige, sowie die Wiederaufnahme des unterbrochenen Verfahrens kann auch durch mündliche Erklärung in der Sitzung geschehen.

G. A. d. K. d. A. II S. 273. 279. 290. 291. 352. 353. IV S. 111. 115. 336.
K. d. R. II S. 259. 260. IV S. 63.

1) Was die Unterbrechung des Verfahrens betrifft, so gelten die Bestimmungen der Art. 490—494, deren Fassung schon so eingerichtet ist, daß sie auch für den Parteiprozeß paßt, und kann im Allgemeinen auf die Bemerkungen zu jenen Artikeln Bezug genommen werden.

Hinzugefügt wird die der Natur des Parteiprozesses entsprechende Bestimmung, daß die Anzeige, welche der Prozeßbevollmächtigte vom Eintritte der Unterbrechung macht (Art. 491 Abs. 2), sowie die Wiederaufnahme des Verfahrens durch mündliche Erklärung in der Sitzung geschehen dürfe; ferner eine die Behinderung des Einzelnrichters betreffende Bestimmung, welche im Verfahren vor Collegialgerichten entbehrlich erschien. Abg. II 281 (v. Neumayr).

Schließlich wird Art. 495 in einer der Natur des Parteiprozesses entsprechenden Weise durch Art. 534 ersetzt.

2) Ist ein Prozeßbevollmächtigter nicht bestellt, was beim einzelnrichterlichen Verfahren die Regel ist, so tritt die Unterbrechung in den Fällen des Art. 491 Ziff. 1—3 mit der Thatsache des Todes, des Verlusts der Rechtsfähigkeit 2c. von Rechtswegen ein, und alle nach diesem Zeitpunkte von den Parteien oder vom Gerichte vorgenommenen Prozeßhandlungen sind nach Maßgabe der Bestimmungen des Art. 492 nichtig. Es liegt hierin eine Mahnung zur Vorsicht für die Parteien und für die Gerichte.

Was die Behinderung des Einzelnrichters betrifft, so wird in Folge derselben das Verfahren in jenen Fällen unterbrochen, wo nach Art. 41 Mittheilung an das Obergericht nöthig ist, d. h. wo der Einzelnrichter keinen Stellvertreter hat. Die Unterbrechung tritt im Augenblicke ein, wo der Behinderungsgrund entsteht (Art. 41 Abs. 3), und hat die nemliche Wirkung und Tragweite, wie im Falle der Ablehnung nach Art. 490. Daß hier von Unterbrechung des Fristenlaufs nicht besonders die Rede ist wie in Art. 490, erscheint ohne Belang. Bemerk. zu Art. 490 Nr. 1.

3) Die Wiederaufnahme des unterbrochenen Verfahrens wird erzwungen durch Zustellung einer Aufforderung.

Handelt es sich bloß um Fortsetzung eines vorbereitenden Verfahrens, z. B. eines Beweisverfahrens, so genügt die Aufforderung, um Verfahren und Fristen wieder in Gang zu bringen; ist jedoch die Sache zur Verhandlung reif, so ist zugleich Vorladung (Art. 501 Ziff. 2) in eine Gerichtssitzung zu geben. Ein besonderer Ausspruch des Richters, daß das Verfahren als wiederaufgenommen gelte, ist auch hier nicht nöthig.

4) Eine wohl zu beachtende Eigenthümlichkeit der Bestimmungen des Art. 534 liegt darin, daß nicht, wie nach Art. 495, vom Zeitpunkte der Aufforderung an eine Erscheinungsfrist läuft und erst, nachdem diese verstrichen ist, das Verfahren seinen Fortgang nimmt, sondern daß sofort mit der Aufforderung die Unterbrechung aufhört und die neuen Fristen ihren Lauf beginnen.

Dies ist offenbar der Gedanke, welcher der jetzigen Fassung zu Grunde liegt, mag auch die ursprüngliche Fassung (Abg. II 290) von anderer Anschauung ausgegangen sein.

5) Eine weitere Eigenthümlichkeit des Art. 534 ist darin zu finden, daß die in der Hauptsache zu nehmenden Anträge nicht zugleich mit der Aufforderung zugestellt werden müssen. Man sollte glauben, es sei dies im Parteiprozesse gerade so nöthig, ja vielleicht noch nöthiger, als im Anwaltsprozesse.

Uebrigens versteht sich nach dem Zwecke der Aufforderung von selbst, daß dieselbe wenigstens den Prozeß, welcher unterbrochen ist und fortgesetzt werden soll, genau bezeichnen müsse. Es wird geeignet sein, immer das Datum der Klage und ihren wesentlichen Inhalt anzuführen. Auch das unterbrechende Ereigniß und die Eigenschaft, in welcher die aufgeforderte Person in das Verfahren eintreten soll, sind zu bezeichnen.

Ist die Aufforderung mangelhaft, so hat das Gericht im Falle des Nichterscheinens dies ebenso wie bei der Ladung, von Amtswegen zu beachten (Art. 520 Abs. 1 u. 2).

6) Bezüglich des Abstandes ist einfach auf die Bemerkungen zu Art. 496—498 zu verweisen.

Gemeinsame Bestimmungen.

Art. 536. — **Die Hinterlegung von Anträgen ist im Verfahren vor den Handels- und Einzelngerichten nicht geboten. Den Parteien ist jedoch gestattet, vor Abschluß der Verhandlung die dabei gestellten Anträge dem Vorsitzenden oder Einzelnrichter schriftlich zu überreichen.**

Art. 537. — **Soweit Bestimmungen für das Verfahren bei den Bezirksgerichten auch im Verfahren vor Handels- oder Einzelngerichten Anwendung finden, ist das dort von den Anwälten der Parteien Gesagte von den Parteien selbst oder ihren Gewalthabern, das von Anwaltsakten und von Zustellungen an den Gegenanwalt Gesagte von Gerichtsvollzieherakten und von Zustellungen an die Gegenpartei selbst oder ihren Zustellungsbevollmächtigten zu verstehen.**

Was dort von dem Senatsvorstande oder Vorsitzenden gesagt ist, gilt bei den Einzelngerichten von dem Einzelnrichter.

G. A. d. K. d. A. II S. 273. 279. 353. IV S. 111. — K. d. R. II S. 259. IV S. 63.

1) Im Parteiprozesse ist das mündliche Verfahren ganz rein durchgeführt und es werden daher die Anträge, welche die Parteien in der Sitzung stellen, ja unter Umständen die Klage selbst (Art. 504) nur mündlich vorgebracht und vom Richter im Urtheile beurkundet. Daß es gestattet und in vielen Fällen sehr sachgemäß sei, wenn die Parteien ihre Anträge schriftlich überreichen, ist begreiflich; ebenso, daß in diesem Falle die schriftliche Notiz maßgebend und bei der Abfassung des Urtheils zu Grunde zu legen sei. Bemerk. zu Art. 506 Nr. 4.

2) Die Vorschriften in Art. 537 regeln die Uebertragung der im Anwaltsprozesse für das Beweisverfahren gegebenen Bestimmungen auf den Parteiprozeß und bedürfen keiner Erläuterung.

Besichtigung von Waaren.

Art. 538. — **Will Jemand auf Grund einer Bestimmung des Handelsgesetzbuchs den Zustand einer Waare oder eines sonstigen Gegenstands durch Sachverständige feststellen lassen, so hat er das Ansuchen um Ernennung von Sachverständigen an das Handelsgericht des Orts, wo die Waare oder der Gegenstand sich befindet oder, falls im Bezirke des Einzelngerichts, zu welchem der Ort gehört, kein Handelsgericht seinen Sitz hat, an das betreffende Einzelngericht zu richten.**

Das Gesuch muß die Gegenstände kurz bezeichnen und ist entweder schriftlich einzureichen oder auf der Gerichtsschreiberei zu Protokoll zu erklären.

Die Ernennung von Sachverständigen erfolgt bei den Handelsgerichten in geheimer Sitzung, in dringenden Fällen durch den Gerichtsvorstand. In der Regel sind drei Sachverständige zu ernennen, bei unbedeutenden Gegenständen genügt einer.

Die Sachverständigen können nicht abgelehnt werden. Sie sind durch ein Mitglied des Handelsgerichts, beziehungsweise durch den Einzelnrichter über den Auftrag zu belehren und, falls sie nicht zu Begutachtungen dieser Art schon im Allgemeinen in Pflicht genommen sind, zu beeidigen.

Vernehmung der Gegenpartei über das Ansuchen um Ernennung von Sachverständigen und Vorladung derselben zur Einweisung oder Untersuchung ist nur nöthig, wo das Handelsgesetzbuch sie vorschreibt.

Das Gutachten der Sachverständigen, bei welchem im Uebrigen die Bestimmungen des Art. 445 zur Anwendung kommen, wird von ihnen, wenn sie es nicht schriftlich abgeben, auf der Gerichtsschreiberei zu Protokoll erstattet und bleibt ein wie andernfalls dort aufbewahrt, bis das Gericht, bei welchem über den Gegenstand ein Rechtsstreit anhängig wird, die Ablieferung veranlaßt.

G. A. d. K. d. A. II S. 279—281. 353. — K. d. R. II S. 259.

1) Das deutsche Handelsgesetzbuch räumt an verschiedenen Stellen (Art. 348, 365, 407) ein Recht ein, den Zustand von Waaren, wegen deren Streit zu entstehen droht, durch gerichtlich ernannte Sachverständige feststellen zu lassen. Durch Art. 538 soll das Verfahren für diese Fälle bestimmt werden; in sonstigen nicht auf Bestimmungen des Handelsgesetzbuches beruhenden Fällen, wo etwa der Zustand einer Sache festzustellen ist, sind daher die allgemeinen Vorschriften über den Beweis zum ewigen Gedächtnisse maßgebend.

2) Zuständiges Gericht ist das Handelsgericht oder Einzelngericht nach den näheren Bestimmungen in Abs. 1.

Das Verfahren ist einseitig, soweit nicht das Handelsgesetzbuch ausdrücklich ein Beiziehen der Gegenpartei vorschreibt, wie in Art. 407.

Die betreffende Partei wendet sich an das zuständige Gericht mit einem Gesuche, welches die zu besichtigenden Gegenstände zu bezeichnen und selbstverständlich auch den Sachverhalt darzustellen hat, soweit dies nöthig ist, um darzuthun, daß der Fall des Gesetzes gegeben sei.

Auf dieses Gesuch hin, welches von der Partei schriftlich einzureichen oder auf der Gerichtsschreiberei zu Protokoll zu geben ist, erfolgt die Ernennung der Sachverständigen. Ist dasselbe an das Handelsgericht gerichtet, so kann in dringenden Fällen der Gerichtsvorstand verfügen, und zwar tritt dessen Befugniß ein, sobald er sich überzeugt, es sei die anzuordnende Maßregel so dringend, daß es nicht thunlich sei, eine Entschließung des ganzen Gerichts einzuholen. Ob solche Dringlichkeit vorliege, hat der Gerichtsvorstand zu ermessen.

3) Die Wahl der Sachverständigen ist ganz in die Hand des Richters gegeben, welcher in Betracht, daß die Gegenpartei nicht vertreten ist, mit großer Vorsicht zu Werke gehen muß, insbesondere etwaigen Vorschlägen des Gesuchstellers gegenüber. In der Regel sind drei Sachverständige zu ernennen, bei unbedeutenden Gegenständen genügt einer.

Eine Eigenthümlichkeit ist es, daß diese Sachverständigen nicht abgelehnt werden können. Man fand diese Bestimmung im Interesse einer schnellen ungehinderten Erledigung geboten, jedoch ist durch dieselbe nicht ausgeschlossen, daß etwa bestehende Ablehnungsgründe später, wenn die Beweiskraft des Gutachtens zu würdigen ist, berücksichtigt werden können.

Zugleich mit der Ernennung der Sachverständigen ist eine Tagfahrt zu deren Belehrung, d. h. Einweisung und zur Beeidigung festzusetzen. Es folgt dies aus Art. 525, aus der Natur des Parteiprozesses überhaupt und schließlich aus der auf möglichst schnelle und einfache Erledigung gerichteten Tendenz des Art. 538. Deßhalb wird auch für den Fall keine Ausnahme zu machen sein, wo das Handelsgericht verfügt und eines seiner Mitglieder mit der Einweisung beauftragt.

4) Ob die richterliche Verfügung in Urschrift abzugeben oder auszufertigen sei, könnte fraglich erscheinen, und steht diese Frage mit der weiteren in Verbindung, ob hier die Vorschriften von Hauptst. XXV wegen einfacher Vorstellungen gelten?

Es läßt sich sagen:

Nach dem Willen des Gesetzgebers (Art. 642 u. Abg. II 441) sollen die Bestimmungen von Hauptst. XXV nur gelten, wo das Gesetz den technischen Ausdruck: „einfache Vorstellung" gebraucht. Es wurden demgemäß alle einschlägigen Bestimmungen der Prozeßordnung in diesem Sinne berichtigt, namentlich auch die vom Beweise zum ewigen Gedächtniß handelnden Art. 347—352. Hat man nun hier den Ausdruck „Gesuch" stehen lassen, so zeigt dies, daß man die Anwendung des Hptst. XXV nicht wollte.

Dagegen läßt sich jedoch bemerken:

Alle Vorbedingungen, wie sie das Gesetz nach den vom kgl. Minist.-Commissär (Abg. II 441) vorgetragenen Motiven für einfache Vorstellungen verlangt, sind hier vollständig gegeben. Offenbar lag auch kein Grund vor, hier strengere Anforderungen zu stellen, als beim Beweise zum ewigen Gedächtnisse, vielmehr war eher Anlaß gegeben, hier weniger förmlich zu verfahren, da sich die richterliche Thätigkeit auf die Bezeichnung der Sachverständigen beschränkt und der Fall immer dringlich ist. Hierzu kommt, daß die Verfügung auch vom Gerichtsvorstande ausgehen kann, und diese Art der Erledigung sogar zur Regel gemacht worden wäre, hätte man sich nicht durch den Wortlaut des Handelsgesetzbuches gebunden erachtet (Abg. II 441), daß aber bei Verfügungen einzelner Gerichtsmitglieder unsere Prozeßordnung die Hinausgabe in Urschrift als selbstverständlich ansieht, wie dies denn z. B. bei der Bewilligung der Ladung auf kurze Frist (Art. 259) oder bei Festsetzung der Tagfahrt zu einer Beweisaufnahme (Art. 338, 406, 438) nicht bezweifelt werden kann.

Letztere Gründe erscheinen mir überwiegend, und bin ich daher der Ansicht, daß der Gesetzgeber hier ebenso wie im Falle des Art. 213 die Berichtigung im Sinne des Art. 642 übersehen habe.

5) Die Sachverständigen werden in der Regel auf mündliche oder briefliche Einladung freiwillig vor dem Richter erscheinen; sollte dies nicht geschehen, so hätte Vorladung zu erfolgen. Ueber Einweisung und Beeidigung errichtet der Richter ein kurzes Protokoll.

Nähere Vorschriften über die Art, wie die Sachverständigen zu verfahren haben, sind in Art. 538 nicht gegeben, und auch die Bestimmungen des Art. 444 dürfen nicht zur Anwendung kommen, da nur auf Art. 445 Bezug genommen ist. Es ist daher so zu verfahren, wie es der Natur der Sache entspricht.

Die Sachverständigen sind verpflichtet, nach Maßgabe der vom Richter ertheilten Weisungen ihre Prüfung und Feststellung vorzunehmen, und zwar so rasch, als es den Umständen nach nöthig und möglich ist, indem sie nach Uebernahme der Mission für Versäumungen haftbar gemacht werden können. Die Parteien brauchen, soweit nicht etwa das Handelsgesetzbuch anders verfügt, weder anwesend zu sein, noch beigerufen zu werden. Vgl. Art. 350 Abs. 2 mit Art. 538 Abs. 5.

6) Ist ausnahmweise die Gegenpartei zu vernehmen, wie es z. B. Art. 407 des Handelsgesetzbuches für den Fall vorschreibt, wo diese am Orte anwesend ist, so wäre das natürliche Verfahren, sie unter Zustellung des Gesuches in eine vom Richter zu bestimmende geheime Sitzung zu laden, in welcher dann beide Parteien das Für und Wider entwickeln könnten.

Uebrigens scheint mir weder das Handelsgesetzbuch noch unsere Prozeßordnung ein derartiges Verfahren im Auge zu haben, vielmehr möchte anzunehmen sein, daß man nur eine Zustellung des Gesuches mit der Aufforderung, innerhalb gewisser Frist Gegenerinnerungen auf der Gerichtsschreiberei einzugeben, voraussetzte, wie dies in ähnlichen Fällen, wo die Verhandlung in geheimer Sitzung stattfindet, zur Vorschrift gemacht ist, z. B. in Art. 35.

7) Was die Abfassung des Protokolles betrifft, so verweist das Gesetz auf die Vorschriften des Art. 445 und bestimmt, daß das Protokoll beim Gerichte, wo es aufgenommen ist, verwahrt bleibe, bis etwa später vom Prozeßgerichte die Ablieferung begehrt werde.

Dritter Abschnitt.

Außerordentliches Verfahren.

XVIII. Hauptstück.

Wechselprozeß.

Wechsel.

Art. 539. — **In Wechselsachen finden die Vorschriften über das Verfahren vor den Handelsgerichten Anwendung, soweit nicht die Art. 540 — 551 Abweichungen enthalten.**

G. A. d. K. d. A. II S. 378. 401. 402. IV S. 111. — K. d. R. II S. 260. IV S. 63.

1) Unter dem alten Prozesse war ein besonderes Verfahren in Wechselsachen unentbehrlich, unter dem neuen Prozesse jedoch ist es weit weniger Bedürfniß, da schon das gewöhnliche Verfahren Mittel und Wege bietet, auch den Bedürfnissen des Wechselverkehres Rechnung zu tragen.

Es könnte sich sogar die Frage aufwerfen, ob überhaupt ein besonderer Wechselprozeß noch nöthig sei, und zieht man die Erfahrung zu Rathe, so möchte man diese Frage eher verneinen als bejahen. In Frankreich z. B. gibt es keinen Wechselprozeß, ja nicht einmal einzelne Ausnahmsverfügungen für Wechselsachen, vielmehr begnügt man sich mit dem gewöhnlichen handelsgerichtlichen Verfahren und hat sich meines Wissens nie das Bedürfniß eines besonderen Wechselprozesses gezeigt. Dabei ist zu beachten, daß das handelsgerichtliche Verfahren dort in manchen Beziehungen, z. B. was das Beweisverfahren, die Appellabilität von Interlokuten betrifft, umständlicher ist, als das unsrige. Wenn nun in einem Lande, wo der Wechselverkehr so stark ist, ein Zustand über 60 Jahre lang besteht und man damit zufrieden ist, so sollte man denken, er könne nicht schlecht sein.

2) Geht man auf eine nähere Prüfung der Mittel ein, welche unser Gesetz gibt, um Wechselverbindlichkeiten schnell zum Vollzuge zu bringen, so sind dieselben in gewisser Beziehung sehr energisch, sogar bis zur Härte; allein dennoch führen sie nicht zum Ziele, denn es bleibt die Möglichkeit, frivole Einwände wegen Zahlung, Fristgestattung, Irrthum, Betrug rc. vorzubringen, und durch mehr oder minder langwierige Beweisverfahren die Sache in die Länge zu ziehen.

Meiner Meinung nach hätte eine ganz einfache Bestimmung genügt, um den Vollzug von Wechselverbindlichkeiten gegen Chikane zu sichern, nemlich wenn man den Richter befugt erklärt hätte, eine *provisorische Verurtheilung* auszusprechen, d. h. eine Verurtheilung, bei welcher nicht die Nachklage, sondern die Weiterklage, die Fortsetzung des bereits anhängigen Verfahrens vorbehalten würde.

3) Wenn das Gesetz für „*Wechselsachen*“ die besonderen Vorschriften dieses Hauptstücks anwendbar erklärt, so sind hier wohl nicht ganz die nemlichen Gesichtspunkte maßgebend, als dort, wo es sich bloß um die Zuständigkeit handelt. Bemerk. zu Art. 7 Nr. 63 — 65. Offenbar lassen sich die Vorschriften dieses Hauptstückes,

nach ihrem Inhalte und nach dem Zwecke des Gesetzes, nur anwenden auf Fälle, wo der Vollzug einer wechselrechtlichen Verpflichtung in Frage steht, worunter allerdings auch Klagen auf Sicherheitsleistung (Art. 26 der Wechsel-O.) begriffen sind.

Art. 540. — **Wo nicht die Wechselordnung etwas anderes mit sich bringt, muß der Kläger den Wechsel, den dazu gehörigen Protest und die etwa sonst zur Begründung seines Anspruchs erforderlichen Urkunden mit der Klage zustellen lassen und bei der Verhandlung in Urschrift vorlegen.** G. A. d. K. d. A. II S. 378—380. 401. 402. 453. — K. d. R. II S. 260.

1) Für die Vorladung sind im Wechselprozesse außer den gewöhnlichen noch zwei besondere Formen vorgeschrieben, nemlich 1) daß der Wechsel oder überhaupt diejenigen Urkunden, welche nach Maßgabe der Wechselordnung zur Begründung des wechselrechtlichen Anspruches nöthig sind (Art. 26 der W.O.), mit der Klage zugestellt werden müssen, und 2) daß dem Beklagten anzukündigen ist, er müsse, falls er die Unterschrift auf dem Wechsel abläugnen wolle, persönlich erscheinen, oder sofort Nachweis seiner Verhinderung vorlegen (Art. 541).

Es frägt sich nun: welches sind die Folgen, wenn die eine oder die andere dieser besonderen Vorschriften nicht beobachtet wird?

2) Die beiden in Frage stehenden Vorschriften sind gegeben im Hinblicke auf die strengen Anforderungen, welche im Wechselprozesse an den Beklagten gestellt werden, sich persönlich in der ersten Sitzung einzufinden und hier sofort zu erklären, ob er die Urkunde anerkenne oder ob er den Diffessionseid schwören wolle, sowie überhaupt im Hinblicke auf die besonderen Nachtheile, welche sich in diesem Prozesse an das Nichterscheinen des Wechselschuldners knüpfen (vgl. Art. 551). Der Beklagte soll schon in der Vorladung die nöthigen Mittheilungen und Warnungen erhalten, und nur unter der Voraussetzung, daß dies vorschriftsmäßig geschehen, sollen die betreffenden gesetzlichen Vermuthungen und Rechtsverlustigungen eintreten.

Hieraus folgt, daß im Falle des Nichterscheinens des Beklagten die Vorladung als nicht nach den gesetzlichen Vorschriften erhoben im Sinne des Art. 520 Abs. 1 zu betrachten ist, wenn die eine oder die andere der besagten Förmlichkeiten fehlt, und daß der Richter gehalten ist, diesen Mangel von Amtswegen zu beachten. Dabei möchte ich die Gerichtsvollzieher darauf hinweisen, daß sie, um sicher zu gehen, gut thun, wenn sie bei der dem Beklagten zu gebenden Ankündigung genau sich an die Worte halten, wie sie Art. 541 gebraucht.

3) Man würde jedoch irren, wollte man aus dem Vorgesagten folgern, es müsse in derartigen Fällen die Klage als unstatthaft abgewiesen werden. Es ist zu beachten, daß der Wechselgläubiger nicht gezwungen ist, den bloß zu seinem Vortheile geschaffenen Nebenweg des Wechselprozesses zu wählen, daß es ihm vielmehr freisteht, seinen Anspruch im gewöhnlichen handelsgerichtlichen Verfahren zu verfolgen, und daß anzunehmen ist, es sei dies seine Absicht, wenn er die für den Wechselprozeß nöthige Form der Ladung nicht beobachtet hat. Wenn daher der Kläger Zuspruch seiner Klage verlangt und es sind die Voraussetzungen dazu nach den allgemeinen Prinzipien des Art. 520 gegeben, so muß diesem Begehren entsprochen werden; jedoch hat selbstverständlich das ergehende Urtheil nicht die besonderen Wirkungen eines im Wechselprozesse ergangenen Urtheiles und ist insbesondere der Einspruch gegen dasselbe nicht ausgeschlossen.

4) Im Falle des Erscheinens des Beklagten dürfen die dem Wechselprozesse eigenthümlichen Rechtsverlustigungen, wie sie eintreten, wenn der Beklagte nicht persönlich erscheint, sich nicht zum Eide erbietet 2c., der mangelhaften Ladung gegenüber nicht sofort ausgesprochen werden; allein es erscheint sachgemäß und im Geiste der Bestimmungen des Art. 220 Abs. 2 begründet, ist auch ausgesprochener Wille des Gesetzgebers (Abg. II 378 Sp. 2), hier wenn nöthig durch Vertagung zu helfen.

Gibt der Beklagte oder sein Vertreter sofort die Aechtheit der betreffenden Unterschrift zu, so liegt nicht einmal Anlaß zu einer Vertagung vor, wenigstens läßt sich aus den Mängeln der Ladung kein solcher herleiten.

5) Tritt Vertagung ein, so ist in der Regel eine nachträgliche Zustellung auf Kosten des Klägers oder des betreffenden Gerichtsvollziehers anzuordnen und namentlich muß dies in Fällen geschehen, wo für den Beklagten bloß ein Prozeßbevollmächtigter aufgetreten war.

War der Beklagte persönlich erschienen und wurde ihm die betreffende Urkunde in der Sitzung zur Prüfung und Anerkennung vorgelegt, so wird einfache Vertagung mit Hinweisung auf die Nothwendigkeit des wiederholten persönlichen Erscheinens oder des sofortigen Nachweises der Verhinderung (Art. 541) genügen.

In Fällen dieser Art hört natürlich der Prozeß nicht auf, Wechselprozeß zu sein, und finden daher alle Bestimmungen über denselben Anwendung.

Art. 541. — **Der Beklagte, welcher die ihn verbindende Unterschrift auf dem Wechsel eidlich abläugnen will, muß in der Sitzung persönlich erscheinen, falls ihm aber dies wegen Krankheit oder anderer unabwendbarer Verhinderung nicht möglich ist, sofort in dieser Sitzung den Nachweis seiner Verhinderung liefern. Auf diese Bestimmung ist in der Vorladung ausdrücklich aufmerksam zu machen.**

Art. 542. — **Der Beklagte hat sich bei der Verhandlung sofort zu erklären, ob er die ihn verbindende Unterschrift auf dem Wechsel anerkenne oder nicht. Letztern Falls muß er sich zugleich erbieten, zu beschwören, daß er sie weder selbst beigesetzt habe, noch durch einen Andern in seinem Namen habe beisetzen lassen, falls aber die Unterschrift von einem Dritten herrühren soll, daß ihm nicht bekannt sei, daß sie von diesem Dritten herrühre, und daß er nach sorgfältiger Benützung der ihm zu Gebote stehenden Ueberzeugungsmittel sie als ächt anzuerkennen nicht vermöge.**

Soll die Unterschrift von einem Dritten herrühren, so hat sich der Beklagte zugleich darüber zu erklären, ob er anerkenne, daß der Dritte ihn durch seine Unterschrift rechtlich habe verpflichten können.

Art. 543. — **Wenn der Beklagte nicht erscheint, so ist die Unterschrift für anerkannt und im Falle des Art. 542 Abs. 2 auch die Haftbarkeit des Beklagten für die aus der Unterschrift des Dritten sich ergebenden Verpflichtungen als zugestanden zu erachten.**

Art. 544. — **Die Unterschrift ist auch dann für anerkannt zu erachten, wenn der erschienene Beklagte die in Art. 542 Abs. 1 erwähnte Erklärung verweigert oder wenn er zwar die Unterschrift bestreitet, sich jedoch nicht zur eidlichen Abläugnung erbietet.**

Gleiches gilt, wenn ein Bevollmächtigter die Unterschrift bestreitet und zwar damit die Erklärung verbindet, daß der Beklagte sie eidlich abzuläugnen bereit sei, jedoch nicht zugleich darthut, daß es demselben wegen Krankheit oder anderer unabwendbarer Verhinderung unmöglich war, zur sofortigen Eidesleistung persönlich in der Sitzung zu erscheinen.

Art. 545. — **Der Kläger ist nicht gehalten, es auf den Eid des Beklagten ankommen zu lassen, sondern kann die Aechtheit der Unterschrift auf gewöhnlichem Wege beweisen.**

Läßt er es auf den Eid ankommen, so hat das Gericht dem Beklagten den Eid entweder sofort abzunehmen oder, falls hiegegen Bedenken oder Hindernisse bestehen, das weitere Sachgemäße zu verfügen.

Im andern Falle finden die Vorschriften des Art. 371 Abs. 2, Art. 376 – 383 und Art. 385 Anwendung.

Art. 546. — **Verweigert im Falle des Art. 542 Abs. 2 der Beklagte die dort erwähnte Erklärung, so ist seine Haftbarkeit für die aus der Unterschrift des Dritten sich ergebenden Verpflichtungen als zugestanden zu erachten.**

Bestreitet im erwähnten Falle der Beklagte, daß der Dritte ihn durch seine Unterschrift rechtlich habe verpflichten können, so hat der Kläger vorerst letzteres zu beweisen.

G. A. d. K. d. A. II S. 378—380. 401. 402. 453. 454. — K. d. R. II S. 260.

1) Für das Verfahren in der Sitzung sind die Fälle zu unterscheiden, wo der Beklagte persönlich erscheint, wo er bloß durch Bevollmächtigten erscheint und wo er gar nicht erscheint.

a) Persönliches Erscheinen.

2) Das Streben des Gesetzes ist dahin gerichtet, in kürzester Frist den Hauptpunkt, auf welchen es bei Wechselsachen anzukommen pflegt, die Aechtheit der Wechselunterschrift, festzustellen. Deßhalb wird verlangt, daß der Wechselbeklagte, welcher jene Unterschrift abläugnen oder, besser gesagt, in Abrede stellen will, persönlich erscheinen oder seine Verhinderung sofort nachweisen müsse (Art. 541), und gilt diese Vorschrift sowohl für den Fall, wo die Unterschrift vom Beklagten selbst, als wo sie von einem Dritten herrühren soll.

Ist nun der Beklagte persönlich erschienen, so ist ihm der Wechsel sofort vorzulegen und er hat zu erklären, ob er die ihn verpflichtende Unterschrift anerkenne oder nicht (Art. 542), wie dies schon im gewöhnlichen Verfahren (Art. 506) zur Regel gemacht, hier aber noch strenger vorgeschrieben ist.

Erkennt der Beklagte die Unterschrift nicht an, so muß er sich sofort zum Schwure (Diffessionseide) erbieten nach der Formel, wie sie Art. 542 Abs. 1 vorschreibt. Es geht also hier die Eidesannahme der Eideszuschiebung voraus.

Die Natur des mündlichen Verfahrens bringt es mit sich, daß der Richter sich diesen Verpflichtungen des Beklagten gegenüber nicht passiv verhalte, sondern daß er ihn frage, ob er sich zur Eidesleistung erbieten wolle, und ihn auf die gesetzlichen Folgen der Unterlassung dieses Erbietens aufmerksam mache.

3) Verweigert der Beklagte die Erklärung über die Aechtheit, oder erbietet er sich nicht zu dem besagten Eide, so wird nach Art. 544 Abs. 1 die Unterschrift für anerkannt erachtet. Diese gesetzliche Vermuthung läßt sich auch auf dem Wege der Berufung nicht mehr beseitigen (Art. 707).

Hat jedoch der Beklagte die fraglichen Bedingungen erfüllt, und will es Kläger auf den Eid ankommen lassen, so hat das Gericht, wie schon in Art. 531 angeordnet ist und in Art. 545 Abs. 2 wiederholt wird, den Eid in der Regel sofort abzunehmen, kann aber, wenn Bedenken oder Hindernisse bestehen, auch vertagen oder selbst einen Richter beauftragen (Art. 478, 479).

Will der Kläger die Aechtheit der Unterschrift auf anderem Wege darthun, so sind die allgemeinen Vorschriften über den Beweis der Aechtheit von Urkunden maßgebend.

b) Erscheinen durch Bevollmächtigten.

4) Will der Beklagte die Unterschrift nicht bestreiten so kann er wie in jeder andern Sache sich durch einen Bevollmächtigten vertreten lassen, vorbehaltich der Befugniß des Gerichts das persönliche Erscheinen anzuordnen. In der Thatsache, daß er nicht persönlich, sondern durch Bevollmächtigten erscheint, liegt, vorausgesetzt, daß die Ladung den gesetzlichen Vorschriften entspricht, ein Verzicht auf das Recht, die Aechtheit der Unterschrift zu bestreiten, welche gemäß Art. 543 für anerkannt zu erachten ist.

Eine Ausnahme greift jedoch Platz und es kann die Bestreitung der Aechtheit auch durch einen Bvollmächtigten erfolgen, wenn in der Weise, wie es Art. 541 verlangt, sofort der Nachweis der Verhinderung erbracht wird. Zu beachten ist in dieser Beziehung, daß nur Krankheit oder andere unabwendbare Verhinderung entschuldigen und Nachweis verlangt wird, also Bescheinigung nicht genügt.

5) Auch in diesem Ausnahmsfalle hat übrigens, nach den allgemeinen Vorschrifen des Art. 506 und nach den besonderen der Art. 542 Abs. 1 und 544 Abs. 2, der Bevollmächtigte sich sofort darüber zu erklären, ob die Unterschrift anerkannt werde und ob der Beklagte bereit sei, den Diffessionseid zu leisten.

Glaubt er Grund zu haben, um eine Vertagung zu erbitten, welche nach Maßgabe von Art. 548 allerdings gewährt werden darf, so stellt er ein bezügliches Ansuchen und verbindet damit für den Fall der Verwerfung die betreffenden Erklärungen.

6) Was insbesondere den Fall betrifft, wo die Wechselunterschrift von einem Dritten herrührt, so ist der Beklagte, wenn er bloß seine Haftung in Abrede stellen, nicht aber die Aechtheit der Unterschrift bestreiten will, nicht verpflichtet, persönlich zu erscheinen. Das Gesetz sagt zwar in Art. 542 Abs. 2, daß der Beklagte mit der Erklärung über die Aechtheit sofort auch diese Erklärung zu verbinden habe, und setzt in Art. 546 eine Rechtsverlustigung auf die Versäumung; es sagt aber nirgends, daß zur Bestreitung des Wechsels in dieser Richtung das persönliche Erscheinen oder das Erbieten zur Eidesleistung nöthig sei.

Es kann diese Bestreitung also auch durch einen Bevollmächtigten erfolgen. Dieser Bevollmächtigte ist jedoch ebenso wie der Beklagte, welcher persönlich erscheint, verpflichtet, sich sofort zu erklären, ob die Unterschrift als verpflichtend anerkannt werde, und wenn er dies versäumt, so tritt die in Art. 546 gedrohte gesetzliche Vermuthung der Anerkennung ein.

c) Nichterscheinen.

7) Erscheint der Beklagte nicht, so soll nach Art. 543 die Unterschrift als anerkannt gelten, und im Falle sie von einem Dritten herrührt, auch die Haftung des Beklagten für zugestanden.

Das Gesetz hat hier dasjenige Erscheinen im Auge, welches den Umständen nach nöthig ist, so daß also die beiden Sätze dieses Artikels eine verschiedene Tragweite haben, indem der erste ein persönliches Erscheinen voraussetzt, der letzte aber ein Erscheinen überhaupt im Sinne des Art. 520.

8) Der erste Satz umfaßt natürlich auch den Fall, wo der Beklagte gar nicht erscheint, d. h. auch nicht durch Bevollmächtigten, was insofern nicht ohne Bedeutung erscheint, als aus der Verbindung von Art. 540 a. E. und Art. 543 sich ergibt, daß auch in diesem Falle der Kläger verpflichtet sei, den Wechsel vorzulegen, der Richter aber durch Prüfung desselben sich zu überzeugen habe, ob die Voraussetzungen des Wechselprozesses gegeben seien. Es genügt also hier

nicht, wie nach gewöhnlichem Verfahren (Art. 520), daß der Kläger bloß Thatsachen behaupte. Folge hiervon ist, daß im Sachverhalte des Versäumungsurtheiles die Thatsache, daß der Wechsel vorgelegt worden, beurkundet werden muß.

9) Auch hier ist zu bemerken, daß es dem Wechselgläubiger nicht verwehrt ist, von den besonderen Formen und Vortheilen des Wechselprozesses abzusehen und den Weg des gewöhnlichen Verfahrens zu wählen.

Art. 547. — Der Beklagte kann sich nur solcher Einreden bedienen, welche entweder die wesentlichen Erfordernisse des Verfahrens betreffen oder unter Art. 82 der Wechselordnung fallen.

G. A. d. K. d. A. II S. 380—385. 401. 402. — K. d. R. II S. 260.

1) Dieser Artikel ist für den Wechselprozeß eigentlich nur durch das, was er nicht sagt, von Erheblichkeit, nemlich insofern aus demselben sich ergibt, daß es auf die Frage, ob eine vorgebrachte Einrede liquid sei oder nicht, ferner nicht mehr ankomme. Was er sagt, ist theils selbstverständlich, theils enthält es eine einfache Bezugnahme auf die Bestimmungen der Wechselordnung.

Wenn es heißt, der Beklagte dürfe sich solcher Einreden bedienen, welche die wesentlichen Erfordernisse des Verfahrens betreffen, so sind hiermit alle Einreden getroffen, welche sich aus prozessualen Vorschriften herleiten. Wo Einreden dieser Art gesetzlich gegeben sind, handelt es sich auch um wesentliche Erfordernisse des Verfahrens. Vgl. Art. 218 Abs. 2. Solche Einreden sind insbesondere diejenigen der Unzuständigkeit, des Mangels der Prozeßvollmacht und der Nichtigkeit der Ladung.

2) Was die Bestimmungen von Art. 82 der Wechselordnung betrifft, auf welche Art. 547 Bezug nimmt, so sprechen dieselben ausschließlich von Einreden, welche dem Wechselrechte angehören, welche also die Frage betreffen, ob der wechselrechtliche Anspruch als solcher erhoben werden könne. Sie sind daher im Grunde dem Wechselprozesse fremd. Trotzdessen erscheint es sachgemäß, eine Erörterung derselben nicht zu umgehen, da sie an sich von großer Wichtigkeit sind und wenigstens mittelbar auch in das Gebiet des Prozesses hinüberwirken.

3) Art. 82 der W. O. erklärt zwei Arten von Einreden wechselrechtlich zulässig, nemlich 1) solche, welche aus dem Wechselrechte selbst hervorgehen, und 2) solche, welche dem Wechselschuldner unmittelbar gegen den jedesmaligen Kläger zustehen.

Unter den Einreden erster Art sind jene zu verstehen, welche auf die besonderen Bestimmungen der Wechselordnung sich gründen, also die Wechselfähigkeit (§ 1), die Aechtheit der Wechselunterschrift (§ 75), Form und Inhalt der Wechselerklärung (§ 4 ff.), Beobachtung der zur Sicherung des Wechselrechts vorgeschriebenen Formen (§ 41, 45 ff.), Verjährung der Wechselklage (§ 77 ff.) 2c. betreffen. Solche Einreden haften am Wechsel selbst und können jedem, der ihn geltend macht, entgegengehalten werden.

4) Unter den Einreden der zweiten Art sind civilrechtliche Einreden zu verstehen.

Das Gesetz unterscheidet, ob diejenige Person klagend auftritt, welcher gegenüber der Wechselanspruch entstanden ist, oder aber ein Erwerber dieses Anspruchs, ein dritter Wechselinhaber. Letzteren schützt es gegen civilrechtliche Einreden, welche sich aus der Zeit vor ihrem Erwerbe oder aus der Person früherer Besitzer des Wechsels herleiten. Es kann ihm weder entgegengehalten werden, daß der Wechselanspruch aus civilrechtlichen Gründen (wegen Irrthums, Betrugs 2c.) nicht giltig entstanden, oder daß er einem früheren Wechselinhaber gegenüber wieder erloschen sei.

Was nun aber den ursprünglichen Wechselgläubiger betrifft, so entsteht die Frage, ob ihm alle civilrechtlichen Einreden ohne Ausnahme entgegengehalten werden können, wie dies der Wortlaut des Art. 82 gestatten würde, oder aber ob gewisse Einreden als unzulässig auszuscheiden seien.

Diese Frage ist eine sehr schwierige und vielbestrittene, eine Frage von größter Wichtigkeit für das Wechselrecht und mittelbar auch für den Wechselprozeß, insofern je nach ihrer Beantwortung das Gebiet der Zwischenstreite, über welche sich der Wechselprozeß erstreckt, ein engeres oder weiteres ist. Man muß, um sie zu lösen, auf die Natur der Wechselverpflichtung zurückgehen und fragen: Was hat man im Sinne unserer Wechselordnung unter einer wechselmäßigen Haftung zu verstehen?

5) Es lassen sich zwei verschiedene Ansichten aufstellen.

Nach der ersten Ansicht sind alle civilrechtlichen Einreden statthaft, und sprechen für dieselbe folgende Erwägungen:

Jede Wechselverpflichtung setzt irgend ein Rechtsverhältniß voraus, in welchem sie nach den Grundsätzen des Civilrechts ihren Verpflichtungsgrund findet. Da nun Civilrecht und Wechselrecht sich wie Regel und Ausnahme gegenüberstehen, so ist selbstverständlich, daß die Grundsätze des Civilrechts überall durchgreifen und wirksam werden müssen, wo sie nicht durch ausdrückliche Bestimmungen der Wechselordnung beseitigt sind. Nirgends ist nun in der Wechselordnung bestimmt, daß der Wechselgläubiger gegen Einreden civilrechtlicher Natur, welche ihm selbst gegenüber zustehen, geschützt sein solle, bloß deßhalb, weil dieselben aus dem der Wechselverpflichtung zu Grunde liegenden Rechtsverhältnisse sich herleiten.

Hätte die Wechselordnung bestimmen wollen, daß unter wechselmäßiger Verpflichtung eine solche zu verstehen sei, welche vom Zusammenhange des Wechselversprechens mit sonstigen Rechtsverhältnissen ganz absehe, so würde sie nicht unterlassen haben, dies auszusprechen. Sie wäre sicher nicht verlegen gewesen, den Ausdruck dafür zu finden. Das Stillschweigen des Gesetzgebers führt nun aber offenbar zur Annahme, daß er alle einem bestimmten Kläger gegenüber bestehenden civilrechtlichen Einreden zulassen wollte, und es dem Wechselprozesse überlassen bleiben sollte, gewisse Einreden, z. B. illiquide, mit Vorbehalt der Nachklage auszuscheiden.

Auch aus dem Geiste des Gesetzes lassen sich Gründe für diese Ansicht geltend machen.

Die ganze Frage hat offenbar nur Bedeutung für trockene Wechsel und für die Fälle, wo der Wechselschuldner dem ursprünglichen Wechselgläubiger gegenübersteht. Nun müssen zwar trockene Wechsel den gezogenen ganz gleichstehen, sofern sie in den Verkehr gelangt sind und in dritter Hand sich befinden; allein es liegt kein genügender Grund vor, auch dem ursprünglichen Gläubiger gegenüber das Eingehen auf die Art und Weise der Entstehung des Wechsels abzuschneiden. Ein Privileg dieser Art ist kein Bedürfniß des kaufmännischen Verkehrs, wohl aber leistet es schlechten und verbotenen Geschäften Vorschub, welchen die Wechselform als Deckmantel dient.

Schließlich ist zu bemerken, daß dem Schuldner jedenfalls das Recht zugestanden werden müßte, das, was er im Wechselprozesse zu zahlen verurtheilt wurde, im ordentlichen Prozesse als sine causa gezahlt zurückzufordern; nun ist aber nicht abzusehen, warum dem klagenden Wechselgläubiger nicht sofort dürfe der Grundsatz entgegengehalten werden: »dolo facit, qui petit, quod redditurus est.«

Von diesen Anschauungen geht die französische Gesetzgebung aus, welche nur den gezogenen Wechsel kennt und nur in gewisser Richtung auch dem billet à ordre wechselrechtliche Wirkungen einräumt. Vgl. Bemerk. zu Art. 7 Nr. 34.

Von der nemlichen Anschauung gehen aus die Oberappellationsgerichte in Stuttgart (Seuff. Archiv Bd. XII Nr. 191), Celle (Bd. XV Nr. 69, Bd. XX Nr. 65), Kassel (Bd. XV Nr. 70, Bd. XIX Nr. 184) und Rostock (Bd. XVIII Nr. 41a). Sie wird vertreten durch Hofmann (Erläut. der allg. d. W.O. S. 101).

6) Nach einer zweiten Ansicht scheidet sich ein großer Theil der civilrechtlichen Einreden aus, und zwar nach folgenden Gesichtspunkten.

Während man früher die wechselrechtlichen Grundsätze aus dem Vertragsrechte herzuleiten suchte, hat sich in neuerer Zeit eine neue Lehre vom Wesen der Wechselverpflichtung herausgebildet, welche dieselbe als ein für sich bestehendes, von der Geschichte seiner Entstehung sich loslösendes, den Verpflichtungsgrund in sich allein tragendes formales Zahlungsversprechen auffaßt. Zwar gehen bei Charakterisirung dieses selbstständigen Verpflichtungsaktes die Ansichten auseinander, indem Einert von einem „kaufmännischen Papiergelde", Thöl von einem „Summenversprechen", Liebe von einem „Formalakte" spricht, allein im Wesen führen sie zum nemlichen Ziele.

Diese neue Lehre war bereits anerkannt, als unsere Wechselordnung entstand; die Motive zum preußischen Entwurfe (S. 35) sprechen sie scharf und entschieden aus, und es läßt sich nicht bezweifeln, daß sie auch von der Leipziger Commission, zu deren Mitgliedern ihre Gründer zählten, als maßgebend betrachtet worden sei, wie sie denn namentlich Anlaß gab, daß man die Erwähnung der Valuta beseitigte. Bei den bezüglichen Verhandlungen (Sitzung vom 25. Okt. 1847 S. 11) wurde ausgesprochen, „daß das Wechselgeschäft ein formelles sei, bei welchem die causa debendi zurücktrete."

Deßhalb wurde fragliche Anschauung denn sofort von Brauer, einem Mitgliede der Leipziger Commission, in seinem Commentare zur d. W.O. S. 5 u. 25 als diejenige des Gesetzes erklärt. Dieselbe ist vertreten von Bluntschli (Dollmanns Gesetzgeb. des K. B. Bd. I S. 5) und in einer sehr lichtvollen Abhandlung der Bl. f. R. Bd. XXVI S. 371 ff. Sie findet Anerkennung in einer Reihe von Urtheilen des Obertribunals in Berlin (Seuff. Archiv Bd. IX Nr. 68, Bd. XI Nr. 292, Bd. XII Nr. 191, Bd. XIV Nr. 60, Bd. XIX Nr. 66), dann durch das O.L.G. in Wien (Seuff. Archiv Bd. XX Nr. 257) und d. O.A.G. in Wolfenbüttel (Bd. XII Nr. 191). Namentlich aber haben sich die Gerichte in Bayern von jeher in diesem Sinne ausgesprochen, wie aus einer Reihe appellationsgerichtlicher Entscheidungen sich ergibt, welche in der Zeitschrift für G. u. R. abgedruckt sind (Vgl. Bd. II S. 483, 485, 496. Bd. IV S. 433, 434. Bd. IX S. 583. Bd. X S. 337. Bd. XII S. 123, neue Folge Bd. I S. 247. Bd. II S. 146.

7) Aus dieser Feststellung des Begriffes einer Wechselverpflichtung leiten sich sehr gewichtige Folgen ab.

Da diese Verpflichtung eine für sich bestehende Rechtshandlung und ihr Zweck einzig und allein dahin gerichtet ist, dem Wechselgläubiger zur bestimmten Zeit die bestimmte Geldsumme zu sichern, so ist es gleichgiltig, ob die erfolgende Zahlung als Tilgung einer eignen oder fremden Schuld, ob sie als ein zurückzuzahlender Vorschuß, oder als Schenkung zu betrachten sei. Dies sind Fragen, um welche sich das Wechselrecht nicht bekümmert. Nach Wechselrecht können vielmehr nur folgende Fragen erhoben werden: Sind die Formen des Wechselrechts eingehalten? War der Wechselschuldner fähig, Wechselverpflichtungen überhaupt einzugehen? Erscheint die Wechselerklärung selbst als Ausfluß einer ernstlichen und freien Willensäußerung?

Hieraus ergibt sich weiter, daß eine wechselrechtliche Verurtheilung das Rechtsverhältniß unter den Parteien nicht endgiltig ordnet, daß vielmehr eine spätere Regelung vorbehalten bleiben und es gestattet sein muß, die civilrechtlichen Einwände, welche der Wechselverpflichtung gegenüber wirkungslos waren, in einer besonderen Klage zur Geltung zu bringen. Vgl. Bemerk. zu Art. 550.

Auch für die Frage der Wechselfähigkeit, d. h. für die Tragweite des § 1 der d. W. O., ergeben sich wichtige Folgen. Erscheint nemlich das wechselmäßige Zahlungsversprechen als ein freistehendes, den wechselrechtlichen Verpflichtungsgrund in sich selbst tragendes Rechtsgeschäft, so kann es weder eine Schenkung, noch eine Verbürgung, noch sonst ein besonderes Civilgeschäft sein. Wechselfähig ist dann jeder, welcher im Allgemeinen fähig ist, ein Zahlungsversprechen zu geben, und es kann demgemäß eine Wechselverpflichtung nicht deßhalb angefochten werden, weil sie von einer Ehefrau zum Zwecke einer Verbürgung, oder von einem Haussohne wegen eines Darlehens eingegangen worden sei. Vgl. Seuff. Archiv Bd. X Nr. 79, Bd. XII Nr. 191. Zeitschrift für G. u. R. Bd. II S. 483, 485. Bd. IV S. 433, 434.

8) Frägt man, welche der beiden erörterten Ansichten den Vorzug verdiene, so glaube ich mich für die letztere, als die dem Willen des Gesetzgebers entsprechende, aussprechen zu müssen.

Es spricht für sie noch der besondere Grund, daß sie offenbar bei den Verhandlungen über unsere Prozeßordnung die leitende gewesen ist. Vgl. Abg. II 384 (Schmitt), 385 (Völk).

Nur unter dieser Voraussetzung konnte der Gesetzgeber es wagen, alle Einreden, welche das Wechselrecht zuläßt, ohne jegliche Rücksicht auf Liquidität auch im Wechselprozesse zuzulassen. Vergenwärtigt man sich Fälle, wo der Wechsel für eine Theilungsherausgabe, einen Rechnungsrezeß, einen Immobiliarkaufpreis, eine Aussteuer rc. ausgestellt wurde, so leuchtet sofort ein, daß es der Wille des Gesetzgebers nicht sein konnte, alle civilrechtlichen Einreden, welche sich aus den beregten Rechtsverhältnissen herleiten, im Wechselprozesse verhandeln zu lassen. Es ist dies so klar und greifbar, daß man bei Annahme der ersteren Ansicht sich einen Nothweg bahnen und alle Einreden, welche sich zur Aburtheilung durch Handelsgerichte nicht eignen, als selbständige Zwischenpunkte im Sinne des Art. 9 vor's Civilgericht verweisen müßte, ein Verfahren, welches natürlich nichts weniger als geeignet wäre, dem Wechselprozesse einen raschen Fortgang zu verschaffen.

Schließlich läßt auch der Inhalt des Art. 550 die Anschauung, von welcher die Prozeßordnung ausgeht, klar erkennen, denn nachdem der Wechselprozeß keinen Anlaß zu einer Nachklage mehr gibt, kann derselbe nur im Wechselrechte gesucht werden. Vgl. Abg. II 385 (Völk).

Art. 548. — **Alle Fristen, deren Bestimmung vom Gerichte abhängt, sind nur nach den Anforderungen des unabweislichen Bedürfnisses festzusetzen.**

Die Vertagung der Verhandlung ist ohne Einwilligung des Klägers nur wenn besonders dringende und vollständig nachgewiesene Umstände sie nothwendig machen und nur auf möglichst kurze Zeit zu bewilligen.

Vertagung aus Anlaß einer Streitverkündung oder Gewährschaftsklage ist immer nur mit Einwilligung des Klägers zulässig.

Art. 549. — **Die einstweilige Vollstreckung des Urtheils ist auf Verlangen des Klägers, wenn der Wechselverpflichtete die Aechtheit der ihn verbindenden Unterschrift auf dem Wechsel nicht bestritten hat, ohne vorgängige Sicherheitsleistung zu verfügen. Andernfalls bleibt es dem Ermessen des Gerichts anheimgegeben, ob eine solche Sicherheitsleistung anzuordnen sei.**

G. A. d. K. d. A. II S. 379. 385. 386. 402. 407. 454. IV S. 111.
K. d. R. II S. 260. 261. IV S. 63.

1) Bei der auf rasche Erledigung dringenden Tendenz des Wechselprozesses ist es natürlich, daß alle Fristen so kurz als möglich bemessen werden müssen und Vertagungen gegen den Willen des Klägers nur in seltenen Fällen eintreten dürfen.

Wenn das Gesetz sagt, die Fristen seien nur nach den Anforderungen des unabweislichen Bedürfnisses festzusetzen, so möchte hieraus zu folgern sein, daß die Befugniß des pfälzischen Richters, Fristen für den Vollzug seines Urtheils zu gestatten, in Wechselsachen wegfalle, denn eine solche Fristgestattung kann nie unabweisliches Bedürfniß sein. Uebrigens läßt sich auch aus dem Wesen der Wechselverpflichtung und aus den Bestimmungen des Art. 549 die Unstatthaftigkeit solcher Fristbewilligungen folgern. Vgl. Bemerk. zu Art. 207 u. 208 Nr. 6.

Was Vertagungen anbelangt, so ist hervorzuheben, daß vollständiger Nachweis der veranlassenden Umstände verlangt wird.

2) Eine beachtenswerthe Bestimmung ist diejenige in Abs. 3 des Art. 548, welche Vertagung zum Zwecke der Streitverkündung und Gewährschaftsklage verbietet, wenn nicht der Kläger einwilligt.

Da die Erscheinungsfrist in Handelssachen sehr kurz ist und selten Zeit übrig bleibt, um vor der Verhandlung eine Streitverkündung oder Gewährschaftsklage wirksam vorzunehmen, so erleiden hier die allgemeinen Vorschriften der Art. 69 ff. zu Gunsten des Wechselprozesses eine Ausnahme und zwar sowohl was die Rechte, als was die Pflichten des Gewährschäftsberechtigten betrifft. Uebrigens ist darauf hinzuweisen, daß wegen des Regresses in Wechselsachen besondere Vorschriften bestehen. W.O. § 45 ff.

3) Bezüglich der vorläufigen Vollstreckbarkeit der Urtheile (Art. 268 u. 513) gibt das Gesetz zwei Ausnahmsbestimmungen, nemlich:

1) daß in Fällen, wo die Aechtheit der Unterschrift nicht bestritten ist, die einstweilige Vollstreckung ohne Sicherheitsleistung verfügt werden müsse, wenn Kläger es verlangt, und

2) daß in sonstigen Fällen es im Ermessen des Gerichts stehe, Sicherheitsleistung anzuordnen.

Bei der ersten Ausnahme ist nicht davon die Sprache, daß die Aechtheit der Unterschrift zugestanden, sondern daß sie nicht bestritten sei; es sind daher auch die Fälle begriffen, wo sie wegen Nichterscheinens des Beklagten oder wegen Verweigerung der erforderlichen Erklärungen als anerkannt gilt.

Aus der zweiten Ausnahme folgt, daß auch in jenen Fällen, wo in sonstigen Handelssachen nach Art. 513 Abs. 3 Sicherheitsleistung nöthig ist, deren Auflage vom Ermessen des Richters abhängt.

Abgesehen vom Falle der Nichtbestreitung der Aechtheit der Wechselunterschrift, entscheidet daher bei Wechselsachen in allen Fällen das richterliche Ermessen darüber, ob Sicherheitsleistung einzutreten habe oder nicht. Für jenen Fall, von welchem Art. 268 Abs. 1 spricht, ist keine weitere Ausnahme zu machen, da er die Nichtbestreitung der Unterschrift voraussetzt.

Art. 550. — **Die Nachklage wird im Wechselprozesse weder besonders vorbehalten, noch findet Anordnung einer Sicherheitsleistung für dieselbe statt.**

G. A. d. K. d. A. II S. 385. 386. 402. — K. d. R. II S. 261.

1) Wie schon zu Art. 125 Nr. 2 bemerkt, verstand man unter Nachklagen bis jetzt Klagen, vermittelst deren Punkte, über welche in einem bestimmten Prozesse nach der Natur der besonderen Prozeßart nicht entschieden werden konnte, zum Austrage gebracht werden.

Der Entwurf gab zu Nachklagen dieser Art Anlaß im Exekutivprozesse und im Wechselprozesse, indem er bei diesen Prozeßarten nur Einreden, welche sofort urkundlich erwiesen werden konnten, zuließ (Art. 527 u. 621 des E.); allein nachdem der Exekutivprozeß beseitigt ist, im Wechselprozesse aber auch illiquide Einreden zugelassen werden, kann von einer prozessualen Nachklage nicht mehr die Rede sein.

2) Da nun Art. 550 trotzdem von einer Nachklage spricht, so kann nur jene aus dem Wechselrechte sich ergebende Nachklage gemeint sein, welche zuzulassen ist, wenn man der oben (zu Art. 547 Nr. 6, 7, 8) entwickelten Ansicht über die Natur der Wechselverpflichtung huldigt. Es liegt nemlich auf flacher Hand, daß die Wechselverpflichtung nicht die Kraft haben könne, alle Grundsätze des Civilrechts umzustoßen, aus weiß schwarz zu machen, zu bewirken, daß was verboten ist erlaubt und was nichtig ist giltig werde; vielmehr kann die Wechselstrenge civilrechtliche Einreden nur mit dem Vorbehalte beseitigen, sie im Wege besonderer Klage nachträglich zur Geltung zu bringen.

Ob man diese Nachklage als condictio sine causa zu charakterisiren habe oder wie sonst, erscheint als eine müßige Frage; sicher ist, daß sie statthaft sein müsse. Ebensowenig wie der Wechsel selbst sich bloß nach den Begriffen des gemeinen Rechts beurtheilen läßt, ist dies auch bezüglich dieser seiner Natur entspringenden Nachklage der Fall, insbesondere aber dürfte man nicht untersuchen, ob nach den Lehren des gemeinen Rechts eine Rückforderung begründet wäre. Jenen Fall, wo das Gesetz nicht erlaubt, eine Einrede, obgleich sie besteht, zur Geltung zu bringen, darf man nicht demjenigen gleichstellen, wo Jemand eine Verpflichtung, gegen welche eine Einrede gegeben war, freiwillig erfüllt hat.

3) Die Nachklage des Art. 550 wäre demnach eine Klage, vermittelst deren Punkte, über welche im Wechselprozesse nach der besonderen Natur des Wechselrechtes nicht entschieden werden kann, zum Austrage gebracht werden.

Der Charakter der Nachklage, wie ihn der seitherige Prozeß anerkannte, hat sich hierdurch im Wesen nicht geändert, wie denn eine aus dem Wechselrechte sich herleitende Nachklage auch seither schon zugelassen werden mußte und zugelassen wurde (Bl. f. R. Bd. XXXII S. 18); nur hat die Nachklage ihr prozessuales Gebiet verloren und die Definition, wie sie Seuffert a. a. O. gibt, ist jetzt nicht mehr passend.

4) Aus der Verfügung des Art. 550 geht hervor, daß die Nachklage sich überall, wo Anlaß dazu gegeben ist, auch ohne besonderen Vorbehalt des Gerichts oder des Beklagten, von selbst verstehe, sowie ferner, daß eine Sicherheitsleistung, wie sie Art. 125 für den Fall einer Nachklage vorbehält, nicht stattfinde. Hiermit ist allerdings zugleich ausgesprochen, daß die Bestimmungen, welche Art. 125 bezüglich der Nachklage gibt, geradezu gegenstandslos sind.

Art. 551. — Gegen Versäumungsurtheile findet kein Einspruch statt.

G. A. d. K. d. A. II S. 386. 402. IV S. 111. — K. d. R. II S. 261. 262. IV S. 63.

1) Die Bestimmung, daß gegen Versäumungsurtheile im Wechselprozesse kein Einspruch stattfinde, enthält eine große Härte, zu welcher um so weniger Grund vorlag, nachdem man so nachsichtig gewesen war, selbst illiquide Einreden zuzulassen und dem Schuldner die Mittel zur Prozeßverzögerung in die Hand zu geben. Besser und praktischer wäre es gewesen, den Einspruch zu gestatten, jedoch zu verfügen, daß er den Vollzug nie hemme.

Die Verfügung des Art. 551 ist ganz allgemein, trifft also Versäumungsurtheile jeder Art, ohne Unterschied, ob sie gegen den Beklagten oder gegen den Kläger gesprochen wurden, ob sie in der ersten Verhandlung oder nach einer Beweiserhebung erfolgten, ob sie eine Vorfrage oder die Hauptsache betreffen. Abg. II 386 Sp. 1.

2) Eine schwierige Frage ist es, ob bei gegebenen Voraussetzungen die Wiedereinsetzung in den vorigen Stand an Stelle des versagten Einspruches treten könne.

Daß Wiedereinsetzung erwirkt werden könne, wenn in Folge der Einlegung eines Rechtsmittels, namentlich der Berufung, eine neue Aburtheilung stattfindet, erleidet keinen Zweifel; allein fraglich ist, ob jenes Auskunftsmittel auch dann zu Gebot stehe, wenn ein Rechtsmittel, in dessen Gefolge es auftreten könnte, nicht gegeben ist, m. a. W. ob es selbst die Stelle eines Rechtsmittels vertreten könne.

Liest man, was bei den Verhandlungen (Abg. II 386 Sp. 1 und 402) über die Zuläßigkeit der Wiedereinsetzung gesagt worden ist, insbesondere folgende Aeußerung: „Einspruch und Wiedereinsetzung stehen selbständig für sich, so daß, wenn der Einspruch versäumt ist, Wiedereinsetzung nachgesucht werden kann,“ so sollte man es für zweifellos halten, daß die aufgeworfene Frage zu bejahen sei; allein faßt man die Prinzipien ins Auge, sowie die Bestimmungen des Entwurfs und die Aeußerungen in der Kammer der Reichsräthe, so entstehen gewichtige Bedenken und muß sich schließlich die Ueberzeugung vom Gegentheile ergeben.

3) Die Wiedereinsetzung in den vorigen Stand, soweit sie von unserer Prozeßordnung beibehalten wurde, ist kein Rechtsmittel und kann auch nicht an Stelle eines solchen treten.

Schon im alten Prozesse hielt man am Grundsatze fest, daß durch die restitutio contra lapsum termini für sich allein keine der Rechtskraft fähige Entscheidung aufgehoben werden könne. Wenn Seuffert (Comm. Bd. IV S. 203) gegen Versäumungsurtheile die Restitution zuläßt, so rechtfertigt er dies unter dem Gesichtspunkte einer Remonstration und sagt: „Nur gegen das Versäumniß wird hier Restitution gesucht, die Bitte um die Zurücknahme des Erkenntnisses hat die Natur einer Remonstration.“ Hieraus folgt, daß wenn irgendwo verfügt wäre, es finde gegen eine gewisse Entscheidung keine Remonstration statt, hiermit selbstverständlich auch das Nachsuchen um Restitution vor dem nemlichen Richter ausgeschlossen wäre. Vgl. Gönner Comm. zur Novelle von 1819 S. 281 ff. 293.

Noch entschiedener muß im neuen Prozesse an diesem Grundsatze festgehalten werden, indem jetzt die Restitution gegen die Versäumung von Tagfahrten und Fristen und die Restitution gegen Urtheile noch viel schärfer, selbst der Benennung nach, getrennt sind als früher, und die Art und Weise, wie Urtheile angefochten und aufgehoben werden können, erschöpfend geregelt ist.

Ein Urtheil, welches der Rechtskraft fähig ist, kann nach den Grundsätzen der Prozeßordnung nur aufgehoben werden auf Grund eines der im Buche III bezeichneten Rechtsmittel, oder aber in jenen Fällen, wo sonst eine ausdrückliche Verfügung des Gesetzes es gestattet, z. B. auf Grund der Nichtigkeitsklage des Art. 98 oder des Einspruchs gegen Versäumungsurtheile. Auch der Fall des Art. 566 läßt sich hierher ziehen.

In den von der Wiedereinsetzung handelnden Artikeln 216 und 217 ist nun aber mit keiner Sylbe davon die Rede, daß hier ein Mittel gegeben werden solle, um Urtheilssprüche aufzuheben.

Es versteht sich dies auch keineswegs von selbst, denn der Spruch des Urtheils ist von der Thatsache der Versäumung der Tagfahrt wohl zu trennen. Nur gegen die Versäumung gibt Art. 216 Restitution, nicht gegen das in Folge derselben ergangene Urtheil. Von derselben könnte etwa die Rede sein, wenn am Tage, auf welchen Vorladung erging, bloß die Versäumung beurkundet wird, der Spruch des Urtheils aber später erfolgt und noch vor demselben die säumige Partei erscheint; allein sie ist ausgeschlossen, sobald das Urtheil gesprochen ist. Allerdings wird sich das Urtheil in der Regel auf die Versäumung stützen, es wird diese einen wesentlichen Theil der Entscheidungsgründe bilden; allein es ist bekannter Grundsatz, daß der Nachweis, es beruhe ein Richterspruch auf irrigen, unhaltbaren thatsächlichen Voraussetzungen, nicht genügt, ihn umzustoßen, falls nicht Rechtsmittel gegeben sind oder sonst eine ausdrückliche Verfügung des Gesetzes es erlaubt.

Hätte man die unverschuldete Versäumung einer Tagfahrt oder Frist als Grund zur Anfechtung eines sonst rechtskräftigen Urtheils anerkennen wollen, so hätte Artikel 761 davon sprechen müssen, welcher jedoch nur die Ausnahmsfälle begreift, wo der Gegner durch Betrug die Versäumung veranlaßt oder wo ein Vormund Gefährde geübt hat.

4) Daß man bei den Art. 216 u. 217 nicht an die Anfechtung von Urtheilen dachte, geht auch klar aus dem Verfahren hervor, wie es Art. 217 vorschreibt.

Es ist dort nur davon die Rede, daß die Verhinderungsursache anzugeben und zu beweisen sei, wird aber nicht angedeutet, daß auch die Gründe für Aufhebung des Urtheils zu entwickeln seien, wie dies für den Einspruch (Art. 312 u. 522) vorgeschrieben und wie es nöthig ist, wenn ein richterlicher Spruch umgestoßen werden soll. Es genügt nemlich zu diesem Zwecke nicht, die Nichtverschuldung der Versäumung darzuthun, sondern es ist auch zu prüfen, ob und in wie weit die Versäumung von Einfluß auf die Entscheidung gewesen und ob überhaupt Grund gegeben sei, diese Entscheidung zu ändern.

5) Ein Versäumungsurtheil hat, abgesehen von der Eigenheit, dem Einspruche unterworfen zu sein, ganz die nemliche Natur wie ein contradiktorisches Urtheil. Insofern es die Klage zu- oder aberkennt, liegt ebensogut ein der Rechtskraft fähiges Endurtheil vor, als wäre die Aburtheilung eine contradiktorische.

Wollte man die Wiedereinsetzung gegen Versäumungsurtheile zulassen, so müßte man sie überhaupt bei allen Urtheilen ohne Unterschied zulassen, um die Folgen des Nichterscheinens bei einer Verhandlung zu beseitigen. Sie könnte also nicht bloß erwirkt werden gegen Urtheile auf wiederholtes Ausbleiben (Art. 315) und gegen Urtheile, welche in Folge eines Verbindungsurtheiles ergehen (Art. 317), sondern auch bei rein contradiktorischen Urtheilen, insofern eine Partei, welche bei Hinterlegung der Anträge (Art. 240) oder bei der Vertagung zur Fortsetzung der Verhandlung (Bemerk. zu Art. 520) erschienen war, bei der späteren Verhandlung aber ausbleibt, Wiedereinsetzung begehren könnte, um jene Aenderungen und Zusätze zu machen, jene neuen Mittel des Angriffs oder der Vertheidigung zur Geltung zu bringen, wie sie das Gesetz bis zum Schlusse der Verhandlung gestattet.

Ferner müßte man in Fällen, wo das Recht des Einspruchs besteht, die Wahl zwischen Einspruch und Wiedereinsetzung lassen, was nicht ohne Belang ist, da für letztere die Formen des Einspruchs wegfallen würden, ebenso wie die Verpflichtung in die nächste Sitzung zu laden (Art. 522). Auch würde sich geltend machen lassen, daß die Wiedereinsetzung das Urtheil ganz beseitige, während der Einspruch ihm eine bedingte Geltung läßt. Bemerk. zu Art. 309—315 Nr. 17.

6) Nach vorstehenden Erörterungen bin ich der Ansicht, daß man, ohne den Prinzipien offene Gewalt anzuthun, auch im Wechselprozesse der Wiedereinsetzung in den vorigen Stand die Natur und Wirkung eines Rechtsmittels nicht einräumen dürfe.

Eine Bestärkung findet diese Ansicht im Entwurfe, welcher nirgends andeutete, daß die Wiedereinsetzung auch gegen Urtheile wirksam sein könne, welcher vielmehr in Art. 529a ganz richtig und den Prinzipien entsprechend verfügte, daß im Wechselprozesse der Einspruch nur stattfinde, wenn die Voraussetzungen der Wiedereinsetzung gegeben seien. Ebenso ließ er in Art. 273 Wiedereinsetzung wegen Versäumung der Einspruchsfrist, nicht aber der Vorladungsfrist zu.

Ferner ist wichtig, daß im Ausschusse der K. d. R. vom Referenten und vom Correferenten auf die in Versagung des Einspruchs liegende Härte hingewiesen und namentlich betont wurde: „es könne der Fall sein, daß der Beklagte zu „einer Zeit geladen werde, wo er sich gar nicht „zu Hause befindet, weit entfernt ist und „durch die Unzulässigkeit des Einspruchs ohne „Verschulden sehr benachtheiligt werde," nichtsdestoweniger aber der kgl. Minist.-Commissär sich nicht veranlaßt fand, auf das Mittel der Wiedereinsetzung hinzuweisen. R. R. II S. 261. 262. Auch bei den Verhandlungen zweiter Lesung wurde der Wiedereinsetzung nicht mehr erwähnt. Referat zu Hauptst. XVIII Art. 13 und Abg. IV 111.

Es läßt sich daher nicht annehmen, daß die obberegten Aeußerungen die Meinung aller Gesetzgebungsfaktoren darstellen; wäre dies aber auch der Fall, so ist eine bloße Meinung noch kein Gesetz.

7) Hieraus ergibt sich die Folge, daß in Fällen, wo kein Recht der Berufung besteht, das Versäumungsurtheil im Wechselprozesse sofort rechtskräftig ist, und es läßt sich nicht verkennen, daß hierin eine sehr große Härte liegt.

Beim ersten Anblicke erscheint der Mißstand so groß, daß man glaubt nach einem Nothwege suchen zu müssen, allein bei näherer Betrachtung zeigt sich denn doch, daß die Folgen nicht gar so schlimm seien. Es ist nemlich zu beachten:

1) daß die Spezialbestimmung des Art. 520 Abs. 2 auch im Wechselprozesse anwendbar und durch die Verfügungen des Art. 548 nicht beseitigt erscheint;

2) daß der Wechsel dem Richter vorzulegen und dieser zu prüfen hat, ob die Voraussetzungen einer wechselrechtlichen Haftung gegeben seien;

3) daß bei falschen Wechseln Wiederaufnahme des Verfahrens statthaft ist (Art. 761 Ziff. 5);

4) daß endlich, was das Wichtigste ist, wie bei Art. 547 erörtert, die Verurtheilung nach Wechselrecht die civilrechtliche Regelung des Rechtsverhältnisses freiläßt.

8) Falls Berufung zuläsig ist, können nach den Prinzipien der Prozeßordnung (Art. 707) alle Mittel des Angriffs und der Vertheidigung, bezüglich deren eine Verlustigung nicht eingetreten ist, in der Berufungsinstanz geltend gemacht werden.

Was insbesondere das Recht der Abläugnung der Unterschrift anbelangt, so muß dasselbe nach Art. 541 in der Sitzung, auf welche geladen ist, von dem persönlich erschienenen Beklagten ausgeübt werden; es erscheint daher verwirkt, wenn nicht in der Berufungsinstanz Wiedereinsetzung gegen die Versäumung besagter Tagfahrt erlangt wird. Ebenso kann die Rechtsverlustigung, welche dadurch eingetreten ist, daß der erschienene Beklagte die erforderlichen Erklärungen (Art. 542) abzugeben verweigert, durch die Berufung nicht beseitigt werden.

Was jedoch die allgemeine Rechtsvermuthung des Geständnisses anbelangt, welche Art. 520 für den Fall des Nichterscheinens ausspricht, so begründet dieselbe, meiner Ansicht nach, keine Rechtsverlustigung im Sinne des Art. 707 a. E., wie zu diesem Artikel näher erörtert werden wird. Es können daher vor dem Berufungsrichter ebenso wie im Einspruchsverfahren nicht bloß alle Einreden vorgebracht, sondern auch die früher als zugestanden betrachteten Thatsachen bestritten werden und zwar ohne Wiedereinsetzung in den vorigen Stand. Es liegt dies im Geiste des ganzen Verfahrens, namentlich auch des Art. 707. Vgl. Referat zu den Art. 647, 658 u. 660 des Entwurfs.

9) Schließlich ist darauf hinzuweisen, daß der Einspruch nur ausgeschlossen ist, insofern die Verurtheilung im Wechselprozesse erfolgte. Der Wechselprozeß ist bloß zu Gunsten des Wechselgläubigers eingeführt, dieser aber ist nicht gezwungen, diesen näheren Seitenweg zu gehen, sondern kann den gewöhnlichen Weg des handelsgerichtlichen Verfahrens einschlagen.

Geht nun aus dem Urtheile hervor, daß nicht nach den besonderen Vorschriften der Wechselordnung verfahren worden ist, z. B. weil die Ladung nicht den Vorschriften der Art. 540 und 541 entsprach, so ist der Einspruch nicht ausgeschlossen.

Kaufmännische Anweisungen.

Art. 552. — Das Verfahren in Wechselsachen findet auch Anwendung auf Klagen aus kaufmännischen Anweisungen. G. A. d. K. d. A. II S. 378. 382. 402. — K. d. R. II S. 262.

Die kaufmännische Anweisung unterscheidet sich laut des Gesetzes vom 29. Juni 1851 vom gezogenen Wechsel nur unbedeutend, nemlich was die Form betrifft dadurch, daß statt des Wortes „Wechsel" das Wort „Anweisung" gebraucht wird, und was die Wirkungen betrifft, dadurch, daß der Protest Mangels Annahme und die Wechselhaft wegfallen. Im Uebrigen finden die nemlichen Grundsätze Anwendung, insbesondere jene, welche die Wechselfähigkeit, sowie die Folgen der Wechselverpflichtung betreffen.

Durch vorstehenden Artikel wird die Gleichstellung auch für das Verfahren ausgesprochen, und gilt daher alles, was in den vorausgehenden Artikeln bezüglich des Wechsels bestimmt ist, auch für die kaufmännische Anweisung.

XIX. Hauptstück.

Verfahren mittelst bedingter Zahlungsbefehle.

Zulässigkeit.

Art. 553. — **Wegen persönlicher Forderungen, welche an Geld oder vertretbaren Sachen den Betrag oder Werth von hundertfünfzig Gulden in der Hauptsache ohne Einrechnung von Zinsen und Kosten nicht übersteigen, kann der Gläubiger bei dem Einzelnrichter, vor welchem der Schuldner seinen allgemeinen Gerichtsstand hat, die Erlassung eines bedingten Zahlungsbefehls verlangen.**

Zur Erlassung eines solchen Zahlungsbefehles wird vorausgesetzt, daß nach dem Vortrage des Gläubigers die Forderung dem Gegenstande nach gewiß, fällig und unbestritten, und daß der allgemeine Gerichtsstand für den betreffenden Fall nicht ausgeschlossen ist.

G. A. d. K. d. A. II S. 432—436. 446. IV S. 111. 112. — K. d. R. II S. 262—266.

1) Ob es sachgemäß gewesen, das bedingte Mandat auch im neuen Verfahren, welches den Weg zur Erlangung eines Urtheils so sehr erleichtert und abkürzt, beizubehalten, möchte fraglich sein, besonders wenn erwogen wird, daß die Vervielfältigung der Prozeßarten an und für sich als Mißstand zu betrachten ist.

Die einzigen Vortheile, welche dieses Ausnahmsverfahren bietet, sind: 1) die Bequemlichkeit für den Gläubiger, nicht in der Gerichtssitzung erscheinen oder sich vertreten lassen zu müssen, und 2) eine kleine Kostenersparung. Dem entgegen ergibt sich der Nachtheil, daß die einfache Protestation des Schuldners genügt, das ganze Verfahren zu vereiteln und den Weg zur Gewinnung einer Verurtheilung länger, umständlicher und kostspieliger zu machen.

Eine praktische Bedeutung läßt sich daher dem betreffenden Verfahren nur zugestehen in Fällen, wo als *sicher* anzunehmen ist, daß der Schuldner nicht protestiren werde.

2) Das Verfahren mittelst bedingter Zahlbefehle ist nur für die Einzelngerichte gegeben und auch bei diesen nur für *Bagatellsachen*, nemlich für Forderungen, welche in der Hauptsumme den Werth von 150 Gulden nicht übersteigen.

Da das Gesetz ganz allgemein von Forderungen, die nicht über 150 Gulden gehen, spricht, es jedoch auch Fälle gibt, wo solche Forderungen nicht zur *Zuständigkeit* der Einzelngerichte gehören, wie z. B. Wechselforderungen oder jene Forderungen, von welchen in Art. 5 Ziff. 4 die Sprache ist, so wirft sich sofort die Frage auf, ob zur Erlassung eines bedingten Zahlungsbefehls die Zuständigkeit des Einzelnrichters *in der Sache selbst* zu erkennen vorausgesetzt werde.

Einerseits läßt sich der Wortlaut des Gesetzes anführen, auf den Umstand hinweisen, daß Art. 553 sonstige Competenzbestimmungen enthalte und geltend machen, es handle sich nur um einen *Versuch*, die Sache ohne förmliche Verhandlung und Aburtheilung zu erledigen, welcher füglich auch einem sonst unzuständigen Richter übertragen werden könne.

Anderseits ist jedoch, wohl mit besserem Rechte, hervorzuheben, daß der Gesetzgeber hier überhaupt keine die *sachliche* Zuständigkeit betreffende Verfügung treffen wolle, diese Zuständigkeit vielmehr als gegeben voraussetze, daß ferner die Erläuterungen des kgl. Minist.-Commissärs (Abg. II 433 u. 435) dann die Verhandlungen, namentlich aber die Verfügung des Art. 566 Abs. 3, welche sofortige *Verhandlung in der Sache* selbst anordnet, klar zu erkennen geben, daß die Zuständigkeit in der Sache vorausgesetzt werde.

3) Hieraus ergibt sich die Folge, daß auch die Bestimmungen des Art. 3 Abs. 2 über Zusammenrechnen verschiedener gleichzeitig verfolgter Forderungen Anwendung zu finden habe.

Es könnte sich sogar fragen, ob nicht fragliches Prinzip hier bei *allen* Forderungen, also auch denjenigen, von welchen Art. 6 spricht, zu gelten habe, weil überall der Werth von 150 Gulden entscheidet; allein offenbar läßt sich nicht annehmen, daß der Gesetzgeber hier abweichende Grundsätze habe einführen wollen, und müssen daher, sowohl was Zusammenrechnen als was Getrennthalten der einzelnen Forderungen betrifft, die allgemeinen Grundsätze maßgebend sein, wie sie zu Art. 3 Nr. 14—17 entwickelt wurden. Wenn demnach für ein Darlehen von 100 Gulden und einen Miethzins von 100 Gulden bedingter Zahlungsbefehl verlangt wird, so ist der Einzelnrichter zuständig, ihn zu erlassen.

4) Zuständig zur Erlassung des Zahlungsbefehles ist derjenige Einzelnrichter, vor welchem der Schuldner seinen allgemeinen Gerichtsstand im Sinne der Art. 12—20 hat, vorausgesetzt, daß dieser Gerichtsstand für den betreffenden Fall nicht ausgeschlossen ist. Letzteres ist z. B. der Fall bei den Forderungen, von welchen Art. 28 spricht, jedoch nicht dort, wo der Kläger das Recht hat, zwischen dem besonderen und allgemeinen Gerichtsstande zu wählen.

Selbst in jenen Fällen, wo der besondere Gerichtsstand allein maßgebend ist, möchte fragliche Ausnahme nicht Platz greifen, wenn er zufällig mit dem allgemeinen Gerichtsstande zusammenfällt; denn der Grund, warum der Gesetzgeber so besonderes Gewicht auf diesen letzteren Gerichtsstand legt, ist nur darin zu suchen, daß dem Schuldner die Protestation, welche durch Erklärung auf der Gerichtsschreiberei geschieht, erleichtert werden soll.

5) Das Gesetz setzt eine persönliche Forderung an Geld oder vertretbaren Sachen voraus; Vindikationen sind daher ausgenommen, auch wenn es sich um bewegliche Sachen oder gar um Geld handelt.

Die Forderung rückständiger Grundrenten ist eine persönliche und gehört zur Zuständigkeit des Einzelngerichts, so lange die Rente selbst nicht bestritten ist; es steht daher der Erlassung eines bedingten Zahlungsbefehls wegen derselben nichts im Wege.

Eine Sache ist vertretbar, wenn sie nur ihrer Art und Beschaffenheit nach bestimmt ist, so daß jede gleichgeartete Sache zur Leistung genügt, wie z. B. Geld, Waaren bestimmter Art ꝛc. Wie aus Art. 554 Abs. 4 und Art. 556 Abs. 2 hervorgeht, muß die vertretbare Sache in Geld angeschlagen werden und der Zahlungsbefehl es in die Wahl des Schuldners stellen, den Geldanschlag zu zahlen. Hiermit ist zugleich die Zuständigkeit geregelt. Art. 4 Abs. 2.

6) Es wird vom Gläubiger keine Bescheinigung seiner Forderung verlangt, sondern ist verfügt, daß der Zahlungsbefehl zu erlassen sei, wenn nach dem Vortrage des Gläubigers die Forderung dem Gegenstande nach gewiß, fällig und unbestritten sei.

Mit den Worten: „dem Gegenstande nach gewiß" soll gesagt sein, es müsse aus den vorgetragenen Thatsachen bestimmt hervorgehen, wie groß die Summe des zu Leistenden sei; es sind also Fälle ausgeschlossen, wo erst eine richterliche Schätzung stattzufinden hat, wie in der Regel bei Entschädigungsforderungen. Ursprünglich hieß es: „dem Betrage nach gewiß" (Entwurf Art. 635 und Abg. II 432), die Aenderung aber erfolgte bloß aus redaktionellen Gründen, wahrscheinlich weil der Ausdruck „Betrag" zu „vertretbaren Sachen" nicht recht zu passen schien. Abg. II 446.

Die Forderung muß ferner fällig sein, d. h. es müssen die Voraussetzungen zur Einklagung derselben gegeben sein (Bemerk. zu Art. 224 Nr. 2—10). Bestanden ursprünglich Bedingungen oder Fristen, so muß aus dem Vortrage hervorgehen, daß die Bedingungen erfüllt, die Fristen verstrichen sind.

Schließlich wird verlangt, es solle die Forderung unbestritten sein. Hiermit soll nur gesagt sein, es dürfe nicht aus dem Vortrage des Gläubigers sich ergeben, daß der Schuldner die Forderung bestreite, keineswegs aber wird die Behauptung der Unbestrittenheit oder gar die Darlegung besonderer Thatsachen begehrt, aus denen die Nichtbestreitung sich ergebe. Fand früher eine Bestreitung statt, so wird vermuthet, daß sie fortdauere, falls nicht Thatsachen vorgetragen werden, aus denen klar hervorgeht, daß sie aufgegeben worden sei.

7) Sind die in Artikel 553 aufgestellten Voraussetzungen gegeben, ist also das Verlangen statthaft, so ist der Einzelnrichter verpflichtet, Zahlungsbefehl zu erlassen, und es steht nicht in seiner Macht, ihn aus Gründen der Zweckmäßigkeit oder weil die vorgetragenen Thatsachen nicht glaubhaft seien, zu verweigern. Allerdings ist er auch hier nicht gezwungen, etwas als wahr vorauszusetzen, was notorisch (Art. 320) sich anders verhält. Hat der Gläubiger durch falsche Darstellung des Sachverhalts sich einen Zahlungsbefehl, welcher bei Angabe der Wahrheit unstatthaft gewesen wäre, erschlichen, so sind ihm die hierdurch verursachten zwecklosen Kosten zur Last zu legen.

Uebrigens ist zu bemerken, daß gegen den abweisenden Beschluß des Richters Rechtsmittel nicht zulässig sind (Art. 564).

Antrag des Gläubigers und Verfahren darauf.

Art. 554. — **Das Gesuch um Erlassung eines bedingten Zahlungsbefehls kann von der Partei oder ihrem Bevollmächtigten, wie auch von dem mit Verfolgung der Sache beauftragten Gerichtsvollzieher schriftlich oder mündlich angebracht werden. Gerichtsvollzieher und Advokaten bedürfen hiebei keines Nachweises der Bevollmächtigung.**

Wird das Gesuch mündlich angebracht, so ist darüber durch den Einzelrichter oder den Gerichtsschreiber ein Protokoll aufzunehmen.

In dem Gesuche sind die zur Würdigung der Statthaftigkeit desselben und zur Abfassung des Zahlungsbefehls erforderlichen Angaben zu machen.

Ist die Forderung auf vertretbare Sachen gerichtet, so müssen diese im Gesuche zugleich in Geld angeschlagen sein.

Art. 555. — **Erscheint das Gesuch statthaft, so ist der Zahlungsbefehl sofort zu erlassen, andernfalls ist das Gesuch abzuweisen.**

Im einen wie im andern Falle ist der Beschluß auf die schriftliche Eingabe oder das errichtete Protokoll zu setzen und dem Gläubiger auf Anmelden in Urschrift auszuhändigen.

Ist das Gesuch abgewiesen worden, so bleibt dem Gläubiger vorbehalten, seinen Anspruch im ordentlichen Verfahren zu verfolgen.

Art. 556. — **Der Zahlungsbefehl hat zu enthalten:**

1) **die Bezeichnung des Gläubigers und des Schuldners nach Vor- und Familiennamen, Stand oder Gewerbe und Wohnort;**
2) **die Angabe des Betrags der Forderung und des Sachverhältnisses, aus welchem sie entspringt;**
3) **die Auflage an den Schuldner binnen einer Frist von fünfzehn Tagen, vom Tage der Zustellung des Zahlungsbefehls an gerechnet, bei Vermeidung sofortiger Zwangsvollstreckung entweder den Gläubiger für Hauptsumme, etwaige Zinsen und die Kosten des Verfahrens zu befriedigen oder Protestation gegen den Zahlungsbefehl bei Gericht zu erheben.**

Ist die Forderung auf eine vertretbare Sache gerichtet, so ist dem Schuldner die Wahl zu lassen, ob er diese oder den im Gesuche enthaltenen Geldanschlag dafür leisten wolle.

Art. 557. — **Der Gläubiger hat den Zahlungsbefehl dem Schuldner zustellen zu lassen. Damit ist die Zustellung der das Gesuch enthaltenden Eingabe oder des über das mündlich angebrachte Gesuch errichteten Protokolles zu verbinden.**

Mit der Zustellung des Zahlungsbefehls treten die nach Art. 179 an die Zustellung der Klage geknüpften Wirkungen ein.

G. A. d. K. d. A. II S. 432. 436. 437. 446. IV S. 112. 115. — K. d. R. II S. 266. IV. S. 63.

1) Das Verfahren, welches das Gesetz hier vorzeichnet, ist ein sehr einfaches.

Die Partei kann selbst oder durch einen beliebigen Bevollmächtigten ihr Gesuch schriftlich oder mündlich vorbringen, und ist der Bevollmächtigte ein Advokat oder ein Gerichtsvollzieher, so bedarf es nicht einmal der Vorlage einer Vollmacht.

Wird das Gesuch mündlich gestellt, so ist entweder durch den Einzelrichter selbst oder durch den Gerichtsschreiber ein kurzes Protokoll aufzunehmen, woraus zugleich folgt, daß vor jedem dieser Beamten die Erklärung giltig geschehen kann.

Das Gesuch muß selbstverständlich alles enthalten, was nach Art. 553 zu seiner Begründung gehört, sowie ferner, was zur Abfassung des Zahlungsbefehles nöthig ist, also insbesondere die genaue Bezeichnung von Gläubiger und Schuldner.

Ist die Forderung auf vertretbare Sachen gerichtet, so sind diese in Geld anzuschlagen, und dieser Anschlag macht zufolge der Bestimmung in Art. 556 Abs. 2 die Forderung zu einer alternativen. Der Gläubiger bestimmt in dieser Weise sofort die Geldentschädigung, welche er für den Fall der Nichtleistung zu fordern habe.

2) Der Richter hat nur zu prüfen, ob das Gesuch statthaft sei, d. h. den Anforderungen des Art. 553 genüge. Muß er dies bejahen, so hat er den Zahlungsbefehl zu erlassen, andernfalls zu verweigern. In beiden Fällen ist sein Beschluß ein endgiltiger (Art. 564).

Wird das Gesuch abgewiesen, so ist es dem Gläubiger nicht verwehrt, unter Hebung der formellen Mängel oder auf Grund neu vorgebrachter Thatsachen ein wiederholtes Gesuch zu stellen. Die durch das erste Gesuch verursachten Kosten bleiben ihm natürlich zur Last.

Eine Form ist für den Abweisungsbeschluß nicht vorgeschrieben, insbesondere findet die Bestimmung in Art. 651, welche bei Beschlüssen auf einfache Vorstellungen Entscheidungsgründe verlangt, keine Anwendung; jedoch erscheint es sachgemäß und deßhalb Pflicht des Richters, daß er die Gründe kurz anführe, welche die Abweisung veranlaßten.

Sowohl im Falle der Abweisung als im Falle der Bewilligung hat der Einzelnrichter seinen Beschluß auf das schriftliche Gesuch oder die Protokollarerklärung zu setzen und dem Gläubiger in Urschrift auszuhändigen, letzteres auf Anmelden, d. h. es bleibt dem Gläubiger überlassen, den Beschluß auf der Gerichtsschreiberei, wo er für ihn bereit liegt, selbst oder durch Bevollmächtigten in Empfang zu nehmen. Abg. II 436 Sp. 2, 437 Sp. 1. In der Regel wird der Gerichtsvollzieher, welcher mit der Zustellung beauftragt ist, sich den Beschluß aushändigen lassen, und bedarf dieser hierzu keiner Vollmacht. Bemerk. zu Art. 102 Nr. 2.

3) Die Form des bewilligenden Beschlusses, d. h. des bedingten Zahlbefehls, ist durch Art. 556 vorgezeichnet.

Es sind hier keine Entscheidungsgründe nöthig, sondern wird bloß eine genaue Bezeichnung von Gläubiger und Schuldner, Angabe des Betrags der Forderung und des ihr zu Grunde liegenden Sachverhaltes verlangt. Diese Formen, namentlich die Darstellung des Sachverhaltes, müssen schon deßhalb sehr wesentlich erscheinen, weil der Zahlungsbefehl nach Art. 557 Abs. 2 eine Klage ersetzen soll.

Offenbar wollte übrigens der Gesetzgeber, indem er fragliche Vorschriften gab, dem Richter nicht die Befugniß nehmen, sich auf die im Gesuche enthaltenen Angaben zu beziehen, im Gegentheile ergibt sich aus den Verhandlungen, daß man gerade zum Zwecke, um den Richter zu erleichtern, d. h. ihm eine Bezugnahme möglich zu machen, in Art. 557 gleichzeitige Zustellung des Gesuches vorschrieb. Abg. II 436 Sp. 1 (v. Weiß). Für die Bezeichnung des Gläubigers und die Darstellung des Sachverhalts wird daher in der Regel die Bezugnahme auf das Gesuch genügen und der Zahlungsbefehl sich sehr einfach gestalten, etwa wie folgt:

> Vorstehendem Gesuche stattgebend, wird dem — — die Auflage gemacht (der Befehl ertheilt), binnen fünfzehn Tagen 2c. entweder den Gesuchsteller zu befriedigen, indem er demselben die gemäß seiner Angabe geschuldete Hauptsumme von — nebst Zinsen 2c., sowie die Kosten dieses Verfahrens zahlt, oder Protestation gegen diesen Zahlungsbefehl bei Gericht zu erheben.

Ist die Forderung auf eine vertretbare Sache gerichtet, so hat der Zahlungsbefehl etwa dahin zu lauten:

> indem er demselben die gemäß seiner Angabe geschuldeten Waaren, nemlich — in Natur liefert, oder aber den Anschlag derselben im Betrage von — zahlt, u. s. w.

4) Die fünfzehntägige Frist, welche dem Schuldner zum Zwecke der Protestation gegeben ist, erweitert sich nach Maßgabe des Art. 209 mit Rücksicht auf die Entfernung zwischen dem Wohnorte des Schuldners und dem Sitze des Einzelngerichtes. Es hat dies zwar nur wenig praktische Bedeutung, indem der Ort, wo Jemand wohnt oder sich aufhält, auch in der Regel den allgemeinen Gerichtsstand bestimmt; allein es kann doch auch anders sein, z. B. bei Ausländern, Gesandten 2c. In derartigen Fällen halte ich es für nöthig, jedenfalls sehr rathsam, daß der Richter im Zahlungsbefehle die erweiterte Frist angebe.

5) Sache des Gläubigers ist es, den Zahlungsbefehl durch einen Gerichtsvollzieher zustellen zu lassen. Zu gleicher Zeit ist auch das Gesuch selbst zuzustellen, d. h. Gesuch und Zahlungsbefehl sind als Ganzes zu behandeln, damit das erstere zur Erläuterung des letzteren diene.

Mit dieser Zustellung treten die Wirkungen ein, welche das Gesetz (Art. 179) an die Zustellung einer Klage knüpft, jedoch, wie sich aus Art. 559 ergibt, nur in bedingter Weise.

Protestation gegen den Zahlungsbefehl.

Art. 558. — **Die Protestation gegen den Zahlungsbefehl ist bis zur Erlassung des Vollstreckungsbeschlusses zulässig. Sie ist auf der Gerichtsschreiberei von der Partei selbst oder von ihrem Bevollmächtigten anzumelden. Eine Begründung wird nicht erfordert.**

Die Anmeldung kann mittels Eingabe oder mündlich geschehen.

Der Gerichtsschreiber hat im ersten Falle auf der Eingabe den Tag des Einlaufs zu bemerken, im letzten ein Protokoll aufzunehmen.

Die Eingabe oder das Protokoll wird auf der Gerichtsschreiberei hinterlegt und ist dem Gläubiger auf Verlangen vorzuzeigen.

Art. 559. — **Durch die rechtzeitig erklärte Protestation wird der Zahlungsbefehl wirkungslos und**

der Gläubiger kann seinen Anspruch nur im ordentlichen Verfahren geltend machen. Die nach Art. 557 Abs. 2 eingetretenen Wirkungen erlöschen jedoch nur dann, wenn der Gläubiger nicht innerhalb sechs Monaten, von der Erklärung des Schuldners an gerechnet, die Klage im ordentlichen Verfahren erhebt.

Art. 560. — **War der Zahlungsbefehl wegen mehrerer selbständiger Forderungen erlassen und hat der Schuldner ausdrücklich die Protestation auf die eine oder andere beschränkt, so bleibt der Zahlungsbefehl bezüglich der übrigen in Kraft.**

G. A. d. K. d. A. II S. 432. 437. 438. 446. IV S. 112. 115. — K. d. R. II S. 266. IV S. 63.

1) Die einfache Erklärung des Schuldners, daß er gegen den Zahlungsbefehl protestire, beseitigt das ganze Verfahren und läßt nichts davon übrig, als die Kosten und, in bedingter Weise, die Wirkungen der Anhängigkeit.

Die Protestation ist auch nach Verlauf der im Zahluugsbefehle gesetzten Frist noch zulässig, so lange bis der Vollstreckungsbeschluß erlassen ist; mit Erlaß dieses Beschlusses jedoch ist das Recht der Protestation verwirkt, mag auch der Beschluß dem Gläubiger noch nicht ausgehändigt worden sein (Art. 562 Abs. 3).

2) Obgleich der Schuldner nur aufgefordert ist, zu zahlen oder zu protestiren, so ist ihm doch anzurathen, auch im Falle der Zahlung die Protestation nicht zu unterlassen, weil sonst leicht trotz seiner Zahlung ein Vollstreckungsbeschluß nachgesucht und erlassen werden könnte und in Betracht kommt, daß gegen diese Beschlüsse Rechtsmittel nicht gegeben sind.

3) Die Erklärung der Protestation erfolgt auf der Gerichtsschreiberei des Einzelngerichtes, von welchem der Zahlungsbefehl ausgegangen ist, entweder schriftlich oder mündlich, durch die Partei selbst oder ihren Bevollmächtigten. Die Bestimmung in Art. 554 Abs. 1, daß Advokaten und Gerichtsvollzieher keiner Vollmacht bedürfen, findet hier keine Anwendung.

Die schriftliche Eingabe oder das über die mündliche Erklärung aufgenommene Protokoll bleiben auf der Gerichtsschreiberei hinterlegt und sind dem Gläubiger auf Verlangen vorzuzeigen.

4) Die einzige Wirkung, welche dem Zahlungsbefehle nach eingelegter Protestation noch bleibt, besteht darin, daß er die Anhängigkeit der Sache mit den in Art. 179 bezeichneten Folgen begründet, dies jedoch nur unter der Bedingung, daß der Gläubiger innerhalb 6 Monaten von der Protestation an förmliche Klage erhebe und soweit dies geschieht. Tritt diese Bedingung nicht ein, so ist der Zahlungsbefehl auch in dieser Richtung als nicht geschehen zu betrachten und bleiben ihm bloß die Wirkungen einer gewöhnlichen Aufforderung.

5) Die Bestimmung des Art. 560, daß in Fällen, wo der Zahlungsbefehl wegen mehrerer selbständiger Forderungen erlassen war, der Schuldner aber die Protestation ausdrücklich auf einzelne Forderungen beschränkt, bezüglich der übrigen Forderungen der Zahlungsbefehl in Kraft bleibe, ist dem hannoveranischen Entwurfe (§ 503 Abs. 3) entnommen und erscheint vollkommen sachgemäß, jedoch möchte Anlaß gegeben sein, zu fragen, ob denn in Fällen, wo der Schuldner die Forderung theilweise zugesteht und nur gegen einen Theil derselben protestirt, nicht die nemlichen Gründe eintreten und daher dasselbe zu gelten habe?

Nach dem Wortlaute des Gesetzes ist diese Frage unbedenklich zu verneinen, denn aus dem Umstande, daß nur bezüglich der selbständigen Forderungen eine Ausnahme gemacht ist, folgt, daß eine solche nicht eintrete, wenn es sich um Theile der nemlichen Forderung handelt. Jeder Zweifel ist übrigens dadurch beseitigt, daß der hannov. Entwurf ausdrücklich bestimmt, es verliere der Zahlungsbefehl auch im Falle, wo der Widerspruch nur einen Theil der Forderung betreffe, seine Kraft. Verhdl. S. 3314 — Entw. § 503 Abs. 1 u. 2.

Vollstreckungsbeschluß.

Art. 561. — **Nach Ablauf der in dem Zahlungsbefehle festgesetzten Frist kann der Gläubiger unter Vorlage des Zahlungsbefehls und der Zustellungsurkunde beantragen, daß für den im Zahlungsbefehle bezeichneten Forderungsbetrag sammt Zinsen und Kosten ein Vollstreckungsbeschluß erlassen werde.**

Dieser Antrag muß spätestens innerhalb sechs Monaten von Zustellung des Zahlungsbefehls gestellt werden, widrigenfalls der Zahlungsbefehl seine Kraft verliert und alle Wirkungen desselben erlöschen.

Der Antrag ist in der in Art. 554 Abs. 1 und 2 angegebenen Weise anzubringen. Geschieht dies durch Eingabe, so hat der Gerichtsschreiber auf dieser den Tag des Einlaufs zu bemerken.

Art. 562. — **Erscheint der Antrag auf Erlassung eines Vollstreckungsbeschlusses nicht gerechtfertigt, so weist ihn das Gericht in einem auf den Zahlungsbefehl zu setzenden kurz motivirten Beschlusse zurück.**

Erscheint der Antrag gerechtfertigt, so ist der von dem Richter und Gerichtsschreiber unter Beidrückung des Gerichtssiegels zu unterzeichnende Vollstreckungsbeschluß sofort auf dem Zahlungsbefehle zu erlassen, mit der Ueberschrift: „Im Namen Seiner Majestät des Königs von Bayern" und am Schlusse vor dem Datum mit den Worten: „Vorstehender Beschluß wird für vollstreckbar erklärt."

Im einen wie im andern Falle wird der Beschluß dem Gläubiger auf Anmelden in Urschrift ausgehändigt.

Art. 563. — **Bei Forderungen, die auf eine vertretbare Sache gerichtet sind, ist der Vollstreckungsbeschluß auf den Geldanschlag zu stellen, es bleibt aber dem Schuldner demungeachtet freigestellt, so lange die Vollstreckung nicht wirklich erfolgt ist, sich durch Leistung der vertretbaren Sache von der Zahlung des Geldanschlags zu befreien.**

G. A. d. K. d. A. II S. 432. 438. 446. IV S. 112. 336. — K. d. R. II S. 266. IV S. 64.

1) Nach Ablauf der zur Zahlung oder Protestation gegebenen Frist kann der Gläubiger auf Grund der Vorlage des Zahlungsbefehles und der Zustellungsurkunde Vollstreckungsbeschluß beantragen, der Einzelnrichter aber ist verpflichtet, diesem Antrage zu willfahren, wenn die Frist verstrichen, die Zustellung vorschriftsmäßig geschehen und eine Protestation nicht erklärt ist.

Der Antrag wird auf dieselbe Weise gestellt, wie der frühere auf Erlaß des Zahlungsbefehles (Art. 554 Abs. 1 u. 2), jedoch bedarf er keiner Begründung.

Er muß binnen 6 Monaten von Zustellung des Zahlungsbefehles an vorgebracht werden, widrigenfalls alle besonderen Wirkungen, die mit dem Zahlungsbefehle nach den Vorschriften dieses Hauptstückes verbunden sind, erlöschen. Weder diese Frist, noch die gleiche des Art. 559 unterliegt einer Erweiterung auf Grund des Art. 209.

2) Der Beschluß des Einzelnrichters, mag er abweisen oder bewilligen, wird auf den Zahlungsbefehl gesetzt und dem Gläubiger auf Anmelden in Urschrift ausgehändigt.

Ergeht Abweisungsbeschluß, so ist derselbe kurz zu begründen.

Für den Vollstreckungsbeschluß sind Entscheidungsgründe nicht vorgeschrieben, jedoch wird es in Betracht, daß dieser Beschluß bestimmt ist, die Stelle eines Urtheils zu vertreten, im Geiste des Gesetzes begründet sein, die der Sache entsprechenden kurzen Gründe beizufügen, insbesondere auf die ihm zu Grunde liegenden Urkunden Bezug zu nehmen. Ueberhaupt ist wohl zu beachten, daß es nicht genügt, einfach zu sagen: „Vorstehender Zahlungsbefehl wird für den „Betrag von — vollstreckbar erklärt", wie es in der Pfalz in manchen ähnlichen Fällen Uebung ist, daß vielmehr das Gesetz einen förmlichen die Stelle einer Verurtheilung vertretenden Beschluß verlangt und dieser Beschluß erst durch eine zu Ende beigefügte Formel vollstreckbar erklärt werden soll.

Es möchte ein solcher Beschluß etwa wie folgt zu fassen sein:

Der kgl. Landrichter —

nach Einsicht vorstehenden Zahlungsbefehls und der Zustellungsurkunde des Gerichtsvollziehers — vom —;

nach Einsicht des vom Gläubiger am — eingereichten (zu Protokoll erklärten) Gesuches;

erwägend, daß die Zustellung vorschriftsmäßig erfolgt, die gesetzliche Frist verstrichen und eine Protestation gegen den Zahlungsbefehl nicht (nur bezüglich der Forderung von —) erhoben worden ist;

beschließt:

es sei — schuldig, an — die in vorstehendem Zahlungsbefehle bezeichnete Hauptsumme von — rc. zu zahlen, sowie die Kosten dieses Verfahrens, bis jetzt betragend —.

München, rc.

Rechtsmittel.

Art. 564. — **Gegen die in Art. 555 und 562 Abs. 2 erwähnten richterlichen Verfügungen finden keine Rechtsmittel statt. Gegen den in Art. 562 Abs. 1 bezeichneten Beschluß ist das Rechtsmittel der Beschwerde zulässig.**

G. A. d. K. d. A. II S. 433. 438. 439. 446. IV S. 112. — K. d. R. II S. 266. IV S. 64.

1) Gegen den bedingten Zahlungsbefehl sowohl, als gegen den Vollstreckungsbeschluß finden Rechtsmittel nicht statt.

Was den Zahlungsbefehl betrifft, so erscheint diese Bestimmung ganz sachgemäß, da das Mittel der Protestation alle Rechtsmittel unnöthig macht, allein was den Vollstreckungsbeschluß anbelangt, so muß ich gestehen, daß ich nicht begreife, wie man zu einer so harten, die Prinzipien so verletzenden Maßregel sich hat veranlaßt sehen können.

Um die Wichtigkeit und Tragweite fraglicher Verfügung zu erkennen, ist es nöthig, die Natur und die rechtlichen Wirkungen des Vollstreckungsbeschlusses ins Auge zu fassen.

2) Es kann kein Zweifel obwalten, daß nach dem Willen des Gesetzes der in Frage stehende Vollstreckungsbeschluß nicht etwa bloß eine vorsorgliche Verurtheilung darstellen soll, bei welcher die Regelung des Rechtsverhältnisses im gewöhnlichen Verfahren vorbehalten wäre, sondern daß es sich allerdings um eine Endentscheidung handelt, daß der Schuldner aller Einwände gegen die Forderung verlustig werden und der Vollstreckungsbeschluß die Wirkung eines rechtskräftigen Urtheils haben soll. — Es wurde dies bei den Verhandlungen klar ausgesprochen, wie es denn auch den Prinzipien des bedingten Mandatprozesses, an dessen Stelle das in Frage stehende Verfahren getreten ist, entspricht. Abg. II 439 Sp. 1 (v. Neum.), Abg. IV 112 Sp. 1 (v. Weiß).

Der Vollstreckungsbeschluß ist also als ein auf einmalige Vorladung ergangenes Versäumungsurtheil zu betrachten, gegen welches weder Einspruch noch sonstige Rechtsmittel zugelassen werden, welches also, abgesehen von der in Art. 565 vorgesehenen Wiedereinsetzung in den vorigen Stand, sofort unanfechtbar wird!

3) Erwägt man nun, daß weder Beweis noch Bescheinigung vom Gläubiger verlangt wird, sondern sein einseitiger Vortrag als Wahrheit gelten muß, daß ferner nicht einmal Dringlichkeit vorzuliegen braucht, erwägt man weiter, daß der Einzelnrichter möglicherweise verfügt in Fällen, wo er gar keine Zuständigkeit hat, oder wo ein Klagerecht gesetzlich gar nicht gegeben ist, so wird man zugestehen müssen, daß es zu weit geht, hier Rechtsmittel zu versagen, welche sogar im Wechselprozesse trotz des Vorbehalts der Nachklage gestattet sind. Es macht einen sonderbaren Gegensatz, wenn es einerseits dem Schuldner so leicht gemacht wird, durch die einfache Erklärung: „ich protestire“ das Vorgehen des Gläubigers zu vereiteln, daß aber anderseits, sowie er diese zwei Worte versäumt, sei es auch in Folge der leichtesten Verschuldung, man sofort in der schonungslosesten Weise gegen ihn verfährt.

4) Nur gegen den Beschluß, welcher das Gesuch um Erlassung eines Vollstreckungsbeschlusses abweist, ist ein Rechtsmittel gegeben und zwar dasjenige der Beschwerde. — Man fand sich hierzu veranlaßt in der Erwägung, daß der Gläubiger ein wohlerworbenes Recht habe, Rechtsverlustigungen, welche etwa zu seinen Gunsten bereits eingetreten sind, aussprechen zu lassen.

Wiedereinsetzung.

Art. 565. — **Sucht der Schuldner Wiedereinsetzung in den vorigen Stand gegen die Versäumung der für die Protestation gegen den Zahlungsbefehl gestatteten Frist nach, so muß die Zustellung, welche nach Art. 217 zu geschehen hat, zugleich Vorladung des Gläubigers in die nächste Sitzung des Einzelngerichts, welches den Vollstreckungsbeschluß erlassen hat, jedoch unter Beobachtung der Bestimmungen des Art. 502 enthalten.**

Die Vollstreckung wird durch diese Zustellung so lange nicht aufgehalten, als nicht vom Einzelngerichte die Einstellung verfügt wird.

Art. 566. — **Erscheint der Schuldner in der in Art. 565 bezeichneten Sitzung nicht, so wird seine nachträgliche Protestation unter Verurtheilung in die Kosten verworfen.**

Erscheint der Gläubiger nicht, so wird der Vollstreckungsbeschluß aufgehoben, vorbehaltlich für den Gläubiger, seinen Anspruch im ordentlichen Verfahren zu verfolgen.

Wird nach gepflogener Verhandlung die nachträgliche Protestation für zulässig erklärt, so ist, wenn der Gläubiger es beantragt, sofort oder in einer hiezu festgesetzten spätern Sitzung in der Sache selbst zu verhandeln.

Gegen die in den Fällen der Abs. 1 und 2 erlassenen Versäumungsurtheile ist Einspruch nicht zulässig.

G. A. d. K. d. A. II S. 433. 439. 446. IV S. 112. 336. — K. d. R. II S. 266. IV S. 64.

1) Das einzige Mittel, um gegen die Versäumung der Protestationsfrist und den in Folge derselben ergangenen Vollstreckungsbeschluß aufzukommen, ist die Wiedereinsetzung in den vorigen Stand, welche selbstverständlich nur innerhalb der Frist und unter den sonstigen Voraussetzungen verlangt werden kann, wie es Art. 216 bestimmt.

Da hier der Weg der Wiedereinsetzung zugleich dienen soll, eine gerichtliche Entscheidung aufzuheben, so ist vorgeschrieben, daß ebenso wie beim Einspruche (Art. 522), Vorladung in die nächste Gerichtssitzung, jedoch mit Einhaltung der in Art. 502 bestimmten Erscheinungsfrist gegeben werden solle.

2) Gegenüber der Härte des alle Rechtsmittel versagenden Gesetzes wird der Richter keine allzu strengen Forderungen bezüglich der Wiedereinsetzung machen und diese überall zulassen müssen, wo es der Geist des Gesetzes irgendwie gestattet.

So wird insbesondere die Wiedereinsetzung zu bewilligen sein, wenn der Schuldner in Folge des Zahlungsbefehls den Gläubiger befriedigt hat, nichtsdestoweniger aber ein Vollstreckungsbeschluß ergangen ist, was bei unredlichen Gläubigern leicht eintreten kann, da der Richter von Zahlungen nichts erfährt. Der Schuldner ist nemlich bloß aufgefordert zu zahlen oder zu protestiren; für den Fall, wo er zahlt, ist er also gar nicht aufgefordert zu protestiren und kann also ebensowenig im Zustande einer Versäumung sein, als wenn ihn die Zustellung gar nicht erreicht hätte.

Ferner wird eine schuldhafte Versäumung nicht angenommen werden können, wenn etwa der Gläubiger selbst durch betrügliche Kunstgriffe den Schuldner veranlaßt hat, die Protestation zu unterlassen.

3) Mit der Vorladung hat der Schuldner gemäß Art. 217 die Erklärung zu verbinden, daß er gegen den Zahlungsbefehl protestire und zugleich die Verhinderungsursache genau anzugeben.

Das Ansuchen ist dahin zu richten, ihm gegen die Versäumung der besagten Frist Wiedereinsetzung in den vorigen Stand zu bewilligen, demgemäß die nachträgliche Protestation für zulässig zu erklären und den Vollstreckungsbeschluß aufzuheben.

Im Falle des Nichterscheinens des einen oder des anderen Theils entscheidet der Richter in der Weise, wie es in Art. 566 Abs. 1 und 2 vorgeschrieben ist, und können diese Versäumungsurtheile durch Einspruch nicht angefochten werden.

Im Falle des Erscheinens beider Theile zeigt sich die nachträgliche Protestation entweder zulässig oder nicht, und hat der Richter das Eine oder das Andere auszusprechen.

Bei der ersten Voraussetzung gestattet der Gesetzgeber, erwägend, daß beide Theile doch einmal vor dem zuständigen Richter stehen, die sofortige Aburtheilung der Sache selbst. Es ist zwar der Vollstreckungsbeschluß aufzuheben, allein, falls der Gläubiger es beantragt, entweder sofort oder in einer festzusetzenden späteren Sitzung in der Sache selbst zu verhandeln, wobei die Zustellung des Zahlungsbefehls die Vorladung vertritt.

Bei den Urtheilen, welche die Wiedereinsetzung in den vorigen Stand zulassen oder verweigern, sind Rechtsmittel nicht ausgeschlossen.

Kosten.

Art. 567. — Findet wegen einer vom Schuldner erhobenen Protestation Verhandlung und Entscheidung der Sache im ordentlichen Verfahren statt, so ist hiebei auch über die in Folge des Gesuchs um Erlassung eines bedingten Zahlungsbefehls entstandenen Kosten zu entscheiden. Die durch eine nachträgliche Protestation und die darüber gepflogene Verhandlung verursachten Kosten fallen jedoch immer, und zwar selbst im Falle des Art. 566 Abs. 2 dem Schuldner zur Last.

Gemeinsame Bestimmung.

Art. 568. — Der Gerichtsschreiber hat ein Register zu führen, in welchem die Gesuche um Erlassung eines bedingten Zahlungsbefehls, die hierauf ergangenen Entschließungen und die Aushändigung der letztern vorgemerkt werden. Ueber die erfolgte Aushändigung hat sich der Gerichtsschreiber in dem Register oder in sonstiger entsprechender Weise Bescheinigung ertheilen zu lassen. G. A. d. K. d. A. II S. 433. 439. 446. VI S. 115. — K. d. R. II S. 266. IV S. 64.

1) Das Gesetz regelt in Art. 567 die Entscheidung bezüglich der Kosten für die Fälle, wo es wegen eingelegter Protestation zu einem Vollstreckungsbeschlusse nicht kommt, oder wo auf Grund einer nachträglichen Protestation dieser Beschluß wieder aufgehoben wird.

Im ersten Falle wird das versuchte Ausnahmsverfahren als vorbereitend für das später eingeleitete ordentliche Verfahren betrachtet und vorgeschrieben, es solle der Richter bei Entscheidung der Sache zugleich über die betreffenden Kosten entscheiden. Für diese Entscheidung gelten die allgemeinen Grundsätze, d. h. der am Ende unterliegende Theil trägt die Kosten, falls nicht wegen besonderer Verschuldung, z. B. weil der Gläubiger durch unwahre Darstellung des Sachverhalts den Zahlungsbefehl erschlichen hatte, eine Ausnahme zu machen ist. Art. 106 Abs. 2.

2) Im zweiten Falle sollen die Kosten, welche durch die nachträgliche Protestation und die

darüber gepflogene Verhandlung verursacht sind, immer, also auch wenn sich ergibt, daß die Versäumung eine vollständig unverschuldete war, oder der Gläubiger nicht erscheint, um den Vollstreckungsbeschluß aufrecht zu erhalten, dem Schuldner zur Last fallen. Auch hier wiederum liegt eine ganz ungerechtfertigte Härte vor. Wenn sogar beim gewöhnlichen Einspruche gegen Versäumungsurtheile, obgleich derselbe nicht den geringsten Nachweis einer Verhinderung voraussetzt, der Richter nach den allgemeinen Prinzipien über die Kosten zu erkennen hat, warum gerade hier, wo der Nachweis der Nichtverschuldung vorliegt, ihm Fesseln anlegen?

3) Wenn Art. 568 vorschreibt, daß die Gerichtsschreiber an den Einzelngerichten Register zu führen haben, in welche die Gesuche um Erlassung bedingter Zahlungsbefehle, die hierauf ergangenen Entschließungen und die Aushändigung der letzteren vorzumerken seien, so findet diese Vorschrift ihre Begründung in der Thatsache, daß alle Beschlüsse des Richters, namentlich aber der so wichtige Vollstreckungsbeschluß in Urschrift hinausgegeben werden.

Uebrigens erscheint die Fassung des Gesetzes mangelhaft, denn offenbar will es auch, daß die Gesuche um Erlassung von Vollstreckungsbeschlüssen und die Entschließungen auf diese Gesuche im nemlichen Register vorgemerkt werden. Vgl. die Erläuterungen des kgl. Minist.-Commissärs. Abg. II 439 (zu Art. 643a).

XX. Hauptstück.

Aufforderung zur Klage.

Allgemeine Bestimmungen.

Art. 569. — **Aufforderung zur Klage findet statt:**

1) **wider denjenigen, welcher mündlich oder schriftlich behauptet, an den Auffordernden einen bestimmten klagbaren Anspruch zu haben;**
2) **wenn der Auffordernde der Klage eine die Sache selbst betreffende Einrede entgegenzusetzen hat, welche bei längerer Verzögerung der Klagestellung ihre Zulässigkeit oder Wirksamkeit verlieren würde.**

Steht dem Auffordernden selbst eine Klage in der Hauptsache zu, befindet im Falle der Ziff. 1 der Aufgeforderte sich im Besitze des angesprochenen Rechts oder handelt es sich im Falle der Ziff. 2 nur um die Gefahr, Beweismittel zu verlieren, so ist die Aufforderung unzulässig.

Art. 570. — **Wer zur Klage aufgefordert hat, kann der in Folge davon erhobenen Klage die Einrede, daß der Anspruch noch nicht fällig sei, nicht entgegensetzen.**

G. A. d. K. d. A. II S. 425. 426. 447. — K. d. R. II S. 266—268.

1) Die provocatio ex lege Diffamari und die provocatio ex lege Si contendat tragen zwar ihre Namen von bestimmten römischen Gesetzen (c. 5 Cod. [7. 14] und l. 28 Dig. [46. 1]), sind aber im Grunde Schöpfungen der Praxis und des Gewohnheitsrechtes. Es läßt sich auch in der That nicht läugnen, daß sie beide einem praktischen Bedürfnisse entsprechen.

Auch in Frankreich, wo Provokationsklagen unbekannt sind, ist dieses Bedürfniß anerkannt und wird ihm in anderer, meiner Ansicht nach entsprechenderer Weise Rechnung getragen. Man erblickt nemlich in der Berühmung eines Anspruches, wenn sie entschieden und förmlich auftritt, z. B. in einer Ladung vor's Vermittlungsamt oder in einer sonstigen Zustellung, eine Rechtsverletzung, einen trouble de droit, und gestattet eine direkte Klage auf Aberkennung des angemaßten Rechtes. cass. 7. Nov. 1832 — Grenoble 15. Febr. 1816 — Metz 14. Nov. 1816 — Nîmes 5. Juni 1835 — Journal du Pal. (action) No. 281.

Was die provocatio ex lege Si contendat anbelangt, so wird ihr Zweck erreicht durch die Bestimmungen des Art. 2032 Code civ., welcher dem Bürgen ein direktes Klagerecht zu seiner Sicherung gibt.

2) Es wäre wohl sachgemäßer gewesen, den Ideen des französischen Rechtes folgend, hier mit zivilrechtlichen Bestimmungen, welche geradewegs zum Ziele führen, zu helfen, statt ein unbehilfliches, ganz im Geiste des alten Prozesses wurzelndes Verfahren wieder aufzufrischen, welches das nemliche Ziel auf großem Umwege, mit Aufwand von Zeit und Kosten erreicht.

Das Wesen der Provokationsklage ex lege Diffamari liegt doch wohl darin, daß derjenige, gegen welchen ein Rechtsanspruch auch bloß behauptet worden ist, ein Klagerecht haben solle, um das Bestehen oder Nichtbestehen des

Anspruches sofort in Gewißheit zu setzen. Was hindert nun den Gesetzgeber, geradezu auf den Kern der Sache loszugehen und eine Klage auf Aberkennung des beanspruchten Rechtes zu geben, d. h. die Prinzipien der Negatorienklage entsprechend auszudehnen?

Der Kläger hätte seine Klage durch Nachweis der Berühmung zu begründen, der Beklagte aber entweder den Anspruch aufzugeben, oder auf demselben zu beharren und seine Beweise zu führen. Alles dies würde zusammen verhandelt und erledigt und der ganze schwerfällige Apparat mit Aufforderungsklage, Androhung ewigen Stillschweigens und Erhebung der Hauptklage wäre erspart."

3) Unsere Prozeßordnung führt die beiden erwähnten Provokationsklagen im Wesentlichen so ein, wie sie das gemeine Recht bis jetzt kannte, und läßt daher eine Aufforderungsklage zu a) wegen Berühmung und b) wegen Gefahr des Verlustes von Einreden.

a) Aufforderung wegen Berühmung.

4) Die Aufforderungsklage wegen Berühmung wird vom Gesetze gegen jeden gegeben, welcher mündlich oder schriftlich behauptet, an den Auffordernden einen bestimmten klagbaren Anspruch zu haben.

Es ist zwar nicht ausdrücklich gesagt, möchte sich aber nach dem Geiste des Gesetzes von selbst verstehen, daß in der Behauptung, welche Anlaß zu einer Aufforderungsklage geben soll, die Absicht eines Angriffes sich kundgeben müsse; eine solche Absicht läßt sich aber nicht annehmen bei Aeußerungen, welche bei einer zeugschaftlichen Vernehmung oder überhaupt auf obrigkeitliches Befragen, oder zum Zwecke der Abwehr eines vom Gegner selbst ausgehenden Angriffes gemacht worden sind. Vgl. Bl. f. R. Bd. VI S. 282 — Seuff. Archiv Bd. III Nr. 386.

Ebenso erscheint selbstverständlich, daß die Aeußerungen sich als ernstlich gemeint ankündigen müssen. Ob sie aber öffentlich erfolgten oder nicht, ist ohne Belang.

5) Die Aeußerungen, welche zur Aufforderungsklage berechtigen, müssen vom Aufforderungsbeklagten ausgegangen sein. Es frägt sich, ob hiermit nur die Person des Beklagten gemeint sei, oder ob auch Berühmungen des Erblassers Anlaß zu einer Aufforderungsklage gegen die Erben geben könne.

Diese Frage war bis jetzt strittig.

Für Einschränkung auf die Person sprachen sich aus Seuff. Commentar Bd. IV S. 159 und ein Erkenntniß des kgl. O.A.G. München vom 18. März 1847 (Seuff. Archiv Bd. II Nr. 235). Dagegen sprach sich aus ein Plenarerkenntniß des O. A. G. zu Dresden (Seuff. Archiv Bd. VI Nr. 93).

Insofern die Berühmung ein Recht zur Klage gibt und nirgends gesagt wird, dieses Recht beschränke sich auf die Person, nehme ich an, daß die allgemeinen Prinzipien Maß zu geben haben, d. h. daß die letztere Ansicht die richtige sei. Jedenfalls ginge es zu weit, mit dem erst-erwähnten Erkenntnisse anzunehmen, daß eine bereits ausgesprochene Verurtheilung zur Klagerhebung gegen die Erben nicht wirke.

6) Es muß ein bestimmter klagbarer Anspruch behauptet worden sein und zwar gegen den Aufforderungskläger. Der Fall muß also so gelagert sein, daß gegen letzteren Klage erhoben werden könnte, wenn die Behauptung begründet wäre. Ein Anspruch dieser Art liegt z. B. nicht vor, wenn ein Gläubiger ein Pfandrecht oder einen sonstigen Vorzug vor anderen Gläubigern in Anspruch nimmt, denn es stünde ihm nicht zu, sofort Klage auf Anerkennung oder Feststellung seines Vorzugsrechtes gegen diese Gläubiger zu erheben. Seuff. Commentar B. II S. 158.

Die Klagbarkeit eines Anspruches setzt eigentlich voraus, daß seine Geltendmachung weder von einer aufschiebenden Bedingung, noch von einer Frist abhänge, vielmehr sofort Klage erhoben werden könne; aus Art. 570 geht jedoch hervor, daß ausnahmsweise auch auf die Behauptung einer noch nicht fälligen, d. h. noch von einer Frist abhängigen Forderung eine Aufforderungsklage gegründet werden könne, was insofern natürlich ist, als in der Aufforderung zu klagen der Verzicht auf den Einwand der Nichtfälligkeit liegt.

Der behauptete Anspruch muß nicht bloß klagbar, sondern auch bestimmt sein. Allgemeine Behauptungen, welche nur darauf hinausgehen, daß Ansprüche überhaupt, oder ein Anspruch bestimmter Art, z. B. ein Darlehen bestehe, ohne daß jedoch eine Summe genannt und sonst der Anspruch näher bezeichnet wäre, begründen eine Aufforderungsklage nicht.

7) Nach unserer Prozeßordnung ist die Aufforderungsklage wesentlich subsidiärer Natur; sie ist nur gegeben, wo sich kein anderer Weg darbietet. Steht daher dem Auffordernden selbst ein Klagerecht zur Seite, so ist er auf dieses verwiesen und ist nicht befugt, den Gegner zur Klagerhebung aufzufordern.

In Fällen, wo jeder Theil klagberechtigt ist, z. B. bei Klagen auf Theilung, Grenzberichtigung zc., kann daher, wenn nicht das ganze Recht bestritten wird, die Aufforderungsklage nicht Platz greifen, ferner kann derjenige, welchem eine besondere Klage auf Vernichtung eines Vertrages gegeben ist (Art. 1304 ff. Code civ.) nicht verlangen, daß der Gegner auf Erfüllung dieses Vertrages klage, und ebenso kann Jemand, welchem eine Negatorienklage zusteht, den Gegner nicht auffordern, confessorisch zu klagen. Soweit das französische Civilrecht eine Klage auf Aberkennung eines Rechtes zuläßt (s. oben Nr. 1), besteht dieselbe natürlich in der Pfalz auch jetzt noch fort und sind die Bestimmungen des Hauptst. XX gegenstandlos.

Selbstverständlich erscheint es, daß wenn ein Rechtsstreit bereits anhängig ist, in welchem auf dem Wege der Widerklage, oder sonst anschlußweise eine Entscheidung über den in Frage stehenden Anspruch veranlaßt werden kann, der Weg der Provocationsklage nicht offen steht.

8) Als eine Folge des eben erörterten Grundsatzes ist es zu betrachten, daß die Aufforderung unzulässig ist, wenn der Aufgeforderte sich im Besitze des beanspruchten Rechtes befindet. Wer im Besitze ist, braucht nicht zu klagen und rühmt sich daher keines Klaganspruches; anderseits aber steht demjenigen, welcher ihm gegenüber ein Recht auf Besitz oder Eigenthum in Anspruch nimmt, ein Klagerecht zur Seite; es liegt somit ein doppelter Grund vor, die Aufforderungsklage hier auszuschließen.

Offenbar ist bloß der jüngste Besitz entscheidend, denn kann der Aufgeforderte sich auf diesen berufen, so fällt ihm die Rolle des Beklagten, dem Kläger aber die Rolle des Klägers zu.

b) Aufforderung wegen Gefahr des Verlustes einer Einrede.

9) Die zweite Aufforderungsklage ist gegeben zur Wahrung von Einreden, welche nur innerhalb bestimmter Frist geltend gemacht werden können, wie z. B. früher die exceptio non numeratae pecuniae, oder welche im Verlaufe der Zeit ihre Wirksamkeit verlieren, wie die Einreden der Vorausklage und Theilung, welche werthlos erscheinen, nachdem der Hauptschuldner bezw. Mitbürge zahlungsunfähig geworden ist.

Die Gerichtsordnung gab diese Aufforderungsklage nur ad replicandum, d. h. in der Weise, daß die Frage des Bestehens der Einrede in einem besonderen Verfahren festgestellt, die Einrede perpetuirt wurde; unsere Prozeßordnung jedoch gibt sie, dem gemeinen Rechte folgend, zur Klagstellung.

10) Das Gesetz erklärt diese Aufforderung unstatthaft, wenn es sich nur um die Gefahr handelt, Beweismittel zu verlieren. Man war der Ansicht, daß in dieser Richtung der Beweis zum ewigen Gedächtnisse genüge, allein völlig richtig ist dies nicht, da jenes Verfahren nicht dazu dienen kann, die Eideszuschiebung zu sichern.

Diese Aufforderung ist ferner unstatthaft, wenn dem Auffordernden ein Klagrecht zusteht, mittelst dessen er das Nemliche erreichen kann.

11) Zufolge dieser Prinzipien verliert die in Frage stehende Aufforderungsklage einen großen Theil ihres früheren Wirkungskreises.

Ihre Anwendung wird sich diesseits nahezu auf die erwähnten beiden Einreden des Bürgen beschränken, in der Pfalz aber erscheint sie gegenstandslos, da dort das Civilgesetz überall die zur Sicherung von Einreden nöthigen Klagen gibt. So hat insbesondere der Bürge, sobald die Forderung fällig ist, ein direktes Klagerecht gegen den Schuldner, um sich sicher zu stellen (Art. 2032 C. civ.).

12) Es ergibt sich schließlich die Frage, wie Art. 570 auf diese Aufforderungsklage anzuwenden sei?

Der Sinn dieses Artikels ist der, daß eine Aufforderungsklage wegen Berühmung zulässig sei, auch wenn es sich um eine noch nicht fällige Forderung handle (Referat zu Art. 604 des Entwurfs). — Der allgemeinen Fassung dieser Bestimmung gemäß sollte man nun denken, sie gelte ebenso unbedingt für den Fall, wo eine Einrede zu wahren ist, als für den Fall der Berühmung, allein bei näherer Erwägung zeigt sich, daß dies nicht richtig sein könne.

Gerade in jenen Fällen, wo fragliche Aufforderungsklage jetzt noch praktisch ist, bei den Einreden des Bürgen, setzt die Einschreitung gegen den Bürgen die Ausklagung des Hauptschuldners bezw. Mitbürgen voraus, und es liegt in der Aufforderung zur Klage gegen den Bürgen zugleich eine indirekte Aufforderung zur Klage gegen besagte dritte Personen. Es kann nun aber der Bürge durch seine Aufforderung dem Gläubiger nicht das Recht geben, gegen jene dritten Personen klagend aufzutreten.

Hieraus folgt, daß der Gläubiger der Aufforderungsklage mit dem Einwande entgegentreten darf, es sei die Forderung noch nicht fällig. Er kann diesen Einwand jedoch nur mit Bezugnahme auf die Rechte besagter dritter Personen erheben; haben diese auf die Frist verzichtet oder sind sie derselben aus irgend einem Grunde verlustig geworden, so besteht ein Einwand nicht mehr und es treten die Bestimmungen des Art. 570 in Wirksamkeit.

Zuständigkeit.

Art. 571. — Die Aufforderungsklage ist bei dem in der Hauptsache zuständigen Gerichte, falls aber deren mehrere sind, bei einem derselben zu erheben.

Dem Aufgeforderten wird hiedurch bei Anstellung der Hauptklage das Wahlrecht zwischen den mehreren zuständigen Gerichten nicht entzogen.

G. A. d. K. d. A. II S. 426. 447. — K. d. R. II S. 268.

1) Unsere Prozeßordnung betrachtet in Uebereinstimmung mit der Gerichtsordnung die Aufforderungsklage nur als eine Einleitung zu der hervorzurufenden Hauptklage, als ein Zubehör derselben und verfügt demgemäß, daß sie immer bei dem in der Hauptsache zuständigen Gerichte anzubringen sei.

Dies gilt ebensowohl für die *sachliche* als für die *örtliche* Zuständigkeit (Bemerk. zu Art. 38 Nr. 2). Sind in letzterer Beziehung mehrere Gerichte gleich zuständig, sei es weil Streitgenossen, die in verschiedenen Gerichtsbezirken wohnen, zu belangen sind, sei es weil die Wahl zwischen dem allgemeinen und einem besonderen Gerichtsstande freisteht, so hat der Auffordernde zwar die Wahl, kann aber hiermit das Wahlrecht des Aufgeforderten bei Anstellung der Hauptklage nicht beeinträchtigen.

Auch in Fällen, wo die Aufforderung nur von *einem* der Streitgenossen ausgeht, der Aufgeforderte aber es für sachgemäß hält, auch die anderen Streitgenossen zu belangen, ist diesem sein Wahlrecht unverkümmert.

2) Wie sich hieraus ergibt, wird es hie und da vorkommen, daß die Hauptklage vor einem anderen Gerichte zur Verhandlung kommt, als die Aufforderungsklage. Es ist dies ein Mißstand, der leicht hätte vermieden werden können, wenn man in allen Fällen, wo nicht die Sache selbst den Gerichtsstand bestimmt, den allgemeinen Gerichtsstand des Aufgeforderten als maßgebend für Durchführung *beider* Klagen erklärt hätte.

Derjenige, welchem die Vergünstigung zu Theil wird, auf eine bloße Aeußerung hin Jemanden vor Gericht ziehen zu dürfen, kann sich nicht beschwert finden, wenn ihm zur Bedingung gemacht wird, dem Gerichtsstande seines Gegners zu folgen. Es steht ja nur bei ihm, eine Aufforderungsklage zu erheben oder zu unterlassen.

3) Der Fall, wo nicht der nemliche Richter über die Hauptklage und über die Aufforderungsklage erkennt, kann auch eintreten, wenn sich inzwischen die thatsächlichen Verhältnisse, welche den Gerichtsstand bestimmen, geändert haben, oder wenn sich später ergibt, daß eine von Amtswegen zu beachtende Unzuständigkeit vorliege.

In letzterer Beziehung war man zwar unter der Herrschaft der G.O. der Ansicht, daß der Provokant gegen die Zuständigkeit desjenigen Gerichts, bei welchem er die Provokationsklage erhoben, keinen Einwand mehr machen könne (Seuff. Comm. Bd. II S. 252 Note 7); allein wenn dies auch für Fälle, wo Vereinbarung statthaft ist, auch jetzt noch richtig sein mag, so steht doch in sonstigen Fällen die leidige Bestimmung des Art. 265 entschieden im Wege.

4) Was insbesondere die Aufforderungsklage des *Bürgen* zur Wahrung seiner Einreden anbelangt, so ist die Hauptklage, welche die Zuständigkeit bestimmt, nicht etwa die gegen den Hauptschuldner oder den Mitbürgen, sondern nur die gegen den auffordernden Bürgen selbst anzustellende Klage. Unsere Prozeßordnung kennt nemlich eine direkte Aufforderung zur Anstellung einer Klage gegen *Dritte* nicht, wie sie allerdings nach gemeinem Rechte von manchen Rechtslehrern zugelassen wurde. Glück Commentar VI S. 509 ff.

Verfahren.

Art. 572. — Erscheint die Aufforderung als begründet, so ist bei Bezirksgerichten dem Aufgeforderten eine angemessene, vom Tage der Rechtskraft des Urtheils an laufende Frist zur Anstellung der Klage unter Androhung des Rechtsnachtheils vorzusetzen, daß nach fruchtlosem Ablaufe der Frist das Klagerecht für erloschen erklärt würde.

Art. 573. — Wird die Hauptklage bei dem nämlichen Bezirksgerichte erhoben, welches über die Aufforderung erkannt hat, so gelten die in dem Aufforderungsverfahren erfolgten Anwaltsbestellungen auch für die Hauptklage, die Klageschrift ist auf Betreiben des Anwalts des Hauptklägers dem Anwalte des Hauptbeklagten ohne die in Artikel 226 vorgesehene Aufforderung zuzustellen und die Frist für den motivirten Antrag des Beklagten läuft von der Zustellung der Klageschrift.

Art. 574. — Wird im Verfahren vor Bezirksgerichten die Klage innerhalb der vorgesetzten Frist nicht erhoben, so kann der Auffordernde beantragen, daß das behauptete Klagerecht für erloschen erklärt werde. Solange dieser Antrag nicht zugestellt ist, kann die Klage auch nach Ablauf der Frist noch wirksam erhoben werden.

Art. 575. — **Wird die bei einem Handels- oder Einzelngerichte erhobene Aufforderungsklage als begründet erkannt, so ist in dem Urtheile zugleich eine Sitzung anzuberaumen, in welcher der Aufgeforderte die Hauptklage mündlich erheben und entwickeln muß, widrigenfalls das Klagerecht auf Antrag des Auffordernden für erloschen erklärt wird.**

Ist für die Hauptklage noch ein anderes Gericht zuständig, so genügt der Nachweis, daß die Klage dort erhoben worden sei.

Art. 576. — **Die Entscheidung über die Kosten des Aufforderungsverfahrens ist, wenn die Aufforderung als begründet erklärt wird, einstweilen vorzubehalten.**

Art. 577. — **Gegen die auf Aufforderungsklagen und auf Anträge, das Klagerecht wegen Nichterhebung der Klage für erloschen zu erklären, ergangenen Endurtheile findet Berufung statt, wenn sie in der Hauptsache zulässig ist.**

Art. 578. — **Im Uebrigen gelten für Aufforderungsklagen und für das Verfahren auf solche die allgemeinen gesetzlichen Bestimmungen.** G. A. d. K. d. A. II S. 426. 427. 447. — K. d. R. II S. 268.

1) Im Allgemeinen gelten für Aufforderungsklagen und für das Verfahren auf solche die gewöhnlichen Prinzipien (Art. 578).

Zur Klagbegründung nach Maßgabe des Art. 225 gehört 1) die Thatsache der Berühmung bezw. der Gefahr des Verlustes bestimmter Einreden, 2) die Behauptung, daß der Anspruch, dessen sich der Gegner berühmte, unbegründet bezw. die Einrede begründet sei und 3) in Fällen, wo es auf den Besitz ankommt, die Behauptung, daß der Auffordernde sich im Besitze befinde.

Das Gesuch ist dahin zu richten, daß dem Gegner eine Frist gesetzt werde zur Erhebung der bestimmten Klage, widrigenfalls das Klagerecht als erloschen erklärt würde.

2) Erscheint die Aufforderung unbegründet, so ist die Klage abzuweisen und Kläger in die Kosten zu verurtheilen.

Erscheint die Aufforderung begründet, so ist nach Art. 576 die Entscheidung über die Kosten vorzubehalten und wird im Erkenntnisse, welches die Klage erloschen erklärt, oder aber im Erkenntnisse, welches in der Hauptsache ergeht, auch über die Kosten des einleitenden Prozesses entschieden, wobei es keinen Unterschied macht, ob der nemliche oder ein anderer Richter in der Hauptsache zu erkennen habe.

3) Die Urtheile, welche im Provokationsprozesse ergehen, können nach allgemeinen Prinzipien durch Rechtsmittel angefochten werden; ebenso ist auch gegen Versäumnungsurtheile Einspruch zulässig.

Das Urtheil, welches die Aufforderungsklage für begründet erklärt und demgemäß eine Frist zur Klagerhebung setzt, ist ein Endurtheil im Sinne des Art. 682, ebenso wie das weitere Urtheil, welches das Klagerecht für erloschen erklärt; beide Urtheile unterliegen daher der Berufung.

Was nun die besonderen Erfordernisse zur Zulässigkeit dieser Berufung betrifft, so ist gemäß Art. 577 in dieser Beziehung die Hauptsache maßgebend, sowie sie sich nach Maßgabe der Aufforderungsklage darstellt, d. h. es ist die Berufung statthaft, wenn der behauptete Anspruch die Berufungssumme erreicht, oder in der Hauptsache Berufung ohne Rücksicht auf den Werth des Streitgegenstandes zulässig ist. Abg. II 426 Sp. 1.

Auch für die Berufung gegen Zwischenurtheile, wo diese statthaft ist, z. B. wenn es sich um die Frage der Zuständigkeit oder um eine Eidesleistung handelt, muß Art. 577 analoge Anwendung finden.

4) Die Bestimmung der Frist zur Anstellung der Hauptklage ist ganz dem Ermessen des Richters überlassen, welcher die Umstände des Falles berücksichtigen wird, namentlich ob dem Aufgeforderten das Recht zustehe, die Klage vor einem anderen Gerichte zu erheben. Er wird Sorge tragen, daß bei der Verhandlung über die Aufforderungsklage die Parteien ihre bezüglichen Wünsche geltend machen und die nöthigen Anhaltspunkte liefern.

Reicht die festgesetzte Frist nicht aus, so kann nach Maßgabe des Art. 213 Abs. 2 u. 3 die Frist verlängert bezw. die Tagfahrt verlegt werden.

5) Was insbesondere den Fall betrifft, wo der Bürge zur Wahrung seiner Einreden zur Klage auffordert, so ergeben sich Schwierigkeiten.

Das Gesetz will auch hier, daß nicht für die Klage gegen Hauptschuldner oder Mitbürgen, sondern für die Klage gegen den Bürgen eine Frist gesetzt werde. Nun führt aber eine solche Klage in der Regel nicht zum Ziele; denn wenn auch fragliche Einreden entgegengesetzt und als begründet befunden werden, so sind sie doch nur dilatorisch; es kann also der Gläubiger nach erfolgter Ausklagung des Hauptschuldners bezw. Mitbürgen wiederholt gegen den Bürgen auftreten. Es wird sich demnach im Grunde doch nur darum handeln, eine Frist zur Erhebung und Durchführung der Klage gegen besagte dritte Personen zu geben.

Bei dieser Sachlage wird wie folgt zu verfahren sein. Erklärt der Gläubiger, den Hauptschuldner ausklagen zu wollen, so ist die Frist zur Klagestellung gegen den Bürgen so zu bemessen, daß diese Ausklagung vollständig stattfinden kann, und falls der Gläubiger darthut, daß die Frist zu diesem Zwecke nicht ausreiche, so ist dieselbe zu verlängern. Erklärt jedoch der Gläubiger, daß er sofort bereit sei, den Ungrund der Einrede (die Unzahlfähigkeit des Hauptschuldners) darzuthun, so ist eine kürzere Frist zu setzen.

6) Im Falle, wo die Aufforderung für begründet erklärt wird, gestaltet sich sowohl die Fassung des Urtheils als das spätere Verfahren verschieden, je nachdem die Sache sich im Anwaltsprozesse oder im Parteiprozesse bewegt.

a) Verfahren im Anwaltsprozesse.

7) Im Anwaltsprozesse setzt das Urtheil eine Frist fest zur Anstellung der Klage mit der Androhung, daß nach fruchtlosem Ablaufe dieser Frist das Klagerecht für erloschen erklärt werde. Offenbar legt das Gesetz Werth darauf, daß diese ausdrückliche Androhung im Urtheile enthalten sei, und müßte dieses bei Mangel derselben als unvollständig betrachtet werden.

Die bestimmte Frist läuft vom Tage der Rechtskraft des Urtheils an, d. h. vom Tage an, wo dasselbe weder durch Einspruch noch durch Berufung mehr angefochten werden kann.

8) Es frägt sich, ob Letzteres auch zu gelten habe bei Urtheilen, welche sofort mit dem Spruche rechtskräftig sind, sei es weil die bezüglichen Rechtsmittel nicht statthaft, sei es weil sie bereits erschöpft sind.

Der Wortlaut spricht dafür, der Geist des Gesetzes aber entschieden entgegen. Der Gesetzgeber kann nicht wollen, daß auch in Fällen, wo der Anwalt der verurtheilten Partei bei Spruch des Urtheils nicht zugegen war, oder wo der Anwalt erster Instanz in Folge eines in der Berufungsinstanz gesprochenen Urtheils handeln soll, oder endlich gar, wo Klage vor einem anderen Gerichte durch einen neu zu bestellenden Anwalt erhoben werden soll, die Frist immer sofort vom Augenblicke des Urtheilsspruches an laufe!

Mit den Worten: „vom Tage der Rechtskraft des Urtheils an," welche im Entwurfe (Art. 605) nicht vorkamen, welche vielmehr erst der neue Vorschlag des kgl. Minist.-Commissärs (Abg. II 426) brachte, und welche ohne jede Bemerkung belassen wurden, sollte daher nur gesagt sein, daß die Frist nie eher beginne, als bis das Urtheil rechtskräftig geworden sei. Im Uebrigen sind die allgemeinen Prinzipien des Art. 208 Abs. 1 maßgebend, gemäß deren die Fristen von der Zustellung an laufen.

9) Es entsteht nun aber die Frage, ob auch Art. 210 Abs. 3 Anwendung finde, welcher vorschreibt, daß bei Endurtheilen der Fristenlauf, soweit das Gesetz nicht anders bestimme, erst mit der Zustellung an die Partei beginne.

Da das Urtheil, welches die Aufforderungsklage für begründet erklärt, ohne Zweifel ein Endurtheil ist (vgl. Referat zu Art. 605 des Entwurfs u. Abg. II 427 Sp. 1), so wird diese Frage zu bejahen sein, und zwar um so sicherer, als die Fristen für Einspruch und Berufung auch nur von Zustellung an die Partei laufen.

Uebrigens sprechen noch besondere Gründe dafür, daß die hier in Frage stehende Frist erst von der Zustellung an die Partei laufe. Für jene Fälle nemlich, wo die Klage an einem anderen Gerichte anzustellen, dort erst ein Anwalt zu beauftragen ist, liegt es auf flacher Hand, daß ein Handeln der Partei nöthig sei und vom Gesetze vorausgesetzt werde; was aber für diese Fälle gilt, muß allgemein gelten, da das Gesetz nicht unterscheidet. Zwar sind Ausnahmsbestimmungen gegeben für Fälle, wo die Klage am nemlichen Gerichte anzubringen ist, allein diese beziehen sich nur auf die Art der Erhebung der Klage (Art. 573 u. 574), nicht aber auf den Fristenlauf, von welchem Art. 572 spricht. Daß Art. 573 das Mandat der Anwälte fortdauern läßt, ist für sich ohne Belang, denn auch bei den Zwischenurtheilen, von welchen Art. 683 spricht, ist dies der Fall.

Da dem Gesagten zufolge das Gesetz voraussetzt, daß die Partei selbst in Verzug gesetzt werde, so müssen folgerichtig auch die Art. 209 und 211 wegen Erweiterung und Unterbrechung der Frist zur Anwendung kommen.

10) Was die Einleitung der Klage betrifft, so gelten für den Ausnahmsfall, wo sie an einem anderen Gericht erhoben wird, die gewöhnlichen Regeln, für den gewöhnlichen Fall aber, wo die Klagestellung am nemlichen Gerichte erfolgt, ist das Verfahren sehr vereinfacht. Es wird der neue Prozeß als Fortsetzung des Provokationsprozesses behandelt und gelten die im letzteren bestellten Anwälte auch als berechtigt zur Vertretung im ersteren.

Eine Klageschrift ist allerdings nöthig und muß dieselbe allen Anforderungen entsprechen, wie sie für sonstige Fälle gestellt sind; allein es genügt die Zustellung von Anwalt zu Anwalt, um den Rechtsstreit abhängig zu machen in ähnlicher Weise, wie bei Zwischenstreiten. Hiermit fällt selbstverständlich die Aufforderung zur Bestellung eines Anwalts, sowie die zu diesem Zwecke gegebene Erscheinungsfrist nebst ihren Erweiterungen hinweg und ergibt sich die Folge, daß die Frist für den motivirten Antrag des Beklagten von Zustellung der Klageschrift an läuft. Ferner verbindet sich hiermit der Vortheil, daß eine einzige Abschrift für alle durch den nemlichen Anwalt vertretene Beklagten genügt (Art. 203 Abs. 3).

11) Ist innerhalb der nach vorstehenden Erörterungen sich ergebenden Frist die Klage nicht erhoben worden, so hat der Aufforderungskläger das Recht, zu beantragen, daß das Klagerecht für erloschen erklärt werde.

Dieser Antrag ist immer an das Gericht, bei welchem die Aufforderungsklage anhängig ist, zu richten, wie denn überhaupt das bezügliche Verfahren nur als eine Fortsetzung des Prozesses und der Ausspruch der Klagerlöschung nur als Ergänzung des Urtheils, welches dieselbe androht, zu betrachten ist.

Auch nach Ablauf der Frist und bis zu der von Anwalt zu Anwalt erfolgenden Zustellung des bezüglichen Antrags kann die Klage noch giltig erhoben werden; nach dieser Zustellung jedoch ist dieses Recht verwirkt und der Gegner hat ein Recht, die Klagerlöschung aussprechen zu lassen, falls nicht Wiedereinsetzung in den vorigen Stand erwirkt wird.

b) Verfahren im Parteiprozesse.

12) Im Parteiprozesse ist das Verfahren ein wesentlich anderes.

Das Urtheil bestimmt die Frist nur in der Art, daß es sofort eine Sitzung festsetzt, in welcher die Klage mündlich anzubringen oder der Nachweis, daß sie an einem andern Gerichte angebracht sei, vorzulegen ist. Wird dies versäumt, so ist auf Antrag des Auffordernden in der nemlichen Sitzung die Klage für erloschen zu erklären.

Es entsteht nun die Frage, ob das Urtheil, welches die Rechtsverlustigung androht, zuzustellen sei und wann?

13) Durch Bezugnahme auf die Art. 508 und 525 läßt sich diese Frage nicht beseitigen, denn das fragliche Urtheil enthält weder eine einfache Vertagung zur Verhandlung, noch ordnet es eine Beweiserhebung an, vielmehr ist es ein Endurtheil, welches vollzogen werden soll.

Unterstellt man den Fall, es sei dasselbe ein Versäumungsurtheil, so springt sofort in die Augen, daß es nicht angehe, in der anberaumten Sitzung das Klagerecht für erloschen zu erklären, ohne dem Aufgeforderten von der Anberaumung der Sitzung Kenntniß zu geben und ihn in die Lage zu versetzen, Einspruch einzulegen; daß also eine Zustellung nöthig sei, ohne welche eine Rechtsverlustigung nicht eintreten könne. Muß man nun zugeben, daß es Fälle gebe, wo die Urtheilszustellung stattfinden müsse, so folgt, daß Art. 575 nicht beabsichtigte, eine Ausnahme von den allgemeinen Grundsätzen einzuführen, gemäß deren Endurtheile sowie überhaupt Urtheile, gegen welche selbständige Rechtsmittel zulässig sind, zugestellt sein müssen, bevor sie in Vollzug gesetzt werden können (Art. 192 und Bemerk. dazu Nr. 9).

Diese Zustellung ist im Geiste des Gesetzes hauptsächlich auch deßhalb nöthig, weil das Gesetz nicht will, daß der Vollzug solcher Urtheile erzwungen werden könne, bevor die Fristen für die Rechtsmittel nicht wenigstens in Lauf gesetzt seien, und es kommen in dieser Beziehung nicht bloß die ordentlichen Rechtsmittel (Einspruch und Berufung), sondern auch die außerordentlichen (Wiederaufnahme des Verfahrens und Nichtigkeitsbeschwerde) in Betracht, deren Zulässigkeit gleichfalls durch die Zustellung bedingt ist (Art. 770 Abs. 3, Art. 797).

Ich nehme daher an, daß in allen Fällen das Urtheil vor der anberaumten Sitzung zugestellt sein müsse.

14) Es frägt sich nun weiter, ob für diese Zustellung eine gewisse Frist einzuhalten sei?

Liegt ein Versäumungsurtheil vor, so fühlt man, daß es nicht genügen könne, die Zustellung am Tage vor der Sitzung zu bethätigen, und man ist versucht, die gewöhnliche Erscheinungsfrist des Art. 503 zu beanspruchen, da der Fall, wo Jemand aufgefordert ist, sich gegen eine Klage zu vertheidigen, und der Fall, wo Jemand aufgefordert ist, bei Strafe des Verlustes seines Rechts Klage zu erheben, sich ziemlich ähnlich verhalten.

Ich halte es jedoch für gewagt, in der analogen Anwendung des Gesetzes so weit zu gehen, und glaube, daß andere Gesichtspunkte maßgebend sein müssen.

Der gegebene Fall ist demjenigen gleich zu achten, wo das Gericht erlaubt, ohne Rücksicht auf die gewöhnliche Erscheinungsfrist in eine bestimmte Sitzung zu laden (Art. 259 u. 502 Abs. 2). Wie in jenen Fällen der Richter befugt und verpflichtet ist, zu prüfen, ob die Zustellung bzw. Vorladung rechtzeitig erfolgt sei oder nicht, unter Umständen aber den Ausspruch des Versäumungsurtheils zu verweigern und neue Vorladung anzuordnen (Art. 300 u. 520 Abs. 2), so wird dies auch hier anzunehmen sein.

Binnen der neueröffneten Frist kann, falls der Gegner bereits Verlustigungserklärung beantragt hatte, Wiedereinsetzung gegen die Versäumung der Tagfahrt begehrt werden, welche bei Unzureichendheit der Frist nicht verweigert werden darf. Das Nemliche gilt auch für den Fall, wo das Urtheil ein contradiktorisches ist, jedoch bietet die Wiedereinsetzung größere Schwierigkeit.

15) Inconsequenter Weise hat das Gesetz beim Parteiprozesse auf die Frage, ob das Urtheil rechtskräftig geworden sei oder nicht, keinen Werth gelegt; es kann daher, trotzdessen daß am anberaumten Sitzungstage noch Berufung gegen dasselbe statthaft ist, die Erlöschung des Klagerechts wegen Nichterhebung der Klage begehrt und ausgesprochen werden.

Uebrigens wird der Umstand, daß die Frist zur Ergreifung der Berufung noch im Laufe ist, in der Regel Anlaß zu einem Gesuche um Verlegung der Tagfahrt geben. Nach dem Geiste des Gesetzes, welches im Parteiprozesse auf die Reihenfolge des Vorbringens kein Gewicht gelegt haben will (Art. 507 Abs. 2), möchte ein solches Gesuch rechtzeitig erscheinen, wenn es nur überhaupt in der Sitzung gestellt wird, mag auch der Gegner vorher erklärt haben, daß er Ausspruch der Verlustigung beantrage.

Ist am bestimmten Sitzungstage die Berufung bereits erklärt, oder die Einspruchsfrist noch im Laufe, so hat die Fixirung keinen Werth und muß später auf Anrufen des Aufforderungsklägers von Neuem eine Sitzung bestimmt und in dieselbe vorgeladen werden.

XXI. Hauptstück.

Verfahren zur Feststellung der Aechtheit von Privaturkunden.

Klage auf Aechtheitserklärung.

Art. 579. — **Der Inhaber einer Privaturkunde kann, wenn der aus derselben sich ergebende Anspruch noch nicht klagbar ist, gegen die als Aussteller der Urkunde bezeichnete Person bei dem für den Anspruch zuständigen Gerichte zu dem Zwecke Klage erheben, damit die Urkunde für ächt erklärt werde.**

Art. 580. — **Mit der Klage auf Aechtheitserklärung ist Abschrift der betreffenden Urkunde zuzustellen.**

Art. 581. — **Hat der Beklagte die Aechtheit der Urkunde nicht bestritten, so fallen alle Kosten, soweit sie nicht durch Verschulden des Beklagten veranlaßt sind, dem Kläger zur Last, gleichviel ob der Beklagte erschienen ist oder nicht.**

Art. 582. — **Im Uebrigen finden bezüglich des Verfahrens die allgemeinen Bestimmungen Anwendung.**

G. A. d. K. d. A. II S. 431. 447. — K. d. R. II S. 269.

1) Das Verfahren, welches Gegenstand dieses Hauptstückes bildet, ist dem französischen Rechte entlehnt (Art. 193—195 Code de proc.). Die Wichtigkeit des Urkundenbeweises im französischen Rechte, die Unsicherheit des Beweises durch Privaturkunden, so lange deren Aechtheit noch nicht feststeht, endlich der Umstand, daß das französische Recht einen Beweis zum ewigen Gedächtnisse nicht kennt, erklären es, wie der französische Gesetzgeber dazu kam, einen besonderen Weg zur Feststellung der Aechtheit von Privaturkunden zu geben. Mit dieser Feststellung verband er den weiteren Vortheil, daß sie gleich einer Verurtheilung Generalhypotheke bewirkte (Art. 2123 C. civ.), eine Wirkung, welche jedoch durch ein Gesetz vom 3. Sept. 1807 dahin eingeschränkt wurde, daß eine Hypothekeneinschreibung erst giltig genommen werden kann, nachdem die Forderung einklagbar geworden ist.

Besondere praktische Bedeutung hatten diese Bestimmungen nicht, wenigstens nicht in der Pfalz. Nur selten wurde von ihnen Gebrauch gemacht und dann nur in Fällen, wo die Forderung bereits fällig war, und es sich darum handelte, möglichst wohlfeil und schnell eine Generalhypotheke zu erlangen.

Für diesseits hat dieses Ausnahmsverfahren nur insofern einigen Werth, als es für Urkunden den Beweis zum ewigen Gedächtnisse ersetzt oder vielmehr ergänzt, indem es dazu dient, gewisse dem Aechtheitsbeweise eigenthümliche Beweisbehelfe — Beiladung des Ausstellers (Art. 371 Abs. 2), Erhebung von Vergleichsschriften (Art. 380), Eide — zu sichern.

2) Die Bestimmungen unserer Prozeßordnung weichen wesentlich von den Bestimmungen des französischen Prozesses ab.

Zum Ersten wird fragliches Ausnahmsverfahren nur zugelassen, wenn der Anspruch noch nicht klagbar ist, ist also ausgeschlossen, wenn auf Grund der Urkunden sofort Klage erhoben werden kann.

Es frägt sich hierbei, was zu gelten habe, wenn die Ansprüche, welche aus der Urkunde hervorgehen, nur theilweise klagbar sind, z. B. eine einzelne Zielfrist? — Da res judicata bezüglich der Frage der Aechtheit nur entsteht, wenn dieselbe Gegenstand eines Zwischenstreites, d. h. der unmittelbaren oder mittelbaren Aburtheilung wird, da ferner in der Pfalz der Gläubiger Interesse hat, Generalhypotheke auch bezüglich der nicht fälligen Beträge zu erlangen, so wird im unterstellten Falle die Klage auf Aechtheitserklärung nicht ausgeschlossen sein, jedoch wird sie sich der Einklagung der fälligen Ansprüche anschließen müssen.

3) Eine weitere sehr eingreifende Neuerung besteht darin, daß nach unserer Prozeßordnung die Klage sich gegen die als Aussteller der Urkunde bezeichnete Person richtet, während sie sich nach französischem Rechte gegen diejenige Person richten muß, gegen welche der Anspruch geltend gemacht wird. Es ist dies nichts weniger als einerlei, denn Aussteller ist im Sinne der Prozeßordnung auch derjenige, welcher eine Urkunde nur für fremde Rechnung unterzeichnet hat, als Vormund, Verwalter, Bevollmächtigter, gegen welchen also, falls er innerhalb seines Mandates gehandelt, ein Klagerecht nicht gegeben ist.

Ob es ein glücklicher Gedanke war, das französische Recht in diesem Punkte verbessern zu wollen, möge aus nachstehenden Erörterungen bemessen werden.

4) Der Gläubiger will, wenn er diese Klage anstellt, seinem Schuldner gegenüber die Aechtheit der Unterschrift rechtskräftig festgestellt haben; zur Erreichung dieses Zweckes ist ihm aber mit einem Klagerechte gegen dritte Personen wenig oder gar nicht gedient.

Ferner ist es aber auch prinzipwidrig, gegen Personen einen selbständigen Prozeß zu eröffnen, welche die Sache gar nichts angeht.

Schließlich frägt es sich, was zu geschehen habe, wenn der Aussteller nicht mehr lebt oder verschollen oder unter Vormundschaft gestellt ist? Fällt dann das Klagerecht, als an der Person haftend, hinweg, oder kann es auch den Erben und gesetzlichen Vertretern gegenüber geltend gemacht werden?

In Fällen, wo eine dritte Person der Aussteller war, muß offenbar der Umstand, daß sie verstorben ist oder wegen Interdiktion rc. Erklärungen mit rechtlicher Wirkung nicht mehr machen kann, das Klagerecht beseitigen, weil der gesetzliche Boden dafür fehlen würde, hier ausnahmsweise die Klage nicht gegen den Aussteller, sondern gegen den Interessenten zu richten, d. h. zum richtigen Prinzipe zurückzukehren.

In Fällen, wo der Interessent selbst der Aussteller war, würde ich jedoch, obgleich man auch hier den Wortlaut des Gesetzes entgegenhalten könnte, die Klage gegen den Rechtsnachfolger zulassen.

Schließlich glaube ich, daß der Vormund, Bevollmächtigte rc., welcher als Aussteller belangt ist, das Recht habe, des Kostenersatzes wegen den Interessenten auf Gewährschaft beizuladen.

5) Zuständig für die Klage auf Aechtheitserklärung ist dasjenige Gericht, welches für die Ansprüche, welche auf die Urkunde gegründet werden können, zuständig ist, und finden hier, was die materielle Competenz betrifft, die Grundsätze Anwendung, wie sie zu Art. 528 näher erläutert sind. Es kann daher die Klage unter Umständen auch vor dem Handelsgerichte oder Einzelngerichte erhoben werden.

6) Zweck der Klage ist bloß die Feststellung der Aechtheit, d. h. der Thatsache, daß die Privaturkunde von dem Beklagten ausgestellt worden sei.

In der Regel wird es sich bloß um die Unterschrift handeln; allein es kann auch der sonstige Inhalt in Frage kommen, z. B. bei Urkunden, welche vom Aussteller nicht unterzeichnet sind (Art. 357), bei olographischen Testamenten in der Pfalz, welche ganz von der Hand des Erblassers herrühren müssen, bei Schuldscheinen, welche der Gutschrift bedürfen (Art. 1326 C. civ.).

Das Klagebegehren ist dahin zu richten, daß die Urkunde als ächt erklärt werde. Obgleich dies nach den Worten des Gesetzes genügt, so möchte es doch unter Umständen räthlich sein, das Gesuch zu spezialisiren, z. B. dahin: es möge erkannt werden, daß die fragliche Schrift von der Hand des Beklagten herrühre, daß Unterschrift und Gutschrift oder die ganze Urkunde von ihm herrühre rc.

Alle anderen Fragen, welche die Begründung der aus der Urkunde herzuleitenden Ansprüche betreffen, bleiben vorerst unberührt.

7) Für das Verfahren gelten die allgemeinen Bestimmungen, also insbesondere auch die Vor-

schriften über den Inhalt der Klageschrift, über Erscheinungsfrist 2c.; nur ist vorgeschrieben (Art. 580), daß mit der Klage sofosort Abschrift der Urkunde zuzustellen sei.

Bezüglich der Kosten gilt die besondere Bestimmung, daß in allen Fällen, wo der Beklagte die Aechtheit nicht bestreitet, selbst wenn er gar nicht erscheint, also sein Zugeständniß bloß auf einer Rechtsvermuthung beruht, alle Kosten dem Kläger zur Last fallen, soweit sie nicht etwa durch besonderes Verschulden des Beklagten veranlaßt sind (Art. 106 Abs. 2). Diese Bestimmung, welche allerdings vollkommen gerechtfertigt ist, wird meinen Erfahrungen nach hinreichen, das ganze Verfahren unpraktisch zu machen.

8) Schließlich ist hervorzuheben, daß die Bestimmung des Art. 2123 Code civ., gemäß welcher das Urtheil, welches eine Privaturkunde für ächt erklärt, eine Generalhypotheke begründet, auch unter dem neuen Prozeßrechte gilt, ebenso wie die beschränkende Verfügung des erwähnten Gesetzes vom 3. September 1807.

Dabei ist jedoch zu bemerken, daß ein Urtheil, welches nur gegen den dritten Aussteller einer Urkunde ergeht, kein solches ist, welches eine Hypotheke begründen kann, weder gegen diesen Aussteller, welcher nicht verpflichtet ist, noch gegen den angeblich Verpflichteten, welcher nicht im Prozesse war.

Anerkennung vor dem Vermittlungsamte.

Art. 583. — Erkennt der Aussteller einer Urkunde vor dem einzelngerichtlichen Vermittlungsamte (Art. 222 Abs. 2) die Urkunde als ächt an, so ist hierüber Protokoll aufzunehmen, das Anerkenntniß auf der Urkunde vorzumerken und die Vormerkung von dem Richter und Gerichtsschreiber unter Beidrückung des Gerichtssiegels zu unterzeichnen.

Solche Anerkenntnisse haben gleiche Wirkung, wie ein rechtskräftiges Urtheil, durch welches die Urkunde für ächt erklärt wurde.

G. A. d. K. d. A. II S. 431. 447. — K. d. R. II S. 269.

1) Die Klage auf Aechtheitserklärung unterliegt in der nemlichen Weise, wie jede andere Klage, dem Sühneversuche, wenn der Kläger es geeignet findet, davon Gebrauch zu machen.

Vorstehender Artikel bestimmt nun, daß wenn der Einzelnrichter zur Vermittlung angegangen und vor demselben die Aechtheit der Urkunde anerkannt werde, dieses Anerkenntniß vollkommen gleiche Wirkung habe, wie ein rechtskräftiges Urtheil, welches eine Urkunde für ächt erklärt. Namentlich steht außer Zweifel, daß in der Pfalz eine Generalhypotheke daraus entsteht. Abg. II 447 Sp. 2.

Es versteht sich von selbst, daß sowohl die Vorbedingungen zur Erhebung der Klage auf Aechtheitserklärung (Nichtfälligkeit des Anspruchs, Belangen der Person des Ausstellers), als die Vorbedingungen für den Sühneversuch bei dem betreffenden Einzelnrichter (Art. 222) gegeben sein müssen, wenn das Anerkenntniß besagte Wirkung äußern soll.

2) Ueber die Anerkennung der Aechtheit ist Protokoll aufzunehmen und dieselbe auf der Urkunde selbst vorzumerken, diese Vormerkung aber vom Richter und Gerichtsschreiber unter Beidrückung des Gerichtssiegels zu unterzeichnen.

Bezieht sich die Anerkennung der Aechtheit nur auf einzelne Unterschriften, oder auf eine einzelne von verschiedenen auf demselben Blatte Papier vereinigten Urkunden, so ist dies in der Vormerkung bestimmt hervorzuheben.

3) Wenn das Gesetz sagt, solche Anerkenntnisse hätten gleiche Wirkung wie ein rechtskräftiges Urtheil, so geht es viel weiter, als in Art. 223 Abs. 2, wo nur ausgesprochen ist, die Erklärungen vor dem Vermittlungsamte seien vollstreckbar gleich rechtskräftigen Urtheilen, ihnen aber im Uebrigen nur die Wirkung von Notariatsurkunden gegeben ist.

Es geschah dies, wie aus den Aeußerungen des kgl. Minist.=Commissärs (Abg. II 447 Sp. 2) hervorgeht, um keinen Zweifel zu lassen, daß solche Anerkenntnisse in der Pfalz eine Generalhypotheke bewirken; allein offenbar schoß man, um diesen Zweck zu erreichen, weit über das Ziel hinaus, denn gelten solche Anerkenntnisse in allen Beziehungen als Urtheile, so unterliegen sie auch in gleicher Weise wie diese den Rechtsmitteln der Wiederaufnahme des Verfahrens und der Nichtigkeisbeschwerde, und können in anderer Weise nicht angefochten werden. Faßt man aber auch nur den nächsten Zweck, die Bewirkung einer Generalhypotheke, in's Auge — was lagen für Gründe vor, hier, wo es sich bloß von nichtfälligen Forderungen und von Entscheidung eines bloßen Zwischenpunktes handelt, an die Erklärungen vor dem Vermittlungsamte eine Generalhypotheke zu knüpfen, welche man in Fällen, wo eine bereits fällige Forderung in Frage ist und wo das Recht selbst anerkannt wird, versagt? —

XXII. Hauptstück.

Besitzprozeß.

Vorbemerkung für die Pfalz.

Laut Einführungsgesetzes Art. 67 findet dieses ganze Hauptstück in der Pfalz keine Anwendung, und bleiben dort die Art. 3 Ziff. 2 und die Art. 23—27 Code de proc. in Kraft.

Die Bestimmungen in Art. 606 Ziff. 4 ff., welche dem Richter gestatten, durch eine Vorsichtsverfügung einer Partei den Besitz vorläufig zuzusprechen, gelten auch für die Pfalz, und ist durch dieselben ein neues Mittel zum Schutze des Besitzes gegeben.

Die Klage in der Hauptsache, welche nach Art. 630 anzustellen ist und von welcher auch die Zuständigkeit zum Erlasse der Vorsichtsverfügung abhängt (Art. 619 Abs. 2), ist die Besitzklage, falls nicht etwa der Gesuchsteller vorzieht, sofort petitorisch zu klagen.

Allgemeine Bestimmungen.

Art. 584. — **Die Voraussetzungen für die Statthaftigkeit der Besitzklagen sind nach den Vorschriften des bürgerlichen Rechts zu beurtheilen.**

G. A. d. K. d. A. II S. 429. 430. 447. 418. IV S. 115. — K. d. R. II S. 269. IV S. 64.

1) Die Bestimmungen dieses Artikels, sowie überhaupt des Hauptstücks, dessen Einleitung er bildet, gelten von Besitzklagen jeder Art, also sowohl von solchen, welche, sich auf einen vorausgängigen Besitz gründend, dessen Erhaltung oder Wiedererlangung bezwecken (die remedia retinendae et recuperandae possessionis), als von solchen, welche bloß auf Erlangung des Besitzes sich richten (remedia adipiscendae possessionis).

Auf Erhaltung des Besitzes sind gerichtet die interdicta uti possidetis und utrubi, auf Wiedererlangung das interdictum unde vi und die ihm verwandte aus dem canonischen Rechte sich herleitende Spolienklage, auf Erlangung des Besitzes endlich das remedium ex lege ult. Cod. de edicto d. Hadriani tollendo und das interdictum quorum bonorum.

2) Durch die Reichsgesetzgebung (K.G.O. p. II tit. 21) wurde ein possessorium summariissimum eingeführt, welches, ohne auf die Güte des Besitzes Rücksicht zu nehmen, den jüngsten Besitz schützt und dem unterliegenden Theile die gewöhnliche Besitzklage vorbehält. Die Gerichtsordnung (Cap. III § 5) hat dieses Ausnahmsverfahren in der Weise beibehalten, daß derjenige, welcher Jahr und Tag vor entstandener Irrung in ruhigem Besitze gewesen, darin geschützt werden solle, bis in possessorio plenario oder petitorio ein anderes dargethan sei.

Es frägt sich, ob diese Klage auf Schutz im jüngsten Besitze noch bestehe?

Daß das possessorium summariissimum als besondere Prozeßart aufgehört habe, steht außer Zweifel, allein hiermit ist die Frage nicht gelöst, ob auch der civilrechtliche Theil jener Bestimmung der Gerichtsordnung beseitigt sei, m. a. W. ob ein ruhiger Annalbesitz nicht auch jetzt noch ein Klagerecht eröffne, welches im gewöhnlichen Verfahren zur Geltung zu bringen wäre.

Auch der Umstand, daß das Gesetz in Art. 606 Vorsichtsverfügungen zur Regelung des Besitzes zuläßt, erscheint für sich allein nicht von Gewicht, denn durch Eröffnen eines neuen Rechtsweges werden in der Regel die schon bestehenden Wege nicht geschlossen, namentlich nicht, wenn sie besondere Vortheile bieten. Letzteres ist nun aber hier der Fall, denn es ist durchaus nicht gleichgiltig 1) ob unter gewissen Voraussetzungen ein Recht auf den Besitz gegeben sei, oder ob nach freiem richterlichen Ermessen verfügt werde, und 2) ob die in Besitz gesetzte Person zuwarten dürfe, bis der Gegner Klage erhebe, oder ob sie genöthigt werde, selbst klagend aufzutreten, wie dies Art. 620 vorschreibt.

Wäre bloß der Wortlaut des Gesetzes maßgebend, so müßte man das Fortbestehen der betreffenden Klage annehmen, allein aus den Verhandlungen geht klar hervor, daß nach dem Willen des Gesetzgebers dieselbe wegfallen und an deren Stelle die besagte Vorsichtsverfügung treten solle, wie dies denn auch die sachentsprechende Lösung ist. Vgl. Referat zu Art. 23 Ziff. 11 des Entw. (S. 296), zu Art. 614—619 des Entwurfs und zum Einführungsgesetze S. 125 u. 126 — Abg. II 429, 430 (v. Weiß), IV 115 Sp. 2 u. 394 Sp. 2. Auch der hannoveranische Entwurf hielt diese Ansicht fest. Vhdl. S. 3461 ff.

3) Im Hinblicke auf das Wegfallen der Klage auf Schutz im jüngsten Besitze hob das Einführungsgesetz (Art. 26) die Beschränkungen, welche das bayr. Landrecht (Th. II Cap. VII § 9

Ziff. 5 u. 6) bezüglich der Zulässigkeit der gewöhnlichen Besitzklage bei Grunddienstbarkeiten aufstellt, auf und änderte dem entsprechend in Art. 27 die Fassung von Th. II Cap. VII § 11 Ziff. 2.

Art. 585. — Die Besitzklage kann mit oder neben der Klage, wodurch das Recht selbst verfolgt wird, nicht erhoben werden.

Wer die Klage, wodurch das Recht verfolgt wird, erhoben hat, kann von der Besitzklage keinen Gebrauch mehr machen.

Wer die Besitzklage erhoben hat, kann jederzeit zur Klage auf das Recht selbst übergehen, er unterwirft sich aber dadurch allen Folgen des Unterliegens im Besitzprozesse.

Art. 586. — Gegen die Besitzklage sind Einreden oder eine Widerklage, welche auf das Recht selbst gerichtet sind, nicht zulässig.

G. A. d. K. d. A. II S. 429. 447. 448. IV S. 115. 116. — K. d. R. II S. 269—273. IV S. 64.

1) Die Bestimmungen dieser Artikel sind mehr civilrechtlicher als prozessualer Natur und enthalten nicht unwesentliche Aenderungen des bestehenden Rechtes.

Bis jetzt waren Possessorium und Petitorium nicht so streng geschieden. Die Gerichtsordnung gestattete die Cumulirung beider Klagen, erlaubte insbesondere auch, daß der Beklagte, welcher wegen Besitzstörung belangt war, sofort auf dem Wege einer Widerklage das Recht selbst geltend machte. Ferner waren Einwände, welche aus dem Rechte selbst hergenommen waren, nicht unbedingt ausgeschlossen, und selbst der Spolienklage gegenüber durfte nach bayerischem Landrechte das Recht selbst zur Geltung gebracht werden, falls es „augenscheinlich und offenbar" war, »quia dolo petit, quod statim iterum restiturus est.« Anmerk. von Kreitmayer zu L. R. Th. II Cap. V § 11 Ziff. 6 lit. e.

Unsere Prozeßordnung nahm die strengen Normen des französischen Rechtes zum Muster und verfügte im Einklange mit Code de proc. Art. 25 u. 27:

1) daß Possessorium und Petitorium nie cumulirt werden dürfen;

2) daß gegen die Besitzklage Einreden oder eine Widerklage, welche das Recht selbst betreffen, nicht zulässig sind.

2) Meiner Ansicht nach sind die hierin liegenden Neuerungen vom praktischen Standpunkte aus eher als Rückschritt denn als Fortschritt zu betrachten, und hätte eher Grund vorgelegen, unter Ausdehnung der Bestimmungen der Gerichtsordnung die Cumulirung unbedingt zuzulassen, als sie ganz zu verbieten.

Im französischen Rechte, wo die Aburtheilung von Possessorium und Petitorium verschiedenen Gerichten übertragen und die bezügliche Zuständigkeit so streng geschieden ist, daß sie sogar durch Vereinbarung nicht verrückt werden kann, ist diese Strenge wenn auch nicht nöthig, doch erklärlich, allein diesseits, wo der nemliche Richter über beide Klagen zu erkennen hat, erscheint sie mir nicht gerechtfertigt. Es sind mir in der Praxis Fälle vorgekommen, wo sich aus Erwerbsurkunden, Ortsplänen und Ortsbesichtigung sofort das Recht das wegen Besitzstörung Belangten klar herausstellte, nichtsdestoweniger aber die Besitzklage zugesprochen und das Besitzurtheil vollzogen werden mußte, ehe das vor Augen liegende Recht zur Anerkennung gebracht werden konnte. Ein derartiges Verfahren verletzt das Rechtsgefühl des Volkes, welches keinen Sinn für juristische Feinheiten hat, zufolge deren das wirkliche Recht von der Schwelle gewiesen wird und das scheinbare Recht den Sieg behält.

Es erschiene mir deßhalb ebenso praktisch als dem Rechtsgefühle entsprechend, wenn demjenigen, welcher mit einer Besitzklage belangt ist, gestattet wäre, widerklagsweise das Eigenthum geltend zu machen.

3) Die weiteren Bestimmungen, daß im Ergreifen des Petitoriums ein Verzicht auf das Possessorium liege, und daß derjenige, welcher die Besitzklage erhoben hat, zwar auf das Petitorium übergehen könne, jedoch sich hierdurch den Folgen des Unterliegens im Besitzstreite unterwerfe, galten auch schon im früheren Rechte.

Verfahren.

Art. 587. — Wird ein Urtheil auf Schutz im Besitze oder auf Einsetzung oder Wiedereinsetzung in denselben erlassen, so kann das Gericht auf Antrag der obsiegenden Partei gegen Sicherheitsleistung die einstweilige Vollstreckung des Urtheils ohne Rücksicht auf Einspruch oder Berufung verfügen.

Art. 588. — Wer im Besitzprozesse unterlegen ist, kann die Klage auf das Recht erst dann erheben, wenn er dem gegen ihn ergangenen Urtheile vollständig Genüge geleistet hat.

Weist der unterlegene Theil nach, daß eine Zögerung hiebei durch den Gegner veranlaßt sei, so bestimmt das Gericht zur Beseitigung der Hinderungsgründe eine angemessene Frist, nach deren Ablauf die Klage zugelassen wird.

Art. 589. — **Im Uebrigen finden auf Besitzklagen bezüglich des Verfahrens die allgemeinen Vorschriften Anwendung.** G. A. d. K. d. A. II S. 429. 430. 447. 448. IV S. 112. 116. 118. 336. 368. K. d. R. II. S. 273—278. IV S. 64. 65.

1) Die Eigenthümlichkeit des Besitzprozesses besteht nur in den zwei besonderen Bestimmungen, welche die Artikel 587 und 588 enthalten, in allem Uebrigen gelten die allgemeinen Vorschriften.

2) In Art. 587 werden die Vorschriften des Art. 268 Abs. 3 etwas erweitert, indem das Gericht die vorläufige Vollstreckbarkeit des den Besitz zusprechenden Urtheils unbedingt, also ohne Eingehen auf die Frage, ob ein unersetzlicher oder unverhältnißmäßiger Nachtheil drohe, verfügen darf.

Selbstverständlich soll diese Ausnahmsbestimmung nur erweiternd nicht aber beschränkend sein, und bleiben daher die allgemeinen Vorschriften bestehen, sofern sie die vorläufige Vollstreckung erleichtern, z. B. im Falle ausdrücklichen Anerkenntnisses (Art. 268 Abs. 1).

Zu erwähnen ist, daß in Art. 587 absichtlich eine Fassung gewählt wurde, welche die drei Arten der Besitzklagen umfaßt. Abg. II 448.

3) Die Bestimmung in Art. 588, daß diejenige Partei, welche im Besitzprozesse unterliegt, die petitorische Klage nicht erheben dürfe, bevor sie dem gegen sie ergangenen Urtheile vollständig Genüge geleistet, entspricht der Verfügung in Ger.-O. Cap. III § 4 Ziff. 11.

Meiner Meinung liegt auch hierin eine ungerechtfertigte Härte und zwar um so mehr, nachdem man die Cumulirung von Petitorium und Possessorium verboten hat. Zum Beweise beziehe ich mich auf die oben (zu Art. 585 Nr. 2) erwähnten praktischen Fälle, in welchen die Eigenthumsklage vor dem Bezirksgerichte erhoben war, jedoch zurückgewiesen werden mußte, obgleich sich sofort bei der ersten Verhandlung auf Grund der Urkunden sowie der Erhebungen im Besitzprozesse die völlige Begründung derselben ergeben hatte. Es ist diese dilatorische Einrede um so mißlicher, als sich, wie die Erfahrung lehrt, häufig ein besonderer Vorprozeß über die Frage entspinnt, ob dem Besitzurtheile völlig genügt sei oder nicht.

Daß es dem Unterliegenden freisteht, die Vollstreckung des Besitzurtheiles im Zwangswege herbeizuführen und dies zwar trotz der Erhebung der petitorischen Klage, hätte meiner Ansicht nach vollkommen genügt.

4) Uebrigens gehen auch in anderer Beziehung die Bestimmungen dieses Artikels zu weit.

Offenbar liegt dem Gesetze nur der Gedanke zu Grunde, daß das Unrecht, welches durch die Besitzstörung oder Vorenthaltung des Besitzes geübt worden sei, vorerst wieder gut gemacht werden müsse, ehe der Beklagte befugt sei, sein Recht zu verfolgen. Um nun diesem Gedanken Worte zu geben, hätte der Gesetzgeber nur vom unterliegenden Beklagten sprechen dürfen, wie es Seitens des französischen Gesetzgebers in Art. 27 Code de proc. geschieht, es lag aber nicht der geringste Grund vor, den unterliegenden Kläger nicht eher zur petitorischen Klage zuzulassen, als bis er dem gegen ihn ausgesprochenen Verurtheilungen zu den Kosten ꝛc. nachgekommen sei.

Unter Umständen, z. B. wenn die Kosten groß sind und die Partei im Armenrechte geklagt hat, kann diese principwidrige Bestimmung die Erhebung der Klage geradezu unmöglich machen.

5) Die Gerichtsordnung sagt, daß die Einlassung in petitorio verweigert werden dürfe, Art. 588 aber, daß die Klage nicht erhoben werden dürfe, und man könnte hieraus folgern, daß die Klage immer unbedingt abzuweisen sei, falls nicht der vorausgängige Vollzug des Besitzurtheiles dargethan werden könne, daß also ein nachträglicher Vollzug nichts nütze, allein dies ist offenbar nicht der Sinn des Gesetzes, wie aus Art. 185 hervorgeht (vgl. Bemerk. zu diesem Art. Nr. 6).

6) Wurde der Nichtvollzug durch den Gegner selbst verschuldet, z. B. weil er seine Kosten nicht taxiren läßt oder nicht kund gibt, so ist nach Art. 588 Abs. 2 vom Gerichte eine Frist zur Beseitigung des Hindernisses zu bestimmen, nach deren Ablauf die (bereits erhobene) Klage zugelassen wird.

XXIII. Hauptstück.

Verfahren bei Klagen auf Ersatz des bei Aufläufen verursachten Schadens.

Zulässigkeit und Zuständigkeit.

Art. 590. — **Klagen, welche in den Landestheilen diesseits des Rheins in Gemäßheit des Gesetzes vom 12. März 1850, die Verpflichtung zum Ersatze des bei Aufläufen verursachten Schadens betreffend, in der Pfalz in Gemäßheit des Gesetzes vom 10. Vendémiaire IV über die innere Polizei in den Gemeinden, gegen Gemeinden oder gegen den Staat auf Ersatz des Schadens, der durch Verbrechen oder Vergehen, welche von einer zusammengerotteten Menge oder von Einzelnen aus derselben mit offener Gewalt gegen Personen oder das Eigenthum verübt wurden, verursacht worden ist, erhoben werden, gehören ohne Rücksicht auf die Größe der angesprochenen Entschädigung zur Zuständigkeit des Bezirksgerichts, in dessen Sprengel der Schaden verursacht wurde.**

Art. 591. — **Die Klage muß bei Verlust des Anspruchs innerhalb eines Jahrs vom Tage der Beschädigung an gerechnet zugestellt werden.**

G. A. d. K. d. A. III S. 385. 594. 595. 610—612. IV S. 118. — K. d. R. II S. 280. 281. IV S. 65.

1) Es wird sich nicht leicht Anlaß bieten, das Ausnahmsverfahren dieses Hauptstückes zur Anwendung zu bringen (in der Pfalz trat der Fall meines Wissens nie ein), und es scheint fast, als habe man im Hinblicke hierauf der Fassung des ersten Artikels geringere Sorgfalt zugewendet, als wünschenswerth gewesen wäre.

Dieser Artikel sagt, daß Entschädigungsklagen, welche auf Grund des Ges. vom 12. März 1850, in der Pfalz auf Grund des Ges. v. 10. Vend. IV, tit. 4, gegen Gemeinden oder gegen den Staat erhoben werden, ohne Rücksicht auf die Größe des Anspruchs, zur Zuständigkeit desjenigen Bezirksgerichts gehören, in dessen Sprengel der Schaden verübt wurde.

In Art. 1 des Ges. vom 12. März 1850 ist bestimmt, daß jede politische Gemeinde, in deren Bezirke von einer zusammengerotteten oder unbewaffneten Menge oder von Einzelnen aus derselben mit offener Gewalt Verbrechen oder Vergehen gegen Personen oder Eigenthum verübt wurden, verpflichtet sei, den hierdurch verursachten Schaden zu ersetzen.

Das Nemliche, fast mit den nemlichen Worten, ist verfügt in tit. 4 art. 1 des Ges. v. 10. Vend. IV.

Das Gesetz vom 12. März 1850 macht in Art. 2 Ausnahmen für Fälle, wo 1) die Menge überwiegend aus Personen einer anderen Gemeinde besteht und die Einwohner der Gemeinde, wo die That verübt wurde, außer Stand waren, die Beschädigung zu hindern, und wo 2) die Menge überwiegend aus nicht beurlaubten Soldaten besteht. Im ersteren Falle haftet die fremde Gemeinde, im zweiten Falle der Staat.

Ist die Klage gegen mehrere in verschiedenen Gerichtsbezirken liegende Gemeinden zu richten, was der Fall sein kann, wenn die Thätlichkeiten sich über mehrere Gemeindebezirke ausdehnten, oder wenn mehrere fremde Gemeinden haften, so findet die allgemeine Bestimmung des Art. 29 Anwendung, zufolge welcher in solchen Fällen dem Kläger die Wahl freisteht. Abg. III 595 (v. Weiß). — R.R. II 290 u. 291.

Der besondere Gerichtsstand, welchen hier das Gesetz bestimmt, ist ein ausschließlicher und kann selbst durch Vereinbarung nicht verrückt werden (Art. 38 Ziff. 6).

2) In Art. 591 wird verfügt, daß die Klage bei Verlust des Anspruches innerhalb Jahresfrist erhoben werden müsse, und ist hiermit die Bestimmung des Ges. vom 12. März 1850 Art. 5 auch auf die Pfalz ausgedehnt. Noch sachgemäßer wäre es gewesen, das ganze Gesetz auf die Pfalz auszudehnen.

Die hier gedrohte Rechtsverlustigung wird abgewendet durch ein Schuldbekenntniß, welches geeignet ist als selbständiger Klaggrund zu dienen. Vgl. Art. 8 des Ges. vom 12. März 1850.

Verfahren.

Art. 592. — **Ist die Haftungsverbindlichkeit mehrerer Gemeinden begründet, so sind die Ansprüche gegen dieselben in einer und derselben Klage zu verbinden.**

Art. 593. — **In der Klageschrift sind die Zeugen, durch welche der Kläger die von ihm behaupteten Thatsachen erforderlichen Falls darthun will, unter Angabe der durch die einzelnen Zeugen zu beweisenden Thatsachen zu benennen.**

In gleicher Weise hat der Beklagte hinsichtlich seiner Zeugen und der durch sie zu

beweisenden Thatsachen in dem motivirten Antrage, welchen er auf die Klage zustellen läßt, zu verfahren.

Art. 594. — Nach Zustellung des motivirten Antrags des Beklagten — falls aber für letzteren ein Anwalt nicht aufgestellt wurde oder der aufgestellte einen motivirten Antrag nicht hat zustellen lassen, nach Ablauf der betreffenden Fristen — hinterlegt der Anwalt des Klägers die Akten sammt den durch den motivirten Antrag des Beklagten etwa veranlaßten Bemerkungen auf der Gerichtsschreiberei.

Art. 595. — Das Gericht prüft in geheimer Sitzung nach schriftlicher Vernehmung des Staatsanwalts auf Vortrag eines vom Gerichtsvorstande ernannten Berichterstatters, ob noch weitere Erhebungen über den Thatbestand, die Größe des Schadens oder die Umstände, unter welchen er zugefügt wurde, nöthig erscheinen.

Das Gericht hat hiebei außer den vom Kläger übergebenen Akten die von der Polizeibehörde gemachten Erhebungen, welche durch den Staatsanwalt zu erholen und dem Gerichte vorzulegen sind, sowie die etwaigen strafrechtlichen Untersuchungsakten zu berücksichtigen.

Art. 596. — Erachtet das Gericht weitere Erhebungen nicht für nothwendig, so setzt es sofort eine Sitzung zur Verhandlung fest.

Art. 597. — Erachtet das Gericht weitere Erhebungen für nothwendig, so ordnet es an, daß dieselben in der für Voruntersuchungen in Verbrechenssachen vorgeschriebenen Form durch ein damit beauftragtes Gerichtsmitglied von Amtswegen gemacht werden.

Sind die Erhebungen außerhalb des Gerichtssitzes zu machen, so kann damit auch das betreffende Einzelngericht beauftragt oder nach Art. 335 verfahren werden.

Hiebei können auch andere als die von den Parteien benannten Zeugen vernommen werden.

Soweit es ohne Verzögerung der Sache geschehen kann, ist den Anwälten Mittheilung zu machen, wann und wo die Erhebungen vorgenommen werden. Anwälte und Parteien können der Vornahme derselben beiwohnen.

Sind die Erhebungen gepflogen, so setzt das Gericht eine Sitzung zur Verhandlung fest.

Eine Mittheilung der gepflogenen Erhebungen an die Anwälte findet nicht statt. Diese sind jedoch befugt, davon, sowie auch von den vom Gerichte außerdem benützten Aktenstücken auf der Gerichtsschreiberei Einsicht zu nehmen.

Art. 598. — Von der Festsetzung der Sitzung zur Verhandlung (Art. 596 und 597 Abs. 5) hat der Gerichtsschreiber den Anwalt des Klägers in Kenntniß zu setzen. Dieser hat die Sache zum Eintrage in das Hauptverzeichniß anzumelden und dem Gegenanwalte, wenn ein solcher aufgestellt ist, eine Aufforderung zum Erscheinen in der Sitzung zustellen zu lassen. Dem Beklagten, welcher keinen Anwalt aufgestellt hat, sind keine Zustellungen zu machen.

Zustellung eines motivirten Antrags des Klägers (Art. 231) ist nicht geboten.

Hinterlegung von Anträgen findet nur bei der Verhandlung statt.

Art. 599. — Bei der Verhandlung wird zuvörderst durch ein vom Senatsvorstande zu bestimmendes Gerichtsmitglied das Ergebniß der über den Thatbestand, die Größe des Schadens und die Umstände, unter welchen er zugefügt wurde, vorliegenden Erhebungen — nöthigenfalls unter Ablesung der betreffenden Aktenstücke — vorgetragen, worauf die Anwälte ihre Anträge zu stellen und zu entwickeln haben.

Beweisführung der Parteien und richterliche Eidesauflage finden nicht statt.

Das Gericht hat auch dann, wenn bei der Verhandlung nur eine der Parteien erscheint, das Urtheil nach Maßgabe der Sachlage und des Ergebnisses der gepflogenen Erhebungen zu erlassen. Gegen solche im ersten Rechtszuge ergangene Urtheile ist Einspruch nicht zulässig.

Erlassung von Verbindungsurtheilen findet nicht statt.

Art. 600. — Ergibt sich bei der Verhandlung die Nothwendigkeit weiterer Erhebungen, so ordnet das Gericht dieselben in der in Art. 597 angegebenen Weise an.

Art. 601. — Kosten, welche durch die von dem Gerichte angeordneten Erhebungen veranlaßt werden, sind von dem Kläger vorläufig auszulegen.

Art. 602. — **Hinsichtlich des Vollzugs der gegen die Beklagten ergehenden Urtheile bleibt es bei den Bestimmungen der in Art. 590 angeführten Gesetze.**

Art. 603. — **Im Uebrigen gelten für die im gegenwärtigen Hauptstücke behandelten Klagen und für das Verfahren auf solche die allgemeinen gesetzlichen Bestimmungen.**

G. A. d. K. d. A. III S. 594—598. 611. 612. IV S. 118. 336. 368. — K. d. R. II S. 281—287. IV S. 65.

1) Das hier vorgezeichnete Verfahren weicht sehr erheblich vom gewöhnlichen Verfahren ab. Es enthält eine Verschmelzung des Verhandlungsprinzipes, wie es im Wesen des Civilprozesses liegt, und des Untersuchungsprinzipes, wie es im Strafverfahren waltet, — eine Verschmelzung, welche in ähnlicher Weise vielleicht auch in sonstigen Fällen, wo das öffentliche Interesse betheiligt ist — bei Ehescheidungen, Verschollenheitserklärungen, Interdiktionen etc. — Verwendung finden könnte.

a) Einleitung des Verfahrens.

2) Abweichend von den allgemeinen Prinzipien, welche es in's Ermessen des Gläubigers stellen, mehrere Mitschuldner zusammen oder getrennt zu verfolgen und welche der exceptio plurium litisconsortium nur beschränkte Wirksamkeit gestatten (Art. 65), macht es Art. 592 dem Kläger zur Pflicht, sämmtliche Gemeinden, welche ihm haften, gleichzeitig zu verfolgen. Da übrigens eine Rechtsverlustigung nicht gedroht ist, so wird aus der Nichtbeobachtung dieser Vorschrift nur folgen, daß die belangte Gemeinde ein Recht auf Beiziehung der mithaftenden Gemeinden habe (Art. 65) und daß dem Kläger die Mehrkosten zur Last fallen.

3) Für Erhebung der Klage, Erscheinungsfrist und Zustellung des motivirten Antrags des Beklagten gelten die allgemeinen Regeln, jedoch sind in der Klagschrift bezw. im Antrage des Beklagten sofort die Zeugen, sowie die Thatsachen, worüber jeder Zeuge aussagen soll, zu bezeichnen.

Da gemäß Art. 603 die allgemeinen Prinzipien gelten, soweit sie nicht ausgeschlossen sind, so steht der beklagten Partei das Recht zu, Gewährschaftsklage zu erheben, sei es gegen andere Gemeinden, welche ihrer Behauptung nach mithaften, sei es gegen die Urheber der That (Ges. vom 12. März 1850 Art. 14). Auch für die Gewährschaftsbeklagten gilt die Vorschrift, daß sie ihre Zeugen sofort zu benennen haben.

b) Untersuchung.

4) Nachdem der Beklagte seinen Antrag zugestellt hat, oder die für Anwaltsbestellung bezw. für Zustellung seines Antrages gegebene Frist verstrichen ist, tritt die Sache in das Stadium des Untersuchungsverfahrens. Ein Versäumungsurtheil kann daher nicht genommen werden.

Der Kläger hinterlegt seine Akten auf der Gerichtsschreiberei, das Gericht aber prüft in geheimer Sitzung, nach schriftlicher Vernehmung des Staatsanwalts, auf Vortrag eines Berichterstatters, ob weitere Erhebungen über den Thatbestand geboten seien, oder ob genügende Aufschlüsse zur Aburtheilung der Sache aus den Akten des Klägers, aus den durch die Erklärungen der beklagten Partei sich darbietenden Anhaltspunkten und aus den von Amtswegen beizuziehenden polizeilichen oder strafrichterlichen Erhebungen hervorgehen.

Werden weitere Erhebungen für nöthig befunden, so wird ein Richter beauftragt, dieselben von Amtswegen zu machen und zwar in den für Voruntersuchungen in Verbrechenssachen vorgeschriebenen Formen. Da das Gesetz keine bestimmte Vorschriften gibt, so steht es dem Gerichte frei, nur einzelne zu bezeichnende Erhebungen anzuordnen, oder seinen Auftrag allgemein zu geben „zur Vornahme der zur Aufklärung der Sache nöthigen Erhebungen". Das Letztere wird in der Regel das Sachgemäßere sein, da sich meist im Verlaufe der Untersuchung erst ergibt, in welcher Richtung die Erhebungen stattzufinden haben.

5) Die Zeugen, welche von den Parteien bezeichnet wurden, sind natürlich vorzugsweise zu vernehmen, allein der Richter ist nicht auf dieselben beschränkt, hat vielmehr volle Freiheit, zu thun, was er sachgemäß findet.

Anwälte und Parteien dürfen den Erhebungen beiwohnen, allein es ist nicht nothwendig, sie dazu beizuladen, vielmehr schreibt das Gesetz nur vor, es solle, so weit es ohne Verzögerung geschehen könne, den Anwälten Mittheilung gemacht werden. Diese Mittheilung kann in entsprechender Weise sowohl schriftlich als mündlich geschehen. Die Parteien können, falls sie den Erhebungen beiwohnen, dem Richter ihre Wünsche zu erkennen geben und die Frage bezeichnen, welche sie an Zeugen oder Sachverständige gestellt wünschen, jedoch widerstrebt es der Natur des Untersuchungsverfahrens, daß sie den amtlichen Erhebungen des Richters durch Erhebung von Zwischenstreiten hindernd in den Weg treten.

Die Kosten, welche durch die amtlichen Erhebungen veranlaßt werden, sind hier nicht gemeinschaftlich von den Parteien zu tragen (Art. 105 Abs. 2), sondern vom Kläger vorläufig auszulegen (Art. 601), und ist in dieser Beziehung auf die Bestimmung in Art. 343 Abs. 2 hinzuweisen.

c) Verhandlung der Sache.

6) Werden weitere Erhebungen nicht für nöthig befunden (Art. 596), oder haben dieselben stattgefunden (Art. 597 Abs. 5), so setzt das Gericht sofort von Amtswegen eine Sitzung zur Verhandlung fest.

Der Gerichtsschreiber gibt sofort dem klägerischen Anwalte hievon Kenntniß, dieser aber läßt die Sache in's Hauptverzeichniß eintragen und fordert den Gegenanwalt, wenn ein solcher aufgestellt ist, nach Maßgabe der Bestimmungen des Art. 233 zum Erscheinen auf.

Die Anwälte nehmen von den gepflogenen Erhebungen und den erhobenen Akten auf der Gerichtsschreiberei Einsicht.

Motivirte Anträge sind nicht weiter zuzustellen. Wenn Art. 598 Abs. 2 nur vom Antrage des Klägers spricht, so geschieht es, weil der Beklagte seinen motivirten Antrag bereits zugestellt hat (Art. 593), und durch die inzwischen erfolgten amtlichen Erhebungen ein neues Prozeßstadium nicht begründet wird. Indem das Gesetz nur sagt: „ist nicht geboten", deutet es an, daß, wie in den Fällen der Art. 260 Ziff. 2 und Art. 344, das Zustellen motivirter Anträge nicht verwehrt sein soll, wenn es sich sachgemäß zeigt.

Hatte der Beklagte keinen Anwalt aufgestellt, so sind ihm keine Zustellungen zu machen, fällt insbesondere die Aufforderung zum Erscheinen in der Sitzung weg.

7) Da sofort eine Sitzung zur Verhandlung festgesetzt wird, so findet natürlich, ebenso wie im Falle des Art. 259, eine besondere Hinterlegung der Anträge nicht statt.

Die Verhandlung beginnt mit der Berichterstattung eines Gerichtsmitgliedes, in der Regel des Richters, welcher die Untersuchung geführt hat, nach welcher sofort die Anwälte ihre Anträge stellen und begründen.

Die Entscheidung erfolgt bloß auf Grund der vorliegenden Akten und Erhebungen, und kann es zu Auflagen von Beweisen oder Eiden nicht kommen; findet jedoch das Gericht die Sache nicht genügend aufgeklärt, so kann es weitere Erhebungen anordnen (Art. 600).

Auch wenn nur eine der Parteien erscheint, entscheidet der Richter nach Maßgabe der Sachlage, unter Zugrundlage der zugestellten Anträge, wie im Falle des Art. 346, jedoch ist hier bei Urtheilen im ersten Rechtszuge der Einspruch ausgeschlossen. Aus gleichen Gründen sind Verbindungsurtheile ausgeschlossen.

Erscheint keine der Parteien, so erfolgt nach allgemeinen Vorschriften die Streichung der Sache vom Hauptverzeichnisse.

8) Nach Spruch des Urtheils sind die Parteiakten zurückzugeben, namentlich auch diejenigen des Klägers, denn selbstverständlich hat die Hinterlegung, von welcher Art. 594 spricht, nicht den Sinn, als ob die Akten hinterlegt bleiben sollten. Ich möchte sogar annehmen, daß sofort nach Schluß der amtlichen Erhebungen der klägerische Anwalt seine Akten zurückverlangen könne, natürlich nur unter der Verpflichtung, sie dem Richter zur Berichterstattung rechtzeitig wieder vorzulegen.

Was die Fertigung des Sachverhalts und die Einlegung von Rechtsmitteln betrifft, so gelten die allgemeinen Prinzipien. R. R. II 287.

d) Vor- und Zwischenfragen.

9) Wie in jedem Prozesse, so können auch hier Prozeßeinreden vorgeschützt, Legitimationsfragen angeregt und Zwischenstreite erhoben werden. Es erleidet auch keinen Zweifel, daß die allgemeinen Prinzipien, wonach bevorzugte Prozeßeinreden (Art. 185 u. 186) von der Pflicht zur Streiteinlassung befreien, und solche Einreden oder Präjudizialsachen zur gesonderten Aburtheilung gebracht werden können (Art. 190, 232), auch hier gelten.

Es frägt sich nun, wie diese Prinzipien mit den Spezialvorschriften dieses Hauptstückes in Einklang zu bringen seien.

Offenbar soll und kann sich das Untersuchungsverfahren nur auf jene Vorgänge erstrecken, welche der Klage zu Grunde liegen. Nur in dieser Richtung hat auch das Gericht in geheimer Sitzung (Art. 595) die Sachlage zu prüfen, und es wäre nicht seine Aufgabe, amtliche Erhebungen zur Klarstellung von Prozeßeinreden oder Präjudizialpunkten anzuordnen.

Es kann ferner auch nicht Wille des Gesetzes sein, daß unter allen Verhältnissen zuerst die Untersuchung über den Thatbestand stattfinde und erst bei der darauffolgenden Verhandlung die Prozeßeinreden und sonstigen Vorfragen zur Geltung zu bringen seien. Ein solches Verfahren wäre nicht bloß höchst unpraktisch, sondern in jenen Fällen, wo der Beklagte die Einlassung verweigert hat, nicht einmal möglich.

Bei dieser Sachlage ist anzunehmen, daß der Gesetzgeber bei seinen Bestimmungen nur den Fall im Auge hatte, wo es nach der Regel geht und sofort der Grund der Sache zur Sprache kommt, daß also, wenn Vorfragen sich erheben, diese vorher bereinigt werden müssen, und zwar nach Art. 603 im gewöhnlichen Verfahren. Sollten solche Vorfragen Beweise nöthig machen, welche die für die amtliche Untersuchung gezogene Grenze überschritten, so wären dieselben auf gewöhnlichem Wege zu erheben und fände das Verbot des Art. 599 Abs. 2 keine Anwendung.

e) Vollzug des Urtheils.

10) Was den Vollzug der gegen die Beklagten ergehenden Urtheile betrifft, so gelten gemäß Art. 602 die Ausnahmsbestimmungen der Gesetze vom 12. März 1850 Art. 8 und vom 10. Vend. IV tit. 5 art. 7—9 fort.

Wenn im ersten Gesetze gesagt ist, das Gericht müsse der Verwaltungsbehörde, welche den Vollzug zu betreiben habe, eine Abschrift des Urtheils zufertigen, so wird dies im Geiste des neuen Verfahrens eine Aenderung dahin erleiden, daß der Kläger der Verwaltungsbehörde eine Urtheilsausfertigung mit der Bitte um Vollzug vorlege.

Ausdehnende Bestimmung.

Art. 604. — Die Bestimmungen des gegenwärtigen Hauptstücks finden analoge Anwendung auf Klagen, mittels welcher der k. Fiskus den Ersatz der mit dem Einschreiten der bewaffneten Macht verbundenen Kosten in Gemäßheit des hierauf bezüglichen Gesetzes vom 4. Mai 1851 Art. 14 von den betreffenden Gemeinden in Anspruch nimmt.

G. A. d. K. d. A. III S. 595. 598. 611. 612. — K. d. R. II S. 287.

Durch das Gesetz vom 4. Mai 1851, welches das Einschreiten der bewaffneten Macht bei Aufläufen regelt, ist in Art. 14 verfügt, daß hinsichtlich der mit diesem Einschreiten verbundenen Kosten die Bestimmungen der Gesetze vom 12. März 1850 bezw. vom 10. Vend. IV zur Anwendung kommen.

Da, was das Verfahren betrifft, die Bestimmungen dieser Gesetze geändert wurden, so hielt man es für sachgemäß, ausdrücklich zu verfügen, daß diese Aenderung auch für das Gesetz vom 4. Mai 1851 Geltung habe.

XXIV. Hauptstück.

Vorsichtsverfügungen.

Vorbemerkungen.

1) Vorsichtsverfügungen sind bestimmt, Rechtsverhältnisse einstweilen und auf so lange zu regeln, bis im gewöhnlichen Verfahren Entscheidung ergeht oder Rechtshilfe gewährt wird. Sie haben daher ihrer Natur nach nur eine zeitlich beschränkte Wirksamkeit, welche sofort von selbst aufhört, wenn die definitive Regelung eintritt.

2) Die Gerichtsordnung enthielt keine allgemeinen Vorschriften über Provisorien, setzte vielmehr deren Zulässigkeit als selbstverständlich voraus und gab in dieser Voraussetzung Bestimmungen über Rechtskraft (Cap. XIV § 11 Ziff. 3) und über Rechtsmittel (Cap. XV § 3 Ziff. 2).

In ähnlicher Weise setzt auch der Code de proc. als selbstverständlich voraus, daß der Richter im Laufe eines Rechtsstreites provisorische Maßregeln anordnen dürfe, und beschränkt sich auf die Vorschrift des Art. 134, welche dem Richter zur Pflicht macht, nicht gesondert über das Provisorium zu erkennen, wenn die Hauptsache reif zur Entscheidung sei.

Was jedoch die außerhalb eines anhängigen Rechtsstreites zulässigen Provisorien betrifft, so enthält der Code de proc. spezielle Bestimmungen. Er gestattet 1) in gewissen Fällen, daß eine Beschlagnahme dem Rechtsstreite vorausgehe, z. B. in Art. 557 (saisie-arrêt), in Art. 819 (s.-gagerie), in Art. 822 (s.-foraine), in Art. 826 (s.-revendication), sieht ferner 2) Fälle vor, wo Anstände im Vollstreckungsverfahren oder bei der nichtstreitigen Rechtspflege zu beseitigen sind (Art. 554, 607, 786, 843, 845, 852, 921, 922, 944 u. 948 Code de proc.), weist endlich 3) dem Präsidenten des Bezirksgerichts die Anordnung provisorischer Maßregeln in allen Fällen zu, wo Gefahr auf dem Verzuge steht (Art. 806—811 Code de proc.).

3) Unsere Prozeßordnung faßt die Vorsichtsverfügungen jeder Art, sei es daß der Anlaß dazu sich im Laufe eines Rechtsstreites oder eines Vollstreckungsverfahrens ergibt, sei es, daß er vor Einleitung eines gerichtlichen Verfahrens entsteht, zusammen und gibt darüber allgemeine und erschöpfende Bestimmungen.

Hieraus folgt, daß Vorsichtsverfügungen nur unter den im Hauptstücke XXIV bestimmten Voraussetzungen statthaft sind und nur auf dem hier vorgezeichneten Wege erwirkt werden können, soweit nicht besondere Bestimmungen des Gesetzes oder die Natur der Sache Ausnahmen bedingen.

Besondere Ausnahmsbestimmungen gibt die Prozeßordnung an verschiedenen Stellen, z. B. in Art. 54 Abs. 4 und in Art. 190 Abs. 2. Als aus der Natur der Sache folgend läßt sich die Befugniß des Richters betrachten, in Fällen, wo er ein Beweisverfahren anordnet, zugleich dasjenige zu verfügen, was zum Zwecke der Beweisführung sachgemäß, z. B. daß der strittige Gegenstand, über welchen Sachverständige ihr Gutachten abgeben sollen, an einen bestimmten Ort zu verbringen sei, um dort beobachtet und untersucht zu werden.

Für die Pfalz enthält das Einführungsgesetz mehrfache Ausnahmen durch Beibehaltung von Sonderbestimmungen des französischen Rechts, nemlich in Art. 98 (saisie-revendication), Art. 99 (saisie-gagerie) und Art. 111 (Refereverfahren). Vgl. auch Art. 69 Ziff. 4.

4) Was zuerst diese Ausnahmsbestimmungen für die Pfalz betrifft, so hätten sie, wenigstens größtentheils, füglich entbehrt werden können; denn die Bestimmungen des Hauptst. XXIV sind so umständlich und für alle Fälle erschöpfend, daß concurrirende Sonderbestimmungen nicht nöthig waren.

Art. 98 des Einf.-G. bestimmt:

„Die Beschlagnahme von Mobiliargegen-„ständen zur Wahrung des Eigenthumsrechtes „(Art. 826 Code de proc.) ist auch fernerhin „zulässig und kommen bezüglich derselben die „Bestimmungen des Hauptstückes XXIV der „neuen P.O. zur Anwendung."

Da Artikel 606 Ziff. 2 der P.O. die Beschlagnahme beweglicher Sachen als Vorsichtsverfügung zuläßt, so könnte diese Bestimmung des Einf.-G. fast überflüssig erscheinen, jedenfalls aber hat sie nur eine höchst geringfügige Bedeutung. Sie hat nemlich zur Folge, daß für diese Beschlagnahme nur die Voraussetzungen gegeben sein müssen, wie sie Art. 826 Code de proc. im Sinne hat, daß also dem Richter freierer Spielraum gegönnt ist und derselbe nicht zu untersuchen braucht, ob die Beschlagnahme sich im Sinne von Art. 605 der P.O. als nothwendig darstelle.

Art. 99 des Einf.-G. erhält, unter Beifügung einiger Abänderungen, die Bestimmungen des Art. 2102 Ziff. 1 Code civ. und der Art. 819 bis 821 Code de proc. über die Vorrechte der Verpächter und Vermiether und deren Geltendmachung aufrecht. Da in Abs. 1 bemerkt ist: „Soweit sich das Verfahren nach allgemeinen Vorschriften zu richten hat, kommen die Bestimmungen der neuen P.O. zur Anwendung," so ist Art. 821, welcher auf die allgemeinen Vorschriften des Code de proc. über Beschlagnahme verweist, ziemlich gegenstandslos und kann höchstens insofern Anwendung finden, als er bestimmt, daß ausnahmsweise der Gepfändete selbst als Hüter bestellt werden dürfe. Vgl. Art. 915 der P.O.

Art. 111 des Einf.-G. bestimmt:

„Für diejenigen Fälle, in welchen „durch die in der Pfalz in Wirksamkeit ver-„bleibenden gesetzlichen Bestimmungen die pro-„visorische Entscheidung von Streitigkeiten oder „sonstigen sich ergebenden Anständen dem Prä-„sidenten des Bezirksgerichts übertragen ist, „bleiben die Vorschriften der Art. 806—811 „Code de proc. in Kraft."

Nach dem Laute dieses Artikels sollte man meinen, es sei dem Präsidenten die fragliche Entscheidung nur für gewisse Fälle übertragen, allein dem ist nicht so, denn der Art. 806, welcher aufrecht erhalten wird, sagt: »Dans tous les cas d'urgence, ou« etc. Es ist hiernach nicht ganz klar, was der Gesetzgeber sagen will. Will er einfach sagen: Die Befugnisse, welche Art. 806 oder sonstige Spezialgesetze dem Präsidenten geben und das in Art. 807 — 811 bezeichnete Verfahren bleiben auch fernerhin (concurrirend mit den Bestimmungen des Hauptstücks XXIV) in Kraft, oder will er sagen: Wo Spezialgesetze der Pfalz, welche durch die P.O. nicht berührt werden oder durch das Einf.-G. beibehalten worden sind, dem Präsidenten fragliche Befugniß geben, sollen für das Verfahren die Art. 807—811 in Kraft bleiben? Ich glaube, daß Letzteres das richtige sei und sprechen hiefür insbesondere auch die Motive zu Art. 111 des Einf.-G.

Demgemäß würde das Refereverfahren nur noch Anwendung finden in Fällen der nichtstreitigen Rechtspflege (Art. 843, 845, 852, 921, 922, 944, 948 Code de proc.), für welche es sich allerdings von selbst verstanden hätte. Fälle der streitigen Rechtspflege wüßte ich nicht anzuführen, da Art. 926 Code de proc., welchen der Entwurf des Einf.-G. (Art. 100) aufrecht erhalten wollte und welchen man vielleicht im Auge hatte, beseitigt worden ist.

5) Was die obberegten Fälle betrifft, in welchen die Prozeßordnung selbst die Zulässigkeit vorsorglicher Verfügungen besonders ausspricht,

so ist der nächste Gedanke, daß jene besonderen Bestimmungen nur den Zweck haben, Eigenthümlichkeiten bezüglich der Zuständigkeit, des Einschreitens von Amtswegen &c. festzusetzen, daß aber dem Wesen nach die getroffenen Maßregeln Vorsichtsverfügungen seien und im Uebrigen die allgemeinen Bestimmungen des Hauptst. XXIV zur Anwendung zu kommen haben. Von diesem Gedanken geleitet sprach man in dem jetzigen Art. 683 Ziff. 2 ursprünglich von Vorsichtsverfügungen im Allgemeinen und war der Ansicht, daß hiermit jene Ausnahmsbestimmungen mitgetroffen seien (Abg. III 77 — R. R. III 8—11); bei der zweiten Lesung aber machte sich die entgegengesetzte Ansicht geltend und wurde deßhalb die allgemeinere Fassung: „vorsorgliche Verfügungen“ gewählt (Abg. IV 171).

Es entspricht daher dem Willen des Gesetzes, daß die Bestimmungen von Hauptst. XXIV auf jene Ausnahmsbestimmungen keine Anwendung finden.

Zulässigkeit.

Art. 605. — Vorsichtsverfügungen können sowohl vor der Einleitung eines Rechtsstreits oder Vollstreckungsverfahrens als im Laufe eines solchen getroffen werden, wenn sie sich als nothwendig darstellen:

1) um die künftige Vollstreckung zu sichern, oder

2) um drohender Privatgewalt vorzubeugen, oder

3) weil wegen Gefahr auf dem Verzuge die im gewöhnlichen Verfahren zu hoffende Rechtshilfe ohne wesentlichen Nachtheil nicht abgewartet werden kann.

Dadurch, daß der Anspruch noch nicht fällig ist, wird die Erlassung von Vorsichtsverfügungen nicht ausgeschlossen. Wegen Ansprüchen, die von einer aufschiebenden, nicht blos die Zeit der Fälligwerdung betreffenden Bedingung abhängen, finden Vorsichtsverfügungen nicht statt.

G. A. d. K. d. A. II S. 411—413. 448. IV S. 161. 218. 219. K. d. R. II S. 288. IV S. 65.

1) Das Gesetz bezeichnet hier ebenso einfach und klar als erschöpfend die Vorbedingungen zum Erlasse von Vorsichtsverfügungen.

Wie bereits erwähnt, sind solche Verfügungen in jeder Lage der Sache statthaft, sowohl vor Einleitung eines Rechtsstreites oder Vollstreckungsverfahrens, als im Laufe eines solchen, bis eine endliche Regelung eingetreten ist, welche sie als gegenstandslos erscheinen läßt.

Sie können daher auch in der Berufungsinstanz begehrt werden, ja sogar während die Sache am obersten Gerichtshofe anhängig ist, falls die Nichtigkeitsbeschwerde gegen ein Zwischenurtheil, z. B. ein Urtheil, welches auf Eid erkannte, gerichtet ist. Auch der Umstand, daß ein Urtheil vorläufig vollstreckbar erklärt ist, macht Vorsichtsverfügungen nicht gegenstandslos, insofern diese Vollstreckung nur gegen Sicherheitsleistung stattfindet.

In Fällen, wo Gefahr auf dem Verzuge ist, insbesondere, wo betrügerische Beseitigungen zu befürchten sind, kann selbst für denjenigen Gläubiger, welcher eine unbedingt vollstreckbare Urkunde in Händen hat, Interesse vorliegen, eine Vorsichtsverfügung zu erwirken, weil ihm diese nach Art. 845 erlaubt, sofort zuzugreifen, während er im gewöhnlichen Verfahren eine dreitägige Frist vom Befriedigungsgebote an abwarten muß.

2) Allgemeine Vorbedingung zum Erlasse einer Vorsichtsverfügung ist, daß sie nothwendig sei zur Erreichung der in Art. 605 bezeichneten Zwecke.

Hiemit sind bloße Rücksichten der Zweckmäßigkeit entschieden ausgeschlossen; allein die Frage, unter welchen Umständen eine Nothwendigkeit anzunehmen sei, gibt immerhin dem weisen Ermessen des Richters großen Spielraum. Es werden in dieser Beziehung, namentlich aber auch was die erforderliche Bescheinigung betrifft, strengere Anforderungen zu stellen sein, wenn es sich um Maßregeln handelt, welche in die Rechtsverhältnisse des Betroffenen tief eingreifen, ihn möglicherweise stark beschädigen, als wenn Maßregeln in Frage sind, welche nur unbedeutend belästigen.

Indem das Gesetz sagt, Vorsichtverfügungen seien nur zuzulassen, wenn sie nothwendig seien, sagt es mittelbar auch, insoweit sie nothwendig seien, und erscheinen daher die Bestimmungen der Art. 610 ff. nur eine Erläuterung dessen, was schon in Art. 605 liegt.

3) Das Gesetz bezeichnet drei Zwecke, zu deren Erreichung Vorsichtsverfügungen erwirkt werden können, nemlich

1) um die künftige Vollstreckung zu sichern;
2) um drohender Privatgewalt vorzubeugen und
3) um vorläufige Rechtshilfe zu gewähren in Fällen großer Dringlichkeit.

Die beiden ersten Fälle sind spezieller Art, der dritte aber geht in's Allgemeine, und eben deßhalb glaubte der Gesetzgeber, um Mißbräuchen zu begegnen, möglichst nachdrucksvoll hervorheben zu müssen, daß strenge Anforderungen gestellt werden, daß nemlich Gefahr auf dem Verzuge liegen und ein wesentlicher Nachtheil zu befürchten sein müsse. Das Ergreifen der Maßregel muß zugleich dringlich und wichtig sein. Eine nähere Erläuterung zum letzteren Erfordernisse gibt Art. 610 Abs. 3.

4) Vorsichtsverfügungen, welche bestimmt sind, die künftige Vollstreckung zu sichern, sind die gewöhnlichsten. Es hat hiebei der Gesetzgeber nicht bloß die Beitreibung von Geldforderungen im Auge (Art. 607), sondern auch die Vollstreckung von Urtheilen, welche Besitz, Eigenthum oder sonstige Rechte an beweglichen oder unbeweglichen Sachen zusprechen.

In Fällen dieser letzteren Art ist zu beachten, daß der Gläubiger ein Recht auf die Sache selbst hat und sich nicht auf die Entschädigung braucht verweisen zn lassen, welche im Falle der Nichtleistung an die Stelle tritt. Ist daher die begehrte Maßregel nothwendig, um die Sache selbst zu sichern, so ist sie im Sinne des Gesetzes gerechtfertigt.

5) Vorsichtsverfügungen, um drohender Privatgewalt vorzubeugen, ergeben sich namentlich bei Besitzstreitigkeiten und treten hier, wie bereits zu Art. 584 Nr. 2 bemerkt, an Stelle des Schutzes im jüngsten Besitze.

Uebrigens beschränkt sich die Anwendung dieser Gesetzesstelle keineswegs auf Besitzstreite, tritt vielmehr überall ein, wo der Richter findet, daß sein Dazwischentreten nöthig sei, um Gewaltthätigkeiten zu verhüten. Insbesondere dienen Vorsichtsverfügungen auch zum Ersatze der früheren Attentatenbeschwerden.

6) Vorsichtsverfügungen, um rasche Rechtshilfe bei Gefahr auf dem Verzuge zu gewähren, sind geboten in Fälleu, wo es nicht sowohl auf eine Leistung überhaupt, als darauf ankommt, daß sie schnell geschehe, z. B. wenn es sich um Räumung von Miethlokalitäten, Herstellung dringender Reparaturen, Beseitigung gefahrdrohender Bauten oder Vorrichtungen, Einspruch gegen Neubauten rc. handelt.

7) Wer eine Vorsichtsverfügung erwirken will, der muß seiner Geschichtserzählung nach (die nach Art. 608 u. 609 zu bescheinigen ist) ein Recht haben, und zwar ein solches, dessen Bestehen von keiner aufschiebenden Bedingung abhängt.

Daß der Anspruch noch nicht fällig ist, d. h. erst nach einer gewissen Frist das Recht mit Klage verfolgt werden darf, steht dem Erlasse einer Vorsichtsverfügung nicht im Wege, selbst nicht, wenn der Zeitpunkt der Fälligkeit ungewiß, z. B. vom Ableben einer Person bedingt ist. Es genügt, daß das Bestehen des Rechts sicher sei.

Art. 606. — **Die Vorsichtsverfügungen können vorbehaltlich der in den Gesetzen enthaltenen besondern Bestimmungen und der sonst durch die eigenthümlichen Verhältnisse des Falls bedingten Anordnungen bestehen:**

1) **in dem Verbote der Vornahme bestimmter Handlungen oder in der einstweiligen Verurtheilung zu einer bestimmten Leistung oder Handlung;**
2) **in der einstweiligen Beschlagnahme von Forderungen oder beweglichen Gegenständen;**
3) **in dem Verbote der Veräußerung oder weitern Belastung unbeweglicher Güter;**
4) **in der Ueberweisung des vorläufigen Besitzes streitiger Sachen an eine der Parteien;**
5) **in der Hinterlegung beweglicher Sachen bei Gericht;**
6) **in der Uebergabe einer Sache zur Verwahrung oder Verwaltung an einen Dritten (Sequester);**
7) **in der Verhaftung des Schuldners.**

Art. 607. — **Insbesondere kann zur Sicherstellung einer Geldforderung oder eines sonstigen in Geld anschlagbaren Anspruchs dem Gläubiger die Ermächtigung, in seinen Händen befindliche Sachen des Schuldners oder an diesen zu leistende Zahlungen bis auf weitere Verfügung zurückzubehalten, Forderungen oder sonstiges bewegliches Vermögen desselben mit Beschlag belegen oder den Schuldner verhaften zu lassen, ertheilt, dem Schuldner die Veräußerung oder weitere Belastung unbeweglicher Güter verboten, die Hinterlegung beweglicher Sachen bei Gericht verfügt oder die Sequestration beweglicher oder unbeweglicher Sachen angeordnet werden (Arrest).**

Solche Arrestverhängung ist auch zu Gunsten eines Ausländers gegen einen Ausländer und zwar selbst dann zulässig, wenn der sicherzustellende Anspruch nicht in Bayern entstanden ist. G. A. d. K. d. A. II S. 413. 414. 418. IV S. 118. 119. — K. d. R. II S. 288. IV S. 65.

1) Unsere Prozeßordnung unterscheidet zwischen gewöhnlichen Vorsichtsverfügungen und Arrest. Letzterer bildet eine eigenthümliche Unterart der Vorsichtsverfügungen im Allgemeinen.

Art. 606 bezeichnet die Maßregeln, welche überhaupt als Vorsichtsverfügungen getroffen werden können, Art. 607 aber beschäftigt sich ausschließlich mit dem Arreste.

a) Vorsichtsverfügungen im Allgemeinen.

2) Indem Art. 606 eine Reihe von Maßregeln aufzählt, welche als Vorsichtsverfügungen zulässig seien, schließt er hiemit das Gebiet dieser Maßregeln keineswegs ab, denn er macht ausdrücklichen Vorbehalt für die sonst durch die eigenthümlichen Verhältnisse des Falls bedingten Anordnungen. Bei der Mannigfaltigkeit der sich darbietenden Verhältnisse wäre es auch gewagt gewesen, eine erschöpfende Aufzählung zu versuchen.

Die Maßregeln, welche der Gesetzgeber besonders hervorhebt, vertheilen sich nach den Zwecken, welche im Art. 605 bezeichnet sind, in drei Hauptarten, nemlich:

1) in Hemmung der freien Verfügung des Schuldners über gewisse Sachen;
2) in Regelung des Besitzstandes und
3) in der Auflage gewisser Leistungen oder Unterlassungen.

3) Was das Verbot der Vornahme bestimmter Handlungen betrifft (Ziff. 1), so dient diese Vorsichtsverfügung hauptsächlich dazu, den Einspruch gegen die Errichtung eines neuen Werkes (novi operis nunciatio), sowie das Verbot von Neuerungen im Laufe eines Rechtsstreites (Attentatenbeschwerde) zu ersetzen. Vgl. Referat zu Art. 618 des Entwurfs.

Die einstweilige Verurtheilung zu bestimmten Leistungen oder Handlungen (Ziff. 1) findet insbesondere auch Anwendung auf Geldleistungen, z. B. auf den einstweiligen Zuspruch einer Alimentation bei Alimentations- oder Ehescheidungsklagen. Bemerk. zu Art. 8 Nr. 4.

Es ist diese Vorsichtsverfügung wohl die weitgreifendste unter allen denjenigen, welche das Gesetz bezeichnet, und muß der Richter mit besonderer Vorsicht zu Werke gehen, namentlich beachten, daß im Geiste des Gesetzes solche Vorsichtsverfügungen nicht benützt werden dürfen, um die Vorschriften über vorläufige Vollstreckbarkeit von Urtheilen zu umgehen.

4) Die Vorsichtsverfügung, welche den vorläufigen Besitz strittiger Sachen überweist (Ziff. 4) ersetzt, wie zu Art. 584 Nr. 2 dargethan, die Klage auf Schutz im jüngsten Besitze.

Wenn auch der Richter das muthmaßliche Recht der einen Partei, namentlich das Recht auf Besitz, vor Allem ins Auge zu fassen und seiner Entscheidung zum Grunde zu legen hat, so ist doch durch diese Entscheidung für die Stellung der Parteien im Prozesse, namentlich für die Frage der Beweislast nichts präjudizirt (Art. 641 Abs. 1). Im Zweifel wird der jüngste Besitz zu schützen sein. Zu beachten ist, daß in Art. 610 Abs. 1 dem Richter ausdrücklich zur Pflicht gemacht wird, eine Veränderung oder Beschränkung des Besitzstandes ohne dringende Noth nicht anzuordnen.

b) Arrest.

5) Diejenige Vorsichtsverfügung, welche das Gesetz mit dem technischen Ausdrucke „Arrest“ bezeichnet, ist eine bezüglich des Verfahrens begünstigte Unterart der Vorsichtsverfügungen. Ihr Hauptvorzug besteht darin, daß sie auf einseitiges Ansuchen bewilligt wird (Art. 618 Abs. 3).

Da es sich nur um eine zum Vortheile des Gläubigers geschaffene Ausnahme handelt, so versteht sich von selbst, daß auch in Fällen, welche sich zur Arrestanlage eignen, gewöhnliche Vorsichtsverfügungen erwirkt oder der für dieselbe vorgezeichnete Weg eingeschlagen werden kann.

Zu bemerken ist, daß die Prozeßordnung dem Worte „Arrest“ noch eine andere technische Bedeutung gibt, nemlich um die Beschlagnahme auf Forderungen zu bezeichnen (Art. 966). Der Arrest als Vorsichtsverfügung wird jenem Arreste gegenüber als „Sicherheitsarrest“ bezeichnet (Art. 1002).

6) Vorbedingung des Arrestes ist, daß es sich um die Sicherstellung einer Geldforderung oder eines sonstigen in Geld anschlagbaren Anspruches handle. Vgl. weiter Art. 611.

Eine Geldforderung ist gegeben, wenn der um Arrest nachsuchende Gläubiger in der erhobenen oder in Aussicht stehenden Klage in der Hauptsache eine bestimmte Geldsumme verlangt oder verlangen kann, mag dieselbe auch noch nicht liquid gestellt sein, sondern richterlicher Feststellung bedürfen; ebenso, wenn wegen einer bestimmten Geldsumme die Vollstreckung eingeleitet ist oder werden kann.

Ein in Geld anschlagbarer Anspruch ist gegeben, wenn die Klage zwar zunächst nur auf Erfüllung einer Verbindlichkeit gerichtet ist, diese jedoch sich im Falle der Nichterfüllung in eine Geldentschädigung auflöst. Der Zweck des Gläubigers muß unmittelbar oder mittelbar auf Eintreibung einer Geldsumme gerichtet sein.

Daß die Bezeichnung „in Geld anschlagbar“ bloß in diesem Sinne gemeint, nicht aber allgemein zu nehmen sei, erscheint klar und ergibt sich schon aus der Natur der Maßregeln, welche das Gesetz als „Arrest“ zuläßt. Wollte man diese Bezeichnung allgemein nehmen, so wären nahezu sämmtliche Vorsichtsverfügungen darunter begriffen, denn mit Ausnahme etwa der vorsorglichen Gestattung der Trennung bei Ehescheidungen oder der vorsorglichen Zuweisung der Erziehung von Kindern gibt es wohl keine solche Verfügung, bei welcher das Interesse sich nicht in Geld anschlagen läßt.

7) Das Gesetz sagt bloß „anschlagbar“, nicht „anzuschlagenden“, geht also jedenfalls von anderen Voraussetzungen aus, als beim bedingten Zahlungsbefehle (Art. 554 Abs. 4 und Art. 556 Abs. 2); ob aber hieraus zu folgern sei, daß das Gesuch oder die richterliche Verfügung eine bestimmte Summe nicht anzugeben brauche, wird bei Art. 618 erörtert werden.

8) Wie schon angedeutet, sind die Maßregeln, welche das Gesetz als Arrest zuläßt, sämmtlich darauf berechnet, die Eintreibung von Geldforderungen zu sichern, dem Gläubiger den Zugriff auf das Vermögen des Schuldners oder auf gewisse Vermögenstheile zu sichern. Es handelt sich um Sicherung derjenigen Vollstreckungsmittel, welche Art. 856 für Eintreibung von Geldforderungen vorsieht und welche Gegenstand der Verfügungen in Hauptst. XXXII bis XXXVII sind.

Was insbesondere die Zurückbehaltung der in Händen des Gläubigers befindlichen Sachen oder Einhaltung der an diesen zu leistenden Zahlungen betrifft, von welchen Maßregeln Art. 606 nicht spricht, so liegt darin im Grunde nur eine Beschlagnahme, welche der Gläubiger bei sich selbst anlegt.

9) In Art. 607 Abs. 2 ist verfügt, daß Arrest auch von Ausländern gegen Ausländer erwirkt werden könne, und zwar selbst dann, wenn der sicherzustellende Anspruch nicht in Bayern entstanden sei. Man hat hierin bloß eine Ausdehnung der Bestimmung des Art. 19 zu erblicken, welche, wie schon zu jenem Artikel Nr. 3 a. E. bemerkt, zur Folge hat, daß nunmehr auch der Ausländer das Recht der Klagestellung erwirkt, welches ihm ohne die Arrestanlage nicht zugestanden hätte.

Es ist selbstverständlich, daß diese Bestimmung dem Ausländer bloß Rechte geben, ihn aber nicht in den Rechten, welche ihm schon nach allgemeinen Prinzipien zustehen, verkürzen will. Man dürfte daher nicht folgern, weil das Gesetz nur bezüglich des Arrestes den Ausländer dem Inländer gleichstelle, seien die gewöhnlichen Vorsichtsverfügungen demselben versagt, vielmehr kann der Ausländer in allen Fällen, wo ihm kraft Gesetzes ein Klagrecht verliehen ist, auch die zur Sicherung desselben dienenden Vorsichtsverfügungen erwirken. Es ist in dieser Beziehung auf die Erörterungen zu Art. 19 zu verweisen.

Art. 608. — In dem Gesuche um Erlassung einer Vorsichtsverfügung sind der Anspruch oder das Rechtsverhältniß, wegen dessen die Verfügung beantragt wird, und die thatsächlichen Verhältnisse, welche ihre Erlassung rechtfertigen sollen, darzulegen und, vorbehaltlich der Bestimmung des Art. 609 Abs. 1, soweit sie nicht schon aus den Umständen als wahrscheinlich sich ergeben, zu bescheinigen.

Das Gesuch muß ferner ein bestimmtes Begehren enthalten und die Gegenstände, an welchen die Vorsichtsverfügung vollzogen werden soll, sowie gegebenen Falls die dritten Personen, bei denen dies zu geschehen hat, soweit möglich bezeichnen.

Art. 609. — Mangelt die in Art. 608 Abs. 1 vorgeschriebene Bescheinigung, so kann die Vorsichtsverfügung gleichwohl getroffen werden, wenn der Gesuchsteller wegen der daraus dem Gegner drohenden Nachtheile eine von dem Richter nach den Umständen des Falls zu bestimmende Sicherheit leistet oder nach richterlichem Ermessen durch seine persönlichen und Vermögensverhältnisse genügende Sicherheit bietet.

Der Richter kann, auch wenn die Bescheinigung geliefert ist, den Vollzug der zu erlassenden Vorsichtsverfügung von einer Sicherheitsleistung abhängig machen.

Auf die in diesem Artikel bezeichneten Sicherheitsleistungen finden die Vorschriften des Art. 127 nur dann Anwendung, wenn die Sicherheit auf Grund eines richterlichen Urtheils zu leisten ist. Andernfalls wird sie von dem Imploranten einseitig bestellt und läßt dieser bei der Vollstreckung der Vorsichtsverfügung in den Fällen des Art. 126 Ziff. 1—3 die über die Sicherheitsleistung ausgefertigte Bescheinigung, im Falle des Art. 126 Ziff. 4 die betreffende Notariatsurkunde zustellen.

G. A. d. K. d. A. II S. 415. 416. 448. — K. d. R. II S. 288.

1) Es ergibt sich aus den allgemeinen Prinzipien des Prozesses und ist auch durch die Fassung des Art. 608 Abs. 2 anerkannt, daß Vorsichtsverfügungen nicht von Amtswegen an-

geordnet werden dürfen, vielmehr begehrt werden müssen, und daß der Richter über das Begehren der Partei nicht hinausgehen dürfe.

Nur wo das Gesetz ausdrücklich anders verfügt, oder wo es sich nach dem Geiste des Gesetzes von selbst versteht, erleidet diese Regel eine Ausnahme. So z. B. kann es keinem Anstande unterliegen, daß jene vorsorglichen Verfügungen, von welchen Art. 190 Abs. 2 spricht, von Amtswegen ergehen dürfen, denn da der Richter von Amtswegen die Verhandlung aussetzen darf, so ist es nur eine einfache logische Folgerung, daß er auch die hierdurch veranlaßten vorsorglichen Maßregeln von Amtswegen anordnen dürfe.

2) Die Natur der Sache bedingt es, daß das Gesuch um Erlassung einer Vorsichtsverfügung alle diejenigen thatsächlichen Angaben enthalten müsse, welche erforderlich sind, um dasselbe im Sinne der Art. 605 — 607 zu begründen. Findet der Richter in demjenigen, was der Gesuchsteller ihm vorträgt, nicht diejenigen Anhaltspunkte, welche ihn bestimmen können, dem Gesuche zu willfahren, und welche ihn in den Stand setzen, seine Verfügung so vollständig wie es das Gesetz verlangt zu erlassen, so weist er es ab. Vgl. übrigens die Bemerk. zu Art. 619. Handelt es sich um einen Arrest (Art. 607), so müssen insbesondere auch Anhaltspunkte dafür gegeben sein, daß die Forderung im behaupteten Betrage gegründet oder daß sie in einem bestimmten Betrage zu Geld anzuschlagen sei. Vgl. Art. 615 und Bemerk. zu Art. 618.

3) Ebenso liegt es in der Natur der Sache, daß ein die Maßregeln genau bezeichnendes Begehren gestellt werde.

Insbesondere ist vorgeschrieben, daß die Gegenstände, an welchen die Vorsichtsverfügung vollzogen werden soll, d. h. welche beschlagnahmt, mit Veräußerungsverbot belegt, sequestrirt, hinterlegt werden sollen, sowie die dritten Personen, bei welchen Forderungen des Schuldners an Geld oder beweglichen Sachen mit Beschlag belegt werden sollen (Art. 966), bezeichnet werden, jedoch dies nur, soweit möglich.

Es ist also nicht unbedingt verwehrt, Maßregeln dieser Art auch unbestimmt zu erlassen, also zu gestatten, daß die sich vorfindenden Mobilien, die zu ermittelnden Ausstände beschlagnahmt werden, jedoch muß wahrscheinlich gemacht sein, daß eine genaue Bezeichnung nicht möglich gewesen sei, daß z. B. genauere Ermittlungen vom Gegner verhindert worden oder wegen Dringlichkeit der Sache nicht möglich gewesen seien. Es tritt manchmal der Fall ein, daß der Gläubiger nicht genau weiß, in welcher dritten Hand sich die mit Beschlag zu belegenden Gelder befinden, ob bei dem ursprünglichen Schuldner oder bei einem Bevollmächtigten (Notar), welcher mit der Auszahlung beauftragt ist, und in solchen Fällen kann ohne Anstand die Beschlagnahme bei einer oder der anderen Person begehrt und bewilligt werden.

4) Es genügt übrigens nicht, daß der Gesuchsteller die zur Begründung seines Gesuches erforderlichen Thatsachen behaupte, er muß sie der Regel nach auch bescheinigen. S. Einleitung zu Hauptst. IX Nr. 2 u. 3.

Welche Anforderungen an diese Bescheinigung zu stellen seien, hat der Richter nach Lage der Umstände frei zu ermessen. Besondere Strenge verlangt das Gesetz hier nicht, wie daraus hervorgeht, daß es ausdrücklich verfügt, es sei eine Bescheinigung nur nöthig, soweit nicht schon aus den Umständen sich das Vorgetragene als wahrscheinlich ergebe. Wichtigkeit der Maßregel einerseits und Dringlichkeit derselben andererseits werden von wesentlichem Einflusse sein. Bemerk. zu Art. 605 Nr. 2.

5) Ausnahmsweise gestattet das Gesetz von jeder Bescheinigung Umgang zu nehmen, wenn der Gesuchsteller wegen der dem Gegner drohenden Nachtheile Sicherheit leistet, oder durch seine persönlichen und Vermögensverhältnisse Sicherheit bietet.

Solche Sicherheitsleistung kann der Richter selbst dann anordnen, wenn Bescheinigung geliefert ist.

Die Sicherheitsleistung, welche die Bescheinigung ersetzen soll, ist natürlich im Gesuche anzubieten. Der Richter bestimmt in Erwägung der Umstände des Falles nach freiem Ermessen die Summe, für welche Sicherheit zu leisten ist; im Uebrigen aber ist Art. 130 maßgebend, d. h. es finden die Bestimmungen der Art. 125 — 129 Anwendung, auf welche jener Artikel verweist.

Die Vorschriften des Art. 127 lassen sich ihrer Natur nach nur in Fällen anwenden, wo die Sicherheit auf Grund eines richterlichen Urtheiles, d. h. einer nach Verhandlung in der Sitzung ergehenden Entscheidung zu leisten ist; für jene Fälle aber, wo auf einseitiges Ansuchen oder nach vorausgegangener Verhandlung von einem einzelnen Richter, außer den Formen des gewöhnlichen Prozesses, verfügt wird, trifft Art. 609 in Abs. 3 entsprechende Abänderungen.

Art. 610. — Die Vorsichtsverfügung darf über das zur Erreichung des Zwecks Nothwendige nicht hinausgehen und namentlich darf eine Veränderung oder Beschränkung des Besitzstands ohne dringende Noth nicht angeordnet werden.

Unter mehreren an sich zulässigen Vorsichtsverfügungen ist die für den Imploraten mindest beschwerliche zu wählen.

Ist die auf Grund des Art. 605 Ziffer 3 nachgesuchte Vorsichtsverfügung dem Imploraten nachtheiliger oder gleich nachtheilig, als deren Unterlassung für den Gegner, so ist sie unstatthaft.

Art. 611. — Arrest kann nur verfügt werden, wenn nach den Umständen anzunehmen ist, daß die wirksame Geltendmachung des Anspruchs ohne solche Maßregel unmöglich oder doch erheblich erschwert sein werde. Letzteres ist bei Klagen von Inländern namentlich dann anzunehmen, wenn außerdem die Vollstreckung im Auslande stattfinden müßte.

Art. 612. — Die Verhaftung des Schuldners kann vorbehaltlich der Bestimmung des Art. 614 nur wegen einer bereits klagbaren Forderung und nur unter der Voraussetzung verfügt werden, daß der Schuldner Ausländer ist und in Bayern unbewegliches Vermögen, dessen hypothekfreier Werth dem Betrage der Forderung entspricht, nicht besitzt.

Dem Ausländer steht in dieser Beziehung der Inländer gleich, welcher auf der Flucht befindlich oder derselben dringend verdächtig ist oder dauernden Aufenthalt im Auslande genommen hat oder zu nehmen im Begriffe ist.

Durch Staatsvertrag kann auch die Verhaftung der Angehörigen eines auswärtigen Staats für unstatthaft erklärt werden. Ist dies geschehen, so ist auch die Verhaftung von Inländern, welche in diesem Staate dauernden Aufenhalt genommen haben oder zu nehmen beabsichtigen, nicht mehr statthaft.

G. A. d. K. d. A. II S. 413— 415. 424. 448. III S. 334. IV S. 119. 336.
K. d. R. II S. 288. IV. S. 65. 66.

1) Das Gesetz gibt in diesen drei Artikeln besondere, die Zulässigkeit von Vorsichtsverfügungen betreffende Vorschriften, und zwar zum Theil bloße Weisungen für den Richter (Vollzugsvorschriften zu Art. 605), theilweise auch zusätzliche Bestimmungen.

2) Art. 610 ertheilt drei allgemeine Weisungen, nemlich:

1) die Vorsichtsverfügung darf über das zur Erreichung des Zweckes Nothwendige nicht hinausgehen;

2) unter mehreren an sich zulässigen Vorsichtsverfügungen ist die für den Imploraten mindest beschwerliche zu wählen;

3) ist die auf Grund des Art. 605 Ziff. 3 nachgesuchte Vorsichtsverfügung dem Imploraten nachtheiliger oder gleich nachtheilig, als deren Unterlassung für den Gegner, so ist sie unstatthaft.

Die erste Vorschrift erscheint selbstverständlich und bedarf keiner näheren Erläuterung.

Was die zweite betrifft, so ist die Ansicht des Gesetzgebers nicht bloß dahin gerichtet, daß unter mehreren beantragten Vorsichtsverfügungen der Richter die mindest beschwerliche zu wählen, sondern daß er ganz unabhängig von der Antragstellung zu prüfen habe, welches die für den gegebenen Fall passende Maßregel sei. Abg. II 448 Sp. 2. Wurde diese Maßregel beantragt, so ist sie zuzulassen; wurde sie nicht beantragt, so ist das Begehren mit entsprechender Motivirung abzuweisen.

Uebrigens dürfte nicht gefolgert werden, daß der Richter unter mehreren zulässigen Vorsichtsverfügungen immer nur eine einzelne zu wählen habe. Dies ist nur für den Fall gesagt, wo eine einzelne Maßregel zur Sicherung des Gläubigers hinreicht; ist dies aber nicht der Fall, so dürfen auch mehrere Vorsichtsverfügungen zugelassen werden.

Was die dritte Weisung anbelangt, so ist hervorzuheben, daß sie sich auf jene Fälle, wo es sich um die Sicherung der künftigen Vollstreckung oder um Abwendung von Privatgewalt handelt (Art. 605 Ziff. 1 u. 2), nicht erstreckt, sondern nur den Fall trifft, wenn die Vorsichtsverfügung sich bloß auf Art. 605 Ziff. 3 gründet.

3) Beim Arreste stellt Art. 611 als Vorbedingung auf, daß die wirksame Geltendmachung des Anspruchs ohne solche Maßregel unmöglich oder doch erheblich erschwert sein würde. Es erscheint hiemit das Prinzip des Art. 605 nicht bloß erläutert, sondern auch etwas erweitert, indem eine bloße Erschwerung der Geltendmachung, auch wenn sie erheblich ist, nach Art. 605 nicht hinreichen würde.

Eine erhebliche Erschwerung liegt nach ausdrücklicher Verfügung des Gesetzes darin, daß bei Klagen von Inländern die Vollstreckung im Auslande stattfinden müßte. Ausländer können daher einen Arrest nicht bloß deshalb begehren, weil die Vollstreckung im Auslande stattfinden müßte, mag der Gegenstand der Klage sein, welcher er wolle, und mag die Vollstreckung in der Heimath des Ausländers oder in einem anderen Lande zu geschehen haben.

4) Die Maßregel der Verhaftung läßt das Gesetz nur unter der Bedingung zu, daß die Forderung bereits klagbar sei, und verlangt weiter, daß der Schuldner ein Ausländer sei, welcher in Bayern unbewegliches Vermögen, dessen hypothekenfreier Werth dem Betrage der Forderung entspricht, d. h. für Hauptsumme und Zubehör genügende Deckung bietet, nicht besitze.

Dem Ausländer steht in dieser Beziehung der Inländer gleich, welcher der Flucht dringend verdächtig ist, oder welcher dauernden Aufenthalt im Auslande genommen hat oder zu nehmen im Begriffe steht. Auch hier ist die Verhaftung nicht erlaubt, wenn der inländische Immobiliarbesitz genügende Sicherheit bietet.

Schließlich macht das Gesetz Vorbehalt für Staatsverträge, durch welche auch die Verhaftung der Angehörigen eines auswärtigen Staates für unstatthaft erklärt werden kann.

Offenbar ist der Sinn dieses Vorbehalts nur der, daß der Ausländer dem Inländer gleichgestellt, das Ausland als dem Inlande gleichgeltend erklärt werden könne, und es wäre daher nicht statthaft, durch Staatsverträge dem Ausländer Vorrechte einzuräumen, welche dem Inländer gesetzlich nicht zustehen. Es erleidet daher trotz scheinbar entgegenstehender Aeußerungen (Abg. IV 119 Sp. 1) keinen Zweifel, daß der Ausländer, welcher sich in einen dem Inlande nicht gleichstehenden Staat flüchten will oder dort seinen dauernden Aufenthalt nimmt, der Verhaftung unterworfen ist. Eine bessere Fassung des Gesetzes hätte übrigens nichts geschadet.

Wegen der Vorbedingungen der Verhaftung vgl. auch das Gesetz vom 6. April 1869, dessen Bestimmungen in die Prozeßordnung aufgenommen und durch sie ersetzt sind.

Art. 613. — **Soweit die Vorsichtsverfügungen in Maßregeln bestehen, welche das Gesetz auch als Vollstreckungsmittel bezeichnet, finden alle für letztere gesetzlich vorgesehenen Ausnahmen und Beschränkungen, vorbehaltlich besonderer Bestimmung des Gesetzes, auch Anwendung auf die betreffenden Vorsichtsverfügungen.**

Art. 614. — **Für den Fall der Nichtbefolgung einer Vorsichtsverfügung können, wenn dies nach der Beschaffenheit der Verfügung und den sonstigen Umständen angemessen erscheint, unbeschadet der nach allgemeinen Bestimmungen zulässigen Vollstreckung auch Geldstrafen und selbst Verhaftung angedroht werden.**

Art. 615. — **Vorsichtsverfügungen wegen einer Geldforderung oder eines in Geld anschlagbaren Anspruchs kann der Imploraт, wo sich dies mit der Erreichung des Zwecks verträgt, durch Sicherheitsleistung abwenden. Hiebei kommen die Bestimmungen des Art. 126 Ziff. 1—4, Art. 127 Abs. 2—5, Art. 128 und 129 Abs. 1 zur Anwendung.**

Der Betrag, für welchen die Sicherheit zu leisten ist, muß, soweit möglich, schon in der Vorsichtsverfügung unter Berücksichtigung des Anspruchs in Haupt- und Nebensache festgesetzt werden. Die hiezu erforderlichen Anhaltspunkte sind in dem Gesuche um Erlassung der Vorsichtsverfügung anzugeben.

Art. 616. — **Statt der Verhaftung des Schuldners kann auf seinen Antrag die Beigebung einer Wache oder die einfache Polizeiaufsicht verfügt werden, wenn dadurch hinreichende Sicherheit geboten ist und der Schuldner die Kosten vorschießt.**

Art. 617. — **Der auf Grund der Bestimmungen des Art. 607 Verhaftete ist auf seinen Antrag der Haft zu entlassen, wenn er glaubhaft darthut, daß er keine Mittel zur Befriedigung seines Gläubigers besitzt. Vermögenstheile, welche nach Hauptstück XXXII, XXXIV oder XXXV nicht Mittel der Vollstreckung für die betreffende Forderung sein können, bleiben hiebei außer Betracht.**

G. A. d. K. d. A. II S. 413—417. 448. IV S. 119. 336.
K. d. R. II S. 288. IV S. 67. 81—84.

1) Das Gesetz gibt hier eine Reihe besonderer Bestimmungen, welche die zu verfügenden Maßregeln, namentlich auch den Vollzug derselben betreffen.

a) Vorsichtsverfügungen, welche zugleich Vollstreckungsmittel sind.

2) Die Natur der Sache bringt es mit sich, daß Vorsichtsverfügungen nicht weiter gehen, als die definitive Regelung. Werden daher gewöhnliche Vollstreckungsmittel vorläufig zugelassen, so versteht es sich eigentlich von selbst, daß sie sich innerhalb der Grenzen halten müssen, welche das Gesetz für den Fall der definitiven Vollstreckung gezogen hat, es müßte denn ausdrücklich eine Ausnahme gemacht sein. Dies ist

nun in Art. 613 auch ausdrücklich vorgeschrieben. Die Bestimmungen darüber, welche Sachen gepfändet, welche Forderungen mit Arrest belegt, unter welchen Voraussetzungen Früchte auf der Wurzel gepfändet werden dürfen (Art. 901, 957, 967—969), gelten daher auch für Vorsichtsverfügungen.

b) Androhung von Strafen.

3) Gewisse Vorsichtsverfügungen, wie z. B. das Verbot der Vornahme gewisser Handlungen oder das Gebot irgend etwas zu thun, lassen sich nicht durch direkten Zwang zum Vollzuge bringen, der Gesetzgeber hielt es daher für sachgemäß, indirekte Zwangsmittel durch Androhung von Strafen zu gestatten.

Das Gesetz läßt Geldstrafe und Verhaftung zu.

Die Geldstrafe ist eine reine Strafe, also nicht etwa eine auf die Forderung zu verrechnende Zahlung, und wird nach Maßgabe der Bestimmungen in Art. 146 u. 147 eingetrieben und verwendet. Die Verhaftung ist natürlich nur soweit zu verhängen, als sie zur Erreichung des Zweckes unbedingt nöthig erscheint.

Bezüglich des Vollzugs der Androhungen ist Art. 640 maßgebend.

c) Sicherheitsleistung zur Abwendung von Vorsichtsverfügungen (Art. 615).

4) Jede Vorsichtsverfügung, welche direkt oder indirekt die Sicherung einer Geldforderung bezweckt, mag es sich um Arrest oder eine sonstige Vorsichtsverfügung handeln, kann durch Sicherheitsleistung abgewendet werden. Das Gesetz setzt hinzu: „wo sich dies mit der Erreichung des Zweckes verträgt"; allein da es sich immer um Sicherung einer Geldforderung handelt, so wird nicht wohl ein Ausnahmsfall sich ergeben können.

Der Betrag, für welchen die Sicherheit zu leisten ist, muß, soweit möglich, schon in der Vorsichtsverfügung, von wem diese auch ausgehen möge, festgesetzt werden, und deshalb muß das Gesuch die nöthigen Anhaltspunkte zu dieser Festsetzung bieten. Die Zulassung der Vorsichtsverfügung wird dadurch von vornherein eine bedingte.

Mit den Worten: „wo möglich" scheint der Gesetzgeber nur einzelne Ausnahmsfälle bezeichnen zu wollen, in denen ein annähernd richtiger Geldanschlag von vornherein nicht geschehen kann, z. B. wenn es sich um Rechnungspflicht handelt. Abg. IV 416 Sp. 2 (v. Weiß). Vgl. Bemerk. zu Art. 618 Nr. 8 und Art. 632.

d) Aufhebung der Verhaftung (Art. 616 u. 617).

5) Statt der Verhaftung des Schuldners kann auf dessen Antrag die Beigebung einer Wache oder die einfache Polizeiaufsicht verfügt werden, wenn er die Kosten der Bewachung und Aufsicht vorschießt und der Richter die hierdurch gebotene Sicherheit hinreichend findet. Es unterliegt keinem Bedenken, daß auch eine schon verfügte Verhaftung unter diesen Voraussetzungen aufgehoben, d. h. eine Umwandlung der Verfügung stattfinden kann (Art. 631).

Wer auf Grund von Art. 607, d. h. zur Sicherung einer Geldsumme verhaftet ist, muß auf Antrag aus der Haft entlassen werden, wenn er glaubhaft darthut, daß er keine Mittel zur vollen oder theilweisen Befriedigung seines Gläubigers besitze. Daß hierbei Vermögenstheile, welche nicht Mittel der Vollstreckung für die betreffende Forderung sein können, auf welche also der Gläubiger kein Recht hat, außer Betracht bleiben, versteht sich von selbst.

Zuständigkeit und Verfahren.

Art. 618. — **Das Arrestgesuch (Art. 607) ist anzubringen:**

1) wenn wegen der Sache ein Vollstreckungsverfahren eingeleitet ist, bei dem Vorstande des Vollstreckungsgerichts;

2) wenn dies nicht der Fall, aber die Hauptsache bei Gericht im ersten Rechtszuge oder in jenem der Berufung anhängig ist, bei dem Vorstande des Prozeßgerichts beziehungsweise des betreffenden Senats;

3) in allen andern Fällen bei dem Vorstande des in der Hauptsache zuständigen Gerichts.

Bei dringender Gefahr können die Arrestgesuche auch bei dem Einzelnrichter angebracht werden, in dessen Bezirk der Arrest vollzogen werden soll.

Die Verfügung erfolgt durch den Gerichts- oder Senatsvorstand beziehungsweise den Einzelnrichter ohne vorläufige Mittheilung des Gesuchs und ohne Vernehmung des Imploraten.

G. A. d. K. d. A. II S. 417. 448. IV S. 336. 337. — K. d. R. II S. 288. IV S. 84. 85. V. S. 9.

1) Dieser Artikel behandelt Zuständigkeit und Verfahren für den Arrest (Art. 607). Wegen Anbringung der Gesuche, Vertretung der Parteien, Form der Entschließungen und Rechtskraft derselben sind jedoch die allgemeinen Verfügungen der Art. 637 bis 639 maßgebend.

a) Zuständigkeit.

2) Die Arrestgesuche sind der Regel nach an den Vorstand desjenigen Gerichtes, welches in der Hauptsache zuständig ist, d. h. über die zu sichernde Forderung zu erkennen hat (des Bezirks-, Handels-, Einzelngerichts) zu richten. Vgl. Abg. IV 337 Sp. 1 (v. Neumayr).

Ausnahmsweise ist zuständig:

1) der Vorstand des Prozeßgerichts, wenn die Hauptsache in erster oder zweiter Instanz anhängig ist, bezw. der Vorstand des Senats, welchem der Prozeß zugetheilt ist (Art. 238);

2) der Vorstand des Vollstreckungsgerichts (Bezirks- oder Einzelngerichts), falls wegen der betreffenden Forderung ein Vollstreckungsverfahren bereits eingeleitet ist (Art. 842).

Ist in Folge Widerspruchs (Art. 868) ein Prozeß anhängig, so ist Ziff. 1 maßgebend. Abg. IV 337 Sp. 1 (v. Neumayr).

Eine allgemeine Ausnahme macht Art. 618 Abs. 2 für den Fall dringender Gefahr, in welchem der Arrest auch beim Einzelnrichter des Bezirks, wo er vollzogen werden soll, erwirkt werden darf, also eine concurrirende Zuständigkeit eintritt.

3) Besteht für Anstellung der Hauptklage ein Wahlrecht, so gilt dies auch für das Arrestgesuch.

Ist eine Klage ihrer Natur nach geeignet, gegen mehrere Streitgenossen gerichtet zu werden, so erscheint es ohne Belang, wenn die Maßregel des Arrestes nur einzelnen Streitgenossen gegenüber begehrt wird. Beabsichtigt z. B. ein Gläubiger eine Reihe von Erben seines Schuldners zu belangen und zwar beim Gerichte, wo der größte Theil der Erben wohnt, findet es jedoch nur nöthig, gegen einen der Erben Arrest zu erwirken, so ist er nicht gezwungen, den Vorstand des Gerichts, wo dieser Erbe wohnt, anzugehen, kann vielmehr sich an den Vorstand jenes Gerichts wenden, bei welchem er Klage erheben will.

Wenn nun aber der Gläubiger für die Arrestanlage eine Wahl getroffen, z. B. den Ort, wo der betreffende Erbe wohnt, gewählt hat, ist er gehalten, auch bei Erhebung der Klage sich darnach zu richten, oder steht ihm hier noch die Wahl frei? Da das Gesetz keinen Anhaltspunkt für eine Beschränkung bietet, es überhaupt dessen Geiste entspricht, hier nicht allzustreng zu sein, so wird diese Frage zu bejahen sein. Vgl. Art. 641.

4) Es können Fälle vorkommen, wo für mehrere Forderungen, welche theilweise schon im Prozesse oder in einer Vollstreckung begriffen sind, theilweise noch nicht, Arrest erwirkt werden soll, oder wo sogar bei Theilen der nemlichen Forderung (z. B. bei Zielfristen, die theils fällig sind, theils nicht), eine solche Verschiedenheit eintritt.

Es lassen sich hier verschiedene Ansichten aufstellen, nemlich: 1) daß jeder Theil vor den zuständigen Richter zu bringen sei, also mehrfache Arreste erwirkt werden müßten, oder 2) daß bloß der anhängige Theil, oder 3) daß bloß der nicht anhängige Theil entscheide, oder endlich 4) daß der Gläubiger die Wahl habe.

Ich würde das Letztere als dem Willen des Gesetzes entsprechend ansehen, weil es das Praktischere ist und weil, wie gesagt, Strenge hier nicht am Platze wäre, da es nicht von besonderer Wichtigkeit erscheint, ob der Arrest gerade vom nemlichen Richter, der in der Hauptsache erkennt, bewilligt wird oder nicht. Nur dürfte nicht aus den Umständen hervorgehen, daß es bei Häufung der Forderungen nur auf Umgehung des Gesetzes abgesehen sei, z. B. dem Richter, bei welchem die Sache anhängig ist und welcher die Sachlage kennt, die Entscheidung zu entziehen.

Wo Dringlichkeit vorliegt, wird es übrigens in solchen Fällen immer rathsam sein, sich an den Einzelnrichter, wo der Vollzug stattfinden soll, zu wenden.

5) Die Vorschrift, daß der Vorstand des Gerichts, wo der Prozeß anhängig ist, vorzugsweise zuständig sei, hat ihren sehr triftigen Grund darin, daß derselbe zur Zeit am besten in der Lage ist, den Werth des Anspruches und die Nothwendigkeit der Maßregel zu beurtheilen.

Diese Zuständigkeit besteht sowohl für die erste als für die zweite Instanz, also nicht für den obersten Gerichtshof. So lange daher eine Sache beim obersten Gerichtshofe anhängig ist, läßt sich die Ausnahme der Ziff. 2 des Art. 618 nicht anwenden, tritt somit die Regel der Ziff. 3 in Kraft, gemäß deren der Vorstand des Gerichts erster Instanz zu verfügen hat.

Diese Zuständigkeit des Richters erster Instanz muß überhaupt überall Platz greifen, wo die Voraussetzungen der Ziff. 1 u. 2 nicht eintreffen, also z. B. nach Spruch eines Endurtheils zweiter Instanz bis zur Einleitung der Vollstreckung oder vom Spruche des Endurtheiles erster Instanz bis zur Zustellung der Berufung.

Daß die eingelegte Berufung oder die ergriffene Nichtigkeitsbeschwerde bloß ein Zwischenurtheil oder einen Präjudizialpunkt zum Gegenstande haben, wird ohne Belang sein. Zur Zeit sind die unteren Gerichte nicht mehr mit der Sache befaßt, und ob sie an dieselbe zurückgelange, ist zweifelhaft.

b) Verfahren.

6) Beim Arreste verfügt der Richter auf einseitiges Ansuchen des Gläubigers, ohne daß der Schuldner vorher gehört oder ihm Kenntniß vom Gesuche gegeben werde. Falls, wie es in der Regel geschieht, ein schriftliches Gesuch eingereicht wird, setzt der Richter seine Verfügung, sei sie bewilligend oder abweisend, sofort auf dieses Gesuch und dieselbe wird dem Gesuchsteller in Urschrift ausgehändigt (Art. 637 Abs. 5 u. 6). Bei mündlich erklärten Gesuchen hat er dieselben im Eingange seiner Verfügung kurz zu beurkunden.

7) Die richterliche Verfügung muß natürlich die zu gestattende Maßregel so bestimmt als möglich bezeichnen. Schon die allgemeine Vorschrift, daß Vorsichtsverfügungen nur soweit zuzulassen sind, als sie nothwendig erscheinen (Art. 605 u. 610), bringt dies mit sich; allein der Wille des Gesetzes erscheint noch bestimmter ausgesprochen in Art. 608, denn was dort über den Inhalt des Gesuches vorgeschrieben ist, hat mittelbar auch Geltung für die richterliche Verfügung.

Es ist daher so bestimmt wie möglich anzugeben, auf welche Ausstände, welche Mobilien Beschlag gelegt werden dürfe, jedoch ist es, abgesehen von besonderen Vorschriften (z. B. in Art. 624 Abs. 1) nicht gerade verboten, solche Maßregeln auch mehr oder minder unbestimmt zu gestatten. Vgl. Bemerk. zu 608 Nr. 3. Bei der Beschlagnahme von Mobilien wird sogar die Unbestimmtheit fast Regel werden, da der Gerichtsvollzieher nur pfänden kann, was er vorfindet, hierüber aber im Voraus sich der Regel nach nichts bestimmen läßt. Es ist in dieser Beziehung alles dem weisen Ermessen des Richters überlassen.

8) Insbesondere ist es auch Pflicht des Richters, die Geldsumme zu bezeichnen, für welche er die Arrestanlage gestattet, und zwar ist dies schon deshalb geboten, weil die Maßregeln des Art. 607 fast ausnahmslos solche sind, welche eine der Summe nach bestimmte Forderung voraussetzen.

Bei Veräußerungsverboten schreibt Art. 625 Abs. 2 ausdrücklich die Bezeichnung der Summe vor, allein auch bei Beschlagnahmen von Mobilien und von Forderungen ist sie nöthig, denn Art. 859 Abs. 2 weist den Gerichtsvollzieher an, mit der Pfändung einzuhalten, sobald die beschlagnahmten Gegenstände zur Tilgung der Forderung hinreichen, und nach Art. 972 Ziff. 3 u. 4, sowie Art. 1002 Abs. 2, ist beim Sicherheitsarrest auf Forderungen die Forderung des Arrestklägers genau zu bezeichnen und zu erklären, daß bis zum Betrage seines Guthabens die Arrestanlage stattfinde.

Wenn Art. 615 nur bestimmt, es solle der Betrag der Forderung soweit möglich schon in der Vorsichtsverfügung festgestellt werden, damit Sicherheit geleistet werden könne (vgl. Art. 632), so ist zu beachten, daß jener Artikel von Vorsichtsverfügungen überhaupt, nicht bloß vom Arreste spricht, daß übrigens auch unter den Maßregeln des Arrestes einige vorkommen, welche einen vorausgehenden Anschlag der Forderung in Geld nicht nothwendig voraussetzen, z. B. die Ermächtigung zur Rückbehaltung bestimmter beweglicher Sachen, oder die Verfügung der Hinterlegung bestimmter Sachen.

Art. 619. — **Anträge auf Erlassung von Vorsichtsverfügungen, bei welchen es sich nicht um Arrestanlegung handelt, sind, wenn die Vorsichtsverfügung eine bei Gericht anhängige Sache betrifft oder mit einer solchen im Zusammenhange steht, in der für Zwischenstreite vorgeschriebenen Weise zu stellen.**

Besteht diese Voraussetzung nicht, so sind derartige Anträge, wenn wegen der Sache, auf welche sich die Vorsichtsverfügung bezieht, ein Vollstreckungsverfahren eingeleitet ist, bei dem Vorstande des Vollstreckungsgerichts, andernfalls bei dem Vorstande des in der Hauptsache zuständigen Gerichts zu stellen. Der Gerichtsvorstand hat sofort anzuordnen, daß über den Antrag zwischen den Parteien vor ihm verhandelt werde, und hiezu möglichst nahe Tagfahrt anzuberaumen.

Art. 620. — **Bei dringender Gefahr können in den Fällen des Art. 619 Abs. 1 durch den Vorstand des Gerichts oder Senats, bei dem der Rechtsstreit anhängig ist, und selbst durch den Einzelnrichter, in dessen Bezirk die Verfügung vollzogen werden soll, auf einseitiges Gesuch einer Partei einstweilige Verfügungen erlassen werden, welche aber unbeschadet**

ihrer sofortigen Vollstreckbarkeit (Art. 639 Abs. 2) unverzüglich der Gegenpartei zuzustellen sind, der es freisteht, die Aufhebung oder Abänderung in der für Zwischenstreite vorgeschriebenen Weise bei Gericht nachzusuchen.

Unter derselben Voraussetzung können in den Fällen des Art. 619 Abs. 2 solche sofort vollstreckbare einstweilige Verfügungen von dem zur Erlassung der Vorsichtsverfügung zuständigen Gerichtsvorstande schon sogleich bei Anberaumung der Tagfahrt und außerdem auch von dem Einzelnrichter, in dessen Bezirk die Verfügung zu vollziehen ist, erlassen werden. Im letztern Falle sind aber das betreffende Gesuch und die erlassene einstweilige Verfügung von dem Gesuchsteller dem nach Art. 619 Abs. 2 zuständigen Gerichtsvorstande vorzulegen, der zu der vor ihm zu pflegenden Verhandlung möglichst nahe Tagfahrt festzusetzen hat.

Art. 621. — Zu der in Art. 619 Abs. 2 und Art. 620 Abs. 2 bezeichneten Verhandlung hat der Antragsteller die Gegenpartei unter Zustellung der Tagfahrtsfestsetzung, sowie der etwa erlassenen einstweiligen Verfügung so zeitig vorladen zu lassen, daß deren Erscheinen bei der Verhandlung möglich ist.

Erscheinen beide Theile, so sind sie über den Sachverhalt zu vernehmen und ist dieser durch sachgemäße Fragen möglichst aufzuklären. Es ist sodann, wenn dies nach Lage der Sache angemessen erscheint, ein Sühneversuch vorzunehmen und in Ermangelung eines Vergleichs das den Sachverhältnissen Entsprechende zu verfügen. Die etwa erlassene einstweilige Verfügung ist je nach den Umständen zu bestätigen, abzuändern oder aufzuheben.

Erscheint der Antragsteller nicht, so ist sein Gesuch abzuweisen und die von ihm etwa erwirkte einstweilige Verfügung aufzuheben.

Erscheint der Imploral gehöriger Vorladung ungeachtet nicht, so ist auf Grund des Vorbringens des Antragstellers das Sachgemäße zu verfügen.

G. A. d. K. d. A. II S. 417. 448. 449. VI S. 337. 338. — K. d. R. II S. 288. IV S. 67. 85—87. V S. 10.

1) Diese drei Artikel regeln Zuständigkeit und Verfahren bei gewöhnlichen Vorsichtsverfügungen. Auch hier ist in letzterer Beziehung auf die allgemeinen Vorschriften der Art. 637—639 zu verweisen.

a) Zuständigkeit.

2) Bei gewöhnlichen Vorsichtsverfügungen ist zu unterscheiden, ob sie eine bei Gericht anhängige Sache betreffen oder mit einer solchen im Zusammenhange stehen, oder aber nicht.

Im ersteren Falle sind die bezüglichen Anträge in der für Zwischenstreite (Art. 483) vorgeschriebenen Weise zu stellen. Die Vorsichtsverfügung bildet ein Zubehör zur anhängigen Sache und das Prozeßgericht ist ausschließlich für dieselbe zuständig. Dies gilt auch für den Fall, wo die Sache in der Berufungsinstanz anhängig ist (Art. 705 Ziff. 3).

Der oberste Gerichtshof, dessen Zuständigkeit überhaupt exceptionell ist und sich der Regel nach nur auf die Frage beschränkt, ob eine Nichtigkeitsbeschwerde statthaft und begründet sei oder nicht, hat keine Zuständigkeit zur Verfügung von Vorsichtsverfügungen. Falls daher die Sache vor ihm anhängig ist, sowie überhaupt in allen Fällen, wo eine Instanz über den Grund der Sache nicht anhängig, ist Art. 619 Abs. 2 maßgebend. Vgl. die Bemerk. zu Art. 618 Nr. 5.

3) In letzterem Falle ergeht die Entscheidung durch einen einzelnen Richter, und zwar, wenn ein Vollstreckungsverfahren eingeleitet ist und die Vorsichtsverfügung darauf Bezug hat, durch den Vorstand des Vollstreckungsgerichts (Bezirks- oder Einzelngerichts); ist aber dies nicht der Fall, durch den Vorstand des in der Hauptsache zuständigen Gerichts erster Instanz.

4) Bei dringender Gefahr kann die Vorsichtsverfügung in allen Fällen durch den Vorstand des Gerichts oder Senats, bei welchem die Sache anhängig ist, erlassen werden, oder durch den Einzelnrichter, in dessen Bezirke sie zu vollziehen ist (Art. 620 Abs. 1 u. 2). Die besondere Dringlichkeit muß, wenn sie nicht aus den Umständen hervorgeht, nach Art. 608 bescheinigt sein, oder nach Art. 609 Sicherheitsleistung angeordnet werden.

b) Verfahren in gewöhnlichen Fällen.

5) In den gewöhnlichen Fällen, d. h. in jenen, wo keine dringende Gefahr vorliegt, gestaltet sich das Verfahren verschieden, je nachdem die Vorsichtsverfügung, sich an einen anhängigen Prozeß anschließend, Gegenstand eines Zwischenstreites zu bilden hat (Art. 619 Abs. 1) oder nicht; immer aber ist es contradiktorisch.

Im ersteren Falle ist das für Zwischenstreite vorgeschriebene Verfahren zu beobachten, also das

Begehren mittelst motivirten Antrages (Art. 484) oder in der Sitzung (Art. 510) zu stellen und gleichzeitig mit der Hauptsache zu verhandeln und zu entscheiden, falls nicht der Dringlichkeit wegen gesonderte Aburtheilung geboten erscheint (Art. 484, 157 u. 259).

6) Im zweiten Falle wird contradiktorisch vor dem betreffenden Vorstande des Gerichts (Bezirks-, Handels-, Einzelngerichts) verhandelt. Derselbe verfügt, falls das Gesuch nicht schon in sich als unbegründet erscheint, daß in einer möglichst nahe anzuberaumenden Tagfahrt über den Antrag zwischen den Parteien vor ihm verhandelt werde.

Der Antragsteller läßt sofort die Gegenpartei unter Zustellung der Tagfahrtsbestimmung zur Verhandlung vorladen und zwar so zeitig, daß deren Erscheinen möglich ist. Ob letzterer Bedingung genügt sei, hat der Richter frei zu würdigen, unter Umständen aber wiederholte Vorladung anzuordnen (Art. 220, 300, 520 Abs. 1).

7) Die Vorladung soll erfolgen, damit über den Antrag verhandelt werde, und es ergibt sich hieraus, daß auch der Antrag bezw. das Gesuch, mag es schriftlich eingereicht oder vom Richter in seiner Verfügung beurkundet sein, zugestellt werden müsse.

Das Gesetz schreibt dies zwar nicht ausdrücklich vor, setzt es jedoch offenbar voraus, denn die Tagfahrtsfestsetzung findet nur unter Bezugnahme auf das Gesuch und sich demselben anschließend statt, und es bildet also das Gesuch einen Bestandtheil der Tagfahrtsbestimmung. Aus demselben Grunde, warum in Fällen, wo auf dem Wege des Zwischenstreites verfahren wird, ein motivirter Antrag gefordert wird, muß hier die Zustellung des Gesuches, welches diesen Antrag ersetzt, erfolgen, und es wäre höchst ungeeignet und sachwidrig, eine Partei zu einer Verhandlung zu laden, ohne ihr mitzutheilen, worüber verhandelt werden soll.

Wenn in Art. 621 Abs. 4 für den Fall des Nichterscheinens des Gegners vorgeschrieben ist, es solle auf Vorbringen des Antragstellers das Sachgemäße verfügt werden, so heißt dies nicht, der Antragsteller dürfe im Verhandlungstermine begehren, was er wolle, sondern es seien die vorgetragenen Thatsachen als wahr zu betrachten und demgemäß auf den Antrag zu verfügen. Vgl. Art. 297 u. 520.

Allerdings kann jedoch im Falle, wo der Gegner erscheint, der Gesuchsteller nach den allgemeinen Prinzipien (Art. 180 ff. u. 506) seinen Antrag ändern.

8) Da für diese Verhandlungen die Oeffentlichkeit nicht ausgeschlossen ist (vgl. Art. 341 u. 649), so wird nach den allgemeinen Prinzipien (Art. 148) Niemanden verwehrt werden können, dabei anwesend zu sein; jedoch ist es nicht nöthig, dieselbe im gewöhnlichen Sitzungssaale vorzunehmen, vielmehr wird der Richter in der Regel eine andere Räumlichkeit (die Rathskammer, sein Arbeitszimmer) dazu wählen.

Wenn Art. 621 vorschreibt, der Richter solle die Parteien hören, ihnen sachgemäße Fragen stellen, unter Umständen die Sühne versuchen, wenn sich aber kein Vergleich erzielen lasse, seine Verfügung treffen, so hätte sich dies Alles wohl von selbst verstanden.

Eine Verkündung des Beschlusses ist nicht vorgeschrieben, jedoch erscheint es sachgemäß, daß der Richter den Parteien kundgebe, was er verfüge, und falls die Aushändigung nicht sofort erfolgt, dem Antragsteller eröffne, daß er den Beschluß beim Gerichtsschreiber in Empfang nehmen könne. Vgl. Bemerk. zu Art. 634 Nr. 11.

Schließlich trifft Art. 621 Vorsorge für den Fall des Nichterscheinens der einen oder der andern Partei. Erscheint der Antragsteller nicht, so wird das Gesuch abgewiesen; erscheint der Gegner nicht, so wird, den allgemeinen Prinzipien entsprechend, das Vorbringen des Antragstellers als wahr betrachtet und demgemäß verfügt.

c) Verfahren im Falle der Dringlichkeit.

9) Liegt dringende Gefahr vor (Art. 620), so darf der Richter auf einseitiges Verlangen eine einstweilige Vorsichtsverfügung erlassen, welche sofort vollstreckbar ist — ein Provisorium im Provisorium.

Unverzüglich nach Erwirkung einer solchen Verfügung ist jedoch das gewöhnliche contradiktorische Verfahren anzubahnen, damit entschieden werde, ob das einstweilige Provisorium zu bestätigen, abzuändern oder aufzuheben sei (Art. 621 Abs. 2).

Ist auf dem Wege des Zwischenstreites zu verfahren (Art. 619 Abs. 1), so genügt es, dem Gegner sofort die einstweilige Verfügung zuzustellen, indem diesem freisteht, den Zwischenstreit anzuregen und in die Sitzung zu bringen.

Ist der Weg des selbständigen Verfahrens einzuhalten und ist es der nach Art. 619 Abs. 2 zuständige Gerichtsvorstand, welcher die einstweilige Vorsichtsverfügung erläßt, so bestimmt dieser bei Erlaß der Verfügung zugleich Tagfahrt zur contradiktorischen Verhandlung.

Wurde jedoch fragliche Verfügung von einem Einzelnrichter erlassen, welcher außer dem Falle dringender Gefahr nicht zuständig gewesen wäre, so schreibt Art. 619 Abs. 2 vor, daß Gesuch und Verfügung dem zuständigen Gerichtsvorstande (also möglicherweise auch einem anderen Einzelnrichter) vorzulegen seien und dieser möglichst nahe Tagfahrt festzusetzen habe. Bei erster Lesung war auch hier vorgeschrieben, es habe die Vorlage unverzüglich zu geschehen, bei zweiter Lesung (R. R. IV 86, 87) ließ man jedoch bei Umgestaltung der ganzen Fassung diese Vorschrift weg; allein sie versteht sich wohl von selbst. Da übrigens das Gesetz es ganz dem Ermessen des Richters anheimstellt, die nachgesuchte Maßregel zu bewilligen oder nicht, so kann derselbe seine Bewilligung auch mit der Auflage verbinden, binnen bestimmter Frist die fragliche Vorlage zum Zwecke der Bestätigung der Maßregel zu bethätigen.

10) Wurden die nach Art. 620 Abs. 1 u. 2 vorgeschriebenen Zustellungen und Vorlagen nicht rechtzeitig gemacht, so ist auf Antrag der Gegenpartei die Aufhebung der einstweiligen Vorsichtsverfügung auszusprechen (Art. 633).

Was das weitere Verfahren betrifft, so ist nur zu erwähnen, daß die einstweilige Verfügung bei der Ladung zur contradiktorischen Verhandlung zuzustellen ist, wie sich dies, da die Bestätigung derselben in Frage ist, im Grunde von selbst versteht.

Schließlich erscheint selbstverständlich, daß der Richter, welcher angegangen wird, eine einstweilige Vorsichtsverfügung zu erlassen, jedoch dringende Gefahr nicht gegeben erachtet, unter Abweisung dieses Antrages sofort Tagfahrt zur Verhandlung festsetzen kann, wenn er anders für dieselbe zuständig ist.

Art. 622. — **Wird eine Sequestration verfügt, so ist der Sequester, wenn die Parteien über die Wahl eines solchen nicht übereingekommen sind, sogleich in der Verfügung zu ernennen. Auch sind zugleich die etwa nöthigen Verwaltungsvorschriften zu ertheilen.**

Art. 623. — **Wird der Antrag auf Erlassung einer Vorsichtsverfügung abgewiesen, so ist der Antragsteller zugleich in die Kosten und zum Ersatze des dem Gegner durch den Vollzug einer etwa früher erlassenen einstweiligen Verfügung verursachten Schadens zu verurtheilen. In allen andern Fällen wird vorbehaltlich der Bestimmung des Art. 636 Abs. 1 die Entscheidung über Kosten- und Schadensersatz dem Erkenntnisse in der Hauptsache vorbehalten.**

G. A. d. K. d. A. II S. 417. 448. 449. — K. d. R. II S. 288.

1) Art. 622 gibt für den Fall, wo eine Sequestration verfügt wird, dem Richter die Weisung, sofort in der Verfügung den Sequester zu ernennen, falls die Parteien sich nicht wegen der Wahl einigen — ein Fall, der natürlich nur bei contradiktorischer Verhandlung eintreten kann. Es ist bei Verfügungen auf einseitiges Gesuch Sache des Gesuchstellers, bei contradiktorischer Verhandlung Sache beider Parteien, dem Richter die Anhaltspunkte zur Wahl eines geeigneten Sequesters durch Bescheinigungen zu geben.

Ist der Richter nicht im Stande, sofort einen Sequester zu bezeichnen, so ist nach dem Willen des Gesetzes die Verfügung auszusetzen, d. h. entweder die Verhandlung selbst oder der Ausspruch der Verfügung zu vertagen. Abg. II 417 (v. Weiß).

Ferner wird der Richter angewiesen, sofort die etwa nöthigen Verwaltungsvorschriften zu ertheilen, d. h. in seine Verfügung aufzunehmen. Es können diese Vorschriften allgemeiner oder spezieller Art sein, je nach dem Bedürfnisse des Falles und unter Einhaltung des Prinzipes, daß alle Vorsichtsverfügungen sich streng innerhalb der Grenzen des Nothwendigen halten müssen.

2) Art. 623 trifft Bestimmungen bezüglich derjenigen Kosten, welche zur Zeit der Bescheidung des bezüglichen Antrags entstanden sind. Er verfügt, daß in Fällen, wo der Antrag auf Erlaß einer Vorsichtsverfügung abgewiesen wird, der Antragsteller in die entstandenen Kosten, sowie zum Ersatze des durch eine etwa vollzogene einstweilige Vorsichtsverfügung verursachten Schadens verurtheilt werden solle. Diese Verfügung ist allgemein, gilt also auch für den Fall, wo die Vorsichtsverfügung im Wege eines Zwischenstreites aufgehoben wird, und liegt hierin eine Aenderung des allgemeinen Prinzipes (Art. 111), gemäß dessen es sonst im Ermessen des Richters steht, die Kosten von Zwischenstreiten auszuscheiden oder dem Endurtheile vorzubehalten.

Kosten und Schaden hat der Richter sofort zu liquidiren.

In allen anderen Fällen ist die Entscheidung über Kosten- und Schadensersatz dem Erkenntnisse in der Hauptsache vorzubehalten. Dies wird bezüglich der Kosten auch dann zu geschehen haben, wenn der Antrag nur theilweise abgewiesen oder eine einstweilige Vorsichtsverfügung bloß geändert wird. Vgl. Art. 636 Abs. 1 u. Bemerk. dazu.

Vollstreckung.

Art. 624. — Soweit die Vorsichtsverfügungen in Maßregeln bestehen, welche das Gesetz zugleich als Vollstreckungsmittel bezeichnet, richtet sich deren Vollstreckung, sowie das weitere Verfahren, soferne gesetzlich nicht anders bestimmt ist, nach den für das betreffende Vollstreckungsmittel bestehenden Vorschriften. Die Vorsichtsverfügung ist vorbehaltlich besonderer gesetzlicher Bestimmungen bei der Vollstreckung zuzustellen, falls deren Zustellung nicht schon früher stattgefunden hat.

Art. 625. — Das Verbot der Veräußerung und weitern Belastung unbeweglicher Güter wird dadurch vollstreckt, daß der Imploraut dasselbe in der gesetzlich vorgeschriebenen Weise in das Hypothekenbuch eintragen und davon, daß dies geschehen, der Gegenpartei durch Gerichtsvollzieherakt unter Zustellung der erlassenen Vorsichtsverfügung Mittheilung machen läßt. Diese Mittheilung muß spätestens innerhalb acht Tagen — falls sie in einem andern Bezirksgerichtssprengel als demjenigen, wo der Eintrag erfolgt ist, zu geschehen hat, spätestens innerhalb fünfzehn Tagen — vom Tage des Eintrags in das Hypothekenbuch erfolgen.

Die Güter, auf welche sich das Verbot erstreckt, müssen in der Vorsichtsverfügung einzeln beschrieben und der Eintrag im Hypothekenbuche muß so beschaffen sein, daß sie aus letzterem ersichtlich sind.

Wurde das Verbot zur Sicherstellung einer Geldforderung oder eines in Geld anschlagbaren Anspruchs erlassen, so muß der Betrag, für welchen der Schuldner, um die erlassene Vorsichtsverfügung abzuwenden, Sicherheit zu leisten hat, sowohl in der Verfügung als auch in dem Hypothekenbuche angegeben sein.

Art. 626. — Gegen Dritte wirkt das Verbot der Veräußerung und weitern Belastung unbeweglicher Güter von dem Zeitpunkte des Eintrags in das Hypothekenbuch. Veräußerungen und Belastungen mit Dienstbarkeiten oder Reallasten, welche nach diesem Zeitpunkte stattgefunden haben, sowie Hypotheken, welche nach demselben in das Hypothekenbuch eingetragen worden sind, haben demjenigen, der das Verbot erlangt hat, gegenüber keine Wirksamkeit.

Dritte, zu deren Gunsten nach dem bezeichneten Zeitpunkte Hypotheken eingetragen wurden oder der Schuldner Veräußerungen oder Belastungen vorgenommen hat, können die deshalb gegen sie gerichteten Ansprüche des Gläubigers jederzeit dadurch beseitigen, daß sie den in Art. 625 Abs. 3 bezeichneten Betrag bei Gericht erlegen.

Art. 627. — Die angeordnete Hinterlegung beweglicher Sachen bei Gericht, sowie die Uebergabe solcher Sachen an einen Sequester wird, soferne sich der Implorant im Besitze der betreffenden Sachen befindet, durch die Hinterlegung oder Uebergabe vollstreckt, andernfalls durch die dem Besitzer unter Mittheilung der Verfügung zugestellte Aufforderung, die Hinterlegung oder Uebergabe unverzüglich zu bewirken.

Die Vollstreckung der Verfügung, welche die Uebergabe unbeweglicher Güter zur Verwaltung an einen Sequester anordnet, erfolgt dadurch, daß die Verfügung auf Betreiben des Imploranten dem ernannten Sequester mit der Aufforderung zugestellt wird, die Verwaltung sofort zu übernehmen.

Art. 628. — Ist einer Partei der einstweilige Besitz überwiesen oder ein Gläubiger in Gemäßheit des Art. 607 ermächtigt worden, in seinen Händen befindliche Sachen des Schuldners oder an diesen zu leistende Zahlungen vorläufig zurückzubehalten, oder ist einer Partei die Vornahme bestimmter Handlungen verboten oder eine bestimmte Leistung oder Handlung auferlegt worden, so liegt in der Zustellung der betreffenden Verfügung die Vollstreckung derselben.

Art. 629. — Die Vollstreckung sonstiger Vorsichtsverfügungen richtet sich nach der Natur der betreffenden Verfügung. G. A. d. K. d. A. II S. 417—421. 448. 449. IV S. 119. 337. 338. K. d. R. II S. 288. IV S. 87. 88.

1) Die Vollstreckung von Vorsichtsverfügungen richtet sich im Allgemeinen und soweit nicht besondere gesetzliche Vorschriften, insbesondere die Art. 624—628 Maß geben, nach der Natur der betreffenden Verfügungen und — läßt sich hinzufügen — nach den besonderen vom Richter etwa gegebenen Weisungen (Art. 629).

Als eine allgemeine, sämmtliche Vorsichtsverfügungen treffende Vorschrift hat ferner zu gelten, daß die Verfügungen bei der Vollstreckung zuzustellen seien, falls dies nicht schon früher geschehen ist, und vorbehaltlich besonderer Ausnahmen. Vgl. Art. 625 Abs. 1 u. Art. 832 Abs. 2.

2) Für Fälle, wo die Vorsichtsverfügung in Maßregeln besteht, welche das Gesetz zugleich als Vollstreckungsmittel bezeichnet, richtet sich deren Vollstreckung, sowie das weitere Verfahren, sofern gesetzlich nichts anderes bestimmt ist, nach den für die betreffenden Vollstreckungsmittel bestehenden Vorschriften (Art. 624). Was hier im Einklange mit Art. 613 verfügt ist, erscheint sehr natürlich, denn die Vorsichtsverfügung stellt sich in solchen Fällen nur als eine vorläufige Vollstreckung dar, bestimmt, soweit durchgeführt zu werden, als es der Zweck der Sicherung bedingt, und später in eine definitive Vollstreckung überzugehen.

Selbstverständlich ist, daß die Vorschriften über das Verfahren bei der Vollstreckung nur soweit Anwendung finden, als sie nicht nach dem Zwecke der Vorsichtsverfügungen, welcher mit Sicherung der Vollstreckungsmittel erreicht ist, gegenstandslos erscheinen. Von Versteigerung gepfändeter Mobilien, Zuweisung von Erlösen rc. kann daher, so lange die Vorsichtsverfügung nicht in die wirkliche Vollstreckung übergegangen ist, nicht die Rede sein.

Das Gesetz gibt übrigens bei Regelung des Vollstreckungsverfahrens verschiedene Bestimmungen, welche bloß den Vollzug von Vorsichtsverfügungen betreffen, und auf welche sich die Worte des Art. 624: „sofern gesetzlich nicht anders bestimmt ist“ beziehen. So verfügt Art. 845, daß bei Vorsichtsverfügungen die Vollstreckung immer zugleich mit dem Befriedigungsgebote erfolgen dürfe, gibt ferner Art. 922 Vorschriften über den Anschluß auf Grund von Vorsichtsverfügungen, wird endlich in Art. 1002 bis 1006 das Verfahren beim Sicherheitsarreste auf Forderungen und in Art. 1172 das Verfahren bei Verhaftungen, welche auf Grund von Vorsichtsverfügungen stattfinden, geregelt.

Ferner enthält das Gesetz besondere Bestimmungen bezüglich des Uebergangs von Vorsichtsverfügungen in die wirkliche Vollstreckung und bezüglich Concurrenz solcher Verfügungen mit Vollstreckungen. Vgl. Art. 902, 909, 1005.

3) In den Art. 856—865 werden die Vollstreckungsmittel in solche eingetheilt, welche die Beitreibung von Geldforderungen bezwecken, und in solche, welche sonstige Leistungen zum Gegenstande haben.

Spricht man von Vollstreckungsmitteln, so denkt man zunächst nur an jene der ersteren Art, und sie allein sind auch Gegenstand besonderer Vorschriften in den Hauptstücken XXXIII bis XXXVII. Es frägt sich nun, ob auch Art. 624 nur diese besondere Vollstreckungsmittel im Auge habe?

Das Gesetz spricht allgemein, und so wird eine solche Beschränkung nicht statthaft sein. Sie wäre übrigens auch nicht sachgemäß, wie zu Art. 627 u. 628 näher erörtert werden wird. Vgl. Abg. IV 218 Sp. 2 (Barth).

a) Verbot der Veräußerung und Belastung.

1) Diesseits.

4) Die Art. 625 und 626 geben besondere Vorschriften über Form und Vollzug der Vorsichtsverfügung, welche die Veräußerung und weitere Belastung unbeweglicher Güter verbietet, sowie über die Tragweite dieser Verfügung — Vorschriften, welche in der Pfalz nur im Sinne von Art. 68 des Einf.-Ges. Anwendung finden.

5) Es müssen in der Verfügung die betroffenen Güter einzeln beschrieben und muß auch der Eintrag ein spezieller sein. Uebrigens werden bezüglich der Spezialität des Eintrags keine weitergehenden Forderungen gemacht, als sie das Hypothekengesetz stellt. Abg. II 118.

Handelt es sich bloß um Sicherung eines Geldanspruches, nicht aber dinglicher oder persönlicher Rechte auf die Güter selbst, so muß der Betrag des Anspruches in der Verfügung sowohl, als im Eintrage angegeben sein. Durch Erlegung dieses Betrages können dritte Personen die Wirkungen des Eintrags sofort beseitigen (Art. 626 Abs. 2).

Die Vollstreckung erfolgt durch den sofort, ohne vorausgehende oder gleichzeitige Zustellung der Vorsichtsverfügung, vorzunehmenden Eintrag in's Hypothekenbuch.

Innerhalb acht Tagen vom Eintrage an muß von diesem der Gegenpartei durch Gerichtsvollzieherakt Mittheilung gegeben werden. Hiermit ist die Zustellung der Vorsichtsverfügung zu verbinden (Art. 626 Abs. 1), und falls die Sache noch nicht anhängig oder die Vollstreckung noch nicht eingeleitet ist, die Zustellung der Klage bezw. des Befriedigungsgebotes (Art. 630 Abs. 5). Hat die Mittheilung in einem anderen Bezirksgerichtssprengel zu geschehen, so erweitert sich die Frist auf 15 Tage.

Sind diese Fristen nicht eingehalten, so ist auf Begehren die Aufhebung der Maßregel auszusprechen (Art. 633).

6) Die Bestimmungen, welche Art. 626 über die Wirkungen des in Frage stehenden Eintrages gibt, sind Spezialbestimmungen, für deren

Auslegung der besondere Zweck, welchen der Gesetzgeber erreichen will, maßgebend ist, und dieser Zweck ist die vollkommene Sicherstellung des Antragstellers gegen Beschädigungen, welche aus der Einräumung dinglicher Rechte an dritte Personen für ihn entstehen können.

Das Gesetz unterscheidet zwischen Hypotheken und dinglichen Rechten sonstiger Art.

In ersterer Beziehung verfügt es, daß alle Einträge von Hypotheken, welche nach dem Eintrage des Verbotes erfolgen, wirkungslos seien; bezüglich der sonstigen dinglichen Rechte aber sagt es nur, daß Veräußerungen und Belastungen, welche nach diesem Eintrage geschehen, keine Wirksamkeit haben. Rechte, welche auf Grund solcher Veräußerungen und Belastungen zur Zeit, wo der Eintrag des Verbotes erfolgte, bereits giltig erworben sind, bleiben also (vorbehaltlich der Anfechtung wegen Betrugs) unberührt, selbst wenn bezüglich derselben ein Eintrag im Hypothekenbuche nicht besteht, oder dieser erst später stattfindet. Abg. II 419 (v. Weiß). Hieraus ergibt sich jedoch, daß die Bestimmung, welche später eingetragene Hypotheken für unwirksam erklärt, nicht wörtlich zu nehmen sei, denn wenn frühere Erwerbungen aufrecht erhalten werden, so versteht sich von selbst, daß auch die von den früheren Erwerbern bestellten Hypotheken nicht wirkungslos sein können. Dem Gläubiger, welcher kein Recht auf das betreffende Grundstück selbst hat, mangelt auch jedes Interesse, die bestellten Hypotheken anzufechten.

7) Das in Frage stehende Verbot enthält eine Dispositionsbeschränkung und ist als solche in der zweiten Rubrik vorzutragen. Ist für das betreffende Grundstück ein Folium noch nicht eröffnet, so ist es zum Zwecke des Eintrages zu eröffnen. Abg. II 418 u. 419.

Vom Falle, wo eine vorsorgliche Hypotheke (Hypotheken-Vormerkung) als Vorsichtsverfügung gestattet wird, soweit eine solche vorkommen kann (Hyp.-G. § 30), spricht hier das Gesetz nicht. In diesem Falle hat natürlich der Eintrag in dritter Rubrik zu geschehen und gelten bezüglich der Wirkungen die allgemeinen Prinzipien des Hypothekengesetzes. Abg. II 419 (Schmitt, v. Weiß, v. Neumayr). Auch die Prinzipien über Protestationen (Hyp.-G. § 28 ff.) bleiben unberührt.

Die Dispositionsbeschränkung, von welcher hier die Rede ist, wirkt dem Wortlaute des Gesetzes und ihrem Zwecke nach unbedingt, auch soweit es sich nicht bloß um das Hypothekenwesen handelt, und namentlich werden auch Grunddienstbarkeiten davon getroffen. Vgl. übrigens Referat zu Art. 15 des Entw. (S. 456) und die Aeußerungen des Referenten Abg. II S. 417 u. 418.

8) Wie natürlich, ist die Wirkung des Verbotes nur eine relative; sie tritt nur ein zu Gunsten des Gläubigers, welcher dasselbe erwirkt hat, und soweit es zu dessen Sicherung nöthig erscheint. Es sind daher Einträge auf Grund von Veräußerungen und weiteren Belastungen jeder Art nicht verwehrt, jedoch ist deren Wirkung nur eine bedingte, d. h. davon abhängig, daß das Verbot wieder aufgehoben oder der Anspruch, zu dessen Sicherung es dient, beseitigt werde.

Stehen Geldforderungen in Frage, so gestattet das Gesetz (Art. 626 Abs. 2) dem Gläubiger durch Hinterlegung des angegebenen Betrages bei Gericht die Wirkungen des Verbots zu beseitigen

2) In der Pfalz.

9) Für die Pfalz bestimmt Art. 68 des Einführungsgesetzes:

„Die Vorsichtsverfügung des Verbots der „Veräußerung und weiteren Belastung unbe„weglicher Güter (Art. 606 Ziff. 3 der P.O.), „ist in der Pfalz nur zur Sicherung von Geld„forderungen oder sonstigen in Geld anschlag„baren Ansprüchen gestattet. Der nach Art. 625 „der P.O. zu bewirkende Eintrag hat daselbst „unter analoger Anwendung der Vorschriften „der Art. 2148—2150 Code civil zu ge„schehen."

Diese Sonderbestimmung wurde im Hinblicke auf die eigenthümlichen Prinzipien des pfälzischen Rechtes gegeben, gemäß deren das Hypothekenbuch nicht die Aufgabe hat, das Eigenthum festzustellen, und für denjenigen, welcher darin als Eigenthümer vorgetragen ist, eine für das ganze Hypothekenwesen wirksame Rechtsvermuthung zu schaffen, vielmehr nur bestimmt ist, Wirkung und Rang der Hypotheken unter der Voraussetzung zu sichern, daß der Besteller wirklich Eigenthümer sei. Deßhalb konnten, ohne gewaltsames Eingreifen in das bestehende Recht, dem Eintrage einer Dispositionsbeschränkung nur solche Wirkungen gegeben werden, welche denjenigen eines gewöhnlichen Hypothekareintrages ähnlich sind, und mußte folgegemäß sich die Maßregel auf Fälle beschränken, wo es sich darum handelt, für Geldforderungen den Zugriff auf das Immobiliarvermögen zu sichern.

10) Der Eintrag erfolgt in der nemlichen Weise, wie bei gewöhnlichen Hypothekareinschreibungen, jedoch nur analog, da Zweck und Natur des Verbotes Abweichungen erheischen.

Den Titel, auf Grund dessen die Einschreibung erfolgt, bildet die Vorsichtsverfügung, und es ist unbedingt nothwendig, zu erklären, daß dieselbe das Verbot der Veräußerung und weiteren Belastung der zu bezeichnenden Grundstücke enthalte, denn hierdurch kennzeichnet sich die Natur und Wirkung dieser Einschreibung zum Unterschiede einer Hypothekareinschreibung. Es wird hiermit zugleich der Forderung des Art. 2148 Ziff. 3 (Bezeichnung der Natur des Titels) genügt.

11) Was die Wirkungen des Verbots betrifft, so sind die Verfügungen des Art. 626 maßgebend, soweit es sich mit dem Sinne fraglicher Ausnahmsbestimmung verträgt.

Hiernach sind Hypotheken, welche von dem in der Einschreibung bezeichneten Schuldner ausgehen und nach dem Eintrage des Verbotes eingeschrieben werden, sowie Veräußerungen und Belastungen, welche dieser Schuldner nach diesem Eintrage vornimmt, dem betreffenden Gläubiger gegenüber ohne Wirkung. Ob Veräußerungen, Hypothekebestellungen und sonstige Belastungen dritter Personen giltig seien, bleibt eine offene Frage.

Es lassen sich die Wirkungen des Verbotes in der Pfalz kurz dahin bezeichnen:

> Soweit es sich um Verhütung von Veräußerungen und Belastungen handelt, wirkt das Verbot gleich einer vorsorglichen Hypotheke.

Diese Wirkung tritt auch gegenüber von Hypotheken ein, welche früher giltig bestellt waren, jedoch erst später eingeschrieben wurden. Art. 834 Code de proc. ist hier nicht anwendbar, denn die Dispositionsbeschränkung läßt sich nicht als Veräußerung betrachten.

12) Es könnte sich fragen, ob dem Verbote nicht unbedingt die Wirkung einer vorsorglichen Hypotheke zukomme, also auch in dem Sinne, daß der Gläubiger ein Vorrecht vor später eingeschriebenen Hypothekargläubigern erlange.

Diese Frage ist zu verneinen.

Vorsichtsverfügungen sind ihrer Natur nach nur auf Sicherung gerichtet. Sie sollen verhüten, daß andere Personen Vorrechte zum Schaden des Antragstellers erlangen, es liegt aber ihrem Zwecke fern, dem einen Gläubiger den Vorzug vor dem andern zu verleihen. Zudem wurde bei den Verhandlungen anerkannt, daß es sich hier nicht um Eintrag eines Hypothekarrechts handle. S. oben Nr. 7.

Vormerkungen von Hypotheken sind dem pfälzischen Rechte unbekannt, dürften übrigens als Vorsichtsverfügung nie vorkommen, um eine Hypotheke, welche noch nicht besteht, einzuräumen, sondern höchstens, um in Fällen, wo das Bestehen zweifelhaft ist und die Einschreibung vom Hypothekenbewahrer verweigert wird, diese vorläufig und vorbehaltlich der Entscheidung über deren Werth zu gestatten.

b) Hinterlegung und Sequestrirung (Art. 627).

13) Die Vorsichtsverfügung, welche die Hinterlegung beweglicher Sachen bei Gericht oder deren Uebergabe an einen Sequester verfügt, soll in Fällen, wo nicht der Gesuchsteller selbst Besitzer ist, dadurch vollstreckt werden, daß dem Besitzer die Verfügung mit der Aufforderung zugestellt wird, der Vorsichtsverfügung unverzüglich zu genügen.

Es klingt dies etwas naiv, etwa als ob man sagte: Urtheile werden dadurch vollstreckt, daß man ein Befriedigungsgebot zustellt. Offenbar will das Gesetz nur sagen, es werde auf diese Weise die Vollstreckung angebahnt, es müsse besagte Aufforderung vorausgehen, bevor ein weiteres Einschreiten Platz greife. Zugleich ist hiermit genau der Zeitpunkt bezeichnet, von welchem an die Frist zur Klagerhebung (Art. 630 Abs. 1) läuft.

14) Leistet der Besitzer der Aufforderung keine Folge und ist in der Vorsichtsverfügung für diesen Fall eine Strafe gedroht (Art. 614), so kann gemäß Art. 640 sofort die Verhängung dieser Strafe begehrt werden.

In Fällen, wo Jemand besonderen Werth darauf legt, die Sache selbst zu erhalten, zu verhüten, daß sie beseitigt, beschädigt, verändert werde, ist mit einer Strafandrohung wenig gedient und wird es keinem Anstande unterliegen, nach Analogie der Bestimmungen in Art. 860 die Wegnahme der Sache durch den Gerichtsvollzieher und deren Ueberlieferung an das Gericht oder an den Sequester vornehmen zu lassen.

Uebrigens wird es bei der Unklarheit des Gesetzes rathsam sein, in Fällen dieser Art die Vorsichtsverfügung dahin zu erlassen, daß gestattet werde, die Sache in Beschlag nehmen und bei Gericht hinterlegen bezw. einem Sequester aushändigen zu lassen. Da die Maßregel der Beschlagnahme nicht auf den Fall der Sicherung von Geldforderungen beschränkt ist, also auch bei Vindikationen 2c. verfügt werden kann (Art. 606 Ziff. 2), so ist eine derartige Vorsichtsverfügung wohl statthaft, und verbindet sich mit derselben noch der weitere, gerade in den unterstellten Fällen sehr schwerwiegende Vortheil, daß eine vorausgängige Aufforderung nicht nöthig ist, vielmehr sofort mit dem Befriedigungsgebote die Beschlagnahme erfolgen kann (Art. 845).

15) Die Vollstreckung der Vorsichtsverfügung, welche die Uebergabe unbeweglicher Güter zur Verwaltung an einen Sequester anordnet, erfolgt nach Art. 627 Abs. 2 dadurch, daß diesem Sequester die Verfügung mit der Aufforderung zugestellt wird, die Verwaltung zu übernehmen. Zu gleicher Zeit wird übrigens auch dem Gegner die Vorsichtsverfügung zuzustellen sein, gegebenen Falls mit der Aufforderung, den Besitz zu räumen (Art. 624).

Leistet der Gegner nicht Folge, so liegt es wohl nicht im Willen des Gesetzes, daß der Sequester sich eigenmächtig in Besitz setze, oder daß ein Urtheil erwirkt werde, welches die Räumung anordne, vielmehr kann nach Analogie von Art. 861 sofort die Hülfe des Gerichtsvollziehers beansprucht werden.

In der Regel wird übrigens für den Fall der Unfolgsamkeit Strafe angedroht sein.

c) Besitzüberweisung und Auflage von Leistungen.

16) Ist einer Person der einstweilige Besitz überwiesen, oder sind bestimmte Handlungen geboten oder verboten, so liegt gleichfalls die Vollstreckung in der Zustellung. Es gilt hier, was oben (Nr. 13) bemerkt wurde.

Was das Verbot oder Gebot von Handlungen betrifft, so ist hier der Natur der Sache nach nur indirekter Zwang durch Strafandrohung statthaft. Leistet der Verpflichtete der mit der Zustellung zu verbindenden Aufforderung, das Betreffende zu lassen oder zu thun, nicht Folge, so kann sofort der Ausspruch der gedrohten Strafe beantragt werden (Art. 640).

Anders verhält es sich bei Besitzüberweisungen, wo allerdings auch direkter Zwang möglich und unter Umständen sachgemäß, ja nothwendig ist. Räumt daher der Verpflichtete nicht freiwillig den Besitz ein, so ist nach Art. 861 gewaltsame Besitzentsetzung statthaft und kann die Anwendung dieses Artikels um so weniger Anstand finden, als das Gesetz, wo es von Vollstreckung spricht, im Zweifel auch die Vollstreckung von Vorsichtsverfügungen im Auge hat. Art. 624 und Abg. IV 218 Sp. 2 (Barth).

Betreibung der Hauptsache.

Art. 630. — Ist eine Vorsichtsverfügung vollstreckt worden, die sich auf eine Sache bezieht, welche bei Gericht noch nicht anhängig und wegen welcher auch ein Vollstreckungsverfahren noch nicht eingeleitet ist, so ist der Implorant verpflichtet, innerhalb acht Tagen von der Vollstreckung entweder die bezügliche Klage zu erheben oder das Vollstreckungsverfahren in der Hauptsache einleiten und dieses ohne Unterbrechung fortführen zu lassen.

Ist der Anspruch noch nicht fällig, so kann die Klage vorbehaltlich der Bestimmung des Art. 836 gleichwohl erhoben werden.

Die in Abs. 1 bezeichnete Frist beträgt fünfzehn Tage, wenn an einem Orte, der außerhalb des Bezirksgerichtssprengels, in welchem die Vorsichtsverfügung vollzogen wurde, liegt, die Klage zuzustellen oder das Vollstreckungsverfahren einzuleiten ist.

Sind Forderungen des Schuldners oder ihm gehörige bewegliche Sachen, die sich in den Händen eines Dritten befinden, mit Beschlag belegt worden, so läuft die in Abs. 1 und 3 bezeichnete Frist vom Tage der Beschlagnahme an.

In dem in Art. 625 vorgesehenen Falle muß die Zustellung der Klage oder des Befriedigungsgebots mit der daselbst vorgeschriebenen Mittheilung an die Gegenpartei verbunden werden.

Bei den von einem Gerichtsvorstande oder Einzelnrichter in Gemäßheit des Art. 620 Abs. 2 erlassenen einstweiligen Verfügungen läuft, wenn sie bereits vor der nach Art. 621 zu pflegenden Verhandlung vollstreckt worden sind, die in Abs. 1 und 3 bezeichnete Frist erst von dem Tage, an welchem die Verfügung in Gemäßheit des Art. 621 bestätigt wurde.

G. A. d. K. d. A. II S. 421. 448. 449. III S. 244—246. IV S. 119. 218. 219. 337. 338.
K. d. R. II S. 288. IV S. 68—70.

1) Provisorische Zustände dürfen nur möglichst kurz dauern; es ist daher natürlich, wenn das Gesetz an den Vortheil der Gestattung einer Vorsichtsverfügung zugleich die Verpflichtung knüpft, für schleunige Herbeiführung des definitiven Zustandes Sorge zu tragen.

Je nach der Sachlage ist diese Verpflichtung eine verschiedene.

2) Hat der Gläubiger bereits ein vollstreckbares Endurtheil oder eine sonstige sofort vollstreckbare Urkunde in Händen, so ist innerhalb 8 Tagen das wirkliche Vollstreckungsverfahren einzuleiten (Art. 842) und ohne Unterbrechung fortzuführen.

Die Nichterfüllung dieser Vorschriften zieht Aufhebung der Vorsichtsverfügung nach sich, jedoch mit folgender Unterscheidung. Wurde die zur Einleitung der Vollstreckung gegebene Frist versäumt, so muß auf Antrag die Aufhebung ausgesprochen werden, bis zur Stellung dieses Antrags kann jedoch das Versäumte nachgeholt werden (Art. 215 Abs. 2); hat hingegen eine Versäumung bloß bezüglich der Fortführung des Vollstreckungsverfahrens stattgefunden, so kann das Gericht auch nach Stellung des Antrages eine einmalige kurze Frist bewilligen (Art. 633).

Bei Versäumung dieser letzteren Frist ist auf Antrag die Aufhebung auszusprechen. Auf Fälle, wo sich in einem späteren Stadium des Verfahrens eine neue Verzögerung ergibt, möchten die Worte: „einmalige Frist" nicht zu beziehen sein, allerdings jedoch wird das Gericht nicht leicht Jemanden eine Frist bewilligen, der trotz früherer Warnung rückfällig geworden ist.

3) Die Vorschrift, daß das Verfahren ohne Unterbrechung fortzuführen sei, hat, soweit nöthig, auch für die seltenen Fälle zu gelten, wo im Laufe eines bereits eingeleiteten Vollstreckungsverfahrens, z. B. innerhalb der vom Befriedigungsgebote an laufenden Frist (Art. 845, 1039), eine Vorsichtsverfügung erwirkt wird.

4) Befindet sich der Gläubiger zwar nicht in der Lage, ein Vollstreckungsverfahren einleiten zu können, ist jedoch wegen der Sache ein Rechtsstreit anhängig, in erster oder zweiter Instanz oder am obersten Gerichtshofe, so steht es nach den Prinzipien unseres Prozesses in der Gewalt jeder Partei, die Sache zu betreiben, um die Entscheidung herbeizuführen; es war daher, soweit es sich bloß um Durchführung des Rechtsstreites handelt, eine Vorschrift nicht nöthig.

Es ist nun aber zu beachten, daß die Erwirkung eines Endurtheiles nicht immer die Vorsichtsverfügung als solche beseitigt, diese vielmehr häufig bestehen bleibt, bis sie durch die Vollstreckung gegenstandslos gemacht wird. Für diesen Fall trifft das Gesetz keine Vorsorge, nach seinem Geiste jedoch ist die Annahme gerechtfertigt, daß der Gläubiger verpflichtet sei, ohne Verzug das Vollstreckungsverfahren einzuleiten und fortzuführen. Auch hier die Einleitung an Einhaltung der achttägigen Frist zu knüpfen, möchte nicht angehen.

5) Ist weder der Fall zur Einleitung eines Vollstreckungsverfahrens gegeben, noch ein Rechtsstreit anhängig, so muß wegen des Anspruchs, zu dessen Sicherung die Vorsichtsverfügung erging, binnen acht Tagen Klage erhoben werden, und bei Versäumung dieser Frist gilt, was oben (Nr. 2) gesagt ist.

Diese Klage ist, abgesehen von einzelnen Ausnahmen (z. B. in Art. 1002, Einf.-Ges. Art. 99 Abs. 4), nicht auf Rechtfertigung oder Giltigerklärung der Maßregel zu richten, sondern bloß auf Zuspruch des Rechtes. Der Antrag auf Giltigerklärung, wie ihn der französische Prozeß in ähnlichen Fällen fordert, kann daher füglich wegbleiben.

6) Das Gesetz bestimmt, daß die bezügliche Klage auch erhoben werden dürfe, wenn der Anspruch noch nicht fällig sei, und zwar hat diese Bestimmung nicht bloß den Sinn, daß einstweilen nur das Bestehen der Forderung rechtskräftig hergestellt werde, die Vollstreckung aber verschoben bleibe, bis die Fälligkeit eintrete, vielmehr geht aus der Bezugnahme auf Art. 836 und aus den Verhandlungen (Abg. IV 217—219) zweifellos hervor, daß man einen vor dem Zeitpunkt der Fälligkeit eintretenden Vollzug im Auge hatte.

Die Vorsichtsverfügung überschreitet in diesem Falle das Gebiet der bloßen Sicherung, sie nimmt dem Schuldner wohlerworbene Rechte, und liegt hierin eine Mahnung für den Richter, überall, wo es sich um eine noch nicht fällige Forderung handelt, mit äußerster Vorsicht zu Werke zu gehen, und Vorsichtsverfügungen nur zu gestatten, wenn ähnliche Gründe vorliegen, wie im Falle des Art. 830. Da übrigens das Klagerecht in Fällen dieser Art seine Grundlage in der Vorsichtsverfügung findet, so fällt es hinweg, und ist die Klage als verfrüht abzuweisen, wenn diese Verfügung sich als nicht gerechtfertigt darstellt.

In Fällen, wo eine an sich vollstreckbare Urkunde vorliegt, die Forderung aber noch nicht fällig ist, und auch keiner der Ausnahmsfälle des Art. 830 vorliegt, ist die Klagerhebung nicht zu umgehen (Abg. III 246). Es bezweckt dieselbe bei dieser Sachlage zugleich Giltigerklärung der Vorsichtsverfügung, d. h. Entscheidung darüber, daß der Fall sofortiger Einklagbarkeit und mittelbar auch Vollstreckbarkeit des Anspruches gegeben sei.

7) Wurde die Vorsichtsverfügung wegen verschiedener Forderungen oder verschiedener Theile der nemlichen Forderung, welche in verschiedenen Stadien sich befinden, erlassen, so versteht sich von selbst, daß bezüglich jeden Theiles das ihm entsprechende Verfahren zu beobachten sei, und ist, falls die Versäumung bloß einen Theil betrifft, auch nur für diesen Theil die Aufhebung gerechtfertigt.

8) Die Frist von acht Tagen läuft von Vollstreckung der Vorsichtsverfügung an, und ist dieses Wort in dem durch die Art. 624—628 bestimmten Sinne zu nehmen.

Wenn das Gesetz (Art. 630 Abs. 4) erklärt, daß bei Beschlagnahmen von Forderungen und beweglichen Sachen in den Händen dritter Personen die Frist von der Beschlagnahme an laufe, so ist hierin wohl nur eine Erläuterung des Gesetzes, nicht aber eine Ausnahme zu erblicken. Vgl. Art. 832 Abs. 2.

Hat die Klagerhebung oder die Einleitung des Vollstreckungsverfahrens in einem anderen Bezirksgerichtssprengel zu geschehen, als demjenigen, wo der Akt der Vollstreckung, welcher die Frist in Lauf setzt, stattfindet, so erweitert sich dieselbe auf fünfzehn Tage.

Bei einstweiligen Vorsichtsverfügungen, welche nach Maßgabe von Art. 620 Abs. 2 der Bestätigung bedürfen, beginnt der Lauf der Frist nie vor dieser Bestätigung.

Aufhebung oder Abänderung.

Art. 631. — **Ist eine Vorsichtsverfügung ohne vorausgegangene Verhandlung erlassen worden und will der Imploral beantragen, daß die Verfügung aufgehoben oder abgeändert, oder daß er in Gemäßheit des Art. 617 der Haft entlassen, oder daß der Gegenpartei aufgegeben werde, innerhalb einer bestimmten Frist Sicherheit oder eine größere als die früher angeordnete Sicherheit zu leisten, oder daß die gemäß Art. 607 in den Händen des Gläubigers belassenen Beträge oder Sachen gerichtlich hinterlegt oder letztere an einen Sequester übergeben werden, so hat er diesen Antrag, wenn die Vorsichtsverfügung eine bei Gericht anhängige Sache betrifft oder mit einer solchen im Zusammenhange steht, in der für Zwischenstreite vorgeschriebenen Weise, andernfalls bei dem Gerichts- oder Senatsvorstande, der die Verfügung erlassen hat, anzubringen. Im letztern Falle erfolgt die Entscheidung auf Grund einer vor dem Gerichts- oder Senatsvorstande nach Maßgabe der Bestimmungen des Art. 621 zu pflegenden Verhandlung.**

Art. 632. — **Will der Imploral in den Fällen des Art. 615 die getroffene Vorsichtsverfügung durch eine seinerseits zu leistende Sicherheit beseitigen und ist der Betrag der letztern in der Vorsichtsverfügung nicht festgesetzt, so soll dieser Betrag auf Antrag des Imploraten, und zwar, wenn die Vorsichtsverfügung eine bei Gericht anhängige Sache betrifft oder mit einer solchen im Zusammenhange steht, in der für Zwischenstreite vorgesehenen Weise, andernfalls durch den Gerichts- oder Senatsvorstand, welcher die Verfügung erlassen hat, nach Vernehmung der Gegenpartei festgesetzt werden.**

Art. 633. — **Derjenige, gegen welchen eine Vorsichtsverfügung erlassen wurde, kann, gleichviel ob deren Erlassung eine Verhandlung vorausgegangen ist oder nicht, jederzeit Aufhebung der Verfügung in der in Art. 631 angegebenen Weise verlangen, wenn die Gegenpartei die ihr gesetzlich obliegenden Verpflichtungen nicht erfüllt hat, insbesondere wenn die angeordnete Sicherheit nicht in genügender Weise oder nicht in der festgesetzten Frist geleistet wurde, wenn im Falle des Art. 630 die Erhebung der Klage oder Einleitung des Vollstreckungsverfahrens nicht rechtzeitig stattgefunden hat oder letzteres nicht ohne Unterbrechung fortgeführt wurde, oder wenn die in Art. 620 und 625 Abs. 1 vorgeschriebenen Vorlagen, Zustellungen und Mittheilungen nicht in der gesetzlich bestimmten Weise und Frist erfolgt sind.**

Ist der Antrag auf Aufhebung der Vorsichtsverfügung nur darauf gestützt, daß die angeordnete Sicherheit nicht in genügender Weise geleistet oder daß ein eingeleitetes Vollstreckungsverfahren nicht ohne Unterbrechung fortgeführt wurde, so kann zur Ergänzung der Sicherheit, soweit eine solche als nöthig erkannt wird, beziehungsweise zur Fortführung des Vollstreckungsverfahrens eine einmalige kurze Frist bewilligt werden. In allen andern Fällen kann die Aufhebung der Vorsichtsverfügung, sobald der Antrag darauf gestellt ist, durch nachträgliche Erfüllung der betreffenden Verpflichtungen nicht verhindert werden.

Art. 634. — **Wer sich durch eine Entschließung beschwert erachtet, welche in Bezug auf eine Vorsichtsverfügung von dem Vorstande eines Collegialgerichts oder einem Senatsvorstande nach vorausgegangener Verhandlung erlassen worden ist, kann sich an das Gericht beziehungsweise den betreffenden Senat mit dem Antrage auf Aufhebung oder Abänderung wenden.**

Im Anwaltsprozesse ist diese Beschwerde in einem motivirten Antrage auszuführen, den der Beschwerdeführer, nachdem durch den Gerichts- oder Senatsvorstand auf dem ihm zu diesem Behufe vorzulegenden Antrage eine möglichst nahe Sitzung zur Verhandlung festgesetzt worden, der Gegenpartei mit Vorladung in diese Sitzung zustellen zu lassen hat.

Bei den Handelsgerichten hat der Beschwerdeführer die Gegenpartei in eine der nächsten Sitzungen durch Gerichtsvollzieherakt vorladen zu lassen, in welchem die Beschwerdepunkte und das Gesuch zu bezeichnen sind.

Die in Abs. 2 und 3 erwähnten Zustellungen müssen spätestens innerhalb fünfzehn Tagen, vom Tage der angefochtenen Entschließung an, erfolgen.

Art. 635. — Vorsichtsverfügungen können außerdem in der in Art. 631 angegebenen Weise auf Antrag einer jeden Partei jederzeit aufgehoben oder abgeändert werden, wenn sich die Umstände geändert haben, durch welche die Verfügung veranlaßt wurde.

Auch ohne solche Aenderung der Umstände kann das Gericht, bei welchem die Sache anhängig ist, die in derselben erlassenen Vorsichtsverfügungen auf Grund der vor ihm gepflogenen Verhandlungen und der daraus geschöpften Aufklärungen auf Antrag einer Partei jederzeit aufheben oder abändern.

Eine oberrichterlich erlassene oder bestätigte Vorsichtsverfügung kann von dem Untergerichte auf Grund der Bestimmung des Abs. 2 nicht aufgehoben werden.

Eine von einem Einzelnrichter, welcher nicht zugleich in der Hauptsache zuständig ist, in Gemäßheit des Art. 620 Abs. 2 erlassene einstweilige Verfügung kann von diesem nur solange aufgehoben oder abgeändert werden, als sie dem nach Art. 619 Abs. 2 zuständigen Gerichtsvorstande noch nicht vorgelegt worden ist.

Art. 636. — Wird eine Vorsichtsverfügung als ursprünglich nicht begründet aufgehoben, so ist derjenige, welcher sie erwirkt hat, zugleich in sämmtliche Kosten und zum Ersatze des dem Imploraten verursachten Schadens zu verurtheilen.

Wird eine Vorsichtsverfügung dem auf ihre Aufhebung oder Abänderung gestellten Antrage entgegen aufrecht erhalten, so ist der Antragsteller in die durch seinen Antrag verursachten Kosten zu verfällen.

In allen andern Fällen der Entscheidung über Aufhebung oder Abänderung von Vorsichtsverfügungen wird das Urtheil über Kosten- und Schadensersatz dem in der Hauptsache ergehenden Endurtheile vorbehalten.

G. M. d. K. d. A. II S. 416. 417. 421. 422. 448. 449. III S. 115. 116. IV S. 119. 337. 338.
K. d. R. II S. 288. IV S. 70. 71. 88—91.

1) Die Bestimmungen vorstehender Artikel, denen man nicht vorwerfen kann, allzu einfach zu sein, lassen sich der Hauptsache nach auf folgende Sätze zurückführen, nemlich:

1) Jede Vorsichtsverfügung ist widerruflich auf Grund besserer Aufklärung, welche die Verhandlung des betreffenden Rechtsstreits ergibt (Art. 635 Abs. 2).

2) Jede Vorsichtsverfügung kann aufgehoben oder geändert werden, wenn sich die Umstände ändern, welche sie veranlaßt haben (Art. 635 Abs. 1).

3) Jede Vorsichtsverfügung kann aufgehoben werden, wenn derjenige, zu dessen Gunsten sie erging, die ihm obliegenden Verpflichtungen nicht erfüllt (Art. 633).

4) Vorsichtsverfügungen können angefochten werden und zwar:

a) wenn sie auf einseitiges Ansuchen ergingen, durch Herbeiführung einer contradiktorischen Verhandlung, also durch eine Art von Einspruch (Art. 631);

b) wenn sie nach vorausgegangener Verhandlung durch ein einzelnes Gerichtsmitglied (Vorstand des Gerichts, Senats) erlassen wurden, durch Berufung an das Gericht (Art. 634).

Für die durch Urtheil getroffenen Verfügungen gelten die gewöhnlichen Rechtsmittel (Art. 638 Abs. 1).

a) Widerruf.

2) Das Gericht, bei welchem die Sache anhängig ist, kann, auf Antrag einer Partei, jede in dieser Sache erlassene Vorsichtsverfügung, auf Grund der vor ihm gepflogenen Verhandlung und der hieraus geschöpften Aufklärung, aufheben oder abändern, auch wenn die Umstände sich seitdem nicht geändert haben.

Jede Vorsichtsverfügung, mag sie vom Gerichte selbst im Laufe eines Rechtsstreites oder bloß von einem einzelnen Richter erlassen sein, ist daher ihrer Natur nach widerruflich, falls bei Verhandlung der Hauptsache der Richter die Ueberzeugung gewinnt, daß keine Gründe vorlagen, sie überhaupt oder in dem Umfange, wie geschehen, zu erlassen. Es ist hierbei ohne Belang, ob sie vom nemlichen Richter herrühre oder von einem anderen Richter, sowie zu welcher Zeit der Rechtsstreit anhängig geworden sei, vielmehr genügt es, daß zur Zeit ein Rechtsstreit anhängig ist und daß die Vorsichtsverfügung die anhängige Sache betrifft. Soweit Letzteres der Fall, ist die Zuständigkeit zum Widerrufe gegeben.

Diese Befugniß steht dem Richter auch zu in Fällen, wo Einspruch oder Berufung statthaft ist (Art. 638 Abs. 1), und obgleich diese Rechtsmittel versäumt wurden; jedoch ist es dem Unterrichter untersagt, eine vom Oberrichter erlassene oder bestätigte Vorsichtsverfügung ohne Aenderung der Umstände aufzuheben (Art. 635 Abs. 3). Dem Oberrichter selbst steht, falls die Hauptsache in irgend einer Weise an ihn gelangt, die Befugniß des Widerrufes ohne Zweifel zu. Vgl. Art. 705 Ziff. 3.

b) Aufhebung wegen Aenderung der Umstände.

3) Vorsichtsverfügungen können auf Antrag jeder Partei jederzeit aufgehoben oder abgeändert werden, wenn sich die Umstände ändern, durch welche sie veranlaßt wurden. Welches diese Umstände gewesen seien, ist aus den Entscheidungsgründen der Verfügung zu entnehmen.

Die Aenderung kann den Anspruch selbst betreffen, z. B. daß derselbe in Folge Eintritts einer Resolutivbedingung, einer Zahlung &c. ganz oder theilweise weggefallen ist, oder aber die Nothwendigkeit der Maßregel im Sinne von Art. 605.

4). Was Zuständigkeit und Verfahren betrifft, so ist zu unterscheiden, ob die Vorsichtsverfügung eine zur Zeit anhängige Sache betrifft oder nicht. Ersteren Falls ist in der für Zwischenstreite (Art. 483) vorgeschriebenen Weise zu verfahren, letzteren Falls hat derjenige Gerichts- oder Senatsvorstand (unter Umständen auch ein Einzelnrichter), welcher die Verfügung erlassen hat, zu entscheiden, wobei natürlich nur der jeweilige Vorstand gemeint und auf die Person des Richters kein Gewicht zu legen ist.

Das Verfahren ist das in Art. 621 vorgezeichnete. Der Gesuchsteller reicht seinen zu begründenden Antrag beim betreffenden Richter ein und dieser setzt Tagfahrt zur Verhandlung fest, zu welcher die Gegenpartei unter Zustellung der Tagfahrtsfestsetzung nebst Antrag vorzuladen ist. Vgl. Bemerk. zu Art. 621 Nr. 8.

Handelt es sich um eine einstweilige Vorsichtsverfügung, welche der Bestätigung bedarf (Art. 620 Abs. 2), so fällt die Zuständigkeit des Einzelnrichters zur Aenderung seiner Verfügung mit dem Augenblicke hinweg, wo diese dem Gerichtsvorstande zur Bestätigung vorgelegt wird (Art. 635 Abs. 4).

c) Aufhebung zur Strafe.

5) Dem Gläubiger, welcher eine Vorsichtsverfügung erwirkt hat, sind je nach den Umständen des Falles verschiedene Verpflichtungen (Sicherheitsleistung, Zustellungen, Klagerhebung &c.) auferlegt, oder können solche auferlegt werden, welche als Bedingungen anzusehen sind, unter denen ihm der betreffende Vortheil eingeräumt ist. Kommt derselbe diesen Verpflichtungen nicht nach, so erwächst aus dieser Versäumniß für den Schuldner das Recht, die Aufhebung der Maßregel zu verlangen.

Dieses Recht ist in der Regel erworben, d. h. die Aufhebung ist ohne Rücksicht auf nachträgliche Erfüllung auszusprechen, sobald der Antrag gestellt ist, während bis zur Antragstellung die Erfüllung noch wirksam geschehen kann (Art. 215 Abs. 2).

Das Gesetz sagt: „sobald der Antrag gestellt ist," und dies bedeutet für den Fall, wo der Weg des Zwischenstreites einzuhalten ist, ohne Zweifel: „sobald der motivirte Antrag zugestellt bezw. der Antrag in der Sitzung gestellt ist" (Art. 483 u. 510); für den Fall aber, wo nach Art. 619 Abs. 2 zu verfahren, können Zweifel entstehen, ob nicht die Eingabe des Antrages beim Gerichtsvorstande gemeint sei. Nach den allgemeinen Prinzipien treten Anträge ebenso wie Klagen der Gegenpartei gegenüber erst ins Leben durch die Zustellung, und dies ist gewiß auch der Sinn des gleichlautenden Art. 215 Abs. 2. Die Eingabe des Antrages beim Gerichtsvorstande bezweckt nur die Festsetzung einer Tagfahrt, ebenso wie die Einreichung der Klagschrift im Falle des Art. 259 Abs. 2, und ebenso wie dort die Klagschrift wird hier der Antrag erst Wirkung äußern von der Vorladung an. Ich nehme daher an, daß erst die Vorladung, welche zugleich Zustellung des Antrags enthält (s. oben Nr. 4), das Recht auf Aufhebung gebe.

6) Für zwei Fälle macht das Gesetz eine Ausnahme, nemlich: 1) wenn die angeordnete Sicherheitsleistung nicht in genügender Weise geschehen, und 2) wenn das Vollstreckungsverfahren nicht ohne Unterbrechung fortgeführt worden ist. In diesen Fällen kann zur Ergänzung der Sicherheit bezw. zur Fortführung der Vollstreckung eine einmalige Frist bewilligt werden. Vgl. im Uebrigen Bemerk. zu Art. 630 Nr. 2.

Hervorzuheben ist, daß der Fall, wo die Sicherheitsleistung nicht in der festgesetzten Frist geschah (Art. 631), von der Ausnahme nicht getroffen wird.

7) Was die einzelnen Verpflichtungen anbelangt, deren Versäumung die Aufhebung nach sich zieht, so zählt sie Art. 633 Abs. 1 auf; übrigens ist zu den betreffenden Artikeln das Nöthige bemerkt.

Bezüglich der Sicherheitsleistung hat das Gesetz jene Fälle im Auge, wo erst mit der Vollstreckung der Vorsichtsverfügung der Gegner Kenntniß davon erhält (Art. 609 Abs. 3), oder wo sie nachträglich angeordnet wird (Art. 631).

Zu erwähnen ist, daß die Aufhebung auch verlangt werden kann wegen Verpflichtungen, für welche keine bestimmte Frist gegeben ist, z. B. in den Fällen des Art. 620 Abs. 1 u. 2, wo unverzügliche Zustellung bezw. Vorlage angeordnet ist. Der Richter hat in solchen Fällen zu würdigen, ob im Sinne des Gesetzes und nach vorliegenden Umständen eine Versäumung anzunehmen sei oder nicht. Eine nachträgliche Erfüllung darf er auch hier nur berücksichtigen, wenn er annimmt, es habe zur Zeit der Antragstellung eine schuldhafte Versäumung noch nicht vorgelegen.

d) Anfechtung.

8) Vorsichtsverfügungen, welche ohne vorausgegangene Verhandlung erlassen wurden, kann der Schuldner anfechten, um ihre Aufhebung oder Aenderung zu bewirken, und zwar, je nachdem ein Rechtsstreit zur Zeit anhängig ist oder nicht, im Wege des Zwischenstreites oder in dem durch Art. 621 vorgezeichneten Verfahren vor dem Richter, welcher die Verfügung erlassen hat. S. oben Nr. 4.

Die Worte: „ohne vorausgegangene Verhandlung" begreifen auch den Fall, wo eine Verhandlung anberaumt, der dazu geladene Schuldner aber nicht erschienen war — Abg. II 422 (v. Weiß); sie bedeuten daher soviel als: „auf einseitiges Ansuchen."

Handelt es sich um eine vom Einzelrichter erlassene einstweilige Vorsichtsverfügung, welche der Bestätigung bedarf, so wird wohl auch hier die Zuständigkeit des Einzelrichters wegfallen, sobald die Vorlage zur Bestätigung erfolgt ist, nicht sowohl auf Grund des Art. 635 Abs. 4, als weil es in der Natur der Sache liegt.

9) Wer sich durch eine Entschließung beschwert erachtet, welche in Bezug auf eine Vorsichtsverfügung von dem Vorstande eines Collegialgerichts oder einem Senatsvorstande nach vorausgegangener Verhandlung erlassen worden ist, kann sich an's Gericht bezw. den Senat um Aufhebung oder Abänderung wenden (Art. 634 Abs. 1).

Dieses Recht der Berufung vom einzelnen Richter an's Collegium gilt für alle bezüglichen Entschließungen, mögen sie auf den ersten Antrag ergangen sein (Art. 619 Abs. 2), oder auf den Antrag, welcher Aufhebung oder Abänderung der Vorsichtsverfügung bezweckte (Art. 631), und jede Partei, welche sich beschwert erachtet, kann davon Gebrauch machen.

Fraglich könnte sein, ob Art. 634 auch für Entschließungen gelte, welche den Antrag auf Erlaß einer Vorsichtsverfügung abweisen.

Man kann sagen, es habe für diesen Fall Art. 638 Abs. 2 zu gelten, welcher die Erneuerung abgewiesener Anträge unbedingt zulasse, kann ferner darauf hinweisen, daß in den Art. 631 — 635 überall nur von Aufhebungen und Abänderungen von Vorsichtsverfügungen die Rede sei und insbesondere die Eingangsworte von Art. 635 andeuten, daß auch Art. 634 nichts Anderes meine.

Dem ist jedoch entgegenzuhalten der Wortlaut des Art. 634, welcher im Gegensatze zur Fassung der vorausgehenden und nachfolgenden Artikel von einer Entschließung spricht, welche in Bezug auf Vorsichtsverfügungen ergehen, sowie von Aufhebung und Aenderung dieser Entschließung. Was den Art. 638 Abs. 2 betrifft, so begründet es einen großen Unterschied, ob ich mich mit dem nemlichen Antrage an den nemlichen Richter wenden muß, oder ob ich bei einem andern Richter Recht suchen darf.

Wollte man hervorheben, es sei kein Grund gegeben, für fragliche Abweisungsbeschlüsse einen Rechtsweg zu geben, während bei jenen Abweisungsbeschlüssen, welche auf einseitiges Ansuchen erfolgen, ein solcher versagt sei, so wäre zu entgegnen, daß auch kein Grund vorliege, solche Beschlüsse, wenn sie nach Verhandlung in der Sitzung erfolgen, zu bevorzugen, der Richter nichtsdestoweniger aber die Abweisung dann für so wichtig hält, daß er selbständige Berufung dagegen zuläßt (Art. 683 Ziff. 2). Strenge Consequenz darf man überhaupt in dieser Materie nicht suchen.

Ich nehme daher an, daß Art. 634 auch auf abweisende Beschlüsse Anwendung finde, wie dies übrigens auch der Sinn der entsprechenden Bestimmung im Gesetzesentwurfe gewesen ist. Vgl. ursprüngl. Entwurf Art. 601 (S. 214) und späterer Entwurf Art. 23 (S. 462).

10) Voraussetzung der Zulässigkeit der Berufung an's Gericht ist, daß die angefochtene Entschließung nach vorausgegangener Verhandlung erlassen wurde, d. h. nicht auf einseitiges Ansuchen, mag auch ein Theil bei der Verhandlung nicht erschienen sein. Abg. II 422 (v. Weiß).

Für Vorsichtsverfügungen, welche der Einzelnrichter erlassen hat, ist dieser Rechtsweg nicht gegeben, wohl aber dann, wenn eine einstweilige Vorsichtsverfügung des Einzelnrichters vom Gerichtsvorstande bestätigt worden ist (Art. 620 Abs. 2).

11) Die Entscheidung erfolgt auf Grund einer Verhandlung in der Sitzung, also durch Urtheil, gegen welches die gewöhnlichen Rechtsmittel zulässig sind. Art. 638 Abs. 1 — Abg. II 422 (v. Weiß. Barth).

Soll das Bezirksgericht entscheiden, so ist vom betreffenden Anwalte ein motivirter Antrag zu fertigen und dem Vorstande des Gerichtes bezw. Senates vorzulegen, welcher eine möglichst nahe Sitzung zur Verhandlung festsetzt. Das Verfahren ist also dasselbe wie bei der Ladung auf kurze Frist (Art. 259) und haben die bezüglichen Prinzipien analoge Anwendung zu finden.

Soll das Handelsgericht entscheiden, so ist in eine der nächsten Sitzungen vorzuladen und sind in der Ladung die Beschwerdepunkte und das Gesuch zu bezeichnen. Von Einhaltung einer Vorladungsfrist spricht das Gesetz nicht, und es läßt sich daher annehmen, daß es die Dringlichkeit von Rechtswegen, ohne Verfügung des Richters, als gegeben erachtet und Art. 502 Abs. 2 maßgebend ist. Rathsam ist es übrigens, die dreitägige Ladungsfrist einzuhalten.

12) Die Vorladung muß innerhalb 15 Tagen vom Tage der angefochtenen Entschließung erfolgen. Ist diese Frist, welche jedoch durch Uebereinkunft der Parteien erstreckt werden kann, versäumt, so ist das Recht der Anfechtung verwirkt.

Dieselbe läuft von der Entschließung, also nicht deren Zustellung an, woraus zugleich hervorgeht, daß der Gerichtsvorstand verpflichtet ist, seine Entschließung den Parteien zu verkünden, denn eine stillschweigende Aushändigung an den Antragsteller kann unmöglich genügen, den Gegner in Verzug zu setzen.

e) Beseitigung durch Sicherheitsleistung.

13) Durch Art. 615 wird bestimmt, daß Vorsichtsverfügungen wegen Ansprüchen, die in Geld anschlagbar sind (s. Bemerk. zu Art. 607 Nr. 6), durch Sicherheitsleistung beseitigt werden können. Art. 632 trifft nun, jenen Artikel ergänzend, für den Fall Vorsorge, wo die Verfügung den Betrag der Ansprüche nicht festsetzt, indem er vorschreibt, es solle diese Festsetzung im Wege contradiktorischen Verfahrens nachträglich erwirkt werden können. Bezüglich des Verfahrens gilt, was oben Nr. 4 gesagt ist. Gegen die Festsetzung kann, falls sie vom Vorstande eines Collegialgerichtes ausging, Berufung an's Gericht ergriffen werden (Art. 634).

f) Kosten.

14) Nachdem Art. 623 bestimmt hat, wie es mit den Kosten zu halten sei, welche bei Bescheidung des ersten Antrags erwachsen sind, faßt Art. 636 den Zeitpunkt in's Auge, wo ein Antrag auf Aufhebung oder Abänderung einer Entschließung beschieden wird.

Wird eine Vorsichtsverfügung als ursprünglich nicht begründet aufgehoben, so ist derjenige, welcher sie erwirkt hat, in sämmtliche Kosten, namentlich auch die früher vorbehaltenen, sowie zum Schadensersatze zu verurtheilen.

Die Fassung dieser Gesetzesstelle erscheint insofern nicht ganz klar, als sie den Fall, wo die Aufhebung zur Strafe, also aus einem formellen Grunde erfolgt, auszunehmen scheint, obgleich sie denselben ohne Zweifel begreift. Nur jene Fälle, wo die Aufhebung wegen Aenderung der Umstände, Sicherheitsleistung, Nachweis der Mittellosigkeit (Art. 617) erfolgt, sollten ausgeschlossen sein. Abg. II 421 Sp. 2.

Auf den Fall einer theilweisen Aufhebung oder einer bloßen Abänderung findet fragliche Vorschrift keine Anwendung, jedenfalls nicht bezüglich der Kosten. Abg. II 421 Sp. 2. Vgl. im Uebrigen die Bemerk. zu Art. 623 Nr. 2.

15) In gleicher Weise ist sofort über die Kosten des Zwischenstreits zu erkennen, wenn der Antrag auf Aufhebung oder Abänderung vollständig abgewiesen wird.

In allen anderen Fällen ist die Entscheidung über Kosten und Schadenersatz dem Endurtheile in der Hauptsache vorzubehalten.

Gemeinsame Bestimmungen.

Art. 637. — **Alle in Bezug auf Vorsichtsverfügungen an Gerichts- oder Senatsvorstände oder an Einzelrichter zu richtenden Gesuche und Anträge können von der Partei selbst oder ihrem Bevollmächtigten, sowie von jedem bayerischen Advokaten und von dem mit der Vollstreckung beauftragten Gerichtsvollzieher mündlich oder schriftlich gestellt werden.**

Bei allen Verhandlungen, welche in Bezug auf Vorsichtsverfügungen vor Gerichts- oder Senatsvorständen oder Einzelrichtern stattfinden, können die Parteien ohne Anwälte in Person oder durch Bevollmächtigte mit oder ohne Beistand erscheinen. Auch können sie sich durch jeden bayerischen Advokaten oder durch den mit der Vollstreckung der Vorsichtsverfügung beauftragten Gerichtsvollzieher vertreten lassen.

Advokaten und Gerichtsvollzieher bedürfen in den in Abs. 1 und 2 bezeichneten Fällen keines Nachweises der Bevollmächtigung.

Wenn der Gesuchsteller sich nicht in dem Bezirksgerichtssprengel, wo er sein Gesuch stellt, befindet, so hat er im Gesuche einen innerhalb dieses Sprengels wohnhaften Zustellungsbevollmächtigten zu bezeichnen.

Die Verfügungen sind mit möglichster Beschleunigung zu erlassen und mit Entscheidungsgründen zu versehen. Vertagungen sollen nur im Falle dringender Nothwendigkeit stattfinden.

Die von Einzelrichtern, Gerichts- oder Senatsvorständen erlassenen Verfügungen sind dem Gesuchsteller in Urschrift auszuhändigen.

G. A. d. K. d. A. II S. 422. 423. 448. 449. IV S. 338. — K. d. R. II S. 288. IV S. 92.

1) Ueberall, wo über Anträge in Bezug auf Vorsichtsverfügungen vom Gerichte selbst zu entscheiden ist, gelten die gewöhnlichen Regeln des Verfahrens, und zwar je nach Umständen diejenigen des Anwaltsprozesses oder diejenigen des Parteiprozesses. Es gilt dies sowohl für die Fälle, wo ein Prozeß anhängig und in demselben auf dem Wege des Zwischenstreites zu verfahren ist, als für jene Fälle, wo gegen die Entschließung von Gerichts- oder Senatsvorständen Berufung an's Gericht ergriffen wird (Art. 634).

Insbesondere gelten auch bezüglich des Rechtes der Parteien, in Person zu handeln, und bezüglich ihrer Vertretung die allgemeinen Prinzipien.

In letzterer Beziehung ist die Fassung des Art. 637 Abs. 1 u. 2 insofern einer Mißdeutung fähig, als bei den getroffenen Ausnahmsbestimmungen allgemein von Verhandlungen vor Einzelnrichtern gesprochen wird, während es keinem Zweifel unterliegen kann, daß über einen Antrag auf Erlassung oder Abänderung einer Vorsichtsverfügung, welcher im Wege des Zwischenstreits vor den Einzelnrichter gebracht ist, nach den Prinzipien des gewöhnlichen Verfahrens zu entscheiden sei. Man dürfte z. B. das Verfahren vor dem Einzelngerichte nicht spalten und für die Anträge, welche sich auf die Vorsichtsverfügung beziehen, einen Advokaten oder Gerichtsvollzieher ohne Vollmacht zulassen, für die Anträge aber, welche die Hauptsache betreffen, eine solche verlangen. Es ist daher der Ausdruck „Einzelnrichter" im Gegensatze vom „Einzelngericht" zu nehmen.

2) Für die Fälle, wo die Vorsichtsverfügung Gegenstand selbständiger Verhandlung und zwar vor einem einzelnen Richter ist, also für das besondere Verfahren bei Provisorien, gibt das Gesetz Ausnahmsbestimmungen, welche bezwecken, dasselbe möglichst einfach zu machen und aller unnöthigen Formen zu entkleiden. Es sind dies folgende:

3) Alle Gesuche und Anträge können von der Partei selbst oder ihrem Bevollmächtigten sowohl mündlich als schriftlich gestellt werden. Ueber mündliche Gesuche ist kein Protokoll aufzunehmen, jedoch versteht es sich von selbst, daß der Richter bei der Begründung seiner Verfügung bezw. als Einleitung zur Tagfahrtsbestimmung das Vorbringen des Gesuchstellers kurz beurkunde.

4) Bei allen Verhandlungen können die Parteien in Person oder durch Bevollmächtigten erscheinen, mit oder ohne Beistand.

Aufnahme eines Protokolls findet auch hier nicht statt, jedoch erscheint es sachgemäß, daß in der Verfügung ähnlich wie in einem Urtheile das Wesentlichste constatirt werde, z. B. wie folgt:

In Gemäßheit vorstehender Tagfahrtsbestimmung erschienen heute vor mir —: 1) der Gesuchsteller A; 2) die Gegenpartei B.

A wiederholte den in vorstehendem Gesuche gestellten Antrag, B jedoch beantragte Abweisung desselben, eventuell Anordnung einer Sicherheitsleistung.

Nach Anhörung beider Parteien;

In Erwägung, daß 2c.

Daß das Verfahren geheim sein solle, ist nicht gesagt; nach allgemeinen Prinzipien wäre daher anzunehmen, daß fremden Personen der Zutritt nicht verwehrt werden könne. Vgl. Bemerk. zu Art. 621 Nr. 8. Uebrigens erscheint die Frage ohne praktische Bedeutung und zwar um so mehr, als Rechtsmittel ausgeschlossen sind (Art. 638 Abs. 2), also von einer Anfechtung auf Grund von Art. 788 Ziff. 5 nicht die Rede sein kann, und auch im Falle der Anfechtung der Entschließung auf Grund von Art. 631 oder 634 immer über das Materielle der Sache zu entscheiden sein wird.

5) Bei Stellung von Gesuchen sowohl als bei Verhandlungen bedürfen Advokaten, sowie diejenigen Gerichtsvollzieher, welche mit der Vollstreckung beauftragt sind, keines Nachweises der Bevollmächtigung, und ist hierbei zu bemerken, daß Gerichtsvollzieher in der Regel auch für die Thatsache, daß sie zur Vollstreckung beauftragt sind, einer Vollmacht nicht bedürfen. Ausnahmen enthalten die Art. 1041 Abs. 5 und Art. 1145 Abs. 1. Vgl. Bemerk. zu Art. 102 Nr. 2.

6) Wenn der Gesuchsteller sich nicht in dem Bezirksgerichtssprengel, wo er sein Gesuch stellt, befindet, so hat er im Gesuche einen dort wohnhaften Zustellungsbevollmächtigten zu bezeichnen, widrigenfalls sein Gesuch zurückzuweisen ist.

Es beruht diese Vorschrift auf gleichen Gründen, wie die Vorschrift in Art. 851, daß der betreibende Theil im Vollstreckungsverfahren einen Zustellungsbevollmächtigten aufzustellen habe, jedoch ist dort gesagt: „wenn sie nicht im Sprengel des Vollstreckungsgerichts wohnen," hier aber: „sich befinden." Der Zweck des Gesetzes ist offenbar in beiden Fällen derselbe, nemlich im Hinblicke auf die vorliegende Dringlichkeit, sowie darauf, daß die Parteien nicht durch Anwälte vertreten sind (Abg. II 449), der Gegenpartei die Zustellung für solche Fälle zu erleichtern, wo diese im Sprengel eines anderen Gerichtes stattfinden müßte. Unter Festhaltung dieses Gesichtspunktes erscheint Art. 851 besser gefaßt als Art. 637, denn die Thatsache, daß sich Jemand irgendwo befindet, gibt noch kein Recht, ihm dort Zustellungen zu machen, während umgekehrt die Zustellung giltig in der Wohnung geschehen kann, auch wenn sich der Requisit dort nicht befindet. Vgl. Bemerk. zu Art. 195 Nr. 2.

7) Das Gesetz spricht von „dem Gesuchsteller" und meint wohl hiermit diejenige Partei, welche das Gesuch um Erlassung einer Vorsichtsverfügung stellt, d. h. wie in Art. 851 den betreibenden Theil; es wäre also die Gegenpartei, welche Anträge auf Aufhebung oder Aenderung einer Vorsichtsverfügung stellt, nicht genöthigt, einen Zustellungsbevollmächtigten zu bezeichnen.

Uebrigens ist es doch nicht vollkommen sicher, ob das Gesetz nicht auch der Gegenpartei diese Pflicht auferlegen wollte, ob es nicht insbesondere bei Bestimmung der Frist des Art. 634 Abs. 4 von der Unterstellung, daß die betreffenden Zustellungen immer an einen Zustellungsbevollmächtigten gemacht werden könnten, ausgegangen sei, und ich würde daher anrathen, auch in den Gesuchen der Gegenpartei fragliche Förmlichkeit zu beobachten.

Die Bestellung eines Zustellungsbevollmächtigten wirkt für das ganze auf die in Frage stehende Vorsichtsverfügung bezügliche Verfahren; es können daher alle Zustellungen, welche die Anfechtung, Aufhebung und Aenderung der Vorsichtsverfügung, den Vollzug der Sicherheitsleistung 2c. nöthig machen, beim Zustellungsbevollmächtigten geschehen.

Ist im Gesuche ein Zustellungsbevollmächtigter nicht bestellt, so hat der Richter die Erlassung einer Vorsichtsverfügung zu verweigern, jedoch nur wenn er auf einseitiges Ansuchen zu verfügen hat, denn sonst wird wohl die Bestellung auch noch bei der Verhandlung nachgetragen werden können.

Verlegt der Gesuchsteller, welcher bei Einreichung des Gesuches im Gerichtssprengel wohnte, später seinen Wohnsitz in einen Ort außerhalb desselben, so wird er im Sinne des Gesetzes verpflichtet sein, nachträglich einen Zustellungsbevollmächtigten zu bezeichnen.

8) Die bezügliche Vorschrift gilt, wie der Ausdruck „Gesuchsteller" andeutet und aus den bei den Verhandlungen (Abg. II 449) bezeichneten Motiven hervorgeht, nicht für den Fall, wo ein Prozeß anhängig und die Vorsichtsverfügung im Wege des Zwischenstreits beantragt wird. Uebrigens ist doch zu bemerken, daß sie auch hier nicht ganz gegenstandslos erscheint, und zwar nicht bloß für den Parteiprozeß, sondern auch für den Anwaltsprozeß, insofern sich der Fall ereignen kann, daß zur Zeit, wo ein Prozeß nicht mehr anhängig ist, die Aufhebung der Verfügung wegen Nichterfüllung der Bedingungen oder wegen Aenderung der Umstände begehrt wird.

9) Alle bezüglichen Verfügungen, mögen sie abweisen oder bewilligen, mögen sie auf Antrag der einen oder der andern Partei ergehen, mögen sie vom Gerichte oder vom einzelnen Richter ausgehen, mag endlich eine Verhandlung vorausgegangen sein oder nicht, sind mit Entscheidungsgründen zu versehen.

Die bloße Festsetzung einer Tagfahrt (Art. 619 Abs. 2) ist übrigens als eine Verfügung in diesem Sinne nicht zu erachten.

Ueber die Form der Verfügungen bestehen keine Vorschriften; es ist also dem Richter überlassen, das Sachgemäße zu wählen. Bei Entschließungen des einzelnen Richters ist die Mitwirkung des Gerichtsschreibers, da das Gesetz sie nicht vorschreibt (vgl. Art. 562 u. 651), nicht nöthig; hieraus folgt jedoch nicht, daß der Gerichtsschreiber seine Aushilfe ablehnen könne, wenn der Richter sie beansprucht (Einf.-G. Art. 130).

Obgleich die Erlasse des Richters sofort vollstreckbar sind (Art. 639 Abs. 2), so ist es doch nicht nöthig, die Vollstreckbarkeitsklausel beizufügen, da das Gesetz es hier nicht, wie in ähnlichen Fällen (Art. 562 u. 651), verlangt, und erscheint dies um so zweifelloser, als eine bezügliche Vorschrift des ursprünglichen Entwurfs (Art. 588) beseitigt wurde. Die Vollstreckbarkeit liegt in der Natur der Verfügung.

10) Das Gesetz verfügt schließlich, daß die von Einzelnrichtern, Gerichts- oder Senatsvorständen erlassenen Verfügungen dem Gesuchsteller

in Urschrift auszuhändigen seien. Es gilt dies von allen Verfügungen, ob sie auf Antrag der einen oder der anderen Partei ergehen; jedoch ist auch hier wieder hervorzuheben, daß das Wort „Einzelnrichter" im Gegensatze von „Einzelngericht" zu nehmen ist (s. oben Nr. 1).

Hat eine contradiktorische Verhandlung stattgefunden, so ist es selbstverständlich Pflicht des Richters, den Laut seiner Entschließung beiden Parteien mündlich zu verkünden. Vgl. Bemerk. zu Art. 634 Nr. 11.

Art. 638. — **Bei den in Bezug auf Vorsichtsverfügungen von den Gerichten erlassenen Urtheilen finden hinsichtlich des Einspruchs und der Rechtsmittel die allgemeinen Bestimmungen Anwendung.**

Gegen die auf Vorsichtsverfügungen sich beziehenden Erlasse der Einzelnrichter, Gerichts- und Senatsvorstände finden unbeschadet der nach Art. 615—617, dann 631—635 zulässigen Anträge auf Aufhebung oder Abänderung weder Einspruch noch Rechtsmittel statt, die durch einen solchen Erlaß abgewiesenen Anträge können aber jederzeit erneuert werden.

G. A. d. K. d. A. II S. 423. 448. 449. IV S. 119. 338. — K. d. R. II S. 288. IV S. 71. 92.

1) Bei den in Bezug auf Vorsichtsverfügungen von den Gerichten erlassenen Urtheilen finden hinsichtlich des Einspruchs und der Rechtsmittel die allgemeinen Bestimmungen Anwendung. Dem entsprechend ist in Art. 683 Ziff. 2 verfügt, daß Urtheile, welche vorsorgliche Verfügungen treffen oder verweigern, hinsichtlich der Zulässigkeit der Berufung den Endurtheilen gleichstehen, und hieraus folgt weiter, daß auch das Rechtsmittel der Nichtigkeitsbeschwerde (Art. 788) statthaft ist.

Die Fälle, auf welche diese Bestimmung Anwendung findet, sind jene, wo über die betreffenden Anträge im Wege eines Zwischenstreites verhandelt und entschieden wird, sowie jene, wo von der Entscheidung eines Gerichts- oder Senatsvorstandes Berufung an das Gericht ergriffen wird (Art. 634).

Trotz dieser Zulässigkeit aller Rechtsmittel erlangen die fraglichen Urtheile, insofern sie eine Vorsichtsverfügung treffen, nie vollkommene Rechtskraft. Vgl. Bemerk. zu Art. 635 Nr. 2.

2) Gegen Erlasse einzelner Richter finden weder Einspruch noch Rechtsmittel statt; sie können nur unter den besonderen Voraussetzungen und auf den besonderen Wegen, wie es die Art. 615 — 617 sowie 631 — 635 bestimmen, angefochten und aufgehoben werden.

Anderseits erlangen hier auch abweisende Erlasse keine Rechtskraft und können die gestellten Anträge jederzeit erneuert werden, ein Prinzip, welches, da das Gesetz allgemein spricht, von den Anträgen beider Parteien zu gelten hat. Es erscheint diese Bestimmung etwas weitgehend, namentlich da nicht verlangt wird, daß irgend neue Behauptungen aufgestellt werden müssen, und wäre es vielleicht sachgemäß gewesen, zu verfügen, daß Gesuche, welche sich auf die nemlichen, bereits untersuchten und gewürdigten Thatsachen stützen, a limine abgewiesen werden dürfen. Thatsächlich wird von Wiederholung des nemlichen Gesuchs nur dann Erfolg zu hoffen sein, wenn ein anderer Richter zu erkennen hat.

Art. 639. — **Erlasse von Vorständen von Collegialgerichten, durch welche eine bereits vollstreckte Vorsichtsverfügung ganz oder theilweise aufgehoben wird, sind erst dann vollstreckbar, wenn die in Art. 634 Abs. 4 bestimmte Frist abgelaufen ist, ohne daß der Gegner einen Antrag auf Aufhebung oder Abänderung des Erlasses hat zustellen lassen.**

Im Uebrigen sind die auf Vorsichtsverfügungen sich beziehenden Erlasse der Einzelnrichter, Gerichts- oder Senatsvorstände kraft des Gesetzes sofort vollstreckbar und die Vollstreckung wird auch durch wirklich gestellte Anträge auf Aufhebung oder Abänderung nicht gehemmt.

Die von den Gerichten in Bezug auf Vorsichtsverfügungen erlassenen Urtheile können als ohne Rücksicht auf Einspruch oder Berufung vorläufig vollstreckbar erklärt werden und zwar, je nach den Umständen, gegen oder ohne Sicherheitsleistung. Ist dies nicht geschehen, so können Urtheile, durch welche eine bereits vollstreckte Vorsichtsverfügung ganz oder theilweise aufgehoben wird, wenn dagegen eine Frist zur Einlegung des Einspruchs oder der Berufung läuft, erst vollstreckt werden, nachdem die Frist abgelaufen ist, ohne daß der Einspruch oder die Berufung erhoben wurde.

G. A. d. K. d. A. II S. 423. 448. 449. III S. 91. 92. 103. IV S. 338. — K. d. R. II S. 288. IV S. 92.

1) Art. 639 regelt die Vollstreckung von Urtheilen und Erlassen, welche sich auf Vorsichtsverfügungen beziehen, und zwar sowohl derjenigen, welche solche treffen, als derjenigen, welche solche aufheben.

2) Alle Erlasse einzelner Richter sind in der Regel sofort vollstreckbar und kann deren Vollstreckung selbst durch wirklich gestellte Anträge auf Aufhebung oder Abänderung nicht gehemmt werden.

Nur für den Fall, wo durch Erlaß des Vorstandes eines Collegialgerichts eine bereits vollstreckte Vorsichtsverfügung ganz oder theilweise aufgehoben wird, ist eine Ausnahme dahin gemacht, daß dieser Aufhebungsbeschluß erst vollstreckbar wird, wenn die in Art. 634 Abs. 4 zur Berufung an's Gericht gegebene Frist von 15 Tagen unbenützt verstrichen ist. War die Vorsichtsverfügung noch nicht vollzogen, so tritt also diese Ausnahme nicht ein, und eine nachträgliche Vollstreckung wäre unstatthaft.

Es frägt sich, ob auch hier der durch die Art. 627 u. 628 für die Vollstreckung fixirte Zeitpunkt maßgebend sei? Ich würde annehmen, es sei das Gesetz so zu nehmen, als wenn es hieße: „soweit eine Vorsichtsverfügung bereits vollstreckt ist."

3) Die von den Gerichten, insbesondere auch den Einzelngerichten in Bezug auf Vorsichtsverfügungen erlassenen Urtheile können als ohne Rücksicht auf Einspruch oder Berufung vorläufig vollstreckbar erklärt werden, und zwar je nach Umständen mit oder ohne Sicherheitsleistung. Offenbar liegt keine Consequenz darin, daß Vorsichtsverfügungen, welche in Urtheilen getroffen werden, nur vorläufig vollstreckbar erklärt werden können, während die nemlichen Vorsichtsverfügungen, wenn sie der einzelne Richter erläßt, obgleich dessen Erlasse der Anfechtung unterliegen (Art. 634), es von Rechtswegen sind.

Ein Urtheil, welches eine bereits vollstreckte Vorsichtsverfügung ganz oder theilweise aufhebt, jedoch noch durch Einspruch oder Berufung angefochten werden kann, darf, falls es nicht vorläufig vollstreckbar erklärt ist, erst nach Ablauf der Fristen für diese Rechtsmittel vollstreckt werden. Bezüglich der Berufung erleiden daher die allgemeinen Prinzipien, gemäß deren erst die Einlegung des Rechtsmittels den Vollzug hemmt, hier eine Ausnahme.

Art. 640. — Die Bestimmungen der Art. 619, 621, 634 und 637—639 finden auch dann Anwendung, wenn wegen Nichtbefolgung einer Vorsichtsverfügung die Verurtheilung einer Partei in die nach Art. 614 angedrohte Strafe oder die Ermächtigung zu ihrer Verhaftung beantragt wird.

Die in einem solchen Falle erwachsenen Kosten sind, wenn der Antrag abgewiesen wird, dem Antragsteller, andernfalls der Gegenpartei zu überbürden.

Wird eine Geldstrafe verhängt, so ist zugleich eine höhere Geldstrafe für den Fall weiterer Nichtbefolgung der Vorsichtsverfügung anzudrohen, auch kann für diesen Fall die Verhaftung selbst dann angedroht werden, wenn sie früher nicht angedroht war.

G. A. d. K. d. A. II S. 423. 448. 449. — K. d. R. II S. 288.

1) Ist in einer Vorsichtsverfügung für den Fall der Nichtbefolgung derselben Geldstrafe oder Verhaftung gedroht (Art. 614), so kann, unbeschadet der sonstigen Vollstreckungsmittel, im Falle der Säumigkeit sofort der Ausspruch der gedrohten Geldstrafe oder die Anordnung der Verhaftung beantragt werden. Ueber diesen Antrag wird auf dem für den Erlaß gewöhnlicher Vorsichtsverfügungen vorgezeichneten Wege contradiktorisch entschieden.

Bis zum Erlasse des betreffenden Spruches kann durch nachträglichen Vollzug die Verhängung der in Frage stehenden Maßregeln, welche ja nur indirekte Zwangsmittel sein sollen, abgewendet werden; ist aber die Geldstrafe ausgesprochen, so kann, da hier eine ähnliche Bestimmung wie in Art. 432 Abs. 2 nicht gegeben ist, diese auch durch sofortige Erfüllung nicht beseitigt werden.

2) Die Beitreibung der ausgesprochenen Geldstrafe erfolgt nach Maßgabe des Art. 147, für die Verhaftung aber sind die Bestimmungen von Hauptst. XXXVII maßgebend, insbesondere Art. 1172. Die Freilassung kann verlangt werden, sobald der Vorsichtsverfügung Folge geleistet und hiermit der Zweck der Verhaftung erreicht ist.

Mit der Verhängung der Geldstrafe ist zugleich eine höhere Geldstrafe für den Fall weiterer Unfolgsamkeit anzudrohen und kann sogar nachträglich die Verhaftung verfügt werden.

Art. 641. — Vorsichtsverfügungen haben auf die Entscheidung der Sache, auf welche sie sich beziehen, und auf die mit dem Besitze verbundenen Rechte keinen Einfluß.

Die Zuständigkeit für die Hauptsache wird durch Vorsichtsverfügungen nur in dem in Art. 32 bezeichneten Falle begründet. G. A. d. K. d. A. II S. 423. 424. 448. 449. — K. d. R. II S. 288.

1) Es liegt in der Natur der Vorsichtsverfügungen, daß sie auf die endliche Entscheidung der Sache keinen Einfluß äußern. Dies gilt nicht bloß in solchen Richtungen, wo der Richter wegen

ungenügender Aufklärung nicht im Stande ist, sich ein sicheres Urtheil zu bilden, sondern auch dort, wo er sofort mit vollkommener Sachkenntniß entscheiden könnte, z. B. bei Würdigung von reinen Rechtsfragen.

Insbesondere ist auch die Ueberweisung des Besitzes ohne allen Einfluß für die Frage, wer Klage zu erheben und Beweis zu führen habe. In dieser Richtung ersetzt also die betreffende Vorsichtsverfügung die Klage auf Schutz im jüngsten Besitze nicht.

2) Die Zuständigkeit in der Hauptsache wird durch Vorsichtsverfügungen nur im Falle des Art. 32 begründet, welcher Artikel ein forum arresti anerkennt gegenüber von Ausländern sowie von Inländern ohne Wohnsitz.

Es folgt hieraus zugleich, daß die Wahl, welche bei Beantragung einer Vorsichtsverfügung unter verschiedenen zuständigen Gerichten getroffen wird, für die Anstellung der Hauptklage nicht bindend ist.

XXV. Hauptstück.

Verfahren bei gerichtlichen Entscheidungen auf einfache Vorstellungen.

Zulässigkeit.

Art. 642. — **Entscheidungen auf einfache Vorstellungen und ohne vorgängige mündliche Verhandlung können nur in den Fällen erlassen werden, für welche das Gesetz dies ausdrücklich bestimmt.**

Verfahren.

Art. 643. — **Wo das Gesetz eine solche Entscheidung zuläßt, richtet sich das Verfahren dabei, soweit nicht für einzelne Fälle etwas anderes vorgesehen ist, nach den Bestimmungen der Art. 644 — 654.** G. A. d. K. d. A. II S. 439. 440. 441. 449. 450. IV S. 110. — K. d. R. II S. 288. IV S. 71.

1) Prozeß- und Vollstreckungserfahren bieten eine Reihe von Fällen, in denen der Richter nicht auf Grund mündlicher Verhandlung, sondern auf schriftliches Gesuch hin verfügt oder entscheidet.

Im Entwurfe waren über das in solchen Fällen einzuhaltende Verfahren keine allgemeinen Vorschriften gegeben; bei den Berathungen fand man jedoch solche Vorschriften sachgemäß, und es wurde deßhalb das Hauptstück XXV eingefügt. Abg. II 439. Dasselbe faßt diejenigen Fälle zusammen, wo ohne vorgängige mündliche Verhandlung, auf bloßes Gesuch hin, vom Gerichte entschieden wird, und bezeichnet sie als solche, in welchen gerichtliche Entscheidung auf einfache Vorstellung ergeht. Diese Bezeichnung soll eine technische sein, d. h. es soll das vorgeschriebene Verfahren ausschließlich nur dort Anwendung finden, wo die Prozeßordnung den Ausdruck „einfache Vorstellung“ gebraucht, also nicht, wo sie bloß von „Gesuchen“ oder „Anträgen“ spricht. Man unterwarf dem entsprechend das ganze Gesetzbuch einer Durchsicht und setzte überall, wo man das betreffende Verfahren eingehalten wissen wollte, den technischen Ausdruck ein; so in den Art. 34, 45, 54, 116, 292, 347, 392, 656, 659, 664, 769, 864, 881, 892, 940, 1016, 1048, 1049, 1052, 1078, 1121, 1126, 1141, 1189, 1194, 1209 u. 1314 der Prozeßordnung und in den Art. 35 u. 97 des Einf-Ges. zur P. O. Vgl. auch Art. 743 u. 758.

2) Es ist erklärlich, daß bei einer so umfangreichen, alle Theile des Gesetzbuches umfassenden Berichtigung leicht hie und da ein Fall, auf welchen nach dem Geiste des Gesetzes das betreffende Verfahren Anwendung zu finden hätte, übersehen werden konnte, und es sind in diesem Commentare bereits zwei Fälle bezeichnet, bei denen ein solches Uebersehen anzunehmen sein möchte. Bemerk. zu Art. 213 Nr. 4 und zu Art. 538 Nr. 4.

Nimmt man Anstand, in Fällen dieser Art die Bestimmungen des Hauptst. XXV geradezu anzuwenden, weil der technische Ausdruck fehlt, so mangelt eine maßgebende Vorschrift, weil das für die mündlichen Verhandlungen vorgezeichnete Verfahren offenbar nicht Platz greifen kann. Es würde also die Sachlage die nemliche, als wenn die Vorschriften des Hauptst. XXV nicht beständen, d. h. man käme darauf, daß dasjenige zu geschehen habe, was naturgemäß ist und dem vermuthbaren Willen des Gesetzgebers entspricht. Auf diesem Wege würde man so ziemlich zum nemlichen Resultate gelangen, wie bei direkter Anwendung des Hauptst. XXV. Die einzige wesentlichere Abweichung bestünde wohl darin, daß die Mitwirkung des Staatsanwaltes wegfiele.

3) Die Nothwendigkeit, bei Mangel besonderer Vorschriften, sich bloß durch die Natur der Sache leiten zu lassen, tritt übrigens auch bei jenen Gesuchen ein, welche nicht an das ganze Gericht, sondern an einen einzelnen Richter

(Gerichtsvorstand, beauftragten Richter) gerichtet sind. Das Gesetz enthält bei Gesuchen dieser Art manchmal eingehendere Vorschriften, z. B. in Art. 555; in den meisten Fällen aber fehlen solche, wie z. B. bei den Gesuchen um Festsetzung von Tagfahrten zu Beweisaufnahmen (Art. 406, 438 etc.) oder bei Gesuchen um Fristabkürzung (Art. 259, 502).

Es kann wohl keinem Zweifel unterliegen, daß in allen Fällen dieser Art im Sinne des Gesetzes möglichst einfach zu verfahren sei und nur das zu geschehen habe, was sich als nöthig und naturgemäß ergibt. Offenbar verlangt das Gesetz bei solch einfachen Verfügungen, die zudem meist dringlich sind, weder eine Mitwirkung des Gerichtsschreibers noch eine Ausfertigung der Verfügung; es läßt sich daher als allgemeiner Grundsatz aufstellen, daß bei allen Gesuchen der bezeichneten Art die Beschlüsse vom Richter sofort auf das Gesuch selbst niedergeschrieben und dem Gesuchsteller in Urschrift ausgehändigt werden. So wird es auch im französischen Prozesse gehalten und zwar gleichfalls ohne besondere Vorschrift des Gesetzes, weil es eben selbstverständlich erschien.

4) Für die Pfalz ergibt sich die besondere Frage, wie es mit jenen, die freiwillige Gerichtsbarkeit betreffenden Gesuchen zu halten sei, welche man seither in öffentlicher Sitzung zu erledigen pflegte, wie z. B. die Gesuche um Rektifikation von Civilstandsregistern, um Ernennung von Curatoren für Abwesende und andere. Vgl. Bemerk. zu Art. 160 Nr. 10.

Die bezüglichen Bestimmungen und Prinzipien des französischen Rechtes werden insofern von der Prozeßordnung nicht berührt, als es sich um Akte der freiwilligen Gerichtsbarkeit handelt, sind übrigens für eine Reihe von Fällen durch das Einführungsgesetz (Art. 83—97) ausdrücklich für fortgeltend erklärt. Statt nun in allgemeiner Weise zu bestimmen, daß Entscheidungen auf Gesuche in Fällen der nichtstreitigen Rechtspflege in der Pfalz fortan nach dem in Hauptst. XXV vorgezeichneten Verfahren zu erfolgen haben, wie es sachgemäß gewesen wäre, hat das Einführungsgesetz in kasuistischer Weise bald gesagt, es sei auf einfache Vorstellung hin zu entscheiden, bald, es sei in geheimer Sitzung zu entscheiden, bald, es seien, soweit sich das Verfahren nach allgemeinen Prozeßvorschriften zu richten habe, die Vorschriften der neuen Prozeßordnung anzuwenden.

Aus diesen Bestimmungen des Einführungsgesetzes läßt sich ein Prinzip in sicherer Weise nicht ableiten; allein unter Beihilfe der Anschauungen, welche sich im französischen Rechte selbst in neuerer Zeit geltend machten, glaube ich mit Grund als Prinzip aufstellen zu dürfen, daß alle Gesuche in Fällen der nichtstreitigen Rechtspflege in geheimer Sitzung zu erledigen seien.

5) Früher galt in Frankreich die, insbesondere auch bei mehreren Gerichten der Pfalz bis zur jüngsten Zeit festgehaltene Ansicht, daß alle Verhandlungen und Entscheidungen der Gerichte, welche nicht durch eine ausdrückliche Bestimmung des Gesetzes in die Rathskammer verwiesen seien, in öffentlicher Sitzung stattzufinden hätten. Man glaubte auch auf diesem Gebiete das Prinzip der Oeffentlichkeit als Regel aufrecht halten zu müssen.

In neuerer Zeit hat sich nun aber das entgegengesetzte Prinzip Bahn gebrochen, d. h. man nimmt an, daß Verhandlungen und Entscheidungen der Gerichte, welche die nichtstreitige Rechtspflege (die juridiction gracieuse) betreffen, ihrer Natur nach in der Rathskammer zu erledigen seien, und Ausnahmen hievon nur eintreten, wo das Gesetz ausdrücklich in die Sitzung verweise.

Diese Ansicht, welcher schon Favard de Langlade huldigte, ist sehr entschieden vertreten von Bertin (chambre du conseil), sowie von de Belleyme in der Vorrede zu diesem Werke; sie fand auch in der Praxis allgemeine Anerkennung. Journal du Pal. suppl. (chambre du conseil) No. 14 ff. Bertin führt als Fälle, welche sich zur Entscheidung in der Rathskammer eignen, unter anderen auf: rectifications des actes de l'etat civil — absents — envoie en possesion de succession — administrateurs judiciaires etc.

Dieses neuere Prinzip wird jetzt in der Pfalz um so mehr das maßgebende sein müssen, als es dem Geiste der neuen Prozeßordnung vollkommen entspricht.

Uebrigens folgt hieraus nicht, daß in den fraglichen Fällen nunmehr alle Bestimmungen des Hauptstückes XXV zur Anwendung zu kommen hätten, vielmehr behaupten die Prinzipien des französischen Rechtes, soweit sie eine Abweichung nothwendig bedingen, ihre Geltung. So wird z. B. die Beschränkung der Befugnisse des Staatsanwaltes, wie sie Art. 646 Abs. 2 ausspricht, hier keine Anwendung finden.

1) bei den Bezirks- und Appellationsgerichten und dem obersten Gerichtshofe;

Art. 644. — **Bei den Bezirks- und Appellationsgerichten, sowie bei dem obersten Gerichtshofe müssen die Vorstellungen, auf welche eine gerichtliche Entscheidung erfolgen soll, auf der Gerichtsschreiberei eingereicht werden.**

Sie müssen von einem bei dem betreffenden Gerichte zur Anwaltspraxis berechtigten Advokaten gefertigt sein, und außer der Bezeichnung des Gesuchstellers nach Vor- und Familiennamen, Stand oder Gewerbe und Wohnort, sowie des angerufenen Gerichts, eine gedrängte, aber vollständige und deutliche Darstellung der das Gesuch begründenden thatsächlichen Verhältnisse, den Rechtsgrund, auf welchen das Gesuch gestützt wird, und ein bestimmtes Begehren enthalten.

Wo das Gesetz gestattet, die Vorstellung vor dem Gerichtsschreiber zu Protokoll zu geben, kann dies auch von der Partei selbst oder einem Bevollmächtigten derselben geschehen.

Sind zur Begründung des Gesuchs Urkunden erforderlich, so sind sie in Urschrift oder in beglaubigter Abschrift beizulegen. In der Vorstellung kann sowohl zur Bezeichnung der Gesuchsteller, wenn deren mehrere sind, als auch bei Darstellung der thatsächlichen Verhältnisse auf diese Urkunden soweit Bezug genommen werden, als sich aus denselben das Erforderliche ergibt.

G. A. d. K. d. A. II S. 439. 440. 442. 449. 450. IV S. 119. — K. d. R. II S. 288. IV S. 71.

1) Bei jenen Gerichten, für welche der Anwaltsprozeß vorgeschrieben ist, besteht auch für einfache Vorstellungen der Anwaltszwang, und zwar unbedingt und ohne Unterschied, ob in der Sache ein Prozeß zur Zeit anhängig ist, oder nicht. In gleicher Weise gilt auch das Prinzip der Lokalisirung der Anwälte für die Gerichte, bei denen es besteht.

Eine Ausnahme besteht nur für jene Fälle, wo ausdrücklich gesagt ist, die Partei dürfe das Gesuch persönlich fertigen, z. B. in Art. 952, 1116, 1126, sowie dort, wo das Gesetz gestattet, daß die Vorstellung vor dem Gerichtsschreiber zu Protokoll erklärt werde, wie z. B. in Art. 45, 1016, 1049, 1120, 1141. In letzteren Fällen kann die Erklärung durch die Partei selbst oder ihren Bevollmächtigten erfolgen (Art. 644 Abs. 3).

Der Gerichtsvollzieher, welcher in Fällen dieser Art als Bevollmächtigter auftritt, muß, falls nicht eine Ausnahme gemacht ist, wie z. B. in Art. 952, Vollmacht vorlegen, da die Präsumtivvollmacht, welche er kraft Gesetzes für seine amtliche Thätigkeit hat, hier nicht wirkt. Vgl. Art. 637 Abs. 3 und Bemerk. dazu.

2) Die Vorstellungen sind auf der Gerichtsschreiberei einzureichen. Sie müssen die Person des Gesuchstellers in der Weise, wie bereits in Art. 165 vorgeschrieben, bezeichnen, müssen ferner gleich Klagschriften (Art. 225) ein bestimmtes Begehren enthalten und dasselbe thatsächlich und rechtlich begründen.

Eine Nichtigkeit folgt aus der Nichtbeobachtung dieser Vorschriften nur, sofern Art. 218 Abs. 2 anwendbar erscheint. Bei unwesentlicheren Mängeln wird der Staatsanwalt oder Berichterstatter im Sinne des Art. 648 Erläuterungen oder Ergänzungen veranlassen.

3) Stützt sich das Gesuch nicht auf Thatsachen, welche notorisch sind (Art. 320), so sind zu dessen Begründung Urkunden beizulegen und zwar entweder in Urschrift oder in beglaubigter Abschrift.

Der Umfang dieser Verpflichtung richtet sich natürlich nach den Anforderungen, welche im gegebenen Falle das Gesetz stellt; in der Regel werden Bescheinigungen genügen. Vgl. Einleitung zu Hauptst. IX.

Um unnöthige Schreibereien zu vermeiden, fand der Gesetzgeber geeignet, ausdrücklich zu bestimmen, daß in der Vorstellung auf den Inhalt der Urkunden Bezug genommen werden dürfe, und zwar selbst zur Bezeichnung der Gesuchsteller, falls deren mehrere seien.

In dieser letzteren Beziehung ist jedoch zu beachten, daß die Urkunden nicht bestimmt sind, immer mit der Vorstellung und der auf dieselbe zu setzenden gerichtlichen Entscheidung verbunden zu bleiben. Wo daher die Vorstellung selbst eine vollständige Bezeichnung der Gesuchsteller nicht enthält, muß eine solche jedenfalls in die Entscheidung aufgenommen werden, weil aus derselben sicher hervorgehen muß, zu wessen Gunsten sie erlassen sei.

Art. 645. — **Der Gerichtsschreiber legt die Vorstellung, nachdem er, soferne sie schriftlich eingereicht wurde, den Tag des Einlaufs darauf bemerkt hat, dem Gerichtsvorstande vor.**

Der Gerichtsvorstand ernennt auf der Vorstellung einen Berichterstatter und verordnet, daß sie durch den Gerichtsschreiber dem Staatsanwalte zur etwaigen Antragstellung mitgetheilt werde. Der Gerichtsvorstand kann die Berichterstattung auch selbst übernehmen.

Art. 646. — **Der Staatsanwalt hat, wenn er nichts zu erinnern findet, dies auf der Vorstellung kurz zu bemerken, andernfalls einen schriftlichen Antrag zu stellen, der, soweit erforderlich, zu begründen und unter die Verfügung des Gerichtsvorstands zu setzen ist.**

Wo das Gesetz die Vernehmung des Staatsanwalts nicht besonders vorschreibt und es sich auch nicht um einen der in Art. 160 bezeichneten Gegenstände handelt, darf der Staatsanwalt einen Antrag nur insoweit stellen, als er das im gegenwärtigen Hauptstücke vorgesehene Verfahren für unstatthaft hält.

Art. 647. — **Sobald der Staatsanwalt die Akten zurückgestellt hat, sind sie durch den Gerichtsschreiber dem ernannten Berichterstatter zu übergeben.**

Art. 648. — **Der Staatsanwalt sowohl als der Berichterstatter kann den Gesuchsteller von kurzer Hand veranlassen, Aufklärungen und Urkunden, welche noch nöthig erscheinen, nachträglich beizubringen. Derlei Nachträge sind ohne weitere Förmlichkeit der Vorstellung beizufügen.**

G. A. d. K. d. A. II S. 440. 442—444. 449. 450. IV S. 119. 120. 338—340.
K. d. R. II S. 288. 289. IV S. 70—72.

1) Das Verfahren, welches hier zur Vorbereitung der gerichtlichen Entscheidung vorgezeichnet wird, und zwar zunächst für diejenigen Gerichte, an welchen Staatsanwälte bestehen, ist der Natur der Sache entsprechend sehr einfach. Es ist im Wesen dasjenige, wie es bis jetzt in der Pfalz geübt wurde.

Der Gerichtsschreiber legt die schriftlich eingereichte Vorstellung oder das von ihm aufgenommene Protokoll dem Gerichtsvorstande vor, welcher einen Berichterstatter ernennt und anordnet, daß die Vorstellung dem Staatsanwalte zur Antragstellung mitgetheilt werde. Der Gerichtsvorstand darf auch selbst die Berichterstattung übernehmen, d. h. sich selbst als Berichterstatter bezeichnen, wozu in sehr dringlichen Fällen Anlaß gegeben sein wird.

2) Unmittelbar unter diese Verfügung setzt der Staatsanwalt seinen Antrag, und ist zu beachten, daß das Gesetz in Art. 646 Abs. 1 vorschreibt, der Staatsanwalt habe entweder zu bemerken, daß er nichts zu erinnern finde, oder Antrag zu stellen.

Wo es sich nicht um jene Fälle handelt, in welchen durch Art. 160 dem Staatsanwalte das Recht zur Antragstellung eingeräumt ist, oder wo nicht für die in Frage stehende Vorstellung die Vernehmung des Staatsanwaltes besonders vorgeschrieben ist (z. B. in Art. 48, 672), darf derselbe einen Antrag nur soweit stellen, als es die Frage betrifft, ob der Weg der einfachen Vorstellung überhaupt statthaft sei oder nicht.

Diese Beschränkung des Antragrechtes, einer übergroßen, für den Richterstand fast beleidigenden Furcht vor dem Einflusse der Staatsanwaltschaft entsprungen, hat wenig praktischen Werth, denn sollte der Staatsanwalt auch hie und da einmal aus Versehen einen weitergehenden Antrag stellen, so könnte hieraus eine Nichtigkeit nicht gefolgert werden. Ein solcher Antrag wäre nur als nicht genommen zu betrachten, wie dies im Grunde jeder Antrag des Staatsanwaltes ist, wenn das Gericht dessen Ansicht nicht theilt. Selbst wenn der Staatsanwalt soweit gegangen wäre, die Nachbringung von Aufklärungen oder Urkunden zu veranlassen, könnte hieraus kein Nachtheil erwachsen, im Gegentheile wären solche Nachträge, wenn auch nur als zufällige Ergebnisse, vom Gerichte zu berücksichtigen.

3) Nachdem der Staatsanwalt die Akten zurückgegeben, sind dieselben sofort dem Berichterstatter einzuhändigen, welchem selbstverständlich die Pflicht obliegt, so schnell als möglich für Erledigung der Sache und Anberaumung einer Sitzung zur Berichterstattung zu sorgen. In der Pfalz pflegte bis jetzt der Gerichtsvorstand sofort den Tag der Berichterstattung zu bezeichnen und denselben, wenn die Zeit ausnahmsweise nicht hinreichte, durch einfache Correktur zu verlegen — ein Verfahren, welches einer geordneten raschen Erledigung sehr förderlich ist und sich zur Nachahmung empfohlen hätte.

Der Staatsanwalt sowohl als der Berichterstatter können den Gesuchsteller von kurzer Hand veranlassen, Aufklärungen oder Urkunden nachzubringen. Es genügt, wenn der Beamte den betreffenden Anwalt, sei es mündlich, sei es durch Zusenden einer Notiz, von seinen Wünschen in Kenntniß setzt. In der Regel wird die Vermittlung des Gerichtsschreibers beansprucht werden.

Art. 649. — **Die Entscheidung erfolgt auf Vortrag des Berichterstatters in geheimer Sitzung und zwar bei Gerichten, welche in Senate abgetheilt sind, bei dem Senate, dem der Berichterstatter angehört.**

Die Sitzung wird auf mündliche Anzeige des Berichterstatters durch den Vorstand ohne Förmlichkeit anberaumt.

Das Gericht kann den Staatsanwalt einladen, der Sitzung beizuwohnen, wenn es dessen Anwesenheit für zweckmäßig hält.

Art. 650. — Hält das Gericht weitere Aufklärungen oder Urkunden für nothwendig, so kann es durch einen Beschluß dem Gesuchsteller die bezügliche Auflage machen.

Art. 651. — Alle Beschlüsse und Entscheidungen in diesem Verfahren sind mit Entscheidungsgründen zu versehen. Sie werden auf die Vorstellung gesetzt und von dem Vorsitzenden und Gerichtsschreiber unter Beidrückung des Gerichtssiegels unterzeichnet, wobei eintretenden Falls die Bestimmungen des Art. 280 Abs. 6 zur Anwendung kommen.

Die Beschlüsse und Entscheidungen werden dem Gesuchsteller auf dessen Anmelden mit den vorgelegten Urkunden in Urschrift ausgehändigt. Schreibt das Gesetz in einem Falle vor, daß die Entscheidung auf der Gerichtsschreiberei hinterlegt bleiben solle, so finden bezüglich der den Betheiligten zu ertheilenden Ausfertigungen die Bestimmungen der Art. 288 — 292 analoge Anwendung.

Entscheidungen, welche in Urschrift auszuhändigen sind, erhalten, wenn nach ihrem Inhalte darauf ein Vollstreckungsverfahren eingeleitet werden kann, die Ueberschrift: „Im Namen Seiner Majestät des Königs von Bayern" und am Schlusse den Beisatz: „Vorstehende Entschließung wird hiemit für vollstreckbar erklärt."

Art. 652. — Der Gerichtsschreiber hat ein Register zu führen, in welchem die Vorstellungen und die darauf erfolgten Beschlüsse und Entscheidungen vorgemerkt werden und die Gesuchsteller den Empfang der ihnen ausgehändigten Akten zu bescheinigen haben.

G. A. d. K. d. A. II S. 440. 444. 445. 449. 450. IV S. 120. 340. — K. d. R. II. S. 289. 290. IV S. 72.

1) Sobald der Berichterstatter die Sache als reif zum Vortrage erachtet, hat er dies mündlich dem Gerichtsvorstande anzuzeigen und die Anberaumung einer Sitzung zu veranlassen, welche ohne Förmlichkeit, d. h. gleichfalls mündlich, erfolgt.

Offenbar ist es auch erlaubt, ohne vorausgängige Festsetzung einer Sitzung Bericht zu erstatten, wenn das Gericht gerade versammelt ist und sich Zeit dazu ergibt, und es wird wohl dieses Verfahren in der Praxis das gewöhnliche werden. Unbedeutendere Sachen wird man unmittelbar vor oder nach der Sitzung erledigen, je nachdem gerade freie Zeit sich ergibt; bei bedeutenderen Sachen aber wird man die Zeit wählen, wo das Gericht zur Berathung der zu fällenden Urtheile sich in seinem Berathungszimmer versammelt. Vgl. Bemerk. zu Art. 269 ff. Nr. 3.

2) Die Entscheidung erfolgt auf Vortrag des Berichterstatters in geheimer Sitzung und zwar in demjenigen Senate, welchem der Berichterstatter angehört. Ist also der Berichterstatter aushilfsweise in einem anderen Senate verwendet, so darf er dort nicht vortragen.

Hält das Gericht weitere Aufklärungen oder Urkunden für nothwendig, so erläßt es einen Beschluß, in welchem dem Gesuchsteller die bezügliche Auflage gemacht wird. Dieser Beschluß ist nach Art. 651 mit Entscheidungsgründen zu versehen und dem Gesuchsteller in Urschrift auszuhändigen; Letzteres allerdings nur, um später mit den Ergänzungen wieder in Vorlage gebracht zu werden.

In der Regel wird man viel einfacher verfahren können; es wird nemlich genügen, die Entscheidung vorerst auszusetzen und dem Berichterstatter die Erhebungen nach Maßgabe von Art. 648 zu überlassen.

3) Alle Beschlüsse und Entscheidungen, welche im Verfahren auf einfache Vorstellung ergehen, sind mit Entscheidungsgründen zu versehen.

Sie werden, an den Antrag des Staatsanwaltes anschließend, auf die Vorstellung bezw. ein dieser angefügtes Papier gesetzt, und gleich den Urtheilen (Art. 280 Abs. 5 u. 6) vom Vorsitzenden und Gerichtsschreiber bezw. den Stellvertretern derselben unterzeichnet. Zugleich ist mit Rücksicht darauf, daß alle derartigen, oft nicht unwichtigen Entscheidungen in Urschrift hinausgegeben werden, die Beidrückung des Gerichtssiegels vorgeschrieben.

Kann nach dem Inhalte der Entscheidung auf Grund derselben ein Vollstreckungsverfahren eingeleitet werden, wie z. B. im Falle der Art. 1015 u. 1016 und wohl auch der Art. 1140 und 1141, so ist die gewöhnliche Vollstreckungsklausel beizufügen. Der Gesetzgeber war hier, wie in Art. 562, veranlaßt, dies besonders vorzuschreiben, da die Bestimmung des Art. 882 nur Entscheidungen (d. h. Urtheile in öffentlicher und Erkenntnisse in geheimer Sitzung), welche ausgefertigt werden, im Auge hat.

4) Wo in einzelnen Fällen das Gesetz verfügt, es solle die Entschließung des Gerichts nicht in Urschrift abgegeben werden, sondern bei Gericht hinterlegt bleiben, wie dies in Art. 656, 659, 751, 940, 1126 ausdrücklich, in Art. 35 aber stillschweigend geschieht, so hat der Gesuchsteller sich Ausfertigung ertheilen zu lassen, und finden überhaupt die Bestimmungen der Art. 288 bis 292 Anwendung.

Diese Ausfertigung trifft zwar zunächst nur die Entscheidung mit ihren Gründen, allein sofern die Entscheidung auf die vorausgehende Vorstellung Bezug nimmt, bildet diese einen Bestandtheil derselben, gleichsam den Sachverhalt, und ist mit auszufertigen. Jedenfalls muß die Bezeichnung der Personen der Gesuchsteller vollständig in der Ausfertigung enthalten sein und wäre dieselbe, soweit nöthig, aus der Vorstellung zu ergänzen.

5) Das Hauptverzeichniß, welches Art. 236 vorsieht, ist nur für den Eintrag von Prozessen bestimmt; für die Erledigung von einfachen Vorstellungen schreibt daher Art. 652 ein besonderes Register vor, welches zugleich bestimmt ist, die Bescheinigung der Gesuchsteller bezw. der Anwälte derselben über Rückempfang ihrer Akten aufzunehmen.

2) bei den Handels- und Handels-Appellationsgerichten,

Art. 653. — **Die Bestimmungen der Art. 644 — 652 finden, mit Ausnahme der auf die Staatsanwaltschaft bezüglichen, auch bei den Handelsgerichten und Handels-Appellationsgerichten Anwendung, bei den erstern jedoch mit der Abweichung, daß die Vorstellungen, auf welche eine gerichtliche Entscheidung erfolgen soll, von der Partei selbst oder ihrem Bevollmächtigten schriftlich einzureichen oder dem Gerichtsschreiber zu Protokoll zu erklären sind.**

3) bei den Einzelngerichten.

Art. 654. — **Vorstellungen, auf welche Entscheidung durch ein Einzelngericht erfolgen soll, können von der Partei oder deren Bevollmächtigten schriftlich eingereicht oder zu Protokoll gegeben werden. Letzteres kann sowohl bei dem Einzelnrichter als bei dem Gerichtsschreiber geschehen.**

Hält der Einzelnrichter noch Aufklärungen oder Urkunden für nöthig, so kann er entweder der Partei durch einen Beschluß die bezügliche Auflage machen oder sie veranlassen, ihm das Erforderliche von kurzer Hand zu übergeben.

Im Uebrigen finden die Bestimmungen der Art. 644, 651 und 652 auch bei den Einzelngerichten Anwendung.

G. A. d. K. d. A. II S. 440. 445. 449. 450 IV S. 120. — K. d. R. II S. 290. 291. IV S 72.

1) Für die Handelsappellationsgerichte ändert sich das Verfahren nur insofern, als die Mitwirkung der Staatsanwaltschaft wegfällt.

Für die Handelsgerichte erster Instanz tritt die weitere durch die Natur des Parteiprozesses bedingte Aenderung ein, daß die Partei selbst oder deren Bevollmächtigter handelt, und zwar entweder, indem sie das Gesuch schriftlich einreichen oder es dem Gerichtsschreiber zu Protokoll erklären. Advokaten und Gerichtsvollzieher bedürfen, wo nicht eine besondere Bestimmung eine Ausnahme bedingt, einer Vollmacht.

2) Bei Einzelngerichten gilt das Nemliche, wie bei Handelsgerichten, nur mit dem Unterschiede, daß das Gesuch auch dem Einzelnrichter selbst zu Protokoll erklärt werden darf, und mit den weiteren Abweichungen, wie sie sich durch das Wegfallen eines Collegiums von selbst ergeben. Auch die Bestimmung, daß der Einzelnrichter die Wahl habe, ob er weitere Aufklärungen von kurzer Hand erheben oder einen Beschluß deßhalb fassen wolle, erscheint im Grunde selbstverständlich, da er ja Berichterstatter und entscheidendes Gericht in einer Person ist.

XXVI. Hauptstück.

Verfahren bei den protestantischen Ehegerichten in den Landestheilen diesseits des Rheins.

Allgemeine Bestimmung.

Art. 655. — **Das Verfahren vor den protestantischen Ehegerichten in den Landestheilen diesseits des Rheins ist dasselbe wie vor den Bezirksgerichten, soweit nicht in den Artikeln 656 bis 681 Abweichungen bestimmt sind.**

G. A. d. K. d. A. II S. 386. 387. 402. 403. IV S. 120. — K. d. R. II S. 291—298. IV S. 72.

1) Das Verfahren vor den protestantischen Ehegerichten diesseits des Rheins ist dasselbe, wie bei den Bezirksgerichten, mit den Abweichungen, wie sie die Art. 656 — 681 bestimmen. Es gilt also an diesen Gerichten der Anwaltsprozeß.

Auch bei Ehestreitigkeiten gegen Dissidenten findet nach den Bestimmungen des Gesetzes vom 2. Mai 1868 Art. 17 u. 21 dieses Verfahren Anwendung. Art. 22 jenes Gesetzes, welcher besondere Vorschriften bezüglich des Sühneversuches enthielt, wurde durch Art. 3 Ziff. 15 des Einführungsgesetzes wieder aufgehoben.

2) In der Pfalz bleiben die Sonderbestimmungen, welche der Code civil in Art. 234—311 und der Code de proc. in Art. 875 bis 880 über das Verfahren bei Ehescheidungen und Trennungen von Tisch und Bett enthält, in Giltigkeit, soweit nicht durch Art. 69 des Einf.-Gesetzes Abänderungen getroffen sind. Dabei ist zu erwähnen, daß die auf die Strafe des Ehebruchs bezüglichen Bestimmungen der Art. 298, 308 u. 309 Code civil bereits durch das Einführungsgesetz zum Strafgesetzbuche aufgehoben wurden.

3) Im Allgemeinen ist hervorzuheben, daß nur die Sonderbestimmungen jener Artikel aufrecht erhalten worden sind, daß jedoch, soweit bisher die allgemeinen Prozeßvorschriften galten, was beim Ehescheidungsverfahren erster Instanz nur ergänzungsweise der Fall war, bei der Trennung von Tisch und Bett jedoch nach Art. 879 Code de proc. die Regel bildete, die Bestimmungen der neuen Prozeßordnung maßgebend sind. Einf.-Ges. Art. 69 Ziff. 5.

Die Vorschrift des Art. 879 Code de proc., daß bei Trennungen von Tisch und Bett der Staatsanwalt gehört werden müsse, ist als eine fortgeltende Sonderbestimmung zu erachten, und zwar um so mehr, als sie mit den Bestimmungen der neuen Prozeßordnung in Art. 672 u. 674 im Einklange steht. Art. 160 Ziff. 6, welcher die Antragstellung des Staatsanwalts nur fakultativ erklärt, findet daher in der Pfalz nur Anwendung bei Klagen auf Nichtigerklärung von Ehen, diesseits aber in Fällen, wo nicht die Ehegerichte, sondern die gewöhnlichen Gerichte entscheiden. Vgl. Bemerk. zu Art. 8 Nr. 7.

4) Die erste Abänderung, welche Art. 69 des Einf.-Ges. trifft, besteht darin, daß es die auf Zeugenreprochen bezüglichen Artikel 250 und 251 Code civil aufhebt und dafür die Bestimmungen der Art. 400 u. 401 der P.O. für maßgebend erklärt. Es fallen daher auch im Ehescheidungsverfahren die Zeugenreprochen im engeren Sinne hinweg und besteht nur die Verwerfung der Zeugen wegen Untüchtigkeit (Art. 400), sowie das Recht der Verweigerung der Zeugschaft (Art. 401).

Zwischenstreite, welche sich bezüglich der Untüchtigkeit oder des Rechtes der Zeugschaftsverweigerung ergeben, werden, da Art. 250 Code civ. aufgehoben ist, am Tage der Zeugenvernehmung verhandelt und entschieden, wie dies denn in letzterer Beziehung gar nicht anders der Fall sein kann.

Die Geltung des Art. 400 der P.-O. hat zur Folge, daß auch die mit demselben im unmittelbaren Zusammenhange stehenden Art. 411 u. 429 der P.-O., welche die Erwirkung der Ermächtigung für öffentliche Beamte und deren Befreiung von der Pflicht des Erscheinens betreffen, zur Anwendung kommen. Die Bestimmungen der Art. 413 u. 415 der P.-O. über Beibringung neuer Zeugen können jedoch den Vorschriften des Art. 249 Code civ. gegenüber keine Anwendung finden, wie denn überhaupt das Verfahren für Zeugenvernehmungen in Ehescheidungen so in's Einzelne gehend vorgezeichnet ist, daß Ergänzungen aus den Bestimmungen der Prozeßordnung nicht nöthig erscheinen.

5) Weiter ist abändernd bestimmt, daß in Fällen, wo die beklagte Partei zugegen oder vertreten war, die Zustellung der Ordonnanz, welche den Tag zur Verhandlung in öffentlicher Sitzung bestimmt (Art. 256 Code civ.), zu unterbleiben habe, sowie daß die Fristen für Einlegung der zulässigen Rechtsmittel sich nach den Bestimmungen der neuen Prozeßordnung richten.

Endlich ist eine Streitfrage des französischen Rechtes bezüglich des Verfahrens bei Anordnung der durch die Art. 268 — 270 Code civ. zugelassenen provisorischen Maßregeln, in dem Sinne entschieden, wie sie in neuerer Zeit dem Wesen nach auch schon durch die Praxis gelöst worden war, nemlich dahin, daß solche Maßregeln ohne jede Zustellung mündlich in der Sitzung gestellt werden dürfen, und zwar selbst im Falle des Nichterscheinens des Beklagten. Solche Zwischenfragen bilden daher vollständig einen Theil des Ehescheidungsprozesses und unterliegen dem für dasselbe bestehenden Verfahren.

Hervorzuheben ist, daß das Gesetz sagt, sie könnten in jeder zur Verhandlung im Ehescheidungsprozesse anberaumten Sitzung gestellt werden, so daß also auch die Verhandlungen in geheimer Sitzung darunter begriffen sind.

Ehescheidung.

Art. 656. — **In Ehescheidungsprozessen ist die Klage vor der Zustellung dem Ehegerichte mittels einfacher Vorstellung zur vorläufigen Prüfung und Beschlußfassung über ihre Zulassung zu übergeben.**

Das Gericht hat nur seine Zuständigkeit und die Erheblichkeit der geltend gemachten Thatsachen zu prüfen.

Der Beschluß bleibt auf der Gerichtsschreiberei hinterlegt.

Art. 657. — **Hat nach dem bestehenden Eherechte der Klagestellung ein Rückkehr- oder Besserungsbefehl vorauszugehen, so steht die Erlassung desselben dem Einzelngerichte des Wohnsitzes der Eheleute zu.**

Die gesetzlichen Befugnisse der Polizeibehörden werden hiedurch nicht berührt.

Art. 658. — **Im Falle der böslichen Verlassung ist bei unbekanntem Aufenthalte des betreffenden Ehetheils auf Antrag des andern eine öffentliche Aufforderung zur Rückkehr vom Einzelnrichter zu erlassen. Sie darf erst ergehen, nachdem vom Zeitpunkte der Entfernung sechs Monate verstrichen sind, und das Ehegericht darf die Klage auf Scheidung wegen böslicher Verlassung erst zulassen, nachdem vom Datum des Blattes, in welchem die Aufforderung zuerst erfolgte, weitere sechs Monate abgelaufen sind.**

Diese Vorschriften finden Anwendung, auch wenn das einschlägige Eherecht die Aufforderung nicht vorschreibt. Dagegen treten alle Bestimmungen der Eherechte, welche noch weitere Aufforderungen oder die Erfüllung sonstiger Förmlichkeiten vorschreiben oder andere Fristen festsetzen, außer Geltung.

G. A. d. K. d. A. II S. 387. 388. 395. 396. 402. 403. 454. IV S. 120. — K. d. R. II S. 298. IV S. 72.

1) In Art. 657 u. 658 sind Bestimmungen getroffen, welche nicht das Ehescheidungsverfahren selbst, sondern die Begründung der Ehescheidungsklage zum Gegenstande haben.

Verschiedene Eherechte, z. B. das preußische Landrecht Thl. II Tit. I § 675, 685, 709, 712, die Nürnberger Ehescheidungsordnung v. 25. Nov. 1803 § 11, 14, 19, 22, 27, und die im Oettingen-Spielbergischen Gebiete geltende Eheordnung vom 2. Jan. 1660 Abs. 4, schreiben vor, daß Ehescheidungen nur begehrt werden können, nachdem ein Befehl zur Rückkehr bez. Besserung vorausgegangen und fruchtlos geblieben sei.

Für Befehle dieser Art bestimmt nun Art. 657 die Zuständigkeit, und zwar dahin, daß er dieselben dem Einzelngerichte des Wohnsitzes der Eheleute zuweist.

2) Für den besonderen Fall, wo die Ehescheidung auf Grund böslicher Verlassung begehrt wird und der Aufenthalt des schuldigen Ehegatten unbekannt ist, regelt Art. 658 die Vorbedingungen der Zulässigkeit der Ehescheidungsklage in allgemeiner, alle abweichenden Bestimmungen der einzelnen Eherechte aufhebenden Weise.

In diesem Falle ist auf Antrag des verlassenen Ehegatten eine öffentliche Aufforderung zur Rückkehr vom Einzelnrichter zu erlassen. Zu diesem Zwecke bedarf es natürlich weder eines schriftlichen Gesuches noch einer Beurkundung der mündlich gestellten Bitte, vielmehr ordnet der Einzelnrichter ohne weitere Förmlichkeit die öffentliche Aufforderung an.

Es erscheint als selbstverständliche Voraussetzung des Gesetzes und theilweise auch durch dessen Wortlaut angedeutet, daß die Aufforderung in einem oder mehreren öffentlichen Blättern erfolge, daß der Einzelnrichter diese Blätter zu bestimmen habe, und daß endlich die Einrückung nicht etwa auf Betreiben des Ehegatten oder seines Anwaltes stattfinde, sondern vom Einzelnrichter selbst ausgehe.

3) Die Aufforderung darf erst ergehen, nachdem vom Zeitpunkte der Entfernung sechs Monate verstrichen sind.

Diese Vorschrift, bestimmt, übereilte Aufforderungen dieser Art zu verhüten, beruht auf sehr wichtigen Gründen der öffentlichen Ordnung, und es folgt hieraus, daß der Einzelnrichter sich nicht mit der bloßen Angabe, welche der Ehegatte bezüglich des Zeitpunktes der Entfernung macht, begnügen dürfe, sondern sich eine sicherere Bürgschaft dafür verschaffen müsse, daß die Voraussetzungen des Gesetzes gegeben seien. Falls ihm selbst nicht zufällig die Thatsachen bekannt sind, wird er Bescheinigungen (Zeugnisse des Ortsvorstandes 2c.) zu verlangen nicht nur berechtigt, sondern auch verpflichtet sein.

Ist dennoch eine Aufforderung zu früh erlassen worden, so wird dies später die Rückweisung der Ehescheidungsklage zur Folge haben; denn die Ehescheidung ist nur begründet, insofern eine dem Gesetze entsprechende öffentliche Aufforderung vorausgegangen, und der Zeitpunkt der Aufforderung ist für die Frage, ob der abwesende Ehegatte präsumirt werden dürfe, Kenntniß von derselben zu haben, von entscheidendem Einflusse.

Die Klage auf Scheidung darf im fraglichen Falle erst zugelassen werden, nachdem vom Datum desjenigen Blattes, in welchem die Aufforderung **zuerst** erfolgte, weitere sechs Monate abgelaufen sind.

4) Die **Einleitung** des Ehescheidungsverfahrens erfolgt dadurch, daß der Anwalt des klagenden Theils, unter Vorlage der Klageschrift, eine **einfache Vorstellung** einreicht, worin er bittet, die Ehescheidungsklage zuzulassen. Es hat dieses vorbereitende Verfahren, für welches die Vorschriften des Hauptst. XXV gelten, den Zweck, offenbar **frivole** Ehescheidungsklagen schon von vornherein zu beseitigen, ehe noch der andere Ehegatte in Streit gezogen ist.

Das Gericht hat, laut Vorschrift des Art. 656, nur zu prüfen: 1) ob seine Zuständigkeit gegeben sei, und 2) ob die geltend gemachten Thatsachen erheblich, d. h., ihre Wahrheit vorausgesetzt, geeignet seien, die Ehescheidung zu begründen, und auch diese Prüfung ist nur eine **vorläufige** und schließt nicht aus, daß später die nemlichen Fragen von neuem geprüft und anders entschieden werden. Uebrigens ergibt sich aus Art. 658, daß das Gericht im Falle der Ehescheidung wegen böslichen Verlassens noch ferner zu prüfen habe, ob die dort bezeichnete Frist verstrichen sei, und versteht es sich wohl von selbst, daß in diesem Falle es nicht genüge, die Thatsache der öffentlichen Aufforderung zu behaupten, vielmehr die öffentlichen Blätter, in welchen sie enthalten ist, mit der Klage vorzulegen seien.

Erscheint der Klagvertrag so allgemein und vag, daß er den Anforderungen des Art. 225 nicht entspricht und das Gericht nicht im Stande ist, sich ein Urtheil darüber zu bilden, ob die behaupteten Thatsachen zur Begründung der Ehescheidung genügend erscheinen, so hat es die Klage nicht zuzulassen, in welchem Fall natürlich nichts im Wege steht, eine verbesserte Klage einzureichen.

5) Der Beschluß, durch welchen die Ehescheidungsklage zugelassen oder deren Zulassung verweigert wird, bleibt auf der Gerichtsschreiberei hinterlegt; es hat sich daher derjenige Theil, welcher seiner bedarf, wie z. B. der klagende Theil, wenn er später die Klage zustellen will (Art. 665), Ausfertigung ertheilen zu lassen.

Gegen einen **abweisenden** Beschluß steht nach Art. 738 das Rechtsmittel der **Beschwerde** offen, und wurde eine bezügliche ausdrückliche Bestimmung als selbstverständlich gestrichen. Abg. IV 120.

Art. 659. — **Nach Zulassung der Scheidungsklage kann das Ehegericht den einen Ehetheil auf seinen Antrag für befugt erklären, während des Prozesses von dem andern getrennt zu leben.**

Wird der Antrag vor der Zustellung der Scheidungsklage gestellt, so hat dies mittels einfacher Vorstellung zu geschehen. Die Entscheidung bleibt auf der Gerichtsschreiberei hinterlegt. Wird dem Antrage entsprochen, so ist in der Entscheidung zugleich eine Frist zu bestimmen, mit deren Ablauf die ertheilte Befugniß außer Kraft tritt, soferne die Zustellung der Klage bis dahin nicht erfolgt ist.

G. A. d. K. d. A. II S. 396. 398 399. 403. 454. IV S. 120. — K. d. R. II S. 298. IV S. 72.

1) Die Gestattung vorläufiger Trennung der Ehegatten ist ihrer Natur nach eine **Vorsichtsverfügung**, welche jedoch sowohl was die Zuständigkeit zum Erlasse derselben, als was das einzuhaltende Verfahren betrifft, besonderen Vorschriften unterworfen ist.

Zuständig ist nur das betreffende **Ehegericht**, das Verfahren aber ist verschieden, je nachdem das Begehren **vor** oder **nach** Zustellung der Ehescheidungsklage gestellt wird.

Im ersteren Falle ist der Weg der **einfachen Vorstellung** vorgezeichnet, jedoch verfügt, daß die Entscheidung nicht in Urschrift hinauszugeben sei, sondern auf der Gerichtsschreiberei hinterlegt bleibe (Art. 651 Abs. 2). Gegen einen abweisenden Beschluß ist Beschwerde statthaft (Art. 738).

Im letzteren Falle gelten die allgemeinen Prinzipien, d. h. es ist das für Zwischenstreite (Art. 483) bestimmte Verfahren einzuhalten. Die Worte des Art. 659 Abs. 1: „auf seinen Antrag“ besagen daher nur, daß fragliche Maßregel nicht von Amtswegen zu erlassen sei, und dürften nicht dahin mißverstanden werden, daß immer eine einseitige Antragstellung genüge. Die ergehenden Urtheile unterliegen der Berufung und Nichtigkeitsbeschwerde. Art. 683 Ziff. 2.

2) Das Gesetz erklärt **jeden** Ehetheil befugt, die einstweilige Trennung zu beantragen, also kann die bezügliche Verfügung unter Umständen auch auf Antrag des **beklagten** Ehetheiles erlassen werden.

Ferner ist ebenso der Mann als die Frau berechtigt, dieses Verlangen zu stellen. Für ersteren handelt es sich um Aufhebung der Pflicht, die Frau bei sich aufzunehmen, für letztere um Aufhebung der Pflicht, bei dem Manne zu wohnen.

Da nicht verfügt ist, es habe das Gericht die Wohnung des sich trennenden Ehegatten zu bezeichnen, wie dies der Art. 268 Code civil bezüglich der Frau vorschreibt, so hat sich der richterliche Spruch auf die Erlaubniß getrennt zu leben zu beschränken.

Für die Frage des gesetzlichen Wohnsitzes der Ehefrau ist die einstweilige Trennung ohne Einfluß, für die Frage aber, wo spätere Zustellungen zu bewirken seien, kann sie von Belang sein. Vgl. Bemerk. zu Art. 195 Nr. 3.

3) Das Gesetz sagt nur: „das Ehegericht kann die Trennung gestatten," stellt es also unbedingt dem richterlichen Ermessen anheim, zu gestatten oder zu verweigern, ohne zu unterscheiden, in welcher Periode des Verfahrens der Antrag gestellt wird und von welcher Seite. Offenbar wird aber das Gericht nur in Fällen, wo es Grund hat, die Ehescheidungsklage für frivol zu erachten, veranlaßt sein, die erbetene Erlaubniß zu verweigern, namentlich wenn der Antrag von der Ehefrau ausgeht.

War der Antrag vor Zustellung der Scheidungsklage gestellt und wurde demselben stattgegeben, so ist zugleich eine Frist zu setzen, innerhalb welcher, bei Strafe der Erlöschung der ertheilten Erlaubniß, die Klage zuzustellen sei.

4) Die ertheilte Erlaubniß wirkt für den ganzen Prozeß, also so lange, bis ein rechtskräftig gewordenes Erkenntniß vorliegt.

Wurde sie auf einfache Vorstellung gegeben, so kann sie selbstverständlich später im Wege eines Zwischenstreites wieder aufgehoben werden.

Für Fälle anderer Art entsteht jedoch die Frage, ob das Prinzip, daß Vorsichtsverfügungen auf Grund erlangter besserer Aufklärung oder wegen veränderter Umstände jeder Zeit zurückgenommen werden können (Art. 635), auch hier seine Anwendung finde. Da es sich dem Wesen nach um eine Vorsichtsverfügung handelt, so werden, soweit nicht Art. 659 Ausnahmen macht, die bezüglichen allgemeinen Prinzipien allerdings Maß geben, wird also die gestellte Frage zu bejahen sein. Vgl. Abg. II 398, 399 (v. Weiß).

5) Der Entwurf (Art. 25) wies den Ehegerichten ausdrücklich auch die Entscheidung über die der Ehefrau während des Prozesses zu verabreichenden Alimente zu; allein man hielt es schließlich sachgemäßer, es in dieser Beziehung bei den allgemeinen Prinzipien, wie sie für Vorsichtsverfügungen gelten, zu belassen und die bezügliche Bestimmung zu streichen. Abg. II 398, 399. Man war dabei der Ansicht, es trete in Folge dieser Streichung die Zuständigkeit der gewöhnlichen Gerichte ein, und es war mit einer der Bestimmungsgründe für die Streichung, daß der Richter des Wohnortes die bezüglichen Fragen besser zu würdigen verstehe. Derselben Ansicht gemäß sprach man aus, daß etwaige abweichende Vorschriften des preußischen Landrechts, namentlich Thl. II Tit. I § 729, zu streichen seien. Vgl. Einf.-Ges. Art. 48 und Abg. II 399 Sp. 2 (v. Weiß).

Diese Ansicht zeigt sich nun aber insofern irrig, als, wie zu Art. 8 Nr. 4 bemerkt, die Jurisprudenz sich entschieden dahin fixirt hat, daß die Zusprechung vorsorglicher Alimente eine Nebensache des Ehescheidungsprozesses bilde und als solche zur Zuständigkeit der Ehegerichte gehöre.

Die Frage, ob diese Zuständigkeit noch fortbestehe, ist in Folge besagter Aeußerungen im Gesetzgebungsausschusse eine ziemlich schwierige geworden, und die Controverse, welche als erledigt galt, ist von Neuem ins Leben gerufen. Einerseits ist die bestimmt ausgesprochene Ansicht des Gesetzgebers zu beachten, anderseits ist zu betonen, daß das Gesetz nicht bezweckte, etwas Neues zu verfügen, und eine geäußerte Ansicht des Gesetzgebers, so schwer sie unter Umständen in's Gewicht fallen mag, doch kein Gesetz ist.

Ich halte letztere Gründe für überwiegend und gebe ihnen um so lieber den Vorzug, als das Resultat, zu welchem sie führen, das praktischere ist und mit den Bestimmungen über Vorsichtsverfügungen besser im Einklange steht. Offenbar ist es nemlich ein Mißstand, wenn wegen eines unbedeutenden Nebenpunktes, der sich im Wege des Zwischenstreites so leicht erledigen läßt, ein besonderes Verfahren vor einem anderen Gerichte anhängig gemacht werden muß; allein abgesehen hiervon werden manche Bestimmungen über Vorsichtsverfügungen, z. B. daß sie auf Grund besserer Aufklärung vom Gerichte, bei welchem die Sache anhängig ist, jeder Zeit aufgehoben oder geändert werden dürfen (Art. 635 Abs. 2), geradezu gegenstandslos, wenn man die Zuständigkeit des Ehegerichts nicht annimmt.

Dabei ist schließlich zu beachten, daß sich die besagte Jurisprudenz bloß auf Grund der allgemeinen Bestimmungen der Gerichtsordnung gebildet hat, und es daher ohne Belang erscheint, wenn der angeführte § 729 des preuß. Landrechts, welcher übrigens eine Competenzbestimmung nicht enthält, durch das Einf.-Ges. (Art. 48) aufgehoben worden ist.

Art. 660. — **Vorbehaltlich der Bestimmung des Art. 664 ist in Ehescheidungssachen, nachdem die Klage zugelassen worden und vor der Zustellung derselben, der Sühneversuch vorzunehmen.**

Dies geschieht durch den Vorstand des Ehegerichts oder ein von ihm beauftragtes Gerichtsmitglied; der Vorstand des Ehegerichts ist aber auch befugt, den Vorstand des Bezirksgerichts, in dessen Sprengel die Eheleute wohnen, um die Vornahme zu ersuchen, und dieser kann statt seiner ein Mitglied des Bezirksgerichts — im Falle Krankheit oder sonstiger unabwendbarer Verhinderung eines der Ehetheile auch das betreffende Einzelngericht — damit beauftragen.

Die Tagfahrt wird von dem mit dem Sühneversuche befaßten Richter bestimmt.

Die Parteien haben dabei in Person und ohne Beistand zu erscheinen.

Art. 661. — Der mit dem Sühneversuche befaßte Richter muß auf Antrag des Beklagten und kann auch von Amtswegen einen Seelsorger — bei gemischten Ehen einen solchen von jeder der beiden Religionsparteien — dazu beiziehen.

Art. 662. — Die Vorladung des Beklagten zu dem Sühneversuche liegt dem Kläger ob. Erscheint der vorgeladene Beklagte nicht, so ist die Sühne als mißlungen zu betrachten, der Beklagte aber an Geld bis zu fünfzig Gulden zu bestrafen.

Art. 663. — Erscheint bei dem Sühneversuche der Kläger nicht oder hat er die Vorladung des Beklagten unterlassen, so kann er innerhalb dreißig Tagen bei dem damit befaßten Richter die Festsetzung einer neuen Tagfahrt nachsuchen. Nach Ablauf dieser Frist, sowie wenn der Kläger die neuerliche Tagfahrt abermals vereitelt, gilt die Klage als nicht angebracht, kann jedoch von Neuem erhoben werden.

Art. 664. — Ist der Aufenthalt des Beklagten im Auslande oder unbekannt, so unterbleibt der Sühneversuch.

Das Gericht kann auch in andern Fällen auf das mittels einfacher Vorstellung anzubringende Gesuch des einen oder andern Theils bei oder nach Zulassung der Klage den Sühneversuch für entbehrlich erklären, wenn diesem schwer zu beseitigende und von dem Kläger nicht verschuldete Hindernisse entgegenstehen.

G. A. d. K. d. A. II S. 387—389. 391. 392. 395. 398. 403. 404. 454. IV S. 120.
K. d. R. II S. 298. IV S. 72.

1) Der nächste Schritt nach Zulassung der Klage ist der Sühneversuch, welcher, abgesehen von nachbezeichneten Ausnahmen, der Zustellung der Scheidungsklage, d. h. der Einleitung des eigentlichen Scheidungsprozesses, immer vorausgehen muß.

Von dieser Regel macht das Gesetz zwei Ausnahmen.

Der Sühneversuch hat 1) gemäß Art. 664 Abs. 1 zu unterbleiben, wenn der Aufenthalt des beklagten Theils im Auslande oder unbekannt ist. Wie zu beachten, ist hier nur vom Aufenthalte, nicht vom Wohnsitze die Rede, wenn auch der Regel nach beide zusammenfallen.

Das Gericht kann 2) gemäß Art. 664 Abs. 2 den Sühneversuch erlassen, wenn schwer zu beseitigende und zugleich vom Kläger nicht verschuldete Hindernisse entgegenstehen. Hindernisse dieser Art sind z. B. Geisteskrankheit, unter Umständen auch körperliche Krankheit, Haft an einem entfernten Orte. Diese Erlassung erfolgt auf einfache Vorstellung des einen oder des anderen Theils, und kann das betreffende Gesuch auch mit dem Gesuche um Zulassung der Scheidungsklage verbunden werden.

2) Zur Vornahme des Sühneversuches ist der Vorstand des Ehegerichts zuständig, welcher jedoch in der Weise, wie dies in Art. 660 Abs. 2 näher bezeichnet ist, seine Befugnisse auf andere Richter übertragen kann, und zwar von Amtswegen. In den meisten Fällen wird es sachgemäß sein, den Sühneversuch dem Richter des Wohnortes, und zwar dem Einzelnrichter, zu übertragen.

Die Einleitung des Verfahrens wird in der Regel der Art erfolgen, daß der Anwalt des klagenden Theils beim Vorstande des Ehegerichts ein Gesuch um Festsetzung einer Tagfahrt zum Sühneversuche einreicht, mit Beifügung einer etwaigen Bitte um Beauftragung des Richters des Wohnortes. Auf dieses Gesuch setzt der Vorstand den entsprechenden Beschluß und gibt ihn in Urschrift hinaus. Wird ein anderer Richter beauftragt, so ist an diesen ein neues Gesuch zu richten.

Uebrigens ist ein schriftliches Gesuch nicht vorgeschrieben, und genügt es daher, daß der Richter in irgend einer Weise veranlaßt werde, die Tagfahrt festzusetzen. Das Gesetz verlangt nicht einmal einen förmlichen Beschluß, jedoch erscheint ein solcher mindestens sachgemäß, da, wie Art. 663 zeigt, an die Festsetzung der Tagfahrt sich rechtliche Folgen knüpfen.

3) Dem klagenden Theile liegt ob, den beklagten Theil zum Sühneversuche vorzuladen.

Ueber die einzuhaltende Frist ist nichts bestimmt und wird daher, wie bei Ladungen auf kurze Frist, nur die allgemeine Erwägung Maß geben, daß die Frist genügen müsse, um das persönliche Erscheinen möglich zu machen. Rathsam möchte es jedenfalls sein, die gewöhnliche Erscheinungsfrist (Art. 225 u. 209) einzuhalten.

Findet der Richter die Frist nicht genügend und ist der Vorgeladene nicht erschienen, so wird die Sachlage so anzusehen sein, als sei die Vorladung unterlassen, und wird neue Tagfahrt festzusetzen sein, für welche der Richter die Erscheinungsfrist bestimmt. (Vgl. Art. 300 und Art. 520 Abs. 2.) Zu Letzterem erscheint mir nemlich der Richter vollkommen befugt, und steht daher auch nichts im Wege, sofort bei der ersten Tagfahrtsbestimmung geeignete Weisung zu geben. Vgl. Bemerk. zu Art. 259 Nr. 6.

Daß der Beschluß, welcher die Tagfahrt festsetzt, mit der Vorladung zuzustellen sei, ist zwar nicht vorgeschrieben, möchte jedoch nach allgemeinen Prinzipien anzunehmen, mindestens sachgemäß sein. Geschähe es nicht, so müßte wenigstens in der Vorladung die richterliche Festsetzung angeführt werden, denn der Gegner muß erfahren, daß es eine vom Richter festgesetzte Tagfahrt sei, zu welcher er erscheinen soll.

Daß die Vorladung ausdrücklich die Aufforderung enthalten müsse, zum Zwecke des Sühneversuchs wegen einer Scheidungsklage zu erscheinen, erscheint selbstverständlich. Eine Mittheilung der Ehescheidungsgründe ist nicht geboten.

4) Beim Sühneversuch müssen die Parteien in Person und ohne Beistand erscheinen.

Erscheint auf gehörige Vorladung der beklagte Theil nicht, so ist der Sühneversuch als mißlungen zu betrachten und der Nichterschienene in eine Geldstrafe bis zu fünfzig Gulden zu verurtheilen.

Erscheint der klagende Theil nicht, so ist die Tagfahrt vereitelt, mag der beklagte Theil erschienen sein oder nicht, jedoch kann innerhalb 30 Tagen die Festsetzung einer neuen Tagfahrt nachgesucht werden. Wurde diese letztere Frist versäumt, oder bleibt der klagende Theil wiederholt aus, so gilt die Klage als nicht angebracht, d. h. die Klagzulassung verliert ihre Wirkung.

Dem Nichterscheinen des Klägers steht in beiden Fällen das Unterlassen der Vorladung gleich, und zwar ist hierunter das Unterlassen einer den Vorschriften des Gesetzes entsprechenden Vorladung zu verstehen. Vgl. Art. 297 Abs. 1.

Das Nichterscheinen des Beklagten hat natürlich bei der zweiten Tagfahrt die nemliche Folge, wie bei der ersten.

5) Der Richter darf, wenn er es geeignet findet, von Amtswegen einen Seelsorger beiziehen; beantragt aber der beklagte Theil diese Beiziehung, so muß sie stattfinden. Die Wahl des Seelsorgers ist in beiden Fällen Sache des Richters, der Begriff bringt es jedoch mit sich, daß der Seelsorger der Religion der Ehegatten angehören müsse.

Der bezügliche Antrag kann schon vor dem Sühneversuche gestellt werden, erscheint aber noch rechtzeitig angebracht, wenn er auch erst bei Gelegenheit desselben gestellt wird. In diesem Falle bestimmt der Richter, falls die Beiziehung nicht sofort erfolgen kann, eine weitere Tagfahrt, in welcher die Eheleute ohne neue Ladung zu erscheinen haben. Die Form der Beiziehung des Seelsorgers ist Sache des Richters und hat dieselbe durch einfache Einladung zu geschehen.

Bei gemischten Ehen soll für jeden Ehetheil ein eigener Seelsorger beigezogen werden, jedoch wird in Fällen, wo der Richter nur von Amtswegen handelt, diese Vorschrift nicht bindend sein.

6) Das Verfahren ist seiner Natur nach ein geheimes. Bleibt der Sühneversuch fruchtlos, so ist, wie es die Natur der Sache mit sich bringt und auch aus Art. 665 hervorgeht, ein förmliches Protokoll zu errichten, und das Nemliche wird zu geschehen haben, wenn der Versuch wegen Nichterscheinens des Klägers vereitelt worden ist. Aus den Bestimmungen des Art. 166 läßt sich folgern, daß auch die Beiziehung eines Gerichtsschreibers nöthig sei, jedenfalls ist es dem Richter nicht verwehrt, einen solchen beizuziehen.

Das Protokoll hat selbstverständlich nicht die Vorhalte des Richters und Seelsorgers und die gegenseitigen Aeußerungen der Parteien zu beurkunden, sondern nur im Allgemeinen den Gang der Verhandlung, die Thatsache des Nichterscheinens des einen oder andern Theils und die Thatsache, daß eine Versöhnung nicht zu Stande kam, festzustellen.

Erfolgt Versöhnung, so ist es nicht nöthig, jedoch sachgemäß, Protokoll zu errichten.

Art. 665. — Die Klagezustellung hat nur dann die gesetzlichen Wirkungen einer solchen, wenn damit die Zustellung des Beschlusses über die Zulassung der Klage und, abgesehen von den Fällen des Art. 664, auch die Zustellung des Protokolles über den fruchtlos angestellten Sühneversuch verbunden wird.

Art. 666. — Der Kläger ist befugt, bis zum Endurtheile noch andere Ehescheidungsgründe geltend zu machen, als in der Klage angeführt sind.

Der Beklagte darf eine Widerklage nur stellen, wenn diese gleichfalls auf Scheidung gerichtet ist.

Sowohl rücksichtlich der neuen Ehescheidungsgründe des Klägers als für die Widerklage des Beklagten ist weder ein vorgängiger Beschluß des Gerichts über ihre Zulassung, noch ein Sühneversuch erforderlich.

Art. 667. — Thatsachen, welche von der Gegenpartei in einer Urkunde oder bei der Verhandlung zugestanden worden oder nach gesetzlicher Vorschrift als zugestanden zu betrachten sind, darf das Gericht nur soweit für richtig annehmen, als es durch das Ergebniß der Verhandlung die Ueberzeugung von der Richtigkeit derselben gewonnen hat oder die Erhaltung der Ehe dadurch nicht gefährdet ist.

Art. 668. — Die bösliche Verlassung ist, auch wenn der Beklagte den gerichtlichen Rückkehrbefehl nicht befolgt oder der öffentlichen Aufforderung nicht entsprochen und auch auf die Zustellung der Klage einen Anwalt nicht bestellt hat, doch nur in so ferne als erwiesen anzunehmen, als sich das Ehegericht aus den sonstigen Umständen des Falls von ihrem Vorhandensein überzeugt.

Dabei kann das Gericht, wenn die Aufforderung erfolglos geblieben ist, vor Erlassung des Erkenntnisses dem klagenden Theile zu beschwören aufgeben, daß ihm über den Aufenthalt des Beklagten nichts oder nichts Weiteres, als er angegeben hat, bekannt sei.

Art. 669. — Die Erlassung eines zurückgeschobenen oder vom Gerichte auferlegten Eides ist unstatthaft, wenn es sich um einen Beweis handelt, durch welchen der Antrag auf Scheidung begründet werden soll.

Art. 670. — Ist die Ehescheidung nicht auf Grund eines Ehebruchs begehrt und hält das Gericht die Wiederaussöhnung der Parteien für nicht unwahrscheinlich, so kann es die Aussetzung des Verfahrens auf bestimmte Zeit anordnen. Diese Anordnung kann bei jeder Verhandlung, jedoch auf Grund der vorstehenden Bestimmung im Laufe des ganzen Prozesses nur einmal und nicht auf länger als sechs Monate getroffen werden.

Art. 671. — Solange der Prozeß nicht durch rechtskräftiges Urtheil erledigt ist, kann der Kläger die Klage zurücknehmen.

Die Zurücknahme hat die gleiche Wirkung wie die Abweisung.

G. A. d. K. d. A. II S. 389. 390. 392—396 404. 405. 454. VI S. 120.
K d. R II S 298. IV S 72

1) Das Verfahren im Ehescheidungsprozesse ist, soweit nicht abweichende Bestimmungen ausdrücklich gegeben sind, ganz das nemliche, wie im gewöhnlichen Anwaltsprozesse. Insbesondere ist das persönliche Erscheinen der Ehegatten vor Gericht, auf welches im französischen Ehescheidungsverfahren so viel Gewicht gelegt wird, nicht nöthig und hat, wie in sonstigen Prozessen, nur stattzufinden, wenn das Gericht es nach Art. 155 anordnet. Uebrigens möchte hier besonderer Anlaß vorliegen, solche Anordnung zu erlassen, ebenso wie sich häufig Veranlassung ergeben möchte, die Oeffentlichkeit der Verhandlung zu beschränken (Art. 149).

a) Klagezustellung.

2) Die Klage darf erst zugestellt werden, nachdem sie vorher zuzulassen und der Sühneversuch, wo solcher nöthig, fruchtlos geblieben ist. Damit dies sicher beobachtet werde, ist vorgeschrieben, daß der Zulassungsbeschluß sowie das Protokoll über den Sühneversuch mit der Klage zuzustellen seien, und ist ausgesprochen, daß, falls dies nicht geschehe, die Klagezustellung die gesetzlichen Wirkungen einer solchen nicht habe, d. h. daß sie als nichtig zu betrachten sei.

Nach der Fassung des Gesetzes erleidet es keinen Zweifel, daß diese auf Gründen der öffentlichen Ordnung beruhende Nichtigkeit von Amtswegen zu berücksichtigen sei, auch wenn die Gegenpartei keinen Einwand daraus herleitet.

Ferner wird nach der Ausdrucksweise des Gesetzes, sowie nach dem Zwecke der getroffenen Verfügung, der formelle Charakter der gedrohten Nichtigkeit streng aufrecht zu halten sein, so daß es weder genügt, wenn später durch Vorlage der betreffenden Urkunden der Nachweis, daß dem Gesetze Genüge geschehen, geführt wird, noch wenn die Zustellung dieser Urkunden ohne neue Klagezustellung nachträglich erfolgt.

3) Der bezügliche Mangel der Klage kann natürlich vom Gerichte erst berücksichtigt werden, wenn die Sache — sei es im Versäumungsfalle, sei es contradiktorisch — zur Verhandlung kommt. Bei Hinterlegung der Anträge handelt es sich nur um Festsetzung der Sitzung zur Verhandlung, und ist daher das Gericht nicht berufen, sich über die fragliche Prozeßeinrede auszusprechen, jedoch kann und wird es allerdings nach Art. 241 Abs. 7 die sofortige Verhandlung anordnen.

Wurde auf Grund von Art. 664 Abs. 2 der Sühneversuch erlassen, so ist bei Zustellung der Klage der betreffende Beschluß, da er die Zulässigkeit der Klage bedingt, also zur Klagbegründung im weiteren Sinne gehört, anzuführen.

b) Neue Entscheidungsgründe.

4) Es ließe sich die Frage aufwerfen, ob neue Ehescheidungsgründe, namentlich solche, welche Thatsachen derselben Art betreffen, unter den Gesichtspunkt von Klagänderungen (Art 180) fallen, oder ob sie nur als Thatsachen, welche zur besseren Begründung der nemlichen Klage neu vorgebracht werden (Art. 707) zu betrachten seien. Diese Frage wird dadurch gegenstandslos, daß das Gesetz die Geltendmachung neuer Ehescheidungsgründe jeder Art ausdrücklich gestattet, wie dies schon in Consequenz der Bestimmungen des Art. 673 geschehen mußte.

Das Nachbringen neuer Ehescheidungsgründe darf stattfinden bis zum Endurtheile, also auch nach dem Beweisinterlokute und selbst nach beendigtem Beweisverfahren. In solchen Fällen ordnet das Gericht, falls es die neuen Gründe erheblich erachtet und das vorhandene Material nicht bereits hinreicht, neuen Beweis an. Unter dem Endurtheile ist wohl nur das Endurtheil erster Instanz zu verstehen, und wäre also die Anwendung des Art. 707, soweit es sich um neue Ehescheidungsgründe handelt, unbedingt ausgeschlossen.

Neue Zulassung der Klage und neuer Sühneversuch sind nicht erforderlich.

c) Widerklagen.

5) Eine Widerklage ist der Scheidungsklage gegenüber nur statthaft, wenn mittelst derselben gleichfalls die Scheidung verlangt wird. Der beklagte Theil dürfte daher nicht im Wege der Widerklage die Nichtigkeit der Ehe geltend machen, wohl aber wird nichts im Wege stehen, eine Trennung von Tisch und Bett als das Mindere zu verlangen. Vgl. Abg. II 392 Sp. 1.

Auch bei der Widerklage ist weder neuer Zulassungsbeschluß noch neuer Sühneversuch erforderlich.

Im Uebrigen gelten die gewöhnlichen Grundsätze, insbesondere fällt nach Art. 31 Abs. 2 die Zuständigkeit des betreffenden Ehegerichts für die Widerklage hinweg, wenn diese als selbständige Klage nicht vor dasselbe hätte gebracht werden können, was bei gemischten Ehen in der Regel der Fall sein wird. Vgl. Art. 38 Ziff. 1.

Die Bestimmung, daß neue Ehescheidungsgründe bis zum Endurtheile nachgebracht werden können, muß ebenso für die Widerklage wie für die Hauptklage gelten.

d) Beweis.

6) Da Ehescheidungen durch Uebereinkunft nicht erlaubt sind, so ist klar, daß es nicht in der Willkür einer Partei liegen dürfe, durch Zugeständnisse oder durch die gleichwirkenden Handlungen der Verweigerung oder Erlassung eines Eides die Scheidung herbeizuführen. Es liegt daher hier einer jener Fälle vor, von welchen in Art. 324 Abs. 2 die Sprache ist, und hätte sich schon aus allgemeinen Grundsätzen dasjenige ableiten lassen, was Art. 667 ausdrücklich bestimmt, nemlich daß das Geständniß hier den Beweis nicht ersetzen, sondern nur als ein vom Richter zu würdigendes Beweismoment, als eine gewöhnliche Vermuthung dienen könne.

Dies gilt jedoch nur in so fern, als das Geständniß die Folge haben soll, die Scheidung zu begründen, in jeder anderen Richtung aber gelten die gewöhnlichen Grundsätze, so insbesondere, wenn es sich darum handelt, eine Versöhnung nachzuweisen oder sonst einen Beweis zu führen, welcher die Zurückweisung der Scheidungsklage zur Folge haben soll. Selbst für den Fall, wo es sich um Wegräumung eines Einwandes gegen die sonst begründete Scheidungsklage handelt, z. B. um Beseitigung der Einrede der Versöhnung durch Ausschwörung des bezüglich zugeschobenen Eides, tritt eine Ausnahme nicht ein. Vgl. Referat zu Art. 12 (S. 445).

7) Die Eideszuschiebung ist auch bei Thatsachen, von denen der Anspruch der Scheidung abhängt, zulässig, jedoch wirkt die Eidesverweigerung nicht sachentscheidend, denn es kann dem in ihr liegenden stillschweigenden Geständnisse keine stärkere Wirkung zukommen, als einem ausdrücklichen

Geständnisse. Vgl. Bemerk. zu Art. 449 Nr. 3 und zu Art. 465 Nr. 1.

Aus dem nemlichen Grunde kann umgekehrt die Ausschwörung eines zurückgeschobenen Eides keine sachentscheidende Wirkung äußern.

Im Einklange hiemit steht die Bestimmung des Art. 669, daß die Erlassung eines zurückgeschobenen oder gerichtlich auferlegten Eides unstatthaft sei, wenn hierdurch die Scheidung begründet werden solle. Uebrigens möchte diese Bestimmung, insoweit sie sich auf den zurückgeschobenen Eid erstreckt, nicht ganz zu billigen sein, denn warum soll es der Partei, welcher es freistand, den Eid nicht zurückzuschieben, verwehrt sein, die Zurückschiebung zu widerrufen und hierdurch die Leistung eines möglicherweise falschen Eides zu verhindern, welcher, selbst wenn er geschworen wird, nicht sachentscheidend erscheint?

8) Für den besonderen Fall, wo die Ehescheidung auf die Thatsache der böslichen Verlassung gegründet wird, gibt Art. 668 verschiedene Vorschriften, welche den Zweck verfolgen, Collusionen unter den Eheleuten zur Herbeiführung einer gütlichen Scheidung möglichst zu vereiteln.

Dem Richter wird die Vorschrift gegeben, daß er aus dem bloßen Stillschweigen oder Nichterscheinen des beklagten Ehegatten nie die bösliche Verlassung folgern dürfe, vielmehr den Beweis hierfür aus den sonstigen Umständen des Falles zu entnehmen habe. Dabei kann dem klagenden Theile der besondere Eid darüber auferlegt werden, daß er vom Aufenthalte des anderen Theils nichts oder nichts Weiteres, als was er schon angegeben, wisse.

e) Aussetzung des Verfahrens.

9) Wird die Ehescheidung weder in der Hauptklage noch in der Widerklage auf Grund eines Ehebruches begehrt, und hält das Gericht eine Aussöhnung für nicht unwahrscheinlich, so kann es die Aussetzung des Verfahrens anordnen, jedoch nur einmal und auf höchstens sechs Monate.

Diese Aussetzung kann bei jeder Verhandlung im Laufe des Prozesses ausgesprochen werden, mag es sich bei dieser Verhandlung um Vorfragen und Zwischenpunkte oder um die Hauptsache handeln, und mag der Prozeß in erster oder zweiter Instanz anhängig sein, und zwar überall von Amtswegen.

Wenn das Gesetz sagt: „auf Grund der vorstehenden Bestimmung nur einmal," so hat es Fälle im Auge, wo aus anderen Gründen, z. B. weil die Nichtigkeit der Ehe geltend gemacht wird, oder das Ergebniß eines Strafverfahrens abzuwarten ist, die Aussetzung des Verfahrens geboten erscheint.

Es versteht sich von selbst, daß etwaige vorsorgliche Maßregeln ihre Wirkung auch während der Zeit, wo das Verfahren ruht, behaupten.

Berufung ist gegen die in Frage stehende Verfügung nicht statthaft, da sie ihrer Natur nach nur ein Zwischenbescheid ist und Art. 683 Ziff. 3 diesen Fall nicht begreift.

f) Zurücknahme der Klage.

10) Zu jeder Zeit, so lange der Prozeß nicht durch rechtskräftiges Urtheil erledigt ist, kann die Scheidungsklage zurückgenommen werden, und gilt dies selbstverständlich ebensowohl von der Widerklage als von der Hauptklage. Im französischen Ehescheidungsverfahren erstreckt sich dieses Recht sogar noch über die Rechtskraft des Urtheils hinaus (Art. 266 Code civ.), und es ist hervorzuheben, daß Fälle, wo erst in diesem Stadium die Versöhnung erfolgt, gar nicht selten sind.

Die Zurücknahme der Ehescheidungsklage gilt immer gleich einer Abweisung derselben, d. h. sie enthält immer einen Verzicht auf das Recht, die Ehescheidung zu verlangen, und läßt den Vorbehalt neuer Klagerhebung nicht zu. Offenbar ist es nemlich der Wille des Gesetzes nicht, daß neben der Zurücknahme im Sinne des Art. 671 auch noch der Klagabstand im Sinne des Art. 496 bestehen solle, und muß daher die Zurücknahme, welche vor der ersten Verhandlung erfolgt, ebenso einer Abweisung der Klage gleichgelten, als diejenige, welche später erfolgt. Die Zulassung eines bloßen Klagabstandes erschien einestheils unpassend, weil die Vervielfältigung der Ehescheidungsprozeduren nicht zu begünstigen, und anderntheils unnöthig, weil das Nachbringen neuer Ehescheidungsgründe unbedingt gestattet ist.

Sowie der klagende Ehegatte die ganze Klage zurücknehmen kann, so kann er natürlich auch nur theilweise auf dieselbe verzichten. Abg. II 405 Sp. 1.

Art. 672. — **Der Staatsanwalt hat vor jeder Entscheidung, welche in Ehescheidungssachen auf einfache Vorstellung erfolgt, sowie bei jeder Verhandlung seine Ansicht über die zu treffende Entscheidung oder das zu erlassende Urtheil vorzutragen. Er ist befugt, zum Zwecke der Aufrechthaltung der Ehe Thatsachen geltend zu machen, welche von den Parteien nicht**

angeführt sind, sowie Beweise anzubieten und zu führen. Er kann der Beweisaufnahme anwohnen, auch wenn er die Beweisführung nicht übernommen hat.

Das Recht zur Einlegung von Rechsmitteln steht dem Staatsanwalte nicht zu.

G. A. d. K. d. A. II S. 389. 390. 392. 394–396. 405. 454. — K. d. R. II S. 298.

1) Im Ehescheidungsverfahren sind dem Staatsanwalte größere Befugnisse eingeräumt, als irgend sonst auf dem Gebiete des Civilprozesses, abgesehen von den Klagen auf Nichtigerklärung von Ehen.

Derselbe ist bei allen Verhandlungen in der Sitzung zu hören, und seine Antragstellung ist hier nicht bloß geduldet, sondern vorgeschrieben. Seine Rolle beschränkt sich ferner nicht auf gutachtliche Aeußerungen, sondern er wird in gewisser Beziehung als Partei betrachtet, indem ihm das Recht eingeräumt ist, zum Zwecke der Aufrechthaltung der Ehe neue Thatsachen geltend zu machen, ja selbst Beweise anzubieten und zu führen.

Es kann daher keinen Zweifel erleiden, daß eine Verhandlung im Ehescheidungsverfahren, bei welcher der Staatsanwalt nicht anwesend war oder nicht gehört wurde, an einem wesentlichen, die Giltigkeit der Verhandlung und des darauf sich gründenden Urtheils in Frage stellenden Mangel leidet (Art. 218 Abs. 2).

2) Wenn auch dem Staatsanwalte in einer bestimmten Richtung die Rechte einer Partei zustehen, so schreibt doch das Gesetz nicht vor, daß ihm im Allgemeinen gleich einer Partei Zustellungen zu machen, namentlich die motivirten Anträge zuzustellen seien. Ja nicht einmal zur Mittheilung der Akten, welche der französische Prozeß in Fällen, wo der Staatsanwalt zu hören ist, vorschreibt, sind die Parteien verpflichtet.

Es ist nun allerdings nicht sachgemäß, wenn der Staatsanwalt erst in der Sitzung von der Sache nähere Kenntniß erhält, denn in der Regel wird er sich dann nicht in der Lage befinden, selbständige Beweisanträge zu stellen, oder auch nur zu beurtheilen, ob ein selbständiges Eingreifen seinerseits geboten sei, wird sich vielmehr beschränken müssen, eine Vertagung zu beantragen. Mit Rücksicht hierauf möchte es rathsam erscheinen, wenn das Gericht bei Hinterlegung der Anträge auf das mögliche Eingreifen des Staatsanwaltes geeignete Rücksicht nehmen, die Tagfahrt zur Verhandlung im Hinblicke auf die vom Staatsanwalte etwa zu bethätigenden Nachforschungen festsetzen und veranlassen würde, daß die hinterlegten Anträge sofort dem Staatsanwalte zur Einsicht mitgetheilt würden.

3) Das Recht des Staatsanwaltes, selbständige Beweise zu führen, bedingt anderseits seine Pflicht, überall, wo Anlaß gegeben erscheint, namentlich, wo Verdacht obwaltet, es möchten die Ehegatten im Einverständnisse handeln, von Amtswegen die nöthigen Nachforschungen und Ermittelungen vornehmen. Besonderer Anlaß hierzu wird in Fällen gegeben sein, wo die Ehescheidungsklage auf Grund böslichen Verlassens erhoben wird.

4) So lange der Staatsanwalt sich bloß darauf beschränkt, seine gutachtliche Ansicht auszusprechen, oder Punkte, welche die Parteien unbeachtet ließen, hervorzuheben, tritt er nicht förmlich in die Rolle einer Partei, und es genügt daher, im Urtheile zu erwähnen, daß er gehört worden sei, ohne daß es nöthig wäre, seinen Antrag wörtlich anzuführen. Vgl. Art. 817 Ziff. 3.

Sobald aber der Staatsanwalt selbständige Beweisanträge nimmt, wird er auch der Form nach Partei und ist sowohl im Beweisurtheile als im Beweisverfahren als solche zu behandeln. Es ist also in den Sachverhalt des Urtheils auch der Antrag des Staatsanwaltes aufzunehmen (Art. 285 Ziff. 3) und der Sachverhalt auch diesem zuzustellen, bezw. zur Genehmigung vorzulegen. Ebenso ist das Beweisurtheil dem Staatsanwalte zuzustellen, und gelten die Formen und Fristen des in Frage stehenden Beweisverfahrens auch für und gegen den Staatsanwalt.

5) Da das Gesetz dem Staatsanwalte ausdrücklich ein Recht gibt, der Beweisaufnahme beizuwohnen, auch wenn er die Beweisführung nicht übernommen hat, so ist ihm selbstverständlich von Beweisaufnahmen außerhalb der Sitzung besondere Kenntniß zu geben, und es wird dem Willen des Gesetzes entsprechen, ihm die Tagfahrtsfestsetzung unter Einhaltung der in Art. 338 bestimmten Frist zuzustellen.

Es könnte sich dabei die Frage aufwerfen, ob nicht der Staatsanwalt, auch wenn er keinen selbständigen Beweis erboten hat, zur besseren Führung eines auf Antrag des beklagten Ehetheils zugelassenen Beweises, Zeugen benennen und vernehmen lassen könne. Ich würde nach dem Grundsatze, daß in der größeren Befugniß die kleinere enthalten ist, dies für zulässig erachten, natürlich unter der Bedingung, daß die für die Partei selbst geltenden Formen und Fristen eingehalten werden.

Sicherer handelt der Staatsanwalt jedenfalls, wenn er auch in Fällen, wo er bloß beabsichtigt, besondere Zeugen vernehmen zu lassen, sich zum Beweis erbietet bezw. sich das Beweisanerbieten des Beklagten förmlich aneignet.

6) Die Betheiligung des Staatsanwaltes am Prozesse in der Rolle einer Partei ist nur eine vorübergehende, sich auf das Beweisverfahren beschränkende. Sobald dieses vorüber ist, tritt er in seine gewöhnliche Stellung zurück, namentlich aber erklärt das Gesetz, daß ihm nie ein Recht zur Einlegung von Rechtsmitteln zustehe.

Art. 673. — Wird die Scheidungsklage abgewiesen, so ist der Kläger nicht befugt, eine neue Klage auf Thatsachen, welche er im früheren Prozesse geltend zu machen im Stande gewesen wäre, als ausschließenden Klagegrund zu stützen.

Gleiches gilt für den Widerkläger in Betreff der Thatsachen, auf welche er seine Widerklage zu gründen vermochte. G. A. d. K. d. A. II S. 395 405. – K. d. R. II S. 298.

1) Ist ein Ehescheidungsverfahren einmal anhängig, so verlangt das Gesetz, daß die Frage, ob Grund zu einer Scheidung gegeben sei, erschöpfend erörtert und erledigt werden, und sucht es möglichst zu verhüten, daß unter den Ehegatten wiederholt über die Frage der Ehescheidung verhandelt werde.

In dieser Absicht wollte man ursprünglich sogar den beklagten Ehetheil nöthigen, Widerklage zu erheben, wenn er die ihm zur Seite stehenden Ehescheidungsgründe nicht verlieren wolle (Abg. II 395), beschränkte sich jedoch schließlich auf die Bestimmung, daß weder der als Kläger noch der als Widerkläger auftretende Ehegatte eine neue Klage ausschließlich auf Thatsachen gründen dürfe, welche im früheren Prozesse hätten geltend gemacht werden können. Hierunter sind alle Thatsachen begriffen, welche dem betreffenden Ehegatten zur Zeit der dem Endurtheile vorausgehenden Verhandlung bereits bekannt waren, mögen sie aus der Zeit vor oder nach der Klagstellung herrühren, da diese sämmtlichen Thatsachen nach Art. 666 zur Geltung gebracht werden dürfen.

2) Da nur gesagt ist, es dürften solche Thatsachen nicht ausschließlich zur Begründung einer neuen Ehescheidungsklage benützt werden, so ist klar, daß nichts im Wege stehe, sie zur Unterstützung neu sich ergebender Ehescheidungsgründe herbeizuziehen.

Selbst Thatsachen, welche wirklich zur Begründung einer Ehescheidungsklage geltend gemacht, jedoch als nicht genügend beseitigt worden waren, können unter Umständen in einer neuen Ehescheidungsklage benützt werden. Ueberhaupt ist als Grundsatz anzuerkennen, daß, wenn neue Thatsachen, welchen an sich die Eigenschaft von Ehescheidungsgründen zukommt, geltend gemacht werden, zu deren Unterstützung auch ältere Thatsachen jeder Art beigezogen werden dürfen, damit der Richter ein Gesammtbild des ehelichen Lebens gewinne.

Deßhalb möchte ich annehmen, daß auch Ehescheidungsgründe, wegen deren eine Versöhnung stattgefunden, im Vereine mit neuen, der Versöhnung nachgängig entstandenen Ehescheidungsgründen geltend gemacht werden dürfen, obgleich das Gesetz dies nicht ausdrücklich ausspricht, wie es in Art. 273 Code civil geschieht.

Art. 674 — Die Bestimmungen für den Ehescheidungsprozeß finden auch Anwendung bei Klagen auf Trennung von Tisch und Bett. G. A. d. K. d. A. II S. 396. 405. – K. d. R. II S. 298.

Obgleich dieser Artikel nur davon spricht, daß für die Klagen auf Trennung von Tisch und Bett das nemliche Verfahren einzuhalten sei, wie für Klagen auf Ehescheidung, so sind doch aus der engen Verwandtschaft beider Klagen noch weitere Folgerungen zu ziehen.

Die Trennung von Tisch und Bett erscheint nemlich ihrem Wesen nach bloß als ein niederer Grad der Scheidung. Während diese das Band der Ehe vollständig löst, beschränkt sich jene darauf, die Ehe thatsächlich, ihrer äußeren Erscheinung nach aufzuheben. Daß insbesondere das Gesetz von dieser Anschauung ausgehe, ist dadurch angedeutet, daß es unter der allgemeinen Ueberschrift: „Ehescheidung" auch von der Trennung von Tisch und Bett spricht

Es wird demnach anzunehmen sein, daß einer Klage auf Trennung von Tisch und Bett mit einer Widerklage auf Scheidung geantwortet werden könne, und umgekehrt. Ebenso möchte die Vorschrift des Art. 673 über die Zulässigkeit älterer Thatsachen nicht dadurch umgangen werden können, daß man in der neuen Klage statt einer Scheidung eine Trennung von Tisch und Bett verlangte, oder umgekehrt.

Art. 675. — Sucht der protestantische Ehetheil in dem in Art. 2 der Verordnung vom 28. Juli 1818 vorgesehenen Falle die Auflösung der Ehe bei dem protestantischen Ehegerichte nach, so ist bei diesem die Sache in dem für die Bezirksgerichte vorgeschriebenen Verfahren ein-

zuleiten und zu verhandeln und finden die Bestimmungen der Art. 656—674 keine Anwendung.

Das protestantische Ehegericht hat seiner Entscheidung die bei dem katholischen festgestellten Thatsachen zu Grunde zu legen.

G. A. d. K. d. A. II S. 399—401 405. 454. IV S. 120. — K. d. R. II S. 298. IV S. 72.

1) Wie zu Art. 8 Nr. 8 bemerkt, ist durch eine Verordnung vom 28. Juli 1818 die Zuständigkeit für Scheidungsklagen bei gemischten Ehen dahin geregelt, daß die Religion des beklagten Ehegatten maßgebend sei.

Art. 2 jener Verordnung bestimmt weiter:

„Wurde hingegen die Klage bei der katholischen geistlichen Behörde angebracht „und von derselben auf Scheidung von Tisch „und Bett erkannt, so steht dem protestantischen Ehegerichte frei, in Ansehung des „protestantischen Ehetheils, wenn dieser die „Auflösung der Ehe nachsuchen würde, auf „dessen Beschwerde zu beschließen, was es dem „protestantischen Eherechte in dieser Hinsicht „gemäß finden würde."

In dem hier bezeichneten Falle soll nun, obgleich es sich im Grunde um eine Klage auf Ehescheidung handelt, dennoch nicht das für diese vorgezeichnete Ausnahmsverfahren stattfinden, sondern im Wege des gewöhnlichen Anwaltsprozesses zu verfahren sein. Es fallen also die vorläufige Zulassung der Klage, der Sühneversuch, sowie die besonderen Befugnisse des Staatsanwaltes hinweg.

2) Das protestantische Ehegericht hat seiner bezüglichen Entscheidung die bei dem katholischen festgestellten Thatsachen zu Grunde zu legen; seine Aufgabe besteht also einzig und allein in Entscheidung der Frage, ob auf Grund der bereits festgestellten Thatsachen nach protestantischem Eherechte die Scheidung auszusprechen sei oder nicht.

Unter welchen Voraussetzungen in diesem besonderen Falle die Scheidung ausgesprochen werden dürfe, ob namentlich die Thatsache, daß das katholische Ehegericht die Trennung von Tisch und Bett auf unbestimmte Zeit ausgesprochen, genüge, ist nach den bezüglich geltenden Rechtsgrundsätzen zu beurtheilen, an welchen der Gesetzgeber hier nichts ändern wollte. Abg. II 400 a. E. Neue Thatsachen dürfen vor dem protestantischen Ehegerichte nicht vorgebracht werden, jedoch ist eine nach dem Spruche des katholischen Ehegerichts eingetretene Versöhnung allerdings zu berücksichtigen.

Ungiltige und nichtige Ehen

Art. 676. — **Die Bestimmungen der Art. 659, 666, 667 und 669—673 sind auch für die Klagen maßgebend, mittels deren beantragt wird, eine Ehe auf Grund des allgemeinen preußischen Landrechts oder einer sonstigen gesetzlichen Bestimmung für ungiltig zu erklären.**

Eine Widerklage ist in diesem Falle nur in so ferne zulässig, als sie gleichfalls darauf gerichtet ist, die Ehe für ungiltig zu erklären.

G. A. d. K. d. A. II S. 396. 397 405. 406 — K. d. R. II S. 298.

1) Das preußische Landrecht unterscheidet zwischen ungiltigen und nichtigen Ehen und kennzeichnet in Theil II Tit. I § 933 u. 934 diesen Unterschied in folgender Weise:

§ 933. — Ehen, welche wegen obwaltender Verbotsgesetze niemals bestehen können, heißen nichtig.

§ 934. — Ehen, welchen zwar von Anfang an gesetzliche Hindernisse im Wege standen, die aber doch in der Folge durch Hebung dieser Hindernisse verbindliche Kraft erlangen können, werden ungiltig genannt.

Ungiltig sind also solche Ehen, welche nur von bestimmten Personen angefochten werden können und bei Mangel dieser Anfechtung, für welche das preußische Landrecht kurze Fristen von sechs Monaten bezw. sechs Wochen setzt, sowie in Folge von Genehmigung, von Ursprung an giltig werden. Das preußische Landrecht zählt eine Reihe solcher Fälle a. a. O. § 968—1000 auf, darunter insbesondere Zwang, Betrug oder Irrthum beim Eheabschluß, Mangel der Einwilligung von Eltern oder Vormundschaftsbehörden, unreifes Alter 2c., während es in § 935—967 die Fälle der Nichtigkeit anführt.

Unsere Prozeßordnung schreibt nun für jede dieser beiden Arten der Anfechtung einer Ehe ein besonderes Verfahren vor, indem sie im Falle bloßer Ungiltigkeit auf die Möglichkeit einer Versöhnung geeignete Rücksicht nimmt, im Falle absoluter Nichtigkeit aber der Amtsthätigkeit des Staatsanwaltes eine ungewöhnliche Ausdehnung gibt.

2) Der nemliche Unterschied im Verfahren soll auch eintreten, soweit andere Ehegesetzgebungen oder das gemeine protestantische Eherecht, in gleicher Weise wie das preußische Landrecht,

zwischen Ehen, die bloß ungiltig, und solchen, die nichtig sind, unterscheiden, und kann es dabei selbstverständlich nur auf die Natur des in Frage stehenden Anfechtungsgrundes ankommen, nicht aber darauf, ob das besondere Eherecht gerade die nemlichen Kunstausdrücke gebrauche, wie das preußische Landrecht. Abg. II 396 Sp. 2.

Die Frage, in welchen Fällen außerhalb des preußischen Landrechts eine Ehe als ungiltig und in welchen als nichtig zu betrachten sei, ist sehr wichtig, da, je nachdem man sie in dem einen oder dem andern Sinne löst, ein ganz verschiedenes Verfahren einzuhalten ist; sie ist zugleich nicht ohne Schwierigkeiten.

3) Faßt man nun das Wesen der Sache in's Auge, so gelangt man dahin, daß jede Nichtigkeit, welche nur von bestimmten Personen geltend gemacht werden darf und durch ausdrückliche oder stillschweigende Genehmigung dieser Personen geheilt werden kann, als eine bloße Ungiltigkeit im Sinne von Art. 676 zu betrachten sei, im Gegensatze zu jenen absoluten Nichtigkeiten, welche, als auf Gründen der öffentlichen Ordnung beruhend, nicht geheilt werden können und von Jedermann geltend gemacht werden dürfen. Es entspricht diese Unterscheidung auch vollständig der Verschiedenheit des Verfahrens, denn nur bei Nichtigkeiten der ersten Art lassen sich die Bestimmungen der Art. 670, 671 und 673 anwenden, während anderseits die weitgehenden Befugnisse des Staatsanwaltes, wie sie die Art. 678—680 feststellen, nur für absolute, im öffentlichen Interesse wurzelnde Nichtigkeiten Anwendung finden können.

Was Zweifel erregen könnte, ist die Bestimmung in Art. 678, welcher auch bei Nichtigkeiten den Fall vorsehen zu müssen glaubt, wo die Geltendmachung des Nichtigkeitsgrundes vom Willen der betheiligten Ehegatten abhängt, denn es läßt sich nicht verkennen, daß in Fällen dieser Art eine Nichtigkeit im strengen Sinne des preußischen Landrechts nicht angenommen werden könnte. Trotzdessen wird an der aufgestellten Ansicht festzuhalten sein, wenn man nicht in's Prinziplose gerathen will.

Uebrigens ist zu bemerken, daß fragliche Bestimmung in Art. 678 nur der Vorsicht wegen nachträglich eingefügt wurde, um keinen Zweifel darüber zu lassen, daß an den Beschränkungen, welche die einzelnen Civilrechte bezüglich der Geltendmachung von Nichtigkeiten enthalten, nichts geändert werden wollte. Offenbar hätte man jedoch, um diesem Gedanken vollen Ausdruck zu geben, noch einen Schritt weiter gehen und auch die in Art. 679 und 680 dem Staatsanwalte verliehenen Befugnisse, durch Stellen vollständiger Anträge und Einlegen von Rechtsmitteln die Vernichtung der Ehe herbeizuführen, entsprechend beschränken müssen.

4) Das Verfahren in Fällen, wo es sich bloß um die Ungiltigkeit von Ehen handelt, ist das nemliche, wie bei der Ehescheidung, nur fällt die vorläufige Zulassung der Klage und der Sühneversuch hinweg. Insbesondere hat der Gesetzgeber im Hinblicke darauf, daß durch den Verzicht der klagenden Partei die Ungiltigkeit der Ehe gehoben werden kann, jene Bestimmungen des Ehescheidungsverfahrens, welche darauf abzielen, die Ursachen zur Aufhebung der Ehe zu beseitigen, z. B. über Aussetzung des Verfahrens (Art. 670), über Zurücknahme der Klage, auch hier beibehalten. Auch die Mitwirkung der Staatsanwaltschaft ist dieselbe, wie bei der Ehescheidung, und darf dieselbe auch hier nur zum Zwecke der Erhaltung der Ehe selbständig auftreten.

Was die Art. 667 und 673 betrifft, welche gleichfalls für anwendbar erklärt sind, so gilt, was dort von Ehescheidungsgründen gesagt ist, hier natürlich von Ungiltigkeitsgründen. Neue Ungiltigkeitsgründe, welche der klagenden Person zustehen, dürfen also bis zum Endurtheile nachgetragen werden, während anderseits auch alle Anfechtungsgründe dieser Art, welche nicht zur Geltung gebracht wurden, für immer ausgeschlossen sind.

Was die Widerklagen anbelangt, so erklärt sie Art. 676 Abs. 2 ausdrücklich nur zulässig, insofern sie ebenfalls dahin gerichtet sind, die Ehe für ungiltig zu erklären. Hiermit sind nicht bloß Widerklagen auf Scheidung oder Trennung von Tisch und Bett, sondern auch Widerklagen auf Nichtigerklärung der Ehe im Sinne von Art. 677 ff. ausgeschlossen.

Art. 677. — Ueber die Nichtigkeit einer Ehe darf, so lange beide Ehetheile leben, nur verhandelt und erkannt werden, wenn mittels einer besondern Klage beantragt wird, die Ehe für nichtig zu erklären.

Art. 678. — Soweit die Geltendmachung des Nichtigkeitsgrundes nicht gesetzlich von dem Willen der betheiligten Ehegatten abhängt, kann die Klage auf Nichtigerklärung einer Ehe außer von einem der Eheleute auch von dem bei dem Ehegerichte angestellten Staatsanwalte,

ingleichen von einem Dritten, welcher ein rechtliches Interesse daran hat, daß die Ehe für nichtig erklärt werde, erhoben werden.

Wird die Nichtigkeitsklage von dem Staatsanwalte oder einem Dritten erhoben, so ist sie gegen beide Ehegatten zu richten.

Art. 679. — Der Staatsanwalt hat ohne Unterschied, ob die Nichtigkeitsklage von ihm erhoben ist oder nicht, bei allen gerichtlichen Verhandlungen wie im Ehescheidungsprozesse mitzuwirken. Er ist außerdem befugt, wie eine Partei den Prozeß zu betreiben, sowie selbständig behufs Aufrechthaltung oder Vernichtung der Ehe Anträge zu stellen und gegen die ergehenden Urtheile Rechtsmittel einzulegen, das Letztere auch dann, wenn seinen Anträgen gemäß erkannt war.

Art. 680. — Legt der Staatsanwalt ein Rechtsmittel ein, so ist dieses gegen beide Eheleute und gegen den etwa im Prozesse befindlichen Dritten zu richten.

Legt der Dritte ein Rechtsmittel ein, so hat er es gegen beide Eheleute zu richten.

Art. 681. — Die Bestimmungen der Art. 659, 667 und 669 gelten auch für die Klage, mittels welcher beantragt wird, eine Ehe für nichtig zu erklären.

G. A. d. K. d. A. II S. 397. 406. — K. d. R. II S. 298.

1) Was im Sinne dieser Artikel unter der Nichtigkeit einer Ehe zu verstehen sei, wurde bereits zu Art. 675 Nr. 1—3 näher erörtert.

Das Gesetz setzt bei der Klage, von welcher es hier spricht, überall nur den Fall voraus, daß beide Ehegatten noch am Leben sind, und verfügt dem entsprechend, daß Klage und Rechtsmittel gegen die beiden Eheleute zu richten seien. Vgl. auch Entwurf Art. 31 (S. 452) und Referat dazu (S. 448).

Für den Fall, wo die Nichtigkeit der Ehe geltend gemacht werden soll, nachdem Einer der Ehegatten bereits gestorben ist, besteht also die besondere Klage, welche Gegenstand der Art. 677—681 ist, nicht, und fällt folgeweise auch die Zuständigkeit des Ehegerichtes hinweg (Abg. II 406 Sp. 1). Es muß dann die Frage, ob die Ehe bestehe oder nicht, als Zwischenpunkt in den Prozessen, für welche sie von Erheblichkeit ist, behandelt und entschieden werden, und zwar mit Beschränkung der Rechtskraft auf die betreffenden Parteien.

2) Für die Fälle nun, welche das Gesetz hier im Auge hat, bestimmt es, daß die Frage der Nichtigkeit der Ehe nie als Zwischenpunkt eines anderen Prozesses behandelt werden dürfe, sondern daß selbständige Klage deßhalb vor dem Ehegerichte zu erheben sei, für deren Durchführung die Vorschriften der Art. 677 bis 681 Maß geben.

Diese Klage kann gestellt werden:

1) von einem Ehegatten gegen den anderen;
2) vom Staatsanwalte oder einem Dritten, welcher rechtliches Interesse an der Vernichtung der Ehe hat, gegen beide Eheleute.

Ein rechtliches Interesse besteht z. B. im Falle der Bigamie für den ersten Ehegatten, oder im Falle, wo in Frage steht, ob Kinder aus der Ehe erbberechtigt seien, für die gefährdeten Notherben. Selbstverständlich haben solche Personen auch das Recht, zu interveniren.

3) Aus dem Ehescheidungsverfahren sind für diese Klage nur die Bestimmungen über die Wirkungen von Geständnissen und Eiden, sowie über die provisorischen Maßregeln für anwendbar erklärt, die sonstigen Sonderbestimmungen finden keine Anwendung. Es gelten also bezüglich der Zulässigkeit von Klagänderungen, sowie bezüglich der Zulässigkeit und Wirkung des Klagabstandes die Grundsätze des gewöhnlichen Prozesses.

Auch hinsichtlich der Widerklagen ist hier keine Ausnahmsbestimmung gegeben, es möchte daher nichts im Wege stehen, eine Widerklage auf Ungiltigerklärung der Ehe im Sinne des Art. 676 zu erheben.

4) Dem Staatsanwalte ist hier ein großes Gebiet der Thätigkeit eröffnet, und zeigen schon die hierauf bezüglichen Bestimmungen des Gesetzes, daß dasselbe ausschließlich nur Fälle im Auge hat, wo die Ehe absolut nichtig und das öffentliche Interesse bei Vernichtung derselben betheiligt ist.

Wie bereits erwähnt, hat der Staatsanwalt das Recht, selbst auf Vernichtung der Ehe zu klagen, und zwar indem er seine Klagen gegen beide Ehegatten richtet.

Es versteht sich von selbst, daß er in diesem Falle im ganzen Prozesse gleich einer andern Partei behandelt wird und die Rechte einer solchen hat, jedoch könnte in Frage gezogen werden, ob ihm auch die Eigenschaft eines Anwaltes zukomme, wie dies im französischen Prozesse, sowie nach preußischem Rechte (Verordnung vom 25. Juni 1844) ohne Zweifel der Fall ist. Nach dem Wortlaute von Art. 79 käme man allerdings dahin, daß der Staatsanwalt, gleich jedem anderen gesetzlichen Vertreter, einen Anwalt aufstellen und durch denselben den Prozeß führen, ja selbst in der Sitzung vertreten lassen müßte. Ich glaube jedoch, daß dies nicht in der Absicht des Gesetzgebers gelegen sei, daß vielmehr hier, wie überhaupt überall, wo das Gesetz ein selbständiges Eingreifen des Staatsanwalts in den Prozeß — Stellen von Beweisanträgen (Art. 672), Stellen selbständiger Anträge auf Aufrechthaltung oder Vernichtung der Ehe (Art. 679) — zuläßt, es voraussetze, daß er selbst handle, nicht aber durch das Organ eines Anwaltes.

5) Auch in Fällen, wo der Staatsanwalt die Klage auf Nichtigkeit nicht selbst gestellt hat, ist er befugt, wie eine Partei den Prozeß zu betreiben, selbständige Anträge selbst behufs Vernichtung der Ehe zu nehmen und selbständig Rechtsmittel einzulegen, Letzteres sogar dann, wenn seinen Anträgen gemäß erkannt worden war.

Indem er in dieser Weise selbständig in den Prozeß eingreift, wird er Partei in demselben und ist von da an als Intervenient zu behandeln.

Ende der ersten Abtheilung.

Druck von C. R. Schurich in München.

www.ingramcontent.com/pod-product-compliance
Lightning Source LLC
LaVergne TN
LVHW081355011026
849161LV00013BA/2817